October 26-30, 2015
Brisbane, Australia

Association for
Computing Machinery

Advancing Computing as a Science & Profession

MM'15

Proceedings of the 2015 ACM Multimedia Conference

Sponsored by:

ACM SIGMM

Supported by:

The University of Queensland, NSF, FX PAL, Baidu, UESTC, Google, QUT, Alibaba Group, University of Sydney, Brisbane, HUAWEI, IBM Research, Microsoft Research, HTC, Facebook, Yahoo! Labs, & cisra

Association for
Computing Machinery

Advancing Computing as a Science & Profession

The Association for Computing Machinery
2 Penn Plaza, Suite 701
New York, New York 10121-0701

Notice to Past Authors of ACM-Published Articles
ACM intends to create a complete electronic archive of all articles and/or other material previously published by ACM. If you have written a work that has been previously published by ACM in any journal or conference proceedings prior to 1978, or any SIG Newsletter at any time, and you do NOT want this work to appear in the ACM Digital Library, please inform permissions@acm.org, stating the title of the work, the author(s), and where and when published.

ISBN: 978-1-4503-3459-4 (Digital)

ISBN: 978-1-4503-4111-0 (Print)

Additional copies may be ordered prepaid from:

ACM Order Department
PO Box 30777
New York, NY 10087-0777, USA

Phone: 1-800-342-6626 (USA and Canada)
+1-212-626-0500 (Global)
Fax: +1-212-944-1318
E-mail: acmhelp@acm.org
Hours of Operation: 8:30 am – 4:30 pm ET

Printed in the USA

General Chairs' Welcome

It is our great pleasure to welcome you to the *2015 ACM MULTIMEDIA* Conference, the premier conference for multimedia experts and practitioners from across academia and industry. This year we are in beautiful Brisbane, Australia, our first time in this wonderful country and we're delighted to be here and looking forward to experiencing some of the delights and treasures this great country has to offer.

This year's conference is the 23rd in the annual series continues our tradition to bring together a wide and diverse set of activities including panel sessions, tutorials, a series of workshops, technical demos, an open source software competition, a doctoral symposium, an interactive art exhibition, a video program and of course scientific papers and posters including special sessions on brave new ideas and grand challenges, as well as "regular" topics. What a busy week we are going to have!

One of the great parts of the program that we have lined up for you is the two keynote talks. On Tuesday October 27th, Judy Kay from the University of Sydney will talk about "*Harnessing Big Personal Data, with scrutable user modeling for privacy and control*", bringing her extensive background in Human-Computer Interaction to the really topical issue of personal data, and how to manage and use it for good and practical purposes. On Thursday October 29th, Zhengyou Zhang from Microsoft Research will talk about *"Vision-enhanced Immersive Interaction and Remote Collaboration with Large Touch Displays"* where he will address issues like telepresence and computer supported cooperative work and how those technologies have, and continue to develop.

We are immensely grateful to the University of Queensland, our hosts and local organizers, for inviting us here to Brisbane and for organizing such a great event. We also thank our gold sponsors ACM SIGMM, the University of Queensland, the National Science Foundation, FXPAL, Baidu, and the University of Electronic Science and Technology China, our silver sponsors Google, Queensland University of Technology, the Alibaba Group, the University of Sydney and Brisbane Marketing, and our bronze sponsors Huawei, IBM Research, Microsoft Research, HTC, Facebook and Yahoo! Labs. Without their support this conference would simply not be what it is today.

Of course putting together *MULTIMEDIA 2015* was a team effort and there are large number of people we should thank including authors, the program committee, area chairs, chairs of a myriad of other conference-related functions, local organizers and volunteers. We would like to make a special call out to Roger Zimmerman and Yongdong Zhang, our proceedings chairs, for the enormous amount of work they have done in the background to bring all this material together into one volume.

Finally, we hope that you will find the program for *Multimedia 2015* interesting and thought-provoking and that you use the opportunity to share and exchange ideas with other researchers and practitioners from around the world.

Welcome to Brisbane.

Xiaofang Zhou
The University of Queensland, Australia

Alan F. Smeaton
Dublin City University, Ireland

Qi Tian
The University of Texas at San Antonio, USA

ACM MULTIMEDIA '15 General Chairs

Message from Technical Program Chairs

We are pleased to introduce to you the Technical Program for the ACM International Conference on Multimedia (ACM Multimedia) 2015, for its first appearance in the Southern hemisphere. While adopting the best practices from previous ACM Multimedia conferences, this year we also introduced some changes on the research areas, the review process, and the conference program to reflect and ensure the greatest interests of researchers in our multimedia community.

Fifteen research areas of interest were grouped into four research themes, including a System Theme (covering Multimedia Telepresence and Virtual/Augmented Reality, Multimedia Systems and Middleware, Multimedia Transport and Delivery, Mobile Multimedia), an Experience Theme (covering Multimedia for Collaboration in Education & Distributed Environments, Multimedia HCI and Quality of Experience, Music, Speech and Audio Processing in Multimedia, Multimedia Authoring and Enrichment), an Understanding Theme (covering Deep Learning for Multimedia, Multimodal Analysis and Description, Multimedia and Vision), and an Engagement Theme (covering Multimedia Art, Entertainment and Culture, Multimedia Search and Recommendation, Social Multimedia, Emotional and Social Signals In Multimedia). In particular, the area of Multimedia and Vision was introduced to reach out to the relevant community that mainly deals with processing vision-related multimedia data.

This year, CMT was used to manage paper submissions and each research theme was set up as a track in the system. While CMT worked well for most steps in the review process, moving submissions across tracks was not allowed. In CMT, the Conflict of Interest (CoI) was easily handled by authors who had to specify the conflicting domains, Area Chairs and reviewers before they could make submissions.

Each research theme was overseen by one Technical Program Chair. For each area, a team of Area Chairs (ACs) of one to five members was recruited to handle the paper review process. In total, 37 ACs were appointed. Technical Program Chairs firstly assigned three or four reviewers and one or two ACs to each full and short submission. ACs then monitored the review process, coordinated discussions based on feedback, assessed the submissions based on reviews, and provided meta-recommendations as the inputs for the Technical Programme Committee (TPC) meeting.

While the general practices for ACs as stated in previous ACM Multimedia conferences were followed, this year we introduced the pairing relationship between two ACs to look at all borderline papers. If a submission received an initial borderline recommendation, another AC with relevant expertise was brought in to provide another examination of the submission before a final decision was made.

Regarding the paper submission and review process,

- As in 2014, there was no pre-submission of abstracts. Submissions of full and short papers were separated from each other, with the short paper submission deadline being one month later than the deadline for full paper submissions.
- As in 2014, for full papers, a two-stage review process was applied. Authors were invited to submit a rebuttal based on the first stage reviews. The reviewers were then asked to consider the rebuttal, to revise their reviews accordingly, and to enter discussion with other reviewers aiming to improve review consensus on each paper. The results of the second round reviews and discussion were then summarized by the ACs into meta-reviews, which included

tentative recommendations, to be discussed and finalized during the TPC meeting. In the second stage review, authors had the opportunity to talk to the Authors' Advocate if they felt they had issues with the reviews.

- For any submission with a borderline recommendation, an additional AC was paired with the initially assigned AC to provide a second recommendation, to be further discussed and finalized during the TPC meeting.
- Submissions from Technical Program Chairs and ACs were handled personally by non-conflicting Technical Program Chairs.
- In total, 252 full and 386 short paper submissions were received by their respective deadlines and entered the regular review process.
- The table below gives the exact submission numbers across research areas.

Area	**Full**	**Short**
Multimedia Telepresence and Virtual/Augmented Reality	12	11
Multimedia Systems and Middleware	16	23
Multimedia Transport and Delivery	11	8
Mobile Multimedia	16	15
Multimedia for Collaboration in Education & Distributed Environments	8	5
Multimedia HCI and Quality of Experience	16	17
Music, Speech and Audio Processing in Multimedia	7	18
Multimedia Authoring and Enrichment	3	8
Deep Learning for Multimedia	8	34
Multimodal Analysis and Description	26	43
Multimedia and Vision	43	94
Multimedia Art, Entertainment and Culture	16	11
Multimedia Search and Recommendation	40	59
Social Multimedia	18	17
Emotional and Social Signals In Multimedia	12	23
Total	**252**	**386**

Decisions on full and short paper acceptances were made at the one-day TPC meeting held at Fudan University on 22 June 2015. All four Technical Program Chairs attended the meeting and handled their own themes in four different rooms separately. The emphasis of the TPC meeting was on high-score, borderline, and controversial paper submissions. The discussion was intensive, taking into account all the available data, including reviews, the authors' rebuttals, the discussions, the initial recommendations by the ACs (in the form of a meta review) and the reviews performed by other ACs during the meeting. Technical Program Chairs and ACs were requested to leave the room when a conflicting submission was discussed.

After the meeting, the four TPC Chairs met to make final decisions, taking quality and balance of different tracks into consideration. By end of the day, we accepted 56 full and 117 short papers, leading to acceptance rates of 22.2% and 30.3% for full and short papers, respectively. Eight high quality full paper submissions had also been suggested to be accepted as short papers.

In a change from previous years, we also arranged a poster session for orally presented papers, including full and BNI papers, to be presented as posters to increase interactions among conference attendees. A number of TOMM papers published in 2014 were also invited to be presented in this poster session, to promote their research results as reported in TOMM.

The Technical Program Committee has worked really hard to ensure that the technical program of the conference is of the highest possible quality. Unfortunately, we couldn't include every single quality paper into the program. We really appreciate all the efforts and inputs from ACs and reviewers towards the exciting technical program.

We look forward to seeing you in the season of Spring, in Brisbane, Australia.

Dick C.A. Bulterman
FXPal, USA

Heng Tao Shen
The University of Queensland, Australia

Ketan Mayer-Patel
The University of North Carolina, USA

Shuicheng Yan
National University of Singapore

Message from SIGMM Chair

T-Shaped Vision, New Initiative, and Great Tradition

Different from other professional societies, the technical activities in ACM are organized around SIG, which stands for Special Interest Group. Each SIG is focused on a specific disciplinary area. In our case, it's *Multimedia*, a relatively broad but vaguely defined field covering a wide spectrum of aspects surrounding multimedia – computing, communications, and applications. However, there is a unique force that makes our community continue to excel and thrive: it's the dynamic *cross-disciplinary* nature of the intellectual pursuit of novel solutions in response to grand challenges facing the community at various times, starting with streaming and storage of multimedia data in the 90's, to rich media interaction (including overcoming the semantic gap in accessing web-scale multimedia), large-scale media sensing and processing over distributed platforms (including Internet of Things), collaborative environments incorporating rich sensory data and peta-scale networks, finally to the emerging cognitive multimedia systems involving affective computing and sociopsychological study.

The outcomes of such dynamic interdisciplinary efforts are both deep and broad, underscoring an important theme identified in the recent SIGMM retreat held in November 2014. A concrete recommendation made by 28 volunteer leaders in that retreat was ***the T-shaped vision for SIGMM*** - SIGMM should continue to embrace both depth (the vertical line of T) and breadth (the horizontal bar of T). We should welcome and encourage research of "X and Multimedia" (X being works from other individual "narrow" disciplines), while aiming to develop the core foundation of our field, including but not limited to multimedia integration, experience, representation, devices, contexts, and distributed computing.

I am delighted to see this upcoming ACM Multimedia Conference demonstrates excellent execution of the above T-shaped vision. The technical program, including an impressive array of regular and special activities, fully embodies the balanced spirit. You can find in-depth studies of foundational topics as well as applications of multimedia solutions in many practical domains.

This year also marks the launching of an important initiative – the inaugural ***SIGMM Multimedia Frontiers Workshop***, featuring 12 rising star researchers in multimedia. These speakers will share their achievements and visions through invited talks, followed by open dialogs with senior members in the community. These rising members are at the height of their career and, together with the senior colleagues, in perfect positions to shape the future direction of the community. The workshop has been organized with broad input from the Executive Committee and many other volunteers, but the list of speakers is by no means complete. We look forward to continuing this new initiative in the future to benefit from views from other rising members.

A great tradition at ACMMM is celebration of the extraordinary achievements of SIGMM members. This year we are privileged to recognize the exceptional achievements of the following members: Dr. Tat-Seng Chua for SIGMM Technical Achievement Award, Dr. Yu-Gang Jiang for SIGMM Rising Star Award, and Dr. Ting Yao for SIGMM Best Ph.D. Thesis Award. These are the prestigious honors bestowed upon members for their outstanding contributions. Each recipient will address the conference audience in plenary presentations to share their exciting accomplishments. We thank the award committees (chaired by Rainer Lienhart and Shin'ichi Satoh) for their hard work in making the selections from the nominations.

Finally, we are all profoundly indebted to the organizing team of ACM Multimedia 2015 for their devoted efforts that make ACMMM15 possible and more importantly sustains the success of SIGMM. We salute them for their invaluable leadership and contributions!

Shih-Fu Chang
Columbia University, USA
ACM SIGMM Chair

Table of Contents

Panel 1
Session Chairs: Shih-Fu Chang *(Columbia University)* and David A. Shamma *(Yahoo Labs)*

Panel 2
Session Chair: Yung-Hsiang Lu *(Purdue University)*

Session 1: Multimedia Indexing and Search
Session Chair: Heng Tao Shen *(The University of Queensland)*

Session 2: Social Multimedia
Session Chair: Tao Mei *(Microsoft Research Asia)*

Session 3: Emotional and Social Signals in Multimedia
Session Chair: Hayley Hung *(Technical University of Delft)*

Session: Multimedia Grand Challenge

Session: Brave New Ideas

Session 4: Multimedia and Vision

Session Chair: Mohan S. Kankanhalli *(National University of Singapore)*

Session 5: Multimedia Art, Entertainment and Culture

Session Chair: Phoebe Chen *(La Trobe University)*

Session 6: Telepresence, Virtual, and Augmented Reality

Session Chair: Klara Nahrstedt *(UIUC)*

Session: Session 7: Actions and Events

Session Chair: Nicu Sebe *(University of Trento)*

Doctoral Symposium

Session Chairs: Hervé Jégou *(Facebook AI Research)* and Cees G. M. Snoek *(University of Amsterdam)*

Open Source Software Competition

Session Chairs: Tao Mei *(Microsoft Research Asia)*, Marco Bertini *(University of Florence)*, and Xian-Sheng Hua *(Alibaba)*

Art Exhibit

Videos/Demos 1

Demos 2

Session Chair: Zheng-Jun Zha *(Hefei Institute of Intelligent Machines, Chinese Academy of Sciences)*

Poster Session 1

Session Chair: Jun Zhou *(Griffith University)*

Poster Session 2

Session Chair: Dian Tjondronegoro *(Queensland University of Technology)*

Tutorials

Workshop Summaries

MM 2015 Conference Organization

General Chairs: Xiaofang Zhou *(The University of Queensland, Australia)*
Alan F. Smeaton *(Dublin City University, Ireland)*
Qi Tian *(The University of Texas at San Antonio, USA)*

Technical Program Committee Chairs: Dick C.A. Bulterman *(FXPAL, USA)*
Heng Tao Shen *(The University of Queensland, Australia)*
Ketan Mayer-Patel *(The University of North Carolina, USA)*
Shuicheng Yan *(National University of Singapore, Singapore)*

Author's Advocate: Wei Tsang Ooi *(National University of Singapore, Singapore)*

Brave New Idea Chairs: Yong Rui *(Microsoft Research Asia, China)*
Nicu Sebe *(University of Trento, Italy)*
Xuelong Li *(OPTical IMagery Analysis and Learning (OPTIMAL), China)*

Multimedia Grand Challenge Chairs: Michael Lew *(Leiden University, The Netherlands)*
Jie Yang *(National Science Foundation, USA)*

Technical Demo Chairs: Alejandro Jaimes *(Yahoo!, Spain)*
Zheng-Jun Zha *(Hefei Institute of Intelligent Machines, Chinese Academy of Sciences, China)*

Interactive Arts Chairs: Stephen Viller *(The University of Queensland, Australia)*
Ann Morrison *(Aalborg University, Denmark)*

Panel Chairs: Chang Wen Chen *(University at Buffalo, USA)*
Zhi-Hua Zhou *(Nanjing University, China)*

Open Source Software Competition Chairs: Marco Bertini *(University of Florence, Italy)*
Xian-Sheng Hua *(Alibaba, China)*
Tao Mei *(Microsoft Research Asia, China)*

Video Program Chairs: Shin'ichi Satoh *(National Institute of Informatics, Japan)*
Meng Wang *(Hefei University of Technology, China)*
Jinman Kim *(The University of Sydney, Australia)*

Doctoral Symposium Chairs: Cees G. M. Snoek *(University of Amsterdam & Qualcomm Research Netherlands, The Netherlands)*
Hervé Jégou *(Facebook AI Research, France)*

Tutorials Chairs: Rainer Lienhart *(University of Augsburg, Germany)*
Thomas Plagemann *(University of Oslo, Norway)*
Zhiyong Wang *(The University of Sydney, Australia)*

Workshop Chairs: Alan Hanjalic *(Delft University of Technology, The Netherlands)*
Lexing Xie *(Australian National University, Australia)*
Svetha Venkatesh *(Deakin University, Australia)*

Sponsorship Chairs: Abdulmotaleb El Saddik *(University of Ottawa, Canada)*
Rong Yan *(Snapchat Inc, USA)*
Kiyoharu Aizawa *(University of Tokyo, Japan)*
Zhengyou Zhang *(Microsoft Research, USA)*

Travel Grant Chairs: Xiangjian (Sean) He *(University of Technology Sydney, Australia)*
Yang Yang *(University of Electronic Science and Technology, China)*

Publicity Chairs: Jiebo Luo *(University of Rochester, USA)*
Lei Zhang *(Microsoft Research, USA)*
Weidong Cai *(The University of Sydney, Australia)*

History Preservation Chairs: K. Selçuk Candan *(Arizona State University, USA)*
Chong-Wah Ngo *(City University of Hong Kong, Hong Kong)*

Local Organization Chairs: Xue Li *(University of Queensland, Australia)*
Dian Tjondronegoro *(Queensland University of Technology, Australia)*

Finance Chair: Zi Huang *(The University of Queensland, Australia)*

Proceedings Chairs: Roger Zimmermann *(National University of Singapore, Singapore)*
Yongdong Zhang *(Chinese Academy of Science, China)*

Web and Social Media Chairs: Lorna Macdonald *(The University of Queensland, Australia)*
Jun Zhou *(Griffith University, Australia)*

MM 2015 Area Chairs

Multimedia Telepresence and Virtual/Augmented Reality: Klara Nahrstedt *(UIUC, USA)*
Wanmin Wu *(Ricoh Innovations, USA)*

Multimedia Systems and Middleware: Wu-Chi Feng *(Portland State University, USA)*
Kuan-Ta Chen *(Academia Sinica, Taiwan)*

Multimedia Transport and Delivery: Ali C. Begen *(Cisco Systems, USA)*
Christian Timmerer *(Alpen-Adria-University Klagenfurt, Austria)*

Mobile Multimedia: Jochen Huber *(MIT Media Lab, USA)*
Winston Hsu *(National Taiwan University, Taiwan)*

Multimedia for Collaboration in Education & Distributed Environments: Matt Cooper *(FXPAL, USA)*

Multimedia HCI and Quality of Experience: Bart Thomee *(Yahoo, USA)*

Music, Speech and Audio Processing in Multimedia: Ye Wang *(National University of Singapore, Singapore)*

Multimedia Authoring and Enrichment: Pablo Cesar *(CWI, The Netherlands)*

Deep Learning for Multimedia: Greg Corrado *(Google, USA)*
Ming Yang *(Facebook, USA)*

Multimodal Analysis and Description: Mohan S. Kankanhalli *(National University of Singapore, Singapore)*
Xian-Sheng Hua *(Microsoft Research, USA)*
Qiong Liu *(FXPAL, USA)*
Guo-Jun Qi *(University of Central Florida, USA)*
Benoit Huet *(Eurecom, France)*

Multimedia and Vision: Nicu Sebe *(University of Trento, Italy)*
Gang Hua *(Stevens Institute of Technology, USA)*
Yaser Sheikh *(CMU, USA)*
Meng Wang *(Hefei Institute of Technology, China)*
Cees G. M. Snoek *(University of Amsterdam & Qualcomm Research Netherlands, The Netherlands)*

Multimedia Art, Entertainment and Culture: James Z. Wang *(Pennsylvania State University, USA)*
Vincent Oria *(New Jersey Institute of Technology, USA)*

Multimedia Search and Recommendation: John R. Smith *(IBM, USA)*
Jingdong Wang *(Microsoft Research Asia, China)*
Phoebe Chen *(University of Latrobe, Australia)*
Chunhua Shen *(Adelaide University, Australia)*
Zi Huang *(University of Queensland, Australia)*

Social Multimedia: Mei Tao *(Microsoft Research Asia, China)*
Peng Cui *(Tsinghua University, China)*

Emotional and Social Signals In Multimedia: Hayley Hung *(Technical University of Delft, The Netherlands)*
Hatice Gunes *(Queen Mary University of London, UK)*
Mohammad Soleymani *(University of Geneva, Switzerland)*
Emily Mower Provost *(University of Michigan, USA)*

MM 2015 Program Committee

Lyndon Kennedy
Maha Abdallah
Marc Cavazza
Marcel Worring
Marcio Ferreira Moreno
Marco Cristani
Maria da Graca Campo Pimentel
Maria-Luisa Sapino
Marianna Obrist
Mario Montagud
Mark Cartwright
Mark Claypool
Mark Hasegawa-Johnson
Mark Liao
Marko Tkalcic
Markus Schedl
Martha Larson
Marwin Schmitt
Massimo Piccardi
Mathew Magimai Doss
Mathias Lux
Matt Cooper
Maurizio Mancini
Meihui Zhang
Meng Wang
Michael Gurevich
Michel Valstar
Michele Merler
Ming Li
Ming Yang
Mingkui Tan
Mingli Song
Mingsong Dou
Mohamed Chetouani
Mohamed Hefeeda
Mohammad Soleymani
Mohan S. Kankanhalli
Mu Qiao
Munmun De Choudhury
Nabil Sarhan
Nadia Berthouze
Nicholas Race
Nicu Sebe
Niloo Dezfuli
Nitendra Rajput
Noel C. F. Codella
Oliver Nina
Omar Niamut
Oya Celiktutan
Pablo Cesar
Pål Halvorsen
Paris Smaragdis
Pascal Mettes
Patrick Lucey
Pavel Korshunov
Pei-Yu Chi
Peng Cui
Peng Wang
Peter Bajcsy
Peter Carr
Peter Grosche
Philipp Fechteler
Phoebe Chen
Pinar Duygulu Sahin
Preeti Rao
Qi Wang
Qiong Liu
Ram Vasudevan
Raoul Rivas
Raphael Troncy
Raymond Fu
Reid Porter
Remi Trichet
Rene Kaiser
Richang Hong
Rodrigo Laiola Guimarães
Roger Zimmermann
Ronald Poppe
Rongrong Ji
Rufael N. Mekuria
Saad Ali
Sabina Barakovic
Salman Khokhar
Samira Ebrahimi Kahou
Sean Banerjee
Shang-Hong Lai
Shannon Chen
Shervin Shirmohammadi
Shiguang Shan
Shih-Fu Chang
Shin'ichi Satoh
Shoou-I Yu
Shu Shi
Si Liu
Sileye Ba
Songqing Chen
Sorin Hermon
Stavros Petridis
Stefanos Vrochidis
Stefanos Zafeiriou
Stephan Kopf
Stevan Rudinac
Steven Hoi
Surender Chandra
Susanne Boll
Suzanne Little
Symeon Papadopoulos
Tao Mei
Tat-Jen Cham
Teresa Chambel
Thomas Mensink
Thomas Steiner
Tiago Falk
Tim Althoff
Ting Yu
Tobias Hossfeld
Touradj Ebrahimi
Ulrich Engelke
Vasileios Mezaris
Vincent Oria
Vittorio Baroncini
Wanmin Wu
Wei Liu
Wei Tong
Wei Tsang Ooi
Wei Wang
Wengang Zhou
Wen-Hsiao Peng
Wen-Huang Cheng
Winston H. Hsu
Wolfgang Huerst
Wu-Chi Feng
Xi Li
Xiangyang Xue
Xian-Sheng Hua
Xiaofei He
Xiaofeng Zhu
Xiaoqiang Lu
Xinbo Gao
Xin-Jing Wang
Xinmei Tian
Xin-shun Xu
Xirong Li
Xubo Yang
Xueliang Liu
Xuelong Li
Yadong Mu
Yahong Han
Yan Tong
Yan Yan
Yang Yang
Yannis Kalantidis
Yanwei Pang
Yan-Ying Chen
Yao Hu
Yao Liu
Yao Zhao
Yaser Sheikh
Yashar Moshfeghi
Ye Wang
Yelin Kim
Yi Li
Yi Yang
Yiannis Kompatsiaris
Yi-Hsuan Yang
Yonggang Wen
Yoshiharu Ishikawa
Yue Ming
Yu-Gang Jiang
Yu-Hsun Lin
Zan Gao
Zheng Liu
Zheng-Jun Zha
Zhenxing Niu
Zhenyang Li
Zhenzhong Lan
Zhifeng Li
Zhigang Ma
Zhiyong Wang
Zhongfei Zhang
Zhu Liu
Zi Huang
Zixia Huang
Zuofu Cheng

MM 2015 Grand Challenge Program Committee

Chairs: Michael Lew *(Leiden University, The Netherlands)*
Jie Yang *(National Science Foundation, USA)*

Program Committee: **IBM – New York City 360°**
John Smith *(IBM, USA)*
Liangliang Cao *(IBM,USA)*
Michele Merler *(IBM, USA)*
Yuan-Chi Chang *(IBM,USA)*

Microsoft – MSR-Bing Image Retrieval Challenge
Hongzhi Li *(Columbia University, USA)*
Yuxiao Hu *(Microsoft, USA)*
Zhangyang Wang *(UIUC, USA)*

Yahoo – Yahoo-Flickr Event Summarization Challenge
Adrian Popescu *(CEA-LIST, France)*
Bart Thomee *(Yahoo Labs, USA)*
Bogdan Ionescu *(LAPI, University Politehnica of Bucharest, Romania)*
Debanjan Mahata *(University of Arkansas at Little Rock, USA)*
Raphael Troncy *(Eurecom, France)*
Vasileios Mezaris *(CERTH-ITI, Greece)*

MM 2015 Doctoral Symposium Program Committee

Chairs: Cees G. M. Snoek *(University of Amsterdam & Qualcomm Research Netherlands, The Netherlands)*
Hervé Jégou *(Facebook AI Research, France)*

Program Committee: Relja Arandjelovic *(Inria, France)*
Susanne Boll *(University of Oldenburg, Germany)*
Dick C.A. Bulterman *(FXPAL, USA)*
Shih-Fu Chang *(Columbia University, USA)*
Tat-Seng Chua *(National University of Singapore, Singapore)*
Alan Hanjalic *(Delft University of Technology, The Netherlands)*
Xian-Sheng Hua *(Alibaba Group, China)*
Alexis Joly *(Inria, France)*
Thomas Mensink *(University of Amsterdam, The Netherlands)*
Bernard Merialdo *(Eurecom, France)*
Dinh Phung *(Deakin University, Australia)*
Georges Quénot *(Laboratory of Informatics of Grenoble, France)*
Miriam Redi *(Yahoo! Research, UK)*
Shin'ichi Satoh *(NII, Japan)*
Ronan Sicre *(Inria, France)*
Giorgos Tolias *(Inria, France)*
Lexing Xie *(Australian National University, Australia)*

MM 2015 Technical Demos Program Committee

Chairs: Alejandro Jaimes *(Yahoo!, Spain)*
Zheng-Jun Zha *(Hefei Institute of Intelligent Machines, Chinese Academy of Sciences)*

Program Committee: Marco Beritini *(ESADE, Spain)*
Junjie Cai *(University of Texas at San Antonio, USA)*
Yang Cao *(University of Science and Technology of China, China)*
Shu-Ching Chen *(Florida International University, USA)*
Jian Chen *(Institute of Automation, CAS, China)*
Wen-Huang Cheng *(Academia SINICA, Taiwan)*
Cheng Deng *(Xidian University, China)*
Lu Fang *(University of Science and Technology of China, China)*
Alex Hauptman *(Carnegie-Mellon University, USA)*
Steven Hoi *(Singapore Management University, Singapore)*
Wolfgang Hurst *(Utrecht University, Netherlands)*
Ichiro Ide *(Nagoya University, Japan)*
Alejandro Jaimes *(Yahoo!, USA)*
Yannis Kalantidis *(Yahoo!, USA)*
Yiannis Kompatsiaris *(Informatics and Telematics Institute, Greece)*
Hyowon Lee *(Singapore University of Technology and Design, Singapore)*
Liang Li *(University of Chinese Academy of Sciences, China)*
Dong Liu *(University of Science and Technology of China, China)*
Vasileios Mezaris *(CERTH-ITI, Greece)*
Bingbing Ni *(Advanced Digital Sciences Center, Singapore)*
Naoko Nitta *(Osaka University, Japan)*
Vincent Oria *(New Jersey Institute of Technology, USA)*
Stefan Rueger *(The Open University, UK)*
Jitao Sang *(Institute of Automation, CAS, China)*
Shin'ichi Satoh *(National Institute of Informatics, Japan)*
Klaus Schoeffmann *(Klagenfurt University, Austria)*
Xinmei Tian *(University of Science and Technology of China, China)*
Changhu Wang *(Microsoft Research Asia, China)*
Qi Wang *(Northwestern Polytechnical University, China)*
Jinqiao Wang *(Institute of Automation, CAS, China)*
Xiangyu Wang *(Institute for Infocomm Research, Singapore)*
Zilei Wang *(University of Science and Technology of China, China)*
Marcel Worring *(University of Amsterdam, Netherlands)*
Yang Yang *(University of Electronic Science and Technology of China)*
Kuiyuan Yang *(Microsoft Research Asia, China)*
Xin Yang *(Huazhong University of Science and Technology, China)*

Program Committee (continued):

Ting Yao *(Microsoft Research Asia, China)*
Zheng-Jun Zha *(Hefei Institute of Intelligent Machines, CAS, China)*
Hanwang Zhang *(National University of Singapore, Singapore)*
Shiliang Zhang *(Beijing University, China)*
Yan-Tao Zheng *(Snapchat Inc., USA)*
Wengang Zhou *(University of Science and Technology of China, China)*
Roger Zimmermann *(National University of Singapore, Singapore)*

MM 2015 Open Source Software Competition Organization Committee

Chairs: Marco Bertini *(University of Florence, Italy)*
Xian-Sheng Hua *(Alibaba, China)*
Tao Mei *(Microsoft Research Asia, China)*

Program Committee: Andreas Girgensohn *(FXPAL, USA)*
Anthony Vetro *(Mitsubishi Electric Research Laboratories, USA)*
Samson Cheung *(University of Kentucky, USA)*
Steven Hoi *(Singapore Management University, Singapore)*
Peng Cui *(Tsinghua University, China)*
Chia-Wen Lin *(National Tsing Hua University, Taiwan)*
Dan Ellis *(Columbia University, USA)*
Meng Wang *(Hefei University of Technology, China)*
Junfeng He *(Facebook, USA)*
Ichiro Ide *(Nagoya University, Japan)*
Yangqing Jia *(Google, USA)*
Jingdong Wang *(Microsoft Research Asia, China)*
Rongrong Ji *(Xiamen University, China)*
Kuiyuan Yang *(Microsoft Research Asia, China)*
Lei Zhang *(Microsoft Research, USA)*
Liangliang Cao *(Yahoo! Labs, USA)*
Qiong Liu *(FXPAL,USA)*
Marco Bertini *(University of Florence, Italy)*
Ioannis Pitas *(University of Thessaloniki, Greece)*
Kuan-Ta Chen *(Academia Sinica, Taiwan)*
Kwang-Ting (Tim) Cheng *(University of California, Santa Barbara, USA)*
Vicky Zhao *(University of Alberta, Canada)*
Winston Hsu *(National Taiwan University, Taiwan)*
Lynn Wilcox *(FXPAL, USA)*
Xiaoyan Sun *(Microsoft Research Asia, China)*
Yan-Yin Chen *(FXPAL, USA)*
Yi Yang *(University of Technology, Sydney, Australia)*
Yimin Zhang *(Intel, China)*
Yu-Gang Jiang *(Fudan University, China)*
Zhou Wang *(University of Waterloo, Canada)*

MM 2015 Brave New Idea Organization Committee

Chairs: Yong Rui *(Microsoft Research Asia, China)*
Nicu Sebe *(University of Trento, Italy)*
Xuelong Li *(OPTical IMagery Analysis and Learning (OPTIMAL), China)*

Program Committee: Abdulmotaleb El Saddik *(University of Ottawa, Canada)*
Benoit Huet *(Eurecom, France)*
Bo Du *(Wuhan University, China)*
Bo Luo *(University of Kansas, USA)*
Bruno Lepri *(FBK, Italy)*
Cha Zhang *(Microsoft Research, USA)*
Cheng Deng *(Xidian University, China)*
Chong-Wah Ngo *(Hong Kong University of Science & Technology, Hong Kong)*
Dong Liu *(Columbia University, USA)*
Gene Cheung *(National Institute of Informatics, Japan)*
Gerald Friedland *(International Computer Science Institute, USA)*
Jacopo Staiano *(UPMC-Sorbonne Universitees, France)*
Jian Zhang *(University of Technology Sydney, Australia)*
Jianfei Cai *(Nanyang Technological University, Singapore)*
Jiebo Luo *(University of Rochester, USA)*
Kaiqi Huang *(Chinese Academy of Sciences, China)*
Kuan-Ta Chen *(Academia Sinica, Taiwan)*
Lei Zhang *(Microsoft Research Asia, China)*
Lexing Xie *(Australian National University, Australia)*
Ling Shao *(Northumbria University, UK)*
Lyndon Kennedy *(Yahoo Labs, USA)*
Marco Cristani *(University of Verona, Italy)*
Martha Larson *(TU Delft, Netherlands)*
Mohammad Soleymani *(University of Geneva, Switzerland)*
Munmun De Choudhury *(Georgia Tech, USA)*
Nannan Wang *(Xidian University, China)*
Peng Cui *(Tsinghua University, China)*
Ramanathan Subramanian *(Advanced Digital Sciences Center, Singapore)*
Raymond Fu *(Northeastern University, USA)*
Shin'ichi Satoh *(National Institute of Informatics, Japan)*
Stefan Winkler *(Advanced Digital Sciences Center, Singapore)*
Tao Mei *(Microsoft Research Asia, China)*
Ting Yao *(Microsoft Research Asia, China)*
Vasileios Mezaris *(CERTH-ITI, Greece)*
Winston Hsu *(National Taiwan University, Taiwan)*
Xian-Sheng Hua *(Microsoft Research, USA)*
Xiaogang Wang *(The Chinese University of Hong Kong, Hong Kong)*
Xing Xie *(Microsoft Research Asia, China)*
Yi Yang *(University of Technology Sydney, Australia)*
Yongsheng Dong *(Chinese Academy of Sciences, China)*

MM 2015 Sponsor & Supporters

Sponsor:

Gold Supporters:

Silver Supporters:

Bronze Supporters:

HUAWEI

IBM Research

Microsoft Research

htc quietly brilliant

facebook

YAHOO! LABS

Supporter:

cisra

ACM SIGMM/TOMM 2015
Award Announcements

The ACM Special Interest Group in Multimedia (SIGMM) and ACM Transactions on Multimedia Computing, Communications and Applications (TOMM) are pleased to announce the following awards for 2015 recognizing outstanding achievements and services made in the multimedia community.

SIGMM Technical Achievement Award
Dr. Tat-Seng Chua, National University of Singapore

SIGMM Rising Star Award
Dr. Yu-Gang Jiang, Fudan University

SIGMM Best Ph.D. Thesis Award
Dr. Ting Yao, City University of Hong Kong (currently Microsoft Research)

TOMM Nicolas D. Georganas Best Paper Award
"A Quality of Experience Model for Haptic Virtual Environments" by Abdelwahab Hamam, Abdulmotaleb El Saddik, and Jihad Alja'am, published in TOMM, Vol. 10, Issue 3, 2014

TOMM Best Associate Editor Award
Dr. Pradeep K. Atrey, State University of New York, Albany

Additional information of each award and recipient is available: http://www.sigmm.org/

Awards will be presented in the annual SIGMM event, ACM Multimedia Conference, held in Brisbane, Australia during October 26-30, 2015.

ACM is the professional society of computer scientists, and SIGMM is the special interest group on multimedia. TOMCCAP is the flagship journal publication of SIGMM.

ACM Multimedia 2016

Photo (cc) by Benutzer:AlterVista

The 24th ACM International Conference on Multimedia
October 15-19, 2016 Amsterdam, The Netherlands

About ACM Multimedia 2016

Since the founding of ACM SIGMM in 1993, ACM Multimedia has been the worldwide premier conference and a key world event to display scientific achievements and innovative industrial products in the multimedia field. At ACM Multimedia 2016, we will celebrate its twenty-forth iteration with an extensive program consisting of technical sessions covering all aspects of the multimedia field in forms of oral and poster presentations, tutorials, panels, exhibits, demonstrations and workshops, bringing into focus the principal subjects of investigation, competitions of research teams on challenging problems, and also an interactive art program stimulating artists and computer scientists to meet and discover together the frontiers of artistic communication. Details and updates will be published on the conference's website: www.acmmm.org/2016.

Call for Contributions

ACM Multimedia 2016 solicits submissions of contributions for the following programs (partial list, please visit the website for details):

- Regular scientific papers
- Brave new idea papers
- Interactive art exhibition
- Open source software competition
- Multimedia grand challenge competition
- Tutorials
- Panels
- Doctoral symposium
- Technical demonstrations
- Workshops

Important Dates

The dates for submissions to the abovementioned contribution categories and other key dates will be provided on the conference website. Please check the website frequently for the latest news and updates.

Conference Location – Amsterdam, The Netherlands

The conference will be held at the *Tuschinski Theater* in Amsterdam, a beautiful 1921 historic building in Jugendstil style. Amsterdam is a renowned tourist destination with its famous canals, museums and relaxed atmosphere. It has optimal accessibility by plane from almost everywhere in the world. It also has a very extensive public transport system, although the city center is small enough to make walking a rewarding experience.

Accommodation caters for any budget from 5 star hotels to youth hostels all in close vicinity of the conference venue. Amsterdam is in the top-5 of creative hotspots in the world and is hosting the head offices for leading international companies such as Philips, Booking.com and TomTom.

Photo (cc) by AAron Metcalfe

ACMmultimedia XXX 2016

Association for Computing Machinery

SIGMM

Harnessing Big Personal Data, with Scrutable User Modelling for Privacy and Control

Judy Kay
Human Centred Technology Cluster, The University of Sydney
Sydney, Australia
Judy.Kay@sydney.edu.au

ABSTRACT

My work aims to enable people to harness, control and manage their big personal data. This is challenging because people are generating vast, and growing, collections of personal data. That data is captured by a rich personal digital ecosystems of devices, some worn or carried, and others are fixed or embedded in the environment. Users explicitly store some data but systems also capture the user's digital footprints, ranging from simple clicks and touches, to images, audio and video. This personal data resides in a quite bewildering range of places, from personal devices to cloud stores, in multitudes of silos.

Big personal data differs from the scientific big data in important ways. Because it is personal, it should be handled in ways that enable people to ensure it is managed and used as they wish. It may be of modest size compared with scientific big data, but people consider their data stores as big, because they are complex and hard to manage.

A driving goal for my research has been to tackle the challenges of big personal data by creating infrastructures, representations and interfaces that enable a user to scrutinize and control their personal data in a scrutable user model.

One important role for users models is personalisation, where the user model is a dynamic set of evidence-based beliefs about the user. This is the foundation for personalization, ranging from recommenders to teaching systems. User models may represent anything from the user's attributes to their knowledge, beliefs, goals, plans and preferences. Some user modeling evidence comes directly from the user; for example, people typically provide dating sites with rich (if not entirely accurate) descriptions of themselves and about the people they believe that would like. Much commercial user modeling evidence comes from observing the user; for example, a personalized teaching system observes the learner's interactions, as they use learning resources and tackle problem and from this data the system infers what the learner knows. Typically, a user model refines raw data about the user and combines it with other knowledge. For example, teaching systems make use of a knowledge model of the domain and recommenders use collaborative filters based on user models of many people. A scrutable user model is designed to enable people to scrutinize their own user model, the processes used to form it and the ways that it is used.

A second important role for the user model is as an independent first class citizen; user models can be valuable in their own right, independently of whether they are used by any personalised system. Such user models have the potential to support diverse forms of learning. This is because they can mirror salient aspects of the user over the long term, and when there is a suitable interface to these models, they can provide a valuable resource. In education, this is described in terms of important self-regulated learning processes, such as reflection, self-monitoring and planning. Some broader uses are central to the Quantified Self movement.

The talk presents a series of four linked case studies of my work:

1. Infrastructures for scrutable user modeling that are designed to people to determine what it in the user model and how it is collected, used, managed and forgotten [3, 1];
2. Open Learner Models [2] that can be independent or within personalized teaching systems and MOOCs [4];
3. Harnessing personal data to tackle the Sisyphean challenge of lifelong self-regulated activity needed for health and wellness;
4. Harnessing rich streams of depth images, video, audio, touch using surface computing to create collaboration technologies that support collaborative learning [5].

MM'15, October 26–30, 2015, Brisbane, Australia.
ACM 978-1-4503-3459-4/15/10.
DOI: http://dx.doi.org/10.1145/2733373.2806280.

Categories and Subject Descriptors

H.1.2 [**User/Machine Systems**]: Human factors; H.3.4 [**Systems and Software**]: User profiles and alert services

General Terms

User model; user modelling; personalisation; user control; privacy

1. SPEAKER BIO

Judy Kay is Professor of Computer Science. She leads the multi-disciplinary Human Centred Technology Research Cluster, based in the Faculty of Engineering and Information Technologies at the University of Sydney, Australia. Her own lab, CHAI (Computer Human Adapted Interaction) aims to create new technologies for human computer interaction (HCI). Her personalisation research has created the Personis user modelling framework. This is a unified mechanism for keeping and managing people's long-term personal data from diverse sources. This is the foundation for building personalised systems. Personis models are distinctive in that they were designed to be scrutable, because interfaces enable the user to scrutinise their user model and personalisation processes based on it. In learning contexts, she has created interfaces for Open Learner Models that make this personal data available in useful forms for long-term learning and self-monitoring. In other recent interface research, her team has created the Cruiser Natural User Interaction (NIU) software framework. This provides new ways for people to make use of large interactive tabletops and wall displays. By mining the digital footprints of such interaction, this research is creating new ways for people to learn to collaborate, and to learn and work more collaboratively.

She has extensive publications in venues such as the conferences Ubicomp, Pervasive, Computer Human Interaction (CHI), Interactive Tabletops and Surfaces User Modeling (UM, AH, UMAP), AIED and journals, such as IEEE Transactions on Knowledge and Data Engineering, International Journal of Artificial Intelligence in Education (IJAIED), User Modeling and User-Adapted Interaction (UMUAI), IEEE Transactions on Learning Technologies (IEEE TLT), Personal and Ubiquitous Computing, Communications of the ACM, Computer Science Education.

2. REFERENCES

[1] D. Barua, J. Kay, B. Kummerfeld, and C. Paris. Theoretical foundations for user-controlled forgetting in scrutable long term user models. In *Proceedings of the 23rd Australian Computer-Human Interaction Conference*, pages 40–49. ACM, 2011.

[2] S. Bull and J. Kay. Open learner models as drivers for metacognitive processes. In *International Handbook of Metacognition and Learning Technologies*, pages 349–365. Springer, 2013.

[3] J. Kay and B. Kummerfeld. Creating personalized systems that people can scrutinize and control: Drivers, principles and experience. *ACM Transactions on Interactive Intelligent Systems (TiiS)*, 2(4):24, 2012.

[4] J. Kay, P. Reimann, E. Diebold, and B. Kummerfeld. MOOCs: So Many Learners, So Much Potential... *IEEE Intelligent Systems*, (3):70–77, 2013.

[5] R. Martinez-Maldonado, A. Clayphan, K. Yacef, and J. Kay. MTFeedback: Providing Notifications to Enhance Teacher Awareness of Small Group Work in the Classroom. *IEEE Transactions on Learning Technologies*, 8(2):187–200, April–June 2015.

Vision-enhanced Immersive Interaction and Remote Collaboration with Large Touch Displays

Zhengyou Zhang
Microsoft Research, Redmond, WA, USA
zhang@microsoft.com

ABSTRACT

Large displays are becoming commodity, and more and more, they are touch-enabled. In this keynote, we describe a system called *ViiBoard* (Vision-enhanced Immersive Interaction with touch Board) that enables natural interaction and immersive remote collaboration with large touch displays by adding a commodity color plus depth sensor. It consists of two parts.

The first part is called *VTouch* that augments touch input with visual understanding of the user to improve interaction with a large touch-sensitive display such as Microsoft Surface Hub. An RGBD sensor such as Microsoft Kinect adds the visual modality and enables new interactions beyond touch. Through visual analysis, the system understands where the user is, who the user is, and what the user is doing even before the user touches the display. Such information is used to enhance interaction in multiple ways. For example, a user can use simple gestures to bring up menu items such as color palette and soft keyboard; menu items can be shown where the user is and can follow the user; hovering can show information to the user before the user commits to touch; the user can perform different functions (for example writing and erasing) with different hands; and the user's preference profile can be maintained, distinct from other users. User studies are conducted and the users very much appreciate the value of these and other enhanced interactions.

The second part is called *ImmerseBoard.* ImmerseBoard is a system for remote collaboration through a digital whiteboard that gives participants a 3D immersive experience, enabled by an RGBD sensor mounted on the side of a large touch display (the same setup as in VTouch). Using 3D processing of the depth images, life-sized rendering, and novel visualizations, ImmerseBoard emulates writing side-by-side on a physical whiteboard, or alternatively on a mirror. User studies involving three tasks show that compared to standard video conferencing with a digital whiteboard, ImmerseBoard provides participants with a quantitatively better ability to estimate their remote partners' eye gaze direction, gesture direction, intention, and level of agreement. Moreover, these quantitative capabilities translate qualitatively into a heightened sense of being together and a more enjoyable experience. ImmerseBoard's form factor is suitable for practical and easy installation in homes and offices.

MM 2015, October 26-30, 2015, Brisbane, Australia.
ACM 978-1-4503-3459-4/15/10.
DOI: http://dx.doi.org/10.1145/2733373.2817845

Categories and Subject Descriptors

H.1.2 [User/Machine Systems]: Human factors; H.4.3 [[Information Systems]: Communications Applications; H.5.1 [Information Systems]: Multimedia Information Systems; I.2.10 [Computing Methodologies]: Vision and Scene Understanding

Keywords

Computer-Supported Cooperative Work; Telepresence; Videoconferencing; Tele-immersion; Natural interaction; Immersive Collaboration; Computer Vision; Interactive whiteboard

BIO

Zhengyou Zhang received the B.S. degree in electronic engineering from Zhejiang University, Hangzhou, China, in 1985, the M.S. degree in computer science from the University of Nancy, Nancy, France, in 1987, and the Ph.D. degree in computer science and the Doctorate of Science (Habilitation à diriger des recherches) from the University of Paris XI, Paris, France, in 1990 and 1994, respectively.

He is a Principal Researcher with Microsoft Research, Redmond, WA, USA, and the Research Manager of the "Multimedia, Interaction, and Experiences" group. Before joining Microsoft Research in March 1998, he was a Senior Research Scientist with INRIA (French National Institute for Research in Computer Science and Control), France. In 1996-1997, he spent a one-year sabbatical as an Invited Researcher with the Advanced Telecommunications Research Institute International (ATR), Kyoto, Japan. He has published over 200 papers in refereed international journals and conferences, and has coauthored the following books: 3-D Dynamic Scene Analysis: A Stereo Based Approach (Springer-Verlag, 1992); Epipolar Geometry in Stereo, Motion and Object Recognition (Kluwer, 1996); Computer Vision (Chinese Academy of Sciences, 1998, 2003, in Chinese); Face Detection and Adaptation (Morgan and Claypool, 2010), and Face Geometry and Appearance Modeling (Cambridge University Press, 2011). He is an inventor of more than 100 issued patents. He has given a number of keynotes in international conferences and invited talks in universities.

Dr. Zhang is an IEEE Fellow and an ACM Fellow. He is the Founding Editor-in-Chief of the IEEE Transactions on Autonomous Mental Development, and has served on the editorial board of IEEE TPAMI, IEEE TCSVT, IEEE TMM, IJCV, IJPRAI, MVA, among others. He has served as a program chair, a general chair, and a program committee member for numerous international conferences in the areas of computer vision, audio and speech signal processing, multimedia, human-computer interaction, and autonomous mental development. He is serving as a General Chair of International Conference on Multimodal Interaction (ICMI) 2015, and a General Chair of IEEE Conference on Computer Vision and Pattern Recognition (CVPR) 2017. He received the IEEE Helmholtz Test of Time Award at ICCV 2013 for his paper published in 1999 on camera calibration, now known as Zhang's method.

REFERENCES

1. Y. Chen, Z. Liu, P.A. Chou, and Z. Zhang, "Vtouch: Vision-Enhanced Interaction for Large Touch Displays", in *Proc. IEEE International Conference On Multimedia And Expo* (ICME 2015), Torino, Italy, June 29 - July 3, 2015.
2. K. Higuchi, Y. Chen, P.A. Chou, Z. Zhang, and Z. Liu, "ImmerseBoard: Immersive Telepresence Experience Using a Digital Whiteboard", in *Proc. the 33rd Annual ACM Conference on Human Factors in Computing Systems* (ACM CHI 2015), pages 2383-2392, Seoul, Korea, April 18-23, 2015.

Analyzing Free-standing Conversational Groups: A Multimodal Approach

Xavier Alameda-Pineda
University of Trento
Trento, Italy
xavier.alamedapineda@unitn.it

Yan Yan
Univ. of Trento / ADSC, UIUC
Trento, Italy / Singapore
yan.yan@unitn.it

Elisa Ricci
FBK / Univ. of Perugia
Trento, Italy / Perugia, Italy
eliricci@fbk.eu

Oswald Lanz
Fondazione Bruno Kessler
Trento, Italy
lanz@fbk.eu

Nicu Sebe
University of Trento
Trento, Italy
sebe@disi.unitn.it

ABSTRACT

During natural social gatherings, humans tend to organize themselves in the so-called free-standing conversational groups. In this context, robust head and body pose estimates can facilitate the higher-level description of the ongoing interplay. Importantly, visual information typically obtained with a distributed camera network might not suffice to achieve the robustness sought. In this line of thought, recent advances in wearable sensing technology open the door to multimodal and richer information flows. In this paper we propose to cast the head and body pose estimation problem into a matrix completion task. We introduce a framework able to fuse multimodal data emanating from a combination of distributed and wearable sensors, taking into account the temporal consistency, the head/body coupling and the noise inherent to the scenario. We report results on the novel and challenging SALSA dataset, containing visual, auditory and infrared recordings of 18 people interacting in a regular indoor environment. We demonstrate the soundness of the proposed method and the usability for higher-level tasks such as the detection of F-formations and the discovery of social attention attractors.

1. INTRODUCTION

Several wearable sensing devices became available for the general public in the past few years. Often, such consumer platforms include several sensors, *e.g.* microphone, accelerometer or blue-tooth. Investigating methods to process the data gathered with wearable devices is worthwhile for many reasons. First of all, considering that modern consumer platforms, such as smart-phones or smart-watches, are at the reach of the general public, many are already using them for data acquisition. Second, these platforms are inherently multimodal, thus they provide a rich description of the environment. Third, since these devices are easy-to-wear, the continuous flow of information emanating from them is a precious resource to study casual situations of the real life, far from laboratory-controlled conditions.

MM'15, October 26–30, 2015, Brisbane, Australia.
 ISBN 978-1-4503-3459-4/15/10 ...$15.00.
DOI: http://dx.doi.org/10.1145/2733373.2806238.

Figure 1: People interacting naturally organized in free-standing conversational groups during a poster session. The social interplay is captured by a distributed camera network and by sociometric badges worn by each participant (small white boxes).

Importantly, wearable technologies are complementary to distributed sensor networks. For example, when analyzing social interactions, wearable sensing devices can be exploited *inter alia* to localize people and to roughly estimate their activities. However, a fine-grained analysis of the social scene requires additional information gathered with alternative distributed sensing networks, *e.g.* visual data [29]. Developing methods that robustly fuse data from wearable devices and distributed networks remains largely unexplored, and many challenges arise in this context. As with any consumer device, data gathered with wearable technology are corrupted by severe noise. Therefore, unimodal approaches fail to provide a robust and accurate representation of the environment and smart multimodal fusion strategies need to be developed [27]. Moreover, these strategies should also account for the specificities of the combination of a distributed sensor network and the wearable technology.

The focus of this research study is the analysis of spontaneous social interactions in natural indoor environments, see Figure 1. In such social events, human beings tend to

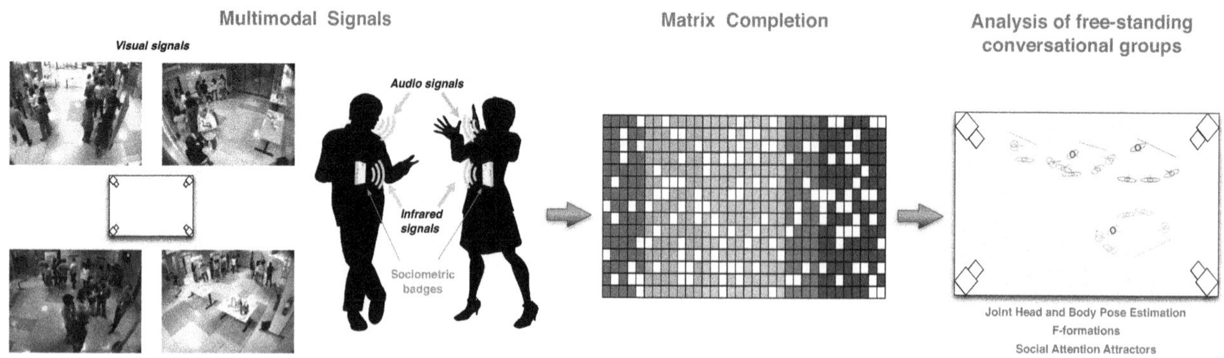

Figure 2: Overview of the proposed approach for detection of attentional patterns. The scene is captured by a distributed camera network and sociometric badges worn by each participant. The estimation of the head and body poses, required to further extract F-formations and social attention attractors, is cast into a matrix completion problem. The HBPE are used to provide a higher-level description of the social interplay.

organize themselves in free-standing conversational groups (FCGs). Contrary to the staticity proper to round-table meetings, FCGs are dynamic by nature (they increase and decrease in size, move and split) and therefore their analysis is inherently difficult [11, 33]. In this context, robust human pose estimates can ease the further mining of higher-level descriptions, such as F-formations or attentional patterns. In this paper we are expressly interested in analyzing FCGs using head and body pose estimates obtained through the processing of the multimodal flow of data emanating from a distributed camera network and sociometric badges [10] worn by each participant.

Providing a complete description of the human pose (positions of the limbs) is chimeric in video surveillance settings, *i.e.* when people are monitored with distant and large field-of-view cameras. Indeed, the low-resolution images and the numerous occlusions have a relentless negative effect on current approaches. Fortunately, the head and body pose can be used as a surrogate of the full pose when analyzing free-standing conversational groups. Indeed, *all* features delineating group social interplays, are often extracted from head and body pose estimates (HBPE). More precisely, accurate and robust HBPEs are the prelude to detect face-to-face interactions, identify the potential addressee and addresser, describe the geometric structure of the group (or F-formation) and recognize personality traits. Many research studies focused on HBPE from visual data in the recent past, and demonstrated the synergistic effect of joint head and body pose estimation, when compared to independent estimation [9]. Furthermore, as previously discussed, wearable sensing devices provide a complementary source of information to the surveillance distributed camera network. Nowadays, up to the authors' knowledge, there are no existing research studies that address the challenging task of head and body pose estimation in crowded indoor environments using multimodal data gathered with a combination of distributed visual sensors and wearable devices.

In this paper we propose to integrate multimodal signals acquired in regular indoor environments to robustly extract HBPE of several people naturally arranged in FCG. More precisely, we use auditory and proximity (infrared) information to automatically label visual features of head and body respectively. All this information, together with the visual features extracted from the surveillance camera network, are pulled together into a linear classification problem. Seeking for the non-available labels, *i.e.* estimating the head and body pose of all people, is cast into a matrix completion problem. Within this framework, the joint head and body pose estimation adds an additional coupling term to the formulation. Similarly, the temporal structure inherent to the problem is induced by means of a Laplacian matrix that regularizes the matrix completion task. The resulting HBPE are then used to infer the F-formations and to further retrieve the social attention attractors. Figure 2 shows an overview of the proposed approach.

The main contributions of this study are: (i) address multimodal HBPE within the analysis of FCGs (ii) propose a framework versatile enough to handle not only data coming from different modalities, but also to process features extracted with both wearable sensors and a distributed camera network (iii) cast HBPE into a matrix completion problem, accounting for the noisy multimodal labels, and the inherent temporal structure of the head and body poses (iv) induce joint HBPE by coupling the two incomplete matrices (v) derive a novel optimization approach to solve for the matrix completion task and (vi) conduct an extensive evaluation of the proposed method on the novel SALSA dataset, showing the usability of the HBPE for detecting F-formations and discovering social attention attractors.

The rest of the paper is structured as follows. Related approaches for head and body pose estimation are discussed in the next section. The proposed matrix completion model, accounting for noise, temporal regularization and joint head and body pose estimation is presented in Section 3, together with the associated optimization algorithm. Extensive evaluations of the proposed approach, and comparisons with the state of the art are reported in Section 4, before concluding and delineating future research directions in Section 5.

2. RELATED WORK

The applicative context of the present study is the multimodal analysis of social interactions in informal gatherings. Special focus is given to the estimation of the head and body pose, easing the automatic study of free-standing conversational groups. Moreover, the proposed solution is based on a matrix completion framework.

2.1 Multimodal analysis of social interactions

Combining data from heterogeneous modalities is of utmost importance for understanding human behaviors [36]. Approaches relying on audio-visual cues are probably the most popular and successful examples [18, 30, 37, 1]. In

[18], the role of non-verbal cues for the automatic analysis of face-to-face social interactions is investigated. Social interactions in political debates are studied in [37]. A multimodal approach for detecting laughter episodes from audio-visual data and a novel dataset for studying this problem are introduced in [30]. In the last few years, mobile and wearable devices opened novel opportunities for multimodal analysis of social interactions [6, 16, 15, 28]. In [15] a probabilistic approach is proposed to automatically discover interaction types from large-scale dyadic data (*e.g.* proximity blue-tooth data, phone call network or email network). In [28] social interactions on a small spatio-temporal scale combining proximity data and accelerometers are analyzed.

On the one hand, traditional distributed camera and microphone networks are able to capture subtle features of human behavior, but their performance drops significantly when dealing with a crowded scene. On the other hand, wearable devices permit the ubiquitous localization of people for a long time span, as they typically embed proximity sensors, but they fail to provide accurate and detailed descriptions of the ongoing interplay. Therefore, it is obvious that the nuances and the complexity of social interactions require leveraging information from both wearable and traditional sensors. This paper develops from this intuition and, to our knowledge, it is the first work jointly employing sociometric badges and external cameras for HBPE.

2.2 Head and body pose estimation

As already outlined, the analysis of the human behavior will definitely benefit from automatic human pose estimation. Multimodal approaches based on RGB-D data [35, 42], eventually combined with audio [17], and with visual-inertial sensors [13], have recently proved very successful in tracking human limbs. However, the former methods are appropriate when only one or few people move in proximity of the camera, while the latter approaches are often not practical solutions, as they require to instrument the person's body with multiple sensors. In addition, the robust estimation of the full human pose is chimeric in crowded scenes, which is typically the case of informal social gatherings. Consequently, when considering social interactions among several people, the head and body pose can be used as a surrogate of the full human pose.

Previous research has demonstrated that head and body orientations can be successfully detected from visual data [3, 9, 41, 31] and used as primary cues to infer high level information, such as visual focus of attention [38] and conversational groups [11]. In order to alleviate the human annotation effort, previous research has focused on using related cues to estimate head and body pose. For example, head pose labels generated using walking direction are considered by Benfold and Reid [3]. Similarly, coupling of head and body pose due to anatomical constraints is enforced by Chen and Odobez [9]. The body orientation is considered as a link between walking direction and head pose in [32, 25]. A transfer learning framework for head pose estimation under target motion is proposed in [31]. In [41] a multi-task learning approach is introduced for accurate estimates of the head pose from large field-of-view surveillance cameras. More recently, approaches to specifically cope with label noise [19] and integrate temporal consistency [14] are introduced. Audio-visual head pose estimation is attempted in [8]. However, up to the authors' knowledge, there are no research studies combining visual features from a distributed camera network with multimodal cues extracted from wearable sensors to jointly estimate the head and body poses.

2.3 Matrix Completion

We propose to cast multimodal head and body pose estimation into a matrix completion problem, which has been shown to be equivalent to learning a classifier in a transductive setting [21]. This formulation is particularly advantageous when data and labels are noisy or in the case of missing data. In the computer vision and multimedia communities, this fact has been exploited in several applications, such as multi-label image classification [5], image retrieval [40] and facial expression analysis [39]. A recent study [24] extends the matrix completion problem to take into account an underlying graph structure inducing a weighted relationship between the columns and between the rows of the matrix. We also utilize this structure to model the temporal smoothness of the head and body pose estimates. However, from the technical point of view our approach is novel because: (i) we address two matrix completion problems (for the head and body poses) that are coupled and cannot be reduced to a joint matrix completion problem, (ii) the proposed framework is able to deal with data coming from multiple modalities, handling signals generated from different types of sensing devices (distributed and wearable).

3. MATRIX COMPLETION FOR MULTIMODAL POSE ESTIMATION

The technical challenge of the present study is the robust estimation of the body and head pose in crowded scenarios for further analysis of FCGs. We assume a regular indoor environment populated with K people and captured with a distributed camera network and by sociometric badges [10] worn by the participants. On the one hand, we extract visual features of the head and body of all the participants, localized in the scene thanks to a multi-target visual tracking algorithm. On the other hand, since manual annotation is tedious and resource-demanding, we automatically label part of the sequence using the information gathered with the sociometric badges. The full preprocessing pipeline is described in Section 4.2, but we outline here the main insights and notations used in our research.

The visual descriptors of the head and body of person k at time t are denoted by $\mathbf{v}^{\mathrm{h}}_{kt} \in \mathbb{R}^{d_{\mathrm{h}}}$ and by $\mathbf{v}^{\mathrm{b}}_{kt} \in \mathbb{R}^{d_{\mathrm{b}}}$ respectively, where d_{h} and d_{b} are the features' dimension. Similarly, the head and body orientations of person k at time t are denoted by θ^{h}_{kt} and θ^{b}_{kt}. Inspired by previous research on the topic [9], we discretize the space of angular orientations into C sectors. Therefore the body and head orientations are C-dimensional vectors. $\left(\theta^{\mathrm{b}}_{kt}\right)_c$ should be understood as the probability that the associated body visual feature lies in the cth sector (analogously for the head). For instance, $\theta^{\mathrm{b}}_{kt} = [1, 0, \ldots, 0]$, means that θ^{b}_{kt} belongs to the first sector.

As outlined before, we assume the existence of a labeled training set $\mathcal{L}$ containing the raw features and noisy labels of the head and body pose of all the K persons involved in the interaction for $T_0 < T$ frames, where T is the total number of frames. That is: $\mathcal{L} = \left\{\mathbf{v}^{\mathrm{b}}_{kt}, \theta^{\mathrm{b}}_{kt}, \mathbf{v}^{\mathrm{h}}_{kt}, \theta^{\mathrm{h}}_{kt}\right\}_{k=1,t=1}^{K,T_0}$. Complementary, the set of unlabeled features is defined as: $\mathcal{U} = \left\{\mathbf{v}^{\mathrm{b}}_{kt}, \mathbf{v}^{\mathrm{h}}_{kt}\right\}_{k=1,t=T_0+1}^{K,T}$. It is important to remark that part of the training set is manually annotated and the rest

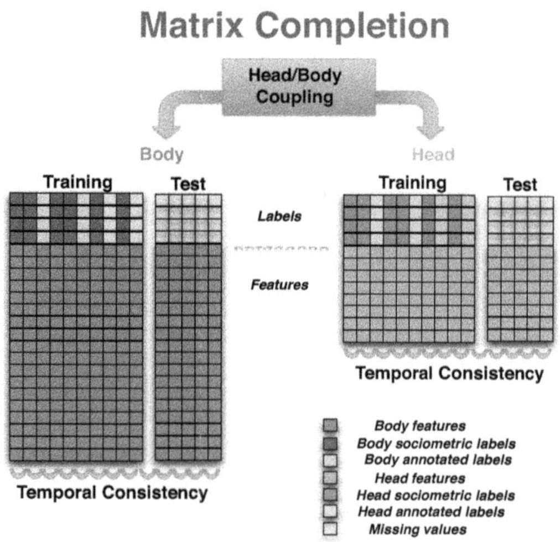

Figure 3: Illustration of the proposed matrix completion framework for multimodal head and body pose estimation (MC-HBPE). Two matrix completion problems, for the head and body poses, are regularized to account for the temporal consistency and for head/body coupling.

is automatically labeled. More precisely, we use the infrared detections as a proxy for the body pose and auditory correlations to automatically label the head pose. Indeed, it is reasonable to assume that the audio signals have a strong influence on the gaze direction of the targets, while the infrared detections naturally correlate with the body orientation. Finally, it is worth noticing that while visual data are continuously available, audio and infrared signals are sparse observations. In the following we describe the proposed approach for fusing these multiple modalities, so to robustly estimate the head and body poses of all participants.

3.1 The Model

Recent theoretical results and practical advances in matrix completion theory [5, 21], motivated us to consider the head and body problem from this perspective. We thoroughly cast the estimation into a matrix completion problem, thus introducing Matrix Completion for Head and Body Pose Estimation (MC-HBPE), a graphical illustration of which is shown in Figure 3. In the following, in order to ease the exposition, all the claims, definitions and properties are stated only for the body pose, but they remain true for the head pose, unless it is explicitly written otherwise. Before describing the model, we set a few useful notations: the matrices of labeled and unlabeled body features of person k, $\mathbf{V}^{\mathrm{b}}_{\mathcal{L},k} = [\mathbf{v}^{\mathrm{b}}_{kt}]_{t=1}^{T_0}$ and $\mathbf{V}^{\mathrm{b}}_{\mathcal{U},k} = [\mathbf{v}^{\mathrm{b}}_{kt}]_{t=T_0+1}^{T}$; their concatenation, $\mathbf{V}_k = [\mathbf{V}^{\mathrm{b}}_{\mathcal{L},k}\mathbf{V}^{\mathrm{b}}_{\mathcal{U},k}] = [\mathbf{v}^{\mathrm{b}}_{kt}]_{t=1}^{T}$; and the concatenation over all persons, *i.e.* , the concatenation of all body visual features, $\mathbf{V}^{\mathrm{b}} = [\mathbf{V}^{\mathrm{b}}_k]_{k=1}^{K}$. The matrices $\mathbf{\Theta}^{\mathrm{b}}_{\mathcal{L},k}$, $\mathbf{\Theta}^{\mathrm{b}}_{\mathcal{U},k}$, $\mathbf{\Theta}^{\mathrm{b}}_k$ and $\mathbf{\Theta}^{\mathrm{b}}$ are analogously built from θ^{b}_{kt}.

The objective is to estimate the matrix $\mathbf{\Theta}_{\mathcal{U}} = [\mathbf{\Theta}^{\mathrm{b}}_{\mathcal{U},k}]_{k=1}^{K}$, under the assumption of a linear classifier:

$$\mathbf{\Theta}^{\mathrm{b}} = \mathbf{W}^{\mathrm{b}} \begin{bmatrix} \mathbf{V}^{\mathrm{b}} \\ \mathbf{1}^{\top} \end{bmatrix}, \tag{1}$$

with $\mathbf{W}^{\mathrm{b}} \in \mathbb{R}^{C\times(d_{\mathrm{b}}+1)}$. Remarkably, the joint feature-label matrix $\mathbf{J}_{\mathrm{b}} = \left[\mathbf{\Theta}^{\mathrm{b}\top}\mathbf{V}^{\mathrm{b}\top}\mathbf{1}\right]^{\top} \in \mathbb{R}^{(C+d_{\mathrm{b}}+1)\times KT}$ is low rank, since the linear classifier in (1) imposes a linear dependency between the rows of $\mathbf{J}_{\mathrm{b}}$. Therefore, we set the following optimization problem for $\mathbf{\Theta}^{\mathrm{b}}_{\mathcal{U}}$:

$$\mathbf{\Theta}^{\mathrm{b}*}_{\mathcal{U}} = \underset{\mathbf{\Theta}^{\mathrm{b}}_{\mathcal{U}}}{\operatorname{argmin}} \ \operatorname{rank}(\mathbf{J}_{\mathrm{b}}). \tag{2}$$

Minimizing the rank of a matrix is a NP-hard problem, but it can be exactly relaxed by means of the nuclear norm [7]. Indeed, since the nuclear norm $\|\cdot\|_*$ is the tightest convex envelope of the rank, the previous optimization problem is equivalent to:

$$\mathbf{\Theta}^{\mathrm{b}*}_{\mathcal{U}} = \underset{\mathbf{\Theta}^{\mathrm{b}}_{\mathcal{U}}}{\operatorname{argmin}} \ \|\mathbf{J}_{\mathrm{b}}\|_*. \tag{3}$$

In real applications both the observations and the training labels are noisy. Therefore, it is of crucial importance to account for the observational and label noise. In practice, we assume $\widetilde{\mathbf{J}}_{\mathrm{b}} = \mathbf{J}_{\mathrm{b}} + \mathbf{E}_{\mathrm{b}}$, where $\widetilde{\mathbf{J}}_{\mathrm{b}}$ represents the noisy features and labels, and $\mathbf{E}_{\mathrm{b}}$ represents the noise. The objective is to estimate the low-rank matrix $\mathbf{J}_{\mathrm{b}}$ that best approximates the observed matrix $\widetilde{\mathbf{J}}_{\mathrm{b}}$. This is done by constraining (3), and relaxing it into [21]:

$$\min_{\mathbf{J}_{\mathrm{b}}} \nu_{\mathrm{b}} \|\mathbf{J}_{\mathrm{b}}\|_* + \frac{\lambda_{\mathrm{b}}}{2} \left\| P^{\mathrm{b}}_{\mathcal{O}}\left(\widetilde{\mathbf{J}}_{\mathrm{b}} - \mathbf{J}_{\mathrm{b}}\right)\right\|^2_{\mathcal{F}}, \tag{4}$$

where ν_{b} and λ_{b} are regularization parameters, $\|\mathbf{X}\|^2_{\mathcal{F}} = \operatorname{Tr}\left(\mathbf{X}^{\top}\mathbf{X}\right)$ denotes the Frobenius norm of $\mathbf{X}$ and $P^{\mathrm{b}}_{\mathcal{O}}$ denotes the projection onto the "set of observations", defined as $P^{\mathrm{b}}_{\mathcal{O}}\left(\left[\mathbf{\Theta}^{\mathrm{b},\top}\mathbf{V}^{\mathrm{b},\top}\mathbf{1}\right]^{\top}\right) = \left[[\mathbf{\Theta}^{\mathrm{b},\top}_{\mathcal{L},k}\ \mathbf{0}]_{k=1}^{K}\mathbf{V}^{\mathrm{b},\top}\mathbf{1}\right]^{\top}$, and thus setting to zero all elements associated to $\mathbf{\Theta}^{\mathrm{b}}_{\mathcal{U}}$. We remark that this *unitary* regularization term, encompasses the error on the visual features as well as on the training labels.

One of the prominent factors alleviating the matrix completion problem with noisy observations is the inherent temporal structure of the problem. Intuitively, we would expect the labels to be *smooth* in time, that is $\theta^{\mathrm{b}}_{kt} \approx \theta^{\mathrm{b}}_{kt+1}$, $\forall k, t$. We reinforce this intuition through a set of *binary* regularization terms, grouped in the following loss function:

$$T_{\mathrm{b}}(\mathbf{J}_{\mathrm{b}}) = \frac{1}{2}\operatorname{Tr}\left(P^{\mathrm{b}}_{\Theta}(\mathbf{J}_{\mathrm{b}})^{\top}\mathbf{T}_{\mathrm{b}}P^{\mathrm{b}}_{\Theta}(\mathbf{J}_{\mathrm{b}})\right), \tag{5}$$

where P^{b}_{Θ} is the projection onto the labels, $\mathbf{\Theta}_{\mathrm{b}}$, defined as $P^{\mathrm{b}}_{\Theta}\left(\left[\mathbf{\Theta}^{\mathrm{b},\top}\mathbf{V}^{\mathrm{b},\top}\mathbf{1}\right]^{\top}\right) = \left[\mathbf{\Theta}^{\mathrm{b},\top}\mathbf{0}\ \mathbf{0}\right]^{\top}$, and $\mathbf{T}_{\mathrm{b}} \in \mathbb{R}^{KT\times KT}$ is the Laplacian matrix associated to the graph encoding the relations between the variables. In our case, $\mathbf{T}_{\mathrm{b}} = \mathbf{I}_K \otimes \mathbf{L}$, where $\mathbf{I}_K$ is the K-dimensional identity matrix, $\otimes$ is the Kronecker product and $\mathbf{L} \in \mathbb{R}^{T\times T}$ is a tri-diagonal matrix defined as follows: the elements of the two subdiagonals are set to -1, and the elements of the main diagonal are set to 2, except $\mathbf{L}_{11} = \mathbf{L}_{TT} = 1$. In practice this means that only contiguous pose labels of the same person are embolden to be equal.

Until this point, we discussed the problem of body and head pose estimation separately. However, previous research studies in head and body pose estimation demonstrated the synergistic effect of joint estimation [9]. Subsequently, the estimation of head and body pose benefits from a coupling structure, in addition to the temporal structure already discussed. We write, $\theta^{\mathrm{b}}_{kt} \approx \theta^{\mathrm{h}}_{kt}$ and formalize the coupling structure by means of the following regularization term:

$$C(\mathbf{J}_{\mathrm{b}}, \mathbf{J}_{\mathrm{h}}) = \frac{1}{2}\left\| P^{\mathrm{b}}_{\Theta}(\mathbf{J}_{\mathrm{b}}) - P^{\mathrm{h}}_{\Theta}(\mathbf{J}_{\mathrm{h}})\right\|^2_{\mathcal{F}}, \tag{6}$$

where P^{h}_{Θ} is defined analogously[1] as P^{b}_{Θ}.

Summarizing, the head and body pose estimation is cast into a matrix completion problem encompassing the temporal and coupling structural constraints, by considering the following optimization problem:

$$\begin{aligned}\min_{\mathbf{J}_{\mathrm{b}},\mathbf{J}_{\mathrm{h}}} \quad & \nu_{\mathrm{b}} \|\mathbf{J}_{\mathrm{b}}\|_* + \frac{\lambda_{\mathrm{b}}}{2} \left\|P^{\mathrm{b}}_{\mathcal{O}}\left(\tilde{\mathbf{J}}_{\mathrm{b}} - \mathbf{J}_{\mathrm{b}}\right)\right\|^2_{\mathcal{F}} \\ & + \nu_{\mathrm{h}} \|\mathbf{J}_{\mathrm{h}}\|_* + \frac{\lambda_{\mathrm{h}}}{2} \left\|P^{\mathrm{h}}_{\mathcal{O}}\left(\tilde{\mathbf{J}}_{\mathrm{h}} - \mathbf{J}_{\mathrm{h}}\right)\right\|^2_{\mathcal{F}} \\ & + \frac{\tau_{\mathrm{b}}}{2}\mathrm{Tr}\left(P^{\mathrm{b}}_{\Theta}(\mathbf{J}_{\mathrm{b}})^\top \mathbf{T}_{\mathrm{b}} P^{\mathrm{b}}_{\Theta}(\mathbf{J}_{\mathrm{b}})\right) + \frac{\tau_{\mathrm{h}}}{2}\mathrm{Tr}\left(P^{\mathrm{h}}_{\Theta}(\mathbf{J}_{\mathrm{h}})^\top \mathbf{T}_{\mathrm{h}} P^{\mathrm{h}}_{\Theta}(\mathbf{J}_{\mathrm{h}})\right) \\ & + \frac{\lambda_c}{2}\left\|P^{\mathrm{b}}_{\Theta}(\mathbf{J}_{\mathrm{b}}) - P^{\mathrm{h}}_{\Theta}(\mathbf{J}_{\mathrm{h}})\right\|^2_{\mathcal{F}}.\end{aligned} \tag{7}$$

This is a non-linear convex optimization problem whose critical points cannot be expressed in closed-form solution. In the following we describe the proposed optimization algorithm to find the optimal solution for (7).

3.2 Optimization method

The alternating-direction method of multipliers (ADMM) is a well-known optimization procedure, and a review of theoretical results, practical implementation considerations and applications can be found in [4]. Recently, an ADMM-based optimization procedure for the matrix completion problem has been presented [24]. We also considered ADMM to solve the matrix completion problem. However, the proposed method is intrinsically different from previous approaches because of two reasons:

- First, we consider a coupled matrix completion problem, which is different from solving for the concatenated head/body matrix. Absolutely, completing the concatenation matrix implicitly assumes, not only that the body and head visual features have the same dimension, but also that the linear classifier for the body and head poses are equal $\mathbf{W}^{\mathrm{b}} = \mathbf{W}^{\mathrm{h}}$. Therefore, the method developed in [24] cannot be used in our case. Instead, we propose and develop a *Coupled Alternating Direction Method of Multipliers (C-ADMM)*.
- Second, the temporal structure of the problem is modeled with a column-wise regularizer on the matrices, which is a particular case of [24]. Importantly, as will be shown in the following, column-wise regularization can be solved in closed-form, while the formulation of [24] cannot. Consequently, all the steps of the proposed C-ADMM have a closed-form solution, and the convergence is guaranteed.

Classically, the ADMM arises from the construction of the *augmented Lagrangian* [4], which in our case writes:

$$\begin{aligned}\mathfrak{L} = \quad & \nu_{\mathrm{b}} \|\mathbf{J}_{\mathrm{b}}\|_* + \frac{\lambda_{\mathrm{b}}}{2} \left\|P^{\mathrm{b}}_{\mathcal{O}}\left(\tilde{\mathbf{J}}_{\mathrm{b}} - \mathbf{K}_{\mathrm{b}}\right)\right\|^2_{\mathcal{F}} \\ & + \nu_{\mathrm{h}} \|\mathbf{J}_{\mathrm{h}}\|_* + \frac{\lambda_{\mathrm{h}}}{2} \left\|P^{\mathrm{h}}_{\mathcal{O}}\left(\tilde{\mathbf{J}}_{\mathrm{h}} - \mathbf{K}_{\mathrm{h}}\right)\right\|^2_{\mathcal{F}} \\ & + \frac{\tau_{\mathrm{b}}}{2}\mathrm{Tr}\left(P^{\mathrm{b}}_{\Theta}(\mathbf{K}_{\mathrm{b}})^\top \mathbf{T}_{\mathrm{b}} P^{\mathrm{b}}_{\Theta}(\mathbf{K}_{\mathrm{b}})\right) + \frac{\tau_{\mathrm{h}}}{2}\mathrm{Tr}\left(P^{\mathrm{h}}_{\Theta}(\mathbf{K}_{\mathrm{h}})^\top \mathbf{T}_{\mathrm{h}} P^{\mathrm{h}}_{\Theta}(\mathbf{K}_{\mathrm{h}})\right) \\ & + \frac{\lambda_c}{2}\left\|P^{\mathrm{b}}_{\Theta}(\mathbf{K}_{\mathrm{b}}) - P^{\mathrm{h}}_{\Theta}(\mathbf{K}_{\mathrm{h}})\right\|^2_{\mathcal{F}} + \frac{\phi_{\mathrm{b}}}{2}\|\mathbf{K}_{\mathrm{b}} - \mathbf{J}_{\mathrm{b}}\|^2_{\mathcal{F}} + \frac{\phi_{\mathrm{h}}}{2}\|\mathbf{K}_{\mathrm{h}} - \mathbf{J}_{\mathrm{h}}\|^2_{\mathcal{F}} \\ & + \langle \mathbf{M}_{\mathrm{b}}, \mathbf{J}_{\mathrm{b}} - \mathbf{K}_{\mathrm{b}}\rangle + \langle \mathbf{M}_{\mathrm{h}}, \mathbf{J}_{\mathrm{h}} - \mathbf{K}_{\mathrm{h}}\rangle.\end{aligned} \tag{8}$$

[1]Even if P^{b}_{Θ} and P^{h}_{Θ} are conceptually equivalent, they are formally different since the features' dimension is different in general, $d_b \neq d_h$.

The Lagrangian $\mathfrak{L}$ has to be minimized with respect to $\mathbf{J}_{\mathrm{b}}$, $\mathbf{J}_{\mathrm{h}}$, $\mathbf{K}_{\mathrm{b}}$, $\mathbf{K}_{\mathrm{h}}$, $\mathbf{M}_{\mathrm{b}}$ and $\mathbf{M}_{\mathrm{h}}$, where the last two are matrices of Lagrangian multipliers, $\mathbf{K}_{\mathrm{b}}$ and $\mathbf{K}_{\mathrm{h}}$ are auxiliary variables, and $\langle \mathbf{A}, \mathbf{B}\rangle = \sum_{ij} \mathbf{A}_{ij}\mathbf{B}_{ij}$ is the scalar product in the matrix space.

At iteration $r+1$, the C-ADMM updates are:

$$\left(\mathbf{J}^{r+1}_{\mathrm{b}}, \mathbf{J}^{r+1}_{\mathrm{h}}\right) = \arg\min_{\mathbf{J}_{\mathrm{b}},\mathbf{J}_{\mathrm{h}}} \mathfrak{L}(\mathbf{J}_{\mathrm{b}}, \mathbf{J}_{\mathrm{h}}, \mathbf{K}^r_{\mathrm{b}}, \mathbf{K}^r_{\mathrm{h}}, \mathbf{M}^r_{\mathrm{b}}, \mathbf{M}^r_{\mathrm{h}}), \tag{9}$$

$$\left(\mathbf{K}^{r+1}_{\mathrm{b}}, \mathbf{K}^{r+1}_{\mathrm{h}}\right) = \arg\min_{\mathbf{K}_{\mathrm{b}},\mathbf{K}_{\mathrm{h}}} \mathfrak{L}\left(\mathbf{J}^{r+1}_{\mathrm{b}}, \mathbf{J}^{r+1}_{\mathrm{h}}, \mathbf{K}_{\mathrm{b}}, \mathbf{K}_{\mathrm{h}}, \mathbf{M}^r_{\mathrm{b}}, \mathbf{M}^r_{\mathrm{h}}\right), \tag{10}$$

$$\mathbf{M}^{r+1}_{\mathrm{b}} = \mathbf{M}^r_{\mathrm{b}} + \phi_{\mathrm{b}}\left(\mathbf{J}^{r+1}_{\mathrm{b}} - \mathbf{K}^{r+1}_{\mathrm{b}}\right), \tag{11}$$

$$\mathbf{M}^{r+1}_{\mathrm{h}} = \mathbf{M}^r_{\mathrm{h}} + \phi_{\mathrm{h}}\left(\mathbf{J}^{r+1}_{\mathrm{h}} - \mathbf{K}^{r+1}_{\mathrm{h}}\right). \tag{12}$$

From (8) it is straightforward that the coupling term does not have any effect on (9), but only on (10). Therefore, solving for (9) the two matrices $\mathbf{J}^{r+1}_{\mathrm{b}}$ $\mathbf{J}^{r+1}_{\mathrm{h}}$ can be computed independently. Furthermore, the optimal solution of (9) is:

$$\mathbf{J}^{r+1}_{\mathrm{b}} = \mathbf{U}_{\mathrm{b}} S_{\frac{\nu_{\mathrm{b}}}{\phi_{\mathrm{b}}}}(\mathbf{D}_{\mathrm{b}})\,\mathbf{V}_{\mathrm{b}} \tag{13}$$

where $\mathbf{U}_{\mathrm{b}}\mathbf{D}_{\mathrm{b}}\mathbf{V}_{\mathrm{b}}$ is the singular-value decomposition of the matrix $\mathbf{K}^r_{\mathrm{b}} - \frac{1}{\phi_{\mathrm{b}}}\mathbf{M}^r_{\mathrm{b}}$ and $S_\lambda(x) = \max(x-\lambda, 0)$ is the shrinkage operator with constant λ applied element-wise to the diagonal matrix of singular values, $\mathbf{D}_{\mathrm{b}}$. $\mathbf{J}^{r+1}_{\mathrm{h}}$ is found analogously. The details of the derivation can be found in the supplementary material.

The second C-ADMM update, *i.e.* (10), is also solved in closed-form. The critical point is computed by canceling the derivative of the objective function in (10) with respect to $\mathbf{K}_{\mathrm{b}}$ and $\mathbf{K}_{\mathrm{h}}$. As shown in the supplementary material, these derivatives lead to block-diagonal linear systems that can be efficiently solved. In order to sketch the proof, we define $\mathbf{k}_{\mathrm{b}} = \mathrm{vec}(\mathbf{K}_{\mathrm{b}})$ as the row-vectorization of $\mathbf{K}_{\mathrm{b}}$. The same notation stands for all other matrices involved. Moreover, we define $\mathbf{k}_{\mathrm{b},kc} = [(\theta^{\mathrm{b}}_{kt})_c]^T_{t=1}$, as the T-dimensional vector composed of the coordinate c of the angle labels of person k over time. Likewise, $\mathbf{k}_{\mathrm{b},\mathbf{v}}$ stands for the $KT(d_{\mathrm{b}}+1)$-dimensional row vectorization of the rest of the matrix $\mathbf{K}_{\mathrm{b}}$, that is the part corresponding to the visual features $\mathbf{V}^{\mathrm{b}}$. With these notations, the vector $\mathbf{k}_{\mathrm{b}}$ rewrites:

$$\mathbf{k}_{\mathrm{b}} = \left[\mathbf{k}^\top_{\mathrm{b},11} \ldots \mathbf{k}^\top_{\mathrm{b},KC}\ \mathbf{k}^\top_{\mathrm{b},\mathbf{v}}\right]^\top,$$

and analogously for all other row-vectorized matrices.

Each of the KC variables for body and head, $\mathbf{k}_{\mathrm{b},kc}$ and $\mathbf{k}_{\mathrm{h},kc}$, are independently solved:

$$\mathbf{k}_{\mathrm{b},kc} = \left(\mathbf{L}_{\mathrm{h}}\mathbf{L}_{\mathrm{b}} - \mathbf{I}_T\right)^{-1}\left(\mathbf{L}_{\mathrm{h}}\overline{\mathbf{k}}_{\mathrm{b},kc} + \overline{\mathbf{k}}_{\mathrm{h},kc}\right), \tag{14}$$

$$\mathbf{k}_{\mathrm{h},kc} = \mathbf{L}_{\mathrm{b}}\mathbf{k}_{\mathrm{b},kc} - \overline{\mathbf{k}}_{\mathrm{h},kc}, \tag{15}$$

where all matrices and vectors are precisely defined in the supplementary material. The vector $\overline{\mathbf{k}}_{\mathrm{b},kc}$ is computed from $\tilde{\mathbf{j}}_{\mathrm{b},kc}$, $\mathbf{m}^r_{\mathrm{b},kc}$ and $\mathbf{j}^{r+1}_{\mathrm{b},kc}$ and thus depends on the iteration (analogously for the head). Importantly, the matrices $\mathbf{L}_{\mathrm{b}}$ and $\mathbf{L}_{\mathrm{h}}$, computed from $\mathbf{L}$ and the regularization parameters, do not depend on the iteration. Therefore, the inversion can be computed before the iterative procedure of the C-ADMM starts, leading to an efficient algorithm. The system involving $\mathbf{k}_{\mathrm{b},\mathbf{v}}$ and $\mathbf{k}_{\mathrm{h},\mathbf{v}}$ is simpler since there is no

Algorithm 1 The coupled alternating-directions method of multipliers solving for the derived matrix completion for multimodal HBPE.

1: **Input**:
  Observation $\widetilde{\mathbf{J}_\mathbf{h}}$, $\widetilde{\mathbf{J}_\mathbf{b}}$ and Laplacian $\mathbf{T}_\mathbf{h}$, $\mathbf{T}_\mathbf{b}$ matrices. Regularization parameters.
2: **Output**:
  Optimized $\mathbf{J}_\mathbf{h}$, $\mathbf{J}_\mathbf{b}$.
3: Randomly initialize $\mathbf{M}_\mathbf{b}$, $\mathbf{M}_\mathbf{h}$, $\mathbf{K}_\mathbf{b}$, $\mathbf{K}_\mathbf{h}$;
4: **Repeat**
    Solve for $\mathbf{J}_\mathbf{h}$, $\mathbf{J}_\mathbf{b}$ in (9) using (13);
    Solve for $\mathbf{K}_\mathbf{h}$, $\mathbf{K}_\mathbf{b}$ in (10) using (14)-(17);
    Solve for $\mathbf{M}_\mathbf{h}$, $\mathbf{M}_\mathbf{b}$ using (11)-(12);
  Until Convergence

coupling between body and head features and there is no temporal regularization:

$$(\lambda_\mathrm{b} + \phi_\mathrm{b})\mathbf{k}_{\mathrm{b},\mathbf{v}} = \lambda_\mathrm{b}\tilde{\mathbf{j}}_{\mathrm{b},\mathbf{v}} + \mathbf{m}^r_{\mathrm{b},\mathbf{v}} + \phi_\mathrm{b}\mathbf{j}^{r+1}_{\mathrm{b},\mathbf{v}} \quad (16)$$

$$(\lambda_\mathrm{h} + \phi_\mathrm{h})\mathbf{k}_{\mathrm{h},\mathbf{v}} = \lambda_\mathrm{h}\tilde{\mathbf{j}}_{\mathrm{h},\mathbf{v}} + \mathbf{m}^r_{\mathrm{h},\mathbf{v}} + \phi_\mathrm{h}\mathbf{j}^{r+1}_{\mathrm{h},\mathbf{v}}. \quad (17)$$

Equations (14)-(17) provide the critical point sought in (10) and conclude the derivation of the proposed C-ADMM. As it is classically the case, the complexity bottle-neck of the matrix-completion solver is in the computation of the singular-value decomposition required in (13). The complete C-ADMM algorithm is shown in Algorithm 1.

4. EXPERIMENTS

In this section, we show the results of our experimental evaluation conducted on the novel SALSA (Synergistic sociAL Scene Analysis) dataset [2]. Then, we provide a detailed description of our experimental setup and show the results of our extensive evaluation, demonstrating the effectiveness of the proposed MC-HBPE method. Finally, we perform further experiments on the analysis of social interaction in SALSA, showing that the computed head and body orientations are accurate and robust so to efficiently detect F-formations and discover social attention attractors.

4.1 SALSA

The SALSA dataset records a two-part social event involving 18 participants. While the first half consists on a poster presentation session (see Fig.1), the second half consists on a cocktail party over food and beverages. The scene of SALSA is captured by a distributed camera network and by sociometric badges worn by the participants. Specifically, visual data are recorded by four synchronized static RGB cameras operating at 15 FPS. The sociometric badges are equipped with a microphone and an infrared (IR) beam and detector. Importantly, these wearable devices are battery-powered and store the data on a USB card without the need of any wired connection, thus guaranteeing a natural social interplay. SALSA also comprises manual annotations every 3 seconds of position, head and body orientation of each target as well as F-formations.

4.2 Experimental setup

In order to extract the visual features for body and head, $\mathbf{v}^\mathrm{b}_{tk}$ and $\mathbf{v}^\mathrm{h}_{tk}$, the participants can be tracked on the visual stream with multi-target tracking algorithms with state-of-the-art occlusion handling such as [26]. The estimates of the ground positions are used together with the camera calibration to retrieve the bounding box of the head and body of all participants for each camera view. We used those frames in which all participants are seen from all four cameras. Inspired by [9], we choose to describe each bounding box with a Histogram of Oriented Gradient (HOG) descriptors [12]. More precisely, the head and body images are first normalized to 20×20 and 80×60 pixel images, respectively, from which we extract HOG in non-overlapping cells of 4×4 pixels. Finally, the descriptors for all the four views are concatenated and the dimensionality of the head and body descriptors is reduced using Principal Component Analysis, keeping 90% of the variance. In all, the head and body visual features extracted from the four cameras for each participant ($\mathbf{v}^\mathrm{b}_{tk}$ and $\mathbf{v}^\mathrm{h}_{tk}$) are roughly 100–dimensional.

As outlined in Section 3, the infrared and auditory information from the sociometric badges are processed in order to automatically extract body and head pose labels, respectively. Indeed, the different nature of the infrared and auditory signals carries a rich representation of the badge's owner with respect to the other participants. On one side, if the badge of person k detects the infrared beam of person l, most likely k's body orientation points to l, since the badge settles on its owner's chest. On the other side, if the auditory signal of k's badge is highly correlated with the one of l, it is likely that l is speaking towards k, and that therefore the head of l points towards k. It is worth noticing that, whilst visual features are extracted in a continuous manner, infrared and auditory labels are sparse. Finally, inspired by [9], we discretize the angular space to $C = 8$ sectors (corresponding to an angular resolution of 45°) for both head and body labels.

4.3 Head and body pose estimation

To experimentally validate the technical core of the present study, *i.e.* the MC-HBPE, we considered those frames of SALSA in which all the participants are in the field of view of the four cameras. In practice, we use 340 frames of the poster session (17 minutes approximately), resulting in a data set comprising 6120 head/body samples. We split this set into two equal parts, and use only the annotations of the first part for training: 10% of manual annotations and 90% of weak annotations obtained with the sociometric badges, when available. In essence, we have 5% of manual annotations for head and body pose, and therefore the labels are sparse. We report the classification accuracy of the test samples, *i.e.* the second half of the data set. In all our experiments, and for both our approach and the baseline methods, the regularization parameters are set with cross-validation.

Figure 4 shows the performance obtained with our method when the training labels come from different modalities. At the light of the results, we can clearly state that using multimodal labels significantly improves the accuracy of both head and body pose estimates. Interestingly, when considering only ground truth and auditory labels (*i.e.* no additional labels for body pose), not only the accuracy of the head pose estimates improves, but also the accuracy of body pose estimates. This is an important and remarkable effect of the head/body coupling term introduced in the proposed formulation. We notice the analogous effect with the performance rise of, not only body pose estimates, but also head pose estimates, when adding the infrared labels (*i.e.* with no additional labels for head pose). It is worth noticing that

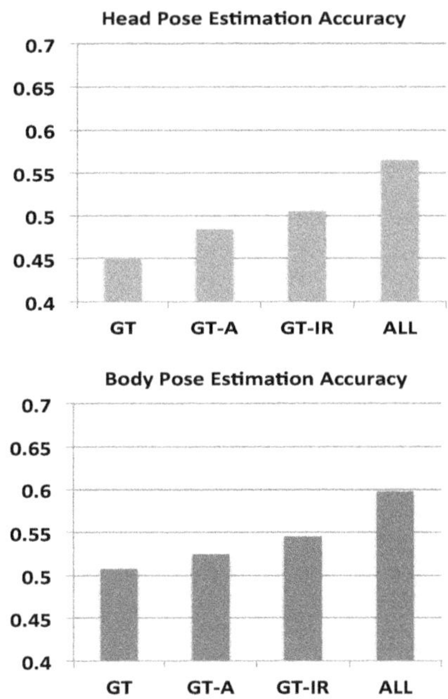

Figure 4: Accuracy of the head (top) and body (bottom) pose estimates obtained with the proposed MC-HBPE approach using visual features and labels from different modalities: ground truth annotations (GT), GT and audio data (GT-A), GT and infrared data (GT-IR), all modalities (ALL).

infrared labels have a significantly more positive effect than auditory labels. We ascribe this fact to the higher accuracy of the infrared labels (87%) compared to the auditory labels (70%). when compared to the manual annotations. Importantly, we highlight the synergistic effect of jointly using auditory, infrared and visual data to robustly solve the head and body pose estimation problem by means of matrix completion techniques. Finally, the implementation of the proposed methodology needs roughly 0.5 seconds to estimate the head and body poses of one person.

Table 1 reports the classification accuracy of several methods. First of all, the proposed MC-HBPE method considering different configurations regarding the head/body coupling and the temporal consistency (from top to bottom): (i) only with head-body coupling $\tau_b, \tau_h = 0$ in (7); (ii) only with temporal consistency λ_c equal to 0 in (7) and (iii) with both types of constraints. The comparison with the state-of-the-art is particularly difficult in our case, since there is no existing methodology for head and body pose estimation using multimodal data. That is why we chose to compare with the state-of-the-art on *visual-only* HBPE [9]. Notably, the conversational flavor of SALSA is challenging for [9], since when analyzing FCG the direction of motion cannot be considered as a proxy for the body pose, as done in [9]. Moreover, given that the proposed learning methodology belongs to the class of transductive learning approaches, and [9] does not, we perform additional comparisons with Transductive Support Vector Machines (TSVM) [23]. It is worth noting that neglecting the coupling and the temporal consistency terms in MC-HBPE, *i.e.* $\tau_b, \lambda_c, \tau_h = 0$ in (7), is similar to the work of Goldberg *et al.* [21]. Therefore, MC-HBPE could be seen as a generalization of the transductive methodology presented in [21]. Results in Table 1 demonstrate the advantageous performance obtained when enforcing temporal consistency or coupling the head and body pose estimates. Importantly, the effect of both regularizations is impressive, increasing by approximately 20% the classifiers' accuracy. Our understanding, is that this is the main reason for which the complete method we presented outperforms the baselines up to a large extent. In order to show the complexity of the task, we show the original image of one of the cameras and the estimated poses plot in a bird's eye view in Figure 5. Finally, we evaluate the robustness of the approach to the amount of training and of manually annotated data in Figure 6, where we remark the 40% accuracy obtained with only 1% of manually annotated data (plus the noisy labels from the sociometric badges).

Table 1: Classification accuracy of different methods for HBPE.

Method	C	T_b, T_h	Body	Head
	✓		0.515	0.465
MC-HBPE		✓	0.548	0.515
	✓	✓	**0.597**	**0.567**
Chen *et al.* [9]			0.524	0.475
TSVM [23]			0.481	0.429
Golberg *et al.* [21]			0.479	0.439

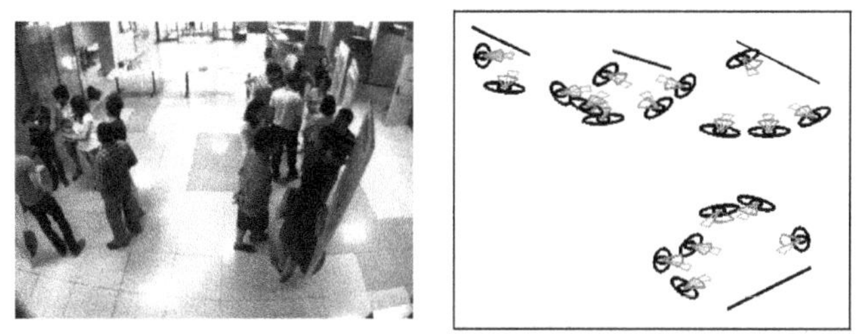

Figure 5: Frame example: (left) the original image of one of the cameras, (right) the head–green and body–red pose estimates plot in bird view.

4.4 F-formation detection

One of the prominent applications of robust estimation of the head and body poses when analyzing FCGs is the detection of F-formations. We evaluate three state-of-the-art approaches for F-formation detection, namely: the Hough voting method (HVFF-lin) in [11], its multi-scale extension (HVFF-ms) [33] and the graph cut approach in [34]. We chose these methods because their implementation is publicly available[2]. All these approaches compute the F-formation independently frame by frame, from the targets' position and pose. The rationale behind the Hough voting methods is that each target generates a set of samples in front of him/her, which are candidates of the F-formation centers. By aggregating these samples into a discrete number of cells, F-formations are detected by finding local maxima in the discretized space. Conversely, in the graph-cut algorithm [34], an optimization problem is solved, discovering directly the coordinates of the F-formations.

Previous works [22] have acknowledged the importance of accurate body pose estimates for detecting F-formations. However, one of the inherent difficulties within the analysis of FCGs in crowded indoor environments is the adverse im-

[2]`http://profs.sci.univr.it/~cristanm/ssp/`

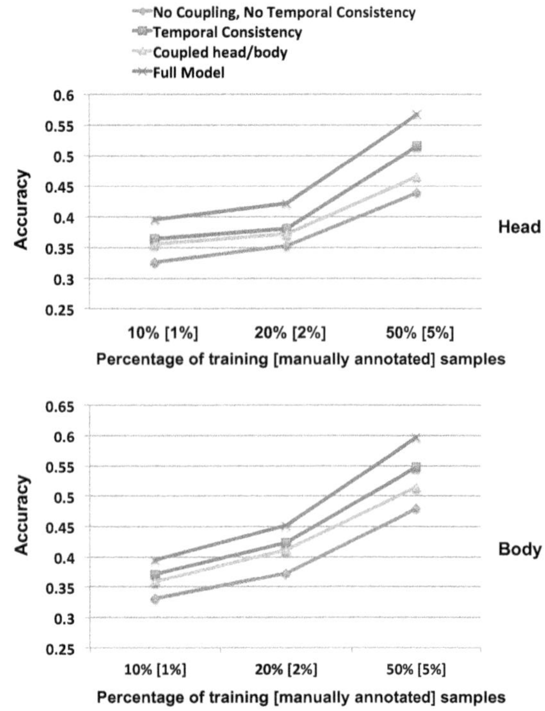

Figure 6: Classification accuracy for different percentage of training samples and of manually annotated samples (in square brackets).

pact of highly occluded body images, which empower strong noise and outliers in the estimated body poses. Classically, the head pose is used as a surrogate to the body pose, and the F-formation are detected from the head pose. In Section 4.3, we demonstrate that the proposed MC-HBPE approach can be effectively used to accurately infer the body pose, thus making possible to use the body pose for F-formation detection and therefore improving the quality of the analysis of FCGs.

We implement the validation protocol defined in [11], and report F-formation precision, recall and F1-measure in Table 2. At each frame, we consider a group as correctly estimated if at least $T \cdot |G|$ of the members are correctly found, and if no more than $1 - T \cdot |G|$ non-members are wrongly identified, where $|G|$ is the cardinality of the group G, and $T = 2/3$. Table 2 shows the performance measures using body (first three rows) and head (fourth and fifth rows) pose. We compare the estimates obtained with MC-HBPE to the body pose ground truth and the body estimates computed with [9]. Regarding the head pose, in addition to our approach, we also used the transductive SVM approach in [23] to emulate previous works on F-formation detection that used head pose estimates. The results clearly confirm that accurate inference of the body pose using the MC-HBPE framework is advantageous for the detection of F-formations.

4.5 Retrieving Social Attention Attractors

Automatically discovering attentional patterns from multimodal data is an unexplored area of research. Interestingly, retrieving the person who holds the attention of the other members in the group can be helpful for other higher-level tasks. In the short-term it can be used to describe who is leading the conversation. In the mid-term, it can describe the role of the person during the interaction. And in

Table 2: Performance of state-of-the-art approaches on F-formation detection from different estimations of the head and body pose. Each table cell contains precision, recall and F1-measure, in this order.

	HVFF lin [11]	HVFF ms [33]	GC [34]
Our-B	0.62 / 0.61 / 0.62	0.66 / 0.64 / 0.66	0.69 / 0.66 / 0.67
[9]-B	0.56 / 0.58 / 0.58	0.59 / 0.62 / 0.61	0.62 / 0.61 / 0.62
GT-B	0.66 / 0.65 / 0.65	0.72 / 0.69 / 0.71	0.74 / 0.72 / 0.73
Our-H	0.61 / 0.59 / 0.60	0.64 / 0.63 / 0.63	0.65 / 0.64 / 0.64
[23]-H	0.58 / 0.58 / 0.58	0.59 / 0.58 / 0.59	0.62 / 0.59 / 0.61
GT-H	0.65 / 0.63 / 0.64	0.70 / 0.67 / 0.69	0.72 / 0.70 / 0.71

the long-term it is related to personality. In this particular study we are interested in interactions that last several minutes, thus we focus on role analysis. In practice, we analyze the scientific poster session of SALSA to automatically find out who are the poster presenters.

In order to do that we introduce the first computational model for the *social attention holding power* (SAHP), which is defined as "the ability to direct favorable attention to the self" [20]. Intuitively, in our scenario the people with high SAHP are likely to be the sought poster presenters, or someone interacting with the presentation *e.g.* asking a question. Within the context of FCGs, SAHP can be computed as the percentage of the F-formation members that are looking towards a particular person.

We consider that if person k is looking to person l, the estimated head pose of person k at time t ($\hat{\theta}^{\text{h}}_{tk}$) lies within $\theta^{\max}$ degrees of the direction from k to l at time t. This provides us a binary vector $\mathbf{A}_{kl}$ of size T, in which $(\mathbf{A}_{kl})_t$ is one if k is looking at l at time t and zero otherwise. However this binary matrix is insufficient, since we are interested in the ability of *holding* the attention. Therefore, we consider that holding someone's attention for more than $T_N = 5$ seconds is positive, but holding it for less than the same amount, meaning that the attention was not held long enough, is negative. These allows us to split the attentional periods into two groups $\mathcal{T}_{kl}^{+} \subset \{t|(\mathbf{A}_{kl})_t = 1\}$ the temporal frames with an ongoing long held attention (positive SAHP) and $\mathcal{T}_{kl}^{+} \subset \{t|(\mathbf{A}_{kl})_t = 1\}$ the temporal frames with an ongoing short held attention (negative SAHP). Formally, the social attention holding power of person l is computed as:

$$\text{SAHP}_l = \sum_{t=1}^{T} \frac{1}{|\mathcal{G}_{tl}|} \sum_{k \in \mathcal{G}_{tl}} \left(\mathbb{I}(t \in \mathcal{T}_{kl}^{+}) - \mathbb{I}(t \in \mathcal{T}_{kl}^{-}) \right), \quad (18)$$

where $\mathbb{I}$ is the indicator function and $\mathcal{G}_{tl}$ is the F-formation to which person l belongs at time t.

In the addressed scenario, however, part of the attention is held by the posters themselves. Intuitively, the attention given to the poster corresponds to the poster presenter or to an attendee who just took part into the discussion (*e.g.* asking a question). Therefore, we add the attention given to the poster after participation of person l, to the previously computed SAHP_l. Moreover, since we know that there are four posters, we seek the four highest values of SAHP, and we refer to these participants as *social attention attractors*.

We performed an extensive set of experiments to systematically evaluate the robustness of the proposed computational formulation of SAHP against errors in the estimation of the head pose and the detection of F-formations. First, we computed the attention vectors $\mathbf{A}_{kl}$ with an angular threshold of $\theta^{\max} \in \{5°, 10°, 15°, 20°\}$, and the positive

Table 3: Accuracy results of the social attention attractor detector built from the proposed computational model for the SAHP.

Parameters		Simulated Data			Real Data			
W	$\theta^{\max}$	5°	20°	55°	HP	F-f.	Both	Pos
1′	5°	0.92	0.77	0.74	0.71	0.90	0.71	0.73
	10°	0.92	0.82	0.76	0.72	0.92	0.73	0.70
	15°	0.94	0.87	0.78	0.75	0.90	0.73	0.70
	20°	0.95	0.87	0.82	0.75	0.90	0.75	0.70
2′	5°	0.93	0.78	0.77	0.70	0.91	0.68	0.70
	10°	0.92	0.83	0.77	0.70	0.88	0.69	0.69
	15°	0.94	0.89	0.83	0.77	0.92	0.76	0.71
	20°	0.96	0.90	0.87	0.79	0.92	0.79	0.74
4′	5°	0.96	0.81	0.82	0.70	0.89	0.68	0.71
	10°	0.96	0.88	0.76	0.76	0.91	0.72	0.67
	15°	0.96	0.94	0.85	0.79	0.96	0.78	0.69
	20°	0.98	0.93	0.88	0.79	0.98	0.77	0.76

and negative held attentional periods from them. Thirdly, we calculated the SAHP within a sliding window of length $W \in \{1, 2, 4\}$ minutes. Finally we compare the retrieved social attention attractors with the ones obtained applying the same procedure to the ground truth data. This evaluation procedure is applied to simulated and to real data. In the former case, we corrupted the head pose ground truth values with uniform random noise of amplitude 5°, 20° and 55°. In the latter case, we evaluate the effect of the estimation procedure of the proposed MC-HBPE together with the F-formation detection state-of-the-art graph-cut method [34] (since it provided the best performance with our data). Finally, we compare our computational model to the straightforward strategy of selecting the person closest to the poster.

We report the accuracy for all combinations of the parameter values in Table 3. The two group columns correspond to the experiments with simulated and real data respectively. In the case of real data we consider three subcases: when only the head pose is estimated (HP), when only the F-formation is estimated (F-f.) and when both are estimated (Both). Last single column corresponds to the strategy of selecting the person closest to the poster (Pos). We first notice that, in the case of simulated data, the noise notably decreases the performance of the social attention attractor detector: in severe noise conditions, the accuracy drops down roughly to 0.75. Importantly, we also remark that part of this performance loss can be recovered if we choose the right value for the parameters. Indeed, in severe noise conditions, the right choice of parameters make the performance increase by 0.14. Moreover, the effect of the parameter choice in the robustness against noise is intuitive. On the one side, when the integration window W is longer, we expect short errors to be smoothed out. On the other side, a larger angular threshold allows to account for low-accuracy estimates of the head pose. We performed experiments with larger values of W (up to 30′) and of $\theta^{\max}$ (up to 40°), and the accuracy results follow the same trend. Regarding the real data, we remark that the effect of estimating the head pose is more critical than detecting the F-formations. In addition, the proposed model outperforms the Pos strategy probably because: (i) the person closest to the poster is not necessarily the social attractor at a given time (ii) the poster presenter is not systematically the social attractor. The results confirm this fact since the accuracy of the head estimates is lower than the accuracy of the detected F-formations. Remarkably, the effect of the parameters follows the same trend as in the case of simulated data. At the light of this results we conclude that, there is still room for improvement in the estimation of the head and body poses within FCGs in crowded environments. Furthermore, since robust estimation of head and body pose is useful for higher-level analysis, and no previous methodologies exist to fuse multimodal data flows emanating from a combination of distributed and wearable sensor networks, we believe it is worth pursuing further this line of research.

5. CONCLUSIONS AND FUTURE WORK

The focus of this research study is the analysis of free-standing conversational groups from multimodal estimates of head and body pose. We propose a framework able to (i) combine data emanating from a distributed camera network and from sociometric badges worn by each participant, (ii) fuse data from different modalities to boost the estimation of head and body pose, (iii) alleviate the annotation process thanks to the multimodal labels provided by the sociometric badges, (iv) handle noisy features and labels by means of the matrix completion framework, (v) account for the temporal consistency and head/body coupling inherent to the scenario and (vi) provide robust estimates of the head and body poses that have proven to be useful for higher-level tasks, such as the detection of F-formations and the discovery of social attention attractors.

At the light of the results obtained through the extensive experimental evaluation of the presented methodology, we believe that this study opens the door to several interesting future research directions. First of all, the links with other related tasks should be exploited in a bidirectional way. Indeed, the estimation of the head and body poses can ease the tracking of multiple people. Similarly, the recognition of F-formations and discovery of social attention attractors can help the estimation of head and body poses. Second, the spectrum of applications should be enlarged to address personality recognition. Importantly, the analysis of personality traits could require longitudinal studies (*i.e.* extend the recordings to days or weeks), and the current methodology should be adapted to this scenario. Finally, from the technical point of view, one could focus on speeding up the current MC-HBPE algorithm and develop incremental matrix completion strategies, so to adapt the proposed methodology to real-time processing.

Acknowledgments

This work has been partially supported by the MIUR Cluster project Active Ageing at Home, the EC project ACANTO and the A*STAR Singapore Human-Centered Cyber-physical Systems (HCCS) grant.

6. REFERENCES

[1] X. Alameda-Pineda and R. Horaud. Vision-guided robot hearing. *IJRR*, 34(4-5):437–456, 2015.

[2] X. Alameda-Pineda, J. Staiano, R. Subramanian, L. Batrinca, E. Ricci, B. Lepri, O. Lanz, and N. Sebe. Salsa: A novel dataset for multimodal group behavior analysis. *arXiv:1506.06882*, 2015.

[3] B. Benfold and I. Reid. Unsupervised learning of a scene-specific coarse gaze estimator. In *ICCV*, 2011.

[4] S. Boyd, N. Parikh, E. Chu, B. Peleato, and J. Eckstein. Distributed optimization and statistical learning via the alternating direction method of multipliers. *Foundations and Trends in Machine Learning*, 3(1):1–122, 2011.
[5] R. Cabral, F. De la Torre, J. Costeira, and A. Bernardino. Matrix completion for multi-label image classification. *TPAMI*, 37(1):121–135, 2014.
[6] A. T. Campbell, S. B. Eisenman, N. D. Lane, E. Miluzzo, and R. A. Peterson. People-centric urban sensing. In *Int. Work. on Wireless Internet*, 2006.
[7] E. J. Candès and T. Tao. The power of convex relaxation: Near-optimal matrix completion. *IEEE Trans. Inf. Theory*, 56(5):2053–2080, 2010.
[8] C. Canton-Ferrer, C. Segura, J. R. Casas, M. Pardas, and J. Hernando. Audiovisual head orientation estimation with particle filtering in multisensor scenarios. *EURASIP Jour. on Adv. in Sig. Proc.*, 2008.
[9] C. Chen and J.-M. Odobez. We are not contortionists: coupled adaptive learning for head and body orientation estimation in surveillance video. In *CVPR*, 2012.
[10] T. Choudhury and A. Pentland. Sensing and modeling human networks using the sociometer. In *Inter. Sym. on Wearable Comp.*, 2003.
[11] M. Cristani et al. Social interaction discovery by statistical analysis of F-formations. In *BMVC*, 2011.
[12] N. Dalal and B. Triggs. Histograms of oriented gradients for human detection. In *CVPR*, 2005.
[13] F. De la Torre et al. Guide to the Carnegie Mellon University multimodal activity (CMU-MMAC) database. Technical report, 2009.
[14] M. Demirkus, D. Precup, J. J. Clark, and T. Arbel. Probabilistic temporal head pose estimation using a hierarchical graphical model. In *ECCV*, 2014.
[15] T. M. T. Do and D. Gatica-Perez. Human interaction discovery in smartphone proximity networks. *Personal and Ubiquitous Computing*, 17(3):413–431, 2013.
[16] N. Eagle and A. Pentland. Reality mining: sensing complex social systems. *Personal and Ubiquitous Computing*, 10(4):255–268, 2006.
[17] S. Escalera, X. Bar, J. Gonzlez, M. A. Bautista, M. Madadi, M. Reyes, V. Ponce, H. J. Escalante, J. Shotton, and I. Guyon. Chalearn looking at people challenge 2014: Dataset and results. In *ECCV Workshops*, 2014.
[18] D. Gatica-Perez. Automatic nonverbal analysis of social interaction in small groups: A review. *Image and Vision Computing*, 27(12):1775–1787, 2009.
[19] X. Geng and Y. Xia. Head pose estimation based on multivariate label distribution. In *CVPR*, 2014.
[20] P. Gilbert, J. Price, and S. Allan. Social comparison, social attractiveness and evolution: How might they be related? *New Ideas in Psychology*, 13(2), 1995.
[21] A. Goldberg, B. Recht, J. Xu, R. Nowak, and X. Zhu. Transduction with matrix completion: Three birds with one stone. In *NIPS*, 2010.
[22] H. Hung and B. Kröse. Detecting F-formations as dominant sets. In *ICMI*, 2011.
[23] T. Joachims. Transductive inference for text classification using SVM. In *ICML*, 1999.
[24] V. Kalofolias, X. Bresson, M. Bronstein, and P. Vandergheynst. Matrix completion on graphs. *arXiv:1408.1717*, 2014.
[25] N. Krahnstoever, M.-C. Chang, and W. Ge. Gaze and body pose estimation from a distance. In *AVSS*, 2011.
[26] O. Lanz. Approximate bayesian multibody tracking. *TPAMI*, 28:1436–1449, 2006.
[27] F. Lingenfelser, J. Wagner, E. André, G. McKeown, and W. Curran. An event driven fusion approach for enjoyment recognition in real-time. In *ACMMM*, 2014.
[28] A. Matic, V. Osmani, A. Maxhuni, and O. Mayora. Multi-modal mobile sensing of social interactions. In *PervasiveHealth*, 2012.
[29] M. Pantic, N. Sebe, J. F. Cohn, and T. Huang. Affective multimodal human-computer interaction. In *ACMMM*, 2005.
[30] S. Petridis, B. Martinez, and M. Pantic. The mahnob laughter database. *Image and Vision Computing*, 31(2):186–202, 2013.
[31] A. K. Rajagopal, R. Subramanian, E. Ricci, R. L. Vieriu, O. Lanz, and N. Sebe. Exploring transfer learning approaches for head pose classification from multi-view surveillance images. *IJCV*, 109(1-2):146–167, 2014.
[32] N. Robertson and I. Reid. Estimating gaze direction from low-resolution faces in video. In *ECCV*, 2006.
[33] F. Setti, O. Lanz, R. Ferrario, V. Murino, and M. Cristani. Multi-scale F-formation discovery for group detection. In *ICIP*, 2013.
[34] F. Setti, C. Russell, C. Bassetti, and M. Cristani. F-formation detection: Individuating free-standing conversational groups in images. *arXiv:1409.2702*, 2014.
[35] J. Shotton et al. Real-time human pose recognition in parts from single depth images. *Communications of the ACM*, 56(1):116–124, 2013.
[36] Y. Song, L.-P. Morency, and R. Davis. Multimodal human behavior analysis: learning correlation and interaction across modalities. In *ICMI*, 2012.
[37] A. Vinciarelli, A. Dielmann, S. Favre, and H. Salamin. Canal9: A database of political debates for analysis of social interactions. In *ICACII*, 2009.
[38] M. Voit and R. Stiefelhagen. 3d user-perspective, voxel-based estimation of visual focus of attention in dynamic meeting scenarios. In *ICMI*, 2010.
[39] B. Wu, S. Lyu, B.-G. Hu, and Q. Ji. Multi-label learning with missing labels for image annotation and facial action unit recognition. *Pattern Recognition*, 2015.
[40] L. Wu, R. Jin, and A. K. Jain. Tag completion for image retrieval. *TPAMI*, 35(3):716–727, 2013.
[41] Y. Yan, E. Ricci, R. Subramanian, O. Lanz, and N. Sebe. No matter where you are: Flexible graph-guided multi-task learning for multi-view head pose classification under target motion. In *ICCV*, 2013.
[42] Y. Yan, E. Ricci, R. Subramanian, G. Liu, and N. Sebe. Multitask linear discriminant analysis for view invariant action recognition. *IEEE Transactions on Image Processing*, 23(12):5599–5611, 2014.

An Affordable Solution for Binocular Eye Tracking and Calibration in Head-mounted Displays

Michael Stengel[1], Steve Grogorick[1],
Martin Eisemann[2], Elmar Eisemann[3], Marcus Magnor[1]
[1]TU Braunschweig, Germany [2]TH Köln, Germany [3]TU Delft, Netherlands
{stengel,grogorick,magnor}@cg.cs.tu-bs.de, martin.eisemann@fh-koeln.de, e.eisemann@tudelft.nl *

ABSTRACT

Immersion is the ultimate goal of head-mounted displays (HMD) for Virtual Reality (VR) in order to produce a convincing user experience. Two important aspects in this context are motion sickness, often due to imprecise calibration, and the integration of a reliable eye tracking. We propose an affordable hard- and software solution for drift-free eye-tracking and user-friendly lens calibration within an HMD. The use of dichroic mirrors leads to a lean design that provides the full field-of-view (FOV) while using commodity cameras for eye tracking. Our prototype supports personalizable lens positioning to accommodate for different interocular distances. On the software side, a model-based calibration procedure adjusts the eye tracking system and gaze estimation to varying lens positions. Challenges such as partial occlusions due to the lens holders and eye lids are handled by a novel robust monocular pupil-tracking approach. We present four applications of our work: Gaze map estimation, foveated rendering for depth of field, gaze-contingent level-of-detail, and gaze control of virtual avatars.

Categories and Subject Descriptors

C.3 [**Computer Graphics**]: Special-Purpose and Application-based Systems - Real-time and embedded systems; I.3.1 [**Computer Graphics**]: Hardware Architecture - Input devices; I.3.7 [**Computer Graphics**]: 3D Graphics and Realism - Virtual Reality; I.3.8 [**Computer Graphics**]: 3D Graphics and Realism - Applications

Keywords

eye tracking; gaze; wearable; virtual reality; head-mounted display; mobile

1. INTRODUCTION

Virtual Reality (VR) has become a well-established field in research and industrial applications, e.g., for simulations, scientific visualization, or gaming. Previously, high hardware costs prevented a wide-spread application and development. But recent advances in the mobile device market, lead to high-quality, low-cost virtual reality hardware (*Oculus Rift, HTC Vive, Sony PS4 HMD*, etc.). These low-weight, low-latency head-mounted displays (HMDs), in combination with a wide field of view (FOV), enable a never before experienced *immersion* and *presence* within a virtual environment. Future developments of HMDs will include even higher resolution displays, higher refresh rates, and wider FOVs [8].

Commodity HMDs mostly use fixed hardware setups. However, preconfigured HMDs are often difficult to parameterize for individuals, e.g., to account for differing interocular distances; both, in horizontal and vertical direction (previously often ignored and known as Hypertropia [17]). Further, existing software calibration is often unsatisfactory and cumbersome with current HMDs. This limitation can lead to non-frontal relative positioning of the eye and non-converging lenses inside the HMD, resulting in reduced perceived sharpness, and an increased likelihood of motion sickness and headaches for the user.

The wide adoption of VR equipment makes it crucial to investigate methods to simplify calibration and to improve the experience for each user. Here, analyzing user behavior in virtual environments can deliver many insights: What is drawing attention? What emotional response results from certain content?

For a desktop setup congeneric findings are usually investigated involving an eye tracker (measuring pupil size for emotions or focus points of interests on the screen). Unfortunately, when using an HMD setup, the integration of eye tracking is not straightforward and existing solutions are not convenient for commodity HMDs.

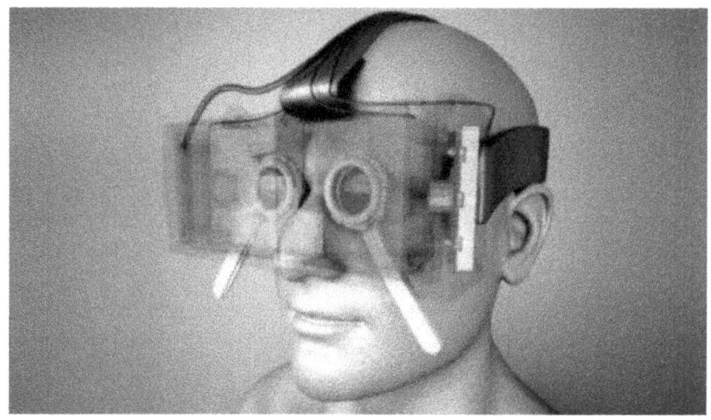

Figure 1: **Prototype visualization.** A rendering of our self-contained eye tracking head-mounted display. Based on a system of dichroic mirrors (red), infrared light illuminating lense holders (white) and tracking cameras (yellow) the device captures the user's eye motion for binocular eye-tracking while he is fully immersed in the virtual world.

*Video and further paper details available under:
`http://graphics.tu-bs.de/publications/stengel2015acmmm/`

MM'15, October 26–30, 2015, Brisbane, Australia.
© 2015 ACM. ISBN 978-1-4503-3459-4/15/10 ...$15.00.
DOI: http://dx.doi.org/10.1145/2733373.2806265.

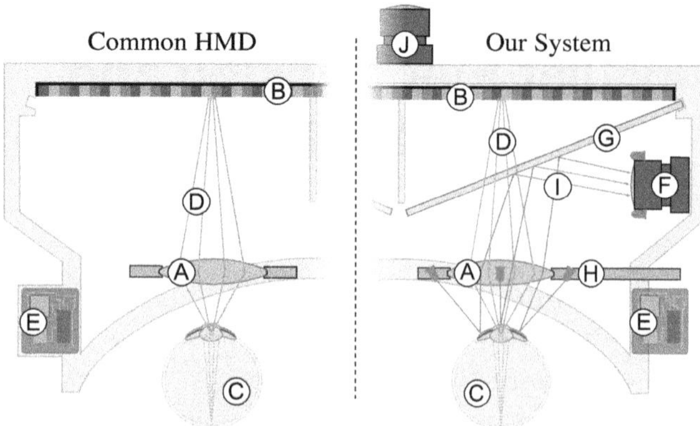

Figure 2: **HMD design comparison.** Common HMDs setup (left part): converging lens (A), display (B), eye ball (C), visible light (D), orientation tracker (E); Our system adds (right part): eye tracking cameras (F), dichroic mirrors (G), lens controller with infrared LEDs (H), infrared light (I), positional tracking camera (J).

Stationary solutions for eye tracking are state-of-the-art with regard to tracking quality and mostly applied to estimate scan paths (fixations and saccades) [26, 36]. The user's head is locked in a position using a rigid positioner and a camera records the eye. While the systems are very accurate at a high tracking sample rate, the fixed viewing position is not an option for immersive VR and even small head movements lead to drifts if recalibration is not frequently performed.

Mobile eye-tracking solutions overcome the motion restrictions. In this case, an integration into a headgear or special-glasses frame enables free head movement (e.g., SMI Eye Tracking Glasses, Arrington Research 3DViewPoint™, Biopac Systems, Inc. HMD). However, due to the smaller form factor it is significantly more ambitious to integrate such a solution into an HMD: The tracking relies on a camera, whose position is constrained by the HMD lenses and lens holders, which would block the view partially. Hence, a point right below the eyes is chosen, where precision is unfortunately non-uniform. An alternate more-frontal placement inadvertently reduces the FOV, which is often not an option because the feeling of immersion only starts at a horizontal FOV of 80°and increases quickly until 110°[8, 14]. Such an eye tracking procedure is further complicated since typical corneal-reflection-based eye-tracking algorithms [23] are not applicable, as they would produce disturbing reflections on the lenses.

Our work addresses these limitations and works towards gaining more insights into the VR experience. We propose an affordable, drift-free, and binocular eye-tracking solution, which is usable within the limited space of current HMD hardware designs without FOV reduction (Fig. 1). Throughout this paper, we will show how to overcome the challenges involved in designing such a VR system and solve several other issues, for instance calibration and adaptation to the user. Specifically, our contributions are:

1. a personalizable lens positioning system (horizontal and vertical) for HMDs and an integration of an unobtrusive camera setup for eye tracking in a lens-based HMD based on a specialized infra-red lighting (Sec. 3);

2. a model-based gaze estimation algorithm and calibration procedure to adjust the system to the user (Sec. 4);

3. a robust monocular pupil-tracking algorithm, which can deal with partial eye occlusions due to the lens holders and eye lid (Sec. 5);

We present applications showing the potential of our (binocular) eye tracking HMD, which are foveated rendering for depth of field, gaze-contingent level-of-detail, gaze map creation and realistic gaze control of virtual characters. In general, these applications illustrate the ability of our system to also perform psychophysical experiments and to extend the experience in immersive environments (Sec. 6). To validate our proposed system, we performed an objective comparison with a state-of-the-art pupil-tracking algorithm for near-field eye-trackers [31] and conducted a user evaluation (Sec. 7). We discuss the limitations of the current setup and give an outlook on future work (Sec. 8) before concluding this paper (Sec. 9).

2. RELATED WORK

Head-mounted Eye Trackers The success of the Oculus-Rift HMD led to a renewed interest in VR for the consumer market. The most-evolved HMDs in this low-cost sector, Crystal Cove (Oculus VR) and HTC Vive, offer a display resolution of at least Full-HD as well as positional and rotational tracking. Eye tracking is a natural next step and gained much attention in the research and development sector (e.g., FOVE Inc., Arrington Research, ASL Eye-Trac 6, SR Research, or Senso Motoric Instruments (SMI)). Even though first attempts have been undertaken in the year 2000 [20], current prototypes are still far from being consumer-ready with prices up to 15,000$ (SMI's eye tracker in the Oculus Rift case). One major cost factor are the miniature cameras and specialized digital processors for tracking at high speed. While the interior design of these Eye-tracking HMDs (ETHMD) is mostly kept secret, the comparatively low vertical FOV could suggest that the camera is placed inside the user's FOV occluding parts of the display. Our eye-tracking HMD setup has several benefits. It is a low-cost solution (approximately 450$), which offers the full FOV of current state-of-the-art HMDs.

Closest to our design is the EyeSeeCam [37]. This wearable eye tracker is used to align the focus of an external camera and the user in real-time for medical applications, surgery, or behavioral sciences. We similarly use dichroic mirrors to reflect infrared light from the eyes back to the cameras located outside the FOV. The custom-built EyeSeeCam can rely on traditional eye-tracking algorithms, but is also more expensive. We propose a customization, but it implies additional challenges to be solved, such as partial occlusions by the lens holders and view distortions by the lenses.

Eye-Tracking Algorithms Eye-tracking algorithms have a long research history and are often optimized for specialized setups which vary greatly in their design. A more general survey on eye tracking, including the employed eye models can be found in [23], while methods to evaluate eye-tracking quality are presented in [27]. Here, we will focus on the most-related work.

An essential step for feature-based eye tracking is the pupil detection. It forms the darkest part of the eye if illuminated from an off-axis view, and the brightest part if illuminated from a near-camera-axis view. Consequently, it is often well-separable from the surrounding iris. Most techniques rely on edge or contour detection of the pupil followed by an ellipse fitting. The main challenge is to deal with glints and reflections [30, 16], blinks [15], or noise [31], especially for near-eye devices, as e.g. Google Glasses [15, 11]. The gaze is then often estimated using the Purkinje effect (a bright glint appearing in the recorded infrared image resulting from the reflection of a spotlight LED used for illumination) in conjunction with camera and LED positions [18]. A taxonomy of the different approaches is given in [39].

In an HMD the Purkinje effect cannot be directly applied due to the converging lenses. LED illumination in front of the lenses (camera side) results in visible reflections from the lenses themselves, while a placement behind the lenses (closer to the eye) has the drawback that glints will not always be visible for the targeted wide FOV. We will show how to overcome this challenge.

Appearance-based methods do not extract features (pupil or glints) but use the complete input image to estimate the observed screen position. Several approaches built upon this idea in form of multilayer networks [10], Gaussian processes [40] or manifold learning [38]. While flexible (requiring only a calibration step), these techniques are often computationally costly and less applicable for VR scenarios, where high tracking rates are required. We make use of a novel approach combining image features with an underlying simulation model of our HMD; we detect the pupil in the recorded views, calibrate our HMD model, and derive the observed screen pixel position using a physical eye model.

3. EYE-TRACKING HMD

In the following, we describe our low-cost low-weight and personalizable design for immersive VR with unobtrusive eye tracking. After a general overview, we describe the details of each of the HMD's main components (Sec. 3.1).

3.1 Device Construction

General The most important elements are visualized in Fig. 2 and the working prototype in Fig. 3a–b. Our basic setup resembles a classic HMD with converging lenses (A) to focus the view on the display (B). The difference lies in infrared cameras at the outer boundary of the body case (F), dichroic mirros (G) and a circular LED-light array along the adjustable lens holders (H) to illuminate the eye (C). Reflected infrared light passes through the converging lenses and is reflected towards the cameras via two tilted dichroic mirrors (G). Display light (D) passes unhindered towards lenses and eye. An additional front camera (J) is used for markerless positional tracking and an integrated Inertial Measurement Unit (E) for orientation [21]. The electronic components are wired to a single harness connected to an external box with the display controller, an Arduino for orientation tracking, and the LED power supply [3].

Body Case The body case encapsulates all internal components (Fig. 2). A central barrier with a gap for the nose divides the display (C) into two disjoint symmetric parts, one for each eye. The case is firmly closed and tightened with foamed material to avoid exterior stray light and covered with comfortable tissue, except at the nose tip to enable normal breathing. The dimensions of the body were determined by fitting it to several 3D head scans (Fig. 3c).

Display We integrated a 5.6" LCD (1280×800 pixel resolution) with a refresh rate of 60 Hz. As indicated before, display controller and display are separated, which reduces the HMD weight.

Converging Lenses We use converging lenses of an Oculus Rift (DK1) to increase the perceived field of view [6]. Hereby, we also maintain compatibility to the Oculus Rift. Our prototype offers a horizontal field of view of 86°per eye. We provide dedicated controllers to adjust the position of the lenses in both horizontal and vertical direction for optimal lens placement (Fig. 1). Compared to a traditional HMD with interchangeable lens cups, our design makes more flexible and precise adjustments for varying head anatomy possible. For calibration, a circular IR reflecting ring is located on the backside of the lens holders.

Dichroic Mirrors We use two dichroic flat surfaces (also known as *hot mirrors*), which reflect light at wavelengths longer than 730 nm (infrared), while short wavelengths (< 720 nm) are entirely transmitted. They redirect infrared light reflected by the illuminated eyes towards the integrated cameras, which allows us to track the gaze without obscuring the field of view of the user.

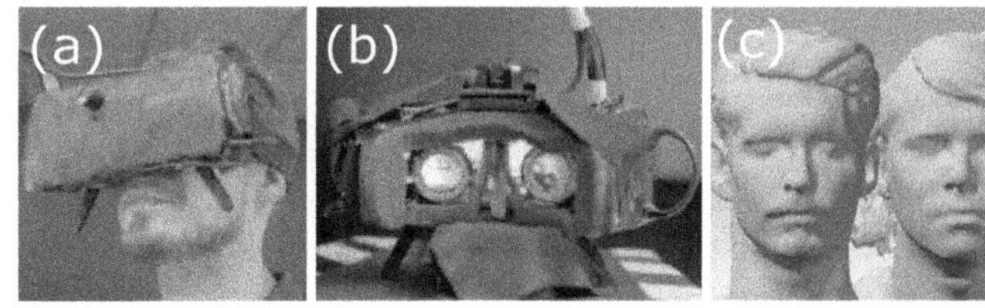

Figure 3: **HMD design and assembly**. User wearing the eye tracking HMD (a), working prototype (b), 3d scans of different human heads used for case dimensioning (c).

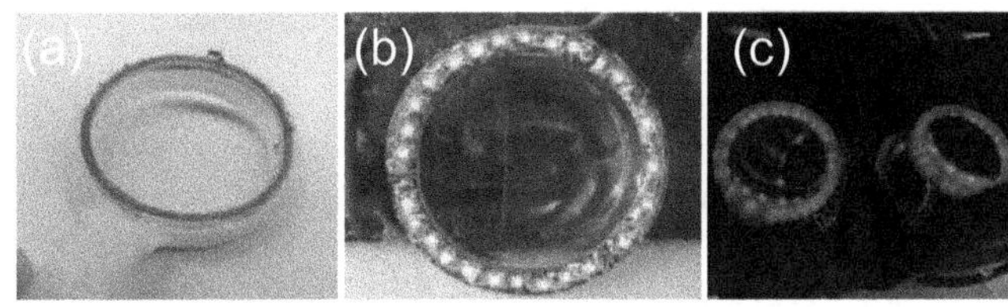

Figure 4: **Eye illuminating lense holder.** 3d printed lense holder with manufactured circuit board (a), working infrared SMD-LED array (b), illumination units within the HMD (c).

The dichroic mirrors have a size of $80 \times 80 \times 2$ mm with central cutouts for the nose and an inclination angle of 19.5°along the vertical axis. The angle is a tradeoff between space and optimal view on the eye (45°inclination). Higher inclination angles increase the necessary screen distance and, thus, screen size and weight. Smaller inclination angles lead to partly occluded views on the eye, which need to be dealt with during the pupil tracking.

Infrared Illumination Unit Twenty-five infrared LEDs mounted on a ring circuit lead to a uniform eye illumination from all directions (Fig. 4). The circuit has an inner diameter of 37 mm and width of 1.5 mm to minimize the lens controller size. The LEDs radiate with a wavelength of 830 nm over a wide angle of 140°. This infrared light enhances the pupil's contour in comparison to the contour of the limbus, but is outside the visible spectrum, thus, invisible to the user. We ensure safety of the user with regard to the impact on the user's exposure to the involved infrared radiation. An analysis can be found in the supplemental material.

Eye Tracking Cameras For binocular eye tracking, we integrated two low-cost cameras focusing at the distance of the user's eyes and having a fixed diagonal field of view of 56°. We exchanged their infrared filters with a long-pass filter blocking all but infrared light, in form of a single layer of a raw film negative. The cameras have fixed positions in the HMD (Fig. 2 (F)) and record at a 640×480 pixel resolution in grayscale at 75 Hz with a delay of 13 ms due to the internal image processor. This sampling rate suffices to track *fixations* and *smooth pursuit eye movements*.

Head Tracking For the viewpoint estimation in a virtual environment the rotational and translational component of the HMD are required as well. To this extent, we integrated an orientation sensor into the HMD and perform positional tracking via a head-mounted front camera. This combined setup is inexpensive and enables the required 6-degrees-of-freedom head tracking with sufficiently high precision and low latency.

We include an inertial measurement unit (IMU) holding multiple sensors connected to an Arduino microcontroller board to track the orientation (Yaw-Pitch-Roll). The IMU consists of an accelerometer, a gyro sensor and a digital motion processor (DMP). We set the update rate to 200 Hz to avoid a noticeable delay when moving the head and to reduce motion sickness.

The DMP supports automatic self-calibration and the angular drift of the IMU is less than 1° per minute, which is sufficient for longer usage. The positional tracking of the IMU could suffer from an integration error over time, resulting in an accumulated drift. However, over short periods of time, the IMU delivers sufficiently precise data. Our tracking solution combines the low-latency IMU output with markerless camera tracking, which results in a robust low-latency positional tracking with good precision. The pose estimation of the HMD front camera in world space is based on SLAM-feature tracking, implemented in the Metaio SDK [21, 2]. Our pose estimation proceeds as follows: The world frame is oriented and positioned automatically after a few seconds of feature initialization. Features are then detected and refined adaptively over time during tracking. Since world scale cannot be estimated from the tracker, it is automatically adjusted in the initialization phase, such that the camera-tracker results share the magnitude of the velocity measured by the IMU. This positional tracking takes ≈ 23 ms in our setup (13 ms for frame transmission, 10 ms for pose estimation).

4. CALIBRATION

This section describes calibration and reconstruction procedures for the different HMD components (Sec. 4.1) and the user-specific calibration (Sec. 4.2). Both are required for precise eye tracking, gaze estimation, and personalized adjustments. It is an important step in adapting the device to the user, which, ultimately, leads to a better VR experience. We describe the setup for one eye, the second eye is handled equivalently. The eye tracking implementation will be described in Sec.5.

4.1 HMD Calibration

To avoid motion sickness and create a convincing 3D impression, we require precise knowledge about each component in our HMD projection chain, meaning the relative position and orientation of the eye-tracking camera, the dichroic mirror, the lens and lens holder, as well as the refractive properties of the converging lens, and the intrinsic parameters of the eye-tracking camera. As a reference point $\mathbf{o}_H$ for all components of the HMD, we use the horizontal center of the HMD's front-most point.

Eye-Tracking Camera Calibration. We estimate both the intrinsic and extrinsic parameters for the eye-tracking camera. Intrinsics are derived via the technique by Bouguet [13]. Providing image resolution and sensor size is sufficient to transform a recording of a checkerboard or circle pattern of known size on a flat surface into focal length, principal point, as well as radial and tangential lens distortion.

The extrinsic camera parameters are derived during production as follows. Before the dichroic mirror is inserted into the body case, we cover the screen with a checkerboard calibration pattern, which is carefully adjusted to align with the edges of the body case. The eye tracking camera records the pattern and the extrinsic parameters are derived in relation to the pattern. We use the same CAD model, which we used to print the body case, and transform the extrinsic camera parameters into $\mathbf{o}_H$, the coordinate system of the HMD [24]. This virtual/real-world relationship will be exploited for the calibration. For validation, we compare the captured image with a rendered version of the checkerboard using the derived camera parameters. The reprojection error is less than 3 pixels and would be further reduced in an industrial production setting.

Mirror Calibration. After the camera has been calibrated the dichroic mirror is inserted and calibrated. We cover the mirror with a carefully aligned calibration pattern, to later match it to the CAD model, and capture it from the eye-tracking cameras. Performing the same calibration procedure as for the cameras this gives us the camera parameters in relation to the mirror position, and vice versa. We then transform this relative mirror position into $\mathbf{o}_H$. Again, we validate the correctness of the derived parameters by rendering the checkerboard and comparing it with the captured image. In our prototype, the rotation angles of the mirrors were $\sim 18.9^\circ$ and $\sim 19.5^\circ$ for the left and right mirror, respectively. The slight asymmetry was due to a fabrication imperfection when printing the HMD.

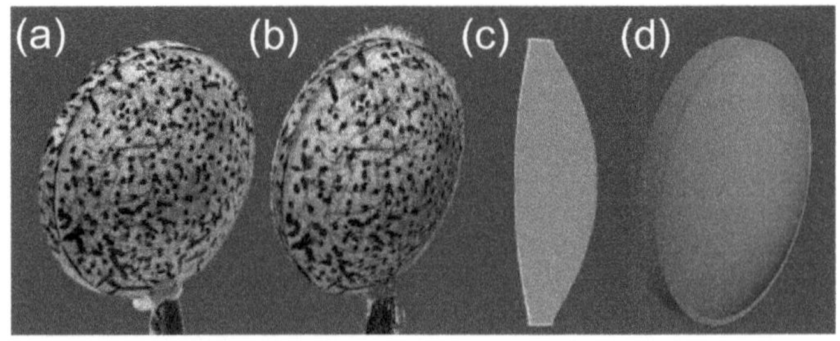

Figure 5: **Lens reconstruction**. Converging lens with artificial surface features (a), reconstructed 3d point cloud (b), derived lens profile (c), smooth reconstructed model (d).

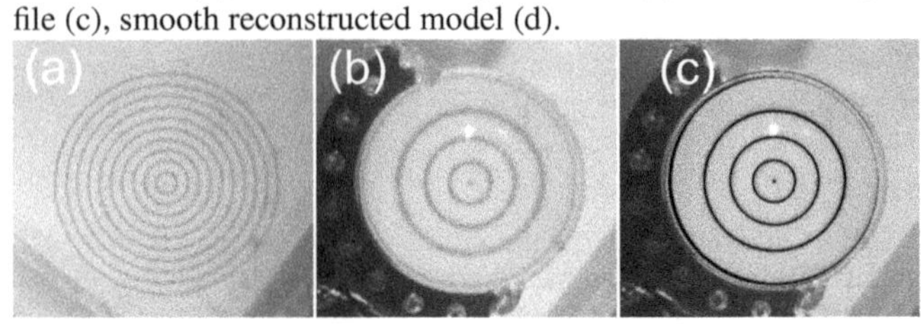

Figure 6: **Refractive index estimation**. Calibration object (a), ground truth refraction through the lens (b), rerendered calibration object (c) rendered on top of (b).

Lens Reconstruction. We require an accurate geometric model of the aspheric lens as well as the index of refraction (IOR) to support the user calibration later on. In our case, details about the used optics have not been available and accordingly had to be reconstructed. As this is the situation for most lens models in HMDs, we describe our lens reconstruction approach in the following.

Lens Geometry To avoid a complicated reconstruction of a transparent surface, we artificially colorize the lens with ink and create a set of discriminative features (Fig. 5a). We then reconstruct a lens-surface point cloud based on different input views [1], which we capture at high quality and resolution using a DSLR camera (Fig. 5b). As a point cloud may contain holes, we fit a parametric lens model (Fig. 5c) as follows. We assume a disc-like and radially-symmetric shape. The mean positional vector μ of the point cloud and the eigenvectors $\mathbf{e}_1, \mathbf{e}_2, \mathbf{e}_3$ provide a convenient coordinate space for the lens reconstruction, as μ is equal to the center of the lens and together with $\mathbf{e}_3$ describes the rotation axis $\mathbf{r} = \mu + t\mathbf{e}_3$. Because of the symmetry assumption, we only need to derive the 2D profile (Fig. 5c). It can be conveniently described by two 2nd order polynomials for the front and back curvature. We rotate each point of the point cloud around $\mathbf{r}$ onto the plane centered at μ and spanned by $\mathbf{e}_1, \mathbf{e}_3$. We then fit two 2nd order polynomials to the point cloud, one for the front facing points and one for the backfacing points [33]. This approach also increases robustness as the symmetry assumption leads to a better use of the redundancy in the point cloud. The lens is then reconstructed from this parameterized profile (Fig. 5d).

Index of Refraction Since the lens' index of refraction (IOR) is wavelength-dependent, we estimate it for infrared and the visible spectrum to incorporate both light paths in our HMD (Fig. 2). The following procedure is the same for both, only the recording camera is exchanged. We apply an analysis-by-synthesis approach based on the lens' geometric properties. First, we record a front view of a circular calibration pattern (Fig. 6a) having an outer diameter of 50mm at a known distance and calibrate the cameras as before. After adding the lens between camera and pattern we take several images at different known distances between pattern and lens (Fig. 6b). We then optimize the IOR by comparing synthetically rendered scenes of the lens and calibration pattern (Fig. 6c) using the physically-correct and wavelength-dependent Maxwell Renderer [5] to the recorded camera images. We estimated an IOR $N_I = 1.472$ for the wavelength $\lambda = 950nm$ and $N_V = 1.515$ for $\lambda = 560nm$ which are typical values for materials like Acrylite, Lucite or Plexiglass.

4.2 User Calibration

Most components of our system can be calibrated at production time (Sec. 4.1). User-specific components, such as the lens holder position, interpupillary distance, and eye-to-lens distance need to be estimated for every user separately. These are important for a natural 3D impression and meaningful eye-tracking results, as they are essential to predict the virtual viewpoint, which can otherwise only be roughly estimated. The components of the gaze simulation model being calibrated are visualized in Fig. 7a. First, the user adjusts the lenses parallel to the screen, to have a frontal view when looking straight. Next, the lens distance is adjusted until the screen appears sharp.

Lens-Holder Localization. To detect the lens-holder position, and, hereby, the lens' position, we use the white IR reflecting ring on the backside of the lens holder (Fig. 7a). Additionally added infrared LEDs are located around the eye tracking camera solely for illuminating the ring (Fig. 2 (F), red LEDs at the camera). When turning off the screen and the interior LED ring, the lens holder can be detected by thresholding the image captured by the eye-tracking camera. We then derive its center and eccentricity [22]. We compute the 3D position and orientation of this ring again via an analysis-by-synthesis procedure; we render a model of the ring and iteratively optimize its position and rotation via a gradient-descent approach based on the difference between the ellipse centers, size and eccentricity, which proved fast and accurate.

Eye Calibration. Next, we estimate the eye's distance to the lens. The main problem is that a view of the eye does not provide useful information regarding scale, as eye sizes differ. Further, the view might be distorted in complex ways by the converging lenses. Analysis-by-synthesis can again help us in this situation. The LED ring in the lens holders produces a characteristic reflection on an eye, also known as glint (Fig. 7b–c). This reflection can be used to determine the distance between lens and eye. Nonetheless, to make this step possible we need a physically-plausible eye model.

Eye Model The eye ball of a healthy adult human has a quite consistent shape [9]. The main part can be modeled as a sphere rotating around its center with a diameter of 24mm and only few individual deviations (Gaussian distribution with a standard deviation of ± 1mm). The cornea forms an additional spherical surface above the sclera with a smaller radius of 7.8mm. The direct light reflected from the sclera produces the most prominent glints. We set the IOR of the cornea to $N_D = 1.2$ and the eye fluids to $N_D = 1.276$ [9].

Eye Registration We extract the glints using a simple threshold $t_G = 0.9$. When a user looks along the optical axis of the eye tracking camera (taking the reflection from the dichroic mirror into account) the glints form an almost perfect circle on the sclera, otherwise this circle is distorted. The shape of the glints can, thus, be used in a feedback loop to guide the user's view towards the optical axis (Fig. 7b–c). To this extent, the user is asked to focus on a marker on the screen. The glints from the resulting image are extracted and an ellipse is fitted to it [22]. The marker is then moved and the ellipse is evaluated again. The movement of the marker is given by $\alpha(c_g - c_p)$ where c_g is the glint-ellipse center in pixel coordinates and c_p the estimated pupil-center position. The process is computationally cheap and α can be small, which lets the marker smoothly move over the screen until the algorithm converges.

We then derive the eye-lens distance and the absolute 3d position of the eye based on the eye model. In practice, we rendered the characteristic positions, where the glints are as circular as possible, for different eye distances and positions and record the diameter and center of the fitted ellipse. The result is a Look-Up table, which allows us to calibrate for the eye position quickly.

Gaze Calibration. Finally, for the gaze estimation, we need a mapping from pupil positions in the eye-tracking camera to screen positions. We rely on our virtual HMD model configured with the derived calibration values and estimated eye position. Here, we compute the light path from a pixel, representing a detected pupil center, of the eye-tracking image over the dichroic mirrors, through the lens towards the eye. By construction, this ray has to cross the eye at the pupil center (Fig. 2 red light paths). We can, thus, map eye-tracking camera pixels to an eye rotation. Similarly, the eye rotation can be used to determine a screen position by computing the light path from the eye through the lenses onto the screen (Fig. 2 green light paths). This mapping is precomputed for approximately 1300 virtual eye rotations per eye covering the full motion range of the human eye (Fig. 8k, black and red dots). Using barycentric interpolation, we can then map each potential pupil position c_p in the eye-tracking camera (Fig. 8k, green dot), to a view vector $\vec{v}$ and a pixel position on the display c_s.

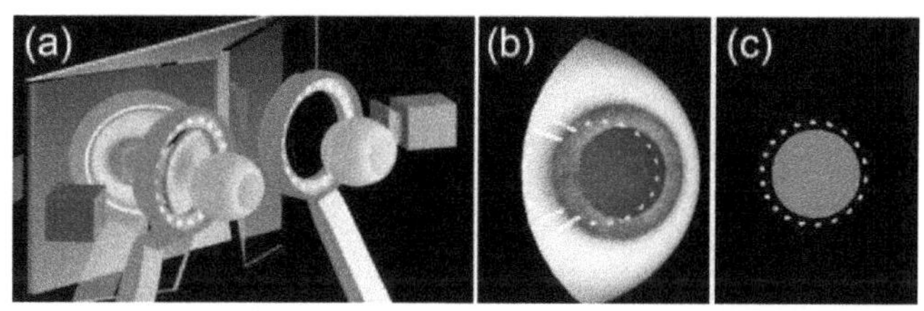

Figure 7: **Simulated gaze model**. Virtual gaze setup (a), realistic synthetic eye (b), glints and pupil mask for characteristic gaze (c).

5. MONOCULAR PUPIL TRACKING

Our gaze estimation (Sec. 4) relies on the current pupil position in the eye-camera image. The pupil extraction is described in this section, for which noise, (partial) occlusions by the eye lid or lashes, and dust or smears on the lens or mirror need to be handled.

Since our off-axis illumination units result in a *dark pupil*, we detect low intensities, which differ significantly from the high amount of reflected infrared light from the sclera and limbus. The limbus only absorbs more light in the visible light spectrum.

For the pupil tracking (Alg. 1), we rely on the grayscale-image $\mathbf{I}$ normalized to $[0, 1]$ and a binary mask $\mathbf{M}_L$ indicating pixels belonging to the lens, which is obtained during the calibration step. For real-time performance and robustness, we first determine whether the eye is closed, open or halfway closed. Each configuration is dealt with separately (Alg. 1).

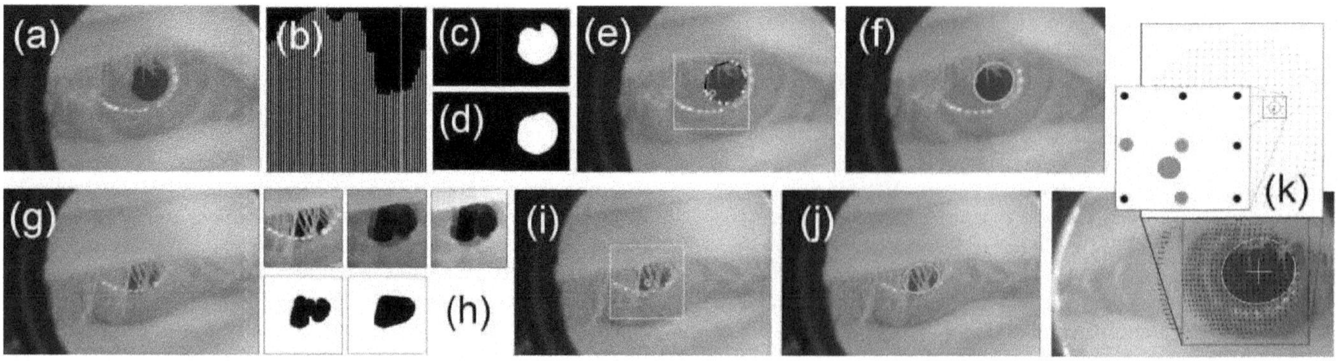

Figure 8: **Pupil detection pipeline.** Top row: Visible pupil case, Alg. 4. Captured image (a), histogram for threshold estimation (b), pupil binarization (c), pupil closing (d), contour filtering (e), pupil ellipse fitting (f). Bottom row: Partially occluded pupil case, Alg. 5. Captured image (g), pupil filtering and binarization (h), contour point filtering (i), pupil ellipse fitting (j). Barycentric interpolation for pupil-to-screen mapping (green: current pupil position, black: precomputed positions, red: closest samples used for interpolation) (k).

Algorithm 1 Pupil Tracking $(\mathbf{I}, \mathbf{M}_L)$

$\tilde{p} \leftarrow$ Approximate Pupil Position $(\mathbf{I}, \mathbf{M}_L)$ ▷ Alg. 2
if $\mathbf{I}(\tilde{p}) > t_{visibility}$ **then**
  Eye is closed
else
  $\theta \leftarrow$ Compute Pupil Occlusion $(\mathbf{I}, \mathbf{M}_L, \tilde{p})$ ▷ Alg. 3
  if $\theta < t_{occlude}$ **then**
    $\{p, e_x, e_y, \phi\} \leftarrow$ Detect Visible Pupil $(\mathbf{I}, \mathbf{M}_L)$ ▷ Alg. 4
  else
    $\{p, e_x, e_y, \phi\} \leftarrow$ Detect Occluded Pupil $(\mathbf{I}, \mathbf{M}_L)$
    ▷ Alg. 5
  end if
end if
return $\{p, e_x, e_y, \phi\}$

Approximate Pupil Position To make a fast guess of whether the eye is closed or not we approximately locate the pupil position as follows (Alg. 2):

Algorithm 2 Approximate Pupil Position $(\mathbf{I}, \mathbf{M}_L)$

$p_{cum} \leftarrow (0,0) \quad w_{cum} \leftarrow 0$
for $p \in \mathbf{M}_L$ **do**
  $w \leftarrow (1 - \mathbf{I}(p))^{\gamma}$
  $p_{cum} \leftarrow p_{cum} + p \cdot w$
  $w_{cum} \leftarrow w_{cum} + w$
end for
return $\tilde{p} \leftarrow p_{cum} / w_{cum}$

We accumulate a weighted average of all pixel positions p within the lens mask $\mathbf{M}_L$. Each pixel p contributes with a weight w determined by $(1 - \mathbf{I}(p))^{\gamma}$ with $\gamma = 10$. Hence, darker pixels (higher likelihood to be the pupil) will contribute more. The weighted-average position is our initial pupil-position guess $\tilde{p}$.

Occlusion Estimation If the intensity in a 70×70 pixels wide window around the initial pupil position is above the threshold $t_{visibility} = 0.4$, the eye is regarded as being closed. If the eye is not completely closed, we further refine our strategy by classifying it as either completely visible or partially occluded. The amount of occlusion is defined by two measures m_1 and m_2 (Alg. 3). While not being sufficient on their own the combination is significantly more robust. The first m_1 estimates the presence of eye lashes. The second m_2 tries to detect the amount of non-pupil pixels. Based on their combination, the eye is declared visible or partially visible and the corresponding detection algorithms are run.

To compute m_1 and m_2, we first remove glints by inpainting all pixels with a higher intensity than $t_G = 0.9$ [12]. These appear especially in the 1.5 – 2 mm transition zone of the curvature of the sclera and the curvature of the corneal surface that forms an external and internal surface groove (*scleral sulcus*) [9]. For more conservative results we slightly dilate the inpainted area $\mathbf{M}_{Glints}$.

We then detect eye lashes occluding the pupil in the resulting image $\mathbf{I}_{NoGlints}$. We restrict our computations to a small area $\mathbf{M}_{ROI}$ of radius $r = 35$ pixels around $\tilde{p}$. Then a morphological opening filter is applied (minimum before maximum filter) to $\mathbf{I}_{NoGlints}$ with a kernel size $k_{MinMax} = 13$, removing finer structures, such as eye lashes. The first term m_1 is then defined as the sum of absolute intensity values of the difference image $\mathbf{I}_{\Delta} = |\mathbf{I}_{MinMax} - \mathbf{I}_{NoGlints}|$.

The second term aims at estimating the number of non-pupil pixels, which are brighter. To this extent, the gray value range $[0.4, 0.7]$ in $\mathbf{I}_{NoGlints}$ is linearly mapped to the range $[0, 1]$. Other values are clamped accordingly. The second term m_2 is then defined as the sum of the resulting intensities inside $\mathbf{M}_{ROI}$. Both terms are combined into the final occlusion score $\theta = 0.5 \cdot (1/3 m_1 + 2/3 m_2)$. If $\theta < t_{occlude} = 0.3$ the eye is considered visible otherwise as partially occluded. The corresponding detection algorithm is applied.

Algorithm 3 Compute Pupil Occlusion $(\mathbf{I}, \mathbf{M}_L, \tilde{p})$

$\mathbf{M}_{Glints} \leftarrow \{p \in \mathbf{M}_L \mid \mathbf{I}(p) > t_G\}$ ▷ Glint Mask
$\mathbf{M}_{Glints} \leftarrow F_{\text{Dilate}}(\mathbf{M}_{Glints})$
$\mathbf{I}_{NoGlints} \leftarrow F_{\text{Inpainting}}(\mathbf{I}, \mathbf{M}_{Glints})$ ▷ Glints removed
$\mathbf{I}_{MinMax} \leftarrow F_{\text{Min}}(\mathbf{I}_{NoGlints}, k_{MinMax})$ ▷ Eye lashes removed
$\mathbf{I}_{MinMax} \leftarrow F_{\text{Max}}(\mathbf{I}_{EyeLashes}, k_{MinMax})$
$\mathbf{I}_{\Delta} \leftarrow |\mathbf{I}_{MinMax} - \mathbf{I}_{NoGlints}|$
$\mathbf{M}_{ROI} \leftarrow F_{\text{circMask}}(\mathbf{I}, \tilde{p}, r_1) \cap \mathbf{M}_L$
$\mathbf{I}_{\Delta} \leftarrow \text{Normalize}(\mathbf{I}_{\Delta} \cap \mathbf{M}_{ROI})$
$m_1 \leftarrow \sum_{p \in \mathbf{M}_{ROI}} \mathbf{I}_{\Delta}(p) / |\mathbf{M}_{ROI}|$ ▷ First Metric
$\mathbf{I}_{EyeLashes} \leftarrow F_{\text{(Tonal Correction)}}(\mathbf{I}_{NoGlints}, [0.4, 0.7])$
$\mathbf{M}_{ROI} \leftarrow F_{\text{circMask}}(\mathbf{I}, \tilde{p}, r_2) \cap \mathbf{M}_L$
$m_2 \leftarrow \sum_{p \in \mathbf{M}_{ROI}} \mathbf{I}_{EyeLashes}(p) / |\mathbf{M}_{ROI}|$ ▷ Second Metric
$\theta \leftarrow (m_1 \cdot w_1 + m_2 \cdot w_2) \cdot 0.5$ ▷ Combined Metric
return θ

Visible Pupil We will now describe how to localize a visible or moderately-occluded pupil (Alg. 4). We build upon the observation that pupil pixels in comparison to its surrounding are well separated in an image histogram (Fig. 8a–b). We thus compute a histogram

Algorithm 4 Detect visible pupil $(\mathbf{I}, \mathbf{M}_L)$

$\mathbf{I}_{BP} \leftarrow 1 - \mathbf{I}$ $\triangleright$ Inverts to bright pupil image
$\mathbf{H} \leftarrow \text{Histogram}(\mathbf{I}_{BP}, \mathbf{M}_L)$
$\mathbf{H} \leftarrow F_{\text{Median}}(\mathbf{H}, k_{HistMedian})$
$h \leftarrow \text{findGrayvalueOfBrightestLocalMinimum}(\mathbf{H})$
$\mathbf{M}_{PupilSeg} \leftarrow \{p \in \Omega \mid \mathbf{I}_{BP}(p) > h\}$
$\mathbf{B} \leftarrow \text{Blob Detection}(\mathbf{M}_{PupilSeg})$
$\mathbf{b} \leftarrow \text{argmax}_{\tilde{b} \in \mathbf{B}} \text{HullArea}(\tilde{b})$
if $\text{HullArea}(\mathbf{b}) < t_b \cdot \sum_{\tilde{b} \in \mathbf{B}} \text{HullArea}(\tilde{b})$ **then** $\triangleright$ Merge blobs
    $\mathbf{b} \leftarrow \mathbf{b} \cup \{\tilde{b} \in \mathbf{B} \mid \|\text{Centroid}(\mathbf{b}) - \text{Centroid}(\tilde{b})\| < d\}$
end if
$\mathbf{C} \leftarrow \text{Convex Hull Contour}(\mathbf{b})$
$\mathbf{C} \leftarrow \text{Remove Close Points}(\mathbf{C})$
$\mathbf{C} \leftarrow \text{Remove Colinear Points}(\mathbf{C})$
$\{p, e_x, e_y, \phi\} \leftarrow \text{Ellipse Fit}(\mathbf{C})$
return $\{p, e_x, e_y, \phi\}$

Algorithm 5 Detect occluded pupil $(\mathbf{I}, \mathbf{M}_L)$

$\mathbf{I} \leftarrow 2 \cdot \mathbf{I} - G * \mathbf{I}$
$\mathbf{I} \leftarrow F_{\text{Min}}(\mathbf{I}_{Filt}, k_{Min})$
$\bar{\mathbf{I}} \leftarrow \text{Normalize}(\mathbf{I})$
$\mathbf{M}_{PupilSeg} \leftarrow \{p \in \Omega \mid \bar{\mathbf{I}}(p) > t_{Pupil}\}$
$\mathbf{B} \leftarrow \text{Blob Detection}(\mathbf{M}_{PupilSeg})$
$\mathbf{C} \leftarrow \text{Convex Hull Contour}(\mathbf{B})$
$\mathbf{C} \leftarrow F_{\text{Erode}}(\mathbf{C})$
$\{p, e_x, e_y, \phi\} \leftarrow \text{Ellipse Fit}(\mathbf{C})$
return $\{p, e_x, e_y, \phi\}$

$\mathbf{H}$ on the inverted input image $\mathbf{I}_{BP} = 1 - \mathbf{I}$ with 64 bins. A median filter of size $k_{HistMedian} = 2$ removes outliers. Marking pixels brighter than a threshold h separates the pupil well. Following our observations, we set h to be the grayvalue belonging to the brightest local minimum within $\mathbf{H}$ (Fig. 8b, red bar in histogram).

Next, we want to clean up the derived pupil pixels and perform a blob detection ($\mathbf{B}$) to find connected components. Inspired by Chen *et al.* [15], we work on the convex hull for every blob in $\mathbf{B}$ to remove residues of the glint removal. In difference to [15], we check if the blob detection already detected the pupil. We assume this to be the case if the largest convex hull of each blob covers more than 70 % of the summed area of all blobs. Otherwise, we merge blobs whose center is closer to the center of the largest blob (Fig. 8c) than half the maximum extent of the largest blob d. The contour of the convex hull of the merged blobs then gives us a first estimate of the pupil contour $\mathbf{C}$ (Fig. 8d). We refine this contour by first removing any point closer than 5 pixels to each other and secondly removing colinear points since those are probably generated by the (mostly) straight geometry of the eye lid (Fig. 8e). Finally, we fit an ellipse to the remaining contour points to obtain position p, eccentricity e_x and e_y and angle ϕ of the projected pupil (Fig. 8f).

Partially Occluded Pupil The last case to treat is a strongly occluded pupil (Alg. 5). Here, we boost the contrast using unsharp masking; $\mathbf{I} = 2 \cdot \mathbf{I} - G * \mathbf{I}$ (Fig. 8h), where G is a Gaussian and $*$ the convolution operator. We then apply a minimum filter with radius $k_{Min} = 21$ pixels to remove eye lashes. By normalizing the input image $\mathbf{I}$ to the range $[0, 1]$, we can detect pupil segments by an adaptive thresholding. Setting the threshold to $t_{Pupil} = 0.12 + (\|\tilde{p} - p_E\|)^{0.5}$ derives an approximate mask of the pupil fragments, where p_E is the pixel position of the center of the eye ball. We chose this formula to countervail an observed vignette effect at the border of the eye.

As in Alg. 4, we perform the blob detection and merge the resulting blobs to estimate the convex hull of the result (Fig. 8h). To counteract the minimum filter, we erode the result with a similar kernel of size k_{Min}. Finally, we extract the contour of the blob and again perform an ellipse fitting to obtain the ellipse parameters of the projected pupil (Fig. 8j).

6. APPLICATIONS

We implemented several application for our HMD with integrated eye tracker, based on the freely-available Unreal Engine and game content [4]. **Adaptive Depth of Field Rendering** We simulate the accommodation reflex inspired by previous studies for desktop applications [25, 32]. In reality, accommodation allows us to focus on objects at arbitrary distances by flexing our eye lens. In consequence, other objects are naturally blurred. To compute the focus distance, we cast a ray into the scene starting at the viewpoint and directed by the estimated viewing direction from our gaze estimation of one eye. We then determine the distance to the surface the ray hits first (Fig. 9) and render the scene with the appropriate depth-of-field effect turned on. When thin objects are very close to the viewer a binocular eye tracking is required, where the convergence point of both viewing rays defines the focal distance. Nonetheless, in most scenarios the increase of computational effort seems unnecessary.

Figure 9: **Real-time Gaze-contingent Rendering.** Foveated rendering (left): Rendering quality and saturation is decreased for peripheral vision. Adaptive depth-of-field effect (center, right): near and far focus distances. Gaze vector shown as red marker.

Foveated Rendering In the second application, we show that our gaze tracker enables simulation of a gaze-contingent display. Previous work showed the potential of this techniques [35, 19]. Due to the rapid acuity fall-off from foveal to peripheral vision rendering could massively benefit from Gaze-contingency. We demonstrate the effect by rendering the scene with five different resolutions describing circles of different radii on the screen. The highest resolution is used in the foveal region where the user is looking at. The render resolution is reduced by a factor of two for each following circle. We smoothly blend between each render resolution to avoid visible resolution seams.

Our current implementation is just a simulated Foveated Rendering and does not lead to an actual performance boost for the renderer we employed. When using a path tracer the number of samples per pixel could be reduced in the peripheral vision whereas in a rasterizer a lower level-of-detail or less texture lookups could be performed (Fig. 9).

Additionally, similar techniques could be used to simulate various visual field defects, such as hemianopia (partial blindness), color blindness, retinitis pigmentosa (night blindness, blurring of vision, loss of central vision, and others) or pigmentary retinopathy (deposits of pigments) (Fig. 9, left).

Gaze Transfer for Avatars In this application, we enhance immersion by mapping the gaze direction and head movements of the user onto an avatar standing virtually in front of him. The eyes of the avatar rotate as the user rotates his eyes and the avatar blinks as the user blinks (Fig. 10). This increases perceived realism for every entity in VR and offers novel opportunities for self-expression. Gaze transfer can be a valuable extension for telepresence applications or user-to-user communication within VR applications.

Gaze Maps are an effective visualization of the user's gaze over time and an effective tool for user experience studies [36]. For a demonstration using our binocular eye tracker, we implemented a player for stereoscopic movies and recorded the gaze for multiple users when watching the video. The gaze maps have been derived by plotting and filtering the estimated screen positions for all the viewers. The result is shown for one frame of the movie in Fig. 11. Most viewers fixated the person in foreground as well as the picture in the background and the table. We used a temperature color coding for visulization (hot areas are fixated more than cool areas).

Figure 10: **Gaze Transfer and Avatar Animation.** (Left, center) Eye tracking enables more expressive and natural character animation. The estimated pupil size and blink event can also be used to animate eye adaptation and blinks instantly (right).

Figure 11: **Gaze visualization.** Gaze maps for images or videos show the fixated display area averaged over time or users. Temperature color scheme represents fixation quantity.

7. EVALUATION

In this section, we evaluate our method by estimating tracking quality and performance. We tested our pupil detection algorithms against two other state-of-the-art algorithms [31, 15]. We conclude the section with a user study with 33 participants.

Performance Evaluation We have implemented our eye tracking framework in C++ using the OpenCV algorithm library [7]. Our primarily CPU-based processing pipeline achieves a total end-to-end latency from capturing the eyes by the cameras until a rendered frame is visible to the user of 32 ms on current hardware (i7-4930K @ 3.4 Ghz, GeForce GTX 780 Ti). The pupil estimation of both eyes and the camera capture threads run in parallel on multiple cores of the CPU. Some of the preprocessing filters

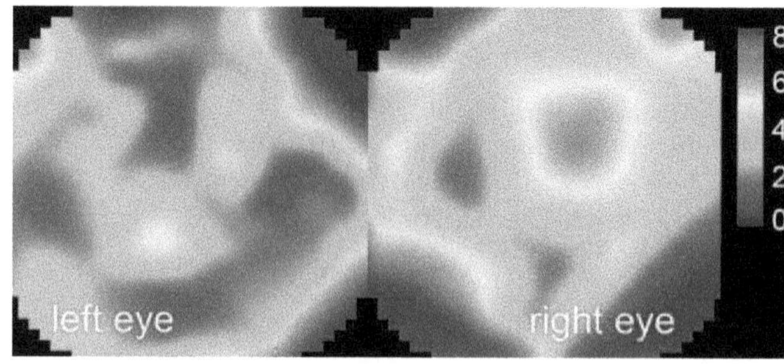

Figure 12: **Gaze direction error.** The absolute error for both eyes over the available FOV, given in screen pixels.

(sharpening, blur) run in CUDA on GPU. The eye-tracking camera resolution is 640×480 pixels at 75 frames per second. Timings for each step of the processing pipeline are given in Table 1.

Process step	*Duration (milliseconds)*
Frame grabbing (@75 Hz)	≈ 13
Pupil estimation	≈ 9
Gaze estimation	< 1
Rendering (Application)	≈ 10
Total Latency	≈ 32

Table 1: **End-to-end latency estimation.**

Tracking Quality In this section, we evaluate our pupil-tracking algorithm in terms of tracking stability and tracking precision. After having calibrated the eye tracker for the two different male users with corrected to normal vision, we measured the tracking precision. We conducted a fair-minded comparison to the *STARBURST* eye tracking algorithm of Li *et al.* [31] and the auto-threshold algorithm of Chen *et al.* [15] working for near-field eye tracking without relying on the corneal reflection. As input we used the glint-free images as these are required by all algorithms.

T1 Pupil Position and Size We test the pupil position and size objectively against ground-truth data derived from manually created pupil masks of a 1987 frames video recorded with both eye tracking cameras. The error values for pupil position and size are computed by the differences of the extracted pupil-ellipse position and eccentricity. The result of the test is summarized in Table 2. The pupil position error ε_{Pos} is computed as the average pixel deviation of the computed position p_e from the reference position p_{gt}:

$$\varepsilon_{Pos} = \frac{1}{n}\sum_{i=1}^{n}\left(|p_e - p_{gt}|\right) \tag{1}$$

and the pupil size error by the equation

$$\varepsilon_{Size} = \frac{1}{n}\sum_{i=1}^{n}\left(|e_x - e_{x,gt}| + |e_y - e_{y,gt}|\right), \tag{2}$$

where e_x, e_y are the eccentricities of the estimated ellipse. In terms of accuracy, our algorithms clearly outperforms the competitors as they can hardly deal with partially occluded pupils in which case our algorithm clearly stands out. Independent from the used pupil detection algorithm the pupil size is closest to the real pupil size for a central view. The pupil size artificially increases as the view tilts towards the sides due to the increasing lens distortion resulting in partial magnification of the projected pupil.

Test	ε_{Size} (px)	ε_{Pos} (px)
Ours	**0.04**	**2.16**
Auto-threshold [15]	0.63	21.67
Starburst [31]	0.24	13.15

Table 2: **Pupil position and pupil size accuracy.**

T2 Gaze Direction Error We also evaluate the difference of the screen position returned by the eye tracker and the reference screen position set by a visible marker on screen as

$$\varepsilon_{Screen} = \frac{1}{n}\sum_{i=1}^{n} |s_e - s_{gt}| \qquad \varepsilon_{Ang} = \tan^{-1}\frac{\varepsilon_{Screen}}{d_{EyeScreen}} \quad (3)$$

where s_e and s_{gt} are the estimated and reference screen positions and n the number of tracking samples (n = 30 in our test). The pixel error is then transformed into the angular error by estimating $d_{EyeScreen}$ via ray tracing using the calibrated model. The error is evaluated for thirty different positions.

The error ranges from $\varepsilon_{Ang} \approx 0.5$ °to $\varepsilon_{Ang} \approx 3.5$ °, being generally higher at the borders of the screen due to stronger occlusion and therefore aggravated pupil position estimation. The interpolated screen position error is visualized in Fig. 12.

User Study We tested our eye tracker with 33 participants (25 males, 8 females); 15 had normal vision, but 18 had corrected-to-normal vision. The current prototype does not support wearing glasses when using the HMD. However, the lenses can be adjusted to compensate for a wide variety of ametropia and hypertropia [17]. Every person started with the user calibration procedure and then was able to use the Adaptive Depth-of-Field application (Sec. 6).

Afterwards, we asked the users to rate certain aspects of the device (update rate, latency, stability, accuracy) and the application (naturalness, usefulness, user experience). The complete questionnaire and evaluated numbers are included in the supplemental material. The evaluation of the user feedback is visualized in Fig. 13.

Summarizing the results the user feedback was very positive with regard to the user experience and evaluation of the usefulness of the system. Every user mentioned that they can think about and want gaze usage in many application using the presented HMD.

The stability and accuracy was rated positive but not completely convincing yet. There were two major issues, which explain the reduced rating. The system is currently an early prototype, and it includes disturbing redundant cables from the cameras, as well as an inflexible display cable, which resulted in slight shifts of the HMD when turning the head, which reduced the accuracy of the gaze estimation. Another issue for some participants was the usage of mascara on the eye lashes which negatively influenced our pupil estimation resulting in a reduced user experience.

8. DISCUSSION AND FUTURE WORK

Limitations The concept of adjustable lens controllers provides a sharp vision even for people usually wearing glasses. Wearing glasses inside the HMD is an open problem as this would require larger lens-to-eye distance, larger lenses, and a larger screen for the same view. A strict positioning of the HMD with respect to the head is also crucial. Otherwise a recalibration becomes necessary.

Long-term user study In this work, we tested the tracking quality of our gaze estimation algorithm just for a small number of people and a limited time (several minutes) of usage. In the future, we plan a larger user study to improve the hardware design and software of our prototype. Additional studies with longer usage sessions will provide more information about robustness, usability and wearing comfort.

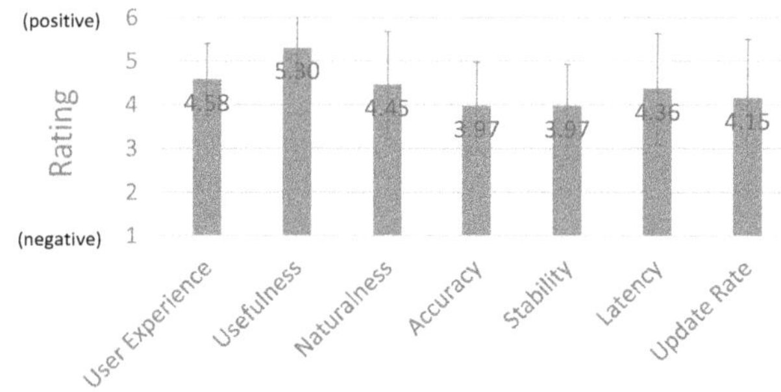

Figure 13: **User study results.** Blue bars show user ratings concerning specific aspects (entitled on the left). Scale ranging from [1, 6] (negative/positive). Black bars represent standard deviation.

Auto-calibration In the literature there are software methods for auto-calibration that rely on natural scan pathes of the environment and provide a seamless transition between calibration and interaction phase [34]. These concepts may be beneficial for our system. However, to the best of our knowledge none of those methods have been tested within an HMD yet. Alternatively, by using additional hardware, it might be possible that the calibration process can be largely simplified or completely automated. Klefenz et al. and Kohlbecher et al. exploit the precalibration in a stereoscopic camera setup to track the pupil without additional user calibration [28, 29]. Alternatively a depth sensor could provide valuable information about the actual anatomy of the individual eye. An automated calibration process seems interesting, even if additional hardware would increase weight and complexity of the device.

Applications With the presented applications we only scratch the surface of possible VR scenarios. Many other applications are enabled with instant knowledge of the users gaze or at least could benefit from this input, e.g., gaze-based selection and manipulation or studies on user interfaces.

Perception studies can assess the potential of eye tracking to exploit or examine the perception of the human visual system or an individual user. These insights may lead to methods, which will improve viewing experience or accelerate the rendering process. Perception studies also enable evaluation of simulations in VR, e.g., in the fields of assembly processes or training for aerospace, military or surgery, psychological therapy, or eye disease simulation.

Using eye tracking as an input device enables novel gaze-based interaction metaphors, hands-free interaction with Attentive User Interfaces (AUIs) or an additional communication channel. The user is able to express his interest naturally by gaze. With additional cameras our HMD prototype could be extended for Augmented Reality usage (AR) where hands-free interaction is beneficial and precise IPD estimation and calibration are very important. Instead of using a closed body, the mirror-based setup, and gaze-estimation technique could also be used for See-Through HMDs.

9. CONCLUSION

We have presented a complete binocular eye-tracking solution for head-mounted displays. Our system relies on low-cost components that should be affordable for every user group. This aspect opens the door for a large variety of novel applications and contributes to progress in research. The prototype has been tested by a small group of subjects. For the future, we will work with a larger group of people in order to improve pupil detection and user comfort. We also plan to investigate new ways for continuous and automatic user calibration.

10. ACKNOWLEDGMENTS

The research leading to these results has received funding from the European Union's Seventh Framework Programme FP7/2007-2013 under grant agreement no. 256941, Reality CG. We thank Lorenz Rogge, Pablo Bauszat and Günther Stengel for supporting us with the project. We also thank Epic Games, Inc. for making the Unreal Engine and the stock footage openly available.

11. REFERENCES

[1] Agisoft PhotoScan, 2014. agisoft.com , vis. 12-20-2014.

[2] metaio SDK, 2014. dev.metaio.com/sdk, vis. 1-5-2015.

[3] Arduino microprocessor, 2015. arduino.cc, vis. 03-12-2015.

[4] Epic Games, Inc., Unreal Engine, 2015. unrealengine.com, vis. 03-12-2015.

[5] Next Limit S.L., Maxwell Render, 2015. maxwellrender.com, vis. 03-12-2015.

[6] Oculus VR Oculus Rift, 2015. oculus.com, vis. 03-12-2015.

[7] OpenCV Library, 2015. opencv.org, vis. 03-12-2015.

[8] M. Abrash. What VR could, should, and almost certainly will be within two years. Steam Dev Days, Seattle, 2014.

[9] F. H. Adler, P. L. Kaufman, L. A. Levin, and A. Alm. *Adler's Physiology of the Eye*. Elsevier Health Sciences, 2011.

[10] S. Baluja and D. Pomerleau. Non-intrusive gaze tracking using artificial neural networks. In *Machine Learning in Computer Vision: What, Why and How?*, 1993.

[11] P. Bazanov and T. Järvenpää. Gaze estimation for near-eye display based on fusion of starburst algorithm and fern natural features. In *FRUCT 2011*, pages 1–8, 2011.

[12] M. Bertalmio, A. L. Bertozzi, and G. Sapiro. Navier-stokes, fluid dynamics, and image and video inpainting. In *CVPR 2001. Proceedings*, volume 1, pages I–355. IEEE, 2001.

[13] J.-Y. Bouguet. Camera calibration toolbox for matlab, 2010. vision.caltech.edu/bouguetj, vis. 08-10-2014.

[14] D. A. Bowman, E. Kruijff, J. J. LaViola Jr, and I. Poupyrev. *3DUI: theory and practice*. Addison-Wesley, 2004.

[15] S. Chen and J. Epps. Efficient and robust pupil size and blink estimation from near-field video sequences for human machine interaction. *IEEE Transactions on Cybernetics*, 44(12):2356–2367, Dec 2014.

[16] T. Dera, G. Boning, S. Bardins, and E. Schneider. Low-latency video tracking of horizontal, vertical, and torsional eye movements as a basis for 3dof realtime motion control of a head-mounted camera. In *SMC'06, Proceedings*, volume 6, pages 5191–5196. IEEE, 2006.

[17] J. E. Doble, D. L. Feinberg, M. S. Rosner, and A. J. Rosner. Identification of binocular vision dysfunction in traumatic brain injury patients and effects of individualized prismatic spectacle lenses. *PM&R*, 2(4):244–253, 2010.

[18] A. Duchowski. *Eye tracking methodology: Theory and practice*, volume 373. Springer, 2007.

[19] A. T. Duchowski and A. Çöltekin. Foveated gaze-contingent displays for peripheral lod management, 3d visualization, and stereo imaging. *TOMCCAP'07*, 3(4):6, 2007.

[20] A. T. Duchowski, V. Shivashankaraiah, T. Rawls, A. K. Gramopadhye, B. J. Melloy, and B. Kanki. Binocular eye tracking in virtual reality for inspection training. In *ETRA'00, Proceedings*, pages 89–96. ACM, 2000.

[21] H. Durrant-Whyte and T. Bailey. Simultaneous localization and mapping: part i. *Robotics & Automation Magazine, IEEE*, 13(2):99–110, 2006.

[22] A. W. Fitzgibbon, R. B. Fisher, et al. A buyer's guide to conic fitting. *DAI*, 1996.

[23] D. W. Hansen and Q. Ji. In the eye of the beholder: A survey of models for eyes and gaze. *PAMI'10*, 32(3):478–500, 2010.

[24] R. Hartley and A. Zisserman. *Multiple View Geometry in Computer Vision*. Cambridge University Press, 2003.

[25] S. Hillaire, A. Lécuyer, R. Cozot, and G. Casiez. Using an eye-tracking system to improve camera motions and depth-of-field blur effects in virtual environments. In *VR'08, Proceedings*, pages 47–50. IEEE, 2008.

[26] K. Holmqvist, M. Nyström, R. Andersson, R. Dewhurst, H. Jarodzka, and J. Van de Weijer. *Eye tracking: A comprehensive guide to methods and measures*. Oxford University Press, 2011.

[27] K. Holmqvist, M. Nyström, and F. Mulvey. Eye tracker data quality: what it is and how to measure it. In *ETRA'12, Proceedings*, pages 45–52. ACM, 2012.

[28] F. Klefenz, P. Husar, D. Krenzer, and A. Hess. Real-time calibration-free autonomous eye tracker. In *ICASSP'10, Proceedings*, pages 762–765. IEEE, 2010.

[29] S. Kohlbecher, S. Bardinst, K. Bartl, E. Schneider, T. Poitschke, and M. Ablassmeier. Calibration-free eye tracking by reconstruction of the pupil ellipse in 3d space. In *ETRA'08, Proceedings*, pages 135–138. ACM, 2008.

[30] N. Kumar, S. Kohlbecher, and E. Schneider. A novel approach to video-based pupil tracking. In *SMC'09, Proceedings*, pages 1255–1262. IEEE, 2009.

[31] D. Li, D. Winfield, and D. J. Parkhurst. Starburst: A hybrid algorithm for video-based eye tracking combining feature-based and model-based approaches. In *CVPR 2005, Proceedings of*, pages 79–79. IEEE, 2005.

[32] M. Mauderer, S. Conte, M. A. Nacenta, and D. Vishwanath. Depth perception with gaze-contingent depth of field. In *CHI'14, Proceedings*, pages 217–226. ACM, 2014.

[33] F. Moisy. Ezyfit: a free curve fitting toolbox for matlab. *U. Paris Sud. Version 2*, 2011.

[34] K. Pfeuffer, M. Vidal, J. Turner, A. Bulling, and H. Gellersen. Pursuit calibration: Making gaze calibration less tedious and more flexible. In *UIST'13, Proceedings*, pages 261–270. ACM, 2013.

[35] E. M. Reingold, L. C. Loschky, G. W. McConkie, and D. M. Stampe. Gaze-contingent multiresolutional displays: An integrative review. *HFES Journal*, 45(2):307–328, 2003.

[36] A. Schall. *Eye tracking in user experience design*. Morgan Kaufmann, 2014.

[37] E. Schneider, T. Villgrattner, J. Vockeroth, K. Bartl, S. Kohlbecher, S. Bardins, H. Ulbrich, and T. Brandt. Eyeseecam: An eye movement–driven head camera for the examination of natural visual exploration. *Annals of the NY Academy of Science*, 1164(1):461–467, 2009.

[38] K.-H. Tan, D. Kriegman, and N. Ahuja. Appearance-based eye gaze estimation. In *WACV 2002, Proceedings*, pages 191–195, 2002.

[39] C. Topala and C. Akinlara. An adaptive algorithm for precise pupil boundary detection using the entropy of contour gradients. 2013. Elsevier preprint.

[40] O. Williams, A. Blake, and R. Cipolla. Sparse and semi-supervised visual mapping with the S3GP. In *CVPR'06, Proceedings*, volume 1, pages 230–237, 2006.

SINGA: Putting Deep Learning in the Hands of Multimedia Users

Wei Wang†, Gang Chen§, Tien Tuan Anh Dinh†, Jinyang Gao†
Beng Chin Ooi†, Kian-Lee Tan†, Sheng Wang†
†School of Computing, National University of Singapore, Singapore
§College of Computer Science, Zhejiang University, China
†{wangwei, dinhtta, jinyang.gao, ooibc, tankl, wangsh}@comp.nus.edu.sg,
§cg@zju.edu.cn

ABSTRACT

Recently, deep learning techniques have enjoyed success in various multimedia applications, such as image classification and multi-modal data analysis. Two key factors behind deep learning's remarkable achievement are the immense computing power and the availability of massive training datasets, which enable us to train large models to capture complex regularities of the data. There are two challenges to overcome before deep learning can be widely adopted in multimedia and other applications. One is usability, namely the implementation of different models and training algorithms must be done by non-experts without much effort. The other is scalability, that is the deep learning system must be able to provision for a huge demand of computing resources for training large models with massive datasets. To address these two challenges, in this paper, we design a distributed deep learning platform called SINGA which has an intuitive programming model and good scalability. Our experience with developing and training deep learning models for real-life multimedia applications in SINGA shows that the platform is both usable and scalable.

Categories and Subject Descriptors

I.5.1 [**Pattern Recognition**]: Models—*Neural Nets*;
H.3.4 [**Information Storage and Retrieval**]: Systems and Software—*Distributed System*

General Terms

Design, Experimentation, Performance

Keywords

Deep learning; Multimedia application; Distributed training

1. INTRODUCTION

In recent years, we have witnessed successful adoptions of deep learning in various multimedia applications, such as image and video classification [14, 29], content-based image retrieval [24], music recommendation [27] and multi-modal data analysis [25, 9, 33]. Deep learning refers to a set of feature learning models which consist of multiple layers. Different layers learn different levels of abstractions (or features) of the raw input data [15]. It has been regarded as a re-branding of neural networks developed twenty years ago, since it inherits many key neural networks techniques and algorithms. However, deep learning exploits the fact that high-level abstractions are better at representing the data than raw, hand-crafted features, thus achieving better performance in learning. Its recent resurgence is mainly fuelled by higher than ever accuracy obtained in image recognition [14]. Two key factors behind deep learning's remarkable achievement are the immense computing power and the availability of massive training datasets, which together enable us to train large models to capture the regularities of data more efficiently than twenty years ago.

There are two challenges in bringing deep learning to wide adoption in multimedia applications (and other applications for that matter). The first challenge is *usability*, namely the implementation of different models and training algorithms must be done by non-experts without much effort. Many deep learning models exist, and different multimedia applications may use different models. For instance, the deep convolution neural network (DCNN) is suitable for image classification [14], recurrent neural network (RNN) for language modelling [17], and deep auto-encoders for multi-modal data analysis [25, 9, 33]. Most of these models are too complex and costly to implement from scratch. An example is the GoogleNet model [23] which comprises 22 layers of 10 different types. Training algorithms are also intricate in details. For instance the Back-Propagation [16] algorithm is notoriously difficult to debug.

The second challenge is *scalability*, that is the deep learning system must be able to provision for a huge demand of computing resources for training large models with massive datasets. It has been shown that larger training datasets and bigger models lead to better accuracy [3, 15, 23]. However, memory requirement for a deep learning model may exceed the memory capacity of a single CPU or GPU. In addition, computational cost of training may be unacceptably high for a single, commodity server. For instance, it takes 10 days [30, 20] to train the DCNN [14] with 1.2 million training images and 60 million parameters using one GPU [1].

Addressing both usability and scalability challenge requires a distributed training platform that supports various deep learning models, that comes with an intuitive programming model (similar to MapReduce [7], Spark [31] and epiC [12] in spirit), and that is scalable. A recent deep learning system, called Caffe [11], addresses the first challenge but falls short at the second challenge (it

[1]According to the authors, with 2 GPUs, the training still took about 6 days.

MM'15, October 26–30, 2015, Brisbane, Australia.

ACM 978-1-4503-3459-4/15/10 ...$15.00.
DOI: http://dx.doi.org/10.1145/2733373.2806232 .

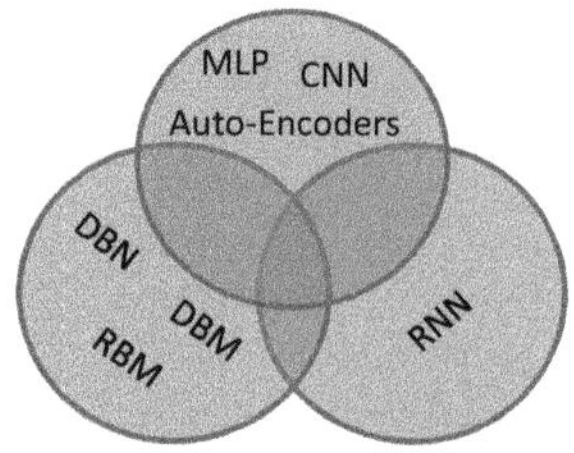

Figure 1: Deep learning model categorization.

is not designed for distributed training). There are systems supporting distributed training [20, 30, 13], but they are model specific and do not generalize well to other models. General distributed platforms such as MapReduce and Spark achieve good scalability, but they are designed for generic data processing. As a result, they lack both the programming model and system optimizations specific to deep learning, hindering the overall usability and scalability. Recently, there are several specialized distributed platforms [6, 4, 1] that exploit deep learning specific optimizations and hence are able to achieve high training throughputs. However, they forgo usability issues: the platforms are closed-source and no detail of their programming models is given, rendering them unusable by multimedia users.

In this paper, we present our effort in bringing deep learning to the masses. In particular, we design and implement an open source distributed deep learning platform, called SINGA[2], which tackles both usability and scalability challenge at the same time. SINGA runs on commodity servers and provides a simple, intuitive programming model which makes it accessible even to non-experts. SINGA's simplicity is driven by the observation that both the structures and training algorithms of deep learning models can be expressed using a simple abstraction: the neuron layer (or layer). In SINGA, the user defines and combines layers to create the neural network model, and the runtime takes care of issues pertaining to the distributed training such as partitioning, synchronization and communication. SINGA achieves scalability via its hybrid architecture design which consists of groups of workers (and servers). Worker groups run asynchronously over different data partitions (*data parallelism*) to improve the convergence rate, and workers within a group run synchronously over one model replica (*model parallelism*) to improve the efficiency of each iteration. SINGA enables users to find an optimal cluster setting (e.g., group size) that trades off between the convergence rate and efficiency to minimize the training time to reach certain accuracy.

In summary, this paper makes the following contributions:

1. We present a distributed platform called SINGA which is designed to train deep learning models for multimedia and other applications. SINGA offers a simple and intuitive programming model based on the layer abstraction.

2. We describe SINGA's distributed architecture which runs on commodity servers. The architecture achieves scalability via hybrid parallelism. SINGA runtime handles the communication and synchronization between nodes transparently.

[2]http://singa.incubator.apache.org/, http://www.comp.nus.edu.sg/~dbsystem/singa/

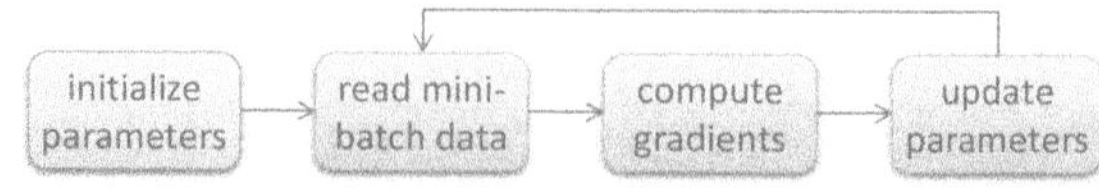

Figure 2: Flow of stochastic gradient descent algorithm.

3. We demonstrate SINGA's usability by describing the implementation of three multimedia applications: multi-modal retrieval, dimensionality reduction and language modelling.

4. We evaluate SINGA's performance by comparing with other open-source systems. The results show that SINGA is scalable and it outperforms other systems with respect to training time.

The rest of this paper is organized as follows. Section 2 provides the background on training deep learning models. An overview of SINGA as a platform follows in Section 3. The programming model is discussed in Section 4. Section 5 describes the implementations of multimedia applications in SINGA. We discuss SINGA architecture in Section 6, and the model partitioning in Section 7. The experimental study and related works are presented in Section 8 and Section 9 respectively before we conclude in Section 10.

2. DEEP LEARNING

Deep learning is considered as a feature learning technique. One deep learning model typically consists of multiple layers, each associated with a feature transformation function. After going through all layers, raw input features (e.g., pixels of images) are converted into high-level features that are used for tasks such as classification.

We group popular deep learning models into three categories based on the connection types between layers, as shown in Figure 1. Category *A* consists of *feed-forward models* wherein the layers are directly connected. The extracted features at higher layers are fed into prediction or classification tasks, e.g., image classification [14]. Example models in this category include Multi-Layer Perceptron (MLP), Convolution Neural Network (CNN) and Auto-Encoders. Category *B* contains models whose layer connections are undirected. These models are often used to pre-train other models [10], e.g., feed-forward models. Deep Belief Network (DBN), Deep Boltzmann Machine (DBM) and Restricted Boltzmann Machine (RBM) are examples of such models. Category *C* comprises models that have recurrent connections. These models are called Recurrent Neutral Networks (RNN). They are widely used for modelling sequential data in which prediction of the next position is affected by previous positions. Language modelling [17] is a popular application of RNN.

A deep learning model has to be trained to find the optimal parameters for the transformation functions. The training quality is measured by a loss function (e.g., cross-entropy loss) for each specific task. Since the loss functions are usually non-linear and non-convex, it is difficult to get closed-form solutions. A common approach is to use the Stochastic Gradient Descent (SGD) algorithm shown in Figure 2. SGD initializes the parameters with random values, and then iteratively refines them to reduce the loss based on the computed gradients. There are three typical algorithms for gradient computation corresponding to the three model categories above: Back-Propagation (BP), Contrastive Divergence (CD) and Back-Propagation Through Time (BPTT).

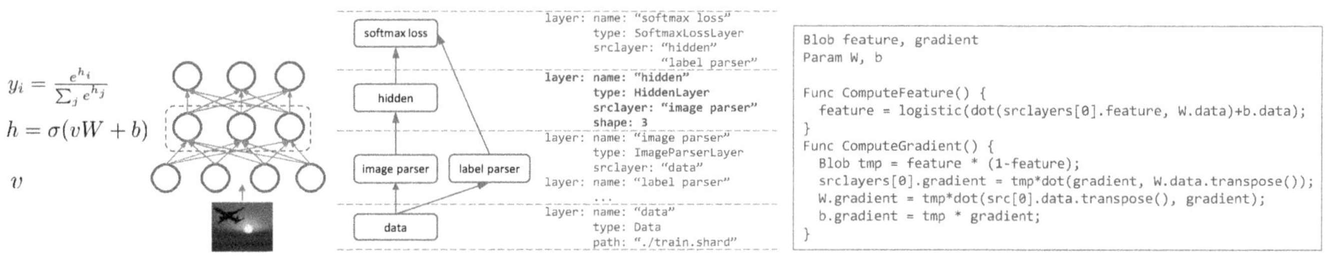

(a) Sample MLP. (b) NeuralNet configuration. (c) Hidden layer implementation.

Figure 4: Running example using an MLP.

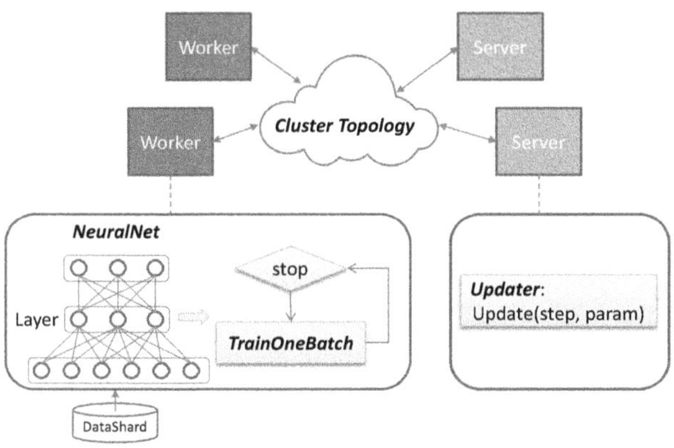

Figure 3: SINGA overview.

3. OVERVIEW

SINGA trains deep learning models using SGD over the worker-server architecture, as shown in Figure 3. Workers compute parameter gradients and servers perform parameter updates. To start a training job, the user (or programmer) submits a job configuration specifies the following four components:

- A *NeuralNet* describing the neural network (or neural net) structure with the detailed layers and their connections. SINGA comes with many built-in layers (Section 4.1.2), and users can also implement their own layers.
- A *TrainOneBatch* algorithm for training the model. SINGA implements different algorithms (Section 4.1.3) for all three model categories.
- An *Updater* defining the protocol for updating parameters at the servers (Section 4.1.4).
- A *Cluster Topology* specifying the distributed architecture of workers and servers. SINGA's architecture is flexible and can support both synchronous and asynchronous training (Section 6).

Given a job configuration, SINGA distributes the training tasks over the cluster and coordinates the training. In each iteration, every worker calls *TrainOneBatch* function to compute parameter gradients. *TrainOneBatch* takes a *NeuralNet* object representing the neural net, and it visits (part of) the model layers in an order specific to the model category. The resultant gradients are sent to the corresponding servers for updating. Workers then fetch the updated parameters at the next iteration.

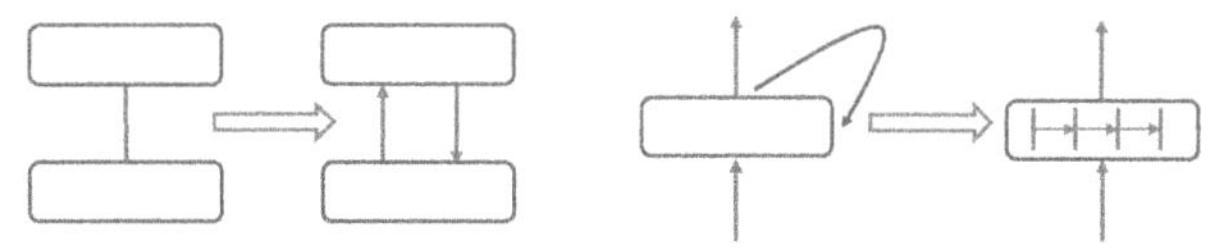

(a) Convert undirected connection. (b) Unroll recurrent connection.

Figure 5: Unified representation of connections.

4. PROGRAMMING MODEL

This section describes SINGA's programming model, particularly the main components of a SINGA job. We use the MLP model for image classification (Figure 4a) as a running example. The model consists of an input layer, a hidden feature transformation layer and a Softmax output layer.

4.1 Programming Abstractions

4.1.1 NeuralNet

NeuralNet represents a neural net instance in SINGA. It comprises a set of unidirectionally connected layers. Properties and connections of layers are specified by users. The *NeuralNet* object is passed as an argument to the *TrainOneBatch* function.

Layer connections in *NeuralNet* are not represented explicitly; instead each layer records its own source layers as specified by users (Figure 4b). Recall that different model categories have different types of layer connections. However, they can be unified using directed edges as follows. For feed-forward models, nothing needs to be done as their connections are already directed. For undirected models, users need to replace each edge with two directed edges, as shown in Figure 5a. For recurrent models, users can unroll a recurrent layer into directed-connecting sub-layers, as shown in Figure 5b.

4.1.2 Layer

Layer is a core abstraction in SINGA. Different layer implementations perform different feature transformations to extract high-level features. In every SGD iteration, all layers in the *NeuralNet* are visited by the *TrainOneBatch* function during the process of computing parameter gradients.

Figure 6 shows the definition of a base layer. It has two fields and two functions. The *srclayer* field represents in-coming edges to the layer. The *feature* field is a set of feature vectors (blob) computed from the source layers. Some layers may require parameters (e.g., a weight matrix) for their feature transformation functions. In this case, these parameters are represented by a *Param* object containing a *data* field for the parameter values and a *gradient* field for the gradients. The *ComputeFeature* function evaluates the feature blob by transforming features from the source layers. The *Com-*

```
Layer:
Vector<Layer> srclayer
Blob feature
Func ComputeFeature()
Func ComputeGradient()

Param:
Blob data, gradient
```

Figure 6: Layer abstraction.

puteGradient function computes the gradients associated with this layer. These two functions are invoked by the *TrainOneBatch* function during training (Section 4.1.3).

SINGA provides a variety of built-in layers to help users build their models. Table 1 lists the layer categories in SINGA. For example, the data layer loads a mini-batch of records via the *ComputeFeature* function in each iteration. Users can also define their own layers for their specific requirements. Figure 4c shows an example of implementing the hidden layer h in the MLP. In this example, besides the basic feature blob there is another gradient blob storing the loss gradients with respect to the feature blob. There are two *Param* objects: the weight matrix W and the bias vector b. The *ComputeFeature* function rotates (multiply W) , shifts (plus b) the input features and then applies non-linear (logistic) transformations. The *ComputeGradient* function computes the layer's parameter gradients, as well as the source layer's gradients that will be used for evaluating the source layer's parameter gradients.

Table 1: Layer categories.

Category	Description
Data layers	Load records from file, database or HDFS.
Parser layers	Parse features from records, e.g., pixels.
Neuron layers	Feature transformation, e.g., convolution.
Loss layers	Compute objective loss, e.g., cross-entropy loss.
Other layers	Connect layers when neural net is partitioned.

4.1.3 *TrainOneBatch*

The *TrainOneBatch* function determines the sequence of invoking *ComputeFeature* and *ComputeGradient* functions in all layers during each SGD iteration. SINGA implements two *TrainOneBatch* algorithms for the three model categories. For feed-forward and recurrent models, the BP algorithm is provided. For undirected modes (e.g., RBM), the CD algorithm is provided. Users simply select the corresponding algorithm in the job configuration. Should there be specific requirements for the training workflow, users can define their own *TrainOneBatch* function following a template shown in Algorithm 1. Algorithm 1 implements the BP algorithm which takes a *NeuralNet* object as input. The first loop visits each layer and computes their features, and the second loop visits each layer in the reverse order and computes parameter gradients. More details on applying BP for RNN models (i.e., BPTT), and the CD algorithm are available in [19].

4.1.4 *Updater*

Once the parameter gradients are computed, workers send these values to servers to update the parameters. SINGA implements several parameter updating protocols, such as AdaGrad[8]. Users can also define their own updating protocols by overriding the *Update* function.

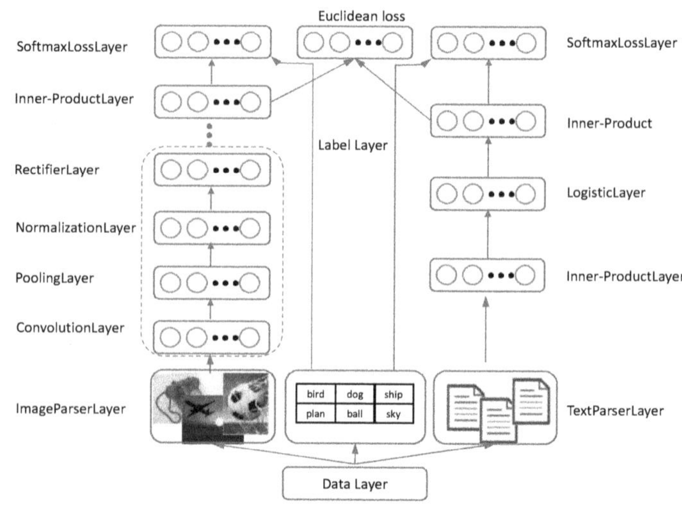

Figure 7: Structure of MDNN.

4.2 MLP Example

To train the MLP model shown in Figure 4a, the first step is to prepare a training dataset and the corresponding layers, e.g., the data layer and parser layer. Since all layers used by the MLP example are provided as built-in layers in SINGA, users do not need to implement them on their own. Next, the neural net should be configured to connect all layers as shown in Figure 4b. After configuring the *TrainOneBatch* function using BP and the updater using AdaGrad, users can submit the job for single node training. In Section 6, we shall discuss how to configure SINGA for distributed training.

Algorithm 1: BPTrainOneBatch

Input: net

foreach *layer in net.layers* **do**
  Collect(layer.params()) `// receive parameters`
  layer.ComputeFeature() `// forward prop`
foreach *layer in reverse(net.layers)* **do**
  layer.ComputeGradient()`// backward prop`
  Update(layer.params())`// send gradients`

5. MULTIMEDIA APPLICATIONS

This section demonstrates the use of SINGA for multimedia applications. We discuss the training of three deep learning models for three different applications: a multi-modal deep neural network (MDNN) for multi-modal retrieval, a RBM for dimensionality reduction, and a RNN for language modelling.

5.1 MDNN for Multi-modal Retrieval

Feed-forward models such as CNN and MLP are widely used to learn high-level features in multimedia applications, especially for image classification [14]. Here, we demonstrate the training of the MDNN [26], which combines a CNN and a MLP. MDNN is used for extracting features for the multi-modal retrieval task [25, 9, 22] that searches objects from different modalities. In MDNN, the CNN [14] is used to extract image features, and the MLP is used to extract text features. The training objective is to minimize a weighted sum of (1) the error of predicting the labels of image

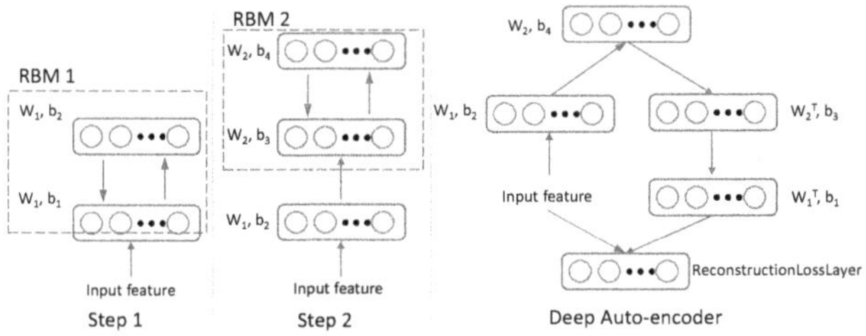

Figure 8: Structure of RBM and deep auto-encoder.

and text documents using extracted features and (2) the distance between features of relevant image and text objects. As a result, the learned features of semantically relevant objects from different modalities are similar. After training, multi-modal retrieval is conducted using the learned features.

Figure 7 depicts the user configured neural net of MDNN model in SINGA. We can see that there are two parallel paths: one for text modality and the other for image modality. The data layer reads in records of semantically relevant image-text pairs. The image layer, text layer and label layer then parse the visual feature, text feature (e.g., tags of the image) and labels respectively from the records. The image path consists of layers from DCNN [14], e.g., the convolution layer and pooling layer. The text path includes inner-product (or fully connected) layer, logistic layer and loss layer. The Euclidean loss layer measures the distance of the feature vectors extracted from these two paths. All except the parser layers, which are application specific, are SINGA's built-in layers. Since this model is a feed-forward model, the BP algorithm should be selected for the *TrainOneBatch* function.

5.2 RBM for Dimensionality Reduction

RBM is often employed to pre-train parameters for other models. In this example application, we use RBM to pre-train a deep auto-encoder [10] for dimensionality reduction. Multimedia applications typically operate with high-dimensional feature vectors, which demands large computing resources. Dimensionality reduction techniques, such as Principal Component Analysis (PCA), are commonly applied in the pre-processing step. Deep auto-encoder is reported [10] to have better performance than PCA.

Generally, the deep auto-encoder is trained to reconstruct the input feature using the feature of the top layer. Hinton et al. [10] use RBM to pre-train the parameters for each layer, and fine-tune them to minimize the reconstruction error. Figure 8 shows the model structure (with parser layer and data layer omitted) in SINGA. The parameters trained from the first RBM (RBM 1) in step 1 are ported (through checkpoint) into step 2 wherein the extracted features are used to train the next model (RBM 2). Once pre-training is finished, the deep auto-encoder is unfolded for fine-tuning. SINGA applies the contrastive divergence (CD) algorithm for training RBM and back-propagation (BP) algorithm for fine-tuning the deep auto-encoder.

5.3 RNN for Language Modelling

RNN models are good at modelling sequential data (e.g., music, videos and text sentences) in multimedia applications. We use SINGA to train the RNN model [17] for language modelling, which can then be exploited to learn word embedding, generate sentences, etc.

The model structure (i.e., *NeuralNet*) of the RNN is configured as shown in Figure 9. This model is trained to predict the next word in a sentence given its previous words. Each sentence is parsed as a sequence of word indices in the parser layer. The embedding layer

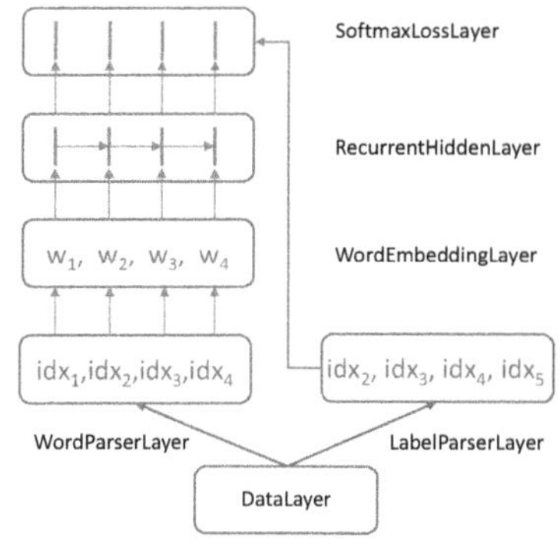

Figure 9: Structure of RNN for language modelling.

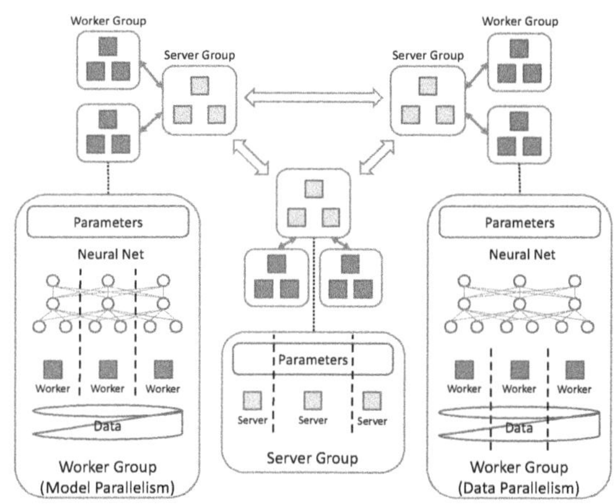

Figure 10: Logical architecture of SINGA.

outputs the feature vector of each word. The hidden feature of each word is computed from the word feature and the hidden feature of the previous word. The label layer passes the word indices into the loss layer which calculates the prediction error. In each iteration, the BP algorithm forwards and backwards through all layers. The *ComputeFeature* function of the recurrent layer evaluates all unrolled features in time-order, while the *ComputeGradient* function computes the gradients in a reverse time-order. Consequently, the training is conducted as the BPTT algorithm.

6. DISTRIBUTED TRAINING

In this section, we introduce SINGA's architecture, and discuss how it supports a variety of distributed training frameworks.

6.1 System Architecture

Figure 10 shows the logical architecture. The architecture consists of multiple server groups and worker groups, and each worker group communicates with only one server group. Each server group maintains a complete replica of the model parameters, and is responsible for handling requests (e.g., get or update parameters) from worker groups. Neighboring server groups synchronize their parameters periodically. Typically, a server group contains a number of servers, and each server manages a partition of model parameters. Each worker group trains a complete model replica against a partition of the training dataset (i.e. data parallelism), and is responsible for computing parameter gradients. All worker groups run and communicate with the corresponding server groups asynchronously. However, inside each worker group, the workers syn-

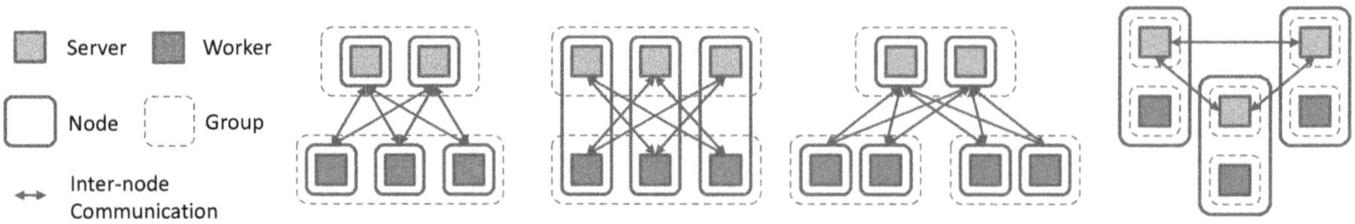

(a) Sandblaster. (b) AllReduce. (c) Downpour. (d) Distributed Hogwild.

Figure 11: Training frameworks in SINGA.

chronously compute parameter updates for the model replica. There are two strategies to distribute the training workload among workers within a group: by model or by data. More specifically, each worker can compute a subset of parameters against all data partitioned to the group (i.e., model parallelism), or all parameters against a subset of data (i.e., data parallelism). SINGA also supports hybrid parallelism (Section 7).

In SINGA, servers and workers are execution units running in separate threads. They communicate through messages. Every process runs the main thread as a stub that aggregates local messages and forwards them to corresponding (remote) receivers. If two units manage the same parameter partition and they are in the same process, it is possible for them to leverage the shared memory to reduce communication cost, as discussed later in Section 6.3.

6.2 Training Frameworks

In SINGA, worker groups run asynchronously and workers within one group run synchronously. Users can leverage this general design to run both synchronous and asynchronous training frameworks. In specific, users control the training framework by configuring the cluster topology, i.e., the number of worker (resp. server) groups and worker (resp. server) group size. In the following paragraphs, we will discuss the realization of popular distributed training frameworks in SINGA, including Sandblaster and Downpour from Google's DistBelief system [6], AllReduce in Baidu's DeepImage system [28] and the distributed Hogwild implementation in Caffe [11].

6.2.1 *Synchronous Training*

A synchronous framework is realized by configuring the cluster topology with only one worker group and one server group. The training convergence rate is the same as that on a single node.

Figure 11a shows the Sandblaster framework implemented in SINGA. A single server group is configured to handle all requests from workers. A worker computes on its partition of the model, and only communicates with servers handling related parameters. Figure 11b shows the AllReduce framework in SINGA, in which we bind each worker with a server on the same node, so that each node is responsible for maintaining a partition of parameters and collecting updates from all other nodes.

The synchronous training is typically limited to a small or medium size cluster , e.g. fewer than 100 nodes. When the cluster size is large, the synchronization delay is likely to be larger than the computation time. Consequently, the training cannot scale well.

6.2.2 *Asynchronous Training*

An asynchronous framework is implemented by configuring the cluster topology with more than one worker group. The training convergence is likely to be different from single-node training, because multiple worker groups are working on different versions of parameters [32].

Figure 11c shows the Downpour [6] framework implemented in SINGA. Similar to the synchronous Sandblaster, all workers send requests to a global server group. We divide workers into several worker groups, each running independently and working on parameters from the last *update* response. Figure 11d shows the distributed Hogwild framework, in which each node contains a complete server group and a complete worker group. Parameter updates are done locally, so that communication cost during each training step is minimized. However, the server group must periodically synchronize with neighboring groups to improve the training convergence. The topology (connections) of server groups can be customized by users (the default topology is all-to-all connection).

Asynchronous training can improve the convergence rate to some degree. But the improvement typically decreases when there are more and more model replicas. A more scalable training framework should combine both the synchronous and asynchronous training. In SINGA, users can run a hybrid training framework by launching multiple worker groups that run asynchronously to improve the convergence rate. Within each worker group, multiple workers run synchronously to accelerate one training iteration. Given a fixed budget (e.g., number of nodes in a cluster), there lies the opportunity to find one optimal hybrid training framework that trades off between the convergence rate and efficiency to achieve the minimal training time.

6.3 Parameter Sharing

In SINGA, each server group and worker group have a *ParamShard* object representing a complete model replica. If workers and servers resident in the same process, their *ParamShard* (partitions) can be configured to share the same memory space. In this case, the messages transferred between different execution units just contain pointers to the data, which reduces the communication cost. For other cases, the messages have to include the parameter values (or gradients).

7. NEURAL NETWORK PARTITIONING

In this section, we describe how SINGA partitions the neural net to support data parallelism, model parallelism, and hybrid parallelism within one worker group.

SINGA partitions a neural net at the granularity of layer. Every layer's feature blob is considered a matrix whose rows are feature vectors. Thus, the layer can be split on two dimensions. Partitioning on dimension 0 (also called batch dimension) slices the feature matrix by rows. For instance, if the mini-batch size is 256 and the layer is partitioned into 2 sub-layers, each sub-layer would have 128 feature vectors in its feature blob. Partitioning on this dimension has no effect on the parameters, as every *Param* object is replicated in the sub-layers. Partitioning on dimension 1 (also called feature dimension) slices the feature matrix by columns. For example, suppose the original feature vector has 50 units, after partitioning into 2 sub-layers, each sub-layer would have 25 units. This

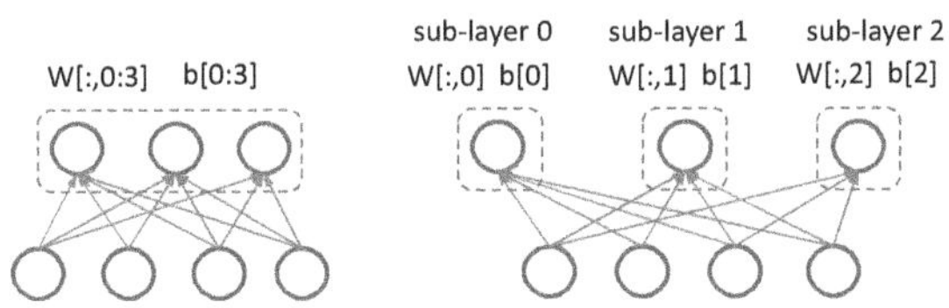

Figure 12: Partition the hidden layer in Figure 4a.

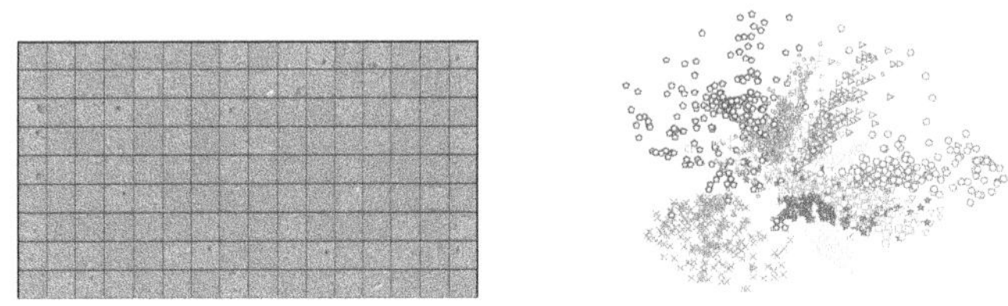

(a) Bottom RBM weight matrix. (b) Top layer features.

Figure 14: Visualization of the weight matrix in the bottom RBM and top layer features in the deep auto-encoder.

partitioning may result in *Param* object being split, as shown in Figure 12. Both the bias vector and weight matrix are partitioned into two sub-layers (workers).

SINGA partitions the layers when creating the *NeuralNet* instance. Each sub-layer is assigned a location ID, based on which it is dispatched to one worker. Some connection layers are automatically inserted to connect the sub-layers. For instance, if two connected sub-layers are located at two different workers, then a pair of bridge layers is inserted to transfer the feature (and gradient) blob between them. When two layers are partitioned on different dimensions, a concatenation layer which concatenates feature rows (or columns) and a slice layer which slices feature rows (or columns) would be inserted. These connection layers help making the network communication and synchronization transparent to the users.

Users can specify the partition decision in two places. The first is in the neural net configuration. A *partition_dim* field determines the partition dimension for every layer. The second place is in the layer configuration which overwrites the *partition_dim* in the neural net configuration. Advanced users can also directly specify the location ID for each layer to control the dispatching of layers to workers. For the MDNN model in Figure 7, users can configure the layers in the image path with location ID 0 and the layers in the text path with location ID 1, making the two paths run in parallel.

When every worker computes the gradients of the entire model parameters, we refer to this process as data parallelism. When different workers compute the gradients of different parameters, we call this process model parallelism. Particularly, partitioning on dimension 0 results in data parallelism, while partitioning on dimension 1 results in model parallelism. SINGA supports hybrid parallelism wherein some workers compute the gradients of the same subset of model parameters while other workers compute on different model parameters. For example, to implement the hybrid parallelism in [13] for the CNN model, we set *partition_dim = 0* for lower layers and *partition_dim = 1* for higher layers.

8. EXPERIMENTAL STUDY

We evaluated SINGA with real-life multimedia applications. Specifically, we used SINGA to train the models discussed in Section 5, which requires little effort since SINGA comes with many built-in layers and algorithms. We then examined SINGA's training performance in terms of efficiency and scalability. SINGA is more efficient than three other open-source systems, and it is scalable for both synchronous and asynchronous training.

8.1 Applications of SINGA

We implemented the multi-modal retrieval and dimensionality reduction applications using SINGA. Due to space constraint, we omit the experiment for language modelling.

Multi-modal Retrieval. We trained the MDNN model for multi-modal retrieval application as described in Section 5.1. We used NUS-WIDE dataset [2], which has roughly 180,000 images after removing images without tags or from non-popular categories. Each image is associated with several tags. We used Word2Vec [18] to learn a word embedding for each tag and aggregated the embeddings of all the tags from the same image as a text feature. Figure 13 shows sample search results. We first used images as queries to retrieve similar images and text documents. It can be seen that image results are more relevant to the queries. For instance, the first image result of the first query is relevant because both images are about architecture, but the text results are not very relevant. This can be attributed to the large semantic gap between different modalities, making it difficult to locate semantically relevant objects in the latent (representation) space.

Dimensionality Reduction. We trained RBM models to initialize the deep auto-encoder for dimensionality reduction as discussed in Section 5.2. We used the MNIST[3] dataset consisting of 70,000 images of hand-written digits. Following the configuration used in [10], we set the size of each layer as 784→1000→500→250→2. Figure 14a visualizes sample columns of the weight matrix of the bottom (first) RBM. We can see that Gabor-like filters are learned. Figure 14b depicts the features extracted from the top-layer of the auto-encoder, wherein one point represents one image. Different colors represent different digits. We can see that most images are well clustered according to the ground truth, except for images of digit '4' and '9' (central part) which have some overlap (in practice, handwritten '4' and '9' digits are fairly similar in shape).

8.2 Training Performance Evaluation

This section presents SINGA's performance in terms of its efficiency and scalability for distributed training. We evaluated both synchronous and asynchronous training frameworks on a single multi-core node and a commodity cluster.

8.2.1 Methodologies

The deep convolution neural network[4] for image classification was used as the training model for benchmarking. The training was conducted over the CIFAR10 dataset[5] which has 50,000 training images and 10,000 test images.

For the single-node setting, we used a 24-core server with 500GB memory. The 24 cores are distributed into 4 NUMA nodes (Intel Xeon 7540). Hyper-threading is turned on. For the multi-node setting, we used a 32-node cluster. Each cluster node is equipped with a quad-core Intel Xeon 3.1 GHz CPU and 8GB memory. The cluster nodes are connected by a 1Gbps switch.

SINGA uses Mshadow[6] and OpenBlas[7] to accelerate linear algebra operations (e.g., matrix multiplication). Caffe's im2col and pooling code [11] is adopted to accelerate the convolution and pool-

[3]http://yann.lecun.com/exdb/mnist/
[4]https://code.google.com/p/cuda-convnet/
[5]http://www.cs.toronto.edu/ kriz/cifar.html
[6]https://github.com/dmlc/mshadow
[7]http://www.openblas.net/

Figure 13: Multi-Modal Retrieval. Top 5 similar text documents (one line per document) and images are displayed.

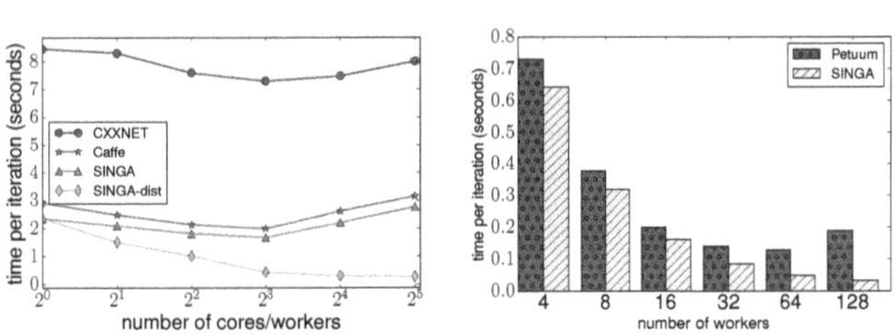

(a) On a single node .

(b) In a cluster of 32 nodes.

Figure 15: Synchronous training.

ing operations. We compiled SINGA using GCC with optimization level O2.

8.2.2 *Synchronous training*

We compared SINGA with CXXNET[8] and Caffe [11]. Both systems were compiled using their default optimization levels: O3 for CXXNET and O2 for Caffe. Since synchronous training has the same convergence rate as sequential SGD, all systems would run the same number of iterations (i.e., mini-batches) to converge. The difference of total training time between different systems lies in the efficiency of a single iteration. Thus, the efficiency comparison was conducted against the training time for one iteration. For each system, we ran 100 iterations and averaged the time over 50 iterations, i.e., from 30th to 80th, to avoid the influence of starting and ending phases.

We first conducted the training on the 24-core single node with 256 images per mini-batch. All three systems use OpenBlas to accelerate matrix multiplications. We varied the number of threads used by OpenBlas as shown in Figure 15a. SINGA-dist denotes the running of SINGA by setting the number of OpenBlas threads to 1[9]; SINGA-dist was configured with the cluster topology as one server group with four servers and one worker group with varying number of worker threads (Figure 15a). Consequently, SINGA ran as the in-memory Sandblaster framework. We can observe that SINGA-dist has the best overall performance: it is the fastest for each number of threads, and it is also the most scalable. All systems using multi-threading OpenBlas have poor scalability. This is because OpenBlas has little awareness of the application, and hence cannot be fully optimized. For example, it may only parallelize operations such large matrix multiplications. In contrast, SINGA-dist partitions the 256 images in one mini-batch equally. Workers run in parallel for the whole iteration, instead of only for some matrix multiplication operations. Another limitation of OpenBlas, as shown in Figure 15a, is that when the number of threads is larger than 8, the overhead caused by cross-CPU memory access starts to affect the training performance.

Next, we performed experiments on a 32-node cluster comparing with Petuum [5]. Petuum is a distributed machine learning framework. It runs Caffe as an application to train deep learning models. It implements a parameter server to conduct updates from workers (clients), while all workers run synchronously. We used a larger mini-batch size (512) and disabled OpenBlas multi-threading. We configured the cluster topology to realize the AllReduce framework for SINGA. Specifically, there is one worker group and one server

[8]https://github.com/dmlc/cxxnet

[9]OPENBLAS_NUM_THREADS=1

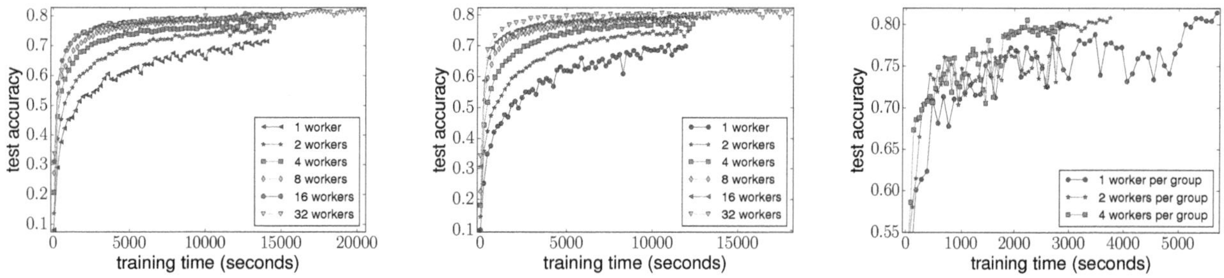

(a) Caffe on a single node.

(b) SINGA on a single node.

(c) SINGA in a cluster of 32 nodes.

Figure 16: Asynchronous training.

group, and in each node there are 4 workers and 1 server. We varied the size of worker group from 4 to 128, and the server group size from 1 to 32. Figure 15b shows that SINGA achieves almost linear scalability. Petuum scales up to 64 workers, but becomes slower when 128 workers are launched. It might be caused by the communication overhead in the parameter server as well as the synchronization delays among workers. One drawback of the synchronous distributed training is that it cannot scale to too many nodes because the mini-batch size is typically fewer than 1024. Consequently, we cannot launch more than 1024 workers (nodes); otherwise some workers will not be assigned any image to train.

8.2.3 Asynchronous training

Both SINGA and Caffe support in-memory asynchronous training. Particularly, Caffe implements the in-memory Hogwild [21] framework, and SINGA implements the in-memory Downpour framework. Their main difference is that parameter updates are done by workers in Caffe and by a single server (thread) in SINGA. Figure 16a and Figure 16b show the model accuracy versus training time for Caffe and SINGA with different numbers of worker groups (i.e. model replicas). Every worker processes 16 images per iteration, for a total of 60,000 iterations. It can be seen that SINGA is faster than Caffe. Both systems scale well as the number of workers increases, with respect to (1) the time to reach the same accuracy and (2) the final converged accuracy. Another observation is that the training takes longer with more workers. This is because the context-switching overhead increases when there are more threads (workers). Finally, the performance difference becomes smaller when the cluster size (i.e., the number of model replicas) reaches 16. This implies that there would be little benefit in having too many model replicas. Thus, we fixed the number of model replicas (i.e., worker groups) to 32 in the following experiments for the distributed asynchronous training.

For the multi-node setting, we still used mini-batch of 16 images per worker group and 60,000 training iterations. The distributed Downpour framework was configured: there were 32 worker groups, 32 servers per server group (one server thread per node). We varied the number of workers within one group as shown in Figure 16c. We can see that with more workers, the training is faster, since each worker processes fewer images. However, the training is not as stable as in the single-node setting. This may be attributed to the delay of parameter synchronization between workers. Whereas in single-node training, each worker's update is immediately visible to other workers as they share the memory. The final stage of training (i.e., last few points of each line) is stable because there is only one worker group running during that time, namely the testing group. We note that using a warm-up stage, which trains the model using a single worker group at the beginning, may help to stabilize the training as reported in Google's DistBelief system [6].

9. RELATED WORK

Due to its outstanding capabilities in capturing complex regularities of multimedia data (e.g., image and video), deep learning techniques are being adopted by more and more multimedia applications. It has been shown that deep learning models can learn high-level semantic features from raw image data [15]. Based on this, Ji and et al. [24] apply deep learning techniques to learn high-level image features to bridge the 'semantic gap' that exists between the high-level semantic concepts perceived by human and low-level image pixels captured by machines. The learned features are effective for content-based image retrieval. Zhang et al. [33] also exploit deep learning to learn the high-level, shared representations across textual and visual modalities. The learned representations encode strong visual and semantic evidence for visual attributes discovery. Other applications of deep learning include language modelling [17] , and multi-modal retrieval [26, 25], etc. (Section 5).

Different applications use different deep learning models. It is essential to provide a general deep learning system for non-experts to implement their models without much effort. In addition, deep learning training requires a huge amount of computing resources to process large scale multimedia data. Hence, a general distributed deep learning training system is essential. Recently, some distributed training approaches have been proposed, for examples [20, 30, 13]. They are specifically optimized for training the AlexNet model [14], thus cannot generalize well to other models. The general distributed deep learning platforms [6, 4, 1] exploit deep learning specific optimizations and hence are able to achieve a high training throughput. However, they are closed-source and there are no details of the programming model, rendering them unusable to developers.

10. CONCLUSION

In this paper, we proposed a distributed deep learning platform, called SINGA, for supporting multimedia applications. SINGA offers a simple and intuitive programming model, making it accessible to even non-experts. SINGA is extensible and able to support a wide range of multimedia applications requiring different deep learning models. The flexible training architecture gives the user the chance to balance the trade-off between the training efficiency and convergence rate. We demonstrated the use of SINGA for representative multimedia applications, and showed that the platform is both usable and scalable.

11. ACKNOWLEDGMENTS

This work was in part supported by the National Research Foundation, Prime Minister's Office, Singapore under its Competitive Research Programme (CRP Award No. NRF-CRP8-2011-08) and A*STAR project 1321202073. Gang Chen's work was supported by National Natural Science Foundation of China (NSFC) Grant No. 61472348. We would like to thank the SINGA team members and NetEase for their contributions to the implementation of the Apache SINGA system, and the anonymous reviewers for their insightful and constructive comments.

12. REFERENCES

[1] T. Chilimbi, Y. Suzue, J. Apacible, and K. Kalyanaraman. Project adam: Building an efficient and scalable deep learning training system. In *OSDI*, pages 571–582. USENIX Association, Oct. 2014.

[2] T.-S. Chua, J. Tang, R. Hong, H. Li, Z. Luo, and Y.-T. Zheng. NUS-WIDE: A real-world web image database from National University of Singapore. In *CIVR'09*, July 8-10, 2009.

[3] D. C. Ciresan, U. Meier, L. M. Gambardella, and J. Schmidhuber. Deep big simple neural nets excel on handwritten digit recognition. *CoRR*, abs/1003.0358, 2010.

[4] A. Coates, B. Huval, T. Wang, D. J. Wu, B. C. Catanzaro, and A. Y. Ng. Deep learning with cots hpc systems. In *ICML (3)*, pages 1337–1345, 2013.

[5] W. Dai, J. Wei, X. Zheng, J. K. Kim, S. Lee, J. Yin, Q. Ho, and E. P. Xing. Petuum: A framework for iterative-convergent distributed ML. *CoRR*, abs/1312.7651, 2013.

[6] J. Dean, G. Corrado, R. Monga, K. Chen, M. Devin, Q. V. Le, M. Z. Mao, M. Ranzato, A. W. Senior, P. A. Tucker, K. Yang, and A. Y. Ng. Large scale distributed deep networks. In *NIPS*, pages 1232–1240, 2012.

[7] J. Dean and S. Ghemawat. Mapreduce: Simplified data processing on large clusters. In *(OSDI 2004), San Francisco, California, USA, December 6-8, 2004*, pages 137–150, 2004.

[8] J. C. Duchi, E. Hazan, and Y. Singer. Adaptive subgradient methods for online learning and stochastic optimization. *Journal of Machine Learning Research*, 12:2121–2159, 2011.

[9] F. Feng, X. Wang, and R. Li. Cross-modal retrieval with correspondence autoencoder. In *ACM Multimedia*, pages 7–16, 2014.

[10] G. Hinton and R. Salakhutdinov. Reducing the dimensionality of data with neural networks. *Science*, 313(5786):504 – 507, 2006.

[11] Y. Jia, E. Shelhamer, J. Donahue, S. Karayev, J. Long, R. Girshick, S. Guadarrama, and T. Darrell. Caffe: Convolutional architecture for fast feature embedding. *arXiv preprint arXiv:1408.5093*, 2014.

[12] D. Jiang, G. Chen, B. C. Ooi, K. Tan, and S. Wu. epiC: an extensible and scalable system for processing big data. *PVLDB*, 7(7):541–552, 2014.

[13] A. Krizhevsky. One weird trick for parallelizing convolutional neural networks. *CoRR*, abs/1404.5997, 2014.

[14] A. Krizhevsky, I. Sutskever, and G. E. Hinton. Imagenet classification with deep convolutional neural networks. In *NIPS*, pages 1106–1114, 2012.

[15] Q. V. Le, M. Ranzato, R. Monga, M. Devin, G. Corrado, K. Chen, J. Dean, and A. Y. Ng. Building high-level features using large scale unsupervised learning. In *ICML*, 2012.

[16] Y. LeCun, L. Bottou, G. B. Orr, and K. Müller. Effiicient backprop. In *Neural Networks: Tricks of the Trade*, pages 9–50, 1996.

[17] T. Mikolov, S. Kombrink, L. Burget, J. Cernocký, and S. Khudanpur. Extensions of recurrent neural network language model. In *ICASSP*, pages 5528–5531. IEEE, 2011.

[18] T. Mikolov, I. Sutskever, K. Chen, G. S. Corrado, and J. Dean. Distributed representations of words and phrases and their compositionality. In *NIPS*, pages 3111–3119, 2013.

[19] B. C. Ooi, K.-L. Tan, S. Wang, W. Wang, Q. Cai, G. Chen, J. Gao, Z. Luo, A. K. H. Tung, Y. Wang, Z. Xie, M. Zhang, and K. Zheng. SINGA: A distributed deep learning platform. In *ACM Multimedia*, 2015.

[20] T. Paine, H. Jin, J. Yang, Z. Lin, and T. S. Huang. GPU asynchronous stochastic gradient descent to speed up neural network training. *CoRR*, abs/1312.6186, 2013.

[21] B. Recht, C. Re, S. J. Wright, and F. Niu. Hogwild: A lock-free approach to parallelizing stochastic gradient descent. In *NIPS*, pages 693–701, 2011.

[22] H. T. Shen, B. C. Ooi, and K. Tan. Giving meanings to WWW images. In *ACM Multimedia*, pages 39–47. ACM, 2000.

[23] C. Szegedy, W. Liu, Y. Jia, P. Sermanet, S. Reed, D. Anguelov, D. Erhan, V. Vanhoucke, and A. Rabinovich. Going deeper with convolutions. *CoRR*, abs/1409.4842, 2014.

[24] J. Wan, D. Wang, S. C. H. Hoi, P. Wu, J. Zhu, Y. Zhang, and J. Li. Deep learning for content-based image retrieval: A comprehensive study. In *ACM Multimedia*, pages 157–166, 2014.

[25] W. Wang, B. C. Ooi, X. Yang, D. Zhang, and Y. Zhuang. Effective multi-modal retrieval based on stacked auto-encoders. *PVLDB*, 7(8):649–660, 2014.

[26] W. Wang, X. Yang, B. C. Ooi, D. Zhang, and Y. Zhuang. Effective deep learning-based multi-modal retrieval. *The VLDB Journal*, pages 1–23, 2015.

[27] X. Wang and Y. Wang. Improving content-based and hybrid music recommendation using deep learning. In *ACM Multimedia*, pages 627–636, 2014.

[28] R. Wu, S. Yan, Y. Shan, Q. Dang, and G. Sun. Deep image: Scaling up image recognition. *CoRR*, abs/1501.02876, 2015.

[29] Z. Wu, Y. Jiang, J. Wang, J. Pu, and X. Xue. Exploring inter-feature and inter-class relationships with deep neural networks for video classification. In *ACM Multimedia*, pages 167–176, 2014.

[30] O. Yadan, K. Adams, Y. Taigman, and M. Ranzato. Multi-GPU training of convnets. *CoRR*, abs/1312.5853, 2013.

[31] M. Zaharia, M. Chowdhury, T. Das, A. Dave, J. Ma, M. McCauly, M. J. Franklin, S. Shenker, and I. Stoica. Resilient distributed datasets: A fault-tolerant abstraction for in-memory cluster computing. In *NSDI*, pages 15–28, 2012.

[32] C. Zhang and C. Re. Dimmwitted: A study of main-memory statistical analytics. *PVLDB*, 7(12):1283–1294, 2014.

[33] H. Zhang, Y. Yang, H. Luan, S. Yang, and T. Chua. Start from scratch: Towards automatically identifying, modeling, and naming visual attributes. In *ACM Multimedia*, pages 187–196, 2014.

Weakly-Shared Deep Transfer Networks for Heterogeneous-Domain Knowledge Propagation

Xiangbo Shu
Nanjing University of Science and Technology, P.R. China
shuxb104@gmail.com

Guo-Jun Qi
University of Central Florida
USA
guojun.qi@ucf.edu

Jinhui Tang*
Nanjing University of Science and Technology, P.R. China
jinhuitang@njust.edu.cn

Jingdong Wang
Microsoft Research
P.R. China
jingdw@microsoft.com

ABSTRACT

In recent years, deep networks have been successfully applied to model image concepts and achieved competitive performance on many data sets. In spite of impressive performance, the conventional deep networks can be subjected to the decayed performance if we have insufficient training examples. This problem becomes extremely severe for deep networks with powerful representation structure, making them prone to over fitting by capturing nonessential or noisy information in a small data set. In this paper, to address this challenge, we will develop a novel deep network structure, capable of transferring labeling information across heterogeneous domains, especially from text domain to image domain. This *weakly-shared Deep Transfer Networks* (DTNs) can adequately mitigate the problem of insufficient image training data by bringing in rich labels from the text domain.

Specifically, we present a novel architecture of DTNs to translate cross-domain information from text to image. To share the labels between two domains, we will build multiple weakly shared layers of features. It allows to represent both shared inter-domain features and domain-specific features, making this structure more flexible and powerful in capturing complex data of different domains jointly than the strongly shared layers. Experiments on real world dataset will show its competitive performance as compared with the other state-of-the-art methods.

Categories and Subject Descriptors

I.4.7 [**Learning**]: Parameter learning, Concept learning, Knowledge acquisition; H.2.5 [**Database Applications**]: Image Representation

*Corresponding author.

MM'15, October 26–30, 2015, Brisbane, Australia.

DOI: http://dx.doi.org/10.1145/2733373.2806216.

Keywords

Heterogeneous-domain knowledge propagation, cross-domain label transfer, deep transfer network, image classification

1. INTRODUCTION

Deep networks [11] formed by multiple layers of non-linear transformations can simulate the perception of human brain to represent high-level abstractions. Existing deep network architectures include *Deep Belief Networks* (DBNs) [11], *Convolutional Neural Networks* (CNNs) [11], *Stacked Auto-Encoders* (SAEs) [3], *Deep Boltzmann Machines* (DBMs) [27], as well as many of their variants. These deep networks have achieved a tremendous success in many areas, such as image classification [16], feature learning [25], collaborative filtering [28], face verification [32], etc.

However, these general deep networks are so powerful that they are prone to overfitting into minor and often noisy variations in a relatively small size of data set. This problem becomes extremely severe when we attempt to build deep networks to model images and their concepts without sufficient amount of data. Several strategies have been proposed to avoid the overfitting by reducing the unnecessary network complexity, e.g., dropout technique for randomly omitting some hidden units with a constant probability [12], corrupted input [33], greedy layer-wise training with sparse filtering [17, 19], alternative convolution and pooling layers as previous layers [16]. Although these strategies have achieved better generalization performance, they often sacrifice the representation power of deep networks to varying degrees.

Instead of trading the representation power of deep networks for reduced overfitting risk, we will consider another way to address this challenge of insufficient training data by bringing in labeling information from other modality, namely, the text document. We aspire to answer the question – How can the cross-modal data help model image concepts? We find it beneficial to explore the text information for at least twofold reasons: 1) the word features of text data are more directly related to semantic concepts inherent in class labels and interpret its concept intuitively; 2) abundant labeled text documents are more widely available on the websites. They inspire the heterogenous transfer of discriminative knowledge from web text space (i.e., source domain) to image space (i.e., target domain). By transferring the feature representation and labeling information from text space, we will learn a semantic-intensive image feature representation directly related to image concepts, which can greatly improve the performance of image classification tasks. In other words, the rich information transferred from text can help

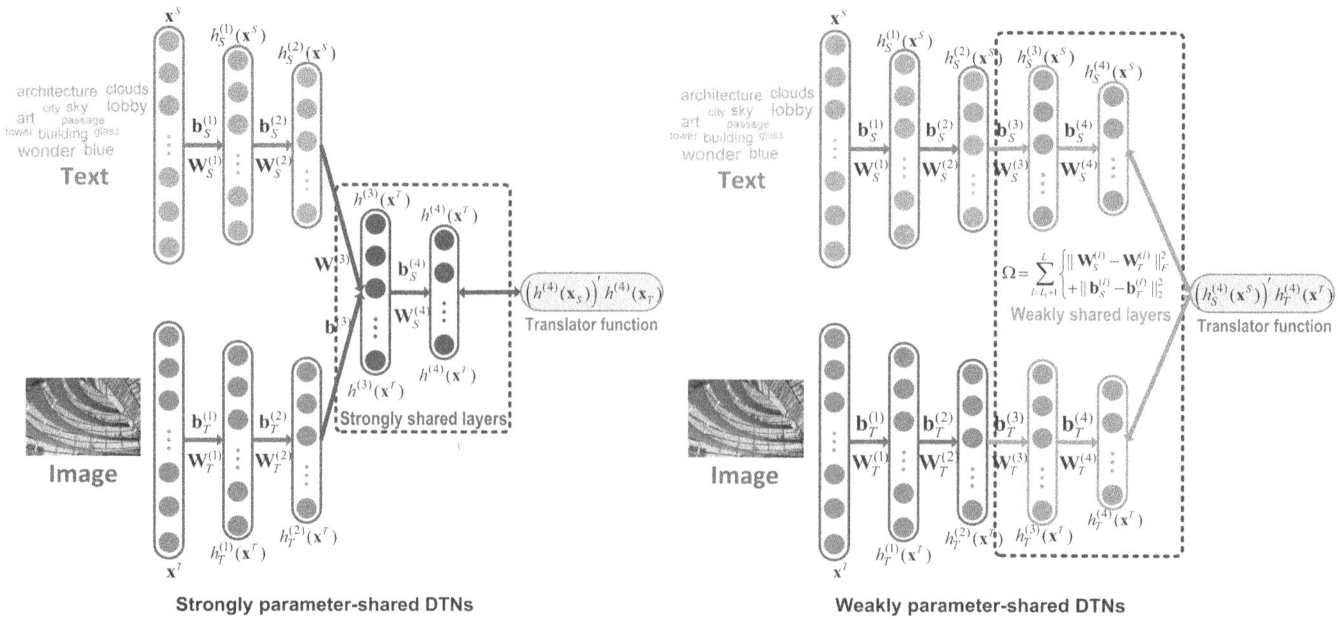

Figure 1: Architecture of *weakly-shared Deep Transfer Networks* (DTNs) with strongly parameter-shared layers (left figure) and weakly parameter-shared layers (right figure). In the left figure, DTNs use the parameter-shared layers (Layer 3 and 4) to model a set of shared features for two domains. On the contrary, in the right figure, weakly parameter-shared DTNs relax this constraint, allowing to use separate series of layers to model the features for two domains. These layers are weakly parameter-shared by imposing a regularizer that decides the extent to which they should be shared. This structure is much flexible, enabling to represent both domain-specific features and the shared features across domains.

train complex image deep networks even with little supervised image data. This is contrary to the popular strategy of trading the representation power of the deep networks for a better generalization performance in the literature. In this paper, we will present how to use transferred cross-modal information to train a powerful deep network without sacrificing structural richness, which will yield much competitive performance on image classification tasks.

To this end, we propose a novel deep network structure that hierarchically learns to transfer the semantic knowledge from web texts to images [23], namely *weakly-shared Deep Transfer Networks* (DTNs) in this paper. As a hierarchically non-lineal model, DTNs differ from existing shallow transfer learning algorithms in the literature [37, 8, 24, 26] which learn the heterogeneous feature presentations by linear mathematics models, such as matrix factorization, subspace learning, and linear translator function. In DTNs, we model two SAEs that take a pair of text and image as input respectively, followed by multiple **parameter-sharing** network layers at the top. The output of the shared layer in DTNs yields the translator function that can be used to transfer cross-modal information. To the best of our knowledge, existing methods in literature like multimodal deep networks [20] are **representation-sharing**. Our parameter sharing scheme makes our networks more flexible, especially when the application requires more modality-specific features are learned. In other words, by sharing parameters, we allow deviation exists between the feature representations of different modalities. In contrast, in "representation-sharing structure", a set of common features are constructed, which usually overestimates the importance of modality-specific features.

In this paper, we highlight the difference between the *strongly* parameter-shared layers and the *weakly* parameter-shared layers as shown in Figure 1. Different from the strongly-shared layers, the weakly-shared layers allow the use of separate layers for different domains. The extent to which these layers are weakly-shared is adjustable by a regularizer modeling their difference. The benefit of weakly-shared layers is the flexibility of representing shared inter-domain features as well as domain-specific ones, making it more powerful in modeling complex data of multiple domains than strongly-shared layers.

We will show that DTNs are trained in a novel way that minimizes the errors incurred by a cross-modal information transfer process. In our experiments, we use image classification task to evaluate the effectiveness of trained DTNs. In testing phase, the test image without neither text nor label/tag can be represented by trained DTNs, and then assigned the class label by the trained translator. Extensive experiments on real world data sets show the effectiveness of DTNs compared with the other state-of-the-art methods. Figure 1 presents an overview of our proposed networks.

2. RELATED WORK

We briefly review some related works on deep learning and transfer learning in this section.

2.1 Deep Learning

Deep learning has been comprehensively reviewed and discussed in [1]. As one of the variants of deep learning models, SAEs have been widely used for face recognition [15], motion detection [35], multimedia retrieval [22, 9], etc. The classical SAEs linearly stack multiple layers of *Auto-Encoders* together to learn higher-level representation. The high-level representation output by SAEs can be used as input to a stand-alone supervised learning algorithm, e.g.,

Support Vector Machine, *Softmax*, *Logistic Regression*, *etc*. Consider their superior performance in feature learning, we will adopt SAEs as basic building blocks to model multi-modal representations upon which a novel multi-layered translator function will be built to transfer discriminative information across heterogeneous domains.

2.2 Transfer Learning

Transfer learning [23] aims to improve a learning task with little or no additional supervised information in a target domain by propagating the knowledge from the other source domains in which there are usually abundant training data. Transfer learning can be mainly categorized two subsets: homogeneous transfer learning (domain adaptation) [7, 18, 21, 14] in a single domain but with different distributions in training and testing sets, and heterogenous transfer learning [37, 8, 24] across different modalities. Most of existing transfer learning algorithms focus on the former class of transfer learning problem, while the latter one is more challenging. In this paper, we will focus the second class of transfer learning problem. Our focus is a novel transfer learning scenario where the heterogenous data in different domains is not aligned, and a cross-modal alignment must be learned before information can be transferred across different modalities. This will make the transfer learning problem more challenging as compared with the existing scenarios.

2.3 Alliance of Deep Learning and Transfer Learning

Deep learning has been explored to marry the transfer learning in literature [2]. For example, Glorot *et al.* [10] employed *Stack Denoising Autoencoders* (SDAs) to learn hidden feature representation for homogeneous cross-domain sentiment classification. Zhang *et al.* [36] proposed a deep neural network for domain adaptation by modeling and matching both the marginal and the conditional distribution between two homogeneous data. To reduce high computational cost and enhance the scalability of SDAs, Chen *et al.* [4] proposed marginalized SDAs. Socher et al. [29] first attempted to study heterogenous transfer learning, though they focused on learning a zero-shot image representation than directly transferring cross-modal information. On the contrary, the proposed DTNs will consider a practical heterogeneous transfer learning scenario where the image concepts can be directly modeled from the text labels. This way, we can fully explore the rich cross-modal information to train densely connected deep transfer models while avoiding the overfitting problem.

The related deep representation networks (i.e., multimodal deep learning [20, 30], multimodal learning with DBMs [31], etc.) learning joint representations across multiple modalities are only shared on top of layers of modality-specific sub-networks. Deeply coupled auto-encoder networks [34] learn two deep networks embedded intra-class compactness and inter-class penalty with each other in each layer. **The key difference is that these existing models are "sharing representation", while our method is "sharing parameters", which makes our networks are more robust for modality-specific features**.

3. PROBLEM DEFINITION

First, we consider text as source domain and image as target domain in this paper in this paper. Then we are given a labeled text data set $\mathcal{D}_S = \{(\bar{\mathbf{x}}_j^S, \bar{y}_j^S)\}_{j=1}^{N_S}$ in text domain, in which $\bar{\mathbf{x}}_j^S \in \mathbb{R}^a$ is the text data of source domain and $\bar{y}_j^S \in \{+1, -1\}$ is the corresponding label [1]. Our goal is to transfer the labels from the text data set to the target image domain for a classification task. To facilitate the label transfer process, we also have another co-occurrence set of paired texts and images $\mathcal{C} = \{(\mathbf{x}_i^S, \mathbf{x}_i^T)\}_{i=1}^{N_C}$, where $\mathbf{x}_i^S \in \mathbb{R}^a$ and $\mathbf{x}_i^T \in \mathbb{R}^b$ denote one text and image respectively. By exploring this co-occurrence set, we can reveal the alignment between texts and images, which will facilitate the label transfer between these two domains.

In particular, in this paper, we will jointly learn the deep representation of texts and images to effectively transfer the discriminative information from the source text domain to the target image domain. At the core of the deep transfer learning process is an efficient cross-modal translator which can transform the labels from text domain to image domain, even with the challenge of scarcely labeled target-domain data. By leveraging the learned deeply translator, we can solve the image classification task with extremely insufficient training data.

4. PROPOSED NETWORKS

4.1 The Architecture

For an input vector $\mathbf{x}_0$, the formulation of a classical *Auto-Encoder* is comprised of an encoder function $h(\mathbf{x}) = s_e(\mathbf{W}\mathbf{x} + \mathbf{b})$ and a counterpart decoder function $\tilde{h}(\mathbf{x}) = s_d(\tilde{\mathbf{W}}\mathbf{x} + \tilde{\mathbf{b}})$ to minimize the reconstruction error of loss function $loss(\mathbf{x}_0, \tilde{h}(h(\mathbf{x}_0)))$. $s_e(\cdot)$ and $s_d(\cdot)$ are the non-linear activation function and decoder's activation function respectively. Several auto-encoders can be consecutively stacked to form the *Stacked Auto-Encoders* (SAEs) by feeding the hidden representation of the *l*-th auto-encoder into the *l+1*-th auto-encoder.

Built upon SAEs, we propose a Deep Transfer Networks for information transfer across two domains, whose structure [2] is shown in Figure 1. First we pre-train two SAEs for text and image respectively, which output hidden representations of these two domains via the multiple layers of nonlinear encoding. Assume that these two SAEs have L_1 layers, where they are structured and built separately. After the first L_1 layers, the two SAEs begin to share their structure where L_2 shared layers are constructed as shown in Figure 1. These shared layers provide a way to transfer the information across two different domains represented by the two SAEs. In this case, the input into the shared layers is the (additive or multiplicative) mixture of outputs of the bottom L_1 layers by two SAEs.

However, we find this sort of *strongly* parameter-shared layers tend to over-mix the features learned from two heterogeneous domains, namely text and images. In other words, although there exist many shared features across different domains, it is risky to completely ignore the domain-specific features through the shared layers, since text and images often contain many elements that cannot be expressed by the same set of the neurons in the shared layers. In this paper, we relax such strongly shared structure, and propose to use *weakly* parameter-shared layers, which balance between the shared features and domain-specific ones.

Formally, there are $L{+}1$ layers in DTNs, where $L = L_1 + L_2$. Given a pair of input text $\mathbf{x}_i^S$ and image $\mathbf{x}_i^T$, we use $\mathbf{x}_{S_i}^{(l)} \in \mathbb{R}^{a_l}$ and $\mathbf{x}_{T_i}^{(l)} \in \mathbb{R}^{b_l}$ to denote the latent representation of a hidden layer l

[1]We reserve S and T in the superscript to denote the source domain and target domain respectively throughout of this paper.

[2]It is worth pointing out that the SAEs for each domain can be built upon another deep network. For example, we can create a Convolutional Neural Networks whose output is ingested into the SAEs for image domain. However, to avoid notational and illustration clutters, we do not explicitly show this structure.

for the two SAEs respectively. At the first layer, we set $\mathbf{x}_{S_i}^{(0)} = \mathbf{x}_i^S$ and $\mathbf{x}_{T_i}^{(0)} = \mathbf{x}_i^T$ as inputs. For easy of presentation, we drop the subscripts i of $\mathbf{x}_{S_i}^{(l-1)}$ and $\mathbf{x}_{T_i}^{(l-1)}$ $(l = 1, 2, \cdots, L)$ in the following. For $l = 1, 2, \cdots, L$, the layer-wise processing of these two inputs through the whole network is defined as follows

$$\begin{aligned} \mathbf{x}_S^{(l)} &\triangleq h_S^{(l)}(\mathbf{x}^S) = s_e(\mathbf{W}_S^{(l)}\mathbf{x}_S^{(l-1)} + \mathbf{b}_S^{(l)}) \in \mathbb{R}^{a_l}, \\ \mathbf{x}_T^{(l)} &\triangleq h_T^{(l)}(\mathbf{x}^T) = s_e(\mathbf{W}_T^{(l)}\mathbf{x}_T^{(l-1)} + \mathbf{b}_T^{(l)}) \in \mathbb{R}^{b_l}, \end{aligned} \tag{1}$$

where $h_S^{(l)}(\cdot)$ and $h_T^{(l)}(\cdot)$ denote the l-th layer hidden representation in text and image SAEs respectively, $\{\mathbf{W}_S^{(l)}, \mathbf{b}_S^{(l)}\}_{l=1}^L$ and $\{\mathbf{W}_T^{(l)}, \mathbf{b}_T^{(l)}\}_{l=1}^L$ are the parameters in text and image SAEs respectively.

The first L_1 layers are expected to learn the representations of text and image respectively, while the last L_2 layers provide shared representations. Under *weakly parameter-sharing* assumption, the parameters of the last L_2 layers should be set to be equal to a certain degree in order to trade off between modeling the shared cross-domain features and preserving necessary domain-specific details. Therefore, we propose the following penalty term Ω to quantify such trading-off

$$\Omega = \sum\nolimits_{l=L_1+1}^{L} (||\mathbf{W}_S^{(l)} - \mathbf{W}_T^{(l)}||_F^2 + ||\mathbf{b}_S^{(l)} - \mathbf{b}_T^{(l)}||_2^2). \tag{2}$$

Minimizing this term will minimize the difference of parameters in the last L_2 layers of two SAE networks. It will be added to the proposed objective function in the next section. A positive value of balancing coefficient will be multiplied with it in the objective function, which reflects the above trading-off for the weakly shared layers.

4.2 Deeply Transfer Mechanism

The goal of the proposed heterogenous domain transfer algorithm is to transfer the labels annotated on the source domain data set $\mathcal{D}_S$ to annotate an arbitrary test data $\mathbf{x}^T$ in the target domain. For this purpose, for a pair of image $\mathbf{x}^T$ and text $\bar{\mathbf{x}}_j^S$ in $\mathcal{D}_S$, we define a translator function as the inner product $(h_S^{(L)}(\bar{\mathbf{x}}_j^S))' h_T^{(L)}(\mathbf{x}^T)$ between their weakly shared features output from the two SAEs, where $'$ denotes transpose operation in this paper. This translator function is used to propagate the labels from the source domain to the target domain as follows

$$f(\mathbf{x}^T) = \sum_j^{N_S} \bar{y}_j^S \left(h_S^{(L)}(\bar{\mathbf{x}}_j^S)\right)' h_T^{(L)}(\mathbf{x}^T), \tag{3}$$

which combines all the source labels weighted by the corresponding translator functions. For the binary classification task considered in this paper, $f(\mathbf{x}^T)$ is also a discriminant function, whose sign predicts the class of the corresponding target domain data $\mathbf{x}^T$.

We learn the parameters in the proposed DTNs by minimizing the loss incurred by the above label transfer process, as well as maximizing the consistency between a set of co-occurrence pairs of texts and images to capture the cross-domain alignment information. We elaborate these two criteria below.

- **Empirical loss on the auxiliary set.** We have a small size of auxiliary training set $\mathcal{A}_T = \{(\tilde{\mathbf{x}}_t^T, \tilde{y}_t^T)\}_{t=1}^{\tilde{N}_T}$ in the target domain, where $\tilde{\mathbf{x}}_t^T \in \mathbb{R}^b$ of the target space and $\tilde{y}_t^T \in \{+1, -1\}$ is the label. We wish to minimize the training errors incurred by the label transfer function f on this set. We define the training errors on $\mathcal{A}_T$ as

$$\operatorname*{argmin}_{\Theta} J_1 = \sum_{t=1}^{\tilde{N}_T} \ell\left(\tilde{y}_t^T \cdot f(\tilde{\mathbf{x}}_t^T)\right), \tag{4}$$

where we adopt a logistic loss function $\ell(x) = \log(1 + \exp(-x))$ to measure the cross-domain label transfer error.

The set of parameters of DTNs over which we will minimize J_1 include $\Theta = \{\mathbf{W}_S^{(l)}, \mathbf{b}_S^{(l)}, \mathbf{W}_T^{(l)}, \mathbf{b}_T^{(l)}\}_{l=1}^L$ at each layer, which will determine the obtained weakly shared feature representations.

- **Empirical loss on co-occurrence pairs.** Given a set of co-occurrence pairs $\mathcal{C} = \{(\mathbf{x}_i^S, \mathbf{x}_i^T)\}_{i=1}^{N_C}$ of texts and images, we wish to maximize the alignment between each pair of examples in this set, yielding a translator function that can well capture the alignment between these co-occurrence pairs. Mathematically, we minimize the following objective function

$$\operatorname*{argmin}_{\Theta} J_2 = \sum_{i=1}^{N_C} \chi\left(\left(h_S^{(L)}(\mathbf{x}_i^S)\right)' h_T^{(L)}(\mathbf{x}_i^T)\right), \tag{5}$$

where $\chi(x) = \exp(-x)$ is an exponential loss function, which can be seen as a measurement of mis-alignment between co-occurrence pairs caused by the translator function. Clearly, minimizing this loss function will ensure a large response of translator function over the co-occurrence set $\mathcal{C}$.

Algorithm 1 Training of Weakly-Shared Deep Transfer Networks

Input: $\mathcal{D}_S = \{(\bar{\mathbf{x}}_j^S, \bar{y}_j^S)\}_{j=1}^{N_S}$, $\mathcal{C} = \{(\mathbf{x}_i^S, \mathbf{x}_i^T)\}_{i=1}^{N_C}$, $\mathcal{A}_T = \{(\tilde{\mathbf{x}}_t^T, \tilde{y}_t^T)\}_{t=1}^{\tilde{N}_T}$, L_1, L_2, γ, λ, μ, dimension per layers and maxIter.
Output: Parameter set Θ.
Initialization: Initialize parameters in set Θ, $iter \leftarrow 1$.

```
// pre-training
for l = 1, 2, ..., L do
    Pre-train text and image SAEs with inputs {x_i^S}_{i=1}^{N_C} and {x_i^T}_{i=1}^{N_C} respectively.
end for
Extract hidden representations on pre-trained DTNs for all text and image examples.
// dual fine tuning
repeat
    for l = 1, 2, ..., L do
        Update W_S^(l), b_S^(l) with Eq. (7) and (8).
        Update W_T^(l), b_T^(l) with Eq. (9) and (10).
    end for
    for l = 1, 2, ..., L_1 do
        Fine tune W_T^(l), b_T^(l) with the back-propagated errors from the softmax output layer of image SAEs.
    end for
    Extract hidden representations on DTNs for all text and image examples.
    iter ← iter + 1.
until Convergence or iter > maxIter.
```

4.3 Objective Function and Optimization

After the above analyses, we propose the following objective function to learn the parameters of deep semantic translator as input of the top-layers of DTNs

$$\operatorname*{argmin}_{\Theta} J = J_1 + \eta J_2 + \frac{\gamma}{2}\Omega + \frac{\lambda}{2}\Psi, \tag{6}$$

where $\Psi = \sum_{l=1}^{L}(||\mathbf{W}_S^{(l)}||_F^2+||\mathbf{b}_S^{(l)}||_2^2+||\mathbf{W}_T^{(l)}||_F^2+||\mathbf{b}_T^{(l)}||_2^2)$ is the regularization term. The parameters λ, γ and η weigh the importance of different terms. In particular, η is the importance weight on alignment between the co-occurrence pairs, γ adjusts the weakly shared structure, and λ weighs the the regularization term.

To train the DTNs, we first pre-train each layer per time in a greedy fashion by using the unsupervised data as in conventional auto-encoder algorithms. The pre-trained DTNs set up a good starting point that can be fine tuned according to the objective function (6) by employing the available supervision information.

We implement a back propagation process starting from the top output layers down through the whole DTNs to adjust all parameters. Each parameter in Θ is updated by stochastic gradient descent in back propagation algorithm below:

$$\mathbf{W}_S^{(l)} = \mathbf{W}_s^{(l)} - \mu\frac{\partial J}{\partial \mathbf{W}_S^{(l)}}, \quad (7)$$

$$\mathbf{b}_S^{(l)} = \mathbf{b}_s^{(l)} - \mu\frac{\partial J}{\partial \mathbf{b}_S^{(l)}}, \quad (8)$$

$$\mathbf{W}_T^{(l)} = \mathbf{W}_T^{(l)} - \mu\frac{\partial J}{\partial \mathbf{W}_T^{(l)}}, \quad (9)$$

$$\mathbf{b}_T^{(l)} = \mathbf{b}_T^{(l)} - \mu\frac{\partial J}{\partial \mathbf{b}_T^{(l)}}, \quad (10)$$

where μ is the learning rate. In more detail, the gradient of the objective function J with respect to the parameters $\{\mathbf{W}_S^{(l)}, \mathbf{b}_S^{(l)}, \mathbf{W}_T^{(l)}, \mathbf{b}_T^{(l)}\}_{l=1}^{(L)}$ of the weakly shared layers can be computed as that:

(1) for $l = 1, 2, \ldots, L_1$, we have

$$\frac{\partial J}{\partial \mathbf{W}_S^{(l)}} = \sum_{t=1}^{\tilde{N}_T}\frac{\partial \ell(u_t)}{\partial \mathbf{W}_S^{(l)}} + \eta\sum_{i=1}^{N_C}\frac{\partial \chi(v_i)}{\partial \mathbf{W}_S^{(l)}} + \lambda\mathbf{W}_S^{(l)}, \quad (11)$$

$$\frac{\partial J}{\partial \mathbf{b}_S^{(l)}} = \sum_{t=1}^{\tilde{N}_T}\frac{\partial \ell(u_t)}{\partial \mathbf{b}_S^{(l)}} + \eta\sum_{i=1}^{N_C}\frac{\partial \chi(v_i)}{\partial \mathbf{b}_S^{(l)}} + \lambda\mathbf{b}_S^{(l)}, \quad (12)$$

$$\frac{\partial J}{\partial \mathbf{W}_T^{(l)}} = \sum_{t=1}^{\tilde{N}_T}\frac{\partial \ell(u_t)}{\partial \mathbf{W}_T^{(l)}} + \eta\sum_{i=1}^{N_C}\frac{\partial \chi(v_i)}{\partial \mathbf{W}_T^{(l)}} + \lambda\mathbf{W}_T^{(l)}, \quad (13)$$

$$\frac{\partial J}{\partial \mathbf{b}_T^{(l)}} = \sum_{t=1}^{\tilde{N}_T}\frac{\partial \ell(u_t)}{\partial \mathbf{b}_T^{(l)}} + \eta\sum_{i=1}^{N_C}\frac{\partial \chi(v_i)}{\partial \mathbf{b}_T^{(l)}} + \lambda\mathbf{b}_T^{(l)}; \quad (14)$$

(2) for $l = L_1 + 1, L_1 + 1, \cdots, L$, we have

$$\frac{\partial J}{\partial \mathbf{W}_S^{(l)}} = \sum_{t=1}^{\tilde{N}_T}\frac{\partial \ell(u_t)}{\partial \mathbf{W}_S^{(l)}} + \eta\sum_{i=1}^{N_C}\frac{\partial \chi(v_i)}{\partial \mathbf{W}_S^{(l)}} + \gamma(\mathbf{W}_S^{(l)} - \mathbf{W}_T^{(l)}) + \lambda\mathbf{W}_S^{(l)}, \quad (15)$$

$$\frac{\partial J}{\partial \mathbf{b}_S^{(l)}} = \sum_{t=1}^{\tilde{N}_T}\frac{\partial \ell(u_t)}{\partial \mathbf{b}_S^{(l)}} + \eta\sum_{i=1}^{N_C}\frac{\partial \chi(v_i)}{\partial \mathbf{b}_S^{(l)}} + \gamma(\mathbf{b}_S^{(l)} - \mathbf{b}_T^{(l)}) + \lambda\mathbf{b}_S^{(l)}, \quad (16)$$

$$\frac{\partial J}{\partial \mathbf{W}_T^{(l)}} = \sum_{t=1}^{\tilde{N}_T}\frac{\partial \ell(u_t)}{\partial \mathbf{W}_T^{(l)}} + \eta\sum_{i=1}^{N_C}\frac{\partial \chi(v_i)}{\partial \mathbf{W}_T^{(l)}} + \gamma(\mathbf{W}_T^{(l)} - \mathbf{W}_S^{(l)}) + \lambda\mathbf{W}_T^{(l)}, \quad (17)$$

$$\frac{\partial J}{\partial \mathbf{b}_T^{(l)}} = \sum_{t=1}^{\tilde{N}_T}\frac{\partial \ell(u_t)}{\partial \mathbf{b}_T^{(l)}} + \eta\sum_{i=1}^{N_C}\frac{\partial \chi(v_i)}{\partial \mathbf{b}_T^{(l)}} + \gamma(\mathbf{b}_T^{(l)} - \mathbf{b}_S^{(l)}) + \lambda\mathbf{b}_T^{(l)}. \quad (18)$$

(a) (b)

Figure 2: Examples of *birds* images from NUS-WIDE and ImageNet. (a) *birds* images from NUS-WIDE; (b) *birds* images from ImageNet.

We define $u_t = \tilde{y}_t^T \cdot f(\tilde{\mathbf{x}}_t^T)$ and $v_i = (h_S^{(L)}(\mathbf{x}_i^S))' h_T^{(L)}(\mathbf{x}_i^T)$ in above Eq. (11)$\sim$(18). The derivatives of $\ell(u_t)$ and $\chi(v_i)$ over the network parameters can be computed in a similar back propagation fashion as for the conventional neural networks. The gradient of the objective function J over the network parameters of the first L_1 layers of two separate SAEs can be computed similarly as in the above equations, expect for the third term of RHS of each equation which accounts for the weakly shared layers only.

The above fine tuning strategy is more effective to update the text SAE than its image counterpart, since more number of text labels are involved to tune the networks. To more adequately tune the image SAE in conjunction with the tuning of text SAE, we exploit the supervision information in the training set $\mathcal{A}_T$ to directly tune the image SAE. Specifically, we add an additional softmax layer upon image SAE that outputs the image labels. Then the labeled images in $\mathcal{A}_T$ are used to compute the back-propagated errors to tune the parameters in the image SAE. These back-propagated errors are different from those computed from the objective function J that is based on label transfer process. Here the back-propagated errors only arise from the image labels that are intended to enhance the tuning of image SAE. This can avoid unbalanced tuning of text and image SAEs when much more text labels are used in label transfer process.

We alternate between the above two fine tuning strategies – minimizing the objective function J and tuning image SAE with labeled examples in $\mathcal{A}_T$. We call such mixed strategy *dual-fine tuning* in this paper. This is contrary to *single-fine tuned DTNs* (sigDTNs) that only trains the DTNs by minimizing J. We will compare these two methods in experiments. The detailed procedure of *dual-fine tuned DTNs* (duftDTNs) is described in Algorithm 1. The convergence criterion is that the iteration steps shall end when the number of iterations reaches the max or the relative cost of objective function is smaller than a predefined threshold.

5. EXPERIMENTS

5.1 Datasets

We conduct our experiments on NUS-WIDE data set [5], which consists of 269,648 Flickr images and the associated text parts containing the user tags and comments annotated on each image. In our experiments, we use ten categories to evaluate the effectiveness on the image classification task, including *birds*, *building*, *cars*, *cat*, *dog*, *fish*, *flowers*, *horses*, *mountain* and *plane*. To train DTNs, we collect 1,500 co-occurrence pairs of text and image for each category. The co-occurrence pairs of image and text with top-10 high-frequency words for 10 categories are shown in Table 1. The text descriptions of user tags in this co-occurrence set are labeled

birds	*building*	*cars*	*cat*	*dog*	*fish*	*flowers*	*horses*	*mountain*	*plane*
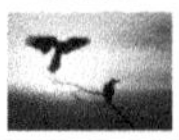				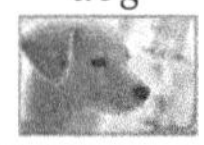				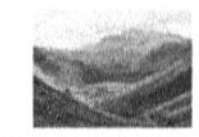	
bird	sky	car	cat	dog	fish	flower	horse	mountain	airplane
nature	night	street	kitty	beach	sea	plant	foal	landscape	aircraft
sky	city	road	kitten	puppy	water	rose	nature	nature	plane
animal	architecture	locomotive	animal	pet	nature	color	bravo	cloud	aviation
wildlife	water	automobile	cute	running	color	spring	brazil	sky	airport
water	clouds	traffic	pet	animal	dark	nature	brasil	now	flying
flight	blue	vehicle	feline	water	pet	pink	argentina	blue	jet
animal	building	city	tabby	blue	ocean	grass	cloud	lake	sky
blue	sunset	police	nature	cute	swimming	cute	sky	water	flight
sea	skyline	train	white	nature	blue	beautiful	animal	tree	fighter

Table 1: Exhibition of co-occurrence pair of image and text with top-10 high-frequency words for all 10 categories.

♯ training images	Single-Dataset (SD) setting						Cross-Dataset (CD) setting					
	SVM	SAEs	HTL	TTI	sigDTNs	duftDTNs	SVM	SAEs	HTL	TTI	sigDTNs	duftDTNs
2	58.05	59.11	63.81	71.21	75.52	**77.64**	59.01	60.54	66.22	71.69	76.62	**80.01**
3	59.58	62.25	65.97	71.47	75.69	**78.95**	60.65	63.34	67.23	72.16	77.14	**80.30**
4	62.97	65.21	67.21	71.38	76.02	**79.27**	61.97	65.07	68.22	72.44	77.50	**80.63**
5	63.91	66.04	69.20	71.57	76.34	**79.46**	63.33	66.23	69.28	72.82	77.86	**81.05**
6	65.45	67.25	70.10	71.69	76.70	**79.50**	64.94	66.84	70.17	73.26	78.28	**81.53**
7	66.76	68.95	71.00	71.66	76.27	**79.82**	66.48	68.09	71.01	73.40	78.53	**81.67**
8	67.29	68.60	71.36	72.02	77.54	**80.04**	67.19	69.32	71.64	73.56	78.80	**81.90**
9	67.73	69.94	71.86	72.14	77.68	**80.21**	68.07	69.89	72.25	73.93	79.24	**82.31**
10	67.83	70.66	72.52	72.35	77.95	**80.72**	68.76	71.19	72.62	74.04	79.41	**82.50**

Table 2: Average accuracy (%) of various algorithms vs. number of training images in SD and CD settings.

by these ten categories. These text labels are transferred by the trained DTNs to label the images. A test set of images without any co-occurred texts are annotated with ground truth labels on NUS-WIDE dataset for evaluation purpose.

5.2 Experiment Settings

We consider two different experiment settings to evaluate the performance of the proposed DTNs.

- **Single-Dataset (SD) setting:** In this setting, we use NUS-WIDE data set to train the DTNs model. Then we use the trained DTNs to transfer the text labels to annotate the test images in NUS-WIDE data set. This is a challenging image annotation task since the images in Flickr are taken out of focus by amateur photographers. These images often have a wide range of resolution sizes, ranging from extremely small sizes (tens of pixels in each dimension) to very large sizes; many of them contain cluttered backgrounds. All of these factors make it difficult to model images with only limited visual information. To address this challenge, we use DTNs to transfer the text labels to enhance the discriminant information for modeling images in Flickr.

- **Cross-Dataset (CD) setting:** In this setting, we train the DTNs model with NUS-WIDE data set, but then use the trained DTNs to transfer the text labels from NUS-WIDE to annotate the images in ImageNet [6]. This setting can test the generalization ability of DTNs across different image data sets. For the sake of fair comparison, we test on ImageNet with the same set of ten image categories and their subcategories as in NUS-WIDE. Figure 2 shows some examples of *birds* images from NUS-WIDE and ImageNet. We can see that the images from NUS-WIDE are visually diverse, while those images of the same category from ImageNet are more visually consistent with each other.

The performance of the proposed DTNs (with sigDTNs and duftDTNs) are compared with a set of state-of-the-art algorithms below. (1) SVMs: they are conventional shallow structured classifiers and set as the baseline for comparison; (2) SAEs: they represent deep structured network. SAEs model image content, and we connect them to a logistic output layer that directly gives the predicted labels on images. Both SVMs and SAEs only use image content, without any text labels involved. We also compare with the other heterogeneous transfer learning algorithms exploring text labels. (3) *Heterogeneous Transfer Learning* (HTL) [37]: it maps each image into a latent vector space via a formulated implicit distance function. HTL also makes use of the occurrence information between images and text documents as well as images and visual words. (4) *Translator from Text to Image* (TTI) [24]: it learns a translator on co-occurred pairs of text and images as well as a small size of training images and effectively convert the semantics from texts to images for image classification task. Both of these two algorithms explore the text labels to model images. TTI has been reported to achieve the state-of-the-art performances over Flickr dataset, however it only considers a shallow label transfer structure.

We compare the performances of different algorithms with varying numbers of training images, ranging from 2 to 10. In both experimental settings, SD and CD, the training images are random-

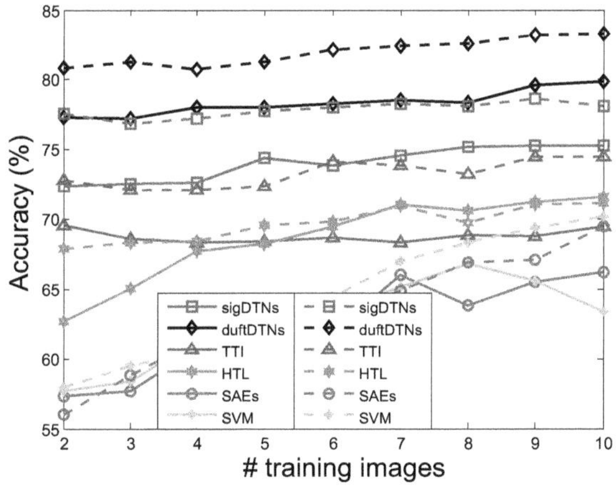

(a) *birds*

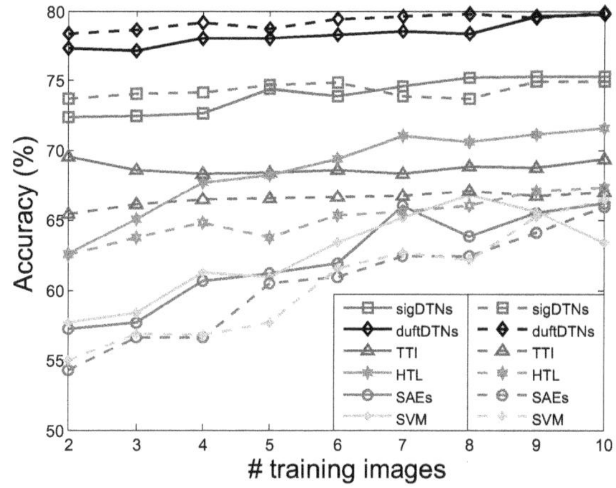

(b) *building*

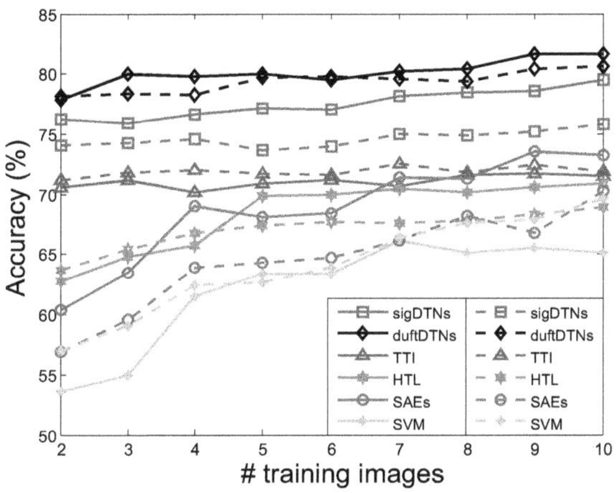

(c) *cars*

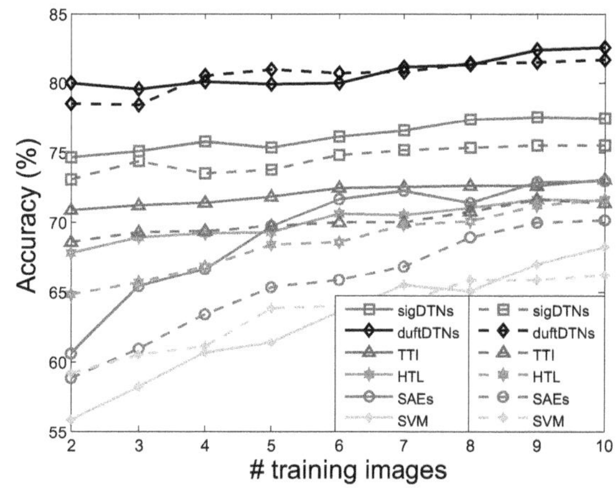

(d) *cat*

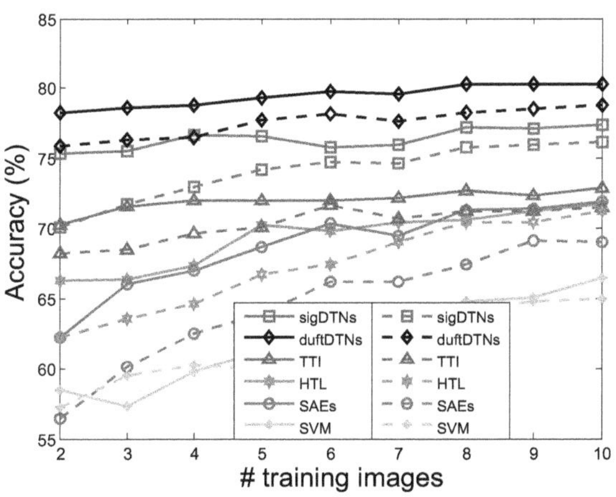

(e) *dog*

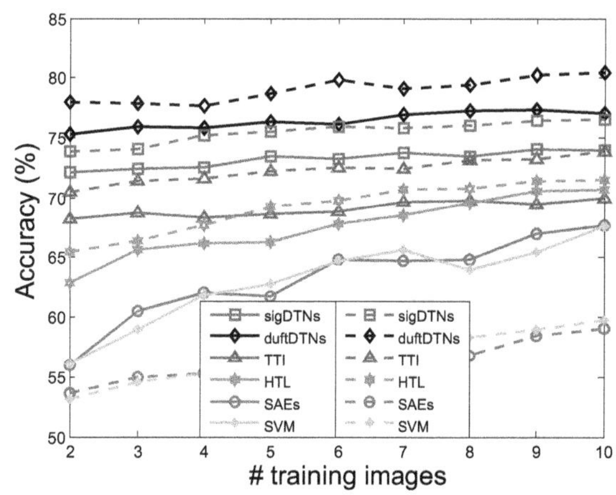

(f) *fish*

Figure 3: Accuracy (%) of different algorithms with number of auxiliary labeled images. Solid line and dotted line denote the two experiment settings *SD* and *CD*, respectively. This figure is followed by Figure 4.

ly selected, and the process is repeated ten times, and the average performance is reported.

We also compare the accuracy of the compared algorithms with the varying numbers of co-occurrence text-image pairs. All the parameters in our model are tuned based on a 2-fold cross-validation procedure on the training set, and the parameters are selected when the best performance is achieved.

5.3 Results

In this paper, we train 5-layer DTNs, in which the number of neurons are $1226 \rightarrow 618 \rightarrow 128 \rightarrow 128 \rightarrow 60$ and $1000 \rightarrow 512 \rightarrow 128 \rightarrow 128 \rightarrow 60$ at each layer from bottom up in iamges SAEs and text SAEs, respectively. The last three ones are weakly shared layers. At the input layers of DTNs, $1,000$ words are extracted and stemmed from the text parts and their frequencies are input into text

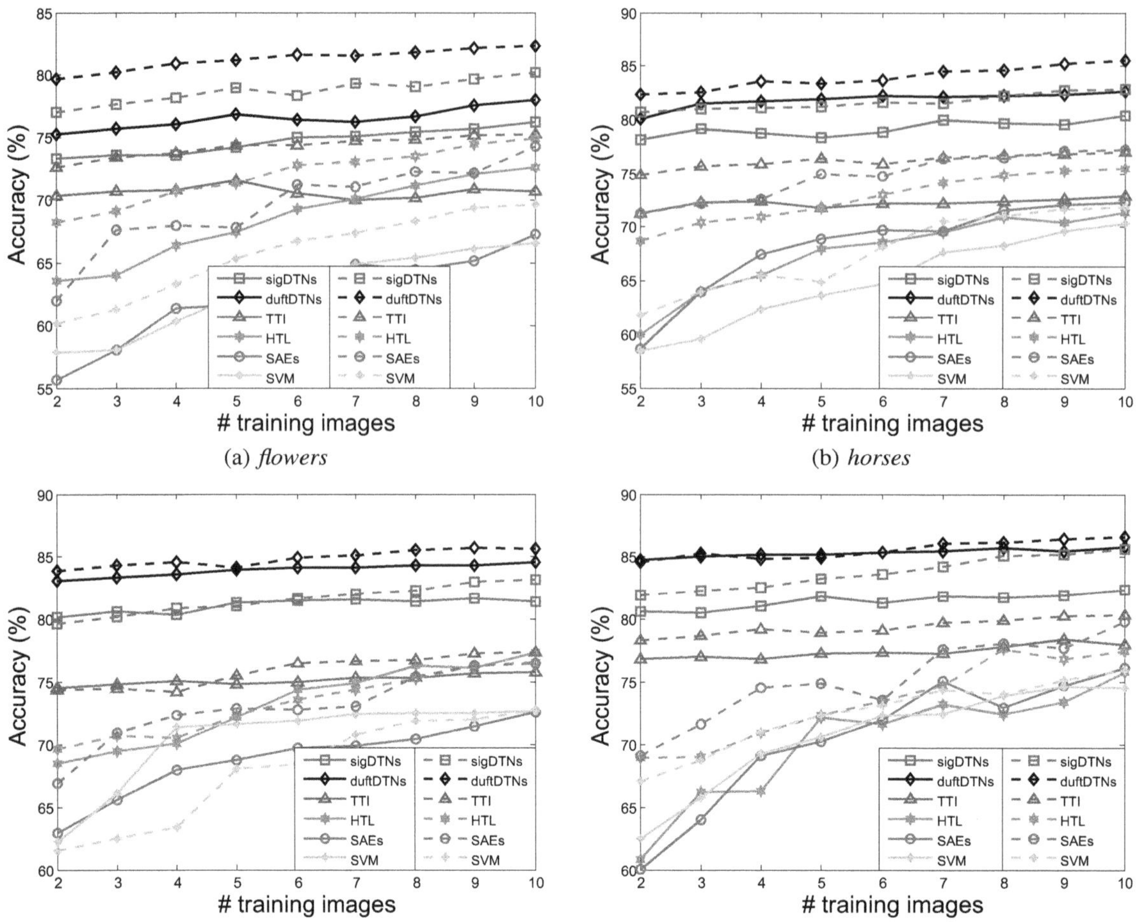

(a) *flowers* (b) *horses*

(c) *mountain* (d) *plane*

Figure 4: Accuracy (%) of different algorithms with number of auxiliary labeled images. Solid line and dotted line denote the two experiment settings SD and CD, respectively. This figure follows Figure 3.

SAEs. We extract the 4096 dims CNN features as an visual features for images by AlexNet [16, 13], and then reduce the dimensionality of CNN features into the 1226 dims by PCA.

The accuracies over all categories with varying number of auxiliary training examples are plotted in Figure 3 and Figure 4. Either in SD setting or CD setting, the accuracy of traditional SVMs and SAEs algorithms is the lowest among all the compared algorithms no matter how many training images are used, since neither of them explores the heterogeneous domain. The performance of the compared transfer learning algorithms, including TTI, HTL and the proposed DTNs, is improved to different degrees. Among them, both of two proposed training algorithms, sigDTNs and duftDTNs, have performed the best.

All the subplots in Figure 3 and 4 show that the proposed DTNs, with both training algorithms of sigDTNs and duftDTNs, outperform the other compared algorithms. It illustrates the amazing advantages of the proposed DTNs when there are an extremely little amount of training data. This is also consistent with our earlier assertions that our DTNs can work well even in the insufficiency of auxiliary training examples, by exploring the co-ocurrence information between text and image. We also observe that duftDTNs often performs better than sigDTNs. This is due to the fact that duftDTNs use an extra step to tune the image SAEs with the training images. This better balances between the fine tuning of text and image SAEs, when the text labels are much more than image labels.

Table 2 also reports the average accuracies of various methods over all 10 categories with varying number of training images. Results in both of two experiment settings are reported in this table. An interesting discovery is the accuracy in cross-dataset (CD) setting is much comparable with that in single-dataset (SD) setting. This suggests that the DTNs trained with one data set (NUS-WIDE) are well generalized to transfer the labels between data sets (i.e., from NUS-WIDE to ImageNet). This is a very useful property in many real applications when we have to handle data from different sources.

The above results for DTNs are obtained by using $3,000$ co-occurrence pairs of text and image. Since the co-occurrence pairs play an important role as a bridge to connect heterogeneous domains in our proposed DTNs, we examine the effect with varying number of co-occurrence pairs of text and image in Figure 5, where the number of training images is fixed to 10. The average accuracy of TTI and DTNs in both SD and CD settings are increased with an increasing number of co-occurrence text-image pairs. This suggests that more co-occurrence pairs tend to provide more information to better model DTNs with improved performance.

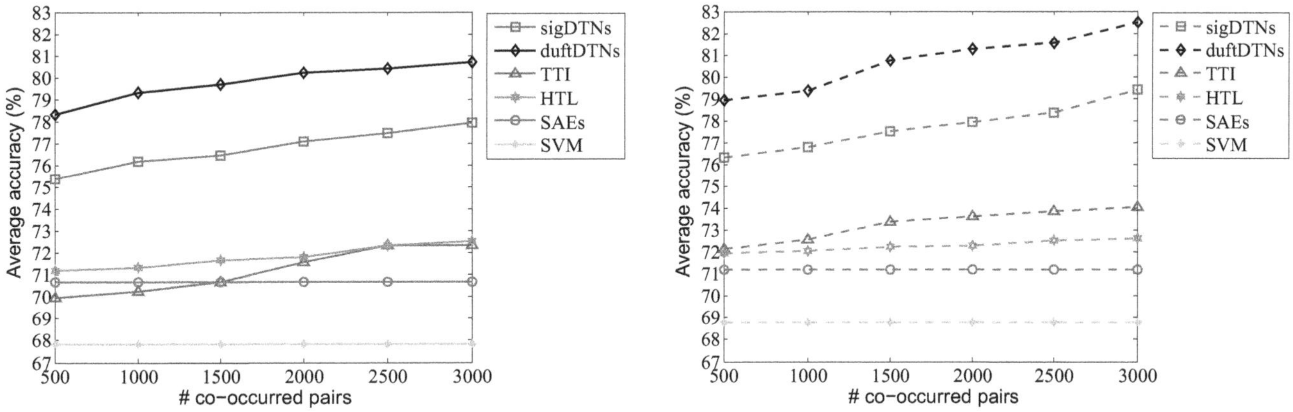

(a) Experiment setting *SD*

(b) Experiment setting *CD*

Figure 5: Number of co-occurrence pairs vs. average accuracy (%) in SD and CD settings. (a) and (b) denote the two experiment settings *SD* and *CD* respectively.

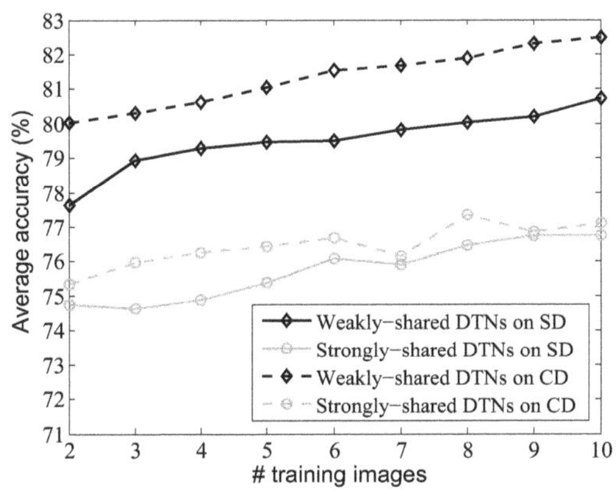

Figure 6: Comparison results of DTNs with weakly shared layers and strongly parameter-shared layers.

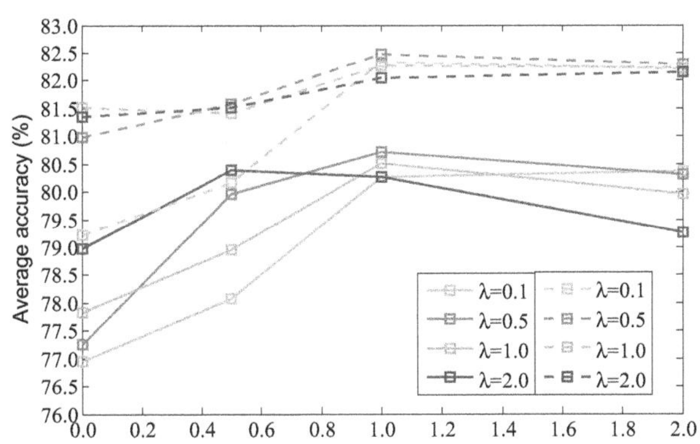

Figure 7: Parametric sensitivity vs. average accuracy (%) with different parameters γ and λ on 10 training images. Solid line and dotted line denote the SD and CD settings, respectively.

5.4 Strongly Parameter-Shared vs. Weakly Parameter-Shared Layers

To illustrate the superiority of the weakly parameter sharing, we also compare the performances of DTNs with strongly parameter-shared layers and weakly parameter-shared layers. For strongly parameter-shared layers, we set $\mathbf{W}_S^{(l)} = \mathbf{W}_T^{(l)}$ and $\mathbf{b}_S^{(l)} = \mathbf{b}_T^{(l)}$ for text and image SAEs for the top layers $l = L_1+1, \cdots, L$. In other words, these layers share the same neuron connections between two successive layers.

In this experiment, we also set the number of training images from 2 to 10. Figure 6 compares the performances of weakly parameter-shared layers and strongly parameter-shared layers. We can see that the performances of DTNs with weakly shared layers are further improved as compared with DTNs with strongly shared layers in both SD and CD settings. This confirms that proposed weakly shared layers are more suitable to model the DTNs than strongly shared layers.

5.5 Parameter Sensitivity

In the experiments, parameters γ and λ of object function J in Eq. (6) are chosen $\gamma \in \{0, 0.5, 1.0, 2.0\}$ and $\lambda \in \{0.1, 0.5, 1.0, 2.0\}$ respectively by a cross-validation procedure. Conventionally, we set $\eta = 1$ to equally weigh the two types of loss terms. Here, we study their impacts on the performances in Figure 7. When $\gamma = 0$, the average accuracy is the lowest. This is because in this case the text and image SAEs are completely independent without any shared layers. This structure fails to model the joint image and text representation, and is unable of transferring labels across heterogenous domains. The accuracy increases rapidly when γ becomes large. On the other hand, λ can also improve the accuracy when it is set to a proper value to regularize the model. The best accuracy in both SD and CD settings is achieved when $\gamma = 1$ and $\lambda = 0.5$. The accuracies with different values of parameters are not varied very much, which suggests that DTNs are not very sensitive to these model parameters.

6. CONCLUSION

In this paper, we propose a type of novel *weakly-shared Deep Transfer Networks* (DTNs) to translate cross-domain information from text domain to image domain. The proposed DTNs with weekly parameter-shared layers can more powerfully capture complex representation of data of different domains with both shared inter-domain and domain-specific knowledge than the strongly parameter-shared layers. The DTNs are trained in a novel way that directly minimizes the loss incurred by a label transfer function. This yields a *dual-fine tuning* strategy to train DTNs from top down with back-propagated errors that are derived from the label transfer loss alongside the loss from softmax output layer of image SAE to avoid unbalanced tuning. We show superior results of the proposed DTNs on extensive experiments as compared with the baselines and the other state-of-the-art methods.

7. ACKNOWLEDGEMENTS

This work was partially supported by the 973 Program (Project No. 2014CB347600), the National Natural Science Foundation of China (Grant No. 61402228), the Program for New Century Excellent Talents in University under Grant NCET-12-0632 and the Natural Science Fund for Distinguished Young Scholars of Jiangsu Province under Grant BK2012033.

8. REFERENCES

[1] Y. Bengio. Learning deep architectures for ai. *Foundations and trends® in Machine Learning*, 2(1):1–127, 2009.

[2] Y. Bengio. Deep learning of representations for unsupervised and transfer learning. In *ICML*, pages 17–36, 2012.

[3] Y. Bengio, P. Lamblin, D. Popovici, and H. Larochelle. Greedy layer-wise training of deep networks. *NIPS*, 19:153, 2007.

[4] M. Chen, Z. Xu, F. Sha, and K. Q. Weinberger. Marginalized denoising autoencoders for domain adaptation. In *ICML*, pages 767–774, 2012.

[5] T.-S. Chua, J. Tang, R. Hong, H. Li, Z. Luo, and Y. Zheng. Nus-wide: a real-world web image database from national university of singapore. In *CIVR*, page 48, 2009.

[6] J. Deng, W. Dong, R. Socher, L.-J. Li, K. Li, and L. Fei-Fei. Imagenet: A large-scale hierarchical image database. In *CVPR*, pages 248–255, 2009.

[7] J. Donahue, J. Hoffman, E. Rodner, K. Saenko, and T. Darrell. Semi-supervised domain adaptation with instance constraints. In *CVPR*, pages 668–675, 2013.

[8] L. Duan, D. Xu, and I. W. Tsang. Learning with augmented features for heterogeneous domain adaptation. In *ICML*, pages 711–718, 2012.

[9] F. Feng, X. Wang, and R. Li. Cross-modal retrieval with correspondence autoencoder. In *ACM Multimedia*, pages 7–16, 2014.

[10] X. Glorot, A. Bordes, and Y. Bengio. Domain adaptation for large-scale sentiment classification: A deep learning approach. In *ICML*, pages 513–520, 2011.

[11] G. Hinton, S. Osindero, and Y.-W. Teh. A fast learning algorithm for deep belief nets. *Neural Computation*, 18(7):1527–1554, 2006.

[12] G. E. Hinton, N. Srivastava, A. Krizhevsky, I. Sutskever, and R. R. Salakhutdinov. Improving neural networks by preventing co-adaptation of feature detectors. *arXiv*, 2012.

[13] Y. Jia, E. Shelhamer, J. Donahue, S. Karayev, J. Long, R. Girshick, S. Guadarrama, and T. Darrell. Caffe: Convolutional architecture for fast feature embedding. In *ACM Multimedia*, pages 675–678, 2014.

[14] Y.-G. Jiang, C.-W. Ngo, and S.-F. Chang. Semantic context transfer across heterogeneous sources for domain adaptive video search. In *ACM Multimedia*, pages 155–164, 2009.

[15] M. Kan, S. Shan, H. Chang, and X. Chen. Stacked progressive auto-encoders (spae) for face recognition across poses. In *CVPR*, pages 1883–1890, 2014.

[16] A. Krizhevsky, I. Sutskever, and G. E. Hinton. Imagenet classification with deep convolutional neural networks. In *NIPS*, pages 1097–1105, 2012.

[17] H. Lee, C. Ekanadham, and A. Y. Ng. Sparse deep belief net model for visual area v2. In *NIPS*, pages 873–880, 2008.

[18] M. Long, J. Wang, G. Ding, J. Sun, and P. S. Yu. Transfer joint matching for unsupervised domain adaptation. In *CVPR*, pages 1410–1417, 2014.

[19] J. Ngiam, Z. Chen, S. A. Bhaskar, P. W. Koh, and A. Y. Ng. Sparse filtering. In *NIPS*, pages 1125–1133, 2011.

[20] J. Ngiam, A. Khosla, M. Kim, J. Nam, H. Lee, and A. Y. Ng. Multimodal deep learning. In *ICML*, pages 689–696, 2011.

[21] J. Ni, Q. Qiu, and R. Chellappa. Subspace interpolation via dictionary learning for unsupervised domain adaptation. In *CVPR*, pages 692–699, 2013.

[22] X. Ou, L. Yan, H. Ling, C. Liu, and M. Liu. Inductive transfer deep hashing for image retrieval. In *ACM Multimedia*, pages 969–972, 2014.

[23] S. J. Pan and Q. Yang. A survey on transfer learning. *TKDE*, 22(10):1345–1359, 2010.

[24] G.-J. Qi, C. Aggarwal, and T. Huang. Towards semantic knowledge propagation from text corpus to web images. In *WWW*, pages 297–306, 2011.

[25] S. Rifai, P. Vincent, X. Muller, X. Glorot, and Y. Bengio. Contractive auto-encoders: Explicit invariance during feature extraction. In *ICML*, pages 833–840, 2011.

[26] S. D. Roy, T. Mei, W. Zeng, and S. Li. Socialtransfer: cross-domain transfer learning from social streams for media applications. In *ACM Multimedia*, pages 649–658, 2012.

[27] R. Salakhutdinov and G. E. Hinton. Deep boltzmann machines. In *AISTATS*, pages 448–455, 2009.

[28] R. Salakhutdinov, A. Mnih, and G. Hinton. Restricted boltzmann machines for collaborative filtering. In *ICML*, pages 791–798, 2007.

[29] R. Socher, M. Ganjoo, C. D. Manning, and A. Ng. Zero-shot learning through cross-modal transfer. In *NIPS*, pages 935–943, 2013.

[30] K. Sohn, W. Shang, and H. Lee. Improved multimodal deep learning with variation of information. In *NIPS*, pages 2141–2149, 2014.

[31] N. Srivastava and R. Salakhutdinov. Multimodal learning with deep boltzmann machines. In *NIPS*, pages 2222–2230, 2012.

[32] Y. Taigman, M. Yang, M. Ranzato, and L. Wolf. Deepface: Closing the gap to human-level performance in face verification. In *CVPR*, pages 1701–1708, 2014.

[33] P. Vincent, H. Larochelle, Y. Bengio, and P.-A. Manzagol. Extracting and composing robust features with denoising autoencoders. In *ICML*, pages 1096–1103, 2008.

[34] W. Wang, Z. Cui, H. Chang, S. Shan, and X. Chen. Deeply coupled auto-encoder networks for cross-view classification. *arXiv*, 2014.

[35] P. Xu, M. Ye, X. Li, Q. Liu, Y. Yang, and J. Ding. Dynamic background learning through deep auto-encoder networks. In *ACM Multimedia*, pages 107–116, 2014.

[36] X. Zhang, F. X. Yu, S.-F. Chang, and S. Wang. Deep transfer network: Unsupervised domain adaptation. *arXiv*, 2015.

[37] Y. Zhu, Y. Chen, Z. Lu, S. J. Pan, G.-R. Xue, Y. Yu, and Q. Yang. Heterogeneous transfer learning for image classification. In *AAAI*, 2011.

Opportunities and Challenges of Industry-Academic Collaborations in Multimedia Research

Shi-Fu Chang
Columbia University
sfchang@ee.columbia.edu

Matt Cooper
FXPal
cooper@fxpal.com

Denver Dash
Magic Leap
ddash@magicleap.com

Funda Kivran-Swaine
Facebook
fundaks@fb.com

Jia Li
Snapchat
lijiali@cs.stanford.edu

David A. Shamma
Yahoo Labs
aymans@acm.org

ABSTRACT

This ACM MM panel aims to redefine the state of research between Academia and Industry.

Categories and Subject Descriptors

H.4.0 [**Information Systems**]: Information Systems Applications—*General*; H.5.m. [**Information Interfaces and Presentation (e.g. HCI)**]: Miscellaneous

Keywords

Multimedia, Industry, Academia, Panel

1. INTRODUCTION

There have been several rapid advancements in large-scale multimedia computing in the past 5 years. As the sheer volume of online photos and other multimedia data has increased and there have been recent optimizations in deep learning; many industry technologies have become the focus of research, application, and press [1]. However, there is much that remains unsolvable and that is likely beyond industrial reach. In this panel, we aim to illuminate the hard questions for the future as well as discuss the intersections and collaboration opportunities that exists to bridge and grow the vital communities across both academia and industry. Given the vibrant participation from industry, ACMMM is the natural community for industry and academia to jointly explore this intersection topic. A panel with such focus will help ACMMM to continue its preeminent position in leading such fruitful joint efforts. We aim for this panel to be discussion lead with 4 industry recognized panelists from a diverse background as not to just skew to a single multimedia perspective. The two organizers will carry the conversation and questions forward and invite audience discussion and participation from the start.

MM'15, October 26–30, 2015, Brisbane, Australia.
ACM 978-1-4503-3459-4/15/10.
http://dx.doi.org/10.1145/2733373.2806281.

2. PANELISTS

Matt Cooper Dr. Cooper is a senior research scientist at FX Palo Alto Laboratory, where he leads the social and enterprise media group. He received the BS, MS, and DSc degrees in Electrical Engineering from Washington University in St. Louis. His primary research focus is developing content analysis techniques that enable interactive multimedia information management and retrieval applications. He is a senior member of both the IEEE and the ACM.

Denver Dash Dr. Dash is a Principal Engineer at Magic Leap co-leading the applied Machine Learning effort. Prior to that he was at Intel where he was part of three novel academic funding models over the span of 10 years: Strategic Research Projects, the Intel Lablet at Carnegie Mellon University, and the Intel Science & Technology Center on Embedded Computing (ISTC-EC) at CMU. He has over 40 peer-reviewed publications in Machine Learning, AI, Causality, Graphical Models and Computer Vision, a book chapter and is co-inventor on 6 patents.

Funda Kivran-Swaine Ms. Kivran-Swaine leads the user experience research team for media in Facebook. She is an information scientist, and a PhD candidate in Rutgers University, School of Communication and Information. She earned her B.Sc. in computer science and engineering from Sabanci University in Istanbul, Turkey, and previously worked as a UX designer.

Jia Li Dr. Li is the Head of Research at Snapchat, leading the research innovation effort. Before joining Snapchat, she led the Visual Computing and Learning Group at Yahoo! Labs. She was selected to receive the Super Star award at Yahoo!, the highest award at the company and awarded the Master Inventor Award for innovations in Computer Vision and Machine Learning. She is the Industry Relationship Chair of CVPR 2016 and the Associate Editor of the Visual Computer: International Journal of Computer Graphics by Springer.

3. REFERENCES

[1] B. Thomee, D. A. Shamma, G. Friedland, B. Elizalde, K. Ni, D. Poland, D. Borth, and L.-J. Li. YFCC100M: The new data in multimedia research. *Communications of the ACM*, 2015. To appear.

Opportunities and Challenges of Global Network Cameras

Joanna Batstone
IBM
batstone@us.ibm.com

Touradj Ebrahimi
EPFL
touradj.ebrahimi@epfl.ch

Tiejun Huang
Peking University
tjhuang@pku.edu.cn

Yung-Hsiang Lu
Purdue University
yunglu@purdue.edu

Yonggang Wen
Nanyang Technological University
ygwen@ntu.edu.sg

Since the introduction of consumer digital cameras, user-created multimedia content has become increasingly popular. Digital cameras, together with inexpensive editing tools, and free hosting sites have made multimedia an integral part of everyday life. Today, hundreds of hours video are uploaded to hosting sites every minute. Video-on-demand through wireless networks and smartphones have profoundly changed how people consume multimedia content. Meanwhile, the widely deployed network cameras can provide live views of many parts of the world. These cameras can provide rich sources creating multimedia content. This panel will explore the opportunities and discuss the challenges using global network cameras for creating multimedia contents and understanding the world.

Every year, millions of network cameras are deployed. The data from some of these network cameras are publicly available, continuously streaming live views of national parks, city halls, streets, highways, and shopping malls. A person may see multiple tourist attractions through these cameras, without leaving home. Researchers may observe the weather in different cities. Using the data from the cameras, it is possible to observe natural disasters, such as volcano eruption or tsunami, at a safe distance. News reporters may obtain instant views of an unfolding riot without risking their lives. A spectator may watch a celebration parade from multiple locations using the street cameras. Despite the many promising applications, the opportunities of using global network cameras for creating multimedia content have not been fully exploited.

The opportunities also bring forth many challenges. Managing the large amount of data would require fundamentally new thinking. The data from network cameras are unstructured and have few (if any at all) metadata describing the content. Searching the relevant content would be a challenge. Moreover, many network cameras are stationary watching the same scenes continuously (even though some have pan-tilt-zoom). The data from outdoor cameras have repetitive content due to the periodic daylight (with gradual seasonal changes or sudden changes due to storms); storing the data efficiently may require new compression techniques. Because network cameras continuously produce data, processing must be able to handle the streaming data. This imposes stringent requirements of the performance. The panelists will present their views about how network cameras could be utilized and what new technologies are needed to realize the potential from the cameras.

MM'15, October 26-30, 2015, Brisbane, Australia
ACM 978-1-4503-3459-4/15/10.
http://dx.doi.org/10.1145/2733373.2806282.

Joanna Batstone is the Vice President and Lab Director, IBM Research-Australia and Chief Technology Officer, IBM Australia and New Zealand. Previously she was Vice President, Architecture & Technical Solution Design, IBM Global Technology Services, Ireland, and Director for Distributed Computing in IBM Research - Watson, with worldwide strategy responsibility for Distributed Computing. Her IBM career has included a variety of technical and business leadership roles across different IBM Lines of Business, including Healthcare & Life Sciences, Sensors & Actuators, Physical Sciences and Application and Integration Middleware. She received a B.Sc., in Chemical Physics and a Ph.D., in Physics from The University of Bristol, UK, followed by postdoctoral work at AT&T Bell Laboratories, NJ, and a Lectureship in the Department of Materials Science and Engineering at the University of Liverpool, UK, before joining IBM Research. She received the '95 Burton Medal from the Microscopy Society of America, the '91 Robert Lansing Hardy Gold Medal from The Minerals, Metals and Materials Society and the '89 Cosslett Award from the Microbeam Analysis Society.

Touradj Ebrahimi is a Professor at EPFL heading its Multimedia Signal Processing Group. He was also adjunct Professor with the Center of Quantifiable Quality of Service at Norwegian University of Science and Technology (NTNU) between 2008 and 2012. In 1993, he was a research engineer at the Corporate Research Laboratories of Sony Corporation in Tokyo, where he conducted research on advanced video compression techniques for storage applications. In 1994, he served as a research consultant at AT&T Bell Laboratories working on very low bitrate video coding. He has been the recipient of various distinctions and awards, such as the IEEE and Swiss national ASE award, the SNF-PROFILE grant for advanced researchers, Four ISO-Certificates for key contributions to MPEG-4 and JPEG 2000, and the best paper award of IEEE Transactions on Consumer Electronics. He became a Fellow of the international society for optical engineering (SPIE) in 2003. He has initiated more than two dozen National, European and International cooperation projects with leading companies and research institutes around the world. He is also the head of the Swiss delegation to MPEG, JPEG and SC29, and acts as the Chairman of Advisory Group on Management in SC29. He is a co-founder of Genista SA, a high-tech start-up company in the field of multimedia quality metrics. In 2002, he founded Emitall SA, start-up active in the area of media security and surveillance. In 2005, he founded EMITALL Surveillance SA, a start-up active in the field of privacy and protection. He is or has been associate Editor with various IEEE, SPIE, and EURASIP journals, such as IEEE Signal Processing Magazine, IEEE Transactions on Image Processing, IEEE Transactions on Multimedia, EURASIP Image Communication Journal, EURASIP Journal of Applied Signal Processing, SPIE Optical Engineering Magazine. Prof. Ebrahimi is a member of Scientific Advisory Board of various start-up and established companies in the general field of Information Technology. He has served as Scientific Expert and Evaluator for Research Funding Agencies such as those of European Commission, The Greek Ministry of Development, The Austrian National Foundation for Scientific Research, The Portuguese Science Foundation, as well as a number of Venture Capital Companies active in the field of Information Technologies and Communication Systems. His research interests include still, moving, and 3D image processing and coding, visual information security (rights protection, watermarking, authentication, data integrity, steganography), new media, and human computer interfaces (smart vision, brain computer interface).

Tiejun Huang is a professor and the director of the Institute for Digital Media Technology, the School of Electronic Engineering and Computer Science, Peking University. He is also the vice director of the National Engineering Lab for Video technology of China from 2009. He was awarded as the New Century Excellent Talents by the Ministry of Education of China in 2011. He is a member of the Advisory Board of IEEE Computing Now, the Board of Director Digital Media Project, and the Editorial Board of Springer 3D Research Journal. In China, he is a council member of Chinese Institute of Electronics, the head of the China delegation of MPEG, a senior member of China Computer Federation. He is also the member of China National Standardization Theory and Methodology Standardization Technical Committee and the Multimedia subgroup of the China National Informational Technology Standardization Technical Committee. His research areas are video coding, image understanding, digital right management (DRM) and digital library. In the last ten years, as the principal investigator, he led ten research projects funded by the Ministry of Science and Technology, Natural Science Foundation, Ministry of Education of China. He involved in three cooperation projects between China and USA, Europe and Korea.

Yung-Hsiang Lu is an associate professor in the School of Electrical and Computer Engineering and (by courtesy) the Department of Computer Science of Purdue University. He is an ACM distinguished scientist and ACM distinguished speaker. His research areas include computer systems, mobile and cloud computing, image processing, and robotics. He is an organizing member of the IEEE Rebooting Computing Working Group. He is the chair of the Multimedia Communication Systems Interest Group in IEEE Multimedia Communications Technical Committee; he was a vice-chair of the ACM SIGDA Low Power Technical Committee. He obtained the Ph.D. from the Department of Electrical Engineering at Stanford University.

Yonggang Wen is an assistant professor with school of computer engineering at Nanyang Technological University, Singapore. He received his PhD degree in Electrical Engineering and Computer Science from Massachusetts Institute of Technology, Cambridge, USA. Previously he has worked in Cisco to lead product development in content delivery network, which had a revenue impact of 3 Billion US dollars globally. His work in Multi-Screen Cloud Social TV has been featured by global media (more than 1600 news articles from over 29 countries) and received ASEAN ICT Award 2013 (Gold Medal). His work on Cloud3DView for Data Centre Life-Cycle Management, as the only academia entry, has made into the Top 4 finalist on Data Centre Dynamics Awards 2014-APAC. He has also received Best Paper Awards at IEEE WCSP 2014, IEEE Globecom 2013 and IEEE EUC 2012. He serves on editorial boards for IEEE Transactions on Multimedia, IEEE Transactions on Signal and Information Processing over Networks, IEEE Access Journal and Elsevier Ad Hoc Networks, and was elected as the Chair for IEEE ComSoc Multimedia Communication Technical Committee (2014-2016). His research interests include cloud computing, green data center, big data analytics, multimedia network and mobile computing.

Fast and Accurate Content-based Semantic Search in 100M Internet Videos

Lu Jiang[1], Shoou-I Yu[1], Deyu Meng[2],
Yi Yang[3], Teruko Mitamura[1], Alexander G. Hauptmann[1]
[1] Carnegie Mellon University, [2] Xi'an Jiaotong University, [3] University of Technology Sydney
{lujiang, iyu, teruko, alex}@cs.cmu.edu, dymeng@mail.xjtu.edu.cn

ABSTRACT

Large-scale content-based semantic search in video is an interesting and fundamental problem in multimedia analysis and retrieval. Existing methods index a video by the raw concept detection score that is dense and inconsistent, and thus cannot scale to "big data" that are readily available on the Internet. This paper proposes a scalable solution. The key is a novel step called concept adjustment that represents a video by a few salient and consistent concepts that can be efficiently indexed by the modified inverted index. The proposed adjustment model relies on a concise optimization framework with interpretations. The proposed index leverages the text-based inverted index for video retrieval. Experimental results validate the efficacy and the efficiency of the proposed method. The results show that our method can scale up the semantic search while maintaining state-of-the-art search performance. Specifically, the proposed method (with reranking) achieves the best result on the challenging TRECVID Multimedia Event Detection (MED) zero-example task. It only takes 0.2 second on a single CPU core to search a collection of 100 million Internet videos.

Categories and Subject Descriptors

H.3.1 [**Information Storage and Retrieval**]: Content Analysis and Indexing; I.2.10 [**Vision and Scene Understanding**]: Video analysis

General Terms

Algorithms, Experimentation, Performance

Keywords

Internet Video Search; Semantic Search; Big Data; Content-based Retrieval; Multimedia Event Detection; Zero Example

1. INTRODUCTION

Searching semantic content in Internet videos has long been a goal of multimedia analysis and retrieval. This fundamental problem is a building block for many tasks such as video visualization, recommendation and summarization. As opposed to merely searching user-generated metadata, such as titles and descriptions, content-based semantic search strives to leverage concepts that are automatically detected in the video, such as objects/scenes/actions. For example, in order to search for videos depicting a "birthday party", we might look for visual concepts like "cake", "gift" and "kids", and audio concepts like "birthday songs" and "cheering sounds". This semantic search relies on extensive video understanding, and requires neither metadata nor example videos. According to the National Institute of Standards and Technology (NIST), semantic search in video is also known as zero-example search (0Ex). A benchmark task called Multimedia Event Detection (MED) 0Ex, which was initiated by NIST TRECVID in 2013, is to detect the occurrence of a main event, e.g. "making a sandwich" or "rock climbing", occurring in a video clip without any user-generated metadata or example videos.

A number of studies have demonstrated promising progress in this direction [17, 9, 22, 42, 14, 21, 1]. However, existing methods index a video by the raw concept detection score that is dense and inconsistent. This solution is mainly designed for analysis and search over a few thousand of videos, and cannot scale to big data collections required for real world applications. For example, in order to search the semantics in YouTube videos, a system must be able to search over billions of Internet videos [35]. The scale problem is well beyond the scope of the existing work, and thus, as shown in the experiments in Section 7, their solutions will simply fail as the data grows. Large-scale semantic search, though challenging, opens possibilities for many interesting applications. For example, a currently nonexisting functionality is to search videos on social media platforms such as Facebook or Twitter. 12 million videos are posted on Twitter every day that have either no text or only a few words with little relevance to the visual content. It is extremely difficult to find meaningful information without content-based semantic search. Another example relates to in-video advertising. Currently, it may be hard for companies to effectively place in-video advertisements as the user-generated metadata typically does not describe the video content, let alone concept occurrences in time. However, a solution may be achieved by putting the advertisement into the top-ranked relevant videos returned by the semantic search. For example, a sport shoe company may use the query "(running OR jumping) AND urban_scene AND parkour" to select parkour videos for special shoe ads.

MM'15, October 26–30, 2015, Brisbane, Australia.
© 2015 ACM. ISBN 978-1-4503-3459-4/15/10 ...$15.00.
DOI: http://dx.doi.org/10.1145/2733373.2806237.

Even though a modern text retrieval system can already search over billions of text documents, the task is still very challenging for semantic video search. The main reason is that semantic concepts are quite different from the text words, and indexing of semantic concepts is still an understudied problem. Specifically, concepts are automatically extracted by detectors with limited accuracy. The raw detection score associated with each concept is inappropriate for indexing for two reasons. First, the distribution of the scores is dense, i.e. a video contains every concept with a non-zero detection score, which is analogous to a text document containing every word in the English vocabulary. The dense score distribution hinders effective inverted indexing and search. Second, the raw score may not capture the complex relations between concepts, e.g. a video may have a "puppy" but not a "dog". This type of inconsistency can lead to inaccurate search results.

To address this problem, we propose a novel step called concept adjustment that aims at producing video (and video shot) representations that tend to be consistent with the underlying concept representation. After adjustment, a video is represented by a few salient and consistent concepts that can be efficiently indexed by the inverted index. In theory, the proposed adjustment model is a general optimization framework that incorporates existing techniques as special cases. In practice, as demonstrated in our experiments, the adjustment increases the consistency with the ground-truth concept representation on the real world TRECVID dataset. Unlike text words, semantic concepts are associated with scores that indicate how confidently they are detected. We propose an extended inverted index structure that incorporates the real-valued detection scores and supports complex queries with Boolean and temporal operators.

To the best of our knowledge, our study is the first effort devoted to applying the semantic video search techniques [18] to million-scale search applications. Compared to existing methods, the proposed method exhibits the following three benefits. First, it advances the text retrieval method for video retrieval. Therefore, while existing methods fail as the size of the data grows, our method is scalable, extending the current capability of semantic search by a few orders of magnitude while maintaining state-of-the-art performance. The experiments in Section 6.2 and Section 7 validate this argument. Second, we propose a novel component called concept adjustment in a common optimization framework with solid probabilistic interpretations. Finally, our empirical studies shed some light on the tradeoff between efficiency and accuracy in a large-scale video search system. These observations will be helpful in guiding the design of future systems on related tasks such as video summarization, recommendation or hyperlinking [1].

The experimental results are promising on three datasets. On the TRECVID Multimedia Event Detection (MED), our method achieves comparable performance to state-of-the-art systems, while reducing its index by a relative 97%. The results on the TRECVID Semantic Indexing dataset demonstrate that the proposed adjustment model is able to generate more accurate concept representation than baseline methods. The results on the largest public multimedia dataset called YCCC100M [37] show that the method is capable of indexing and searching over a large-scale video collection of 100 million Internet videos. It only takes 0.2 seconds on a single CPU core to search a collection of 100 million Internet videos. Notably, the proposed method with reranking is able to achieve by far the best result on the TRECVID MED 0Ex task, one of the most representative and challenging tasks for semantic search in video. In summary, our contribution is threefold:

- We propose a scalable solution that extends the current capability of semantic video search by a few orders of magnitude of data while maintaining state-of-the-art accuracy.
- We propose a novel optimization framework that represents a video with relatively few salient and consistent concepts. Several related techniques can be regarded as its special cases.
- Our paper is the first work that addresses a long-lasting challenge of content-based semantic search in 100 million Internet videos on a single core.

2. RELATED WORK

Traditional content-based video retrieval methods have demonstrated promising results in a number of large scale applications, such as SIFT matching [34, 25] and near duplicate detection [43]. The search mainly utilizes the low-level descriptors that carry little semantic meaning. On the other hand, semantic video search aims at searching the high-level semantic concepts automatically detected in the video content. Compared with traditional methods, semantic search relies on understanding about the video content. This line of study first emerged in a TRECVID task called Semantic Indexing [27], the goal of which is to search the occurrence of a single or a pair of concepts [36]. A concept can be regarded as a visual or acoustic semantic tag on people, objects, scenes and actions in the video content [26].

With the advance in object and action detection, people started to focus on searching more complex queries called events. An event is more complex than a concept as it usually involves people engaged in process-driven actions with other people and/or objects at a specific place and time [13]. For example, the event "rock climbing" involves video clips such as outdoor bouldering, indoor artificial wall climbing or snow mountain climbing. A benchmark task on this topic is called TRECVID Multimedia Event Detection (MED). Its goal is to detect the occurrence of a main event occurring in a video clip without any user-generated metadata. MED is divided into two scenarios in terms of whether example videos are provided. When example videos are given, a state-of-the-art system first train classifiers using multiple features and fuse the decision of the individual classification results [7, 40, 11, 28, 32, 2, 39, 10, 3].

This paper focuses on the other scenario named zero-example search (0Ex) where no example videos are given. 0Ex mostly resembles a real world scenario, in which users start the search without any example. As opposed to training an event detector, 0Ex searches semantic concepts that are expected to occur in the relevant videos, e.g. we might look for concepts like "car", "bicycle", "hand" and "tire" for the event "changing a vehicle tire". A few studies have been proposed on this topic [9, 22, 42, 17, 14, 21]. A closely related work is detailed in [18], where the authors presented their lessons and observations in building a state-of-the-art semantic search engine for Internet videos. Existing solutions are promising but only for a few thousand videos because they cannot scale to big data collections. Therefore, the biggest collection in existing studies contains no more than 200 thousand videos [18, 29].

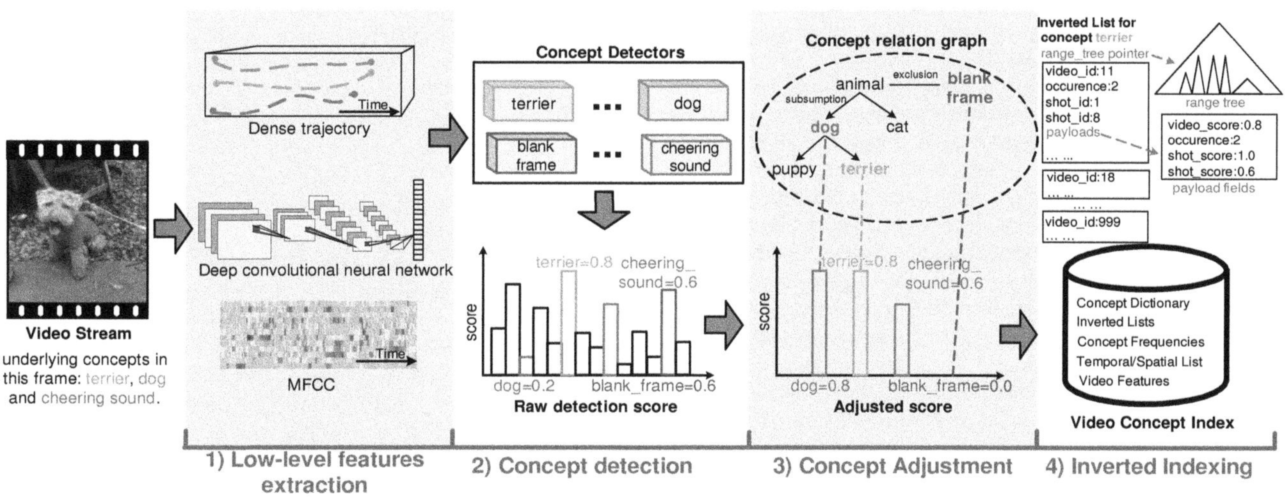

Figure 1: Pipeline for the offline video indexing.

3. OVERVIEW

There is an offline stage called video semantic indexing before one can perform any online search. The stage aims at indexing the semantic content in a video for efficient online search. As illustrated in Fig. 1, there are four major components in this video semantic indexing pipeline, namely, low-level feature extraction, concept detection, concept adjustment and inverted indexing, in which the concept adjustment component is first proposed in this paper.

A video clip is first represented by low-level visual or audio features. Common features include dense trajectories [41], deep learning [20] and MFCC features. The low-level features are then fed into the off-the-shelf detectors to extract the semantic concept features, where each dimension corresponds to a confidence score of detecting a semantic (audio and visual) concept in a video shot. The dimensionality is equal to the number of unique detectors in the system. The semantic concept is a type of high-level feature [13] that can be used in search. The high-level features also include Automatic Speech Recognition (ASR) [23, 24] and Optical Character Recognition (OCR) [45].

We found that raw concept detection scores are inappropriate for indexing for two reasons: *distributional inconsistency* and *logical inconsistency*. The *distributional inconsistency* means that the distribution of the raw detection score is inconsistent with the underlying concept distribution of the video. The underlying concept representation tends to be sparse but the distribution of the detection score is dense, i.e. a video contains every concept. Indexing the dense representation by either dense matrices or inverted indexes is known to be inefficient. For example, Fig. 1 illustrates an example in which the raw concept detection contains 14 nonzero scores but there are only three concepts in the underlying representation: "dog", "terrier", and "cheering sound". As we see, the dense distribution of the raw detection score is very different from the underlying distribution.

The *logical inconsistency* means that the detection scores are not consistent with the semantic relation between concepts, e.g. a video contains a "terrier" but not a "dog". This type of inconsistency results from that 1) the detectors are usually trained by different people using different data, features and models. It is less likely for them to consider the concept consistency that is not in their vocabulary; 2) even within a concept vocabulary, many classification models cannot capture complex relation between concepts [4]. The inconsistent representation can lead to inaccurate search results if not properly handled. For example, in Fig. 1, the score of "dog" 0.2 is less than the score of "terrier" 0.8; the frame is detected as "blank frame", which means a empty frame, and a "terrier".

To address the problem of distributional and logical inconsistencies, we propose a novel step called concept adjustment. It aims at generating consistent concept representations that can be efficiently indexed and searched. We propose an adjustment method based on the recently proposed label relation graph [4] that models the hierarchy and exclusion relation between concepts (see Step 3 in Fig. 1). After adjustment, a video is represented by a few salient concepts, which can be efficiently indexed by the inverted index. In addition, the adjusted representation is logically consistent with the complex relation between concepts.

An effective approach is to index the adjusted representation by the inverted index in text retrieval. However, unlike text words, semantic concepts are associated with scores that indicate how confidently they are detected. The detection score cannot be directly indexed by the standard inverted index. As a result, the scores are usually indexed by dense matrices in existing methods [42, 18]. To this end, we modify the inverted index structure so that it can index the real-valued adjusted score. The modified index contains inverted indexes, frequency lists that store the concept statistics used in the retrieval model, temporal lists that contain the shot information, and video feature lists that store the low-level features. The extended index structure is compatible to existing text retrieval algorithms. More details are given in Section 5.

4. CONCEPT ADJUSTMENT

4.1 Concept Adjustment Model

In this paper, we make no assumption on the training process of the off-the-shelf concept detectors. The detectors may be trained by any type of features, models or data. We relax the assumption [4] that detectors must be "re-trainable" by particular training algorithms because this is usually impossible when we do not have the access to the training data, the code or the computational resource.

Concept adjustment aims at generating video (or video shot) representations that tend to be consistent to the underlying concept representation and meanwhile can be searched efficiently. An ideal video representation tends to be similar to the underlying concept representation in terms of the distributional and logical consistency. To this end, we propose an optimization model to find consistent video representations of the given raw concept detection output. Formally, let $\mathbf{D} \in \mathbb{R}^{n \times m}$ denote the raw scores outputted by the concept detectors, where the row represents the n shots in a video, and the column represents the m visual/audio concepts. The prediction score of each concept is in the range between 0 and 1, i.e. $\forall i, j$, $\mathbf{D}_{ij} \in [0, 1]$. We are interested in obtaining a consistent representation $\mathbf{v} \in \mathbb{R}^{m \times 1}$, which can be obtained by solving the following optimization problem:

$$\begin{aligned} \arg\min_{\mathbf{v}\in[0,1]^m} \frac{1}{2}\|\mathbf{v} - f_p(\mathbf{D})\|_2^2 + g(\mathbf{v}; \alpha, \beta) \\ \text{subject to } \mathbf{A}\mathbf{v} \leq \mathbf{c} \end{aligned} \quad (1)$$

where

$$f_p(\mathbf{D}) = (1 - (\frac{m-1}{m})^p)[\|\mathbf{d}_1\|_p, \dots, \|\mathbf{d}_m\|_p]^T \quad (2)$$

and $\mathbf{D} = \begin{bmatrix} | & & | \\ \mathbf{d}_1 & \cdots & \mathbf{d}_m \\ | & & | \end{bmatrix}$. Each element of $f_p(\mathbf{D})$ is the p-norm of the column vector of $\mathbf{D}$. $g(\mathbf{v}; \alpha, \beta)$ is a regularizer of $\mathbf{v}$ with the parameters α and β. $g(\cdot)$ imposes the distributional consistency, and will be discussed in Section 4.1.1. $\mathbf{A}$ and $\mathbf{c}$ are a constant matrix and a constant vector, which model the logical consistencies and will be discussed in Section 4.1.2. It is easy to verify that when $p = \infty$ and $p = 1$, the operator $f_p(\mathbf{D})$ corresponds to the max and the average pooling operator. Usually $g(\cdot)$ is convex, and thus Eq. (1) can be conveniently solved by the standard convex programming toolbox [8]. The raw prediction score may diminish during the concept adjustment. It is usually helpful to normalize the optimal value of $\mathbf{v} = [v_1, \cdots, v_m]$ by:

$$\hat{v}_i = \min(1, \frac{v_i}{\sum_{j=1}^m v_j} \sum_{j=1}^m f_p(\mathbf{D})_j I(v_j)), \quad (3)$$

where $I(v)$ is an indicator function equalling 1 when $v > 0$, and 0 otherwise. Here we define $0/0 = 0$.

In order to obtain the shot-level adjusted representation, we can treat a shot as a "video" and let $\mathbf{D}$ be a single row matrix containing the detection score of the shot. Eq. (1) can be used but with an extra integer set in the constraints (see Section 4.1.2).

4.1.1 Distributional Consistency

For the distributional consistency, a regularization term $g(\mathbf{v}; \alpha, \beta)$ is introduced that produces sparse representations while taking into account that certain concepts may co-occur together. A naive implementation is to use the l_0 norm:

$$g(\mathbf{v}; \alpha, \beta) = \frac{1}{2}\beta^2\|v\|_0. \quad (4)$$

This regularization term presents a formidable computational challenge. In this paper we propose a more feasible and general regularization term. Suppose the concepts are divided into q non-overlapping groups. A group may contain a number of co-occurring concepts, or a single concept if it does not co-occur with others. Such sparsity and group sparsity information can be encoded into the model by adding a convex regularization term $g(\mathbf{v})$ of the l_1 norm and the sum of group-wise l_2 norm of $\mathbf{v}$:

$$g(\mathbf{v}; \alpha, \beta) = \alpha\beta\|\mathbf{v}\|_1 + (1-\alpha)\sum_{l=1}^{q} \beta\sqrt{p_l}\|\mathbf{v}^{(l)}\|_2, \quad (5)$$

where $\mathbf{v}^{(l)} \in \mathbb{R}^{p_l}$ is the coefficient for the lth group where p_l is the length of that group. $\alpha \in [0, 1]$ and β are two parameters controlling the magnitude of the sparsity.

The parameter α balances the group-wise and the within-group sparsity. When $\alpha = 1$, $g(\mathbf{v})$ becomes *lasso* [38] that finds a solution with few nonzero entries. When $\alpha = 0$, $g(\mathbf{v})$ becomes *group lasso* [46], that only yields nonzero entries in a sparse set of groups. If a group is included then all coefficients in the group will be nonzero. Sometimes, the sparsity within a group is also needed, i.e. if a group is included, only few coefficients in the group will be nonzero. This is known as *sparse-group lasso* [33] that linearly interpolates *lasso* and *group lasso* by the parameter α.

In the context of semantic concepts, *lasso* is an approximation to the corresponding l_0 norm regularization problem which is computationally expensive to solve. *Lasso* and the l_0 norm term assume the concepts are independent, and works well when the assumption is satisfied, e.g. the 1,000 concepts in ImageNet challenges where the concepts are manually selected to be exclusive labels [4]. On the other hand, *Group lasso* assumes the there exist groups of concepts that tend to be present or absent together frequently, e.g. "sky/cloud", "beach/ocean/waterfront" and "table/chair". The group may also include multimodal concepts such as "baby/baby noises". Since co-occurring concepts may not always be present together, the within-group sparse solution is needed sometimes, i.e. only few concepts in a group are nonzero. This can be satisfied by *sparse-group lasso* that makes weaker assumptions about the underlying concept distribution.

4.1.2 Logical Consistency

The concept relation is modeled by Hierarchy and Exclusion (HEX) graph. Deng et al. [4] recently introduced label relation graphs called Hierarchy and Exclusion (HEX) graphs. The idea is to infer a representation that maximizes the likelihood and do not violate the label relation defined in the HEX graph. Following Deng et al. [4], we assume that the graph is given beforehand. According to [4], a HEX graph is defined as:

DEFINITION 1. *A HEX graph $G = (N, E_h, E_e)$ is a graph consisting of a set of nodes $N = \{n_1, \cdots, n_m\}$, directed edges $E_h \subseteq N \times N$ and undirected edges $E_e \subseteq N \times N$ such that the subgraph $G_h = (N, E_h)$ is a directed acyclic graph and the subgraph $G_e = (N, E_e)$ has no self-loop.*

Each node in the graph represents a distinct concept. A hierarchy edge $(n_i, n_j) \in E_h$ indicates that concept n_i subsumes concept n_j in the concept hierarchy, e.g. "dog" is a parent of "puppy". An exclusion edge $(n_i, n_j) \in E_e$ indicates concept n_i and n_j are mutually exclusive, e.g. a frame cannot be both "blank frame" and "dog". Based on Definition 1, we define the logically consistent representation as:

DEFINITION 2. *$\mathbf{v} = [v_1, \cdots, v_m]$ is a vector of concept detection scores. The ith dimension corresponds to the concept node $n_i \in N$ in the HEX graph G. $\mathbf{v} \in [0, 1]^m$ is logically consistent with G if for any pair of concepts (n_i, n_j):*

1. if $n_i \in \alpha(n_j)$, then $v_i \geq v_j$;

2. if $\exists n_p \in \bar{\alpha}(n_i)$, $\exists n_q \in \bar{\alpha}(n_j)$ and $(n_p, n_q) \in E_e$, then we have $v_i v_j = 0$;

where $\alpha(n_i)$ is a set of all ancestors of n_i in G_h, and $\bar{\alpha}(n_i) = \alpha(n_i) \cup n_i$.

Definition 2 indicates that a logically consistent representation should not violate any concept relation defined in its HEX graph G. This definition generalizes the legal assignments in [4] to allow concepts taking real values. We model the logical consistency by the affine constraints $\mathbf{Av} \leq \mathbf{c}$. The constant matrix $\mathbf{A}$ and vector $\mathbf{c}$ can be calculated from Algorithm 1. For each edge in the graph, Algorithm 1 defines a constraint on values the two concepts can take. A hierarchy edge $(n_i, n_j) \in E_h$ means that the value of a parent is no less than the value of its children, e.g. "puppy=0.8" but "dog=0.2" is inconsistent. For each exclusion edge, Algorithm 1 introduces an affine constraint $v_i + v_j = 1$ and $v_i, v_j \in \{0, 1\}$ to avoid the case where two concepts both have nonzero values. Note that the solution of the exclusion constraint complies with the binary legal assignments in [4] that for any $(n_i, n_j) \in E_e$, $(v_i, v_j) \neq (1, 1)$. It is unnecessary to propagate an exclusion constraint to its children nodes because the hierarchy constraint guarantees the score of the children nodes is no more than their parent. According to Definition 2, it is easy to prove that the optimal solution of Eq. (1) is logically consistent with a given HEX graph. The problem with integer constraints can be solved either by the mixed-integer convex programming toolbox, or by the constraint relaxation [6].

THEOREM 1. *The optimal solutions of Eq. (1) (before or after normalization) is logically consistent with its given HEX graph.*

Algorithm 1: Constraints for logical consistency.

input : A HEX graph $G = (V, E_h, E_e)$
output: A constant matrix $\mathbf{A}$ and a constant $\mathbf{c}$.

$n = |E_h| + |E_e|$; $m = |V|$; $k = 0$;
$\mathbf{A} = \mathbf{0}_{n \times m}$, $\mathbf{c} = \mathbf{0}_{n \times 1}$;
foreach $(n_i, n_j) \in E_h$ **do**
  $\mathbf{A}_{ki} = -1$; $\mathbf{A}_{kj} = 1$; $\mathbf{c}_k = 0$;
  k++;
end
Define an integer constraint set $\mathbb{I} \leftarrow \phi$;
foreach $(n_i, n_j) \in E_e$ **do**
  $\mathbf{A}_{ki} = 1$; $\mathbf{A}_{kj} = 1$; $\mathbf{c}_k = 1$;
  add n_i, n_j to $\mathbb{I}$;
  k++;
end
return $\mathbf{A}$, $\mathbf{c}$, $\mathbb{I}$;

4.2 Discussions

The proposed model can produce a representation that tends to be both distributionally and logically consistent to the underlying concept representation. A nice property of the model in Eq. (1) is that it can degenerate to several existing methods. For example, it is easy to verify that the max and the average pooling results are optimal solutions of Eq. (1) in special cases. Theorem 1 indicates that the optimal solution of adjusted representations complies with the logical consistency definition. Theorem 2 indicates that the thresholding and the top-k thresholding results are optimal solutions of Eq. (1) in special cases. The thresholding method preserves scores only above some threshold. In some cases, instead of using an absolute threshold, one can alternatively set the threshold in terms of the number of concepts to be included. This is known as the top-k thresholding. The proof is provided in the supplementary materials.

THEOREM 2. *The thresholding and the top-k thresholding results are optimal solutions of Eq. (1) in special cases.*

The proposed model also provides common interpretations of what are being optimized. The physical meaning of the optimization problem in Eq. (1) can be interpreted as a maximum a priori model. The interpretation is provided in the supplementary materials.

The choice of the proposed model parameters depends on the underlying distribution of the semantic concepts. For the manually exclusive concepts, such as the 1,000 concepts in the ImageNet challenge [31], the l_0 norm or the l_1 norm without any HEX constraint should work reasonably well. In addition, as the model is simple, the problem can be efficiently solved by the closed-form solution. When the concepts are of concrete hierarchical or exclusion relations, such as the concepts in TRECVID SIN [29], incorporating the HEX constraint tends to be beneficial. The group-lasso and the sparse-group lasso play a role when groups of concepts tend to co-occur together frequently. It can be important for the multimodal concept detectors that capture the same concept by multiple features, e.g. audio or visual. An approach to derive the co-occurring concepts is by clustering the concepts in their labeled training data. We observed big clusters tend to include more loosely coupled concepts, e.g. sky/cloud is a good group, but sky/cloud/helicopter is not. To be prudent, we recommend limiting the group size in clustering.

Note the exclusion relation between concepts only makes sense at the shot-level adjustment, as in the video-level representation the scores of exclusive concepts can be both nonzeros. Solving a mixed integer convex programming problem takes more time than solving a regular convex programming problem. So when the proposed method is applied on shot-level features, it is useful to use some type of constraint relaxation techniques. Besides, in the current model, we assume the concept detectors are equally accurate. A simple extension to embed this information is by discounting the squared loss of inaccurate concepts in Eq. (1).

5. INVERTED INDEXING & SEARCH

The dense raw detection scores are usually indexed by dense matrices in existing methods [42, 18]. This simple solution, though preserves all detection scores, is not scalable. In comparison, the proposed adjustment method represents a video by a few salient and consistent concepts. To index the adjusted representation, we modify the structure of inverted index so that it can incorporate real-valued detection scores. In this section, we discuss video indexing and search, using the proposed inverted indexes.

5.1 Inverted Indexing

After adjustment, a video is represented by a few salient and consistent concepts. In analogy to words in a text document, concepts can be treated as "words" in a video. Unlike text words, concepts are associated with scores that indicate how confidently they are detected. The real-valued scores are difficult to be directly indexed in the standard inverted index designed for text words. A naive approach is by binning, where we assign real values to the bins representing the segment covering the numerical value. The concepts are duplicated by the number of its filled bins. However, this solution creates hallucinating concepts in the index, and cannot store the shot-level concept scores.

To solve the problem in a more principled way, we propose a modified inverted index to incorporate the real-valued detection scores. In text retrieval, each unique text word has a list of *postings* in the inverted index. A *posting* contains a document ID, the term frequency, and the term positions in the document. The term frequency is used in the retrieval model, and the position information is used in the proximity search. Inspired by this structure, in our system, the concept with a nonzero score in the adjusted representation is indexed to represent a video. Each unique concept has a list of *video postings* and a range search tree. An example index structure is illustrated in Step 4 in Fig. 1. A *video posting* contains a video ID, the number of concept occurrence in the video, a video-level detection score, and a list of video shots in which the concept occurs. It also has a payload to store the real-valued detection score for each shot. The query that searches for the video-level score of a certain range can be handled by the range tree, e.g. "videos that contain dog > 0.5"; the query that searches for the shot-level score can be handled by the payload in the posting, e.g. "shots that contain dog > 0.5"; otherwise, the query can be processed in a similar way as in text retrieval using the adjusted video-level score, e.g. videos that contain "dog AND cat".

5.2 Video Search

A search usually contains two steps: retrieving a list of *video postings* and ranking the postings according to some retrieval model. In our system, we consider the following query operators to retrieve a *video posting* list:

- **Modality query**: Searching a query term in a specified modality. For example, "visual:dog" returns the videos that contain the visual concept "dog"; "visual:dog/[score s_1, s_2]" returns the videos that have a detection score of "dog" between s_1 and s_2. "visual" is the default modality. The other modalities are "asr" for automatically recognized speech, "ocr" for recognized optical characters, and "audio" for audio concepts.
- **Temporal query**: Searching query terms that have constraints on their temporal occurrences in a video. The constraints can be specified in terms of the absolute timestamp like "videos that contain dog between the time t_1 and t_2", the relative sequence like "videos in which dog is seen before cat", or the proximity relations like "videos that contain dog and cat within the time window of t_1". A temporal query can be handled in a similar fashion as the proximity search in text retrieval.
- **Boolean query**: Multiple terms can be combined together with Boolean operators to form a more complex query. Our system supports three operators: "AND", "OR" and "AND NOT", where the "OR" operator is the default conjunction operator.

A Boolean query can be handled by the standard algorithms in text retrieval, as Theorem 1 guarantees that the adjusted representation is logically consistent. However, the query may be accelerated by utilizing the concept relation in the HEX graph. For example, it is unnecessary to run a query to realize that ("dog" AND "animal") = "dog". Suppose the query is expressed in the disjunctive normal form. Given a HEX graph G and two concepts $n_i, n_j \in V$, for each term in the disjunctive normal form, we apply: (n_i AND n_j) = n_i if $n_j \in \alpha(n_i)$, where $\alpha(n_i)$ is the set of all ancestors of n_i in G_h; (n_i AND NOT n_j) = ϕ if $\exists n_p \in \bar{\alpha}(n_i)$, $\exists n_q \in \bar{\alpha}(n_j)$ and $(n_p, n_q) \in E_e$. The simplified query can be then used to retrieval the *video postings*.

After retrieving a *video posting* list, the next step is to rank the postings according to some retrieval model. A retrieval model can have substantial impact on the performance, and following [18], we adopt the Okapi BM25 model that work reasonably well for concept retrieval. Suppose the input query is $Q = q_1, \cdots, q_n$, the model ranks a video d by:

$$\mathrm{s}(d|Q) = \sum_{i=1}^{n} \log \frac{|C| - df(q_i) + \frac{1}{2}}{df(q_i) + \frac{1}{2}} \frac{tf(q_i, d)(k_1 + 1)}{tf(q_i, d) + k_1(1 - b + b\frac{len(d)}{\overline{len}})}, \tag{6}$$

where $|C|$ is the total number of videos. $tf(q_i, d)$ returns the score of the concept q_i in the adjusted representation of video d. $df(\cdot)$ calculates the sum of adjusted score of q_i in the video collection. $len(d)$ calculates the sum of adjusted scores for video d, and $\overline{len}$ is the average length across all videos. k_1 and b are two parameters to tune. Note the statistics are calculated by the adjusted concept score rather than the raw detection score.

6. EXPERIMENTS

6.1 Setups

Dataset and evaluation: The experiments are conducted on two TRECVID benchmarks called Multimedia Event Detection (MED): MED13Test and MED14Test [29]. The performance is evaluated by several metrics for a better understanding, which include: P@20, Mean Reciprocal Rank (MRR), Mean Average Precision (MAP), and MAP@20, where the MAP is the official metric used by NIST. Each set includes 20 events over 25,000 test videos. The official NIST's test split is used. We also evaluate each experiment on 10 randomly generated splits to reduce the split partition bias. All experiments are conducted without using any example or text metedata.

Features and queries: Videos are indexed by high-level features including semantic concepts, Automatic Speech Recognition (ASR), and Optical Character Recognition (OCR). These features are provided in [18]. For semantic concepts, 1,000 ImageNet concepts are trained by the deep convolution neural networks [20]. The remaining 3,000+ concepts are directly trained on videos by the self-paced learning pipeline [15, 16] on around 2 million videos using improved dense trajectories [41]. The video datasets include Sports [19], Yahoo Flickr Creative Common (YFCC100M) [37], Internet Archive Creative Common (IACC) [29] and Do it Yourself (DIY) [44]. The details of these datasets can be found in Table 1. The ASR module is built on Kaldi [30, 23]. OCR is extracted by a commercial toolkit. Three sets of queries are used: 1) *Expert* queries are obtained by human experts; 2) *Auto* queries are automatically generated by the Semantic Query Generation (SQG) methods in [18] using ASR, OCR and visual concepts; 3) *AutoVisual* queries are also automatically generated but only includes the visual concepts. The *Expert* queries are used by default.

Configurations: The concept relation released by NIST is used to build the HEX graph for IACC features [26][1]. The adjustment is conducted at the video-level average ($p = 1$ in Eq. (1)) so no shot-level exclusion relations are used. For other concept features, since there is no public concept relation specification, we manually create the HEX graph. The HEX graphs are empty for Sports and ImageNet features as there is no evident hierarchical and exclusion relation in their concepts. We cluster the concepts based on the correlation of their training labels, and include concepts that frequently co-occur together into a group. The parameters are tuned on a validation sets, and then are fixed across all experiment datasets including MED13Test, MED14Test and YFCC100M. Specifically, the default parameters in Eq. (1) are $p = 1$, $\alpha = 0.95$. β is set as the top k detection scores in a video, and is different for each type of features: 60 for IACC, 10 for Sports, 50 for YFCC100M, 15 for ImageNet, and 10 for DIY features. CVX optimization toolbox [8] is used to solve the model in Eq. (1). Eq. (6) is used as the retrieval model for concept features, where $k_1 = 1.2$ and $b = 0.75$.

6.2 Performance on MED

We first examine the overall performance of the proposed method. Table 2 lists the evaluation metrics over the two benchmarks on the standard NIST split and on the 10 randomly generated splits. The performance is reported over three set of queries: *Expert*, *Auto*, and *AutoVisual*.

Table 3 compares the performance of the raw and the adjusted representation on the 10 splits of MED13Test. *Raw* lists the performance of indexing the raw score by dense matrices; *Adjusted* lists the performance of indexing the adjusted concepts by the proposed index which preserves the real-valued scores. As we see, although *Raw* is slightly better than *Adjusted*, its index in the form of dense matrices is more than 33 times bigger than the inverted index in *Adjusted*. The comparison substantiates that the adjusted representation has comparable performances with the raw representation but can be indexed by a much smaller index.

An interesting observation is that *Adjusted* outperforms *Raw* on 8 out of 20 events on MED13Test (see the supplementary materials). We inspected the results and found that concept adjustment can generate more consistent representations. Fig. 2 illustrates raw and adjusted concepts on three example videos. Since the raw score is dense, we only list the top ranked concepts. As we see, the noisy concept in the raw detection may be removed by the logical consistency, e.g. "snow" in the first video. The missed concept may be recalled by logical consistencies, e.g. "vehicle" in the third video is recalled by "ground vehicle". The frequently co-occurring concepts may also be recovered by distributional consistencies, e.g. "cloud" and "sky" in the second video. Besides, we also found that Boolean queries can boost the performance. For example, in "E029: Winning a race without a vehicle", the query of relevant concepts such as swimming, racing or marathon can achieve an AP of 12.5. However, the Boolean query also containing "AND NOT" concepts such as car racing or horse riding can achieve an AP of 24.5.

We then compare our best result with the published results on MED13Test. The experiments are all conducted on the NIST's split, and thus are comparable to each other. As we see in Table 4, the proposed method has a comparable

[1] http://www-nlpir.nist.gov/projects/tv2012/tv11.sin.relations.txt

Table 2: Overview of the system performance.

(a) Performance on the NIST's split

Dataset	Query	Evaluation Metric P@20	MRR	MAP@20	MAP
MED13Test	Expert	0.355	0.693	0.280	0.183
	Auto	0.243	0.601	0.177	0.118
	AutoVisual	0.125	0.270	0.067	0.074
MED14Test	Expert	0.228	0.585	0.147	0.172
	Auto	0.150	0.431	0.102	0.100
	AutoVisual	0.120	0.372	0.067	0.086

(b) Average Performance on the 10 splits

Dataset	Query	Evaluation Metric P@20	MRR	MAP@20	MAP
MED13Test	Expert	0.325	0.689	0.247	0.172
	Auto	0.253	0.592	0.187	0.120
	AutoVisual	0.126	0.252	0.069	0.074
MED14Test	Expert	0.219	0.540	0.144	0.171
	Auto	0.148	0.417	0.084	0.102
	AutoVisual	0.117	0.350	0.063	0.084

Table 3: Comparison of the raw and the adjusted representation on the 10 splits.

Method	Index	Evaluation Metric P@20	MRR	MAP@20	MAP
MED13 Raw	385M	0.312	0.728	0.230	0.176
MED13 Adjusted	11.6M	0.325	0.689	0.247	0.172
MED14 Raw	357M	0.233	0.610	0.155	0.185
MED14 Adjusted	12M	0.219	0.540	0.144	0.171

performance to the state-of-the-art methods. Notably, the proposed method with one iteration of reranking [14] is able to achieve the best result. The comparison substantiates that our method maintains state-of-the-art accuracy. It is worth emphasizing that the baseline methods may not scale to big data sets, as the dense matrices are used to index all raw detection scores [42, 14, 18].

Table 4: MAP ($\times$ 100) comparison with the published results on MED13Test.

Method	Year	MAP
Composite Concepts [9]	2014	6.4
Tag Propagation [22]	2014	9.6
MMPRF [17]	2014	10.1
Clauses [21]	2014	11.2
Multi-modal Fusion [42]	2014	12.6
SPaR [14]	2014	12.9
E-Lamp FullSys [18]	2015	20.7
Our System	2015	18.3
Our System + reranking	**2015**	**20.8**

The parameters α and β in Eq. (1) control the magnitude of sparsity in the concept adjustment, i.e. the percentage of concepts with nonzero scores in a video representation. A sparse representation reduces the size of indexes but hurts the performance at the same time. As we will see later, β is more important than α in affecting the performance. Therefore, we fix α to 0.95 and study the impact of β. Fig. 3 illustrates the tradeoff between accuracy and efficiency on the 10 splits of MED13Test. By tuning β, we obtain different percentages of nonzero concepts in a video representation. The x-axis lists the percentage in the log scale. $x = 0$ indicates the performance of ASR and OCR without semantic concept features. We discovered that we do not need many concepts to index a video, and a few adjusted concepts already preserve significant amount of information for search. As we see, the best tradeoff in this problem is 4% of the total

Table 1: **Summary of the semantic concept training sets. ImageNet features are trained on still images, and the rest are trained on videos.**

Dataset	#Samples	#Classes	Category	Example Concepts
DIY [44]	72,000	1,601	Instructional videos	Yoga, Juggling, Cooking
IACC [29]	600,000	346	Internet archive videos	Baby, Outdoor, Sitting down
YFCC100M [37]	800,000	609	Amateur videos on Flickr	Beach, Snow, Dancing
ImageNet [5]	1,000,000	1000	Still images	Bee, Corkscrew, Cloak
Sports [19]	1,100,000	487	Sports videos on YouTube	Bullfighting, Cycling, Skiing

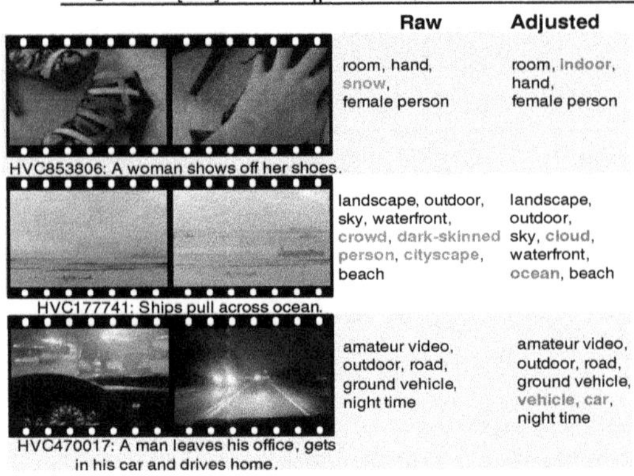

Figure 2: Comparison of raw and adjusted concepts.

concepts (i.e. 163 concepts). Further increasing the number of concepts only leads to marginal performance gain.

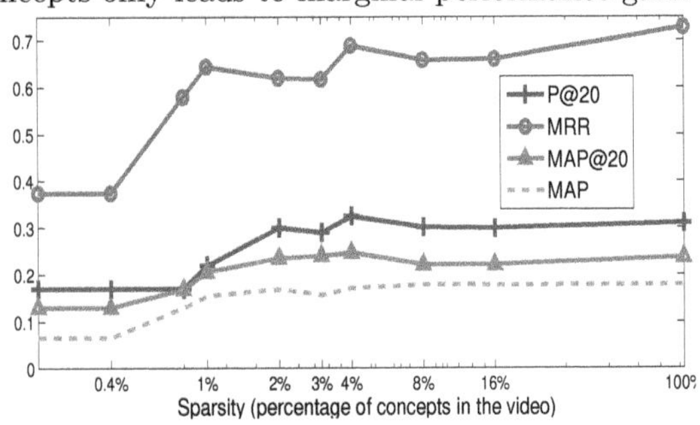

Figure 3: The impact of parameter β. $x = 0$ indicates the performance of ASR and OCR without semantic concepts.

6.3 Accuracy of Concept Adjustment

Generally the comparison in terms of retrieval performance depends on the query words. A query-independent way to verify the accuracy of the adjusted concept representation is by comparing it to the ground truth representation. To this end, we conduct experiments on the TRECVID Semantic Indexing (SIN) IACC set, where the manually labeled concepts are available for each shot in a video. We use our detectors to extract the raw shot-level detection score, and then apply the adjustment methods in Section 4 to obtain the adjusted representation. The performance is evaluated by Root Mean Squared Error (RMSE) to the ground truth concepts for the 1,500 test shots in 961 videos.

We compare our adjustment method with the baseline methods in Table 5, where HEX Graph indicates the logical consistent representation [4] on the raw detection scores (i.e. $\beta = 0$), and Group Lasso denotes the representation yield by Eq. (5) when $\alpha = 0$. We tune the parameter in each baseline method and report its best performance. As the ground truth label is binary, we let the adjusted scores be binary in all methods. As we see, the proposed method outperforms all baseline methods. We hypothesize the reason is that our method is the only one that combines the distributional consistency and the logical consistency. As discussed in Section 4.2, the baseline methods can be regarded as special cases of the proposed model.

We study the parameter sensitivity in the proposed model. Fig. 4 plots the RMSE under different parameter settings. Physically, α interpolates the group-wise and within-group sparsity, and β determines the number of concepts in a video. As we see, the parameter β is more sensitive than α, and accordingly we fix the value of α in practice. Note the parameter β is also an important parameter in the baseline methods including thresholding and top-k thresholding.

Table 5: Comparison of the adjusted representation and baseline methods on the TRECVID SIN set. The metric is Root Mean Squared Error (RMSE).

Method	RMSE
Raw Score	7.671
HEX Graph Only	8.090
Thresholding	1.349
Top-k Thresholding	1.624
Group Lasso	1.570
Our method	**1.236**

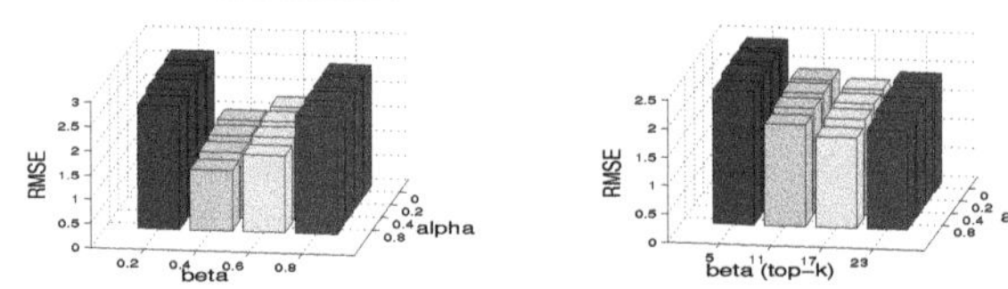

(a) Thresholding (b) Top-k thresholding

Figure 4: Sensitivity study on the parameter α and β in our model.

7. APPLICATION ON YFCC100M

We apply the proposed method on YFCC100M, the largest public multimedia collection that has ever been released [37]. It contains about 0.8 million Internet videos (approximately 12 million key shots) on Flickr. For each video and video shot, we extract the improved dense trajectory, and detect 3,000+ concepts by the off-the-shelf detectors in Table 1. We implement our inverted index based on Lucene [12], and a similar configuration described in 6.1 is used except we set $b = 0$ in the BM25 model. All experiments are conducted without using any example or text metedata. It is worth emphasizing that as the dataset is very big. The offline video indexing process costs considerable amount of computational resources in Pittsburgh super-computing center. To this end, we share this valuable benchmark with our community `http://www.cs.cmu.edu/~lujiang/0Ex/mm15.html`.

To validate the efficiency and scalability, we duplicate the original videos and video shots, and create an artificial set of 100 million videos. We compare the search performance of the proposed method to a common approach in existing studies that indexes the video by dense matrices [42, 18]. The experiments are conducted on a single core of Intel Xeon 2.53GHz CPU with 64GB memory. The performance is evaluated in terms of the memory consumption and the online search efficiency. Fig. 5 (a) compares the in-memory index as the data size grows, where the x-axis denotes the number of videos in the log scale, and the y-axis measures the index in GB. As we see, the baseline method fails when the data reaches 5 million due to lack of memory. In contrast, our method is scalable and only needs 550MB memory to search 100 million videos. The size of the total inverted index on disk is only 20GB. Fig. 5 (b) compares the online search speed. We create 5 queries, run each query 100 times, and report the mean runtime in milliseconds. A similar pattern can be observed in Fig. 5 that our method is much more efficient than the baseline method and only costs 191ms to process a query on a single core. The above results verify scalability and efficiency of the proposed method.

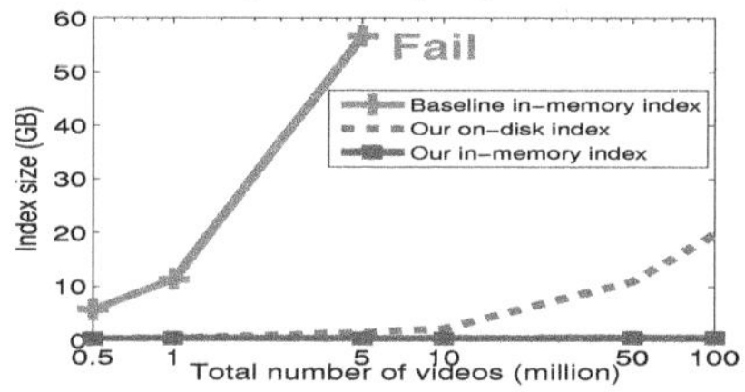

(a) Index (in GB)

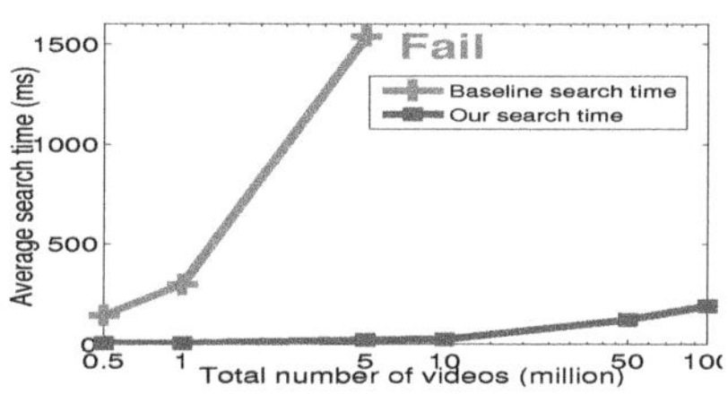

(b) Search Time (in ms)

Figure 5: The scalability and efficiency test on 100 million videos. Baseline method fails when the data reaches 5 million due to the lack of memory. Our method is scalable to 100 million videos.

As a demonstration, we use our system to find relevant videos for commercials. The search is on 800 thousand Internet videos. We download 30 commercials from the Internet, and manually create 30 semantic queries only using semantic visual concepts. See detailed results in the supplementary materials. The ads can be organized in 5 categories. As we see, the performance is much higher than the performance on the MED dataset in Table 2. The improvement is a result of the increased data volumes. Fig. 6 plots the top 5 retrieved videos are semantically relevant to the products in the ads. The results suggest that our method may be useful in enhancing the relevance of in-video ads.

8. CONCLUSIONS

This paper is the first work that addresses a long-lasting challenge of content-based search in 100 million Internet videos. We proposed a scalable solution for large-scale semantic search in video. Our method extends the current capability of semantic video search by a few orders of magnitude while maintaining state-of-the-art retrieval performance. A key in our solution is a novel step called concept adjustment that aims at representing a video by a few salient and consistent concepts which can be efficiently indexed by the modified inverted index. We introduced a novel adjustment model that is based on a concise optimization framework with solid interpretations. We also discussed a solution that leverages the text-based inverted index for video retrieval. Experimental results validated the efficacy and the efficiency of the proposed method on several datasets. Specifically, the experimental results on the challenging TRECVID MED benchmarks validate the proposed method is of state-of-the-art accuracy. The results on the largest multimedia set YFCC100M set verify the scalability and efficiency over a large collection of 100 million Internet videos.

Table 6: Average performance for 30 commercials on the YFCC100M set.

Category	#Ads	Evaluation Metric		
		P@20	MRR	MAP@20
Sports	7	0.88	1.00	0.94
Auto	2	0.85	1.00	0.95
Grocery	8	0.84	0.93	0.88
Traveling	3	0.96	1.00	0.96
Miscellaneous	10	0.65	0.85	0.74
Average	30	0.81	0.93	0.86

Acknowledgments

This work was partially supported by the Intelligence Advanced Research Projects Activity (IARPA) via Department of Interior National Business Center contract number D11PC20068. The U.S. Government is authorized to reproduce and distribute reprints for Governmental purposes notwithstanding any copyright annotation thereon. Disclaimer: The views and conclusions contained herein are those of the authors and should not be interpreted as necessarily representing the official policies or endorsements, either expressed or implied, of IARPA, DoI/NBC, or the U.S. Government. This work used the Extreme Science and Engineering Discovery Environment (XSEDE), which is supported by National Science Foundation grant number OCI-1053575. It used the Blacklight system at the Pittsburgh Supercomputing Center (PSC).

9. REFERENCES

[1] E. Apostolidis, V. Mezaris, M. Sahuguet, B. Huet, B. Červenková, D. Stein, S. Eickeler, J. L. Redondo Garcia, R. Troncy, and L. Pikora. Automatic fine-grained hyperlinking of videos within a closed collection using scene segmentation. In *MM*, 2014.

[2] S. Bhattacharya, F. X. Yu, and S.-F. Chang. Minimally needed evidence for complex event recognition in unconstrained videos. In *ICMR*, 2014.

[3] E. F. Can and R. Manmatha. Modeling concept dependencies for event detection. In *ICMR*, 2014.

[4] J. Deng, N. Ding, Y. Jia, A. Frome, K. Murphy, S. Bengio, Y. Li, H. Neven, and H. Adam. Large-scale object classification using label relation graphs. In *ECCV*, 2014.

[5] J. Deng, W. Dong, R. Socher, L.-J. Li, K. Li, and L. Fei-Fei. Imagenet: A large-scale hierarchical image database. In *CVPR*, 2009.

[6] M. L. Fisher. The lagrangian relaxation method for solving integer programming problems. *Management science*, 50(12):1861–1871, 2004.

[7] N. Gkalelis and V. Mezaris. Video event detection using generalized subclass discriminant analysis and linear support vector machines. In *ICMR*, 2014.

Figure 6: Top 5 retrieved results for 3 example ads on the YFCC100M dataset.

[8] M. Grant, S. Boyd, and Y. Ye. CVX: Matlab software for disciplined convex programming, 2008.

[9] A. Habibian, T. Mensink, and C. G. Snoek. Composite concept discovery for zero-shot video event detection. In *ICMR*, 2014.

[10] A. Habibian, T. Mensink, and C. G. Snoek. Videostory: A new multimedia embedding for few-example recognition and translation of events. In *MM*, 2014.

[11] A. Habibian, K. E. van de Sande, and C. G. Snoek. Recommendations for video event recognition using concept vocabularies. In *ICMR*, 2013.

[12] E. Hatcher and O. Gospodnetic. Lucene in action. In *Manning Publications*, 2004.

[13] L. Jiang, A. Hauptmann, and G. Xiang. Leveraging high-level and low-level features for multimedia event detection. In *MM*, 2012.

[14] L. Jiang, D. Meng, T. Mitamura, and A. G. Hauptmann. Easy samples first: Self-paced reranking for zero-example multimedia search. In *MM*, 2014.

[15] L. Jiang, D. Meng, S.-I. Yu, Z. Lan, S. Shan, and A. G. Hauptmann. Self-paced learning with diversity. In *NIPS*, 2014.

[16] L. Jiang, D. Meng, Q. Zhao, S. Shan, and A. G. Hauptmann. Self-paced curriculum learning. In *AAAI*, 2015.

[17] L. Jiang, T. Mitamura, S.-I. Yu, and A. G. Hauptmann. Zero-example event search using multimodal pseudo relevance feedback. In *ICMR*, 2014.

[18] L. Jiang, S.-I. Yu, D. Meng, T. Mitamura, and A. G. Hauptmann. Bridging the ultimate semantic gap: A semantic search engine for internet videos. In *ICMR*, 2015.

[19] A. Karpathy, G. Toderici, S. Shetty, T. Leung, R. Sukthankar, and L. Fei-Fei. Large-scale video classification with convolutional neural networks. In *CVPR*, 2014.

[20] A. Krizhevsky, I. Sutskever, and G. E. Hinton. Imagenet classification with deep convolutional neural networks. In *NIPS*, 2012.

[21] H. Lee. Analyzing complex events and human actions in" in-the-wild" videos. In *UMD Ph.D Theses and Dissertations*, 2014.

[22] M. Mazloom, X. Li, and C. G. Snoek. Few-example video event retrieval using tag propagation. In *ICMR*, 2014.

[23] Y. Miao, L. Jiang, H. Zhang, and F. Metze. Improvements to speaker adaptive training of deep neural networks. In *SLT*, 2014.

[24] Y. Miao and F. Metze. Improving low-resource cd-dnn-hmm using dropout and multilingual dnn training. In *INTERSPEECH*, 2013.

[25] D. Moise, D. Shestakov, G. Gudmundsson, and L. Amsaleg. Indexing and searching 100m images with map-reduce. In *ICMR*, 2013.

[26] M. Naphade, J. R. Smith, J. Tesic, S.-F. Chang, W. Hsu, L. Kennedy, A. Hauptmann, and J. Curtis. Large-scale concept ontology for multimedia. *MultiMedia, IEEE*, 13(3):86–91, 2006.

[27] M. R. Naphade and J. R. Smith. On the detection of semantic concepts at trecvid. In *MM*, 2004.

[28] S. Oh, S. McCloskey, I. Kim, A. Vahdat, K. J. Cannons, H. Hajimirsadeghi, G. Mori, A. A. Perera, M. Pandey, and J. J. Corso. Multimedia event detection with multimodal feature fusion and temporal concept localization. *Machine vision and applications*, 25(1):49–69, 2014.

[29] P. Over, G. Awad, M. Michel, J. Fiscus, G. Sanders, W. Kraaij, A. F. Smeaton, and G. Quéenot. TRECVID 2014 – an overview of the goals, tasks, data, evaluation mechanisms and metrics. In *TRECVID*, 2014.

[30] D. Povey, A. Ghoshal, G. Boulianne, et al. The kaldi speech recognition toolkit. In *ASRU*, 2011.

[31] O. Russakovsky, J. Deng, H. Su, J. Krause, S. Satheesh, S. Ma, Z. Huang, A. Karpathy, A. Khosla, M. Bernstein, et al. Imagenet large scale visual recognition challenge. *arXiv preprint arXiv:1409.0575*, 2014.

[32] B. Safadi, M. Sahuguet, and B. Huet. When textual and visual information join forces for multimedia retrieval. In *ICMR*, 2014.

[33] N. Simon, J. Friedman, T. Hastie, and R. Tibshirani. A sparse-group lasso. *Journal of Computational and Graphical Statistics*, 22(2):231–245, 2013.

[34] J. Sivic and A. Zisserman. Video google: Efficient visual search of videos. In *Toward Category-Level Object Recognition*, 2006.

[35] J. R. Smith. Riding the multimedia big data wave. In *SIGIR*, 2013.

[36] C. Snoek, K. van de Sande, D. Fontijne, A. Habibian, M. Jain, S. Kordumova, Z. Li, M. Mazloom, S. Pintea, R. Tao, et al. Mediamill at trecvid 2013: Searching concepts, objects, instances and events in video. In *TRECVID*, 2013.

[37] B. Thomee, D. A. Shamma, G. Friedland, B. Elizalde, K. Ni, D. Poland, D. Borth, and L.-J. Li. The new data and new challenges in multimedia research. *arXiv preprint arXiv:1503.01817*, 2015.

[38] R. Tibshirani. Regression shrinkage and selection via the lasso. *Journal of the Royal Statistical Society. Series B (Methodological)*, pages 267–288, 1996.

[39] W. Tong, Y. Yang, L. Jiang, et al. E-LAMP: integration of innovative ideas for multimedia event detection. *Machine Vision and Applications*, 25(1):5–15, 2014.

[40] F. Wang, Z. Sun, Y. Jiang, and C. Ngo. Video event detection using motion relativity and feature selection. In *TMM*, 2013.

[41] H. Wang and C. Schmid. Action recognition with improved trajectories. In *ICCV*, 2013.

[42] S. Wu, S. Bondugula, F. Luisier, X. Zhuang, and P. Natarajan. Zero-shot event detection using multi-modal fusion of weakly supervised concepts. In *CVPR*, 2014.

[43] X. Wu, A. G. Hauptmann, and C.-W. Ngo. Practical elimination of near-duplicates from web video search. In *MM*, 2007.

[44] S.-I. Yu, L. Jiang, and A. Hauptmann. Instructional videos for unsupervised harvesting and learning of action examples. In *MM*, 2014.

[45] S.-I. Yu, L. Jiang, Z. Xu, et al. Informedia@ trecvid 2014 med and mer. In *TRECVID*, 2014.

[46] M. Yuan and Y. Lin. Model selection and estimation in regression with grouped variables. *Journal of the Royal Statistical Society: Series B (Statistical Methodology)*, 68(1):49–67, 2006.

Visual Coding in a Semantic Hierarchy

Yang Yang[†], Hanwang Zhang[‡], Mingxing Zhang[†], Fumin Shen[†], Xuelong Li[§]
[†]University of Electronic Science and Technology of China
[‡]National University of Singapore
[§]Chinese Academy of Sciences
{dlyyang, hanwangzhang, zhangmingxing, fumin.shen}@gmail.com; xuelong_li@opt.ac.cn

ABSTRACT

In recent years, tremendous research endeavours have been dedicated to seeking effective visual representations for facilitating various multimedia applications, such as visual annotation and retrieval. Nonetheless, existing approaches can hardly achieve satisfactory performance due to the scarcity of fully exploring semantic properties of visual codes. In this paper, we present a novel visual coding approach, termed as *hierarchical semantic visual coding* (HSVC), to effectively encode visual objects (*e.g.*, image and video) in a semantic hierarchy. Specifically, we first construct a semantic-enriched dictionary hierarchy, which is comprised of dictionaries corresponding to all concepts in a semantic hierarchy as well as their hierarchical semantic correlation. Moreover, we devise an on-line semantic coding model, which simultaneously 1) exploits the rich hierarchical semantic prior knowledge in the learned dictionary, 2) reflects semantic sparse property of visual codes, and 3) explores semantic relationships among concepts in the semantic hierarchy. To this end, we propose to integrate concept-level group sparsity constraint and semantic correlation matrix into a unified regularization term. We design an effective algorithm to optimize the proposed model, and a rigorous mathematical analysis has been provided to guarantee that the algorithm converges to a global optima. Extensive experiments on various multimedia datasets have been conducted to illustrate the superiority of our proposed approach as compared to state-of-the-art methods.

Categories and Subject Descriptors

H.3.1 [**Content Analysis and Indexing**]: Abstracting methods

General Terms

Algorithm

MM'15, October 26–30, 2015, Brisbane, Australia.
 ISBN 978-1-4503-3459-4/15/10 ...$15.00.
DOI: http://dx.doi.org/10.1145/2733373.2806244.

Keywords

semantic hierarchy; dictionary hierarchy; visual coding; group lasso

1. INTRODUCTION

Recent years have witness the power of multimedia techniques to facilitate various real-world applications, such as visual retrieval [32], visual annotation [29, 30], etc. Over the past two decades, visual representation (or features) has undergone the transition from simple raw feature extraction, to higher-level feature statistics such as Bag-of-Words, and today, to more complex but generic feature extraction pipelines. For example, one of the most popular pipelines extracts hand-crafted descriptors (*e.g.*, SIFT or HOG) from local visual patches, and then encodes these descriptors into certain over-complete representation using various algorithms such as k-means or sparse coding; after coding stage, global visual representations are formed by spatially pooling the coded local descriptors. Finally, the global representations of visual samples are fed into task-dependent classifiers. Another promising pipeline has been growing its popularity with the recent advances in deep learning. In general, it is a deep neural network with repeated feature detection and pooling layers. The output of the top layer is regarded as the ultimate visual features, which are then fed into the final classification layer. Although these two pipelines are motivated differently, they are both shown to achieve the state-of-the-art performance in most image classification benchmarks.

However, as compared to our humans, who can easily recognize more than tens of thousands objects, the above artificial pipelines are obviously inferior. Deng *et al.* [5] have shown that when they tried to classify ten thousand objects, the accuracy is only around 3.7%. Admittedly, it is still unclear how to computationally model human vision system, nevertheless, we can observe the following three crucial defects in current visual representation designs.

- First, one of the core stages of the pipelines is the generation of elementary feature representations (*e.g.*, codebook, dictionary or convolutional kernels), which are learned or sampled globally over the whole dataset. However, this may lose fine-grained details that are specific object categories during the sample bias. For example, if the number of crucial elementary features of "dog" is smaller than that of other objects, then the resultant codebook is less capable to represent "dog" images.

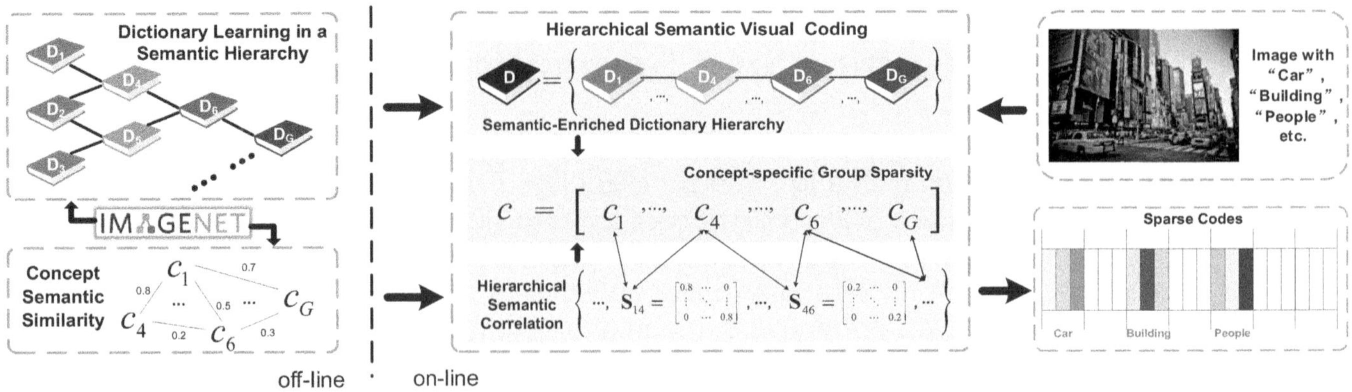

Figure 1: The proposed hierarchical semantic visual coding (HSVC) pipeline. In the off-line part, we learn dictionaries for every concept in a semantic hierarchy. Each dictionary is learned by the training samples belonging to the referenced concept. In the on-line part, we aggregate the set of learned dictionaries as a holistic semantic-enriched dictionary hierarchy, which provides fundamental feature basis for HSVC. Meanwhile, we also explore semantic properties of visual codes, including sematic sparsity and semantic correlation. The resultant sparse visual codes are the visual representation used in subsequent specific tasks such as visual annotation and visual retrieval.

- Second, these pipelines neglect to consider the relationships between different object categories, which is the most appealing ability that human vision system possesses. For example, when a human is trying to recognize a "puma", she may transfer some visual knowledge from "pet cat". By this way, our vision system can generalize well to objects unseen in the training samples.
- Moreover, real-world visual objects usually contain multiple objects and scenes, which are correlated through certain semantics. For example, "people" and "dog" are more likely to appear in the same scene than "dog" and "fish", since the former two have closer semantic relationship than the latter. However, to the best of our knowledge, seldom existing visual representation methods take this observation into account.

In this paper, we propose a novel sematic visual representation extraction pipeline, termed as *hierarchical semantic visual coding* (HSVC), which encodes visual objects in accordance with a semantic hierarchy. As illustrated in Figure 1, the proposed pipeline comprises an off-line part and an online part. Suppose we have a semantic hierarchy populated with training samples referenced to each concept (*e.g.*, ImageNet [6]). In the off-line part, we embed rich hierarchial semantic information into dictionary learning process to construct a semantic-enriched dictionary hierarchy. For each individual concept in the sematic hierarchy, we extract visual features (*e.g.*, DeCAF [8], Bag-of-Words, *etc.*) for all the attached training samples and learn a concept-specific dictionary; then the dictionaries corresponding to all concepts in the hierarchy are concatenated to form a holistic dictionary. Moreover, in order to facilitate the subsequent on-line visual coding, we preliminarily compute semantic similarities (or correlations) of concepts in the hierarchy as well. In the on-line part, we devise a novel semantic coding approach by fully exploring semantic properties of visual codes, including rich hierarchical semantic information in the learned dictionary, semantic sparsity of concepts, as well as semantic relationships among concepts in the semantic hierarchy. In order to achieve this goal, we incorporate a novel semantically structured regularization term, which not only induces concept-level group sparsity to preserve semantic purity of visual samples, but also employs hierarchical semantic cues to retain semantic correlations among concepts and enhance the representative power of visual codes. The generated sparse codes are considered as the final visual representation and further used in specific tasks. We conduct extensive experiments on real-world large-scale datasets, and the promising results demonstrate that the proposed visual codes are more effective in supporting fundamental applications, such as visual annotation and retrieval, as compared to state-of-the-art methods.

We highlight the three major contributions of the proposed coding pipeline as follows:

- **Dictionary Learning in a Semantic Hierarchy**. In order to prepare dictionaries for generating effective visual representation, we propose a novel dictionary learning approach in a semantic hierarchy. We learn a concept-specific dictionary for every concept using all its attached visual samples. The constructed dictionary comprises elementary features that are most representative for the referenced concept. By aggregating the dictionaries of all concepts in the semantic hierarchy, we can obtain a holistic semantic-enriched dictionary hierarchy.
- **Concept-specific Group Sparsity**. We obverse that real-world visual objects normally contain very sparse semantic concepts. For instance, an image of "car" may only correspond to a small number of concepts such as "car", "road", "building". Hence, encoding information of all the concepts into an individual visual sample may affect semantic purity of visual samples and lead to imprecise representation. In order to avoid such problem, we propose to impose concept-level sparsity on the desired codes. Each concept is the part of dictionary (i.e., a group of base elements) that corresponds to a specific semantic concept, and the induced sparsity will lead to sparse codes with a reasonable number of concepts.
- **Hierarchical Semantic Correlation**. In order to enable sparse codes to be more meaningful and representative, we further exploit the semantic relationships

among concepts when coding visual objects. By exploiting the explicit semantic information of concepts in the hierarchy, we are able to calculate semantic similarity (or correlation) and incorporate such information into the coding process. For instance, we may punish the coincidence of the codes of "people" and "dog" lighter than that of "fish" and "dog". Therefore, the resultant visual codes would be more semantically informative.

The rest of the paper is organized as follows. Section 2 reviews related work. Section 3 describes dictionary learning in a semantic hierarchy. Section 4 details the proposed hierarchical semantic visual coding pipeline, including the formulation, algorithms and a rigorous mathematical proof. Experimental results and analysis are reported in Section 5, followed by conclusions in Section 6.

2. RELATED WORK

2.1 Visual Coding for Representation

State-of-the-art visual representation comprises the following stages. First, raw visual feature descriptors (*e.g.*, color, texture or shape) are extracted from local patches; then, these features are encoded into an over-complete representation. One general coding approach is described as below:

$$\begin{aligned} &\min_{\mathbf{c}} \ \|\mathbf{x} - \mathbf{D}\mathbf{c}\|_2^2, \\ &\textbf{s.t.} \ \ \mathbf{c} \in \mathcal{F}, \end{aligned} \tag{1}$$

where $\mathbf{x} \in \mathbb{R}^d$ is the feature vector of a visual sample, and d is the dimensionality of the feature space. $\mathbf{D} \in \mathbb{R}^{d\times M}$ is an over-complete dictionary (*i.e.*, $M \geq d$), M is the number of bases in the dictionary, $\mathbf{c} \in \mathbb{R}^M$ is the sparse codes, and $\mathcal{F}$ is certain feasible region. For example, when $\mathcal{F} = \{\mathbf{c}|\mathbf{c} \in \{0,1\}, \|\mathbf{c}\|_1 = 1\}$, the coding reduces to the well-known k-means method [9]; when $\mathcal{F} = \{\mathbf{c}|\|\mathbf{c}\|_1 \leq \gamma\}$, where $\gamma > 0$ is a constant, it becomes the popular sparse coding [17]. After the coding stage, global image representations are formed by spatially *pooling* the coded local descriptors [16]. Finally, such global representations are used in specific tasks such as classification and retrieval. Methods following such a pipeline have achieved state-of-the-art performance on several benchmark datasets. Recently, convolutional neural network (CNN) has been shown a successful alternative in learning image representations, achieving a significant boost in image classification task [8,15,24]. These two pipelines both follow a hierarchical feature extraction philosophy, but the core difference is that CNN automatically learns features while the other one is manually designed. However, they do not conflict since we can use the learned image representation as an input to the manually designed pipeline in order to further boost the performance [8].

As compared to local feature-level coding methods for image representation, our work falls into the image-level coding, where feature $\mathbf{x}$ is a global representation of an image (*e.g.*, we use DeCAF feature in this paper). In this way, we relate to some recent work. Zheng *et al.* [34] exploited the geometry structure of the data space, casting the image-level sparse coding problem into a graph embedding one. Huang *et al.* [13] proposed an efficient sparse coding methods for image annotation, where the dictionary is the feature matrix of the whole training images. Some studies used coding methods with group sparsity, which tackles the problem that the ℓ_1-norm sparse coding implicitly assumes that an element in the dictionary is independent of all others. Essentially, group sparsity motivates to integrate correlations among the dictionaries. Zhang *et al.* [33] used group sparsity in selecting useful features of the same type for image annotation. Bengio *et al.* [1] proposed to use group sparse coding for jointly encoding the group of visual descriptors within the same image to achieve image-level sparsity. Yang *et al.* [28] considered regions of an image as a group, used to achieve region-level image annotation. Gao *et al.* [11] extended the meaning of group into "class", "tag" and "instance" levels and proposed a multi-layer group sparse coding algorithm for image annotation. Formally, given a dictionary $\mathbf{D} = \{\mathbf{D}_1, \mathbf{D}_2, ..., \mathbf{D}_G\}$, where $\mathbf{D}_i$ is a group (or subset) of the entire dictionary $\mathbf{D}$, the sparse coding with group sparsity (a.k.a. Group Lasso [31]) can be formulated as

$$\min_{\mathbf{c}} \left\| \mathbf{x} - \sum_{i=1}^{G} \mathbf{D}_i \mathbf{c}_i \right\|_2^2 + \lambda \sum_{i=1}^{G} \|\mathbf{c}_i\|_2, \tag{2}$$

where λ is the trade-off constant and $\mathbf{c}_i$ is the coding coefficient corresponding to the i-th group. In fact, the group sparsity constraint $\sum_{i=1}^{G} \|\mathbf{c}_i\|_2$ can be considered as the ℓ_1-norm of the vector $[\|\mathbf{c}_1\|_2, \|\mathbf{c}_2\|_2, \ldots, \|\mathbf{c}_G\|_2]^T$. In this paper, we consider a group as a concept-specific dictionary.

2.2 Semantic Hierarchy

A semantic hierarchy is a formally defined taxonomy or ontology, where each node represents a semantic concept, such as WordNet [10], ImageNet [6], or LSCOM [20], *etc.* It organizes semantic concepts from general to specific and has been shown to be effective in boosting visual recognition [18] and retrieval [4,7].

In this paper, we predict the semantic path of images by hierarchical concept classifiers. As compared to a bag of flat classifiers (*e.g.*, a bag of one-vs-all classifiers), hierarchical classifiers exploit the ontological relationship and thus significantly reduce the prediction time while producing comparatively good accuracy. For example, [12] automatically built classification trees which achieve significant speedup at a small performance drop. There are also studies which found that hierarchical top-down prediction using local classifiers can retain the same performance as one-vs-all classifiers [18]. Here, "local" is a concept classifier training strategy that considers the images of the concept itself as positive and those of its siblings as negative. However, local classifiers may suffer severely from the error propagation problem. If a classifier at higher levels fails, it is hard for the successive classifiers at lower levels to stop the error (*e.g.*, classify the error as negative) since they have never seen such an error as a negative sample. In order to alleviate this problem, [3] developed a structure learning method that optimizes the performance of all local classifiers in a semantic hierarchy. However, the training cost of the method is prohibitive in the large-scale semantic hierarchy as employed in this work. For efficiency, we adopt an hierarchical one-vs-all training strategy to learn local concept classifiers as in [23].

Most recent work exploits semantic hierarchy for image retrieval and designs certain semantic similarity function that embeds hierarchical information. In [7], given two images, their visual nearest neighbor images were first found, and their semantic distance was computed as a distance between the concepts of their neighbors. [4] developed an hierarchical bilinear similarity function for image retrieval. They first represented an image as a semantic vector $\mathbf{z}$ consisting of its relevances to a set of concepts, and defined the bilinear similarity between any two images as $\mathbf{z}_i^T \mathbf{S} \mathbf{z}_j$, where $\mathbf{S}$ is a matrix encoding the pairwise semantic affinities among the concepts. They have shown that this method achieves state-of-the-art performance of image retrieval on ImageNet. Recently, in [27], a new method was proposed to associate separated visual similarity metrics for every concept in a hierarchy and then learn the metrics jointly through an aggregated hierarchical metric. In our work, we use the semantic similarities between the concepts in a semantic hierarchy to regularize the semantic coding. By doing this, we cannot only achieve semantic group sparsity which boost the discriminative power of the sparse codes, but also enrich the semantic descriptiveness of them.

3. DICTIONARY LEARNING IN A SEMANTIC HIERARCHY

Dictionary learning [22, 25] plays a vital role in multimedia applications. The premise of our visual coding pipeline is to construct a semantic-enriched dictionary hierarchy in accordance with certain hierarchy. As shown in Figure 1, for each concept in the hierarchy, we learn a dictionary from visual samples that belong to the concept. Without loss of generality, for any concept c, we learn a dictionary $\mathbf{D}_c$ from the training samples as follows:

$$\min_{\mathbf{C}, \mathbf{D}_c} \|\mathbf{X} - \mathbf{D}_c \mathbf{C}\|_F^2, \tag{3}$$

where $\mathbf{X} = [\mathbf{x}_1, ..., \mathbf{x}_{N_c}] \in \mathbb{R}^{d \times N_c}$ is the matrix of the training samples, N_c is the number of the training samples, $\mathbf{x}_i \in \mathbb{R}^d$ is the i-th sample, and $\mathbf{C}$ is the matrix of the corresponding codes for all training visual samples. $\|\cdot\|_F$ is the Frobenius norm of a matrix. Fortunately, the solution we are interested in, the dictionary $\mathbf{D}_c$, can be obtained through Singular Value Decomposition (SVD) of the visual sample matrix $\mathbf{X} = \mathbf{D}_c \mathbf{\Sigma} \mathbf{C}^T$, where $\mathbf{\Sigma}$ is a diagonal matrix of the singular values, $\mathbf{D}_c$ and $\mathbf{C}$ are the the matrix concatenation of the left and right singular vectors, respectively. Therefore, the ultimate dictionary with respect to the entire semantic hierarchy can be obtained by concatenating all the concept-specific dictionaries:

$$\mathbf{D} = [\mathbf{D}_1, ..., \mathbf{D}_c, ..., \mathbf{D}_G], \tag{4}$$

where G is the number of semantic concepts in the hierarchy.

Dictionary $\mathbf{D}_c$ can be considered as a base matrix that spans an intrinsic subspace for the visual information of concept c. The advantages of our concept-specific dictionary learning are two folds. First, since we will eventually combine these dictionaries, the size of each dictionary should be small otherwise it will cause prohibitive computation problem. Fortunately, the SVD solution $\mathbf{D}_c$ leads to compact base matrix depicting the characteristics of a specific concept. In this work, we set the number of base features to 10, which means only the top 10 visual variances are captured. Note that each dictionary is only responsible for its own concept, therefore we merely need to retain the principal variances in the dictionary since the "entire" picture will be eventually emerged by aggregating all the "local" pictures.

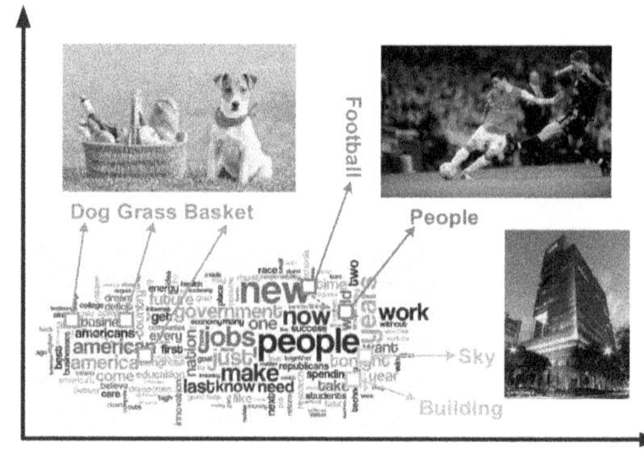

Figure 3: Illustration of **semantic sparsity** and **semantic correlation** among concepts. As shown, due to limited amount of content, an individual image can only cover a small proportion of semantic concepts in the whole semantic space, which implies that within the image, the semantic information should be sparse enough at concept level. On the other hand, concepts co-occurring in the same image (*e.g.*, "sky" and "building") should be semantically correlated, and thus should mutually reinforce/influence weights of each other's codes.

Figure 2 illustrates the semantic meanings of the dictionaries we learned. Second, computing $\mathbf{D}_c$ is very efficient, especially when the number of training samples is large-scale. This is very common when learning dictionaries for more general concepts who possess many more samples. In fact, no matter how large the number of the samples (*i.e.*, the column dimension of $\mathbf{X}$) is, we can always efficiently obtain $\mathbf{D}_c$ by computing the singular eigenvectors for $\mathbf{X}^T$, which has a smaller column dimension, i.e., the dimension of the original visual feature.

4. CODING VISUAL OBJECTS IN A SEMANTIC HIERARCHY

After we harvest the concept-dependent dictionaries as aforementioned, we are ready to encode visual objects into sparse codes while exploring the semantic properties in the hierarchy. In this way, we expect the sparse codes not only provide efficient sparse visual representations but also can be explicitly interpreted as semantic meanings such as objects and relationships among them. As aforementioned in Eq. (2), a straightforward way is to formulate the coding problem into a Group Lasso problem. However, this formulation treats the codes of each semantic concepts independently and thus neglects the hierarchical semantic relationships between them. In fact, concepts are semantically intercorrelated to each other in the semantic space. Furthermore, for an individual visual object, its related semantics should be sparse due to limited amount of content. In this section, we show how to efficiently and effectively encode visual objects in a semantic hierarchy by jointly considering semantic sparsity and semantic correlation.

4.1 Formulation

If we inspect Eq. (2), we can easily find that the Group Lasso term ($\sum_{i=1}^{G} \|\mathbf{c}_i\|_2$) fails to incorporate the relationship between $\mathbf{c}_i$ and $\mathbf{c}_j$. For example, if the semantic similarity $s_{dog,people}$ of "dog" and "people" is large, we should consider

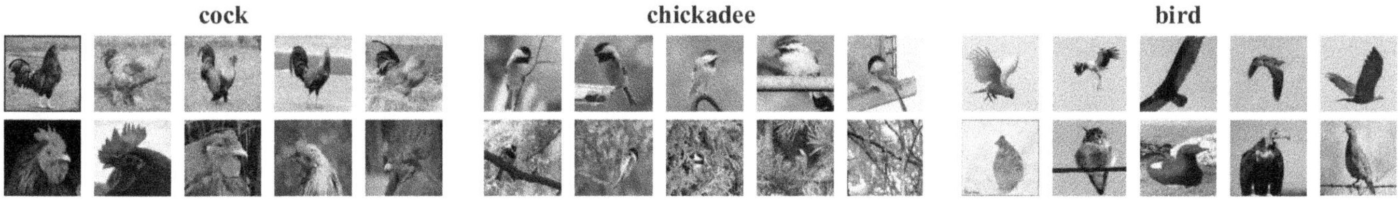

Figure 2: The illustration of concept-specific dictionary. By Eq. (3), the learned dictionary only captures the intrinsic semantic of the concept. For concept "cock" (ImageNetID: n01514668), "chickadee" (ImageNetID: n01592084), and "bird" (ImageNetID: n01503061), we choose the dimension of the dictionary with the largest singular value, and we map all the images in one concept into this dimension. The top and bottom images are largest and smallest mapped values, respectively, representing semantic meanings. For example, the dimension in "bird" dictionary captures birds with/without wings.

them jointly and expect them to co-occur in the sparse codes with a relatively high probability; if $s_{dog,fish}$ of concepts "dog" and "fish" is small, it is reasonable to neglect their joint sparsity since they are semantically far away. In general, we propose to jointly consider the sparsity of the codes through a similarity weight s_{ij} between concepts $\mathbf{c}_i$ and $\mathbf{c}_j$:

$$\min_{\mathbf{c}} \left\| \mathbf{x} - \sum_{i=1}^{G} \mathbf{D}_i \mathbf{c}_i \right\|_2^2 + \lambda \sum_{i=1}^{G} \sum_{j=1}^{G} \left(\mathbf{c}_i^T \mathbf{S}_{ij} \mathbf{c}_j \right)^{1/2}, \quad (5)$$

where $\mathbf{S}_{ij}$ is a diagonal matrix whose diagonal entries are s_{ij}. In particular, we can see that the original Group Lasso in Eq. (2) is only a special case such that $s_{ij} = 1$ if $i = j$ and $s_{ij} = 0$ otherwise. Specifically, s_{ij} can be defined $s_{ij} = f(\pi(i,j))$, where $\pi(i,j)$ is the lowest common ancestor of concepts $\mathbf{c}_i$ and $\mathbf{c}_j$, and $f(\cdot)$ is some real function that is non-decreasing going down the hierarchy, *i.e.*, the lower the lowest shared ancestor is, the more similar concepts i and j are. For example, "dog" is much more similar to "people" than "car" because "dog" shares a lower level common ancestor "mammal" with "people" than "object" with "car". Figure 3 illustrates semantic sparsity and semantic correlation. Note that there are other ways to obtain s_{ij}, *e.g.*, mining from the Internet corpus or exploiting crowd sourcing [21].

In [19], it has shown that the generalized form of Group Lasso in Eq. (5) is an intermediate regularizer between the ℓ_1-norm in the Lasso and the ℓ_2-norm in ridge regression. This indicates that our visual coding formulation encourages concept-level sparsity when taking hierarchical semantic prior knowledge into consideration.

4.2 Solution

Note that our coding formulation in Eq. (5) is non-smooth because it contains the square root to impose concept-level sparsity. In this part, we propose an efficient iterative algorithm to solve the optimization problem in Eq. (5).

To illustrate the algorithm, at each iteration, we reformulate Eq. (5) into an alternative quadratic and smooth form by dividing the Group Lasso term at the previous iteration,

$$\min_{\mathbf{c}^{(t)}} \left\| \mathbf{x} - \sum_{i=1}^{G} \mathbf{D}_i \mathbf{c}_i^{(t)} \right\|_2^2 + \lambda \sum_{i=1}^{G} \sum_{j=1}^{G} \frac{\mathbf{c}_i^{(t)T} \mathbf{S}_{ij} \mathbf{c}_j^{(t)}}{2 \left(\mathbf{c}_i^{(t-1)T} \mathbf{S}_{ij} \mathbf{c}_j^{(t-1)} \right)^{1/2}}. \quad (6)$$

The re-weighting term $\left(\mathbf{c}_i^{(t-1)T} \mathbf{S}_{ij} \mathbf{c}_j^{(t-1)} \right)^{1/2}$ can be considered as a constant term since we assume that we have already obtained $\{\mathbf{c}_i\}_{i=1}^{G}$ at the previous iteration. Eq. (6) can be rewritten into a more compact form as

$$\min_{\mathbf{c}^{(t)}} \left\| \mathbf{x} - \mathbf{D}\mathbf{c}^{(t)} \right\|_2^2 + \lambda \mathbf{c}^{(t)T} \mathbf{S}^{(t-1)} \mathbf{c}^{(t)}, \quad (7)$$

where $\mathbf{D} = [\mathbf{D}_1, \ldots, \mathbf{D}_G]$, $\mathbf{c} = [\mathbf{c}_1^T, \ldots, \mathbf{c}_G^T]^T$, and

$$\mathbf{S}^{(t-1)} = \begin{pmatrix} \mathbf{S}_{11}^{(t-1)} & \cdots & \mathbf{S}_{1G}^{(t-1)} \\ \vdots & \ddots & \vdots \\ \mathbf{S}_{G1}^{(t-1)} & \cdots & \mathbf{S}_{GG}^{(t-1)} \end{pmatrix}, \qquad \mathbf{S}_{ij}^{(t-1)} = \frac{\mathbf{S}_{ij}}{2 \left(\mathbf{c}_i^{(t-1)T} \mathbf{S}_{ij} \mathbf{c}_j^{(t-1)} \right)^{1/2}}. \quad (8)$$

It is easy to see that Eq. (7) has a closed form solution:

$$\mathbf{c}^{(t)} = \left(\mathbf{D}^T \mathbf{D} + \lambda \mathbf{S}^{(t-1)} \right)^{-1} \mathbf{D}^T \mathbf{x}. \quad (9)$$

This equation is the resultant iterative updating rule for the ultimate hierarchical semantic sparse codes $\mathbf{c}^*$. A detailed algorithm is illustrated in Algorithm 1.

In the next section, we elaborate detailed analysis of the proposed algorithm and provide a rigorous mathematical verification of the convergence.

Algorithm 1: Hierarchical Semantic Visual Coding

Input : A visual feature $\mathbf{x}$, dictionary matrix $\mathbf{D}$ and similarity matrix $\mathbf{S}$ w.r.t. a semantic hierarchy, trade-off parameter λ;
Output: Hierarchical semantic sparse codes $\mathbf{c}^*$;

```
Initialization: Randomly initialize sparse codes c^(0) with ||c^(0)||_2 = 1, t = 0;
repeat
    t ← t + 1;
    Calculate S^(t-1) according to Eq. (8);
    c^(t) = (D^T D + λ S^(t-1))^(-1) D^T x;
until there is no change to c^(t);
Return: c* = c^(t);
```

5. ALGORITHMIC ANALYSIS

In this section, we prove that Algorithm 1 converges to a global minimum of Eq. (5) and analyze its computational complexity. We first show the Algorithm 1 converges to a limiting point and then show this point is a stationary point of Eq. (5), which is therefore a global minimum due to the convexity of Eq. (5). We start from the following lemma.

LEMMA 1. *For nonzero vectors* $\mathbf{c}$ *and* $\mathbf{b}$, *and symmetric positive definite matrix* $\mathbf{S}$, *we have*

$$\left(\mathbf{c}^T\mathbf{S}\mathbf{c}\right)^{1/2} - \frac{\mathbf{c}^T\mathbf{S}\mathbf{c}}{2\left(\mathbf{b}^T\mathbf{S}\mathbf{b}\right)^{1/2}} \leq \left(\mathbf{b}^T\mathbf{S}\mathbf{b}\right)^{1/2} - \frac{\mathbf{b}^T\mathbf{S}\mathbf{b}}{2\left(\mathbf{b}^T\mathbf{S}\mathbf{b}\right)^{1/2}}. \tag{10}$$

PROOF. Since $\mathbf{S}$ is symmetric positive definite, we have $\mathbf{S} = \mathbf{L}^T\mathbf{L}$ by Cholesky decomposition, and for any nonzero vectors we have $\mathbf{c}^T\mathbf{S}\mathbf{c} > 0$. Denote $\widehat{\mathbf{b}} = \mathbf{L}\mathbf{b}$ and $\widehat{\mathbf{c}} = \mathbf{L}\mathbf{c}$, since $(\|\widehat{\mathbf{c}}\|_2 - \|\widehat{\mathbf{b}}\|_2)^2$, we have

$$\|\widehat{\mathbf{c}}\|_2 - \frac{\|\widehat{\mathbf{c}}\|_2^2}{2\|\widehat{\mathbf{b}}\|_2} \leq \|\widehat{\mathbf{b}}\|_2 - \frac{\|\widehat{\mathbf{b}}\|_2^2}{2\|\widehat{\mathbf{b}}\|_2}, \tag{11}$$

which therefore proves Lemma 1. □

THEREOM 1 (CONVERGENCE OF ALGORITHM 1). *The iterative update in Algorithm 1 guarantees that the objective function in Eq.* (5) *converges to a global minimum.*

PROOF. Since the solution in Eq. (9) minimizes the value of the objective function in Eq. (7), we have

$$\begin{aligned} &\left\|\mathbf{x} - \sum_{i=1}^{G}\mathbf{D}_i\mathbf{c}_i^{(t)}\right\|_2^2 + \lambda\sum\nolimits_{i,j}\frac{\mathbf{c}_i^{(t)T}\mathbf{S}_{ij}\mathbf{c}_j^{(t)}}{2\left(\mathbf{c}_i^{(t-1)T}\mathbf{S}_{ij}\mathbf{c}_j^{(t-1)}\right)^{1/2}} \\ \leq &\left\|\mathbf{x} - \sum_{i=1}^{G}\mathbf{D}_i\mathbf{c}_i^{(t-1)}\right\|_2^2 + \lambda\sum\nolimits_{i,j}\frac{\mathbf{c}_i^{(t-1)T}\mathbf{S}_{ij}\mathbf{c}_j^{(t-1)}}{2\left(\mathbf{c}_i^{(t-1)T}\mathbf{S}_{ij}\mathbf{c}_j^{(t-1)}\right)^{1/2}}. \end{aligned} \tag{12}$$

By applying Lemma 1, we have

$$\begin{aligned} &\left(\mathbf{c}_i^{(t)T}\mathbf{S}_{ij}\mathbf{c}_j^{(t)}\right)^{1/2} - \frac{\mathbf{c}_i^{(t)T}\mathbf{S}_{ij}\mathbf{c}_j^{(t)}}{2\left(\mathbf{c}_i^{(t-1)T}\mathbf{S}_{ij}\mathbf{c}_j^{(t-1)}\right)^{1/2}} \\ \leq &\left(\mathbf{c}_i^{(t-1)T}\mathbf{S}_{ij}\mathbf{c}_j^{(t-1)}\right)^{1/2} - \frac{\mathbf{c}_i^{(t-1)T}\mathbf{S}_{ij}\mathbf{c}_j^{(t-1)}}{2\left(\mathbf{c}_i^{(t-1)T}\mathbf{S}_{ij}\mathbf{c}_j^{(t-1)}\right)^{1/2}}. \end{aligned} \tag{13}$$

By summing Ineq. (13) over i and j, multiplying by λ, and adding it to Ineq. (12), we have

$$\begin{aligned} &\left\|\mathbf{x} - \sum_{i=1}^{G}\mathbf{D}_i\mathbf{c}_i^{(t)}\right\|_2^2 + \lambda\sum_{i=1,j=1}^{G}\left(\mathbf{c}^{(t)T}_i\mathbf{S}_{ij}\mathbf{c}_j^{(t)}\right)^{1/2} \\ \leq &\left\|\mathbf{x} - \sum_{i=1}^{G}\mathbf{D}_i\mathbf{c}_i^{(t-1)}\right\|_2^2 + \lambda\sum_{i=1,j=1}^{G}\left(\mathbf{c}^{(t-1)T}_i\mathbf{S}_{ij}\mathbf{c}_j^{(t-1)}\right)^{1/2}. \end{aligned} \tag{14}$$

Ineq. (14) shows that the updating rule in Eq. (9) decreases the value of the objective function in Eq. (5), denoted as $F(\mathbf{c}^{(t)}) \leq F(\mathbf{c}^{(t-1)})$. Since $F(\cdot)$ is bounded above zero, we can conclude that $F(\mathbf{c}^{(t)})$ converges to a limiting point F^* when $t \to \infty$. Moreover, note that $F(\cdot)$ is Lipschitz continuous, we can conclude that $\lim_{t\to\infty}\mathbf{c}^{(t)} = \mathbf{c}^*$. Further, it is easy to verify that when $\mathbf{c}^t = \mathbf{c}^{(t-1)} = \mathbf{c}^*$, Eq. (9) assures $\mathbf{c}^*$ is a stationary point of Eq. (6), hence it is also a stationary point of Eq. (5). Due to the convexity of Eq. (5), we conclude that $\mathbf{c}^*$ is a global minimum of Eq. (5). □

In practice, we use an efficient algorithm to avoid tackling the large-scale $\left(\mathbf{D}^T\mathbf{D} + \lambda\mathbf{S}^{(t-1)}\right)$. To this end, we exploit the symmetric positive definite nature of $\mathbf{S}^{(t-1)}$, using Cholesky decomposition $\mathbf{S}^{(t-1)} = (\mathbf{L}^{(t-1)})^T\mathbf{L}^{(t-1)}$. Here, $(\mathbf{L}^{(t-1)})^T$ is an upper triangular matrix with strictly positive diagonal entries, which is efficiently invertible. By denoting $\widehat{\mathbf{c}}^{(t)} = \mathbf{L}^{(t-1)}\mathbf{c}^{(t)}$, $\mathbf{D}^{(t-1)} = \mathbf{D}(\mathbf{L}^{(t-1)})^{-1}$, the new iterative updating rule is

$$\widehat{\mathbf{c}}^{(t)} = \left((\mathbf{D}^{(t-1)})^T\mathbf{D}^{(t-1)} + \lambda\mathbf{I}\right)^{-1}(\mathbf{D}^{(t-1)})^T\mathbf{x}. \tag{15}$$

Here, in order to inverse $\left((\mathbf{D}^{(t-1)})^T\mathbf{D}^{(t-1)} + \lambda\mathbf{I}\right)$, we can first apply eigen decomposition for $\mathbf{D}^{(t-1)}(\mathbf{D}^{(t-1)})^T$, and then inverse the matrix by only inversing the eigenvalue diagonal matrix. Suppose d is the feature dimension of a visual sample $\mathbf{x}$ and $d \ll N$, its complexity $\mathcal{O}(d^3)$ is much smaller than the former $\mathcal{O}(N^3)$. Note that the only overhead is the Cholesky decomposition for $\mathbf{S}^{(t-1)}$. Fortunately, due to the extreme sparse form of $\mathbf{S}^{(t-1)}$, this overhead is almost a very small constant.

6. EXPERIMENT

In this section, we systematically evaluate the effectiveness of our proposed HSVC approach on two classic multimedia tasks, namely visual annotation and content-based retrieval, as compared to several baselines and state-of-the-art visual coding methods over various multimedia datasets.

6.1 Experimental Settings

6.1.1 Data

In our experiments, three real-world visual datasets are utilized for evaluation. The first one is from ImageNet [6], which is one of the largest well-organized image datasets publicly-available. All images on ImageNets were collected from the Web and organized in accordance with the structure of WordNet hierarchy. Each concept in the hierarchy is depicted by hundreds to thousands of images. We used a subset of ImageNet with 1,000 concepts and 1.27 million images, which were used for ILSVRC 2012[1]. This dataset contains partial hierarchy of WordNet and some new nodes that are not in WordNet. In our evaluation, ImageNet is used for constructing semantic-enrich dictionary as depicted in Section 3. For each individual concept, its attached images are employed for learning concept-specific dictionary according to Eq. (3). The number of base features in each concept-specific dictionary is set to 10, and thus we have 10,000 base features in total in the aggregated dictionary.

To the end of evaluating the effectiveness of the proposed HSVC approach, we chose to perform two classic multimedia applications, namely visual annotation and content-based image/video retrieval, on one Flickr[2]-based image set **NUS-WIDE** and one YouTube[3]-based video set Columbia Consumer Video (**CCV**) database [14]. While the former one contains 269,648 images annotated with 81 concepts, the latter is comprised of 9,317 YouTube video clips associated

[1]http://www.image-net.org/challenges/LSVRC/2012/index
[2]http://www.flickr.com/
[3]http://www.youtube.com/

Table 1: Overall performance (mean Average Precision) of Classeme, PiCodes, DeCAF, Lasso, Group Lassoand HSVC for visual annotation on NUS-WIDE and CCV datasets.

Dataset \ Method	Classeme	PiCodes	DeCAF	Lasso	Group Lasso	HSVC
NUS-WIDE	24.09%	20.29%	36.04%	37.42%	38.01%	**40.15%**
CCV	47.60%	50.08%	61.02%	64.30%	65.62%	**67.32%**

to 20 categories. For annotation task, we follow the original setting of "train/test", i.e., "161,789/107,859" for NUS-WIDE and "4,659/4,658" for CCV. For retrieval task, we randomly selected 10% test samples from each concept as query examples to search the results in training samples.

For all three visual datasets, we adopted the 4,096-D DeCAF generic visual feature [8], which is the activations of the 6-th layer of a deep CNN trained in a fully supervised fashion on ImageNet. It has shown that this feature is very effective for multimedia tasks on various benchmark data sets. For each individual video sample in CCV dataset, we averaged visual features of all its keyframes to form a video-level representation. All features are ℓ_2-normalized.

For evaluation metrics, we chose commonly used mAP (mean Average Precision) over all concepts for visual annotation evaluation. For visual retrieval, we adopt Average Precision at top K retrieved results (AP@K), which is defined as

$$\text{AP@K} = \frac{1}{min(R, K)} \sum_{j=1}^{K} \frac{R_j}{j} \times I_j,$$

where R is the number of relevant visual samples within the dataset and R_j is the number of relevant visual samples among top j search results. I_j is set to 1 if the j-th visual sample is relevant, and 0 otherwise. We averaged AP@K over all queries to obtain mAP@K as overall evaluation metric, where $K \in \{1, 2, \ldots, 100\}$.

6.1.2 Comparison Methods

In order to illustrate the representative power of our proposed **HSVC** approach, we compared it to several state-of-the-art semantic coding methods, including

- **Classeme** [26], which uses the output of 2,659 image classifiers trained on images retrieved from Bing Image Search engine[4] according to 2,659 query concepts from LSCOM [20];
- **PiCodes** [2], which gathers 2048 binary codes by optimizing the classification processes of 2,659 classifiers on ImageNet;
- **DeCAF** [8], which utilizes the output of the 6-the layer in a CNN deep learning architecture learned from ImageNet.

To demonstrate the effects of different components (*e.g.*, semantic sparsity and semantic correlation) of HSVC, we further compared to two baselines, namely **Lasso** and **Group Lasso**. For both of the above coding baselines, we used the same semantic-enriched dictionary hierarchy as in HSVC. For **Lasso**, we did not consider any semantic sparsity constraint and semantic correlation among concepts. For **Group Lasso**, visual codes follow the same constraint as HSVC, but do not take semantic correlation into consideration.

For visual annotation task, we chose to train concept classifiers using SVM based on the generated codes of different comparison methods. In our implementation, liblinear[5] toolbox was used. For visual retrieval experiments, all the query samples and the gallery samples were represented using these comparison visual codes and then the retrieval was then performed by similarity search. In particular, we used ℓ_1-norm distance for Classeme, DeCAF and our proposed HSVC Hamming distance for PiCodes since its outputs are binary codes.

For all comparison methods, we tuned parameters, such as λ in HSVC, Lasso, Group Lasso and C in SVM, in the range of $\{10^{-6}, 10^{-4}, \ldots, 10^{6}\}$.

6.2 Experimental Results I: Visual Annotation

In this part, we report and analyze the experiments on visual annotation task. We compare HSVC to the other state-of-the-arts approaches and show the effects of the use of semantic properties. In particular, Table 1 shows overall performance (mAP) of all comparison approaches over all concepts in NUS-WIDE and CCV datasets. Figure 4 and Figure 5 reports detailed performance (AP) of individual concepts on NUS-WIDE and CCV, respectively.

From the results, we can observe that HSVC consistently achieves the best performance among all comparison coding algorithms. Specially, in NUS-WIDE, HSVC outperforms Classeme, PiCodes and DeCAF semantic features by around 16%, 20% and 4%, respectively; and in CCV, the improvements are about 20%, 17% and 6%, respectively. The underlying reasons are in two folds. First of all, the dictionary of HSVC are derived from existing knowledge base containing rich semantic and hierarchical information, thereby establishing a favourable foundation for effective visual representation of visual semantics. Second, our proposed HSVC fully explores semantic properties of visual codes, including semantic sparsity and semantic correlation. Such considerations are rarely reflected in all above semantic features. On the one hand, semantic sparsity of visual data is significant to visual coding since it deeply reveals the genuine patterns of visual world, i.e., within a visual object, only a small part of the entire semantic space is touched. On the other hand, semantic correlation captures intrinsic relationships (*e.g.*, co-occurrence) among concepts, which leads to exerting mutually reinforcing effects on the qualities of the resultant visual codes.

The comparison of the results of Lasso, Group Lasso and HSVC can further shed light on the effectiveness of semantic sparsity and semantic correlation. As seen, HSVC and Group Lasso always performs better than Lasso. Although Lasso applies ℓ_1-norm to induce feature-level sparsity, it can

[4]https://www.bing.com/images/

[5]http://www.csie.ntu.edu.tw/~cjlin/liblinear/

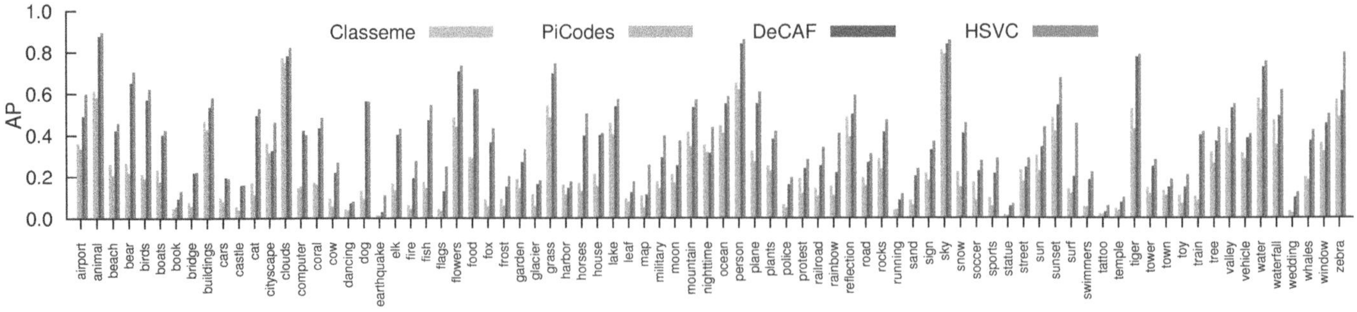

Figure 4: Detailed performance (Average Precision) of individual concepts of Classeme, PiCodes, DeCAF and HSVC on visual annotation over NUS-WIDE dataset.

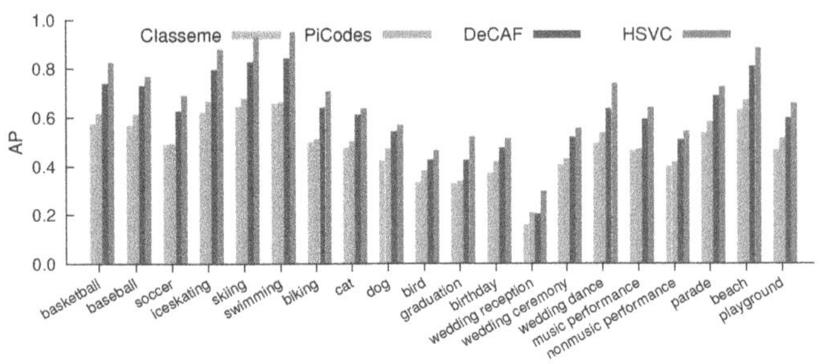

Figure 5: Detailed performance (Average Precision) of individual concepts of Classeme, PiCodes, DeCAF and HSVC on visual annotation over CCV dataset.

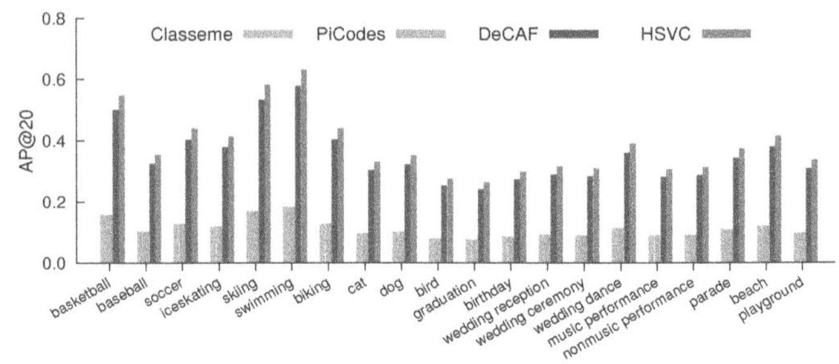

Figure 8: Detailed performance (mAP@20) of individual concepts of Classeme, PiCodes, DeCAF and HSVC for visual retrieval on CCV datasets.

easily propagate non-zero weights to irrelevant concepts, resulting in influencing semantic purity of visual codes. Moreover, HSVC consistently obtains superior visual annotation results than Group Lasso. A reasonable explanation is that HSVC takes semantic correlation into consideration and thus acquires more internal mutual promotion of code quality.

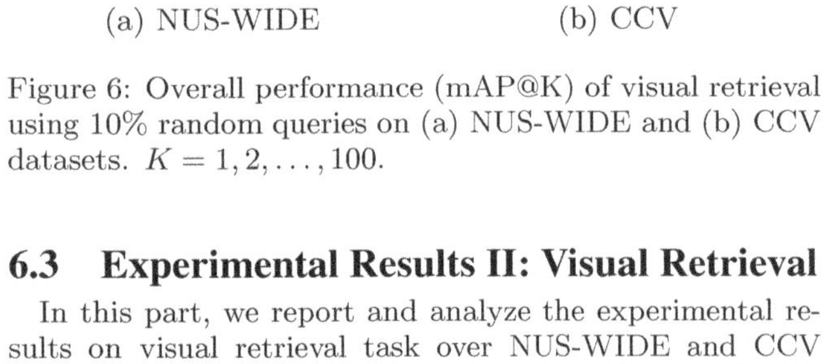

(a) NUS-WIDE (b) CCV

Figure 6: Overall performance (mAP@K) of visual retrieval using 10% random queries on (a) NUS-WIDE and (b) CCV datasets. $K = 1, 2, \ldots, 100$.

6.3 Experimental Results II: Visual Retrieval

In this part, we report and analyze the experimental results on visual retrieval task over NUS-WIDE and CCV datasets. As illustrated, Figure 6.(a) and 6.(b) give mAP@K ($K = 1, 2, \ldots, 100$) curves of all comparison approaches over all concepts in NUS-WIDE and CCV datasets, respectively. Figure 7 and Figure 8 report detailed performance (AP) of individual concepts on NUS-WIDE and CCV, respectively.

We can observe from the results that HSVC can achieve obvious improvements in terms of retrieval performance over all the other comparison methods on both of the evaluated datasets. For instance, on NUS-WIDE, HSVC improves the performance of Classeme, PiCodes and DeCAF by around 18%, 17% and 5% in terms of mAP@20; and on CCV, our method can perform better than Classeme, PiCodes and DeCAF in terms of mAP@20 by approximately 27%, 28% and 3%, respectively. The above phenomenons of performance boost can be reasonably attributed to the deep exploration of semantic aspects in our proposed approach. While the construction of semantic-enrich dictionary in the hierarchical fashion guarantees a reliable basis for generating effective visual codes, semantic sparsity and semantic correlation provides a better understanding of the essence of visual worlds. By naturally connecting visual and semantic worlds through the proposed semantic coding method, HSVC is able to retrieve more useful results for users.

6.4 Parameter Sensitivity

In this part, we empirically test the parameter sensitivity in our approach. Specifically, we evaluate the effects of λ on visual annotation and visual retrieval over the two evaluated datasets. We tune λ in the range of $\{10^{-6}, 10^{-4}, \ldots, 10^{4}, 10^{6}\}$. The experimental results are illustrated in Figure 9.(a) and 9.(b) for NUS-WIDE and CCV, respectively. As we can see, generally speaking, our approach is not obviously sensitive to different values of λ; nonetheless, we may still observe certain patterns of variation trends from the results. For instance, as shown in Figure 9.(a), when λ gradually grows from 10^{-6} to 10^{2}, we can see an increasing trend of the annotation performance for NUS-WIDE dataset; as λ keeps

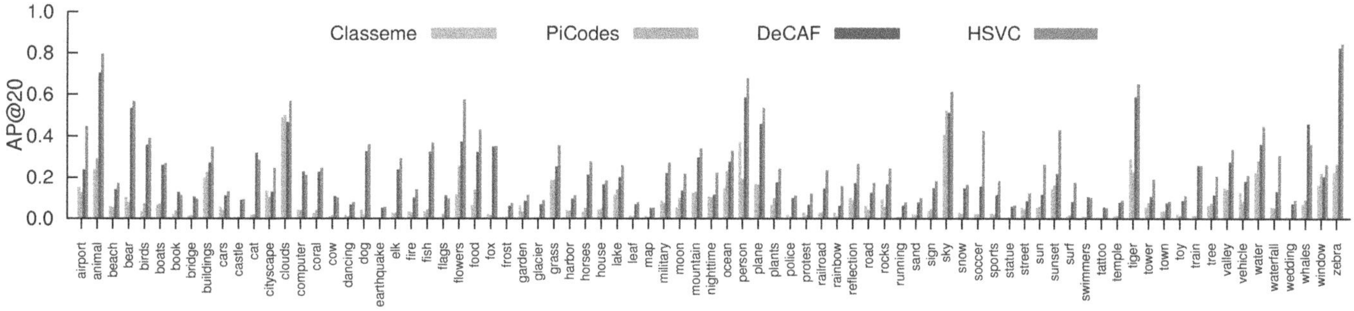

Figure 7: Detailed performance (mAP@20) of individual concepts of Classeme, PiCodes, DeCAF and HSVC for visual retrieval on NUS-WIDE datasets.

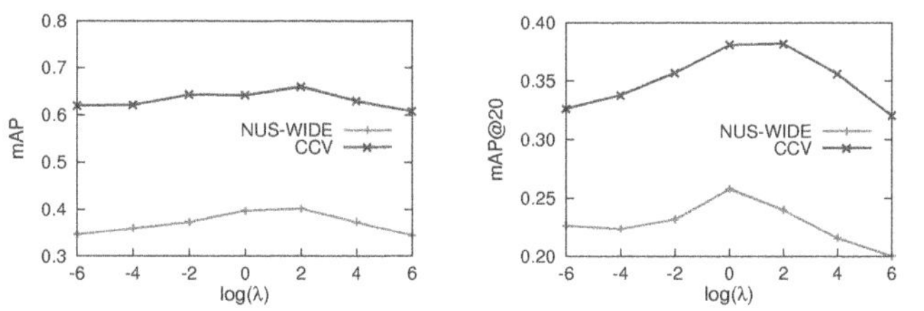

(a) Annotation (b) Retrieval

Figure 9: Evaluation of effects of λ on (a) visual annotation (mAP) and (b) visual retrieval (mAP@20) over NUS-WIDE and CCV datasets.

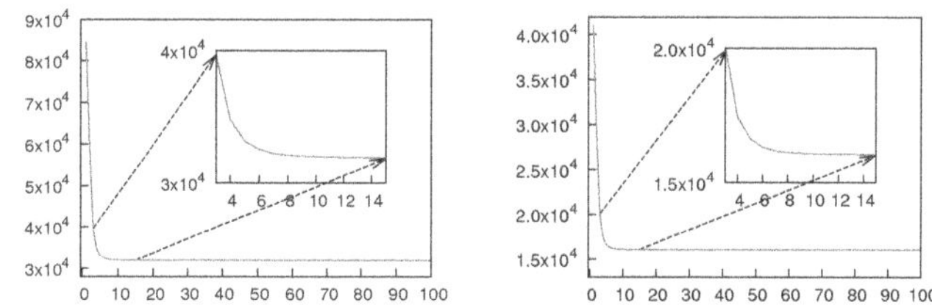

(a) NUS-WIDE (b) CCV

Figure 10: Convergence analysis on the two evaluated datasets: (a) NUS-WIDE and (b) CCV. For illustration, we fix $\lambda = 1$.

increasing to 10^6, the performance starts to drop. Such phenomenon hints us that neither large nor small value of λ can help to achieve the best performance. This is because when λ is too large, the effect of hierarchical semantic information in the dictionary may be suppressed; and small λ probably causes seldom reflection of semantic sparsity and semantic correlation in HSVC.

6.5 Convergence Analysis

As depicted in Section 5, the rigorous mathematical analysis guarantees that Algorithm 1 is able to converge to a global optimal solution as $t \to \infty$. In this part, we conduct empirical study on the convergence in both of the evaluated datasets. Figure 10 illustrate the results on the two datasets. Here, we fix the tradeoff parameter λ to 1. As we can see, in experiments, our algorithm can quickly converge within only a few iterations, which clearly shows its efficiency for practical use. We analyze that our designed iterative updating rule in Eq. (9) can almost always detect a fast "path" from initial point to the global optimal.

7. CONCLUSION

In this paper, we introduced a novel visual coding approach, termed as *hierarchical semantic visual coding* (HSVC), to effectively encode visual objects in a semantic hierarchy. Following the designed pipeline, we generated a semantic-enriched dictionary hierarchy, which contains dictionaries corresponding to all concepts in a semantic hierarchy as well as their hierarchical semantic information. We also developed an on-line semantic coding model, which jointly exploits the rich hierarchical semantic information in the learned dictionary as well as considers various semantic properties of visual objects, including semantic sparsity and semantic correlations among concepts in the semantic hierarchy. We proposed to combine concept-level sparsity constraint and semantic similarity into a unified regularization term. An effective algorithm was devised for solving the optimization problem in the proposed model, and a rigorous mathematical analysis has been provided to guarantee the algorithm converges to the global optima. Extensive experiments have been conducted to show the effectiveness of our approach.

Although HSVC has achieved superior performance as compared to several baselines and state-of-the-art methods, it still leaves the following open problem to be further handled. The representative power of the learned dictionary heavily relies on existing hand-crafted semantic hierarchy, which may not be suitable for constantly-evolving visual worlds. In the future, we will further investigate an automatic way for discovering representative concepts and building semantic dictionary from both the visual and textual data, such that visual semantics could be identified in a more precise manner.

8. REFERENCES

[1] S. Bengio, F. Pereira, Y. Singer, and D. Strelow. Group sparse coding. In *NIPS*, pages 82–89, 2009.

[2] A. Bergamo, L. Torresani, and A. W. Fitzgibbon. Picodes: Learning a compact code for novel-category recognition. In *NIPS*, pages 2088–2096, 2011.

[3] A. Binder, K.-R. Müller, and M. Kawanabe. On taxonomies for multi-class image categorization. *IJCV*, 99(3):281–301, 2012.

[4] J. Deng, A. C. Berg, and L. Fei-Fei. Hierarchical semantic indexing for large scale image retrieval. In *CVPR*, pages 785–792, 2011.

Figure 11: Illustration of retrieval examples using our proposed HSVC on NUS-WIDE and CCV. The top two lines are results of NUS-WIDE while the bottom two are from NUS-WIDE.

[5] J. Deng, A. C. Berg, K. Li, and L. Fei-Fei. What does classifying more than 10,000 image categories tell us? In *ECCV*, pages 71–84. 2010.

[6] J. Deng, W. Dong, R. Socher, L.-J. Li, K. Li, and L. Fei-Fei. Imagenet: A large-scale hierarchical image database. In *CVPR*, pages 248–255. IEEE, 2009.

[7] T. Deselaers and V. Ferrari. Visual and semantic similarity in imagenet. In *CVPR*, pages 1777–1784, 2011.

[8] J. Donahue, Y. Jia, O. Vinyals, J. Hoffman, N. Zhang, E. Tzeng, and T. Darrell. Decaf: A deep convolutional activation feature for generic visual recognition. *arXiv preprint arXiv:1310.1531*, 2013.

[9] C. Elkan. Using the triangle inequality to accelerate k-means. In *ICML*, volume 3, pages 147–153, 2003.

[10] C. Fellbaum. Wordnet. *Theory and Applications of Ontology: Computer Applications*, 2010.

[11] S. Gao, L.-T. Chia, and I. W. Tsang. Multi-layer group sparse coding – for concurrent image classification and annotation. In *CVPR*, pages 2809–2816, 2011.

[12] G. Griffin and P. Perona. Learning and using taxonomies for fast visual categorization. In *CVPR*, pages 1–8, 2008.

[13] J. Huang, H. Liu, J. Shen, and S. Yan. Towards efficient sparse coding for scalable image annotation. In *ACM Multimedia*, pages 947–956. ACM, 2013.

[14] Y.-G. Jiang, G. Ye, S.-F. Chang, D. Ellis, and A. C. Loui. Consumer video understanding: A benchmark database and an evaluation of human and machine performance. In *ICMR*, page 29, 2011.

[15] A. Krizhevsky, I. Sutskever, and G. E. Hinton. Imagenet classification with deep convolutional neural networks. In *NIPS*, pages 1097–1105, 2012.

[16] S. Lazebnik, C. Schmid, and J. Ponce. Beyond bags of features: Spatial pyramid matching for recognizing natural scene categories. In *CVPR*, volume 2, pages 2169–2178, 2006.

[17] H. Lee, A. Battle, R. Raina, and A. Y. Ng. Efficient sparse coding algorithms. In *NIPS*, pages 801–808, 2006.

[18] M. Marszałek and C. Schmid. Semantic hierarchies for visual object recognition. In *CVPR*, pages 1–7, 2007.

[19] L. Meier, S. Van De Geer, and P. Bühlmann. The group lasso for logistic regression. *JRSS-B*, 70(1):53–71, 2008.

[20] M. Naphade, J. R. Smith, J. Tesic, S.-F. Chang, W. Hsu, L. Kennedy, A. Hauptmann, and J. Curtis. Large-scale concept ontology for multimedia. *IEEE Multimedia*, 13(3):86–91, 2006.

[21] M. Rohrbach, M. Stark, G. Szarvas, I. Gurevych, and B. Schiele. What helps where–and why? semantic relatedness for knowledge transfer. In *CVPR*, pages 910–917, 2010.

[22] L. Shao, R. Yan, X. Li, and Y. Liu. From heuristic optimization to dictionary learning: A review and comprehensive comparison of image denoising algorithms. *TCYB*, 44(7):1001–1013, 2014.

[23] Y. Song, M. Zhao, J. Yagnik, and X. Wu. Taxonomic classification for web-based videos. In *CVPR*, pages 871–878, 2010.

[24] Y. Sun, X. Wang, and X. Tang. Deep convolutional network cascade for facial point detection. In *CVPR*, pages 3476–3483, 2013.

[25] J. Tang, L. Shao, and X. Li. Efficient dictionary learning for visual categorization. *CVIU*, 124:91–98, 2014.

[26] L. Torresani, M. Szummer, and A. Fitzgibbon. Efficient object category recognition using classemes. In *ECCV*, pages 776–789. 2010.

[27] N. Verma, D. Mahajan, S. Sellamanickam, and V. Nair. Learning hierarchical similarity metrics. In *CVPR*, pages 2280–2287, 2012.

[28] Y. Yang, Y. Yang, Z. Huang, H. T. Shen, and F. Nie. Tag localization with spatial correlations and joint group sparsity. In *CVPR*, pages 881–888, 2011.

[29] Y. Yang, Y. Yang, and H. T. Shen. Effective transfer tagging from image to video. *TOMM*, 9(2):14, 2013.

[30] Y. Yang, Z.-J. Zha, Y. Gao, X. Zhu, and T.-S. Chua. Exploiting web images for semantic video indexing via robust sample-specific loss. *TMM*, 16(6):1677–1689, 2014.

[31] M. Yuan and Y. Lin. Model selection and estimation in regression with grouped variables. *JRSS-B*, 68(1):49–67, 2006.

[32] H. Zhang, Z.-J. Zha, Y. Yang, S. Yan, Y. Gao, and T.-S. Chua. Attribute-augmented semantic hierarchy: towards bridging semantic gap and intention gap in image retrieval. In *ACM Multimedia*, pages 33–42, 2013.

[33] S. Zhang, J. Huang, H. Li, and D. N. Metaxas. Automatic image annotation and retrieval using group sparsity. *TCYB*, 42(3):838–849, 2012.

[34] M. Zheng, J. Bu, C. Chen, C. Wang, L. Zhang, G. Qiu, and D. Cai. Graph regularized sparse coding for image representation. *TIP*, 20(5):1327–1336, 2011.

Deep Compositional Cross-modal Learning to Rank via Local-Global Alignment

Xinyang Jiang, Fei Wu, Xi Li, Zhou Zhao, Weiming Lu, Siliang Tang, Yueting Zhuang
College of Computer Science and Techonology
Zhejiang University
{xinyangj, wufei, xilizju, zhaozhou, luwm, siliang, yzhuang}@zju.edu.cn

ABSTRACT

Cross-modal retrieval is a very hot research topic that is imperative to many applications involving multi-modal data. Discovering an appropriate representation for multi-modal data and learning a ranking function are essential to boost the cross-media retrieval. Motivated by the assumption that a compositional cross-modal semantic representation (pairs of images and text) is more attractive for cross-modal ranking, this paper exploits the existing image-text databases to optimize a ranking function for cross-modal retrieval, called *deep* compositional cross-modal learning to rank (C^2MLR). In this paper, C^2MLR considers learning a multi-modal embedding from the perspective of optimizing a pairwise ranking problem while enhancing both *local alignment* and *global alignment*. In particular, the local alignment (i.e., the alignment of visual objects and textual words) and the global alignment (i.e., the image-level and sentence-level alignment) are collaboratively utilized to learn the multi-modal embedding common space in a max-margin learning to rank manner. The experiments demonstrate the superiority of our proposed C^2MLR due to its nature of multi-modal compositional embedding.

Categories and Subject Descriptors

H.3.3 [**Information Search and Retrieval**]: Retrieval Models

Keywords

learning to rank; local-global alignment; compositional embedding

1. INTRODUCTION

This paper focuses on the learning to rank problem in information retrieval, which is to sort the retrieved documents according to their relevance to a given query. In the traditional information retrieval literature, queries and documents are typically from the same modality. However, the ranking in cross-media retrieval (e.g., *image-query-text* or *text-query-image*) according to the relevance of multi-modal data, which is imperative to many real-world applications (e.g., to find a set of most relevant images that visually best illustrates a given text description), is still a challenging task. This kind of tasks is called cross-modal learning to rank. In this paper, we propose to solve the cross-modal ranking problem for two specific modalities, i.e., the image modality and the text modality. Like all the cross-modal retrieval tasks, the ranking of multi-modal data faces great challenges, which requires appropriate understanding of the semantics in multi-modal data and accurate discovering of their complicated correlations based on their semantics. In general, the procedure of cross-modal ranking can be divided into three stages. First a common representation is learned for multi-modal data, and then the multi-modal relevance is evaluated by calculating their similarity in the learned common space, and finally a ranking function is devised to generate a ranking list and preserve the order of the relevance between multi-modal data.

In cross-modal learning to rank, there is a heterogeneity-gap between data from different modalities (images and text in this paper), so the learning of a common representation shared by data with different modalities plays an important role. In recent years, a great deal of research has been devoted to the development of algorithms for learning a optimal common representation for the data with different modalities. The learning of a multi-modal common representation can be mainly classified into two categories. One type of methods embeds images and text respectively into a common space where the correlation between a pair of highly relevant multi-modal data is minimized, such as canonical correlation analysis (CCA) [9] and multi-modal dictionary learning [28, 20, 31]. In this way, each pair of highly relevant multi-modal data is individually represented in this common space. The other type of methods embeds the pairs of images and text as one single feature vector in the common space (i.e., the joint representation of multi-modal data). For example, probabilistic models are often used to discover the latent structures (*topics*) of images and text, and generate their joint representation of pairs of image-text data in terms of topics (i.e., the bag-of-topics), such as the correspondence Latent Dirichlet Allocation (corr-LDA) [2] and dual-wing harmoniums (DWH) [27].

In this paper, we focus on using learning to rank framework to learn the common space for multi-modal data. Learning to rank [3, 23, 22] attempts to train a ranking-based loss function (evaluation criterion) to preserve the orders of

MM'15, October 26–30, 2015, Brisbane, Australia.
© 2015 ACM. ISBN 978-1-4503-3459-4/15/10 ...$15.00.
DOI: http://dx.doi.org/10.1145/2733373.2806240.

the retrieved documents according to a given query (e.g., relevant documents should have higher ranking scores than irrelevant ones). Many approaches [8, 1, 17, 25, 30] have been proposed to learn the common space of multi-modal data from the perspective of solving an optimized ranking function.

Motivated by the fact that the existing pairs of image-text data can be employed to boost the learning of the common space of multi-modal data, this paper focuses on learning multi-modal common space specifically for images and text. Given a pair of semantically relevant image and text (e.g., the image and the describing sentence "a black dog is running with two sheep in a grassy field" in Figure 1), the compositional semantics in the image and text data is collaboratively grounded. That is to say, the semantics of the text is visually-grounded by its illustrated image, and meanwhile the semantics of the image is literally grounded by its describing text. Moreover, the visually-literally grounded semantics are further highlighted both in local structure (i.e., visual objects in images and textual entities in texts) and global structure (i.e, image-level semantics and sentence-level semantics). As a result, it is more attractive to exploit the local structure and global structure in pairs of images and text to learn a better common space for multi-modal data. Therefore, this paper proposes that two type of common spaces can be learned to embed the collaboratively grounded semantics in local structure and global structure respectively.

In particular, the semantics of visual objects and the textual words in local structure is embedded into a local common space, where the visual objects and their relevant textual words are aligned with each other. We refer this kind of embedding as the local alignment. For example, in Figure 1, the textual word "dog " in the sentence and the bounding-box region of a dog in the image are aligned with each other in the local common space. Similarly, the global alignment embeds the image-level and text-level compositional semantics into a global common space, where each image and its relevant text are aligned with each other. For example, in Figure 1, since the image and the sentence saying "a black dog is running with two sheep in a grassy field" are relevant, their embeddings are near each other in the global common space. In conclusion, we propose that the common space for multi-modal data is learned in two ways, i.e., local alignment and global alignment.

Obviously, most of the traditional approaches to learning a common space for multi-modal data are conducted in a global alignment manner. For example, Deep visual-semantic embedding (DeViSE) [7] directly learns a common space of images (encoded by the convolutional neural network) and their labels (encoded by the skip-gram model) and disregards the local alignment of multi-modal data (i.e., the alignment of visual objects and textual words). Recently, Deep Fragment Alignments(DeepFE) [13] is proposed to use local alignment to embed the visual objects in images (encoded by the region-based convolutional neural network [7]) and the phrases in sentences into a common space. In general, DeepFE learns the common space of multi-modal data in terms of local alignment but does not fully consider the compositional semantics in multi-modal data. Furthermore, for cross-modal learning to rank, most of the proposed methods such as Passive-Aggressive Model for Image Retrieval (PAMIR) [8] and Supervised Semantic Indexing (SSI) [1] use global alignment to learn the common space so that text-image relevance is measured based on their global structure.

In this paper, we propose a deep compositional cross-modal learning to rank (C^2MLR) model that aims to model the intrinsic local-global structural properties of images and text to boost the learning of a common space for multi-modal data. C^2MLR not only constructs a local common space for visual objects and textual words via the local alignment, but also learns a global common space for the compositional semantics in image and text via global alignment. Furthermore, C^2MLR generates the compositional semantics embeddings of an image and text from the isolated semantics embeddings of visual objects in the image and textual words in the text, so the learned global common space by C^2MLR preserves not only the relevance between an image and text, but also the relevance between visual objects and textual words. After obtaining common representations of images and text in both local and global common space, C^2MLR predicts the ranking list by evaluating the relevance between an image and text based on both local and global alignment. The algorithm framework (both training and prediction) of C^2MLR is shown in Figure 1.

In order to effectively perform both local alignment and global alignment, a max-margin learning to rank framework is devised in C^2MLR. As shown in Figure 1, in the training process, C^2MLR can be seen as a two-level network. Compared to traditional networks, C^2MLR trains the model parameters by back propagating (BP) the ranking loss in three ways. C^2MLR not only back propagates the ranking loss from higher level (global common space) to the lower level (local common space) to update the parameters in both levels like traditional networks, but also propagates the ranking loss into both levels directly to update the parameters in each level respectively.

The rest of the paper is organized as follows. In section 2, we describe the previous work relating to our method. In section 3, we describe our proposed C^2MLR in detail. In section 4, we compare C^2MLR with other cross-modal ranking approaches. The section 5 concludes this paper.

2. RELATED WORK

Much research has been conducted to learn the common space of multi-modal data via the global alignment [26, 29, 28, 20, 24]. For example, CCA finds the linear projection that maximally preserve the mutual correlations among multi-modal data, so data from different modalities are mapped into the same space. Rather than a linear projection via Pearson coefficient, lots of methods like DeViSE [7] and Correspondence Autoencoder [6] have been proposed to use a nonlinear projection of the images and text[18, 12, 5]. Motivated by the fact that the dictionary learning (DL) methods have the intrinsic power of dealing with the heterogeneous features by generating different dictionaries for multi-modal data, some research [28, 20, 31] proposes to find a representation for multi-modal data by jointly learning multi-modal dictionaries.

Several probabilistic approaches also achieve a considerable progress in learning multi-modal representation by global alignment. Since Latent Dirichlet Allocation (LDA) uses a hierarchical Bayesian probability model to discover the latent structures (i.e.,*topics*) of documents and can provide a low-dimensional embedding representation of documents in

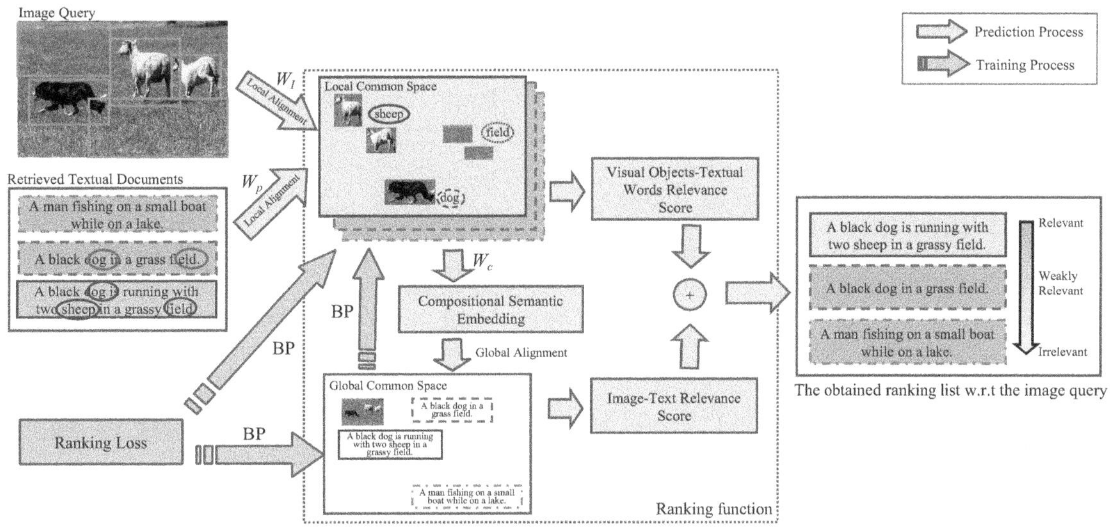

Figure 1: An illustration of the deep compositional multi-modal learning to rank via local-global alignments in C^{2}MLR (both training and prediction). An example of image ranking text is given. Given one query image and the retrieved text, the local alignment is first employed to map visual objects in the query image and the textual entities (i.e., noun words) in retrieved text into a *local common space* by W_p and W_I respectively, so that each visual object is aligned to its most relevant textual entity. After generating the compositional semantics embeddings of the query image and the retrieved text by W_c, the global alignment is then conducted by mapping the query image and the retrieved text into a *global common space*, so that the query image is aligned with its relevant description text. The ranking function parameterized by W_p, W_I and W_c obtains the ranked text w.r.t the query image by evaluating the relevance between image and text in both local and global common space. For the training process, C^{2}MLR not only back propagates (BP) the ranking loss from higher level (global common space) to the lower level (local common space) like traditional networks, but also propagates the loss into both levels directly.

terms of topics, LDA has been extended to learn the joint distribution of multi-modal data (e.g., text and image) such as the Corr-LDA and Multi-modal mutual topic reinforce model (M^{3}R)[24]. In order to simplify the inference process, DWH and Deep Boltzmann Machines [21] assume the conditional independence among the hidden topics and use an undirected graph to model the relationship among the variables.

As to the local alignment, several works have achieved great advance in bilingual language translation [32, 14], which learns the common space for the bilingual words, so that the bilingual words with the same meanings are aligned to each other. Deep Fragment Alignments (DeepFE) is proposed in [13] to learn the common space of multi-modal data in a deep learning manner. In DeepFE, the region-based convolutional neural network [7]) is used to encode visual objects in images and the dependency triplets are used to encode entities as well as their attributes or interactions in sentences. Then the fragment alignment is utilized in DeepFE to learn the multi-modal common space.

In order to perform cross-modal ranking, one appealing way is to directly learn a ranking function in terms of a ranking-based loss function (evaluation criterion) so as to preserve the orders of the relevance instead of the purely absolute values of similarity (dis-similarity) between multi-modal data. Some approaches have been proposed to jointly learn the common space of multi-modal data and the ranking function at the same time [8, 1, 17, 25, 30]. A discriminative method PAMIR is proposed to solve the problem of cross-modal ranking by adopting the Passive-Aggressive algorithm in a "pair-wise ranking" manner. However, the ranking performance of PAMIR is limited by the distribution of the pairs of items and the skewed data may deteriorate the ranking result. Rather than learning a mapping from the query space to the document space in PAMIR, Supervised Semantic Indexing [1] discovers a common space for queries and documents, and embeds the multi-modal data in this low-dimensional latent space for the cross-lingual retrieval. Bi-directional cross-media ranking is employed in [17, 25] to learn the embedding of multi-modal data by optimizing a list-wise ranking problem. DeepRank [16] proposes to use neural network as a non-linear mapping for the multi-modal data, which is proved to be more effective than a mere linear projection.

3. THE ALGORITHM

3.1 Local alignment for objects and words

C^{2}MLR uses the local alignment to map visual objects in images and textual words in text into a local common space, where the relevant objects and words are near each other.

Given a feature vector $\mathbf{r}$ extracted from an object region, the visual object inside the object region is mapped into a local common space by a non-linear projection as follows:

$$v_1(\mathbf{r}) = f(W_I\mathbf{r} + \mathbf{b}_I) \tag{1}$$

where $\mathbf{r}$ is a d_r-dimensional feature vector, W_I is a $d \times d_r$ matrix that maps the visual object into a d-dimensional local common space via local alignment, $\mathbf{b}_I$ are the biases. In the experiments, the region-based convolutional neural network

(R-CNN) [7]) pre-trained on Image-Net [15] is used to detect object regions and extract their **r**-dimensional features respectively.

As to the local alignment for textual words, C^{2}MLR proposes to align textual words in text in different ways. For example, some words (i.e., nouns) explicitly denote visual objects (e.g., a person or a car) in images and some words (i.e., verbs or adjectives) describe the attributes or states of an visual object (e.g., the appearance or action of one visual object) in images. For a given particular grammatical class p of words (e.g., the part of speech), we will learn a mapping matrix to embed all of words belonging to this grammatical class p into the local common space as follows:

$$h_1(\mathbf{w}) = f(W_p\mathbf{w} + \mathbf{b}_p) \tag{2}$$

where W_p is a $d \times d_w$ matrix that maps each d_w-dimensional vector $\mathbf{w}$ into a d-dimensional vector, $\mathbf{b}_p$ are biases. In practice, the d_w-dimensional vector $\mathbf{w}$ is obtained by Word2Vec [19] or one-hot representation according to their specific applications. Note that different parts-of-speech p can have their own set of weights W_p, and in our experiments we only learn two sets of weights: one is for nouns (to identify visual objects), another is for adjectives and verbs (to describe attributes and states of visual objects).

After the visual objects and textual words are mapped into a local common space by W_I and W_p with local alignment respectively, given a pair of image containing a set of objects I and text containing a set of words S, the relevance score between I and S in terms of their local structure is obtained by: 1) aligning each visual object $\mathbf{r}$ in I with the textual word $\mathbf{w}$ whose semantic embedding has the highest cosine similarity with $\mathbf{r}$, and 2) summing up the cosine similarity of all the aligned visual objects and textual words as the overall relevance score between the image I and the text S:

$$s_1(S, I) = \sum_{\mathbf{w} \in S} \max_{\mathbf{r} \in I} h_1(\mathbf{w})^T v_1(\mathbf{r}) \tag{3}$$

Later we will introduce the optimization of parameters W_I, $\mathbf{b}_I$, W_p and $\mathbf{b}_p$ respectively in a learning to rank framework.

3.2 Global alignment for image and text

C^{2}MLR uses the global alignment to embed the compositional semantics of images and text into a global common space. The compositional semantics of the image I is encoded by a *compositional semantics embedding* matrix W_c as follows:

$$v_2(I) = f(\frac{1}{|I|} \sum_{\mathbf{r} \in I} W_c v_1(\mathbf{r})) \tag{4}$$

where W_c is a $d_c \times d$ matrix that maps the image I into a d_c-dimensional global common space, and the operator $|\cdot|$ is the cardinality of a set. Note that C^{2}MLR models the compositional semantics of an image as a nonlinear composition of all the visual objects inside this image.

Similarly, the compositional semantics of S is encoded as follows:

$$h_2(S) = f(\frac{1}{|S|} \sum_{\mathbf{w} \in S} W_c h_1(\mathbf{w})) \tag{5}$$

As a result, the relevance score between image I and text S in the global common space is obtained by computing the cosine similarity between their compositional semantic embeddings:

$$s_2(S, I) = h_2(S)^T v_2(I) \tag{6}$$

Later we will introduce the optimization of parameter W_c in a learning to rank framework.

Algorithm 1 Ranking list prediction in C^{2}MLR

Input: the given query S; the retrieved documents set $\mathcal{I}$; tradeoff parameter $\alpha > 0$
Output: ranking list Y
  for $\mathbf{w} \in S$ **do**
    Using local alignment to obtain $h_1(\mathbf{w})$ with Eq. (2)
  end for
  Using global alignment to obtain $h_2(S)$ with Eq. (5)
  for $i = 1$ **to** $|\mathcal{I}|$ **do**
    for $\mathbf{r} \in I_i$ **do**
      Using local alignment to obtain $v_1(\mathbf{r})$ with Eq. (1)
    end for
    Using global alignment to obtain $v_2(I_i)$ with Eq. (4)
    Obtain relevance score $s_1(S, I_i)$ with Eq. (3)
    Obtain relevance score $s_2(S, I_i)$ with Eq. (6)
    Obtain total relevance score $s(S, I_i)$ with Eq. (9)
  end for
  Obtain Y by sorting the documents based on the relevance scores.
  return Y

3.3 Image-Text Learning to Rank

In this section, we introduce the image-text ranking function in C^{2}MLR that generates the rank list given a query. There are two search directions in image-text ranking, i.e., *image-query-text* and *text-query-image*. Here we use text-query-image as an example.

Given a textual query S from the textual query set $\mathcal{S}$, our method aims at sorting a set of retrieved images $\mathcal{I} = \{I_i\}_{i=1}^{|\mathcal{I}|}$, to generate a ranking list, denoted as R, where R is a set of relations over $\mathcal{I} \times \mathcal{I}$, and if I_i ranked higher w.r.t S than I_j, then $(I_i, I_j) \in R$.

Given the textual query S, a ranking function g is learned to predict a ranking list for the retrieved images:

$$R = g(S, \mathcal{I}) \tag{7}$$

To efficiently optimize the ranking function $g(\cdot)$ and well generalized $g(\cdot)$ beyond the training data, C^{2}MLR devises a multi-modal ranking function $g(\cdot)$ as follows:

$$(I_i, I_j) \in g(S, \mathcal{I}) \Leftrightarrow s(S, I_i) > s(S, I_j) \tag{8}$$

where, $s(\cdot)$ is the relevance score between the textual query and the retrieved images.

As mentioned before, due to the nature that compositional semantics of multi-modal data is visually-literally grounded in terms of the local structure and the global structure, the relevance induced by the local alignment and the global alignment are combined to obtain the overall relevance between a textual query S and an image document I as follows:

$$s(S, I) = \alpha s_1(S, I) + (1 - \alpha) s_2(S, I) \tag{9}$$

where α is a hand-tuned tradeoff parameter to reflect the different impacts of two relevance scores upon the overall relevance between a pair of image and text, which is determined by cross-validation and is set to 0.7 in our experiments.

Given a new textual query, ranking function f predicts the ranking list by sorting the retrieved images based on the relevance score s in a descending order. The higher the score is, the more ahead the retrieved image is in the ranking list. Algorithm 1 shows the whole procedure of the proposed C^{2}MLR to predict a ranking list given a query S and a set of retrieved images $\mathcal{I}$. For each pair of image and text, the computation complexity of global and local alignment is $O(|S||I|)$, which is the same as the recent state-of-art algorithms (e.g. DeepFE). The running time of algorithm 1 is 8.4 ms for each query on a PC with an Intel i5 CPU. The running time can be further largely improved by parallelization.

3.4 Parameter Estimation

Two sets of parameters will be learned in ranking function g, namely W_I, $\mathbf{b}_I$, W_p and $\mathbf{b}_p$ in *local alignment*, as well as W_c in *global alignment*. In this section, we introduce the learning of these parameters in a max-margin learning to rank framework.

For the learning of a *text-query-image* ranking function, there is a collection of training samples denoted as $\mathcal{T} = \{(S^{(k)}, Y^{(k)}, \mathcal{I}^{(k)}) : k = 1, ..., N\}$, where $Y \in \mathcal{Y}$ such that $\mathcal{Y} \subset \{-1, 0, +1\}^{|\mathcal{I}|\times|\mathcal{I}|}$. For each $Y^{(k)} \in \mathcal{Y}$, each element $Y_{ij}^{(k)}$ in $Y^{(k)}$ indicates a pairwise ranking score for documents $I_i \in \mathcal{D}$ and $I_j \in \mathcal{D}$ w.r.t the query $S^{(k)}$. Namely, $Y_{ij}^{(k)} = +1$ leads to the fact that I_i is ranked ahead of I_j given the query $S^{(k)}$; $Y_{ij} = 0$ leads to the fact that I_i and I_j have an equal ranking score; otherwise, $Y_{ij} = -1$.

According to Eq. (8), for each textual query, the documents ranked in a higher position should have higher relevance score than the documents ranked in a lower position. As a result, given a textual query $S^{(k)}$, each pair of image documents (I_i, I_j) should fulfill following inequality:

$$Y_{ij}^{(k)}(s(S^{(k)}, I_i) - s(S^{(k)}, I_j)) > 0 \tag{10}$$

Following the idea in support vector machine [4], we turn the inequalities above into a ranking SVM problem by introducing slack variables $\xi_{i,j,k}$ in the objective, and it leads to following optimization problem:

$$\min_W \frac{\lambda}{2}||W||^2 + C\sum_{i,j,k} \xi_{i,j,k}, \tag{11}$$

subject to:

$$\begin{aligned} \forall i, j, k : & Y_{ij}(s(S^{(k)}, I_i) - s(S^{(k)}, I_i)) > 1 + \xi_{i,j,k} \\ & \xi_{i,j,k} \geq 0 \end{aligned} \tag{12}$$

where W denotes two sets of model parameters for both local alignment and global alignment.

Given the above optimization problem, we propose to solve it with a stochastic gradient descent algorithm. First, the above optimization problem is equivalently converted to the following unconstrained problem:

$$\min_W \frac{\lambda}{2}||W||^2 + \sum_{k=1}^{N}\sum_{ij} L(S^{(k)}, \mathcal{I}^{(k)}, Y^{(k)}, i, j) \tag{13}$$

where,

$$L = \max(0, Y_{ij}(s(S^{(k)}, I_i^{(k)}) - s(S^{(k)}, I_j^{(k)}) + \Delta)) \tag{14}$$

Then, the gradients of the above cost function are computed by back propagation. Finally the model parameters are updated iteratively until convergence. In each iteration, we sample a small batch of training data, and uses the gradient to update the parameters. Algorithm 2 describes the parameter estimation procedure.

Next, we introduce the way to obtain the gradients for optimization. Here we present the computation of derivatives of the cost function L w.r.t. W_I when its value is greater than 0 as an example. The derivatives with respect to the other two sets of parameters W_p and W_c can be computed in the similar way. Note that the biases $\mathbf{b}_I$ and $\mathbf{b}_p$ can be seen as extra columns of W_I and W_p by adding one extra dimension valued 1 in the input features. The derivatives of L w.r.t. W_I is computed as follows:

$$\begin{aligned} \frac{\partial L}{\partial W_I} = & Y_{ij}(\frac{\partial s_1(S, I_i)}{\partial W_I} + \frac{\partial s_2(S, I_i)}{\partial W_I} \\ & - \frac{\partial s_1(S, I_j)}{\partial W_I} - \frac{\partial s_2(S, I_j)}{\partial W_I}) \end{aligned} \tag{15}$$

From the derivatives above, we can see that the cost function value is back propagated into two types of derivatives, namely $\frac{\partial s_1(S,I)}{\partial W_I}$ and $\frac{\partial s_2(S,I)}{\partial W_I}$. As $s_1(S, I)$ contains a maximization function (i.e., Eq. (3)), a sub-gradient is used to obtain $\frac{\partial s_1(S,I)}{\partial W_I}$ as follows:

$$\frac{\partial s_1(S, I)}{\partial W_I} = \sum_{\mathbf{w}\in S}(h_1(\mathbf{w}) \odot f'(W_I\mathbf{r}' + \mathbf{b}_I))(\mathbf{r}')^T \tag{16}$$

where $\odot$ denotes the element-wise multiplication, $f'(\cdot)$ denotes the derivatives of $f(\cdot)$ w.r.t its input, and $\mathbf{r}'$ is obtained by using the model parameters from the previous iteration as follows:

$$\mathbf{r}' = \arg\max_{\mathbf{r}\in I} h_1(\mathbf{w})^T v_1(\mathbf{r}) \tag{17}$$

$\frac{\partial s_2(S,I)}{\partial W_I}$ is computed as follows:

$$\begin{aligned} \frac{\partial s_2(S, I)}{\partial W_I} = & \sum_{\mathbf{r}\in I} W_c^T(h_2(S) \odot f'(\sum_{\mathbf{r}\in I} W_c v_1(\mathbf{r}))) \\ & \odot f'(W_I\mathbf{r} + \mathbf{b}_I)\mathbf{r}^T \end{aligned} \tag{18}$$

Algorithm 2 Parameter Estimation in C^{2}MLR

Input: the given ranking examples $\mathcal{T}$; the retrieved images set $\mathcal{I}$; tradeoff control parameter $\lambda > 0$, $\alpha > 0$; Mini-batch size M;
Output: parameters W
```
repeat
  Select a mini-batch with M training samples
  for k = 1 to M do
    for I_i, I_j in |I^(k)| do
      computing the derivatives of L w.r.t. W
    end for
  end for
  Sum up the derivatives of L and add the derivatives of
  the regularization term
  Estimate the step size with a line search algorithm
  Update W with the new gradients
until convergence
return W
```

---

4. EXPERIMENTS

4.1 Experimental Setup

4.1.1 Datasets Configuration

We evaluate the cross-modal ranking performance on two benchmark datasets, namely Pascal VOC'07 (Pascal07) [11] and Flickr8K [10].

Pascal07 is a benchmark dataset commonly used for evaluating multi-modal information retrieval. There are 10,000 images labeled with 804 tags from 20 different categories. We remove those images without tags and obtain 9587 images for the experiments. For the comparing approaches in terms of image-level and sentence-level alignment (i.e., global alignment), each image is represented as a 4096-dimensional feature vector extracted by convolutional neural network and the corresponding text description is represented as a 804-dimensional vector (each dimension indicates if a tag appears or not). For the comparing approaches in terms of visual objects and textual words alignment (i.e, local alignment), we use R-CNN to detect the object regions and extract CNN features for each object region, and each tag is represented as a *one-hot* vector. The network trained on ImageNet is used, and the 4096-dimensional features extracted by the full-connected layer before the classification layer is kept as the object features. For each image, top 20 objects with the highest detection scores are kept to train our model. In order to generate a ranking list for each query as the ground truth, we define the relevant documents of a query as the documents that belong to at least one category with the query.

There are 8000 images in Flickr8k and each image in Flickr8k has 5 related sentences that describe the semantics in this image. Therefore, for each ranking list of a image query, there are 5 relevant textual documents. For the comparing approaches that use global alignment, we represent the images and description text in the same way as in Pascal07. For the comparing approaches that use local alignment, each word in the sentences is represented as a word vector.

For Pascal07, 2000 images and the associated tags are randomly selected as the training set, and both the testing set and the validation set are randomly selected with 2000 images and tags. For Flickr8K, we randomly use 6000 images and their corresponding sentences for training, 1000 for validation and the rest for testing. For every training sample, 150 documents are selected to generate the ranking list for the query.

4.1.2 Datasets Comparison

Pascal07 and Flickr8k have their own characteristics. Figure 2 shows some examples of the two datasets. As shown in Figure 2, compared to Flickr8k, the alignments between annotated tags and the visual objects in Pascal07 is more intuitive, since some of annotated tags in Pascal07 likely express high-level concepts instead of directly describing the specific visual objects in images, such as "nature" and "Christmas". On the contrary, in Flick8k, most of the words (especially nouns, adjectives and verbs) in each sentence describe specific visual objects as well as their attributes and interactions in the image, such as "cars","race" and "three". Since the visual semantics and literal semantics are collaboratively grounded in a finer level (via local alignment) and a compositional level (via global alignment) to a certain extent, the appropriate adoption of local alignment and global alignment can naturally boost the learning of multi-modal common space.

(a) Pairs of image-text examples in Pascal07

(b) Pairs of Image-text examples in Flickr8k

Figure 2: The pairs of image-text examples in Pascal07 and Flickr8k. Compared to Flickr8k, the alignments between annotated tags and the visual objects in Pascal07 is more intuitive.

4.1.3 Performance Metrics

We use Mean Average Precision (MAP) as the performance evaluation. Given the true ranking list Y and the predicted ranking list $\bar{Y}$, let $p = score(Y)$ and $\bar{p} = score(Y)$, where $score(\cdot)$ return the relevance scores for all retrieved documents, the Average Precision is defined as

$$AP(p, \bar{p}) = \frac{1}{rel} \sum_{j=1}^{R} Prec(j) Rel(j) \qquad (19)$$

where, L is the number of the relevant retrieved documents, $Prec(\cdot)$ is the percentage of the relevant documents in the top j documents in the predicted ranking, $Rel(\cdot)$ is the indicator function equaling to 1 if the document at rank j is relevant, and R is the number of retrieved documents to be examined in the ranking list. In our experiments, we report the MAP performance when $R = 5$ and $R = 10$ as well as when the value of R is the number of all the retrieved documents, denoted as MAP@5, MAP@10 and MAP@all respectively.

4.2 Performance Comparison

Following four approaches are used as the the comparison in our experiments:

- **PAMIR**[8]: PAMIR is a state-of-art cross-media ranking method using global alignment to learn the image-text common space in a pairwise ranking manner. A linear projection is used to embed images and texts into a global common space in our experiments.
- **DeepRank**[16]: DeepRank is a state-of art cross-media ranking method that also uses global alignment to learn the image-text common space, and it uses a non-linear projection (neural network) to embed images and text into a global common space.
- **DeepFE**[13]: To demonstrate the advantage of utilizing both local and global alignment, we also compare our method with DeepFE which is a state-of-art retrieval method only using local alignment. In fact,

Table 1: The ranking performance comparison in terms of MAP over Pascal07. The performances of *text-query-image* and *image-query-text* are given respectively. The results shown in boldface are the best. Note that C^{2}MLR can be seen as a generalized version of DeepFE and C^{2}MLR-.

	Image Query Text			Text Query Image		
	MAP@5	MAP@10	MAP@all	MAP@5	MAP@10	MAP@all
PAMIR	0.6685	0.6574	0.4791	0.6122	0.6000	0.4261
DeepRank	0.6666	0.6405	0.4061	0.6454	0.6276	**0.4661**
DeepFE	0.5721	0.5675	0.4889	0.7337	0.6809	0.4113
C^{2}MLR-	0.5709	0.5762	0.4928	0.7869	0.7722	0.4326
C^{2}MLR	**0.6963**	**0.6868**	**0.5384**	**0.8027**	**0.7745**	0.4339

Table 2: The ranking performance comparison in terms of MAP over Flickr8K. The performances of *text-query-image* and *image-query-text* are given respectively. The results shown in boldface are the best. Note that C^{2}MLR can be seen as a generalized version of DeepFE and C^{2}MLR-.

	Image Query Text			Text Query Image		
	MAP@5	MAP@10	MAP@all	MAP@5	MAP@10	MAP@all
PAMIR	0.0691	0.0752	0.0445	0.0692	0.0787	0.0951
DeepRank	0.0919	0.0990	0.0602	0.1012	0.1136	0.1297
DeepFE	0.1601	0.1657	0.0963	0.1269	0.1408	0.1583
C^{2}MLR-	0.1496	0.0953	0.0597	0.0896	0.1308	0.1496
C^{2}MLR	**0.1647**	**0.1687**	**0.0992**	**0.1343**	**0.1448**	**0.1665**

DeepFE can be seen as a simplified version of C^{2}MLR by setting α to 1 .

- **C^{2}MLR-**: This method is another simplified version of C^{2}MLR, which only uses the global alignment to learn the common space of image-text data and discards the local alignment. That is to say, α in Eq. (9) is set to 0. Different from PAMIR and DeepRank, C^{2}MLR- represents the images and text by compositional semantics embeddings (via the nonlinear composition of all visual objects in each image or all textual words in each text).

Table 1 shows the performance of cross-modal ranking in terms of MAP over Pascal07 Dataset. Following conclusions are made based the observation of the performance comparison over Pascal07:

- Our proposed method (C^{2}MLR) outperforms the other methods on both search directions in terms of most of the performance metrics.
- We observe that those methods merely utilizing local alignment achieve a poor performance over Pascal07. For example, DeepFE achieves the lowest performance in terms of MAP@5 and MAP@10 on image-query-text direction, and achieves the lowest performance in terms of MAP@all on text-query image direction. This observation verifies that many annotated tags of images in Pascal07 dataset do not explicitly align with visual objects in images, so using global alignment to discover compositional grounded semantics in images and annotated tags is more effective. As a result, the ranking approaches merely adopting the global alignment (i.e., PAMIR and DeepRank) achieve better performance on this dataset than those merely adopting local alignment like DeepFE .
- PAMIR achieves the second best performance on image-query-text direction because PAMIR maps the images into the textual space and the high-level semantics delivered by the textual space is reasonable enough on Pascal07 to achieve good performance on ranking text.

Table 2 shows the performance of cross-modal ranking in terms of MAP over Flickr8k Dataset. We can observe from the given results:

- C^{2}MLR outperforms the other methods on both search direction in terms of all the performance metrics.
- We observe that the ranking methods adopting local alignment achieve good performance over Flickr8k. For example, DeepFE achieves the second best performance in terms of all the performance measure on both query directions. This is because that most images and their description sentences on Flickr8k have a explicit alignments between visual objects and textual words. Therefore, the ranking algorithm that adopting local alignment (i.e., DeepFE and C^{2}MLR) will achieve better performance on this dataset than those only adopting global alignments.

By comparing the performance of different ranking methods on both datasets, we make following conclusions:

- By combining both global and local alignment, C^{2}MLR achieve good performance on both datasets, which validates that mere local alignment or global alignment does not suffice. The appropriate combination of local alignment and global alignment is essential because visual semantics and literal semantics are collaboratively grounded in a subtle interaction (i.e., a object/word finer level or a compositional image/sentence level).
- C^{2}MLR- outperforms the other global alignment ranking methods (PAMIR and DeepRank) most of the time (i.e., text-query-image on Pascal07 as well as text-query-image and image-query-text on Flickr8K). This

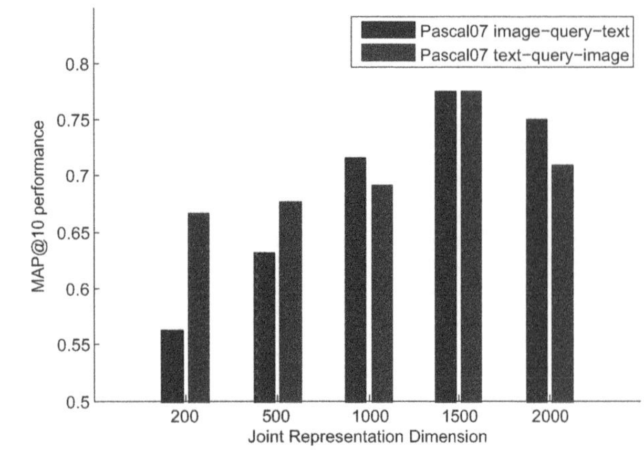

Figure 3: The performance of C^2MLR in terms of MAP@10 when the dimension of the global common space is set to different values on Pascal07. C^2MLR achieves the highest performance on both search directions when the number of dimension is set to 1500. Furthermore, the ranking performance is more sensitive on the text-query-image search direction than the image-query-text direction.

observation verifies that a compositional semantics embedding (a non-linear composition in this paper) from visual objects and textual words like C^2MLR can achieve better performance than traditional embedding directly from the whole image or the whole sentence like PAMIR and DeepRank.

- DeepRank outperforms PAMIR most of the time. Compared to PAMIR, DeepRank introduces a nonlinear projection to map the multi-modal data into a common space. This observation verifies that a nonlinear projection for multi-modal learning achieves better performance than a linear projection.

As a whole, C^2MLR outperforms the other ranking methods due to its two decent aptitudes: first C^2MLR conducts the compositional semantic embeddings for an image and text from visual objects in the image and words in the text; second our method adopts both global alignment and local alignment for multi-modal embedding.

We also report the different ranking performance of our method when the dimension of a global common space is set to different values. As shown in Figure 3, the performance of our method in terms of MAP@10 on Pascal07 is reported. From Figure 3, we observe that C^2MLR achieves the highest performance on both search direction when the number of dimensions is set to 1500, and the ranking performance is more sensitive on the image-query-text search direction than the text-query-image direction. As shown in Figure 3, the ranking performance is much lower on image-query-text direction when the number of feature dimension is small (e.g., 200 and 500). This is because the textual documents on Pascal07 contains uncontrolled richer semantics, so a larger feature dimension is more attractive for ranking text.

4.3 Local Alignments Analysis

In this section we will present some examples of ranking textual documents with image query using C^2MLR. By analysing the alignments between the object regions and the textual words discovered by our method, the benefits of adopting local alignment in learning multi-modal common space as well as the future work to further improve C^2MLR will be discussed.

Figure 4 shows three examples of the ranking results as well as the alignments between objects and words from Flickr8K dataset. Several local alignments with the highest similarity scores are selected. The aligned object regions and words from a pair of image-text data are framed and highlighted with the same color. From the three examples in Figure 4, we have following observation:

- The local alignment in our method is able to successfully align the valid visual objects with their most relevant textual words in the sentence. For example, the "boy" and "tire" in Figure 4 (a), "black" and "boy" in in Figure 4 (b), as well as "brown" and "car" in Figure 4 (c).

- Sometimes, even the results of object detections are not accurate, our method still manages to find a correct alignment between the textual words and their most relevant objects located in the slightly incorrect bounding boxes. For example, in Figure 4 (b), although our method detects the region of two boys wearing backpack instead of the actual region of the backpack, our approach is still able to align the word "backpack" with this region. Same thing happens to the word "dog" in the second sentence in Figure 4 (b).

- In our experiments, one query image has five most relevant sentences in Flickr8k dataset. Figure 4 gives some examples to analyze the situations that C^2MLR does not perfectly work. In Figure 4, the sentences irrelevant to the query image are underlined. For example, as shown in Figure 4 (a), the second and the third sentences are irrelevant to the query image. The reason why the second and the third sentences are ranked more ahead than other relevant sentences is that the word "swing" and "tire" in these two sentences are already aligned to their valid visual objects in the query image with a high confident score, so that even the algorithm does not find the alignments for other words such as "two" or "park", it still determines these two sentences to be relevant, although the compositional semantics in these two sentences are irrelevant to the query image. These mistaken ranking can be resolved by penalizing the missing local alignment (i.e., the the alignment of quantifiers words "two") in our future work.

In the experiments, C^2MLR uses two separate sets of parameters to embed words with different parts-of-speech into a local common space. One set of parameters is used for nouns that describe visual objects in images, and another is for adjectives/verbs expressing the attributes or states of visual objects. Figure 5 shows some examples of these two types of words and the object regions aligned to them. As shown in the Figure 5, the nouns are often aligned to specific visual objects in images, such as tire, boy, train and dog. The adjectives/verbs/quantifiers are usually aligned to the objects or regions with certain attributes (e.g, colors like green, black, white or quantities like "three") or states (e.g. actions like swing).

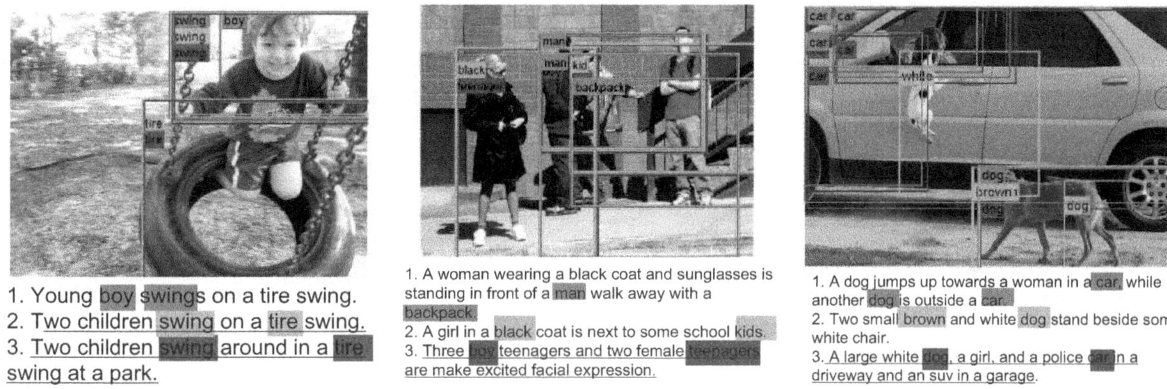

(a) (b) (c)

Figure 4: Examples of the ranking results as well as the alignments of visual object/textual words from Flickr8K dataset. Three image queries as well as the top-three retrieved sentences for each query are reported. Several visual objects aligned with textual words by the highest similarity scores are selected. The aligned object regions and textual words from a pair of image-text data are framed and highlighted with the same color. The sentences irrelevant to the image query are underlined

(a) The local alignments for words describing visual objects

(b) The local alignments for words expressing attributes of visual objects

Figure 5: Examples of local alignments of textual words-visual objects in terms of parts-of-specch.

5. CONCLUSION

This paper proposes a new method for cross-modal ranking called C^{2}MLR. The proposed C^{2}MLR uses the local alignment to embed visual objects and textual words into a local common space, and employs the global alignment to map images and text in a global common space after obtaining the image-level and sentence-level compositional semantics embeddings of multi-modal data from the visual objects and textual words. The local common space, the compositional semantics and the global common space are learned jointly in a max-margin learning to ranking manner. Experiments show that using both local alignment and global alignment for cross-modal ranking is able to boost the ranking performance.

6. ACKNOWLEDGEMENTS

This work was supported in part by the National Basic Research Program of China (2012CB316400), NSFC (61472353, 61402401), 863 Program (2012AA012505), the China Knowledge Centre for Engineering Sciences and Technology, the Fundamental Research Funds for the Central Universities.

7. REFERENCES

[1] B. Bai, J. Weston, D. Grangier, R. Collobert, K. Sadamasa, Y. Qi, O. Chapelle, and K. Weinberger. Learning to rank with (a lot of) word features. *Inf. Retr.*, 13(3):291–314, June 2010.

[2] D. M. Blei and M. I. Jordan. Modeling annotated data. In *Proceedings of Internetional ACM SIGIR Conference on Research and Development in Informaion Retrieval*, pages 127–134, 2003.

[3] C. Burges, T. Shaked, E. Renshaw, A. Lazier, M. Deeds, N. Hamilton, and G. Hullender. Learning to rank using gradient descent. In *ICML*, pages 89–96, New York, NY, USA, 2005. ACM.

[4] C. Cortes and V. Vapnik. Support-vector networks. *Machaine Learning*, 20(3):273–297, Sept. 1995.

[5] J. Donahue, L. A. Hendricks, S. Guadarrama, M. Rohrbach, S. Venugopalan, K. Saenko, and T. Darrell. Long-term recurrent convolutional networks for visual recognition and description. *arXiv preprint arXiv:1411.4389*, 2014.

[6] F. Feng, X. Wang, and R. Li. Cross-modal retrieval with correspondence autoencoder. In *ACM MM*, pages 7–16, New York, NY, USA, 2014. ACM.

[7] A. Frome, G. S. Corrado, J. Shlens, S. Bengio, J. Dean, M. A. Ranzato, and T. Mikolov. Devise: A deep visual-semantic embedding model. In C. Burges, L. Bottou, M. Welling, Z. Ghahramani, and K. Weinberger, editors, *NIPS*, pages 2121–2129. Curran Associates, Inc., 2013.

[8] D. Grangier and S. Bengio. A discriminative kernel-based approach to rank images from text queries. *TPAMI*, pages 1371–1384, 2008.

[9] D. R. Hardoon, S. R. Szedmak, and J. R. Shawe-taylor. Canonical correlation analysis: An

overview with application to learning methods. *Neural Computing*, pages 2639–2664, 2004.

[10] M. Hodosh, P. Young, and J. Hockenmaier. Framing image description as a ranking task: Data, models and evaluation metrics. *J. Artif. Int. Res.*, 47(1):853–899, May 2013.

[11] M. J. Huiskes and M. S. Lew. The mir flickr retrieval evaluation. In *Proceedings of the 1st ACM International Conference on Multimedia Information Retrieval*, pages 39–43, 2008.

[12] A. Karpathy and L. Fei-Fei. Deep visual-semantic alignments for generating image descriptions. In *CVPR*, June 2015.

[13] A. Karpathy, A. Joulin, and F. F. F. Li. Deep fragment embeddings for bidirectional image sentence mapping. In Z. Ghahramani, M. Welling, C. Cortes, N. Lawrence, and K. Weinberger, editors, *NIPS*, pages 1889–1897. Curran Associates, Inc., 2014.

[14] A. Klementiev, I. Titov, and B. Bhattarai. Inducing crosslingual distributed representations of word. In *COLING*, pages 1459–1474. The COLING 2012 Organizing Committee, 2012.

[15] A. Krizhevsky, I. Sutskever, and G. E. Hinton. Imagenet classification with deep convolutional neural networks. In F. Pereira, C. Burges, L. Bottou, and K. Weinberger, editors, *NIPS*, pages 1097–1105. Curran Associates, Inc., 2012.

[16] X. Lu, F. Wu, X. Li, Y. Zhang, W. Lu, D. Wang, and Y. Zhuang. Learning multimodal neural network with ranking examples. In *ACM MM*, pages 985–988, New York, NY, USA, 2014. ACM.

[17] X. Lu, F. Wu, S. Tang, Z. Zhang, X. He, and Y. Zhuang. A low rank structural large margin method for cross-modal ranking. In *ACM MM*, pages 433–442, 2013.

[18] J. Mao, W. Xu, Y. Yang, J. Wang, Z. Huang, and A. Yuille. Deep captioning with multimodal recurrent neural networks (m-rnn). In *ICLR*, 2015.

[19] T. Mikolov, I. Sutskever, K. Chen, G. S. Corrado, and J. Dean. Distributed representations of words and phrases and their compositionality. In C. Burges, L. Bottou, M. Welling, Z. Ghahramani, and K. Weinberger, editors, *NIPS*, pages 3111–3119. Curran Associates, Inc., 2013.

[20] G. Monaci, P. Jost, P. Vandergheynst, B. Mailhe, S. Lesage, and R. Gribonval. Learning multimodal dictionaries. *TIP*, pages 2272–2283, 2007.

[21] N. Srivastava and R. R. Salakhutdinov. Multimodal learning with deep boltzmann machines. In F. Pereira, C. Burges, L. Bottou, and K. Weinberger, editors, *NIPS*, pages 2222–2230. Curran Associates, Inc., 2012.

[22] X. Tian, L. Yang, J. Wang, Y. Yang, X. Wu, and X.-S. Hua. Bayesian video search reranking. In *ACM MM*, pages 131–140, New York, NY, USA, 2008. ACM.

[23] X. Tian, Y. Yang, J. Wang, X. Wu, and X.-S. Hua. Bayesian visual reranking. *TMM*, 13(4):639–652, Aug 2011.

[24] Y. Wang, F. Wu, J. Song, X. Li, and Y. Zhuang. Multi-modal mutual topic reinforce modeling for cross-media retrieval. In *ACM MM*, pages 307–316, New York, NY, USA, 2014. ACM.

[25] F. Wu, X. Lu, Z. Zhang, S. Yan, Y. Rui, and Y. Zhuang. Cross-media semantic representation via bi-directional learning to rank. In *ACM MM*, pages 877–886, New York, NY, USA, 2013. ACM.

[26] F. Wu, H. Zhang, and Y. Zhuang. Learning semantic correlations for cross-media retrieval. In *ICIP*, pages 1465–1468, Oct 2006.

[27] E. P. Xing, R. Yan, and A. G. Hauptmann. Mining associated text and images with dual-wing harmoniums. In *UAI*, pages 633–641, 2005.

[28] J. Yang, J. Wright, T. Huang, and Y. Ma. Image super-resolution via sparse representation. *TIP*, pages 2861–2873, 2010.

[29] Y. Yang, Y. Zhuang, F. Wu, and Y.-H. Pan. Harmonizing hierarchical manifolds for multimedia document semantics understanding and cross-media retrieval. *TMM*, 10(3):437–446, April 2008.

[30] J. Yu, Y. Rui, and D. Tao. Click prediction for web image reranking using multimodal sparse coding. *TIP*, 23(5):2019–2032, May 2014.

[31] Y. Zhuang, Y. F. Wang, F. Wu, Y. Zhang, and W. Lu. Supervised coupled dictionary learning with group structures for multi-modal retrieval. In *AAAI*, 2013.

[32] W. Y. Zou, R. Socher, D. Cer, and C. D. Manning. Bilingual word embeddings for phrase-based machine translation. In *EMNLP*, 2013.

Effective Multi-Query Expansions: Robust Landmark Retrieval

Yang Wang†, Xuemin Lin†, Lin Wu§♯ and Wenjie Zhang†

†The University of New South Wales, Kensington, Sydney, Australia

§The University of Adelaide, SA, Australia ♯Australian Centre for Robotic Vision

{wangy, lxue, zhangw}@cse.unsw.edu.au, lin.wu@adelaide.edu.au

ABSTRACT

Given a query photo issued by a user (q-user), the landmark retrieval is to return a set of photos with their landmarks similar to those of the query, while the existing studies on the landmark retrieval focus on exploiting geometries of landmarks for similarity matches between candidate photos and a query photo. We observe that the same landmarks provided by different users may convey different geometry information depending on the viewpoints and/or angles, and may subsequently yield very different results. In fact, dealing with the landmarks with low quality shapes caused by the photography of q-users is often nontrivial and has never been studied.

Motivated by this, in this paper we propose a novel framework, namely multi-query expansions, to retrieve semantically robust landmarks by two steps. Firstly, we identify the top-k photos regarding the latent topics of a query landmark to construct multi-query set so as to remedy its possible low quality shape . For this purpose, we significantly extend the techniques of Latent Dirichlet Allocation. Secondly, we propose a novel technique to generate the robust yet compact pattern set from the multi-query photos. To ensure redundancy-free and enhance the efficiency, we adopt the existing minimum-description-length-principle based pattern mining techniques to remove similar query photos from the $(k+1)$ selected query photos. Then, a landmark retrieval rule is developed to calculate the ranking scores between mined pattern set and each photo in the database, which are ranked to serve as the final ranking list of landmark retrieval. Extensive experiments are conducted on real-world landmark datasets, validating the significantly higher accuracy of our approach.

Categories and Subject Descriptors

H.3.3 [**Information Storage and Retrieval**]: Information Search and Retrieval

MM'15, October 26–30, 2015, Brisbane, Australia.

ACM 978-1-4503-3459-4/15/10 ...$15.00.

DOI: http://dx.doi.org/10.1145/2733373.2806233.

Keywords

Landmark Photo Retrieval; Multi-Query Expansions

1. INTRODUCTION

The popularity of personal digital photography has led to an exponential growth of photos with landmarks, *e.g.,*

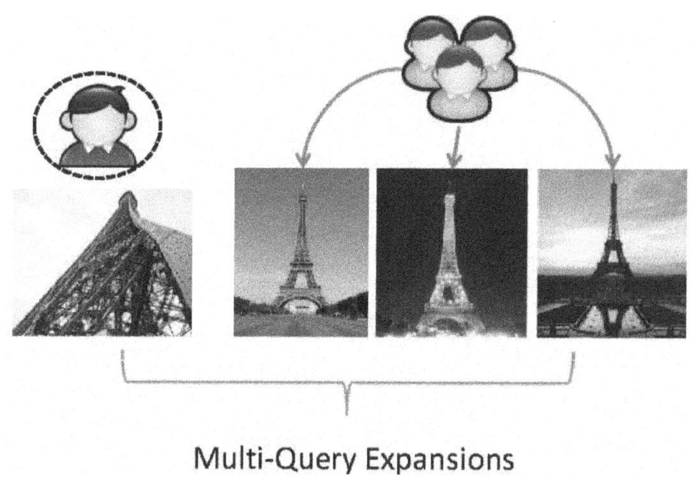

Figure 1: A q-user has issued a biased landmark photo of Eiffel Tower in Paris in the left most photo. Multiple users with the same latent topic as the q-user are selected to recommend three more landmark photos taken at the same place, that complement the given query landmark to construct a multi-query set.

panoramio.com and Picasa Web Album[1]. This highly demands for the research in the area of efficient and effective retrieval of photos based on landmarks (*e.g.,* tower and churches), namely *landmark retrieval.* Given a query photo, the landmark retrieval returns the set of photos with their landmarks highly similar to that of the query photo.

Unlike the conventional image retrieval that performs within the low-level feature spaces (*e.g.,* color and texture), the landmark retrieval is conducted based on geometry information of landmarks. A number of paradigms [8, 10, 14] have been proposed to perform the landmark retrieval under the heterogeneous feature spaces, including the paradigms based on patch level region features [8], mid-level attributes [10], and the combination of low-level features [14].

[1]picasa.google.com

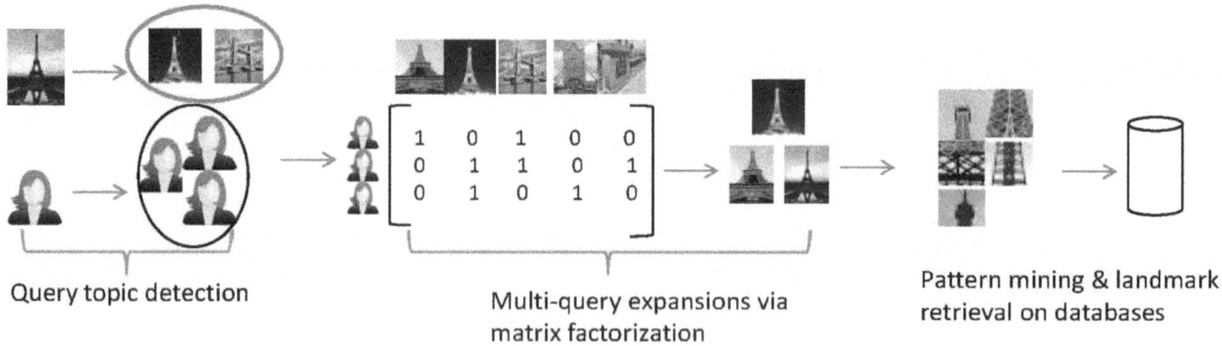

Figure 2: The flow chart of our framework. Our framework comprises three main phases: 1) query landmark based topic and user community discovery; 2) select multiple landmark photos from user-query photo matrix to form a multi-query set; and 3) Mining robust and compact pattern set to represent the multi-query set, and calculate the ranking score between such pattern set and each photo in the database, which further lead to the ranking retrieval result for landmark retrieval.

Among the existing techniques, there is one critical assumption: a high quality of query photo is always provided; that is, the landmark captured from a query photo always provides a shape with high quality. Nevertheless, such an assumption is not always true in practice. Indeed, the landmark of a query photo may provide shape with low quality due to various reasons, such as personal preference, photography, etc. For example, as illustrated in Fig. 1, the left most photo taken by a q-user gives the landmark Eiffel Tower with a very low quality shape . Consequently, the existing methods may not be able to return the set of photos that contain the Eiffel Tower since the geometry quality of the landmark in the query photo is too low.

Motivated by this, in this paper we propose a novel method, depicted in Fig. 2, for a robust landmark retrieval through a novel paradigm based on multi-query expansions. Firstly, we propose to identify a set of photos that share the similar latent topics with the query landmark by adopting the Latent Dirichlet Allocation (LDA) techniques [4]. Then, we propose a localized matrix factorization technique over the user-photo matrix that encodes the information from the selected photos. Based on that, a ranking strategy is proposed to generate the top-k photos; this gives the multi-query set with the size $k+1$ by including the original given query.

We observe that if k is too small then the selected query photos may not be representative, while if k is too large then it will be too expensive to learn robust pattern set (multi-query). Moreover, the multi-query set may contain many similar photos; that is, their landmarks have very similar geometric shapes. To resolve these, we propose to set-up a large k, then adopt the existing minimum-description-length-principle [12] based pattern mining techniques to remove similar query photos from the $(k+1)$ selected query photos. Afterwards, we develop an effective retrieval rule to calculate the ranking score, which represents the similarity between each photo in the database and mined pattern set for multi-query. Finally, the landmark retrieval is performed based on the ranking score of each photo to return the final ranking list.

To sum up, our major contributions are below:

- We propose to tackle the problem of landmarks in query photos with low quality shapes . We present a novel method based on an effective multi-query expansion paradigm.
- A novel strategy is proposed to generate an effective multi-query set. To remove similar photos in the multi query set, we adopt the existing minimum-description-length-principle based pattern mining technique to generate a robust patten set to represent the multi-query. Then, we propose a novel strategy to calculate the ranking score between each photo and pattern set. The final landmark retrieval result is the ranking list of photos as per their ranking score.
- We conducted extensive experiments over real-world landmark photo datasets, validating the higher accuracy of our approach.

The rest of this paper is structured as follows. We review the related work in Section 2. Then, we describe our proposed technique in Section 3, for user communities discovery and multiple queries expansion in Sections 3.1 and 3.2, respectively. A minimum length based pattern mining technique is presented in Section 3.3. We experimentally validate the performance of our approach in Section 4, and conclude this paper in Section 5.

2. RELATED WORK

In this section, we mainly review the related work on landmark retrieval and related query argumentation technique.

2.1 Feature Learning for Landmark Retrieval

The increasing amount of landmark photos has resulted in numerous methods for landmark retrieval [14, 36, 8, 10]. Hays *et al.* [14] presented a feature matching approach to return the K nearest neighbors with respect to the query landmark photo where a query photo and photos in database are represented by aggregating a set of low-level features to perform landmark retrieval. Zhu *et al.* [36] proposed to learn the landmark feature by combining low-level features while assisted with Support Vector Machine (SVM). In [8], a region based recognition method is proposed to detect discriminative landmark regions at patch level, which is seen as the feature for landmark retrieval. To augment semantic interpretation on landmark representation, Fang *et al.* [10] presented an effective approach, namely GIANT, to discover both discriminative and representative mid-level attributes for landmark retrieval. However, these approaches are still using a single query photo for landmark retrieval whilst our approach is focusing on mining robust patterns of landmark photos from an expanded multi-query set.

2.2 Query Argumentation Technique

In [7], a query expansion technique is brought into the visual domain in which a strong spatial constraint between a query image and each result allows for an accurate verification of each return, improving image retrieval performance. This simple method of well-performing query expansion is referred to as Average Query Expansion [7] (AQE) where given a query image, images are ranked using tf-idf scores and corresponding visual words in these images are averaged together with the query visual words, and this resulting query expanded visual word vector is recast to be a new query to re-query the database. Observing that AQE is lack of discrimination, Arandjelovic *et al.* [2] enhanced it using a linear SVM to discriminatively learn a weight vector for re-querying yields a significant improvement over the standard average query expansion method, called DQE. The most related work to ours is [11] (PQE), where a query expansion approach for a particular object retrieval is presented. Our method is different from them in terms of multi-query construction. Zhu *et al.* [37] propose to perform landmark classification with a hierarchical multi-modal exemplar features. There are also research [17] aiming at developing the feature representations for diverse landmark search.

These methods are commonly based on the idea that those particular multiple queries are manually selected or simply retrieved from top-k similar items whilst we automatically determine helpful queries by exploring the latent topics of query landmark as well as the informative user communities. Besides, previous query expansion pipelines are not applicable in the context of social media networks. In other words, this problem cannot be addressed by simple variations of methods in literature.

2.3 Geo-tagging by Exploring User Community

Geo-tagging refers to adding geographical identification metadata into various multimedia data such as images [13] and videos [6] in websites, blogs, and photo-sharing web-services [1, 21, 35]. Associating time and location information (latitude/longitude) with pictures can facilitate geotagging-enabled information services in terms of finding location-based news, photos, or other resources [3, 32, 33, 16]. There are also a number of approaches [15] trying to learn the location based visual codebook for landmark search. Similar to our method, such research area also explore the user communities. However, this kind of research is apparently different from landmark retrieval studied in this paper.

3. PROPOSED TECHNIQUE

In this section, we formally present our techniques with three steps as depicted in Fig. 1.

3.1 Query Topics and User Group Discovery

We aim to discover the latent topics of the query landmark by modeling the relationship between the query landmark and latent topics inherent over entire photo set uploaded by users. To this end, we use Latent Dirichlet Allocation (LDA) [4] to discover a set of latent topics where each topic contains a set of photos describing the similar landmarks. As a byproduct, we construct the user group that consists of the users, who upload the landmark photos sharing the similar topics as the query landmark, which is further utilized to perform multi-query expansions on Section 3.2.

Before shedding lights on how to transfer LDA to detect the latent topics of query landmark photo over the entire photo database, we firstly introduce some preliminaries on some notations and latent topics.

3.1.1 Preliminaries

Formally, given a set of users U, each of which is associated with their landmark photos. We assume that these observed photos can be grouped into clusters as per their latent topics, where each latent topic consists of the set of landmarks; for example, *e.g.,* the photo containing the landmark "Eiffel tower" may belong to the latent topic "architecture"; the landmark "Himalayas" may belong to the topic "mountain". Suppose a set of topics for query landmark have been detected, each photo can be then modeled as a probabilistic distribution over these topics. Based on that, it can also be seen as a generative model where each user album, denoted as d, is composed of a number of topics, and the generation for each photo is probabilistically determined by the topics of the album.

Now, we are ready to reformulate the problem of query photo topic discovery as a LDA model. Denote α, β as the parameter of the Dirichlet prior on the per-album topic distributions (per-topic photo distribution), θ_d as the topic distribution on album d, and ϕ_z as the photo distribution on topic z. LDA assumes the following generative process for a corpus D consisting of $|D|$ user albums:

1. Choosing the number of topics: $|Z|$
2. Choosing $\theta_d \sim Dir(\alpha)$, $d \in \{1, \ldots, |D|\}$
3. Choosing $\phi_z \sim Dir(\beta)$, $z \in \{1, \ldots, |Z|\}$
4. For each photo ω in album d
   - Choosing a topic $z_{\omega d} \sim Multinomial(\theta_d)$
   - Choosing a photo $\omega \sim Multinomial(\phi_{z_{\omega d}})$.

Fig.3 depicts a graphical model for this representation.

As such, the output of LDA over D, denoted as LDA(D), can be seen as a partition of D into multi-groups, each of which consists of a photo set characterizing the same latent topic.

3.1.2 Detecting the candidate latent topics for query landmark

We propose to detect the possible latent topics for query landmark from the entire photo database, and group photos as per each topic z in album d, where each d is described as a mixture of a fixed number of topics Z with topic z having the probability of $P(z|d)$. Each topic z has the probability of generating various photos containing the query photo q in z, denoted as $P(q|z)$. Commonly, we set a probability threshold λ to decide the candidate latent topics for query landmark q. That is, $P(q|z) \geq \lambda$ indicates that z could be one candidate topic for q. Therefore, we further have the following cases regarding probability threshold λ:

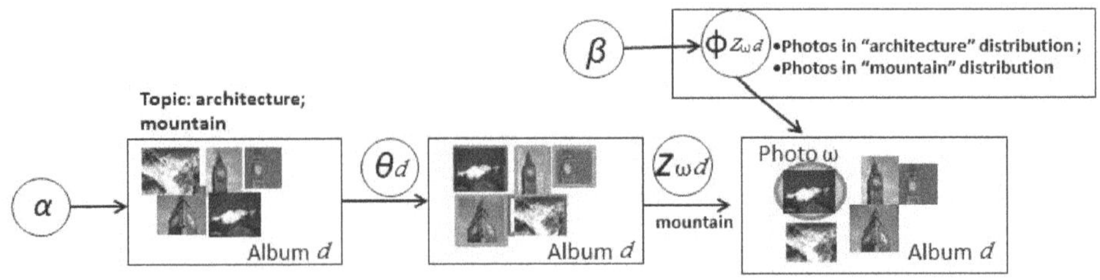

Figure 3: The LDA model of graphical representation on landmark photo distributions. A topic distribution θ_d (*e.g.*, "architecture" and "mountain") on album d is chosen by Dirichlet prior $Dir(\alpha)$, and photo distribution ϕ_z on topic z is chosen by $Dir(\beta)$. Then each image ω from d can be modeled as a distribution on its topic $z_{\omega d}$ ($\omega \sim Multinomial(\phi_{z_{\omega d}})$) with topic $z_{\omega d}$ characterized by $z_{\omega d} \sim Multinomial(\theta_d)$.

1. if λ is small, we may generate a lot of candidate latent topics, resulting into non-relevant latent topics regarding the query landmark q.
2. if λ is large, the size of candidate topic set may be quite small, which may be not inclusive to involve the true topic for q.

We learn the trade-off value for λ from our empirical studies, which is critical to decide the topic set regarding the query landmark q.

Once the query topic set is determined, it is plausible to recommend a few photos sharing the similar topics to the query photo. To this end, we propose to utilize user communities to assist multi-query set construction. Specifically, a user is seen to have a similar landmark of interest as q-user, if she upload the photos sharing at least one of the similar topics with that of the q-user. Based on that, a user-photo matrix is naturally constructed. Let $M \in \mathbb{R}^{|U|\times|J|}$ be a user-photo matrix that contains $|U|$ users and $|J|$ photos, in which U is the user set, J is the photo set, and $u_q \in U$ where u_q represent the q-user. In M, we have $M(u,j) = 1$ if a user $u \in U$ uploaded a photo j into J, and $M(u,j) = 0$, otherwise.

In next section, we will elaborate the details on selecting the Top-K photos to complement the query landmark to be multi-query set.

3.2 Multi-Query Expansions

To find the appropriate photo set for query expansions, we propose to conduct a non-negative matrix factorization [18] on the user-photo matrix M, where the users (include q-user) and relevant photos are detected by LDA mentioned above. By factorizing the M into a lower-dimensional latent space, each photo's possibility of being recommended to the query user u_q is computed based on the factorized result. Then, photos with top-K highest relevant scores (possibility to share the similar topic with query landmark) are calculated and selected, together with the original single query, to form a robust multi-query set.

Specifically, we perform the non-negative matrix factorization on M by minimizing the objective function below.

$$\arg\min_{P,V} ||M - PV||_F, P \geq 0, V \geq 0, \quad (1)$$

where $||\cdot||_F$ denotes the Frobenius norm. Two low-rank factor matrices $P \in R^{|U|\times L}$ and $V \in R^{L\times|J|}$ are obtained by solving Eq.(1), where P models the mapping of users in the low-dimensional latent space with L dimensions, and V defines the mappings of photos to the same latent space. That is, each user u is represented as the u-th row vector of P denoted by p_u, while each photo j is encoded by the j-th column vector of V denoted by v_j. For a q-user $u_q \in U$, we compute a score as the possibility that photo j will be recommended to u_q from M. The possibility is calculated by the inner product of $P(u_q,.)$ and $V(.,j)$ as follows

$$S(u_q, j) =< P(u_q,\cdot), V(\cdot,j) >, \quad (2)$$

where $P(u_q,\cdot)$ and $V(\cdot,j)$ denote the row vector of P corresponding to u_q and j-th column vector of V corresponding to photo j, respectively.

We determine a number of photos to form a multi-query set by ranking all $S(u_q, j)$ scores in descending order and select up to K photos with highest scores, together with q to expand to a new multi-query set. The advantage of using non-negative matrix factorization over a user-photo matrix is: it avoids a brute-force evaluation on each photo's similarity to the query photo; instead, this factorization strategy is more efficient in determining multiple queries.

The landmark retrieval is then performed against a landmark database with respect to this multi-query set. Given multiple queries, a naive way of generating a retrieval list is to issue each query in the set individually, and then combine their retrieved results. However, such a fusion fashion is highly computational demanding when the size of ranking list is large. By contrast, we present a pattern mining method that mines a landmark-specific pattern set as the mid-level representation to represent multi-query set. After that, we aim at calculating the similarity score between such pattern set and each photo in the database. The final ranking retrieval result is formed by ranking all these scores of corresponding photos.

3.3 Multi-Query based Pattern Mining

3.3.1 *Why Pattern Mining on Multi-Query?*

Although an expanded multi-query set can be obtained by the aforementioned steps, it may fail to form the robust feature representation for multi-query landmark photo set due to the following facts:

1. The multi-query set may cause rather redundancy due to the fact that multiple photos might describe the same landmark from the same perspective but different angles and lighting conditions. Thus, they are not helpful to better represent the landmark.

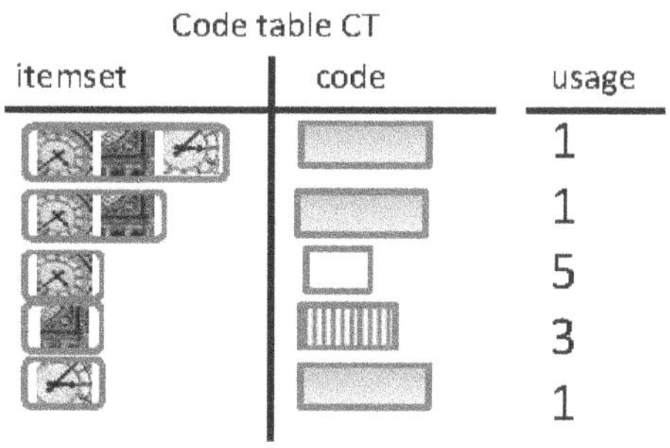

Figure 4: Example on a code table. The lengths of codes represent their lengths in encoding. Note that the usage column is not part of code table, but shown here as illustration: in optimal compression, more shorter the codes should be the more often they are used.

2. The multi-query set may contain the photos characterizing the inconsistent latent topics with the query landmark.

To address the above challenge, we propose to employ a pattern mining strategy to discover the complementary but compact feature representation from a multi-query set, which can serve to be landmark specific mid-level representation to conduct landmark retrieval effectively.

3.3.2 *Learning robust pattern set for multi-query set*

To faithfully represent a landmark of interest, we mine the frequent patterns among multi-query. A frequent pattern only describes a part of the query set Q, thus, we aim to find a set of patterns that can best describe Q. To this end, we employ an effective pattern mining technique of minimal description length (MDL) [12], which is able to find set of frequent patterns that yield the best compression of Q. Nonetheless, MDL still suffers from the high computational cost in all possible combinations of permutations on patterns. To address this issue, we further deploy the existing KRIMP algorithm [23] which introduces a few heuristic strategies to reduce the complexity of MDL algorithm.

In the following, we will present the technical details based on the principle of minimum description length (MDL), followed by KRIMP algorithm to yield the final robust pattern set to be mid-level representation for multi-query set.

3.3.3 *The MDL algorithm*

A pattern, denoted as h, consists of a set of items, and each item denotes a patch from a photo. In the rest of paper, we would interchangeably use patch and item. In our case, the multi-query set Q can be regarded as a transaction collection where each photo is treated as a transaction t containing a set of items (patches). The size of a patch is set to be 16×16 and we use root-SIFT descriptors extracted from Hessian-affine regions [22]. A single pattern h can describe only part of the query landmark and a pattern h is considered to be matched/mapped into transaction t if $h \subseteq t$. A set of patterns that together describe a query landmark is referred to as a model H. That is, we want to find the best set of (frequent) itemsets, H^*, to describe Q the best. Essentially, the best model is featured to be able to compress Q the best. To this end, we use the Minimal Description Length Principle (MDL) to seek a set of patterns which are the characteristic of Q.

The key idea of compression is the code table CT, which is a simple two-column translation table that has itemsets on the left-hand side and a code for each itemset on its right-hand side. With such as a code table we find through MDL, the set of itemsets that together optimally describe the multi-query set Q.

DEFINITION 1. *Let I be a set of items and C a set of code words. A code table CT over I and C is a two-column table such that: The first column contains itemsets,* i.e., *subsets over I. The second column contains code words from C such that each code word occurs at most once.*

An itemset X drawn from the powerset of I, *i.e.*, $X \in P(I)$ occurs in CT, denoted by $X \in CT$ if X appears in the first column of CT. For $X \in CT$, $code_{CT}(X)$ denotes its code, *i.e.*, the corresponding element in the second column.

EXAMPLE 1. *We show an example on code table in Fig4. The first and second columns in the code table present the itemsets and corresponding codes, respectively. Each bar represents a code and its width shows the code length. The usage column is actually not part of code table, however, it is shown for illustrative purposes and will be used later to calculate optimal code length.*

To encode a transaction t from Q over I with code table CT, we require a cover function $cover(CT, t)$ that identifies which elements of CT are used to encode t. The result of a cover function is a disjoint set of elements of CT that cover t. We omit the details on how to compute a cover function, which can be found in [23] [2]. To encode the query set Q using CT, we simply replace each transaction $t \in Q$ by the codes of the itemsets in the cover of t, that is,

$$t \rightarrow \{code_{CT}(X) | X \in cover(CT, t)\}. \qquad (3)$$

Since MDL is concerned with the best compression, the codes in CT should be chosen such that the most often used code has the shortest length. Due to the correspondence between code lengths and probability distributions [19], we can calculate the code length $L(d)$ of code d through the following equation:

$$L(d) = -\log(P(d)), \qquad (4)$$

where the probability distribution P on Q induced by a cover function is given by the relative usage frequency of each of the itemsets in the code table. To achieve this, we define the usage count of an itemset $X \in CT$ as the number of transactions t from Q where X is used to cover. This normalized frequency represents the probability that the code d is used in the encoding of a transaction $t \in Q$. Then, the optimal code length is $-\log(P(d))$, denoted by $L(code_{CT}(X))$ and a code table is optimal if all its codes have their optimal length.

EXAMPLE 2. *As illustrated in Fig.4, for the third itemset X, its probability distribution over Q is $P(X|Q) = \frac{5}{11}$, and $L(code_{CT}(X)) = -\log(\frac{5}{11}) = 0.788$, thus X is assigned a code of length 0.788 bits.*

[2] Let h, m be patterns ($h, m \in H$) and t a transaction ($t \in B$). A cover function has three important properties: 1) $h \in cover(H, t) \implies h \in H$; 2) $h, m \in cover(H, t) \implies (h = m)$ or $(h \cap m = \oslash)$; 3) $t = \cup_{h \in cover(H,t)} h$.

For any $t \in Q$, its encoded length, in bits, denoted by $L(t|CT)$ is $L(t|CT) = \sum_{X \in cover(CT,t)} L(code_{CT}(X))$, and the encoded size of Q in bits, is

$$L(Q|CT) = \sum_{t \in Q} L(t|CT). \tag{5}$$

To use MDL, we need to know $L(CT)$, *i.e.*, the encoded size of a code table. The size of CT in bits, denoted by $L(CT|Q)$ is given by

$$L(CT|Q) = \sum_{X \in CT} L(code_{ST}(X)) + L(code_{CT}(X)), \tag{6}$$

where ST denotes the standard code table for Q which contains only the singleton itemsets, and we do not take itemsets with zero usage into account, that is, $usage_Q(X) \neq 0$.

Let multi-query set Q be a transaction collection over I, let CT be a code table that is code-optimal for Q and *cover* a cover function. The total compressed size of the encoded Q and CT, in bits, denoted by $L(Q, CT)$ is computed as $L(Q, CT) = L(Q|CT) + L(CT|Q)$. Now we can state our problem using MDL.

Problem statement from MDL principle. The problem of minimal coding set on landmark queries: Let I be a set of items (patches) and Q be transaction set over I, $cover(\cdot)$ a cover function, and F be a candidate set which contains at least all singleton itemsets of I, our goal is to find the a subset of F, denoted by H^* such that for the corresponding code table CT, the total compressed size $L(Q, CT)$ is minimal.

The solution to the above problem allows us to find the best pattern set H^* to describe Q.

3.3.4 The KRIMP Algorithm

To find a set of patterns H^* that best describe the multi-query set Q, we need to examine all $|CT|!$ possible permutations for one transaction (one photo in Q), which is practically impossible. Thus, we employ the KRIMP algorithm that can reduce the computational burden by

- using a heuristic to consider the code table in a fixed order, referred as Standard Cover Order;
- ordering the candidate itemsets such that long, frequently occurring itemsets are given priority, referred as Standard Candidate Order.

We summarize applying KRIMP algorithm to seek the compact patterns for a multi-landmark query in Algorithm 1.

Algorithm 1: The KRIMP algorithm to discover compact set of patterns from a multi-query set Q.

Input: A multi-query set Q (transaction collection), a candidate set F, both cover a set of items I.
Output: The best set of patterns H^*

```
Initialize CT ← StandardCodeTable(Q);
F_0 ← F in Standard Candidate Order;
for F ∈ F_0\I do
    CT_c ← (CT ∪ F) in Standard Cover Order;
    if L(Q, CT_c) < L(Q, CT) then
        CT ← CT_C;
H* ← CT;
Return H*;
```

3.3.5 Landmark Retrieval Rule

Once the optimal pattern $H^* = \{I_1, \ldots, I_N\}$ regarding multi-query set is mined where I_i denotes the i-th patch(item) set, we aim at calculating the similarity score for each photo based on H^*. To resolve this, we use term frequency and inverse document frequency to (tf-idf) to generate a weight for each patch set I_i that appears in each photo y from a database. We use the term-frequency $tf_{I_i,y}$ to count the number of I_i occurs in photo y (**As aforementioned in section 3.3.3, each patch is generated with** 16×16**, we therefore pre-segment each photo** y **to be a patch set via such size.**). However, because some patch sets can appear in many photos frequently, without giving enough weight to the more meaningful patch sets in the query photo (*e.g.*, some visual patches of London bridge are common architecture features that can be commonly seen in other bridges). Hence, an inverse document frequency factor, idf_{I_i}, is incorporated which diminishes the weight of patch sets that occur very frequently in the database and increases the weight of patch set that occur rarely. Then its tf-idf weighting scheme that assigns the itemset I_i a weight in photo y is given by

$$w^i = tf \cdot idf_{I_i,y} = tf_{I_i,y} \times idf_{I_i}, \tag{7}$$

where we define $tf_{I_i,y} = 1$ if I_i occurs in y and 0 otherwise, and the idf_{I_i} is a measure of how much information I_i provides, that is, whether I_i is common or rare across all photos in a database. Specifically, we define $idf_{I_i} = \log \frac{|\Omega|}{|\{y: I_i \in y\}|}$, where, as aforementioned, Ω denotes the size of the whole photo database and $|\{p : I_i \in p\}|$ is the number of photos where I_i appears (*i.e.*, $tf_{I_i,y} \neq 0$), from which we can see the larger $|\{y : I_i \in y\}|$ implies more photos where the patch set I_i occurs, the idf_{I_i} will be smaller.

Thus, we may view each photo y as a vector with i-th entry corresponding I_i in H^*, together with a weight given by Eq.(7), which can be seen as a similarity score between between I_i and y. Based on that, we can calculate the total similarity between y and all patch set $I_i (i = 1, 2, \cdots, N)$ below:

$$\mathbf{w} = \{w^i\}_{i=1}^{N}. \tag{8}$$

It can be seen to be similarity between y and H^*(multi-query set). Based on Eq.(8), we define the L_2 normalized overlap score measure $score(y, Q)$ below.

$$score(y, Q) = \sqrt{\sum_{i=1}^{N} |w^i|^2}. \tag{9}$$

The final output of landmark retrieval is to return the ranking list according to Eq.(9) based on expanded multi-query set Q.

To sum up, we give the entire framework in Algorithm 2.

3.4 Complexity Analysis

Besides applying the efficient Minimal Description Length Principle Pattern Mining techniques to do feature coding, we will analyze the major cost of Algorithm 2 coming from detecting latent topics of query landmark by LDA and non-negative matrix factorization operation. Firstly, for LDA, assume we have $|D|$ user albums, Ω photos, and Z topics.

Algorithm 2: Multi-query expansion and pattern mining based landmark retrieval.

Input: User set U.
Photo set Ω.
Query photo q.
Query user u_q.
Topic detection threshold λ.
Number of photos to construct multi-query set K.
Number of reduced lower dimensions or latent factors by matrix factorization L.
Final ranking retrieval list Re.
Output: Ranked list R from Ω.

$D = \emptyset$;
for $u \in U$ **do**
  $d_u = \{\omega | u \in U \wedge u \ \ uploaded \ \ \omega \in \Omega\}$;
  $D = D \cup d_u$;
/*Query landmark latent topic set detected by LDA*/
$Z \longleftarrow LDA(D)$;
$C = \emptyset$;
while $z \in Z$ **do**
  $T \longleftarrow \emptyset$;
  if $P(q|z) > \lambda$ **then**
    $T = T \cup z$;
Construct the user-photo matrix M;
/*Form robust multi-query set*/
Perform matrix factorization on M using Eq.(1);
for *photo j sharing at least one of topic set for q* **do**
  Compute $S(u_q, j)$ using Eq.(2);
Select top-K highest $S(u_q, j)$ to form a multi-query set Q;
/* Pattern mining and landmark retrieval */
Call Algorithm 1 to obtain the robust compact patterns H^* that can best describe Q;
for *photo* $y \in \Omega$ **do**
  Build patch set on y with size of each one to be 16×16 ;
  Compute $score(y, Q)$ according to Eq.(9);
Ranking $score(y, Q)$ to select top-Re to be R;
Return R;

The computational complexity of LDA is $\mathcal{O}(|D|Z\Omega)$. In non-negative matrix factorization, the overall cost for optimizing P in Eq.(1) is $\mathcal{O}(|U||J|L)$ where $|U|$ and $|J|$ represent the number of users and photos in user-photo matrix M, and L is the dimensions of factorized low-dimensional latent space. Optimizing Q has the same time cost. Thus, matrix factorization over M costs $\mathcal{O}(|U||J|L)$. Selecting top-K items by using Eq.(2) costs $|J|$, where $|J|$ is the number of photos encoded in M. Hence, the complexity of the first step is $\mathcal{O}(|U||J|L + |J|)$.

4. EXPERIMENTS

In this section, we first present our experimental settings, and then report the experimental results to verify the effectiveness and efficiency of our approach.

4.1 Datasets and Features

Two datasets are constructed by collecting photos from websites of **Flickr** and **Picasa Web Album**. They are suitable for landmarks retrieval because they contain both user information and corresponding landmark photos.

Table 1: Statistics of datasets.

Dataset	Flickr	Picasa Web Album
# Landmark	55	16
# Photo per landmark	nearly 1,000	100 ~ 300
# Total photo	49,840	4,100
# User	7,332	577

Figure 5: Example landmarks photos from our manually collected Flickr dataset.

Flickr. We use the **Flickr** API to retrieve landmark photos taken at a city posted by a large number of users. We sort out 11 cities: London, Paris, Barcelona, Sydney, Singapore, Beijing, Tokyo, Taipei, Cairo, New York city, and Istanbul. In each city, such as Paris, we obtained photos by querying the associated text tags for famous landmarks such as "Paris Eiffel Tower" or "Paris Triomphe" [3]. Example photos containing a variety of landmarks from this dataset are shown in Fig. 5.

Picasa Web Album. Providing rich information about interesting tourist attractions, this source contains a vast amount of GPS-tagged photos uploaded by users who have visited the landmarks, along with their text tags. We manually download a fraction of photos and their user information on 6 cities: London, Paris, Beijing, Sydney, Chicago, and Barcelona.

The statistics for user information and their uploaded photos over the two datasets are summarized in Table 1. In the training stage, the SIFT descriptor [20] is used as a local descriptor due to its excellent performance in object recognition [5]. Specifically, we adopt a dense sampling strategy to select the interest regions from which SIFT descriptors are extracted. To test the generalization of our framework in which test data differs from the dataset used to generate the quantization, we adopt another dataset. The **Oxford** dataset is used for constructing the vocabulary book [4], upon which local bag-of-words are encoded as representations. The **Oxford Building** dataset contains 5,062 photos, which is a standard set of particular objects for retrieval. The reason for choosing Oxford landmarks is that the photos have the scenes similar to, rather than identical landmarks, those in the two test databases (e.g., buildings, often with some similarities in the architectural style).

[3]In Paris, 12 queries were used to collect the photos from Flickr: La Defense Paris, Eiffel Tower Paris, Hotel des Invalides Paris, Louvre Paris, Moulin Rouge Paris, Musee d'Orsay Paris, Notre Dame Paris, Pantheon Paris, Pompidou Paris, Sacre Coeur Paris, Arc de Triomphe Paris, Paris

[4]http://www.robots.ox.ac.uk/ vgg/data/oxbuildings/

4.2 Settings

Evaluation Metric. We choose precision-recall as the metrics to evaluate both our model and state-of-the-art methods over top-100 retrieval ranked list based on each query landmark. In each landmark, we issue 20 queries and an average precision score is computed for all queries, and these are averaged to obtain a mean Average Precision (mAP) for the each landmark category.

Competitors. In our experiment, we consider the following competitors:

- K-NN [14]: A feature matching approach to return the K nearest neighbors with respect to the query landmark photo where a query photo and photos in database are represented by aggregating a set of low-level features to perform landmark retrieval.
- LF+SVM: Low-level features [36] combined with SVM;
- DRLR [8]: A region based location recognition method that detects discriminative regions at the patch-level.
- GIANT [10]: A method to discover geo-informative attributes that are discriminative and useful for location recognition.
- AQE [7]: Average Query Expansion method that proceeds as follows: given a query region, it ranks a list of photos using tf-idf scores. Bag-of-Word vectors corresponding to these regions are averaged with BoW vectors of the query, resulting in an expanded vector used to re-query the database.
- DQE [2]: Discriminative Query Expansion that enriches a query in the exactly same way as AQE. It considers photos with lower tf-idf scores as negative data to train a linear SVM for further rankings and retrievals.
- PQE [11]: A Pattern based Query Expansion algorithm that combines top-K retrieved photos with a query to find a set of patterns.

4.3 Learning Parameters

In this section, we learn three important parameters for our technique,

- K: the number for queries after matrix factorization in multi-query set.
- λ: threshold to determine the latent topic set for query landmark.
- L: reduced dimension or latent factor number for matrix factorization.

We tuning the parameters over two dataset via the following fashion: that is, we vary one parameter at a time while fixing the others. For instance, when we test the sensitivity of K, we try different values of K within a range of [10,55] while the other two parameters λ and L are fixed to be 0.4 and 64. We adopt mAP as the evaluation metric. For each landmark category, we randomly select 20 distinct queries to yield the mAP value.

The following observations are made:

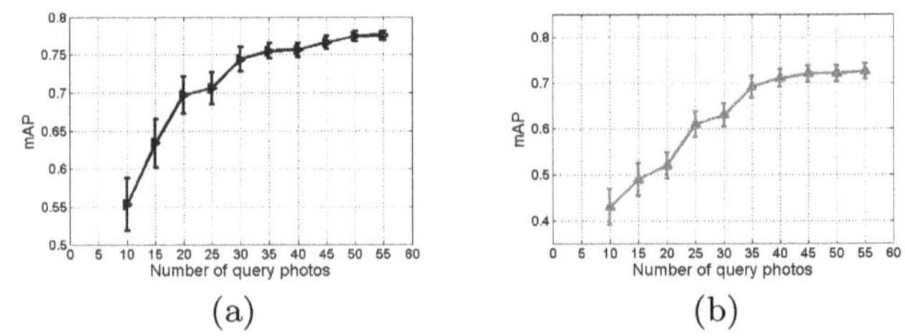

Figure 6: Results on mAP scores by varying the number of photos recommended from each user community. (a) mAP scores vs. varied K values over Flickr dataset. (b) mAP scores vs. varied K values over Picasa dataset.

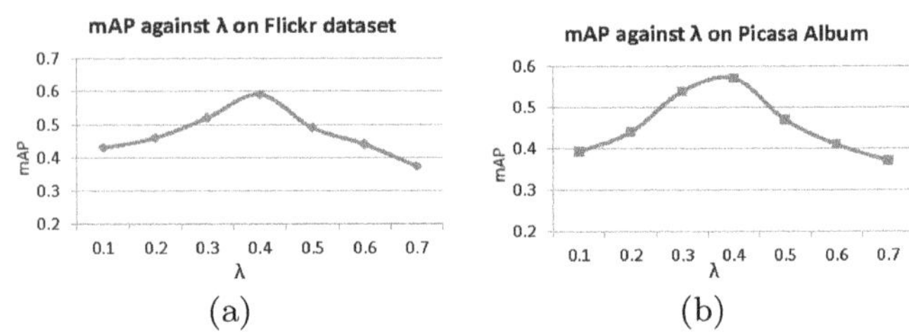

Figure 7: Results on mAP scores by varying the λ. (a) mAP scores vs. varied λ values over Flickr dataset. (b) mAP scores vs. varied λ values over Picasa dataset.

- Fig. 6 depicts the mAP scores against a variety of K values, which indicates that as the number of query photos increases, the values of mAP by our method become higher. This is because a larger query set may be more representative for the queried landmark. As such, our approach is more robust against occlusion or bias-viewpoint captures. However, it may also result in a higher running time. Therefore, we set the value of K to 40 as a trade-off option.
- Fig. 7 reports the mAP scores against varied λ value. Interestingly, as the value of λ increases within a relative small beginning point, the mAP value will be increased as well, since it will prune some topics with a very small probability yielded by LDA. However, when keeping enhanced, the performance will be downgrade, since the larger λ is more likely to prune more topics, which may result into the missing of true topics with a large probability. Within our expectation, the above results over two dataset are consistent with our discussions in section 3.1.2. From our results, we finalize λ to be 0.4.
- Figs. 8 and 9 show the mAP score and running time against varied L value over two datasets, from which we can see the larger L is, the **pros** is that the larger mAP score can be achieved as more original information can be preserved; the **cons** comes from the larger running time for matrix factorization. To achieve a trade-off in terms of effectiveness and efficiency, we set L to be 64 in our experiments.

Based on the above, we just select K to be 40, λ to be 0.4 and L to be 64 for our method, which leads to the corresponding results in the remaining of experimental results for our multi-query expansions.

Table 2: **The mAP values of selected landmarks by different approaches against Flickr dataset.**

Method	London bridge	Triumphal arch	Sagrada familia	Sydney bridge	Singapore city	Temple heaven	Tokyo skytree	Taipei 101	Cairo tower	Brooklyn bridge	Maiden's tower	mAP
K-NN	46.75	32.03	33.55	38.93	29.83	54.33	17.21	32.39	44.37	22.56	64.58	38.78
LF+SVM	40.52	52.35	45.78	36.09	29.17	61.23	38.96	15.99	34.55	33.58	62.33	40.96
DRLR	52.45	35.65	51.48	34.58	40.33	62.45	42.33	40.24	44.58	38.34	57.35	45.52
GIANT	53.15	42.44	50.89	39.15	42.36	64.37	46.73	43.59	47.21	37.82	64.58	49.29
Ours	**57.83**	**64.76**	**57.33**	**45.59**	**63.48**	**68.38**	**60.48**	**59.32**	**70.04**	**54.58**	**72.38**	**61.29**

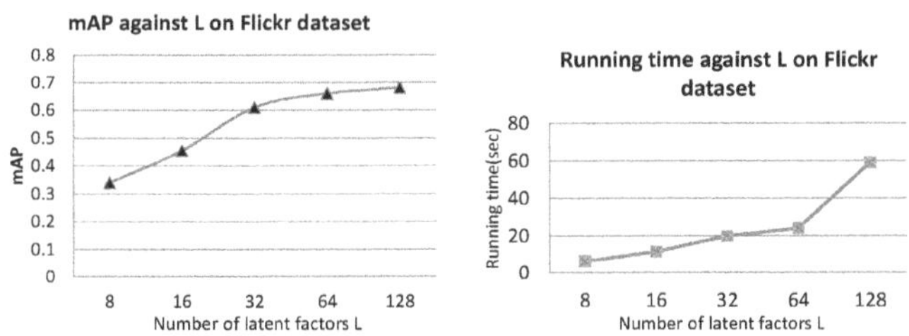

(a) (b)

Figure 8: (a) The mAP value for landmark retrieval over Flickr dataset against latent factor number L (b) The running time for landmark retrieval over Flicker dataset against latent factor number L.

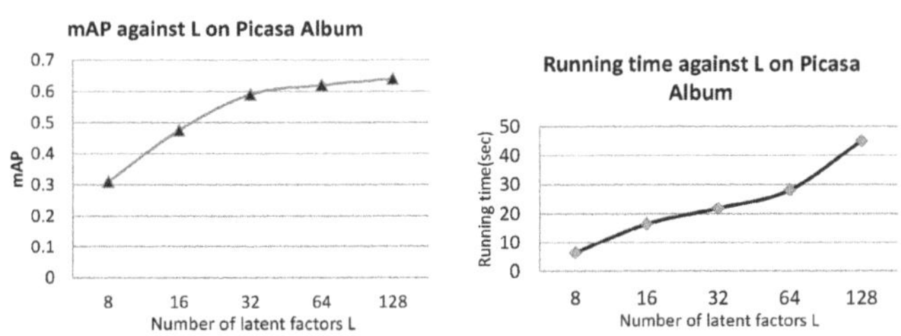

(a) (b)

Figure 9: (a) The mAP value for landmark retrieval over Picasa Web Album dataset against latent factor number L (b) The running time for landmark retrieval over Flicker Picasa Web Album against latent factor number L.

4.4 Landmark Retrieval and Ranking

We evaluate precision-recall and mAP for our approach and competitors. For each landmark in **Flickr** and **Picasa Web Album**, we randomly sample 20 query photos for each landmark and perform landmark retrieval to return the ranking list, where we obtain the precision-recall value and plot a precision-recall curve, plotting precision $p(r)$ versus the recall r. In our experiment, the average precision-recall is calculated by averaging their values on 20 query photos of each landmarks, and the average values of $p(r)$ over the internal from $r = 0$ to $r = 1$ are shown in Fig.10.

For each dataset, we also use mAP as the evaluation metric to examine the performance of each approach. For a query q, the average precision (AP) is defined as $AP(q) = \frac{1}{L_q} \sum_{r=1}^{n} P_q(r)\theta_q(r)$, where L_q is the ground-truth neighbors of query q in database, n is the number of photos in ranked list, we set $n = 100$, $P_q(r)$ denotes the precision of the top r retrieved photos, and $\theta_q(r) = 1$ if the r-th retrieved photo is a ground-truth within this landmark category and $\theta_q(r) = 0$, otherwise. In our case, given 20 query photos for each landmark, the mAP is defined over all 20 queries for

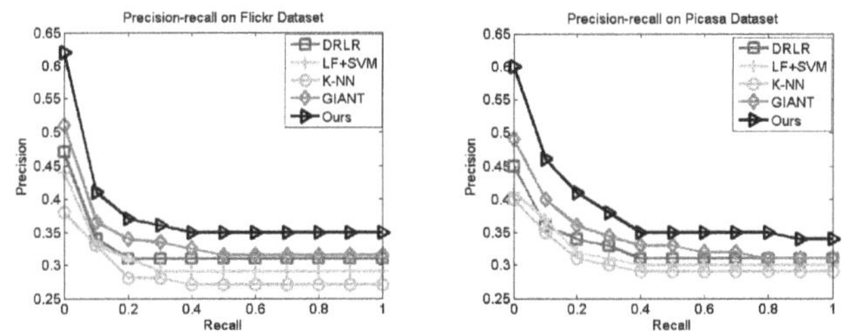

Figure 10: Comparison on average precision-recall curve on top-10 returned photo list over two databases.

each landmark as: $mAP = \frac{1}{20} \sum_{i=1}^{20} AP(q_i)$. In the step of multi-query expansions, by default, the multi-query set Q are composed of 40 recommended photos.

Fig.10 shows the average precision-recall curve over two benchmarks. We can see that our method consistently performs better than all competitors. The compared landmark retrieval results with mAP values are shown in Table 2 and Table 3. We observe that: (1) Our method outperforms all competitors, due to the effectiveness of exploiting the complementation of multiple queries as well as the use of the robust yet compact pattern mining technique; (2) The large intra-class variance limits the performance of LF+SVM and K-NN, especially for the **Flickr** dataset; and (3) DRLR detects discriminative regions from a single query photo, which degrades its performance when a query photo was shot from a bad viewpoint. Although GIANT also performs better but second to us, it only utilizes user-generated content to obtain visual attributes. This also demonstrates the need of exploiting user information to assist query understanding.

4.5 Comparing Query Expansion Approaches

Unlike AQE and DQE where plausible queries are selected via a low-level feature matching procedure, our strategy of selecting a multi-query set exploits latent topics and assistance from users to complement a q-user. While PQE uses a similar approach to expanding a single query into a multiple query set with pattern mining being used subsequently, its multi-query set is determined by manual selection. To demonstrate the superiority of our method over existing multiple query methods that can be adopted for landmark retrieval, we compare our method against the above three state-of-the-art approaches with query expansion, which are AQE, DQE, and PQE. Results are shown in Fig.11. We conclude that our multi-query based pattern mining approach outperforms AQE, DQE, and PQE for landmark retrieval by a large margin in terms of mAP values in two databases.

5. CONCLUSIONS AND FUTURE WORK

In this paper, we motivate the problem of landmark retrieval with possibly "ill-shaped" query landmark to be is-

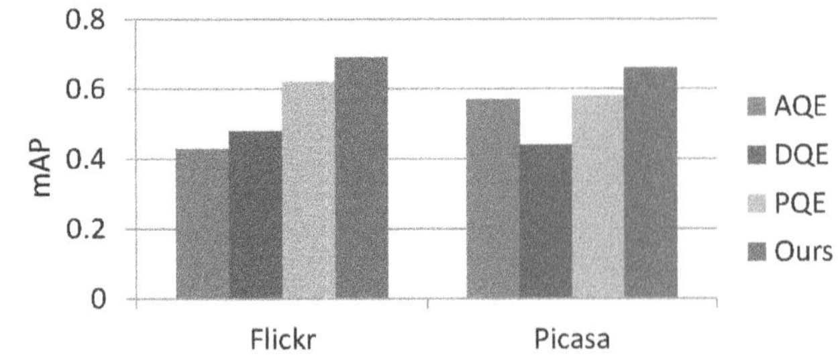

Figure 11: Comparison of query expansion methods.

Table 3: The mAP values of selected landmarks by different approaches against Picasa Web Album dataset.

Landmark	K-NN	LF+SVM	DRLR	GIANT	Ours
London clock	58.37	50.03	60.65	62.20	**71.89**
Eiffel tower	51.24	51.05	46.77	52.13	**61.71**
Forbidden city	44.04	55.28	58.57	58.94	**70.68**
Opera house	49.26	33.48	46.88	48.48	**61.74**
Catalunya plaza	24.87	12.37	21.67	23.23	**42.83**
Chicago plaza	35.48	38.38	33.76	38.74	**50.84**
mAP	43.87	40.09	44.73	47.28	**59.94**

sued. For this purpose, we propose an effective multi-query expansions paradigm to form a multi-photo query set, which sharing the highly similar latent topics with query landmark. Based on such multi-query set, we propose a novel technique to generate the robust pattern set (photo patch set regarding multi-query set). To ensure bias-free and enhance the efficiency, we adopt the existing minimum-description-length-principle based pattern mining techniques to remove similar query photos from the selected multi-query photos, leading to a compact set with smaller size. Then an effective retrieval rule is developed to calculate the similarity score between each photo in the database and mined pattern set (multi-query set). All these similarity scores are ranked to be the final ranking list of landmark retrieval based on query landmark. Experimental results on real-world datasets validate the significantly higher accuracy of our proposed method.

Our future work will investigate learning the deep features for landmark retrieval, such as DeCAF [9], which has been demonstrated to be powerful in many visual recognition applications. We would like to improve the current performance by addressing such gap. Another directions may go to leveraging the multi-view features [29, 30, 28, 27, 24, 34]. Zhu *et al.* [38] propose to learn the hypergraph structure of landmark photos for content based landmark retrieval, which inspires us to explore the (hyper) graph structure [31, 25, 26] of landmarks to improve the performance of landmark retrieval upon our proposed feature learning technique in this paper.

Acknowledgement. Xuemin Lin's research is supported by ARC DP120104168, ARC DP140103578, ARC DP150102728 and NSFC 61232006. Wenjie Zhang's research is supported by ARC DP150103071 and ARC DP150102728.

6. REFERENCES

[1] E. Amitay, N. Harel, R. Sivan, and A. Soffer. Web-a-where: geotagging web content. In *ACM SIGIR*, 2004.

[2] R. Arandjelovic and A. Zisserman. Three things everyone should know to improve object retrieval. In *CVPR*, 2012.

[3] S. Arslan, S. Kim, M. He, and R. Zimmermann. Relevance ranking in georeferenced video search. *Multimedia Systems*, 2010.

[4] D. M. Blei, A. Y. Ng, and M. I. Jordan. Latent dirichlet distribution. *J. Mach. Learn. Res.*, 2003.

[5] Y. Boureau, F. Bach, Y. Cun, and J. Ponce. Learning mid-level features for recognition. In *CVPR*, 2010.

[6] X. Cao, L. Wu, Z. Rasheed, H. Liu, T. Choe, F. Guo, and N. Haering. Automatic geo-registration for port surveillance. *International Journal of Pattern Recognition and Artificial Intelligence*, 2010.

[7] O. Chum, J. Philbin, J. Sivic, M. Isard, and A. Zisserman. Total recall: automatic query expansion with a generative feature model for object retrieval. In *ICCV*, 2007.

[8] C. Doersch, S. Singh, A. Gupta, J. Sivic, and A. A. Efros. What makes paris look like paris? *ACM Trans. Graph.*, 2012.

[9] J. Donahue, Y. Jia, O. Vinyals, J. Hoffman, N. Zhang, E. Tzeng, and T. Darrell. Decaf: A deep convolutional activation feature for generic visual recognition. In *arXiv:1310.1531*, 2013.

[10] Q. Fang, J. Sang, and C. Xu. Giant: Geo-informative attributes for location recognition and exploration. In *ACM Multimedia*, 2013.

[11] B. Fernando and T. Tuytelaars. Mining multiple queries for image retrieval: on-the-fly learning of an object-specific mid-level representation. In *ICCV*, 2013.

[12] P. D. Grunwald. *The minimum description length principle.* The MIT press, Cambridge, Massachusetts, USA, 2007.

[13] C. Hauff and G.-J. Houben. Geo-location estimation of flickr images: Social web based enrichment. In *Proceedings of ECIR 12*, 2012.

[14] J. Hays and A. A. Efros. im2gps: estimating geographic information from a single image. In *CVPR*, 2008.

[15] R. Ji, L. Duan, J. Chen, H. Yao, J. Yuan, and W. Gao. Location discriminative vocabulary coding for mobile landmark search. *International Journal of Computer Vision*, 96:290–314, 2012.

[16] E. Kalogerakis, O. Vesselova, J. Hays, A. A. Efros, and A. Hertzmann. Image sequence geolocation with human travel priors. In *Proceedings of ICCV 09*, pages 253–260, 2009.

[17] L. Kennedy and M. Naaman. Generating diverse and representative image search results for landmarks. In *Proceedings of WWW 08*, 2008.

[18] Y. Koren, R. Bell, and C. Volinsky. Matrix factorization techniques for recommender systems. *Computer*, 2007.

[19] M. Li and P. Vitanyi. *An introduction to Kolmogorov complexity and its applications.* Springer, 1993.

[20] D. Lowe. Object recognition from local scale-invariant features. In *ICCV*, 1999.

[21] J. Luo, D. Joshi, J. Yu, and A. Gallagher. Geotagging in multimedia and computer vision-a survey. *Multimedia Tools and Applications*, 2011.

[22] O. C. M. Perdoch and J. Matas. Efficient representation of local geometry for large scale object retrieval. In *CVPR 09*, 2009.

[23] J. Vreeken, M. Leeuwen, and A. Siebes. Krimp: mining itemsets that compress. *Data Min. Knowl. Discov*, 2011.

[24] Y. Wang, M. A. Cheema, X. Lin, and Q. Zhang. Multi-manifold ranking: Using multiple features for better image retrieval. In *PAKDD*, 2013.

[25] Y. Wang, X. Lin, L. Wu, and Q. Zhang. Shifting hypergraphs by probabilistic voting. In *PAKDD*, 2014.

[26] Y. Wang, X. Lin, L. Wu, Q. Zhang, and W. Zhang. Shifting multi-hypergraphs via collaborative probabilistic voting. *Knowledge and Information Systems, DOI 10.1007/s10115-015-0833-8*, 2015.

[27] Y. Wang, X. Lin, L. Wu, W. Zhang, and Q. Zhang. Exploiting correlation consensus: Towards subspace clustering for multi-modal data. In *ACM Multimedia*, 2014.

[28] Y. Wang, X. Lin, L. Wu, W. Zhang, and Q. Zhang. Lbmch: Learning bridging mapping for cross-modal hashing. In *ACM SIGIR*, 2015.

[29] Y. Wang, X. Lin, L. Wu, W. Zhang, Q. Zhang, and X. Huang. Robust subspace clustering for multi-view data by exploiting correlation consensus. *IEEE Transactions on Image Processing, DOI 10.1109/TIP.2015.2457339*, 2015.

[30] Y. Wang, X. Lin, and Q. Zhang. Towards metric fusion on multi-view data: a cross-view based graph random walk approach. In *ACM CIKM*, 2013.

[31] Y. Wang, J. Pei, X. Lin, Q. Zhang, and W. Zhang. An iterative fusion approach to graph-based semi-supervised learning from multiple views. In *PAKDD*, 2014.

[32] L. Wu and X. Cao. Geo-location estimation from two shadow trajectories. In *CVPR*, 2010.

[33] L. Wu, X. Cao, and H. Foroosh. Camera calibration and geo-location estimation from two shadow trajectories. *Computer Vision and Image Understanding*, 2010.

[34] L. Wu, Y. Wang, and J. Shepherd. Efficient image and tag co-ranking: a bregman divergence optimization method. In *ACM Multimedia*, 2013.

[35] Y. Zheng, L. Zhang, X. Xie, and W. Ma. Mining interesting locations and travel sequences from gps trajectories. In *Proceedings of World Wide Web*, 2009.

[36] J. Zhu, S. C. H. Hoi, M. R. Lyu, and S. Yan. Near-duplicate keyframe retrieval by nonrigid image matching. In *ACM Multimedia*, 2008.

[37] L. Zhu, J. Shen, H. Jin, L. Xie, and R. Zheng. Landmark classification with hierarchical multi-modal exemplar feature. *IEEE Transactions on Multimedia*, 2015.

[38] L. Zhu, J. Shen, H. Jin, R. Zheng, and L. Xie. Content-based visual landmark search via multimodal hypergraph learning. *IEEE Transactions on Cybernetics*, 2015.

What are Popular: Exploring Twitter Features for Event Detection, Tracking and Visualization

Hongyun Cai [#], Yang Yang [†], Xuefei Li [#], Zi Huang [#]
[#] The School of Information Technology and Electrical Engineering, The University of Queensland, Australia
[†] Computer Science and Engineering, University of Electronic Science and Technology of China, China
h.cai2@uq.edu.au, dlyyang@gmail.com, x.li14@uq.edu.au, huang@itee.uq.edu.au

ABSTRACT

As one of the most representative social media platforms, Twitter provides various real-life information on social events in real time. Despite that social event detection has been actively studied, tweet images, which appear in around 36 percent of the total tweets, have not been well utilized for this research problem. Most existing event detection methods tend to represent an image as a bag-of-visual-words and then process these visual words in the same way as textual words. This may not fully exploit the visual properties of images. State-of-the-art visual features like convolutional neural network (CNN) features have shown significant performance gains over the traditional bag-of-visual-words in unveiling the image's semantics. Unfortunately, they have not been employed in detecting events from social websites. Hence, how to make the most of tweet images to improve the performance of social event detection and visualization remains open. In this paper, we thoroughly study the impact of tweet images on social event detection for different event categories using various visual features. A novel topic model which jointly models five Twitter features (text, image, location, timestamp and hashtag) is designed to discover events from the sheer amount of tweets. Moreover, the evolutions of events are tracked by linking the events detected on adjacent days and each event is visualized by representative images selected on three predefined criteria. Extensive experiments have been conducted on a real-life tweet dataset to verify the effectiveness of our method.

Categories and Subject Descriptors

H.3.1 [**Information Storage and Retrieval**]: Content Analysis and Indexing

Keywords

Twitter Event Detection; Event Tracking; Event Visualization

1. INTRODUCTION

With the ever-accelerating development of modern technologies, social networking services have become increasingly popular nowadays. Among them, Twitter plays a leading role in providing a worldwide information sharing platform. All this up-to-date information describes the miscellaneous events which are happening all over the world. Event detection has long been a popular research topic which aims at discovering meaningful events from the sheer amount of raw tweets data. The correctly detected events can benefit many important applications such as emergency management, business marketing, public opinion survey, etc. How to detect events from Twitter thus becomes of great importance.

Different from the traditional text documents such as web pages, tweets contain a large number of meaningless and polluted content and are usually short. These characteristics present two challenges to the event detection task. First, the limitation that a tweet has maximum 140 characters leads to a problem that most existing topic models may not work any more for Twitter event detection. For example, Latent Dirichlet Allocation (LDA) [3] has been widely used for semantic-based event detection. Although LDA is a classic yet effective algorithm, its assumption that each document is a mixture of several topics is not valid for short tweets. Intuitively, a single tweet is usually about one topic [1]. Second, tweets are often overwhelmed by meaningless words and irrelevant images [25]. Existing detection methods such as LTT [28] and MMLDA [1] take no measures to filter those noisy contents.

Along with these challenges, tweets data also bring opportunities which are not found in conventional media. Apart from the textual content, tweets contain other features such as image, timestamp, location and hashtag. The benefits of incorporating different features into event detection are twofold. First, these features provide supplemental information that facilitates the event detection model. Second, different features describe the detected events from different aspects, which enables users to have a better understanding with more vivid visualizations. Recent studies have already started to consider some of these features. However, existing methods have the following two main limitations. First, although a fast-growing percentage of tweets contain images now, few efforts have been devoted to study these images in tweets and utilize them in the event detection task. [4] is the first attempt to discover the correlations between the tweet's image and its text. It classifies the image tweets into the visually-relevant and visually-irrelevant tweets. Existing image-involved Twitter event detection methods (e.g., [1, 23]) tend to use the whole image collections in their models despite that not all images are relevant and useful. Furthermore, the way they utilize images is to apply the bag-of-visual-words model on the extracted SIFT feature and then handle the generated visual words in the same way as textual words. This straightforward process of images may fail to fully capture the rich visual information embedded in images. Second, even though different Twitter features have been utilized in different models (e.g., spatio-temporal information [28], images [1, 2], hashtag [18]), no one has comprehensively ex-

MM'15, October 26–30, 2015, Brisbane, Australia.
© 2015 ACM. ISBN 978-1-4503-3459-4/15/10 ...$15.00.
DOI: http://dx.doi.org/10.1145/2733373.2806236.

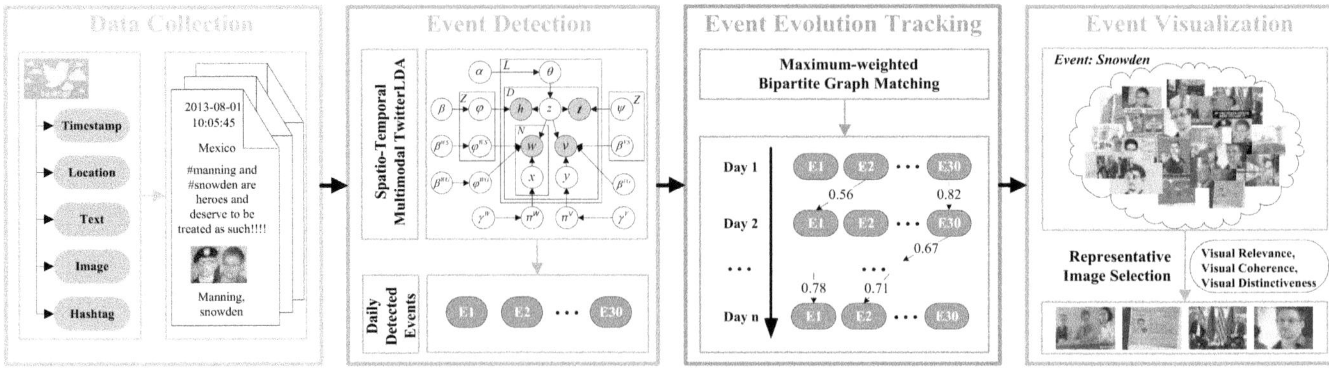

Figure 1: The Proposed Framework for Twitter Event Detection, Tracking and Visualization. Spatio-temporal multimodal TwitterLDA is first applied for event detection from the collected tweets data, followed by adopting the maximum-weighted bipartite graph matching for event evolution tracking. Finally, the representative images are selected for event visualization.

ploited all these features in one framework.

To tackle the above challenges and overcome the limitations, we propose a novel Twitter event detection approach termed **S**patio-**T**emporal **M**ultimodal TwitterLDA (STM-TwitterLDA). The framework is illustrated in Fig. 1. Five different Twitter features including text, image, timestamp, location and hashtag, are extracted from the raw tweets stream and input to our STM-TwitterLDA model. Notably, only text is compulsory and the other four features may not be necessarily present. Events are then periodically detected. The event evolution tracking is achieved by applying the maximum-weighted bipartite graph matching on the events discovered in consecutive periods. In the final step, the events are visualized by summarizing images of all the tweets related to the events, where the representative images are selected based on our defined three criteria. Different from the traditional topic models, in our STM-TwitterLDA each short tweet is generated from one topic rather than a mixture of topics. Importantly, we apply an SVM classifier as a preliminary filter to remove noisy images, followed by a latent filter in our STM-TwitterLDA model which classifies the images as general images and specific images. Only the specific images are used for event detection. In other words, the first filter (SVM classifier) removes the stop images and the second filter (latent in the STM-TwitterLDA) removes the general images. More details on the three image types are introduced in Section 3.1. We also take advantage of the state-of-the-art visual feature generated by convolutional neural networks (CNN) [10] and specifically design a component in our STM-TwitterLDA model to maximize the profit from tweet images.

The main contributions of this paper are summarized as follows:

- We design a novel generative probabilistic model for effective event detection in Twitter which jointly models various Twitter features. The intrinsic correlations among these features are fully explored for the performance improvements.
- We extensively study the impact of images on the Twitter event detection performance and propose a two-layer filter framework to address the issue of the noisy tweet images.
- We define three criteria to select the representative images for event visualization and verify its quality by a case study.
- We conduct comprehensive experiments on a large real-world tweet dataset. The results prove the advantages of our STM-TwitterLDA over existing studies.

The remainder of this paper is organized as follows. In Section 2, we review the related work on Twitter event detection and event visualization. Our proposed Twitter event detection model is presented in Section 3, followed by the event evolution tracking and visualization approach in Section 4. The experimental results are shown in Section 5 and Section 6 concludes the paper.

2. RELATED WORK

2.1 Topic Models for Twitter Event Detection

Event detection in Twitter has been extensively studied in recent years. As mentioned in [1], majority of these methods can be categorized into frequency-based, semantic-based, graph-based and machine learning-based. In this paper, we focus on the semantic-based methods. More specifically, a literature review is conducted on the Twitter event detection via LDA-based topic model. Latent Dirichlet Allocation (LDA) [3] was first proposed for topic discovery in 2003. Ever since that, many extensions and variants (e.g., [26, 20]) have been proposed due to its effectiveness and high degree of modularity. Labeled LDA [18] presents a partitially supervised learning model and incorporates hashtags as labels for their model. However, not all topics in Twitter include hashtags. TwitterLDA is proposed in [27] as the first topic model specifically designed for tweets data. Different from the traditional formal documents, tweets are short and noisy. In view of this, TwitterLDA makes two major corresponding adjustments. First, instead of representing a document as a distribution of multiple topics, they think that each tweet is only mapped to one topic. Second, they classify the words into background words and topic words. Background words are the noisy words commonly used in all tweets while topic words are the meaningful words from some topics. Inspired by TwitterLDA, TimeUserLDA [6] extends TwitterLDA via utilizing the time factor in addition to the text for bursty topics discovery. MMLDA [1] is another extension of TwitterLDA, which appends the tweet images in their model. SIFT features are extracted from the images in tweets, and the visual words are generated by applying the bag-of-visual-words model on these SIFT features. After that, the visual words are treated in the same way as textual words in their MMLDA model. However, images in tweets are not necessarily relevant to the text [4]. Moreover, representing an image as a bag-of-visual-words may not fully exploit the visual properties existing in images, given that recent visual features generated from sophisticated methods such as convolutional neural networks (CNN) can represent images more effectively than traditional features like SIFT features in many recognition tasks [12]. In [28], a Location-Time constrained Topic (LTT) model is proposed by extending the TOT model [22] and considering the latitude and longitude information. Three tweet features are considered in their

Location-Time constrained Topic (LTT) model, including text, time and geography information. Nevertheless, LTT follows the standard LDA framework and the problem caused by the above two characteristics of the tweets are not addressed in their model. Besides, tweet images are ignored in their work.

2.2 Representative Image Selection

Images provide users a more vivid description of an event and representative image selection is an effective way to summarize a set of images for event visualization. Different summarization objectives are considered in existing work. In [24], authors design three criteria: relevance, visual consistency and burstiness to personalize trending image search suggestion. However, the diversity is not considered. [9] improves the diversity of the search results by ranking the set of near-duplicate video clusters. Similarly, [1] applies normalized cut for images clustering and then adopts manifold ranking algorithm to rank the images within each cluster. The most representative image is selected from each cluster to construct the representative images set. Diversity is also considered in [21] to measure the concept subgraph redundancies. However, for Twitter event visualization, tweet images are quite noisy and some images are not relevant enough to represent the event [4]. These less relevant images should be removed from the images set first. In this sense, a visual coherence based filter should be built before the image diversity is taken into account. In our work, we use a random walk process [8] to get the visual coherence score, which is considered together with a visual relevance score to filter out the less relevant images. After that, the bipartite graph hitting time [14] is adopted to achieve image result diversity.

Our work is different from the existing work in the following important ways. First, our topic model is specifically designed for the tweets data. Although TwitterLDA has tackled the problem of short and noisy tweets contents, many other features such as images are not taken into account. Our model is capable of jointly modelling five different Twitter features with the noisy words and images filtered. Second, we use the CNN feature in our model rather than the bag-of-visual-words feature as in previous studies. CNN feature has been proved to generate consistent superior results compared to others for a wide range of visual recognition and classification tasks on different datasets [17, 19]. Furthermore, our model is well designed to be fit for the CNN feature. Third, we propose three criteria for representative image selection. In contrast to other algorithms, our schema first generates a candidate set based on the visual relevance and coherence in order to remove the less relevant images. This is very important for the messy tweet images. After that, the representative images are selected from the candidates with the consideration of diversity which is omitted in [24].

3. TWITTER EVENT DETECTION

In this section, we first formally define some concepts in this paper and then present the proposed STM-TwitterLDA model for event detection from Twitter.

3.1 Notations and Definitions

Table 1 summarizes the notations used in this paper for our proposed topic model and the corresponding descriptions.

Tweet. A tweet is a five-tuple (d, v, t, h, l) that denotes a tweet is posted with text d, tweet image v and hashtag h at time t in location l. The scale of the location is adjustable, which could be a country, a state or even a user-defined area. It is set as country in this paper.

Word Type. The words from tweets are categorized into three types: the stop word, the general word and the specific word. The stop words are a set of predefined words to be removed in the data pre-process phase, for example "a", "we", "haha" etc. The general words are the noisy words frequently and uniformly appearing in many events and thus not useful for event detection. The specific words are the distinguishable words for describing different events. The general words and specific words are automatically recognized by our topic model.

Notation	Description
L	Total number of locations
D_l	Total number of tweets in location l
$N_{l,d}, C_{l,d}$	Total number of words and hashtags in l's d-th tweet
M	Dimensionality of the visual feature
Z, W, H	Total number of topics, words, and hashtags
z, w, h	Label for topic, word, and hashtag
v, t	Visual feature vector and timestamp
x, y	Indicator of general or specific for word and image
φ^{WG}, β^{VG}	General word and image distribution
φ^{WS}, β^{VS}	Specific word and image distribution
φ	Hashtag distribution
θ	Location-specific topic distribution
π^W, π^V, ψ	Bernoulli and Beta distribution
$\beta, \beta^{WG}, \beta^{WS}, \alpha, \gamma^W, \gamma^V$	Dirichlet priors

Table 1: Notation

Image Type. Three types of tweet images are defined, namely, the stop image, the general image and the specific image. The definition of each image type is similar to the corresponding word type. The only difference is that stop images are defined as a set of images belonging to some predefined categories since we cannot list all the exact images to be filtered in the data pre-process step. The stop images must meet two requirements: they are visually similar to each other when they appear in different events, and they must be easily recognized by certain methods. After analysing the tweet images, we define the following four categories including cartoon, landscape, diagram and the screenshot of text as the stop images categories and use an SVM classifier to identify them. The general images are the noisy images which bring negative effect on event detection. The noises could be caused by the users (the irrelevant images) or the characteristics of images (the unidentifiable images for events). The specific images are meant to describe the event visually. Only the specific images are used for event detection.

Topic. Given a collection of tweets, a topic z generated by our topic model is a combination of a multinomial word distribution φ_z^{WS}, a multinomial hashtag distribution φ_z, a Beta timestamp distribution ψ_z, and a Dirichlet image distribution β_z^{VS}. All the above four distributions are location-specific.

Event. An event is a set of tweets which are semantically coherent to each other. Specifically, an event is defined as a group of tweets labelled as the same topic z by the topic model.

3.2 Spatio-Temporal Multimodal TwitterLDA

Suppose we are given a continuous tweet stream as the input, and each tweet consists of five features: text, image, timestamp, location and hashtag. The objective of this work is to model the topics latent in the tweets data by exploiting different Twitter features so as to detect events from these tweets automatically. Afterwards, the evolutions of these events along the timeline are tracked and each event is visualized using the summarized information and the representative images. In this paper, STM-TwitterLDA is proposed as a novel topic model for Twitter event detection. Its graphical model is shown in Fig. 2.

Formally, we assume that there are Z topics in total in tweets data. In contrast to the original LDA, each tweet is only assigned to one topic in our model. Unlike TwitterLDA which presumes that each single user has a specific topic distribution, we assume that

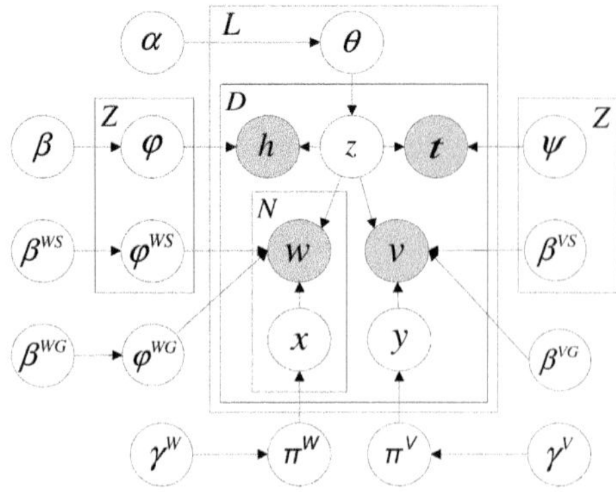

Figure 2: Graphical Model of STM-TwitterLDA

users in the same location share the same topics of interest (considering that these users usually share the similar cultural background and live in the same environment), hence the tweets collected from the same location share one topic distribution θ, i.e., a location-specific topic distribution. Our assumption is more applicable for the general event detection because the tweets from each single user are very sparse in the whole tweets collection. In our model, words (images) are divided into general words (images) and specific words (images). Two latent random variables x and y work as the general/specific indicators for words and images. Each topic z in our model has a mixture of four distributions decided by four Twitter features: a multinomial hashtag distribution φ_z, a multinomial distribution over specific words φ_z^{WS}, a Beta timestamp distribution ψ_z, and a Dirichlet distribution over specific images β_z^{VS}. Note that instead of representing images as bag-of-visual-words and sampling visual words using the Dirichlet-multinomial distribution as in existing image-involved topic models, we adopt the state-of-the-art CNN feature to represent images and model the normalized CNN feature by the Dirichlet distribution. As shown in Fig. 2, there are three distributions not conditioned on the topic z: the Dirichlet-multinomial distributions over general words β^{WG} and φ^{WG}, and the Dirichlet distribution over general images β^{VG}. These are the topic-independent distributions shared by the general words and images because they do not belong to any specific topics.

The proposed STM-TwitterLDA is different from TwitterLDA mainly from two aspects. First, STM-TwitterLDA models topics as location-specific distributions while TwitterLDA uses user-specific distributions. Second, STM-TwitterLDA utilizes multiple Twitter features including location, time, text, hashtag, and image, while TwitterLDA considers user and text only.

3.3 The Generative Process

When a tweet is generated, a topic is first assigned based on the topic distribution from the user's location. Next, given the topic, the word(s), image, hashtag(s), timestamp are then generated based on their own distributions. Notably, when the words and image are generated, they are selected from either the general or the specific sets of words and images. The generative process for all tweets is as follows, where Dir() and Multi() represent Dirichlet and multinomial distributions respectively.

1. Draw $\varphi^{WG} \sim$ Dir(β^{WG}) indicating the general word distribution. Draw $\pi^W \sim$ Dir(γ^W) and $\pi^V \sim$ Dir(γ^V) denoting the Bernoulli distributions that determine the selections between the general words and specific words, and between the general images and specific images.
2. For each topic $z = 1, \cdots, Z$, draw $\varphi_z^{WS} \sim$ Dir(β_z^{WS}) and $\varphi_z \sim$ Dir(β_z), denoting the specific word and hashtag distribution for topic z.
3. For each location $l = 1, \cdots, L$
   (a) Draw $\theta_l \sim$ Dir(α), indicating distribution of topics over the tweets collection in location l.
   (b) For the d-th tweet in location l, $d = 1, \cdots, D_l$
      i. Draw $z_{l,d} \sim$ Multi(θ_l), corresponding to the topic assigned for each tweet.
      ii. For the n-th word in the tweet, $n = 1, \cdots, N_{l,d}$
         - Draw a variable $x_{l,d,n} \sim$ Bernoulli(π^W) as an indicator for general or specific word;
         - Draw $w_{l,d,n} \sim$ Multi (φ^{WG}) if $x_{l,d,n} = 0$, and $w_{l,d,n} \sim$ Multi ($\varphi^{WS}_{z_{l,d}}$) if $x_{l,d,n} = 1$.
      iii. For the c-th hashtag of the tweet, $c = 1, \cdots, C_{l,d}$
         - Draw $h_{l,d,c} \sim$ Multi ($\varphi_{z_{l,d}}$), a Multinomial distribution conditioned on the topic $z_{l,d}$.
      iv. Draw a timestamp $t_{l,d} \sim$ Beta($\psi_{z_{l,d}}$), a Beta distribution conditioned on the topic $z_{l,d}$.
      v. Draw a variable $y_{l,d} \sim$ Bernoulli(π^V) as an indicator for general or specific image.
      vi. Draw $v_{l,d} \sim$ Dir(β^{VG}) if $y_{l,d} = 0$, and $v_{l,d} \sim$ Dir ($\beta^{VS}_{z_{l,d}}$) if $y_{l,d} = 1$.

3.4 Inference

In our proposed STM-TwitterLDA, there are three latent variables to be inferred from the observed Twitter features $\{w, v, t, h\}$, including the topic z, the general-specific (word and image) indicators x and y. Collapsed Gibbs sampling [7] is adopted as in other topic models for the approximate model inference to obtain these latent variables due to its effectiveness and simplicity.

3.4.1 *Sampling* $z_{l,d}$

We firstly sample the topic label for the d-th tweet in location l. Let i denote $\{l, d\}$, we use the following equation to sample z_i:

$$p(z_i|\boldsymbol{Z}_{\neg i}, \boldsymbol{W}, \boldsymbol{V}, \boldsymbol{X}, \boldsymbol{Y}, \boldsymbol{T}, \boldsymbol{H}) \propto \frac{p(\boldsymbol{Z}, \boldsymbol{W}, \boldsymbol{V}, \boldsymbol{X}, \boldsymbol{Y}, \boldsymbol{T}, \boldsymbol{H}|\Theta)}{p(\boldsymbol{Z}_{\neg i}, \boldsymbol{W}_{\neg i}, \boldsymbol{V}_{\neg i}, \boldsymbol{X}_{\neg i}, \boldsymbol{Y}_{\neg i}, \boldsymbol{T}_{\neg i}, \boldsymbol{H}_{\neg i}|\Theta)} \tag{1}$$

where Θ is the set of all the parameters.

To derive the above conditional probability, we start with computing the following joint probability:

$$\begin{aligned} & p(\boldsymbol{Z}, \boldsymbol{W}, \boldsymbol{V}, \boldsymbol{X}, \boldsymbol{Y}, \boldsymbol{T}, \boldsymbol{H}|\Theta) \\ & = p(\boldsymbol{W}|\boldsymbol{Z}, \boldsymbol{X}, \beta^{WG}, \beta^{WS}) p(\boldsymbol{X}|\gamma^W) p(\boldsymbol{V}|\boldsymbol{Z}, \boldsymbol{Y}, \beta^{VG}, \beta^{VS}) \\ & \quad \times p(\boldsymbol{Y}|\gamma^V) p(\boldsymbol{T}|\boldsymbol{Z}, \psi) p(\boldsymbol{H}|\boldsymbol{Z}, \beta) p(\boldsymbol{Z}|\alpha) \\ & = \frac{\Delta(n^{\boldsymbol{W}}_{x=0} + \beta^{WG})}{\Delta(\beta^{WG})} \prod_{z=1}^{Z} \frac{\Delta(n^{\boldsymbol{W}}_{z,x=1} + \beta^{WS})}{\Delta(\beta^{WS})} \frac{\Delta(n^{\boldsymbol{X}}_{(.)} + \gamma^W)}{\Delta(\gamma^W)} \\ & \quad \times \prod_{l=1}^{L} \prod_{d=1}^{D} p(v_i|\beta^{VG}) \prod_{l=1}^{L} \prod_{d=1}^{D} p(v_i|\beta^{VS}_{z_i}) \frac{\Delta(n^{\boldsymbol{Y}}_{(.)} + \gamma^V)}{\Delta(\gamma^V)} \\ & \quad \times \prod_{l=1}^{L} \prod_{d=1}^{D} p(t_i|\psi_{z_i}) \prod_{z=1}^{Z} \frac{\Delta(n^{\boldsymbol{H}}_z + \beta)}{\Delta(\beta)} \prod_{l=1}^{L} \frac{\Delta(n^{\boldsymbol{Z}}_l + \alpha)}{\Delta(\alpha)} \end{aligned} \tag{2}$$

where $n^{\boldsymbol{W}}_{x=0}$ and $n^{\boldsymbol{W}}_{z,x=1}$ denote two W-dimensional vectors in which each value is the number of times every word is sampled as general word and the number of times each word is sampled as specific word with topic z respectively. $n^{\boldsymbol{X}}_{(.)}$ is a 2-dimensional vector denoting the number of times $x = 0$ and $x = 1$ occurs respectively. Similarly, $n^{\boldsymbol{Y}}_{(.)}$ is the counter for y. $n^{\boldsymbol{H}}_z$ is a H-dimensional vector and each value in it denotes the number of times each hashtag is sampled as topic z. $n^{\boldsymbol{Z}}_l$ is a Z-dimensional vector in which each element denotes the number of times that each topic occurs in the tweets from location l. v_i and t_i represent the normalized visual feature vector and the timestamp of the d-th tweet in location l.

Given Eqn. 1 and Eqn. 2, the probability of assigning a topic z to z_i can be estimated as follows:

$$\begin{aligned} & p(z_i = z|\boldsymbol{Z}_{\neg i}, \boldsymbol{W}, \boldsymbol{V}, \boldsymbol{X}, \boldsymbol{Y}, \boldsymbol{T}, \boldsymbol{H}) \\ & \propto \frac{\prod_{w=1}^{W}\prod_{p=1}^{n_i^w}(n_{z,x=1}^w+\beta^{WS}-p)}{\prod_{q=1}^{N_i}(\sum_{w=1}^{W} n_{z,x=1}^w+W\beta^{WS}-q)} \frac{\prod_{m=1}^{M} v_{i,m}^{\beta_{z,m}^{VS}-1}}{\Delta(\beta_z^{VS})} \\ & \times \frac{(1-t_i)^{\psi_{z1}-1} t_i^{\psi_{z2}-1}}{B(\psi_{z1},\psi_{z2})} \frac{\prod_{h=1}^{H}\prod_{p=1}^{n_i^h}(n_z^h+\beta-p)}{\prod_{q=1}^{C_i}(\sum_{h=1}^{H} n_z^h+H\beta-q)} \frac{n_{l,\neg i}^z+\alpha}{\sum_{z=1}^{Z} n_l^z+T\alpha-1} \end{aligned} \tag{3}$$

where N_i and C_i denote the number of words and hashtags occurs in the d-th tweet from location l. n_i^w and n_i^h denote the number of times word w and hashtag h occur in the d-th tweet from location l. $n_{z,x=1}^w$ and n_z^h are the number of times specific word w and hashtag h is sampled as topic z. $n_{l,\neg i}^z$ is the number of times topic z occurs in the tweets from location l not including the d-th tweet. t_i and $v_{i,m}$ are the timestamp and the m-th dimension of the visual feature vector for the d-th tweet from location l.

3.4.2 *Sampling $x_{l,d,n}$ and $y_{l,d}$*

Next, we sample the general-specific indicators x and y. Let i be $\{l, d\}$ and j be $\{l, d, n\}$, given Eqn. 2, x_j is sampled as follows:

$$\begin{aligned} & p(x_j|\boldsymbol{X}_{\neg j}, \boldsymbol{Z}, \boldsymbol{W}, \boldsymbol{V}, \boldsymbol{Y}, \boldsymbol{T}, \boldsymbol{H}) \\ & \propto \frac{p(\boldsymbol{Z},\boldsymbol{W},\boldsymbol{V},\boldsymbol{X},\boldsymbol{Y},\boldsymbol{T},\boldsymbol{H}|\ominus)}{p(\boldsymbol{Z},\boldsymbol{W}_{\neg j},\boldsymbol{V},\boldsymbol{X}_{\neg j},\boldsymbol{Y},\boldsymbol{T},\boldsymbol{H}|\ominus)} \\ & \propto \frac{\Delta(n_{x=0}^{\boldsymbol{W}}+\beta^{WG})}{\Delta(n_{x=0,\neg j}^{\boldsymbol{W}}+\beta^{WG})} \prod_{z=1}^{Z} \frac{\Delta(n_{z,x=1}^{\boldsymbol{W}}+\beta^{WS})}{\Delta(n_{z,x=1,\neg j}^{\boldsymbol{W}}+\beta^{WS})} \frac{\Delta(n_{(.)}^{\boldsymbol{X}}+\gamma^W)}{\Delta(n_{\neg j}^{\boldsymbol{X}}+\gamma^W)} \end{aligned} \tag{4}$$

Accordingly, the probability of assigning a binary label 1 to x_j as a specific word indicator is estimated as below:

$$\begin{aligned} & p(x_j = 1|\boldsymbol{X}_{\neg j}, \boldsymbol{Z}, \boldsymbol{W}, \boldsymbol{V}, \boldsymbol{Y}, \boldsymbol{T}, \boldsymbol{H}) \\ & \propto \frac{n_{\neg j}^{x=1}+\gamma^W}{\sum_{x=0}^{1} n_{\neg j}^x+2\gamma^W} \frac{n_{z_i,x=1,\neg j}^{w_j}+\beta^{WS}}{\sum_{w=1}^{W} n_{z_i,x=1,\neg j}^w+W\beta^{WS}} \end{aligned} \tag{5}$$

where $n_{\neg j}^{x=1}$ denotes the number of times $x = 1$ occurs for the tweets set not including the n-th word in the d-th tweet from location l. $n_{z_i,x=1,\neg j}^{w_j}$ denotes the number of times the specific word w_j is sampled as topic z_i for the tweets set not including the n-th word in the d-th tweet from location l.

The probability of assigning a binary label 0 to x_j is similar to Eqn. 5 by replacing β^{WS}, $n_{\neg j}^{x=1}$ and $n_{z_i,x=1,\neg j}^{w_j}$ with β^{WG}, $n_{\neg j}^{x=0}$ and $n_{x=0,\neg j}^{w_j}$ correspondingly. $n_{\neg j}^{x=0}$ and $n_{x=0,\neg j}^{w_j}$ denotes the number of times $x = 0$ occurs and the number of times word w_j is sampled with label 0 for the tweets set not including the n-th word in the d-th tweet from location l.

Next we will introduce the process of sampling $y_{l,d}$. Given Eqn. 2, to sample y_i, the following equation is used:

$$\begin{aligned} & p(y_i|\boldsymbol{Y}_{\neg i}, \boldsymbol{W}, \boldsymbol{V}, \boldsymbol{X}, \boldsymbol{Z}, \boldsymbol{T}, \boldsymbol{H}) \\ & \propto \frac{p(\boldsymbol{Z},\boldsymbol{W},\boldsymbol{V},\boldsymbol{X},\boldsymbol{Y},\boldsymbol{T},\boldsymbol{H}|\ominus)}{p(\boldsymbol{Z}_{\neg i},\boldsymbol{W}_{\neg i},\boldsymbol{V}_{\neg i},\boldsymbol{X}_{\neg i},\boldsymbol{Y}_{\neg i},\boldsymbol{T}_{\neg i},\boldsymbol{H}_{\neg i}|\ominus)} \\ & \propto p(v_i|\beta^{VG}) \prod_{z=1}^{Z} p(v_i|\beta_z^{VS}) \frac{\Delta(n_{(.)}^{\boldsymbol{Y}}+\gamma^V)}{\Delta(\gamma^V)} \end{aligned} \tag{6}$$

Accordingly, the probability of assigning a binary label 1 to y_i is estimated as below:

$$p(y_i = 1|\boldsymbol{Y}_{\neg i}, \boldsymbol{Z}, \boldsymbol{W}, \boldsymbol{V}, \boldsymbol{Y}, \boldsymbol{T}, \boldsymbol{H}) \propto \frac{n_{\neg i}^{y=1}+\gamma^V}{\sum_{y=0}^{1} n_{\neg i}^y+2\gamma^V} \frac{\prod_{m=1}^{M} v_{i,m}^{\beta_{z_i,m}^{VS}-1}}{\Delta(\beta_{z_i}^{VS})} \tag{7}$$

where $n_{\neg i}^{y=1}$ denotes the number of times $y = 1$ occurs for the tweets set not including the d-th tweet from location l.

Similarly, the probability of assigning a binary label 0 to y_i can be derived by using β^{VG}, $n_{\neg i}^{y=0}$ corresponding to $\beta_{z_i}^{VS}$ and $n_{\neg i}^{y=1}$ in Eqn. 7. $n_{\neg i}^{y=0}$ denotes the number of times $y = 0$ occurs for the tweets set not including the d-th tweet from location l.

3.5 Parameter Estimation

We use the following variational EM [5] procedure to estimate the parameters of our STM-TwitterLDA model.

1. (E-step) For each tweet, use Gibbs sampling as described before to find the optimizing values of the variational parameters θ, φ^{WS}, φ^{WG}, φ, π^W and π^V.
2. (M-step) Maximize the joint likelihood of the model with respect to the model parameters α, ψ, γ^W, γ^V, β, β^{WG}, β^{WS}, β^{VS} and β^{VG} given the variational parameters fixed as computed in the E-step.

Notably, the parameters of some well-studied Dirichlet distribution are set fixed as $\alpha = 50/T$, $\beta^{WG} = \beta^{WS} = 0.1$ for simplicity as in existing work [28]. The other variational parameters updated after each Gibbs sampling iteration are estimated as following [1].

$$\begin{cases} \psi_{z1} = \bar{t}_z(\frac{\bar{t}_z(1-\bar{t}_z)}{s_z^2} - 1), \\ \psi_{z2} = (1 - \bar{t}_z)(\frac{\bar{t}_z(1-\bar{t}_z)}{s_z^2} - 1), \\ \theta_{l,z} = \frac{n_l^z+\alpha}{\sum_{z=1}^{Z} n_l^z+Z\alpha}, \\ \varphi_w^{WG} = \frac{n_{(.)}^w+\beta^{WG}}{\sum_{w=1}^{W} n_{(.)}^w+W\beta^{WG}}, \\ \varphi_{z,w}^{WS} = \frac{n_z^w+\beta^{WS}}{\sum_{w=1}^{W} n_z^w+W\beta^{WS}}, \\ \pi_x^W = \frac{n_{(.)}^x+\gamma^W}{\sum_{x=0}^{1} n_{(.)}^x+2\gamma^W}, \\ \varphi_{z,h} = \frac{n_z^h+\beta}{\sum_{h=1}^{H} n_z^h+H\beta}, \end{cases} \tag{8}$$

where $\bar{t}_z$ and s_z^2 are the sample mean and the biased sample variance of the timestamps belong to topic z respectively. Note that these two values can be maintained incrementally by their zeroth, first and second order moments (denoting as M_0, M_1 and M_2) as $\bar{t}_z = M_1/M_0$ and $s_z^2 = M_2/M_0 - (M_1/M_0)^2$. n_l^z is the number of times topic z is sampled for the tweets from location l. $n_{(.)}^w$ is the number of times word w is sampled. n_z^w and n_z^h are the number of times w and h are sampled given the topic z. $n_{(.)}^x$ is the number of times label x is sampled. The estimation of π_y^V is similar to π_x^W, with counting $n_{(.)}^y$ as the number of times label y is sampled.

To estimate the parameter β^{VS} and β^{VG}, the Newton-Raphson method is applied due to its linear time performance in computing the inverse of Hessian matrix [15]. The update rule for parameter

[1]The estimation of ψ_z utilizes the method of moments.

β^{VG} is as follows:

$$\beta_m^{VG\,new} = \beta_m^{VG\,old} - (\boldsymbol{H}^{-1}\boldsymbol{g})_m = \beta_m^{VG\,old} - \frac{g_m - b}{q_{m,m}} \quad (9)$$

where $b = \frac{\sum_{m=1}^{|M|}(g_m/q_{m,m})}{1/(N^{VG}\Psi'(\sum_{m=1}^{|M|}\beta_m^{VG}))}$ and $g_m = N^{VG}(\Psi(\sum_{m=1}^{|V|}\beta_m^{VG}) - \beta_m^{VG}) + \sum_{i \in GeneralImage} v_{i,m}$. N^{VG} is the number of general images, Ψ, Ψ' and δ denote the digamma function, the trigamma function and the delta function. The update rule for β^{VS} is similar, with N_z^{VS} being the number of images sampled as topic z.

4. EVENT TRACKING AND VISUALIZATION

The social events are dynamically changing over time, hence tracking the event evolution is no less important than detecting events. Besides, event visualization is also of great importance for providing users a vivid and intuitive presentation of an event.

4.1 Event Evolution Tracking

Inspired by [13], the maximum-weighted bipartite graph matching (MWBGM) is applied for tracking the evolution of events in consecutive days. Formally speaking, a bipartite graph $G = (V, E)$ is constructed with two sets of nodes which correspond to the two sets of events detected in two successive days. The edge between two nodes represents the relevance between two events. In this work, each event is represented as a set of words, among which each word has a value showing its probability of being assigned to this event. The event relevance score between two events (i.e., the weight of the edge in the graph) is then defined as $event\ relevance = \sum_{w \in I} p(w) / \sum_{w \in U} p(w)$, where I represents the intersection set of words in the two events and U denotes the union word set. $p(w)$ is the maximum probability value of the word w being assigned to the two events. The objective of MWBGM is to find a subset of the events from the graph so that each event is only linked to at most one event in the adjacent day and the multiplication of the weights between the final event pairs is maximized. The linkages between those events in the final event pairs indicate the evolutions of these events. For instance, event 1 is detected on day 1 and event 2 is detected on the next day. If event 1 and event 2 form an event pair after applying MWBGM, it means that event 1 evolves into event 2 on the second day. Finally, the event evolutions over time are tracked by the event chains formed from the individual event pairs. In this work, the MWBGM problem is addressed by the Kuhn-Munkres algorithm [16] which estimates the maximum sum of the log probabilities of the final event pairs' weights.

4.2 Event Visualization

In addition to provide supplemental information for event detection, images can be further used for event visualization since they describe the event in a much more straightforward way. How to select the most representative images for an event from a large number of disordered candidates is the key for event visualization.

4.2.1 *Representative Image Selection*

Three aspects are considered when choosing the representative images to visualize a target event: visual relevance, visual coherence and distinctiveness.

Visual Relevance When discussing an event, a same image might be posted by different users. The more times an image is tweeted, the more relevant it is to the event. In other words, the visual relevance $P_r(I_k)$ is determined by the occurrence number N_k of an image I_k. Therefore the visual relevance $P_r(I_k)$ is defined as $P_r(I_k) = \frac{N_k}{M}$, where M is the total number of images in the images set of the event.

Visual Coherence An image with more near neighbours is more coherent to the event and should have a higher probability to be the representative image. Visual coherence is defined under the above assumption as in [24] and is calculated by a random walk process [8] in this work. Each node I_k represents an image. There exists an edge $e_{k,l}$ between I_k and I_l if I_l is one of the K-nearest neighbours of I_k. The weight of the edge $e_{k,l}$ is calculated as the visual similarity $Sim(I_k, I_l)$ divided by the sum of visual similarities among I_k and all its K-nearest neighbours. Visual coherence $P_c(I_k)$ is formulated as $P_c(I_k) = (\alpha E + \frac{(1-\alpha)}{M}\Lambda^T)P_c(I_k)$, where E is the transition matrix constructed by $e_{i,j}$, and Λ is a column vector with the i-th element being the textual similarity between the tweet that image I_i belongs to and the target event. M is the total number of images in the image set of the event. The optimal solution is the eigenvector of $(\alpha E + \frac{(1-\alpha)}{M}\Lambda^T)$ with the largest eigenvalue. Notably, in [24] the initial scores for random walk are set to be equal for all the images while we define the initial score as the textual score of the tweet that each image belongs to for boost.

Distinctiveness Intuitively, a set of images with diverse contents are more informative than images with duplicate contents. This makes distinctiveness an important criterion for representative image selection. The visual relevance and visual coherence score are summed up (i.e., $P_r(I_k) + P_c(I_k)$) to get a representative image candidates set containing the more relevant images. Suppose a total of K representative images are needed. We firstly select the most representative image as the one with the largest sum of visual relevance and coherence value. After that, the remaining $K - 1$ representative images are selected from the image candidates set of the event one by one. The remaining images must carry diverse contents in order to describe the event from different perspectives. In [11], the bipartite graph hitting time is applied to personalized query suggestion with diversity awareness. Similarly, to achieve the representative images diversity, we construct a bipartite graph $G = (V, E)$ by two sets of nodes $V = V_1 \cup V_2$. One set (V_2) is the images which have already been selected as the representative images and the other set (V_1) contains all the rest images. A random walk is performed on this bipartite graph where the transition probability is defined as $p_{ij} = \sum_{k \in V_2} \frac{w(i,k)}{d_i}\frac{w(k,j)}{d_k}$, and $d_i = \sum_{k \in V_2} w(i,k)$.

The following linear system is obtained for computing the hitting time [14]:

$$\begin{cases} h_i = 0, & \text{if} i \in V_2 \\ h_i = 1 + \sum_{j \notin V_2} p_{ij}h_j, & \text{if} i \notin V_2 \end{cases} \quad (10)$$

The hitting time of an image in the image set V_1 is the number of steps before the random walk first reaches the selected image set V_2. At each iteration, the image in the set V_1 with the largest hitting time is chosen as the next representative image and moved from V_1 to the selected image set V_2. This avoids picking the near neighbours of those already selected images in V_2, leading to the diversity of the representative images in V_2. Finally, a list of K diverse representative images is generated.

5. EXPERIMENTS

In this section, we experimentally evaluate the performance of our proposed STM-TwitterLDA model on a large real-life tweet dataset. The experiments are designed to verify the effectiveness of the three main components of our framework: Twitter event detection, event evolution tracking and event visualization.

5.1 Dataset

Our experiments are conducted on a large real-life dataset which consists of 10,681,232 tweets posted from August to November

Vocabulary size	569741
Number of tweets	10681232
Number of images	2130562
Number of stop words	816
Number of stop images	594829
Number of countries	16
Average number of words per tweet	5
Percentage of tweets with hashtag	48%
Percentage of tweets with latitude/ longitude	7%

Table 2: Statistics of the Tweet Dataset.

in 2013. The tweets are collected by Twitter Search API given a list of search terms. The reason we choose Search API instead of Stream API is that the latter one only returns a small fraction of the total volume of tweets at any given moment, based on which events can rarely be detected. The search terms list we used is constructed by including a set of predefined event-relevant words (e.g., accident, earthquake, etc.), as well as the top 10 hottest trending words from the G20 countries provided by Twitter in real time. For each crawled tweet, five features (text, image, location, timestamp, hashtag) are recorded. The text of each tweet is preprocessed by removing the stop words, stemming and obtaining nouns and verbs only using the Stanford POS Tagger[2]. As for the images, convolutional neural networks (CNNs) have become more and more popular for extracting visual features from images recently. In this work, we use the widely used 'ImageNet network' which is trained on 1.3 million images [12]. Specifically, Caffe [10] is used to extract a 4096 dimensional visual feature from the layer (named "fc") before the classification layer. This visual feature is referred as "CNN" feature in this work. We define four categories including cartoon, landscape, diagram and the screenshot of text as the stop image categories and manually labelled 6600 images to train an SVM classifier for the stop image filtering. Specifically, 4600 images are used to train an SVM classifier with Gaussian kernel and the trained classifier is tested on the rest 2000 images showing a satisfying result (i.e., accuracy: 0.9017, precision: 0.8892 and recall: 0.9642). More details on the statistics of this dataset are summarized in Table 2.

5.2 Comparisons

Four competitor approaches are compared in our experiments to demonstrate the effectiveness of the event detection performance.

- **LDA**[3]:The original LDA is implemented as a baseline model. We adopt the same strategy as in LTT [28] to form events from the topics detected by LDA.
- **TwitterLDA**[27]: TwitterLDA is the first topic model specifically designed for tweets data. They assume that each short tweet is only assigned to one topic.
- **MMLDA**[1]: This is a topic model for Twitter subtopic discovery. Tweet images are first considered in this work, where each image is represented as a bag-of-visual-words derived from SIFT feature. We compare MMLDA to verify the superiority of the CNN feature in our proposed model over the traditional SIFT feature based methods.
- **LTT**[28]: This is the state-of-the-art work in topic modelling for Twitter event detection, which considers geographic information in addition to the text and time factor.

5.3 Performance on Event Detection

In this section, we first introduce the ground truth for event detection and the three performance indicators. After that, we study the impact of different Twitter features on event detection performance and evaluate the effectiveness of our event detection model in different aspects.

5.3.1 *Ground Truth Generation*

Due to the lack of ground truth for social event detection, we build up the ground truth (i.e., the top K hottest events on a particular day) based on the search terms used for collecting the tweets. Intuitively, the more tweets crawled based on a search term, the hotter the event related to this term is. We calculate the sum of retweeted numbers for every search term in the daily collected tweets as the mentioned times. The K search terms with the top K largest mentioned times constitute the K ground truth events for that day.

5.3.2 *Evaluation Metrics*

Mean average precision (MAP) for a set of queries is the mean of the average precision for each query. In this paper, we detect a list of ranked events daily. MAP is then calculated as the mean of the average event detection precision value of each day.

$$MAP = (\sum\nolimits_{q=1}^{Q} \text{AveP}(q))/Q \qquad (11)$$

where Q is the number of days we recommend events and the average precision (AveP) is defined as $AveP = \frac{\sum_{i=1}^{K}(\text{Precision}(i)\times\text{rel}(i))}{\text{number of relevant events}}$, where K is the number of detected events and Precision(i) is the precision at the top i events in the detected list. rel(i) equals to one if the the i-th event in the list is a relevant event, zero otherwise.

MAP evaluates the performance of the top K events recommendation, while the following two metrics verify the quality of one event. For a specific event, the tweets which should be assigned to this event are the *targets*, and all the other tweets are *nontargets*.

Probability of missed tweet detections (P_{Miss}) is the fraction of *missed tweet detections* over all targets:

$$P_{Miss} = \frac{\text{number of missed tweet detections}}{\text{number of targets}} \qquad (12)$$

where a missed tweet detection is defined as a target tweet that is not assigned to the corresponding event.

Probability of false tweet alarm errors (P_{Fa}) is the percentage of *false tweet alarms* over all nontargets:

$$P_{Fa} = \frac{\text{number of false tweet alarms}}{\text{number of nontargets}} \qquad (13)$$

where a nontarget tweet that is falsely detected in the corresponding event is called a false tweet alarm.

It is obvious that an effective event detection algorithm should have a large MAP but small P_{Miss} and P_{Fa}.

5.3.3 *Effect of Time, Location and Hashtag*

To evaluate the impact of different Twitter features in the proposed model, we provide five groups of results, including the original TwitterLDA as a baseline, TwitterLDA with time, TwitterLDA with location, Spatio-temporal TwitterLDA and Spatio-temporal TwitterLDA with hashtag. The effect of images will be verified separately in the next two subsections as it is a main contribution of this work. As shown in Fig. 3, each Twitter feature improves the performance of the text-only based event detection (i.e., the original TwitterLDA) on all the three measurements. Among them, location information brings bigger improvements than the time factor, especially for P_{Miss} and P_{Fa} (i.e., relative 24% and 6% further declines respectively). With the consideration of the hashtag, MAP further increases around 3% when $K < 20$. Notably, the combination of all these features consistently generates the best results. This demonstrates the importance of each factor and the power of fusing them when detecting events from Twitter.

[2]http://nlp.stanford.edu/software/tagger.shtml

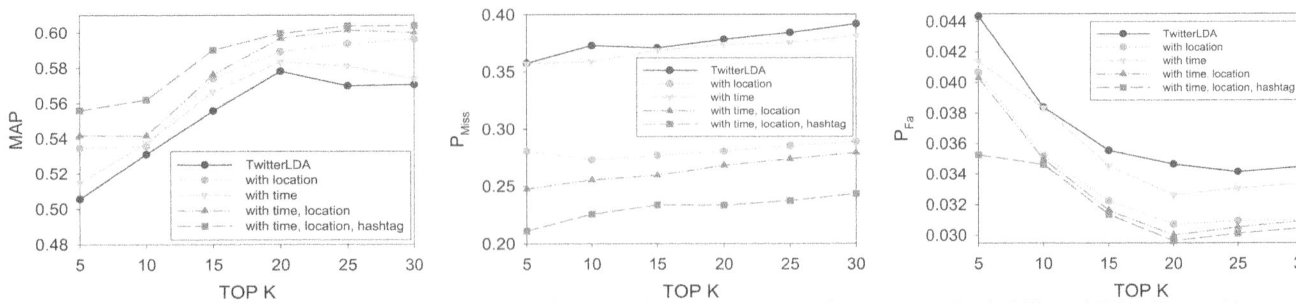

(a) Mean Average Precision (b) Probability of Missed Tweet Detections (c) Probability of False Tweet Alarms

Figure 3: Effect of Time, Location and Hashtag

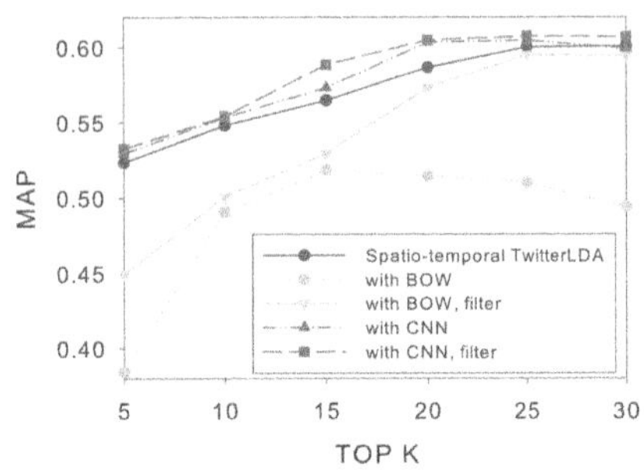

Figure 4: Effect of Visual Features

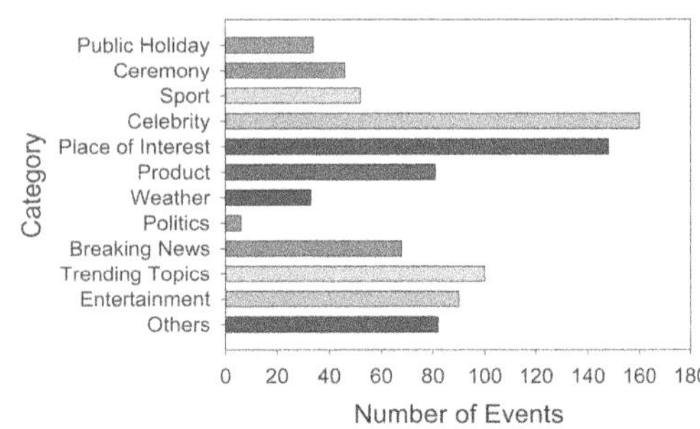

Figure 5: Category Distribution of the Ground Truth Events

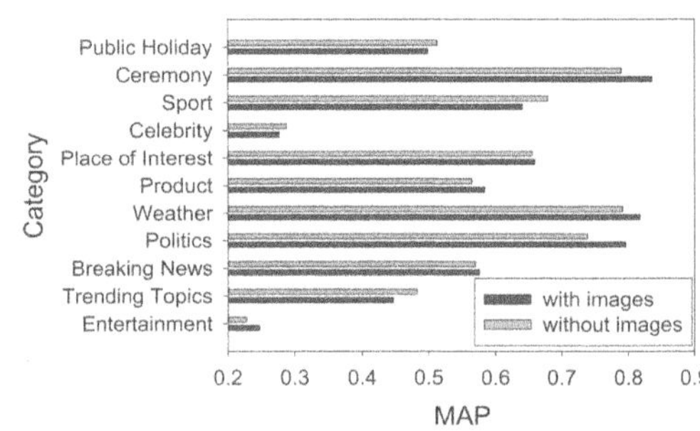

Figure 6: Effect of Images on Different Categories

5.3.4 *Effect of Visual Feature*

Image is one of the key factors in the proposed model and the choice of visual feature to represent images is thus of great importance. To test the effect of visual feature, we conduct experiments on all image tweets (i.e., tweets which contain images). Two different visual features are tested. One is the bag-of-visual-words derived from the SIFT feature as generally used in existing studies and the other is the state-of-the-art CNN feature. Moreover, to demonstrate the advantage of the stop image filter component, the results for the whole image set and for the filtered image set are shown respectively. As illustrated in Fig. 4, the bag-of-visual-words model on SIFT feature even deteriorates the performance. This shows that representing tweet images as visual words and straightforwardly processing them in the same way as textual words are inapplicable for Twitter event detection. Moreover, for the bag-of-visual-words model, the lack of stop image filter even causes a fall in MAP when $K > 15$, which demonstrates that the noisy images affect the performance more seriously for larger K values. In contrast to the bag-of-visual-words model, CNN feature benefits the event detection by improving the MAP by 2% to 5%. In addition, using the stop image filter further increases the MAP by up to 3%.

5.3.5 *Effect of Images on Different Categories*

Images are supposed to have diverse impacts on the events in different categories. We manually divide all ground truth events in August 2013 into eleven major categories, including public holiday, ceremony, sport, celebrity, place of interest, product, weather, breaking news, trending topics, entertainment and politics. The distribution of the ground truth events in different categories is shown in Fig. 5. To show the impact of images on different categories, the event detection performances for different categories with and without images are demonstrated in Fig. 6. We can observe that images bring negative effect on four categories, including public holiday, sport, celebrity and trending topics. The reason is that, in these four categories, images are either visually similar to each other (for sport, celebrity) or containing too many noises (for public holiday, trending topics). Hence these images do not benefit the event detection process. Among all the other categories, ceremony and politics benefit most from tweet images (5.8% and 7.8% improvements in MAP respectively). This is because that the intra-event image similarity within an event and inter-event image diversity across events in these two categories are larger than those in other categories.

5.3.6 *Effectiveness of Event Detection*

In this part, we compared different event detection methods. Note that all of our collected tweets comprise country information, but only a small fraction of them (as shown in Table 2) contain latitude and longitude information. To test the algorithm LTT which requires the detailed geographical information, we construct a dataset named "Geo-labelled Data" consisting of a subset of our collected tweets which contain latitude and longitude. We then conduct two series of comparisons on both the "Geo-labelled Data" (for LTT) and "All Data" (to show the consistent superiority on a large dataset). The results are shown in Fig 7 and Fig 8 respectively. We can see that our method performs the best in both MAP and P_{Miss} on both datasets. As in Fig 7(a), LTT is relatively 7% lower than our approach in MAP. Fig 7(b) shows that our method achieves remarkably smaller P_{Miss} compared to LTT (0.21 vs. 0.31 in average). The reason LTT gets a relatively lower P_{Fa} is that the events de-

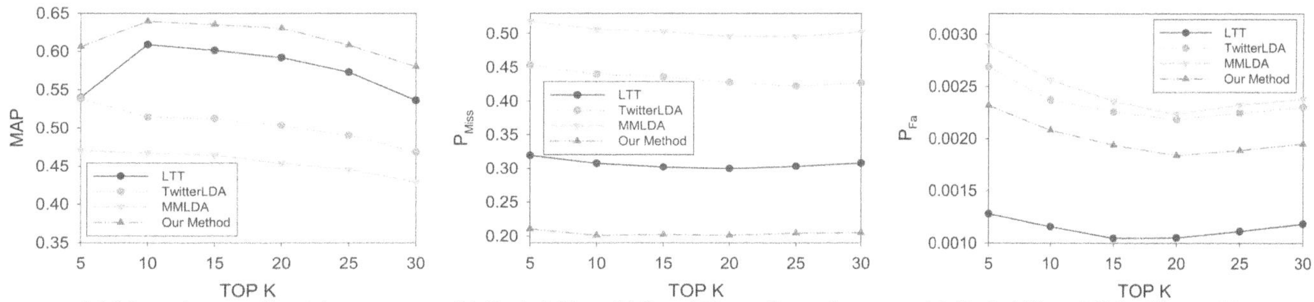

(a) Mean Average Precision (b) Probability of Missed Tweet Detections (c) Probability of False Tweet Alarms

Figure 7: Event Detection Performance on Geo-labelled Data

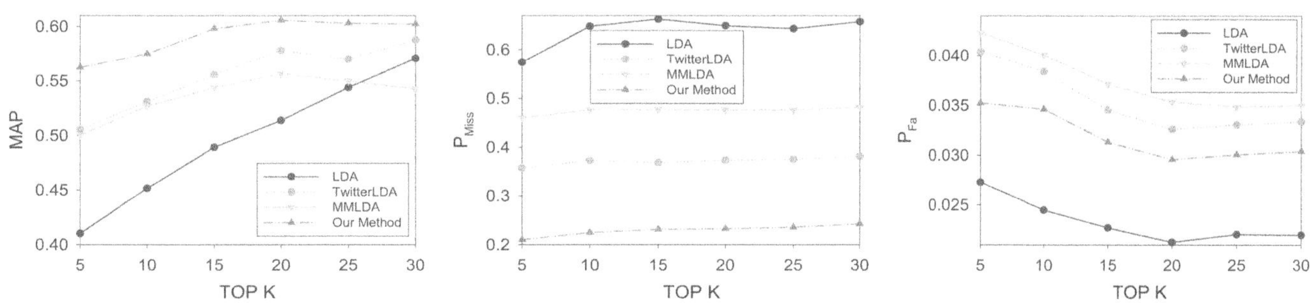

(a) Mean Average Precision (b) Probability of Missed Tweet Detections (c) Probability of False Tweet Alarms

Figure 8: Event Detection Performance on All Data

tected by LTT are much smaller than ours. This makes LTT less likely to generate false alarms since the number of tweets in each event is limited. It is the same for LDA (Fig. 8(c)) due to the same event detection strategy as LTT. However, a big event may be separated into several small events in their methods. Moreover, comparing the performance of LTT and our method on P_{Miss}, we can observe the small events detected by LTT also causes many missed tweet detections. And as indicated by MAP, our method outperforms LTT in terms of the overall event detection performance. MMLDA is originally designed for subtopic discovery under the assumption that all the images are relevant to a certain topic. The noisy images in our collected tweet data result in the unsatisfactory event detection performance of MMLDA. LDA presents a marked increase in MAP with the increase of K. This demonstrates that when discussing the top few hottest events in Twitter, people are more focused and tend to concentrate on just one topic. However, for the less popular events, there might exist diverse discussions in one single tweet.

5.4 Event Evolution Tracking Study

We conduct a case study on the event "Snowden" to show the performance of event evolution tracking and event visualization. Table 3 illustrates the events related to "Snowden" detected by our framework, where the first column is the date when the event happened and the second column displays the top ten words for each event as well as their probabilities assigned to the event. This table shows the evolution of event "Snowden" in three consecutive days, from August 1, 2013 to August 3, 2013. On the first day, people were talking about Snowden's stay in the airport in Moscow and his temporary asylum issued by Russia. On the next day, the discussion shifted to that Snowden left the airport after his lawyer read the formal document. On the third day, the Russia president Putin and the warner Putin received from NSA became the foci of this event. This case study shows that the event detected from tweets can truly reflect what happens in real life. However, it is difficult to quantitatively evaluate such performance mainly due to the subjectiveness on event understanding.

Date	Event Words
Aug 1, 2013	snowden 0.039, russia 0.038, **asylum** 0.016, **temporary** 0.014, moscow 0.012, **confirm** 0.010, airport 0.010, edward 0.009, paper 0.009, break 0.009
Aug 2, 2013	snowden 0.055, russia 0.032, **nsa** 0.021, asylum 0.017, edward 0.015, **read** 0.012, **leave** 0.011, **airport** 0.011, moscow 0.010, netflix 0.007
Aug 3, 2013	snowden 0.035, russia 0.033, **nsa** 0.012, moscow 0.010, edward 0.010, cbs 0.008, **russian** 0.008, **putin** 0.007, cable 0.007, **warner** 0.006

Table 3: Evolution of the Event "Snowden": Snowden received temporary asylum from Russia, Snowden left Moscow airport and then Putin was at the forefront of public discussion.

5.5 Event Visualization Study

We compare our event visualization results for the example event "Snowden" with two baseline methods and a spectral clustering based method [1]. Observed from Fig 9, our method generates the most relevant and diverse representative images for the event "Snowden". As we mentioned in Section 2.2, there exist a certain number of images which are less relevant to the event, and existing cluster-and-rank methods (e.g., [1]) lack the strategy to deal with these images, as shown in Fig 9(a). Fig. 9(b) and 9(c) show the results based on the criterion *visual relevance* and *visual coherence* respectively. Fig. 9(d) demonstrates the importance of considering *distinctiveness* in addition to visual relevance and visual coherence.

6. CONCLUSIONS AND FUTURE WORK

In this paper, we have presented a novel topic model named Spatio-Temporal Multimodal TwitterLDA for effective Twitter event detection. Five different Twitter features are fully exploited for performance improvements. Tweet images are thoroughly studied and

(a) Spectral Clustering Based

(b) Visual Coherence Only

(c) Visual Relevance Only

(d) Our Method

Figure 9: Representative Image Selection for Event "Snowden"

a two-filter strategy is specifically designed for eliminating the impact of noisy tweet images. Extensive experiments are conducted on a real-life tweet dataset to demonstrate the effectiveness of our method from different aspects. For the future work, we plan to dynamically detect the granularity of the time interval and location area of the events and utilize them in our model for more accurate event detection and tracking.

7. REFERENCES

[1] J. Bian, Y. Yang, and T.-S. Chua. Multimedia summarization for trending topics in microblogs. In *CIKM*, pages 1807–1812, 2013.

[2] J. Bian, Y. Yang, and T.-S. Chua. Predicting trending messages and diffusion participants in microblogging network. In *SIGIR*, pages 537–546, 2014.

[3] D. M. Blei, A. Y. Ng, and M. I. Jordan. Latent dirichlet allocation. *J. Mach. Learn. Res.*, 3:993–1022, 2003.

[4] T. Chen, D. Lu, M.-Y. Kan, and P. Cui. Understanding and classifying image tweets. In *ACM MM*, pages 781–784, 2013.

[5] A. P. Dempster, N. M. Laird, and D. B. Rubin. Maximum likelihood from incomplete data via the EM algorithm. *J. Roy. Statist. Soc. Ser. B*, 39:1–38, 1977.

[6] Q. Diao, J. Jiang, F. Zhu, and E.-P. Lim. Finding bursty topics from microblogs. In *ACL*, pages 536–544, 2012.

[7] S. Geman and D. Geman. Stochastic relaxation, gibbs distributions, and the bayesian restoration of images. *IEEE Trans. Pattern Anal. Mach. Intell.*, 6(6):721–741, 1984.

[8] W. H. Hsu, L. S. Kennedy, and S.-F. Chang. Video search reranking through random walk over document-level context graph. In *ACM MM*, pages 971–980, 2007.

[9] Z. Huang, B. Hu, H. Cheng, H. T. Shen, H. Liu, and X. Zhou. Mining near-duplicate graph for cluster-based reranking of web video search results. *ACM Trans. Inf. Syst.*, 28(4):22:1–22:27, 2010.

[10] Y. Jia, E. Shelhamer, J. Donahue, S. Karayev, J. Long, R. Girshick, S. Guadarrama, and T. Darrell. Caffe: Convolutional architecture for fast feature embedding. *arXiv preprint arXiv:1408.5093*, 2014.

[11] D. Jiang, K. W. Leung, J. Vosecky, and W. Ng. Personalized query suggestion with diversity awareness. In *ICDE*, pages 400–411, 2014.

[12] A. Khosla, B. An, J. J. Lim, and A. Torralba. Looking beyond the visible scene. In *CVPR*, pages 3710–3717, 2014.

[13] R. Long, H. Wang, Y. Chen, O. Jin, and Y. Yu. Towards effective event detection, tracking and summarization on microblog data. In *WAIM*, pages 652–663, 2011.

[14] Q. Mei, D. Zhou, and K. Church. Query suggestion using hitting time. In *CIKM*, pages 469–478, 2008.

[15] T. Minka. Estimating a Dirichlet distribution. Technical report, MIT., 2000.

[16] J. Munkres. Algorithms for the assignment and transportation problems. *J. Soc. Ind. Appl. Math.*, 5(1):32–38, 1957.

[17] M. Oquab, L. Bottou, I. Laptev, and J. Sivic. Learning and transferring mid-level image representations using convolutional neural networks. In *CVPR*, pages 1717–1724, 2014.

[18] D. Ramage, S. T. Dumais, and D. J. Liebling. Characterizing microblogs with topic models. In *ICWSM*, pages 130–137, 2010.

[19] A. S. Razavian, H. Azizpour, J. Sullivan, and S. Carlsson. CNN features off-the-shelf: an astounding baseline for recognition. *arXiv preprint arXiv:1403.6382*, 2014.

[20] S. D. Roy, T. Mei, W. Zeng, and S. Li. Socialtransfer: Cross-domain transfer learning from social streams for media applications. In *ACM MM*, pages 649–658, 2012.

[21] B.-S. Seah, S. S. Bhowmick, and A. Sun. Prism: Concept-preserving social image search results summarization. In *SIGIR*, pages 737–746, 2014.

[22] X. Wang and A. McCallum. Topics over time: A non-markov continuous-time model of topical trends. In *KDD*, pages 424–433, 2006.

[23] Z. Wang, P. Cui, L. Xie, H. Chen, W. Zhu, and S. Yang. Analyzing social media via event facets. In *ACM MM*, pages 1359–1360, 2012.

[24] C.-C. Wu, T. Mei, W. H. Hsu, and Y. Rui. Learning to personalize trending image search suggestion. In *SIGIR*, pages 727–736, 2014.

[25] Y. Yang, Z. Zha, Y. Gao, X. Zhu, and T. Chua. Corrections to "exploiting web images for semantic video indexing via robust sample-specific loss". *IEEE Trans. Multimedia*, 17(2):256, 2015.

[26] H. Yin, B. Cui, L. Chen, Z. Hu, and Z. Huang. A temporal context-aware model for user behavior modeling in social media systems. In *SIGMOD*, pages 1543–1554, 2014.

[27] W. X. Zhao, J. Jiang, J. Weng, J. He, E.-P. Lim, H. Yan, and X. Li. Comparing twitter and traditional media using topic models. In *ECIR*, pages 338–349, 2011.

[28] X. Zhou and L. Chen. Event detection over twitter social media streams. *The VLDB Journal*, 23(3):381–400, 2014.

Cross-Domain Collaborative Learning in Social Multimedia

Shengsheng Qian[1], Tianzhu Zhang[1], Richang Hong[2], Changsheng Xu[1]
[1]National Lab of Pattern Recognition, Institute of Automation, CAS, Beijing 100190, China
[2]School of Computer and Information, Hefei University of Technology
{shengsheng.qian, tzzhang, csxu}@nlpr.ia.ac.cn, hongrc@hfut.edu.cn

ABSTRACT

Cross-domain data analysis is one of the most important tasks in social multimedia. It has a wide range of real-world applications, including cross-platform event analysis, cross-domain multi-event tracking, cross-domain video recommendation, etc. It is also very challenging because the data have multi-modal and multi-domain properties, and there are no explicit correlations to link different domains. To deal with these issues, we propose a generic Cross-Domain Collaborative Learning (CDCL) framework based on non-parametric Bayesian dictionary learning model for cross-domain data analysis. In the proposed CDCL model, it can make use of the shared domain priors and modality priors to collaboratively learn the data's representations by considering the domain discrepancy and the multi-modal property. As a result, our CDCL model can effectively explore the virtues of different information sources to complement and enhance each other for cross-domain data analysis. To evaluate the proposed model, we apply it for two different applications: cross-platform event recognition and cross-network video recommendation. The extensive experimental evaluations well demonstrate the effectiveness of the proposed algorithm for cross-domain data analysis.

Categories and Subject Descriptors

H.3.5 [**Online Information Services**]: Web-based services

Keywords

social media, cross-domain collaborative learning, multi-modality

1. INTRODUCTION

With the rapid development of Internet, there are more and more social media sites (e.g., Flickr, YouTube, Facebook, and Google News), which make people be able to conveniently generate and share rich social multimedia content online, including multimedia documents, social links. As a result, a popular event topic that is happening around us and around the world can spread very fast in different media sites, and there are substantial amounts of media data with multi-modality (e.g., images, videos, and text). For example, as shown in Figure 1(a), a hot topic (e.g., United States Presidential Election) emerges, there are many relevant documents (images and text) in different platforms, such as Goodle News, Flickr. These documents have different perspectives, official on Google News, and personal comments and interesting photos on Flickr. If we aggregate the relevant data across different platforms, they can complement and enhance each other, especially when the strengths of one domain complement the weaknesses of the other. For example, a lot of interesting comments and photos by Web users on Flickr can complement few official reports on Google News. Moreover, the images of official reports generally captured by journalists can focus on the targets of a specific event perfectly on Google News, while most uploaded images which are typically captured by users are not professional on Flickr. To better understand what happens across multiple platforms, it is better to make use of the virtues of different information sources via collaborative learning algorithm. In social multimedia, the cross-domain collaborative learning (CDCL) is an important task for knowledge mining as it aims at discovering collective and subjective information, which may be more beneficial to users than a single domain in many applications such as cross-platform event analysis [1], cross-domain multi-event tracking [2], cross-domain collaboration recommendation [3].

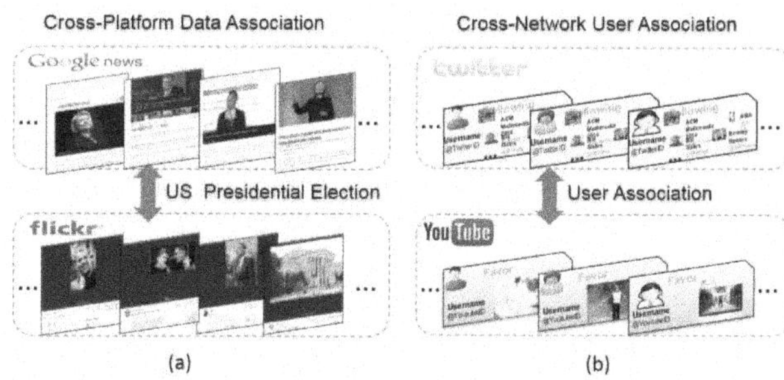

Figure 1: Two different cross-domain scenarios: (a) cross-platform data association (b) cross-network user association(All photos via Flickr under Creative Commons License).

In real-world scenarios, different domains can bridge the domain gap via the shared domain information, such as event topics, social links. As shown in Figure 1, we illustrate a toy example and show two different cross-domain scenarios including cross-platform data association and cross-network user association. In Figure 1(a), we show an example about the cross-platform data association. Here, Google News and Flickr are regarded as two domains, and their documents are associated via the shared event topic "United States Presidential Election". In Figure 1(b), it shows an example about the cross-network user association. In the two different network-

MM'15, October 26-30, 2015, Brisbane, Australia.

DOI: http://dx.doi.org/10.1145/2733373.2806234.

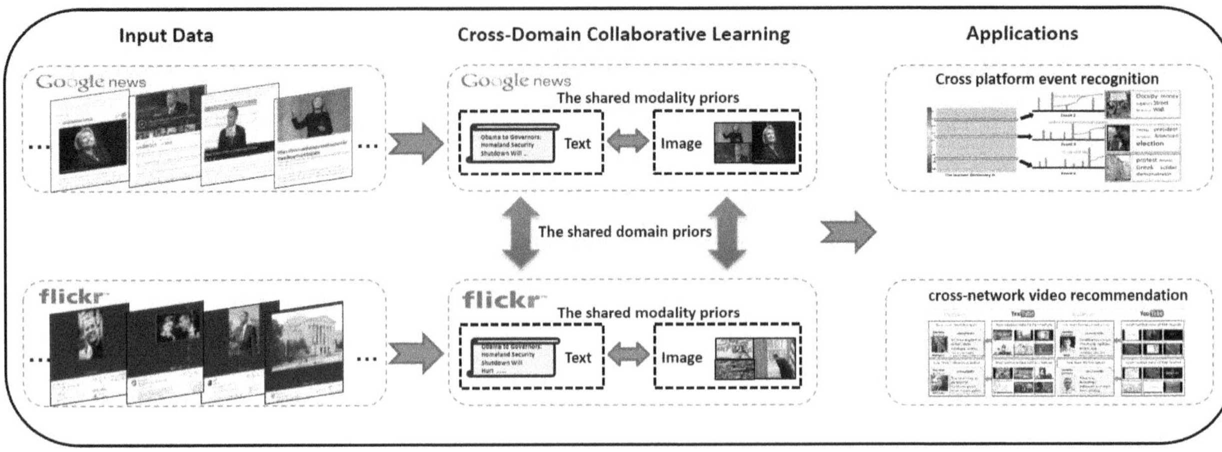

Figure 2: Illustration of the key idea of our cross-domain collaborative learning. For simplicity, we only show an example for cross-platform data association. Here, there are two domains (Google News and Flickr) with two modalities (Text and Image)(All photos via Flickr under Creative Commons License).

s Twitter and YouTube, there are many social links by users. For each user, he/she will have video-related behaviors on YouTube and tweeting behaviors on Twitter, and we explore the overlapped user account linkage between Twitter and YouTube to realize cross-network user association. Even though the shared domain information can help bridge the domain gap, it is still a challenging problem to find the most effective way to explore the useful information, as the data are inherently heterogeneous, noisy and ambiguous.

Recently, how to explore useful information via cross domain collaborative learning in social multimedia has attracted much research interest. Basically, there are two major research topics: (1) cross-domain feature learning in multimedia by adopting a cross-domain constraint to make different domains share a common feature space [1, 4, 5]. For example, Yang et al. [1] propose a cross-domain feature learning algorithm based on stacked denoising autoencoders, and apply the learned features for three important applications: sentiment classification, spam filtering, and event classification. (2) personalization recommendation in social links by modeling cross-network user behaviors [6, 7]. For example, a cold-start recommendation solution is proposed by aggregating user profiles in Flickr, Twitter, and Delicious [6]. Yan et al. investigate into cross-network social relation and behavior information to address the cold-start friend recommendation problem [7]. These two topics focus on feature learning and user modeling in cross domain analysis by combining the virtues of different domains to complement each other. They are both challenges and benefits. (1) The media data (e.g., event topics, social links) have **multi-domain** property. As shown in Figure 1, the media data can come from multiple domains (e.g., Flickr, Google News, YouTube, and Twitter), and they can complement each other, but also have domain discrepancy. (2) The media data have **multi-modal** property. As shown in Figure 1(a), each data instance in social media sites can be described with images and texts simultaneously, and the textual and visual information can also complement each other. (3) The media data have **sparse** property. For example, the social behaviors of the users in one social network are sparse. In particular, most users have no chance to browse or review most images and videos. When a new user registers on Youtube, the system knows nothing about his/her interactions on videos and cannot conduct video recommendation.

In this paper, motivated by the previous work, we propose a novel generic Cross-Domain Collaborative Learning (CDCL) framework based on non-parametric Bayesian dictionary learning model for cross-domain data analysis. In our CDCL, the non-parametric Bayesian dictionary learning model can explore the multi-domain, multi-modality, and sparse properties jointly. (1) To deal with the domain discrepancy, we adopt the shared domain priors across multiple domains to make them share a common feature space. (2) To make use of the multi-modal property, we learn the sparse representation of multi-modal data by introducing the shared modality priors to infer the sparse structure shared among different modalities of media data. (3) To deal with the sparsity of the media data, we learn the shared dictionary space to bridge cross-domain information. Due to the sparsity of user behavior in one social network, we exploit social relations and behaviors of users in the auxiliary social network to help estimate their preferences on other social network by learning the shared dictionary space, which can perform the cold-start recommendation task. The details of our CDCL algorithm is shown in Figure 2. For simplicity, we only show an example for cross-platform data association. There are two domains (Google News and Flickr) with two modalities (Text and Image) related to the event "United States Presidential Election". In the left panel of Figure 2, the related data associated with the event include textual and visual information. Here, each social event instance contains text and its corresponding images. Since the multi-modal data among different domains have their own characteristics but also have their commonalities, we can collaboratively learn the shared feature representation by adopting the shared domain priors and modality priors across multiple domains as shown in Figure 2. As a result, the proposed CDCL can effectively combine the virtues of different information sources to complement each other for cross-domain multi-modal data analysis. The proposed generic framework can be applied for many applications, such as cross-platform event recognition and cross-network video recommendation. The cross-platform event recognition is to use multi-modal data from multiple domains to conduct social event recognition. And the cross-network video recommendation is to leverage users' rich cross-network activity data to help estimate their preferences on other social platforms. For example, by using the overlapped user account linkage between Twitter and YouTube, and considering both the Twitter tweeting activities and historical interactions with YouTube videos, we design a cold-start recommendation task for the new YouTube user by the proposed CDCL method. We evaluate our method on these two applications and the results demonstrate its effectiveness in social multimedia. Compared with the existing methods, the contributions of this work are threefold.

- We propose a generic cross-domain collaborative learning framework based on non-parametric Bayesian dictionary learning model for cross-domain data analysis, and the proposed CDCL can effectively make use of the virtues of different information sources to complement and enhance each other.
- The proposed non-parametric Bayesian dictionary learning model can effectively adopt the shared domain and modality priors to collaboratively learn the shared feature representation to deal with the domain discrepancy with considering the multi-modal property.
- We evaluate the proposed CDCL method on two different applications in social multimedia and demonstrate that it achieves much better performance than existing methods. Besides, we collect a large-scale dataset for research on multi-modality cross-domain social event analysis, and will release it for academic use.

The rest of the paper is organized as follows. In Section 2, the related work is reviewed. Section 3 introduces the formulation of the CDCL. Two cross-domain applications are presented in Section 4. In Section 5, we report and analyze extensive experimental results. Finally, we conclude the paper with future work in Section 6.

2. RELATED WORK

In this Section, we briefly review previous methods which are most related to our work including cross-domain feature learning and cross-network collaborative learning in multimedia.

Cross-domain Feature Learning: In cross-domain feature learning, most of the existing methods aim to propagate the knowledge from an auxiliary domain to a target domain, which can learn feature representation by using data from one domain space to enhance the learning tasks of other domain spaces. In these methods, the auxiliary domain can be considered as the prior knowledge and experience guidance to perform new learning task on target domain. To achieve this goal, many methods adopt a cross-domain constraint to make different domains share a common feature space [1, 4, 5, 8]. Blitzer et al. [4] introduce structural correspondence learning to automatically induce correspondences among features from different domains by modeling their relations with pivot features that appear frequently in both domains. In [5], it reduces the distance across two domains by learning a latent feature space where domain similarity is measured through maximum mean discrepancy. With the explosive growth of multi-media data on the Web, cross-media learning [9, 10, 11, 12, 13] also has drown much attention in the past few years. Bian et al. [12] propose the CM-LDA method to model the relations among different media types by introducing a shared latent variable Z. Yang et al. [9] integrate semi-supervised learning and transfer learning techniques to exploit manually-labeled images for video tagging.

Different from the existing methods, the proposed CDCL algorithm adopts a shared dictionary space learning strategy to bridge different domains. There are some existing dictionary learning approaches. In [14], a novel coupled dictionary training method is proposed for single image super-resolution based on patch-wise sparse recovery, where the learned couple dictionaries can connect the low with high-resolution image patch spaces. Semi-coupled dictionary learning model is proposed to solve such cross-style image synthesis problems [15]. In these dictionary learning methods, the sparse coefficient is estimated by assuming the reconstructed residual error or the sparsity level. However, we usually do not know the residual error or sparsity level. If the settings do not agree with the ground truth, the performance can significantly degrade. Instead, Zhou et al. [16] and Yuan et al. [17] introduce a non-parametric Bayesian model to address these problems. In [16], the dictionary learning method with the non-parametric beta process is presented, where the beta process is employed as a prior for learning the dictionary, and this non-parametric method can naturally infer an appropriate dictionary size. In [17], a novel multi-task sparse learning model is proposed for human action recognition. In these two methods, the non-parametric Bayesian methods perform well in image denoising, image inpainting, compressive sensing, and human action recognition. In this paper, motivated by the previous work, we propose a novel non-parametric Bayesian dictionary learning model for cross-domain data analysis by using the shared domain and modality priors in social multimedia. Different from the proposed method, in [16], it mainly adopts beta process prior to model the image's sparse structure information and does not consider the cross-domain information. While our goal is to model cross-domain information with the shared domain and modality priors to complement and enhance each other.

Cross-network Collaborative Learning: The cross-network collaborative learning has recently attracted broad attentions. Most of the existing methods are devoted to taking advantage of different social networks' information towards collaborative applications. Suman et al. [18] exploit the real-time and socialized characteristics of the Twitter tweets to facilitate video applications on YouTube. Abel et al. [19] investigate tag profiles for the same user on Flickr, Twitter and Delicious, and discover consistency and replication characteristics in cross-platform user behavior.

The challenge in cross-network collaborative learning is how to bridge the domain gap by the shared content information, which is to make the strengths of one domain complement the weaknesses of the others. In terms of cross-network collaborative learning in social media, our work is related to [7] and [20]. In [7], the cross-network social relation and behavior information are adopted to address the cold-start friend recommendation problem. Different from [7], our work focuses on applying cross-network collaborative learning method to a YouTube video recommendation applications to deal with the cold-start problem. This work is also different from [20] which uses coupled dictionary learning method to conduct the cross-network topic association to meet the YouTube video promotion demand. Instead of the coupled dictionary learning method, we introduce the non-parametric Bayesian dictionary learning model by using the shared domain priors to collaboratively learn the shared dictionary space. Moreover, the proposed CDCL method is a generic framework for cross-domain data analysis, and the cross-network collaborative learning is only one of our applications in social multimedia.

3. OUR APPROACH

In this Section, we will first introduce the details of the proposed cross-domain collaborative learning algorithm, and then show its model inference.

3.1 Cross-Domain Collaborative Learning

The cross-domain collaborative learning is to explore the virtues of different information sources to complement and enhance each other for cross-domain data analysis. To achieve this goal, we propose a generic collaborative learning framework via non-parametric Bayesian dictionary learning model. In the proposed model, it can effectively explore the multi-domain property and the multi-modality property of cross-domain data to collaboratively learn the shared feature representation to deal with the domain discrepancy and help bridge the domain gap. For cross-domain data analysis, without loss of generality, we can assume that the data have J do-

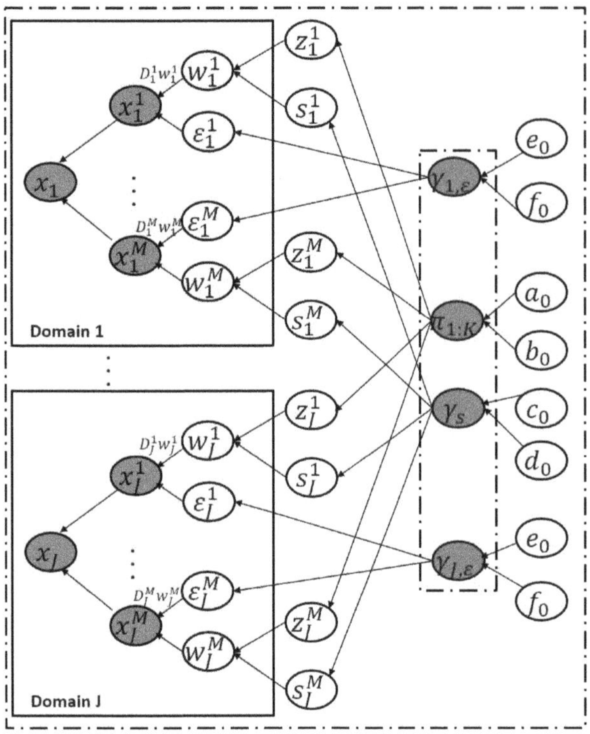

Figure 3: The graphical representation of our cross-domain collaborative learning algorithm. The red circles represent the shared priors to associate with the relevant information and collaboratively learn the shared feature space in different domains. For details, please refer to the corresponding text in Section 3.1.

mains with M modalities. Let $\mathbf{X} = [\mathbf{x_1}, \ldots, \mathbf{x_j}, \ldots, \mathbf{x_J}]$ denote the data instances in J domains. Here, $\mathbf{x_j} = [\mathbf{x_j^1}, \cdots, \mathbf{x_j^M}]$ denote M modalities in the j-th domain, and $\mathbf{x_j^m} \in \mathbf{R^{n_j^m}}$. The n_j^m is the dimensionality of the feature of the m-th modality in the j-th domain. In this paper, these instances $\mathbf{X}$ can be either social event data or user information, such as social events described by images and texts or the user account linkages between Twitter and YouTube.

To model these data, sparse representation has shown encouraging performance in traditional methods [21]. Given an instance $\mathbf{x_j^m}$ in the j-th domain with the m-th modality, it can be represented as a linear combination of elements in dictionary $\mathbf{D}_j^m$ with an error term ε_j^m as shown in Eq.(1).

$$\mathbf{x}_j^m = \mathbf{D}_j^m \mathbf{w}_j^m + \varepsilon_j^m \tag{1}$$

Here, the columns of the matrix $\mathbf{D}_j^m \in \mathbf{R}^{n_j^m \times K}$ represent the K elements of the dictionary, the $\mathbf{w}_j^m$ is the sparse feature coefficient, and the ε_j^m represents measurement noise with the m-th modality in the j-th domain. The sparse representation in Eq.(1) only models an instance with single modality in one domain. To improve it for modeling instance with multi-modality in cross-domain, we should take into account the following issues: (1) How to make use of the multi-modality and multi-domain properties to learn cross-domain data representations; (2) How to make the coefficient $\mathbf{w}_j^m$ have a sparse constraint; (3) How to learn a shared dictionary space $\mathbf{D}_j^m$ to bridge the domain gap; To deal with the above issues, we propose an effective cross-domain collaborative learning algorithm by introducing the non-parametric Bayesian dictionary learning model as shown in Figure 3. In the proposed model, (1) To deal with the domain discrepancy, we add the the shared domain priors π, γ_s to associate with the information across multiple domains. Meanwhile, the shared modality priors $\gamma_{j,\varepsilon}, \pi_j, \gamma_{j,s}$ are adopted to associate with the multi-modality information in the j-th domain. (2) The sparseness is achieved by introducing the Beta Process priors. Since different domains may favor different sparse reconstruction coefficients, the constraint of joint sparsity across different domains is necessary, which is to enforce the robustness in the sparse coefficient estimation. Due to the shared priors, our model can realize joint sparsity across different domains. (3) The shared dictionary space is learned by using the shared domain and modality priors, and it can bridge the domain gap for cross-domain data analysis.

In the non-parametric Bayesian dictionary learning model, the beta process is employed as a prior to learn the dictionary $\mathbf{D}_j^m$, and the number of dictionary elements across all domains and their relative importance can be inferred non-parametrically. As a result, the sparseness of the coefficient can be achieved via the Beta process priors rather than the computationally expensive ℓ_1 norm penalty. The Beta process (BP) is developed in [22], and the BP with parameters $a_0 > 0$, $b_0 > 0$, and base measure H_0, is represented as $BP(a_0, b_0, H_0)$. The stick-breaking construction of a beta process $H \sim BP(a_0, b_0, H_0)$ is represented as:

$$H(\psi) = \sum_{k=1}^{K} \pi_k \delta_{\psi_k}(\psi) \tag{2}$$

Here, $\pi_k \sim Beta(a_0/K, b_0(K-1)/K)$ and $\psi_k \sim H_0$. The $H(\psi)$ represents a vector of K probabilities, with each associated with a respective atom ψ_k, and ψ_k is the atom distributed according to H_0. When $K \to \infty$, $H(\psi)$ corresponds to an infinite-dimensional vector of probabilities, and each probability has an associated atom ψ_k drawn i.i.d. from H_0. In the proposed model, we set the sparse feature coefficient $\mathbf{w}_j^m = \mathbf{z}_j^m \odot \mathbf{s}_j^m$, where $\odot$ represents the Hadamard (element-wise) multiplication of two vectors, the binary vector $\mathbf{z}_j^m \in \{0,1\}^K$ denotes which of the K columns of D_j^m are used to represent the instance $\mathbf{x}_j^m$, and the weights $\mathbf{s}_j^m \sim N(0, \gamma_s^{-1}\mathbf{I}_K)$ are introduced to impose that the reconstruction coefficients of the dictionary are not always binary, where γ_s is the precision or inverse variance. That is to say, let the atoms ψ_k correspond to the candidate members of our dictionary D_j^m, and the k-th component of the binary vector $\mathbf{z}_j^m$ is drawn $\mathbf{z}_{j,k}^m \sim \text{Bernoulli}(\pi_k)$. As shown in Figure 3, the shared priors $\pi, \gamma_s, \gamma_\varepsilon$ are utilized to learn the shared dictionary space and the feature representation of instances across multiple domains. The hierarchical form of the cross-domain collaborative learning method can be described as:

$$\begin{aligned} &\mathbf{x}_j^m = \mathbf{D}_j^m \mathbf{w}_j^m + \varepsilon_j^m, m = 1, \ldots, M, j = 1, \ldots, J \\ &\mathbf{D}_j^m = [d_{j,1}^m, \cdots, d_{j,K}^m] \\ &\mathbf{w}_j^m = \mathbf{z}_j^m \odot \mathbf{s}_j^m \\ &\varepsilon_j^m \sim N(0, \gamma_{j,\varepsilon}^{-1} \mathbf{I}_{n_j^m}), \end{aligned} \tag{3}$$

where $d_{j,k}^m \sim N(0, n_j^{m(-1)} \mathbf{I}_{n_j^m})$, $\mathbf{z}_j^m \sim \prod_{k=1}^{K} \text{Bernoulli}(\pi_k)$, $\pi_k \sim \text{Beta}(a_0/K, b_0(K-1)/K)$, $\mathbf{s}_j^m \sim N(0, \gamma_s^{-1}\mathbf{I}_K)$, $\gamma_s \sim \Gamma(c_0, d_0)$, and $\gamma_{j,\varepsilon} \sim \Gamma(e_0, f_0)$. The gamma hyper-priors placed on γ_s and $\gamma_{j,\varepsilon}$ are typically non-informative. Note that, for simplicity, independent conjugacy Gaussian priors for $d_{j,k}^m$, $\mathbf{s}_j^m$, and ε_j^m are adopted. As a result, the proposed CDCL method can effectively not only make use of the information of each domain, but also combine the virtues of other domains to complement and enhance each other by the shared domain and modality priors.

3.2 Model Inference

In the proposed CDCL method, the full likelihood probability can be factorized as:

$$P(X, D, Z, S, \pi, \gamma_s, \gamma_\varepsilon) =$$

$$\prod_{j=1}^{J}\prod_{m=1}^{M} N(x_j^m; D_j^m(s_j^m \odot z_j^m), \gamma_{j,\varepsilon}^{-1} I_{n_j^m})$$

$$\prod_{j=1}^{J}\prod_{m=1}^{M}\prod_{k=1}^{K} N(d_{j,k}^m; 0, n_j^{m(-1)} I_{n_j^m})\text{Bernoulli}(z_{j,k}^m;\pi_k)$$

$$\prod_{k=1}^{K} \text{Beta}(\pi_k; a_0,b_0) \prod_{j=1}^{J} \Gamma(\gamma_{j,\varepsilon}; e_0,f_0)\Gamma(\gamma_s; c_0,d_0). \quad (4)$$

An exact model inference is often intractable in many non-parameter Bayesian models, and some appropriate methods must be used, such as variational inference [23] and Gibbs sampling [24]. To estimate the latent variables conditioned on the observed variables, namely $\mathbf{D}$, $\mathbf{Z}$, $\mathbf{S}$, π, γ_s, γ_ε, we employ Gibbs sampling method to obtain samples of latent variables and estimate unknown parameters in our model. In a Gibbs sampler, it iteratively samples new assignments of latent variables by drawing from the distributions conditioned on the previous state of the model. We list the update rules for latent variables $\mathbf{D}$, $\mathbf{Z}$, $\mathbf{S}$, π, γ_s, γ_ε as follows:

We first sample the dictionary variable $\mathbf{D}_j^m = [d_{j,1}^m, \cdots, d_{j,K}^m]$ according to the posterior probability as shown in Eq.(5).

$$P(d_{j,k}^m|-) \propto N(x_j^m; D_j^m(s_j^m \odot z_j^m), \gamma_{j,\varepsilon}^{-1} I_{n_j^m}) \; N(d_{j,k}^m; 0, n_j^{m(-1)} I_{n_j^m}) \quad (5)$$

Here, the $d_{j,k}^m$ can be drown from a normal distribution $p(d_{j,k}^m|-) \sim N(u_{d_{j,k}^m}, \Sigma_{d_{j,k}^m})$.

Then, we sample the binary vector $\mathbf{z}_j^m = [z_{j,1}^m, \cdots, z_{j,K}^m]$ according to the following posterior probability,

$$P(z_{j,k}^m|-) \propto N(x_j^m; D_j^m(s_j^m \odot z_j^m), \gamma_{j,\varepsilon}^{-1} I_{n_j^m})\text{Bernoulli}(z_{j,k}^m;\pi_k) \quad (6)$$

Here, when $z_{j,k}^m = 1$, the $P_1 \propto N(x_j^m; D_j^m(s_j^m \odot z_j^m), \gamma_{j,\varepsilon}^{-1} I_{n_j^m}) \cdot \pi_k$; when $z_{j,k}^m = 0$, the $P_0 = 1 - \pi_k$. We can draw $z_{j,k}^m$ according to the Bernoulli distribution $z_{j,k}^m \sim \text{Bernoulli}(\frac{P_1}{P_1+P_2})$.

Next, we sample the weight variable $\mathbf{s}_{j,k}^m = [s_{j,1}^m, \cdots, s_{j,K}^m]$ as in Eq.(7).

$$P(s_{j,k}^m|-) \propto N(x_j^m; D_j^m(s_j^m \odot z_j^m), \gamma_{j,\varepsilon}^{-1} I_{n_j^m}) N(s_j^m; 0, \gamma_s^{-1} I_K) \quad (7)$$

Here, as $d_{j,k}^m$, the $s_{j,k}^m$ can be drown from a normal distribution $p(s_{j,k}^m|-) \sim N(u_{s_{j,k}^m}, \Sigma_{s_{j,k}^m})$.

Finally, we sample the shared priors $\pi, \gamma_s, \gamma_\varepsilon$ with the following updating rules.

$$P(\pi_k|-) \propto \text{Beta}(\pi_k; a_0, b_0) \prod_{j=1}^{J}\prod_{m=1}^{M} \text{Bernoulli}(z_{j,k}^m; \pi_k) \quad (8)$$

$$P(\gamma_s|-) \propto \Gamma(\gamma_s; c_0, d_0) \prod_{j=1}^{J}\prod_{m=1}^{M} N(s_j^m; 0, \gamma_s^{-1} I_K) \quad (9)$$

$$P(\gamma_{j,\varepsilon}|-) \propto \Gamma(\gamma_{j,\varepsilon}; e_0, f_0) \prod_{j=1}^{J}\prod_{m=1}^{M} N(x_j^m; D_j^m(s_j^m \odot z_j^m), \gamma_{j,\varepsilon}^{-1} I_{n_j^m}) \quad (10)$$

Algorithm 1 The proposed CDCL method for cross-platform event recognition.

Input: data in auxiliary domain D_a; training and testing data in target domain D_t; Iteration number T_{gibbs};
Output: predict class labels for testing documents in D_t.

// Learn the shared domain priors in auxiliary domain D_a.
1: Initialize the dictionary variable via the K-SVD
2: Initialize latent variables $\mathbf{z}, \mathbf{s}, \pi, \gamma_s, \gamma_\varepsilon$
3: **for** $t := 1 \rightarrow T_{gibbs}$ **do**
4: Run Gibbs sampling strategy for all instances in the auxiliary domain D_a according to Eq.(5) $\sim$ Eq.(10)
5: **end for**
// Predict class labels for testing samples in D_t
6: Initialize the domain priors with the learned values in D_a
7: Learn the sparse representation $\mathbf{w}$ for all instances in D_t
8: Predict class labels of testing data using Linear SVM.

Note that, the priors π, γ_s are shared across multiple domains, while the prior γ_ε is only shared across multiple modalities in a single domain.

4. APPLICATIONS

In this Section, we introduce how to leverage our generic model for two cross-domain applications: *cross-platform event recognition* and *cross-network video recommendation*.

4.1 Cross-platform Event Recognition

The cross-platform event recognition is to make use of the virtues of different domains to learn the shared feature representation for social event recognition. A popular social event that is happening around us can spread very fast. As a result, there are a large amount of social events with multi-modality (e.g., images, videos, and text) in many different domains (e.g., Flickr and Google News). Therefore, it is important to automatically identify and recognize the interesting social events from massive social media data. The critical challenge is how to make use of the cross-domain multi-modality social event data. The social event recognition is normally studied with textual features. In addition to textual information, social events also have rich visual information. For an event in different sites, it may have different textual descriptions (comments, tags, etc.) due to different users. However, it may have very similar visual information, such as images or videos, which are useful for social event recognition across time and sites. For example, the event "United States Presidential Election", its stories with the picture of Obama are highly related. Therefore, multi-modality fusion is useful for social event recognition. In addition, different platforms can complement and enhance each other. For example, most events on Google News are from the official, but they have a lot of comments by web users on Flickr. The images on Google News are generally captured by professional journalists while the images on Flickr are typically captured by common users, who may upload images which do not focus on the targets of a specific event perfectly. Therefore, social events in different domains can help each other, especially when the strengths of one domain complement the weaknesses of the other.

Next, we will introduce how to apply the proposed CDCL algorithm for the cross-platform event recognition by considering two domains (Google News and Flickr) with two modalities (text and image). Here, each social event has many documents, and each document is an event instance (event sample) including text and images. Our goal is to classify each document by using the information from Google News and Flickr. In general, these two domains can be viewed as auxiliary domain and target domain, respectively. The auxiliary domain can be modeled as the prior knowledge and experience to perform new learning task on target domain, which can be facilitated to improve the classification accuracies, especially when the size of available labeled training samples on target domain is not large enough. The overall procedure for cross-domain social event recognition is depicted in Algorithm 1. We first learn the shared domain priors of the proposed CDCL model by alternately sampling instances from the auxiliary domain. Here, the data from the auxiliary domain are used to infer the shared domain and modality priors $\pi, \gamma_s, \gamma_\varepsilon$. Then, we use the learned priors to train the proposed CDCL model and learn the sparse feature representation $\mathbf{w}$ for all instances in the target domain D_t. Then, the Linear SVM [25] is trained and used to predict class labels of the testing data in D_t. Here, a half of instances in the target domain are randomly sampled to train the SVM classifiers, and the other half of the instances are used for testing.

4.2 Cross-network Video Recommendation

The cross-network video recommendation is to leverage users' rich cross-network activity data to help estimate their preferences on other social network, especially for a new user or the users with few records. In this paper, we exploit social relations and behaviors of users in the auxiliary social platform, and apply our CDCL method to help another platform conduct the cold-start recommendation task. Specifically, we employ Twitter and YouTube as the two platforms, which are connected due to the overlapped user account linkage between Twitter and YouTube. When a new user registers on Youtube, the system knows nothing about his/her interactions on the videos and cannot conduct video recommendation. By considering both the Twitter tweeting activities and historical interactions with YouTube videos, the proposed CDCL algorithm can present a YouTube video recommendation application to deal with the cold-start problem.

In cross-network video recommendation, each user $u \in U$ can be represented as a 2-dimensional tuple $< \mathbf{u}^T, \mathbf{u}^Y >$ when given a set of overlapped users U, where the user u is considered as an instance, the $\mathbf{u}^T$ represents the user' tweet information in Twitter, and the $\mathbf{u}^Y$ represents that the user u has interacted with the videos in Youtube. Here, we consider each user's tweet history information as one document and employ the standard Latent Dirichlet Allocation to the corpus composed by all the Twitter users. Feature description of $\mathbf{u}^T$ can be represented as $\mathbf{u}^T = \{u_1^T, \cdots, u_{K_T}^T\}$, where K_T is the number of topics in the latent Twitter topic space. Similarly, YouTube user's feature representation $\mathbf{u}^Y$ can be obtained with his/her interested video set. We consider all the video set as the feature items of the YouTube users and take the commonly used vector space model to represent the YouTube user. The $\mathbf{u}^Y$ can be represented as $\mathbf{u}^Y = \{u_1^Y, \cdots, u_{K_Y}^Y\}$, where K_Y is the number of YouTube videos in our dataset, and $u_n^Y = 1$ denotes that the YouTube user u has been interested in the n-th YouTube video and $u_n^Y = 0$ otherwise. The task of cross-network video recommendation is, for a given new user $u \in U$ on YouTube, to recommend a ranking list of videos V_u according to the user' interest by considering the user' tweet activities $\mathbf{u}^T$ on Twitter.

The proposed cross-network video recommendation solution consists of two steps, i.e., cross-network dictionary learning and video recommendation for the new YouTube users, as shown in Algorithm 2. At the first step, with the obtained Twitter and YouTube user feature representation $\mathbf{u}^T, \mathbf{u}^Y$, we utilize the proposed CDCL method to discover the shared latent structure among different networks. Specifically, given the user feature representation $\mathbf{u}^T = \{u_1^T, \cdots, u_{K_T}^T\}$ and $\mathbf{u}^Y = \{u_1^Y, \cdots, u_{K_Y}^Y\}$, we can learn the shared dictionary space for the users across different domains and obtain the dictionary variables $\mathbf{D}^T = \{d_1^T, \cdots, d_K^T\}$ and $\mathbf{D}^Y = \{d_1^Y, \cdots, d_K^Y\}$ on Twitter and YouTube, respectively. With the derived shared dictionary spaces $\mathbf{D}^T$ and $\mathbf{D}^Y$, we are able to realize the transfer of user's feature distribution between different networks. Therefore, we can conduct video recommendation for new user on YouTube by his/her tweet history information in Twitter. The second step is to recommend a ranking list of videos V_u for a given new user in YouTube based on the learned $\mathbf{D}^T$ and $\mathbf{D}^Y$. Specifically, given a new user on YouTube, we can obtain the user's feature representation $\mathbf{u}^T \in R^{K_T \times 1}$ on Twitter by his/her tweet history information. Then, we can estimate the user's sparse feature coefficient $\mathbf{w}$ via Eq.(11) for $\mathbf{u}^T$.

Algorithm 2 The proposed CDCL method for cross-network video recommendation.

Input: User representation $\mathbf{u}^T \in U$ on Twitter; User representation $\mathbf{u}^Y \in U$ on YouTube; Candidate YouTube videos $v_t \in V$; A test user $u_t \in U_t$ on YouTube.
Output: A ranked list of videos V_u for u_t.

// Do the cross-network dictionary learning
1: Learn the shared dictionary space $\mathbf{D}^T = \{d_1^T, \cdots, d_K^T\}$ on Twitter according to Eq.(5) $\sim$ Eq.(10)
2: Learn the shared dictionary space $\mathbf{D}^Y = \{d_1^Y, \cdots, d_K^Y\}$ on YouTube according to Eq.(5) $\sim$ Eq.(10)
//Recommend videos for a new YouTube user u_t
3: Obtain $\mathbf{u}^T \in R^{K_T \times 1}$ by the user's tweet history information
4: Estimate the corresponding sparse coefficient $\mathbf{w}$ by Eq.(11)
5: Obtain the feature representation $\mathbf{u}^Y$ via Eq.(12)
6: Recommend a ranked list of videos V_u for u_t by Eq.(13)

$$\mathbf{u}^T = \mathbf{D}^T \mathbf{w} + \varepsilon_j \tag{11}$$

Since the unique user across different domains has the shared dictionary space ($\mathbf{D}^T$ and $\mathbf{D}^Y$) and sparse feature coefficient ($\mathbf{w}$), we can adopt these learned parameters to help conduct the transfer of user's feature distribution between the Twitter and YouTube. Therefore, the new user's YouTube feature representation can be defined as:

$$\mathbf{u}^Y = \mathbf{D}^Y \mathbf{w} \tag{12}$$

As a result, given the new user $\mathbf{u}^Y$ and candidate YouTube videos $\mathbf{v}_t \in V$ represented in the same feature space, the recommended videos from YouTube are ranked by Eq.(13).

$$sim(\mathbf{u}^Y, \mathbf{v}_t) =< \mathbf{u}^Y, \mathbf{v}_t >= \sum_{k=1}^{K_T} u_k^T \cdot v_{k,t} \tag{13}$$

5. EXPERIMENTS

In this Section, we evaluate the performance of the proposed CDCL algorithm on two different applications: cross-platform event recognition and cross-network video recommendation. The extensive results demonstrate the effectiveness of our CDCL algorithm for cross-domain collaborative learning in social multimedia.

5.1 Cross-platform Event Recognition

5.1.1 *Dataset Collection*

For social event recognition, the evaluation dataset is constructed from online social platforms. Nowadays, there are already some

Table 1: **Illustration of the event name, duration time, and number of documents for each event in our collected social event dataset.**

Event ID	Event Name	Start Time	End Time	Google News		Flickr	
				#Images	#Text	#Images	#Text
1	Senkaku Islands dispute	2008.06	2012.12	3743	2495	6617	6617
2	Occupy Wall Street	2011.09	2012.09	5601	3108	7151	7151
3	United States Presidential Election	2009.10	2013.01	5169	3446	7352	7352
4	War in Afghanistan	2001.10	2012.08	5373	2915	7172	7172
5	North Korea nuclear program	2000.01	2012.04	3969	2640	8635	8635
6	Greek protests	2011.05	2012.04	3900	2630	7385	7385
7	Mars Reconnaissance Orbiter	2005.04	2012.08	3901	2600	7188	7188
8	Syrian civil war	2011.01	2013.01	4899	3266	7426	7426

Table 2: The event classification accuracy of different methods.

Methods	Accuracy	
	#Google News	#Fickr
BOW	0.797	0.857
CCA	0.758	0.861
SRC-L1	0.820	0.857
SRC-L1-DL	0.843	0.862
CDCL-s	0.834	0.861
CDCL-c	**0.848**	**0.877**
CDCL	**0.876**	**0.885**

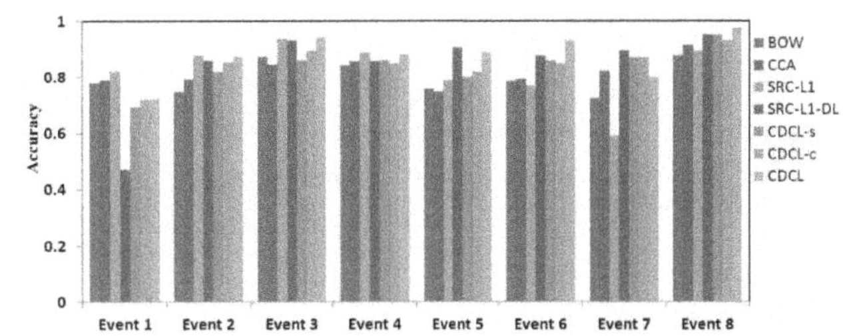

Figure 4: The classification accuracy for each event on Google News.

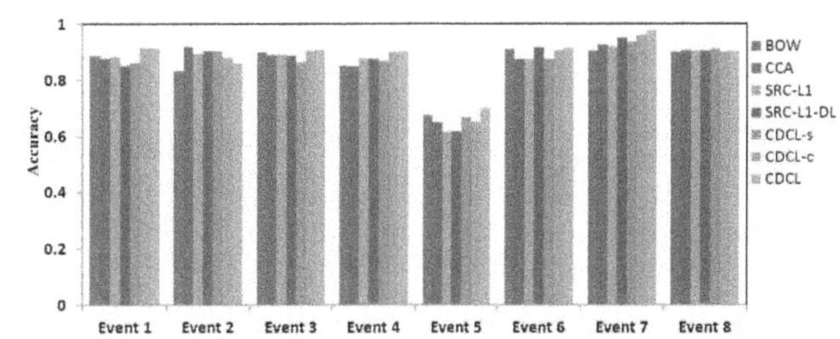

Figure 5: The classification accuracy for each event on Flickr.

public event datasets, such as the MediaEval social event detection(SED) [26]. However, the existing MediaEval SED dataset include only social media content created by people and do not have current hot social events. Besides, the existing MediaEval SED dataset do not have multi-modality cross-domain information. To analyze event data with the multi-modal and multi-domain properties, we mainly focus on 8 complex and public social events happened in the past few years, and collect the dataset by ourselves from Google News and Flcikr. For these 8 events, we manually create the introduction page of each event or download it from the Wikipedia page[1], which contains the whole stories of each event. We then search and download related text and its corresponding images from Google News and Flickr based on the keywords in the whole timeline of each social event. The detail of our collected dataset is shown in Table 2. The collected 8 social events cover a wide range of topics including politics, economics, military, society, and so on. For each social event, there are about 2000 to 9000 documents including text and its corresponding images.

5.1.2 Feature Extraction

For textual description, we use stemming method and stop words elimination and remove words with a corpus frequency less than 15 in the whole stories of the event, and take the commonly used vector space model to represent the textual information. For visual description, we adopt the popular sparse coding method [27]. In our implementation, we densely sample SIFT points from images, and adopt K-means to build a codebook. For each SIFT point, the Localized Soft-assigment Coding (LSC) is adopted to obtain its descriptor. Then, the max pooling and the Spatial Pyramid Matching (SPM) strategy are adopted to obtain image representation.

5.1.3 Results and Analysis

In our experiment setting, the K is set to 100. Note that not all K dictionary elements are used in the model. The number of shared dictionary elements will be determined by the shared domain priors. The hyperparameters within the gamma distributions are set as $c_0 = d_0 = e_0 = f_0 = 10^{-6}$ as in [16]. Since the data overwhelms these prior values when calculating posterior distributions, our algorithm is robust to the initial values. We set $T_{gibbs} = 100$ and use the results of the last iteration.

To demonstrate the effectiveness of the proposed CDCL model for cross-domain event analysis, we compare it with the most related baseline methods (BOW, CCA, SRC-L1, SRC-L1-DL):

- BOW: It is to concatenate the textual and visual features as discussed in Section 5.1.2 to represent each event document.
- Canonical Correlation Analysis (CCA) [28]: The CCA is a classical method in cross modal retrieval by learning a common space across multi-modal data. The text and image features are obtained by the maximally correlated subspace.
- SRC-L1: It is to adopt the sparse representation based on traditional ℓ_1 regularization and the dictionary is learned via the traditional K-SVD method.
- SRC-L1-DL: It is to adopt the sparse representation based on traditional ℓ_1 regularization and the dictionary is learned by the proposed non-parametric Bayesian model with the auxiliary domain as in Algorithm 1.

[1] http://www.wikipedia.org

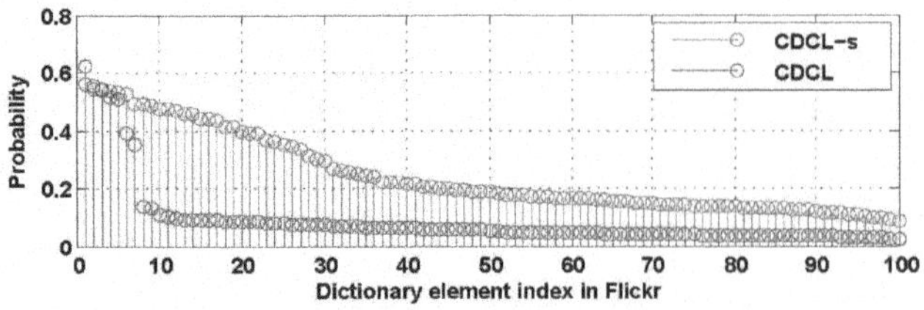

(a) Dictionary weights π_k (Flickr)

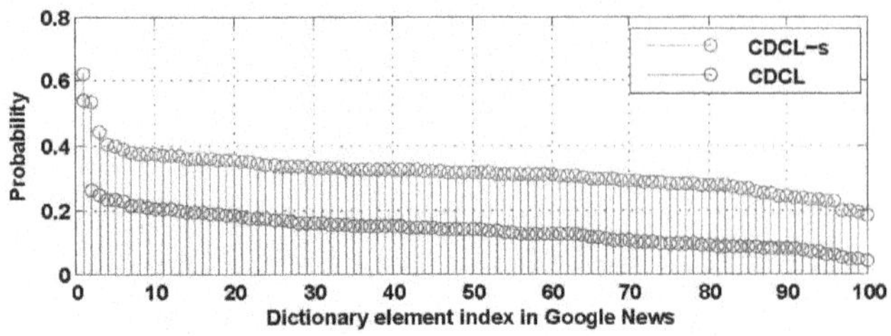

(b) Dictionary weights π_k (Google News)

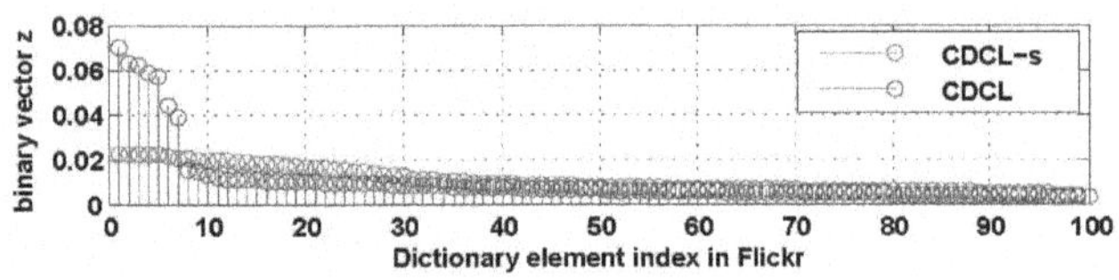

(c) Statistics of binary vector z (Flickr)

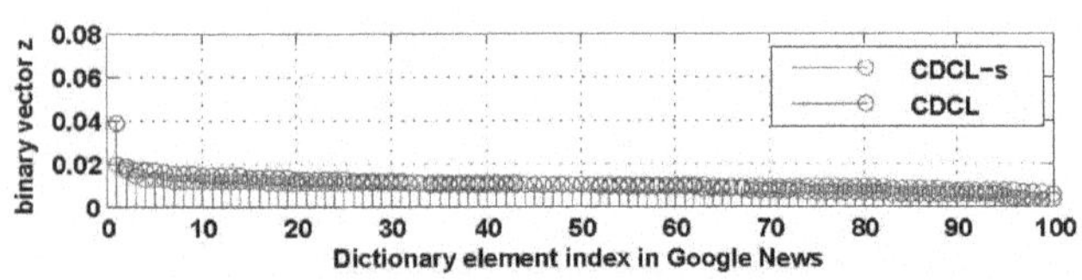

(d) Statistics of binary vector z(Google News)

Figure 6: The shared dictionary learning results by CDCL-s and CDCL. (a-b) the comparison of dictionary weights π_k on Flickr and Google News, respectively. (c-d) the statistics results of binary vector z on Flickr and Google News, respectively.

For the cross-platform event analysis, our goal is to classify the event instances on Google News/Flickr domain with the help of the auxiliary domain Flickr/Google News, respectively. With different experimental settings, we have 3 methods CDCL-s, CDCL-c, and CDCL. The CDCL-s is only trained in the single domain without the help of the auxiliary domain, and the shared priors is initialized with random values. The CDCL-c is trained with the help of the auxiliary domain, but ignores the multi-modal constraint by directly concatenating the textual and visual features. The CDCL is trained by using the auxiliary domain with multi-modal property to obtain the shared domain priors and modality priors. After learning the representations, the Linear SVM is utilized as the classifier.

The classification results of different methods are shown in Table 2, and the accuracy comparison of each event class is given in Figure 4 and Figure 5. Based on these results, we have the following observations. (1) The BOW model shows inferior classification performance. This is because the BOW models textual and visual words obscurely and cannot differentiate the associations between multi-modal data. (2) The CCA and our CDCL achieve better performance than the BOW, which shows that it is useful to model and fuse the textual and visual information. (3) The SRC-L1-DL achieves better average classification accuracy than the SRC-L1, which shows that the dictionary learning method by adopting the auxiliary domain can obtain a more compact and representative dictionary to improve the average performance. (4) Overall, the proposed CDCL method consistently outperforms other existing methods based on the average classification accuracy. The major reason is that the proposed non-parametric Bayesian dictionary learning model can adopt the shared domain priors and modality priors to collaboratively learn the feature representation by considering the domain discrepancy and the multi-modal property. We also observe that our CDCL method is much worse than the SRC-L1 for the event 1 in Figure 4 and the event 2 in Figure 5, respectively. This is may be because the superposition of cross-domain information has no effect on the event 1 and event 2. As a result, it can effectively combine the virtues of different information sources to complement and enhance each other.

In Figure 6, we give a detailed analysis about the proposed model. In Figure 6(a) and Figure 6(b), we show the comparison of the dictionary weights π_k (ordered in the probability) to be used by CDCL-s and CDCL on Flickr and Google News, respectively. We observe that most dictionary elements are used with a low probability in our CDCL, especially after the eighth dictionary element on Flickr. While the probability values of most dictionary elements used in CDCL-s are greater than 0.2. As a result, the learned feature representation of our CDCL is much more sparse. This shows that our model can effectively utilize the prior knowledge and experience of the auxiliary domain to learn a compact shared dictionary space and obtain the sparse representation. In Figure 6(c) and Figure 6(d), we show the statistics results of binary vector **z** by calculating the expected number of binary factors on Flickr and Google

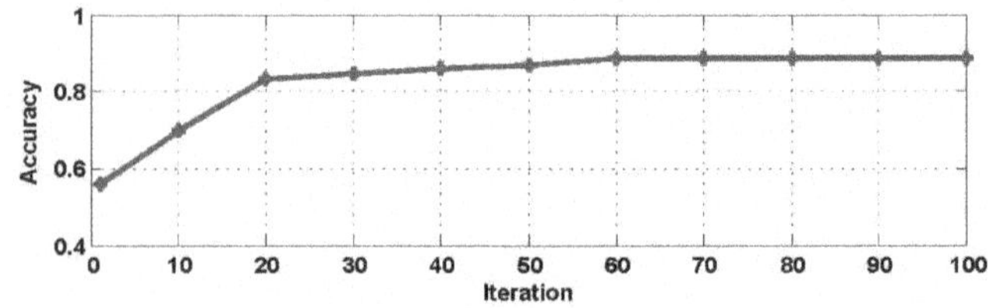

(a) On Flickr

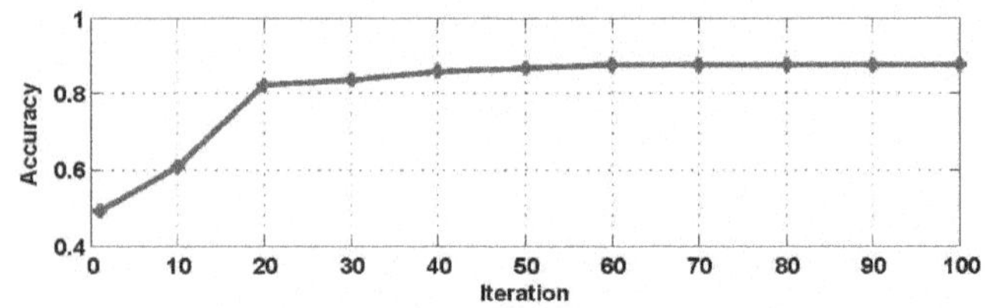

(b) On Google News

Figure 7: The classification accuracy with the iteration of Gibbs sampling on Flickr data and Google News data, respectively.

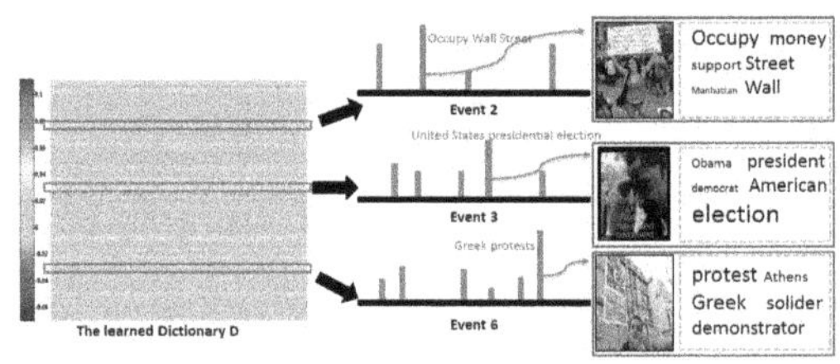

Figure 8: The visualization of the 100 learned dictionary elements. Each row corresponds to one element. The red color indicates the highest statistics results of binary vector z in each event set, and the corresponding dictionary element is shown with the image and text(All photos via Flickr under Creative Commons License).

News, respectively. We can see that the statistics results of binary vector $\mathbf{z}$ are consistent with the dictionary weights π_k, which shows that our model is reasonable. In Figure 7, we show the classification accuracies with the iteration of Gibbs sampling on Flickr and Google News, respectively. We can see that our CDCL can achieve accessible results after 20 iterations. As shown in Figure 8, we analyze the statistics results of binary vector $\mathbf{z}$ in each event and show the corresponding dictionary element (images and text) with the highest confidence score.

5.2 Cross-network Video Recommendation

5.2.1 *Dataset Collection*

For the cross-network video recommendation, we use the cross-network dataset [20]. This is a cross-network dataset with user account linkage between YouTube and Twitter, which contains 143,259 Google+ users, among which 38,540 users provide YouTube account, 39,400 users provide Twitter account, and 11,850 users provide both accounts. However, the dataset do not have the behavioral information of these users on Twitter. Therefore, we download the most recent 1,000 tweets generated by each user via the official APIs according to the users ID provided by [20]. In order to better evaluate the recommendation results, we only use the users providing both the YouTube and Twitter accounts, and keep only the cross-network users who interacted with at least 8 different videos on YouTube. As a result, we obtain 1655 cross-network users and 5105 videos in total for this experiment evaluation.

In our experiment setting, the proposed video recommendation solution is expected to facilitate cold-start recommendation for the new YouTube user. In the first stage of our cross-network video recommendation, we randomly select 900 active users to construct the training dataset, which is to learn the shared dictionary space. The remaining 755 users are considered as the cold-start users on YouTube, denoted as U^{new}. For the testing user $u_t \in U^{new}$, all the observed video-related interactions are hidden in the second stage and taken as ground truth for evaluation.

5.2.2 *Evaluation Metrics*

In practical video recommender system, users are basically only concerned about the top-ranked recommendation results and the available space to present the results on YouTube is also limited. The aim of the personalized video recommendation is to provide each user a ranking list of videos. Similar to traditional information retrieval task, we use Precision@K, Mean Average Precision (MAP@K) to measure the quality of the ranking list of recommended videos. For each new user $u \in U^{new}$ in the test set, Precision@K is defined as $Precision@K = \sum_{k=1}^{K} r_k/K$, and the MAP@K is the mean of average precision scores over test users U^{new} and is defined as:

$$MAP@K = \frac{1}{U^{new}} \sum_{u=1}^{U^{new}} \frac{\sum_{k=1}^{K} Precision@uk * r_{u,k}}{L_u}, \quad (14)$$

where r_k is the relevance level at position k, which is 0 for "Not Relevant" and 1 for "Relevant" in our experiment. The $r_{u,k}$ is the relevance level at position k for user u. The $Precision@uk$ is the precision at position k for user u, and K is the truncation level. L_u is the number of relevant data in the recommended set. The evaluation result is obtained by checking whether the recommended videos are truly in u's interested video set. In our study, we set $K \in 10, 20, 30, 40, 50, 60, 70, 80, 90, 100$.

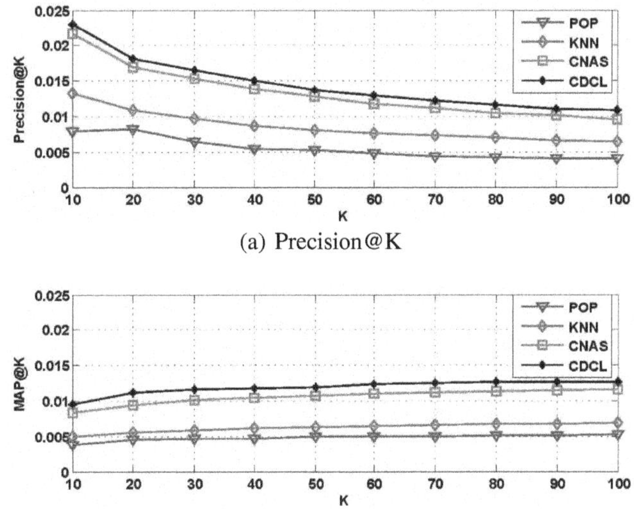

(a) Precision@K

(b) MAP@K

Figure 9: The Precision and MAP of cross-network video recommendation for new YouTube users.

5.2.3 *Results and Analysis*

We compare the proposed model with three baseline methods:

- Popularity(POP): This approach provides the same recommendation list of the videos to all new users according to this video's popularity. Here, we consider the view counts of the video as its popularity.

- KNN: For a new YouTube user, the KNN uses his/her Twitter information to obtain the most related Twitter users. Then the relevant videos can be obtained by the most related users.

- Cross-network Association (CNAS) [20]: The CNAS uses a coupled dictionary learning method to learn a pair of dictionary spaces by the same users across different networks.

The evaluation results of different methods are shown in Figure 9. From the results, we have the following conclusions: (1) The POP method shows inferior performance. This is due to its incapability of learning user's personalized needs and considering cross-network user behaviors. (2) The KNN and CNAS methods achieve better results. This shows that it is useful to adopt the auxiliary domain and consider the cross-network collaboration for the cold start recommendation task. (3) The proposed CDCL method outperforms the CNAS and the KNN, and achieves the best recommendation performance in terms of precision and MAP under all values of K computed. This is because the proposed model can collaboratively learn the shared dictionary space with the shared domain priors, which can better leverage users' cross-network activity data to address the user cold-start recommendation problem.

In Figure 10, we show four new YouTube users with their twitter history information on Twitter and the corresponding recommended video list from YouTube. Take the test user "Daniel Rodriguez" as an example, we can see that this new user is a software engineer and likes music and science. The corresponding recommended video list from YouTube includes some science technology, game design, and popular music, which better satisfies the interest of the new YouTube user. These results demonstrate the effectiveness of the proposed cross-domain collacross-network video recommendation method.

Figure 10: Four examples on cross-network video recommendation from Twitter to YouTube users(All photos via Flickr under Creative Commons License).

6. CONCLUSION

In this paper, we propose a generic cross-domain collaborative learning framework based on non-parametric Bayesian dictionary learning model for cross-domain data analysis. The proposed model can effectively adopt the shared domain priors and modality priors to collaboratively learn the feature representation by considering the domain discrepancy and the multi-modal property. The extensive experimental results on two different applications (cross-platform event recognition and cross-network video recommendation) demonstrate the effectiveness of the proposed model. In the future, we will investigate more applications with the proposed generic framework, such as cross-domain event summarization and cross-domain attribute mining.

7. ACKNOWLEDGMENT

This work is supported in part by National Basic Research Program of China (973 Program No. 2012CB316304), and National Natural Science Foundation of China (No.61225009, 61432019, 61303173, 61472115, 61472379, U1435211).

8. REFERENCES

[1] Xiaoshan Yang, Tianzhu Zhang, and Changsheng Xu. Cross-domain feature learning in multimedia. *IEEE Transactions on Multimedia*, 17(1):64–78, 2015.

[2] Tianzhu Zhang and Changsheng Xu. Cross-domain multi-event tracking via co-pmht. *ACM Trans. Multimedia Comput. Commun. Appl.*, 10(4):31:1–31:19, 2014.

[3] Jie Tang, Sen Wu, Jimeng Sun, and Hang Su. Cross-domain collaboration recommendation. In *KDD '12*, 2012.

[4] John Blitzer, Ryan McDonald, and Fernando Pereira. Domain adaptation with structural correspondence learning. In *EMNLP '06*, 2006.

[5] Sinno Jialin Pan, Ivor W. Tsang, James T. Kwok, and Qiang Yang. Domain adaptation via transfer component analysis. In *IJCAI'09*, 2009.

[6] Fabian Abel, Samur Araújo, Qi Gao, and Geert-Jan Houben. Analyzing cross-system user modeling on the social web. In *Web Engineering - 11th International Conference, ICWE 2011, Paphos, Cyprus, June 20-24, 2011*, pages 28–43, 2011.

[7] Ming Yan, Jitao Sang, Tao Mei, and Changsheng Xu. Friend transfer: Cold-start friend recommendation with cross-platform transfer learning of social knowledge. In *Proceedings of the 2013 IEEE International Conference on Multimedia and Expo, ICME 2013, San Jose, CA, USA, July 15-19, 2013*, pages 1–6, 2013.

[8] Xiaoshan Yang, Tianzhu Zhang, Changsheng Xu, and Ming-Hsuan Yang. Boosted multifeature learning for cross-domain transfer. *TOMCCAP*, 11(3):35:1–35:18, 2015.

[9] Yang Yang, Yi Yang, and Heng Tao Shen. Effective transfer tagging from image to video. *ACM Trans. Multimedia Comput. Commun. Appl.*, 9(2):14:1–14:20, 2013.

[10] Yang Yang, Zheng-Jun Zha, Yue Gao, Xiaofeng Zhu, and Tat-Seng Chua. Exploiting web images for semantic video indexing via robust sample-specific loss. *IEEE Transactions on Multimedia*, 16(6):1677–1689, 2014.

[11] Xiaoshan Yang, Tianzhu Zhang, Changsheng Xu, and M. Shamim Hossain. Automatic visual concept learning for social event understanding. *IEEE Transactions on Multimedia*, 17(3):346–358, 2015.

[12] Jingwen Bian, Yang Yang, Hanwang Zhang, and Tat-Seng Chua. Multimedia summarization for social events in microblog stream. *IEEE Transactions on Multimedia*, pages 216–228, 2015.

[13] Shengsheng Qian, Tianzhu Zhang, Changsheng Xu, and M. Shamim Hossain. Social event classification via boosted multimodal supervised latent dirichlet allocation. *TOMCCAP*, 11(2):27:1–27:22, 2014.

[14] Jianchao Yang, Zhaowen Wang, Zhe Lin, Scott Cohen, and Thomas S. Huang. Coupled dictionary training for image super-resolution. *IEEE Transactions on Image Processing*, 21(8):3467–3478, 2012.

[15] Shenlong Wang, Lei Zhang, Yan Liang, and Quan Pan. Semi-coupled dictionary learning with applications to image super-resolution and photo-sketch synthesis. In *CVPR*, pages 2216–2223, 2012.

[16] Mingyuan Zhou, Haojun Chen, John William Paisley, Lu Ren, Guillermo Sapiro, and Lawrence Carin. Non-parametric bayesian dictionary learning for sparse image representations. In *NIPS'09*, pages 2295–2303, 2009.

[17] Chunfeng Yuan, Weiming Hu, Guodong Tian, Shuang Yang, and Haoran Wang. Multi-task sparse learning with beta process prior for action recognition. In *CVPR'13*, pages 423–429, 2013.

[18] Suman Deb Roy, Tao Mei, Wenjun Zeng, and Shipeng Li. Socialtransfer: cross-domain transfer learning from social streams for media applications. In *MM'12*, pages 649–658, 2012.

[19] Fabian Abel, Eelco Herder, Geert-Jan Houben, Nicola Henze, and Daniel Krause. Cross-system user modeling and personalization on the social web. *User Model. User-Adapt. Interact.*, 23(2-3):169–209, 2013.

[20] Ming Yan, Jitao Sang, and Changsheng Xu. Mining cross-network association for youtube video promotion. In *MM '14*, 2014.

[21] John Wright, Allen Y. Yang, Arvind Ganesh, S. Shankar Sastry, and Yi Ma. Robust face recognition via sparse representation. *IEEE Trans. Pattern Anal. Mach. Intell.*, 31:210–227, 2009.

[22] John Paisley and Lawrence Carin. Nonparametric factor analysis with beta process priors. In *ICML '09*, pages 777–784, 2009.

[23] David M. Blei, Andrew Y. Ng, and Michael I. Jordan. Latent dirichlet allocation. *JMLR*, 3:993–1022, 2003.

[24] T. L. Griffiths and M. Steyvers. Finding scientific topics. *Proceedings of the National Academy of Sciences*, 101:5228–5235, 2004.

[25] Rong-En Fan, Kai-Wei Chang, Cho-Jui Hsieh, Xiang-Rui Wang, and Chih-Jen Lin. Liblinear: A library for large linear classification. *J. Mach. Learn. Res.*, 9:1871–1874, 2008.

[26] Timo Reuter, Symeon Papadopoulos, Georgios Petkos, Vasileios Mezaris, Yiannis Kompatsiaris, Philipp Cimiano, Christopher M. De Vries, and Shlomo Geva. Social event detection at mediaeval 2013: Challenges, datasets, and evaluation. In *MediaEval*, 2013.

[27] L. Liu, L. Wang, and X. Liu. In defense of softassignment coding, 2011. In ICCV.

[28] Nikhil Rasiwasia, Jose Costa Pereira, Emanuele Coviello, Gabriel Doyle, Gert R.G. Lanckriet, Roger Levy, and Nuno Vasconcelos. A new approach to cross-modal multimedia retrieval. In *MM '10*, pages 251–260, 2010.

Learning Socially Embedded Visual Representation from Scratch

Shaowei Liu, Peng Cui, Wenwu Zhu and Shiqiang Yang
Computer Science Department, Tsinghua University, China
Tsinghua National Laboratory for Information Science and Technology
liu-sw11@mails.tsinghua.edu.cn, cuip/wwzhu/yangshq@tsinghua.edu.cn

ABSTRACT

Learning image representation by deep model has recently made remarkable achievements for semantic-oriented applications, such as image classification. However, for user-centric tasks, such as image search and recommendation, simply employing the representation learnt from semantic-oriented tasks may fail to capture user intentions. In this paper, we propose a novel Socially Embedded VIsual Representation Learning (*SEVIR*) approach, where an Asymmetric Multi-task CNN (*amtCNN*) model is proposed to embed user intention learning task into semantic learning task. Specifically, to address the sparsity and unreliability problems in social behavioral data, we propose to use user clustering, reliability evaluation, random dropout in output layer in our *amtCNN*. With its the partially shared network architecture, the learnt representation can capture both semantics and user intentions. Comprehensive experiments are conducted to investigate the effectiveness of our approach in applications of user favoring prediction, personalized image recommendation, and image reranking. Compared to the state-of-the-art image representation techniques, our approach achieves significant improvement in performance.

Categories and Subject Descriptors

H.3.3 [**Information Search and Retrieval**]: Retrieval models

General Terms

Algorithms, Experimentation, Performance

Keywords

user intention; user behavior; multi-task CNN; image search and recommendation

MM'15, October 26–30, 2015, Brisbane, Australia.
© 2015 ACM. ISBN 978-1-4503-3459-4/15/10 ...$15.00.
DOI: http://dx.doi.org/10.1145/2733373.2806247.

1. INTRODUCTION

Image representation learning is a fundamental task in various image-related applications. In past years, a tons of research works have been conducted to learn image representations with the goal of bridging the semantic gap between low-level features and high-level semantics. The learnt image representations have gained great success in content-centric applications, such as image classification, object detection, motion tracking, etc. In recent years, user-centric image platforms (such as Flickr and Pinterest) are more and more prevalent, where images are generated, disseminated and consumed by users. How to proactively provide images according to users' intentions (*e.g.*, interests) has become a critical problem, which subsequently posits a significant challenge to image representations: besides semantics, can image representations also reflect user intentions?

Recently, a paucity of works attempt to embed social signals into visual representations to capture user intention, where social signals such as user behaviors and social relations are commonly used to capture user intentions [15, 28]. They usually learn a linear or kernel variation of traditional hand-crafted descriptors, such as SIFT, HOG, bag-of-features representations, *etc*, to make the learnt representations consistent to social signals. However, these methods can hardly bridge the gap between low-level features and high-level user intentions because the hand-crafted features pose serious limit on how much intention information can be embedded. These hand-crafted features are designed for identifying image semantics, and cannot work well in reflecting user intentions, because these two factors cover different aspects of image contents.

Then can we learn image representations incorporating both semantics and user intentions from scratch rather than hand-crafted features? The recent progress in deep learning models, such as Convolutional Neural Network, offers an optimistic answer. These methods have demonstrated their superiority in learning image representations from scratch and attained significant improvement than hand-crafted features. However, existing deep learning based methods are usually designed for semantic-oriented tasks, *e.g.* image classification. How to embed both semantic-related information and intention-related information into deep models is still an unexplored problem.

Learning image representations to capture both semantics and user intentions still entail following challenges:

- **Multiple and asymmetric learning tasks.** In user-centric image applications, such as image search and recommendation, semantics is an important factor to determine whether a user will like an image or not. Other factors in user intention, such as visual style and emotion will also play important roles. These two factors are complementary, but they have different characteristics and thus need different learning paths from raw data to supervised information. How to design an asymmetric architecture to jointly fuse semantics learning and intention learning tasks is challenging.

- **The sparsity and unreliability of social behavioral data.** In social media platform, the number of images and users is huge. But a user can only see a tiny proportion of the whole images. Thus, the real user-image behaviors are very sparse. Furthermore, the social behavioral information is sometimes unreliable due to some "fake" users and noisy information. How to make the right use of social behavioral data is critical and challenging for image representation learning.

To address the above challenges, we propose a novel *Socially Embedded VIsual Representation learning (SEVIR)* method. It aims at learning mid-level image representation that can capture both semantics and user intention based on Convolutional Neural Network. The framework is illustrated in Figure 1. In our approach, user intention is evaluated based on social behavioral data. An Asymmetric Multi-task CNN (*amtCNN*) model is proposed to embed user intention learning task into semantic learning task. In *amtCNN*, semantic meaning is learnt from labeled image classification datasets, such as ImageNet. And user intention is learnt from the social images with quantified intention labels. In particular, we consider data reliability issue and conduct dropout on the output layer to address the sparsity and unreliability problems in social behavioral data, and thus avoid overfitting problem. As the output, the activations in mid-layers of *amtCNN* can be utilized as image representations, where both semantics and user intention are incorporated. We perform extensive experiments to demonstrate the effective of our approach. Figure 2 is a showcase, in which the curves in the left part denote the performance in *Precision@k* on our image recommendation dataset. And the representations learned for a image by different methods are visualized in the right part. Intuitively, we can observe from Figure 2 that the representations learned by *SEVIR* and semantic-oriented CNN are apparently different, and *SEVIR* performs significantly better than traditional representations, which is attributed to its capability of fusing semantics and intentions into image representations.

The contributions of the proposed approach can be summarized as follows:

1) In contrast with traditional semantic-oriented representation learning methods, we investigated an unexplored problem of learning socially embedded visual representations from scratch, where the learned representation can well capture both the semantics of images and users' intentions over the images.

2) We propose a novel Asymmetric Multi-task CNN (*amtCNN*) model to address the challenges of multiple and asymmetric learning tasks, as well as the sparsity and unreliability of social behavioral data, where two different pathways are designed to learn semantics and user intentions respectively with partially shared network architecture and data reliability in user intention learning pathway is considered.

3) We conducted comprehensive experiments on real application scenarios. Compared to the state-of-the-art baseline methods, our approach can achieve significant improvement, i.e., it performs at least 15% better in image recommendation and reranking tasks, which demonstrates its superiority in user-centric image applications.

The rest of the paper is organized as follows: Section 2 gives a brief introduction and comparison of related works. Section 3 introduces the framework of the proposed approach. In Section 4, we present the architecture of the proposed asymmetric multi-task CNN model and the strategies for training. Then, we report the experimental results to show the effectiveness of our approach in Section 5. Finally, Section 6 summarizes the paper.

2. RELATED WORK

2.1 CNN based Image Representation Learning

To bridge the gap between low-level features and high-level semantics, a series of works focus on learning image representation to capture semantic meaning of images. In image classification task, Convolutional Neural Network (CNN) [12, 25] has shown is superiority to traditional methods based on hand-crafted features such as Bag-of-Visual-Word features (BoW) [33] since 2012. Furthermore, in other computer vision problems, such as tracking and object detection, CNN also showed its strength [4, 6]. Not only it performs well in the above areas, but also the layer before the output layer can naturally be used as image representation. However, to date, there is few deep learning based approaches designed for image retrieval or recommendation tasks. Although some works [23, 1, 27] explore to use the codes learnt from image classification datasets for image retrieval, they can only retrieve the images in object level, where user intention, an important factor for human, is ignored.

2.2 Learning User Intention for Image Representaion

Aiming at capturing user intention to improve the performance of image retrieval and recommendation, query log analysis [8, 7, 21] and relevance feedback [24, 32] are proposed in the past years. However, users' query log in image search engines can be hardly accessed for common users and researchers. Besides, the frequent operation in relevance feedback methods may sometimes reduce user satisfaction. With the development of social media, the information in social platforms, such as image tags [13], user behaviors [30] and user relationships, are utilized to analyze user interests. Cui *et al.* [3] proposed a social-sensed image search framework, which first summarizes user interests based on his favorite images in Flickr, and then reranks the search results based on his interests to realize personalized search. Liu *et al.* [15] learns an image distance metric based on social behavioral information to evaluate image similarity of user intention. However, traditional works based on social information usually use "shallow models". Thus, their ability in bridging semantic gap and intention gap can still be strengthened by deep models. Although in [30], Yuan *et al.* explore to learn latent features of social entities (*e.g.* users, images, tags) by deep model, this work only focuses on learning the relationship between pair-wised social entities (*e.g.* user-image and image-tag). For an image that

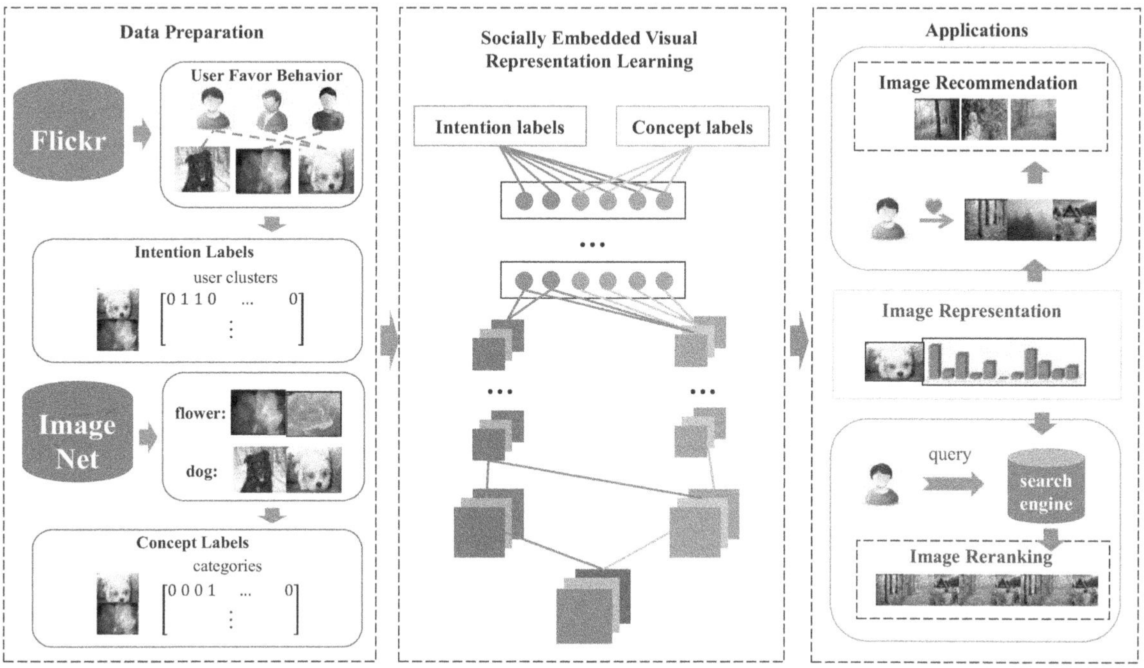

Figure 1: The conceptual framework of the proposed Socially Embedded VIsual Representation Learning approach.

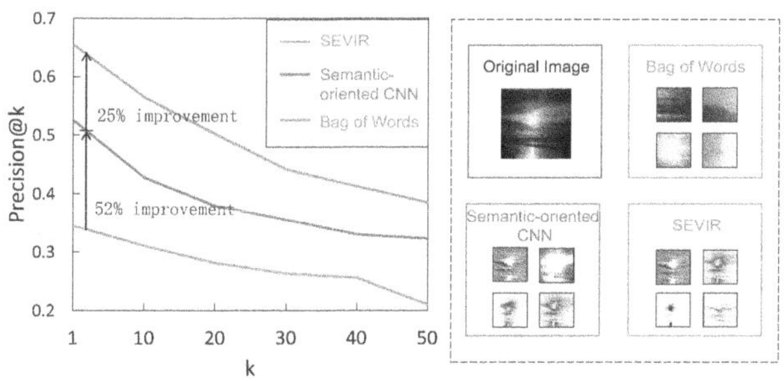

Figure 2: A showcase of the performance in *Precision@k* for image recommendation tasks (left) and the visualized features (right, best viewed in color).

has multi-modal information, such as faves, tags, there is no common representation for this image. In another word, when user intention is learnt based on user-image relationship, the semantic meaning in image-tag relationship will be ignored. Furthermore, as other social-sensed works show [14], the pair-wised relationships in social platforms are usually unreliable because social information is very sparse and noisy. To make image representation robust, it must completely capture both semantics and user intention.

2.3 Multi-task Deep Learning

Multi-task learning is typically applied when there are multiple related learning tasks on multiple datasets. Deep model based multi-task learning has been proven effective in many computer vision problems, such as face recognition [34], human tracking [26, 29], ontology concept learning [5], and video semantic embedding [16]. The main idea of multi-task is to share part of network structures or add some common constraints to the parameters in each task. Most of previous works aim at learning multiple subproblems in a given problem. However, in our problem, the goal is to learn two different aspects in image representation, *i.e.*, semantic aspect and intention aspect. Therefore, we cannot simply apply traditional multi-task models but have to consider the different characteristics in different task.

3. THE FRAMEWORK OF SEVIR

3.1 Overview

In this paper, we propose a Socially Embedded VIsual Representation Learning *SEVIR* approach to capture both semantic meaning and user intention in image representation. In our approach, we first prepare and pre-process two training datasets: an image classification dataset for semantic learning and a user favor behavior[1] dataset in social platforms for user intention learning. Then, a Symmetric Multi-task CNN (*amtCNN*) is designed to embed user intention learning task into traditional semantic learning CNN model. Therefore, the image representation learnt in mid-layers in *amtCNN* can be applied to user-centric applications, such as image search and recommendation.

In image classification task, we usually use category label vector to represent the semantic meaning of images. To make user behavior learning task aligned to classification task, we need to restructure the favor behavior into the form of label vector which is called intention label in data preprocessing stage. For an image, its intention label is defined

[1]In Flickr, user can click "favor" button for an image, which denotes this is his/her favorite image.

as the distribution of user interests. In our approach, we divide user into different clusters with respect to the images they favor. Thus, each user cluster can represent a user interest. We can evaluate whether the current image will be liked for each user cluster based on our user favor behavior data. Furthermore, we evaluate the confidence score of the intention label to solve the sparsity and unreliability problems in social information.

After the data are pre-processed, we have two datasets: a classification dataset $\mathcal{D}_1 = \{I_1, \cdots, I_m\}$ with category label z_i for each image I_i; a social dataset $\mathcal{D}_2 = \{I'_1, \cdots, I'_n\}$ with intention y_i and confidence score t_i for each image I_i. Then, we use the proposed *amtCNN* model to learn an image representation $f(\cdot)$, so that: 1) for any $I_i \in \mathcal{D}_1$, its features $f(I_i)$ includes the knowledge in z_i, i.e., there exists $g(\cdot)$, so that $g(f(I_i)) \approx z_i$; 2) for any $I'_i \in \mathcal{D}_2$, its features $f(I'_i)$ includes the knowledge in y_i, i.e., there exists $h(\cdot)$, so that $h(f(I_i)) \approx y_i$.

In this section, we introduce how to conduct user clustering, as well as generate intention labels y_i and confidence score t_i for social images in detail. The proposed amtCNN model will be introduced in Section 4.

3.2 Intention Label for Social Images

In most of social multimedia platforms, such as Flickr, a user can "favor" some images, which indicates that the user likes this image. By collecting all images that a user favors, we can estimate his/her interests. By dividing n users into k clusters, we can regard each cluster as a interest. Thus, a social image can be represented as the distribution of the clusters whose users like it, which is called intention labels in our work. Intuitively, the images that are liked by similar user clusters should be similar in user intention aspect. Therefore, the image representations that are learnt from intention labels can capture user intention aspect. Here, we generate intent labels based on user clusters rather than independent users due to two main reason. First, social behavior information is very sparse, using independent users may make the label vector very sparse and high-dimensional. Second, when new users come, we hope the intent label to be stable in dimensionality. We first introduce how to divide users into k clusters in this section.

Inspired by [15], given n users and their favorite images, we conduct user clustering to partition the users into k clusters. First, each user u_i is represented by the set of his favorite images $\mathcal{I}m(u_i)$. Then, the pair-wised user similarity of u_i and u_j can be evaluated by the *Jaccard* similarity of $\mathcal{I}m(u_i)$ and $\mathcal{I}m(u_j)$:

$$sim(u_i, u_j) = \frac{|\mathcal{I}m(u_i) \cap \mathcal{I}m(u_j)|}{|\mathcal{I}m(u_i) \cup \mathcal{I}m(u_j)|}. \quad (1)$$

Then, we can conduct Spectral Clustering [19] on the similarity graph. Finally, we can obtain the users in each cluster, which is denoted as C_i.

However, we cannot judge that users in the same cluster must have the same interests, and vise versa. It is mainly because the data in social platforms are usually sparse and unreliable. For some active users who favor a lot of images that he/she really likes, we can understand his/her interests well. Oppositely, for the ones who favor few images or randomly favor some images, the clustering results may have some error. Therefore, for each cluster, we give a reliability score to each user in it to denote the confidence that it belongs to the cluster. In our approach, we use the centrality score calculated by PageRank [20] model as the reliability score. r_i denotes the vector of reliability scores of these users. Then, r_i can be iteratively updated by:

$$r_i(t) = d \cdot P_i \cdot r_i(t-1) + (1-d)e, \quad (2)$$

where $r_i(t)$ is the pagerank score in the tth iteration. P_i is the transaction matrix, which is normalized from pair-wised user similarity of the users in $\mathcal{C}_i$ to make the sum of each column to be 1, d is the damping factor to guarantee the connectivity of the similarity graph, and e is a normalized n-dimension vector whose elements are all $1/n$. In traditional PageRank model [20], the empirical value of d is about 0.8. Thus, we adopt this value in our approach. After $r_i(t)$ converged to $\tilde{r}_i$, the final reliability score r_i is normalized to make the maximum value to be 1:

$$r_i = \frac{\tilde{r}_i}{max(\tilde{r}_i)}. \quad (3)$$

Thus, for user u_i, we have known that he/she should belong to cluster c_i with reliability r_i.

For an image I_i, we use $\mathcal{U}_i$ to denote the set of users who favor it. Thus, we can map $\mathcal{U}_i$ to a k-dimensional vector y_i to represent the intention label for I_i:

$$y_{ij} = \begin{cases} 1, & \mathcal{U}_i \cap \mathcal{C}_j \neq \phi \\ 0, & \text{otherwise.} \end{cases} \quad (4)$$

In this equation, if there is at least one user in cluster j that favors image I_i, the jth element in y_i will be 1. However, for different 1 in y_i, we have different confidence because the users have different reliability. We use t_{ij} to denote the confidence score that image I_i is favored by cluster j. If $y_{ij} = 1$, we can know that users $\mathcal{U}_i \cap \mathcal{C}_j$ favored I_i in $\mathcal{C}_j$. Thus, the confidence score t_{ij} is defined as the average of these users' reliability score. Thus, the confidence score t_{ij} is defined as follows,

$$t_{ij} = \begin{cases} \frac{\sum_{u \in \mathcal{U}_i \cap \mathcal{C}_j} r_j(u)}{|\mathcal{U}_i \cap \mathcal{C}_j|}, & y_{ij} = 1 \\ 1, & \text{otherwise.} \end{cases} \quad (5)$$

Note that, although we define $t_{ij} = 1$ when $y_{ij} = 0$, we just know that there is no user in cluster j that favors image i. However, we do not know that the users in cluster j dislike image i. This problem will be discussed in detail in the next section.

Based on the above formulation process, for an image I_i, we can obtain two k-dimensional vectors y_i and t_i. y_i denotes which clusters of users favor the image, and t_i represents the corresponding confidence.

4. ASYMMETRIC MULTI-TASK CNN

In the last section, we introduced how to pre-process the social behavioral datasets to construct intention labels. Meanwhile, for traditional image classification task, we usually use a 1-of-k vector to denote the category that an image belongs to. Therefore, we have two datasets after data preprocessing stage: classification dataset D_1 with category labels z for semantic learning and user favor behavior dataset D_2 with intention labels y and confidence scores t for user intention learning. We now use the proposed Asymmetric Multi-task CNN (*amtCNN*) model to learn an effective image representation, in which semantic meaning and user intention are captured.

4.1 Network Architecture

We design the multi-task convolutional neural network based on the previous problem definition, which is illustrated in Figure 3. In Figure 3, there are two pathways for two tasks. The pathway in the top dash box is designed for image classification task, and the other is designed for user intention learning task. "conv", "pool" and "fc" denote convolutional layer, pooling layer, and fully connected layer in CNN correspondingly. The layer name that ends with "i_j" denotes it is the ith layer in the jth pathway. For example, "conv3_1" indicates that it is the third layer in the first pathway (for image classification task), and it is a convolutional layer.

In the first pathway, there are five convolutional layers and three fully connected layers, where the first, second and fifth convolutional layers are followed by pooling layers. This setting refers to AlexNet [12], which is one of typical CNN architectures in image classification area. The size of convolution kernels in the convolution layers and the number of neurons in the fully connected layers are illustrated over each layer. The setting of stride and padding is also similar to AlexNet. In this pathway, we do not adjust much from AlexNet because it is for typical image classification task. Therefore, in the forward propagation stage, the transaction function from the $(l-1)^{th}$ layer to the lth layer can be formulated as follows,

$$x_l^1 = \sigma(W_{l-1}^1 x_{l-1}^1 + b_{l-1}^1), \qquad 1 < l \leq 8, \tag{6}$$

where $\sigma(\cdot)$ is the activation function, where we use RELU [12] in our network, where $\sigma(x) = x$ when $x > 0$ and 0 otherwise. Here superscript "1" refers to the first pathway; x_l^1 denotes the output of the lth layer; W_{l-1}^1 denotes the weights from the $(l-1)^{th}$ layer to the ith layer; b_{l-1}^1 is the bias. Equation is suitable for both convolutional layer and fully connected layer. For convolutional layers, x and b are $q_l \times 1$ vectors and W is a $q_{l-1} \times p_{l-1} \times p_{l-1} \times q_l$ tensor, where q_l is the number of feature maps and p_l is the size of convolutional kernel in the lth layer. For fully connection layers, we can regard each neuron as a 1×1 convolution. Thus W is a $q_{l-1} \times q_l$ matrix. Different from the previous layers, the final output layer $\tilde{z}$ is defined as:

$$\tilde{z} = softmax(\sigma(W_8^1 x_8^1 + b_8^1)), \tag{7}$$

where $softmax(\cdot)$ is a function which can generate a distribution from a given vector.

The second pathway is designed to embed social favor behavior. In this pathway, the types of layers are similar to those in the first pathway, but the connections are quite different. A convolutional or fully connected layer in the second pathway is connected to the previous layers in both of the first and the second pathway, *i.e.*,

$$x_l^2 = \sigma(W_{l-1}^{2,1} x_{l-1}^1 + b_{l-1}^{2,1} + W_{l-1}^{2,2} x_{l-1}^2 + b_{l-1}^{2,2}), 1 < l \leq 8, \tag{8}$$

where $W_{l-1}^{2,i}$ $(i = 1, 2)$ refers to the weights from the ith pathway's $l-1$ layer to the second pathway's l layer, and $b_{l-1}^{2,i}$ is the corresponding bias. In the second pathway, the output layer $\tilde{y}$ is defined as:

$$\tilde{y} = \sigma'(W_8^{2,1} x_8^1 + b_8^{2,1} + W_8^{2,2} x_8^2 + b_8^{2,2}), \tag{9}$$

where $\sigma'(\cdot)$ is sigmoid function, which is defined as $\sigma'(x) = \frac{1}{1+e^{-x}}$. Compared to Equation 7, we do not use softmax+RELU but sigmoid function. It is mainly because in the first pathway, the groudtruth label is z_i, which is a 1-of-k indicator. However, in the second pathway, the groundtruth is y_i, which have multiple 1s. Therefore, the softmax (a probability distribution) is not suitable.

In this work, we call the layers in the first pathway "semantic layers" and the second pathway "social layers". Therefore, we can observe that a semantic layer is only determined by the last semantic layer, while a social layer is determined by both of the last semantic layer and the last social layer. This is because user intention, *i.e.*, which kind of users will like this image, is first determined by the semantic meaning of the image, and also determined by other emotional or social aspects. Based on this setting, we can embed the user intention learning task into traditional image classification task. From Figure 3, we can observe that the final size of each social layer is half of the size of corresponding semantic layer to achieve the best performance. There are two reasons for this phenomenon. First, semantic layer has included a lot of useful information which will effect user intention. Thus, we do not need so much social nodes. Second, for image classification task, ImageNet is a very big dataset to pre-train our network. On the other hand, the Flickr dataset is crawled by ourselves and thus does not have a very huge amount. If the size of social layers is too big, the network may face under-fitting problem due to the lack of training samples.

4.2 Training

Based on the architecture in Figure 3, our target is to derive the optimal weights in the network. For each image, the input data x_1 is the pixel data of RGB channels, *i.e.*, $x_1 =< I_i^R, I_i^G, I_i^B >$. In the first pathway, *i.e.*, image classification task, we expect the output layer $\tilde{z}_i$ to be close to the classification label vector z_i. In ImageNet ILSVRC-2012 dataset, there are 1000 categories in total. Thus, z_i is a 1000-D vector where only one element is 1 and the others are 0. We define the loss function for this task as L_1, which can be computed according to the loss function of regression:

$$L_1 = \frac{1}{2}\sum_{i=1}^{N}(z_i - \tilde{z}_i)^2 + \frac{\lambda}{2}\sum_{l=1}^{8}\|W_l^1\|_F^2, \tag{10}$$

where $\tilde{z}_i$ is the output $\tilde{z}$ in Equation 7 for image I_i; λ is the factor to balance the loss and regularization to previous overfitting.

For the second user intention learning task, the supervised label is y_i. Here, the loss function should be re-defined because we have different confidence for the elements in y_i. In Section 3, we compute the confidence score t_i for y_i. As mentioned, when $y_{ij} = 1$, t_{ij} denotes the confidence that users in cluster j like image i. However, $y_{ij} = 0$ only denotes "unknown" but not "dislike". If we use all 0s in y_i for training, it may bring a lot of noise. Here we refer to the idea of dropout to solve this problem. For all the js that make $y_{ij} = 0$, we only select part of them for back propagation. Therefore, we first modify the confidence score in Equation 5 as follows,

$$t'_{ij} = \begin{cases} t_{ij}, & y_{ij} = 1 \\ 1, & y_{ij} = 0 \text{ and } j \text{ is selected} \\ 0, & \text{otherwise.} \end{cases} \tag{11}$$

In this work, the dropout rate is 0.2, *i.e.*, we only select 20% 0s in y_i for back propagation. Then, the loss function for

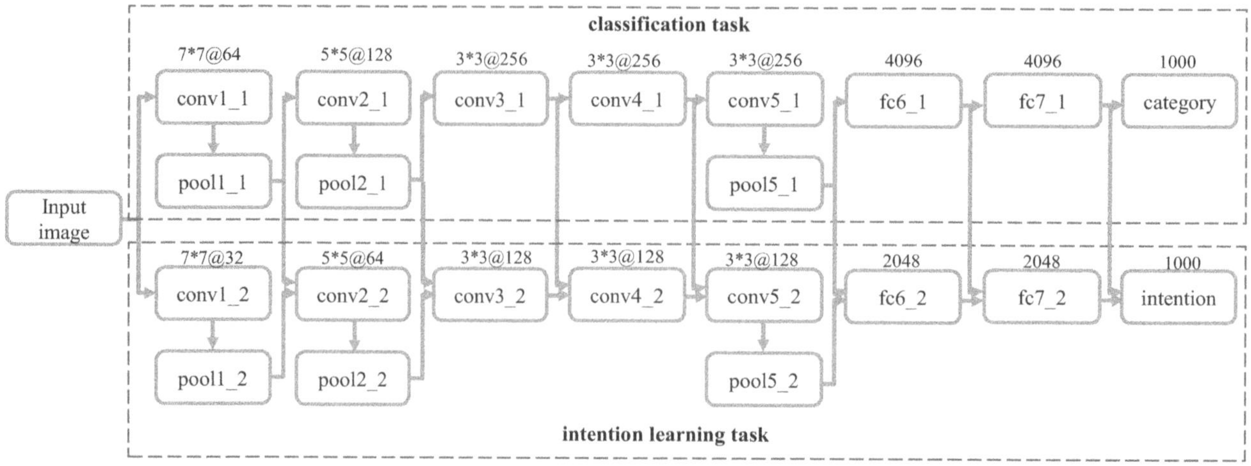

Figure 3: The architecture of the proposed network. The top dash line box is designed for image classification task and the bottom one is for favor behavior learning task. The arrow line between two layers denotes that these two layers are fully connected.

this task is defined as,

$$L_2 = \frac{1}{2}\sum_{i=1}^{N} t_i'(y_i - \tilde{y}_i)^2 + \frac{\lambda}{2}\sum_{l=1}^{8}(\|W_l^{2,1}\|_F^2 + \|W_l^{2,2}\|_F^2). \quad (12)$$

Using Equation 12, only the weights connected to the selected neuron in the output layer will be updated in the back propagation stage.

We use batch mode in the training stage. We first select a batch of images in classification dataset D_1, and use L_1 to update the weights W^1. Second, we select a batch of images in social image dataset D_2, and user L_2 to update the weights $W^{2,1}$ and $W^{2,2}$. We iteratively repeat the above two operations until the errors converge on both of the validation sets for two tasks.

When the training processed is finished, we can use the combination of mid-level fully connect layers, *i.e.*, the $fc6$ to $fc7$, as the learnt representation. In our approach, we find $fc7$ performs the best on the validation set. Therefore, for image I_i, its representation in our network $f(I_i)$ is $< x_{i,7}^1, x_{i,7}^2 >$.

4.3 Algorithm

We summarize the algorithm of the whole Socially Embedded Visual Representation Learning approach as described in Algorithm 1.

Our approach has three main steps. First, we divide n users into k clusters. Then, we compute the k-dimensional vector y and t for each social image. Finally, we train our *amtCNN* model based on the pre-processed data.

5. EXPERIMENTS

In this section, we first introduce the experimental settings in this work. Then we evaluate the proposed approach in three application scenarios: user favor behavior prediction, personalized image recommendation, as well as image reranking. Finally, we give some observations of the learnt image representation.

5.1 Experimental Setup

5.1.1 Datasets

In our experiments, we have prepared four datasets, including:

Training dataset. The training dataset consists of two sub sets: D_1 for classification and D_2 for user intention learning. In this work, D_1 is a subset of ILSVRC-2012 dataset in ImageNet and D_2 is crawled from Flickr. We do not use the whole ILSVRC-2012 dataset as D_1 bacause its amount is much more than D_2. We first use the whole ILSVRC-2012 to pre-train the weights in classification pathway in our network. Then, we use D_1 and D_2 for fine-tuning. We randomly select 128,000 images from ILSVRC-2012 dataset as D_1, where there are 1000 categories in total and each category has 128 images. To construct D_2, we select 128,000 images from *Yahoo Flickr Creative Commons WebScope* dataset [2] with popular tags [3]. Then, we crawl the users who favor them through Flickr API. Finally, there are 97,513 users in total and each image is favored by 4 users in average. For each of D_1 and D_2, we use 90% for training and remained 10% for test.

Favor behavior prediction dataset. We crawl other 10,000 images that are favored by the users in training dataset in Flickr. The user intention labels y_i computed by Equation 4 is used as groundtruth to predict which clusters of users will favor them. This dataset can be regarded as the test dataset after training.

Recommendation dataset. We also prepare a recommendation dataset for image recommendation. We crawled 1,000 users' favorite images in Flickr. The number of the images in total is 17,935. All of the selected users have at least 80 favorite images. For each user, we randomly select 40 of his favorite images as ground truth for test and the remained favorite image for training. Then we randomly

[2]http://webscope.sandbox.yahoo.com/catalog.php?datatype=i&did=67

[3]https://www.flickr.com/photos/tags/

Algorithm 1: *SEVIR*

Input: Image Classification dataset $\mathcal{D}_1 = \{I_1, \cdots, I_m\}$ with label z_i for each I_i;
User favorite images $\mathcal{D}_2 = \{I'_1, \cdots, I'_n\}$ with favored users $\mathcal{U}_i$ for each I'_i;
Output: The trained CNN model, which can obtain the representation $f(I_i)$ for any image I_i.

```
for pair-wised users (u_i, u_j) do
    Compute user similarity sim(u_i, u_j) by Eq. 1;
end
Conduct spectral clustering on the similarity graph;
for each cluster C_i do
    for user u ∈ C_i do
        Compute the reliability score r(u) by Eq. 3;
    end
end
for each image I_i ∈ D_2 do
    Compute intention labels y_i by Eq. 4;
    Compute confidence score vector t_i by Eq. 5;
end
repeat
    Select batch of images B_1 ⊆ D_1;
    Compute loss L_1 along the first pathway by Eq. 10;
    Conduct back propagation for the first pathway;
    Select batch of images B_2 ⊆ D_2;
    Compute loss L_2 along the second pathway by Eq.
    12 with dropout;
    Conduct back propagation for the second pathway;
until errors for both two pathways converged;
```

sample other 160 images from the whole image dataset as candidates for testing.

MSR dataset. We utilize Bing Image Retrieval Grand Challenge (MSR) dataset [7] to prove that our distance learning method can improve the performance of image reranking. In this dataset, the images under a given query are labeled as "Excellent", "Good" or "Bad" with respect to the click count. Different from traditional image retrieval datesets, MSR dataset is based on user click data, which can capture not only semantic relevance but also human cognition.

To the best of our knowledge, there is no public benchmark including user behavioral information for image recommendation. Thus, we crawled the data from Flickr for the first three datasets. In our image reranking method, a public dataset is utilized to make our approach comparable to others.

5.1.2 *Model Implementation*

We train the network introduced in Section 4 on our training dataset. Our training strategy follows the practice of the previous works on CNN [12, 31]. In our training set, each image is resized to 256×256. Five 224×224 crops are cropped from the center and the four corners of the resized image. We also conduct horizonal flipping and vertical flipping for each cropped sample. Following AlexNet [12], dropout with probability 0.5 is used in the first two fully connection layers in each task in learning process. The learning rate starts from 0.02 for all layers. It is divided by 10 when the error rate stops reducing. Our model is modified based on the public code of Caffe [9]. It is trained on a single GeForce Tesla K40 GPU with 12GB memory. The training process will cost about 3 days.

5.2 Favor behavior Prediction

In our CNN model, for any image I, we can compute the output $\tilde{y}$ in the second pathway using Equation 9. For an image in our favor behavior prediction dataset, y means which clusters of users will like it. Therefore, we can use $\tilde{y}$ to predict users' favor behavior. In this experiment, for each image I in favor behavior prediction dataset, we evaluate the similarity between the prediction result $\tilde{y}$ and groundtruth y in metrics of $RMSE$ (Root Mean Square Error), *Precision@k*, and $Kendall-\tau$ [11]. Here $RMSE$ reflects the error in value; *Precision@k* reflects the accuracy when we recommend the image to k clusters of users; and $Kendall - \tau$ evaluates the performance in ranking point of view. For $RMSE$, lower value is better. For the other metrics, the higher the better.

To compare with our approach, we use the following methods as baselines:

- **Logistic Regression with Bag-of-Words feature (BOW) [33].** In this method, we first train a logistic regression model on the training dataset D_2. Bag-of-Words features are extracted based on SIFT descriptors [17]. Then we use the favor prediction dataset to evaluate the performance using the trained logistic regression model.
- **Logistic Regression with SIDL (SIDL).** SIDL [15] is a distance learning method which incorporates social behavioral information. The learned image distance metric can map the original image feature to a new space. Like the previous baseline, we train a logistic regression model based on the mapped features.
- **AlexNet.** AlexNet [12] is a CNN model proposed for image classification on ImageNet which captures semantic information. We use the last layer before the output layer as image representation.
- **Social task in SEVIR (SEVIR_soc).** Here we only use the second pathway in our proposed SEVIR Network. The network is trained on Flickr dataset D_2 and the last layer before the output layer is used as image representation.

In our experiments, we mark our proposed method as $SEVIR\_soc + sem$ because it captures social information and semantic information at the same time. Table 1 shows the results.

Table 1: The performance on favor behavior prediction dataset in $RMSE$, *Precision@k*, and $Kendall - \tau$ for different image representation methods.

	$RMSE$	$P@3$	$P@10$	$Kendall - \tau$
BoW [33]	0.4368	0.1201	0.2855	0.057
SIDL [15]	0.3345	0.2347	0.3451	0.3939
AlexNet [12]	0.347	0.2099	0.3362	0.3467
SEVIR_soc	0.3199	0.2289	0.353	0.3751
SEVIR_soc+sem	**0.2857**	**0.2556**	**0.4061**	**0.4277**

From Table 1, it can be observed that the proposed method $SEVIR\_soc + sem$ achieves the best performance in all of the metrics. BoW performs the worst because it is extracted only based on visual contents. Thus, it does not include adequate information for semantic and intention. Although SIDL also embeds social behavioral information, it performs worse than $SEVIR\_soc$ because the linear model (logistic regression) cannot bridge low-level feature and high-level favor behavior well. Intuitively, favor behavior is more related to user intention than semantic meaning of images. However, we can observe that AlexNet performs better than $SEVIR\_soc$. To our understanding, it is mainly because the social data are very sparse and unreliable. Thus the model that fits the training social data very much may reduce the performance on test data on the contrary due to overfitting.

5.3 Image Recommendation

In the image recommendation dataset, we have 1,000 users' favorite images in Flickr. We divide part of them for training and rest for test. In test stage, our task is to recommend 40 images from 200 candidate images for each user. In this experiment, we use the following recommendation methods to show the effectiveness of our approach:

- **Content-based Filtering using Bag-of-Words Features (BoW).** Content-based Filtering [22] is one of the most popular content based recommendation methods. The idea is to rank the candidate images according to their similarity to the training images of a given user. Here we use Bag-of-Words features to evaluate image similarity.
- **Content-based Filtering based on SIDL, AlexNet, SEVIR_soc, SEVIR_soc+sem.** Respectively, we use SIDL, AlexNet, SEVIR_soc, SEVIR_soc+sem to evaluate image similarity for Content-based Filtering.
- **Content-boosted Collaborative Filtering based on SIDL, AlexNet, SEVIR_soc, SEVIR_soc+sem.** Collaborative Filtering [2] is a typical recommendation method which uses user behavioral information. To demonstrate that our content-based method and CF are competitive. We adopt the approach in [18] to combine Content-based Filtering with Collaborative Filtering. Here we use the proposed SEVIR to evaluate content similarity of images.

We use $Precision@k$ to evaluate the performance of the above recommendation methods. Figure 4 shows the results for image recommendation. In Figure 4, (a) illustrates the performance of content-based methods of our proposed SEVIR and baseline methods; (b) illustrates the performance of combining content-based methods with collaborative filtering. From Figure 4 (a), we can see that the proposed SIVIR_soc+sem performs the best, which is consistent to the previous experiments. When combined with Collaborative Filtering (CF), we can observe from Figure 4 (b) that the hybrid method CF+SEVIR (here SEVIR means SIVIR_soc+sem) still performs the best. It indicates that although the pure CF produces relatively good performance, our proposed SEVIR is still an effective image representation which is competitive to CF.

5.4 Image Reranking

In this experiment, we follow the method in [10] to rerank the images for a given query in MSR dataset. In this method, pair-wised image similarity is computed to build the similarity graph. Then, PageRank [20] is used to compute the

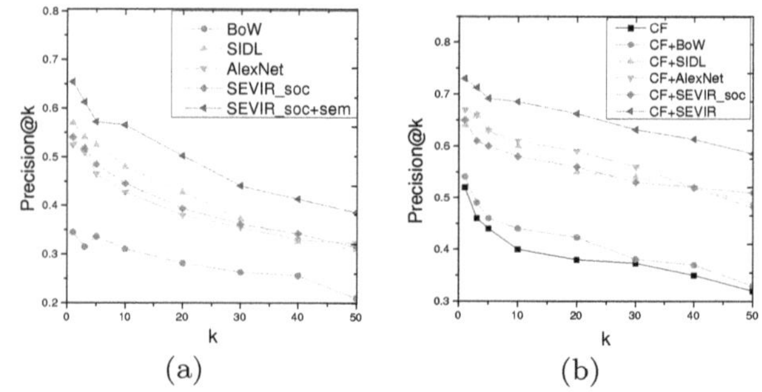

Figure 4: The performance on recommendation dataset in $Precision@k$ with different number of top k images using (a) content-based methods (b) hybrid methods of content-based filtering and collaborative filtering.

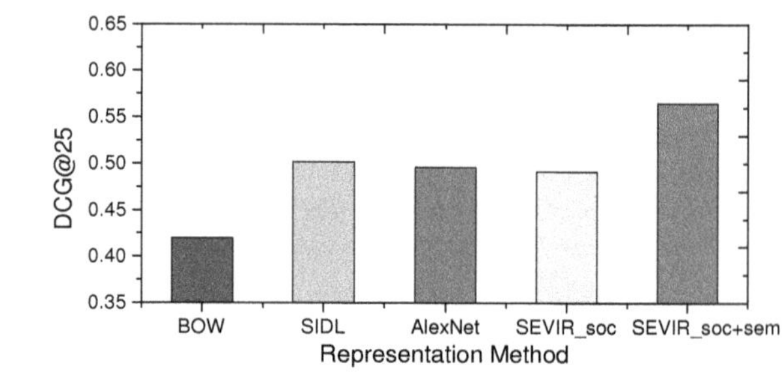

Figure 5: The performance on the MSR dataset in terms of $DCG@25$ with using different image representations in the PageRank model.

centrality scores for each image. Therefore, the image with high PageRank score is similar to most of other images. Following the measurements in ACM Multimedia Grand Challenge 2013, we use Discounted Cumulated Gain of the top 25 images ($DCG@25$) to evaluate the performance. When the rank order is given, the $DCG@25$ for each query is calculated as:

$$DCG@25 = 0.01757 \sum_{i=1}^{25} \frac{2^{rel_i} - 1}{\log_2(i+1)}, \quad (13)$$

where rel_i is the relevance score of the ith ranked image (Excellent=3, Good=1, Bad=0), 0.01757 is to normalize the value of $DCG@25$ up to 1. Note that the $DCG@25$ of a perfect ranking may also be less than 1 when there are some non-excellent images in top 25. For the queries with fewer than 25 images, we simply supply some "Bad" images after the original ranking list. We use the baseline methods similar to favor behavior prediction task to evaluate image similarity. Figure 5 shows the results of our experiments. From Figure 5, we can observe that our approach has remarkable superiority to the other baseline methods. SIDL, AlexNet, and SEVIR_soc produce similar performance because they include different aspects of information: SIDL uses both users' favor behavior and image tags, but it is a shallow learning model; AlexNet considers semantic categories; SEVIR_soc only uses favor behavior but it is a deep learning model. Therefore, it is reasonable that our approach, which uses deep learning model and captures both user intention and semantic information achieves 0.5649 in $DCG@25$. Note that, here we just use the development dataset in MSR. Thus, the reranking method is unsupervised. However, the performance is comparable to the state-of-the-art methods that are supervised by training dataset. It indicates that our approach trained by Flickr images can indeed capture user intention information, which is independent to training data.

5.5 Discussions

In our approach, we are very curious about what we have learned from the classification task and the behavior learning task. Therefore, we visualize some representative activations in our CNN model. We first select 3 images that have the similar semantic meaning of "flower". Then, we compute the activations of bottom convolutional layers (conv1) and top convolutional layers (conv5) for social task and semantic task. Figure 6 illustrates representative activations that we obtain.

Although the selected 3 images are all about flowers, they have quite different favored users in Flickr. The first two images are from a flower lover's album, so that the favored users are similar. The third image is a photo in a party. Thus, it has no overlap with the previous two images in user dimension. From Figure 6, we have some interesting observations. For conv1, the activations in semantic task are very close to the original image, but the ones in social task have been abstract. It indicates that the features extracted in behavior learning task are relatively latent but not intuitive. For conv5, the activations in semantic task describe the outline of the flowers, while the ones in social task seem to be some very detailed aspects, such as texture of pistil or petal. For the activations of conv5 in semantic task, three images are very similar, which leads to the same classification result "flower". While when we observe the activations of conv5 in social task, the third image is obviously different with the first two images. Intuitively, for the third image, the activations of conv5 in social task deliver the information about "many" because there are many black "dots" in them. However, for the first and the second images, the activations are relatively pure. Therefore, we can find that we really learned some extra information in social task that differs from classification task.

6. CONCLUSION

In this paper, we explore learning image representation to capture both semantics and user intention for user-centric applications, such as image search and recommendation. A Socially Embedded VIsual Representation Learning (*SEVIR*) approach is proposed, in which an Asymmetric Multi-task Convolutional Neural Network (*amtCNN*) model is designed to embed user intention learning task into semantic learning task. In user intention learning task, we first compute intention labels with confidence scores based on favor behavior in social platforms. Then, the loss function is specifically designed to tackle the sparsity and unreliability challenges in social behavioral information. The experimental results in user behavior prediction and image reranking applications indicate that our representation learning approach includes more intention level information than baseline methods. The experiment for image recommendation demonstrate that the learnt representation can make the performance of content-based filtering method comparable to collaborative filtering methods. In all of the experiments, our approach performs at least 15% better than baseline methods, which is remarkably better than baseline methods. From the visualization of the learning results, we observed that learnt features in social task are quite different with the ones in classification task.

This work is an effort to embed social information into deep CNN model. We have a long way to go because the quality of social data is much worse than well-labeled classification data. To our understanding, this is the main reason that we can just observe the difference of the features in visualization part, but we cannot give a good intuitive explanation. In the future, we will explore to better organize social information and design a more reasonable deep model for embedding to make image representation learning more intelligent and more personalized. Furthermore, we can incorporate multi-modal social information to better understand user intention.

7. ACKNOWLEDGEMENT

This work is supported by the National Basic Research Program of China, No. 2015CB352300; National Natural Science Foundation of China, No. 61370022 and No. 61210008; International Science and Technology Cooperation Program of China, No. 2013DFG12870. Thanks for the support of NExT Research Center funded by MDA, Singapore, under the research grant, WBS:R-252-300-001-490 and the research fund of Tsinghua-Tencent Joint Laboratory for Internet Innovation Technology.

8. REFERENCES

[1] A. Babenko, A. Slesarev, A. Chigorin, and V. Lempitsky. Neural codes for image retrieval. In *ECCV*, pages 584–599. Springer, 2014.

[2] J. S. Breese, D. Heckerman, and C. Kadie. Empirical analysis of predictive algorithms for collaborative filtering. In *Uncertainty in artificial intelligence*, pages 43–52. Morgan Kaufmann Publishers Inc., 1998.

[3] P. Cui, S.-W. Liu, W.-W. Zhu, H.-B. Luan, T.-S. Chua, and S.-Q. Yang. Social-sensed image search. *ACM TOIS*, 32(2):8, 2014.

[4] J. Fan, W. Xu, Y. Wu, and Y. Gong. Human tracking using convolutional neural networks. *TNN*, 21(10):1610–1623, 2010.

[5] X. Geng, H. Zhang, Z. Song, Y. Yang, H. Luan, and T.-S. Chua. One of a kind: User profiling by social curation. In *ACM Multimedia*, pages 567–576. ACM, 2014.

[6] R. Girshick, J. Donahue, T. Darrell, and J. Malik. Rich feature hierarchies for accurate object detection and semantic segmentation. In *CVPR*, pages 580–587. IEEE, 2014.

[7] X.-S. Hua, L. Yang, J. Wang, J. Wang, M. Ye, K. Wang, Y. Rui, and J. Li. Clickage: towards bridging semantic and intent gaps via mining click logs of search engines. In *ACM Multimedia*, pages 243–252, 2013.

[8] B. J. Jansen. Search log analysis: What it is, what's been done, how to do it. *Library & information science research*, 28(3):407–432, 2006.

[9] Y. Jia, E. Shelhamer, J. Donahue, S. Karayev, J. Long, R. Girshick, S. Guadarrama, and T. Darrell. Caffe: Convolutional architecture for fast feature embedding. *arXiv preprint arXiv:1408.5093*, 2014.

[10] Y. Jing and S. Baluja. Visualrank: Applying pagerank to large-scale image search. *PAMI*, 30(11):1877–1890, 2008.

[11] M. G. Kendall. A new measure of rank correlation. *Biometrika*, 1938.

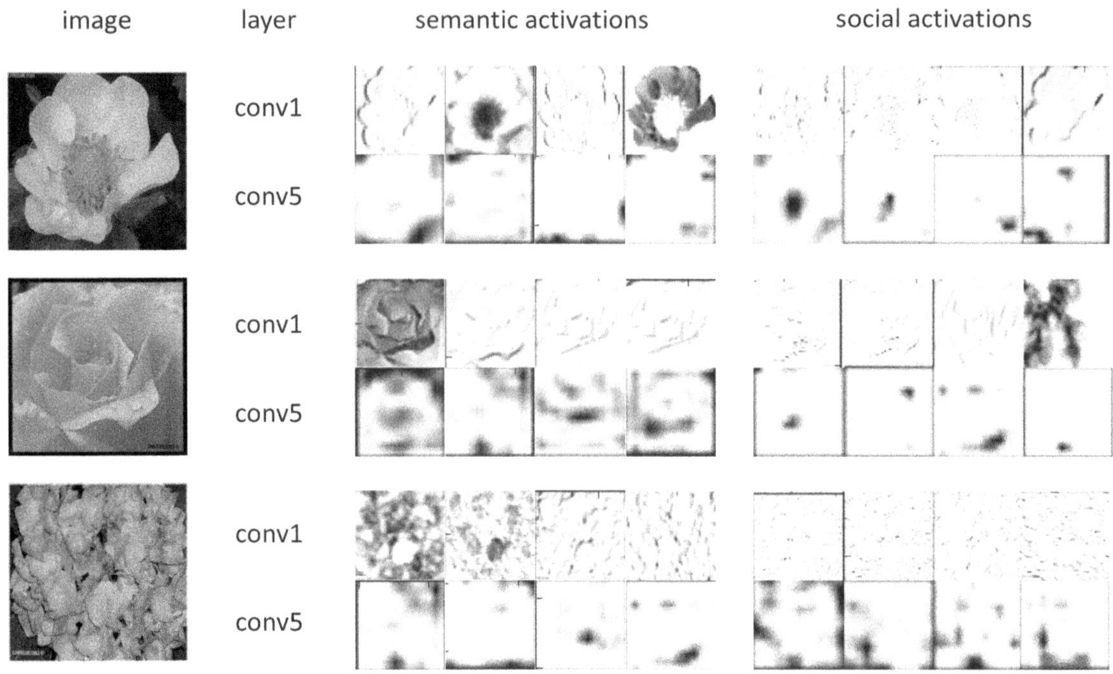

Figure 6: The illustration of representative activations of bottom convolutional layers (conv1) and top convolutional layers (conv5) for social task and semantic task.

[12] A. Krizhevsky, I. Sutskever, and G. E. Hinton. Imagenet classification with deep convolutional neural networks. In *NIPS*, pages 1097–1105, 2012.

[13] X. Li, C. G. Snoek, and M. Worring. Learning social tag relevance by neighbor voting. *TMM*, 11(7):1310–1322, 2009.

[14] S. Liu, P. Cui, H. Luan, W. Zhu, S. Yang, and Q. Tian. Social visual image ranking for web image search. In *MMM*, pages 239–249. Springer, 2013.

[15] S. Liu, P. Cui, W. Zhu, S. Yang, and Q. Tian. Social embedding image distance learning. In *ACM Multimedia*, pages 617–626. ACM, 2014.

[16] W. Liu, T. Mei, Y. Zhang, C. Che, and J. Luo. Multi-task deep visual-semantic embedding for video thumbnail selection. In *CVPR*, pages 3707–3715, 2015.

[17] D. G. Lowe. Object recognition from local scale-invariant features. In *ICCV*, volume 2, pages 1150–1157. Ieee, 1999.

[18] P. Melville, R. J. Mooney, and R. Nagarajan. Content-boosted collaborative filtering for improved recommendations. In *AAAI*, pages 187–192, 2002.

[19] A. Y. Ng, M. I. Jordan, Y. Weiss, et al. On spectral clustering: Analysis and an algorithm. *NIPS*, 2:849–856, 2002.

[20] L. Page, S. Brin, R. Motwani, and T. Winograd. The pagerank citation ranking: Bringing order to the web. 1999.

[21] Y. Pan, T. Yao, T. Mei, H. Li, C.-W. Ngo, and Y. Rui. Click-through-based cross-view learning for image search. In *SIGIR*, pages 717–726. ACM, 2014.

[22] M. J. Pazzani. A framework for collaborative, content-based and demographic filtering. *Artificial Intelligence Review*, 13(5-6):393–408, 1999.

[23] A. S. Razavian, H. Azizpour, J. Sullivan, and S. Carlsson. Cnn features off-the-shelf: an astounding baseline for recognition. In *CVPR Workshop*, pages 512–519. IEEE, 2014.

[24] Y. Rui, T. S. Huang, M. Ortega, and S. Mehrotra. Relevance feedback: a power tool for interactive content-based image retrieval. *CSVT*, 8(5):644–655, 1998.

[25] K. Simonyan and A. Zisserman. Very deep convolutional networks for large-scale image recognition. *arXiv preprint*, 2014.

[26] J. J. Tompson, A. Jain, Y. LeCun, and C. Bregler. Joint training of a convolutional network and a graphical model for human pose estimation. In *NIPS*, pages 1799–1807, 2014.

[27] J. Wan, D. Wang, S. C. H. Hoi, P. Wu, J. Zhu, Y. Zhang, and J. Li. Deep learning for content-based image retrieval: A comprehensive study. In *ACM Multimedia*, pages 157–166. ACM, 2014.

[28] G. Wang, D. Hoiem, and D. Forsyth. Learning image similarity from flickr groups using fast kernel machines. *Pattern Analysis and Machine Intelligence, IEEE Transactions on*, 34(11):2177–2188, 2012.

[29] N. Wang and D.-Y. Yeung. Learning a deep compact image representation for visual tracking. In *NIPS*, pages 809–817, 2013.

[30] Z. Yuan, J. Sang, Y. Liu, and C. Xu. Latent feature learning in social media network. In *ACM Multimedia*, pages 253–262. ACM, 2013.

[31] M. D. Zeiler and R. Fergus. Visualizing and understanding convolutional networks. In *ECCV*, pages 818–833. Springer, 2014.

[32] H. Zhang, Z.-J. Zha, S. Yan, J. Bian, and T.-S. Chua. Attribute feedback. In *ACM Multimedia*, pages 79–88. ACM, 2012.

[33] S. Zhang, Q. Tian, G. Hua, Q. Huang, and S. Li. Descriptive visual words and visual phrases for image applications. In *ACM Multimedia*, pages 75–84. ACM, 2009.

[34] Z. Zhang, P. Luo, C. C. Loy, and X. Tang. Facial landmark detection by deep multi-task learning. In *ECCV*, pages 94–108. Springer, 2014.

Spatial-aware Multimodal Location Estimation for Social Images

Jiewei Cao[1], Zi Huang[1], and Yang Yang[2]
[1]The University of Queensland, Australia
[2]University of Electronic Science and Technology of China, China
j.cao3@uq.edu.au, huang@itee.uq.edu.au, dlyyang@gmail.com

ABSTRACT

Nowadays the locations of social images play an important role in geographic knowledge discovery. However, most social images still lack the location information, driving location estimation for social images to have recently become an active research topic. With the rapid growth of social images, new challenges have been posed: 1) data quality of social images is an issue because they are often associated with noises and error-prone user-generated content, such as junk comments and misspelled words; and 2) data sparsity exists in social images despite the large volume, since most of them are unevenly distributed around the world and their contextual information is often missing or incomplete. In this paper, we propose a spatial-aware multimodal location estimation (SMLE) framework to tackle the above challenges. Specifically, a spatial-aware language model (SLM) is proposed to detect the high quality location-indicative tags from large datasets. We also design a spatial-aware topic model, namely spatial-aware regularized latent semantic indexing (SRLSI), to discover geographic topics and alleviate the data sparseness problem existing in language modeling. Taking multi-modalities of social images into consideration, we employ the learning to rank approach to fuse multiple evidences derived from textual features represented by SLM and SRLSI, and visual features represented by bag-of-visual-words (BoVW). Importantly, an ad hoc method is introduced to construct the training dataset with spatial-aware relevance labels for learning to rank training. Finally, given a query image, its location is estimated as the location of its most relevant image returned from the learning to rank model. The proposed framework is evaluated on a public benchmark provided by MediaEval 2013 Placing Task, which contains more than 8.5 million images crawled from Flickr. Extensive experiments on this dataset demonstrate the superior performance of the proposed methods over the state-of-the-art approaches.

MM'15, October 26–30, 2015, Brisbane, Australia.
 ISBN 978-1-4503-3459-4/15/10 ...$15.00.
DOI: http://dx.doi.org/10.1145/2733373.2806249.

Categories and Subject Descriptors

H.3.3 [**Information Search and Retrieval**]: Retrieval models; Information filtering

Keywords

Location Estimation; Geotagging; Multimodal

1. INTRODUCTION

In recent years, driven by the proliferation of GPS-enabled devices and media-sharing platforms such as Flickr, Twitter, YouTube and Foursquare, people have been creating large collections of online multimedia content with coordinates. It has been reported that 62% of on-the-go consumers publish social sharing images, videos or posts with geo-tags, which are either manually labeled or automatically assigned by GPS-enabled devices [21]. Such georeferenced community-contributed content has been attracting extensive attention from both industry and research communities [18].

However, publicly-visible location annotations are remarkably sparse in online data. It has been estimated that only about 5% of the existing multimedia content on the Internet is actually geotagged [7]. Specifically, only 2.5% of the most-viewed videos on YouTube and approximately 4.3% of Flickr images are tagged with coordinates. Therefore, multimedia location estimation has become an active research topic. This task is also known as *geocoding* in the geographic information retrieval community and *geotagging* or *georeferencing* in the multimedia field [18]. In this paper, we are focused on the social image location estimation by utilising both the visual and textual information.

Location estimation based on visual content has been widely studied. The intuition is that the locations of two images might be close to each other if they share highly similar visual content. Early visual-based methods make the estimation within a geographically constrained area, such as urban environments or city-scale areas [29, 23]. [11] is among the first to address the images location estimation at the global level and [16] introduces a geo-visual ranking method to further improve the accuracy. Both work employ content-based image retrieval (CBIR) techniques to search the visually-nearest-neighbors with respect to a geotagged image corpus, and estimate the location of an image according to the coordinators of its neighbors.

The main drawback of the visual-based methods lies in the low prediction accuracy. They require images to contain landmarks with highly discriminative visual patterns, which rarely happens for many social images. Therefore, textual

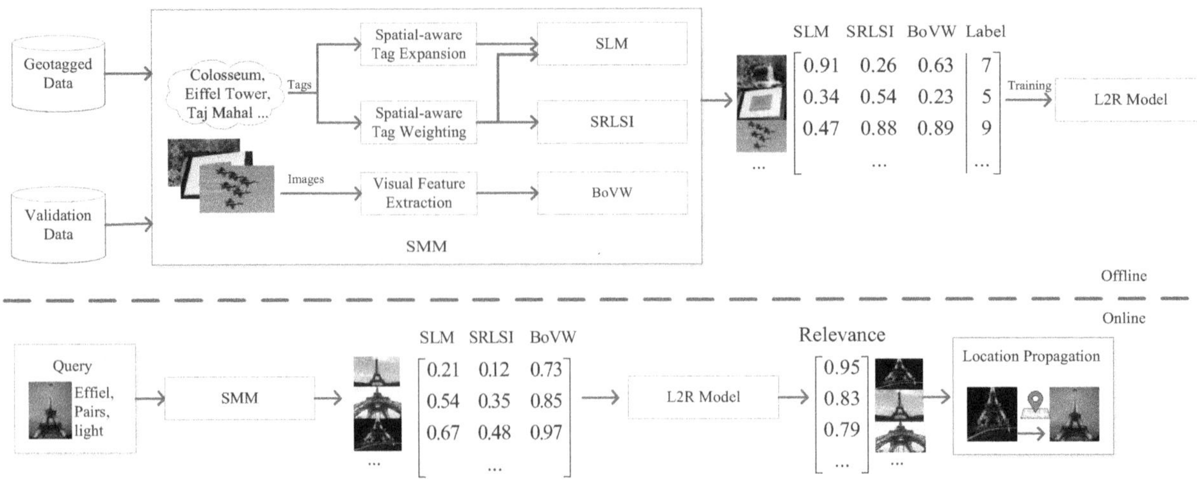

Figure 1: The proposed spatial-aware multimodal location estimation framework.

information is involved naturally, which aims to make an accurate estimation by exploiting the metadata including tags, titles and descriptions associated with social images. It has been found that language modeling (LM) approaches are particularly suitable [24, 25]. While gazetteers have traditionally been the main tool to assess the geographic scope of textual resources, they are limited to manually compiled lists of toponyms. As a compensation, large collections of georeferenced text, such as the associated tags of geotagged Flickr images, can be used to identify correlations between occurrences of terms and particular places. A vital step for these approaches is to extract spatial-aware terms [19] that are most indicative of geographic locations from a given text collection. Language model *smoothing* is required due to data sparseness. However, traditional smoothing techniques are not well tailored to the location estimation problem. In this paper, we propose a spatial-aware topic model to discover compact and readable geographic topics from georeferenced text. Integrated with language modeling, this topic model can serve as an effective smoothing technique to alleviate the data sparseness problem.

Inspired by the aforementioned observations and analysis, here we propose a spatial-aware multimodal location estimation (SMLE) framework for location estimation of social images. As illustrated in Fig. 1, the framework has an offline process and an online process. In the offline process, learning to rank (L2R) is employed to combine three lists of relevance scores computed from the spatial-aware multi-modeling module (SMM) which consists of three models, namely spatial-aware language model (SLM), spatial-aware regularized latent semantic indexing model (SRLSI) and bag-of-visual-words image retrieval model (BoVW). Given a geotagged dataset, such as Flickr images and their tags, SMM handles these data by three models accordingly. Tags are preprocessed with spatial-aware tag weighting and tag expansion, and then consumed by SLM and SRLSI. And images are used by the BoVW model for visual word dictionary construction and indexing. To effectively train learning to rank, we introduce an ad hoc method to construct the training dataset with spatial-aware relevance labels. In the online process, given a query (or test) image, it is firstly processed by SMM to generate three lists of relevance scores from database images, which are then fused by the learning to rank model to generate the final ranking list. The final location estimation is conducted by propagating the top one image's location to the query image.

Our main contributions are summarized as follows: 1) the location is estimated by considering multimodal relevance scores obtained from three different models including SLM, SRLSI and BoVW; 2) the visibility of location-indicative tags is enhanced by spatial-aware tag weighting and tag expansion; 3) a novel topic model is designed to learn geographic topics from social images according to their location-indicative tags; 4) an ad hoc method is developed to construct the training dataset with spatial-aware relevance labels for learning to rank training; 5) an extensive performance study is conducted on a large-scale benchmark dataset to prove the effectiveness of our framework, in comparison with the state-of-the-art methods.

The rest of the paper is organized as follows. Related work is reviewed in Section 2. The proposed SMM and its methodologies are presented in Section 3, followed by learning to rank in Section 4. Section 5 reports the results and the paper is concluded in Section 6.

2. RELATED WORK

In this paper, we focus on the location estimation for social images on a global scale. More comprehensive surveys about geotagging in multimedia and computer vision domains and its applications can be found in [18] and [4]. In this section, we divide related work into three categories according to the modalities they utilized.

The first group is visual-based location estimation. Early work simplifies the problem to do estimation within a highly geographically constrained area. Given an urban images dataset, Zhang et al. [29] first select the best visually similar candidates based on SIFT keypoints matching and then estimate the location by performing position triangulation on top two best reference views selected by the camera motion estimation. Schindler et al. [23] work on a city-scale images dataset, and point out that the accuracy can be greatly improved by choosing the most informative visual features during vocabulary construction and efficiently increasing the branching factor in vocabulary tree searching.

Hays and Efros [11] address the image location estimation in a global level. They first collect 6 million of geotagged Flickr images and extract various visual features. For each query image, they calculate its aggregated feature distances against the whole referenced dataset in order to find the nearest-neighbors, and estimate the location according to these neighbors' coordinates. Li et al. [16] further refine the visually similar candidates by considering their geo-visual neighbors which are both geographically nearby and visually similar.

The second group is textual-based location estimation. Serdyukov et al. [24] estimate the locations of Flickr images by using a language model purely based on the tags assigned by users. They further improve the model by location-aware form of smoothing which utilized the spatial distribution of tags. Van Laere et al. [25] propose a two-step approach which first determines the most possible area for the query image based on language model and then performs similarity search within this area to find the most textually similar candidate for final location estimation. They further improve the classification accuracy by spatial-aware terms selection [19] which reduces the negative impact of noisy tags by detecting the most location-indicative tags from the whole corpus. Another approach to improve the language model is to combine it with geographic topic model. For example, Eisenstein et al. [6] propose a multi-level generative model to discover coherent topics and their regional variants which reveal topic-specific regional distinctions.

The third group is multimodal location estimation. Friedland et al. [7] introduce the concept of multimodal location estimation which leverages cues from the visual and the acoustic content of a video as well as from the given metadata. They attempt to classify which city a video comes from by matching videos containing audio from ambulance sirens in different cities. User specific modeling approaches utilize social relationship for location estimation. For example, since most social images are home-style, [13] incorporates user home location prior to favor location which is closed to user's home and shows great accuracy improvement. On the other hand, most users nowadays use Twitter to share their experiences while traveling, Hauff et al. [9] show that extracting location information from users' microblog stream can also benefit images locating.

3. SPATIAL-AWARE MULTI-MODELING

In this section, we give a detailed description of the proposed spatial-aware multi-modeling module (SMM) in the proposed spatial-aware multimodal location estimation framework, including its three models: spatial-aware language model, spatial-aware topic model, and BoVW image retrieval model. The relevance scores computed from the above three models will be used in learning to rank for both offline training and online location estimation.

3.1 Spatial-aware Language Model

To estimate the location of a query image, a straightforward solution is to find the most similar image from the database and assign its location to the query image. Given that each image is associated with a set of tags, it can be represented by its tags as a *document*. Usually, this document is short as images are generally assigned with a limited number of tags. Traditionally, this image textual representation only treats the associated tags with equal weights, which limits the advantage of taking into account the significant location information carried by the location-indicative tags. For the problem of location estimation, we improve the image textual representation by considering: 1) spatial-aware tag weighting, which assigns high weights to the location-indicative tags; and 2) spatial-aware tag expansion, which alleviate the problem that short text documents yield little in the way of term frequency information.

3.1.1 Spatial-aware Tag Weighting

In order to increase the weights of the tags that carry geographical cues, we apply the method proposed in [19] to calculate the spatial-aware weight for each tag. Given a tag t and the image set $\mathbf{L}_t$ consisting of the images with this tag, the weight of t, denoted as $s(t)$, is computed as:

$$s(t) = logN_t \cdot \frac{\sum_{\mathbf{p}\in\mathbf{L}_t}(|\{\mathbf{q}|\mathbf{q}\in\mathbf{L}_t, \mathbf{q}\neq\mathbf{p}, dist(\mathbf{p},\mathbf{q})\leq\lambda\}|)^w}{N_t^2}, \tag{1}$$

where $N_t = |\mathbf{L}_t|$ is the total number of occurrences of tag t, $\mathbf{p}$ and $\mathbf{q}$ are images in $\mathbf{L}_t$, $dist(\cdot)$ is the geographic distance (e.g., Haversine distance), λ is the distance threshold, and w is the hyper-parameter controlling the weight to favor tags whose occurrences are centered around only a few locations. The weight $s(t)$ is calculated in the way similar to "tf-idf", where the first part $logN_t$ prefers tags with high frequencies in the corpus and the second part will downgrade the $s(t)$ if tag t spreads all over the world and vise verse. Specifically, when $w = 1$, if all the images with tag t are clustered in a small region (controlled by λ), then the second part will be close to 1, otherwise, close to 0. For each tag in the corpus, we calculate its spatial-aware weight by Eq.1 and apply it in the language model and topic model later on.

3.1.2 Spatial-aware Tag Expansion

Given that each image is represented as a short document consisting of its tags, it is assumed that document closeness may indicate geographical closeness of images, if those tags are location-indicative. However, similarity search in short documents is challenging for traditional retrieval models because most tags occur only once in a single document. It is difficult to accurately estimate the relevance of documents in terms of term frequency. There are two ways to address such problem: 1) apply document clustering during language model smoothing; and 2) document expansion, which modifies each document by adding additional terms from its neighborhood documents. The latter one is particularly useful to the retrieval of short and noisy documents, where the additional terms can enrich the document content.

We propose the following method to expand the tags of each image in the whole corpus to enhance their location visibility. For each image represented by $\mathbf{d}_i$ in the image corpus $\mathbf{D}$, we find a set of its neighbors $\mathbf{D}_i$ which satisfies:

$$\mathbf{D}_i = \{\mathbf{d}_j|\forall\mathbf{d}_j\in\mathbf{D}, j\neq i, dist(\mathbf{d}_i,\mathbf{d}_j)\leqslant\lambda_1, |\mathbf{d}_i\cap\mathbf{d}_j|\geqslant\lambda_2\}, \tag{2}$$

where $dist(\cdot)$ is the geographic distance between the locations of the corresponding images $\mathbf{d}_i$ and $\mathbf{d}_j$, and $|\mathbf{d}_i\cap\mathbf{d}_j|$ is the number of their overlapping tags. We expand $\mathbf{d}_i$ by duplicating the tags which also appear in its neighborhood images. In details, for any $\mathbf{d}_j\in\mathbf{D}_i$, its overlapping tags with $\mathbf{d}_i$ will be duplicated in $\mathbf{d}_i$. For example, given $\mathbf{d}_i$={Paris, Eiffel, flower} and its two neighbors $\mathbf{d}_j^{'}$={Eiffel, night} and $\mathbf{d}_j^{''}$={Eiffel, sunny}, $\mathbf{d}_i$ will be expanded to {Paris, Eiffel,

Eiffel, Eiffel, flower} as "Eiffel" appear twice in two neighboring images. In this case, the tags in $\mathbf{d}_i$ are not unique any more. The duplicate tags in $\mathbf{d}_i$ are assigned with the same weight as computed in Eq.1 and assumed to be of high importance to their belonging images in location estimation. It can be understood that such tag expansion actually increases the frequency of location-indicative tags in image's textual representation. We conduct the spatial-aware tag expansion on all the images in the corpus $\mathbf{D}$.

3.1.3 Language Model Relevance Calculation

Given a query image $\mathbf{q}$ represented by its tags, we apply the query likelihood retrieval model [20] to calculate the relevance between the query $\mathbf{q}$ and any image $\mathbf{d}$ from the corpus where spatial-aware tag weighting and tag expansion is applied. In the query likelihood retrieval model, the language model score, denoted as $P(\mathbf{q}|\mathbf{d})$, is formally defined as follows:

$$P(\mathbf{q}|\mathbf{d}) = \prod_{t \in \mathbf{q}} (P(t|\mathbf{d}) \times s(t)), \tag{3}$$

$$P(t|\mathbf{d}) = \frac{tf_{t,\mathbf{d}} + \mu P(t|\mathbf{D})}{|\mathbf{d}| + \mu}, \tag{4}$$

where t stands for a tag, and μ is the Dirichlet prior parameter that needs to be tuned.

The language model score $P(\mathbf{q}|\mathbf{d})$ is used to measure the relevance between $\mathbf{q}$ and $\mathbf{d}$, which is based on the tag matching between the query image and the corpus images. For easy illustration in the rest of the paper, we denote the the relevance score between $\mathbf{q}$ and $\mathbf{d}$ computed from our spatial-aware language model as $s_{lm}(\mathbf{q}, \mathbf{d})$. In other words, $s_{lm}(\mathbf{q}, \mathbf{d}) = P(\mathbf{q}|\mathbf{d})$. This spatial-aware language model (SLM) is one of the three models in the proposed SMM. The relevance score computed from SLM is one of the three scores to be fused in learning to rank.

3.2 Spatial-aware Topic Model

Besides the language model score, we define the topic model score in this subsection. Essentially, the SLM is based on the tag matching (or term matching). The advantage of incorporating the topic model is to alleviate the "term mismatch" problem. Traditional text retrieval models, such as vector space model, language model and BM25, are all based on term matching. The term mismatch problem arises when the documents and the query use different terms to describe the same concept, and thus relevant documents may get low ranking scores. It is beneficial to integrate the topic matching scores with the term matching scores, to leverage both broad topic relevance and specific term relevance. Here we consider using the topic model to further improve the accuracy of textual-based location estimation. However, existing topic models are not well suited for location estimation, since they do not consider the location property of tags associated with social images.

In this subsection, we present a spatial-aware tag representation instead of using traditional term score vector (e.g., tf-idf) for latent topics learning, based on which a spatial-aware topic model named spatial-aware regularized latent semantic indexing (SRLSI) is proposed to discover geographic topics by incorporating image location factors during the topic learning phase.

3.2.1 Spatial-aware Tag Representation

Existing topic modeling methods represent a document as a M-dimensional vector, where the mth entry denotes the score of the mth term, such as a boolean value indicating occurrence, term frequency, tf-idf score, and joint probability of the term and document. The term score is designed to indicate the importance of a term in a specific document. Therefore, in the context of location estimation, we replace the traditional term score with the spatial-aware tag representation. Specifically, we use the tag weight calculated by Eq.1 to represent each image $\mathbf{d} = (d^{(1)}, ..., d^{(M)})$ in corpus $\mathbf{D}$ as follows:

$$d^{(m)} = \begin{cases} s(t_m) & t_m \in \mathbf{T_d} \\ 0 & \text{otherwise} \end{cases}, m \in [1, M], \tag{5}$$

where t_m is the mth tag in the tag vocabulary, $\mathbf{T_d}$ is the set of tags in image $\mathbf{d}$, and M is the size of the tag vocabulary of the entire corpus. Experimental results in Section 5.3.2 show that this representation significantly improves the location estimation accuracy compared with the traditional representations.

3.2.2 Regularized Latent Semantic Indexing

There are various topic modeling methods [2], such as Latent Semantic Indexing (LSI), Probabilistic Latent Semantic Indexing (PLSI), and Latent Dirichlet Allocation (LDA). In real-world applications, however, the usefulness of the topic modeling is often limited due to the scalability issue. Most solutions require drastic steps such as vastly reducing the size of term vocabulary to achieve efficient modeling. Regularized Latent Semantic Indexing (RLSI) [26] can scale to large datasets without reducing the term vocabulary. Given an image corpus $\mathbf{D}$, RLSI aims to solve the following optimization objective function:

$$\min_{\mathbf{U}, \{\mathbf{v}_n\}} \sum_{n=1}^{N} ||\mathbf{d}_n - \mathbf{U}\mathbf{v}_n||_2^2 + \lambda_1 \sum_{k=1}^{K} ||\mathbf{u}_k||_1 + \lambda_2 \sum_{n=1}^{N} ||\mathbf{v}_n||_2^2, \tag{6}$$

where $\mathbf{U} = [\mathbf{u}_1, ..., \mathbf{u}_K]$ is the latent topics, K is the number of topics, $\mathbf{V} = [\mathbf{v}_1, ..., \mathbf{v}_N]$ is the topic representations of each image in $\mathbf{D}$, and λ_1 and λ_2 are the parameters that control the effects of their regularization terms. By optimizing the above objective function, RLSI simultaneously learns the latent topics as well as topic representations. Based on RLSI, we propose the Spatial-aware RLSI (SRLSI) to calculate the geographic topic relevance between images.

3.2.3 Spatial-aware RLSI

To utilize the location cue of each image, the intuition of SRLSI is that: given two images $\mathbf{d}_i$ and $\mathbf{d}_j$, if $|\mathbf{d}_i \cap \mathbf{d}_j| > \theta_1$ and $dist(\mathbf{d}_i, \mathbf{d}_j) < \theta_2$, then the Euclidean distance $||\mathbf{v}_i - \mathbf{v}_j||_2$ should be small. In other words, if two images are geographically closed to each other and share a certain number of common tags, their latent topic representations $\mathbf{v}_i$ and $\mathbf{v}_j$ should be similar. Therefore, we propose the objective function of SRLSI as follows:

$$\min_{\mathbf{U}, \{\mathbf{v}_n\}} (\sum_{n=1}^{N} ||\mathbf{d}_n - \mathbf{U}\mathbf{v}_n||_2^2 + \lambda_1 \sum_{k=1}^{K} ||\mathbf{u}_k||_1 + \lambda_2 \sum_{n=1}^{N} ||\mathbf{v}_n||_2^2 + \lambda_3 \sum_{i,j=1}^{N} w_{ij} ||\mathbf{v}_i - \mathbf{v}_j||_2^2), \tag{7}$$

where the non-negative weight $w_{ij} > 0$ controls the effects of the latent topic representation distances among different image pairs, and λ_3 controls the effects of the whole corpus' latent topic representation similarity among all the image pairs. If $w_{ij} = 0$, the distance of $\mathbf{v}_i$ and $\mathbf{v}_j$ will not be considered. If w_{ij} is large, it will penalize the image pairs with large latent topic representation distance, and as a result, the objective function will flavor smaller $||\mathbf{v}_i - \mathbf{v}_j||_2^2$ during each optimization iteration.

By embedding location closeness in the weighted adjacency matrix $W{=}(w_{ij})_{i,j=1,\ldots,N}$, we are able to discover geographic topics which are geographically close. By setting a proper W, we can learn similar geographic topic representations for certain image pairs. Specifically, we set:

$$w_{ij} = \begin{cases} e^{-\frac{dist(\mathbf{d}_i,\mathbf{d}_j)}{2\sigma_{dist}^2}} & \text{if } |\mathbf{d}_i \cap \mathbf{d}_j| \geqslant \theta_1 \text{ and } dist(\mathbf{d}_i, \mathbf{d}_j) \leqslant \theta_2 \\ 0 & \text{otherwise} \end{cases}, \quad (8)$$

where the parameter σ_{dist} controls the width of the spatial neighborhoods, θ_1 is the constraint of the minimum number of overlapping tags, and θ_2 is the maximum allowable geographic distance.

We regard the above topic model as a spatial-aware topic model to discover geographic topics. The optimization of Eq.7 is convex with respect to $\mathbf{U}$ when $\mathbf{V}$ is fixed and is convex with respect to $\mathbf{V}$ when $\mathbf{U}$ is fixed. However, it is not convex with respect to both of them. Following the practice in sparse coding, we optimize the objective function by alternately minimizing it with respect to tag-topic matrix $\mathbf{U}$ and topic-image matrix $\mathbf{V}$. This procedure is summarized in Algorithm 1.

Algorithm 1 Spatial-aware RLSI

Require: $\mathbf{D} \in \mathbb{R}^{M \times N}$
$\mathbf{V}^{(0)} \in \mathbb{R}^{K \times N} \leftarrow$ random matrix
for $t = 1 : T$ **do**
  $\mathbf{U}^{(t)} \leftarrow Update\mathbf{U}(\mathbf{D}, \mathbf{V}^{t-1})$
  $\mathbf{V}^{(t)} \leftarrow Update\mathbf{V}(\mathbf{D}, \mathbf{U}^{t})$
end for
return $\mathbf{U}^{(T)}, \mathbf{V}^{(T)}$

Algorithm 2 $Update\mathbf{U}$

Require: $\mathbf{D} \in \mathbb{R}^{M \times N}, \mathbf{V} \in \mathbb{R}^{K \times N}$
$\mathbf{S} \leftarrow \mathbf{V}\mathbf{V}^T$
$\mathbf{R} \leftarrow \mathbf{D}\mathbf{V}^T$
for $m = 1 : M$ **do**
  $\bar{\mathbf{u}}_m \leftarrow \mathbf{0}$
  repeat
    for $k = 1 : K$ **do**
      $w_{mk} \leftarrow r_{mk} - \sum_{l \neq k} s_{kl} u_{ml}$
      $u_{mk} \leftarrow \frac{(|w_{mk}| - \frac{1}{2}\lambda_1)_+ sign(w_{mk})}{s_{kk}}$
    end for
  until convergence
end for
return U

Holding $\mathbf{V}$ fixed, the update of $\mathbf{U}$ is illustrated in Algorithm 2. With $\mathbf{U}$ fixed, the update of $\mathbf{V}$ amounts to the following optimization problem:

$$\min_{\{\mathbf{v}_n\}} \sum_{n=1}^{N} ||\mathbf{d}_n - \mathbf{U}\mathbf{v}_n||_2^2 + \lambda_2 \sum_{n=1}^{N} ||\mathbf{v}_n||_2^2 + \lambda_3 \sum_{i,j=1}^{N} w_{ij} ||\mathbf{v}_i - \mathbf{v}_j||_2^2. \quad (9)$$

Applying the spectral clustering graph construction [27, 28] on the last weighted sum component of Eq.9, we have:

$$\min_{\mathbf{V}} ||\mathbf{D} - \mathbf{U}\mathbf{V}||_F^2 + \lambda_2 ||\mathbf{V}||_2^2 + \lambda_3 Tr(\mathbf{V}\mathbf{L}\mathbf{V}^T), \quad (10)$$

where $\mathbf{L}$ is the graph Laplacian matrix. There are several variants of graph Laplacians, while we use the unnormalized graph Laplacian defined as:

$$\mathbf{L} = \tilde{\mathbf{D}} - \mathbf{W}, \quad (11)$$

where $\tilde{\mathbf{D}}$ is the diagonal matrix $\tilde{\mathbf{D}}_{ii} = \sum_j w_{ij}$. Now the update of $\mathbf{V}$ amounts to solving the optimization problem Eq.10. Let its differentiation w.r.t $\mathbf{V}$ to zero, we have:

$$(\mathbf{U}^T\mathbf{U} + \lambda_2 \mathbf{I})\mathbf{V} + \lambda_3 \mathbf{V}L = \mathbf{U}^T\mathbf{D}. \quad (12)$$

Eq.12 is a Sylvester equation which can be solved in parallel by parallel explicitly blocked Bartels-Stewart algorithm [8].

3.2.4 *Topic Model Relevance Calculation*

Given a query image $\mathbf{q}$ and a corpus image $\mathbf{d}$, we calculate their relevance in the geographic topic space as follows. The query is represented in the geographic topic space as:

$$\mathbf{v}_q = arg \min_{\mathbf{v}} ||\mathbf{q} - \mathbf{U}\mathbf{v}||_2^2 + ||\mathbf{v}||_2^2, \quad (13)$$

where vector $\mathbf{q}$ is a weighted representation (e.g., tf-idf, spatial-aware weighting, etc.) of the query in the tag space. $\mathbf{d}$ is represented as $\mathbf{v}_d$ in the geographic topic space in the similar way. Their geographic topic relevance, denoted as $s_{tm}(\mathbf{q}, \mathbf{d})$, is then calculated as:

$$s_{tm}(\mathbf{q}, \mathbf{d}) = \frac{\langle \mathbf{v}_q, \mathbf{v}_d \rangle}{||\mathbf{v}_q||_2 \cdot ||\mathbf{v}_d||_2}, \quad (14)$$

which will be used in the final ranking step.

3.3 BoVW Relevance Calculation

The proposed two textual-based models have been discussed in Section 3.1 and 3.2. Here we also consider the visual relevance of social images in addition to the textual relevance. The typical SIFT feature and the bag-of-visual-words (BoVW) representation are applied. To construct our visual word dictionary, we extract SIFT features from images and post-process them to RootSIFT [1] in order to boost the retrieval performance. Fast approximate k-means clustering algorithm is implemented to build the visual codebook. We build the vocabulary of one million visual words for the whole image corpus. The inverted file is used to index all the corpus images to achieve efficient retrieval.

This bag-of-visual-words image retrieval model is regarded as the third model in the SMM. The visual relevance between a query image $\mathbf{q}$ and a corpus image $\mathbf{d}$ is measured by the cosine similarity of tf-idf weighting based on the BoVW representation, denoted as $s_{bovw}(\mathbf{q}, \mathbf{d})$.

4. LEARNING TO RANK

Given a query image, we can get three lists of relevance scores generated by the three models in the SMM, as described in Section 3. How to fuse these result lists and generate the final ranking list is the question to be answered in this section.

Learning to rank (L2R) is widely applied for ranking creation in modern information retrieval system, which leverages machine learning technologies to innovate more effective ranking models [14]. In this paper, we adopt the listwise L2R model [3] to fuse three result lists. In the listwise L2R model, suppose that for a query image $\mathbf{q}$, its related candidate images $\mathbf{d}_1, \mathbf{d}_2, ..., \mathbf{d}_n$ retrieved by the SMM, and the relevance grade labels $\mathbf{y} = \{y_1, y_2, ..., y_n\}$ for each corresponding candidate are given. The vector $\mathbf{x}_i$ for each candidate image $\mathbf{d}_i$ is a triplet of the three models' relevance scores: $\mathbf{x}_i = \langle s_{lm}(\mathbf{q}, \mathbf{d}_i), s_{tm}(\mathbf{q}, \mathbf{d}_i), s_{bovw}(\mathbf{q}, \mathbf{d}_i)\rangle$. Let $\mathbf{X} = \{\mathbf{x}_1, \mathbf{x}_2, ..., \mathbf{x}_n\}$ represent the list of all the candidates with their relevance scores. Each $(\mathbf{X}, \mathbf{y})$ pair w.r.t a given query $\mathbf{q}$ is regarded as one training instance. Given a number of m training instances $\mathbf{I} = \{(\mathbf{X}_1, \mathbf{y}_1), ..., (\mathbf{X}_m, \mathbf{y}_m)\}$, listwise L2R can be formalized as minimizing the following empirical risk function $\hat{R}$:

$$\hat{R}(F) = \frac{1}{m}\sum_{i=1}^{m} L(F(\mathbf{X}_i), \mathbf{y}_i), \tag{15}$$

where $F(\cdot)$ is the ranking function, and $L(\cdot, \cdot)$ is the loss function that evaluates the prediction accuracy of $F(\mathbf{X})$ against the corresponding grades $\mathbf{y}$. The goal of the learning task is to automatically learn a function $\hat{F}(\cdot)$ minimizing $\hat{R}$.

The first step of learning to rank for our location estimation task is to prepare a high-quality training dataset $\mathbf{I}$ with spatial-aware relevance labels $\mathbf{y}$ for each list $\mathbf{X}$ in order to learn an effective ranking model. Most commercial search engines obtain the ground truth relevance labels by mining users' click logs during searching or browsing behaviors, which is cheap to obtain. However, in location estimation, there is no such log data for mining. Although we can obtain training data by asking human annotators to label the relevance of a candidate image $\mathbf{d}$ w.r.t a query image $\mathbf{q}$, it is extremely time-consuming to generate sufficient training data for effective learning. Here we introduce an ad hoc method to construct a training dataset with spatial-aware relevance labels for listwise L2R training in the context of location estimation.

We randomly select a number of images from the training dataset as pseudo-queries. For each pseudo-query image $\mathbf{q}$, we generate the list $\mathbf{X}$ by combining the three relevance score lists of candidate images derived from the SMM. The corresponding spatial-aware relevance label for each candidate image $\mathbf{d}_i$ is calculated as follows:

$$y_i = \sum_{g=1}^{G} \alpha_g \chi_{A_g}(dist(\mathbf{q}, \mathbf{d}_i)), \tag{16}$$

$$\chi_{A_g}(dist(\mathbf{q}, \mathbf{d}_i)) = \begin{cases} 1 & \text{if } dist(\mathbf{q}, \mathbf{d}_i) \in A_g \\ 0 & \text{if } dist(\mathbf{q}, \mathbf{d}_i) \notin A_g \end{cases}, \tag{17}$$

where G is the number of different relevance grades, α_g is the defined relevance grade value, A_g is distance interval, and χ_{A_g} is the indicator function of A_g. For example, given $A_1 = [0, 10)$ as a distance interval of 0 to 10 meters and $\alpha_1 = 10$, if $dist(\mathbf{q}, \mathbf{d}_i) \in A_1$, then y_i will be assigned with the relevance grade value of $y_i = \alpha_1 = 10$. Different relevance grades can be defined to flavor different distance intervals. We go though all pseudo-query images to generate a training dataset $\mathbf{I}$ with spatial-aware relevance labels for listwise L2R model training.

When conducting the location estimation, given a query image, we first retrieve a list of the most relevant image candidates (e.g., top 100) from each of the three models in the SMM, and then merge them into one list (i.e., $\mathbf{X}$) by combining the same image candidate's multimodal scores into a triplet vector. The non-existence of a candidate image represents zero relevance score in one list. The merged list is then taken the input of the trained L2R model to predict the final relevance score of each candidate image. The final location of the query image is estimated as the location of the candidate image with the highest relevance score computed from the trained listwise L2R model.

5. EXPERIMENT

In this section, we evaluate the performance of the proposed methods on location estimation. To this end, we use the following two metrics: 1) *accuracy at x km* is the percentage of test images estimated within x km of the ground truth location. The values of x can be 1 km, 10 km, and 100 km etc.. As the estimated location is represented by latitude and longitude, the great-circle (Haversine) distance is applied in our experiments; 2) *median error distance (MER)* is the error distance that no more than half of the test images exceed. The first metric measures the accuracy at different levels of location granularity. The median error distance, on the other hand, presents the overall performance by a single value, which is convenient for overall comparisons.

In the following, we first describe the evaluation benchmark and data preprocess. As the proposed framework involves multi-modalities in the final ranking for the location estimation, we conduct comprehensive experiments to observe the effects of each model in the SMM separately, followed by the fused results from the trained listwise L2R model. Finally, we compare our whole framework with existing methods. All the experiments are conducted on a Linux server with 40 3.0GHz CPU cores and 256GB memories.

5.1 Benchmark and Data Preprocess

Placing Task has been introduced in MediaEval[1] evaluation campaign since 2010. This task requires the participants to estimate the locations (i.e., longitude and latitude) of Flickr resources (images/videos) based on their associated tags, visual features, and metadata information. *Accuracy at x km* is used in this task for the performance evaluation. In 2013, they provided a dataset with more than 8.5 million training images and 250,000 test images [10]. We use this benchmark for evaluation in the following experiments.

For textual-based location estimation, not all the images in the training dataset are useful. We carry out two standard preliminary filter steps on it: 1) images without tags are removed; 2) Flickr users are allowed to upload multiple images with the same tags or metadata at once. In order to mitigate the negative effect of bulk upload [24], for images uploaded on the same date with identical tag set and coordinates, we only keep the first uploaded image in the training dataset as their representative.

As a result, we generate a preprocessed training dataset with 4,539,384 images. In order to avoid overfitting on test dataset, for parameters tuning of the proposed spatial-ware

[1]http://www.multimediaeval.org/

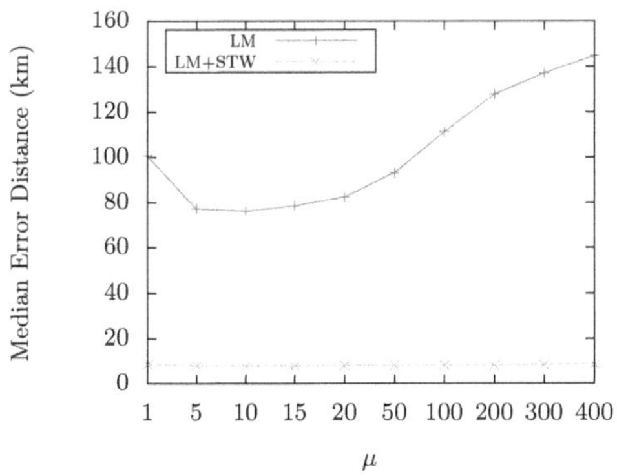

Figure 2: Comparison of the baseline (LM) and language model with spatial-aware tag weighting (LM+STW).

language model (SLM) and topic model (SRLSI), we randomly sample 50,000 images from the training dataset as a validation dataset, and the rest are used for training. Note that when separating the validation dataset from the training dataset, we ensure all the images from the same user are either in the training dataset, or in the validation dataset, in order to avoid an unfair exploitation of user-specific tags [19]. This validation dataset is also used for training the listwise L2R model. The 250,000 test images are used for the final location estimation performance evaluation.

5.2 Performance of SLM

The location of a query image is estimated as the location of the query's most relevant image from the database. To evaluate the effectiveness of the proposed SLM, we can only consider the query and database images which have textual tags. The baseline language model used for the comparison is derived by [20], where the relevance score is calculated similarly to Eq.3 by setting the weight of each tag $s(t)$ to be 1. This model treats the weights of all tags equally without the consideration of their location indication. The effects of the spatial-aware tag weighting (STW) and the performance gains after applying the spatial-aware tag expansion (STE) are discussed in the following sections respectively.

5.2.1 Spatial-aware Tag Weighting

Following [19], we set $w = 1$ and $\lambda = 40$ km in Eq.1 to favor tags that are clustered around a small number of locations. Given a query image, the baseline LM method considers all its tags as a plain text query for retrieval. In contrast, with STW, we assign different weights to each tag.

Fig.2 presents the median error distance of the baseline LM and the LM with STW regarding different Dirichlet prior μ values in Eq.4. The lowest median error distance for the baseline method is obtained when $\mu \in [5, 10]$ because most images contain five to ten tags, which means that the average text length is rather short. Comparing with the baseline LM method, we observe that LM with STW reduces the median error distance significantly and performs much stable than the baseline regarding to different μ values. This observation confirms that location-indicative tags play a much more important role than other tags in location estimation.

5.2.2 Spatial-aware Tag Expansion

We preprocess the corpus images with STE described in Section 3.1.2, and then apply the same language model (i.e., Eq.3) to find the most relevant image. The neighbor selection in Eq.2 is controlled by two thresholds: the maximum geographic distance λ_1 (in meters) and the minimum number of overlapping tags λ_2. For the ease of experiment, we discretize and restrict these two thresholds into certain values: $\lambda_1 \in [100, 200, 300, 400, 500]$ and $\lambda_2 \in [1, 2, 3, 4, 5]$.

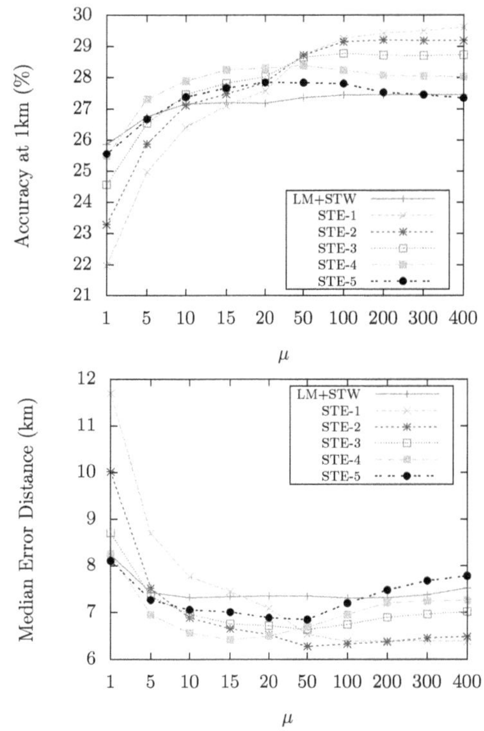

Figure 3: The influence of the parameter λ_2 in Eq.2 on spatial-aware tag expansion ("STE-k" means $\lambda_2 = k$).

Compared with the language model with STW, we study the performance improvement after applying STE. Fig.3 shows the comparisons when $\lambda_1 = 100$ for different λ_2 values (e.g., STE-1 represents the results of applying STE on LM+STW for λ_2=1). We observe similar patterns when λ_1 equals to other values and hence do not show them here. From Fig.3, as μ increase, generally speaking the accuracy increases while the median error distance drops. The reason is that STE assigns more tags to each image, which requires a larger μ for the language model smoothing. STE consistently improves LM+STW for relatively large μ values (e.g., μ >15) in terms of both accuracy and median error distance, which confirms the positive impact of increasing the frequencies of location-indicative tags in representing social images for their location estimation. However, when μ becomes very large (e.g., μ >50), the improvements for some λ_2 values start shrinking, mainly because μ gets much larger than the average number of expanded tags for each image. Considering the improvements of both accuracy and median error distance from Fig.3, we set the default values of λ_2 and μ to be 2 and 50 respectively.

5.3 Performance of SRLSI

5.3.1 SRLSI Parameters Tuning

There are three parameters controlling the weighted adjacency matrix W construction (in Eq.8): band width σ_{dist},

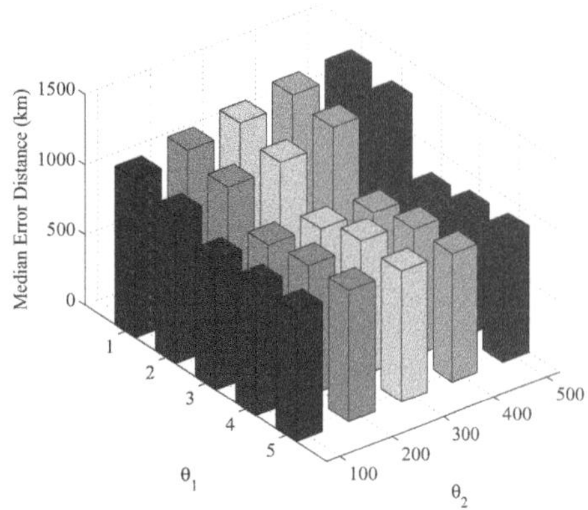

Figure 4: SRLSI performance w.r.t different θ_1 and θ_2.

minimum number of overlapping terms θ_1 and maximum geographic distance θ_2 (in meters). For the ease of experiment, we discretize and restrict these parameters into certain values: $\theta_1 \in [1, 2, 3, 4, 5]$, $\theta_2 \in [100, 200, 300, 400, 500]$ and $\sigma_{dist} \in [1, 5, 10, 15, 20]$. Similarly, we discretize the parameters λ_1, λ_2 and λ_3 in SRLSI's objective function (in Eq.7) in the range of $[0.2, 0.4, ..., 1]$. Since there are six parameters in total and we aim to improve the location estimation performance, our strategy for parameters tuning is: evaluate one or two parameters at a time and keep others fixed or assign default values, then we select the optimal values which achieve lowest median error distance on the validation dataset.

The first step is to construct matrix W. We set default values for parameters in SRLSI model: $\lambda_1 = \lambda_2 = \lambda_3 = 0.6$, and keep $\sigma_{dist} = 10$ fixed. The performance results of different combinations of θ_1 and θ_2 are shown in Fig.4. As we can see, when $\theta_1 = 1$ or 2, the median error distance is much higher than other settings. The reason is that the smaller the minimum number of overlapping tags is, the denser W is, which will introduce unexpected penalties while optimizing the objective function. The lowest median error distance is obtained when $\theta_1 = 3$ and $\theta_2 = 500$. We obtain the optimal values for the other four parameters in a similar way, and the lowest median error distance is obtain when $\sigma_{dist} = 20$, $\lambda_1 = 0.6$, $\lambda_2 = 0.4$ and $\lambda_3 = 0.4$. We use these settings in the following experiments.

5.3.2 *Spatial-aware Tag Representation*

Here, we compare SRLSI with the traditional LSI and RLSI as the baselines. For different topic models, we compare their performances with different tag representations, including tf-idf representation $\mathbf{D}_{tfidf}$ and spatial-aware tag representation $\mathbf{D}_{spatial}$. The superiority of our proposed spatial-aware tag representation outperforms the traditional tf-idf representation across all topic models, which is explicitly shown in Table 1. Besides, our SRLSI achieves the best estimation accuracy and the lowest median error distance compared with LSI and RLSI. This demonstrates the effectiveness of our spatial-aware topic model which incorporates location factors during latent geographic topic learning.

SRLSI's advantages in terms of topic readability can be observed from Table 2 which contains the topics generated by non-spatial-aware topic model LSI-$\mathbf{D}_{tfidf}$ and the topics generated by SRLSI-$\mathbf{D}_{spatial}$. We randomly show five topics with their top five weighted tags. It is obvious that the topics generated by SRLSI-$\mathbf{D}_{spatial}$ are less noisy and more relevant to specific locations. For example, the tags in Topic 1 generated by SRLSI-$\mathbf{D}_{spatial}$ are related to UK, while the tags in the topics generated by LSI-$\mathbf{D}_{tfidf}$ are less geo-related. The effectiveness of the proposed spatial-aware topic model is visualized in Fig.5. For each topic in Table 2, we randomly select 500 training images that contain its top five tags. Each image is represented by a spot on the figure. Different colors and shapes of the spots stand for different topics that the corresponding images belong to. By applying our SRLSI topic model, the images which are geographically close mostly share the same topic. It is a strong evidence to support that the SRLSI topic closeness indicates the geographical closeness of their images.

Table 1: Performance comparisons of topic models on the validation dataset, including accuracy at x km and mean error distance (ME). LSI-$\mathbf{D}_{tfidf}$ means LSI topic model with tf-idf representation, and so on.

	acc@1km	acc@10km	acc@100km	ME (km)
LSI-$\mathbf{D}_{tfidf}$	5.15	18.61	26.53	1263.93
LSI-$\mathbf{D}_{spatial}$	7.33	22.49	32.47	798.38
RLSI-$\mathbf{D}_{tfidf}$	6.30	20.40	28.13	1154.09
RLSI-$\mathbf{D}_{spatial}$	7.17	24.36	34.40	711.66
SRLSI-$\mathbf{D}_{tfidf}$	8.36	24.52	34.36	942.99
SRLSI-$\mathbf{D}_{spatial}$	**9.43**	**24.75**	**34.83**	**683.06**

Table 2: Topics learned by LSI-$\mathbf{D}_{tfidf}$ and SRLSI-$\mathbf{D}_{spatial}$.

	Topic 1	Topic 2	Topic 3	Topic 4	Topic 5
LSI-$\mathbf{D}_{tfidf}$	budapest	castle	croatia	hagiasophia	scotland
	hungary	nikon	dubrovnik	streetart	baltimore
	2007	2009	fountain	mannheim	glasgow
	pisa	athens	czechrepublic	badenwürttemberg	edinburgh
	lasvegas	greece	sign	ny	arizona
SRLSI-$\mathbf{D}_{spatial}$	london	edinburgh	dublin	netherlands	atlanta
	england	greenwich	ireland	holland	dragoncon
	uk	thames	salzburg	nederland	finland
	londres	england	montreal	amsterdam	helsinki
	unitedkingdom	greaterlondon	dublincastle	paysbas	montmartre

Table 3: Visual-based location estimation performance comparison on the test dataset.

	acc@1km	acc@10km	acc@100km
SOTON [5]	0.34	0.56	0.10
RECOD [15]	0.37	0.80	1.69
CERTH [12]	0.76	1.16	2.04
Delft [17]	**2.80**	**3.70**	**4.70**
ours	2.04	2.75	3.84

5.4 Performance of BoVW

We evaluate the BoVW model directly on the test dataset without tuning any parameter. Table 3 compares the BoVW model with MediaEval 2013 Placing Task participants' best visual-based location estimation results which are also evaluated based on this benchmark. As we can see, although the BoVW model achieves comparable performance compared with the best result [17], the accuracy of visual-based location estimation is rather low, since most of the images do not have visually similar images within their geo-neighborhood as described in [16]. Therefore, visual representations can only be used as supplementary information for location estimation in this benchmark.

5.5 Performance of L2R

In this experiment, we study the performance of fusing multi-modalities using the listwise L2R model. As described in Section 4, in order to construct the training dataset for

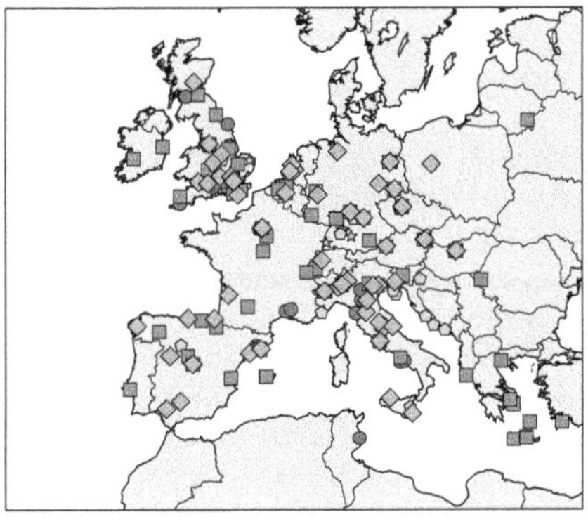

(a) LSI-$\mathbf{D}_{tfidf}$

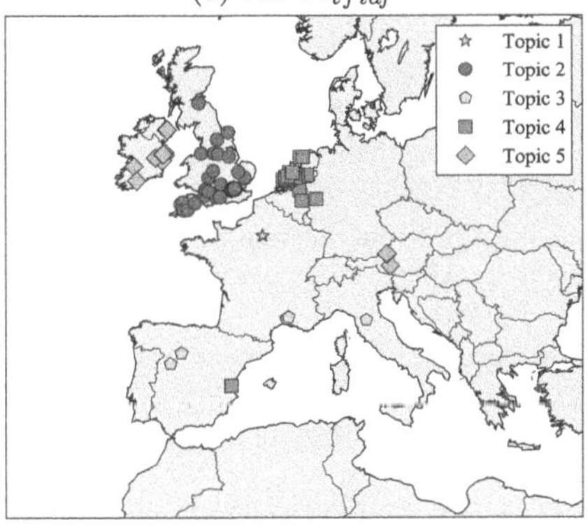

(b) SRLSI-$\mathbf{D}_{spatial}$

Figure 5: Location distribution of the 5 topics in Table 2. (a) is the distribution of topics generated by LSI-$\mathbf{D}_{tfidf}$; (b) is the distribution of topics generated by SRLSI-$\mathbf{D}_{spatial}$.

Table 4: Predefined relevance grades α and the corresponding distance intervals A in Eq.16.

g	1	2	...	10	11
Interval A_g (in meter)	$[0, 100]$	$(100, 200]$	...	$(900, 1000]$	$(1000, \infty)$
Grades α_g	10	9	...	1	0

the listwise L2R model, we sample 50,000 images as pseudo-queries from the whole training dataset. We define the relevance grades as shown in Table 4. For example, given a query $\mathbf{q}$, if the geographic distance between $\mathbf{q}$ and its relevant image candidate $\mathbf{d}_i$ is within 100 meters ($dist(\mathbf{q}, \mathbf{d}_i) \in A_1$), then the relevant grade value of this candidate image is $y_i = \alpha_1 = 10$ according to Eq.16. The higher grade an image has, the more relevant the image is. We select and merge the top 100 candidates retrieved by each models in the SMM, and remove candidates whose grade label is zero in order to avoid noises and reduce the size of training dataset. We eventually obtain a training dataset with 2.6 million labeled data for training the listwise L2R model.

We choose ListNet [3] as our listwise L2R model and evaluate the influence of individual model on the final location estimation by incorporating one or more models at a time during the training. Table 5 shows the performance of the trained listwise L2R model tested on the validation dataset with different model combinations. An obvious observation is that all the models and their combinations consistently reach higher estimation accuracies at larger location granularities, which is easy to understand. For two textual-based location estimation models, SLM achieves much better performance than SRLSI does, which demonstrates that the specific tag relevance matching is more capable to precisely locate an image than the topic relevance matching. The BoVW model alone has the worst estimation performance as expected. From the above observations, we consider topic relevance and visual relevance as supplementary information when performing models fusion in listwise L2R model. When SLM combines with SRLSI or BoVW, the combination achieves a higher accuracy in locating images within 1 km and a lower median error distance. When all the models are combined, we achieve the highest estimation accuracy and the lowest median error distance. This means we can locate the images more precisely by incorporating more information from other models. Especially, the improvement on smaller location granularities (e.g., 1 km) are more significant. In practice, location estimation within a finer location granularity is more useful for real-world applications.

Table 5: Multimodal performance comparisons on the validation dataset. *SLM*, *SRLSI*, and *BoVW* are each model's performance before fusion. *SLM+SRLSI* means both SLM score list and SRLSI score list are used in the listwise L2R model, etc. *All* means all three models' score lists are used in the listwise L2R model.

	acc@1km	acc@10km	acc@100km	ME(km)
SLM	28.72	53.63	66.29	6.28
SRLSI	11.21	25.41	38.67	338.72
BoVW	1.99	2.55	3.42	5391.87
SLM + SRLSI	29.31	53.52	65.21	6.23
SLM + BoVW	29.13	53.69	65.95	6.24
All	**31.22**	**54.13**	**67.05**	**5.89**

5.6 Comparison with Existing Methods

In this experiment, we evaluate our proposed framework SMLE's location estimation performance on the whole test dataset containing 250,000 images, compared with [13] and the methods developed by all the groups participating in MediaEval 2013 Placing Task. For a fair comparison, we report the best results achieved by each method that are based on the provided 8.5M training dataset only, without using external data.

Table 6 shows the comparison results on the whole test dataset. The CERTH [12] team uses both visual and textual data, while the others use textual data only. Our proposed framework SMLE surpasses all the methods in terms of both the estimation accuracy and the median error distance. When compared with the CEA LIST's method and the GHENT's method, which also apply the language model to find probable location, our spatial-aware multimodal framework improves the estimation accuracy by up to 34% relatively, and reduces the median error distance significantly from the second best performer GHENT's 51.07 to 32.29km only. This demonstrates the benefits of incorporating more information from different model. The CERTH's method simply applies a fallback strategy to combine the visual and textual information: if the test image had no tag associated with it, then the visual feature is employed to find the most relevant neighbor. In contrast, our multimodal relevance scores are fused and candidate images are ranked by the trained listwise L2R model, which provides much better estimation results. The above comparisons verify the supe-

Table 6: Performance comparison on the test dataset.

	acc@1km	acc@10km	acc@100km	ME(km)
CERTH [12]	10.37	23.70	36.22	681.00
SOTON [5]	23.15	37.70	43.82	451.89
CEA-LIST [22]	26.00	43.00	50.00	98.80
GHENT [13]	20.26	41.96	53.15	51.07
SMLE	**27.22**	**44.99**	**54.98**	**32.29**

riority of the proposed spatial-aware multimodal framework in terms of both the estimation accuracy and the median error distance. Note that the performance of our framework on the test dataset in Table 6 is not as good as the performance when tested on the validation dataset in Table 5. The reason is that all the images in the validation dataset are associated with tags while 13% images in the test dataset have no tags at all, which suggest that we can only estimate those non-tagged images via visual relevance ranking only.

6. CONCLUSION

In this paper, we propose a spatial-aware multimodal location estimation framework to address the social image's location estimation problem. We propose a spatial-aware language model to improve textual-based location estimation by utilizing spatial-aware tag weighting and tag expansion. We also design a spatial-aware topic model to discover geographic topics which can further facilitate the estimation. A learning to rank model is adopted and effectively trained to fuse multiple textual and visual models to generate a refined ranking list for final location estimation. Extensive experiments illustrate the advantages of the proposed framework over the state-of-the-art approaches.

7. REFERENCES

[1] R. Arandjelovic and A. Zisserman. Three things everyone should know to improve object retrieval. In *CVPR*, pages 2911–2918, 2012.

[2] D. M. Blei. Probabilistic topic models. *Commun. ACM*, 55(4):77–84, 2012.

[3] Z. Cao, T. Qin, T.-Y. Liu, M.-F. Tsai, and H. Li. Learning to rank: from pairwise approach to listwise approach. In *ICML*, pages 129–136, 2007.

[4] J. Choi and G. Friedland. *Multimodal Location Estimation of Videos and Images*. Springer, 2015.

[5] J. Davies, J. Hare, S. Samangooei, J. Preston, N. Jain, D. Dupplaw, and P. H. Lewis. Identifying the geographic location of an image with a multimodal probability density function. In *MediaEval*, 2013.

[6] J. Eisenstein, B. O'Connor, N. A. Smith, and E. P. Xing. A latent variable model for geographic lexical variation. In *EMNLP*, pages 1277–1287, 2010.

[7] G. Friedland, O. Vinyals, and T. Darrell. Multimodal location estimation. In *ACM MM*, pages 1245–1252, 2010.

[8] R. Granat and B. Kågström. Evaluating parallel algorithms for solving sylvester-type matrix equations: Direct transformation-based versus iterative matrix-sign-function-based methods. In *PARA*, pages 719–729, 2004.

[9] C. Hauff and G.-J. Houben. Placing images on the world map: a microblog-based enrichment approach. In *SIGIR*, pages 691–700, 2012.

[10] C. Hauff, B. Thomee, and M. Trevisiol. Working notes for the placing task at mediaeval 2013. In *MediaEval*, 2013.

[11] J. Hays and A. A. Efros. Im2gps: estimating geographic information from a single image. In *CVPR*, pages 1–8, 2008.

[12] G. Kordopatis-Zilos, S. Papadopoulos, E. S. Xioufis, A. L. Symeonidis, and Y. Kompatsiaris. CERTH at mediaeval placing task 2013. In *MediaEval*, 2013.

[13] O. V. Laere, S. Schockaert, and B. Dhoedt. Georeferencing flickr resources based on textual meta-data. *IS*, 238(0):52 – 74, 2013.

[14] H. Li. Learning to rank for information retrieval and natural language processing. *Synthesis HLT*, 4(1):1–113, 2011.

[15] L. T. Li, J. Almeida, O. A. B. Penatti, R. T. Calumby, D. C. G. Pedronette, M. A. Gonçalves, and R. da Silva Torres. Multimodal image geocoding: The 2013 RECOD's approach. In *MediaEval*, 2013.

[16] X. Li, M. Larson, and A. Hanjalic. Geo-visual ranking for location prediction of social images. In *ICMR*, pages 81–88, 2013.

[17] X. Li, M. Riegler, M. Larson, and A. Hanjalic. Exploration of feature combination in geo-visual ranking for visual content-based location prediction. In *MediaEval*, 2013.

[18] J. Luo, D. Joshi, J. Yu, and A. Gallagher. Geotagging in multimedia and computer vision - a survey. *MTAP*, 51(1):187–211, 2011.

[19] O. Van Laere, J. A. Quinn, S. Schockaert, and B. Dhoedt. Spatially aware term selection for geotagging. *TKDE*, 26(1):221–234, 2014.

[20] D. Metzler and W. B. Croft. Combining the language model and inference network approaches to retrieval. *IPM*, 40(5):735–750, 2004.

[21] NinthDecimal. Ninthdecimal mobile audience Q2 2012 insights report, 2012.

[22] A. Popescu. CEA LIST's participation at mediaeval 2013 placing task. In *MediaEval*, 2013.

[23] G. Schindler, M. Brown, and R. Szeliski. City-scale location recognition. In *CVPR*, pages 1–7, 2007.

[24] P. Serdyukov, V. Murdock, and R. van Zwol. Placing flickr photos on a map. In *SIGIR*, pages 484–491, 2009.

[25] O. Van Laere, S. Schockaert, and B. Dhoedt. Finding locations of flickr resources using language models and similarity search. In *ICMR*, pages 48:1–48:8, 2011.

[26] Q. Wang, J. Xu, H. Li, and N. Craswell. Regularized latent semantic indexing: a new approach to large-scale topic modeling. *TOIS*, 31(1):1–44, 2013.

[27] Y. Yang, Y. Yang, Z. Huang, H. T. Shen, and F. Nie. Tag localization with spatial correlations and joint group sparsity. In *CVPR*, pages 881–888, 2011.

[28] Y. Yang, Z.-J. Zha, Y. Gao, X. Zhu, and T.-S. Chua. Exploiting web images for semantic video indexing via robust sample-specific loss. *TMM*, 16(6):1677–1689, 2014.

[29] W. Zhang and J. Kosecka. Image based localization in urban environments. In *3DPVT*, pages 33–40, 2006.

Collaborative Fashion Recommendation: A Functional Tensor Factorization Approach

Yang Hu†, Xi Yi‡, Larry S. Davis§
Institute for Advanced Computer Studies, University of Maryland, College Park, MD 20742
eeyanghu@gmail.com†, yixi@cs.umd.edu‡, lsd@umiacs.umd.edu§

ABSTRACT

With the rapid expansion of online shopping for fashion products, effective fashion recommendation has become an increasingly important problem. In this work, we study the problem of personalized outfit recommendation, i.e. automatically suggesting outfits to users that fit their personal fashion preferences. Unlike existing recommendation systems that usually recommend individual items, we suggest sets of items, which interact with each other, to users. We propose a functional tensor factorization method to model the interactions between user and fashion items. To effectively utilize the multi-modal features of the fashion items, we use a gradient boosting based method to learn nonlinear functions to map the feature vectors from the feature space into some low dimensional latent space. The effectiveness of the proposed algorithm is validated through extensive experiments on real world user data from a popular fashion-focused social network.

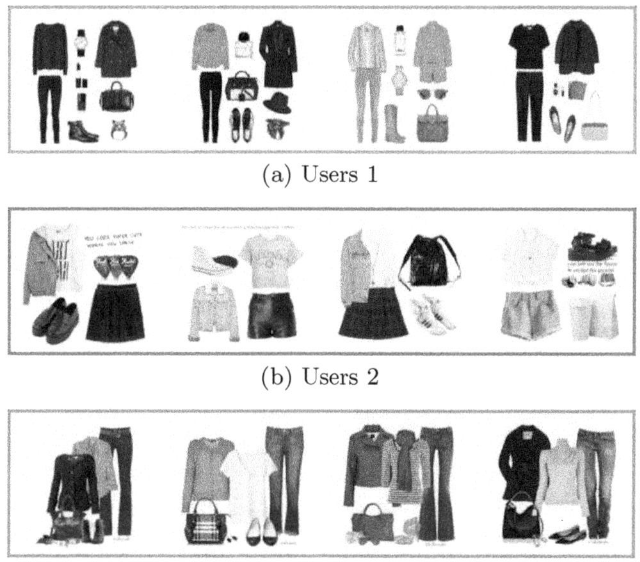

(a) Users 1

(b) Users 2

(c) Users 3

Figure 1: Examples of fashion sets created by three Polyvore users. Different users have different style preferences. Our task is to automatically recommend outfits to users that fit their personal taste.

Categories and Subject Descriptors

H.3.3 [**Information Search and Retrieval**]: Retrieval models; I.2.6 [**Learning**]: Knowledge acquisition

Keywords

Recommendation systems; Collaborative filtering; Tensor factorization; Learning to rank; Gradient boosting

1. INTRODUCTION

With the proliferation of social networks, people share almost everything in their daily life online nowadays. They share the dinners they had, the movies they watched, the music they listened to, the places they visited, and also, the outfits they wore. There are numerous fashion-focused online communities, such as Polyvore[1], Chictopia[2], Lookbook[3], where people showcase their personal styles and connect to others that share similar fashion taste. With this rising trend, a larger share of the fashion industry has moved online, which triggers a strong demand for intelligent fashion analysis techniques.

Many recent works have begun to study fashion related problems, e.g. clothing parsing [29, 28, 30, 7], clothing recognition [4, 13], clothing retrieval [26, 20], and clothing recommendation [11, 18, 12]. In this work, we are interested in the problem of fashion recommendation, which is a key problem for promoting people's interest and participation in online shopping. There are two kinds of fashion recommendation problems. One is recommending whole outfits that people may be interested in. The other is recommending fashion items that make good matches with some given items. We mainly focus on the first problem. However the model we learned can also be applied to solve the second task.

[1] http://www.polyvore.com/
[2] http://www.chictopia.com/
[3] http://lookbook.nu/

MM'15, October 26–30, 2015, Brisbane, Australia.
 ISBN 978-1-4503-3459-4/15/10 ...$15.00.
DOI: http://dx.doi.org/10.1145/2733373.2806239.

One crucial point that has not been addressed in previous work is recommendation should be *personal.* Figure 1 shows examples of fashion sets created by three users on Polyvore. It is obvious that different people have different preferences of styles, which is a reflection of their ages, occupations, cultural background, place of living, etc. Therefore, for different users, an effective recommender system should recommend different outfits.

To generate good recommendations, we need to learn from people's past behavior. The outfits a person has created or worn reveal his or her fashion taste. However, the number of outfits we observe for a single person may be small. On the other hand, there are a large number of outfits shared by other people who have similar fashion taste. These outfits could give a person a broader glimpse of the clothing in stock. Therefore, for effective recommendation, we should also learn from the behavior of others. This is the basic idea of collaborative filtering, which is a common strategy for recommendation problems.

Collaborative filtering analyzes relationships between users and interdependencies among items to identify new user-item associations. However, previous work mostly restricted attention to recommending individual items like movies and music. We, on the other hand, want to recommend sets of items to users. In addition to matching user preferences, the fashion items in an outfit should also match with each other.

Compared with movies and music, the number of fashion items is extremely huge. Each item may have only been chosen by very few or even no users. Therefore collaborative filtering methods that only use user-item associations to characterize items are inapplicable. It is important to use auxiliary information about the fashion items to capture the relationships amongst items. There is rich information about fashion items on the web. For example, visual features related to style can be extracted from the images of the items. Sellers often provide properties of the fashion products through text descriptions. Other information, such as the price and the popularity of the items, may also be available. It is important to design a model that can effectively handle these heterogeneous features.

With these considerations in mind, we propose a functional tensor factorization model for fashion recommendation. We decompose the high order interactions between users and the fashion items into a set of pairwise interactions in some latent space. We use the idea of gradient boosting to learn nonlinear functions to map the multi-modal feature vectors of the fashion items from the feature space into the latent space. A learning to rank formulation is used to learn the model. We collect real world user data from a popular fashion-focused social network. Comprehensive experiments have been conducted to verify the effectiveness of the proposed algorithm.

Moving from individual items to item sets opens a new area for the studying of recommendation systems. Besides fashion, it has potential applications to other problems. For example, on Polyvore, users are also interested in creating collages of furniture. Using this data, the proposed method may also be used to help people design their rooms.

2. RELATED WORK

Fashion analysis techniques have drawn much attention in the computer vision and multimedia communities [19]. Recent papers have studied problems including clothing parsing, recognition, retrieval, as well as fashion recommendation.

Clothing parsing predicts pixel-wise labeling for garment items, which provides a foundation for other tasks. Several solutions have been proposed in the literature [29, 28, 7, 30]. For clothing recognition, Chen et al. [4] described clothing appearance by semantic attributes using a CRF based approach. Kiapour et al. [13] designed an online game to crowd source human judgements of fashion styles and used the data collected to train models for between-class and within-class classifications of styles. Clothing retrieval attempts to find similar clothing to a given query. Wang et al. [26] designed a retrieval system by using color and attribute information. Liu et al. [20] considered the cross-scenario retrieval problem of finding similar clothing in online stores given a daily human photo captured in the wild.

There are only a handful of attempts to solve the problem of fashion recommendation. For item recommendation, Iwata et al. [11] proposed a probabilistic topic model for learning information about fashion coordinates. In [12], Jagadeesh et al. proposed two classes of recommenders, namely deterministic and stochastic fashion recommenders. They mainly focused on color modeling for recommendation. Liu et al. [18] studied both outfit and item recommendation problems. They designed a latent SVM based model for occasion-oriented clothing recommendation, i.e. given a user-input occasion, suggest the most suitable clothing, or recommend items to pair with the reference clothing. For outfit recommendation, they only considered outfits with two clothing items. None of these works considered the personal issue, as we do.

Besides recommendation, there is increasing interest in building personalized models for other learning problems. Personalized tags are annotated for photos [24] and songs [23]. In [27] Weston et al. studied the collaborative retrieval problem. Latent models were learned for recommending items to a user with respect to a given query. Yue et al. [31] presented a clustering analogue to collaborative filtering, called personalized collaborative clustering.

Factorization techniques have shown great success in recommender systems. Various models have been proposed to factorize the user-item rating matrix [15]. To further enhance the performance of the models, the use of auxiliary information in matrix factorization has been studied. In [1, 22, 27], linear functions have been used to map the feature vectors in the feature space into a latent space. Recently, Chen et al. [5] proposed using gradient boosting to automatically construct feature functions in matrix factorization. We extend Chen et al.'s work to tensor factorization. Also, instead of using regression, a learning to rank formulation is used in our work.

3. COLLABORATIVE FASHION RECOMMENDATION

3.1 Problem Formulation

In personalized outfit recommendation, we recommend a list of outfits, each of which consists of a set of fashion items, to a user. Assume the fashion items can be grouped into N categories. For example, the three most essential fashion categories are tops, bottoms and shoes. Let $\mathcal{I}^{(n)} = \{\boldsymbol{x}_1^{(n)}, \ldots, \boldsymbol{x}_{L^{(n)}}^{(n)}\}, n = 1, \ldots, N$ be the set containing items in the n-th category. $L^{(n)}$ is the total number of items in $\mathcal{I}^{(n)}$. $\boldsymbol{x}_l^{(n)} \in \mathbb{R}^{M^{(n)}}, l = 1, \ldots, L^{(n)}$ denotes the feature vector of the l-th item in the n-th category. $M^{(n)}$ is the dimension of $\boldsymbol{x}_l^{(n)}$. An outfit with N items can be represented as $\mathcal{O}_{\boldsymbol{t}} = \{\boldsymbol{x}_{t_1}^{(1)}, \ldots, \boldsymbol{x}_{t_N}^{(N)}\}$, $\boldsymbol{t} = \{t_1, \ldots, t_N\}$ denotes the indexes of the items in $\mathcal{O}_{\boldsymbol{t}}$. Assume there are U users in total. The level of affection a user u, $u = 1, \ldots, U$, has for $\mathcal{O}_{\boldsymbol{t}}$ is denoted by a rating score $r_{u,\mathcal{O}_{\boldsymbol{t}}}$. Our problem is to learn a model so that the score for any pair of user u and outfit $\mathcal{O}_{\boldsymbol{t}}$ can be predicted. Then we recommend those with highest $r_{u,\mathcal{O}_{\boldsymbol{t}}}$ to user u.

3.2 Functional Pairwise Interaction Tensor Factorization

$r_{u,\mathcal{O}_{\boldsymbol{t}}}$ can be viewed as an entry in a $(N+1)$-th order tensor, with N dimensions corresponding to the N fashion categories and the remaining one corresponding to the users. We need to decompose this tensor so that unobserved entries in it can be predicted.

Tensor decomposition has been intensively studied in the literature [14]. Higher order interactions between the components are considered in many works. In our problem, the tensor we observed is extremely sparse. Among all possible outfits, each user can only rate a very small number of them. It would be difficult to learn effective high order interactions from such a limited number of observations. We therefore model $r_{u,\mathcal{O}_{\boldsymbol{t}}}$ by factoring it into a set of pairwise interactions in some latent space:

$$r_{u,\mathcal{O}_{\boldsymbol{t}}} = \sum_{n=1}^{N} \boldsymbol{v}_u^{(n)} \cdot \boldsymbol{h}^{(n)}(\boldsymbol{x}_{t_n}^{(n)}) + \sum_{n=1}^{N} \sum_{m=n+1}^{N} \boldsymbol{h}^{(nm)}(\boldsymbol{x}_{t_n}^{(n)}) \cdot \boldsymbol{h}^{(mn)}(\boldsymbol{x}_{t_m}^{(m)}) . \quad (1)$$

In the first summation, we model users' affection for individual fashion items. $\boldsymbol{v}_u^{(n)} \in \mathbb{R}^D$ characterizes user u's preference for items from the n-th category. D is the dimensionality of the latent space. $\boldsymbol{h}^{(n)}(\boldsymbol{x}_{t_n}^{(n)}) \in \mathbb{R}^D$ contains outputs from D functions, i.e.

$$\boldsymbol{h}^{(n)}(\boldsymbol{x}_{t_n}^{(n)}) = [h_1^{(n)}(\boldsymbol{x}_{t_n}^{(n)}), \ldots, h_D^{(n)}(\boldsymbol{x}_{t_n}^{(n)})]^T . \quad (2)$$

The functions $h_d^{(n)}(\boldsymbol{x}^{(n)}), d = 1, \ldots, D$ map the features of the n-th category items to the latent space for matching with users. In the second summation, the matches between items from two different categories are measured. $\boldsymbol{h}^{(nm)}(\boldsymbol{x}_{t_n}^{(n)}) \in \mathbb{R}^D$ also contains outputs from D functions:

$$\boldsymbol{h}^{(nm)}(\boldsymbol{x}_{t_n}^{(n)}) = [h_1^{(nm)}(\boldsymbol{x}_{t_n}^{(n)}), \ldots, h_D^{(nm)}(\boldsymbol{x}_{t_n}^{(n)})]^T . \quad (3)$$

$h_d^{(nm)}(\boldsymbol{x}^{(n)}), d = 1, \ldots, D$ map the features of the n-th category items to a latent space in which their matches with items from the m-th category can be evaluated. To make the discussion concise, $\boldsymbol{h}^{(n)}(\boldsymbol{x}^{(n)})$ will also be referred to as $\boldsymbol{h}^{(nn)}(\boldsymbol{x}^{(n)})$ in the following.

The use of this simple factorization model in Eq.(1) effectively avoids overfitting. It also leads to more efficient algorithm for learning. A similar pairwise factorization method has been successfully used for personalized tag recommendation [23] where a third-order tensor was decomposed. However, in that application, they solved a conventional tensor factorization problem where no auxiliary information of the items was used. Due to the introduction of the functions $\{\boldsymbol{h}^{(nm)}(\boldsymbol{x}^{(n)})\}_{n,m=1}^{N}$, we refer to Eq.(1) as *Functional Pairwise Interaction Tensor Factorization* (FPITF).

Note that, if available, we may also utilize auxiliary information about the users, such as their ages and occupations, to help predict user' preferences, i.e., instead of using $\{\boldsymbol{v}_u^{(n)}\}_{n=1}^{N}$, a set of functions are used to map these features into the latent space just like the use of the functions $\{\boldsymbol{h}^{(nm)}(\boldsymbol{x}^{(n)})\}_{n,m=1}^{N}$ for the fashion items. Here, we adopt conventional representation for the users and keep our focus on the analysis of the fashion items.

Notation	Explanation
$\boldsymbol{x}_l^{(n)}$	Feature vector of the l-th item in the n-th fashion category
$\boldsymbol{v}_u^{(n)}$	Latent space representation of user u's preference for items from the n-th category
$\boldsymbol{h}^{(n)}(\cdot)$	Functions to map the n-th category items to the latent space for matching with users
$\boldsymbol{h}^{(nm)}(\cdot)$	Functions to map the n-th category items to the latent space for matching with the m-th category items
N	Number of fashion categories, i.e. number of items in an outfit
$M^{(n)}$	Number of features for the n-th category items
$L^{(n)}$	Number of n-th category items
U	Number of users
D	Dimension of latent space
$\boldsymbol{t}$	Indexes of the items in an outfit
$\mathcal{O}_{\boldsymbol{t}}$	Outfit with items indexed by $\boldsymbol{t}$
$r_{u,\mathcal{O}_{\boldsymbol{t}}}$	Rating score of outfit $\mathcal{O}_{\boldsymbol{t}}$ given by user u
$\mathcal{P}$	The set of preference pairs

Table 1: Notation

3.3 The Optimization Problem

To learn the model in Eq.(1), we assume that, for each user, the preference orderings between some pairs of outfits are given as training data, i.e.

$$\mathcal{P} \equiv \{(i,j) | u_i = u_j, r_{u_i,\mathcal{O}_{\boldsymbol{t}_i}} > r_{u_j,\mathcal{O}_{\boldsymbol{t}_j}}\}, i, j = 1, \ldots, Z \quad (4)$$

Z is the total number of user outfit tuples $(u, \mathcal{O}_{\boldsymbol{t}})$ involved in the training set. The i-th and j-th tuples make a pair if they concern the same user and the user likes outfit $\mathcal{O}_{\boldsymbol{t}_i}$ more than he or she likes outfit $\mathcal{O}_{\boldsymbol{t}_j}$. The actual values of the ratings $r_{u_i,\mathcal{O}_{\boldsymbol{t}_i}}$ and $r_{u_j,\mathcal{O}_{\boldsymbol{t}_j}}$ are not needed. In fact, for different users the absolute values of the ratings may be highly biased. The use of preference pairs as training data avoids the need to calibrate the ratings and has become a popular approach for learning ranking function.

With the above training data, we use the following objective function for our learning problem

$$\frac{1}{2}\Omega + C \sum_{(i,j)\in\mathcal{P}} \log(1 + \exp(-(r_{u_i,\mathcal{O}_{\boldsymbol{t}_i}} - r_{u_j,\mathcal{O}_{\boldsymbol{t}_j}}))) , \quad (5)$$

Algorithm 1: Coordinate descent for solving Eq.(5)

Randomly initialize $\{\boldsymbol{h}^{(nm)}(\boldsymbol{x}^{(n)})\}_{n,m=1}^{N}$ and $\{\boldsymbol{v}_u^{(n)}\}_{n=1}^{N}$;
while *not converged* **do**
  for $n = 1$ **to** N **do**
    for $m = 1$ **to** N **do**
      for $d = 1$ **to** D **do**
        Update $h_d^{(nm)}(\boldsymbol{x}^{(n)})$ with functional gradient descent
      end
    end
  end
  for $u = 1$ **to** U **do**
    Update $\{\boldsymbol{v}_u^{(n)}\}_{n=1}^{N}$ by solving the optimization problem in Eq.(25)
  end
end

where $r_{u_i,\mathcal{O}_{t_i}}$ and $r_{u_j,\mathcal{O}_{t_j}}$ are computed by Eq.(1). Ω denotes the regularization term and is defined as

$$\Omega = \sum_{u=1}^{U}\sum_{n=1}^{N} \|\boldsymbol{v}_u^{(n)}\|^2 + \sum_{n=1}^{N}\sum_{m=1}^{N}\sum_{l=1}^{L^{(n)}} \|\boldsymbol{h}^{(nm)}(\boldsymbol{x}_l^{(n)})\|^2 . \quad (6)$$

Eq.(5) applies a regularized logistic regression model to pairwise classification, i.e. we are learning to classify a pair (i, j) into two classes, where class label $y_{(i,j)} = 1$ means $r_{u_i,\mathcal{O}_{t_i}} > r_{u_j,\mathcal{O}_{t_j}}$ and $y_{(i,j)} = -1$ corresponds to the contrary. The loss term in Eq.(5) is the negative log-likelihood of observing the training data, using a logistic function as the probability model, i.e.

$$\begin{aligned} &P(y_{(i,j)}|r_{u_i,\mathcal{O}_{t_i}}, r_{u_j,\mathcal{O}_{t_j}}) \quad (7)\\ =&(1+\exp(-y_{(i,j)}(r_{u_i,\mathcal{O}_{t_i}} - r_{u_j,\mathcal{O}_{t_j}})))^{-1} . \end{aligned}$$

To obtain good generalization ability, the regularization term controls the complexity of the model by penalizing the magnitudes of $\boldsymbol{v}_u^{(n)}$ and the functions $\boldsymbol{h}^{(nm)}(\boldsymbol{x}^{(n)})$. A detailed Bayesian analysis of a similar optimization criterion for individual item recommendation can be found in [21].

We use coordinate descent to minimize the objective function in Eq.(5). Assume all other terms are fixed for all users, we first minimize Eq.(5) with respect to functions $\{\boldsymbol{h}^{(nm)}(\boldsymbol{x}^{(n)})\}_{n,m=1}^{N}$. Then assuming $\{\boldsymbol{h}^{(nm)}(\boldsymbol{x}^{(n)})\}_{n,m=1}^{N}$ are fixed, we minimize Eq.(5) with respect to $\{\boldsymbol{v}_u^{(n)}\}_{n=1}^{N}$ for all $u = 1, \ldots, U$. The general procedure is shown in Algorithm 1. In the following two sections, we explain these two steps in details.

3.4 Learning $\{\boldsymbol{h}^{(nm)}(\boldsymbol{x}^{(n)})\}_{n,m=1}^{N}$ with Functional Gradient Descent

In general, we can choose a parameterized model for each function $h_d^{(nm)}(\boldsymbol{x}^{(n)})$. For example, $h_d^{(nm)}(\boldsymbol{x}^{(n)})$ can be a linear function of $\boldsymbol{x}^{(n)}$ so that $h_d^{(nm)}(\boldsymbol{x}^{(n)}) = \boldsymbol{w}_d^{(nm)} \cdot \boldsymbol{x}^{(n)}$. However, the features in $\boldsymbol{x}^{(n)}$ may come from multiple modalities. We can extract low level visual features from the images of the fashion items. Products for online shopping also have an abundance of other information on the web. Figure 2 shows an example web page for a fashion item on Polyvore. It provides the category, name and price of the item. Moreover, a paragraph of text providing detailed description of the item is also available. A linear model cannot handle such heterogeneous information effectively. We therefore use a functional gradient descent method [9] to learn non-linear models that can inherently integrate the multi-modal information in $\boldsymbol{x}^{(n)}$.

Figure 2: Example web page for a fashion item.

3.4.1 *Functional Gradient Descent*

Let $\Phi(h(\boldsymbol{x}))$ be a general loss function, where $h \in \mathcal{H}$ is the function we seek to find, and $\mathcal{H}$ is a pre-defined function space. The gradient boosting method [9] applies gradient descent in function space to minimize $\Phi(h(\boldsymbol{x}))$, i.e., compute the gradient of $\Phi(h(\boldsymbol{x}))$ with respect to $h(\boldsymbol{x})$ at the current estimation $h_k(\boldsymbol{x})$ and form the next estimate as

$$h_{k+1}(\boldsymbol{x}) = h_k(\boldsymbol{x}) - \alpha_k \nabla\Phi(h(\boldsymbol{x})) . \quad (8)$$

However, we can not compute $\nabla\Phi(h(\boldsymbol{x}))$ at all $\boldsymbol{x}$, but rather we can only compute it at a finite data sample $\{\nabla\Phi(h(\boldsymbol{x}_i))\}$. So the gradient boosting method finds a function that interpolates/approximates these sample values and thus obtains an approximation of the negative gradient $-\nabla\Phi(h(\boldsymbol{x}))$ to form the next iterate.

In the following, we consider the learning of $h_d^{(n)}(\boldsymbol{x}^{(n)})$ for some n and d as an example to show how functional gradient descent can be applied to our problem. All other functions in $\{\boldsymbol{h}^{(nm)}(\boldsymbol{x}^{(n)})\}_{n,m=1}^{N}$ are learned the same way.

3.4.2 *Learning* $h_d^{(n)}(\boldsymbol{x}^{(n)})$

Let $\{\hat{\boldsymbol{v}}_u^{(n)}\}_{n=1}^{N}$ and $\{\hat{\boldsymbol{h}}^{(nm)}(\boldsymbol{x}^{(n)})\}_{n,m=1}^{N}$ be the current estimates of $\{\boldsymbol{v}_u^{(n)}\}_{n=1}^{N}$ and $\{\boldsymbol{h}^{(nm)}(\boldsymbol{x}^{(n)})\}_{n,m=1}^{N}$ respectively. The corresponding score for tuple $(u_i, \mathcal{O}_{t_i})$ with these estimates is $\hat{r}_{u_i,\mathcal{O}_{t_i}}$. Let

$$\hat{s}_i = \hat{r}_{u_i,\mathcal{O}_{t_i}} - \hat{v}_{u_i,d}^{(n)} \hat{h}_d^{(n)}(\boldsymbol{x}_{t_{i,n}}^{(n)}) . \quad (9)$$

Optimizing Eq.(5) with respect to $h_d^{(n)}(\boldsymbol{x}^{(n)})$ is equivalent to minimizing

$$\begin{aligned} \Phi(h_d^{(n)}(\boldsymbol{x}^{(n)})) = \frac{1}{2}\sum_{l=1}^{L^{(n)}}(h_d^{(n)}(\boldsymbol{x}_l^{(n)}))^2 + C \sum_{(i,j)\in\mathcal{P}} \log(1+ \quad (10)\\ \exp(-(\hat{v}_{u_i,d}^{(n)} h_d^{(n)}(\boldsymbol{x}_{t_{i,n}}^{(n)}) - \hat{v}_{u_j,d}^{(n)} h_d^{(n)}(\boldsymbol{x}_{t_{j,n}}^{(n)}) + \hat{s}_i - \hat{s}_j))) . \end{aligned}$$

The gradient with respect to $h_d^{(n)}(\boldsymbol{x}_l^{(n)})$ is

$$
\begin{aligned}
g_l =& [\frac{\partial \Phi(h_d^{(n)}(\boldsymbol{x}^{(n)}))}{\partial h_d^{(n)}(\boldsymbol{x}_l^{(n)})}]_{h_d^{(n)}(\boldsymbol{x}_l^{(n)})=\hat{h}_d^{(n)}(\boldsymbol{x}_l^{(n)})} \quad (11)\\
=& C \sum_{(i,j)\in\mathcal{P}} (\sigma_{i,j}-1)(\hat{v}_{u_i,d}^{(n)} 1(t_{i,n}=l) - \hat{v}_{u_j,d}^{(n)} 1(t_{j,n}=l))\\
&+ \hat{h}_d^{(n)}(\boldsymbol{x}_l^{(n)}),\ l=1,\ \ldots,\ L^{(n)},
\end{aligned}
$$

where

$$\sigma_{i,j} = (1+\exp(-(\hat{r}_{u_i,\mathcal{O}_{t_i}} - \hat{r}_{u_j,\mathcal{O}_{t_j}})))^{-1}. \quad (12)$$

$1(\cdot)$ is indicator function that has value 1 if its argument is true, and zero otherwise.

We then construct a training set with $\{(\boldsymbol{x}_l^{(n)}, -g_l)\}_{l=1}^{L^{(n)}}$ as the samples and learn a regression function from it. Specifically, a small decision tree regressor is learned here [8]. Compared to other learning methods, the decision tree has the advantage of inherently being able to handle the heterogeneous features in $\boldsymbol{x}^{(n)}$. Let $\{R_q\}_{q=1}^{Q}$ be the terminal nodes of the tree learned, and let $\{e_q\}_{q=1}^{Q}$ be the corresponding coefficients for the nodes. According to Eq.(8) the update of $h_d^{(n)}(\boldsymbol{x}^{(n)})$ becomes

$$h_d^{(n)}(\boldsymbol{x}^{(n)}) = \hat{h}_d^{(n)}(\boldsymbol{x}^{(n)}) + \alpha_k \sum_{q=1}^{Q} e_q 1(\boldsymbol{x}^{(n)} \in R_q). \quad (13)$$

Note that since the negative gradients $\{-g_l\}_{l=1}^{L^{(n)}}$ are used to learn the regressor, the operator before α_k is changed to plus. Eq.(13) can be alternatively expressed as

$$h_d^{(n)}(\boldsymbol{x}^{(n)}) = \hat{h}_d^{(n)}(\boldsymbol{x}^{(n)}) + \sum_{q=1}^{Q} \gamma_q 1(\boldsymbol{x}^{(n)} \in R_q) \quad (14)$$

with $\gamma_q = \alpha_k e_q$. Eq.(14) can be viewed as adding Q separate basis functions at each step $\{1(\boldsymbol{x}^{(n)} \in R_q)\}_{q=1}^{Q}$. We can further improve the quality of the fitting by using the optimal coefficients for each of these basis functions. These optimal coefficients are the solution to

$$
\begin{aligned}
\arg \min_{\boldsymbol{\gamma}=[\gamma_1,\ldots,\gamma_Q]^T} & \frac{1}{2} \sum_{l=1}^{L^{(n)}} \sum_{q=1}^{Q} 1(\boldsymbol{x}_l^{(n)} \in R_q)(\hat{h}_d^{(n)}(\boldsymbol{x}_l^{(n)}) + \gamma_q)^2 \quad (15)\\
&+ C \sum_{(i,j)\in\mathcal{P}} \log(1+\exp(-(\hat{v}_{u_i,d}^{(n)} \sum_{q=1}^{Q} \gamma_q 1(\boldsymbol{x}_{t_{i,n}}^{(n)} \in R_q)\\
&- \hat{v}_{u_j,d}^{(n)} \sum_{q=1}^{Q} \gamma_q 1(\boldsymbol{x}_{t_{j,n}}^{(n)} \in R_q) + \hat{r}_{u_i,\mathcal{O}_{t_i}} - \hat{r}_{u_j,\mathcal{O}_{t_j}}))),
\end{aligned}
$$

which substitutes $h_d^{(n)}(\boldsymbol{x}^{(n)})$ in Eq.(10) with Eq.(14). Following [9], we obtain the approximated solution to Eq.(15) by a single Newton-Raphson step, using a diagonal approximation to the Hessian. The result is

$$\gamma_q = -\Psi_{\gamma_q}/\Psi_{\gamma_q\gamma_q},\ q=1,\ \ldots,Q, \quad (16)$$

where Ψ_{γ_q} and $\Psi_{\gamma_q\gamma_q}$ are the first and the second order derivatives of the objective function in Eq.(15) (denoted as $\Psi(\{\gamma_q\}_{q=1}^{Q})$) with respect to γ_q evaluated at $\boldsymbol{\gamma}=0$ respectively, i.e.

$$
\begin{aligned}
\Psi_{\gamma_q} =& [\frac{\partial \Psi(\{\gamma_q\}_{q=1}^{Q})}{\partial \gamma_q}]_{\boldsymbol{\gamma}=0} \quad (17)\\
=& \sum_{l=1}^{L^{(n)}} \hat{h}_d^{(n)}(\boldsymbol{x}_l^{(n)}) 1(\boldsymbol{x}_l^{(n)} \in R_q)\\
&+ C \sum_{(i,j)\in\mathcal{P}} (\sigma_{i,j}-1)(\hat{v}_{u_i,d}^{(n)} 1(\boldsymbol{x}_{t_{i,n}}^{(n)} \in R_q)\\
&- \hat{v}_{u_j,d}^{(n)} 1(\boldsymbol{x}_{t_{j,n}}^{(n)} \in R_q))
\end{aligned}
$$

$$
\begin{aligned}
\Psi_{\gamma_q\gamma_q} =& [\frac{\partial^2 \Psi(\{\gamma_q\}_{q=1}^{Q})}{\partial^2 \gamma_q}]_{\boldsymbol{\gamma}=0} \quad (18)\\
=& \sum_{l=1}^{L^{(n)}} 1(\boldsymbol{x}_l^{(n)} \in R_q)\\
&+ C \sum_{(i,j)\in\mathcal{P}} \sigma_{i,j}(1-\sigma_{i,j})(\hat{v}_{u_i,d}^{(n)} 1(\boldsymbol{x}_{t_{i,n}}^{(n)} \in R_q)\\
&- \hat{v}_{u_j,d}^{(n)} 1(\boldsymbol{x}_{t_{j,n}}^{(n)} \in R_q))^2
\end{aligned}
$$

$\sigma_{i,j}$ is computed by Eq.(12).

We summarize the procedure for updating $h_d^{(n)}(\boldsymbol{x}^{(n)})$ in Algorithm 2. The time complexities for calculating the gradient $\boldsymbol{g}$ with Eq.(11) and the terminal node coefficients $\boldsymbol{\gamma}$ with Eq.(16) are $O(P + L^{(n)})$ and $O(P + L^{(n)} + Q)$ respectively, where $P = |\mathcal{P}|$ is the total number of preference pairs in $\mathcal{P}$. The cost to construct a decision tree is $O(L^{(n)} M^{(n)} \log L^{(n)})$ [8].

Algorithm 2: Update $h_d^{(n)}(\boldsymbol{x}^{(n)})$ with functional gradient descent

---

1. For $l = 1,\ \ldots,\ L^{(n)}$, compute the gradient g_l with Eq.(11);
2. Construct a training set with $L^{(n)}$ samples

$$\{(\boldsymbol{x}_1^{(n)}, -g_1),\ \ldots, (\boldsymbol{x}_{L^{(n)}}^{(n)}, -g_{L^{(n)}})\}, \quad (19)$$

and learn a decision tree regressor from it;
3. Update the terminal node coefficients of the tree with Eq.(16);
4. Update $h_d^{(n)}(\boldsymbol{x}^{(n)})$ with

$$h_d^{(n)}(\boldsymbol{x}^{(n)}) \leftarrow \hat{h}_d^{(n)}(\boldsymbol{x}^{(n)}) + \nu \sum_{q=1}^{Q} \gamma_q 1(\boldsymbol{x}^{(n)} \in R_q), \quad (20)$$

$0 < \nu \leq 1$ is a shrinkage parameter.

3.5 Learning $\{\boldsymbol{v}_u^{(n)}\}_{n=1}^{N}$

To learn $\{\boldsymbol{v}_u^{(n)}\}_{n=1}^{N}$ for user u, we concatenate them into a single vector $\boldsymbol{w}_u$ that

$$\boldsymbol{w}_u = [\boldsymbol{v}_u^{(1)T},\ \ldots,\ \boldsymbol{v}_u^{(N)T}]^T. \quad (21)$$

Assume $\mathcal{P}_u \equiv \{(i,j)|u_i = u_j = u, r_{u_i,\mathcal{O}_{t_i}} > r_{u_j,\mathcal{O}_{t_j}}\}$ is the subset of $\mathcal{P}$ that only contains preference pairs concerning user u. Let $(u_i, \mathcal{O}_{t_i})$ be a tuple involved in $\mathcal{P}_u$, i.e. $u_i = u$.

We define

$$\boldsymbol{x}_i = [\hat{\boldsymbol{h}}^{(1)T}(\boldsymbol{x}^{(1)}_{t_{i,1}}), \ldots, \hat{\boldsymbol{h}}^{(N)T}(\boldsymbol{x}^{(N)}_{t_{i,N}})]^T \qquad (22)$$

be the concatenation of the mappings of the fashion items involved in $(u_i, \mathcal{O}_{t_i})$ using the currently learned functions $\{\hat{\boldsymbol{h}}^{(n)}(\boldsymbol{x}^{(n)})\}_{n=1}^N$. Also let

$$b_i = \sum_{n=1}^{N} \sum_{m=n+1}^{N} \hat{\boldsymbol{h}}^{(nm)}(\boldsymbol{x}^{(n)}_{t_{i,n}}) \cdot \hat{\boldsymbol{h}}^{(mn)}(\boldsymbol{x}^{(m)}_{t_{i,m}}) \,. \qquad (23)$$

The rating score $r_{u_i,\mathcal{O}_{t_i}}$ can be rewritten as

$$r_{u_i,\mathcal{O}_{t_i}} = \boldsymbol{w}_u^T \boldsymbol{x}_i + b_i \,. \qquad (24)$$

Then optimizing Eq.(5) with respect to $\{\boldsymbol{v}_u^{(n)}\}_{n=1}^N$ reduces to minimizing the following objective function

$$f(\boldsymbol{w}_u) = \frac{1}{2}\boldsymbol{w}_u^T \boldsymbol{w}_u + C \sum_{(i,j)\in\mathcal{P}_u} \log(1+ \exp(-(\boldsymbol{w}_u^T \boldsymbol{x}_i - \boldsymbol{w}_u^T \boldsymbol{x}_j + b_i - b_j))) \,. \qquad (25)$$

We modify the trust region Newton method for logistic regression in [17] to solve this optimization problem.

4. EXPERIMENTS

4.1 Dataset and features

We use data from the popular fashion website Polyvore[4] to evaluate our recommendation algorithm. We collect a dataset consisting of image collages (called "Sets" on Polyvore) created by 150 users. In this evaluation, we assume an outfit contains three items, i.e. one top, one bottom and a pair of shoes. There are 38,800 tops, 21,833 bottoms and 24,619 pairs of shoes in total in our datasets.

On Polyvore, product images, which have clean background and only contain individual items, are available for most of the fashion items. This is a big advantage since we do not need to extract them from street snaps by clothes parsing, which is still a challenging computer vision problem. We therefore can more clearly study the performance of the recommendation algorithms.

We extract low level visual features from the item images. We first use the salient region detection method in [6] to precisely locate the the items in the images (region of interest (ROI)). Then features are extracted from the ROIs. The features we used include color histograms in RGB and LAB spaces, dense multi-scale SIFT descriptors (PHOW) [25] and Pyramid of HOG (PHOG) [3]. The total number of features is 7262. We use PCA to reduce the dimensionality so that 95% of the energy is preserved. The resulting dimensions are around 100 for the three item categories.

The text information we use includes the categories, names and descriptions of the fashion items on the web pages (Figure 2). For each type of information, after removing the stop words and perform stemming, we discard the words that occur less than 5 times in the dataset. Then word counts are used to construct the feature vectors. Finally, latent dirichlet allocation (LDA) [2] is applied to reduce the dimensionality of the features. In particular, the 20 most informative topics for each type of text information are selected by LDA.

[4]http://www.polyvore.com/

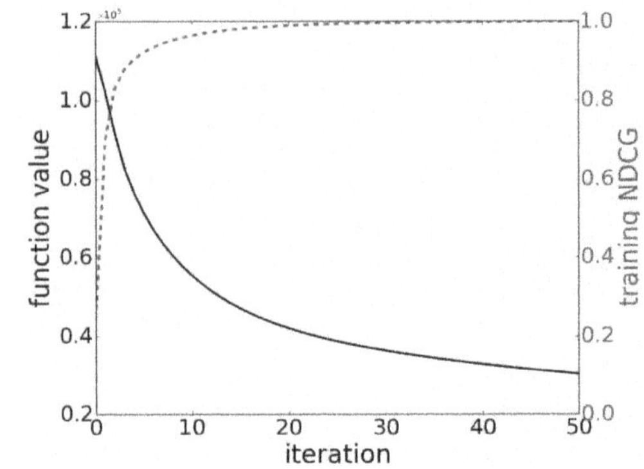

Figure 3: Objective function value in Eq.(5) (black solid line) and training NDCG (blue dashed line) along iteration in one run of the training algorithm.

And the posterior Dirichlet parameters associated with each item are used as the low dimensional features.

4.2 Baselines

To the best of our knowledge, this is the first work to study personalized outfit recommendation. The methods that can be compared against are very limited. We use the following methods as baselines for comparison, which include both personalized and non-personalized methods.

In the first method, outfits that are similar to the outfits a user liked in the past are recommended, which is the basic idea of content-based filtering. The similarity between two outfits is measured by the sum of similarities between individual items in the outfits, i.e.

$$\text{Sim}(\mathcal{O}_{t_i}, \mathcal{O}_{t_j}) = \sum_{n=1}^{N} \exp(-\|\boldsymbol{x}^{(n)}_{t_{i,n}} - \boldsymbol{x}^{(n)}_{t_{j,n}}\|) \,. \qquad (26)$$

Letting $\mathcal{S}_u$ contains all the outfits user u has created and therefore liked, the score for any new outfit $\mathcal{O}_t$ is defined as the average similarities between $\mathcal{O}_t$ and those in $\mathcal{S}_u$, i.e.

$$(r_{u,\mathcal{O}_t})_{\text{Mean}} = \frac{1}{|\mathcal{S}_u|} \sum_{\mathcal{O}_{t_j}\in\mathcal{S}_u} \text{Sim}(\mathcal{O}_t, \mathcal{O}_{t_j}) \,. \qquad (27)$$

We refer to this method as CF Mean.

The idea of the second method is similar to the first one, except that the similarity between a new outfit and the outfits in $\mathcal{S}_u$ is measured in a slightly different way. For each item in $\mathcal{O}_t$, it first finds the item most similar to it in $\mathcal{S}_u$, then the score is computed as the sum of item similarities

$$(r_{u,\mathcal{O}_t})_{\text{NN}} = \sum_{n=1}^{N} \max_{\mathcal{O}_{t_j}\in\mathcal{S}_u} \exp(-\|\boldsymbol{x}^{(n)}_{t_n} - \boldsymbol{x}^{(n)}_{t_{j,n}}\|) \,. \qquad (28)$$

We refer to this method as CF NN since it is based on the nearest neighbors of the items.

The recommendation of outfits involves finding the outfits whose constituent items match well with each other. In the third method, the multi-view extension of canonical correlation analysis (CCA) is used to learn a set of matrices $\{W_n\}_{n=1}^N$ that project the feature vectors of the items from each fashion category into a low-dimensional common space

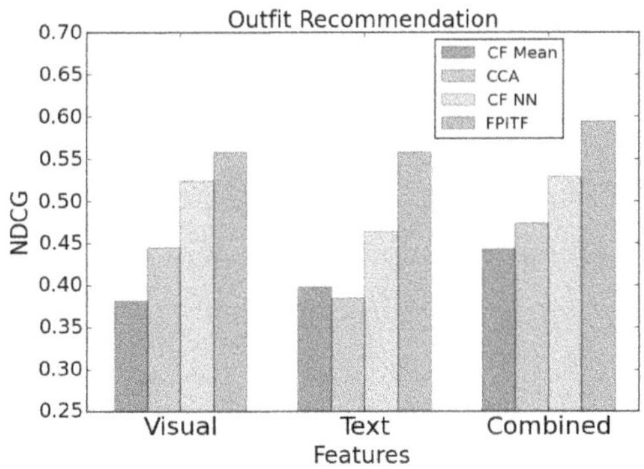

Figure 4: Comparison of recommendation methods. Different feature settings are tested, i.e. only using visual features, only using text features, and using both visual and text features (Combined).

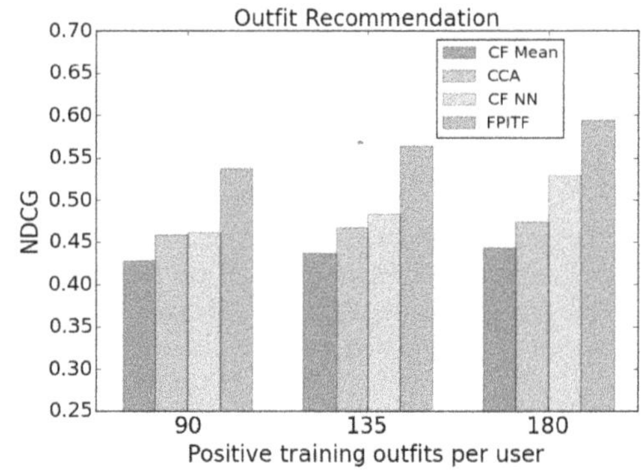

Figure 5: Comparison of recommendation methods with different numbers of training outfits. The number of positive outfits for each user is set to 90, 135 and 180 respectively. The neutral outfits are five times the positive ones for each user.

such that, for the user created outfits, the sums of the correlations between pairs of items in the common space are maximized. We use the multi-view CCA implementation in [10] to learn the models. During training, outfits created by all users are used together to learn a global model for creating outfits. We also tried the method of learning a personalized model for each user only using his/her own outfits. The performance was quite poor due to the very limited number of training samples for each user.

4.3 Outfit recommendation

For training our model, we consider two rating levels for the outfits. The outfits created by a user are taken as positive outfits for that user. And we assume that outfits with randomly mixed top, bottom and shoes are neutral outfits for any user (We do not use the word "negative" here since it is more appropriate for outfits that are disliked by a user, which is not necessarily the case for the random outfits). It is possible that a neutral outfit may happen to match a user's taste. However, considering the huge number of outfits that can be obtained by random mixturing, this possibility is relatively small. Therefore, it is reasonable to assume that a user likes a positive outfit more than a neutral one, i.e. they form a preference pair for training. Our training set contains 180 positive outfits and 900 neutral outfits for each user. For testing, 45 positive outfits and 450 neutral outfits not included in the training set are used per user.

During evaluation, for each user, the positive and neutral outfits in the testing set are ranked in descending order of their scores $r_{u,\mathcal{O}_t}$. The performance is measured by mean NDCG, a widely used criteria for comparing ranked lists. We follow the NDCG definition used in [16]. Letting π' be the ordering being evaluated, the NDCG at the m-th position is

$$\text{NDCG@m} = (N_m)^{-1} \sum_{i=1}^{m} \frac{(2^{y_{\pi'(i)}} - 1)}{\log_2(\max(2, i))}, \qquad (29)$$

where N_m is the score of an ideal ordering, $y_{\pi'(i)}$ is 1 for positive outfits and 0 for neutral ones. Mean NDCG is the mean of NDCG@m for $m = 1, \ldots, M$ with M being the length of the ordering. We report the average of mean NDCG over all users and refer to it as NDCG for short in the following.

We first verify experimentally the convergence of our learning algorithm. We show the changes of the objective function in Eq.(5) and the training NDCG during one run of the training algorithm in Figure 3. We can see that both values change smoothly as a function of iteration. They also change very quickly in early iterations.

Method	$D = 6$	$D = 12$	$D = 18$	$D = 24$	$D = 30$
Visual	.5309	.5460	.5518	.5550	.5576
Text	.5246	.5432	.5439	.5497	.5578
Combined	**.5550**	**.5785**	**.5822**	**.5902**	**.5941**

Table 2: Changing the dimensionality of the latent space for the FPITF method.

In Figure 4, we compare the performance of the four methods for outfit recommendation. Results using different kinds of features for the fashion items, i.e. only using visual features, only using text features and using both visual and text features, are shown. We set the latent space dimension $D = 30$ for FPITF in this experiment. Among the two methods that only use a user's own training outfits for calculating $r_{u,\mathcal{O}_t}$, CF NN performs much better than CF Mean. CF NN also outperforms the multi-view CCA method that trains a universal model for all users. Our method, which considers both personalization and utilizing the outfits created by other users, achieves the best results. For FPITF, the NDCGs with visual and text features only are very close. By combining them together, we obtain significant performance gain. This shows the effectiveness of our method for fusing different kinds of features. On the other hand, the CF NN method, which ranks second, doesn't shown much performance improvement with the addition of text features to visual features.

We show the performance of our method with different dimensions of the latent space in Table 2. This dimension parameter affects test performance, training and evaluation time, as well as storage requirements. We can see that FPITF performs better than the other methods even with $D = 6$. Higher dimension is needed for more complex features. So FPITF with the combined features obtains larger performance gains when moving from $D = 6$ to $D = 30$ than those with visual or text features only.

Figure 5 compares the performance of the four methods with different numbers of training outfits. Both visual and

Method	Top	Bottom	Shoe
CF WMean	0.4336	0.3876	0.4246
CF NN	0.3946	0.3560	0.3770
Multi-view CCA	0.3327	0.3359	0.3105
FPITF	**0.2605**	**0.2377**	**0.2548**

Table 3: Comparison of item retrieval results. Each column corresponds to the search of the item in the column title given the other two items. The smaller the values, the better the results.

text features are used for all methods. We set the number of positive outfits for each user to 90, 135 and 180 respectively. The number of neutral outfits for each user is five times the positive number for each setting. FPITF outperforms the other methods in all cases. The improvements of CF Mean and multi-view CCA are relatively small with the doubling of the training outfits, but both FPITF and CF NN enjoy large performance improvements.

We show in Figure 7 some examples of the top recommendations. For each user, the top 10 outfits obtained by the four methods using combined features are shown respectively. We can see that for different users, FPITF has recommended outfits with quite different styles. It also has recommended more user created sets than the other methods. As a non personalized method, the recommendations by CCA exhibit much weaker personalization than the other three methods. Although CF Mean and CF NN are able to generate personalized recommendations, since they only consider outfits previously created by the the same user, their results tend to lack diversity (note how similar jeans dominate in their recommendations for User 1 and User 2). By also borrowing ideas from other users, FPITF is able to generate diversified recommendations that are consistent with users' taste. Among its recommendations, even those not marked by red boxes are very likely to also be liked by the users and be taken as good references for their future attire.

4.4 Personalized item retrieval

Besides recommending whole outfits to users, the model learned by FPITF can also be used to recommend individual fashion items to a user with respect to some given items. This is the problem of personalized retrieval. Here we show the performance of FPITF for this task.

For comparison, we also adapt the baseline methods in Section 4.2 for this retrieval problem. Assume we need to find an appropriate item from the n-th category to match with the given items for user u. We can still use $r_{u,\mathcal{O}_t}$ as the score of item $\boldsymbol{x}_{t_n}^{(n)}$. Note that except for $\boldsymbol{x}_{t_n}^{(n)}$, the other items in $\mathcal{O}_t$ are given as query. Direct use of CF Mean results in a method that computes the score as the average of the similarities between $\boldsymbol{x}_{t_n}^{(n)}$ and the n-th category items involved in $\mathcal{S}_u$. The query is actually not considered. We therefore modify CF Mean to use weighted average similarities, where the weight is determined by how similar the items in the query are to the corresponding items in $\mathcal{O}_{t_j} \in \mathcal{S}_u$, i.e.

$$(r_{u,\mathcal{O}_t})_{\text{WMean}} = \sum_{\mathcal{O}_{t_j} \in \mathcal{S}_u} w_j \exp(-\|\boldsymbol{x}_{t_n}^{(n)} - \boldsymbol{x}_{t_{j,n}}^{(n)}\|) , \quad (30)$$

where $w_j \sim \sum_{l \neq n} \exp(-\|\boldsymbol{x}_{t_l}^{(l)} - \boldsymbol{x}_{t_{j,l}}^{(l)}\|)$ and the sum of $\{w_j\}_{j=1}^{|\mathcal{S}_u|}$ is normalized to 1.

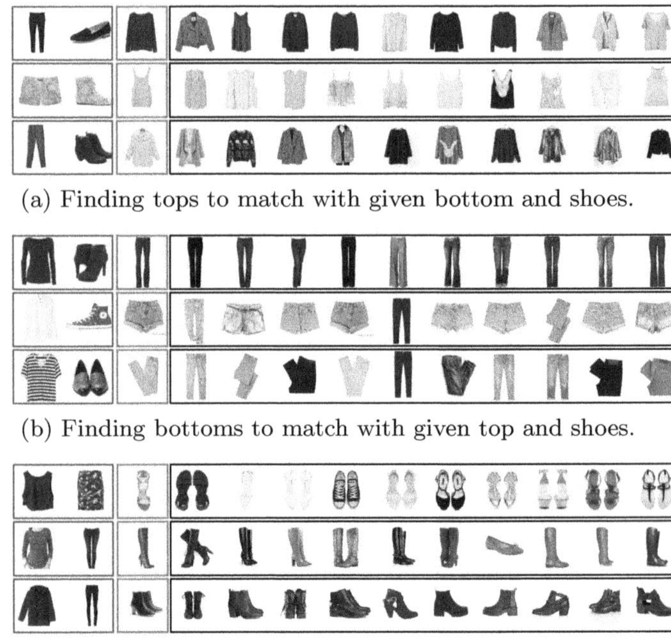

(a) Finding tops to match with given bottom and shoes.

(b) Finding bottoms to match with given top and shoes.

(c) Finding shoes to match with given top and bottom.

Figure 6: Examples of top 10 recommended items with respect to the given query using the FPITF model. The two items in purple boxes are the query. The items in red boxes are the ground truth items.

For CF NN, the score becomes

$$(r_{u,\mathcal{O}_t})_{\text{NN}} = \max_{\mathcal{O}_{t_j} \in \mathcal{S}_u} \exp(-\|\boldsymbol{x}_{t_n}^{(n)} - \boldsymbol{x}_{t_{j,n}}^{(n)}\|) . \quad (31)$$

For multi-view CCA and FPITF, we just need to omit the pairwise interactions in $r_{u,\mathcal{O}_t}$ that do not involve $\boldsymbol{x}_{t_n}^{(n)}$.

For each user, all the positive outfits in the testing set are used to form the queries. For each outfit, $N-1$ items in it are used as the query. The remaining item in that outfit is taken as the ground truth. Assume we are searching for an item from the n-th category. We compute scores for all the n-th category items in the testing set and rank them in descending order of the scores. The position of the ground truth item in the ordering is used as the performance measurement. We divide the position by the total number of items in the ordering to normalize it to range of $[0, 1]$. In an ideal ordering, the ground truth item is ranked as the first item and has a position measurement of 0. Therefore, the smaller the measurement value, the better the ordering.

Table 3 compares the four methods for item retrieval. Each column corresponds to the search of one item. For example, the column "Top" contains results of recommending a top to a user with respect to the given bottom and shoes. The combined features are used in the experiments. The latent space dimensionality of FPITF is set to 30. Note that we directly apply the FPITF model learned for outfit recommendation to the retrieval task here. Again, FPITF obtains the best results among the four methods. Multi-view CCA, which explicitly optimizes the matching between pairs of items, outperforms the other two CF methods.

Note that although the results of FPITF are around 0.25, which is a bit far from the optimal value 0, this measurement is an underestimate of the true quality of the results. Items that are similar to the ground truth item may rank high in the ordering. Although treated as negative items during evaluation, they are actually good alternatives to the ground truth item. This can be seen in Figure 6, which shows the top recommended items for some example queries.

5. CONCLUSION

In this work, we have studied the problem of personalized fashion recommendation, where outfits catering to users' personal fashion taste are automatically recommended. We propose a functional tensor factorization method to model the user-item and item-item interactions. To handle the multi-modal features of the fashion items, a gradient boosting based method was used to learn the nonlinear functions that map the feature vectors from the feature space to a latent space. The effectiveness of the proposed method has been shown through extensive experiments. As a first attempt to approach a new recommendation problem, there are some remaining issues worth exploring, such as the cold start problem and incorporating social information from social networks to enhance performance. We will investigate these problems in the future.

6. ACKNOWLEDGMENTS

This work was supported by the NSF Grant (12621215) EAGER: Video Analytics in Large Heterogeneous Repositories.

7. REFERENCES

[1] D. Agarwal and B.-C. Chen. Regression-based latent factor models. In *KDD*, 2009.

[2] D. Blei, A. Ng, and M. Jordan. Latent dirichlet allocation. *JMLR*, 3:993–1022, 2003.

[3] A. Bosch, A. Zisserman, and X. Munoz. Representing shape with a spatial pyramid kernel. In *CIVR*, 2007.

[4] H. Chen, A. Gallagher, and B. Girod. Describing clothing by semantic attributes. In *ECCV*, 2012.

[5] T. Chen, H. Li, Q. Yang, and Y. Yu. General functional matrix factorization using gradient boosting. In *ICML*, 2013.

[6] M.-M. Cheng, J. Warrell, W.-Y. Lin, S. Zheng, V. Vineet, and N. Crook. Efficient salient region detection with soft image abstraction. In *ICCV*, 2013.

[7] J. Dong, Q. Chen, X. Shen, J. Yang, and S. Yan. Towards unified human parsing and pose estimation. In *CVPR*, 2014.

[8] F. Pedregosa et al. Scikit-learn: Machine learning in Python. *JMLR*, 12:2825–2830, 2011.

[9] J. H. Friedman. Greedy function approximation: A gradient boosting machine. *The Annals of Statistics*, 29(5):1189–1232, 2001.

[10] Y. Gong, Q. Ke, M. Isard, and S. Lazebnik. A multi-view embedding space for modeling internet images, tags, and their semantics. *IJCV*, 106:210–233, 2014.

[11] T. Iwata, S. Watanabe, and H. Sawada. Fashion coordinates recommender system using photographs from fashion magazines. In *IJCAI*, 2011.

[12] V. Jagadeesh, R. Piramuthu, A. Bhardwaj, W. Di, and N. Sundaresan. Large scale visual recommendations from street fashion images. In *KDD*, 2014.

[13] H. Kiapour, K. Yamaguchi, A. C. Berg, and T. L. Berg. Hipster wars: Discovering elements of fashion styles. In *ECCV*, 2014.

[14] T. G. Kolda and B. W. Bader. Tensor decompositions and applications. *SIAM REVIEW*, 51(3):455–500, 2009.

[15] Y. Koren, R. Bell, and C. Volinsky. Matrix factorization techniques for recommender systems. *IEEE Computer*, 42:30–37, 2009.

[16] C.-P. Lee and C.-J. Lin. Large-scale linear ranksvm. *Neural Computation*, 26:781–817, 2014.

[17] C.-J. Lin, R. C. Weng, and S. S. Keerthi. Trust region newton method for large-scale logistic regression. *JMLR*, 9:627–650, 2008.

[18] S. Liu, J. Feng, Z. Song, T. Zhang, H. Lu, C. Xu, and S. Yan. "Hi, magic closet, tell me what to wear!". In *ACM Multimedia*, 2012.

[19] S. Liu, L. Liu, and S. Yan. Fashion analysis: Current techniques and future directions. *IEEE MultiMedia*, 21(2):72–79, 2014.

[20] S. Liu, Z. Song, G. Liu, C. Xu, H. Lu, and S. Yan. Street-to-shop: Cross-scenario clothing retrieval via parts alignment and auxiliary set. In *CVPR*, 2012.

[21] S. Rendle, C. Freudenthaler, Z. Gantner, and L. Schmidt-Thieme. BPR: Bayesian personalized ranking from implicit feedback. In *UAI*, 2009.

[22] S. Rendle, Z. Gantner, C. Freudenthaler, and L. Schmidt-Thieme. Fast context-aware recommendations with factorization machines. In *SIGIR*, 2011.

[23] S. Rendle and L. Schmidt-Thieme. Pairwise interaction tensor factorization for personalized tag recommendation. In *WSDM*, 2010.

[24] B. Sigurbjörnsson and R. van Zwol. Flickr tag recommendation based on collective knowledge. In *WWW*, 2008.

[25] A. Vedaldi and B. Fulkerson. VLFeat: An open and portable library of computer vision algorithms. `http://www.vlfeat.org/`, 2008.

[26] X. Wang, T. Zhang, D. Tretter, and Q. Lin. Personal clothing retrieval on photo collections by color and attributes. *IEEE Trans. on Multimedia*, 15(8):2035–2045, 2013.

[27] J. Weston, C. Wang, R. Weiss, and A. Berenzweig. Latent collaborative retrieval. In *ICML*, 2012.

[28] K. Yamaguchi, H. Kiapour, and T. L. Berg. Paper doll parsing: Retrieving similar styles to parse clothing. In *ICCV*, 2013.

[29] K. Yamaguchi, H. Kiapour, L. E. Ortiz, and T. L. Berg. Parsing clothing in fashion photographs. In *CVPR*, 2012.

[30] W. Yang, P. Luo, and L. Lin. Clothing co-parsing by joint image segmentation and labeling. In *CVPR*, 2014.

[31] Y. Yue, C. Wang, K. El-Arini, and C. Guestrin. Personalized collaborative clustering. In *WWW*, 2014.

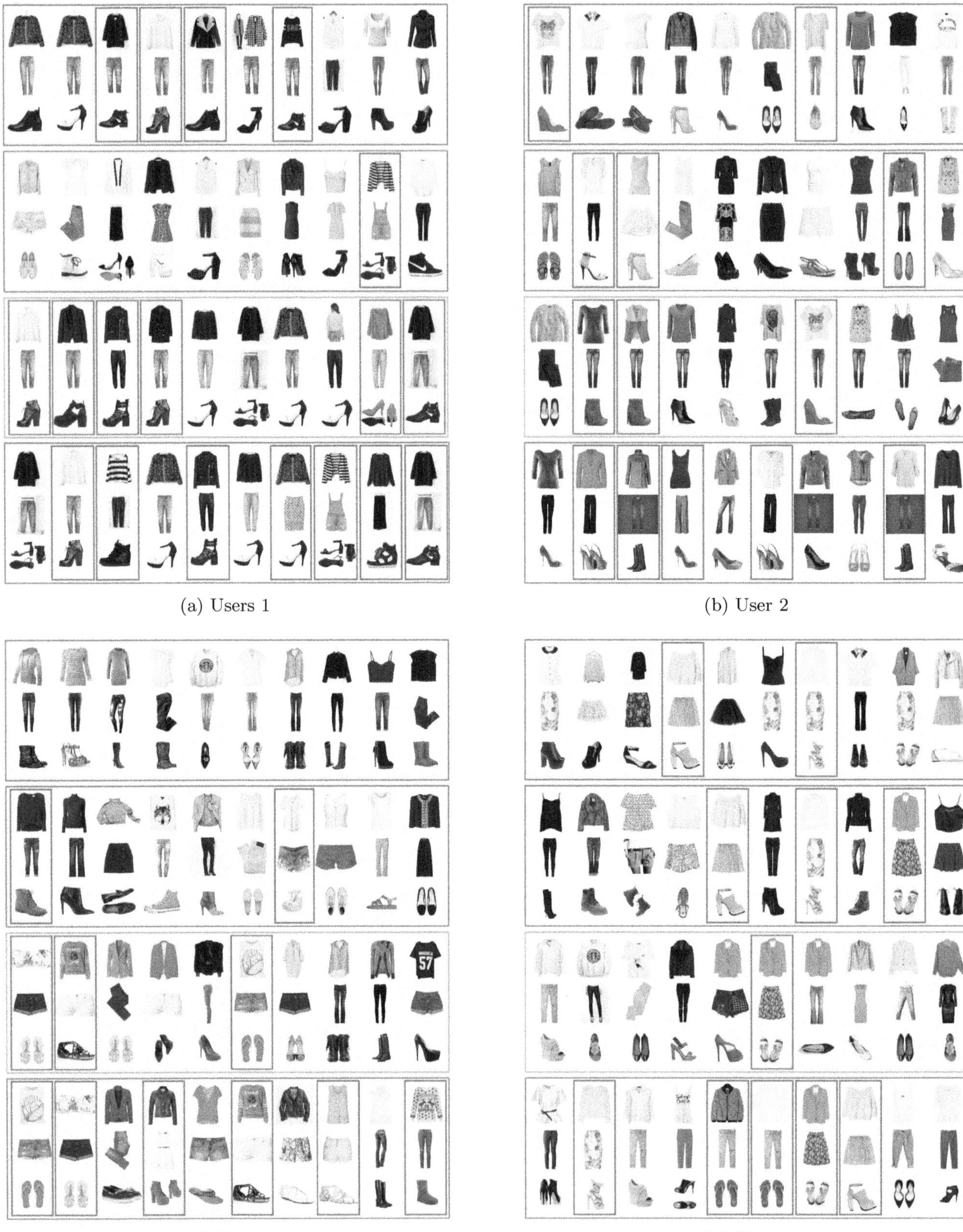

(a) Users 1 (b) User 2

(c) User 3 (d) User 4

Figure 7: Examples of top 10 recommended outfits. For each user, the results from top to bottom are obtained by CF Mean (purple), CCA (green), CF NN (blue) and FPITF (grey) respectively. The outfits marked with red boxes were created by the users.

Predicting and Understanding Urban Perception with Convolutional Neural Networks

Lorenzo Porzi
FBK, Trento, Italy
University of Perugia
Perugia, Italy

Samuel Rota Buló
FBK, Trento, Italy

Bruno Lepri
FBK, Trento, Italy

Elisa Ricci
FBK, Trento, Italy
University of Perugia
Perugia, Italy

ABSTRACT

Cities' visual appearance plays a central role in shaping human perception and response to the surrounding urban environment. For example, the visual qualities of urban spaces affect the psychological states of their inhabitants and can induce negative social outcomes. Hence, it becomes critically important to understand people's perceptions and evaluations of urban spaces. Previous works have demonstrated that algorithms can be used to predict high level attributes of urban scenes (*e.g.* safety, attractiveness, uniqueness), accurately emulating human perception. In this paper we propose a novel approach for predicting the perceived safety of a scene from Google Street View Images. Opposite to previous works, we formulate the problem of learning to predict high level judgments as a ranking task and we employ a Convolutional Neural Network (CNN), significantly improving the accuracy of predictions over previous methods. Interestingly, the proposed CNN architecture relies on a novel pooling layer, which permits to automatically discover the most important areas of the images for predicting the concept of perceived safety. An extensive experimental evaluation, conducted on the publicly available Place Pulse dataset, demonstrates the advantages of the proposed approach over state-of-the-art methods.

1. INTRODUCTION

Cities are shaped by and affects the life of their inhabitants. Several studies have shown that cities' visual appearance plays a central role in human perception and response to the surrounding environment. A notable example is the *Broken Windows Theory* suggesting that visual signs of environmental disorder, such as broken windows, abandoned cars, litter and graffiti, can induce negative social outcomes and increase crime levels [17]. Interestingly, the

MM'15, October 26–30, 2015, Brisbane, Australia.

ACM 978-1-4503-3459-4/15/10 ...$15.00.
DOI: http://dx.doi.org/10.1145/2733373.2806273 .

Figure 1: Given the images above showing specific details extracted from pictures of urban scenes, a human observer can easy choose which group corresponds to safe areas and which to unsafe ones.

Broken Windows Theory has greatly influenced public policy strategies leading to aggressive police tactics to control the manifestations of social and physical disorder. Moreover, the visual qualities of urban spaces affect the psychological states of their inhabitants [22]. For example, urban scenes with vegetation tend to produce positive feelings [37], while urban disorder induces psychological distress [33]. Hence, it becomes critically important to understand people's perceptions and evaluations of urban spaces.

In *The Image of the City* [23], Kevin Lynch introduced the city's mental map, indicating the city elements that are distinguished among hundreds, thousands, or millions of other city artifacts by their unique shapes, sizes, colors, etc. Traditionally, researchers have studied the city's mental map by interviewing city residents and manually reviewing photographs and videotapes: a tedious process, involving considerable collective efforts [26]. While this was unavoidable at the time of Lynch's study, today, modern information technology permits to analyze the image of the city in a quantitative manner. In particular, recent works have shown that modern crowdsourcing platforms can be used to collect millions of users' opinions about places and advanced machine learning approaches are very accurate in predicting human judgements of urban scenes, even in case of previously unseen locations. Moreover, geo-tagged images publicly available from Google Street View and from social network platforms, such as Flickr or Foursquare, represent an invaluable resource to study human perceptions of places. Recently, few works [31, 25, 2, 27] have proposed computational methods to automatically infer high level perceptual attributes from geo-referenced images of urban spaces.

In this paper we propose a novel approach for predicting human opinions about places. Specifically, confirming the recent findings in [27, 25], we demonstrate that a computer vision algorithm can emulate human perception and reliably predict judgments of safety from pictures of urban scenes. For a human observer it is generally hard to quantify the absolute degree of safety of a scene, while relative judgements (*e.g.* "*this looks safer than that*") are more natural [7]. Indeed, most crowdsourcing platforms collecting annotations of high levels human judgments[1] operate on image pairs. Previous works presented solutions based on a two-steps approach: first the pairwise annotations are used to calculate a set of absolute safety scores, then a regression model is learned to predict these scores. We believe that this indirect approach rises some fundamental issues, which are thoroughly discussed in Subsection 4.2.1. For these reasons we propose to adopt a ranking framework, which directly operates on relative judgements. The prediction algorithm we propose relies on a Convolutional Neural Network specifically designed for ranking tasks. Experiments conducted on the Place Pulse dataset [32] demonstrate that our approach is superior to state-of-the-art regression methods.

Previous works [27, 25] presented computational models capable of answering the question "*does this place look safe?*". In this paper we also tackle a second fundamental aspect about the way humans judge a place from a picture: "*what makes this place look safe?*". Our proposed CNN is based on a set of latent detectors, which are optimally combined for predicting urban safety. Each detector is asked to select specific parts of the images, correlating them with the concepts of perceived safety/unsafety. Indeed, a human observer can guess the degree of safety of a specific urban scene by simply looking at some parts of it (Figure 1). Importantly, the proposed detectors are designed in order to capture complementary information: some aim to discover very localized areas, thus focusing on discriminative objects (*e.g.* residential windows and trees, graffiti), while others are meant to capture spread areas, focusing on large objects and more diffuse patterns (*e.g.* roads and vegetation).

In summary, the main contributions of this study are: (i) we propose a ranking approach to predict human perceptions of safety from geo-tagged images of urban spaces. Our analysis and experimental evaluation demonstrates the advantages of a ranking-based framework over previous regression methods; (ii) To our knowledge, this is the first work based on CNN for predicting high level judgements of urban spaces. Previous works have considered traditional feature representations or descriptors derived from a pre-trained CNN. Differently, in this paper we propose a novel CNN architecture, demonstrating improved performance over state-of-the art methods; (iii) Our approach permits to automatically discover the parts of the image, which correlate with the concept of perceived safety. No previous works have proposed computational models to address this issue.

[1]`http://pulse.media.mit.edu/,http://urbangems.org/`

The rest of the paper is structured as follows. Related work for analysing patterns of human perception are discussed Section 2. The proposed approach for predicting the perceived safety from geo-tagged images of urban scenes is presented in Section 3. Extensive evaluations and comparisons with state-of-the-art methods are reported in Section 4. Finally, Section 5 is devoted to conclusions and future works.

2. RELATED WORK

In this section, we review key works from two research fields: urban perception and automatic scene recognition.

2.1 Urban Perception

Since the seminal study of Lynch [23], several works in urban studies and environmental psychology have investigated people's preferences for certain environments and their aesthetic judgments of urban scenes, such as streets, parks, buildings [38]. In particular, the urban activist Jane Jacobs discussed extensively, in *The Death and Life of Great American Cities*, the role played by streets as principal visual scenes in a city [14]. In particular, research has shown seven environmental features as prominent in human evaluation of places: naturalness, complexity, order, novelty, openness, historical significance, and upkeep [26]. More specifically, people prefer vegetation and dislike obtrusive signs, intense land uses and traffic. Weber and colleagues identified uniformity in architectural style, symmetry, scale and presence of vegetation as primary factors driving the aesthetic judgments of urban spaces [38]. Again, several studies highlights people notice and prefer order. Dilapidation and disorder such as trash, boarded up buildings, abandoned property and cars, and litter, which researchers refer to as *physical incivilities*, also contribute to a perception of the breakdown of social controls, fear of crime, and crime [36, 17]. For example, Schroeder and Anderson found vacant buildings and graffiti associated with judgements of low safety [35]. Based on videotaping and systematic rating of more than 23,000 street segments in Chicago, Sampson and Radenbausch [34] constructed scales of social and physical disorder for 196 neighborhoods. In particular, graffiti, abandoned cars, garbage or litter on street or sidewalk were recognized by raters as visual signs of physical disorder. Another set of environmental cues evoking the possibility that an area is unsafe are related with *entrapment*, referring to the difficulty a person would have escaping, and *physical concealment*, referring to a visual occlusion of space big enough to hide potential offenders. Thus, people usually consider safer places offering open vistas [26]. The studies described above were mostly based on interviews or visual surveys where people were asked to rate images of streets and neighborhoods on a 1-10 scale. Nowadays, the large amount of geo-tagged images publicly available on Google Street View and in social network platforms such as Flickr or Foursquare opens a new way to study human perceptions of places. Our work represents one of the first attempts in this novel research direction.

2.2 Automatic Scene Recognition

In the last few years there has been significant progress in the area of automatic scene recognition [21, 39, 40]. However, previous research on scene understanding has mainly focused on traditional problems such as place classification or analysis of scene composition (*i.e.* the detection and recognition of the objects present in the scene). This paper tackles a different problem: we are interested in learning to infer human high level (safety) judgments of places. Perceptual prediction from images has received an increased interest recently in the vision and multimedia community. However, previous works have focused mainly on tasks such as assessing automatically the interestingness and the aesthetic quality of images [10, 24] or discovering the style of a city or an object [8]. These tasks are substantially different from ours, as we focus on predicting high level judgments of urban areas from geo-tagged images and specifically from pictures depicting outdoor street level scenes.

Geo-tagged images are an invaluable resource for researchers in multimedia analysis and have been exploited for many tasks, such as for automatic localization of non geo-referenced pictures [12], for photo trip pattern mining [1], for augmented reality [30, 29], for developing personalized travel recommendations [6]. Prediction of human judgments from geo-tagged images depicting urban spaces has been attempted only very recently. Quercia *et al.* [31] used crowdsourcing to collect a dataset of street level images and the associated perceptual attributes, corresponding to the concepts of attractiveness, happiness and quiet. They also investigated the role of different visual features (*i.e.* color, texture and compositional features) for automatic high level judgments prediction. Naik *et al.* [25] proposed an approach based on support vector regression to predict three perceptual characteristics of scenes, *i.e.* safety, wealth and uniqueness). Their analysis is performed on the Place Pulse dataset [32], consisting of about 4K images downloaded from Google StreetView and corresponding to four different cities (New York, Boston, Linz and Salzburg). Human annotations have been collected with crowdsourcing, asking users to decide, among two scene images, which picture corresponds to the most safe/upper-class/unique place. The Place Pulse dataset has been used in [27], where deep convolutional activation features [20] have been shown superior to traditional descriptors (*e.g.* GIST, Dense and Sparse SIFT, HOG) for high level judgments prediction. In this paper we also consider the Place Pulse dataset, but differently from previous works based on regression [25, 27], we propose a ranking framework, showing that our approach guarantees more accurate estimates of human perceptions.

The problem of automatically identifying visual elements (*i.e.* small image patches) that correlate with high level non-visual attributes has been rarely considered. Notable exceptions are the works in [2, 18]. Arietta *et al.* [2] proposed a computational model, based on support vector regression, to predict non-visual attributes (crime rate, housing prices) from images and to automatically discover visual elements correlated with the predicted attributes. However, they did not consider human annotations obtained with crowdsourcing and the annotated data are derived from public databases of city municipalities. Khosla *et al.* [18] presented an approach to *look beyond the visible scene* and used deep learning features extracted from visual data to infer properties about the environment (*e.g.* crime rate). They also proposed an approach based on sparse coding to analyze the importance of different image regions for predicting high level attributes. To our knowledge, no previous work have considered the problem of discovering mid-level visual elements responsible for human perceptual judgments in the context of Convolutional Neural Networks.

3. PREDICTING THE PERCEIVED SAFETY OF URBAN SPACES

In this section, we first describe the Place Pulse dataset, then we present the proposed ranking method for learning the perceived safety of urban places. Specifically, we first show an approach based on Support Vector Machines (SVM) and precomputed feature descriptors, then we introduce a novel method based on CNNs. Additionally, we discuss the challenges of learning from human judgments, analyzing the noise of users annotations in the Place Pulse dataset.

3.1 Place Pulse 1.0

We consider the publicly available Place Pulse 1.0 dataset [32]. This dataset contains 4,136 geo-tagged images for the cities of New York (including Manhattan and parts of Queens, Brooklyn and The Bronx), Boston (including parts of Cambridge), Linz and Salzburg. As typical for images downloaded from Google Street View, these are captured from a vehicle in the early morning, thus depicting mostly empty sidewalks, little traffic and limited human activity.

For each image, the scores for perceived safety, wealth and uniqueness are provided. These scores were computed from user preferences using the Microsoft Trueskill algorithm [11]. User preferences were collected with crowdsourcing through an online website[2]. Participants were shown two randomly chosen images from the dataset and were asked to choose one of the two in response to the question: *Which place looks safer/more upper-class/more unique?*. In total, user annotations corresponding to 208,738 votes were obtained between August and November 2011. 7,872 unique users from 91 countries took part to the survey. The user preferences, *i.e.* the votes corresponding to pairwise comparisons, are publicly available only for the attribute of safety. Therefore, in this work we only consider this attribute. However, it is worth nothing that our approach is general and can be used for predicting arbitrary high level judgments.

3.2 Learning to Predict the Perceived Safety

It is hard for a human observer to quantify the degree of safety of a place given a single picture, while it may be relatively easy to give judgments over image pairs. In confirmation of this, in the Place Pulse dataset, as well as in other studies on urban perception [31], annotations are collected in the form of votes on couples of images. Therefore, in this paper we propose to formulate the problem of learning to predict the perceived safety of places as a ranking task.

More formally, we consider a setting, where we observe judgments about the relative safeness of pairs of images. Each judgment consists of a triplet $(I, J, y) \in \mathcal{I} \times \mathcal{I} \times \mathcal{Y}$, where $I, J \in \mathcal{I}$ are images and $y \in \mathcal{Y} = \{+1, -1\}$ is a label that indicates whether image I is perceived by a human as safer ($y = +1$) or unsafer ($y = -1$) than image J.[3] We assume the judgments to follow an unknown distribution P, which is in general noisy due to inconsistencies that exist among humans' perceptions. We denote by $\mathcal{D}_\mathsf{n} \subseteq \mathcal{I} \times \mathcal{I} \times \mathcal{Y}$ a training set of n judgments, being *i.i.d.* samples from P.

The goal of the learning task is to estimate from the training set $\mathcal{D}_\mathsf{n}$ a function $f \in \mathcal{I} \to \mathbb{R}$ that provides for each im-

[2]http://pulse.media.mit.edu/

[3]To facilitate comparison with previous methods we have excluded ties in our analysis, but in principle they could be added as a third class.

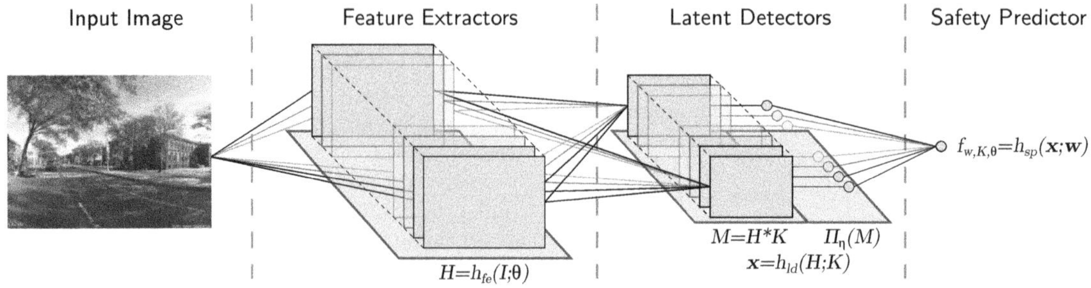

Figure 2: Schematic representation of the three blocks composing our rCNN architecture.

age $I \in \mathcal{I}$ a real value $f(I)$ that reflects the degree of safety perceived by a human. The prediction function f is sought within a subset of feasible functions $\mathcal{F} \subseteq \mathcal{I} \to \mathbb{R}$ (*a.k.a.* hypothesis space) following the regularized, empirical risk minimization principle. This yields the following optimization problem

$$f^\star \in \arg\min_{f \in \mathcal{F}} \lambda\, \Omega(f) + R_{\text{emp}}(f)\,, \quad (1)$$

where $\Omega(f)$ is a regularization term penalizing complex functions to prevent overfitting, λ is a nonnegative trade-off parameter and $R_{\text{emp}}(f)$ is the empirical risk term, which is given by:

$$R_{\text{emp}}(f) = \frac{1}{|\mathcal{D}_\mathsf{n}|} \sum_{(I,J,y)\in\mathcal{D}_\mathsf{n}} L(y, f(I), f(J))\,.$$

In the empirical risk, the quality of a prediction function with respect to the observed data is assessed via a *loss function.* Each loss term $L(y, z_I, z_J)$ represents the cost one incurs by assigning image I and J a safety degree of z_I and z_J, respectively, given that y is the true, relative safety label.

The loss function that is typically regarded as the reference loss, and that is used in practice at test time to measure the errors committed by the learning algorithm, is the *binary loss*, which is defined as

$$L_{\text{bin}}(y, z_I, z_J) = \begin{cases} 1 & \text{if } y(z_I - z_J) \le 0 \\ 0 & \text{otherwise.} \end{cases}$$

At training time, however, the binary loss is typically replaced with some other convex, surrogate loss that renders the optimization of (1) easier. Later in this section, we will consider differentiable, convex losses such as the squared hinge loss and the logistic-loss.

In the following we present two different learning settings for the problem at hand: in Subsection 3.2.1 we present a solution based on the well-known SVM; in Subsection 3.2.2 we propose a Convolutional Neural Network (CNN) architecture, which includes a new type of pooling unit. Finally, in Subsection 3.3 we discuss the problem of optimizing the empirical risk in the case of a binary loss and unconstrained function space, with the purpose of determine the intrinsic noise level of a given dataset.

3.2.1 RankingSVM

We describe a learning machine for our task that is known as RankingSVM [13, 5]. In this setting, the hypothesis space $\mathcal{F}_{\text{SVM}}$ comprises linear, generalized decision functions of the following form:

$$\mathcal{F}_{\text{SVM}} = \{f_{\boldsymbol{w}} = I \mapsto \boldsymbol{w}^\top \phi(I) \,:\, \boldsymbol{w} \in \mathbb{R}^\mathsf{m}\} \subset \mathcal{I} \to \mathbb{R}\,.$$

where $\phi \in \mathcal{I} \to \mathbb{R}^\mathsf{m}$ is a pre-defined *feature map* that provides a vector-valued feature abstraction for image I. Functions $f_{\boldsymbol{w}} \in \mathcal{F}_{\text{SVM}}$ are penalized by means of an ℓ_2-regularization of the parameter vector $\boldsymbol{w}$, *i.e.*

$$\Omega_{\ell_2}(f_{\boldsymbol{w}}) = \|\boldsymbol{w}\|_2^2\,,$$

and the loss function we consider is given in terms of the squared hinge loss as follows:

$$L_{\text{hinge}^2}(y, z_I, z_J) = |1 - y(z_I - z_J)|_+^2\,,$$

where $|x|_+ = \max(x, 0)$. With this loss, one incurs no penalization if $y = +1$ and $z_I > z_J + 1$, or if $y = -1$ and $z_J > z_I + 1$, *i.e.* when the image deemed as safer has indeed a safety degree that is at least 1 point better than the one of the other image.

Under this setting, the optimization in (1) is convex in $\boldsymbol{w}$ and a global solution can be recovered using the algorithm in [5]. Once the learned parameters $\boldsymbol{w}$ are obtained, the degree of safety for a novel image $\hat{I}$ can be computed as $f_{\boldsymbol{w}}(\hat{I})$.

3.2.2 Convolutional Neural Networks

A drawback of the SVM-based approach is its dependence on a pre-defined feature mapping ϕ. To overcome this limitation, we consider a richer hypothesis space in which functions admit a compositional factorization of the type $f = h_\mathsf{k} \circ \cdots \circ h_1$, such as those implemented by multilayer neural networks. In the specific, the architecture we propose can be organized into three compositional blocks (Figure 2):

Feature extractor

$$h_{fe}(\cdot;\theta) \in \mathcal{I} \to \mathbb{R}^{\mathsf{r}\times\mathsf{s}\times\mathsf{t}}$$

This block maps an input image I to an intermediate $\mathsf{r} \times \mathsf{s} \times \mathsf{t}$-dimensional representation. It consists of the first 2/3 layers (we tried both settings) of the deep convolutional network proposed in [20] and known as AlexNet. All the parameters of the block are held by θ;

Latent detectors

$$h_{ld}(\cdot;K) \in \mathbb{R}^{\mathsf{r}\times\mathsf{s}\times\mathsf{t}} \to \mathbb{R}^\mathsf{m}\,, \quad K = (K_1, \ldots, K_\mathsf{m})$$

This block takes the output H of the feature extractor and returns the scalar responses of m detectors of latent visual concepts. The i-th detector performs the convolution of the input H with a linear filter $K_i \in \mathbb{R}^{\mathsf{u}\times\mathsf{v}\times\mathsf{t}}$, followed by a ReLU non-linearity, obtaining a matrix. This matrix is then fed to a pooling operator $\Pi_{\eta_i}(\cdot)$, parametrized by $0 \le \eta_i \le 1$, to obtain a single scalar. The pooling parameters $(\eta_1, \ldots, \eta_\mathsf{m})$ are model choices to be fixed a priori. In our experiments we use linear filters of spatial dimensions $\mathsf{u} = \mathsf{v} = 3$, corresponding to a receptive window of 99×99

Figure 3: Visual representation of our pooling method. Given different values of the η parameter we show the areas of four images that concur to the output value of the pooling function, *i.e.* those corresponding to the $1 + \lceil \eta(\mathsf{wz} - 1) \rceil$ largest elements in its input M. Each pixel's intensity is scaled according to the magnitude of its corresponding element in M.

pixels in the input image. The pooling operator $\Pi_\eta(M)$ that we propose generalizes the well-known max-pooling and average-pooling operators. It takes as input a matrix $M \in \mathbb{R}^{\mathsf{w} \times \mathsf{z}}$ and depends on a parameter $0 \leq \eta \leq 1$. It computes the average of the $1 + \lceil \eta(\mathsf{wz} - 1) \rceil$ largest elements in M. If $\eta = 0$ then it returns the largest element as the max-pooling operator, while if $\eta = 1$ it returns the average of the elements in M as the average-pooling operator. Intuitively, this pooling operator selects a variable-sized portion of the input image as the most relevant for the detector's response. In other words, the proposed structure for latent detectors permits to discover the regions of the image which are discriminative with respect to the perceived safety/unsafety. A graphical representation of this intuition is shown in Figure 3.

In summary, this block takes the following form:

$$h_{ld}(H; K) = (\Pi_{\eta_1}(|H * K_1|_+), \ldots, \Pi_{\eta_{\mathsf{m}}}(|H * K_{\mathsf{m}}|_+)) ,$$

where $|M|_+$ returns M with negative elements set to 0.

Previous works [4, 19] have investigated similar parametric pooling methods, which allow a smooth transition between average and max-pooling. However, none of these works have focused specifically on CNN architectures for automatic scene analysis.

Safety predictor

$$h_{sp}(\cdot; \boldsymbol{w}) \in \mathbb{R}^{\mathsf{m}} \to \mathbb{R}$$

This block is a linear decision function with parameter $\boldsymbol{w} \in \mathbb{R}^{\mathsf{m}}$ applied to the responses $\boldsymbol{x} \in \mathbb{R}^{\mathsf{m}}$ of the latent detectors, *i.e.*

$$h_{sp}(\boldsymbol{x}; \boldsymbol{w}) = \boldsymbol{w}^\top \boldsymbol{x} .$$

The final form of the safety prediction function is

$$f_{\boldsymbol{w},K,\theta} = h_{sp}(\cdot; \boldsymbol{w}) \circ h_{ld}(\cdot; K) \circ h_{fe}(\cdot; \theta) ,$$

where $\boldsymbol{w} \in \mathbb{R}^{\mathsf{m}}$, $K \in \mathbb{R}^{\mathsf{u} \times \mathsf{v} \times \mathsf{t} \times \mathsf{m}}$ and $\theta \in \Theta$, Θ being the set of all possible parametrizations of the h_{fe}. The corresponding hypothesis space is thus given by

$$\mathcal{F}_{\text{rCNN}} = \left\{ f_{\boldsymbol{w},K,\theta} \,:\, \boldsymbol{w} \in \mathbb{R}^{\mathsf{m}}, K \in \mathbb{R}^{\mathsf{u} \times \mathsf{v} \times \mathsf{t} \times \mathsf{m}}, \theta \in \Theta \right\} \subset \mathcal{I} \to \mathbb{R} .$$

Functions in $\mathcal{F}_{\text{rCNN}}$ are regularized as usually done for neural networks through an ℓ_2-penalization of the parameters in each layer. As for the loss function, we adopt the so-called logistic loss, which is given by

$$L_{\text{logistic}}(y, z_I, z_J) = \log(1 + \exp(z_J - z_I)) .$$

As opposed to the SVM case, the optimization of (1) in this scenario is non-convex and we rely on Stochastic Gradient Descent (SGD). Specifically, we adopt an SGD solver with momentum $\mu = 0.9$ and learning rate $\alpha = 0.01$ (or $\alpha = 0.001$ for fine-tuned layers), scheduling a tenfold decrease of the learning rate every 6 training epochs.

As a final remark, it is worth noting that, comparing our CNN with recent deep learning approaches popular in the vision community [20, 40], the proposed architecture is relatively shallow. Our choice is motivated by the fact that, with the proposed latent detectors, we aim to discover mid-level visual representations (*i.e.* small image regions), which are discriminative with respect to the perceived safety. Importantly, our experimental results demonstrate that this choice does not imply a decrease in terms of prediction accuracy.

3.3 Determining the training set noise

The learning task that we address has a data distribution that is by nature affected by noise, because humans, to some degree, tend to provide inconsistent judgements regarding the relative safety of image pairs. For this reason, it is interesting to quantify the smallest error that can be achieved for some data $\mathcal{D}_{\mathsf{n}}$. To this end, we setup a learning task under an unconstrained hypothesis space $\mathcal{F}$ consisting of explicit mappings of images in $\mathcal{D}_{\mathsf{n}}$ to real values, without regularization (*i.e.* $\lambda = 0$) and with a binary loss. By doing so, the solution to (1) yields an error, which corresponds to the intrinsic noise of the dataset.

Unfortunately, the ERM optimization under this setting is NP-hard, as it is substantially equivalent to the *Minimal Feedback Arc Set* (MFAS) problem [16], which asks for the minimum set of edges that should be removed from a directed graph to obtain an acyclic graph. The directed graph $G = (\mathcal{V}, \mathcal{E})$ we refer to can be constructed from the training set by considering the set of images in $\mathcal{D}_{\mathsf{n}}$ as the vertex set $\mathcal{V}$, and for each judgement $(I, J, y) \in \mathcal{D}_{\mathsf{n}}$ we have an edge $(I, J) \in \mathcal{E}$ if $y = +1$, or $(J, I) \in \mathcal{E}$ if $y = -1$.

From the MFAS of G, denoted by $\mathcal{A} \subset \mathcal{E}$, we can directly recover the optimal empirical error as $R_{\text{emp}}(f^\star) = |\mathcal{A}|/|\mathcal{E}|$. As for the minimizer $f^\star$, there are uncountably many possible solutions that belong to the set

$$\mathcal{F}^\star = \{ f \in \mathcal{F} \,:\, f(I) > f(J), \forall (I, J) \in \mathcal{E} \setminus \mathcal{A} \} .$$

To construct an arbitrary function $f \in \mathcal{F}^\star$, we initialize f_I for all $I \in \mathcal{V}$ with a random real number. Then, we visit the directed acyclic graph $G' = (\mathcal{V}, \mathcal{E} \setminus \mathcal{A})$ in breadth-first order starting from the source vertices, *i.e.* those ones having no incoming edge. Each time a new vertex $I \in \mathcal{V}$ is visited, we set $f_J \leftarrow \max(f_J, f_I + r)$ with r a random positive number for each vertex $J \in \mathcal{V}$ that is adjacent to I, *i.e.* such that (I, J) is an edge of G'. At the end of the graph visit, f represents an arbitrary function in $\mathcal{F}^\star$ and, therefore, a minimizer of (1). Since solving the MFAS problem exactly is in general NP-hard, we rely on the heuristic algorithm of Berger and Shor [3] to find a possibly good solution. In the following section we show the results of this analysis on the Place Pulse dataset.

4. EXPERIMENTAL RESULTS

4.1 Experimental setup

As mentioned above, our experimental evaluation is conducted on the Place Pulse 1.0 dataset. We implemented Convolutional Neural Networks approaches using the Caffe package [15] and run them using a NVIDIA Tesla K40 GPU. For RankingSVM, we adopted a publicly available implementation[4], while for Support Vector Regression (SVR) we used LIBLINEAR [9]. In all our experiments, the regularization parameters of RankingSVM and SVR have been chosen with a five-fold cross-validation. The performance of the tested methods has been evaluated in terms of the share of correctly predicted users' votes on pairs of images.

4.2 Prediction of Perceived Urban Safety

In this section we demonstrate that a ranking approach can be successfully used to learn a function that automatically predicts the perceived safety of places from images.

4.2.1 Ranking vs Regression

In Section 3 we have shown that we can learn from the users' judgements a real-valued function that assigns a score to each image. This function induces a total ordering (*a.k.a.* ranking) on the set of images, which should be as consistent as possible with the pairwise relations gathered from the users. Although the true source of information for the Place Pulse dataset is given by the users' pairwise judgements, previous works [25, 27] have focused on training their algorithms in a way to mimic a "ground-truth" image scoring function, which has been computed by the Place Pulse creators from the users' annotations through the Microsoft Trueskill algorithm. In this way, the attention has been shifted from the original ranking problem based on the users' judgements to a regression problem relying on the provided "ground-truth" scoring function.

In our opinion, this drift raises two important issues. First of all, the ability of an algorithm to mimic the provided scoring function *weakly* correlates with the ability of the algorithm to explain the true data distribution, which consists of the users' pairwise annotations, being the only, true, physical observations one can rely on. Indeed, there are uncountably many possible scoring functions (see, Subsection 3.3) performing equally well, but being arbitrarily different, that could potentially have been taken as a "ground-truth" scoring function. Moreover, errors measured for the regression task on the scoring function do not properly map to errors relative to the true data distribution (*i.e.* violations of the users' annotations). A second issues is that, according to the previous point, the only reliable way to measure how well a trained algorithm performs for the safety prediction task on the Place Pulse dataset is via an error measurement on the true data distribution. However, any attempt in this direction will be intrinsically biased, if the algorithm has been trained using the "ground-truth" scoring function. This is because the "ground-truth" scoring function has been constructed using all the users' annotations and, hence, any algorithm trained for regression on those scores is a function of the whole dataset, thus leaving no independent piece of information for a proper error assessment.

We also found out that the "ground-truth" scoring function based on Microsoft Trueskill, which is used in [25, 27], is not the best representative for the users' annotations. Indeed, it yields an accuracy of 72.87%, which is smaller than what we obtain with a scoring function constructed using the procedure described in Subsection 3.3, namely 76,9%.

For the aforementioned reasons, we do not find reliable to train an algorithm for regression on the "ground-truth" scoring function provided with the Place Pulse dataset: it will hinder the possibility of a more principled error assessment via the users' annotations, *i.e.* the true data distribution. We consider instead more appropriate to train our algorithm directly on the users' votes.

Table 1: RankingSVM: Performance with different features representations.

Features	Average Accuracy (std)
GIST	65.42% (±0.95)
HOG	65.82% (±0.79)
ImageNet	62.02% (±1.15)
PLACES	66.34% (±1.16)
SSIM	64.48% (±1.03)
SUN	65.97% (±1.04)

4.2.2 RankingSVM

In this section we analyze the performance of a ranking approach, *i.e.* RankingSVM, when different types of features are considered: **GIST**, Histogram of Oriented Gradients (**HOG**) and Self-similarity descriptors (**SSIM**), as described in [28]; features extracted from the sixth layer of the Caffe reference network, trained on the 1.2 million images of **ImageNet** (ILSVRC 2012) [15]. These features have been used in previous related works [25, 27]. We also propose two additional feature representations: (i) features extracted from the sixth layer of a CNN having the same architecture as the Caffe reference network, trained on the recent **PLACES** [40] dataset; and (ii) features derived from the **SUN** Attribute dataset [28]. Specifically, we used as high-level features the scores computed by predicting the presence of each of the 102 crowd-sourced scene attributes available in the SUN Attribute dataset [28]. The 102 attributes are quite heterogeneous and span materials, surface properties, functions or affordances, and spatial envelope properties. The prediction of attributes is obtained following the approach described in [28] using a publicly available code.[5]

The results shown in Table 1 demonstrate that, despite the many challenges inherent to the task, a ranking approach can be used to learn to predict human judgements of safety. Table 1 also shows that the best performance is obtained using the features derived from the pre-trained Places-CNN. This is somehow expected, as these features represent state-of-the-art descriptors for scene recognition problems [40]. However, confirming the findings of previous works on the

[4]`http://olivier.chapelle.cc/primal/`

[5]`http://cs.brown.edu/~gen/sunattributes.html`

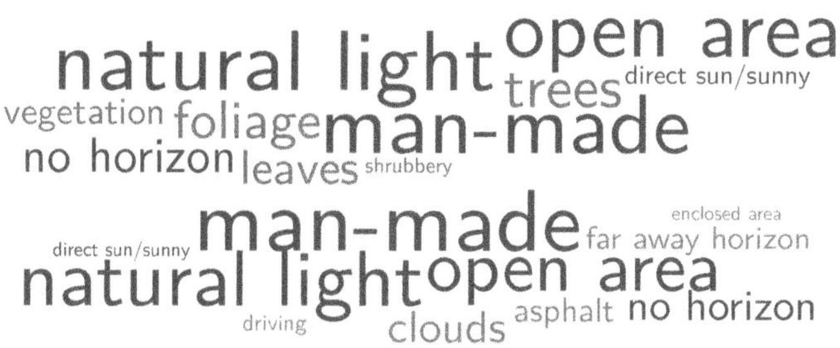

Figure 4: Word clouds of SUN attributes. Top, green: safe, bottom, red: unsafe.

Table 2: Comparison between different ranking methods.

	Method	Accuracy
	rCNN$_2$[m $= 24, \eta_A$]	70.25%
	rCNN$_3$[m $= 24$, max]	69.12%
CNN	AlexNet-noinit	66.85%
	AlexNet-ImageNet	67.15%
	AlexNet-PLACES	70.65%
	GIST	66.18%
	HOG	66.37%
SVM	ImageNet	63.01%
	PLACES	65.93%
	SSIM	64.56%

Place Pulse dataset [27], we did not observe a significant increase in accuracy when using pre-trained CNN-derived features with respect to more traditional descriptors. It is worth noting that, discarding CNN-based features, the best performance is obtained considering SUN attributes.

Looking at SUN features, it is also interesting to try to interpret these data, by analyzing which of the SUN attributes correlate with the concept of perceived safety/unsafety. To this aim we performed a simple experiment. Given the ranking scores computed with the algorithm described in Section 3.3, we took the 100 images corresponding to places perceived as safe and 100 pictures associated with the most unsafe locations. For each of the SUN attributes we analyzed the distribution of the scores computed as in [28] and we selected the 10 most represented attributes in both sets. Figure 4 shows these attributes in the form of a word cloud, where the size of each attribute's name is proportional to the number of images in which it was detected. It is interesting to see that, among attributes being discriminative of a specific set, those corresponding to vegetation are associated to safe areas, while concepts like clouds or asphalt correlate with non-safe places. As expected, common attributes involve aspects like natural light, man-made structures and open area, indicating general concepts related to outdoor scenes.

4.2.3 *Ranking with CNN*

In this section we analyze the performance of the proposed CNN architectures for ranking (rCNN). Specifically we consider the following configurations (*cfr.* Section 3.2.2):

- rCNN$_2$[m $= 24, \eta_A$], rCNN$_2$[m $= 32, \eta_A$]: 2-layers feature extractor, respectively 24 and 32 latent detectors split into four groups with pooling factors $\eta_A = (0, 0.01, 0.05, 0.1)$;
- rCNN$_2$[m $= 24, \eta_B$], rCNN$_2$[m $= 32, \eta_B$]: 2-layers feature extractor, respectively 24 and 32 latent detectors split into four groups with pooling factors $\eta_B = (0, 0.1, 0.25, 0.5)$;
- rCNN$_2$[m $= 24$, max], rCNN$_2$[m $= 32$, max]: 2-layers feature extractor, respectively 24 and 32 latent detectors with max pooling ($\eta = 0$);
- rCNN$_3$[m $= 24$, max], rCNN$_3$[m $= 32$, max]: 3-layers feature extractor, respectively 24 and 32 latent detectors with max pooling ($\eta = 0$).

Table 3: Comparison between different regression methods using the same split as Table 2.

Features	Accuracy
GIST [25, 27]	65.29%
HOG [25]	66.04%
ImageNet [27]	66.79%
PLACES	67.93%
SSIM [25]	63.93%

Table 4: Comparison among the proposed CNNs.

Method	Accuracy
rCNN$_2$[m $= 24, \eta_A$]	70.25%
rCNN$_2$[m $= 32, \eta_A$]	69.44%
rCNN$_2$[m $= 24, \eta_B$]	69.70%
rCNN$_2$[m $= 32, \eta_B$]	69.73%
rCNN$_2$[m $= 24$, max]	66.87%
rCNN$_2$[m $= 32$, max]	68.39%
rCNN$_3$[m $= 24$, max]	69.12%
rCNN$_3$[m $= 32$, max]	68.98%

The feature extractor layers of all configurations are fine-tuned from AlexNet trained on the Places dataset [40], while all other layers are learned from scratch. Due to the long training time of CNNs, the results presented in this section refer to a single random split of the data, where 80% of the images and their votes are used for training and 20% for testing. We do not expect significant differences in the results when a different split is chosen.

In a first series of experiments we compare the two best performing configurations of our CNN architecture with RankingSVM and state-of-the-art deep learning methods. In particular, we adapt the well-known AlexNet architecture [20] to our task: we keep the original topology for the bottom 6 layers (5 convolutional, 1 fully connected) and attach a final fully connected layer that outputs the ranking score. The resulting network is trained both from scratch (denoted as AlexNet-noinit) and by fine-tuning the bottom six layers from two publicly available models learned on object recognition [20] (AlexNet-ImageNet) and scene recognition [40] (AlexNet-PLACES) tasks. Table 2 reports the results of this comparison. It is immediately clear that CNN approaches outperform SVM-based ones, confirming the advantages of deep learning for predicting human perception over previous works based on traditional features descriptors [25, 27]. By comparing the accuracy of our CNNs with the AlexNet-derived ones, we observe that AlexNet-PLACES slightly outperforms our approach. Indeed, a deeper network typically guarantees improved performance when sufficient training data is available. The requirement for considerable amounts of training data is reflected by the results obtained for AlexNet-noinit, which shows the worst performance among the CNN approaches. Finally, we note that AlexNet-ImageNet achieves a lower accuracy than both AlexNet-PLACES and our CNNs. We think that this depends on the scene recognition task on which AlexNet-PLACES was pre-trained begin closer to our safety-prediction task, as opposed to the object recognition task in ImageNet.

Figure 5: The most important patterns correlated with perception of safety discovered by the network rCNN$_2$[m = 24, η_B]

Figure 6: The most important patterns correlated with perception of safety discovered by the network rCNN$_2$[m = 32, η_A]

Figure 7: The most important patterns correlated with perception of unsafety discovered by the network rCNN$_2$[m = 24, η_B]

Figure 8: The most important patterns correlated with perception of unsafety discovered by the network rCNN$_2$[m = 32, η_A]

For the sake of comparison, we also report the results obtained on the same data split using SVR (Table 3). Note that the values in Table 3 suffer from the score bias discussed in Section 4.2.1. Nevertheless, Table 3 clearly shows that the proposed CNN outperforms previous regression-based methods [25, 27], independently from the feature representation used. Table 4 reports a comparison among the aforementioned configurations of our CNN architecture. We observe an advantage in terms of accuracy for the mixed-pooling configurations compared to the max-only ones. In particular, rCNN$_2$[m = 24, η_A] achieves the best overall result with an accuracy of 70.25%, while rCNN$_2$[m = 24, max] shows the worst with an accuracy of 66.87%, suggesting that both localized and diffused features are more informative for the prediction of perceived safety. Looking at the effects of changing the number of latent detectors, only slight differences in accuracy are observed between m = 24 and m = 32. We did not report results for m > 32 as they typically correspond to a decrease in accuracy as well as a less clear separation between safe/unsafe visual patterns.

4.3 Visualizing Patterns of Safety/Unsafety

In this section we analyze the ability of the proposed CNN approaches to automatically discover visual patterns associated with the perception of safety. With reference to Section 3.2.2, we use the learned weights $\boldsymbol{w}$ to characterize the latent detectors. Intuitively, since a latent detector's output is always greater than or equal to zero, its positive or negative contribution to the predicted image safety only depends on the sign of the corresponding entry of $\boldsymbol{w}$. Thus, we mark as "safe" the detectors associated with learned positive weights and "unsafe" the others, while we use the weight's magnitude to determine how discriminative the detector is.

As a first visualization approach, we select the four most discriminative "safe" and "unsafe" latent detectors from the two best performing CNNs of Table 4: rCNN$_2$[m = 24, η_A] and rCNN$_2$[m = 24, η_B]. Then, we extract from the dataset the 10 patches showing the highest response on each detector and collect them (arranged row-wise) in Figures 5-8. Looking at Figures 5 and 6, we can see a prevalence of residential single houses, and, in particular, windows of residential houses. Another interesting aspect is the presence of trees and portions of gardens. Interestingly, Quercia *et al.* [31] found residential trees and residential windows as visual words associated with quiet images. The prevalence of residential trees and residential gardens is also in line with the results obtained in environmental psychology [38], highlighting the positive influence of vegetation, particularly gardens, parks and residential trees, on judgements about urban spaces. Finally, in some of the patches are represented crosswalks. Turning now our attention to the four most discriminative "unsafe" latent detectors (Figures 7 and 8), we can see the presence of gates, graffiti and other signs of vandalism. As pointed out by the *Broken Windows Theory*, graffiti contribute to a perception of breakdown of social order [17] and usually are associated with judgments of low safety [35]. Moreover, *Broken Windows Theory* suggested a positive relationship not only between signs of disorder and perception of unsafety, but also between disorder and crime rates. Another emerging sign from the images associated with judgments of unsafety is the presence of empty roads, electricity and communication pylons. Finally, the buildings are mainly council houses and industrial buildings and their selected portions represent usually the roofs.

As mentioned in Section 3.2.2, the output of the pooling operator adopted in our rCNN networks only depends on a portion of the input image. Depending on the η parameter the size of this portion varies from a single patch to the whole image. This observation suggests an effective way to visualize the internal representation learned by each of our latent detectors, which is exploited to generate the images in Figure 9. Here we chose three "safe" and three "unsafe" detectors from $\text{rCNN}_2[\mathsf{m} = 24, \eta_A]$, each having a different pooling parameter, and study their output on some of the images that exhibit the strongest response on each detector. For each image we show the portions that concurred to the detectors' output and scale the pixel intensities according to the local detector response. As expected, the images corresponding to a small value of the pooling parameter depict very localized features of the environment, like roofs and windows. Increasing values of η shift the detectors' attention towards bigger areas, comprising sidewalks, roads, facades or entire buildings. The same observations concerning the nature of the features associated with safety and unsafety reported in the previous paragraphs also apply here (presence of residential gardens and trees, and residential single houses for safety, while council houses and industrial buildings for unsafety). It is also interesting to note how the aspect ratio of the image regions selected by the "unsafe" detectors tends to be wider, highlighting horizontal structures typical of industrialized open areas.

5. CONCLUSIONS AND FUTURE WORK

We presented a novel approach for predicting the perceived safety of urban scenes from Google Street View images. Our extensive experimental evaluation, conducted on the publicly available Place Pulse dataset, demonstrates that the proposed method, combining a ranking framework with the representational power of CNNs, is more accurate than state of the art methods. Moreover, our CNN-based approach permits to discover automatically mid-level visual patterns correlated with urban perception. To our knowledge, this is the first work that introduces a computational model for addressing the issue: *What makes a place look safe?*. Future works include extending the proposed approach to prediction of other high level attributes and analyzing the difference among scenes of various geographic areas (Europe vs USA).

Acknowledgments

We would like to thank Cesar Hidalgo and Nikhil Naik for the insightful discussion, as well as for sharing the data of Place Pulse 1.0. We also thank NVIDIA Corporation for providing us a K40 GPU.

6. REFERENCES

[1] Y. Arase, X. Xie, T. Hara, and S. Nishio. Mining people's trips from large scale geo-tagged photos. In *ACM Multimedia*, 2010.

[2] S. M. Arietta, A. A. Efros, R. Ramamoorthi, and M. Agrawala. City forensics: Using visual elements to predict non-visual city attributes. *IEEE Trans. on Visualization and Computer Graphics*, 2014.

[3] B. Berger and P. W. Shor. Approximation alogorithms for the maximum acyclic subgraph problem. In *ACM-SIAM symposium on Discrete algorithms*, 1990.

[4] Y.-L. Boureau, J. Ponce, and Y. LeCun. A theoretical analysis of feature pooling in visual recognition. In *International Conference on Machine Learning*, 2010.

[5] O. Chapelle and S. S. Keerthi. Efficient algorithm for ranking with svms. *Information Retrieval*, 13(3):201–215, 2010.

[6] Y.-Y. Chen, A.-J. Cheng, and W. H. Hsu. Travel recommendation by mining people attributes and travel group types from community-contributed photos. *IEEE Trans. on Multimedia*, 15(6):1283–1295, 2013.

[7] H. David. *The method of paired comparisons.* Hodder Arnold, 1988.

[8] C. Doersch, S. Singh, A. Gupta, J. Sivic, and A. Efros. What makes paris look like paris? *ACM Transactions on Graphics*, 31(4), 2012.

[9] R.-E. Fan, K.-W. Chang, C.-J. Hsieh, X.-R. Wang, and C.-J. Lin. Liblinear: A library for large linear classification. *The Journal of Machine Learning Research*, 2008.

[10] H. Grabner, F. Nater, M. Druey, and L. Van Gool. Visual interestingness in image sequences. In *ACM Multimedia*, 2013.

[11] T. Graepel, T. Minka, and R. T. Herbrich. A bayesian skill rating system. *Neural Information Processing Systems*, 2007.

[12] J. Hays and A. A. Efros. Im2gps: estimating geographic information from a single image. In *Computer Vision and Pattern Recognition*, 2008.

[13] R. Herbrich, T. Graepel, and K. Obermayer. Large margin rank boundaries for ordinal regression. *Advances in Large Margin Classifiers*, pages 115–132, 2000.

[14] J. Jacobs. *The death and the life of great american cities.* Random House, 1961.

[15] Y. Jia. Caffe: An open source convolutional architecture for fast feature embedding. *http://caffe.berkeleyvision.org*, 2013.

[16] R. Karp. Reducibility among combinatorial problems. In *Complexity of Computer Computations*, The IBM Research Symposia Series, pages 85–103. 1972.

[17] G. Kelling and C. Coles. *Fixing broken windows: Restoring order and reducing crime in our community.* Free Press, 1998.

[18] A. Khosla, B. An, J. J. Lim, and A. Torralba. Looking beyond the visible scene. In *Computer Vision and Pattern Recognition*, 2014.

[19] P. Koniusz, F. Yan, and K. Mikolajczyk. Comparison of mid-level feature coding approaches and pooling strategies in visual concept detection. *Computer Vision and Image Understanding*, 117(5):479–492, 2013.

[20] A. Krizhevsky, I. Sutskever, and G. E. Hinton. Imagenet classification with deep convolutional neural networks. In *Neural Information Processing Systems*, 2012.

[21] S. Lazebnik, C. Schmid, and J. Ponce. Beyond bags of features: Spatial pyramid matching for recognizing natural scene categories. In *Computer Vision and Pattern Recognition*, 2006.

[22] P. Lindal and T. Hartig. Architectural variation, building height, and the restorative quality of urban residential streetscapes. *Journal of Environmental Psychology*, 2012.

[23] K. Lynch. *The image of the city*, volume 11. MIT press, 1960.

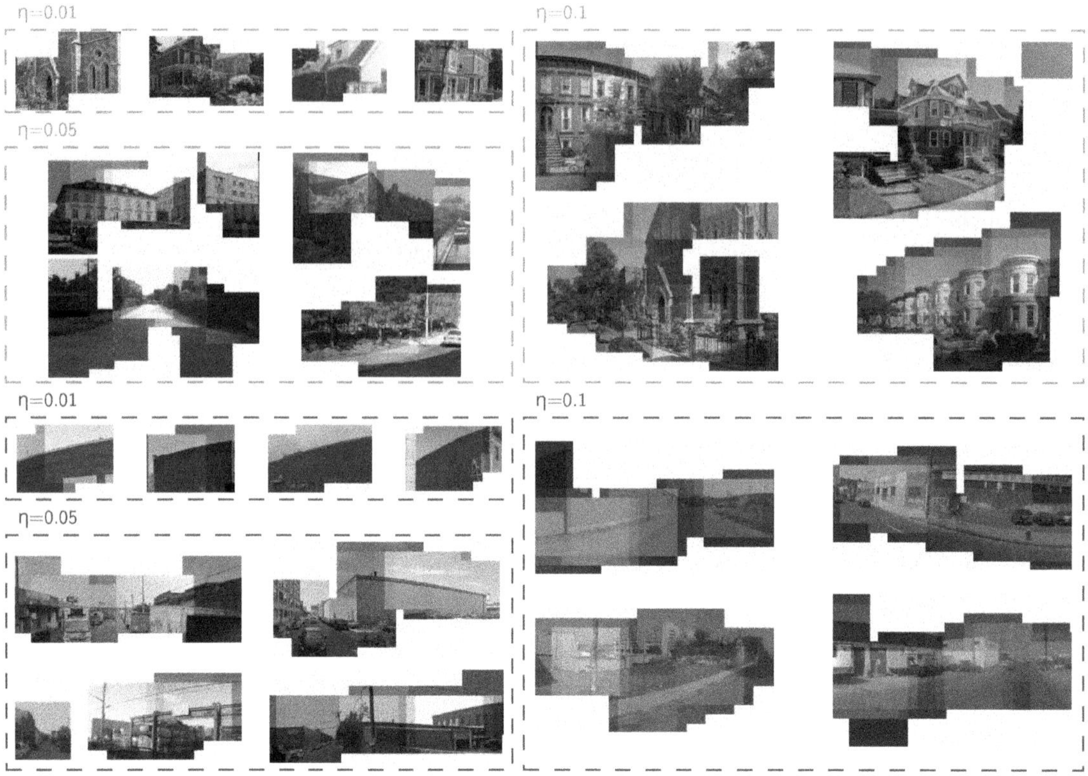

Figure 9: Visualization of the responses of latent detectors associated to safe (green boxes) and unsafe areas (red boxes) from our rCNN$_2$[m $= 24, \eta_A$] network. For each image we show the regions that concur to a detector's output after the pooling function with the shown η value is applied.

[24] L. Marchesotti, F. Perronnin, D. Larlus, and G. Csurka. Assessing the aesthetic quality of photographs using generic image descriptors. In *International Conference on Computer Vision*, 2011.

[25] N. Naik, J. Philipoom, R. Raskar, and C. Hidalgo. Streetscore–predicting the perceived safety of one million streetscapes. In *Computer Vision and Pattern Recognition Workshops*, 2014.

[26] J. Nasar. *The evaluative image of the city.* Sage Publications, 1997.

[27] V. Ordonez and T. L. Berg. Learning high-level judgments of urban perception. In *European Conference on Computer Vision.* 2014.

[28] G. Patterson, C. Xu, H. Su, and J. Hays. The sun attribute database: Beyond categories for deeper scene understanding. *International Journal of Computer Vision*, 108(1-2):59–81, 2014.

[29] L. Porzi, S. R. Buló, P. Valigi, O. Lanz, and E. Ricci. Learning contours for automatic annotations of mountains pictures on a smartphone. In *International Conference on Distributed Smart Cameras*, 2014.

[30] L. Porzi, E. Ricci, T. Ciarfuglia, and M. Zanin. Visual-inertial tracking on android for augmented reality applications. In *IEEE Workshop on Environmental, Energy and Structural Monitoring Systems*, 2012.

[31] D. Quercia, N. K. O'Hare, and H. Cramer. Aesthetic capital: what makes london look beautiful, quiet, and happy? In *ACM Computer supported cooperative work & social computing*, pages 945–955, 2014.

[32] P. Salesses, K. Schechtner, and C. A. Hidalgo. The collaborative image of the city: mapping the inequality of urban perception. *PloS one*, 8(7):e68400, 2013.

[33] R. J. Sampson, J. Morenoff, and T. Gannon-Rowley. Assessing 'neighborhood effects': Social processs and new directions in research. *Annual Review of Sociology*, 2002.

[34] R. J. Sampson and S. W. Raudenbush. Systematic social observation of public spaces: A new look at disorder in urban neighborhoods. *American Journal of Sociology*, 105(3):603–651, 1999.

[35] H. Schroeder and L. Anderson. Perception of personal safety in urban recreation sites. *Journal of Leisure Research*, 16:177–194, 1983.

[36] W. Skogan. *Disorder and decline: Crime and the spiral of decay in American neighborhoods.* University of California Press, 1990.

[37] R. Urlich. Visual landscapes and psychological well-being. *Landscape Research*, 4:17–23.

[38] R. Weber, J. Schnier, and T. Jacobsen. Aesthetics of streetscapes: Influence of fundamental properties on aesthetic judgments of urban space. *Perceptual and Motor Skills*, 106:128–146, 2008.

[39] J. Xiao, J. Hays, K. A. Ehinger, A. Oliva, and A. Torralba. Sun database: Large-scale scene recognition from abbey to zoo. In *Computer Vision and Pattern Recognition*, 2010.

[40] B. Zhou, A. Lapedriza, J. Xiao, A. Torralba, and A. Oliva. Learning deep features for scene recognition using places database. In *Neural Information Processing Systems*, 2014.

A Multimodal Predictive Model of Successful Debaters or How I Learned to Sway Votes

Maarten Brilman
University of Twente
Drienerlolaan 5, 7522 NB
Enschede, The Netherlands
m.f.brilman@alumnus.utwente.nl

Stefan Scherer
USC Institute for Creative Technologies
12015 Waterfront Drive
Playa Vista, CA 90094, United States
scherer@ict.usc.edu

ABSTRACT

Interpersonal skills such as public speaking are essential assets for a large variety of professions and in everyday life. The ability to communicate in social environments often greatly influences a person's career development, can help resolve conflict, gain the upper hand in negotiations, or sway the public opinion. We focus our investigations on a special form of public speaking, namely public debates of socioeconomic issues that affect us all. In particular, we analyze performances of expert debaters recorded through the Intelligence Squared U.S. (IQ2US) organization. IQ2US collects high-quality audiovisual recordings of these debates and publishes them online free of charge. We extract audiovisual nonverbal behavior descriptors, including facial expressions, voice quality characteristics, and surface level linguistic characteristics. Within our experiments we investigate if it is possible to automatically predict if a debater or his/her team are going to sway the most votes after the debate using multimodal machine learning and fusion approaches. We identify unimodal nonverbal behaviors that characterize successful debaters and our investigations reveal that multimodal machine learning approaches can reliably predict which individual (~75% accuracy) or team (85% accuracy) is going to win the most votes in the debate. We created a database consisting of over 30 debates with four speakers per debate suitable for public speaking skill analysis and plan to make this database publicly available for the research community.

Categories and Subject Descriptors

H.4 [**Information Systems Applications**]: Miscellaneous; J.4 [**Social and Behavioral Sciences**]

General Terms

Experimentation; Human Factors

MM'15, October 26–30, 2015, Brisbane, Australia.

ACM 978-1-4503-3459-4/15/10 ...$15.00.
DOI: http://dx.doi.org/10.1145/2733373.2806245.

Keywords

Machine Learning; Multimodal; Public Speaking; Nonverbal Behavior; Information Fusion

1. INTRODUCTION

The art of public speaking was practiced long before the Greeks wrote about it in their treatises more than 2500 years ago. For the Greek, it was a way of life, a way of being. The ancient Greeks were the first to systematize the art of public speaking, which they called *rhetoric*; the art of discourse. This art aimed to improve the capability of writers, lawyers, or politicians to inform, persuade, or motivate their audiences. An attest to the timeless role of public speaking in our culture are statistics accrued by online platforms such as Youtube[1], TED[2], or Intelligence Squared U.S.[3] providing access to historic and contemporary public speeches, debates, and arguments. In fact, public speeches to this day are an integral part of our lives and the ability to communicate in social environments often greatly influences a person's career development, can help build relationships, resolve conflict, gain the upper hand in negotiations, or sway the public opinion.

Proficient public speaking requires a different method of delivery than informal everyday conversations. While decisive arguments and a well-structured train of thought are important for a good public speaking performance, nonverbal behavior are just as, if not more, important for a speaker's success [27]. Relevant nonverbal behaviors include facial expressions, eye contact, posture, and gestures, as well as acoustic characteristics of the voice and speech, known as paralinguistic characteristics. These consist of voice quality, i.e. the coloring or timbre of the voice, as well as prosodic features, comprising pitch, rhythm, and intonation. An important aspect that is closely related to these behaviors is the display of emotion and affect. The importance of nonverbal behavior was shown in many domains that require proficiency in interpersonal skills, including healthcare, education, and negotiations where nonverbal communication was shown to be predictive of patient and user satisfaction [9], negotiation performance [29, 37] and proficiency in public speaking [38, 36, 35, 4, 7].

Within this work, we focus our investigations on a special form of public speaking, namely public debates of socioeconomic issues that affect us all. In particular, we analyze

[1] `http://youtube.com`
[2] `http://ted.com/talks`
[3] `http://intelligencesquaredus.org/`

performances of expert debaters recorded through the Intelligence Squared U.S. (IQ2US) organization. IQ2US invites subject matter experts on a regular basis to discuss issues of global and national impact in the Oxford style debate format, consisting of opening and closing statements, as well as a question and answer section. IQ2US collects high-quality audiovisual recordings of these debates and publishes them free of charge online. We mined this publicly available dataset and prepared it for automatic analysis. We extract audiovisual nonverbal behavior descriptors, including facial expressions, voice quality characteristics and a surface level linguistic analysis of sentiment and choice of words [40]. Within our experiments we investigate if it is possible to automatically predict if a debater or his/her team are going to sway the most votes after the debate - the Oxford style debating win condition - using automatic behavior analysis as well as multimodal machine learning and fusion approaches. Specifically, we identified three main research questions that we address within this work:

Q1: What nonverbal behaviors are indicative of successful debate performances and can we automatically and reliably extract such behaviors?

Q2: Which modality (audio, visual or the surface level linguistic analysis) is most indicative of successful debate performances and performs best in subject independent classification experiments?

Q3: Is it possible to reliably predict which individual is part of or what team is going to win the debate, i.e. sway the most votes, using multimodal information fusion?

The remainder of the paper is organized as follows. In Section 2 we provide an overview of related work. In Section 3 we go into detail on the creation of the dataset. In Section 4 we provide information about the feature extraction methods. In Section 5 we give a statistical evaluation of the features. In the following section (Section 6) we discuss our machine learning method. And in the remaining sections we provide the discussion and a conclusion.

2. RELATED WORK

Public speaking anxiety has received a lot of attention [32], but rather little work has been done on automatic assessment of public speaking skills. And to the best of our knowledge there is no work out there that attempts to automatically predict outcomes of debates similar to ours based on audiovisual nonverbal behavior descriptors, surface level linguistic analysis, and multimodal machine learning approaches. In the following, we summarize some of the related work found on automatic public speaking performance assessment and characterization.

Strangert and Gustafson [38] found in their study that the subjectively highest rated Swedish parliamentarians had a greater mean, standard deviation (SD) and range of the fundamental frequency (f_0) than the lower rated ones. This work is backed up by Hirschberg and Rosenberg [19], who observed a positive correlation between a greater mean and standard deviation of f_0 and charisma ratings for American politicians. Hincks [18] found that a greater f_0 standard deviation characterized speaker liveliness in her thesis studying computer aided pronunciation training.

Pfister and Robinson [31] developed a system that could classify between nine affective states. The same system was also used to detect six speech qualities in public speaking.

Scherer et al. [35] used the acoustic feature set in [38] along with measures of pause timings (i.e. average pause) and voice quality parameters. They identified that more tense voices are correlated with more persuasive and better political speeches overall. They furthermore analyzed motion energy on a global scale and found that it was positively correlated with the speaker's rating.

Weninger et al. [45] addressed the automatic assignment of 14 affective ratings to lectures from the TED talks website based on the relation between linguistic features and the ratings given by the audience on the website. They also performed a study to automatically determine different dimensions of leadership on a manually annotated YouTube corpus utilizing linguistic and acoustic features [44].

Chen et al. [7] used features for speech delivery, speech content (using transcripts) and non-verbal behavior to predict human holistic scores. They selected a subset of their features based on the Pearson correlation with the human rating scores on the entire data set.

Apart from trying to correlate subjective ratings with automatically extracted parameters, there has also been some effort put into creating systems that can automatically assess the speaker's skill and provide feedback. The results from our research can potentially be used to improve these type of systems.

In [24] a presentation coaching system was developed that detects the duration of utterances, the pitch (f_0) and the filled pauses. It furthermore uses a speech recognition engine to detect the speech rate. Face position and face orientation is tracked with the help of a marker. Both online and offline feedback is given to the user.

Cicero [4] is a platform that aims to train public speaking skills by providing automated feedback while speaking to a virtual audience. The system measures various vocal features such as pitch variety, volume and voice breathiness. It also tracks global arm and leg movement as well as gaze.

MACH (My Automated Conversation coacH) [20] is a system designed for social skill training. In particular the system was built for job interview training. It automatically reads facial expressions, speech, and prosody and responds via a virtual agent in real time. The researchers further developed their algorithms and developed an application using Google Glass to give online feedback to the user during a presentation based on their volume and speaking rate [39].

3. DATASET COLLECTION

We collected 36 debates published by the Intelligence Squared U.S. (IQ2US) organization from 2011 to 2014. We gathered video footage with audio of the debates, as well as manual transcripts provided by IQ2US. Voting results of each debate were also collected as well as the gender of the speakers. Debates were chosen solely on video quality, proper camera angles and audio quality. Twenty-three of the videos have a resolution of 720p (1280 by 720 pixels) and the remaining thirteen are 360p (640 by 360 pixels). All videos were extracted from the IntelligenceSquared Debates YouTube page[4]. Example motions include "Break up big banks" and "Genetically modify food". A full list of the debates is provided online[5].

[4]https://www.youtube.com/user/IntelligenceSquared

[5]http://tinyurl.com/noof6vr

3.1 Debate Structure

Debates are held in Oxford-style, a style derived from the Oxford Union society. In our case two teams of two are arguing the motion; two debating for and two against the motion. Both teams consist of professionals that have a significant amount of experience with public speaking and are leading experts in the field of the debated motion.

A strict structure is followed for these debates (Figure 2). Prior to any debate, the audience members cast their vote (for, against, or undecided) on the motion, which is shortly introduced by the organizer of the debate. Then each panelist takes turns in giving an uninterrupted opening statement. After the opening statements a question round takes place where the moderator presents the panelists with questions from both himself and the audience. In the final round each presenter gives a short closing statement. Finally the audience cast their post-debate vote. The winner is declared by looking at which team swayed the most audience members, based on the difference between the voting percentages before and after the debate. Speakers have a maximum of seven minutes for their opening statements and two minutes for their closing statement. For a few debates the maximum duration of the opening speech is six minutes. The question round varies in duration, but lasts around 45 minutes on average. Opening speeches were held standing up behind a lectern, while closing speeches were held sitting down behind a table (see Figure 1). The team debating for the motion always debated on the left for the audience and the other team on the right. The debates were held in large venues. Most debates took place in either the Merkin Concert Hall or Miller Theatre in New York, who seat 449 and 688 people respectively.

Figure 1: a) An overview of the stage. b) A typical frontal camera angle for the opening speech. c) A typical frontal camera angle for the closing speech. d) Example voting results.

3.2 Preprocessing

We decided not to include the question round in our work. During this question round speakers quickly change and interruptions take place. Given that this question round lasts a long time this would result in many short fragmented segments per speaker. However, we acknowledge it might be important to the outcome of the debates and plan to incorporate this round in our future investigations.

The opening and closing speech time frames have been annotated in ELAN [46][6] for all debates. These speeches have also been annotated on whether or not the camera had a frontal view of the speaker. Then, utilizing the slice functionality present in the SALEM toolbox [15], we extracted the time frames from the ELAN annotations to Matlab. As a next step we used the Matlab FFmpeg toolbox[7] to extract all the segments. The eight statement videos per debates where converted to 16 kHz mono wav audio files using FFmpeg[8]. From the transcripts we copied each statement to an individual text file. These transcriptions are clean versions, meaning that for example hesitations are not included. Transcripts are not time aligned with the audio files. The resulting files include for each speaker:

- Audio segments for the closing and opening statements.
- Full transcript for the closing and opening statements.
- All video segments with frontal data for the closing and opening statements.

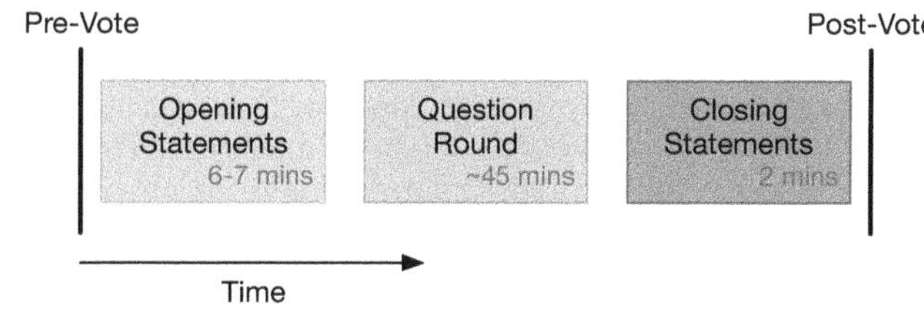

Figure 2: Oxford style debating overview figure. Prior to the start of the debate the audience votes on the motion. This motion is followed by opening statements by each speaker in turn. The opening statements are followed by a question round and the debate is closed by individual closing statements. After these statements a second vote is conducted. The team that swayed the most votes in their favor wins the debate.

3.3 Final Dataset

For our study we excluded six debates with the lowest voting difference (ranging from six to two) as these debates are close to being ties, i.e. it is unclear who the winner would be. This left thirty debates with a mean voting difference of 21.77 (SD=14.44) with a minimum difference of eight percentage points. We included all 120 speakers (19 female, 101 male) in our dataset from these debates, originating from various ethnicities and nationalities.

Ten females debated for a motion and nine against. A different group of ten females won the debate while nine lost. Furthermore the teams proposing the motion won fifteen times in total; the same amount as the teams opposing the motion. Four males partook in two debates, each time with a different partner. Two of these persons won both debates, one lost both and one won once and lost the other.

4. FEATURE EXTRACTION

4.1 Audio Features

Using COVAREP(v1.3.2), a freely available open source Matlab and Octave toolbox for speech analyses, we extracted several audio feature [8][9]. A large number of voice feature

[6] `http://tla.mpi.nl/tools/tla-tools/elan`

[7] `http://www.mathworks.com/matlabcentral/fileexchange/42296-ffmpeg-toolbox`

[8] `https://www.ffmpeg.org`

[9] `http://covarep.github.io/covarep/`

extraction methods have been implemented in this toolbox based on notable papers. We extracted the pitch, first and second formant as well as seven features that characterize voice qualities on a breathy to tense dimension. Breathy voice and tense voice are often considered to be on the opposite ends of the voice quality continuum [13].

- **Fundamental frequency (f_0)**: The fundamental frequency, or pitch, is tracked using the method suggested in [10] based on residual harmonics. This method simultaneously detects if a segment is voiced or unvoiced and is especially suitable for noisy conditions.
- **Formants (F_1 and F_2)**: [5] introduces the tracking of formants in detail. The first and second formants (F1 and F2) identify and characterize primarily vowels. These formants are the vocal tract frequencies that describe the first two spectral peaks with the lowest frequencies of the speech signal.
- **Normalized Amplitude Quotient (NAQ)**: The use of time-base parameters is one of the most common methods for glottal flow parameterization, which is used for voice quality estimation. Two commonly used parameters are the open quotient (OQ), the ratio between the open phase of the glottal pulse and the length of the fundamental period and the closing quotient (CQ), the ratio between the glottal closing phase and the length of this period.
  The NAQ [1] is a method to parametrize the glottal closing phase. It describes the ratio between the maximum of glottal flow and the minimum of its derivative, after being normalized by the fundamental frequency.
- **Quasi-Open Quotient (QOQ)**: The QOQ is related to the OQ and thus describes the relative open time of the glottis. It is measured by detecting the duration during which the glottal flow is 50% above the minimum flow. This is then normalized by the local glottal period [34].
- **H1-H2 ratio**: The H1-H2 parameter describes the amplitude of the fundamental frequency relative to that of the second harmonic. It is used as an indication of the open quotient [16].
- **Parabolic Spectral Parameter (PSP)**: The PSP is derived by fitting a parabolic function to the low-frequency part of the glottal flow spectrum. It provides a single value that describes how the spectral decay of an obtained glottal flow behaves with respect to a theoretical limit corresponding to maximal spectral decay [2].
- **Maxima Dispersion Quotient (MDQ)**: The MDQ is a parameter that quantifies the extent of the dispersion of the maxima derived from the wavelet decomposition of the glottal flow in the vicinity of the glottal closure instant (GCI) [22]. This dispersion is larger for a breathy voice than for a tense voice.
- **Peak Slope (PS)**: The PS involves decomposition of the speech signal into octave bands and then fitting a regression line to the maximum amplitudes at the different scales. The slope coefficient of this line is a measure for the voice breathiness [21].
- **Liljencrants-Fant model parameter Rd**: The final measure is one of the R-parameters of the Liljencrants-Fant model characterizing the glottal source [12]. The Rd captures most of the covariation of the LF model parameters. In [8] it was shown that the Rd confidence score also has discriminatory properties with respect to emotions and is therefore included in our work as a separate feature. We set the confidence threshold for the Rd parameter to 0.6. Rd values below this threshold are filtered out.

For all the above mentioned features we computed the mean and standard deviation over the entire opening or closing statement after removing the unvoiced data. Furthermore we computed the range of the f_0, F_1 and F_2 between the 25th and 75th percentile of these features. This gives a total of 25 audio features per segment.

4.2 Video Features

Paul Ekman showed in his studies that people can universally recognize the expressions of seven emotions. We extracted evidence for the presence of these seven basic emotions (joy, anger, surprise, fear, sadness, disgust and contempt) using Facet[10] from the frontal videos. Evidence for two more advanced emotions, confusion and frustration, was also extracted. Three overall sentiments were estimated as well; positive, neutral and negative. Due to the nature of the database baselining the application, feeding it neutral expressions per video, was not feasible. Therefore the results should be interpreted as facial expressions, rather than pure emotions. Nineteen features that describe elementary facial muscle actions, called action units (AU) in the Facial Action Coding System (FACS) [41], were computed as well. After combining the features from all the frontal video for each speaker we computed the mean and standard deviation over these features for a total of 46 features per statement.

Using Okao[11] we extracted nine more video features. These include horizontal and vertical face direction, face roll as well as horizontal and vertical gaze. The openness of the mouth and the level of smiling were also measured. We again computed the mean and standard deviation over these features. We ended up not using the mean of the horizontal gaze and face direction. This is due to the fact that those features are biased towards on which side of the stage the debater presented (see Figure 1a). This results in 16 remaining features.

4.3 Text Features

We applied a text analysis method called LIWC2007 [30] to extract features belonging to psychological and structural categories. LIWC is software that is developed to assess emotional, cognitive and structural text samples using a psychometrically validated internal dictionary [40, 42]. The software calculates the relative frequency to which a text sample belongs to a category. We used all 32 relevant categories, namely various pronouns, articles, as well as several psychological processes divided into social processes, affective processes, cognitive processes and perceptual processes[12] resulting in 32 features.

5. STATISTICAL EVALUATION

In order to investigate research question **Q1**, we conducted statistical analysis with the extracted audiovisual

[10]`http://www.emotient.com/products/emotient-analytics/`

[11]`http://www.omron.com/r_d/coretech/vision/okao.html`

[12]`http://www.liwc.net/descriptiontable1.php`

and surface level linguistic features. For each feature we computed a two tailed t-test as well as the effect size, using Hedges' g, over all segments. The g value denotes the estimated difference between the two population means in magnitudes of standard deviations [17]. Hedges' g is a commonly used standardized mean difference measure that can be transferred into other measures like Cohen's d [11]. In this section we summarize the features that differentiate the groups the most based on these tests. Due to the relatively small number of females we analyzed males and females together as one group, rendering the sample more heterogeneous. Given that the groups are balanced this shouldn't affect the results.

Table 1 summarizes the result of this statistical evaluation with respect to winning vs. losing debate performance characteristics and lists observed mean values, standard deviations, and effect sizes. Below we report major findings with respect to each modality separately.

Audio: The audio feature that distinguishes the winners and the losers the most is the pitch (f_0) range ($p<0.01$) and f_0 standard deviation ($p<0.01$). Furthermore the frequency of the second formant (F2) is higher for winners ($p<0.05$). The voice quality parameter that showed the biggest difference between the two groups is the QOQ with a near significant p-value of 0.0638. Given that winning speakers have an overall lower value than losing speakers, this indicates that voices of losers are more breathy. We also notice a larger standard deviation for H1-H2 and MDQ ($p<0.05$) for winners and a higher standard deviation of the confidence level for the Rd parameter ($p<0.05$) for losers.

Video: We found that the winning teams express less joy than the losing teams ($p<0.01$) this goes together with showing less overall positive expressions ($p<0.05$). Winners also show a larger standard deviation of evidence for disgust ($p<0.05$). Evidence for two action units, 18 and 20, showed significant differences between the two groups. Action unit 18 (*lip puckerer*) was detected more in the winning group, while action unit 20 (*lip stretcher*) was detected more in the losing group[13]. Action unit 20 its standard deviation also differs greatly between the two groups ($p<0.01$), being higher for the winners.

Utilizing Okao software we find that the standard deviation for the horizontal face movement is larger for the winners ($p<0.05$), while the deviation for the horizontal gaze movement is lower ($p<0.05$).

Text: Winners use more personal pronouns (e.g. *we* or *you*) than losers ($p<0.05$). Furthermore they use more words belonging to the discrepancy category such as *would*, *could* and *should* ($p<0.05$). Losers include more words from the perceptual category ($p<0.01$) and in particular related to the hearing (i.e. *listen*, *hearing*, $p<0.05$) category. Finally winners use somewhat more language involving social subjects ($p = 0.0742$) using words such as *mate*, *child*, and *story*.

When we compare the opening and the closing statements to each other we found a large number of differences between the two, which was expected due to their different nature (i.e. seated vs. standing, 2 mins vs. 6-7 mins, etc.). We opted to not include the results for this comparison within this work, as this is outside the scope of this paper. We, however, provide the results of the statistical tests between winners and losers on only the opening and closing speeches separately in Table 1. The observed values for both opening and closing statements separately indicate similar trends as shown with the Hedges' g values. In particular, positive g values represent a higher observation for the respective feature for the winners and lower values for losing debaters, vice versa for negative g values respectively.

[13]Examples of action units are found here: `http://www.cs.cmu.edu/~face/facs.htm`

6. EXPERIMENTS

In order to investigate research questions **Q2** and **Q3** we conduct speaker and debate team independent unimodal (**Q2**) and multimodal (**Q3**) machine learning experiments.

6.1 Method

Using all the features described in Section 4, we built a classifier to automatically determine the winning team of a debate. Given the large differences between the opening speech and closing speech features we decided to keep them separate in our work. Making use of the LIBSVM [6][14] package we trained eight separate support vector machine classifiers using second order polynomial kernels after testing Gaussian, linear, and several polynomial kernels.

We perform leave-one-debate-out testing where one debate with four speakers is kept for testing and the remaining 29 debates are used for training and validation. We conduct this validation approach in order to investigate the automatic classifier performance independent of the debate topic, debate teams, as well as individual debaters. All training data is scaled using min-max normalization. This same normalization is then applied to the test data.

In order to find the optimal regularization parameter (C-parameter) we perform 5-fold cross validation on the training set automatically searching in a range from 2^{-5} to 2^{20} with a step size of $2^{0.5}$. The C-value resulting in the highest performance is then chosen. This process is repeated 30 times, once for each debate excluded from the training set. We then take the median value of these 30 C-parameters as our one optimal C-parameter to train the classifier with. This final step essentially takes out outlying C-parameters that might have been the result of a random optimal 5 fold split, but aren't necessarily representative for the entire data set. This last step provides us with a more robust C-values for all cases.

Individual Debaters: In the next step eight models - one for each modality or data source and for opening and closing statements separately (see Figure 3) - are trained based on the leave-one-debate-out validation, i.e. each time with leaving out a different debate for classification. This provides us with eight labels per person that can then be used for decision fusion utilizing majority voting on an individual debater level. Given that we have an even number of inputs for the decision fusion classifier a tie might occur. In case a tie happens we take the best scoring initial classifier as having the final decision. This decision fusion step provides us with one label per person.

Debate Teams: For each debate, we then fuse the individual debater labels once more to come to a final conclusion on which team won the debate. As we have four speakers per debate a tie can also occur here. Such a tie occurs when all four persons in the debate are classified as either being winners, being losers, or if one person in each time is being

[14]`http://www.csie.ntu.edu.tw/~cjlin/libsvm`

Table 1: **Winning speakers versus losing speakers. Significance is denoted with * ($p < .05$) and ** ($p < .01$). The last two columns indicate the values when only including the opening or closing speeches.**

Feature	Winner mean (SD)	Loser mean (SD)	Hedges' g	Hedges' g Opening	Hedges' g Closing
Audio Features					
f_0 Range	41.88 (15.10)	35.80 (13.71)	0.4203**	0.3893*	0.4696*
f_0 SD	32.45 (9.74)	29.02 (9.57)	0.3540**	0.2871	0.4374*
Rd Confidence SD	0.0595 (0.010)	0.0626 (0.009)	-0.3285*	-0.2606	-0.3879*
MDQ SD	0.0091 (0.0022)	0.0085 (0.0016)	0.3214*	0.2740	0.3641*
H1-H2 SD	2.786 (0.661)	2.620 (0.526)	0.2776*	0.2438	0.3121
Mean F2	1540.60 (61.60)	1523.16 (60.81)	0.2841*	0.3735*	0.2141
Mean QOQ	0.505 (0.062)	0.519 (0.058)	-0.2396	-0.2516	-0.2281
Video Features					
AU20 Evidence SD	0.455 (0.105)	0.415 (0.084)	0.4161**	0.4807**	0.3482
Mean AU20 Evidence	-0.1520 (0.311)	-0.030 (0.358)	-0.3628**	-0.4701*	-0.2683
Mean AU18 Evidence	-0.817 (0.684)	-1.045 (0.626)	0.3491**	0.4124*	0.3072
Mean Joy Evidence	-1.587 (0.720)	-1.333 (0.745)	-0.3460**	-0.4721*	-0.2388
Disgust Evidence SD	0.530 (0.168)	0.480 (0.142)	0.3244*	0.2987	0.3841*
Mean Positive Evidence	-0.177 (0.583)	0.018 (0.635)	-0.3191*	-0.4165*	-0.2326
Horizontal Face Direction SD	10.585 (3.055)	9.703 (3.458)	0.2695*	0.2539	0.3023
Horizontal Gaze Direction SD	17.990 (7.085)	20.423 (10.800)	-0.2655*	-0.3066	-0.2236
Text Features					
Perceptual Processes	1.273 (0.710)	1.596 (1.036)	-0.3628**	-0.2785	-0.4296*
Hear Category	0.550 (0.484)	0.732 (0.688)	-0.3055*	-0.2985	-0.3106
Discrepancy Category	2.006 (1.031)	1.751 (0.926)	0.2597*	0.2791	0.2636
Personal Pronouns	7.900 (2.810)	7.292 (2.276)	0.2551*	-0.0272	0.5325**
Social Category	10.318 (2.810)	9.693 (2.600)	0.2300	0.0944	0.3767*

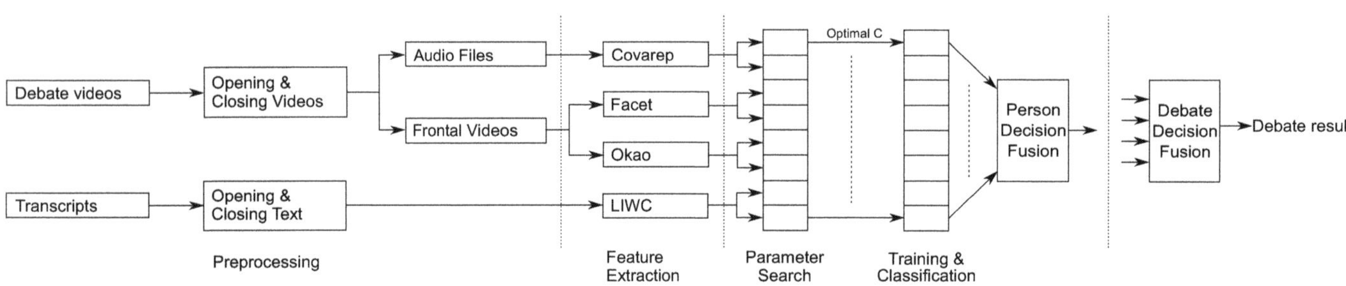

Figure 3: An overview of the entire system from preprocessing (Section 3), feature extraction (Section 4) to classification (Section 6). Opening and closing statements are individually processed, resulting in a total of eight initial classifiers.

classified as a winner. We do not further try to solve for these ties, but rather interpret them as being 50% correct as there are only two possible outcomes for each debate[15]. Alternatively, these ties could also be interpreted as reject cases, when no conclusive decision can be found by the classifier.

6.2 Results

The results of each unimodal classifier are presented in Table 2. The first column of numbers indicate the percentage of persons that were correctly classified by each individual support vector machine. The second column indicate the results from each individual classifier on a debate level. Overall, the support vector machine utilizing the acoustic domain features extracted using Covarep outperforms the other individual modalities for both the opening and closing statements (opening: 67.5% accuracy; closing: 65.0% accuracy). This result is considerably above chance level which is due to the setup of the dataset at 50% for all levels of investigation. We see that although a classifier might score the same as another on an individual level, it could score different on the debate level. This is due to the way the correctly classified persons are distributed over all the debates.

As a next step we combine multiple modalities to one label per person as discussed in the previous section. The number of correctly classified individuals for the different combinations is provided in Table 3. Both the fusion of audio and video as well as all three available modalities perform the best with 75.8% accuracy in both cases.

Table 3 further provides prediction accuracy on which team won the debate when fusing multimodal individual labels again. The debate team classification can either be correct, incorrect, or a tie might occur. In this case, the multimodal fusion over all modalities performs the best with 85.0% accuracy.

[15]This assumption statistically should also hold as a classifier could randomly choose the winner among these reject cases and still be correct about 50% of the time.

In total 22 debates are correctly classified, the classification of seven debates results in a tie and only one debate is misclassified. Figure 4 summarizes and visualizes the results of the multimodal fusion for both the individual debaters and the debate teams.

Table 2: The accuracy for each of the eight initial classifiers. The numbers in the brackets indicate (correct-tie-false) on the debate level.

Feature Group	Individual	Debate
Video		
Okao Opening	58.33%	61.7% (12-13-5)
Okao Closing	58.33%	61.7% (13-11-6)
Facet Opening	58.33%	66.7% (14-12-4)
Facet Closing	58.33%	60.0% (12-12-6)
Audio		
Covarep Opening	**67.50%**	71.7% (18-7-5)
Covarep Closing	65.00%	**73.3%** (15-14-1)
Text		
LIWC Opening	55.00%	53.3% (11-10-9)
LIWC Closing	60.00%	70.0% (19-4-7)

Table 3: The accuracies for individual speaker decision fusion and full debate decision fusion. The numbers in the brackets indicate (correct-tie-false).

Modalities	Individual	Debate
Video + Text	60.0%	66.7% (14-12-4)
Audio + Text	72.5%	76.7% (20-6-4)
Audio + Video	**75.8%**	83.3% (22-6-2)
Audio + Video + Text	**75.8%**	**85.0%** (22-7-1)

7. DISCUSSION

In this section, we discuss our results with respect to the research questions previously introduced:

7.1 Q1 - Nonverbal Indicators

Our first research question aims at identifying behavior indicators from audio, video and the surface level linguistic analysis. Our statistical evaluations revealed several interesting findings that we discuss in the following.

Audio: Based on the acoustic analysis we found that increased fundamental frequency (f_0) both measured as range as well as standard deviation is indicative of a successful debate performance. Intuitively, both measures indicate that a speaker with an increased expressivity is more successful than a speaker that sounds more monotonous. In fact, expressive speakers have been found to be more engaging and better overall in related work [38, 19, 35]. In addition, we could identify that speakers with less breathy voice quality are more likely to be in a winning team. This finding is confirmed in prior work that investigated political speakers in the German parliament [35]. The researchers found that speakers with tenser voice qualities were rated better overall and more persuasive and less insecure than those with more breathy voice qualities. While we already found a good number of interesting features with respect to the acoustic characteristics of successful debate performances, we believe there is plenty of room for improvement. For example we have not at all investigated timing based features (e.g. pause timings) or intensity features within our

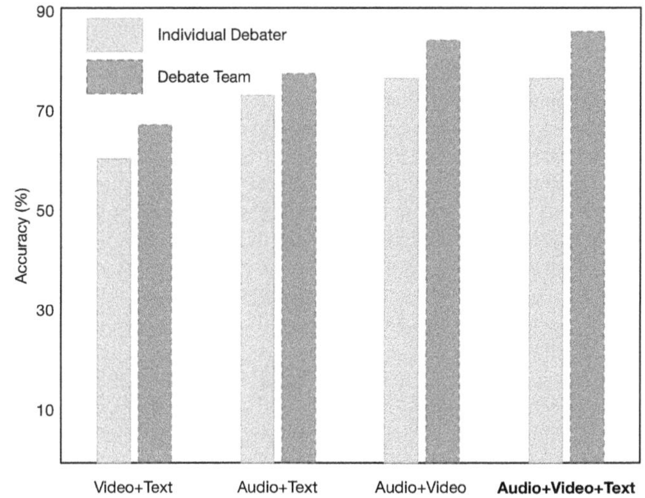

Figure 4: Results of the multimodal fusion in accuracy in % for both individual debaters as well as entire debate teams. Overall the multimodal fusion of all available modalities shows the most promising results and outperforms the other subsets of modalities.

work that have been found to be of relevance in the past [35]. We plan to incorporate such indicators in forthcoming investigations.

Video: With respect to video based behavioral descriptors we found that a decreased display of joy and less positive emotional displays overall are indicative of a successful debate performance. While this might sound counterintuitive, it is possible that a debater that performs more seriously during the opening and closing statements is regarded as more professional. A serious speaker might be regarded as having more powerful arguments than someone that appears to mask insecurity in his/her argument through the display of joy [3, 33].

We further found some interesting behavior indicators that are related to gaze patterns and debate performances. It appears that individuals that win their debates shift their entire face when addressing the audience during their opening and closing statements, while individuals on the losing teams shift their gaze more with their eye movement rather than gross head movements. This finding is in line with other work that has identified gestures and overall coarse body motion has a large impact on public speaking performances and their effect on audiences. Nguyen et al. [28] for example, state that emotion expression through body language is the most important cue to asses a speaker and built a system around this fact using the skeleton data from the Microsoft Kinect. Gross movement of the body was also identified to be related to proficient public speaking in political debates [23, 35]. In the future, we plan to incorporate behavioral features in our investigations as well. In particular, we aim to analyze gestures jointly with acoustic features. For example, visual beat gestures to emphasize a point should be temporally coordinated with acoustic emphasis in order to maximize the conveyed effect. We seek to identify behavioral factors that reveal synergies across modalities to explain qualitatively observed behavioral concepts, such as increased anxiety, reduced expressivity, or lack of competence.

Text: With our limited surface level linguistic analysis using the software LIWC [40], we could only identify a few indicators of successful performances. For example increased use of words such as *should*, *would* and *could* is associated with a higher chance of success in the debate. However, it is difficult to assess the relevance of such findings given the small statistical difference between winners and losers. Our future analysis will aim to unravel more complex features such as argument structure or thought processes. In particular, the identification of the use of metaphors, examples, arguments, or facts could be of use. We plan to investigate novel natural language processing algorithms that have been successfully employed in a wide range of applications, such as document vectorization approaches to identify such patterns in language [26, 25].

7.2 Q2 - Unimodal Debate Classification

Our second research question is aimed at finding out which modality (audio, visual, or surface linguistic features) is most indicative of successful debate performances based on classification experiments.

In order to do so we trained eight separate support vector machines (one for each data source). We trained the opening and closing statements separately as our analysis indicated that there were significant differences between the two.

Audio: We found that audio was the best modality at differentiating winning speakers from those that lose. With the audio features we achieved an accuracy for individual debaters of 65.0% for the closing statement and 67.5% for the opening statement respectively. This result shows an accuracy, which is considerably above chance level (50%). On a debate level, the accuracy increases slightly to above 70% accuracy for both opening and closing statements. The opening statements appear to yield slightly improved results for the individual debater classification; for debate level classification this trend is reversed.

Given the promising results from these audio features we plan to investigate them further using more advanced machine learning methods. We plan to investigate sequential learning techniques such as recurrent neural networks. In particular the recurrent neural network toolkit that supports processing on GPU's called CURRENNT, allowing for much faster processing times, is of interest to us [43]. Recurrent neural networks have shown promising results in the modeling of speech and human behavior in general [14].

Video: From the video modality we extract two separate groups of features. While both feature sets originate from the same modality, i.e. video, they are qualitatively quite different, as one focuses on emotions, while the other focuses on head and gaze movement (cf. Section 4).

Our two types of video features both achieve an accuracy of 58.33% over both the opening and closing statements for the individual debater classification. We attempted to fuse both feature sets early (i.e. combining the features before classification), this however led to a lower performance than the initial 58.33%. This might indicate that both feature sets are able to classify a different set of speakers correctly, which holds a lot of potential for multimodal fusion techniques and error correcting algorithms (cf. Research question **Q3**).

On a debate level the classification results improve slightly, with the best performance observed for the emotion relevant features (i.e. Facet features) in the opening statement. This can be interpreted in a way that emotional display is in particular important for the opening statements of the debate rather than the closing statements.

Text: Utilizing the surface level linguistic analysis provided by the software LIWC [40], we find that in particular closing statements appear to be important to distinguish winning from losing debaters as well as teams respectively. For the opening statements, we barely reach accuracies above chance level, which indicates that these surface features (i.e. broad word categories) are not specific enough or do not capture important aspects of the performances. In fact, the opening statements are about three times as long as the closing statements and hence comprise a lot more data, which intuitively should result in better classification results. This, however, is not the case. We believe that the classification approach utilizing the debate transcripts has the largest potential for improvement in the future.

7.3 Q3 - Multimodal Debate Classification

Our third research question aimed to answer the question if we could improve classification results by combining modalities. In order to do so we applied decision (or late) fusion on the eight initial classifiers to obtain one label for each individual speaker. We then fused these labels once more to obtain a result on a debate level.

We found that using all three modalities (audio, video, and text) showed the most promising results with an accuracy of 75.8% on individuals and 85.0% on debates. Using only video and audio information also resulted in an accuracy of 75.8% on individuals, but gave slightly worse results on debates (83.33%; cf. Table 3 and Figure 4). This indicates that the text features do not add a lot of information to the fusion. Now while it is certainly possible to extract different text features, as explained in the discussion for **Q1**, our results in fact also indicate that it is possible to reliably determine the winners of debates without having access to manual transcripts of the debates, but merely based on nonverbal behavior. However, as argued earlier we consider linguistic information, such as argument structure, a very important source of information to determine successful debaters. In the present work, we only utilize surface level linguistic features.

The multimodal fusion further underlines the discussed importance of audio features in our investigations (cf. Discussion for question **Q2**), as the accuracy drops to only 60.0% on individuals and 66.7% on debates when using only surface linguistic and visual features. This is below that of using an unimodal approach based on the audio features.

When investigating the debates that led to wrong or undecided results we find the following: For the debates that aren't correctly classified we find that their average voting difference in percent of votes (mean 14.25) is well below that of the overall database (mean 21.77). With the one debate that is being misclassified, "Break up big banks", having the lowest voting difference in the dataset being eight percentage points. For the seven debates that are being classified as ties or undecided we found that one has a difference of 9 percentage points and three of them a difference of 10. This in fact indicates that in particular the close debates are difficult to classify. This can be explained intuitively as the speakers' performances in these debates in fact might be quite similar and on par across teams. Therefore the difficulty of the classification is increased. In addition, it might be argued that in the closer debates one speaker is carrying their team, while his/her partner might be considered a poorer speaker and does not add to the team. As the debates are evaluated in teams both speakers are always given the same label. We plan to investigate individual speaker performances using post-hoc annotations per speaker at a later stage.

8. CONCLUSION

In this paper we investigated public speaking in the context of team based debates on a large variety of socioeconomic issues. The debates follow the standard Oxford style debating model in which the winner is decided by the percentage amount of swayed votes between a pre-debate and a post-debate vote. This paper aims to provide four additions to the state of the art on public speaking research: (1) we conduct a thorough analysis of nonverbal behavioral indicators of successful debate performances. Our findings confirm those of related work and extend the pool of features investigated considerably. (2) We identified that within our analysis the acoustic modality might have the strongest discriminative faculty and resulted in the highest observed accuracies for single modalities. We, however, acknowledge that there is considerable room for improvement in our work especially in the visual modality (e.g. behavioral information, gestures) and the linguistic analysis (e.g. argument structure, use of facts, blame, etc.). (3) A multimodal fusion approach was found to reliably predict winners of debates automatically both for individual debaters as well as debate teams with accuracies of around 75% for individuals and 85% for teams respectively. (4) In addition to the conducted investigations, we collected a novel multimodal database that we plan to make publicly available to help further research on public speaking assessment and evaluation. The database is based on a very active online platform named Intelligence Squared U.S. and the organization is publishing a novel debate online every few weeks, which renders the proposed database extensible and ever more challenging in the future.

Acknowledgements

We would like to thank Intelligence Squared U.S. for the immensely interesting debates and the excellent resource that they provide online. This material is based upon work supported by the National Science Foundation under Grants No. IIS-1421330 and U.S. Army Research Laboratory under contract number W911NF-14-D-0005. Any opinions, findings, and conclusions or recommendations expressed in this material are those of the author(s) and do not necessarily reflect the views of the National Science Foundation or the Government, and no official endorsement should be inferred.

9. REFERENCES

[1] P. Alku, T. Bäckström, and E. Vilkman. Normalized amplitude quotient for parametrization of the glottal flow. *the Journal of the Acoustical Society of America*, 112(2):701–710, 2002.

[2] P. Alku, H. Strik, and E. Vilkman. Parabolic spectral parameter–A new method for quantification of the glottal flow. *Speech Communication*, 22(1):67–79, 1997.

[3] J.-A. Bachorowski, M. J. Smoski, and M. J. Owren. The acoustic features of human laughter. *Journal of the Acoustical Society of America*, 110(3):1581–1597, 2001.

[4] L. Batrinca, G. Stratou, A. Shapiro, L.-P. Morency, and S. Scherer. Cicero - towards a multimodal virtual audience platform for public speaking training. In *Proceedings of Intelligent Virtual Agents (IVA) 2013*, pages 116–128. Springer, 2013.

[5] B. Bozkurt, B. Doval, C. d'Alessandro, and T. Dutoit. Improved differential phase spectrum processing for formant tracking. pages 2421–2424, 2004.

[6] C.-C. Chang and C.-J. Lin. LIBSVM: A library for support vector machines. *ACM Transactions on Intelligent Systems and Technology*, 2:27:1–27:27, 2011.

[7] L. Chen, G. Feng, J. Joe, C. W. Leong, C. Kitchen, and C. M. Lee. Towards automated assessment of public speaking skills using multimodal cues. In *Proceedings of the 16th International Conference on Multimodal Interaction*, pages 200–203. ACM, 2014.

[8] G. Degottex, J. Kane, T. Drugman, T. Raitio, and S. Scherer. Covarep - a collaborative voice analysis repository for speech technologies. In *Proceedings of IEEE International Conference on Acoustics, Speech and Signal Processing (ICASSP 2014)*, pages 960–964, 2014.

[9] M. R. DiMatteo, R. D. Hays, and L. M. Prince. Relationship of physicians' nonverbal communication skill to patient satisfaction, appointment noncompliance, and physician workload. *Health Psychology*, 5(6):581, 1986.

[10] T. Drugman and A. Abeer. Joint robust voicing detection and pitch estimation based on residual harmonics. In *Proceedings of Interspeech 2011*, pages 1973–1976. ISCA, 2011.

[11] J. A. Durlak. How to select, calculate, and interpret effect sizes. *Journal of Pediatric Psychology*, 34(9):917–928, 2009.

[12] G. Fant, J. Liljencrants, and Q. Lin. A four parameter model of glottal flow. *KTH, Speech Transmission Laboratory, Quarterly Report*, 4:1–13, 1985.

[13] C. Gobl and A. N. Chasaide. Acoustic characteristics of voice quality. *Speech Communication*, 11(4):481–490, 1992.

[14] A. Graves. *Supervised sequence labelling with recurrent neural networks*, volume 385. Springer, 2012.

[15] M. Hanheide, M. Lohse, and A. Dierker. SALEM-statistical analysis of ELAN files in Matlab. *Multimodal Corpora: Advances in Capturing, Coding and Analyzing Multimodality*, pages 121–123, 2010.

[16] H. M. Hanson and E. S. Chuang. Glottal characteristics of male speakers: Acoustic correlates and comparison with female data. *The Journal of the Acoustical Society of America*, 106(2):1064–1077, 1999.

[17] L. V. Hedges. Distribution theory for glass's estimator of effect size and related estimators. *Journal of Educational Statistics*, 6(2):107–128, 1981.

[18] R. Hincks. *Computer support for learners of spoken English.* PhD thesis, Royal Institute of Technology, 2005.

[19] J. B. Hirschberg and A. Rosenberg. Acoustic/prosodic and lexical correlates of charismatic speech. In *Proceedings of Eurospeech 2005*, pages 513–516, 2005.

[20] M. E. Hoque, M. Courgeon, J.-C. Martin, B. Mutlu, and R. W. Picard. MACH: My automated conversation coach. In *Proceedings of the 2013 ACM international joint conference on Pervasive and ubiquitous computing*, pages 697–706. ACM, 2013.

[21] J. Kane and C. Gobl. Identifying regions of non-modal phonation using features of the wavelet transform. In *Proceedings of Interspeech 2011*, pages 177–180. ISCA, 2011.

[22] J. Kane and C. Gobl. Wavelet maxima dispersion for breathy to tense voice discrimination. *IEEE Transactions on Audio, Speech, and Language Processing*, 21(6):1170–1179, 2013.

[23] M. Koppensteiner and K. Grammer. Motion patterns in political speech and their influence on personality ratings. *Journal of Research in Personality*, 44(3):374–379, 2010.

[24] K. Kurihara, M. Goto, J. Ogata, Y. Matsusaka, and T. Igarashi. Presentation sensei: a presentation training system using speech and image processing. In *Proceedings of the 9th international conference on Multimodal interfaces*, pages 358–365. ACM, 2007.

[25] Q. Le and T. Mikolov. Distributed representations of sentences and documents. In *Proceedings of The 31st International Conference on Machine Learning*, pages 1188–1196, 2014.

[26] T. Mikolov, I. Sutskever, K. Chen, G. Corrado, and J. Dean. Distributed representations of words and phrases and their compositionality. In *Proceedings of NIPS*, 2013.

[27] A.-T. Nguyen, W. Chen, and M. Rauterberg. Feedback system for presenters detects nonverbal expressions. *SPIE Newsroom*, 2012.

[28] A.-T. Nguyen, W. Chen, and M. Rauterberg. Online feedback system for public speakers. In *IEEE Symp. e-Learning, e-Management and e-Services*, 2012.

[29] S. Park, P. Shoemark, and L.-P. Morency. Toward crowdsourcing micro-level behavior annotations: the challenges of interface, training, and generalization. In *Proceedings of the 18th International Conference on Intelligent User Interfaces (IUI '14)*, pages 37–46. ACM, 2014.

[30] J. W. Pennebaker, C. K. Chung, M. Ireland, A. Gonzales, and R. J. Booth. The development and psychometric properties of LIWC2007, 2007.

[31] T. Pfister and P. Robinson. Real-time recognition of affective states from nonverbal features of speech and its application for public speaking skill analysis. *IEEE Transactions on Affective Computing*, 2(2):66–78, 2011.

[32] C. B. Pull. Current status of knowledge on public-speaking anxiety. *Current opinion in psychiatry*, 25(1):32–38, 2012.

[33] S. Scherer, M. Glodek, F. Schwenker, N. Campbell, and G. Palm. Spotting laughter in natural multiparty conversations: a comparison of automatic online and offline approaches using audiovisual data. *ACM Transactions on Interactive Intelligent Systems: Special Issue on Affective Interaction in Natural Environments*, 2(1):4:1–4:31, 2012.

[34] S. Scherer, Z. Hammal, Y. Yang, L.-P. Morency, and J. F. Cohn. Dyadic behavior analysis in depression severity assessment interviews. In *Proceedings of the 16th International Conference on Multimodal Interaction*, pages 112–119. ACM, 2014.

[35] S. Scherer, G. Layher, J. Kane, H. Neumann, and N. Campbell. An audiovisual political speech analysis incorporating eye-tracking and perception data. In *Proceedings of the Eight International Conference on Language Resources and Evaluation (LREC'12)*, pages 1114–1120. ELRA, 2012.

[36] L. M. Schreiber, D. P. Gregory, and L. R. Shibley. The development and test of the public speaking competence rubric. *Communication Education*, 61(3):205–233, 2012.

[37] H. S. Shim, S. Park, M. Chatterjee, S. Scherer, K. Sagae, and L.-P. Morency. Acoustic and paraverbal indicators of persuasiveness in social multimedia. In *Proceedings of IEEE International Conference on Acoustics, Speech and Signal Processing*, 2015.

[38] E. Strangert and J. Gustafson. What makes a good speaker? Subject ratings, acoustic measurements and perceptual evaluations. In *Proceedings of Interspeech 2008*, pages 1688–1691. ISCA, 2008.

[39] M. I. Tanveer, E. Lin, and M. E. Hoque. Rhema: A real-time in-situ intelligent interface to help people with public speaking. In *Proceedings of the 20th International Conference on Intelligent User Interfaces*, pages 286–295. ACM, 2015.

[40] Y. R. Tausczik and J. W. Pennebaker. The psychological meaning of words: LIWC and computerized text analysis methods. *Journal of language and social psychology*, 29(1):24–54, 2010.

[41] Y.-l. Tian, T. Kanade, and J. F. Cohn. Recognizing action units for facial expression analysis. *IEEE Transactions on Pattern Analysis and Machine Intelligence*, 23(2):97–115, 2001.

[42] A. Tumasjan, T. O. Sprenger, P. G. Sandner, and I. M. Welpe. Predicting elections with twitter: What 140 characters reveal about political sentiment. In *International AAAI Conference on Weblogs and Social Media*, volume 10, pages 178–185, 2010.

[43] F. Weninger, J. Bergmann, and B. Schuller. Introducing CURRENNT–the Munich open-source CUDA RecurREnt Neural Network Toolkit. *Journal of Machine Learning Research*, 16:547–551, 2015.

[44] F. Weninger, J. Krajewski, A. Batliner, and B. Schuller. The voice of leadership: Models and performances of automatic analysis in online speeches. *IEEE Transactions on Affective Computing*, 3(4):496–508, 2012.

[45] F. Weninger, P. Staudt, and B. Schuller. Words that fascinate the listener: Predicting affective ratings of on-line lectures. *International Journal of Distance Education Technologies (IJDET)*, 11(2):110–123, 2013.

[46] P. Wittenburg, H. Brugman, A. Russel, A. Klassmann, and H. Sloetjes. ELAN: a professional framework for multimodality research. In *International Conference on Language Resources and Evaluation*, pages 1556–1559, 2006.

Visual Affect Around the World: A Large-scale Multilingual Visual Sentiment Ontology

Brendan Jou*
Columbia University
New York, NY USA
bjou@ee.columbia.edu

Tao Chen*
Columbia University
New York, NY USA
taochen@ee.columbia.edu

Nikolaos Pappas*
Idiap Research Institute/EPFL
Martigny, Switzerland
npappas@idiap.ch

Miriam Redi*
Yahoo Labs
London, UK
redi@yahoo-inc.com

Mercan Topkara*
JW Player
New York, NY USA
mercan@jwplayer.com

Shih-Fu Chang
Columbia University
New York, NY USA
sfchang@ee.columbia.edu

ABSTRACT

Every culture and language is unique. Our work expressly focuses on the uniqueness of culture and language in relation to human affect, specifically sentiment and emotion semantics, and how they manifest in social multimedia. We develop sets of sentiment- and emotion-polarized visual concepts by adapting semantic structures called adjective-noun pairs, originally introduced by Borth et al. [5], but in a multilingual context. We propose a new language-dependent method for automatic discovery of these adjective-noun constructs. We show how this pipeline can be applied on a social multimedia platform for the creation of a large-scale multilingual visual sentiment concept ontology (MVSO). Unlike the flat structure in [5], our unified ontology is organized hierarchically by multilingual clusters of visually detectable nouns and subclusters of emotionally biased versions of these nouns. In addition, we present an image-based prediction task to show how generalizable language-specific models are in a multilingual context. A new, publicly available dataset of >15.6K sentiment-biased visual concepts across 12 languages with language-specific detector banks, >7.36M images and their metadata is also released.

Categories and Subject Descriptors

H.5.4 [**Information Interfaces and Presentation**]: Hypertext/Hypermedia; I.2.10 [**Artificial Intelligence**]: Vision and Scene Understanding

Keywords

Multilingual; Language; Cultures; Cross-cultural; Emotion; Sentiment; Ontology; Concept Detection; Social Multimedia

*Denotes equal contribution.

MM'15, October 26–30, 2015, Brisbane, Australia.
© 2015 ACM. ISBN 978-1-4503-3459-4/15/10 ...$15.00.
DOI: http://dx.doi.org/10.1145/2733373.2806246.

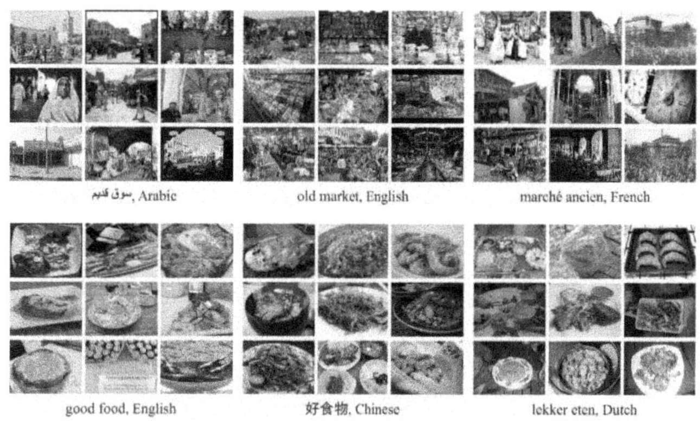

Figure 1: Example images from "around the world" organized by affective visual concepts. Top set shows images of *old market* concept from three different cultures/languages; and the bottom, images of *good food*. Even though conceptual reference is the same, each culture's sentimental expression of these concept may be adversely different.

1. INTRODUCTION

If you scoured the world and took several people at random from major countries and asked them to fill in the blank "_____ love" in their native tongue, how many unique adjectives would you expect to find? Would people from some cultures tend to fill it with *twisted*, while others *pure* or *unconditional* or *false*? All over the world, we daily express our thoughts and feelings in culturally isolated contexts; and when we travel abroad, we know that to cross a physical border also means to cross into the unique behaviors and interactions of that people group – its cultural border. How similar or different are our sentiments and feelings from this other culture? Or the thoughts and objects we tend to talk about most? Motivated by questions like this, our work explores the computational understanding of human affect along cultural lines, with focus on visual content. In particular, we seek to answer the following important questions: (1) how are images in various languages used to express affective visual concepts, e.g. *beautiful place* or *delicious food*? And (2) how are such affective visual concepts used to convey different emotions and sentiment across languages?

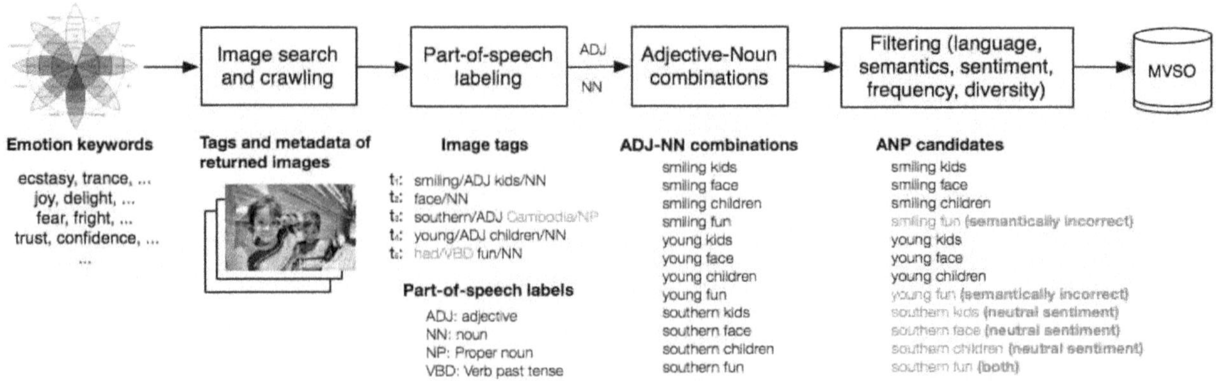

Figure 2: The construction process of our multilingual visual sentiment ontology (MVSO) begins with crawling images and metadata based on emotion keywords. Image tags ($t_1, \ldots, t_5$) are labeled with part-of-speech tags, and adjectives and nouns are used to form candidate adjective-noun pair (ANP) combinations [5], while others are ignored (in red). Finally, these candidate ANPs are filtered based on various criteria (Sec. 3.2) which help remove incorrect pairs (in red), forming a final MVSO with diversity and coverage.

In Psychology, there are two major schools-of-thought on the connection between cultural context and human affect, i.e. our experiential feelings via our sentiments and emotions. Some believe emotion to be culture-specific [29], that is, emotion is dependent on one's cultural context, while others believe emotion to be universal [16], that is, emotion and culture are independent mechanisms. For example, while this paper is written in English, there are emotion words/phrases in other languages for which there is no exact translation in English, e.g., *Schadenfreude* in German refers to the pleasure at someone else's expense. Do English-speakers not feel those same emotions or do they simply refer to them in a different way? Or even if the reference is the same, perhaps the underlying emotion is different?

In Affective Computing [33] and Multimedia, we often refer to the *affective gap* as the conceptual divide between the low-level visual stimuli, like images and features, and the high-level, abstracted semantics of human affect, e.g. *happy* or *sad*. In one attempt to bridge sentiment and visual media, Borth et al. [5] developed a *visual sentiment ontology* (VSO), a set of 1,200 mid-level concepts using structured semantics called adjective-noun pairs (ANPs). The noun portion of the ANP allows for computer vision detectability and the adjective serves to polarize the noun toward a positive or negative sentiment, or emotion, e.g. so instead of having visual concepts like *sky* or *dog*, we have *beautiful sky* or *scary dog*. Many works like this that have built algorithms, models and datasets on the assumption of the psychology theory that emotions are universal. However, while such works provide great research contributions in that native language, their applicability and generalization to other languages and cultures remains largely unexplored.

We present a large-scale multilingual visual sentiment ontology (MVSO) and dataset including adjective-noun pairs from 12 languages of diverse origins: Arabic, Chinese, Dutch, English, French, German, Italian, Persian, Polish, Russian, Spanish, and Turkish. We make the following contributions: **(1)** a principled, context-aware pipeline for designing a multilingual visual sentiment ontology, **(2)** a Multilingual Visual Sentiment Ontology mined from social multimedia data end-to-end, **(3)** a MVSO organized hierarchically into noun-based clusters and sentiment-biased adjective-noun pair sub-clusters, **(4)** a multilingual, sentiment-driven visual concept detector bank, and **(5)** the release of a dataset containing MVSO and large-scale image collection with benchmark cross-lingual sentiment prediction[1].

2. RELATED WORK

We address the general challenge of *affective image understanding*, aiming at both recognition and analysis of sentiment and emotions in visual data, but from a multilingual and cross-cultural perspective. Our work is closely related to Multimedia and Vision research that focus on visual aesthetics [22], interestingness [14], popularity [23], and creativity [35]. Our work also relates to research in Cognitive and Social Psychology, especially emotion and culture research [11, 30, 34], but also neuroaesthetics [41], visual preference [41, 44], and social interaction [28].

Progressive research in "visual affect" recognition was done in [42] and [27] where image features were designed based on art and psychology principles for emotion prediction. And such works were later improved in [18] by adding social media data in semi-supervised frameworks. From this research effort in visual affect understanding, several affective image datasets were released to the public. The International Affective Picture System (IAPS) dataset [25] is a seminal dataset of ~1,000 images, focused on induced emotions in humans for biometric measurement. The Geneva Affective PicturE Database (GAPED) [8] consists of 730 pictures meant to supplement IAPS and tries to narrow the themes across images. And recently, in [5], a *visual sentiment ontology* (VSO) and dataset was created from Flickr image data, resulting in a collection of adjective-noun pairs along with corresponding images, tags and sentiment. One major issue with these datasets and existing methods is that they do not consider the *context* in which emotions are felt and perceived. Instead, they assume that visual affect is universal, and do not account for the influence of culture or language. We explicitly tackle visual affect understanding from a multi-cultural, multilingual perspective. In addition, while existing works often use handpicked data, we gather our data "in the wild" on a popular, multilingual social multimedia platform.

[1] `mvso.cs.columbia.edu`

English	joy	trust	fear	surprise	sadness	disgust	anger	anticipation
Spanish	alegría	confianza	miedo	sorpresa	tristeza	asco	ira	previsión
Italian	gioia	fiducia	paura	sorpresa	tristezza	disgusto	rabbia	anticipazione
French	bonheur	confiance	peur	surprise	tristesse	dégoût	colère	prévision
German	Freude	Vertrauen	Angst	Überraschung	Traurigkeit	Empörung	Ärger	Vorfreude
Chinese	歡樂	信任	害怕	震驚	悲	討厭	憤怒	預期
Dutch	vreugde	vertrouwen	angst	verrassing	verdriet	walging	woede	anticipatie

Table 1: Most representative keywords according to native/proficient speakers for eight basic emotions and for 7 of our 12 languages, chosen and shown top-to-bottom in decreasing no. of discovered visual affect concepts, or adjective-noun pairs.

The study of emotions across language and culture has long been a topic of research in Psychology. A main contention in the area concerns whether emotions are culture-specific [29], i.e. their perception and elicitation varies with the context, or universal [16]. In [36], a survey of cross-cultural work on semantics surrounding emotion elicitation and perception is given, showing that there are still competing views as to whether emotion is pan-cultural, culture-specific, or some hybrid of both. Inspired by research in this domain, we are the first to investigate the relationship between visual affect and culture[2] from a multimedia-driven and computational perspective, as far as we know.

Other work in cross-lingual research comes from text sentiment analysis and music information retrieval. In [3] and [31], they developed multilingual methods for international text sentiment analysis in online blogs and news articles, respectively. In [26] and [17], they presented approaches to indexing digital music libraries with music from multiple languages. Specific to emotion, [17] tried to highlight differences between languages by building models for predicting the musical mood and then cross-predicting in other languages. Unlike these works, we propose a multimedia-driven approach for cross-cultural visual sentiment analysis in the context of online image collections.

It is important to distinguish our work from that of Borth et al. on VSO [5] and its associated detector bank, SentiBank [4]. Their mid-level representation approach has recently proven effective in a wide range of applications in emotion prediction [4, 21], social media commenting [7], etc. However, in addition to lack of multilingual support, there are several technical challenges with VSO [4, 5] that we seek to improve on via (1) detection of adjectives and nouns with language-specific part-of-speech taggers, as opposed to a fixed list of adjectives and nouns, (2) automatic discovery of adjective-noun pairs correlated with emotions, as opposed to "constructed" pairs from top frequent adjectives and nouns, and (3) stronger selection criterion based on image tag frequency, linguistic and semantic filters and crowdsource validation.. Our proposed MVSO discovery method can be easily extended to any language, while achieving greater coverage and diversity than VSO.

3. ONTOLOGY CONSTRUCTION

An overview of the proposed method for multilingual visual sentiment concept ontology construction is shown in Figure 2. In the first stage, we obtain a set of images and their tags using seed emotion keyword queries, selected according to emotion ontologies from psychology such as [34] or [11]. Next, each image tag is labeled automatically by a language-specific part-of-speech tagger and adjective-noun combinations are discovered from words in the tags. Then, the combinations are filtered based on language, semantics, sentiment, frequency and diversity filters to ensure that the final set of ANPs have the following properties: (a) are written in the target language, (b) they do not refer to named entities or technical terms, (c) reflect a non-neutral sentiment, (d) are frequently used, and (e) are used by a non-trivial number of users of the target language.

The discovery of affective visual concepts for these languages using adjective-noun pairs poses several challenges in lexical, structural and semantic ambiguities, which are well-known problems in natural language processing. Lexical ambiguity is when a word has multiple meanings which depend on the context, e.g. *sport jaguar* or *forest jaguar.* Structural ambiguity is when a word might have different grammatical interpretation depending on the position in the context, e.g. *ambient light* or *light room.* Semantic ambiguity is when a combination of words with the same syntactic structure have different semantic interpretation, e.g. *big apple.* We selected languages in our MVSO according to the availability of public natural language processing tools and sentiment ontologies per language so that automatic processing was feasible. In addition, we sought to cover a wide range of geographic regions from the Americas to Europe and to Asia. We settled on 12 languages: Arabic, Chinese, Dutch, English, French, German, Italian, Persian, Polish, Russian, Spanish, and Turkish.

We applied our proposed data collection pipeline to a popular social multimedia sharing platform, Yahoo! Flickr[3], and collected public data from November 2014 to February 2015 using the Flickr API. We selected Flickr because there is an existing body of multimedia research using it in the past, and in particular, [20] describes how Flickr satisfies two conditions for making use of the "wisdom of the social multimedia": popularity and availability. We do not repeat the argument in [20], but note that in addition to those benefits, Flickr has multilingual support and the use of Flickr facilitates a natural comparison to the seminal VSO [5] work.

3.1 Adjective-Noun Pair Discovery

As our seed emotion ontology, we selected the *Plutchik's Wheel of Emotions* [34]. This psychology ontology was selected because it consists of graded intensities for multiple basic emotions providing a richer set of emotional valences compared to alternatives like [11]; it has also been shown to be useful for VSO [5]. The Plutchik emotions are organized by eight basic emotions, each with three valences: ecstasy > joy > serenity; admiration > trust > acceptance; terror > fear > apprehension; amazement > surprise > distraction; grief > sadness > pensiveness; loathing > disgust

[2]Note that we use *language* and *culture* interchangeably often. We define language as the "lens" through which we can observe culture. So while the two can be distinguished, for simplicity, we use them interchangeably.

[3]`www.flickr.com`

	#images	#tags	#cand	#anps (final)
Arabic	116,125	958,435	15,532	29
Chinese	895,398	3,919,161	50,459	504
Dutch	260,093	4,929,581	1,045,290	348
English	1,082,760	26,266,484	2,073,839	4,421
French	866,166	22,713,978	1,515,607	2,349
German	528,454	10,525,403	854,100	804
Italian	548,134	10,425,139	1,324,076	3,349
Persian	128,546	1,304,613	103,609	15
Polish	294,821	5,261,940	141,889	70
Russian	60,108	1,518,882	30,593	129
Spanish	827,396	15,241,679	925,975	3,381
Turkish	332,609	4,717,389	73,797	231
#total	5,940,610	107,782,684	8,154,766	15,630

Table 2: Ontology refinement statistics over 12 languages. Beginning with many images from seed emotion keywords denoted by #images, we extracted tags from these images #tags, and performed adjective-noun pair (ANP) discovery for candidate combinations #cand. Through a series of filters – frequency, language, semantics filter, sentiment filter and diversity – and after crowdsourcing, we got our final visual sentiment concepts #anps.

> boredom; rage > anger > annoyance; and, vigilance > anticipation > interest.

Multilingual Query Construction: To obtain seeds for each language, we recruited 12 native and proficient language speakers to provide a set of translated or synonymous keywords to those of the 24 Plutchik emotions. Speakers were allowed to use any number of keywords per emotion since the possible synonyms per emotion and language can vary, but they were asked to rank their chosen keywords along each emotion seed. They were also allowed to use tools like Google Translate[4] or other resources to enrich their emotion keywords. Table 1 lists top ranked keywords according to speakers for 7 out of 12 languages in each emotion.

Given the set of keywords $E^{(l)} = \{e_{ij}^{(l)} \mid i = 1 \ldots 24, j = 1 \ldots n_i\}$ describing each emotion i per language l, where n_i is the number of keywords per emotion i, we performed tag-based queries on tags with the Flickr API to retrieve images and their related tags. Like [5], for each emotion, we chose to sample only the top 50K images ranked by Flickr relevance to simply limit the size of our results, but if an emotion had less than 50K images, we extended the search to additional metadata, i.e. title and description.

Part-of-speech Labeling: To identify the type of each word in a Flickr tag, we performed automatic part-of-speech labeling using pre-trained language-specific taggers which achieve high accuracy (>95% for most languages), namely TreeTagger [37], Stanford tagger [39], HunPos tagger [15] and a morphological analyzer for Turkish [13]. Though not all the tags contained multiple words, the average number of words was always greater than the average number of tags for all languages, so word context was almost always taken into account. From the full set of part-of-speech labels, we retained identified nouns, adjectives and other part-of-speech types which can be used as adjectives, such as simple or past participle (e.g. *smiling face*) in English.

Discovery Strategy: We based our discovery strategy for ANPs on co-occurrence in image tags, that is, if an adjective-noun pair is relevant to the specific emotion it should appear at least once as that exact pair phrase in the crawled images for that emotion. To validate the completeness of our strategy we compared with VSO and found that ~86% of ANPs discovered by VSO [5] overlap with the English ANPs discovered by our method.

[4]translate.google.com

3.2 Filtering Candidate Adjective-Noun Pairs

From these discovered ANPs, we applied several filters to ensure they satisfied the following criteria: (a) written in the target language, (b) do not refer to named entities, (c) reflect a non-neutral sentiment, (d) frequently used and (e) used by multiple speakers of the language.

Language & Semantics: We used a combination of language dictionaries[5] instead of language classifiers to verify the correctness of the ANP as the performance of using the latter was low for short-length text, especially for Romance languages which share characters. All of the English ANPs were classified as indeed English by the dictionary, while for other languages, ANPs were removed if they passed the English dictionary filter but not the target language dictionary. The intuition for this was that most candidate ANPs in other languages were mixed mostly with English. We removed candidate pairs which referred to named entities or technical terms, where named entities were detected using several public knowledge bases such as Wikipedia and dictionaries for names[6], cities, regions and countries[7], and technical terms were removed via a manually created list of words specific to our source domain, Flickr, containing photography-related (e.g. *macro*, *exposure*) and camera-related words (e.g. *DSLR*).

Non-neutral Sentiment: To filter out neutral candidate adjective-noun pairs, each ANP was scored in sentiment using two publicly available sentiment ontologies: SentiStrength [38] and SentiWordnet [12]. SentiStrength ontology supported all the languages we considered, but since SentiWordnet could only be used directly for English, we passed in automatic translations in English from all other languages to it, following previous research on multilingual sentiment analysis in machine translation [1, 2][8]. We computed the ANP sentiment score $S(anp) \in [-2, +2]$ as:

$$S(anp) = \begin{cases} S(a) & : sgn\{S(a)\} \neq sgn\{S(n)\} \\ S(a) + S(n) & : \text{otherwise} \end{cases} \quad (1)$$

where $S(a) \in [-1, +1]$ and $S(n) \in [-1, +1]$ are the sentiment scores of the individual adjective and noun words, respectively, each of which are given by the arithmetic mean of SentiStrength and SentiWordnet scores on the word, and *sgn* is the sign of the scores. The piecewise condition essentially says that if the signs of the sentiment scores of the adjective and noun differ, then we ignore the noun. This highlights our belief that adjectives are the dominant sentiment modifiers in an adjective-noun pair, so for example, even if a noun is positive, like *wedding*, an adjective such as *horrible* would completely change the sentiment of the combined pair. And so, for these sign mismatch cases, we chose the adjective's sentiment alone. In the other case, when the sign of the adjective and noun were the same, whether both

[5]www.winedt.org

[6]www.wikipedia.org and www.ssa.gov, respectively

[7]www.geobytes.com

[8]For four non-English languages with the highest ANP counts, we have verified only a small percentage of non-neutral ANPs (less than 2%) reverse sentiment polarity after translation, confirming similar observations in the previous work.

positive (e.g. *happy wedding*) or both negative (e.g. *scary spider*), we simply allowed the ANP sentiment score to be the unweighted sum of its parts. ANP candidates with zero sentiment score were filtered out.

Frequency: Good ANPs are those which are actually used together. Here, we loosely defined an ANP's "frequency" of usage as its number of occurrences as an image tag on Flickr. When computing counts for each pair, we accounted for language-specific syntax like the ordering of adjectives and nouns. Following anthropology research [10], we followed two dominant orderings (91.5% of the languages worldwide): adj-noun and noun-adj. We also "merged" simplified and traditional forms in Chinese by considering them to be from the same language pool but distinct characters sets. In addition, we considered the possible intermediate Chinese character 的 during our frequency counting. For all non-English languages, we retained all ANPs that occurred at least once as an image tag; but for English, since Flickr's most dominant number of users are English-speaking, we set a higher frequency threshold of 40.

Diversity: The shear frequency of an adjective-noun pair occurrence alone was not sufficient to ensure a pair's pervasive use in a language. We also checked if the ANP was used by a non-trivial number of distinct Flickr users for a given language. We identified the number of users contributing to uploads of images for each ANP and found a power law distribution in every language. To avoid this uploader bias, we removed all ANPs with less than three uploaders. Many removed candidate pairs came from companies and merchants for advertising and branding.

To further ensure diversity in our MVSO, we subsampled nouns in every language by limiting to the 100 most frequent ANPs per adjective so that we do not have, for example, the adjective *surprising* modifying every possible noun in our corpus. In addition, we performed stem unification by checking and including only the inflected form (e.g. singular/plural) of an ANP that was most popular in usage as a tag on Flickr. This unification did also filter some candidate ANPs as some "duplicates" were present but simply in different inflected forms.

3.3 Crowdsourcing Validation

A further inspection of the corpus after the automatic filtering process showed that some issues could not completely be solved in an automatic fashion. Common errors included many fundamental natural language processing challenges like confusions in named entity recognition (e.g. *big apple*), language mixing (e.g. adjective in English + noun in Turkish), grammar inconsistency (e.g. adj-adj, or verb-noun) and semantic incongruity (e.g. *happy happiness*). So to refine our multilingual visual sentiment ontology, we crowdsourced a validation task. For each language, we asked native speaking workers to evaluate the correctness of ANPs post automatic filtering. We collected judgements using CrowdFlower[9], a crowdsourcing platform that distributes small tasks to a large number of workers, where we limited workers by their language expertise. We note that while we elected to perform this additional stage of crowdsourcing, other researchers may find a fully automatic pipeline more desirable, so in our public release, we also release the pre-crowdsourced version of our MVSO.

[9] `www.crowdflower.com`

	#cand	#users	#coun	%correct	%agree
Arabic	81	10	7	0.57	0.90
Chinese	1055	56	24	0.63	0.83
Dutch	1874	45	2	0.23	0.92
English	5369	223	52	0.78	0.84
French	5840	152	37	0.43	0.86
German	3360	119	27	0.32	0.90
Italian	4996	216	42	0.57	0.88
Persian	65	6	6	0.37	0.86
Polish	159	6	1	0.52	0.93
Russian	294	13	3	0.70	0.89
Spanish	4992	190	30	0.70	0.89
Turkish	701	61	22	0.66	0.84

Table 3: Crowdsourcing results via no. of input candidate ANPs #cand, #users, countries #coun, and perc. of ANPs accepted %correct and annotator agreement %agree.

3.3.1 Crowdsourcing Setup

We required that each ANP was evaluated by at least three independent workers. To ensure high quality results, we also required workers to be (1) native speakers of the language, for which CrowdFlower had its own language competency and expertise test for workers, and (2) have a good reputation according to the crowdsourcing platform, measured by workers' performance on other annotation jobs. For whatever reasons, for three languages (Persian, Polish and Dutch), the CrowdFlower platform does not evaluate workers based on their language expertise, so we filtered them by provenience, selecting the countries according to the official language spoken (e.g. Netherlands, Belgium, Aruba and Suriname for Dutch).

Task Interface: The verification task for workers consisted of simply evaluating the correctness of adjective-noun pairs. At the top of each page, we gave a short summary of the job and tasked workers: "*Verify that a word pair in* `<Language>` *is a valid adjective-noun pair.*" Workers were provided with a detailed definition of what an adjective-noun pair is and a summary of the criteria for evaluating ANPs, i.e. it (1) is grammatically correct (adjective + noun), (2) shows language consistency, (3) shows generality, that is, commonly used and does not refer to a named entity, and (4) is semantically logical. To guide workers, examples of correct and incorrect ANPs were provided for each criteria, where these ground truths were carefully judged and selected by four independent expert annotators. In the interface, aside from instructions, workers were shown five ANPs and simply chose between "yes" or "no" to validate ANPs.

Quality Control: Like some other crowdsourcing platforms, CrowdFlower provides a quality control mechanism called *test questions* to evaluate and track the performance of workers. These test questions come from pre-annotated ground truth, which in our case, correspond to ANPs with binary validation decisions for correctness. To access our task at all, workers were first required to correctly answer at least seven out of ten such test questions. In addition though, worker performance was tracked throughout the course of the task where these test questions were randomly inserted at certain points, disguised as normal units. For each language, we asked language experts to select ten correct and ten incorrect adjective-noun pairs from each language corpus to serve as the test questions.

3.3.2 *Crowdsourcing Results*

To measure the quality of our crowdsourcing, we looked at the annotator agreement along each validation task. For all languages, the agreement was very strong with an average annotator agreement of 87%, where workers agreed on either the correctness or incorrectness of ANPs. We found that workers tended to agree more that ANPs were correct than that they were incorrect. This was likely due to the wide range of possible criteria for rejecting an ANP where some criteria are easy to evaluate (e.g. language consistency), while others, such as general usage versus named entity, may cause disagreement among users due to the cultural background of the worker. For example, not all workers may agree that an ANP like *big eyes* or *big apple* refers to a named entity. However, for languages where the agreement on the incorrect ANPs was high, namely Arabic, German, and Polish, the average annotator agreement as a percentage of all ANP for that language were greater than 90%.

On average, our crowdsourcing validated that a vast number of the input candidate ANPs from our automatic ANP discovery and filtering process were indeed correct ANPs. English, Spanish and Russian were the top three for which the automatic pipeline performed the best, where every three in five ANPs were approved by the crowd judgements. However, for certain languages, including German, Dutch, Persian and French, the number of ANPs rejected by the crowd was actually greater than accepted ANPs due to a higher occurrence of mixed language pairs, e.g. *witzig humor*. In Table 3, we summarize statistics from our crowdsourcing experiments according to the number of ANPs, percentage of correct/incorrect ANPs by worker majority vote, and average agreement.

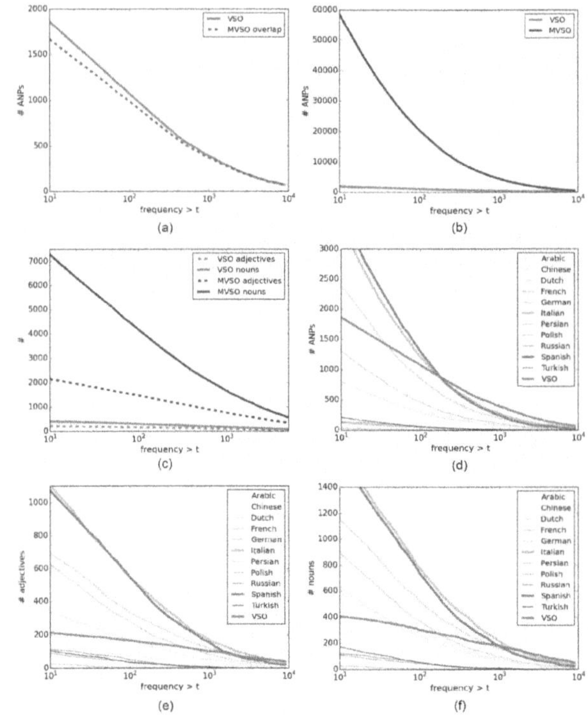

Figure 3: Comparison of our English MVSO and VSO [5] in Figures (a), (b) and (c), in terms of ANP overlap, no. of ANPs, adjectives and nouns; and with all other languages in Figures (d), (e) and (f), in terms of the no. of ANPs, adjectives and nouns when varying the frequency threshold t from 0 to 10,000 (on log-scale), respectively.

4. DATASET ANALYSIS & STATISTICS

Having acquired a final set of adjective-noun pairs for each of the 12 languages, we downloaded images by querying the Flickr API with ANPs using a mix of tag and metadata search. To limit the size of our dataset, we downloaded no more than 1,000 images per ANP query and also enforced a limit of no more than 20 images from any given uploader on Flickr for increased visual diversity. The selected 1,000 images were selected from the pool of retrieved image tag search results, but in the event that this pool is less than 1,000, we also enlarged the pool to include searches on the image title and description, or metadata. Selections from the pool of results were always randomized and a small number of images which Flickr or uploaders removed or changed privacy settings midway were removed. In total, we downloaded 7,368,364 images across 15,630 ANPs for the 12 languages, where English (4,049,507), Spanish (1,417,781) and Italian (845,664) contributed the most images.

4.1 Comparison with VSO [5]

To verify and test the efficacy of our MVSO, we provide a comparison of our extracted English visual sentiment ontology with that of VSO [5] along dimensions of size (number of ANPs) and diversity of nouns and adjectives (Figure 3). In Figure 3a, the overlap of English MVSO with VSO is compared with VSO alone after applying all filtering criteria except subsampling which might exclude ANPs belonging to VSO. As mentioned previously, about 86% overlaps between them. As we vary a frequency threshold t (as described in Sec. 3.2) over image tag counts, the overlap converges to 100%. This confirms that the popular ANPs covered by VSO are also covered by MVSO, an interesting finding given the difference in the crawling time periods and approaches. In Figure 3b, we show that there are far greater number of ANPs in our English MVSO compared to VSO ANPs throughout all the possible values of frequency threshold, after applying all filtering criteria. Similarly, as shown in Figure 3c, given there are more adjectives and nouns in our English MVSO, we also achieve greater diversity than VSO.

In Figure 3d, we compare the number of ANPs for the remaining languages in MVSO with VSO after applying all filtering criteria. The curves show that VSO has more ANPs than all the languages for most of the languages over all values of t, except from Spanish, Italian and French in the low values of t. Our intuition is that this is due to the popularity of English on Flickr compared to other languages. In Figures 3e and 3d, we observe that these three languages have greater diversity of adjectives and nouns than VSO for $t \leq 10^3$, German and Dutch have greater diversity than VSO for smaller values of threshold t, while the rest of the languages have smaller diversity over most values of t.

4.2 Sentiment Distributions

Returning to our research motivation from the Introduction, an interesting question to ask is which languages tend to be more positive or negative in their visual content. To answer this, we computed the median sentiment value across all ANPs of each language and ranked languages as in Fig. 4.

Here, to take into account the popularity difference among ANPs, we replicated each ANP k times, with k equal to the number of images tagged with the ANP, up to an upper limit $L = \alpha \times Avg_i$, where Avg_i is the average image count per ANP in the ith language. Varying α value will result in different medians and distributions, but the trend in differentiating positive languages from negative ones was quite stable. We show the case when $\alpha = 3$ in Fig. 4, indicating that there is an overall tendency toward positive sentiment across all languages, where Spanish demonstrates the highest positive sentiment, followed by Italian. This surprising observation is in fact compatible with previous research showing that there is a universal positivity bias over languages with Spanish being the most relatively positive language [9]. The languages with the lowest sentiment were Persian and Arabic, followed by English.

The sentiment distributions (Fig. 4: right) also showed interesting phenomena: Spanish being the most positive language also has the highest variation in sentiment, while German has the most concentrated sentiment distribution. Even for languages that have the lowest median sentiment values, the range of sentiment was concentrated in a small range near zero (between 0 and -0.1).

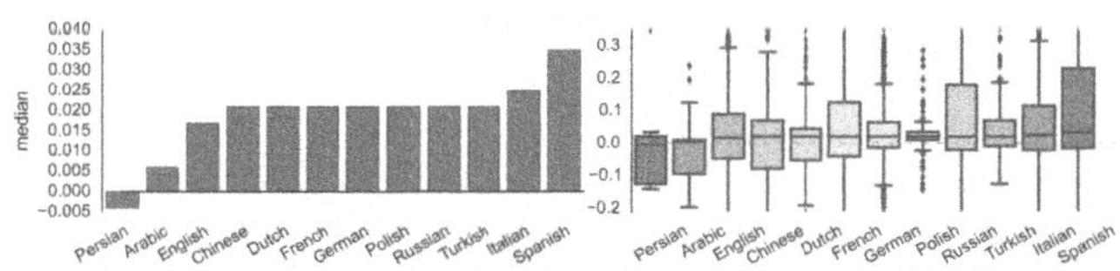

Figure 4: Median sentiment computed over all ANPs per language is shown on left, and the sentiment distribution using box plots on the right (zoomed at 90% of the distributions). On right, languages are sorted by median sentiment in ascending order (from the left).

4.3 Emotion Distributions

Another interesting question arises when considering co-occurrence of ANPs with the emotions in different languages. While our adjective-noun pair concepts were selected to be sentiment-biased, emotions still represent the root of our framework since we built MVSO out from seed emotion terms. So aside from sentiment, which focuses on only positivity/negativity, what are probable mappings of ANPs to emotions for each language? What emotions are most frequently occurring across languages? Given the set of keywords $E^{(l)} = \{e_{ij}^{(l)} \mid i = 1 \dots 24, j = 1 \dots n_i\}$ describing each emotion i per language l, where n_i is the number of keywords per emotion i, the set of ANPs belonging to language l, noted as $x \in X^{(l)}$, and the number of images tagged with both ANP x and emotion keyword e_{ij}, $C^{(x)} = \{c_{ij}^{(x)} \mid i = 1 \dots 24, j = 1 \dots n_i\}$, we define the probabilities of emotion for each ANP x in language l as:

$$\text{emo}^i(x) = \frac{\frac{1}{n_i}\sum_{j=1}^{n_i} c_{ij}^{(x)}}{\sum_{i=1}^{24} \frac{1}{n_i}\sum_{j=1}^{n_i} c_{ij}^{(x)}} \in [0, 1] \qquad (2)$$

Note the model in (2) does not take into account correlation among emotions, where for example, by an image tagged with "ecstasy," users may also imply "joy" even though the latter is not explicitly tagged. These correlations can be easily accounted for by smoothing co-occurrence counts c_{ij}

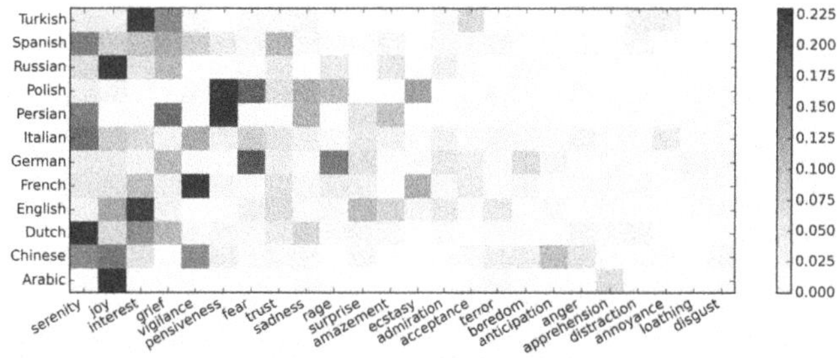

Figure 5: Probabilities of emotions per language with respect to their visual sentiment content. Emotions are ordered by the sum of their probabilities across languages (left to right) and clipped for better visualization. Each row sums to 1.

over correlated emotions, e.g. the co-occurrence counts of an ANP tagged with "ecstasy" can be included partially in the co-occurrence count of "joy." Regardless, still based on (2), we compute a normalized emotion score per language l and emotion i as:

$$\text{score}^i(l) = \frac{\sum_{x=1}^{|X^{(l)}|} \text{emo}^i(x) \cdot \text{count}(x)}{\sum_{i=1}^{24}\sum_{x=1}^{|X^{(l)}|} \text{emo}^i(x) \cdot \text{count}(x)} \in [0, 1] \qquad (3)$$

Figure 5 shows these scores per language and Plutchik emotion [34] on a heatmap diagram. Scores in each row sum to 1 (over 24 emotions). The emotions are ordered by the sum of their scores across languages. The top-5 emotions across all languages are *joy*, *serenity*, *interest*, *grief* and *fear*. And the highest ranked emotion is *joy* in Russian, Chinese and Arabic. Two other emotions in the top-5 were also positive: *serenity*, being high ranked emotion for Dutch, Italian, Chinese and Persian, and *interest* for English, Turkish and Dutch. The remaining two emotions in the top-5 were negative: *grief* for Persian and Turkish, and *fear*, which was high ranked in German and Polish. We also observed that *pensiveness* was top ranked for Persian and Polish, *vigilance* for French, *rage* for German, while *apprehension* and *distraction* for Spanish. We note that these results are more concrete for languages with many ANPs (>1000) and less conclusive for those with few ANPs like Arabic and Persian.

5. CROSS-LINGUAL MATCHING

To get a gauge on the topics commonly mentioned across different cultures and languages, we analyzed alignments of translations for each ANP to English as a basis. Two approaches were taken to study this: exact and approximate alignment. We ensured that translations of ANPs also passed all our validation filters described in Sec. 3.2 for this analysis.

Exact Alignment: We grouped ANPs from each language that have the exact same translation. For example, *old books* was the translation for one or more ANPs from seven languages, including 老書 (Chinese), *livres anciens* (French), *vecchi libri* (Italian), Старые книги (Russian), *libros antiguos* (Spanish), *eski kitaplar* (Turkish). The translation covered by the greatest number of languages was *beautiful girl* with ANPs from ten languages. Figure 6 (left) shows a correlation matrix of the number of times ANPs from pairs of languages appeared together in a set with the exact same translation, e.g. out of all the translations that German ANPs were translated to (782), more of them were

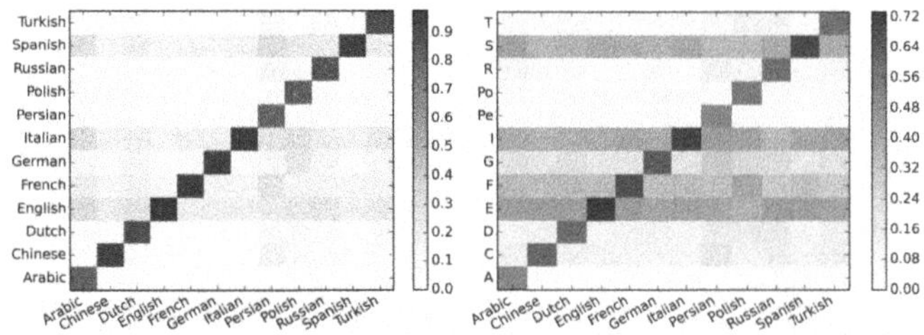

Figure 6: Percentage of times ANPs from one language (columns) were translated to [Left] the same phrase, or to [Right] the phrase in the same cluster as in another language (rows).

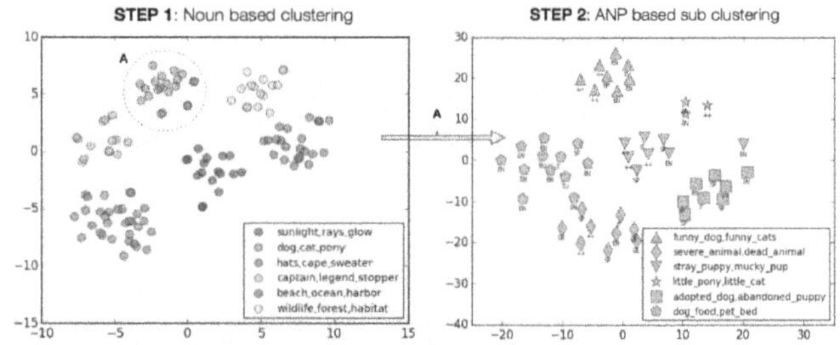

Figure 7: Examples of noun clusters (left) and ANP sub-clusters (right) from our two-stage clustering for cross-lingual matching. For visualization, word2vec [32] vectors were projected to $\mathbb{R}^2$ using t-SNE [40].

translated to the same phrase with the ANPs used by Dutch speakers (39) than with the ANPs used by Chinese speakers (23). This was striking given that there were less (340) translation phrases from Dutch than from Chinese (473).

Approximate Alignment: Translations can be inaccurate, especially when capturing underlying semantics where context is not provided. And so, we relaxed the strict condition for exact matches by approximately matching using a hierarchical two-stage clustering approach instead. First, we extracted nouns using TreeTagger [37] from the list of translated phrases and discovered 3,099 total nouns. We then extracted word2vec [32] features, a word representation trained on a Google News[10] corpus, for these translated nouns (188 nouns were out-of-vocabulary), and performed k-means clustering (k=200) to get groups of nouns with similar meaning. The number of clusters was picked based on the coherence of clusters; and we picked the number where the inertia value of the clustering started saturating while gradually increasing k. In the second stage of our hierarchical clustering, we split phrases from the translations into different groups based on the clusters their nouns belonged to. We extracted word2vec [32] features from the full translated phrase in each cluster and ran another round of k-means clustering (adjusting k based on the number of phrases in each cluster, where phrases in each noun-cluster ranged from 3 to 253). This two-stage clustering enables us to create a hierarchical organization of our ANPs across languages and form a multilingual ontology over visual sentiment concepts (MVSO), unlike the flat structure in VSO [5]. We discovered 3,329 sub-clusters of ANP concepts, e.g. resulting in clusters containing *little pony* and *little horse* as in Figure 7. This approach also yielded a larger intersection between languages, where German and Dutch share 118 clusters, and German and Chinese intersect over 101 ANP clusters.

The correlation matrix from this approximate matching is shown in Figure 6, along with one subtree from our ontology by hierarchical clustering in Figure 7. For Figure 7, we projected data to $\mathbb{R}^2$ using t-SNE dimensionality reduction [40]. On the left, six clusters composed of different sets of nouns are shown with clusters of *sunlight-rays-glow* and *dog-cat-pony*. On the right, we show the sub-clustering of ANPs for the *dog-cat-pony* cluster in **A**, giving us noun groupings modified by sentiment-biasing adjectives to get ANPs like *funny dog-funny cats* and *adopted dog-abondoned puppy.*

6. VISUAL SENTIMENT PREDICTION

To test the effectiveness of a vision-based approach for visual affect understanding when crossing languages, we designed and built language-specific sentiment predictors using the data collected with MVSO. Inspired by work in [17], we studied the extent to which the visual sentiments of a given language can be predicted by sentiment models of other languages. We chose to focus on a sentiment prediction task, i.e. predicting whether an image is of positive or negative sentiment, because there is a large body of work expressly focused on sentiment (e.g. [5, 42, 43]) for its simplicity, compared to emotion prediction. More importantly, we wanted to reduce the number of variables to be analyzed since our primary goal was to uncover cross-lingual differences.

We first constructed a bank of visual concept detectors like in [4] for our final MVSO adjective-noun pairs. For simplicity, we focused on the six languages with the most ANPs and associated images in our dataset: in decreasing order, English, Spanish, Italian, French, German and Chinese. Combined these six languages account for 94.7% of the ANPs in MVSO and 98.4% of the images in our dataset. However, to ensure that there were enough training images for each ANP, only the ANPs with no less than 125 images were selected for model training and prediction. This reduced the combined ANP coverage to 63.5% but still ensured 92.0% coverage for images. For each ANP, the images were split randomly 80/20% train/test, respectively.

6.1 Visual Sentiment Concept Detectors

To construct our bank of visual concept detectors of ANPs, we used convolutional neural networks (CNNs), in particular, adopting an AlexNet-styled architecture [24] for its good performance on large-scale vision recognition and detection tasks. To train our detector bank, we fined-tuned six models, one for each language, where network weights were initialized with DeepSentiBank [6], an AlexNet model trained on the VSO [5] dataset. This fine-tuning approach ensures that each network begins with weights that are already somewhat "affectively" biased. The base learning rates were set to 0.001 and the number of output neurons in the last fully connected layer were set to the number of training ANPs of each language. Step sizes for reducing the learning rate in the second stage were set proportional to the number of training images per language. For a single language, fine-tuning took between 12 and 40 hours for convergence on a single NVIDIA GTX 980 GPU implemented with Caffe [19]. From Table 4, as expected we achieve higher top-1 and top-5 accuracies than DeepSentiBank [6], even when the numbers of output neurons in English and Spanish are higher than those in [6]. Top-k accuracy refers to the percentage of classifications that the true class is in the top k predicted ranks.

[10] `news.google.com`

Figure 8: Example top-5 classification results from our multilingual visual sentiment detector bank. Translations to English provided for convenience.

6.2 Sentiment Prediction on Flickr

We used the CNN-based visual concept models trained for each language to extract image features and use the sentiment scores of ANPs as supervised labels to learn sentiment prediction models. We compared different layers of the CNN models as image features. To simplify the process, we binarized the ANP sentiment scores computed with Eq. (1), i.e. into positive and negative classes, and learned a binary classifier using linear SVMs, one for each language. The training images are those associated with ANPs of strong sentiment scores (absolute values higher than 0.05). Splits of training and test sets were stratified across all languages so that the amount of training and testing for positive and negative sentiment classes was the same for fair cross-lingual experiment comparison.

We found that the softmax output features from the penultimate layer outputs of each language's CNN model performed the best for all languages, and we show resulting sentiment prediction results in Figure 9. Each language expectedly did better in predicting test samples from its own language, but in addition, Chinese generally was the most difficult to predict by models trained from other languages; and using a sentiment model trained over Chinese images to predict the sentiment in other languages was also the worst in average. We speculate that this is due to the difference in the visual sentiment portrayal from Eastern and Western cultures. Interestingly, the classification of French and Italian sentiments was the most consistent using models from all languages. We also observed good performance in cross-lingual prediction for Latin languages, i.e. Spanish, Italian and French, where Italian was the best cross-lingual classifier for Spanish and French sentiment, and Spanish was best for Italian sentiment, followed by French. Despite not performing as well as others in average, the English-specific sentiment model had the least variance in its accuracy across all languages, likely from the pervasiveness of English world-wide and across cultures.

	#ANPs	#train	#test	lrs (K)	time (hr)	top-1	top-5
English	4,342	3,236,728	807,447	50	40	10.1%	21.7%
Spanish	2,382	1,085,678	270,400	40	35	12.4%	25.4%
Italian	1,561	602,424	149,901	30	30	17.0%	30.9%
French	1,115	462,522	115,112	30	26	17.7%	35.5%
German	275	108,744	27,048	20	12	30.1%	52.8%
Chinese	243	102,740	25,575	20	15	27.1%	45.0%
DSB [6]	2,089	826,806	41,113	-	-	8.2%	19.1%

Table 4: Adjective-noun pair (ANP) classification performance on Flickr images for six major languages in MVSO and compared to DeepSentiBank (DSB) [6]. No. of visual sentiment concepts #ANPs, #train and #test images along with learning rate step size (lrs, in thousands) are shown with training times (in hours), top-1 and top-5 accuracies.

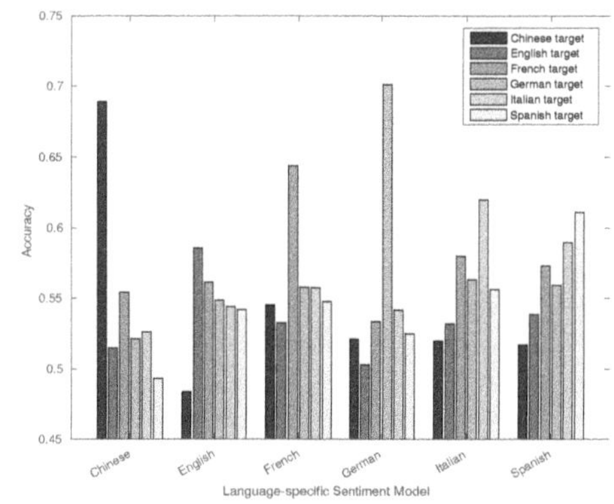

Figure 9: Image-based, cross-lingual domain transfer sentiment prediction results with language-specific models applied on cross-lingual examples.

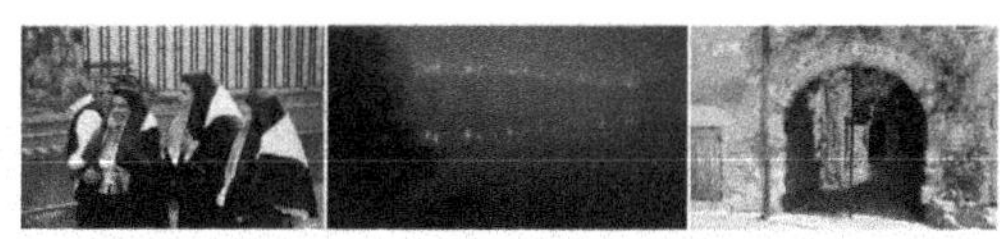

Original Language	Italian	English	French
Adj-Noun Pair	costumi tradizionali (traditional costume)	foggy morning	beau village (beautiful village)
Prediction Model	German	Chinese	Spanish
Truth/Predicted	positive/negative	negative/positive	positive/positive

Figure 10: Classification examples from cross-lingual sentiment prediction. The model from a source language is used to predict the sentiment of a target language image where the true label comes from the sentiment of the associated ANP.

In Figure 10, we show three classification example results from our cross-lingual sentiment prediction. On the left, an image from the Italian test set representing the *costumi tradizionali* concept was labeled as positive via sentiment scoring, but was predicted by the German model to be negative; this may be due to differences in cultural perceptions of traditional clothing. In the center, the Chinese model wrongly predicted an image from the English test set of *foggy morning* as positive, possibly for its resemblance to a Chinese painting. And on the right, an image of a *beau village* from the French test set was successfully classified as positive with the Spanish sentiment predictor. These examples and preliminary experiments highlight some similarities and differences in how visual sentiment is expressed and perceived by various cultures.

7. CONCLUSION & FUTURE WORK

We proposed a new multilingual discovery method for visual sentiment concepts and showed its efficacy on a social multimedia platform for 12 languages. We based our approach on the psychology theory that emotions are culture-specific and carry inherent linguistic context, and so we showed how to use language-specific part-of-speech labeling along with progressive filtering to achieve coverage and diversity of visual affect concepts in multiple languages. In addition, we presented a two-stage hierarchical clustering approach to unify our ontology across languages. And we make our Multilingual Visual Sentiment Ontology (MVSO), pre-crowdsourcing as well as post, and image dataset, available to the public. A cross-lingual analysis of our large-scale MVSO and image dataset using semantic matching and visual sentiment prediction hint that emotions are not necessarily culturally universal. Our preliminary results show that there are indeed commonalities, but also distinct separations, in how visual affect is expressed and perceived, where other works assumed only commonalities. We believe these point to the colorful diversity of our world, rather than our inability to understand one another.

In the future, we plan to explore differences along other human factors which can be collected from self-reported user metadata like age group, gender, profession, etc. We will also adopt our approach to other language-specific social multimedia platforms to counter the insufficient data for some languages like Arabic, Persian and Chinese. In addition, while we discussed culture and languages in this work, we have not yet performed an in-depth study on geo-location data in MVSO, often provided along with uploaded images on Flickr. While such information could be useful to distinguish between sub-cultures speaking the same languages (e.g. Spanish vs. South-Americans), we omitted such a study here because of the noise that geo-location data can add. For example, an American traveling in China uploading pictures is still more likely to use their native tongue to tag and sentimentally describe their content. The trade-off is that while their semantics are culturally American, the uploaded visual content is now from another culture, so there is still much to be explored from geo-location and user metadata.

8. ACKNOWLEDGMENTS

Research was sponsored by the U.S. Defense Advanced Research Projects Agency (DARPA) under the Social Media in Strategic Communication (SMISC) program, Agreement Number W911NF-12-C-0028. The views and conclusions contained in this document are those of the author(s) and should not be interpreted as representing the of official policies, either expressed or implied, of the U.S. Defense Advanced Research Projects Agency or the U.S. Government. The U.S. Government is authorized to reproduce and distribute reprints for Government purposes notwithstanding any copyright notation here-on. B. Jou was supported by the Department of Defense (DoD) through the National Defense Science & Engineering Graduate Fellowship (NDSEG) Program. N. Pappas was supported by the InEvent (FP7-ICT n. 287872) and MODERN Sinergia (CRSII2 147653) projects.

9. REFERENCES

[1] A. Balahur and M. Turchi. Multilingual sentiment analysis using machine translation? In *WASSA*, 2012.

[2] C. Banea, R. Mihalcea, J. Wiebe, and S. Hassan. Multilingual subjectivity analysis using machine translation. In *EMNLP*, 2008.

[3] M. Bautin, L. Vijayarenu, and S. Skiena. International sentiment analysis for news and blogs. In *ICWSM*, 2008.

[4] D. Borth, T. Chen, R. Ji, and S.-F. Chang. SentiBank: Large-scale ontology and classifiers for detecting sentiment and emotions in visual content. In *ACM MM*, 2013.

[5] D. Borth, R. Ji, T. Chen, T. Breuel, and S.-F. Chang. Large-scale visual sentiment ontology and detectors using adjective noun pairs. In *ACM MM*, 2013.

[6] T. Chen, D. Borth, T. Darrell, and S.-F. Chang. DeepSentiBank: Visual sentiment concept classification with deep convolutional neural networks. *arXiv preprint arXiv:1410.8586*, 2014.

[7] Y.-Y. Chen, T. Chen, W. H. Hsu, H.-Y. M. Liao, and S.-F. Chang. Predicting viewer affective comments based on image content in social media. In *ICMR*, 2014.

[8] E. S. Dan-Glauser and K. Scherer. The Geneva affective picture database: A new 730-picture database focusing on valence and normative significance. *Behav. Res. Meth.*, 43(2), 2011.

[9] S. Dodds and et al. Human language reveals a universal positivity bias. *PNAS*, 112(8), 2015.

[10] M. S. Dryer and M. Haspelmath, editors. *WALS Online*. Max Planck Institute for Evolutionary Anthropology, 2013. http://wals.info/chapter/87.

[11] P. Ekman. Facial expression and emotion. *American Psychologist*, 48(4), 1993.

[12] A. Esuli and F. Sebastiani. SENTIWORDNET: A publicly available lexical resource for opinion mining. In *LREC*, 2006.

[13] Z. Güngördü and K. Oflazer. Parsing Turkish using the lexical functional grammar formalism. In *ACL*, 1994.

[14] M. Gygli, H. Grabner, H. Riemenschneider, F. Nater, and L. V. Gool. The interestingness of images. In *ICCV*, 2013.

[15] P. Halácsy, A. Kornai, and C. Oravecz. HunPos: An open source trigram tagger. In *ACL*, 2007.

[16] M. G. Haselton and T. Ketelaar. Irrational emotions or emotional wisdom? The evolutionary psychology of affect and social behavior. *Affect in Soc. Think. and Behav.*, 8(21), 2006.

[17] X. Hu and Y.-H. Yang. Cross-cultural mood regression for music digital libraries. In *JCDL*, 2014.

[18] J. Jia, S. Wu, X. Wang, P. Hu, L. Cai, and J. Tang. Can we understand van Gogh's mood?: Learning to infer affects from images in social networks. In *ACM MM*, 2012.

[19] Y. Jia, E. Shelhamer, J. Donahue, S. Karayev, J. Long, R. Girshick, S. Guadarrama, and T. Darrell. Caffe: Convolutional architecture for fast feature embedding. In *ACM MM*, 2014.

[20] X. Jin, A. Gallagher, L. Cao, J. Luo, and J. Han. The wisdom of social multimedia: Using Flickr for prediction and forecast. In *ACM MM*, 2010.

[21] B. Jou, S. Bhattacharya, and S.-F. Chang. Predicting viewer perceived emotions in animated GIFs. In *ACM MM*, 2014.

[22] Y. Ke, X. Tang, and F. Jing. The design of high-level features for photo quality assessment. In *CVPR*, 2006.

[23] A. Khosla, A. Das Sarma, and R. Hamid. What makes an image popular? In *WWW*, 2014.

[24] A. Krizhevsky, I. Sutskever, and G. E. Hinton. ImageNet classification with deep convolutional neural networks. In *NIPS*, 2012.

[25] P. Lang, M. Bradley, and B. Cuthbert. International Affective Picture System (IAPS): Technical manual and affective ratings. Technical report, NIMH CSEA, 1997.

[26] J. H. Lee, J. S. Downie, and S. J. Cunningham. Challenges in cross-cultural/multilingual music information seeking. In *ISMIR*, 2005.

[27] J. Machajdik and A. Hanbury. Affective image classification using features inspired by psychology and art theory. In *ACM MM*, 2010.

[28] H. R. Markus and S. Kitayama. Culture and the self: Implications for cognition, emotion, and motivation. *Psychological Review*, 98(2), 1991.

[29] E. D. McCarthy. The social construction of emotions: New directions from culture theory. *Social Perspectives on Emotion*, 2, 1994.

[30] B. Mesquita, N. H. Frijda, and K. Scherer. Culture and emotion. In J. W. Berry, P. R. Dasen, and T. S. Saraswathi, editors, *Handbook of Cross-cultural Psychology*, volume 2. Allyn & Bacon, 1997.

[31] R. Mihalcea, C. Banea, and J. Wiebe. Learning multilingual subjective language via cross-lingual projections. In *ACL*, 2007.

[32] T. Mikolov, I. Sutskever, K. Chen, G. Corrado, and J. Dean. Distributed representations of words and phrases and their compositionality. In *NIPS*, 2013.

[33] R. W. Picard. *Affective Computing*. MIT Press, 1997.

[34] R. Plutchik. *Emotion: A Psychoevolutionary Synthesis*. Harper & Row, 1980.

[35] M. Redi, N. O'Hare, R. Schifanella, M. Trevisiol, and A. Jaimes. 6 Seconds of sound and vision: Creativity in micro-videos. In *CVPR*, 2014.

[36] J. A. Russell. Culture and the categorization of emotions. *Psychological Bulletin*, 110(3), 1991.

[37] H. Schmid. Probabilistic part-of-speech tagging using decision trees. In *Intl Conf. on New Methods in Language Proc.*, 1994.

[38] M. Thelwall, K. Buckley, G. Paltoglou, and D. Cai. Sentiment strength detection in short informal text. *Jour. Ameri. Soci. for Info. Sci. & Tech.*, 61(12), 2010.

[39] K. Toutanova, D. Klein, C. D. Manning, and Y. Singer. Feature-rich part-of-speech tagging with a cyclic dependency network. In *NAACL*, 2003.

[40] L. van der Maaten and G. E. Hinton. Visualizing high-dimensional data using t-SNE. *JMLR*, 9, 2008.

[41] E. A. Vessel, J. Stahl, N. Maurer, A. Denker, and G. G. Starr. Personalized visual aesthetics. In *SPIE-IS&T Electronic Imaging*, 2014.

[42] V. Yanulevskaya, J. van Gemert, K. Roth, A. Herbold, N. Sebe, and J. M. Geusebroek. Emotional valence categorization using holistic image features. In *ICIP*, 2008.

[43] Q. You, J. Luo, H. Jin, and J. Yang. Robust image sentiment analysis using progressively trained and domain transferred deep networks. In *AAAI*, 2014.

[44] R. B. Zajonc. Feeling and thinking: Preferences need no inferences. *American Psychologist*, 35(2), 1980.

Learning Deep Features For MSR-bing Information Retrieval Challenge

Qiang Song[1], Sixie Yu[2], Cong Leng[1]
JiaXiang Wu[1], Qinghao Hu[1], Jian Cheng[1*]
National Laboratory of Pattern Recognition
Institute of Automation, Chinese Academy of Sciences
Beijing, China
{qiang.song, cong.leng, jiaxiang.wu, qinghao.hu, jcheng}@nlpr.ia.ac.cn[1]
bit.yusixie@gmail.com[2]

ABSTRACT

Two tasks have been put forward in the MSR-bing Grand Challenge 2015. To address the information retrieval task, we raise and integrate a series of methods with visual features obtained by convolution neural network (CNN) models. In our experiments, we discover that the ranking strategies of Hierarchical clustering and PageRank methods are mutually complementary. Another task is fine-grained classification. In contrast to basic-level recognition, fine-grained classification aims to distinguish between different breeds or species or product models, and often requires distinctions that must be conditioned on the object pose for reliable identification. Current state-of-the-art techniques rely heavily upon the use of part annotations, while the bing datasets suffer both abundance of part annotations and dirty background. In this paper, we propose a CNN-based feature representation for visual recognition only using image-level information. Our CNN model is pre-trained on a collection of clean datasets and fine-tuned on the bing datasets. Furthermore, a multi-scale training strategy is adopted by simply resizing the input images into different scales and then merging the soft-max posteriors. We then implement our method into a unified visual recognition system on Microsoft cloud service. Finally, our solution achieved top performance in both tasks of the contest

Categories and Subject Descriptors

H.3.3 [**Information Search and Retrieval**]: Retrieval models

Keywords

Information retrieval, visual recognition

*corresponding author

MM'15, October 26–30, 2015, Brisbane, Australia.
 ISBN 978-1-4503-3459-4/15/10 ...$15.00.
DOI: http://dx.doi.org/10.1145/2733373.2809928.

1. INTRODUCTION

MSR-bing Grand Challenge 2015 tries to deal with the following 2 tasks: 1) how can we build a system to assess the relevance of a text query and its returned image list? 2) how to develop an image recognition system based on the bing datasets provided by the Challenge to recognize a wide range of dog breeds.

As for the first task: the key point lies in choosing a better search engine which can successfully meet users' requirements. The dataset of MSR-bing Grand Challenge contains 11.7 million queries and 1 million images which were collected from the user click logs of bing image search in the EN-US market[3]. Participants are asked to produce a floating point score on each image-query pair that can reflect how relevant the image matches the given query, with higher numbers indicating higher relevance.

A large number of methods [10, 11, 12] have been put forward in the previous Challenges. In general, two feasible proposals have been carried out in these methods: image content based model and text based model. The former[11] firstly retrieves images and their associated queries by computing the visual similarities between the images, and then calculates the final relevance scores based on the textual similarities between the corresponding queries. However, the proposal is hard to retrieval reliable visually similar images in such a massive number of image collection with a crowd of noisy samples. The latter [10, 12] concentrates on firstly retrieving semantically similar queries and then computing the visual similarity between the corresponding images. Specifically, for instance, Wu [11] proposed a modified PageRank model for ranking images, with an assumption that the majority of images under a same query are relevant to the query and the higher similarity to other images, the higher relevance score the image should be obtained. This method worked pretty well and achieved the first place in the competition. The assumption is also widely followed by later participants [10, 12].

In this paper, we raise and integrate a series of methods to deal with the Challenge, with visual features obtained by convolution neural network (CNN) models. We discover that the ranking strategies of Hierarchical clustering and PageRank methods are mutually complementary.

The second task is a new task of the Grand Challenges this year. Contestants are asked to develop an image recognition system based on the bing datasets provided by the Challenge to recognize a wide range of dog breeds. Generally, the problem of visual fine-grained classification can be extremely challenging due to the subtle differences in the appearance of certain parts across related categories. Localizing the parts in an object is therefore central to establishing correspondence between object instances and discounting object pose variations and camera view position. Previous work [2, 8] has investigated part-based approaches to this problem. Farrell et al.[2] proposed a pose-normalized representation using poselets. Liu et al.[8] put forward an exemplar-based geometric method to detect dog faces and extract highly localized image features from keypoints to differentiate dog breeds. However, the bottleneck for many pose-normalized representations is indeed accurate part localization. Without any ground truth information, it's difficult to adopt these part-based strategies.

Thus, in this paper, we propose a method only using image-level information. Our CNN model is pre-trained on a collection of clean datasets and fine-tuned on the bing datasets. Furthermore, a multi-scale learning strategy is adopted by simply resizing the input images into different scales. We then implement our method into a unified visual recognition system on Microsoft cloud service. Fortunately, our team achieved the third prize in task 1 and the first prize in task 2.

2. OUR APPROACH

2.1 Web Image Retrieval

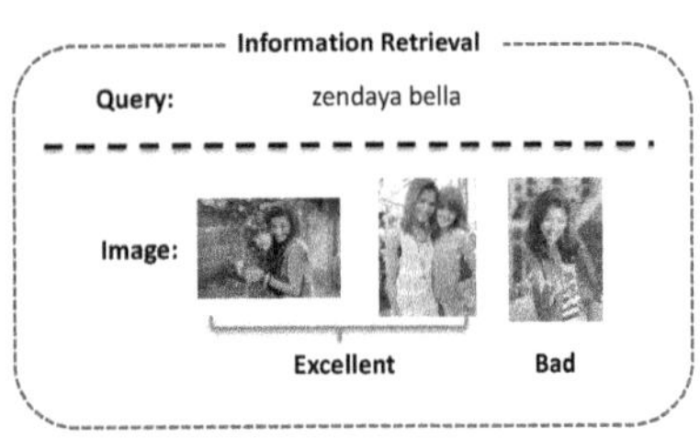

Figure 1: Web image retrieval

Shown in Figure 1, the web image retrieval task is to produce a floating point score on each image-query pair that can reflect how relevant the image matches the given query, with higher numbers indicating higher relevance. In this paper, we deal with the task by systematic strategies, including feature extraction, query matching and ranking.

2.1.1 *Feature Extraction*

Recently deep neural networks obtain astonishing performance at many vision tasks, outperforming the algorithms based on hand-designed features. Among variety of deep neural network architectures, Convolutional Neural Networks(CNN) have attracted much attention. A deep CNN together with large databases has achieved remarkable results[6]. Moreover, with huge amount of training data, CNN has shown to learn high-level image representation from raw pixels[13].

2.1.2 *Query Match Strategy*

As mentioned in [3], the original queries suffer some issues, such as meaningless words, e.g., 'picture' and 'image'. Similar to [10], we also utilize an open source tool OpenNLP[1] to remove those meaningless words and get the stems of each query. As a result, the number of distinct query triads in training dataset decreases from 23,094,502 to 8,766,023. Besides, instead of applying some traditional textual feature models in query analysis [4], e.g., 'BM25' and 'Tf-Idf', we calculate the Jaccard index to measure similarities between queries. Since query information is not long enough to extract more efficient textual features, those traditional textual feature models may not be much helpful for retrieval tasks but increase the time complexity. Furthermore, some textual expansion approaches are introduced with aims of matching possible queries. For instance, query 'hat' can be extended to 'cap' or 'chapeau'. We also discover that the queries in the dataset are written in several languages, e.g., query 'capicola' comes from Italian language, which has the same meaning as 'pork' in English. Finally, applying the above strategy in the development set obtains 450 completely matched queries and 550 partly matched queries. As for each query in the completely matched list, we sort the click count of images in descending order and select top 5 images in training dataset as the templates. As for each query in the partly matched list, we obtain top 5 similar queries in training dataset and pick images with highest click count in these 5 queries as the templates.

2.1.3 *Ranking Strategies*

A K-means clustering is implemented on the development set and their corresponding templates. We then sort images based on the distances to their cluster center and the number of template neighbors. Besides, we also penalize the images by the variance of their clusters. We consider that compact cluster means a higher relevance. The above method is formulated as follows:

$$score(I_i) = \frac{e^{-(D_i+\alpha Var_i)}}{1+e^{-CN_i}} \tag{1}$$

where I_i denotes the ith image, D_i, Var_i and CN_i denote the distances to the cluster center, the variance of the cluster and the number of neighbors belonging to the templates respectively. α is a trade-off parameter. We simply vary the number of the clusters and use the bagging strategy to obtain a final ranking result.

In data mining, hierarchical clustering is a method of cluster analysis which seeks to build a hierarchy of clusters.

Besides, similar to [11, 12], we also implement a modified PageRank method to obtain the ranking of images. It is reasonable to assign the relevance score to an image based on its connections (or similarities) with others. The stronger the connections are, the higher the score should be. The relevance scores are formulated as follows:

$$score(I) = (\beta P + (1-\beta)\mathbf{1}^T)score(I) \tag{2}$$

where β denotes a trade-off parameter.

2.2 Visual Recognition

Imagine the following case: a user may have seen many lovely dogs, but can hardly tell all their names. Our target is to design a dog breeds recognition system, whose core algorithm is running on our own servers. And with the help of Microsoft cloud service, the system will be accessible to

[1]http://opennlp.apache.org/index.html

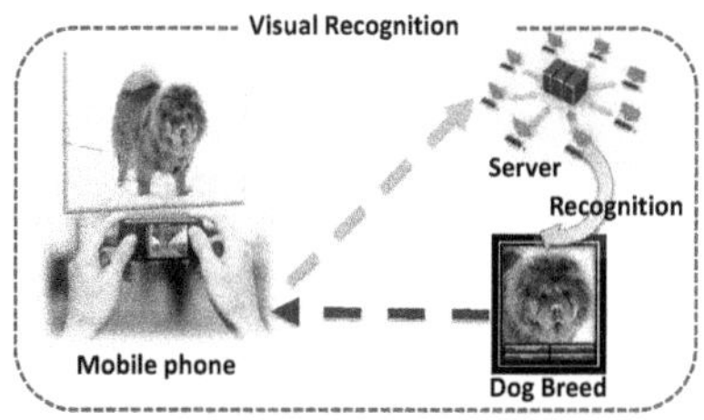

Figure 2: Visual recognition.

Table 1: Detailed descriptions of dataset.

Dataset	Category	Amount
Stanford	120	20,580
Columbia	133	8351
MM2015	344	42,886

public users.(Figure 2) In this paper, we deal with the visual recognition task by first carrying out data analysis and then building a deep learning model-based system.

2.2.1 Data Analysis

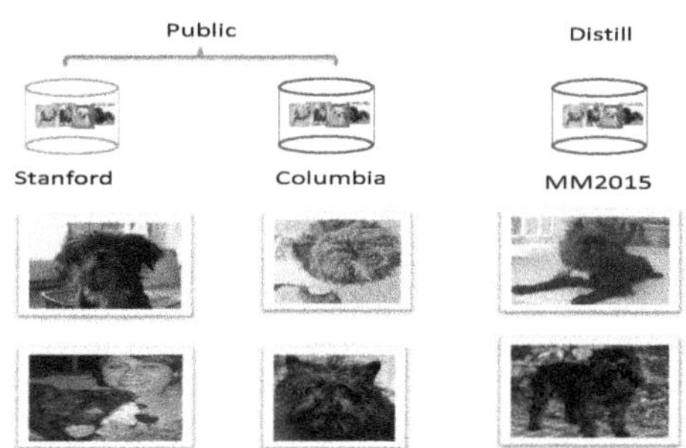

Figure 3: Images of distinct datasets.

Three distinctive datasets are utilized in our experiments, including two public real-world datasets, namely Stanford[1] and Columbia [8] respectively. The rest one is a collection on the Clickture-Full of MSR-bing dataset. Specifically, M-M2015 is a public released dataset with our post-denoising process. Detailed descriptions are shown in Table 1. After analyzing images of these distinct datasets (Figure 3), we have discovered the following observations (where $\succ$ denotes as 'is superior to'):

- Clarity: Columbia $\succ$ Stanford $\succ$ MM2015
- Complexity: MM2015 > Stanford > Columbia
- Slant degree of samples: Stanford>Columbia>MM2015
- Category: MM2015>Columbia>Stanford

2.2.2 Dog Breeds Recognition System

Convolutional Neural Network has recently obtained great success on several visual recognition and detection Challenges. With CNN pre-trained on large amount of data, we can fine-tune the trained CNN on our own datasets so as to accomplish specific tasks. In our model, we utilized the architecture proposed by VGG group, which is a 19-layer convolutional neural network[9] pre-trained on ILSVR-C dataset. In order to generalize this CNN to dog breeds classification, we pre-trained it on two datasets, Stanford Dogs Dateset[1] and Columbia Dogs with Parts[8]. Stanford Dataset contains images of 120 breeds of dogs from ImageNet and Columbia Dataset contains images of 133 breeds of dogs downloaded from Google, ImageNet and Flickr. The 120 breeds of Stanford Dogs Dataset are included in 133 breeds of Columbia Dogs with Parts. Therefore we de-

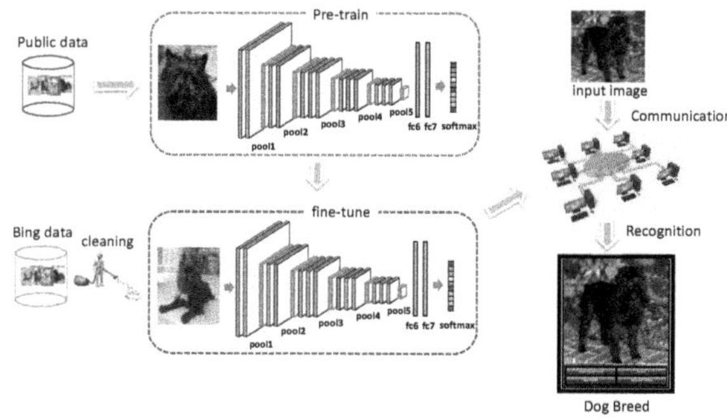

Figure 4: A flow chart of our system.

noted the 120 breeds as our targeted categories. For each category we selected 200 images as training data and 30 images as testing data. In pre-training stage, our model was pre-trained with dropout(dropout ratio set to 0.5) and regularized by weight decay(The L_2 penalty multiplier set to $5 \cdot 10^{-4}$). The initial learning rate is 0.01 and then decreased by a factor of 10 after each epoch, the learning rate was stopped after 100K iterations(2 epochs). In fine-tuning stage, we first detected dog breeds in MSR-bing query data. We found 344 dog breeds occurred in queries. Then we extracted corresponding images of each breed from MSR-bing training set and removed obviously unrelated images by human, which resulted in 42886 images as training data. Since we noticed that dogs in images can be of different sizes, we followed the multi-scale training proposed in [9] to fine-tune our model. We first rescaled all training images to 256×256 and then fine-tuned our model with these images. Then we rescaled all training images to 384×384, reduced initial learning rate to 10^{-3} and fine-tuned only fully-connected layers. Our data augmentation generally followed [6] and training procedure is the same as that in pre-training stage. We conducted experiments in Caffe[5]. In a word, the synthesized model is shown in Figure 4. For future convenience, we will plan to implement our CNNs model into mobile phones through hashing methods(e.g. [7]).

3. EXPERIMENT

3.1 Web Image Retrieval

We utilized CNNs trained on ImageNet[6] and Places[14] datasets respectively, to extract features that will be used in later stage. Both CNNs have the same architecture, with the only difference is that they are trained on two different large datasets, namely object-centric ImageNet dataset and scene-centric Places dataset[14]. The reason for using the two CNNs is that high-level features learned by them are complementary[14]. We also experimented with 19-layer VGG[9] network. Nevertheless it does not perform well in our experiments. We attribute its inferior performance to absence of fine-tuning such that in later layers it cannot learn meaningful high-level features. We use open source framework Caffe[5] to extract features from 7-th layer(fc7).

We then compare our methods with those proposals in the previous Challenges, and the results are shown in Table 2. We can observe that the $NDCG$ of completely matched queries of our methods outperforms that of partly matched ones. For instance, compared with the Ground-truth, ImageNet(P) achieves 84.34% of completely matched queries and 75.34% of partly matched queries respectively. The PageRank method still surpasses other two methods whatever the CNN features are. Furthermore, although the Hierarchical clustering is not as good as PageRank method, a model fusion with PageRank achieves a great improvement in $NDCG$, indicating that the strategies of these 2 methods do act complementary. However, combining the three models makes the performance a little bit lower, since the ranking strategy of K-means is similar to Hierarchical clustering, and the bagging may weaken the complemental benefit. Besides, we also discover that a simply re-ranking strategy on the top 25 images can improve the performance. The final competition result of our method is: 0.4715.(a little format error occurd in the submission.) We only achieved the third prize in web image retrieval task.

Table 2: Metrics evaluation of different methods on MSR-bing Dev. 'K', 'H' and 'P' are short for K-means, Hierarchical clustering and PageRank respectively. 'Comb' denotes the model fusion of ImageNet and Places. 'Rerank' denotes a re-ranking strategy for the top 25 images.

Method	Comp Match	Part Match	Total
Randomly	-	-	0.4690
Ground-truth	0.8090	0.5800	0.6840
GP[10]	0.6780	0.4330	0.5400
CrossMedia[12]	-	-	0.5608
ImageNet(K)	0.6720	0.4210	0.5340
ImageNet(H)	0.6787	0.4235	0.5383
ImageNet(P)	0.6823	0.4370	0.5474
ImageNet(H+P)	0.6884	0.4456	0.5549
ImageNet(K+H+P)	0.6880	0.4448	0.5542
Comb(H+P)	0.6912	0.4468	0.5567
Comb-Rerank(H+P)	0.6986	0.4440	0.5586

3.2 Visual Recognition

We compare our methods on the two CNN architectures and the results are shown in Table 3. We can observe that the metric of VGG is much higher than that of AlexNet. It demonstrates that deep network has better representation. Furthermore, Multi-scale training improved 1.2% performance during testing, which demonstrates our idea. The final competition results of our method are: Accuracy@1: 57% and Accuracy@5: 85%. Fortunately, we achieved the first prize in fine-grained recognition task.

Table 3: Experiment on MM2015 dataset. where S, C denote as 'Stanford' and 'Columbia' dataset respectively.

CNN Structure	Pre-train	Fine-tune	Accuracy@1(%)
AlexNet	S+C	MM	51.7
VGG	S+C	MM	63.2
Mul-AlexNet	S+C	MM	52.8
Mul-VGG	S+C	MM	64.5

4. CONCLUSION

In this paper, we propose a series of methods to accomplish the two tasks of MSR-bing Challenge. We discover that the Hierarchical clustering and PageRank methods are mutually complementary for information retrieval. Besides, we propose a method only using image-level information for fine-grained visual recognition. Our CNN model is pre-trained on a collection of clean datasets and fine-tuned on the bing datasets. We then implement our methods into a unified visual recognition system on Microsoft cloud service.

5. ACKNOWLEDGMENTS

This work was supported in part by National Natural Science Foundation of China (Grant No. 61332016,61170127), and 863 program (Grant No.2014AA015105).

6. REFERENCES

[1] E. Dataset. Novel datasets for fine-grained image categorization. In *First Workshop on Fine Grained Visual Categorization, CVPR*. Citeseer, 2011.

[2] R. Farrell, O. Oza, N. Zhang, V. Morariu, T. Darrell, L. S. Davis, et al. Birdlets: Subordinate categorization using volumetric primitives and pose-normalized appearance. In *Computer Vision (ICCV), 2011 IEEE International Conference on*, pages 161–168. IEEE, 2011.

[3] X.-S. Hua. Looking into" msr-bing image retrieval challenge. Technical report, Microsoft Research Technical Report MSR-TR-2013–76, 2013.

[4] Y. Hua, J. Shao, H. Tian, Z. Zhao, F. Su, and A. Cai. An output aggregation system for large scale cross-modal retrieval. In *Multimedia and Expo Workshops (ICMEW), 2014 IEEE International Conference on*, pages 1–6. IEEE, 2014.

[5] Y. Jia, E. Shelhamer, J. Donahue, S. Karayev, J. Long, R. Girshick, S. Guadarrama, and T. Darrell. Caffe: Convolutional architecture for fast feature embedding. *arXiv preprint arXiv:1408.5093*, 2014.

[6] A. Krizhevsky, I. Sutskever, and G. E. Hinton. Imagenet classification with deep convolutional neural networks. In *Advances in neural information processing systems*, pages 1097–1105, 2012.

[7] C. Leng, J. Wu, J. Cheng, X. Bai, and H. Lu. Online sketching hashing. In *Proceedings of the IEEE Conference on Computer Vision and Pattern Recognition*, pages 2503–2511, 2015.

[8] J. Liu, A. Kanazawa, D. Jacobs, and P. Belhumeur. Dog breed classification using part localization. In *Computer Vision–ECCV 2012*, pages 172–185. Springer, 2012.

[9] K. Simonyan and A. Zisserman. Very deep convolutional networks for large-scale image recognition. *arXiv preprint arXiv:1409.1556*, 2014.

[10] J. Wang, C. Kang, Y. He, S. Xiang, and C. Pan. Cross modal deep model and gaussian process based model for msr-bing challenge. In *Proceedings of the ACM International Conference on Multimedia*, pages 225–228. ACM, 2014.

[11] C.-C. Wu, K.-Y. Chu, Y.-H. Kuo, Y.-Y. Chen, W.-Y. Lee, and W. H. Hsu. Search-based relevance association with auxiliary contextual cues. In *Proceedings of the 21st ACM international conference on Multimedia*, pages 393–396. ACM, 2013.

[12] Z. Xu, Y. Yang, A. Kassim, and S. Yan. Cross-media relevance mining for evaluating text-based image search engine. In *Multimedia and Expo Workshops (ICMEW), 2014 IEEE International Conference on*, pages 1–4. IEEE, 2014.

[13] M. D. Zeiler and R. Fergus. Visualizing and understanding convolutional networks. In *Computer Vision–ECCV 2014*, pages 818–833. Springer, 2014.

[14] B. Zhou, A. Lapedriza, J. Xiao, A. Torralba, and A. Oliva. Learning deep features for scene recognition using places database. In *Advances in Neural Information Processing Systems*, pages 487–495, 2014.

Image Retrieval by Cross-Media Relevance Fusion

Jianfeng Dong[1]* Xirong Li[2,3]† Shuai Liao[2], Jieping Xu[2,3], Duanqing Xu[1], Xiaoyong Du[2]
[1]College of Computer Science and Technology, Zhejiang University
[2]Key Lab of Data Engineering and Knowledge Engineering, Renmin University of China
[3]Multimedia Computing Lab, School of Information, Renmin University of China
danieljf24@zju.edu.cn, xirong@ruc.edu.cn

ABSTRACT

How to estimate cross-media relevance between a given query and an unlabeled image is a key question in the MSR-Bing Image Retrieval Challenge. We answer the question by proposing *cross-media relevance fusion*, a conceptually simple framework that exploits the power of individual methods for cross-media relevance estimation. Four base cross-media relevance functions are investigated, and later combined by weights optimized on the development set. With DCG_{25} of 0.5200 on the test dataset, the proposed image retrieval system secures the first place in the evaluation.

Categories and Subject Descriptors

H.3.3 [**INFORMATION STORAGE AND RETRIEVAL**]: Information Search and Retrieval

Keywords

Image retrieval challenge, Cross-media relevance fusion

1. INTRODUCTION

A well-educated native speaker of English is known to have a vocabulary of about 17,000 base words [3]. Image queries as varied combinations of these words are countless. Putting subjective queries like "*happy new year*" aside, even a query with strong visual clues like "*girl with long brown hair and blue eye with eyeliner on*" remains challenging for state-of-the-art visual object recognition. By all standards, finding relevant images for an unconstrained query is difficult.

In this paper we tackle the image retrieval problem in the context of the MSR-Bing Image Retrieval Challenge (IRC). In this challenge, a contesting system is asked to produce a real-valued score on each image-query pair that reflects how relevant the query could be used to describe the given image, with higher numbers indicating higher relevance. A sample of Bing user click log with 1M images and over 11M queries, called Clickture-lite [4], is provided for developing the system. While the images come from the web, contextual information such as filename, URL, and surrounding text that could be used for relevance estimation has been removed by the task organizers. Hence, how to effectively estimate cross-media relevance for a given image-query pair is essential for conquering the challenge.

As image and query are of two distinct modalities, they have to be represented in a common space so that cross-media relevance can be computed. Depending on the choice of the common space, we categorize existing works into three groups, namely image2text, text2image, and semantic embedding. In the first group, the image is represented by a bag-of-word vector, either by label propagation from visual neighbors [12, 13] or by a deep neural network that maps images into a bag-of-words space [1]. The second group reverses the mapping direction, representing the query by a set of images. The images are retrieved either from Clickture-lite by tag-based image retrieval [2], or from the other test images of the given query [13, 14]. Consequently, the cross-media relevance is implemented by aggregating the visual similarity between the retrieved images and the given image. Lastly, semantic embedding based methods project both image and query into a *learned* space. Four methods for constructing such a space are investigated in [11], where Canonical Correlation Analysis and its variant are found to be the best.

The three groups of methods may complement each other, due to their different mechanisms for cross-media relevance estimation. By directly matching with query logs, image2text and text2image are more suited for instance search, e.g., finding images of a specific celebrity. Semantic embedding has an effect of dimension reduction and topic discovery, and thus works for category search. Following this argument, fusion of cross-media relevance scores generated by different methods seems appealing.

While efforts have been made along the line of fusion [2, 11], the fact that none of these systems has ever won the challenge is somewhat discouraging. The winning team of the IRC 2013 edition even concludes that fusion has little influence on the performance [13]. Notice that in [11], the results to be combined are all generated by semantic embedding methods. This may make the results less diverse and thus less complementary. Moreover, the fusion weights are either set to be equal [11] or chosen by hand [2]. All this

*Work performed at Renmin University of China.
†Corresponding author

MM'15, October 26–30, 2015, Brisbane, Australia.

ACM 978-1-4503-3459-4/15/10 ...$15.00.
DOI: http://dx.doi.org/10.1145/2733373.2807419.

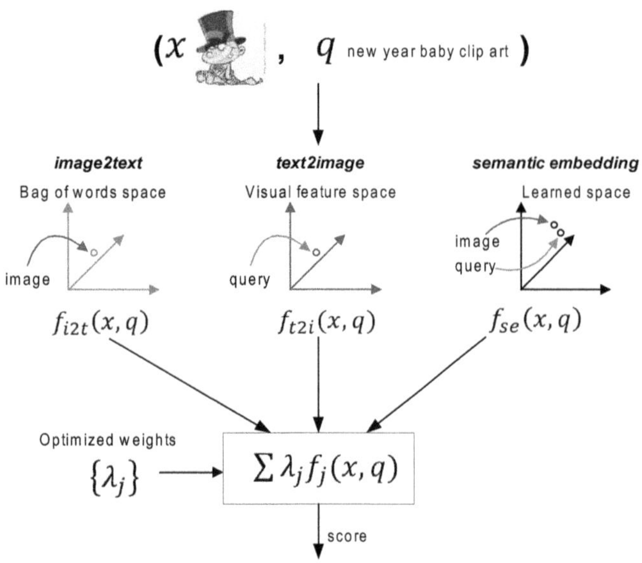

Figure 1: A conceptual diagram of the proposed cross-media relevance fusion (best viewed in color).

makes us believe that the potential of fusion has not been well explored.

Our contribution is a solution to IRC by cross-media relevance fusion, which is ranked the 1st according to the official evaluation. A conceptual diagram of the proposed solution is illustrated in Fig. 1.

The remaining sections are organized as follows. We describe the new solution in Section 2, followed by evaluation in Section 3. Conclusions are given in Section 4.

2. PROPOSED SOLUTION

Given an unlabeled image x and a textual query q, we aim to construct a real-valued function $f(x, q)$ that outputs a cross-media relevance score for the given pair. As discussed in Section 1, we opt for a fusion-based solution that exploits the power of the individual methods for cross-media relevance estimation. In what follows, we depict our choices of the methods, and present a strategy for optimizing the fusion weights.

2.1 Cross-Media Relevance Estimation

In order to generate relevance scores that complements each other, we adopt three different types of methods, i.e., image2text, text2image, and semantic embedding.

1) image2text $f_{i2t}(x, q)$. Inspired by the label propagation algorithm [12], for a given image x, we retrieve its k nearest visual neighbors, denoted as $\{x_1, \ldots, x_k\}$, from Clickture-lite. Relevance between x and a given query q is computed as a weighted sum of the textual similarity between q and queries associated with each of the k neighbor images. In particular, we have

$$f_{i2t}(x, q) := \frac{1}{k} \sum_{i=1}^{k} sim(x, x_i) \cdot sim_t(x_i, q), \quad (1)$$

where $sim(x, x_i)$ is a visual similarity, and

$$sim_t(x_i, q) := \frac{1}{m_i} \sum_{j=1}^{m_i} sim(q, q_{i,j}) \cdot \log(click_{i,j}), \quad (2)$$

where m_i is the number of queries associated with x_i in Clickture-lite, $click_{i,j}$ is click count x_i received with respect to query $q_{i,j}$, and $sim(q, q')$ is a query-wise similarity. Viewing each query as a set of tags, we use the Jaccard similarity coefficient to realize $sim(q, q')$.

For the visual similarity, we extract off-the-shelf CNN features and use the cosine similarity. Specifically, we employ two pre-trained Caffe models, using their fc7 layer as features. One model was learned from examples of 1,000 visual object classes in the Large Scale Visual Recognition Challenge (LSVRC) [5], and thus describes what objects are present in an image. The second model was learned from examples of 205 scene classes [15], and thus describes what scenes the image captures. For the ease of reference, we term the two models and corresponding features as LSVRC-CNN and Places-CNN.

2) text2image $f_{t2i}(x, q)$. We propose to realize text2image in a dual form of image2text. For a given query q, we first retrieve the top k most similar queries, denoted as $\{q_1, \ldots, q_k\}$, from Clickture-lite. Relevance between x and q is computed as a weighted sum of the visual similarity between x and images associated with each of the neighbor queries. In particular, we have

$$f_{t2i}(x, q) := \frac{1}{k} \sum_{j=1}^{k} sim(q, q_j) \cdot sim_v(x, q_j), \quad (3)$$

where

$$sim_v(x, q_j) := \frac{1}{n_j} \sum_{i=1}^{n_j} sim(x, x_{i,j}) \cdot \log(click_{i,j}), \quad (4)$$

and n_j is the number of images associated with q_j in the query log.

3) text2image as Parzen window $f_{pw}(x, q)$. As an extreme case of Eq. 3, we set the similar query to be the test query itself. In this case, the click count of the log item in Eq. 4 will not be available. Therefore, the relevance score is computed as the averaged similarity between the given image and the other test images of the given query. Such a simplified formula has played a key role in the previous winning systems [1, 13, 14]. Note that the averaged similarity is essentially a specific form of Parzen window density estimation. The Parzen window version of text2image is expressed as

$$f_{pw}(x, q) := \frac{1}{n_q} \sum_{i=1}^{n_q} K_h(x - x_i^q), \quad (5)$$

where n_q is the number of test images corresponding to q, x_i^q indicates a specific test image, $K(\cdot)$ is the kernel parameterized by the bandwidth h. We use the normal kernel.

4) semantic embedding $f_{se}(x, q)$. We utilize ConSE [10], a deep learning based semantic embedding method originally developed for zero-shot learning. The key idea of ConSE is to first construct a semantic space by a neural language model [9] trained on millions of web documents. Each dimension of the space corresponds to a specific word, which is associated with a unique real-valued vector. Since the training process of the language model is highly scalable and efficient, the size of the vocabulary can easily be hundreds of thousands. This is an advantage compared to semantic embedding methods that have been investigated in the context of IRC, where the vocabulary size is typically limited to 50k for the scalability concern [1, 11].

An image is embedded into the same space, by first predicting relevant tags using an existing image annotation system (either LSVRC-CNN or Places-CNN in this work), and then taking the convex combination of the embedding vectors of the predicted tags. Let $\{y_1, \ldots, y_T\}$ be the top T most relevant tags predicted for a given image, the image embedding vector is obtained by

$$\mathbf{v}(x) := \frac{1}{Z} \sum_{i=1}^{T} p(y_i|x) \cdot \mathbf{v}(y_i) \tag{6}$$

where $p(y_i|x)$ is the relevance score of y_i given x, $Z = \sum_{i=1}^{T} p(y_i|x)$ is a normalization factor, and $\mathbf{v}(y_i)$ is the word embedding vector. We adopt word vectors from [6], which were trained on many Flickr tags and found to better capture visual relationships compared to word vectors learned from web documents.

To embed a query of arbitrary length, we use average pooling of the vectors of the query words. Consequently, the cross-media relevance is computed as the cosine similarity between the embedding vectors of the query and the image:

$$f_{se}(x, q) := cosine(\mathbf{v}(x), \mathbf{v}(q)). \tag{7}$$

2.2 Relevance Fusion with Optimized Weights

Given the above four methods and two CNN models, eight scores are computed per image-query pair. Without loss of generality, we use $\{f_i(x, q)|i = 1, \ldots, d\}$ to denote a d-dimensional score vector of a given pair. Linear fusion is applied for its effectiveness and efficiency:

$$f(x, q) := \sum_{i=1}^{d} \lambda_i f_i(x, q), \tag{8}$$

where $\{\lambda_i\}$ are weights to be optimized.

Formalization as Eq. 8 opens the way for a number of learning to rank algorithms. We employ Coordinate Ascent, initially developed for document retrieval [8], and later shown to be effective for combining multiple sources of ranking features for image retrieval [7]. Per iteration the algorithm optimizes a chosen weight by a bi-direction line search with increasing steps, with the remaining weights fixed. The search process requires no gradient computation, so a non-differentiable performance metric, e.g., DCG_{25} specified by IRC, can be directly optimized.

3. EVALUATION

3.1 Setup

Datasets. We use Clickture-lite as the training set to derive $f_{i2t}(x, q)$, $f_{t2i}(x, q)$, $f_{pw}(x, q)$, and $f_{se}(x, q)$, and the provided dev set for optimizing the weights $\{\lambda_i\}$. The test dataset, with 9.4K queries and 147K images, is significantly larger when compared to the previous editions. Moreover, a considerable amount of irrelevant image-query pairs are added, making the task even more challenging. As shown in Table 1, while the dev and test sets have similar upper bound, the random baseline of the test set is much lower.

Query preprocessing. We conduct standard text preprocessing: removing punctuation and lemmatizing words by NLTK. Meaningless words such as "image" and "picture" and standard English stopwords are removed also. Consequently, some queries are merged, resulting in 9M unique queries in the training set.

Table 1: Performance comparison.

Method	Dev set	Test set
random baseline	0.4702	0.4260
Upper bound	0.6852	0.6924
image2text + LSVRC-CNN	0.4992	–
image2text + Places-CNN	0.4967	–
text2image + LSVRC-CNN	0.5157	0.4897
text2image + Places-CNN	0.5086	–
Parzen window + LSVRC-CNN	0.5428	–
Parzen window + Places-CNN	0.5347	–
semantic embedding + LSVRC-CNN	0.4857	–
semantic embedding + Places-CNN	0.4795	–
fusion-feat6-avg	0.5139	–
fusion-feat6	0.5201	0.4929
fusion-feat8-avg	0.5369	–
fusion-feat8	0.5529	0.5200

Performance metric. Following the evaluation protocol, DCG_{25} is reported.

Naming convention. We name each run using the corresponding method plus feature name. E.g., image2text + LSVRC-CNN means using relevance scores produced by the image2text method with the LSVRC-CNN feature. The runs start with "fusion" correspond to cross-media relevance fusion, while fusion-feat8 means all the 8 scores are combined, and fusion-feat6 does not include two scores related to $f_{pw}(x, q)$. The difference between fusion-feat8 and fusion-feat8-avg is that the latter uses equal weights.

3.2 Results

Performance comparison on the dev set. As shown in Table 1, all methods outperform the random baseline. Concerning the choice of the visual features, LSVRC-CNN is better than Places-CNN. This is probably because Places-CNN focuses on scene classes, making its features less effective for representing the visual content of generic images. We attribute the relatively lower performance of semantic embedding to the fact that the LSVRC 1,000 object classes are not specifically designed for describing generic queries. The result that fusion-feat6-avg and fusion-feat8-avg are worse than the best single method shows the importance of weight optimization. Fig. 2 shows top 10 results of query "new year baby clip art" retrieved by different methods. In this example, fusion improves over Parzen Window in terms of both accuracy and diversity.

Performance comparison on the Test Set. We submitted three runs, i.e., text2image, fusion-feat6, and fusion-feat8. Our runs lead the evaluation, as shown in Fig. 3. Similar to the dev set, the Parzen window method is important. Adding it increases DCG_{25} from 0.4929 to 0.5200.

Concerning efficiency, our prototype system runs at a speed of approximately 0.8 image-query pair per second on a common GPU.

4. CONCLUSIONS

Our experiments with IRC support conclusions as follows. Among the four methods we have investigated, Parzen win-

Figure 2: Top 10 results of query "new year baby clip art" returned by different methods.

dow remains the most effective. Fusion leads to the best performance. But the superiority is achieved only when appropriate care is taken to optimize fusion weights.

Acknowledgments. This work was supported by the National Natural Science Foundation of China (No. 61303184), the Fundamental Research Funds for the Central Universities and the Research Funds of Renmin University of China (No. 14XNLQ01), the National Key Technology Support Program (No. 2012BAH70F02), and the National Social Science Fundation of China (No. 12&ZD141).

5. REFERENCES

[1] Y. Bai, W. Yu, T. Xiao, C. Xu, K. Yang, W.-Y. Ma, and T. Zhao. Bag-of-words based deep neural network for image retrieval. In *ACM MM*, 2014.

[2] Q. Fang, H. Xu, R. Wang, S. Qian, T. Wang, J. Sang, and C. Xu. Towards msr-bing challenge: Ensemble of diverse models for image retrieval. In *MSR-Bing IRC 2013 Workshop*, 2013.

[3] R. Goulden, P. Nation, and J. Read. How large can a receptive vocabulary be? *Applied Linguistics*, 11(4):341–363, 1990.

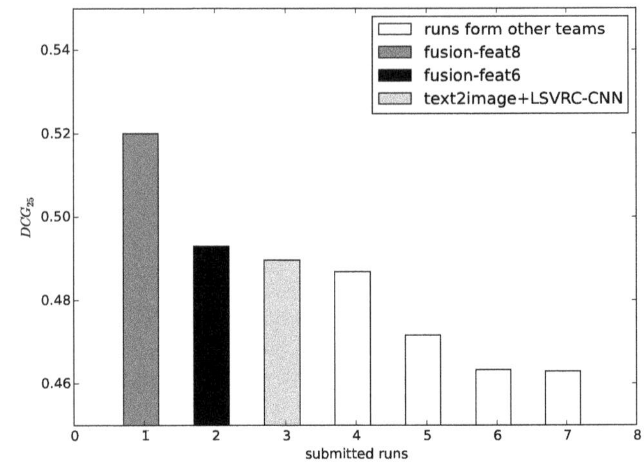

Figure 3: Performance on the test dataset. Our submissions lead the evaluation.

[4] X. S. Hua, L. Yang, J. Wang, J. Wang, M. Ye, K. Wang, Y. Rui, and J. Li. Clickage: Towards bridging semantic and intent gaps via mining click logs of search engines. *ACM MM*, 2013.

[5] Y. Jia, E. Shelhamer, J. Donahue, S. Karayev, J. Long, R. Girshick, S. Guadarrama, and T. Darrell. Caffe: Convolutional architecture for fast feature embedding. *arXiv:1408.5093*, 2014.

[6] X. Li, S. Liao, W. Lan, X. Du, and G. Yang. Zero-shot image tagging by hierarchical semantic embedding. *SIGIR*, 2015.

[7] X. Li, C. Snoek, M. Worring, and A. Smeulders. Fusing concept detection and geo context for visual search. In *ICMR*, 2012.

[8] D. Metzler and B. Croft. Linear feature-based models for information retrieval. *Inf. Retr.*, 10(3):257–274, 2007.

[9] T. Mikolov, K. Chen, G. Corrado, and J. Dean. Efficient estimation of word representations in vector space. In *ICLR*, 2013.

[10] M. Norouzi, T. Mikolov, S. Bengio, Y. Singer, J. Shlens, A. Frome, G. Corrado, and J. Dean. Zero-shot learning by convex combination of semantic embeddings. *ICLR*, 2014.

[11] Y. Pan, T. Yao, X. Tian, H. Li, and C.-W. Ngo. Click-through-based subspace learning for image search. In *ACM MM*, 2014.

[12] Y. Pan, T. Yao, K. Yang, H. Li, C.-W. Ngo, J. Wang, and T. Mei. Image search by graph-based label propagation with image representation from dnn. In *ACM MM*, 2013.

[13] C.-C. Wu, K.-Y. Chu, Y.-H. Kuo, Y.-Y. Chen, W.-Y. Lee, and W. H. Hsu. Search-based relevance association with auxiliary contextual cues. In *ACM MM*, 2013.

[14] Z. Xu, Y. Yang, A. Kassim, and S. Yan. Cross-media relevance mining for evaluating text-based image search engine. In *ICME*, 2014.

[15] B. Zhou, A. Lapedriza, J. Xiao, A. Torralba, and A. Oliva. Learning deep features for scene recognition using places database. *NIPS*, 2014.

Who are the Devils Wearing Prada in New York City?

KuanTing Chen
National Taiwan University,
Taipei, Taiwan
ktchen@cmlab.csie.ntu.edu.tw

Kezhen Chen*
University of Rochester,
Rochester, New York, USA
kchen33@u.rochester.edu

Peizhong Cong
University of Rochester,
Rochester, New York, USA
cong314159@gmail.com

Winston H. Hsu
National Taiwan University,
Taipei, Taiwan
whsu@ntu.edu.tw

Jiebo Luo
University of Rochester,
Rochester, New York, USA
jluo@cs.rochester.edu

ABSTRACT

Fashion is a perpetual topic in human social life, and the mass has the penchant to emulate what large city residents and celebrities wear. Undeniably, New York City is such a bellwether large city with all kinds of fashion leadership. Consequently, to study what the fashion trends are during this year, it is very helpful to learn the fashion trends of New York City. Discovering fashion trends in New York City could boost many applications such as clothing recommendation and advertising. Does the fashion trend in the New York Fashion Show actually influence the clothing styles on the public? To answer this question, we design a novel system that consists of three major components: (1) constructing a large dataset from the New York Fashion Shows and New York street chic in order to understand the likely clothing fashion trends in New York, (2) utilizing a learning-based approach to discover fashion attributes as the representative characteristics of fashion trends, and (3) comparing the analysis results from the New York Fashion Shows and street-chic images to verify whether the fashion shows have actual influence on the people in New York City. Through the preliminary experiments over a large clothing dataset, we demonstrate the effectiveness of our proposed system, and obtain useful insights on fashion trends and fashion influence.

Categories and Subject Descriptors

H.4.0 [**Information Systems Applications**]: General; I.4.8 [**Scene Analysis**]: Color, Shape, Object recognition; I.5.4 [**Applications**]: Computer vision

Keywords

Fashion trend; clothing attributes; clothing style

*KuanTing Chen and Kezhen Chen contributed equally to this work.

MM'15, October 26–30, 2015, Brisbane, Australia.
© 2015 ACM. ISBN 978-1-4503-3459-4/15/10 ...$15.00.
DOI: http://dx.doi.org/10.1145/2733373.2809930.

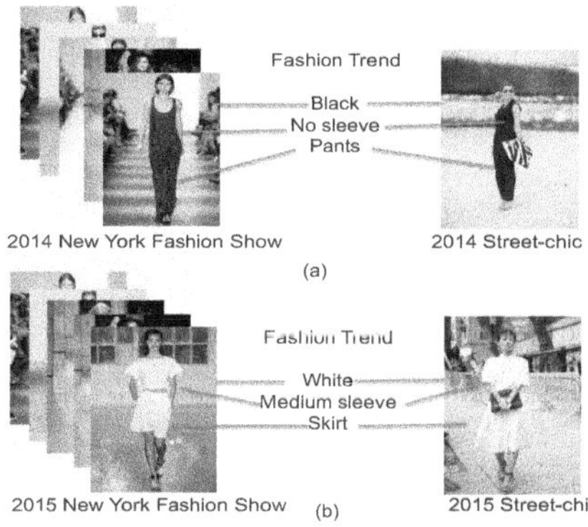

Figure 1: Examples for the influence of New York Fashion Show on the public.

1. INTRODUCTION

"The devil wears Prada" is a very popular fashion related movie which describes the story between a recent college graduated girl and the diabolic fashion magazine editor Miranda Priestly. Although Miranda's grim manner of management is impressive, we also admire her unique foresight and aesthetics of fashion. In modern times, a growing number of people pay more attention to fashion and the mass has the penchant to emulate what large city residents and celebrities wear. Moreover, investigating fashion trends has become a great interest for the industry and academia [8][14][15][13] because of its promising opportunity for boosting many emerging applications such as clothing recommendation, advertising by clothing brand association, etc. Consequently, learning the fashion trends every year is very important for the industry as well as sociology and psychology.

Indisputably, New York City is one of the most famous fashion metropolises and the New York Fashion Week is one of the four most significant fashion weeks around the world [6][2][4]. The New York Fashion Show consists of almost 300 catwalk shows which are attended by more than 100,000 people [6]. The New York City Economic Development Corporation reported that the local economy is boosted by 850 million dollars by the New York Fashion Week [5].

A traditional way to discover fashion trend in the New York Fashion Week would be relying on the domain knowledge of the clothing designers and experts. However, it is very time consuming and the fashion trends vary with the

Year	#designer	#images	Year	#designer	#images
2014	27	4000	2015	20	3914

(a) New York Fashion Shows

Year	#images	Year	#images
2014	471	2015	575

(b) Street-Chic

Figure 2: Examples from two data resources for clothing style analysis, (a) New York Fashion Show and (b) Street-chic.

season. Hidayati et al. [12] proposed to exploit fashion elements by clustering visual patches in the video frames of the fashion show. In contrast to this work, we focus on learning the clothing fashion trends by fashion attribute discovery. Moreover, to our best knowledge, this is the first work to address the question "Does the fashion trend in the New York Fashion Show actually influence the clothing styles of the public?" (cf. Figure).

In this paper, we first construct a large clothing dataset from two resources: (1) a large number of images from fashion shows during the annual New York Fashion Week. (2) Street-chic images after New York Fashion Shows in order to gauge whether the fashion trends have influence on people's daily life. Next, we analyze 2014 and 2015 fashion show images and extract the fashion attributes. More specifically, for every image, we automatically extract 60 clothing attributes such as collar, necktie, pants, etc. Using semantic clothing attributes to represent fashion trends can tell people the most popular style, which is not only a good way to learn fashion trends for research, but also is a specific fashion reference for people to choose. Finally, we utilize these attributes as our predicted clothing fashion style and compare these attributes with attributes from street-chic. In our experimental results, we demonstrate the effectiveness of the clothing attributes and the correlation of clothing style between fashion shows and street-chic.

2. DATASET CONSTRUCTION

In this work, we mainly exploit the fashion trend in 2015 and the influence of fashion trends on people's daily life. In our dataset, in order to study the fashion influence on people's daily life, we collect two datasets. **(1) Street-chic dataset.** This dataset contains 471 street-chic images in New York from April 2014 to July 2014 and 575 street-chic images in New York from April 2015 to July 2015 [1][3]. It is worth noting that the number of images from street chic is not very large in each year, but these images are high quality and representative (cf. Figure 2) **(2) New York Fashion Show.** As these street-chic images are all from summer/spring season, we collected 3914 images from 2014 summer/spring New York Fashion Show and 4000 images from 2015 summer/spring New York Fashion Show, respectively [7]. The 7914 images from 2014 and 2015 New York Fashion Shows are used to extract features and fashion attributes to analyze fashion trends. We summarize and illustrate examples of our datasets in Figure 2.

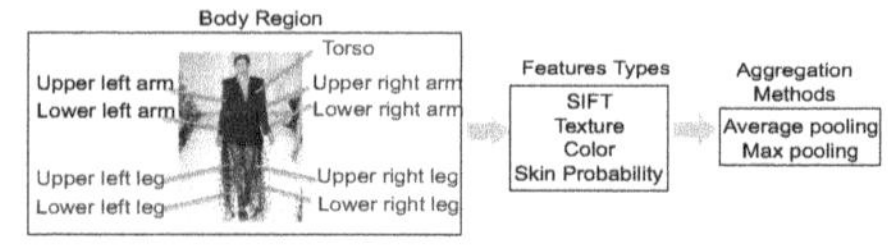

Figure 3: An illustration of the visual features we extracted from photos.

3. FASHION STYLE DISCOVERY

To provide a significant and specific clothing fashion reference, an effective framework for exploring clothing style representation is required. Using an appropriate clothing representation, we could offer a semantic and intuitive way for people to determine what fashion style they would like to choose. Inspired by the paper [10], a learning-based clothing attributes approach was carried out to describe clothing style. In the research [10], Chen et al. only detected 42 upper body clothing attributes. However, we observe the clothing information in the lower body is an essential clue for fashion trends understanding (e.g. wearing pants or skirt). Different from this research [10], we proposed to exploit a 60-attribute semantic representation to describe both upper and lower body clothing attributes. In the following, we briefly describe the adopted approaches for learning the clothing attribute. Table 1 shows the details of clothing attributes.

3.1 Feature Extraction

Before learning the 60 clothing attributes, we need to extract clothing features beforehand to train classifiers for every attribute. Thanks for Marcin Eichner's team [11], we apply their pose estimation software to detecting the model's pose and retrieve the body region of the model. More clearly, the pose estimation process is to segment body into nine parts: torso, upper left arm, upper right arm, lower left arm, lower right arm, upper left leg, upper right leg, lower left leg and lower right leg. Next, we extract four different kinds of features (e.g. color, texture, SIFT, and skin) and utilize two different aggregation methods to generate a visual feature vector for all the parts of the body. An example is illustrated in Figure 3.

3.2 Fashion Attribute Learning

In order to determine whether an fashion element is present in an image, we adopt a Support Vector Machine (SVM) [9] with a Chi-square kernel to learning fashion attributes (cf. Table 1). The most intuitive way for training each fashion attribute is concatenating 72 features (cf. Section 3.1) into a long vector that becomes the full body visual feature vector. However, the influence of different types of feature on each attributes may vary. For example, texture features might have a great effect on pattern based attributes. Consequently, we compute the classification performance of each feature to represent the importance of features as weights towards individual attributes. As a result, a weighting parameter can be applied to vectors from different features to emphasize the importance of different features.

3.3 Attribute Relation Inference

In section 3.2 the fashion elements are considered as isolated attributes. However, it is highly possible that some attributes appear in pairs (or groups). For example, we ob-

Table 1: A summary of Fashion attributes.

Style	Gender	Bags	Accessories	Skin Exposure
	Necktie	Collar	Neckring	Belt
	Placket	Pant	Skirt	
Upper -body	Pattern		Color	
	floral, graphics, plaid, solid, spot, stripe		black, blue, brown, cyan, gray, green, purple, red, white, yellow, multicolor	
Lower -body	Pattern		Color	
	floral, graphics, plaid, solid, spot, stripe		black, blue, brown, cyan, gray, green, purple, red, white, yellow, multicolor	

Table 2: The summary of attributes percentage appeared in spring/summer fashion shows.

Style

Attribute	2014	2015	Attribute	2014	2015	Attribute	2014	2015	Attribute	2014	2015
Bags accessories	21.9%	22.7%	Necktie	0.7%	1.1%	Medium (Knee Length)	48.8%	43.4%	T-shirt (category)	6.1%	7.7%
Skirt	**74.0%**	**71.0%**	Placket	29.6%	34.1%	Long (Knee Length)	45.3%	52.7%	Outwear (category)	44.6%	49.1%
Pants	26.0%	29%	Skin Exposure	30%	27.4%	V-shape (Neckline)	15.4%	18.9%	Suit (category)	2.0%	2.2%
Belt	21.4%	20.4%	No Sleeve	35.2%	29.6%	Round (Neckline)	60.0%	59.1%	Tank Top (category)	28.1%	34.0%
Collar	39.5%	43.6%	Short Sleeve	18.5%	20.8%	Other (Neckline)	19.6%	18.1%	Dress (category)	43.7%	37.4%
Male	2.1%	2.3%	Long Sleeve	56.6%	61.0%	Shirt (category)	2.6%	3.2%			
Neckring	5.4%	6.2%	Short (Knee Length)	27.6%	22.1%	Sweater (category)	3.8%	3.5%			

Color

Attribute (Upper-body)	2014	2015	Attribute (Upper-body)	2014	2015	Attribute (Lower-body)	2014	2015	Attribute (Lower-body)	2014	2015
Black	**20.9%**	**19.2%**	Purple	3.2%	3.1%	Black	**27.7%**	**28.5%**	Purple	0.8%	1.1%
Blue	8.9%	11.7%	Red	4.1%	5.4%	Blue	5.7%	6.8%	Red	9.0%	8.9%
Brown	4.0%	4.4%	White	**32.6%**	**32.1%**	Brown	6.5%	5.5%	White	**29.9%**	**29.3%**
Cyan	10.4%	11.8%	Yellow	14.6%	11.7%	Cyan	0.3%	0.5%	Yellow	6.3%	4.3%
Gray	**18.9%**	**18.4%**	Multicolor	14.2%	16.3%	Gray	**15.7%**	**15.7%**	Multicolor	36.4%	35.5%
Green	7.1%	6.9%				Green	2.1%	1.6%			

Pattern

Attribute (Upper-body)	2014	2015	Attribute (Upper-body)	2014	2015	Attribute (Lower-body)	2014	2015	Attribute (Lower-body)	2014	2015
Floral	12.7%	10.0%	Solid	**46.4%**	**50.4%**	Floral	8.9%	8.7%	Solid	**59.1%**	**62.4%**
Graphics	14.7%	13.7%	Spotted	3.1%	3.2%	Graphics	20.0%	19.5%	Spotted	1.7%	1.2%
Plaid	0.5%	0.3%	Striped	2.6%	3.3%	Plaid	0.6%	0.5%	Striped	1.5%	2.1%

serve that a plaid shirt might have more than two colors. Note that inter-attribute dependencies are not always symmetric. For example, while a plaid shirt strongly suggests the presence of more than two colors, more than two colors do not necessarily suggest a shirt being plaid. We adopt a Conditional Random Fields (CRF) approach to inference the relation betweens attributes. More specifically, each attribute acts as a node in the CRF framework and the edge connecting every two nodes indicates the joint probability of these two attributes. We build a fully connected CRF with all the attributes pairwise connected.

4. EXPERIMENTAL RESULTS

We conduct experiments on a large clothing dataset collected from the New York Fashion Shows and Street-chic photos.

We conduct several experiments to gain understanding of the performance of the attributes. The overall accuracy of attributes is 62.6%. The examples in Figure indicate that the extracted attributes was effective for clothing style representation. An interesting observation is that some categories suffer from worse results (e.g. 42% accuracy of belt, 56% accuracy of accessories) since the objects are relatively small compared to the entire body. In the future, we could segment the body into more parts to improve the accuracy of the attributes detection. For example, we could segment the middle body for belt and the neck part for the accessories.

Table 2 shows the attributes percentage detected on the 2014 New York Fashion Shows and 2015 New York Fashion Shows. We divide these attributes into three categories, color, pattern and clothing style. We observe that there are always some classic colors, patterns or styles that have a large amount of clothing images in the fashion shows of every year. For example, in upper body color, both 2014 and 2015 fashion images have a large amount of white, gray and black colors. In upper body and lower body patterns, solid pattern is the classic pattern and solid pattern clothes always dominate every year's fashion shows. In the style attribute category, there are many images with skirt in spring/summer fashion shows. These examples indicate that the results generated by attribute description methods are very reasonable and these results can be a very significant reflection for the fashion shows styles.

Besides these classic cloth styles, we are also interested in the changes in the fashion trend. These changes in attributes could indicate special fashion trends for the specific year. Note that we remove the classic style attributes, black, white and gray in the color category, solid pattern in the pattern category and skirts in the style category to present the changes more clearly. Figure 4 shows the change of fashion trend between the 2015 fashion shows and the 2014 fashion shows. From this figure, we could tell the unique fashion trends for 2015. In the color category, attributes with larger changes in the upper body are blue, multicolor, cyan and red; attributes with larger changes in the lower body are blue and purple. In the pattern category, attribute with larger changes in the upper body is striped; attribute with larger changes in the lower body is striped. In the style category, long knee length, tank top, placket, outwear and collar are most significant attributes in 2015. These attributes with larger changes could be regarded as the unique fashion attributes trends shown in 2015.

In order to analyze the influence from the New York Fashion Shows on people's daily life, we analyze the clothing attributes from the street chic images. As we mainly focus on the spring and summer fashion show influence, we collected 471 street chic images in 2014 and 575 street chic images in 2015 that were taken in New York from April to July and utilize these images as our street-chic data for fashion influence analysis. The changes of these attributes between 2014 and 2015 are shown in Figure 4. As shown in Figure 4, some changing trends of attributes are the same in fashion shows and in street chic. For example, there is a significant rise in both placket and tank top of the style category. In the pattern category, striped pattern in the upper body increased substantially. In the color category, blue in the lower body, blue, cyan, red and multicolor in the upper body showed an upward trend in both fashion show and street chic images. Consequently, we could tell that many people have the penchant to emulate clothing styles shown in the fashion shows. Some examples are shown in Figure 5. Interestingly, there are some different changes of fashion elements between the fashion shows and street chic images. For instance, we observe that the difference between the fashion shows and street chic lies in the long knee sleeve and outwear. We discovered that summer 2014 is the coldest in a decade, and people tended to wear outwear to keep warm. Another interesting observation is that people tend to wear bright-colored clothes in both the upper body and the lower body instead of wearing in only the upper body as shown in the fashion shows. A reasonable explanation is that light-colored clothes can absorb less sun light and keep people cooler; therefore, people are tempted to wear light color clothes in order to keep them cooler in the hotter weather in 2015. In summary, it seems clear that fashion trends from fashion shows indeed provide people a clothing reference and have significant influence on people's daily life. However, so-

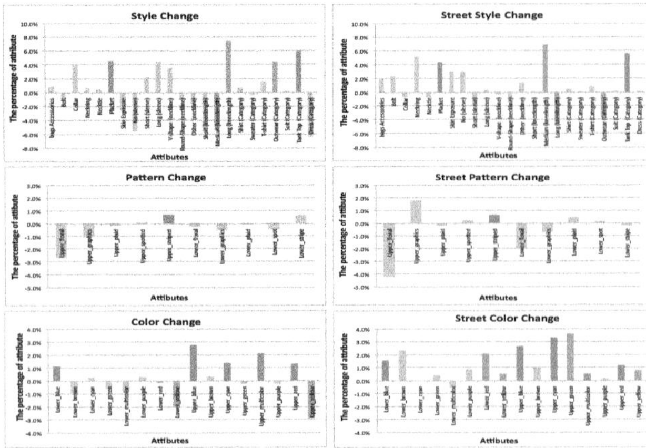

Figure 4: Quantitative fashion style changes in 2015 shown in the New York Fashion Shows (left column) and street-chic (right column). The correlation coefficients between the two columns are (style: -0.32, pattern: 0.64, color: 0.28). Note that the positively correlated attributes are marked red and the negatively correlated attributes are marked green. In terms of style, there are positively correlated attributes even though the overall correlation is negative, revealing both correlation and distance between stage and reality.

cial condition and natural conditions, such as weather, could be important factors for people to determine what they are likely to wear. Furthermore, analysis of street chic images also has benefit to inspire fashion designers to come up with more main-stream designs.

5. CONCLUSIONS

In this work, we construct a large dataset from the New York Fashion Shows and street-chic in order to investigate the possible clothing fashion trends in New York. In addition, we investigate a learning based method to automatically detect fashion attributes as the representation of fashion trends. We further demonstrate that the proposed framework is effective in fashion trend discovery. Furthermore, we compare the analysis result from the New York Fashion Shows and street-chic images in order to investigate whether and to what extent the fashion shows have influence on New York people. In the future, we plan to collect more images to increase the data set for more comprehensive studies. Moreover, there is also keen interest in exploring the proper fashion outfits to recommend users by aggregating user preference in clothing style and one future direction would be to incorporate these elements into the existing model and the scope will be extending and applying our system to practical applications, for example clothing style and product recommendation. Besides, the concept of clustering will also be one of the options as it will be interesting to automatically learning unseen clothing elements [12].

6. ACKNOWLEDGMENTS

This work was generously supported in part by Google, Yahoo, Adobe, TCL, and New York State CoE CEIS and IDS. KuanTing Chen is supported by a scholarship by the Taiwan Government NSC Study Abroad Program grants 103-2917-I-002-159.

Figure 5: The examples of the similarity of fashion trends shown both in (a) New York Fashion Show and (b) Street-chic.

7. REFERENCES

[1] Pinterest. http://pinterest.com.

[2] In vogue: How does catwalk influence the main street. http://www.bbc.com/news/magazine-14984468.

[3] Flickr. http://www.flickr.com.

[4] The 14 best trends of new york fashion week. http://www.marieclaire.com/fashion/g2359/new-york-fashion-week-spring-2015-trends/.

[5] The new york city economic development corporation. http://www.nycedc.com/.

[6] The new york times. http://www.nytimes.com/.

[7] Vogue. http://www.vogue.com/.

[8] L. D. Bourdev, S. Maji, and J. Malik. Describing people: A poselet-based approach to attribute classification. In *IEEE ICCV 2011, Barcelona, Spain, November 6-13, 2011*, pages 1543–1550, 2011.

[9] C.-C. Chang and C.-J. Lin. Libsvm: A library for support vector machines. *ACM Trans. Intell. Syst. Technol.*, 2(3):27:1–27:27, May 2011.

[10] H. Chen, A. Gallagher, and B. Girod. Describing clothing by semantic attributes. In *ECCV 2012*, volume 7574, pages 609–623, 2012.

[11] M. Eichner and V. Ferrari. Appearance sharing for collective human pose estimation. In *Computer Vision - ACCV 2012*, pages 138–151, 2012.

[12] S. C. Hidayati, K.-L. Hua, W.-H. Cheng, and S.-W. Sun. What are the fashion trends in new york? In *Proceedings of the ACM International Conference on Multimedia*, MM '14, pages 197–200. ACM, 2014.

[13] S. Liu, J. Feng, C. Domokos, H. Xu, J. Huang, Z. Hu, and S. Yan. Fashion parsing with weak color-category labels. *IEEE Transactions on Multimedia*, 16(1):253–265, 2014.

[14] S. Liu, Z. Song, G. Liu, C. Xu, H. Lu, and S. Yan. Street-to-shop: Cross-scenario clothing retrieval via parts alignment and auxiliary set. In *IEEE CVPR 2012*, pages 3330–3337, 2012.

[15] T. V. Nguyen, S. Liu, B. Ni, J. Tan, Y. Rui, and S. Yan. Sense beauty via face, dressing, and/or voice. In *Proceedings of the 20th ACM Multimedia Conference, MM '12*, pages 239–248, 2012.

What Makes New York So Noisy? Reasoning Noise Pollution by Mining Multimodal Geo-Social Big Data*

Hsun-Ping Hsieh
National Taiwan University
Taipei, Taiwan
d98944006@csie.ntu.edu.tw

Tzu-Chi Yen
Sensoro Technology Co., Ltd.,
Beijing, China
junipertcy@gmail.com

Cheng-Te Li
Academia Sinica
Taipei, Taiwan
ctli@citi.sinica.edu.tw

ABSTRACT

Noise pollution in modern cities is getting worse and sound sensors are sparse and costly, but it is highly demanded to have a system that can help reason and present the noise pollution at any region in urban areas. In this work, we leverage multimodal geo-social media data on Foursquare, Twitter, Flickr, and Gowalla in New York City, to infer and visualize the volume and the composition of noise pollution for every region in NYC. Using NYC 311 noise complaint records as the approximation of noise pollution for validation, we develop a joint inference and visualization system that integrates multimodal features, including geographical, mobility, visual, and social, with a graph-based learning model to infer the noise compositions of regions. Experimental results show that our model can achieve promising results with substantially few training data, compared to state-of-the-art methods. A NYC Urban Noise Diagnotor system is developed and allowed users to understand the noise composition of any region of NYC in an interactive manner.

Categories and Subject Descriptors

H.4.0 [**Information Systems Applications**]: General

Keywords

urban noises; multimodal data; geo-social media; big data

1. INTRODUCTION

With the prosperity of geo-social media, like Flickr, Twitter, Facebook and Foursquare, the volume of data that sensors and records the urban dynamics has increased dramatically. Geo-social media data is essentially *multimodal* since it is a mixture of geographical information (venue and location attributes), mobility footprints (check-in data), visual snapshots (consumer-contributed photos), and social interactions (social network). Data collected from geo-social media can be extensively considered as a kind of *sensors* that monitor urban human activities, and can be applied to urban-driven applications, such as detecting natural hazards events [7], tracking disease activities [8], and inferring air quality [10]. In current big cities like New York City, noise pollution had become a major problem [9] that affects the work efficiency and the sleep quality, and damages the mental health of people [1]. To tackle noise pollution of a certain urban region, the first step is to understand the elements and causes that produce the noise. If the composition of noise of any place in a city can be unveiled, such as "*in evening rush hour, 60% noise come from vehicle traffic, 30% from loud music, and 10% from loud talking*" on weekdays at Time Square, the government agencies can make the policies to cope with the problems, and the residents can plan their daily routines to prevent themselves from noise disturbance.

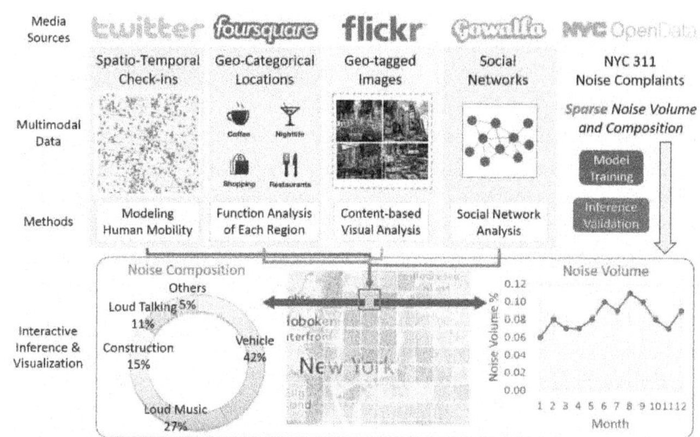

Figure 1: Exploiting multimodal data for urban noise pollution analysis and visualization.

In this paper, we aim to leverage multimodal geo-social media data to reason urban noises of regions in NYC. It is a challenging problem because both the magnitude and the composition of noise pollution vary by places and change over time. One might think installing sound sensors everywhere in the city is an approach. However, sound sensors are costly, limited to very small areas, and hard to help diagnose the reasons that produce noises. Since it is infeasible to access the noise information of all the urban regions, we resort to use the noise complaint records of the NYC 311 service, which is a platform allowing people to report the locations, time, and categories of their near-by annoyed events via phone calls, as an approximate of urban noises at some regions and time. Then we are allowed to analyze the noise

*This is the system version of our ACM MM 2015 Short Paper [5].

MM '15, October 26–30, 2015 Brisbane, Australia

DOI: http://dx.doi.org/10.1145/2733373.2809931.

composition of any region in a city. Nevertheless, the NYC 311 noise complaint data is sparse and gathered in a few number of regions. A model is needed to infer the noise composition of any region in the city.

Given the regions in NYC, in which a limited number of regions have sufficient noise composition information derived from 311 noise data, and multimodal geo-social media data, including check-in records in Twitter, geographical locations with categories in Foursquare, geo-tagged images in Flickr, and location-based social network in Gowalla, as illustrated in Figure 1, our goal is to infer the noise compositions of the remaining regions. The NYC 311 noise data is used as labeled data for model training and inference validation. Then based on the inferred results, we develop a visualization system that allows users to understand the noise compositions of regions in an interactive manner. To deal with the inference task, we devise a novel model, *Urban Noise Diagnotor* (UND). In UND, for each of the noise-labeled regions (marked ones) and the unlabeled regions, we use the geo-social sensor data to extract four heterogeneous features: geographical features from Foursquare, mobility features from Gowalla check-in data, visual features from Flickr geo-tagged photos, and social features from Gowalla location-based social network. Then a three-stage inference method is devised: constructing *region association map* (RAM), modeling the similarity values between regions, and a *noise propagation* algorithm to infer the noise composition of a region.

2. URBAN NOISE DIAGNOTOR

2.1 Geo-Social & NYC 311 Noise Datasets

We extract the noise complaint records from the open data of the NYC 311 service[1]. From Jan 2010 to Mar 2015, there are 196,631 complaint records of urban noise. The noise composition consists of 14 categories, in which the top-4 categories with the largest proportions are *Loud Music/Party*, *Construction*, *Loud Talking*, and *Vehicle*. On the other hand, we collect check-in records from Twitter[2], venue data with location categories from Foursquare[3] and the location-based social network (LBSN) data from Gowalla[4]. There are totally 47,581 venues/locations, 196,591 users, 950,327 social connections between users, and 6,442,890 check-in records. For geo-tagged photos, we use Flickr tourist photos whose GPS coordinates are in NYC, collected by Chen and Grauman [3]. Totally there are 57,200 images. According to a well-known study of urban noise analysis [4], we partition the geographical area of NYC into a number of *regions*, in which the size of each region is 1 km × 1 km. Totally there are 560 regions in NYC.

2.2 Multimodal Features

Geographical Features (G) are devised to describe the spatial and category distribution and the geographical interactions between venues because the type of noise can be related to the urban business environment. Regions with more/less venues or more/less venue categories can have different effects on the composition of noise. We extract two kinds of features for a region r.

- *Volume-based* features (**G-V**) use the *region density* and the *venue closeness* as the feature values. Region density $\mathcal{F}_d(r)$ is the number of venues in a region. Venue closeness $\mathcal{F}_{vc}(r)$ is the average geographical distance between venues in region r.
- *Category-based* features (**G-C**) consider the categories of venues, such as `food`, `shops`, `outdoors`, and `nightlife`, to characterize the activities of a region. We propose two category-based features. The first is *category entropy* measuring the diversity of a region, given by $\mathcal{F}_e(r) = -\sum_{a\in A} f_a \cdot \log(f_a)$, where a is a venue category, A is the set of all categories, and f_a is the fraction of venues with category a in region r. The second is *competitiveness* estimating the extent that venues with the same category gather in a region, given by $\mathcal{F}_b(r) = |\{l_i, l_j \in r : a(l_i) = a(l_j)\}|/\mathcal{F}_d(r)$, where l_i is a check-in venue, and $a(l_i)$ is the category of l_i.

Mobility Features (M) are developed to model the human moving dynamics among venues in a region. Regions with larger volume of visits, higher density of movement, and more incoming movements can produce more noises. Hence we use check-in data to propose the following features to characterize the human mobility.

- *Region Popularity* (**M-P**), denoted by $\mathcal{F}_p(r)$, is the number of check-ins in region r at a certain time.
- *Movement Density* (**M-D**) is the density of transitions between venues in region r. By denoting the set of consecutive check-ins from venue l_i and l_j in region r as TS_r, ($\langle l_i, l_j\rangle \in TS_r$), the movement density $\mathcal{F}_{md}(r)$ is defined as the size of TS_r.
- *Incoming Flow* (**M-F**) estimates the transitions from venues outside r to venues in r. The incoming flow value of r is given by: $\mathcal{F}_{if}(r) = |\{\langle l_i, l_j\rangle \in TS : l_i \notin L(r) \text{ and } l_j \in L(r)\}|$, where TS is the set of all consecutive check-ins, $L(r)$ is the set of all venues in r.

Visual Features (V). We combine the global features of colors and texture and local geometric features to model the visual contents of photos. The global features capture the photographic visual composition while the local ones identify the actual structural elements of objects. Such mixed global and local features have been shown to provide significant complementary information in recognition tasks [2].

- *Global* (**V-G**). We extract color histograms $\mathcal{F}_{ch}(r)$ and color moments $\mathcal{F}_{cm}(r)$ as global features of photos to capture theirs visual and spatial color distributions. We also utilize the Gabor textures $\mathcal{F}_{gt}(r)$ to model the textural information. Feature vectors are produced for each photo by concatenating these features. The similarity between two photos is calculated according to normalized Euclidean distance.
- *Local* (**V-L**). We represent photos by local interest point descriptors, given by the scale-invariant feature transform (SIFT) with a Difference of Gaussian (DoG) process. Given two photos p_i and p_j with the descriptor vectors, $D_i = (d_i^1, d_i^2, ..., d_i^m)$ and $D_i = (d_j^1, d_j^2, ..., d_j^n)$,

[1] https://nycopendata.socrata.com/Social-Services/311-Service-Requests-from-2010-to-Present/erm2-nwe9
[2] https://dev.twitter.com/
[3] https://developer.foursquare.com/
[4] https://snap.stanford.edu/data/loc-gowalla.html

we define the similarity between two photos as the number interest points shared between two photos divided by their average number of interest points.

Social Features (**S**) are designed to characterize the social interactions for people who had ever been in the region. Some public regions are crowded while people who tend to be unacquainted with each other while other regions favor friends or family gathering together. Different social interactions can lead to various levels of noises with distinct compositions of noise. Therefore, we compute features from the location-based social network.

- *Centrality Metrics* (**S-C**). We employ network centrality metrics $\mathcal{F}_{cm}(r)$, including degree, closeness, betweenness, *PageRank*, and *SimRank*, and geo-social influence measures [6] $\mathcal{F}_{im}(r)$, including spatial degree, spatial closeness, node novelty, and geographic clustering coefficient, over users who had ever visit region r as feature values. The maximum, minimum, and average values for these nine features are computed.
- *Group Measures* (**S-G**). We characterize the extent of cohesion or separation for people who visit venues in region r, by modeling the structure connectivity of the graph $\mathbb{G}[r]$ induced by users who had ever visited venues in r. We compute the values of density, clustering coefficient, the number of communities, and the number of components in $\mathbb{G}[r]$ as group features $\mathcal{F}_g(r)$.

2.3 Region Association Map

We construct the *Region Association Map* (RAM) to model the correlation between regions. We first introduce the noise composition and RAM, then describe how to exploit the extracted features to derive region similarities as edge weights.

The noise composition of a region r, denoted by $\mathbf{n}(r)$ is a vector, in which each element $n_c(r)$ is the percentage of a certain noise category c happening to region r. The dimension of $\mathbf{n}(r)$ is the number of noise categories, and $\sum_{c \in C} n_c(r) = 1$, where C is the set of all noise categories.

A *RAM* is a multi-layer weighted connected graph $G = \langle G^{t_1}, G^{t_2}, ..., G^{t_n} \rangle$, in which t is the total number of layers for time periods $t_1, t_2, ..., t_n$, and $G^{t_i} = (V, E, W)$ is the layer graph in at the t_i-th time period, where V is the set of regions, E is the set of edges between regions, and $W = W^{t_i} + W^{t_i,t_j}$ is the matrix representing edge weights, where W^{t_i} and W^{t_i,t_j} are edge weights learned from nodes within time period t_i and across time periods t_i and $t_j (i \neq j)$ respectively. The node set V consists of (a) regions whose noise compositions have known from NYC 311 noise complaint records, termed by **labeled nodes** $V_\bullet$, and (b) regions whose noise compositions are unknown, termed by **unlabeled nodes** $V_\circ$, where $V = V_\bullet \cup V_\circ$. Each labeled node $v_\bullet$ is associated with the corresponding noise composition $\mathbf{n}(v_\bullet)$, and the noise composition $\mathbf{n}(v_\circ)$ of each unlabeled node $v_\circ$ is initialized as a zero vector. The edge set E also consists of two parts: the set of edges $E_{\circlearrowleft}$ connecting nodes within each layer graph G^{t_i}, and the set of edges $E_{\curvearrowright}$ connecting the same nodes across different layer graphs G^{t_i} and $G^{t_j} (i \neq j)$, where $E = E_{\circlearrowleft} \cup E_{\curvearrowright}$.

The construction of RAM consists of three parts. First, since we aim to infer the noise composition of unlabeled regions from labeled ones, we connect each $v_\circ \in V_\circ$ to all $u_\bullet \in V_\bullet$ in each layer graph. Second, owing to the fact that the noise composition of a region can be highly correlated to its history, we connect each $v_\circ$ within time period t_j to the corresponding unlabeled node at time period $t_i (i < j)$ whose noise composition had ever observed. Third, since the noise composition of near-by regions tends to be similar (due to sharing similar characteristics), each $v_\circ \in V_\circ$ is connected to the direct near-by $u_\circ \in V_\circ$.

2.4 Region Similarity

Learning edge weights in RAM from features plays a key role in the inference of noise compositions for unlabeled nodes. We model the similarity between regions as edge weights. The idea is that for a certain time period, if two regions with higher similarity in terms of features, they tend to have similar noise composition. While various features can contribute different degree of effect on the similarity for noise composition, the importance of each feature should be considered separately.

Given a certain feature $\mathcal{F}_k$, we compute the corresponding individual region similarity $rs_{\mathcal{F}_k}(u(t_i), v(t_j))$ between nodes u and v in time periods t_i and t_j respectively from their feature difference $\Delta\mathcal{F}_k(u(t_i), v(t_j))$, where $\Delta\mathcal{F}_k$ is their feature difference, defined by $\Delta\mathcal{F}_k = \|\mathbf{f_k}(u(t_i)) - \mathbf{f_k}(v(t_j))\|$, and $\mathbf{f_k}(u(t_i))$ is $u(t_i)$'s feature vector of feature $\mathcal{F}_k$. Then, given a set of features $F = \{\mathcal{F}_1, \mathcal{F}_2, ..., \mathcal{F}_m\}$, we can derive the combined region similarity $rs(u(t_i), v(t_j))$ via the weighted sum of $rs_{\mathcal{F}_k}$, given by $rs(u(t_i), v(t_j)) = \exp(-\sum_{k=1}^{m} \pi_k \times rs_{\mathcal{F}_k}(u(t_i), v(t_j)))$, where π_k is the weight of feature $\mathcal{F}_k$. The combined region similarity is considered as the edge weight $M(u, v, t_i, t_j) = rs(u(t_i), v(t_j))$ between $u(t_i)$ and $v(t_j)$ $((u(t_i), v(t_j)) \in E)$. We will empirically learn the feature weight π_k from the validation set.

2.5 Noise Random Walk

We infer the noise composition of each unlabeled region using RAM. The idea is to apply the random walk mechanism to iteratively update the noise composition $\mathbf{n}(v_\circ)$ of each unlabeled node $v_\circ$ until the change of its noise composition converges. The noise composition $\mathbf{n}(v_\circ)$ of $v_\circ$ is computed from its neighboring labeled or unlabeled nodes in RAM, given by: $n_c(v_\circ) = \sum_{u \in \Gamma(v_\circ)} w_{v_\circ,u} \times n_c(u), c \in C$, where $\Gamma(v_\circ)$ is the set of neighboring nodes in RAM. That said, we aggregate the noise composition of $v_\circ$'s neighbors via edge weights. Note that the noise composition for each labeled node $v_\bullet$ will not be updated (i.e., they are fixed). Since RAM provides the benefit on modeling the region similarities between nodes, a near-by region u with higher similarity with unlabeled node $v_\circ$ can contribute more weights on the propagation of noise to $v_\circ$.

3. EXPERIMENTS

The experiments consists of two parts: show the effectiveness of our UND model, understand the performance under time intervals, and report how various features affects the results. First, we control the percentage of regions used as the training set from 10% to 90%, fix 5% as the validation set, and use the remaining as the test set. Second, we present the performance of each feature set. As for evaluation metrics, we use Normalization Root Mean Square Error (NRMSE) that measure the difference between ground-truth and inferred noise compositions, and Average Accuracy that is defined by whether the inferred noise category with the highest percentage of an unlabeled region is its correspond-

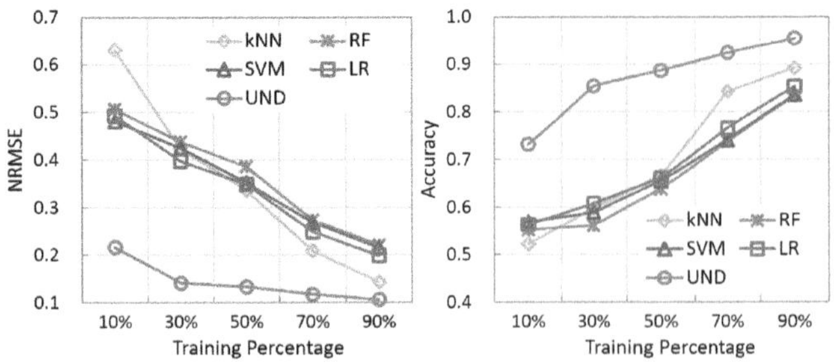

Figure 2: Results by varying training percentages.

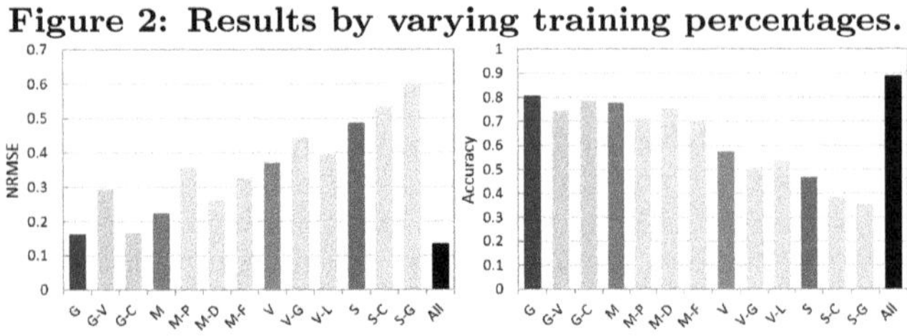

Figure 3: Results of different sets of features.

ing ground-truth category in average. We compare UND with several typical supervised learning methods, including Support Vector Machine (SVM), Random Forest (RF), L_1 logistic regression (LR), and k-nearest neighbor (kNN) (averaging the noise composition from the top-k most similar labeled regions using features, $k = 5$).

The main results are shown in Figure 2. We can find that our UND model outperforms the competitors in every case, especially when the training percentage is higher than 50%. The best accuracy (above 0.90) exhibits that UND can accurately identify the major noise category of an unlabeled region. In addition, we use UND to examine the accuracy of each feature set in Figure 3, and find that the geographical features are more influential. Though it may result from that the semantics of locations can reflect human activities in geography, we think this deserve more effort to investigate the correlation between urban noise and fine-grained geographical and mobility factors.

4. SYSTEM DEMONSTRATION

We develop the proposed model as an Urban Noise Diagnotor system[5]. A snapshot is shown in Figure 4. The essential function is to visualize the degree of noise pollution (highlighted by different colors) for each grid in New York City. The noise pollution is derived from the volume of noise complaints, which are either obtained from both the NYC 311 noise data (for grids having adequate noise complaints) and the inferred noise composition by our UND model (for grids without or having rare complaints). When users select a certain grid, the corresponding noise composition will be displayed. The corresponding multimodal geo-social media information will be presented as well, including the category distribution of locations from Foursquare, the number of check-ins from Twitter, and few representative venue names with photos from Flickr. Moreover, users are allowed to input the addresses to understand the noise pollution of their nearby areas, and choose the time period of interest (i.e., seasons, weekday/weekend, and hours of day) to observe how noise pollution varies in the selected grid.

[5]http://uwalk.elasticbeanstalk.com/noise

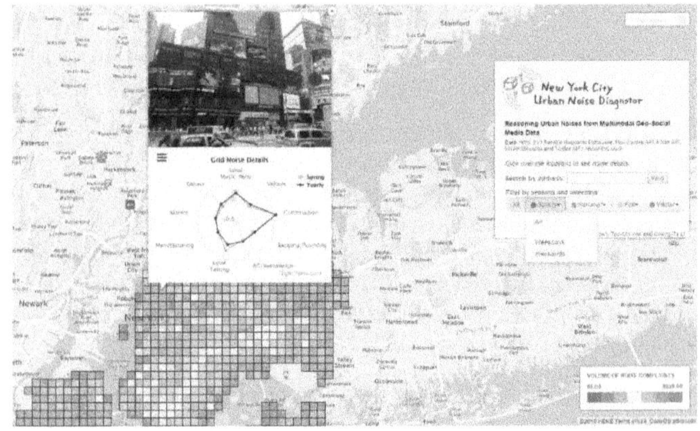

Figure 4: A snapshot of Urban Noise Diagnotor.

5. CONCLUSIONS

The contribution of this paper is four-fold. First, we extract a series of features from multimodal geo-social media data to characterize urban noise dynamics. Second, we develop the UND model that is validated to accurately infer the noise compositions of unlabeled regions. Third, we show that the visual feature of geo-tagged photos is the most important factor on inferring urban noises, and such finding can encourage future advanced analysis on this direction. Fourth, an Urban Noise Diagnotor system is developed for users to understand what make NYC so noisy.

6. ACKNOWLEDGEMENTS

This work was sponsored by Ministry of Science and Technology of Taiwan under grant 104-2221-E-001-027-MY2. This work is also supported by Multidisciplinary Health Cloud Research Program: Technology Development and Application of Big Health Data, Academia Sinica, Taipei, Taiwan under grant MP10212-0318. In addition, we especially thank Qiao Lin, Xiaodong Liu, and Shijing Wu for their fruitful discussions as well as the Sensoro team for the open research atmosphere.

7. REFERENCES

[1] D. Butler. Noise management: Sound and vision. *Nature*, 2004.
[2] S. Chang, W. Hsu, L. Kennedy, L. Xie, A. Yanagawa, E. Zavesky, and D. Zheng. Columbia university trecvid-2005 video search and high-level feature extraction. In *NIST TRECVID Workshop*, 2005.
[3] C.-Y. Chen and K. Grauman. Clues from the beaten path: Location estimation with bursty sequences of tourist photos. In *IEEE CVPR*, 2011.
[4] E. D'Hondt, M. Stevens, and A. Jacobs. Participatory noise mapping works! an evaluation of participatory sensing as an alternative to standard techniques for environmental monitoring. *Pervasive and Mobile Computing*, 2013.
[5] H.-P. Hsieh, R. Yan, and C.-T. Li. Dissecting urban noises from heterogeneous geo-social media and sensor data. In *ACM MM*, 2015.
[6] A. Lima and M. Musolesi. Spatial dissemination metrics for location-based social networks. In *ACM UbiComp*, 2012.
[7] T. Sakaki, M. Okazaki, and Y. Matsuo. Earthquake shakes twitter users: Real-time event detection by social sensors. In *WWW*, 2010.
[8] A. Signorini, A. M. Segre, and P. M. Polgreen. The use of twitter to track levels of disease activity and public concern in the u.s. during the influenza a h1n1 pandemic. *PLoS ONE*, 2011.
[9] Y. Zheng, L. Capra, O. Wolfson, and H. Yang. Urban computing: concepts, methodologies, and applications. *ACM TIST*, 2014.
[10] Y. Zheng, F. Liu, and H.-P. Hsieh. U-air: When urban air quality inference meets big data. In *ACM SIGKDD*, 2013.

EventBuilder: Real-time Multimedia Event Summarization by Visualizing Social Media

Rajiv Ratn Shah
School of Computing, National University of Singapore, Singapore
rajiv@comp.nus.edu.sg

Anwar Dilawar Shaikh
Department of Computer Engineering, Delhi Technological University, India
anwardshaikh@gmail.com

Yi Yu
Digital Content and Media Sciences Research, National Institute of Informatics, Japan
yiyu@nii.ac.jp

Wenjing Geng
Department of Computer Science & Technology, Nanjing University, China
wjgeng@smail.nju.edu.cn

Roger Zimmermann
School of Computing, National University of Singapore, Singapore
rogerz@comp.nus.edu.sg

Gangshan Wu
Department of Computer Science & Technology, Nanjing University, China
gswu@nju.edu.cn

ABSTRACT

Due to the ubiquitous availability of smartphones and digital cameras, the number of photos/videos online has increased rapidly. Therefore, it is challenging to efficiently browse multimedia content and obtain a summary of an event from a large collection of photos/videos aggregated in social media sharing platforms such as Flickr and Instagram. To this end, this paper presents the EventBuilder system that enables people to automatically generate a summary for a given event in real-time by visualizing different social media such as Wikipedia and Flickr. EventBuilder has two novel characteristics: (i) leveraging Wikipedia as event background knowledge to obtain more contextual information about an input event, and (ii) visualizing an interesting event in real-time with a diverse set of social media activities. According to our initial experiments on the YFCC100M dataset from Flickr, the proposed algorithm efficiently summarizes knowledge structures based on the metadata of photos/videos and Wikipedia articles.

Categories and Subject Descriptors

H.3.1 [**Information Storage and Retrieval**]: Content Analysis and Indexing; H.5.1 [**Information Interfaces and Presentation**]: Multimedia Information Systems

Keywords

Event detection; event summarization; event visualization

1. MOTIVATION AND BACKGROUND

The EventBuilder system presented in this study is our solution to the ACM Multimedia 2015 Grand Challenge on automatic event summarization from a large collection of photos/videos. EventBuilder[1] is a real-time multimedia event summarization system which produces an event summary by visualizing social media such as Flickr. The number of photos/videos on social media sites has increased rapidly due to the advancement in smartphone and digital camera technologies and affordable network connectivity. However, obtaining an overview of an event from a large collection of photos/videos, such as the YFCC100M dataset (Đ), is still a very challenging task due to the following reasons: (i) the existence of much noise in Flickr metadata, (ii) the big size of such datasets, and (iii) the difficulty in capturing the semantics of photos/videos. EventBuilder leverages metadata such as user tags, descriptions, spatial information, *etc.*, of all photos/videos in Đ, and content of Wikipedia articles, using a feature-pivot approach to build the indices of event-datasets in Đ. Moreover, EventBuilder introduces a summarization system which considers aspects such as quality, diversity, coverage, and redundancy, during the building process. The summarization system consists of three steps: (i) the identification of important *concepts* which should be described in the event summary, (ii) the composition of a text digest which covers the maximal number of important *concepts* by selecting the minimal number of sentences from available texts, within the desired summary length, and (iii) the geo-graphical visualization of the event on Google Maps.

For efficient and fast processing, we compute scores of all multimedia contents in Đ for the given events and build indices for event datasets ($\mathcal{F}$) during pre-processing. We include only those photos/videos in $\mathcal{F}$ whose scores are above a threshold δ. Next, we formulate the problem and introduce a solution to produce text summaries of events by employing a sentence selection algorithm inspired by the greedy algorithm [3]. In the summarization process we consider a representative set of $\mathcal{M}$ photos/videos ($\mathcal{R}$) from $\mathcal{F}$ with the highest scores. In this way, the proposed EventBuilder system provides an overview of events through text summaries and improves the visualization of events by displaying only multimedia contents and their descriptions from $\mathcal{R}$.

[1]URL: eventbuilder.geovid.org

MM '15, October 26–30, 2015, Brisbane, Australia.
Copyright 2015 ACM 978-1-4503-3459-4/15/10.
http://dx.doi.org/10.1145/2733373.2809932.

Since EventBuilder detects events from photos/videos offline rather than at search time, our system is time-efficient and scales well to large repositories. Since we use Wikipedia as background knowledge for more contextual information about the event to be summarized, our system can work well for new events by constructing feature vectors for those events by leveraging information from Wikipedia. An event summarization system can schedule event detection algorithms for newly uploaded photos/videos at regular time intervals to update event datasets.

2. RELATED WORK

There exists significant prior work in the area of event modeling, detection, and understanding from multimedia [5, 7, 10, 11]. Earlier methods [4, 9, 15] leveraged metadata such as user tags, spatial and temporal information to detect events automatically from a large collection of photos/videos such as Flickr. Rattenbury *et al.* [9] extracted place and event semantics for tags using Flickr metadata. Raad *et al.* [8] presented a clustering algorithm for automatically detecting personal events from photos shared online on the social network of a specific user by defining an event model that captures event triggers and relationships that can exist between events. They also detected multi-site, multi-day, and multi-person events using the appropriate time-space granularities. Fabro *et al.* [2] presented an algorithm for the summarization of real-life events based on community-contributed multimedia content using photos from Flickr and videos from YouTube. They evaluated the coverage of the produced summaries by comparing them with Wikipedia articles that report on the corresponding events. Atrey *et al.* [1] presented the detection of surveillance events such as human movements and objects being abandoned, by exploiting visual and aural information. Shah *et al.* [12] presented the ATLAS system which detects events such as slide transitions in a lecture video by exploiting its visual content and audio transcription. Low level visual features are often used for event detections or the selection of representative images from a collection of images/videos [7]. Recently, Papagiannopoulou and Mezaris [6] presented a clustering approach to produce an event-related image collection summarization using trained visual concept detectors based on image features such as SIFT, RGB-SIFT and OpponentSIFT. Wang *et al.* [14] summarized events based on the minimum description length principle, which is achieved through learning an HMM from the event data. Filatova and Hatzivassiloglou [3] proposed a set of event-based features which not only offers an improvement in summary quality over words as features (based on *tf-idf* scores), but also avoids redundancies in event summaries.

3. SYSTEM OVERVIEW

Figure 1 shows the system framework of EventBuilder. First, it performs event-wise classification and indexing of all photos/videos in social media datasets such as YFCC100M (Đ). Next, it solves the problem formulation of event summarization based on a greedy algorithm using event-based features which represent *concepts* (*i.e.*, important event-related information), as described by Filatova and Hatzivassiloglou [3]. *Concepts* associate the actions described in texts extracted from user descriptions and Wikipedia articles through verbs or action nouns labeling the event itself. Hence, an event summarization can be formulated as a maximum coverage problem. However, this problem is NP-hard, as it can be reduced to the well-known set cover problem. Thus, event summarization can be solved only in polynomial time by approximation algorithms.

Notations. Let N_e, T_e, S_e, and K_e be the feature vectors for event name, temporal information, spatial information, and keywords of an event e, respectively. The keywords of e are selected from the noun phrases used in the Wikipedia article of e. Let D be the list of 1080 camera models from Flickr, which are ranked based on their sensor sizes. Let N_i, T_i, S_i, K_i, and D_i be the feature vectors of photo/video i in Đ for event name, temporal information, spatial information, keywords, and camera model, respectively, and let $\xi(N_i, N_e)$, $\lambda(T_i, T_e)$, $\gamma(S_i, S_e)$, $\mu(K_i, K_e)$, and $\rho(D_i, D)$ be their corresponding similarity scores with e. Let $\mathcal{R}$ be the representative set for e, consisting of the top $\mathcal{M}$ photos/videos with the highest scores in an event dataset $\mathcal{F}$. Let $\mathcal{T}$ be the set of all sentences which are extracted from the description of photos/videos in $\mathcal{R}$ and contents of the Wikipedia article of e, and are used to produce a text summary $\mathcal{S}$. Let $|\mathcal{S}|$ and $\bar{\mathcal{L}}$ be the current word count and the word limit for $\mathcal{S}$, respectively. Let $\mathcal{K}$ and $\mathcal{Y}$ be the set of all *concepts* (c_k) of e and the set of corresponding weights (y_k), respectively. Let $v(s)$ be the score for a sentence s, which is the sum of the weights of all concepts it covers. Let $t(i)$ be the upload time of i. Let $\omega_{(s)}$ be a binary indicator variable which indicates if s is selected in the summary or not. Let $d(i)$ be a binary indicator variable which specifies if i has a description or not. Let $p(c, s)$ and $\beta(s, i)$ be 1 if $c \in s$ and $s \in i$, respectively, or otherwise 0.

Event Dataset and Experimental Settings. The score $u(i, e)$ of i for e is computed by a linear combination of similarity scores as follows: $u(i, e) = (w_1\ \xi(N_i, N_e) + w_2\ \lambda(T_i, T_e) + w_3\ \gamma(S_i, S_e) + w_4\ \mu(K_i, K_e) + w_5\ \rho(D_i, D))$, where $w_{i'}{}_{i'=1}^{5}$ are weights for different similarity scores such that $\sum_{i'=1}^{5} w_{i'} = 1$. We construct the event dataset $\mathcal{F}$ by indexing only those photos/videos of Đ whose scores $u(i, e)$ are above threshold δ. We set the weights as follows: $w_1 = 0.40$, $w_2 = 0.20$, $w_3 = 0.15$, $w_4 = 0.20$, and $w_5 = 0.05$, after initial experiments on the development set for event detection. We allocate only 5% of the total score for the camera model based on the heuristic that a good camera leads to a better quality photo/video which results in a better visualization of the event. All similarity scores, thresholds, and other scores are normalized to values [0, 1]. Let $\bar{\mathcal{L}}$ and $\mathcal{M}$ be system parameters to limit the summary length (number of words) and the number of photos/videos to be considered in the event summarization, respectively.

Problem Formulation for Text Summary. An event summary $\mathcal{S}$ is produced by extracting some sentences from $\mathcal{T}$, which cover important *concepts*. With the above notations and functions, we write the problem formulation for the event summarization as follows:

$$\min \sum_{(s\in\mathcal{T})\wedge(i\in\mathcal{R})} \omega(s)\beta(s,i) \tag{1a}$$

$$\text{s.t.} \sum_{s\in\mathcal{T}} \omega(s)\ p(c,s) \geq 1,\ \forall\ c \in \mathcal{K} \tag{1b}$$

$$v(s) \geq \eta,\ \ \forall\ s \in \mathcal{T} \tag{1c}$$

$$|\mathcal{S}| \leq \bar{\mathcal{L}}, \tag{1d}$$

$$d(i) = 1,\ \forall\ i \in \mathcal{R} \tag{1e}$$

$$t(i) \leq \tau,\ \forall\ i \in \mathcal{R} \tag{1f}$$

$$\omega(s) \in \{0, 1\},\ \forall\ s \in \mathcal{T} \tag{1g}$$

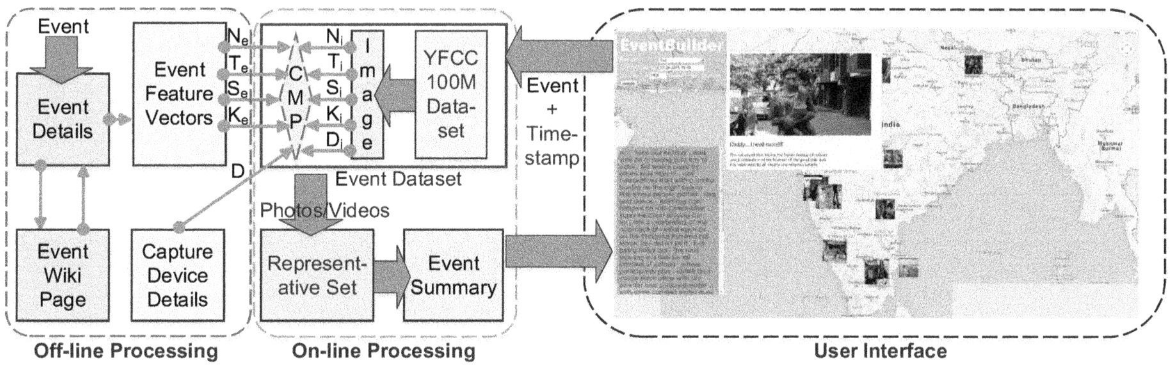

Figure 1: System framework of EventBuilder.

	c_1	c_2	c_3	c_4	...	$c_{\|\mathcal{K}\|}$
s_1	1	1	0	1	...	1
s_2	0	1	1	0	...	0
...	...	...	...	...	...	...
$s_{\|\mathcal{T}\|}$	1	0	0	1	...	1

Table 1: Matrix model for event summarization.

$$p(c, s) \in \{0, 1\}, \forall\ s \in \mathcal{T}, \forall\ c \in \mathcal{K} \quad \text{(1h)}$$

$$\beta(s, i) \in \{0, 1\}, \forall\ s \in \mathcal{T}, \forall\ i \in \mathcal{R} \quad \text{(1i)}$$

The objective function in Eq. (1a) solves the problem of event summarization and selects the minimal number of sentences which cover the maximal number of important concepts within the desired length of a summary. Eqs. (1b) and (1c) ensure that each concept is covered by at least one sentence with a score above threshold η. Eq. (1d) assures that the length constraint of the summarization is met. Eqs. (1e) and (1f) ensure that i has a description and is uploaded before the given timestamp τ. Eqs. (1g), (1h), and (1i) ensure that a concept, sentence, and photo is either present or absent in the sentence selected for the summarization.

Algorithm 1 Event summarization algorithm.

procedure EVENTSUMMARIZATION
  INPUT: An event e and a time stamp τ
  OUTPUT: A text summary $\mathcal{SV}$
  $\bar{\mathcal{K}} = []$, $|\mathcal{S}| = 0$, $\bar{\mathcal{S}} = 200$ ▷ initialization.
  $(\mathcal{K}, \mathcal{Y})$ = getEventConceptsAndWeights(e) ▷ see [3].
  $\mathcal{F}$ = getEventDataset(e) ▷ pre-processed event dataset.
  $\mathcal{R}$ = getRepresentativeSet(e, $\mathcal{F}$) ▷ representative photos.
  $\mathcal{T}$ = getSentences(e, $\mathcal{R}$) ▷ user description, Wiki texts.
  while $((|\mathcal{S}| \leq \bar{\mathcal{L}}) \wedge (\mathcal{K} \neq \bar{\mathcal{K}}))$ **do** ▷ $\bar{\mathcal{K}}$ is covered concepts.
    c = getUncoveredConcept($\mathcal{K}$, $\bar{\mathcal{K}}$) ▷ important c first.
    s = getSentence(c, $\mathcal{Y}$, $\bar{\mathcal{K}}$, $\mathcal{T}$) ▷ $c \in s \wedge v(s)$ is max.
    updateCoveredConceptList(s, $\bar{\mathcal{K}}$) ▷ add all $c \in s$ to $\bar{\mathcal{K}}$.
    addToEventTextSummary(s, $\mathcal{S}$) ▷ add s to summary.
    for each sentence $s \in \mathcal{T}$ **do** ▷ say, $s \in$ photo/video i.
      updScr(s, $\mathcal{Y}$, $\bar{\mathcal{K}}$) ▷ $v(s) = u(i, e) \times \sum_{c \in s, c \notin \bar{\mathcal{K}}} y$.

Solution. A greedy algorithm is reportedly the best possible polynomial approximation algorithm to solve NP-hard problems such as the set cover problem (*i.e.*, an event summarization problem in our case). We introduce a greedy algorithm which iteratively adds sentences to the event summary $\mathcal{S}$, until it either achieves the desired length $\bar{\mathcal{L}}$ or covers all *concepts*. Hence, the maximal number of important *concepts* are covered in the summary. Every time, when a new sentence is added to the summary, we check whether it contains enough new important *concepts* to avoid redundancy. We have formulated the problem of event summarization in terms of a matrix model, as shown in Table 1. Sentences and important concepts are mapped onto a $|\mathcal{T}| \times |\mathcal{K}|$ matrix. An entry of this matrix is 1 if the concept (column) is present in the sentence (row), otherwise it is 0. We take advantage of this model matrix to avoid redundancy by globally selecting the sentences that cover the most important concepts (*i.e.*, information) present in user descriptions and Wikipedia articles. Using the above matrix, it is possible to formulate the event summarization problem as equivalent to extracting the minimal number of sentences which cover all the important concepts. In our approximation algorithm, we constrain the total length of the summary with respect to the total weight of covered concepts, in order to handle the cost of long summaries. Our adaptive greedy algorithm for the event summarization is motivated by the summarization algorithm presented by Filatova and Hatzivassiloglou [3].

Algorithm 1 presents our summarization algorithm. First, we determine all event-related important concepts and their weights, as described by Filatova and Hatzivassiloglou [3]. Next, we extract all sentences from the user description of photos/videos in the representative set and texts in the Wikipedia article of an event e. We compute the score of a sentence by multiplying the sum of weights of all concepts it covers and the score of the photo/video which this sentence belongs to. Since each concept has different importance, we cover important concepts first. We consider only those sentences that contain the concept with the highest weight that has not yet been covered. Among these sentences, we choose the sentence with the highest total score and add it to the final event summary. Then we add the concepts which are covered by this sentence to the list of covered concepts $\bar{\mathcal{K}}$ in the final summary. Before adding further sentences to the event summary, we recalculate the scores of all sentences by not considering the weight of all the concepts that are already covered in the event summary. We continue adding sentences to $\mathcal{S}$ until we obtain a summary of the desired length $\bar{\mathcal{L}}$ or a summary covering all concepts.

4. EVALUATION

Dataset. The YFCC100M [13] (Yahoo! Flickr Creative Commons 100M) dataset, consisting of a total of 100 million photos/videos (approximately 99 million photos and 1 million videos) from Flickr, were provided with several metadata annotations such as user tags, spatial and temporal information, *etc.*, for the Yahoo-Flickr Event Summarization Challenge. To evaluate the proposed automatic summarization systems, the organizers have provided several events and timestamps, as listed in Table 2.

Event Name	Timestamp @ 12:00am UTC	Infor- mative	Exper- ience	Accep- tance	Event Name	Timestamp @ 12:00am UTC	Infor- mative	Exper- ience	Accep- tance
Holi	8 March 2009	3.93	4.13	4.00	Olympic Games	25 June 2012	3.00	2.60	2.80
	1 April 2009	3.80	3.80	3.66		1 Oct 2012	3.33	2.93	3.06
	1 April 2011	3.93	4.00	3.93		1 Jan 2015	3.27	3.13	3.13
	Avg. Rating	3.87	3.98	3.86		**Avg. Rating**	3.20	2.87	3.00
Eyjafjallajökull Eruption	1 April 2010	3.93	3.73	3.80	Batkid	15 Nov 2013	3.93	4.00	3.80
	18 April 2010	3.73	3.73	3.73		16 Nov 2013	3.80	4.00	3.73
	1 Jan 2014	4.06	4.13	4.0		1 Jan 2014	3.73	3.80	3.67
	Avg. Rating	3.91	3.86	3.86		**Avg. Rating**	3.61	3.93	3.76
Occupy Movement	19 Sep 2011	2.46	2.53	2.20	Byron Bay Bluesfest	1 June 2011	3.53	3.53	3.40
	1 Nov 2011	3.60	3.53	2.93		1 Jan 2015	3.53	3.60	3.60
	19 Sep 2012	3.67	3.67	3.67		-	-	-	-
	Avg. Rating	2.40	3.24	2.93		**Avg. Rating**	3.53	3.57	3.50
Hanami	1 Feb 2013	3.60	3.60	3.80	**All Events**	**Avg. Rating**	**3.46**	**3.61**	**3.54**
	1 June 2013	3.80	4.00	3.93					
	Avg. Rating	3.70	3.80	3.87					

Table 2: Evaluation results for the Yahoo-Flickr Event Summarization Challenge (YFCC100M dataset).

Results. The same algorithm was used for all summaries. No event-specific tuning was performed. All event summaries in our evaluation cover the maximal number of important concepts and their summary length is within the desired word limit. Since the summary evaluation is subjective in nature, we evaluated the performance through a user study. We asked fifteen evaluators to assess EventBuilder and provide scores from 1 to 5, with a higher score indicating better satisfaction. We defined three perspectives that evaluators should consider: (i) informativeness, which indicates to what degree a user feels that the summary captures the essence of the event, (ii) experience, which indicates if the user thinks the summary is helpful for understanding the event, and (iii) acceptance, which indicates if a user would be willing to use this event summarization function if Flickr were to incorporate it into their system. The default event summary length $\bar{\mathcal{L}}$ was set to 200 words during evaluation. Experimental results (see Table 2) indicate that users generally think that the summaries are informative and can help them to obtain a quick overview of an event.

5. CONCLUSIONS

The proposed EventBuilder system is a real-time automatic event detection and summarization system. First, it computes event-wise scores for each photo/video in social media datasets such as YFCC100M for the given events and builds event-wise indices. Next, it produces event summaries based on the given events and timestamps in real-time and facilitates efficient access to a large collection of photos/videos. In our future work we plan to extend the approach by exploiting visual contents, in addition to the available texts, using machine learning methods.

ACKNOWLEDGMENTS

This research has been supported by the Singapore National Research Foundation under its International Research Centre @ Singapore Funding Initiative and administered by the IDM Programme Office through the Centre of Social Media Innovations for Communities (COSMIC).

6. REFERENCES

[1] P. K. Atrey, A. El Saddik, and M. S. Kankanhalli. Effective Multimedia Surveillance using a Human-centric Approach. *Springer Multimedia Tools and Applications*, 51(2):697–721, 2011.

[2] M. Del Fabro, A. Sobe, and L. Böszörmenyi. Summarization of real-life events based on community-contributed content. In *MMEDIA*, 2012.

[3] E. Filatova and V. Hatzivassiloglou. Event-based Extractive Summarization. In *ACL Workshop on Summarization*, pages 104–111, 2004.

[4] C. S. Firan, M. Georgescu, W. Nejdl, and R. Paiu. Bringing Order to Your Photos: Event-driven Classification of Flickr Images based on Social Knowledge. In *ACM CIKM*, pages 189–198, 2010.

[5] V. Mezaris, A. Scherp, R. Jain, and M. S. Kankanhalli. Real-life Events in Multimedia: Detection, Representation, Retrieval, and Applications. *Springer Multimedia Tools and Applications*, 70(1):1–6, 2014.

[6] C. Papagiannopoulou and V. Mezaris. Concept-based Image Clustering and Summarization of Event-related Image Collections. In *Workshop on HuEvent at ACM Multimedia*, pages 23–28, 2014.

[7] G. Petkos, S. Papadopoulos, V. Mezaris, R. Troncy, P. Cimiano, T. Reuter, and Y. Kompatsiaris. Social Event Detection at MediaEval: a Three-Year Retrospect of Tasks and Results. In *Workshop on SEWM at ACM ICMR*, 2014.

[8] E. J. Raad and R. Chbeir. Foto2Events: From Photos to Event Discovery and Linking in Online Social Networks. In *IEEE BdCloud*, pages 508–515, 2014.

[9] T. Rattenbury, N. Good, and M. Naaman. Towards Automatic Extraction of Event and Place Semantics from Flickr Tags. In *ACM SIGIR*, pages 103–110, 2007.

[10] A. Scherp and V. Mezaris. Survey on Modeling and Indexing Events in Multimedia. *Springer Multimedia Tools and Applications*, 70(1):7–23, 2014.

[11] A. Scherp, V. Mezaris, B. Ionescu, and F. De Natale. HuEvent '14: Workshop on Human-Centered Event Understanding from Multimedia. In *ACM Multimedia*, pages 1253–1254, 2014.

[12] R. R. Shah, Y. Yu, A. D. Shaikh, S. Tang, and R. Zimmermann. ATLAS: Automatic Temporal Segmentation and Annotation of Lecture Videos Based on Modelling Transition Time. In *ACM Multimedia*, pages 209–212, 2014.

[13] B. Thomee, D. A. Shamma, G. Friedland, B. Elizalde, K. Ni, D. Poland, D. Borth, and L.-J. Li. The New Data and New Challenges in Multimedia Research. *arXiv preprint arXiv:1503.01817*, 2015.

[14] P. Wang, H. Wang, M. Liu, and W. Wang. An Algorithmic Approach to Event Summarization. In *ACM SIGMOD*, pages 183–194, 2010.

[15] M. Zaharieva, M. Zeppelzauer, and C. Breiteneder. Automated Social Event Detection in Large Photo Collections. In *ACM ICMR*, pages 167–174, 2013.

Multimodal Graph-based Event Detection and Summarization in Social Media Streams

Manos Schinas
CERTH-ITI
Thessaloniki, Greece
manosetro@iti.gr

Symeon Papadopoulos
CERTH-ITI
Thessaloniki, Greece
papadop@iti.gr

Georgios Petkos
CERTH-ITI
Thessaloniki, Greece
gpetkos@iti.gr

Yiannis Kompatsiaris
CERTH-ITI
Thessaloniki, Greece
ikom@iti.gr

Pericles A. Mitkas
Aristotle University of
Thessaloniki, Greece
mitkas@eng.auth.gr

ABSTRACT

The paper describes a multimodal graph-based system for addressing the Yahoo-Flickr Event Summarization Challenge of ACM Multimedia 2015. The objective is to automatically uncover structure within a collection of 100 million photos/videos in the form of detecting and identifying events, and summarizing them succinctly for consumer consumption. The presented system uses a sliding window over the stream of multimedia items to build and maintain a multimodal same-event image graph and applies a graph clustering algorithm to detect events. In addition, it makes use of a graph-based diversity-oriented ranking approach and a versatile event retrieval mechanism to access summarized instances of the events of interest. A demo of the system is online at `http://mklab.iti.gr/acmmm2015-gc/`.

Categories and Subject Descriptors

H.4 [**Information Systems Applications**]: Miscellaneous

General Terms

Experimentation, Algorithms

Keywords

Event Detection, Clustering, Event Summarization

1. INTRODUCTION

As a result of the widespread use of media capturing devices and social media sharing platforms, a growing amount of diverse multimedia content is available online. Hence, there is a profound need for information systems that can effectively organize such content. As real-world events are a key part of social life, the detection of events and the organization of content around them is an effective way for navigating and searching large multimedia collections.

MM'15, October 26–30, 2015, Brisbane, Australia.

ACM 978-1-4503-3459-4/15/10 ...$15.00.
DOI: http://dx.doi.org/10.1145/2733373.2809933 .

Event detection in social media is a challenging task due to the nature and characteristics of social multimedia: There is a large number of multimedia items that are of personal nature and/or not relevant with respect to an event. Also, many items have missing fields, e.g., title or taken date, that make difficult their linking to an already known event. Additionally, the order of magnitude of available media content creates excessive computational costs and calls for scalable and efficient solutions. Furthermore, the presentation of detected events poses additional challenges as the volume of images for large scale events e.g., the Olympic Games, could be massive. Not every image is of the same importance for an event and long-running events can be quite complex containing many aspects and numerous sub-events. Thus, there is a need for event-based summarization methods that can produce concise visual summaries for any time interval of the event, covering its main aspects.

In this paper, we describe a prototype system addressing the Yahoo-Flickr Event Summarization Challenge of ACM Multimedia 2015. We detect events from a set of about 100 million images [12] and then summarize each detected event by presenting only a representative and diverse subset of images. Although the system uses Flickr images, it could be applied to any multimedia collection with a similar set of metadata. To handle the massive scale of the dataset, the system uses a sliding time-window that enables the discovery of new events or their merging into previously detected events. During the procedure, an image graph is constructed and updated on the fly, and a graph-based clustering algorithm is applied periodically to detect dense subgraphs that correspond to events. In order to keep track of evolving or periodic events, a graph of events is also generated incrementally. To perform summarization, the system takes advantage of the image graph and applies per event a graph-based ranking algorithm that produces a diverse set of images, ranked by their importance.

2. RELATED WORK

Numerous approaches have recently appeared in the literature on the problems of event detection tracking and summarization in social media content. There are two general event detection and tracking approaches: *document-pivot* [1, 9] and *feature-pivot methods* [4]. The former aim to cluster items related to the same event. The latter aim to first identify the representative features (e.g., tags) of the underlying events in the collection (typically by detecting bursty frequency patterns along time or space) and then detect events by leveraging these representative features.

The core idea of the majority of works in event summarization is the segmentation of items set into coherent topics or sub-events and the selection of the most representative documents in each segment. For event segmentation several approaches have been proposed, ranging from Hidden Markov Models [3] to LDA extensions [2]. Regarding selection of representative documents, either centroid-based [10] or graph-based ranking approaches [5] have been considered.

3. SYSTEM OVERVIEW

The proposed system consists of three main components: event detection and tracking, event summarization, and event retrieval and presentation. The event detection and tracking component identifies events per timeslot and keeps track of their evolution from timeslot to timeslot. The summarization component calculates a score for each image per event by applying a graph-based ranking algorithm. Finally, event retrieval and presentation is the online component of the system, used to present the detected events to end users.

3.1 Event Detection and Tracking

The system utilizes a sliding time-window to detect and keep track of events. As the window moves along the timeline, new images are inserted into the window while others are removed. As days are a meaningful unit of time for events, we set the step of the time-window to one day and its length to three days. In other words, there is a significant overlap of two days between successive timeslots. We use this overlap to keep track of evolving and long-running events as will be described in the next sections.

For images within a given timeslot we use what is termed the Same Event Model (SEM) [7]. The SEM takes as input the set of per modality similarities between two images and predicts how likely it is that these two images belong to the same event. A graph of images $\mathcal{G}_I$ is constructed, in which the existence of an edge between a pair of images denotes the positive prediction of the SEM. Subsequently, a graph-based clustering algorithm is applied on $\mathcal{G}_I$ to obtain a full clustering. Finally, the method either merges these clusters into events from previous timeslots or creates new events.

3.1.1 *Same Event Model*

To implement the SEM, a Support Vector Machine (SVM) with a linear kernel is utilized. An independent training dataset from the 2014 MediaEval Social Event Detection task (SED 2014) [8] was used for building the model. The SED 2014 dataset contains 362,578 Flickr images that are associated with 17,834 events. Several variations were considered for building the models, including: a) different ways of sampling the training and test data, b) different sets of features and feature similarities, and c) different values of the classification threshold.

According to [9], sampling of the training and testing data was found to be a critical factor for the usefulness of the learned SEM. The problem arises because in reality, there are pairs of images that have some similarity, according to at least some modalities, e.g., time, but do not actually represent the same event. However, it is rather unlikely that random sampling of negative instances, picks pairs of items that are even marginally similar to each other. An alternative is to sample negative pairs so that the chosen pairs of items are similar according to some modality. Empirically, we observed that by doing this, although training accuracy dropped test accuracy increased because the model was more effective on difficult (borderline) cases compared to a model that would have been trained on purely randomly selected data. To be more specific, the models that were eventually used were trained with 80% randomly selected data and 20% non-randomly selected data. Each data point that was not randomly selected involved the examination of a single modality at a time, and all used modalities were equally considered for sampling the 20% of non-randomly selected data. The single-modality similarities were based on the following features:

- **Taken time:** Four similarity scores are extracted. The first is the absolute difference in days between the two image timestamps. The other three are binary indicators signifying whether the difference between the time each of the images was taken is smaller than 3 hours, 12 hours and 24 hours respectively.
- **Text:** Three text metadata fields are used, namely title, description, and tags. For each field, we compute a $tf \cdot idf$ vector and the corresponding cosine similarity. Additionally, we extract named entities from these fields by using Stanford NLP library[1] and include three additional similarity measures based on the number of common locations, organizations and names of people.
- **Image:** We used SURF+VLAD using the implementation of [13]. In particular, we extract SURF features from the raw image content and aggregated them using the VLAD scheme. We then used the L_2 distance between VLAD vectors to compute similarities.

The third variation that we explored for building the SEMs was to tune the classification threshold. Intuitively, for each image, the SEM will be evaluated against far more images than the average event size. In a typical scenario, the "real negative" evaluations of the SEM are expected to be much more than the "real positive" ones. Therefore, in order to produce a "clean" graph with not too many spurious edges, it is useful to increase the true negatives rate. This can be achieved by increasing the classification threshold for positive predictions, at the cost of a lower true positives rate. According to our experiments, this significantly improves the clustering performance. The test accuracy of the model when the threshold is not tuned is 98.65% for positives and 98.81% for negatives (average 98.73%). When the threshold for positive classification is set to 0.9, test accuracy for positives drops to 95.12%, while accuracy on negatives increases to 99.87% (average accuracy is 97.49%).

3.1.2 *Generation of Image Graph*

As the time-window moves forward, new images are inserted into the image graph $\mathcal{G}_I$. At the same time, the out-of-window images and the corresponding edges are removed from the graph. For the newly inserted images, edges between them and images already in the graph are calculated based on the SEM as described in section 3.1.1. To limit the number of SEM evaluations and make the approach more

[1]http://nlp.stanford.edu/software/CRF-NER.shtml

scalable, we apply a candidate neighbor selection step [9]. For each image, we utilize appropriate indices to obtain the most similar images according to each modality and evaluate the SEM only for them. More specifically, for each image we retrieve all the nearest images in terms of textual and visual content provided that they exceed a predefined threshold and are within the current timeslot. Then, we calculate the same event score only for the union of these two sets. For text we used an indexing scheme based on Locality Sensitive Hashing, while for visual content, we used Product Quantization on top of the SURF+VLAD representation.

To detect the events in a time window we opted for a graph clustering algorithm, namely the Structural Clustering Algorithm for Networks (SCAN) [14]. We apply SCAN on $\mathcal{G}_I$ to identify dense sub-graphs of images. These subgraphs represent the events in the set of images of this time window, i.e. each event $e \in E$ is represented as a set $\mathcal{G}_e$ of highly connected images on the graph. However, a substantial amount of images is kept outside of the detected clusters. These images are divided into two categories, *hubs* and *outliers*. Hubs are bridges to more than one clusters, while outliers are images that may be connected to images of a cluster but do not belong to any of them. We add hubs to the clusters to which they are connected under the condition that the number of edges exceed a predefined threshold (10 edges). Note that after this step hubs may belong to more than one clusters. Once the set of events E are detected, we use images associated with each $event_i \in E$ to calculate an aggregated representation of the event. Namely, for each event, we compute the minimum, maximum and average taken time of the images and calculate three merged $tf \cdot idf$ vectors that describe the aggregated textual content of title, description and tags. As named entities are expected to be particularly relevant for each event, we also aggregate persons, locations and organizations.

3.1.3 Event Tracking

As new events are detected, the system tries to link them with detected events from earlier timeslots. To identify that two clusters are referring to the same event we use the structural similarity between the underlying sub-graphs, expressed as the Jaccard coefficient of their edges. If this similarity exceeds a certain threshold (0.6), we merge the two clusters into a single event. Intuitively in our case, if two sub-graphs of successive timeslots share a significant amount of edges, the later sub-graph is arising from the previous one. Note that the overlap of edges is feasible due to the content overlap (of two days) between successive timeslots. When such a similarity is detected, the new event is merged into the older. Namely, the images of the new event are added to the previous event and its aggregated representation is updated accordingly. Furthermore, we also check for *inactive* events. As inactive, we define the events that have no new inserted images for the last three days. As the length of the timeslot is also three days, it is unlikely that these events will have any overlap with events in the following windows. We remove those from the set of active events and discard events with less than 10 images. For the rest, we calculate whether they are *local*, *regional* or *global*. More specifically, for each event we find a median point and an average radius based on the latitude and longitude of its images. Events with radius <100km are considered to be local. Between 100 and 500km they are classified as regional, while events with average radius >500km are defined as global. Also, events with images from a single user are tagged as *personal*. Finally, we calculate the significance scores of images as will be described in the next section, and we store and index them in MongoDB and Solr respectively.

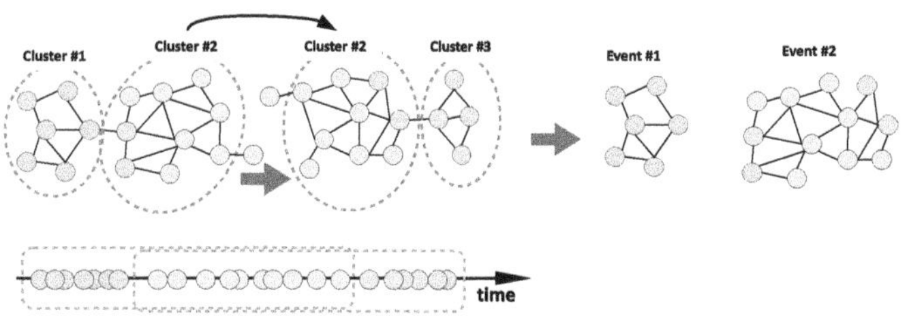

Figure 1: Event tracking in successive timeslots.

3.2 Event Summarization

Our goal is to generate a concise summary of a selected event e for an arbitrary time-frame. A summary is a set of representative images depicting the key aspects of the selected time interval. To support this at retrieval time, we calculate a significance score for each event image according to its position on the sub-graph $\mathcal{G}_e$. This calculation is based on the *MGraph* summarization method [11], which first finds sub-events within the event and uses these sub-events to calculate a prior score for each image. Then, to incorporate diversity into image scoring, it uses DivRank [6], a variant of PageRank that aims at diversity. In our case, instead of finding sub-events within an event by clustering its images, we perform time-based segmentation. Namely, we create segments/clusters corresponding to one-day timeslots, and apply scoring in the same way as done in [11]. At the end of this process, for an event lasting D days, we have a rank of the images within each time-slot $t_i, i = 1...D$.

3.3 Event Retrieval and Presentation

At retrieval time, there are two main tasks: The first is to obtain a set of events that match a specific query q. The second is to use the calculated DivRank scores to generate a summary of arbitrary length.

Regarding retrieval, the initial query q is usually short, e.g., `olympic games`, and although this usually yields results of high relevance, it cannot fully capture the underlying information need of the user. To improve the expressive power of q and increase recall, query expansion is applied: $q \rightarrow q_{ext}$. For this purpose we use the tags and named entities of the retrieved events to expand the query with new terms. As single tags and named entities could yield noisy results, we combine them in pairs. The final query is the logical OR between the aforementioned pairs.

For each retrieved event e with associated images I, the user can select to see a summary of length L for a specific time-frame $\mathcal{F}$. To this end, we use the scores described in section 3.2. To achieve this, we keep images $I_{\mathcal{F}}$ within $\mathcal{F}$ and iterate over the timeslots of $\mathcal{F}$ to form a summary following a greedy approach. We first calculate the compression rate $CR = L/|I_F|$, needed to achieve a summary of length L. Then, for each timeslot $t_j \in \mathcal{F}$, we get the corresponding images I_j and find the number of images that need to be selected to meet the budget of L messages. Namely, the local target for timeslot t_j , is $L_j = CR \cdot |I_j|$ messages.

Table 1: Details of predefined events

Event	#events	#items	i/ev	u/ev
Occupy Movement	120	9,814	81	3.45
Batkid	2	624	312	2
Olympic Games	117	11,535	98	5.2
Eyjafjallajokull Eruption	12	588	49	1.7
Holi, festival of colors	2	52	26	1
Byron Bay Bluesfest	9	707	78	2.4
Hanami	16	3106	194	6.6

Table 2: Basic Statistics of event detection process between 1/1/2009 and 1/1/2014

Statistics	Personal	Social	Total
Events	23,184	45,729	68,913
Avg. items/event	39	47	44
Avg. users/event	1	5.25	3.82
Local	17,334	24,453	41,787
Regional	765	11,196	11,961
Global	171	7,929	8,100
Avg duration (hours)	19.11	42.9	34.84
Max duration (days)	9.83	19.25	19.25

The algorithm iterates through the images in I_j sorted by their DivRank score and selects the top L_j images provided that the value of Equation 1 is below a predefined threshold R_{th}. As the maximum possible L_2 distance is $\sqrt{2}$ we set $R_{th} = \sqrt{2}/2 \simeq 0.7$. In case that the length of a local summary is still below than the desired one, we re-calculate the compression rate to select more images from the next timeslots.

$$Redundancy(im) = \min_{im' \in S} L_2(im, im') \quad (1)$$

The score of Equation 1 measures the redundancy introduced by an image im with respect to the set of already selected images. To this end, we compute its minimum visual distance, based on L_2, to the already selected images. Filtering based on redundancy during image selection ensures that no visual duplicates are including in the summary.

4. RESULTS

Table 1 presents some statistics for the set of seven predefined events. The number of sub-events in each event and the number of associated items exhibits high variance. Large scale real-world events, such as the `Occupy Movement` and the `Olympic Games`, consist of several sub-events and the number of items per event is high. Also, the average number of users per event is higher as more users are engaged in these events. On the other hand, single day events, such as the `batkid` case, consist of a small number of sub-events with many associated items.

Table 2 presents some basic statistics for all the events detected in the YFCC dataset between 1/1/2009 and 1/1/2014. In total, there are 68,913 events, of which 45,729 are social events, i.e. the multimedia content for the same event comes from more than two users. Regarding the characteristics of personal and social events, a marked difference is the following: personal events are typically tagged as local, since it is unlikely that the same user can post content for the same event from different locations. At the same time, the ratio of events tagged as regional and global is considerably higher for social events.

5. ACKNOWLEDGMENTS

This work was supported by the REVEAL project, partially funded by the European Commission, under contract number FP7-610928.

6. REFERENCES

[1] H. Becker, M. Naaman, and L. Gravano. Learning similarity metrics for event identification in social media. In *Proceedings of the Third ACM International Conference on Web Search and Data Mining*, WSDM '10, pages 291–300, New York, NY, USA, 2010. ACM.

[2] J. Bian, Y. Yang, and T.-S. Chua. Multimedia summarization for trending topics in microblogs. In *Proceedings of the 22nd ACM international conference on Conference on Information and Knowledge Management*, CIKM '13, pages 1807–1812, NY, USA, 2013. ACM.

[3] D. Chakrabarti and K. Punera. Event summarization using tweets. *ICWSM*, 11:66–73, 2011.

[4] L. Chen and A. Roy. Event detection from flickr data through wavelet-based spatial analysis. In *Proceedings of the 18th ACM Conference on Information and Knowledge Management*, CIKM '09, pages 523–532, New York, NY, USA, 2009. ACM.

[5] G. Erkan and D. R. Radev. Lexrank: Graph-based lexical centrality as salience in text summarization. *J. Artif. Int. Res.*, 22(1):457–479, Dec. 2004.

[6] Q. Mei, J. Guo, and D. Radev. Divrank: The interplay of prestige and diversity in information networks. In *Proceedings of the 16th ACM SIGKDD International Conference on Knowledge Discovery and Data Mining*, KDD '10, pages 1009–1018, NY, USA, 2010. ACM.

[7] G. Petkos, S. Papadopoulos, and Y. Kompatsiaris. Social event detection using multimodal clustering and integrating supervisory signals. In *Proceedings of the 2nd ACM International Conference on Multimedia Retrieval*, ICMR '12, pages 23:1–23:8, New York, NY, USA, 2012. ACM.

[8] G. Petkos, S. Papadopoulos, V. Mezaris, and Y. Kompatsiaris. Social event detection at mediaeval 2014: Challenges, datasets, and evaluation. In *Working Notes Proceedings of the MediaEval 2014 Workshop, Barcelona, Catalunya, Spain, October 16-17*, 2014.

[9] G. Petkos, S. Papadopoulos, E. Schinas, and Y. Kompatsiaris. Graph-based multimodal clustering for social event detection in large collections of images. In *Proceedings of the 20th Anniversary International Conference on MultiMedia Modeling - Volume 8325*, MMM 2014, pages 146–158, New York, NY, USA, 2014. Springer-Verlag New York, Inc.

[10] D. R. Radev, H. Jing, M. Styś, and D. Tam. Centroid-based summarization of multiple documents. *Information Processing & Management*, 40(6):919–938, 2004.

[11] M. Schinas, S. Papadopoulos, Y. Kompatsiaris, and P. Mitkas A. Visual event summarization on social media using topic modelling and graph-based ranking algorithms. In *Proceedings of the ACM International Conference on Multimedia Retrieval*, ICMR 2015, 2015.

[12] B. Thomee, D. A. Shamma, G. Friedland, B. Elizalde, K. Ni, D. Poland, D. Borth, and L.-J. Li. The new data and new challenges in multimedia research. *arXiv preprint arXiv:1503.01817*, 2015.

[13] E. S. Xioufis, S. Papadopoulos, Y. Kompatsiaris, G. Tsoumakas, and I. P. Vlahavas. A comprehensive study over VLAD and product quantization in large-scale image retrieval. *IEEE Transactions on Multimedia*, 16(6):1713–1728, 2014.

[14] X. Xu, N. Yuruk, Z. Feng, and T. A. J. Schweiger. Scan: A structural clustering algorithm for networks. In *Proceedings of the 13th ACM SIGKDD International Conference on Knowledge Discovery and Data Mining*, KDD '07, pages 824–833, New York, NY, USA, 2007. ACM.

Evento 360: Social Event Discovery from Web-scale Multimedia Collection

Jaeyoung Choi[1,3], Eungchan Kim[2], Martha Larson[3], Gerald Friedland[1], Alan Hanjalic[3]

[1]International Computer Science Institute, Berkeley, CA, USA
[2]Oracle America, Inc., USA [3]Delft University of Technology, Delft, Netherlands

[1]{jaeyoung, fractor}@icsi.berkeley.edu
[2]chan.kim@oracle.com [3]{m.a.larson, a.hanjalic}@tudelft.nl

ABSTRACT

We present *Evento 360°*[1], an online interactive social event browser, which allows the user to explore events detected within a web-scale multimedia corpus. The system addresses five key aspects of social multimedia event detection and summarization: multimodality, scale, diversity of representations, noise of multimedia items, and missing metadata. The detection algorithm uses unsupervised clustering approach that exploits temporal, spatial and textual metadata. For each detected event cluster, to choose the best subset of photos that meet both relevance and diversity criteria, the system uses hierarchical clustering that exploits both visual and audio information. Evento 360°'s user interface provides a search feature that is not limited to a certain set of events, but rather can handle an arbitrary event query. It allows the user to retrieve and explore relevant events. The system scales well and is effective in producing high-quality summaries of the detected events.

Categories and Subject Descriptors

H.3.3 [**Information Storage and Retrieval**]: Information Search and Retrieval; H.3.5 [**Information Storage and Retrieval**]: Online Information Services

Keywords

social event detection, event summarization, topic models

1. INTRODUCTION

The ACM Multimedia 2015 Yahoo-Flickr Event Summarization Challenge is a call for solutions capable of automatically finding detecting and identifying events in a collection of 100 Million photos, and creating event summaries suited for user consumption. Our solution, called Evento 360°, consists of a social event browser and an underlying event detection/summarization engine. This system allows users to search and browse events in a completely unconstrained manner. It is capable of accepting an arbitrary keyword query entered by a user. For each event, the system provides the user with an event summary containing representative photos and videos and an accompanying visualization of spatial and temporal and spatial properties of the event.

Our solution is specifically designed to address what we consider the five most critical and challenging aspects of the 2015 Yahoo-Flickr Event Summarization challenge: *multimodality*, *scale*, *diversity*, *noise* and *missing metadata*. Here, we briefly cover each in turn.

We address *multimodality* using a combination of metadata (user ID, timestamp, geo-coordinates, textual metadata) and content-based visual information. In the case of the videos, we also exploit audio information. We address *scale* by developing an algorithm that has two separate steps: Event detection and event summarization. Event detection is carried out in the computationally inexpensive clustering step, which uses metadata. More computational power is invested where it can be most useful, namely, in the summarization step, which exploits audio and visual content.

Our use of audio and visual content is directed at the challenge of ensuring the *diversity* content chosen for the event summaries, while at the same time ensuring relevance and reducing *noise*. Here, our insight is that the combination of multiple metadata sources in the event detection step can constrain images or videos being associated with events for which they are not actually relevant. Building on the event detection step, content-based features can deliver their full potential for diversification in the summary step without introducing irrelevant images or videos into the summaries. Finally, we address *missing metadata* by automatically predicting the geo-coordinates of images and videos in the collection that do not already have geo-tags.

Our approach delivers events which are highly relevant to user queries, and provide good coverage of all aspects of the events displayed by the system. It has the advantage of carrying out discovery of event structure automatically, and does not require extensive training or parameter tuning.

The remainder of the paper is structured as follows. Section 2 covers related work and Section 3 briefly describes the dataset. Section 4 presents the algorithmic details of the system and Section 5 describes the user interface. Finally, Section 6 concludes.

[1]`http://evento360.info`

MM'15, October 26–30, 2015, Brisbane, Australia.

ACM 978-1-4503-3459-4/15/10 ...$15.00.
DOI: http://dx.doi.org/10.1145/2733373.2809934 .

2. RELATED WORK

2.1 Event Detection

In recent years, event detection in multimedia collections has become a topic that has attracted a lot of interest. Event detection in text streams of social media such as Twitter are discussed in [14] [17]. For the case where all input images depict events and the list of interested event is given, supervised clustering approach can be used [9, 11]. Some approaches use structured online resources to retrieve description of events such as *last.fm* and *Upcoming* [7]. Using some form of external resource to retrieve structured information may help increase the performance, however, some events may not have a formal description and thus it is not feasible to use external resource for all cases. MediaEval workshop hosted a *social event detection* task [10] on a collection of Flickr images. At a very high level, two types of approaches were used among participants . The first type of approach was to apply a sequence of unsupervised clustering operations according to textual, temporal, or spatial similarity [18] [8] without considering the visual similarity. The second type of approach uses clustering based on the visual or multimodal similarity matrix between images [12]. The event detection step of *Evento 360°* is inspired by the first type of approach using a sequence of clustering steps using only the metadata as the simplicity of approach makes it easier to scale to the large size of the multimedia collection while still providing better performance than the similarity matrix based clustering approaches.

2.2 Event Summarization

Social photo retrieval system should present results with both the diversity and relevance. Diversification widens the pool of possible results and allows the system to address sub-topics involved in queries. However, relevance and diversity need to be well-balanced, as too much diversification may result in losing relevant items and focusing only on the relevance will produce near duplicate information as a result. Although a large amount of relevance and diversification literature exists, however, the topic still remains as an important one, especially in handling social media contents. One recent contribution [13] presents a graph-based approach that provides a photo summary of a geographic area by using both machine-tagged and user-contributed metadata collected from content-sharing websites. Location and event summarization have been addressed at MediaEval workshop as *Retrieving Diverse Social Images* task [4, 5]. In top-performing submissions, pre-filtering, clustering, reranking, optimization-based and relevance feedback methods were used and showed good quality results [3, 15].

3. DATASET

We used Yahoo Flickr Creative Commons 100M dataset [16]. The dataset contains a list of photos and videos under Creative Commons license compiled from data available on Flickr [2]. We are interested in all possible and meaningful events embedded in the dataset. Note that the dataset is not hand-curated or filtered in any way, therefore some of the media items may not correspond to any event. Since clustering based on temporal information is a crucial component in our approach, the small percentage of items that do not have valid timestamps were filtered out, leaving us with 99,998,544 items. According to the *capture device* metadata, the majority of photos and videos (74.3% or more) uploaded to Flickr were captured by stand-alone cameras, while mobile devices such as iPhone and Android phones comprised 3.6% and 2.1% of the entire collection, respectively. Standalone cameras are capable of capturing more diversified aspects of scenes due to better optical zoom capability, and wider choice of lenses, etc.

About half of the items (48.5 millions) are geo-tagged. Photos and videos captured with mobile devices have a higher percentage of geo-tag (69%) whereas about 49% of the ones captured with camera devices have geo-tag. This is understandable as majority of the stand-alone camera devices are not equipped with a geo-tagging feature.

[2] `https://www.flickr.com/`

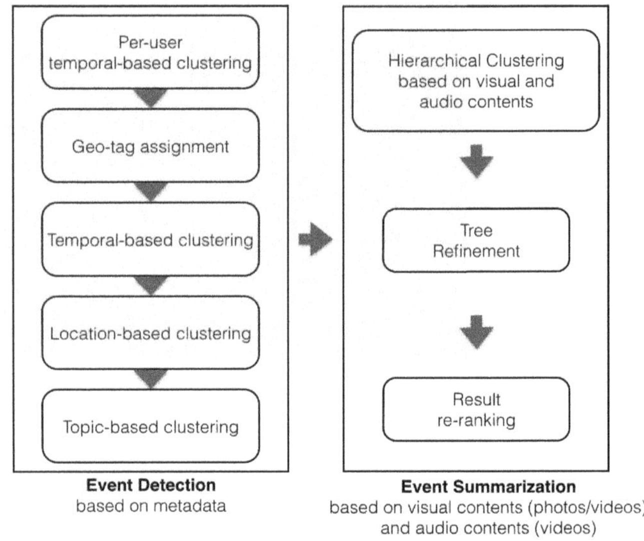

Figure 1: Overview of the event detection / event summarization pipeline

4. TECHNICAL APPROACH

After the initial text preprocessing, our approach is follows its two steps: event detection, where unsupervised clustering of media items is performed, and event summarization, where relevance and diversity is taken into account to choose a representative media subset. We describe each step in detail.

4.1 Text Preprocessing

User-contributed textual metadata—*title, usertags*, and *description*—were preprocessed to reduce ambiguity. Stop words and words related to media capture (e.g., 2011, photo, iphone4s) were removed using a predefined list compiled automatically on the basis of TF-IDF information. Words appearing only once in the metadata collection were removed as well. The preprocessing applied here is a general approach and is not hand-tailored for event detection or summarization.

4.2 Event Detection

Initially, each image is assigned to a single item cluster. Then, unsupervised item clustering using temporal informa-

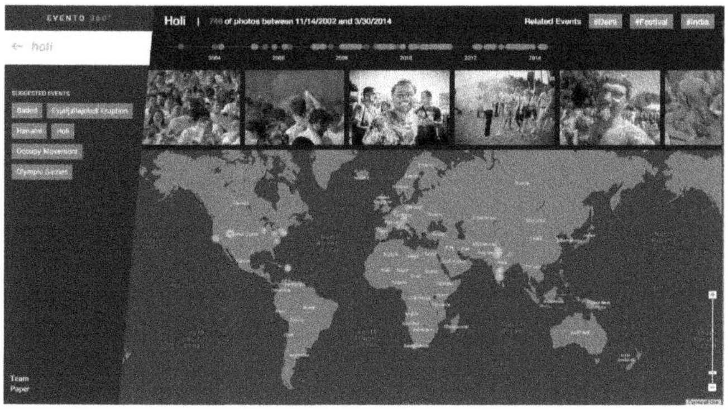

Figure 2: The screenshot of the event *holi*. The heatmap shows where the event occurs: predominantly in India with some presence in other locations. The pattern shown in the timeline at the top of the screen provides more insight into when this event occurs:t annually around Spring.

tion is carried out for each user's media stream. We leverage physical limitations, which dictate that a user can only be at a single event within a certain predefined time span. We look at time difference between items in each individual user's media stream. If the difference between two items is less then a predefined threshold, the items are assigned to the same cluster.

After the per-user time-based clustering step, we next address missing metadata. Specifically, we apply automatic geo-tagging to the items without geo-tags. As a first step, if the temporal difference between the tag-less item and the closest geo-tagged item is smaller than a time threshold, we propagate the geo-tag from the geo-tagged item. If this step fails, we infer the location of the tag-less item using a probabilistic location model, similar to the one proposed in [2], that is learned from the collection's *usertags* metadata.

After the geo-tags have been assigned, the same temporal-based clustering method used for each user's stream is applied globally to all clusters in the collection. For each of the event clusters that are the result of this temporal clustering process, a representative location is identified and assigned. The representative location is the location of the media item with the minimum sum of distances to all other geo-tagged items in the same cluster.

Once the temporal clustering is finished, we apply spatial clustering. If the representative locations of two clusters are within a separation threshold, these clusters are merged and the representative location is updated.

The last step is the refinement of clusters using the textual metadata. Latent Dirichlet Allocation [1] is used to extract topics and term dictionaries from the user-contributed textual metadata. Clusters with the similar textual descriptions are then merged iteratively using both topic and term similarity. Term dictionary is saved with each cluster and used later in the search step.

4.3 Event Summarization

Event summarization is processed in three steps. First, we cluster items with a hierarchical algorithm based on visual features. Photos with similar global visual features are assigned to the same cluster. Weighted distance of Fuzzy Color and Texture Histogram (FCTH), Color Edge Directivity Descriptor (CEDD), and Gist feature were used for visual similarity calculation. In the second step, isolated clusters are merged with other branches in the hierarchical tree. In the final step, we pick the first photo that is closest to the centroid from a cluster with the largest number of photos. The next photo is subsequently selected from the next largest cluster and is the one having the largest visual distance from the previously picked photo. This repeats until all clusters are visited. When all clusters are processed, we have a re-ranked subset of photos that best represent the event cluster.

Videos go though a similar scheme except that they are first clustered using the audio contents only. An i-Vector representation [6], a compact global feature proven to be effective at speaker or scene recognition task, is extracted from each video's audio track. Pairwise i-Vector similarity scores are computed and used for the same hierarchical algorithm. Again, the tree refinement step is carried out in order to merge isolated clusters with other branches. In the final step, we extract the temporal median frame from each video to use as its representative *keyframe*. We select the video from each cluster whose keyframe has the least visual distance to the re-ranked photo list that was previously obtained. The intuition behind this approach with videos is to have more acoustic diversity while maintaining visual interestingness.

5. USER INTERFACE & RESULT

The flow of the user interface within the *Evento 360°* is composed of three steps.

1) Main screen: The first step is browsing of events in the main screen. User can either type in a search keyword to retrieve a list of the events that are most relevant to the query, or choose one of the events in the list of suggested events.

2) Event summary screen: When users select an event, they are shown the event summary screen, including a timeline interface, photo and video thumbnails, as well as a heatmap on a map (cf. Figure 2). The timeline interface permits refinement of the time range of the search. According to the refinement, the thumbnail list and map heatmap will be updated. Each photo and video thumbnail can be clicked to see an individual photo/video display screen.

3) Photo/video display screen: This screen shows the photo or video in detail along with its metadata.

The summarization results shown in Figure 3 are representative of the hight quality detection and summarization that our system achieves.

6. CONCLUSION

We have presented *Evento 360°*, an event summarization system that allows users to explore events detected within an enormous collection of social media photos and videos. The system addresses five challenging aspects of the 2015 Event Summarization challenge: *multimodality, scale, diversity, noise* and *missing metadata.* The underlying system detects events with an unsupervised clustering algorithm using temporal, spatial, and topic information derived from the metadata. It then chooses representative media items for each event cluster by exploiting visual and audio features.

Figure 3: Each row shows the top-4 photos from the photo summary of each event cluster when queries are given as *Olympic Games* and *Eyjafjallajokull Eruption*, respectively.

The proposed approach scales well, while also providing results that impress users with their quality.

7. ACKNOWLEDGMENTS

This research is supported in part by NSF grant 1065240 "TC:Medium:Understanding and Managing the Impact of Global Inference on Online Privacy" and NSF grant 1251276, "BIGDATA: Small: DCM: DA: Collaborative Research: SMASH: Scalable Multimedia content AnalysiS in a High-level language".

8. REFERENCES

[1] D. M. Blei, A. Y. Ng, and M. I. Jordan. Latent dirichlet allocation. *J. Mach. Learn. Res.*, 3:993–1022, Mar. 2003.

[2] J. Cao, Z. Huang, Y. Yang, and H. T. Shen. UQ-DKE's participation at MediaEval 2014 placing task. In *MediaEval Workshop 2014*, 2014.

[3] D. Dang-Nguyen, L. Piras, G. Giacinto, G. Boato, and F. De Natale. Retrieval of diverse images by pre-filtering and hierarchical clustering. In *MediaEval Workshop 2014*, 2014.

[4] B. Ionescu, A. L. Gînscă, B. Boteanu, A. Popescu, M. Lupu, and H. Müller. Retrieving diverse social images at MediaEval 2015: Challenge, dataset and evaluation. In *MediaEval 2015 Workshop*, to appear.

[5] B. Ionescu, A. Popescu, M. Lupu, A. L. Gînscă, and H. Müller. Retrieving diverse social images at MediaEval 2014: Challenge, dataset and evaluation. In *MediaEval 2014 Workshop*, 2014.

[6] A. Kanagasundaram, R. Vogt, D. Dean, S. Sridharan, and M. Mason. I-vector based speaker recognition on short utterances. In *Proceedings of the 12th Conference of the ISCA*, pages 2341–2344, 2011.

[7] X. Liu, R. Troncy, and B. Huet. Finding media illustrating events. In *Proceedings of the 1st ACM ICMR*, pages 58:1–58:8, 2011.

[8] D. Manchon Vizuete, I. Gris-Sarabia, X. Giró Nieto, et al. UPC at MediaEval 2014 social event detection task. In *MediaEval Workshop 2014*, 2014.

[9] G. Petkos, S. Papadopoulos, and Y. Kompatsiaris. Social event detection using multimodal clustering and integrating supervisory signals. In *Proceedings of the 2nd ACM ICMR*, 2012.

[10] G. Petkos, S. Papadopoulos, V. Mezaris, and Y. Kompatsiaris. Social event detection at MediaEval 2014: Challenges, datasets, and evaluation. In *MediaEval 2014 Workshop*.

[11] T. Reuter and P. Cimiano. Event-based classification of social media streams. In *Proceedings of the 2nd ACM ICMR*, 2012.

[12] M. Riga, G. Petkos, S. Papadopoulos, E. Schinas, and Y. Kompatsiaris. CERTH@ MediaEval 2014 social event detection task. In *MediaEval Workshop 2014*.

[13] S. Rudinac, A. Hanjalic, and M. Larson. Generating visual summaries of geographic areas using community-contributed images. *Multimedia, IEEE Transactions on*, 15(4):921–932, June 2013.

[14] H. Sayyadi, M. Hurst, and A. Maykov. Event detection and tracking in social streams. In *Proceedings of the ICWSM. AAAI*, 2009.

[15] E. Spyromitros-Xioufis, S. Papadopoulos, Y. Kompatsiaris, and I. Vlahavas. Socialsensor: Finding diverse images at MediaEval 2014. In *MediaEval Workshop 2014*, 2014.

[16] B. Thomee, D. A. Shamma, G. Friedland, B. Elizalde, K. Ni, D. Poland, D. Borth, and L.-J. Li. The new data and new challenges in multimedia research. *arXiv preprint arXiv:1503.01817*, 2015.

[17] J. Weng. Event detection in Twitter. In *Proceedings of the 5th International Conference on Weblogs and Social Media*, 2011.

[18] M. Zaharieva, M. Schopfhauser, M. Del Fabro, and M. Zeppelzauer. Clustering and retrieval of social events in flickr. In *MediaEval 2014 Workshop*, 2014.

Unsupervised Latent Aspect Discovery for Diverse Event Summarization*

Wen-Yu Lee, Yin-Hsi Kuo, Peng-Ju Hsieh, Wen-Feng Cheng, Ting-Hsuan Chao,
Hui-Lan Hsieh, Chieh-En Tsai, Hsiao-Ching Chang, Jia-Shin Lan, Winston Hsu
National Taiwan University, Taipei, Taiwan

ABSTRACT

Recently, the fast growth of social media communities and mobile devices encourages more people to share their media data online than ever before. Analyzing data and summarizing data into useful information have become increasingly popular and important for modern society. Given a set of event keywords and a dataset, this paper performs event summarization, aiming to discover and summarize what people may concern for each event from the given dataset. More specifically, this paper extracts latent sub-events with diverse and representative attributes for each given event. This paper proposes effective methods on detecting events with (1) human attribute discovery, such as human pose and clothes, (2) scene analysis, (3) image aspect discovery, and (4) temporal and semantic analysis, to provide people different perspectives for the events they are interested in. For practical implementation, this paper studied and conducted experiments on YFCC100M, which is a dataset with 100 million of photos and videos, provided by Yahoo!. Finally, a comprehensive and complete system is created accordingly to support diverse event summarization.

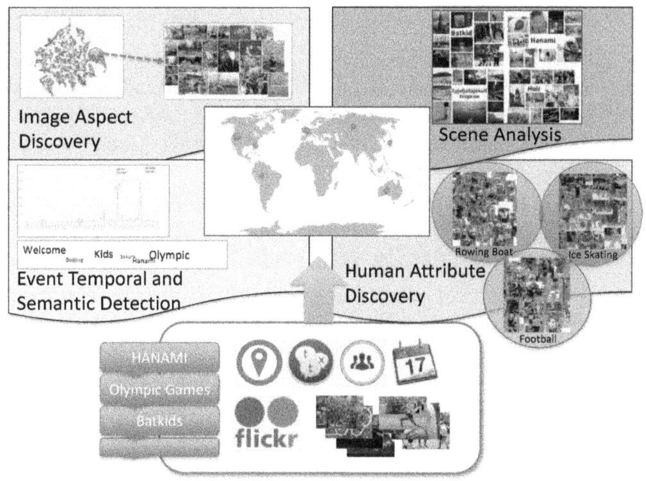

Figure 1: A system framework of extracting various perspectives for a large-scale dataset from the Flickr website.

Categories and Subject Descriptors

H.4.0 [**Information Systems Applications**]: General

Keywords

Event summarization, multimodal, visualization

1. INTRODUCTION

As the growth of social media, more and more people like to share their daily life and activities through social websites. Over the decades, thousands of photos and videos per minute have been uploaded to social photography sharing websites. Contributed by different people, the photos and videos on the cloud do offer rich information. As a result, detecting events of interest from large media collection has been receiving increasing attention for various media applications, such as earthquake detection by Twitter tweets [8]. Mostly, event detection attempts to answer the questions, "What are popular/happened?", "What they are doing?", and "What can be found?". As a global solution, event summarization gathers results of event detection and then combines useful information so as to provide summarized results to people. Event summarization automatically uncovers the structure of a large collection of photos and videos in terms of detecting and identifying events, followed by summarizing them succinctly.

This work focuses on event summarization. We consider a dataset of Flickr, with 100 million photos and videos. We extract (1) image contents, (2) locations, (3) time information, and (4) texts (e.g., title and user tags), and expected to unify them for summarization. Compared to previous works, our work not only detects special events, but also summarizes sub-events for each event. We then develop an effective system [1], see Figure 1, that discovers multiple diverse attributes and contents from the given dataset. Meanwhile, we present new methods to handle and leverage a massive amount of user-contributed data, including more than 100 million photos and videos. To sum up, the contributions of the paper include (1) developing new methods to unify and summarize different complementary information for data analytics, (2) discovering the latent behaviors, such as human poses and clothes (i.e., human attributes), (3) applying image aspect analysis and scene analysis to recognize and visualize the view of the given events which would be like, (4) performing unsupervised mining on the image contents of random top-

*The work was supported in part by MOST 103-2622-E-002-034, MediaTek, and Intel-NTU Connected Context Computing Center.

MM'15, October 26–30, 2015, Brisbane, Australia.
© 2015 ACM. ISBN 978-1-4503-3459-4/15/10 ...$15.00.
DOI: http://dx.doi.org/10.1145/2733373.2809935.

[1]http://bit.ly/1DwJnTN

Figure 2: Given an event, such as Olympics, we observed that we can automatically discover sub-events by analyzing human factors such as clothing.

ics to describe the given events, (5) showing robust detection and learning methods for massive and noisy user-contributed data, and (6) providing diverse contents for the given events.

2. MINING SPECIAL EVENT FROM FLICKR

2.1 Scene Diversity Analysis

Scene recognition can uncover the distribution of places representation among images in a specific event. It is important for users to quickly grasp the concept (e.g., outdoor, indoor) of an event's attribute. Deep convolutional neural networks (CNNs) show excellent results [4, 12] on scene recognition and they can transfer the generic representation from public scene datasets to our task (i.e., by the fine-tuning approach). Hence, for learning scene concepts, we train a deep convolutional neural network using Caffe [3] with the Places [12] pre-trained model, which we denote by Places-CNN. The Places dataset contains about 2.5 million scene-centric images from 205 scene categories. Finally, we use the activations of the last fully-connected layer as our scene feature.

In order to demonstrate the diversity of the places representation, we use KL-divergence

$$D_{KL}(I_A||I_B) = \sum_i P_{I_A}(i) \ln \frac{P_{I_A}(i)}{P_{I_B}(i)},$$

where $P_I(i)$ is the probability of image I to be categorized as scene i. In the beginning, for each event, we draw an image which is closest to centroid of image pool as our first image into candidate pool. Then, we greedily draw the image with maximum KL-divergence against remaining images in image pool into candidate pool until we have enough images. With our method, we can ensure images in candidate pool to have large diversity, allowing users to understand the event with only a few images.

2.2 Automatic Aspect Discovery

Given an event, we attempt to discover various aspects automatically. Inspired by [1] which utilizes latent Dirichlet allocation (LDA) to solve multi-document summarization problem, we propose an automatic aspect discovery for event summarization. LDA, a powerful and unsupervised generative model, is a very promising technique in computer vision tasks such as object recognition [7] and human activity recognition [6]. Meanwhile, with the huge success of deep learning in computer vision [5], we integrate deep CNN features as semantic visual representations with LDA. That is to say, each image now becomes a document consist of a set of semantic visual words. We then apply LDA on images for discovering latent aspects. Moreover, we can further analyze the discovered aspects from those semantic visual representations. We will demonstrate how this important attribute of LDA benefit our event-aspects discovery task in Section 3.4.

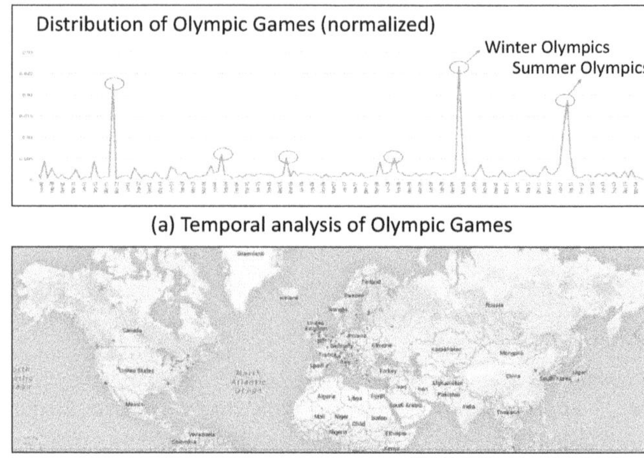

(a) Temporal analysis of Olympic Games

(b) Location analysis of Olympic Games

Figure 3: Illustration of (a) temporal analysis and (b) location analysis on the given dataset for a pre-selected event, Olympic Games. Based on the results, it is most likely that Olympic Games were held around the time associated to the peaks shown in (a). The Olympic Games are likely to be closely related to the venues shown in (b).

2.3 Human Pose and Clothing Analysis

Instead of focusing on text and image analysis, human action and activity are also essential factors to understand an event. As shown in Figure 2, for example; in Olympics, people participate in different games would have specific poses, clothes, etc. Hence, we attempt to investigate and cluster what people are doing during the event based on human pose and clothing analysis. For clothing detection, we apply pose estimator [11] to obtain the positions for arms and legs, and then trim the body box by four limbs. For pose analysis, followed by [2], we apply poselet, a body part detector, to find action patterns. Empirically, we only retain those high confidence results as action patterns. Based on clothing and action pattern detection, similar to prior section, we extract CNN features for obtaining semantic visual representations, and concatenate them for further unsupervised sub-event discovery.

3. VISUALIZATION AND APPLICATIONS

3.1 Data Preprocessing

Before the demonstration of our system, we first introduce our dataset as a preliminary. We used the YFCC100M dataset [9], which was provided by Yahoo! and was generated through data processing and data extraction from the Flickr website. Totally, the dataset contains 100 million of photos and videos. Based on our analysis, for the dataset, the timestamps of most data are between 2004 and 2014, about 48% data have location information, about 32% data have text description, and about 69% data have tags.

Figure 4: We apply Places-CNN to extract scene features and use it to select a set of images with the highest diversity by KL-divergence. Top-10 images are shown with corresponding event's name. Diverse aspects of place information make users quickly grasp the attributes of an event. For the event 'batkid', scene diversity analysis can reveal that this event took place in *streets*, *stadium*, *city hall*, etc.

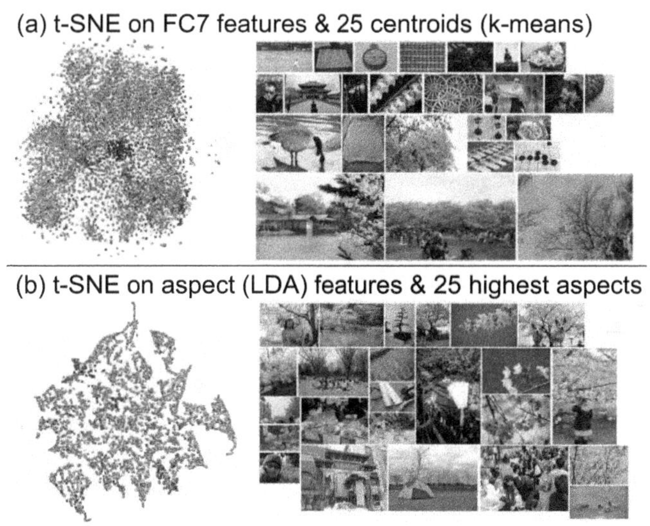

Figure 5: We apply t-SNE to visualize the effect of latent aspect discovery. (a) We observe that it might be hard to discover various aspects from the original deep CNN features. (b) However, after applying the proposed automatic aspect discovery, we can obtain more obvious aspects (topics) for the 'Hanami' event. We also provide the top-25 representative images from both features.

3.2 Temporal and Location

Consider temporal analysis and spatial analysis of an event. For temporal analysis, we found that an event may be composed of several sub-events, and the temporal distribution of the sub-events may be diverse. Some sub-events may last for only a few hours, while some sub-events may continue for several months. It is challenging to find a generic way for temporal summarization. An intuitive way is to draw timestamps of data along with a time axis. However, it might be hard to visualize the result when the distribution of the data points is too dense or sparse. As a result, we use time slots. Empirically, the size of time slots is first set to be one month. We then reduce the size to be one week for the months with peaks. For spatial analysis, we consider data title, data descriptions, and user tags of data. More specifically, for each event, we extracted the location information of a place if any of the title, description, and user tags, cover the event. Figure 3 illustrates the idea.

3.3 Scene Diversity Analysis

Scene diversity analysis can demonstrate the high diverse place information of an event and help users quickly grasp the attributes of an event. Figure 4 shows the results of some events (i.e., "Batkid", "Hanami", "Eyjafjallajokull Eruption", "Holi"). In these sets of top-10 images, we find that they can be divided into two parts, which is outdoor scene and indoor or building scene. For outdoor scene, the event "Batkid" mainly took place on *street*, "Hanami" on *sakura field*, "Eyjafjallajokull Eruption" on *iceberg/volcano*, and "Holi" on *playground*. For indoor or building scene, the event "Batkid" took place in *city hall*, "Hanami" in *washitsu*, "Eyjafjallajokull Eruption" in *train station*, and "Holi" in *religion buildings*. We also can discover other attributes such as *flavor meal* in "Hanam"" and *flag of Island* in "Eyjafjallajokull Eruption". Scene diversity analysis allows users to discriminate the semantic content in similar attributes (e.g., outdoor, indoor) and understand the event with only a few images.

3.4 Automatic Aspect Discovery

We first conduct experiments on "Hanami" event. We collect images with "Hanami" hash tag, and extract FC7 features using AlexNet described in [5]. To demonstrate the effect of the proposed latent aspect discovery, we utilize t-distributed stochastic neighbor embedding (t-SNE) [10] to reduce the dimension and visualize the relation between images. As shown in Figure 5, after LDA aspect discovery, it is more obvious to see the clustering effect. We claim LDA clustering would perform better on selecting representative images compared to k-means. Since we are discovering aspects within images related to a given event, the visual features tend to be consistent and less noise. LDA takes cooccurrence into consideration in the learning step; hence, it is more suitable to describe the common and distinctive aspects (topics).

3.5 Human Pose and Clothing Analysis

As mentioned in Section 2.3, we attempt to automatically cluster human activities for massive consumer photos. Based on the clothing and pose detection and analysis, we can roughly uncover sub-events from different dressing styles or action patterns. As shown in Figure 2, the players would have some specific actions, and wear particular clothes in the different Olympic Games. Therefore, we conduct experiments on Olympics related photos. We first search text that related to Olympics in 2012, and apply the framework described as previous. We then concatenate clothes features

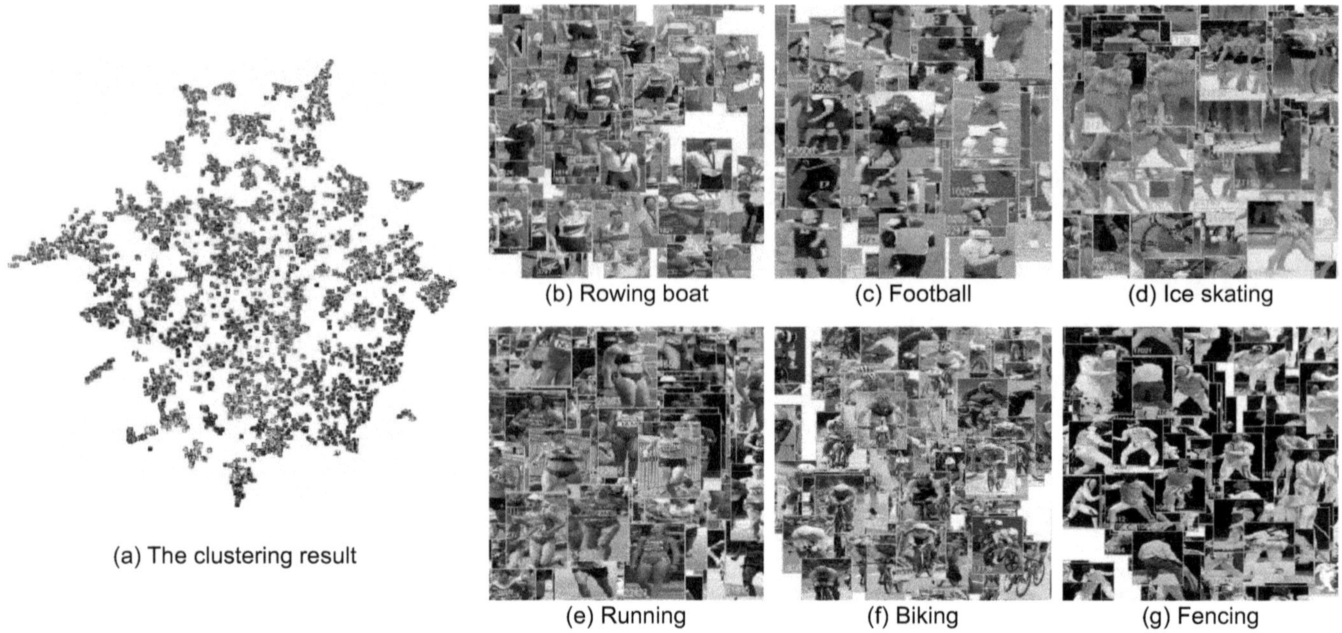

Figure 6: Based on the clothing and pose detection and semantic feature extraction, we can automatically uncover various sub-events for Olympic Games without specifying any target sub-event names. The idea is that people tend to wear similar clothing (e.g., fencing) or act similar poses (e.g., running, biking) for those sub-events. Therefore, we can provide various perspectives for a given event and generate more diverse event summarization.

and action pattern features to perform unsupervised image clustering by LDA. As shown in Figure 6, it is interesting to find that some specific clothes, including fencing suit, running sportwears, and biking are easy to recognize. Furthermore, we also notice the special backgrounds, such as football field (green grass) and fencing venues (black background), help to distinguish different sub-events using CNN features. Based on the summarized results, we analyzed what people in the images are doing. Generally, people participating in different games have different poses and different clothes. We detected human poses and extracted clothing features of visual content from user-contributed photos. Based on our experimental result, we concluded that the analysis of human poses and clothes is useful for the events that many people are participating in. As a result, we can detect some sub-events accordingly.

4. CONCLUSIONS AND FUTURE WORK

To tackle the challenges of event summarization, we investigate various perspectives for a given event, and propose unsupervised sub-event discovery to uncover latent aspects from text, visual content, and human activities. Compared to previous works on event detection, our work can not only detect events, but also sub-events, based on the given dataset. Experiment results demonstrate that the automatically discovered aspects can provide more distinctive and representative images for sub-events. Meanwhile, by analyzing human activities, we are able to realize the clothing styles and action patterns for those specific sub-events. In the future, we attempt to integrate the results from multimodality and further associate them together for achieving a more comprehensive event summarization.

5. REFERENCES

[1] R. Arora and B. Ravindran. Latent Dirichlet allocation based multi-document summarization. In *AND*, 2008.

[2] L. Bourdev and J. Malik. Poselets: Body part detectors trained using 3D human pose annotations. In *ICCV*, 2009.

[3] Y. Jia et al. Caffe: Convolutional architecture for fast feature embedding. In *MM*, 2014.

[4] M. Koskela and J. Laaksonen. Convolutional network features for scene recognition. In *MM*, 2014.

[5] A. Krizhevsky et al. Imagenet classification with deep convolutional neural networks. In *NIPS*. 2012.

[6] J. C. Niebles et al. Unsupervised learning of human action categories using spatial-temporal words. *IJCV*, 79(3):299–318, 2008.

[7] B. C. Russell et al. Using multiple segmentations to discover objects and their extent in image collections. In *CVPR*, 2006.

[8] T. Sakaki et al. Earthquake shakes Twitter users: real-time event detection by social sensors. In *WWW*, 2010.

[9] B. Thomee et al. The new data and new challenges in multimedia research. *arXiv preprint:1503.01817*, 2015.

[10] L. van der Maaten and G. Hinton. Visualizing high-dimensional data using t-SNE. *JMLR*, 9:2579–2605, 2008.

[11] Y. Yang and D. Ramanan. Articulated pose estimation with flexible mixtures-of-parts. In *CVPR*, 2011.

[12] B. Zhou et al. Learning deep features for scene recognition using places database. In *NIPS*, 2014.

How Was It? Exploiting Smartphone Sensing to Measure Implicit Audience Responses to Live Performances

Claudio Martella[1]*, Ekin Gedik[2]*, Laura Cabrera-Quiros[2,4]*, Gwenn Englebienne[3], Hayley Hung[2]
[1]VU University Amsterdam, Netherlands
[2]Delft University of Technology, Netherlands
[3]University of Amsterdam, Netherlands
[4]Instituto Tecnológico de Costa Rica, Costa Rica
c.martella@vu.nl, {e.gedik, l.c.cabreraquiros, h.hung}@tudelft.nl, g.englebienne@uva.nl

ABSTRACT

In this paper, we present an approach to understand the response of an audience to a live dance performance by the processing of mobile sensor data. We argue that exploiting sensing capabilities already available in smart phones enables a potentially large scale measurement of an audience's implicit response to a performance. In this work, we leverage both tri-axial accelerometers, worn by ordinary members of the public during a dance performance, to predict responses to a number of survey answers, comprising enjoyment, immersion, willingness to recommend the event to others, and change in mood. We also analyse how behaviour as a result of seeing a dance performance might be reflected in a people's subsequent social behaviour using proximity and acceleration sensing. To our knowledge, this is the first work where pervasive mobile sensing has been used to investigate spontaneous responses to predict the affective evaluation of a live performance. Using a single body worn accelerometer to monitor a set of audience members, we were able to predict whether they enjoyed the event with a balanced classification accuracy of 90%. The collective coordination of the audience's bodily movements also highlighted memorable moments that were reported later by the audience. The effective use of body movements to measure affective responses in such a setting is particularly surprising given that traditionally, physiological signals such as skin conductance or brain-based signals are the more commonly accepted methods to measure implicit affective response. Our experiments open interesting new directions for research on both automated techniques and applications for the implicit tagging of real world events via spontaneous and implicit audience responses during as well as after a performance.

Categories and Subject Descriptors

H.1.2 [**Models and Principles**]: User/Machine Systems—*Human Information Processing*; H.3.1 [**Information Storage and Retrieval**]: Content Analysis and Indexing—*Indexing Methods*; G.3 [**Probability and Statistics**]: Time Series Analysis

*C. Martella, E. Gedik, and L. Cabrera-Quiros contributed equally to this article

MM'15, October 26-30 2015, Brisbane, Australia
© 2015 ACM. ISBN 978-1-4503-3459-4/15/10 ...$15.00.
DOI: http://dx.doi.org/10.1145/2733373.2806276.

Keywords

Human behavior, proximity sensing, wearable sensors, accelerometers, arts, dance, audience response, mobile phones.

1. INTRODUCTION

Art and cultural events such as dance, art exhibitions, and concerts have an inherent value [14], which some studies have shown are correlated with a perceived quality of life [25] as well as self-rated health levels [26]. Driven by the high reward that such information would have for the art and cultural industry, the aim of this paper is to investigate ways of automatically measuring the response to the experience of art and cultural events as a means of enhancement for both consumers and practitioners.

As public subsidies for the arts and culture reduce, we argue that society loses a significant contribution to public life in both intellectual, emotional, and social stimulation. Art and cultural institutions increasingly find that they must be able to quantify the service they provide for monetary investment. The quantification of the effect of such events has the potential to benefit society by providing members of the public with a more targeted enhancement of art and cultural experiences and a way of showing that such experience on their own contribute significantly to the improvement of people's social lives. While this may appear to be a luxury to have in society, numerous studies have shown the benefits of art and cultural events for stimulating the social life of public spaces [42], and health and mental wellbeing [27, 32, 14].

In this paper, we target the task of quantifying people's experience and automatically predicting factors related to watching a modern dance performance. We show experimental results based on two different public modern dance performances. However, unlike prior works that have used biosignals or physiological sensing [36, 13], we hypothesise that behaviour, as sensed by sensors that one would find in smart phones, could also be used to sense affective responses to a performance. Our experiments show that using more pervasive sensors opens up huge possibilities for implicit affective sensing on a large scale in the wild.

By working closely for the last 2 years with Holland Dance (HD)[1], an organization whose role is to promote dance in The Netherlands, we have identified some key challenges to measuring audience response:

The limits of survey responses: Organisers of live performances are always interested to gauge audience opinions about the performance they organise — if they enjoyed a performance or enjoy dance performances in general, they are more likely to recommend it to others, thus sustaining the popularity of the art form. Such responses must also be obtained after the performance and do not therefore

[1]http://www.holland-dance.com

capture the spontaneous response of the performance audience to specific moments. Note that sentiment about a performance can also be assessed via social media but again requires audience members to actively participate in putting forward an opinion publicly [38].

Obtaining implicit measurements on a large scale: To our knowledge, most related work that tries to use implicit responses to visual stimuli such as movies [36, 13] or live performances [41] have tended to rely on physiological or brain activity measurements. While such signals are considered fairly reliable, equipment that is able to sense this data is still not particularly pervasive. As social norms would dictate, one tries to stay as quiet and still as possible when sitting and watching a live dance performance, so measuring implicit and measurable responses from pervasive sensors are likely to be even more challenging.

Obtaining detailed audience responses on a large scale: Even when survey responses are available for a performance, typical Likert scale questions cannot provide detailed insights into what moments of a performance could have triggered someone to dislike or like it. One way to circumvent this problem involves using free text answers, which can provide richer but still incomplete information about someone's experience that need to be manually processed. Going further, interviews can also be used, but provide more unstructured responses for those few who are willing to spend more time reflecting on their experience. They are, therefore, limited to an even smaller subset of an entire audience.

Quantifying the impact of a Performance on our Social Lives To our knowledge, most works focus on measurements obtained solely during the performance, measuring direct responses to it. However, the value of a performance can stretch beyond this period to its affect afterwards. For instance, it could affect ones mood, serve as a topic of stimulating discussion over drinks, leading to positive feelings about the entire performance and socialising experience. In an ideal case, its effects should last beyond the performance itself, perhaps even providing lasting memories that are recalled collectively by friends. This is perhaps the most difficult challenge but, if answered, even in part, would provide a broader metric to quantify the value of arts and cultural events.

More concretely, we make the following novel contributions; we show that (i) even when people are sitting and watching a live dance performance, they spontaneously react it via body movements that can be captured from a standard acceleration sensor, (ii) moments of common spontaneous bodily reaction correspond to memorable events in the performance as reported by survey responses relating to the performance, (iii) their reactions can be used to predict their enjoyment of the performance, whether they felt immersed in the experience, would recommend it to others, or thought dance performance changed their mood positively, (iv) and finally by considering the social context that surrounds the activity of going to a live dance performance, we also provide initial results using acceleration and proximity sensors, that suggest that a change in the mood of a person as a result of watching a live dance performance is reflected in their general body behaviour while mingling.

2. RELATED WORK

Traditional methods to investigate the response of an audience to a live dance performance make use of self-reports, such as surveys and interviews [6, 30]. Digital technologies can overcome the limitations of surveys and interviews, by giving more direct and fine-grained insights into the response of an audience. For example, the explosion in popularity of the social media, e.g. Twitter, and mobile computing has broadened the borders of a live performance, as fans comment and post information and opinions live to the online community [4]. Practitioners are interested in the activity of their audience through the social media to understand both their response and to leverage their activities as marketers of their performances [21, 20]. For example, some theatres, including Broadway, have experimented with so-called "tweet-seats" reserved for customers who promised to tweet about the performance live [1].

Other rather less pervasive technologies can also overcome the granularity issues of surveys using sensors. For example, work in neuroaesthetics use fMRI scanning to relate viewer responses to the aesthetics of the performance [5, 9, 7]. Moreover, tracking of eye gaze from video has been used when trying to distinguish novice from expert observers of dance [37]. Finally, physiological sensing such as galvanic skin response (GSR) sensors, have been investigated to measure the arousal of individuals watching a video of a dance performance, and its relationship with the individuals' self-reports [19]. Similarly, GSRs have been used also to measure the response to other types of live performance, such as comedy [41] and movies in a cinema [13].

These attempts show an increasing interest in quantifying the experience of arts and cultural events, such as live dance performances. Unlike these approaches, we advocate the use of pervasive sensors which are readily available in smartphones, which enable less obtrusive measurements and on a massive scale, compared to those obtained via physiological sensing. In particular, in this work, we focus on using acceleration and proximity sensors to measure people's reactions to live performance, which have been used thus far to measure very different phenomena.

Specifically, most work that consider accelerometers and people have addressed the problem of activity recognition of daily activities such as walking, running, sitting, climbing the stairs [18], daily household activities including eating or drinking, vacuuming or scrubbing, lying down [2], or identifying modes of transportation taken [31]. There is a trend moving towards the detection of medically relevant events, such as fall detection [11, 44], but all of these approaches focus resolutely on physical activities where the behaviour can be represented directly by quite specific movements of the body. It is possible to classify these types of activities with excellent performance, yet these activities are very different to analysing the response to a live performance. Few works do exist where less specific body movements have been classified. For example, Matic et al. also used acceleration to detect speaking status by strapping an accelerometer to the chest so that vibrations directly caused by speaking could be detected [24], Hung et al. [17] used body movements to predict socially relevant actions with a device hung loosely round the neck or for detecting conversations[16]. Such works highlight the potential of measuring spontaneous bodily responses to external stimuli using more pervasive sensing.

Apart from focusing on different activities and tasks, the above-mentioned works measure behaviour in environments that are far less challenging than a theatre where the audience sits in silence, and where the link between activity and behaviour is not as direct. The most similar work to our own was presented by Englebienne and Hung [12] who found that they were able to identify audience members as professors and non-professors from their behaviour while attending an inaugural lecture. Although they were sitting, the small movements made in reaction to parts of the lecture demonstrated implicit responses of interest to particular moments and content delivered during the lecture. However, they did not analyse whether reactions from the audience to the lecture correlated with enjoyment of the lecture, for example. Another closely related work where the audience response was measured was presented by Bao et al. [3] who investigated how users watching movies on abuffer tablet could have their implicit responses sensed by a wide variety of modalities from the tablet itself including the video, audio, tablet interactions, and accelerometer. In this case, movements from the tablet whilst the user was holding it were used to gauge responses. Using a multimodal approach they were able to predict the rating of users to movies they watched on the tablet. However, in this case, the user sat alone to watch the movies and was not inhibited by the social norms usually adhered to in an auditorium.

Proximity sensors have been used to study the interactions between individuals with approaches more similar to complex network analysis. Cattuto et al. [8] have used wearable sensors to analyse social interactions in crowded social settings, by means of proximity data collected through RFIDs. Martella et al. [23] used data collected through a series of wearable proximity sensors to identify the different communities attending a multi-disciplinary ICT conference. Roggen et al. [33] and Wirz et al. [43] proposed the usage of wearable sensors to discover spatio-temporal relationships between a number of individuals in the context of crowd dynamics. While these studies show that social relationship between individuals can be captured by means of spatio-temporal information, none of these works focus on the measurement of spatio-temporal relationship information in the context of arts and cultural events.

3. CASE STUDY 1: DIRECT RESPONSES TO A PERFORMANCE

To inspect whether it is possible to predict responses to a performance by using data collected with wearable sensors, we have conducted an experiment in an actual dance performance. We start this section by explaining the characteristics of the performance and the resulting dataset we obtained. Then, we describe the features we used in the data analysis and classification experiments. The next two sections present the qualitative analysis and classification experiments we did based on questionnaire responses. The qualitative analysis aims to show that the movements of the audience are informative of their reactions to the performance. We do this by showing that the captured activity of the participants and common responses correspond to the salient events happening in the performance. The classification experiments present our methodology for automatically predicting a participant's evaluation of the event. The performance and further analysis presented show that the proposed method is indeed promising and worth investigating further.

3.1 Data Collection

The sensor set-up: We organised a data collection experiment during a dance performance. This event consisted of almost an hour and a half of performance without intermission. It mainly consisted of dancing but also included monologues by the performers in Italian, while the music was mainly based on live cello arrangements but also included pre-recorded songs. Using triaxial acceleration and IR cameras (for additional data verification), we recorded 41 participants watching the performance. The accelerometers were located in a custom-made device hung around every participant's neck. These devices recorded at 20Hz and were synchronised to a global time obtained by communicating through a wireless network. However, due to hardware malfunctions, only 32 accelerometers recorded data. In addition, the performance was recorded using a GoPro Hero +3 to analyse salient moments (i.e. favourite moments that were reported by the participants).

Survey responses: To evaluate the experience, a questionnaire was filled in by all 41 participants after the performance. Each questionnaire had 12 questions, where each group of three questions aimed to measure one aspect of the experience. The four aspects were "enjoyment", "recommendation (to a friend)", "immersion" and "mood changes". Each participant evaluated these aspects of the performance on a ten-point Likert scale, where one means "I completely disagree" and ten means "I completely agree". For measuring enjoyment, we adapted and selected questions presented in [35]. For the task of immersion, we selected involvement questions from the Igroup Presence Questionnaire [34]. For recommendation we used items from O'Brien's questionnaire [28]. Each of these questions were carefully chosen to measure each task and slightly adapted to match our scenario. We formed the questions regarding mood by ourselves. Given that the majority of the audience members were Dutch, we used a back-translation procedure to ensure that each questionnaire item was accurately describing the original English wording. This involved finding three different Dutch speakers to translate the questions from English to Dutch, then from Dutch to English and then from English to Dutch again ensuring that the finally chosen words best matched the original English. The complete set of questions asked in this questionnaire in both English and Dutch are listed in the Appendix 9. From the total number of participants, 32 responded with the Dutch questionnaire and 9 to the English one.

Of the 32 participants with working accelerations, 25 reported a favourite moment of the performance. Two moments were particularly memorable: the *motorcycle sequence* was declared as favourite by 32% of the participants, and the *bolero finale*, favourite of 52% of the subjects. Note that in some cases that participants declared more than one favorite moment.

3.2 Feature Extraction

We used the variance of the accelerometer readings, which is expected to act as a proxy for the physical activity level of the participants. Our assumption was that both subtle as well as more expansive movements of the the participants is related to the experience of the event. We expect participants with different evaluations of the event to have different movement patterns throughout the event, especially during salient parts of the performance. We calculate the variance in a sliding window of 2 seconds with 1 second shift, which corresponds to 40 samples for each window with a shift of 20 samples. This window size is carefully selected to capture the subtle and short variations in motion while still preserving a fine time scale and is empirically proven to perform well.

We extract features from an interval of $\sim$79 minutes, starting just before the first piece, when all participants are seated and ending when the final piece of the performance finishes. With this we obtain 4705 different variance values for each axis. Before calculating the variance along each axis, each axis is normalised by computing the z-score to remove interpersonal differences. We also calculate the variance of the magnitude, resulting in 4 different variance values for each interval. For the qualitative analysis, we only use the variance of the magnitude. For classification, we treat the variance values of each axis as well as the magnitude as our features, resulting in a 18820 dimensional feature vector for each participant. This feature choice restricts the representation to be temporally dependent. Therefore we may not capture cases where two participants liked (or disliked) the event during different parts of the performance. With another formulation of the problem, like using bag-of-words or a multiple instance learning approach, temporal dependence can be avoided. Although such cases are quite probable, in this experiment we assume that participants with similar evaluations of the performance tend to respond similarly during salient parts of it.

3.3 Data Analysis

The variance in magnitude signals from all the participants were compared against each other to create a pairwise co-occurrence measurement over time using Mutual Information (MI). These signals were calculated over a sliding window (size of 60 samples) shifted

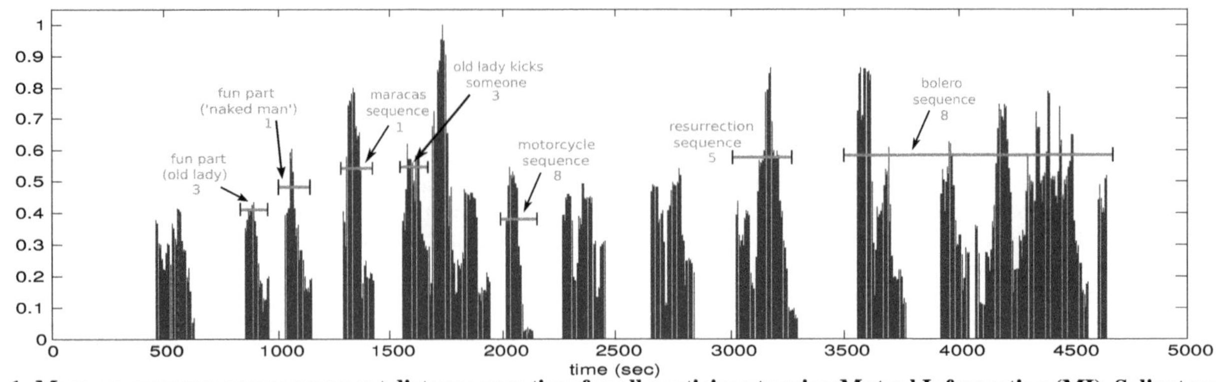

Figure 1: Mean co-occurrence measurement distance over time for all participants using Mutual Information (MI). Salient moments are highlighted in red with number of appearance

by one sample, resulting in a vector of co-occurrence over time between two participants. The mean mutual information at each time interval was calculated, allowing us to evaluate the collective response of the participants to the performance over time. We hypothesised that salient moments would correspond to a high MI among all participants. These moments were chosen using a Otsu threshold [15] on the values of the computed signal. Figure 1 shows these salient moments captured by points where the mutual information goes beyond the threshold (blue), as well as the frequency of the reported favorite moments (red) that appeared in the free text survey responses. The time stamps were generated by manually identifying the time period(s) where the reported favourite moments occured. Notice that the two moments declared as favourites for the majority of participants (*motorcycle* and *bolero finale*) are captured . This shows that memorable moments for people during these events can be captured by their coordinated movements, as they share the experience.

Furthermore, the role of music during the performance is also interesting and we want to understand its effect, if any, on the collective behaviour of the participants. To do so, we looked at the sound intensity of the performance as obtained from the video and annotated song changes. Figure 2 shows the sound intensity of the performance (green) compared to the normalized co-occurrence measurement for MI (blue). The performance's songs are also highlighted in this figure in red. Here, it can be seen that although the music had a correlation with the response of the public in a performance in certain sequences, other moments of high mean MI are also correlated with acts with no music. This suggests that the music may not have been the main factor stimulating coordination between our participants. For this reason, we decided that the song changes would not be useful for the following classification experiments and have focused solely on acceleration data instead.

With this preliminary qualitative information, the next subsection describes our classification experiments using the four questionnaire tasks mentioned in Section 3.3.

3.4 Classifying Experience

Labelling samples

We use a standard pattern recognition approach to automatically predict the responses of participants. We start by labelling our participants according to the questionnaire answers they gave. For each group of three questions, we obtained one numerical value by averaging and rounding the three answers. This way, we obtain four different labels for our participants, where each label corresponds to the one of the tasks. We divided the participants into two classes

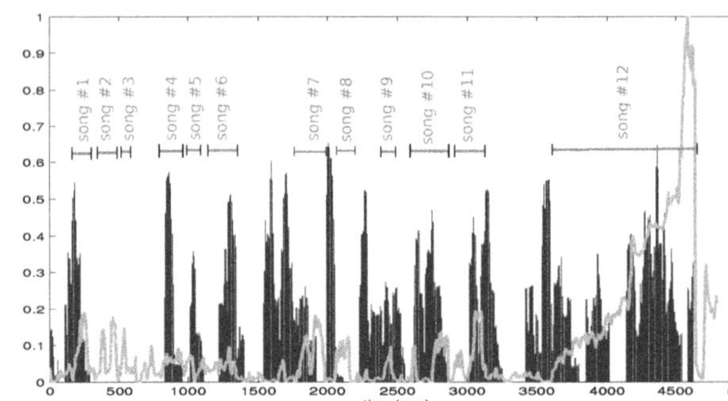

Figure 2: Sound intensity of the performance (green) compared against the normalized co-occurrence measurement calculated by MI (blue).

for each task corresponding to a "positive" and "negative" report on their experience of the performance. Participants whose averaged answer to any group of questions was below 5 was placed in the negative class for that task, meaning this participant, either did not enjoy the event, would not recommend the performance, did not feel immersed throughout the performance or did not think the performance uplifted their mood. The positive class thus contains participants who gave positive responses to the questions.

In this study, we mainly focus on enjoyment and recommendation, since these two are questions with clearer indications, but still provide results for immersion and the mood changes as we believe they can help in obtaining a general understanding of the performance's effects on the participants. After defining the classes for each task, our class distributions were not always balanced. For "enjoyment" and "recommendation", the majority of participants (26) gave positive answers. 22 participants thought "the performance affected their mood positively". Therefore, for these tasks, the problem becomes challenging for the smaller negative classes. These imbalance in class distributions also affected our choices of performance measure; in addition to accuracy, we also provide the balanced accuracy so each classes contributes equally to the final measure. The distribution for the "immersion" task is more balanced with 17 participants in the positive class.

Methodology

To emphasise the connection between the information contained in the motion data and the participants' experience of the event, in our classification experiments we focus on a simple set of features and a well-understood classifier. More precisely, our features are the variance of acceleration along each axis and of acceleration magnitude, extracted with the aforementioned setup. We selected a Linear SVM as our classifier. Since the number samples is limited, we chose to use a model with few parameters . For evaluating the performance of our method, we used leave-one-out cross validation, training with 31 samples and with the remaining one is used for testing. The hyperparameters of the SVM are also selected using cross validation on the training set.

As stated in Section 3.2, representing the features using the whole performance would require classification on a 18820-dimensional feature vector for each participant. Since we do not expect all intervals to be equally informative and to avoid the curse of dimensionality, we decided to use a filtering approach which selects the informative intervals before feature extraction.

To do so, we selected a Dynamic Time Warping (DTW) distance computed over a window (sizes were set from 20 to 60 samples) with a shift size of 1 sample . Similar to the mean MI co-occurrence vector used in Section 3.3. Our assumption here is that if we select the intervals where the average DTW distance between each pair is significantly higher than the rest, we should end up with time intervals that are more discriminative than the rest. In an ideal scenario, intra-class distances should stay relatively stable throughout the event, so the parts where the average DTW distance between pairs is high coorespond to intervals where the intra-class distances are maximised. We hypothesise that using this metric provides better discrimination between classes compared to using mutual information where moments of high mutual information could also correspond to moments where the mean DTW is low and both classes would be almost indistinguishable . Empirical results using a threshold on the mean MI supported this claim, with performance scores significantly lower than the proposed method for the majority of tasks.

Using the same setup explained in Section 3.3, we detect the intervals where pairwise DTW distances are significantly higher than the rest and extract variance features for each person from these intervals only. The number of remaining intervals after filtering depends on the window size selection. In our experiments, where we have used windows of 20 to 60 samples, the number of selected intervals ranged from 86 to 830. Finally, after interval selection and feature extraction, we perform further dimensionality reduction by applying principal component analysis (PCA) to the feature vectors. We keep the principal components which preserve the 99 percent variance of features and use them for training and testing our model. This resulted in 12 and 19 resulting feature dimensions.

Results

The performance obtained by the proposed method, with different window size selections when using the thresholded DTW distance to pre-filter the salient intervals, are presented in Table 1. This table also includes the performance scores obtained without interval selection. The statistically significant results between those using interval selection and those using whole event are specified with a sign '*'.

<table>
<tr><th>Method \ BAcc | Acc(%)</th><th>Enjoyment</th><th>Recommend</th><th>Immerse</th><th>Mood</th></tr>
<tr><td>DTW IS(20 Sample)</td><td>60 | 66*</td><td>61 | 78</td><td>63 | 63</td><td>60 | 63*</td></tr>
<tr><td>DTW IS(40 Sample)</td><td>90 | 94**</td><td>70 | 81</td><td>53 | 53</td><td>55 | 66*</td></tr>
<tr><td>DTW IS(60 Sample)</td><td>78 | 84**</td><td>71 | 84</td><td>49 | 50</td><td>48 | 63*</td></tr>
<tr><td>Whole Event</td><td>36 | 38</td><td>74 | 78</td><td>51 | 50</td><td>38 | 38</td></tr>
</table>

(→ p<0.05) (** → p<0.01)*

Table 1: Performance scores obtained with different methods

The performance obtained without interval selection, which are reported in the final row of Table1, are unsatisfactory in general. Any task other than predicting recommendation has an accuracy lower than or equal to the proposed method, regardless of the window size.

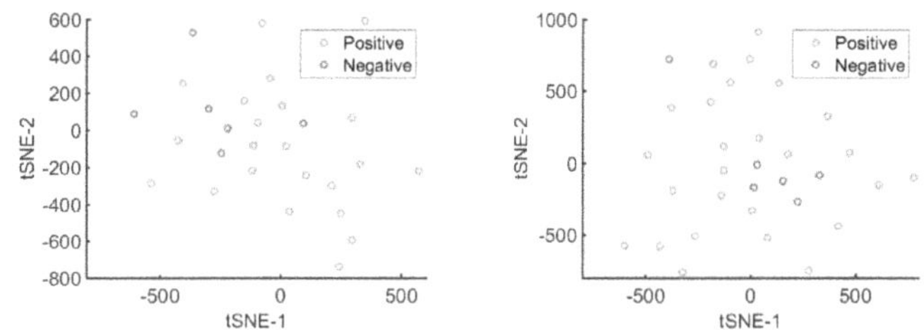

(a) (b)

Figure 3: Non-linear embedding of feature vectors for the enjoyment class for (a) the whole event and (b) using interval selection with a 40 sample window.

We should note that we did also apply PCA to the feature vectors for the non-filtered method. However, these scores showed that the extracted principal components were still affected by variance features extracted from many non-informative intervals, supporting our claim of interval selection is necessary.

The performance obtained with different window sizes have some interesting implications. For the tasks of immersion and mood, we obtained the highest performance with a window of 20 samples, corresponding to one second. With the increasing window size, our performance for these tasks dropped below random. We can see that this same window size is not optimal for the enjoyment and recommendation tasks. This could suggest that some tasks are shorter in time scale than others. However, we need more data to draw solid conclusions about such implications. It should be also noted that for the mood task, our proposed method always provides a significantly better result than the whole interval method, regardless of the window size.

Another interesting implication can be seen in the performance scores for "recommendation". For this task, the highest performance score is obtained when the whole event was used. Supporting this idea, the performance for this task increases as the window size increases. We should note that using a wider window may not always guarantee that more intervals are selected for classification. None of the results presented for the recommendation task showed significant improvement over the whole event baseline. However, the recommendation accuracy is very high for the whole event, suggesting that the behaviour of people who are interested in recommending dance performance to others could be distinguished from those who did not tend to recommend dance performances to others, and that this was independent of any particular moments during a performance.

Finally, we can see that for enjoyment, one of our most important tasks, we obtain relatively high performance, with the highest score of 94% accuracy and 90% balanced accuracy. With a window size of 40 samples, only one sample from each class is misclassified, resulting in high precision and recall scores for both classes. This result is significantly better than the whole interval method (p>0.01). To further investigate how the interval selection affects the distribution of samples, we visualise the filtered set of feature vectors of each participant using t-SNE [39], a non-linear embedding technique. The resultant two-dimensional embedding shown in Figure 3 illustrates that interval selection allows data points in the negative class to be clustered together in the feature space.

We also experimented with computing DTW distances on the raw accelerometer magnitude signal, instead of the variance. This experiment resulted in performance scores that were worse than random for "enjoyment", "immersion" and "mood". For "recommendation", we obtained a balanced accuracy score of 85 percent. This result is quite interesting, since the highest performance we obtained for "recommendation" in Table 1 was the case where the whole event was used. However, in general it can be said that this experiment empirically supported our claim that the variance in acceleration is a valid feature for our experiments, both as a feature and for the interval selection using the thresholded DTW distance.

3.5 Further Analysis of Salient Moments

This section aims to further explain the salient moments of the performance, now relating these with the classes identified in Section 3.4. For space reasons, we focus on the enjoyment task as it has given us the best performance. The pairwise similarity measurements from the previous qualitative analysis were separated into two groups for each task: the ones who completely agreed with the statement and everyone else. For each group, the same unified similarity measurement as described in Section 3.3 was calculated and the salient moments were obtained using the Otsu threshold level. Since the goal is to asses the similarity of people within the same class, pairs of different classes are left out.

Figure 4 shows the measurements of mean MI over time for both classes in the enjoyment task (where the negative class was plotted below the positive class). Notice how the two moments considered as favorites for the majority of participants (*motorcycle sequence* and *bolero finale*) reappears for the mean MI in the group that enjoyed the performance but not for those who disliked it. Actually, there is almost no overlap between the salient moments for the classes 1 and 2. This reaffirms that specific acts or sequences in a performance (or movie) can have a significant impact in the final assessment of enjoyment.

Furthermore, Figure 5 shows the mean DTW distance for members within the 'Enjoy' class (blue), the 'Not Enjoy' class (green) and all pairs in opposing classes (red). The 'Not Enjoy' class resulted in a higher overall DTW distance, over the complete performance, compared to the 'Enjoy' class. This might indicate a lack of synchrony among people who dislike the performance, which echoes findings by Wang and Cesar with Galvanic Skin Response measures to an audience's reaction to a live performance [40].

4. CASE STUDY 2: IMPACT OF A PERFORMANCE ON SOCIAL BEHAVIOUR

Section 3 provided interesting insights into how the response to a dance performance can be measured with pervasive sensing. However, while working with HD, we came across a different perspective on the problem. Can we quantify the influence of a performance on the audience even after the performance is over?

There is clearly a context that surrounds the event itself — typically, people will attend a performance with friends and/or family, may come for a drink beforehand and stay for drink afterwards. We hypothesised that people's social behaviour (as measured through proximity and acceleration) could also be affected by watching a dance performance. As a business model HD was already co-organising networking events around dance performances together with two local networking organizations. The idea was that the dance performance could be an occasion to enhance the networking event, and the co-located networking event would encourage more people to watch dance.

To investigate this hypothesis, we decided to investigate whether we could measure differences in how people socialized during the event. Hence, we measured mingling behavior during two networking sessions, one right before a dance performance and another right after it. With HD and regional networking groups, we co-organised a networking event with 48 volunteers. The same sensing devices described in Section 3 were used. An example snapshot of the mingling data is shown in Figure 6.

Figure 6: Snapshots of the instrumented mingling room.

Although a networking event is not exactly the same as the more casual ways that people might attend dance performances socially, we believe this initial investigation provides a feasibility study for larger scale less controlled studies in the future.

Similar to previous work using proximity sensors to analyse social behaviour in conferences [23], musea [8], and work-places [29], we used proximity sensors as proxies for face-to-face social interactions, together with accelerometer data as described above. Two months after the experiment, we published sensor analysis results for the volunteers and asked them to answer a survey about their experience of the dance performance and the networking event.

4.1 Setup

Each device we used during the previous study is also equipped with a wireless radio, which we used to broadcast the device's unique identifier (ID) every second up to a distance of some 2-3 meters. The reception of such broadcast by the devices nearby is considered a proximity detection. Since the device lies on the front of the torso, the radio transmission is shielded by the body, hence restricting the proximity sensing mostly towards the front of the individual. The device logs each detection on the on-board storage along with their timestamps. We used an energy-efficient MAC protocol [10] to allow the devices to communicate their IDs and detect each other's proximity. Because of the unreliability of the wireless medium, we used a density-based filtering technique to increase the sensitivity of the signal for detecting face-to-face proximity [22].

To measure whether people were interacting or not, we processed the proximity detections collected by the devices as follows. For each pair of individuals, we computed the intervals where pairs were continuously facing each other, formally $[t_i, t_j]$ where t_i is the timestamp of the first detection and t_j is the timestamp of the last detection of the interval. Because pairs can be close for multiple non-overlapping time intervals during the same measurement, we computed multiple intervals for the same pair. Here, we refer to an interval of proximity between any pair as an *interaction*. For our experiments we considered only intervals of proximity longer than 60s to indicate interactions.

4.2 Results

Since some attendees did not attend the entire event, only the data from 35 of the participants was available for analysis. We first hypothesized a difference in the length or the number of interactions between the two sessions. For example, one could imagine that individuals would interact in longer conversations, or with more people. In Figure 7(a) we present the distribution of the length of the interactions for the two sessions (from here on referred to as round 1 and round 2) across all the individuals. In both rounds shorter interactions are predominant. Note that as drinks were served at the bar, during both rounds often individuals left a conversation to fill their glass and went back right afterwards to the same conversation, which would be measured as two distinct interactions. No significant mean difference was seen between the distribution in interaction length for the two rounds. In Figure 7(b) we present the distribution of the number of distinct interactions for round 1 and round 2 across all the individuals.

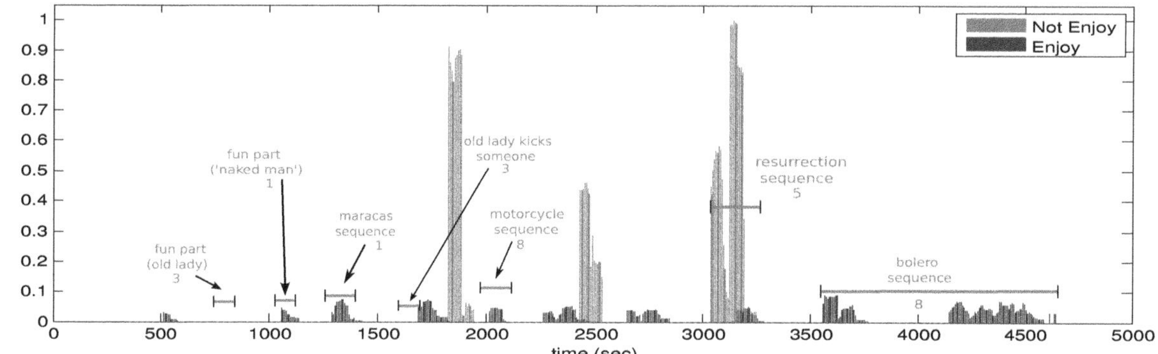

Figure 4: Salient moments from mean MI discriminating people in class 'Enjoy' and 'Not Enjoy'

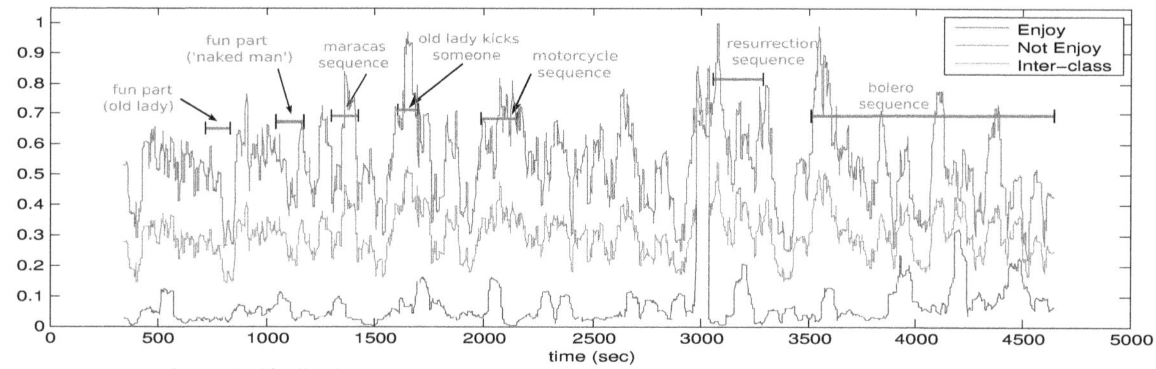

Figure 5: Similarity measurement using DTW for each class in the enjoyment task.

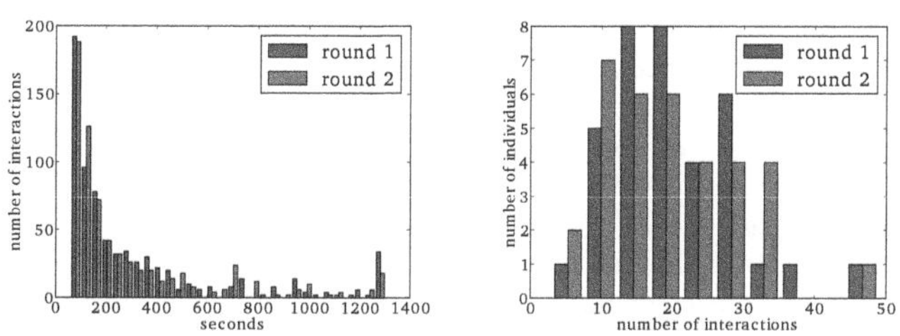

(a) interaction lengths (b) interaction numbers

Figure 7: (a) Distribution of the lengths of the interactions during the two rounds. (b) Distribution of the number of interactions for round 1 and round 2 across all the individuals.

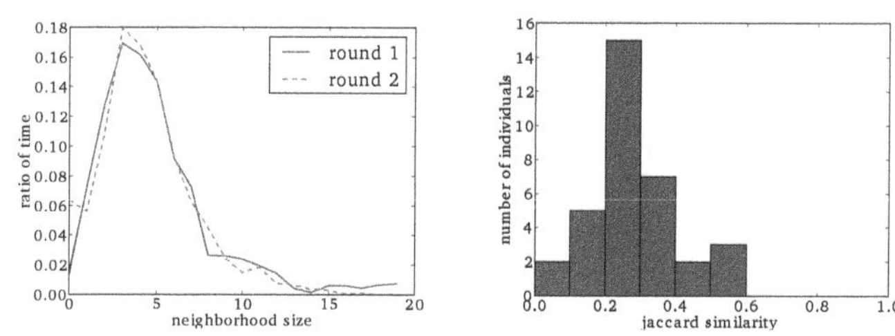

(a) conversational group sizes (b) change in partners

Figure 8: (a) Relative amount of time sensors detected a certain number of other sensors (at a specific moment in time). (b) Distribution of the jaccard similarity across the individuals.

A second difference we hypothesized was in the size of conversational groups. For example, people could be engaged in conversations involving more people, or conversely more one-to-one conversations, perhaps to discuss the content of the performance. We define a *neighborhood* as the set of nodes a sensor a detects at a given moment in time, i.e. the individuals in physical proximity of the individual wearing sensor a. In Figure 8(a) we present the distribution of neighborhood size with respect to the amount of time they were observed together, expressed as a ratio over the round duration. In other words, it represents the amount of time individuals have spent in proximity to another n individuals. The results show a peak around four individuals, a reasonable group size for a conversation. Similar to the interaction lengths, the two distributions look very similar.

The third hypothesis regarded changes in conversational partners. For example, people could be interacting with the same individuals as before the performance, or be stimulated to engage with others. To this end, for each individual we computed the *Jaccard similarity* between the set of participants an individual has interacted with during the two rounds. Given two sets of IDs R_1 and R_2, the Jaccard similarity function is defined as $J(R_1, R_2) = \frac{|R_1 \cap R_2|}{|R_1 \cup R_2|}$ and computes a value in the interval $[0, 1]$. Figure 8(b) presents the distribution of the Jaccard similarity across all individuals between round 1 and round 2. The results show that although the mingling pattern of the individuals did not change between the two rounds, they did interact with different individuals. In particular, they changed at least 50% of their interaction partners between round 1 and round 2 (mean 0.278 and standard deviation 0.121).

4.2.1 *Acceleration*

The image emerging from the pure proximity measurement is that of an ordinary mingling event. Overall, these results indicate that the volunteers, as a group, applied a consistent pattern in their mingling behavior during the two rounds, a pattern that they used, however, to target different conversational partners between the two rounds. The measurement pictures a socializing context, but it is difficult to reach conclusions about the impact of the performance. For this reason, we focused on the acceleration data as well.

Similar to the direct approach, we used variance in the acceleration magnitude as the main feature. We then correlated the participant's self-reported behavior with our findings. Correlation between the answers to question "Do you think the performance had an effect on your mood? Yes|No" and the difference between the acceleration magnitude variance in round 1 and 2 is computed. Since not all participants filled in the post event survey and some accelerometers failed due to a firmware bug, we were only able to use the accelerometer data from 14 participants.

The variance values are extracted using the whole intervals for round 1 and 2. A statistically significant ($p = 0.02$) positive correlation value of 0.60 wass obtained as a result. This correlation supports our hypothesis that the mood change can be linked to implicit behaviour as measured by acceleration, though we would like to verify this with a larger dataset later. In conclusion, the results suggest that while individuals acted similarly as a group in terms of networking behaviour captured by the proximity sensors, the quality of those interactions seemed different between the two sessions, as captured by the accelerometers.

5. DISCUSSION

Our experiments show that using sensors commonly available in smart phones, we are able to leverage group dynamics in the audience to predict an audience's experience of a dance performance and that their implicit responses to the performance can automatically highlight salient moments in it.

In addition, to our knowledge, it is the first time that the context surrounding a performance has also been analysed. Our results suggest that measureable changes in social behaviour before and after watching a dance performance are correlated with an audience's perceptions of how a performance can affect their willingness to socialise as well as their mood. Given that the problem of automatically analysing and quantifying the experience of audience members of live performances is a difficult and multi-faceted domain to conduct experiments, we believe that our first steps show much potential for further devising automated methods to enrich live artistic performances via implicit responses.

5.1 Opportunities

Our experiments shed light on the huge and under-explored potential of linking implicit responses from pervasive sensing to augment digital signals that already connect with live performance such as verbal expressions of sentiment via social media. Given the potential of acceleration and proximity to be measured pervasively, we identify a number of key areas in which this information, when coupled with multimedia systems could be of real societal benefit.

Enriching the experience of a live performance Live performances tend already to have much multi-media data associated with them such as advertisements of the event on the Internet, video or audio recordings from smart phones, the associated social media, critical reviews of a performance in news or blog posts, attendees and their associated social media profiles, to name but a few. However, in all cases, online responses to an event requires an active and declarative response by audience members. One could easily imagine an audience member's experience of an event could be further enriched by seeing whether their responses to the performance matched that of others in the audience.

Live performance recommendation By using the acceleration signal generated by the sensor data, we were able to capture spontaneous responses. Our experiments show that the temporal characteristics of the variation in acceleration were similar for people who enjoyed the performance and sufficiently different for those that didn't. An immediate question following this would be whether such response signatures could be used for recommendation via collaborative filtering – if person A who responded similarly at particular moments of a live performance to a person B also like other performances that person B enjoyed?

Benefitting performers One could easily imagine that the salient moments in the performance that were identified automatically in our experiments could be used to verify or highlight key moments of audience response. While our analysis was performed afterwards offline, one could also imagine that such information could be provided in real time to the performers while they are performing. Moreover, the implicit responses from multiple audience members show that even if they do not report certain salient events in the performance to be memorable, their implicit responses can still provide supporting evidence for more sparse explicit survey responses.

Benefitting organisers of live performances For many, going to a live performance involves both the experience of the performance as well as the social event surrounding going to the performance. The national dance organisation that we worked with is aware of this and needs quantitative proof of its benefit. Importantly, from both events that we organised, volunteers paid to take part so they saw inherent value in it. Both experiments that we carried out show that dance performances can have an effect on how people behave and that these responses reflect positive experiences to the performance. This suggests that further studies should be carried out to investigate what triggers people to recommmend dance performance in general and using pervasive sensing provides a realistic means of doing this.

5.2 Open Challenges

Based on our experiences, it seems that ordinary members of the public are interested in being measured about their responses to a dance performance and having their sensed responses given back to them. However, working with real events with members of the public in dynamic and uncontrolled environments leads to a number of open challenges.

From controlled to uncontrolled large scale measurement First, to obtain large scale measures, we would need to use people's personal smart phones to record their behaviour. Like in our experiments, better responses can probably be gained from hanging their phones around their neck rather than keeping it in a pocket or handbag. Aside from requiring a special pouch to hang the phone around the neck (which could be easily made at low cost and large scale), we are not able to prevent, for example, tampering with the phone during the performance. Moreover, to investigate the role that live performances could have in improving people's social lives, we must also be able to measure their behaviour before and after the performance, which requires further collaboration by audience members unless some other method of incentivisation is provided.

Handling low numbers of explicit responses Implicit responses to a live performance can only be better understood when coupled with survey responses. However, as reported by HD, people tend not to answer surveys about a performance voluntarily unless they have extreme views about it. There are two ways of considering the problem. One perspective is to address how to more easily obtain even light declarative forms of sentiment about a performance (e.g. 'like' vs. 'dislike') – perhaps socialised incentives could lead to more willingness to report such information. Another perspective would be to consider label propagation techniques to estimate the reaction of the larger unlabelled data.

Subjectivity of responses Perhaps one of the biggest challenges remains in the fact that even if a set of people enjoyed a performance, it is highly probable that they enjoyed different parts. There is no guarantee that responses to the dance performance will be the same for everyone, particular if performances are unstructured or more abstract. Fortunately, the performance that we analysed was less abstract, having quite specific components that could be easily referred to. It remains an open question as to how more abstract performances would be responded to and whether they would as easily analysed.

6. CONCLUSIONS

We have made a first investigation of how a seated audience's perception of a performance can be perceived and measured from their body movements using an accelerometer that exists typically in smart phones. We analysed whether subtle and complex concepts such as "enjoyment", "immersion", an in improvement in mood as results of the performance, and whether participants would "recommend" dance in general, would be reflected in body motion using a simple accelerometer hung around the neck. Using the variance of the acceleration, we were already able to predict with 90% accuracy whether somebody enjoys the performance, which performed significantly above a random baseline.

Importantly, joint coordination in the variance in acceleration helps to distinguish salient from non-salient moments, which lead to significant improvements over using each person's body movements from the entire performance period. As well as the obvious usefulness to the entertainment industry of such direct measurements of an audience's reaction, we have also made a first attempt to measure the role that a live performance can have on the social behaviour that precedes and follows it. Our experiments shows huge promise in enabling us to measure the implicit responses of people while watching a live performance without the need for more traditional sensing approaches using physiological or brain signals. However, and perhaps more importantly, our experiments demonstrate the potential of quantifying the experience of 'a cultural night out', highlighting the relevance of the social context in moderating an individual's enjoyment of an event.

7. ACKNOWLEDGEMENTS

For the case study presented in Section 3, we would like to thank the Distributed & Interactive Systems group (`http://www.dis.cwi.nl`) at CWI for their involvement in designing, preparing, and executing the event. Thanks to Jesse Krijthe and Wouter Kouw for assisting with the back translations of the questionnaires, and Julian Kooij for assisting with the translation of the Dutch free text survey responses. We would also like to thank the staff at the Lucent Theatre for their logistic support. Thanks to the board of the networking groups Young the Hague, JongOCW, and Teater aan het Spui for their assistance in the logistics the case study in Section 4. Thanks to Djana Eminovic from Holland Dance for her assistance in the preparation and execution of both studies described in Sections 3 and 4. We thank all the anonymous volunteers who took part in both studies. This publication was partially supported by the Dutch national program COMMIT, the European Commission under grant agreement number 601033 - MOnarCH, the Costa Rican Institute of Technology, and is affiliated with the Delft Data Science Consortium.

8. REFERENCES

[1] USA Today. Providence theater experiments with 'tweet seats', 2013. `http://www.usatoday.com/story/tech/2013/01/27/theater-tweet-seats/1868693/`.

[2] L. Bao and S. Intille. Activity recognition from user-annotated acceleration data. *Pervasive Computing*, page 1Ű17, 2004.

[3] X. Bao, S. Fan, A. Varshavsky, K. Li, and R. Roy Choudhury. Your Reactions Suggest You Liked the Movie: Automatic Content Rating via Reaction Sensing. In *Proceedings of the 2013 ACM International Joint Conference on Pervasive and Ubiquitous Computing*, UbiComp '13, page 197Ű206, New York, NY, USA, 2013. ACM.

[4] L. Bennett. Patterns of listening through social media: online fan engagement with the live music experience. *Social Semiotics*, 22(5):545Ű557, 2012.

[5] B. Bläsing, B. Calvo-Merino, E. S. Cross, C. Jola, J. Honisch, and C. J. Stevens. Neurocognitive control in dance perception and performance. *Acta psychologica*, 139(2):300Ű308, 2012.

[6] A. S. Brown and J. L. Novak. *Assessing the intrinsic impacts of a live performance*. WolfBrown San Francisco, CA, 2007.

[7] B. Calvo-Merino, C. Jola, D. E. Glaser, and P. Haggard. Towards a sensorimotor aesthetics of performing art. *Consciousness and cognition*, 17(3):911Ű922, 2008.

[8] C. Cattuto, W. Van den Broeck, A. Barrat, V. Colizza, J. Pinton, and A. Vespignani. Dynamics of Person-to-Person Interactions from Distributed RFID Sensor Networks. *PLOS ONE*, 5(7):e11596, 07 2010.

[9] E. S. Cross, L. Kirsch, L. F. Ticini, and S. Schütz-Bosbach. The impact of aesthetic evaluation and physical ability on dance perception. *Frontiers in human neuroscience*, 5, 2011.

[10] M. Dobson, S. Voulgaris, and M. van Steen. Merging ultra-low duty cycle networks. In *Proceedings of the 41st International Conference on Dependable Systems & Networks (DSN 2011)*, 2011.

[11] C. Doukas, I. Maglogiannis, P. Tragas, D. Liapis, and G. Yovanof. Patient fall detection using support vector machines. *Artificial Intelligence and Innovations 2007: from Theory to Applications*, page 147Ű156, 2007.

[12] G. Englebienne and H. Hung. Mining for motivation: using a single wearable accelerometer to detect people's interests. In *Proceedings of the 2nd ACM international workshop on Interactive multimedia on mobile and portable devices*, IMMPD '12, page 23Ű26, New York, NY, USA, 2012. ACM.

[13] J. Fleureau, P. Guillotel, and I. Orlac. Affective Benchmarking of Movies Based on the Physiological Responses of a Real Audience. In *Proceedings of the 2013 Humaine Association Conference on Affective Computing and Intelligent Interaction*, ACII '13, page 73Ű78, Washington, DC, USA, 2013. IEEE Computer Society.

[14] D. Fujiwara, L. Kudrna, and P. Dolan. Quantifying and Valuing the Wellbeing Impacts of Culture and Sport. Technical report, UK Department of Culture, Media and Sport, Apr. 2014.

[15] R. Gonzalez and R. Woods. *Digital Image Processing*. Prentice Hall, 2008.

[16] H. Hung, G. Englebienne, and L. Cabrera Quiros. Detecting conversing groups with a single worn accelerometer. In *Proceedings of the 16th International Conference on Multimodal Interaction*, page 84Ű91. ACM, 2014.

[17] H. Hung, G. Englebienne, and J. Kools. Classifying Social Actions with a Single Accelerometer. In *Ubicomp*, page 207Ű210, 2013.

[18] J. R. Kwapisz, G. M. Weiss, and S. A. Moore. Activity recognition using cell phone accelerometers. *ACM SIGKDD Explorations Newsletter*, 12(2):74Ű82, 2011.

[19] C. Latulipe, E. A. Carroll, and D. Lottridge. Love, hate, arousal and engagement: exploring audience responses to performing arts. In *Proceedings of the SIGCHI Conference on Human Factors in Computing Systems*, page 1845Ű1854. ACM, 2011.

[20] A. Leask, A. Hassanien, and P. C. Rothschild. Social media use in sports and entertainment venues. *International Journal of Event and Festival Management*, 2(2):139Ű150, 2011.

[21] M. R. Lockstone, L. Olga Junek, S. Hudson, and R. Hudson. Engaging with consumers using social media: a case study of music festivals. *International Journal of Event and Festival Management*, 4(3):206Ű223, 2013.

[22] C. Martella, M. Dobson, A. van Halteren, and M. van Steen. From Proximity Sensing to Spatio-Temporal Social Graphs. In *Pervasive Computing and Communications (PerCom), 2014 IEEE International Conference on*, 2014.

[23] C. Martella, A. van Halteren, M. van Steen, C. Conrado, and J. Li. Crowd Textures as Proximity Graphs. In *IEEE Communications Magazine*, 2014.

[24] A. Matic, V. Osmani, A. Maxhuni, and O. Mayora. Multi-modal mobile sensing of social interactions. In *Pervasive computing technologies for healthcare (PervasiveHealth), 2012 6th international conference on*, page 105Ű114. IEEE, 2012.

[25] A. C. Michalos and P. M. Kahlke. Arts and the perceived quality of life in British Columbia. *Social indicators research*, 96(1):1Ű39, 2010.

[26] T. Nenonen, R. Kaikkonen, J. Murto, and M.-L. Luoma. Cultural services and activities: The association with self-rated health and quality of life. *Arts & Health*, 0(0):1Ű19, 0.

[27] C. L. Nightingale, C. Rodriguez, and G. Carnaby. The Impact of Music Interventions on Anxiety for Adult Cancer Patients A Meta-Analysis and Systematic Review. *Integrative cancer therapies*, 12(5):393Ű403, 2013.

[28] H. L. O'Brien and E. G. Toms. The development and evaluation of a survey to measure user engagement. *Journal of the American Society for Information Science and Technology*, 61(1):50Ű69, 2010.

[29] A. Pentland, T. Choudhury, N. Eagle, and P. Singh. Human dynamics: computation for organizations. *Pattern Recognition Letters*, 26(4):503Ű511, 2005.

[30] M. Reason and D. Reynolds. Kinesthesia, empathy, and related pleasures: An inquiry into audience experiences of watching dance. *Dance Research Journal*, 42(02):49Ű75, 2010.

[31] S. Reddy, M. Mun, J. Burke, D. Estrin, M. Hansen, and M. Srivastava. Using mobile phones to determine transportation modes. *ACM Transactions on Sensor Networks (TOSN)*, 6(2):13, 2010.

[32] M. Ritter and K. G. Low. Effects of dance/movement therapy: A meta-analysis. *The Arts in Psychotherapy*, 23(3):249Ű260, 1996.

[33] D. Roggen, M. Wirz, D. Helbing, and G. Tröster. Recognition of Crowd Behavior from Mobile Sensors with Pattern Analysis and Graph Clustering Methods. *Networks and Heterogeneous Media*, 6, 2011.

[34] T. Schubert, F. Friedmann, and H. Regenbrecht. The experience of presence: Factor analytic insights. *Presence*, 10(3):266Ű281, 2001.

[35] E. W. See-To, S. Papagiannidis, and V. Cho. User experience on mobile video appreciation: How to engross users and to enhance their enjoyment in watching mobile video clips. *Technological Forecasting and Social Change*, 79(8):1484Ű1494, 2012.

[36] M. Soleymani, J. Lichtenauer, T. Pun, and M. Pantic. A multimodal database for affect recognition and implicit tagging. *Affective Computing, IEEE Transactions on*, 3(1):42Ű55, 2012.

[37] C. Stevens, H. Winskel, C. Howell, L. Vidal, J. Milne-Home, and C. Latimer. Direct and indirect methods for measuring audience reactions to contemporary dance. 2009.

[38] M. Thelwall, K. Buckley, and G. Paltoglou. Sentiment in Twitter Events. *JOURNAL OF THE AMERICAN SOCIETY FOR INFORMATION SCIENCE AND TECHNOLOGY*, 62(2):406Ű418, 2011.

[39] L. Van der Maaten and G. Hinton. Visualizing Data using t-SNE. *Journal of Machine Learning Research*, 9(11), 2008.

[40] C. Wang and P. Cesar. Do we react in the same manner?: comparing GSR patterns across scenarios. In *Nordic Conference on Human-Computer Interaction: Fun, Fast, Foundational*, 2014.

[41] C. Wang, E. Geelhoed, P. Stenton, and P. S. Cesar Garcia. Sensing A Live Audience. In *Proceedings of ACM CHI Conference on Human Factors in Computing Systems 2014 (CHI 0)*, page 1909Ű1912. ACM, 2014.

[42] W. H. Whyte. *The Social Life Of Small Urban Spaces*. Project for Public Spaces Inc, Jan. 1980.

[43] M. Wirz, D. Roggen, and G. Tröster. A Methodology towards the Detection of Collective Behavior Patterns by Means of Body-Worn Sensors. In *Workshop at the 8th International Conference on Pervasive Computing (Pervasive 2010)*, 2010.

[44] T. Zhang, J. Wang, P. Liu, and J. Hou. Fall detection by embedding an accelerometer in cellphone and using KFD algorithm. *International Journal of Computer Science and Network Security*, 2006.

9. APPENDIX

Post-event Questionnaire (English)

1 . The dance performance was interesting.(*)
2 . The dance performance was exciting.(*)
3 . The dance performance was enjoyable.(*)
4 . I lost track of the world while I was watching the dance performance.(**)
5 . I still paid attention to my surroundings while I was watching the dance performance.(**)
6 . I was completely captivated by the dance performance.(**)
7 . I will definitely want to come to another dance performance again.(***)
8 . I will recommend dance performances to my friends.(***)
9 . Dance performance was worthwhile.(***)
10 . This dance performance uplifted my mood.(****)
11 . This dance performance energized me.(****)
12 . This dance performance made me feel more cheerful.(****)
13 . It was natural for me to wear the sensors during the performance
14 . Did you came with friends or family?
15 . Did you have a favorite moment? If yes, please describe it.

Post-event Questionnaire (Back-translated Dutch)

1. De voorstelling was interessant.(*)
2. De voorstelling was opwindend.(*)
3. De voorstelling was aangenaam.(*)
4. Ik vergat de wereld om me heen gedurende de voorstelling.(**)
5. Ik had gedurende de voorstelling aandacht voor mijn omgeving.(**)
6. Ik was volledig in de ban van de voorstelling.(**)
7. Ik kom zeker terug voor een andere dansvoorstelling.(***)
8. Ik zal dansvoorstelling aan mijn vrienden aanraden.(***)
9. Dansvoorstellingen zijn de moeite waard.(***)
10. Deze dansvoorstelling heeft me opgebeurd.(****)
11. Deze dansvoorstelling heeft me een energetisch gemaakt.(****)
12. Deze dansvoorstelling eeft me blij gemaakt.(****)
13. De sensoren voelden gedurende de voorstelling niet onnatturlijk ann
14. Bent u met wrienden of familie gekomen?
15. Had u een favoriet moment? Zo ja, gelieve dit te omschrijven:

(*)Enjoyment [35], (**)Immersion [34], (***)Recommendation [28], (****)Mood.

Loud and Trendy: Crowdsourcing Impressions of Social Ambiance in Popular Indoor Urban Places

Darshan Santani
Idiap Research Institute
EPFL, Lausanne, Switzerland
dsantani@idiap.ch

Daniel Gatica-Perez
Idiap Research Institute
EPFL, Lausanne, Switzerland
gatica@idiap.ch

ABSTRACT

New research cutting across architecture, urban studies, and psychology is contextualizing the understanding of urban spaces according to the perceptions of their inhabitants. One fundamental construct that relates place and experience is ambiance, which is defined as "the mood or feeling associated with a particular place". We posit that the systematic study of ambiance dimensions in cities is a new domain for which multimedia research can make pivotal contributions. We present a study to examine how images collected from social media can be used for the crowdsourced characterization of indoor ambiance impressions in popular urban places. We design a crowdsourcing framework to understand suitability of social images as data source to convey place ambiance, to examine what type of images are most suitable to describe ambiance, and to assess how people perceive places socially from the perspective of ambiance along 13 dimensions. Our study is based on 50,000 Foursquare images collected from 300 popular places across six cities worldwide. The results show that reliable estimates of ambiance can be obtained for several of the dimensions. Furthermore, we found that most aggregate impressions of ambiance are similar across popular places in all studied cities. We conclude by presenting a multidisciplinary research agenda for future research in this domain.

Categories and Subject Descriptors: H.4.m [Information Systems Applications]: Miscellaneous

Keywords: Ambiance; Urban Perception; Indoor Places; Crowdsourcing; Foursquare; Social Media

1. INTRODUCTION

Cities are unique expressions of human activity and, at their core, are the intersection of physical spaces and the people who live in them. Cities are buildings and roads, but also the people who use them and create new knowledge through their continuous interaction and exchange of ideas [15]. Public places in cities have played a central role in facilitating a socio-cultural habitat for people to counterbalance the grind of daily life, an environment away from home and work [42, 6].

MM'15, October 26–30, 2015, Brisbane, Australia.

ACM 978-1-4503-3459-4/15/10 ...$15.00.
http://dx.doi.org/10.1145/2733373.2806277.

In this context, new research cutting across architecture, urban studies, and psychology is contextualizing the understanding of the urban space according to the perceptions of their inhabitants, which are rooted in both socio-economic factors and psychological constructs [14]. Studying cities from this multidisciplinary perspective is fundamental, as research is finding connections between psychological features of cities and key indicators like well-being and prosperity [29, 1]. Given the inevitable growth of urban life worldwide and the connections between place and well-being, an urgent goal is the development of scientific methodologies to provide "a better idea of how people perceive and experience places" [14].

One fundamental construct that relates place and experience is ambiance, defined as "the mood or feeling associated with a particular place" [26] or "the character and atmosphere of a place" [12]. As soon as we walk into a place, we can tell if it is made for us. We ubiquitously judge restaurants, cafes, or bars according to their ambiance – whether the venue is energetic, bohemian, loud, or trendy. In other words, we form place impressions combining perceptual cues that involve most senses (vision and hearing, but also smell, taste, and touch) as well as prior knowledge of both the physical space and its inhabitants [16]. As urban dwellers, we rely on ambiance to make decisions that have long-term impact, defining our favourite social hangouts and shaping our discoveries, including the kind of people we might end up meeting and interacting with.

The understanding of place ambiance in cities is a brave new topic for which multimedia research can play a pivotal role for several reasons:

1. Social media represents a crowdsourced mechanism to document urban places like restaurants, bars, clubs, and cafes. Due to the growth of sensor-rich mobile devices, online directory services like Yelp, Foursquare, and TripAdvisor are all popular today. These platforms provide users with functionalities to search for places in a given region and to leave feedback in the form of reviews and comments about their experience [3]. These services co-exist with integrated services like Google Places, Facebook Places, and Instagram. In all of them, users often take photos at venues and share them publicly. As a result, millions of images documenting places across the globe are available. The move by Google to acquire Zagat (one the most prestigious restaurant review services) and Hoppit service [19] are two examples of the increasing interest in industry to provide their users with detailed descriptions of places.

2. There is previous work in urban studies, architecture, psychology, and design that has studied connections between places and human perception, and that show that ambiance is a human way of relating to places [2, 17, 35]. This provides theoretical grounds for new computational research. However, most previous studies

in these disciplines have faced the challenge represented by the difficulty to obtain place impressions. A standard approach involves physically visiting a place and gather impressions making silent observations about its atmosphere. Clearly, this approach is neither scalable nor captures contextual aspects of venues like time, by which a place might be ideal for a business lunch, but then turns into a trendy loud bar at night. In contrast, gathering place impressions based on images or videos shared on social media, where observers rate ambiance after viewing media items coming from a venue, has the advantages of being scalable, allowing the study of contextual factors like time, and spanning national boundaries to examine geographic and cultural differences in ambiance perception.

3. A holistic study of indoor place ambiance would involve the interpretation of multiple sources of information (images and videos, sound, text, and contextual metadata) in socially meaningful ways. Each of these modalities involve real challenges. As an example, visual cues used by venue owners to convey ambiance (and by patrons to perceive it) can be subtle, including colour schemes, lighting, spatial design, wall decorations and artwork, flooring and carpeting [2, 35, 18]. These visual categories pose many challenges for state-of-art computer vision algorithms. Similar points can be made for text or audio analysis.

4. Multimedia has over two decades of history of research on recognition of real-life visual scenes, moving from the original indoor/outdoor approaches in the late 1990s [36] to the recognition of functional place categories (like offices, corridors, etc) in the 2000s [33], and the recent use of Google Street View or Panoramio images to discover salient visual features in outdoor scenes in cities [13, 41]. Research on ubiquitous computing has also contributed to functional place categorization by focusing on other data inputs [24, 8]. Multimedia research has a younger history of understanding social and affective constructs from people [5] and media [10]. This said, little has been done so far to develop methodologies that allow to conceptualize and operationalize multimedia approaches to study social perception of urban places in general, and social ambiance of indoor places in particular.

We argue that a multimedia research agenda to study place ambiance is needed. Relying on a combination of social media data collection, image crowdsourcing, and data analysis, we contribute research resources and findings towards the understanding of how social ambiance can be systematically studied by the multimedia community. We address two research questions:

RQ1: What types of social media images best convey the ambiance of popular indoor places?

RQ2: Can the ambiance of an indoor place be reliably assessed by observers of social media images? If so, for what dimensions of ambiance?

The paper has five contributions:

1. Using Foursquare, we collect 50,000 images from 300 popular places from six metropolitan cities worldwide in three world regions – North America (New York City, Seattle, and Mexico City), Europe (Barcelona and Paris) and Asia (Singapore) (Section 3). In addition to geographic and cultural diversity, these cities are chosen because of their active user population on Foursquare. The focus of our collection is on *popular* places in Foursquare rather than on arbitrary places (see examples in Figure 1).

2. We design an image crowdsourcing experiment on Amazon's Mechanical Turk (MTurk) to assess the suitability of image categories that are most appropriate to describe the ambiance of a place (Section 4). Research in both psychology and computing has confirmed the feasibility of crowdsourcing as a way to conduct behavioral studies when appropriate incentives and mechanisms for quality control are established [22]. Using statistical tests, the results show that images with clear views of the environment are perceived by crowdworkers as being more informative of ambiance than other image categories, like food and drinks, or groups of people. Based on the crowdsourcing results, we build a refined image corpus suitable for indoor ambiance characterization.

3. A priori, the social ambiance of places is not known to zero-acquaintance visitors or observers. We design a second crowdsourcing experiment to assess how people perceive places from the perspective of ambiance (Section 5). We asked crowdworkers to rate indoor ambiance along 13 different physical and psychological dimensions where images served as stimuli to form place impressions. The ambiance categories include romantic, bohemian, formal and trendy, among others.

4. Based on the results obtained from the latter experiment, we find that reliable estimates of ambiance can be obtained using social media images, suggesting the presence of strong visual cues to form place impressions. Furthermore, while we identify a few statistically significant differences across cities along four ambiance dimensions, most aggregate impressions of ambiance are similar across popular places in all cities, which open relevant questions about the roles that geography and background knowledge of observers might be playing (Section 6).

5. We conclude by presenting a research agenda for future research in this domain along multiple axes of interest, some of which are multidisciplinary (Section 7). The resources we generated (data and annotations) are available to the research community. Overall, our work contributes to define multimedia approaches to understand the social perception of urban places in cities.

2. RELATED WORK

Given the multifaceted nature of our research questions, we review the related work along five axes: ubiquitous and multimedia computing, social media, hospitality research, social psychology, and urban computing.

The existing work on place characterization in ubiquitous computing, computer vision, and audio processing has examined several aspects including physical properties of places like their geographic location [21]; place composition, including the scene layout and the objects present in the scene [27]; place function, i.e., home, work, or leisure places; and place occupancy and noise levels [37]. This research has used both automatic [24, 8] and semi-automatic approaches [39] and a variety of data sources often studied in isolation, including images, sensor data like GPS/Wifi, and RF data. Works like [24, 8] have used audio or audio-visual data to characterized places through phone apps. The studied place categories (personal places in [24], home, work in [8]) differ significantly from ours. A recent work [37] investigates the recognition of physical ambiance categories (occupancy, human chatter, noise and music levels) using standard audio features collected in-situ by users. In contrast, our work examines social images as source of data, impressions of people who are not physically at the places, and a much larger number of social ambiance categories.

(a) Food/Drinks (b) People/Group

(c) Physical Environment (d) None of these

Figure 1: Sample images from *Random Image* corpus. Based on online annotations, a random set of four images which were classified as (a) Food/Drinks, (b) People/Group, (c) Physical Environment, and (d) None of these. For privacy reasons, images showing faces have been pixelated.

The emergence of social multimedia platforms, which allow users to take and share photos using mobile devices, have gained wide spread adoption. In the social multimedia literature, the work in [40] studies the problem of recommending locations based on mobility traces extracted from GPS and social links, without using image information. In contrast, the work in [7] uses geo-localized images, travel blog text data, and manual user profiles to suggest trips. Other works involving social images include [13] and [9]. These cases are focused on outdoor places and do not address the atmosphere dimensions we studied here. Due to the availability of large amount of images on Flickr or Instagram, researchers have analyzed these platforms (recent examples include [20, 4]). In [4], using a corpus of one million Instagram images, the authors studied the relationship between photos containing a face and its social engagement factors and found that photos with faces are more likely to receive likes and comments. As it relates to our work, an interesting result is that only 20% of images were found to contain faces, which suggests that many other image categories (related to food, places, etc.) exist (for an example, refer to the small-scale coding study in [20]).

In hospitality and retail studies, there has been significant interest to examine the effect of physical ambiance cues or "atmospherics" such as color, lighting, layout, and furnishing on customer perception and quality inferences [2, 35]. In a study conducted in a retail store, it was found that ambient (such as music, lighting, smell), design (such as color, ceilings, spatial layout) and social factors present in the store environment contribute towards higher merchandise and service quality [2]. In another study [18] the role of atmospherics across 10 full-service restaurants in Hong Kong was investigated. Using five dimensions of restaurant atmospherics (facility aesthetics, ambiance, spatial layout, employee factors, and view from the window) it was found that these dimensions have a significant influence on patrons' dining experience, and their willingness to pay more and recommend the restaurant to others. Similar results were obtained in another related work conducted across ethnic restaurants in the U.S. [23]. However, most of these studies are either done on controlled laboratory settings or based on questionnaires, which may have limitations with respect to ecological validity or recall biases.

Unlike the above research, we take a different direction examining the social perception of places (the ambiance impressions that people form about venues). Our proposed research is most closely related to work in social psychology [29, 16] which has investigated first impressions of places in connection to the personality of their inhabitants, mostly in controlled settings. A key first study [17] investigated the reliability (in terms of inter-rater agreement) of impressions of place ambiance and patron personality formed by (a) observers physically present at a number of indoor places, and (b) observers of Foursquare user profiles who visited those places (as opposed to views of places as we do). The results suggest that people do indeed form consistent impressions of ambiance and patrons traits. The study, however, only examined 49 places in one city (Austin, TX) and involved personally visiting every venue. In contrast, we study places in six cities.

An urban computing study [31] measured the perception of three variables (safety, class, and uniqueness) using 4,136 geo-tagged *outdoor* images in four cities, two each in the US and Austria. Images for the US cities were obtained via Google Street View, while manual collection was performed for the Austrian cities. The authors claimed differences in the range of perceptions of these dimensions between American cities and their Austrian counterpart. In a similar study on *outdoor* urban perception, judgments from over 3000 individuals were collected to study simple visual cues that could correlate outdoor places with three dimensions (beauty, quietness, and happiness) [28]. In both studies, dedicated websites were used to collect annotations, as opposed to common crowdsourcing platforms like MTurk. Our research differs from these previous work on two specific grounds. First, we are interested in examining indoor places as opposed to outdoor spaces. These are clearly different categories from the urban design and urban studies perspectives. Second, we study 13 dimensions of social ambiance (including artsy, bohemian, loud, trendy, romantic, etc.), appropriate for the indoor setting, as opposed to dimensions studied in [31, 28], which reflect pedestrian or street-level characteristics.

3. SELECTION OF PLACES AND IMAGES

In this section we describe our methodology to select the list of popular places and their associated images across six cities.

3.1 Place Selection

We ground our analysis on data collected from Foursquare, a popular location-based social network. In Foursquare, users typically visit a place, announce their arrival (*check-in*) and share information about their visits to places with their friend circle. As per Foursquare rules, a place or a venue is a geographical location with fixed spatial coordinates, i.e., latitude and longitude. Throughout this paper, we will use place and venue interchangeably in the context of Foursquare.

City	Ratings	Photos	Visitors
Barcelona	8.66 (0.67)	309.58 (383.53)	1,874.34 (2,371.43)
NYC	9.31 (0.41)	463.62 (387.31)	8,272.16 (6,208.76)
Paris	8.55 (0.63)	220.98 (254.16)	1,685.76 (1,433.14)
Seattle	8.95 (0.38)	240.7 (147.94)	3,533.54 (1,815.34)
Singapore	8.29 (0.86)	304.88 (206.58)	3,457.64 (3,916.89)
Mexico City	8.78 (0.49)	361.34 (374.85)	3,692.56 (3,578.84)

Table 1: Summary statistics of Foursquare data. For each city, mean scores of attributes of popular places is shown, along with their standard deviations (shown in brackets.)

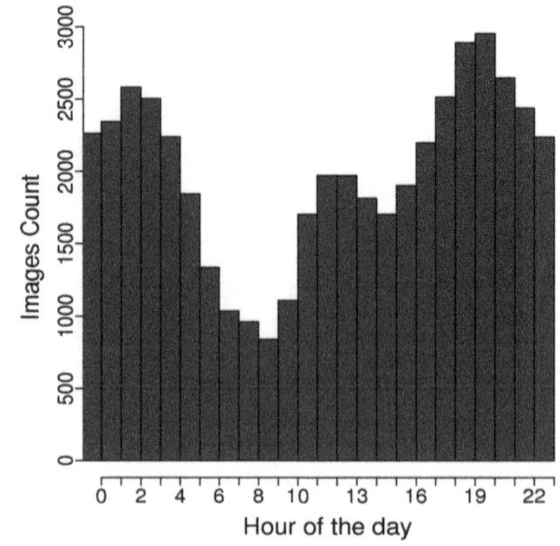

Figure 2: Histogram showing the frequency of images taken during different times of the day.

Each place on Foursquare maintains a profile page, which contains general information about the place (address, directions, phone number, etc.), in addition to Foursquare-specific data such as its popularity, total number of check-ins and past visitors, and a collection of images uploaded by users. Foursquare allows developers to obtain most of this information using its public API, which we used to gather all the relevant information for a given place [1].

For our analysis, we studied popular places on Foursquare for six cities around the world – Barcelona, Mexico City, New York City, Paris, Seattle, and Singapore. These cities were chosen for two reasons. First, they all are large cities in diverse world regions, and are known to have a vibrant urban life. Second, they all have an active user population on Foursquare. For each city, we chose 50 of the most popular places in each city which fall under the Foursquare-defined category of either being "Food" or "Nightlife Spots", which means cafes, restaurants, or bars. Table 1 lists the mean values of Foursquare data for all 50 places in each city. As stated in Section 1, we are focused on studying popular indoor places as opposed to arbitrary places (i.e., indoor or outdoor, and that might or might not be represented on Foursquare.)

Place selection was performed manually by the first author, taking into account place popularity, number of checkins, number of past visitors and number of available images. As image quality was an important criterion while selecting a place, we ignored all popular places which did not had any good-quality images such as dark images. In Table 1, using data obtained from Foursquare API, we notice that the user-generated mean rating of places selected for our study is above 8.2 (on a scale from 1 to 10) for all cities, confirming the popularity of places. Moreover, we also observe that these places are frequently visited by a large visitor population.

3.2 Image Selection

The second important consideration was the selection of images for each chosen place. We decided to select a small number of images per place to illustrate the place's atmosphere. This decision was motivated by the need to account for the variability in image quality, while at the same time providing general views of a place, without complicating the annotation process. Moreover, having more than one image for a place gives us the flexibility to show the place at different times of the day. Our hypothesis is that images of the physical environment will often be more representative of the place ambiance, so to test our hypothesis we built two image corpora, which are described in the next subsection.

[1]Foursquare has changed its mobile application and API significantly since our data collection.

3.2.1 Random Image Corpus

Given that each place in our database has on average more than 300 user-contributed images (see Table 1), it is challenging to select a small number of representative images that can accurately describe the ambiance of a place. One approach is to randomly select them given the collection of all images available for a place. We follow this approach to build a *random image* corpus.

Images for a place listed on Foursquare can be obtained via the API, but due to rate limits imposed by the API, we have access to at most 200 publicly visible images per place. We gathered a total of 50,023 images for all 300 places. This gives an average of 166 images per place, which is lower than the average estimated from the profile metadata ($\geq$ 300), yet it remains a large number. In addition to gathering the images, the API also provides information on the image source (i.e., the application used to generate the photo), creation time, and other attributes such as image height and width. However, due to API restrictions we had access to metadata information for only 47,980 images.

Using the metadata information, we found that the median height and width of an image in our collected corpus is 720 pixels, with 55% of images taken via iPhone, 19% via an Android device, and 22% uploaded via Instagram. We also plot the distribution of image creation times in Figure 2. We identify three distinctive peaks – the first one occurs during the lunch hour (11am–1pm), the second peak around dinner time (6–8pm), and the last one occurs after midnight and early hours of the morning (nightlife). This result confirms our intuition that social media images provide a well-suited medium to capture places during different times of the day.

For the study described in this section, since we are interested in only a few images to represent each place, we randomly sampled three images per place from our corpus, to build a *random image* corpus of 900 images for all 300 places. Refer to Figure 1 for a sample of selected images from this corpus.

3.2.2 Physical Environment Image Corpus

Our second approach is to build an image corpus with clear views of the physical environment. We manually select a small number of images per place that satisfy this condition. Although this task can potentially be automated, we have chosen to manually control the quality of data for the crowdsourcing experiment. The selection was performed by the first author after browsing through all the user-contributed images. During the process, we opted for images with a view clearly showing the space from different angles (with or without the presence of visitors.) To the best of our ability, we avoided images where one can potentially identify faces, to protect

Figure 3: Sample images from *Physical Environment Image* corpus. Based on MTurk annotations, images which scored the **highest** on (a) Artsy, (b) Creepy, (c) Loud, and (d) Trendy; and **lowest** on (e) Artsy, (f) Creepy, (g) Loud, and (h) Trendy. For privacy reasons, images showing faces have been pixelated.

the privacy of individuals. Moreover, we ensured that images that showed the venue name or any other information that explicitly revealed the identity of the place were discarded e.g., an image showing Starbucks or Hard Rock Cafe logos, to reduce any bias while characterizing the place ambiance. See Figure 3 for a sample of selected images from this corpus. Note that all these attributes cannot be controlled for while choosing images randomly.

The *physical environment image* corpus also contains 900 images for all 300 places (three images per place). The manual selection was constrained by the quality of Foursquare images. At times, we encountered images which were not optimally bright or clear. However, this setting is realistic due to the absence of any beautified or vendor-provided images, which can potentially add biases to the impressions.

4. EXPERIMENT 1: SUITABILITY OF IMAGES TO CONVEY AMBIANCE

In this section we address RQ1, i.e., we use both image corpora to judge which approach results in better "ambiance quality", that is, images which are more adequate to convey ambiance according to crowd judgements. On one hand, random selection of images is a realistic "in the wild" setting that provides an automated way to collect images. However, it will represent a valid approach only if it results in a collection of images which provide sufficient visual cues to characterize place ambiance. On the other hand, the manual selection of physical environment images is a controlled setting that satisfies the criteria described in the previous paragraphs.

4.1 Crowdsourcing Image Impressions

Our hypothesis is that many images in the *random image* corpus might not be perceived by crowdworkers as ideal to characterize a place's ambiance, as they do not contain visual cues to gauge a place's physical environment. In our exploratory inspection, most of these random images contain food items or show groups of people. To answer RQ1, we conducted a crowdsourcing study to gather the perceived ability of both image corpora – *random* and *physical environment*, to describe a place's ambiance and physical environment. For crowdsourcing, we used MTurk and chose US-based workers with at least 95% approval rate for historical HITs (Human Intelligence Tasks). In addition, to increase the potential reliability of MTurk annotations, we only chose "Master" annotators, which typically involves a worker pool with an excellent track record of completing tasks with precision.

For each HIT annotation task, we picked a set of five images per place, consisting of two from the *physical environment image* corpus, and three from the *random image* corpus. We ensured that images from the two sets do not overlap. In each HIT, workers were asked to view these five images and then answer three questions. In the first question, the workers were asked to rank the images based on how informative they were of the ambiance of the place. In the second one, workers were asked to rank the same set of images based on their degree of information about the physical environment of the place. The third question asked workers to categorize the images in four classes: a) Food/Drinks, b) People/Group, c) Physical Environment, and d) None of these. For these questions, no explicit definitions of ambiance, physical environment, food/drinks or people were provided, as we wanted the workers to rely on their internal representation of these concepts.

In the two ranking questions, images cannot be given the same rank, each image needed to have a different rank. For the image categorization task, the workers were asked to choose exactly one category for each image. If the images had the same rank or fell into one or more categories, we asked the annotators to pick the rank or category that for them was the best choice. We collected 10 annotations for each HIT across all 300 places, for a total of 3,000 responses for every question.

We also gathered crowdworkers' demographics via an email-based survey. We asked workers about their age group, gender,

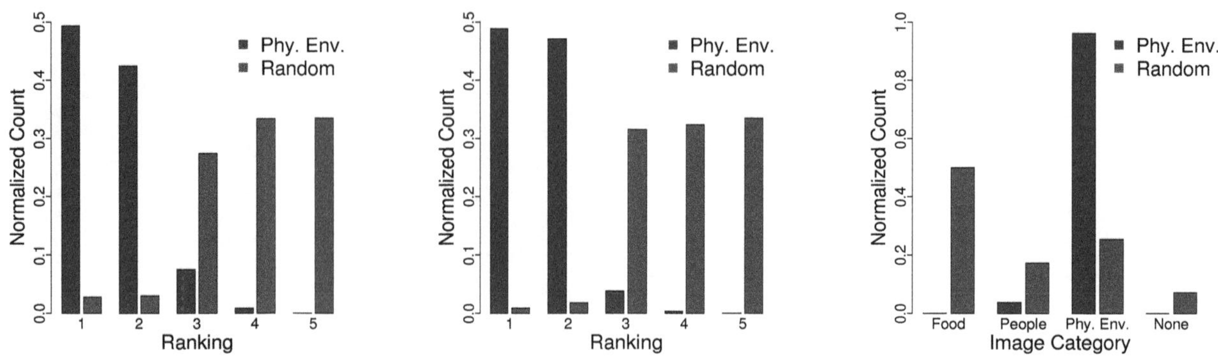

(a) Ambiance (b) Physical Environment (c) Image Category

Figure 4: Results for *Majority Vote* aggregation technique. Plot showing the histograms for a) Ambiance, b) Physical Environment, and c) Image Category, for both *Physical Environment Image* and *Random Image* corpus.

Method	Physical Environment				Random			
	Top 2		Bottom 3		Top 2		Bottom 3	
	Ambiance	Phy. Env.	Ambiance	Phy. Env.	Ambiance	Phy. Env.	Ambiance	Phy. Env.
Majority Vote	91.7%	95.8%	8.3%	4.2%	5.8%	2.7%	94.2%	97.3%
Median	89.7%	94.7%	10.3%	5.3%	4.1%	2.0%	95.9%	98.0%

Table 2: Table showing the summary statistics for each aggregation method. For each method, we show the percentage of images from both image corpora which are either in Top 2 ranks (rank 1 or 2), or ranked in Bottom 3 (ranks 3,4,5).

education level, current place of residence (categorized as either rural, suburbs, small-sized town, mid-sized town or city), and any experience of living in a big city. We also inquired them about their typical frequency to go out for food or drinks (almost every day, 2-3 times per week, once a week, 1-2 times a month, or less than once a month). These questions were designed to understand the ability of workers to rate images for ambiance and physical environment based on previous experiences.

4.2 Results

In this section, we present the results of our first crowdsourcing experiment.

4.2.1 Worker Participation and Demographics

For a total number of 3,000 HITs available for this experiment, we observe that a typical worker completed an average of 39 HITs. While 50% of the workers submitted less than 9 HITs, the worker with the highest number of HITs completed 295 assignments. We observe a long-tailed distribution in HIT completion times (mean: 114 secs, median: 88 secs, max: 593 secs). It is worth noting that we allocated a maximum of 10 minutes per HIT.

We had a pool of 101 workers who responded to our HITs. Of all HIT respondents, 32% replied to our demographics survey. We notice a balanced gender ratio (50% of workers being female), which corroborates earlier findings in the literature [30]. While only 34% of our worker pool currently lives in a big city, 75% of them have already experienced city living in the past. Furthermore, 56% of them go out for food or drinks at least once a week. These findings provide evidence that the majority of respondents are likely capable to assess ambiance in urban environments. We also notice that the worker population is relatively not so young with the most popular category (53%) being the age group of 35-50 years old. Note that the worker demographics reported here encompasses the worker population in both crowdsourcing experiments of this paper.

4.2.2 Analysis of Annotations

Now we turn our focus towards assessing the suitability of each image corpus to convey ambiance. As mentioned earlier, for each HIT we collected 10 impressions per place. Thus, it becomes important to consider the role of different aggregation methods in analyzing the results. Aggregation is used to create a composite score per place given the 10 responses for each question. In other words, for every question, aggregation is performed at the place-level. We use two different aggregation techniques. The first one is the *majority vote*, where we compute the majority score given the 10 impressions for each place. We then summarize the results based on 300 majority impressions. For the *median* method, we compute the median as the composite score across 10 impressions for each place.

Table 2 lists the summary statistics for the two aggregation techniques. For each aggregation technique and each corpus, we report the percentage of images which are in Top 2 ranks (ranks 1,2) and Bottom 3 ranks (ranks 3,4,5). We list these statistics for both the ambiance and physical environment questions. For the *majority vote* technique, manually selected images (*physical environment image* corpus) are in Top 2 ranks 91.7% for ambiance and 95.8% for physical environment, while random images are in Bottom 3 ranks for 94.2% and 97.3%, respectively. Note that a random ranking method would assign the manually selected image in the Top 2 rank with a probability of $1/10$ $(1/\binom{5}{2})$. We also plot the histogram of rankings for image sets from both corpora in Figures 4a and 4b. These results show that manually selected images are associated with higher ranks, while the random set of images are associated with lower ranks for both ambiance and physical environment, irrespective of the aggregation technique.

In addition to asking annotators to rank images, we also asked them to classify images into one of the four categories (food/drinks, people/group, physical environment, and none of these), as described in Section 4.1. In Figure 4c, we plot the assigned category for the *majority vote* technique. We observe that images from the *physical environment image* corpus are labeled as describing the physical environment in 96.2% of the cases. In contrast, im-

Label	Barcelona	New York City	Paris	Seattle	Singapore	Mexico City	Combined	Graham [17]
Artsy	0.81	0.66	0.69	0.72	0.80	0.76	0.76	0.63
Bohemian	0.63	0.58	0.54	0.54	0.66	0.66	0.62	0.67
Conservative	0.67	0.77	0.78	0.67	0.70	0.85	0.76	0.77
Creepy	0.54	0.62	0.60	0.57	**0.32**	0.62	0.59	0.81
Dingy	0.74	0.81	0.59	0.69	0.67	0.81	0.74	0.74
Formal	0.76	0.93	0.93	0.89	0.89	0.90	0.91	0.82
Sophisticated	0.68	0.91	0.90	0.85	0.80	0.87	0.86	0.70
Loud	0.80	0.81	0.76	0.74	0.82	0.82	0.80	0.74
Old-fashioned	0.82	0.46	0.78	0.45	0.72	0.67	0.72	0.67
Off the beaten path	0.58	0.62	0.39	0.54	0.61	0.59	0.58	0.73
Romantic	0.38	0.84	0.86	0.80	0.83	0.86	0.82	0.63
Trendy	0.69	0.71	0.50	0.43	0.68	0.85	0.69	0.58
Up-scale	0.69	0.91	0.90	0.85	0.81	0.85	0.86	0.76

Table 3: $ICC(1,k)$ scores of 13 ambiance dimensions for each city. $ICC(1,k)$ scores obtained in [17] are also shown in the last column for comparison. Cells marked in **bold** are **not** statistically significant at $p < 0.01$.

ages from the *random image* corpus are representative of either food/drinks, or people, or other in 74.6% of cases combined, and showing food items or people in 67% of cases.

Statistical Comparison: We perform a statistical comparison of rankings between both image corpora for ambiance and physical environment dimensions. We performed the Wilcoxon signed-rank statistical test, which is a non-parametric test to compare the mean ranks of two populations [38]. At the 99% confidence level, we obtained a p-value $< 2.2 \times 10^{-16}$ for both dimensions, validating the hypothesis that manually selected images are perceived by crowdworkers as better describing ambiance and physical environment.

In summary, these results provide an answer to RQ1, validating that images with clear views of the environment from Foursquare places are perceived as more suitable to characterize indoor ambiance than other image categories, as they contain visual cues to gauge a place's ambiance and physical environment. Please note that in this section we report the summary statistics across all cities combined. Individual trends for each city are similar to the overall trends and are omitted due to space restrictions.

5. EXPERIMENT 2: DIMENSIONS OF PLACE AMBIANCE

A priori, the ambiance of places is not known to zero-acquaintance observers. In this section, we address our second question (RQ2) i.e., whether reliable estimates of ambiance can be obtained using Foursquare images. Based on the *physical environment image* corpus of 900 images across 300 places, we design a second crowdsourcing experiment and asked crowd workers to rate indoor ambiance along 13 different physical and psychological dimensions where images served as stimuli to form place impressions.

5.1 Selection of Ambiance Categories

In order to select dimensions to characterize place ambiance, we base our methodology on prior work [17]. The authors proposed a rating instrument consisting of 41 dimensions for ambiance characterization. In our work, we chose 13 dimensions for which the corresponding intraclass correlations were amongst the highest as reported in [17]. Note that many dimensions in [17] did not reach sufficient inter-annotator agreement. We used a five-point Likert scale ranging from *strongly disagree* (1) to *strongly agree* (5) to judge the ambiance labels, while [17] used a 3-point categorical scale (yes, maybe, no). We will use the terms dimensions and labels interchangeably in the context of ambiance categories. The list of selected labels is shown in alphabetical order in Table 3.

5.2 Crowdsourcing Ambiance Impressions

To answer RQ2, crowdsourcing was employed to gather ambiance impressions. We used MTurk with the same worker qualification requirements as the first study. In each HIT, the workers were asked to view three images corresponding to a place, and then rate their personal impressions of the place ambiance based on what they saw. As part of the annotation interface, we ensured that workers viewed images in high resolution (and not just the image thumbnails). People were given a previous definition of each ambiance category. Moreover, workers were not informed about the city under study to reduce potential bias and stereotyping associated to the city identity. We collected 10 annotations for each dimension across all 300 places, for a total of 3,000 responses.

5.3 Results

For the 3,000 available HITs in this experiment, a typical worker completed an average of 56 HITs, with one worker completing 270 HIT assignments. When compared to the first experiment, similar results were obtained for HIT completion times (mean: 97 secs, median: 68 secs, max: 596 secs).

We turn our focus towards assessing the reliability of the annotations. We measure the inter-annotator consensus by computing intraclass correlation (ICC) among ratings given by the worker pool. Our annotation procedure requires every place to be judged by k annotators randomly selected from a larger population of K workers ($k = 10$, while K is unknown as we have no means to estimate the MTurk worker population). Consequently, $ICC(1,1)$ and $ICC(1,k)$ values, which respectively stand for single and average ICC measures [32], are computed for each ambiance dimension across all cities.

Table 3 reports the $ICC(1,k)$ values for all cities (due to space constraints, we omit $ICC(1,1)$ values.) In addition to listing the individual scores for each city and label, we also report the combined $ICC(1,k)$ scores for each label for the whole dataset, where we have combined all places across cities. We observe acceptable inter-rater reliability for many labels, with all the scores being statistically significant (p-value < 0.01), with the exception of *creepy* label in Singapore. Furthermore, we notice that the inter-rater reliability for labels *formal*, *sophisticated*, *romantic*, and *up-scale* is typically high (above 0.8) for most of the cities. Using correlation analysis between labels (which is presented in Section 6.2), we find that these four labels are collinear, with pairwise correlations exceeding 0.8. It is interesting to note that label *loud* achieved high agreement from images not showing any sound (0.8 combined

Label	Barcelona	Mexico City	NYC	Paris	Seattle	Singapore	Combined
Artsy	2.54 (0.78)	2.20 (0.69)	2.14 (0.56)	2.36 (0.69)	2.05 (0.59)	2.46 (0.72)	2.29 (0.69)
Bohemian	2.34 (0.60)	1.94 (0.58)	2.07 (0.49)	2.09 (0.55)	1.99 (0.44)	2.04(0.57)	2.08 (0.55)
Conservative	2.04 (0.58)	2.36 (0.81)	2.33 (0.70)	2.17 (0.71)	2.37 (0.57)	2.28 (0.59)	2.26 (0.67)
Creepy	1.33 (0.31)	1.37 (0.38)	1.21 (0.27)	1.20 (0.27)	1.21 (0.27)	1.18 (0.19)	1.25 (0.29)
Dingy	1.68 (0.52)	1.61 (0.60)	1.60 (0.58)	1.49 (0.40)	1.57 (0.46)	1.49 (0.42)	1.57 (0.50)
Formal	1.60 (0.50)	2.13 (0.91)	2.14 (0.97)	2.01 (0.96)	1.95 (0.75)	1.62 (0.68)	1.91 (0.84)
Sophisticated	2.09 (0.56)	2.41 (0.90)	2.42 (0.96)	2.37 (0.93)	2.20 (0.74)	2.15 (0.70)	2.27 (0.82)
Loud	2.30 (0.67)	2.45 (0.78)	2.51 (0.72)	2.09 (0.68)	2.33 (0.62)	2.49 (0.83)	2.36 (0.73)
Old-fashioned	2.20 (0.77)	2.30 (0.62)	2.33 (0.46)	1.90 (0.67)	2.44 (0.41)	2.16 (0.56)	2.22 (0.61)
Off the beaten path	2.27 (0.51)	1.88 (0.53)	2.06 (0.52)	1.89 (0.46)	1.99 (0.45)	1.96 (0.48)	2.01 (0.50)
Romantic	1.77 (0.37)	2.09 (0.81)	1.95 (0.72)	1.92 (0.78)	1.86 (0.62)	1.80 (0.65)	1.90 (0.68)
Trendy	2.34 (0.65)	2.55 (0.89)	2.55 (0.66)	2.49 (0.55)	2.45 (0.47)	2.54 (0.64)	2.49 (0.65)
Up-scale	1.93 (0.56)	2.36 (0.85)	2.39 (0.93)	2.36 (0.91)	2.13 (0.70)	2.01 (0.69)	2.20 (0.80)

Table 4: Means and standard deviations (in brackets) of annotation scores for each city and label.

score). On the other hand, labels *creepy* and *off the beaten path* are the labels with the lowest ICC (below 0.6 for the combined score.)

Importantly, these reliability scores are comparable to the ones obtained by Graham et al. [17], who conducted a similar study, but where the raters physically visited every venue (see section 2 and last column of Table 3), while in our case online images act as a stimuli. To summarize, these results provide an answer to RQ2 as they suggest that consistent impressions of place ambiance can be formed based upon images contributed in social media, which further suggests that there might be strong visual cues present for annotators to form accurate place impressions. The investigation of what specific cues contribute to impression formation will be the subject of future work.

6. AMBIANCE ACROSS CITIES

In this section we present descriptive statistics and study differences across cities for each ambiance label.

6.1 Descriptive Statistics

Table 4 lists the descriptive statistics (mean score and standard deviation) for each city and label. The mean scores are derived as follows: first, for every place we compute the mean score for each ambiance label, using the 10 annotations per label for each place; we then compute the mean scores and standard deviations for each city and label using the 50 places for each city. At the level of individual annotations, minimum and maximum values are 1 and 5 respectively for all each city and label, showing that the full scale is used by the crowd-workers. Note that the mean value obtained for all labels and all cities is below 3, which indicates a trend towards disagreement with the corresponding label. On the other hand, each city has venues that score high for each dimension.

In all cities, except Barcelona, the mean score for *trendy* is the highest amongst all labels; Barcelona places score the maximum on being *artsy*. *Creepy* scores the lowest (along with the lowest variance) for all cities, which is not surprising given that all places are popular places in their respective cities. From Table 4, we do not observe much variation in the mean values across cities, but a few differences stand out. For instance, the mean differences of the *formal* attribute between NYC and Barcelona, and the *old fashioned* attribute between Paris and Seattle exceed 0.5, potentially suggesting differences in place perceptions. We explore this further in Section 6.3.

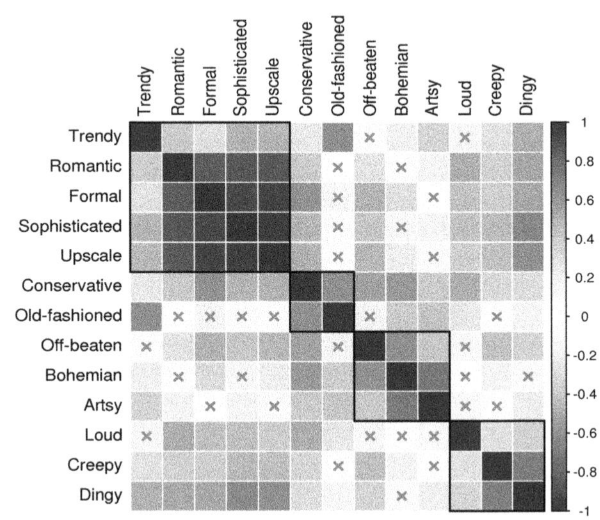

Figure 5: Plot showing the correlation matrix between ambiance dimensions. Black rectangular borders indicate the four distinct clusters found in the correlation matrix. Cells marked **X** are **not** statistically significant at $p < 0.01$.

6.2 Correlation Analysis

To look for linear relationship between ambiance labels, we perform correlation analysis using the mean annotation scores for all ambiance labels. Figure 5 visualizes the correlation matrix across all ambiance dimensions. We have used hierarchical clustering to re-order the correlation matrix in order to reveal its underlying structure. We color code the matrix instead of providing numerical scores to facilitate the discussion. We observe four distinct clusters. Starting from top left in the first cluster, labels *formal*, *sophisticated*, *romantic* and *up-scale* are highly collinear with pairwise correlations exceeding 0.8. The second cluster consists of places which are either *conservative* or *old-fashioned*, and the third cluster consists of *off-beaten*, *bohemian* or *artsy* places. The fourth cluster (bottom-right) lies on the opposite spectrum with respect to cluster one, and consists of *loud*, *dingy* and *creepy* places. Each of these four clusters clearly correspond to different ambiances. Furthermore, we can also observe significant negative correlations between dimensions in cluster one and cluster four and between clusters two and three.

Label	City Pair	Mean Difference	$p-$value $\times 10^{-3}$
Old Fashioned	SEA–PAR	$+0.544$	9.9×10^{-2} (7.4×10^{-3})
Artsy	SEA–BCN	-0.492	4.26 (6.18)
Old Fashioned	PAR–NYC	-0.434	4.09 (0.67)
Bohemian	MEX–BCN	-0.398	3.70 (**39.68**)
Off the beaten path	MEX–BCN	-0.386	1.43 (0.051)
Off the beaten path	PAR–BCN	-0.376	2.11 (0.67)

Table 5: Tukey's HSD and KS test statistics. $p-$values obtained from KS test are shown in brackets in the last column. Values marked in **bold** are **not** statistically significant at $p < 0.01$

6.3 Statistical Comparison

To better understand whether mean differences across cities for some of these ambiance labels are statistically significant, we perform the Tukey's honest significant difference (HSD) test. Tukey's HSD test is a statistical procedure for groups which compares all possible pairs of mean values for each group, the null hypothesis being that the mean values being compared are drawn from the same population [34]. We perform the HSD test to compute pairwise comparisons of mean values between cities for each ambiance label, which result in a total of 195 comparisons (15 city-wise pairs across 13 dimensions). Table 5 lists only the significant results of the Tukey's HSD test, where the differences in the observed means are statistically significant at p-value < 0.01. Based on these statistics and commenting only on results where differences is larger than 0.4, we observe that:

1. Popular places in Seattle are perceived as less *artsy* compared to places in Barcelona;

2. Popular places in Paris are perceived as less *old fashioned* compared to New York City and Seattle.

To validate the statistical significance of the Tukey's HSD test, we perform a series of pairwise Kolmogorov-Smirnov test (KS test) across all cities and labels. The KS test is a non-parametric test to compare the empirical distributions of two samples, with the null hypothesis being that the two samples are drawn from the same distribution [25]. We perform the KS test to compare the cumulative distribution functions of each city-pair across each dimension (195 comparisons). We report the $p-$values for the KS test in Table 5 for a statistical level $\alpha = 0.01$. Results from the KS test confirms most of the results from the Tukey's HSD test.

To conclude this subsection, our study shows that most of the differences across cities for each of the ambiance dimensions are not statistically significant. This result is interesting in itself as it might suggest that popular places in social media in cosmopolitan cities have many points in common. To our knowledge, this is a result that has not been reported before in social media research, but that could have some support from literature that discusses the "uniformization of taste" in globalized cities [11] and social media content. This said, any possible interpretation would have to be further validated with more data and a combination of further data analysis and ethnography. In addition, these results highlight the need to study other venues, including not so popular places on Foursquare and places not represented on Foursquare because of well-known socio-economic biases in social media.

7. AN AGENDA FOR FUTURE RESEARCH

We presented an emerging subject in social media, namely the study of psychological dimensions of the urban space from social media content under the construct of ambiance. Using over 50,000 Foursquare images collected from 300 popular indoor places across six cities, we first assessed the suitability of social images as data source to convey place ambiance, and found through a crowdsourcing experiment that images with clear views of the environment were significantly perceived by people as being more informative of ambiance than other image categories. Second, we demonstrated through another crowdsourcing experiment involving 13 ambiance dimensions that reliable estimates of ambiance for several dimensions can be obtained using Foursquare images, suggesting the presence of strong visual cues to form place impressions. Furthermore, we found that most aggregated impressions of popular places are similar across cities, with a few statistically significant differences across four ambiance dimensions (*bohemian*, *artsy*, *old fashioned*, and *off the beaten path*).

This topic extends multimedia research through the connection of "traditional" multimedia research with emerging themes like multimedia crowdsourcing and psychology of both social media and cities. We close the paper by defining a research agenda, which would include (and could extend beyond) the following issues:

1. The understanding of what specific cues in an indoor venue people use to judge a place and form ambiance impressions when looking at social media content – color, lighting scheme, spatial layout, interior design, or customers – is a fundamental open issue. This topic requires the integration of psychology research (e.g. models of cue utilization and validity) and of existing knowledge in hospitality, design, and marketing (known as atmospherics in those domains). Multimedia research could further use computer vision or audio processing algorithms to extract and reason about some of these cues.

2. The automatic recognition of ambiance is another key open issue. While there is a variety of potentially informative cues (visual cues from images or video, acoustic cues that could be collected on-site, text from comments, tips, and metadata), the specific connections of these features with ambiance still need to be established. We hypothesize that some of the studied dimensions have the potential to be automatically recognized, and would like to explicitly propose a challenge to the multimedia community on this topic.

3. The long tail (of non-popular places) is a third issue. The intrinsic biases of social media result in few places being richly represented (as the ones studied here), but the majority of urban indoor venues that are poorly represented (if at all) could be also studied under the ambiance lens. Could significant differences in impressions between popular and non-popular venues be quantified? Could one devise transfer learning approaches that could be used to learn from popular places and adapted for non-popular ones? These are just a couple of research questions that ought to be investigated.

4. The possibility of global studies of place ambiance is a fourth key dimension. Our results showed few significant differences among the impressions of observers across the six cities we studied. There is a need to expand and explain this concrete result, but more importantly there is open space to think about bigger questions that relate ambiance, culture, and economics at the collective level. Are the tastes of "global" social media users being uniformized, and if so is this being reflected in the media

they collect and the judgements they make? Or are the socio-economic biases in social media hiding the diversity of venues that one could expect to exist across cities and cultures? Research in this domain could integrate multimedia analysis with cross-cultural studies.

5. Finally, the applications derived from the above research are manifold. On the user side, this could include hyper-local, ambiance-driven place search and discovery in online platforms, where users could search for places by its ambiance e.g., a *formal* place for a family dinner, or a *romantic* place for a date. This could complement existing sources of information like place reviews. As a second application domain, on the side of venue owners, this could include data-driven tools to deepen the understanding of the impressions that their venues evoke in potential and real customers, and recommendations about improving the appearance and style of their venues.

To conclude, as a concrete step towards advancing the above agenda, we are making the dataset (data and annotations) publicly available for research here: `https://www.idiap.ch/dataset/place-ambiance`

8. ACKNOWLEDGEMENTS

This work has been supported by the SNSF Youth@Night project. We thank anonymous reviewers for their valuable feedback and MTurk workers for their participation in our study.

9. REFERENCES

[1] World Happiness Report by Sustainable Development Solutions Network (UN). `http://bit.ly/1hWociG`, 2013.

[2] J. Baker, D. Grewal, and A. Parasuraman. The influence of store environment on quality inferences and store image. *Journal of the Academy of Marketing Science*, 1994.

[3] S. Bakhshi et al. Demographics, weather and online reviews: A study of restaurant recommendations. In *Proc. WWW*, 2014.

[4] S. Bakhshi et al. Faces engage us: photos with faces attract more likes and comments on Instagram. In *Proc. CHI*, 2014.

[5] J. Biel et al. The YouTube Lens: Crowdsourced Personality Impressions and Audiovisual Analysis of Vlogs. *IEEE Trans. on Multimedia*, 2013.

[6] S. Carr. *Public Space*. Cambridge Press, 1992.

[7] Y. Chen et al. Travel Recommendation by Mining People Attributes and Travel Group Types From Community Contributed Photos. *IEEE Trans. on Multimedia*, 2013.

[8] Y. Chon et al. Automatically characterizing places with opportunistic crowdsensing using smartphones. In *Proc. UbiComp*, 2012.

[9] D. J. Crandall et al. Mapping the world's photos. In *Proc. WWW*, 2009.

[10] M. Cristani et al. Unveiling the Multimedia Unconscious: Implicit Cognitive Processes and Multimedia Content Analysis. In *Proc. ACM MM*, 2013.

[11] H. Cuadra Montiel. *Globalization-Approaches to Diversity*. InTech, 2012.

[12] O. Dictionary. `http://bit.ly/1dAy80r`.

[13] C. Doersch et al. What makes Paris look like Paris? *ACM Trans. Graph.*, 2012.

[14] R. Florida et al. Place and well-being. *Designing positive psychology: Taking stock and moving forward*, 2011.

[15] E. Glaeser. *Triumph of the city: How our greatest invention makes us richer, smarter, greener, healthier and happier*. Macmillan, 2011.

[16] S. D. Gosling et al. First impressions based on the environments we create and inhabit. *First impressions*, 2008.

[17] L. Graham et al. Can the ambiance of a place be determined by the user profiles of the people who visit it? In *Proc. ICWSM*, 2011.

[18] V. Heung et al. Influence of restaurant atmospherics on patron satisfaction and behavioral intentions. *International Journal of Hospitality Management*, 2012.

[19] Hoppit. `http://www.hoppit.com`.

[20] Y. Hu et al. What We Instagram: A First Analysis of Instagram Photo Content and User Types. In *Proc. ICWSM*, 2014.

[21] D. H. Kim et al. Discovering semantically meaningful places from pervasive RF-beacons. In *Proc. Ubicomp*, 2009.

[22] A. Kittur, E. H. Chi, and B. Suh. Crowdsourcing user studies with mechanical turk. In *Proc. CHI*, 2008.

[23] Y. Liu et al. The effects of dining atmospherics: an extended mehrabian–russell model. *International Journal of Hospitality Management*, 2009.

[24] H. Lu et al. Soundsense: scalable sound sensing for people centric applications on mobile phones. In *MobiSys*, 2009.

[25] F. J. Massey Jr. The Kolmogorov-Smirnov test for goodness of fit. *Journal of the American Statistical Association*, 1951.

[26] Merriam-Webster. `http://bit.ly/1Ivgs23`.

[27] A. Quattoni et al. Recognizing indoor scenes. In *Proc. CVPR*, 2009.

[28] D. Quercia et al. Aesthetic Capital: What Makes London look Beautiful, Quiet, and Happy? In *Proc. CSCW*, 2014.

[29] P. J. Rentfrow. The Open City. *Handbook of Creative Cities*, 2011.

[30] J. Ross et al. Who are the crowdworkers?: Shifting demographics in mechanical turk. In *Proc. CHI*, 2010.

[31] P. Salesses et al. The Collaborative Image of The City: Mapping the Inequality of Urban Perception. *PLoS ONE*, 2013.

[32] P. E. Shrout and J. L. Fleiss. Intraclass correlations: uses in assessing rater reliability. *Psychological bulletin*, 1979.

[33] A. Torralba et al. Describing Visual Scenes using Transformed Dirichlet Processes. In *Proc. NIPS*, 2005.

[34] J. W. Tukey. The philosophy of multiple comparisons. *Statistical science*, 1991.

[35] L. W. Turley et al. Atmospheric effects on shopping behavior: a review of the experimental evidence. *Journal of Business Research*, 2000.

[36] A. Vailaya et al. Image classification for content-based indexing. *IEEE Trans. on Image Processing*, 2001.

[37] H. Wang et al. Local business ambience characterization through mobile audio sensing. In *Proc. WWW*, 2014.

[38] F. Wilcoxon. Individual comparisons by ranking methods. *Biometrics*, 1945.

[39] M. Ye et al. On the semantic annotation of places in location-based social networks. In *Proc. KDD*, 2011.

[40] Y. Zheng et al. Recommending friends and locations based on individual location history. *ACM Trans. on the Web*, 2011.

[41] B. Zhou et al. Recognizing City Identity via Attribute Analysis of Geo-tagged Images. In *Proc. ECCV*. 2014.

[42] S. Zukin. *The cultures of cities*. Blackwell Oxford, 1995.

Bringing Deep Causality to Multimedia Data Streams

Laleh Jalali
Computer Science
University of California, Irvine
Irvine, CA 92617
lalehj@ics.uci.edu

Ramesh Jain
Computer Science
University of California, Irvine
Irvine, CA 92617
jain@ics.uci.edu

ABSTRACT

We live in a data abundance era. Availability of large volume of diverse multimedia data streams (ranging from video, to tweets, to activity, and to PM2.5) can now be used to solve many critical societal problems. Causal modeling across multimedia data streams is essential to reap the potential of this data. However, effective frameworks combining formal abstract approaches with practical computational algorithms for causal inference from such data are needed to utilize available data from diverse sensors. We propose a causal modeling framework that builds on data-driven techniques while emphasizing and including the appropriate human knowledge in causal inference. We show that this formal framework can help in designing a causal model with a systematic approach that facilitates framing sharper scientific questions, incorporating expert's knowledge as causal assumptions, and evaluating the plausibility of these assumptions. We show the applicability of the framework in a an important Asthma management application using meteorological and pollution data streams.

Categories and Subject Descriptors

H.4 [**Information Systems Applications**]: Miscellaneous; D.2.8 [**Software Engineering**]: Metrics—*complexity measures, performance measures*

General Terms

Causal Modeling, Multimedia, Multimodal Data Streams

Keywords

Causal Analysis; Causal Patterns; Asthma Risk Factor Recognition

1. INTRODUCTION

A common topic in multimedia content analysis is detecting events and understanding relationships among those events from video streams, audio streams, and text. More recently other data modalities such as wearable and environmental sensory streams have attracted attention in multimedia community. Detecting low-level events (e.g. tracked objects appearing in certain spatial relationships) and higher-level events (e.g. from surveillance videos and news) are well studied research topics in multimedia. Today with instantaneously accessible data from wireless sensors, biosensors, and mobile apps other fields such as medical research, biology, and physiology are catching up with it and are offering even more challenging problems in understanding relations between domain-level events from disparate streams. So we are facing a unique situation of abundance of multimedia data that can be used to solve challenging societal problems. Most of our existing techniques and concepts are rooted in the time when we had scarcity of data and limited computing and communication technology. But with the emergence of multimedia Big Data our challenge has shifted towards handling this abundance and harnessing the true potential of this ever-growing data. This data spreads over heterogeneous sources containing unstructured, semi-structured, or structured information. Before any analysis, unified signals need to be created from asynchronous, multivariate, and mixed-modality information. Then conceptual models are constructed to account for data in different application domains.

From signal processing perspective, sensory data streams are continuous numerical time-series. Signal models entail a mathematical representation of data so as to extract desirable information from signals. Signal models have been successfully used in various problems that include image processing, speech processing, signal filtering and prediction. These models generate encouraging results in low-level perceptual and signal processing tasks. However, their success is limited in higher cognitive areas where data streams are heterogeneous and symbolic modeling and reasoning are required.

Whenever one talks about models, prediction is presumed to be the end goal. However there are other benefits in creating models. Models *explain* a phenomenon, which is quite different from prediction. For example, in healthcare domain, a model can explain the relation between multiple asthma risk factors (i.e. air pollution, pollen, and weather fluctuation) and asthma attack and not necessarily predict when attack might happen. Also models raise new questions and in the processing of finding answers, interesting insight might be discovered. Most importantly models are used to

MM'15, October 26–30, 2015, Brisbane, Australia.
 ISBN 978-1-4503-3459-4/15/10 ...$15.00.
DOI: http://dx.doi.org/10.1145/2733373.2806278.

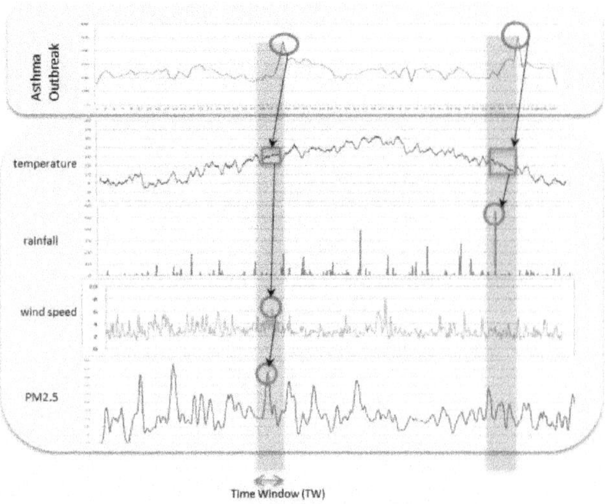

Figure 1: Causal relation between asthma outbreak and environmental data.

understand causes of a problem. So causal analysis is the artifact of models.

Inferring causal relationships is one of the central tasks of science, it is a topic that has been heavily debated in philosophy, statistics, and scientific disciplines. We all have a mental model of cause and effect that helps reasoning about daily life. Individuals prefer explanations for phenomena couched in terms of cause and effect [9]. Causes can be actions, states, or state transitions. So we use the general term *event* that include any potential cause or effect. In most applications there is not a simple or a linear causal relationship between events and the meaning of causal assertions depend on *temporal constraints* between a set of events.

Consider Fig. 1 as an example of causal relation between multiple data streams. The first data stream is measured from tweets, and depicts the burstiness of *asthma topic* in a specific geo-location (Tokyo city). Other streams are measured by physical sensors in the same location, and represents meteorological and pollution data. Once a burst in asthma related messages is detected, physical sensory data within a preceding TW time window is analyzed to find a set of complex causal patterns that might have resulted in the burst. From this figure two causal patterns can be inferred: 1) *pollution increases suddenly* followed by *high wind* while *temperature increases slightly* will cause an asthma outbreak. 2) A *thunderstorm* followed by *temperature decreases steadily* will cause an asthma outbreak. Of course, finding such patterns within one dataset doesn't **prove** the validity of a causal model, but it lends credibility to it. If we repeatedly test this model on more data and in diverse related datasets (e.g from other cities) and find good matches to the data, then the inferred causal model gain more credibility.

Building models involve many decisions such as determining model selection strategy, defining a model structure, defining criteria for model goodness, selection of data and transformation applied to it, just to name a few. Most of these decisions involve reliance on theoretical or empirical results, that is expert's domain knowledge, and cannot be learned by a system itself solely from available input data. Moreover, causal inference is not simple. There is not an easy answer for problems where analyst wants to estimate a causal pathway between a sequences of causes while some minor causes might happen in parallel as well (will elaborate on this in section 2). So it is often necessary to incorporate human judgment into this modeling process. When we encounter large volumes of disparate information, data-driven discovery techniques are quite useful in refining human judgment. So when scientist doesn't have any idea what hypothesis to generate or how to proceed with data analysis task, automatic data-driven techniques provide significant insight. By seeding a hypothesis based on this insight, analyst can incorporate her own domain knowledge and formulate a refined hypothesis quickly, systematically, and 'grow' a hypothesis iteratively to generate a comprehensive model. The former is called 'unknown-unknown' problem and the latter is called 'known-unknown' problem. The best practice is to create a balance between these two. We believe a comprehensive modeling technique should keep human in the loop while taking advantage from new data-driven modeling techniques.

1.1 Problems with Current Approaches

The avalanche of sensory data has led scientists to envision a future in which automated modeling techniques, or 'data-driven discovery' will eventually rival the traditional hypothesis-driven research that has dominated research areas for at least the past century. Most researchers are fascinated by deep learning to model high level abstractions in data. These methods are computationally expensive and there are many training parameters need to be considered. Also they still lack ways of representing causal relationships and have no obvious ways of performing logical inferences.

Situated with temporal data mining research domain causal inference is reduced to finding significant serial or parallel temporal patterns in time-series data. In serial patterns, events occur in a specific order while there is no ordering between events in parallel patterns. Many algorithms are proposed to mine time points [16, 1] or time interval [19, 18] patterns. But handling incomplete and partial information has been less studied. Interestingly the majority of these algorithms deal with serial and parallel patterns *separately*. So cause-effect patterns cannot contain both sequential and parallel components simultaneously, as depicted in Fig. 3. Also significance of a pattern is decided based on its frequency alone and analyst cannot use her domain expertise to guide the analysis. Temporal data mining products (e.g. Theme [1]) work as a black box. They don't involve human in the analysis process and their input is limited to numerical time-series.

In general, bypassing the analyst and carrying out causal analysis as a black box via learning or statistical techniques have several problems:

- Hiding the inference from the analysts reduce their understanding of the model. Also lack of understanding might result in overconfidence, with potentially catastrophic consequences when learned models actually fail in real-world situations.
- Available methods typically cannot give advise to the analyst as how to refine the model and what to do next.

[1]http://www.noldus.com/human-behavior-research/products/theme

- By using available products, it is easy to fall into two traps: either the system acts at a very high level, and it is difficult to deviate from the way the developers of the product thought was the proper way to approach the problem, or the system acts at a very low level, and the analyst has to know a great deal in order to use the system meaningfully.
- Changing even a small parameter in a learned causal model, either for specific circumstances or for including individual judgment, is difficult and needs the whole model to be re-learned. Even if the source code is available, the persons qualified to do the changes may not have the time to tap into the code successfully.

To tackle these problems, we propose an appropriately designed causal modeling platform with 3 principles in mind: 1) There should be a balance between data-driven and hypothesis driven modeling techniques, when one complements the other. 2) Analyst needs to understand causal patterns descriptively. 3) For each causal hypothesis, analyst needs to perform a separate analysis which results in a causal model. At the end, multiple causal models describe the end goal of the analysis.

1.2 Brave New Idea

We present a causal modeling technique that facilitates deep computational understanding and model building in different domains using traditional as well as emergent new multimedia big data streams. It is a new tool for empirical research and offers a natural environment for the study of structural and temporal inter-relations between multiple heterogeneous data sources. The novelty of our approach are: 1) Abstracting data streams to conceptual events as a unified data representation that is understandable for experts and facilitates the manipulation of a model's structure; 2) Design a high-level declarative language which allows for definition of complex causal patterns from the combination of a unique set of well-defined operators. The language is very concise, contains a small number of operators, and is still very expressive; 3) Provide data-driven processing techniques, using a combination of basic operators and visual analytics to generate an insight in unknown-unknown situations. 4) Design a framework and a comprehensive GUI that engage analysts in an interactive, online process, allows them to iteratively use their knowledge to generate and evaluate a causal hypotheses to build a model.

Fig. 2 demonstrates our evolving system's UI. Analyst can import pre-processed data (i.e. event streams) and choose visual data-driven operators to explore data, generate a basic model and derive a preliminary insight. Then analyst can seed a hypothesis and grow it step by step using provided operators. A good hypothesis is not the one that is necessarily correct, but one that opens up a new path of investigation. In complex problem domains this path cannot be fully perceived in advance. So analyst must be provided with appropriate operators to carry out new analyses based on the original hypothesis.

The proposed causal modeling approach has the important effect of coupling both data-driven and hypothesis-driven modeling, keeping human in the loop while taking advantage of data-driven analytics when needed. In this sense, it is a new hybrid modeling approach. This is a general platform and can be applied to different problem domains. In the evaluation section we demonstrate the applicability of such platform in a healthcare application.

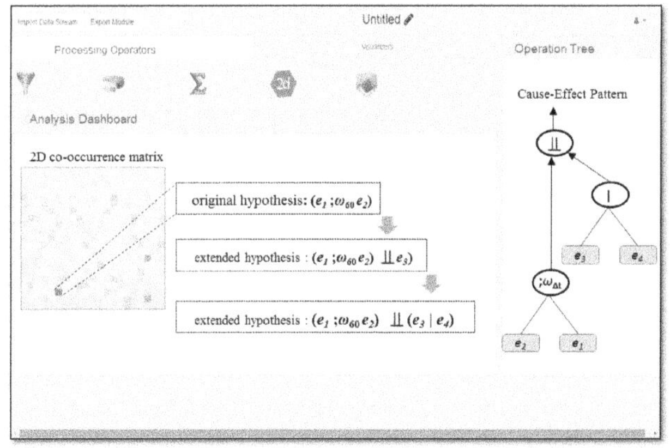

Figure 2: Analytical dashboard of causal modeling framework.

2. CAUSAL MODELIING

The most popular data representation is N-dimensional numerical vectors. Hence, modeling is usually carried out in R^N based on algebraic semantics. For non-numeric data such as survey entries or computer logs, the general practice is to transform them to R^N and force a real vector observation into the problem. However, a data transformation to R^N typically abandons original data semantics. Therefore, the ability to carry out computations beyond R^N could be valuable for developing useful models while retaining original problem semantics. One one hand, data representation needs to have representational power to capture the necessary aspects of a complex model. On the other hand, it has to be understandable for experts to facilitate the manipulation of a model's structure. Some complex representations might hinder such understanding and manipulation. As suggested in [5], in a pre-processing phase, different machine learning, discretization, statistical and mathematical, mapping, and natural language processing techniques can be used to convert raw heterogeneous measurements to events (and event's attributes). These events are application dependent and they abstract sensory data into a higher conceptual level. Then causal patterns can be formulated by applying a set of operators on these events.

Fig. 3 shows a sample complex causal pattern. Multiple ordered events with time lags in between generate a *sequential causal pattern.* Also some events are minor causes and when coupled with other events at the same time (e.g. occur in parallel) results in an effects, that is so called *concurrent causal pattern.* Bringing an example from asthma management problem, a causal pattern of asthma attack can be: ([*e1*: patient did not take medication] *within* 60 minutes *followed by* [*e2*: engaged in an intense exercise]) *while* ([*e3*: pollution is high] *or* [*e4*: temperature is below 20° C]) *within* 15 minutes *followed by* [asthma attack].

$$\Big(\big(\ e1\ ;\omega_{60}\ e2\ \big) \amalg \big(\ e3 \mid e4\ \big)\Big);\omega_{15}\ e5$$

We provide a high level causal pattern language that contain a set of operators to formulate such complex patterns. Bellow is the asthma attack causal pattern translated into events and operators. The semantics of these operators are explained in section 2.3.

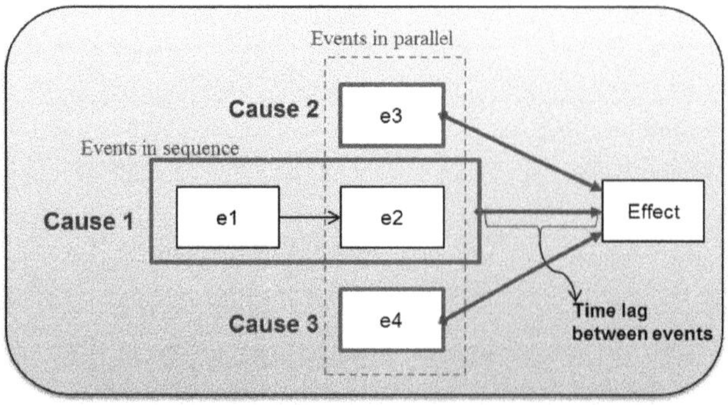

Figure 3: A sample structure of multiple causes and an effect. Causes might happen in a sequential order or concurrent.

2.1 Time Model

For the purpose of temporal reasoning Allen formalized temporal logic on intervals by specifying 13 interval relations [2]. These temporal relations have been used by the majority of research on mining time-interval data [12, 14, 6, 3, 6]. However, researchers identified problems using Allen's relations such as ambiguousness in the pattern representation and lack of robustness to noise because small shifts of time points lead to different patterns [15, 19]. After Allen, Freksa revisited interval relationships at the semi-interval level [4]. He generalized the interval relations by using semi-intervals with the following 11 operators: *older, younger, head to head, survives, survived by, tail to tail, precedes, succeeds, contemporary, born before death,* and *died before birth.* Semi-intervals allow a flexible representation where partial or incomplete knowledge need to be handled since operations are on parts of an interval and not the whole.

In temporal data mining, very little work has focused on using semi-intervals. The most notable was conducted by Morchen et al. in [13] where they explored semi-intervals for unsupervised pattern mining and proved that semi-interval patterns are more flexible than patterns over full intervals. In our work, we use semi-interval to represent temporal facet of an event. We adopt a time point representation of time intervals [19] in which intervals are represented with their start and end time point.

Definition 1 (*Time Domain*). A time domain $\mathbb{T}$ is a discrete, linearly ordered, countably infinite set of time instants $t \in \mathbb{T}$. We assume that $\mathbb{T}$ is bounded in the past, but not necessarily in the future.

Definition 2 (*Time Interval*). A time interval is a triple $[\partial, t_s, t_e]$ where $\partial \in \Sigma$ is a unique symbol and $t_s, t_e \in \mathbb{T}$ and $t_s \leq t_e$. The finite set of all time intervals is noted $I = \{ [t_s, t_e] | t_s \leq t_e \}$. If $[t_s, t_e] \bigcap [t'_s, t'_e] \neq \emptyset$, intervals are overlapped.

Definition 3 (*Semi Interval*). A semi interval is a tuple $[\partial^{+/-}, t]$ where $\partial \in \Sigma$ is a unique symbol and interval boundaries are represented with + and signs where ∂^+ and ∂^- are corresponding to the start and end of the interval respectively. $[\partial^+, t]$ represent a semi interval where start time is available and $[\partial^-, t]$ represent a semi interval where end time is available. Using the semi-interval definition, an interval can also be represented with its interval boundaries. Formally in a time interval $[\partial, t_s, t_e]$, $\partial.t_s = \partial^+$ and $\partial.t_e = \partial^-$ and duration of the interval is $d(\partial) = \partial^- - \partial^+$. Also an instantaneous time point can be considered as an interval with zero duration where $\partial^- = \partial^+$.

The most important criteria in any cause-effect pattern (as depicted in Fig. 3)is that an effect always occurs after a set of causes within a time lag. Two situations need to be considered: 1)The causes occur in a particular order with specific time lag in between. 2) The order is not important but there has to be a notion of concurrency.

We define two temporal relations to meet these requirements. Then we use semi-interval operators to represent these temporal relations.

1. Order: is the sequential occurrence of time points or time intervals. In Freska's formalism *younger, succeeds, survives,* and *born after death* relations fall in this category.
2. Concurrency: is a nonempty time period where two or more temporal events occur in no particular order. In Freska's formalism *head to head, tail to tail,* and *contemporary* relations fall in this category.

2.2 Event Model

An event is either an instantaneous occurrence or spans over time. The former is called point event and the latter is called interval event. Sometimes we have a semi-interval event where information about the event is not complete. For example we might know when event starts but there is no information available about when it ends or vice versa. Event model has a schema $\mathbb{S}$ that describes a set of attributes a class of events must contain.

Definition 3 (*Point Event*). A point event (pE) is an event that occurs at an instantaneous point in time. It is a tuple $e = (v, [E, t])$ consists of the name of its type, denoted by an upper-case letter (e.g., 'E'), the time of occurrence $t \in \mathbb{T}$, and a set of values $v \in \mathbb{S}$.

Definition 4 (*Interval Event*). An interval event (iE) is an event that spans over time. It is a tuple $e = (v, [E, t_s, t_e])$ consists of the name of its type, start and end time $[t_s, t_e] \in I$, and a set of values $v \in \mathbb{S}$.

Definition 5 (*Semi-interval Event*). A semi-interval event (sE) is a special case of interval event when one of the event boundaries is missing. It is a tuple $e = (v, [E^{+/-}, t])$ consists of the name of its type, start time or end time $t \in \mathbb{T}$, and a set of values $v \in \mathbb{S}$.

These three categories of events with their graphical illustration are shown in Table 1.

Definition 6 (*Event Stream*). An event stream $ES^{(i)} = \{e_1^{(i)}, e_2^{(i)}, ..., e_n^{(i)}\}$ is an ordered set of events where $e_k \in \{pE, iE, sE\} (1 \leq k \leq n)$.

Definition 7 (*Multi-Event Stream*). A multi-event stream $ES = \{ES^{(1)}, ES^{(2)}, ..., ES^{(|I|)}\}$ is a finite set of event streams. Events from multiple event streams have a total order based on their start time so they can be overlapped. The alphabet of multi-event stream is $\Sigma = \{\Sigma^{(1)} \bigcup \Sigma^{(2)} \bigcup ... \bigcup \Sigma^{(|I|)}\}$.

Take an example from Fig. 4(a), $ES^{(1)}$ is an event stream with 3 disparate events. E_1 is an interval event represented with E_1^+ and E_1^- for start and end points, E_2 is a point event where $E_2^+ = E_1^-$, and E_3 is a semi-interval event represented with E_3^+ for start point. The events that belong to the same event stream cannot have overlaps. However, as shown in Fig. 4(b), events from multiple event streams might be overlapping. This brings us to the next question: How to encode a multi-event stream with overlapping events so the ordering and temporal structures between events are preserved? As explained before, we seamlessly represent semi interval

Table 1: Three event categories with their data model and graphical illustration.

Category	Event Model	Time Model	Graphic
Point Event (pE)	(A , t)	$A^+ = A^-$	A
Interval Event (iE)	(B, t_s, t_e)	$B^+ = B.t_s$ $B^- = B.t_e$	B^+ B^-
Semi-interval Event (sE)	($C^{+/-}$, t)	If $C.t_s \neq$ NA then $C^+ = C.t_s$ If $C.t_e \neq$ NA then $C^- = C.t_e$	C^+ C^-

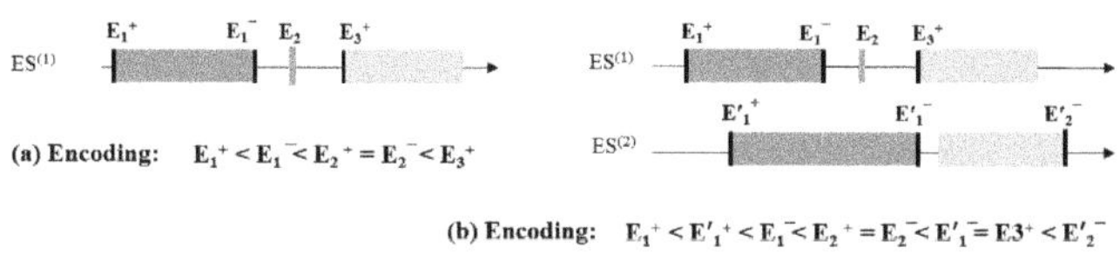

Figure 4: (a) Example encoding of a sequence of events. E_1^+ and E_1^- represent the start and end times of event E_1, respectively. Relational operators are used to indicate the ordered relations between start/end times. (b) Example of encoding a multi-event stream from two sequence of events.

and interval events using instantaneous time points in the interval boundaries. A simple schema similar to that of [6] can be used to encode a multi-event stream in a single linear data stream (Fig. 4) without any ambiguity with respect to the temporal relation between overlapping events. Event E_1 ends before E_2 occurs (<), or an event E'_1 ends at the same time E_2 starts (=).

2.3 Processing Operators

We formally define our language by defining an operation algebra for causal pattern formulation. These operators are aimed to be the basic operations, combination of which can be used for arbitrarily sophisticated pattern formulation and pattern querying on event streams. Due to space limitation, the semantic of the operators are removed from this version and available in the extended version of our paper [2].

Arbitrary patterns can be defined by applying operators on individual event types. Each pattern consists of a number of participating events. Suppose pattern ρ has k participating events E_i $(1 \leq i \leq k)$, size of the pattern denotes $|\rho| = k$, start and end timestamps of the pattern denotes $\rho.t_s$ and $\rho.t_e$ respectively and defined as follows:

$$\rho^+ = \rho.t_s = min\{E_1.t_s, E_2.t_s, ..., E_k.t_s\} \quad (1)$$

$$\rho^- = \rho.t_e = max\{E_1.t_e, E_2.t_e, ..., E_k.t_e\} \quad (2)$$

Definition 8 (*Pattern*). A pattern ρ is represented as $\rho = (X_1 \odot_1 X_2 \odot_2 ... \odot_{k-1} X_k)$ where X_i is an event, $X_i \in \{pE, iE, sE\}(1 \leq i \leq k)$, and $\odot_i \in \{;, ;\omega_{\Delta t}, \amalg, |\}(1 \leq i \leq k-1)$ is a pattern formulation operation. In case there are multiple occurrences of a X_i in a pattern, it is necessary to distinguish which two event boundaries (e.g. X_i^+ and X_i^-) represent the same X_i occurrence. However, we assume that each event type has only one occurrence in a pattern and X_i^+ and X_i^- are coming from the same occurrence of X_i. Our language supports a hierarchy of complex patterns by feeding the output of one operator as an input to another. So a pattern operator not only connects events but also connects a number of pattern expressions to form a new expression. Frequency of a pattern is the number of occurrences of the pattern in an event stream.

Selection Operation σ_P : This operator filters pattern expression on predicate P, where P refers to event attributes contained in the pattern.
$\sigma_P(\rho) \equiv \exists\, T = [t_s, t_e]$ such that $\rho(T) \wedge P$

Sequence Operation $(\rho_1; \rho_2; ...; \rho_k)$: This operator detects if pattern expression ρ_1 is followed by pattern expression ρ_2 and so on. The operator specifies a particular order in which the patterns of interest should occur.

Conditional Sequence Operation $(\rho_1 ;\omega_{\Delta t_1} \rho_2 ;\omega_{\Delta t_2} ... ;\omega_{\Delta t_{k-1}} \rho_k)$: It detects if pattern expression ρ_1 is followed by pattern expression ρ_2 *within* Δt time units. Δt is called the time lag or temporal restriction between two successive patterns.

Concurrency Operation $(\rho_1 \amalg \rho_2 \amalg ... \amalg \rho_k)$: Concurrency detects multiple patterns occur in parallel, and succeeds only if all patterns are detected. Unlike sequence, any order is allowed, and there has to be a non-empty overlap interval among the patterns.

Alternation $(\rho_1|\rho_2|...|\rho_k)$: This operator detects if any pattern expressions ρ_1 to ρ_k matches the input event stream.

Time $(\omega_{\Delta t}\rho)$: This operator requires a pattern ρ to occur within a certain time interval $\Delta t = [\delta_1, \delta_2]$.

Co-occurrence $(CO_{\rho_1,\rho_2}[\Delta t])$: These operator computes if ρ_2 is co-occuring with ρ_1 within Δt time lag. Formally it defines as:

$$CO_{\rho_1,\rho_2}[\Delta t] = \frac{Count(\rho_1; \omega_{\Delta t}\rho_2)}{Count(\rho_1)} \quad (3)$$

with $CO_{\rho_1,\rho_2}[\Delta t] \in [0, 1] and max|CO_{\rho_1,\rho_2}[\Delta t]| = 1$ means that ρ_1 and ρ_2 are always co-occurring within Δt time lag, while values close to zero indicate that there is no co-occurrence within the specified time lag. To check for a significant time lag between ρ_1 and ρ_2 we define:

$$\Delta t^{max} = \underset{\Delta t}{\text{argmax}}(CO_{\rho_1,\rho_2}[\Delta t])$$

with $\Delta t \in \{1, 2, ..., \lambda_{CO}\}$ where λ_{CO} is a design parameter indicating the maximum possible time lag between patterns.

2.4 Visualization Operators

Temporal data mining methods often identify frequently occurring patterns. However, the context in which these patterns occur is typically lost. Also complex patterns that contain both sequential and concurrent components cannot be formulated. So we define visualization operators that combines both mining and visualization techniques.

2D Co-occurrence Matrix: In image processing a co-occurrence matrix or co-occurrence distribution is a matrix that is defined over an image to be the distribution of co-occurring values at a given offset to measure the texture of the image. In our work, we use co-occurrence matrix in a different way. Consider two event streams $ES^{(1)}$ and $ES^{(2)}$ with $N = |\Sigma^{(1)}|$ and $M = |\Sigma^{(2)}|$ denote the number of event types in each event stream. Co-occurrence matrix C is an $N \times M$ matrix where each cell (i, j) is the co-occurrence value calculated from definition 3 for a pair of events E_i and E_j:

$$C_{\Delta t}(i, j) = CO_{E_i,E_j}[\Delta t] \;\forall i = 1, ...N \;, j = 1, ...M \quad (4)$$

[2]http://www.ics.uci.edu/~lalehj/MMBNI2015-jalali.pdf

In future, we will introduce a 3D Co-occurrence matrix operator that captures causal association between 3 event streams.

3. PROCESSING TECHNIQUE

The processing operators defined in the previous section are the basic building blocks of causal pattern recognition. These operators need to be compiled to a processing unit. We chose Finite State Automaton (FSA) as the underlying processing technique and each operator translates to its corresponding automaton (as shown in Table 2) to detect instances of a specific pattern in the input stream. The theory of finite-state automata is rich and finite-state automata techniques have been used in a wide range of domains, such as pattern matching, pattern recognition, speech processing, hand writing recognition, encryption algorithm, and data compression. So in our framework the pattern recognition component employs an extended FSA that supports a time model to address temporal restrictions that are needed in causal analysis. This automaton contains of a finite number of states and state transitions. There are two types of states: ordinary states and time states. Ordinary state is analogous to states in traditional finite automata. It consume an event from event stream, apply an EVALUATE() function and make a transition to the next state if the evaluation is successful. Time state on the other hand keeps track of time constraint requirement by applying a SET() function on boundaries of time lag (δ_1, δ_2) that is going to be used in the evaluation function of the next ordinary state. Ordinary state is represented by an event type $E_i \in \Sigma$ and it means that the FSA is waiting for E_i to be seen in the input event stream.

Definition 9 (*Automaton*): A finite-state automata (FSA) is a 5-tuple (OS, TS, Ed, s_0, s_f), consisting of a finite set of ordinary states (OS), time states (TS), transitions between states (Ed), a start state $s_0 \in OS$, and a final or acceptance state $s_f \in OS$.

The underlying processing technique is same for both hypothesis driven and data-driven analysis. However, hypothesis driven emphasis on an interactive reasoning using expert's knowledge. First, analyst seeds a causal hypothesis using pattern operators and create a causal pattern. Then this pattern translates to its corresponding automaton. Finally a processing algorithm is used to find instances of that pattern in the input event streams. Fig. 5 demonstrates an initialized FSA corresponding to pattern $\rho_1 = (E_5; \omega_{[10]} E_1; \omega_{[3]} E_4)$. During run time $E_i.t_s$ and $E_i.t_e$ substitute with start and end time of an instance of event E_i from the input event stream. The strategy for counting occurrences of a pattern is straight forward. For a pattern, say ρ, an automaton FSA_ρ is initialized. The initialization process includes translating event types and temporal constraints to ordinary states and time states, and allocating

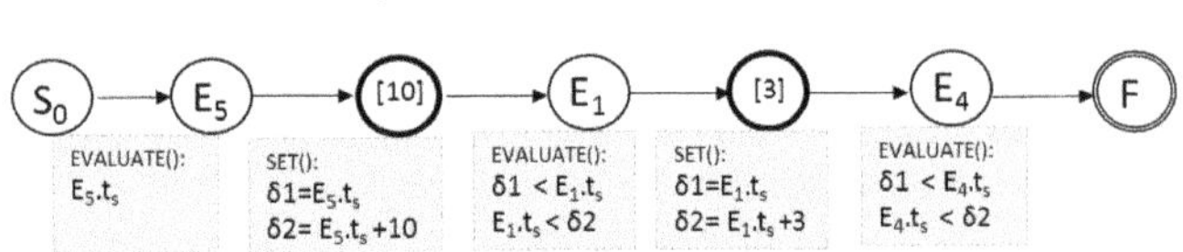

Figure 5: The automaton corresponding to pattern $\rho 1$ with 3 event components. It demonstrates 3 ordinary states, 2 time states, and EVALUATE() and SET() functions associated with each state.

Table 2: Corresponding automaton for each operation. (Note: For simplicity and without the loss of generality, operators are depicted between two events only)

Operation	Automaton
$\sigma_P(E_i)$	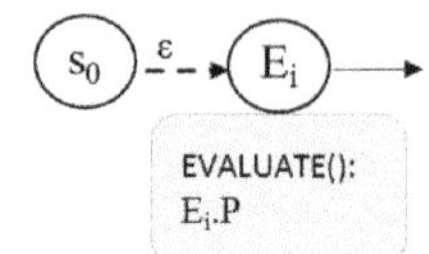
$(E_i; E_j)$	
$(E_i^+; E_j^+)$	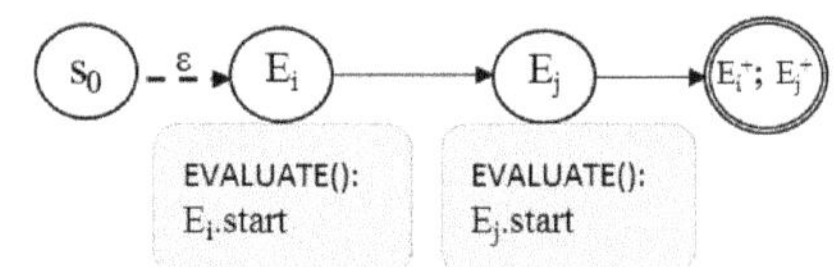
$(E_i ;\omega_{\Delta t} E_j)$	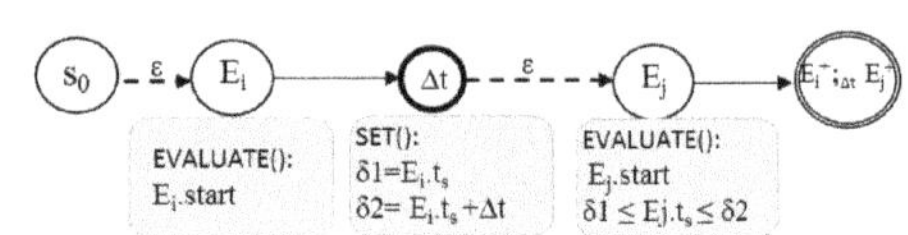
$(E_i \perp\!\!\!\perp E_j))$	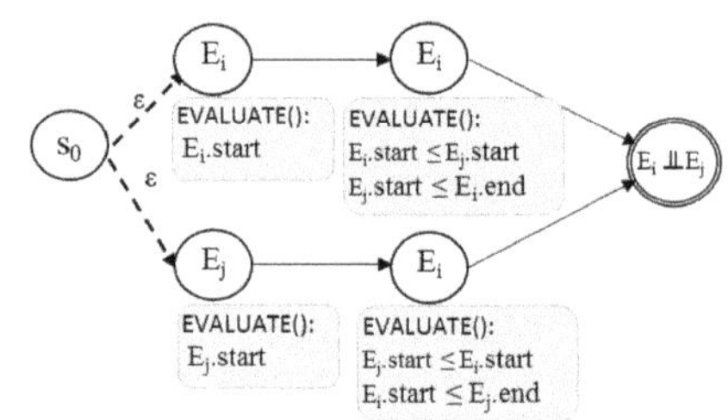
$(E_i \| E_j)$	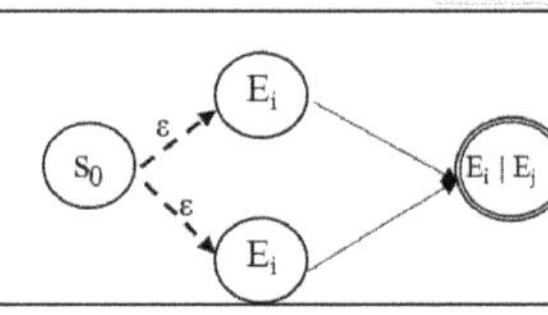
$(\omega_{\Delta t} E))$	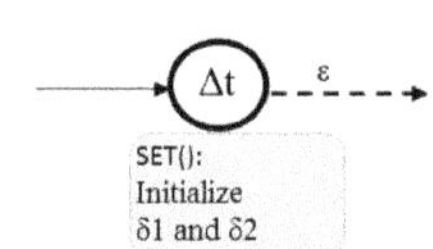

a buffer for EVALUATE() and SET() functions within each state. As we read data from event stream, by considering the output of EVALUATE(), automaton makes earliest possible transitions into the next successive state. Once it reaches its final state, an occurrence of the pattern is recognized and its frequency is increased by one. A fresh automaton is initiated for this pattern when an event corresponding to its first event appears again in the event stream.

In order to process complex patterns that are combination of multiple operators, we use a logical operator tree. The logical operator tree for a given causal pattern specifies the processing operators used and their order. Nodes in the operator tree represent configured operators (refer to the side panel in Fig. 2), and directed edges between nodes denote the the event streams flow. Analyst sequentially configure operators as a part of designing a causal hypothesis. This operator tree is then parsed, instantiated and converted to a run-time operator tree.

In data-driven analysis our goal is knowledge discovery, finding novel, interesting and interpretable patterns. As op-

Algorithm 1. Pseudocode for counting conditional sequential patterns

```
1: Input: Event Streams E(1),E(2),...E(N)
2:        A set of patterns P
3: ES = merge (E(1),E(2),...E(N))
4: Σ = Σ(1) U Σ(2) U...U Σ(N)
5: for all event types E in Σ
6:     waits(E) = φ  // Initialize waits(.) index
7: end
8: for all patterns ρ in P
9:     Initialize an automaton FSAρ = (OSρ, TSρ, Ed, s0, sf)
10:         Create a list of ordinary states OSρ
11:         Create a list of time states TSρ
12:         ρ.freq = 0
13:         Add (FSAρ , 1) to waits(OSρ[1].EventType)
14: end
15: for i =1 to n read the next event ei from ES
16:     Let E = ei.type
17:     for all (FSAρ , x) pointed by waits(E)
18:         if OSρ[x].EVALUATE() = TRUE
19:             Proceed to TSρ[x] state
20:             Execute TSρ[x].SET()
21:             Let x'= x , x = x+1
22:             Proceed to OSρ[x]
23:             Remove (FSAρ , x') from waits(E)
24:             if OSρ[x].type=final
25:                 ρ.freq++ , x = 1
26:             Add (FSAρ , x) to waits(OSρ[x].EventType)
27:         else  // temporal conditions are violated
28:             x=1  // start matching again
29:     end
30: end
31: return P
```

posed to hypothesis driven, where a single complex pattern was analyzed, in data-driven analysis a batch processing is performed on a collection of patterns. Then the result of the analysis is presented in visual graphics so analyst can explore data visually in order to extract information. For this batch analysis, our processing algorithm is a fast automaton based frequency counter that counts the frequency of **a collection** of patterns efficiently with only one pass through event streams. Algorithm 1 shows the pseudo-code of processing algorithm for conditional sequential patterns. We will present the algorithms for other types of patterns in our future work. For each pattern an automaton is initialized (line 9-12). A conditional sequential pattern ρ has an automaton FSA_ρ where OS_ρ is a list of ordinary states TS_ρ is a list of time states. $OS_\rho[x]$ is the xth ordinary state with *EventType* and *StateType* attributes and *EVALUATE()* method. Similarly, $TS_\rho[x]$ is the xth time state with a *SET()* method to set time constraint boundaries.

To efficiently access all automata, we index them using a *waits(.)* list. For each event type E, the automata that are waiting for E are linked together in a list pointed by *waits(E)*. Giving an example from figure 5, ρ_1 is added to $waits(E_5)$ (line 13). Each element of this list is a pair (FSA_ρ, x) indicating that FSA corresponding to pattern ρ is in its xth ordinary state, waiting for $OS_\rho[x].EventType$ to be seen in the input stream. The idea of efficiently indexing automata through a *waits(.)* list was introduced in the windows-based frequency counting algorithm [10] with the difference that the list was used to manage up to N automata per a pattern of size N. The algorithm we present here requires just one automaton per pattern. The main loop in the algorithm looks at each event, say e_i, in the input stream and makes necessary changes to the list of automata pointed by $waits(e_i.type)$. If an automaton reaches its final state, frequency of the pattern increases by one. At any state, if the validation function fails, automaton will not proceed with the current match and goes back to its start state. This algorithm is very efficient because it goes through the multi-event stream only once to count the frequency of all input patterns.

4. THE FRAMEWORK FOR COMBINING HYPOTHESIS-DRIVEN AND DATA-DRIVEN ANALYSIS

As mentioned, in an appropriately designed causal modeling platform, there should be a balance between data-driven and hypothesis-driven modeling techniques where the former helps in knowledge discovery and the latter keeps human in the loop for reasoning and causal modeling. In this section we explain how casual modeling framework can be used as an exploration environment through 3 experiments: 1) Visual discovery 2) Interactive pattern growth. 2) Hypothesis refinement.

The experiments are performed on synthetic data that is generated by embedding some causal patterns. At this point, we have only used conditional sequential operator to generate sample patterns. Each pattern to be embedded in the dataset, consists of a specific ordered sequence of events and time lags between them. Data generation process is as follow: There is a timer that specifies the current time instant. Each time an event is generated, this timer specifies event's start time. The duration of each event is picked from a normal distribution with a mean value μ . After generating an event, timer is incremented with a small random integer. Each time the next event is to be generated, two decisions should be made. 1) Whether the event is going to have both start and end timestamps, or one of them might be missing randomly. This is controlled by the parameter α , which is the probability that the next event has its both interval boundaries. If α = 1 then generated event stream contains only events having complete intervals. 2) Whether the next event is to be generated randomly with uniform distribution over all event types or according to one of temporal patterns to be embedded. This is controlled by the parameter β , which is the probability that the next event is generated randomly. If β = 1 then data contains only noise with no sequential temporal patterns embedded. If it decides that the next event is to be from one of the patterns to be embedded, then we have a choice of continuing with a pattern that is already embedded partially or starting a new pattern.

4.1 Visual Discovery

Following the synthesized data generation approach, dataset1 is generated with total number of events n $= 10^6$, number of event types $|\Sigma| = 22$, $\alpha = 0.3$, and $\beta = 0.2$. While generating the data, the following three patterns were injected:

$\rho_1 = (E_3 \overset{15}{\longrightarrow} E_6 \overset{30}{\longrightarrow} E_{10})$

$\rho_2 = (E_8 \overset{30}{\longrightarrow} E_{19})$

$\rho_3 = (E_{13} \overset{60}{\longrightarrow} E_9 \overset{15}{\longrightarrow} E_{20})$

(a) Co-occurrence patterns $(E_3;\omega_{15}E_6)$= 0.92 and $(E_9;\omega_{15}E_{20})$=0.85

(b) Co-occurrence patterns $(E_8;\omega_{30}E_{19})$=0.84 and $(E_6;\omega_{30}E_{10})$=0.88

(c) Co-occurrence pattern $(E_{13};\omega_{60}E_9)$=0.82

Figure 6: Co-occurrence matrices with different temporal offsets. (a) Δt=15 min, (b) Δt=30 min ,(c) Δt=60 min

Data generation with β=0.2 means that with 20% probability the next event is generated randomly and with 80% probability pattern ρ_i $(i = 1, 2, 3)$ is continued or a new occurrence of ρ_i is started. Suppose analyst doesn't know what to look for and needs some preliminary knowledge about the data (unknown-unknown problem). Using 2D co-occurrence matrix operation and by changing temporal offset, multiple 22×22 co-occurrence matrices can be computed. Three of these matrices are demonstrated in Fig. 6. Such a visualization facilitates browsing co-occurrence characteristics in event streams, formulating hypothesis regarding those characteristics, and investigating potential causal relationships between events. Considering the visualization, analyst finds 5 causal patterns that seeds the following hypotheses: 1)$h1 = (E_3\ ;\omega_{15}\ E_6)$. 2)$h2 = (E_6\ ;\omega_{30}\ E_{10})$. 3)$h3 = (E_8\ ;\omega_{30}\ E_{19})$. 4)$h4 = (E_{13}\ ;\omega_{60}\ E_9)$. 5)$h5 = (E_9\ ;\omega_{15}\ E_{20})$.

4.2 Interactive Pattern Growth

Analyst can use the knowledge discovered in the previous section and interactively formulate and analyze more complex patterns. This interaction cannot be displayed in the form of snapshots. So we explain a simple case of growing a pattern. Suppose analyst wants to find causal patterns of size 3 in the form of $E_i \rightarrow E_j \rightarrow E_k$. With 22 event types, there are 9240 sequential patterns of size 3 (same event type cannot occur twice in a pattern). If we restrict the time lag $\Delta t \in \{15, 30, 60\}$, in case of conditional sequential patterns of size 3, the total number of patterns reaches **55440**. However, by performing visual analytics in the previous step and formulating hypothesis $h1$ to $h5$, we only need to analyze **300** candidate patterns to find significant causal patterns of size 3. These candidate patterns are generated as follow:

$E_3 \xrightarrow{15} E_6 \xrightarrow{\Delta t} E_i\ \forall i \in \{1, 2, ...22\}, i \neq 3, 6$

$E_6 \xrightarrow{30} E_{10} \xrightarrow{\Delta t} E_i\ \forall i \in \{1, 2, ...22\}, i \neq 6, 10$

$E_8 \xrightarrow{30} E_{19} \xrightarrow{\Delta t} E_i\ \forall i \in \{1, 2, ...22\}, i \neq 8, 19$

$E_{13} \xrightarrow{60} E_9 \xrightarrow{\Delta t} E_i\ \forall i \in \{1, 2, ...22\}, i \neq 13, 9$

$E_9 \xrightarrow{15} E_{20} \xrightarrow{\Delta t} E_i\ \forall i \in \{1, 2, ...22\}, i \neq 9, 20$

So by incorporating experts knowledge from previous step, the search space for finding embedded patterns has significantly reduced. The frequency of these patterns are displayed graphically and analyst can easily recognize the significance of $(E_3 \xrightarrow{15} E_6 \xrightarrow{30} E_{10})$ and $(E_{13} \xrightarrow{60} E_9 \xrightarrow{15} E_{20})$.

4.3 Hypothesis Refinement

Suppose analyst has a vague hypothesis in her mind where E_1 is the effect and E_2 , E_3 , E_4 are presumed to be causes of E_1 in a specified order. Also the time lag between events are unknown but her domain expertise indicate that $\Delta t \in \{15, 30, 60\}$. Hypothesis refinement is beneficial in investigating which events are the true causes and what temporal precedence and restriction exists between them. So, using sequence operation, analyst can formulate a vague hypothesis as: h = $E_2; E_3; E_4; E_1$. For refining this hypothesis, system automatically generates the following causal patterns:

$\rho_1 = E_2 \xrightarrow{\Delta t} E_1$, $\rho_2 = E_3 \xrightarrow{\Delta t} E_1$ $\rho_3 = E_4 \xrightarrow{\Delta t} E_1$, $\rho_4 = E_2 \xrightarrow{\Delta t} E_3 \xrightarrow{\Delta t} E_1$, $\rho_5 = E_2 \xrightarrow{\Delta t} E_4 \xrightarrow{\Delta t} E_1$, $\rho_6 = E_3 \xrightarrow{\Delta t} E_4 \xrightarrow{\Delta t} E_1$

Then the frequency of these patterns are computed and graphically displayed. Analyst can easily select the most significant ones and repeat the refinement if needed.

5. EXPERIMENT: ASTHMA RISK FACTOR MODELING

In this section we present the applicability of our causal modeling framework in extracting expressive causal rules in the context of a healthcare application, asthma management. Exposure to air pollution specifically Particular Matter (PM2.5) is linked with asthma exacerbation; however, the role played by meteorological factors such as temperature, humidity, rainfall, wind, and the complicated interrelations between these factors and asthma attacks are not well understood. Temporal structure and order relation between these environmental factors and their effect on asthma exacerbation comprise complex patterns called *asthma risk factors*. By extracting such causal patterns we create an asthma risk model that is important both for an asthmatic patient and public health.

From our causal modeling framework we use conditional sequential operator to formulate and recognize complex risk factors. First unified event streams are construct by abstracting trends of data streams using Symbolic Aggregate approXimation (SAX) method [8]. Then algorithm 1 is applied on multiple event streams to recognize significant complex patterns that encode asthma risk factors. We use meteorological, pollution and tweet data collected for 18 months in Tokyo (as shown in Fig.1). The result of our experiment is presented as descriptive rules (32 causal patterns) that are easily understandable by an expert. Expert might perceive some insight within these rules or decide to seed a new hypothesis based on them and dig deeper to find even more interesting causal patterns.

Mizunuma et al. [11] shows that there is a strong relationship between real world events and what people tweet about. So, tweets can be leveraged for recognizing a situa-

Table 3: Definition of events assigned to each SAX-code

Symbol	SAX-code	Event Definition
Low Value Level=a	ab / bc	increase
	ac	suddenly increase
Medium Value Level=b	ca	suddenly decrease
	cb / ba	decrease
High Value Level=c	aaa	stay low
	ccc	stay high

tion in the real world. Once we have recognized a real world phenomenon from social messages then we can look for digital footprints of potential triggers of the phenomenon in physical sensory data (e.g. air pollution and meteorological factors).

5.1 Topic Modeling

KeyGraph [17], a network of keywords based on their co-occurrence in documents, is used to build a topic detector E_v. The KeyGraph is the set of non-overlap sub-graphs, call communities; each community is considered as one topic. The significance of this methodology is that there is no need to define the number of topics beforehand. In order to build E_v for *asthma* topic, we first collect a set of documents relate to asthma, from the Internet (e.g. Wikipedia, medical organizations), and scientific journal archives (e.g. ojphi.org). Then, we use KeyGraph to build a set of communities. Finally, we pick a community that contains *asthma* keyword and collect all keywords that connect directly to this keyword as the E_v. We assume that an incoming tweet that contains at least one of the keyword in E_v might be related to asthma.

5.2 Event Stream Modeling

First we need to extract meaningful events from data streams and generate corresponding event streams. Event model explained in section 2.2 is used to create an abstraction level on top of sensory data streams to mask the heterogeneity of the underlying data. For human sensory data, a burst detector [7] is applied to find bursting points on the topic histogram to generate asthma outbreaks event stream (*effect* events). Since physical sensory data is a time-series data stream, trend analysis plays a major role. It not only facilitates prediction of a new value of data within a certain interval of time, but also gives a holistic view of changing values. Therefore, instead of raw data, trend data is used to extract information. The Season-Trend Decomposition by Loess (STL) method, introduced in [8], is taken into account to decompose original time-series data into Trend, Seasonal, and Remainder streams. Then, SAX algorithm with alphabet size equal to 3 (a,b,c symbols) is applied to trend data in order to create SAX-code streams. Given the specifications of our application, we are interested in capturing not only state transitions (e.g. pollution level increases or decreases, point events) but also maintaining a specific state value for a duration of time (e.g. pollution level stays high, interval events). To do so, we define 6 event types for each stream. Table 3 shows a list of SAX codes and the corresponding event definition assigned to them. Using this encoding, each SAX-code trend data stream is converted to an event stream.

As explained earlier we are interested in finding the interrelation between multiple asthma triggers, mainly PM2.5 and meteorological factors. Complex risk factors are pat-

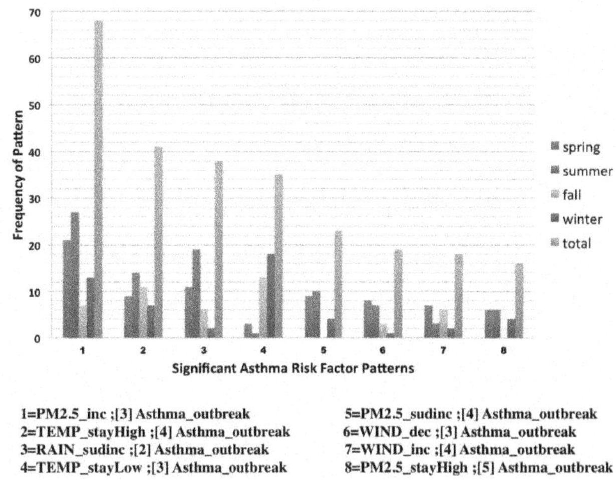

Figure 7: Frequency of asthma risk factors of size 2. "$PM2.5\_inc; \omega_{[3]} Asthma\_outbreak$" reads: once PM2.5 increases, an asthma outbreak happens within 3 days.)

terns characterizing by structural order and temporal constraints between events from multiple event streams. Going back to the definition of a pattern $(X_1 \odot_1 X_2 \odot_2 \dots \odot_{k-1} X_k)$, X_k is burst in tweets (an indication of asthma outbreak), X_1 to X_{k-1} are event types from air pollution and meteorological event streams, and $\odot_i$ $(1 \le i \le k-1)$ is considered to be $;\omega_{\Delta t}$ where Δt is 1 to 7 day time lag.

5.3 Causal Pattern Extraction

For extracting and evaluating asthma risk factor patterns we have used data collected for 18 months, from 2013-July-01 to 2014-Dec-30, in Tokyo city. Continuous hourly-average PM2.5, temperature, rainfall, and wind speed data are available for multiple sampling locations in Tokyo. Since asthma risk factors are quite different between different seasons, dataset is divided into 4 seasons: Spring (March -May), summer (June - August), autumn (September - November), and winter (December - February).

Fig. 7 demonstrates the most significant asthma risk factors of size 2 with their frequency in total and for each season as well. From this analysis we have found that although PM2.5 has the most impact on asthma outbreak in general, its effect is not noteworthy in the fall and winter seasons. Also, temperature fluctuation has the most impact in the fall and winter seasons and it is not a risk factor during spring or summer. Another insight is that during spring and summer, when rain suddenly increases to a very high level, an asthma outbreak is more probable. This might sound counter intuitive, since rain by itself should not effect asthma, unless it is combined with some other factors that we have not been included in our causal model. However, a pulmonologist suggested that thunderstorms are associated with an increase in asthma exacerbation. This is because high concentrations of allergens, specially pollen, are found to coincide with thunderstorms. Our experiments do not account for the effect of allergens such as pollen on asthma outbreaks since reliable data was not available. This impacts the quality of some causal patterns and reflects its effect on the accuracy of our model.

Fig. 8 shows 17 significant patterns of size 3 and 6 significant patterns of size 4. These patterns encode relations

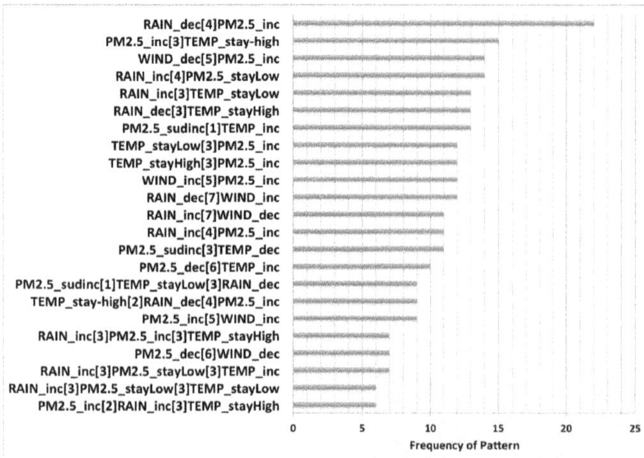

Figure 8: Frequency of asthma risk factors of size 3 and 4

between two or three events as well as the time lag between them and asthma exacerbation (e.g. when rain decreases followed by PM2.5 increase within 4 days, then asthma outbreak is probable.) Our results suggest some interesting patterns: when PM2.5 increases followed by temperature stay high within 3 days, then asthma outbreak is probable; or when wind decreases followed by PM2.5 increases within 5 days, then asthma outbreak is probable. Recognizing the time lags between events is one of the most important contributions of our approach. To the best of our knowledge this aspect of correlation between different risk factors has never been studied systematically before in causal modeling for health care applications.

6. CONCLUSION

In this paper we presented a causal modeling technique that facilitates deep computational understanding and model building in different domains using traditional as well as emergent new multimedia big data streams. We argued that there should be a balance between data-driven and hypothesis-driven modeling techniques since they complement each other. A formal causal pattern language consists of processing and visualization operators was defined and an extended FSA was applied as the underlying processing technique. By using this framework, on one hand analyst can benefit from visual operators for knowledge discovery and on the other hand she can perform separate analysis for each causal assumption and interactively refine the generated hypothesis. Some preliminary results using conditional sequence operator for asthma risk factor recognition is presented. In future we apply this framework to build a comprehensive user model (objective self [5]) from personal data streams.

7. REFERENCES

[1] R. Agrawal and R. Srikant. Mining sequential patterns. In *Data Engineering, 1995. Proceedings of the Eleventh International Conference on*, pages 3–14. IEEE, 1995.

[2] J. F. Allen. An interval-based representation of temporal knowledge. In *IJCAI*, volume 81, pages 221–226, 1981.

[3] P. R. Cohen. Fluent learning: Elucidating the structure of episodes. In *Advances in Intelligent Data Analysis*, pages 268–277. Springer, 2001.

[4] C. Freksa. Temporal reasoning based on semi-intervals. *Artificial intelligence*, 54(1):199–227, 1992.

[5] R. Jain and L. Jalali. Objective self. *MultiMedia, IEEE*, 21(4):100–110, 2014.

[6] P.-s. Kam and A. W.-C. Fu. *Discovering temporal patterns for interval-based events*. Springer, 2000.

[7] J. Kleinberg. Bursty and hierarchical structure in streams. *Data Mining and Knowledge Discovery*, 7(4):373–397, 2003.

[8] J. Lin, E. Keogh, L. Wei, and S. Lonardi. Experiencing sax: a novel symbolic representation of time series. *Data Mining and knowledge discovery*, 15(2):107–144, 2007.

[9] K. Manktelow and M. C. Chung. *Psychology of reasoning: Theoretical and historical perspectives*. Psychology Press, 2004.

[10] H. Mannila, H. Toivonen, and A. I. Verkamo. Discovery of frequent episodes in event sequences. *Data Mining and Knowledge Discovery*, 1(3):259–289, 1997.

[11] Y. Mizunuma, S. Yamamoto, Y. Yamaguchi, A. Ikeuchi, T. Satoh, and S. Shimada. Twitter bursts: Analysis of their occurrences and classifications. In *ICDS 2014, The Eighth International Conference on Digital Society*, pages 182–187, 2014.

[12] F. Moerchen. Algorithms for time series knowledge mining. In *Proceedings of the 12th ACM SIGKDD international conference on Knowledge discovery and data mining*, pages 668–673. ACM, 2006.

[13] F. Moerchen and D. Fradkin. Robust mining of time intervals with semi-interval partial order patterns. In *SDM*, pages 315–326, 2010.

[14] C. Mooney and J. F. Roddick. Mining relationships between interacting episodes. In *SDM*, pages 1–10. SIAM, 2004.

[15] F. Mörchen and A. Ultsch. Efficient mining of understandable patterns from multivariate interval time series. *Data Mining and Knowledge Discovery*, 15(2):181–215, 2007.

[16] J. Pei, J. Han, B. Mortazavi-Asl, H. Pinto, Q. Chen, U. Dayal, and M.-C. Hsu. Prefixspan: Mining sequential patterns efficiently by prefix-projected pattern growth. In *2013 IEEE 29th International Conference on Data Engineering (ICDE)*, pages 0215–0215. IEEE Computer Society, 2001.

[17] H. Sayyadi and L. Raschid. A graph analytical approach for topic detection. *ACM Transactions on Internet Technology (TOIT)*, 13(2):4, 2013.

[18] E. Winarko and J. F. Roddick. Armada–an algorithm for discovering richer relative temporal association rules from interval-based data. *Data & Knowledge Engineering*, 63(1):76–90, 2007.

[19] S.-Y. Wu and Y.-L. Chen. Mining nonambiguous temporal patterns for interval-based events. *Knowledge and Data Engineering, IEEE Transactions on*, 19(6):742–758, 2007.

Analytic Quality: Evaluation of Performance and Insight in Multimedia Collection Analysis

Jan Zahálka
Intelligent Systems Lab Amsterdam
University of Amsterdam
Amsterdam, The Netherlands
j.zahalka@uva.nl

Stevan Rudinac
Intelligent Systems Lab Amsterdam
University of Amsterdam
Amsterdam, The Netherlands
s.rudinac@uva.nl

Marcel Worring
Intelligent Systems Lab Amsterdam
University of Amsterdam
Amsterdam, The Netherlands
m.worring@uva.nl

ABSTRACT

In this paper, we present *analytic quality* (*AQ*), a novel paradigm for the design and evaluation of multimedia analysis methods. *AQ* complements the existing evaluation methods based on either machine-driven benchmarks or user studies. *AQ* includes the notion of user insight gain and the time needed to acquire it, both critical aspects of large-scale multimedia collections analysis. To incorporate insight, *AQ* introduces a novel user model. In this model, each simulated user, or *artificial actor*, builds its insight over time, at any time operating with multiple categories of relevance. The methods are evaluated in timed sessions. The artificial actors interact with each method and steer the course by indicating relevant items throughout the session. *AQ* measures not only precision and recall, but also throughput, diversity of the results, and the accuracy of estimating the percentage of relevant items in the collection. *AQ* is shown to provide a wide picture of analytic capabilities of the evaluated methods and enumerate how their strengths differ for different purposes. The *AQ* time plots provide design suggestions for improving the evaluated methods. *AQ* is demonstrated to be more insightful than the classic benchmark evaluation paradigm both in terms of method comparison and suggestions for further design.

Categories and Subject Descriptors

H.3.4 [**Information Storage and Retrieval**]: Systems and Software—*Performance evaluation (efficiency and effectiveness)*

General Terms

Measurement; Performance; Experimentation

Keywords

Evaluation; multimedia search and exploration; interactivity; user insight

MM'15, October 26–30, 2015, Brisbane, Australia.
 ISBN 978-1-4503-3459-4/15/10 ...$15.00.
DOI: http://dx.doi.org/10.1145/2733373.2806279.

1. INTRODUCTION

The abundance of multimedia collections has given data analysts in diverse fields a rich new resource. For instance, multimedia collections provide forensic evidence in cases of child abuse or terrorism. In many scientific fields, such as physics, new discoveries are made and validated using various observations and simulations, which are decidedly multimedia data. In the business domain, news media companies often find entire stories to cover in the content of social media platforms. In arts, multimedia applications are instrumental in navigating and exploring cultural heritage collections. In most data analytics use cases, timeliness of the results is a critical factor as insight in the data has to lead to an action as fast as possible. For instance, a forensics expert has 48 hours to decide whether a suspect should be detained further. Likewise, a media expert looking for stories connected to a globally-important event like the Charlie Hebdo attack cannot wait weeks before publishing them. In such cases, decisions are based on millions of multimedia data items and thus difficult. In short, analysts from diverse fields of expertise need to gain understanding of increasingly large and complex multimedia collections, and they need to gain this understanding fast. So what is needed to support the analytics process for multimedia collections?

To support multimedia *analytics* tasks, sophisticated underlying multimedia *analysis* tools and techniques are needed. A solid basis of multimedia analysis tool has been presented within the multimedia community, including algorithms like active SVM [33] or tools like Caffe [13]. In recent years, such multimedia analysis methods have reached the state of being able to truly support insightful multimedia analytics: the features are short enough to allow smooth interaction and sufficiently descriptive to allow the algorithms to operate on high semantic levels with high accuracy. In combination with hardware developments, time is ripe for multimedia analytics. However, which multimedia analysis techniques are the best and how to optimize or develop them further for multimedia analytics?

To answer this question we should carefully consider the goal of data analytics: gaining understanding about the data. This understanding, or *insight*, as it is called in the fields of information visualization and visual analytics [31], is complex and requires interplay of a number of factors. Insight builds up on itself and over time, requires all or most data at hand and is often serendipitous [20]. Interaction is thus crucial: the analyst needs to navigate the collection through intelligent interactions in order to gradually build

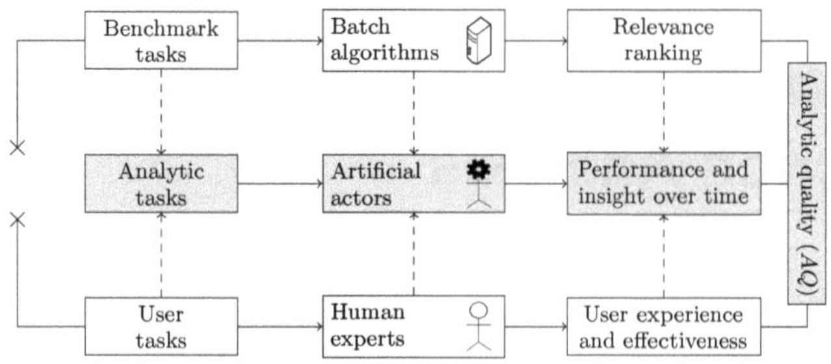

Figure 1: The novelty of analytic quality (AQ), the framework proposed in this paper.

insight and not to get overwhelmed by the scale of the data. In the case of multimedia data, analytic tasks involve a combination of exploration and search, and in order to build insight, the analyst needs to be able to organically move back and forth between the two [38]. Hence, it is imperative that techniques behind multimedia analytics support both exploration and search, as well as take into account the various aspects of insight.

Evaluation is a necessary part of designing any good-quality system. The abovementioned works, while providing a theoretical basis for insight, do not provide any means of actually evaluating it. In the multimedia community, we are heavily relying on a number of benchmarks and datasets enabling evaluation of the individual methods. Examples include MediaEval [14], TRECVID [22], MSR-Bing IRC [7], or visual sentiment ontology [1]. These benchmarks are instrumental in establishing, comparing, and improving the quality of the analysis. Most benchmarks focus on the relevance of the results. Indeed, higher relevance improves analytics in general. However, the underlying user model is only implicit and very simple: the notion of relevance is fixed, users process the top ranked results only, and the time for the analysis is unlimited. Do the benchmarks paint the complete picture with respect to the analytic process in which experts are interacting with the data to gain insight?

One way to look at the support of the process of gaining insight is the large body of multimedia research on human-centered interaction and computing [11]. The bulk of the evaluation in this human-centered field is done through user studies, where groups of real users large enough to yield statistically significant results typically assess two well-defined conditions through detailed interviews or questionnaires. This methodology allows for gauging user experience and effectiveness of the evaluated method with regard to the user tasks. From the perspective of multimedia analytics systems design, however, the space of options and possible design paths for future systems is vast and not all these paths can be explored by full user studies. Human-computer interaction studies are appropriate when close to a final design, but different mechanisms are needed in earlier stages.

In order to be truly able to design and assess the analytic potential of multimedia analysis techniques, a new evaluation paradigm is needed. It should not only evaluate the relevance of the returned results, but also the insight gain and the time needed to acquire it. In this paper, we therefore propose *analytic quality (AQ)*, a time-based evaluation framework which evaluates the system performance and at the same time estimates the user insight. AQ uses a novel artificial user model, which simulates the behaviour of an analyst striving to gain data understanding. As illustrated in Figure 1, AQ brings the worlds of relevance-based benchmarks and user studies closer together. Hence, AQ is a significant first step towards evaluation covering both performance and insight aspects of multimedia analytics.

The rest of the paper is organized as follows. Section 2 summarizes the related work. In Section 3, the AQ framework is developed along with all its constituent components. Section 4 showcases AQ evaluation. Section 5 concludes the paper.

2. RELATED WORK

This section summarizes the related work on evaluation in the multimedia community and the related fields such as computer vision or information retrieval. Namely, we investigate the relevance-based benchmarks, evaluation of interactivity, and existing work on evaluation paradigms going beyond relevance alone.

The dominant paradigm are relevance-based benchmarks. Evaluation sessions are usually not timed and fully automatic with no user involvement. The dominant evaluation metrics are the classic and well-known accuracy, precision, recall, and average precision. These gained traction in the information retrieval benchmarks such as TREC [3] and are now also widely used in computer vision benchmarks, for example ILSRVC [26], Pascal VOC [5], or TRECVID [22]. Some MediaEval tracks also involve these metrics [4]. For a good reason: the main reason for employing a multimedia analysis algorithm is to get results relevant to our intent.

Gaining insight rarely boils down to just going over a list of retrieved results. A visual analytics study by North et al. shows that insight-based evaluation provides richer feedback, and thus much more valuable lessons to the method designers, than the feedback obtained from benchmark-based evaluation [21]. The human cognitive model of visual analytics by Green et al. sheds light on user insight by establishing that a human analyst keeps a categorical model with up to 7 ± 2 categories when reasoning about new data[6]. The carrier of analyst's multidimensional intent is interaction, extensively investigated by Pike et al. [24]. Interactivity is actively researched also by the multimedia community. The key techniques are summarized in a survey by Thomée and Lew [32]. Considering evaluation, interactivity is explicitly considered for example by the Video Browser Showdown, a competition between user-centered video search engines [28]. Extending the visual analytics and interaction theory, Zahálka and Worring model multimedia analytics insight as a set of categories of relevance defined by the analyst herself [38]. However, [38] presents only a theoretical model and does not provide any means of actually evaluating system performance and multimedia analytic quality. All in all, while relevance rightfully takes a spotlight with regard to insight, there are more aspects that contribute to the user's understanding of the data.

The multimedia-related fields are well-aware of the imperfections of relevance alone. Indeed, the gap between relevance metrics and user preferences was confirmed by Sanderson et al. [27]. Numerous metrics expand the classic binary relevance paradigm, mostly originating in the field of information retrieval. The notion of graded relevance is embodied in discounted cumulative gain (DCG) by Järvelin and Kekäläinen [12]. The expected reciprocal rank (ERR) of Chapelle et al. extends graded relevance to include a sim-

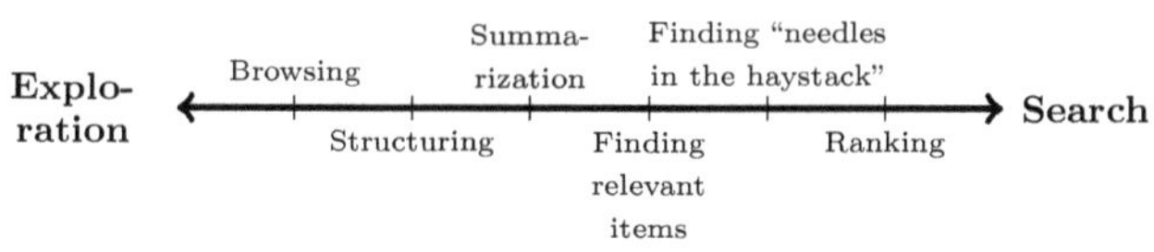

Figure 2: The exploration-search axis with example multimedia analytics (sub)tasks [38].

ple user model, measuring retrieval quality as the inverse expected effort by the user to satisfy her information need [2]. Smucker and Clarke introduce the crucially important notion of time to IR effectiveness measures, making the notion of information gain dependent on time the user needs to reach the item, rather than its position in the list alone [29]. By modelling the correlation between the position of the item in the list and the time the user needs to reach it, this work is one of the first ones to consider time explicitly. These metrics are already being used in text-based benchmarks, including a number of TREC tracks, for example the federated Web search track [3]. Research on evaluation reaching beyond simple benchmark relevance is thus gaining momentum in recent years.

Multimedia analytics tasks consist not only of search, but also of exploration. Hence, to truly evaluate the analytic capabilities of multimedia analysis methods, the exploration component has to be taken into account. In the multimedia domain, exploration is strongly tied to summarization: the analyst gains understanding about the structure of the collection by seeing relevant, representative, and diverse results. The metrics evaluating the quality of summarization again originate in the field of information retrieval, the most prominent examples including BLEU by Papineni et al. [23], ROUGE by Lin [18], Meteor by Lavie and Agarwal [15], and pyramid score by Nenkova et al. [19]. CIDEr by Vedantam et al. automatically measures image description consensus [35]. Some of those metrics have been adapted by the multimedia community. VERT by Li and Merialdo is an extension of BLEU and ROUGE [17], while Rudinac et al. have extended the pyramid score to visual summaries [25]. The increasing importance of diversity is reflected in a number of benchmarks, such as ImageCLEF 2009 [16] or MediaEval Diverse Social Images [9]. The latter resulted in Div400, a diversity benchmark dataset [10].

Overall, the research on evaluation metrics for multimedia is active. There are metrics covering aspects of either search or exploration. Yet multimedia analytics is an intricate interplay of *both*. The main drawback we perceive in most current paradigms is the absence of interaction. Currently, each evaluated method analyzes the entire collection using a relevance indication (e.g., a query or class annotation) and returns a list of results, the entirety of which is used to compute the respective relevance metric. In addition, the notion of relevance is static from the beginning to the end. Time is rarely considered, and few approaches take into account the time the analyst needs to invest to reach a particular result. These shortcomings, combined with the fact that gaining analytical insight is an open-ended task involving both exploration and search in all its phases, is the motivation for our evaluation method developed further in the paper.

3. METHOD

This section presents the *AQ* evaluation framework. Section 3.1 discusses the analytic task model and its implications for *AQ*. Section 3.2 describes the artificial actors, i.e., the user model used by *AQ*. Section 3.3 outlines the details of the *AQ* evaluation process. Section 3.4 presents the evaluation measures used by *AQ*. Finally, Section 3.5 provides guidelines for interpreting the results of *AQ* evaluation.

3.1 Evaluating analytic tasks

Our evaluation method, *AQ*, is built on the notion of the exploration-search axis [38], illustrated in Figure 2. A user analyzing a collection builds insight over time, i.e., her needs, intent, and the notion of relevance are changing over the course of the analysis. Moreover, the user will be tilting back and forth between exploration and search as the insight builds up. To complete her analytic task, the user will be *interacting* with the collection, undertaking (sub)tasks based on the *current* notion of relevance. Examples of these (sub)tasks are depicted on the exploration-search axis in Figure 2. *Analytic categorization*, i.e., the task of assigning individual items into categories defined by the analyst, is the umbrella task for the exploration-search axis task model [38]. These categories can be completely different than any categories associated with the dataset itself, such as class labels or annotations. An example of such a category could be for example "suspicious activity" in forensic research. This category can encode multiple aspects in multiple modalities: e.g., presence of firearms in the image, text description inciting terrorism, or geo location corresponding to terrorist training camps. In order to support the evaluation of analytic tasks, the artifical actors in the *AQ* user model need to be able to create analytic categories of relevance, further denoted simply "categories."

To define categories, an artificial actor needs to "make sense" of the content of the individual items in the analyzed collection. For the individual artificial actors to be able to do that, the items need to be annotated with content annotations, e.g., "this image contains a person, a car, and a house", or "the topics in the text are politics and USA." However, in the analytic context, we cannot expect the collection to be annotated. Hence, we need to collect these annotations ourselves.

To this end, we employ a so called *arbiter*, i.e., a black box producing content annotations for each item in the analyzed collection. An arbiter needs to be:

- *Consistent.* Inputting the same item twice yields identical annotations.
- *Semantic.* A human can interpret the annotations and judge their presence in the item.
- *Autonomous.* The arbiter is self-contained, providing the annotations without any involvement of the evaluated methods.
- *Mostly accurate.* The error rate of the arbiter annotation assignment is as low as possible.

The *consistency* condition prevents randomness and ensures repeatability of the results. The *semantic* condition is necessary for *AQ* to simulate actual human behaviour. It would be technically possible for artificial actors to operate on low-level machine features, but given that humans rarely think in terms of these features, such approach would hardly measure analytic quality. The *autonomous* condition ensures fairness: an artificial actor explicitly using the same data model as one of the evaluated methods would have an innate edge over the other evaluated methods. The requirement for autonomy does not ensure full independence of the annotations. For example, it may occur that a visual arbiter's concept dictionary overlaps with that of one (or more) evaluated methods. Given that the arbiter is autonomous, the underlying features might be correlated, but are not identical. Bearing in mind that this correlation is hard to measure, we conjecture that having non-identical data representations is enough to treat the method's data model as autonomous from the arbiter data model for the purposes of evaluation. The fourth condition requires that the arbiter annotations have to be *accurate* enough. This condition is also hard to assert. However, we conjecture that the level of the state of the art in visual and text analysis algorithms is high enough to provide meaningful annotations. This has been shown by a number of applications, for example in interactive venue recommendation [37].

The arbiter annotation process itself has two steps. The first one is selecting the arbiter. There is an abundance of excellent tools allowing fast and meaningful content annotation. In the visual domain, Caffe by Jia et al. can be used to obtain concepts from a convolutional deep network trained on another dataset [13]. In the text domain, a solid option for content annotation is extracting the LDA topics using the Gensim framework [36]. The second step involves crisp assignment of content annotations to individual items. If the arbiter produces scores for each annotation, these need to be thresholded to determine annotations present on each item. An example of such crisp assignment is assigning those concept annotations reaching at least 80% of the maximum confidence score for each item. Once each item is associated with arbiter annotations, the candidate analytic categories for the actors can be generated.

The candidate categories (C_c) are created from the arbiter annotations as follows. Let $\mathcal{A}_i = \{a_1, a_2, \cdots, a_{|\mathcal{A}_i|}\}$ be the set of visual, text, and metadata annotations associated with item i in the analyzed multimedia collection I. Each category $C \in C_c$ is composed of the arbiter annotations associated with the category ($\mathcal{A}_C$) and the set of all items belonging to the category (denoted I_C):

$$C = \{\mathcal{A}_C, I_C\} \tag{1}$$

The categories of each item $i \in I$ correspond to all subsets of $\mathcal{A}_i$ except the empty set. Indeed, if we take for instance an item i with $\mathcal{A}_i = \{\texttt{blood}, \texttt{firearms}\}$, we want to associate it not only with the category $\{\texttt{blood}, \texttt{firearms}\}$, but also the category $\{\texttt{blood}\}$ and the category $\{\texttt{firearms}\}$. Let $\mathcal{P}(\mathcal{A}_i)$ denote the power set of $\mathcal{A}_i$ and $\mathcal{A}_I = \bigcup_{i \in I} \mathcal{P}(\mathcal{A}_i)$. C_c is then:

$$C_c = \bigcup_{\mathcal{A}_C \in \mathcal{A}_I \setminus \varnothing} \{\mathcal{A}_C, \{i \mid i \in I \wedge \mathcal{A}_C \subseteq \mathcal{A}_i\}\} \tag{2}$$

If necessary, C_c can be further pruned to contain only those categories $C \in C_c$ for which $|I_C|$ is above a certain threshold. All actors will draw their categories from C_c. In the further text, random draw from C_c is a shorthand for uniformly drawing an item from the set and removing it. The removal is done to foster the diversity of the individual artificial actors. The resulting set of candidate categories C_c is the source of analytic categories for the artificial actors described in the next section.

3.2 Artificial actors

The *AQ* user model operates with *artificial actors*, i.e., computer agents interacting with the evaluated method and simulating user behaviour. The artificial actors are built on three cornerstones: analytic categories, changing notion of relevance, and limited time. The analytic categories are obtained from the candidate categories set (C_c) defined in Section 3.1. The actors change their categories of relevance over time, modelling the dynamic nature of insight. The limited time adresses the real-life need for timely analysis. The conjunction of these factors addresses the aspects of insight by North [20]. Providing arbiter annotations of multiple modalities and defining analytic categories as compounds of these annotations simulates *complexity*, since the actors are using all of the data channels or at least most of them. The artificial actor model allows for both incremental evolution of the categories (*depth*) and abrupt category changes (*serendipity*). *Relevance* is embodied in the very mode of interaction, where each actor guides the evaluation session based on what items are relevant to the current category definitions. In this section, we describe the four-step probabilistic process of generating the artificial actors.

Step 1: Initial actor categories. In the first step, the set of categories of relevance (C^a) is established for each actor $a \in A$. As mentioned in Section 2, a study by Green et al. indicates that a human analyst can operate with up to 7 ± 2 categories of relevance [6]. Each artificial actor's number of initial categories is thus an integer uniformly drawn from the $[1, 9]$ interval. Each of the initial categories is in turn uniformly drawn from C_c.

Step 2: Number of insight changes. Once the initial C^a is established, we need to determine the number of insight changes, or *breakpoints*, the actor will make throughout the session (denoted as n_B). The maximum number of these breakpoints ($n_B^{\max}$) is a parameter to be chosen based on the domain of expertise: for example, a casual user browsing celebrity photos will typically have a shorter attention span and focus than a medical scientist analyzing a medical dataset, resulting in a higher $n_B^{\max}$. In our method, we account for different kinds of users within the same domain of expertise. To this end, we propose a simple user behaviour model. A portion of the actors is *single-minded*, with a clear purpose from start to end, i.e., $n_B^{\max} = n_B = 0$. The rest is *volatile* and have their n_B determined in a probabilistic manner. We treat a breakpoint as a rarely occurring event, and hence draw n_B from an exponential distribution with $\lambda = \frac{\ln 10}{n_B^{\max}}$. This distribution ensures that increasingly large values of n_B are drawn with decreasing probability (a number of volatile actors will actually be single-minded with $n_B = 0$). The value of λ ensures that 90% of the actors will have their $n_B < n_B^{\max}$. The remaining 10% accounts for the unpredictability of user behaviour; we cannot assume a crisp upper bound for n_B in any domain.

Step 3: Insight change times. For each breakpoint $b \in \{b_1, \ldots, b_{n_B}\}$, we need to determine the time when it occurs (t_b). The value of t_b is again probabilistic: since insight is serendipitous, occuring unexpectedly [20], it is not fully predictable. However, insight is also deep and it takes time to build it [20]. Thus, given n_B, we can expect the session to be divided in $n_B + 1$ segments of roughly equal length. Let $t_{seg}^{eq} = \frac{t_s}{n_B+1}$ denote the length of each segment assuming the breakpoints are equidistant. For the i-th breakpoint b_i, we draw t_b from a normal distribution $\mathcal{N}_i(\mu_i, \sigma)$, setting $\mu_i = i \cdot t_{seg}^{eq}$ and $\sigma = \frac{1}{6} t_{seg}^{eq}$. The value of μ_i expresses the centering of individual breakpoints on equidistant time ticks. The value of σ is motivated by the desire to leave sufficient time between breakpoints to build up insight (the "deep" characteristic). To assert sufficient segment length, we want the majority of the t_b draws to fall within $\frac{1}{2} t_{seg}^{eq}$ seconds of the mean. Using the three sigma rule, setting $3\sigma = \frac{1}{2} t_{seg}^{eq}$ ensures that 99.7% of the drawn values fall within the desired time interval.

Step 4: Insight change actions. The last aspect of the actor's insight scenario to be determined is the type of the insight change and the associated action. These actions have to account for both depth and serendipity of building insight: the changes can range from incremental to abrupt [20]. Thus, in our actor model, we account for 6 distinct insight change events with equal probabilities for each breakpoint:

Action 1: Add category. If $|C^a| < 9$, a category is randomly drawn from C_c and added to the C^a. Otherwise, "replace category" is performed.

Action 2: Remove category. If $|C^a| > 1$, a category is uniformly drawn from C^a and removed from the set. Otherwise, "replace category" is performed, with the removal step being enforced.

Action 3: Replace category. Performs "remove category" followed by "add category."

Action 4: Expand category. Replaces category $C \in C^a$ with a category whose associated annotations are a superset of those associated with C. For example, the {**dog**} category will get replaced by the {**dog**, **house**} category. C^{sup} is established as the set of "annotation superset" categories:

$$C^{\text{sup}} = \{C_k \in C_c \mid \exists C \in C^a : \mathcal{A}_C \subset \mathcal{A}_{C_k}\} \tag{3}$$

Then, a category is uniformly drawn from C^{sup}, replacing that category in C^a whose annotation superset it corresponds to. If there are multiple such categories in C^a, one is selected randomly with uniform probability. If $C^{\text{sup}} = \varnothing$, "add category" is performed instead.

Action 5: Reduce category — Replaces category $C \in C^a$ with a category whose associated annotations are a *sub*set of those associated with C. For example, the {**forest**, **river**} category will get replaced by the {**forest**} category. The reduction process is an analogy to the expand process: C^{sub} is established as the set of "annotation subset" categories:

$$C^{\text{sub}} = \{C_k \in C_c \mid \exists C \in C^a : \mathcal{A}_C \supset \mathcal{A}_{C_k}\} \tag{4}$$

Then, a category is uniformly drawn from C^{sub} to replace a category whose annotation subset it corresponds to. If there are multiple candidates for replacement, the reduced category is again uniformly drawn. If $C^{\text{sub}} = \varnothing$, *remove category* is performed instead.

Action 6: Change category — Replaces category $C \in C^a$ with a category $C_i \in C_c$ whose associated annotations are of the same size and contain at least one annotation associated with category C. For example, the {**parrot**, **rainforest**} category will get replaced by the {**parrot**, **savanna**} category. C^{ch}, the set of candidate replacements, is formally defined as:

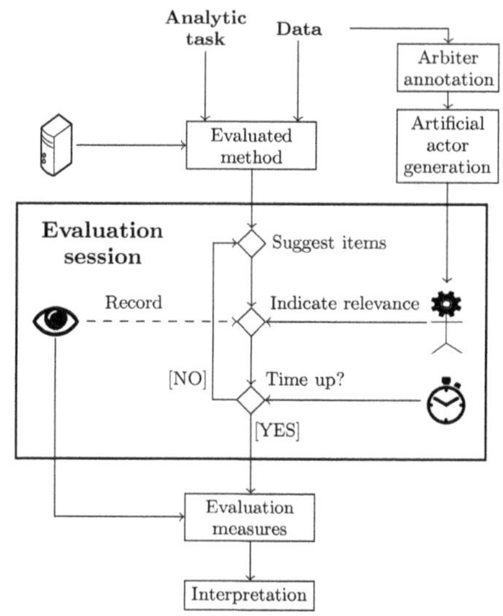

Figure 3: The *AQ* evaluation method pipeline.

$$C^{\text{ch}} = \left\{ C_k \in C_c \mid \exists C \in C^a : \begin{array}{c} |\mathcal{A}_C| = |\mathcal{A}_{C_k}| \\ \mathcal{A}_C \cap \mathcal{A}_{C_k} \neq \varnothing \end{array} \right\} \tag{5}$$

Once C^{ch} is established, an existing category $C \in C^a$ is replaced. If $C^{\text{ch}} = \varnothing$, *replace category* is performed instead.

The artificial actors capture all key aspects of the multimedia analytics process. They operate with multiple categories of relevance, which are not defined by the evaluated method, but externally, using arbiter annotations. This simulates the real user's ability to define the categories herself. Moreover, the artificial actors address all enumerable characteristics of insight as defined by North [20]. The artificial actor model thus provides a user model conforming to multimedia analytics task and interaction theory.

3.3 Evaluation pipeline

The pipeline of *AQ* is depicted in Figure 3. In the preparation phase, we need to generate candidate categories of relevance (cf. Section 3.1) and construct the artificial actors (cf. Section 3.2). Each method is evaluated using the same session time (t_s) and the same set of actors (A, the number of actors to be generated is denoted n_A). The value of t_s depends on the domain and/or purpose of the evaluated method. For instance, the sessions in a system for casual exploration of social network content will typically be shorter than forensic investigations, warranting a smaller t_s. Considering n_A, we posit the default $n_A = 100$. This value is a trade-off between having enough actors to capture nuances in the insight gaining process and offset the stochastic generation process on the one hand, and not having too many so that the evaluation time stays reasonable. The third *AQ* parameter to be considered is the time it takes an actor to process one item (t_1^a). This simulates the time cost of processing individual items by a human analyst, which is certainly higher than if the machine would be allowed to iterate over results uninhibited. Indeed, even in rapid serial visual presentation (RSVP), users have been shown to only be able to perform basic processing (e.g., "is this an orange?") on 5–15 images per second, as shown by Van der

Corput and Van Wijk [34]. To the best of our knowledge, there is no decisive study on the "correct" value of t_1^a. For AQ, however, the main implication is that t_1^a remains the same across all methods. For simplicity, we posit the default $t_1^a = 1\ s$. If necessary for the domain of expertise, n_A and t_1^a can be both treated as a free parameter. Once the actors are generated and the session time is established, the evaluation itself can start.

Each evaluation session is first divided into *segments*, i.e., time periods between the insight changes by the actors when the actor's categories of relevance are constant. A subsession is ran for each segment, and each involves two parallel execution threads:

- *Actor thread* executes the artificial actor's interaction with the evaluated method.
- *Observer thread* records the progression of the actor.

Each session starts with the first query by the artificial actor and runs uninterrupted until t_s is reached. The time the evaluated method takes to produce the results is thus included in the session time.

The actor thread starts with the evaluated method suggesting items to the actor. Then, the actor indicates which items are relevant according to the current categories of relevance. An item is marked as relevant if it belongs to at least one category of relevance, and as not relevant otherwise. After processing each item, the actor sleeps for t_1^a seconds before proceeding further to simulate the time needed by a real user to process the item. Once the actor has given a complete relevance indication over all items suggested by a method, a time check is performed. If the elapsed time is greater or equal to t_s, the actor thread stops and records the set of all items ($\widehat{I}(t)$) and the set of all relevant items ($\widehat{I}_r(t)$) seen by the actor in the segment. Otherwise, the thread goes back to the first step, asking for new suggestions from the evaluated method.

The observer thread records the progression of the actor thread at certain equidistant time points further called *ticks*. The length of each tick, t_T, depends on t_s, and as such is also dependent on the domain and/or purpose of the evaluated method. At each tick t, the observer thread snapshots two sets: the set of all items seen by the user ($\widehat{I}(t)$), and the set of all relevant items seen by the user ($\widehat{I}_r(t)$). Note that the ticks start counting at the start of the session, rather than the start of each segment. The recorded values per ticks and segments are used to compute the results of AQ.

Once all sessions are complete, the AQ measures are computed. The measures, described in Section 3.4, take into account relevance, as well as other characteristics of multimedia analytic quality, namely the speed of the method, the diversity of the suggested items, and how well is the analyst able to estimate the percentage of relevant items in the collection. Finally, in Section 3.5, we explain how to interpret the results.

3.4 Evaluation measures

In this section, we describe the evaluation measures collected by AQ. Since AQ is a time-based evaluation method, each of the measures is a function of time. This allows for unbiased test of the analytic capabilities of the evaluated methods: measuring performance by recall steps does not reflect the computational efficiency of the evaluated method. AQ provides a clear overview of the methods' performance with respect to both relevance and efficiency.

The natural starting point is judging the relevance of the items suggested to the user by the evaluated method. For this, we use the classic metrics which have been the cornerstone of multimedia analysis evaluation for years: recall and precision. Let I_r be the set of relevant items in the collection and $\widehat{I}_r(t)$ the set of relevant items seen by the actor up until time t. I denotes the entire collection, and $\widehat{I}(t)$ corresponds to the set of items seen by the actor up until time t. RECALL ($R(t)$) is defined as:

$$R(t) = \frac{|\widehat{I}_r(t)|}{|I_r|} \tag{6}$$

PRECISION ($P(t)$) is:

$$P(t) = \frac{|\widehat{I}_r(t)|}{|\widehat{I}(t)|} \tag{7}$$

These two metrics have time and again proved their mettle with respect to judging the relevance of the results. Another analytic consideration is the diversity of the results, as already considered by the diversity benchmarks and datasets mentioned in Section 2. An exploring analyst will want to see as many different kinds of items as possible. In general, it is difficult to evaluate diversity. Fortunately, for AQ, we can utilize the arbiter annotations. Let $\mathcal{A}$ denote the set of all arbiter annotations, and $\widehat{\mathcal{A}}(t)$ the set of annotations encountered in the seen items up until time t. The measure of DIVERSITY ($D(t)$) of results shown to the actor is then defined as:

$$D(t) = \frac{|\widehat{\mathcal{A}}(t)|}{|\mathcal{A}|} \tag{8}$$

A notion which is rarely taken into account by benchmarks is the evaluated method's speed with respect to producing the results, despite efficiency and responsiveness being a crucial requirement for many multimedia analytics systems. Since the evaluation sessions in AQ run uninterrupted, the time the evaluated method takes to produce results occupies an important portion of t_s and as such should be evaluated. Let $|\widehat{I}(t)|^{\max} = \lfloor \frac{t}{t_1^a} \rfloor$ denote the maximum number of items that the actor could have processed by time t, given the time to process 1 item (t_1^a). The THROUGHPUT ($T(t)$) measure is then the ratio of the true number of items seen by the actor to the theoretical maximum:

$$T(t) = \frac{|\widehat{I}(t)|}{|\widehat{I}(t)|^{\max}} \tag{9}$$

The last important concern that we consider in this work is the ability to estimate the ratio of relevant items per category to the size of the entire collection. This ratio has been shown to greatly affect the perception of precision-recall results [8], so it is imperative that AQ reports it. Giving the user a correct impression about the ratio is also important for analytic purposes. For example, consider a medical scientist wanting to establish the percentage of patients with cancer. An analytic tool that she uses to explore the collection of body scans should be able to give her a correct estimate throughout the exploration. Let $RS_C = \frac{|I_C|}{|I|}$ denote the size of the set of the items in category $C \in C^a$ relative to the entire collection I and $\widehat{RS}_C(t) = \frac{|\widehat{I_C}(t)|}{|\hat{I}(t)|}$ denote the relative size estimate based on what the actor has seen up until time t. Using these values, we can enumerate how much the relative size estimate over- and underestimates the true value by computing $\frac{\widehat{RS}_C(t)}{RS_C}$ and $\frac{RS_C}{\widehat{RS}_C(t)}$, respectively. For the purposes of our measure, we treat over- and underestimation equally. The RELEVANCE PERCENTAGE ESTIMATE ($RPE(t)$) measure for actor a is then the minimum of these two values, averaged over all relevance categories of the actor:

$$RPE(t) = \frac{1}{|C^a|} \sum_{C \in C^a} \min \left(\frac{\widehat{RP}_C(t)}{RP_C}, \frac{RP_C}{\widehat{RP}_C(t)} \right) \quad (10)$$

For each of those measures, a value per each actor needs to be determined. Let $\bar{X}^a$ denote the final value of measure X for actor a. T and D are computed for the entire session at once by design, and hence $\bar{T}^a = T(t_s)$ and $\bar{D}^a = D(t_s)$. For R, P, and RPE, the value for actor a is the average over all segments seg in the actor's set of segments (denoted S_a):

$$\bar{X}^a = \frac{1}{|S_a|} \sum_{seg \in S_a} X(t_{seg}), \quad X \in \{R, P, RPE\} \quad (11)$$

Let $\bar{X}$ denote the final value of measure X. The final value for each measure $X \in \{R, P, D, T, RPE\}$ is then the average of values per actor:

$$\bar{X} = \frac{1}{n_A} \sum_{a \in A} \bar{X}^a, \quad X \in \{R, P, D, T, RPE\} \quad (12)$$

The analytic quality measure ($\mathbf{aq}_m$) of the evaluated method m is then the vector of the individual final values:

$$\mathbf{aq}_m = (\bar{R}, \bar{P}, \bar{D}, \bar{T}, \overline{RPE}) \quad (13)$$

3.5 Interpretation

Rather than being a single metric, AQ is a *collection* of metrics. Each of them captures a different aspect of the analytics process and can be easily interpreted. Apart from the classic presentation of the results in a table, an especially strong tool for interpreting results is the *time plot*, plotting time on the x axis and the individual measures on the y axis. For the time plots, individual values are computed per observer time tick, showing the development of the measures with respect to time with fine detail. The time frame provides a fair analytic comparison of individual methods by showing the naked truth about what the analyst sees and can work with at time t. The traditional recall-step-based plots, on the other hand, can easily disguise shortcomings with respect to key analytic aspects. For example throughput: as long as the method provides more relevant results, it is always shown to be the best, even if it is unusably slow. This can result in a warped view of the performance of the individual methods.

Comparing two sets of measures to assess ranking of multiple evaluated methods might be difficult. To tackle this problem, we propose AQ^{svm}, which learns the key aspects of the interplay between individual AQ measures. Let $\mathbf{aq}^a_m$ denote the vector of AQ measures corresponding to method m and actor a:

$$\mathbf{aq}^a_m = (\bar{R}^a, \bar{P}^a, \bar{D}^a, \bar{T}^a, \overline{RPE}^a) \quad (14)$$

Computing AQ^{svm}_m for method m then involves the following steps:

1. Collect AQ^a_{rand}, the set containing the AQ vectors for all actors $a \in A$ obtained by a random baseline, which always suggest a uniform random sample from the collection (without repetition):

$$AQ^a_{\text{rand}} = \bigcup_{a \in A} \mathbf{aq}^a_{\text{rand}} \quad (15)$$

2. Collect AQ^a_M, the set containing the AQ vectors for all actors $a \in A$ for all evaluated methods $m \in M$:

$$AQ^a_M = \bigcup_{\substack{m \in M \\ a \in A}} \mathbf{aq}^a_m \quad (16)$$

3. Train a linear SVM model using the vectors in AQ^a_M as positive training data and the vectors in AQ^a_{rand} as negative training data.

4. For each method m, AQ^{svm}_m is equal to the SVM score assigned to $\mathbf{aq}_m$ by the model trained in the previous step.

The intuition behind AQ^{svm} is as follows. The linear SVM model fits a separating hyperplane into the space of AQ measures such that the margin between positives (the actual evaluated methods) and the random baseline is maximal. We want our evaluated methods to be as far from this separating hyperplane (and thus, from the random baseline), as possible. Hence, comparing two methods, the one with higher AQ^{svm} wins. The difference between the AQ^{svm} values of the random baseline and the evaluated methods also indicate the benefit of using the methods over a simple random baseline: the higher the difference, the better. AQ^{svm} thus provides easy, powerful, and non-parametric aggregation of the AQ measures for easy comparison of methods.

Overall, using AQ measures has a number of distinct advantages. They provide rich information beyond simple relevance. Taken into account separately, they shed light on the evaluated methods' performance with respect to distinct key analytic aspects. Time plot analysis provides a fair comparison of methods, and it is easy to compare how the individual methods fare in different stages of the analytic session. AQ^{svm} provides a simple way to aggregate AQ measures for the purpose of ranking of individual methods. Moreover, individual AQ measures can be selected or discarded based on their importance to a specific purpose. This applies to all interpretation techniques presented in this section. Combining the time-based nature of the AQ measures with the insight-centered artificial actor model employed to obtain them yields a much broader and richer perspective of the evaluated methods' capabilities than the classic benchmark paradigm and shedding light on the potential insight gain by a real user.

4. SHOWCASE

In this section, we demonstrate the capabilities of AQ on an example analytic task. Note that AQ itself is independent of this showcase example, both in terms of task definition and the evaluated methods. For the showcase task, an

Table 1: Showcase AQ results.

Method	R	P	T	D	RPE
`random`	0.037	0.014	**0.999**	**0.443**	**0.405**
`vis`	**0.263**	0.134	0.532	0.218	0.105
`txt`	0.186	0.070	0.977	0.397	0.271
`mm`	0.203	**0.138**	0.465	0.239	0.108

Table 2: AQ^{svm} results for *search* (precision and recall) and *exploration* (precision and diversity).

Method	AQ^{svm}, *search*	AQ^{svm}, *exploration*
`random`	-0.11	0.12
`vis`	**1.73**	0.85
`txt`	1.02	0.45
`mm`	1.39	**0.87**

urban planner employed by the municipality of Amsterdam has downloaded a dataset of 20,000 Flickr images with their associated text related to Amsterdam. Her task is to quickly assess neighbourhood decay: deserted and/or poorly maintained buildings, graffiti, waste, loiterers etc. She wants to discover which neighbourhoods are problematic and what the problems are. The analytic session starts with the analyst providing three relevant examples of a multimedia item capturing a problematic aspect, i.e., with a query by example. Then, the session proceeds with the analyst going over the multimedia items provided by the analytic system, exploring the collection and interacting with the system throughout the session, steering the flow of the task by her current notion of relevance.

In our showcase, we want to see whether it is more beneficial for the analyst to use a system guiding her using a simple interactive learning algorithm, or if she is better off just selecting items at random. As designers, we want to see the build-up of quick insight, setting t_s to 15 minutes. For the other two parameters, number of actors (n_A) and time to process 1 item (t_1^a), we use the defaults, i.e., $n_A = 100$, $t_1^a = 1\ s$. To evaluate the methods, we employ AQ. We are interested in the overall picture AQ paints. Since neighbourhood decay is a wide semantic notion, we will be looking at the performance of the individual methods with respect to using a broad image concept/topic dictionary. More specifically, we want to assess individual methods' capabilities with respect to both exploration and search, as the analyst in our case will need both: exploring the city and seeing diverse neighbourhoods, but also being able to search for specific signs of neighbourhood decay matching her relevance criteria.

The data processing step involved collecting the arbiter annotations and the visual and text features to be used for the interactive learning method. Since we are interested in the methods' performance on varying images, we opt for arbiter models that have been shown to work well on natural images and general text corpora. As the arbiter visual annotations, we used the 1000 ImageNet visual concepts provided by the Inception convolutional deep net conceived by Szegedy et al. [30], the winning entry of ILSRVC 2014. As the arbiter text annotations, we employed latent Dirichlet allocation to extract 100 latent topics using the Gensim framework [36]. As the visual features for the interactive learning method, we use 15k concepts provided by a custom Inception network retrained to provide annotations for all ImageNet classes with more than 200 examples. The text features for the interactive learning method are 300 latent topics again extracted using Gensim [36].

The random baseline (further denoted as `random`) simply returns a uniform random sample of the collection. The interactive learning method we use is a simple linear SVM model trained on the visual modality only (further denoted as `vis`), a linear SVM trained on the text modality only (`txt`); or two linear SVM models, one per modality, whose results are fused using Borda count (`mm`). The interactive learning method is seeded by three relevant examples provided by the user before the start of the session. After each relevance indication by the user, the interactive learning algorithm updates the positives and negatives, retrains the model accordingly, and provides its item suggestions based on the retrained model. All methods return 5 results at a time for the user to process. Each item can be seen up to one time, i.e., the user sees no repeated suggestions.

The AQ results are summarized in Table 1. If we would look at the results through the optics of the classic relevance-based paradigm, the clear winner is `vis`, winning over all competitors significantly in recall while being a very close second to `mm` on precision. All intelligent learning approaches dominate the `random` baseline on precision and recall. However, a broader look at all the components of AQ reveals that there are analytic components like diversity and relevance percentage estimation where `random` ranks first. These seem to be correlated to throughput, emphasizing that important elements of analytic quality can be dependent on the performance of the algorithm. In addition, `random`, due to it's fairness in selecting suggestions, covers a wider range of different kinds of items in the collection. These aspects of multimedia analytics are neither shown nor enumerated by the classic evaluation approaches.

To judge the exploration and search capabilities of individual methods, we obtain the respective AQ^{svm} scores. We aggregate precision and recall for the search AQ^{svm}, following the classic relevance-based paradigm. For the exploration AQ^{svm}, we use precision and diversity. The AQ^{svm} scores are summarized in Table 2. AQ^{svm} confirms the intuition with respect to search, which is purely relevance-based: `vis` comes out strongly on top, `mm` second, `txt` third. The `random` baseline is scored far from the intelligent learning methods, confirming the big gap with respect to relevance. In the exploration case, `mm` pulls slightly ahead of `vis`, which exactly reflects the situation when looking at D and P individually in Table 1. The gap between `random` and the winner is much smaller than in the case of search. This reflects that the `random` baseline is actually very strong in one of the characteristics and it is not as easy to discriminate `random` from the intelligent learning methods as in the case of search. AQ^{svm} is thus shown to provide a meaningful, comprehensive purpose-based ranking of methods.

The time plot of individual AQ metrics (Figure 4) gives additional insights with respect to the development of the metrics over time. Let $t = 150\ s$ be roughly the boundary of the early stage of exploration. Drawing this boundary, as shown in Figure 4, allows easy comparison of individual methods in the early vs. the late stage. In the precision plot, we notice that `mm` is strongly dominant in the early stage. After that point, the precision of `mm` and `vis` remains similar until the end of the session. This can be interpreted

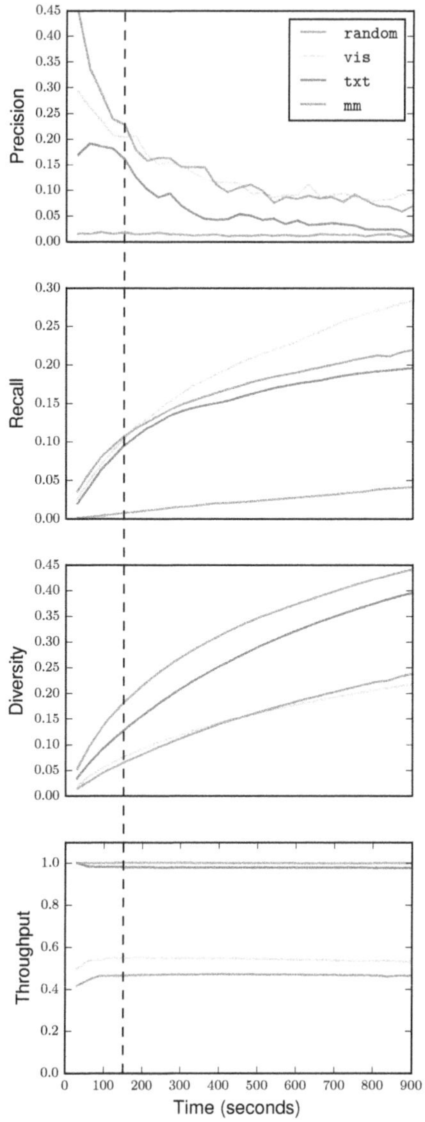

Figure 4: *AQ* time plots with $t = 150\ s$ marking the boundary of the early stage of the session.

as mm being very strong in the "pure query response" phase when the notion of relevance is constant. At the same time, it is lackluster in adapting to the insight changes, since it experiences the sharpest drop out of all intelligent learning methods. This gives a suggestion for improvement: since the model works well with a small number of positives/negatives and much worse with more, introducing decay to keep only the last few relevance indications might improve the performance. The recall plot confirms the modality synergy of the mm algorithm in the early stage and shows that mm is being significantly dragged down by the underperforming txt method in the later stages. The diversity plot reveals that the solid txt performance is not reflected in the mm method at all. The recall and diversity analyses give yet another suggestion: since the text modality is beneficial only initially, switching it off in the mm algorithm after a certain time might be considered to increase performance. As a side effect, this would increase throughput, which is also desirable. Overall, the time plot analysis reveals key strengths and weaknesses of individual algorithms, providing design insight into what to improve and what to exploit.

Compared with the classic evaluation taking into account only precision and recall or derivations thereof (mAP, F-measure etc.), *AQ* offers a much broader overview. In our case, it was able to characterize the four evaluated algorithms, pinpointing which techniques are more suitable for exploration and which for search. Moreover, the *AQ* analysis highlighted particular aspects to focus on in the case of mm method, which can be used to further improve its performance. This would not have been possible by just comparing individual values across evaluated methods, as is the case in the classic benchmark paradigm. *AQ* thus not only reveals *which* method is the best, but, unlike the classic evaluation approaches, also gives insights into the *why*.

5. CONCLUSION

In this paper, we presented *AQ* (analytic quality), a novel paradigm for multimedia analysis method design and evaluation. It significantly expands on the classic relevance evaluation paradigm by adding a number of real-life analytic considerations to the table, namely time, interactivity, and user insight. The time-based nature of *AQ* provides both the method designers and the end users with a picture about the analytic capabilities in a realistic time-limited setting, removing the strong assumption that the analyst will go over all the results. Including interactivity and evolving insight into the user model mimicks real user behaviour. This, in conjunction with using multiple evaluation metrics, each capturing a different aspect of the method, provides a much more detailed feedback and conclusions for further design improvement than just comparing two values of mean average precision. Another distinct advantage is the modularity of *AQ*. Metrics of interest can be selected for different method purposes, and new ones can be easily collected from the artificial actor sessions on demand. Moving multimedia analysis evaluation towards realistic analytic settings involving end users is certainly desirable. *AQ* is a leap forward on this path, bringing new challenges to the multimedia community which the computer vision and machine learning communities cannot yet address.

6. ACKNOWLEDGMENTS

This research is supported by the Dutch Technology Foundation STW, which is part of the Netherlands Organisation for Scientific Research (NWO), and which is partly funded by the Ministry of Economic Affairs.

7. REFERENCES

[1] D. Borth, R. Ji, T. Chen, T. Breuel, and S.-F. Chang. Large-scale visual sentiment ontology and detectors using adjective noun pairs. In *ACM MM*, pages 223–232, 2013.

[2] O. Chapelle, D. Metlzer, Y. Zhang, and P. Grinspan. Expected reciprocal rank for graded relevance. In *ACM CIKM*, pages 621–630, 2009.

[3] T. Demeester, D. Trieschnigg, D. Nguyen, K. Zhou, and D. Hiemstra. Overview of the TREC 2014 federated Web search track. In *TREC*, 2014.

[4] M. Eskevich, R. Aly, R. Ordelman, S. Chen, and G. J. F. Jones. The search and hyperlinking task at MediaEval 2013. In *MediaEval*, 2013.

[5] M. Everingham, L. V. Gool, C. K. I. Williams, J. Winn, and A. Zisserman. The PASCAL Visual Object Classes (VOC) challenge. *IJCV*, 88(2):303–338, 2010.

[6] T. M. Green, W. Ribarsky, and B. Fisher. Building and applying a human cognition model for visual analytics. *InfoVis*, 8(1):1–13, Mar. 2009.

[7] X.-S. Hua, Y. Ming, and J. Li. Mining knowledge from clicks: MSR-Bing image retrieval challenge. In *IEEE ICMEW*, pages 1–4, 2014.

[8] D. P. Huijsmans and N. Sebe. How to complete performance graphs in content-based image retrieval: Add generality and normalize scope. *IEEE TPAMI*, 27(2), Feb. 2005.

[9] B. Ionescu, M. Menéndez, H. Müller, and A. Popescu. Retrieving diverse social images at MediaEval 2013: Objectives, dataset, and evaluation. In *MediaEval*, 2013.

[10] B. Ionescu, A.-L. Radu, M. Menéndez, H. Müller, A. Popescu, and B. Loni. Div400: A social image retrieval result diversification dataset. In *ACM MMSys*, pages 29–34, 2014.

[11] A. Jaimes, N. Sebe, and D. Gatica-Perez. Human-centered computing: A multimedia perspective. In *ACM MM*, pages 855–864, 2006.

[12] K. Järvelin and J. Kekäläinen. Cumulated gain-based evaluation of IR techniques. *ACM TOIS*, 20(4):422–446, Oct. 2002.

[13] Y. Jia, E. Shelhamer, J. Donahue, S. Karayev, J. Long, R. Girshick, S. Guadarrama, and T. Darrell. Caffe: Convolutional architecture for fast feature embedding. In *ACM MM*, pages 675–678, 2014.

[14] M. A. Larson, B. Ionescu, X. Anguera, M. Eskevich, P. Korshunov, M. Schedl, M. Soleymani, G. Petkos, R. F. E. Sutcliffe, J. Choi, and G. J. F. Jones, editors. *Working Notes Proceedings of the MediaEval 2014 Workshop*, 2014.

[15] A. Lavie and A. Agarwal. Meteor: An automatic metric for mt evaluation with high levels of correlation with human judgments. In *StatMT*, pages 228–231.

[16] M. Lestari Paramita, M. Sanderson, and P. Clough. Diversity in photo retrieval: Overview of the ImageCLEF photo task 2009. In *Multilingual Information Access Evaluation II. Multimedia Experiments*, pages 45–59. 2010.

[17] Y. Li and B. Merialdo. VERT: Automatic evaluation of video summaries. In *ACM MM*, pages 851–854, 2010.

[18] C.-Y. Lin. ROUGE: A package for automatic evaluation of summaries. In *ACL*, pages 74–81, 2004.

[19] A. Nenkova, R. Passonneau, and K. McKeown. The pyramid method: Incorporating human content selection variation in summarization evaluation. *ACM TSLP*, 4(2), May 2007.

[20] C. North. Towards measuring visualization insight. *IEEE TCGA*, 26(3):6–9, 2006.

[21] C. North, P. Saraiya, and K. Duca. A comparison of benchmark task and insight evaluation methods for information visualization. *InfoVis*, 10(3):162–181, July 2011.

[22] P. Over, A. F. Smeaton, and G. Awad. The TRECVid 2008 BBC Rushes summarization evaluation. In *ACM TRECVid Video Summarization Workshop*, ACM MM, pages 1–20, 2008.

[23] K. Papineni, S. Roukos, T. Ward, and W.-J. Zhu. BLEU: A method for automatic evaluation of machine translation. In *ACL*, pages 311–318, 2002.

[24] W. A. Pike, J. Stasko, R. Chang, and T. A. O'Connell. The science of interaction. *InfoVis*, 8(4):263–274, 2009.

[25] S. Rudinac, M. Larson, and A. Hanjalic. Learning crowdsourced user preferences for visual summarization of image collections. *IEEE TMM*, 15(6), Oct. 2013.

[26] O. Russakovsky, J. Deng, H. Su, J. Krause, S. Satheesh, S. Ma, Z. Huang, A. Karpathy, A. Khosla, M. Bernstein, A. C. Berg, and L. Fei-Fei. ImageNet Large Scale Visual Recognition Challenge. *arXiv:1409.0575*, 2014.

[27] M. Sanderson, M. L. Paramita, P. Clough, and E. Kanoulas. Do user preferences and evaluation measures line up? In *ACM SIGIR*, pages 555–562, 2010.

[28] K. Schoeffmann. A user-centric media retrieval competition: The video browser showdown 2012-2014. *IEEE Multimedia*, 21(4):8–13, 2014.

[29] M. D. Smucker and C. L. A. Clarke. Time-based calibration of effectiveness measures. In *ACM SIGIR*, pages 95–104, 2012.

[30] C. Szegedy, W. Liu, Y. Jia, P. Sermanet, S. Reed, D. Anguelov, D. Erhan, V. Vanhoucke, and A. Rabinovich. Going deeper with convolutions. *arXiv:1409.4842*, 2014.

[31] J. J. Thomas and K. A. Cook. *Illuminating the Path: The Research and Development Agenda for Visual Analytics*. IEEE Computer Society, 2005.

[32] B. Thomée and M. S. Lew. Interactive search in image retrieval: a survey. *Int J of MIR*, 1(2):71–86, July 2012.

[33] S. Tong and E. Chang. Support vector machine active learning for image retrieval. In *ACM MM*, pages 107–118, 2001.

[34] P. van der Corput and J. J. van Wijk. Effects of presentation mode and pace control on performance in image classification. *IEEE TVCG*, 20(12):2301–2309, Dec. 2014.

[35] R. Vedantam, C. L. Zitnick, and D. Parikh. CIDEr: Consensus-based image description evaluation. *arXiv:1411.5726*, 2015.

[36] R. Řehůřek and P. Sojka. Software framework for topic modelling with large corpora. In *LREC*, pages 45–50, 2010.

[37] J. Zahálka, S. Rudinac, and M. Worring. New Yorker Melange: Interactive brew of personalized venue recommendations. In *ACM MM*, pages 205–208, 2014.

[38] J. Zahálka and M. Worring. Towards interactive, intelligent, and integrated multimedia analytics. In *IEEE VAST*, pages 3–12, 2014.

Dancing with *Turks*

I-Kao Chiang[◇] Ian Spiro[†] Seungkyu Lee[⋆] Alyssa Lees[†] Jingchen Liu[‡]
Chris Bregler[†] Yanxi Liu[‡]
[◇]Dept. of Computer and Information Science, University of Pennsylvania, Philadelphia, PA, USA
[†]Dept. of Computer Science, Courant Institute, New York University, New York, NY, USA
[⋆]Dept. of Computer Engineering, KyungHee University, Yongin-si, South Korea
[‡]School of Electrical Engineering and Computer Science,
The Pennsylvania State University, University Park, PA, USA
{igorchiang,ispiro,seungkyu74,alyssa.lees,jasonliu401,chris.bregler}@gmail.com
yanxi@cse.psu.edu (corresponding author)

ABSTRACT

Dance is a dynamic art form that reflects a wide range of cultural diversity and individuality. With the advancement of motion-capture technology combined with crowd-sourcing and machine learning algorithms, we explore the complex relationship between perceived dance quality/dancer's gender and dance movements/music respectively. As a feasibility study, we construct a computational framework for an analysis-synthesis-feedback loop using a novel multimedia *dance-music texture* representation. Furthermore, we integrate crowd-sourcing, music and motion-capture data, and machine learning-based methods for dance segmentation, analysis and synthesis of new dancers. A quantitative validation of this framework on a motion-capture dataset of 172 dancers evaluated by more than 400 independent on-line raters demonstrates significant correlation between human perception and the algorithmically intended dance quality or gender of synthesized dancers. The technology illustrated in this work has a high potential to advance the multimedia entertainment industry via *dancing with Turks*.

Categories and Subject Descriptors

I.2.6 [**Computing Methodologies**]: ARTIFICIAL INTELLIGENCE—*Learning*

Keywords

Dance perception; Crowd-sourcing; Motion-capture; Dance-texture; Feature selection; Regression; Dance-texture synthesis; Animation

1. INTRODUCTION

As digital media comes of age, massive multi-media data sets have become commonplace while computational tools to discover their intricate relations are scarce. With the introduction of crowd-sourcing technology, human perception-driven algorithms become more feasible. In social (non-choreographed) dance, perception by others plays an important role to our understanding of social dynamics among dancers and viewers. Our goal in this work is to develop a computational framework and associated tools for dance perception, driven by active, on-line audience participation. The feasibility of our framework has been validated on a multi-media, multi-dimensional data set composed of motion capture data of 172 Jamaican dancers of both genders free-dancing to the same music. Our initial investigation focuses on the dance quality (good, bad) and dancer's gender (masculine, feminine), since the perception of these two attributes has a direct impact on social dynamics reflected in social dance across different cultures.

We combine a suite of signal processing, machine learning, animation and social media technology to discover mappings between human dance perception and a set of measurable, isolatable and controllable human body joint parameters. More specifically, from an initial set of 25 human ratings per dancer, we use a weakly supervised learning method to learn dance ability and dancer's gender discriminative features composed of subsets of body joints (angular displacement, velocity and acceleration) and to construct a multivariate regression model that captures human-perceived dance quality and dancer's gender. We then employ these learned features as "control knobs" for music-motion-correlated dance segments to synthesize ability or gender-targeted new dancers. To close the loop, the synthesized dancers are re-evaluated via crowd-sourcing by hundreds of online Mechanical Turk workers (Figure 1). The main contributions of our work:
(1) a novel machine learning-based, human perception-driven computational framework for dance analysis, synthesis and validation from multimedia data (music, motion-capture data and human ratings);
(2) a novel spatiotemporal *dance texture* and *music texture* joint representation, and a novel dance texture synthesis algorithm, confirmed to be visually convincing by Mechanical Turks with statistical significance;
(3) an effective human-in-the-loop initiative that uses crowd-sourcing both as an initialization for machine learning and as a validation for the dance analysis and synthesis algorithms (Figure 1).

MM'15, October 26–30, 2015, Brisbane, Australia.
 ISBN 978-1-4503-3459-4/15/10 ...$15.00.
DOI: http://dx.doi.org/10.1145/2733373.2806220.

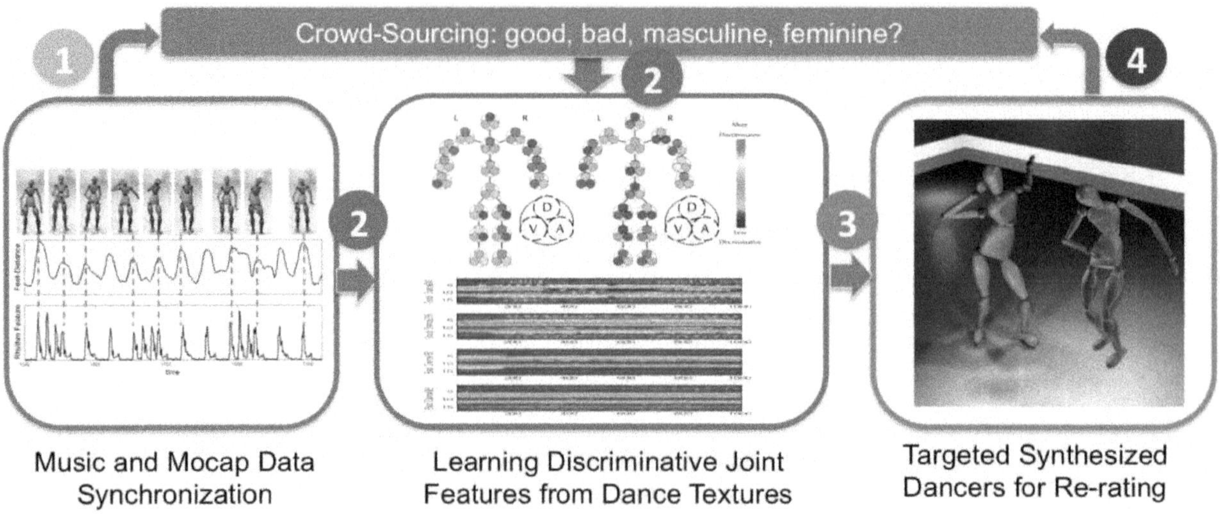

Figure 1: The outline of our multi-media computational framework: after computing the synchronization between the raw mocap and music data (Section 3.1) we (1) obtain a set of initial human ratings via crowd-sourcing on dance ability and dancer's gender; (2) input both synchronized mocap/music data and the human ratings for analysis (Section 3.2), where we discover, automatically, the most discriminative human joint feature subsets (D: displacement, V: velocity, A: acceleration) for dance ability and dancer's gender respectively; (3) synthesize targeted new dancers (for example: a level-5 (highest level) dancer or a female dancer) using learned discriminative body joint features (Section 3.3); and (4) feed the newly synthesized targeted dancers to on-line human raters (the Mechanical Turks) for re-evaluation of dance ability and dancer's gender (Section 3.4). Finally, we compare the statistical consistency between human perception and the intended/targeted dancer's ability and gender (Table 2).

2. RELATED WORK

"Human in the loop" applications span many research disciplines from the creation of simulation software like flight simulators to the more active solicitations of human feedback for image retrieval [37, 27]. Using crowd-sourcing to improve the performance of computer vision algorithms has become more feasible in recent years, especially for those data sets with visually distinct objects, such as identification of birds, and parts of a bird[1]. Many research disciplines such as machine learning, mathematical optimization, automatic control, cyber-physical systems, and autonomic computing rely on feedback to achieve goals such as autonomy, learning, adaptation, stabilization, robustness, or performance optimization[2]. Our effort differs from these in that the human perception of dance we use is at a *general impression* level instead of specific object instance/parts or feature labeling by the human users. The localization details (which body joints) are learned automatically in our work. Many *motion perceptual experiments* are relevant to our work, dating back to the famous Johannsson Experiments [14], particularly those perceptual experiments on gender classification [16, 30]. There is also a vast literature on automatic motion analysis techniques [8] beyond the scope of this paper.

Previous work in style transfer (e.g. transforming from "happy" to "sad" while preserving walking to location A) has looked at applying user-specified style to an existing motion sequence [34, 13, 32, 7, 28], or existing style in a motion capture database to new motion paths [12, 1, 15, 17, 26, 33, 36]. Most of the recent techniques build a graph structure out of large amounts of motion capture data [1, 15] and have been inspired by earlier systems in speech recognition [23], video face animations [4], and video textures [29]. Related to style transfer are methods that integrate stylistic variables into generative models to synthesize stylized motion directly. Brand and Hertzmann [3] modeled style and content using HMMs whose emission distributions depend on stylistic parameters learned from data. More sophisticated models have been introduced using other HMM extensions, Gaussian Processes and hierarchical models applied to style variations [18, 35, 25]. The most complex architecture, based on so called "deep networks", has been introduced by Taylor and Hinton using explicit stylistic variables to modulate the interactions of binary latent variables modeling dynamics and real-valued variables representing pose [31].

Different from example-based motion synthesis, our work depends on fuzzy input from human raters that may or may not agree with each other. We face both the question of how to use such inconsistent labeling as well as figuring out what body motion attributes dominate human perceptual evaluation.

Directed graphs have been used, e.g. [15], as a primary motion/dance representation with edges corresponding to clips of motion and nodes as choice of connecting points. Other dance representations are typically one dimensional along the time axis [18, 26]. Our *dance texture* proposed in this work is a true 2-dimensional image (Section 3.1). Our dance texture synthesis algorithm is the first to adapt the "*Markov properties*", employed in image-based near-regular texture synthesis [11, 19, 22], into a multimodal audio-spatio-temporal *dance texture* space.

[1] http://www.vision.caltech.edu/visipedia/

[2] *The Feedback Computing workshop 2013*

3. OUR APPROACH

We start with a given piece of music, *Elephant Man*, sampled at a standard 44.1 kHz stereo, and a set of *asynchronized* motion capture (mocap) data of 172 Jamaican (teenage) dancers of both genders (equal distribution) free-dancing to the same music[3]. Independently, we collected 25 human ratings for each dancer on both the perceived dance-ability and the perceived gender, where each human rater is shown a replay of a dancer's mocap data on a computer screen, and asked to provide a score between 0 (female) and 1 (male) for gender; and a score between 1 (bad) and 5 (good) for dance quality or dancer's ability. We use the average of ability (gender) ratings for each dancer in our subsequent analysis.

Our goal is to develop computational means that can (1) learn the most discriminative body-joint features for regression models best corresponding to human ratings; (2) use this knowledge to generate new dancers with intended dance ability or gender; and (3) validate the synthesized dancers via human perception using independent human raters (Mechanical Turks).

To facilitate the discovery of the intricate relationships between human perception and the body movements, we first propose a spatiotemporal representation of mocap data, *Dance Texture* (Figure 2), and synchronize the 2-dimensional dance texture with the 1-dimensional music texture along the time axis.

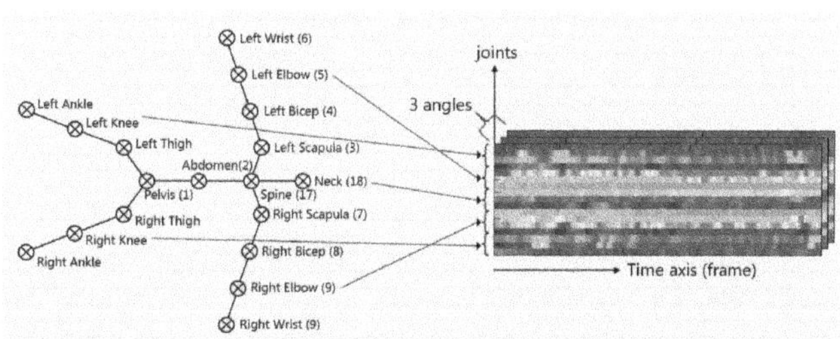

Figure 2: Left: The 18 body joints captured by the motion capture data. Right: A dance texture of three layers, $P_{axis}(time, joints)$, $axis : X, Y, Z$, capturing joint rotation angles about each axis. P is a 2D frieze-like pattern/image, extending along the (horizontal) time axis bilaterally centered about the four mid-body-joints: neck, spine, abdomen, and pelvis.

3.1 Dance Texture and Music Texture

Dance Texture

Since human motion capture (mocap) data captures joint rotation angles about the corresponding joint axes X, Y, Z respectively [5, 24], we define a dance texture $P_{axis}(time, joints)$, where $axis : X, Y, Z$. Each P_{axis} is 2D frieze-like pattern extending along the time axis horizontally from left to right (Figure 2). Since the human body presents a natural bilateral symmetry, we place the left-right body joints correspondingly around the four mid-body joints. Each point on the dance texture P_{axis} denotes the twist angle value about its rotation axis $X(Y, Z)$, represented here in the color scheme of $[R, G, B]$. Each column of $P_{axis}(time = i, :)$ represents a pose of the dancer at time i and each row of $P_{axis}(:, joint = j)$ represents the angular values of a specific body joint j along time axis. For simplicity, we sometimes omit the rotation axis indicator X, Y, Z in $P_{axis}(i, j)$ by summing by up all twist angles at i,j as $P(i, j)$.

Music Texture

When transforming music input into the frequency domain using conventional Fourier transform, the frequencies corresponding to integer multiples of 0.44 Hz and 0.88 Hz i.e. harmonics of 0.44 Hz, stand out in the music power spectrum and the average dancer power spectrum respectively (Fig.3 (A)). This clearly suggests that the music and the dancers have commensurate periodicity and the ratio between the fundamental frequencies is 2 (0.88 Hz/0.44 Hz).

Dance Texture and Music Texture Synchronization

The corresponding periods in the dance and music textures are captured computationally, while the alignment between dance and music remains ambiguous. Exploring different body joints, a strong correlation between the feet separation and the up-beat is observed and captured computationally. Since the music and body-motion signals have shared cycle lengths, we only need to compute the offset within a single period T. The beat signal $b(t)$ is obtained by passing the music signal through an anti-aliasing low pass filter and then downsampling to the same $30Hz$ sampling rate as the mocap data. The music beat signal (down sampled), between-feet distance and their correlations are displayed in Figure 3 (B).

3.2 Analysis

To further explore the discriminative power of body joints in relation to human ratings, we define and extract measurements from dance texture beyond angular joint values.

Dance Texture Features

We extract from three types of dance textures: angular Displacement (D), angular Velocity (V), and angular Acceleration (A). Given a dance texture $P^d(i, j)$ for a specific dancer d with i indicating the frame number (time) and j body joint, the total number of raw features is 3 (D,V,A) $\times$18 (body joints) $\times$# frames = 54 $\times$ # frames (Figure 2). One approximation of these features is an accumulated movement of each joint $j \in [1...18]$ over the entire dance segment: $P^d_\Sigma(j) = \sum_{i=1}^{n} P^d(i, j)$ and all the possible subsets of 18, from a single joint to nine joints (and their complements), to form our initial feature set $F^d_{Displacement}$ short as F^d_D: $|F_D| = \sum_{j=1}^{9} \binom{18}{j} = 155,381$. Including angular displacements (D), angular velocity (V) and acceleration (A) measurements in an analogous manner, we obtain a feature set F^d_{DVA}, short as F^d with $|F^d| = 155,381 \times 3 = 466,143$. Since every dance has the same set of features, we can drop d and use F to express this total feature set from dancer mocap data of 172 data points (dancers) where each data point has 466,143 feature dimensions.

Dimensionality Reduction for Regression

Given the distribution of human ratings (green circles in Figure 6) for dance quality and dancers gender respectively, we propose to construct a linear regression model to approximate human perceptual labels. It is obvious that some dimensionality reduction of the dance-texture feature set F is necessary for us to learn and compute a model capturing the most relevant parameters of human perception of dance. We have experimented with multiple methods for dimensionality reduction in this work. We can summarize

[3]We obtained the raw motion capture dataset from [6] where it was used for human visualization only.

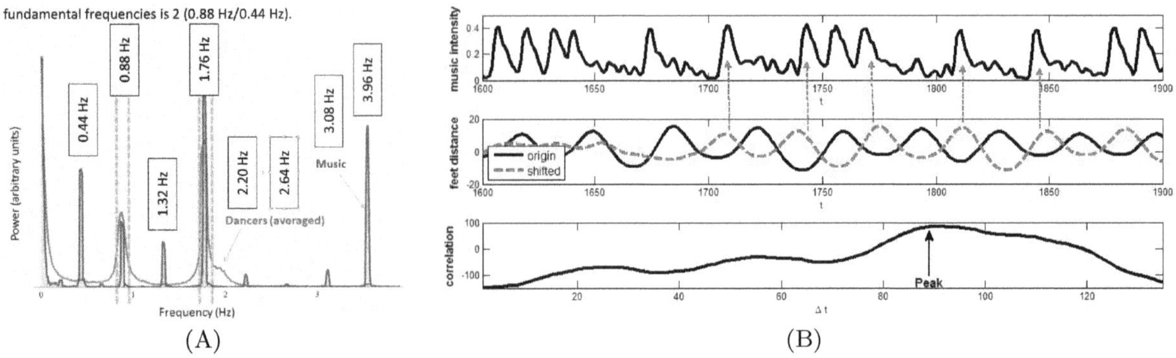

Figure 3: (A) Using the conventional Fourier transform spectral method to show representative power spectra of the music and the mocap of the dancers. The red line corresponds to the intensity averaged across all 172 dancers. The green dotted lines indicate the two regions where the integrated intensity is correlated to dancer ability. (B) Alignment of the music (30Hz sampling rate, top), between-feet distance (30Hz sampling rate, middle), and correlation score (bottom).

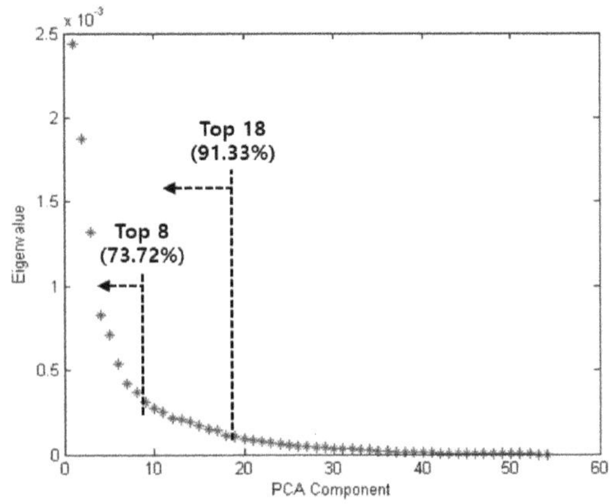

Figure 4: Eigenvalues versus Eigenvectors plot from a principle component analysis (PCA) of the dancers mocap data set. For dimensionality reduction, we experimented with taking the top 8 and top 18 eigenvectors to construct two corresponding linear regression models (Figure 6).

them into two basic categories: Principle Component Analysis (PCA)-based and machine learning-based methods.

PCA-based: For dimensionality reduction, we apply Principle Component Analysis on the raw mocap features of angular displacements for all subjects. Figure 4 shows the eigenvalue versus eigenvector plot. Using the top-8 (73% variance) and top-18 (91.33% variance) eigenvectors respectively, we built and evaluated two linear regression models against human ratings (Tabel 1, Figure 6). We pick top-8 eigenvectors since previous works using PCA methods report 8 principle components (PCs) as sufficient for capturing human motions such like gaits; and top-18 is due to the fact that 18 different body joints are captured in the dance mocap data set (Figure 2). It is worth noting that PCA is an unsupervised approach for data analysis, thus the human ratings associated with the data set play no role in the construction of the PCA-based linear regression models.

Machine Learning-based: Supervised learning is an active branch of research in general machine learning to automatically find the most discriminative features that separate different classes of data given the class labels [2]. In our case, perceptual ratings of multiple human raters are readily available, the average ratings are however not necessary discrete 'class labels' to train a classifier. We have experimented with two discriminative feature subset selection measures, which are used to select the highest ranked features to construct linear regression models for predicting human ratings on dance quality and dancer's gender respectively, achieving dimensionality reduction at the same time.

Learning-based Method #1: The first method is to find a continuous correlation value between human ratings and feature values in the dance-texture feature set F. For a feature of dancer d, $f^d \in F$, its relation to perceived rating R^d_{gender} of dancer d can be expressed as: $f = a \times R_{gender} + b$, and solved for a, b using all dancers. A $(R, p\text{-}value)$ pair can thus be computed for all features $f \in F$ and used to rank all features by their correlation value R to the perceived dancer ability or gender ratings respectively. We then pick the top N features as the most discriminative features for gender (dance ability) separation and build a pair of linear regression models that are quantitatively compared with the PCA-based regression models above (Table 1, Figure 6).

Learning-based Method #2: Alternatively, we train a set of binary-class classifiers by modifying the given human ratings. We sample a data subset where only the dancers with human ratings in the extreme ranges (say thresholds at ratings $> 75\%$ as class 1 and $\leq 25\%$ as class 0) are chosen, and use them to form a binary classification problem with discrete class labels.

Table 1: Comparisons of three regression models measured by Root-Mean-Squares (RMS) against human ratings, the RMS value is the smaller the better. Also see Figure 6.

PCA (variance captured)	Ability	Gender
Top-8 Eigenvectors (73.72%)	0.0077	0.0321
Top-18 Eigenvectors (91.33%)	0.0048	0.0218
Proposed Method	**0.0009**	**0.0087**

We use an *augmented variance ratio* (AVR) as a criteria to compute and rank discriminative features for these two classification problems (ability and gender) respectively. AVR is a variant of Fisher criterion [10] and has been used in many other biomedical image applications, e.g. [20, 21]. To make the features more compact, we perform PCA on the top N most discriminative features. A multivariate linear regression model is then constructed using the PCs found above. This regression model is trained and cross-validated using leave-one-out (LOO) on the same dance segments (500 frames/segment) the *MTurkers* have rated. We have obtained the average error rates of $12 \pm 8.6\%$ for dance ability and $14.58 \pm 10.66\%$ for gender.

The machine learning-based methods have helped us to gain new insights on the human perception of dancers:

(1) *Which body features are important?*

Figure 5 illustrates three different feature selection results demonstrating, qualitatively and quantitatively, which body joints and what type of joint measures (Displacement, Velocity, Acceleration) are discriminative for human perception of dancer quality and/or dancer's gender.

(2) *How to label/rate a given dancer algorithmically that mimics a human rater?*

The regression models built from the selected discriminative features provide a higher level, dance quality/dancer's gender *predictor* that maps an arbitrary length of dance (mocap data) into a pair of perceptual labels. This function will be used extensively in our new dance synthesis algorithm next.

Automatic Dance Texel Segmentation and Rating

As a result of music texture and dance texture synchronization (Section 3.1), we are able to segment a dance texture into a sequence of equal sized **dance-texture texels** along the time axis. Dance-texture texels are the smallest dance-texture units, each of which has the length of one music beat/measure (Figure 3), that can also be used as the building blocks for synthesizing new dancers. Since each dance texel is a short dance (one measure long), we can map it to the discriminative feature space and use our machine learning-based linear regression model to rate each dance texel on its dance quality and its dancer's gender. As a result, we have a collection of dance texels that are unit length and are automatically labeled in both dance quality and dancer's gender.

This computational *decomposition* of a long dance texture into small pieces (texels) of short dances, and the semantic labeling of each dance texel play a crucial role in: (1) Perception – each dance/dancer can be viewed as a composition of many dance texels; each texel can have its independent labels in dance quality and dancer's gender. Thus, during a long dance, it is possible to perceive a dancer as sometimes good and sometimes bad, sometimes more masculine and sometimes more feminine; (2) Synthesis – these dance texels, associated with their own ratings from our learned regression model, form the perfect dance texture synthesis *building blocks* to generate new dancers with the desired perceptual effect. Therefore, the dance-synthesis process with desired perceived gender and ability becomes a dance-texel composition procedure of mixing and matching texels from **different** dancers selectively.

3.3 Synthesis

A unique aspect of our approach is to treat dance as a 2D texture, enabling the generation of a new dance via tex-

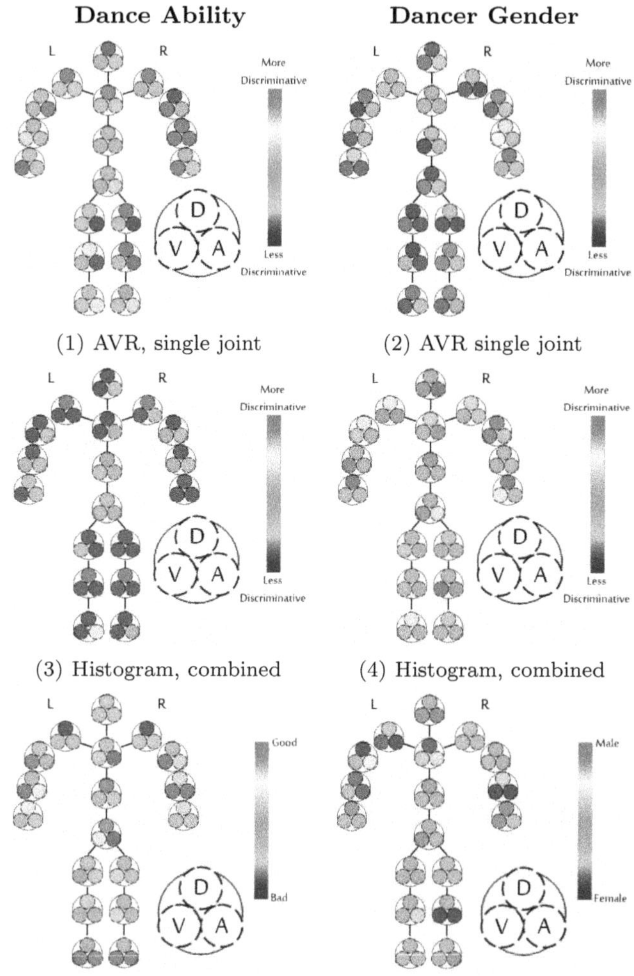

(1) AVR, single joint (2) AVR single joint

(3) Histogram, combined (4) Histogram, combined

(5) correlation, combined (6) correlation, combined

Figure 5: Using D (displacement), V (velocity), and A (acceleration) body joint features, we demonstrate the most discriminative features learned algorithmically using three different computable measures. (1, 2) are the single joint features (D,V,A) ranked and color-coded (red: most discriminative) by its respective Augmented Variance Ratio (AVR). (3,4) are combined-joint features evaluated using the histogram of the most selected (highly frequent) body joint features (from ten random splits of data into training/testing subsets). (5,6) are the feature ranking results from the correlation between *feature-subset* (D,V,A) values and the human raters labels. Several corresponding body joint features are found across three different discriminative feature selection measures. For example, all three find that left and right knee displacement and ankle velocity/acceleration in particular are most discriminative for dance quality; while the right (and left) wrist joint angel displacement, the head/neck angle velocity/acceleration, abdomen angle displacement, and pelvis angle velocity/acceleration (mostly upper body joints) highly discriminative for dancer's gender perception. Interestingly, many of these automatically found, discriminative joint features are also acknowledged by some human raters (Table 2).

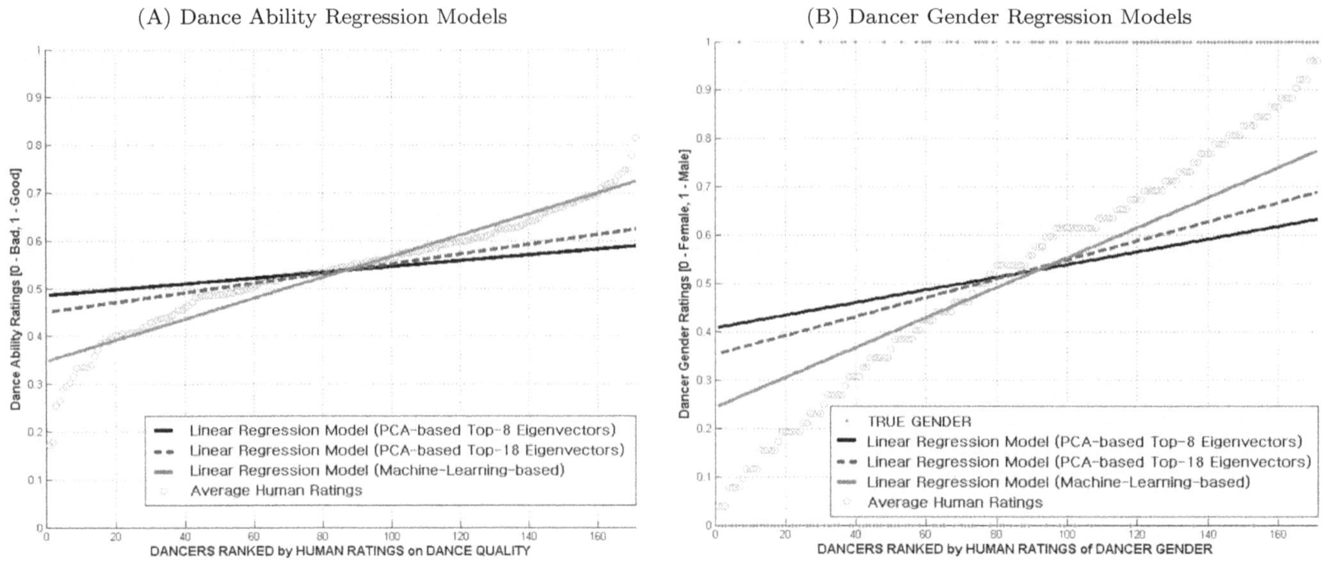

Figure 6: We compare our proposed supervised-learning-based linear regression model against non-supervised PCA-based dimensionality reduction linear models, where different top-N eigenvectors with the highest eigenvalues are used (top-8, top-18). The horizontal axes above are ranked dancers in non-decreasing order of their average human ratings (25) of dancer ability and dancer's gender respectively: bad dancer=0, good dancer=1; female=0, male=1. The three overlaid linear regression model plots, two from PCA-method using top-8 and top-18 eigenvectors respectively and one from our feature-selection method, illustrate that our proposed machine learning-based regression models align the best with human perception of dancers in terms of their dance ability and demonstrated gender; while our dance ability regression model has a better fit with human ratings than the regression model for dancers genders. Table 1 shows the root-mean-square (RMS) measures between these regression models and human ratings. It is worth noting that (1) the average human ratings (green circles) are not strictly linear either for dance quality (left) or for dancer's gender (right); and (2) the average accuracy of human gender rating with respect to dancers' true genders (red dots) is only $64.78\% \pm 7.6\%$.

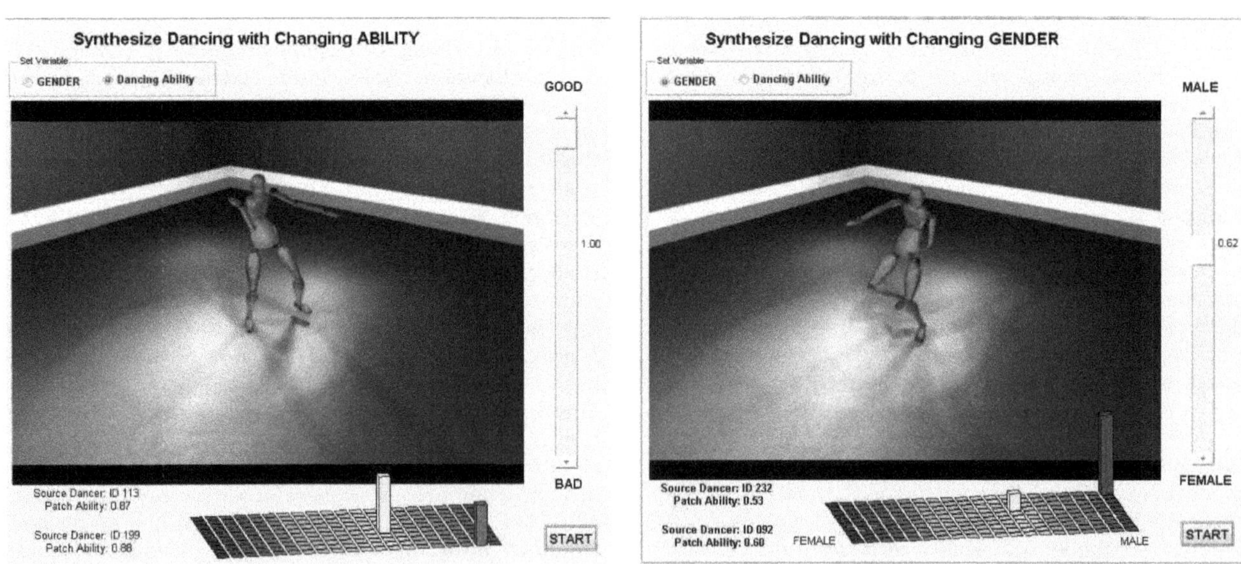

Figure 7: The user interface where the dance ability and gender of the synthesized dancer can be controlled and visualized. Each colored-square corresponds to a dancer with ranked (color-coded) label for dance quality or for dancer gender. The synthesized dance transits across smoothened dance texels/patches from different dancers (see the two color bars in transition coming out for the plane.

ture synthesis. The analogy between creating new, targeted dance animations from existing mocap data and image-based texture synthesis on 2D textures is motivated by the similarity of a common goal: to generate new (synthesized) texture samples that are *visually* and *statistically similar* to the given texture's regularity [11, 19, 22]. Dance texture/texel plays the similar *dual function* of representing spatial transformations (18-body-joint motion space) as well as a 2D color-image such like the *geometric deformation-field texture* does in the near-regular texture synthesis algorithm [19]. We map back and forth between a 2D dance texture and a motion space, guided by the intended/targeted semantic ratings.

Different from general texture synthesis however, the regularity of a music texture guides us to segment a dance texture into unit-length dance texels. The basic idea for our dance texture synthesis algorithm is: given a desired level of dance ability (gender), our algorithm generates a piece of dance texture that meets the goal by choosing from the candidate dance texels with the highest *visual similarity* as well as the closest gender or dance quality compatibility.

Dance Texture Synthesis Method

We have developed a novel similarity function for implementing a dance texture synthesis algorithm, adapted from image quilting [11] and near-regular texture synthesis [19, 22]. Here we define a *texture patch* as a pair of consecutive texels for the use of feathering during the synthesis process. The two-texel-length patches are used to achieve feathering for smooth transitions between dance patches overlapping on one texel. The similarity function for the best matched patches requires: 1) compatibility between consecutive patches and 2) class (ability or gender) and level (high or low) compatibility of each patch. The compatibility of the consecutive patches determines the smoothness of the dance; if tolerance in pixel-wise overlapping texels difference is too high (e.g. > 0.5 degree), the resultant dance motion may contain abrupt rotations. Hence, we first randomly pick and filter dance patches for compatibility to yield smooth body motion transitions. Second, as the classification of each patch determines the perceived rating of the entire dance, we filter out patches with undesired rankings. In addition, higher weights are placed on the more perception discriminative body joint features (Figure 5), leading to a body joint-sensitive similarity metric. Figures 7 and 8 show the dance texture synthesis process and the interface where the dance ability and dancer's gender are controlled independently. The texture synthesis process has three steps: 1) patch-finding for most similar texel pairs, 2) patch pool screening for a specified targeted rating, and 3) feathering adjacent patches for smooth dance movement transition.

Synthesize Dance To New Music

Let the basic period of origin music be T_0; to synthesize dancing with music having a different basic period T we resample (warp) the dancing texture with ratio T/T_0 to make the dancing faster or slower to go with the new music. The same alignment is done as described in the pre-processing stage.

Sample movies of synthesized dancers can be found here: http://vision.cse.psu.edu/research/MTurkDancing/index.shtml

3.4 Human Perception Validation

We validate the results of our dance synthesis with crowdsourcing. Mechanical Turk (MT) provides a general platform for deploying units of informational labor (called human intelligence tasks, or HITs) to users on the Internet who are paid for their efforts. Our user interface, built in Flash, functions in the same way for the dance quality and dancer gender assessments (Figure 9). At the beginning, the user is shown a sample video that contains thumbnail versions of four dances. The dance quality of these dances cover the extreme ends of our 1-5 range. The user is required to watch the sample video for 20 seconds and can then begin the labeling task. For each assessment, a single video is shown. The user can click the quality or gender radio buttons at any time and change the answer any number of times, but the 'Next' button is disabled until 20 seconds have elapsed. The user repeats this for 10-12 assessments before the HIT is over. The order of the sample videos is randomized per user. For the gender assessment task the order of the videos is randomized and the order of male/female buttons is also randomized at the start of each HIT.

To ensure rating consistency, we have each user perform assessments twice, though the user is not informed of this fact. This is similar to an approach used previously [9] in which all shape perception HITs were presented twice to each MT user as means of assessing consistency. In our case, we ask for 5 or 6 unique assessments, and each appears twice. Numerical consistency of the user is computed as the average of the squared differences between each pair of responses. The number lets us assess user consistency on a relative scale per task. We can then remove all data from users who have highly inconsistent scores.

A user could complete the task in a trivially consistent way by always clicking the same response. Therefore, we also look at the variance of a user's assessment scores. If the variance is too low, the user is either not attempting the task in earnest, or is failing to see significant differences between the input videos.

A final metric we can use for assessing the work quality is the 'click time.' Because we built the assessment interface, we are free to track numerous details of the user interaction, including timing information and tentative, non-final responses. If the user clicks a particular answer, then changes the answer, this is recorded and sent to our server, including the amount of time that has passed with each click. We want the user to form his/her opinion based on a reasonable length of video, not just a couple seconds. So we can throw out any work by users who click their final assessment too quickly. We do not penalize users for making multiple assessments or for making a non-final assessment too quickly.

To turn the aggregated MT results into an assessment of our ability to synthesize videos, we look at the correlation (R) between our targeted scores and MT assessed scores. We perform thresholding as described above to exclude disqualified HIT results, and then compute the correlation on the remaining values with a null-hypothesis that there is no correlation between the intended synthesized dancer quality/gender and human ratings. The numerical results shown in Table 2 suggest strong agreement between our synthesized dancers ability/gender and human raters; especially for dance quality assessment where the correlation score is strongly linear (R-value $= 0.7251$) and statistically significant (p-value is very low). Dancer's gender assessment from the MTs shows significant positive correlation with the computer targeted dancer genders, but the linear relationship is only moderate (R-value $= 0.451$).

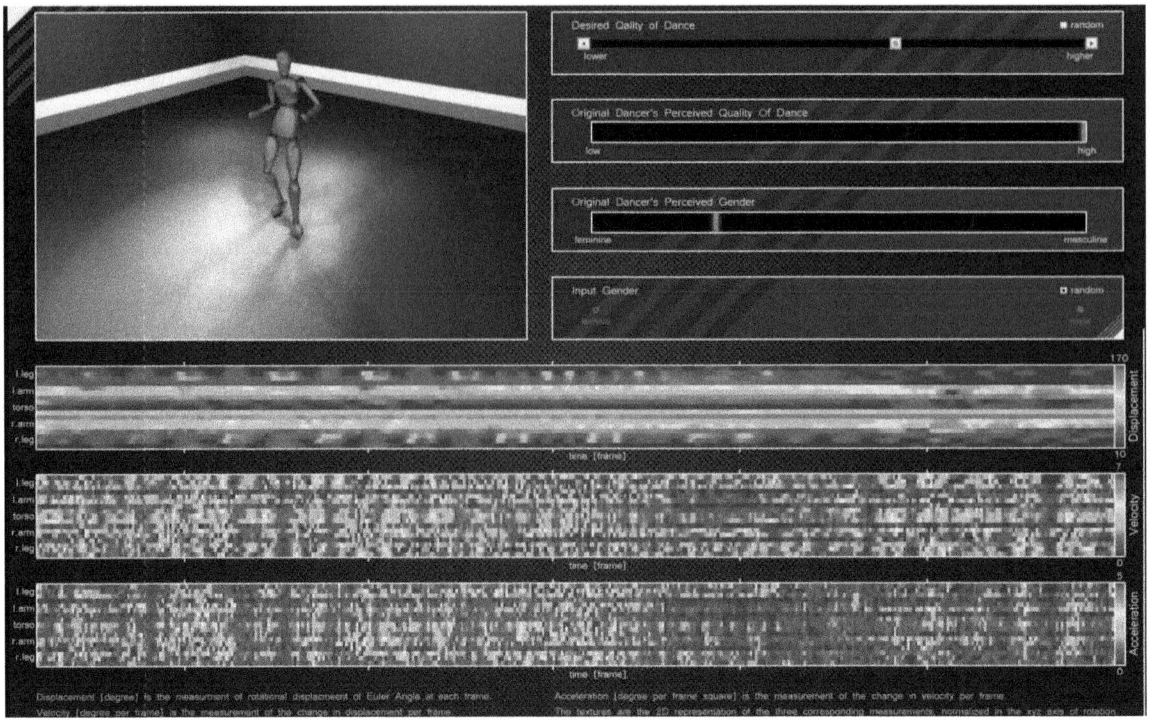

Figure 8: Dance-synthesizer at work: the bottom three rows demonstrate the three dynamic dance textures (Displacement, Velocity and Acceleration); top right displays the user desired dance quality; the two sliders below show the original data point (dancer) information of both perceived dance quality and perceived dancer's gender. Movies of synthesized dancers can be found here: http://vision.cse.psu.edu/research/MTurkDancing/index.shtml

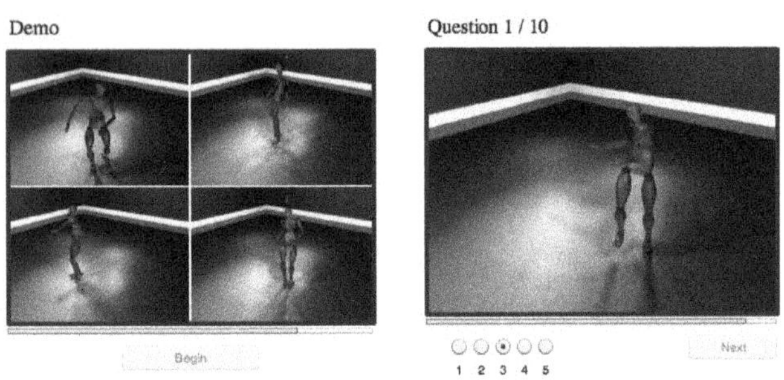

Figure 9: The interface for Mechanical Turk

Table 2: Summary of the Mechanical Turk Assessments of Synthesized Dancers

	Dance Quality	Dancer Gender
Total HITs	302	260
Unique workers (effective size)	232	189
Accepted HITs	244	200
R-value	**0.7251**	**0.451**
P-value	3e-216	0

4. SUMMARY AND DISCUSSION

We have proposed an effective framework for music and motion capture dance analysis, synthesis and evaluation. We have built a dance-synthesizer (Figure 8) and we have validated this framework on a mocap dataset containing 172 dancers, an asychronized piece of music, 25 initial human raters and more than 400 independent online raters.

Quantitative results from Table 2 provide a justification of our approach and its outcome. Starting with human input, analyzing the mocap data in a weakly supervised manner, and synthesizing the dancers based on learned discriminative features, we have produced promising output (synthesized dancers with certain targeted ability/gender scoring) that are confirmed by the human raters at a statistically significant level.

4.1 Motivated Raters

From a large amount of enthusiastic feedback of MTs (samples are shown in Table 3), it seems obvious that the raters are highly motivated: they personalize the computer (synthesized) animated dancers and treat the evaluation as a form of entertainment. These positive reactions are encouraging signs that *dancing with Turks* has a high potential to become a human-computer interactive game. With the support of the advanced technology, we expect our work lead to a rewarding experience for both the dancers and the actively participating audience (raters).

4.2 Dancer Ability versus Gender Perception

To our surprise, human perception of gender from dance animation (motion alone) of real dancers turns out to be rather challenging. From the 25 initial raters, the human

Table 3: **Sample Comments from Anonymous Mechanical Turks (Gender, Age-range, Country, Self-rating, Comment)**

F,31-40,CA,4,	"One of the most interesting HIT's I've done yet. You have made me very curious as to your study/project."
M,25-30,IN,3,	"Its bit difficult to find out the gender. "
F,18-24,US,1,	"The videos looked super cool!"
M,25-30,IN,4,	"Awesome job TNT"
F,31-40,US,1,	"I think the males tend to dance with pelvis forward"
M,25-30,US,3,	"Most of the dances seemed to have a salsa tone to them."
F,18-24,US,4,	"This hit was AWESOME!!!!"
M,31-40,IN,4,	"WANT MORE HITS LIKE THIS"
M,18-24,AU,2,	"Love the last dance."
F,31-40,IN,3,	"It was a nice entertainment."
M,18-24,IN,4,	"great animated dance"
M,31-40,BE,1,	"This was a nice HIT to do. What will you use it for exactly?"
M,18-24,PH,3,	**"the hands determine my choice of the dancers gender."**
F,18-24,US,1,	"The music used is addictive!"
M,41-50,US,5,	"professional theatrical dancer. None earned a 5 for me. Criteria Used: **level of energy exhibited, range of motion, variety in patterns**"
M,18-24,CA,4,	"good movements , to me the **best ones were the ones where it starts slow and requires a lot of foot work** with some body movements as it goes with the music"
F,41-50,US,2,	"amusing"
M,31-40,CA,3,	"great job! Lots of fun !"
F,31140,CA,4,	"Great HIT! Don't know if it helps, but I find usually women are more inclined to make larger movements, and cover more floor space than men when dancing. "
M,25-30,IN,3,	"Its bit difficult to find out the gender. However,i have done my best.Tnx"
M,51-60,US,2,	"Wow, very interesting!!!"
F,18-24,US,1,	"Fun to watch!!"
M,18-24,PH,4,	"Awesome!These is great!Love it very much.Break hit!"
M,41-50,US,1,	"I thought the animations were awesome and I actually was learning moves by watching"

gender classification rate is 64.78% ± 7.6% with approximately equal performance on both genders. For computers, discriminating and synthesizing gender specific subjects is also less agreed up by MTs than controlling the levels of dance quality (Table 2). This challenge may arise from the nature of gender as a binary variable; a 0.5 rating value in ability means the dancer is an *average* dancer, while a 0.5 value in gender means 'either' male or female, therefore the variance is potentially much higher. In the context of relatively easy recognition of gender through human gaits [14], this issue of gender recognition in free-form dancing is of high social and scientific interest.

4.3 Future Work

So far, we have explored the gender and dance ability of a dancer separately. Future work to test our methodology will include both gender and dance ability jointly. Finding the dance texture patch that matches both ratings the best within the training data pool allows the resultant motion to have more than one controllable characteristic.

Furthermore, although we closed the loop in this work in one cycle, our learning-evaluation cycle can continue evolving. Synthesized results can further be reclassified by human raters (Section 3.4) and fed back into our analysis/learning system. This will allow the machine to learn and adjust itself accordingly over time, as if in a back-and-forth dance with the *Turks*.

5. ACKNOWLEDGMENTS

I-Kao Chiang (first author) worked on this project for his BS honors thesis while at PSU. Brian VanLeeuwen contributed to Figure 3(A). We thank the authors of [6] for sharing their motion capture data. This work is supported in part by NSF grants IIS-1248076 and IIS-1144938.

6. REFERENCES

[1] O. Arikan and D. Forsyth. Interactive motion generation from examples. *ACM Transactions on Graphics*, 21(3):483–490, 2002.

[2] C. M. Bishop. *Neural Networks for Pattern Recognition*. Clarendon Press, 1995. ISBN:0198538499.

[3] M. Brand and A. Hertzmann. Style machines. In *Proc. Conf. on Comp. Graph. and Int. Techn.*, pages 183–192, 2000.

[4] C. Bregler, M. Covell, and M. Slaney. Video rewrite: Driving visual speech with audio. In *Proceedings of SIGGRAPH 97*, pages 353–360, August 1997.

[5] C. Bregler and J. Malik. Tracking people with twists and exponential maps. In *IEEE Computer Society Conference on Computer Vision and Pattern Recognition*, pages 8–15. Citeseer, 1998.

[6] W. M. Brown, L. Cronk, K. Grochow, A. Jacobson, K. Liu, Z. Popović, and R. Trivers. Dance reveals symmetry especially in young men. *Nature*, 438, 2006. Retracted December 2013.

[7] A. Bruderlin and L. Williams. Motion signal processing. In *Proceedings of the 22nd annual conference on Computer graphics and interactive techniques*, page 104. ACM, 1995.

[8] C. Cedras and M. Shah. A survey of motion analysis from moving light displays. In *1994 IEEE Computer Society Conference on Computer Vision and Pattern Recognition, 1994. Proceedings CVPR'94.*, pages 214–221, 1994.

[9] F. Cole, K. Sanik, D. DeCarlo, A. Finkelstein, T. Funkhouser, S. Rusinkiewicz, and M. Singh. How well do line drawings depict shape? In *ACM Transactions on Graphics (Proc. SIGGRAPH)*, volume 28, Aug. 2009.

[10] R. Duda, P. Hart, and D. Stork. *Pattern Classification*. John Wiley & Sons, New York, 2001.

[11] A. Efros and W. Freeman. Image quilting for texture synthesis and transfer. In *SIGGRAPH*, pages 35–42, 2001.

[12] K. Grochow, S. Martin, A. Hertzmann, and Z. Popović. Style-based inverse kinematics. *ACM Transactions on Graphics (TOG)*, 23(3):522–531, 2004.

[13] E. Hsu, K. Pulli, and J. Popović. Style translation for human motion. In *Proceedings of the 32nd annual conference on computer graphics and interactive techniques (SIGGRAPH 2005)*, pages 1082–1089. ACM Press, 2005.

[14] G. Johansson. Visual perception of biological motion and a model for its analysis. *Perceiving events and objects*, 3, 1973.

[15] L. Kovar, M. Gleicher, and F. Pighin. Motion graphs. *ACM Transactions on Graphics (TOG)*, 21(3):473–482, 2002.

[16] L. Kozlowski and J. Cutting. Recognizing the sex of a walker from a dynamic point-light display. *Perception & Psychophysics*, 21(6):575–580, 1977.

[17] J. Lee, J. Chai, P. Reitsma, J. Hodgins, and N. Pollard. Interactive control of avatars animated with human motion data. *ACM Transactions on Graphics*, 21(3):491–500, 2002.

[18] Y. Li, T. Wang, and H. Shum. Motion texture: a two-level statistical model for character motion synthesis. In *Proceedings of the 29th annual conference on Computer graphics and interactive techniques*, pages 465–472. ACM, 2002.

[19] Y. Liu, W. Lin, and J. Hays. Near-regular texture analysis and manipulation. *ACM Transactions on Graphics (SIGGRAPH)*, 23(3):368–376, August 2004.

[20] Y. Liu, K. Schmidt, J. Cohn, and S. Mitra. Facial asymmetry quantification for expression invariant human identification. *Computer Vision and Image Understanding Journal*, 91(1/2):138–159, Special issue on face recognition, Martinez, Yang and Kriegman (Eds.). July/August 2003.

[21] Y. Liu, L. Teverovskiy, O. Carmichael, R. Kikinis, M. Shenton, C. Carter, V. Stenger, S. Davis, H. Aizenstein, J. Becker, O. Lopez, and C. Meltzer. Discriminative mr image feature analysis for automatic schizophrenia and alzheimer's disease classification. In *7th International Conference on Medical Imaging Computing and Comptuer Assisted Intervention (MICCAI 2004)*, pages 378–385. Springer, October 2004.

[22] Y. Liu, Y. Tsin, and W. Lin. The promise and perils of near-regular texture. *International Journal of Computer Vision*, 62(1-2):145,159, April 2005.

[23] E. Moulines, P. Emerard, D. Larreur, J. L. S. Milon, L. L. Faucheur, F. Marty, F. Charpentier, and C. Sorin. A real-time french text-to-speech system generating high-quality synthetic speech. In *Proc. Int. Conf. Acoustics, Speech, and Signal Processing*, 1990.

[24] R. Murray, Z. Li, and S. Sastry. *A mathematical introduction to robotic manipulation*. CRC, 1994.

[25] W. Pan and L. Torresani. Unsupervised hierarchical modeling of locomotion styles. In *Proceedings of the 26th Annual International Conference on Machine Learning*, pages 785–792. ACM, 2009.

[26] K. Pullen and C. Bregler. Motion capture assisted animation: Texturing and synthesis. *ACM Transactions on Graphics (TOG)*, 21(3):508, 2002.

[27] T. Qin, X.-D. Zhang, T.-Y. Liu, D.-S. Wang, W.-Y. Ma, and H.-J. Zhang. An active feedback framework for image retrieval. *Pattern Recogn. Lett.*, 29(5):637–646, Apr. 2008.

[28] C. Rose, M. Cohen, and B. Bodenheimer. Verbs and adverbs: Multidimensional motion interpolation. *IEEE Computer Graphics and Applications*, 18(5):32–40, 1998.

[29] A. Schödl, R. Szeliski, D. H. Salesin, and I. Essa. Video textures. In *Proceedings of ACM SIGGRAPH 2000*, pages 489–498, July 2000.

[30] S. Sumi. Upside-down presentation of the Johansson moving light-spot pattern. *Perception*, 13(3):283–286, 1984.

[31] G. W. Taylor and G. E. Hinton. Factored conditional restricted boltzmann machines for modeling motion style. In *Proc. Int. Conf. on Mach. Learn.*, pages 1025–1032, 2009.

[32] L. Torresani, P. Hackney, and C. Bregler. Learning motion style synthesis from perceptual observations. In *Adv. in Neural Inf. Proc. Sys.*, pages 1393–1400, 2007.

[33] M. Unuma, K. Anjyo, and R. Takeuchi. Fourier principles for emotion-based human figure animation. In *Proceedings of the 22nd annual conference on Computer graphics and interactive techniques*, pages 91–96. ACM, 1995.

[34] R. Urtasun, P. Glardon, R. Boulic, D. Thalmann, and P. Fua. Style-based Motion Synthesis. *Computer Graphics Forum*, 23(4):1–14, 2004.

[35] J. Wang, D. Fleet, and A. Hertzmann. Multifactor gaussian process models for style-content separation. In *Proc. Int. Conf. on Mach. Learn.*, pages 975–982, 2007.

[36] A. Witkin and Z. Popovic. Motion warping. In *Proceedings of the 22nd annual conference on Computer graphics and interactive techniques*, pages 105–108. ACM, 1995.

[37] X. S. Zhou and T. S. Huang. Relevance feedback in image retrieval: A comprehensive review. *Multimedia Systems*, 8(6):536–544, 2003.

Single Image Spectral Reconstruction for Multimedia Applications

Antonio Robles-Kelly
NICTA, Locked Bag 8001, Canberra ACT 2601, Australia
antonio.robles-kelly@nicta.com.au

ABSTRACT

In this paper, we present a method which can perform spectral reconstruction and illuminant recovery from a single colour image making use of an unlabelled training set of hyperspectral images. Our method employs colour and appearance information to drive the reconstruction process subject to the material properties of the objects in the scene. The idea is to reconstruct the image spectral irradiance making use of a set of prototypes extracted from the training set. These spectra, together with a set of convolutional features are hence obtained using sparse coding so as to reconstruct the image irradiance. With the reconstructed spectra in hand, we proceed to compute the illuminant power spectrum using a quadratic optimisation approach. We provide a quantitative analysis for our method and compare to a number of alternatives. We also show sample results on illuminant substitution and transfer, film simulation and image recolouring using mood board colour schemes.

Categories and Subject Descriptors

I.4 [**Computing Methodologies**]: Image Processing and Computer Vision; I.5 [**Computing Methodologies**]: Pattern Recognition

General Terms

Algorithms, Experimentation, Performance

Keywords

Spectral reconstruction, Sparse coding, Image reproduction and enhacement

1. INTRODUCTION

In multimedia, computer vision, video and graphics, we rely upon cameras and rendering contexts to capture and reproduce colour image data. Furthermore, the accurate reproduction and capture of the scene colour across different devices is an important and active area of research spanning camera simulation [19], sensor design [5] and white balancing [14].

The manner in which colour data is presented to the user is central to multimedia applications since the imagery is often delivered to the user based upon a rendering intent, *i.e.* colorimetric, perceptual, etc., which can determine the processing to be undertaken or the display medium. To this end, several methods have been proposed whereby making use of reflectance and illuminant measurements, colorimetric simulations and comparisons can be effected using quadratic programming [6], monochromators [31], spectrophotometers [21] or fluorescence [10]. Other camera radiometric calibration methods such as that in [14] require the scene irradiance to be in hand or make assumptions regarding the scene.

Note that, even when the camera has been radiometrically calibrated, the image raw colour values are sensor specific [24]. Moroever, raw-to-raw colour mappings between cameras are generally limited to linear transformations [24]. The problem here stems from the fact that, in practice, cameras often do not abide to the Luther condition, *i.e.* the camera spectral sensitivity functions are a linear transformation of the CIE colour matching functions [22]. This induces a nonlinear transformation between camera colour spaces which depends on both, the spectral sensitivity functions and the image irradiance [12].

Thus, and despite being a challenging task, the spectral reconstruction of the spectral irradiance from a single colour image opens up the possibility of exploiting the relationship between the scene spectral reflectance, illuminant power spectrum and sensor sensitivity functions for applications such as material-specific colour rendition [8], accurate colour reproduction [28] and material reflectance substitution [9].

It is important to note that existing spectral reconstruction approaches are eminently pixel-based, disregarding the object material properties and reconstructing the image irradiance solely based upon colour information. For instance, Nguyen et al. [25] have attempted to reconstruct the scene reflectance by mapping the RGB values yielded by a trichromatic camera to the scene reflectance spectra. Maloney [20] and Agahian *et al.* [2] have used a PCA basis to model of the surface reflectance. Romero *et al.* [26] also used a linear basis to represent the illuminant in the scene. In [1], the authors use look-up tables to reconstruct reflectance data using linear interpolation. Zhao and Berns [36] have used a Karhunen-Loeve transformation, *i.e.* the matrix $\mathbf{R}$ method, to perform spectral reflectance reconstruction using a calibration target.

MM'15, October 26-30, 2015, Brisbane, Australia

DOI: http://dx.doi.org/10.1145/2733373.2806223.

2. CONTRIBUTION

Here, we present a method for spectral reconstruction that allows images to be reproduced and presented with a look and feel in better accordance to the rendering intent. For instance, a warm or cooler feeling can be conveyed by substituting the illuminant (Figures 2 and 3) or more complex emotions through mood boards (Figure 5). Moreover, our method is also suitable for emulation of other cameras and films (Figure 4), which can be used to give a sense of realism, authenticity or artistic choice in multimedia settings.

We note that, by using the material properties of the objects in the image, the effects of metamers (surfaces with different spectral reflectance but identical colour) can be reduced and, hence, a better spectral reconstruction can be obtained. This hinges in the notion that the image reflectance is a photometric invariant which is intrinsic to the object material. Thus, here we employ features often used for classification and recognition in computer vision in combination with a set of training images to reconstruct the spectral irradiance. This contrasts with other methods for spectral reconstruction in the sense that they do not attempt to model the object material properties but rather reconstruct the reflectance from colour information alone.

The method presented here is quite general, making the following assumptions

- The spectral sensitivity function of the camera used to acquire the colour image is known.
- The colour image can be white balanced using existing methods.
- The scene in the colour image is illuminated by a single illuminant.
- The illuminant power spectra for the training data set is available.

We would like to stress these are not overly restrictive, being akin to those in [25].

In Figure 1, we show a diagram of the training and testing phases of our method. At training, the dataset of hyperspectral images is used to obtain spectral and convolutional features. We then use these features to recover the prototype set using a constrained sparse coding approach. Since these prototypes correspond to spectral samples in the training dataset and their corresponding material properties, they can be employed at testing to reconstruct the image spectra. Finally, once the spectral reconstruction is effected, we compute the illuminant power spectrum making use of a quadratic optimisation approach.

The paper is organised as follows. In Section 3, we provide background material on the relationship between the image irradiance and colour. In Section 4, we present the constrained sparse coding approach used at training and elaborate upon the reconstruction of the image irradiance. We also introduce our illuminant power spectrum recovery step. In Section 5, we provide implementation details and further discussion on our method. We show experiments in Section 6 and conclude in Section 7.

3. IMAGE IRRADIANCE AND COLOUR

Throughout the paper, we employ the relationships between spectral irradiance, illuminant power spectrum, spectral sensitivity functions, colour and chromaticity. Thus, we

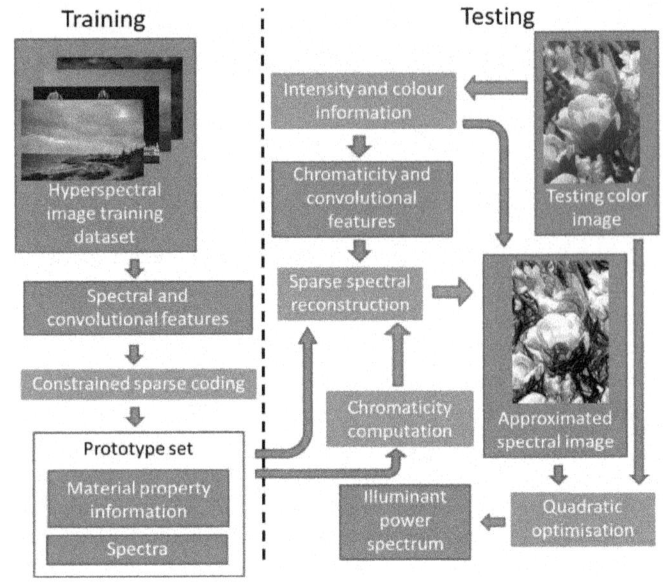

Figure 1: Our method takes at input a single colour image and recovers the spectra and illuminant making use of a training dataset.

commence by providing some useful background on these and express the image irradiance at wavelength λ and pixel u as follows

$$I(u,\lambda) = L(\lambda)R(u,\lambda) \tag{1}$$

where $L(\lambda)$ is the power spectrum of the light impinging on the object surface and $R(u,\cdot)$ is the product of the mean scattered power in the direction of the viewer and the surface reflectance spectrum.

Equation 1 is important since it permits expressing the value of the colour channel $c = \{R, G, B\}$ at pixel u as

$$I_c(u) = \int_\Lambda L(\lambda)Q_c(\lambda)R(u,\lambda)d\lambda \tag{2}$$

where $Q_c(\lambda)$ is the spectral sensitivity function of the imager for the colour channel c and Λ is the wavelength interval spanning the visible spectrum. Note that, in practice, spectra is sampled in a set of n discrete wavelength indexed values λ_k. As a result, the integral above becomes a sum given by

$$I_c(u) = g(u) \sum_{\lambda_k \in \Lambda} L(\lambda_k)Q_c(\lambda_k)r(u,\lambda_k) \tag{3}$$

where $g(u) = |R(u,\cdot)|_2$ is the L-2 norm of $R(u,\cdot)$ across the wavelength domain, *i.e.* the radiosity at pixel u[1], such that $R(u,\lambda) = g(u)r(u,\lambda_k)$.

With the notation above, it becomes straightforward to define the colour pixel values in the rg-chromaticity space

[1]Note that radiosity is often called intensity in some areas of physics. This is also in good accordance with the intuitive use of the term in computer vision and image processing and, hence, we use it throughout the paper

as follows

$$K_c(u) = \frac{I_c(u)}{\sum_{q=\{R,G,B\}} I_q(u)} = \frac{\sum_{\lambda_k \in \Lambda} L(\lambda_k) Q_c(\lambda_k) r(u,\lambda_k)}{\sum_{q=\{R,G,B\}} \sum_{\lambda_k \in \Lambda} L(\lambda_k) Q_q(\lambda_k) r(u,\lambda_k)} \quad (4)$$

where $c = \{R, G, B\}$.

4. SPECTRAL RECONSTRUCTION

Note that, if a set $\mathcal{I}$ of training images is in hand and both, the spectral sensitivity functions and illuminant power spectra are known, for each pixel u, it becomes straightforward to compute both, the intensity $g(u)$ and its corresponding rg-chromaticity values. This is important since intensity values are traditionally used in computer vision to obtain textons [17]. We follow the intuition that these textons are indicative of local object surface properties [33] and, hence, apply the filter banks in [33] to recover a convolutional feature for each pixel u. Our choice of a convolutional feature vector with local support follows the notion that, in this manner, object specific information is ignored so as to capture material properties devoid of the object itself [27].

4.1 Spectra and Convolutional Features

The use of convolutional features allows for a treatment where the image irradiance can be used to recover a set of prototypes for spectral reconstruction. To see this more clearly, recall that the convolutional features are computed using a set of filters. If the ith filter in our set is applied to the kth wavelength indexed band across the image lattice, we can write

$$f_{i,\lambda_k} = I_{\lambda_k} * h_i = L(\lambda_k) r_{\lambda_k} \circ (g * h_i) \quad (5)$$

where the right-hand side of the equation follows the distributive property of the convolution. In Equation 5, we have omitted the pixel indices as a matter of convenience ($I_{\lambda_k} \equiv I(\cdot, \lambda_k)$, $g(\cdot) \equiv g$ and $r_{\lambda_k} \equiv r(\cdot, \lambda_k)$), h_i is the filter mask and, as usual, $*$ and $\circ$ indicate the convolution and Hadamard products, respectively.

As a result, for each wavelength-indexed band in our training set, the spectra becomes a multiplicative constant as applied to the convolutional features computed from the image intensities. Thus, for our spectral reconstruction approach we use the vectors given by

$$\gamma(u) = [r(u,\lambda_1)\mathbf{v} \;||\; r(u,\lambda_2)\mathbf{v} \;||\; \dots \;||\; r(u,\lambda_N)\mathbf{v}] \quad (6)$$

where $\mathbf{v}$ is a row vector whose i^{th} entry corresponds to the filter response $g * h_i$ at pixel u, N is the number of wavelength-indexed bands in our training imagery and we have written $||$ to imply vector concatenation.

The use of the vectors in Equation 6 for our reconstruction approach has two main advantages. Firstly, it permits a consistent treatment of both, our hyperspectral image training set and our colour testing image. Secondly, it allows for a constrained sparse coding scheme to be used to recover prototypes that can then be employed to perform the spectral reconstruction. This is since we can always convert the vectors $\gamma(u)$ to their rg-chromaticity analogues by extracting the values of $r(u, \cdot)$ so as to apply Equation 4. This can be done in a straightforward manner by noting that the value of $r(u, \lambda_1)$ repeats over the length of the convolutional features across the vector $\gamma(u)$.

4.2 Constrained Sparse Coding

Here, we view the problem in hand as that of representing the vectors $\gamma(u)$ using a set Φ of prototypes such that

$$\gamma(u) = \sum_{\phi \in \Phi} \alpha_\phi(u)\phi \quad (7)$$

where $\alpha_\phi(u)$ can be seen as the "abundance" of the prototype ϕ in $\gamma(u)$.

This treatment responds to a twofold motivation. Firstly, we exploit the fact that, in this manner, the set of prototypes can be obtained using sparse coding. Secondly, Equation 7 implies that the prototype ϕ should have a structure akin to that of $\gamma(u)$. This is important since the spectral and convolutional feature components in ϕ can then be used to reconstruct the testing image making use of its chromaticity information.

We will elaborate upon this later on. For now, we focus on the recovery of the prototype set Φ. To this end, we aim at solving the optimization problem given by

$$\min_{\Phi, A} \left\{ \sum_{u \in \mathcal{I}} |\gamma(u) - \alpha(u)^T \Phi|_2 + \tau_1 \sum_{u \in \mathcal{I}} |\alpha(u)|_1 \right\} \quad (8)$$

subject to

$$|\alpha(u)|_2 \leq \kappa \quad \forall \quad u \in \mathcal{I}$$
$$\alpha_\phi(u) \geq 0 \quad \forall \quad \alpha_\phi(u) \in \alpha(u)$$

where $|\cdot|_p$ denotes the p-norm, A is the set of column weight vectors $\alpha(u)$ for all the pixels in our training data, κ is a bounding positive constant and τ_1 is a scalar that accounts for the contribution of the second term in Equation 8 to the minimisation in hand. Note that we have added the positivity constraint on the vector $\alpha(u)$ following the notion that the contributions of the primitives to the pixel spectrum correspond to an additive process. This is consistent with the notion that the weight vector entry $\alpha_\phi(u)$ can be seen as the "abundance" of the prototype ϕ in $\gamma(u)$. Also, we have imposed a norm constraint in order to avoid the possibility of degenerate cases involving linear transformations of $\alpha(u)$. Note that this is akin to the approach taken in [16].

4.3 Reconstructing the Image Irradiance

With the prototypes in hand, we now turn our attention to the spectral reconstruction of a testing image I^*. To reconstruct the spectra, we commence by computing the intensity of the testing image. With the intensity in hand, we proceed to compute the chromaticity values $K_c(v)$, $c = \{R, G, B\}$ and the convolutional feature $\mathbf{w}$ for each pixel v in the testing image.

Recall that each of the prototypes $\phi \in \Phi$ shares its structure with that of $\gamma(u)$ as defined in Equation 6. This is as a result of the linear relationship in Equation 7 and the positivity constraint introduced in our sparse coding approach. This is important since we can write

$$\phi = [s(\lambda_1)\mathbf{x} \;||\; s(\lambda_2)\mathbf{x} \;||\; \dots \;||\; s(\lambda_N)\mathbf{x}] \quad (9)$$

where $s(\cdot)$ can be viewed as the spectral component of ϕ whereas $\mathbf{x}$ arises from the convolutional features.

With these ingredients, we aim at recovering the weight vector $\rho(v)$ such that the spectral reconstruction of the testing pixel v becomes

$$R(v, \cdot) = g(v)\rho(v)^T \mathbf{S} \quad (10)$$

such that $\mathbf{w} = \rho(v)^T \mathbf{X}$, where $\mathbf{X}$ and $\mathbf{S}$ are matrices whose rows correspond to the vectors $\mathbf{x}$ and $s(\cdot)$ as defined in Equation 9 and $g(v)$ is the intensity at pixel v.

Thus, both, the convolutional feature $\mathbf{w}$ and the spectral reconstruction of the pixel v are given by the linear combination of the spectral and convolutional components of the prototypes $\phi \in \Phi$. To determine the weight vector $\rho(v)$, we note that the relationship in Equation 10 applies also to the chromaticity values. That is, the chromaticity $K_c(v)$ of the testing pixel is given by

$$K_c(v) = \rho(v)^T \mathbf{K}_c \tag{11}$$

where $\mathbf{K}_c$ is a matrix whose rows correspond to the chromaticities $K_c(s)$, $c = \{R, G, B\}$ of the vectors $s(\cdot)$.

Thus, we construct the vectors

$$\beta(v) = [K_R(v)\mathbf{w} \mid\mid K_G(v)\mathbf{w} \mid\mid K_B(v)\mathbf{w}] \tag{12}$$

for each of the pixels v in the testing image and solve the optimisation

$$\min_{\rho(v)} \left\{ |\beta(v) - \rho(v)^T \Omega|_2 + \tau_2 |\rho(v)|_1 \right\} \tag{13}$$

subject to

$$\rho(v)^T \Omega \geq 0 \qquad \forall \ \ \rho(v)_\omega \in \rho(v)$$

where τ_2 is a scalar that controls the degree of sparsity in the resulting weight vector, Ω is a matrix whose rows are given by the vectors

$$\omega = [K_R(s)\mathbf{x} \mid\mid K_G(s)\mathbf{x} \mid\mid [K_B(s)\mathbf{x}] \tag{14}$$

and $\rho_\omega(v)$ is the entry of $\rho(v)$ corresponding to ω.

Here, we have added the positivity constraint on the weight column vector $\rho(v)$ following the notion that the spectra cannot exhibit negative values. The vectors $\omega \in \Omega$ are analogue to the prototypes $\phi \in \Phi$ presented in Section 4.1. The main difference, however, is that these are defined in the rg-chromaticity space rather than the image spectral irradiance. This is not a problem, however, since the rg-chromaticity values for $s(\cdot)$ can be computed in a straightforward manner using Equation 4 if the illuminant power spectrum for the training imagery and spectral sensitivity functions for the testing image are known.

4.4 Illuminant Power Spectrum Recovery

With the spectra in hand, we can recover the illuminant power spectrum $L(\cdot)$ for the testing image I^* making use of the colour information for each of the colour channels $I_c^*(\cdot)$, $c = \{R, G, B\}$. Making use of Equation 3, and since the spectral sensitivity function $Q_c(\cdot)$ is known, we can solve the following non-negative optimization problem

$$\min_{L(\cdot)} \left\{ \sum_{\substack{v \in I^* \\ c \in \{R,G,B\}}} |I_c^*(v) - \sum_{\lambda_k \in \Lambda} L(\lambda_k) Q_c(\lambda_k) R(v, \lambda_k)|_2 \right\} \tag{15}$$

subject to $L(\lambda_k) \geq 0$ for all $\lambda_k \in \Lambda$.

5. IMPLEMENTATION AND DISCUSSION

In Algorithm 1 we show the pseudocode for the training stage of our approach. There are a number of traits that merit further discussion. Note that the algorithm takes at input a dataset of training hyperspectral images with the illuminant removed. This is, for each of the images in the training data set, we use

$$R(u, \lambda_k) = \frac{I(u, \lambda_k)}{L(\lambda_k)} \tag{16}$$

as an alternative to the image irradiance $I(u, \lambda_k)$ at input. This is reflected in Line 3, of Algorithm 1. We have done this since the illuminant power spectrum $L(\cdot)$ for the training images is assumed to be known and, hence, $R(u, \lambda_k)$ can be computed in a straightforward manner.

For the convolutional features, we have used the three filter banks in [33]. It is also worth noting that the constrained sparse coding problem in Equation 8 can be solved in a number of ways. Here, we have opted for a basis pursuit [30] where the non-negative constraint is enforced explicitly. For initialisation, we have used the mode seeking method in [34]. This follows the intuition that the prototypes are expected to correspond to the modes of the distribution of the vectors $\gamma(u)$ over the training images.

In Line 12 of the the algorithm we recover, for each prototype, the corresponding spectral and convolutional components. This can be done via a simple division following by a normalisation step. The reason being that, for convolutional features of length M, the first M elements of ϕ will account for $s(\lambda_1)\mathbf{x}$. As a result, by concatenating these N times, *i.e.* the number of wavelength-indexed bands in our training images, we can employ the Hadamard product and Equation 9 so as to write

$$\phi \circ \zeta^{-1} = \left[\mathbf{1} \mid\mid \frac{s(\lambda_2)}{s(\lambda_1)} \mathbf{1} \mid\mid \ \ldots \ \mid\mid \frac{s(\lambda_N)}{s(\lambda_1)} \mathbf{1} \right] \tag{17}$$

where $\mathbf{1}$ is a vector whose dimensionality is the same as the convolutional features and ζ is a vector comprised of the first M elements of ϕ concatenated N times.

From Equation 17 is straightforward to note that the ith unique value in $\phi \circ \zeta^{-1}$ will account for the quantity $\frac{s(\lambda_i)}{s(\lambda_1)}$. That is, these values are proportional to the spectral components $s(\lambda_i)$ up to the inverse of $s(\lambda_1)$. At this point, we also note that, by definition, $r(u, \cdot)$ is normalised to unity. Hence, it follows that, once the values $\frac{s(\lambda_i)}{s(\lambda_1)}$ are in hand, they can be normalised such that $|s(\cdot)|_2 = 1$ so as to recover the spectral component of ϕ. Once $s(\cdot)$ is computed, the convolutional component $\mathbf{x}$ can be retrieved using the equation

$$\frac{1}{s(\lambda_1)} \zeta = [\mathbf{x} \mid\mid \mathbf{x} \mid\mid \ldots \mid\mid \mathbf{x}] \tag{18}$$

and noting that $\mathbf{x}$ repeats N times on the right-hand side of the expression above.

In Algorithm 2, we show the step sequence for the testing phase of our algorithm. In our code, we have also used basis pursuit for the solution of the optimisation in Equation 13. Also, in our implementation, the intensity of the testing image is given by the lightness dimension, *i.e.* L, of the image in the CIELab colour space. For the optimisations in Equations 8 and 13 we have set $\tau_1 = \tau_2 = 1/N$, *i.e.* the inverse of the number of wavelength indexed bands in our training imagery, and $\kappa = 1$.

Regarding our illuminant recovery step, it is worth noting in passing that the optimisation in Equation 15 is somewhat similar to the expression used in [25]. The main difference stems from the lack of a regularisation term which imposes a smoothness constraint on the illuminant power spectrum.

Algorithm 1 Training

Require: $\mathcal{I}$: Dataset of training hyperspectral images with the illuminant removed
for Every image in $\mathcal{I}$ **do**
  for Every pixel u in the image **do**
    Compute the image intensity $g(u) = |I(u, \cdot)|_2$
  end for
  Compute the convolutional features using the image intensities
  for Every pixel u in the image **do**
    Construct $\gamma(u)$ making use of Equation 6.
  end for
end for
Compute Φ by solving Equation 8
for Every prototype ϕ in Φ **do**
  Recover the spectral and convolutional components so as to satisfy Equation 9.
end for
return Set of spectral components of Φ and set X of convolutional components of Φ.

Algorithm 2 Testing

Require: Input colour image, set of spectral components of Φ, set X of convolutional components of Φ, spectral sensitivity functions $Q_c(\cdot)$ for the sensor used to acquire the testing image
White balance the input image
for Every $\phi \in \Phi$ in the prototype set **do**
  Compute the chromaticity values using Equation 4.
  Construct the vector ω using Equation 14.
end for
for Every pixel v in the input image **do**
  Compute the chromaticity values using Equation 4.
  Compute the image intensity $g(v)$
end for
Compute the convolutional features using the image intensities
for Every pixel v in the input image **do**
  Construct the vector $\beta(v)$ as per Equation 12.
  Recover the weight vector $\rho(v)$ by solving the optimisation problem in Equation 13.
  Compute the spectrum $R(v, \cdot)$ using Equation 10.
end for
Compute the illuminant power spectrum by solving the optimisation in Equation 15
return The reconstructed spectra and the illuminant power spectrum for the testing image

Note that the number of variables in $L(\lambda)$ is given by the number of wavelength indexed bands comprising the spectra $R(v, \cdot)$. For N discrete wavelengths $\lambda_1, \ldots, \lambda_N$, the recovered image spectra has a dimension of $P \times N$, where P is the number of pixels in the testing image. The optimisation problem in Equation 15 is generally well-formed if there are more pixels in the image than the number of wavelength indexed channels, *i.e.* $P \geq N$. As a result, the minimisation in hand can be solved using standard non-negative least squares methods.

6. EXPERIMENTS

6.1 Datasets and Settings

In this section, we commence by elaborating on the datasets used in our experiments. Later on, we present a quantitative analysis for our approach and illustrate its utility for illuminant substitution and transfer, film simulation and mood board colour transfer.

For the experiments presented in this section, we use a number of hypersepctral image datasets of rural and urban environments for both, training and testing. For our experiments, we also use the spectral sensitivity functions for commercial camera models presented in [18][2], spectral sensitivity functions for Fuji and Kodak film, real-world imagery acquired RAW with a Nikon D80 and Nikon D5100 cameras and reflectance and illuminant power spectra captured in house using a spectrometer.

On the hyperspectral datasets used here, the first of these is comprised by the reflectance images of 16 scenes captured by Foster *et al.* [7][3]. These images were acquired with a Peltier-cooled digital camera and a fast VariSpec tunable liquid-crystal filter producing a spatial resolution of 1344×1024 pixels and a spectral resolution of 10 nm over the wavelength range $[400nm, 720nm]$. The intensity response was recorded with 12-bit precision and was linear to the image irradiance. To compute image reflectance, the illumination spectrum was obtained from a grey Munsell surface placed in the scene.

The second of our datasets is that presented in [25][4]. The dataset is comprised of 64 images acquired using a Specim camera with a spectral resolution of 10 nm in the visible spectrum. It is worth noting that the dataset has been divided into testing and training sets. Here, all our experiments have been effected using the latter of these for training our method.

Finally, we have also employed a subset of the Scyllarus Series A dataset of spectral images[5]. Our subset is given by the 52 images in the full dataset which contain a Spectralon calibration target in the scene and, hence, the image reflectance can be computed from the irradiance. These images were acquired with a Liquid Crystal Tunable Filter (LCTF) tuned at intervals of 10 nm in the visible spectrum. The intensity response was recorded with a low distortion intensified 12-bit precision camera.

For our quantitative experiments and presentation of results, unless otherwise noted, we have employed the CIE colour sensitivity functions proposed by Judd [13]. All the spectral reconstructions performed herein cover the range $[400nm, 700nm]$ in $10nm$ steps. Also, note that using the full set of pixels from the 40 training images is, in practice, infeasible. As a result, for our method and the alternatives in [2] and [1] we have used the Markov chain Monte Carlo (MCMC) sampling strategy in [4] and set the number of prototypes delivered by our sparse coding approach to $11,800$. For the method in [25], we have followed the authors and used k-means to obtain $16,000$ reflectance samples.

[2] Accessible at http://www.cis.rit.edu/jwgu/research/camspec/

[3] The imagery can be accessed at: http://personalpages.manchester.ac.uk/staff/d.h.foster/

[4] The dataset can be downloaded from: http://www.comp.nus.edu.sg/~whitebal/spectral_reconstruction/

[5] Downloadable at: http://www.scyllarus.com

		Foster	Scyllarus	NUS
Abed et al. [1]	GW	28.96	26.85	18.69
	WP	<u>26.98</u>	<u>23.93</u>	<u>16.82</u>
	General GW	27.94	25.92	17.96
	1st GE	27.17	24.96	17.20
	2nd GE	27.03	24.48	16.91
Agahian et al. [2]	GW	58.98	44.24	38.19
	WP	<u>49.08</u>	<u>39.42</u>	<u>33.65</u>
	General GW	53.79	42.91	37.53
	1st GE	50.67	41.92	35.81
	2nd GE	50.75	41.87	35.98
Nguyen et al. [25]	GW	25.67	23.98	18.85
	WP	21.62	<u>18.76</u>	14.91
	General GW	23.71	20.75	16.46
	1st GE	21.95	19.73	<u>14.87</u>
	2nd GE	<u>21.59</u>	19.36	15.07
Our approach	GW	17.81	14.23	13.21
	WP	14.32	**12.66**	11.61
	General GW	15.07	13.99	12.81
	1st GE	**14.14**	13.34	11.31
	2nd GE	14.45	13.19	**11.23**

Table 1: Average per-pixel spectral reconstruction errors (in degrees) yielded by our approach and the three alternatives for the datasets under study and a number of white balancing methods. The absolute lowest error per dataset is in bold font. We have underlined the lowest error for each of the alternatives as applied to each dataset.

6.2 Quantitative Evaluation

We commence by showing quantitative results on both, the spectral reconstruction and the illuminant recovery for our method and a number of alternatives. These are the method presented in [25], which is based on a Radian Basis Function (RBF) network, the weighted PCA algorithm in [2] and the linear interpolation approach of Abed *et al.* [1].

For all the methods, we have used the training images provided in the NUS [25] dataset and quantified the spectral reconstruction error using the Euclidean angle in degrees between the ground truth and the reconstructed values of $R(u, \cdot)$. We opt for this error measure as it is widely used in previous works [32]. Note that the other error measure used elsewhere is the RMS error [25]. It is worth noting, however, that the Euclidean angle and the RMS error are correlated when the spectra is normalised to unit L2-norm.

In Table 1, we show the angular errors for the spectral reconstruction on the three datasets and the methods under study when the grey world (GW) assumption [3], white patch (WP) algorithm [15] and the 1st and 2nd order grey edge (GE) methods [32] are used to perform white balancing at testing. Note that the absolute best (in bold), is always yielded by our method, followed by the approach in [25].

In Table 2 we show the angular error for the recovered illuminant for both, our method and the alternative in [25]. This is since the other alternatives do not aim at recovering the illuminant. Note that, again, our method consistently delivers the lowest angular error. Moreover, the results in the table are quite consistent with those in Table 1.

Here, we also quantify the difference in pseudocolor, *i.e.* the reconstructed image converted into colour using the colour sensitivity functions in [13]. between the reconstructed image spectra and the input testing imagery. We do this following the intuition that a good spectral reconstruction should yield a pseudocolor image whose colour difference with respect to the ground truth is small. To quantify the colour difference, we have used the CIEDE2000 colour difference [29]. In Table 3, we show the colour difference per dataset for each of the alternatives and white balancing strategies. Note that the colour difference for our method is the lowest, consistently being about 1 unit, which is within the just noticeable chromatic difference.

Finally, we use the dataset in [18] to evaluate the effect of different spectral sensitivity functions in our method and the alternatives. To this end, we have tested the methods using pseudocolour images, *i.e.* colour imagery generated using the hyperspectral images and spectral sensitivities for the 28 camera models in [18] for each of the datasets. In Table 4, we show the mean and standard deviation for the

		Foster	Scyllarus	NUS
Nguyen et al. [25]	GW	27.86	23.98	19.18
	WP	26.21	<u>21.66</u>	16.88
	General GW	25.17	23.52	17.99
	1st GE	22.53	22.06	<u>16.71</u>
	2nd GE	<u>22.32</u>	21.73	17.28
Our approach	GW	18.56	15.11	14.06
	WP	15.67	**13.35**	12.47
	General GW	15.22	15.12	13.47
	1st GE	**14.23**	14.62	12.67
	2nd GE	15.01	14.01	**12.25**

Table 2: Illuminant angular error (in degrees) yielded by our approach and the alternative in [25] for the datasets under study. The absolute lowest error per dataset is in bold font. We have underlined the lowest error for each of the two methods as applied to each dataset.

		Foster	Scyllarus	NUS
Abed et al. [1]	GW	9.11	7.85	5.89
	WP	<u>7.99</u>	<u>6.99</u>	<u>5.12</u>
	General GW	8.54	7.44	5.20
	1st GE	8.18	7.11	5.37
	2nd GE	8.05	7.23	5.62
Agahian et al. [2]	GW	<u>15.82</u>	12.78	9.99
	WP	12.85	<u>9.56</u>	<u>8.47</u>
	General GW	14.78	11.43	9.32
	1st GE	13.67	9.87	9.19
	2nd GE	12.99	10.76	8.92
Nguyen et al. [25]	GW	5.69	6.18	3.93
	WP	6.54	5.58	3.59
	General GW	7.48	5.73	3.77
	1st GE	5.63	4.68	3.32
	2nd GE	<u>4.43</u>	<u>4.52</u>	<u>3.29</u>
Our approach	GW	2.57	2.32	2.14
	WP	1.42	**1.03**	**1.02**
	General GW	2.21	2.43	1.02
	1st GE	1.32	1.21	1.09
	2nd GE	**1.08**	1.34	1.04

Table 3: Average per-pixel CIEDE2000 colour difference for the three datasets. The absolute lowest difference per dataset is in bold font. We have underlined the lowest error for each of the alternatives as applied to each dataset.

	Abed et al. [1]	Agahian et al. [2]
	Spectra	Spectra
Foster	27.04±3.56 (WP) 29.24±4.06 (GW)	49.12±2.68 (WP) 58.95±3.63 (GW)
Scyllarus	24.24±3.25 (WP) 26.94±3.79 (GW)	39.35±3.96 (WP) 44.20±4.29 (GW)
NUS	16.14±3.27 (WP) 19.48±3.72 (GW)	33.37±3.47 (WP) 39.09±3.45 (GW)
	Nguyen et al. [25]	
	Spectra	Illuminant
Foster	21.14±2.32 (2nd GE) 26.36±2.98 (GW)	22.18±1.32 (2nd GE) 28.42±3.31 (GW)
Scyllarus	19.05±1.29 (WP) 23.82±2.16 (GW)	21.95±1.68 (WP) 23.82±2.16 (GW)
NUS	14.48±1.98 (1st GE) 18.12±1.28 (GW)	16.75±1.07 (1st GE) 19.94±2.58 (GW)
	Our approach	
	Spectra	Illuminant
Foster	**14.21±1.28 (1st GE)** 18.45±2.84 (GW)	**14.08±1.43 (1st GE)** 19.45±3.43 (GW)
Scyllarus	**12.82±1.69 (WP)** 14.29±2.31 (GW)	**13.88±1.95 (WP)** 15.11±2.01 (General GW)
NUS	**11.17±1.29 (2nd GE)** 13.43±1.29 (GW)	**12.19±1.09 (2nd GE)** 14.16±1.18 (GW)

Table 4: Per-pixel angular difference for the three datasets when the spectral sensitivity functions of commercial cameras are used to generate the testing imagery. The white balancing methods (in parenthesis) shown are those that previously delivered the best and worst performance. Absolute best per dataset are in bold fonts.

per-pixel angular error for each of the alternatives yielded by the best and worst performing white balancing algorithm. In the table, the corresponding white balancing method is in parenthesis. We only show the illuminant recovery results for our method and the approach in [25], which do deliver the illuminant at output.

It is worth noting in passing that, as expected, in the tables, all the alternatives do better in the NUS dataset. This is since we have used the NUS subset for training. Nonetheless, our method is able to deliver good results on the other datasets regardless. This hints that our approach can generalise well, being trained in a particular dataset and then used to process imagery from other sources.

6.3 Illuminant Substitution and Transfer

Now, we turn our attention to a sample application relevant to image editing. In this section, we show how the reconstructed spectra and recovered illuminant power spectrum can be used to substitute or transfer the illuminant from one scene to another. This stems from the observation that, once the spectra $R(u, \cdot)$ and the illuminant power spectrum are in hand, we can recover the new image in a straighforward manner by evaluating Equation 3.

For our experiments, we have used two widely available commercial cameras. These are a Nikon D80 and a Nikon D5100. The imagery presented here has all been acquired in RAW format and, for our method, we have performed white balancing using the 2nd order grey edge method [32]. The spectral sensitivity functions are those in [18] and the training set is, again, the subset of spectral imagery taken from the NUS dataset.

In Figure 2, we show two sets of images where the illuminant has been transferred from one on to the other. In the figure, the top row shows the images used for extracting the illuminant transferred to the imagery in the second row. The third row shows the white balanced imagery. We have included these since it can be interpreted as true "white" light. The bottom row shows the illuminant substitution results when the power spectrum of the light in the images on the top row is used to compute the colour for the ones in the second row. Note that, in the figure, the changes in the imagery on the left are quite subtle whereas those in the right-hand side are much more evident. Nonetheless, we can appreciate that the tones on the stainless steel escalator are in good accordance with the metallic surfaces in the top image and the green walls appear more yellow.

Finally, in Figure 3, we show a set of images where the illuminant has been substituted by that of a tungsten (middle column) and fluorescent lamp (right-hand column). We have acquired the power spectrum of these light sources in house using a spectrometer equipped with an integrating sphere. Here, we also see the expected effects due to the changes in the illuminant. Note that the middle column imagery is "warmer", which is a common effect of incandescent and tungsten lamps. The right-hand panels, in the other hand, show shifts of the colour balance towards the green channel.

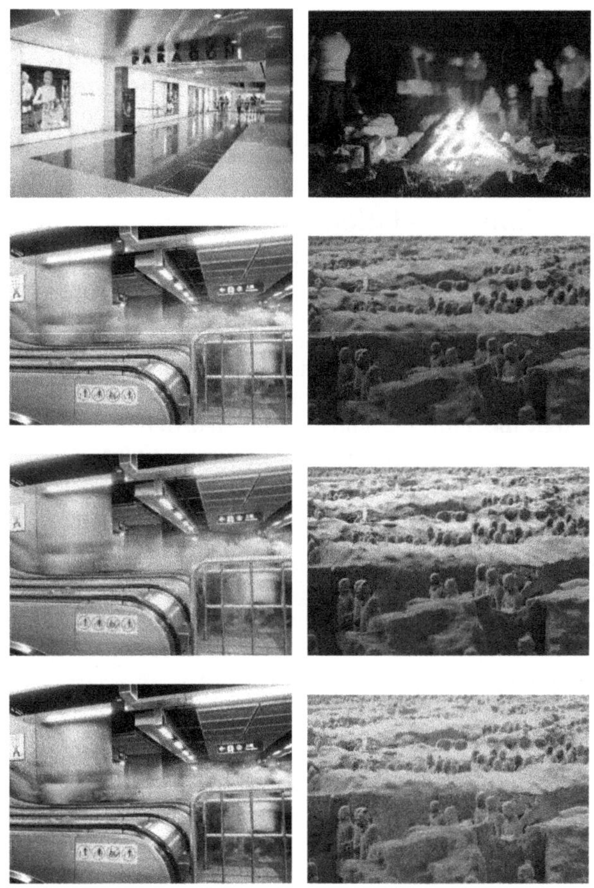

Figure 2: Illuminant transfer results. We have transferred the illuminant from the imagery in the top row to that in the second rows The third row shows the images in the second row after white balancing. The bottom two rows show the images in the second row lit by the illuminant in the top images.

Figure 3: Illuminant substitution results. Left-hand column: Input images; Middle column: Images when the illuminant has been subsituted by an incandescent light; Right-hand column: Images with the illuminant substituted by a fluorescent lamp.

6.4 Film Simulation

We now turn our attention to the use of spectral sensitivity functions other than that of the sensor used to acquire the image to present the scene to the user. This can be done in a straightforward manner by setting $Q_c(\cdot)$ in Equation 3 to an alternative. This, in effect, allows for the presentation of the image to the user with the colour rendition of a completely different medium, *i.e.* film as compared to digital.

To illustrate the effects of doing this, in Figure 4 we have taken two sample pictures acquired with a Nikon D80 and recovered their spectral reconstruction using our method. As done in the previous section, for all our images, we have performed white balancing using the 2nd order grey edge method [32]. For all the imagery, we have produced colour imagery using the spectral sensitivity function corresponding to the Fujichrome 64T Type II Professional[6] and the Kodak HD 400[7] and T-MAX 100 films[8].

Note that, in the figure, the images produced using the Fujichrome 64T Type II Professional show a very faint greenish colour tint whereas the ones produced using the sensitivity function of the Kodak HD 400 appear to be better colour balanced. This is consistent with the Fujichrome 64T film being a tungsten film as compared to the Kodak HD 400, which is a daylight film. This is also consistent with the notion that different types of film will deliver distinctive colours with particular look and feel. In the other hand, the imagery produced using the sensitivity functions for the Kodak T-MAX 100 has a very different character as compared to the colour panels in the figure.

6.5 Mood Board Colour Transfer

Finally, we explore the use of a mood board for recolouring the image accordingly. Mood boards are collections of colours, filters or images that convey a mood or feeling. These are used by arts and media professionals as part of the creative process. Here, we have used a set of tiles from an XRite ColorChecker Digital SG to create a mood board in a manner akin to that used for Lee filters[9].

For each of our two mood boards, we have selected a set of tiles from the colour chart. We have then acquired the reflectance of these tiles in house with a StellarNet spectrometer and used these reflectance spectra to "unmix" the reconstructed image irradiance for three sample scenes captured with a Nikon D5100. Spectral unmixing is widely used in remote sensing so as to express the relative abundance of primordial materials, *i.e.* end members, in multispectral or hyperspectral imagery. Thus, here, after performing our spectral reconstruction, we have applied the method in [11] so as to recover the spectral reflectance. With the reflectance in hand, we have then used the unmixing method in [23] so as to recover the abundances of the mood board spectra that account for the best linear approximation of the image reflectance, *i.e.* the abundances of the XRite ColorChecker tiles whose reflectance best mixes into the image spectra.

In Figure 5, we show the results of applying the two mood boards to our input images. As in the previous section, we have used, for our approach, the 2nd order grey edge white balancing method [32]. Note that, in principle, the same unmixing approach can be applied in a straightforward manner to the image colour in the rg-chromaticity space. As a result, in the figure, we have also included the results yielded by the unmixing in the chromaticity space rather than in the spectral domain.

Note that the colour-based results are much more similar to one another than those yielded by our spectral reconstruction. This is due to the fact that, as a result of Grassmann's law [35], any value inside the simplex formed by the mood board colours on the CIE XY chromaticity diagram will be reproduced by the unmixing process. This contrasts with the spectral domain, where each of the pixel colours arises from the application of Equation 3 to the mixed spectra and, hence, it does not abide to Grassmann's law. This can be clearly appreciated in the figure, where the results yielded by our spectral reconstruction have clearly acquired the colour scheme of the corresponding mood boards.

7. CONCLUSIONS

In this paper, we have presented a method to perform spectral reconstruction from a single colour image making use of training data. The method presented here is based upon a set of spectral and convolutional features. This is an important trait of our approach, leveraging material appearance information to better capture the reflectance properties of objects in the training set. We have also shown how the illuminant power spectrum can be recovered via a quadratic optimisation step. We have performed a qualitative analysis and compared against a number of alternative methods. We

[6] Available at http://www.fujifilmusa.com/support/ServiceSupportProduct.do?prodcat=238599

[7] Accessible at http://www.kodak.com/global/en/consumer/products/techInfo/e7013/e7013.shtml

[8] Downloadable from http://www.kodak.com/global/en/professional/support/techPubs/f32/f32c.jhtml

[9] See http://www.leefilters.com/lighting/moods.html

Figure 4: Film simulation results. We have performed spectral reconstruction on the images in the right-hand column and simulated three commercial films. The second column shows the white balanced images. The remaining columns show the result of applying a uniform irradiance illuminant and the spectral sensitivity functions for Fujichrome 64T Type II Professional, Kodak HD 400 and Kodak T-MAX 100, respectively.

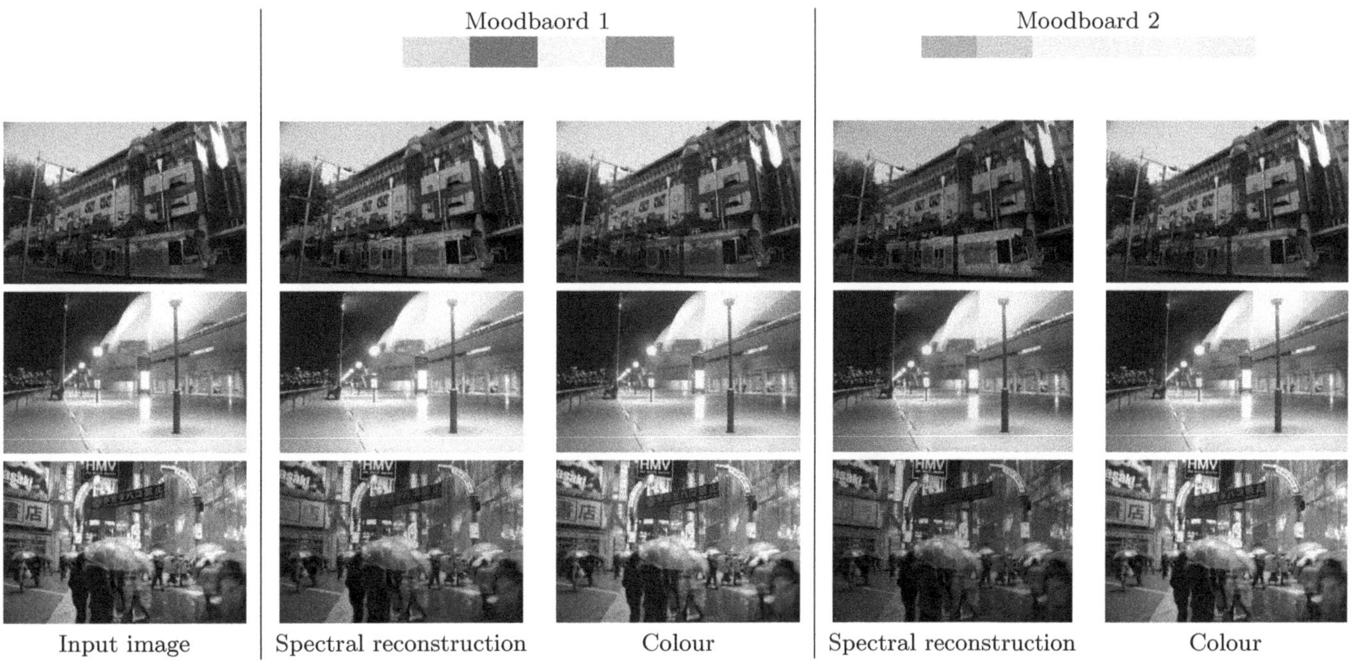

Figure 5: Mood board colour transfer results. We have performed spectral reconstruction on the images in the right-hand column and used the spectral reflectance of the mood board tiles to further decompose the scene reflectance. In the figure, we show results for two mood board tile sets. We also show results when the unmixing is effected in the rg-chromaticity space ("Colour" labelled columns) rather than on the spectral reconstruction.

have also illustrated the utility of our approach for illuminant transfer and substitution, film look and feel simulation and the application of mood board colour schemes to novel imagery.

Acknowledgements

NICTA is funded by the Australian Government through the Department of Communications and the Australian Research Council through the ICT Centre of Excellence Program.

8. REFERENCES

[1] F. M. Abed, S. H. Amirshahi, and M. R. M. Abed. Reconstruction of reflectance data using an interpolation technique. *Journal of the Optical Society of America A*, 26(3):613–624, 2009.

[2] F. Agahian, S. A. Amirshahi, and S. H. Amirshahi. Reconstruction of reflectance spectra using weighted principal component analysis. *Color Research & Application*, 33:360–371, 2008.

[3] G. Buchsbaum. A spatial processor model for object colour perception. *Journal of the Franklin Institute*, 310(1):337–350, 1980.

[4] J. Domke and X. Liu. Projecting ising model parameters for fast mixing. In *Neural Information Processing Systems*, pages 665–673, 2013.
[5] T. Ejaz, T. Horiuchi, G. Ohashi, and Y. Shimodaira. Development of a camera system for the acquisition of high-fidelity colors. *IEICE Trans. on Electronics*, E89–C(10):1441–1447, 2006.
[6] G. Finlayson, S. Hordley, and P. Hubel. Recovering device sensitivities with quadratic programming. In *Proceedings of the IS&T/SID Color Imaging Conference*, pages 90–Ű95, 1998.
[7] D. H. Foster, K. Amano, S. M. C. Nascimento, and M. J. Foster. Frequency of metamerism in natural scenes. *Journal of the Optical Society of America A*, 23(10):2359–2372, 2006.
[8] L. Gu, C. P. Huynh, and A. Robles-Kelly. Material-specific user colour profiles from imaging spectroscopy data. In *IEEE International Conference on Computer Vision*, 2011.
[9] L. Gu, A. Robles-Kelly, and J. Zhou. Efficient estimation of reflectance parameters from imaging spectroscopy. *IEEE Trans. on Image Processing*, (99):1–1, 2013.
[10] S. Han, Y. Matsushita, I. Sato, T. Okabe, and Y. Sato. Camera spectral sensitivity estimation from a single image under unknown illumination by using fluorescence. In *Computer Vision and Pattern Recognition*, 2012.
[11] C. P. Huynh and A. Robles-Kelly. A solution of the dichromatic model for multispectral photometric invariance. *International Journal of Computer Vision*, 90(1):1–27, 2010.
[12] J. Jiang, D. Liu, J. Gu, and S. Süsstrunk. What is the space of spectral sensitivity functions for digital color cameras? In *Workshop on Applications of Computer Vision*, pages 168–179, 2013.
[13] D. B. Judd. Report of U.S. secretariat committee on colorimetry and artificial daylight. page 11, 1951.
[14] R. Kawakami, H. Zhao, R. Tan, and K. Ikeuchi. Camera spectral sensitivity and white balance estimation from sky images. *International Journal of Computer Vision*, 105(3):187–204, 2013.
[15] E. H. Land and J. J. Mccann. Lightness and retinex theory. *Journal of the Optical Society of America*, 61:1–11, 1971.
[16] H. Lee, A. Battle, R. Raina, and A. Y. Ng. Efficient sparse coding algorithms. In *Neural Information Processing Systems (NIPS)*, pages 801–808, 2006.
[17] T. Leung and J. Malik. Representing and recognizing the visual appearance of materials using three dimensional textons. *International Journal of Computer Vision*, 43(1):29–44, 2001.
[18] H. T. Lin, S. J. Kim, S. Süsstrunk, and M. S. Brown. Revisiting radiometric calibration for color computer vision. In *International Conference on Computer Vision*, pages 129–136, 2011.
[19] P. Longere and D. H. Brainard. Simulation of digital camera images from hyperspectral input. In *Vision Models and Applications to Image and Video Processing*.
[20] L. Maloney. Evaluation of linear models of surface spectral reflectance with small numbers of parameters. *Journal of the Optical Society of America A*, 50(1):1673–1683, 1983.
[21] R. Martin, Z. Arno, and K. Reinhard. Practical spectral characterization of trichromatic cameras. In *SIGGRAPH Asia*, 2011.
[22] J. Nakamura. *Image Sensors and Signal Processing for Digital Still Cameras*. CRC Press, 2006.
[23] J. M. P. Nascimento and J. M. B. Dias. Vertex component analysis: A fast algorithm to unmix hyperspectral data. *IEEE Trans. on Geoscience and Remote Sensing*, 43(4):898–910, 2005.
[24] R. M. H. Nguyen, D. K. Prasad, and M. S. Brown. Raw-to-raw: Mapping between image sensor color responses. In *Computer Vision and Pattern Recognition*, 2014.
[25] R. M. H. Nguyen, D. K. Prasad, and M. S. Brown. Training-based spectral reconstruction from a single RGB image. In *European Conference on Conputer Vision*, pages 186–201, 2014.
[26] J. Romero, A. García-Beltrán, and J. Hernández-Andrés. Linear basis representation of natural and artificial illuminants. *Journal of the Optical Society of America*, 15:2913–2920, 1997.
[27] G. Schwartz and K. Nishino. Visual material traits: Recognizing per-pixel material context. In *Proc. of Color and Photometry in Computer Vision*, 2013.
[28] G. Sharma, M. J. Vrhel, and H. J. Trussell. Color imaging for multimedia. *Proceedings of the IEEE*, 86(6):1088–1108, 1998.
[29] G. Sharma, W. Wu, and E. N. Dalal. The CIEDE2000 color-difference formula: implementation notes, supplementary test data, and mathematical observations. *Color Research & Application*, 30(1):21–30, 2005.
[30] R. Tibshirani. Regression shrinkage and selection via the lasso. *Journal of the Royal Statistical Society, Series B*, 58:267–288, 1994.
[31] P. Urban, M. Desch, K. Happel, and D. Spiehl. Recovering camera sensitivities using target-based reflectances captured under multiple led-illuminations. In *Proceedings of the Workshop on Color Image Processing*, page 916, 2010.
[32] J. van de Weijer, T. Gevers, and A. Gijsenij. Edge-based color constancy. *IEEE Trans. on Image Processing*, 16(9):2207–2214, 2007.
[33] M. Varma and A. Zisserman. Classifying images of materials: Achieving viewpoint and illumination independence. In *European Conf. on Computer Vision*, volume 3, pages 255–271, 2002.
[34] A. Vedaldi and S. Soatto. Quick shift and kernel methods for mode seeking. In *European Conference on Computer Vision*, pages 705–718, 2008.
[35] G. Wyszecki and W. Stiles. *Color Science: Concepts and Methods, Quantitative Data and Formulae*. Wiley, 2000.
[36] Y. Zhao and R. S. Berns. Image-based spectral reflectance reconstruction using the matrix R method. *Color Research & Application*, 32(5):343–351, 2007.

SkyStitch: a Cooperative Multi-UAV-based Real-time Video Surveillance System with Stitching

Xiangyun Meng, Wei Wang and Ben Leong
School of Computing
National University of Singapore
idmmeng@nus.edu.sg, weiwang@comp.nus.edu.sg, benleong@comp.nus.edu.sg

ABSTRACT

Recent advances in unmanned aerial vehicle (UAV) technologies have made it possible to deploy an aerial video surveillance system to provide an unprecedented aerial perspective for ground monitoring in real time. Multiple UAVs would be required to cover a large target area, and it is difficult for users to visualize the overall situation if they were to receive multiple disjoint video streams. To address this problem, we designed and implemented *SkyStitch*, a multiple-UAV video surveillance system that provides a single and panoramic video stream to its users by stitching together multiple aerial video streams. SkyStitch addresses two key design challenges: (i) the high computational cost of stitching and (ii) the difficulty of ensuring good stitching quality under dynamic conditions. To improve the speed and quality of video stitching, we incorporate several practical techniques like distributed feature extraction to reduce workload at the ground station, the use of hints from the flight controller to improve stitching efficiency and a Kalman filter-based state estimation model to mitigate jerkiness. Our results show that SkyStitch can achieve a stitching rate that is 4 times faster than existing state-of-the-art methods and also improve perceptual stitching quality. We also show that SkyStitch can be easily implemented using commercial off-the-shelf hardware.

Categories and Subject Descriptors

I.4 [**Image processing and computer vision**]: [Applications]; I.2.9 [**Robotics**]: [Autonomous vehicles]

Keywords

UAV; stitching; real-time

1. INTRODUCTION

The proliferation of commodity UAV technologies like quadcopters has made it possible to deploy aerial video surveillance systems to achieve an unprecedented perspective when monitoring a target area from the air. UAV-based surveillance systems have a broad range of applications including firefighting [2], search and rescue [3], and border monitoring [8].

MM'15, October 26–30, 2015, Brisbane, Australia.
© 2015 ACM. ISBN 978-1-4503-3459-4/15/10 ...$15.00.
DOI: http://dx.doi.org/10.1145/2733373.2806225.

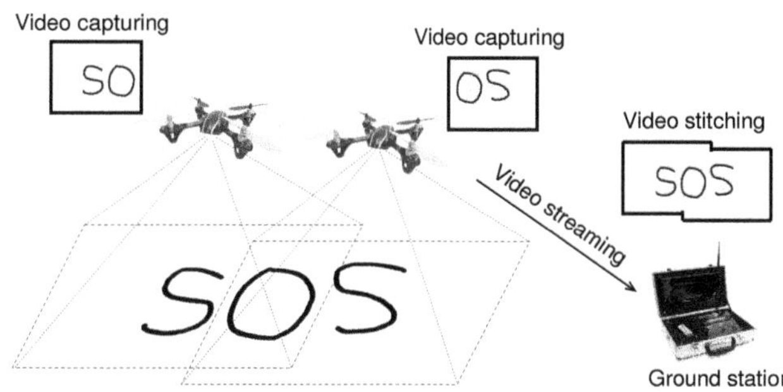

Figure 1: Illustration of SkyStitch. Each quadcopter transmits a live video stream to the ground station, which stitches them together to provide a single composite view of the target area.

For example, a UAV could be deployed to hover over a bushfire to transmit a live video feed to firefighters using wireless links to allow them to appraise the situation from an aerial perspective. However, because on-board cameras have only a limited field of view, multiple UAVs would be required to cover a large target area. If the firefighters were to receive multiple disjoint video streams from each UAV, it would be difficult for them to put together a consistent view of the situation on the ground.

To address this problem, we designed and implemented SkyStitch, a quadcopter-based HD video surveillance system that incorporates *fast video stitching*. With SkyStitch, users on the ground would receive a single composite live video feed produced from the video streams from multiple UAVs. This is illustrated in Figure 1, where an SOS sign is marked on the ground by victims trapped in a bushfire.

Although the high-level idea of SkyStitch is relatively straightforward, there are two practical design challenges. The first challenge is that image stitching inherently has a very high computational cost. Existing stitching algorithms in both industry and academia [5, 26, 13] were designed for better stitching quality rather than shorter stitching time. Although some algorithms can achieve shorter stitching times [6, 27, 31], they impose an additional requirement that the cameras be in fixed relative positions, which is infeasible in our operating scenario as the cameras are mounted on moving quadcopters. The other challenge is that existing image stitching algorithms are designed for static images, and not video. We found that even though the individual frames produced by image stitching algorithms might look fine, the video obtained by naively stitching them together would usually suffer from perspective distortion, perspective jerkiness and frame drops.

To address these challenges, we made a few key observations about our unique operating environment and developed several practical techniques to improve both stitching efficiency and quality. One observation is that, although each UAV has only a limited payload, each on-board computer has a fair amount of computational power. In SkyStitch, we divide the video stitching process into several tasks and offload some pre-processing to the UAVs. In this way, we can improve the speed of stitching by reducing the workload of the ground station, which would be a potential bottleneck when there are a large number of UAVs. Another observation is that we can exploit the hints from instantaneous flight information like UAV attitude and GPS location from the on-board flight controller to greatly improve the efficiency of stitching and rectify perspective distortion. Our third observation is that image stitching and optical flow have complementary properties in terms of long-term stability and short-term smoothness. Therefore, a Kalman filter-based state estimation model can be applied by incorporating optical flow information to significantly reduce perspective jerkiness.

We deployed SkyStitch on a pair of low-cost self-assembled quadcopters and evaluated its performance for two ground scenarios with very different feature distributions. Our experiments showed that SkyStitch achieves a shorter stitching time than existing methods with GPU acceleration [26], e.g., SkyStitch is up to 4 times faster for 12 concurrent aerial video sources. In other words, for a fixed frame rate, SkyStitch can support many more video sources and thus cover a much larger target area in practice. For example, at a stitching rate of 20 frames per second (fps), SkyStitch is able to stitch videos from 12 quadcopters while existing methods can only support three with the same hardware. In addition, SkyStitch is able to achieve better stitching quality by rectifying perspective distortion, recovering stitching failures and mitigating video jerkiness. Furthermore, SkyStitch can be easily implemented using commercial off-the-shelf hardware thereby reducing the cost of practical deployment.

The rest of this paper is organized as follows. In Section 2, we present the prior work related to SkyStitch. In Section 3, we discuss the design details of SkyStitch, followed by its implementation in Section 4. In Section 5, we present the performance evaluation of SkyStitch. Finally, we conclude this paper in Section 6.

2. RELATED WORK

Image stitching has been widely studied in the literature. Most available stitching algorithms are focused on improving stitching quality without considering stitching time [26, 16, 13]. Recently, image stitching algorithms have been applied in UAV-based incremental image mosaicking [32]. Basically, a UAV flies over a target area along a pre-planned route and continuously takes images, which are transmitted to a ground station and incrementally stitched to produce a large image of the target area. Unlike SkyStitch, such applications do not have a stringent requirement on stitching rate. Wischounig et al. improved the responsiveness of mosaicking by first transmitting meta data and low-resolution images in the air, and only transmitting the high-resolution images at a later stage, i.e., after landing [30]. There are also commercial systems for UAV-based image mosaicking. The company NAVSYS claims that its system can achieve a stitching rate of one image per second [12].

There are several existing video stitching algorithms that can achieve fast stitching rate, but most of them only work for a static camera array like the one used by Google Street View [10]. Tennoe et al. developed a real-time video stitching system using four static HD cameras installed in a sports stadium [27]. The key idea of their design is to pipeline the stitching process and implement it in GPU, and it is able to achieve a stitching rate of 30 fps. Adam et al. utilized belief propagation to obtain depth information of images captured on a pair of fixed cameras [9]. Their GPU-based implementation is able to achieve a rate of 37 fps when stitching two 1600×1200 images, but it requires a calibration process to compute the overlapping region of the camera views. Another GPU-based method relied on specific photogrammetric procedure to find the cameras' orientation and translation relative to a common coordinate system, and it could support a stitching rate up to 360 fps when stitching four 1360×1024 images [15]. A CPU-based method of video stitching can be found in [31]. Although these methods achieve fast stitching rates, they assume that the cameras are in a static position and require system calibration and are thus not applicable to stitching videos from highly dynamic UAVs.

As smartphones become ubiquitous, some researchers have tried in recent times to improve viewers' viewing experience by managing video streams from multiple smartphones. Kaheel et al. proposed a system called Mobicast which could stitch several 352×288 video streams from smartphones that captured the same event [22]. While the frame rate of Mobicast was able to meet real-time requirements, its stitching quality in real experiments was generally poor, with a stitching failure rate of some 60%. El-Saban et al. improved the frame rate of a similar system by considering the temporal correlation of frames [17]. Since most smartphones are equipped with various sensors, we believe that the methods proposed in this paper could potentially also be applied to improve the performance of smartphone-based video stitching systems.

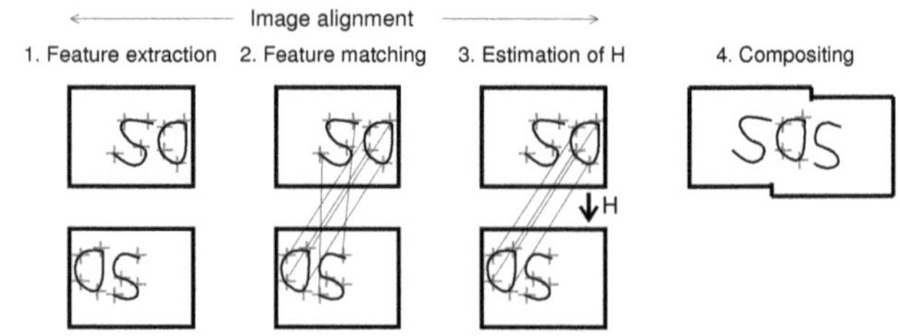

Figure 2: Overview of image stitching.

3. REAL-TIME VIDEO STITCHING

Image stitching involves the alignment and blending of a pair of images with some overlap into a single seamless image. Video stitching is effectively the stitching of a series of image pairs (i.e., video frame pairs). Image stitching is computationally expensive and it takes several seconds to stitch a pair of HD images using Hugin [5], a popular image stitching software, on a workstation with a 3.4 GHz CPU. The challenge of real-time video stitching is to ensure that we can stitch a set of video frames within the required video frame interval. In this paper, we will use image and video frame interchangeably. In this section, we describe the steps required in image stitching and explain how SkyStitch improves the efficiency and quality of video stitching.

The key task in image stitching is to find the transformation between two images. Assume the ground is a planar surface, and let each pixel location in an aerial image be represented by a *homogeneous coordinate* $(x, y, 1)$. Then the pixel locations of the overlapping area in the two images are related by

$$[x'\ y'\ 1]^T \sim \mathbf{H} \cdot [x\ y\ 1]^T \quad (1)$$

where $\mathbf{H}$ is a 3×3 homography matrix for transformation. In order to align two images, we need to estimate $\mathbf{H}$.

The most popular method for $\mathbf{H}$ estimation is the *feature*-based method illustrated in Figure 2. Features refer to the unique parts in an image, e.g., corners are often considered as features. A feature is usually represented using a high-dimensional vector, called *feature descriptor*, which encodes feature information like gradient and orientation histogram in the neighborhood. A feature-based method for estimating $\mathbf{H}$ generally consists of the following three steps: (i) feature extraction, (ii) feature matching and (iii) robust homography estimation (e.g., using RANSAC [18]).

Once the image alignment (i.e., $\mathbf{H}$) is determined, it remains to combine the images into a single composite image while minimizing visual artefacts such as seams, blurring and ghosting. A more detailed discussion on image stitching can be found in [26].

The challenge of video stitching is that most of the abovementioned steps in image stitching are computationally expensive. Our main contributions in SkyStitch are several techniques to reduce the processing time of video frame stitching to the scale of tens of milliseconds, while maintaining good stitching quality, as follows: (i) we reduce the workload of the ground station by offloading feature extraction to quadcopters (§ 3.1); (ii) we exploit flight status information to speed up feature matching and rectify perspective distortion (§ 3.2); (iii) we propose an efficient GPU-based RANSAC implementation (§ 3.3); and (iv) we utilize optical flow and Kalman filtering to improve video smoothness (§ 3.4). Finally, we developed a new approach for closing loops when stitching multiple video sources (§ 3.5).

3.1 Offloading Feature Extraction

In traditional image stitching systems, feature extraction and the subsequent processing steps are all performed on a single computer. However, such an approach might be problematic for SkyStitch because the ground station would become the computation bottleneck, especially when the number of quadcopters is large.

We noticed that there is an on-board computer in each quadcopter, and thus we can offload feature extraction to the quadcopters to reduce the amount of computation at the ground station. In other words, instead of transmitting only a video frame to the ground station, a quadcopter would also compute and append the corresponding features, which are simply a series of high-dimensional vectors, for each frame.

The computer on our quadcopters is an NVIDIA Jetson TK1 board. We implemented feature extraction using its GPU, which has 192 CUDA cores. We adopted the latest ORB method [25] for feature extraction, as it has been shown to achieve comparable accuracy to other methods such as SIFT [23] and SURF [11] but at a much lower computational cost. Profiling shows that extracting 1,000 features from a 1280×1024 image takes less than 35 ms.

3.2 Exploiting Flight Status Information

It is difficult to achieve short stitching time and high stitching quality at the same time. First, because of wind turbulence, the on-board camera will not always be pointing vertically downwards. Consequently, the images taken from a tilted camera will almost certainly have some amount of perspective distortion, which affects the quality of stitching.

Second, feature matching between two images is time-consuming since all the features have to be pairwise compared. For example, matching the features from two images with 1,000 features each would require one million pairwise comparisons of feature descriptors. This would take around 16 ms on a workstation with a 3.4 GHz CPU. Furthermore, for each feature in an image, there is at most one correct feature match in the corresponding image. This means that the probability of incorrect matching will be high when the number of features is large. If there are many mismatched features, the quality of stitching will suffer.

We observed that we have more information about the images to be stitched compared to conventional image stitching. In particular, because quadcopters are equipped with various on-board sensors for flight control, we are able to derive a relationship between the two images from the flight status information. We can detect and correct for perspective distortion and determine the region of overlap between two images to significantly reduce the target region in the images for feature matching.

3.2.1 Orthorectification of Perspective Distortion

Perspective distortion occurs when the camera is not pointing vertically downwards to the ground. With orthorectification, we can transform the image so that it looks as if the camera is pointed vertically downwards.

Since the degree of camera tilt is determined by the angles of roll and pitch, we can correct for the resulting perspective distortion using the attitude information from the flight controller. Let θ_r, θ_p and θ_y be the Euler angles of roll, pitch and yaw in the coordinate system of the flight controller, respectively (see Figure 3). Then the transformation matrix (denoted by the matrix $\mathbf{R}$) to map from strictly downwards camera direction to the tilted direction can be expressed as follows:

$$\mathbf{R} = \begin{bmatrix} 1 & 0 & 0 \\ 0 & \cos\theta_r & \sin\theta_r \\ 0 & -\sin\theta_r & \cos\theta_r \end{bmatrix} \begin{bmatrix} \cos\theta_p & 0 & -\sin\theta_p \\ 0 & 1 & 0 \\ \sin\theta_p & 0 & \cos\theta_p \end{bmatrix} \begin{bmatrix} \cos\theta_y & \sin\theta_y & 0 \\ -\sin\theta_y & \cos\theta_y & 0 \\ 0 & 0 & 1 \end{bmatrix} \quad (2)$$

We include the yaw angle in $\mathbf{R}$ so that orthorectification can also align the two images to a common orientation (i.e., to the north).

As the angles in the attitude information are with respect to the flight controller itself, we need another two simple transformations for orthorectification. One is needed to transform the pixel locations of an image (originally in pixel coordinates) into world coordinates that is centered at the camera. This can be easily achieved using *camera intrinsic matrix* $\mathbf{K}$. The other transformation (denoted by matrix $\mathbf{B}$) is needed to map from the world coordinates centered at the camera to the world coordinates centered at the flight controller. Both $\mathbf{K}$ and $\mathbf{B}$ can be easily obtained via calibration.

In summary, the orthorectification process consists of (i) mapping the pixels of an image into the world coordinates system of the flight controller (using matrices $\mathbf{K}$ and $\mathbf{B}$), (ii) correcting for the effect due to camera tilt (using matrix $\mathbf{R}$), and (iii) mapping them back to pixel coordinates (again using matrices $\mathbf{K}$ and $\mathbf{B}$). The orthorectification matrix (denoted by $\mathbf{M}$) can be expressed as,

$$\mathbf{M} = \mathbf{KBR}^{-1}\mathbf{B}^{-1}\mathbf{K}^{-1} \quad (3)$$

Let $(x, y, 1)$ be the original homogeneous pixel coordinates. Then the corresponding pixel coordinates after orthorectification (x', y', z') can be expressed using matrix multiplication,

$$[x'\ y'\ z']^T = \mathbf{M}\,[x\ y\ 1]^T \quad (4)$$

3.2.2 Search Region Reduction for Feature Matching

To reduce feature matching time, we take the spatial locations of features into consideration. Like image orthorectification, we exploit the available flight status information to find the mapping of pixel locations between two images. We first transform the pixel locations from pixel coordinates to a world coordinate system, with the center of the camera sensor as the origin, and merge the two world coordinate systems using the reported GPS locations (see Figure 4). Recall (x', y', z') are the coordinates of a pixel location after orthorectification. Let s be the number of meters represented by the side of a pixel, $W \times H$ be the image resolution (in pixels), θ_f be the angle of horizontal field of view in the camera, and h be the quadcopter altitude. Then,

$$s = 2h\tan(\frac{\theta_f}{2})/W \quad (5)$$

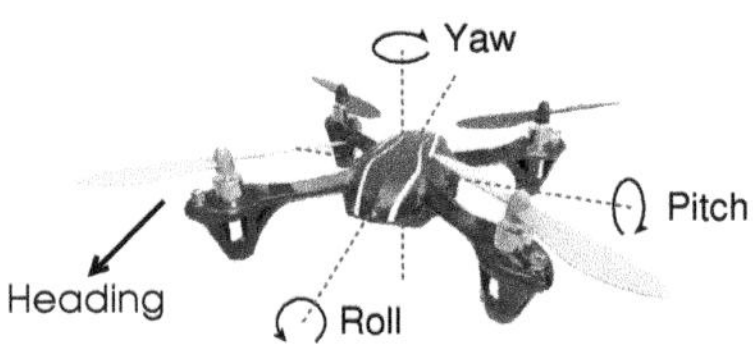

Figure 3: Flight attitude of quadcopter: roll, pitch and yaw.

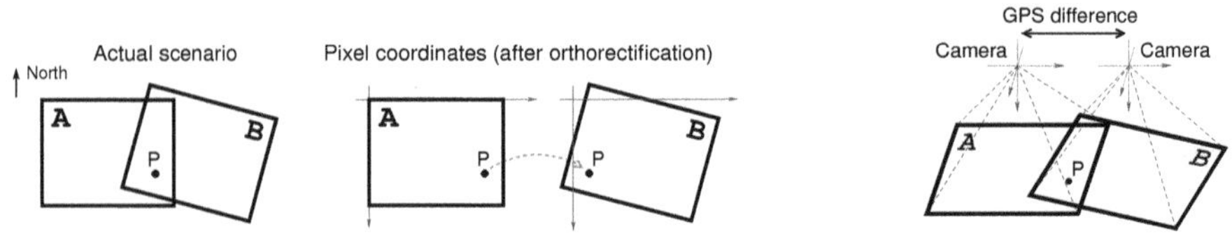

(a) Mapping a pixel location from one image to another.

(b) Merging coordinate systems.

Figure 4: Overlap determination using flight status information.

Then the final world coordinates (x_w, y_w, z_w) can be obtained by,

$$\begin{cases} x_w = s\,(\frac{x'}{z'} - \frac{W}{2}) \\ y_w = s\,(\frac{y'}{z'} - \frac{H}{2}) \\ z_w = h \end{cases} \tag{6}$$

In other words, each pixel of an image is mapped to a point (x_w, y_w) on the ground, with the center of the camera sensor as the coordinate origin. The two world coordinate systems can then be correlated using the difference in the GPS locations. With such information, we only need to search in a small local neighborhood for the matched feature. Because the area of the local neighborhood is often much smaller than the whole image, we can significantly reduce the search time of feature matching as compared with the traditional method of searching the entire image for the target feature.

This simple idea is illustrated in Figure 5. P is the location in Image 2 that we map for a feature point from Image 1, and r is the search radius for the matched feature. Since an image covers a finite 2D space, a grid indexing approach is preferred. We divide Image 2 into 50×40 bins. 50×40 was chosen because it is proportional to the aspect ratio of the image and it yields bins that are small enough. We would use more bins for a bigger image. If a bin is within a distance r from P (i.e., the colored bin), all the features in the bin will be considered as candidates for feature matching.

It remains for us to determine an appropriate value for the search radius r. Fortunately, the simple approach of setting a fixed and conservative value for r based on empirical experiments seems to be sufficient. In particular, we found that $r = 200$ pixels was sufficient in our implementation. In Section 3.4, we show that r can be further reduced if we estimate and compensate for GPS errors.

3.3 Optimizing RANSAC

The step after feature matching is to use the standard RANSAC method [18] to remove outliers. RANSAC arbitrarily selects four matched features to compute a homography matrix $\mathbf{H}$, applies this estimated $\mathbf{H}$ on all the matched features, repeats it for N iterations and finds the one with the most inliers. In challenging cases where the inlier ratio is low, we often set N to a large value (e.g., 500) in the hope that at least one subset of the four matched features would not contain any outliers.

While a large N improves RANSAC's likelihood of finding the correct homography, it also increases its computation time. For example, it takes about 11 ms to perform a 512-iteration RANSAC on a computer with a 3.4 GHz Intel CPU. This means that it is impossible to stitch more than 4 videos at 30 fps. In order to speed up RANSAC, we noticed that the traditional Singular Value Decomposition (SVD) method is unnecessary for 4-point homography and can be replaced with Gauss-Jordan elimination. The Gauss-Jordan method runs efficiently on GPU due to its simple and branchless structure, whereas an SVD implementation is usually much more complicated and GPU-unfriendly. Finally, we implemented an OpenCL-based RANSAC homography estimator that can compute a 512-iteration RANSAC in 0.6 ms.

To further improve RANSAC performance when the number of image pairs is large, we maximize parallelism and minimize IO overhead by performing RANSAC on all image pairs in one pass (Figure 6). First, candidate homographies of all image pairs are computed in a single kernel execution. The candidate homographies are then routed to corresponding image pairs for reprojection error computation and inlier mask generation. Finally, the scores and inlier masks of all candidate homographies are downloaded to main memory. Our RANSAC pipeline has only four CPU-GPU memory transactions and the amount of parallelism at each stage is much higher than performing RANSAC sequentially for each image pair.

In addition to execution speed, we also made improvements to the accuracy of RANSAC. Traditionally, each RANSAC iteration is scored based on the number of inliers. While this approach works well most of the time, we found that when the inliers are concentrated in a particular region, it may result in a bad estimation of $\mathbf{H}$. To mitigate this problem, we modified the score by taking into consideration the distribution of inliers. Specifically, we use a score that is a function of both the number of inliers and the standard deviations of their locations:

$$score = N_{inliers}\,\sigma_x\,\sigma_y \tag{7}$$

This score can be efficiently computed on the GPU during inlier mask generation. The RANSAC iteration with the highest score under this new metric was used to provide the inliers for the final $\mathbf{H}$ estimation.

3.4 Optimizing Video Stitching Quality

Given the set of inliers identified by RANSAC, we can proceed to compute the homography matrix $\mathbf{H}$ using least squares and then composite the two images based on $\mathbf{H}$ [26]. However, even though the set of inliers appears to be the best that we can find, it is possible for the resulting $\mathbf{H}$ to be ill-formed and to produce a stitched image with some perceptual artefacts. In particular, part of a stitched video frame may suddenly "jerk" when compared to the video frames before and after it.

There are two common causes for such "stitching failures". One is that the overlapping area between the two images is too small, and the resulting matched features are not sufficient to produce a good estimate of $\mathbf{H}$. Our experiments showed that the stitched images generally start exhibiting a certain degree of perceptual distortion when the number of inliers is smaller than 30. An example is shown in Figure 7(a). The other cause is that the original set of inliers selected by RANSAC are concentrated in a small region, and the resultant $\mathbf{H}$ becomes less stable, causing distant regions of images to be misaligned. An example is shown in Figure 7(b).

As human vision is sensitive to sudden scene change, we need to detect ill-formed $\mathbf{H}$ and prevent them from affecting the perceptual experience. In particular, we first determine whether there are sufficient inliers produced by $\mathbf{H}$. If the number of inliers is smaller than 30 (which we had determined from empirical experiments), we consider it as a failure and discard the current frame.

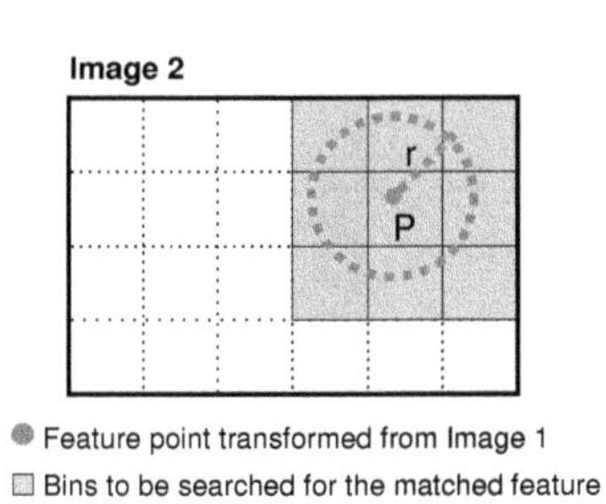

Figure 5: Search region reduction for feature matching.

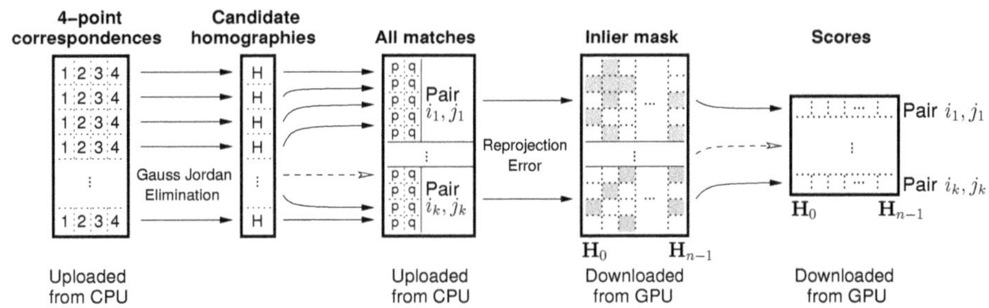

Figure 6: RANSAC GPU Pipeline

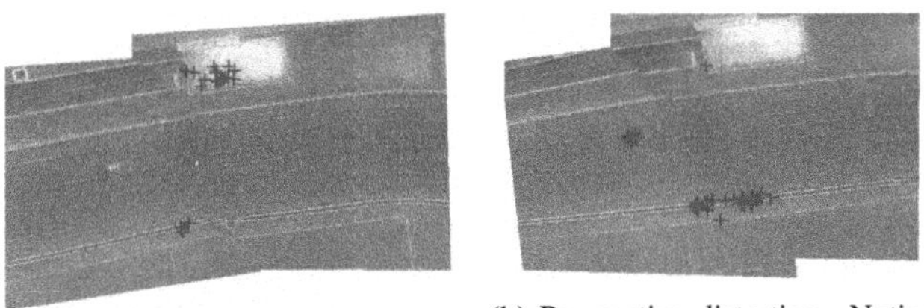

(a) Inaccurate rotation. Notice the broken and bent touchline of the football field, below the running track.

(b) Perspective distortion. Notice that the left part of the image is erroneously warped and cannot be perfectly aligned with the right image.

Figure 7: Examples of perceptual distortion. Each blue cross represents a feature point.

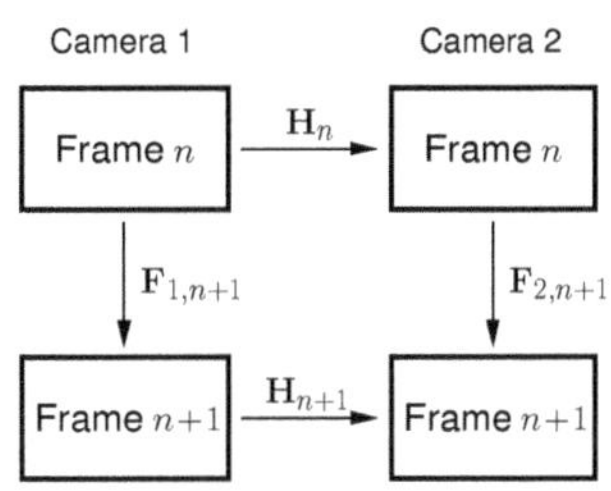

Figure 8: Predict $\mathbf{H}_{n+1}$ using optical flow when $\mathbf{H}_{n+1}$ is ill-formed.

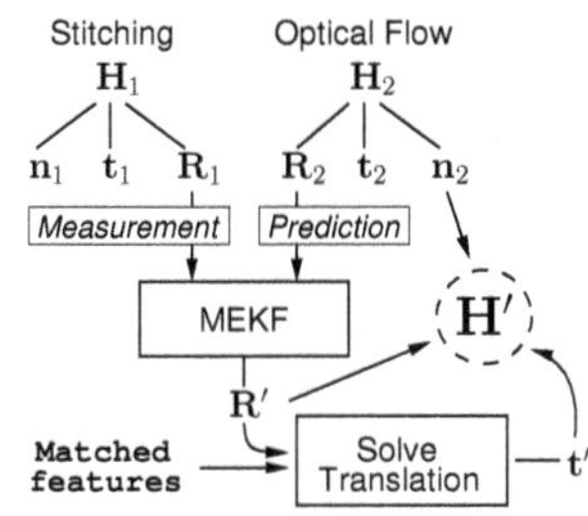

Figure 9: Fusing information from both stitching and optical flow.

When there are sufficient inliers, we also check whether $\mathbf{H}$ badly warps the images and introduces perspective distortion. Let θ be the angle between the two image planes after orthorectification using $\mathbf{M}$. Ideally, θ should be zero, but in practice it could be a small non-zero value due to the errors in the readings of our on-board sensors. To find θ we do homography decomposition on $\mathbf{H}$ [24]

$$\mathbf{H} = \mathbf{R} + \mathbf{t}\,\mathbf{n}^T \tag{8}$$

$\mathbf{R}$ is a 3×3 rotation matrix that transforms camera from the reference image to the target image. We are concerned about the angle between the reference xy-plane and the target xy-plane, which is simply the angle between the reference z-axis and the target z-axis:

$$cos(\theta) = r_{33} \tag{9}$$

By analyzing 300 stitched frames that do not exhibit noticeable perspective distortion (i.e., $\mathbf{H}$ is well-formed), we found that 90% of them have $|\theta| \leq 5°$. Thus, we use θ of 5° as the threshold to determine whether $\mathbf{H}$ is erroneously estimated.

3.4.1 Recovering from Failed Stitching

While discarding ill-formed $\mathbf{H}$ alleviates jerkiness in the stitched video frames, it also leads to frame drops and viewers may notice discontinuity in the video. To reduce frame drops, we use an alternative method to "predict" $\mathbf{H}$ when the original method fails, by utilizing the optical flow of adjacent frames.

This prediction method is illustrated in Figure 8. $\mathbf{F}$ is the 3×3 homography matrix of optical flow, which can be accurately and efficiently computed on each quadcopter as adjacent frames usually have large overlap. $\mathbf{F}_{n+1}$ is transmitted together with frame $n+1$ to the ground station, which will predict $\mathbf{H}_{n+1}$ as follows:

$$\mathbf{H}_{n+1} = \mathbf{M}_{2,n+1}\,\mathbf{F}_{2,n+1}\,\mathbf{M}_{2,n}^{-1}\,\mathbf{H}_n\,\mathbf{M}_{1,n}\,\mathbf{F}_{1,n+1}^{-1}\,\mathbf{M}_{1,n+1}^{-1} \tag{10}$$

where $\mathbf{M}$ is the orthorectification matrix described in Section 3.2.1 and $\mathbf{H}_n$ is the transformation matrix of the previous stitching which was not ill-formed. We check that $\mathbf{H}_{n+1}$ is not ill-formed according to the criteria described in the previous section.

3.4.2 Fusing Stitching and Prediction

In cases where stitching succeeds, we have two homography solutions: one is from pairwise stitching and the other is from prediction by optical flow. Stitching is independently performed for each pair of frames so it does not take temporal information into consideration. Optical flow makes use of previous results to estimate current homography but it could suffer from drift errors in the long term. The property of stitching is like an accelerometer: stable in long term but noisy in short term. Optical flow is like a gyroscope: accurate in the short term but prone to drift over time. This implies that sensor filtering techniques can be applied to achieve a better estimate by considering both stitching and prediction results.

The fusion procedure is shown in Figure 9. First, the two homography matrices are decomposed into rotations and translations (eq. 8). The rotation matrices $\mathbf{R}_1$ and $\mathbf{R}_2$ are converted to quaternions and fed into a Multiplicative Extended Kalman Filter (MEKF) [28]. The quaternion produced by stitching acts as a measurement vector and the quaternion produced by optical flow is used to generate a state transition matrix. We chose not to filter both the rotation and translation at the same time because the filtered homography would generate noticeable misalignment. Instead, the filtered rotation $\mathbf{R}'$ is used to compute a least-squares solution of translation $\mathbf{t}'$ using matched features. Finally, the filtered rotation $\mathbf{R}'$ and recomputed translation $\mathbf{t}'$ are combined to form a new homography matrix $\mathbf{H}'$.

3.4.3 GPS Drift Compensation

We explained in Section 3.2.2 that we can improve the speed of feature matching by focusing on a small search region with radius r. The purpose of r is to tolerate the potential errors when mapping pixels between two images since there are likely errors in the flight status information from on-board sensors, i.e., GPS drift errors.

We observed that when two images are successfully stitched, we will know the ground truth of the transformation. By comparing the ground truth with the transformation which relies on GPS locations

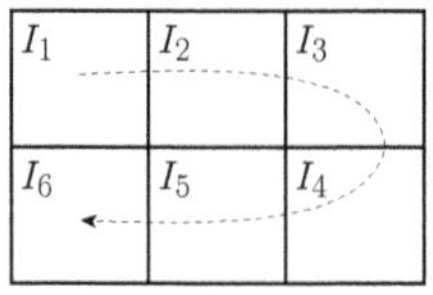

Figure 10: A loop sequence of stitching 6 images.

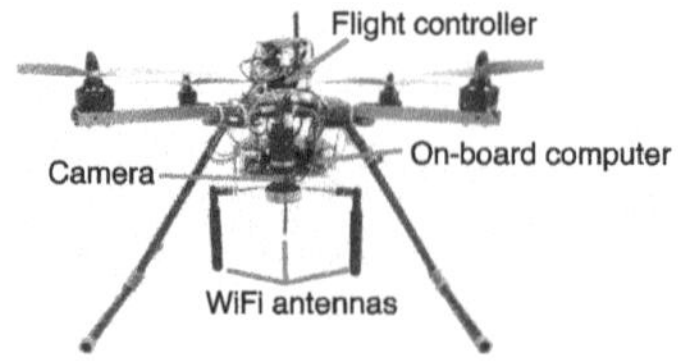

Figure 11: Our self-assembled quadcopter.

(Section 3.2.2), we can estimate the GPS error. Subsequently, we feed this estimated GPS error to feature matching and reduce r by subtracting the GPS error for the next round of stitching. Experimental results show that r can be reduced to smaller than 30 pixels, which makes the search area less than $^1/_{300}$ of total image size. If stitching fails, we reset r to the original conservative value.

3.5 Multiple Video Sources

Stitching multiple video frames can be considered as iteratively performing pairwise stitching. One problem is to decide which image pairs can be stitched. Previous approaches perform pairwise feature matching for all the images to identify the pairs of overlapping images based on matched features [13]. Such exhaustive search is too costly for SkyStitch. Instead, we make use of available flight status information to identify overlapping images and find a sequence of images for stitching. If we assume the quadcopters hover in a grid-like pattern, a simple stitching sequence would be a loop that traverses all the images as shown in Figure 10.

While such loop-based stitching is simple, stitching errors will gradually accumulate along the loop. Consequently, there could be significant distortion between the first and last images, e.g., between images I_1 and I_6 in Figure 10. To address this problem, our solution is to perform adjustment on every pairwise stitching along the loop so that the distortion can be gradually corrected.

Suppose we want to stitch four images in Figure 10, according to the sequence I_1, I_2, I_5 and I_6. Let $\mathbf{H}_1$, $\mathbf{H}_2$, $\mathbf{H}_3$ and $\mathbf{H}_4$ be the homography matrices of image pairs $\langle I_1, I_2\rangle$, $\langle I_2, I_5\rangle$, $\langle I_5, I_6\rangle$ and $\langle I_6, I_1\rangle$ respectively. Ideally, we should have

$$\mathbf{M}_1\mathbf{p} \sim \mathbf{H}_4\mathbf{H}_3\mathbf{H}_2\mathbf{H}_1\mathbf{M}_1\mathbf{p}$$

where $\mathbf{p}$ is a feature point in image I_1 and $\mathbf{M}_1$ is the orthorectification matrix of I_1. However, in practice, $\mathbf{H}_4\mathbf{H}_3\mathbf{H}_2\mathbf{H}_1$ is often not an identity matrix (even after scaling) because of errors in the homography matrices. To make the above relationship hold, we can introduce a correction matrix $\mathbf{H}$ such that:

$$\mathbf{M}_1\mathbf{p} \sim \mathbf{H}\mathbf{H}_4\mathbf{H}_3\mathbf{H}_2\mathbf{H}_1\mathbf{M}_1\mathbf{p}$$

Then we decompose $\mathbf{H}$ into four "equal" components and distribute them among the original four homography matrices. One way to decompose $\mathbf{H}$ is RQ decomposition:

$$\mathbf{H} = \mathbf{A}\mathbf{R}$$

Here $\mathbf{A}$ is an upper triangular matrix (affine) and $\mathbf{R}$ is a 3D rotation matrix. $\mathbf{A}$ can be further decomposed as follows:

$$\mathbf{A} = \mathbf{T}\mathbf{S}\mathbf{D}$$

where $\mathbf{T}$ is a 2D translation matrix, $\mathbf{S}$ is a scaling matrix and $\mathbf{D}$ is a shearing matrix along x-axis. $\mathbf{T}, \mathbf{S}, \mathbf{D}$ can be taken nth real root where n is number of images in the loop. We can write $\mathbf{H}$ as

$$\mathbf{H} = \mathbf{T}'^4\mathbf{S}'^4\mathbf{D}'^4\mathbf{R}'^4$$

Since the reference image is well orthorectified, $\mathbf{A}$ and $\mathbf{R}$ have geometric meanings. They represent how a camera should be rotated and translated to match the reference camera frame. We move each element from $\mathbf{H}$ into $\mathbf{H}_1, \cdots, \mathbf{H}_4$ to slightly adjust each camera's rotation and translation. For example, we move one $\mathbf{R}'$ into $\mathbf{H}_1$ so that the rotational error is reduced by $^1/_4$. In this way, we can partially correct the errors at each stitching step along the loop to mitigate the distortion between images I_1 and I_6. Note that for a 6-image stitching loop as in Figure 10, we can also perform a similar adjustment to correct the distortion between images I_2 and I_5.

Comparison with Bundle Adjustment. The classical method to close loops is to do bundle adjustment [13]. We tested bundle adjustment in SkyStitch and noticed that it has a few limitations. First, bundle adjustment requires pairwise matching information to be available. This is not always possible because pairwise stitching may fail and have to be predicted by optical flow, in which case bundle adjustment is unusable. Second, bundle adjustment does not take any temporal information into consideration so perspective jerkiness can be introduced between consecutive frames. Our loop closing approach works even when pairwise feature matching information is missing; there is very little jerkiness since cameras are smoothly and coherently adjusted. Even though we cannot prove that our approach will always reduce reprojection errors, we found that in practice, it introduces less perspective jerkiness and is much faster, while visually, it performs as well as bundle adjustment for small loops.

Table 1: Major components used in our quadcopter. The total weight (including components not listed) is 2.1 kilograms, and the total cost is about USD1,200.

Components	Model
Flight controller	APM 2.6
GPS receiver	uBlox LEA-6H
Motor	SunnySky X3108S
Electronic speed controller	HobbyWing 30A OPTO
Propeller	APC 12×3.8
Airframe	HobbyKing X550
On-board computer	NVIDIA Jetson TK1
Camera	PointGrey BlackFly 14S2C
Lens	Computar H0514-MP2
WiFi adapter	Compex WLE350NX

4. SYSTEM IMPLEMENTATION

The implementation of the SkyStitch system involves the integration of UAV design, computer vision and wireless communication. In this section, we describe the key implementation details of SkyStitch.

While there were commercial quadcopters available in the market, we chose to assemble our own quadcopter because it offered the greatest flexibility for system design and implementation. The components used in our quadcopter assembly are listed in Table 1, and our self-assembled quadcopter is shown in Figure 11. We built two identical quadcopters of the same design.

We used ArduPilot Mega (APM) 2.6 [1] as the flight controller. APM 2.6 has built-in gyroscope, accelerometer and barometer, and both its hardware and software are open source. The on-board computer is a 120-gram NVIDIA Jetson TK1, featuring a 192-core GPU and a quad-core ARM Cortex A15 CPU. The GPU is dedicated for feature extraction, while the CPU is mainly used for data transmission and optical flow computation. Jetson TK1 also has a built-in hardware video encoder, which we used for H.264 encoding. The Jetson TK1 board runs Ubuntu 14.04.

Each quadcopter is equipped with a PointGrey BlackFly camera, which has a $^1/_3$ inch sensor with 1280×1024 resolution. The external lens we added to the camera has a 62.3° diagonal field of view.

To avoid seam artefacts caused by the imaging process, we applied the same exposure parameters to the cameras and each quadcopter periodically broadcasts its white balance values to neighbors so that videos from both quadcopters have consistent colors.

The ground station consists of an Advantech MIO-2260 board, which acts as a wireless router, and a commodity computer that performs video stitching. The computer, which runs Ubuntu 12.04, has a quad-core 3.4 GHz Intel CPU and is connected to the router through Ethernet. Our implementation uses only a single thread to do video stitching, while the rest of the CPU resources are used for other tasks such as video decoding. The computer also has a GTX 670 graphics card which has 1,344 CUDA cores, much higher than the 192 CUDA cores in the Jetson TK1. We also implemented seam finding and image blending on the GPU. The seam finder is based on Voronoi diagram and is implemented in OpenCL. We adopted the classical multi-resolution approach for image blending and implemented it in OpenGL shaders. We optimized these two stages so that it takes 6 ms to composite two HD images and 30 ms to composite 12 HD images.

Video Synchronization. An implicit requirement for high-quality video stitching is that the video frames to be stitched should be captured at exactly the same instant. Without accurate video synchronization, a mobile object on the ground would appear at different locations from different cameras, which is commonly known as "ghosting" artefacts. Software-based synchronization methods are intrinsically inaccurate since they do not consider the non-negligible delay from the time when photons hit the sensor to the time when the host computer receives the video frame [19].

In SkyStitch, we adopt a hardware-based approach for video synchronization. Our key observation is that each quadcopter is equipped with a GPS receiver for flight control, which also provides an accurate time source. In particular, we connected the GPS receiver's time pulse pin to the external shutter trigger of the camera, and set the GPS receiver to issue a triggering pulse at desired frame rate. When issuing the very first pulse, the GPS receiver also sends the corresponding UTC time to the on-board computer through the flight controller. In this way, the on-board computer can associate every video frame with an accurate UTC time, which will be transmitted to the ground station along with the corresponding video frame. Offline ground truth measurement using a logic analyzer showed that our hardware-based approach could reduce video synchronization errors down to smaller than 10 μs.

5. EVALUATION

In this section, we evaluate the performance of SkyStitch on both stitching time and stitching quality. We conducted our experiments over two types of ground with different distributions of features. One venue was a grass field in a park, covered by yellow leaves and a few wooden blocks ("Grass field"). Due to the scattered yellow leaves, the images taken over this field were rich in features. These features were similar to each other and could lead to many feature mismatches, thereby degrading stitching quality. The other venue was a running track, which did not have many good features ("Running track").

In our experiments, the two quadcopters hovered at an altitude of 20 m, equivalent to the height of a 6-storey building. We did not typically fly higher for safety reasons. That said, we did some simple experiments to verify that altitude did not have a significant effect on performance. The benchmarks we used for comparison are the popular OpenCV implementations [7] of commonly-used stitching algorithms [26].

5.1 Stitching Time

The time required to stitch a pair or batch of frames directly determines the maximum frame rate (or stitching rate) that a stitching algorithm can support. A higher frame rate generally results in better user experience. On the other hand, given a particular frame rate, a shorter stitching time also allows a stitching algorithm to support more video sources. In this section, we show that SkyStitch achieves shorter stitching times than existing methods.

The 12 video traces used in our evaluation were collected by our quadcopters in a 2×6 grid pattern (for the Grass field venue). The resolution of the traces is 1280×1024 and the overlap between adjacent traces is about 80%. The duration of each video trace is 15 seconds at a frame rate of 20 fps. We ran both the CPU-based and GPU-based implementations of the benchmarks at the ground station. One exception is that we used the GPU-based implementation in [20] to benchmark RANSAC, for which OpenCV lacks the GPU-based implementation. We selected OpenCV's BruteForceMatcher method (instead of the KD-tree method) as a benchmark for feature matching, as we found the KD-tree method has little speed advantage when feature database is small. The number of iterations in all the RANSAC implementations was set to 512. The CPU in the ground station is a 3.4 GHz quad-core CPU, and the GPU is a GTX 670 graphics card with 1,344 cores (see Section 4).

Execution time of individual step. We varied the number of video sources N from 2 to 12 and measured the execution time of each individual step. Figure 12(a) compares the average execution time of feature extraction for SkyStitch to the two benchmarks (i.e., the CPU-based and GPU-based implementations). The standard deviation of the results are not included as they are very small. As expected, we find that SkyStitch is scalable to many video sources because feature extraction is offloaded to each quadcopter. On the other hand, the execution time of benchmarks is proportional to the number of video sources. Even though the GPU benchmark uses a more advanced GPU (1,344 cores) than SkyStitch (192 cores), it has a worse execution time than SkyStitch when the number of video sources is large ($N > 6$).

Figure 12(b) illustrates the execution time of feature matching. SkyStitch is approximately 4 times faster than the GPU-accelerated benchmark and up to 70 times faster than the CPU benchmark (not shown in the figure as it is too slow). Such large gain of SkyStitch over CPU benchmark is mostly due to the reduction of the search space, as feature matching in SkyStitch runs in CPU as well. We believe that a GPU implementation of feature matching in SkyStitch could further reduce its execution time. Note that when $N > 7$, the slopes of both methods become steeper. The reason is that our 12 video traces are in a 2×6 grid pattern and more pairwise stitchings are needed when processing the second row of video sources.

The execution time of RANSAC is shown in Figure 12(c). SkyStitch is up to 18 times faster than the GPU benchmark and 24 times faster than the CPU benchmark. Surprisingly, the gap between the GPU benchmark and the CPU benchmark is not large. One reason is that a typical SVD solver (e.g., Jacobian SVD) does not run efficiently on GPU cores and the speedup due to high parallelism is partially offset by its poor performance per core. Another reason is that sequentially performing RANSAC for each image pair requires many CPU-GPU memory transactions and thus introduces significant IO overhead. In contrast, SkyStitch's RANSAC GPU pipeline is much more efficient. Even with 12 video sources, its execution time is below 10 ms.

Stitching rate. We calculate stitching rate by taking the reciprocal of the total execution time for stitching a batch of frames. Let $T_{extract}$ denote feature extraction time and T_{others} denote the total

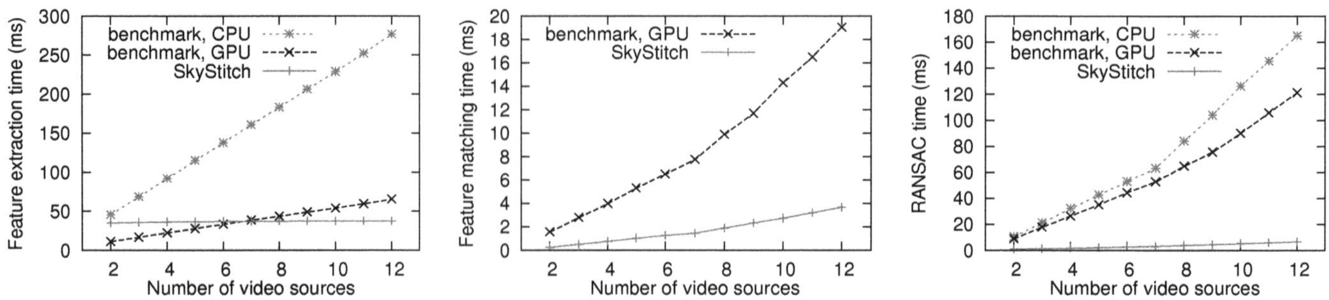

(a) Feature extraction. (b) Feature matching. (c) RANSAC.

Figure 12: Execution time of each step of video stitching. The number of features extracted from every frame is 1,000.

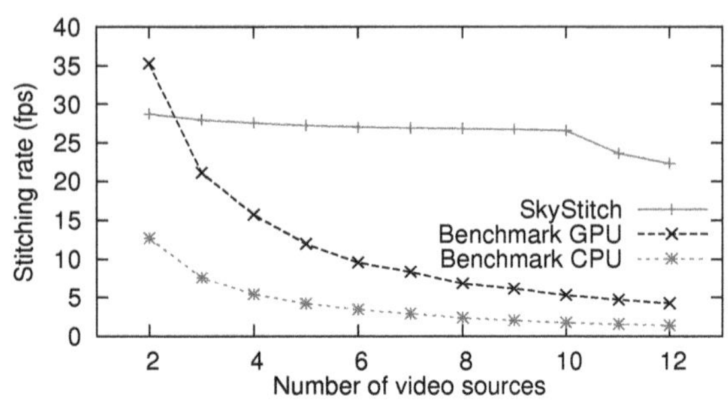

Figure 13: Stitching rate (in terms of frames per second) with respect to the number of video sources.

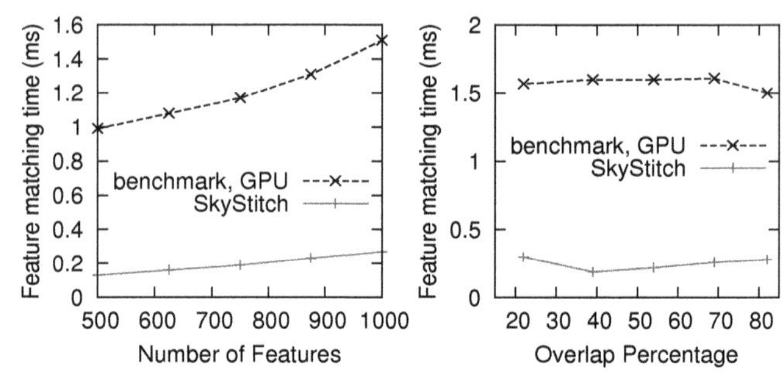

(a) Impact of feature count. (b) Impact of overlap.

Figure 14: Impact of feature count and overlap percentage on the execution time of feature matching.

time of the remaining steps (i.e., feature matching, RANSAC and image compositing). Then the execution time per stitching is equal to $max(T_{extract}, T_{others})$ for SkyStitch and $T_{extract} + T_{others}$ for the benchmarks.

Figure 13 shows that SkyStitch achieves a stitching rate up to 4 times faster than the GPU benchmark and up to 16 times faster than the CPU benchmark. The stitching rates of both benchmarks drop sharply as N increases due to the fact that all computations are performed at the ground station. SkyStitch, however, offloads feature extraction to the UAVs to greatly reduce the workload at the ground station. When $N \leq 10$, SkyStitch's stitching rate is solely determined by the feature extraction time, which is around 28 fps. When $N > 10$, the bottleneck of SkyStitch shifts to the ground station and the stitching rate starts to drop. Nevertheless, we estimate that SkyStitch will be able to support a stitching rate of 22 fps when $N = 12$ while the two benchmarks could not maintain such stitching rate when $N > 3$.

Impact of feature count and overlap percentage. In the above experiments, the number of extracted features is fixed at 1,000 and the overlap between two adjacent video sources is about 80%. We found that these two factors do not affect stitching time except the time of feature matching. Figure 14(a) shows the impact of feature count on the time of feature matching, for the case of two video sources. We can see that the feature matching time of both SkyStitch and the GPU benchmark increases with feature count, but the rate of increase for SkyStitch is slower. This is expected since the GPU benchmark requires pairwise comparison for all the features while SkyStitch only needs to search in a small area for the potential match.

The impact of overlap percentage on feature matching time is shown in Figure 14(b). Generally the time of SkyStitch increases with overlap since more features in the overlapping area need to be matched. The exception is at the overlap of 20%, where feature matching time does not follow the trend. Upon closer inspection, we found that it is because when the overlap is small there are more stitching failures which lead to a larger search radius r (see Section 3.4.3). The feature matching time of the GPU benchmark appears to be independent of the overlapping area and is much longer than SkyStitch.

5.2 Stitching Quality

In this section, we show that SkyStitch produces high-quality stitching results. In particular, we evaluate the number of inliers, the stitching success rate and the degree of frame jerkiness and also the incidents of ghosting artefacts. Sample videos of stitching can be found in [4].

Number of inliers. The number of inliers is a basic measure of goodness for stitching algorithms. More inliers generally leads to a better $\mathbf{H}$ estimate. Figure 16 shows the number of inliers at different degrees of overlap. For both types of ground, SkyStitch generates more inliers than the benchmark. The reason is that the feature matching step in the benchmark uses pairwise comparison among all the features and the probability of false matching is high. In contrast, the feature matching in SkyStitch only searches in a small target area and thus it is less likely to have false matching. From Figure 16 we can also see that the slope of Grass field is steeper than that of Running track. This is likely because these two types of ground have different feature distributions.

Success rate of stitching. In Section 3.4, we define the failure of stitching (or ill-formed $\mathbf{H}$) based on the number of inliers and the angle θ. In SkyStitch, failed stitching can be potentially recovered using optical flow. We calculate the success rate of stitching for the above experiment, as shown in Figure 17. For both types of ground, we can see that SkyStitch has higher success rate than the benchmark, because of the recovery using optical flow.

Frame jerkiness. Stitching every frame independently could introduce perspective jerkiness which degrades visual quality. To quantify perspective jerkiness and show how our approach can reduce jerkiness, we measure the rotation component in the homography matrix, which is directly related to camera perspective. To

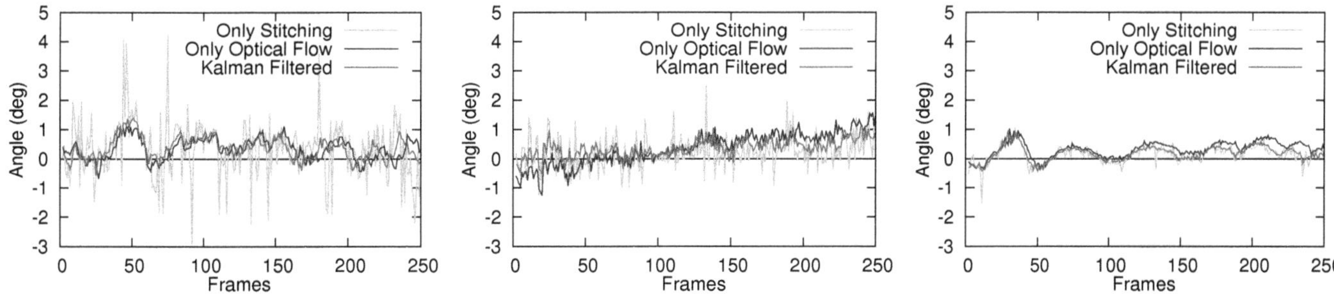

(a) Roll (b) Pitch (c) Yaw

Figure 15: Jerkiness of rotation components in computed homographies

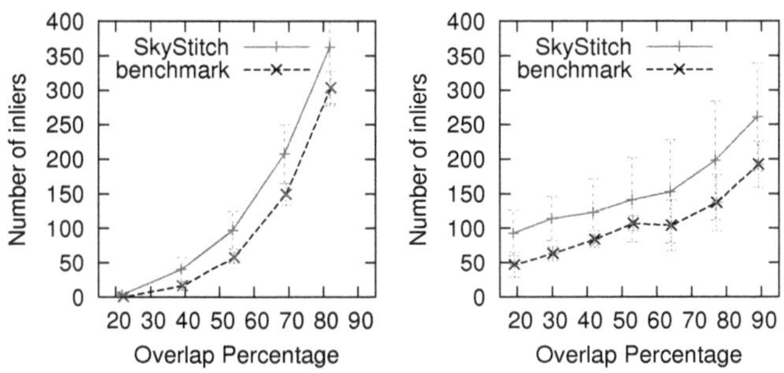

(a) Grass field. (b) Running track.

Figure 16: Impact of overlap percentage on the number of inliers. The number of features extracted from every frame is 1,000.

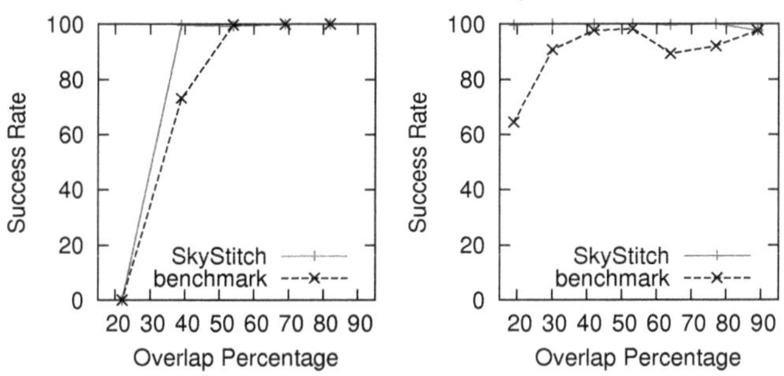

(a) Grass field. (b) Running track.

Figure 17: Impact of overlap percentage on success rate.

make things more intuitive, we convert the rotation matrix into Euler angles yaw, pitch and roll. We stitched a pair of video sequences (40% overlap) in the Running Track scene. Figure 15 shows the Euler angles extracted in the estimated homographies. Note that "Only stitching" produces very significant jerkiness in pitch and roll angles. In contrast, "Only optical flow" method is much smoother but suffers from drift especially in yaw and pitch angles. The "Kalman filtered" angles are not prone to either of the problems. It follows closely the results of "Only stitching" while mitigating most of the jerkiness. The perceptual difference can be seen from our demo videos [4].

Multiple video sources. In Section 3.5, we proposed a loop closing method for multi-image stitching. Figure 18 illustrates the effect of alleviating the misalignment between the first and the last image during multi-image stitching. The six images were collected from the Running track scene. We can see in Figure 18(a) that there is a discernible misalignment along the stitching seam between the first and the last image. By applying the loop closing method discussed in Section 3.5, we were able to mitigate the misalignment so that the viewers could hardly notice it (see Figure 18(b)). A sample video can be found in [4].

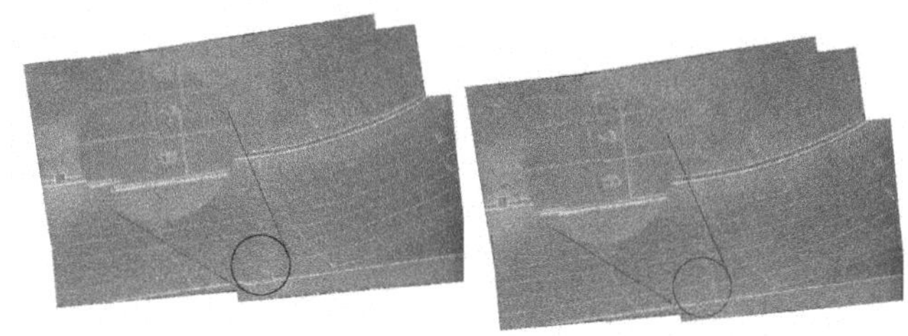

(a) No loop closing. (b) With loop closing.

Figure 18: Effect of loop closing for 6-image stitching.

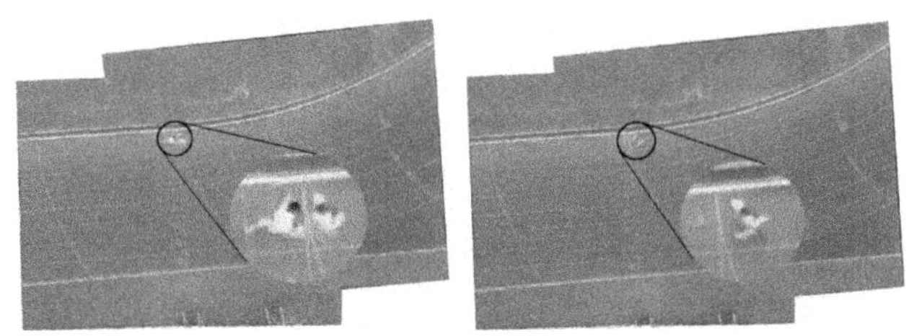

(a) Unsynchronized frames. (b) Synchronized frames.

Figure 19: Effect of video synchronization on ghosting artefacts.

We follow a similar method to that in Section 3.4 to determine the success rate of multi-image stitching. Specifically, if any pairwise stitching is found to have an ill-formed $\mathbf{H}$, we consider the multi-image stitching as a failure. Using the above trace with six video sources, we found that the success rate of SkyStitch is about 97%, while the success rate of the benchmark is only 32%.

Elimination of Ghosting Artefacts. In Section 4, we explained that our hardware-based method for video synchronization is important to ensure good stitching quality when there are mobile objects. Figure 19 illustrates the effectiveness of our synchronization method. The source images were taken from two quadcopters with hardware-based synchronization, while a man was jogging on the running track. Figure 19(a) is stitched from two video images that are 200 ms apart in capturing time. We can see a clear ghosting artefact around the stitching seam, i.e., two running men instead of one. In practice, such ghosting artefact will affect the viewers' assessment of the actual situation on the ground. In Figure 19(b), the image is stitched from two video frames synchronized by GPS. We can see that our hardware-based synchronization method is sufficiently accurate to eliminate distracting ghosting artefacts.

6. CONCLUSION

In this paper, we present the design and implementation of SkyStitch, a multi-UAV-based video surveillance system that supports real-time video stitching. To improve the speed and quality of video stitching, we incorporated several practical and effective techniques into SkyStitch, including feature extraction offloading, utilization of flight status information, efficient GPU-based RANSAC implementation and jerkiness mitigation by Kalman filtering. By implementing SkyStitch using a pair of quadcopters, we demonstrate that it can achieve stitching rate 4 times faster than state-of-the-art GPU accelerated methods, while ensuring good stitching quality.

Although SkyStitch is developed for quadcopters, its design principles and techniques can also be applied to other types of hovering aircraft such as blimps [14] which are more vulnerable to wind but have longer flight time. In addition, SkyStitch is currently only a proof-of-concept prototype and there is significant room for future work. For example, we would like to understand how other types of features (like color feature [29] or low-dimensional feature [21]) affect the performance of SkyStitch; it is also interesting to see how SkyStitch performs in challenging environments such as over rough ground with buildings.

7. ACKNOWLEDGMENTS

This work was supported by the Singapore Ministry of Education grant T1 251RES1204.

8. REFERENCES

[1] ArduPilot Mega 2.6. http://ardupilot.com.

[2] Assisting firefighting with a quadcopter. http://tinyurl.com/o5gxvmv.

[3] Civilians with drones lead charge in search and rescue. http://tinyurl.com/oq3zcob.

[4] Demo videos for SkyStitch. http://tinyurl.com/oz8ftc4.

[5] Hugin, panorama photo stitcher. http://hugin.sourceforge.net.

[6] Kolor. http://www.kolor.com.

[7] OpenCV. http://opencv.org.

[8] TCOM's aerostat systems help U.S. border patrol. http://tinyurl.com/ovnwgbr.

[9] M. Adam, C. Jung, S. Roth, and G. Brunnett. Real-time stereo-image stitching using GPU-based belief propagation. In *Proceedings of the Vision, Modeling, and Visualization Workshop, 2009*, Nov. 2009.

[10] D. Anguelov, C. Dulong, D. Filip, C. Frueh, S. Lafon, R. Lyon, A. Ogale, L. Vincent, and J. Weaver. Google street view: Capturing the world at street level. *Computer*, 43(6):32–38, 2010.

[11] H. Bay, T. Tuytelaars, and L. Van Gool. SURF: Speeded up robust features. In *Proceedings of ECCV '06*, May 2006.

[12] A. Brown, C. Gilbert, H. Holland, and Y. Lu. Near real-time dissemination of geo-referenced imagery by an enterprise server. In *Proceedings of the GeoTec Event*, Jun. 2006.

[13] M. Brown and D. G. Lowe. Automatic panoramic image stitching using invariant features. *International Journal of Computer Vision*, 74(1):59–73, 2007.

[14] M. Burri, L. Gasser, M. Kach, M. Krebs, S. Laube, A. Ledergerber, D. Meier, R. Michaud, L. Mosimann, L. Muri, et al. Design and control of a spherical omnidirectional blimp. In *Proceedings of the IEEE/RSJ International Conference on Intelligent Robots and Systems (IROS '13)*, Nov. 2013.

[15] J. de Villiers. Real-time photogrammetric stitching of high resolution video on COTS hardware. In *Proceedings of International Symposium on Optomechatronic Technologies (ISOT '09)*, Sep. 2009.

[16] A. Eden, M. Uyttendaele, and R. Szeliski. Seamless image stitching of scenes with large motions and exposure differences. In *Proceedings of CVPR '06*, Jun. 2006.

[17] M. El-Saban, M. Izz, and A. Kaheel. Fast stitching of videos captured from freely moving devices by exploiting temporal redundancy. In *Proceedings of ICIP '10*, Sep. 2010.

[18] M. A. Fischler and R. C. Bolles. Random sample consensus: a paradigm for model fitting with applications to image analysis and automated cartography. *Communications of the ACM*, 24(6):381–395, 1981.

[19] R. Hill, C. Madden, A. v. d. Hengel, H. Detmold, and A. Dick. Measuring latency for video surveillance systems. In *Proceedings of Digital Image Computing: Techniques and Applications (DICTA '09)*, Dec. 2009.

[20] N. Ho. GPU RANSAC homography. http://nghiaho.com/?page_id=611.

[21] G. Hua, M. Brown, and S. Winder. Discriminant embedding for local image descriptors. In *Proceedings of ICCV '07*, Oct. 2007.

[22] A. Kaheel, M. El-Saban, M. Refaat, and M. Ezz. Mobicast: a system for collaborative event casting using mobile phones. In *Proceedings of the International Conference on Mobile and Ubiquitous Multimedia (MUM '09)*, Nov. 2009.

[23] D. G. Lowe. Distinctive image features from scale-invariant keypoints. *International Journal of Computer Vision*, 60(2):91–110, 2004.

[24] E. Malis and M. Vargas. Deeper understanding of the homography decomposition for vision-based control. 2007.

[25] E. Rublee, V. Rabaud, K. Konolige, and G. Bradski. ORB: an efficient alternative to SIFT or SURF. In *Proceedings of ICCV '11*, Nov. 2011.

[26] R. Szeliski. Image alignment and stitching: A tutorial. *Foundations and Trends in Computer Graphics and Vision*, 2(1):1–104, 2006.

[27] M. Tennoe, E. Helgedagsrud, M. Næss, H. K. Alstad, H. K. Stensland, V. R. Gaddam, D. Johansen, C. Griwodz, and P. Halvorsen. Efficient implementation and processing of a real-time panorama video pipeline. In *Proceedings of the IEEE International Symposium on Multimedia*, Dec. 2013.

[28] N. Trawny and S. I. Roumeliotis. Indirect Kalman filter for 3D attitude estimation. *University of Minnesota, Dept. of Comp. Sci. & Eng., Tech. Rep*, 2, 2005.

[29] K. E. van de Sande, T. Gevers, and C. G. Snoek. A comparison of color features for visual concept classification. In *Proceedings of the International Conference on Content-based Image and Video Retrieval*, Jul. 2008.

[30] D. Wischounig-Strucl, M. Quartisch, and B. Rinner. Prioritized data transmission in airborne camera networks for wide area surveillance and image mosaicking. In *Proceedings of CVPRW '11*, Jun. 2011.

[31] W. Xu and J. Mulligan. Panoramic video stitching from commodity HDTV cameras. *Multimedia Systems*, 19(5):407–426, 2013.

[32] S. Yahyanejad, D. Wischounig-Strucl, M. Quaritsch, and B. Rinner. Incremental mosaicking of images from autonomous, small-scale UAVs. In *Proceedings of the IEEE International Conference on Advanced Video and Signal Based Surveillance (AVSS '10)*, Aug. 2010.

Eye of the Dragon: Exploring Discriminatively Minimalist Sketch-based Abstractions for Object Categories

Ravi Kiran Sarvadevabhatla
Video Analytics Lab
Supercomputer Education and Research Centre
Indian Institute of Science, Bangalore, India
ravikiran@ssl.serc.iisc.in

Venkatesh Babu R
Video Analytics Lab
Supercomputer Education and Research Centre
Indian Institute of Science, Bangalore, India
venky@serc.iisc.in

ABSTRACT

As a form of visual representation, freehand line sketches are typically studied as an end product of the sketching process. However, from a recognition point of view, one can also study various orderings and properties of the primitive strokes that compose the sketch. Studying sketches in this manner has enabled us to create novel sparse yet discriminative sketch-based representations for object categories which we term *category-epitomes*. Concurrently, the epitome construction provides a natural measure for quantifying the sparseness underlying the original sketch, which we term epitome-score. We analyze *category-epitomes* and epitome-scores for hand-drawn sketches from a sketch dataset of 160 object categories commonly encountered in daily life. Our analysis provides a novel viewpoint for examining the complexity of representation for visual object categories.

Categories and Subject Descriptors

I.5.4 [**Applications**]: Computer Vision

General Terms

Experimentation

Keywords

freehand sketch; object category recognition; deep learning

1. INTRODUCTION

A master painter in ancient China was once painting an elaborate dragon. His son, carefully observing his father's craft, noticed that the eye of the dragon had not been painted. When he pointed it out, the painter replied: "My son, adding the eye will make the dragon come alive and fly out of the painting".

A fascinating spectrum – from realistic depictions to sparsely drawn sketches – exists for hand-drawn art depicting objects[27, 3]. Across this spectrum, the level of detail in the artwork usually correlates with the confidence in recognizing the object. However, an interesting phenomenon is observed for freehand sketches : even with minimal stroke detail (see Figure 1), the underlying subject can be easily recognized by us. This suggests an inherent sparseness driving the human neuro-visual representation mechanism. Therefore, studying such sparsely detailed sketches can aid our understanding of the cognitive processes involved and spur the design of efficient representations and visual classifiers for objects.

Figure 1: A sketch belonging to category **cup**. In spite of minimal detail, we can recognize the sketch easily and correctly.

Typically, freehand line sketches are studied as an end product of the sketching process. Indeed, sketches have been utilized *in-toto* in the context of classification and content-based retrieval problems [11, 13, 22]. However, from a recognition point of view, we believe it is instructive to study the primitives (strokes) that compose the sketch, starting with the first hand-drawn stroke until the last stroke which finalizes the sketch. Our belief originates in a discovery we have made : for a given sketch of an object and an associated sketch classifier, there exists a minimal subset of strokes which ensures consistent and correct identification of the object category. We term this new sketch, constructed using the minimal stroke subset, as a *category-epitome*. Figure 2 shows examples of freehand line sketches and their corresponding sparse *category-epitomes*. In this paper, we explore the multi-faceted ways in which *category-epitomes* convey insights into the nature of visual object category representation. In the spirit of the dragon story mentioned at the beginning, we wish to examine sketches at the moment they come "alive".

MM'15, October 26–30,2015,Brisbane,Australia.
© 2015 ACM 978-1-4503-3459-4/15/10 ...$15.00.
DOI: http://dx.doi.org/10.1145/2733373.2806230.

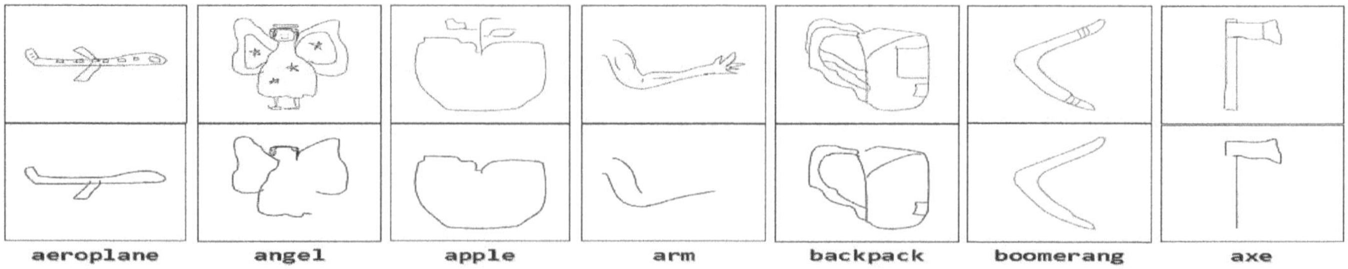

Figure 2: Original sketches (top row) and corresponding *category-epitomes* (bottom row) for various object categories.

We summarize our contributions below:

- Via *category-epitomes*, we introduce a novel representation for visual object categories. The freehand sketch of an object is already a sparse representation of the object category. *Category-epitomes* take this sparsification to the extreme while guaranteeing recognizability (Section 4). This guarantee provision is a unique feature which sets our method apart from other methods of sparse sketch generation and sketch simplification[19, 22, 24, 20].

- We show that *category-epitomes* can be constructed based on various philosophies of visual abstraction (Section 4.4). Our analysis of the resulting epitomes (Section 5.1) suggests that the longest sketch strokes best capture the "signature" sparsity of object categories in general.

- The measure we use to quantify the sparseness underlying a sketch is simple to understand and arises naturally out of its *category-epitome* construction (Section 4.3). Our analysis demonstrates that the distribution of epitome-scores can be used to quantify semantic level of detail in object categories (Section 5.2).

- To represent sketches, we propose novel features obtained from Alexnet, a popular deep-learning network [15]. Utilizing these features, we achieve state-of-the-art results for sketch classification on a challenging sketch dataset (Section 3.3).

2. RELATED WORK

The notion of a sparse, sketch-like representation for generic images was proposed in the seminal work of Marr [18] who coined the term *primal sketch* for the same. Primal sketch-like representations have been used as features for object detection [13], texture characterization [9] and for super resolution [25]. The idea of generating sketches from one or more source images, without any reference to the notion of primal sketch, has been explored by Qi et al. [22] and Marvaniya et al. [19]. In all these works, photographic images serve as the starting point. In contrast, our starting point is the sketch stroke data generated by human beings. This creates the possibility that the sparse neuro-visual representation is transferred to the sketch in the process of drawing by humans, at least in part. Though we do not survey the domain for reasons of space and focus, a significant body of work from Computer Graphics has also examined simplification of artistic renderings, including line art. The work of Ravish et al. [20] on abstraction of 3D-geometric models can be considered a representative example.

In addition to the artificial (i.e. not generated by human hand) nature of sketch generation, the works mentioned above do not attempt to quantify the sparseness of the resulting sketch nor do they examine the temporal nature of sketch composition. In contrast, recent work by Berger et al. [12] analyzes the temporal aspect of sketching in the context of mimicking artist style. However, their emphasis is on synthesizing abstract facial sketches rather than recognition. Moreover, their sketches are produced by professional artists. In contrast, our sketches have been generated by crowdsourcing and therefore, are more representative of object depictions by humans in general. The idea of identifying and utilizing a discriminative subset of strokes was employed by Karteek et al. [14] for classifying online handwritten data. The work of Eitz et al. [3] examines how humans tend to draw objects by analyzing a large number of sketches spread across commonly encountered object categories. We use their database of sketches in this paper.

The basic premise of sparse, sketch-like drawings being adequate for visual category recognition has also been acknowledged by the neuroscience community. As early as 1960, Gollin [7] used a series of drawings containing progressively more information as a measure of visual development and to examine long-term memory in amnesic patients. Dirk et al. [26] performed a functional MRI based study of participants viewing photographs and line drawings of natural scene categories. Their interesting conclusion was that the neural activity of the visual system in response to viewing line drawings is virtually the same as when coloured photographs are viewed, which indicates that line drawings capture the most important elements of a scene. Ghosh and Petkov [5] studied the robustness of contour based shape recognition algorithms to different kinds of contour incompleteness. While their work bears some resemblance to ours, the stroke segments they use are artificially created and do not correspond to natural breaks since temporal information is not captured. Moreover, as with some of the works we previously mentioned, their sketch-like representations are artificially generated, i.e. not generated by human hand.

3. BUILDING THE SKETCH CLASSIFIER

We first describe the sketch database used in our experiments. Subsequently, we describe sketch feature extraction (Sec. 3.2) and conclude the section with a discussion on the performance of our sketch classifier (Sec. 3.3). In the next section (Sec. 4), we describe how the sketch classifier is actually used to construct *category-epitomes*.

Figure 3: An ambiguously drawn sketch (left) with two plausible categorizations - `tyre` (middle) and `donut` (right). The figure is from the work of Schneider et al. [23].

3.1 The sketch database

The sketches in our study have been taken from the publicly available freehand line sketch database of Eitz et al. [3]. This database contains a curated set of 20,000 hand-drawn sketches evenly distributed across 250 object categories. These sketches have been obtained by crowdsourcing across the general population. Therefore, they are a good starting point for analyzing the underpinnings of the sketching process by humans. Significantly, the temporal stroke information (i.e. the sequential order in which the strokes were drawn) for sketches is also available. As we will see subsequently, this plays a crucial role in obtaining *category-epitomes* involving temporal stroke ordering. A few examples from the sketch database can be seen in the top row of Figure 2.

While the database of Eitz et al. is quite comprehensive and general in coverage of object categories, it has its share of shortcomings, a number of which have been analyzed by Schneider et al. [23]. One of the major shortcomings is the presence of ambiguously drawn sketches whose identity is difficult to discern even for fellow human beings (See Figure 3. Is the sketch on the left depicted by the two concentric shapes a `tyre` or a `donut` ?). To address this situation, [23] employ a human-evaluation based technique and identify a subset containing 160 non-ambiguous object categories which can be utilized as a more reliable benchmark database for evaluating sketch recognition systems (Refer to Section 5 of [23] for details). For our experiments and analysis, we utilize the sketches from this curated set of 160 object categories. Furthermore, following [23], we uniformly consider 56 sketches from each category for the purpose of sketch classifier training and evaluation.

To increase the number of sketches per category for classification and improve performance[1], we perform data augmentation by applying geometric and morphological transformations to each sketch. Specifically, each sketch is initially subjected to image dilation ("thickening") using a 5×5 square structuring element. A number of transforms are applied to this thickened sketch – mirroring (across vertical axis), rotation ($\pm 5, \pm 15$ degrees), systematic combinations of horizontal and vertical shifts ($\pm 5, \pm 15$ pixels), central zoom ($\pm 3\%, \pm 7\%$ of image height). As a result, 30 new sketches are generated per original sketch. The data augmentation procedure results in $30 \times 56 = 1680$ sketches per category, for a total of $1680 \times 160 = 268,800$ sketches across 160 categories.

In the context of the sketches being processed by CNNs, the reason for sketch dilation must be pointed out. As each sketch gets processed by deeper layers of the CNN, fine details tend to get eliminated. To minimize the impact of detail loss, the sketches are subjected to thickening (dilation) which helps preserve detail better.

3.2 Feature Extraction and Classification

The sketch features are extracted using pre-trained Convolutional Neural Networks (CNNs). For our experiments, we utilize the pre-trained Alexnet CNN as described by Krizhevsky et al [15]. Our choice was motivated by the fact that features extracted from Alexnet have resulted in impressive performance across a variety of challenging computer vision problems [6, 8], surpassing the performance of hand-crafted features. The sketch features are obtained by tapping the output of layer conventionally denoted as fc_7 of the pre-trained Alexnet with the sketch as the input. Eventually, for an input sketch image, a 4096-dimensional feature vector is obtained.

The entire database of sketches is divided into training and test sets. Features from training set sketches are passed to a multi-class linear Support Vector Machine (SVM) classifier [4] whose parameter C has been empirically set to 0.5. The principled manner of choosing the SVM parameters would be to try different kernels and related parameter settings via cross-validation. Serendipitously, however, our choice of parameter C resulted in state-of-the-art sketch classifier performance (Section 3.3). Therefore, in order to focus on our objective of constructing *category-epitomes* and analyzing epitome properties, we deferred the task of kernel and parameter selection.

3.3 Evaluation of sketch classifier

For comparable evaluation, we utilize the methodology and test set described in [23]. We summarize this procedure next. To begin with, the curated dataset contains 160 sketch categories, each containing 56 sketches. Since some of the categories contain more than 56 sketches, we randomly select a 56-sized subset from these categories. The number of sketches utilized for training is progressively increased, starting from 8 sketches per category in steps of 8 up to 48 of the 56 sketches. The rest of the sketches are utilized for testing[1]. The entire data is randomly shuffled thrice and for each shuffle, it is split according to one of the training and testing splits mentioned above. For each shuffle, precision is calculated over test data. The resulting precision values are then averaged. This procedure of shuffling thrice and computing average precision is repeated for each of the 8 train/test splits considered. For the SVM classifier, parameter C is empirically set to 0.5.

The results can be seen in Figure 4. Our Alexnet feature-based recognition system consistently outperforms the hitherto best results in [23] – the improvement in average precision ranges from 3% to 11%. It must be conceded that the performance of the method in [23] is based on unaugmented data. However, they employ Fisher vector feature

[1]Note that for training, data augmented variants (Section 3.1) of each sketch are used while testing is done only on the original sketch subjected to dilation and not on the data augmented variants. As an example, when 32 of the original sketches are used, the actual number of training sketches is $32 \times 30 \times 160 = 153,600$ while the number of test sketches is $24 \times 160 = 3840$.

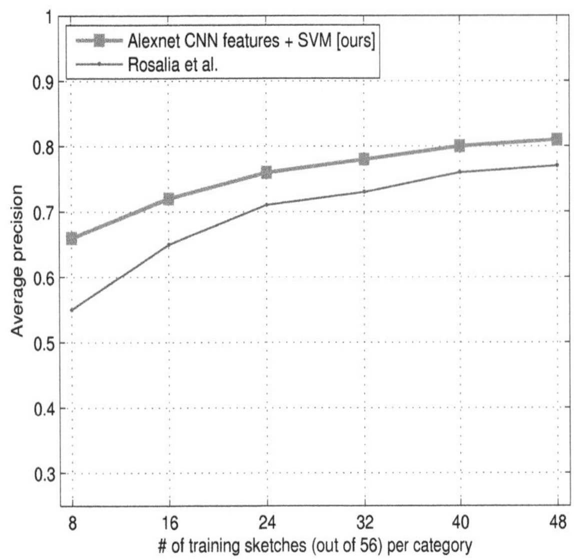

Figure 4: Comparing the performance of our sketch classifier with that of Schneider et al. [23]. The x-axis shows the number of sketches (subset size) used for training.

representation whose dimensions[2] are larger than our 4096-dimensional feature vectors by a factor of about 10. This would result in prohibitively large memory requirements and training times. In contrast, our feature vectors are faster to process. Therefore, they are also a good candidate for related applications such as sketch-based image retrieval [11].

A classifier with good performance, as in our case (Figure 4), translates to a larger percentage of sketches from the test set being classified correctly. This, in turn, translates to a larger set of *category-epitomes* for analysis since the epitomes can only be constructed for correctly classified sketches, as we will see shortly. In the next section, we shall see how this sketch classifier is utilized in the construction of *category-epitomes*.

4. OBTAINING THE *CATEGORY-EPITOME*

As the first step in determining the *category-epitome*, for each correctly classified test sketch, we construct a cumulative sketch sequence from its strokes (Section 4.1). Each of the sketches in this sequence is labeled using the sketch classifier. The resulting sequence of labels is analyzed to determine the *category-epitome* of the sketch. Our procedure for obtaining the *category-epitome* also provides a natural measure, termed epitome-score, for quantifying the sparseness of the original, full sketch (Section 4.3).

The temporal sequence in which the strokes are added is, by default, the basis for construction of sketch image sequences of cumulative strokes. However, other plausible stroke orderings exist. These stroke orderings optionally utilize the length of strokes in the construction of *category-epitomes*. Towards the end of this section (Section 4.4), we describe how these additional stroke ordering based sketch image sequences are created.

[2]The Fisher vector feature dimension is estimated based on the description of feature extraction process in [23].

4.1 Constructing Cumulative Stroke Sequences

As the first step in determining the *category-epitome*, we construct sequences of cumulative strokes derived from correctly classified test sketches. Suppose the sequence of strokes in the temporal order they were drawn in a sketch is given by $S_t = \{s_1, s_2 \dots s_N\}$ where N is the total number of strokes in the sketch. To construct the corresponding cumulative stroke sequence, we begin with a blank canvas. Strokes from the given sketch are successively added to the blank canvas in the temporal order. As each stroke is added, intermediate canvases $S_1, S_2, \dots, S_N$ are created. Specifically, the intermediate canvases are given by $S_1 = \{s_1\}, S_2 = \{s_1, s_2\}, \dots, S_N = \{s_1, s_2, \dots, s_N\}$. At the end of this process, we obtain the cumulative stroke sequence $CSS_T = \{S_1, \dots, S_N\}$ for the temporal stroke order. Figure 5 illustrates the creation of cumulative stroke sequence for a sketch from `airplane` category.

4.2 Constructing the *category-eptiome*

Having generated the cumulative stroke sequence for a sketch as described above, the *category-epitome* can be constructed. To begin with, each intermediate canvas of the cumulative stroke sequence is classified to obtain a binary labeling – the label is 1 if the sketch category is correctly identified by the sketch classifier and 0 otherwise. Thus, we obtain a binary label sequence $\mathcal{L} = \{l_1, l_2, \dots, l_N\}$ corresponding to each canvas of the cumulative stroke sequence CSS_T (see Figure 5).

Note that the final canvas S_N corresponds to the original test sketch since all the strokes have been added to the canvas at that point. Therefore, the final classification label l_N must be 1 since we are working with correctly classified test sketches. Now, consider the product sequence $\mathcal{P} = \{P_1, P_2 \dots . P_N\}$ formed by cumulative multiplication of labels $l_i \in \mathcal{L}, i = 1, 2 \dots N$:

$$P_i = \prod_{j=i}^{N} l_j \tag{1}$$

Then, the *category-epitome* corresponds to canvas S_e of the cumulative stroke sequence such that

$$e = \min_{1 \leq i \leq N} \{i | P_i = 1\} \tag{2}$$

Informally, the *category-epitome* S_e is the sequentially earliest, correctly classified canvas whose successors are classified correctly as well. Using the example in Figure 5, the classification label sequence is $\mathcal{L} = \{0, 1, 0, 1, 1, 1, 1, 1, 1\}$. From Equation (1), the product sequence is computed as $\mathcal{P} = \{0, 0, 0, 1, 1, 1, 1, 1, 1\}$. From Equation (2), we obtain $e = 4$. In other words, canvas S_4 (outlined by a cyan rectangle in Figure 5) corresponds to the *category-epitome*: the sequentially earliest, correctly classified canvas whose successors $S_5 \dots S_9$ are classified correctly as well. Figure 2 shows sketches from various categories and their corresponding *category-epitomes*.

4.3 Epitome-score : Quantifying the *category-epitome*

Our procedure for obtaining the *category-epitome*, described above, also provides a natural method for quantifying the "epitome"-ness of the original, full sketch. Using e obtained

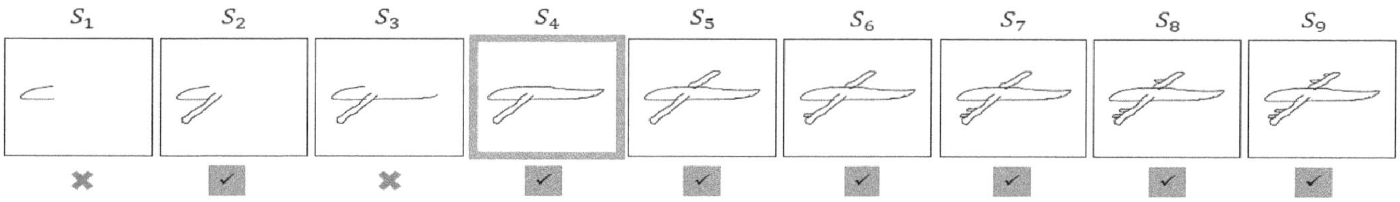

Figure 5: Constructing the TEMPORAL *category-epitome* for an **airplane** sketch: The sketch has 9 strokes. $S_1 - S_9$ are the cumulative stroke sequence canvases. A red cross mark indicates a misclassification(0) while a green tick mark indicates correct classification(1). Canvas S_4 outlined by a cyan rectangle is the *category-epitome*. Note that even though canvas S_2 is classified correctly, we consider *category-epitome* as canvas S_4, the sequentially earliest, correctly classified canvas whose successors are classified correctly as well.

from Equation (2), we define the epitome-score $\mathcal{E}$ of a sketch as :

$$\mathcal{E} = \begin{cases} \frac{e}{N}, e \neq 1 \\ 0, \; e = 1 \end{cases} \tag{3}$$

where N is the total number of strokes in the sketch. $e = 1$ corresponds to the situation where merely drawing the first stroke conveys the epitome-ness of the sketch. Therefore, for consistency across sketches, we define the corresponding epitome-score $\mathcal{E}$ to be 0. Our definition of epitome-score $\mathcal{E}$ essentially conveys the sparseness underlying the sketch – the smaller its value, the more sparser the sketch is likely to be. Epitome-scores very close to 1, on the other hand, indicate that very few strokes in the original sketch are perceptually irrelevant. Fortunately, very high epitome-scores are not the norm, as we will see – sparsity is pervasive across categories. Referring once again to Figure 5, the epitome-score for the **airplane** sketch is computed as $\mathcal{E} = \frac{4}{9} = 0.44$ (see Equation 3).

4.4 Additional Stroke Sequence Orderings

The temporal sequence in which the strokes are added is, by default, the basis for construction of cumulative stroke sequence. However, apart from temporal stroke order, we propose other plausible stroke orderings. For completeness, we include the previously introduced temporal stroke ordering as well.

1. TEMPORAL : Strokes are accumulated in the order they were drawn temporally (see top row of Figure 6). Using the notation for sketch strokes defined in Section 4.1, the intermediate canvases are given by $S_1 = \{s_1\}, S_2 = \{s_1, s_2\}, \ldots, S_N = \{s_1, s_2, \ldots, s_N\}$. The resulting sketch sequence $CSS_T = \{S_1, S_2 \ldots, S_N\}$ reflects the hypothesis that the natural order in which people draw sketch strokes best captures the epitome-ness of the sketch.

2. LENGTH : Strokes are accumulated in the order of non-increasing length, i.e. longer strokes are accumulated before adding the shorter ones(second row of Figure 6). Suppose the sorted-by-non-increasing-length version of the original temporal sequence S_t is $S_l = \{s_{l_1}, s_{l_2} \ldots s_{l_N}\}$. Then, the intermediate canvases are $S_1 = \{s_{l_1}\}, S_2 = \{s_{l_1}, s_{l_2}\}, \ldots S_N = \{s_{l_1}, s_{l_2}, \ldots, s_{l_N}\}$. The resulting sequence $CSS_L = \{S_1, S_2 \ldots S_N\}$ reflects the hypothesis that longest strokes best capture the epitome-ness of the sketch.

3. ALTERNATE : Strokes are accumulated by alternately adding strokes of non-increasing length and strokes considered in reverse temporal order (see third row of Figure 6). In this case, the intermediate canvases are $S_1 = \{s_{l_1}\}, S_2 = \{s_{l_1}, s_N\}, S_3 = \{s_{l_1}, s_N, s_{l_2}, \ldots\}$ which in turn generate $CSS_A = \{S_1, S_2 \ldots, S_N\}$. Note that in constructing the sequence, strokes are removed from S_t (temporal sequence) and S_l (non-increasing length sequence) upon being added to CSS_A. This sequence reflects the hypothesis that the longest strokes *and* decorative elements (finishing touches) typically added towards the end of the drawing best capture the epitome-ness of the sketch.

The stroke sequence orderings essentially capture various philosophies of visual abstraction as manifested in *category-epitomes*. Once the cumulative sketch sequence (CSS_T or CSS_L or CSS_A) of a correctly classified full sketch is obtained, the procedure for determining the *category-epitome* (Section 4.2) and epitome-score (Section 4.3) is essentially the same.

The *category-epitomes* can be viewed at
`http://val.serc.iisc.ernet.in/eotd/epitome_images`.

5. ANALYSIS

For our experiments, we utilize the classifier obtained by training with 24 (out of 56) sketches from each category. The ensuing accuracy of the classifier is 76% (see Figure 4). While it is certainly possible to consider many other training and test splits of data, we chose a split which provides a classifier with acceptable performance while maximizing the potential number of *category-epitomes* obtained.

5.1 Epitome-scores across categories for various sketch orderings

We begin our analysis by computing the median of epitome-scores for correctly classified sketches on a per-category basis. The median epitome scores are computed for all the three sketch orderings described in Section 4.4 viz. TEMPORAL, LENGTH and ALTERNATE. The median epitome scores along with corresponding error bars are presented in Figure 8 for correctly classified test sketches across the 160 object categories.

The first heartening aspect is that most of the median-epitome scores are small (i.e. not close to 1). As Figure 7 shows, the percentage of categories which have median epitome-scores below 0.5 ranges between 57% and 87% for various sketch stroke orderings. These trends suggest the

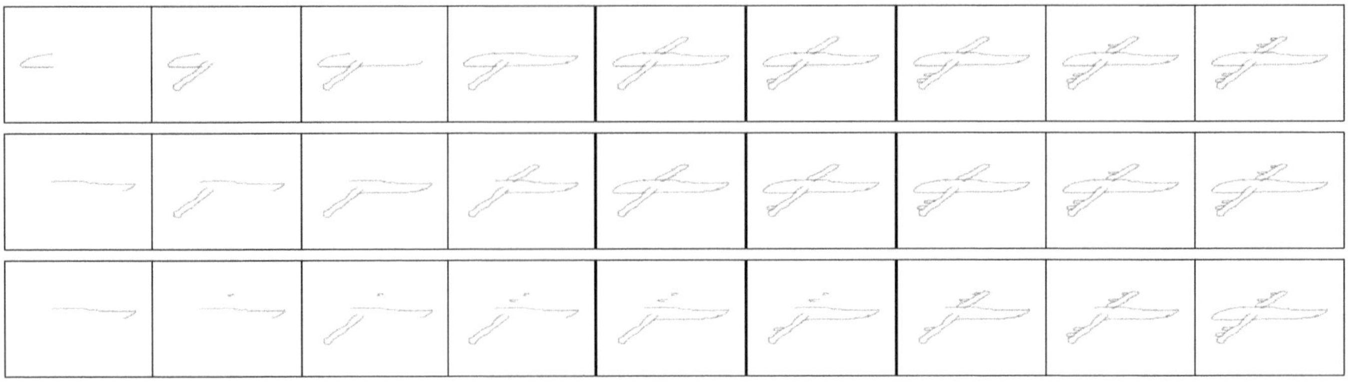

Figure 6: A sketch from **airplane** category and its cumulative stroke sequence canvases for the stroke orderings TEMPORAL (top row), LENGTH (middle row) and ALTERNATE (bottom row).

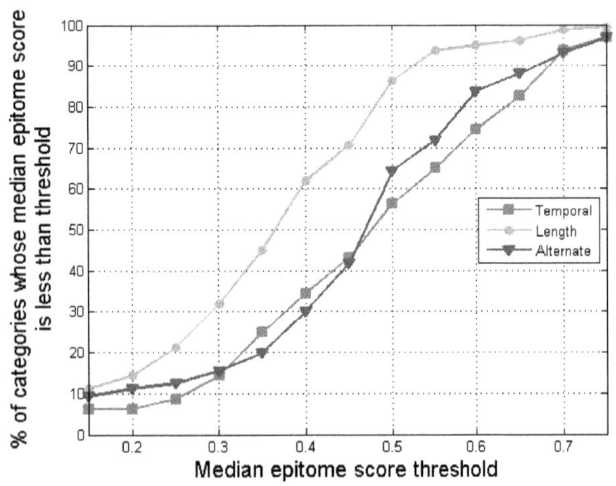

Figure 7: Most of the median epitome-scores are small: The figure shows the % of total categories whose median epitome-score is below a certain threshold. The plots are depicted for the three sketch orderings.

viability of *category-epitomes*. More significantly, they suggest an inherent sparseness for visual representation of object categories because the smaller the epitome-score, the sparser the *category-epitome* sketch typically.

If we examine the scores closely, the epitome-scores for some of the categories (e.g. **apple** and **nose** of TEMPORAL sketch order in Figure 8, topmost row, leftmost column) are 0. For these categories, the sketches are typically drawn such that a dominant stroke or two essentially captures the epitome-ness of the category (See also Equation 3).

The varying lengths of error bars in Figure 8 indicates the variability in depiction across categories. For example, the sketches of the category **sun** (topmost row, middle column in Figure 8) are drawn with a fairly consistent appearance by humans. This consistency influences the sketch classifier and can cause it to produce *category-epitomes* which exhibit a minor amount of variations, thus resulting in a compact distribution of epitome-scores (shorter error bars). In contrast, the variety in sketches of a category such as **flying bird** (same plot as that of **sun**) is reflected in the corresponding *category-epitomes* and by extension, in the longer error bars of its epitome-score.

If we compare the median epitome scores across sketch orderings (Figures 7 and 8), it is easy to see that the LENGTH sketch ordering (adding strokes in decreasing order of length) produces the sparsest epitomes. The result is very interesting since it runs contrary to intuition – we expect people to somehow draw the most discriminative strokes first (i.e. in TEMPORAL stroke ordering). Thus, temporal information does not seem to play any role in obtaining the sparsest epitomes. This throws the door open for analysis of additional freehand sketch datasets where temporal information is absent [21, 16]. The results also demonstrate that the next viable ordering (ALTERNATE) is not good enough. An interleaving of longest strokes with the decorative strokes (typically added temporally towards the end of the sketching process) does result in sparser epitomes compared to temporal order, but an even sparser yet recognizable sketch can be obtained if the strokes are added in order of decreasing length.

5.2 Epitome-score as a proxy for semantic level of detail

A different perspective can be gained by examining categories for a given value of epitome-score. For each category, we count the number of test sketches whose epitome-score is less than a threshold and normalize by the number of test sketches in the category. To facilitate analysis and avoid visual clutter, we select 10 prototypical categories for display. The plot that results by varying the threshold can be viewed for various sketch stroke schemes in Figures 9, 10, 11. The 10 categories are chosen as follows : The AUC (area-under-the-curve) is computed for each category's plot. The AUCs are sorted across categories. Finally, the categories corresponding to the top 4, bottom 4 and the middle 2 AUC values are chosen for representation.

The epitome-score can be considered as a proxy for semantic level-of-detail. Viewed in this light, the plots mentioned above suggest the varying epitome-score budgets across categories. Some categories require a considerable level of detail before their epitomal avatars are revealed. These are typically categories whose plots are towards the lower right in the figures (e.g. **monkey**, **angel**). On the other hand,

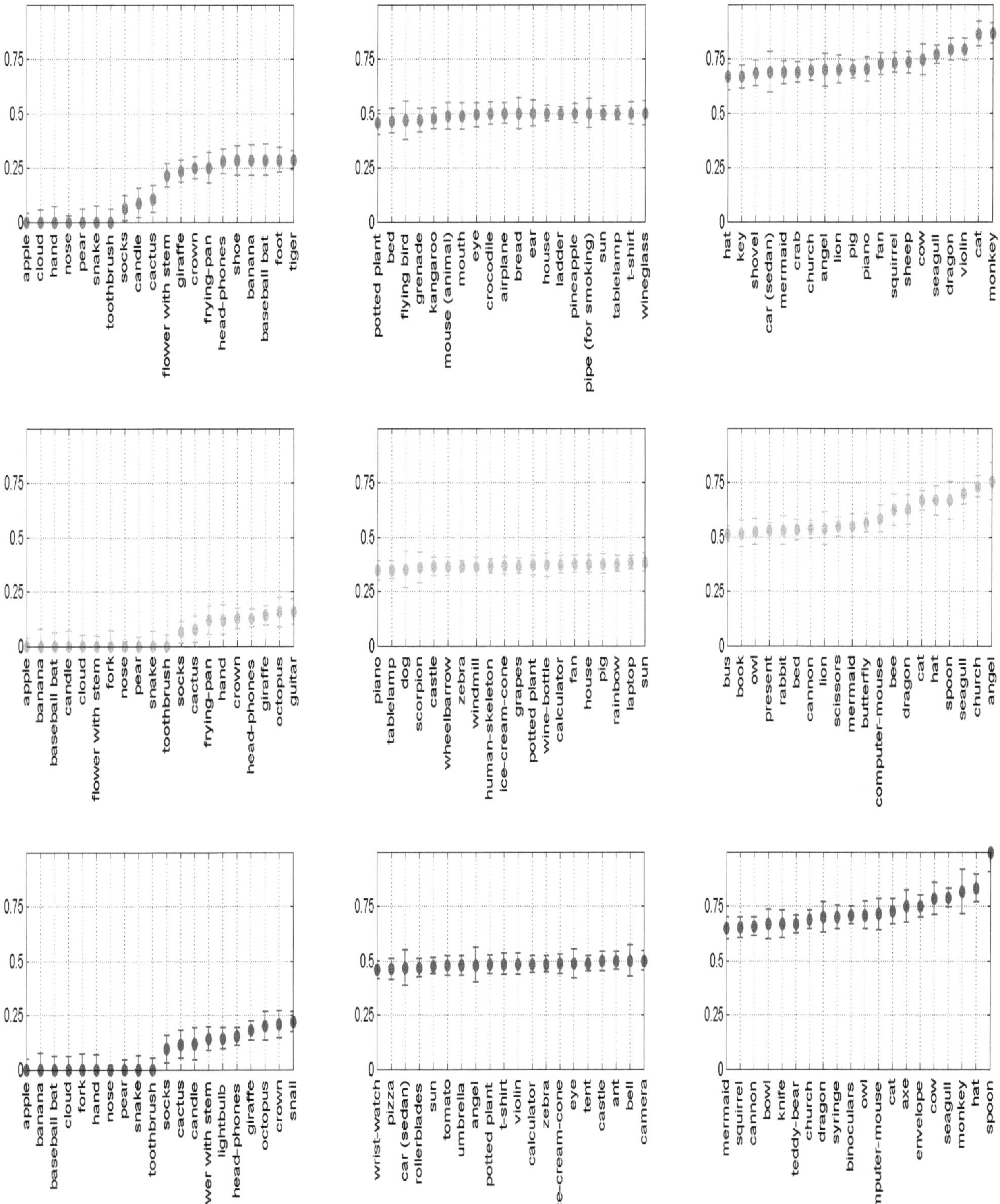

Figure 8: Sorted median epitome-scores (y-axis) and corresponding error bars for 160 object categories(x-axis). For clarity, only the first, middle and last 20 categories of the sorted order are shown. The standard errors are clamped to $[0, 1]$ – the range of epitome-scores. The median scores are shown as filled circles. The plots above depict the trends for the three different philosophies of abstraction – Temporal (topmost plot, magenta), Length (middle plot, green) and Alternate (bottom plot,blue). Plots for the full set of 160 categories can be viewed at `http://val.serc.iisc.ernet.in/eotd/`.

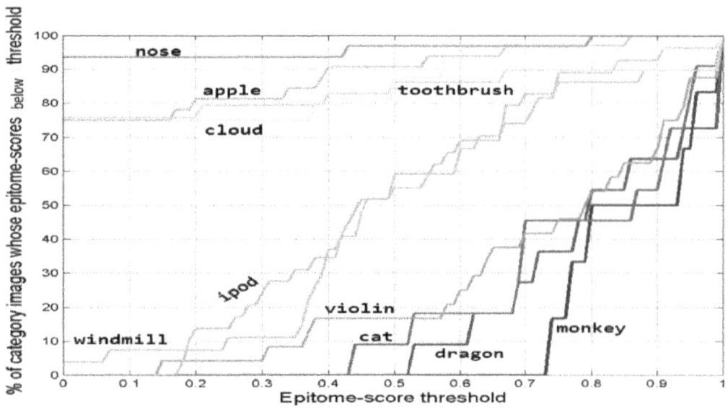

Figure 9: Effect of budgeting epitome-score on category recognition rate using data from 10 selected categories (TEMPORAL ordering). The values of epitome-score thresholds are shown on x-axis. The % of images in each category whose epitome scores are below a particular value of the epitome-score threshold are shown on y-axis. The 10 category names are shown adjacent to their respective plots.

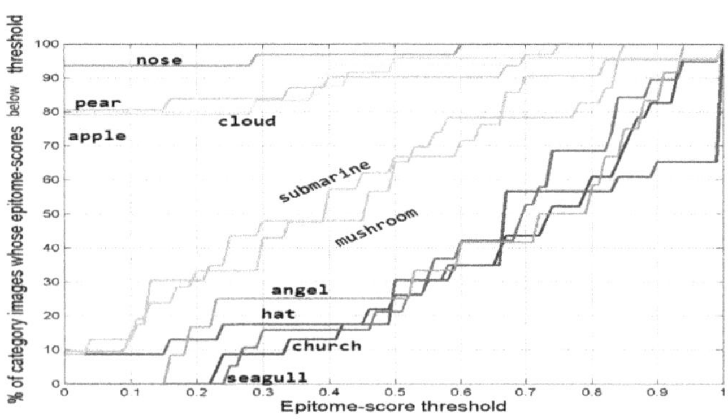

Figure 10: Effect of budgeting epitome-score on category recognition rate using data from 10 selected categories (LENGTH ordering). The values of epitome-score thresholds are shown on x-axis. The % of images in each category whose epitome scores are below a particular value of the epitome-score threshold are shown on y-axis. The 10 category names are shown adjacent to their respective plots.

categories with plots towards the upper left corner (e.g. `apple`,`nose`) have relatively less stringent demands on level of detail.

6. DISCUSSION

In this paper, we have presented a preliminary exploration of *category-epitomes* as a sparse yet discriminative representation of visual object categories. Our analysis of *category-epitomes* and their epitome-scores provides a novel viewpoint for studying the complexity of representation for object categories. Our method of constructing the *category-epitome* has a unique feature which sets it apart from other methods of sparse sketch generation and sketch simplification [22, 19, 24, 20]: It guarantees that the most fundamental primitives (strokes) which enable category recognition (discrimination) are retained. Since the construction of *category-epitomes* renders them incomplete yet recognizable sketches, they can also be used to benchmark the robustness of sketch features and sketch classification pipelines. In addition, epitome-score of the *category-epitomes* can serve as a quantitative measure for evaluation of Non-Photorealistic Rendering methods, a need sorely felt by the researchers active in the area [17, 10, 2].

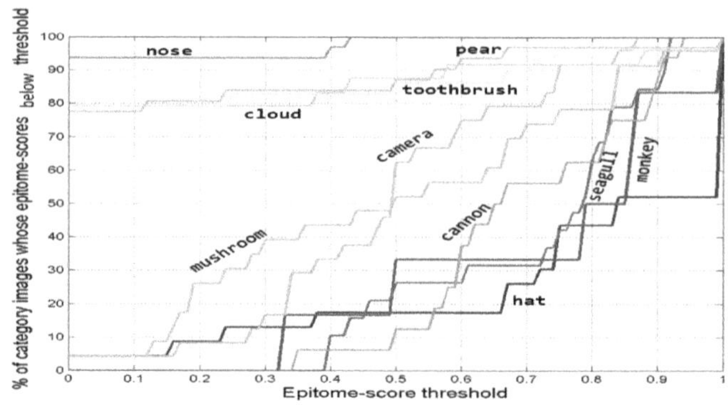

Figure 11: Effect of budgeting epitome-score on category recognition rate using data from 10 selected categories (ALTERNATE ordering). The values of epitome-score thresholds are shown on x-axis. The % of images in each category whose epitome scores are below a particular value of the epitome-score threshold are shown on y-axis. The 10 category names are shown adjacent to their respective plots.

A practical application domain for *category-epitomes* is the field of neuro healthcare. Partially drawn sketches of objects are used to analyze the extent of visual agnosia: a neurological disorder in which object recognition is impaired in humans [7]. The epitome-score provides an additional measure for medical practitioners to monitor and characterize the disorder.

Comparison with the work of Schneider et al. [23]: Suppose a sketch has n strokes. Schneider et al. [23] determine a stroke's contribution (positive, negative, no effect) on object recognizability by removing the stroke and retaining the remaining $(n-1)$ strokes. However, to truly determine stroke importance, other (smaller than $(n-1)$ strokes) subsets must also be considered. For example, the petal strokes of a flower sketch, when removed individually, may be grouped as negative contributors. However, a smaller subset of strokes which contains both petals and other strokes can result in correct classification, as our results suggest. Also, the analysis by [23] is qualitative. We additionally provide a novel quantitative measure (epitome-score) for sketches. Finally, our method also results in sparse yet recognizable representation for objects.

7. FUTURE WORK

A number of other directions exist for future work. One such would be to compare the performance across various Convolutional Neural Networks and analyze the effect of tapping features from different layers of such networks. More generally, we hope that our work will spur interest in analysis of sketches utilizing cutting-edge tools of the deep learning methodology.

By the nature of their generation, sketches have an inherent sequential structure (of strokes). The classifier we use does not exploit this information. Therefore, another direction of work would be to utilize classifiers similar in spirit to Hidden Markov Models (HMM) which can exploit such information for improved sketch recognition. On a related note, it would be worthwhile to explore if classifiers whose performance is relatively superior produce sparser epitomes.

In our work, we have analyzed *category-epitomes* arising out of three different methods of visual abstraction (stroke ordering). The methods are by no means exhaustive. Other methods, such as those based on stroke curvature and randomized stroke data occlusion [5] are potential candidates for constructing *category-epitomes* as well. However, we defer the related study.

In this paper, the results and analysis rely on a machine classifier trained on sketches. A natural extension would be to analyze *category-epitomes* obtained when humans are asked to identify sketches given only a subset of strokes from the original sketch. Comparing the resulting epitomes and epitome-scores would delineate the differences between humans and machines in terms of the cognitive load imposed by partial sketch recognition. In fact, the epitomes and intermediate predictions generated by humans and the machine classifier could be used to conduct a Turing test to quantify the aforementioned difference. To this end, we have deployed a web app where users are randomly shown sketches in different stroke sequence orderings and asked to recognize the sketch. At the time of writing, the web app has been successfully used by about 500 people and has enabled us to collect recognition data for nearly 9000 sketches.

Given their minimalist appearance, *category-epitomes* can also be considered "stylized" yet recognizable depictions of objects. To evaluate the style factor as perceived by humans, we are currently developing an app which tracks user preferences for various philosophies of sketch abstraction (stroke orderings). The resulting statistics would reflect the degree of human agreement on style-quotient of machine-generated abstract art.

8. ACKNOWLEDGMENTS

We wish to acknowledge the anonymous reviewers for their feedback. In addition, we thank the members of Video Analytics Lab, IISc for their feedback during various stages of the draft preparation. Ravi Kiran Sarvadevabhatla would like to acknowledge Victor Ng-Thow-Hing for relating anecdotes which served to inspire the paper's title and the opening story. We would also like to acknowledge NVIDIA Corporation for their donation of Tesla K40 GPU.

9. REFERENCES

[1] K. Chatfield, K. Simonyan, A. Vedaldi, and A. Zisserman. Return of the devil in the details: Delving deep into convolutional nets. In *BMVC*, 2014.

[2] F. Cole, K. Sanik, D. DeCarlo, A. Finkelstein, T. Funkhouser, S. Rusinkiewicz, and M. Singh. How well do line drawings depict shape? In *SIGGRAPH*, 2009.

[3] M. Eitz, J. Hays, and M. Alexa. How do humans sketch objects? *SIGGRAPH*, 2012.

[4] R. Fan, K. Chang, C. Hsieh, X. Wang, and C. Lin. LIBLINEAR: A library for large linear classification. *J. Mach. Learn. Res.*, 9:1871–1874, 2008.

[5] A. Ghosh and N. Petkov. A cognitive evaluation procedure for contour based shape descriptors. *Int. J. Hybrid Intell. Syst.*, 2(4):237–252, Dec. 2005.

[6] R. Girshick, J. Donahue, T. Darrell, and J. Malik. Rich feature hierarchies for accurate object detection and semantic segmentation. In *CVPR*, 2014.

[7] E. S. Gollin. Developmental studies of visual recognition of incomplete objects. *Perceptual and Motor Skills*, 11:289–298, 1960.

[8] Y. Gong, L. Wang, R. Guo, and S. Lazebnik. Multi-scale orderless pooling of deep convolutional activation features. In *ECCV*. 2014.

[9] R. Haralick, L. T. Watson, and T. J. Laffey. The topographic primal sketch. *The International Journal of Robotics Research*, 2(1):50–72, March 1983.

[10] A. Hertzmann. Non-photorealistic rendering and the science of art. In *NPAR*, 2010.

[11] R. Hu and J. Collomosse. A performance evaluation of gradient field hog descriptor for sketch based image retrieval. *CVIU*, 117(7):790–806, July 2013.

[12] I.Berger, A. Shamir, M. Mahler, E. Carter, and J. Hodgins. Style and abstraction in portrait sketching. *SIGGRAPH*, 2013.

[13] I.Kokkinos, P. Maragos, and A. Yuille. Bottom-up and top-down object detection using primal sketch features and graphical models. In *CVPR*, 2006.

[14] A. Karteek, P. S. Lahari, and C. V. Jawahar. Discriminant substrokes for online handwriting recognition. In *ICDAR*, 2005.

[15] A. Krizhevsky, I. Sutskever, and G. E. Hinton. Imagenet classification with deep convolutional neural networks. In *NIPS*, 2012.

[16] L. J. Latecki, R. LakÃd'mper, and U. Eckhardt. Shape descriptors for non-rigid shapes with a single closed contour. In *CVPR*, 2000.

[17] H. Li, D. Mould, and J. Davies. Structure and aesthetics in non-photorealistic images. In *Proceedings of Graphics Interface*, 2013.

[18] D. Marr. Chapter 2: Representing the image. In *Vision*, pages 54–79. The MIT Press, 2010.

[19] S. Marvaniya, S. Bhattacharjee, V. Manickavasagam, and A. Mittal. Drawing an automatic sketch of deformable objects using only a few images. In *ECCV. Workshops and Demonstrations*, 2012.

[20] R. Mehra, Q. Zhou, J. Long, A. Sheffer, A. Gooch, and N. J. Mitra. Abstraction of man-made shapes. In *ACM SIGGRAPH Asia*, 2009.

[21] S. Nene, S. K. Nayar, and H. Murase. Columbia Object Image Library (COIL-20). Technical report, 1996.

[22] Y. Qi, J. Guo, Y. Li, H. Zhang, T. Xiang, and Y. Song. Sketching by perceptual grouping. In *ICIP*, 2013.

[23] R. G. Schneider and T. Tuytelaars. Sketch classification and classification-driven analysis using fisher vectors. *SIGGRAPH Asia*, 2014.

[24] A. Shesh and B. Chen. Efficient and dynamic simplification of line drawings. *Comput. Graph. Forum*, 27(2):537–545, 2008.

[25] J. Sun, N.Zheng, H.Tao, and H. Y. Shum. Image hallucination with primal sketch priors. In *CVPR*, 2003.

[26] D. B. Walther, B. Chai, E. Caddigan, D. M. Beck, and L. Fei-Fei. Simple line drawings suffice for functional mri decoding of natural scene categories. *PNAS*, 108(23):9661–9666, 2011.

[27] W. Zhang, X. Wang, and X. Tang. Lighting and pose robust face sketch synthesis. In *ECCV*, 2010.

A Distributed Theatre Experiment with Shakespeare

Doug Williams & Ian Kegel
BT
Adastral Park,
IPSWICH, Suffolk, UK
doug.williams@bt.com

Marian Ursu
University of York
Theatre, Film and Television
Baird Lane, York, UK
marian.ursu@york.ac.uk

Pablo Cesar & Jack Jansen
CWI
Science Park 123, 1098 XG
Amsterdam P.O. Box 94079,
NL-1090 GB Amsterdam, NL
p.s.cesar@cwi.nl

Erik Geelhoed
Falmouth University
The Air Building,
Penryn, Cornwall, UK
erik.geelhoed@falmouth.ac.uk

Andras Horti
Joanneum Research
Steyrergasse 17
A-8010 Graz Austria
andras.horti@joanneum.at

Michael Frantzis
Goldsmiths,
University of London
New Cross, London.
m.frantzis@gold.ac.uk

Bill Scott
Miracle Theatre Company
Redruth, UK
bill@miracletheatre.co.uk

ABSTRACT

This paper reports on an experimental production of *The Tempest* that was developed in collaboration with Miracle Theatre Company realised as a distributed performance from two separate stages through a dynamically configured telepresence system. The production allowed an exploration of the way a range of technologies, including consumer grade broadband, cameras and projection technologies could affect the development and delivery of live theatre by regional touring company.

The architecture of the communication platform used to deliver the performance is introduced as are two novel software tools that are used to describe and control the way the play should be captured and represented. The experimental production was thoroughly evaluated and the feedback from audience and theatre professionals is presented in some detail.

A considered observation of the process and the way it differs from film, TV and theatre suggest that distributed theatre can be treated as a new genre of storytelling.

Categories and Subject Descriptors

Computer applications: ARTS AND HUMANITIES: Performing Arts

General Terms: Design, Experimentation. Measurement

Keywords: Distributed theatre; Broadband

1. INTRODUCTION

Shakespeare's plays have been performed on stage for over 400 years, but the way they are presented is often adapted to take advantage of new technologies. Innovations in staging, lighting, costumes, sound effects and props have all been used to re interpret the plays of the bard in ways that are meant to be attractive to audiences.

MM'15, October 26 - 30, 2015, Brisbane, Australia

ACM 978-1-4503-3459-4/15/10…$15.00
DOI: http://dx.doi.org/10.1145/2733373.2806272

This paper describes a detailed case study that explores how a range of technologies, including consumer grade broadband, cameras and projection technologies could affect the development and delivery of live theatre through an experimental production of The Tempest that was developed in collaboration with Miracle Theatre Company[1]. Miracle Theatre Company is a small, well established regional touring company that produces both familiar and new work across the South West of England. Since their goal is to bring theatre to people, they often perform in small outdoor locations using simple staging and lighting and sometimes in small community venues such as village halls. This approach enables them to reach remote venues but requires a form of theatre which places limited demands on staging, lighting, props and costume.

1.1 Motivations

The work described in this paper is motivated primarily by enquiry from commercial and artistic perspectives. The drive from these quarters creates a rare opportunity for scientific investigation with high ecological validity. To underscore and embed that opportunity the performance, carried out by a commercial theatre company with a reputation to maintain, took place in front of a paying audience. The complex blend of ambition, responsibility and jeopardy created a poignant mix of dread and excitement.

1.2 Artistic Motivation

Miracle Theatre Company's interest in this project was to explore the extent to which consumer grade fast broadband connections, cameras and screens can be used to help them to achieve their stated purpose i.e. to *produce a rich mix of touring theatre, always with a unique comic style, joyful use of language and an immediate visual appeal. It embraces digital technology, nurtures new writers, performers, venues and promoters. Miracle works to build audiences by bringing 'big' shows to little venues. Miracle is committed to touring work which is innovative, but not intimidating, to communities in the far flung corners of the UK.'*

The motivation for this work was thus to establish whether consumer grade fast broadband, cameras, and projection technologies could be used to deliver an engaging amusing performance to a paying audience whilst also exploring the extent to which it could extend audience reach, bring something new to

---

[1] www.miracletheatre.co.uk

the theatre and even hint at new forms of creative artistic expression.

We also anticipated that consumer grade high speed broadband connections and the use of audio and video links would enable a different form of rehearsal practice, in which actors did not have to be co-located.

The play selected (*The Tempest*) was one the troupe had recently performed and that the Artistic Director felt lent itself to being performed in two locations; we could not afford to produce a brand new performance. *The Tempest* (1610-1611) is believed to be the last play that William Shakespeare wrote alone. It is set on a remote island where a magician named Prospero, the once Duke of Milan, lives with his daughter Miranda, having been exiled there by his younger brother Alonso. Prospero and Miranda share the island with Ariel, a nymph like spirit, and Caliban, a magical monster, both of whom are controlled by Prospero. Prospero, on sensing that his brother is sailing past the island, conjures a storm that shipwrecks Alonso, the King (with whom Alonso is travelling), and a number of their acolytes. The plot centres on Prospero who, using magic, exposes his brother's dishonest ascent to power and yet chooses to forgive him. It is filled with beautiful language and many comedic passages.

Figure 1 Schematic of the performance challenge, two performance spaces and an audience at home

In the distributed production, the actors are split between two locations but together deliver a single performance mediated by the cameras, consumer grade high speed broadband and projection technologies. This had an immediate appeal to the Artistic Director of Miracle Theatre Company as he envisaged being able to *"give an extra dimension to the production of The Tempest by placing Prospero into some quite dramatic natural surrounding - like a cliff with the sea pounding behind him... and having the rest of the play taking place in a theatre with Prospero there on a screen and gently transporting the theatre to an environment that you wouldn't normally be able to do."* This vision, whilst still valid, was moderated during the development stage.

Another motivation was to explore how the technology could allow the creative team to emphasise the nature and capabilities of the characters. Prospero, for example, can be seen as an eccentric, slightly reclusive but immensely powerful even God-like character. Ariel's magical qualities can likewise be enhanced using affordances of the distributed performance and the technology.

1.3 Technical Motivation

We selected Cornwall in the UK as the location of the performances because Cornwall was enjoying an accelerated deployment of fast broadband connection through the Superfast Cornwall Project[2]. This project was exploring the impact of the deployment in terms of the way it affected education, industry, tourism, culture and employment. In this work we explore how consumer grade fast broadband connections could have an impact on live performance.

There were two main technical objectives; the first was to establish whether it was possible to stream live theatre over consumer grade fast broadband connections; the second was to explore the capabilities of a system based on controllable cameras that semi-automatically develop simultaneous live streams, based on a scripted set of camera selections, for three different audiences (two theatres and the Internet audience).

Filming and broadcasting theatre began in the 1930s [1]. Live streaming theatre to cinemas, using satellite technology, is a practice used today by large theatre companies like the Metropolitan Opera and NT Live. It is reported to strengthen their brand and enhances all forms theatre attendance [2]. However it is expensive and only really viable for the larger, more successful, theatre companies. Distributed theatre experiments have shown what is possible using advanced high speed networks [3]. This exploration sought to explore what could be achieved using consumer grade fast broadband connections [4]. Through separating the performance of an established touring play between two locations, and mediating that performance using technology it is clear that the performances have to be adapted: the actors can no longer deliver the performance they use for the single stage performance. This production explores how this can be done with unmanned relatively low cost cameras and explores the degree to which the semi-automated cameras can enhance the storytelling for both the audiences in the performance venues and the online audience.

1.4 Scientific motivation

Part of the scientific motivation of this work was inherited from the Vconect project that developed the technology. The Vconect project[3], sought to improve ad hoc communication between groups and the video communication platform developed by the Vconect project [5] was used in this distributed theatrical performance.

The project postulated that changing the way audio and video were captured, transmitted and presented could positively affect group communication by improving the quality of mediated communication and by enabling more complex communication setups to be supported. To test this, its sophisticated video communication platform was deployed in two diverse setups. One in the context of an online social network [6] and this trial in distributed theatre. The use of the technology in these settings

[2] Superfast Cornwall is a programme funded by the EU, BT and Cornwall Council, and managed by Cornwall Development Company, a local authority company controlled by Cornwall Council.

[3] Vconect received funding from the European Community's Seventh Framework Programme (FP7/2007-2013) under grant agreement no. ICT-2011-287760

allowed us to explore, in an holistic experiential way, whether this postulation was valid.

The distributed nature of this performance also allowed us to explore, in an ecologically valid context, the differences in the responses to live theatre of remote and local audiences. This is an important component of developing satisfying and sustainable theatrical performance that can be enjoyed at a distance.

1.5 Experimental Approach

The approach adopted in this work is represented in Figure 1; it depicts two performance spaces (the Dogbite Studio and the Maritime Museum) each with a local audience, plus an audience watching live video streamed over the Internet.

The Dogbite Studio performance space was host to Prospero and his assistant Ariel. The second location, the Maritime Museum, played host to the remainder of the cast. Ariel, who is sometimes invisible can easily move between the two locations. In this production the role of Ariel was performed by two actors, one in each location.

The Dogbite Studio consisted of a simple stage, two screens and two cameras. Prospero and Ariel could be seen on the stage and the action taking place in the Maritime Museum could be observed on one screen. On occasions Prospero found himself in conversation, through the screen, with Ariel in the Maritime Museum. At other times he merely observed the action. The other screen was used to overlay recorded video onto the physical performance space.

In the Maritime Museum the actors had a stage, a screen and four cameras. The screen here showed Prospero in conversation with Ariel but also illustrated portions of the story that took place in Prospero's location.

In order to evaluate this case study we provided questionnaires for the audiences and also took the time to interview key participants from the theatre company to better understand the experience from their perspective. We also encouraged all of the technical team to be aware of, and to reflect upon, the things that went well, things that surprised them and things that did not work so well. All these sources of information were collated and provide a rich insight into the experiment.

2. RELATED WORK

Performance artists have creatively made use of physical and, more recently, digital illusionary tools: *"there is nothing in cyberspace and the screened technologies of the virtual that has not been already performed on the stage. The theatre has always been virtual, a space of illusory immediacy."* [7]. It is not our intention to survey all the various efforts from artists to exploit technology to enhance performances, since [8] and [9] already provide comprehensive overviews. Nevertheless, there are a number of recent pieces that showcase current directions and challenges. "Skype Duet" [10] is a distributed live performance between New York and Berlin. Organisations like "Dimanche Rouge" promote experimental performances that have included actors and dancers accompanied by pre-recorded video and other multimedia work that has been streamed live between Paris and New York providing opportunities for distributed audiences to interact, give feedback and even co-create [11]. "Discovering Pasolini: Notes on an unborn movie" [12] is a project that was developed and performed with telepresence technology at Teatro La Pergola Firenze. In "Graphic Ships" [13] musicians and a dancer are distributed across locations. Visuals are created based on the movements of the dancer, captured by motion sensing, and create a graphic score from which the live musicians improvise the musical accompaniment. The audience sees the live movement of the local dancer, the visualization her movement creates and simultaneous projections of the multi-sited musicians themselves. Finally, "The Return" [14] shows one performance, which happened simultaneously (with audience) in two spaces, and with people that followed the live streaming from different parts of the world.

All these pieces connect two or more locations with the aim of creating a single performance. With the emergence of pervasive low cost videoconferencing systems, such as Skype, perspectives in the mediated performance space have been broadened. With the technology becoming so much more accessible there has been an increase in mediated performances. Cinzia Cremona [15] puts it succinctly: *"Skype communication and video-performance have been converging into a set of art practices that adopts the screen as a relational device."* Our work is significantly different. From an artistic perspective the goal was not so much on experimental theatre, but on understanding how a local theatre company could appropriate novel technologies for the transformation of a single-stage play into a distributed performance. From a technical perspective, we took the conscious decision of not using commercial systems like Polycom and Skype (except the out of band channels used by the production team, where Google+ Hangouts was used). Instead we built our own infrastructure over which we had full control. The infrastructure was somewhat based on the one we have previously used for enabling remote gaming between homes [16] so it provided a low delay communication and rich composition capabilities. Unlike other research approaches that take advantage of very fast networks between universities [3] and simulations [17], this experiment uses consumer grade fast broadband products. At the aesthetics level, our system provides rich composition capabilities, beyond existing videoconferencing systems, for combining a variety of video inputs (including pre-recorded media) for a variety of outputs: the other theatre, online audiences, etc.

Companies such as The National Theatre live stream one-stage productions to cinemas [18]. As a one-way communication system, they miss information about the reaction of the audience [19], [20] and do not provide means for the audience to interact, except out of band using system like the social network Twitter. Previous works have considered interactivity based on mobile phone usage [21] or messages [22]. In our case, we provide audience awareness between the locations based on the audiovisual communication. One key innovation, which brings the overall budget for a production down, when compared to services such as NTLive, is our innovative mechanism for scripted automatic control of the cameras that capture the play and the audience.

3. TECHNOLOGY PLATFORM

The video communication platform developed by the Vconect project [5] to address the challenge of supporting complex use cases for multimedia communication between ad hoc groups incorporates three innovations over state-of-the-art video communication systems:

- The use of communication modelling and automatic reasoning, which we call orchestration, to determine how best to employ the capabilities of a given system (cameras, microphones and displays) to meet the communication needs of each participant.
- Multimedia composition functions which enable real-time streams and pre-recorded content to be synchronised and rendered just-in-time at multiple clients, under the control of a central orchestration system.
- A 'service-aware' network in which the selection and routing of media streams is dynamically adapted in order to balance

quality of experience against the cost and capabilities of the resources available.

The Vconect platform was deployed and extended for our trial of *The Tempest*, using the architecture shown in Figure 2. The figure is divided into three layers which represent groups of physical locations: the two performance venues (top), private homes (bottom) and the Vconect platform, hosted in London (middle). In the platform architecture, audio and video are carried in separate streams and are processed independently, while the system as a whole is tuned to ensure correct synchronisation. Audio processing components such as the Audio Communication Engine (ACE) and the Multi-point Control Unit (ACE-MCU) are shown in purple. Video processing components such as: the Studio Client; the Video Router and the Video Bridge are shown in blue. Components associated with orchestration and control of the service-aware network such as: Sync Control, Performance Orchestration Engine and Optimiser are shown in green. The platform uses a message broker, based on Apache ActiveMQ, for mediating control messages between all components. Control messages include communication cues, commands, signalling, synchronisation and network monitoring data. The architecture achieves the dual goals of linking two theatre environments and presenting a coherent experience to remote audiences joining over broadband. A Web Streamer component relays audio and video streams from the platform to an external web broadcasting service (not shown) for onward delivery to viewers in their homes.

3.1 Audiovisual Capture and Presentation

A key challenge for audio in a distributed theatre setting is forestalling feedback and echo effects from delayed playout at each location. We addressed this by using miniature directional body-worn microphones which were relatively immune to audio from the PA loudspeakers. The audio mix in each location (including additional pre-recorded effects and music) was captured and transmitted by the Audio Communication Engine (ACE), a Voice-over-IP (VoIP) client allowing multichannel audio and echo control with low delay (<50ms end-to-end) and full audio bandwidth (24kHz). The audio system design was significantly more complex than a single theatre environment, but only standard equipment was required in addition to the ACEs.

Professional video conferencing cameras were used due to their high quality optics, good low-light performance and Pan/Tilt/Zoom heads which could be remotely controlled. HD video projectors displayed images on fabric screens in each location; the screens were about 3m in diagonal. Video capture and rendering was managed by the Vconect Studio Client, a set of applications that together implement a highly customisable platform for video conferencing. Based on the Ambulant multimedia document player, the Studio Client used SMIL [23] documents to define and render composition layouts for live streams and pre-recorded video, plus transitions and animations. The SMIL language can easily capture composition requirements, both *spatial composition* (*where* things will appear on screen) and *temporal composition* (*when* they will appear). The SMIL document structure was further extended to store details about available camera positions and video encoder settings, as well as the location and relative position of the available projector screens. Video captured by the cameras was H.264-encoded using HD (720p) resolution, at a frame rate of 25fps and a target bandwidth of 2Mbits/s. During the performance, each Studio Client controlled the PTZ head of each of its connected cameras in order to reframe shots when instructed by the Performance Orchestration Engine.

3.2 Audiovisual Transmission and Routing

The Vconect platform provided a hybrid transmission and routing architecture to suit the needs of a distributed theatre performance. For audio, the ACE-MCU is a full-bandwidth audio bridge which provides an appropriate mix of incoming streams for each connected client, thus allowing the Web Streamer to transmit audio from both sets of actors to home viewers while at the same time connecting audio between each performance location.

Video streams were connected between each performance location using a Video Router, a highly-efficient UDP packet switch capable of handling multiple incoming video streams and switching or duplicating them to various outputs at any time in response to instructions from the Optimiser. The platform also included a Video Bridge, which performed a similar function to traditional bridges used in video conferencing today. The Video Bridge was used to render a single composite version of the performance at both locations at any one moment. This was forwarded via the Video Router to the Web Streamer for onward delivery to the home viewers. The combination of Video Router and Video Bridge offers further benefits which were not fully explored during *The Tempest* trial, including the ability to render a preview of all available video sources for presentation on preview monitors for members of the crew.

In the Vconect platform, the Optimiser component is responsible for monitoring low-level information about network performance and working in conjunction with the Orchestration Engine to dynamically adapt the configuration of video streams to cost-effectively deliver the best Quality of Experience. However, for *The Tempest* trial, the capabilities of the consumer grade fast broadband network connections in each performance location were known well in advance, and exclusive access was negotiated for the duration of the performances. This meant that the Studio Clients could be pre-configured to the optimum settings and dynamic adaptation within this part of the system was unnecessary. The main role of the Optimiser was therefore to provide reliable setup of connections between the two Studio Clients, the Video Router, the Video Bridge and the Web Streamer, and to enable monitoring and debugging at runtime.

3.3 Orchestration and Composition

Theatre is scripted and this changes significantly the way we think about how to choose which camera views to select for transmission. In live systems used to represent video communications, complex algorithms can be developed that dynamically determine how best to represent the conversation [24]. But in theatre the director can select, in advance, the best camera shots. This is similar to film (the action is scripted) but also has similarities to live television where there is no "take 2"; as such the production team have to develop a filmic language based on a limited number of possible camera views, selected live during the performance.

The precise timings of events in theatre will change from night to night even if the sequence should not. For this reason a system had to be developed that would control the cameras, moving them in sync with the theatrical script so that they framed the action in the way that the director viewed was best for the audience.

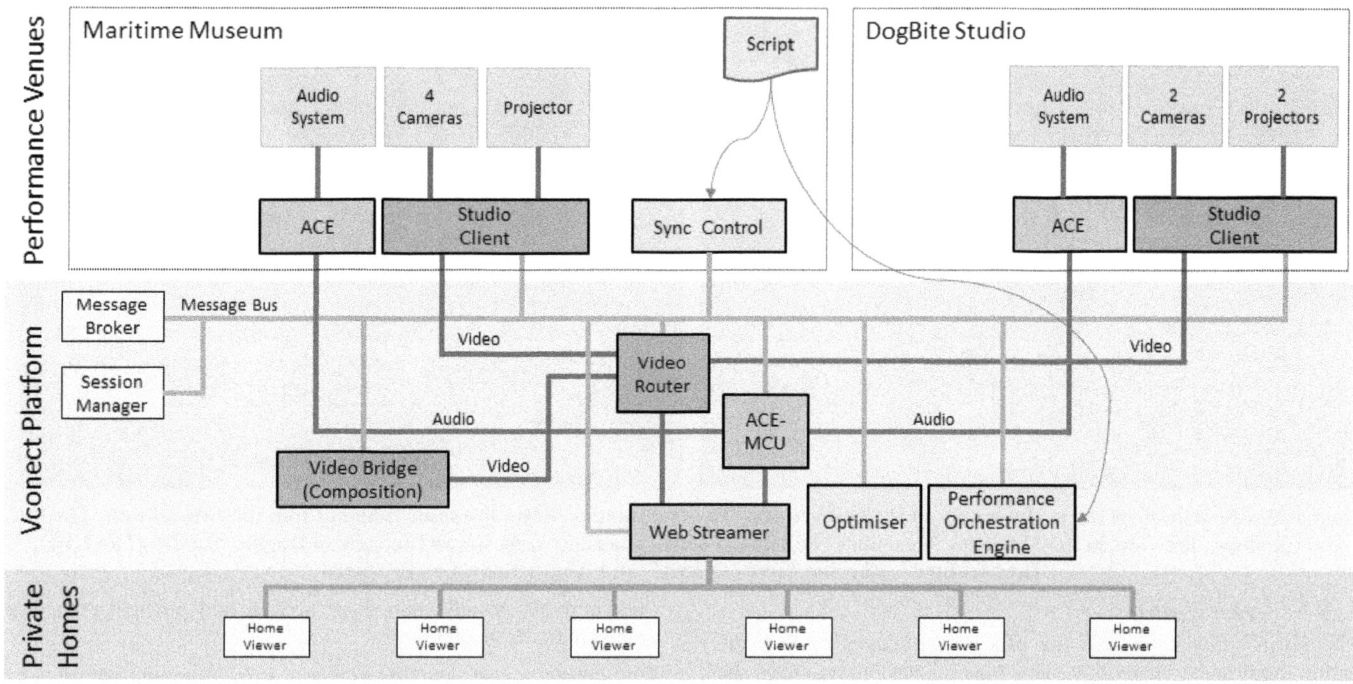

Figure 2 The Vconect platform as implemented for *The Tempest* trial

The requirement was for tools which can take a theatrical script and link it, via a set of cues, to editable audiovisual representation instructions. These instructions exist as a script which can be executed by the Performance Orchestration Engine. The components need to achieve this, some of which are in Figure 2, include:

1. A set of *PTZ (Pan/Tilt/Zoom) positions*, camera configurations which have been predetermined to capture the creative intention of the director at certain points in time.
2. A set of *Composition Layouts*, each determining where live streams are displayed, possibly augmented with pre-recorded media and visual effects.
3. A *Script Editor*. A software tool which was used to create a description of the way the play should be represented on the screens in the audience locations. We call this description the "representation script". Representation scripts are both readable/editable by operators, and can also be executed automatically by the Sync Control component.
4. A *Sync Control* component. This component displays, in a user-friendly form, the representation script and allows an operator to synchronize the devices in each theatre with the stage performance.
5. A *Visual Composition Engine* per theatre and one for the home audience. These engines execute the PTZ position and composition layout commands, under control of the Sync Control component. Each Studio Client contains a Visual Composition Engine, as well as the Video Bridge.

A significant aspect of the system is the user interface for the Script Editor. The model chosen to achieve this also borrowed from existing methods in cinema, specifically for the user interface for a script editor. The standard interface, which appears in many modern non-linear editing (NLE) systems of a timeline with parallel tracks on which material can be placed, served as a useful model. However the tracks in the Vconect system differ from those in an NLE in two important respects, which make it a much richer model. Firstly, the timeline is not a sequence in minutes and seconds, but a sequence of cues which correspond to moments on a theatrical script. Each cue can trigger multiple actions. Secondly, the parallel tracks on the timeline do not represent media items but rather sets of instructions to different components – screens, layouts and cameras.

It is worth noting that, besides meeting the technical requirements for building the creative artefact via the relationship between creative professional and the Performance Orchestration Engine, the Vconect architecture supports some important functionalities required to help the director and actors achieve their goals in the context of the final mediated environment. For example, additional video feeds can be required for monitoring the performance, or the audio channels can support communication between director and performers in a number of different locations. These were not part of the initial system, but emerged as requirements during the trial.

3.3.1 PTZ positions and Composition Layouts

Early in the production, placeholder decisions were made about how things would appear on the on-stage screens and for the home audience. In each location (where for the purpose of composition we consider the feed to the home viewers as one location) there can be a combination of pre-recorded media and live feeds from specific camera angles. To these media items and live feeds visual effects can be applied, such as crossfading, semi-transparent overlays, etc.

These layouts are then encoded into SMIL fragments. Each SMIL fragment may contain any number of pre-recorded media items such as video clips or images, to be played out at a certain time after the activation of the fragment, and any number of placeholders for live streams. Each layout is named to reflect the intent of the layout and to make their role clear when they appear in the Script Editor. Names such as "*FullScreen*" and "*Prerecorded clip with pillar fading into live feed*" are examples that worked well.

Figure 3 Illustration of the performance in the two venues. The two images shows the same moment fom the two venues. The left image shows the view in the Maritime Museum (The Island) whilst the right view shows the view in Dogbite Studio (The Lair). They feature Catherine Lake (as Ariel) and Angus Brown as Prospero

3.3.2 Script Editor

The Script Editor used the notion of scenes and cues to locate the script representation within the play. Each scene may be punctuated by cues which were labelled uniquely. For each cue sufficient information was provided to unambiguously define what each camera is capturing and what is being shown on the screens in each of the performance locations. These include:

- Narrative - a human description of the scene's events (e.g. "Miranda watching sea")
- A description, for each Camera, of what is being captured (for example "Island-Camera3_Wide"). A descriptive term, such as "Wide", corresponds to a specific triple of Pan, Tilt and Zoom settings for that camera. Any number of descriptive names and triples can be described for each camera; these may be general, such as "Wide", or related to a specific scene such as "CloseUp (Ariel double and Prospero with puppet)".
- A description, for each of the audience locations (Dogbite, Maritime museum and the Home viewers), of what is being shown. The screen content is described using a layout description and the identifiers of the cameras that are displayed within this layout.

For example, at a specific cue, the script editor will indicate that Island-Camera3 is being shown full screen in DogBite studio

3.3.3 Sync Control

The Sync Control component allowed an operator to synchronise the execution of the representation script with the pace of the performance. The design focus was simplicity, usability and ways to recover from a technical breakdown during a live performance. The user interface included one area that showed the representation script in natural language and one area that showed the controlling view i.e. an area that showed information about the previous, current and next performance sections. This controlling area included identifiers such as the cue name and the narrative text together with all the camera and screen commands that correspond to the cue. This technical description combined with the information from the natural language script helped the operator to ensure that the chosen cue entry corresponded to the action on the stage and that the system components were all running correctly. A "Send Cue" button sends the data of the cue shown in the middle horizontal section and positions the user interface to the next cue.

The interface also included a "Go to Cue" function that allowed the operator to jump to a specific cue – an essential feature in the event that, due to human or technical error, the representation script became desynchronised with the performance. In case of emergency there were two "panic" configurations which shift the representation to a wide shot.

3.3.4 Visual Composition Engine

Each Visual Composition Engine (whether embedded within the Studio Clients or the Video Bridge) is responsible for rendering live streams and pre-recorded media to one or more screens or encoded output streams. It receives three types of instructions from the Sync Control component:

- switch to a new layout,
- switch a particular live stream within the current layout to another camera,
- position a specific camera to another PTZ angle.

The Visual Composition Engine is responsible for maintaining accurate synchronization of media items, and for displaying all media items at the right place on the screens, with the right visual effects, and at the right time. This separation of responsibilities between the composition engine and the Sync Control has the effect that Sync Control does not have hard real-time requirements because these are handled by the Visual Composition Engine. And the composition engine is not responsible for story line sequencing because this is handled by Sync Control.

4. OUTCOMES

4.1 The Performance

The Tempest, was performed on Tuesday September 8th 2014 and appeared as illustrated in Figure 3. The total audience was about 60; with about 40 being seated at the 'Island' location (the Maritime Museum), and about 20 in 'The Lair' (Dog Bite studio) and further 30 or so watching on line. A handful watched from both performance locations – swapping locations at the interval

Throughout the development of this play the theatre company had communicated with its audience with a tag line "*expect the unexpected*" and expectations were again set when the Artistic Director, during his introduction to the performance, wryly commented that, *"...given the large numbers of computers involved I shall be bold. I will not say that something may go wrong I shall say something will go wrong."*

Remarkably, given the known jeopardy, this daring distributed performance of *The Tempest* to a paying audience worked. The play suffered only one short stoppage and this was because a microphone was not switched on; it did not materially affect people's enjoyment of the play and was not commented on in the feedback sheets. As the General Manager of Miracle Theatre Company commented: *"I could not believe that when we came to do the actual thing it literally worked the whole time when it hadn't gone for more than about 15 minutes in all the run ups."*

Results are presented from three main sources. The first source is system performance measurements; the second source is the responses to the audience feedback questionnaires, these are mixture of quantifiable subjective assessment and qualitative subjective assessments. The third source is the reflections of those involved in the production. They include extensive interviews with members of the Miracle Theatre Company which took place a few months after the performance.

4.2 System Performance Metrics

Bandwidth measurements of 76Mbits/s downstream and 18Mbits/s upstream were made in each of the two venues using a standard web-based speed test tool[4]. Given that we chose an encode rate of 2Mbits/s per stream during the rehearsals, this bandwidth was nominally enough to support all the traffic we anticipated generating.

Analysis of the video showed that the action as displayed in the remote location lagged the action in the local location by 320ms. Transmission delays were dominated by delays in the capture, encoding and packetisation; transit over the broadband link (to London and back, about 500km) amounts to only 3ms.

Delay in the audio transmission can be made much shorter than the delays in the video transmission. In this set up we had the option of adding delay into the audio chain to achieve good synchronization between the audio and the video.

4.3 Audience Response Metrics

Audience members were invited to indicate their responses to a range of questions by making a mark on a scale that ranged between 'Not at all' and 'Very' see Figure 4. The marks were recorded as normalized values between 0 and 100 based on the location of the mark respondents made on the scale.

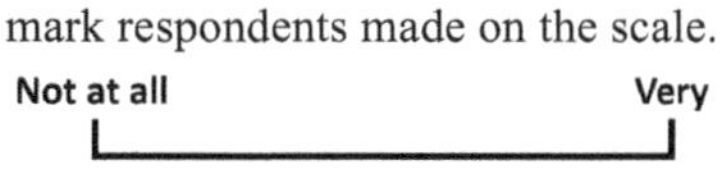

Figure 4 Response scale used to collect audience responses

The questionnaire offered respondents an opportunity to add comments. We received 47 questionnaire responses. The questions included:

1. Overall: How much did you enjoy the performance?
2. How immersed were you in the action that took place in the room where you were?
3. How immersed were you in the action that took place in the remote location?
4. How close did you feel to the actors in the room where you were?
5. How close did you feel to the actors in the remote location?
6. How close did you feel to the audience in the room where you were?
7. How close did you feel to the audience in the remote location?
8. How well did the action flow between the two locations?
9. How well could you see the action in the remote location?
10. How well could you hear the actors in the remote location?
11. How loud did you clap at the end of the performance?

In Figure 5 these results are reported with a colour code that illustrates whether the questions related to the performance overall, to the co-located part of the experience (i.e. to do with the performance in the venue in which the respondent watched the play) or to do with the performance from the remote venue.

4.4 Interviews with Experts

Video recordings of three interviews with key members of Miracle Theatre Company were made. These included the Artistic Director, the General Manager and an actor. These interviews provided about 2 hours of loosely structured conversation exploring their reflections on the experience. Further telephone interviews were carried with the operator of the sync control UI and with other members of the technical team some of whom also offered written reflections on the performance and of the experiment.

5. RESULTS AND DISCUSSION

5.1 System Performance Metrics

Whilst the speedtest.net results suggested we had plenty of bandwidth, we found we could not transmit traffic without modifications to the router settings. Firstly, because the broadband router had a short keep-alive timeout which was conflicting with the VClient's NAT traversal implementation, we set up a static port mapping for UDP video streams to the Studio VClient internal IP address. Secondly after observing poor long term stability we identified that the broadband router performed traffic shaping on long lived connections in order to prioritise more normal tasks like file transfer. This feature had to be turned off.

5.2 Audience Response

In Figure 5, the average score for each of the questions are arranged in rank order (error bars are the 95% confidence interval). It is clear that the scores receiving the lowest scores related to the performance in the remote location. Question 7 *"How close did you feel to the audience in the remote location?"* received the lowest score (about 16). This is not surprising, no systems were in place to attempt to build any awareness between the audiences in the two locations. This response therefore can be taken as a baseline, a function of the scoring method and factors that have nothing to do with the technology set up. The other scores all relate to questions where the system was designed to address the issue in hand. These scores ranged from 55 to 80, on a scale of 100, which we interpret as generally positive. Gratifyingly one of the highest scoring responses was question 11 *"How loud did you clap at the end of the performance?"*

These responses are subjective and whilst quantitative they do not provide much insight into why our paying audience made these assessments. We gained more insights about what the

[4] The network testing tool we used was www.speedtest.net, other tools that work in a similar way are also available. We do not think the selection of tool is critical.

respondents were thinking through the comments. Through a detailed treatment of the questionnaire results, that included covariance analysis and a multi-dimensional scaling analysis (to be reported elsewhere) it emerged that the variable which co-varied most strongly with other variables was question 2 – the one about remote immersion.

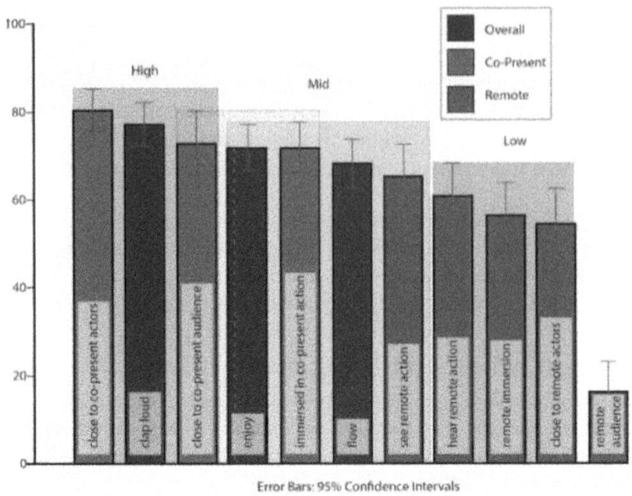

Figure 5 Questionnaire responses, colour-coded to highlight responses related to the performance overall, to the co-located performance only and to the remote performance only.

To help highlight the difference in commentaries provided by those who reported feeling immersed and those who were not immersed we ordered the responses with respect to the response to questions 2 and then reviewed the comments of those in the upper quartile of this rank and of those in lower quartile of this rank. The comments from those in this upper quartile included: *"Novel experience to highlight real possibility & remote theatre being experienced as close to live as possible."*

"Really great idea, loved how seamlessly the characters transferred between on screen and real life. Amazing how it all worked out looking at the amount of tech. Great!"

"Exciting, innovative, captivating, unexpected. Marvelled at the skill of the direction & acting as it was so slick despite the many technical elements. Atmospheric lighting. Great set. Adored the delightful puppets. Dazzled by the clever technical/visual tricks. All the different camera angles kept your attention, so that it was impossible to drift. I feel kids would hugely benefit from this facet of the experience. A lot going on, so hard to get bored!"

In the same vein, we looked at what the bottom 25%, those who scored remote immersion below 36, did not like; i.e. those for whom it did not work.

"Film less engaging - did not always join together smoothly & therefore disrupted the narrative. Prospero's reading from the script detracted from the fantasy & upset the eye contact between him & the players."

"The engagement between characters off screen to on screen, very disjointed & difficult for the actors to truly connect. Voice delay was a little distracting. Music & sound from other venue very distant. Story lost its strength, difficult to engage with the performance as a whole. I sense that the experiment probably had more strength in the other venue. Good luck xxx"

"The sound quality - that prevented a sense of immersion more than any disparity between visuals. Get the sound quality up and it would be truly brilliant (but I'm sure you know that!!)"

Although we distilled the quotes above to illustrate the differences between high and low immersion participants, we also inspected all the like and dislike quotes; overall it is not easy to distinguish between them. Some comments are about the sense the distributed play made. We saw these comments in particular from those who also saw the (open air) stage version. Most of the 'likes' reflect how much they are fans of Miracle Theatre Company; there is a lot of good will whether people thought it was a success or not. Other comments are about the technology per se. This is partly to be expected as the audience were invited to an experiment with technology. The real success of applying this kind of technology, one might argue, would lie in an audience not noticing the technology. However, that is beyond the experimental nature of the trial.

5.3 Expert Interviews

The interviews and written feedback from members of the creative and technical teams have been analysed. A number of themes have emerged which form the frame for this section of the results. They include broad reflections on:

- the system supporting natural communication
- applications to future theatre practice
- stories suited to distributed performance
- the experience for the audience

5.3.1 ..on supporting natural communication.

The system worked well and provided a very clear communication channel which the creative team used without thinking. In this use case, objective measures of the system's performance do not tell the whole story. Obviously delays in the video transmission system had to be low enough that parties in each performance location could converse in a way that seemed natural to the audience and delay has an impact on the ability to communicate naturally but the 320ms delay we measured does not tell us how natural the interactions were. Tests that attempt to provide objective measures of conversational analysis, looking for things like double starts and double talk are being developed for more controlled conditions [25], in this case we report observations of the actors, directors and crew as they used the system; and they seemed to use the system very naturally. This perception was shared by the Artistic Director who recalled that: *"People started behaving as if they were in the same room very quickly, when you're in down time they all start fooling round telling jokes teasing each other that sort of thing absolutely as if they were in the same space".*

5.3.2 ...on application to future theatre practice

One of the remarkable discoveries was that the communication system could be used in the daily working practice of the Miracle Theatre Company to support distributed working. The General Manager observed: "The thing I.. enjoyed most was seeing the working practice between the two spaces, the rehearsal, and the way people were interacting between the two spaces using the technology....we were using the technology in our real practice and I thought this was really working well...you know - if [the Artistic Director] was in New York we could use that for rehearsals for a week if you had to... and that would be quite exciting."

Similarly both one of the actors and the Artistic Director felt comfortable with the prospect of using the technology as a means for conducting remote rehearsals. The actor believed it could be suitable for *"Theatrical groups that couldn't meet otherwise, whether you do a collaboration between countries, whether it is a telepresence rehearsal process"* and the Artistic Director commented: *"this set up, if you were to try and do a co-production with a theatre company in another country or at the other end of this country, where it wouldn't be financially viable or practical to work together you could actually work using this technology really easily. People started behaving as if they were in the same room, very quickly".*

Figure 6 Left to Right: Hannah Stevens (as Miranda) and Ciaran Clarke (as Prince Ferdinand) and Angus Brown (as Prospero), showing how close-up of Prospero helps convey a God-like omnipotence.

5.3.3 ... on stories suited to distributed performance

There were limitation with the approach taken here. Specifically we tried to impose upon a well-established single stage production the artifice of two performance spaces. Some virtue could be found in this and some compelling shot choices could deliver a "*mesmerising effects"* but on reflection the creative team knew that, were they to attempt another distributed production, then that production should, from the beginning, integrate the technology into the production. At times, the creative team struggled with the technology as there was a tension between technology push from the project team and the lack of predetermined requirements from an artistic perspective. The push was for a deterministic representation of an imagines performance.

Our scripting tools started with a user interface based on a timeline representation that looked like a non-linear editing tool. This was extended with elements such as abstract shot types and screen layout templates. During the course of the production it became clear that the creative team needed additional technology elements such as preview and pre-visualisation which would support a much more iterative approach. It also became clear that the tools and the associated scripting language were an integral part of the creative artefact. We regard this as analogous to the way in which non-linear editing suites, and the language they use, define many aspects of film and television. Our use of new tools, technology and language to define and create video-mediated distributed theatre suggests a new genre of media; one that cannot be supported entirely using concepts and approaches from existing genres. The tension between technology and creativity was allowing this technologically-enabled genre to emerge. And it raises the question: is this a new genre?

Our work was at its most rewarding when the creative team, of their own accord, validated the idea of the emergence of a genre, by speculating about specific productions which could be supported by the emerging toolset. The Artistic Director speculated on the stories that could be told:

"I have been thinking about it. I have got quite a specific thing really, I thought it would be nice to do an end of World War One project with a German theatre company and to use the technology for rehearsals but also for each to use the technology in their own way as part of the production"

We believe this is one of the most exciting developments to emerge from the production. This will be explored in more detail in a separate publication.

5.3.4 ...the experience for the audience

This production did not seek to "*'faithfully' and tediously broadcast from the theatre*" [26] but to use screen language learned from TV and film to tell the story differently, as never told before and possibly, better. Whilst we struggled for time and the Artistic Director was aware of some shot choices that did not work as well as he would have liked, some shots worked really well.

The Artistic Director anticipated that the best audience experience would be in the Maritime Museum where there were 5 actors and 3 cameras. He anticipated that the experience in Dogbite studio, where Prospero was located, would be a lesser experience. He commented *"I always thought that the main TV experience, you know where the five actors were... I always thought that would be a much more interesting audience experience but I am not sure it was in the end, they were both interesting...when the camera script was working well* (the performance in the smaller venue) *was really watchable, you were getting close into the action and you have a real live Prospero and a structured intimate view of what is happening in the other".*

6. CONCLUSION

We have described an experiment in which we have used a novel communications technology platform to support a distributed performance of *The Tempest*. The scientific motivation was to test, in a highly situated and ecologically valid way, the postulation from the Vconect project that changing the way audio and video were captured transmitted and presented could positively affect group communication. The artistic challenge was to use the technology to emphasise some the nature of the characters and to explore how low cost technologies would be appropriated by a regional touring company in pursuit of their aims. There were two main technical objectives; the first was to establish whether it was possible to stream live theatre over consumer grade fast broadband connections; the second was to explore the capabilities of a system based on controllable cameras that semi-automatically develop simultaneous live streams, based on a scripted set of camera selections, for three different audiences (two theatres and the Internet audience).

The work focused on developing a performance for a paying audience and used audience feedback questionnaires, and in depth interviews with key practitioners to learn from the event. The audience feedback whilst overwhelmingly positive highlighted that the audience was likely to comment more favourably about aspects of the performance that related to their location, giving lower marks for the remote aspects of the performance. The audience response to the overall event was very positive.

Key observations emerging from the in depth interviews supported the Vconect project's postulation and suggested that the communication system would make a very effective tool for remote rehearsals; it also highlighted the need to develop, from scratch, stories that needed to be performed or rehearsed from split locations.

The difficulties the creative team had in developing the production were largely addressed through a set of tools and an approach that were developed during the process. The fact that the difficulty existed at all, and that the tools and language used in existing genres of media were not sufficient to address the difficulties, suggests that distributed theatre may well need its own toolsets and its own language to thrive. The same was true for the pioneering days of film and television. This hints at a rather bold observation: that distributed theatre can be considered and treated as a new genre.

This new genre, supported by the technology we created, can be really attractive; according to the Artistic Director, it was able to create compelling new forms of theatre ...(in parts it was) *really mesmerising; you were completely drawn into it and the image was telling you stuff and it was playing a part in your experience".*

7. REFERENCES

1. Jacobs, J. 2000 "The Intimate Screen. Early British Television Drama." *Oxford University Press.*
2. Bakshi, H and Whitby A. 2014 "Estimating the Impact of Live Simulcast on Theatre Attendance: An Application to London's National Theatre." *NESTA, 2014. Working Paper No. 14/04.*
3. Sheppard, R.M., Kamali, M., Rivas, R., Tamai, M., Yang, A., Wu, W., Nahrstedt, K. 2008 "Advancing interactive collaborative mediums through tele-immersive dance (TED): a symbiotic creativity and design environment for art and computer science." *Proceedings of the 16th ACM international conference on Multimedia, 579-588.*
4. Broadband Commission, The State of Broadband 2014: Broadband for all. *broadbandcommission.org.*
5. Stevens, T., Kegel, I., Williams, D., Cesar, P., Kaiser, R., Farber, N., Torres, P., Stenton, P., Ursu, M., and Falekalis, M. "Video communication for networked communities: Challenges and opportunities." 2012. *Proceedings 16th International Conference on Intelligence in Next Generation Networks.*
6. Ursu, M.F., Stollenmayer, P., Williams, D., Torres, P., Cesar, P., Farber, N., and Geelhoed, E. "Smart Video Communications for Social Groups - The Vconect Project." *Integrating Social Media with Video Communications (ed Kaiser R.,) IEEE Computer Society Special Technical Community on Social Networking E-LetteR.* June 2014, Vol. 2, 2.
7. Causey, M. 1999 "The Screen Test of the Double: The Uncanny Performer in the Space of Technology." *Theatre Journal, Vols. 51, 4, pp. 383-394.*
8. Birringer, J. 2008 "Thinking Images: Paul Kaiser and Marc Downie in conversation with Johannes Birringer." *Performance, Technology & Science. (30) 2.*
9. Dixon, S. 2007. "Digital Performance, a history of new media in theatre, dance, performance art, and installation." *Cambridge MA : MIT,*
10. Stinehelfer, B., Lugo, A.C., Martinson, Z., and Schneider, N. 2011. "Skype Duet." [dir.] Nikolaus Schneider. [perf.] Brina Stinehelfer. New York & Berlin. Per Aspera Productions,
11. Dimanche Rouge. Dimanche Rouge. [Online] [Cited: 14 July 2015.] www.dimancherouge.org.
12. Quacquarelli, A.J., Paciotto, A., and Yoo, M. 2011. "Discovering Pasolini." [dir.] A Garbagnati. La MaMa,
13. Ricke, J. and Lee, L. 2014. "Graphic Ships." [prod.] Jesse Ricke. *3rd Networked Music Festival, Birmingham : CultureHub Inc, 26-28 September*
14. Lee, T. 2014. "The Return." New York, La Mama, Culture Hub, https://www.youtube.com/watch?v=YJy3ME9bc5I.
15. Cremona, C. 2011 "Skype and videoperformance: relational screens." *Proceedings of the International Symposium on Electronic Art.*
16. Kegel, I., Cesar, P., Jansen, J., Bulterman, D.C.A., Kort, J., Stevens, T. and Farber, N. Enabling 'Togetherness' in High-Quality Domestic Video Conferencing. 2012. *Proceedings of the 20th ACM international conference on Multimedia 159-168.*
17. Chen, S.,Gao, Z., Nahrstedt, K., and Gupta, I. 3DTI Amphitheater: Towards 3DTI Broadcasting. 2015. *ACM TOMM, 11(2s): article 47.*
18. National Theatre. 2010. "NT Live Digital broadcast of theatre. Learning from the pilot season." London : NESTA,
19. Latulipe, C., Carroll,E.A., and Lottridge, D. 2011 "Love, hate, arousal and engagement: exploring audience responses to performing arts." *Proceedings of ACM CHI: 1845-1854.*
20. Wang, C., E. Geelhoed, E., Stenton, P., and Cesar, P. 2014 "Sensing a Live Audience." *Proceedings ACM CHI: 1909-1912.*
21. Tseng, Y.C., Huang, Y.C., Wu, K.Y., Chin, C.P. 2012. "Dinner of Luciérnaga: an interactive play with iPhone app in theater." *Proceedings of ACM Multimedia: 559-568.*
22. Cerratto-Pargman, T., C. Rossitto, C., Barkhuus, L. 2014 "Understanding audience participation in an interactive theater performance." *Proceedings of the Nordic Conference on Human-Computer Interaction*: 608-617.
23. Bulterman, D.C.A. et al. 2008. "Synchronized Multimedia Integration Language (SMIL 3.0)." W3C. [Online] 2008. http:// www.w3.org/TR/SMIL/.
24. Ursu, M., Falekalis, M., Groen, M., Kaiser, R., and Frantzis, M.. 2015 "Experimental Enquiry into Automatically Orchestrated Live Video Communication". *Proceedings of ACM International Conference for Television and Online Video pp63-72* (TVX 2015).
25. Schmitt, M., Gunkel, S., Cesar, P., and Hughes, P., "A QoE Testbed for Socially-Aware Video-Mediated Group Communication." *International Workshop on Socially-Aware Multimedia Workshop, ACM Multimedia 2013.*
26. Gardner, C and Wyver, J. 1983 "From Reithian Reverence to Cost Accounting and Censorship." *Screen* 24:4-5, 1983, pp. 114-129.

Image Profiling for History Events on the Fly

Jia Chen* [1], Qin Jin† [2], Yong Yu[1], Alexander G. Hauptmann[3]
[1]Dept. of Computer Science & Engineering, Shanghai Jiao Tong University
{chenjia, yyu}@apex.sjtu.edu.cn
[2] School of information, Renmin University of China
qjin@ruc.edu.cn
[3]School of Computer Science, Carneige Mellon University
alex@cs.cmu.edu

ABSTRACT

History event related knowledge is precious and imagery is a powerful medium that records diverse information about the event. In this paper, we propose to automatically construct an image profile given a one sentence description of the historic event which contains where, when, who and what elements. Such a simple input requirement makes our solution easy to scale up and support a wide range of culture preservation and curation related applications ranging from wikipedia enrichment to history education. However, history relevant information on the web is available as "wild and dirty" data, which is quite different from clean, manually curated and structured information sources. There are two major challenges to build our proposed image profiles: 1) unconstrained image genre diversity. We categorize images into genres of documents/maps, paintings or photos. Image genre classification involves a full-spectrum of features from low-level color to high-level semantic concepts. 2) image content diversity. It can include faces, objects and scenes. Furthermore, even within the same event, the views and subjects of images are diverse and correspond to different facets of the event. To solve this challenge, we group images at two levels of granularity: iconic image grouping and facet image grouping. These require different types of features and analysis from near exact matching to soft semantic similarity. We develop a full-range feature analysis module which is composed of several levels, each suitable for different types of image analysis tasks. The wide range of features are based on both classical hand-crafted features and different layers of a convolutional neural network. We compare and study the performance of the different levels in the full-range features and show their effectiveness on handling such a wild, unconstrained dataset.

*The work was done when the author was visiting Renmin University of China.

†Qin Jin is the corresponding author

MM'15, October 26–30, 2015, Brisbane, Australia.

ACM 978-1-4503-3459-4/15/10 ...$15.00.
DOI: http://dx.doi.org/10.1145/2733373.2806242.

(a) wikipedia image

(b) generated image profile (images are grouped by boxes)

Figure 1: Illustration of image profiling for history event on the fly: input text sentence is "At 9:40 a.m. on Saturday, July 28, 1945, a B-25 Mitchell bomber, piloted in thick fog by Lieutenant Colonel William Franklin Smith, Jr., crashed into the north side of the Empire State Building, between the 79th and 80th floors.".

General Terms

H.3.3 Information Search and Retrieval

Keywords

image profiling; history event

1. INTRODUCTION

"What is history? An echo of the past in the future; a reflex from the future on the past" once said by Victor

Hugo [2]. Knowledge of history is valuable. Some of this knowledge is recorded in text form containing exact information about"where", "when", "who" and "what" (the 4Ws of an event) while the majority of information is recorded in image media such as photo snapshots, art paintings and maps. There currently are many well organized text resources about historic events. However, images embody a wealth of information recorded and transmitted by various means including paper, artistic expression (e.g. painting) and camera. We find there are relatively few organized image resources about historic events but there are many image resources related to these events scattered around the web which can be found through a combination of different keyword queries on image search engines. This big gap between organized image resources for historic events and available image resources online makes automatic image profiling of historic events desirable and valuable. An example is the famous "B-25 Empire State Building crash" event. On Wikipedia, there is an individual page describing this event [1] with two illustrating images as shown in Figure 1(a). The image profile constructed by our algorithm from online resources is shown in Figure 1(b). It not only covers far more photos with acceptable quality, but also different genres of images such as newspaper reports and diagrams. Such historic event profiles facilitate better understanding and preservation of historical knowledge.

In our proposed image profiles, photos function as vivid snapshots of historic events, paintings provide an artistic subjective view, while document/maps supplement background information. These profiles benefit a wide range of cultural preservation and curation related applications covering history education, wikipedia enrichment, material supplement for museums, and false historic event photo detection.

The input requirement of the image profiling system is extremely simple: a sentence describing a historic event containing the 4Ws. This simple requirement makes it extremely easy to apply our approach to many types of historic events and the resulting image profile corpus can grow rapidly. However, there are two major challenges in building an image profile for an event.

Unconstrained Image Genres: Unlike most computer vision datasets which focus only on photos, photos are just one of many image genres that record historic event related materials. Related material can be in the form of images of a scanned document, an original manuscript, a hand crafted map, an oil painting, a portrait, a sketch and so on. We divide images into three general genres: documents/maps (recording history on paper), paintings (recording history through artistic expression) and photos (recording history with cameras). Furthermore, within each genre, there are many variants. The document/map genre includes scanned documents, original manuscripts and hand-drawn maps. Paintings can include a variety of styles from Renaissance to Realism. The variations in photo genres have already been well recognized [4]. Because of such diversity, genre classification requires a full range of feature analysis methods from low-level color distribution and edge detection to high-level semantic content identification. Our approach utilizes the multiple layers of a neural network image processing model [14][9] to effectively classify genres.

Diverse Image Content: Most well-known computer vision research datasets focus on a single aspect of computer vision such as faces[11], objects[5], scenes[35] and so on. However, in historic event image profiling, the content of related images are unconstrained. Furthermore, even for the same event, the related images can be quite diverse, describing different facets of the event. One goal of our system is to aggregate images portraying various facets of an event to provide diversity in the profile. We solve this challenge by grouping images at two levels of granularity: iconic image grouping and facet image grouping. We achieve these two-level groupings via ***iconic image detection*** and ***image diversification***, respectively. Iconic images are classic event images that have been propagated to multiple places on the web. In the propagation process, images may be cropped or edited, which makes iconic image detection even more challenging. Image diversification for historic events is more difficult than image search result diversification of object queries since the visual appearance of images within the same group is more varied and images only share similar semantics of content. The two levels of granularity require different types of feature analysis ranging from near exact matching to content semantic similarity.

The solution for both challenges requires a broad-range of feature analysis from low-level pixels to the high-level content semantics. Our approach leverages the hierarchy of layers in a convolutional neural network where different layers can be considered as different levels of feature analysis. Technically, we view each layer's output in a convolutional neural network as a feature map extracted on a dense grid. We construct different level feature descriptors upon different layer's raw features and fuse these feature descriptors to solve the above two challenges. We also include classical hand-crafted features as the bottom level in our full-range feature approach. We do not apply fine-tuning to adapt the convolutional neural network in this work for two reasons: First, fine-tuning needs a significant amount of labelled image data to work well. This is not available in our image profiling setting, since the amount of available images is relatively small. Second, our feature extractor view of a convolutional neural network might only need pre-trained models. Different from work in [6][24] which focuses on directly using the output of the last two hidden fully connected layers for high-level vision tasks, we focus on constructing a wide range of features to solve different types of visual classification tasks such as genre classification and image grouping.

We make the following contributions:

1. we propose a novel system to automatically construct an image profile given a one-sentence description of the historic event, which has many potential applications related to cultural preservation and curation. For this, we develop a flexible approach making efficient use of DCNNs to facilitate classification and labeling for this work.
2. we construct a full-range feature analysis framework to study the best level or level combinations for different tasks such as shown in Figure 3. This helps us to better understand differences between tasks and guides us to improve the performance accordingly.
3. we apply this framework to genre classification and find that level 5 (the middle level) feature works best, which is very different from traditional object detection tasks where high level features usually work best.
4. we also apply this framework for image grouping and find that the level 0 (hand-crafted) feature works best for iconic

image grouping while level 6 (high level) works best for facet image grouping.

The remainder of the paper is organized as follows. Section 2 presents related work. Section 3 presents the detailed process of image profiling for historic events based on the full range of features. Section 4 discusses detailed evaluation on image profiling and does case study to show the effectiveness of the proposed full-range of features. Section 5 concludes the paper.

2. RELATED WORK

2.1 Genre Classification

Genre classification has not been extensively studied. The most related work is distinguishing paintings from photographs [4]. A bunch of hand-crafted features, most of which are based on color, are designed in work [4]. The features are shown to be effective on a dataset composed of paintings from archive websites and photos from photography library website. However, in our collected historic events dataset, the designed features don't work well. Based on our analysis, there are two reasons for the dramatic performance drop using these features on our dataset. First, the images in our dataset are wild and much more difficult, i.e. there are few typical paintings and few typical photos. Color based features do not have much discriminative power for such difficult dataset. Second, these features seem to be over-tuned for the dataset used in work [4]. We propose to design a wide range of features based on the rich information contained in the different layers of a pre-trained convolutional neural network to solve the genre classification problem. We show that such features are robust for a wild genre classification dataset.

There are much work on processing document/map images [29][13] but little on distinguishing it from other genres. In historic event related images, document images include not only cleanly scanned black-white document but also photos of old faded newspapers, hand written manuscripts and hand-crafted colored maps. Given the diversity of images in document genre, it is not a trivial task. We apply our wide range of features to classify document/map, painting and photo genres simultaneously.

2.2 Image Search Result Diversification

Image search result diversification is useful to improve the quality of text-based image retrieval [32][30]. Most of the queries studied in these papers are object queries with ambiguity such as apple and jaguar. Image results for such queries can be diversified based on low-level features such as color and texture. However, diversified image grouping for historic events relies much more on the content semantic and images within the same group may be diverse on low-level features. We show that low-level color, edge and texture features don't work well in this challenging task. We propose to exploit the semantic expressive power of the wide range of features combined with region proposal to match images within a group.

2.3 Convolutional Neural Network

Convolutional neural network has been shown to be the state-of-the-art on a variety of high-level computer vision tasks such as object classification [14] and object detection [9]. Pre-trained convolutional neural network has also been used as a feature extractor for generic visual recognition [6][24]. However, the focus is on the semantic discriminative power via directly using the output of last several layers for recognition tasks. Features based on rich information of other layers for different vision tasks have not been well unexplored. Work in [6] only considers the output of last three layers as the authors think that only the output of these three layers are activations fully propagated through the convolutionl layers of the network, which is true only in direct use of layer outputs. Work in [24] evaluates all the layer outputs only in the recognition task and then only applies the output of last two hidden layers in other vision tasks. Different from these works, we design a wide range of features based on the output of different layers in the network rather than directly using the output layer. They are more compact particularly for intermediate convolutional layer outputs. Based on this compact representation, we compare and study the performance of different levels in the wide range of features on genre classification and diversified image grouping on our challenging historic event dataset.

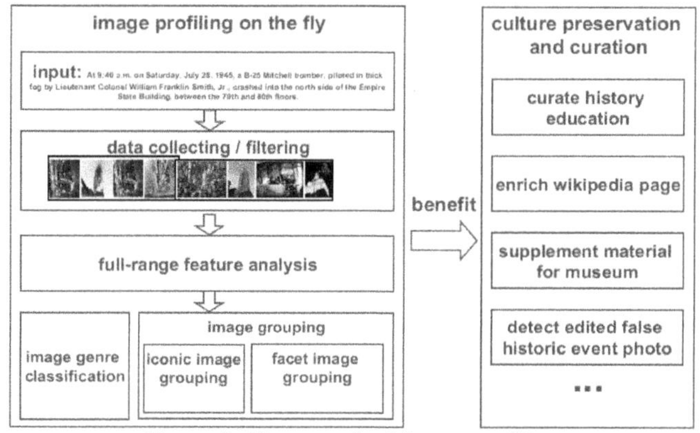

Figure 2: Framework of image profiling

3. SYSTEM DESCRIPTION

The overall system framework is composed of four modules: data collection and filtering, full-range feature analysis, image genre classification and image grouping as shown in Figure 2. In this section, we present the detailed implementation for each module in our image profiling system. We first describe the data collection and filtering procedure, which gathers data from the web and filters out clearly irrelevant images. We then explain the full range of feature analysis, which will be used in both genre classification and image grouping modules. Later in the genre classification, we show the robustness of the full range of features compared to hand-crafted features and study the performance of different levels in the wide range of features. Finally in the image grouping, we consider grouping at two levels of granularity: iconic image grouping and facet image grouping. Different versions of the iconic images will be categorized into a single group. Images that share similar content semantics are grouped into the same facet group and different facet groups correspond to different facets of a historic event (see also Figure 1).

3.1 Data Collection and Filtering

Data Collection: For each input sentence, we run named entity detection using Stanford NLP toolbox [20] and iden-

tify "who", "where" and "when" elements. We also extract noun phrases, verbs and other named entities as key phrase candidates for query construction. Some examples of the key phrase candidates are highlighted in Table 1.
For each event, we construct queries by combining each keyword with the "when" and "where" elements to collect related images for the historic event.

Data Filtering: Even for a human being without very good background knowledge, it may be difficult to tell whether an image is really relevant to a specific event or not. Therefore, we only attempt to filter out clearly irrelevant images, which is a much easier task that does not require too much knowledge of the event. Based on observations of our collected data, a majority of definitely irrelevant images are contemporary landmark photos retrieved by the "where" element in the query. Thus we construct additional background queries which contain only the "where" element. Images retrieved by "where" only queries are classic contemporary landmark photos. We measure the similarity between a candidate image and these classic contemporary landmark photos using the level 6 in our full-range features. We remove images that are too similar to classic contemporary landmark photos according to a similarity threshold. We note that the data filtering can not be reduced to a simple color filtering task, which would initially seem to be a tempting thing to do. Since the images we are handling include different genres such as documents/maps , paintings and photos, we cannot simply remove colourful images even for events that happened before the invention of color camera. Furthermore, the definition of the relevance of an image to an event is vague and subjectively changes from person to person and event to event. Thus, we choose to remove only those contemporary images which are obviously irrelevant.

3.2 Full-range Feature Analysis

The full-range feature is composed of several levels. Level 0 is composed of all the hand-crafted features. Some are classic general purpose features such as sift [18]. Others are features designed for special purposes such as image quality. Features in level 0 will be introduced later when used.

Features in the rest levels are based on the output of different layers in a convolutional neural network. All the three state-of-the art convolutional neural networks (CNN) [14][36][28] share a similar layer architecture of 5 convolutional layers (conv1-5) and 3 fully-connected layers (full6-8). We do not consider the output of the last fully-connected layer in designing our full-range feature since it is the softmax for category prediction. We do not consider the output of the first layer either since it has been shown to be similar to edge features, which are covered by our features in level 0. For the remaining layers, we construct one level-feature from the output of each layer. The construction process for the level-features is different for the convolutional layer and fully-connected layer.

For a convolutional layer, its output is actually n channels of $m \times m$ feature maps. Each channel corresponds to a filter. Each element in the feature map corresponds to the response of that filter on a particular region in the original image. Directly using the output leads to a feature with very high dimensions ($n \times m \times m$), which is usually at the scale of hundreds of thousands. We construct a compact feature representation (21 dimension) by a three-level pyramid average pooling on grids 1x1, 2x2, 4x4 on each feature map.

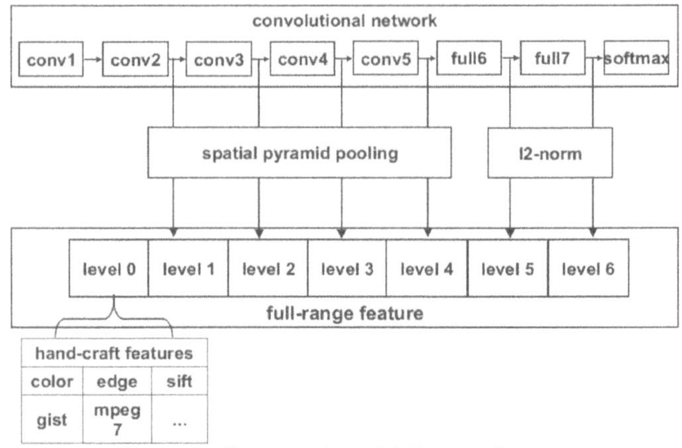

Figure 3: Construction of full-range features

Then we concatenate the compact feature representation by channels into a $21 \times n$ dimensional level-feature. For the two hidden fully-connected layers, we normalize their output by $l2-norm$ to get the corresponding level-features. In a summary, our full-range feature is composed of 7 levels. Level 0 is composed of all the hand-crafted features. The next 4 levels are constructed on the outputs of conv2-4 layers and the last 2 levels are constructed on the outputs of full6-7 layers. The construction of the full-range feature is summarized in Figure 3.

The dimension of each level-feature in the full-range feature is around tens of thousands, which is rather compact compared to that of commonly used HoG features. This enables us to enumerate the performance of different levels to find out best level feature for different tasks at a relatively low cost. In implementation, we construct the full-range feature based on the pre-trained CNN-M [33]. The full-range features can also be constructed upon other pre-trained CNNs as long as they follow the same architecture.

Level analysis of full-range features: In previous research of art, history and culture [25][17][38], authors typically design various hand-crafted features based on different principals and prior knowledge of certain domain. Different from these approaches, in our task the relevant information is available as a "wild and dirty" dataset, which makes hand-crafting specific features based on principles and prior knowledge almost impossible. Therefore, we build our solution as a mixture of hand-crafted general features and different layer outputs from a CNN. Lower levels usually capture pixel information while higher levels usually reflect soft content semantics. We apply level analysis by comparing performance of different level-features on the two challenges (genre classification and image grouping) in image profiling for historic events.

3.3 Image Genre Classification

We consider three genres: document/map, painting and photo in this work. Document/map genre includes scanned document photos, maps drawn by hand and other documentary records saved in image format. Painting genre includes oil painting, watercolour, sketch and other artistic records. Photo genre includes natural photos. To distinguish document/map from photo, we usually rely on the content semantics of the image. To distinguish paintings from photos, we rely on not only the content semantics but also low-level

Event ID	Where	When	Who	What (event description)
E12	Paris	1987	A.J. Hackett	1987: {*A.J. Hackett*} made {*one of his first bungee jumps*} from the top of the Eiffel Tower, using {*a special cord*} he had helped develop.
E66	Paris	1885	Victor Hugo	Prior to {*burial*} in {*the Pantheon*}, {*the body of Victor Hugo*} was exposed under {*the Arc*} during the night of 22 May 1885.

Table 1: Two historic event descriptions: key phrases used to construct queries are emphasized in italics

name	function
color edge	the removal of color eliminates more visual information from a painting than from a photograph of a real scene.
spatial variation of color	color changes to a larger extent from pixel to pixel in paintings than in photographs.
number of unique colors	paintings appear to have a larger color palette than photographs.
pixel saturation	paintings tend to contain a larger percentage of highly saturated pixels where as photographs contains more unsaturated pixels.
pixel distribution in RGBXY space	Paintings use a larger color palette and also have larger spatial variation of color, resulting in larger singular values for the covariance matrix of RGBXY space.

Table 2: List of level 0 features used in image genre classification

name	granularity	function
sift	iconic image grouping	it is shown to provide robust matching across a a substantial range of affine distortion, change in 3D viewpoint, addition of noise, and change in illumination.
gist	facet image grouping	it is found to be effective in grouping images by perceptual similarity [10] and it describes global image structure.
mpeg7	facet image grouping	it has been widely used in image search result diversification [32] and it includes color layout, scalable color and edge histogram.

Table 3: List of level 0 features used in image grouping

features such as color edge and color distribution as stated in work [4].

The genre classification problem is a multi-class classification task, which is usually solved by ensembles of several one-vs-one or one-vs-all binary classifiers. In this work, we use one-vs-one binary classifier ensembles so that we can study which is the best level-feature to distinguish each pair of genres. Since the class number is 3, ensembles of one-vs-one binary classifiers is quite efficient. To be specific, we study feature levels from 0 to 6. In level 0, we implement the features described in work [4], which were used to distinguish paintings from photos. The list of implemented features is shown in Table 2. Thus, we only evaluate its performance in the painting vs photo classifier.

To create ensembles of binary classifiers, we apply three strategies as follows.

single level-feature: all the three binary classifiers use the same level-features and we select the best level-feature for each of them on the validation set.

late fusion: each binary classifier is tuned to its best level-features on the validation set and classification is achieved with each binary classifier using its own best level-feature.

early fusion: the best level-features for each binary classifier are selected on the validation set and fused into one feature at the feature construction stage.

3.4 Image Grouping

In image grouping, we organize images at two levels of granularity: iconic image grouping and facet image grouping. Iconic image grouping requires partial duplication within a group and is useful to find classical event images that have been propagated at multiple places on the web. Facet image grouping requires content semantics consistency within a group and is useful to construct different facets for the image profile of a historic event. Similar to genre classification, we also exploit different levels in the full-range features for grouping. Low-level features are expected to work well in iconic image grouping while facet image grouping needs high-level semantic features to get a descent performance.

The level 0 features used in image grouping involves SIFT [18], GIST [22] and Mpeg7 features [27].

3.4.1 Iconic Image Grouping

An iconic image is an image that is propagated to multiple places on the web. During the propagation, its content may be edited or cropped, but the major content is preserved. In historic event related images, iconic images appear frequently as famous classic photos for a historic event. Different from classic partial duplication solutions which usually focus on the dataset scale, the dataset scale of our partial duplication grouping is small and we focus on a high precision and recall since historic event photos are rare and precious. The dataset scale of iconic image grouping is the number of candidate images retrieved from several queries, which is typically around a few hundreds.

For all the level-features used in iconic image grouping, we follow a common pipeline as in [16]: matching image pairs and extracting connected components of matched pairs. The matching algorithms differ for different level-features.

level 0 (SIFT + RANSAC): we match points in an image pair based on descriptors and then estimate the underlying affine transformation using RANSAC [3] algorithm. In our task, we simplify the underlying affine transformation to 4 degree of freedom: scale change on x, y axis and translation on x, y axis. Rotation rarely happens in iconic image grouping in our collected dataset while cropping and editing is the major issue. Thus, such simplification helps reduce the hypothesis space and improve the estimated affine transformation quality. We get matched region from inlier pairs after affine transformation and its confidence can be measured by the number of matched pairs. Applying threshold on the inlier number can remove unmatched pairs.

level 0 (SIFT + RANSAC + salient region): This technique has proven to work well if the query region is given [23]. However, in iconic image grouping, the query region is not given beforehand and the matched region may be a background region as illustrated in Figure 4. This may be considered as a correct case in partial duplication grouping but incorrect for iconic image grouping. To solve this problem, we extract salient regions [37] and calculate the coverage of the matched region in the salient regions. Now the confidence of the iconic image pair is related to both the coverage and the inlier number. We also set a threshold for

genre	training	validation	test
doc/map	imagenet (1,402)	history (176)	history (404)
painting	archive (966)	history (259)	history (420)
photo	history (1,000)	history (2,187)	history (3,427)

Table 4: Split strategy of training, validation and test data for genre classification: the number in the bracket is the number of images from the corresponding source

level	doc/map vs painting	doc/map vs photo	painting vs photo
0	NA	NA	0.0/81.2/81.2
1	81.3/88.9/85.1	54.9/98.4/91.9	42.3/93.6/86.9
2	85.2/89.5/87.5	63.9/98.5/94.0	**50.1/94.1/88.9**
3	86.1/89.0/87.6	64.3/98.4/94.0	**50.0/94.6/88.9**
4	85.0/88.9/87.1	**65.7/98.5/94.3**	41.2/94.2/86.3
5	**88.1/87.8/87.9**	65.1/98.5/94.2	37.4/94.5/84.4
6	87.3/82.8/84.7	55.6/98.2/92.0	35.1/93.1/84.5

Table 5: Study of best level-features for genre classification on one-vs-one binary classifiers. The three numbers in each table element are precision of the first class, precision of the second class and overall precision.

coverage to further remove background matched pairs.
levels 1 − 4 *(SPM):* the features in level 1 − 4 are constructed by spatial pyramid pooling. Naturally, we can match them by spatial pyramid matching [15].
levels 5 − 6 *(Cosine):* feature vectors are matched by calculating cosine similarity.

3.4.2 Facet Image Grouping

The related images of a historic event are diverse and different images are associated with different keyword facets of a historic event description. It is difficult for the users to find out what these images are about if they are mixed together. Thus it is necessary to group images into different groups for different event facets. This task is similar to image search diversification, in which image candidates of ambiguous queries are grouped to different facets. Such grouping usually uses different kinds of low-level features to group images and get reasonable results [32]. The queries studied are usually ambiguous about objects, which leads to the fact that resulting images containing a single major object and having coherent visual appearance within a group and distinguished visual appearance between groups. However, in historic event image profiling, images usually contain multiple objects and images within the same facet are more coherent on content semantics rather than their visual appearance. We use affinity propagation [8] for facet image grouping since it can handle different types of distances through pairwise similarities. We study the following distances on different level-features.
level 0 *(Mpeg7 + dist):* the similarity is the negative of the distance function implemented in LIRE [19].
level 0 *(GIST + euclidean):* the similarity is the negative of euclidean distance.
levels 1 − 4 *(SPM):* the similarity is calculated using spatial pyramid matching [15].
levels 5 − 6 *(Cosine):* cosine similarity between feature vectors is computed.

(a) spatial match by ransac (inlier number: 12)

(b) spatial match by ransac (inlier number: 13)

(c) salient region post-process (coverage: 0.06)

(d) salient region postprocess (coverage: 0.21)

Figure 4: An example of adding salient region post-process for matching level 0 feature sift.

4. EXPERIMENT

4.1 Dataset

We parse events from Wikipedia pages[1]. The detailed process includes two steps: first, we get "where" by parsing pages of landmarks from the landmark list[2]; second, we get "when" by extracting sentences with year information in history sections on Wilipedia. Each sentence corresponds to the text description of one historic event. We discard events that happened after 2004 according to our definition of a historic event. We also discard events that happened too early, i.e. before the birth of photography(1816)[3]. In the end, 615 events and their corresponding descriptions are extracted. We crawl 40,912 candidate images for these 615 events and 17,504 images are classified as relevant images automatically.

4.2 Genre Classification

We randomly sample 6,693 images from the automatically filtered history corpus and labelled genre ground-truth using Amazon Mechanical Turk (mturk)[4], which includes 580 doc/maps, 679 paintings and 5,434 photos. We create the training data for document/map and painting genres by collecting additional images from other sources such as the imagenet and art archive websites. Specifically, 1,402 images under category document (synset n06470073) and map (synset n03720163) from imagenet, 966 painting images from an art archive website (archive)[5] are collected in addition. The training and test data split strategy is listed in Table 4. Both the validation and test data are only composed of images from our historic event corpus.

We can see from Table 5 that the best feature lies in level 5, 4 and 3 for doc/map vs painting, doc/map vs photo and

[1] `http://en.wikipedia.org/`
[2] `http://www1.i2r.a-star.edu.sg/~yzheng/landmark/1000_landmarks.html`
[3] `http://en.wikipedia.org/wiki/History_of_the_camera`
[4] `https://www.mturk.com/mturk/`
[5] www.archive.com

method	precision
single level-feature (level 3)	65.3/47.4/93.5/85.2
late fusion	**70.6/48.1/92.9/86.0**
early fusion	**69.6/47.8/93.0/86.0**

Table 6: Evaluation on genre classification: The four numbers in each table element are precision of doc/map, precision of painting, precision of photo and overall precision. Late fusion is done by combining classifier doc/map vs painting on level 5, classifier doc/map vs. photo on level 5, classifier painting vs. photo on level 3. Early fusion is done by fusing level 3 and level 5 features

level	matching strategy	P_{pair}	R_{pair}
0	SIFT + RANSAC	0.95 ± 0.10	0.98 ± 0.02
0	SIFT + RANSAC + salient region	$\mathbf{0.98 \pm 0.06}$	$\mathbf{0.98 \pm 0.02}$
$1-4$	SPM	0.70 ± 0.15	0.83 ± 0.13
$6-7$	Cosine	0.33 ± 0.30	0.49 ± 0.29

Table 7: Evaluation on iconic image grouping

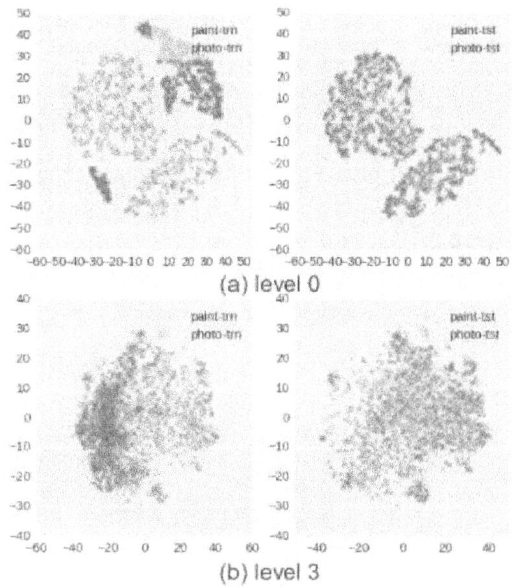

Figure 5: Visualization of level 0 and level 3 features on training (left) and test (right) data of the painting vs. photo classifier

painting vs photo classifiers respectively, which is shallower than the best feature level widely reported in recognition tasks [28]. Furthermore, the best feature layer for painting vs photo classifier is shallower than the rest two binary classifiers, which is in accordance with our conjecture in section 3.3. Distinguishing doc/map from photo or painting is easier than distinguish painting from photo. The performances on feature levels $2-5$ only slightly differ in the two easy binary classifiers.

Surprisingly, the level 0 features predict all the images as photos on our history dataset. We visualize level 0 features on the training and test data by using t-SNE algorithm [31] to embed features on a two dimensional plane in Figure 5(a). We can see that the hand-crafted level 0 features designed in work [4] works perfectly in separating paintings from photos on the training data. However, these features are entirely mixed for photos and paintings on the test data. We also visualize the level 3 features in Figure 5(b) as a comparison. From the comparison, we observe two phenomena. First, the embedded points of paintings in the training data are more dense than those in the test data in both figures. Our explanation is that the paintings in the training data are more typical as they are collected from a particular archive website. Second, only level 0 features exhibit dramatic difference on the two datasets. We suspect that the hand-crafted features are over-tuned as all the experiments in [4] were conducted on paintings from the same website.

We also compare the three fusion strategies on the full genre classification in Table 6. We see that both early and late fused predictors perform better than single level-feature predictor, which indicates that different levels of features are complementary. We illustrate some top predicts for each genre in Figure 6.

4.3 Image Grouping

4.3.1 Iconic Image Grouping

We use pairwise P_{pair} and R_{pair} metrics as they have been widely used in iconic image grouping [34][7]. Larger P_{pair} and R_{pairs} mean higher precision and recall. We sample 46 events for iconic image labelling and label 65 ground-truth iconic image groups with 4.43 images in each group on average. We calculate P_{pair} and R_{pair} for each event. For the images that are detected by the algorithm but not labelled in the ground-truth iconic image grouping, we assign each of them to a new different group ID. That is, we don't consider them to be in the same group with any other images.

We compare all the four matching algorithms with different levels of features: SIFT + RANSAC on level 0, SIFT + RANSAC + salient region on level 0, SPM on level $1-4$ and cosine on level $5-6$. As shown in Table 7, each method is shown in mean $\pm$ std (standard deviation) format based on different events. Each method is tuned to its best performance on matching thresholds. Paired t-test shows that the improvement of SIFT + RANSAC + salient region over SIFT + RANSAC is significant at 0.05 p-value.

We study four typical modified versions in historic event image profiles on two automatically detected iconic image groups in Figure 7. We select the image with highest resolution as the iconic one on the left and list modified versions in the same iconic image group on the right. The registration of modified versions are highlighted by red boxes in the iconic one.

cropping: a2, a3 and b4 are cropped versions. They don't have higher resolution on the corresponding regions compared to the iconic one. For the cropped version, iconic image grouping can be used to recover the original high resolution one.

editing: a1 seems to be a cropped version but after careful comparison with the iconic one we find that the military on the right is erased from a1. We indicate the position of this military man by a blue box in a1. For the edited version, iconic image grouping can be used to remind users such images may be inconsistent with the historical fact.

composition: b2 is a manual composition of different history photos. Such composition helps enrich the context of the iconic image. The red arrow in the manually added image illustrates which level of the tower the man jumped from.

higher resolution of detail: b1 and b3 are higher resolution version of corresponding region in the iconic one. They give us a detailed look of the parachute the man wearing.

(a) doc/map (4.8, 2.7) (b) painting (2.3, 1.1) (c) photo (6.1, 4.9)

Figure 6: Top predicts for each genre: the predicted score is shown in the bracket.

(a) (b)

Figure 7: Example of iconic image groups: the selected iconic image is shown on the left and its different modified versions on the web are shown on the right

level	distance	consensus groundtruth				diverse groundtruth			
		ARI	AMI	HM	CM	ARI	AMI	HM	CM
0 (mpeg7)	dist	0.058	0.089	0.327	0.245	0.146	0.188	0.397	0.370
0 (gist)	euclidean	0.056	0.082	0.311	0.246	0.130	0.180	0.364	0.370
$1-4$	SPM	0.118	0.167	0.407	0.323	0.253	0.306	0.481	0.474
$5-6$	cosine	**0.121**	**0.184**	**0.444**	**0.325**	**0.294**	**0.344**	**0.536**	**0.496**

Table 8: Comparison of matching strategies for different feature levels on profile diversification: the parameter in affinity propagation is tuned to its best performance.

4.3.2 Facet Image Grouping

We use ARI [12], AMI [21], HM [26] and CM [26] metrics in evaluating diversified facet image grouping. If the label assignment is entirely random, ARI and AMI values are 0 , which can be used as a baseline value in comparison. ARI and AMI give a normalized (regard to random baseline) single value for evaluation while HM and CM can be used to qualitatively analyze for what "kind" of mistakes are made in the assignment. Facet image grouping is a relatively subjective task and we use mturk to collect the ground-truth, assigning 3 workers per hit. Our instructions for the hit are: 1. At most 5 groups are required. 2. a group should consist of at least 2 images. 3. Not all images are required to be labelled (there may be outliers). For 75 events, we collect 3.84 image groups under each event on average and 6.06 images under each group on average. This indicates the diversity of historic event images.

We note that multiple manual labels for clustering related hit hasn't been well studied yet. Here we propose two ground-truths from multiple labelling of clusters. The first ground-truth is called consensus ground-truth, which includes only images and labels agreed by all the labellers. The second ground-truth is called diverse ground-truth, which comprises three label tracks from three workers respectively.
Details of consensus ground-truth: First we remove images that are labelled by less than 3 workers. On the remaining images, we intersect the groups from all the 3 worker labels. This may result in singular groups which contains only one image and we remove such singular groups. The images in the rest groups are used in evaluation.
Details of diverse ground-truth: The predicted grouping is compared to each track and we report the best evaluated score among the three comparisons. For each track in this ground-truth, we preserve images labelled by the corresponding worker to get evaluation score.

We compare all the proposed different matching strategies on different levels in the full-range features in Table 8. The details of performance change within level $1-4$ and level $5-6$ are not shown due to the limit of space. Within level $1-4$, the best performance is achieved at level 3 while within level $5-6$, the best performance is achieved at level 6. We can see that cosine distance of level 6 performs best on both consensus and diverse ground-truths. Its performance doubles that of level 0 features. This indicates that image profile diversification relies more on content semantics than visual appearance. To further illustrate the semantic coherence within each group, we present case study of image profile diversification on two events in Figure 8. For the event shown at the top, the first group contains portraits

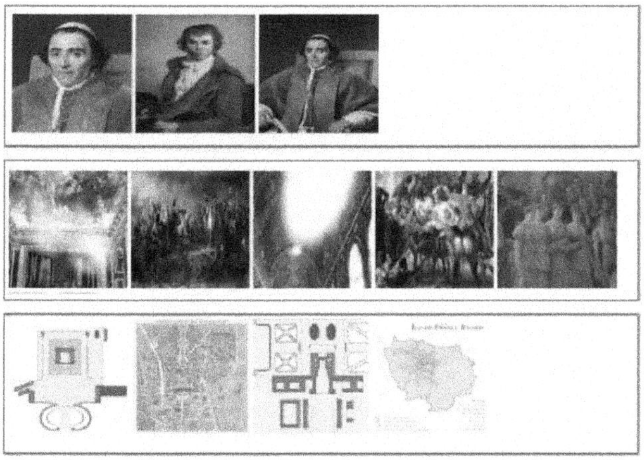

(a) Nevertheless, on 3 January 1805, Pope Pius VII, who came to France to officiate at Napoleon's coronation, visited the palace and blessed the throng of people gathered on the parterre d'eau from the balcony of the Hall of Mirrors (Mauguin, 1940-1942).

(b) During the 1850s the Smithsonian Institution's librarian Charles Coffin Jewett aggressively tried to move that organization towards becoming the United States' national library.

Figure 8: Case study of facet image grouping

for figures in the event; the second group shows the Hall of Mirrors; the third group contains various maps, from indoor balcony and hall map to outdoor Palace of Versailles map. For the event shown at the bottom, the first group shows portraits of the librarian; the second group shows the documents in the library; the third group shows the librarian photos; the fourth group shows the activities and posters of events hosted by the library.

5. CONCLUSION

In this paper, we proposed to automatically construct image profiles for historic events given only a one sentence description with 4Ws. This extremely simple input requirement makes it easy to apply the method to many different historic events and support a wide range of cultural preservation and curation applications ranging from wikipedia enrichment to history education. However, it is also an extremely challenging task which must process relevant information from a wild and unconstrained sources directly. We tackle two major challenges in this work: unconstrained image genres and diversity of image content. Different genres represent different methods of recording history through the image medium. The image content of a historic event can include any type of visual information including faces, objects and scenes, corresponding to a wide range of computer vision tasks. Within an event, images are different in content which reflects different facets of the event. We analyze the data using a full-spectrum of image features including classical hand-crafted low-level features and the rich information in different layers of a convolutional neural network. Comprehensive experiments show the effectiveness of different levels of features from a full-range of features ranging from pixel level to semantic level analysis to solve these challenges. In our future work, we will perform a formal user study and expand the dataset to cover more historic events.

6. ACKNOWLEDGMENTS

This research was partially supported by the Fundamental Research Funds for the Central Universities and the Research Funds of Renmin University of China (No. 14XNLQ01), the Beijing Natural Science Foundation (No. 4142029), and the Scientific Research Foundation for the Returned Overseas Chinese Scholars, State Education Ministry. This research was also supported in part by the National Science Foundation (NSF) under grant number IIS-1251187. Any opinions, findings, and conclusions or recommendations expressed in this material are those of the authors and do not necessarily reflect the views of the funding agencies.

7. REFERENCES

[1] B-25 empire state building crash. http://en.wikipedia.org/wiki/B-25_Empire_State_Building_crash.

[2] Victor hugo quotes. http://www.brainyquote.com/quotes/quotes/v/victorhugo385868.html.

[3] O. Chum and J. Matas. Optimal randomized RANSAC. *IEEE Trans. Pattern Anal. Mach. Intell.*, 30(8):1472–1482, 2008.

[4] F. Cutzu, R. I. Hammoud, and A. Leykin. Estimating the photorealism of images: Distinguishing paintings from photographs. In *2003 IEEE Computer Society Conference on Computer Vision and Pattern Recognition (CVPR 2003), 16-22 June 2003, Madison, WI, USA*, pages 305–312, 2003.

[5] J. Deng, W. Dong, R. Socher, L. Li, K. Li, and F. Li. Imagenet: A large-scale hierarchical image database. In *2009 IEEE Computer Society Conference on Computer Vision and Pattern Recognition (CVPR 2009), 20-25 June 2009, Miami, Florida, USA*, pages 248–255, 2009.

[6] J. Donahue, Y. Jia, O. Vinyals, J. Hoffman, N. Zhang, E. Tzeng, and T. Darrell. Decaf: A deep convolutional activation feature for generic visual recognition. In *Proceedings of the 31th International Conference on Machine Learning, ICML 2014, Beijing, China, 21-26 June 2014*, pages 647–655, 2014.

[7] Z. Feng, J. Chen, X. Wu, and Y. Yu. Aggregation-based probing for large-scale duplicate image detection. In *Web Technologies and Applications - 15th Asia-Pacific Web Conference, APWeb 2013, Sydney, Australia, April 4-6, 2013. Proceedings*, pages 417–428, 2013.

[8] B. J. Frey and D. Dueck. Clustering by passing messages between data points. *Science*, 315:972–976, 2007.

[9] R. B. Girshick, J. Donahue, T. Darrell, and J. Malik. Rich feature hierarchies for accurate object detection and semantic segmentation. In *2014 IEEE Conference on Computer Vision and Pattern Recognition, CVPR 2014, Columbus, OH, USA, June 23-28, 2014*, pages 580–587, 2014.

[10] J. Hays and A. A. Efros. Scene completion using millions of photographs. *ACM Trans. Graph.*, 26(3):4, 2007.

[11] G. B. Huang, M. Ramesh, T. Berg, and E. Learned-Miller. Labeled faces in the wild: A database for studying face recognition in unconstrained environments. Technical Report 07-49, University of Massachusetts, Amherst, October 2007.

[12] L. Hubert and P. Arabie. Comparing partitions. *Journal of Classification*, 2(1):193–218, 1985.

[13] H. il Koo and N. I. Cho. Rectification of figures and photos in document images using bounding box interface. In *The Twenty-Third IEEE Conference on Computer Vision and Pattern Recognition, CVPR 2010, San Francisco, CA, USA, 13-18 June 2010*, pages 3121–3128, 2010.

[14] A. Krizhevsky, I. Sutskever, and G. E. Hinton. Imagenet classification with deep convolutional neural networks. In *Advances in Neural Information Processing Systems 25: 26th Annual Conference on Neural Information Processing Systems 2012. Proceedings of a meeting held December 3-6, 2012, Lake Tahoe, Nevada, United States.*, pages 1106–1114, 2012.

[15] S. Lazebnik, C. Schmid, and J. Ponce. Beyond bags of features: Spatial pyramid matching for recognizing natural scene categories. In *2006 IEEE Computer Society Conference on Computer Vision and Pattern Recognition (CVPR 2006), 17-22 June 2006, New York, NY, USA*, pages 2169–2178, 2006.

[16] X. Li, C. Wu, C. Zach, S. Lazebnik, and J. Frahm. Modeling and recognition of landmark image collections using iconic scene graphs. In *Computer Vision - ECCV 2008, 10th European Conference on Computer Vision, Marseille, France, October 12-18, 2008, Proceedings, Part I*, pages 427–440, 2008.

[17] M. Lin, Z. Hu, S. Liu, M. Wang, R. Hong, and S. Yan. eheritage of shadow puppetry: creation and manipulation. In *ACM Multimedia Conference, MM '13, Barcelona, Spain, October 21-25, 2013*, pages 183–192, 2013.

[18] D. G. Lowe. Distinctive image features from scale-invariant keypoints. *International Journal of Computer Vision*, 60(2):91–110, 2004.

[19] M. Lux and S. A. Chatzichristofis. Lire: lucene image retrieval: an extensible java CBIR library. In *Proceedings of the 16th International Conference on Multimedia 2008, Vancouver, British Columbia, Canada, October 26-31, 2008*, pages 1085–1088, 2008.

[20] C. D. Manning, M. Surdeanu, J. Bauer, J. Finkel, S. J. Bethard, and D. McClosky. The Stanford CoreNLP natural language processing toolkit. In *Proceedings of 52nd Annual Meeting of the Association for Computational Linguistics: System Demonstrations*, pages 55–60, 2014.

[21] X. V. Nguyen, J. Epps, and J. Bailey. Information theoretic measures for clusterings comparison: Variants, properties, normalization and correction for chance. *Journal of Machine Learning Research*, 11:2837–2854, 2010.

[22] A. Oliva and A. Torralba. Modeling the shape of the scene: A holistic representation of the spatial envelope. *International Journal of Computer Vision*, 42(3):145–175, 2001.

[23] J. Philbin, O. Chum, M. Isard, J. Sivic, and A. Zisserman. Object retrieval with large vocabularies and fast spatial matching. In *2007 IEEE Computer Society Conference on Computer Vision and Pattern Recognition (CVPR 2007), 18-23 June 2007, Minneapolis, Minnesota, USA*, 2007.

[24] A. S. Razavian, H. Azizpour, J. Sullivan, and S. Carlsson. CNN features off-the-shelf: An astounding baseline for recognition. In *IEEE Conference on Computer Vision and Pattern Recognition, CVPR Workshops 2014, Columbus, OH, USA, June 23-28, 2014*, pages 512–519, 2014.

[25] E. Roman-Rangel, C. P. Gayol, J. Odobez, and D. Gatica-Perez. Searching the past: an improved shape descriptor to retrieve maya hieroglyphs. In *Proceedings of the 19th International Conference on Multimedia 2011, Scottsdale, AZ, USA, November 28 - December 1, 2011*, pages 163–172, 2011.

[26] A. Rosenberg and J. Hirschberg. V-measure: A conditional entropy-based external cluster evaluation measure. In *EMNLP-CoNLL 2007, Proceedings of the 2007 Joint Conference on Empirical Methods in Natural Language Processing and Computational Natural Language Learning, June 28-30, 2007, Prague, Czech Republic*, pages 410–420, 2007.

[27] P. Salembier and T. Sikora. *Introduction to MPEG-7: Multimedia Content Description Interface*. John Wiley & Sons, Inc., New York, NY, USA, 2002.

[28] P. Sermanet, D. Eigen, X. Zhang, M. Mathieu, R. Fergus, and Y. LeCun. Overfeat: Integrated recognition, localization and detection using convolutional networks. *CoRR*.

[29] C. Simon, Williem, J. Choe, I. D. Yun, and I. K. Park. Correcting photometric distortion of document images on a smartphone. In *IEEE Conference on Computer Vision and Pattern Recognition, CVPR Workshops 2014, Columbus, OH, USA, June 23-28, 2014*, pages 199–200, 2014.

[30] K. Song, Y. Tian, W. Gao, and T. Huang. Diversifying the image retrieval results. In *Proceedings of the 14th ACM International Conference on Multimedia, Santa Barbara, CA, USA, October 23-27, 2006*, pages 707–710, 2006.

[31] L. van der Maaten. Accelerating t-sne using tree-based algorithms. *Journal of Machine Learning Research*, 15(1):3221–3245, 2014.

[32] R. H. van Leuken, L. G. Pueyo, X. Olivares, and R. van Zwol. Visual diversification of image search results. In *Proceedings of the 18th International Conference on World Wide Web, WWW 2009, Madrid, Spain, April 20-24, 2009*, pages 341–350, 2009.

[33] A. Vedaldi and K. Lenc. Matconvnet – convolutional neural networks for matlab. *CoRR*, abs/1412.4564, 2014.

[34] B. Wang, Z. Li, M. Li, and W. Ma. Large-scale duplicate detection for web image search. In *Proceedings of the 2006 IEEE International Conference on Multimedia and Expo, ICME 2006, July 9-12 2006, Toronto, Ontario, Canada*, pages 353–356, 2006.

[35] J. Xiao, J. Hays, K. A. Ehinger, A. Oliva, and A. Torralba. SUN database: Large-scale scene recognition from abbey to zoo. In *The Twenty-Third IEEE Conference on Computer Vision and Pattern Recognition, CVPR 2010, San Francisco, CA, USA, 13-18 June 2010*, pages 3485–3492, 2010.

[36] M. D. Zeiler and R. Fergus. Visualizing and understanding convolutional networks. In *Computer Vision - ECCV 2014 - 13th European Conference, Zurich, Switzerland, September 6-12, 2014, Proceedings, Part I*, pages 818–833, 2014.

[37] J. Zhang and S. Sclaroff. Saliency detection: A boolean map approach. In *IEEE International Conference on Computer Vision, ICCV 2013, Sydney, Australia, December 1-8, 2013*, pages 153–160, 2013.

[38] S. Zhao, Y. Gao, X. Jiang, H. Yao, T. Chua, and X. Sun. Exploring principles-of-art features for image emotion recognition. In *Proceedings of the ACM International Conference on Multimedia, MM '14, Orlando, FL, USA, November 03 - 07, 2014*, pages 47–56, 2014.

Modeling Perspective Effects in Photographic Composition

Zihan Zhou[†] Siqiong He[†] Jia Li [‡] James Z. Wang[†]
[†]College of Information Sciences and Technology
[‡]Department of Statistics
The Pennsylvania State University, University Park, PA, USA
zzhou@ist.psu.edu, hesiqiong@gmail.com, {jiali, jwang}@psu.edu

ABSTRACT

Automatic understanding of photo composition is a valuable technology in multiple areas including digital photography, multimedia advertising, entertainment, and image retrieval. In this paper, we propose a method to model geometrically the compositional effects of linear perspective. Comparing with existing methods which have focused on basic rules of design such as simplicity, visual balance, golden ratio, and the rule of thirds, our new quantitative model is more comprehensive whenever perspective is relevant. We first develop a new hierarchical segmentation algorithm that integrates classic photometric cues with a new geometric cue inspired by perspective geometry. We then show how these cues can be used directly to detect the dominant vanishing point in an image without extracting any line segments, a technique with implications for multimedia applications beyond this work. Finally, we demonstrate an interesting application of the proposed method for providing on-site composition feedback through an image retrieval system.

Categories and Subject Descriptors

I.4.8 [**Image Processing and Computer Vision**]: Scene Analysis

General Terms

Algorithms; Experimentation; Human Factors

Keywords

Perspective Effect; Composition Modeling; Image Segmentation; Vanishing Point Detection; Photo Retrieval

1. INTRODUCTION

With the rapid advancement of digital camera and mobile imaging technologies, we have witnessed a phenomenal increase of both professional and amateur photographs in the past decade. Large-scale social media companies, *e.g.*, Flickr, Instagram, and Pinterest, enable their users to share photos with people all around the world. As millions of new photos are added daily on the Internet, the demand increases for creating automatic systems to manage, assess, and edit such content. Consequently, *photo composition understanding* has emerged as a new research area, attracting attention of the multimedia community lately.

In photography, composition is the art of positioning or organization of objects and visual elements (*e.g.*, color, texture, shape, tone, motion, depth) within an photo. Principles of organization include balance, contrast, Gestalt perception and unity, geometry, rhythm, perspective, illumination, and viewing path. Automated understanding of photo composition has been shown to benefit a number of applications such as summarization of photo collections [25] and assessment of image aesthetics [26]. It can also be used to render feedback to the photographer on the photo aesthetics [36, 35], and suggest improvements to the image composition through image re-targeting [21, 4, 7]. Moreover, the capability to understand compositions has broad implications beyond photography. For example, in multimedia advertising, designers often need to come up with interesting compositions to attract the attention or to influence the emotions of the viewers. Also, composition analysis can potentially be used to assist movie directors by providing feedback on the scene composition.

In the literature, most work on image composition understanding has focused on design rules such as the simplicity, visual balance, golden ratio, the rule of thirds, and the use of diagonal lines. These rules are mainly concerned with the 2D rendering of objects or simple ways of dividing the image frame. They are by no means exhaustive for capturing the wide variations in photographic composition.

The Use of Perspective Effect in Photography. Perspective effect is one of the most commonly used techniques in photo composition. As illustrated by the examples in Figure 1, during photographic creation, experienced photographers often make use of the linear perspective effect to emphasize the sense of 3D space in a 2D photo. It not only reveals the appearance of objects in space and their relationships to each other, but also tells us our angle of perception and our position as an observer. In this regard, perspective is credited with recognizing the viewer as a specific unique individual in a distinct place with a point of view [18].

According to the perspective camera geometry, all parallel lines in 3D converge to a single point, the vanishing point, in the image. However, only the vanishing point lying within or near the image frame and associated with the

MM'15, October 26–30, 2015, Brisbane, Australia.
© 2015 ACM. ISBN 978-1-4503-3459-4/15/10 ...$15.00.
DOI: http://dx.doi.org/10.1145/2733373.2806248.

Figure 1: The use of perspective effects in photography. Top two rows: natural landscape. Bottom two rows: urban scenes.

dominant structures of the scene (*e.g.*, grounds, large walls, bridges) convey a strong impression of 3D space or depth to the viewers. Figure 2(a) shows some examples. We regard such a vanishing point as the *dominant vanishing point* of the particular image. By placing the dominant vanishing point at different image locations and choosing how each composition region in the image relates to this point, an experienced photographer could produce various image compositions that convey different messages or impressions to the viewers.

Modeling Perspective Effects Automatically. Based on the above discussion, we argue that, in order to obtain a comprehensive understanding of composition, it is necessary to develop automatic systems to examine the perspective effects in the photos. To this end, we propose to *partition an image into photometrically and geometrically consistent regions according to the dominant vanishing point.* In our work, we assume that each geometric region can be roughly modeled by a flat surface, or a plane. As shown in Figure 2(c), such a partition naturally provides us with a novel *holistic* yet *compact* representation of the 3D scene geometry that respects the perspective effects of the scene the image captured in, and allows us to derive a notion of relative depth and scale for the objects. Nevertheless, obtaining such a representation is a challenging problem for the following reasons.

First, given any two adjacent geometric regions in an image, there may not be a distinguishable boundary in terms of photometric cues (*e.g.*, color, texture) so that they can be separated. For example, the walls and the ceiling in the second photo of Figure 2 share the same building material. Because existing segmentation algorithms primarily depend on the photometric cues to determine the distance between regions, they are often unable to separate these regions from each other (see Figure 2(b) for examples). To resolve this issue, we propose a novel hierarchical image segmentation algorithm that leverages significant geometric information about the dominant vanishing point in the image. Specifically, we compute a geometric distance between any two adjacent regions based on the similarity of the angles of the two regions in a polar coordinate system, with the dominant vanishing point being the pole. By combining the geometric cues with conventional photometric cues, our method is able to preserve essential geometric regions in the image.

(a) (b) (c)

Figure 2: Geometric image segmentation. (a) The original image with the dominant vanishing point detected by our method (shown as a yellow round dot). (b) Region segmentation map produced using a state-of-the-art method. (c) Geometric image segmentation map produced by our method.

Second, detecting the dominant vanishing point from an image itself is a nontrivial task. Typical vanishing point detection methods assume the presence of a large number of strong edges in the image. However, for many photos of natural outdoor scenes, such as the image of an arbitrary road, there may not be adequate clearly-delineated edges that converge to the vanishing point. In such cases, the detected vanishing points are often unreliable and sensitive to image noise. To overcome this difficulty, we observe that while it may be hard to detect the local edges in these images, it is possible to directly infer the location of the vanishing point by aggregating the aforementioned photometric and geometric cues over the entire image (Figures 2 and 7). Based on this observation, we develop a novel vanishing point detection method which does not rely on the existence of strong edges, hence works better for natural images.

Application to On-Site Composition Feedback. Since our region-based model captures rich information about the photo composition, it may benefit many composition-based applications. As an illustrative example, we apply it to an image retrieval application which aims to provide amateur users with on-site feedback about the composition of their photos, in the same spirit as Yao *et al.* [35]. In particular, given a query image taken by the user, the system retrieves exemplar photos with similar compositions from a collection of photos taken by experienced photographers. These exemplar photos can serve as an informative guide for the users to achieve good compositions in their photos.

Our Contributions. In summary, we have made the following contributions:

- *Composition modeling:* We model the composition of an image by examining the perspective effects and partitioning the image into photometrically and geometrically consistent regions using our novel hierarchical image segmentation algorithm.
- *Dominant vanishing point detection:* By aggregating the photometric and geometric cues used in our segmentation algorithm, we develop an effective method to detect the dominant vanishing point in an arbitrary image.
- *On-site composition feedback:* We demonstrate that our region-based model can be used to provide amateur users with on-site composition feedback by retrieving images with similar composition as the query image from a collection of photos taken by experienced photographers.

Nevertheless, our framework does not attempt to model *all* potential compositions in the photos, especially when there is a lack of strong perspectivity. While in this paper we focus on the use of perspective geometry in the photography, we point out that there are many works which study other important aspects of composition, including the semantic features (*e.g.*, buildings, trees, roads) [14, 15, 9, 10]. It would be ideal to integrate all these features in order to gain a deeper understanding of the image composition, but such a comprehensive work is beyond the scope of this paper.

2. RELATED WORK

Standard composition rules such as the rule of thirds, golden ratio and low depth of field have played important roles in early works on image aesthetics assessment [5, 22]. Obrador *et al.* [26] later showed that by using only the composition features, one can achieve image aesthetic classification results that are comparable to the state-of-the-art. Recently, these rules have also been used to predict high-level attributes for image interestingness classification [6], recommend suitable positions and poses in the scene for portrait photography [36], and develop both automatic and interactive cropping and retargeting tools for image enhancement [21, 4, 7]. In addition, Yao *et al.* [35] proposed a composition-sensitive image retrieval method which classifies images into horizontal, vertical, diagonal, textured, and centered categories, and uses the classification result to retrieve exemplar images that have similar composition and visual characteristics as the query image. However, as we mentioned before, these features or categories are all about 2D rendering, with 3D impression not taken into account.

Meanwhile, various methods have been proposed to extract 3D scene structures from a single image. The GIST descriptor [27] is among the first attempts to characterize the global arrangement of geometric structures using simple image features such as color, texture and gradients. Following this seminal work, a large number of supervised machine learning methods have been developed to infer approximate 3D structures or depth maps from the image using carefully designed models [14, 15, 9, 31, 24] or grammars [10, 11]. In addition, models tailored for specific scenarios have been studied, such as indoor scenes [19, 12, 13] and urban scenes [3]. However, these works all make strong assumptions on the structure of the scene, hence the types of scene they can handle in practice are limited. Despite the above efforts, obtaining a good estimation of perspective in an arbitrary image remains an open problem.

Typical vanishing point detection algorithms are based on clustering edges in the image according to their orientations. Kosecka and Zhang proposed an Expectation Maximization (EM) approach to iteratively estimate the vanishing points and update the membership of all edges [17]. Recently, a non-iterative method is developed to simultaneously detect multiple vanishing points in an image [33]. These methods assume that a large number of line segments are available for each cluster. To reduce the uncertainty in the detection results, a unified framework has been proposed to jointly optimize the detected line segments and vanishing points [34]. For images of scenes that lack clear line segments or boundaries, specifically the unstructured roads, texture orientation cues of all the pixels are aggregated to detect the vanishing points [29, 16]. But it is unclear how these methods can be extended to general images.

Image segmentation algorithms commonly operate on low-level image features such as color, edge, texture and the position of patches [32, 8, 20, 2, 23]. But it was shown in [30] that given an image, images sharing the same spatial composites can help with the unsupervised segmentation task.

3. GEOMETRIC IMAGE SEGMENTATION

Since our segmentation method follows the classic hierarchical segmentation framework, we give an overview of the framework and some of the state-of-the-art results in Section 3.1. In Section 3.2, we introduce our geometric distance measure for hierarchical image segmentation, assuming the location of the dominant vanishing point is known. The proposed geometric cue is combined with traditional photometric cues in Section 3.3 to obtain a holistic representation for composition modeling. In Section 3.4, we further show how the proposed distance measure, when aggregated over the entire image, can be used to detect the dominant vanishing point in an image.

3.1 Overview of Hierarchical Segmentation

Generally speaking, the segmentation method can be considered as a greedy graph-based region merging algorithm. Given an over-segmentation of the image, we define a graph $\mathcal{G} = (\mathcal{R}, \mathcal{E}, W(\mathcal{E}))$, where each node corresponds to one region, and $\mathcal{R} = \{R_1, R_2, \ldots\}$ is the set of all nodes. Further, $\mathcal{E} = \{e_{ij}\}$ is the set of all edges connecting adjacent regions, and the weights $W(\mathcal{E})$ are a measure of dissimilarity between regions. The algorithm proceeds by sorting the edges by their weights and iteratively merging the most similar regions until certain stopping criterion is met. Each iteration consists of three steps:

1. Select the edge with minimum weight:
$$e^* = \arg\min_{e_{ij} \in \mathcal{E}} W(e_{ij}).$$
2. Let $R_1, R_2 \in \mathcal{R}$ be the regions linked by e^*. Set $\mathcal{R} \leftarrow \mathcal{R} \setminus \{R_1, R_2\} \bigcup \{R_1 \bigcup R_2\}$ and update the edge set $\mathcal{E}$ accordingly.
3. Stop if the desired number of regions K is reached, or the minimum edge weight is above a threshold δ. Otherwise, update weights $W(\mathcal{E})$ and repeat.

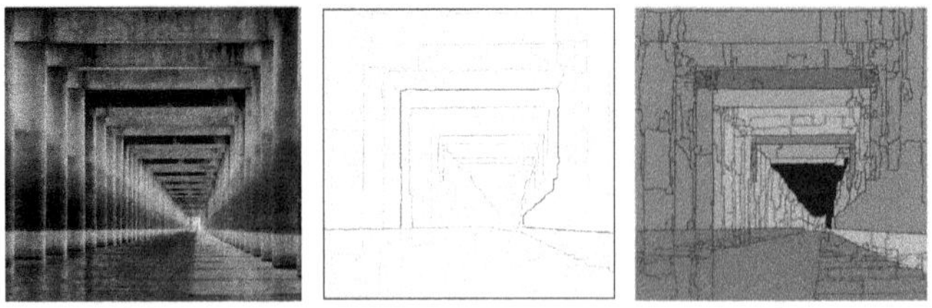

(a) (b) (c)

Figure 3: Hierarchical image segmentation using photometric cues only. (a) The original image. (b) The ultrametric contour map (UCM) generated by [2]. (c) The segmentation result obtained by thresholding the UCM at a fixed scale.

Various measures have been proposed to determine the distance between two regions, such as the difference between the intensity variance across the boundary and the variance within each region [8], and the difference in coding lengths [23]. Recently, Arbelaez *et al.* proposed a novel scheme for contour detection which integrates *global photometric information* into the grouping process via spectral clustering [2]. They have shown that this globalization scheme can help identify contours which are too weak to be detected using local cues. The detected contours are then converted into a set of initial regions (*i.e.*, an over-segmentation) for hierarchical image segmentation. We show an example of the segmentation result obtained by [2] in Figure 3. In particular, in Figure 3(b), we visualize the entire hierarchy of regions on an real-valued image called the ultrametric contour map (UCM) [1], where each boundary is weighted by the dissimilarity level at which it disappears. In Figure 3(c), we further show the regions obtained by thresholding the UCM at a fixed scale. It is clear that because the weights of the boundaries are computed only based on the photometric cues in [2], different geometric regions could be merged at early stages in the hierarchical segmentation process if they have similar appearances.

Motivated by this problem, we take the over-segmentation result generated by [2] (*i.e.*, by thresholding the UCM at a small scale 0.05) as the input to our algorithm, and develop a new distance measure between regions which takes both photometric and geometric information into consideration.

3.2 Geometric Distance Measure

We assume that a major portion of the scene can be approximated by a collection of 3D planes parallel to a dominant direction in the scene. The background, *e.g.*, the sky, can be treated as a plane at infinity. The dominant direction is characterized by a set of parallel lines in the 3D space which, when projected to the image, converge to the dominant vanishing point. Consequently, given the location of the dominant vanishing point, our goal is to segment an image so that each region can be roughly modeled by one plane in the scene. To achieve this goal, we need to formulate a dissimilarity measure which yields small values if the pair of adjacent regions belong to the same plane, and large values otherwise.

We note that any two planes that are parallel to the dominant direction must intersect at a line which passes through the dominant vanishing point in the image. Intuitively, this observation provides us with a natural way to identify adjacent regions that could potentially lie on different planes: If the boundary between two regions is parallel to the dominant direction (hence passes through the dominant vanishing point), these two regions are likely to lie on different planes. However, in the real world, many objects are not completely planar, hence there may not be a clear straight line that passes through the dominant vanishing point between them. As an example, if we focus our attention on the three adjacent regions R_1, R_2 and R_3 in Figure 4, we notice that R_1 and R_3 belong to the vertical wall and R_2 belongs to the ceiling. However, the boundaries between the pair (R_1, R_2) and the pair (R_1, R_3) both lie on the same (vertical) line. As a result, it is impossible to differentiate these two pairs based on only the orientation of these boundaries.

To tackle this problem, we propose to look at the angle of each region from the dominant vanishing point in a polar coordinate system, instead of the orientation of each boundary pixel. Here, the angle of a region is represented by the distribution of angles of all the pixels in this region. Mathematically, let the dominant vanishing point P be the pole of the polar coordinate system, for each region R_i, we compute the histogram of the angle value $\theta(X)$ for all the pixels $X \in R_i$, as illustrated in Figure 4.

Let $c_i(\theta)$ be the number of the pixels in R_i that fall into the θ-th bin. We use 360 bins in our experiments. We say that one region R_i *dominates* another region R_j at angle θ if $c_i(\theta) \geq c_j(\theta)$. Our observation is that if one region R_i always dominates another region R_j at almost all angles, these two regions likely belong to the same plane. Meanwhile, if one region has larger number of pixels at some angles whereas the other region has larger number of pixels at some other angles, these two regions likely lie on different planes. This observation reflects the fact a plane converging to the vanishing point often divides along the direction perpendicular to the dominant direction because of architectural or natural structures, e.g., columns and trees. Because perpendicular separation of regions has little effect on the polar angles, the histograms of angles tend to overlap substantially.

Based on this observation, we define the geometric distance between any two regions R_i and R_j as follows:

$$W_g(e_{ij}) = 1 - \max\left(\frac{\sum_\theta \min(c_i(\theta), c_j(\theta))}{|R_i|}, \frac{\sum_\theta \min(c_i(\theta), c_j(\theta))}{|R_j|}\right),$$

where $|R_i|$ and $|R_j|$ are the total numbers of pixels in regions R_i and R_j, respectively. For example, as illustrated in Figure 4(c), R_1 dominates R_3 at all angles and hence we have $W_g(e_{1,3}) = 0$. Meanwhile, R_1 and R_2 dominate each other at different angles and their distributions have very small overlap. As a result, their geometric distance is large: $W_g(e_{1,2}) = 0.95$. In Figure 4(d), we show all the boundaries weighted by our geometric distance. As expected, the boundaries between two regions which lie on different planes tend to have higher weights than other ones. This suggests that, by comparing the angle distributions of two adjacent regions, we can obtain a more robust estimate of the boundary orientations than directly examining the orientations of boundary pixels.

Here, a reader may wonder why we don't simply normalize the histograms and use popular metrics like KL divergence or the earth mover's distance to compare two regions. While our intuition is indeed to compare the distributions of angles of two regions, we have found in practice that computing the normalized histograms could be highly unstable for

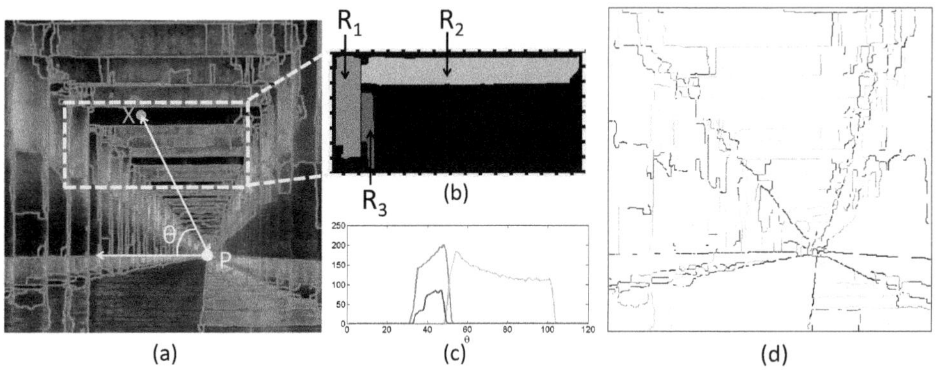

Figure 4: Illustration of the the computation of the geometric distance. (a) The over-segmentation map with the polar coordinate system. (b) Three adjacent regions from the image. (c) The histograms of angle values for the three regions. (d) The boundary map weighted by the geometric distance between adjacent regions.

small regions, especially at the early stages of the iterative merging process. Thus, in this paper we propose an alternative geometric distance measure which avoids normalizing the histograms, and favors large regions during the process.

3.3 Combining Photometric and Geometric Cues

While our geometric distance measure is designed to separate different geometric structures, *i.e.*, planes, in the scene, the traditional photometric cues often provide additional information about the composition of images. Because different geometric structures in the scene often have different colors or texture, the photometric boundaries often coincide with the geometric boundaries. On the other hand, in practice it may not always be possible to model all the structures in the scene by a set of planes parallel to the dominant direction. Recognizing the importance of such structures to the composition of the image due to their visual saliency, it is highly desirable to integrate the photometric and geometric cues in our segmentation framework to better model composition. In our work, we combine the two cues by a linear combination:

$$W(e_{ij}) = \lambda W_g(e_{ij}) + (1 - \lambda) W_p(e_{ij}), \qquad (1)$$

where $W_p(e_{ij})$ is the photometric distance between adjacent regions, and can be obtained from any conventional hierarchical image segmentation method. Here we adopt the contour map generated by [2].

In Figure 5, we show the segmentation results of an image using our method with different choices of λ and a fixed number of regions K. Note that when $\lambda = 1$, only the geometric cues are used for segmentation; when $\lambda = 0$, the result is identical to that obtained by the conventional method [2]. It can be seen that using the geometric cues alone ($\lambda = 1$), we are able to identify most of the structures in the scene. Some of the boundaries between them may not be accurate enough (*e.g.*, the boundary between the bridge on the left and the sky area). However, when $\lambda = 0$, the algorithm tends to merge regions from different structures early in the process if they have similar colors. By combining the two cues (*e.g.*, λ is 0.4 or 0.6), we are able to eliminate the aforementioned problems and obtain satisfactory result. Additional results are provided in Figures 6. Our method typically achieves the best performance when λ is in the range of $[0.4, 0.6]$. We fix λ to 0.6 for the remaining experiments.

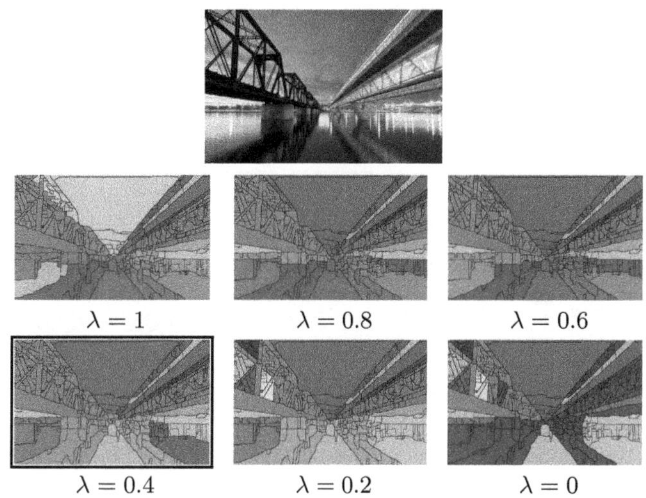

Figure 5: Image segmentation results by integrating both photometric and geometric cues. Different values of weighting parameter λ have been used.

3.4 Enhancing Vanishing Point Detection

In the previous subsection we demonstrated how the knowledge about the dominant vanishing point in the scene can considerably improve the segmentation results. However, detecting the vanishing point in an arbitrary image itself is a challenging problem. Most existing methods assume that (1) region boundaries in the image provide important photometric cues about the location of the dominant vanishing point, and (2) these cues can be well captured by a large number of line segments in the image. In practice, we notice that while the first assumption is generally true, the second one often fails to hold, especially for images of natural outdoor scenes. This is illustrated in Figure 7: although human can easily infer the location of the dominant vanishing point from the orientations of the aggregated region boundaries, existing line segment detection algorithms may fail to identify these boundaries. For this reason, any vanishing point detection method relying on the detected line segments would also fail.

To alleviate this issue, we propose to use our geometric distance measure $W_g(e_{ij})$ to obtain a more robust estimation of the orientation of each boundary and subsequently develop a simple exhaustive search scheme to detect the

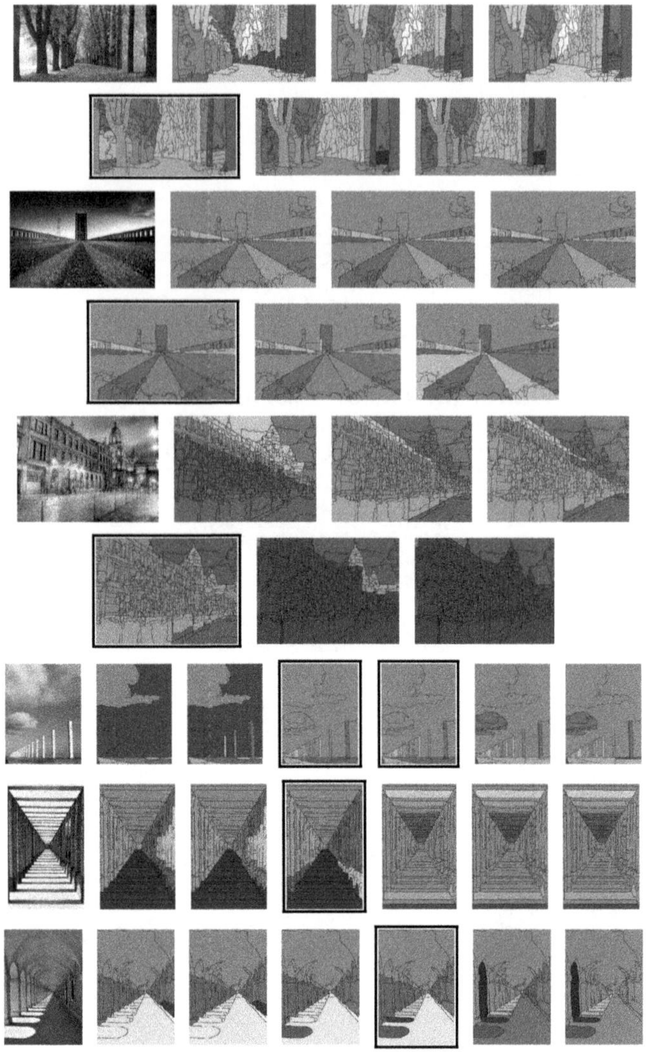

Figure 6: Additional segmentation results. For each original image, we show the results in the order of λ =1, 0.8, 0.6, 0.4, 0.2 and 0.

dominant vanishing point. In particular, given a hypothesis of the dominant vanishing point location, we can obtain a set of boundaries which align well with the converging directions in the image by computing $W_g(e_{ij})$ for each pair of adjacent regions. These boundaries then form a "consensus set". We compute a score for the hypothesis by summing up the strengths of the boundaries in the consensus set (Figure 7(c) and (d)). Finally, we keep the hypothesis with the highest score as the location of the dominant vanishing point (Figure 7(e)). Our algorithm can be summarized as follows:

1. Divide the image by an $m \times n$ uniform grid mesh.
2. For each vertex P_k on the grid, we compute the geometric distance $W_g(e_{ij})$ for all the boundaries in an over-segmentation of the image. Then, the consensus score for P_k is defined as: $f(P_k) = \sum_{e_{ij} \in \mathcal{E}} W_p(e_{ij}) W_g(e_{ij})$.
3. Select the point with the highest score as the detected dominant vanishing point: $P^* = \arg\max f(P_k)$.

Here, the size of the grid may be chosen based on the desired precision for the location of the vanishing point. In practice,

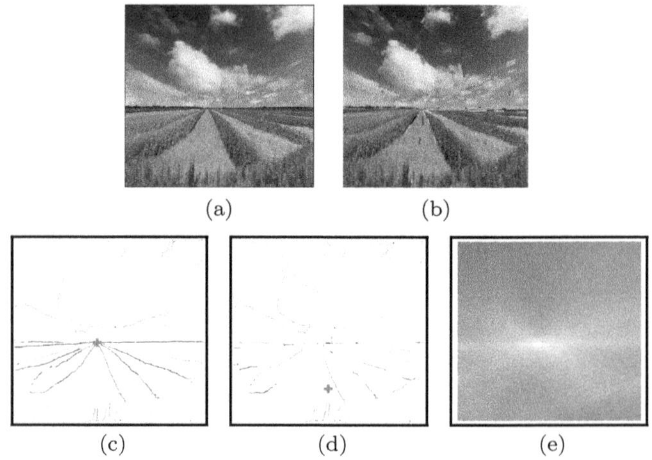

Figure 7: Enhancing vanishing point detection. (a) Original image. (b) Line segment detected. (c) and (d) The weighted boundary map for two different hypotheses of the dominant vanishing point location. (e) The consensus score for all vertices on the grid.

our algorithm can find the optimal location in about one minute on a 50×33 grid on a single CPU. We also note that the time may be reduced using a coarse-to-fine procedure.

In addition, we assume that the dominant vanishing point lies in the image frame because, as we noted before, only the vanishing point which lies within or near the frame conveys a strong sense of 3D space to the viewer. But our method can be easily extended to detect vanishing points outside the frame using a larger mesh grid.

4. QUANTITATIVE EVALUATIONS

We systematically evaluate the proposed geometric image segmentation algorithm and vanishing point detection algorithm in Section 4.1 and 4.2, respectively.

4.1 Evaluation on Image Segmentation

In this section, we compare the performance of our method with the state-of-the-art image segmentation method, *gPb*-owt-ucm [2]. For this experiment, we assume known dominant vanishing point locations. We emphasize that our goal here is not to compete with [2] as a generic image segmentation algorithm, but to demonstrate that information about the vanishing point (*i.e.*, the geometric cue), if properly harnessed, can empower us to get better segmentation results.

To quantitatively evaluate the methods, we use three popular metrics to compare the result obtained by each algorithm with the manually-labeled segmentation: Rand index (RI), variation of information (VOI) and segmentation covering (SC). First, the RI metric measures the probability that an arbitrary pair of samples have the same label in two partitions. The range of RI metric is $[0, 1]$, higher values indicating greater similarity between two partitions. Second, the VOI metric measures the average condition entropy of two clustering results, which essentially measures the extent to which one clustering can explain the other. The VOI metric is non-negative, with lower values indicating greater similarity. Finally, the SC metric measures the overlap between the region pairs in two partitions. The range of SC metric is $[0, 1]$, higher values indicating greater similarity. We refer interested readers to [2] for more details about these metrics.

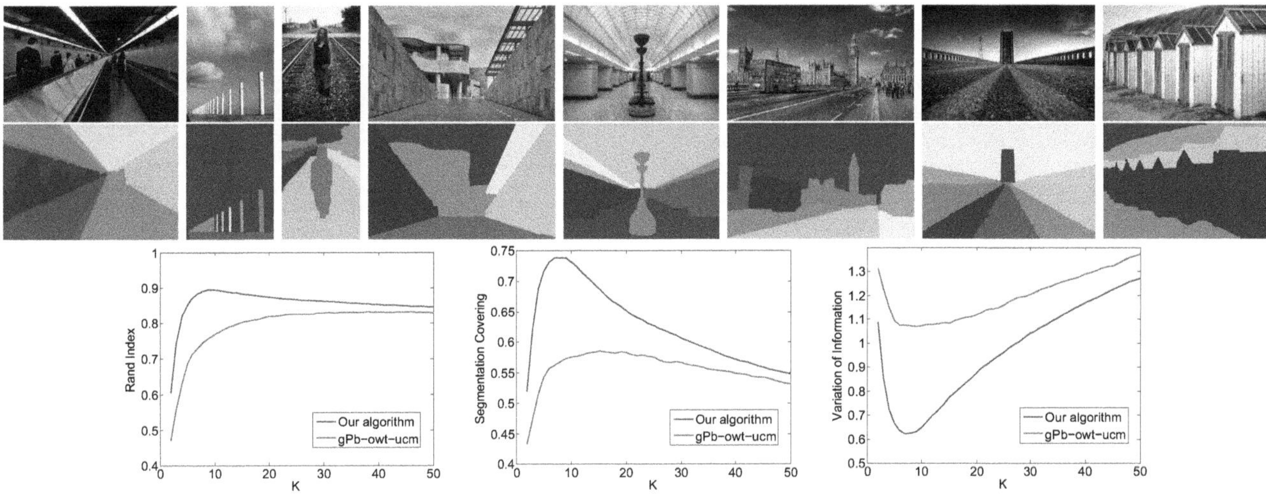

(a) Rand Index (b) Segmentation Covering (c) Variation of Information

Figure 8: Segmentation benchmarks. K is the number of regions. Top rows show some example test images with the manually labeled segmentation maps.

For this experiment, we manually labeled 200 images downloaded from `flickr.com`. These images cover a variety of indoor and outdoor scenes and each has a dominant vanishing point. During the labeling process, our focus is on identifying all the regions that differ from their neighbors either in their geometric structures or photometric properties. We show some images with the hand-labeled segmentation maps in Figure 8.

Figure 8 also shows the benchmark results of both methods. Our method significantly outperforms *gPb*-owt-ucm on all metrics. This is consistent with the example results in Figures 5 and 6, suggesting that our method is advantageous in segmenting the geometric structures in the scene.

4.2 Evaluation on Vanishing Point Detection

Next, we compare our vanishing point detection method with two state-of-the-art methods proposed by Tardif [33] and Tretiak *et al.* [34], respectively. As discussed earlier, both methods rely on the line segments to generate vanishing point candidates. Then, a non-iterative scheme similar to the popular RANSAC technique is developed in [33] to group the line segments into several clusters, each corresponding to one vanishing point. Using the vanishing points detected by [33] as an initialization, [34] further propose a non-linear optimization framework to jointly refine the extracted line segments and vanishing points.

In this experiment, we use 400 images downloaded from `flickr.com` whose dominant vanishing points lie within the image frame. All images are scaled to size 500×330 or 330×500. To make the comparison fair, for [33] and [34] we only keep the vanishing point with the largest support set among all hypotheses that also lie within the image frame. We consider a detection successful if the distance between the detected vanishing point and the manually labeled ground truth is smaller than certain threshold t, and plot the success rates of all methods w.r.t. the threshold t in Figure 9. As one can see, our method outperforms existing methods as long as the threshold is not too small ($t \geq 10$ pixels), justifying its effectiveness for detecting the dominant vanishing point in arbitrary images. When t is small, our method does not perform well because its precision in locating the vanishing point is limited by the size of the grid mesh. Nevertheless, this issue can be alleviated using a denser grid mesh at the cost of more computational time. Also, we note that while the joint optimization scheme proposed in [34] can recover weak line segments and vanishing points for urban scenes, its improvement over [33] is quite small in our case.

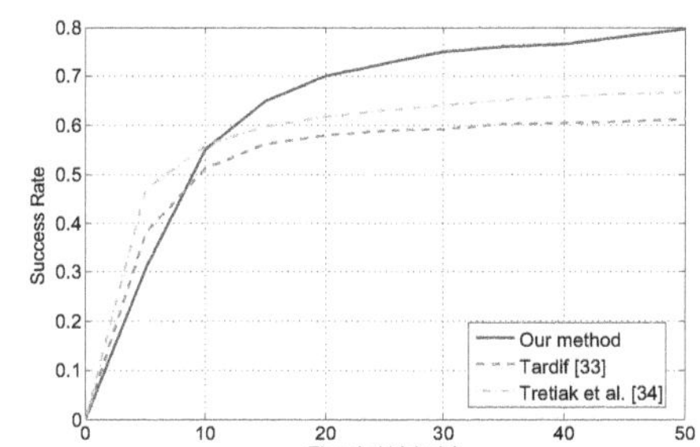

Figure 9: Comparison of vanishing point detection algorithms.

5. ON-SITE COMPOSITION FEEDBACK TO PHOTOGRAPHERS

The segmentation results obtained by our method capture rich information about the composition of images, hence can be used to facilitate various composition-driven applications. We now discuss one such application, which aims at providing amateur users with on-site feedback about the composition of their photos.

As we know, good composition highlights the object of interest in a photo and attract the viewer's attention immediately. However, it typically requires years of practice and training for a photographer to master all the necessary composition skills. An effective way for an amateur or an enthusiast to learn photography is through observing masterpieces and building models about photography. Nowadays, thanks to increased popularity of online photo sharing services such as `flickr.com` and `photo.net`, one can easily access millions of photos taken by people all around the world. Such resource naturally provides us with opportunities to develop new and more efficient ways for the beginners to learn the composition skills.

Specifically, given a photo taken by the user, we propose to find photos with similar compositions in a collection of photos taken by experienced or accomplished photographers. These photos are rendered as feedback to the user. The user can then examine these exemplar photos and consider re-composing his/her own photo accordingly. Yao *et al.* pioneered this direction in [35], but the types of composition studied there are limited to a few categories which are predefined based on simple 2D rules.

In this paper, we take a completely different approach and develop a similarity measure to compare the composition of two images based on their geometric image segmentation maps. Our observation is that, experienced photographers often are able to achieve different compositions by placing the dominant vanishing point at different image locations, and then choosing how the main structures of the scene are related to it in the captured image. In addition, while the difference in the dominant vanishing point locations can be simply computed as the Euclidean distance between them, our geometric segmentation result offers a natural representation of the arrangement of structures with respect to the dominant vanishing point. Specifically, given two images I_i and I_j, let P_i and P_j be the locations of dominant vanishing points and S_i and S_j be the segmentation results generated by our method for these two images, respectively, we define the similarity measure as follows:[1]

$$D(I_i, I_j) = F(S_i, S_j) + \alpha \|P_i - P_j\|, \tag{2}$$

where $F(S_i, S_j)$ is a metric to compare two segmentation maps. We adopt the Rand index [28] for its effectiveness. In addition, α controls the relative impact of the two terms in Eq. (2). We empirically set $\alpha = 0.5$.

To obtain a dataset of photos which make good use of the perspective effect, we collect 3,728 images from `flickr.com` by querying the keyword "vanishing point". When collecting the photos, we use the sorting criterion of "interestingness" provided by `flickr.com`, so that the retrieved photos are likely to be well-composed and taken by experienced or accomplished photographers. Each photo is then scaled to size 500×330 or 330×500. To evaluate the effectiveness of our similarity measure (Eq. (2)), we manually label the dominant vanishing point and then apply our geometric image segmentation algorithm (with the proposed distance measure $W(e_{ij})$ and the stopping criteria $\delta = 0.55$) to obtain a segmentation for each image.

In Figure 10, we show the retrieved images for various query images. The results clearly show that the proposed measure is not only able to find images with similar dominant vanishing point locations, but also effectively captures how each region in the image is related to the vanishing point. For example, the images in the 4th, 6th, and 7th rows of Figure 10 all have similar vanishing point locations (around the image center), but very different scene structure compositions, hence convey very different impressions to the viewer.

6. DISCUSSION AND FUTURE WORK

We have developed a new method for modeling visual composition by analyzing the perspective effects and segmenting the image based on photometric and geometric cues.

[1]Here, we assume the two images have the same size, after rescaling.

Figure 11: Composition modeling with complex perspective geometry. First row: photos with multiple dominant vanishing points. Second row: photos with foreground objects.

The method has been demonstrated for its effectiveness in detecting the dominant vanishing point from an arbitrary scene. Among a variety of potential applications, we have illustrated how our model can be used to build a composition-sensitive image retrieval system capable of providing on-site feedback to photographers.

Our work opens up several future directions. First, we may extend our geometric image segmentation and vanishing point detection algorithms to images with two or more dominant vanishing points, often found in man-made environments (Figure 11, first row). Here, our goal is to detect all the dominant vanishing points in an image and to group the regions according to the corresponding vanishing points.

Second, one challenge in composition recognition for real-world photos is the presence of large foreground objects (Figure 11, second row). They typically correspond to regions which are not associated with any vanishing point in the image. We will analyze the composition of these images by first separating the foreground objects from the background. We note that, while our analysis of the perspective geometry provides valuable information about the 3D space, many popular composition rules studied in early work, such as the simplicity of the scene, golden ratio, rule of thirds, and visual balance have focused on the arrangement of objects in the 2D image plane. We believe that combining the strength of both approaches will enable us to obtain a deeper understanding of the composition of these images.

Finally, besides providing on-site feedback to photographers, the proposed method has many potential real-world applications. For example, it can be used to retrieve images with similar composition in a large-scale image database. Here, a major challenge is to assess the relevance of the perspective effect in the overall composition of a photo. Possible solutions include using the metadata from photo-sharing websites, and developing new automatic methods (*e.g.*, via the detection of strong vanishing points). As another example, the proposed method can be employed to further summarize the query results. When a query results in a large number of images that have similar levels of visual similarity or aesthetic quality, the query results can be structured as a tree with levels of refinement in terms of composition by grouping the images using a hierarchical clustering scheme.

7. REFERENCES

[1] P. Arbelaez. Boundary extraction in natural images using ultrametric contour maps. In *POCV*, 2006.

[2] P. Arbelaez, M. Maire, C. Fowlkes, and J. Malik. Contour detection and hierarchical image segmentation. *IEEE Trans. Pattern Anal. Mach. Intell.*, 33(5):898–916, 2011.

[3] O. Barinova, V. Konushin, A. Yakubenko, K. Lee, H. Lim, and A. Konushin. Fast automatic single-view 3-d reconstruction of urban scenes. In *ECCV (2)*, pages 100–113, 2008.

[4] S. Bhattacharya, R. Sukthankar, and M. Shah. A framework for photo-quality assessment and enhancement based on visual aesthetics. In *ACM Multimedia*, pages 271–280, 2010.

[5] R. Datta, D. Joshi, J. Li, and J. Z. Wang. Studying aesthetics in photographic images using a computational approach. In *ECCV (3)*, pages 288–301, 2006.

[6] S. Dhar, V. Ordonez, and T. L. Berg. High level describable attributes for predicting aesthetics and interestingness. In *CVPR*, pages 1657–1664, 2011.

[7] C. Fang, Z. Lin, R. Mech, and X. Shen. Automatic image cropping using visual composition, boundary simplicity and content preservation models. In *ACM Multimedia*, pages 1105–1108, 2014.

[8] P. F. Felzenszwalb and D. P. Huttenlocher. Efficient graph-based image segmentation. *International Journal of Computer Vision*, 59(2):167–181, 2004.

[9] S. Gould, R. Fulton, and D. Koller. Decomposing a scene into geometric and semantically consistent regions. In *ICCV*, pages 1–8, 2009.

[10] A. Gupta, A. A. Efros, and M. Hebert. Blocks world revisited: Image understanding using qualitative geometry and mechanics. In *ECCV (4)*, pages 482–496, 2010.

[11] F. Han and S. C. Zhu. Bottom-up/top-down image parsing by attribute graph grammar. In *ICCV*, pages 1778–1785, 2005.

[12] V. Hedau, D. Hoiem, and D. A. Forsyth. Recovering the spatial layout of cluttered rooms. In *ICCV*, pages 1849–1856, 2009.

[13] V. Hedau, D. Hoiem, and D. A. Forsyth. Thinking inside the box: Using appearance models and context based on room geometry. In *ECCV (6)*, pages 224–237, 2010.

[14] D. Hoiem, A. A. Efros, and M. Hebert. Automatic photo pop-up. *ACM Trans. Graph.*, 24(3):577–584, 2005.

[15] D. Hoiem, A. A. Efros, and M. Hebert. Recovering surface layout from an image. *International Journal of Computer Vision*, 75(1):151–172, 2007.

[16] H. Kong, J.-Y. Audibert, and J. Ponce. Vanishing point detection for road detection. In *CVPR*, pages 96–103, 2009.

[17] J. Kosecká and W. Zhang. Video compass. In *ECCV (4)*, pages 476–490, 2002.

[18] D. A. Lauer and S. Pentak. *Design Basics*. Cengage Learning, 2011.

[19] D. C. Lee, M. Hebert, and T. Kanade. Geometric reasoning for single image structure recovery. In *CVPR*, pages 2136–2143, 2009.

[20] J. Li. Agglomerative connectivity constrained clustering for image segmentation. *Statistical Analysis and Data Mining*, 4(1):84–99, 2011.

[21] L. Liu, R. Chen, L. Wolf, and D. Cohen-Or. Optimizing photo composition. *Comput. Graph. Forum*, 29(2):469–478, 2010.

[22] Y. Luo and X. Tang. Photo and video quality evaluation: Focusing on the subject. In *ECCV (3)*, pages 386–399, 2008.

[23] H. Mobahi, S. Rao, A. Y. Yang, S. S. Sastry, and Y. Ma. Segmentation of natural images by texture and boundary compression. *International Journal of Computer Vision*, 95(1):86–98, 2011.

[24] V. Nedovic, A. W. M. Smeulders, A. Redert, and J.-M. Geusebroek. Stages as models of scene geometry. *IEEE Trans. Pattern Anal. Mach. Intell.*, 32(9):1673–1687, 2010.

[25] P. Obrador, R. de Oliveira, and N. Oliver. Supporting personal photo storytelling for social albums. In *ACM Multimedia*, pages 561–570, 2010.

[26] P. Obrador, L. Schmidt-Hackenberg, and N. Oliver. The role of image composition in image aesthetics. In *ICIP*, pages 3185–3188, 2010.

[27] A. Oliva and A. Torralba. Modeling the shape of the scene: A holistic representation of the spatial envelope. *International Journal of Computer Vision*, 42(3):145–175, 2001.

[28] W. M. Rand. Objective criteria for the evaluation of clustering methods. *Journal of the American Statistical Association*, 66(336):846–850, 1971.

[29] C. Rasmussen. Grouping dominant orientations for ill-structured road following. In *CVPR (1)*, pages 470–477, 2004.

[30] B. C. Russell, A. A. Efros, J. Sivic, B. Freeman, and A. Zisserman. Segmenting scenes by matching image composites. In *NIPS*, pages 1580–1588, 2009.

[31] A. Saxena, M. Sun, and A. Y. Ng. Make3d: Learning 3d scene structure from a single still image. *IEEE Trans. Pattern Anal. Mach. Intell.*, 31(5):824–840, 2009.

[32] J. Shi and J. Malik. Normalized cuts and image segmentation. *IEEE Trans. Pattern Anal. Mach. Intell.*, 22(8):888–905, 2000.

[33] J.-P. Tardif. Non-iterative approach for fast and accurate vanishing point detection. In *ICCV*, pages 1250–1257, 2009.

[34] E. Tretiak, O. Barinova, P. Kohli, and V. S. Lempitsky. Geometric image parsing in man-made environments. *International Journal of Computer Vision*, 97(3):305–321, 2012.

[35] L. Yao, P. Suryanarayan, M. Qiao, J. Z. Wang, and J. Li. Oscar: On-site composition and aesthetics feedback through exemplars for photographers. *International Journal of Computer Vision*, 96(3):353–383, 2012.

[36] Y. Zhang, X. Sun, H. Yao, L. Qin, and Q. Huang. Aesthetic composition represetation for portrait photographing recommendation. In *ICIP*, pages 2753–2756, 2012.

Figure 10: Composition-sensitive image retrieval results. Each row shows a query image (first image from the left) and the top-6 or top-8 ranked images retrieved.

Who's Afraid of Itten: Using the Art Theory of Color Combination to Analyze Emotions in Abstract Paintings

Andreza Sartori[1,2], Dubravko Culibrk[1,4], Yan Yan[1,3], Nicu Sebe[1]
[1]DISI, University of Trento, Italy
[2]Telecom Italia - SKIL, Trento, Italy
[3]ADSC, Singapore
[4]FTS, University of Novi Sad, Serbia
{andreza.sartori, dubravko.culibrk, yan, sebe}@disi.unitn.it

ABSTRACT

Color plays an essential role in everyday life and is one of the most important visual cues in human perception. In abstract art, color is one of the essential means to convey the artist's intention and to affect the viewer emotionally. However, colors are rarely experienced in isolation, rather, they are usually presented together with other colors. In fact, the expressive properties of two-color combinations have been extensively studied by artists. It is intriguing to try to understand how color combinations in abstract paintings might affect the viewer emotionally, and to investigate if a computer algorithm can learn this mechanism.

In this work, we propose a novel computational approach able to analyze the color combinations in abstract paintings and use this information to infer whether a painting will evoke positive or negative emotions in an observer. We exploit art theory concepts to design our features and the learning algorithm. To make use of the color-group information, we propose inferring the emotions elicited by paintings based on the sparse group lasso approach. Our results show that a relative improvement of between 6% and 8% can be achieved in this way. Finally, as an application, we employ our method to generate Mondrian-like paintings and do a prospective user study to evaluate the ability of our method as an automatic tool for generating abstract paintings able to elicit positive and negative emotional responses in people.

Categories and Subject Descriptors

J.5 [**Computer Applications**]: Arts and Humanities - fine arts; I.2 [**Artificial Intelligence**]: Vision and Scene Understanding; H.3.1 [**Information Search and Retrieval**]: Content Analysis and Indexing

General Terms

Algorithms, Experimentation, Theory

MM'15, October 26–30, 2015, Brisbane, Australia.

DOI: http://dx.doi.org/10.1145/2733373.2806250.

Keywords

Visual Art, Abstract Paintings, Emotion Recognition, Color Combination

1. INTRODUCTION

Color has a strong influence on human perception and is commonly used to convey aesthetic information. It can affect people on an emotional level and determine the preferences, interpretation, memorization and reactions of people. Different amounts of one or more colors convey different messages – a mechanism which is closely connected with the mental and emotional states [6]. The relationship between emotion and color has been widely studied in many fields, such as psychology, art, design, marketing and other areas.

Artists such as Kandinsky, Itten, Albers and others, studied how the presence of colors, in different proportions and combinations, affects the viewer emotionally, and applied these studies to their artworks: "Discovery of relationships, mediated by the eye and brain, between color agents and color effects in man, is a major concern of the artist." [5].

Johannes Itten, a notable expressionist painter, theorist and professor of the Bauhaus School[1] studied and taught the aesthetic and expressive aspects of colors and their interpretation. In his studies on the relationship between the chromatic scale and the spiritual evolution, he provided a set of rules of colors and color combinations he called the "objective principles of colors" [5]. Itten stated that "The concept of color harmony should be removed from the realm of subjective attitude into that of objective principle." The fact that many paintings induce similar emotions in the viewer, suggests that there may be some consistency in the way people perceive colors in abstract paintings.

In this paper, we use state-of-the-art computer vision techniques to understand the contribution of colors and two-color combinations in evoking positive or negative emotions in viewers of abstract paintings. We focus on abstract paintings because they present low semantic content (e.g., color, shape and texture), thus color, in these paintings, is one of the most important elements used to convey emotion. Our study into the effect of color combinations is based on Itten's theory of color expression, which states that it is difficult to define the expressive properties of a color without relating it to other colors [5]. Guided by this principle, in his theory of

[1]The Bauhaus School was a German art school which has a "...strong influence of scientific studies of color on the development of abstraction..." [1]

color expression, Itten observed and defined the emotional aspects of two-color combinations, which we explored computationally in the present study.

The main contributions of this work are: (1) we study the role of color combinations on positive and negative emotions induced by abstract paintings; (2) we propose a novel approach which recognizes color combinations in abstract paintings and classifies them in positive and negative emotions, and tested our models in two different datasets of abstract artworks; (3) we are the first to infer color-group information based on sparse group lasso, increasing the relative classification accuracy by 6% to 8% over the approaches that do not use the group structure; (4) we apply our color visual vocabulary (Color Palette) to automatically generate Mondrian-like paintings and provide an empirical study which shows that our method can be used as a tool to generate paintings which evoke positive and negative emotions in people.

The rest of the paper is structured as follows. Section 2 presents the related work covering the color theory and the existing emotion recognition approaches using computer vision techniques. In Section 3 we describe the two datasets of Professional and Amateur abstract paintings, and describe the Relative Scaling method employed to annotate artworks as emotionally positive or emotionally negative. Section 4 presents the details of our proposed approach and Section 5 provides the respective evaluations and results. In Section 6 we describe the learning approach proposed which infers the emotions elicited by paintings based on the sparse group lasso. In Section 7 we present an empirical study to prove that our proposed approach is able to predict emotional response of people. Our last section is devoted to the final discussion and conclusions.

2. RELATED WORK

This section presents previous studies on color and art theory as well as the existing emotion recognition approaches using computer vision techniques and relate these approaches with our work.

2.1 Color Theory

Color is one of the most salient elements of an image and it is the subject of study in many areas, including physics, psychology, philosophy, neuroscience, art, computing and many others. These and other fields attempt to understand the nature of color, how it is constituted, how people perceive it, and how it influences people's life. Initially, Newton [13] observed the physical aspects behind the perception of color and discovered that if some wavelengths of light are reflected better than others, then the object appears colored: "When light falls on an object, some is absorbed. The light that isn't absorbed is reflected off the object's surface; this is the light we see." [10]. Opposed to Newton, Goethe proposed a color wheel based on physiological experiences (e.g., afterimage[2]) and psychological aspects (e.g., moral associations, symbolic and mystic use of colors) to describe complementary colors: "The chromatic circle... [is] arranged in a general way according to the natural order... for the colors diametrically opposed to each other in this diagram are those which reciprocally evoke each other in the eye. Thus, yellow demands

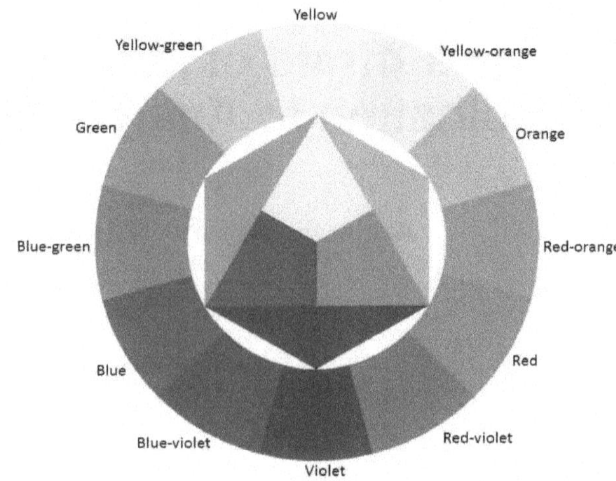

Figure 1: Itten's Color Wheel (taken from [5])

purple; orange, blue; red, green; and vice versa: thus... all intermediate gradations reciprocally evoke each other; the simpler color demanding the compound, and vice versa." [21]. These and subsequent physiological and psychological theories of the effects of color, were used by famous painters and are still used today in order to improve the aesthetic aspects of paintings.

In abstract paintings, colors have an essential role. They are particularly studied and used by artists to convey the emotional message to the beholder. Kandinsky describes the emotional effects of individual colors, stating that it depends on two factors: a physical impression, "one of pleasure and contentment at the varied and beautiful colors" and a psychic effect, in which colors "produce a corresponding spiritual vibration, and it is only as a step towards this spiritual vibration that the elementary physical impression is of importance" [7].

More recently, Itten observed that it is difficult to define the expressive properties of a color without relating it to other colors [5]. Indeed, he formalized theories on the emotional effects of two-color combinations and their properties to generate harmonious artworks [5]. He describes the emotional values of the color combination hues defined on the 12-color circle (Figure 1). Itten's color wheel is widely used in art studies and is composed of 12 hues of primaries, secondary and tertiary colors which are respectively: yellow, red, blue, orange, violet, green, yellow-orange, red-orange, red-violet, blue-violet, blue-green and yellow-green. For Itten, the two diametrically opposed colors in the wheel are complementary, forming a harmonious dyad, for instance red/green, blue/orange, yellow/ violet, etc. These 12 hues are varied by five levels of luminance and three levels of saturation and are represented by Itten in a Color Sphere with a total of 180 colors. In the Color Sphere, the 12 hues are located in the equatorial zone, the luminance varies along the meridians, and the horizontal sections contain the degrees of saturation: "If I use the color sphere, I can get an indefinite number of harmonious dyads. The only requirement is that the two tones be symmetrical with respect to the center of the sphere. Thus if I take a tint of red, the corresponding green must be shaded in the same degree as the red is lightened" [5].

[2] Afterimage refers to an image continuing to appear in one's vision after the exposure to the actual image has ended.

Using Itten's theory of color expression described in [5], we investigate how color combinations can be exploited to improve machine learning approaches to classify the emotions elicited by abstract paintings. In addition we discuss how the insight gained can, potentially, be used to revise and enhance the original theory.

2.2 Emotion Recognition

Recently there is a growing interest from different research communities in understanding the emotional response of the viewer while viewing colors in images, artworks, etc. A psychological study on the effects of colors on emotions based on Pleasure, Arousal and Dominance model concludes that brighter colors are more pleasant, less arousing, and induce less dominance than the darker colors [19]. Ou *et al.* investigate how eleven emotional scales are associated with three color-emotion factors (i.e., color activity, color weight and color heat) of single colors [14] and two-color combinations [15] determined by means of the factor analysis method. These studies show that there is consistency in the way people perceive colors.

From a computational perspective, color, along with shape and texture has been extensively used as a feature in the research focusing on artworks. Yanulevskaya et al. [23] proposed an emotion categorization system for masterpieces based on the assessment of local image statistics, applying supervised learning of emotion categories using Support Vector Machines. Machajdik and Hanbury [11] employed low-level features and combined them with concepts from psychology and art theory to categorize images and artworks emotionally. They obtained better accuracy in affective categorization of semantically rich images than abstract paintings. In [24] a Bag-of-Visual-Words model was trained to classify abstract paintings into those eliciting positive or negative emotions. With the backprojection technique, the authors determined which parts of the paintings evoke positive or negative emotion and concluded that, for instance, light colors and smooth shapes generate a positive emotion, whereas dark colors and sharp edges generate a negative emotion. Recently, sparse learning models have been used in different multimedia problems [22, 16, 9]. Sartori *et al.* [16] proposed to use both visual and text information in a joint learning model for abstract painting emotion recognition. Liu *et al.* [9] proposed a multi-task learning approach for painting style analysis. Zhao *et al.* [25] extracted emotion features of images based on the principles of art, including balance, emphasis, harmony, variety, gradation, and movement, which were shown to be effective for emotion classification of images. In our work, we analyse the emotional effects of color combinations present in abstract paintings.

3. DATASETS AND GROUND TRUTH COLLECTION

We conduct our analysis on two datasets of abstract paintings, which differ from each other in terms of the artists' background: one contains works by professional and the other by amateur artists[3]. Each dataset is composed of 500 abstract paintings. In the following subsections we detail the painting selection process, as well as the nature of each dataset.

[3]The datasets with their respective ground truths are publicly available at: http://disi.unitn.it/~sartori/datasets/

3.1 MART Dataset: A Dataset of Professional Abstract Paintings

The MART dataset was collected in our previous work [24, 17] from the electronic archive of the Museum of Modern and Contemporary Art of Trento and Rovereto (MART). The selected paintings have been created by a total of 78 artists between 1913 and 2008. Most of these artists are Italians, however there are also European and American artists. Some of the artists present in this set, such as Wassily Kandinsky, Josef Albers, Paul Klee and Luigi Veronesi, are known for their studies on abstract art in terms of color, shapes and texture.

3.2 deviantArt Dataset: A Dataset of Amateur Abstract Paintings

The amateur collection of abstract paintings has been collected in our previous work [17] from the deviantArt (dA) website[4], an online social network devoted to user-generated art. DeviantArt is one of the largest online art communities with more than 280 million artworks and 30 million registered users. We selected the artworks that were under the category Traditional Art/Paintings/Abstract, and downloaded 8,000 artworks. We used the information reflecting how many times an artwork was favored as a parameter to downsize the collection from 8000 to 500 paintings[5]. We selected the paintings with the highest and least scores in terms of favourites, as well as added a random selection of paintings scoring in the middle range. Thus the collection has 500 paintings by 406 different authors.

3.3 User Study to Analyse Emotions Evoked by Artworks

To collect our ground truth for elicited emotions we used a relative score method from our previous work [17], in which we asked people to choose the more positive painting in a pair. The annotation was done online and we provided the following instructions to each annotator: "Which painting in the pair looks more positive to you? Let your instinct guide you and follow your first impression of the paintings."

We follow the method of TrueSkill ranking system described in [4, 12] to annotate and calculate the emotional scores from the paintings. The TrueSkill ranking system, developed by Microsoft Research for Xbox Live, recognizes and ranks the skills of the players in a game and matches players with similar skills for a new game. With this method, the annotation task is more manageable, as it gives a representative annotation with only 3,750 pairs of paintings, instead of 124,750 comparisons ($500*(500-1)*0.5$), in case each painting is compared with all the remaining paintings in the dataset.

During the annotation process, we consider that all paintings initially have the same 'skill' and the painting which is chosen as more positive in a single trial wins a 'game'. Then, the rankings of the compared paintings are updated. Afterwards, the paintings with similar rankings are compared, until each painting is compared with at least 15 other paintings. We consider the results as emotional scores of the paintings, in which lower values correspond to negative feelings and the higher values to positive feelings.

[4]http://www.deviantart.com/

[5]We selected only 500 paintings to construct the deviantArt dataset in order to make an impartial comparison with the MART dataset.

In total, 25 subjects (11 females, 14 males) participated in the annotation of the MART dataset. Each person annotated from 19 to 356 pairs of paintings, 145 paintings on average. For the deviantArt dataset 60 people participated in the annotation process, 27 females and 33 males, respectively. Each participant annotated from 2 to 436 pairs of paintings, 63 paintings on average. The participants were anonymous and they participated in this annotation voluntarily, without getting any reward. There was no time-limit to the annotation procedure: each participant was free to annotate whenever he/she had time to do it.

Figure 2 shows a plot of the TrueSkill scores distribution for the MART and DeviantArt datasets. The mean score (μ) obtained for the MART dataset is slightly higher, while the standard deviation (σ) is slightly lower. The two distributions naturally differ, but not extensively so. The third distribution shown in the figure corresponds to synthetic images discussed in Section 7.

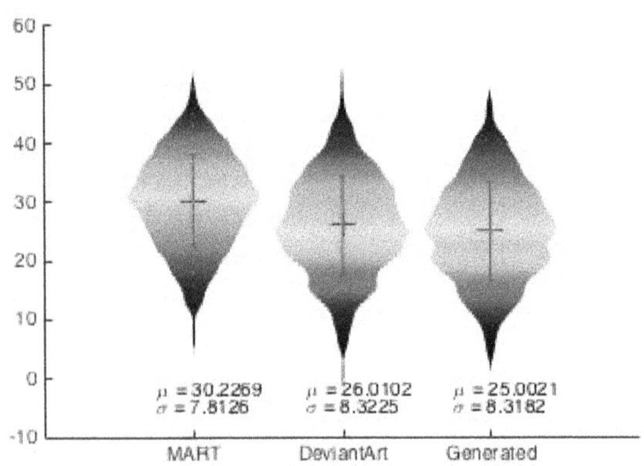

Figure 2: Distribution of TrueSkill scores for different datasets.

To compose the ground truth of both datasets, a threshold was defined to separate the paintings into those eliciting positive and and those eliciting negative emotions. As each painting was compared 15 times, we assume that the threshold should be related to one of the paintings which was chosen 8 times as more positive. Therefore, we consider the TrueSkill ranking values of these paintings, which are the ratings resulted from the comparisons of paintings by using the TrueSkill algorithm. The paintings with TrueSkill ranking equal or lower than the threshold are defined as negative and paintings with ranking higher than the threshold are defined as positive.

As a result, for the MART dataset, the painting with TrueSkill ranking value equal to 25.1 is used as threshold. We obtain a total of 131 paintings in the negative class and 369 in the positive class. To compose the ground truth for deviantArt, we considered as threshold the painting with TrueSkill ranking equal to 21.0. In total, 140 paintings were assigned to negative class and the 360 to the positive class.

4. PROPOSED APPROACH

In this section we provide details on how we use color combinations to automatically classify abstract paintings in positive and negative emotions. Specifically, we analyse the contribution of adjacent colors in a painting and use segmentation to generate the color combinations features to emotionally classify abstract paintings.

An overview of the proposed approach is shown in Figure 3. We first collect the database and the corresponding ground truth of positive and negative emotions evoked by abstract paintings. Afterwards, we use the method of van de Weijer *et al.* [20] to map the paintings into Color Name features and then cluster the entire dataset into 180 clusters (i.e., the largest number of colors in Itten's model) which were used as our *Color Palette.* Then, we calculate the closest value between the Color Palette and each pixel of the painting, and generate a new painting to segment. The segmentation yields blobs of uniform color that are further used to extract our features for image classification.

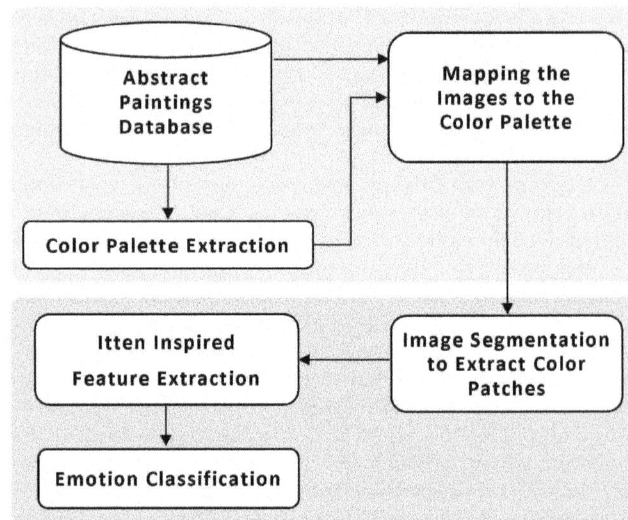

Figure 3: Overview of the proposed approach

4.1 Color Features

In this work, we propose a novel framework to analyze two-color combinations in abstract paintings and use this information to classify the images into those eliciting positive and negative emotions in the viewers. We use the Color Naming method of van de Weijer *et al.* [20] to create a visual vocabulary (Color Palette) able to model the human perception of colors.

van de Weijer *et al.* [20] describe colors through the confidence that a color can be described by 11 linguistic labels. These 11 linguistic labels are considered the ones which humans use to express the colors in the world (i.e., 'blue', 'red', 'yellow', etc.). The Color Name method shows to be more effective compared with photometric invariant descriptions, mainly with the description of achromatic colors such as white, black and grey which is harder to distinguish from a photometric invariance perspective [8, 18].

Algorithm 1 is used to extract the Color Palette. We use the method of [20] to extract initial color features, that should correspond to the way the colors are perceived by the viewers. Each painting in the RGB-color space was mapped to a corresponding image in the Color Names Feature (CNF) space. We used the default parameters of [20], calculating the mean of the patches with 21 pixels each, as the final value of the pixel in the CNF space.

```
Algorithm 1: Color palette extraction
Data: images
Result: color_palette
color_set ← {}
for I ∈ images do
    cni ← color_name_features(I); for color ∈ cni do
        | color_set ← color_set ∪ color;
    end
end
color_palette ← kmeans(color_set, 180);
```

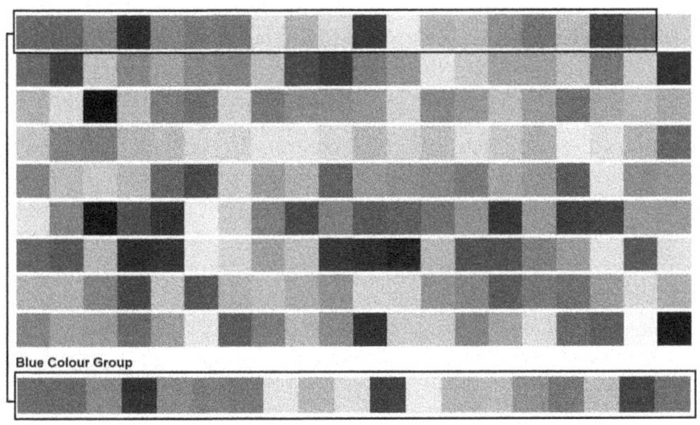

Figure 4: Color Palette extracted from MART dataset with 180 colors. Example of blue color group.

Once all the images have been mapped to the CNF space, we used the k-means algorithm to cluster the CNF values of the entire dataset of abstract paintings into 180 distinct CNF values (those closest to the cluster centroids) to form our CNF Color Palette (i.e., k is 180). The size of our palette matches the largest number of colors in Itten's color model [5].

Figures 4 and 5 display (unsorted) RGB versions of our Color Palettes with 180 colors created for MART and deviantArt datasets, which were subsequently used to represent all the colors in the images. The colors were manually arranged into color groups of blue, brown, orange, yellow, green, red, violet, pink, grey, white and black colors. Such grouping allows the proposed learning algorithm to use the group information to enhance classification performance.

Once our palette (i.e. color vocabulary) has been created for a dataset, the Euclidean distance is then used to to replace all the CNF values in the abstract paintings with the closest value in the palette. Finally the CNF values are mapped back to RGB to enable the use of a standard image segmentation algorithm to perform the segmentation into patches of same color.

Figure 6 shows a sample painting from the MART dataset and the corresponding RGB image after the mapping to our Color Palette.

4.2 Segmentation

To segment the paintings we used the graph-based image segmentation method of Felzenszwalb and Huttenlocher [3]. Their method effectively measures the evidence for a boundary between two regions. We used the publicly available implementation of the algorithm with the parameters $\sigma = 0.8$, the standard deviation of the Gaussian filter to smooth the image, and $k = 100$, which is used to control the threshold function. Figure 7 shows an example of the segmentation result.

Figure 5: Color Palette extracted from deviantArt dataset with 180 colors.

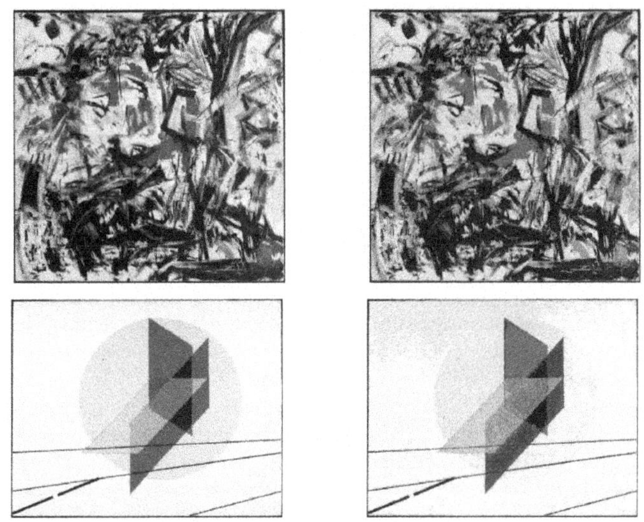

Figure 6: MART paintings repainted with the colors in the derived Color Palette. The images on the left are the original paintings, and the images on the right RGB representations of the repainted paintings. (© *MART - Archivio fotografico e Mediateca*)

4.3 Describing Color Combinations

In this section we detail how we use our computational approach to describe the color combinations in abstract paintings. Based on the art theory of Itten, we consider three aspects: the two-color combinations, the amount of colors and the position of colors. In the design of our features, we were guided by the principles identified by Itten, detailed in this section.

4.3.1 The Color Pairs are Equally Important

We consider that all color pairs are independent from each other and all color pairs are equally important. Indeed, Itten [5] affirms that "[...] the effect of a color is determined by its situation relative to accompanying colors. A color is always to be seen in relation to its surroundings."

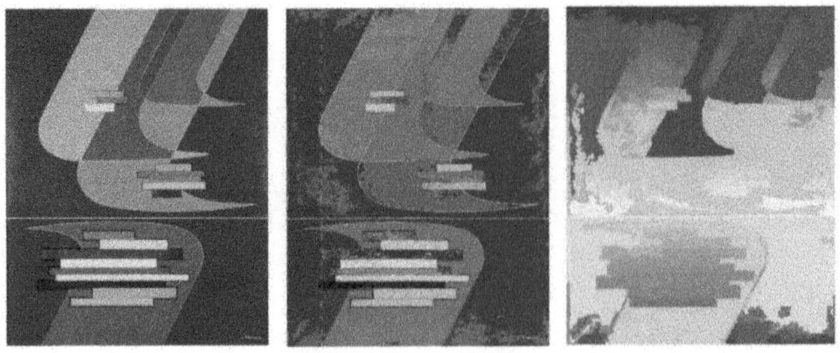

Figure 7: Example of our process of finding color combinations. From the left: (1) the original image (© *MART - Archivio fotografico e Mediateca*); (2) The image repainted with our color palette; (3) Visualization of all segments (patches) of the image. In (3) each color represents one patch.

4.3.2 The Amount of Colors Matters

We assume that the amount of colors affects the emotions elicited by abstract paintings. According to Itten, the harmonic areas of the paintings are generated by a balanced proportions of colors, which yield static, quiet effects. Itten states that the relative areas of two or more color patches, are neutralized when harmonious proportions of colors are used.

Itten gives as an example the work of Piet Mondrian. He points out that "Mondrian paintings employ two elementary resources, contrast of proportion and contrast of hue. [...] The quantitative proportions of the resulting areas assume a peculiarly independent life. Small configurations gain great significance by their placement in the field, while large forms recede and seem as if congealed. High sensitivity to proportion is required to organize all areas of a painting into a balanced whole."

4.3.3 The Position of Colors Matters

We consider that the emotions evoked by abstract paintings depend also on the position of colors. Itten points out that the distribution of colors is important to produce a distinct expression on the painting. In addition, he remarks that each direction in the area of a painting has its peculiar expression [5].

4.3.4 The Distance between the Colors Matters

We assume that the distances between colors might affect the viewer emotionally. In [5], Itten shows that the same color can appear to change in value, depending of the surrounding color.

- The weights of color areas act on either side of that axis. The left side is ordinarily the more passive, the right connoting activity. Right tends onward and upward, while left draws backward and downward.
- The horizontal direction denotes weight, distance, breadth.
- The vertical direction, conversely to the horizontal direction, denotes lightness, height and depth.
- The two directions together give an effect of area, a feeling of equilibrium, solidity and material hardness.
- A strong accent occurs where horizontal and vertical intersect.
- The diagonal directions generate movement and lead into the depth of the picture.

4.4 Feature Selection

We considered two types of features to represent the color combinations in an image:

1. Adjacent color co-occurrence features, which focus solely on the adjacent patches of color and are extracted on the level of the whole painting.
2. Patch-based color-combination features, taking into account the size, position and binary interactions between all the blobs of different color in a painting.

Since the segmentation yields segments (patches) that may not be completely homogeneous, each patch (p) is first assigned the most common value in it (mode), as its true color ($C(p)$).

To extract the adjacent color co-occurrence features, we consider a color combination to be present in the painting, if there are neighboring patches of the two colors in the combination. The adjacent color co-occurrence feature is then a histogram of all color combinations occurring in a painting.

To be able to model all the principles described in this section, we designed a more elaborate patch-level feature, which describes the size of each patch of color (amount of color in the patch), its position and its relationship to patches of other colors, present in the painting. To represent the amount of color contained in each patch, we calculated the relative size ($S(p)$) of each color patch, i.e. the size of each segment in pixels divided by the size of the image in pixels.

To allow for a scalable description of the position of each patch within a painting, the position is represented in relative terms by dividing the horizontal ($X(p)$) and vertical offset ($Y(p)$), from the top left corner of the image, of the center of the mass of the patch with image width (W) and height (H), respectively.

Once the position of all the patches has been determined, we calculate the relative distance of all other colors from a patch ($D(p,c)$) based on Eq. (1).

$$D(p,c) = \sum_{p_i \in P(c)} 1 - \frac{||L(p) - L(p_i)||_2 * S(p_i)}{\sqrt{W^2 + H^2}}, \quad (1)$$

where $P(c) = \{p|C(p) = c\}$ is the set of all patches of color c in the painting and $L(p) = (X(p), Y(p))$ is the absolute location of the patch p within the image.

Our patch-based color-combination feature for a patch p is a concatenation $(X(p), Y(p), S(p), C(p), D(p, c_1), ..., D(p, c_N))$. N is the size of our palette. The painting is described by a set of features extracted for all the color patches in it.

Algorithm 2 outlines our elicited emotion classification approach. The images are first mapped to the corresponding palette, segmented and used to extract features, which are then input into the emotion classifier.

For the simple color co-occurrence features the classifier makes a decision based on a single feature vector extracted for a painting. For the color-combination features, the classifiers attempts to label each patch as positive or negative and the final classification for the painting is the mode of the labels obtained for each patch in the painting.

Algorithm 2: Elicited emotion classification

```
Data: image, color_palette
Result: emotion_label
cni ← color_name_features(image);
for pix_val ∈cni do
  | pix_val ← min(dist(pix_val, color_palette));
end
rgb ← color_name_to_rgb(cni);
patches ← color_segmentation(rgb);
features ← feature_extraction(patches);
emotion_label ← emotion_classifier(features);
```

5. EVALUATION AND RESULTS

In this section we present the experimental results on the classification of abstract paintings into those eliciting positive and negative emotions.

We compare the results of the proposed approach to the state-of-the-art work of Yanulevskaya *et al.* [24], who applied a standard bag-of-words paradigm to extract color-based LAB visual words. They used a grid-based approach to create a color palette (visual vocabulary of colors) containing 343 LAB colors and represented the paintings as histograms of visual word occurrence. Their results show that colors are an important feature for the recognition of emotions elicited by abstract paintings, although they have not considered the effect of color-combinations.

To compare the proposed adjacent color co-occurrence features with those used in the work of Yanulevskaya *et al.* [24], we trained a Support Vector Machine with a linear kernel for supervised learning. The TrueSkill ratings are used as ground truth labels. We tested our model in a 2-fold cross-validation setup, where the images are assigned to folds randomly, and repeat the procedure 1,000 times.

Table 1 shows the classification accuracy results achieved using the adjacent color co-occurrence features approach and using LAB visual words approach of Yanulevskaya *et al.* [24].

Table 1: Linear SVM classification results.

Accuracy	LAB Visual Words	Color Combination
MART	0.673 ± 0.025	0.696 ± 0.028
deviantArt	0.678 ± 0.021	0.691 ± 0.022

Using the color co-occurrence framework, we obtained a 69.6% correct classification rate for the MART dataset. Our method of using color-combination related features improves the performance of the classification, with respect to the pure color-based methodology. Most of the paintings in the MART dataset contain uniform colors (i.e., 781.808 unique colors) which makes it simpler to extract our Color Palette.

The paintings in deviantArt dataset contain a larger amount of colors (i.e., over 4.4 million of unique colors), which made it more difficult to determine derive the Color Palette. To solve this problem, we split the set into smaller blocks of 100,000 colors and applied k-means on each block to get 100 centroids per block. As a result, we got 44.400 centroids from the blocks and then we clustered them into 180 k clusters. Although the deviantArt dataset presents a large amount of colors, the resulting Color Palette seems consistent with the colors represented in this dataset. Indeed, the classification accuracy is 69.1%, which is higher than LAB visual words that achieve 67.8% correct classification rate.

6. LEARNING APPROACH

The patch-level features described in Section 4.4 are specifically designed for inferring emotions elicited by abstract paintings from the color combinations present in the paintings. In order to exploit the structural relationships in the features, we propose inferring the emotions with a sparse group lasso.

6.1 Notation

The Lasso is a shrinkage and selection method for linear regression. It minimizes the usual sum of squared errors, with a bound on the sum of the absolute values of the coefficients. The traditional Lasso problem is formulated as:

$$\arg\min_{\beta} \|Y - X\beta\|_2^2 \qquad s.t. \|\beta\|_1 \leq \sigma \tag{2}$$

where $\sigma > 0$ is a constant which is used for bounding the optimal solution. $Y \in R^n$ is the emotion label vector for n training blob samples (1 for positive feeling and -1 for negative feeling), $X = [x_1, x_2, ..., x_n] \in R^{n \times d}$ is the feature matrix composed of d-dimensional blob feature vectors and $\beta \in R^d$ is the learned coefficient vector. Since the ℓ_1-norm is imposed on β, the learned β has sparse solutions.

6.2 Emotions from Color Combinations with Sparse Group Lasso

Since we have color groups information in our proposed features, we can formulate the problem as a sparse group lasso, where we enforce sparsity on both the group level (location group, color groups) and individual feature level. This is based on the observation that the color blobs can be very different from several groups of color, *e.g.*, red should be more similar to orange groups other than blue groups. To better exploit this group information, we formulate our problem as:

$$\arg\min_{\beta} \|Y - X\beta\|_2^2 + \lambda_1 \sum_{j=1}^{m} \left\|\beta_{G_j}\right\|_2 + \lambda_2 \|\beta\|_1 \tag{3}$$

where the training features are partitioned into m disjoint groups G_1, G_2, ... G_m, $\beta = [\beta_{G_1}, \beta_{G_2}, ... \beta_{G_m}]$ and β_{G_m} denotes the group of weights corresponding to group G_m. The first term in Eq.(3) is the reconstructed error. The second term in Eq.(3) is the combination of ℓ_1 and ℓ_2 norm.The ℓ_2 norm is used for the weights inside the same group, and the ℓ_1 norm is used to sum the results between groups. Using the group structure ensures more robust and accurate weights and still benefits from the sparsity. The third term in Eq.(3) is the ℓ_1 norm to enforce the sparsity on the coefficients in β, which benefits from the sparsity by selecting only a few groups with similar colors.

Testing: Since color blobs in each painting are used for training, the final emotion prediction for a new test painting is based on the majority vote from all blobs in the new test painting.

Table 2 shows the comparison with baseline methods on MART and DeviantArt dataset based on color group feature. In particular, we compared with SVM and Lasso which could not have structure of color groups. From Table 2, we observe that 8% and 6% relative increase in accuracy is achieved using the sparse group lasso approach for MART and DeviantArt dataset respectively. This shows the benefit of properly using color group information.

Table 2: Comparison with baseline methods on MART and DeviantArt dataset.

	MART	DeviantArt
SVM	0.676 ± 0.025	0.687 ± 0.031
Lasso (without group structure)	0.694 ± 0.021	0.701 ± 0.022
Proposed	0.751 ± 0.014	0.745 ± 0.019

7. APPLICATION

As an application, in this section we present an empirical prospective study done on the color combinations generated with our approach. Specifically, we generated Mondrian-like paintings from the Neo-plasticism style, using the colors obtained from our datasets and invited people to emotionally judge these simulated paintings.

Piet Mondrian was a noted Dutch painter and contributor to *De Stijl*, a Dutch artistic movement. The Neo-plasticism style, considered as "the new way of treating the form", is a geometrical style of abstract art which is essentially composed by horizontal and vertical straight black lines filled with primary colors [2]. Moreover, Mondrian's paintings employ the two theories of Itten, which are used in our study: the color combinations theory and the proportion of colors: "Mondrian confined himself to the fundamental colors of yellow, red, blue, white and black. Each of these colors has its unique character and special weight. The position of each color is very important, and so is its orientation, horizontal or vertical." [5]

We selected three Mondrian paintings and randomly changed the colors, replacing them with the colors from the color palette generated from the MART Dataset (Fig. 4). We selected paintings which highlight the aspects we want to analyse in the paintings: distance, amount and the positions of colors.

Figure 8 displays one example of Mondrian-like paintings generated by our algorithm. We refer to the three paintings as simple (Fig. 8 (a)), intermediate (Fig. 8 (b)) and busy (Fig. 8 (c)), based on the quantity of colors and lines depicted in the original painting.

In the original paintings of Mondrian, the painting chosen as simple is composed of three filled small rectangles with primary colors. This painting is mainly composed of small blue, red, yellow and black areas and a large white area. The intermediate painting is composed of a big blue square divided in 3 parts for the black lines and small areas of red, black and yellow. It has also white areas between the colors. The busy painting is composed almost entirely of areas of colored rectangles, which are red, yellow, blue, gray, black and white.

To generate the Mondrian-like paintings we calculated the coordinates size of the horizontal and vertical lines according to the size of the original painting. Then, in the same position where the colors were used by Mondrian in the paintings (i.e., red, yellow, blue, gray and black) we automatically substituted the original colors with a random selection of colors from the color palette extracted from the MART dataset. In total, approximately 15.000 Mondrian-like paintings were generated for each selected Mondrian painting (i.e., simple, intermediate and busy).

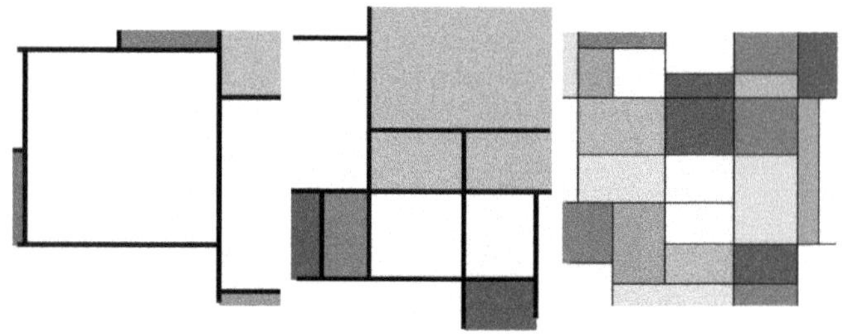

Figure 8: Example of Mondrian-like paintings generated with random colors from the MART Color Palette. From the left: (a) Mondrian Simple: *Tableau 2, 1922*; (b) Mondrian Intermediate: *Composition with Large Blue Plane, Red, Black, Yellow and Grey, 1921*; (c) Mondrian Busy: *Grande composizione A con nero, rosso, grigio, giallo e blu, 1919-1920.*

Afterwards, we applied the same segmentation method detailed in section 4.2 to generate the adjacent color co-occurrence features. We then used the linear Support Vector Machine classifier trained on the MART dataset to classify these images. We select the images with the highest classifier confidence to create a database of 500 Mondrian-like paintings.

7.1 User Study for Assessing Feelings Elicited by Mondrian-like Paintings

To annotate the paintings we use the same relative scale approach described in section 3.3. In total, 35 subjects participated in the annotation task, 18 were females and 17 males. Each subject annotated 104 paintings on average. The subjects participated voluntarily and were free to annotate at any time they wanted.

The distribution of TrueSkill scores obtained is shown in figure 2. As the plot shows, the generated images have almost the same mean and standard deviation of the scores, as the images in the DeviantArt dataset, and the general shape of the distribution matches both DeviantArt and MART datasets.

To define the threshold we use the same procedure of Section 3.3 and choose the TrueSkill score of the painting that was chosen as more positive 8 times. Therefore, the Mondrian-like painting with TrueSkill ranking value equal to 24.7 is used as threshold. In total, 241 paintings were assigned to the negative class and 259 paintings to the positive class. We then compared the TrueSkill ranking values of the Mondrian-like paintings with the results from the classification reported in the previous section. As a result, we have 60.6% correct classification rate using the Mondrian-like paintings with the MART color Palette.

We also matched the TrueSkill ratings obtained at the end of the user study to the individual annotations of the pairs, presented to all the annotators. The results show about 51.58% agreement, which can be considered a representative value of the mean human performance.

At last, Table 3 shows the comparison with baseline methods on Mondrian dataset based on color group feature. In particular, we compared with SVM and Lasso which could not have structure of color groups. From Table 3, we observe that 7% relative increase in accuracy is achieved using sparse group lasso approach on Mondrian dataset. This also shows the benefit of properly using color group information.

Table 3: Comparison with baseline methods on Mondrian dataset.

	Mondrian
SVM	0.576 ± 0.035
Lasso (without group structure)	0.625 ± 0.031
Proposed	0.671 ± 0.021

8. CONCLUSIONS

In this work, we propose novel features and computational approach, aiming to analyze the impact of color combinations on the positive or negative emotions an abstract painting will invoke in an observer.

We exploit art theory concepts to design our features and the learning algorithm. The features proposed allow a baseline classifier to infer the emotions better than the existing state-of-the-art features.

To use the color groups information better, we propose inferring the emotions elicited by paintings based on the sparse group lasso approach. The application of this method is able to increase the accuracy of the classifier even more.

Finally, as an application, we employ the colors extracted from our method to generate Mondrian-like paintings and do a prospective user study to evaluate the ability of our method as a tool for generating paintings able to elicit positive and negative emotional responses in people. The study shows that the proposed approach is able to predict the emotional response of people with accuracy higher than that of the mean human performance.

The limitation of our study is that the focus has been placed on abstract paintings and computational modelling of the art theory of emotions elicited by these paintings. It is unclear to which extent the proposed approach and the theory it is founded on can be applied to other types of paintings and natural images. Future work will focus evaluating possible extensions of the proposed approach to domains beyond abstract art.

Acknowledgments

We thank Victoria Yanulevskaya for the discussions in the initial phases of this work. This work has been partially supported by the MIUR Cluster project Active Ageing at Home, the EC project ACANTO and the A*STAR Singapore Human-Centered Cyber-physical Systems (HCCS) grant.

9. REFERENCES

[1] L. Dickerman, M. Affron, and M. of Modern Art. *Inventing Abstraction, 1910-1925: How a Radical Idea Changed Modern Art.* Museum of Modern Art (New York, N.Y.), 2012.

[2] G. Dorfles and A. Vettese. *Arti visive. Protagonisti e movimenti. VOL.3A: Il Novecento.* Atlas, 2001.

[3] P. F. Felzenszwalb and D. P. Huttenlocher. Efficient graph-based image segmentation. *Int. J. Comput. Vision*, 59(2):167–181, 2004.

[4] R. Herbrich and T. Graepel. Trueskill(tm): A bayesian skill rating system. *no. MSR-TR-2006-80*, 2006.

[5] J. Itten. *The Art of Color: The Subjective Experience and Objective Rationale of Color.* Wiley, 1974.

[6] K. Ivanova, M. Dobreva, P. Stanchev, and G. Totkov, editors. *Access to Digital Cultural Heritage: Innovative Applications of Automated Metadata Generation.*, chapter APICAS - Content-Based Image Retrieval in Art Image Collections Utilizing Colour Semantics, pages 153–202. Univ. Publ. House Paisii Hilendarsk, 2012.

[7] W. Kandinsky. *Concerning the Spiritual in Art.* Dover Books on Art History Series. Dover, 1914.

[8] R. Khan, J. van de Weijer, F. Shahbaz Khan, D. Muselet, C. Ducottet, and C. Barat. Discriminative color descriptors. In *Computer Vision and Pattern Recognition (CVPR), 2013 IEEE Conference on*, pages 2866–2873, June 2013.

[9] G. Liu, Y. Yan, E. Ricci, Y. Yang, Y. Han, S. Winkler, and N. Sebe. Inferring painting style with multi-task dictionary learning. In *International Joint Conferences on Artificial Intelligence (IJCAI)*, 2015.

[10] M. Livingstone. *Vision and art: the biology of seeing.* Harry N. Abrams, 2002.

[11] J. Machajdik and A. Hanbury. Affective image classification using features inspired by psychology and art theory. In *ACM Multimedia*, pages 83–92, 2010.

[12] J. Moser. True skill library. https://github.com/moserware/Skills/, 2010.

[13] I. Newton. *Opticks: Or, a Treatise of the Reflections, Refractions, Inflexions and Colours of Light. Also Two Treatises of the Species and Magnitude of Curvilinear Figures.* S. Smith, and B. Walford, 1704.

[14] L.-C. Ou, M. R. Luo, A. Woodcock, and A. Wright. A study of colour emotion and colour preference. part i: Colour emotions for single colours. *Color Research & Application*, 29(3):232–240, 2004.

[15] L.-C. Ou, M. R. Luo, A. Woodcock, and A. Wright. A study of colour emotion and colour preference. part ii: Colour emotions for two-colour combinations. *Color Research & Application*, 29(4):292–298, 2004.

[16] A. Sartori, Y. Yan, G. Ozbal, A. Salah, A. Salah, and N. Sebe. Looking at mondrian's victory boogie-woogie: What do i feel? In *International Joint Conferences on Artificial Intelligence (IJCAI)*, 2015.

[17] A. Sartori, V. Yanulevskaya, A. A. Salah, J. Uijlings, E. Bruni, and N. Sebe. Affective analysis of professional and amateur abstract paintings using statistical analysis and art theory. *ACM Transactions on Interactive Intelligent Systems*, 5(2):1–27, 2015.

[18] F. Shahbaz Khan, R. Anwer, J. van de Weijer, A. Bagdanov, M. Vanrell, and A. Lopez. Color

attributes for object detection. In *Computer Vision and Pattern Recognition (CVPR), 2012 IEEE Conference on*, pages 3306–3313, June 2012.

[19] P. Valdez and A. Mehrabian. Effects of color on emotions. *Journal of Experimental Psychology: General*, 123(4):394, 1994.

[20] J. van de Weijer, C. Schmid, J. Verbeek, and D. Larlus. Learning color names for real-world applications. *IEEE Transactions on Image Processing*, 18(7):1512–1523, 2009.

[21] J. von Goethe and C. Eastlake. *Goethe's Theory of Colours*. J. Murray, 1840.

[22] Y. Yan, E. Ricci, R. Subramanian, O. Lanz, and N. Sebe. No matter where you are: Flexible graph-guided multi-task learning for multi-view head pose classification under target motion. In *International Conference on Computer Vision (ICCV)*, 2013.

[23] V. Yanulevskaya, J. V. Gemert, K. Roth, A. Herbold, N. Sebe, and J. Geusebroek. Emotional valence categorization using holistic image features. In *IEEE ICIP*, pages 101–104, 2008.

[24] V. Yanulevskaya, J. Uijlings, E. Bruni, A. Sartori, E. Zamboni, F. Bacci, D. Melcher, and N. Sebe. In the eye of the beholder: employing statistical analysis and eye tracking for analyzing abstract paintings. In *ACM Multimedia*, 2012.

[25] S. Zhao, Y. Gao, X. Jiang, H. Yao, T. Chua, and X. Sun. Exploring principles-of-art features for image emotion recognition. In *ACM Multimedia*, pages 47–56, 2014.

Image2Scene: Transforming Style of 3D Room

Xiaowu Chen[1]*, Jianwei Li[1], Qing Li[2], Bo Gao[1], Dongqing Zou[1], Qinping Zhao[1]
[1]State Key Laboratory of Virtual Reality Technology and Systems,
School of Computer Science and Engineering, Beihang University
[2]Beijing Key Laboratory of Information Service Engineering, Beijing Union University
{chen, jianwei.li, gaobo, zoudq, zhaoqp}@buaa.edu.cn, liqing10@buu.edu.cn

ABSTRACT

We propose a style transformation system to transform a 3D room into one that resembles the style of a photograph. We focus on two major components of interior scene style: layout and color. Using an interior image database, we learn the related style guidelines. Given a reference image and a 3D room of two different interior rooms, we first establish semantic correspondence between the two scenes. The styles of the reference image are then extracted in the form of layout constraints and color schemes. Finally, our framework performs layout rearrangement followed by recoloring of the scene to match the learned style of the reference image. We show style transformation results on numerous examples to demonstrate the effectiveness and efficiency of our system.

Categories and Subject Descriptors

I.3.8 [**Computer Graphics**]: Applications; I.3.7 [**Computer Graphics**]: Three-Dimensional Graphics and Realism—*Color, shading, shadowing, and texture*

General Terms

Framework, Algorithms, Experimentation

Keywords

3D indoor scene; style transformation; layout; color

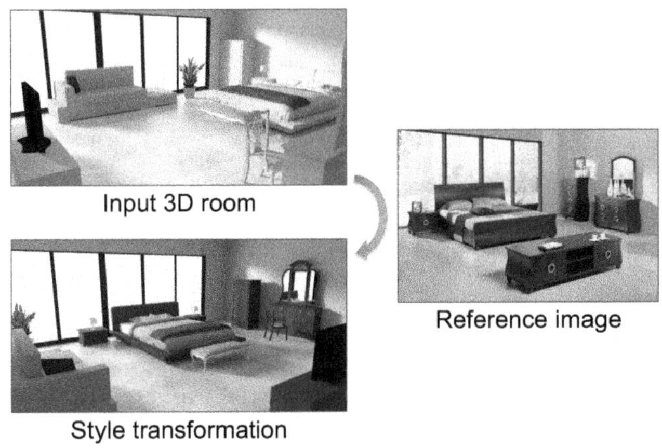

Figure 1: Style transformation of input 3D room involving layout constraints and color schemes based on a reference image.

1. INTRODUCTION

Indoor scene or room modeling has received a great deal of attention lately. Fundamentally speaking, indoor scenes are arguably the most familiar environments to us as we spend most of the time indoors. The ubiquity of indoor scenes in our daily lives demands their uses in many multimedia and graphics applications including virtual reality, game play, design and advertising. The most recent renewed interests in indoor scene modeling have been driven by the increasing ease of acquiring indoor scene data (e.g., using Kinect) and the popularity of data-driven techniques for scene analysis and modeling.

Recent works on indoor scene modeling have focused on two main problems: example- or data-driven scene *synthesis* [22, 34, 9] and approximate *reconstruction* [16, 23, 29], paying most attention to object selection and placement. In this paper, we study a complementary problem. While synthesis seeks to generate a novel scene, e.g., by sampling a probabilistic distribution defined for object arrangements [9], we are interested in working from an existing scene. Beyond merely reconstructing an indoor scene virtually, we are interested in altering its *styles* for design or personalization purposes. For example, we would like to answer the question "can I get my bedroom to have the same style as this other one?", where the "other one" provides the inspiration for the *stylization*.

We pose our problem as that of *style transformation* for 3D room. Given a 3D room, we alter it according to an input style to produce a new 3D scene. As stylization inspiration, we turn to the rich source of online photographs. Professional interior designers often provide a style catalogue filled with images for a customer to choose from. Technically, images provide perhaps the richest source of inspirations to train machine learning algorithms. As well, semantic analysis of images, which is necessary

*Corresponding author: Xiaowu Chen {chen@buaa.edu.cn}

MM'15, October 26–30, 2015, Brisbane, Australia.

DOI: http://dx.doi.org/10.1145/2733373.2806274.

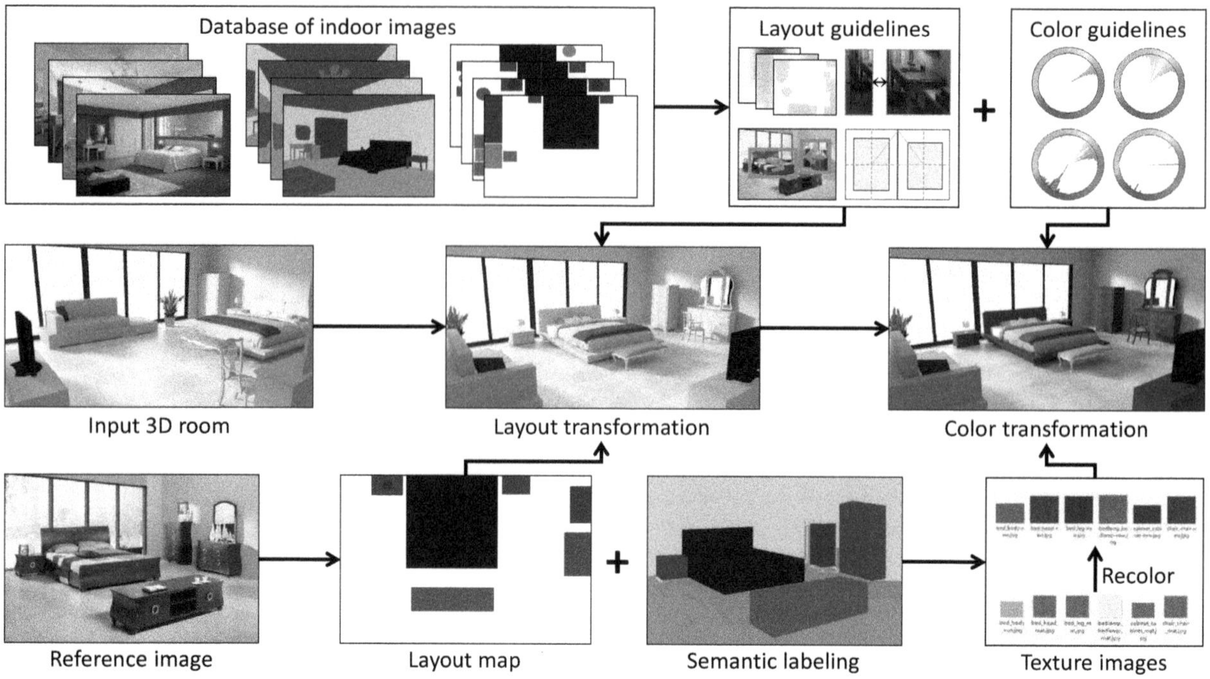

Figure 2: The overview of our style transformation framework. We identify the style, in terms of layout and color, by learning on an interior image database. The identification requires semantic segmentation and layout estimation as the preprocessing. Given a reference image and a 3D room, their correspondence is established based on semantic segmentation. With the style identification, we can transfer the style of a given reference image to the 3D room.

for meaningful style transformation, is an active research problem and has achieved pretty well results [18, 6]. To some extent, the current technology of image semantic analysis can provide basic information for style transformation, and more information can be offered by user interaction if necessary.

The term style encompasses many meanings even when only speaking of indoor scenes; these include color, texture, lighting, layout, use of fabrics, and decorative details of the furniture and other accessories. In our work, we focus on two such styles only, namely furniture layout and color schemes, for a few reasons. First, layout and color are the most visually apparent styles and they are used most prominently by professional designers. Second, compared to other styles, layout and color are relatively easier to extract from images. Lastly, choice of colors depends on layout or spatial arrangements of the colored objects and this implies that a layout-color correlation model is needed. We believe that the framework we propose for layout, color, and correlated layout-color transformation can be generalized to accommodate other styles.

Overview. In this work, we learn the style guidelines, including layout guidelines, color guidelines and layout-color correlation based on an interior image database. Each image in the database has been semantically segmented and annotated by a layout map. These segmentations and maps offer statistical information of layout and color when learning the style guidelines. Based on these guidelines, our system performs style transforming. Given a reference image and a 3D room with semantic labels and texture mapping, the image is first semi-automatically segmented as a semantic label map and a layout map. Thus the objects in the 3D room can establish correspondence to that in the image. Then we extract the layout constraints and color theme of the reference image. For those objects with no correspondence in the 3D room, the guidelines will offer help. With the style information of the reference image and the style guidelines, our system performs furniture arrangement followed by texture recoloring to match the style of the reference image. Figure 2 illustrates the overview of our framework.

Our main contribution is a framework for style transformation of a 3D room according to a reference image. To the best of our knowledge, such a problem has not been explored before. An interior image database is constructed including bedroom and living room with various styles, along with annotated semantic labeling images and layout maps. Layout and color guidelines are learned from the interior image database to guide the style transformation.

2. RELATED WORK

The literature on indoor scene analysis and modeling, both in the image and 3D domains and from the computer vision and graphics communities, is fairly extensive. We would not attempt to enumerate them all but focus on works that produce 3D indoor scenes as output. We will also cover works on style transfer and image-geometry hybrid modeling.

Early methods for interior room layout and furniture arrangement [28, 11] do not take ergonomic elements into consideration. More recent works have made much progress on generating plausible 3D indoor scenes with more complete layout guidelines. Merrel et al. [22] present an interactive system which assists in generating furniture arrangement according to design guidelines, where user interaction plays an important role. Yu et al. [34] present a learning and optimization framework to automatically synthesize a realistic 3D indoor scene which considers various human factors such as visibility and accessibility. Fisher et al. [9] synthesize diverse arrangements of 3D objects based on a small number of example scenes and a larger training set. Yeh et al. [33] present a novel MCMC algorithm to encode complex constraints as factor graphs and synthesize open world layouts. Differently from these works, we tackle the problem of style transformation rather than scene synthesis. What is common between their methods and ours is the data-driven approach. A distinction is that in our work, images, rather than 3D scene models which are relatively scant, serve as training data.

Another line of data-driven approaches have been applied to indoor scene modeling from sparse and noisy captured data, e.g., those obtained using the Kinect camera. What is common about these methods [16, 23, 29, 3] is the utilization of an object database to retrieve and then place the proper models based on a variety of constraints, e.g., certain universal layout guidelines, to populate a captured scene. This approximate reconstruction problem is again different from style transformation. All the works discussed so far focus on generating geometry and not appearance attributes, such as colors.

Matsuda [21] studies color design and put forth eight hue templates and ten tone templates. The tone templates were formed based on feedback from fashion-related questionnaires and the hue templates were provided by fashion companies. Later, Neumann et al. [24] present a quantitative dichromatic harmony formula for any two colors. O'Donovan et al. [25] further develop a color compatibility scheme for five kinds of colors. Although these preset color templates could be applied to an interior scene, they fall far short of the variability offered by online photographs, many of which came from professional designs that do not clearly map to any preset color schemes as described above.

Our color transfer scheme is related to many previous works on the same subject [26, 8, 5, 4]. Reinhard et al. [26] develop a global method for color transform by shifting and scaling the pixel values of the source image to match the mean and standard deviation of the target image. Cohen-or et al. [8] apply the eight hue templates from [21] for color harmonization. Chen et al. [5] perform color transform by considering the manifold structure within the Lab color space. These color transfer methods work well for many kinds of images and videos. Differently from them though, our scheme transfers the color style of a reference image to a 3D scene based on both color guidelines and a learned layout-color correlation model.

Works on style transfer or analogies have appeared before. The classical work on image analogies [15] has inspired many follow-ups. Xu et al. [32] rely on style-content separation for style analysis and present an application for style transfer on 3D man-made shapes, where the style is related to relative part scales. Li et al. [17] study decorative curve styles and apply style transfer as well. In our work, style transfer is applied to layout and color schemes and the transfer crosses

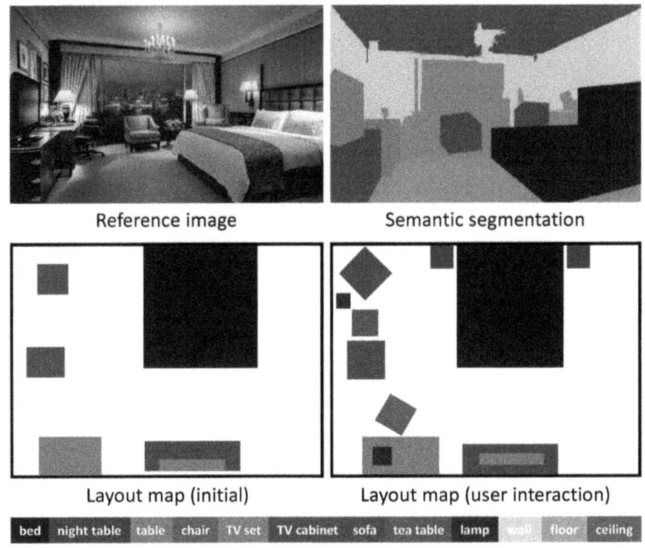

Figure 3: An example of semantic segmentation and layout map for a reference image. User interaction helps to improve the layout map, including adding night tables, chair and lamps which is missing during semantic segmentation, changing the orientation of sofas, adjusting the size and position of several objects and so on. The semantic labels are listed below with color legends.

from the image domain to 3D scene space. There have been many works on image-geometry hybrid analysis and modeling [31, 30, 32, 36], which we would not be able to exhaust here. Our focus is on style transfer rather than semantic image analysis or model/scene reconstruction.

3. INTERIOR STYLE IDENTIFICATION

To transform a 3D scene, we should figure out what makes a style look like a style. Consulting with the professional interior designers, we are informed that the major components of interior scene style are furniture layout and color appearance, which can be extracted from images. These two elements are both identified in an object-level, thereby making the understanding of an image a preprocessing.

3.1 Segmentation and Layout Estimation

Our preprocessing of images includes semantic segmentation and layout estimation, which are two important topics in computer vision. Large numbers of literatures [35, 18, 13, 14, 6, 12, 19] have been focused on these two topics and get promising achievements. However, it still remains a large gap to meet the user requirements for style transformation. Hence, for a given reference image, we provide a semi-automatic way to generate its semantic label map and layout map (Figure 3). We first utilize the available works [13, 6] to recover spatial layout of the room and find the bounding boxes of the objects in it. Using these bounding boxes, we get a semantic segmentation result of the image. Then we project the semantic label map into a layout map according to the principle of perspective and prior knowledge. User interactions will be added here to improve the results. Finally, these maps are used to extract layout and color

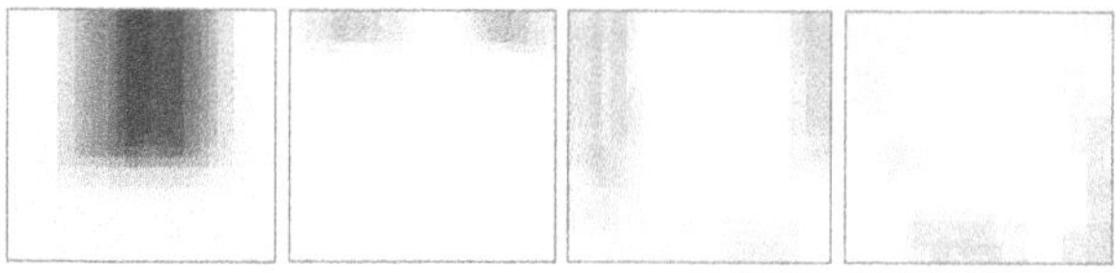

Figure 4: The placement distribution of different categories.

Table 1: Pairwise relationships.

Bedroom	Living room
bed and night table	TV and TV cabinet
TV and TV cabinet	teapoy and sofa
table and chair	teapoy and chair
teapoy and sofa	coffee table and sofa

knowledge to form guidelines or constraints employed during style transformation.

In some cases, the image analysis results generated automatically are too rough to extract useful information, thus we provide an interaction tool for users to improve the semantic segmentation and the layout map. Users can easily edit the maps by adjusting the size and position of objects, changing the orientation of objects, or adding missing objects into the scene. Figure 3 shows an example of layout map generated from a given image and improved by user interaction. In the initial layout map, some objects such as night tables and lamps are absent. There are also mistakes in position, size and orientation of several objects. By simple user interaction, these mistakes are rectified and correct layout map is produced. Note that for images in the database, we manually perform the semantic segmentation and layout map to learn the layout and color guidelines.

3.2 Interior Layout Guidelines

We adopt four layout criteria composed of *placement*, *pairwise relationship*, *orientation* and *accessibility* to define our layout style. These criteria, inspired from previous works [34, 22, 9], consider the function of furniture and the professional knowledge. We learn the distribution of these layout criteria based on the layout map in database. These criteria will be regarded as constraints during the layout transformation.

Placement. The placement of an object for certain categories is not arbitrary, as it represents the functional criteria to some degree. For example, a bed is usually located at the central region of a bedroom and a table is usually located at one side of a room. We regularize all the rooms to the size of 8×6 meters, and experimentally divide the layout map into 32×24 patches. Then we learn the placement distribution on patch-level. The placement of an object i is described by its center coordinate $O_i = (x_i, y_i)$. For each category C, the frequency of objects falling in each patch is calculated to form the placement distribution in the room. The prior mean coordinate of the placement distribution of category C is calculated according to the equation

$$T_{pl}(C) = \frac{1}{k}\sum_{i=1}^{k} f_i O_i^{patch}, \; f_i > \varepsilon, \tag{1}$$

where f_i is the category frequency of patch i, O_i^{patch} is the center coordinate of patch i, and ε represents the frequency threshold. Some distribution examples are visualized in Figure 4, in which darker patch indicates higher frequency.

Note that objects in some categories are not placed on the ground, for example, a TV is usually on a TV cabinet. These objects involve another placement parameter z, which represents the distance from the ground. This parameter is not included in the distribution learning process, as it can be get from the height of the supporting object. For instance, the z of a TV is just the height of the TV cabinet where the TV is located.

Pairwise relationship. It is an intuitive assumption that some furniture are characteristic of pairwise relationships and subject to distance constraints, such as the night table commonly standing beside the bed, the chair usually located next to the table. The pairwise relationships, inspired from professional designers, are listed in Table 1. The user also define its own pairwise relationship in a specific scene to constrain their relative distance and orientation.

Orientation. It is difficult to extract the orientation of an object from an image directly. According to the experience of the professional designers, we simply define the orientation of an object to be related to its nearest wall or pairwise partner. For objects that usually stand close to the wall, they are placed with back surfaces against wall. For objects which have pairwise relationship with others, their orientation is defined as facing each other. For example, a bed is usually placed with its head against the wall, and a chair usually faces its corresponding table. Specifically, we define θ_i as the angle between the back surface of object i and the nearest wall, and θ_{ij} as the angle between two front surfaces of pairwise objects. The orientation of object i will be adjusted by optimizing the parameter θ_i and θ_{ij} when its location is changed.

Accessibility. The accessibility to a furniture should be take into consideration, which allows people walk around and access objects. The description of accessibility in [34] gives us some inspiration. We add accessible space around an object and set this space to be the size of human body. Actually, we set an accessible bounding box for each object when doing our layout transformation. The accessible bounding box includes the object itself and the accessible space for people. We constrain that the accessible bounding boxes of every two objects cannot overlap, making each object accessible. Specifically, we make sure that $\|O_i - O_j\| \geqslant d_i + d_j$, where d_i represents half of the diagonal length of the accessible bounding box for object i.

3.3 Interior Color Guidelines

Based on the experience of professional interior designers and the interior color design knowledge [1], four color guidelines are summarized as: *single primary color*, *analogous colors matching*, *combination of complementary and contrasting colors*, and *black-white-gray combination*. To our knowledge, no work is conducted to extract intrinsic key measures that reflect their distinctiveness in color style. In this work, an experiment is performed to obtain the characteristic color statistics for these four guidelines (i.e. color schemes).

The images in the database are classified into four color categories by professional interior designers. Instead of

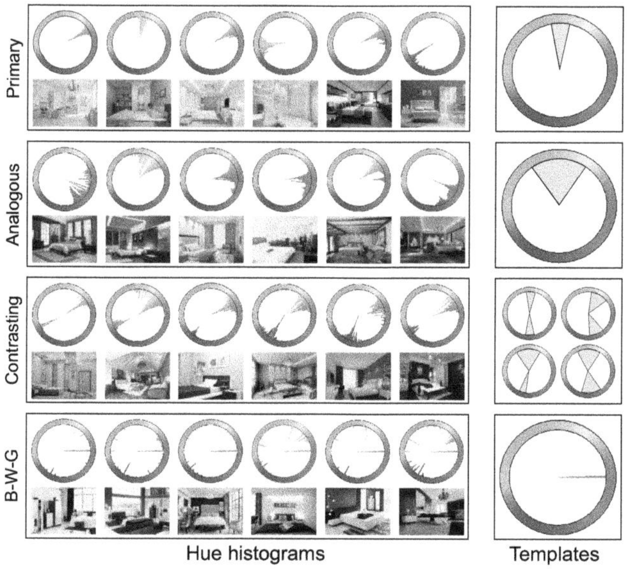

Figure 5: The hue histograms of sample images in each color category and their corresponding templates. It is clear to see that these hue histograms of the four categories are regular in HSV color space.

computing all kinds of statistical measures for each category images, we select a few key statistical measures related to these four color categories in terms of hue, saturation, luminance and color temperature. The actual bounds we use are [0, 360] for hue, [0,1] for saturation, and [0,100] for luminance. Within each category, we compute the mean and standard deviation for each measure. We also calculate the histogram of each property for each image in these four categories. The example histograms of hue property are shown in Figure 5. We can draw that hue is the most distinctive measure while there are no obvious rules to be extracted from other three.

Hue template. We extract the hue distributions of all images in the database and establish schemes for these four categories. The color scheme of each category should be subject to the constraint that the sectors of the hue histogram cover at least 80% pixels for each image in each category. As shown in Figure 5, these hue histograms of the four categories are regularized in HSV color space. The hue values of the images in the first category are distributed compactly in a small sector domain, like an "i" type. The angle of hue histogram in the second category is larger than that of the first category and it looks like a "V". The hue histograms of the images in the third category look like "I", "Y", "L" or "X" types. The images in the last category are black-white-gray images. They don't have so mush colors and the hue values are mostly distributed around zero angle (as gray's hue is zero). According to the statistic of our database, the precise sizes of the hue template sectors are as follows: i type is 5.4% of the whole wheel (19.5°), V is 12% of the wheel (43.16°). X is 50.48°(14%) and the angle between them is 157.35°. The large sector of the type Y is 51.79°(14%) while the small sector is 24.09° (6.7%), and the angle between the centers of the two sectors is 158.46°. I is 6% of the color wheel (21.82°) and the angle between them is 165.46°; L is 49.14°(13.7%) and the angle between them is 93.6°.

3.4 Layout-color Correlation

Our key observation is that, given an interior scene, the color distribution and spatial location of the objects are correlated and the relation lies in a low dimensional space. Thus, we apply the manifold relationship construction [27] to learn the layout-color correlation for a given interior scene.

First of all, according to the layout map, we build a graph representation encoding the spatial arrangement and mutual relations of scene objects. Graph model has been used in many areas successfully [10, 2, 7, 20]. Our graph model is inspired by the graph kernel presented by Fisher et al. [10] for characterizing structural relationships in 3D scenes. However, our model encodes not only the mutual relations but also the absolute positions of scene objects. Specifically, we represent the layout of an interior scene with a hierarchical structure containing three levels of nodes: global, region and object. The entire scene, represented as the global node, is separated into five regions including four wall regions around the four sides of the room and the central region. Objects are partitioned into the nearest wall region. Those objects which is not close to any wall is included in the central region. There are three types of relations, i.e., global-region, region-object and object-object. Global-region and region-object relations indicate inclusion relationship while object-object relations encode the pairwise relationship listed in Table 1.

We define $T_i = (h_i, x_i, y_i)$, where h_i and (x_i, y_i) denote the hue value and the position of object i, respectively. Thus we can build the relation between color and layout through the equation

$$\arg\min_{\{w_{ij}\}} \sum_{i=1}^{n} \left\| T_i - \sum_{j \in N_i} w_{ij} T_j \right\|^2, \quad \text{s.t.} \sum_{j=1}^{K} w_{ij} = 1, \qquad (2)$$

where N_i involves the neighborhood of object i, including the objects directly connected with i (object-object), and the objects sharing the same parent node with i (region-object) in the graph. The parameter n represents the number of objects in the given scene. Each dimension of T is normalized first to unify the metric. The minimization, which can be computed efficiently according to [27], results in a weight matrix $\{w_{ij}\}$ capturing the correlation of furniture layout and color distribution of a given scene.

4. STYLE TRANSFORMATION

Now given a reference image and a 3D scene of interior rooms, with the help of style guidelines learned above, we transform the style of the 3D room to be similar to that of the reference image. We first perform the layout transformation, followed by the color transformation process.

4.1 Layout Transformation

To perform layout transfer from a reference image to the input 3D scene, we need to establish object correspondence between the 3D scene and the image, which can be easily obtained based on the layout map containing semantic label information.

Given an object in the 3D scene which has a corresponding object in the reference image, we rearrange its location according to the arrangement of the corresponding object in image. The layout guidelines learned from the database are involved as constraints. Due to the different scales of the corresponding objects in the 3D scene and the image, the rearrangement may cause incompatibility in the 3D scene, e.g, penetration between adjacent objects. Therefore, our object rearrangement also involves the adjustment of orientation and accessibility. The layout transformation is formulated as the following energy minimization problem:

$$E_l = \alpha_1 E_1 + \alpha_2 E_2 + \alpha_3 E_3 + \alpha_4 E_4, \tag{3}$$

with

$$E_1 = \sum_{i \in \mathcal{R}} \left\| O_i - O_i^{img} \right\|^2 + \sum_{i \in \mathcal{S}-\mathcal{R}} \| O_i - T_{pl}(C_i) \|^2,$$
$$E_2 = \sum_{i \in \mathcal{S}} \| \theta_i - \theta_i' \|^2 + \sum_{\{i,j\} \in \mathcal{P}} \| \theta_{ij} - \theta_{ij}' \|^2,$$
$$E_3 = \sum_{i \in \mathcal{S}} \left\| dist_{wall}(O_i) - \frac{len(i)}{2} \right\|^2,$$
$$E_4 = \sum_{\{i,j\} \in \mathcal{P}} \left(\|O_i - O_j\| - (d_i + d_j) \right)^2,$$

where $\mathcal{S}$ denotes the set of objects in the entire scene, $\mathcal{R} \subseteq \mathcal{S}$ is the set of objects which has a corresponding counterpart in the reference image, and $\mathcal{P}$ is the set of object pairs with pairwise relationship.

The first term E_1 imposes the layout transfer from the reference image to the 3D scene for the corresponding objects, where O_i is the center of object i in the 3D scene and O_i^{img} is that of its corresponding counterpart in the reference image. For those 3D objects which have no correspondence in the reference image, their positions are determined by the category prior $T_{pl}(C)$. The term E_2 determines the orientation of each object, where θ_i represents the angle to the nearest wall, and θ_{ij} is the angle between two pairwise objects. Here we set θ_i' and θ_{ij}' to be zero by default, which means that the objects are parallel to the wall, or to its pairwise object. While users can edit the orientation of any object in the layout map (see Section 3.1 and Figure 3).

The term E_3 preserves the distance from an object to its nearest wall during the layout transfer. The notation $dist_{wall}(\cdot)$ computes the distance between the center of an object and its nearest wall, and $len(i)$ represents the length of the object i in the vertical direction to the nearest wall. That means objects are preferred to be close against the wall. The last term E_4 is the pairwise and accessibility term, which define the distance between object pair to make them accessible. We denote half of the diagonal length of the accessible bounding box as d_i for object i. In all our experiments, we set the weights $\alpha_1 = 15$, $\alpha_2 = 10$, $\alpha_3 = 1$ and $\alpha_4 = 1$, respectively.

4.2 Layout-guided Color Transformation

Color is another important factor of interior design, which is often highly related to furniture layout. Therefore, color transformation should be coupled with layout information. To this end, we propose layout-guided color transformation. In the input 3D room, each model has its texture maps. We perform color transformation by recoloring the color of the texture maps according to the color scheme of the reference

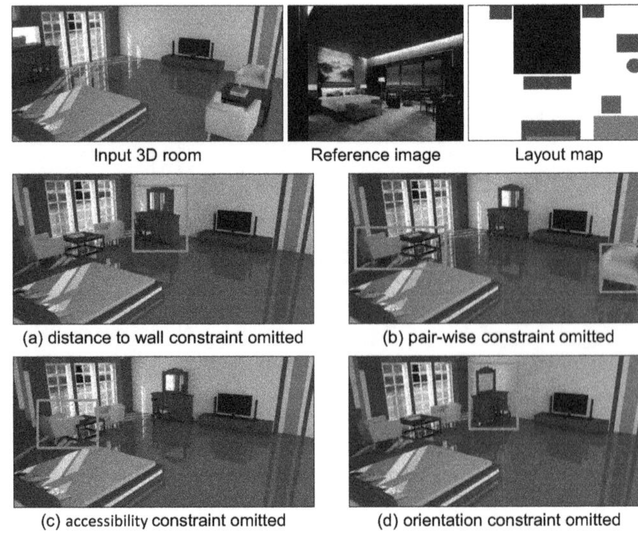

Figure 6: Influence of layout constraints. Without any one of these four constraints, the rearranged results are not reasonable.

image, based on the object correspondence between the image and the 3D room.

To achieve layout-guided color adjustment, we preserve the layout-color correlation learned from the reference image. Such adjustment can lead to more natural color scheme in the resulting 3D scene. For example, it may not be natural to color a furniture golden when its surrounding furnitures are all in silvery, but it may look more comfortable to color it to blue or green [1].

The color transformation is formulated as the following energy minimization problem:

$$E_c = \beta_1 E_1 + \beta_2 E_2 + \beta_3 E_3 + \beta_4 E_4, \tag{4}$$

with

$$E_1 = \sum_{i \in \mathcal{R}} \left\| h_i - h_i^{img} \right\|^2,$$
$$E_2 = \sum_{i \in \mathcal{R}} \left\| h_i - \sum_{j \in N_i} w_{ij} h_j \right\|^2,$$
$$E_3 = \sum_{i \in \mathcal{S}-\mathcal{R}} \left\| h_i - h_i^N \right\|^2,$$
$$E_4 = \sum_{i=1}^{e} \left\| h_i^l - H_i^{edge} \right\|^2,$$

where $\mathcal{S}$ and $\mathcal{R}$ share the same meanings with Eq. (3), h_i denotes the mean hue value of object i in 3D room and h_i^{img} that of its corresponding counterpart in the reference image.

E_1 imposes the color transfer from the reference image to the corresponding objects in the 3D room. Each object in 3D room will have similar color to its corresponding counterpart in the reference image. E_2 imposes layout-guided color adjustment. Specifically, during the 3D room coloring, we preserve the layout-color correlation encoded in the weight matrix $\{w_{ij}\}$ learned from the reference image through Eq. (2). If one object color is changed, other related objects will be changed simultaneously according to their

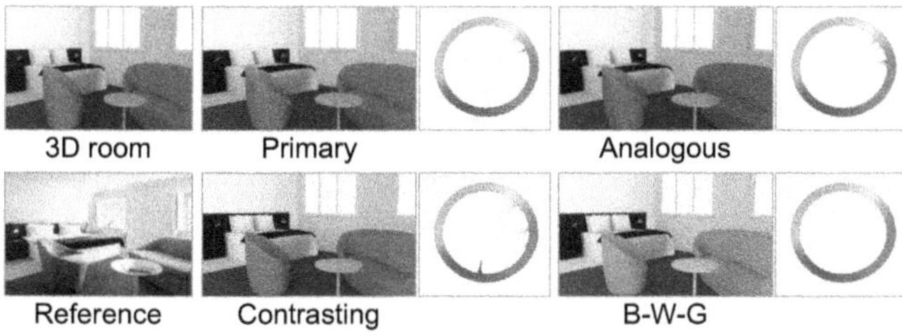

Figure 7: Influence of color schemes. Different recolor results from a same reference image with different hue templates. The first column is the 3D room transferred from the reference image. The most matched recolored result is obtained with contrasting color type.

relationship, leading to a reasonable color distribution of the scene.

For those objects which do not have corresponding counterparts in the reference image, the third energy term E_3 infers an appropriate color h_i by shifting their dominant hue value to match their neighborhoods, similar to [8]. Specifically, given an object i in the 3D scene, we search its k nearest neighbor objects which have corresponding counterparts in the reference image. We extract the dominant hue of these neighboring objects and change the mean hue value of object i to match that of its neighborhood. The symbol h_i^N denotes the dominant hue value of the neighborhood objects.

The term E_4 preserves the hue distribution of objects lying in the hue template of reference image. We identify which template the reference image belongs to (out of the seven hue templates as shown in Fig. 5). The template sector is rotated to cover hues of the reference image as many as possible. Then for each hue value of objects in 3D room, we find its nearest sector edge in template according to the arc length. We shift the farthest hue h^l to its corresponding sector edge H^{edge} of the template. The variable e denotes the number of sector edges in the template. Since the hue relationship is preserved in E_2, all the hues can be shifted into the template sector when h^l is shifted.

In all our experiments, we set the weights $\beta_1 = 5$, $\beta_2 = 1$, $\beta_3 = 1$, and $\beta_4 = 5$, respectively. The minimization problems in both Eq. (3) and Eq. (4) are solved using gradient descent method.

5. EXPERIMENTAL RESULTS

The experiments include three parts: the verification of our layout guidelines and color schemes, the results of image-based scene transformation, and user study evaluations.

5.1 Verification of Guidelines

Layout constraints. In Figure 6, we show the influence of our layout constraints. Each subfigure is a layout transformation result omitted one constraint. In (a), without the position constraint, the dresser is far from wall. In (b), without the pairwise constraint, one sofa is far away from the teapoy. In (c), without accessibility constraint, there is penetration between one sofa and the teapoy. In (d), without orientation constraint, the dresser has an incorrect orientation at its new location.

Color schemes. Figure 7 shows results that are obtained according to different color schemes for the same 3D scene. From this figure we can see that when given different color templates, different color decorated results are generated. Please note that the recolored 3D scene using the guideline "combination of complementary and contrasting colors" is more similar to the reference image. The reason is that the color scheme of the reference image is complementary color scheme, specifically the "X" type.

5.2 Scene Style Transformation Results

We present several style transformation results on bedroom and living room scenes.

Datasets. To test our proposed framework, we have collected 120 online images for bedroom scenes and 80 images for living room scenes to form the training dataset. The images were collected from Google image search. Each image was manually processed with a semantic segmentation and a layout map. The number of 3D indoor scenes collected from Trimble 3D Warehouse is 200, with 100 each for bedrooms and living rooms. The sizes of the mesh models for the 3D scene data range from 50K to 500K vertices.

Style transformation. Figures 8 and 9 show our style transformation results for bedroom and living room scenes, respectively. From left to right, we present the input 3D scenes, the reference images, the layout transformation results and the color transformation results. The furnitures in the input 3D scene are positioned arbitrarily. After layout transformation, the 3D scene has the similar layout to the corresponding reference image. Then we recolor the rearranged scene to make it have the same color scheme to that of the reference image. For example, according to the last row in Figure 8, we observe that in the transferred scenes, the dresser and cabinet are located at the right hand of the bed. Moreover, they are on each side of the door. They have similar locations as in the reference image.

We perform all the experiments on an Intel(R) Core 4 Duo 2.39GHz CPU machine with 4GB memory. For a typical style transformation task with 10 to 30 models in a 3D scene, the processing can be done within 3 seconds after generating the layout map.

5.3 User Study

We perform user study in three aspects, including comparison with stochastic method in layout transformation, the layout-color correlation, and the satisfiability measurement.

Comparison with stochastic sampling. Here we present comparison results between our method and the MCMC-type stochastic sampling method [34] to demonstrate the effectiveness and efficiency of our method. The results in this comparison involves only the layout transformation. Our goal is to change the scene's layout to be similar to that of the reference image while preserving placement rationality. To evaluate the effectiveness of the compared results, we resort to user judgement. We randomly selected 35 scene-reference image pairs. Twenty computer science postgraduates were invited to participate in the study and for each pair, they are asked which result of the two reflects the best layout transfer of the 3D scene according to the reference image. The informal study indicates that in 76.9% of the cases, our method was preferred. Moreover, with the same setting, our layout transformation method completes

Figure 8: Style transformation (both layout and color) results of bedroom scenes. Each row shows an example of a 3D bedroom altered by a reference image. The third column shows the layout transformation results which preserve the color styles of the input 3D room. The last column represents the recolored results which have similar color styles to that of the reference images. All results are rendered in the same view as the reference images. Note that lighting discrepancy between the reference images and rendered 3D scenes may result in perceived differences in colors.

within 3 seconds in average, while the stochastic method takes about 5 minutes. Figure 10 shows an example of the comparison results. In this figure, when using stochastic method, the writing desk and the TV cabinet are in the wrong position compared with that in the reference image, and the sofa and teapoy are not in group. While our method can do it better.

Layout-color correlation. In this experiment, we wish to verify the correlation between layout and color styles and that it is justifiable to perform color transformation after layout transformation. We randomly selected 65 pairs of input scenes and reference images to apply our style transformation algorithm. Two options are used: a) recoloring is applied before layout transformation and (b) recoloring is applied after layout transformation. To rank the goodness of the results, we again resort to user judgement. Twenty computer science graduates, all having normal color vision, participated in the user study. For each style transformation pair, final results from two options are shown, each in three different views with one view the same as that of the reference image. The participants did not know which result was generated with which method; they are asked to tell which result reflects the best style transformation from the reference image. The study reveals that in about 74% of the cases, the users preferred the recoloring results where color transformation was applied after layout transformation. This confirms with our original premise.

Satisfiability. Our motivation is to give user suggestion about style transformation. To justify how our system achieves this goal, we perform the experiment about users' satisfiability. 25 graduates, in different major, participated in this user study. Given the reference image and the input 3D scene, the participants are asked to give scores of how they are satisfied with the style transformation results, where 1 means not satisfied at all and 5 means very satisfied. We provide twenty pairs of input 3D scene and reference image. For each pair, both layout and color transformation

Figure 9: Style transformation results of living room scenes. Each row shows an example of a living room scene altered by a reference image.

Figure 10: Comparison with stochastic sampling in layout transformation.

results are presented. Users would give one score for layout transformation and one for color transformation. The average scores for layout and color transformation are 4.056 and 4.158 respectively, which demonstrate that user are satisfied with our results.

6. LIMITATIONS AND FUTURE WORK

We present a style transformation system to transform the layout and color styles of a 3D indoor scene according to a reference image. To the best of our knowledge, this is the first attempt at tackling this problem and as such, our current method is still limited in several aspects.

Limitations. Our color transformation scheme is only effective for objects having homogenous colors, not a mixture of many colors. In other words, if only one dominant color exists in one object, it can be transferred easily. However, when different parts of a object are in different colors, it has to be addressed by user interaction. Aside from conformation to the layout in the reference image, our object placement scheme does not take into account the full set of available layout guidelines. As a result, certain artifacts, e.g., cluttering of objects, may occur in the obtained layout output. Besides, the constraints such as accessibility of the doors and windows are considered in our system, but the positions of the doors and windows are predefined and fixed during transformation.

Future work. Aside from the technical limitations mentioned above, our current system only considers two particular styles and learns a simple correlation model between the styles. There are some other factors that we do not account for, e.g., the material, the texture, the light and shading. Extending the approach to handle more styles, and defining and applying more sophisticated joint models for style analysis and transformation are both interesting future avenues to pursue. An ultimate task may be to forego the identification of particular styles, but develop a learning framework that is capable of extracting generic and latent styles from training images and then applying them to general style transformation for 3D indoor scenes. Finally, how to best evaluate the style transformation results is a difficult question and we plan to look into that problem in the future work as well.

7. ACKNOWLEDGMENTS

In addition to the anonymous reviewers who provided insightful suggestions, we would like to thank Hao Zhang for his invaluable help in proof reading, and Han Zhang, Yufeng Tang, Feng Ding, Yi Liu, Yu Zhang for their help in experimentation. This work is supported in part by grants from NSFC (61325011) & (61421003), 863 Program (2013AA013801), SRFDP (20131102130002), and Open Funding of VR Lab (BUAA-VR-15KF-18).

8. REFERENCES

[1] ARTSPARX. http://www.artsparx.com/.

[2] J. Chen, Y. Han, X. Cao, and Q. Tian. Object coding on the semantic graph for scene classification. In *ACM Multimedia*, pages 493–496, 2013.

[3] K. Chen, Y.-K. Lai, Y.-X. Wu, R. Martin, and S.-M. Hu. Automatic semantic modeling of indoor scenes from low-quality RGB-D data using contextual information. *ACM Trans. Graph.*, 33(6):208:1–208:12, 2014.

[4] X. Chen, D. Zou, J. Li, X. Cao, Q. Zhao, and H. Zhang. Sparse dictionary learning for edit propagation of high-resolution images. In *CVPR*, pages 2854–2861, 2014.

[5] X. Chen, D. Zou, Q. Zhao, and P. Tan. Manifold preserving edit propagation. *ACM Trans. Graph.*, 31(6):132:1–7, 2012.

[6] W. Choi, Y.-W. Chao, C. Pantofaru, and S. Savarese. Understanding indoor scenes using 3d geometric phrases. In *CVPR*, pages 33–40, 2013.

[7] L. Chu, S. Jiang, S. Wang, Y. Zhang, and Q. Huang. Robust spatial consistency graph model for partial duplicate image retrieval. *IEEE TMM*, 15(8):1982–1996, 2013.

[8] D. Cohen-Or, O. Sorkine, R. Gal, T. Leyvand, and Y.-Q. Xu. Color harmonization. *ACM Trans. Graph.*, 25(3):624–630, 2006.

[9] M. Fisher, D. Ritchie, M. Savva, T. Funkhouser, and P. Hanrahan. Example-based synthesis of 3d object arrangements. *ACM Trans. Graph.*, 31(6):135:1–11, 2012.

[10] M. Fisher, M. Savva, and P. Hanrahan. Characterizing structural relationships in scenes using graph kernels. *ACM Trans. Graph.*, 30(4):34, 2011.

[11] T. Germer and M. Schwarz. Procedural arrangement of furniture for Real-Time walkthroughs. *Computer Graphics Forum*, 28(8):2068–2078, 2009.

[12] Y. Han, F. Wu, J. Shao, Q. Tian, and Y. Zhuang. Graph-guided sparse reconstruction for region tagging. In *CVPR*, pages 2981–2988, 2012.

[13] V. Hedau, D. Hoiem, and D. Forsyth. Recovering the spatial layout of cluttered rooms. In *ICCV*, pages 1849–1856, 2009.

[14] V. Hedau, D. Hoiem, and D. A. Forsyth. Recovering free space of indoor scenes from a single image. In *CVPR*, pages 2807–2814, 2012.

[15] A. Hertzmann, C. E. Jacobs, N. Oliver, B. Curless, and D. H. Salesin. Image analogies. In *SIGGRAPH*, pages 327–340, 2001.

[16] Y. M. Kim, N. J. Mitra, D.-M. Yan, and L. Guibas. Acquiring 3d indoor environments with variability and repetition. *ACM Trans. Graph.*, 31(6):138:1–138:11, 2012.

[17] H. Li, H. Zhang, Y. Wang, J. Cao, A. Shamir, and D. Cohen-or. Curve style analysis in a set of shapes. *Computer Graphics Forum*, 32(6):77–88, 2013.

[18] Q. Li, X. Chen, Y. Song, Y. Zhang, X. Jin, and Q. Zhao. Geodesic propagation for semantic labeling. *IEEE Trans. Image Process.*, 23(11):4812–4825, 2014.

[19] S. Liu, S. Yan, T. Zhang, C. Xu, J. Liu, and H. Lu. Weakly supervised graph propagation towards collective image parsing. *IEEE TMM*, 14(2):361–373, 2012.

[20] X. Liu, D. Zhao, J. Zhou, W. Gao, and H. Sun. Image interpolation via graph-based bayesian label propagation. 23(3):1084–1096, 2014.

[21] Y. Matsuda. *Color Design*. Asakura Shoten, 1995.

[22] P. Merrell, E. Schkufza, Z. Li, M. Agrawala, and V. Koltun. Interactive furniture layout using interior design guidelines. *ACM Trans. Graph.*, 30(4):87:1–87:10, 2011.

[23] L. Nan, K. Xie, and A. Sharf. A search-classify approach for cluttered indoor scene understanding. *ACM Trans. Graph.*, 31(6):137:1–137:10, 2012.

[24] L. Neumann, A. Nemcsics, and A. Neumann. Computational color harmony based on coloroid system. In *Computational Aesthetics*, pages 231–240, 2005.

[25] P. O'Donovan, A. Agarwala, and A. Hertzmann. Color compatibility from large datasets. *ACM Trans. Graph.*, 30(4):63:1–63:12, 2011.

[26] E. Reinhard, M. Ashikhmin, B. Gooch, and P. Shirley. Color transfer between images. *IEEE Comput. Graph. Appl.*, 21(5):34–41, 2001.

[27] S. Roweis and L. Saul. Nonlinear dimensionality reduction by locally linear embedding. *Science*, 290:2323–2326, 2000.

[28] S. Sanchez, O. L. Roux, H. Luga, and V. Gaildrat. Constraint-based 3d-object layout using a genetic algorithm. In *3IA*, 2003.

[29] T. Shao, W. Xu, K. Zhou, J. Wang, D. Li, and B. Guo. An interactive approach to semantic modeling of indoor scenes with an RGBD camera. *ACM Trans. Graph.*, 31(6):136:1–11, 2012.

[30] L. Wang, Y. Yu, K. Zhou, and B. Guo. Example-based hair geometry synthesis. *ACM Trans. Graph.*, 28(3):56:1–9, 2009.

[31] J. Xiao, T. Fang, P. Zhao, M. Lhuillier, and L. Quan. Image-based street-side city modeling. *ACM Trans. Graph.*, 28(5):114:1–114:12, 2009.

[32] K. Xu, H. Zheng, H. Zhang, D. Cohen-Or, L. Liu, and Y. Xiong. Photo-inspired model-driven 3d object modeling. *ACM Trans. Graph.*, 30(4):80:1–80:10, 2011.

[33] Y.-T. Yeh, L. Yang, M. Watson, N. D. Goodman, and P. Hanrahan. Synthesizing open worlds with constraints using locally annealed reversible jump MCMC. *ACM Trans. Graph.*, 31(4):56, 2012.

[34] L.-F. Yu, S. K. Yeung, C.-K. Tang, D. Terzopoulos, T. F. Chan, and S. Osher. Make it home: automatic optimization of furniture arrangement. *ACM Trans. Graph.*, 30(4):86, 2011.

[35] H. Zhang, J. Xiao, and L. Quan. Supervised label transfer for semantic segmentation of street scenes. In *ECCV*, pages 561–574, 2010.

[36] B. Zhou, X. Chen, Q. Fu, K. Guo, and P. Tan. Garment modeling from a single image. *Computer Graphics Forum*, 32(7):85–91, 2013.

Gradient-based 2D-to-3D Conversion for Soccer Videos

Kiana Calagari[2*] Mohamed Elgharib[1] Piotr Didyk[4] Alexandre Kaspar[3]
Wojciech Matusik[3] Mohamed Hefeeda[1]

[1]Qatar Computing Research Institute, HBKU, Doha, Qatar
[2]School of Computing Science, Simon Fraser University, Burnaby, BC, Canada
[3]Computer Science and Artificial Intelligence Laboratory, MIT, Cambridge, MA
[4]MMCI, Saarland University, Saarbrücken, Germany

ABSTRACT

A wide spread adoption of 3D videos and technologies is hindered by the lack of high-quality 3D content. One promising solution to address this problem is to use automated 2D-to-3D conversion. However, current conversion methods, while general, produce low-quality results with artifacts that are not acceptable to many viewers. We address this problem by showing how to construct a high-quality, domain-specific conversion method for soccer videos. We propose a novel, data-driven method that generates stereoscopic frames by transferring depth information from similar frames in a database of 3D stereoscopic videos. Creating a database of 3D stereoscopic videos with accurate depth is, however, very difficult. One of the key findings in this paper is showing that computer generated content in current sports computer games can be used to generate high-quality 3D video reference database for 2D-to-3D conversion methods. Once we retrieve similar 3D video frames, our technique transfers depth gradients to the target frame while respecting object boundaries. It then computes depth maps from the gradients, and generates the output stereoscopic video. We implement our method and validate it by conducting user-studies that evaluate depth perception and visual comfort of the converted 3D videos. We show that our method produces high-quality 3D videos that are almost indistinguishable from videos shot by stereo cameras. In addition, our method significantly outperforms the current state-of-the-art method. For example, up to 20% improvement in the perceived depth is achieved by our method, which translates to improving the mean opinion score from Good to Excellent.

Categories and Subject Descriptors

H.5.1 [**Information Interfaces and Presentation**]: Multimedia Information Systems—*video*

*This work was preformed while the author was an intern at Qatar Computing Research Institute, HBKU, Doha, Qatar.

MM'15, October 26–30, 2015, Brisbane, Australia.
© 2015 ACM. ISBN 978-1-4503-3459-4/15/10 ...$15.00.
DOI: http://dx.doi.org/10.1145/2733373.2806262.

Keywords

2D-to-3D conversion; Depth estimation; 3D video

1. INTRODUCTION

Stereoscopic 3D (S3D) movies are becoming popular with most of big productions being released in this format. However, in practice, most movies are shot in 2D and then they are upconverted to S3D by manually painting depth maps and rendering corresponding views. This process yields very good results but it is extremely costly and time-consuming. S3D production of live events is much harder. Manual upconversion is not possible. Shooting live events, such as soccer games, directly in stereo requires placing multiple stereo rigs in the stadium. This is challenging and it is rarely being attempted. Therefore, a high-quality, automated 2D-to-3D conversion method is highly desired for live events. Current automated conversion methods are lacking. Most of the methods are general – they can be applied to any video stream. However, the output is either marred with artifacts that are not acceptable to many viewers or the upconversion method is extremely conservative – adding only very little depth to the resulting video.

In this paper, we show how to develop high-quality automated 2D-to-3D conversion methods. Our approach is to develop a domain-specific upconversion instead of a general method. In particular, we propose a method for generating S3D soccer video. Our method is data-driven, relying on a reference database of S3D videos. This is similar to previous work [13, 11]; however, our key insight is that instead of relying on depth data computed using computer vision methods or acquired by depth sensors, we can use computer generated depth from current computer sports games for creating a synthetic 3D database. Since the video quality of current computer games has come close to that of real videos, our approach offers two advantages: 1) we obtain a diverse database of video frames to facilitate good matching with input video frames; and 2) for each video frame, we obtain an accurate depth map with perfect depth discontinuities.

Given a query image, we infer its depth based on similar images in the database and their depth maps. We propose to transfer the *depth gradients* (i.e., the rate of change in depth values along the x and y directions) from similar images in the synthetic database to the query image. Specifically, we divide a query into blocks and transfer the depth gradients from matching blocks that may belong to different frames in the synthetic database. This is quite different from previous approaches that use absolute depth over the whole frame [13, 11]. Our approach offers multiple advantages: (i) finer depth assignment to smaller regions/objects (e.g., players), (ii) much smaller database, as we match only small patches not whole frames (frames can have too many varieties), and (iii) more robustness to the (in)accuracy of similar images chosen as references, since we only use individual blocks in the depth calculation. After transferring the depth gradients, we recover the depth from these gradients by using Poisson reconstruction. Poisson reconstruction is a robust technique traditionally used to recover an image from its gradient information by solving a Poisson equation [18, 7]. In addition, to maintain clear player boundaries our method handles depth discontinuities by creating object masks and detecting object boundaries. We show the ability of handling a wide spectrum of soccer video shots, with different camera views, occlusion, close-ups, clutter and motion complexity.

We conduct extensive user studies with diverse video segments. We follow the ITU BT.2021 recommendations [6] in conducting these studies. The results show that: (i) our method produces 3D videos that are almost indistinguishable from videos originally shot in stereo, (ii) the perceived depth quality and visual comfort of videos produced by our method are rated Excellent by the subjects, most of the time, and (iii) our method significantly outperforms the state-of-the-art method [11].

The rest of this paper is organized as follows. Section 2 summarizes the related works in the literature. Section 3 provides an overview of the proposed system, while Section 4 provides the details. Section 5 presents our detailed evaluation, and Section 6 concludes the paper.

2. RELATED WORK

Over the last few years, applications for 3D media have extended far beyond cinema and have become a significant interest to many researchers. Liu et al. [15] discuss 3D cinematography principles and their importance even for non-cinema 3D content. Wu et al. [23] adapt 3D content quality for tele-immersive applications in real-time. Calagari et al. [9] propose a 3D streaming system with depth customization for a wide variety of viewing displays. Yang et al. [24] prioritize 3D content streaming in a tele-immersive environment based on the client viewing angle. While such systems propose useful 3D applications, the limited 3D content remains a main bottleneck for 3D technology. To tackle this issue many researchers have explored 2D-to-3D conversion techniques. However, previous methods are either semi-automatic [19, 26] or cannot handle complex motions [12, 21, 13, 10, 11]. There has not been a 2D-to-3D conversion technique for soccer capable of handling complex motions with variety of scene structures, to the best of our knowledge.

In 2D-to-3D conversion, an image or a sequence of images is augmented with the corresponding depth maps. Using this information stereo image pairs can be synthesized. Depth maps can be computed using traditional computer vision approaches such as structure from motion or depth from defocus. Rzeszutek et al. [19] estimate the background depth based on motion. Zhang et al. [26] propose a semi-automatic 2D-to-3D conversion system based on multiple depth cues including motion and defocus. A survey on automatic 2D-to-3D conversion techniques and depth cues can be found in [25]. Furthermore, strong assumptions are often made on the depth distribution within a given scene. For example, Ko et al. [12] classify shots into long or non-long, where long shots are assumed to have a large field view and a depth ramp is assigned to the whole image, and players are assigned a constant depth. Similarly Schnyder et al. [21] detect players and assign constant depth to them. This, however, generates the well-known 'card-board effect' where objects appear flat when viewed in stereo.

Data-driven methods provide an alternative way of synthesizing depth maps and the corresponding stereo views. Hoiem et al. [10] segment a scene into planar regions, and assign an orientation to each region. This method provides a relatively coarse depth estimation. Konrad et al. [13] infer depth for an input image based on a database of image and depth map pairs. Their work is designed for still images and assumes that images with similar gradient-based features tend to have a similar depth. For a query image, the most similar images from the database are found. The query image depth is estimated as the median over depths of the retrieved images. Karsch et al. [11] extended this approach to image sequences. They also use a large database of image and depth map pairs. For a query frame, they find the most similar images in the database and then warp the retrieved images to the query image. Finally, the warped depth maps are combined to estimate the final depth. The work in [11] is the closest to ours and we compare against it.

There are a few commercial products that provide automated 2D-to-3D conversion, sold as stand-alone boxes (e.g., JVC's IF-2D3D1 Stereoscopic Image Processor, 3D Bee), or software packages (e.g., DDD's TriDef 3D). While the details of these systems are not known, their depth quality is still an outstanding issue [25].

3. SYSTEM OVERVIEW

Fig. 3 shows an overview of our 2D-to-3D soccer video conversion system. Our technique infers depth from a database of synthetically generated depths. This database is collected from video games, which provides high-quality depth maps. We transfer the depth gradient field from the database and reconstruct depth using Poisson reconstruction. In order to maintain sharp and accurate object boundaries, we create object masks and modify the Poisson equation on object boundaries. Finally, the 2D frames and their estimated depth are used to render left and right stereo pairs, using the stereo-warping technique in [11]. In this technique a 2D frame is warped based on its estimated depth such that salient regions remain unmodified, while background areas are stretched to fill dis-occluded regions. In this section, we discuss our synthetic database and object mask creation. Sec. 4 discusses our depth estimation technique.

Synthetic Database: Many databases of RGBD (Red, Green, Blue and Depth) images [2, 1, 5] and videos [11, 3] have been created. The depth channel is acquired using time-of-flight imaging [20] or active stereo (e.g., using Microsoft Kinect). Despite current RGBD databases, none of them can be used for a high-quality 2D-to-3D conversion of sporting events. Acquiring depth maps for a sport event is challenging since depth data needs to be acquired in sunlight conditions in a highly dynamic environment.

In order to address this challenge, we propose to create a Synthetic RGBD (S-RGBD) database from video games, which have very high image quality and from which a large quantity of content can be easily generated. Such database can be used for data-driven 2D-to-3D conversion. We are inspired by the success of Microsoft Kinect Pose Estimation through training on a synthetic database [22]. In our case, we collect our S-RGBD data by extracting image and depth information from FIFA13 video game. We used PIX [4], a Microsoft Directx tool. PIX records all Directx commands called by an application. By re-running these commands it can render and save each of the recorded frames. In addition, PIX allows access to the depth buffer of each rendered frame. The resolution of each extracted frame is 1916×1054 with 10 fps. We extracted 16,500 2D+Depth frames from 40 different sequences. The sequences contain a wide variety of shots expected to occur in soccer matches, with a wide spectrum of camera views, motion complexity and color variation. Two of the 40 sequences are $6-7$ minutes each, containing a half time and designed to capture the common scenes throughout a full game. The remaining sequences are shorter, in the range of $15-60$ seconds, however they focus more on capturing less common events such as close-ups, behind the goal, zoomed on ground views, and so on. Our database includes different teams, stadiums, seasons and camera angles.

Creating Object Masks: In order to better handle depth discontinuities and have a sharp and clear depth on player boundaries, our approach delineates object boundaries by creating object masks. Without specifying object boundaries, the depth of players will be blended with the ground, which degrades the depth quality. To create these masks we automatically detect the objects by pre-processing each video sequence based on motion and appearance. Due to space limitations, we provide a brief description of this step. We propose two different object detection methods: one for close-ups, which are characterized by large player size and small playing area, and another for non close-ups, which have a large field view. Non close-up video segmentation relies on global features such as the playing field color. For these shots, we use a color-based approach to detect the playing field. We train a Gaussian Mixture Model (GMM) on samples collected from the playing field. For close-ups, we rely more on local features such as feature point trajectories [16]. We employ a matting-based approach [14] initialized with feature point trajectory segmentation. We then correct possible misclassification of the playing field using playing area detection.

4. GRADIENT-BASED CONVERSION

The core of our system is depth estimation from depth gradients; for an input 2D video, depth is inferred from our S-RGBD database. Fig. 1 outlines this process. For an examined 2D frame, we find the K nearest frames in our database. We create a matching image for the examined frame. This matching image is created block by block, where we find for each block in the examined frame the best matching block in the K candidate images. We then copy the depth gradients from the matched blocks to the examined frame. We finally reconstruct the depth from its copied gradients by solving a Poisson equation. We use object masks (Sec. 3) to ensure sharp depth discontinuities around object boundaries. We now discuss each step in more detail.

4.1 Block-based Matching

For each frame of the examined video we preform visual search on our S-RGBD database to identify the K ($= 10$ in our work) most similar frames. We use two main features for visual search: GIST [17] and Color. The former favors

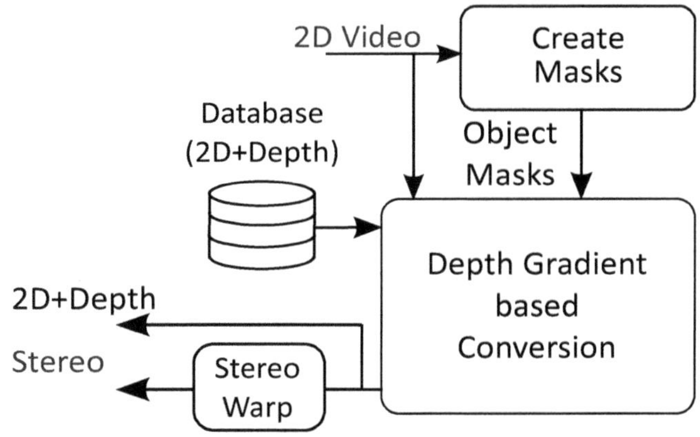

Figure 3: The proposed 2D-to-3D conversion system.

matches with overall similar structure, while the latter favors matches with overall similar color. For color, we use a normalized histogram of hue values, to which we apply a binary thresholding with value 0.1 to represent only dominant colors. The final image search descriptor is the concatenation of GIST and the color histogram. Fig. 2(b) shows 4 samples of the K candidates generated for the frame in Fig. 2(a).

We use the K candidate images to construct an image similar to the examined frame, which we call a matched image. The matched image provides a mapping between the candidates and the examined frame where each pixel in the examined frame is mapped to a corresponding candidate pixel. Karsch et al. [11] use a global approach for such mapping. They warp the candidates to construct images similar to the examined frame. While this approach is robust to local image artifacts, it requires strong similarity between the examined frame and the database. For instance, if the examined frame contains 4 players, the database needs to have an image with similar content. Instead, we use a local approach and construct similar images by block matching. This enables us to preform a more robust matching. For instance, we can have a good matching between two frames despite being shot from different angles, with different number of players and in different locations. This is shown in the example in Fig. 2 where the images in Fig. 2(b) were used to create the high-quality matched image (Fig. 2(c)), which may not have been possible using the global approach in [11]. Our local approach achieves good depth estimation without requiring a massive database size, which is a highly desirable advantage for our method since creating accurate 3D database is difficult as discussed in Sec. 3.

In order to construct the matching image, we first divide the examined frame into $n \times n$ blocks. In all our experiments, n is set to 9 pixels. For each block of the examined frame, we compare it against all possible blocks in the K candidate images. We choose the block with the smallest Euclidean distance as the corresponding block. The candidate images are re-sized to the examined frame size. For block descriptor we use SIFT concatenated with the average RGB value of the block. SIFT descriptor is calculated on a larger patch of size $5n \times 5n$, centered on the block center. This is to capture more representative texture. RGB values are normalized between 0-1. Fig. 2(c) shows the matched image using our block matching approach. Notice that the vertical advertisement boards are all matched to vertical blocks, the horizontal

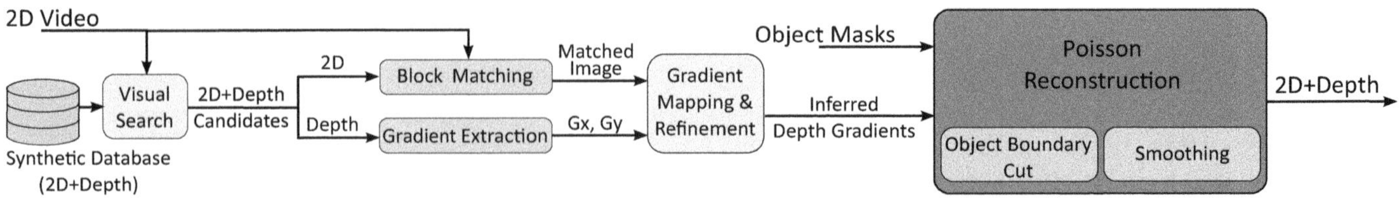

Figure 1: The main components of our data-driven depth estimation.

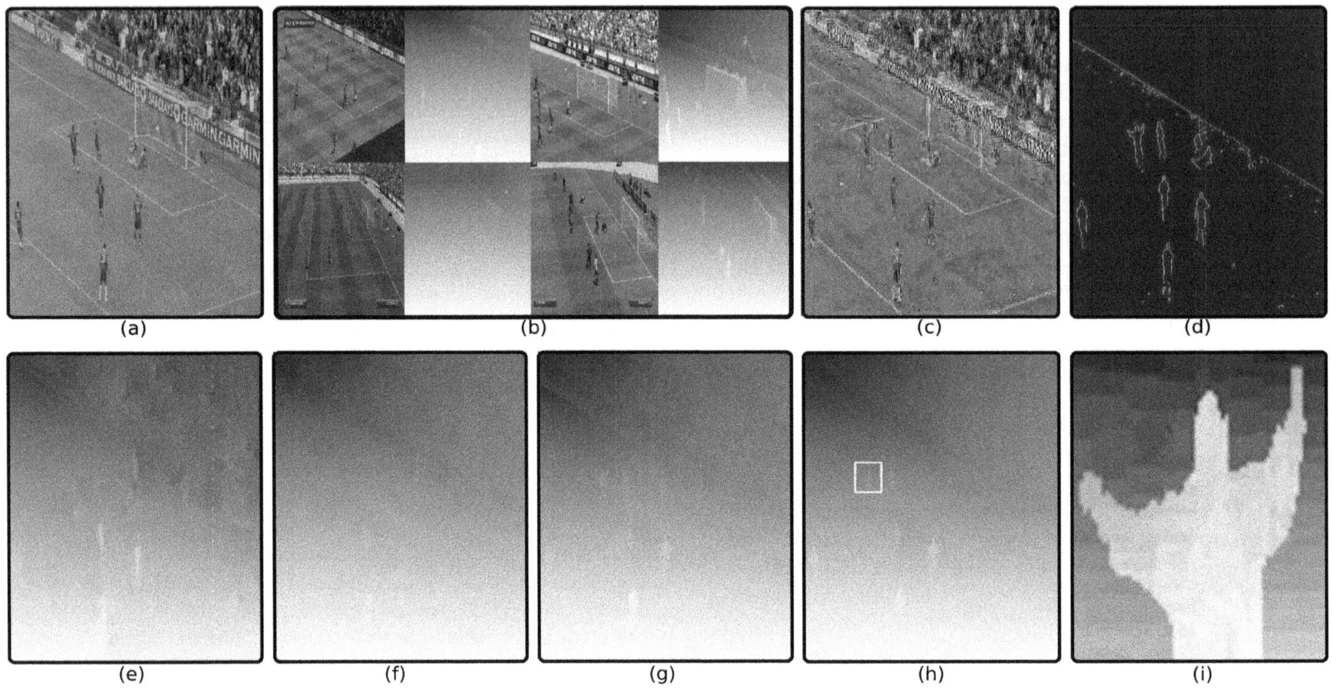

Figure 2: The effect of each step in our depth estimation technique: (a) Query, (b) A subset of its K candidates, (c) Created matched image, (d) Object boundary cuts, (e) Depth estimation using Poisson reconstruction, (f) Gradient refinement and Poisson reconstruction, (g) Depth with object boundary cuts, (h) Final depth estimation with smoothness, and (i) The zoomed and amplified version of the yellow block in h.

playing field is matched to the horizontal playing field, and the tilted audience are also matched to the audience.

4.2 Poisson Depth Estimation

Computing Depth Gradients: Given an input frame and its matched image from S-RGBD, we copy the corresponding depth gradients. We copy the first order spatial derivatives of both horizontal and vertical directions (G_x, G_y). Similar to image matching, we copy the gradients from the corresponding blocks in blocks of $n \times n$ pixels.

Poisson Reconstruction: We reconstruct the depth values from the copied depth gradients using the Poisson equation:

$$\Big(\frac{\partial^2}{\partial x^2} + \frac{\partial^2}{\partial y^2}\Big) D = \nabla \cdot G, \tag{1}$$

where $G = (G_x, G_y)$ is the copied depth gradient and D is the depth we seek to estimate. $\nabla \cdot G$ is the divergence of G:

$$\nabla \cdot G = \Big(\frac{\partial G_x}{\partial x} + \frac{\partial G_y}{\partial y}\Big). \tag{2}$$

In the discrete domain, Eq. (1) and Eq. (2) become Eq. (3) and Eq. (4), respectively:

$$\begin{aligned} D(i, j+1) + D(i, j-1) - 4D(i, j) + \\ D(i+1, j) + D(i-1, j) = \nabla \cdot G(i, j). \end{aligned} \tag{3}$$

$$\begin{aligned} \nabla \cdot G(i, j) = G_x(i, j) - G_x(i, j-1) + \\ G_y(i, j) - G_y(i-1, j). \end{aligned} \tag{4}$$

We formulate a solution in the form of $Ax = b$, where $b = \nabla \cdot G$, $x = D$, and A stores the coefficients of the Poisson equation (Eq. (3)). For an examined image of size $H \times W$, A is a square matrix with size $HW \times HW$, where each row corresponds to a pixel in the examined frame. Values in this row correspond to the coefficients of Eq. (3). Fig. 4(a) illustrates setting up A for a small sample image. Note that extra care should be given to the image boundary pixels as one or more neighbors do not exist. In this case, we update the value of $\nabla \cdot G$ by removing the terms in Eq. (4) that refer to non-existing pixels. Finally, given $Ax = b$, we solve for x. Fig. 2(e)) shows an example of the reconstructed depth (x).

While the overall depth structure is captured, some artifacts are present (see the lower right corner of Fig. 2(e)).

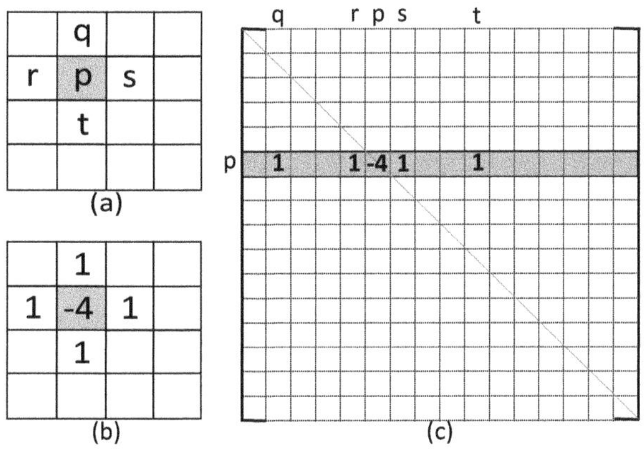

Figure 4: Construction of matrix A of the Poisson equation. (a) An example of 4×4 image showing a sample pixel p and its neighbors. (b) The coefficients of Eq. (3) for pixel p. (c) The non-zero values in matrix A for the row corresponding to pixel p.

Such artifacts are often generated due to inaccurate SIFT matching. For instance, in Fig. 4(c) some field blocks are matched to non-field areas. When a query block from a region which is expected to have smooth depth (such as the field) incorrectly matches a reference block that contains sharp changes in depth (such as the goal or player borders), the sharp gradients transferred from the reference block can introduce small artifacts in the resulting depth. To overcome this problem, before solving for x, we first reduce the large transferred gradients by gradient refinement, and use our object masks to impose depth discontinuities in the proper places instead. These two steps are described in the following.

Gradient Refinement: To reduce the errors introduced due to some incorrect block matchings, we refine depth gradients using:

$$\begin{aligned} G_x &= G_x \times \max(\, 1 - e^{(1 - \frac{1}{\alpha\,|G_x|})},\, 0\,) \\ G_y &= G_y \times \max(\, 1 - e^{(1 - \frac{1}{\alpha\,|G_y|})},\, 0\,) \end{aligned} \tag{5}$$

This maintains low gradients while exponentially reducing large gradients which may be incorrectly estimated. α is a parameter that configures the strength of refinement. A high α can corrupt correct gradients, while a low α can allow artifacts. For all our experiments, α is set to 60. Fig. 2(f) shows the effect of gradient refinement on depth estimation for 2(a). In comparison to 2(e), artifacts are removed and depth becomes smoother.

Object Boundary Cuts: Poisson reconstruction connects a pixel to all its neighbors. This causes most object boundaries to fade, especially after gradient refinement where strong gradients are eliminated (see Fig. 2(f)). To solve this problem, we allow depth discontinuities on object boundaries by modifying the Poisson equation there. Given object masks, we detect edges through the Canny edge detector (see Fig. 2(d)). We then disconnect pixels from the object boundaries by not allowing them to use an object boundary pixel as a valid neighbor. For each pixel neighboring a boundary pixel, we set the corresponding connection in A to 0 and update its $\nabla \cdot G$ value accordingly. Hence, pixels adjacent to object boundaries are treated similar to image boundary pixels.

Note that Poisson reconstruction becomes erroneous if a pixel or a group of pixels are completely disconnected from the rest of the image. This can cause isolated regions to go black and/or can affect depth estimation of the entire image. Hence, it is important to keep object boundary pixels connected to the rest of the image, while ensuring that the two sides of the boundary are still disconnected. To do so, we connect each boundary pixel to either its top or bottom pixel. If a boundary pixel is more similar to its top pixel in the query image, we connect it to the top pixel, otherwise we connect it to the bottom pixel. Thus, each boundary pixel becomes a part of its upper or lower area while keeping the two areas non accessible for each other. We also noticed that holes are frequently found inside the object masks due to segmentation errors. Applying edge detection on such masks will isolate these holes from the rest of the image. To avoid these problems, we fill such holes prior to edge detection. Note however that applying edge detection on the objects themselves will surround them by boundary pixels and hence isolate them from the background. To overcome this problem, we open each object boundary from its bottom (i.e., player legs). This allows Poisson to diffuse depth from the ground to the objects, producing a natural depth while avoiding isolations. Fig. 2(d) shows the object boundaries generated for 2(a). Fig. 2(g) shows the estimated depth when object boundaries are cut during Poisson reconstruction. In comparison to 2(f), the players now are more visible in 2(g).

Smoothness: We add smoothness constraints to the Poisson reconstruction by enforcing the higher-order depth derivatives to be zero. In continuous domain we set

$$\Big(\frac{\partial^4}{\partial x^4} + \frac{\partial^4}{\partial y^4}\Big)D = 0. \tag{6}$$

In the discrete domain this becomes:

$$\begin{aligned} &12D(i,j) + \\ &D(i,j+2) - 4D(i,j+1) - 4D(i,j-1) + D(i,j-2) + \\ &D(i+2,j) - 4D(i+1,j) - 4D(i-1,j) + D(i-2,j) = 0. \end{aligned} \tag{7}$$

We generate A_s, a smoothed version of A. We fill A_s with the new coefficients of Eq. (7). In order to preserve depth discontinuities around object boundaries, we apply the boundary cuts to the smoothness constraints. We then concatenate A with A_s and solve

$$\begin{bmatrix} A \\ \beta \cdot A_s \end{bmatrix} x = \begin{bmatrix} b \\ 0 \end{bmatrix}, \tag{8}$$

instead of the original $Ax = b$. β configures the amount of required smoothness. Large β can cause over-smoothness while a low β can generate weak smoothness. For all experiments, we set $\beta = 0.01$. Note that the effect of smoothness is different from that of gradient refinement. The latter is designed to remove sharp artifacts while keeping the rest of the image intact; smoothness adds a delicate touch to all depth textures. Using smoothness to remove sharp artifacts may cause over-smoothing. In addition, strong gradient refinement will damage essential gradients.

Creating Final Output: The estimated depth (x in Eq. (8)) is normalized between $(0, 255)$ and combined with the query image to form the converted 2D+Depth of our query video. Fig. 2(f) shows the final estimated depth for 2(a), including all steps with smoothness. Our depth is

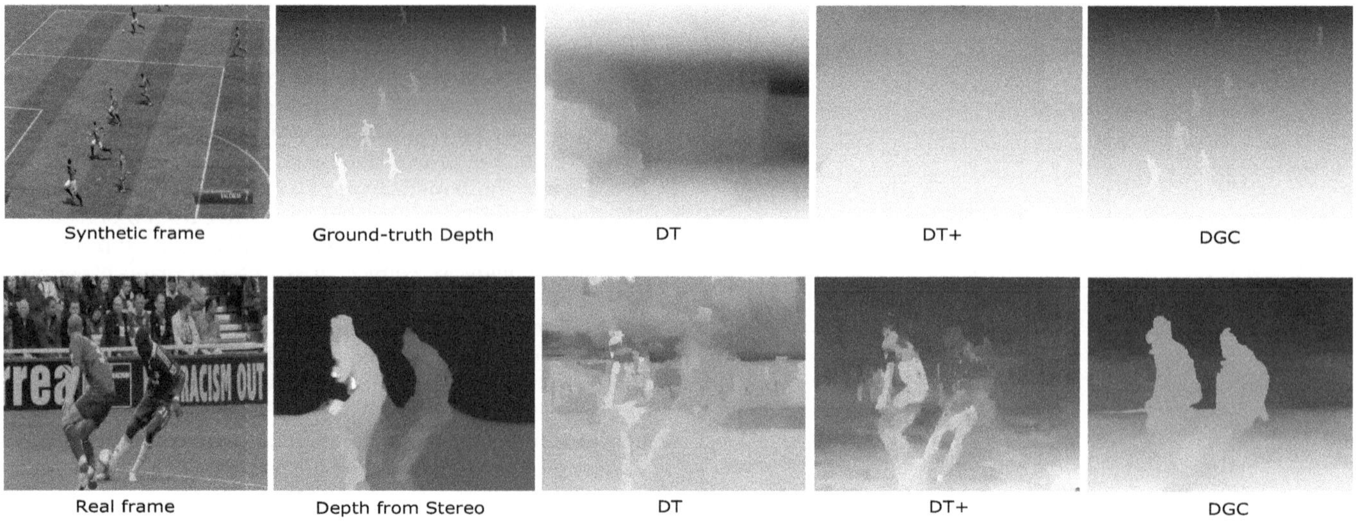

Figure 5: Top row: Frame 3 of a synthetic sequence. Bottom row: Frame 24 of a real sequence. We show the depth extracted using: Ground-truth/Stereo Correspondence [8], DT, DT+ and DGC. Our technique DGC best reassembles the Ground-truth/Stereo Correspondence in both sequences.

smooth and correctly reassembles the depth of the field, audience and players. We also note that our method does not produce 'card-board effect', where each player is assigned the same depth. To show this, we zoom on a depth block from one of the players in Fig. 2(h) and amplify it by normalizing the depth values of the block to the range of $(0, 255)$. Fig. 2(i) shows the zoomed and amplified version of the yellow marked block in 2(h). Note that the player in the marked block has different depth values for its different body parts. This example shows the strength of our gradient-based approach in estimating small depth details.

5. EVALUATION

We have implemented all components of the proposed system, which we refer to in the figures as DGC, short for Depth Gradient-based Conversion. We consider both synthetic and real sequences and we compare against ground-truth where available. We also compare against the closest system in the literature [11], which we refer to as DT (for Depth Transfer). In addition, we show the potential of applying our technique to other field sports, and the results show promising 2D-to-3D conversions for Tennis, Baseball, American Football and Field Hockey.

Note that our method has a few parameters, which are experimentally tuned once for all sequences. Specifically, K (the number of candidate images) is set to 10, n (the block size) is set to 9, α (the gradient refinement parameter) is set to 60, and β (the smoothness parameter) is set to 0.01.

5.1 Examined Methods

We compare our 2D-to-3D conversion technique (DGC) against several techniques.

DT: The Depth Transfer method [11] trained on its own database. Depth Transfer is the state-of-the-art data-driven 2D-to-3D conversion. Its database, MSR-V3D, contains videos captured by Microsoft Kinect, and is available online.

DT+: The Depth Transfer method trained on our synthetic database S-RGBD. As stated in [11], Kinect 2D+Depth capture is limited to indoor environments. This plus its erroneous measurements and poor resolution limits its ability to generate a large soccer database. For rigorous comparison, we compare our technique against Depth Transfer when trained with our soccer database.

Ground-truth Depth: Ground-truth depth maps are extracted from the FIFA13 video game through PIX [4] as described in Sec. 3. This, however, is only available for synthetic data.

Original 3D: The original side-by-side 3D video captured by 3D cameras. We compare results subjectively.

Depth from Stereo: In order to objectively compare results against Original 3D footage, we use stereo correspondence [8] to approximate ground-truth depth. Note that stereo correspondence techniques are not always accurate. However, our results show that sometimes they capture the overall structure of the depth and hence could be useful for objective analysis.

5.2 Test Sequences

We have eight real test sequences: four soccer and four non-soccer. We also have one synthetic soccer sequence (referred to as *Synth*).

Soccer: Our real soccer sequences contain extracted clips from original 3D-shot videos. These sequences are carefully created to include four main categories: long shots, bird's eye view, medium shots and close-ups. In long shots, the camera is placed at a high position and the entire field is almost visible (Fig. 7, top right-most). Bird's eye view is similar but the camera is placed above the field (Fig. 7, bottom right-most). Medium shots have the camera in a lower height, with a smaller field view (Fig. 7, bottom left-most). Close-ups have the camera zoomed on one or few players with a small field view (Fig. 7, top left-most).

Non-soccer: Our real non-soccer sequences contain clips from Tennis, Baseball, American Football and Field Hockey. We use these sequences to assess the potential application of our method on other field sports.

Synth: We extract 120 2D+Depth synthetic frames in a similar manner to S-RGBD creation. Given the ground-truth depth, we compare our technique objectively against DT and DT+ using this synthetic sequence.

5.3 Objective Experiments

We preform objective experiments on both real and synthetic sequences to measure the quality of our depth maps. Fig. 5 (top) shows a frame of the synthetic sequence and its ground-truth depth followed by its estimated depth using DT, DT+ and our DGC. Note that all depth maps are normalized to the range of $(0 - 255)$. DT generates largely erroneous measurements as MSR-V3D hardly resembles soccer data. DT+ generates significantly better results as being trained on our database. Yet most players are not detected. Our technique DGC detects players, generates smooth results and best resembles ground-truth. Fig. 6 shows the Mean Absolute Error (MAE) against ground-truth for the whole 120 frames of **Synth**. The figure shows that our method produces much lower MAE than DT and DT+.

Objective analysis on real sequences is challenging due to the absence of ground-truth depth. In [11], the authors used Kinect depth as ground-truth. However, Kinect is not capable of capturing depth information in outdoor environments and hence it cannot generate ground-truth estimates for soccer matches. Instead, we follow a different approach. Given a soccer sequence shot in 3D, we use stereo correspondence [8] to approximate the ground-truth depth-map. We then compare it against the depth estimated from 2D-to-3D conversion. Fig. 5 (bottom) shows a frame from one of the most challenging soccer test sequences and its extracted depth using stereo correspondence. While far from perfect, the overall depth structure is present and hence can be exploited to infer how good the converted depth is. In Fig. 5 (bottom), we show the estimated depth using DT, DT+ and our DGC. Our technique DGC best reassembles ground-truth. This is also captured objectively over a range of 100 frames, where DGC reduces MAE up to 19% and 86% compared to DT and DT+ respectively. Figure is omitted due to space limitations.

In addition, we performed an experiment to investigate the importance of the synthetic database size. First, we created a synthetic sequence using 120 frames from a wide variety of shots that can occur in soccer matches. We examined six database sizes, 1000, 2000, 4000, 8000, 13000 and 16000 images. Results (figure is omitted due to space limitations) showed that up to a size of 8,000, the performance fluctuates around an MAE of 30, due to the absence of big enough data. However, there is a boost in performance starting from 13,000 images which reduces MAE to around 20. The performance stabilizes around 16,000 images in the database. Hence, we used a database of 16,500 images in our evaluation.

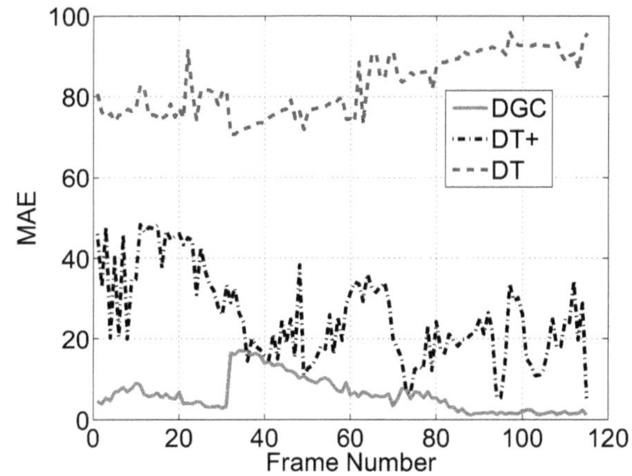

Figure 6: An objective comparison between our method DGC and the closest method in the literature DT, and its extension DT+ on a synthetic soccer sequence.

5.4 Subjective Experiments

We assess the 3D visual perception through several subjective experiments. We compare our technique against DT+ and the original 3D.

5.4.1 Setup

We conduct subjective experiments according to the ITU BT.2021 recommendations [6], which suggests three primary perceptual dimensions for 3D video assessment: picture quality, depth quality and visual (dis)comfort. Picture quality is mainly affected by encoding and/or transmission. Depth quality measures the amount of perceived depth, and visual discomfort measures any form of physiological unpleasantness due to 3D perception, i.e., fatigue, eye-strain, head-ache, and so on. Such discomforts often occur due to 3D artifacts, depth alteration, comfort zone violations and/or cross talk. In our experiments, we measure depth quality and visual comfort. We do not measure picture quality because we do not change any compression or encoding parameters, nor do we transmit the sequences.

Each of our test sequences has a duration between $10 - 15$ seconds according to the ITU recommendations. We display sequences on a 55" Philips TV-set with passive polarized glasses, in low lighting conditions. The viewing distance was around $2\,m$ for 1920×1080 resolution videos and around $3\,m$ for 1280×720 videos according to the ITU recommendations. Fifteen subjects took part in the subjective experiments. They were all computer science students and researchers. Their stereoscopic vision was tested prior to the experiment using static and dynamic random dot stereograms. Prior to the actual experiments, subjects went through a stabilization phase. They rated 4 sequences representative of different 3D quality, from best to worst. Those 4 sequences were not included in the actual test. This step stabilized subjects expectations and made them familiar with the rating protocol. We asked subjects to clarify all their questions and ensure their full understanding of the experimental procedure.

5.4.2 Evaluation of our Technique

We evaluate our 2D-to-3D conversion by measuring the average subject satisfaction when observing our converted sequences. We examine the 4 soccer and the 4 non-soccer sequences. We use the single-stimulus (SS) method of the ITU recommendations to assess depth quality and visual comfort. The sequences are shown to subjects in random order. Each sequence is $10-15$ *sec* and is preceded by a 5 *sec* mid-grey field indicating the coded name of the sequence, followed by a 10 *sec* mid-grey field asking subjects to vote. We use the standard ITU continuous scale to rate depth quality and comfort. The depth quality labels are marked on the continuous scale, and are Excellent, Good, Fair, Poor, and Bad, while the comfort labels are Very Comfortable, Comfortable, Mildly Uncomfortable, Uncomfortable, and Extremely Uncomfortable. Subjects were asked to mark their scores on these continuous scales. We then mapped

Figure 7: Depth estimation for different soccer sequences using our method. Our method handles a wide variety of shots including Close-ups (e.g., top, left-most), Medium Shots (e.g., bottom, left-most), Bird's Eye View (e.g., bottom, right-most) and Long Shots (e.g., top, right-most).

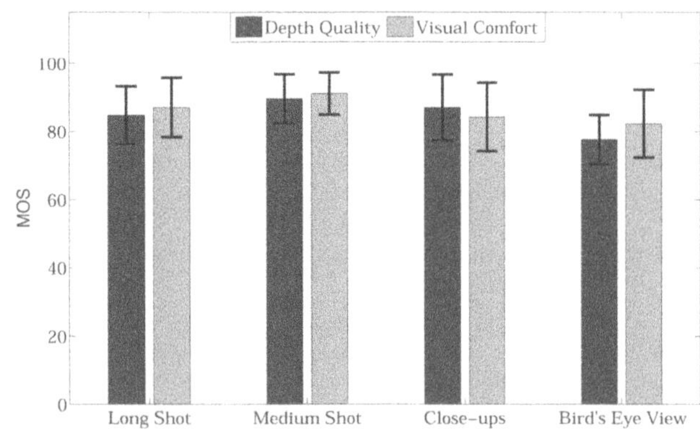

Figure 8: Mean opinion scores of depth perception and visual comfort for different types of soccer scenes.

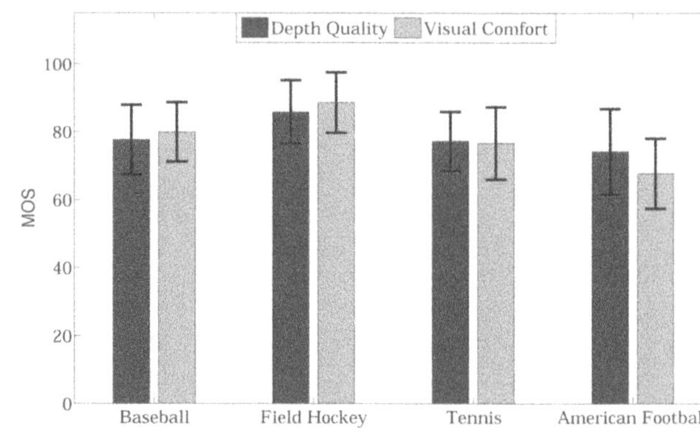

Figure 9: Mean opinion scores of depth perception and visual comfort for different non-soccer field sports.

their marks to integer values between 0-100 and calculated the mean opinion score (MOS).

Fig. 8 shows the MOS for the soccer sequences. In the four soccer sequences most subjects rated DGC in the Excellent range. Fig. 7 shows some of the estimated depth images. Note how we can handle a wide variety of video shots, including different camera views and clutter.

Fig. 9 shows the MOS for the non-soccer sequences. Field Hockey scored the highest as it resembles soccer the most. American Football scored the lowest, however. While some subjects reported very good depth, others reported the difficulty of depth perception due to the high dynamic environment of American Football with strong occlusions and clutter. Those subjects also reported a Mild Discomfort for the same reasons. It is important to note that the results on non-soccer are only meant to show the *potential* of our method, as we actually used the soccer database to convert them. In the future, we will create more diverse database for different sports.

5.4.3 Comparison against Original 3D

We compare our 2D-to-3D conversion against original 3D videos shot using stereo cameras. We use the Double Stimulus Continuous Quality Scale (DSCQS) method of the ITU recommendations for this experiment. Based on DSCQS, subjects view each pair of sequences (our created 3D and original 3D) at least twice before voting so as to assess their differences properly. The sequences are shown in random order without the subjects knowing which is original and which is converted. The subjects were asked to rate both sequences for depth quality and comfort using the standard ITU continuous scale. We then mapped their marks to integer values between 0-100 and calculated the Difference Opinion Score (= score for DGC - score for original 3D). Finally we calculated the mean of the difference opinion scores (DMOS).

A DMOS of zero implies that our converted 3D is judged the same as the original 3D, while a negative DMOS implies our 3D has a lower depth perception/comfort than the original 3D. Fig. 11 shows the DMOS of each of the soccer sequences for both depth quality and visual comfort. Our conversion is comparable to the original 3D, especially in long shots which account for around 70% of a full soccer game [9]. It is interesting to note that some subjects found our conversion more comfortable than the original 3D. They reported that the popping out effect in original 3D was sometimes causing discomfort.

5.4.4 Comparison against State-of-the-Art

We compare our 3D conversion against Depth Transfer DT+ [11]. As in the previous experiments, we use the DSCQS evaluation protocol and calculate DMOS for both depth qual-

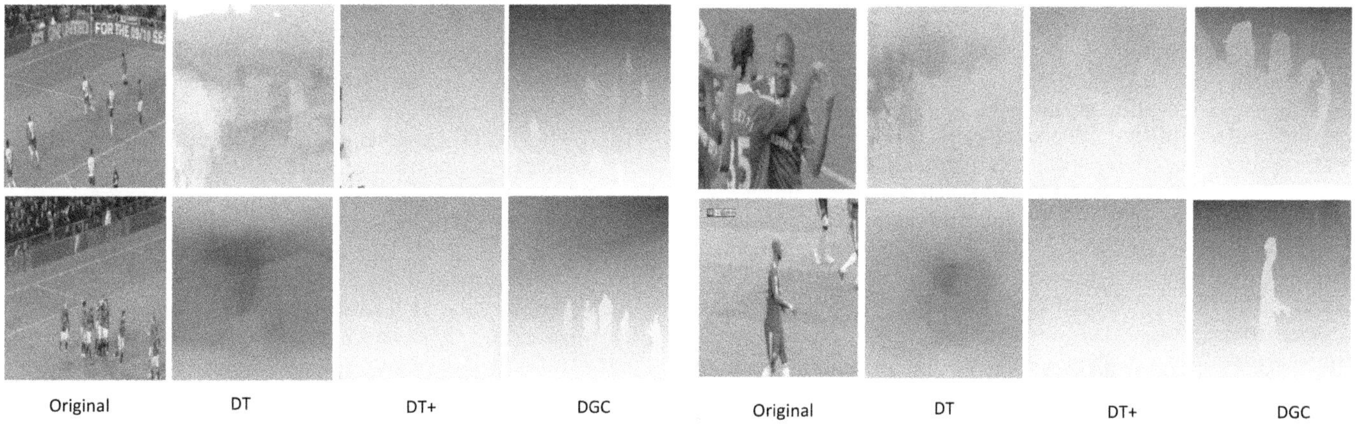

Figure 10: Depth estimation for different sequences using (from left): DT, DT+ and our method DGC. DT generates erroneous estimates, DT+ generates noisy measurements and does not detect players. Our technique outperforms both approaches.

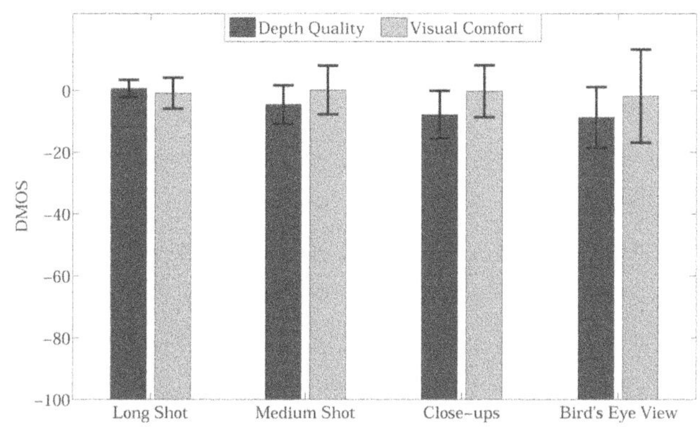

Figure 11: Difference mean opinion score (DMOS) between our converted sequences and the original 3D. Zero implies that our converted sequence is the same as the original 3D.

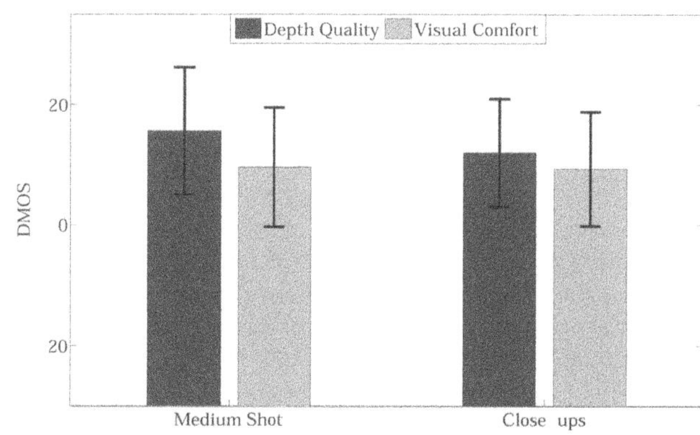

Figure 12: Difference mean opinion score (DMOS) between our converted sequences and Depth Transfer DT+. Positive DMOS means that our technique is preferred over DT+.

ity and visual comfort. We examined the most challenging soccer sequences, close-up and medium shots. Their wide variety of camera angles, complex motion, clutter and occlusion makes them the most challenging sequences for 2D-to-3D conversion. Fig. 12 shows the DMOS of the close-up and medium shot against DT+. Our technique outperforms DT+ by an average of 15 points in medium shots and 12 points in close-ups. In addition, all 15 subjects rated our technique higher or equal to DT+ and the differences reported are statistically significant (p-value < 0.05). Fig. 10 shows some extracted depth maps for DT, DT+ and our DGC. Note that the original implementation of Depth Transfer is DT and this is much worse than DT+ (see Fig. 10). Furthermore, in addition to the lower subjective scores of DT+, their depth is sometimes very noisy (see Fig. 10 and Fig. 5). This could cause eye-strain on the long term.

5.5 Computational Complexity

We measure the running time for DGC and DT+ averaged over 545 close-up frames and 1,726 non close-up frames. The spatial resolution is 960×1080 pixels. DGC takes 3.53 min/frame for close-ups and 1.86 min/frame for non close-ups. The average processing time for DT+ is 15.2 min/frame, which is slower than our technique in both close-ups and non close-ups. DGC requires more time for close-ups due to the more expensive mask creation step. As non close-ups can account for up to 95% of a soccer game [9], we can benefit from the faster non close-up processing. Nevertheless, we cannot ignore close-ups as they often contain rich depth information. Future efforts for improving computational complexity can focus on spatio-temporal multi-resolution schemes for video processing. All numbers are reported from processing on a server with six processors Intel Xeon CPU E5-2650 0 @2.00 GHz, with 8 cores, with a total of 264 GB RAM and 86 GB Cache.

6. CONCLUSIONS AND FUTURE WORK

We presented a 2D-to-3D video conversion method for soccer. Prior methods cannot handle the wide variety of scenes and motion complexities present in soccer matches. Our method is based on transferring depth gradients from a synthetic database and estimating depth through Poisson reconstruction. We implemented the proposed method and evaluated it using real and synthetic sequences. The results show that our method can handle a wide spectrum of video shots present in soccer games, including different camera views, motion complexity, occlusion, clutter and different colors. Participants in our subjective studies rated our created 3D videos Excellent, most of the time. Experimental results also show that our method outperforms state-of-the-art objectively and subjectively, on both real and synthetic sequences.

This paper contributes three *key findings* that can impact the area of 2D-to-3D video conversion, and potentially 3D video processing in general. First, domain-specific conversion can provide much better results than general methods. Second, transferring depth gradient on block basis not only produces smooth natural depth, but it also reduces the size of the required reference database. Third, synthetic databases created from computer-generated content can easily provide large, diverse, and accurate texture and depth references for various 3D video processing applications.

This work can be extended in multiple directions. For example, converting videos of different sports may require creating larger synthetic databases.

7. ACKNOWLEDGMENTS

This research was supported by the QCRI-CSAIL partnership and by the NSF grant IIS-1111415.

8. REFERENCES

[1] Berkeley 3-D object dataset. `http://kinectdata.com/`.

[2] Make3D. `http://make3d.cs.cornell.edu/data.html`.

[3] NYU depth dataset v2. `http://cs.nyu.edu/~silberman/datasets/nyu_depth_v2.html`.

[4] Performance Invistigator for Xbox (PIX). `https://msdn.microsoft.com/en-us/library/windows/desktop/ee663275%28v=vs.85%29.aspx`.

[5] RGB-D object dataset. `http://rgbd-dataset.cs.washington.edu/`.

[6] ITU-R BT.2021, Subjective methods for the assessment of stereoscopic 3DTV systems. Geneva, Switzerland, November 2012. International Telecommunication Union.

[7] P. Bhat, B. Curless, M. Cohen, and C. Zitnick. Fourier analysis of the 2D screened poisson equation for gradient domain problems. In *Proc. of European Conference on Computer Vision (ECCV'08)*, pages 114–128. Marseille, France, October 2008.

[8] T. Brox, A. Bruhn, N. Papenberg, and J. Weickert. High accuracy optical flow estimation based on a theory for warping. In *Proc. of European Conference on Computer Vision (ECCV'04)*, pages 25–36, Prague, Czech Republic, May 2004.

[9] K. Calagari, K. Templin, T. Elgamal, K. Diab, P. Didyk, W. Matusik, and M. Hefeeda. Anahita: A System for 3D Video Streaming with Depth Customization. In *Proc. of ACM Multimedia (MM'14)*, pages 337–346, Orlando, Fl, November 2014.

[10] D. Hoiem, A. A. Efros, and M. Hebert. Automatic photo pop-up. *ACM Transactions on Graphics*, 24(3):577–584, 2005.

[11] K. Karsch, C. Liu, and S. B. Kang. Depth transfer: Depth extraction from video using non-parametric sampling. *IEEE Transactions on Pattern Analysis and Machine Intelligence*, 36(11):2144–2158, 2014.

[12] J. Ko. 2D-to-3D Stereoscopic Conversion: Depth Estimation in 2D Images and Soccer Videos. Master's thesis, Korea Advanced Institution of Science and Technology (KAIST), 2008.

[13] J. Konrad, M. Wang, P. Ishwar, C. Wu, and D. Mukherjee. Learning-based, automatic 2D-to-3D image and video conversion. *IEEE Transactions on Image Processing*, 22(9):3485–3496, 2013.

[14] A. Levin, D. Lischinski, and Y. Weiss. A closed-form solution to natural image matting. *IEEE Transactions on Pattern Analysis and Machine Intelligence*, 30(2):228–242, 2008.

[15] C.-W. Liu, T.-H. Huang, M.-H. Chang, K.-Y. Lee, C.-K. Liang, and Y.-Y. Chuang. 3D cinematography principles and their applications to stereoscopic media processing. In *Proc. of ACM Multimedia Conference (MM'11)*, pages 253–262, Scottsdale, AZ, November 2011.

[16] P. Ochs, J. Malik, and T. Brox. Segmentation of moving objects by long term video analysis. *IEEE Transactions on Pattern Analysis and Machine Intelligence*, 36(6):1187–1200, 2014.

[17] A. Oliva and A. Torralba. Modeling the shape of the scene: a holistic representation of the spatial envelope. *International Journal of Computer Vision*, 42(3):145–175, 2001.

[18] P. Pérez, M. Gangnet, and A. Blake. Poisson image editing. *ACM Transactions on Graphics*, 22:313–318, 2003.

[19] R. Rzeszutek, R. Phan, and D. Androutsos. Depth estimation for semi-automatic 2D to 3D conversion. In *Proc. of ACM Multimedia Conference (MM'12)*, pages 817–820, Nara, Japan, October 2012.

[20] A. Saxena, S. H. Chung, and A. Y. Ng. Learning depth from single monocular images. In *Proc. of Advances in Neural Information Processing Systems (NIPS'05)*, pages 1161–1168, Vancouver, Canada, December 2005.

[21] L. Schnyder, O. Wang, and A. Smolic. 2D to 3D conversion of sports content using panoramas. In *Proc. of IEEE Conference on Image Processing (ICIP'11)*, pages 1961–1964, Brussels, Belgium, September 2011.

[22] J. Shotton, A. Fitzgibbon, M. Cook, T. Sharp, M. Finocchio, R. Moore, A. Kipman, and A. Blake. Real-time human pose recognition in parts from single depth images. In *Proc. of IEEE Conference on Computer Vision and Pattern Recognition (CVPR'11)*, pages 1297–1304, Providence, RI, June 2011.

[23] W. Wu, A. Arefin, G. Kurillo, P. Agarwal, K. Nahrstedt, and R. Bajcsy. Color-plus-depth level-of-detail in 3D tele-immersive video: A psychophysical approach. In *Proc. of ACM Multimedia Conference (MM'11)*, pages 13–22, Scottsdale, Arizona, November 2011.

[24] Z. Yang, W. Wu, K. Nahrstedt, G. Kurillo, and R. Bajcsy. Viewcast: View dissemination and management for multi-party 3D tele-immersive environments. In *Proc. of ACM Multimedia Conference (MM'07)*, pages 882–891, Augsburg, Bavaria, Germany, September 2007.

[25] L. Zhang, C. Vázquez, and S. Knorr. 3D-TV content creation: automatic 2D-to-3D video conversion. *IEEE Transactions on Broadcasting*, 57(2):372–383, 2011.

[26] Z. Zhang, C. Zhou, B. Xin, Y. Wang, and W. Gao. An interactive system of stereoscopic video conversion. In *Proc. of ACM Multimedia Conference (MM'12)*, pages 149–158, Nara, Japan, October 2012.

Ubii: Towards Seamless Interaction between Digital and Physical Worlds

Zhanpeng Huang Weikai Li Pan Hui
HKUST-DT System and Media Laboratory
Hong Kong University of Science and Technology, Hong Kong, China
{soaroc, weikaili, panhui}@ust.hk

ABSTRACT

We present Ubii (**Ubi**quitous **i**nterface and **i**nteraction), an interface system that aims to expand people's perception and interaction from the digital space to the physical world. The centralized user interface is broken into pieces woven in the domain environment. Augmented user interface is paired to the physical objects, where physical and digital presentations are displayed in the same context. The augmented interface and physical affordance respond as one control to provide seamless interaction. By connecting digital interface with physical objects, the system presents a nearby embodiment to afford users sense of awareness to interact with domain objects. Integrated on wearable devices as Google Glass, a less intrusive and more convenient interaction is afforded. Our research illustrates the great potential of direct mapping of interaction between digital interfaces and physical affordance by converging wearable devices and augmented reality (AR) technology.

Categories and Subject Descriptors

H.5.m. [**Information Interfaces and Presentation (e.g. HCI)**]: Augmented and Virtual Realities

General Terms

Design, Human Factor

Keywords

Physical affordance; augmented reality; wearable device; user interface; freehand interaction

Figure 1: Ubii enables users to perform in-situ interactions with physical objects using pinch gestures. Users are able to 1) copy documents between computers, 2) print a document with a printer, 3)share documents on an architecture partition, and 4) display documents on a projector screen by picking, dragging, and dropping AR overlays aligned with① computers, ② printers, ③ architecture partitions, and ④ projector screens at a distance without physical touch.

1. INTRODUCTION

In the past thirty years, we have relied primarily on screen-based Graphical User Interface (GUI) to interact with digital world. No matter whether the screen is placed on a desk (e.g., PC screen), held on a hand (e.g., mobile phone screen), or displayed on a wall (e.g., projection screen), it has cultivated a predominantly visual paradigm of human-computer interaction [36]. However, traditional centralized GUI displays all information in the foreground. The interaction is separated from the physical world that we live in and interact with. It cannot leverage the rich senses and skills that we have acquired from the lifetime interaction with the physical environment [20].

Efforts have been focused on developing direct interaction between physical and digital worlds. As physical objects appeal to be more of our senses, they are redesigned as interaction metaphors. Architectural partition [20], physical props [15], mobile devices [6], and human body [13] are used to afford tangible interaction at a distance. However, physical objects as manipulation metaphor introduces intrusion to user interaction. Particularly, conventional user interface is designed to be irrelevant to the physical affordance of underlying objects. Users have to memorize manipulations like traditional GUI interaction.

As a new interface straddling the real and the digital, AR bridges the gaps between physical and virtual worlds [18]. It supports a sense of shared presence and communal social space. AR has been widely used to help users access additional information for a task without getting distract-

MM'15, October 26–30, 2015, Brisbane, Australia.

ACM 978-1-4503-3459-4/15/10 ...$15.00.
DOI: http://dx.doi.org/10.1145/2733373.2806266.

ed from the task [16][34]. Another baseline leverages AR to provide 3D menu interaction in current view of the real world [24][30]. These works generate egocentric virtual user interface in front of current view, neither breaking of traditional centralized paradigm nor able to interact with physical objects.

Inspired by Weiser's argument that computational services should be delivered through different devices whose design and location are tailored to support a particular task or set of tasks [38], we designed Ubii, a ubiquitous AR-based system to pair tailored interface to the physical affordance of objects. Ubii breaks traditional centralized user interface into individual pieces aligned with the physical objects. It is a directly mapped interface enabling users to perform insitu interactions with the physical objects at a distance. As illustrated in Figure 1, users are able to manipulate physical objects including computers, projector screens, printers, and architecture partitions to complete tasks such as document copy, printing, sharing, and projection display. Individual AR menu overlays are aligned with physical objects to present their physical affordance. Developed on Google Glass, Ubii enables gesture-based freehand interaction with much less intrusion and more convenience.

2. RELATED WORKS

Ubii is built on several technologies including interaction at a distance, freehand interaction, and AR menu.

2.1 Interaction at a distance

Early systems such as PointRight [21] and Perspective Cursor [27] allow distant pointer motion across independently-driven display surfaces that are not organized in a single plane. The systems requires indirecting local input and complicated setups. Other works [39] [25] overcome the problems using absolute pointing techniques, but require additional pointing devices. In these methods motion errors are amplified as distance increases.

Mobile devices have been widely used as physical interface to provide foundation of new interaction paradigm [1]. The relative pointing on mobile devices screen is transferred to distant screens to reduce interaction distance. The Point & Shoot [2] technique employs visual codes to set up an absolute coordinate system for objects selection with mobile phones. To create a self-contained system without fiducial markers, Boring et al. leveraged preformed content arrangement to determine the spatial relationship between the mobile device and display screen [5]. Chang and Li [10] allowed arbitrary content arrangement by matching the captured images with content on display screens. The method does not support continuous interaction as content snapshot are required in advance for further analysis.

Some works support fluent interaction through video stream captured by built-in cameras on mobile devices. Device screens act as portholes of physical world, through which users can interact with the physical objects. The world in miniature metaphor facilitates interaction at a distance. Touch Projector [6] affords bimanual interaction with one hand holding a mobile phone and the other hand interacting with remote screens through live video on the mobile phone. Virtual Projection [3] uses mobile phone as a controllable projection metaphor to interact with content on stationary displays. More works can be referred to survey [26]. As mobile devices have to occupy users' hands when they are used as the manipulation metaphors, these methods can not provide friendlier freehand interaction. Additionally, interaction context is scaled down on smaller display screens, impeding the precision of fine manipulations.

2.2 Freehand interaction

Freehand interaction has been explored to deliver natural and intuitive yet effective interaction [30], especially for non-desktop scenarios (e.g., mid-air interaction) when keyboard and mouse devices are not appropriate or available. Previous works [19] [29] require fiducial markers or digital gloves to track hand gestures. Other works leverage Microsoft Kinect to detect hand poses and movements for freehand menu selection [12] and object manipulation [35]. However, these methods suffer from drawbacks. Instrumented gloves are encumbered and prone to induce fatigue. Fiducial markers and ambient sensors require delicate setups and calibrations.

Image-based methods [40] [4] have also been proposed to detect and recognize hand gestures using image processing technology, which are suitable for both closed and public environments [33]. As mobile devices become powerful, the image-based methods are promising for mobile devices as built-in cameras can be used without resorting to additional devices or sensors.

2.3 AR menu

Menus are widely used in traditional GUI to increase communication bandwidth with computers. However, using menus in the domain of AR is not straightforward, especially when the context is extended to three-dimensional environment. In order to support mid-air operations, non-pull-down menus such as ring menu [23] and tile menu [32] have been designed for manipulation in three-dimensional space.

As traditional mouse and keyboard devices have been discarded to reduce intrusion in AR applications, other inputs are developed for menu manipulation. In Studierstube [41], a tablet-and-pen device is used for menu selection. However, users have to take the tablet and pen with their hands. Some physical props such as fiducial markers [31] and hand fingers are also used to select menu items. The physical props are recognized and tracked using image processing techniques and then mapped for menu manipulation. To capture diverse motions such as wrist tilt and multiple pinch gestures, digital gloves shipped with motion tracking sensors are used [30].

2.4 Rethinking

Early systems provide seamless interaction in order to share the rare computing resources. The problem is partially alleviated as computing devices (e.g. smartphones) become miniaturized and ubiquitous. Mobile devices are promising to provide friendly user interaction when direct touch is unavailable or cross-display interaction is required. Although embedded cameras on mobile devices have been addressed as a suitable input [7], device intrusion disturbs user experiences. Freehand gesture-based method does not introduce much intrusion, but it has the deficiency of low precision [4]. Gesture-based menu system is promising to provide freehand interaction with higher communication bandwidth, but it is difficult to select menu items even with advanced-low pass filters [30].

Our lifetime interaction with the physical world tells that a large part of our interaction is daily operations, which

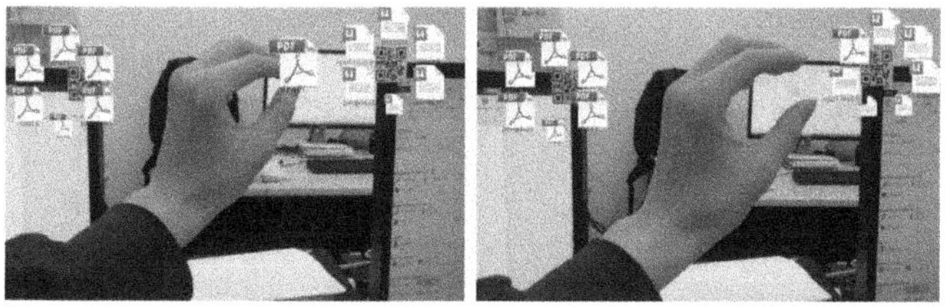

Figure 2: Left panel: a user picks a document item from a computer and drags it towards another computer. Right Panel: the user drops the document item to the other computer to finish document copy.

Figure 3: Left panel: a user is dragging a document item towards a printer. The capture zone of the printer is indicated by a virtual blue overlay. Right Panel: The printer captures the document item and prints out the document.

requires minimal visual attention as the functionality of objects is fully understood and works as expected [17]. An ideal user interface should embrace the richness of human sense and full skills acquired from our daily activities. It appears when and where it is required, otherwise it disappears to minimize visual attention and intrusion. Interaction should be also directly channeled to the physical objects rather than through a single workstation (as traditional GUI), so that it is not separated from the context where we reside and act.

To address the issues, we propose Ubii, a system to be invisible in the ecology of work places. Herein invisibility means it does not intrude user activities. Ubii is similar to the work [17] with a series of improvements. Rather than reprogramming functions of physical objects, we anchor our views on seamless interaction with individual physical objects without intrusion. Wearable devices such as Google Glass replace mobile devices to enable freehand interaction. 3D ring menu is used to support mid-air operations while pinch gesture is adopted to meet required precision of menu manipulation. By converging the technologies together, Uii establishes a direct type of affordance, which is similar to the affordance of direct touch. The aim of our research is to illustrate a concrete interaction approach to move beyond current GUI paradigm which is bounded to computers with flat windows, mice, and keyboards.

3. SYSTEM DESIGN

Designing a system as Ubii requires consideration of physical affordance, which determines the physical objects perceived by the users, the virtual interface presented to the users, and the interaction for users to bridge the virtual interface and the physical objects.

3.1 Physical affordance

All objects present a sort of physical affordance, while we only focus on those that have relations with the digital world in our system. For instance, a computer provides an affordance for entering the cyberspace; a printer exhibits an obvious affordance for printing digital documents. Physical surfaces such as tabletop and architecture partitions (e.g., walls and ceilings) can also act as tangible interface. To name an example, a blank wall can be treated as a virtual bulletin board for sharing information among group members. Authorized members are able view notes and documents on the virtual bulletin board while walk-in visitors only see the blank wall.

Users require interface to interact with the objects. With Ubii users perform the affordance through the interface at a distance without physical touch. Remote operations reduce manipulation distance and facilitate cross-device interaction, which is especially preferable for different groups of objects that have connection with each other. Table 1 lists the physical objects and their applicable interaction which Ubii is interested in. Although the physical objects may be connected through network communication, interaction between the objects is not mutual from the user's point of view. For instance, a user can drag and drop a document from a computer to a printer for printing service, but it is unable or meaningless to transfer anything from a printer to a computer. The applicable interaction between the objects is explained in detail as below:

Table 1: The applicable unidirectional (row to column) interaction between pair devices.

	Computer	Printer	Screen	Surface
Computer	✓	✓	✓	✓
Printer	×	×	×	×
Screen	×	×	✓	✓
Surface	✓	✓	×	✓

Computer: Computers are able to interact with all objects listed in Table 1. Ubii enables a computer to interact with itself for documents and image manipulations (e.g., moving and zooming) at a distance. It can interact with other computers for document copy without portable mass storage devices (e.g., USB devices). A computer can ask a printer for printing documents without users' physical touching. With a single gesture it sends documents for display on a large projector screen. In Ubii system it even can "upload" digital documents to physical surfaces (e.g., walls) for document sharing among multiple users. Figure 2 shows an embodiment of transmitting documents between two computers. A user pinches a document item from a computer, drags and drops towards another computer to finish transmitting the document between the computers, without physically operating the computers.

Printer: Printers are designed to work as passive receivers and do not have much interaction in general. In Ubii printers do not actively interact with other objects. However, as an important output device, it can passively interact with other objects including computers and physical surfaces. As illustrated in Figure 3, a user is dragging a document item from a computer and towards a printer. When the document item is moved near the virtual capture zone of printer affordance, the printer captures the document and starts to print it.

Figure 4: Left panel: a user is dragging an image item from a computer with pinch gesture. Right Panel: the image item is captured by a projector screen and then displayed on the projector screen.

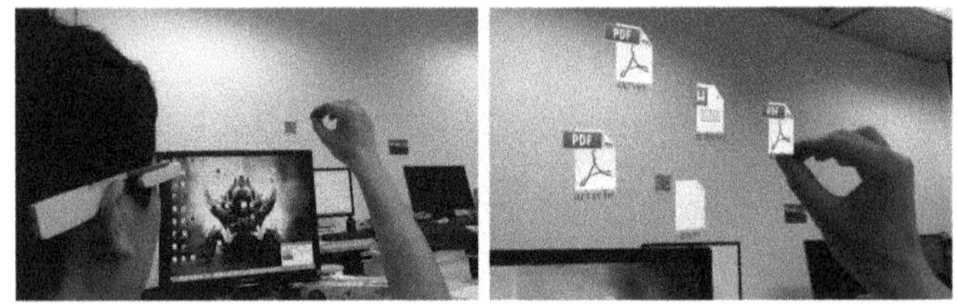

Figure 5: Left panel: a user is moving a document item on a physical surface with pinch gesture. Right Panel: the selected document is moving along with his hand on the physical surface.

Projector Screen: The projector screen presents an implicit affordance of large-screen display. From users' point of view, we directly interact with the projector screen, while it has to collaborate with a projector and a computer to complete the interaction. As a passive display device, the projector screen is unable to actively interact with the computer. However, it can interact with other projector screens and physical surfaces to afford cross-display interaction at a distance. It is possible to ask a printer to print a presented document on a projector screen. However, considering that the document must be stored in a computer, it is easy to turn to the computer and printer for the printing job. Ubii disables the direct interaction between the projector screen and the printer. Figure 4 gives an example of displaying an image on a projector screen. A user pinches an image item from a computer with his fingers. When the image item reaches capture zone of a projector screen, the projector screen captures and displays the image on the screen.

Physical Surface: Acting as document sharing workspace in Ubii, the physical surface enables downloading documents to personal computers, a reversed interaction of uploading documents from computers to the physical surface. Authorized group members are able to drag down a document to a printer to print it out. Ubii disconnects the interaction between the physical surface and the projector screen with private considerations. In the case of projecting a document on a projector screen, users can always resort to a computer where the document is uploaded. Figure 5 shows a user is manipulating a document on an architecture partition with his hand. Documents are oriented and aligned to the partition surface, so that users are able to move documents on the physical surface.

By exploring applicable physical affordance in a typical workspace, we figure out some guidelines of selecting physical objects for our system:

- Physical objects should have connection with digital world. It is possible to add virtual interface to the physical objects isolated from the digital world to enhance the relations with cyberspace, but it requires additional actuators [17] to perform the interaction, which needs to refit functions of the physical objects.
- Only simple and coarse-grained interactions (e.g., document copy and printing) are considered, which have common features of short time, frequent use, and simple input. Complicated and fine-grained interactions (e.g., text editing and fine art creating) that require long-time, precise manipulations, or multiple inputs are not suitable for Ubii.
- The augmented interface should neither redefine the physical affordance nor desensitize users' awareness of the physical affordance, otherwise new users require pre-training before using the system. It should be s-traightforward for most users to perform the operations.

3.2 Menu design

A menu system in the domain of AR applications is not necessarily to be two-dimensional. It is able to feature depth, rotation, and position in 3D space. We follows the criteria in [8] to design an interactive menu for our system:

Placement: Menu placement is classified into four categories [11]. We adopted the object-referenced placement to attach the menu to the physical objects. It is consistent with the design goal of breaking centralized interface into tailored individual interface associated with physical objects. Visual markers tagged on the physical objects are used to anchor the individual menus. The menus move along with the physical objects. Menus' size vary according to relative spatial relations between user and physical objects to indicate depth and distance.

Orientation: Aligning the menu with users' view makes it easy to read but may occlude the environment [8]; Rather, we align the menu with physical object surface which is tagged with the marker to improve readability. In addition, it achieves a better 3D spatial presence of the menu.

Trigger mechanism: A menu may be visible or hidden based on active state of the corresponding object. The menu will be visible if the physical object and its visual marker appear in user's current view. A menu item is triggered whenever a user pinches the item with fingers. A capture zone is activated if a menu item is dropped to its capturing region. All triggers are translated as sockets to perform underlying network communication.

Attributed to the capability of short target-seeking time and low error in selection [9], ring menu is adopted to collaborate with hand-based interaction for freehand menu selection in Ubii. Menu items are distributed on an invisible ring around an anchor determined by the visual marker. Traditional ring menu enlarges the ring size or uses hierarchical structure when it is too crowded to display all menu items in a single ring. Neither method is feasible as items increase to squeeze the space. To solve the problem, we enable menu items to be rotatable along the ring. As illustrated in Figure 6, only a few menu items are active and others are folded. Active items disappear and hidden items appear as the ring menu rotates clockwise.

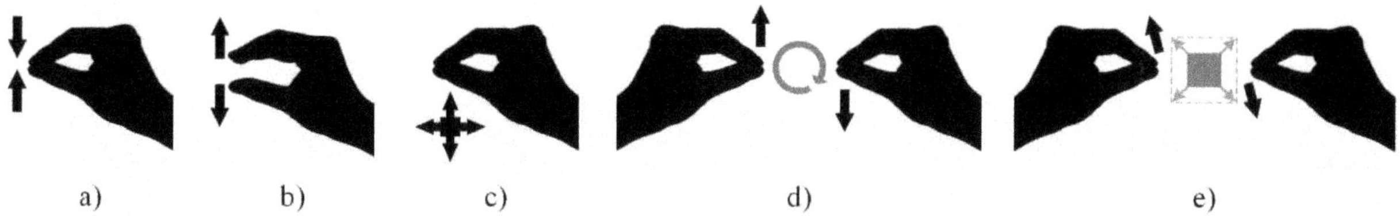

Figure 7: The supported hand gesture based interactions in Ubii.

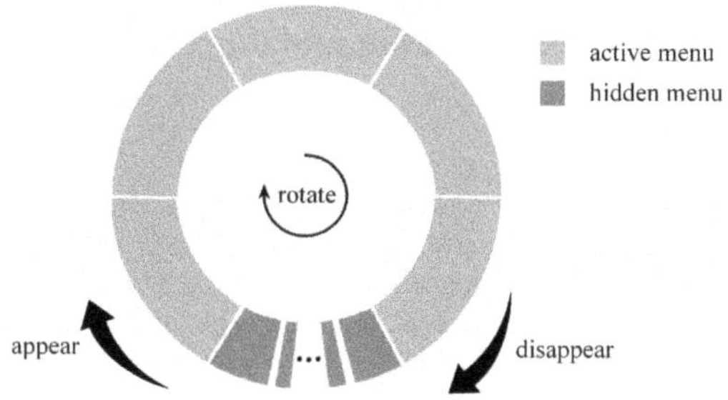

Figure 6: A rotatable and foldable ring menu.

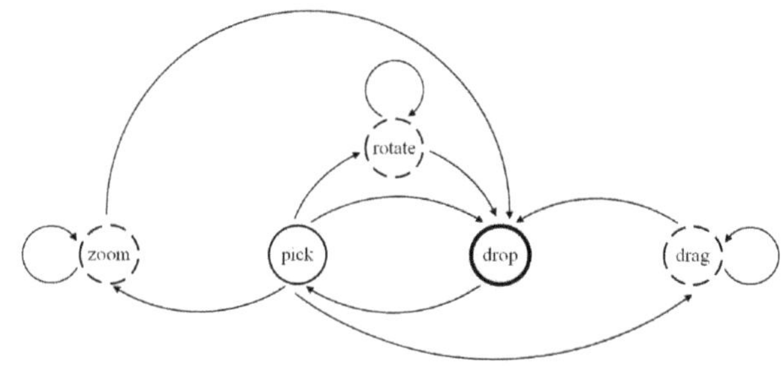

Figure 8: The transition of interaction operations.

Rather than providing operating items (e.g., "translate" and "print"), operated items (e.g., document and image) are defined as menu items as physical affordance of the object items is already understood by users. Users are able to directly perform actions on object items without calling operating commands. For instance, dragging a document item implies copying, printing, or displaying the document according to the target that the document is dropped to.

Capture zone is designed to decrease required precision of interaction. Any menu item dropped to the range of a capture zone is captured by the receiver to trigger underlying commands. For instance, when a user selects a menu item (e.g., a document) of a computer, all printers, projector screens, and predefined physical surfaces in user's current view are overlaid with their capture zones. If the item is dropped to the capture zone of a printer, the printer captures the document and starts to print it out. When the item is dropped to the capture zone of a projector screen, the computer connected with the projector will receive the document, and then asks the projector screen to displays it.

3.3 Interaction design

Uii extends previous video-based interaction to hand gesture interaction without any digital gloves or fiducial marker tracking. However, pointing gesture is difficult for direct positioning operations (e.g., menu selection) because it cannot achieve the same high precision as physical input devices (e.g., mouse and stylus) in free spaces [30]. Directional gesture is ambiguous and error-prone due to lack of distinctive gesture delimiters [37].

Our essential design principle is to leverage multiple discrete gesture inputs to reduce the required precision of continuous hand gesture. The pinch gesture is stable and precise attributed to its discrete and unambiguous states of fingers together and apart [40]. In addition, it appears natural to users as it is evocative of grabbing a physical object [30]. Pinch gesture is suitable for interaction which requires high precision, such as menu picking and dropping. Combined with directional gesture, it also can be used for coarse interaction, such as dragging. Ubii integrates multiple hand gestures to support several types of freehand interaction:

- Pick: a pinch gesture (as illustrated in Figure 7a) is interpreted as a pick operation. The pick operation should be performed on a menu item, otherwise it is invalid.
- Drop: an un-pinch gesture (as illustrated in Figure 7b) acts as dropping the selected item. A pick operation should always finish with a drop operation.
- Drag: triggered when a directional gesture is performed with a pick operation (as illustrated in Figure 7c). The selected item is moved along with directional gesture if only a single drag operation is acted. The drag interaction terminates whenever a drop operation happens.
- Rotate: a combo operation of two pinch gestures that move reversely along the Y direction on screen space (as illustrated in Figure 7d). The interaction is used to rotate a ring menu which is located between the two pinch gestures. Relative distance is mapped as rotation angle. Rotation operation stops whenever either or both pinch gestures end.
- Zoom: a combination of two drag operations performed on the same item (as illustrated in Figure 7e). Relative movement is transferred to scale up and down the item size. As one or both of the drag operations end, the zoom operation is terminated.

The transition of different interactions is illustrated in Figure 8. Pick and drop are instantaneous interactions. All interactions start with the pick and end with the drop operation. The other three start from the pick operation and end to the drop operation. They also enclose self-transitions for continuous interaction.

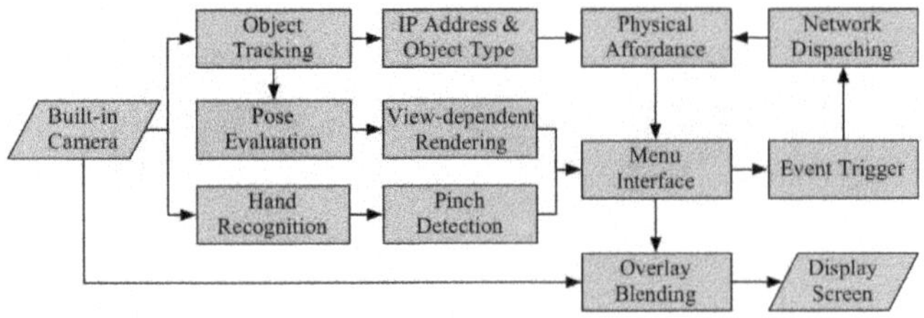

Figure 9: The system workflow of Ubii.

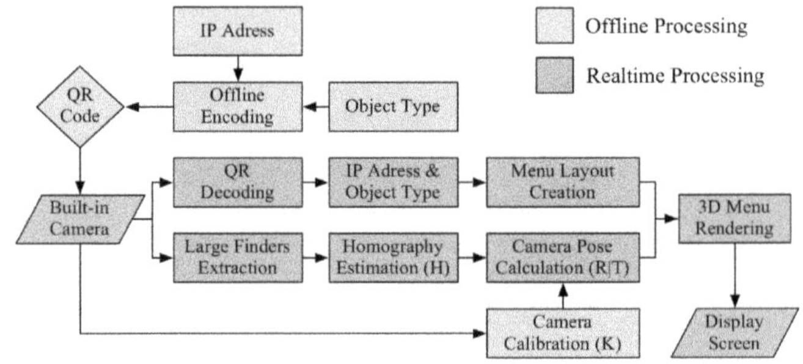

Figure 10: Object tracking and pose estimation with QR markers.

4. IMPLEMENTATION

Implementing our system requires technologies from fields of object tracking and hand gesture recognition. We employed a QR-based method for both object tracking and pose evaluation. A double-threshold algorithm was proposed to accurately detect pinch gestures. Our work explored the synergetic benefits that go beyond the sum of multiple technologies to achieve our design goals.

Figure 9 shows the system workflow. The built-in camera on Google Glass takes live video of the scene around users, which is streamed for image analysis of object tracking and hand recognition. The system extracts object information of IP address and object type from QR code, which is used for physical affordance recognition and network communication. Camera pose is also evaluated by calculating the homography of QR code images. Virtual camera is updated according to the real camera pose to render 3D menus from corresponding viewpoint, making virtual menus align with surfaces of physical objects. Menus are rendered as AR overlays to blend with video stream, and then displayed on Google Glass display prism.

Hand contours are extracted from video stream using a modified inexpensive method based on [40]. The contours are then filtered using double thresholds to determine pinch gestures. Users are able to interact with physical objects through virtual menus using pinch gestures, which are interpreted as socket to perform communication between physical objects through underlying network.

4.1 Object tracking

Ubii heavily relies on the built-in camera on Google Glass to understand the domain environment. The object tracking involves in recognizing object and evaluating spatial relationship between objects and users. Rather than non-intrusive markerless methods such as [22], we adopted the marker-based baseline, which is generally more accurate and robust to image distortion and illumination variation [28]. In our system QR codes are used as fiducial markers to encode additional information for understanding object functions.

As illustrated in Figure 10, object information including IP address and object type is encoded into QR code in advance using the qrcode tool[1]. For non-wired physical objects such as physical surfaces (e.g., wall and tabletop) and projector screens, IP addresses of their counterparts, namely computers storing documents on physical surfaces and computers connected to projectors for projection display, are encoded. Camera calibration is also performed beforehand to calculate the intrinsic matrix K with the classic chess board method [42]. At runtime whenever one or more QR codes appear in the live video stream captured by embedded camera, the system resorts to the integrated Zbar library[2] to decode object information from QR codes. It is then able to determine menu item layout according to the extracted information. The large finders in QR codes are also extracted to get the homography matrix H by solving the coordinate vector-valued function, which is then used to evaluate the pose matrix $R|T = K - \boldsymbol{I} * H$. In practise, we adopted a tricky implementation by using the more efficient and accurate solvePnP method from the library OpenCV4Android[3]. The intrinsic matrix K is mapped to the Normalized Device Coordinates (NDC) in OpenGL ES rendering system for perspective projection, while the pose matrix $R|T$ should be flipped along X axis for consistently locating virtual menus in OpenGL coordinate frame.

In Ubii QR markers are added to the objects, which may be not consistent with our vision of designing a self-contained system. We view QR markers as a temporary and minor violation of our premise, and believe that advances in ubiquitous sensors and smart devices will help us to understand environment without additional annotation in future.

4.2 Hand gesture recognition

Pinch gesture provides a simple and reliable way to detect when interactions start and end without additional gesture delimiters. It can be determined by the thumb and index fingers touching together to make a hole as illustrated in the Figure 11a. We basically follow Wilson's vision-based method [40] to detect one and two-hand pinching gestures, with several improvements in our system.

The first step is to distinguish hands and background using the well-studied segmentation and connected components techniques in computer vision community. In Wilson's method the background of interaction context is constrained to a black computer keyboard. As the background is constantly darker than the foreground hands, the method chooses to separate the background from the image. In Ubii the background varies according to user's view angle. Alternatively, we extract the foreground hands from the image by using hand skin color as reference color. With the same reason in Wilson's method, it is reasonable to take the largest pixel components as hand sections because hands generally occupy the largest region from user-centered perspective.

Contours of hand section are then extracted. The largest one is the outer contour of the hand section as illustrated in Figure 11b. Any inner contour indicates a hole in the hand

[1] https://pypi.python.org/pypi/qrcode

[2] https://github.com/ZBar/ZBar

[3] http://docs.opencv.org/

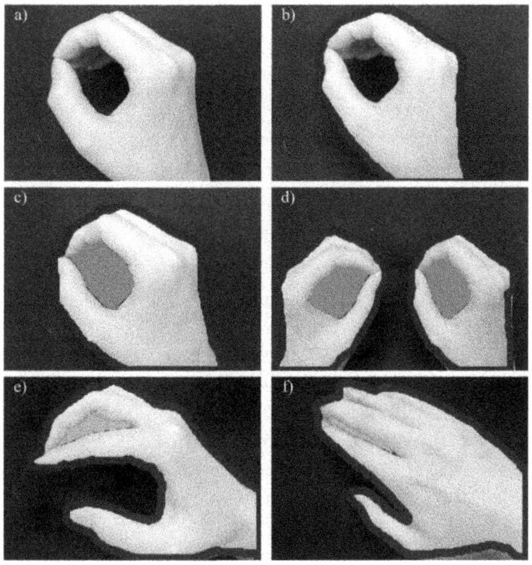

Figure 11: The pinch gesture detection. a) a typical pinch gesture; b) outer contour of hand is extracted; c) and d): red closed regions are recognized as pinch holes; e) and f): green closed regions are eliminated as non-pinch holes.

section. Ambient illumination and other non-pinch gestures may also produce inner contours. Our method adopts contour size to filter out the wrong contours. Any inner contour with size out of given bounds is discarded. The bounds are determined by the acceptance and elimination curves as illustrated in Figure 12. The elimination curve represents accuracy of excluding non-pinch gestures that have inner contours in terms of a lower threshold of the inner contour's size. The inner contours of non-pinch gestures are generally small. The gestures will be more accurately expelled if we set the lower threshold to be larger. Conversely, holes in pinch gestures are normally large. Most pinch gestures detection will pass if the threshold is small, as shown by the acceptance curve that recognition accuracy declines when the threshold gets larger. We chose a lower bound 0.6 and upper bound 0.8 to achieve over 85% accuracy of both pinch gesture detection and non-pinch gesture elimination.

The method works in both one and two-hand pinch gesture detection as shown in Figure 11c and Figure 11d. It is also robust to eliminate other non-pinch gestures. Figure 11e and Figure 11f show two gestures with holes in hand sections, but they are eliminated in our method as the pinch holes are smaller than the given lower bound value. In practise, it is applicable to uncheck the upper bound as result set of a small upper bound always includes result of a large upper bound. However, size of pinch hole is constrained to hand anatomy. A reasonable upper bound guarantees excluding outliers.

The pinch gesture detection relies solely on the hole between thumb and index fingers. The method fails if the hole background is occluded by other curled fingers [40]. It neither works when the hole is invisible to the camera, such as the thumb and index fingers being horizontally coplanar. We see it to be a reasonable compromise for freehand interaction without device intrusion.

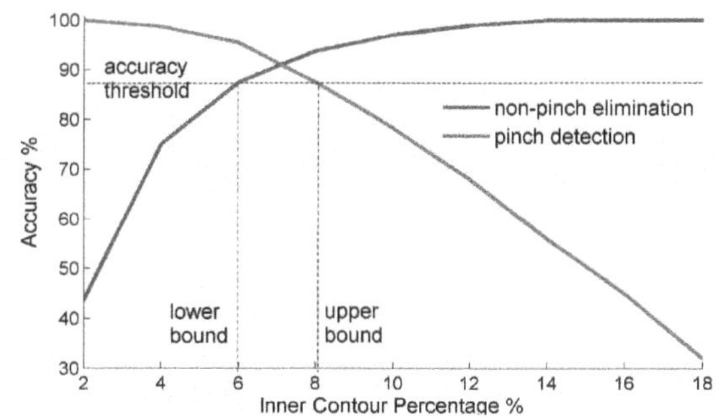

Figure 12: The inner contour acceptance and elimination.

5. EVALUATION

We designed several experiments to evaluate the system from different aspects. Participants were invited to perform the experiments. Their task completion time and failed trials were measured and compared. The participants were asked to answer paper questionnaires after the experiments. A technology acceptance model (TAM) [14] was adopted to evaluate user experience.

5.1 Participants

We invited 10 participants (6 males and 4 females) from other departments in our campus, with ages between 19 and 31. They are frequently computer users and familiar with common computer operations including document copy, print, and projector display. Several (4) have some experience of gesture interaction, including Microsoft Kinect and Wii for computer games. Three of them have experience or hear about AR techniques.

5.2 Experiment design

We designed four tasks in associated with selected physical affordance in Section 3.1. The tasks were conducted in a closed work space with dimensions of about 10m*5m. The work space is equipped with several interconnected computers, printers, and a set of projector and display screen. Several USB devices were available for document copy in our experiments. The computers had installed instant messaging software Skype[4] and share tool Dropbox[5] for transmitting and sharing document. We registered several accounts in advance to use the software. Computers, printers, and projector were running so that participants did not need to login or switch on devices. The computer connected with the projector was also configured beforehand for projection display. Computers' names, and printers' name, document names and paths on computers, were listed on task cards for reference.

Ex1: Copying documents between computers. Participants were required to copy specified documents between assigned computers with USB flash copy, Skype, and Ubii. By using USB flash copy participants had to copy documents between different computers and USB devices. They also needed to find other Skype accounts on target computers in order to transmit documents through Skype. In Ubii, participants needed to perform pick, drag, and drop operations with their

[4]http://www.skype.com/

[5]https://www.dropbox.com/

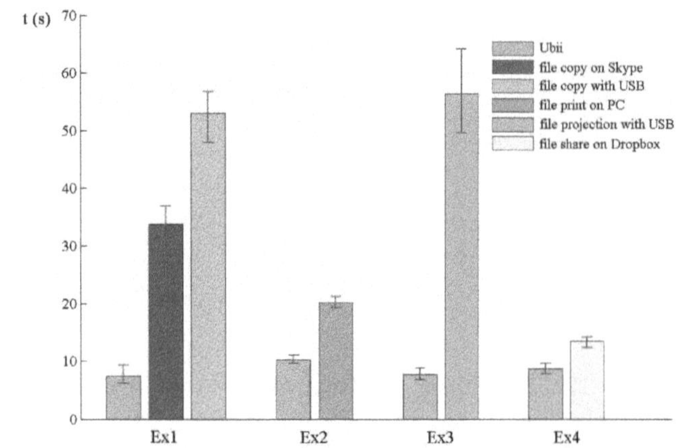

Figure 13: Comparison of task competition time of four experiments by using Ubii and traditional methods.

hands to finish document copy. Rotate operation may be required when the specified document items are folded in menus.

Ex2: Printing documents. Participants were asked to print specified documents on assigned printers by using functions provided by computers and Ubii. In traditional way participants had to select "print" menu item and fill the configuration panel such as assigning printer name. In Ubii participants had to pick, drag, and then drop the specified document item to the capture zone of assigned printer.

Ex3: Displaying documents on projector screens. Participants finished the task of displaying specified documents on the projector screen with traditional USB flash copy and alternative way of Ubii. In traditional way participants copied documents to the computer connected with projector using USB devices, and then opened the document for projection display. Using Ubii system, participants directly interacted with the projector screen rather than the computer connected with the projector.

Ex4: Sharing documents. Participants had to share documents with other participants through Dropbox and Ubii. By using Dropbox participants had to copy specified documents to Dropbox share folders or share Dropbox link, and then wait for documents updating or received. In Ubii participants used an architecture wall as virtual share space for uploading and downloading document with drag and drop interaction.

Each participant was required to perform the four tasks, and each task was performed 4 times. The tasks were presented in random order among the participants. We got a total of 10 (participant) × 4 (task) × 4 (repetition) = 160 times of operations, with each task repeatedly performed 40 times. Each participant completed the whole study within 60 minutes or less.

5.3 Results & discussion

Figure 13 compares participants' task completion time using Ubii system (green bars) and other traditional ways such as document copy through USB devices and Skype, and document share through Dropbox. The time cost of Ubii is much less than other traditional methods in all four tasks. Particulary, it is (M=7440ms, SD=360ms) almost 4 to 7 times faster respectively than transferring on Skype (maroon bar, M=33780ms, SD=3320ms) and USB flash copy (brown bar, M=53475ms, SD=3530ms) in Ex1. It (M=7690ms, S-D=300ms) also achieves high performance gain compared with traditional projection display using USB devices (brown bar, M=56370ms, SD=6510ms). Using USB flash copy requires plugging in, plugging out, and copying documents between USB devices and computers. Ubii simplifies the manipulations without directly physical touch. For document printing Ubii (M=10250ms, SD=380ms) eliminates operations of clicking "print..." menu item and selecting specified printer from printer list required by traditional method (blue bar, M=20250ms, SD=574ms). We found that some participants referenced to task cards when they selected a printer from configuration panel. Ubii (M=8740ms, SD=310ms) is also more efficient in document sharing compared with Dropbox sharing (yellow bar, M=13510ms, SD=1130ms), as it does not require confirming target user's Dropbox account, which is normally not the same as target computer's account.

Table 2: The accumlative failed trials of each expriments.

	failed trial	failed ratio
Ex1	2	5 %
Ex2	3	7.5%
Ex3	3	7.5%
Ex4	4	10%

We compared completion time (green bars) of different tasks using Ubii. The task completion time includes both operation time and document transfer time. The most time-consuming task is printing operation, followed by document copy, projection display, and share. As document printing requires most time due to document transfer between computers and printers, namely almost three times longer (M=6100ms) than that between computers (M=2100ms), it is in fact the fastest operation (M=4200ms, SD=200ms) comparing to document copy (M=4840ms, SD=310ms), projection display (M=5200ms, S=330ms), and document sharing (M=6650ms, SD=300ms).

We measured failed trials and ratios of each task as illustrated in Table 2. All failed trials are induced by failures of Ubii. Document sharing has the highest failed ratio of 10%, and document copy with the lowest of 5%. No participant encountered more than twice failures in single task. The failures mainly lie in the wrong detection of hand gestures, which are caused by fast hand movements and background color.

In addition to profile the system from the aspect of runtime performance, we evaluated user experience of Ubii using the TAM model, which includes four criteria of perceived enjoyment (PE), perceived usefulness (PU), perceived ease of use (PEOU), and intention to use (IOU). We used the Likert scale[6] to quantitatively measure the four criteria, which scale from 1 to 5 scores, with strong disagree (1), disagree (2), neutral (3), agree (4), and strongly agree (5). As illustrated by Figure 14, the four terms in each task are positive in general. In Ex2 (document printing) and Ex3 (projection display) the first quartiles (Q1) pass over 3, and medians (Q2) are not lower than 4. The bottom whiskers also end

[6]http://en.wikipedia.org/wiki/Likert_scale

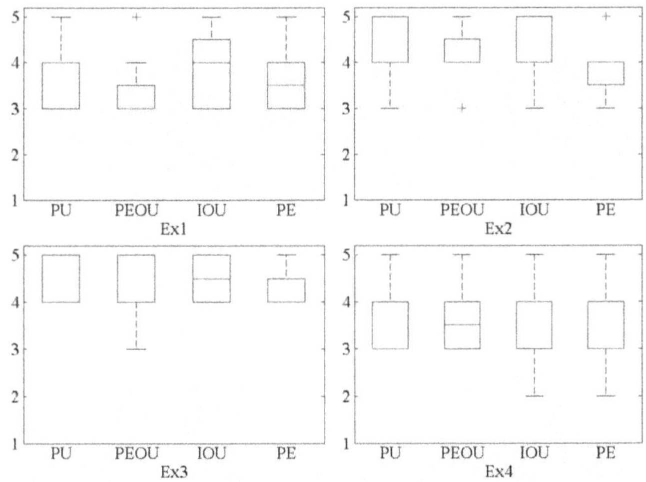

Figure 14: User experience evaluation of four experiments scored with Likert scale.

up at 3 or above, with a few outliers at 3 and 5. Especially, boxes of Ex3 are all located between 4 and 5, indicating strong agreements on all terms. The result can be also found in Ex2, with an exception of weak agreements on PE partly due to the long transfer time between computers and printers. Boxes in Ex1 (document copy) and Ex4 (document sharing) are mainly located between 3 and 4, with bottom whiskers ending above 3, indicating that less than a quarter of participants reserve their opinions on user experience. Particularly, two highlights are easily observed in Ex1 and Ex4: the relatively low and short box of PEOU in Ex1 and bottom whiskers of IOU and PE in Ex4 ending at 2, implying less preference for document copy and sharing. Specifically, participants' opinions on Ex4 are much more diverse, ranging from strong agreement (5) to disagreement (2). From answers to the question of "any comments?" on our questionnaires we discovered a few participants had been used to traditional methods such as IM tools (e.g., Skype) and cloud storage (e.g., Dropbox) for document copy and sharing, and they thought traditional methods were convenient enough for them.

Overall, the results are promising to reduce operation time compared with traditional methods. Most participants are satisfied with the system, albeit occasional failures in their operations. Several said directly operation with physical devices enables them avoid remembering device names. For instance, people have to know the IP address or device name to select the exact one they need from the printer list. With our system they are able to assign print job to any printer they like by directly dragging and dropping the document to the printer without knowing its name or IP address. The projection display is popular among participants as indicated in Figure 14, which lies in the fact that most people only care about document display on projection screen rather than where the document is located. Our system help them simplify the procedure.

6. CONCLUSION

Ubii provides a decentralized interface system for manipulation between the physical and digital worlds. User interface and interaction are delicately designed to afford free-hand user experience. The system is evaluated from both aspects of technical and user experience. By interacting with objects at a high-level of physical affordance rather than underlying digital counterparts, the system helps users perform operations in much convenient and natural way. It has been proved to be useful for simple and frequently-performed manipulations with connected digital devices in closed environments.

In our experiments, we found that most failures were caused by hand gesture detection. The color-based method is chosen to relieve computational cost, but it is not accurate enough in backgrounds with similar color of hand skin. In future we plan to combine depth and visual cameras to improve the accuracy. Another problem is the limitation of poor computational capability and limited power capacity of Google Glass. We will try to leverage device offloading strategies to outsource computationally intensive tasks to companion mobile devices. The method has been proved to improve both real-time performance and runtime sustainability.

7. REFERENCES

[1] R. Ballagas, J. Borchers, M. Rohs, and J. G. Sheridan. The smart phone: a ubiquitous input device. *IEEE Pervasive Computing*, 5(1):70–77, 2006.

[2] R. Ballagas, M. Rohs, and J. G. Sheridan. Sweep and point and shoot: Phonecam-based interactions for large public displays. In *Proceedings of CHI Extended Abstracts*, pages 1200–1203, 2005.

[3] D. Baur, S. Boring, and S. Feiner. Virtual projection: Exploring optical projection as a metaphor for multi-device interaction. In *Proceedings of CHI*, pages 1693–1702, 2012.

[4] H. Benko. Beyond flat surface computing: challenges of depth-aware and curved interfaces. In *Proceedings of ACM Multimedia*, pages 935–944, 2009.

[5] S. Boring, M. Altendorfer, G. Broll, O. Hilliges, and A. Butz. Shoot and copy: Phonecam-based information transfer from public displays onto mobile phones. In *Proceedings of Mobility*, pages 24–31, 2007.

[6] S. Boring, D. Baur, A. Butz, S. Gustafson, and P. Baudisch. Touch projector: mobile interaction through video. In *Proceedings of CHI*, pages 2287–2296. ACM New York, USA, 2010.

[7] S. Boring, M. Jurmu, and A. Butz. Scroll, tilt or move it: Using mobile phones to continuously control pointers on large public display. In *Proceedings of OzCHI*, pages 161–168, 2009.

[8] F. Brudy. Interactive menus in augmented reality environments. Technical report, Media Informatics at the University of Munich, 2013.

[9] J. Callahan, D. Hopkins, M. Weiser, and B. Shneidermann. An empirical comparison of pie vs. linear menus. In *Proceedings of CHI*, pages 95–100, 1988.

[10] T. H. Chang and Y. Li. Deep shot: A framework for migrating tasks across devices using mobile phone cameras. In *Proceedings of CHI*, pages 2163–2172, 2011.

[11] R. Dachselt and A. Hubner. Virtual environments: Three-dimensional menus: A survey and taxonomy. *Computers and Graphics archive*, 31(1):53–65, 2007.

[12] F. Guimbretiere and C. Nguyen. Bimanual marking menu for near surface interactions. In *Proceedings of CHI*, pages 825–828, 2012.

[13] S. G. Gustafson, B. Rabe, and P. M. Baudisch. Understanding palm-based imaginary interfaces: the role of visual and tactile cues when browsing. In *Proceedings of CHI*, pages 889–898. ACM New York, USA, 2013.

[14] A. C. Haugstvedt and J. Krogstie. Mobile augmented reality for cultural heritage: A technology acceptance study. In *IEEE International Symposium on Mixed and Augmented Reality (ISMAR)*, pages 247–255, 2012.

[15] S. J. Henderson and S. Feiner. Opportunistic controls: leveraging natural affordances as tangible user interfaces for augmented reality. In *Proceedings of the ACM symposium on Virtual reality software and technology*, pages 211–218. ACM New York, USA, 2008.

[16] S. J. Henderson and S. K. Feiner. Augmented reality in the psychomotor phase of a procedural task. In *Proceedings of ISMAR*, pages 191–200, 2011.

[17] V. Heun, S. Kasahara, and P. Maes. Smarter objects: using ar technology to program physical objects and their interactions. In *Proceedings of CHI EA*, pages 2817–2818, 2013.

[18] Z. Huang, P. Hui, C. Peylo, and D. Chatzopoulos. Mobile augmented reality survey: A bottom-up approach. Technical report, HKUST Technical Report-20130903-182109-4052 (cite as arXiv:1309.4413), 2013.

[19] W. Hurst and J. Dekker. Tracking-based interaction for object creation in mobile augmented reality. In *Proceedings of ACM Multimedia*, pages 93–101, 2013.

[20] H. Ishii and B. Ullmer. Tangible bits: towards seamless interfaces between people, bits and atoms. In *Proceedings of the ACM SIGCHI*, pages 234–241. ACM Press, 1997.

[21] B. Johanson, G. Hutchins, T. Winograd, and M. Stone. Pointright: experience with flexible input redirection in interactive workspaces. In *Proceedings of UIST*, pages 227–234, 2002.

[22] A. Kanezaki, Y. Kuniyoshi, and T. Harada. Weakly-supervised multi-class object detection using multi-type 3d features. In *Proceedings of ACM Multimedia*, pages 605–608, 2013.

[23] J. Liang and M. Green. A highly interactive 3d modeling system. *Computers & Graphics*, 18(4):499–506, 1994.

[24] A. Marzo and O. Ardaiz. Collart: a tool for creating 3d photo collages using mobile augmented reality. In *Proceedings of ACM Multimedia*, pages 585–588, 2013.

[25] B. Myers, R. Bhatnagar, J. Nichols, C. H. Peck, D. Miller, and A. C. Long. Interacting at a distance: measuring the performance of laser pointers and other devices. In *Proceedings of CHI*, pages 33–40, 2002.

[26] M. A. Nacenta, C. Gutwin, D. Aliakseyeu, and S. Subramanian. There and back again: Cross-display object movement in multi-display environments. *Journal of Human-Computer Interaction*, 24(1):170–229, 2009.

[27] M. A. Nacenta, S. Sallam, B. Champoux, S. Subramanian, and C. Gutwin. Perspective cursor: perspective-based interaction for multi-display environments. In *Proceedings of CHI*, pages 289–298, 2006.

[28] U. Neumann and S. Y. You. Natural feature tracking for augmented reality. *IEEE Transactions on Multimedia*, 1(1):53–64, 1999.

[29] T. Ni, D. Bowman, and C. North. Airstroke: bringing unistroke text entry to freehand gesture interfaces. In *Proceedings of CHI*, pages 2473–2476, 2011.

[30] T. Ni, D. A. Bowman, C. North, and R. P. McMahan. Design and evaluation of freehand menu selection interfaces using tilt and pinch gestures. *Journal International Journal of Human-Computer Studies*, 69(9):551–562, 2011.

[31] I. Poupyrev, D. S. Tan, M. Billinghurst, H. Kato, H. Regenbrecht, and N. Tetsutani. Developing a generic augmented-reality interface. *IEEE Computer*, 35(3):44–50, 2002.

[32] M. Rahman, S. Gustafson, P. Irani, and S. Subramanian. Tilt techniques: investigating the dexterity of wrist-based input. In *Proceedings of CHI*, pages 1943–1952, 2009.

[33] G. Ren and E. O. Neill. 3d selection with freehand gesture. *Computers & Graphics*, 37(3):101–120, 2013.

[34] D. Schmalstieg and D.Wagner. Experiences with handheld augmented reality. In *In Proceedings of Mixed and Augmented Reality, 6th IEEE and ACM International Symposium*, pages 3–18, 2007.

[35] P. Song, W. B. Goh, W. Hutama, C.-W. Fu, and X. Liu. A handle bar metaphor for virtual object manipulation with mid-air interaction. In *Proceedings of CHI*, pages 1297–1306, 2012.

[36] B. Ullmer and H. Ishii. Emerging frameworks for tangible user interfaces. *IBM Systems Journal*, 39(3):579–601, 2000.

[37] Y. Wang and C. MacKenzie. The role of contextual haptic and visual constraints on object manipulation in virtual environments. In *Proceedings of CHI*, pages 532–539, 2000.

[38] M. Weiser. The computer for the 21st century. *Scientific American*, 265(3):94–104, 1991.

[39] A. Wilson and S. Shafer. Xwand: Ui for intelligent spaces. In *Proceedings of CHI*, pages 545–552. ACM New York, USA, 2003.

[40] A. D. Wilson. Robust computer vision-based detection of pinching for one and two-handed gesture input. In *Proceedings of UIST*, pages 255–258, 2006.

[41] Z. Zalavari and M. Gervautz. The personal interaction panel: a two-handed interface for augmented reality. *Computer Graphics Forum*, 16(3):335–346, 1997.

[42] Z. Zhang. A flexible new technique for camera calibration. *IEEE Transactions on Pattern Analysis and Machine Intelligence*, 22(11):1330–1334, 2000.

Smart Beholder: An Open-Source Smart Lens for Mobile Photography

Chun-Ying Huang[1], Chih-Fan Hsu[2], Tsung-Han Tsai[2], Ching-Ling Fan[3], Cheng-Hsin Hsu[3], and Kuan-Ta Chen[2]

[1]Department of Computer Science and Engineering, National Taiwan Ocean University
[2]Institute of Information Science, Academia Sinica
[3]Department of Computer Science, National Tsing Hua University

ABSTRACT

Smart lenses are detachable lenses connected to mobile devices via wireless networks, which are not constrained by the small form factor of mobile devices, and have potential to deliver better photo (video) quality. However, the viewfinder previews of smart lenses on mobile devices are difficult to optimize, due to the strict resource constraints on smart lenses and fluctuating wireless network conditions. In this paper, we design, implement, and evaluate an open-source smart lens, called Smart Beholder. It achieves three design goals: (i) cost effectiveness, (ii) low interaction latency, and (iii) high preview quality by: (i) selecting an embedded system board that is just powerful enough, (ii) minimizing per-component latency, and (iii) dynamically adapting the video coding parameters to maximizing Quality of Experience (QoE), respectively. Several optimization techniques, such as anti-drifting mechanism for video frames and QoE-driven resolution/frame rate adaptation algorithm, are proposed in this paper. Our measurement study shows that Smart Beholder outperforms Altek Cubic and Sony QX100 in terms of lower bitrate, lower latency, slightly higher frame rate, and better preview quality. We also demonstrate that Smart Beholder adapts to network dynamics. Smart Beholder has been made public at `http://www.smartbeholder.org` as an experimental platform for researchers and developers to optimize smart lenses and other embedded real-time video streaming systems.

Categories and Subject Descriptors

H.5 [**Information Systems Applications**]: Multimedia Information Systems

Keywords

Measurements; streaming; wireless networks; cameras; optimization; smartphones; mobile devices; QoE

1. INTRODUCTION

The popularity of smartphones grows dramatically in the past few years, and the growth rate shows no sign of slowing down. For example, a recent report [34] indicates that more than 1 billion smartphones were shipped in 2013, which is equivalent to 38.4% of increase compared to 2012. The smartphones come with cameras, and are used by casual photographers to replace their digital cameras. In fact, we observe clear drops on the number of shipped digital cameras starting from 2012, and the projected shipment volume of digital cameras is only 54 millions in 2014 [14]. Such replacement effect may be attributed to the convenience of smartphones and the shrinking performance gap between smartphone cameras and digital cameras. Nevertheless, there are still well-known reasons that differentiate digital cameras from smartphone cameras [1]. First, smartphones must be compact in order to fit into users' pockets. Therefore, most smartphone cameras are not equipped with bulky optical zoom lenses. The users have to resort to suboptimal digital zooms. Second, smartphones often come with smaller optical sensors due to the space concerns, which lead to inferior photo quality especially under low-light conditions. Third, smartphones do not support interchangeable lenses, and cannot adopt long-focus, macro, fish-eye, and wide-angle lenses for high-quality and more extreme needs. Last, smartphone cameras are not normally adjustable in terms of, e.g., ISO, aperture, and shutter speed, which result in inflexibility. These limitations prevent *mobile photographers* from producing high-quality photos using their smartphones.

Smart lenses, such as Sony QX100 [11], Kodak SL10 [30], and Altek Cubic [2], are detachable lenses connected to mobile devices via wireless networks. Mobile photographers use smartphones (or tablets) to access the smart lenses for: (i) previewing photos (or videos) in live viewfinders, (ii) adjusting various lens configurations, (iii) capturing photo (or video) shots, and (iv) applying digital effects. Since smart lenses are no longer embedded in smartphones, the form factor of smart lenses are not limited by that of smartphones. Therefore, smart lenses are capable to address the aforementioned limitations, closing up the gap of gears between mobile and professional photographers. Moreover, some special shooting angles, such as low-angle and close-up shots, are easier to take with smart lenses as they are detached from viewfinders on smartphones. While smart lenses offer such new opportunities to mobile photographers, delivering good photo taking experience is not an easy task because *smart lenses are connected to smartphones via wireless networks*, which are sensitive to fading, shadowing, and interference in wireless communications. In addition, users have two expectations: (i) low interaction delay and (ii) high graphics quality, which are contracting to each other for several reasons. For example, while complex motion estimation algorithms lead to good graphics quality, they also result in long interaction delay. Last, smart lenses are often implemented on resource-scarce embedded systems, which further complicate the design, development, and

MM'15, October 26–30, 2015, Brisbane, Australia.
© 2015 ACM. ISBN 978-1-4503-3459-4/15/10 ...$15.00.
DOI: http://dx.doi.org/10.1145/2733373.2806261.

Figure 1: The working Smart Beholder prototype.

implementation of smart lenses for diverse applications. However, existing commercial smart lenses are proprietary and closed, and cannot facilitate customizations and parameter tuning to exercise the design space.

In this paper, we design, implement, and evaluate an open-source smart lens, called *Smart Beholder*, or Beholder for short. The term "beholder" is normally used to refer a fictional flying orb with a large eye (commonly seen in AD&D games) [9], in analogy to very portable smart lenses with powerful (but potentially bulky) optical lenses. We carefully design and implement Smart Beholder for cost effectiveness, low interaction delay, and high viewfinder preview quality. This is done by (i) selecting an embedded system board that is just powerful enough, (ii) minimizing per-component latency, and (iii) dynamically adapting the video coding parameters to maximizing Quality of Experience (QoE), respectively. Several optimization techniques, such as anti-drifting mechanism for video frames and QoE-driven resolution/frame rate adaptation algorithm, are proposed and implemented.

Smart Beholder is built to be an *open* platform for researchers and developers to evaluate different design alternatives, so as to make educated, if not optimal, design decisions. Furthermore, we conduct real experiments to compare the performance of Smart Beholder and two commercial products [2, 11], which are the only two smart lenses available when we started this project in 2014. Our experiment results reveal some limitations of the commercial products, e.g., the preview video quality in viewfinders is low, which leaves rooms for improvements. Furthermore, we thoroughly evaluate the performance of a complete Smart Beholder platform as illustrated in Figure 1. In this picture, the server runs on a Raspberry Pi board [29] on the left; the client runs on an Android tablet showing what the webcam on the server points to. Our evaluation results show the practicality and efficiency of the Smart Beholder platform over the considered commercial products.

This paper makes the following contributions:

- We present Smart Beholder, an open-source smart lens project, which is modularized and well documented. Smart Beholder allows researchers, developers, and amateurs to test their new ideas by either adjusting system settings or adding/removing components.
- We develop, implement, and validate a subjective QoE model to support preview adaptation for higher overall user experience. Our evaluation results show that Smart Beholder reduces about 3 Mbps in bitrate and improves at least 0.3 Mean Opinion Score (MOS) in preview quality compared to other commercial products.
- We experimentally compare multiple design choices for better performance and efficiency. The lessons reported in our paper will benefit researchers, developers, and amateurs who work on smart lenses, e.g., using a hardware encoder saves at least 86.5% in energy than using a software encoder.

Smart Beholder is released with two types of software packs: all-in-one and pre-compiled binary packs. In addition, the source codes and complete documents are available on our project website at `http://www.smartbeholder.org`. Users may extend Smart Beholder to support other hardware platforms running embedded Linux. Banana Pi-D1 [3] is an open IP camera project based on a different embedded system board. Compared to Banana Pi-D1, Smart Beholder has been optimized by solving various research problems described in the paper, e.g., constructing QoE model for preview adaptation, and minimizing latency by reducing memory copies. These optimization techniques can also be applied to Banana Pi-D1 and other similar projects.

2. RELATED WORK

Smart lenses are remotely related to mobile photography and camera sensor networks. Mobile photography refers to using smartphones for photo taking, which has attracted considerable attentions in several application domains, such as health care [33] and ethnography [15]. Existing mobile photography studies rely on built-in cameras of smartphones, and can be extended by attaching smart lenses. Camera sensor networks consist of motes with camera sensors and network interfaces, and transmit captured videos over multi-hop wireless networks to one or multiple clients [12, 36]. Camera sensor networks focus more on multi-hop routing, while smart lenses support single-hop transmission of high quality photo (video) to smartphones (tablets).

Remote screen sharing systems impose similar requirements as smart lenses: (i) low interaction delay and (ii) high video quality, but Chang et al. [6] show that earlier screen sharing systems [4, 22, 35] fail to concurrently achieve these two goals. To cope with this limitation, several companies offer streaming-based cloud gaming platforms [13, 26, 32], and multiple research groups also develop open-source cloud gaming [19] and screen sharing [5] platforms. Some platforms adopt adaptive video streaming technology to optimize QoE under various network conditions [17]. These remote screen sharing systems are not designed for resource-scarce smart lenses, and they assume the Internet infrastructure is always available. Our proposed Smart Beholder platform is, in contrast, tailored for smart lenses.

Although the performance evaluations of smart lenses have never been done, similar measurement methodologies have been proposed for remote screen sharing systems [21, 31], cloud gaming platforms [7, 8], and screencast technologies [16, 18]. Nonetheless, the existing measurement methodologies work on videos captured from the frame buffer, while the methodology proposed in this paper considers real-time videos captured from camera sensors. The measurement methodology is useful in its own right, e.g., to evaluate the commercial smart lens products which are proprietary and closed.

3. PROPOSED SYSTEM ARCHITECTURE

The server and client architecture of the proposed Smart Beholder is given in Figure 2. Smart Beholder is inspired by cloud gaming and screen sharing platforms [5, 19], but concentrates on solving the unique challenges of smart lenses, including (i) resource constraints of embedded system boards, (ii) uncertainty of

Table 1: **Candidate Embedded System Boards**

	Arduino	Raspberry Pi (B)	UDOO	BeagleBoard	Pandaboard	Jetson TK1
CPU	ATmegaAVR, ARM Cortex-M3	ARM1176JZF-S	ARM Cortex-A9, ARM Cortex-M3/M4	ARM Cortex-A8	ARM Cortex-A9	ARM Cortex A15
GPU	None	Broadcom VideoCore IV	Integrated graphics	PowerVR SGX530	SGX540 graphics	192 SM3.2 CUDA cores
I/O port	Regular USB	USB 2.0	USB 2.0	USB 2.0	USB 2.0	USB 3.0
HW encoder	None	H.264	H.264	H.264, MPEG4	H.264, MPEG4	H.264, VC-1, VP8
Memory	16 - 512 KB	512 MB	512 MB - 1 GB	256 - 512 MB	1 GB	2 GB
Price	$13 - $60	$35	$135	$49 - $149	$174 - $182	$192
Camera module	Yes	Yes	Yes	Yes	Yes	No

single-hop short-range networks, and (iii) high overhead of external camera modules. The Smart Beholder server runs on an embedded system board, and consists of three software components: AP (Access Point) service, DHCP (Dynamic Host Configuration Protocol) server, and video streamer. The AP service turns the server into an access point, allowing Smart Beholder clients to connect to the server via Wi-Fi (or other wireless networks). The DHCP server assigns IP addresses to connected mobile clients. Meanwhile, the video streamer: (i) captures videos using a camera, (ii) encodes videos using software/hardware codecs, and (iii) streams encoded videos via the RTSP (Real-Time Streaming Protocol) and RTP (Real-Time Protocol) servers.

The Smart Beholder client runs on mobile devices and consists of two components: UI (User Interface) and video streamer. The UI component is composed of the viewfinder and camera controller. The viewfinder renders the live videos received from the Smart Beholder server, and the camera controller sends camera control commands to the server. Possible camera control commands include taking photo, recording video, setting white balance, applying image effects, configuring exposure, and tuning sensitivity. The video streamer contains hardware/software decoders, controller client, and RTSP/RTP client.

4. DESIGN OBJECTIVES

Smart Beholder aims to provide an open platform for researchers and developers to study and build real-time mobile photography applications. The design objectives of the proposed Smart Beholder platform include:

- **Cost effectiveness**. To allow more researchers and developers to use Smart Beholder, we carefully select more cost-effective hardware components. Users are, however, free to swap in/out any of the components to meet their needs.
- **Low latency**. Users will be annoyed by long latency when using mobile photography applications, especially in viewfinder previews. To provide better photo taking experience, we strive to minimize latencies of all components.
- **High quality**. A fundamental requirement for photography is maximizing the photo (video) quality. The photo (video) quality largely depends on the hardware specifications of camera components, which are out of the scope of this work. On the other hand, sending live previews (for both photo and video shots) incurs a huge amount of real-time traffic, and thus leaves more rooms for optimization. Indeed, the quality of live previews significantly affects how a photographer sees and composes photos, especially for portraits and close-up shots. Hence, for higher QoE, we endeavor to maximize the preview video quality.

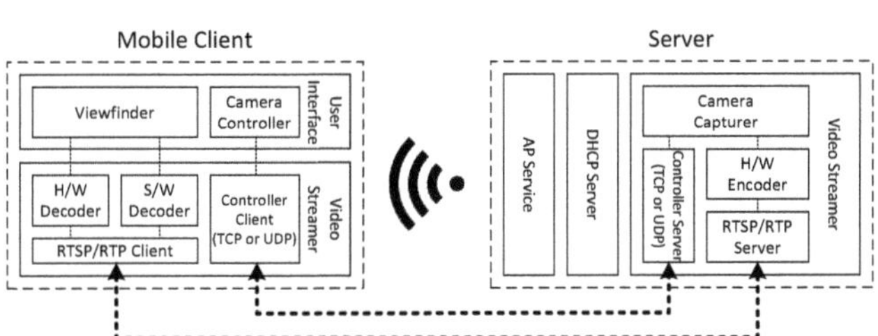

Figure 2: The server and client architecture of Smart Beholder.

We emphasize that concurrently achieving all design goals is no easy task. For example, we have to optimize individual components in the video processing pipeline to minimize the system-wide latency. In addition, we need to consider multiple user-perceived quality metrics, such as graphics quality and interactivity, which further complicates the design of Smart Beholder. We present our approaches to achieve the design goals in the next few sections.

5. HARDWARE PLATFORM

We present the options of main hardware components, and our design decisions.

5.1 Embedded System Boards

Table 1 summarizes the candidate boards. While Arduino is the least expensive board, it does not have enough resources (such as memory) to host Linux OS. This significantly increases the implementation complexity. Moreover, Arduino is not equipped with GPU, which is dictated by real-time video encoding. Hence, we adopt Raspberry Pi, which has a GPU and supports Linux OS and is just powerful enough for Smart Beholder.

5.2 Camera Modules

There are two ways to attach cameras to Raspberry Pi: USB and Camera Serial Interface (CSI). We have experimentally integrated cameras via both interfaces, as detailed below. We adopt *Video4Linux* API to access USB cameras. The API supports UVC (USB Video Class) compatible cameras [25]. The slower `read` system call supports all UVC cameras, while the more efficient `mmap` system call only supports some UVC cameras. Modern webcams like Logitech C525 are supported by `mmap`, but many of them can only capture raw video frames in YUYV (YUV422) format. The YUYV frames are not supported by some encoders, and have to be converted into YUV420 format. We find that Raspberry Pi only achieves 6 to 9 fps (frame per second) at 720p resolution. Hence, USB cameras are less suitable for live previews. CSI cameras, such as Omnivision OV5647, support *Video4Linux* and *OpenMAX IL*. Different from user-space *Video4Linux*, *OpenMAX IL* abstracts a set of multimedia hardware components for developers to use in an efficient way. Therefore, we employ *OpenMAX IL* to access CSI cameras. Doing so increases the 720p frame rate to 15 fps, which is still lower than acceptable. A closer look indicates that

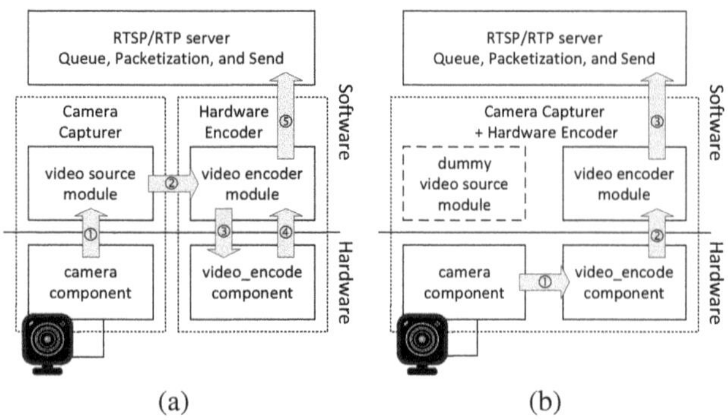

Figure 3: Server software components: (a) unoptimized and (b) optimized.

such inferior frame rate is partially due to expensive (and redundant) memory copies, which are further optimized in Section 6.2.

6. SOFTWARE DESIGN DECISIONS

We minimize the latency of several software components, to minimize the overall latency.

6.1 Hardware Encoder

To reduce the encoding latency, we leverage Raspberry Pi's H.264 hardware encoder via *OpenMAX IL*. This encoder supports various configuration options, and we exercise the following options: profile, bitrate, frame-rate, GoP size, and B frames. One minor issue of Raspberry Pi's hardware encoder is lack of mechanisms to retrieve the SPS (Sequence Parameter Set) and PPS (Picture Parameter Set) parameters associated with an encoder, which are mandatory for correctly setting up the RTSP/RTP server. To cope with this limitation, we first initialize the hardware encoder with a set of parameters P, use it to encode some dummy frames, and then retrieve the SPS and PPS parameters from the encoded video frames. We use those retrieved SPS and PPS parameters to setup the RTSP/RTP server. Next, we re-initialize the encoder with the same set of parameters P in order to ensure that encoded video frames have identical SPS and PPS parameters with the RTSP/RTP server. This allows us to use hardware encoder for lower latency.

6.2 Reduce the Number of Memory Copies

Figure 3(a) presents the software components that are not optimized for low latency. The camera capturer and hardware encoder both span over software and hardware, and thus several memory copies, such as arrows 1 and 3, incur unnecessary overhead. We propose an optimized design in Figure 3(b), which directly passes raw video frames from camera to hardware encoder. By doing so, we significantly increase the capture and encoding rates to 60 fps at 720p and 30 fps at 1080p. This leads to much smoother previews and shorter latency. In addition, the optimized server components are simpler and easier to implement.

6.3 Software Decoder

We have experimentally implemented both software and hardware decoders. Intuitively, hardware decoders run faster than software ones. However, our experiments using Android's *MediaCodec* framework to access hardware decoders on several Sony/HTC mobile devices incur an additional delay between 80 and 100 ms, which is independent to frame resolutions. Some preliminary tests indicate that official Java-based hardware decoder APIs always buffer a couple of frames. The buffer size, however, is not configurable via *MediaCodec* framework. Therefore, we adopt *ffmpeg* software decoder, which achieves 24 fps at 720x480. This is sufficient for live preview on mobile clients. By adopting software decoders, we have full control over the decoding and buffering mechanisms. For minimum delay, we decode a frame whenever we see an end-of-frame mark; consequently, we achieve a ≤ 10 ms buffering time unless the network condition is highly unstable. Currently we adopt the software decoder for shorter latency, but future Smart Beholder may switch to hardware decoders if the extra buffering time can be controlled and eliminated.

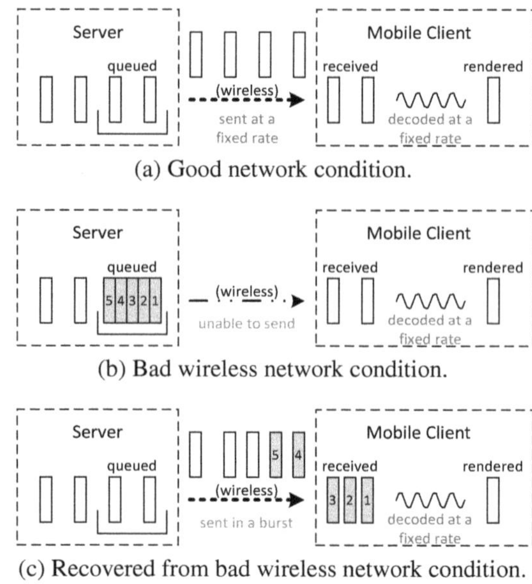

Figure 4: An illustrative example of time-drifted video frames.

6.4 Time-Drifted Video Frames

Our early experiments indicate that playout times of video frames may be drifted. Figure 4 presents an example that causes time-drifted video frames. When network condition is good (Figure 4(a)), server sends video frames at a fixed rate, and mobile client renders video frames at the same rate. When network transmission is stalled due to weak signals or wireless interference (Figure 4(b)), video frames are queued on the server (at IP or MAC layer). Once network condition is recovered (Figure 4(c)), queued video frames are sent in a burst. The decoder at mobile client may fail to keep up with bursty video frames, and renders some video frames too late. This results in time-drifted video frames.

We propose to drop late video frames at mobile clients to address this issue. For this purpose, we attach two timestamps with each video frame: (i) receiving time at client and (ii) sending time at server. For frame i, we denote the receiving timestamp as tr_i and sending timestamp as ts_i, and the time offsets as $\delta tr_i = tr_i - tr_1$ and $\delta ts_i = ts_i - ts_1$. The frame delay is $\Delta f_i = \delta tr_i - \delta ts_i$. We drop a frame i iff $\Delta f_i > L$, where L is a user-configurable threshold. L typically is in the order of tenth of ms, and we use 50 ms if not otherwise specified.

7. ADAPTIVE LIVE PREVIEW

We develop empirical models and then propose an efficient adaptation algorithm to dynamically maximize the QoE of live previews.

7.1 Single-Hop Wi-Fi Network Model

Estimating available bandwidth of an ongoing live preview session is extremely challenging, although several attempts have been made in wired [20, 28] and wireless [24] networks. These approaches send *extra* probing packets, which incur additional overhead on the already tight network resources. In contrast, we develop a customized network model to leverage *existing video packets* for estimating the available bandwidth. Our core idea, inspired by WBest [24], is to keep track of the size and receiving timestamp of packet p as s_p and tr_p. We then compute the dispersion time of every pair of adjacent packets (belonging to the same video frame), and estimate the instantaneous capacity c_p as $c_p = s_{p-1}/(tr_p - tr_{p-1})$. We can use video packets as probing packets, because: (i) Smart Beholder server sends a video frame every 33 ms (assuming a 30-fps configuration), and thus the instantaneous sending bitrate is much higher than the coding bitrate; and (ii) each video frame is composed of several back-to-back packets due to the limited network MSS (Maximum Segment Size). Furthermore, the single-hop Wi-Fi network is dedicated to Smart Beholder, and thus the available bandwidth is the same as estimated capacity. Our initial experiments indicate that c_p fluctuates quite a bit. Therefore, we adopt a sliding window of $W + 1$ packets for de-noising. This is similar to prior studies [20, 24, 28], which employ diverse aggregation approaches, such as mean, medium, and maximum. To be more general and adaptive, we sort all instantaneous capacity values within sliding window (packets $c_{p-W}, c_{p-W+1}, \ldots, c_p$) in the increasing order. We let $\bar{c}_p^\alpha$ be the α-percentile capacity, and use it to estimate the network capacity (available bandwidth).

We have instructed Smart Beholder and conducted experiments to determine the best W and α parameters to better match the estimated capacity with the ground truth given by (intrusive) tools, like `iperf`. We place the sender and client in a hallway, and vary the distance between them between 1 and 40 meters. We measure the network capacity using Smart Beholder and `iperf` at each distance for 1 minute. We then derive the best α parameter based on the ground truth. We first vary the sliding windows size $W = \{375, 750, 1500, 3000\}$ and repeat the experiments 5 times to check the consistency of the best α parameters. We compute the variance of α and find that the variance becomes negligible (at most 8×10^{-4}) with $W = 3000$. Hence, we set W to be 3000. In our experiments, we find that α parameter depends on the *signal strength*, denoted as g, of Wi-Fi. Most OS's, including Android, constantly report Wi-Fi signal strength in dBm, which may be readily used by our adaptation algorithm. Therefore, we conduct additional experiments and log the g values, in order to model α as a function of g. The empirical results reveals that α can be modeled as a piecewise linear function [23] as illustrated in Figure 5. Using adaptive α parameters allow us to better approximate the ground truth from `iperf` without the excessive network overhead. Last, we note that, currently α values are derived offline, while online training of α is also possible.

7.2 Quality of Experience Model

Smart Beholder supports dynamic adjustments of bitrate b, frame rate f, and resolution r of viewfinder previews on-the-fly. However, determining these encoding parameters for high QoE is challenging, and therefore we conduct a user study to derive the model for our adaptation algorithm as follows. We run the sever on a Raspberry Pi and the client on an Xperia tablet in our lab. We vary the encoding configurations in terms of bitrate $b = \{0.5, 1, 2\}$ Mbps, frame rate $f = \{10, 20, 30\}$ fps, and resolution $r = \{$160x120, 352x288, 544x288, 640x480, 864x480$\}$. We recruit subjects on campus and online for the user study. Each subject has

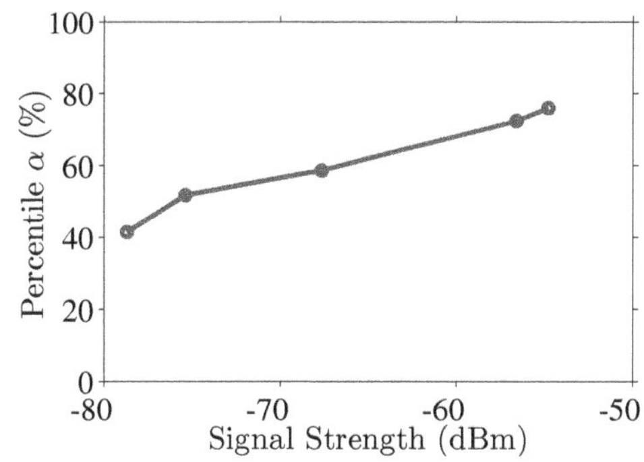

Figure 5: Piecewise linear model of α.

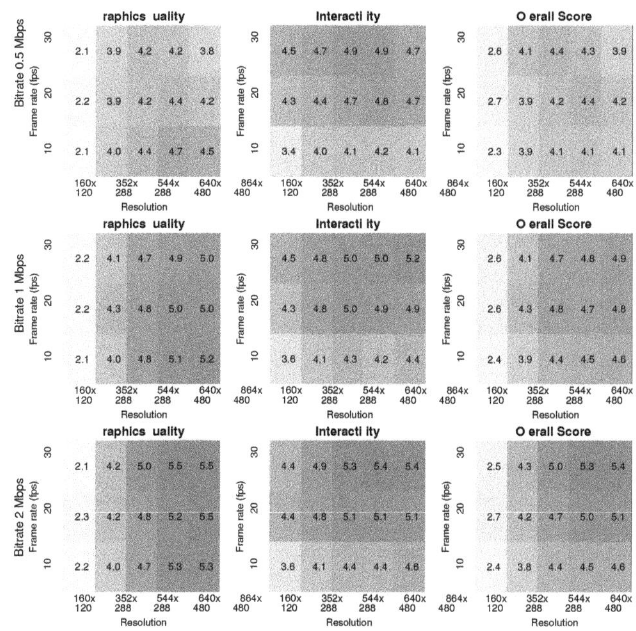

Figure 6: Mean MOS scores from a Smart Beholder testbed.

at most 3 minutes to use Smart Beholder under each configuration. For each configuration, a subject gives three quality scores between 1 (worst) and 7 (best) on: (i) graphics quality, (ii) interactivity, and (iii) overall satisfaction. Subjects are free to terminate 3-minute experiments earlier. We have 30 subjects (63% male) and perform 89 sessions (45 rounds per session) in total. Each session lasts for 31 minutes on average, and the total user study time is almost 46 hours.

We made two observations on the overall MOS scores given in Figure 6. First, when the bitrate is $\geq$ 1 Mbps, higher frame rates and resolutions lead to higher MOS scores. Second, when the bitrate is lower (0.5 Mbps), higher resolutions (such as 864x480) may result in lower MOS scores (than, e.g., 544x288). These two observations show the importance of the QoE model because *higher bitrates, frame rates, and resolutions do not guarantee better QoE.* Based on Figure 6, we let $\mathbf{Q}_b$ be the *overall MOS table* at bitrate b, and $q_b(f, r)$ be the MOS score at b, f, and r. $\mathbf{Q}_b$ table is given in the figure if $b \in \{0.5, 1, 2\}$, but is interpolated/extrapolated otherwise. Then, to get $q_b(f, r)$ we look up table $\mathbf{Q}_b$ with potential inter-

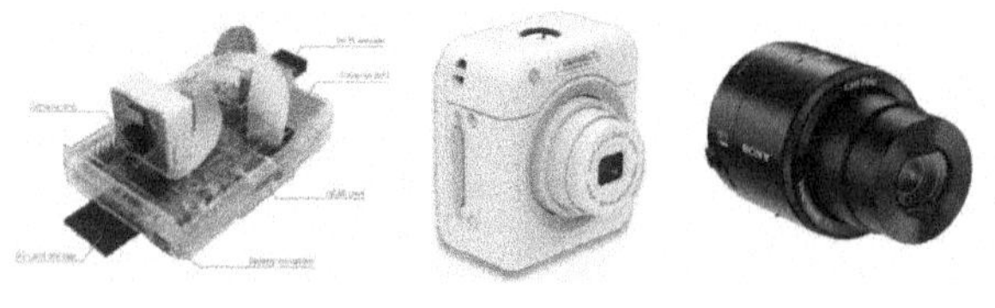

Figure 7: Photos of the considered smart lenses: Smart Beholder (left), Altek Cubic (middle), and Sony QX100 (right).

Algorithm 1 Preview Adaptation Algorithm

1: **for** every T seconds **do**
2: Compute $\bar{c}_p^{\alpha}$ and ρ
3: **if** $b < \bar{c}_p^{\alpha}$ and $\rho < \rho_l$ **then**
4: $b = b + (\bar{c}_p^{\alpha} - b) \times \delta_i$
5: **else if** $b > \bar{c}_p^{\alpha}$ or $\rho > \rho_h$ **then**
6: $b = \gamma_r \times \bar{c}_p^{\alpha}$
7: **end if**
8: Given b, lookup $q_b(f^*, r^*)$ for the highest MOS score
9: Reconfigure video encoder with b, f^*, r^*
10: **end for**

polation/extrapolation as well. The presented QoE model enables us to pick the encoding parameters for optimal user experience.

7.3 Preview Adaptation Algorithm

We develop an efficient algorithm to dynamically adjust the encoding parameters, in order to avoid QoE degradation due to network impairments such as insufficient bandwidth and high packet loss rate. The algorithm runs periodically, evaluating available bandwidth $\bar{c}_p^{\alpha}$ (using the network model developed above) and packet loss rate ρ on mobile client once every T seconds. T is a system parameter, which is set to 10 seconds by default. $\bar{c}_p^{\alpha}$ and ρ are sent back to the server to make decisions on encoding parameters based on four other system parameters: minimum loss rate ρ_l, maximum loss rate ρ_h, bitrate increment step δ_i, and bitrate restoration factor γ_r. If not otherwise specified, we set $\rho_l = 5\%$, $\rho_h = 20\%$, $\delta_i = 0.2$, and $\gamma_r = 0.7$.

Algorithm 1 gives the pseudocode of our algorithm. Line 3 checks whether our encoding bitrate is lower than available bandwidth[1] and packet loss rate is low; if it passes, line 4 increases encoding bitrate. Lines 5 and 6 are similar, but to reduce encoding bitrate by setting it to a certain ratio (i.e., γ_r) times the measured available bandwidth. At line 7, we know the target encoding bitrate b, and employ the QoE model to get the best f^* and r^*. Line 9 reconfigures the video encoder. It is easy to see that our preview adaptation algorithm runs in constant time at the server. At the mobile client, sorting instantaneous capacity values when deriving $\bar{c}_p^{\alpha}$ dominates the time complexity, which is $O(W \log W)$. Given that W is at most a few thousands, the computation complexity is relatively negligible to modern smartphones.

Last, we evaluate the accuracy of the proposed adaptation algorithm by separating the server and client by 1.25, 2.5, 5, 10, and 20 meters. We use Smart Beholder and `iperf` to measure the network capacity for 1 minute at each distance, and repeat the experiments 5 times. Table 2 summarizes the estimated capacity from Smart Beholder and `iperf`. This table shows that Smart Beholder achieves very small deviation compared to the ground truth from `iperf`. The deviation is higher under shorter distances, which however is not a big issue because the available bandwidth is sufficient (e.g., $\sim$ 40 Mbps at 1.25 m) for all practical frame rates and resolutions.

[1]We note that the protocol overhead is considered in our implementation when comparing $\bar{c}_p^{\alpha}$ and ρ. We omit this technical detail in our descriptions for brevity.

Table 2: Average Accuracy of Capacity Measured by Beholder

Distance	1.25 m	2.5 m	5 m	10 m	20 m
Beholder	44.89 Mbps	39.33 Mbps	33.76 Mbps	31.29 Mbps	10.02 Mbps
`iperf`	39.47 Mbps	36.22 Mbps	31.77 Mbps	29.38 Mbps	10.06 Mbps
Deviation	13.7 %	8.5 %	6.3 %	6.5 %	0.4 %

Table 3: Considered Smart Lenses

	Altek Cubic	Sony QX100	Smart Beholder
Model	Altek Cubic C01	Sony DSC-QX100	Raspberry Pi Model B
Image Resolution	2 MP (1600x1200) 13 MP (4160x3120)	5 MP (2592x1944) 18 MP (4864x3648)	5 MP (2592x1944)
Video Resolution	1920x1080 @ 30 fps	1920x1080 @ 30 fps	1920x1080 @ 30 fps

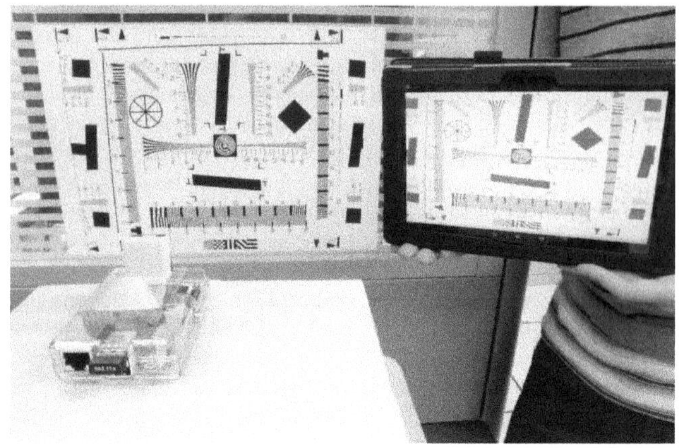

Figure 8: Experiment setup for inferring the preview resolutions of commercial smart lenses.

8. PERFORMANCE EVALUATION

We conduct real experiments to compare Smart Beholder against commercial smart lenses.

8.1 Preview Resolutions of Commercial Smart Lenses

We consider two commercial smart lens products: Altek Cubic and Sony QX100. They both offer in-house mobile apps on Android devices. Figure 7 shows the three smart lenses and Table 3 presents their specifications. Our Smart Beholder is fully configurable, and supports different preview resolutions. The two commercial products only support fixed preview resolutions, which is unknown to users.

We use a PIMA/ISO 12233 Resolution Test Chart [10] to infer the preview resolutions. The experiment setup is presented in Figure 8. We place the smart lens about 30 centimeters away from the test chart, so that the test chart on viewfinder approximately spans the viewable area, and stream preview videos to the tablet on the right. We use only the lower-middle part of the test chart, where 10 numbered blocks with vertical lines in different densities (and widths) are arranged into a row. The block numbers indicate how dense these vertical lines are: from 1 (fewest, thickest lines) to 10 (most, thinnest lines), and we refer to the block number as *line density*. To count the number of lines in blocks with higher line densities, video previews with higher resolutions are needed. We

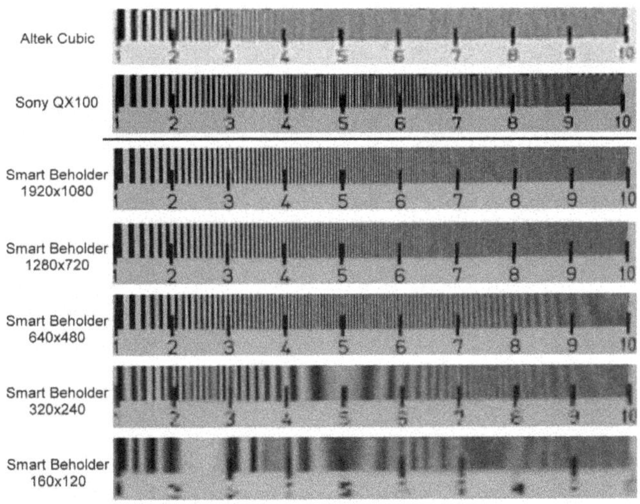

Figure 9: Live preview screenshots of line intensity testing region on the resolution test chart.

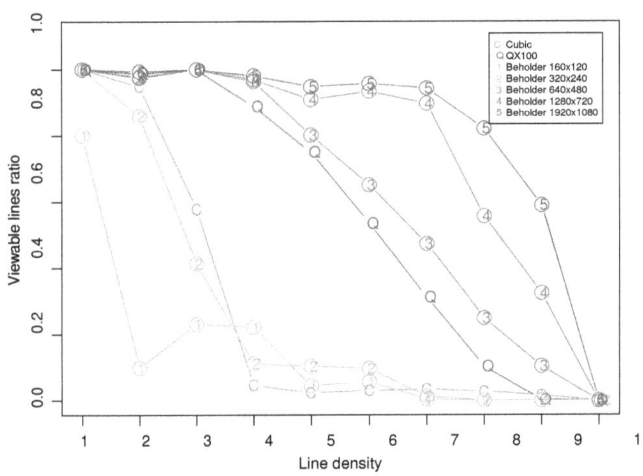

Figure 10: Viewable line ratios of different smart lenses under diverse line densities.

define *viewable line ratio* as the fraction of distinguishable vertical lines over all vertical lines in the test chart.

We then execute the following experiments with Altek Cubic, Sony QX100, and Smart Beholder under 5 different resolutions. For each smart lens (and resolution), we take screenshots of the live preview of the resolution test chart and crop the line intensity testing region, as shown in Figure 9. We then convert the regional screenshots to binary (black and white) using the threshold 128 (with the gray levels ranging from 0 to 255) and programmatically count the numbers of vertical lines in individual blocks (from 1 to 10) in the video previewers in order to calculate the viewable line ratios. We plot the results in Figure 10. This figure shows that Altek Cubic and Sony QX100 achieve very similar viewable line ratios over different line densities as Smart Beholder at 320x240 and 640x480 resolutions, respectively. Hence, we conclude that the preview resolutions of these two commercial products are approximately 320x240 and 640x480, respectively. Even though the quality of camera lenses may be very different, we believe that the (relatively low) resolutions of preview video would dominate how distinguishable the thin lines are.

Figure 11: Testbed setup.

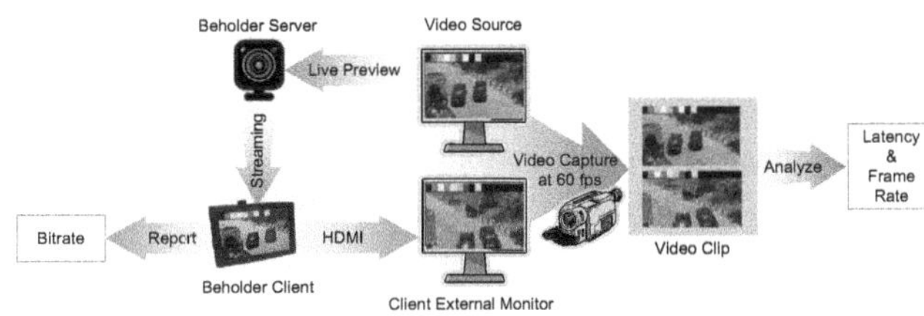

Figure 12: Experimental procedure.

8.2 Setup

We create two video/image datasets for objective and subjective performance metrics. For objective metrics, we use a Canon EOS 600D camera to capture eight segments of 25-sec videos at 720p. Half of the segments are taken indoor (outdoor); and all segments are taken under typical smart lens usage scenarios. We concatenate eight segments into a 216-sec video, in which we insert a 2-sec white screen between any two consecutive videos to reset the video codecs for minimum interference across videos. This dataset represents typical viewfinder previews, and are suitable for objective metrics. It is, however, less suitable for subjective metrics due to the relatively low resolution. For subjective metrics, we collect 9 high-resolution (1080p) popular Creative Commons (CC) photos from Flickr. We play each photo for 10 seconds, and record the viewfinder previews using different smart lenses.

Figure 11 shows the testbed used in our lab. We play the videos on the video source display on the right, put a Smart Beholder (or other smart lenses) server in front of the video source display, and send the previews to the corresponding smart lens client running on a tablet (Sony Xperia). The server and mobile client have a distance of 1 meter. The tablet is connected to an external monitor on the left. Last, we use a Canon EOS 600D camera to capture the videos of the two side-by-side displays at 60 fps. The captured video is then used to derive performance results. We also run `tcpdump` on the tablet to capture and calculate the transmitted bitrate. Figure 12 summarizes the measurement procedure.

For a subjective evaluation of preview quality, we conduct a crowdsourcing-based user study over the Internet via web interface. We present the original images (from Flickr) on the left half of the web page, and the degraded images (extracted from the viewfinder previews) on the right half. For each comparison, a subject gives a DMOS (Differential Mean Opinion Score) between 0 (un-degraded) and 6 (seriously degraded and unacceptable). We

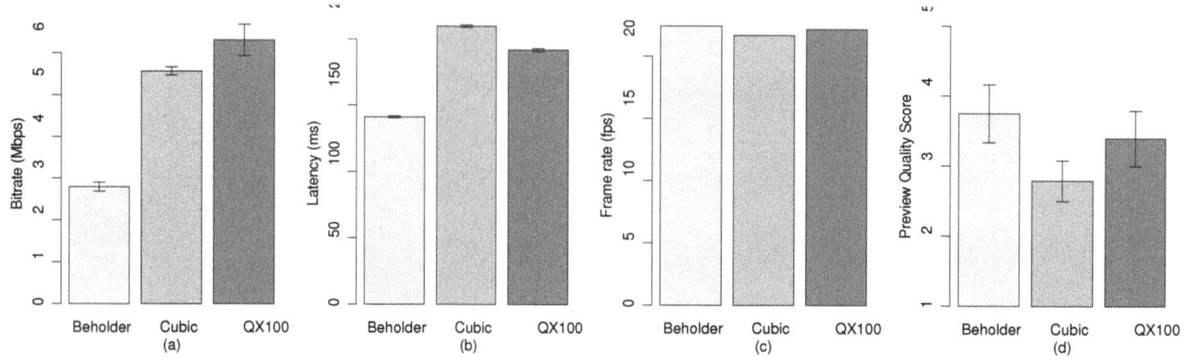

Figure 13: Overall performance comparisons among smart lenses: (a) bitrate, (b) latency, (c) frame rate, and (d) preview quality.

convert the DMOS score to an MOS score by MOS = 7−DMOS and use the resulting MOS score to be the image quality metric. We recruit 52 subjects and perform 117 sessions with a total of 14,410 comparison rounds. The total study duration is 30 hours, where each session lasts for 15 minutes on average.

We consider the following performance metrics:

- **Bitrate**, which is the number of bits sent from the server to mobile client every second.
- **Latency**, which is the delay between capturing and displaying a video frame on mobile client.
- **Frame rate**, which is the number of frames rendered at mobile client every second.
- **Energy consumption**, which is the amount of consumed energy.
- **Preview quality**, which is the MOS score. We focus on previews, because final images/videos are either saved on smart lenses, or transferred to mobile clients in batches at very high quality.

The first four metrics are objective and the last one is subjective. We give mean results with 95% confidence intervals if applicable.

8.3 Results

We first present the results with static Smart Beholder configurations, which are followed by the results with preview adaptation algorithm enabled.

Smart Beholder outperforms other smart lenses. We plot the overall performance in Figure 13. Figure 13(a) shows that Smart Beholder consumes as low as half of the bitrate compared to commercial smart lenses. This conforms to our expectation as we configure Smart Beholder to use an average bitrate of 3 Mbps. Figure 13(b) reveals that Smart Beholder results in at least 50 ms shorter latency, which in turn leads to more responsive user experience. Figure 13(c) depicts that our Smart Beholder achieves comparable, actually slightly higher, frame rate than the two commercial smart lenses. In summary, the Smart Beholder outperforms the two commercial products in all considered objective performance metrics. We report the preview image quality in Figures 13(d), which shows that our Smart Beholder achieves better MOS scores than two commercial smart lenses. More importantly, such higher preview quality does not come with higher network nor system loads as Figures 13(a) and 13(b) show.

Configurability of Smart Beholder. We vary the configurations of Smart Beholder following the parameter values in Table 4 with the default values highlighted in boldface. With each configuration, we measure the system performance using the 216-sec preview video. Two sets of sample results are given below. First, we

Table 4: The System Parameters

Parameter	Values
Frame Rate	6 fps, 12 fps, **24 fps**
Resolution	160x120, 320x240, **640x480**, 1280x720, 1920x1080
Bitrate	1 Mbps, 2 Mbps, **3 Mbps**

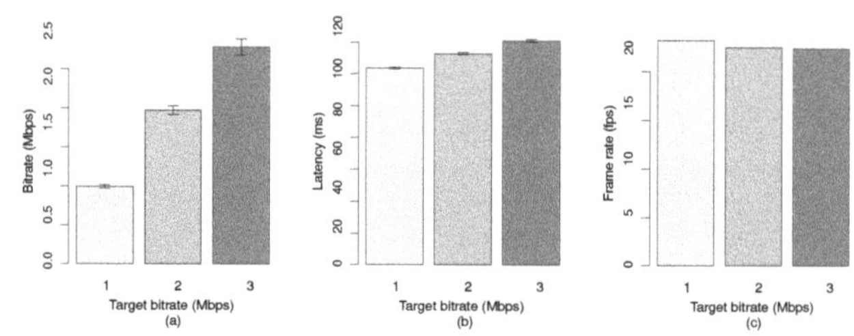

Figure 14: Beholder performance with different target bitrates: (a) achieved bitrate, (b) latency, and (c) frame rate.

adjust the target encoding bitrates and present the results in Figure 14. This figure depicts that when the target bitrate is increased, the achieved bitrate (Figure 14(a)) and the latency (Figure 14(b)) increase, while the frame rate (Figure 14(c)) slightly decreases. We believe the slightly increased latency and slightly decreased frame rate is due to a higher complexity and workload in decoding the preview videos at the client.

Next, we adjust the target frame rate and give the results in Figure 15. Figure 15(c) shows that Smart Beholder always achieves the target frame rates, which reveals the efficiency of its implementation. Figures 15(a) and 15(b) show that higher target frame rates lead to higher bitrate and lower latency, which are consis-

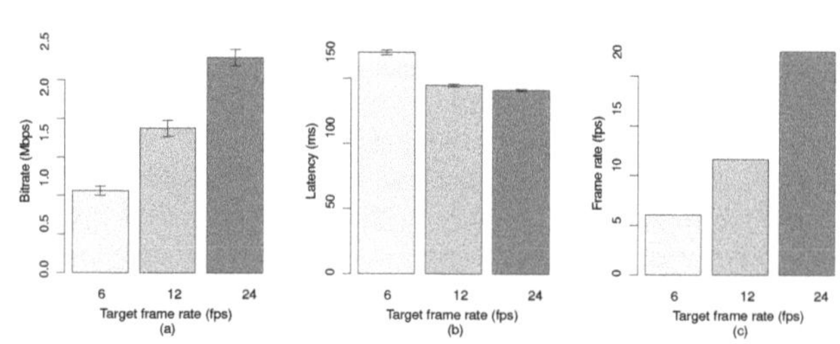

Figure 15: Beholder performance under different target frame rates: (a) bitrate, (b) latency, and (c) frame rate.

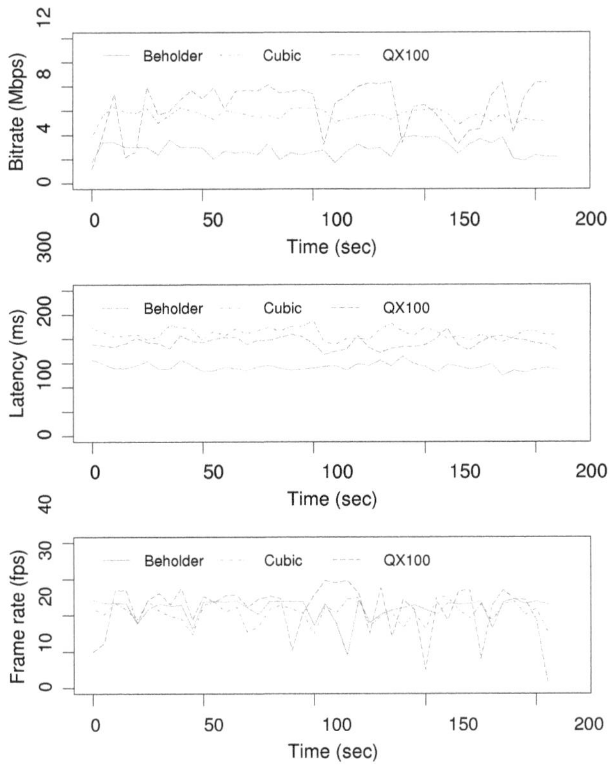

Figure 16: Needs of adaptation algorithm: (a) bitrate, (b) latency, and (c) frame rate over time.

tent with our intuition, as a 6 fps live preview incurs at least 1000 ms $\div$ 6 $\approx$ 166 ms latency. In summary, Figures 14 and 15 demonstrate the configurability of our implementation.

Needs of adaptation algorithm. We zoom into a sample run of the 216-sec video, and report the per-second bitrate, latency, and frame rate in Figure 16. Figures 16(a) and 16(b) show that Smart Beholder constantly results in low bitrate and low latency compared to the two commercial smart lenses. Figure 16(c) shows that Sony QX100 suffers from severe frame rate drops at 150-th, 175-th, and 205-th seconds, due to bad network conditions. Smart Beholder also suffers from a frame rate drop at 110-th second, which demonstrates the needs of preview adaptation algorithm.

Effectiveness of preview adaptation algorithm. We conduct experiments to quantify the performance of our proposed preview adaptation algorithm. We fix the position of the server and move the client following a 3-minute moving pattern of distance from

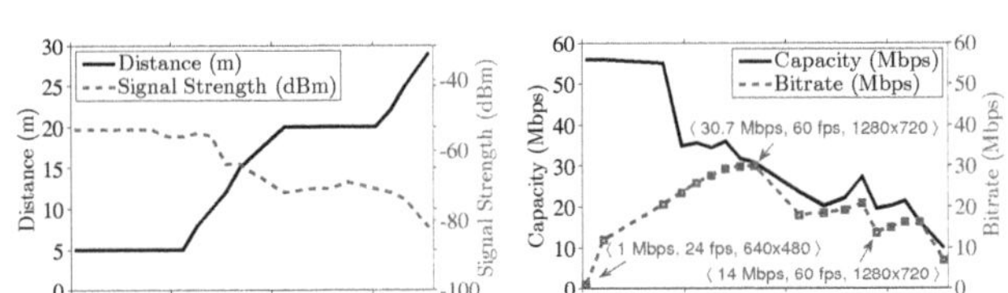

(a) (b)

Figure 17: A sample of 3-minute experiment: (a) distance affects signal strength and (b) reconfiguration (bitrate) decisions are driven by capacity estimation.

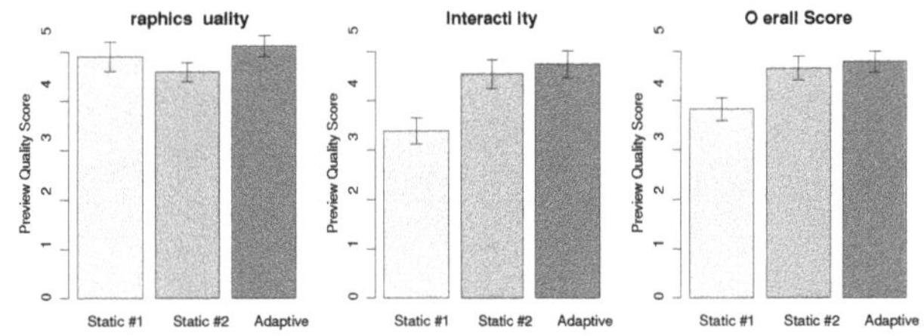

Figure 18: MOS scores of different configurations and preview adaptation algorithm.

5 to 30 m, while configuring Smart Beholder to record the signal strength, capacity, and bitrate. We plot the results in Figure 17. Figure 17(a) shows that the signal strength is inversely proportional to the distance, which is inline with our intuition. At the beginning of the experiment, we set the configuration to be ⟨1 Mbps, 24 fps, 640x480⟩, and trigger the adaptation algorithm once every 10 seconds. Figure 17(b) shows the estimated capacity and the sample bitrate decisions of our adaptation algorithm throughout the experiment. The capacity decreases with the decreasing signal strength. At 140-th second, the signal strength increases a little because the client stays at 20 meters for a while, which makes the network condition more stable. The adaptation algorithm increases the encoding bitrate until it approaches the estimated capacity (at 70-th second). At that moment, our algorithm reconfigures f to 60 fps and r to 1280x720 for the highest MOS score based on the QoE model (Section 7.2). Several other reconfiguration samples are also annotated in Figure 17(b). Last, we note that the resulting bitrate may be lower than the configured bitrate, e.g., at $f = 60$ fps and $r =$ 1280x720, the highest resulting bitrate is 9 Mbps in our experiments.

We next conduct a user study for a subjective evaluation on the preview adaptation algorithm. We compare our algorithm against two configurations: static #1, which is ⟨2 Mbps, 10 fps, 864x480⟩; and static #2, which is ⟨0.5 Mbps, 30 fps, 544x288⟩. We recruit 12 subjects and carry out 60 sessions in total. In each session, we randomly select a configuration and ask the subject to use Smart Beholder for at most 3 minutes, and then score the preview quality. 8 subjects think static #1 outperforms static #2 in graphics quality , and 10 subjects feel static #2 outperforms static #1 in interactivity. Overall, majority of subjects prefer our preview adaptation algorithm, as summarized in Figure 18. Figures 17 and 18 reveal the effectiveness of our preview adaptation algorithm in both objective and subjective metrics.

Energy efficiency. We encode the 216-sec preview video at different frame rates using software and hardware encoders on Raspberry Pi. We repeat each experiment 3 times and clear cache each time for fair comparisons. The average results reported in Table 5 show that using hardware encoder saves at least 86.5% in energy compared to using software encoder. In addition, we use PowerTutor [27] to measure the per-application energy consumption of Smart Beholder client running on an HTC One X. PowerTutor is a popular measurement tool for energy consumption on Android devices. Smart Beholder client averagely consumes about 0.97 W and the LCD display alone is responsible for 0.89 W. This shows that Smart Beholder client is energy efficient.

9. CONCLUSION

In this paper, we have proposed an open-source smart lens platform called Smart Beholder, which is designed with three objectives in mind: cost effectiveness, low latency, and high pre-

Table 5: The Energy Consumption of Beholder Server

Frame Rate	S/W Encoder	H/W Encoder	Saving of H/W Encoder
30 fps	883.44 J	104.98 J	88.1%
20 fps	530.06 J	71.50 J	86.5%
15 fps	421.63 J	42.55 J	89.9%
10 fps	304.78 J	28.51 J	90.6%
5 fps	176.04 J	18.36 J	89.6%

view quality. We have designed, implemented, and evaluated Smart Beholder using off-the-shelf components. Several optimization techniques have been proposed and implemented in this paper. We have compared the performance of Smart Beholder against two commercial smart lens products, and we have found that Smart Beholder achieves lower bitrate, lower latency, slightly higher frame rate, and better preview quality. Our measurement methodology presented in this paper is useful when more commercial smart lenses hit the market. Smart Beholder is released at `http://www.smartbeholder.org`, and can be leveraged by researchers and developers for real experiments to quantify the performance resulted by different design alternatives. We believe that Smart Beholder will lead to optimized smart lenses and other real-time video streaming systems in the future.

Acknowledgements

This work was partially supported by the Ministry of Science and Technology (MOST) of Taiwan under the grants: 103-2221-E-001-023-MY2, 103-2221-E-019-033-MY2, and 102-2221-E-007-062-MY3.

References

[1] 5 areas where cameras still beat smartphones if you want great photo quality. `http://tinyurl.com/n8f5w8d`.

[2] Altek Cubic web page. `http://www.altek.com.tw/cubic/`.

[3] Banana pi, 2014. `http://www.bananapi.org/`.

[4] R. Baratto, L. Kim, and J. Nieh. Thinc: a virtual display architecture for thin-client computing. In *Proc. of ACM Symposium on Operating Systems Principles* (SOSP'05), pages 277–290, Brighton, UK, Oct 2005.

[5] S. Chandra, J. Boreczky, and L. Rowe. High performance many-to-many Intranet screen sharing with DisplayCast. *ACM Transactions on Multimedia Computing, Communications, and Applications*, 10(2):19:1–19:22, Feb 2014.

[6] Y. Chang, P. Tseng, K. Chen, and C. Lei. Understanding the performance of thin-client gaming. In *Proc. of IEEE International Conference on Communications Quality and Reliability Workshop (CQR'11)*, pages 1–6, Naples, FL, May 2011.

[7] K. Chen, Y. Chang, H. Hsu, D. Chen, C. Huang, and C. Hsu. On the quality of service of cloud gaming systems. *IEEE Transactions on Multimedia*, 16(2):480–495, Feb 2014.

[8] M. Claypool, D. Finkel, A. Grant, and M. Solano. Thin to win? network performance analysis of the OnLive thin client game system. In *Proc. of ACM Workshop on Network and Systems Support for Games (NetGames'12)*, pages 1–6, Venice, Italy, Nov 2012.

[9] D. Z. Cook. *Advanced Dungeons & Dragons-Player's Handbook*. TSR, 1989.

[10] Digital camera resolution test procedures. `http://www.gpsinformation.org/jack/photo-test/pics/lens-tests.html`.

[11] DSC-QX100 lens-style camera with 1.0-type sensor. `http://www.sony.co.uk/electronics/cyber-shot-compact-cameras/dsc-qx100`.

[12] M. Farooq and T. Kunz. Wireless multimedia sensor networks testbeds and state-of-the-art hardware: A survey. In *Communication and Networking*, volume 265 of *Communications in Computer and Information Science*, pages 1–14. Springer Berlin Heidelberg, 2012.

[13] Gaikai web page. `http://www.gaikai.com/`.

[14] Global digital camera market decline slowing down in 2014, predicts new report. `http://iphone.tmcnet.com/news/2014/02/07/7667425.htm`.

[15] M. Halpern and L. Humphreys. Iphoneography as an emergent art world. *SAGE New Media and Society*, 2014.

[16] Y. He, K. Fei, G. Fernandez, and E. Delp. Video quality assessment for Web content mirroring. In *Proc. of Imaging and Multimedia Analytics in a Web and Mobile World*, pages 90270C–1–90270C–8, San Francisco, CA, Mar 2014.

[17] H. Hong, C. Hsu, T. Tsai, C. Huang, K. Chen, and C. Hsu. Enabling adaptive cloud gaming in an open-source cloud gaming platform. *IEEE Transactions on Circuits and Systems for Video Technology*, Jun 2015. Accepted to appear.

[18] C. Hsu, T. Tsai, C. Huang, C. Hsu, and K. Chen. Screencast dissected: Performance measurements and design considerations. In *Proc. of ACM Conference on Multimedia Systems (MMSys'15)*, pages 177–188, Portland, OR, Mar 2015.

[19] C. Huang, K. Chen, D. Chen, H. Hsu, and C. Hsu. GamingAnywhere: The first open source cloud gaming system. *ACM Transactions on Multimedia Computing, Communications, and Applications*, 10(1):36–47, Jan 2014.

[20] R. Kapoor, L. Chen, L. Lao, M. Gerla, and M. Y. Sanadidi. Capprobe: A simple and accurate capacity estimation technique. In *Proc. of SIGCOMM'04*, pages 67–78, Portland, OR, Aug 2004.

[21] H. Lagar-Cavilla, N. Tolia, E. de Lara, M. Satyanarayanan, and D. O'Hallaron. Interactive resource-intensive applications made easy. In *Proc. of the ACM/IFIP/USENIX International Conference on Middleware (Middleware'07)*, pages 143–163, Newport Beach, CA, Nov 2007.

[22] A. Lai and J. Nieh. On the performance of wide-area thin-client computing. *ACM Transactions on Computer Systems*, 24:175–209, May 2006.

[23] D. M. Leenaerts and W. M. V. Bokhoven. *Piecewise linear modeling and analysis*. Kluwer Academic Publishers, 1998.

[24] M. Li, M. Claypool, and R. Kinicki. Wbest: a bandwidth estimation tool for ieee 802.11 wireless networks. In *Proc. of IEEE Conference on Local Computer Networks (LCN'08)*, pages 374–381, Montreal, Canada, Oct 2008.

[25] Linux UVC driver and tools. `http://www.ideasonboard.org/uvc/`.

[26] OnLive web page, 2014. `http://www.onlive.com/`.

[27] PowerTutor. `http://ziyang.eecs.umich.edu/projects/powertutor/`.

[28] V. Ribeiro, R. Riedi, R. Baraniuk, J. Navratil, and L. Cottrell. Pathchirp: Efficient available bandwidth estimation for network paths. In *Proc. of Passive and Active Monitoring Workshop (PAM'03)*, volume 4, San Diego, CA, Apr 2003.

[29] M. Richardson and S. Wallace. *Getting Started with Raspberry Pi*. "O'Reilly Media, Inc.", 2012.

[30] Sl10 smart lens camera sl10. `http://kodakcamera.jkiltd.com/Americas/cameras/smartlens/sl10.php`.

[31] N. Tolia, D. Andersen, and M. Satyanarayanan. Quantifying interactive user experience on thin clients. *Computer*, 39(3):46–52, 2006.

[32] Ubitus web page. `http://www.ubitus.net`.

[33] K. Wac. Smartphone as a personal, pervasive health informatics services platform: Literature review. *IMIA Yearbook 2012: Personal Health Informatics*, 7(1):83–93, 2012.

[34] Worldwide smartphone shipments top one billion units for the first time, according to IDC. `http://www.idc.com/getdoc.jsp?containerId=prUS24645514`.

[35] S. Yang, J. Nieh, M. Selsky, and N. Tiwari. The performance of remote display mechanisms for thin-client computing. In *Proc. of USENIX Annual Technical Conference (ATC'02)*, pages 131–146, Monterey, CA, Jun 2002.

[36] S. Yoon, H. Oh, D. Lee, and S. Oh. Virtual lock: A smartphone application for personal surveillance using camera sensor networks. In *Proc. of IEEE International Conference on Embedded and Real-Time Computing Systems and Applications (RTCSA'11)*, pages 77–82, Toyama, Japan, Aug 2011.

Coherent Motion Detection with Collective Density Clustering

Yunpeng Wu, Yangdong Ye*, Chenyang Zhao
School of Information Engineering, Zhengzhou University
No.1, KeXue Road, Zhengzhou, China, 450001
{ieypwu, ieydye}@zzu.edu.cn, iecyzhao@gs.zzu.edu.cn

ABSTRACT

Detecting coherent motion is significant for analysing the crowd motion in video applications. In this study, we propose the Collective Density Clustering(CDC) approach to recognize both local and global coherent motion having arbitrary shapes and varying densities. Firstly, the collective density is defined to reveal the underlying patterns with varying levels of density. Based on collective density, the collective clustering algorithm is further presented to recognize the local consistency, where density-based clustering is more adaptive to recognize clusters with arbitrary shapes. This algorithm has salient properties including single step of clustering process, automatical decision of clustering number and accurate identification of outliers. Finally, the collective merging algorithm is introduced to fully characterize the global consistency. Experiments on diverse crowd scenes, including pedestrians, traffic and bacterial colony, demonstrate the effectiveness for coherent motion detection. The comparisons show that our approach outperforms state-of-the-art coherent detection techniques.

Categories and Subject Descriptors

I.4.8 [**Computing Methodologies**]: Scene Analysis; I.5.3 [**Computing Methodologies**]: Clustering

General Terms

Understanding, Algorithm

Keywords

Collective Behaviour, Coherent Motion Detection, Collective Density Clustering

1. INTRODUCTION

Coherent motion is one of the most ubiquitous phenomenon in nature (*e.g.* Fig.1(A)), which is existing widely from the bacterial colony of biology [6, 24] to the interactive particles in physical field [19, 20]. Detecting coherent motion and understanding the underlying principles have drawn increasing attentions in recent years, since they are of great importance for video applications, such as event recognition [14, 12, 17], activity recognition [5, 4], object counting [15] and crowd tracking [2, 11].

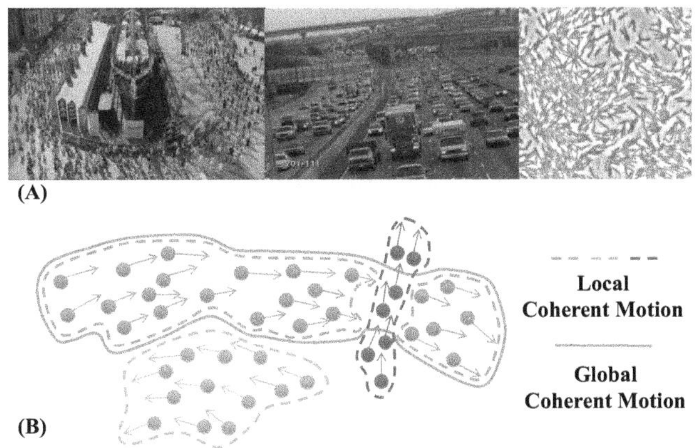

Figure 1: (A) Coherent motion of crowd, traffic and bacterial colony. (B) Both the local and global coherent motion having arbitrary shapes and varying densities make it challenging to detect the collective behaviour.

Coherent motion, which involves both local and global consistency, can be described as the behaviour that individuals act as a union. For the local consistency, each individual has consistent motion with the neighbors in collective subgroup. The global consistency reveals the continuity among different subgroups. Many works have been proposed on detecting coherent motion [1, 10, 22, 8, 23]. However, these methods are not suitable for collective crowd with complex patterns. The latest works [25, 26, 18] model the coherent structures through characterizing the local spatiotemporal relationships, where more satisfying results appear. Meanwhile, they place emphasis on the local spatiotemporal relationships of individuals and are limited to recognizing the global consistency with low-density and disconnected areas(*e.g.* Fig.1(B)).

The collective cluster with arbitrary shapes and varying densities is salient feature of coherent motion. Density-based clustering are adaptive to the clusters with arbitrary shapes.

*The Corresponding Author

MM'15, October 26–30, 2015, Brisbane, Australia.
© 2015 ACM. ISBN 978-1-4503-3459-4/15/10 ...$15.00.
DOI: http://dx.doi.org/10.1145/2733373.2806227.

However, the DBSCAN [7] and density peaks method [16] have their basis in the assumptions that cluster centers are surrounded by the neighbors with lower density. It's difficult for them to reveal the underlying patterns with varying levels of density in collective crowd. Existing works [3, 9] regard the coherent motion as the clustering of motion flow field. However, they are limited to specifying clustering number manually.

Efficiency is another key challenge for the application of coherent motion detection. The diverse events from large amounts of videos require a more efficient way to analyse the collective motion. The existing works [1, 10, 22, 3, 13, 9, 21] mainly extract the motion patterns from optimal flow field. However, the optimal flow considers large amounts of tracking points in both stationary and moving areas, even for an image with low sampling rate. An alternative research is based on local coherent structure [8, 25, 26]. Meanwhile, the time cost for maintaining the topological structure for each individual is expensive. Thus, the methods mentioned above are limited to real-time applications.

In this study, we propose the Collective Density Clustering (CDC) approach to detect coherent motion. The CDC achieves the detection with considering both the local and global coherent motion. Firstly, the collective density is defined with novelty to reveal the collectiveness in coherent motion. Secondly, a novel collective clustering algorithm is presented to recognize the local consistency. The underlying principle is that cluster centers of collective subgroups are characterized by a higher collective density than their neighbors and a relatively large distance or inconsistent orientation from points with higher densities. The proposed algorithm has salient characters: (1) the single step of collective clustering; (2) the automatical decision of clustering centers; (3) the accurate identification of outliers. Finally, the motion with global consistency is fully emerged with the collective merging. The experiments on diverse crowd scenes, including pedestrians, traffic and bacterial colony, demonstrate the high accuracy for coherent motion detection. Compared with the state of the arts, the CDC approach achieves significant improvements on both effectiveness and efficiency. The main contributions of our approach can be concluded as follows:

1. The Collective Density Clustering (CDC) approach is proposed to detect both local and global coherent motion with arbitrary shapes and varying densities. The accuracy and efficiency of CDC guarantee the effectiveness for real-time applications.

2. The collective density is defined with novelty, which describes the collectiveness between individual and its neighbors. Compared with the normal density estimation, the collective density is more adaptive to reveal the underlying patterns of varying densities in coherent motion.

3. Based on collective density, the proposed clustering algorithm has salient properties: (1) the single step of clustering process; (2) the automatic decision of clustering centers; (3) the accurate identification of outliers.

2. RELATED WORKS

Coherent motion attracts many attentions from biology [6, 24] to physics [19, 20]. Especially, detecting coherent motion is significant for the analysis of video applications. Thus, many researchers in multimedia and vision have engaged to recognize the patterns existing in crowd motion. Many works have been proposed on the task of coherent detection. However, they are not mature for detecting the coherent motion accurately and efficiently.

The remarkable solutions focus on extracting coherent motion from the optical flow field. In [3], Brox learned the crowd motion by long term analysis of point trajectories. However, it is not suitable for motions with complex patterns. Ali [1] proposed a lagrangian particle dynamics based segmentation of high density crowd flows. In [13], Mehran *et al.* asserted a streakline framework as a new tool for crowd segmentation. Wu *et al.* [22] proposed a crowd motion partitioning approach based on scattered motion field segmentation. However, the segmentation results have the limitation for global coherent motion. Hu *et al.* [9] detected motion patterns by the clustering of motion flow fields with complex interaction. Meanwhile, the cluster number must be pre-specified. The latest work [21] achieved the coherent detection with thermal energy field and further constructed the semantic regions. However, the pixel-level computation has the limitation of efficiency.

Another distinct solution is based on local coherent structure. In [10], Kratz estimated the pedestrian efficiency to detect unusual events and track individuals in crowded scenes. Ge *et al.* [8] automatically detected small groups of individuals by bottom-up hierarchical clustering. Meanwhile, these methods are not adaptive for the complex patterns. Zhang [23] presented a novel framework to parse collective behaviors for video surveillance applications. The latest works [25, 26, 18] introduced spatial-temporal correlation to model the coherent motion among particles, while more satisfying results appeared. However, there are two limitations: (1) it's not perfect for the complex scenes with global coherent motion; (2) the computation of maintaining the K-Nearest-Neighbor structure is expensive.

The reminder for the rest of paper is organized as follows: In Sec.3, the details of Collective Density Clustering approach are presented, including collective density, collective clustering and collective merging. In Sec.4, the experiments with real videos are illustrated, such as pedestrians, traffic and bacterial colony. Several comparison experiments are also introduced in Sec.4. The conclusions and future work are mentioned in Sec.5.

3. COLLECTIVE DENSITY CLUSTERING APPROACH

Detecting coherent motion involves two factors: (1) local collective subgroups with individuals having similar behaviour; (2) continuous subgroups having global consistent motion. The Collective Density Clustering (CDC) approach achieves the detection with both local and global coherent motion having arbitrary shapes and varying densities. To recognize the local collective subgroups, the collective density and collective clustering are proposed. For the global consistency, the collective merging is introduced. The corresponding algorithms for collective clustering and collective merging are presented respectively.

3.1 Collective Density

The density-based clustering algorithms are adaptive for the arbitrary shapes in coherent motion. However, the nor-

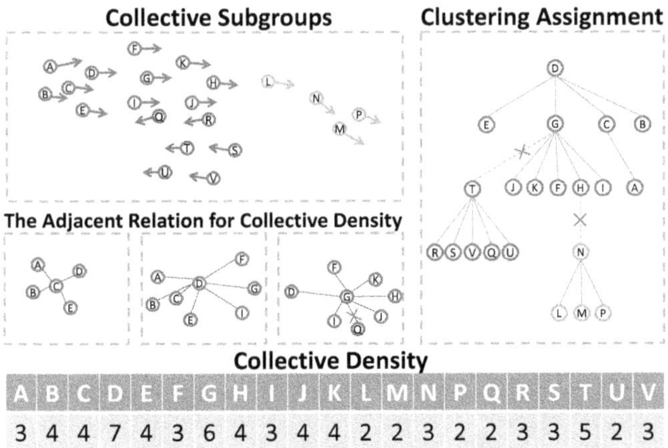

Figure 2: The demonstration of collective density and collective clustering.

mal density estimation is not suitable for the varying densities existing in both local and global coherent motion. The ideal density must be estimated synthetically by factors such as position and orientation in the coherent motion.

In 2-dimensional space $\mathbb{R}^2$, the crowd possessing of $\mathbb{N}$ tracking points is denoted as C, where $|C| = \mathbb{N}$. We mainly consider the spatial position (p_i^x, p_i^y) and orientation p_i^{ori} for point $C_i (i = 1..\mathbb{N})$. These motion features are extracted with the generalized KLT (gKLT) tracker derived from [26]. The similarities of position and orientation between two points C_i and C_j are denoted as

$$\begin{aligned} d_{xy}(i,j) &= \sqrt{(p_i^x - p_j^x)^2 + (p_i^y - p_j^y)^2} \\ d_{ori}(i,j) &= |p_i^{ori} - p_j^{ori}| \end{aligned} \tag{1}$$

Based on these similarities, the definitions of adjacent matrix and collective density are given firstly.

Definition 1. The adjacent matrix represents the collective relation between two points. For each pairs of C_i and C_j, the (i, j) entry of adjacent matrix is denoted as

$$AdjMatrix(i,j) = \begin{cases} 1, & d_{xy}(i,j) \le cut_{xy} * \theta(i,j) \\ 0, & d_{xy}(i,j) > cut_{xy} * \theta(i,j) \end{cases} \tag{2}$$

$$\theta(i,j) = \begin{cases} e^{-(d_{ori}(i,j)/cut_{ori})^2} &, d_{ori}(i,j) \ge cut_{ori} \\ 1 + e^{-(d_{ori}(i,j)/cut_{ori})^2} &, d_{ori}(i,j) < cut_{ori} \end{cases} \tag{3}$$

θ is a amplification factor which is employed to adjust the distance cut-off cut_{xy} dynamically with considering orientation cut-off cut_{ori}. A larger value of θ determined by lower $d_{ori}(i,j)$ will relax the constraint of cutoff distance. Thus, two points with long distance and consistent orientation will be adjacent in coherent motion. Otherwise, a small θ will lead to the result that two points with short distance and inconsistent orientation are nonadjacent. Then collective density is estimated by the sum of adjacent collective neighbors, which can recognize the underlying ordered patterns from the varying levels of density in coherent motion.

Algorithm 1 Collective Clustering

Input: The number of points $\mathbb{N}$, $d_{xy}(i,j)$, $d_{ori}(i,j)$, $AdjMatrix(i,j)$.
Output: For $\forall i$, the clustering result $cluster_i$.
01:$\forall i$, Collective density ρ_i, distance quantity δ_i and its collective neighbor $neigh_i$.
02:Single cluster center $cluster_{max_j(\rho(j)+\delta(j))} = j$, $cluster_i = -1$ otherwise.
03:**For** i = 1 **TO** $\mathbb{N}$ //process in decreasing order of ρ_i
04: Solve $cluster_i$.
05:**END**
06:The outliers:
07:**IF** $\sum(cluster == j) = 1, cluster(j) = -1$ **END**
Return: $cluster$

Definition 2. The collective density for point C_i is

$$\rho_i = \sum_j AdjMatrix(i,j) \tag{4}$$

Another quantity δ is introduced similar to [16], which represents the closest distance from another point with higher collective density. For point C_i, $\delta_i = \min_{j:\rho_j > \rho_i} (d_{xy}(i,j))$. Simultaneously, the collective neighbor is defined as $neigh_i = j$. For point with the highest density, we have that $\delta_i = \max(d_{xy}(i,j))$ and $neigh_i = i$.

The only two parameters of proposed CDC approach are cut_{xy} and cut_{ori}. As a rule of thumb, cut_{xy} is adopted as the k-th smallest element in all pairs of the similarities d_{xy}, where $k = \mathbb{N} * 0.02$ is optimal empirically. The empirical value of cut_{ori} is $\pi/3$. In addition, the discussion of parameters is given in Sec.4.2.

3.2 Collective Clustering

Coherent motion detection can be regraded as the clustering of consistent behaviour. One key problem of the collective clustering is the decision of cluster center for each collective subgroup. According to the definition of collective density, the larger value of ρ_i indicates that point C_i has more neighboring points with consistent behaviour. Simultaneously, δ_i is much larger than the typical nearest neighbor distance only when point C_i is local or global maxima in the density. Thus, the cluster centers in [16] are determined subjectively by the larger ρ and δ. However, there is still a lack of clear decision of the appropriate cluster centers. In the proposed CDC approach, the single initial cluster center is determined by $\max_i(\rho_i + \delta_i)$ and $cluster_i = i$. The final cluster centers will be identified during the process of assignment. Except the initial cluster center, other points are processed by the descending order of ρ. For points C_i and C_j with $\rho_j > \rho_i$, point C_i is assigned to the nearest point C_j when $d_{ori}(i,j) < cut_{ori}$. Otherwise, the point C_i will be an independent cluster center. This is due to that the collective crowd has salient features: (1) Each point should be assigned to the nearest neighbor of higher density; (2) The points in one subgroup should have the consistent orientation. As a result, the number of collective subgroups is determined automatically. The assignment vector $cluster$ is defined as:

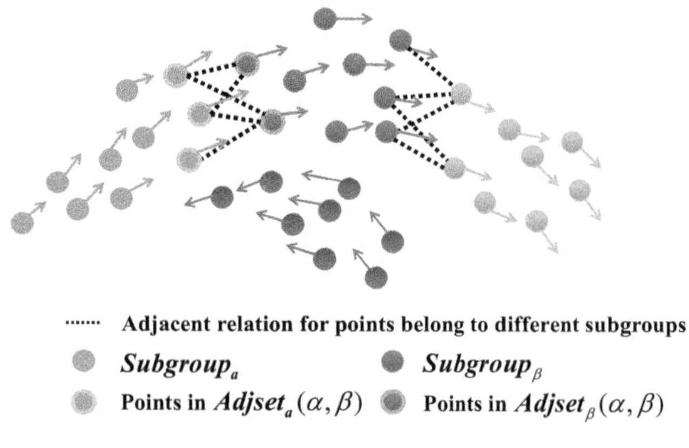

Figure 3: The demonstration of adjacent relation between subgroups, which determines whether they should be merged.

Algorithm 2 Collective Merging

Input: cluster result *cluster*, cluster number Nc, adjacent matrix $AdjMatrix$.

```
FOR α = 1 TO Nc − 1
    FOR β = α + 1 TO Nc
        The adjacent set Adjset_α, Adjset_β.
        Solve the distribution p_α, p_β.
        Compute the expectation E_α, E_β.
        IF |E_α − E_β| ≤ cut_ori
            Merge sub_α, sub_β.
        END
    END
END
```

$$cluster_i = \begin{cases} cluster_j, & \exists \min\limits_{\rho_j > \rho_i, d_{ori}(i,j) < cut_{ori}} (d_{xy}(i,j)) \\ i, & otherwise \end{cases} \tag{5}$$

Another key problem is the identification of outliers resulting from the low quality of videos and tracking. It's difficult to find such border regions mentioned in [16], since (1) the density is not strictly decreasing from the center to border; (2) there exist the inner outliers of clusters. In the CDC approach, an alternative method is proposed to identify the outliers. The outliers appear in two situations that the points with abnormal orientation in a consistent subgroup and a few of subgroups with extremely less points. The outliers have a common character that they will be clustered independently with a single point. With this principle, the outliers can be identified correctly.

Subgroups with local consistency are generated by the collective clustering. The details are shown in Fig.2 and **Algorithm** 1.

3.3 Collective Merging

To adapt for the situations of extremely low density and disconnected areas, the collective merging is presented for the global coherent motion consisting of continuous subgroups. The points in the adjacent area of two subgroups

Figure 4: The demonstration of representative scenes in Collective Motion Database. Scatters and arrows with different colors indicate different clusters of detected coherent motion. Red crosses indicate the outliers.

Figure 5: Continuous frames for two special scenes: (A) An abnormal person among the pedestrians. (B) Two groups of pedestrians pass each other.

determine whether they should be merged. The illustration of collective merging is shown in Fig.3.

The adjacency for two subgroups is defined firstly. For subgroups sub_α and sub_β, if $\exists$ points C_i, C_j ($cluster_i = sub_\alpha, cluster_j = sub_\beta$) satisfy that $cluster_i \neq cluster_j$ (both not equal to -1) and $AdjMatrix(i,j) = 1$, we say that sub_α and sub_β are adjacent. The adjacent sets from sub_α and sub_β are denoted as

$$\begin{aligned} Adjset_\alpha(sub_\alpha, sub_\beta) &= Adjset_\alpha(sub_\alpha, sub_\beta) \cup i \\ Adjset_\beta(sub_\alpha, sub_\beta) &= Adjset_\beta(sub_\alpha, sub_\beta) \cup j \end{aligned} \tag{6}$$

The expectation of orientation distribution in each adjacent set is employed to reveal the main orientation of corresponding adjacent area. The difference between expectations represents the continuity between two subgroups sub_α and sub_β. The less difference between expectations indicates the more possibility to merge them. Without loss of generality, the distribution of orientation for adjacent set $Adjset_\alpha(sub_\alpha, sub_\beta)$ is presented as

$$p_\alpha(\omega = p_i^{ori}) = \chi(p_i^{ori})/N_\alpha \tag{7}$$

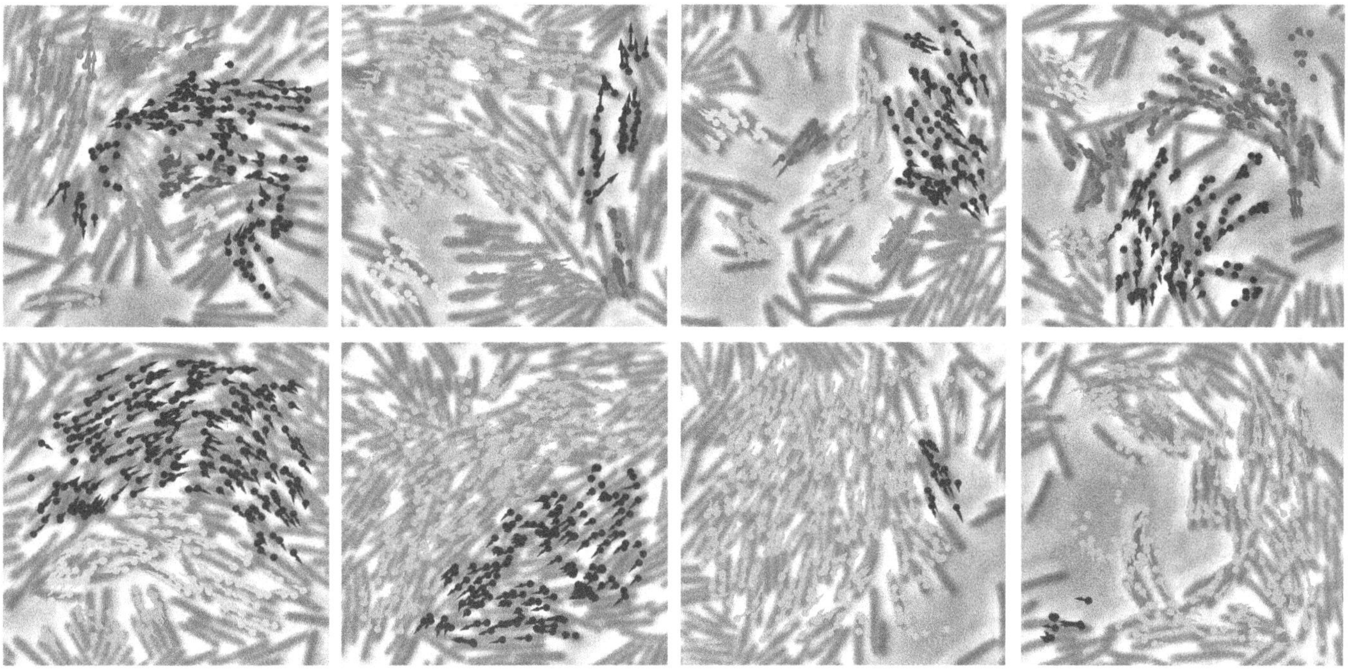

Figure 6: The experiment results on Bacterial Colony Database. Arrows with different colors indicate different clusters of detected collectively moving bacteria. Red crosses indicate the detected outliers.

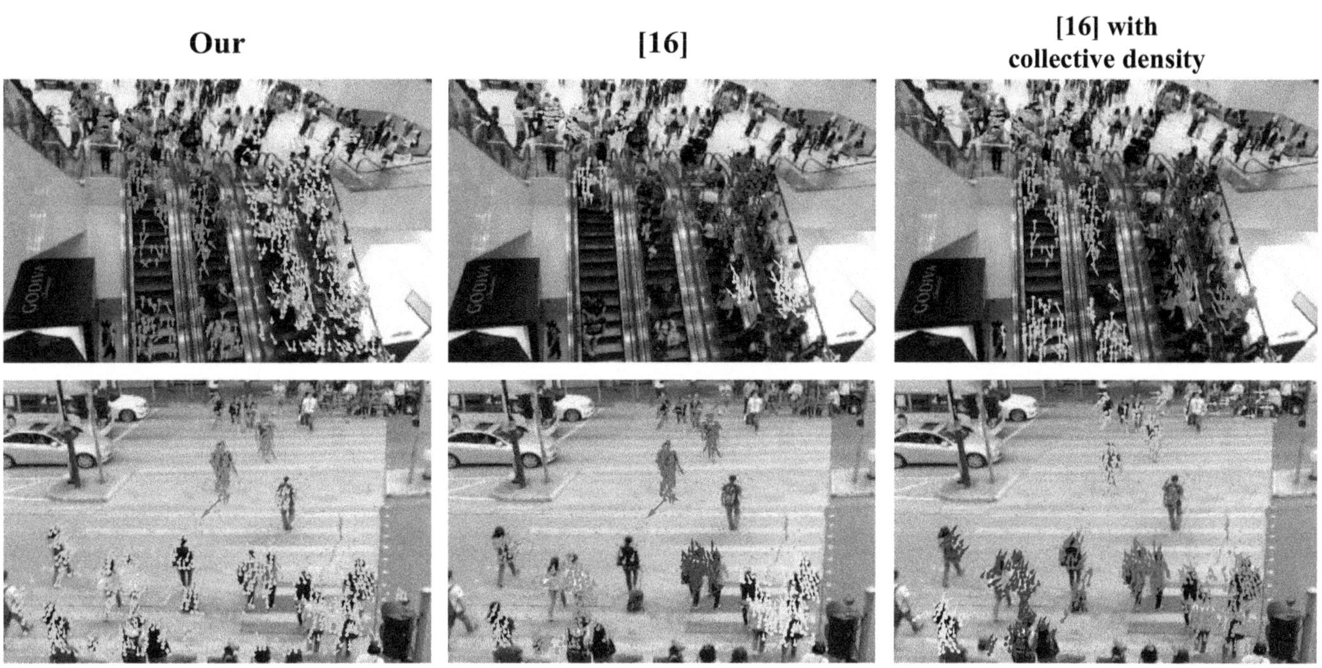

Figure 7: The comparison with density peaks method [16].

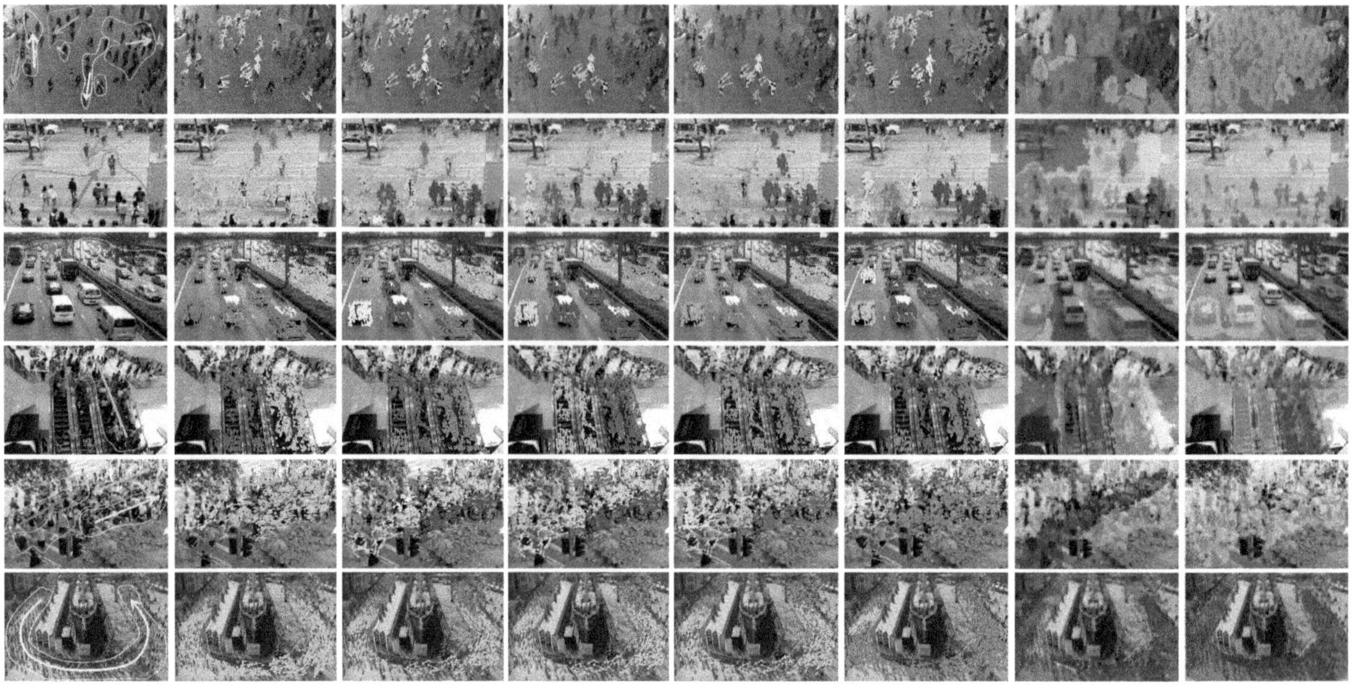

(A) (B) (C) (D) (E) (F) (G) (H)

Figure 8: The comparison results:(A) Ground truth. (B) Ours. (C) [25] with K=10. (D) [25] with K=15. (E) [25] with K=25. (F) [26]. (G) [1]. (H) [13].

where N_α is the number of points in $Adjset_\alpha(sub_\alpha, sub_\beta)$. ω is defined as a discrete random variable with orientation p_i^{ori} and the probability mass function is $p_\alpha(\omega)$. $\chi(p_i^{ori})$ counts the occurrences of value p_i^{ori}. Thus, the expectation is

$$E_\alpha = \sum \omega * p_\alpha(\omega) \tag{8}$$

As a result, the expectations E_α, E_β for subgroups sub_α, sub_β are acquired. The collective subgroups are merged according to the difference between the expectations, where the merging threshold is adopted as the parameter cut_{ori} (mentioned in Sec.3.1). The details of collective merging are shown in **Algorithm** 2.

4. EXPERIMENTS

The proposed CDC is applied to analyze collective motion in diverse videos, such as pedestrians, traffic and bacterial colony. The generalized KLT(gKLT) is adopted as the tracking strategy derived from [26]. The configuration of parameters is given in Sec.3.1.

4.1 Performance

The results on Collective Motion Database [26, 18] are employed to demonstrate the effectiveness. The Collective Motion Database consists of 413 video clips, including various real-world scenes with both low and high density crowds. Some representative frames are shown in Fig.4. The proposed CDC is effective for the different collective scenes: (1) varying levels of density, especially extremely low density and disconnected areas; (2) different scales of collective group with arbitrary shapes. In Fig.5, we further show the results for two special scenes, including an abnormal person among pedestrians and two groups of pedestrians pass each other. For Fig.5(A), the scales of collective groups are extremely imbalanced for the abnormal person and other pedestrians. The accurate detection suggests the proposed method is available for the imbalanced collective clusters. Fig.5(B) indicates the rapid phase transition of a crowd system. The collective patterns become more complicated when some pedestrians walk through the others. The results further verify the effectiveness of CDC approach.

The collective motion of bacterial colony is also introduced, where the real motion data comes from [24]. The bacterial motion is a kind of wild-type *Bacillus subtilis* colony growing on agar substrates. Inside the colony, about 200-

Table 1: The qualitative results compared with density peaks method [16].

Scenario	escalator	crossroad
clusters number		
ground truth	2	2
CDC	2	2
[16]	3	5
[16] with collective density	4	5
outliers number/total number		
CDC	179/774	162/812
[16]	579/774	393/812
[16] with collective density	415/774	289/812

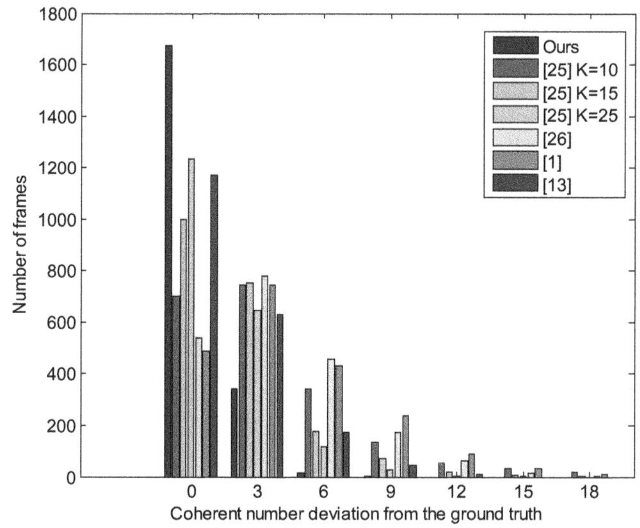

Figure 9: The histogram of difference comparing with the ground truth in 2000+ sampled frames.

400 bacteria swim in a micrometer-thick film of liquid on the agar surface. The confluence and separation appear alternately in the motion of bacteria, which make it more difficult to detect the coherent motion effectively. The result in Fig.6 shows that CDC approach achieves the accurate detection in both local and global coherent motion with arbitrary shapes and varying densities.

4.2 Discussion

The comparison with density peaks method [16] is introduced firstly. There is a conclusion that the proposed CDC approach is effective while the density peaks method [16] is limited for coherent detection. As shown in Fig.7, the results in first column illustrate the accurate detection with CDC approach. In the second column, the original density peaks method with traditional density estimation is employed. Lots of normal points are regarded as the outliers, due to the density peaks method is limited to recognizing the cluster with extremely low density. For the last column, the density peaks method is further evaluated with collective density, where less normal points are identified as outliers. However, there is weakness for both recognizing the global coherent motion and identifying the inner outliers of clusters. The further qualitative comparison with [16] is illustrated in Tab.1. The density peaks method [16] is limited to identifying the right cluster number and accurate outliers.

Fig.8 reveals the comparisons with four state-of-the-art coherent motion detection algorithms, including the coherent filtering approach [25], the collectiveness measurement based approach [18, 26] ([18] is an extension of [26]), the lagrangian particle dynamics approach [1] and the streakline representation of crowd scenes [13]. In particular, the parameter K in [25] has alternative values of $10, 15, 25$, where K is employed in the K-Nearest-Neighbor structure. The parameter K is fixed at 20 in [26]. The experiments with [1, 13] are configured with default parameters mentioned in the each work. The first column is the manually labeled ground truth. We can conclude that the proposed approach achieves better results than the compared methods. Firstly, the proposed approach has a better performance on both local and global coherent motion detection. For example, two traffic flows with varying densities are shown in the second scene. For each traffic flow, the compared methods only recognize the local coherent motion. Secondly, the compared methods make error decisions for the situation of varying densities. In the fifth scenario, two crowds are walking cross the road while one is separated partly by another (The red arrow and green arrow in Fig.8(A)). The results of previous works are not accurate enough for this complicated scene. Moreover, the proposed approach can achieve robust detection with less outliers though the compared methods achieve ideal results in the last marathon scene.

Table 2: The qualitative results compared with the ground truth.

Method	AD	VAR
Ours	**0.807**	**1.043**
[25] with K=10	3.543	12.583
[25] with K=15	2.287	6.271
[25] with K=25	1.604	3.423
[26]	3.839	9.485
[1]	4.358	12.811
[13]	1.862	4.561

Qualitative comparisons on coherent motion detection are also introduced. For the 413 video clips (100 frames per clip) in Collective Motion Database, we manually generate the ground truth of coherent motion number with every 20 frames. More than 2000 frames are sampled in this experiment. Histogram in Fig.9 shows the deviation between the detection results and ground truth. For our approach, the deviation is mainly located in the range $[0, 3]$. The previous works have larger deviation from the ground truth. The further quantitative analysis of consistency between detection result and ground truth is shown in Tab.2. The calculations of Average Difference(AD) and Variance(VAR) are denoted as follows:

$$\begin{aligned} \mathrm{AD} &= \sum_i (Num(i) - Num_{gt}(i)) / \sum_i \\ \mathrm{VAR} &= \sqrt{\sum (|Num(i) - Num_{gt}(i)| - \mathrm{AD})^2 / \sum_i} \end{aligned} \quad (9)$$

For the sampled frame i, $Num(i)$ is the number of detected coherent motion and Num_{gt} is the one for ground truth. $\sum_i$ is the total number of points in the sampled frames. As a result, the lower AD indicates the less deviation from ground truth. Simultaneously, the lower VAR reveals the stability of the proposed approach.

To demonstrate the efficiency of CDC approach, time cost comparisons are also employed. CDC approach and [25, 26] are based on gKLT tracking strategy. The efficiency has great relation with the amount of tracking points. The others [1, 13] are optical flow based, where the size of sampled image is the key factor of efficiency. We introduce two comparison experiments with considering different tracking strategies. In particular, the time cost ignores the tracking stage and only considers the computation of detecting coherent motion. Fig.10(A) scatters the amount of tracking points with time cost, where CDC approach is much more

Table 3: Efficiency comparisons with the optical flow based methods. Each scene consists of 100 frames.

Method	Ours		[1]		[13]	
	tracking points	time per frame (size 1000×670)	time per frame (size 200×134)	time per frame (size 500×335)	time per frame (size 200×134)	time per frame (size 500×335)
scene 1	500	0.027s	1.358s	8.886s	5.433s	38.811s
scene 2	1000	0.197s	1.384s	9.035s	5.397s	39.047s
scene 3	1500	0.412s	1.383s	8.999s	5.385s	38.978s

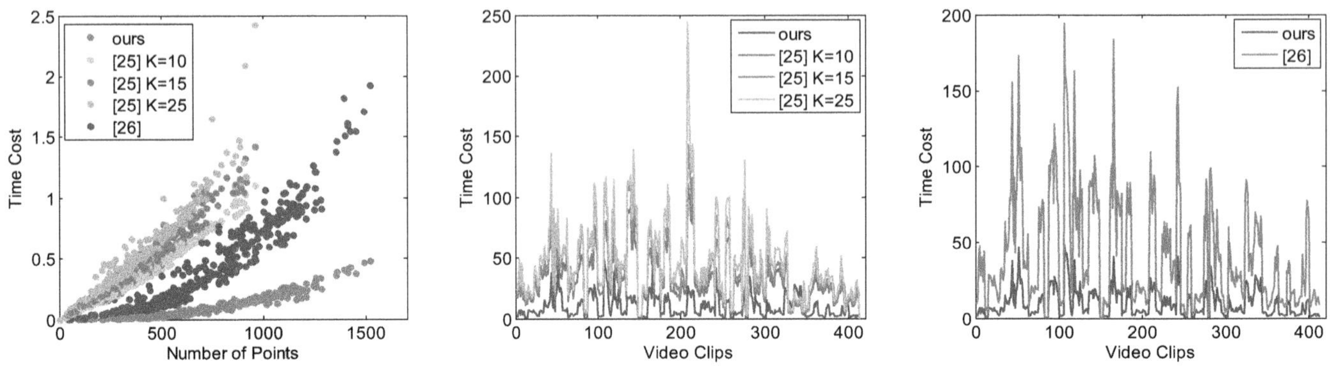

Figure 10: Efficiency comparisons: (A) The scatters of the average amount of points with average time cost for 413 clips in Collective Motion Database(each clip consists of 100 frames). (B) The time cost between ours and [25] in 413 video clips. (C) The time cost between ours and [26] in 413 video clips.

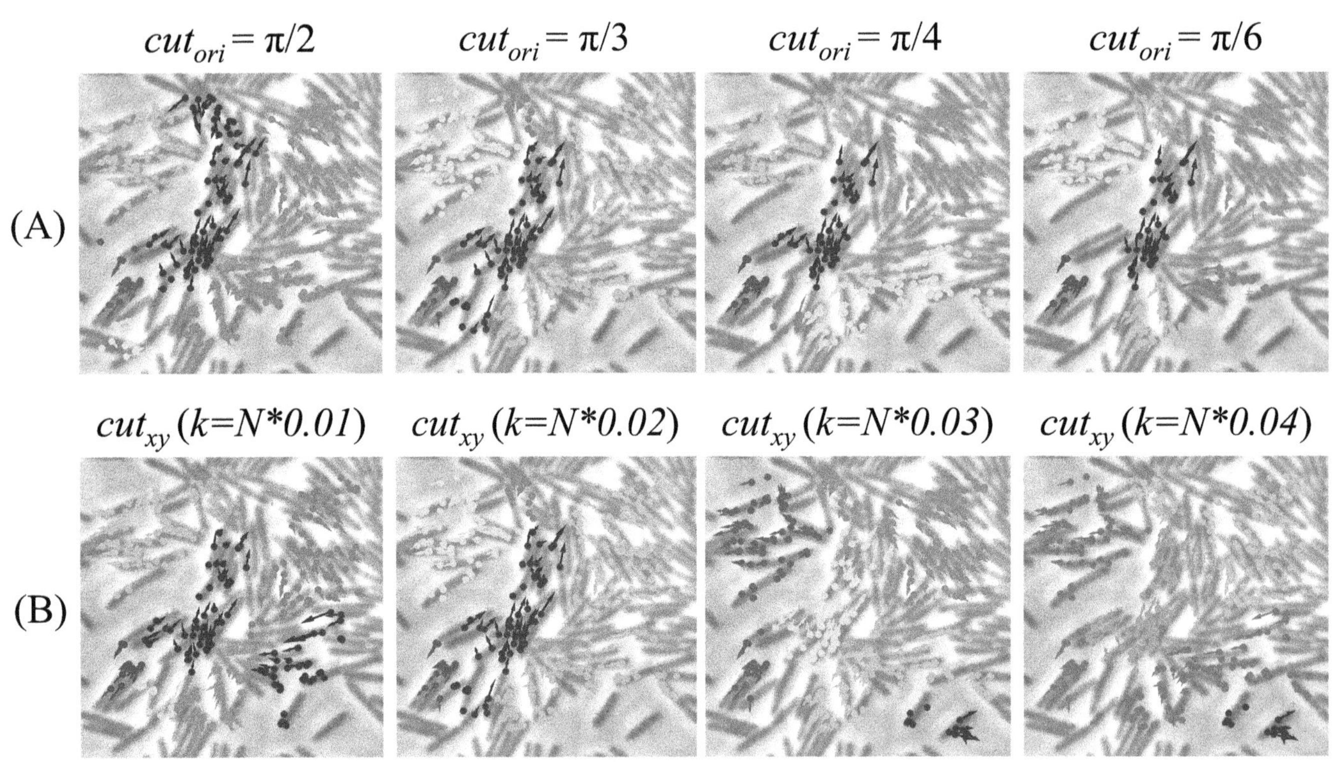

Figure 11: The results with different configuration of parameters.

efficient than previous works with the same points amount. Especially, the tracker with [25] has delicate difference from CDC approach, where less points are tracked in [25](1000 points maximally). Both [26] and CDC approach track more than 1500 points maximally. Fig.10(B) and Fig.10(C) plot the time cost of 413 video clips with the CDC and previous works. With the same amount of tracking points, The CDC approach is optimal than [26]. Moreover, the time cost of CDC is much less than the result of [25], though more points are tracked in CDC. Further comparisons with the optical flow based methods are introduced, as illustrated in Tab.3. There is a conclusion that our approach achieves the best efficiency for coherent motion detection.

The discussion with different configuration of parameters cut_{ori} and cut_{xy} is conducted in this experiment. The default values are given in Sec.3.1. The Bacterial Colony Database is employed for this experiment since it comprises complicated collective subgroups with various levels of density. The cut_{ori} is cutoff parameter to recognize the collective pattern from the orientation aspect. The collective pattern in videos is recognized with keypoint tracking on image plane while human perception of this pattern is based on the ground plane. Thus, the parameter cut_{ori} should have the ability to tolerate the scene perspective distortion between the image and ground plane. As shown in Fig.11(A), the parameter cut_{ori} is changing from $\pi/2$ to $\pi/6$ while cut_{xy} is fixed. A large cut_{ori} brings the excessive assignment in collective clustering and excessive merging in collective merging. A small cut_{ori} makes the collective clustering sensitive to the tiny difference of orientation and brings the limitation of global coherent detection. In our experiments, the $\pi/3$ is optimal for the Collective Motion Database and Bacterial Colony Database, which are two representative databases in coherent detection task. The distance cutoff cut_{xy} is the kth smallest value in all pairs of similarities. Fig.11(B) illustrates the results with changing cut_{xy}. Either too small or too large cut_{xy} will lead the disconnected areas to assign into mistaken clusters, for cut_{xy} is used to identify the collective neighbors. Especially, more outliers are identified as normal points with large cut_{xy}, since the outliers will be assigned to a cluster center even far away from them. Finally, the optimal parameters are adopted as $cut_{ori} = \pi/3$ and $cut_{xy} = N * 0.02$ empirically.

5. CONCLUSIONS AND FUTURE WORK

In this paper, we propose the Collective Density Clustering(CDC) approach to recognize the coherent motion in video applications. The CDC is effective for collective behaviour with arbitrary shapes and varying densities. Based on the definition of collective density, collective subgroups are clustered with the collective assignment for local consistency. The collective merging achieves collective detection with considering the global consistency. Experiments on diverse videos and the comparisons with previous works demonstrate the effectiveness of CDC. The contrast on time cost suggests that the proposed approach achieves the best efficiency.

To further verify the effectiveness and efficiency, we will extend the CDC approach to more applications of video surveillance, such as abnormal detection, activity recognition and analysis of the semantic regions. It is desirable to detect both local and global consistency with the only single step of collective subgroup. The much higher efficiency of CDC approach demonstrates the ability to make extensions for real-time applications.

6. ACKNOWLEDGEMENT

This work is supported by the National Natural Science Foundation of China (Grant No.61170223, 61202207) and Joint Funds of the National Natural Science Foundation of China (Grant No. U1204610). We are grateful to Dr. Bolei Zhou from Computer Science and Artificial Intelligence Laboratory of Massachusetts Institute of Technology for providing significant discussions. We thank Dr. Hepeng Zhang from Institute of Natural Sciences of Shanghai Jiao Tong University for sharing the Bacterial Colony Database.

7. REFERENCES

[1] S. Ali and M. Shah. A lagrangian particle dynamics approach for crowd flow segmentation and stability analysis. *IEEE Conference on Computer Vision and Pattern Recognition*, pages 1–6, 2007.

[2] S. Ali and M. Shah. Floor fields for tracking in high density crowd scenes. *European Conference on Computer Vision*, pages 1–14, 2008.

[3] T. Brox and J. Malik. Object segmentation by long term analysis of point trajectories. *European Conference on Computer Vision*, pages 282–295, 2010.

[4] W. Choi and S. Savarese. Understanding collective activities of people from videos. *IEEE Transactions on Pattern Analysis and Machine Intelligence*, pages 1242 – 1257, 2013.

[5] W. Choi, K. Shahid, and S. Savarese. Learning context for collective activity recognition. *IEEE Conference on Computer Vision and Pattern Recognition*, pages 3273–3280, 2011.

[6] I. Couzin. Collective minds. *Nature*, 445(7129):715–715, 2007.

[7] M. Ester, H.-P. Kriegel, J. Sander, and X. Xu. A density-based algorithm for discovering clusters in large spatial databases with noise. *International Conference on Knowledge Discovery and Data Mining*, 96:226–231, 1996.

[8] W. Ge, R. T. Collins, and R. B. Ruback. Vision-based analysis of small groups in pedestrian crowds. *IEEE Transactions on Pattern Analysis and Machine Intelligence*, 34(5):1003–1016, 2012.

[9] M. Hu, S. Ali, and M. Shah. Learning motion patterns in crowded scenes using motion flow field. *International Conference on Pattern Recognition*, pages 1–5, 2008.

[10] L. Kratz and K. Nishino. Going with the flow: pedestrian efficiency in crowded scenes. *European Conference on Computer Vision*, pages 558–572, 2012.

[11] L. Kratz and K. Nishino. Tracking pedestrians using local spatio-temporal motion patterns in extremely crowded scenes. *IEEE Transactions on Pattern Analysis and Machine Intelligence*, 34(5):987–1002, 2012.

[12] V. Mahadevan, W. Li, V. Bhalodia, and N. Vasconcelos. Anomaly detection in crowded scenes. *IEEE Conference on Computer Vision and Pattern Recognition*, pages 1975–1981, 2010.

[13] R. Mehran, B. E. Moore, and M. Shah. A streakline representation of flow in crowded scenes. *European Conference on Computer Vision*, pages 439–452, 2010.

[14] R. Mehran, A. Oyama, and M. Shah. Abnormal crowd behavior detection using social force model. *IEEE Conference on Computer Vision and Pattern Recognition*, pages 935–942, 2009.

[15] V. Rabaud and S. Belongie. Counting crowded moving objects. *IEEE Conference on Computer Vision and Pattern Recognition*, 1:705–711, 2006.

[16] A. Rodriguez and A. Laio. Clustering by fast search and find of density peaks. *Science*, 344(6191):1492–1496, 2014.

[17] X. Sun, H. Yao, R. Ji, X. Liu, and P. Xu. Unsupervised fast anomaly detection in crowds. *ACM international conference on Multimedia*, pages 1469–1472, 2011.

[18] X. Tang, H. Zhang, B. Zhou, and X. Wang. Measuring crowd collectiveness. *IEEE Transactions on Pattern Analysis and Machine Intelligence*, page 1, 2014.

[19] T. Vicsek, A. Czirók, E. Ben-Jacob, I. Cohen, and O. Shochet. Novel type of phase transition in a system of self-driven particles. *Physical Review Letters*, 75(6):1226, 1995.

[20] T. Vicsek and A. Zafeiris. Collective motion. *Physics Reports*, 517(3):71–140, 2012.

[21] W. Wang, W. Lin, Y. Chen, J. Wu, J. Wang, and B. Sheng. Finding coherent motions and semantic regions in crowd scenes: A diffusion and clustering approach. *European Conference on Computer Vision*, pages 756–771, 2014.

[22] S. Wu and H. San Wong. Crowd motion partitioning in a scattered motion field. *IEEE Transactions on Systems, Man, and Cybernetics, Part B: Cybernetics*, 42(5):1443–1454, 2012.

[23] C. Zhang, X. Yang, J. Zhu, and W. Lin. Parsing collective behaviors by hierarchical model with varying structure. *ACM international conference on Multimedia*, pages 1085–1088, 2012.

[24] H. P. Zhang, A. Be'er, E.-L. Florin, and H. L. Swinney. Collective motion and density fluctuations in bacterial colonies. *Proceedings of the National Academy of Sciences*, 107(31):13626–13630, 2010.

[25] B. Zhou, X. Tang, and X. Wang. Coherent filtering: detecting coherent motions from crowd clutters. *European Conference on Computer Vision*, pages 857–871, 2012.

[26] B. Zhou, X. Tang, and X. Wang. Measuring crowd collectiveness. *IEEE Conference on Computer Vision and Pattern Recognition*, pages 3049–3056, 2013.

Temporal Localization of Fine-Grained Actions in Videos by Domain Transfer from Web Images

Chen Sun* Sanketh Shetty† Rahul Sukthankar† Ram Nevatia*

*University of Southern California
{chensun,nevatia}@usc.edu

†Google, Inc.
{sanketh,sukthankar}@google.com

ABSTRACT

We address the problem of fine-grained action localization from temporally untrimmed web videos. We assume that only weak video-level annotations are available for training. The goal is to use these weak labels to identify temporal segments corresponding to the actions, and learn models that generalize to unconstrained web videos. We find that web images queried by action names serve as well-localized highlights for many actions, but are noisily labeled. To solve this problem, we propose a simple yet effective method that takes weak video labels and noisy image labels as input, and generates localized action frames as output. This is achieved by cross-domain transfer between video frames and web images, using pre-trained deep convolutional neural networks. We then use the localized action frames to train action recognition models with long short-term memory networks. We collect a fine-grained sports action data set FGA-240 of more than 130,000 YouTube videos. It has 240 fine-grained actions under 85 sports activities. Convincing results are shown on the FGA-240 data set, as well as the THUMOS 2014 localization data set with untrimmed training videos.

Figure 1: Fine-grained actions are usually present as a tiny fraction within videos (top). Our framework uses cross-domain transfer from possibly noisy image search results (bottom) and identifies the action related images for both domains (marked in green).

Categories and Subject Descriptors

I.2.10 [**Vision and Scene Understanding**]: Video analysis

General Terms

Algorithms, Experimentation, Measurement

Keywords

Fine-grained action localization, domain transfer, LSTM

1. INTRODUCTION

This paper addresses the problem of fine-grained action localization from unconstrained web videos. A fine-grained action takes place in a higher-level activity or event (e.g., *jump shot* and *slam dunk* in *basketball*, *blow candle* in *birthday party*). Its instances are usually temporally localized within the videos, and share similar context with other fine-grained actions belonging to the same activity or event.

Most existing work on action recognition focuses on action classification using pre-segmented short video clips [25, 14, 23], which assumes implicitly that the actions of interest are temporally segmented during both training and testing. The TRECVID Multimedia Event Recounting evaluation [17] as well as THUMOS 14 Challenge [10] both address action localization in untrimmed video, but the typical approach involves training classifiers on temporally segmented action clips and testing using sliding window on untrimmed video. This setting does not scale to large action vocabularies, when data is collected from consumer video websites. Videos here are unconstrained in length, format (home videos vs. professional videos), and almost always only have video level annotations of actions.

We assume that only video-level annotations are available for the fine-grained action localization problem. The ability to localize fine grained actions in videos has important applications such as video highlighting, summarization, and automatic video transcription. It is also a challenging prob-

MM'15, October 26–30, 2015, Brisbane, Australia.

ACM 978-1-4503-3459-4/15/10 ...$15.00.
DOI: http://dx.doi.org/10.1145/2733373.2806226 .

lem for several reasons: first, fine-grained actions for any high-level activity or event are inherently similar since they take place in similar scene context; second, occurrences of the fine-grained actions are usually short (a few seconds) in training videos, making it difficult to associate the video-level labels to the occurrences.

Our key observation is that one can exploit web images to help localize fine-grained actions in videos. As illustrated in Figure 1, by using action names (*basketball slam dunk*) as queries, many of the image search results offer well localized actions, though some of them are non-video like or irrelevant. Identifying action related frames from weakly supervised videos and filtering irrelevant image tags is hard in either modality by itself; however, it is easier to tackle these two problems together. This is due to our observation that although most of the video frames and web images which correspond to actions are visually similar, the distributions of non-action images from the video domain and the web image domain are usually very different. For example, in a video with a *basketball slam dunk*, non slam dunk frames in the video are mostly from a basketball game. The irrelevant results returned by image search are more likely to be product shots, or cartoons.

This motivates us to formulate a domain transfer problem between web images and videos. To allow domain transfer, we first treat the videos as a bag of frames, and use the feature activations from deep convolutional neural networks (CNN) [13] as the common representation for images and frames. Suppose we have selected a set of video frames and a set of web images for every action, the domain transfer framework goes in two directions: video frames to web images, and vice versa. For both directions, we use the selected images from the source domain to train action classifiers by fine-tuning the top layers of the CNN; we then apply the trained classifiers to the target domain. Each image in the target domain is assigned a confidence score given by its associated action classifier from the source domain. By gradually filtering out the images with low scores, the bidirectional domain transfer can progress iteratively. In practice, we start from the video frames to web images direction, and randomly select the video frames for training. Since the non-action related frames are not likely to occur in web images, the tuned CNN can be used to filter out the non-video like and irrelevant web images. The final domain transfer from web images is used to localize action related frames in videos. We term these action-related frames as *localized action frames* (LAF).

Videos are more than an unordered collection of frames. We choose long short-term memory (LSTM) [8] networks as the temporal model. Compared with the traditional recurrent neural networks (RNN), LSTM has built-in *input gates* and *forget gates* to control its memory cells. These gates allow LSTM to either keep a long term memory or forget its history. The ability to learn from long sequences with unknown size of background is well-suited for fine-grained action localization from unconstrained web videos. We treat every sampled video frame as a time step in LSTM. When we train LSTM models, we label all video frames by their video-level annotation, but use the LAF scores generated by bidirectional domain transfer as weights on the loss for misclassification. By doing this, irrelevant frames are effectively down-weighted in the training stage. The framework can be naturally extended to use video shots as time steps, from which spatio-temporal features can be extracted to capture local motion information.

Fine-grained action localization from untrimmed web videos is a new task. The closest existing data set is THUMOS 2014 with 20 sports categories. It is designed for action localization using segmented videos as training, but has 1,010 untrimmed validation videos. To evaluate the framework in a large scale setting, we collected a new data set from YouTube. We chose 240 fine-grained actions belonging to 85 different sports activities, the total number of videos is over 130,000. Although the evaluated categories are sports actions, this method can be easily extended to other domains. For example, one can easily get *cut cake, eat cake* and *blow candle* images for a *birthday party* event with image search.

Our work makes three major contributions:

- We show that learning temporally localized actions from videos becomes much easier if we combine weakly labeled video frames and noisily tagged web images. This is achieved by a simple yet effective domain transfer algorithm.
- We propose a localization framework that uses LSTM network with the localized action frames to model the temporal evolution of actions.
- We introduce the problem of fine-grained action localization with untrimmed videos, and collect a large fine-grained sports action data set with over 130,000 videos in 240 categories. The data set is available online.[1]

2. RELATED WORK

Most existing work on activity recognition focuses on classifying pre-segmented clips. For example, UCF 101 data set [25] and HMDB 51 data set [14] provide 101 and 51 activity categories respectively. Activity types range from primitive human actions, sports to playing instruments; the typical length of each video clip is 5 to 10 seconds. More recently, Karpathy et al. [11] proposed the Sports-1M data set with more than 1 million untrimmed YouTube videos. Even though it offers 487 sports categories, most of them are high-level activities such as *basketball* and *cricket*. For fine-grained action recognition, Rohrbach et al. [20] collected a cooking action data set with temporal annotation, the videos were shot in an indoor kitchen with static camera. To the best of our knowledge, there is no previous work on fine-grained action localization with untrimmed training videos.

Action recognition typically involves two basic steps: feature extraction and classifier training. The standard approach is to extract hand-designed low-level features, and then aggregate the features into fixed-length feature vectors for classification. Oneata et al. [16] showed that a combination of visual features (SIFT [15]) and motion features (DT [31]) represented using Fisher Vectors [18] produced state-of-the-art activity and event classification performance.

Recent approaches, particularly those based on deep neural networks, jointly learn features and classifiers. Karpathy et al. [11] proposed several variations of convolutional neural net (CNN) architectures that extended Krizhevsky et al.'s

[1] `https://sites.google.com/site/finegrainedactions/`

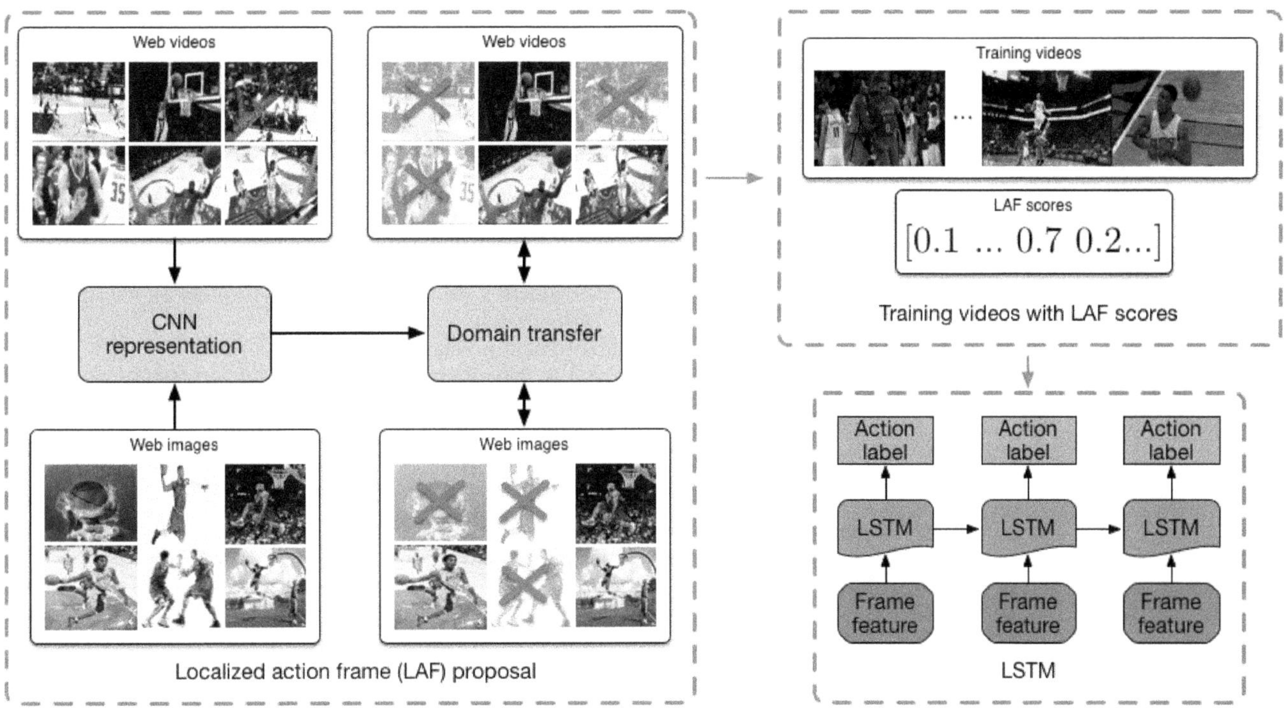

Figure 2: Illustration of the LAF proposal framework for basketball slam dunk videos. We use a cross-domain transfer algorithm to jointly filter out non-video like web images and non-action like video frames. We then learn a LAF proposal model using the filtered images, which assigns LAF scores to training video frames. Finally, we train LSTM based fine-grained action detectors, where the misclassification penalty of each time step is weighted by the LAF score.

image classification model [13] and attempted to learn motion patterns from spatio-temporal video patches. Simonyan and Zisserman [24] obtained good results on action recognition using a two-stream CNN that takes pre-computed optical flow as well as raw frame-level pixels as input.

There have been many attempts to address the action localization problem. Tian et al. [29] proposed a temporal extension of the deformable part model (DPM) for action detection, they used spatio-temporal bounding boxes for training. Wang et al. [33] used dynamic poselets which took motion and pose into account. Jain et al. [9] localized the actions with tubelets. All these approaches require manually annotated spatio-temporal bounding boxes for training. For temporal localization, THUMOS 2014 [10] data set provides trimmed video segments to train action classifiers, the classifiers can be used for localization with temporal sliding windows.

The idea of using images as auxiliary data has also recently been explored. The most common usage is to learn mid-level *concept* detectors for high-level event classification [1, 7, 27]. Yang et al. [36] propose a domain adaptation algorithm from images to videos, but assume perfect image annotation. Divvala et al. [3] learn mixtures of object sub-categories using web images, they achieving this goal by filtering sub-categories with low classification performance.

The long short-term memory network (LSTM) was proposed by Hochreiter and Schmidhuber [8] as an improvement over traditional recurrent neural networks (RNN) for classification and prediction of time series data. Specifically, an LSTM can *remember* and *forget* values from the past, unlike a regular RNN where error gradients decay exponentially quickly with the time lag between events. It has recently shown excellent performance in modeling sequential data such as speech recognition [22, 5], handwriting recognition [6] and machine translation [28]. More recently, LSTM has also been applied to video-level action classification [4, 26, 38] and generate image descriptions [30, 12].

3. OUR APPROACH

Our proposed fine-grained action localization framework uses both weakly labeled videos and noisily tagged web images. It employs the same CNN based representation for web images and video frameworks, and uses a bidirectional domain transfer algorithm to filter out irrelevant images in both domains. A localized action frame (LAF) proposal model is trained from the remaining web images, and used to assign LAF scores to video frames. Finally, we use long short-term memory networks to train fine-grained action detectors, using the LAF scores as the weight of loss for misclassification. The pipeline is illustrated in Figure 2.

3.1 Shared CNN Representation

A shared feature space is required for domain transfer between images and videos. Here we treat a video as a bag of frames, and extract activations from the intermediate layers of a convolutional neural network (CNN) as features for both web images and video frames. Although there is previous work on action recognition from still images using

Figure 3: Top retrieved images from the Google image search engine, using keywords *tennis serve* and *baseball pitch*.

other representations [37], we choose CNN activations for its simplicity and state-of-the-art performance in several action recognition tasks [24, 11].

Training a CNN end-to-end from scratch is time consuming, and requires a large amount of annotated data. It has been shown that CNN weights trained from large image data sets like ImageNet [2] are generic, and can be applied to other image classification tasks by fine-tuning. It is also possible to disable the error back-propagation for the first several layers during fine-tuning. This is equivalent to training a shallower neural network using the intermediate CNN activations as features.

In this paper, we adopt the methodology of fine-tuning the top layers of CNN, and experiment with the AlexNet [13] CNN architecture. It contains five convolution layers and three fully connected layers. Each convolution layer is followed by a ReLU non-linearity layer and a maximum pooling layer. We pre-trained the network on ImageNet data set using the data partitions defined in [21]. We resized the images to 256 by 256, and used the raw pixels as inputs. For the purpose of fine-tuning, we fixed the network weights before its first fully connected layer and only updated the parameters of the top three layers. Feature activations from fc6 serve as the shared representation for web images and video frames, and allow cross-domain transfer between the two.

3.2 LAF Proposal with Web Images

Fine-grained actions tend to be more localized in videos than high-level activities. For example, a *basketball* match video usually consists of *jump shot*, *slam dunk*, *free throw* etc., each of which may be as short as a few seconds. We address the problem of automatically identifying them from minutes-long videos.

Algorithm 1: Domain transfer algorithm for localized action frame proposal.

Input : Images with noisy labels (I_i, a_i), frames with video-level labels (V_i, a_i)
Output: LAF proposal model
Initialize $\mathcal{I}$ and $\mathcal{V}$ to include all image and frame inputs respectively.
while *stopping criteria not met* **do**
1. Fine-tune CNN_v using data in frame set $\mathcal{V}$.
2. Compute $\text{CNN}_v(I)$ for all $I \in \mathcal{I}$.
3. Update $\mathcal{I} = \{I | I \in \mathcal{I}, \text{CNN}_v(I)_{a_I} > \theta_1\}$.
4. Fine-tune CNN_i using data in image set $\mathcal{I}$.
5. Compute $\text{CNN}_i(V)$ for all $V \in \mathcal{V}$.
6. Update $\mathcal{V} = \{V | V \in \mathcal{V}, \text{CNN}_i(V)_{a_V} > \theta_2\}$.

end
return *CNN_i*

Fortunately, we observe that many of the fine-grained actions have *image highlights* on the Internet (Figure 3). They are easily obtained by querying image search engines with action names. However, these images are noisily labeled, and not useful for learning LAF proposal models directly, as they contain:

- Irrelevant images due to image crawling error, for example, a *jogging* image could be retrieved with the keyword *soccer dribbling*.
- Items related to the actions, such as objects and logos.
- Images with the same action but from a different domain, such as advertisement images with clear background, or cartoons.

Filtering the irrelevant web images is a challenging problem by itself. However, it can be turned into an easier problem by using weakly-supervised videos. We hypothesize that applying a classifier, learned on video frames, as a filter on the images removes many irrelevant images and preserves most video-like image highlights. More formally, assume we have video frames in $\mathcal{V}$ and web images in $\mathcal{I}$, and each of them is assigned a fine-grained action label $a = 0, 1, ..., N-1$. We first learn a multi-class classifier $\text{CNN}_v(\cdot) \in \mathbb{R}^N$ by fine-tuning the top layers of CNN using video frames. $\text{CNN}_v(\cdot)$ encodes action discriminative information from the videos' perspective; we apply it to all $I \in \mathcal{I}$, and update

$$\mathcal{I} = \{I | I \in \mathcal{I}, \text{CNN}_v(I)_{a_I} > \theta_1\} \tag{1}$$

where $\theta_1 \in [0, 1]$ is the threshold for minimum softmax output, and $\text{CNN}_v(I)_{a_I}$ corresponds to the a_I-th dimension of $\text{CNN}_v(I)$.

We then use the filtered $\mathcal{I}$ to fine-tune $\text{CNN}_i(\cdot) \in \mathbb{R}^N$, and update $\mathcal{V}$ in a similar manner:

$$\mathcal{V} = \{V | V \in \mathcal{V}, \text{CNN}_i(V)_{a_V} > \theta_2\} \tag{2}$$

We iterate the process and update $\mathcal{V}$ and $\mathcal{I}$ until certain stopping criteria are met. The LAF proposal model $\text{CNN}_i(\cdot)$

is learned using the final web image set $\mathcal{I}$, the LAF score for a video frame V with action label a is given by

$$\text{LAF}(V) = \text{CNN}_i(V)_a \quad (3)$$

The whole process is summarized in Algorithm 1.

Discussion: We initialize the frame set $\mathcal{V}$ by random sampling. Even though many of the sampled frames do not correspond to the actions of interest, they can help filter out the non-video like web images such as cartoons, object photos and logos. In practice, the random sampling of video frames is adequate for this step since the mis-labeled frames rarely appear in the web image collection.

We set the stopping criteria to be: (1) video-level classification accuracy on a validation set starts to drop; or (2) a maximum number of iterations is reached. To be more efficient, we train one-vs-rest linear SVMs using frames in $\mathcal{V}$ after each iteration, and apply the classifiers to video frames in the validation set. We take the average of frame-level classifier responses to generate video-level responses, and use them to compute classification accuracy.

3.3 Long Short-Term Memory Network

Long Short-term Memory (LSTM) [8] is a type of recurrent neural network (RNN) that solves the vanishing and exploding gradients problem of previous RNN architectures when trained using back-propagation. Standard LSTM architecture includes an input layer, a recurrent LSTM layer and an output layer. The recurrent LSTM layer has a set of memory cells, which are used to store real-valued state information from previous observations. This recurrent information flow, from previous observations, is particularly useful for capturing temporal evolution in videos, which we hypothesize is useful in distinguishing between fine-grained sports activities. In addition, LSTM's memory cells are protected by input gates and forget gates, which allow it to maintain a long-term memory and reset its memory, respectively. We employ the modification to LSTMs proposed by Sak et al. [22] to add a projection layer after the LSTM layer. This reduces the dimension of stored states in memory cells, and helps to make the training process faster.

Let us denote the input sequence $\mathbf{X}$ as $\{x_1, x_2, ..., x_T\}$, where in our case each x_t is a feature vector of a video frame with time stamp t. LSTM maps the input sequence into the output action responses $\mathbf{Y} = \{y_1, y_2, ..., y_T\}$ by:

$$i_t = \sigma(W_{ix}x_t + W_{ir}r_{t-1} + W_{ic}c_{t-1} + b_i) \quad (4)$$
$$f_t = \sigma(W_{fx}x_t + W_{rf}r_{t-1} + W_{cf}c_{t-1} + b_f) \quad (5)$$
$$c_t = f_t \odot c_{t-1} + i_t \odot g(W_{cx}x_t + W_{cr}r_{t-1} + b_c) \quad (6)$$
$$o_t = \sigma(W_{ox}x_t + W_{or}r_{t-1} + W_{oc}c_t + b_o) \quad (7)$$
$$m_t = o_t \odot h(c_t) \quad (8)$$
$$r_t = W_{rm}m_t \quad (9)$$
$$y_t = W_{yr}r_t + b_y \quad (10)$$

Here W's and b's are the weight matrices and biases, respectively, and $\odot$ denotes the element-wise multiplication operation. c is the memory cell activation; i, f, o are input gate, forget gate and output gate respectively. m and r are recurrent activation before and after projection. σ is the sigmoid function, g and h are *tanh*. An illustration of the LSTM architecture with a single memory block is shown in Figure 4.

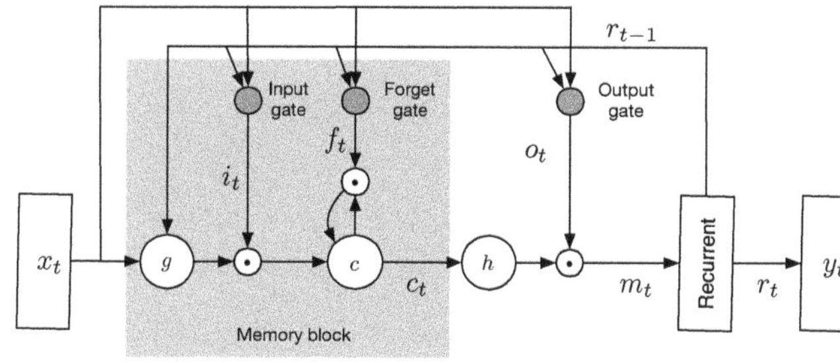

Figure 4: Illustration of LSTM architecture with a single memory block. A recurrent projection layer is added to reduce the number of parameters. Reproduced from [22] with the authors' permission.

Training LSTM with LAF scores. We sample video frames at 1 frame per second and treat each frame as a basic LSTM step. Similar to speech recognition tasks, each time step requires a label and a penalty weight for misclassification. The truncated backpropagation through time (BPTT) learning algorithm [34] is used for training. We limit the maximum unrolling time steps to k and only back-propagate the error for k time steps. Incorporating the LAF scores into the LSTM framework is simple: we first run the LAF proposal pipeline to score all sampled training video frames. Then we set the frame-level labels based on video-level annotation, but use the LAF scores as the penalty weights. Using this method, LSTM is *forced* to make the correct decision after watching a LAF returned by LAF proposal system, and it is not penalized as heavily when gathering context information from earlier frames or misclassifying an unrelated frame.

Computing LAF scores for video shots. For some data sets, it might be desirable to use video shots as the basic LSTM steps, as it allows the use of spatio-temporal motion features for representation. We extend the frame-level LAF scores to shot-level by taking the average of LAF scores from the sampled frames within a certain video shot.

4. EXPERIMENTS

This section first describes the data set we collected for evaluation, and then presents experimental results.

4.1 Data Set

There is no existing data set for fine-grained action localization using untrimmed web videos. To evaluate our proposed method's performance, we collected a Fine Grained Actions 240 (FGA-240) data set focusing on sports videos. It consists of over 130,000 YouTube videos in 240 categories. A subset of the categories is shown in Figure 5. We selected 85 high-level sports activities from the Sports-1M data set [11], and manually chose the fine-grained actions take place in these activities. The action categories cover *aquatic sports*, *team sports*, *sports with animals* and others.

We decided the fine-grained categories for each high-level sports activity using the following method: given YouTube videos and their associated text data such as titles and descriptions, we ran an automatic text parser to recognize sports related entities. The recognized entities which correlate with the high-level sports activities were stored in the

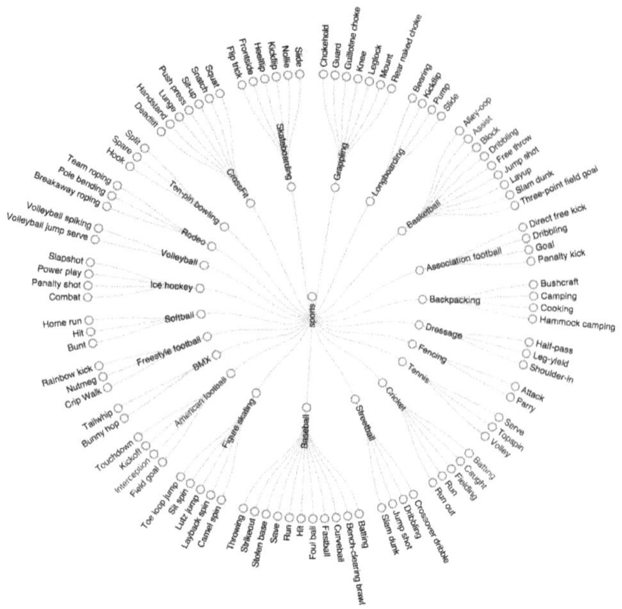

Figure 5: Some of the high-level sports activities and their corresponding fine-grained sports actions in Fine Grained Actions 240 data set. Best viewed under magnification.

pool and then manually filtered to keep only fine-grained sports actions. As an example, for *basketball* the initial entity pool contains not only fine-grained sports actions (e.g., *slam dunk*, *block*), but also game events (e.g., *NBA*) and celebrities (e.g., *Kobe Bryant*). Once the fine-grained categories are fixed, we applied the same text analyzer to automatically assign video-level annotations, and only kept the videos with high annotation confidence. We finally visualized the data set to filter out false annotations and removed the fine-grained sports action categories with too few samples.

Our final data set contains 48,381 training videos and 87,454 evaluation videos. The median number of training videos per category is 133. We used 20% of the evaluation videos for validation and 80% for testing.

For temporal localization evaluation, we manually annotated 400 videos from 45 fine-grained actions. The average length of the videos is 79 seconds.

4.2 Experiment Setup

LSTM implementation. We used the feature activations from pre-trained AlexNet (first fully-connected layer with 4,096 dimensions) as the input features for each time step. We followed the LSTM implementation by Sak et al. [22] which utilizes a multi-core CPU on a single machine. For training, we used asynchronous stochastic gradient descent and set batch size to 12. We tuned the training parameters on the validation videos and set the number of LSTM cells to 1024, learning rate to 0.0024 and learning rate decay with a factor of 0.1. We fixed the maximum unroll time step k to 20 to forward-propagate the activations and backward-propagate the errors.

Video level classification. We evaluated fine-grained action classification results on video level. We sampled test video frames at 1 frame per second. Given T sampled frames from a video, these frames are forward-propagated through time, and produce T softmax activations. We used average fusion to aggregate the frame-level activations over whole videos.

Temporal localization. We generated the frame-level softmax activations using the same approach as video level classification. We used a temporal sliding window of 10 time steps, the score of each sliding window was decided by taking the average of softmax activations. We then applied non-maximum suppression to remove the localized windows which overlap with each other.

Evaluation metric. For classification, we report Hit @k, which is the percentage of testing videos whose labels can be found in the top k results. For localization, we follow the same evaluation protocol as THUMOS 2014 [10] and evaluate mean average precision. A detection is considered to be a correct one if its overlap with groundtruth is over some ratio r.

CNN baseline. We deployed the single-frame architecture used by Karpathy et al. [11] as the CNN baseline. It was shown to have comparable performance with multiple variations of CNNs while being simpler. We sampled the video frames at 1 frame per second, and used average fusion to aggregate softmax scores for classification and localization tasks. Instead of training a CNN from scratch, we used network parameters from the pre-trained AlexNet, and fine-tuned the top two fully-connected layers and a softmax layer. Training parameters were decided using the validation set.

Low-level feature baseline. We extracted low-level features used by [11, 35] over whole videos for classification task, the feature set includes low-level visual and motion features aggregated using bag-of-words. We used the same neural network architecture as [11] with multiple Rectified Linear Units to build classifiers based on the low-level features. Its structure (e.g., number of layers, number of cells per layer) as well as training parameters were decided with validation set.

4.3 Video-level Classification Results

We first report the fine-grained action classification performance on video level.

Comparison with baselines. We compared several baseline systems' performance against our proposed method on FGA-240 data set, the results are shown in Table 1. From the table we can see that systems based on CNN activations outperformed low-level features by a large margin. There are two possible reasons for this: first, CNN learned activations are more discriminative in classifying fine-grained sports actions, even without capturing local motion patterns explicitly; second, low-level features were aggregated on video-level. These video-level features are more sensitive to background and irrelevant video segments, which happens a lot in fine-grained sports action videos.

Among the systems relying on CNN activations, applying LSTM gave better performance than fine-tuning the top layers of CNN. While both LSTM and CNN used the late fusion of frame-level softmax activations to generate video-level classification results, LSTM took previous observations into consideration with the help of memory cells. This shows

Method	Video Hit @1	Video Hit @5
Random	0.4	2.1
Low-level features [35]	30.8	-
CNN [11]	37.3	68.5
LSTM w/o LAF	41.1	70.2
LSTM w/ LAF	**43.4**	**74.9**

Table 1: Video-level classification performance of several different systems on fine-grained actions.

Figure 6: Example actions when LAF is not helpful. The web images retrieved to generate LAF proposals might be beautified (top) or taken from different viewpoint (middle). Sometimes there is a mix of the two issues (bottom).

that temporal information helps classify fine-grained sports actions, and it was captured by LSTM network.

Finally, using LAF proposals helped further improve the video hit @1 by 2.3% and video hit @5 by 4.7%. In Table 2, we show the relative difference in average precision for LSTM with and without LAF proposal. We observe that LAF proposal helps the most when the fine-grained sports actions are likely to be identified based on single frames, and the image highlights on the Internet are visually very similar to the videos. Note that there are still non-video-like and irrelevant images retrieved from the Internet for these categories, but the LAF proposal system is an effective filter. Figure 8 gives the three systems' output on a few example videos.

We also identify several cases when LAF proposals failed to work. The most common case is when most of the retrieved images are non-video like but not filtered out. They could be posed images or beautified images with logos, such as images retrieved for *Parkour:Free running*, or have different viewpoints than videos, such as *Paragliding:Towing*.

Fine-grained sports	Δ AP	Δ AP	Fine-grained sports
Fencing:Parry	0.17	-0.09	Parkour:Free Running
Cricket:Run out	0.15	-0.08	Freestyle soccer:Crip Walk
CrossFit:Deadlift	0.10	-0.08	Paragliding:Towing
CrossFit:Handstand	0.09	-0.07	Freestyle BMX:Stunt
Calisthenics:Push-up	0.09	-0.07	Judo:Sweep
Rings:Pull-up	0.08	-0.06	Basketball:Point

Table 2: Difference in average precision between LSTM with and without LAF proposal. Sorted by top wins (left) and top losses (right).

Method	Video Hit @1	Video Hit @5
Random	1.2	5.9
CNN [11]	69.2	75.9
LSTM w/o LAF	71.7	77.3
LSTM w/ LAF	**73.6**	**79.5**

Table 3: Classification performance when measured on high-level sports activities (e.g., *basketball, soccer*).

Sample video snapshots and web images are shown in Figure 6.

Impact of action hierarchy. A fine-grained sports action could be misclassified to either its sibling or non-sibling leaf nodes in the sports hierarchy. For example, a *basketball slam dunk* can be confused with *basketball alley-oop* as well as *street ball slam dunk.* To study the source of confusion, we decided to measure classification accuracy of high-level sports activities, and check how the numbers compared with fine-grained sports actions.

We obtain the confidence values for high-level sports activities by taking the average of their child nodes' confidence scores. Table 3 shows the classification accuracy with different methods. We can see that the overall trend is the same as fine-grained sports actions: LSTM with LAF proposal is still the best. However, the numbers are much higher than when measured on fine-grained level, which indicates that the major source of confusion still comes from the fine-grained level. In Figure 7, we provide the zoom-in confusion matrices for *ice hockey*, *crossfit* and *basketball.*

4.4 Localization Results

Comparison with baselines. We applied the frameworks to localize fine-grained actions, and varied the overlap ratio r from 0.1 to 0.5 for evaluation. Figure 9 shows the mean average precision over all 45 categories of different systems. We did not include the baseline using low-level features for evaluation as they were computed over whole videos. From the figure we can see that LSTM with LAF proposal outperformed both CNN and LSTM without LAF proposal significantly, the gap grows wider as we increase the overlap ratio. This confirms that temporal information and LAF proposal are helpful for the temporal localization task.

In Table 4, we show the most different average precisions on action level. Some actions have clearly benefited from the introduction of LSTM as well as LAF proposal. We also observed that some actions were completely missed by all three systems, such as *Baseball:Hit*, *Basketball:Three-point field goal* and *Basketball:Block*, possibly due to the video

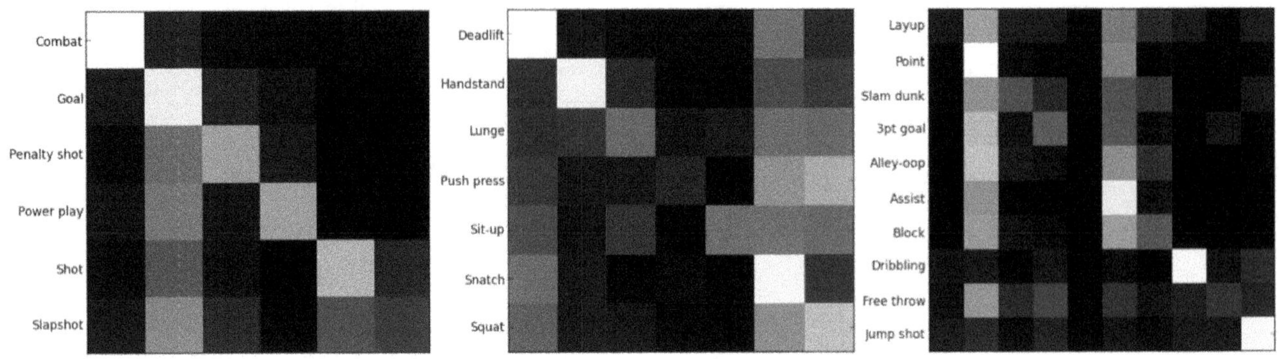

Figure 7: Magnified view of confusion matrices for *ice hockey*, *crossfit* and *basketball*

Figure 8: Classification output for a few videos. The labels under each video were generated by LSTM with LAF proposal, LSTM without LAF proposal and CNN from top to bottom. Correct answers are marked in bold.

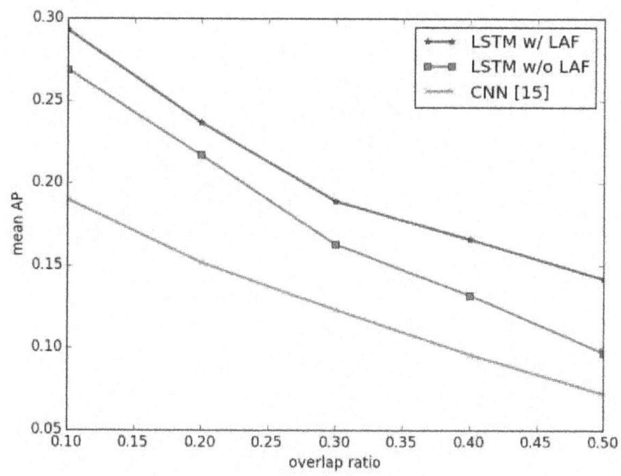

Figure 9: Temporal localization performance on FGA-240 data set.

Fine-grained sports	Δ AP	Δ AP	Fine-grained sports
Soccer:Penalty kick	0.32	-0.06	Baseball:Run
Tennis:Serve	0.25	-0.01	Skateboarding:Kickflip
Basketball:Dribbling	0.21	-0.01	Volleyball:Spiking

Fine-grained sports	Δ AP	Δ AP	Fine-grained sports
Baseball:Brawl	0.52	-0.11	Streetball:Crossovers
Ice hockey:Combat	0.48	-0.05	Ice hockey:Penalty shot
Soccer:Penalty kick	0.33	-0.04	Fencing:Parry

Table 4: Difference in average precision, compared between LSTM with and without LAF proposal (top), LSTM with LAF proposal and CNN (bottom), overlap ratio is fixed to 0.5. A positive number means LSTM with LAF proposal is better.

frames corresponding to these actions not being well localized during training.

4.5 Localization Results on THUMOS 2014

To verify the effectiveness of domain transfer from web images, we also conducted a localization experiment on the THUMOS 2014 data set [10]. This data set consists of over 13,000 temporally trimmed videos from 101 actions, 1,010 temporally untrimmed videos for validation and 2,574 temporally untrimmed videos for testing. The localization annotations cover 20 out of the 101 actions in the validation and test sets. All 20 actions are sports related.

Experiment setup: As this paper focuses on temporal localization of untrimmed videos, we dropped the 13,000 trimmed videos, and used the untrimmed validation videos as the only positive samples for training. We also used 2,500 background videos as the shared negative training data.

To generate LAF scores, we downloaded web images from Flickr and Google using the action names as queries. We also sampled training video frames at 1 frame per second. We used the AlexNet features for domain transfer experiment.

Recently, it has been shown that a combination of improved dense trajectory features [32] and Fisher vector encoding [18] (iDT+FV) offers the state-of-the-art performance on this data set. This motivated us to switch LSTM time steps from frames to video segments, and represent segments with iDT+FV features for the final detector training. We segmented all videos uniformly with a window width of 100 frames and step size of 50 frames. For iDT+FV feature extraction, we took only the MBH modality with 192 dimensions and reduced the dimensions to 96 with PCA. We used the full Fisher vector formulation with the number of GMM cluster centers set to 128. The final video segment representation has 24,576 dimensions.

Method	Overlap ratio 0.1	0.2	0.3	0.4	0.5
Ground truth	0.161	0.152	0.112	0.071	0.044
Video [27, 19]	0.098	0.089	0.071	0.041	0.024
LSTM w/o LAF	0.076	0.071	0.057	0.038	0.024
LSTM w/ LAF	**0.124**	**0.110**	**0.085**	**0.052**	**0.044**

Table 5: Temporal localization on the test partition of THUMOS 2014 dataset. Ground truth uses temporal annotation of the training videos.

Results: We compared the performance of LSTM weighted by LAF scores against several baselines. **LSTM w/o LAF** randomly assigned misclassification penalty for each step of LSTM, where 30% of the steps were set to 1, and others 0. The **Video** baseline used iDT+FV features aggregated over whole videos to train linear SVM classifiers, and applied the classifiers to the testing video shots. It was used by [27, 19] and achieved state-of-the-art performance in event recounting and video summarization tasks. None of these systems require temporal annotations. Finally, **Ground truth** employed manually annotated temporal localizations to set LSTM penalty weights. It is used to study the performance difference between LAF and an oracle with perfect localized actions.

Table 5 shows the mean average precision for the four approaches. As expected, using manually annotated ground truth for training provides the best localization performance. Although LSTM with LAF scores has worse performance than using ground truth, it outperforms LSTM without LAF scores, and the video-level baseline by large margins. This further confirms that LAF proposal by domain transfer from web images is effective in action localization tasks.

5. CONCLUSION

We studied the problem of fine-grained action localization for temporally untrimmed web videos. We proposed to use noisily tagged web images to discover localized action frames (LAF) from videos, and model temporal information with LSTM networks. We conducted thorough evaluations on our collected FGA-240 data set and the public THUMOS 2014 data set, and showed the effectiveness of LAF proposal by domain transfer from web images.

6. ACKNOWLEDGMENTS

We thank George Toderici, Matthew Hausknecht, Jia Deng, Weilong Yang, Susanna Ricco, Tomas Izo, Thomas Leung, Congcong Li and Howard Zhou for helpful comments and discussions. We also thank Bernard Ghanem, Fabian Caba Heilbron and Juan Carlos Niebles for kindly providing us video annotation tools.

7. REFERENCES

[1] J. Chen, Y. Cui, G. Ye, D. Liu, and S. Chang. Event-driven semantic concept discovery by exploiting weakly tagged internet images. In *ICMR*, 2014.

[2] J. Deng, W. Dong, R. Socher, L.-J. Li, K. Li, and L. Fei-Fei. ImageNet: A Large-Scale Hierarchical Image Database. In *CVPR*, 2009.

[3] S. K. Divvala, A. Farhadi, and C. Guestrin. Learning everything about anything: Webly-supervised visual concept learning. In *CVPR*, 2014.

[4] J. Donahue, L. A. Hendricks, S. Guadarrama, M. Rohrbach, S. Venugopalan, K. Saenko, and T. Darrell. Long-term recurrent convolutional networks for visual recognition and description. In *CVPR*, 2015.

[5] A. Graves, A. Mohamed, and G. E. Hinton. Speech recognition with deep recurrent neural networks. In *ICASSP*, 2013.

[6] A. Graves and J. Schmidhuber. Offline handwriting recognition with multidimensional recurrent neural networks. In *NIPS*, 2008.

[7] A. Habibian, K. E. A. van de Sande, and C. G. M. Snoek. Recommendations for video event recognition using concept vocabularies. In *ICMR*, 2013.

[8] S. Hochreiter and J. Schmidhuber. Long short-term memory. *Neural Computation*, 1997.

[9] M. Jain, J. van Gemert, H. Jégou, P. Bouthemy, and C. G. M. Snoek. Action localization with tubelets from motion. In *CVPR*, 2014.

[10] Y.-G. Jiang, J. Liu, A. Roshan Zamir, G. Toderici, I. Laptev, M. Shah, and R. Sukthankar. THUMOS challenge: Action recognition with a large number of classes. `http://crcv.ucf.edu/THUMOS14/`, 2014.

[11] A. Karpathy, G. Toderici, S. Shetty, T. Leung, R. Sukthankar, and L. Fei-Fei. Large-scale video classification with convolutional neural networks. In *CVPR*, 2014.

[12] R. Kiros, R. Salakhutdinov, and R. S. Zemel. Unifying visual-semantic embeddings with multimodal neural language models. *TACL*, 2015.

[13] A. Krizhevsky, I. Sutskever, and G. E. Hinton. Imagenet classification with deep convolutional neural networks. In *NIPS*, 2012.

[14] H. Kuehne, H. Jhuang, E. Garrote, T. Poggio, and T. Serre. HMDB: a large video database for human motion recognition. In *ICCV*, 2011.

[15] D. G. Lowe. Distinctive image features from scale-invariant keypoints. *IJCV*, 2004.

[16] D. Oneata, J. Verbeek, and C. Schmid. Action and Event Recognition with Fisher Vectors on a Compact Feature Set. In *ICCV*, 2013.

[17] P. Over, G. Awad, M. Michel, J. Fiscus, G. Sanders, W. Kraaij, A. F. Smeaton, and G. Queenot. TRECVID 2013 – an overview of the goals, tasks, data, evaluation mechanisms and metrics. In *TRECVID*, 2013.

[18] F. Perronnin and C. Dance. Fisher kernels on visual vocabularies for image categorization. In *CVPR*, 2007.

[19] D. Potapov, M. Douze, Z. Harchaoui, and C. Schmid. Category-specific video summarization. In *ECCV*, 2014.

[20] M. Rohrbach, S. Amin, M. Andriluka, and B. Schiele. A database for fine grained activity detection of cooking activities. In *CVPR*, 2012.

[21] O. Russakovsky, J. Deng, H. Su, J. Krause, S. Satheesh, S. Ma, Z. Huang, A. Karpathy, A. Khosla, M. Bernstein, A. C. Berg, and L. Fei-Fei. ImageNet Large Scale Visual Recognition Challenge, 2014.

[22] H. Sak, A. Senior, and F. Beaufays. Long short-term memory based recurrent neural network architectures for large vocabulary speech recognition. *CoRR*, abs/1402.1128, 2014.

[23] C. Schuldt, I. Laptev, and B. Caputo. Recognizing human actions: A local SVM approach. In *ICPR*, 2004.

[24] K. Simonyan and A. Zisserman. Two-stream convolutional networks for action recognition in videos. In *NIPS*, 2014.

[25] K. Soomro, A. R. Zamir, and M. Shah. UCF101: A dataset of 101 human actions classes from videos in the wild. *CRCV-TR-12-01*.

[26] N. Srivastava, E. Mansimov, and R. Salakhutdinov. Unsupervised learning of video representations using LSTMs. In *ICML*, 2015.

[27] C. Sun, B. Burns, R. Nevatia, C. Snoek, B. Bolles, G. Myers, W. Wang, and E. Yeh. ISOMER: Informative segment observations for multimedia event recounting. In *ICMR*, 2014.

[28] I. Sutskever, O. Vinyals, and Q. V. Le. Sequence to sequence learning with neural networks. In *NIPS*, 2014.

[29] Y. Tian, R. Sukthankar, and M. Shah. Spatiotemporal deformable part models for action detection. In *CVPR*, 2013.

[30] O. Vinyals, A. Toshev, S. Bengio, and D. Erhan. Show and tell: A neural image caption generator. In *CVPR*, 2015.

[31] H. Wang, A. Kläser, C. Schmid, and C.-L. Liu. Dense trajectories and motion boundary descriptors for action recognition. *IJCV*, 2013.

[32] H. Wang and C. Schmid. Action Recognition with Improved Trajectories. In *ICCV*, 2013.

[33] L. Wang, Y. Qiao, and X. Tang. Video action detection with relational dynamic-poselets. In *ECCV*, 2014.

[34] R. J. Williams and J. Peng. An efficient gradient-based algorithm for on-line training of recurrent network trajectories. *Neural Computation*, 1990.

[35] W. Yang and G. Toderici. Discriminative tag learning on youtube videos with latent sub-tags. In *CVPR*, 2011.

[36] Y. Yang, Y. Yang, and H. T. Shen. Effective transfer tagging from image to video. *TOMM*, 2013.

[37] B. Yao and F. Li. Recognizing human-object interactions in still images by modeling the mutual context of objects and human poses. *PAMI*, 2012.

[38] J. Yue-Hei Ng, M. Hausknecht, S. Vijayanarasimhan, O. Vinyals, R. Monga, and G. Toderici. Beyond short snippets: Deep networks for video classification. In *CVPR*, 2015.

Temporal Matching Kernel with Explicit Feature Maps

Sébastien Poullot
National Institute of Informatics and JFLI (CNRS)
Tokyo, Japan
spoullot@nii.ac.jp

Shunsuke Tsukatani
University of Tokyo and National Institute of Informatics
Tokyo, Japan
tsukatani@nii.ac.jp

Anh Phuong Nguyen
MMLab - University of Information Technology
Ho Chi Minh, Vietnam
anhnp@uit.edu.vn

Hervé Jégou
Inria
Rennes, France
herve.jegou@inria.fr

Shin'Ichi Satoh
National Institute of Informatics and University of Tokyo
Tokyo, Japan
satoh@nii.ac.jp

ABSTRACT

This paper proposes a framework for content-based video retrieval that addresses various tasks as particular event retrieval, copy detection or video synchronization. Given a video query, the method is able to efficiently retrieve, from a large collection, similar video events or near-duplicates with temporarily consistent excerpts. As a byproduct of the representation, it provides a precise temporal alignment of the query and the detected video excerpts.

Our method converts a series of frame descriptors into a single visual-temporal descriptor, called a temporal invariant match kernel. This representation takes into account the relative positions of the visual frames: the frame descriptors are jointly encoded with their timestamps. When matching two videos, the method produces a score function for all possible relative timestamps, which is maximized to obtain both the similarity score and the relative time offset.

Then, we propose two complementary contributions to further improve the detection and localization performance. The first is a novel query expansion method that takes advantage of the joint descriptor/timestamp representation to automatically align the first result set and produce an enriched temporal query. In contrast to other query expansion methods proposed for videos, it preserves the localization capability. Second, we improve the localization trade-off between quality and representation size by using several complementary temporal match kernels.

We evaluate our approach on benchmarks for particular event retrieval, copy detection and video synchronization. Our experiments show that our approach achieve excellent detection and localization results.

1. INTRODUCTION

This paper addresses the problem of content-based search in large collections of video clips. Our goal is twofold: (i) identify the content of interest (ii) localize the content of interest within the video clip. We essentially focus on tasks such as particular event retrieval [19], copy detection [15, 25, 7] and video synchronization, for which the temporal consistency is important. Because we want to handle large datasets, the complexity is regarded as a key factor, both in terms of CPU and memory. This disqualifies the numerous approaches that store local image descriptors or spatial-temporal points [15], which are too costly for big datasets.

In contrast, following some recent works for particular event retrieval and video copy detection [19, 8], the input of our approach is a set of compact frame *vectors* produced from local descriptors. A visual frame descriptor is obtained by first encoding the local descriptors of the image with the Fisher vector [16, 17] or another alternative coding approach [24, 12, 2, 14], such as those recently proposed for image classification or search tasks. These vectors are then projected to a few hundreds or thousands components [13, 12] with dimensionality reduction.

With such frame vectors as the initial video representation, the most common options are the following ones:

1. adopt a "bag of frames" shift-invariant representation [8], whose major advantage is to be computationally cheap. The main drawback is that this class of method looses the temporal consistency of the frames, therefore the method is not able to provide the temporal alignment
2. compare videos by matching all the frames of the query video with all the frames of each database video. The potential matching frames are then fed to a Hough temporal matching ensuring that the matches are temporally consistent [7]. However, the complexity of this strategy is quadratic in the length of video clips and is therefore very costly.

To alleviate the quadratic term, the circulant temporal encoding (CTE) of Revaud *et al.* [19] exploits a simple assumption (time translation) on the temporal model to evaluate efficiently, *i.e.*, in the Fourier domain, the cross-correlation of two series of vectors representing two videos. This strategy is inspired by recent works by Henriques *et al.* for efficient detection [10] and tracking [11], who obtained top performances in the VOT2014 object tracking challenge [9]. This approach has the capability of finding the near-duplicates and provides the temporal offset between the videos. Indeed, CTE considers the temporal shift-invariant matching

MM'15, October 26–30, 2015, Brisbane, Australia.

DOI: http://dx.doi.org/10.1145/2733373.2806228.

as matching sequences with all possible shifts, then regards matching sequences with all possible shifts as a convolution. However, this strategy has several shortcomings, the main one being that this method is tailored to a measure of cross-correlation, which is a strong assumption on the time model best fitted to compare videos.

We mention that video recognition based with CTE is outperformed by the recent stable hyper-pooling approach [8]. However hyper-pooling is more costly and, as mentioned previously, does not provide any localization capability, such as the estimation of the temporal offset.

In this paper, we propose a class of *temporal match kernels* which are able to match and align videos efficiently. It can be seen as a generalization of CTE, yet compared to this representation it offers two advantages: (i) the design of the kernel offers degrees of freedom likely to better suit to the particular recognition task ; (ii) the representation has a fixed size and is independent from the video length.

The idea is to encode a set of vectors (the frame descriptors associated with a given video) into a single vector so that the comparison of two videos is performed with dot products, in the spirit of the kernel descriptors of Bo [3], but here specifically adapted to the case of time vector sequences. The design of this encoding strategy, amenable to incorporate the shift-invariance and the capability of finding the temporal offset, relies on explicit feature maps [23]. Compared to kernel descriptors, the main advantage is that we do not have a single score. Instead the comparison outputs a score function for all time-shift hypotheses, in the form of a trigonometric polynomial.

Our paper makes the following contributions:

- We adapt the kernel descriptor framework of Bo [3] to sequences of frames. More specifically, we propose a class of shift-invariant temporal match kernels by gathering the formalism of explicit feature maps [23] and circulant encoding [10, 19]. This strategy is a generalization of CTE, which gives more room to adapt the properties of the matching kernel and limits the approximation artifacts inherent to CTE.
- We propose a query expansion (QE) technique that automatically aligns the videos deemed relevant for the query. The new query is constructed in the Fourier domain and does not require the original frame descriptors. Most importantly and as opposed to possible concurrent QE techniques proposed with compact representations, our method preserves the localization capability of our temporal match kernel.
- We propose a strategy to combine several match kernels into a single one to further improve the trade-off between memory and localization accuracy.

The paper is organized as follows. Section 2 introduces the notation and some preliminary works from which we derive our approach. Section 3 introduces the temporal matching kernels, which is extended to multiple periods to improve the localization in Section 5. Section 4 introduces an original query expansion method for improving the accuracy of the method. The experiments described in Section 6 demonstrate the interest of our approach on public benchmarks for copy detection and particular event retrieval.

2. PRELIMINARIES: FEATURE MAPS

This section briefly introduces a key ingredient of our method, namely the explicit feature maps [23]. It was originally introduced to produce an approximation of a shift-invariant kernel with an explicit mapping, that is, such that the inner product in the embedded space approximates the kernel in the original space. In our case, we employ it to define a class of temporal kernel between set of visual frames.

2.1 Embedding of the kernel function

The idea is to approximate a non-linear kernel $k(\cdot,\cdot) : \mathbb{R}\times\mathbb{R}\rightarrow\mathbb{R}$ by using a mapping function $\boldsymbol{\varphi} : \mathbb{R}\rightarrow\mathbb{R}^{2m+1}$ as

$$k(u,v) \approx \langle \boldsymbol{\varphi}(u)|\boldsymbol{\varphi}(v)\rangle. \tag{1}$$

This is done for shift-invariant kernels, *i.e.*, such that the kernel can be expressed as $k(u,v) = g(u-v)$, by first considering the Fourier approximation of g as

$$g(z) = \sum_{i=0}^{m} a_i \cos\left(\frac{2\pi}{T} iz\right), \tag{2}$$

which approximates g assuming that it is a T-periodic function. Now, let us consider that $z = u-v$. By employing the elementary trigonometric property

$$\cos(u-v) = \cos u \cos v + \sin u \sin v \tag{3}$$

$$= \left\langle \begin{bmatrix}\cos u\\ \sin u\end{bmatrix} \middle| \begin{bmatrix}\cos v\\ \sin v\end{bmatrix}\right\rangle, \tag{4}$$

and further assuming that the coefficients of the Fourier series are all positive, *i.e.*, $\forall i\ a_i > 0$, the approximation (2) is written as

$$g(u-v) \approx \underbrace{\begin{bmatrix}\sqrt{a_0}\\ \sqrt{a_1}\cos\left(\frac{2\pi}{T}u\right)\\ \sqrt{a_1}\sin\left(\frac{2\pi}{T}u\right)\\ \vdots\\ \sqrt{a_m}\cos\left(\frac{2\pi}{T}mu\right)\\ \sqrt{a_m}\sin\left(\frac{2\pi}{T}mu\right)\end{bmatrix}^\top}_{\boldsymbol{\varphi}(u)^\top} \underbrace{\begin{bmatrix}\sqrt{a_0}\\ \sqrt{a_1}\cos\left(\frac{2\pi}{T}v\right)\\ \sqrt{a_1}\sin\left(\frac{2\pi}{T}v\right)\\ \vdots\\ \sqrt{a_m}\cos\left(\frac{2\pi}{T}mv\right)\\ \sqrt{a_m}\sin\left(\frac{2\pi}{T}mv\right)\end{bmatrix}}_{\boldsymbol{\varphi}(v)}, \tag{5}$$

where the interesting property is that $\boldsymbol{\varphi}(u)$ is independent of v. Therefore, it is possible to construct the mapping $\boldsymbol{\varphi}$ to approximate the shift-invariant kernel as proposed in (1). The approximation quality depends on the quality of the approximation of k by Fourier series [23].

2.2 Application to frame time stamps

Considering two videos V_x and V_y that are temporally perfectly aligned, the distance between their time stamps is $t_x - t_y = 0$. In this ideal case, the distance is coded by a Dirac delta function:

$$\begin{aligned} \text{if } t_x = t_y \quad & \text{then } \mathcal{D}(t_x,t_y) = 1\\ & \text{else } \mathcal{D}(t_x,t_y) = 0 \end{aligned} \tag{6}$$

The Fourier transform of a Dirac is a constant function, meaning that all a_i are equal in (2). Using the corresponding embedding function is what implicitly done in the circulant encoding technique of Revaud *et al.* [19]. The Dirac's approximation is the best Fourier expansion, w.r.t. square loss, when the function is evaluated at certain positions ($2\pi iz/T$, $i = 0\ldots m-1$). However, this choice has two drawbacks in our application scenario:

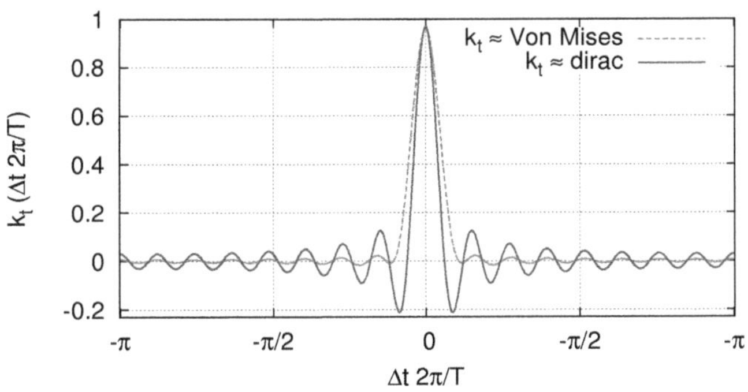

Figure 1: Approximate Dirac and Von Mises: response as a function of the temporal difference when approximating these kernels with finite Fourier series ($m = 16$ frequencies here). As one can observe, the Dirac approximation [19] suffers from oscillations.

1. To get a compact representation, we approximate the temporal kernel with a limited number of frequencies, that is, much smaller that the number of frames to be encoded. The Fourier series we consider are truncated and therefore the approximation obtained when keeping the first components is noisy, suffering strong oscillations around 0, as shown by Figure 1.

2. We want to offer tolerance in time for matching frame by designing a specific shape of the match kernel.

For these reasons, we consider other choices, like the modified Von Mises distribution, a.k.a. the periodic Gaussian, and considered in recent papers [3, 21]. Its Fourier expansion is determined in a close-form manner by the Fourier coefficients

$$a_0 = \frac{B_0(\beta) - e^{-\beta}}{2\sinh(\beta)} \qquad a_i = \frac{B_i(\beta)}{\sinh(\beta)} \text{ for } i \geq 1 \quad (7)$$

where $B_n(\beta)$ is the modified Bessel function of the first kind of order n. Figure 1 clearly shows that the approximate Von Mises temporal kernel gives a flat response out of the target bandwidth, meaning that there are significantly less interferences in the match kernel than with the circulant temporal encoding technique [19].

3. TEMPORAL MATCH KERNELS

This section introduces the class of match kernels proposed in this paper. We first detail the class of kernels that we want to approximate and then show how to approximate them with feature maps encoding. Finally, we show that we can decode them efficiently for any temporal shift. For notation, we denote in bold vectors, tuples and sequences.

3.1 Temporal match kernels with feature maps

Modulating descriptors with timestamps. We consider that each image/frame $\boldsymbol{f_x}$ is associated with a tuple $(\boldsymbol{x}, t_x)$, where $\boldsymbol{x} \in \mathbb{R}^d$ is a d-dimensional vector and t_x is a scalar timestamp. We define a kernel between such tuples that is of the form:

$$k\left(\boldsymbol{f_x}, \boldsymbol{f_y}\right) = k_{\mathrm{f}}(\boldsymbol{x}, \boldsymbol{y})\, k_{\mathrm{t}}(t_x, t_y) \quad (8)$$
$$= \langle \boldsymbol{x} | \boldsymbol{y} \rangle\, k_{\mathrm{t}}(t_x, t_y) \quad (9)$$
$$\approx \langle \boldsymbol{x} | \boldsymbol{y} \rangle\, \varphi(t_x)^\top \varphi(t_y). \quad (10)$$

where we assume that the frame descriptors are normalized and compared with cosine similarity, *i.e.*, $k_{\mathrm{f}}(\boldsymbol{x}, \boldsymbol{y}) = \langle \boldsymbol{x} | \boldsymbol{y} \rangle$. This kernel is further linearized as

$$k\left(\boldsymbol{f_x}, \boldsymbol{f_y}\right) \approx \langle \boldsymbol{x} \otimes \varphi(t_x) | \boldsymbol{y} \otimes \varphi(t_y) \rangle, \quad (11)$$

where $\otimes$ denotes the Kronecker product. In this case, we stress that the tuple $(\boldsymbol{x}, t_x)$ is represented by a single vector $\boldsymbol{x} \otimes \varphi(t_x)$, that serves as the frame descriptor, and which is compared with the inner product. Another way to interpret this joint encoding is to view $\boldsymbol{x}$ as being *modulated* by the timestamp t_x in a continuous manner, so that only frames with the same timestamp can receive a significant contribution: $|k(\mathbf{x}, \mathbf{y})|$ is bounded by $|k_{\mathrm{t}}(t_x, t_y)|$.

Temporal match kernels with feature maps. The expansion in (11) is inspired by the kernel descriptors of Bo *et al.* [3], however it is here based on explicit feature maps instead [23] of efficient match kernels [4]. Following this work, we now consider the context of match kernels. In our case, the goal is to compare two sequences of descriptors $\mathbf{x} = (\boldsymbol{x}_0, \ldots, \boldsymbol{x}_t, \ldots)$ and $\mathbf{y} = (\boldsymbol{y}_0, \ldots, \boldsymbol{y}_{t'}, \ldots)$, where the indices implicitly encode the timestamps[1]. We aim at approximating a kernel on sequences of the form

$$\mathcal{K}_0(\mathbf{x}, \mathbf{y}) = \alpha(\mathbf{x})\alpha(\mathbf{y}) \sum_t k_{\mathrm{f}}(\boldsymbol{x}_t, \boldsymbol{y}_t) \quad (12)$$
$$\propto \sum_{t=0}^{\infty} \boldsymbol{x}_t^\top \boldsymbol{y}_t, \quad (13)$$

where the proportionality factors $\alpha(\cdot)$ are such that $\mathcal{K}_0(\mathbf{x}, \mathbf{x}) = \mathcal{K}_0(\mathbf{y}, \mathbf{y}) = 1$. By convention, we also assume that $\boldsymbol{x}_\tau = \mathbf{0}$ $(\tau > t)$ if the sequence is shorter that t. This kernel is equivalent to

$$\mathcal{K}_0(\mathbf{x}, \mathbf{y}) \propto \sum_{t=0}^{\infty} \sum_{t'=0}^{\infty} \boldsymbol{x}_t^\top \boldsymbol{y}_{t'}\, \delta(t, t'), \quad (14)$$

where $\delta(t, t') = 1$ if $t = t'$, otherwise $\delta(t, t') = 0$. Replacing $\delta(\cdot, \cdot)$ by any temporal kernel $k_{\mathrm{t}}(\cdot, \cdot)$ shows that the circulant temporal embedding [19] is a particular case of our more general formulation, corresponding to the case $k_{\mathrm{t}} = \delta$. Using (11), the kernel is then factorized as

$$\mathcal{K}_0(\mathbf{x}, \mathbf{y}) \propto \underbrace{\Big(\sum_{t=0}^{\infty} \boldsymbol{x}_t \otimes \varphi(t)\Big)}_{\psi_0(\mathbf{x})}^\top \underbrace{\Big(\sum_{t'=0}^{\infty} \boldsymbol{y}_{t'} \otimes \varphi(t')\Big)}_{\psi_0(\mathbf{y})}, \quad (15)$$

where $\psi_0(\mathbf{x})$ is the vector representation of the sequence $\mathbf{x}$. The video representation is a $(1+2m) \times d$ dimensions matrix, where m is the number of coefficient kept from the Fourier series (a_1 to a_m) and d is the initial dimensionality of the frame vectors. It can also be written as

$$\psi_0(\mathbf{x}) = [\mathbf{V}_0{}^\top, \mathbf{V}_{1,c}{}^\top, \mathbf{V}_{1,s}{}^\top, \ldots, \mathbf{V}_{m,c}{}^\top, \mathbf{V}_{m,s}{}^\top]^\top \quad (16)$$

where:

$$\mathbf{V}_0 = a_0 \sum_{t=0}^{\infty} \boldsymbol{x}_t \quad (17)$$
$$\mathbf{V}_{i,c} = a_i \sum_{t=0}^{\infty} \boldsymbol{x}_t \cos\left(\frac{2\pi}{T} t\right)$$
$$\mathbf{V}_{i,s} = a_i \sum_{t=0}^{\infty} \boldsymbol{x}_t \sin\left(\frac{2\pi}{T} t\right)$$

[1]The timestamps are not necessarily integers, any real value is possible. We use integers for the sake of simplicity.

Regularization. The temporal linearity in videos induces a strong self-similarity, and results in interferences when matching two similar videos. Such noise degrades the alignment between two videos. In order to limit this undesirable effect we regularize the kernel descriptors to limit the interferences due to self-similarity in videos. Derived from Winener-Khinchin Theorem, the regularization is done by updating $\psi_0(x)$ as follows:

$$\psi_0(x) := \frac{\psi_0(x)}{\sqrt{\frac{1}{m}\sum_{i=1}^{N}(\mathbf{V}_{i,c}^2 + \mathbf{V}_{i,s}^2)}} \tag{18}$$

This regularization is close to the one introduced in [8]. The main difference is that our regularization is symmetric, applied to both query and database descriptors. In what follows, we use the regularized version for better performance.

3.2 Matching with different timestamps

The temporal similarity in (13) assumes that the sequences are temporally aligned, which prevents from retrieving excerpts that are not synchronous with the query video. We now consider the evaluation of a kernel parametrized by a latent variable Δ controlling the relative offset of two sequences $\mathbf{x}$ and $\mathbf{y}$. The match kernel definition becomes

$$\mathcal{K}_\Delta(\mathbf{x}, \mathbf{y}) \propto \sum_{t=0}^{\infty} \boldsymbol{x}_t^\top \boldsymbol{y}_{t+\Delta}, \tag{19}$$

which, similar to (15), is approximated by

$$\mathcal{K}_\Delta(\mathbf{x}, \mathbf{y}) \propto \Big(\sum_{t=0}^{\infty} \boldsymbol{x}_t \otimes \varphi(t)\Big)^\top \underbrace{\Big(\sum_{t'=0}^{\infty} \boldsymbol{y}_{t'} \otimes \varphi(t'+\Delta)\Big)}_{\psi_\Delta(\mathbf{y})}, \tag{20}$$

where $\psi_\Delta(\mathbf{y})$ indicates that the timestamps of the sequence $\mathbf{y}$ are incremented by the constant Δ. Note that the vector $\psi_\Delta(\mathbf{y})$ corresponds to a translation in the Fourier domain and is therefore obtained from $\psi_0(\mathbf{y})$ by incrementing the phase by the quantity Δ. However, we don't need $\psi_\Delta(\mathbf{y})$ to compute the similarity of the two sequences for any relative time-shift Δ. Instead, similar to Tolias *et al.* [21], we exploit the fact that $\mathcal{K}_\Delta(\mathbf{x}, \mathbf{y})$ is a trigonometric polynomial in Δ, denoted by $\mathcal{K}_{\mathbf{x},\mathbf{y}}(\Delta)$ for clarity, when $\mathbf{x}$ and $\mathbf{y}$ are fixed.

The comparison of two videos proceeds in two steps: (*i*) computation of the coefficients of the polynomial, (*ii*) evaluation of the score at different frame-shifts. Using equations (16) and (17) this trigonometric polynomial of video descriptors $\mathbf{V}(\mathbf{x})$ and $\check{\mathbf{V}}(\mathbf{y})$ is written as

$$\begin{aligned}\mathcal{K}_{\mathbf{x},\mathbf{y}}(\theta) &= \langle \mathbf{V}_0 | \check{\mathbf{V}}_0 \rangle \\ &+ \sum_{n=1}^{N} \cos(n\Delta)(\langle \mathbf{V}_{n,c} | \check{\mathbf{V}}_{n,c} \rangle + \langle \mathbf{V}_{n,s} | \check{\mathbf{V}}_{n,s} \rangle) \\ &+ \sum_{n=1}^{N} \sin(n\Delta)(-\langle \mathbf{V}_{n,c} | \check{\mathbf{V}}_{n,s} \rangle + \langle \mathbf{V}_{n,s} | \check{\mathbf{V}}_{n,c} \rangle)\end{aligned} \tag{21}$$

The coefficients of this polynomial are obtained at the cost of $(1+2m) \times d$ elementary operations, *i.e.*, about twice the cost of an inner product in $\mathbb{R}^d$.

Evaluating the values taken by this score function for all valid frame-shifts Δ has a negligible cost. Figure 2 illustrates the trigonometric polynomials of scores obtained for matching and non-matching sequences. The max peak gives the score $S_{\mathbf{xy}} = \max_\Delta \mathcal{K}_{\mathbf{x},\mathbf{y}}(\Delta)$ and the time offset $\delta_{\mathbf{xy}} = \arg\max_\Delta \mathcal{K}_{\mathbf{x},\mathbf{y}}(\Delta)$ between the sequences $\mathbf{x}$ and $\mathbf{y}$. For each query, the candidates in the database are ordered by decreasing scores.

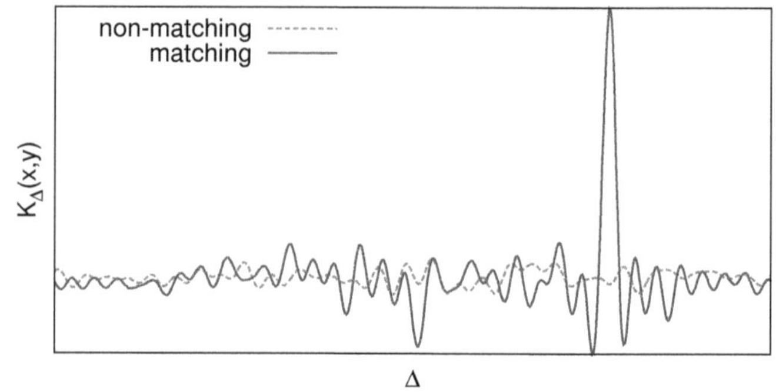

Figure 2: Polynomial of scores $\mathcal{K}_\Delta(\mathbf{x}, \mathbf{y})$ for a matching pair of sequences $(\mathbf{x}, \mathbf{y})$ (blue) and two unrelated sequences (red).

4. TEMPORAL QUERY EXPANSION

Query expansion (QE), a technique initially introduced in text, is an effective mechanism that improves the recall when matching documents can be reliably identified to build an augmented query. In particular object retrieval, it is commonly combined with spatial re-ranking [6, 18, 5]. The most popular is average query expansion (AQE), which constructs the augmented query by averaging the vectors associated with the images deemed positive after spatial verification is applied on an initial short-list. Other variants were recently proposed, such as discriminative query expansion [1].

4.1 Triplet time consistency

In our case, we consider short vector representations of frames that are incompatible with spatial verification based on local descriptors [5, 22]. Therefore we propose a strategy to first check whether the videos returned in the short-list are temporally consistent or not.

Consider a query $\mathbf{q}$ and a database video $\mathbf{x}$, our temporal match kernel returns a temporal offset $\delta_{\mathbf{qx}}$. Within the short-list $\mathcal{N}_1$ of length $|\mathcal{N}_1|$ returned by the ranking strategy, we check the temporal consistency of each result by considering triplets of offsets. The offsets $\delta_{\mathbf{qx}}$ and $\delta_{\mathbf{qy}}$ between the query $\mathbf{q}$ and two videos $\mathbf{x}$ and $\mathbf{y}$ are byproducts of the initial ranking stage. Additionally, we compute the extra offsets $\delta_{\mathbf{xy}}$ between all pairs $(\mathbf{x}, \mathbf{y})$ of videos in the short-list of candidates. These offsets are requested to satisfy the constraint

$$|\delta_{\mathbf{qx}} + \delta_{\mathbf{xy}} + \delta_{\mathbf{yq}}| \leq \varepsilon, \tag{22}$$

where ε is a temporal tolerance related to T. It should be small enough to filter inconsistent matches ($\varepsilon \gg T$) but large enough to tolerate small errors on the estimated offsets. The method is not sensitive to the exact tolerance value. We set $\varepsilon = 100$ frames. Having computed the consistency of each couple of candidates $((|\mathcal{N}_1| - 1)/2$ in total), we produce a per-video consistency measure to partition the short-list as

$$\mathcal{N}_1 = \mathcal{N}_1^{\mathrm{C}} \cup \mathcal{N}_1^{\mathrm{U}}, \tag{23}$$

where $\mathcal{N}_1^{\mathrm{C}}$ is the set of consistent candidates and its supplementary set $\mathcal{N}_1^{\mathrm{U}}$.

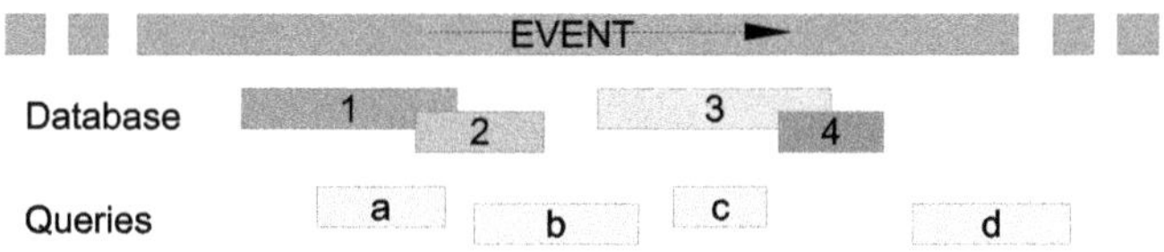

Figure 3: This figure shows how query expansion can retrieve database video clips originally not reachable: in the database video clip **4** is not temporally consistent (and most likely not visually) with any query, however if query **c** returns the database video clip **3** and a new query is generated, based on **c** and **3** then **4** may be reached.

Temporally aligned QE. As discussed in Section 3.2, we compute the descriptor $\psi_\Delta(\mathbf{y})$ to measure the score between $\mathbf{x}$ and $\mathbf{y}$ assuming a time-shift of Δ. We use this property to align the descriptors of $\mathcal{N}_1^{\mathrm{C}}$ in the temporal coordinate system of the query. In other terms, we modify the phase of the candidate i such that its similarity to the query is maximized with time-shift 0 instead of $\delta_{\mathbf{qy}}$. This is done by computing $\psi_{-\delta_{\mathbf{qy}}}(\mathbf{y})$ from the stored vector $\psi_0(\mathbf{y})$. The rationale is that we can now add these vectors to produce an augmented query that still offers localization capabilities. In contrast, we do not align the vectors of $\mathcal{N}_1^{\mathrm{U}}$, as they do not offer any temporal consistency.

4.2 Fusion strategy

We now consider several ways to produce an augmented query. They are inspired by other works on query expansion [6, 8]. The key differences are that we identify a time consistent subset with our triplet consistency and align these videos by performing a translation in the Fourier domain to take into account the relative time-shift with the query. We consider three fusion methods.

1. *Average Query Expansion (AQE).* The top $|\mathcal{N}_1|$ results associated with a query are aligned if time-consistent, and then averaged to produce the augmented query, as

$$\psi_{\mathrm{AQE}}^{\mathcal{C}} = \frac{\psi^{\mathcal{C}}(\mathbf{q}) + \sum_{\mathbf{x}\in\mathcal{N}_1} \psi^{\mathcal{C}}(\mathbf{x})}{1+|\mathcal{N}_1|} \tag{24}$$

$$\psi_{\mathrm{AQE}}^{\mathcal{T}} = \frac{\psi^{\mathcal{T}}(\mathbf{q}) + \sum_{\mathbf{x}\in\mathcal{N}_1^{\mathrm{C}}} \psi^{\mathcal{T}}_{-\delta_{\mathbf{qx}}}(\mathbf{x})}{1+|\mathcal{N}_1|} \tag{25}$$

where $\psi^{\mathcal{C}}(\mathbf{x})$ is for the constant part of the kernel feature $\mathbf{x}$ and $\psi^{\mathcal{T}}(\mathbf{x})$ is for the trigonometric part of the kernel feature $\mathbf{x}$. The final augmented query is the concatenation of these two features:

$$\psi_{\mathrm{AQE}} = [\psi_{\mathrm{AQE}}^{\mathcal{C}}, \psi_{\mathrm{AQE}}^{\mathcal{T}}]. \tag{26}$$

2. *Difference of Neighborhood (DoN).* We combine our automatic alignment with an alternative QE method [8]. It is a variant of AQE where the average vector of close to far $|\mathcal{N}_2|$ neighbors is subtracted to the AQE vector.

$$\psi_{\mathrm{DoN}} = \psi_{\mathrm{AQE}} - \frac{\sum_{\mathbf{x}\in\mathcal{N}_2} \psi_0(\mathbf{x})}{|\mathcal{N}_2|} \tag{27}$$

3. *DoN iterative.* The DoN is iteratively applied I times. Each time the new augmented query replaces the previous one. The score for one candidate for one iteration is averaged with the score at previous iteration.

5. DESIGN WITH MULTIPLE PERIODS

In this section, we propose an approach to improve the localization accuracy while keeping a reasonable size for the video representation. Our motivation is twofold:

- The localization can be done up to a period modulo T only. If a video is longer than this period, our method based on explicit feature maps can not disambiguate the relative offset.

- The localization accuracy depends on the period T (scale dependency). Increasing the modulation period dramatically reduces the localization accuracy for a given number of frequencies (*i.e.*, for a given size of the representation). In other terms, the localization is more precise for a shorter period.

We address these two problems by defining a temporal kernel constructed from multiple explicit feature maps, each being associated with a different period. As opposed to other contexts where the signal is inherently periodic, like angles [21], the choice of the period is a parameter of the method. We want to reduce it to achieve better localization. The main idea in this section is to use multiple elementary match kernels (with different periods), in order to still able to infer the correct time localization for long video.

About periodicity. The property motivating our proposal is that the sum of a T_1-periodic and of a T_2-periodic function is $T_1 \times T_2$-periodic if T_1 and T_2 are relatively prime. More generally, the period is $T_1 \times T_2/\mathrm{gcd}(T_1, T_2)$, where gcd is the greatest common divisor of T_1 and T_2. Said otherwise, if δ_t is a time shift such that $|\delta_t/2| \leq (T_1 \times T_2)/\mathrm{gcd}(T_1, T_2)$, we can determine δ_t if we know $\delta_t \mod T_1$ and $\delta_t \mod T_2$. This property can be generalized to more than two decompositions, which allows us to estimate time shifts for very long videos while keeping a small number of frequencies.

We apply this idea to the temporal match kernels introduced in the previous section to generate very long periods. Figure 4 shows a toy example with two temporal match kernels having distinct periods T_1 and T_2. We consider two synthetic vector sequences of 600 frames each having 100 similar frames in common: the subsequence [100 : 200] in the first sequence corresponds to the subsequence [400 : 500] in the second, which means a 300 frames temporal shift. We first present match kernels with periods ($T_1 = 100, T_2 = 200$) to show that we obtain almost identical peaks due to resonance (top right figure). Unfortunately the higher peak happens at an offset of -500 frames. This is a pathological case that should be avoided because the induced period is only $T_1 \times T_2/\mathrm{gcd}(T_1, T_2) = 200$. In contrast, a proper choice of periods in the other example ($T_1 = 103, T_2 = 227$) does not overlap and a single clear peak appear at 300 frames.

In practice, we use four periods of modulation, T_1 to T_4, all being prime numbers and therefore relatively prime to each other, such that $\mathrm{gcd}(T_1, T_2, T_3, T_4) = 1$. The combined kernel offers a long period. For each decomposition (each being associated with a different period), we compute the polynomial of score $\mathcal{K}_{\Delta,T}$ for each integer value on the interval $[-\max(L_1, L_2), +\max(L_1, L_2)]$, where L_1 and L_2 refer to the durations of the compared videos.

Two fusion operators are then considered to produce a global score function from the polynomial of scores associated with the temporal match kernel. The first is the sum of the polynomials, which itself can be written as a Fourier series. Other alternative are possible, such as taking minimum value of the different score functions. Experimentally,

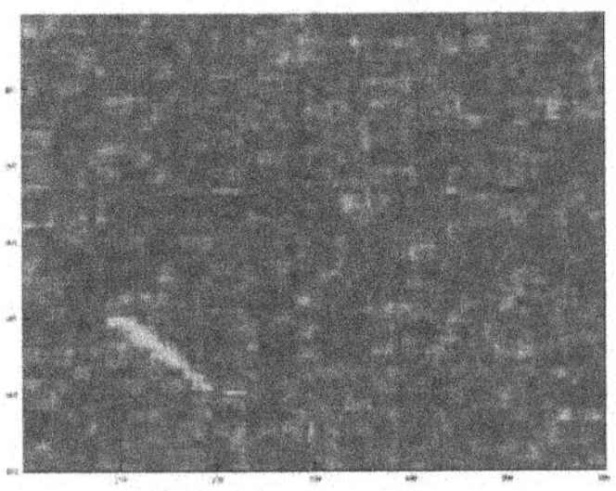

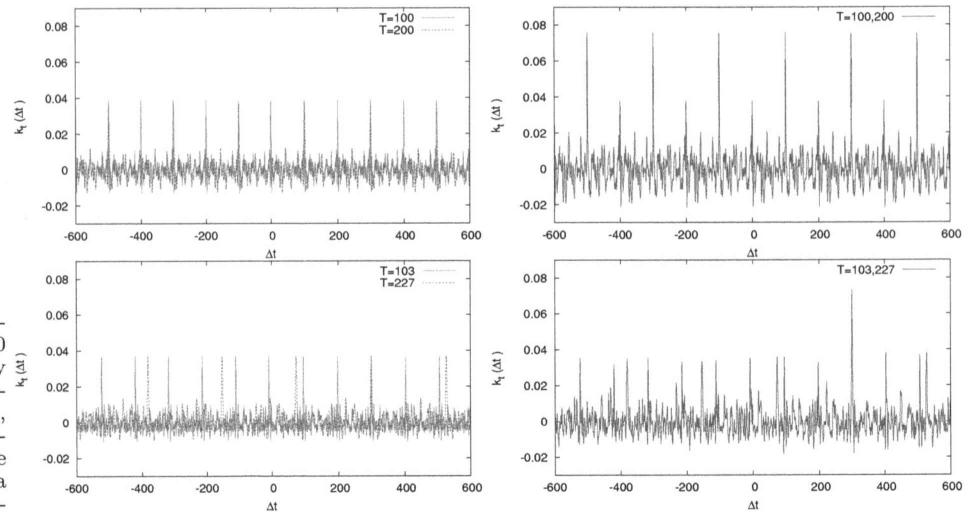

Figure 4: **Top left:** similarity matrix between two synthetic vectors of 600 frames. **Top left plot:** the elementary match kernels $T = \{100, 200\}$ overlap relatively soon, producing a combined (sum, top right plot) match kernel having a relatively short period. In contrast, the other construction (bottom figures) is a better choice: the elementary match kernels $T = \{103, 227\}$ are complementary.

the "sum" and "min" fusion perform similarly for video localization. Therefore we use the sum operator for this Multi-Period Strategy (MPS) in the experimental section.

Figure 9 shows the score function between two matching videos from the EVVE Madonna video set, using a single period $T = 65537$ or four periods $T = [2027, 3019, 5003, 7019]$ with the sum operator and two different settings $m = 4 \times 16$ *vs* $m = 1 \times 64$ and $m = 4 \times 32$ *vs* $m = 1 \times 128$. Observe that the multiple-periods strategy gives a better estimation of the offset. Although we do not have a precise temporal ground-truth on this dataset, we observe that this conclusion seems to be valid in most of the cases we checked: the multiple periods approach gives a better precision.

6. EXPERIMENTS

In this section, we evaluate the temporal match kernel introduced in Section 3, the multi-period variant of Section 5 and our temporally-aligned query expansion (Section 4) for recognition of particular events and for copy detection.

6.1 Event detection

Dataset. We consider the EVVE dataset [19] for particular event detection. The dataset contains videos from 13 particular events grabbed on Youtube™(see in Appendix 9 the details of the events). They are professional or private contents with strong or poor temporal consistency (details are given at the end of this subsection). 620 videos serve as queries, 2375 ones are forming the database.

Frame descriptors and baseline. We use the frame 1024-dimensional multi-VLAD whiten descriptors described in [19], available online, and compare with state-of-the-art methods that use the same input descriptors, namely CTE [19], Mean-MultiVLAD (MMV) [19] and Stable Hyper Pooling (SHP) [8]. CTE is able to provide localization, the two other ones can not. We also include the results achieved by MMV+CTE, which are obtained by adding the normalized scores from MMV and CTE for each query. Our method only involves three dependent parameters: β gives the steepness of the Gaussian approximated by the Fourier coefficient, T the period of modulation, and m the number of Fourier coefficients kept. This last parameter is the most important, as it induces the size of the representation. The method is not very sensitive to small variations of these values.

Event detection performance. Our method performs as well as CTE for the simple EVVE dataset, as shown in Table 1, while SHP remains higher but without alignment capability. Using a longer period of modulation, $T = 65537$ is preferable to a short one $T = 659$: a short period means that long videos will be "folded", consequently cumulated noise may create a peak in the polynomial score that overwhelms the true match. A longer period is safer but induces a less precise alignment for a fixed size of the description. When adding 100000 distractors to the database (+10K), our baseline is as good as MMV+CTE and very close to SHP. The checking of time consistency improves the precision of the method and makes it more robust in a noisy dataset.

Complexity. The modulation is done off-line for the collection. On average (over 10,000 videos, 30,000,000 frames), the modulation with $m = 32$ requires 0.3 s for a video clip comprising 3000 frames. Online, our Matlab implementation of the polynomial score computation requires 1 ms. For $m = 16$ the video descriptor dimensionality is 33792, twice bigger than SHP but still compact. The original CTE video representation depends on the video length [19], leading to a memory footprint of 943 MB for the whole collection, while our method is about 3 times more compact (320 MB).

Query expansion. We evaluate the query expansion methods detailed in Section 4. For this purpose, we consider the baseline descriptors with a unique modulation period $T = 65537$ and $m = 32$ frequencies. The experiments confirm that the proposed phase modification is compatible with the QE framework and does not degrade the results, while preserving the localization ability of the generated queries.

Table 2 compares the three query expansion methods proposed in section 4 to the baseline. Experimentally, parameters are set to $N_1 = 5$, $N_2 = 1000$, *AQE* and *DoN* require one iteration of expansion while *DoN iter* requires three iterations. AQE gives a good improvement but DoN strongly outperforms it. The benefit of the iterative approach is only 0.3% of mAP but is consistent over almost all events. Our best score after three iterations of query expansion is 41.3%. SHP [8] reported up to 44% on this dataset, CTE did not proposed any query expansion method, therefore no fair comparison can be provided (summary in Table 1).

In order to assess the scalability of the approach, 100000 distractors are added to the database (last line of table 1 and

	Ours TE			
m	16		32	
T	659	65537	659	65537
EVVE	0.332	0.334	0.332	**0.335**

state of the art	CTE	MMV	CTE+ MMV	SHP	Ours TE
EVVE	0.352	0.334	**0.376**	0.363	0.335
+QE	-	-	-	**0.440**	0.413
+10K	0.202	0.220	0.254	**0.265**	0.254
+10K+QE	-	-	-	0.331	**0.347**

Table 1: **Top:** Results of our temporal embedding on the EVVE dataset, with two fixed periods of modulation $T = \{659, 65537\}$, two Fourier decompositions $m = \{16, 32\}$, with ($\beta = 32$). **Bottom:** state of the art methods VS ours ($m = 32$, $T = 65537$), with or without +10K distractors, with or without Query Expansion (simple *DoN* for SHP and phase modified *DoN* for Ours).

	baseline	AQE	DoN	DoN iter	+/-
#1	0.243	0.284	0.378	**0.393**	+ 0.15
#2	0.201	0.201	0.193	0.192	- 0.01
#3	0.088	0.056	0.104	0.104	+ 0.02
#4	0.120	0.116	0.151	0.156	+ 0.04
#5	0.235	0.241	0.277	**0.287**	+ 0.05
#6	0.340	0.406	**0.497**	**0.497**	+ 0.16
#7	0.140	0.043	0.110	0.111	- 0.03
#8	0.257	0.258	0.263	0.266	+ 0.01
#9	0.550	0.669	**0.762**	**0.764**	+ 0.21
#10	0.468	0.530	**0.588**	**0.581**	+ 0.11
#11	0.759	**0.815**	**0.814**	**0.806**	+ 0.05
#12	0.363	0.422	**0.484**	**0.494**	+ 0.13
#13	0.589	0.642	**0.712**	**0.721**	+ 0.13
mAP	0.335	0.361	0.410	0.413	+ 0.08

Table 2: Query expansion results – in bold the most significantly improved results for event detection. $N = 65537$, $m = 32$, $\beta = 32$, $N_1 = 5$, $N_2 = 1000$.

	baseline	DoN	DoN iter	+/-
#1	0.219	**0.338**	**0.376**	+ 0.15
#2	0.178	0.173	0.184	+ 0.01
#3	0.077	0.076	0.084	+ 0.01
#4	0.070	0.090	0.093	+ 0.02
#5	0.183	0.204	0.219	+ 0.04
#6	0.248	**0.424**	**0.445**	+ 0.20
#7	0.109	0.091	0.131	+ 0.04
#8	0.228	0.234	0.250	+ 0.02
#9	0.458	**0.657**	**0.665**	+ 0.21
#10	0.451	**0.612**	**0.617**	+ 0.16
#11	0.331	0.373	**0.393**	+ 0.06
#12	0.206	**0.343**	**0.362**	+ 0.16
#13	0.541	**0.663**	**0.689**	+ 0.16
+10K mAP	0.254	0.329	0.347	+ 0.10

Table 3: Query expansion results with +10K – in bold the most significantly improved results for event detection. $N = 65537$, $m = 32$, $\beta = 32$, $N_1 = 5$, $N_2 = 1000$.

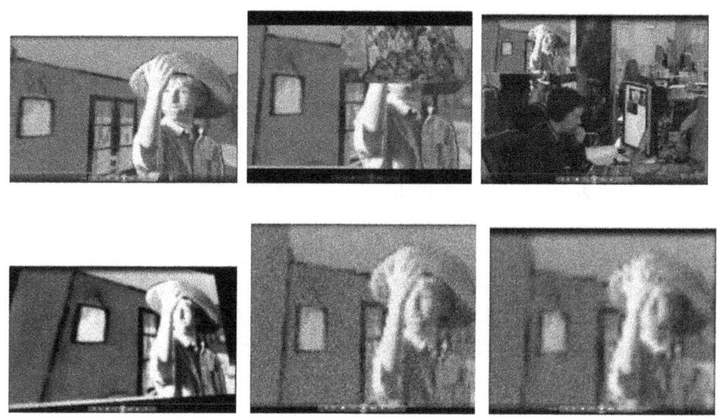

Figure 5: Examples of one video clip (reference is top-left) for which we find all its corresponding copies (5 transformations represented here). For this example, our technique finds the exact offsets (perfect temporal alignement).

details in table 3). The mAP achieves 34.7% after 3 iterations, which is higher than the mAP=33.1% of SHP [8]. This suggests again that the temporal consistency is important to improve the accuracy of the search in larger collections.

Discussion. The events can be separated in two categories, depending on whether they are highly temporally consistent or not. The first group, namely events $\#\{5, 6, 8, 9, 10, 11, 13\}$, mainly contains short live events (concerts, a royal weeding, a political speech, etc), while the second one ($\#\{1, 3, 4, 7, 12\}$) essentially contains edited footage of news (riots, floods, bombing, etc). The improvement of mAP using the iterative query expansion (column *DoN iter*) is 9.5% (12.1% with the distractors) for the first group, 6.5% (7.6% with the distractors) for the second group, which clearly shows that our method takes advantage of the temporal consistency for generating more relevant expanded queries.

6.2 Localization by multi-period

We evaluate the quality of the localization on two benchmarks: 1) The video clip collection introduced for the copy detection task of the TRECVID 2011's evaluation campaign [20] and 2) the Inria CLIMB dataset, which is specifically devoted to evaluate time synchronization in videos. The CTE [19] by Revaud *et al.* is used as the baseline. Recall that SHP [8] can not provide any localization.

TV CBCD 2011 dataset. This set was introduced for the copy detection task of the TRECVID 2011's evaluation campaign [20]. It contains 16776 reference videos and 1608 queries, all extracted at 30 frames per second. The queries were artificially created from 201 videos undergoing 8 different transformations. Some query videos have no corresponding match in the database, while for 134 groups of 8 queries the system is expected to identify the correct video clip and estimates the localization in time.

To evaluate the localization capability of our approach, we match each query with its original reference video. The estimated offset is compared to the ground-truth. We mention than the ground truth is not precise (up to one or two seconds of errors in some cases), likely because of some video encoding errors. Consequently we do not expect a precision at frame level. An example of typical transformations considered in the dataset are presented in Figure 5.

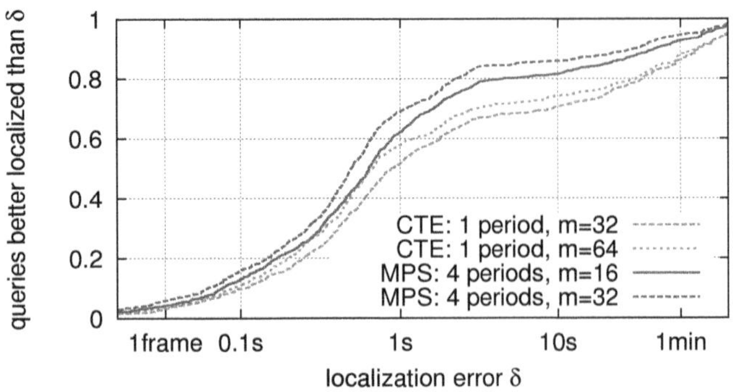

Figure 6: Localization accuracy on CBCD'2011 for CTE and our multi-period strategy (MPS). We show the rate of queries localized better than a tolerance δ (high is better). Note that the size of the representation for CTE with $m = 64$ is similar to that of MPS with 4 periods and $m = 16$.

Frame descriptors. We extract dense PCA-ROOT-sift vectors (step of 5 pixels) and compute an improved Fisher vector [17] for each frame (using a 128 Gaussian Mixture). The 8192-dimensional frame descriptors are further whitened and normalized [12] to produce vectors of 1024 components. As the longer database video clip contains 3694 frames, for the baseline we set $T = 3695$. For our multi-period approach we use the following periods: $\{1777, 2053, 2357, 2731\}$.

Localization performance. Figure 6 reports the localization performance for this copy detection task. Note that the frame rate is constant in this benchmark, which favors the temporal model assumed by CTE. Although for a few videos (about 15%), the localization accuracy is not good because the correct localization is only a local minimum of the score function and not the global one, overall, our multi-period approach clearly outperforms the single-period approach implemented in CTE, and this even when using a similar representation size. This is shown in the figure by comparing MPS with $m = 16$ frequencies against CTE with $m = 64$ frequencies. Using 4 times less frequencies compensates the fact that we use 4 periods w.r.t. complexity, yet gives much better localization accuracy. When manually looking at the alignment, we observe that our method often better aligns the videos than the ground-truth. The reader can also refer to figure 9, it shows how the multiple periods approach improves the localization for the EVVE dataset on a single real data example.

CLIMB dataset. This dataset has been created for the global video alignment task and is available online[2]. This dataset is also used for evaluating the precision of the alignment between pair of videos. The ground truth contains 89 videos at 30 fps. They have been shot, for each event, by different people moving around with different cameras. 452 temporal overlaps exist, however they are not necessarily visual overlaps. The ground truth is more precise than the TV CBCD 2011 one, here the location is at frame level.

The description is done as for the TV CBCD 2011 dataset. The videos of the dataset are longer than in the CBCD dataset, the longer one lasts 37771 frames. Consequently the single period search is set to $T = 37772$. The average video length being much longer than the CBCD dataset, for our MPS approach we set the periods to $\{2731, 4391, 9767, 14653\}$. The results for the localization are given in Figure 7 and

[2]http://pascal.inrialpes.fr/data/evve/index_align.html

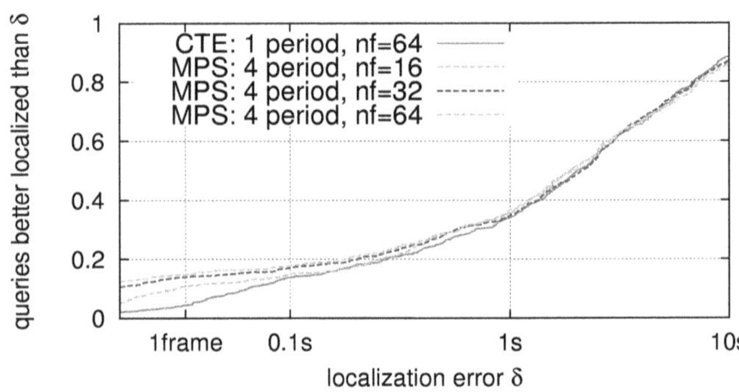

Figure 7: Localization accuracy on CLIMB dataset for CTE and our multi-period strategy (MPS). We show the rate of queries localized better than a tolerance δ (high is better). Note that the size of the representation for CTE with $m = 64$ is similar to that of MPS with 4 periods and $m = 16$.

Figure 8: Captions of couples of video clips well aligned. One column, one couple. On the bottom, first and second ones were initially shot vertically.

illustrations of correctly aligned videos in Figure 8. The database is very challenging, yet the MPS approach clearly outperforms a single period approach and for a negligible extra computational cost (less than 10%). A direct comparison of CTE with $m = 64$ and our MPS method with $m = 4 \times 16$ ensures that the memory footprint is equivalent. In this case, our method is better, especially on small localization errors. Importantly, the accuracy can further be improved by giving more memory budget to our method, as shown when setting $m = 4 \times 32$ and $m = 4 \times 64$.

6.3 Query expansion with multiple periods

Finally, as a concluding experiment, we assess the complementarity of our methods on a event detection task when using all our contributions: the multiple periods match kernel combined with query expansion. The experiments are carried out on the EVVE dataset to allow a direct comparison. The results are reported on Table 4. Observe that they are almost identical to those reported for the single period match kernel with query expansion (Table 2). This suggests that the best option is indeed to combine these methods, as we obtain a similar detection rate with a better alignment.

7. CONCLUSION

This paper proposes a temporal matching kernel for efficient search and localisation of temporally consistent videos. The features, very compact and fast to compute, are also compatible with the query expansion strategies and yet preserve their localization capability. We further propose a multi-period strategy to improve the localisation of the common excerpts at not memory cost and for a very low extra

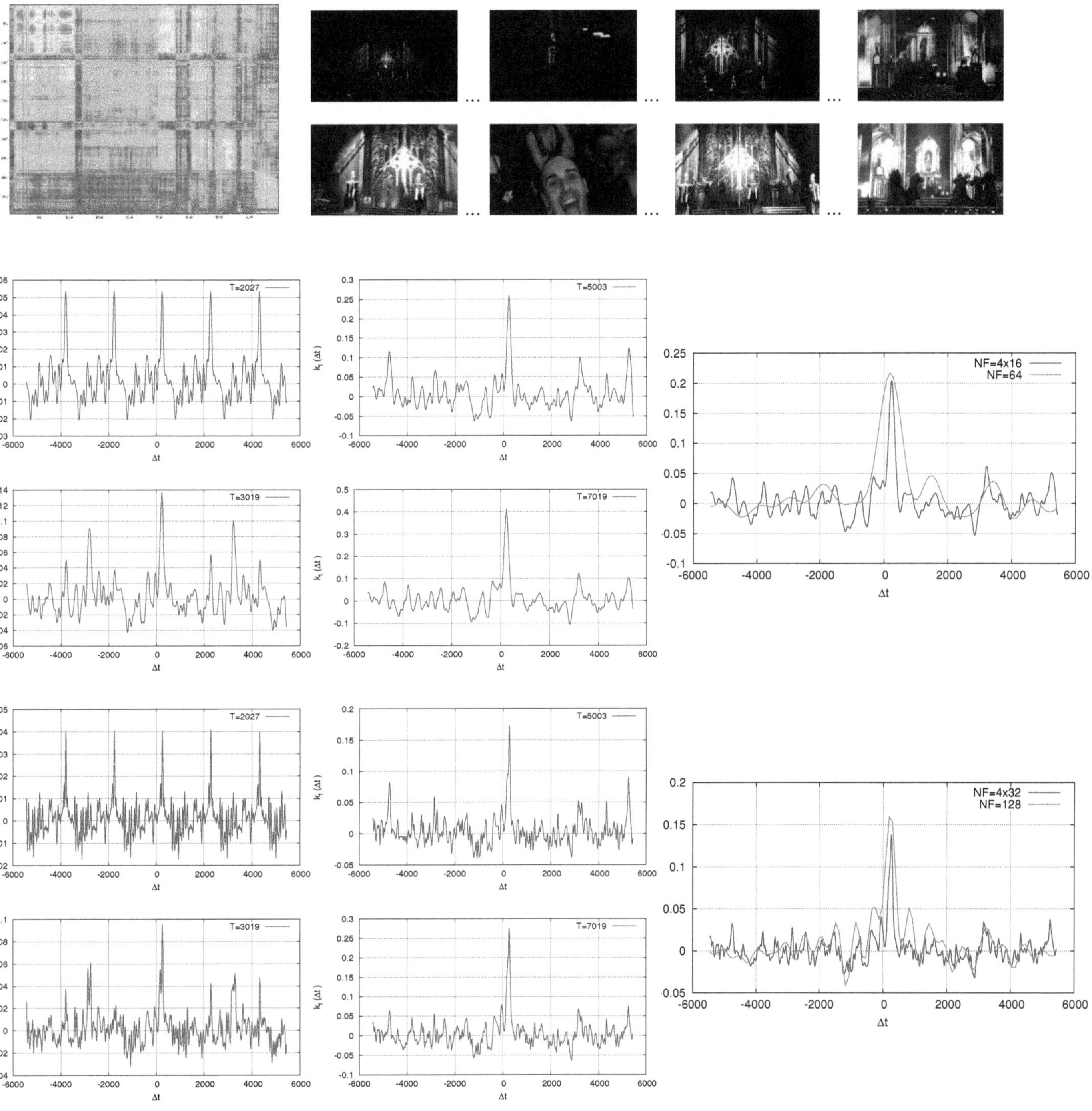

Figure 9: On the top row, on the first column the similarity matrix between two matching videos from the Madonna 2012 Roma concert event (4471 and 5441 frames), beside four captions of each video temporally aligned. It can be seen that it hard to evaluate a visual match between these videos: no clear ridge of high similarity appears in the matrix.
On the second row, the first four figures represent the result of the polynomial for some offsets between the videos for different periods of modulation $T = \{2027, 3019, 5003, 7019\}$ for $m = 16$. Their sum appear on the right figure in blue, while the result of the polynomial for a single period $T = \{65537\}$ for $m = 64$. The multi-period maximal value is observed at 16.3 seconds, the single period one at 12.8 seconds.
On the third row, are represented the same figures for $T = \{2027, 3019, 5003, 7019\}$ for $m = 32$. Their sum appear on the right figure in blue, while the result of the polynomial for a single period $T = \{65537\}$ for $m = 128$. The multi-period maximal value is observed at 17.1 seconds, the single period one at 12.8 seconds.
We visually estimate that the ground-truth offset is 17.5 seconds (+/- 0.5 second). The multi-period approach clearly improves the precision of the localisation.

	baseline	DoN	DoN iter	+/-
#1	0.242	0.383	**0.404**	+ 0.16
#2	0.200	0.194	0.193	- 0.01
#3	0.085	0.091	0.093	+ 0.01
#4	0.120	0.148	0.153	+ 0.03
#5	0.235	0.277	**0.286**	+ 0.05
#6	0.340	**0.502**	**0.498**	+ 0.16
#7	0.115	0.119	0.115	+ 0.00
#8	0.257	0.264	0.268	+ 0.01
#9	0.551	**0.762**	**0.764**	+ 0.21
#10	0.469	**0.587**	**0.580**	+ 0.11
#11	0.756	**0.812**	**0.803**	+ 0.05
#12	0.363	**0.484**	**0.494**	+ 0.13
#13	0.589	**0.714**	**0.723**	+ 0.13
mAP	0.332	0.410	0.413	+ 0.08

Table 4: Combining multi-period and query expansion on EVVE dataset – in bold the most significantly improved results for each event. $N = \{2027, 3019, 5003, 7019\}$, $m = 32$, $\beta = 32$, $N_1 = 5$, $N_2 = 1000$.

computation burden. All these items make the method effective for many tasks, as diverse as event retrieval, copy detection or video synchronization, and outperform state of the art methods that can compete on this range.

8. ACKNOWLEGMENT

This work was partly supported by ERC project Viamass no. 336054, JSPS KAKENHI Grant Numbers 26240016 and 24-02712, and NII International Internship.

9. ANNEX

The events are numbered as follows (alphabetical order): **1.** barcelona riots 2012 **2.** die toten hosen rock am ring 2012 **3.** dsk arrested **4.** egypt Tahrir Square protestors **5.** johnny stade de france 2012 **6.** kate william wedding **7.** marrakech bomb attack **8.** madonna rome 2012 **9.** obama speech victory **10.** shakira live kiev 2011 **11.** strokkur geyser **12.** thailand flood 2011 **13.** universal studios jurassic park ride

10. REFERENCES

[1] R. Arandjelovic and A. Zisserman. Three things everyone should know to improve object retrieval. In *CVPR*, Jun. 2012.

[2] R. Arandjelovic and A. Zisserman. All about VLAD. In *CVPR*, Jun. 2013.

[3] L. Bo, X. Ren, and D. Fox. Kernel descriptors for visual recognition. In *NIPS*, Dec. 2010.

[4] L. Bo and C. Sminchisescu. Efficient match kernel between sets of features for visual recognition. In *NIPS*, Dec. 2009.

[5] O. Chum, A. Mikulik, M. Perdoch, and J. Matas. Total recall II: Query expansion revisited. In *CVPR*, Jun. 2011.

[6] O. Chum, J. Philbin, J. Sivic, M. Isard, and A. Zisserman. Total recall: Automatic query expansion with a generative feature model for object retrieval. In *ICCV*, Oct. 2007.

[7] M. Douze, H. Jégou, C. Schmid, and P. Pérez. Compact video description for copy detection with precise temporal alignment. In *ECCV*, Sep. 2010.

[8] M. Douze, J. Revaud, C. Schmid, and H. Jégou. Stable hyper-pooling and query expansion for event detection. In *ICCV*, Dec. 2013.

[9] M. K. et al. The visual object tracking VOT2014 challenge results. In *ICCV Workshops*, Jun. 2014.

[10] J. F. Henriques, R. Caseiro, P. Martins, and J. Batista. Exploiting the circulant structure of tracking-by-detection with kernels. In *ECCV*, Oct. 2012.

[11] J. F. Henriques, R. Caseiro, P. Martins, and J. Batista. High-speed tracking with kernelized correlation filters. *Trans. PAMI*, 2015. to appear.

[12] H. Jégou and O. Chum. Negative evidences and co-occurences in image retrieval: The benefit of PCA and whitening. In *ECCV*, Oct. 2012.

[13] H. Jégou, F. Perronnin, M. Douze, J. Sánchez, P. Pérez, and C. Schmid. Aggregating local descriptors into compact codes. In *Trans. PAMI*, Sep. 2012.

[14] H. Jégou and A. Zisserman. Triangulation embedding and democratic kernels for image search. In *CVPR*, Jun. 2014.

[15] J. Law-To, L. Chen, A. Joly, I. Laptev, O. Buisson, V. Gouet-Brunet, N. Boujemaa, and F. Stentiford. Video copy detection: a comparative study. In *CIVR*, pages 371–378, 2007.

[16] F. Perronnin and C. R. Dance. Fisher kernels on visual vocabularies for image categorization. In *CVPR*, Jun. 2007.

[17] F. Perronnin, J. Sánchez, and T. Mensink. Improving the Fisher kernel for large-scale image classification. In *ECCV*, Sep. 2010.

[18] J. Philbin, O. Chum, M. Isard, J. Sivic, and A. Zisserman. Lost in quantization: Improving particular object retrieval in large scale image databases. In *CVPR*, Jun. 2008.

[19] J. Revaud, M. Douze, C. Schmid, and H. Jégou. Event retrieval in large video collections with circulant temporal encoding. In *CVPR*, Jun. 2013.

[20] A. F. Smeaton, P. Over, and W. Kraaij. Evaluation campaigns and trecvid. In *MIR*, pages 321–330, 2006.

[21] G. Tolias, T. Furon, and H. Jégou. Orientation covariant aggregation of local descriptors with embeddings. In *ECCV*, Sep. 2014.

[22] G. Tolias and H. Jégou. Visual query expansion with or without geometry: refining local descriptors by feature aggregation. *Pattern Recognition*, Apr. 2014.

[23] A. Vedaldi and A. Zisserman. Efficient additive kernels via explicit feature maps. *Trans. PAMI*, 34(3):480–492, Mar. 2012.

[24] J. Wang, J. Yang, F. L. K. Yu, T. Huang, and Y. Gong. Locality-constrained linear coding for image classification. In *CVPR*, Jun. 2010.

[25] M.-C. Yeh and K.-T. Cheng. Video copy detection by fast sequence matching. In *CIVR*, 2009.

Efficient Activity Retrieval through Semantic Graph Queries

Gregory Castañón
Boston University
gdc1@bu.edu

Yuting Chen
Boston University
yutingch@bu.edu

Ziming Zhang
Boston University
zzhang14@bu.edu

Venkatesh Saligrama
Boston University
srv@bu.edu

ABSTRACT

We present an eff cient retrieval approach for activity detection in large surveillance video datasets based on semantic graph queries. Unlike conventional approaches, our zero-shot retrieval method does not require knowledge of the activity classes contained in the video. We propose a novel user-centric approach that models queries through the creation of sparse semantic graphs based on attributes and discriminative relationships. We then pose search as a ranked subgraph matching problem and leverage the fact that the attributes and relationships in the query have different levels of discriminability to f lter out bad matches. Rather than solving the NP-hard exact subgraph matching problem, we develop a novel maximally discriminative spanning tree (MDST) as the relaxation of a given query graph, and then describe a matching algorithm that recovers matches to this tree in linear time using maximally discriminative subgraph matching (MDSM). We utilize the MDST to minimize the number of possible matches to the original query while guaranteeing that the best matches are within this set. We test this algorithm on two large video datasets: the 35-GB Virat Ground dataset and a 1-TB aerial data collection from Yuma. These datasets yield graphs with 200,000 nodes and 1 million nodes, respectively, with an average degree of 5. Our approach f nds complex, large-scale queries in seconds while maintaining comparable precision and recall to slower current approaches.

1. INTRODUCTION

As cameras become cheaper and more ubiquitous, algorithms that can reason over large video corpora are becoming increasingly vital. An important specialization of large-scale data reasoning is video search, which aims to recover topics of interest from a large volume of video. Video search has applications in many areas such as online video navigation, retail store surveillance, and forensic search of aerial imagery.

The main challenge of surveillance video search is to navigate a large corpus to quickly f nd matches to an a priori unknown query. Unlike typical approaches to search [13, 21, 25], we do not utilize exemplar videos or attempt to learn activity categories a priori. In video search, the *complex vocabulary of activities* renders activity model training both computationally infeasible and practically impossible due to a lack of training examples.

Our approach can be interpreted as zero-shot activity retrieval, a cousin of zero-shot learning [27]. It does not rely on training data or exemplars, nor does it exploit multimedia contextual information such as text or audio since these are not frequently available for surveillance videos. We accomplish zero-shot retrieval by leveraging the fact that activities in certain surveillance videos can be characterized by a relatively small attribute vocabulary $\mathcal{A}$ and a limited relationship vocabulary $\mathcal{R}$ to organize them. Furthermore, this limited vocabulary of attributes and relationships can be easily understood by a user, autonomously extracted in real-time, and stored eff ciently using several well-known hashing schemes. Rather than relying on complex attributes, we make use of the structural relationships of an activity to formulate a query Q as a semantic graph, associating attributes with vertices and relationships with edges. Our search algorithm then tries to match this graph to attributes and relationships in the video data using approximate subgraph matching.

Subgraph matching is an NP-hard [40] problem that is computationally infeasible on large datasets even when the subgraph is relatively small [7]. Our approach is based on data reduction and in this sense is complementary to any large scale video search algorithm. First, we design coarse detectors for attributes and relationships to create a coarse graph C from the archive data, which precludes attributes and relationships that individually could not match vertices and edges in the query graph. The run-time for these detectors scales with $|C|$, the size of the coarse graph, as opposed to the size of the archive data. Second, we leverage the fact that not all attributes and relationships are equally discriminative, and that their discriminability can be calculated in real time. We use this discriminability to calculate the *Maximally Discriminative Spanning Tree* (MDST) T^* for the query graph in $O(|E^q|\log(|V^q|))$ time, where V^q and E^q are the vertices and edges in the query graph, respectively. This is the spanning tree that is expected to yield the smallest possible coarse graph C. We maximize the discriminability of this tree by modeling the distributions of attributes within graphs and solving a spanning tree optimization. Third, we propose a new tree-matching algorithm that f nds a set of solutions in C that match T^*. This process is shown in Figure 1, and is accomplished without the explicit construction of the coarse graph.

Intuitively, our approach is effective on large datasets with different f elds of view and a priori unknown activities because we create simple models from semantic features instead of creating complex models based on high-dimensional features. Thus, while

MM'15, October 26–30, 2015, Brisbane, Australia.

DOI: http://dx.doi.org/10.1145/2733373.2806229.

our models are less tuned than more complex models, they are f exible, easy to generate and have a high probability of detection. In addition, our approach takes advantage of the sparsity of surveillance queries. In order to f nd an activity, we do not have to model each detail - just a series of high-level features which differentiate it from other activities in the dataset. While sliding-window methods [23] struggle to model large-scale complex activities because of the amount of unrelated activity in a broad spatio-temporal window, our subgraph matching approach remains unaffected.

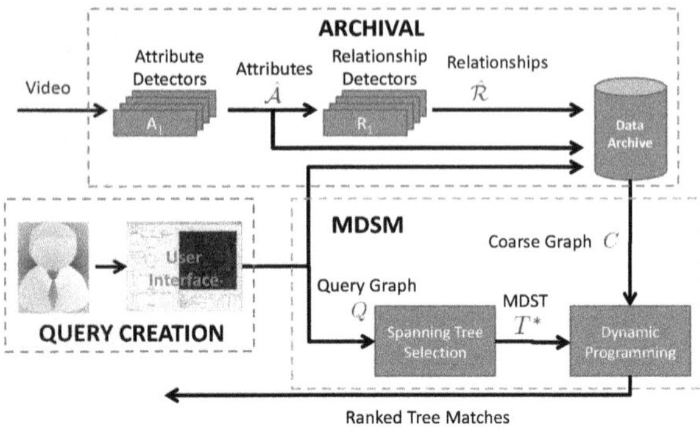

Figure 1: In the archival step, we take in incoming data, extract attributes and relationships and store them in hash tables. In the query creation step, a user utilizes our GUI to create a query graph that is used to extract the coarse graph C from archive data. In the Maximally Discriminative Subgraph Matching (MDSM) step, we calculate the maximally discriminative spanning tree (MDST) T^* from the query graph, retrieve matches to it, and assemble them into ranked search results for the user.

Our contributions are:

Zero-Shot Retrieval: We propose a zero-shot, user-centric approach to model acquistion through the creation of sparse semantic graphs based on attributes and discriminative relationships. This process requires no training data or training step, allowing for the description of novel classes.

Graph Representation: We introduce a graphical approach to query representation. While standard systems learn complete models for each activity, we provide a user with a series of simple semantic concepts and arrange them in a graph. In this graph, nodes represent attributes of an object or scene and edges represent relationships. We use this query in a sub-graph matching approach to identify activity, allowing our algorithm to effectively ignore confuser events and clutter that happen near the activity of interest. This graphical representation also makes the approach relatively agnostic to the duration of the event, allowing it to detect events that take place over several minutes.

MDST: We introduce the calculation of the Maximally Discriminative Spanning Tree, T^* based on the statistics of archive data stored in our indices. We not only exploit, as others do [23, 37], the sparsity of individual elements, but calculate an optimal combination of elements to maximally reduce the archive data using a novel Maximally Discriminative Subgraph Matching (MDSM) algorithm. We show that this approach results in a dramatically smaller corpus over which to search, and prove that the corpus must contain all high-ranking matches to the original graph.

We show that our approach, outlined in Figure 1, works in both airborne and building-mounted surveillance modalities, outperforms previous work and produces results comparable in quality to a brute-force search in a realistic time.

1.1 Related Work

There is extensive work on image and video classif cation [41, 45, 21, 42, 2] that follows a conventional pipeline approach by learning classif ers based on training data. These approaches extract, aggregate and code millions of low-level feature vectors for each image or video clip before learning classif ers for activity classes. Signif cant attention has also been specif cally devoted to activity modeling in videos. Early datasets [35] created an emphasis on bags of local descriptors [13, 21, 25] to model activities. These datasets consist of single clips of isolated actions, with a single class of action appearing in every clip. Later work has moved away from bag of words models and focused on the spatio-temporal relationships of these words [31, 34, 4]. The most recent approaches have extended the focus on relationships to more complex datasets [15] with more activity classes and background noise.

In general it has been recognized that the number of training examples cannot match the increasing complexity of classif ers and activities [33, 20]. While approaches have been developed [32] to artif cially generate training examples, these methods require a sliding window through time and space. The diff culty of model estimation makes activity search particularly challenging - some image search methods [28] rely f rst on classifying the archive data, then classifying a single exemplar provided by the user and returning archived objects from the same class as the exemplar. In summary many of these approaches do not generalize to unseen activities and furthermore their performance degrades in the limit of small training data.

A recent approach that seeks techniques for learning without training data is zero-shot learning [27, 29]. Many of the existing approaches rely on semantic concepts to help generalize to novel classes. These include ontology [30], knowledge transfer [29, 14] and max-margin based methods [44]. In general, these techniques rely on extrapolating activity models from an existing set of classes, while our approach has users summarize their knowledge about activities for search.

There are a number of recent works for video classif cation and retrieval [1, 19, 9, 46, 49] based on video semantic similarity with no prior knowledge or training data. Many of these works are based on exploiting and leveraging multiple modalities such as text, audio and OCR in combination with video. These works attempt to determine semantic similarity between a textual query and a video by employing a multimedia concept lexicon [9, 46] and combining this multimedia information without prior knowledge of the event classes. Unfortunately, this multimedia information is extremely scarce in surveillance video, so our current implementation does not take it into account. Our method, however, can be easily extended into multimedia information retrieval by adding attributes and relationships in those domains.

There is an extensive literature on video retrieval for surveillance applications (see [18, 48, 36, 38, 22, 24]). Much of this literature deals with semantic activity modeling and indexing, where the indexing for motion features is done using keywords and is typically manual. The goal is to perform keyword based retrieval for later use. In contrast, our method does not require human annotation of activities. Our work is closely related to [3] who also create an attribute vocabulary and use the temporal ordering of those attributes to determine likely locations for an activity in the video. However, their approach is extremely limited as they focus primarily on temporal order and lack the ability to accurately model many activities that rely on spatial relationships for discrimination. In contrast our approach allows for arbitrary relationships between objects or attributes and models the uncertainty in those relationships.

Sub-graph and graph matching are also commonly used in image search applications [6, 11] as well as image duplicate detection [50]. In image search and image duplicate detection, the goal is the same: to match the graph extracted from a query image to the graphs extracted from each image in a corpus. Subgraph matching is used to allow these algorithms to be robust to small amounts of clutter. Some papers [5] have adapted this technology to detecting videos with similar events by building a graphical model for the elements of each video. This problem differs signif cantly from ours because their corpus is divisible into a series of relatively small graphs, one for each image or video, it can be solved eff ciently by a series of subgraph matching problems.

In certain video domains, like news broadcasts, the corpus is easily partitionable into segments that can be reasoned over in parallel. In surveillance video, this is rarely the case, as a camera continually produces information, rendering partitioning unrealistic. Current approaches to graph and subgraph matching include semidefinite programming [39], graduated assignment [16] and spectral matching [8]. While the approximations used to solve subgraph matching problems work well on small problems (<1000 vertices per graph), their NP-scaling becomes problematic on a graph with the millions of vertices found in a typical representation of a single large surveillance video. Recent works [37, 12] have explored the idea of using advances in cloud computing to perform massive parallelization. These approaches are promising but have not been extended to attributed relational graphs (ARGs). In contrast, our approach focuses on rapid reduction of the search space to render graph-matching approaches not only feasible, but practical while maintaining similar quality to exact subgraph matching solutions.

2. MODEL

Our model is composed of four parts:

Vocabulary: We def ne an attribute vocabulary $\mathcal{A}$ and a relationship vocabulary $\mathcal{R}$. Our attribute vocabulary consists of pyramidal-binned histograms of pixel-level features, object detectors and low-level motion features extracted from tracked data. Our relationship vocabulary consists of local, pairwise descriptors such as "near to" and "shortly after".

Query: Our query graph, $Q = G(V^q, E^q, A^q, R^q, L^q)$ is a function of f ve elements. For each vertex $v \in V^q$ in the graph, A^q_v is the set of attributes from $\mathcal{A}$ associated with v, and L^q_v is the set of tolerances for each of those attributes. For each edge $(v_1, v_2) \in E^q$, $R^q_{(v_1,v_2)}$ is the set of relationships associated with (v_1, v_2), and $L^q_{(v_1,v_2)}$ is the set of tolerances for each of those relationships. Value and tolerance pairs specify an expected value and the variance in that value that is acceptable to the user.

Scoring: We def ne similarity functions $K_{a,\ell}(a')$ and $K_{r,\ell}(r')$ for the purposes of comparing attributes a and a' with tolerance ℓ, and relationships r and r' with tolerance ℓ.

Storage: We construct an archive representation which stores $\mathcal{A}$ and $\mathcal{R}$ given a maximal tolerance l_{max} for each attribute or relationship. This archive allows us to quickly recover the set of attributes or relationships which could match a query, independent of the specif ed tolerance.

2.1 Vocabulary

The video modality for our datasets is street surveillance, which dictates a specif c set of components that a user might use to construct queries (see Sec. 2.2). We employ four vocabulary elements: three types of attributes in addition to replationships.

1. **Local Descriptors**: These are local descriptors of pixel-level attributes, like those used in [3]. These attributes, like color, size, coarse motion direction, persistence and activity can be computed over tiles made of B by B pixel squares and histogrammed to provide rough descriptors of foreground image properties. This approach is doubly benef cial; histogramming and quantization naturally mitigate low-level measurement noise while simultaneously producing low-dimensional features for eff cient storage.

2. **Object Detections**: The second type of attribute that we utilize comes from object detectors, such as the Viola-Jones detector [43], which work particularly well in video surveillance due to stationary points of view. These detectors are used to f nd objects, people, and vehicles. These features are simple "type" attributes attached to the location where they were generated.

3. **Tracked data**: The third is tracked data [47], from which we can extract properties like identity, object size, direction of motion, and appearance/disappearance. Tracked data serves a dual purpose in our system. First, it enables us to extract motion features in extremely low-resolution/noisy video where accurate pixel-level optical f ow is prohibitively diff cult to compute. It also allows us access to new features indicating that an object appeared or disappeared at a given point in time. We use these descriptors to detect people getting in and out of vehicles, as well as in other scenarios.

4. **Relationships**: In addition to extracting attributes, we compute a relationship vocabulary $\mathcal{R}$ over pairs of extracted attributes $\mathcal{A} \times \mathcal{A}$. We do not, however, store all possible relationships, as the number of potential relationships scales as the square of the number of attributes. Moreover, storing all relationships would be counterproductive to search - a search algorithm is interested in attributes and relationships which discriminate between the activity described in the query and other activities present in the archive data. Instead, we employ a simple visual intuition: important relationships are both sparse and discriminative. They are sparse in that they are relatively rare compared to the number of potential relationships, and discriminative for that same reason. Because of this utility, we precompute sparse relationships like “near” and “the same as”. We use a spatiotemporal index [17] to eff ciently calculate spatiotemporal relationships, and pairwise calculations to evaluate the presence of other relationships. For our datasets, our relationships describe relative positions in space (including proximity), time, and feature space. We also have an identity relationship, indicating if two attributes likely represent the same object.

Some queries may include non-discriminative relationships. The relationship “far” is a good example of a non-discriminative relationship, as most objects in a long video are far from each other in space or time. Likewise, it’s ineff cient to calculate every possible type of spatiotemporal displacement. When we receive queries containing relationships that we have not precalculated we f rst use other precalculated relationships to reduce the data before looking for matches to relationships which we must calculate in real-time.

We discuss specif c examples of $\mathcal{A}$ and $\mathcal{R}$ in Section 4.

2.2 Semantic Graph Query

Effective zero-shot retrieval must bridge the semantic gap between a desired activity and a representation that can be associated to the data with a particular score. To accomplish this, we enable the user to arrange attributes A^q, relationships R^q and uncertainty parameters L^q into query graph $Q = G(V^q, E^q, A^q, R^q, L^q)$. The vertex properties correspond to attributes in $\mathcal{A}$, while the edge properties correspond to relationships in $\mathcal{R}$.

In addition to specifying the attributes and relationships involved in the graph structure, we allow a user to specify sets of parameters L^q_v for the attributes A^q_v in vertex $v \in V^q$ to indicate conf dence in an attribute or tolerance for error. These tolerances are used in the functions that calculate the similarity between pairs of attributes a

and a' and pairs of relationships r and r', $K_{a,\ell}(a')$ and $K_{r,\ell}(r')$, respectively, def ned below in Equation 7. When an attribute $a \in A^q_v$ is something like color or size, we embed it in a real vector space as μ_a. Then we measure the similarity based on RBF kernels $N(\mu_a, \ell^2)$ or employ indicators on the interval $[\mu_a - \ell, \mu_a + \ell]$ with tolerance $\ell \in L^q_v$. For attributes such as object type where a distance metric is not as obvious, these functions merely indicate whether or not the attributes are identical.

Loading Example: Consider the activity of a person loading an object into a car, showing in Figure 2, a user specif es that a vertex has the "car" attribute, and an edge with the "near" relationship with a vertex containing the "small" and "object" attributes. If the user also wanted to see that object earlier, he would add another "small" "object" vertex, with the "same as" and "before" relationships. He might specify an uncertainty parameter for the "before" relationship, indicating that anything within a minute is acceptable. In this way, he uses relationships to f lter out the vast majority of potential attribute matches.

While our attribute and relationship vocabularies, $\mathcal{A}$ and $\mathcal{R}$, may change based on application, we f nd that a relatively small vocabulary is suff cient to characterize a wide range of interesting actions with a surprising degree of nuance.

Graph Creation: The user assembles his or her attributes and relationships using a query GUI. In order to make this assembly simple and intuitive, we ensure that all of the attributes in our attribute vocabulary $\mathcal{A}$ have semantic meaning. This differentiates our approach signif cantly from others [1, 19, 9, 46], which use Histogram of Gradient (HOG) or spatio-temporal interest point (STIP) features to describe their actions. While it is easy for a user to create a graph out of cars, colors, or people, it requires signif cant expertise to create a meaningful assembly out of HOG or STIP features. Our relationships, like "near" and "same as", also represent clear semantic concepts. For common variables like color and motion, we provide intuitive means of user input such as selecting from a color panel or click-and-drag to indicate motion. Anecdotally, this system has been used by members of the armed forces, students and surveillance professionals with little instruction, suggesting that it does not require undue expertise.

Advantages: The advantages of this representation are its simplicity and representational power. Compared to other graphical representations [5], this representation creates far smaller graphs for identical activities. Relative to representations that do not use relationships [23], it is better able to represent long-term activities and events. By reducing an activity to the relevant components, we sparsify activity search.

Meeting example: As evidence, consider an example that would challenge most modern search algorithms: "Three people meet together for f ve minutes". This is a challenging problem because an activity that spans f ve minutes or more represents a signif cant amount of data, and the vast majority of data within that window likely has nothing to do with the activity in question. However, the graphical representation of such a query can be made relatively simple (Figure 3) - all that matters is that the same three people who were all near each other in the beginning remain near eachother f ve minutes later. Because we are going to solving a sub-graph matching problem, this allows us to treat unrelated activity that happens during our activity of interest exactly like we treat unrelated activity the rest of the time, and ignore it. This enables us to search for long-term events without worrying about confuser activity over that time period.

The meeting example highlights both a strength and a weakness of the approach: the graph shown in Figure 3 is not affected by what happened in the intervening f ve minutes between the f rst meet-up and the second meet-up. The group of three could have separated and reconvened, or stayed together the whole time. However, our approach to search focuses not on the perfect modeling of the event we are searching for, but instead discriminating it from other events - and for that, this graph is suff cient.

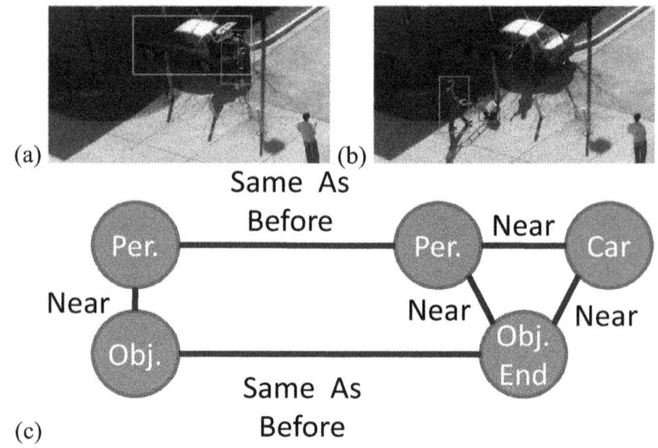

Figure 2: The graphical representation of an "object deposit" event.

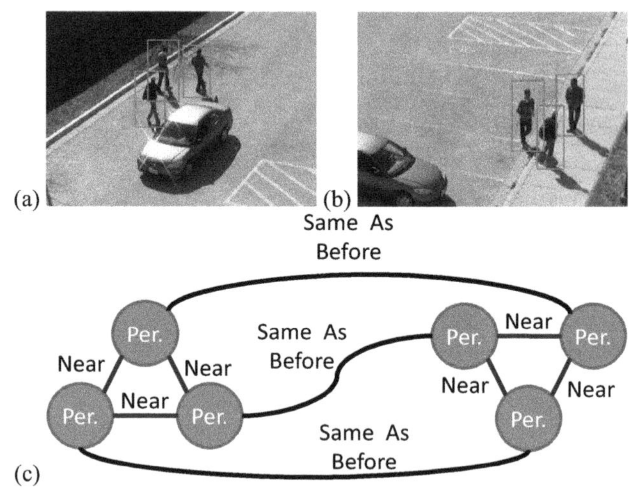

Figure 3: The graphical representation of a "meeting" event.

2.3 Eff cient Indexing

Discriminative attributes and relationships are powerful if you can eff ciently use their sparsity to rule out parts of a video that don't match a provided query. In this section, we describe how to store the attributes and relationships eff ciently so that we can rapidly recover elements that might match a given query $Q = G(V^q, E^q, A^q, R^q, L^q)$.

To accomplish this recovery, we independently hash the locations and values of every attribute we f nd in the video archive to an inverted index. We use Locality Sensitive Hashing (LSH) [10] for attributes like size and color which have computable distances, and employ a standard hash table for discrete attributes like object type. Fuzzy hashing renders our search robust to minor discrepancies in query model, detection model, and storage by retrieving all archived attributes with a certain radius of the query attribute. By computing a hash code for each of a vertex's attributes, A^q_v, and taking the intersection of the bins corresponding to those codes, we can eff ciently retrieve the set of matching locations to vertex $v \in V^q$.

We apply the same logic to the set of relationships. When a relationship exists between a particular pair of locations, we hash it (and its value), to a fuzzy or normal hash table depending on the relationship type. This allows us to retrieve the set of pairs of locations which approximately satisfy a particular relationship in time proportional to the number of satisfying pairs.

The power of this approach is that it allows us to eff ciently downsample the full set of archive data to the set of potentially relevant attributes and relationships, in time proportional to the number of attributes and relationships returned, as opposed to the size of the original data.

3. SEARCH

The goal of search is to rapidly recover from the indexed data the set of attributes and relationships that best match the query graph Q. We accomplish this in three steps: First, we independently look up each attribute and relationship in Q in our data store to retrieve a coarse graph C. Then we calculate discriminative weights for each of the relationships in the query, then calculate the maximally discriminative spanning tree T^* for that query. Finally, we create a matching graph H to encode the possible matches in the coarse graph C for the spanning tree T^* and use a Maximally Discriminative Subgraph Matching (MDSM) approach to recover the ranked matches to T^*.

3.1 Coarse Graph Construction

Given a query graph Q, we construct the coarse archive graph $C = G(V^c, E^c, A^c, R^c)$ in two steps. First, for every vertex $v \in V^q$, we use our data store to retrieve the set of locations where all attributes in A^q_v are present. We add a vertex v_i to V^c for each of those locations and store the attribute values in $A^c_{v_i}$. Second, for every discriminative (hashed) edge $(v_1, v_2) \in E^q$, we retrieve the set of attribute pairs that satisfy every relationship in $R^q_{(v_1,v_2)}$ and whose attributes are in V^c. For each of these pairs, we add an edge to E^c and store the associated relationships in R^c. The computational complexity of this step is proportional to the number of vertices and edges that end up matching the query graph, $O(|V^c| + |E^c|)$.

3.2 Tree Selection

Downsampling the data to the set of potentially relevant vertices and edges provides incredible cost savings, but the result is still frequently a coarse graph with hundreds of thousands of vertices. Modern subgraph matching algorithms for attributed relational graphs only scale to hundreds of vertices [8], absent approximation by massive parallelization. As such, we are obliged to downsample the coarse graph further.

The optimal downsampled graph, C^*_q would contain only vertices and edges that were present in high-ranked matches to query graph Q so as to minimize the time spent performing an expensive search. We approximate C^*_q by selecting a spanning tree T of Q and downsampling the coarse graph C to C_t, the set of vertices and edges involved in high-ranking solutions to that tree. Because the tree effectively relaxes constraints (in the form of edges) of the optimal solution to the query graph, C_t is guaranteed to contain all of the solutions which match the query graph, with added false alarms. To generate such trees, we f rst compute a set of weights indicating the discriminative power of each attribute and relationship in Q, then calculate the spanning tree T which maximizes that discriminative power.

3.2.1 *Weight Computation*

The choice of which spanning tree to select has signif cant runtime implications. Its creation involves the removal of edges from Q, and not all edges are created equal. During the archival process, we assign probabilities $p(a)$ and $p(r)$ to each attribute and relationship that we store. These functions denote the probability that a randomly-chosen attribute or relationship in the archive is a match to the attribute a or relationship r. For example, in a dataset that surveils a highway, the "car" attribute is not particularly discriminative, because almost everything on a highway is a car. The "bicycle" attribute in the same dataset would be extremely discriminative, as it is rare for people to bicycle on the highway. We show the probabilities $p(a)$ for attributes used in the VIRAT [26] data set in Figure 4.

Relationships, in particular, have greater power to be discriminative because the set of potential relationships is $|\mathcal{A}|^2$. Take Figure 2; while the "Person near car" relationship is normally very discriminative, 80% of the dataset is shot in parking lots, where people are frequently near cars. Objects disappear near cars far less less frequently - thus, a tree rooted at the "object disappears" vertex and connecting through the "near" edge to the "car" vertex is more discriminative than one starting elsewhere.

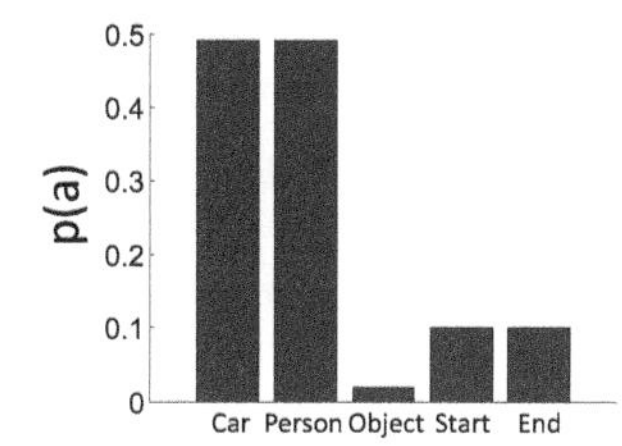

Figure 4: The probabilities associated with f ve of the attributes in the VIRAT dataset. Being an object, as opposed to a car or a person, is the most unlikely attribute and thus the most discriminative.

We compute empirical values for $p(a)$ and $p(r)$ during the archival process by computing the percentage of attributes (and relationships) that are returned by the hash tables described in Section 2.3. If relationships have not been hashed, they are assumed to be nondiscriminative and assigned values of $p(r) = 1$. If it is later determined that these relationships are discriminative, we can revise our estimate of $p(r)$.

3.2.2 *Maximally Descriminative Spanning Tree*

Absent additional information indicating the distribution of relationships and attributes in the video corpus, we assume that all attributes and relationships are generated independently. This model is clearly imperfect, as certain pairs of attributes are more likely to have a particular relationship. A speed attribute of 60 miles per hour is far more likely to be found in the same location as a car object, as opposed to a person object. Given a diverse set of video corpora, one could learn these correlations and adjust our model accordingly, but in this work we assume independence.

Given a query tree $T = G(V^t, E^t, A^t, R^t)$, we compute weights $p(v)$ for all $v \in V^t$ and $p(e)$ for all $e \in E^t$ as the product of the matching probabilities of the attributes in node v or relationships in edge e. That is,

$$p(v) = \prod_{a \in A^t_v} p(a), \quad p(e) = \prod_{r \in R^t_e} p(r) \tag{1}$$

Since nodes and edges in tree T are independent, the total matching probability of the tree $p(T)$ to the archive is:

$$p(T) = \prod_{v \in V^t} p(v) \prod_{e \in E^t} p(e) \quad (2)$$

As noted, we are going to do a search using T instead of the original query graph Q in order to reduce the coarse graph C. We therefore select a tree T which results in the fewest possible matches so as to generate the maximal reduction in the coarse graph. That is our novel maximially discriminative spanning tree.

Def nition (Maximially Discriminative Spanning Tree (MDST)). *We call a tree T^* an MDST of query graph Q with node weights $p(v)\forall v \in V^q$ and edge weights $p(e)\forall e \in E^q$, if the tree satisf es*

$$T^* = \operatorname*{argmin}_{T \in \mathcal{T}} p(T), \quad (3)$$

where $\mathcal{T}$ denotes the set of all possible trees induced from query graph Q.

Lemma 3.1. *Assume that there is no such node in query graph Q that the matching probabilities of the node and all its connected edges are 1. Then the MDST of a query graph Q is equivalent to the minimum spanning tree of Q.*

Proof. Based on the def nition of MDST, we can rewrite Eq. 3 as follows:

$$T^* = \operatorname*{argmin}_{T \in \mathcal{T}} p(T) = \operatorname*{argmin}_{T(V^t, E^t) \in \mathcal{T}} \prod_{v \in V^t} p(v) \prod_{e \in E^t} p(e)$$

$$\equiv \operatorname*{argmin}_{T(V^t, E^t) \in \mathcal{T}} \left\{ \sum_{v \in V^t} \log p(v) + \sum_{e \in E^t} \log p(e) \right\} \quad (4)$$

Since $\forall p(v), \forall p(e)$ are real numbers between 0 and 1, $\forall \log p(v)$ and $\forall \log p(e)$ are all non-positive. Therefore, in order to minimize Eq. 4, all the nodes in Q will be included, and all the specif c edges will be included as well, which (1) form a tree together with all the nodes in Q, and (2) achieve the minimum summation. Deleting any node/edge from the tree will either increase the objective value in Eq. 4 or destroy the tree structure. This is exactly the same as the def nition of minimum spanning tree. □

Lemma 3.1 provides us with a convenient way to calculate the MDST that should produce the fewest possible matches. Notice that by matching with MDST, our method can return all the solutions which satisfy all the nodes and some of the edges in query graph Q. Given that $T^* \neq Q$, we will prove that the set of matches to MDST contains all of the matches to the original query graph.

Lemma 3.2. *Let M denote a match between a query graph $Q = (V^q, E^q)$ and a coarse graph C. Let $S(\cdot, C, M)$ denote the matching score between any query (e.g. graphs, trees, attributes, relationships) and C, and let $Q' = Q - T^* = (\emptyset, E^q - E^t)$ denote the residual of graph Q. We further def ne $S(Q, C, M) = \sum_{v \in V^q} S(v, C, M) + \sum_{e \in E^q} S(e, C, M)$. Then we have*

$$|S(Q, C, M) - S(T^*, C, M)| = \left| \sum_{e \in Q'} S(e, C, M) \right|$$

$$\leq \sum_{e \in Q'} |S(e, C, M)| \leq |Q'| \cdot \max_{e \in Q'} \max_{\tilde{M} \in \mathcal{M}} |S(e, C, \tilde{M})|, \quad (5)$$

where $|Q'|$ denotes the number of edges in Q', and $\mathcal{M}$ denotes the set of possible matches between Q' and C.

Proof. $\max_{e \in Q'} \max_{\tilde{M} \in \mathcal{M}} |S(e, C, \tilde{M})|$ denotes the best possible absolute matching score for an arbitrary edge in Q', which leads to $\forall e \in Q', |S(e, C, M)| \leq \max_{e \in Q'} \max_{\tilde{M} \in \mathcal{M}} |S(e, C, \tilde{M})|$. Together with inequality properties, we can easily prove the lemma. □

Lemma 3.2 shows that the score difference between using query graph Q and using its MDST T^* is upper-bounded. Using this, we can set our parameters to make sure that all good matches to the query graph Q are present in the set of matches to the MDST T^*. We prove this in Lemma 3.3.

Lemma 3.3. *By setting proper thresholds, we guarantee that the matches returned by MDST cover all the matches for the original query graph.*

Proof. Lemma 3.2 shows that the score difference between using query graph Q and using its MDST T^* is upper-bounded. Let $S_Q = \min_{M_Q \in \mathcal{M}_Q} S(Q, C, M_Q)$, where $\mathcal{M}_Q$ denotes the set of possible matches between Q and C, then in the worst case, we can set the matching score threshold δ for returning solutions as

$$\delta = S_Q - \Delta_{Q'} = S_Q - |Q'| \cdot \max_{e \in Q'} \max_{\tilde{M} \in \mathcal{M}} |S(e, C, \tilde{M})|, \quad (6)$$

which is guaranteed to return all the solutions for query graph Q. □

As def ned in Lemma 3.3, δ ensures that every perfect match will be present in the coarse graph C_t. If a user is tolerant of error, they can also set the threshold higher to $\delta + \tau$, guaranteeing that all matches within τ of perfect are preserved. This is the performance/speed tradeoff of the MDST: a higher τ allows for solutions with slightly more error, but it results in a larger coarse graph C_t and thus slower matching. In practice, we have found τ stable and simple to tune.

3.3 Maximally Discriminative Subgraph Matching (MDSM)

3.3.1 Scoring Attributes & Relationships

Because of visual ambiguity, compositional variance and spatiotemporal distortion, we do not want to search for identical matches to the query graph. Not only is it unreasonable to expect a perfect description of an activity from a user, it is improbable that all examples of that activity within the dataset f t a particular description. To this end, we look for a score function with some tolerance for error. This error manifests in two parts - a kernel function on the vertex matches, K_v, and a kernel function on the edges, K_e. For vertex attributes, our similarity functions are the sum of similarities for each attribute belonging to that vertex. Similarity functions for relationships are also the sum of the similarities associated with that edge. For notational convenience, we express vertex attributes, edge relationships, and their corresponding tolerances in terms of binary vectors $A_v \in \{0,1\}^{|\mathcal{A}|}$, $R_e \in \{0,1\}^{|\mathcal{R}|}$, $L_v \in [0,1]^{|\mathcal{A}|}$, $L_e \in [0,1]^{|\mathcal{R}|}$ for any arbitrary vertex v and edge e.

Let v_1 be a vertex in query graph Q, whose value and tolerance for the j-th attribute in $\mathcal{A}$ are given by $a_1(j)$ and $\ell_1(j)$, respectively. Let v_2 be a vertex from the archive graph, whose j-th attribute is given by $a_2(j)$. Let e_1,e_2 represent edges in the archive and query graphs, with values $r_1(j)$ and $r_2(j)$ with tolerance $\ell_1(j)$.

$$K_v(v_1, v_2) = \sum_{j=1}^{|\mathcal{A}|} K_{a_1(j),\ell_1(j)}(a_2(j))$$

$$K_e(e_1, e_2) = \sum_{j=1}^{|\mathcal{R}|} K_{r_1(j),\ell_1(j)}(r_2(j)) \tag{7}$$

Note that we are only provided with tolerance for a given vertex or edge in the query, because the other vertex or edge generally represents archive data.

Given a coarse graph C and the MDST T^*, we want to select a matching $M : V^t \rightarrow V^c$. We select the matching that maximizes our objective function $S(Q, C, M)$ comprised of two parts, vertex and edge potentials

$$S(Q, C, M) = \sum_{v_q \in V^q} K_v(v_q, M(v_q)) + \lambda \sum_{(v_{q1}, v_{q2}) \in E^q} K_e(v_{q1}, v_{q2}, M(v_{q1}), M(v_{q2})) \tag{8}$$

where λ is a weighting parameter determining the relative value of matching vertices and edges.

3.3.2 Matching Graph Creation

We solve for the optimal match between the MDST T^* and archive graph C in two steps. In the f rst step, we build a *matching graph* $H = G(V^h, E^h)$, where each vertex $v \in V^h \subseteq V^t \times V^c$ is a tuple denoting a proposed assignment between a vertex in T^* and a vertex in C, and each edge $e \in E^h$ denotes a relationship between the two assignments. We create H by f rst adding matches for the root, then adding in matches to its successors which satisfy both vertex and edge relationships described in T^*. We then def ne score thresholds τ_v and τ_e to be the minimum score for vertices and edges. This process in described in Algorithm 1, and the expected number of vertices scales as a product of $p(T^*)$ and the size of the archive data.

Algorithm 1 Create Matching Graph

- **procedure** CREATE MATCHING GRAPH($T^*, C, K_v(v_1, v_2), K_e(v_1, v_2, v_3, v_4)$)
  - $H = G(V^h, E^h) \leftarrow \emptyset$
  - Iterate from root to leaves
  - **for all** $v^t \in V^t$ **do**
    - Compute the matches to this vertex
    - $N_{v_t} \leftarrow (v_t, v_c)$ where $K_v(v_t, v_c) > \tau_v$
    - **if** $Parent(v_t) \neq \emptyset$ **then**
      - $E \leftarrow \emptyset$
      - **for all** $(v_{t_p}, v_{c_p}) \in N_{Parent(v_t)}$ **do**
        - $E \leftarrow E \cup (v_t, v_c)$ where $K_e(v_{t_p}, v_{c_p}, v_t, v_c) > \tau_e$
      - **end for**
      - $N_{v_t} \leftarrow N_{v_t} \cap E$
      - $V^h \leftarrow E^h \cup N_{v_t}$
      - $E^h \leftarrow E^h \cup E$
    - **else**
      - $V^h \leftarrow V^h \cup N_{v_t}$
    - **end if**
  - **end for**
- **end procedure**

3.3.3 Retrieval with MDSM

Having traversed T^* from root to leaves to create a matching graph, we traverse it from leaves to root to determine the optimal solution for each root match. For each leaf vertex in T^*, we merge vertices in H with their parents, keeping the one which has the best score. We repeat this process until only matches to root vertices are left, and then sort these root vertices by the score of the best tree which uses them. This process is described in Algorithm 2, and has complexity of $O(|E^h|)$.

Algorithm 2 Solve for Optimal Matches

- **procedure** OPTIMIZE MATCHES(T^*, H)
  - $Score(v) \triangleq K_v(v[0], v[1])$
  - $Score(v_1, v_2) \triangleq K_e(v_1[0], v_1[1], v_2[0], v_2[1])$
  - Iterate from leaves to root
  - **for all** $v_t \in T^*$ **do**
    - **if** $Parent(v_t) \neq \emptyset$ **then**
      - **for all** $v \in V^h$ where $v[0] == Parent(v_t)$ **do**
        - $Score(v) += max_{c \in Children(v)}(Score(c) + Score(v, c))1(c[0] == v_t)$
      - **end for**
    - **end if**
  - **end for**
- **end procedure**

This process yields a set of matches, M_{T^*}, for each potential activity - generally on the order of the number of true matches in the data. We then iterate through each match $m \in M_{T^*}$ and compute $S(Q, C, m)$, f ltering matches that have poor scores for the edges which were not included in the MDST. This allows us to have the speed of the MDSM approach and the effective quality of the full graph-matching result.

4. EXPERIMENTATION

The novelty of this method is its ability to reason over events that are not necessarily extremely time-localized. Other approaches [22, 3, 23] are limited to events which span relatively short amounts of time (seconds), whereas our subgraph matching formulation is agnostic to activity duration. For the purposes of comparison, we compare performance on both local events like dismounts and object loading as well as longer events like group meetings.

4.1 Comparisons

The most comparable approach to our algorithm is the system described in [3]. The authors formulate the optimization purely as a dynamic program and assume that the input graph Q is a line graph. Given a line graph representing a series of temporal events, the system expects events to happen sequentially, but employs dynamic time warping to allow for f exible duration.

Specif cally, given a sequence of vertices $V_1, V_2, ...V_i$, they score activities using a Markov model with three types of f xed transition probabilities. When an activity stays in the same state, the transition probability $P_{i,i}$ is a continuation or a missed detection, depending on evidence support. When the activity moves to the next state, the transition probability $P_{i,i+1}$ is either a match or a deletion, depending on whether or not an archive match exists. Given that their model is a line, they can recover the set of optimal matches in polynomial time.

While this works well for sequential events over relatively short periods of time that always have something happening, it fails at detecting events that have a graph structure, multiple salient objects at a given point in time, or minutes of duration. Specif cally, the linear decay in likelihood that occurs from not seeing the next vertex is a poor model when the next piece of evidence could be minutes away. We compare to the baseline established in this method, and note that we expect comparable performance on short-term chains of events and improved performance in other areas.

We compare this baseline against two other approaches, both utilizing the MDST reduction. In the f rst, we use MDSM to rank matches to the MDST, T^*. We select the top few of these matches, and re-score them using the query graph instead of the MDST. In the second, we evaluate every subgraph in the matching graph H and rank it using query graph Q. By comparing quality against a brute-force approach, we show the error due to modeling.

4.2 Datasets

We evaluate the performance of our algorithm on two data sets representing different surveillance modalities. The f rst is a wide-area persistent surveillance sensor f ying over Yuma, Arizona. This dataset has an extremely low framerate (.66 FPS), combined with large black-and-white frames (64 megapixels) over a large area, totalling to 1 TB of imagery, or a graph with 1 million nodes and 5 million edges. Our hash table stores features averaging .5 MB per GB of data. Because of the size of the area, there are relatively few pixels on a target. Vehicles have roughly 100 pixels and people have around 10. See an example of a u-turn activity in Figure 5.

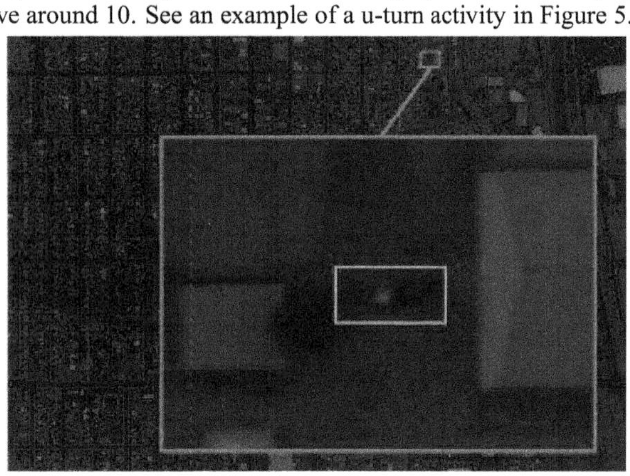

Figure 5: The YUMA video data set features high-resolution imagery taken at significant elevation, leaving few pixels on targets as small as people or vehicles.

Because of the low resolution on target, pixel-level features are extremely noisy in the YUMA dataset. For this dataset, we rely on a very simple tracking approach to generate track IDs, bounding boxes, time-stamps and size. We extract from these tracks a series of locations with the features of object size, motion orientation and magnitude and a start/end attribute denoting the beginning and termination of the track that serve as our attribute vocabulary $\mathcal{A}$, similar to the raw attributes extracted in [18, 3]. We employ object size as a way of disambiguating cars and people - carried objects are not visible at this resolution. The discriminative relationship vocabulary $\mathcal{R}$ contains a "near" operator and an identity operator which provides a conf dence that two elements are from the same object. Because these videos contain no camera zoom, "near" can be def ned in units of pixels. Spatiotemporal and feature displacement are the non-discriminative relationships that are used in queries, but not hashed. For the VIRAT dataset, which has signif cantly higher target resolution, we also include object type as a discrete attribute, as object type can reliably be detected.

The other surveillance modality we explored was street surveillance from building-mounted cameras. For this, we utilized the VIRAT 2.0 Ground Dataset [26], a popular surveillance dataset containing 35 GB of video and represented in a graph of 200,000 nodes and 1 million edges. These are relatively standard 2 megapixel surveillance cameras shooting at 30 frames per second, and we extract 2.5 MB of features per GB of data. Because of the smaller f eld of view, there are far more pixels on target, enabling basic object recognition. As such, we def ne $\mathcal{A}$ to include object type (person, vehicle, bag) as well as the attributes used in the YUMA dataset. The relationship vocabulary $\mathcal{R}$ is identical. To further differentiate it from the YUMA dataset, the VIRAT ground dataset contains 315 different videos covering 11 scenes rather than a single large video covering one scene.

Query	MDST Reduction	Baseline[3]	Brute	Brute (MDST)	DP (MDST)
Long Meeting	85	6.5	*3e25*	4610	2.3
Short Meeting	86	6	*3e25*	10671	2.5
Deposit	<1	12.5	*4.5e16*	5	<1
Removal	<1	14.4	*4.7e16*	4.9	<1
Mount	<1	6.3	*3.7e8*	<1	<1
Dismount	<1	7.7	*3.7e8*	<1	<1
UTurn	<1	2.0269	*6.6e8*	<1	<1
Dismount	<1	<1	<1	<1	<1
Mount	<1	<1	<1	<1	<1
Suspicious Stop	<1	<1	32.2820	<1	<1

Table 1: The run times for baseline [3], brute force and DP algorithms on the VIRAT (top) and YUMA (bottom) datasets. When a brute force algorithm is infeasible, we estimate runtime based on a sub-set of solutions.

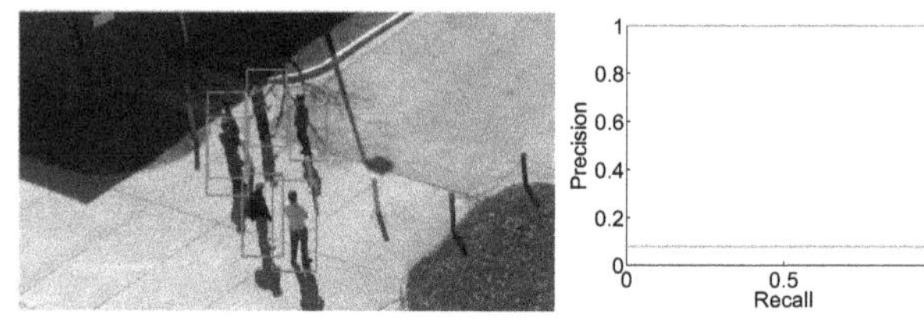

Figure 6: Precision/recall curves for the long-term meeting activities in the VIRAT video dataset. Dynamic programming and brute force recover all three instances as top returns.

4.3 Results

We test our algorithm against a baseline feature-accumulation approach used in [3], as well as a brute-force enumeration of possibilities. Precision/recall curves for the YUMA dataset are shown in Figure 8; the VIRAT results are shown in Figures 7 and 6.

We also show the run-time of our approach in Table 1, demonstrating the futility of solving a large-scale graph search problem without performing intelligent reduction f rst. It should surprise nobody that an algorithm which must explore all $|V^q|$-sized subsets of the data will take forever to run on a large dataset. More relevant is how long it takes us to compute the MDST and downsample the data to the relevant subset: Less than a second with pre-hashed relationships (all examples except meetings), and 80 seconds when we do not have pre-hashed relationships. When we do not have hashed relationships, our algorithm must compute pair-wise relationships, which is expensive to do even when the data is reduced.

The "before" relationship that is used in the meeting events is not hashed because it is not particularly local. Many elements of a dataset satisfy the relationship that one of them comes signif cantly before the other. Therefore, this relationship is not particularly discriminative by itself, so we would have no a-priori reason to calculate it and store it. Here we run into a classic memory vs. runtime trade off, where hashing less-discriminative relationships may turn out to later be valuable, but is prohibitively memory expen-

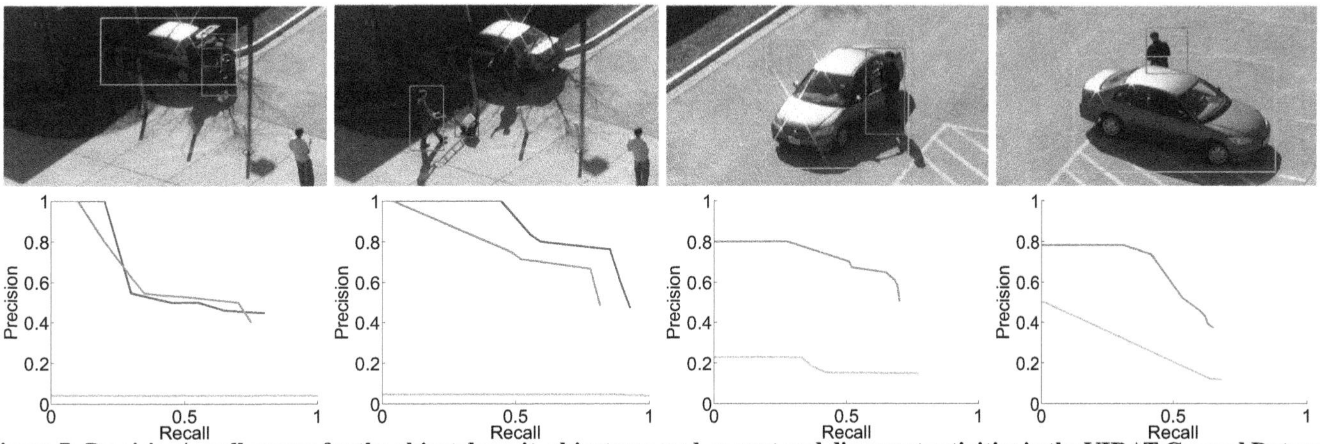

Figure 7: Precision/recall curves for the object deposit, object removal, mount and dismount activities in the VIRAT Ground Dataset. We show baseline [3] search results in green, MDSM results in red, and brute force results in blue when they diverge from MDSM results.

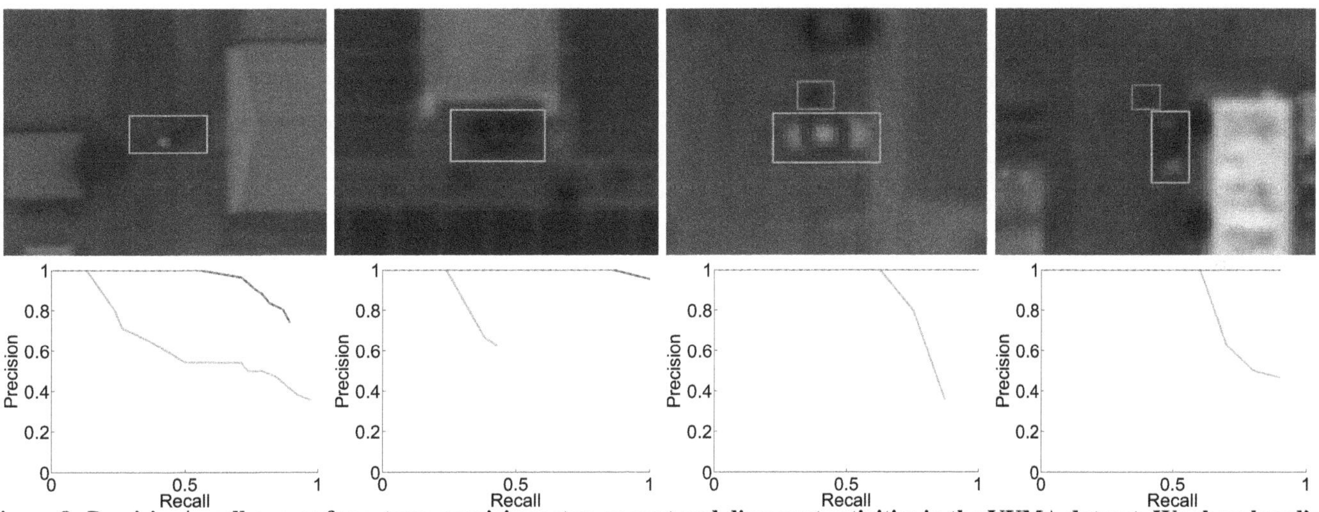

Figure 8: Precision/recall curves for u-turn, suspicious stop, mount and dismount activities in the YUMA dataset. We show baseline [3] search results in green, and unf ltered MDSM results in red. Because these queries are all trees, dynamic programming produces identical results to brute force, shown in the dashed blue and red line.

sive. The "before" attribute becomes discriminative when paired with the "same as" attribute so our algorithm performs successful reduction, albeit slower due to a lack of hashing.

The performance of our approach, compared to baseline and brute force solutions, is shown in Figures 7 and 8. Our algorithm performs extremely favorably relative to the baseline, and comparably to brute force in a number of scenarios. The performance gap for simple, time-localized graphs on the YUMA data is relatively small, so the baseline approach performs relatively well. In addition, the simple/time-localized graphs have relatively few cases of complex spatial relationships that are diff cult to model with time-sequences like those in Figure 2.

The performance of the baseline tails off as the scale of the events begins to grow from pick-up/drop-off to object deposit and withdrawal and widens further as query duration increases. Over a large time scale, the number of unrelated events within the sliding window overwhelms the true information, creating false alarms. The subgraph matching approach remains agnostic to the additional clutter, and performs consistently across all queries.

These experiments convincingly showcase our approach's ability to represent events with multiple entities over multiple time scales while still maintaining strong performance in precision and recall.

5. CONCLUSIONS

In this paper, we presented a practical solution to video search in both run-time and performance quality. Our method has many advantages. First, it is f exible; we are able to model every activity present in our two video corpora, and many activities (such as long-term meetings) that were not intentionally present. Second, it is fast; we downsample the data using the MDST and solve most examples in a matter of seconds using maximally discriminative subgraph matching. Finally, use of a sparse graphical representation of complex activities makes it surprisingly f exible and robust. The subgraph matching formulation allows it to ignore foreground clutter and confusion to identify which elements of the archival data match the query optimally. These attributes combine to make it a powerful new tool in video search.

This material is based upon work supported in part by the U.S. Department of Homeland Security, Science and Technology Directorate,Off ce of University Programs, under Grant Award 2013-ST-061-ED0001, by ONR Grant 50202168 and US AF contract FA8650-14-C-1728. The views and conclusions contained in this document are those of the authors and should not be interpreted as necessarily representing the social policies, either expressed or implied, of the U.S. DHS, ONR or AF.

6. REFERENCES

[1] Y. Aytar, M. Shah, and J. Luo. Utilizing semantic word similarity measures for video retrieval. *Computer Vision and Pattern Recognition*, 2008.

[2] Y. L. Boureau, F. Bach, Y. LeCun, and J. Ponce. Learning mid-level features for recognition. *Computer Vision and Pattern Recognition*, pages 2559–2566, 2010.

[3] G. Castanon and A. Caron. Exploratory search of long surveillance videos. *ACM Multimedia*, 2012.

[4] O. Çeliktutan, C. Wolf, B. Sankur, and E. Lombardi. Real-time exact graph matching with application in human action recognition. *Human Behavior Understanding*, pages 17–28, 2012.

[5] T. E. Choe, H. Deng, F. Guo, M. W. Lee, and N. Haering. Semantic video-to-video search using sub-graph grouping and matching. *International Conference on Computer Vision*, 2013.

[6] W. Christmas, J. Kittler, and M. Petrou. Structural matching in computer vision using probabilistic relaxation. *PAMI*, 17(8), 1995.

[7] L. P. Cordella, P. Foggia, C. Sansone, and M. Vento. A (sub)graph isomorphism algorithm for matching large graphs. *Pattern Analysis and Machine Intelligence*, 26(10):1367–72, Oct. 2004.

[8] T. Cour, P. Srinivasan, and J. Shi. Balanced graph matching. *Advances in Neural Information Processing Systems*, 19:313, 2007.

[9] J. Dalton, J. Allan, and P. Mirajkar. Zero-shot video retrieval using content and concepts. *Information and Knowledge Management*, pages 1857–1860, 2013.

[10] M. Datar, N. Immorlica, P. Indyk, and V. Mirrokni. Locality-sensitive hashing scheme based on p-stable distributions. In *Symposium on Computation Geometry*, pages 253–262. ACM, 2004.

[11] F. De la Torre. Factorized graph matching. *Computer Vision and Pattern Recognition*, pages 127–134, June 2012.

[12] S. Demeyer, T. Michoel, J. Fostier, P. Audenaert, M. Pickavet, and P. Demeester. The Index-Based Subgraph Matching Algorithm (ISMA): Fast Subgraph Enumeration in Large Networks Using Optimized Search Trees. *PLoS ONE*, 8(4), 2013.

[13] P. Dollár and V. Rabaud. Behavior recognition via sparse spatio-temporal features. *Performance Evaluation of Tracking and Surveillance*, pages 65–72, 2005.

[14] M. Elhoseiny, B. Saleh, and A. Elgammal. Write a classif er: Zero-shot learning using purely textual descriptions. *International Conference on Computer Vision*, pages 2584–2591, 2013.

[15] U. Gaur, Y. Zhu, B. Song, and A. Roy-Chowdhury. A "string of feature graphs" model for recognition of complex activities in natural videos. *International Conference on Computer Vision*, 2011.

[16] S. Gold and A. Rangarajan. A graduated assignment algorithm for graph matching. *Pattern Analysis and Machine Intelligence*, 1996.

[17] A. Guttman. R-trees: a dynamic index structure for spatial searching. *SIGMOD '84*, pages 47–57, 1984.

[18] W. Hu, D. Xie, Z. Fu, W. Zeng, and S. Maybank. Semantic-based surveillance video retrieval. *Transactions on Image Processing*, 2007.

[19] M. Y. Jung and S. H. Park. *Semantic Similarity Based Video Retrieval*. 2009.

[20] S. Kwak, B. Han, and J. H. Han. Multi-agent Event Detection: Localization and Role Assignment. *Computer Vision and Pattern Recognition*, pages 2682–2689, June 2013.

[21] I. Laptev. On space-time interest points. *International Journal of Computer Vision*, 64:107–123, 2005.

[22] T.-L. Le, M. Thonnat, A. Boucher, and F. Brémond. Surveillance Video Indexing and Retrieval Using Object Features and Semantic Events. *International Journal of Pattern Recognition and Artif cial Intelligence*, 23(07):1439–1476, 2009.

[23] D. Lin, S. Fidler, C. Kong, and R. Urtasun. Visual Semantic Search : Retrieving Videos via Complex Textual Queries. *Computer Vision and Pattern Recognition*, 2014.

[24] S. Maybank. A Survey on Visual Content-Based Video Indexing and Retrieval. *IEEE Transactions on Systems, Man, and Cybernetics*, 41(6):797–819, 2011.

[25] J. C. Niebles, H. Wang, and L. Fei-Fei. Unsupervised Learning of Human Action Categories Using Spatial-Temporal Words. *International Journal of Computer Vision*.

[26] S. Oh, A. Hoogs, and A. Perera. A large-scale benchmark dataset for event recognition in surveillance video. *Computer Vision and Pattern Recognition*, (2), 2011.

[27] M. Palatucci and D. Pomerleau. Zero-shot learning with semantic output codes. *Neural Information Processing Systems (NIPS)*, 2009.

[28] J. Philbin, O. Chum, M. Isard, J. Sivic, and A. Zisserman. Object retrieval with large vocabularies and fast spatial matching. *Computer Vision and Pattern Recognition*, pages 1–8, June 2007.

[29] M. Rohrbach, M. Stark, and B. Schiele. Evaluating knowledge transfer and zero-shot learning in a large-scale setting. *Computer Vision and Pattern Recognition*, (June):1641–1648, 2011.

[30] O. Russakovsky and L. Fei-Fei. Attribute learning in large-scale datasets. *ECCV*, 6553 LNCS(PART 1):1–14, 2012.

[31] M. Ryoo and J. Aggarwal. Recognition of composite human activities through context-free grammar based representation. *Computer Vision and Pattern Recognition*, 2006(June), 2006.

[32] M. Ryoo and W. Yu. One video is suff cient? Human activity recognition using active video composition. *Workshop on Applications of Computer Vision*, (January), 2011.

[33] M. S. Ryoo and J. K. Aggarwal. Stochastic Representation and Recognition of High-Level Group Activities. *International Journal of Computer Vision*, 93(2):183–200, June 2010.

[34] S. Savarese, A. DelPozo, and J. C. Niebles. Spatial-Temporal correlatons for unsupervised action classif cation. *IEEE Workshop on Motion and Video Computing*, pages 1–8, Jan. 2008.

[35] C. Schuldt, I. Laptev, and B. Caputo. Recognizing human actions: a local SVM approach. *International Conference on Pattern Recognition*, pages 3–7, 2004.

[36] C. G. Snoek and M. Worring. Concept-Based Video Retrieval. *Foundations and Trends in Information Retrieval*, 2009.

[37] Z. Sun, H. Wang, B. Shao, and J. Li. Eff cient subgraph matching on billion node graphs. *Proceedings of the VLDB Endowment*, pages 788–799, 2012.

[38] Y.-L. Tian, A. Hampapur, L. Brown, R. Feris, M. Lu, A. Senior, C.-F. Shu, and Y. Zhai. Event Detection, Query, and Retrieval for Video Surveillance. In *Artif cial Intelligence for Maximizing Content Based Image Retrieval*. 2008.

[39] P. H. S. Torr. Solving Markov Random Fields using Semi Def nite Programming. *Artif cial Intelligence and Statistics*, 2003.

[40] J. R. Ullmann. An Algorithm for Subgraph Isomorphism. *Journal of the ACM*, 23(1):31–42, Jan. 1976.

[41] K. Van De Sande, T. Gevers, and C. Snoek. Evaluating color descriptors for object and scene recognition. *IEEE Transactions on Pattern Analysis and Machine Intelligence*, 32(9):1582–1596, 2010.

[42] J. C. Van Gemert, C. J. Veenman, A. W. M. Smeulders, and J. M. Geusebroek. Visual word ambiguity. *IEEE Transactions on Pattern Analysis and Machine Intelligence*, 32(7):1271–1283, 2010.

[43] P. Viola and M. Jones. Rapid object detection using a boosted cascade of simple features. *Computer Vision and Pattern Recognition*, 2001.

[44] B. H. S. V. N. Vishwanathan. Eff cient Max-Margin Multi-Label Classif cation with Applications to Zero-Shot Learning. *Machine Learning*, 88(1-2):127–155, 2010.

[45] H. Wang, A. Kläser, C. Schmid, L. Cheng-Lin, and L. Cheng. Action Recognition by Dense Trajectories. *Computer Vision and Pattern ...*, pages 3169–3176, 2011.

[46] S. Wu, S. Bondugula, F. Luisier, X. Zhuang, and P. Natarajan. Zero-Shot Event Detection Using Multi-modal Fusion of Weakly Supervised Concepts. *Computer Vision and Pattern Recognition*, pages 2665–2672, June 2014.

[47] T. Yang, S. Z. Li, Q. Pan, and J. Li. Real-time Multiple Objects Tracking with Occlusion Handling in Dynamic Scenes. *Computer Vision and Pattern Recognition*, (60172037), 2005.

[48] J. Yuan, Z.-J. Zha, Y.-T. Zheng, M. Wang, X. Zhou, and T.-S. Chua. Learning concept bundles for video search with complex queries. *ACM Multimedia*, 2011.

[49] J. Yuan, Y. Zhao, H. Luan, M. Wang, and T. Chua. Memory Recall Based Video Search: Finding Videos You Have Seen Before Based on Your Memory. *ACM Trans. Multimedia Comput. Commun. Appl.*

[50] D.-q. Zhang and S.-f. Chang. Stochastic Attributed Relational Graph Matching for Image Near-Duplicate Detection. *ACM Multimedia*, 2004.

Video Killed The Data Store

Extending the n-Dimensional Display Interface for Full Screen Video

Charles D. Estes
University of North Carolina at Chapel Hill
Brooks Computer Science Building, CB 3175
Chapel Hill, NC 27599-3175 USA
cdestes@cs.unc.edu

Ketan Mayer-Patel
University of North Carolina at Chapel Hill
Brooks Computer Science Building, CB 3175
Chapel Hill, NC 27599-3175 USA
kmp@cs.unc.edu

ABSTRACT

Prior research introduced the n-Dimensional Display Interface (NDDI) as a new *"narrow waist"* for the display pipeline. In this paper, we extend the NDDI architecture to provide a blending feature. We then utilize that new feature for full screen video playback, leveraging application-level framing to realize a significant data transmission reduction. We then explore new NDDI configurations for effective rate control under highly constrained transmission budgets.

Categories and Subject Descriptors

C.0 [**General**]: Hardware/software interfaces

General Terms

Design, Algorithms, Performance, Experimentation

Keywords

Display interface, framebuffer, scalable display

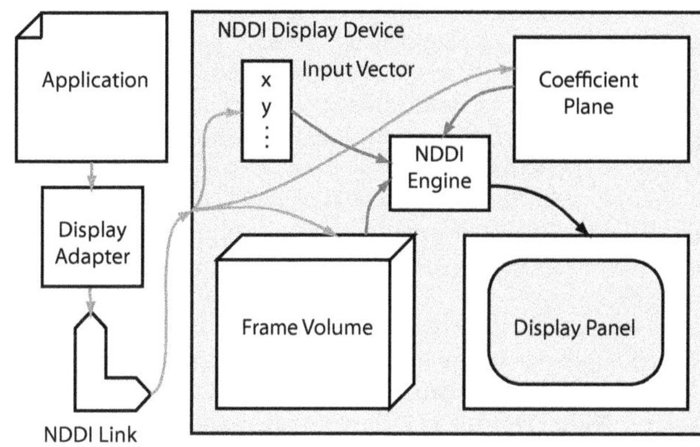

Figure 1: NDDI concept diagram.

1. INTRODUCTION

Ever increasing display resolutions are pushing the limits of framebuffer-based computer/display interfaces. Progressively scanning a framebuffer at 5K display resolutions at a fixed synchronous rate of 60Hz and 24 bits per pixel, for example, requires 19 Gb/s of raw throughput. These data rates are particularly challenging when connecting to a display wirelessly or using mobile devices with a limited battery life. Clearly, these data rates motivate the use of compression in some way. Choosing a single compression standard for communicating with displays, however, is problematic. Different use cases and types of content will require different types of compression techniques. Settling on a single fixed standard limits future innovation and creates interoperability issues.

Our approach to this challenge is to rethink the computer/display abstraction entirely. By replacing the simple framebuffer abstraction with a more general and flexible abstraction that can be used to bring application-level domain knowledge to bear in how display resources are best marshaled. In effect, we have proposed a display architecture that can be used to realize application-specific display compression. We call this abstraction the n-Dimensional Display Interface (NDDI) [7].

One way to think about a display is to consider it a sort of *"big data problem"* where massive amounts of graphical data are mapped and reduced to a 2D array of pixels on a display. NDDI is designed to be a mechanism that allows applications to explicitly express the contents of a display as a collection of map-reduce operations on pixel data. It is intended to act as a *"narrow waist"* abstraction that many different kinds of applications will find different ways of employing.

The NDDI Display concept is illustrated in Figure 1. Instead of a simple framebuffer matching the dimensions of the display, NDDI uses a *Frame Volume* that can be configured to any dimensionality. It serves largely as a store of pixel data on the NDDI device that can be mapped to the *Display Panel.* The mapping is controlled by the *Coefficient Plane*, which is a two-dimensional array of *Coefficient Matrices.* The dimension of the Coefficient Plane match that of the physical Display Panel (i.e., there is a Coefficient Matrix for each pixel on the display). Updates to the display are driven by the *Input Vector.* The *NDDI Engine* houses digital logic that performs calculations necessary to multiply the Input Vector by each pixel's Coefficient Matrix to produce an address tuple. The length of the address tuple matches the dimensionality of the Frame Volume and acts to address a specific pixel value stored in the Frame Volume

MM'15, October 26–30, 2015, Brisbane, Australia.

ACM 978-1-4503-3459-4/15/10 ...$15.00.
DOI: http://dx.doi.org/10.1145/2733373.2806271 .

which is retrieved and placed on the Display Panel. Absent of data dependencies, these calculations can all happen in parallel.

By configuring the size of the Input Vector and dimensionality of the Frame Volume, applications can tailor the display to their needs instead of interacting via a fixed framebuffer. This application-level framing [1] empowers the application to reconfigure the display based on its semantics. For example, a remote kiosk cycling through a set of slides might pre-render its content to the Frame Volume and then slowly switch between advertisements with a single byte written to the appropriate element of the Input Vector. An interactive display with an intricate graphical user interface might configure the Frame Volume as a 4D storage for a variety of content like rendered frames, graphics primitives, icons, fonts, sprites, etc. Compositing could then be performed through appropriate mappings in the Coefficient Plane.

NDDI is not meant as a replacement for a GPU, nor is it a special purpose display optimized for video playback. It is simply a particular type of display that can be connected to a display adapter with a GPU. The GPU can drive the NDDI Display like a framebuffer or in numerous more advanced ways to realize a benefit based on application-level semantics.

Our initial experiments focused on traditional applications with no knowledge of the higher-order functionality provided by NDDI. These experiments simply read out the framebuffer on every refresh cycle and translated the data into NDDI-specific commands to update the memory regions of the NDDI Display. The first significant benefit we demonstrated was to update the NDDI Display only when the contents of the framebuffer changed instead of on a fixed refresh rate of 60 Hz. Subsequent experiments improved these results by using a tiled approach that divided the framebuffer into blocks and updated the Frame Volume on a block-by-block basis, potentially reusing previously transmitted blocks.

The results were very compelling for many different computer applications, save for one. Full screen video playback saw no real benefit beyond updating the NDDI display at 24 fps instead of 60 Hz. Furthermore, the original NDDI Display specification lacked a critical feature: blending. Several use cases require blending to smoothly composite non-rectangular regions. This paper describes a refined NDDI design that adds this critical new feature and uses it in a novel way to revisit rendering of full screen video. The experiments within show a 75% reduction in data transmission cost placing video performance on par with the other computer applications from the prior experiments.

In the remainder of this paper we provide more details on the NDDI in Section 2. In Section 3 we discuss blending extensions needed for advanced compositing. In Section 4 those extensions are used to drive NDDI in a novel video-specific manner. We then extend these ideas in Section 5 to include a multiscale approach that lends itself to constrained bandwidth situations. Related work that inspired these new schemes are described in Section 6 and the paper concludes with a discussion of future work in Section 7.

2. N-DIMENSIONAL DISPLAY INTERFACE

NDDI is a display interface that uses a more complex abstraction to replace the framebuffer. Defining this abstraction required balancing tradeoffs between transmission benefit and flexibility. Our design concept for the new abstraction was driven by a set of guiding principles.

Framebuffer Compatible - Should be fully backward compatible with applications that use a simple framebuffer.

Data-Driven - Should be stateless, updating deterministically based on data alone.

Progressive Benefit - Applications can leverage application-level framing for stronger benefit.

Highly Parallel - Operations should remain independent allowing for massive scalability.

Asynchronous - Should not require a synchronous signal to drive updates.

2.1 NDDI Components

As introduced earlier, the NDDI Frame Volume (**V**) stores 3-channel pixel values transmitted to the display by an application. Once in the Frame Volume, these pixel values can be used in a number of ways, depending on the needs of the driving application. A key innovation of the Frame Volume is that it can be dynamically configured to any n-dimension pixel space ($\mathbb{P}^n$), allowing the pixels to be addressed with a n-tuple matching that dimensionality. This allows applications to explicitly express the contents of a display as a "mapping" of these pixels. With the data now on the display, these mapping operations can scale with the display instead of relying on rendering and transmission components to scale in lockstep.

Specifically, the mapping operations performed by NDDI are driven by the Input Vector (**i**) and controlled by the Coefficient Plane (**C**). The Input Vector is a one dimensional vector with a length (m) that is configureable such that $m \geq 2$. The first two elements i_x and i_y are reserved and logically are set to the x and y coordinates for the pixel being mapped. The remaining values are to be updated by the application on a frame-by-frame basis. The Coefficient Plane is a two-dimensional array matching the physical dimensions of the Display Panel ($w \times h$). The Coefficient Plane holds Coefficient Matrices (**M**). A Coefficient Matrix is a matrix of Coefficients (c) where the size of the matrix is coordinated with the length of the Input Vector and the dimensionality of the Frame Volume ($m \times n$). The purpose of each Coefficient Matrix at location (x, y) in the Coefficient Plane is to perform a mapping that chooses a pixel from the Frame Volume to be composited (i.e., reduced) on to the Display Panel at location (x, y). The mapping is done by performing matrix multiplication of the Input Vector by the Coefficient Matrix, producing an n-tuple that uniquely addresses a pixel value from the framebuffer.

2.2 Pixel Mapping

The pixel mapping operations are deterministic, consisting of highly parallel matrix multiplication. The equations below provide formal definitions. $p_{x,y}$ is the value from pixel space being mapped at location x, y on the Display Panel (2). The Frame Volume (**V**) is configured with n fixed dimensions (an nth-order tensor), a subset of n pixel space (3). The Input Vector (**i**) is an integer vector of length m (4). Each Coefficient Matrix (**M**) is an $m \times n$ matrix of coefficients (c) (6). Coefficients are integers (5). The Coefficient Plane (**C**) is a two dimensional array from coefficient matrix space.

$$\mathbb{P} = \{(r, g, b) | 0 \leq r, g, b < 2^8\} \quad (1)$$

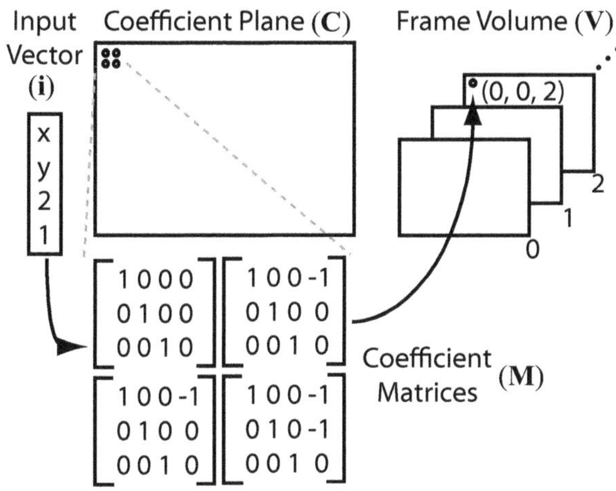

Figure 2: Example NDDI Configuration for simple video player with 4x scaling.

$$p_{x,y} \in \mathbb{P}, x < w, y < h \tag{2}$$

$$\mathbf{V} = V_{i_1 i_2 \dots i_n}, v \in \mathbb{P} \tag{3}$$

$$\mathbf{i} \in \mathbb{Z}^m \tag{4}$$

$$c \in \mathbb{Z} \tag{5}$$

$$\mathbf{M} = \begin{bmatrix} c_{11} & \cdots & c_{1m} \\ \vdots & \ddots & \vdots \\ c_{n1} & \cdots & c_{nm} \end{bmatrix} \tag{6}$$

$$\mathbf{C} = \begin{bmatrix} \mathbf{M_{11}} & \cdots & \mathbf{M_{1w}} \\ \vdots & \ddots & \vdots \\ \mathbf{M_{h1}} & \cdots & \mathbf{M_{hw}} \end{bmatrix}, \mathbf{C}(x,y) = \mathbf{M_{xy}} \tag{7}$$

The Lookup operation takes an n-tuple as an address and retrieves the pixel from that location of the Frame Volume (8). The Map operation accepts a 2-tuple (x, y) and uses the Coefficient Matrix at that location in the Coefficient Plane to multiply by the Input Vector (9). The first two values of the Input Vector will be set to x and y and the remaining values are set by the application.

$$p = \text{Lookup}(\mathbf{V}, (a_1, ..., a_n))) \tag{8}$$

$$(a_1, ..., a_n) = \text{Map}(x, y) = \mathbf{C}(x, y)\mathbf{i} \tag{9}$$

The complete calculation for the pixel $p_{x,y}$ uses the Map operation to produce the address tuple used in the Lookup (10).

$$p_{x,y} = \text{Lookup}(\mathbf{V}, \text{Map}(x, y)) \tag{10}$$

As an example, Figure 2 shows a possible configuration for a scaled video player application. The Input Vector is configured with length four. The Frame Volume is configured with three dimensions and each frame of video is rendered into an x-y plane of the Frame Volume, treating the z dimension like a circular buffer. The Coefficient Matrices are therefore defined to have four columns and three rows. The application chooses coefficients to specify an affine transformation so that the contents of each x-y plane are effectively scaled by four. The third value in the Input Vector is then used to choose which x-y plane is active (i.e., advancing through the circular buffer) and the fourth value is fixed at one as part of the affine transformation.

The following shows the specific calculation for the pixel at $(1, 1)$ of the display using the values from Figure 2. This is the fourth pixel in this group of pixels that are scaled from a single pixel.

$$\text{Map}(1,1) = \begin{bmatrix} 1 & 0 & 0 & -1 \\ 0 & 1 & 0 & -1 \\ 0 & 0 & 1 & 0 \end{bmatrix} \begin{bmatrix} 1 \\ 1 \\ 2 \\ 1 \end{bmatrix} = \begin{bmatrix} 0 \\ 0 \\ 2 \end{bmatrix} \tag{11}$$

$$p_{1,1} = \text{Lookup}(\mathbf{V}, (0, 0, 2)) \tag{12}$$

Map-reduce as a general paradigm is a natural fit for our goal of providing a scalable display interface abstraction. NDDI uses map-reduce at multiple levels in order to arrive at a result. At the coarsest level, NDDI uses the Coefficient Plane to map a pixel value to each Display Panel location. At a finer level, the matrix multiplication of the Input Vector by each Coefficient Matrix can be considered a map-reduce operation producing a tuple that chooses a pixel value from the Frame Volume. Later in the paper, we will refine the NDDI design with another map-reduce layer to provide pixel blending operations that can also be used to support video.

2.3 Application Agnostic Experiments

Our prior experiments assumed the application to be unaware of NDDI and aimed to demonstrate a transmission savings without leveraging any application-level semantics. These experiments served to support backward compatibility by monitoring a framebuffer and translating its changes into the appropriate NDDI commands. The first experiment configured NDDI as a simple framebuffer, while the next two experiments used "tilers" that divided the framebuffer into blocks that could be updated and reused as necessary.

Simple Framebuffer Experiment - Treats the entire framebuffer as a single block, updating the entire region whenever a pixel changes. The Frame Volume is organized into two dimensions matching the Display Panel.

Flat Tiled Experiment - Tiles the framebuffer into blocks and only updates the blocks that change. The Frame Volume is configured to match the Display Panel.

Cached Tiled Experiment - In addition to tiling the framebuffer, the Frame Volume is organized into three dimensions forming a very deep stack of 2D tiles (Figure 3) that act as a cache of blocks. A block is easily mapped to the Display Panel by using an efficient Coefficient Plane fill command for that region of Coefficient Matrices.

These initial experiments were driven with pre-recorded computing sessions at 24 fps. The results for the computing sessions are shown in Figure 4. The results are shown as a ratio of the NDDI data sent versus the amount of data that would be required if the entire display was scanned and transmitted every 60 Hz cycle. As a best case, an *Ideal* mode was introduced. It represents the amount of data required to send over just the individually changed pixels, ignoring the cost of addressing that pixel on the display.

In the Simple Framebuffer experiment, updating the NDDI Display at 24 fps instead of 60Hz provides an immediate

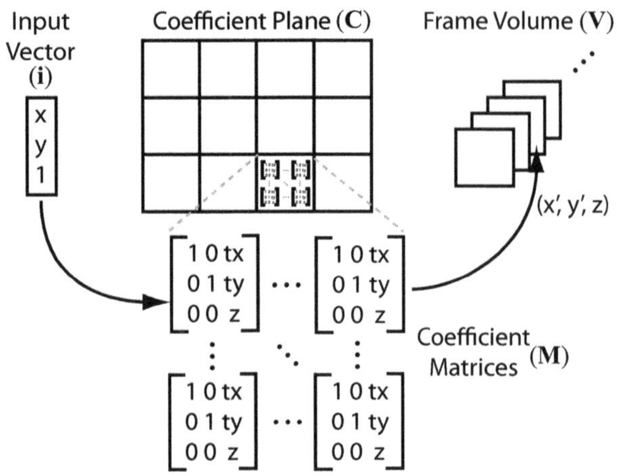

Figure 3: Cached Tiler NDDI configuration.

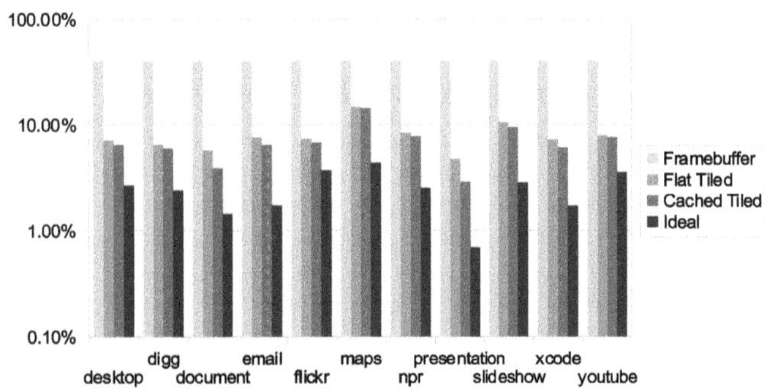

Figure 4: Experiment results for the recorded computing sessions (logarithmic scale).

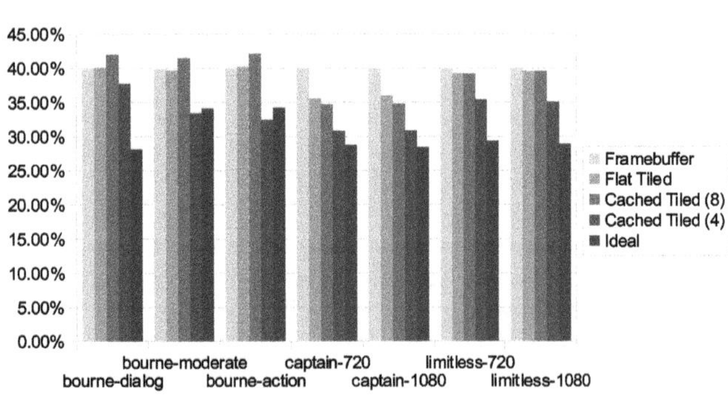

Figure 5: Experiment results for full screen video playback.

benefit by reducing how often data was sent. Furthermore, any time the display was unchanged, no data was sent at all. The Flat Tiled experiment did significantly better for scenarios where the screen was mostly static. The Cached Tiled experiment did marginally better than Flat Tiled. It benefited from efficient fill operations where a single block could be used for several different regions of the display. Additionally scenarios that re-used content such as switching between windows showed a significant benefit.

The results for full screen video playback (Figure 5) were very weak by comparison. In an attempt to realize stronger gains, the Cached Tiler was augmented with a lossy mode where only a certain number of significant bits per pixel channel were used when determining cache matches. Specifically, Cached(8) is lossless (i.e., the match must be exact) and Cached(4) is lossy using only the first 4 bits per channel to match blocks. Using Cached(4) a modest gain was realized while maintaining a reasonable PSNR ranging from 36.71 to 48.73. However, visual artifacts from re-using near matches affected perceived quality.

3. BLENDING

In order to support non-trivial uses cases that require compositing on the display, NDDI must provide a means to blend pixels. The original NDDI design does not do so. To address this shortcoming, we refined the NDDI design while staying true to our guiding principles. Three different approaches were considered.

3.1 Temporal Blending

The first approach requires no modifications to the original NDDI feature set. Temporal Blending exploits image persistence associated with the physical operation of the Display Panel. The driving application renders the planes to be blended into separate planes within the Frame Volume. Pixel blending is then achieved by driving the Input Vector to rapidly switch between those planes using a duty cycle tuned to the desired blending percentage.

Disadvantageously, Temporal Blending is tightly coupled to the technology used in the Display Panel. Different display panel technologies may have vastly different levels of image persistence and may support different refresh rates. Furthermore, it is difficult to blend only sub-regions of the display. Lastly, Temporal Blending is not in keeping with our guiding principle which encourages NDDI to be asynchronous. Driving the Input Vector so precisely and synchronously puts heavy requirements on the quality of service of the connection to the NDDI Display.

3.2 Frame Volume Blending

Frame Volume Blending is perhaps the most intuitive approach. With Frame Volume Blending, pixel values are extended to support an alpha channel. The alpha channel is used with a new NDDI command that alpha blends pixel values from one area of the Frame Volume onto another target area. This blending operation might be implemented by a dedicated digital logic block. The application must direct these operations in order to achieve the desired blended result.

Frame Volume Blending suffers from a number of disadvantages. First, the capabilities of any blender-specific hardware will need to scale with the display in order to blend display-sized or larger areas within the Frame Volume. Second, Frame Volume Blending upsets the ratio of Frame Volume reads to writes. As originally conceived without Frame Volume Blending, large Frame Volume sizes can be supported with an appropriate memory cache hierarchy. Frame Volume Blending now requires more emphasis on Frame Volume write performance and works against caching. In addition to these engineering disadvantages, Frame Volume Blending like Temporal Blending is not in keeping with our guiding principles. Frame Volume Blending requires the application to send over the components of a blended area and to use multiple NDDI commands to composite the result in stages. This uses NDDI as a sort of state machine rather than being entirely data-driven and highly parallel.

3.3 Coefficient Plane Blending

While less obvious, the third approach proved to be the most compatible with our guiding principles while remaining highly flexible. Coefficient Plane Blending extends the NDDI architecture to now provide 64 separate Coefficient Planes and augments every Coefficient Matrix with an associated *Scaler* (13). A Scaler ($\mathbf{s}$) is a 3-tuple representing independent scalers for each color channel (15). Each of the 64 Coefficient Planes still matches the physical dimensions of the display panel.

With this extended architecture, to calculate a pixel value for the Display Panel, the Coefficient Matrices at position (x, y) in each of the 64 Coefficient Planes will map to specific pixel values from the Frame Volume. These 64 pixel values are reduced to a single value by multiplying each by their associated Scaler, accumulating across all 64 planes and dividing by the maximum Scaler ($\mathbf{s}_\gamma$). This is similar to alpha blending, but with a configurable maximum scaler (16) that in our implementation must be a power of two instead of a fixed maximum of 256. This provides a level of flexibility while constraining the maximum to ensure that the division can be implemented efficiently as a shift operation.

$$\mathbf{C_k} = \begin{bmatrix} \mathbf{M_{11}} & \cdots & \mathbf{M_{1w}} \\ \vdots & \ddots & \vdots \\ \mathbf{M_{h1}} & \cdots & \mathbf{M_{hw}} \end{bmatrix}, 0 \le k < 64, \mathbf{C_k}(x, y) = \mathbf{M_{xy}} \tag{13}$$

$$\mathbf{S_k} = \begin{bmatrix} \mathbf{s_{11}} & \cdots & \mathbf{s_{1w}} \\ \vdots & \ddots & \vdots \\ \mathbf{s_{h1}} & \cdots & \mathbf{s_{hw}} \end{bmatrix}, 0 \le k < 64, \mathbf{S_k}(x, y) = s_{xy} \tag{14}$$

$$\mathbf{s} = \{(r, g, b) | -2^{15} < r, g, b < 2^{15}\} \tag{15}$$

$$\mathbf{s}_\gamma = \{(2^\gamma, 2^\gamma, 2^\gamma) | 0 \le \gamma < 15\} \tag{16}$$

Unlike alpha blending, the NDDI scalers are both signed and multi-channel allowing for both positive and negative blending with different values for each color channel. Furthermore, the retrieved pixel values can be treated as unsigned 8-bit values or as signed 7-bit values allowing subtractive masks. The Map operation as defined before is modified slightly to take an additional plane argument (17). The Blend operation simply sums the mapped values multiplied (dot product) by the scalers and then shifts by γ (18).

$$(a_1, ..., a_n) = \mathrm{Map}(x, y, k) = \mathbf{C_k}(x, y)\mathbf{i} \tag{17}$$

Figure 6: Rendered DCT basis functions.

$$(a_1, ..., a_n) = \mathrm{Blend}(x, y) = \frac{\sum_{k=0}^{63} \mathrm{Map}(x, y, k) \cdot \mathbf{S_k}(x, y)}{2^\gamma} \tag{18}$$

While appearing complex, Coefficient Plane Blending is in keeping with the guiding principles – in particular allowing an application to use it in a simple way or to bring to bear application-level semantics to employ it in a more sophisticated manner as is shown in the video use case described in Section 4.

From an engineering perspective, Coefficient Plane Blending does greatly increase the amount of memory required for the Coefficient Planes. That memory, however, can be localized within the per-pixel digital logic. Furthermore, the blending operation itself is just another map-reduce step where the mapping operation performs the scaling and the reduction operation is the accumulate and shift.

4. VIDEO

The refined NDDI architecture to support blending can be used to benefit video content as well. Prior experiments showed lackluster performance on video playback in terms of transmission savings. With *Coefficient Plane Blending* in place, we revisit video playback as a task of blending pre-rendered DCT basis functions (Figure 6) [13]. This new experiment introduces our first scheme for configuring the NDDI Display to benefit a application-specific content model.

We implemented a new tiler called the DCT Tiler. The NDDI display was configured as shown in Figure 7. The Frame Volume is configured to be $8 \times 8 \times 64$ so that it can hold 63 pre-rendered basis functions and a level shift plane as described below. The Input Vector has a length of three with the third value fixed at one. The Coefficient Matrices all have simple affine transforms that map each block of a Coefficient Plane back to an 8×8 area of the Frame Volume with the z component designating a specific plane (i.e., a particular basis function).

For the initial Frame Volume setup, the 63 pre-rendered basis functions were generated as grayscale renderings of a maximum coefficient of 256 clamped to the range $[-127, 127]$. They are arranged in "zig-zag" order which is important

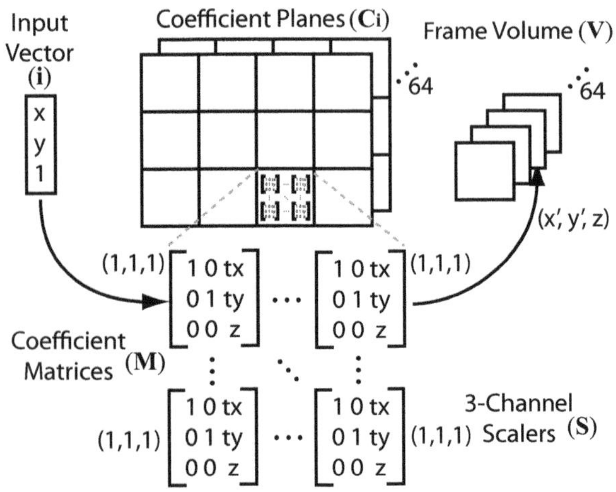

Figure 7: DCT Tiler NDDI configuration.

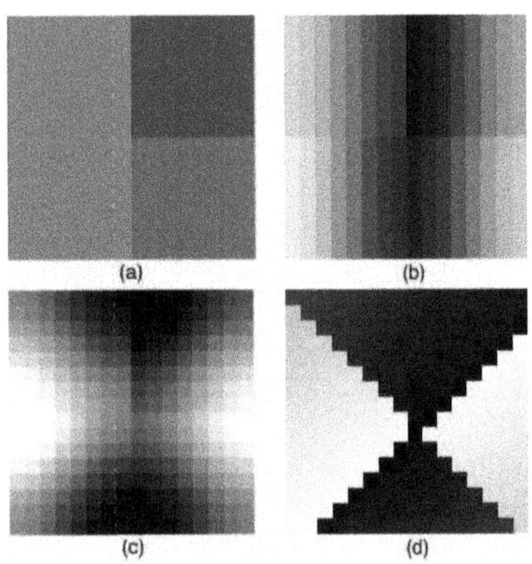

Figure 8: Example blending of weighted basis functions for four 8×8 blocks. (a) shows the rendering with just the DC coefficients for the four blocks. (b) blends the first AC coefficient for each block. (c) blends the second AC coefficient. Finally (d) shows the results of all 63 weighted coefficients blended.

for efficiently updating Scalers associated with a particular block. The final 64th plane is not a pre-rendered basis function, but rather a medium gray plane. This is required because the basis functions are signed and centered at zero. The resulting image must be level shifted to unsigned pixels centered at medium gray.

With the Input Vector, Coefficient Matrices, and Frame Volume initialized, only the Scalers are left uninitialized. The Scalers represent the DCT coefficients. Essentially, the DCT Tiler acts as a simple intra-frame encoder using 8×8 blocks. For each frame, the video is tiled into blocks. Those blocks are transformed to the frequency domain via a DCT. Then the values are quantized with a configurable quality factor.[1] The values are then de-quantized to produce a set of weights. These are arranged into zig-zag order matching the organization of the basis functions already rendered in the Frame Volume and used to set the Scalers for the block.

[1]The quality factor is an integer multiplied by a simple quantization matrix biased against high-frequency components.[15]

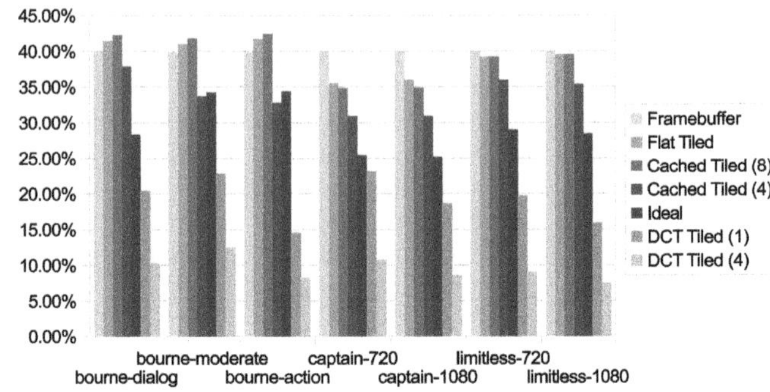

Figure 9: Revised video results with new DCT tiler.

Video	PSNR (1)	PSNR (4)
bourne-dialog	42.49	39.81
bourne-moderate	41.35	37.09
bourne-action	43.91	42.03
captain-720	41.55	37.99
captain-1080	42.66	40.03
limitless-720	42.30	39.55
limitless-1080	43.28	41.24

Table 1: DCT Tiled Mode Statistics using a quality factor of 1 (best) and 4 (modest).

Figure 8 illustrates this process with an example of weighted basis functions being blended over a small 16×16 region of pixels.

Figure 9 shows the results for video using the new DCT tiler alongside the results from the original experiments. The y-axis shows a ratio of the bytes transmitted over the NNDI link for the particular mode compared to the bytes transmitted when the entire framebuffer is sent at 60 Hz. The two additional DCT Tiler runs use a quality factor of 1 producing the highest available quality and 4 which was experimentally determined to reduce the number of surviving coefficients while still producing comparable PSNR scores (see Table 1). The ratio of both of the DCT Tiler runs are far better than Ideal which is a contrived mode that only measures the amount of data associated with pixels that are changed without any addressing overhead. While the DCT Tiler is a lossy mode, video quality remains high.

5. MULTISCALE DCT

The DCT Tiler experiment was our first experiment to exploit application-level semantics to utilize NDDI in a new, more sophisticated way. The next experiment aimed to leverage NDDI more fully to address the issue of rate control based on video content. The DCT Tiler has an adjustable quality factor, but our goal for the Multiscale DCT Tiler experiment was to try to exploit additional savings from more sophisticated configurations of NDDI.

The earlier scaled video player example in Figure 2 is a simple decoder that takes advantage of the Coefficient Plane mapping to scale a source video to 4x by mapping groups of four pixels from the display to a single pixel from the source. The same concept of scaling can be extended to the DCT Tiler such that pre-rendered basis functions are scaled to cover larger than 8×8 blocks on the display. The obvious disadvantage here is that detail is lost when the source video is downscaled for transmission and then upscaled on the display. While this may be acceptable for areas of the frame without fine details, it is not a good scheme for those that do. Advantageously, NDDI affords a level of flexibility such that portions of the display can be rendered at a 1x scale while others are rendered at coarser scales.

NDDI does impose some design constraints that need to be considered. First, reconfiguring areas of the Coefficient Planes is not free. Therefore it is not advisable to do so often as it can impose a heavy penalty on a data transmission budget. To address this, we do not configure areas of the display at particular scales; instead we divide the Coefficient Planes among the different scales. This leads to the next constraint which is the limit of 64 Coefficient Planes. Losing even a few Coefficient Planes for a particular scale means that high frequency details cannot be rendered. In order to maximize quality as seen experimentally through PSNR, the 1x scale must retain a majority of the planes doling out only a few planes to the coarser scales.

Despite the constraints, the Multiscale DCT Tiler does show promise as a means to support rate control while maximizing quality. This is achieved primarily by updating large homogenous regions of the frame using the higher scales. Secondarily, the coarser scales serve as a prediction that can then be refined with the finer scales acting to address the residual differences. Figure 10 illustrates this using a 4x scale with only one Coefficient Plane. In such a configuration, the 1x scale only loses one plane and can therefore represent very fine details. However, the motivation of the Multiscale DCT Tiler is to experimentally find which configurations win out when the rate is reduced dramatically.

5.1 Multiscale Configuration

The Multiscale configuration is specified as a series of scales and number of planes dedicated to that scale. That number of planes is defined as the edge length in a square of basis functions. As an example, a 2 would indicate that 4 planes are reserved for that scale and that the DC coefficient and the AC coefficients at $(1, 0)$, $(0, 1)$, and $(1, 1)$ are used. The choice of the shape is critical, because it allows the higher scales to create effective "checkerboard" outputs where each square of the rendered pattern provides a prediction for one or more finer blocks along perfect boundaries. When using a full 8×8 set of basis functions, it is likely that far fewer than 63 planes will be available. Therefore, the ordering remains zig-zag so that higher frequency AC coefficients are truncated first. The following illustrates the multiscale configuration used for the experiments.

- **1:8** - The only scale (1x) uses all 63 basis functions.
- **16:1, 1:8** - The first scale (16x) uses only the DC basis function. The remaining 62 are used for 1x.
- **2:2, 1:8** - The first scale (2x) uses a 2×2 square of basis functions. The remaining 59 are used for 1x.
- **4:3, 1:8** - The first scale (4x) uses 9 basis functions. The remaining 54 are used for 1x.
- **8:2, 4:2, 1:8** - The first two scales (8x, 4x) each use 4 basis functions. The remaining 55 are used for 1x.

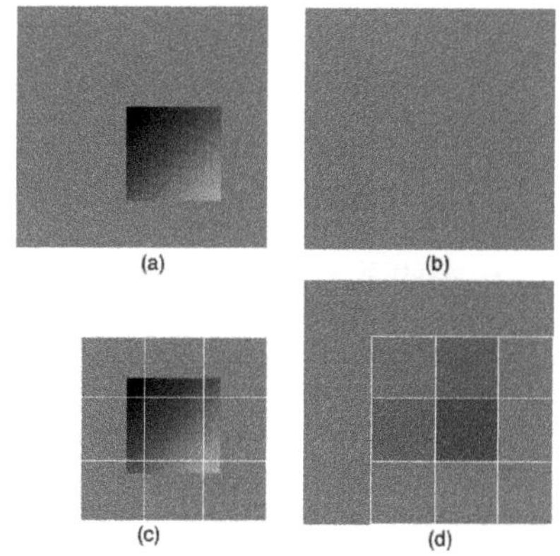

Figure 10: Multiscale DCT example of 16 8×8 blocks. (a) shows the image to be rendered consisting of mostly medium gray. If the first configured scale is 4x with only one plane, then (b) represents the contents of the display after that first layer is rendered. The next configured layer is 1x with the remaining 62 planes. After the first rendering, only 9 of the 16 blocks need to be updated. (c) shows the contents of those four blocks. Of the 9 blocks that are rendered at the 1x scale, 5 did not need to encode the DCT coefficient, because their DCT coefficients matched the coefficient from the 4x layer as seen in (d) which illustrates the DCT component from each of the 16 blocks at the 1x scale.

5.2 Priority Updating Schemes

The Multiscale DCT experiments explore the different multiscale configurations in terms of performance when a transmission budget is enforced. The motivation for this change is that each additional set of planes dedicated to a new scale removes the highest frequency planes from the finest scale thus guaranteeing a loss in quality. Therefore, such a configuration must minimize the number of Scalers that are updated while sacrificing the minimal number of planes from the 1x scale. To minimize the Scalers sent over the wire, we employ four different priority schemes when choosing which Scalers to update.

When considering multiscale configurations and priority updating schemes, it is important to realize another constraint of NDDI. As seen with the DCT Tiler, it is possible to implement an NDDI command to update all of the Scalers for a "stack" of tiled regions of the Coefficient Plane, but it does incur a cost to address the stack and then to specify the size of the tiles and the stack size. Even going from a configuration of just 1x with a stack of one to three scales with three stacks incurs a penalty, but it is mitigated somewhat because the higher scales have fewer blocks. Our priority schemes seek to reduce the size of each stack either through leaving off Scalers for high frequency DCT coefficients from the "bottom" of the stack or the low frequency Scalers from the "top" of the stack as was seen with the example in Figure 10. We explored the following priority updating schemes each with a tunable variable *Delta* or *Plane Count* that is set for every frame in order to ensure that the budget is met.

Trim with a Delta The DCT Tiler trims the unchanged Scalers from the top and bottom of a stack of Scalers before sending them to the NDDI Display. When Trimming with a Delta, then any Scaler where all three channels are within a Delta from the current Scaler is considered unchanged.

Trim with a Plane Count This form of trimming starts with the first unchanged Scaler from the top and trims off enough of the bottom Scalers to a stack height specified by the Plane Count.

Snap to Zero with a Delta In this scheme any Scaler with all three channels within a Delta from zero is set to zero. This is obviously effective for the high frequency AC coefficients at the bottom of the Scaler stack, but it is also beneficial for the DC and low frequency AC coefficients for the finer scales where coarser scales have produced a prediction that drives these coefficients near zero for the residual.

Snap to Zero with a Plane Count While still snapping to zero, this scheme starts with top-most non-zero scaler for each stack and zeroes out the bottom of the stack producing a stack height specified by the Plane Count.

5.3 Multiscale DCT Results

The multiscale configurations and priority schemes were evaluated using various ten-second clips with resolutions ranging from DVD to 4K. For each video source, we estimated the motion by calculating the optical flow using the Lucas-Kanade method with pyramids [12]. We then chose the ten second clips with the highest, lowest, and median flow. Each of the clips was tested with all twenty combinations of configuration and priority scheme using three budgets. The budgets were determined for each video clip using a calculation that used only 8, 4, and 2.5 bits per pixel for low, medium, and high compression. The calculations were adjusted to 4, 3, and 2 bits per pixel for 4K video to better suit the somewhat lower frequency data in the blocks.

Several of the clips exhibited a notable relationship between optical flow and the resulting PSNR. Figure 11 shows the median flow clip of a 720p movie. All twenty runs are shown using the medium (4 bpp) data budget. The flow for each frame is shown as an average that is normalized to $[0, 1000]$ and shown on a separate axis with a logarithmic scale. Nearly every run follows a similar trend; areas of high flow produce better PSNR. This is largely attributed to the motion blur associated with high flow sections. The blur effectively removes high frequency data from each block favoring a multiscale configuration that sacrifices several of the high frequency AC coefficients at the finest (1:8) scale. The low flow areas produced a much lower PSNR than we expected. This particular clip primarily consists of slow sweeping shots, and while the motion is not great this is enough to overcome the simple prediction residual model. Proper motion compensation would likely produce a superior result.

The clips with larger areas of static content performed much better. Figure 12 shows the median flow 4K clip. The top performing two priority schemes were chosen and all three compression settings (4 bpp, 3 bpp, and 2 bpp) were used for each priority scheme. This particular clip is a movie trailer that contains many rapid scene changes with scenes ranging from dialog to high action. Additionally the scene transitions are marked with large black screens with little text. Some of the previous trend is seen with high flow sections yielding higher PSNR, but there was lessened reduction in PSNR for the low flow sections because the flow did not uniformly affect the entire scene. The clip starts with a black screen displaying an actor's name in the center. It then fades to a head shot punctuated later by a fade through

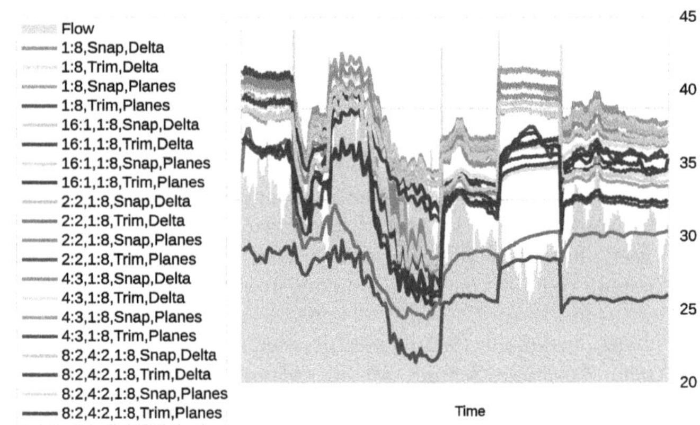

Figure 11: PSNR of all configuration and priority schemes contrasted to optical flow using the medium budget constraint on the Limitless 720p median flow clip.

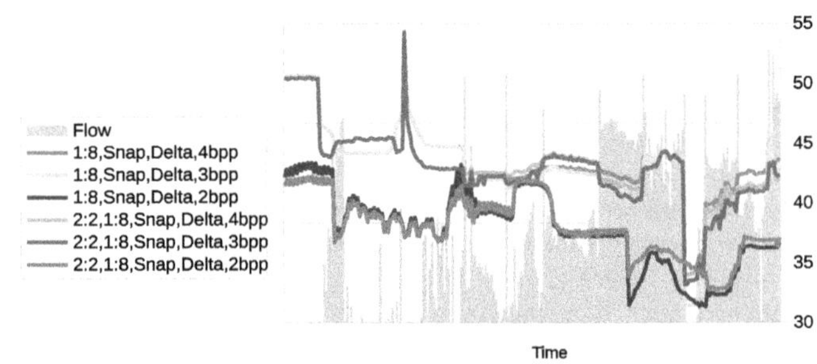

Figure 12: PSNR of best configuration and priority schemes contrasted to optical flow using all three budge constraints on the Elysium 4K median flow clip.

black that produces the very high peak with a PSNR of nearly 64 for the low and medium compression.

The average PSNR for each clip is shown in Tables 2 and 3 alongside the best configuration. For the high and medium data budgets a basic 1:8 scale configuration performed best. For the high data budget the priority schemes performed very similarly, whereas Snap Delta performed best for medium data budgets. Perhaps most interesting, the 2:2 1:8 scale configuration and Snap Delta performed the best for all of the clips when using the low data budget.

The DCT Tiler uses the data budgets as upper bounds when determining either the plane count or delta for each scale. Therefore the data actually transmitted with an 8 bpp budget may not be exactly double that of a 4 bpp budget. Figures 13 and 14 show the total number of bytes sent over the NDDI Link as a ratio to a 60 Hz signal. The larger formats clips generally perform better. The trailer clips (captain and elysium) perform exceptionally well in areas of low flow due to large static frames containing informational text for the audience. In fact, for the 4K elysium clip a majority of the frames were rendered under the tightest budget while still updating all changed Scalers.

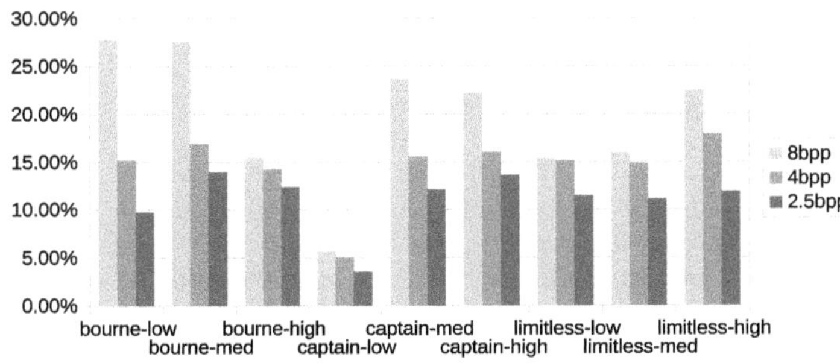

Figure 13: Video results for the DVD, 720p, and 1080p 10s clips using the medium data budget and the configuration and priority scheme that performed best. As with before, the results are a ratio of the byte transmitted over the wire compared to a 60Hz.

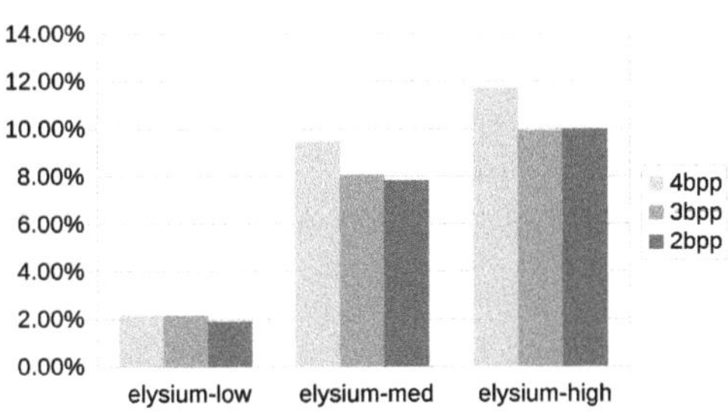

Figure 14: Video results for 4K 10s clips using the medium data budget and the configuration and priority scheme that performed best. As with before, the results are a ratio of the byte transmitted over the wire compared to a 60Hz.

Video / Flow	Budget		
	8 bpp	4 bpp	2.5 bpp
bourne DVD low	35.75 - 1:8 trim delta	33.79 - 1:8 trim delta	31.99 - 2:2 1:8 snap delta
bourne DVD median	38.64 - 1:8 snap planes	36.57 - 1:8 snap delta	34.91 - 2:2 1:8 snap delta
bourne DVD high	44.01 - 1:8 trim planes	43.69 - 1:8 snap delta	41.11 - 2:2 1:8 snap delta
captain 720 low	41.14 - 1:8 trim delta	40.44 - 2:2 1:8 snap delta	38.98 - 2:2 1:8 snap delta
captain 720 median	39.94 - 1:8 snap planes	38.67 - 1:8 snap delta	37.43 - 2:2 1:8 snap delta
captain 720 high	40.52 - 1:8 snap planes	39.79 - 1:8 snap delta	38.72 - 2:2 1:8 snap delta
limitless 1080 low	41.62 - 1:8 snap delta	41.53 - 1:8 snap planes	39.72 - 1:8 snap delta
limitless 1080 median	41.33 - 1:8 snap delta	41.06 - 1:8 snap delta	39.28 - 1:8 snap delta
limitless 1080 high	39.52 - 1:8 trim delta	38.79 - 1:8 snap delta	37.51 - 16:1 1:8 snap delta

Table 2: PSNR and Optimal configuration / scheme for each of the low, medium, and high flow clips. The data budgets are 8, 4, and 2.5 bits per pixel.

Video / Flow	Budget		
	4 bpp	3 bpp	2 bpp
elysium 4K low	48.78 - 1:8 snap delta	48.79 - 1:8 trim planes	48.32 - 2:2 1:8 snap delta
elysium 4K median	43.56 - 1:8 snap delta	43.03 - 1:8 snap delta	38.06 - 2:2 1:8 snap delta
elysium 4K high	43.14 - 1:8 snap delta	42.47 - 1:8 snap delta	41.35 - 2:2 1:8 snap delta

Table 3: PSNR and Optimal configuration / scheme for each of the low, medium, and high flow 4K clips. The data budgets are 4, 3, and 2 bits per pixel.

6. RELATED WORK

In defining the n-Dimensional Display Interface, we sought to redefine a new narrow waist while avoiding the "Wheel of Reincarnation" [14] by just raising the abstraction. Some of the earliest graphics interfaces have tackled the rendering pipeline with highly parallel logic. The framebuffer has survived since the advent of high-density integrated memory in the 1970's with the SuperPaint [18] system from Xerox Parc. As one of the earliest 3D systems, Pixel Planes [8] used programmable logic to realize equations used to render polygons and spheres as well as compute advanced graphics techniques such as shadows, transparency, and anti-aliasing. As 3D rendering became more prevalent, the parallelism became more evident [2]. Slowly the computation moved further from the display. Today GPUs embody much of this parallelism into dedicated hardware distinct from the display. They perform their operations and reduce the result to a single framebuffer that is serialized and sent over the wire.

Today, growing display resolutions and transmission media have led to numerous new standards and technologies to better cope. Digital standards like DVI [20] [4], HDMI [6] [10], and DisplayPort [22] have coped well enough, but they have not used parallelism to address the problem of pixel transmission instead relying on digital compression. Research into large-scale displays and display walls is tackling the problem through more explicit parallelism. IBM's Scaleable Graphics Engine (SGE) [17] introduced a hardware framebuffer allowing separate nodes to render their content. With such high resolutions, collaboratively rendering display content proved promising in systems such as Lightning-2 [19], Chromium [11], SAGE [3], Garuda [16], and Equalizer [5]. These systems each seek to composite the video output from several sources and render it to a single large display or multiple tiled displays. Despite their efficiency, each system still talks to the attached displays as a framebuffer forcing the composited video to be then split amongst displays. A single large NDDI Display can easily be leveraged allowing the sources to write to their own regions of the Frame Volume and Coefficient Planes.

Research into acceleration of large format video on displays has focused primarily on embedding codecs into displays in support of signaling standards such as DPVL [21]. However, certain aspects of video decoding are "embarrassingly parallel" and so GPUs have been leveraged to aid in video decoding [9]. While embedding a GPU on a display can be promising, it raises the abstraction significantly compared to NDDI, which provides basic DCT support at a much lower abstraction.

Perhaps the most similar research in the area is that of the embedded display processor described in the Embedded Function Composition system [23]. This research addresses many of the same challenges as NDDI with a much more sophisticated approach resembling older systems such as Pixel Planes. While is may prove to be more flexible than NDDI, the abstraction is again quite a bit higher and is therefore less suitable as a "narrow waist".

7. CONCLUSIONS AND FUTURE WORK

In prior experiments, NDDI provided little benefit for full screen video when the NDDI Display was configured without regard to application-level framing. Our extension to the NDDI architecture for blending was highly effective for enabling considerable data transmission reduction for full screen video by blending pre-rendered basis functions for each of the 8×8 blocks. With these new extensions, NDDI proved versatile for implementing rate control while maximizing quality, especially for very high resolution 4K video. Despite only using intra-frame data rate control, we were able to maintain strong PSNR under much smaller budgets than any of the earlier experiments. In doing so, we discovered trends in the Multiscale DCT Tiler performance given particular video frame content and types of motion. Future work will employ more realistic inter-frame rate control while supporting mixed media display content as we move into even more specialized uses cases with greater application-level framing.

8. REFERENCES

[1] D. D. Clark and D. L. Tennenhouse. Architectural considerations for a new generation of protocols. *ACM SIGCOMM Computer Communication Review*, 20(4):200–208, 1990.

[2] T. W. Crockett. An introduction to parallel rendering. *Parallel Computing*, 23(7):819–843, July 1997.

[3] M. Deering and D. Naegle. The SAGE Graphics Architecture. In *Proceedings of the 29th Annual Conference on Computer Graphics and Interactive Techniques*, SIGGRAPH '02, pages 683–692, New York, NY, USA, 2002. ACM.

[4] Digital visual interface dvi revision 1.0. Digital Display Working Group, April 1999.

[5] S. Eilemann, M. Makhinya, and R. Pajarola. Equalizer: a scalable parallel rendering framework. In *ACM SIGGRAPH ASIA 2008 courses on - SIGGRAPH Asia '08*, SIGGRAPH Asia '08, pages 1–14, New York, New York, USA, 2008. ACM Press.

[6] P. C. Electronics, B. V. International, S. Image, S. Corporation, and T. Corporation. High-Definition Multimedia Interface, 2006.

[7] C. D. Estes and K. Mayer-Patel. The n-Dimensional Display Interface A More Elastic Narrow Waist for the Display Pipeline. In *MMSYS*, 2012.

[8] H. Fuchs, J. Goldfeather, J. P. Hultquist, S. Spach, J. D. Austin, F. P. Brooks Jr., J. G. Eyles, and J. Poulton. Fast Spheres, Shadows, Textures, Transparencies, and Imgage Enhancements in Pixel-planes. *SIGGRAPH Comput. Graph.*, 19(3):111–120, July 1985.

[9] B. Han and B. Zhou. Efficient video decoding on GPUs by point based rendering. *Proceedings of the 21st ACM SIGGRAPH/EUROGRAPHICS symposium on Graphics hardware - GH '06*, page 79, 2006.

[10] High-definition multimedia interface specification version 1.3a. HDMI Founders, November 2006.

[11] G. Humphreys, M. Houston, R. Ng, R. Frank, S. Ahern, P. D. Kirchner, and J. T. Klosowski. Chromium: a stream-processing framework for interactive rendering on clusters. In *Proceedings of the 29th annual conference on Computer graphics and interactive techniques - SIGGRAPH '02*, SIGGRAPH '02, page 693, New York, New York, USA, 2002. ACM Press.

[12] B. D. Lucas and T. Kanade. An Iterative Image Registration Technique with an Application to Stereo Vision. *Imaging*, 130(x):674–679, 1981.

[13] U. McMillan, L. (Sun Microsystems Inc., Research Triangle Park, NC and L. Westover. A forward-mapping realization of the inverse discrete cosine transform. In *Data Compression Conference*, pages 219 – 228, Snowbird, UT, USA, 1992.

[14] T. H. Myer and I. E. Sutherland. On the design of display processors, 1968.

[15] M. Nelson. *The Data Compression Book*. M&T Books, San Mateo, CA, 1992.

[16] H. Nirnimesh (Institute of Information Technology, P. Harish, and P. Narayanan. Garuda: A Scalable Tiled Display Wall Using Commodity PCs. *Visualization and Computer Graphics, IEEE Transactions on*, 13(5):864 – 877, 2007.

[17] K. A. Perrine and D. R. Jones. Parallel graphics and interactivity with the scaleable graphics engine. In *Proceedings of the 2001 ACM/IEEE conference on Supercomputing (CDROM) - Supercomputing '01*, Supercomputing '01, pages 5–5, New York, New York, USA, 2001. ACM Press.

[18] R. Shoup. SuperPaint: an early frame buffer graphics system. *IEEE Annals of the History of Computing*, 23(2), 2001.

[19] G. Stoll, M. Eldridge, D. Patterson, A. Webb, S. Berman, R. Levy, C. Caywood, M. Taveira, S. Hunt, and P. Hanrahan. Lightning-2: A High-performance Display Subsystem for PC Clusters. In *Proceedings of the 28th Annual Conference on Computer Graphics and Interactive Techniques*, number August in SIGGRAPH '01, pages 141–148, New York, NY, USA, 2001. ACM.

[20] B. Sung, S. H. Hwang, and V. Da Costa. DVI: A Standard for the Digital Monitor Interface, 1999.

[21] Vesa dpvl software interface standard: Version 1. Video Electronics Standards Association, February 2006.

[22] Vesa displayport: Version 1.1. Video Electronics Standards Association, April 2007.

[23] T. Whitted, J. Kajiya, E. Ruf, and R. Bittner. Embedded Function Composition. In *Proceedings of the Conference on High Performance Graphics 2009*, HPG '09, pages 47–50, New York, NY, USA, 2009. ACM.

Dependency-Aware Unequal Error Protection for Layered Video Coding

Mohammad Reza Zakerinasab
University of Calgary
Calgary, Alberta, Canada
mrzakeri@ucalgary.ca

Mea Wang
University of Calgary
Calgary, Alberta, Canada
meawang@ucalgary.ca

ABSTRACT

Layered video coding standards encode a high-quality video into multiple layers of unequal importance. Dependent layers that provide higher quality rely on their respective reference layers for successful reconstruction of transmitted video frames. Hence, if a video packet in a reference layer is corrupted or lost during transmission, all its dependent layers cannot be reconstructed successfully, and the resources consumed to transmit them are wasted. To address this problem, unequal error protection (UEP) techniques have been proposed to provide protection to each layer according to their importance. Nonetheless, the importance of a piece of video content is determined by not only the layering structure, but also visual features and encoding decisions. In this paper, we look deeper into the coding and prediction structure of layered encoded videos and model the the dependency among macroblocks and submacroblocks (the finest processing units of H.264 video coding standard) as a weighted graph. Based on this graph, we propose a dependency-aware UEP model that protects macroblocks according to their importance. Our simulation results show that the proposed UEP model outperforms the conventional UEP models for layered SVC videos by 3.76 dB of peak signal-to-noise ratio (PSNR) when the channel packet loss rate is as high as 28%.

Keywords

unequal error protection, video coding, video streaming

1. INTRODUCTION

Towards optimizing the rate distortion of encoded video sequences, *i.e.*, improving the quality of the encoded video subject to video bitrate and/or communication channel capacity, video encoders exploit the redundancy of visual information in time and scale domains. For example, in the case where a camera pans slowly through the scene or the scenery is stationary, the video sequence may be highly compressed without noticeable loss of quality due to high visual similarity in consecutive frames. In modern layered video coding standards, a *reference picture* refers to the picture (also referred to as frame) whose visual information is used to partially reconstruct past or future pictures. A *dependent picture* refers to the picture that stores differential information from reference picture(s). A picture may be a reference picture for some pictures and may also be a dependent picture depending on some other pictures at the same time. The original pictures are reconstructed based on the reference pictures and dependent pictures. In modern literatures for video encoding, the term *picture* and *frame* are used interchangeably. In this paper, we follow this convention.

MM'15, October 26–30, 2015, Brisbane, Australia.

ACM 978-1-4503-3459-4/15/10 ...$15.00.
DOI: http://dx.doi.org/10.1145/2733373.2806267 .

Reference pictures and dependent pictures may be organized into reference layer(s) or dependent layer(s), respectively. The video bitrate is reduced by storing the residual error of the predicted video signal in dependent layers. Layers are separate substreams inside a video bitstream for independent transmission. Since dependent layers consist of pictures depending on pictures in the reference layers, any noise (lost or corrupted video packets) in a reference layer may hinder the decodability of one ore more dependent layers, even if the dependent layers were received correctly. In this case, the resources consumed to transmit and decode the dependent layers are wasted. To deal with the noise introduced during transmission, unequal error protection (UEP) has been proposed to provide different levels of protection according to the importance of the to-be-protected data [9]. UEP has been applied to layered video streams to better protect video packets in reference layers [2, 5, 8, 13, 24]. However, these proposals do not consider the internal design of the video coding standard. In fact, they confront the problem as a general unequal protection problem between reference and dependent layers where, for example, data partitions in H.264/AVC [22] or multiple descriptions in MDC [3] can be substituted by the concept of layers in scalable video coding (SVC) [21].

In fact, the importance of a piece of video content is determined by not only the layering structure, but also visual features and encoding decisions [27]. To accurately model the importance of visual information in a video sequence, we look deeper into the coding and prediction structure of the state-of-the-art layered video coding standard, *i.e.*, Scalable Video Coding (SVC), and model the dependency among macroblocks and submacroblocks using a weighted dependency graph. In H.264 video coding standard family, macroblocks are rectangular blocks of 16×16 pixels inside each frame. Each macroblock may be divided to rectangular submacroblocks 4×4, 4×8, 8×4, 8×8, 8×16 or 16×8 pixels. Macroblocks and submacroblocks are the finest units processed by video encoders and decoders. Based on the fine granular dependency presented in the proposed dependency graph, we propose a dependency-aware UEP model that protects macroblocks and submacroblocks according to their importance. Our simulation results show that the proposed UEP model outperforms the conventional layer-weighted UEP models by 3.76 dB of peak signal-to-noise ratio (PSNR) for packet loss rates as high as 28%.

The remainder of this paper is organized as follows. Sec. 2 reviews existing proposals on UEP for layered video coding. Sec. 3 provides an overview of coding and prediction structure of SVC. Sec. 4 presents the proposed dependency-aware UEP model, followed by the performance evaluation in Sec. 5. Finally, Sec. 6 concludes the paper.

2. RELATED WORKS

Unequal error protection (UEP) is a special form of forward error correction (FEC) where stronger forward error correction code is used to protect more important data. The application of UEP in data transmission over noisy channels was first proposed in [14]. Since then the notion of unequal protection of data with different importance has been widely investigated. Nonetheless, existing research work on UEP for layer-coded video streaming can be summarized into two focuses: coding paradigms and importance measurements.

Coding paradigms: Any coding technique that can generate code at an arbitrary code rate can be used to provide unequal protection by applying stronger codes with more redundant data to protect important information. This has been verified by a performance comparison of using different random linear coding strategies for UEP of data over lossy packet erasure links [25]. Common coding techniques for UEP include rate-compatible convolutional codes (RCPC) [18], low-density parity-check (LDPC) codes [7], growth codes [20], expanding window fountain codes (EWFC) [16], and Raptor codes [17]. While the aforementioned work are mostly on packet erasure channels, *i.e.*, they set up the UEP mechanism in the application layer, there is a large body of research on UEP in the physical and transport layers using bit-level UEP schemes [10]. Since the focus of this paper is on dependency-aware unequal error protection of layer-coded videos in the application layer, we do not investigate different coding techniques and use general random linear codes as the FEC code in our UEP model.

Importance measures: There are many information in a video sequence that can be used as importance measures when applying UEP.

- *Layer information*: A basic importance measure of a video packet is the position of its corresponding video layer inside the layer dependency structure. For example, a video packet may contain information of a reference or a dependent picture, which can be used as an importance measure [28].
- *Data partitioning*: AVC generates three separate data partitions: header data, intra-predicted macroblocks (macroblocks that are predicted from macroblocks from the same picture), and inter-picture predicted macroblocks (macroblocks that are predicted from other pictures). In [17] and [22], this feature is used as the importance measure of corresponding video packets.
- *Bitrate of video frame*: In [28], the authors considered the bitrate of the encoded video frames as an importance measure. The rational of this design is that larger frames contain more information due to less compression. Similarly, in [16] and [17], the bitrate of video slices (a set of macroblocks) was used for the same purpose.
- *Slice order*: A experimental study showed that early slices are more important than the later ones [15]. Hence, in [15] the order of a slice in a frame can be used as an importance measure.
- *Error propagation zone*: Error propagation zone is the set of processing units (frames, slices, or macroblocks) that depend on a specific reference unit. In [8], error propagation zone of each frame is employed to create a hierarchy of importance levels.
- *Motion information*: In [19], the size of motion information of each slice is used as an importance measure at the slice level. Similarly in [6], motion energy, defined as macroblock size times the motion vector size, is used as the importance measure at the frame level.

In another related research domain, the flexible macroblock ordering (FMO) capability of H.264 family of video coding standards is utilized to dynamically associate the macroblocks to the slices [23]. This mechanism can be used to improve the performance of UEP mechanisms by keeping the macroblocks of the same importance level in the same slice. Due to page limit we do not discuss this problem here and leave it for future research.

We note that none of the proposed UEP mechanisms for layer-coded video streaming consider the internal design of the video codec standard in use. In fact, these UEP mechanisms can be used for any data with different importance levels, such as data partitions in H.264/AVC [26], multiple descriptions in MDC [3], and video layers in SVC [21]. While the generality of the proposed methods can be considered as an advantage, ignoring the internal design of video codec standards leads to less effective UEP due to inaccurate estimation of the importance of visual information encapsulated in each video packet. In this paper, we propose a UEP mechanism that considers the internal design of SVC, the state-of-the-art layered video coding standard.

3. PRELIMINARY

Before proposing the dependency-aware UEP for layered video coding, we need to have a deep understanding of layered video coding by inspecting a real layered video codec standard. Moreover, while the concept of dependency-aware UEP remains the same, as will be shown in Sec. 4, modeling coding dependency and calculating importance of video packets must be tailored for individual codec standard. In this paper, we resort to SVC [21] – the state-of-the-art layered video coding standard.

3.1 General Design of SVC

SVC supports three modes of scalability, *i.e.*, temporal, spatial and quality (SNR) scalability. Every SVC compliant bitstream contains a H.264/AVC compliant base layer and several enhancement layers. The base layer is needed to playback the video at its lowest quality. The quality improves as more enhancement layers become available. The quality of each layer may be denoted by the quality identifier tags: D (for spatial), T (for temporal) and Q (quality). For example, the base layer has $DTQ = (0,0,0)$. Each layer may use visual information from other layers with smaller or equal DTQ identifier tags. This creates a three-dimensional hierarchy of reference and dependent layers. As a part of the H.264 standard family, video compression in SVC is based on dividing each frame into one or more slices, where each slice is composed of a set of macroblocks. Furthermore, each macroblock can be further divided into a set of submacroblocks. Both macroblock and submacroblocks are the basic processing units for encoding and decoding operations in the H.264 standard family.

Each video sequence in SVC starts with an intra-coded picture (or I-frame). This is frame 0 of the base layer ($DTQ = (0, 0, 0)$) in Fig. 1. *Temporal scalability* is achieved by using a hierarchical temporal prediction structure that is defined by the size of group of pictures (GOP). In SVC, a group of pictures is a sequence of consecutive frames that starts with a key-picture (an I-frame or a P-frame, that is predicted from only one picture) and contains $2^n - 1$ bi-directionally predicted pictures (B-frames). Thus, $IB^{n-1}(PB^{n-1})^*$ represents the sequence of frames in a SVC video. In the example depicted in Fig. 1, the GOP size is 8. *Spatial scalability* is achieved through a layered approach, as illustrated in Fig. 1. SVC supports both dyadic and non-dyadic spatial layering. The dyadic configuration enforces the spatial layers to conform to a 2 : 1 resolution scale, and facilitates upsampling of reference spatial layers using bitwise shift operations. Finally, *quality scalability* is achieved by allowing different amount of quality improvement information to be embedded in the SVC video sequence as separate sub-streams.

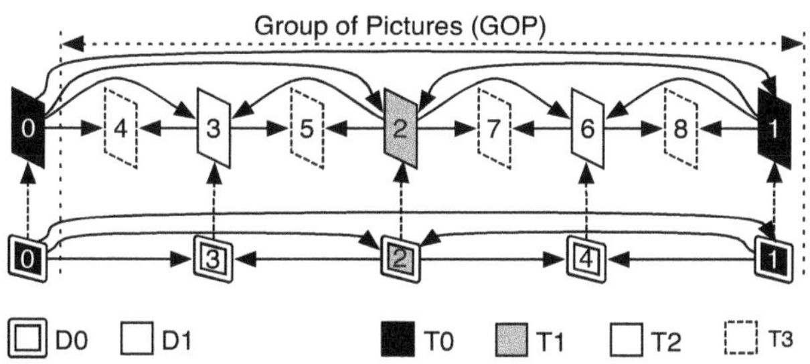

Figure 1: Layering design in a SVC video stream with two spatial and four temporal layers (D={0,1}, T={0,...,3}, Q={0}). Each frame is labelled with the coding order inside the respective spatial layer.

3.2 Coding and Prediction in SVC

Fig. 2 schematically illustrates the prediction in SVC in a tree structure. In SVC, enhancement macroblocks are created based on either temporal or spatial prediction. The quality enhancement information may be included if it is available. Temporal prediction is inherited from the AVC standard, in which the type of the predicted picture determines the possible prediction methods. For example, if the predicted picture is an I-frame, then the slices in this picture are I-slices and the macroblocks within each slice will be predicted from other macroblocks of the same slice. If the predicted picture is a P-frame, the slices in this picture might be I- or P-slices, at the discretion of the encoder. Similarly if the predicted picture is a B-frame, the slices might be I-, P- or B-slices, again at the discretion of the encoder. When encoding P- and B-slices, the intra-picture prediction is augmented with unidirectional and bidirectional inter-picture motion compensated predictions. Moreover, the encoder can also apply special predictions (modules enclosed in boxes with dashed borders in Fig. 2) in the order presented in Fig. 2 to derive motion vectors and reference picture lists from the reference macroblocks.

The general prediction modules available for spatial layering are similar to those for temporal layering, as illustrated in Fig. 2. Inter-layer prediction is used to predict the higher resolution spatial layer from the lower resolution layers. If a slice is an I-slice, inter-layer intra-prediction is used to create enhancement macroblocks. If the slice is a P- or B-slice, inter-layer motion-compensated prediction can be used too. SVC provides three additional inter-layer prediction modules to take advantage of similarities among the spatial layers, namely, motion vector prediction, reference index prediction, and residual signal prediction.

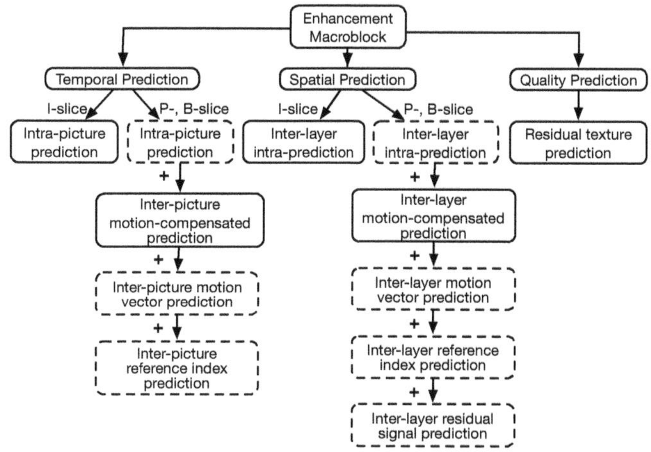

Figure 2: Prediction tree of the scalable video coding standard. The blocks with dashed lines may or may not exist at the discretion of the encoder.

As shown in Fig. 3, in a dyadic setting of spatial layering, each 16×16 macroblock of a dependent layer can be estimated from an 8×8 co-located submacroblock from the reference layer using upsampling operations. If the co-located submacroblock in the reference layer is a part of an intra-coded macroblock, the enhancement macroblock is obtained by inter-layer intra-prediction. If the co-located submacroblock is a part of an inter-picture coded macroblock, then inter-layer motion-prediction can be used. In this case, the enhancement layer contains only a residual signal, and the enhancement macroblock is constructed by upsampling the reference submacroblock and scaling its motion vector components by 2. Furthermore, the upsampled macroblock in dependent layer may extract the reference picture list and motion vectors from the reference submacroblock. Finally, as shown in Fig. 2, the inter-layer residual prediction allows the enhancement block to use the upsampled residual signal of the reference macroblock as a predictor for its own residual signal. Thus, only the difference between the predicted and real residual signal of enhancement macroblocks need to be coded in the enhancement layer.

It is worth to note that while spatial prediction can use a downsampled version of the same macroblock from a lower spatial layer as a reference, this may not always be the best prediction strategy. As a matter of fact, the inter-layer predictor usually has to compete with the temporal predictor. Especially for sequences with slow motion and high spatial detail, the temporal prediction signal likely represents a better approximation of the original signal than the inter-layer predictor does through upsampling a reference macroblock. Hence, the intra-layer dependency imposed by the temporal prediction is more important than the inter-layer dependency generated by the inter-layer predictor. This particular observation is the key motivation for considering macroblock level coding dependency instead of layer dependency when applying UEP to video packets.

For quality prediction, SVC quantizes the residual texture signal of enhancement layers with a relatively smaller quantization parameter (QP) than the one used in the lower quality layers so that more detail is retained in the enhancement

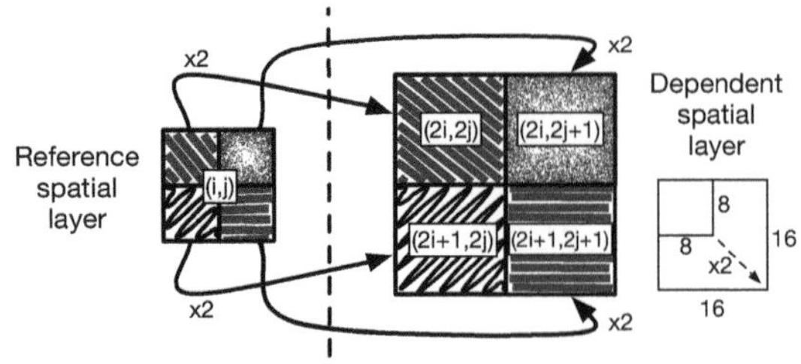

Figure 3: Spatial prediction with dyadic settings in SVC. Each 16×16 rectangle represents a single macroblock.

layer. SVC supports three quality scalable coding modes: CGS (coarse-gain scalable), MGS (medium-grain scalable) and FGS (fine-grain scalable). Since CGS does not provide a proper bitrate adaptability and FGS is computationally extra expensive, MGS is the better choice for most scenarios. MGS allows the transform coefficients of the enhancement layer to be divided into multiple subsets, thus allowing the encoder to create multiple quality enhancement layers from the residual signal and allowing the decoder to partially receive the quality information by dropping some packets.

3.3 Inspecting Macroblock Dependencies

As mentioned in Sec. 1 and Sec. 2, none of the proposed UEP mechanisms for layer-coded video streaming considers the internal design of the video codec standard in use. The brief review of coding and prediction in SVC in Sec. 3.2 reveals that strong dependency exists among pictures within a layer and across layers. We argue that ignoring the internal design of video codec standards leads to less effective UEP for three reasons. First, as mentioned in Sec. 3.2, temporal predictor and spatial predictor modules of SVC compete for the prediction of macroblocks. Hence, not all macroblocks of a frame in the higher spatial layer depend on the co-located submacroblocks in the reference spatial layer. The same dependency property also holds across temporal layers. Second, while P- and B-frames are allowed to use past and future pictures (in playback order) as references, the final coding decision is at the discretion of the encoder. For example, to encode a video with very high motion activity among consecutive frames, the encoder may use I-slices inside of a B-frame since the visual information from past and future pictures are not as useful to predict the current picture. Finally, when using inter-picture and inter-layer motion compensated prediction in temporal and spatial prediction, the encoder may decide to use extra information (such as motion vectors, reference picture lists and the residual signal) from the reference macroblock or submacroblock. Though these observations are drawn from inspecting SVC codec standard, similar observations can be drawn for other codec standards.

To verify the necessity of inspecting macroblock dependencies for more accurate estimation of the importance of video packets, we compare the prediction dependency found in seven raw video sequences. We encode all reference video sequences with a fixed layering configuration of DTQ = (2,4,0). There is no quality layer in this configuration since the quality prediction creates a fixed number of quality dependencies regardless the visual features presented in the video. The results are reported in [27]. The hypothesis of this experiment is that if layering dependency is sufficient to create a portrait of the dependency relations inside a video sequence (as assumed by previous works), all videos should have similar (temporal and spatial) dependency statistics since they are encoded using the same layering configuration. Instead we observe significant variations in temporal and spatial dependency. It is clear that layering dependency cannot properly model the underlying dependency relations of a video sequence. Dependency observed at the macroblock level can lead to an accurate dependency model for a video sequence since all predictions are performed at this level.

In summary, both the deep inspection of coding and prediction structure and the experimental results indicate that the large scale dependency among video layers is not sufficient to determine the importance of video packets or UEP. By considering dependency at the submacroblock/macroblock level (the finest processing unit of the H.264 family), we propose a more effective UEP model that provides a better protection for video packets.

4. DEPENDENCY-AWARE UNEQUAL ERROR PROTECTION

In this section, we present the design of the dependency-aware UEP for SVC. The design is based on a precise model of the dependency structure in the to-be-protected encoded video sequence. In Sec. 4.1 we describe how to model the coding dependency as a weighted acyclic dependency graph. Next, in Sec. 4.2, we illustrate how to calculate the importance of macroblocks and the video packets containing them, and how to use this calculated importance to provide appropriate level of protection for each video packet. At last, we present a practical implementation of the dependency-aware UEP in Sec. 4.3. Please note that although the proposed dependency-aware UEP model is explained in the context of SVC, it can be applied to other video coding standards with minor changes in the calculation of the dependency weight, as will be described in Sec. 4.1.

4.1 Modeling Coding Dependencies

To model the coding dependency in SVC, we introduce a dependency graph $\mathcal{G} = (V, A)$, which is a weighted directed acyclic graph (DAG). Each node $m_i \in V$ represents a macroblock and each directed arc $a_{i,j} \in A$ from m_i (dependent macroblock) to m_j (reference macroblock) indicating that m_i depends on m_j [1] Indirect dependency exists between two macroblocks m_i and m_k if there is a path from m_i to m_k in graph $\mathcal{G}$.

Generating the dependency graph: To generate the dependency graph $\mathcal{G}$, we extract coding dependencies among macroblocks while encoding a video sequence. More specifically, when encoding a new macroblock using SVC encoder, we add a new node to the dependency graph. For each prediction decision made by the encoder, we add an arc to the graph from the dependent macroblock to the reference macroblock. Fig. 4 shows a sample dependency graph with 6 nodes (macroblocks). Due to different prediction mechanisms employed in SVC, the effect of losing a reference macroblock on the dependent macroblocks may be severe or negligible. Therefore, we need to assign a proper weight to each dependency arc to indicate the level of dependency between two macroblocks. The resulting graph is a DAG, *i.e.*, no cycles exist in $\mathcal{G}$ since no two macroblocks can either directly or indirectly mutually depend on each other.

Setting weights of dependency arcs: The SVC encoder is equipped with a rate distortion module that calculates the

[1] Note that this notation is inverse of the traditional notation used in Fig. 1, where the dependency arcs are from reference frames to dependent ones.

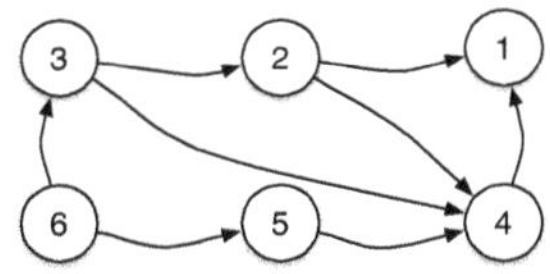

Figure 4: An example of a dependency graph with 6 nodes, where m_1 serves as an absolute reference macroblock and m_6 is not used by any other macroblock.

rate distortion cost of each permissible prediction mode as follows:

$$C_{i,j} = D_{i,j} + 0.85 \times 2^{(QP-12)/3} \times R_{i,j} \quad (1)$$

where i is the index of reference macroblock m_i, j is the index of dependent macroblock m_j, $D_{i,j}$ denotes the sum of absolute difference between pixels in the reference and dependent macroblocks, QP is the quantization parameter, and $R_{i,j}$ is the actual number of bits required to represent the residual signal of m_j. The prediction cost $C_{i,j}$ is inverse proportional to the prediction dependency, *i.e.*, lower prediction cost implies stronger dependency between two macroblocks.

Due to the delicate internal structure of SVC, sometimes the proper weight of a dependency arc in $\mathcal{G}$ cannot be calculated as easy as in Eq. 2. Both temporal and spatial prediction modules may use only a portion of a reference macroblock to predict a dependent macroblock. Moreover, the motion compensated prediction is not limited to the boundaries of the reference macroblocks. The dependency among macroblocks may be categorized into four cases, as illustrated in Fig. 5.

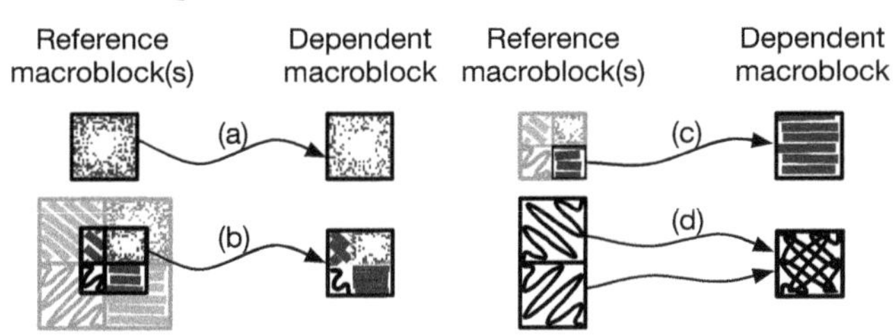

Figure 5: Different types of dependencies among macroblocks in SVC. (a) Using a full macroblock as a reference, (b) Using a macroblock created from portions of 2 or 4 macroblocks as a reference, (c) Using a submacroblock as a reference (after proper upsampling), and (d) Using multiple macroblocks as reference.

The weight of each dependency relation in each case may be calculated as follows:

- Using a full macroblock as a reference (Fig. 5(a)): The simplest prediction form is using a macroblock to predict another macroblock. In this case, we calculate the weight of each dependency relation as the inverse of the prediction cost, *i.e.*:

$$w_{i,j} = \frac{1}{C_{i,j}} \quad (2)$$

- Using a macroblock created from portions of 2 or 4 macroblocks as a reference (Fig. 5(b)): The prediction modules may use a 16×16 area located on the borders of two or four macroblocks as a reference macroblock. In this case, we add a dependency arc from the dependent macroblock to each of the macroblocks serving as a partial reference. The weight of each dependency arc is calculated as follows:

$$w_{i,j} = \frac{1}{C_{i,j}} \times \frac{S_{i,j}}{256} \quad (3)$$

where $S_{i,j}$ is the number of pixels of the reference macroblock that belongs to m_i. Compared to Eqn. 2, the weight of each arc representing a partial dependency is scaled according to the amount of visual information in the dependent macroblock predicted from the partial reference.

- Using a submacroblock as reference (after proper upsampling) (Fig. 5(c)): A submacroblock may be upsampled to serve as a whole reference macroblock. If the reference submacroblock belongs to a macroblock, there is only one arc from the dependent macroblock to the macroblock containing the reference submacroblock, as illustrated in Fig. 5(c). In this case, the weight of the arc is calculated the same way as in the case that a full macroblock is used as a reference. Thus, the weight of the arc is calculated as in Eqn. 2. If the reference submacroblock is located across boundaries of 2 or 4 macroblocks, similar to the case illustrated in Fig. 5(b), we add a dependency arc from the dependent macroblock to each of the macroblocks serving as a partial reference. The weight of each dependency arc is calculated as in Eqn. 3, except that constant in the denominator is 64 (representing the smaller size of 8×8 co-located submacroblock).
- Using multiple macroblocks as reference (Fig. 5(d)): A dependent macroblock may use multiple reference macroblocks and combine the result by, for example, taking an average over the predicted samples. In this case, the importance of each reference macroblock depends on the successful receipt and decoding of the other reference macroblocks. The quality of the reconstructed macroblock improves as more reference macroblocks become available. In this case, we add one dependency arc from the dependent macroblock to each of the reference macroblocks. The weight of each dependency arc is calculated as follows:

$$w_{i,j} = \frac{1}{C_{i,j}} \times \frac{1}{N} \quad (4)$$

where N is the number reference macroblocks. Since the availability of each reference macroblock is not known before transmitting the video packets, all reference blocks are equally important. Thus, each arc has an equal share of the full weight.

Since $C_{i,j}$ is explicitly calculated as a part of the encoding procedure, the calculation of $w_{i,j}$ is very quick in all four scenarios.

4.2 Dependency-aware Unequal Error Protection

Similar to AVC, in SVC, macroblocks of each video frame are grouped into one or more slices, where each slice is encapsulated into a VCL NAL unit and is sent over the network as a video packet. In this section, we propose a new dependency-aware UEP model. The proposed UEP model determines the importance of video packets according to the dependency captured in the dependency graph $\mathcal{G}$. The algorithm involves three steps. First, we calculate the importance of macroblocks according to the dependency graph $\mathcal{G}$. Next, we calculate the importance of video packets based on the importance of the encapsulated macroblocks. At last, we apply UEP to video packets according to their importance. The details of each step are provided below.

Calculating the importance of macroblocks: To calculate the importance of macroblocks, we create a topological sort $\mathcal{T}$, in which m_i is enlisted before m_j if m_i depends on m_j (*i.e.*, there is an arc from m_i to m_j in $\mathcal{G}$). Since $\mathcal{G}$ is a DAG, we can create $\mathcal{T}$ in linear time with complexity of $O(|V| + |A|)$ using algorithms like Kahn's topological sort algorithm [12]. Visiting nodes in $\mathcal{T}$ is the same as traversing $\mathcal{G}$ from macroblocks that are not used as a reference for any other macroblock (nodes with output degree of zero) to macroblocks that do not use any reference macroblock (nodes with input degree of zero).

We note that determining the importance of macroblocks based on the dependency graph resemble the calculation of page scores in information retrieval, where each page in the web is represented by a node and each link in the page is represented by an edge in the graph of web pages. For this reason, we adapt a variation of Page Rank [4] algorithm to determine the importance of all macroblocks.

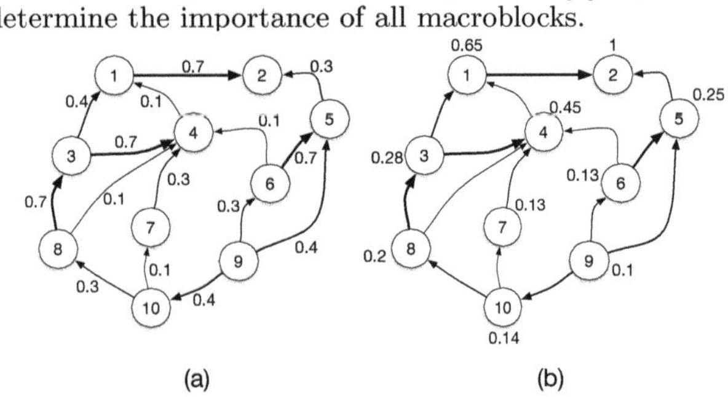

Figure 6: An example of a 10-node weighted dependency graph $\mathcal{G}$. Nodes represent macroblocks and arcs represent the dependencies. (a) Before propagating the weights. (b) After propagating the weights by traversing the nodes in topological order and updating the weight of reference nodes according to Eq. 5.

Given the dependency graph $\mathcal{G} = \{V, A\}$ and the topology sorting $\mathcal{T}$, we set the initial weights of all nodes to $w_{m_i} = 1/|V|$. For the example illustrated in Fig. 6, the initial weight of all 10 nodes is 0.1. We visit nodes in the dependency graph $\mathcal{G}$ according to their order in $\mathcal{T}$. For the 10-node sample dependency graph $\mathcal{G}$ in Fig. 6, one possible topological orders is $\{9, 10, 7, 6, 5, 8, 3, 4, 1, 2\}$. The topological sorting $\mathcal{T}$ guarantees that a reference macroblock is visited after all of its dependent macroblocks. This allows us to calculate the importance of a macroblock reflecting all direct and indirect dependency associated with it. Hence, the computation starts from the edge of the graph (the macroblocks without any dependent) and recursively moves towards the core of the graph (the macroblocks that do not depend on any macroblocks). When visiting a node $m_i \in V$, if there exists an arc $a_{i,j} \in A$, we update the importance of the macroblock j, *i.e.*, w_{m_j} as follows:

$$w_{m_j} = w_{m_j} + \sum_i \frac{w_{m_i} \times w_{i,j}}{\sum_k w_{i,k}} \tag{5}$$

The importance of a macroblock j is the initial weight of macroblock j plus the weighted average of the importance of all of its dependent macroblocks, where the weight of the importance of each dependent macroblock i is a normalized weight of arc $a_{i,j}$ among all outgoing arcs of node i. According to this algorithm, the weight of node 9 in Fig. 6 is 0.1 since it has input degree of zero. The weight of node 10 is $0.1 + (0.4 * 0.1/1.1) = 0.136 \simeq 0.14$. The computation complexity of this algorithm is $O(|A|)$. Once all nodes are visited, the importance values of all macroblocks are calculated.

Calculating the importance of video packets: The SVC encoder puts each video slice in one or sometimes more video packets. Hence, the importance of video packets is the same as the importance of the contained video slice. Since a slice s_i is a collection of macroblocks ($s_i = \{m_j\}$), the importance of s_i is determined by the importance of all macroblocks that form s_i. The average importance of contained macroblocks is a trivial candidate for calculating the importance of a video slice. However, due to different prediction types, the importance measure of video slices obtained from averaging importance of contained macroblocks sparsely distribute in large range. This tricks the UEP model to apply substantial different levels of protection to slices. Therefore, we moderated the importance measure by applying the natural logarithm operator to the average importance of the contained macroblocks as follows:

$$w_{s_i} = \ln(1 + \frac{\sum_j w_{m_j}}{n_{s_i}}) \tag{6}$$

where $m_j \in s_i$, and n_{s_i} is the number of macroblocks contained in s_i. Given the importance of slice s_i, the importance of the container video packet p_i is $w_{p_i} = w_{s_i}$.

There are two other types of video packets that do not contain slice sample data. A video packet may contain important header data for a series of consecutive coded pictures (a coded video sequence) or one or more individual pictures within the series. In this case, the importance of these video packets is the maximum weight of depending slices. A video packet may also contain supplemental enhancement information that can be ignored by the decoder. In this case, importance of such video packets is set to the minimum weight of all slices.

Unequal protection of video packets: The amount of protection bytes (N_{p_i}) associated to each video packet p_i should be proportional to the importance of the packet and packet's length. Thus, we calculate N_{p_i} as follows:

$$N_{p_i} = \frac{w_{p_i} \times l_{p_i}}{\sum_j w_{p_j} \times l_{p_j}} \times N \tag{7}$$

where N is the total number of available protection bytes, and w_{p_i} and l_{p_i} are the importance and length of packet p_i. The iterator j in the denominator iterates over all the video packets, including p_i.

4.3 Practical Implementation of the Proposed UEP Model

Although building the dependency graph and calculating importance measure take $O(|V|+|A|)$, the computation time may still be considerably long since both $|V|$ (number of macroblocks in a video) and $|A|$ (number of dependency links) can be very large. Moreover, the process requires a large amount of memory space to store the dependency graph and to carry out the calculations. In this section, we address these implementation challenges.

As illustrated in Fig. 7, we note that due to the closed GOP structure of H.264 standard family, the proposed dependency graph exhibits a special form of clustering. There is a dependency path among the key pictures in a video sequence, all other dependency arcs are confined between two consecutive key pictures. This clustering property inspires us to implement the algorithm in a divide-and-conquer manner. We may consider dependency among macroblocks from key pictures and dependency of macroblocks within each GOP as a smaller instance of the dependency-aware UEP model. We may solve each instance quickly using very little memory space.

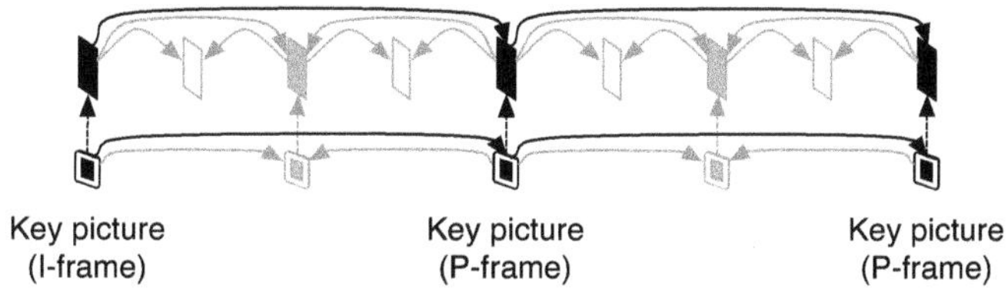

Figure 7: The prediction dependencies in a SVC video sequence with two spatial and three temporal layers. Dependency links between key pictures are shown in black. The grey links represent dependency among pictures between two consecutive key pictures.

Assume that we have the computing power to launch m computing instances of the proposed algorithm in parallel with the video encoder. We dedicate one computing instance to calculate importance of macroblocks from key pictures and importance of corresponding video packets. For clarity, we refer to macroblocks from key pictures as *key macroblocks* from here on. We refer to this computing instance as the main instance since it will run until importance of all video packets are calculated. The calculation of importance of a key macroblock requires the importance of its dependent macroblocks – key macroblocks in future GOPs and macroblocks within the same GOP. Recursively, the calculation of the importance of a key macroblock in a future GOP also requires the importance of key macroblocks in its future GOPs and macroblocks within the same GOP. The recursive relation still requires the main instance to consider all macroblocks in a video sequence. Thus, this instance requires large computing and memory resources. We note that the indirect dependencies decay rapidly as the playback times of two key pictures are more apart. Therefore, when calculating importance of macroblocks, the main instance can consider key macroblocks from n future GOPs and ignore the subsequent ones. We refer to n as the *key picture decay factor*. The value of n may be tuned according to visual features presented in the video sequence. For example, when running the algorithm for high motion video sequences, n can be as small as 4, because the visual similarity between consecutive video frames decays very fast.

When the video encoder proceeds with encoding the GOPs from the beginning of the video, in parallel to the main instance of the proposed algorithm, each of the other $m-1$ instances determines the importance of macroblocks within one GOP and the importance of corresponding video packets. As soon as a computing instance has the importance of macroblocks within one GOP, it passes the results to the main instance so that the importance of key macroblocks of the GOP may be updated. Once the importance of key macroblocks of GOPs $1 \dots n$ is updated, the main instance runs the algorithm on the key macroblocks of GOPs $1 \dots n$ and finalizes the importance of key macroblocks and respective video packets of GOP 1. GOP 1 is then removed from the graph. If $n \geq m-1$, the instance responsible for GOP 1 is re-assigned to the next unprocessed GOP. The same process is repeated for GOPs $2 \dots n+1$ and so on until all GOPs are removed from the graph. In this way, the main instance always keeps track of macroblocks of at most $n+1$ key pictures and other $m-1$ instances always keep track of macroblocks of GOP size plus one pictures.

If $n < m$, when the importance of key macroblocks of GOP n is updated, the main instance runs the algorithm on the key macroblocks of GOPs $1 \dots n$ and finalizes the importance of key macroblocks and respective video packets of GOP 1. Then it removes GOP 1 from the graph, frees the instance responsible for macroblocks of GOP 1, and associates the next available GOP to this instance. In this way, the main instance always keeps track of macroblocks of at most $n+1$ key pictures and other $m-1$ instances always keep track of macroblocks of GOP size plus one pictures. When all GOPs are processed, the main instance will also terminate.

Since the key picture decay factor cuts the continuity of the dependency in the video sequence, the result is suboptimal. In other words, we trade optimality for less computational complexity and the memory usage. For example, if we assume that each macroblock has two outgoing links on average, the proposed algorithm needs 16 GB of memory to store the dependency graph $\mathcal{G}$ for a 2-hour 24 fps HD video sequence. In comparison, the divide-and-conquer implementation requires less than 7 MB of memory when the GOP size and the parameter n are both equal to 8.

5. PERFORMANCE EVALUATION

To evaluate the performance of the proposed dependency-aware UEP model, we conduct a series of experiments using JSVM 9.19.15 software package. JSVM (Joint Scalable Video Model) is a reference software package for scalable video coding that provides encoding, decoding and video analysis tools. As illustrated in Fig. 8, we added two modules (the dependency logger module and the dependency graph module) to the SVC encoder provided by JSVM. The dependency logger module is wiretapped into the main video coding modules of the encoder, including GOP encoder, frame encoder, layer representation encoder, slice encoder, and macroblock encoder. This module extracts all dependency information by monitoring prediction and coding decisions during the encoding process. The dependency graph module uses the macroblocks dependency information compiled by the dependency logger module to generate the dependency graph as described in Sec. 4.1. This module also calculates the importance of video packets using the algorithm presented in Sec. 4.2. We implement the algorithm according to Sec. 4.3 for less computation overhead and memory demand. In these experiments the key picture decay factor is manually tuned.

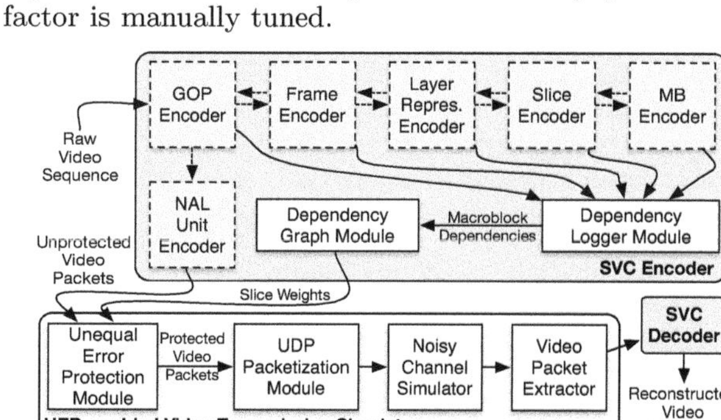

Figure 8: The architecture of the performance evaluation system. Components in grey are modified JSVM components and those in white are developed from scratch.

We also developed a UEP-enabled video transmission simulator, as illustrated in Fig. 8. The simulator consists of four modules: UEP module, UDP packetization module, noisy channel simulator, and video packet extractor. The simulator simulates the transmission of unequally error protected video packets over a noisy network channel. The encoded video packets with respective importance factors are sent to the UEP module. This module associates the proper amount of protection to each video packet using systematic Reed-Solomon codes. Since this paper focuses on determining the importance of a video packet rather than redesigning the coding scheme, an optimal coding scheme (RS) is used with recovery efficiency of 1. The coding scheme can be replaced with any coding scheme like LDPC or Raptor codes. The protected video packets are then sent to the UDP packetization module. This module disperses each video packet in 512-byte UDP datagrams at a rate such that the delay to the decoder is no more than 400 milliseconds. The simulation can be done in TCP as well. With TCP, although there is no end-to-end packet loss, a video packet that arrives after its playback deadline (due to TCP flow or congestion control) are considered lost by the decoder. Simulating the noisy channel in UDP gives us better control on the packet loss rate. Next, UDP datagrams are virtually transmitted over a packet erasure channel, where some packets are randomly dropped according to the channel's packet loss rate. On the receiver side, the video packets are extracted from the received UDP datagrams, and the video stream is reconstructed using a SVC decoder. The decoder is modified to calculate and report the peak signal-to-noise ratio of the reconstructed video.

The seven raw video sequences, as listed in Table 1, are selected from different genres. They also exhibit diverse values of the *detail* and *motion activity* visual features [11]. The detail feature provides a summary of the histogram descriptors in the video sequence, and the motion activity feature primarily captures the degree or intensity of scene changes. The reference raw video sequences are in YUV 4:2:0 format with frame size of 1280×720 pixels and frame rate of 24 fps [1], the standard sampling scheme for H.26x video coding standards. Since it takes hours to analyze a complete video and apply UEP, we select 10 seconds (240 frames) of each video in order to conduct all experiments in a reasonable amount of time. For video sequence that have movie titles at the beginning, *i.e.*, BB and ED, the first 1000 frames are skipped. Otherwise, the frames are selected from the beginning. We also verified that the details and motion activity features of the 10-second represent the average measurements of the corresponding video.

Table 1: Reference video sequences and their properties.

Content	Genre	Detail	Motion Activity
Big Buck Bunny (BB)	Animation	3.52	1.63
Elephants Dream (ED)	Animation	3.73	2.39
Pedestrian Area (PA)	Scene	3.15	4.42
Rush Hour (RH)	Scene	3.17	3.12
Park Joy (PJ)	Scene/Nature	4.24	3.73
Riverbed (RB)	Nature	4.72	4.13
Sunflower (SF)	Nature	4.04	2.57

The modified JSVM package and the transmission simulator enabled us to conduct a series of experiments to determine the effectiveness of the dependency-aware UEP model against the seven reference videos. All experiments are conducted on a server cluster of 10 nodes. Each server node is equipped with four Intel® Xeon® E5640 CPUs with four cores at 2.67GHz and 16GB of 1066MHz memory. To avoid the impact of multi-core operations on core performance and cache hit, we utilize only one core on each CPU and at most three CPUs on each machine.

5.1 Performance of Dependency-aware UEP

To evaluate the performance of the proposed dependency-aware UEP model, we encoded the reference video sequences listed in Table 1 using the fixed layering configuration of $DTQ = (1, 3, 1)$. We set the key picture decay factor to 16, *i.e.*, we assumed the importance of each key picture is negligible for the frames that are more than 16 GOPs away, which is equal to 128 frames or 5.3 seconds in playback. In this experiment, we vary the packet loss rate in the packet erasure channel from 0% to 28% with step size of 4%. In all experiments, the channel capacity is set to the video bitrate plus half of the expected packet loss rate so that there is sufficient bandwidth to carry the video streaming and the corresponding UEP data. To minimize randomness in the results due to random packet drops, we virtually transmitted each video sequence over the channel 10 times and report the average peak signal-to-noise ratio (Y-PSNR) of the received video. In theory, due to better protection of important video packets, the decoded videos should be in higher quality when using the dependency-aware UEP model. For comparison purpose, we implement four other error protection models:

- Equal error protection (EEP): All video packets are associated with the same importance measure for equal protection.
- Packet-weighted UEP (PW-UEP): The importance of each video packet is proportional to the number of bytes used to store the video packet [16, 17]. This model also resembles similar models that use the number of bytes needed to represent a slice or a frame as the importance measure of video packets.
- Layer-weighted UEP (LW-UEP): The importance of each layer is determined by considering the layers that depend on it [8, 28]. This model also resembles the UEP models based on error propagation zone as described in Sec. 2.
- Optimal model (Optimal UEP): The optimal UEP ensures that the most important packets are always protected so that the distortion in playback is minimal. Hence, only the least important packets are affected if losses occur during transmission. To simulate the optimal model, we select and drop the video packets that cause the least rate distortion. The number of packets to be dropped is determined by the channel loss rate.

Implementation of EEP and PW-UEP is straight forward. For LW-UEP, we use the algorithm proposed in [8]. This algorithm involves solving the distortion optimization problem over all video packets of a video sequence using all possible FEC (forward error correction) packets. Since the distortion decrease cannot be determined prior to transmission, we determine the parameter setting for this UEP model by running the algorithm for the RH video sequence with $DTQ = (1, 3, 1)$. Since the algorithm depends on only the layering information and the number of FEC packets, the same parameter setting shall provide the least distortion for other videos that share the same laying configuration. We select video RH because its visual properties and dependency statistics are close to the mean value of the other videos according to Table 1.

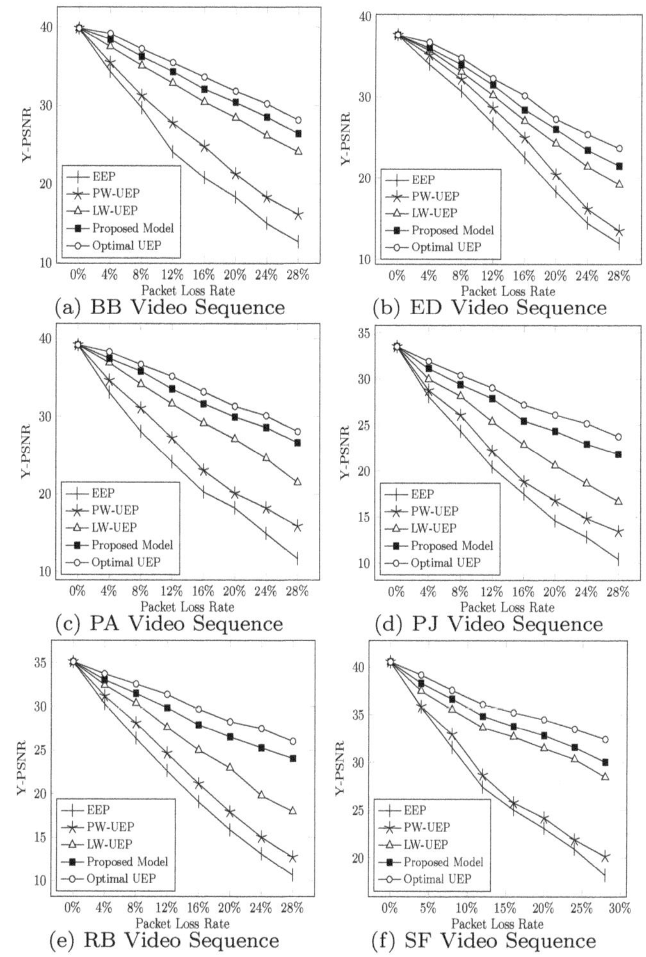

(a) BB Video Sequence (b) ED Video Sequence (c) PA Video Sequence (d) PJ Video Sequence (e) RB Video Sequence (f) SF Video Sequence

Figure 9: Performance of different UEP models over a packet erasure channel with varying packet loss rate and fixed layering configuration of DTQ = (1,3,1).

Fig. 9 provides the Y-PSNR measurements of videos reconstructed from video packets transmitted over channels with different loss rates. As expected, EEP performs the worst since protects all video packets equally. PW-UEP also provides low video quality. This is contributed by large video packets from the quality layer, which out-weights the importance of smaller video packets of other layers. Compared to EEP and PW-UEP, LW-UEP leads to much better video quality since it considers layer dependency and provides more protection to video packets from important layers. This is the improvement observed in existing UEP proposals for layered video coding. For all six videos, the proposed dependency-aware UEP model outperforms EEP, PW-UEP, and LW-UEP, and closely approximates the performance of optimal UEP. More specifically, the average quality of the video transmitted using the proposed model is 3.76 dB, better than that of LW-UEP when the packet loss rate is 28%. Results in Fig. 9 suggest that modeling coding dependencies provides a more accurate importance measure for UEP, which leads to better video quality.

Next, we examine the computation overhead of the proposed dependency-aware UEP model. According to Table 2, while the average computation overhead is less than 2.2%, the overhead noticeably varies among different videos. Consulting the visual properties of the videos in Table 1, we note that there is a strong correlation between the computational complexity and the amount of detail and motion activity of the videos. Hence, there are more dependency among macroblocks in videos with higher detail and motion activity (*i.e.* a dense dependency graph). For these videos, there are more dependency arcs to be processed for those videos. This implies higher computation overhead.

Table 2: Computation overhead of the proposed UEP model

Video Sequence	BB	ED	PA	PJ	RB	SF
Overhead	1.8%	1.6%	2.1%	3.2%	3.4%	2.4%

5.2 Generality of the proposed UEP model

In this section we investigate the sensitivity of the proposed UEP model to the layering configuration and frame size. We compare the Y-PSNR of the received videos under the setting used in Sec. 5.1 with those under two other settings. In one setting, we change only the frame size from HD to 480p, *i.e.* from 1280×720 pixels to 854×480 pixels. In the other setting, we change only the layering configuration from $DTQ = (1,3,1)$ to $DTQ = (2,4,3)$. Due to page limit, we only present the Y-PSNR readings from LW-UEP and the proposed UEP model with 28% packet loss rate in Table 3. Since LW-UEP protects video packets according to the layering dependency, by comparing with LW-UEP, we can determine the sensitivity of the proposed UEP model to layering configuration.

Table 3: Y-PSNR of the transmitted videos when varying the video specification.

Parameters	UEP Model	BB	ED	PA	PJ	RB	SF
HD videos,	LW-UEP	24.1	19.2	21.4	16.6	17.9	28.4
DTQ = (1,3,1)	Proposed	26.4	21.5	26.6	21.8	23.9	30.1
480p videos,	LW-UEP	23.7	16.3	18.9	14.7	17.1	26.0
DTQ = (1,3,1)	Proposed	25.9	18.2	23.1	18.3	22.4	27.6
HD videos,	LW-UEP	27.3	19.9	22.9	17.2	19.7	30.4
DTQ = (2,4,3)	Proposed	29.9	22.6	28.3	23.8	27.2	33.1

From Table 3, we observe that reducing the frame size leads to lower Y-PSNR in the reconstructed videos for both LW-UEP and the proposed UEP model. We also observe that Y-PSNR decreases slightly more when using the proposed UEP model. Hence, the proposed UEP model is more sensitive to changes in frame size. When changing the layering configuration from $DTQ = (1,3,1)$ to $DTQ = (2,4,3)$, the video bitrate increases, resulting in higher video quality. According to Table 3, the Y-PSNR is improved by 1.61 dB and 2.43 dB on average when using LW-UEP model and the proposed model, respectively. The change also leads to an increase in the gap between the average quality from these two models, from 3.76 dB to 4.58 dB. This is because that increasing the number of layers introduces more macroblocks and more dependency relationships. In this case, the proposed dependency-aware UEP model provides more precise UEP for video packets than LW-UEP does.

6. CONCLUSION

In this paper, we proposed a dependency-aware UEP model that protects macroblocks and submacroblocks according to their importance in encoding/decoding a video sequence. In contrast to existing frame-level UEP protection based on layer dependency, the proposed UEP model provides more precise protection for video packets. The performance evaluation of the proposed dependency-aware UEP model confirms that the proposed model outperforms layer-based and other previously proposed UEP models. In future research, we plan to investigate the dynamic adjustment of key picture decay factor. We will also explore how the dependency information may be used to improve other aspects of video streaming.

7. REFERENCES

[1] Xiph.org Test Media collection, http://media.xiph.org.

[2] S. Ahmad, R. Hamzaoui, and M. Al-Akaidi. Unequal Error Protection Using Fountain Codes with Applications to Video Communication. *IEEE Transactions on Multimedia*, 13(1):92–101, 2011.

[3] E. Baccaglini, T. Tillo, and G. Olmo. Image and Video Transmission: A Comparison Study of Using Unequal Loss Protection And Multiple Description Coding. *Multimedia Tools and Applications*, 55(2):247–259, 2011.

[4] S. Brin and L. Page. The Anatomy of a Large-scale Hypertextual Web Search Engine. *Computer Networks and ISDN Systems*, 30(1):107–117, 1998.

[5] H. Cai, B. Zeng, G. Shen, Z. Xiong, and S. Li. Error-Resilient Unequal Error Protection of Fine Granularity Scalable Video Bitstreams. *EURASIP Journal on Advances in Signal Processing*, 2006.

[6] H. Dung and S. Vafi. An Adaptive Unequal Error Protection Based on Motion Energy of H.264/AVC Video Frames. In *IEEE Conference on Wireless Communications and Networking Conference (WCNC'13)*, pages 4594–4599, 2013.

[7] C. Gong, G. Yue, and X. Wang. Message-wise Unequal Error Protection Based on Low-Density Parity-Check Codes. *IEEE Transactions on Communications*, 59(4):1019–1030, 2011.

[8] H. Ha and C. Yim. Layer-weighted Unequal Error Protection for Scalable Video Coding Extension of H. 264/AVC. *IEEE Transactions on Consumer Electronics*, 54(2):736–744, 2008.

[9] U. Horn, K. Stuhlmüller, and M. Link. Robust Internet Video Transmission Based on Scalable Coding and Unequal Error Protection. *Signal Processing: Image Communication*, 15(1):77–94, 1999.

[10] Y. Huo, M. El-Hajjar, and L. Hanzo. Inter-Layer FEC Aided Unequal Error Protection for Multilayer Video Transmission in Mobile TV. *IEEE Transactions on Circuits and Systems for Video Technology*, 23(9):1622–1634, 2013.

[11] S. e. a. Jeannin. MPEG-7 Visual Motion Descriptors. *IEEE Transactions on Circuits and Systems for Video Technology*, 11(6):720–724, June 2001.

[12] A. B. Kahn. Topological Sorting of Large Networks. *Communications of the ACM*, 5(11):558–562, 1962.

[13] E. Maani and A. K. Katsaggelos. Unequal Error Protection for Robust Streaming of Scalable Video over Packet Lossy Networks. *IEEE Transactions on Circuits and Systems for Video Technology*, 20(3):407–416, 2010.

[14] B. Masnick and J. Wolf. On Linear Unequal Error Protection Codes. *IEEE Transactions on Information Theory*, 13(4):600–607, 1967.

[15] S. Nazir, V. Stanković, I. Andonović, and D. Vukobratović. Application Layer Systematic Network Coding for Sliced H.264/AVC Video Streaming. *Advances in Multimedia*, 2012:1–9, 2012.

[16] S. Nazir, V. Stankovic, and D. Vukobratovic. Expanding Window Random Linear Codes for Data Partitioned H.264 Video Transmission over DVB-H Network. In *18th IEEE International Conference on Image Processing (ICIP'11)*, pages 2205–2208, 2011.

[17] S. Nazir, V. Stankovic, and D. Vukobratovic. Unequal Error Protection for Data Partitioned H.264/AVC Video Streaming with Raptor and Random Linear Codes for DVB-H Networks. In *IEEE International Conference on Multimedia and Expo (ICME)*, pages 1–6, 2011.

[18] V. Pavlushkov, R. Johannesson, and V. Zyablov. Unequal Error Protection for Convolutional Codes. *IEEE Transactions on Information Theory*, 52(2):700–708, 2006.

[19] H.-D. Pham and V. Sina. Unequal Error Protection of H. 264/AVC Video Bitstreams Based on Data Partitioning and Motion Information of Slices. In *IEEE International Conference on Signal Processing, Communication and Computing (ICSPCC 2012)*, pages 634–639, Hong Kong, China, August 2012.

[20] R. Razavi, M. Fleury, M. Altaf, H. Sammak, and M. Ghanbari. H.264 Video Streaming with Data-Partitioning and Growth Codes. In *IEEE 16th International Conference on Image Processing*, pages 90–912, 2009.

[21] H. Schwarz, D. Marpe, and T. Wiegand. Overview of the Scalable Video Coding Extension of the H. 264/AVC Standard. *IEEE Transactions on Circuits and Systems for Video Technology*, 17(9):1103–1120, 2007.

[22] T. Stockhammer and M. Bystrom. H.264/AVC Data Partitioning for Mobile Video Communication. In *International Conference on Image Processing (ICIP'04)*, volume 1, pages 545–548, 2004.

[23] N. Thomos, S. Argyropoulos, N. V. Boulgouris, and M. G. Strintzis. Robust Transmission of H.264/AVC Streams using Adaptive Group Slicing and Unequal Error Protection. *EURASIP Journal on Applied Signal Processing*, 2006:1–13, 2006.

[24] D. Vukobratovic and V. Stankovic. Unequal Error Protection Random Linear Coding for Multimedia Communications. In *IEEE International Workshop on Multimedia Signal Processing*, pages 280–285, 2010.

[25] D. e. a. Vukobratovic. Unequal Error Protection Random Linear Coding Strategies for Erasure Channels. *IEEE Transactions on Communications*, 60(5):1243–1252, 2012.

[26] T. Wiegand, G. J. Sullivan, G. Bjontegaard, and A. Luthra. Overview of the H.264/AVC Video Coding Standard. *IEEE Transactions on Circuits and Systems for Video Technology*, 13(7):560–576, 2003.

[27] M. R. Zakerinasab and M. Wang. Inspecting Coding Dependency in Layered Video Coding for Efficient Unequal Error Protection. In *Proc. of the 35th IEEE International Conference on Distributed Computing Systems (ICDCS)*, pages 1–2, Columbus, Ohio, June 29 - July 2 2015.

[28] X. Zhang, X. Peng, D. Wu, T. Porter, and R. Haywood. A Hierarchical Unequal Packet Loss Protection Scheme for Robust H.264/AVC Transmission. In *6th IEEE Consumer Communications and Networking Conference (CCNC 2009)*, pages 1–5. IEEE, January 10-13 2009.

HiFi: A Hierarchical Filtering Algorithm for Caching of Online Video

Shahid Akhtar
Velocix
Alcatel-Lucent
Plano, TX, USA
shahid.akhtar@alcatel-lucent.com

Andre Beck
Bell Labs
Alcatel-Lucent
Naperville, IL, USA
andre.beck@alcatel-lucent.com

Ivica Rimac
Bell Labs
Alcatel-Lucent
Stuttgart, Germany
rimac@bell-labs.com

ABSTRACT

Online video presents new challenges to traditional caching with over a thousand fold increase in number of assets, rapidly changing popularity of assets and much higher throughput requirements.

We propose a new hierarchical filtering algorithm for caching online video—HiFi. Our algorithm is designed to optimize hit-rate, replacement rate and cache throughput. It has an associated implementation complexity comparable to that of LRU.

Our results show that under typical operator conditions, HiFi can increase edge cache byte hit-rate by 5-24% over an LRU policy, but more importantly can increase RAM or memory byte hit-rate by 80% to 200% and reduce replacement rate by 90%! These two factors combined can dramatically increase throughput for most caches. If SSDs are used for storage, the much lower replacement rate may also allow substitution of lower cost MLC based SSDs instead of SLC based SSDs.

We extend previous multi-tier analytical models for LRU caches to caches with filtering. We develop a realistic simulation environment for online video using statistics from operator traces. We show that HiFi performs within a few percentage points from the optimal solution which was simulated by Belady's MIN algorithm under typical operator conditions.

Categories and Subject Descriptors

B.3.2 [**Memory Structures**]: Design Styles—*Cache memories*; C.2.4 [**Computer-Communication Networks**]: Distributed Systems—*Client/server.*

General Terms

Algorithms, Performance, Design.

Keywords

Hierarchical cache, online video, hit-rate, LRU, LFU, GDSF.

1. INTRODUCTION

Online video is now the largest component of Internet traffic [20]. It is kept in small chunks of time of typically between 2 and 10 seconds and each video may be encoded into multiple video quality levels. This chunking technique can increase the number of files that can be requested by end users in a caching system by a thousand fold or more. Increasingly a significant part of the online video is used to rebroadcast recent TV shows or news related programs which are initially quite popular but rapidly drop in popularity [2]. The huge volume of online video requires that caches be extremely scalable, which implies that caching algorithms need to be highly compute efficient. One method which is used for high scalability is SSD memory, which has much faster access times. However SSD memory is known to have a limited number of write cycles in its lifetime. SSD memory with higher number of lifetime write cycles is typically more expensive.

MM '15, October 26-30, 2015, Brisbane, Australia
© 2015 ACM. ISBN 978-1-4503-3459-4/15/10…$15.00
DOI: http://dx.doi.org/10.1145/2733373.2806268

Despite a long history of caching research only simple schemes like Least Recently Used (LRU), Greed Dual Size Frequency (GDSF) or Least Frequently Used with Dynamic Aging (LFU-DA) have been implemented in known caching software such as Apache Traffic Server, Squid or Varnish [23][9]. The key impediments to practical use have been a perceived implementation complexity of the algorithms, which can impede throughput performance, and an expectation that the value of additional caching performance may be outweighed by factors such as ability to adapt to asset popularity changes.

In this paper, we propose a novel algorithm for online video caches—HiFi, that aims to address the above requirements. It achieves near optimal hit-rate and a low replacement rate, has low implementation complexity which is comparable to that of LRU which allows it to scale for caches that have very large number of assets. The main contributions of this paper include: (i) a brief survey of caching schemes with focus on suitability for handling online video; (ii) the design and derivation of the HiFi algorithm and its implementation with *O(1)* compute complexity; (iii) an extension of previous work of an analytical model of LRU caches to represent the impact of using filtering algorithms such as HiFi; (iv) a realistic simulation model for online video using statistics from operators traces; (v) a performance evaluation of HiFi and comparison with prominent state-of-the-art caching schemes and optimal performance using Belady's MIN algorithm [3].

The remainder of the paper is structured as follows. We provide background and a brief survey of caching algorithms in section 2. We then propose our new algorithm and its implementation in section 3, and its analytical model in section 4. We present the simulation methodology in section 5; discuss the results in section 6 and our conclusions and future work in section 7.

2. BACKGROUND

There has been a significant amount of research in making the right or optimal decision to place an asset in a given cache and when to remove it. The right decisions can improve the cache performance in terms of hit-rate, byte hit-rate, replacement rate and how quickly the cache responds to changes in asset libraries. This research can be organized in three main categories: cache eviction algorithms, hierarchical cache asset placement algorithms and cache cooperation algorithms.

Cache eviction algorithms apply to a single cache and try to optimize the decision of evicting the right assets from the cache. Some well known examples are LRU and LFU; LRU is most often used in today's caches.

Hierarchical caching algorithms are an enhancement to the single server cache eviction algorithms. These determine where to place an asset given a hierarchy of caches and a set of demands for each asset at each edge cache. Most practical hierarchies have only few levels, often no more than three [21].

Cache cooperation algorithms control exchange of assets between caches in the same level of hierarchy [13][26]. These allow edge caches to store lower amounts of data than hierarchical caches as they can "co-operate" or ask a neighboring cache when a cache does not have a given asset. However research shows that hierarchical caches produce lower latency and consume less overall bandwidth [18] than cache cooperation algorithms. In addition, many operators prefer to use hierarchical caches since existing operator transport and IP networks are often designed in a hierarchical fashion and their operations are aligned with the hierarchical nature of these networks.

We discuss below caching algorithms for single and hierarchal caches and how well they suit the requirements for online video.

2.1 Single Cache Algorithms

The work in [24] classifies cache eviction algorithms in four categories: recency focused, frequency focused, recency and frequency in equal focus and functional algorithms which typically also use the size and cost of each asset. The cost is a parameter representing the effort required to bring the asset to the cache running the eviction algorithm.

Typically recency based approaches like LRU produce lower hit-rates than other approaches. LRU allows all assets to be inserted in the cache whenever there is a cache miss. This allows unpopular assets to be inserted in the cache, which lowers hit-rate. Perfect LFU, which tracks the popularity of all assets is shown to produce the optimal hit-rate [5][22] when asset popularity is static. With dynamic changes in asset popularity, such as the case with online video, Perfect-LFU does not perform well. Window-LFU [22], on the other hand can produce near optimal results if its window size is optimized for traffic dynamics. However, Window-LFU needs a sorted list of all assets. Since the number of assets for online video can be very large; 100 million assets or more as we explain later, this is a significant issue, both from a storage perspective and a compute perspective as each new asset or asset popularity change requires at least $O(logN)$ time to find the right place in a sorted list.

Window-LFU is an example of recency and frequency based approach since its window acts as a recency filter. Function based approaches introduce the concept of including the cost and size of each asset; GD [19] and GDSF [16] are key examples. However they do not produce near-optimal hit-rates and do not need to track all assets.

There has been some work to develop caching algorithms that have low compute requirements. In [1], the authors show an LFU algorithm data structure that can process a new asset in $O(1)$ time only. The algorithm is based on a data structure that keeps all assets with the same count in a list and this list is connected to a master list which is sorted according to asset count. So when the count of an asset is increased or decreased by one, the algorithm only needs to look at the neighbor in the master list to determine if the asset needs to be moved to the next element in the master list. This algorithm breaks down if the asset count is done for a given time window or if the sorting is based on a more continuous variable such as exponential moving average, when the asset may need to be moved to an arbitrary location away from its current location.

In [5], the authors use a bloom filter to reduce storage requirements for a LFU solution when the number of assets to be tracked is very large. Bloom filters allow reduction in storage at the expense of some errors in asset popularity counts. However, they do require multiple hashes to be calculated per asset. Each hash is quite an expensive operation from a compute perspective – so it does not appear to be a solution for online video where minimizing compute requirement is also an objective.

Size is used in many of these approaches to remove assets of larger size first, which tends to increase overall hit-rate as many smaller sized assets can be accommodated in the cache due to the removal of one larger sized asset. However, this may not increase the byte hit-rate. For online video caches, the individual assets are chunks of video encoded at different transmission rates. Chunks are generally in the 2 to 10 second range. If the cache preferably removes chunks of larger size, which are likely to be for higher Video Quality (VQ) levels, then the client player of the video would often find that chunks of the higher VQ levels are not available at the leaf cache, and would have to fetch these from the higher level caches, which would likely reduce the transmission speed of the larger chunks, and the client may conclude that the higher VQ levels are not sustainable. For this reason, the use of size in the cache eviction algorithms for online video is not recommended.

The use of cost per asset is most valuable if the assets are fetched from different source caches, so the evicting cache could preferably evict assets whose cost is lower. If all the assets are fetched from the same origin server then using a cost parameter per asset may not be as valuable. We do not use cost in our algorithms - we leave that for further work.

2.2 Hierarchical Cache Algorithms

These determine where to optimally, or near optimally place a given asset in a tree based hierarchy of caches. We list some of the key techniques below.

2.2.1 Simple Techniques

Leave Copy Down (LCD) [17] is a technique in which all the caches in every level of hierarchy are required to record a number of requests for the same asset before making the decision to store that asset in the local cache. The most common approach is to use the cache hierarchy number; for example in a three layer hierarchy, the edge cache would not cache until it sees the third request for the same asset.

Move Copy Down (MCD) [17] is similar to LCD, however if all caches at a level have a certain asset, their immediate parent cache would remove that asset from its store. This technique does require some inter cache per asset communication. Practical testing shows slight improvement over LCD, but not in all cases.

The filter algorithm outlined in [7] keeps a characteristic time TC_k per cache in hierarchy level k as well as an average of all assets' inter-arrival time T_{ij} of the ith asset at the edge cache j. The characteristic time is defined as the average time an asset spends in the cache without being requested before it is evicted. According to the algorithm, the asset is kept only in the hierarchy level k if:

$$TC_{k-1} < T_{ij} < TC_k \quad (1)$$

The above equation applies to the hierarchy above edge cache j. We find some problems with this approach. If a higher level cache has multiple caches attached to it at the level immediately below, then the asset inter-arrival time used at the higher level cache should be a function of all those multiple caches' inter-arrival times at the edge. Further, according to the same algorithm, an asset is added to a cache's parent if that asset is removed from it. This is to make sure that an asset always remains in the hierarchy, from the leaf cache to the top cache, but at only one level. However, it is not guaranteed that the edge inter-arrival time T_{ij} of a given asset would be lower than the characteristic time of the immediately higher layer cache in order to satisfy the above equation. The filter algorithm performed significantly worse in a comparison with the LCD and MCD algorithms [17]. We believe the above issues are key contributors to that lower performance.

Another issue with all of the above hierarchical algorithms is that they need to collect information on every asset seen by the cache; in the case of LCD and MCD – number of requests for a given asset and in the case of the filter algorithm, the average inter-arrival time; however unlike Window-LFU, this list of assets does not need to be sorted. With online video caches, the number of assets can become exceeding large, which can make collection of statistics for all assets expensive from a storage perspective. If the statistics for all assets cannot be kept in the memory of a cache, they need to be transferred to disk storage. Frequent access to disk storage can reduce the throughput performance of a cache.

2.2.2 Globally Optimal Techniques

A number of researchers have proposed techniques to obtain an optimal set of asset locations in a set of connected caches; key examples are [11][12]. These techniques have generally very high computational requirements of the order of $O(N^3)$, where N is the typical number of assets in the cache. In online video caches, each asset is a small chunk of the total video and there are multiple video quality levels defined for each video. For a single hour of video with 6 quality levels and 2 second chunks, over 10,000 chunks may be needed. For a 10,000 asset video library, this could amount to over 100 million chunks! Types of adaptive video such as smooth-streaming or Apple's HLS may require different packaging for the same video, which can further add to the number of assets. Algorithms needing more than $O(N)$ with such a large number of assets would typically be infeasible in this environment.

2.2.3 Greedy Techniques

Other researchers have proposed local greedy algorithms to obtain a near optimal set of asset locations [10][14]. In [14], the authors propose that for each request sent upstream in a hierarchy for a given asset; each caching node along the way would add the request rate for that specific asset and the total request rate seen at that node. This combined set of information would be sent to the node that eventually serves the request, which would make a local decision on what locations along the asset path should store the asset based on the collected information along the path.

Another set of researchers have proposed a similar algorithm in the context of energy efficiency [10], which collects information about the energy required for the transport of an asset from each hop that it traverses—in the simplest case the energy is proportional to the hop count. This information is used at the receiving node to derive the energy power benefit, which is defined as the difference between the transport costs for that asset to bring it to the node minus the storage cost for that asset divided by the asset's request inter-arrival time. Assets are sorted and then inserted and evicted based on their power benefit ranking.

These techniques are generally much more feasible than the global optimal techniques. However they rely on information about the path cost of a given asset based on when the request was made. If an asset was evicted from a parent node after the request was made, the path cost of that node in the child would become invalid. Since the asset eviction is based on the average inter-arrival time, they may also require tuning of the period used for calculating the inter-arrival time.

3. A NEW CACHING ALGORITHM

We now define a new caching algorithm for hierarchical caches. We based it on the requirements for caching online video as explained in earlier sections.

This algorithm runs at each cache in a given hierarchy independent of the algorithm in other caches. Each cache estimates the inter-arrival time of each asset locally. Each cache also calculates its characteristic time, which we define as the average time an asset stays in cache without being requested before the asset is evicted. Each cache then only stores assets whose inter-arrival time is smaller than the cache's characteristic time. The eviction policy is the same as LRU, i.e., the least recently requested item is evicted first. We define the algorithm further below.

3.1 Nomenclature

Per-asset variables:

T_{ijk}	Average inter-arrival time of asset i for cache j in hierarchy k.
P_{ijk}	Previous time asset i was requested from cache j in hierarchy k.

Per-cache variables:

TC_{jk}	Characteristic time of cache j in hierarchy k.
TS	Current time.

Parameters for the cache hierarchy:

w_{TC}	Weight for the exponential moving average of the characteristic time.
w_{IA}	Weight for the exponential moving average of inter-arrival times.
GS	Gentle slope parameter on how quickly TC_{jk} is increased over time.

3.2 Hierarchical Filtering (HiFi) Algorithm

Before the main algorithm is run, a few variables are initialized as follows:

- Set all P_{ijk} to the current time TS.
- Set all T_{ijk} to a large number, but smaller than the number used for initial value for the characteristic times TC_{jk}. This allows all assets to be cached until TC_{jk} is updated to a real value.
- Set all TC_{jk} to a large number, larger than the number for T_{ijk}.

At the time of every LRU asset eviction in a given cache, we calculate the exponential moving average (EWMA) of the characteristic time TC_{jk} as follows, assuming asset i was evicted:

$$TC_{jk} = w_{\text{TC}} \times (TS - P_{ijk}) + (1 - w_{\text{TC}}) \times TC_{jk} \tag{2}$$

Whenever an asset is requested from any cache, whether it is a leaf cache or a higher layer cache, we calculate the EWMA of the inter-arrival time of asset i at that cache using the exponential moving average weight w_{IA} as follows:

$$T_{ijk} = w_{\text{IA}} \times (TS - P_{ijk}) + (1 - w_{\text{IA}}) \times T_{ijk} \tag{3}$$

We then set the previous time P_{ijk} to the current time:

$$P_{ijk} = TS \tag{4}$$

At the time of every request for a given asset i; if the asset is not currently in the cache, we check if the asset inter-arrival time T_{ijk} is less than the characteristic time TC_{jk} of the cache, and if yes, we cache that asset; and perform an LRU eviction if there is no space for that asset. If the above test fails we obtain the asset from the cache's parent and deliver to the client without ever storing the asset in the cache, which is often implemented on non-volatile storage such as disks. This provides key value as it allows greatly reduced disk input-output, which is often the bottleneck for most caches. In case the asset is available in the cache, we deliver the asset from the cache.

A peculiar case was observed with this algorithm. Given that an asset is only stored in a cache if its inter-arrival time T_{ijk} is less than the characteristic time TC_{jk}, this would imply that during heavy traffic, the TC_{jk} for a given cache would be lower since the inter-arrival time for all assets is expected to be lower during this time. In the case when this same cache is serving traffic during low traffic, TC_{jk} would remain at this lower level since TC_{jk} is only updated by a LRU asset eviction event. An asset eviction can only happen if the cache tries to store a new asset. During periods of low traffic the check if the inter-arrival time of the asset is lower than the characteristic time of the cache would fail more often. In this case the characteristic time TC_{jk} of the cache may become stuck at a low value. In our scheme the cache characteristic time TC_{jk} of a given cache is always gently increasing to avoid this. We update TC_{jk} at every asset request as follows:

$$TC_{jk} = TC_{jk} + GS \times (TS - P_{ijk}) \tag{5}$$

We limit the total number of assets whose inter-arrival time T_{ijk} is being tracked by the following:

$$T_{ijk} < S_f \times TC_{jk} \tag{6}$$

Where S_f determines a sensitivity factor of how much error is allowed from the best hit-rate achievable from the algorithm. In deriving the above equation, we assume that the inter-arrival time of the same asset is Poisson. This is a good assumption as the inter-arrival time of requests for whole assets is likely to be from different users and therefore should be close to Poisson. A given chunk in an asset is likely to be re-requested from different users, which would make the inter-arrival time of the same chunk also Poisson assuming that the time from the beginning of an asset to a given chunk is approximately deterministic. Then the probability of a single inter-arrival time being less than T_X is given by the following; where T_A is the average inter-arrival time.

$$Pr_i\,(t < T_X) = 1 - e^{-\frac{T_X}{T_A}} \tag{7}$$

If we limit tracking of assets with any single inter-arrival time larger than S_f times TC_{jk}, then the probability that we would miss an asset whose average inter-arrival time is less than or equal to TC_{jk} is:

$$Pr(Miss) \leq e^{-\frac{S_f \times TC_{jk}}{TC_{jk}}} \tag{8}$$

This becomes e to the power of $-S_f$ and using S_f equal to 5 gives a probability of 0.67% for a miss. We use 5 as the value of S_f for the rest of the paper.

3.3 Data-Structures to Support HiFi

We define two lists for maintaining the inter-arrival times. URL_{TRAK} is a list that keeps the EWMA of the inter-arrival time of assets as calculated in equation (3). We define another list URL_{OOL}; a "one occurrence list" which keeps track of assets whose request has only been seen once.

We define an asset block per asset which is shown in Figure 1; it may be accessed via a hash or tree or some other combination data structure based on the URL of the asset, as is typical in today's operating caches where the cache is required to check if a new asset request is currently cached. Such a lookup may not be *O(1)* with respect to the number of assets *N*, however the incremental computation due to the HiFi algorithm is *O(1)*. Each asset block contains a timestamp, when the asset was last requested and also contains pointers to three additional blocks: *OOL*, *TRAK* and *Cache*. Each of these blocks contain two pointers so these blocks can be part of a doubly linked list as well as a pointer back to the main asset block. The *Cache* block may contain details of any asset currently stored in the cache. Such details would typically be stored in operating caches today and are not described here; our proposal is to link such blocks of data to the new blocks, *TRAK* and *OOL*.

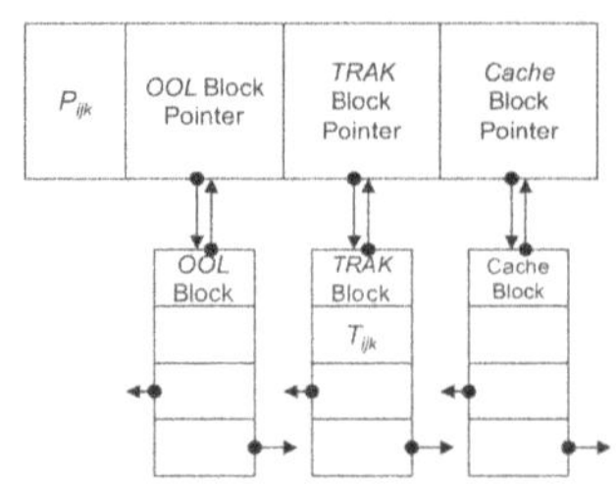

Figure 1: Asset Block

The value of linking the *Cache* block to the asset block is to allow an access data structure to point to all data for a given asset, since running multiple hashes or tree structures can significantly add to the compute time per asset. If a hash structure is used to access the asset, mechanisms may be needed to resolve hash conflicts; we do not describe these here since they are well known and beyond the scope of the paper.

Figure 2 shows how the two doubly linked lists *TRAK* and *OOL* would be arranged. These two lists should never share an asset. Each of these two lists would maintain pointers to their head and tail blocks. Both of these lists would be sorted in the order of the time the last request was seen for that specific asset. Assets would be removed from each of these lists based on the LRU policy as described in the algorithms later. Each block in the list would be connected to the asset block via a bi-directional pointer. The list of *Cache* blocks, which is not shown in Figure 2, would have assets which are a subset of the *TRAK* list. Below are algorithms that show methods to add new assets using the *TRAK, OOL* and *Cache* lists. We do not describe how assets are added or deleted in the *Cache* list as these would be done in typical operating caches today.

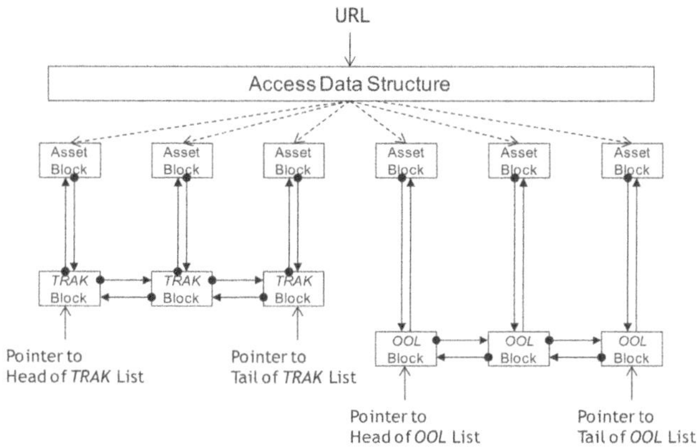

Figure 2: Asset Block with TRAK and *OOL* Lists

Table 1: Parameters used with HiFi Data structures

URL_i	The URL associated with asset *i*.
URL_{TRAK}	A doubly linked list made up of *TRAK* blocks where each block also connects to the asset block via bi-directional pointers.
S_f	A constant that defines the largest inter-arrival time of a given asset that will be allowed to be stored in the URL_{TRAK} list as a function of TC_{jk}.
URL_{OOL}	A doubly linked list made up of *OOL* blocks where each block also connects to the asset block via bi-directional pointers.
TRAK_size	The current size of the URL_{TRAK} list in terms of number of assets, initialized to 0.
TRAK_limit	The maximum size of the URL_{TRAK} list. This allows the operator to set a limit on the memory used for *TRAK* list.
OOL_size	The current size of the URL_{OOL} list in terms of numbers of assets, initialized to 0.
OOL_limit	The maximum size of the URL_{OOL} list. This allows the operator to set a limit on the memory used for *OOL* list.

In addition to the definitions in Table 1, P_{ijk}, *TS*, T_{ijk} and TC_{jk} which are used in the algorithms below are as defined in section 3.1. When a new asset request is seen, its asset block is accessed via an access data structure as described earlier. If an asset block exists, it is determined if the asset is in the URL_{TRAK} list or the URL_{OOL} list or neither based on the blocks attached to the main asset block. Algorithms A, B or C are run based on this result. Algorithm C is also run if no asset block is attached for the asset. In these algorithms, we do not define operations on any doubly-linked lists as these are well known.

Briefly, Algorithm A updates the inter-arrival time of the incoming asset and stores it in the URL_{TRAK} list. Algorithm B removes the asset from the URL_{OOL} list, since the second occurrence of the asset has occurred and adds it to the URL_{TRAK} list if its inter-arrival time meets the required criterion. Algorithm C adds the new asset to URL_{OOL} list.

Algorithm A:

If (URL_i is in URL_{TRAK} list) **begin**
  $P_{ijk}=TS$
  Update T_{ijk} for asset *i* as per equation (3)
  If ($T_{ijk} > S_f \times TC_{jk}$) **begin**
    Remove asset URL_i from URL_{TRAK} List
    TRAK_size--
    For the asset removed from URL_{TRAK} list remove asset block if there is no *Cache* block connected
    end
  else
    Move asset *i* to head of URL_{TRAK} list
  end

Algorithm B:

If (URL_i is in URL_{OOL} list) **begin**
  $P_{ijk}=TS$
  Remove URL_i from URL_{OOL} list
  Remove *OOL* block from asset block *i*
  OOL_size--
  If ($TS-P_{ijk} < S_f \times TC_{jk}$) **begin**
    If ($TRAK\_size \geq TRAK\_limit$) **begin**
      Remove one asset from tail of URL_{TRAK} list
      TRAK_size--
      For the asset removed from URL_{TRAK} list remove its asset block if no *Cache* block is connected to it
      end
    Add *TRAK* block to asset block of asset *i* with $T_{ijk}= TS-P_{ijk}$
    Insert asset *i* to head of URL_{TRAK} list
    TRAK_size++
    end
  else
    Remove asset block for asset *i*
  end

Algorithm C:

if (asset not in URL_{TRAK} or URL_{OOS} lists) **begin**
  If no asset block allocated for *i*, allocate a new one
  $P_{ijk}=TS$
  If ($OOL\_size \geq OOL\_limit$) **begin**
    Remove one asset from the tail of URL_{OOS} list
    OOL_size--
    Remove asset block for this asset
    end
  Insert asset *i* to head of URL_{OOL} list
  OOL_size++
  end

Whenever assets are removed from either of the doubly linked lists URL_{TRAK} or URL_{OOL}, the pointers of the two neighbours of the removed asset are set to point to each other to keep the list continuous. If the asset to be removed is at the head or the tail of the list, the head or the tail pointer is set to point to the neighbour next to the removed asset and its pointer towards the removed asset is set to NULL. Whenever assets are added to either list at the head, the new head pointer points to the new asset and the new asset is connected by bi-directional pointers to the asset previously at the head of the list.

4. Analytical Model for Caches with Filtering

In this section we derive the hit-rates achievable with the LRU and filter policies via analytical means. We define the filter policy as the long term behaviour of the HiFi algorithm without the approximations due to EWMAs, the data structures or equations (5) and (6) and with static popularity of assets. Also all assets are assumed to be the same size; this is to allow analytical tractability of the solution. We do the analysis to compare the hit-rates achievable with the filtering policy with the LRU policy and optimal hit-rates. The analysis is for a two layer cache hierarchy which assumes one edge cache and one parent cache feeding traffic to the edge cache. More complex topologies can derived from the same analysis, we use this simple topology for ease of understanding.

We do not completely show the derivation of the hit-rate for a LRU based cache for either the edge cache or the parent cache, for details on this please refer to [7] and [15], where [15] shows the multi-tier version of the analysis derived in [7]. The following are definitions of variables used in the analysis. We modify the earlier nomenclature for simplicity, the cache location *j,k* is dropped as only two caches are studied.

Table 2: Parameters for Analysis of LRU and filter policies

C	Number of assets that can be stored in the cache, we use the same for both the edge and parent caches.
N	Total number of assets in the library.
M	The asset number where the inter-arrival time of that asset is larger than the characteristic time of the filtering algorithm T_F at the edge cache.
T_i	The average of inter-arrival time of asset i at the edge cache.
T_C	The characteristic time of the edge cache with a LRU policy.
p_i	Probability of a request for asset i among all requests at the edge cache.
T_{F0}	The characteristic time of the edge cache with a filter policy.
T_{F1}	The characteristic time of the parent cache with a filter policy.
f_P	Probability distribution function of the popularity of asset requests at the edge cache.
R_{F1}	Replacement rate ratio at the parent cache with the filter algorithm.
λ_{i0}	The request rate for asset *i* at the edge cache.
λ_{T0}	The total request rate for all assets at the edge cache.
λ_{i1}	The request rate for asset *i* from the edge cache to its parent.
μ_{L0}	The hit-rate for all assets at edge cache with LRU policy.
μ_{F0}	The hit-rate for all assets at edge cache with filter policy.
μ_{F1}	The hit-rate for all assets at parent cache with filter policy.

4.1 LRU based caches

From [7] the following equation is derived to determine the characteristic time T_C:

$$\sum_{i=1}^{N} Pr_i\,(t < T_C) \approx C \tag{9}$$

Where $P_i\,(t<T_C)$ is the probability that the inter-arrival time of the next request for asset *i* is less than T_C and N is large. If we assume Poisson inter-arrival times and that the average inter-arrival time of asset *i* is T_i, then:

$$Pr_i\,(t < T_C) = 1 - e^{-\frac{T_C}{T_i}} \tag{10}$$

The request rate λ_i is calculated based on the request rate for all assets and the fraction of it for asset *i* is as follows:

$$\lambda_{i0} = \lambda_{T0} \times p_i \tag{11}$$

Using the equations (9) (10), (11) and that T_i is $1/\lambda_{i0}$, we solve for T_C numerically. From [7], we note that the request rate of asset *i* by the edge cache from its parent cache is:

$$\lambda_{i1} = \lambda_{i0} \times e^{-\lambda_{i0} T_C} \tag{12}$$

Using the value of T_C obtained from the earlier equations and using equation (12), we obtain the hit-rate at the edge cache as:

$$\mu_{L0} = 1 - \frac{\sum_{i=1}^{N} \lambda_{i0} \times e^{-\lambda_{i0} T_C}}{\sum_{i=1}^{N} \lambda_{i0}} \tag{13}$$

4.2 Filtering Policy based Caches

To derive the hit-rate with the filter policy at the edge cache, we define a characteristic time with the filter policy as T_{F0}. We also assume that the *Mth* asset will have an average inter-arrival time which is just larger than the filter value T_{F0} and that assets are ranked from 1 to N based on their popularity, with 1 being the most popular. Using equation (11) for λ_{i0}, we obtain the following:

$$\frac{1}{\lambda_{T0} \times p_M} \geq T_{F0} \tag{14}$$

From the above and using the inverse of the popularity function, we obtain M as follows:

$$M \geq f_P^{-1}\left(\frac{1}{\lambda_{T0} \times p_M}\right) \tag{15}$$

To obtain T_{F0}, we use the same reasoning as in equation (9), except that the assets which can be stored in the cache are a subset of the total set of assets as assets with inter-arrival time larger than T_{F0} (*Mth* asset and higher) would be rejected. We derive the following assuming M is large:

$$\sum_{i=1}^{M-1} Pr_i\,(t < T_{F0}) \approx C \tag{16}$$

We solve for T_{F0} numerically in a similar manner as the LRU version based on the above equation and equations (15), (10) and (11). Once T_{F0} and M are known we can obtain the hit-rate at the edge cache as:

$$\mu_{F0} = 1 - \frac{\sum_{i=1}^{M-1} \lambda_{i0} \times e^{-\lambda_{i0} T_{F0}} + \sum_{i=M}^{N} \lambda_{i0}}{\sum_{i=1}^{N} \lambda_{i0}} \tag{17}$$

The *Mth* asset and higher will pass right through the edge cache. In a two layer hierarchy, the request rates to the second layer of the hierarchy are given by equation (11) for the LRU case. For the case with the filter policy, the request rates are as below based a single edge cache:

$$\lambda_{i1} = \begin{cases} \lambda_{i0} \times e^{-\lambda_{i0} T_{F0}} & \forall i < M, \\ \lambda_{i0} & \forall i \geq M. \end{cases} \tag{18}$$

These rates are then used in equations similar to the edge cache level to determine the hit-rate, however, since, at the 2nd tier, the probability distribution function of the popularity of asset i is no longer continuously increasing as i increases, we change equation (16) with the following to state that this equation is valid only if the inter-arrival time of asset i to the parent cache is less than T_{F1}, where λ_{i1} is based on equation (18):

$$\sum_{i=1}^{N} Pr_i\,(t < T_{F1}) \approx C \;\forall\; \frac{1}{\lambda_{i1}} < T_{F1} \qquad (19)$$

We use equations (19), (18), (10) and that T_{i1}, the inter-arrival time of asset i at the parent cache, is $1/\lambda_{i1}$ to solve for T_{F1} numerically. T_{F1} should be used in an equation similar to equation (17) to determine the hit-rate, however, since the probability distribution function for the popularity of asset i is no longer continuously increasing with respect to i, we obtain the following for the hit-rate at the parent cache:

$$\mu_{F1} = 1 - \frac{\sum_{i=1,\frac{1}{\lambda_{i1}}<T_{F1}}^{N} \lambda_{i1} \times e^{-\lambda_{i1}T_{F1}} + \sum_{i=1,\frac{1}{\lambda_{i1}}\geq T_{F1}}^{N} \lambda_{i1}}{\sum_{i=1}^{N} \lambda_{i1}} \qquad (20)$$

The replacement rate is defined as the fraction of its downstream traffic requested by the cache from its parent that actually is stored in its cache. The replacement rate with the LRU policy is simple. It is one minus the hit-rate at that cache. The replacement rate with the filter policy is the rate of traffic requested from the upstream cache whose inter-arrival time is less than the filter value since only that traffic is stored in the cache, for example the replacement rate at the parent level with the filter policy is as follows:

$$R_{F1} = \frac{\sum_{i=1,\frac{1}{\lambda_{i1}}<T_{F1}}^{N} \lambda_{i1} \times e^{-\lambda_{i1}T_{F1}}}{\sum_{i=1}^{N} \lambda_{i1}} \qquad (21)$$

4.3 Analytical Performance Comparison

Using the analytical model we simulated a two tier hierarchy of caches to evaluate how well the filter algorithm would perform against the LRU policy in typical operator conditions as well as against a policy which assumes that the most popular C assets are always in the cache, which is optimal for static popularity distributions.

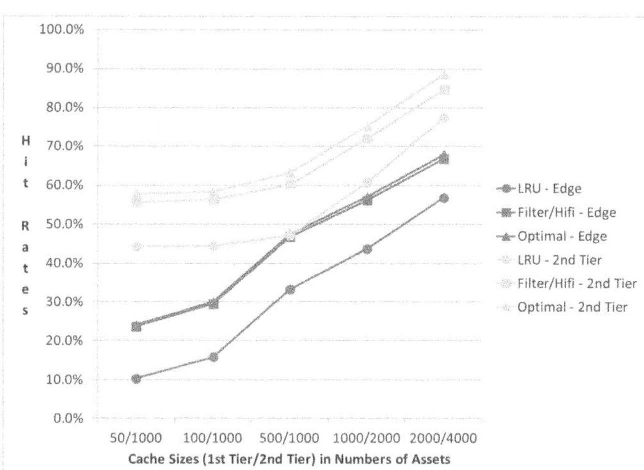

Figure 3: Hit-rate performance using analysis

We assume a 10000 asset library and a popularity function as Zipf with alpha equal to 0.8. A two layer cache hierarchy is used with a single edge cache and a parent cache. Edge cache sizes used were 500, 1000 and 2000 to simulate typical edge cache storage capacities. The cache size used at the parent cache was always two times the size at the edge cache. Two additional combinations were used to simulate the hierarchical caching often implemented in commercial caches where a small cache using RAM or memory is followed by a larger disk cache. For this we used 50 and 100 assets at the RAM cache and 1000 assets at the disk cache.

From Figure 3, a comparison of the filter policy with the LRU policy indicates that for very small cache sizes such as that available in typical RAM based caches, hit-rate can more than double from the LRU policy to the filter policy. With typical edge cache sizes, for example an edge cache size of 1000 or 10% of the total library capacity, hit-rate at the edge cache can increase by 30% as function of the LRU hit-rate and the combined hit-rate for the two tier hierarchy can increase by 20%; also as a function of the LRU hit-rate. A comparison of the filter policy with the optimal policy shows that the filter policy is within 1-2% of the optimal policy for the cache sizes studied.

Running the same analysis with a Zipf popularity function with an alpha value of 0.6, we note that the advantage of the filter policy over the LRU policy significantly improves. We also evaluated the replacement rate difference between the filter and LRU policies as a ratio, for caches sizes of 5% to 40% of the library size; it varied between 10-45 in favour of the filter policy.

5. SIMULATION METHODOLOGY

Simulation of online video caching presents additional challenges since each video is made up of many small chunks. The number of chunks, which would need a discrete event in a simulation, is perhaps 1000 or 10000 times more than a non-chunk based simulation, which makes a simulation using a real trace highly compute intensive if hundreds of simulations runs are required to evaluate multiple caching situations. In our simulation runs, which we explain later, we needed to have each run continue for 35 days of simulation time which would have been prohibitively expensive if each chunk required a discrete event. We build a synthetic simulation environment using statistics form real traces. We match the popularity curve of online videos; the abandonment rate once a client starts watching an online video; the VQ rates and their probability of being requested; the injection rate of new assets and the popularity decay of assets to statistics obtained from real traces.

5.1 Topology

We simulated a two layer caching hierarchy within a single edge cache. The cache is split into a RAM cache and 4 disk caches, with each cache operating its own eviction policy. The selection of a disk for a given asset was based on a hash of its URL. Many real caches operate with this kind of architecture, for example ATS [9]. We simulated two such caches feeding into a higher layer cache; however we did not model an additional RAM cache at the higher layer cache as it will likely not achieve a significant hit-rate. The size of the higher layer cache was always two times the size of the edge cache.

5.2 Modeling Library Dynamics

We model temporal locality in the stream by injecting new assets on a regular basis and decaying their popularity. As reported in [2], statistics from real traces show that the evolution of popularity of an asset is governed by a decaying process. An asset i experiences on the first day τ_i of its lifecycle an initial request rate $R_i(\tau_i)$, which decays exponentially with rate σ_i on the subsequent days.

$$R_i(t) = \begin{cases} 0 & \forall t < \tau_i, \\ R_i(\tau_i) \cdot e^{-\sigma_i(t-\tau_i)} & \forall t \geq \tau_i. \end{cases} \quad (22)$$

During an arbitrary observation window W starting at time τ_L and ending at τ_H, the total number of references for any observed asset in W is given by summing up the above over W:

$$\hat{R}_i = \sum_{t=\tau_L}^{\tau_H} R_i(t) \quad (23)$$

In a static model, asset popularity is typically described by the empirical distribution of asset reference counts observed over a given and large W. It has been shown that asset popularity for online can be approximated sufficiently accurately with a Zipf distribution [8]. Given an empirical popularity distribution (or its approximation), we can extract the number of references $\hat{R}_i$ for any asset i and using power series expansion we derive the following expression for the initial number of requests:

$$R_i(\tau_i) = \hat{R}_i \frac{e^{-\sigma_i \tau_i}(1 - e^{-\sigma_i})}{e^{-\sigma_i \tau_L} - e^{-\sigma_i(\tau_H - 1)}} \quad (24)$$

To simplify the model, we neglect non-stationary effects such as assets ingested before the beginning or at the end of W.

5.2.1 Modeling Asset Lifecycles

We simulate two types of assets, movies and TV shows. All assets are of 60 minutes length and caches. The cache at the second tier was always set to hold two times the number of assets as the leaf caches. We inject assets for 750 TV shows every day and assets for 1250 movies every week, which totals to 7000 assets per week with a shows-to-movies ratio of 4.2:1. We choose the exponential popularity decay rates for all movies uniformly distributed in the range [0.05, 0.2] and for the TV shows uniformly distributed in the range [0.3, 0.5], which seem reasonable values based on the findings reported in [2] and observations from our own data sets.

5.2.2 Modeling Online Video

We model early user abandonment, which can occur with online video by splitting each asset into five parts where the user can abandon watching the asset after any of these parts. We used abandonment rates of 55, 5, 5, 5 and 30 percent after each one of the five parts based on the statistics in [25]. We modeled four VQ levels for adaptive streaming video at 4.5, 3, 1.5 and 0.75 Mbps. The relative percentages of the client requesting each of the above VQ levels was set to 70, 15, 10 and 5 percent respectively based on our own data sets. Both of these two effects together add significant variation in the size of assets requested by the client.

5.2.3 HiFi Parameters

We estimate the best values for the EWMA weights w_{TC} and w_{IA} by considering the marginal asset in the cache, that is the least popular asset expected to be in the cache. This asset would have an inter-arrival time of approximately TC_{jk}. We want to make sure that we have an accurate estimate of its inter-arrival time at least by the time the asset's popularity has halved. We assume λ_A as the decay rate of the marginal asset in days. The decay rate of the average asset is the average of the two kinds of assets movies (average decay rate 0.125) and TV shows (average decay rate 0.4) which comes to 0.347, using the ratio between the two mentioned earlier. Using the above we derive the w_{IA} as:

$$w_{IA} = \frac{\lambda_A \times TC_{jk}}{-\ln(0.5)} \quad (25)$$

Where the value of TC_{jk} is assumed to be in days. We use a value which is 10 times lower for w_{TC} as TC_{jk} variation is very low. We then did a sensitivity analysis of both of these values; varying w_{IA} by a factor of 4 either way did not produce a change in any of the hit-rates by more than 1% and changing w_{TC} by a factor of 10 either way did not produce a change in hit-rates by more than 0.1%.

For setting the gentle slope parameter GS, we set it so that the value of the characteristic time TC_{jk} would double in a 24 hour period, if it is not reset by the latest eviction time from the cache.

5.3 Other Caching Algorithms Simulated

We compare the HiFi algorithm to the performance of the LRU, GDSF and LCD algorithms. We simulate GDSF as it is one of most popular algorithms used in today's operating caches other than LRU [9]. We also simulated the LCD algorithm, which performed the best amongst hierarchical algorithms [17].

6. RESULTS AND DISCUSSION

For the simulation results, we derive the byte hit rate and the replacement rate, which is defined as the percentage of incoming traffic at a given cache that leads to a replacement in its cache. We also discuss cache throughput, which is the maximum traffic a given cache can serve.

6.1 Simulation Setup

We built a simulation environment according to the earlier section and ran an initial simulation with all the different algorithms for 35 days with an average request rate of 130,000 requests per day at each leaf cache. Using the VQ levels, probabilities and early abandonment rates mentioned in section 5.2.2, this corresponds to 10.3 Gbps as the average cache throughput.

We start the simulation with an empty library and continuously increase the library size over this period by injecting new assets as described in section 5.2. We observed relatively stable hit-rates after 7 days, which indicates that the effective library size had approximately become a stationary process. This is reasonable since at this point in time the earlier injected assets produce very few requests as their popularity decays down to negligible levels. Thus, we report all of the simulation statistics between the 7th day and the 35th day of simulations. Using the decay rates from section 5.2.1, and assuming that TV assets decay to negligible levels in 7 days (using the 40% decay rate, they decay to less than 2% of their initial value), we estimate the number of active assets in the library range from 6500 to 11500 between day 8 and day 35, with an average of 9000 assets. With this effective size, asset injection rates as in section 5.2.1 correspond to approximately 10% new assets every day.

6.2 Results

Using a 50 asset RAM cache and 4 250 asset disk caches (sizes based on highest VQ level only), we obtained the byte hit-rates shown in Figure 4 for the edge cache. HiFi significantly outperformed LRU at the RAM level by about 80% to 200%. At the overall edge cache level HiFi improved byte hit-rates by about 20-40% with respect to their values with LRU. It is remarkable that HiFi significantly outperforms the LCD algorithm, even though LCD keeps track of all assets whereas HiFi only tracks a subset of assets. GDSF performed the best amongst the other algorithms for most scenarios.

We show byte hit-rates with different cache sizes, both at the RAM and overall edge cache levels in Figure 5, using a Zipf alpha value of 0.8. Byte hit-rates tended to be very similar to hit-rates in terms of ratios between the different policies, but slightly higher.

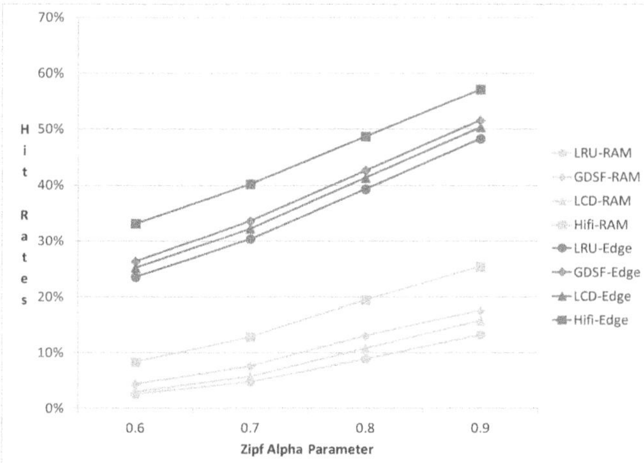

Figure 4: Byte hit-rates with different Zipf alpha values

The improvement in byte hit-rate between the LRU and HiFi policies was between 24% (1000 asset edge cache) to 4.5% (4000 asset edge cache). In the same set of simulations; the byte hit-rate difference between the LRU and HiFi policies for the combined cache hierarchy ranged between 20% (1000 assets) down to 2% (4000 assets).

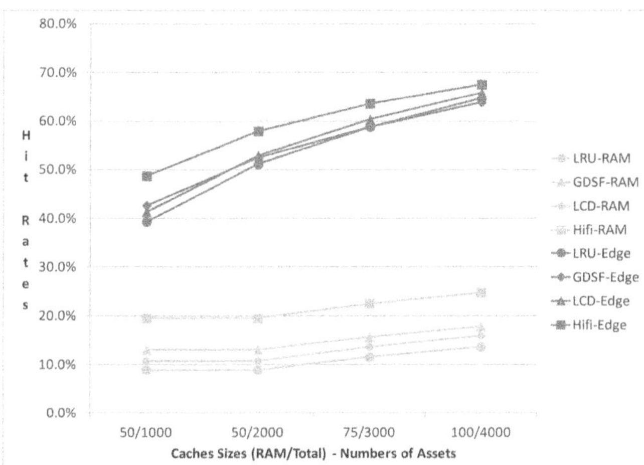

Figure 5: Byte hit-rates with different cache sizes

We report the replacement rates at the both RAM and disk levels in Figure 6, which uses the same set of assumptions as in Figure 4. We note that the replacement rate difference between HiFi and LRU at the RAM level is between 35 and 24 times and at the disk level between 7 and 8 times. We calculate the composite replacement rate for the entire cache, including the RAM as follows:

$$RR_{COMPOSITE} = RR_{RAM} + (1 - BHR_{RAM}) \times RR_{Disk} \qquad (26)$$

Where RR represents replacement rate and BHR, byte hit-rate. We include the replacement rate at the RAM level in the composite level since most caches tend to copy cache contents in the RAM on disk to make sure the cache contents are available in case of a restart. Figure 6 also shows the composite replacement rate which shows a difference between HiFi and LRU policies at a 14 to 15 times improvement. We found at least a 10 times improvement in the composite replacement in all the different scenarios shown in Figures 4 and 5.

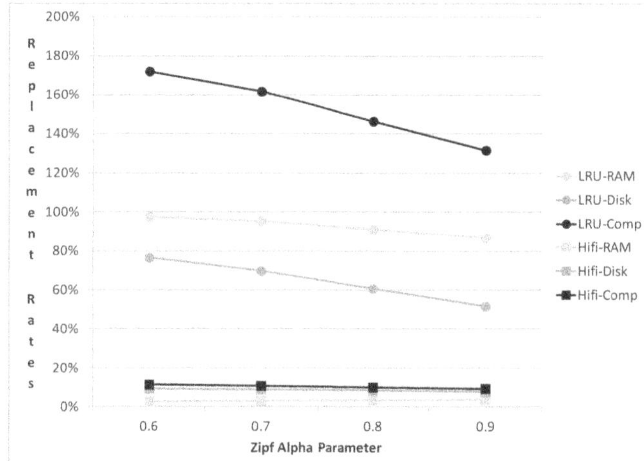

Figure 6: Replacement rates with different Zipf alpha values

6.3 Comparison to Optimal Hit-rates

We simulated Belady's MIN (B-MIN) [3] algorithm for comparison against optimal hit-rates. However, B-MIN is not defined for variable sizes assets, so we ran the simulation without VQ levels, with the same set of assumptions as in Figure 4. We used a total of 2000 asset disk cache and a 50 asset RAM cache, the results of which are shown in Table 3 as a function of Zipf alpha values.

Table 3: Comparison to Belady's MIN

	RAM			Edge Cache		
	LRU	HiFi	B-MIN	LRU	HiFi	B-MIN
0.6	4%	12%	20%	56.8%	64.8%	72.2%
0.7	6%	17%	26%	62.4%	69.3%	75.8%
0.8	11%	25%	33%	68.0%	73.8%	79.8%
0.9	16%	33%	41%	74.0%	78.6%	83.6%

6.4 Discussion

Both the improved RAM hit-rate and the reduced replacement rate reduce disk input-output, which is often the bottleneck in most caches. In order to obtain a rough estimate of the impact of these factors on the throughput of the cache, we assume the following relative throughput rates for a typical cache. From our experience these numbers are fairly representative for a cache with about 20 mechanical disks. These numbers are likely to change for different caches, for examples caches with more disks or caches with SSD disks will likely show a higher throughput for 100% disk access.

Table 4: Estimates for Cache Throughput

Scenario	**Estimated Throughput**
100% RAM hit – all assets are assumed available in RAM and sent to client	X
100% disk hit – all assets are fetched from local disk and sent to client	0.4X
100% miss disk write – all assets are obtained from the parent cache and sent to the client and all assets are inserted into the local disk cache – as per LRU policy	0.25X
100% miss no disk write – all assets are obtained from the parent cache but all assets are sent via RAM to client without ever writing to local disk – as per HiFi policy when the asset fails the characteristic time check	0.35X

We used the above numbers and the hit-rates and replacement rates reported in the previous section to estimate the throughput difference between a cache with HiFi at the RAM and disk layers and a cache with LRU in the same layers. For Zipf values of 0.7, 0.8, 0.9; a 50 asset RAM cache and a 1000 asset total disk cache, we estimate the improvement in cache throughput due to HiFi to be 75%, 65% and 51% from a LRU based cache respectively using linear interpolation for mixes of RAM hit percentage, cache hit percentage and miss percentage. For the 4000 asset disk cache scenario with a Zipf value of 0.8, this number drops to 26%. The major contributor to the throughput improvement is the improved RAM hit-rate when the hit-rate tends to be high and reduction of disk writes, when the hit-rate tends to be low. We implemented HiFi on some of our caches with mechanical drives and were able to observe a substantially higher throughput improvement than the numbers mentioned above in the same set of scenarios. We note that cache throughput has a direct inverse relationship to the amount of caching hardware to be deployed. HiFi also improved overall cache byte hit-rate at the first tier over LRU based caches. Our simulations show this ratio to be between 24% to 4.5% in various scenarios as described in section 6.2; which can save on origin costs or higher tier cache hardware costs as well as network costs. Origin costs tend to be significantly higher than cache server costs.

The substantial reduction in the replacement rate of 10 times or more can reduce SSD costs, if they are used for storage. SSDs are typically either SLC (Single Level Cell) or MLC (Multi Level Cell), where the SLC based SSDs have about 10 times the lifetime [4] of MLC based SSDs and are approximately two or three times the cost. The reduction in replacement rate may allow the use of MLC-based SSDs instead of SLC for a similar level of lifetime write performance. In [6], the authors show a three to four times reduction in disk failure rates due to a 3 times reduction in usage of mechanical disks which also indicates a potential reliability improvement in such disks with reduced disk input-output.

7. CONCLUSIONS AND FUTURE WORK

Many operational caches today still use the LRU policy despite almost 20 years of caching research on improved caching policies. Our results indicate that HiFi can allow such caches to operate near the optimal hit-rate without the performance degradation that comes with policies that have traditionally been attempted for this purpose. Rather, with HiFi, a very significant throughput improvement can be achieved, which leads to a similar reduction in cache hardware costs.

We intend to thoroughly test HiFi with the various types of workloads and conditions found in our operator deployments and also plan to study a cost-based variation of the algorithm. We also plan to test HiFi with general Internet traffic.

8. REFERENCES

[1] Anirban Ketan Shah and Mitra Dhruv Matani. "An O(1) algorithm for implementing the lfu cache eviction scheme." Technical report, 2010. http://dhruvbird.com/lfu.pdf

[2] Athula Balachandran, Vyas Sekar, Aditya Akella, and Srinivasan Seshan, "Analyzing the Potential Benefits of CDN Augmentation Strategies for Internet Video Workloads," in Proc. IMC, New York, NY, USA, 2013, pp. 43-56.

[3] Belady, Laszlo A. "A study of replacement algorithms for a virtual-storage computer." IBM Systems journal 5.2 (1966): 78-101.

[4] Dave Simpson, MLC vs. SLC flash for enterprise SSDs, July 2010, http://www.infostor.com/index/articles/display/1169849064/articles/infostor/disk-arrays/disk-drives/2010/july-2010/mlc-vs__slc_flash.html.

[5] Einziger, Gil, and Roy Friedman. "Tinylfu: A highly efficient cache admission policy." Parallel, Distributed and Network-Based Processing (PDP), 2014 22nd Euromicro International Conference on. IEEE, 2014.

[6] Gerry Cole, Seagate Technology Paper TP-338.1: Estimating drive reliability in desktop computers and consumer electronics systems, November 2000.

[7] Hao Che, Ye Tung, and Z. Wang, "Hierarchical Web caching systems: modeling, design and experimental results," IEEE J. Sel. Areas Commun., vol. 20, no. 7, pp. 1305-1314, Sep 2002

[8] Hongliang Yu, Dongdong Zheng, Ben Y. Zhao, and Weimin Zheng, "Understanding User Behavior in Large-scale Video-on-demand Systems," SIGOPS Oper. Syst. Rev., vol. 40, no. 4, pp. 333-344, #apr# 2006.

[9] https://docs.trafficserver.apache.org/en/4.0.x/admin/configuring-cache.en.html

[10] Jaime Llorca et al., "Dynamic in-network caching for energy efficient content delivery," in Proc. IEEE INFOCOM, 2013, pp. 245-249.

[11] K. Poularakis and L. Tassiulas, "Optimal algorithms for hierarchical web caches," in Proc. IEEE ICC, June 2013, pp. 4073-4077.

[12] K. Poularakis and L. Tassiulas, "Optimal cooperative content placement algorithms in hierarchical cache topologies," in Proc. Ann. Conf. on Inform. Sci. and Syst., March 2012, pp. 1-6.

[13] Kang-Won Lee, Sambit Sahu, Khalil Amiri, and Chitra Venkatramani, "Understanding the Potential Benefits of Cooperation among Proxies: Taxonomy and Analysis," IBM Research, Tech. rep. 2001.

[14] Keqiu Li, Hong Shen, Francis Y. L. Chin, and Si Qing Zheng, Optimal methods for coordinated enroute web caching for tree networks, 2005.

[15] Laoutaris, Nikolaos, Hao Che, and Ioannis Stavrakakis. "The LCD interconnection of LRU caches and its analysis." Performance Evaluation 63.7 (2006): 609-634.

[16] Ludmila Cherkasova, "Improving WWW Proxies Performance with Greedy-Dual-Size-Frequency Caching Policy," HP Computer Systems Laboratory, Tech. rep. 1998

[17] Nikolaos Laoutaris, Sofia Syntila, and Ioannis Stavrakakis, "Meta algorithms for hierarchical Web caches," in Proc. IEEE IPCCC, 2004, pp. 445-452.

[18] Pablo Rodriguez, Christian Spanner, and Ernst W. Biersack, "Analysis of web caching architectures: Hierarchical and distributed caching," IEEE/ACM Trans. Netw., vol. 9, pp. 404-418, 2001.

[19] Pei Cao and Sandy Irani, "Cost-aware WWW proxy caching algorithms," in Proc. USENIX Symp. Internet Technol. Syst., 1997, p. 18.

[20] Sandvine Report, "Exposing the Technical and Commercial Factors Underlying Internet Quality of Experience", Sept 2013.

[21] Sem Borst, Varun Gupta, and Anwar Walid, "Distributed caching algorithms for content distribution networks," in Proc. IEEE INFOCOM, 2010.

[22] Serpanos, Dimitrios N., and George Karakostas. "Exploitation of Different Types of Locality for Web Caches."

[23] Shahab Bakhtiyari, Performance evaluation of the Apache traffic server and Varnish reverse proxies, May 23, 2012.

[24] Stefan Podlipnig and Laszlo Boszormenyi, "A survey of Web cache replacement strategies," ACM Comp. Surv., vol. 35, pp. 374-398, 2003.

[25] Tang, Wenting, et al. "Modeling and generating realistic streaming media server workloads." Computer Networks 51.1 (2007): 336-356.

[26] Yan Chen, Lili Qiu, Weiyu Chen, Luan Nguyen, and Randy H. Katz, "Efficient and adaptive Web replication using content clustering," IEEE J. Sel. Areas Commun., vol. 21, pp. 979-994, 2003.

Exploring QoE for Power Efficiency: A Field Study on Mobile Videos with LCD Displays

Zhisheng Yan, Qian Liu
State University of New York at Buffalo

Tong Zhang
Rensselaer Polytechnic Institute

Chang Wen Chen
State University of New York at Buffalo

ABSTRACT

Display power consumption has become a major concern for both mobile users and design engineers, especially considering the prevalence of today's video-rich mobile services. The power consumption of liquid crystal display (LCD), a dominant mobile display technology, can be reduced by dynamic backlight scaling (DBS). However, such dynamic changes of screen brightness may degrade users' quality of experience (QoE) in viewing videos. How would QoE be impacted by different DBS strategies has not yet been understood clearly and thus obscures the way to achieve systematic power saving. In this paper, we take a first step to explore the QoE of DBS on smartphones and aim at maximally enhancing the display power performance without negatively impacting users' QoE. In particular, we conduct three motivational studies to uncover the inherent relationship between QoE and backlight scaling frequency, magnitude, and temporal consistency, respectively. Motivated by the findings of these studies, we design a suite of techniques to implement a comprehensive DBS strategy. We demonstrate an example application of the proposed DBS designs in a mobile video streaming system. Measurements and user evaluations show that more than 40% system power reduction, or equivalently, 20% more power savings than the non-QoE approaches, can be achieved without QoE impairment.

Categories and Subject Descriptors

H.5.1 [**Multimedia Information Systems**]: Video

General Terms

Design; Experimentation; Human Factors

Keywords

LCD; Mobile Video Streaming; Power Consumption; QoE

1. INTRODUCTION

The proliferation of mobile web access and social networks has dramatically boosted mobile video services. Although mobile computing and storage capabilities have been continuously expanding in order to meet the ever-growing video services, relatively short lifetime of batteries has long been a major complaint by smartphone users. Among the operational components of a mobile phone, display power is one crucial issue that needs to be addressed urgently. Not only have displays been identified as one of the most power-consuming subsystems [1], but display power is also consumed in a broader video-related applications as long as the video is playing on the mobile phone. For example, unlike communication components that consume energy only when video streaming is in session, power dissipation of displays shall occur in both online and offline video viewing.

Liquid crystal display (LCD) is a dominant display technology that is adopted by larger number of modern devices, e.g., Apple iPhone 6/6 Plus, Google Nexus 4/5, and LG G 3/4/Pro. According to a recent study [2], the revenue share of LCD-based mobile phones is expected to reach 70% in 2020. The power consumption of LCD primarily comes from the backlight at the display panel. By dimming the backlight, we could save the display energy. However, dimmed backlight may lead to a lower perceptual luminance of displayed pixels, which would cause video distortion and eventually degrade users' *quality of experience* (*QoE*). Hence, the key principle of LCD power reduction in mobile videos is to dynamically scale the backlight as low as possible without negatively impacting users' QoE. This is commonly termed as *dynamic backlight scaling* (*DBS*).

Despite this general consensus, we observe that our understanding of power-saving strategies for LCD is still limited. This might surprise many experts since DBS has been actively studied in design automation communities. The reason behind this observation is that mobile videos introduce new effects on the QoE of backlight scaling while little is known regarding the optimal backlight under this new context. First, prior backlight scaling schemes for a single image [3–5] cannot be directly applied to the multi-frame videos. Second, most exiting works [6, 7] were implemented using programmable LCD modules, which cannot adequately reflect human perception on smartphones that employ larger screen size and higher pixel-density. Most importantly, prior objective distortion metrics for DBS, e.g., linear relationship between perceptual luminance and backlight levels [4, 8, 9], become inaccurate and need to be replaced by subjective QoE modeling that specifically targets DBS.

On the other hand, although video QoE has been extensively researched in the context of encoding and streaming to improve compression and delivery performance, QoE of

MM'15 October 26–30, 2015, Brisbane, Australia.
© 2015 ACM. ISBN 978-1-4503-3459-4/15/10 ...$15.00.
DOI: http://dx.doi.org/10.1145/2733373.2806269.

backlight-scaled videos for power efficiency has not been studied. In this research, we take a first step to explore QoE when DBS is applied in order to maximally enhance the power performance of LCD-based mobile phones without sacrificing end users' QoE. To achieve this ambitious objective, we are facing several research challenges.

- Finding a suitable *scaling frequency*: How frequently should DBS be applied is fundamentally dependent on both QoE and power. Less frequent scaling will result in more stable viewing experience, but will leave much smaller space for manipulating the backlight dynamics, which diminishes the potential for power saving [8]. When to apply the scaling also matters because abrupt variation of backlight is annoying to users.
- Determining a smallest *scaling magnitude*: For a given segment of video frames, obtaining a smallest scaling magnitude in order to maximally reduce power consumption is a non-trivial task. The inherent relationship between QoE and backlight change has not yet been understood clearly. This is further complicated by the fact that users may express distinct perception for different video contents even under the same backlight condition.
- Applying *temporally consistent* DBS across multiple segments: Simply scaling each segment's backlight individually without inter-segment consideration shall lead to QoE degradation because human eyes are shown to be extremely sensitive to temporally inconsistent videos. For example, adaptive streaming studies [10] have reported that quality switches with high variation frustrate the end users.

In order to tackle these challenges, we have carried out a comprehensive investigation on the QoE of dynamic backlight scaling. We have developed a customized video App, QoEPlayer, to conduct three motivational studies to explore the connection between QoE and scaling frequency, magnitude, and temporal consistency, respectively. By leveraging statistical analysis, we discover that a video shot based scaling frequency is on average 11 times more acceptable by users than other alternative approaches. Accordingly, we design and tune a video shot detection algorithm to decide the best scaling frequency. Furthermore, we observe a content-luminance-dependent logistic relationship (instead of linear) between QoE and backlight levels. We then construct a QoE model using logistic regression in order to determine the best scaling magnitude of a given video shot. Moreover, we find it interesting that users are only sensitive to down-scaled backlight switches rather than up-scaled ones. Therefore, we train a binary classifier to detect those inconsistent down-scaled backlight switches and then properly smooth these variations. Finally, combining all these findings, we develop a systematic strategy for DBS as applied to mobile phones. We demonstrate an example application of the proposed designs in a video delivery system and show that more than 40% system power can be saved, which is equivalent to 20% more power savings than conventional strategies without QoE considerations.

To summarize, the contributions of the proposed research include:

- A open-source video App, *QoEPlayer*, for subjective mobile video studies on Android platform (Section 3).
- A set of motivational studies to explore the intrinsic relation between QoE and scaling frequency, magnitude and temporal consistency (Section 4-6).
- A suite of designs to achieve the most power-efficient DBS strategies without negative effects on user experience (Section 4-6).
- A practical demonstration of the usage of the proposed DBS designs, showing 40% system power reduction, or equivalently, 20% more power savings than non-QoE approaches (Section 7).

2. RELATED WORK

2.1 Dynamic Backlight Scaling

In general, exiting DBS schemes first compute the perceptual luminance of a backlight-scaled image by assuming it is linearly proportional to scaling magnitude and/or original pixel value. Then the backlight keeps scaling down until certain distortion thresholds between the two images are met.

Particularly, Cheng and Pedram scaled the backlight while preserving the image contrast [3]. Chang *et al.* increased the original pixel values to compensate for the scaling distortion and then retained the brightness and contrast [4]. Iranli *et al.* compensated the original image by considering histogram equalization [5]. These single-image level schemes demonstrate the principle of backlight scaling, but they are not directly applicable to mobile videos.

DBS for videos were studied by considering video-related distortion metrics. Structural similarity (SSIM) [7] and peak signal-to-noise ratio (PSNR) [11] based measure were exploited to apply DBS. Visual sensitivity characterization in frequency domain was used to smooth the flicker effect of DBS [6]. Recently, Lin *et al.* optimized the scaling strategies by dynamic programming to minimize power consumption [8]. Liu *et al.* proposed to use GPU to perform luminance compensation and to reduce power effectively [9]. However, these works all rely on objective distortion formulations that are not specifically developed for DBS and therefore lack direct relationship with user experience.

In this paper, we explore the user experience of backlight-scaled videos through subjective user tests on modern smartphones. We aim at uncovering the inherent relations among QoE, backlight and video content, and utilizing them to improve the power performance of mobile phones.

2.2 QoE Studies

Many objective metrics for QoE focus on low-level video features, e.g., PSNR and SSIM [12]. However, whether or not these objective metrics match well with user experience is still controversial and is usually application-dependent [13]. More commonly, QoE is modeled as mean opinion scores obtained from subjective evaluation data. Many efforts were made for different applications, such as general networked video systems [14] and adaptive HTTP streaming [15, 16], and ITU video-telephony [17]. One potential issue of such score-based tests is that participants may be overburdened by the multiple levels of score and may struggle with making a decision [18].

Recently, binary assessment choice was suggested for subjective tests to evaluate the acceptability of videos [13,18,19]. The lowest acceptable video for pleasant viewing can be found using Method of Limits in classical psychophysics [20], where users view a series of videos varied in successive discrete steps with descending or ascending order and submit their binary acceptability choice.

There were also important data-driven works that mine the large-scale network traffic [21] or user engagement data [22] to model QoE in Internet applications. However, this is not feasible for DBS on mobile phones as users need to personally hold the device and view the backlight-scaled video to experience the video display.

All these exiting works explore how QoE is impacted by encoding or transmission parameters, e.g, resolution, bitrate and delay, in order to enhance the networking performance. In this paper, however, our objective is fundamentally different in that we probe into the new QoE space of backlight scaling in order to enhance the power performance.

3. USER STUDY SETUP

In this section, we introduce the general setup of user studies and system demo. Test-dependent setup will be presented in the subsequent sections.

Test Devices. LG Optimus G Pro and Google Nexus 4 are used in all tests except the study of temporal consistency where G Pro and Xiaomi Mi 2 are used. The screen size, resolution, pixel density of G Pro, Nexus 4, and Mi 2 are 5.5 inch/1080x1920/401 ppi, 4.7 inch/768x1280/318 ppi, 4.3 inch/720x1280/342 ppi, respectively. The diverse screen setting allows us to study the impacts for different devices.

Participants. We recruit a total of 50 participants from two universities. Their ages range from 20 to 39. There are 32 males and 18 females. All participants have a normal color vision. We also report that one participant works in the area of mobile display. However, we do not find any significant difference in that particular result. A set of 40 participants take part in the three motivational studies whereas a set of 20 participants evaluate the system application. For each test, participants are divided into two halves and each half uses a different test phone.

Video Sources. We use 15 training sources for motivational studies. There are 5 standard sequences, 2 open movies [23], and 8 movie trailers that are 2015 Oscar nominees for best picture. To validate the designs in system-level application, we also prepare another 4 test sources that are 2015 Oscar nominees for best actor and actress without overlapping with above sources. Such selection concurs with the important principle of user studies that real-world materials should be used [18]. Since we are interested in DBS, we encode all videos identically at a high quality with 1280x720 resolution, 23 quantization parameter, 24 frames/second, and H.264/AVC baseline profile. We also encode all audio materials at AAC format with 44kHz and >180kbps to guarantee that users can understand the content and enjoy the viewing experience. These encoded sources will be split into test clips for the studies in the subsequent sections.

Assessment Objective. Due to the simplicity and comfort of user decision in binary-choice QoE tests, we follow prior works [13,18,19] to adopt this promising method. Participants are asked to identify whether or not a test clip is acceptable. Since we intend to maximally reduce the power without negative effects on users' regular viewing experience, acceptable quality is informed as the quality with tiny/no adjustment of screen brightness that participants would enjoy and thus have a pleasant experience in daily life.

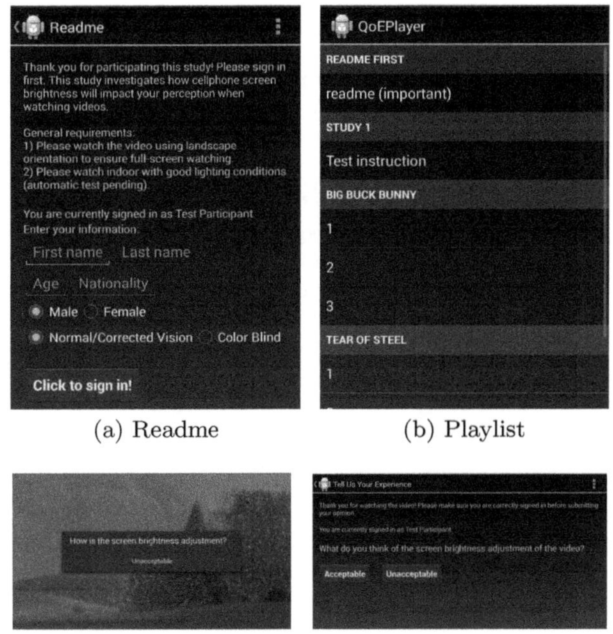

(a) Readme (b) Playlist

(c) Pop-up Dialogue (d) Opinion Form

Figure 1: Screenshots of QoEPlayer.

Test Environment. Human perception of screen brightness might be affected by ambient light. We focus on the ambient light ranging from 100 to 1000 lux, which mimics the indoor residential and working lighting [24]. This is because people spend majority of time on viewing mobile videos in such indoor scenarios. According to the study in [25], 358 out of 663 people watch mobile video at home while 176 at university or working place, 92 at vehicle and 37 at cafe shop, barber and bus station. Although the location distribution within the categories is not known, it is still clear that a greater bulk of mobile viewing occurs indoor.

Test App: QoEPlayer. We implement a open-source[1] Android application for the tests. Initially, participants register at the Readme page (Figure 1a) by providing personal information. They are then asked to randomly select a video clip that has multiple versions differed by a certain stimulus (Figure 1b). The presentation order of multiple versions can be customized as random, ascending, and descending. Once a test version is selected, QoEPlayer will automatically check whether the ambient light meets the requirement via the light sensor in the device. If satisfied, video playback will start. Otherwise, a warning window that instructs users to move to a darker/brighter environment will pop up.

Upon playing the video, QoEPlayer creates a control thread to dynamically adjust the backlight via Android API based on a given scaling profile. It also guarantees that DBS is synchronized with the video and audio codec to support pause, fast forward, etc. During video playback, participants can double tap the screen to initiate a pop-up dialogue (Figure 1c) and submit their decision. Note that this function is only active when allowed by the test protocol. Alternatively, there is always a opinion form (Figure 1d) showing at the end of playback. After the choices are submitted in

[1] `www.cse.buffalo.edu/UBMM/People/zhisheng_yan.html`

either way, QoEPlayer will automatically save the results of participants and return to the playlist.

This automatic process provides participants with a simpler and more immersive viewing experience, which eventually speeds up the studies. We emphasize that QoEPlayer can be modified and ported to any mobile QoE studies.

4. ADDRESSING DBS FREQUENCY

To find a proper scaling frequency, we must identify the requirements in terms of both QoE and power. First, it is desired to let the backlight scaling occur at time points when users pay much less attention to the video. Second, the number of video segments separated by the scaling points should be as many as possible if QoE is not compromised. In fact, more segments allow more rooms for manipulating the backlight dynamics, hence reducing more power [8]. For example, if we mix two segments whose lowest scaling magnitude to maintain QoE are $\mathcal{M}_1$ and $\mathcal{M}_2$, we would need to apply the magnitude $max(\mathcal{M}_1, \mathcal{M}_2)$ to the mixed segment to ensure QoE, which is less power efficient than assigning $\mathcal{M}_1$ and $\mathcal{M}_2$ to each segment, respectively.

4.1 Motivational Study

4.1.1 *Methodology*

Ideally, we should examine the QoE under all combinations of segmentation for a video and then model the scaling frequency versus QoE data and content features of segments. However, this is infeasible as there are too many ways of segmentation, e.g., a 1-second video will have tens of millions options. Therefore, we proceed by comparing several possible approaches and obtain a suboptimal yet acceptable solution. To the best of our knowledge, only two previous works considered DBS frequency. In [8], a constant scaling frequency with certain number of frames was used (denoted as *Const*). In [26], the authors used the rule that the variance of average luminance of frames belonging to a segment should be less than a threshold value (denoted as *GoS*).

In addition, we propose to adopt a *video shot* as one scaling segment and scale the backlight at shot boundaries. A shot refers to a series of consecutive frames played for an uninterrupted period of time. We propose this strategy as there is usually a sudden transition of content when the shot is switched. We anticipate that users might pay much less attention to the shot-boundary frames with sudden switch than to the within-shot frames showing the actual contents. Thereby, the impacts of DBS can be diminished. Note that video scenes in semantic level is a similar idea. We prefer shots as scaling segments since a scene consists of one or more shots and thus leaves us less space for power reduction.

4.1.2 *Results*

We prepare 4 test clips (2 full trailers and 2 movie clips) with average duration 115 seconds. Each clip is dynamically backlight scaled using the above three frequencies. The constant frequency and variance threshold are set to the default value of 10 frames [8] and 40 [26], respectively. Besides, we use a shot detection algorithm to be introduced in the next subsection to find the shot boundaries and manually correct the false/missed detection. For all frequency strategies, the scaling magnitude $\mathcal{M}$ of each segment i is decided using a simple linear mapping that is based on the scheme in [26]. Specifically, if the content of the current segment is darker

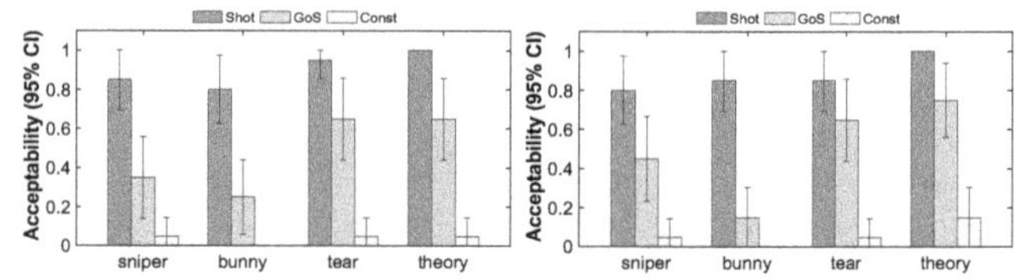

Figure 2: Acceptability under different scaling frequencies on G Pro (left) and Nexus 4 (right).

than the previous segment, its backlight magnitude can be a little less than the previous magnitude without degrading QoE and vice versa, i.e.,

$$\mathcal{M}_i = \begin{cases} \max(\mathcal{M}_{i-1} - \mathcal{M}_{step}, 0) & Y_i < Y_{i-1} \\ \mathcal{M}_{i-1} & Y_i = Y_{i-1} \\ \min(\mathcal{M}_{i-1} + \mathcal{M}_{step}, 1) & Y_i > Y_{i-1} \end{cases} \quad (1)$$

where Y is the average luminance of a segment over all frames and pixels, and $\mathcal{M}_{step}$ is backlight variation step that is 0.2. We choose this $\mathcal{M}_{step}$ to avoid too little or too much backlight variations that may make all or none frequencies strategies acceptable. Participants are asked to watch 3 frequency versions of a clip in a random order and then move to next clip. They can make a "unacceptable" decision during the backlight-scaled playback while they will need to wait until the end of playback to confirm "acceptable".

To better analyze the binary subjective data, we use acceptability $\mathcal{A}$ as in [13,18,25], i.e., $\mathcal{A} = \frac{N_{acc}}{N_{tot}}$, where N_{acc} is the number of acceptable decisions and N_{tot} is the number of total votes. We show the acceptability (95% CI) of 4 clips under different scaling frequencies in Figure 2. We can observe that QoE is clearly impacted by frequency strategies. Chi-square test between frequency strategies and acceptability, $\chi^2 = 167.008$ $df = 2$ $p < 0.001$, further supports that QoE under different scaling frequencies differs significantly from each other in a statistical sense.

It can also be seen from Figure 2 that shot-based scaling frequency achieves the best result for all test clips on both devices. Its average acceptability reaches 88.75%, and is on average 1.82 times and 20.3 times better than the other two methods, respectively. This could be explained as users pay most attentions to the essential parts of a video, such as objects, people, and stories. Subconsciously, they do not quite care about the shot switches. Hence, frequent backlight scaling in the middle of presenting those essential contents is much more annoying than that in shot boundaries. Thereby, we can conclude that shot-based scaling frequency provides a simple yet effective solution to this challenging problem. It is also noted that QoE results are content-dependent, which shall guide us to deliberately set the scaling magnitude of shots based on the content characteristics.

4.2 A Shot Detection Algorithm for DBS

We now present the design of a new shot detection algorithm to determine DBS frequency. Video shot detection have been previously studied [27]. Although none of exiting designs focuses on DBS, they provide the foundations for the proposed algorithm. Shot detection usually consists of two steps [28]: computing discontinuity values for consecutive frames and detecting the shots based on the discontinuity.

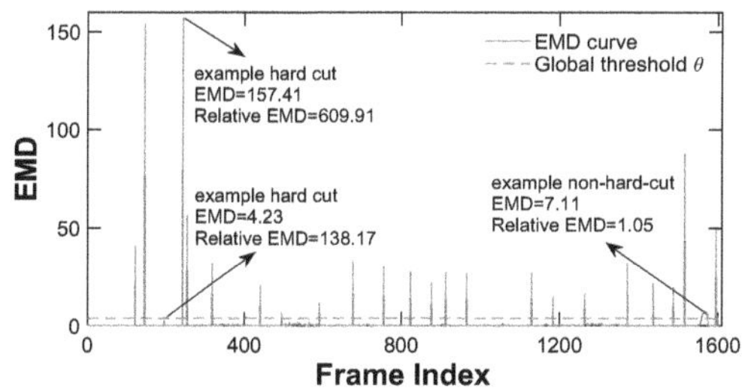

Figure 3: EMD of "sniper" (first 1600 frames)

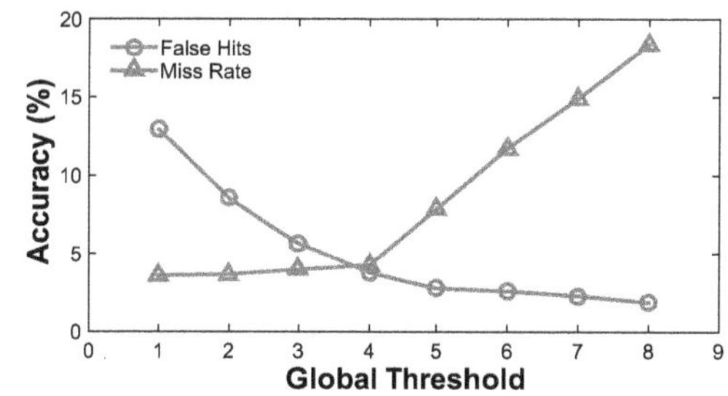

Figure 4: Overall shot detection accuracy

Algorithm 1 Proposed Shot Detection Algorithm

procedure SHOT DETECTION FOR DBS
  $\mathcal{S} \leftarrow 0$, $EMD_{pre} \leftarrow EMD(0, 1)$
  for $k \leftarrow 1; k < LastFrame; k \leftarrow k + 1$ **do**
    if $EMD(k, k+1) > \theta$ & $\frac{EMD(k,k+1)}{EMD_{pre}} > \eta$ **then**
      if $k + 1 - s_{pre} \geq D_{min}$ **then**
        $\mathcal{S} \leftarrow \mathcal{S} \cup \{k + 1\}$, $s_{pre} \leftarrow k + 1$
    $EMD_{pre} \leftarrow EMD(k, k + 1)$
  return $\mathcal{S}$ ▷ $\mathcal{S}$: set of start frames for shots

We propose to adopt the luminance histogram based discontinuity metric in DBS. This is because DBS is more power efficient if we divide a video into segments with distinct luminance feature rather than mixing them together. Furthermore, luminance metric is robust to missed detection in the case of DBS since missed detection could occur only when the luminance strength between two shots are very similar. This is not a problem as we would assign the same scaling magnitude to both shots even if we detected them. Summarizing these discussions, we set the objective to detect hard-cut shots with abrupt luminance change. It is unnecessary to detect those shots with gradual transition like dissolves.

We employ Earth Mover's Distance (EMD) [29], which is commonly used in image retrieval, as the luminance histogram feature. EMD is defined as the minimum cost paid to transform one histogram into the other. Formally, EMD between histogram P and Q is expressed as:

$$\begin{aligned} EMD(P, Q) &= (\min_{f_{ij}} \textstyle\sum_{i,j} f_{ij} d_{ij}) / (\sum_{i,j} f_{ij}) \\ s.t. \quad & f_{ij} \geq 0,\ \textstyle\sum_j f_{ij} \leq P_i,\ \sum_i f_{ij} \leq Q_j \\ & \textstyle\sum_{i,j} f_{ij} = \min(\sum_i P_i, \sum_j Q_j) \end{aligned} \tag{2}$$

where f_{ij} is the flow amount transported from ith bin to jth bin and d_{ij} is ground distance between bin i and j. We choose EMD because it is a cross-bin metric that considers both bin height and inter-bin distance. Unlike bin-to-bin metrics used in conventional shot detection, EMD effectively captures the luminance discontinuity, which makes it a satisfactory metric for DBS.

The proposed shot detection exploits EMD for global thresholding and relative EMD for local thresholding to make the detection decision. This is more flexible than conventional global threshold based methods. The reason is that we observe a wide range of EMD values at true hard-cut positions, as exemplified in Figure 2. By incorporating relative threshold η, we can ensure that non-hard-cut positions with EMD greater than global threshold θ would be dropped. Since most hardware cannot support per-frame scaling, the shot duration should also be greater than a minimum value D_{min}, which is decided to be 5 based on our measurement. Note

Table 1: Detection false hits/miss rate (%)

sniper 0/8.06	bunny 4.72/2.36	birdman 2.63/18.42	boyhood 0/2.86	Budapest 0/4.90
imitation 5.00/7.00	selma 2.07/2.07	tear 11.03/5.15	theory 6.06/0	whiplash 1.57/3.15
ducks 0/0	oldtown 0/0	parkrun 0/0	rushhour 0/0	redkayak 0/0

that shot detection is not sensitive to this hardware limit as most shots last more than 1 second and thus per-shot scaling can be easily supported. The algorithm is summarized in Algorithm 1. Specifically, we first calculate the EMD between frame k and its previous/next frame, respectively. If $EMD(k, k + 1)$ is greater than global threshold and sufficiently larger than $EMD(k - 1, k)$, as well as current shot lasting more than D_{min}, we can decide that a new video shot starts from frame $k + 1$.

We find the proper thresholds by experiments, as commonly done in shot detection research [27, 28]. We observe that all hard-cut positions have a much larger EMD than their neighbors. We go through all 15 training sources and discover that EMD values at hard-cut positions are at least 13.37 times greater than its prior neighbor while the EMDs at non-hard-cut positions are at most 3.21 times greater. Hence, we conservatively set η to 10 for possible hard cuts that have relatively small relative EMD.

Next, we range the global threshold from 1 to 8 and show the overall detection accuracy of all video sources in Figure 4, wherein false hits is the ratio of falsely detected shots to the actual number of shots and miss rate is the ratio of missed shots to the actual number of shots. A larger θ allows less EMD values to pass the global thresholding and thus is less likely for false hits. However, it would also increase the chance of missing true shotsGiven that both curves show stable trends, we can safely determine the optimal θ as 4. The detection results for each source under optimal thresholds are shown in Table 1. The accuracy fulfills the requirement of 5% false hits and miss rate [27] in most cases.

More importantly, we shall report that a false hit is usually found when there is a special lighting in the video, e.g., multiple camera lights repeatedly on. Thereby, false hits are not quite dangerous since people can hardly discern a backlight change under those strong lighting effects. On the other hand, the missed shots usually have very similar content luminance to its neighbors, e.g., a talking man from two shotting angles. Even though those shots are not missed, we would scale the backlight for them similarly as their neighbors. Based on the results and DBS's insensitivity to shot detection accuracy, we conclude that the proposed algorithm can achieve a satisfactory performance for determining scaling frequency.

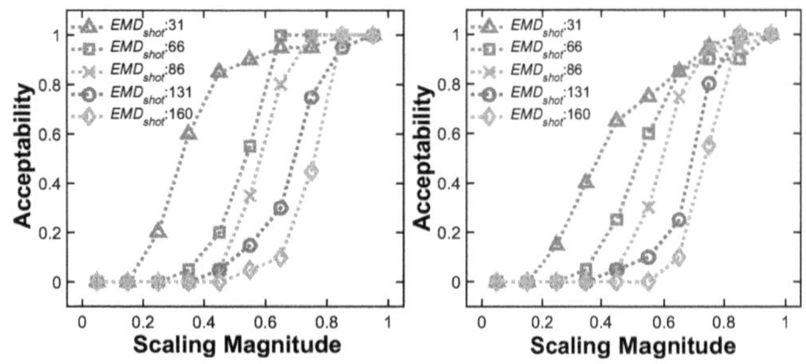

Figure 5: Acceptability under different scaling magnitude on G Pro (left) and Nexus 4 (right).

5. MODELING DBS MAGNITUDE

5.1 Motivational Study

We then proceed to determine the smallest possible scaling magnitude of a given video shot. Recall that both scaling magnitude and content luminance have strong effects on QoE. Hence, we must analyze the acceptability of shots with different content luminance under different backlight levels. It is desired to represent the luminance feature of a shot by using EMD because EMD has shown advantages in characterizing the luminance as discussed previously. However, we shall need to first obtain a shot's histogram in order to compute EMD. Median histogram is a histogram descriptor for a group of frames and has been widely used in multimedia applications [30]. Each bin of the median histogram is computed by the median bin height over all the frame histograms. We select this descriptor since it can effectively eliminate the outlier frames within the shot [30]. Finally, we define the luminance feature of a shot, denoted by EMD_{shot}, as the EMD distance between the shot's median histogram and the constant histogram of a black (zero-intensity) image. A lager EMD_{shot} indicates a brighter content.

We compute EMD_{shot} for all shots in all the training videos. A total of 1014 values are collected and they range from 16 to 185.38. For user study, we divide EMD_{shot} into 5 categories (category 5 darkest) with a step of 34 to represent different luminance strength of a shot. We then prepare 5 test clips accordingly (average duration 9 seconds). Besides, we vary the backlight scaling magnitude from 0.95 to 0.05 at a step of 0.1. The scaling magnitude can span from 0 (turn off) to 1 (full backlight). Overall, we prepare 50 versions of backlight scaled shots (5 EMD_{shot} x 10 $\mathcal{M}$) for this user study. Notice that the backlight is scaled only once at the beginning of the shot and the "acceptable" quality becomes the static brightness that users perceive no/tiny difference compared with the full-backlight version and would enjoy everyday. Participants are first asked to watch a full-backlight version as a reference. Then 10 scaled versions are played either from highest magnitude or from lowest magnitude using Method of Limit as in [13, 18]. Participants will choose whether or not each version is acceptable. They are allowed to confirm acceptable/unacceptable during the playback.

Eventually, we collect 2000 binary data points for this study (40 participants x 50 video versions). To better visualize the binary data and grasp a clear understanding of the data, we convert the binary data into acceptability as in the previous section. We show the raw acceptability data for 5 luminance categories in Figure 5. It is clear that the relationship between QoE and backlight is not linear, indicating past assumptions, e.g., [4, 8, 9], is not accurate. Instead, we observe a sigmoid curve ("S" shape curve) for all luminance categories. Furthermore, the sigmoid curve is horizontally shifted when EMD_{shot} is varied. For example, darker content can enjoy a higher acceptability than brighter content under the same scaling magnitude. Based on the sigmoid curve, we propose to employ a logistic function, an effective option for QoE modeling according to ITU-T [17], to model QoE versus scaling magnitude and luminance feature.

Table 2: Model Coefficients

Term	Estimate	Wald Test	Likehood Ratio Test
Constant	-9.208	$z = -13.69$	NA
EMD_{shot}	-0.081	$z = -13.62$	$\chi^2 = 2526.5$ $df = 1964$
$\mathcal{M}$	28.604	$z = 15.09$	$\chi^2 = 454.1$ $df = 1963$

*All tests are significant at $p < 0.001$.

5.2 Logistic Regression Analysis

Logistic regression is a statistical analysis for binary response data whose probability of being positive is a sigmoid curve. This perfectly matches our data shown in Figure 5. The logistic function can be written as:

$$F(\vec{x}) = \frac{1}{1 + \exp^{-(\alpha+\beta x_1+\gamma x_2+\delta x_3+\cdots)}} \tag{3}$$

where $\alpha, \beta, \gamma, \cdots$ are the coefficients and $\vec{x} = (x_1, x_2, \cdots)$ are the predictor variables. In our user study, the predictor variables are the three stimuli, i.e., shot EMD, scaling magnitude of a shot, and device type. We use maximum likelihood estimation (MLE) to determine the coefficients. Data points that have studentized residuals less than -2 or greater than 2 are identified as outliers, which follows the standard logistic modeling in [31].

The modeling results demonstrate that all the predictors are significant except device type. Specifically, Wald test of device term, $z = -1.313, p = 0.189$, implies that the contribution of device type to model fit is not statistically significant. We also run likelihood ratio test to compare the two models with and without device type. The results, $\chi^2 = 1.734$ $df = 1$ $p = 0.187$, confirm that including device type into the model would not significantly improve model fit in a statistical sense. This is interesting as it is opposed to conventional video QoE for coding, where larger screen size relatively enlarges the coding artifacts and indeed deteriorates QoE. In the proposed scenario, however, people would always have an absolute perception of brightness regardless of screen size or pixel density. Considering that simplicity is always preferred under the same accuracy, we drop the device predictor and re-model the data using the other two predictors. We show the regression results in Table 2. We notice that all the coefficients are now statistically significant by passing Wald test and likelihood ratio test.

After model selection, we evaluate goodness of model fit. We carry out likelihood ratio test of model fit to compare our model with the perfect model that uses all degrees of freedom. The results, $\chi^2 = 454.1$ $df = 1963$ $p > 0.999$, is insignificant and indicate that there is very little unexplained variance and thus good model fit. We also compute multiple metrics of goodness of model fit in Table 3, i.e., root-mean-square error, Nagelkerke pseudo R-squared,

Table 3: Model Evaluations

	RMSE	R^2	r	rho
Proposed	0.079	0.909	0.985	0.915
PSNR	NA	NA	0.798	0.803
SSIM	NA	NA	0.828	0.836

Pearson correlation coefficient (r) and Spearman rank correlation coefficient (rho). The proposed model obtains a small RMSE and close-to-one values for the other three metrics, which implies an accurate and reasonable model.

We also compute the correlation between user experience data and objective metrics in conventional DBS, i.e., PSNR [11] and SSIM [8] between original and backlight-scaled images. The perceptual luminance of backlight-scaled images is calculated by the product of scaling magnitude and original pixel values. The PSNR and SSIM of a shot is the average over the frames within the shot. The results show that the proposed model is 9%~23% more correlated to the subjective data, which provides much more space to exploit user experience and enhance power performance.

Finally, we summarize the user acceptability model of scaling magnitude as

$$\mathcal{A} = \frac{1}{1 + \exp^{-(\alpha + \beta EMD_{shot} + \gamma \mathcal{M})}} \tag{4}$$

where the coefficients are shown in Table 2. Given an acceptability requirement, we would then be able to compute the best scaling magnitude of a given shot.

6. SMOOTHING DBS INCONSISTENCY

6.1 Motivational Study

We now study whether or not the continuous playback of backlight-scaled shots using the proposed scaling magnitude would cause flicker effect and how to smooth such, if any, temporal inconsistency. We proceed by studying the user acceptability of two continuously played shots because this can aid us to understand user experience at the minimum scaling unit. Thereby, we would be able to guarantee QoE for the whole video by individually smoothing the scaling at each shot boundary. Specifically, we aim to identify whether or not the magnitude of the second shot is proper given a known magnitude of the first shot. To this end, we set up a series of test clips of two consecutive shots (average duration 8 seconds), wherein the luminance feature EMD_{shot} of both first shot and second shot spans from category 1 to 5. We exclude the 5 clips whose first and second shots have the same luminance category because, under the same acceptability requirement, the optimal scaling magnitudes of these two shots will be very similar based on (4) and will show smooth variation.

We fix the scaling magnitude for the first shot $\mathcal{M}_{fst}$ at the optimal value obtained from (4) using 0.9 acceptability. For the second shot of down-scaled clips ($\mathcal{M}_{fst,opt} > \mathcal{M}_{sec,opt}$), we reduce the second magnitude $\mathcal{M}_{sec}$ gradually from $\mathcal{M}_{fst}$ at step of 0.1 until reaching the computed optimal magnitude of second shot, i.e., $\mathcal{M}_{sec} = \{\mathcal{M}_{fst} - 0.1, \mathcal{M}_{fst} - 0.2, \cdots, \mathcal{M}_{sec,opt}\}$. We do not include the versions whose second shot is scaled lower than $\mathcal{M}_{sec,opt}$ since those second shots do not have the basic brightness to support user acceptability as shown in the scaling magnitude study. For example, suppose we have a clip with $\mathcal{M}_{fst,opt} = 0.4$ and

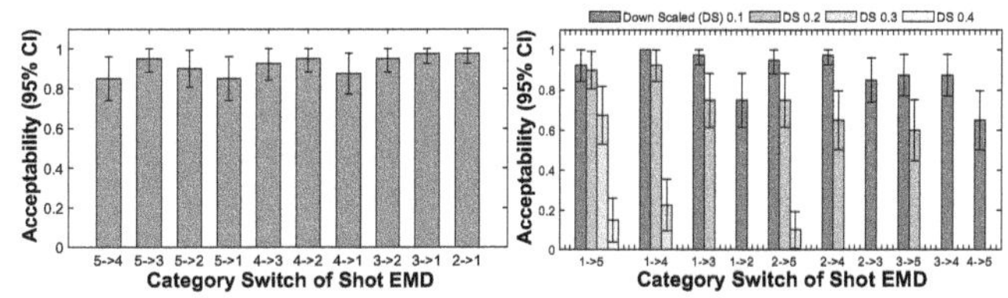

Figure 6: Acceptability of different patterns for up-scaled switch (left) and down-scaled switch (right).

$\mathcal{M}_{sec,opt} = 0.7$ and we scale both shots at 0.4. Even though the backlight scaling is smooth, the second shot is too dark to be accepted because its scaling magnitude was already below 0.7 at the first place. Similarly, there is only one version for those up-scaled clips, i.e., $\mathcal{M}_{sec} = \mathcal{M}_{sec,opt}$. Given these facts, we generate 30 versions of 20 test clips for this user study. Participants follow the same test protocol in scaling frequency test and a total of 1200 binary data points (400 up-scaled and 800 down-scaled) have been collected.

We discover an interesting distinction between the user experience of up-scaled and down-scaled clips. As shown in Figure 6, we see that the acceptability of all up-scaled clips are clearly high. This result is compatible with conventional QoE studies, where low-quality segments followed by high-quality segments was reported to be more preferred [32]. This phenomena might be due to the fact that users subconsciously believe brighter video is better and thus accept those up-scaled clips. Therefore, we decide to directly apply $\mathcal{M}_{opt}$ for up-scaled shots. On the other hand, we observe that QoE of down-scaled clips decreases as the scaling variation increases. Furthermore, QoE under the same level of variation largely depends on luminance features. Considering these inter-related factors, we need to deliberately handle the down-scaled switches. In order to identify and smooth the inconsistent scaling, we propose to train a binary classifier to detect the inconsistency at every down-scaled switch and then smooth it by increasing $\mathcal{M}_{sec}$ accordingly.

6.2 A Classifier for Smooth Scaling

Logistic regression is also a commonly used binary classifier [31]. Since it has been shown to accurately characterize the relation among QoE, content luminance and backlight, we build a logistic binary classifier to detect down-scaled inconsistency. We use the same method as shown in the previous section to process the outliers and fit the model.

Considering the stimuli of the motivational study, many possible features can be used to train the classifier: device type, variation of scaling magnitude $\Delta\mathcal{M}$, variation of luminance feature ΔEMD_{shot}, $\mathcal{M}_{fst}$, $\mathcal{M}_{sec}$, $EMD_{shot,fst}$, and $EMD_{shot,sec}$. We first exclude $\mathcal{M}_{sec}$ and $EMD_{shot,sec}$ because of their direct correlation to $\Delta\mathcal{M}$ and ΔEMD_{shot}, respectively. For example, given $\mathcal{M}_{fst}$, $\mathcal{M}_{sec}$ and $\Delta\mathcal{M}$ can be mutually derived from each other. Besides, we find that the feature of device type does not pass Wald test ($z = 1.672$ $p = 0.094$) and the likelihood ratio test of predictors ($\chi^2 = 488.44$ $df = 765$ $p = 0.093$). This implies that device type is not a significant feature for the classifier. This is expected as we have discussed in the modeling of scaling magnitude. Finally, we obtain a classifier with 4 significant features as shown in Table 4.

Table 4: Classifier Coefficients

Feature	Estimate	Wald Test	Likehood Ratio Test
Constant	-48.930	$z = -3.68$	NA
ΔEMD_{shot}	0.088	$z = 7.05$	$\chi^2 = 848.99$ $df = 769$
$\Delta \mathcal{M}$	-54.775	$z = -10.00$	$\chi^2 = 517.80$ $df = 768$
$EMD_{shot,fst}$	-0.347	$z = -3.73$	$\chi^2 = 507.13$ $df = 767$
$\mathcal{M}_{fst}$	128.060	$z = 3.86$	$\chi^2 = 491.26$ $df = 766$
*All tests are significant at $p < 0.001$.			

Table 5: Classifier Evaluations (%)

	Precision	Recall	F_1
Proposed	87.79	93.09	90.36

To evaluate the classification performance of the classifier, we perform 10-fold cross validation to data points. In Table 5, we show the precision, recall and F1 score ($F_1 = \frac{2 \cdot precision \cdot recall}{precision + recall}$). The results show that the classifier can achieve a reasonably good performance. Hence, we can rely on this classifier to detect the inconsistent down-scaled switches. Then the scaling magnitude of the detected second shot would be increased step by step (step size 0.05) until it can be accepted by the classifier.

7. SYSTEM IMPLEMENTATION

In this section, we demonstrate a practical application of the proposed DBS designs in a HTTP progressive streaming/download system to validate the benefits of QoE-driven power-saving strategy. We choose progressive streaming rather than adaptive streaming because we intend to keep the playing quality of videos unchanged, allowing a more accurate study of user experience in terms of DBS. We first summarize the proposed DBS profiler that addresses the issues in scaling frequency, magnitude and temporal consistency:

1. Determine the scaling boundary of the input video using shot detection via Algorithm 1.
2. Compute the best scaling magnitude for two consecutive shots under a given acceptability requirement using the logistic model in (4).
3. Detect the inconsistent down-scaled switch using the binary classifier and smooth the inconsistency, if needed, by gradually reducing the variation until it is accepted.
4. Iterate step 2 and 3 until all video shots are profiled.

We have implemented the full video-on-demand (VoD) system, where the university server stores encoded videos and users request the video using QoEPlayer. We consider two real-world scenarios. First, users access the video in the university using high-speed campus WiFi, which mimics the enterprise networks. Second, users view the video outside of campus using WiFi of third-party providers, which simulates the typical environment where videos are stored in the near CDN servers. In order to ensure that the QoE evaluation is only impacted by DBS, we choose not to select 3G/4G networks as their relatively unstable network condition and low data rate may cause networking-related distortions.

The server handles the computation of DBS and stores the DBS profile of a video as a separate file. Once a video is selected by the user, QoEPlayer will first download the corresponding DBS profile from the server if it is not already in the local storage and then proceed to the backlight-scaled video playback. By offloading most DBS-related computations to the server side, the proposed DBS profiling can be efficiently treated by modern server clouds. Furthermore, considering that VoD services is time insensitive and a video only needs to be profiled once, we believe such an architecture is feasible and promising for power saving at the system level for massive number of devices.

The potential extra cost of the system lies in the transmission of the profiling file, which may introduce additional delay and power consumption. To investigate this issue, 5 participants are invited to watch clip "ducks" at both on-campus and off-campus environments. We ask them if they perceive any significant initial delay between two scenarios and how is the initial delay compared with their regular viewing. We are happy to report that none of them reports noticeable initial delay in both questions. In fact, this is expected since the file size of the profile is only around 1kB. Based on our measurement, it at most takes a few hundreds of milliseconds to download the file, which can hardly be perceived during the video start-up process. Hence, we conclude that the extra delay is negligible. We will show in the following that the additional power consumption is also marginal and does not compromise the benefits of the proposed designs.

We compare the performance of the proposed DBS designs with a conventional design, which uses the frame luminance variance [26] to decide scaling frequency and SSIM [8] to compute the scaling magnitude. The scaling magnitude of a video segment is computed by iteratively reducing the backlight (step size 0.05) until the minimum SSIM of the frames hits the given threshold. We combine these two schemes as they have been shown in prior sections to achieve better performance than existing approaches. The enhancement over such a strategy will highlight the advantages of the proposed designs. Both acceptability and SSIM requirement are set to be 0.9. The smoothing step size for reducing the down-scaled variation is set to be 0.05.

7.1 QoE Evaluations

We ask the participants to evaluate the acceptability of backlight-scaled videos using both the proposed profiling and the reference profiling. We focus on the on-campus scenario since we need to avoid the potential impact of video buffering on QoE. By using high-speed WiFi (around 4Mbps throughput), the video (bit-rate∼2Mbps) can be playbacked uninterruptedly. Given that 4 full videos (average duration 134 seconds) are tested, we follow the test protocol as in the scaling frequency study.

As shown in Figure 7, the acceptability of the proposed DBS is higher than the reference designs for all clips. This is attributed to the fact that the proposed designs scale the backlight at appropriate time points with pleasing magnitude and smooth transition. In contrast, the reference designs cannot accurately capture the scaling time points and fail to smooth the temporal inconsistency of backlight changes. Although we notice that the average backlight level of videos using reference designs are higher than that of the proposed designs, this fact does not positively contribute to the overall QoE. This is because there is virtually no perceptual difference between the scaling magnitude enforced by the proposed designs and the reference designs. Thus, the high magnitude of reference designs is unnecessary.

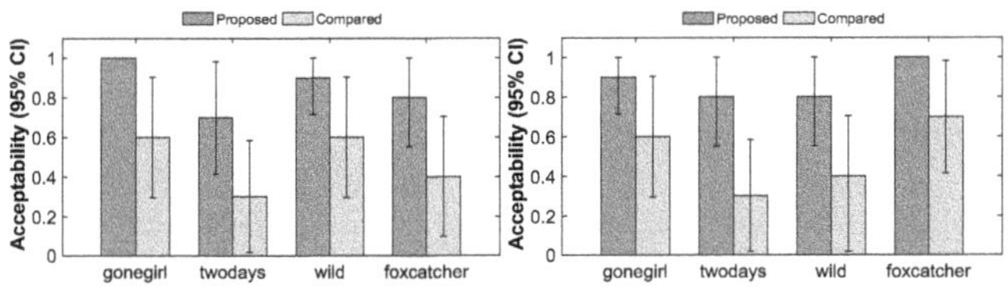

Figure 7: Acceptability on G Pro (left) and Nexus 4 (right).

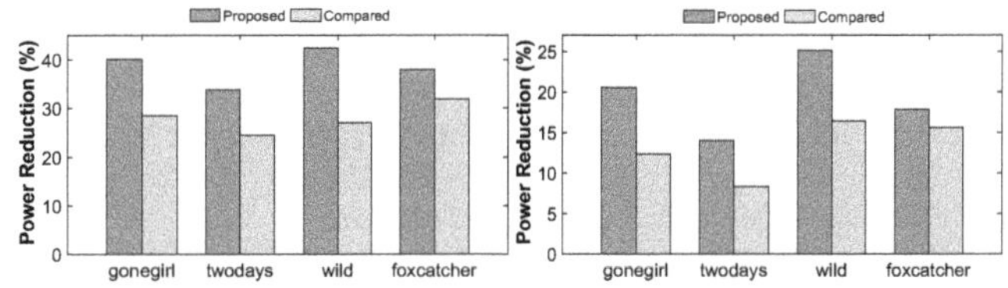

Figure 8: Power Reduction on G Pro (left) and Nexus 4 (right).

7.2 Power Evaluations

In order to measure the battery power, we use Qualcomm Trepn, a measurement tool that directly reads hardware data from the devices. The test devices used in the system level evaluations, i.e., LG Optimus G Pro and Google Nexus 4, have been listed by Qualcomm as the supported devices that enjoy accurate power readings via Trepn [33]. During the system power measuring, we turn off all the unused apps and services. We also close all unnecessary networking activities, such as automatic update and Bluetooth, and only keep video transmission via WiFi active. We measure the power between the moment when users click a video and the moment video playback ends. After every measurement round, we make sure the cache is cleared and the entire video will be transmitted again in the next round.

We obtain the power reduction of different DBS designs based on the measurement method in [34]. First, we perform ten rounds of power measurement for a clip using three different strategies: (1) full backlight without DBS, (2) the proposed DBS, and (3) the reference DBS. Then the average power of a particular strategy can be computed. Finally, the power reduction of DBS over full-backlight playback is expressed as $\frac{P_{full}-P_{DBS}}{P_{full}}$, where P_{full} is the average power without DBS and P_{DBS} is the average power with DBS (either the proposed designs or the reference designs).

We show the results of power reduction in Figure 8. We observe that the proposed DBS designs accomplish a significant power savings. It can reach up to 42.34% power reduction depending on the device and content luminance. If a video is filmed in a darker environment and played on a larger screen, e.g., "wild" on G Pro, more power can be saved. The proposed DBS also outperforms conventional objective distortion based DBS by saving up to 20.95% more power when clip "wild" is tested on LG G Pro. The reason is that those objective distortion assumptions of conventional designs sacrifice much space for DBS and thus cannot maximally exploit the advantages of this technique. Although one may decrease the SSIM threshold to reduce the power of the reference designs, its QoE performance would be further downgraded, which is unacceptable for everyday applications. Therefore, we conclude that the proposed designs achieve best results in terms of both QoE and power.

8. DISCUSSION

Luminance Compensation. To absorb scaling distortion, several schemes have attempted to compensate the pixel luminance first and then scale the backlight. This luminance compensation is not adopted in this research because we would like to focus on the inherent correlation among QoE, backlight scaling, and content luminance at the fundamental level. Adopting additional enhancement techniques, such as luminance compensation that relies on many objective or linear assumptions, into our study shall complicate the issues. Through luminance compensation, many image pixels can be fully compensated and how the resulting contrast distortion in the backlight-scaled image would impact QoE is unknown. It is true that luminance compensation is a complimentary technique to DBS. However, a separate full-scale study is definitely needed. Once the relationship between QoE and luminance compensation is better understood, we expect to achieve an even higher power saving.

VoD System Design. We have shown that the overhead of the extra profiling file is negligible. Alternatively, the profiling information can be easily embedded into the encoded video bitstream as supplemental enhancement information (SEI) of H.264 for DBS at each mobile device to save energy. Such embedding as SEI can be seamlessly integrated into standard VoD systems. This will provide an elegant way to deliver such miniaturized yet essential information.

Note that both adaptive bit-rate streaming and backlight scaling have significant impacts on the overall QoE. They are two independent dimension of QoE. For example, in an adaptive streaming system, when one watches a video with frequently and abruptly scaled backlight, the overall QoE would be bad no matter how high the bit-rate is and how smooth the rate variation is. Although HTTP adaptive streaming is not currently supported in the proposed designs, this can be achieved easily by adopting a similar method to obtain the scaling magnitude and consistency models for different bit-rate/resolution. Similarly, DBS strategy for those rare video viewing scenarios, e.g., brighter outdoor or darker interior, can also be easily obtained.

9. CONCLUSION

In this paper, we have presented a novel approach for tackling the challenges of systematic power reduction on LCD smartphones from the perspective of QoE. We explore the QoE effects when dynamic backlight scaling is applied by conducting three motivational studies. Inspired by the interesting insights derived from these studies, we propose a suite of designs to address the DBS frequency, magnitude and temporal consistency. Through devising a VoD system that adopts the proposed designs, we demonstrate that the proposed DBS can achieve more than 40% system power savings, which represents a 20% improvement over conventional non-QoE schemes, without QoE impairment.

We would like to emphasize that this new approach is fundamentally different from conventional video QoE research which mainly aims to improve encoding and networking performance. This research is indeed a pioneering step towards exploring QoE to enhance power performance. Especially, this approach extends a promising dimension for QoE studies. Furthermore, this research represents a significant attempt to address the prevailing issue of mobile display power in the application layer. The preliminary results have shown that such interdisciplinary research can achieve much desired display power performance in contemporary .

10. ACKNOWLEDGEMENTS

This research is supported by NSF Grants ECCS-1405594 and ECCS-1406154.

11. REFERENCES

[1] A. Carroll and G. Heiser. An analysis of power consumption in a smartphone. In *USENIX annual technical conference (USENIXATC)*, June 2010.

[2] DisplaySearch. http://goo.gl/b56ebH.

[3] W.-C. Cheng and M. Pedram. Power minimization in a backlit tft-lcd display by concurrent brightness and contrast scaling. *IEEE Trans. Consum. Electron.*, 50:25–32, February 2004.

[4] N. Chang, I. Choi, and H. Shim. Dls: dynamic backlight luminance scaling of liquid crystal display. *IEEE Trans. VLSI Syst.*, 12:837–846, August 2004.

[5] A. Iranli, H. Fatemi, and M. Pedram. Hebs: histogram equalization for backlight scaling. In *Proc. of Design, Automation and Test in Europe (DATE)*, March 2005.

[6] A. Iranli, W. Lee, and M. Pedram. Hvs-aware dynamic backlight scaling in tft-lcds. *IEEE Trans. VLSI Syst.*, 14:1103–1116, October 2006.

[7] A. Bartolini, M. Ruggiero, and L. Benini. Hvs-dbs: human visual system-aware dynamic luminance backlight scaling for video streaming applications. In *ACM international conference on Embedded software (EMSOFT)*, October 2009.

[8] C.-H. Lin, P.-C. Hsiu, and C.-K. Hsieh. Dynamic backlight scaling optimization: a cloud-based energy-saving service for mobile streaming applications. *IEEE Trans. Comput.*, 63:335–348, February 2014.

[9] Y. Liu, M. Xiao, M. Zhang, X. Li, M. Dong, Z. Ma, Z. Li, and S. Chen. Content-adaptive display power saving in internet mobile streaming. In *ACM NOSSDAV*, March 2015.

[10] P. Ni, R. Eg, A. Eichhorn, C. Griwodz, and P. Halvorsen. Flicker effects in adaptive video streaming to handheld devices. In *ACM MM*, November 2011.

[11] L. Cheng, S. Mohapatra, M. El Zarki, N. Dutt, and N. Venkatasubramanian. Quality-based backlight optimization for video playback on handheld devices. *Advances in Multimedia*, 2007(1):4–4, 2007.

[12] W. Lin and C.-C. Kuo. Perceptual visual quality metrics: a survey. *Journal of Visual Communication and Image Representation*, 22:297–312, May 2011.

[13] W. Song and D. Tjondronegoro. Acceptability-based qoe models for mobile video. *IEEE Trans. Multimedia*, 16:738–750, April 2014.

[14] F. Zhang, W. Lin, Z. Chen, and K. N. Ngan. Additive log-logistic model for networked video quality assessment. *IEEE Trans. Image Process.*, 16:1536–1547, April 2013.

[15] C. Alberti, D. Renzi, C. Timmerer, C. Mueller, S. Lederer, S. Battista, and M. Mattavelli. Automated qoe evaluation of dynamic adaptive streaming over http. In *IEEE QoMEX*, July 2013.

[16] Z. Yan, J. Xue, and C. W. Chen. QoE continuum driven HTTP adaptive streaming over multi-client wireless networks. In *IEEE International Conference on Multimedia and Expo (ICME)*, July 2014.

[17] Opinion model for video-telephony applications. ITU-T Recommendation G.1070. 2007.

[18] W. Song, D. Tjondronegoro, and M. Docherty. Saving bitrate vs. pleasing users: where is the breakeven point in mobile video quality. In *ACM MM*, November 2011.

[19] H. Knoche, J. McCarthy, and M. Sasse. Can small be beautiful?: assessing image resolution requirements for mobile tv. In *ACM MM*, November 2005.

[20] GT Fechner. Element of psychophysics. *New York: Holt, Rinehart and Winston*, 1966.

[21] A. Balachandran, V. Aggarwal, E. Halepovic, J. Pang, S. Seshan, S. Venkataraman, and H. Yan. Modeling web quality-of-experience on cellular networks. In *ACM MobiCom*, September 2014.

[22] A. Balachandran, V. Sekar, A. Akella, S. Seshan, I. Stoica, and H. Zhang. Developing a predictive model of quality of experience for internet video. In *ACM SIGCOMM*, August 2013.

[23] Xiph. https://media.xiph.org/video/derf/.

[24] DisplayMate. Smartphone displays under bright ambient lighting shoot-out. http://goo.gl/n89Kgo.

[25] W. Song, D. Tjondronegoro, and I. Himawan. Acceptability-based qoe management for user-centric mobile video delivery: a field study evaluation. In *ACM MM*, November 2014.

[26] S. Pasricha, M. Luthra, Shivajit Mohapatra, N. Dutt, and N. Venkatasubramanian. Dynamic backlight adaptation for low-power handheld devices. *IEEE Des. Test. Comput.*, 21:398–405, September 2004.

[27] R. Lienhart. Comparison of automatic shot boundary detection algorithms. In *SPIE Electronic Imaging*, pages 290–301, 1998.

[28] A. Hanjalic. Shot-boundary detection: unraveled and resolved? *IEEE Trans. Circuits Syst. Video Technol.*, 12:90–105, February 2002.

[29] Y. Rubner, C. Tomasi, and L. Guibas. The earth mover's distance as a metric for image retrieval. *International journal of computer vision*, 40:99–121, November 2000.

[30] A M. Ferman, A M. Tekalp, and R. Mehrotra. Robust color histogram descriptors for video segment retrieval and identification. *IEEE Trans. Image Process.*, 11:497–508, May 2002.

[31] R. Christensen. *Log-Linear Models and Logistic Regression.* Springer-Verlag, New York, USA, 1997.

[32] M. Zink, O. Künzel, J. Schmitt, and R. Steinmetz. Subjective impression of variations in layer encoded videos. In *IEEE/ACM IWQoS*, June 2003.

[33] Qualcomm. Devices that report accurate battery power. http://goo.gl/ZecX96.

[34] M. Dong and L. Zhong. Power modeling and optimization for oled displays. *IEEE Trans. Mobile Comput.*, 11:1587–1599, September 2012.

Automatic Image Dataset Construction from Click-through Logs Using Deep Neural Network

Yalong Bai
School of Computer Science and Technology
Harbin Institute of Technology
Harbin, 150001, P. R. China
ylbai@mtlab.hit.edu.cn

Kuiyuan Yang
Microsoft Research
13F, Bldg 2, No. 5, Danling St
Beijing, 100080, P. R. China
kuyang@microsoft.com

Wei Yu
School of Computer Science and Technology
Harbin Institute of Technology
Harbin, 150001, P. R. China
w.yu@hit.edu.cn

Chang Xu
College of Computer and Control Engineering
Nankai University
Tianjin, 300071, P. R. China
changxu@nbjl.nankai.edu.cn

Wei-Ying Ma
Microsoft Research
13F, Bldg 2, No. 5, Danling St
Beijing, 100080, P. R. China
wyma@microsoft.com

Tiejun Zhao
School of Computer Science and Technology
Harbin Institute of Technology
Harbin, 150001, P. R. China
tjzhao@hit.edu.cn

ABSTRACT

Labelled image datasets are the backbone for high-level image understanding tasks with wide application scenarios, and continuously drive and evaluate the progress of feature designing and supervised learning models. Recently, the million scale labelled image dataset further contributes to the rebirth of deep convolutional neural network and bypass manual designing handcraft features. However, the construction process of image dataset is mainly manual-based and quite labor intensive, which often take years' efforts to construct a million scale dataset with high quality. In this paper, we propose a deep learning based method to construct large scale image dataset in an automatic way. Specifically, word representation and image representation are learned in a deep neural network from large amount of click-through logs, and further used to define word-word similarity and image-word similarity. These two similarities are used to automatize the two labor intensive steps in manual-based image dataset construction: query formation and noisy image removal. With a new proposed cross convolutional filter regularizer, we can construct a million scale image dataset in one week. Finally, two image datasets are constructed to verify the effectiveness of the method. In addition to scale, the automatically constructed dataset has comparable accuracy, diversity and cross-dataset generalization with manually labelled image datasets.

Categories and Subject Descriptors

H.2.4 [**Information Systems**]: Systems—*Multimedia databases*

MM'15, October 26–30, 2015, Brisbane, Australia.

DOI: http://dx.doi.org/10.1145/2733373.2806243.

General Terms

Algorithms; Experimentation; Performance

Keywords

Automatic Image Dataset Construction; Image Representation; Word Representation; Deep Learning

1. INTRODUCTION

Image datasets with category labels serve as the backbone for high-level image understanding tasks, and typically used by splitting into training set for model learning and testing set for performance evaluation. With the help of crowdsourcing, ImageNet constructed by manually labeling has reached million scale [7] and acts as one important factor for the great success of deep convolutional neural network by automatically learning visual features [17, 23, 24].

However, the process of manual-based image dataset construction is both time consuming and labor intensive. For example, ImageNet has taken years' efforts to label 21841 categories (nouns from WordNet [19]), which is still far from their goal to label all WordNet nouns, not to mention the continuously emerging categories such as new products and cartoon characters. Even worse, the time cost will cause long latency for application scenarios which require constructing datasets with their own category lists.

To find ways to shorten the construction process, we analyze the whole process by breaking down it into three steps:

1. *Category list generation*, which is often pre-defined according to specific task;
2. *Query formation*, where each category is expanded to a set of queries by referring synonyms in existing ontology such as WordNet, then submitted to image search engines to collect candidate images.
3. *Noisy image removal*, manually verifying each candidate image to removal noisy images.

Obviously, the most time-consuming part comes from step 2 and 3 especially when the number of categories is large.

Step 2 can be bypassed if categories already exist in some predefined ontology, but efforts are required for new emerging categories. While step 3 is extremely time-consuming since there are thousands of images need to be manually verified for each category.

In this work, we propose to relieve the cost by automatizing both step 2 and 3, and construct high quality image datasets in a scalable and timely manner. The proposed method relies on click-through logs from image search engine where lots interactions between queries and images have been associated, and learns both image representation and word representation in a deep learning framework. With the learned representations, word-word similarity and image-word similarity can be effectively calculated. The word-word similarity is used to automatize step 2 by finding similar words for each category. Meanwhile, image-word similarity is used to automatically verify candidate images by removing noisy images that are of low similarity to the category. In the used deep neural network, image representation is modeled by convolutional layers and a fully-connect layer (also some layers without weights such as max-pooling layer), and word representation is formulated as a weight matrix of a fully-connected layer following the fully-connect layer of image representation. To resist heavy tail distribution in click-through logs, we further introduce a regularizer called "Cross Filters Regularization" to speed up the training process.

To verify the effectiveness of the proposed automatic image dataset construction method, we first construct a small scale dataset with 10 categories, and show its cross-dataset generalization ability by comparing with other two manually constructed datasets. Furthermore, to verify the scalability of our method, we construct another large scale dataset with 1000 categories and demonstrate its comparable accuracy and diversity with other human labelled high quality datasets.

Figure 1: A snapshot of click-through logs from Bing image search. Images marked with red boxes are noisy images.

The rest of the paper is organized as follow. We cover related work in Section 2 and then present our automatic method for image dataset construction in Section 3. In Section 4, we apply the proposed method to construct datasets, and analysis characteristics of the constructed datasets in detail. Finally, we discussion conclusions and future work in Section 5.

2. RELATED WORK

Considering the importance of image datasets in the area of image content understanding, lots of efforts have been involved in constructing image datasets. Most works are manually based, while some works explore automatic ways as ours.

2.1 Manual based image dataset construction

The classical way to build an image dataset is manually based (e.g., ImageNet [7], CIFAR-10/100 [16], Pascal VOC series [9], Caltech-101/256 [10, 12], LabelMe [21], SUN [29], etc.). Most of these datasets are built by sending category names to image search engines and aggregating returned images as candidate images, then cleaning candidate images by human judgement. Here, we briefly discuss these works along the steps involved in image dataset construction:

Generating Category List The generation of category list depends on specific tasks. For example, SUN [29] targets on scene recognition task by defining 899 scene categories. Borth *et al.* [2] proposed to detect visual sentiment by constructing a dataset around a category list with strong sentiment. Datasets such as TinyImage [26] and ImageNet [7] directly adopt nouns of WordNet as category list, which cover a large amount of objects but are still far from complete.

Query formation Since most image search engines restrict the number of images returned for each query (in the order of hundreds to one thousand) and only top ranked images are with acceptable precision. To overcome the restriction, synonyms are often used to expand a category into a query set. Moreover, methods such as appending category with popular adjectives and words from its parent category, even translating category to different languages are further used to enrich the query set. All expanded queries will submit to several popular image search engines to collect candidate images from Internet. The method only works for categories defined from existing ontology such as WordNet [19], and cannot generalize to categories that have not been compiled into existing ontology. Recently, word embedding [6, 20] provides a learning based method to compute similarity between words and can be used to bypass the manual compilation of ontology. In this paper, we use learning based method to obtain word representations, and automatically expand a category to a query set.

Noisy image removal The candidate images contains lots noisy images with average accuracy around 10% [7]. Human efforts are involved to remove noisy images by checking candidate images one by one. As this step is quite time consuming and labor intensive, NUS-WIDE only partially labelled the whole dataset [4], while TinyImage [26] and visual sentiment dataset [2] keep all raw candidate images without manual labelling. We are interested in generating high quality image dataset without manual labelling. By leveraging the power of deep neural network, noisy images are automatically removed by calculating image-category similarity with the learned image representation and word representation.

2.2 Learning based image dataset construction

To save labelling cost, some works also explored in the direction of learning based image dataset construction. Collins *et al.* [5] proposed to construct image dataset in a semi-automatic manner by using active learning. Several randomly selected images are firstly labelled by human as seed training set for classifier learning, then the learned classifier is used to examine the unlabelled images to find out unconfident images for manual labelling. The process is iterated until sufficient classification accuracy is obtained.

To further reduce labelling cost, semi-supervised learning is applied to learn classifiers from small amount of labelled images and large amount of unlabelled images. These labelled images can be manually labelled [22] or top-ranked images from image search engines [3, 8, 18]. Schroff *et al.* proposed a multi-modal approach by employing both text, metadata and visual features to remove noisy images. Hua *et al.* [13] proposed clustering based method and propagation based method to remove noisy images, where clustering based method removes large irrelevant image "groups" and propagation based method further removes relatively smaller noises. The human cost of this method lies in labelling clusters to learn cluster level classifier for irrelevant cluster removal.

There are lots of work related to the step of *noisy image removal* though not aiming for dataset construction. To name a few, Weston *et al.* [28] proposed to represent images and annotations jointly in a low dimensional embedding space for relevance estimation, the method is limited by the used low level visual representations. Frome *et al.* [11] proposed to map images into a semantic space learned via word embedding from large scale text corpus. However, the semantic space constructed from text corpus is suitable for NLP tasks while not necessarily reflects visual similarity.

In summary, exiting learning based methods save human cost by leveraging the generalization ability of machine learning models. However, the generalization ability is affected by both quantity and quality of manually labelled images, also models' capability where shallow models are limited. To the best of our knowledge, we are the first to use deep neural network for fully-automatic image dataset construction by gaining generalization ability from large scale click-through logs.

3. AUTOMATIC APPROACH

We are targeting at constructing image dataset in a scalable way while ensuring both accuracy and diversity. The basic idea is to automatize the two most labor cost steps: query formation and noisy image removal. In a computational perspective, the core components for these two steps are two similarity metrics, one is word-word similarity to expand each category to a set of similar words, the other is image-word similarity to remove images not relevant to a category. Furthermore, these two similarity metrics are well defined if word representation and image representation can be effectively obtained. Inspired by the success of deep learning in learning word representation for NLP tasks [6] and image representation for image classification [17], we learn these two representations simultaneously in a deep neural network. To train such a complex model with millions parameters, we resort to large scale click-through logs from image search engine. With the trained model, word representation and image representation are naturally defined, and word-word similarity and image-word similarity are further obtained which are used for automatizing the two labor intensive steps in image dataset construction.

3.1 Representation Learning via DNN

We will first introduce how to model the word representation, image representation and their associations. All these

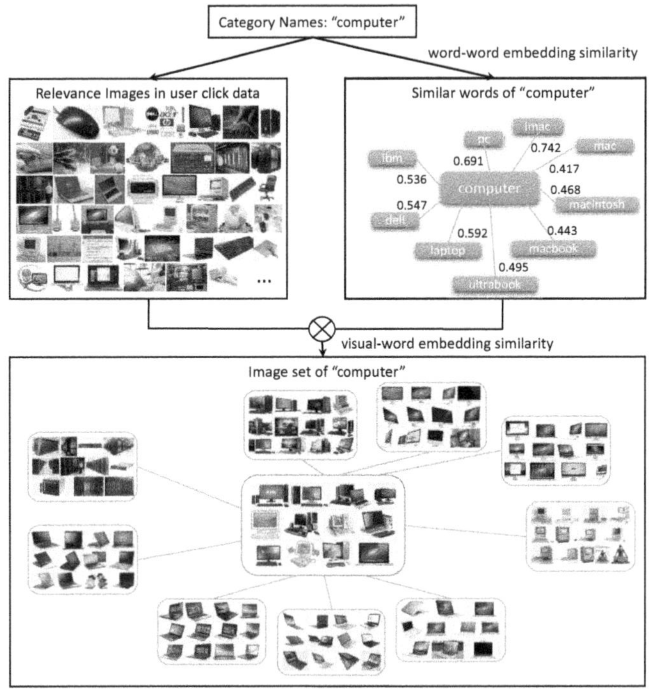

Figure 2: Illustration of our process for automatic image dataset construction. For a given category such as "computer", we first find its similar words with learned word representation, then collect the relevant images from click-through logs according to the similarity between image and similar word set.

computations are then carried by using Bag-of-Words based DNN proposed in [1]. The learning process is performed on the deep neural network through standard method using click-through logs.

3.1.1 *Word Representation*

Similar to word embedding technique which has successfully used in NLP tasks [6], we also represent each word w in vocabulary $\mathcal{V}$ [1] as a vector $\mathbf{e}_w \in \mathbb{R}^{D_w}$ in a continuous space, and denote all word embedding vectors as a matrix E. Instead of learning the representation using text corpus with context constraints which often results only syntactic-level similarity, the word representation will be directly learned using click-through logs together with image representation.

3.1.2 *Image Representation*

Convolutional neural network has demonstrated its superiority in learning image representation from low level to middle level until high level [31]. The network used for image representation learning contains four convolutional layers and one fully-connected layer, three max-pooling layers are used following the first, second and fourth convolutional layers, two local contrast normalization layers are used following the first and second convolutional layers. For image I, its representation is obtained from the output vector $\mathbf{f}(I; \theta_{image}) \in \mathbb{R}^{D_i}$ of the last fully-connected layer, where θ_{image} denotes all parameters in the network for image rep-

[1]In this paper, we use top 50,000 most frequent words in click-through logs as vocabulary

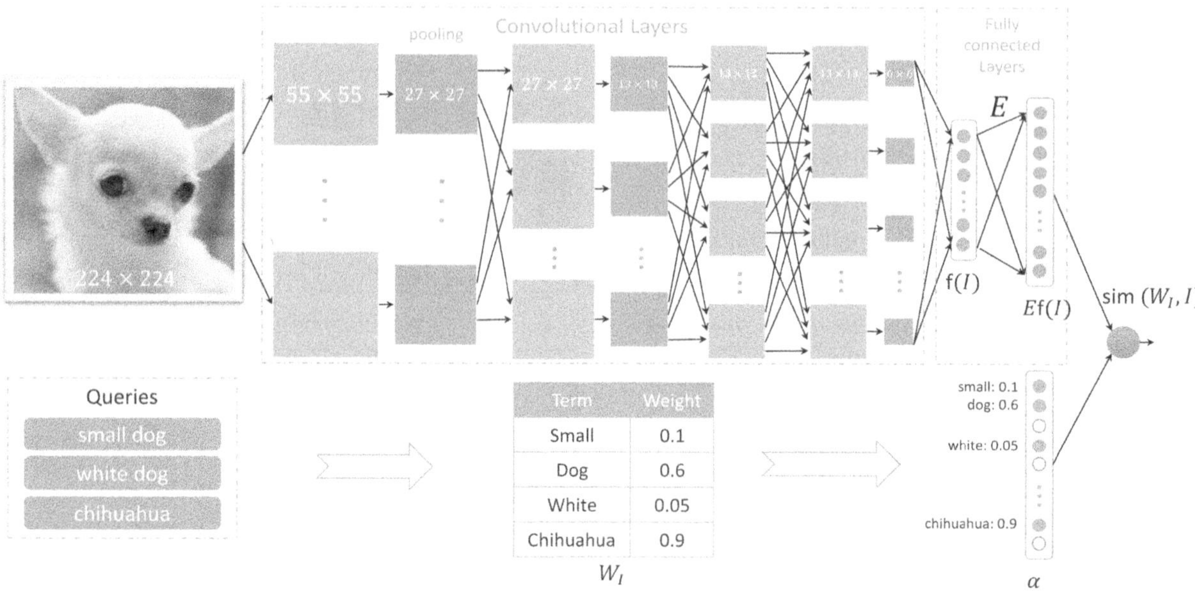

Figure 3: Illustration of the deep neural network for image-query association. The output vector $\mathbf{f}(I)$ of the first fully-connected layer gives the image representation. The weight matrix E encodes word representations in the whole vocabulary. $\boldsymbol{\alpha}$ is the bag-of-textual-words vector generated based on queries.

resentation learning and will be omitted for clarity. Here, we set the dimension of image vector D_i equal to the dimension of word vector D_w for easing image-word similarity caculation.

3.1.3 Image-Query Association

The word representation and image representation are determined by E and θ_{image}, respectively. We follow the standard machine learning pipeline to learn all parameters using supervision from large scale click-through logs. In click-through logs, large number associations are established between queries and images through massive user interactions with image search engine. All queries clicked to image I are merged into a document W_I to form the image's word based representation. Through average composition, document W_I can also be represented as a vector in the same space of word

$$\mathbf{e}_{W_I} = \sum_{w_i \in W_I} \alpha_i \mathbf{e}_{w_i} \tag{1}$$

where α_i is the tf-idf weight for word w_i.

Image I and its associated document W_I is similar based on the judgement of user clicks, should also be similar measured by image representation and word representation, i.e.,

$$\begin{aligned} \text{sim}(W_I, I) &= \langle \mathbf{e}_{W_I}, \mathbf{f}(I) \rangle & (2)\\ &= \Big\langle \sum_{w_i \in W_I} \alpha_i \mathbf{e}_{w_i}, \mathbf{f}(I) \Big\rangle & (3)\\ &= \sum_{w_i \in W_I} \alpha_i \langle \mathbf{e}_{w_i}, \mathbf{f}(I) \rangle & (4)\\ &= \sum_{w_i \in \mathcal{V}} \alpha_i \langle \mathbf{e}_{w_i}, \mathbf{f}(I) \rangle & (5)\\ &= \langle \boldsymbol{\alpha}, E\mathbf{f}(I) \rangle & (6) \end{aligned}$$

Eq(5) summarizes over all words in vocabulary $\mathcal{V}$ where the weights of words not in W_I are zero. $E\mathbf{f}(I)$ can be computed as the output of a fully-connected layer with weight matrix E and input $\mathbf{f}(I)$. Then all computations can be carried in a deep neural network as illustrated in Figure 3.

To avoid trivial solution that maximizes $\text{sim}(W_I, I)$ by simply scaling E or $\mathbf{f}(I)$, we further modify the dot product into cosine similarity

$$\text{sim}(W_I, I) = \frac{\langle \boldsymbol{\alpha}, E\mathbf{f}(I) \rangle}{\|\boldsymbol{\alpha}\| \cdot \|E\mathbf{f}(I)\|} \tag{7}$$

Then the objective function on the whole click-through dataset is defined as

$$J_0(\theta) = -\frac{1}{N} \sum_{i=1}^{N} \text{sim}(W_{I_i}, I_i) + \frac{\beta}{2} \|\theta\| \tag{8}$$

where θ summarizes all parameters in E and θ_{image}.

3.1.4 Cross Convolutional Filters Regularization

The query distribution in click-through dataset has a very long tail. That is only a few of words are frequently appeared, while most words are with low frequency. It also means large amount of similar inputs are fed into DNN frequently during the training process, which leads detection of high-frequency patterns with large neuron responses, and filters in convolutional layers are prone to activate for those highly frequent inputs. Thus, there usually are lots of highly similar filters in convolutional layers at the beginning of training. These highly similar filters not only waste the capacity of the model, but also cause the neural network converge slowly.

To speed up the training process, we add a new regularizer called Cross Convolutional Filters Regularization (CFR) to penalize highly similar filters by adding a regularization term to the objective function. Then the final objective function

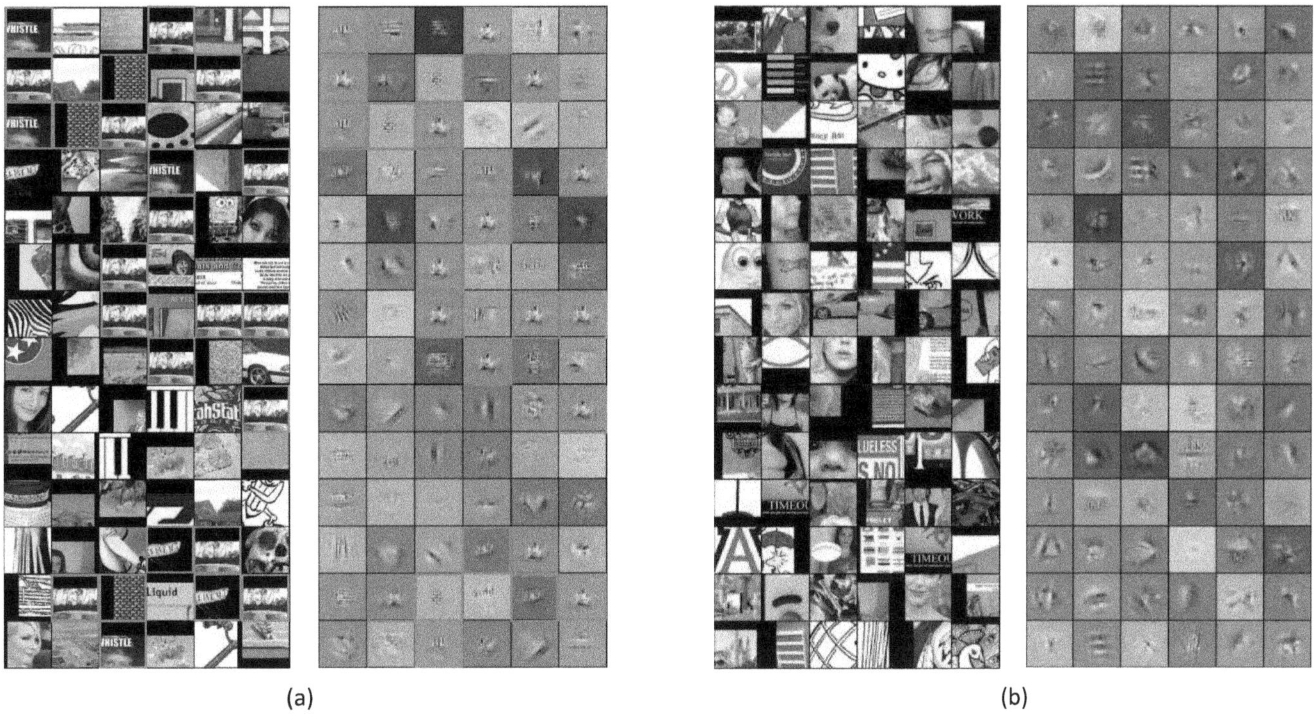

Figure 4: Visualization of filters at the 19th epoch of training. we show the strongest activations in a random subset of the last convolutional layer's feature maps across the click image dataset. The corresponding image patches for each feature map are also shown in the figure: a) DNN, b) DNN+CFR.

is defined as

$$J(\theta) = -\frac{1}{N}\sum_{i=1}^{N} \mathrm{sim}(W_{I_i}, I_i) + \frac{\beta}{2}\|\theta\| + \gamma \sum_{l=1}^{L}\sum_{i=1}^{s_l}\sum_{j=i+1}^{s_l} \langle \theta_i^l, \theta_j^l \rangle \quad (9)$$

where L is the total number of convolutional layers in the neural network, s_l is the number of filters in layer l, and θ_i^l is the parameter vector of the ith filter in layer l. The first term measures the fitness of the neural network on the click-through dataset. The second term is a weight decay term that penalizes weights with large magnitude and used to avoid overfitting. The third term is cross convolutional filters regularization, which aims to penalize highly similar filters.

Figure 4a and 4b visualize the learned filters before and after adding CFR at the early stage of training. The filters are from the last convolutional layer and visualized by image patches with the strongest activations and their deconvolution versions as proposed by [31, 30]. Obviously, CFR can help the network learn more diverse filters, while without CFR, capacity is wasted with lots of similar filters. Figure 5 compares the learning curve of average cosine similarity in the training process, CFR can significantly speed up the training process.

3.1.5 Training Details

The training process of the whole model follows standard training setting of deep neural network. Specifically, we trained our model using stochastic gradient descent with a mini-batch size of 128 samples, weight decay of 5×10^{-4}, cross convolutional filters regularization of 5×10^{-4}, and dropout rate of 0.5 for the first fully-connected layer. The learning rate was initially set to 1, and then decreased by a factor of 10 when average cosine similarity score on validation set stops improving. In total, the learning rate was decreased 4 times.

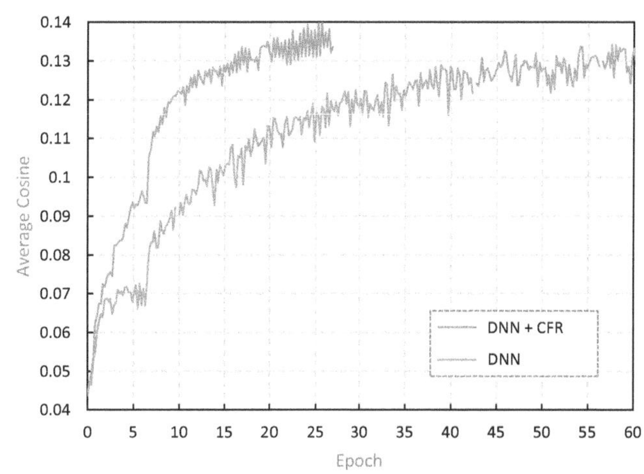

Figure 5: Learning curves of DNN and DNN with CFR. DNN with CFR reaches 0.13 average cosine similarity three times faster than without CFR.

We initialized the weights in each layers from a normal distribution with the zero mean and 0.01 variance. The

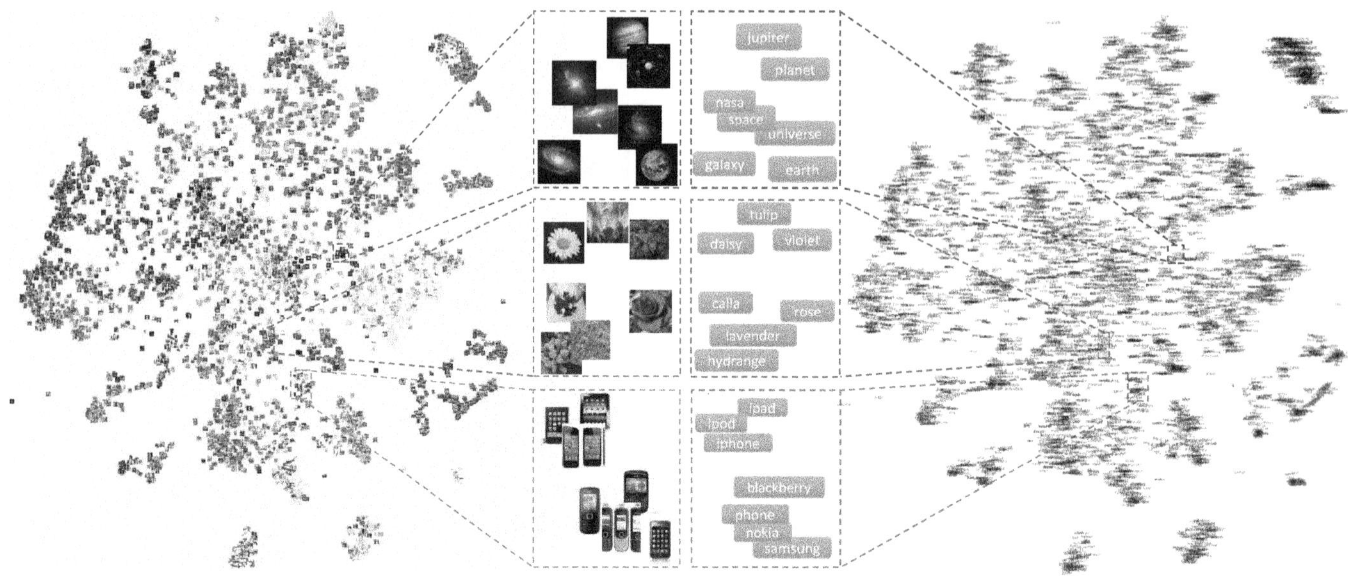

Figure 6: t-SNE visualization of learned word representations of 5,000 randomly selected words, each word is projected as a point in the two dimensional space. Left: each point is pasted with an image clicked by the word. Right: each point is pasted with the string of the word. Middle: Zoom-in to three regions.

neuron biases in the first full-connected hidden layer and the second, fourth convolutional layers were initialized with the constant 1, while the neuron biases in the remaining layers were initialized with zero.

It should be noted that CFR is only used in the early stage of training and removed when learning rate decreased to 0.01. After warm start with less highly similar filters, CFR is removed to let give the objective function more flexility to fit training data.

3.2 Constructing Image Dataset

In this section, we present the automatic way to construct image dataset from click-through logs based on the learned word representation $\mathbf{e}_w$ and image representation $\mathbf{f}(I)$. The process starts with a set of category words $\mathcal{C} = \{c_k\}_{k=1}^{K}$ pre-defined according specific task on hand, and outputs a set of images for each category. Since the process is the same for every category, we will only detail the construction process for category c as an example.

3.2.1 Query Formation

For category c, we first expand it to a set of similar words from vocabulary $\mathcal{V}$. The learned word representation is used for measuring word-word similarity

$$\text{sim}(c, w_i) = \frac{\langle \mathbf{e}_c, \mathbf{e}_{w_i} \rangle}{\|\mathbf{e}_c\| \cdot \|\mathbf{e}_{w_i}\|}. \qquad (10)$$

Accordingly, similar words for category c is defined by

$$\mathcal{S}_c = \{w_i | \text{sim}(c, w_i) > \xi_w, w_i \in \mathcal{V}\} \qquad (11)$$

With the generated similar word set $\mathcal{S}_c$, candidate image set $\mathcal{I}_c$ for category c are collected by aggregating images clicked to queries that contain words in $\mathcal{S}_c$.

3.2.2 Noisy Image Removal

Candidate images still contain many noises, this step is to remove noisy images by leveraging both image representation $\mathbf{f}(I)$ and word representation $\mathbf{e}_w$. Given similar word set $\mathcal{S}_c$ and candidate image set $\mathcal{I}_c$, image set $\mathcal{D}_c$ for category c after noisy removal is obtained by

$$\mathcal{D}_c = \{I | \text{sim}(I, \mathcal{S}_c) > \xi_i, I \in \mathcal{I}_c\} \qquad (12)$$

where similarity between image $I \in \mathcal{I}_c$ and similar word set $\mathcal{S}_c$ is measured as

$$\text{sim}(I, \mathcal{S}_c) = \max_{w \in \mathcal{S}_c} \text{sim}(w, c) \cdot \text{sim}(w, I). \qquad (13)$$

The similarity prefers images that are similar to some word in $\mathcal{S}_c$ and the word is similar to category c. From another perspective, words close to the category have the capacity to keep more images which is consistent with intuition.

The threshold ξ_i for noisy image removal in Eq (12) is set to 0.35 considering the number of images can be collected for each category and ξ_i can be set higher when more click-through logs are available.

4. EXPERIMENTAL RESULTS

We use the click-through logs publicly available from Bing image search [2]. There are two sets of click-through logs: Clickture-Lite and Clickture-Full [14]. Clickture-Lite contains 11.7 million queries and 1 million images, while Clicture-Full is much larger which contains 73.6 million queries and 40 million images. In our experiments, we use Clickture-Lite to train the DNN, and apply the trained DNN on Clickture-Full to construct image dataset. We construct two image datasets to verify our proposed method. The first image dataset named as AutoSet-10 is constructed for 10 categories from CIFAR-10. The second image dataset named as AutoSet-1K, is constructed for 1000 popular categories which were frequently searched by users.

[2]http://research.microsoft.com/en-us/projects/clickture/

Table 1: For six query words, we show their top-10 similar words based on our method and context based word embedding [20]. Words with italic font are visually dissimilar. Our results contains some typos from user queries, but no plurals as we merged plurals in $\mathcal{V}$.

Category	KNN based on visual based word embedding	KNN based on context based word embedding
dog	puppy, dogss, *breed*, hound, spaniel boxer, cocker, retriever, beagle, mastiff	dogs, puppy, *cat*, *pet*, pup canine, puppies, *cats*, *kitten*, terrier
airplane	airplan, aeroplane, boeing, 747, dreamliner lockheed, sukhoi, beechcraft, bomber, fighter	airplanes, aeroplane, plane, *flying*, aircraft planes, takeoff, airliner, helicopter, jet
iphone	ipone, 4s, iphone4s, iphone5, iphon *4gs*, iphone4, *5*, phone5, *otterbox*	*ipad*, *ipod*, 3gs, iphone4, *android* *itouch*, *3g*, ios, iphones, *itunes*
egyptian	pharaoh, egyption, mummification, *horu*, thoth tutankhamun, *heiroglyphic*, bastet, egiptian, mummy.	egypt, *aztec*, egyptians, *arabian*, *greek* egyption, *mayan*, *arabic*, pharaohs, sphinx
universe	hubble, galaxy, supernova, astronomy, *telescope* milkyway, nebula, comet, protostar, andromeda	universes, cosmos, worlds, *existence*, cosmic planet, *infinite*, *realm*, humanity, exist
pokemon	pokeman, *legendary*, victini, bulbasaur, zekrom charizard, pokemoncard, *shiny*, emboar, arceu	*gameboy*, pikachu, *gba*, *nintendo*, *naruto* mew, *yugioh*, *mario*, *zelda*, *digimon*

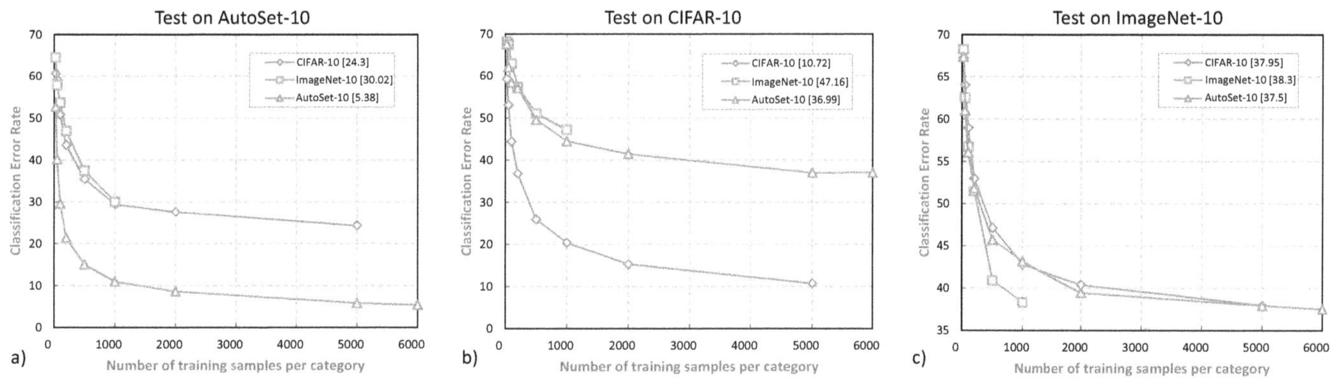

Figure 7: Cross dataset generalization of CNNs trained on AutoSet-10, CIFAR-10 and ImageNet-10, then tested on: a) AutoSet-10, b) CIFAR-10 and c) ImageNet-10.

4.1 Learned Representations

With the learned image representation and word representation, images and words are representated as points in high dimensional space. In Figure 6, we use dimension reduction tool t-SNE [27] to map a set of 5,000 randomly selected words as points in two dimensional space, each point is pasted with an image clicked to the word or string of the word. It can be observed that visually similar words are closely distributed in a meaningful way. For example, words related to handheld are close in the space.

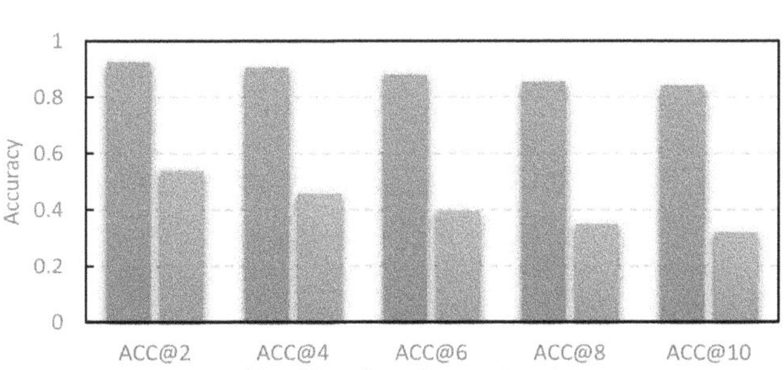

Figure 8: Average accuracy of top-K similar words on 100 randomly words based on our method and context based word embedding [20].

4.2 AutoSet-10

Moreover, we carry a quantitative evaluation for the learned word representation and compare it with state-of-the-art word representation learned from large scale text corpus (including 840 billion tokens) with context constraints [20]. For a set of 100 randomly selected words, we use different word representations to find their top similar words from the vocabulary. The groundtruth of these similar word pairs are manually judged, a pair is labelled as true if the two words are describing the same visual pattern otherwise false. Some exemplar words and their similar words calculated by different word representations are present in Table 1, words with italic font are not visually similar. Obviously, our word representation reflects more about visually similar. Quantitative comparison is based on the following performance metric

$$acc@K = \frac{\sum_{k=1}^{K} 1\{(w_k, w)\}}{K} \tag{14}$$

where $1\{\cdot\}$ is an indicator function, so that it equals to 1 if (w_k, w) is true visually similar word pair and 0 otherwise. Figure 8 shows the average $acc@K$ on the 100 randomly selected words based on the two word representations, and our word representation learned together with image achieved higher accuracy than word representation learned from context based word embedding, thus our word representation

Figure 9: A snapshot of six categories and their sample images in AutoSet-1K.

is more suitable to expand category for image dataset construction.

We first construct a small scale dataset named as AutoSet-10 using the same 10 categories of CIFAR-10 [16]. AutoSet-10 consists of 70000 images in 10 categories, and randomly split into 60000 images as training set and 10000 images as testing set. CIFAR-10 contains 60000 images in total, 50000 images as training set and 10000 images as testing set, which are pre-split. In addition, we construct a subset of ImageNet named as ImageNet-10 using the same 10 categories, and randomly split into 10000 images as training set and 2000 images as testing set.

To compare these three datasets, we conduct a set of image classification experiments to verify their cross-dataset generalization ability [25]. Cross-dataset generalization measures the performance of classifiers learned from one dataset on the other dataset.

The same configuration of convolution neural network is used to build the classifiers, which is modified from [15])(layers-conv-local-11pct.cfg) by replacing local-connected layers with convolutional layers. All images in AutoSet-10 and ImageNet-10 are resized and central cropped into same size as CIFAR-10, i.e., 32×32. Randomly cropped 24×24 image patches with horizontal flips are used as data augmentation for training. Initial learning rate is set to 0.001 and decreased by a factor 10 twice when the validation error stops descreasing.

Figure 7 shows the classification error rates. Each dataset produces one CNN using its training set, and all three CNNs are compared on test set of AutoSet-10 (a), CIFAR-10 (b) and ImageNet-10 (c). In all three cases, at the same number of training samples, the best performance is achieved by training and testing on the same dataset. Since the smallest dataset ImageNet-10 only have 1000 training images per category, we compare the performance of three different dataset at the point of 1000 training samples, it shows that the generalization ability of the three dataset is very close and AutoSet-10 performs slightly better than ImageNet-10 on CIFAR-10. Since AutoSet-10 is larger than the other two datasets, it achieved the best performance on two testing sets when all training samples are used. The comparison at the same number of training samples shows the comparable generalization ability of AuotSet-10 with other two manually constructed datasets, and AutoSet-10 can further get better generalization benefits from its scale up ability.

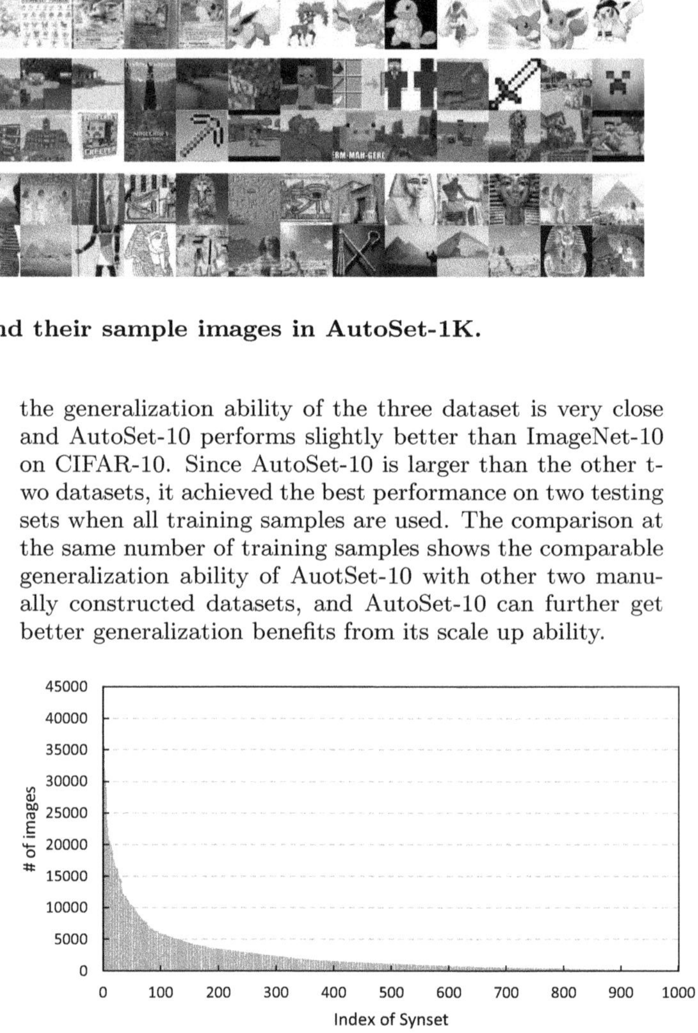

Figure 10: Number of images per category in AutoSet-1K.

4.3 AutoSet-1K

To show the scalability in number of categories, we build a large scale image dataset named as AuotSet-1K consists of 2.5 millions of images for 1000 popular categories that are frequently searched by users. The 1000 categories not only include the long existing categories such as "dog" or other natural objects, but also include many new categories such

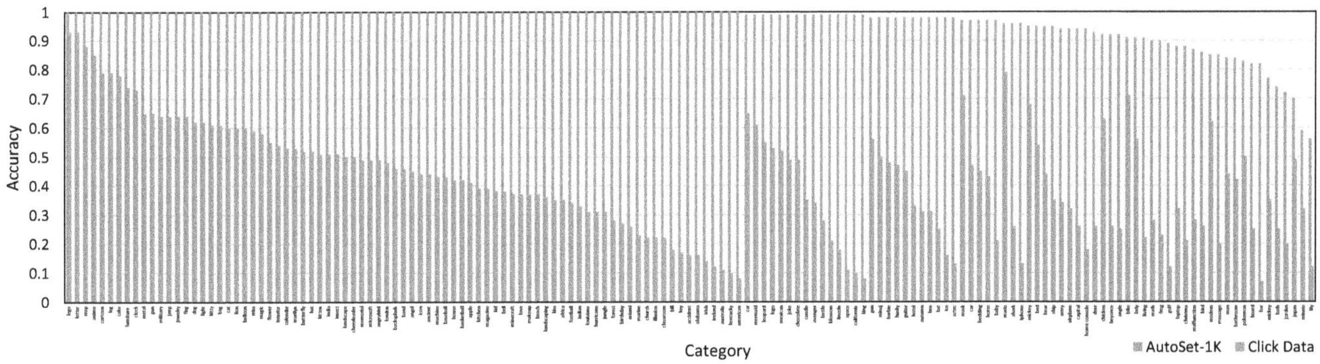

Figure 11: Accuracy of AutoSet-1K and candidate images collected from click-through logs. Randomly sampled 15000 images from AutoSet-1K and 15000 images from click-through logs are manually verified.

Figure 12: Average images and image samples of AutoSet-1K, ImageNet and Caltech-101 from two categories: "elephant" and "airplane". Left chart shows the comparison of the lossless JPG file sizes of average images, we downsampled the average image to 32×32 and sizes are measured in byte. Diverse image set results in a smaller lossless JPG file size.

as products, TV dramas and digital games. Some examplar categories with randomly sampled images are showed in Figure 9. The whole construction process of AutoSet-1K takes a week include the training of deep neural network, which is also an advantage over manually based methods that often need years' efforts to reach datasets with such scale.

In addition to short latency for constructing large scale dataset, we further analysis the quality of AutoSet-1K from three aspects as following.

Scale AutoSet-1K contains 1000 popular categories, and on average over 2500 images for each category. Figure 10 shows the numbers of images per category in AutoSet-1K. Different with static image datasets, AutoSet-1K can be dynamically increased with few efforts.

Accuracy To evaluate accuracy of AutoSet-1K, we randomly sampled 150 categories and 100 images per category. Each category and its images are manually judged, the accuracy on each category are showed in Figure 11. The average accuracy of AutoSet-1K is 95.2% which is much higher than 42.3% of candidate images directly collected from click-through logs, but still little lower than 99.7% achieved by ImageNet. To be noted that, there are several failure categories in AutoSet-1K such as "jordan" with low accuracy 72%, as lots of images about "jordan shoes" instead of "Michael Jordan" exist in click-through logs and mistreated as "jordan" too.

Diversity In order to illustrate the diversity of images belong to a category, we followed the method in [7], which compare the average image of each category and measure lossless JPG file size which reflects the amount of information in an image. Diverse image set should result in a blurrier average image, and the JPG file size of average image of diverse images should be smaller. We resize all images to 256×256, and create average images with randomly selected 60 images for each category. Figure 12 shows the average images of two categories: "elephant" and "airplane", similar to ImageNet, the average image of AutoSet-1K is also very blurrier and hard to recognize out the object, while the average image of Caltech-101 is more structured and sharper. AutoSet-1K has comparable JPG file size with ImageNet, but significantly smaller than Caltech-101.

5. CONCLUSION AND FUTURE WORK

In this paper, we proposed a deep learning based method to automatically construct image dataset from large scale user click-through logs. DNN is used to learn image representation and word representation for calculating word-word similarity and image-word similarity, and further used to automatize two labor costing steps in image dataset construction: query formation and noisy image removal. Moreover, cross convolutional filter regularization is proposed to speed up the training process. The auto-constructed image dataset has no scale up issue, and with high accuracy, diversity and good cross dataset generalization.

One limitation of our method is the unigram based vocabulary, while some categories cannot be represented as unigrams such as "hot dog". In the future, we will replace the unigram based vocabulary with phrase based vocabulary, which will greatly increase the size of vocabulary and require better design of the training system.

6. REFERENCES

[1] Y. Bai, W. Yu, T. Xiao, C. Xu, K. Yang, W.-Y. Ma, and T. Zhao. Bag-of-words based deep neural network for image retrieval. In *Proceedings of the ACM International Conference on Multimedia*, pages 229–232. ACM, 2014.

[2] D. Borth, R. Ji, T. Chen, T. Breuel, and S.-F. Chang. Large-scale visual sentiment ontology and detectors using adjective noun pairs. In *Proceedings of the 21st ACM international conference on Multimedia*, pages 223–232. ACM, 2013.

[3] X. Chen, A. Shrivastava, and A. Gupta. Neil: Extracting visual knowledge from web data. In *Computer Vision (ICCV), 2013 IEEE International Conference on*, pages 1409–1416. IEEE, 2013.

[4] T.-S. Chua, J. Tang, R. Hong, H. Li, Z. Luo, and Y.-T. Zheng. NUS-WIDE: A Real-World Web Image Database from National University of Singapore. In *CIVR*, Santorini, Greece., 2009.

[5] B. Collins, J. Deng, K. Li, and L. Fei-Fei. Towards scalable dataset construction: An active learning approach. In *ECCV*. 2008.

[6] R. Collobert and J. Weston. A unified architecture for natural language processing: Deep neural networks with multitask learning. In *ICML*, 2008.

[7] J. Deng, W. Dong, R. Socher, L.-J. Li, K. Li, and L. Fei-Fei. Imagenet: A large-scale hierarchical image database. In *CVPR*, 2009.

[8] S. K. Divvala, A. Farhadi, and C. Guestrin. Learning everything about anything: Webly-supervised visual concept learning. In *Computer Vision and Pattern Recognition (CVPR), 2014 IEEE Conference on*, pages 3270–3277. IEEE, 2014.

[9] M. Everingham, L. Van Gool, C. K. I. Williams, J. Winn, and A. Zisserman. The PASCAL Visual Object Classes Challenge 2007 (VOC2007) Results.

[10] L. Fei-Fei, R. Fergus, and P. Perona. One-shot learning of object categories. *Pattern Analysis and Machine Intelligence, IEEE Transactions on*, 28(4):594–611, 2006.

[11] A. Frome, G. S. Corrado, J. Shlens, S. Bengio, J. Dean, T. Mikolov, et al. Devise: A deep visual-semantic embedding model. In *Advances in Neural Information Processing Systems*, pages 2121–2129, 2013.

[12] G. Griffin, A. Holub, and P. Perona. Caltech-256 object category dataset. 2007.

[13] X.-S. Hua and J. Li. Prajna: Towards recognizing whatever you want from images without image labeling. AAAI - Association for the Advancement of Artificial Intelligence, January 2015.

[14] X.-S. Hua, L. Yang, J. Wang, J. Wang, M. Ye, K. Wang, Y. Rui, and J. Li. Clickage: Towards bridging semantic and intent gaps via mining click logs of search engines. In *ACM Multimedia*, 2013.

[15] A. Krizhevsky. cuda-convnet2, 2014. `http://code.google.com/p/cuda-convnet2/`.

[16] A. Krizhevsky and G. Hinton. Learning multiple layers of features from tiny images. *Computer Science Department, University of Toronto, Tech. Rep*, 2009.

[17] A. Krizhevsky, I. Sutskever, and G. E. Hinton. Imagenet classification with deep convolutional neural networks. In *NIPS*, 2012.

[18] L.-J. Li and L. Fei-Fei. Optimol: automatic online picture collection via incremental model learning. *International journal of computer vision*, 88(2):147–168, 2010.

[19] G. A. Miller. WordNet: a lexical database for English. *Communications of the ACM*, 38(11):39–41, 1995.

[20] J. Pennington, R. Socher, and C. D. Manning. Glove: Global vectors for word representation. *Proceedings of the Empiricial Methods in Natural Language Processing (EMNLP 2014)*, 12, 2014.

[21] B. C. Russell, A. Torralba, K. P. Murphy, and W. T. Freeman. Labelme: a database and web-based tool for image annotation. *IJCV*, 77(1-3):157–173, 2008.

[22] A. Shrivastava, S. Singh, and A. Gupta. Constrained semi-supervised learning using attributes and comparative attributes. In *ECCV*, pages 369–383. 2012.

[23] K. Simonyan and A. Zisserman. Very deep convolutional networks for large-scale image recognition. *arXiv preprint arXiv:1409.1556*, 2014.

[24] C. Szegedy, W. Liu, Y. Jia, P. Sermanet, S. Reed, D. Anguelov, D. Erhan, V. Vanhoucke, and A. Rabinovich. Going deeper with convolutions. *arXiv preprint arXiv:1409.4842*, 2014.

[25] A. Torralba and A. A. Efros. Unbiased look at dataset bias. In *CVPR*, 2011.

[26] A. Torralba, R. Fergus, and W. T. Freeman. 80 million tiny images: A large data set for nonparametric object and scene recognition. *Pattern Analysis and Machine Intelligence, IEEE Transactions on*, 30(11):1958–1970, 2008.

[27] L. Van der Maaten and G. Hinton. Visualizing data using t-sne. *Journal of Machine Learning Research*, 9(2579-2605):85, 2008.

[28] J. Weston, S. Bengio, and N. Usunier. Wsabie: Scaling up to large vocabulary image annotation. In *IJCAI*, volume 11, pages 2764–2770, 2011.

[29] J. Xiao, J. Hays, K. A. Ehinger, A. Oliva, and A. Torralba. SUN database: large-scale scene recognition from abbey to zoo. In *CVPR*, 2010.

[30] W. Yu, K. Yang, Y. Bai, H. Yao, and Y. Rui. Visualizing and comparing convolutional neural networks. *arXiv preprint arXiv:1412.6631*, 2014.

[31] M. D. Zeiler and R. Fergus. Visualizing and understanding convolutional networks. In *ECCV*. 2014.

DeepFont: Identify Your Font from An Image

Zhangyang Wang[1] Jianchao Yang[3] Hailin Jin[2] Eli Shechtman[2] Aseem Agarwala [4]
Jonathan Brandt [2] Thomas S. Huang [1]
[1]University of Illinois at Urbana-Champaign
[2]Adobe Research
[3]Snapchat Inc [4]Google Inc
{zwang119, t-huang1}@illinois.edu, jianchao.yang@snapchat.com, {hljin, elishe, jbrandt}@adobe.com, aseem@agarwala.org

ABSTRACT

As font is one of the core design concepts, automatic font identification and similar font suggestion from an image or photo has been on the wish list of many designers. We study the Visual Font Recognition (VFR) problem [4], and advance the state-of-the-art remarkably by developing the *DeepFont* system. First of all, we build up the first available large-scale VFR dataset, named *AdobeVFR*, consisting of both labeled synthetic data and partially labeled real-world data. Next, to combat the domain mismatch between available training and testing data, we introduce a Convolutional Neural Network (CNN) decomposition approach, using a domain adaptation technique based on a Stacked Convolutional Auto-Encoder (SCAE) that exploits a large corpus of unlabeled real-world text images combined with synthetic data preprocessed in a specific way. Moreover, we study a novel learning-based model compression approach, in order to reduce the DeepFont model size without sacrificing its performance. The DeepFont system achieves an accuracy of higher than 80% (top-5) on our collected dataset, and also produces a good font similarity measure for font selection and suggestion. We also achieve around 6 times compression of the model without any visible loss of recognition accuracy.

Categories and Subject Descriptors

I.4.7 [**Image Processing and Computer Vision**]: Feature measurement; I.4.10 [**Image Processing and Computer Vision**]: Image Representation; I.5 [**Pattern Recognition**]: Classifier design and evaluation

General Terms

Algorithms, Experimentation

Keywords

Visual Font Recognition; Deep Learning; Domain Adaptation; Model Compression

MM'15, October 26–30, 2015, Brisbane, Australia.

ACM 978-1-4503-3459-4/15/10 ...$15.00.
DOI: http://dx.doi.org/10.1145/2733373.2806219.

1. INTRODUCTION

Typography is fundamental to graphic design. Graphic designers have the desire to identify the fonts they encounter in daily life for later use. While they might take a photo of the text of a particularly interesting font and seek out an expert to identify the font, the manual identification process is extremely tedious and error-prone. Several websites allow users to search and recognize fonts by font similarity, including Identifont, MyFonts, WhatTheFont, and Fontspring. All of them rely on tedious humans interactions and high-quality manual pre-processing of images, and the accuracies are still unsatisfactory. On the other hand, the majority of font selection interfaces in existing softwares are simple linear lists, while exhaustively exploring the entire space of fonts using an alphabetical listing is unrealistic for most users.

Effective automatic font identification from an image or photo could greatly ease the above difficulties, and facilitate font organization and selection during the design process. Such a Visual Font Recognition (VFR) problem is inherently difficult, as pointed out in [4], due to the huge space of possible fonts (online repositories provide hundreds of thousands), the dynamic and open-ended properties of font classes, and the very subtle and character-dependent difference among fonts (letter endings, weights, slopes, etc.). More importantly, while the popular machine learning techniques are data-driven, collecting real-world data for a large collection of font classes turns out to be extremely difficult. Most attainable real-world text images do not have font label information, while the error-prone font labeling task requires font expertise that is out of reach of most people. The few previous approaches [1, 9, 12, 16, 17, 20] are mostly from the document analysis standpoint, which only focus on a small number of font classes, and are highly sensitive to noise, blur, perspective distortions, and complex backgrounds. In [4] the authors proposed a large-scale, learning-based solution without dependence on character segmentation or OCR. The core algorithm is built on local feature embedding, local feature metric learning and max-margin template selection. However, their results suggest that the robustness to real-world variations is unsatisfactory, and a higher recognition accuracy is still demanded.

Inspired by the great success achieved by deep learning models [10] in many other computer vision tasks, we develop a VFR system for the Roman alphabets, based on the Convolutional neural networks (CNN), named *DeepFont*. Without any dependence on character segmentation or content text, the DeepFont system obtains an impressive performance on our collected large real-word dataset, covering

Figure 1: (a) (b) Successful VFR examples with the DeepFont system. The top row are query images from VFR_real_test dataset. Below each query, the results (left column: font classes; right column: images rendered with the corresponding font classes) are listed in a high-to-low order in term of likelihoods. The correct results are marked by the red boxes. (c) More correctly recognized real-world images with DeepFont.

an extensive variety of font categories. Our technical contributions are listed below:

- **AdobeVFR Dataset** A large set of *labeled real-world* images as well as a large corpus of unlabeled real-world data are collected for both training and testing, which is the first of its kind and is publicly released soon. We also leverage a large training corpus of labeled synthetic data augmented in a specific way.
- **Domain Adapted CNN** It is very easy to generate lots of rendered font examples but very hard to obtain labeled real-world images for supervised training. This real-to-synthetic domain gap caused poor generalization to new real data in previous VFR methods [4]. We address this *domain mismatch* problem by leveraging synthetic data to obtain effective classification features, while introducing a domain adaptation technique based on Stacked Convolutional Auto-Encoder (SCAE) with the help of unlabeled real-world data.
- **Learning-based Model Compression** We introduce a novel learning-based approach to obtain a *losslessly compressible model*, for a high compression ratio without sacrificing its performance. An exact low-rank constraint is enforced on the targeted weight matrix.

Fig. 1 shows successful VFR examples using DeepFont. In (a)(b), given the real-world query images, top-5 font recognition results are listed, within which the ground truth font classes are marked out[1]. More real-world examples are displayed in (c). Although accompanied with high levels of background clutters, size and ratio variations, as well as perspective distortions, they are all correctly recognized by the DeepFont system.

[1]Note that the texts are input manually for rendering purposes only. The font recognition process does not need any content information.

Table 1: Comparison of All VFR Datasets

Dataset name	Source	Label?	Purpose	Size	Cl
VFRWild325 [4]	Real	Y	Test	325	9
VFR_real_test	Real	Y	Test	4, 384	6
VFR_real_u	Real	N	Train	197, 396	
VFR_syn_train	Syn	Y	Train	2,383, 000	2,
VFR_syn_val	Syn	Y	Test	238, 300	2,

2. DATASET

2.1 Domain Mismatch between Synthetic and Real-World Data

To apply machine learning to VFR problem, we require realistic text images with ground truth font labels. However, such data is scarce and expensive to obtain. Moreover, the training data requirement is vast, since there are hundreds of thousands of fonts in use for Roman characters alone. One way to overcome the training data challenge is to synthesize the training set by rendering text fragments for all the necessary fonts. However, to attain effective recognition models with this strategy, we must face the domain mismatch between synthetic and real-world text images [4].

For example, it is common for designers to edit the spacing, aspect ratio or alignment of text arbitrarily, to make the text fit other design components. The result is that characters in real-world images are spaced, stretched and distorted in numerous ways. For example, Fig. 2 (a) and (b) depict typical examples of *character spacing* and *aspect ratio* differences between (standard rendered) synthetic and real-world images. Other perturbations, such as background clutter, perspective distortion, noise, and blur, are also ubiquitous.

2.2 The AdobeVFR Dataset

Collecting and labeling real-world examples is notoriously hard and thus a labeled real-world dataset has been absent for long. A small dataset *VFRWild325* was collected in [4], consisting of 325 real-world text images and 93 classes. However, the small size puts its effectiveness in jeopardy.

Chen et. al. in [4] selected 2,420 font classes to work on. We remove some script classes, ending up with a total of 2,383 font classes. We collected 201,780 text images from various typography forums, where people post these images seeking help from experts to identify the fonts. Most of them come with hand-annotated font labels which may be inaccurate. Unfortunately, only a very small portion of them fall into our list of 2,383 fonts. All images are first converted into gray scale. Those images with our target class labels are then selected and inspected by independent experts if their labels are correct. Images with verified labels are then manually cropped with tight bounding boxes and normalized proportionally in size, to be with the identical height of 105 pixels. Finally, we obtain 4,384 real-world test images with reliable labels, covering 617 classes (out of 2,383), as the VFR_real_test set. Compared to the synthetic data, these images typically have much larger appearance variations caused by scaling, background clutter, lighting, noise, perspective distortions, and compression artifacts. Removing the 4,384 labeled images from the full set, we are left with 197,396 unlabeled real-world images which we denote as VFR_real_u.

To create a sufficiently large set of synthetic training data, we follow the same way in [4] to render long English words sampled from a large corpus, and generate tightly cropped, gray-scale, and size-normalized text images. For each class, we assign 1,000 images for training, and 100 for validation, which are denoted as VFR_syn_train and VFR_syn_val, respectively. The entire **AdobeVFR dataset**, consisting of VFR_real _test, VFR_real_u, VFR_syn_train and VFR_syn_val, are made publicly available[2].

The AdobeVFR dataset is the first large-scale benchmark set consisting of both synthetic and real-world text images, for the task of font recognition. To our best knowledge, so far VFR_real_test is the largest available set of real-world text images with reliable font label information (12.5 times larger than VFRWild325). The AdobeVFR dataset is super fine-grain, with highly subtle categorical variations, leading itself to a new challenging dataset for object recognition. Moreover, the substantial mismatch between synthetic and real-world data makes the AdobeVFR dataset an ideal subject for general domain adaption and transfer learning research. It also promotes the new problem area of understanding design styles with deep learning.

[2]http://www.atlaswang.com/deepfont.html

2.3 Synthetic Data Augmentation: A First Step to Reduce the Mismatch

Figure 2: (a) the different characters spacings between a pair of synthetic and real-world images. (b) the different aspect ratio between a pair of synthetic and real-world image

Before feeding synthetic data into model training, it is popular to artificially augment training data using label-preserving transformations to reduce overfitting. In [10], the authors applied image translations and horizontal reflections to the training images, as well as altering the intensities of their RGB channels. The authors in [4] added moderate distortions and corruptions to the synthetic text images:

- **1. Noise:** a small Gaussian noise with zero mean and standard deviation 3 is added to input
- **2. Blur:** a random Gaussian blur with standard deviation from 2.5 to 3.5 is added to input
- **3. Perspective Rotation:** a randomly-parameterized affine transformation is added to input
- **4. Shading:** the input background is filled with a gradient in illumination.

The above augmentations cover standard perturbations for general images, and are adopted by us. However, as a very particular type of images, text images have various real-world appearances caused by specific handlings. Based on the observations in Fig. 2 , we identify two additional font-specific augmentation steps to our training data:

- **5. Variable Character Spacing:** when rendering each synthetic image, we set the character spacing (by pixel) to be a Gaussian random variable of mean 10 and standard deviation 40, bounded by [0, 50].
- **6. Variable Aspect Ratio:** Before cropping each image into a input patch, the image, with heigh fixed, is squeezed in width by a random ratio, drawn from a uniform distribution between $\frac{5}{6}$ and $\frac{7}{6}$.

Note that these steps are not useful for the method in [4] because it exploits very localized features. However, as we show in our experiments, these steps lead to significant performance improvements in our DeepFont system. Overall, our data augmentation includes steps 1-6.

To leave a visual impression, we take the real-world image Fig. 2 (a), and synthesize a series of images in Fig. 3, all with the same text but with different data augmentation ways. Specially, (a) is synthesized with no data augmentation; (b) is (a) with standard augmentation 1-4 added; (c) is synthesized with spacing and aspect ratio customized to be identical to those of Fig. 2 (a); (d) adds standard augmentation 1-4 to (c). We input images (a)-(d) through the

(a) Synthetic, none (c) Synthetic, 5-6

(b) Synthetic, 1-4 (d) Synthetic, 1-6

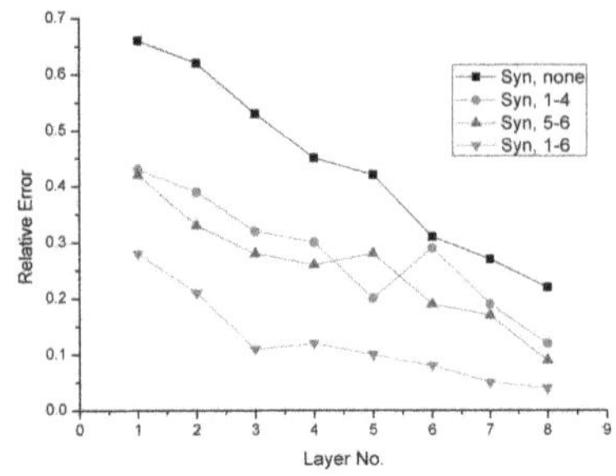

(e) Relative CNN layer-wise responses

Figure 3: The effects of data augmentation steps. (a)-(d): synthetic images of the same text but with different data augmentation ways. (e) compares relative differences of (a)-(d) with the real-world image Fig. 2 (a), in the measure of layer-wise network activations through the same DeepFont model.

trained DeepFont model. For each image, we compare its layer-wise activations with those of the real image Fig. 2 (a) feeding through the same model, by calculating the normalized MSEs. Fig. 3 (e) shows that those augmentations, especially the spacing and aspect ratio changes, reduce the gap between the feature hierarchies of real-world and synthetic data to a large extent. A few synthetic patches after full data augmentation 1-6 are displayed in Fig. 4. It is observable that they possess a much more visually similar appearance to real-world data.

Figure 4: Examples of synthetic training 105×105 **patches after pre-processing steps 1-6.**

3. DOMAIN ADAPTED CNN

3.1 Domain Adaptation by CNN Decomposition and SCAE

Despite that data augmentations are helpful to reduce the domain mismatch, enumerating all possible real-world degradations is impossible, and may further introduce degradation bias in training. In the section, we propose a learning framework to leverage both synthetic and real-world data, using multi-layer CNN decomposition and SCAE-based domain adaptation. Our approach extends the domain adaptation method in [7] to extract low-level features that represent both the synthetic and real-world data. We employs a Convolutional Neural Network (CNN) architecture, which is further decomposed into two sub-networks: a "shared" low-level sub-network which is learned from the composite set of synthetic and real-world data, and a high-level sub-network that learns a deep classifier from the low-level features.

The basic CNN architecture is similar to the popular ImageNet structure [10], as in Fig. 5. The numbers along with the network pipeline specify the dimensions of outputs of corresponding layers. The input is a 105×105 patch sampled from a "normalized" image. Since a square window may not capture sufficient discriminative local structures, and is unlikely to catch high-level combinational features when two or more graphemes or letters are joined as a single glyph (e.g., ligatures), we introduce a **squeezing** operation [3], that scales the width of the height-normalized image to be of a constant ratio relative to the height (2.5 in all our experiments). Note that the squeezing operation is equivalent to producing "long" rectangular input patches.

When the CNN model is trained fully on a synthetic dataset, it witnesses a significant performance drop when testing on real-world data, compared to when applied to another synthetic validation set. This also happens with other models such as in [4], which uses training and testing sets of similar properties to ours. It alludes to discrepancies between the distributions of synthetic and real-world examples. we propose to decompose the N CNN layers into two sub-networks to be learned sequentially:

- **Unsupervised cross-domain sub-network $\mathbf{C_u}$**, which consists of the first K layers of CNN. It accounts for extracting low-level visual features shared by both synthetic and real-world data domains. $\mathbf{C_u}$ will be trained in a unsupervised way, using unlabeled data from both domains. It constitutes the crucial step that further minimizes the low-level feature gap, beyond the previous data augmentation efforts.
- **Supervised domain-specific sub-network $\mathbf{C_s}$**, which consists of the remaining $N-K$ layers. It accounts for learning higher-level discriminative features for classification, based on the shared features from $\mathbf{C_u}$. $\mathbf{C_s}$ will be trained in a supervised way, using labeled data from the synthetic domain only.

We show an example of the proposed CNN decomposition in Fig. 5. The $\mathbf{C_u}$ and $\mathbf{C_s}$ parts are marked by red and green colors, respectively, with $N = 8$ and $K = 2$. Note that the low-level shared features are implied to be independent of class labels. Therefore in order to address the open-ended problem of font classes, one may keep re-using the $\mathbf{C_u}$ sub-network, and only re-train the $\mathbf{C_s}$ part.

Learning $\mathbf{C_u}$ from SCAE Representative unsupervised feature learning methods, such as the Auto-Encoder and the Denoising Auto-Encoder, perform a greedy layer-wise pretraining of weights using unlabeled data alone followed by supervised fine-tuning ([3]). However, they rely mostly on fully-connected models and ignore the 2D image structure. In [13], a Convolutional Auto-Encoder (CAE) was proposed to learn non-trivial features using a hierarchical unsupervised feature extractor that scales well to high-dimensional inputs. The CAE architecture is intuitively similar to the the conventional auto-encoders in [18], except for that their

[3]Note squeezing is independent from the variable aspect ratio operation introduced in Section 2.3, as they are for different purposes.

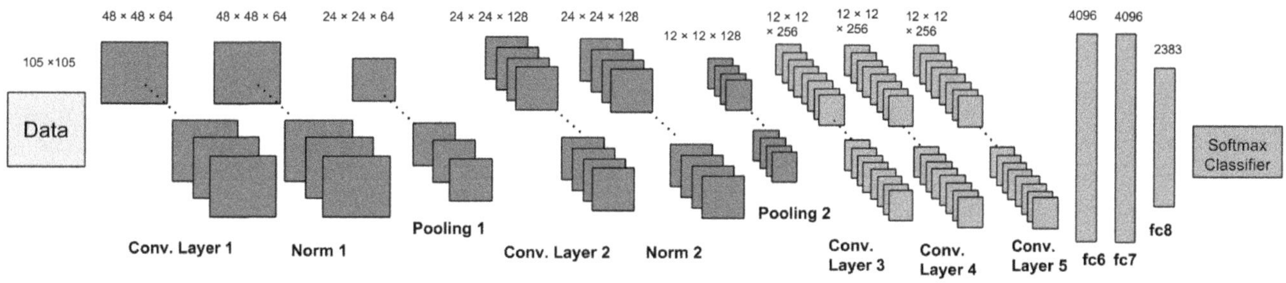

Figure 5: The CNN architecture in the DeepFont system, and its decomposition marked by different colors (N=8, K=2).

weights are shared among all locations in the input, preserving spatial locality. CAEs can be stacked to form a deep hierarchy called the Stacked Convolutional Auto-Encoder (SCAE), where each layer receives its input from a latent representation of the layer below. Fig. 6 plots the SCAE architecture for our $K = 2$ case.

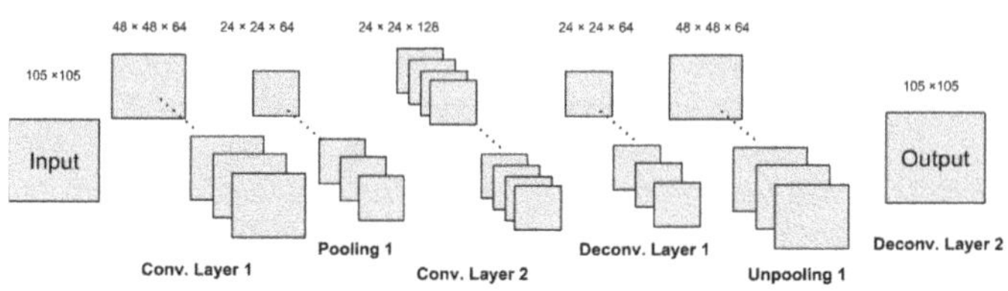

Figure 6: The Stacked Convolutional Auto-Encoder (SCAE) architecture.

Training Details We first train the SCAE on both synthetic and real-world data in a unsupervised way, with a learning rate of 0.01 (we do not anneal it through training). Mean Squared Error (MSE) is used as the loss function. After SCAE is learned, its Conv. Layers 1 and 2 are imported to the CNN in Fig. 5, as the $\mathbf{C_u}$ sub-network and fixed. The $\mathbf{C_s}$ sub-network, based on the output by $\mathbf{C_u}$, is then trained in a supervised manner. We start with the learning rate at 0.01, and follow a common heuristic to manually divide the learning rate by 10 when the validation error rate stops decreasing with the current rate. The "dropout" technique is applied to fc6 and fc7 layers during training. Both $\mathbf{C_u}$ and $\mathbf{C_s}$ are trained with a default batch size of 128, momentum of 0.9 and weight decay of 0.0005. The network training is implemented using the CUDA ConvNet package [10], and runs on a workstation with 12 Intel Xeon 2.67GHz CPUs and 1 GTX680 GPU. It takes around 1 day to complete the entire training pipeline.

Testing Details We adopt multi-scale multi-view testing to improve the result robustness. For each test image, it is first normalized to 105 pixels in height, but squeezed in width by three different random ratios, all drawn from a uniform distribution between 1.5 and 3.5, matching the effects of squeezing and variable aspect ratio operations during training. Under each squeezed scale, five 105×105 patches are sampled at different random locations. That constitutes in total fifteen test patches, each of which comes with different aspect ratios and views, from one test image. As every single patch could produce a softmax vector through the trained CNN, we average all fifteen softmax vectors to determine the final classification result of the test image.

3.2 Connections to Previous Work

We are not the first to look into an essentially "hierarchical" deep architecture for domain adaption. In [15], the proposed transfer learning approach relies on the unsupervised learning of representations. Bengio et. al hypothesized in [2] that more levels of representation can give rise to more abstract, more general features of the raw input, and that the lower layers of the predictor constitute a hierarchy of features that can be **shared** across variants of the input distribution. The authors in [7] used data from the union of all domains to learn their shared features, which is different from many previous domain adaptation methods that focus on learning features in a unsupervised way from the target domain only. However, their entire network hierarchy is learned in a unsupervised fashion, except for a simple linear classier trained on top of the network, i.e., $K = N - 1$. In [19], the CNN learned a set of filters from raw images as the first layer, and those low-level filters are fixed when training higher layers of the same CNN, i.e., $K = 1$. In other words, they either adopt a simple feature extractor ($K = 1$), or apply a shallow classifier ($K = N - 1$). Our CNN decomposition is different from prior work in that:

- Our feature extractor $\mathbf{C_u}$ and classier $\mathbf{C_s}$ are both deep sub-networks with more than one layer (both K and $N - K$ are larger than 1), which means that both are able to perform more sophisticated learning. More evaluations can be found in Section 5.2.
- We learn "shared-feature" convolutional filters rather than fully-connected networks such as in [7], the former of which is more suitable for visual feature extractions.

The domain mismatch between synthetic and real-world data on the lower-level statistics can occur in more scenarios, such as real-world face recognition from rendered images or sketches, recognizing characters in real scenes with synthetic training, human pose estimation with synthetic images generated from 3D human body models. We conjecture that our framework can be applicable to those scenarios as well, where labeled real-world data is scarce but synthetic data can be easily rendered.

4. LEARNING-BASED MODEL COMPRESSION

The architecture in Fig. 5 contains a huge number of parameters. It is widely known that the deep models are heavily over-parameterized [5] and thus those parameters can be compressed to reduce storage by exploring their structure.

For a typical CNN, about 90% of the storage is taken up by the dense connected layers, which shall be our focus for mode compression.

One way to shrink the number of parameters is using matrix factorization [6]. Given the parameter $W \in R^{m \times n}$, we factorize it using singular-value decomposition (SVD):

$$W = USV^T \quad (1)$$

where $U \in R^{m \times m}$ and $V \in R^{n \times n}$ are two dense orthogonal matrices and $S \in R^{m \times n}$ is a diagonal matrix. To restore an approximate W , we can utilize $\widetilde{U}$, $\widetilde{V}$ and $\widetilde{S}$, which denote the submatrices corresponding to the top k singular vectors in U and V along with the top k eigenvalue in S:

$$\widetilde{W} = \widetilde{U}\widetilde{S}\widetilde{V}^T \quad (2)$$

The compression ratio given m, n, and k is $\frac{k(m+n+1)}{mn}$, which is very promising when $m, n \gg k$. However, the approximation of SVD is controlled by the decay along the eigenvalues in S. Even it is verified in Fig. 7 that eigenvalues of weight matrices usually decay fast (the 6-th largest eigenvalue is already less than 10% of the largest one in magnitude), the truncation inevitably leads to information loss, and potential performance degradations, compared to the uncompressed model.

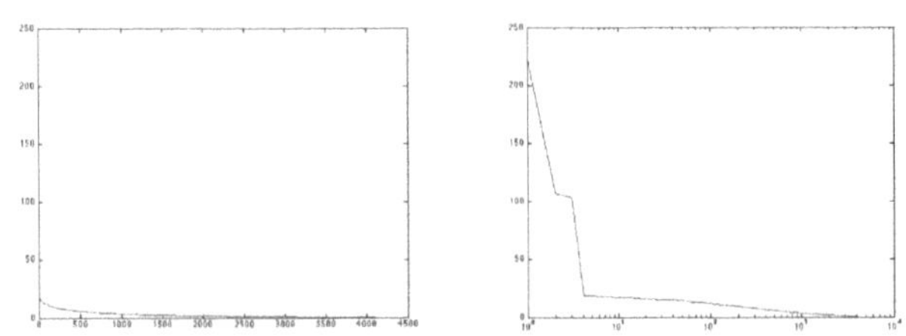

(a) Standard scale (b) Logarithm scale

Figure 7: The plots of eigenvalues for the fc6 layer weight matrix in Fig. 5. This densely connected layer takes up 85% of the total model size.

Instead of first training a model then lossy-compressing its parameters, we propose to directly learn a **losslessly compressible** model (the term "lossless" is referred as there is no further loss after a model is trained). Assuming the parameter matrix W of a certain network layer, our goal is to make sure that its rank is **exactly no more than a small constant** k. In terms of implementation, in each iteration, an extra hard thresholding operation [11] is executed on W after it is updated by a conventional back propagation step:

$$W_k = U\mathcal{T}_k(S)V^T \quad (3)$$

where $\mathcal{T}_k$ will keep the largest k eigenvalues in S while setting others to zeros. W_k is best rank-k approximation of W, as similarly in (2). However, different from (2), the proposed method incorporates low-rank approximation into model training and jointly optimize them as a whole, guaranteeing a rank-k weight matrix that is ready to be compressed losslessly by applying (1). Note there are other alternatives, such as vector quantization methods [8], that have been applied to compressing deep models with appealing performances. We will investigate utilizing them together to further compress our model in the future.

5. EXPERIMENTS

5.1 Analysis of Domain Mismatch

We first analyze the domain mismatch between synthetic and real-world data, and examine how our synthetic data augmentation can help. First we define five dataset variations generated from VFR_syn_train and VFR_real_u. These are denoted by the letters N, S, F, R and FR and are explained in Table 2.

We train five separate SCAEs, all of the same architecture as in Fig. 6, using the above five training data variants. The training and testing errors are all measured by relative MSEs (normalized by the total energy) and compared in Table 1. The testing errors are evaluated on both the unaugmented synthetic dataset N and the real-world dataset R. Ideally, the better the SCAE captures the features from a domain, the smaller the reconstruction error will be on that domain.

As revealed by the training errors, real-world data contains rich visual variations and is more difficult to fit. The sharp performance drop from N to R of SCAE N indicates that the convolutional features for synthetic and real data are quite different. This gap is reduced in SCAE S, and further in SCAE F, which validates the effectiveness of adding font-specific data augmentation steps. SCAE R fits the real-world data best, at the expense of a larger error on N. SCAE FR achieves an overall best reconstruction performance of both synthetic and real-world images.

Fig. 8 shows an example patch from a real-world font image of highly textured characters, and its reconstruction outputs from all five models. The gradual visual variations across the results confirm the existence of a mismatch between synthetic and real-world data, and verify the benefit of data augmentation as well as learning shared features.

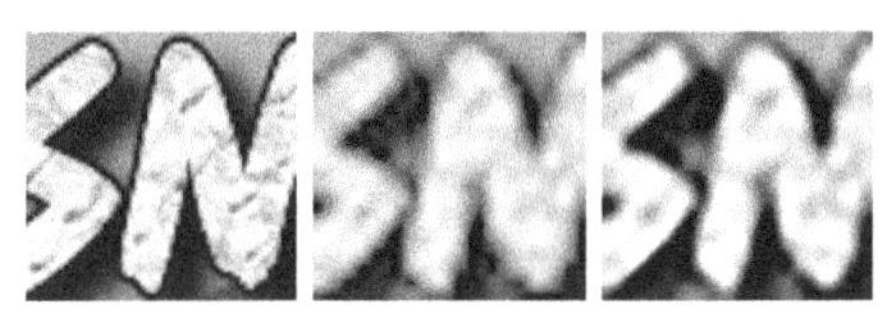

(a) original (b) SCAE N (c) SCAE S

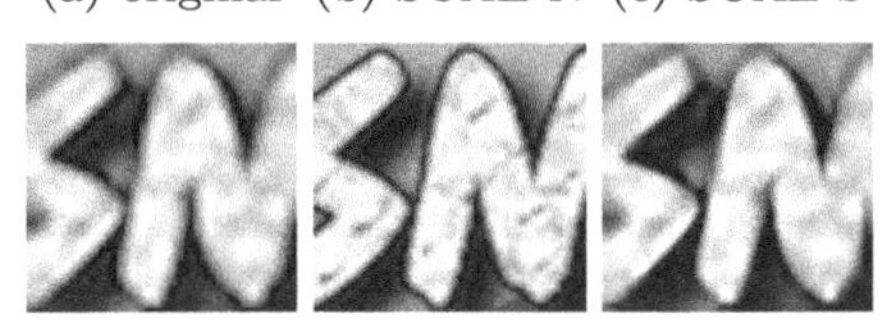

(d) SCAE F (e) SCAE R (f) SCAE FR

Figure 8: A real-world patch, and its reconstruction results from the five SCAE models.

5.2 Analysis of Network Structure

Fixing Network Depth N**.** Given a fixed network complexity (N layers), one may ask about how to best decompose the hierarchy to maximize the overall classification performance on real-world data. Intuitively, we should have sufficient layers of lower-level feature extractors as well as enough subsequent layers for good classification of labeled data. Thus, the depth K of C_u should neither be too small nor too large.

Table 3 shows that while the *classification* training error increases with K, the testing error does not vary monotonically. The best performance is obtained with $K = 2$ (3

Table 2: **Comparison of Training and Testing Errors (%) of Five SCAEs ($K = 2$)**

Methods	Training Data	Train	Test	
			N	R
SCAE N	**N**: VFR_syn_train, no data augmentation	0.02	3.54	31.28
SCAE S	**S**: VFR_syn_train, standard augmentation 1-4	0.21	2.24	19.34
SCAE F	**F**: VFR_syn_train, full augmentation 1-6	1.20	1.67	15.26
SCAE R	**R**:VFR_real_u, real unlabeled dataset	9.64	5.73	10.87
SCAE FR	**FR**: Combination of data from **F** and **R**	6.52	2.02	14.01

Table 3: Top-5 Testing Errors (%) for Different CNN Decompositions (Varying K, $N = 8$)

K	0	1	2	3	4	5
Train	8.46	9.88	11.23	12.54	15.21	17.88
VFR_real_test	20.72	20.31	18.21	18.96	22.52	25.97

Table 4: Top-5 Testing Errors (%) for Different CNN Decompositions (Varying K, $N = K + 6$)

K	1	2	3	4
Train	11.46	11.23	10.84	10.86
VFR_real_test	21.58	18.21	18.15	18.24

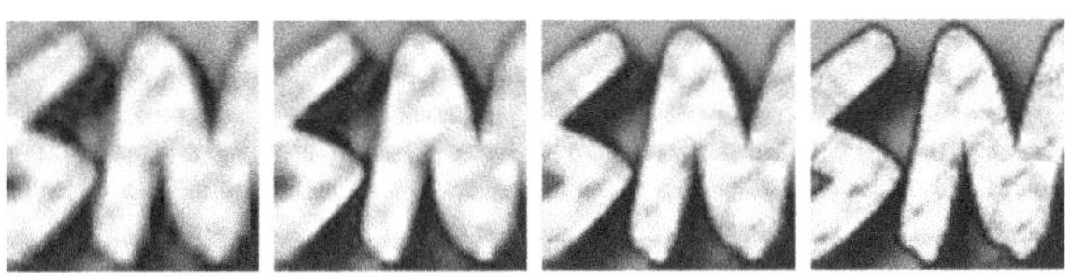

(a) K=1 (b) K=2 (c) K=4 (d) K=5

Figure 9: The reconstruction results of a real-world patch using SCAE FR, with different K values.

slightly worse), where smaller or larger values of K give substantially worse performance. When $K = 5$, all layers are learned using SCAE, leading to the worst results. Rather than learning all hidden layers by unsupervised training, as suggested in [7] and other DL-based transfer learning work, our CNN decomposition reaches its optimal performance when higher-layer convolutional filters are still trained by supervised data. A visual inspection of reconstruction results of a real-world example in Fig. 9, using SCAE FR with different K values, shows that a larger K causes less information loss during feature extraction and leads to a better reconstruction. But in the meantime, the classification result may turn worse since noise and irrelevant high frequency details (e.g. textures) might hamper recognition performance. The optimal K =2 corresponds to a proper "content-aware" smoothening, filtering out "noisy" details while keeping recognizable structural properties of the font style.

Fixing C_s or C_u Depth. We investigate the influences of K (the depth of C_u) when the depth of C_s (e.g. $N - K$) keeps fixed. Table 4 reveals that a deeper C_u contributes little to the results. Similar trends are observed when we fix K and adjust N (and thus the depth ofC_s). Therefore, we choose N= 8, K=2 to be the default setting.

5.3 Recognition Performances on VFR Datasets

We implemented and evaluated the local feature embedding-based algorithm (LFE) in [4] as a baseline, and include the four different DeepFont models as specified in Table 5. The first two models are trained in a fully supervised manner on **F**, without any decomposition applied. For each of the later two models, its corresponding SCAE (SCAE FR for DeepFont CAE_FR, and SCAE R for DeepFont CAE_R) is first trained and then exports the first two convolutional layers to $\mathbf{C_u}$. All trained models are evaluated in term of top-1 and top-5 classification errors, on the VFR_syn_val dataset for validation purpose. Benefiting from large learning capacity, it is clear that DeepFont models fit synthetic data significantly better than LFE. Notably, the top-5 errors of all DeepFont models (except for DeepFont CAE_R) reach zero on the validation set, which is quite impressive for such a fine-grain classification task.

We then compare DeepFont models with LFE on the original VFRWild325 dataset in [4]. As seen from Table 5, while DeepFont S fits synthetic training data best, its performance is the poorest on real-world data, showing a severe overfitting. With two font-specific data augmentations added in training, the DeepFont F model adapts better to real-world data, outperforming LFE by roughly 8% in top-5 error. An additional gain of 2% is obtained when unlabeled real-world data is utilized in DeepFont CAE_FR. Next, the DeepFont models are evaluated on the new VFR_real_test dataset, which is more extensive in size and class coverage. A large margin of around 5% in top-1 error is gained by DeepFont CAE_FR model over the second best (DeepFont F), with its top-5 error as low as 18.21%. We will use DeepFont CAE_FR as the default DeepFont model.

Although SCAE R has the best reconstruction result on real-world data on which it is trained, it has large training and testing errors on synthetic data. Since our supervised training relies fully on synthetic data, an effective feature extraction for synthetic data is also indispensable. The error rates of DeepFont CAE_R are also worse than those of DeepFont CAE_FR and even DeepFont F on the real-world data, due to the large mismatch between the low-level and high-level layers in the CNN.

Figure 10: Failure VFR examples using DeepFont.

Another interesting observation is that all methods get similar top-5 errors on VFRWild325 and VFR_real_test, showing their statistical similarity. However, the top-1 errors of DeepFont models on VFRWild325 are significantly higher than those on VFR_real_test, with a difference of up to 10%. In contrast, the top-1 error of LFE rises more than 13% on VFR_real_test than on VFRWild325. For the small VFRWild325, the recognition result is easily affected by "bad" examples (e.g, low resolution or highly compressed images) and class bias (less than 4% of all classes are covered). On the other hand, the larger VFR_real_test dataset dilutes the possible effect of outliers, and examines a lot more classes.

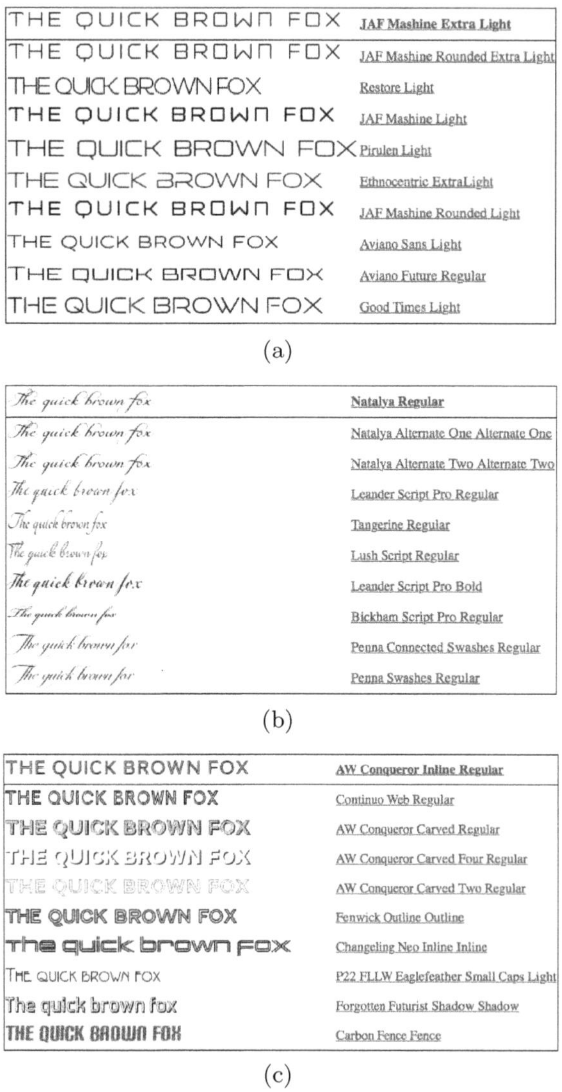

Figure 11: Examples of the font similarity. For each one, the top is the query image, and the renderings with the most similar fonts are returned.

Fig. 10 lists some failure cases of DeepFont. For example, the top left image contains extra "fluff" decorations along text boundaries, which is nonexistent in the original fonts, that makes the algorithm incorrectly map it to some "artistic" fonts. Others are affected by 3-D effects, strong obstacles in foreground, and in background. Being considerably difficult to be adapted, those examples fail mostly because there are neither specific augmentation steps handling their effects, nor enough examples in VFR_real_u to extract corresponding robust features.

5.4 Evaluating Font Similarity using DeepFont

There are a variety of font selection tasks with different goals and requirements. One designer may wish to match a font to the style of a particular image. Another may wish to find a free font which looks similar to a commercial font such as Helvetica. A third may simply be exploring a large set of fonts such as Adobe TypeKit or Google Web Fonts. Exhaustively exploring the entire space of fonts using an alphabetical listing is unrealistic for most users. The authors in [14] proposed to select fonts based on online crowdsourced attributes, and explore *font similarity*, from which a user is enabled to explore other visually similar fonts given a specific font. The font similarity measure is very helpful for font selection, organization, browsing, and suggestion.

Based on our DeepFont system, we are able to build up measures of font similarity. We use the 4096×1 outputs of the fc7 layer as the high-level feature vectors describing font visual appearances. We then extract such features from all samples in VFR_syn_val Dataset, obtaining 100 feature vectors per class. Next for each class, the 100 feature vectors is averaged to a representative vector. Finally, we calculate the Euclidean distance between the representative vectors of two font classes as their similarity measure. Visualized examples are demonstrated in Fig. 11. For each example, the top is the query image of a known font class; the most similar fonts obtained by the font similarity measures are sorted below. Note that although the result fonts can belong to different font families from the query, they share identifiable visual similarities by human perception.

Although not numerically verified as in [14], the DeepFont results are qualitatively better when we look at the top-10 most similar fonts for a wide range of query fonts. The authors of [14] agree per personal communication with us.

5.5 DeepFont Model Compression

Since the fc6 layer takes up 85% of the total model size, we first focus on its compression. We start from a well-trained DeepFont model (DeepFont CAE_FR), and continue tuning it with the hard thresholding (3) applied to the fc6 parameter matrix W in each iteration, until the training/validation errors reach the plateau again.

Table 6 compares the DeepFont models compressed using conventional matrix factorization (denoted as the "lossy" method), and the proposed learning based method (denoted as the "lossless" method), under different compression ratios (fc6 and total size counted by parameter numbers). The last column of Table 6 lists the top-5 testing errors (%) on VFR_real_test. We observe a consistent margin of the "lossless" method over its "lossy" counterpart, which becomes more significant when the compression ratio goes low (more than 1% when $k = 5$). Notably, when $k = 100$, the proposed "lossless" compression suffers no visible performance loss, while still maintaining a good compression ratio of 5.79.

In practice, it takes around 700 megabytes to store all the parameters in our uncompressed DeepFont model, which is quite huge to be embedded or downloaded into most customer softwares. More aggressively, we reduce the output sizes of both fc6 and fc7 to 2048, and further apply the pro-

Table 5: Comparison of Training and Testing Errors on Synthetic and Real-world Datasets (%)

Methods	Training Data		Training	VFR_syn_val		VFRWild325		VFR_real_test	
	$\mathbf{C_u}$	$\mathbf{C_s}$	Error	Top-1	Top-5	Top-1	Top-5	Top-1	Top-5
LFE	/	/	/	26.50	6.55	44.13	30.25	57.44	32.69
DeepFont S	/	F	0.84	1.03	0	64.60	57.23	57.51	50.76
DeepFont F	/	F	8.46	7.40	0	43.10	22.47	33.30	20.72
DeepFont CAE_FR	FR	F	11.23	6.58	0	**38.15**	**20.62**	**28.58**	**18.21**
DeepFont CAE_R	R	F	13.67	8.21	1.26	44.62	29.23	39.46	27.33

Table 6: Performance Comparisons of Lossy and Lossless Compression Approaches

	fc6 size	Total size	Ratio	Method	Error
default	150,994,944	177,546,176	NA	NA	18.21
k=5	204,805	26,756,037	6.64	Lossy	20.67
				Lossless	19.23
k=10	409,610	26,960,842	6.59	Lossy	19.25
				Lossless	18.87
k=50	2,048,050	28,599,282	6.21	Lossy	19.04
				Lossless	18.67
k=100	4,096,100	30,647,332	5.79	Lossy	18.68
				Lossless	18.21

posed compression method ($k = 10$) to the fc6 parameter matrix. The obtained "mini" model, with only 9, 477, 066 parameters and a high compression ratio of 18.73, becomes less than 40 megabytes in storage. Being portable even on mobiles, It manages to keep a top-5 error rate around 22%.

6. CONCLUSION

In the paper, we develop the DeepFont system to remarkably advance the state-of-the-art in the VFR task. A large set of labeled real-world data as well as a large corpus of unlabeled real-world images is collected for both training and testing, which is the first of its kind and will be made publicly available soon. While relying on the learning capacity of CNN, we need to combat the mismatch between available training and testing data. The introduction of SCAE-based domain adaption helps our trained model achieve a higher than 80% top-5 accuracy. A novel lossless model compression is further applied to promote the model storage efficiency. The DeepFont system not only is effective for font recognition, but can also produce a font similarity measure for font selection and suggestion.

7. REFERENCES

[1] C. Avilés-Cruz, R. Rangel-Kuoppa, M. Reyes-Ayala, A. Andrade-Gonzalez, and R. Escarela-Perez. High-order statistical texture analysis: font recognition applied. *PRL*, 26(2):135–145, 2005.

[2] Y. Bengio. Learning deep architectures for ai. *Foundations and trends® in Machine Learning*, 2(1):1–127, 2009.

[3] Y. Bengio, P. Lamblin, D. Popovici, and H. Larochelle. Greedy layer-wise training of deep networks. *NIPS*, 19:153, 2007.

[4] G. Chen, J. Yang, H. Jin, J. Brandt, E. Shechtman, A. Agarwala, and T. X. Han. Large-scale visual font recognition. In *CVPR*, pages 3598–3605. IEEE, 2014.

[5] M. Denil, B. Shakibi, L. Dinh, N. de Freitas, et al. Predicting parameters in deep learning. In *NIPS*, pages 2148–2156, 2013.

[6] E. L. Denton, W. Zaremba, J. Bruna, Y. LeCun, and R. Fergus. Exploiting linear structure within convolutional networks for efficient evaluation. In *NIPS*, pages 1269–1277, 2014.

[7] X. Glorot, A. Bordes, and Y. Bengio. Domain adaptation for large-scale sentiment classification: A deep learning approach. In *ICML*, 2011.

[8] Y. Gong, L. Liu, M. Yang, and L. Bourdev. Compressing deep convolutional networks using vector quantization. *arXiv preprint arXiv:1412.6115*, 2014.

[9] M.-C. Jung, Y.-C. Shin, and S. N. Srihari. Multifont classification using typographical attributes. In *ICDAR*, pages 353–356. IEEE, 1999.

[10] A. Krizhevsky, I. Sutskever, and G. E. Hinton. Imagenet classification with deep convolutional neural networks. In *NIPS*, pages 1097–1105, 2012.

[11] Z. Lin, M. Chen, and Y. Ma. The augmented lagrange multiplier method for exact recovery of corrupted low-rank matrices. *arXiv preprint:1009.5055*, 2010.

[12] H. Ma and D. Doermann. Gabor filter based multi-class classifier for scanned document images. In *ICDAR*, volume 2, pages 968–968. IEEE, 2003.

[13] J. Masci, U. Meier, D. Cireşan, and J. Schmidhuber. Stacked convolutional auto-encoders for hierarchical feature extraction. In *ICANN*, pages 52–59. 2011.

[14] P. O'Donovan, J. Lībeks, A. Agarwala, and A. Hertzmann. Exploratory font selection using crowdsourced attributes. *ACM TOG*, 33(4):92, 2014.

[15] R. Raina, A. Battle, H. Lee, B. Packer, and A. Y. Ng. Self-taught learning: transfer learning from unlabeled data. In *ICML*, pages 759–766. ACM, 2007.

[16] R. Ramanathan, K. Soman, L. Thaneshwaran, V. Viknesh, T. Arunkumar, and P. Yuvaraj. A novel technique for english font recognition using support vector machines. In *ARTCom*, pages 766–769, 2009.

[17] H.-M. Sun. Multi-linguistic optical font recognition using stroke templates. In *ICPR*, volume 2, pages 889–892. IEEE, 2006.

[18] P. Vincent, H. Larochelle, Y. Bengio, and P.-A. Manzagol. Extracting and composing robust features with denoising autoencoders. In *ICML*, pages 1096–1103. ACM, 2008.

[19] T. Wang, D. J. Wu, A. Coates, and A. Y. Ng. End-to-end text recognition with convolutional neural networks. In *ICPR*, pages 3304–3308. IEEE, 2012.

[20] Y. Zhu, T. Tan, and Y. Wang. Font recognition based on global texture analysis. *IEEE TPAMI*, 2001.

Modeling Spatial-Temporal Clues in a Hybrid Deep Learning Framework for Video Classification

Zuxuan Wu, Xi Wang, Yu-Gang Jiang*, Hao Ye, Xiangyang Xue
School of Computer Science, Shanghai Key Lab of Intelligent Information Processing,
Fudan University, Shanghai, China
{zxwu, xwang10, ygj, haoye10, xyxue}@fudan.edu.cn

ABSTRACT

Classifying videos according to content semantics is an important problem with a wide range of applications. In this paper, we propose a hybrid deep learning framework for video classification, which is able to model static spatial information, short-term motion, as well as long-term temporal clues in the videos. Specifically, the spatial and the short-term motion features are extracted separately by two Convolutional Neural Networks (CNN). These two types of CNN-based features are then combined in a regularized feature fusion network for classification, which is able to learn and utilize feature relationships for improved performance. In addition, Long Short Term Memory (LSTM) networks are applied on top of the two features to further model longer-term temporal clues. The main contribution of this work is the hybrid learning framework that can model several important aspects of the video data. We also show that (1) combining the spatial and the short-term motion features in the regularized fusion network is better than direct classification and fusion using the CNN with a softmax layer, and (2) the sequence-based LSTM is highly complementary to the traditional classification strategy without considering the temporal frame orders. Extensive experiments are conducted on two popular and challenging benchmarks, the UCF-101 Human Actions and the Columbia Consumer Videos (CCV). On both benchmarks, our framework achieves very competitive performance: 91.3% on the UCF-101 and 83.5% on the CCV.

Categories and Subject Descriptors

I.5.2 [**Pattern Recognition**]: Design Methodology—*Classifier design and evaluation*

Keywords

Video Classification; Deep Learning; CNN; LSTM; Fusion.

*Corresponding author.

MM'15, October 26–30, 2015, Brisbane, Australia.
© 2015 ACM. ISBN 978-1-4503-3459-4/15/10 ...$15.00.
DOI: http://dx.doi.org/10.1145/2733373.2806222.

1. INTRODUCTION

Video classification based on contents like human actions or complex events is a challenging task that has been extensively studied in the research community. Significant progress has been achieved in recent years by designing various features, which are expected to be robust to intra-class variations and discriminative to separate different classes. For example, one can utilize traditional image-based features like the SIFT [27] to capture the static spatial information in videos. In addition to the static frame based visual features, motion is a very important clue for video classification, as most classes containing object movements like the human actions require the motion information to be reliably recognized. For this, a very popular feature is the dense trajectories [44], which tracks densely sampled local frame patches over time and computes several traditional features based on the trajectories.

In contrast to the hand-crafted features, there is a growing trend of learning robust feature representations from raw data with deep neural networks. Among the many existing network structures, Convolutional Neural Networks (CNN) have demonstrated great success on various tasks, including image classification [22, 38, 34], image-based object localization [7], speech recognition [5], *etc.* For video classification, Ji *et al.* [13] and Karparthy *et al.* [19] extended the CNN to work on the temporal dimension by stacking frames over time. Recently, Simonyan *et al.* [33] proposed a two-stream CNN approach, which uses two CNNs on static frames and optical flows respectively to capture the spatial and the motion information. It focuses only on short-term motion as the optical flows are computed in very short time windows. With this approach, similar or slightly better performance than the hand-crafted features like [44] has been reported.

These existing works, however, are not able to model the long-term temporal clues in the videos. As aforementioned, the two-stream CNN [33] uses stacked optical flows computed in short time windows as inputs, and the order of the optical flows is fully discarded in the learning process (cf. Section 3.1). This is not sufficient for video classification, as many complex contents can be better identified by considering the temporal order of short-term actions. Take "birthday" event as an example—it usually involves several sequential actions, such as "making a wish", "blowing out candles" and "eating cakes".

To address the above limitation, this paper proposes a hybrid deep learning framework for video classification, which is able to harness not only the spatial and short-term motion features, but also the long-term temporal clues. In or-

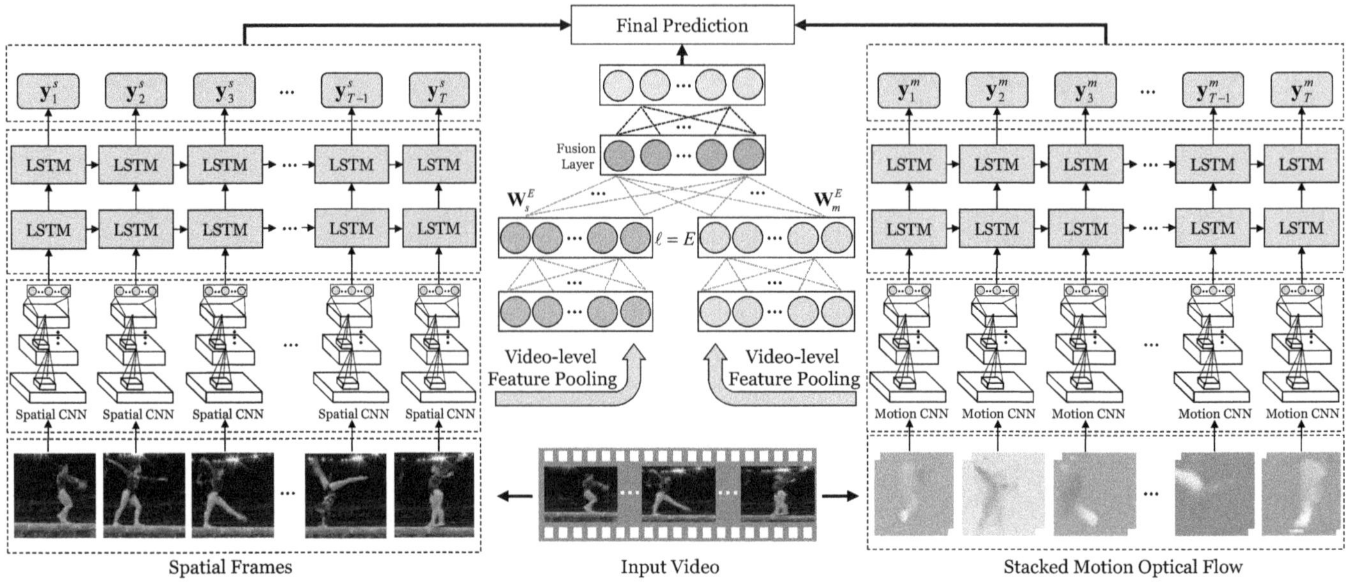

Figure 1: An overview of the proposed hybrid deep learning framework for video classification. Given an input video, two types of features are extracted using the CNN from spatial frames and short-term stacked motion optical flows respectively. The features are separately fed into two sets of LSTM networks for long-term temporal modeling (Left and Right). In addition, we also employ a regularized feature fusion network to perform video-level feature fusion and classification (Middle). The outputs of the sequence-based LSTM and the video-level feature fusion network are combined to generate the final prediction. See texts for more discussions.

der to leverage the temporal information, we adopt a Recurrent Neural Networks (RNN) model called Long Short Term Memory (LSTM), which maps the input sequences to outputs using a sequence of hidden states and incorporates memory units that enable the network to learn when to forget previous hidden states and when to update hidden states with new information. In addition, many approaches fuse multiple features in a very "shallow" manner by either concatenating the features before classification or averaging the predictions of classifiers trained using different features separately. In this work we integrate the spatial and the short-term motion features in a deep neural network with carefully designed regularizations to explore feature correlations. This method can perform video classification within the same network and further combining its outputs with the predictions of the LSTMs can lead to very competitive classification performance.

Figure 1 gives an overview of the proposed framework. Spatial and short-term motion features are first extracted by the two-stream CNN approach [33], and then input into the LSTM for long-term temporal modeling. Average pooling is adopted to generate video-level spatial and motion features, which are fused by the regularized feature fusion network. After that, outputs of the sequence-based LSTM and the video-level feature fusion network are combined as the final predictions. Notice that, in contrast to the current framework, alternatively one may train a fusion network to combine the frame-level spatial and motion features first and then use a single set of LSTM for temporal modeling. However, in our experiments we have observed worse results using this strategy. The main reason is that learning dimension-wise feature correlations in the fusion network requires strong and reliable supervision, but we only have video-level class labels which are not necessarily always related to the frame semantics. The main contributions of this work are summarized as follows:

- We propose a hybrid deep learning framework for video classification, which can model not only the short-term spatial-motion patterns but also the long-term temporal clues with variable-length video sequences as inputs.
- We adopt the LSTM to model long-term temporal clues on top of both the spatial and the short-term motion features. We show that both features work well with the LSTM, and the LSTM based classifiers are very complementary to the traditional classifiers without considering the temporal frame orders.
- We fuse the spatial and the motion features in a regularized feature fusion network that can explore feature correlations and perform classification. The network is computationally efficient in both training and testing.
- Through an extensive set of experiments, we demonstrate that our proposed framework outperforms several alternative methods with clear margins. On the well-known UCF-101 and CCV benchmarks, we attain very competitive performance.

The rest of this paper is organized as follows. Section 2 reviews related works. Section 3 describes the proposed hybrid deep learning framework in detail. Experimental results and comparisons are discussed in Section 4, followed by conclusions in Section 5.

2. RELATED WORKS

Video classification has been a longstanding research topic in multimedia and computer vision [16]. Successful classification systems rely heavily on the extracted video features, and hence most existing works focused on designing robust features. Many video representations were motivated by the advances in image domain, which can be extended to utilize the temporal dimension of the video data. For instance, Laptev [24] extended the 2D Harris corner detector [10] into 3D space to find space-time interest points. Klaser *et al.* proposed HOG3D by extending the idea of integral images for fast descriptor computation [20]. Wang *et al.* reported that dense sampling at regular positions in space and time outperforms the detected sparse interest points on video classification tasks [45]. Partly inspired by this finding, they further proposed the dense trajectory features, which densely sample local patches from each frame at different scales and then track them in a dense optical flow field over time [44]. This method has demonstrated very competitive results on major benchmark datasets. In addition, further improvements may be achieved by using advantageous feature encoding methods like the Fisher Vectors [30] or adopting feature normalization strategies, such as Root-Sift [1]. Note that these spatial-temporal video descriptors only capture local motion patterns within a very short period, and popular descriptor quantization methods like the bag-of-words entirely destroy the temporal order information of the descriptors.

To explore the long-term temporal clues, graphical models have been popularly used, such as hidden Markov models (HMM), Bayesian Networks (BN), Conditional Random Fields (CRF), *etc.* For instance, Li *et al.* proposed to replace the hidden states in HMMs with visualizable salient poses estimated by Gaussian Mixture Models [25], and Tang *et al.* introduced latent variables over video frames to discover the most discriminative states of an event based on a variable duration HMM [39]. Zeng *et al.* exploited multiple types of domain knowledge to guide the learning of a Dynamic BN for action recognition [52]. Instead of using directed graphical models like the HMM and BN, undirected graphical models have also been adopted. Vail *et al.* employed the CRF for activity recognition in [41]. Wang *et al.* proposed a max-margin hidden CRF for action recognition in videos, where a human action is modeled as a global root template and a constellation of several "parts" [46].

Many related works have investigated the fusion of multiple features, which is often effective for improving classification performance. The most straightforward and popular ways are early fusion and late fusion. Generally, the early fusion refers to fusion at the feature level, such as feature concatenation or linear combination of kernels of individual features. For example, in [54], Zhang *et al.* computed non-linear kernels for each feature separately, and then fused the kernels for model training. The fusion weights can be manually set or automatically estimated by multiple kernel learning (MKL) [2]. For the late fusion methods, independent classifiers are first trained using each feature separately, and outputs of the classifiers are then combined. In [50], Ye *et al.* proposed a robust late fusion approach to fuse multiple classification outputs by seeking a shared low-rank latent matrix, assuming that noises may exist in the predictions of some classifiers, which can possibly be removed by using the low-rank matrix.

Both early and late fusion fail to explore the correlations shared by the features and hence are not ideal for video classification. In this paper we employ a regularized neural network tailored feature fusion and classification, which can automatically learn dimension-wise feature correlations. Several studies are related. In [15, 12], the authors proposed to construct an audio-visual joint codebook for video classification, in order to discover and model the audio-visual feature correlations. There are also studies on using neural networks for feature fusion. In [37], the authors employed deep Boltzmann machines to learn a fused representation of images and texts. In [29], a deep denoised auto-encoder was used for cross-modality and shared representation learning. Very recently, Wu *et al.* [47] presented an approach using regularizations in neural networks to exploit feature and class relationships. The fusion approach in this work differs in the following. First, instead of using the traditional hand-crafted features as inputs, we adopt CNN features trained from both static frames and motion optical flows. Second and very importantly, the formulation in the regularized feature fusion network has a much lower complexity compared with that of [47].

Researchers have attempted to apply the RNN to model the long-term temporal information in videos. Venugopalan *et al.* [43] proposed to translate videos to textual sentences with the LSTM through transferring knowledge from image description tasks. Ranzato *et al.* [31] introduced a generative model with the RNN to predict motions in videos. In the context of video classification, Donahua *et al.* adopted the LSTM to model temporal information [6] and Srivastava *et al.* designed an encoder-decoder RNN architecture to learn feature representations in an unsupervised manner [36]. To model motion information, both works adopted optical flow "images" between nearby frames as the inputs of the LSTM. In contrast, our approach adopts stacked optical flows. Stacked flows over a short time period can better reflect local motion patterns, which are found to be able to produce better results. In addition, our framework incorporates video-level predictions with the feature fusion network for significantly improved performance, which was not considered in these existing works.

Besides the above discussions of related studies on feature fusion and temporal modeling with the RNN, several representative CNN-based approaches for video classification should also be covered here. The image-based CNN features have recently been directly adopted for video classification, extracted using off-the-shelf models trained on large-scale image datasets like the ImageNet [11, 32, 53]. For instance, Jain *et al.* [11] performed action recognition using the SVM classifier with such CNN features and achieved top results in the 2014 THUMOS action recognition challenge [17]. A few works have also tried to extend the CNN to exploit the motion information in videos. Ji *et al.* [13] and Karparthy *et al.* [19] extended the CNN by stacking visual frames in fixed-size time windows and using spatial-temporal convolutions for video classification. Differently, the two-stream CNN approach by Simonyan *et al.* [33] applies the CNN separately on visual frames (the spatial stream) and stacked optical flows (the motion stream). This approach has been found to be more effective [51], which is adopted as the basis of our proposed framework. However, as discussed in Section 1, all these approaches [13, 19, 33] can only model short-term motion, not the long-term temporal clues.

3. METHODOLOGY

In this section, we describe the key components of the proposed hybrid deep learning framework shown in Figure 1, including the CNN-based spatial and short-term motion features, the long-term LSTM-based temporal modeling, and the video-level regularized feature fusion network.

3.1 Spatial and Motion CNN Features

Conventional CNN architectures take images as the inputs and consist of alternating convolutional and pooling layers, which are further topped by a few fully-connected (FC) layers. To extract the spatial and the short-term motion features, we adopt the recent two-stream CNN approach [33]. Instead of using stacked frames in short time windows like [13, 19], this approach decouples the videos into spatial and motion[1] streams modeled by two CNNs separately. Figure 2 gives an overview. The spatial stream is built on sampled individual frames, which is exactly the same as the CNN-based image classification pipeline and is suitable for capturing the static information in videos like scene backgrounds and basic objects. The motion counterpart operates on top of stacked optical flows. Specifically, optical flows (displacement vector fields) are computed between each pair of adjacent frames, and the horizontal and vertical components of the displacement vectors can form two optical flow images. Instead of using each individual flow image as the input of the CNN, it was reported that stacked optical flows over a time window are better due to the ability of modeling the short-term motion. In other words, the input of the motion stream CNN is a $2L$-channel stacked optical flow image, where L is the number of frames in the window. The two CNNs produce classification scores separately using a softmax layer and the scores are linearly combined as the final prediction.

Like many existing works on visual classification using the CNN features [32], we adopt the output of the first FC layer of the two CNNs as the spatial and the short-term motion features.

3.2 Temporal Modeling with LSTM

During the training process of the spatial and the motion stream CNNs, each sweep through the network takes one visual frame or one stacked optical flow image, and the temporal order of the frames is fully discarded. To model the long-term dynamic information in video sequences, we leverage the LSTM model, which has been successfully applied to speech recognition [8], image captioning [6], *etc.* LSTM is a type of RNN with controllable memory units and is effective in many long range sequential modeling tasks without suffering from the "vanishing gradients" effect like traditional RNNs. Generally, LSTM recursively maps the input representations at the current time step to output labels via a sequence of hidden states, and thus the learning process of LSTM should be in a sequential manner (from left to right in the two sets of LSTM of Figure 1). Finally, we can obtain a prediction score at each time step with a softmax transformation using the hidden states from the last layer of the LSTM.

More formally, given a sequence of feature representations $(\mathbf{x}_1, \mathbf{x}_2, \ldots, \mathbf{x}_T)$, an LSTM maps the inputs to an output

[1]Note that the authors of the original paper [33] used the name "temporal stream". We call it "motion stream" as it only captures short-term motion, which is different from the long-term temporal modeling in our proposed framework.

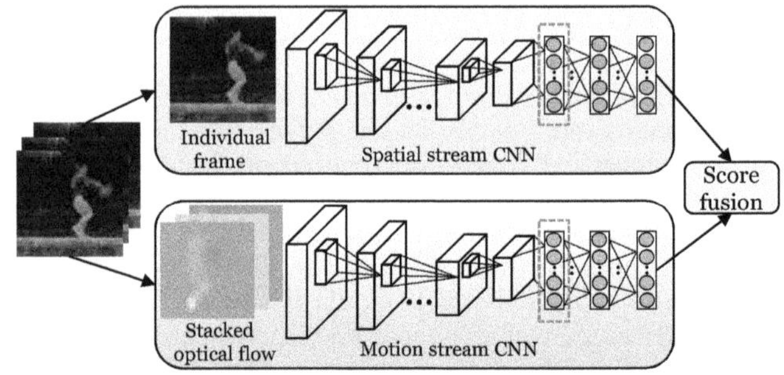

Figure 2: The framework of the two-stream CNN. Outputs of the first fully-connected layer in the two CNNs (outlined) are used as the spatial and the short-term motion features for further processing.

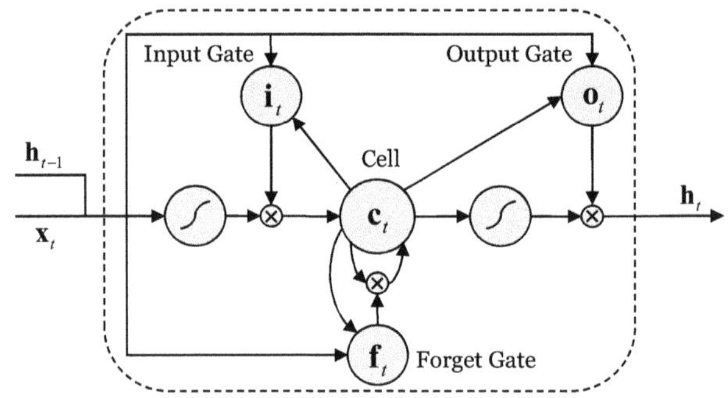

Figure 3: The structure of an LSTM unit.

sequence $(\mathbf{y}_1, \mathbf{y}_2, \ldots, \mathbf{y}_T)$ by computing activations of the units in the network with the following equations recursively from $t = 1$ to $t = T$:

$$\begin{aligned}
\mathbf{i}_t &= \sigma(\mathbf{W}_{xi}\mathbf{x}_t + \mathbf{W}_{hi}\mathbf{h}_{t-1} + \mathbf{W}_{ci}\mathbf{c}_{t-1} + \mathbf{b}_i),\\
\mathbf{f}_t &= \sigma(\mathbf{W}_{xf}\mathbf{x}_t + \mathbf{W}_{hf}\mathbf{h}_{t-1} + \mathbf{W}_{cf}\mathbf{c}_{t-1} + \mathbf{b}_f),\\
\mathbf{c}_t &= \mathbf{f}_t\mathbf{c}_{t-1} + \mathbf{i}_t \tanh(\mathbf{W}_{xc}\mathbf{x}_t + \mathbf{W}_{hc}\mathbf{h}_{t-1} + \mathbf{b}_c),\\
\mathbf{o}_t &= \sigma(\mathbf{W}_{xo}\mathbf{x}_t + \mathbf{W}_{ho}\mathbf{h}_{t-1} + \mathbf{W}_{co}\mathbf{c}_t + \mathbf{b}_o),\\
\mathbf{h}_t &= \mathbf{o}_t \tanh(\mathbf{c}_t),
\end{aligned}$$

where $\mathbf{x}_t, \mathbf{h}_t$ are the input and hidden vectors with the subscription t denoting the t-th time step, $\mathbf{i}_t, \mathbf{f}_t, \mathbf{c}_t, \mathbf{o}_t$ are respectively the activation vectors of the input gate, forget gate, memory cell and output gate, $\mathbf{W}_{\alpha\beta}$ is the weight matrix between α and β (e.g., $\mathbf{W}_{xi}$ is weight matrix from the input $\mathbf{x}_t$ to the input gate $\mathbf{i}_t$), $\mathbf{b}_\alpha$ is the bias term of α and σ is the sigmoid function defined as $\sigma(x) = \frac{1}{1+e^{-x}}$. Figure 3 visualizes the structure of an LSTM unit.

The core idea behind the LSTM model is a built-in memory cell that stores information over time to explore long-range dynamics, with non-linear gate units governing the information flow into and out of the cell. As we can see from the above equations, the current frame $\mathbf{x}_t$ and the previous hidden states $\mathbf{h}_{t-1}$ are used as inputs of four parts at the t-th time step. The memory cell aggregates information from two sources: the previous cell memory unit $\mathbf{c}_{t-1}$ multiplied by the activation of the forget gate $\mathbf{f}_t$ and the squashed inputs regulated with the input gate's activation $\mathbf{i}_t$, the combination of which enables the LSTM to learn to forget information from previous states or consider new information.

In addition, the output gate $\mathbf{o}_t$ controls how much information from the memory cell is passed to the hidden states $\mathbf{h}_t$ for the following time step. With the explicitly controllable memory units and different functional gates, LSTM can explore long-range temporal clues with variable-length inputs. As a neural network, the LSTM model can be easily deepened by stacking the hidden states from a layer $l-1$ as inputs of the next layer l.

Let us now consider a model of K layers, the feature vector $\mathbf{x}_t$ at the t-th time step is fed into the first layer of the LSTM together with the hidden state $\mathbf{h}_{t-1}^1$ in the same layer obtained from the last time step to produce an updated $\mathbf{h}_t^1$, which will then be used as the inputs of the following layer. Denote f_W as the mapping function from the inputs to the hidden states, the transition from layer $l-1$ to layer l can be written as:

$$\mathbf{h}_t^l = \begin{cases} f_W(\mathbf{h}_t^{l-1}, \mathbf{h}_{t-1}^l), & l > 1; \\ f_W(\mathbf{x}_t, \mathbf{h}_{t-1}^l), & l = 1. \end{cases}$$

In order to obtain the prediction scores for a total of C classes at a time step t, the outputs from last layer of the LSTM are sent to a softmax layer estimating probabilities as:

$$prob_c = \frac{\exp(\mathbf{w}_c{}^T \mathbf{h}_t^K + b_c)}{\sum_{c' \in C} \exp(\mathbf{w}_{c'}{}^T \mathbf{h}_t^K + b_{c'})},$$

where $prob_c$, $\mathbf{w}_c$ and b_c are respectively the probability prediction, the corresponding weight vector and the bias term of the c-th class. Such an LSTM network can be trained with the Back-Propagation Through Time (BPTT) algorithm [9], which "unrolls" the model into a feed forward neural net and back-propagates to determine the optimal weights.

As shown in Figure 1, we adopt two LSTM models for temporal modeling. With the two-stream CNN pipeline for feature extraction, we have a spatial feature set $(\mathbf{x}_1^s, \mathbf{x}_2^s, \ldots, \mathbf{x}_T^s)$ and a motion feature set $(\mathbf{x}_1^m, \mathbf{x}_2^m, \ldots, \mathbf{x}_T^m)$. The learning process leads to a set of predictions $(\mathbf{y}_1^s, \mathbf{y}_2^s, \ldots, \mathbf{y}_T^s)$ for the spatial part and another set $(\mathbf{y}_1^m, \mathbf{y}_2^m, \ldots, \mathbf{y}_T^m)$ for the motion part. For both LSTM models, we adopt the last step output $\mathbf{y}_T$ as the video-level prediction scores, since the outputs at the last time step are based on the consideration of the entire sequence. We empirically observe that the last step outputs are better than pooling predictions from all the time steps.

3.3 Regularized Feature Fusion Network

Given both the spatial and the motion features, it is easy to understand that correlations may exist between them since both are computed on the same video (e.g., person-related static visual features and body motions). A good feature fusion method is supposed to be able to take advantages of the correlations, while also can maintain the unique characteristics to produce a better fused representation. In order to explore this important problem rather than using the simple late fusion as [33], we employ a regularized feature fusion neural network, as shown in the middle part of Figure 1. First, average pooling is adopted to aggregate the frame-level CNN features into video-level representations, which are used as the inputs of the fusion network. The input features are non-linearly mapped to another layer and then fused in a feature fusion layer, where we apply regularizations in the learning of the network weights.

Denote N as the total number of training videos with both the spatial and the motion representations. For the n-th sample, it can be written as a 3-tuple as $(\mathbf{x}_n^s, \mathbf{x}_n^m, \mathbf{y}_n)$, where $\mathbf{x}_n^s = \sum_{t=1}^T \mathbf{x}_{n,t}^s \in \mathbb{R}^{d_s}$ and $\mathbf{x}_n^m = \sum_{t=1}^T \mathbf{x}_{n,t}^m \in \mathbb{R}^{d_m}$ represent the averaged spatial and motion features respectively, and $\mathbf{y}_n$ is the corresponding label of the n-th sample.

For the ease of discussion, let us consider a degenerated case first, where only one feature is available. Denote $g(\cdot)$ as the mapping of the neural network from inputs to outputs. The objective of network training is to minimize the following empirical loss:

$$\min_{\mathbf{W}} \sum_{i=1}^{N} \|g(\mathbf{x}_i) - \mathbf{y}_i\|^2 + \lambda_1 \Phi(\mathbf{W}), \tag{1}$$

where the first term measures the discrepancy between the output $g(\mathbf{x}_i)$ and the ground-truth label $\mathbf{y}_i$, and the second term is usually a Frobenius norm based regularizer to prevent over-fitting.

We now move on to discuss the case of fusion and prediction with two features. Note that the approach can be easily extended to support more than two input features. Specifically, we use a fusion layer (see Figure 1) to absorb the spatial and temporal features into a fused representation. To exploit the correlations of the features, we regularize the fusion process with a structural ℓ_{21} norm, which is defined as $\|\mathbf{W}\|_{2,1} = \sum_i \sqrt{\sum_j w_{ij}^2}$. Incorporating the ℓ_{21} norm in the standard deep neural network formulation, we arrive at the following optimization problem:

$$\min_{\mathbf{W}} \mathcal{L} + \lambda_1 \Phi(\mathbf{W}) + \frac{\lambda_2}{2} \left\|\mathbf{W}^E\right\|_{2,1}, \tag{2}$$

where $\mathcal{L} = \sum_{i=1}^N \|g(\mathbf{x}_i^s, \mathbf{x}_i^m) - \mathbf{y}_i\|^2$, $\mathbf{W}^E = [\mathbf{W}_s^E, \mathbf{W}_m^E] \in \mathbb{R}^{P \times D}$ denotes the concatenated weight matrix from the Eth layer (i.e., the last layer of feature abstraction in Figure 1), $D = d_s + d_m$ and P is the dimension of the fusion layer.

Different from the objective in Equation (1), here we have an additional ℓ_{21} norm that is used for exploring feature correlations in the E-th layer. The term $\|\mathbf{W}^E\|_{2,1}$ computes the 2-norm of the weight values across different features in each dimension. Therefore, the regularization attains minimum when $\mathbf{W^E}$ contains the smallest number of non-zero rows, which is the discriminative information shared by distinct features. That is to say, the ℓ_{21} norm encourages the matrix $\mathbf{W}^E$ to be row sparse, which leads to similar zero/nonzero patterns of the columns of the matrix $\mathbf{W}^E$. Hence it enforces different features to share a subset of hidden neurons, reflecting the feature correlations.

However, in addition to seeking for the correlations shared among features, the unique discriminative information should also be preserved so that the complementary information can be used for improved classification performance. Thus, we add an additional regularizer to Equation (2) as following:

$$\min_{\mathbf{W}} \mathcal{L} + \lambda_1 \Phi(\mathbf{W}) + \frac{\lambda_2}{2} \left\|\mathbf{W}^E\right\|_{2,1} + \lambda_3 \left\|\mathbf{W}^E\right\|_{1,1}. \tag{3}$$

The term $\|\mathbf{W}^E\|_{1,1}$ can be regarded as a complement of the $\|\mathbf{W}^E\|_{2,1}$ norm. It provides the robustness of the ℓ_{21} norm from sharing incorrect features among different representations, and thus allows different representations to emphasize different hidden neurons.

Although the regularizer terms in Equation (3) are all convex functions, the optimization problem in Equation (3) is nonconvex due to the nonconvexity of the sigmoid function. Below, we discuss the optimization strategy using the gradient descent method in two cases:

1. For the E-th layer, our objective function has four valid terms: the empirical loss, the ℓ_2 regularizer $\Phi(\mathbf{W})$, and two nonsomooth structural regularizers, *i.e.*, the ℓ_{21} and ℓ_{11} terms. Note that simply using the gradient descent method is not optimal due to the two nonsmooth terms. We propose to optimize the E-th layer using a proximal gradient descent method, which splits the objective function into two parts:

$$p = \mathcal{L} + \lambda_1 \Phi(\mathbf{W}),$$
$$q = \frac{\lambda_2}{2} \left\| \mathbf{W}^E \right\|_{2,1} + \lambda_3 \left\| \mathbf{W}^E \right\|_{1,1},$$

where p is a smooth function and q is a nonsmooth function. Thus, the update of the i-th iteration is formulated as:

$$(\mathbf{W}^E)^{(i)} = \text{Prox}_q((\mathbf{W}^E)^{(i)} - \nabla p((\mathbf{W}^E)^{(i)})),$$

where Prox is a proximal operator defined as:

$$\text{Prox}_q(\mathbf{W}) = \arg\min_{\mathbf{V}} \|\mathbf{W} - \mathbf{V}\| + q(V).$$

The proximal operator on the combination of ℓ_{21}/ℓ_{11} norm ball can be computed analytically as:

$$\mathbf{W}^E_{r\cdot} = \left(1 - \frac{\lambda_2}{\|\mathbf{U}_{r\cdot}\|_2}\right) \mathbf{U}_{r\cdot}, \forall r = 1, \cdots, P, \quad (4)$$

where $\mathbf{U}_{r\cdot} = [|\mathbf{V}_{r\cdot}| - \lambda_3]_+ \cdot sign[\mathbf{V}_{r\cdot}]$, and $\mathbf{W}_{r\cdot}, \mathbf{U}_{r\cdot}, \mathbf{V}_{r\cdot}$ denote the r-th row of matrix $\mathbf{W}, \mathbf{U}$ and $\mathbf{V}$, respectively. Readers may refer to [49] for a detailed proof of a similar analytical solution.

2. For all the other layers, the objective function in Equation 3 only contains the first two valid terms, which are both smooth. Thus, we can directly apply the gradient descent method as in [3]. Denote $\mathbf{G}^l$ as the gradient of $\mathbf{W}^l$, the weight matrix of the lth layer is updated as:

$$\mathbf{W}^l = \mathbf{W}^l - \eta \mathbf{G}^l. \quad (5)$$

The only additional computation cost for training our regularized feature fusion network is to compute the proximal operator in the E-th layer. The complexity of the analytical solution in Equation (4) is $O(P \times D)$. Therefore, the proposed proximal gradient descent method can quickly train the network with affordable computational cost. When incorporating more features, our formulation can be computed efficiently with linearly increased cost, while cubic operations are required by the approach of [47] to reach a similar goal. In sum, the above optimization is incorporated into the conventional back propagation procedure, as described in Algorithm 1.

3.4 Discussion

The approach described above has the capability of modeling static spatial, short-term motion and long-term temporal clues, which are all very important in video content analysis. One may have noticed that the proposed hybrid deep learning framework contains several components that are separately trained. Joint training is feasible but not adopted in this current framework for the following reason. The joint training process is more complex and existing works exploring this aspect indicate that the performance gain is not very significant. In [6], the authors jointly trained the LSTM with a CNN for feature extraction, which only improved the performance on a benchmark dataset from 70.5% to 71.1%. Besides, an advantage of separate training is that the framework is more flexible, where a component can be replaced easily without the need of re-training the entire framework. For instance, more discriminative CNN models like the GoogLeNet [38] and deeper RNN models [4] can be used to replace the CNN and LSTM parts respectively.

Input : $\mathbf{x}^s_n$ and $\mathbf{x}^m_n$: the spatial and motion CNN features of the n-th video sample;
$\mathbf{y}_n$: the label of the n-th video sample;
randomly initialized weight matrices $\mathbf{W}$;

begin
    for *epoch* $\leftarrow$ 1 **to** M **do**
        Get the prediction error with feedforward propagation;
        for $l \leftarrow L$ **to** *1* **do**
            Evaluate the gradients and update the weight matrices using Equation (5);
            if $l == E$ **then**
                Evaluate the proximal operator according to Equation (4);
            end
        end
    end
end

Algorithm 1: The training procedure of the regularized feature fusion network.

In addition, as mentioned in Section 1, there could be alternative frameworks or models with similar capabilities. The main contribution of this work is to show that such a hybrid framework is very suitable for video classification. In addition to showing the effectiveness of the LSTM and the regularized feature fusion network, we also show that the combination of both in the hybrid framework can lead to significant improvements, particularly for long videos that contain rich temporal clues.

4. EXPERIMENTS

4.1 Experimental Setup

4.1.1 Datasets

We adopt two popular datasets to evaluate the proposed hybrid deep learning framework.

UCF-101 [35]. The UCF-101 dataset is one of the most popular action recognition benchmarks. It consists of 13,320 video clips of 101 human actions (27 hours in total). Following [17], we conduct evaluations using 3 train/test splits, which is currently the most popular setting in using this dataset. Results are measured by classification accuracy on each split and we report the mean accuracy over the three splits.

Columbia Consumer Videos (CCV) [18]. The CCV dataset contains 9,317 YouTube videos annotated according to 20 classes, which are mainly events like "basketball", "graduation ceremony", "birthday party" and "parade". We follow the convention defined in [18] to use a training set of 4,659 videos and a test set of 4,658 videos. The performance is evaluated by average precision (AP) for each class, and we report the mean AP (mAP) as the overall measure.

4.1.2 Implementation Details

For feature extraction network structure, we adopt the VGG_19 [34] and the CNN_M [33] to extract the spatial and the motion CNN features, respectively. The two networks can achieve 7.5% [34] and 13.5% [33] top-5 error rates on the ImageNet ILSVRC-2012 validation set respectively. The spatial CNN is first pre-trained with the ILSVRC-2012 training set with 1.2 million images and then fine-tuned using the video data, which is observed to be better than training from scratch. The motion CNN is trained from scratch as there is no off-the-shelf training set in the required form. In addition, simple data augmentation methods like cropping and flipping are utilized following [33].

The CNN models are trained using mini-batch stochastic gradient descent with a momentum fixed to 0.9. In the fine-tuning case of the spatial CNN, the rate starts from 10^{-3} and decreases to 10^{-4} after 14K iterations, then to 10^{-5} after 20K iterations. This setting is similar to [33], but we start from a smaller rate of 10^{-3} instead of 10^{-2}. For the motion CNN, we set the learning rate to 10^{-2} initially, and reduce it to 10^{-3} after 100K iterations, then to 10^{-4} after 200K iterations. Our implementation is based on the publicly available Caffe toolbox [14] with modifications to support parallel training with multiple GPUs in a server.

For temporal modeling, we adopt two layers in the LSTM for both the spatial and the motion features. Each LSTM has 1,024 hidden units in the bottom layer and 512 hidden units in the other layer. The network weights are learnt using a parallel implementation of the BPTT algorithm with a mini-batch size of 10. In addition, the learning rate and momentum are set to 10^{-4} and 0.9 respectively. The training is stopped after 150K iterations for both datasets.

For the regularized feature fusion network, we use four layers of neurons as illustrated in the middle of Figure 1. Specifically, we first use one layer with 200 neurons for the spatial and motion feature to perform feature abstraction separately, and then one layer with 200 neurons for feature fusion with the proposed regularized structural norms. Finally, the fused features are used to build a logistic regression model in the last layer for video classification. We set the learning rate to 0.7 and fix λ_1 to 3×10^{-5} in order to prevent over-fitting. In addition, we tune λ_2 and λ_3 in the same range as λ_1 using cross-validation.

4.1.3 Compared Approaches

To validate the effectiveness of our approach, we compare with the following baseline or alternative methods: (1) **Two-stream CNN**. Our implementation produces similar overall results with the original work [33]. We also report the results of the individual spatial-stream and motion-stream CNN models, namely **Spatial CNN** and **Motion CNN**, respectively; (2) **Spatial LSTM**, which refers to the LSTM trained with the spatial CNN features; (3) **Motion LSTM**, the LSTM trained with the motion CNN features; (4) **SVM-based Early Fusion (SVM-EF)**. χ^2-kernel is computed for each video-level CNN feature and then the two kernels are averged for classification; (5) **SVM-based Late Fusion (SVM-LF)**. Separate SVM classifiers are trained for each video-level CNN feature and the prediction outputs are averaged; (6) **Multiple Kernel Learning (SVM-MKL)**, which combines the two features with the ℓ_p-norm MKL [21] by fixing $p = 2$; (7) **Early Fusion with Neural Networks (NN-EF)**, which concatenates the two features into a long vector and then use a neural network for classification; (8) **Late Fusion with Neural Networks (NN-LF)**, which deploys a separate neural network for each feature and then uses the average output scores as the final prediction; (9) **Multimodal Deep Boltzmann Machines (M-DBM)** [29, 37], where feature fusion is performed using a neural network in a *free* manner without regularizations; (10) **RDNN** [47], which also imposes regularizations in a neural network for feature fusion, using a formulation that has a much higher complexity than our approach.

The first three methods are a part of the proposed framework, which are evaluated as baselines to better understand the contribution of each individual component. The last seven methods focus on fusing the spatial and the motion features (outputs of the first fully-connected layer of the CNN models) for improved classification performance. We compare our regularized fusion network with all the seven methods.

4.2 Results and Discussions

4.2.1 Temporal Modeling

We first evaluate the LSTM to investigate the significance of leveraging the long-term temporal clues for video classification. The results and comparisons are summarized in Table 1. The upper two groups in the table compare the LSTM models with the two-stream CNN, which performs classification by pooling video-level representations without considering the temporal order of the frames. On UCF-101, the Spatial LSTM is better than the spatial stream CNN, while the result of the Motion LSTM is slightly lower than that of the motion stream CNN. It is interesting to see that, on the spatial stream, the LSTM is even better than the state-of-the-art CNN, indicating that the temporal information is very important for human action modeling, which is fully discarded in the spatial stream CNN. Since the mechanism of the LSTM is totally different, these results are fairly appealing because it is potentially very complementary to the video-level classification based on feature pooling.

On the CCV dataset, the LSTM models produce lower performance than the CNN models on both streams. The reasons are two-fold. First, since the average duration of the CCV videos (80 seconds) is around 10 times longer than that of the UCF-101 and the contents in CCV are more complex and noisy, the LSTM might be affected by the noisy video segments that are irrelevant to the major class of a video. Second, some classes like "wedding reception" and "beach" do not contain clear temporal order information (see Figure 4), for which the LSTM can hardly capture helpful clues.

We now assess the performance of combining the LSTM and the CNN models to study whether they are complementary, by fusing the outputs of the two types of models trained on the two streams. Note that the fusion method adopted here is the simple late average fusion, which uses the average prediction scores of different models. More advanced fusion methods will be evaluated in the next subsection.

Results are reported in the bottom three rows of Table 1. We observe significant improvements from model fusion on

	UCF-101	CCV
Spatial CNN	80.1%	75.0%
Spatial LSTM	83.3%	43.3%
Motion CNN	77.5%	58.9%
Motion LSTM	76.6%	54.7%
CNN + LSTM (Spatial)	84.0%	77.9%
CNN + LSTM (Motion)	81.4%	70.9%
CNN + LSTM (Spatial & Motion)	**90.1%**	**81.7%**

Table 1: Performance of the LSTM and the CNN models trained with the spatial and the short-term motion features respectively on UCF-101 and CCV. "+" indicates model fusion, which simply uses the average prediction scores of different models.

	UCF-101	CCV
Spatial SVM	78.6%	74.4%
Motion SVM	78.2%	57.9%
SVM-EF	86.6%	75.3%
SVM-LF	85.3%	74.9%
SVM-MKL	86.8%	75.4%
NN-EF	86.5%	75.6%
NN-LF	85.1%	75.2%
M-DBM	86.9%	75.3%
Two-stream CNN	86.2%	75.8%
RDNN	88.1%	75.9%
Non-regularized Fusion Network	87.0%	75.4%
Regularized Fusion Network	**88.4%**	**76.2%**

Table 2: Performance comparison on UCF-101 and CCV, using various fusion approaches to combine the spatial and the short-term motion clues.

both datasets. On UCF-101, the fusion leads to an absolute performance gain of around 1% compared with the best single model for the spatial stream, and a gain of 4% for the motion stream. On CCV, the improvements are more significant, especially for the motion stream where an absolute gain of 12% is observed. These results confirm the fact that the long-term temporal clues are highly complementary to the spatial and the short-term motion features. In addition, the fusion of all the CNN and the LSTM models trained on the two streams attains the highest performance on both datasets: 90.1% and 81.7% on UCF-101 and CCV respectively, showing that the spatial and the short-term motion features are also very complementary. Therefore, it is important to incorporate all of them into a successful video classification system.

4.2.2 *Feature Fusion*

Next, we compare our regularized feature fusion network with the alternative fusion methods, using both the spatial and the motion CNN features. The results are presented in Table 2, which are divided into four groups. The first group reports the performance of individual features extracted from the first fully connected layer of the CNN models, classified by SVM classifiers. This is reported to study the gain from the SVM based fusion methods, as shown in the second group of results. The individual feature results using the CNN, i.e., the Spatial CNN and the Motion CNN, are already reported in Table 1. The third group of results in Table 2 are based on the alternative neural network fusion methods. Note that NN-EF and NN-LF take the features from the CNN models and perform fusion and classification using separate neural networks, while the two-stream CNN approach performs classification using the CNN directly with a late score fusion (Figure 2). Finally, the last group contains the results of the proposed fusion network.

As can be seen, the SVM based fusion methods can greatly improve the results on UCF-101. On CCV, the gain is consistent but not very significant, indicating that the short-term motion is more important for modeling the human actions with clearer motion patterns and less noises. SVM-MKL is only slightly better than the simple early and late fusion methods, which is consistent with observations in recent works on visual recognition [42].

Our proposed regularized feature fusion network (the last row in Table 2) is consistently better than the alternative neural network based fusion methods shown in the third group of the table. In particular, the gap between our results and that of the M-DBM and the two-stream CNN confirms that using regularizations in the fusion process is helpful. Compared with the RDNN, our formulation produces slightly better results but with a much lower complexity as discussed earlier.

In addition, as the proposed formulation contains two structural norms, to directly evaluate the contribution of the norms, we also report a baseline using the same network structure without regularization ("non-regularized fusion network" in the table), which is similar to the M-DBM approach in its design but differs slightly in network structures. We see that adding regularizations in the same network can improve 1.4% on UCF-101 and 0.8% on CCV.

4.2.3 *The Hybrid Framework*

Finally, we discuss the results of the entire hybrid deep learning framework by further combining results from the temporal LSTM and the regularized fusion network. The prediction scores from these networks are fused linearly with weights estimated by cross-validation. As shown in the last row of Table 3, we achieve very strong performance on both datasets: 91.3% on UCF-101 and 83.5% on CCV. The performance of the hybrid framework is clearly better than that of the Spatial LSTM and the Motion LSTM (in Table 1). Compared with the Regularized Fusion Network (in Table 2), adding the long-term temporal modeling in the hybrid framework improves 2.9% on UCF-101 and 7.3% on CCV, which are fairly significant considering the difficulties of the two datasets. In contrast to the fusion result in the last row of Table 1, the gain of the proposed hybrid framework comes from the use of the regularized fusion, which again verifies the effectiveness of our fusion method.

To better understand the contributions of the key components in the hybrid framework, we further report the per-class performance on CCV in Figure 4. We see that, although the performance of the LSTM is clearly lower, fusing it with the video-level predictions by the regularized fusion network can significantly improve the results for almost all the classes. This is a bit surprising because some classes do not seem to require temporal information to be recognized. After checking into some of the videos we find that there could be helpful clues which can be modeled, even for

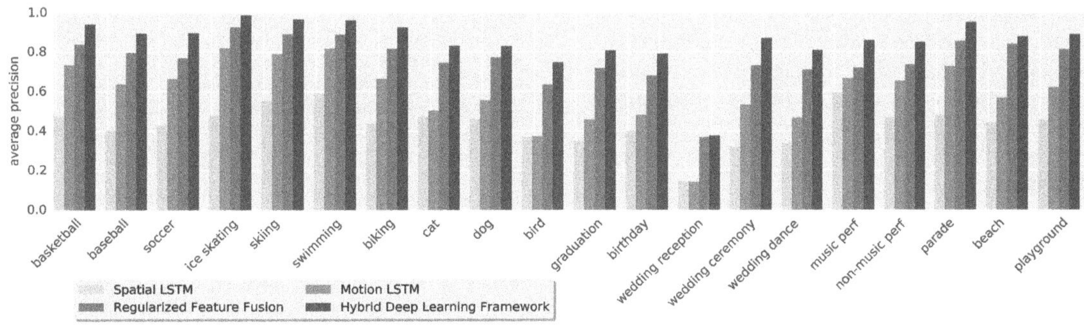

Figure 4: Per-class performance on CCV, using the Spatial and Motion LSTM, the Regularized Fusion Network, and their combination, i.e., the Hybrid Deep Learning Framework.

Figure 5: Two example videos of class "cat" in the CCV dataset with similar temporal clues over time.

UCF-101		CCV	
Donahue *et al.* [6]	82.9%	Xu *et al.* [48]	60.3%
Srivastava *et al.* [36]	84.3%	Ye *et al.* [50]	64.0%
Wang *et al.* [44]	85.9%	Jhuo *et al.* [12]	64.0%
Tran *et al.* [40]	86.7%	Ma *et al.* [28]	63.4%
Simonyan *et al.* [33]	88.0%	Liu *et al.* [26]	68.2%
Lan *et al.* [23]	89.1%	Wu *et al.* [47]	70.6%
Zha *et al.* [53]	89.6%	/	
Ours	**91.3%**	Ours	**83.5%**

Table 3: Comparison with state-of-the-art results.

object-related classes like "cat" and "dog". For instance, as shown in Figure 5, we observe that quite a number of "cat" videos contain only a single cat running around on the floor. The LSTM network may be able to capture this clue, which is helpful for classification.

Efficiency. In addition to achieving the superior classification performance, our framework also enjoys high computational efficiency. We summarize the average testing time of a UCF-101 video (duration: 8 seconds) as follows. The extraction of the frames and the optical flows takes 3.9 seconds, and computing the CNN-based spatial and short-term motion features requires 9 seconds. Prediction with the LSTM and the regularized fusion network needs 2.8 seconds. All these are evaluated on a single NVIDIA Telsa K40 GPU.

4.2.4 Comparison with State of the Arts

In this subsection, we compare with several state-of-the-art results. As shown in Table 3, our hybrid deep learning framework produces the highest performance on both datasets. On the UCF-101, many works with competitive results are based on the dense trajectories [44, 53], while our approach fully relies on the deep learning techniques. Compared with the original result of the two-stream CNN in [33], our framework is better with the additional fusion and temporal modeling functions, although it is built on our implementation of the CNN models which are slightly worse than that of [33] (our two-stream CNN result is 86.2%). Note that a gain of even just 1% on the widely adopted UCF-101 dataset is generally considered as a significant progress. In addition, the recent works in [6, 36] also adopted the LSTM to explore the temporal clues for video classification and reported promising performance. However, our LSTM results are not directly comparable as the input features are extracted by different neural networks.

On the CCV dataset, all the recent approaches relied on the joint use of multiple features by developing new fusion methods [48, 50, 12, 28, 26, 47]. Our hybrid deep learning framework is significantly better than all of them.

5. CONCLUSIONS

We have proposed a novel hybrid deep learning framework for video classification, which is able to model static visual features, short-term motion patterns and long-term temporal clues. In the framework, we first extract spatial and motion features with two CNNs trained on static frames and stacked optical flows respectively. The two types of features are used separately as inputs of the LSTM network for long-term temporal modeling. A regularized fusion network is also deployed to combine the two features on video-level for improved classification. Our hybrid deep learning framework integrating both the LSTM and the regularized fusion network produces very impressive performance on two widely adopted benchmark datasets. Results not only verify the effectiveness of the individual components of the framework, but also demonstrate that the frame-level temporal modeling and the video-level fusion and classification are highly complementary, and a big leap of performance can be attained by combining them.

Although deep learning based approaches have been successful in addressing many problems, effective network architectures are urgently needed for modeling sequential data like the videos. Several researchers have recently explored this direction. However, compared with the progress on image classification, the achieved performance gain on video classification over the traditional hand-crafted features is much less significant. Our work in this paper represents one of the few studies showing very strong results. For future work, further improving the capability of modeling the temporal dimension of videos is of high priority. In addition, audio features which are known to be useful for video classification can be easily incorporated into our framework.

Acknowledgment

This work was supported in part by a National 863 Program (#2014AA015101), a grant from the NSF China (#61201387), a grant from the STCSM, China (#13PJ1400400), and the EU FP7 QUICK project under Grant Agreement No. PIRSES-GA-2013-612652.

6. REFERENCES

[1] R. Arandjelović and A. Zisserman. Three things everyone should know to improve object retrieval. In *CVPR*, 2012.

[2] F. R. Bach, G. R. Lanckriet, and M. I. Jordan. Multiple kernel learning, conic duality, and the smo algorithm. In *ICML*, 2004.

[3] Y. Bengio. Practical recommendations for gradient-based training of deep architectures. In *Neural Networks: Tricks of the Trade*. Springer, 2012.

[4] J. Chung, Ç. Gülçehre, K. Cho, and Y. Bengio. Gated feedback recurrent neural networks. *CoRR*, 2015.

[5] G. E. Dahl, D. Yu, L. Deng, and A. Acero. Context-Dependent Pre-Trained Deep Neural Networks for Large-Vocabulary Speech Recognition. *IEEE TASLP*, 2012.

[6] J. Donahue, L. A. Hendricks, S. Guadarrama, M. Rohrbach, S. Venugopalan, K. Saenko, and T. Darrell. Long-term recurrent convolutional networks for visual recognition and description. *CoRR*, 2014.

[7] R. Girshick, J. Donahue, T. Darrell, and J. Malik. Rich feature hierarchies for accurate object detection and semantic segmentation. In *CVPR*, 2014.

[8] A. Graves, A. Mohamed, and G. E. Hinton. Speech recognition with deep recurrent neural networks. In *ICASSP*, 2013.

[9] A. Graves and J. Schmidhuber. Framewise phoneme classification with bidirectional lstm and other neural network architectures. *Neural Networks*, 2005.

[10] C. Harris and M. J. Stephens. A combined corner and edge detector. In *Alvey Vision Conference*, 1988.

[11] M. Jain, J. van Gemert, and C. G. M. Snoek. University of amsterdam at thumos challenge 2014. In *ECCV THUMOS Challenge Workshop*, 2014.

[12] I.-H. Jhuo, G. Ye, S. Gao, D. Liu, Y.-G. Jiang, D. T. Lee, and S.-F. Chang. Discovering joint audio-visual codewords for video event detection. *Machine Vision and Applications*, 2014.

[13] S. Ji, W. Xu, M. Yang, and K. Yu. 3d convolutional neural networks for human action recognition. In *ICML*, 2010.

[14] Y. Jia, E. Shelhamer, J. Donahue, S. Karayev, J. Long, R. Girshick, S. Guadarrama, and T. Darrell. Caffe: Convolutional architecture for fast feature embedding. In *ACM Multimedia*, 2014.

[15] W. Jiang, C. Cotton, S.-F. Chang, D. Ellis, and A. Loui. Short-term audio-visual atoms for generic video concept classification. In *ACM Multimedia*, 2009.

[16] Y.-G. Jiang, S. Bhattacharya, S.-F. Chang, and M. Shah. High-level event recognition in unconstrained videos. *IJMIR*, 2013.

[17] Y.-G. Jiang, J. Liu, A. Roshan Zamir, G. Toderici, I. Laptev, M. Shah, and R. Sukthankar. THUMOS challenge: Action recognition with a large number of classes. `http://crcv.ucf.edu/THUMOS14/`, 2014.

[18] Y.-G. Jiang, G. Ye, S.-F. Chang, D. Ellis, and A. C. Loui. Consumer video understanding: A benchmark database and an evaluation of human and machine performance. In *ICMR*, 2011.

[19] A. Karpathy, G. Toderici, S. Shetty, T. Leung, R. Sukthankar, and L. Fei-Fei. Large-scale video classification with convolutional neural networks. In *CVPR*, 2014.

[20] A. Klaser, M. Marszałek, and C. Schmid. A spatio-temporal descriptor based on 3d-gradients. In *BMVC*, 2008.

[21] M. Kloft, U. Brefeld, S. Sonnenburg, and A. Zien. Lp-norm multiple kernel learning. *The Journal of Machine Learning Research*, 2011.

[22] A. Krizhevsky, I. Sutskever, and G. E. Hinton. Imagenet classification with deep convolutional neural networks. In *NIPS*, 2012.

[23] Z. Lan, M. Lin, X. Li, A. G. Hauptmann, and B. Raj. Beyond gaussian pyramid: Multi-skip feature stacking for action recognition. *CoRR*, 2014.

[24] I. Laptev. On space-time interest points. *IJCV*, 2007.

[25] W. Li, Z. Zhang, and Z. Liu. Expandable data-driven graphical modeling of human actions based on salient postures. *IEEE TCSVT*, 2008.

[26] D. Liu, K.-T. Lai, G. Ye, M.-S. Chen, and S.-F. Chang. Sample-specific late fusion for visual category recognition. In *CVPR*, 2013.

[27] D. G. Lowe. Distinctive image features from scale-invariant keypoints. *IJCV*, 2004.

[28] A. J. Ma and P. C. Yuen. Reduced analytic dependency modeling: Robust fusion for visual recognition. *IJCV*, 2014.

[29] J. Ngiam, A. Khosla, M. Kim, J. Nam, H. Lee, and A. Ng. Multimodal deep learning. In *ICML*, 2011.

[30] D. Oneata, J. Verbeek, C. Schmid, et al. Action and event recognition with fisher vectors on a compact feature set. In *ICCV*, 2013.

[31] M. Ranzato, A. Szlam, J. Bruna, M. Mathieu, R. Collobert, and S. Chopra. Video (language) modeling: a baseline for generative models of natural videos. *CoRR*, 2014.

[32] A. S. Razavian, H. Azizpour, J. Sullivan, and S. Carlsson. CNN features off-the-shelf: an astounding baseline for recognition. *CoRR*, 2014.

[33] K. Simonyan and A. Zisserman. Two-stream convolutional networks for action recognition in videos. In *NIPS*, 2014.

[34] K. Simonyan and A. Zisserman. Very deep convolutional networks for large-scale image recognition. *CoRR*, 2014.

[35] K. Soomro, A. R. Zamir, and M. Shah. UCF101: A dataset of 101 human actions classes from videos in the wild. *CoRR*, 2012.

[36] N. Srivastava, E. Mansimov, and R. Salakhutdinov. Unsupervised learning of video representations using LSTMs. *CoRR*, 2015.

[37] N. Srivastava and R. Salakhutdinov. Multimodal learning with deep boltzmann machines. In *NIPS*, 2012.

[38] C. Szegedy, W. Liu, Y. Jia, P. Sermanet, S. Reed, D. Anguelov, D. Erhan, V. Vanhoucke, and A. Rabinovich. Going Deeper with Convolutions. *CoRR*, 2014.

[39] K. Tang, L. Fei-Fei, and D. Koller. Learning latent temporal structure for complex event detection. In *CVPR*, 2012.

[40] D. Tran, L. Bourdev, R. Fergus, L. Torresani, and M. Paluri. C3d: Generic features for video analysis. *CoRR*, 2014.

[41] D. L. Vail, M. M. Veloso, and J. D. Lafferty. Conditional random fields for activity recognition. In *AAAMS*, 2007.

[42] A. Vedaldi, V. Gulshan, M. Varma, and A. Zisserman. Multiple kernels for object detection. In *ICCV*, 2009.

[43] S. Venugopalan, H. Xu, J. Donahue, M. Rohrbach, R. J. Mooney, and K. Saenko. Translating videos to natural language using deep recurrent neural networks. *CoRR*, 2014.

[44] H. Wang and C. Schmid. Action recognition with improved trajectories. In *ICCV*, 2013.

[45] H. Wang, M. M. Ullah, A. Klaser, I. Laptev, and C. Schmid. Evaluation of local spatio-temporal features for action recognition. In *BMVC*, 2009.

[46] Y. Wang and G. Mori. Max-margin hidden conditional random fields for human action recognition. In *CVPR*, 2009.

[47] Z. Wu, Y.-G. Jiang, J. Wang, J. Pu, and X. Xue. Exploring inter-feature and inter-class relationships with deep neural networks for video classification. In *ACM Multimedia*, 2014.

[48] Z. Xu, Y. Yang, I. Tsang, N. Sebe, and A. Hauptmann. Feature weighting via optimal thresholding for video analysis. In *ICCV*, 2013.

[49] H. Yang, M. R. Lyu, and I. King. Efficient online learning for multitask feature selection. *ACM SIGKDD*, 2013.

[50] G. Ye, D. Liu, I.-H. Jhuo, and S.-F. Chang. Robust late fusion with rank minimization. In *CVPR*, 2012.

[51] H. Ye, Z. Wu, R.-W. Zhao, X. Wang, Y.-G. Jiang, and X. Xue. Evaluating two-stream cnn for video classification. In *ICMR*, 2015.

[52] Z. Zeng and Q. Ji. Knowledge based activity recognition with dynamic bayesian network. In *ECCV*, 2010.

[53] S. Zha, F. Luisier, W. Andrews, N. Srivastava, and R. Salakhutdinov. Exploiting image-trained cnn architectures for unconstrained video classification. *CoRR*, 2015.

[54] J. Zhang, M. Marszałek, S. Lazebnik, and C. Schmid. Local features and kernels for classification of texture and object categories: A comprehensive study. *IJCV*, 2007.

EventNet: A Large Scale Structured Concept Library for Complex Event Detection in Video

Guangnan Ye*, Yitong Li*, Hongliang Xu, Dong Liu, Shih-Fu Chang
Department of Electrical Engineering, Columbia University, New York, NY 10027, USA
{gy2179, yl3029, hx2168, dl2713, sc250}@columbia.edu

ABSTRACT

Event-specific concepts are the semantic concepts specifically designed for the events of interest, which can be used as a mid-level representation of complex events in videos. Existing methods only focus on defining event-specific concepts for a small number of pre-defined events, but cannot handle novel unseen events. This motivates us to build a large scale event-specific concept library that covers as many real-world events and their concepts as possible. Specifically, we choose WikiHow, an online forum containing a large number of how-to articles on human daily life events. We perform a coarse-to-fine event discovery process and discover 500 events from WikiHow articles. Then we use each event name as query to search YouTube and discover event-specific concepts from the tags of returned videos. After an automatic filter process, we end up with $95,321$ videos and $4,490$ concepts. We train a *Convolutional Neural Network* (CNN) model on the $95,321$ videos over the 500 events, and use the model to extract deep learning feature from video content. With the learned deep learning feature, we train $4,490$ binary SVM classifiers as the event-specific concept library. The concepts and events are further organized in a hierarchical structure defined by WikiHow, and the resultant concept library is called *EventNet*. Finally, the EventNet concept library is used to generate concept based representation of event videos. To the best of our knowledge, EventNet represents the first video event ontology that organizes events and their concepts into a semantic structure. It offers great potential for event retrieval and browsing. Extensive experiments over the zero-shot event retrieval task when no training samples are available show that the proposed EventNet concept library consistently and significantly outperforms the state-of-the-art (such as the $20K$ ImageNet concepts trained with CNN) by a large margin up to 207%. We will also show that EventNet structure can help users find relevant concepts for novel event queries that cannot be well handled by conventional text based semantic analysis alone. The unique two-step approach of first applying event detection models followed by detection of event-specific concepts also provides great potential to improve the efficiency and accuracy of Event Recounting since only a very small number of event-specific concept classifiers need to be fired after event detection.

*Equal contribution.

MM'15, October 26–30, 2015, Brisbane, Australia.
 ISBN 978-1-4503-3459-4/15/10 ...$15.00.
DOI: http://dx.doi.org/10.1145/2733373.2806221.

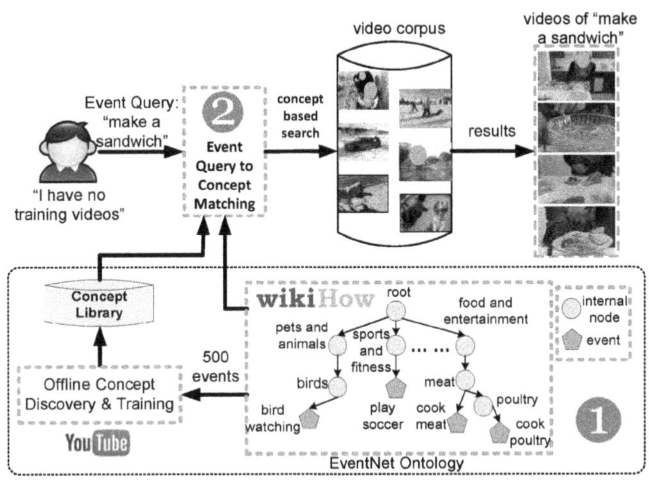

Figure 1: Concept based event retrieval by the proposed large scale structured concept library *EventNet*. This paper presents two unique contributions: (1) A large scale structural event ontology. (2) Effective event-to-concept mapping via the ontology.

Categories and Subject Descriptors

I.2.10 [**ARTIFICIAL INTELLIGENCE**]: Vision and Scene Understanding—*Video Analysis*

Keywords

Multimedia Event Detection, Zero-Shot Retrieval, Structured Concept Ontology, Concept based Video Representation

1. INTRODUCTION

The prevalence of video capture devices and growing practice of video sharing in social media have resulted in enormous explosion of user-generated videos on the Internet. Such video data records daily events related to various aspects of human life. Generally, these events can be categorized into two categories: procedural event and social event. The former includes procedural videos such as "make a cake", "groom a dog" and "change a tire" while the latter includes social activities such as "birthday party" and "flash mob gathering".

Existing video search systems are mostly based on textual descriptions of the videos such as tag keywords, metadata and surrounding text. Recent research in computer vision and multimedia attempts to automatically recognize events in videos, and index event videos based on the learned semantics. A notable example of such effort is TREC Video Retrieval Evaluation (TRECVID) Multimedia Event Detection (MED) [1]. Different from the action recognition task which focuses on primitive human activities such as "walk" and "jump" [13, 25], event detection deals with complicated high-level human activities that interact with objects in a certain scene. The complexity of such event is further increased by the occlusion, motion, and scene transition seen in user generated videos. For example, a video of "land a fish" may contain many semantic concepts such as objects "boat" and "fish", actions "land" and "grab" as well as scenes "pond" and "shore". Most of the early works on event detection focus on building event detection models from low-level features while ignoring the rich semantics in event videos [6, 17, 34]. This makes analysis and interpretation of high-level events difficult, especially when there are only few or zero training videos at hand.

This deficiency has stimulated a new research direction that tries to represent event videos in a high-dimensional semantic space, using each dimension of the space to indicate the likelihood of the occurrence of a concept in the video [16, 32]. A key research problem is how to generate a suitable concept lexicon for events. Existing works can be categorized into two groups. The first is event independent concept lexicon, which directly borrows the object, scene and action concepts from existing works and applies them to video events [32]. However, since these concepts are not specifically optimized for events of interest, they are often insufficient in capturing the rich semantics contained in the events. The second is event driven concept lexicon, which uses the pre-known event definition as query keywords to search external resources such as Flickr and YouTube, and then discover concepts that are specifically relevant to the target events [4]. Although this approach achieves good performance, it can only deal with a small number of target events whose definitions are known beforehand. When a novel unseen event emerges, it is no longer applicable due to the lack of relevant concepts for the unseen event.

To address this problem, we propose to construct a large scale event-driven concept library that covers as many real world events and concepts as possible. Figure 1 illustrates the overall framework of the proposed method, in which we highlight two main challenges addressed in this paper. The first is how to define events and their relevant concepts in order to construct a comprehensive concept library. To achieve this goal, we resort to the external knowledge base called WikiHow [2], a collaborative forum that aims to build the world's largest manual for human daily life events. We define 500 events from the articles of WikiHow website. For each event, we use its name as query keywords to perform text based video search on YouTube, and apply our automatic concept discovery method to discover event-specific concepts from the tags of the returned videos. Then we crawl videos associated with each discovered concept as the training videos to learn deep learning video features using *Convolutional Neutral Network* (CNN) as well as event-specific concept models. This leads to an event-specific concept library composed of $4,490$ concept models trained over $95,321$ YouTube videos. We further organize all events and their associated event-specific concepts into a hierarchical structure defined by WikiHow, and call the resultant concept library *EventNet*.

The second challenge is how to find semantically relevant concepts from EventNet that can be used to search video corpus to answer a new event query. The existing methods address this by calculating the semantic similarity between the event query and the candidate concepts, and then picking up the top ranked concepts with the highest similarities [4, 5, 32]. However, considering that our concepts are event-specific, each concept is associated with a specific event which can be used as contextual information in measuring the similarity between the query event and the concept. Moreover, due to the short text of event names which contain only very few text words, direct measurement of semantic similarity may not be able to accurately estimate semantic relevance, and the concept matching results may become quite unsatisfactory even when EventNet library does contain relevant events and concepts. To solve these issues, we propose a cascaded concept matching method which first matches relevant events and then finds relevant concepts specific to the matched events. For the queries that cannot be well answered by automatic semantic similarity calculation, we propose to leverage the hierarchical structure of EventNet and allow users to manually specify the appropriate high-level category[1] in the EventNet tree structure, and then only perform concept matching under the specified category (cf. Section 7)

We will demonstrate that the proposed EventNet concept library leads to dramatic performance gains in concept based event detection over various benchmark video event datasets. Specially, it outperforms the $20K$ concepts generated from the state-of-the-art deep learning system trained on ImageNet [11] by 207% in zero-shot event retrieval. We will also show that EventNet is able to detect and recount the semantic cues indicating occurrence of an event video. Finally, the video corpus in EventNet can be used as a comprehensive benchmark video event dataset. The browser of EventNet ontology as well as the downloading information of the models and video data can be found at `http://eventnet.ee.columbia.edu`.

This paper presents several major contributions: (1) A systematic framework for discovering a large number of events related to human events (Section 3). (2) Construction of the largest ontology including 500 complex events and $4,490$ event-specific concepts (Section 4 and 6). (3) Rigorous analysis of the properties of the constructed ontology (Section 5). (4) Dramatic performance gains in complex event detection especially for unseen novel events (Task I in Section 8). (5) The benefit of the proposed ontology structure in semantic recounting (Task II in Section 8) and concept matching (Task III in Section 8). (6) A benchmark event video dataset for advancing large scale event detection (Task IV in Section 8).

2. RELATED WORK

There are some recent works that focus on detecting video events using concept-based representations. For example, Wu *et al.* [32] mined concepts from the free-form text descriptions of TRECVID research video set, and applied them as weak concepts of the events in TRECVID MED task. As mentioned earlier, these concepts are not specifically designed for events, and may not capture well the semantics of event videos.

Recent research also attempts to define event-driven concepts for event detection. Liu *et al.* [16] proposed to manually annotate related concepts in event videos, and build concept models with the annotated video frames. Chen *et al.* [4] proposed to discover event-driven concepts from the tags of Flickr images crawled by using keywords of the events of interest. This method is able to find relevant concepts for each event and achieves good performance in various event detection tasks. Despite such promising properties, it heavily relies on the prior knowledge about the target events, and therefore cannot handle novel unknown events that may emerge at

[1]As shown in Figure 1, category nodes in EventNet are high-level categories in WikiHow used to organize articles into a hierarchy, such as "pets and animals", "sports and fitness", etc.

Dataset	EM	PM	RE	NM	Total Class #
MED 10-14 [1]	16	17	15	0	48
CCV [21]	6	5	8	1	20
Hollywood [13]	6	0	1	0	7
KTH [12]	4	1	1	0	6
UCF101 [29]	58	11	20	12	101
Matched Class #	90	34	45	13	182

Table 1: The matching results between WikiHow articles and event classes in the popular event video datasets, where "EM" denotes "Exact Match", "PM" denotes "Partial Match", "RE" denotes "Relevant" and "NM" denotes "No Match".

a later time. Our EventNet library tries to address this deficiency by exploring a large number of events and their related concepts from external knowledge resources, WikiHow and YouTube. A related prior work [5] tried to define a large number of events and discover concepts by using tags of Flickr images. However, as our later experiment will show, concept models trained with Flickr images cannot generalize well to event videos due to the well-known cross-domain data variation [28]. In contrast, our method discovers concepts and trains models based on YouTube videos, which more accurately captures the semantic concepts underlying content of user generated videos.

The proposed EventNet also introduces a benchmark video dataset for large scale video event detection. Current event detection benchmarks typically only contain a small number of events. For example, in the well known TRECVID MED task [1], significant efforts have been made to develop an event video dataset containing 48 events. Columbia Consumer Video (CCV) dataset [21] contains $9,317$ videos of 20 events. Such event categories may also suffer from data bias, and thus fail to provide general models applicable to unconstrained real-world events. In contrast, EventNet contains 500 event categories and $95K$ videos, which covers different aspects of human daily life and is believed to be the largest event dataset up to date. Another recent effort also tries to build a large scale structured event video dataset containing 239 events [20]. However, it does not provide semantic concepts associated with specific events like those defined in EventNet.

3. CHOOSING WIKIHOW AS EVENTNET ONTOLOGY

A key issue in constructing a large scale event driven concept library is to define an ontology that covers as many real-world events as possible. For this, we resort to the Internet knowledge bases constructed from crowd intelligence as our ontology definition resources. Specifically, WikiHow is an online forum that contains a large number of how-to manuals on every aspect of human daily life events, where a user can submit an article in describing how to accomplish a task such as "how to bake sweet potatoes", "how to remove tree stumps", etc. We choose WikiHow as our event ontology definition resource due to the following reasons:

Coverage of WikiHow Articles. WikiHow has a good coverage over different aspects of human daily life events. As of February 2015, it included over $300K$ how-to articles [2], among which some are well-defined video events[2] that can be detected by computer vision techniques, while others such as "how to think" or "how to apply for a passport" do not have suitable corresponding

[2]We define an event as video event when it satisfies the event definition in NIST TRECVID MED evaluation [1], i.e., a complicated human activity interacting with people/object in a certain scene.

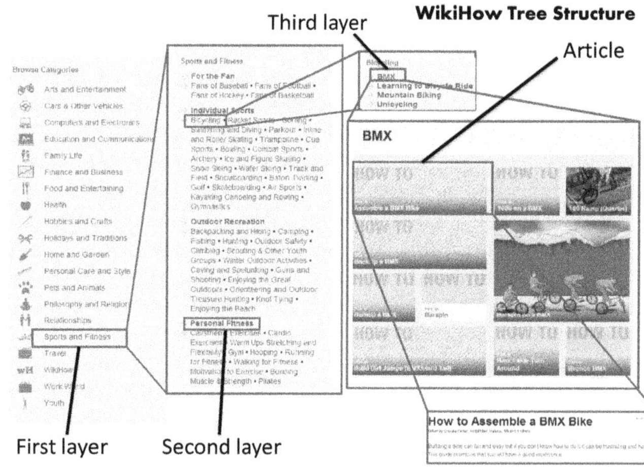

Figure 2: The hierarchial structure of WikiHow.

video events. We expect a comprehensive coverage of video events from such a massive number of articles created by the crowdsourcing knowledge from Internet users.

To verify that WikiHow articles have a good coverage on video events, we conduct a study to test whether WikiHow articles contain the events in the existing popular event video datasets in computer vision and multimedia fields. To this end, we choose the event classes in the following datasets: TRECVID MED 2010-2014 (48 classes) [1], Columbia Consumer Videos (CCV) (20 classes) [21], UCF 101 (101 classes) [29], Hollywood movies (7 classes) [13], KTH (6 classes) [12]. Then, we use each event class name as a text query to search WikiHow and examine the top-10 returned articles, from which we manually pick up the most relevant article title as the matching result. We define four matching levels to measure the matching quality. The first is *exact matching*, in which the matched article title and the event query are exactly matched (e.g., "clap hands" as a matched result to query "hand clapping"). The second is *partial match*, in which the matched article is discussing about a certain case of the query (e.g., "make a chocolate cake" as result to query "make a cake"). The third case is *relevant*, in which the matched article is semantically relevant to the query (e.g., "get your car out of the snow" as result to query "getting a vehicle unstuck"). The fourth case is *no match*, in which we cannot find any relevant articles about the query. The matching statistics can be shown in Table 1. If we count the first three types of matching as successful cases, the coverage rate of WikiHow over these event classes is as high as $169/182 = 93\%$, which confirms the potential of discovering video events from WikiHow articles.

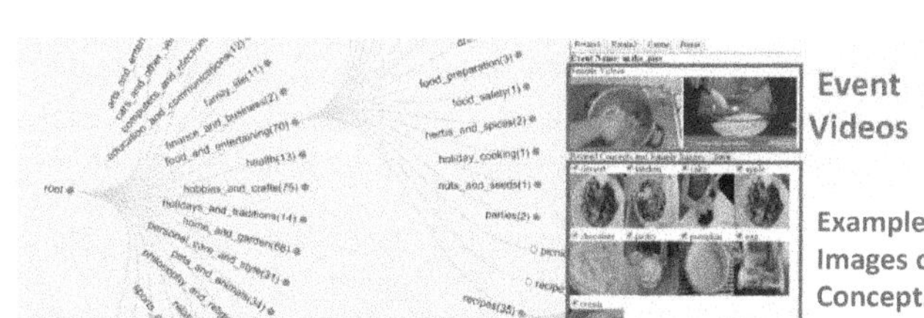

Figure 3: Event and concept browser for the proposed EventNet ontology. The hierarchical structure is shown on the left and the example videos and relevant concepts of each specific event are shown to the right.

Hierarchical Structure of WikiHow. WikiHow categorizes all its articles into 2,803 categories and further organizes all categories into a hierarchical tree structure. Each category contains a number of articles discussing different aspects of the category, and is associated with a node in WikiHow hierarchy. As shown in Figure 2 of the WikiHow hierarchy, the first layer contains 19 high-level nodes ranging from "arts and entertainment", "sports and fitness" to "pets and animal". Each node is further split into a number of children nodes that are subclasses or facets of the parent node with the deepest path from the root to the leaf node containing seven levels. Although such a hierarchy is not based on lexical knowledge, it summarizes human's common practice in organizing daily life events. Typically, a parent category node includes articles that are more generic than those in its children nodes. Therefore, the events residing along similar path in the WikiHow tree hierarchy are highly relevant (cf. Section 4). Such hierarchical structure will help users quickly localize the potential search area in the hierarchy for a specific query that he/she is interested in, and thus improve the concept matching accuracy (cf. Section 7). Besides, such hierarchical structure will also enhance event detection performance by leveraging the detection result of an event in a parent node to boost detection of the events in its children nodes, and vice versa. Finally, such hierarchical structure also allows us to develop an intuitive browsing interface for event navigation and event detection result visualization [33], which can be illustrated in Figure 3.

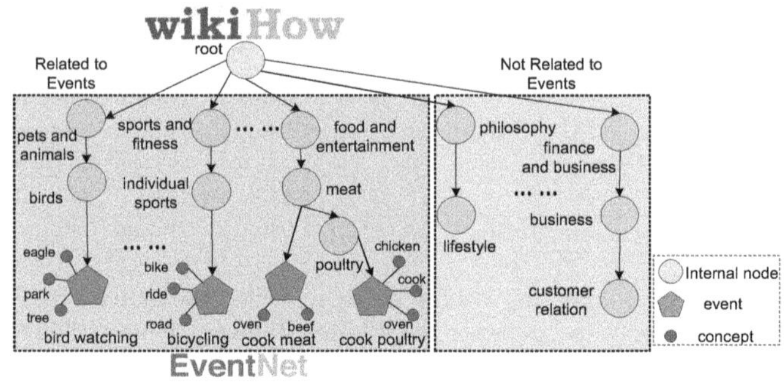

Figure 4: A snapshot of EventNet constructed from WikiHow.

4. CONSTRUCTING EVENTNET

In this section, we describe the procedure used in constructing EventNet, including how to define video events from WikiHow articles and how to discover event specific concepts for each of the events from tags of YouTube videos.

4.1 Discovering Events

First, we aim to discover potential video events from WikiHow articles. Intuitively, this can be done by crawling videos using each article title and then applying the automatic verification technique as that proposed in [3, 4] to determine whether an article corresponds to a video event. However, considering that there are $300K$ articles on WikiHow, it requires massive amount of data crawling and video processing, making it computationally infeasible. For this, we propose a coarse-to-fine event selection approach. The basic idea is to first prune WikiHow categories that do not correspond to video events, and then select one representative event from the article titles within each of the remaining categories. In the following, we will describe the event selection procedure in details.

Step I: WikiHow Category Pruning. Recall that WikiHow contains 2,803 categories, each of which contains a number of articles about this category. We observe that many of the categories are talking about personal experience and suggestions, which do not correspond to video events. For example, the articles in the category of "Living Overseas" are all talking about how to improve living experience in a foreign country and do not satisfy the definition of video event. Therefore, we want to find out such event irrelevant categories and then directly filter out their articles, so that we can significantly prune the number of articles to be verified in the next stage. To this end, we go through 2,803 WikiHow categories and manually remove those that are irrelevant to video events. A category is deemed as event irrelevant when it cannot be visually described by a video, and none of its articles contain any video events. For example, "Living Overseas" is an event-irrelevant category since "Living Overseas" is not visually observable in videos and none of its articles are events. On the other hand, although category "Science" cannot be visually described in a video due to its abstract meaning, it contains some instructional articles corresponding to video events, such as "Make Hot Ice", and "Use a Microscope". As a result, in our manual pruning procedure, we first find a to-be-pruned category name and then carefully review their articles before we decide to remove this category.

Step II: Category Based Event Selection. After category pruning, only event relevant categories and their articles remain. Under each category, there are still a large number of articles that are not corresponding to events. Our eventual goal is to find all video events from these articles and include them into our event collection, which is a long term goal of EventNet project. In the current version, EventNet only includes one representative video event from each category of WikiHow ontology. An article title is considered to be a video event when it satisfies the following four conditions: (1) It defines an event that involves human activity interacting with people/objects in a certain scene. (2) It has concrete non-subjective meanings. For example, "decorating a romantic bedroom" is too subjective since different users may have different interpretation about "romantic". (3) It has consistent observable visual characteristics. For example, a simple method is to use the candidate event name to search YouTube and check whether there are consistent visual tags found in the top returned videos. Tags may be approximately considered visual if they can be found in an existing image ontology such as ImageNet. (4) It is generic, not too detailed. If many article titles under a category share the same verb and direct object, then they can be formed to a generic event name. After this, we end up with 500 event categories as the current event collection in EventNet.

4.2 Mining Event Specific Concepts

We apply the concept discovery method developed in our prior work [4] to discover event-driven concepts from the tags of YouTube videos. For each of the 500 events, we use the event name as query keywords to search YouTube. We check the top 1,000 returned videos and collect the 10 most frequent words appearing in the titles or tags of these videos. Then we further filter the 1,000 videos to only include videos containing at least three of the frequent words. This step helps us remove many irrelevant videos from the searching results. Using this approach, we crawl around 190 videos and their tag lists as concept discovery resource for each event, ending up with 95,321 videos for 500 events. We discover event-specific concepts from the tags of the crawled videos. To ensure the visual detectability of the discovered concepts, we match each tag to the classes of the existing object (ImageNet [7]), scene (SUN [23]) and action (Action Bank [30]) libraries, and only keep the matched words as the candidate concepts. After going through the process, we end up with around nine concepts per event, and in total 4,490 concepts for the entire set of 500 events. Finally, we adopt the hierarchical structure of WikiHow categories and attach each discovered event and its concepts to the corresponding category node. The final event concept ontology is called EventNet, as illustrated in Figure 4.

One may argue that the construction of EventNet ontology heavily depends on subjective evaluation. In fact, we can replace such subjective evaluation with automatic methods from computer vision and natural language processing techniques. For example, we can use concept visual verification to measure the visual detectability of concepts [4], and use text based event extraction to determine whether each article title is an event [24]. However, as the accuracy of such automatic methods is still being improved, currently we focus on design of principled criteria for event discovery and defer incorporation of automatic discovery processes until future improvement.

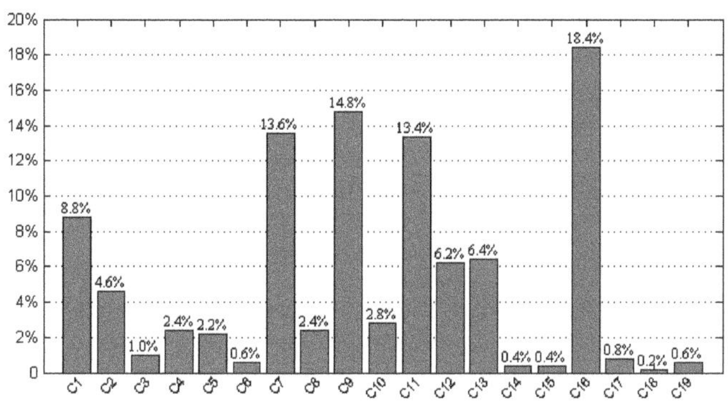

Figure 5: Event distribution over the top-19 categories of EventNet, where C1 to C19 are "arts and entertainment", "cars and other vehicles", "computers and electronics", "education and communications", "family life", "finance and business", "food and entertaining", "health", "hobbies and crafts", "holidays and traditions", "home and garden", "personal care and style", "pets and animals", "philosophy and religion", "relationships", "sports and fitness", "travel", "work world", and "youth".

5. PROPERTIES OF EVENTNET

In this section, we will provide detailed analysis on the properties of EventNet ontology, including basic statistics about the ontology, event distribution over coarse categories, and event redundancy.

EventNet Statistics. EventNet ontology contains 682 WikiHow category nodes, 500 event nodes and $4,490$ concept nodes organized in a tree structure, in which the deepest depth from the root node to the leaf node (the event node) is eight. Each non-leaf category node has four child category nodes in average. Regarding the video statistics in EventNet, the average number of videos per event is 190, and the number of videos per concept is 21. EventNet has $95,321$ videos with an average duration of around 277 seconds ($7,334$ hours in total).

Event Distribution. We show the percentage of the number of events distributed over the top-19 category nodes of EventNet, and the results can be shown in Figure 5. As seen, the top four popular categories including the most number of events are "sports and fitness", "hobbies and craft", "food and entertainment", and "home and garden", while the least four populated categories are " work world", "relationships", "philosophy and religion" and "youth", which are abstract and cannot be described in videos. A further glimpse of the event distributions tells us that the most popular categories reflects user's common interests in video content creation. For example, most event videos captured in human daily life are talking about their life styles reflected in food, fitness, and hobbies. Therefore, we believe that events included in EventNet have the potential to be used as an event concept library to detect popular events in human daily life.

Event Redundancy. We also carry out analysis on the redundancy among the 500 events in EventNet. To this end, we use each event name as a text query, and find its most semantically similar events from other events located at different branches from the query event. Specifically, given a query event e_q, we first localize its category node C_q in EventNet tree structure, and then exclude all events attached under the parent nodes and children nodes of node C_q. The events attached to other nodes are treated as the search base to find similar events of the query based on the semantic similarity described in Section 7. The reason on excluding events at the same branch of the query event is due to the fact that events residing at parent category nodes and children category nodes manifest hierarchical relations such as "cook meat" and "cook poultry". We treat such hierarchical event pairs as a desired property of EventNet library, and therefore do not involve them into redundancy analysis. From the top-5 ranked events for a given query, we ask human annotators to determine whether there is a redundant event talking about the same event as the query. After applying all 500 events as queries, we find zero redundancy among query event and all other events residing at different branches of EventNet structure.

6. LEARNING CONCEPT MODELS FROM DEEP LEARNING VIDEO FEATURES

In this section, we introduce the procedure of learning concept classifiers for EventNet concept library. Our learning framework leverages the recent powerful CNN model to extract deep learning feature from the video content, while employing one-vs-all linear SVM trained on top of the features as concept models.

6.1 Deep Feature Learning with CNN

We adopt the CNN architecture in [11] as deep learning model to perform deep feature learning from the video content. The network takes RGB video frame as input and outputs the score distribution over the 500 events in EventNet. The network has five successive convolutional layers followed by two fully connected layers. The detailed information about the network architecture can be found in [11]. In this work, we apply *Caffe* [18] as the implementation of the CNN model described by [11].

For the training of EventNet CNN model, we evenly sample 40 frames from each video, and end up with four millions frames over all 500 events as the training set. For each of the 500 events, we treat the frames sampled from its videos as the positive training samples of this event. We define the set of 500 events as $E = \{0, 1, ..., 499\}$. Then the prediction probability of k-th event for input sample n is defined as:

$$p_{nk} = \frac{\exp(x_{nk})}{\sum_{k' \in E} \exp(x_{nk'})}, \tag{1}$$

where x_{nk} is the k-th node's output of the n-th input sample from CNN's last layer. The loss funtion L is defined as a multinomial logistic loss of the softmax which is $L = \frac{-1}{N} \sum_{n=1}^{N} \log(p_{n,l_n})$, where $l_n \in E$ indicating the correct class label for input sample n and N is the total number of inputs. Our CNN model is trained on NVIDIA Tesla K20 GPU, and it takes about seven days to finish $450K$ iterations of training. After CNN training, we extract the $4,096$ dimensional feature vector from the second to the last layer of the CNN architecture, and further perform ℓ_2 normalization on

Event Query	without leveraging EventNet structure	with leveraging EventNet structure
landing a fish	landing a plane cook fish	fishing hunt an animal
wedding shower	wedding ceremony take a shower	wedding ceremony make a wedding veil
working on a woodworking project	working out using a rowing machine running	make wood projects make a crochet project

Table 2: Top 2 matched events of some event queries without (2nd column) and with (3rd column) leveraging EventNet structure.

the feature vector as the deep learning feature descriptor of each video frame.

6.2 Concept Model Training

Given a concept discovered for an event, we treat the videos associated with this concept as positive training data and randomly sample the same number of videos from concepts in other events as negative training data. This obviously has the risk of generating false negatives (videos without a certain concept label does not necessarily mean it is negative for the concept). But in view of the prohibitive cost in annotating all videos over all concepts, we follow this common practice used in other image ontologies such as ImageNet [7]. We directly treat frames in positive videos as positive and frames in negative videos as negative to train a linear SVM classifier as the concept model. This is a simplified approach and there are emerging works [17] in selecting more precise temporal segments or frames in videos as positive samples.

To generate concept scores on a given video, we first uniformly sample frames from it and extract the $4,096$ dimensional CNN feature from each frame. Then we apply the $4,490$ concept models on each frame and use all $4,490$ concept scores as the concept representation of this frame. Finally, we average the score vectors across all frames and adopt the average score vector as the video level concept representation.

7. LEVERAGING EVENTNET STRUCTURE FOR CONCEPT MATCHING

In concept based event detection, the first step is to find some semantically relevant concepts that are applicable for detecting videos with respect to the event query. This procedure is called *concept matching* in the literature [4, 32]. To accomplish this task, the existing approaches typically calculate the semantic similarity between the query event and each concept in the library based on the external semantic knowledge bases such as WordNet [8] or ConceptNet [14], and then pick up the top ranked concepts as the relevant concepts for event detection. However, these approaches may not be applicable for our EventNet concept library since the involved concepts are event specific concepts dependent on their associative events. For example, concept "dog" under "feed a dog" and "groom a dog" will be treated as two different concepts due to different event contexts. Therefore, concept matching in EventNet needs to take into account event contextual information.

To this end, we propose a multi-step concept matching approach that first finds relevant events and then chooses concepts from the concepts associated with the matched events. Specifically, given an event query e_q and an event e in EventNet library, we use the textual phrase similarity calculation function developed in [10] to estimate their semantic similarity. The reason to adopt such semantic similarity function is due to the fact that both event query and candidate events in EventNet library are textual phrases, which need sophisticated phrase level similarity calculation supporting word sequence alignment and strong generalization ability achieved by machine learning. However, these properties cannot be achieved by using the standard similarity computation methods based on WordNet or ConceptNet alone. Our empirical studies confirm that the phrase based semantic similarity is able to obtain better event matching results.

However, due to the word sense ambiguity and the limited amount of text information in event names, the phrase similarity based matching approach can also generate wrong matching results. For example, given a query "wedding shower ", event "take a shower" in EventNet will receive a high similarity value since "shower" has an ambiguous meaning, and thus be mistakenly matched as a relevant event. Likewise, the best matching results for query "landing a fish" are "landing an airplane" and "cook fish" rather than "fishing" which is the most relevant. To address these problems, we propose to exploit the structure of EventNet ontology to find relevant events for such difficult query events. Specifically, given the query event, users can manually specify the suitable categories in the top level of EventNet structure. For instance, users can easily specify that the suitable categories for event "wedding shower" is "Family Life" while choosing "Sports and Fitness" and "Hobbies and Crafts" as suitable categories for "landing a fish". After user's specification, the subsequent event matching only needs to be conducted over the events under the specified high-level categories. In this way, the hierarchical structure of EventNet ontology will be helpful in relieving the limitations of short text based semantic matching, and help improve concept matching accuracy. Table 2 shows some difficult events from TRECVID MED and their top matched events with and without leveraging EventNet structure. As seen, our method can achieve more relevant matching results than using phrase based semantic similarity alone. After we get the top matched events, we can further choose concepts based on their semantic similarity to the query event. Quantitative evaluations between the matching methods can be found in Section 8.4.

8. EXPERIMENTS

In this section, we evaluate the effectiveness of EventNet concept library in concept based event detection. We will first introduce the dataset and experimental setup, and then report the performance of different methods in the context of various event detection tasks, including zero-shot event retrieval and semantic recounting. After this, we will study the efforts of leveraging EventNet structure for matching concepts in zero-shot event retrieval. Finally, we will treat the $95K$ videos over 500 events in EventNet as a video event benchmark and report the baseline performance of using the CNN model in event detection.

8.1 Dataset and Experiment Setup

Dataset. We use two benchmark video event datasets as the test sets of our experiments to verify the effectiveness of EventNet concept library. (1) *TRECVID 2013 Multimedia Event Detection (MED)* dataset [1]. It contains $32,744$ videos spanning over 20 event

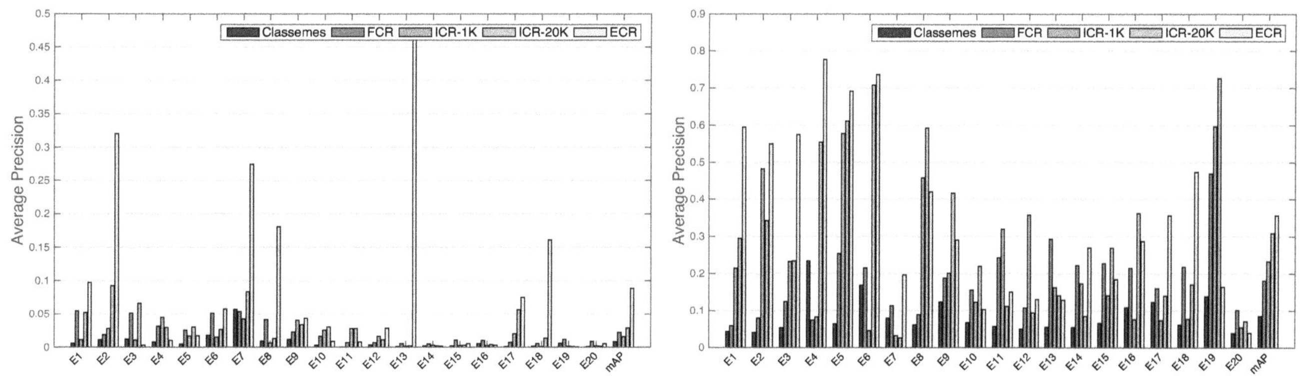

Figure 6: Performance comparisons on zero-shot event retrieval task (left: MED; right: CCV). This figure is best viewed in color.

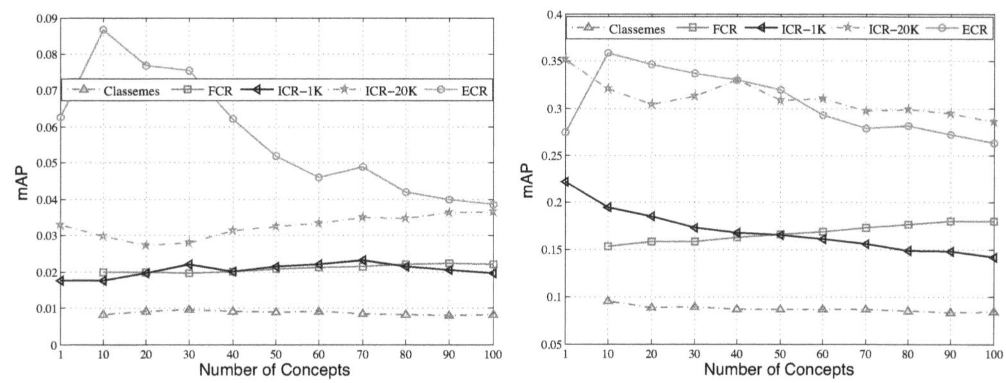

Figure 7: Zero-shot event retrieval performance with different number of concepts (left: MED; right: CCV). The results of Classemes and FCR are from [5], in which the results when concept number is 1 are not reported.

classes and the distracting background, whose names are "E1: *birthday party*", "E2: *changing a vehicle tire*", "E3: *flash mob gathering*", "E4: *getting a vehicle unstuck*", "E5: *grooming an animal*", "E6: *making a sandwich*", "E7: *parade*", "E8: *parkour*", "E9: *repairing an appliance*", "E10: *working on a sewing project*", "E11: *attempting a bike trick*", "E12: *cleaning an appliance*", "E13: *dog show*", "E14: *giving directions to a location*", "E15: *marriage proposal*", "E16: *renovating a home*", "E17: *rock climbing*", "E18: *town hall meeting*", "E19: *winning a race without a vehicle*", "E20: *working on a metal crafts project*". We follow the original partition of this dataset in TRECVID MED evaluation, which partitions the dataset into a training set with $7,787$ videos and a test set with $24,957$ videos. (2) *Columbia Consumer Video (CCV)* dataset [21]. It contains $9,317$ videos spanning over 20 classes, which are "E1: *basketball*", "E2: *baseball*", "E3: *soccer*", "E4: *ice skating*", "E5: *skiing*", "E6: *swimming*", "E7: *biking*", "E8: *cat*", "E9: *dog*", "E10: *bird*", "E11: *graduation*", "E12: *birthday*", "E13: *wedding reception*", "E14: *wedding ceremony*", "E15: *wedding dance*", "E16: *music performance*", "E17: *non-music performance*", "E18: *parade*", "E19: *beach*", "E20: *playground*". The dataset is further split into $4,659$ training videos and $4,658$ test videos. Since we focus on zero-shot event detection, we do not use the training videos in these two datasets, but only test the performance on the test set. For supervised visual recognition, features from deep learning models, e.g., the last few layers of deep learning models learned over ImageNet $1K$ or $20K$) can be directly used to detect events [19]. However, the focus of this paper is on the semantic description power of the event-specific concepts, especially in recounting the semantic concepts in event detection and finding relevant concepts for retrieving events that have not been seen before (zero-shot retrieval).

Feature Extraction. On the two evaluation event video datasets, we extract the same feature as we did on EventNet videos. Specifically, we sample one frame every two seconds from a video, and extract the $4,096$ dimensional deep learning feature from the CNN model trained on EventNet video frames. Then we run SVM-based concept models over each frame, and aggregate the score vectors in a video as the semantic concept feature of the video.

Comparison Methods and Evaluation Metric. We compare different concept based video representations produced by the following methods. (1) **Classemes** [31]. It is a $2,659$-dimensional concept representation whose concepts are defined based on LSCOM concept ontology. We directly extract Classemes on each frame and then average them across the video as video-level concept representation. (2) Flickr Concept Representation (**FCR**) [5]. For each event, the concepts are automatically discovered from the tags of Flickr images in the search results of event query and organized based on WikiHow ontology. The concept detection models are based on the binary multiple kernel linear SVM classifiers trained with the Flickr images associated with each concept. Five kinds of low-level features are adopted to represent Flickr images and event video frames. (3) ImageNet-$1K$ CNN Concept Representation (**ICR-1K**). In this method, we directly apply the network architecture in [11] to train a CNN model over 1.2 million high-resolution images in the ImageNet LSVRC-2010 contest that covers $1,000$ different classes [27]. After model training, we apply the CNN model on the frames from both TRECVID MED and CCV datasets. Concept scores of the individual frames in a video are averaged to form the concept scores of the video. We treat the $1,000$ output scores as the concept based video representation from ImageNet-$1K$. (4) ImageNet-$20K$ CNN Concept Representation (**ICR-20K**). We apply the same network architecture as ICR-1K to train a CNN model over 20 million images spanning over $20,574$ classes from the latest release of ImageNet [7]. We treat the $20,574$ concept scores output from CNN model as the concept representation. Notably, ICR-1K and ICR-20K represent the most successful visual recognition achievements in computer vision area, which can be applied to justify the superiority of our EventNet concept library over the state-of-the-art. (5) Our proposed EventNet-CNN Concept Representation (**ECR**), in which we use our EventNet concept library to generate concept based video representations. (6) Some state-of-the-art results reported in the literature. Regarding the evaluation metric, we adopt Average Precision (AP), which approximates the area under precision/recall curve, to measure the performance on each event in our evaluation datasets. Finally, we calculate mean Average Precision (mAP) over all event classes as the overall evaluation metric.

8.2 Task I: Zero-Shot Event Retrieval

Our first experiment will evaluate the performance of zero-shot event retrieval, in which we do not use any training videos, but completely depend on the concept scores on test videos. To this end, we use each event name in the two video datasets as query to match two most relevant events and choose 15 most relevant EventNet concepts based on semantic similarity, and then average the scores of these 15 concepts as the zero-shot event detection score of video, through which a video ranking list can be generated. Notably, the two most relevant events mentioned above are automatically selected based on the semantic similarity matching method described in Section 7. For Classemes and FCR, we follow the setting in [5] to choose 100 relevant concepts based on semantic similarity using ConceptNet and the concept matching method described in [5]. For ICR-1K and ICR-20K, we choose 15 concepts using the same concept matching method.

Figure 6 shows the performance of different methods on two datasets respectively. From the results, we have the following observations: (1) Event specific concept representations including FCR, ECR outperform the event independent concept representation Classemes. This is due to the fact that the former not only discovers semantically relevant concepts of the event, but also leverages the contextual information about the event in the training samples of each concept. In contrast, the latter only borrows concepts that are not specifically designed for events, and the training images for concept classifiers do not contain the event-related contextual information. (2) Concept representations trained with deep CNN features, including ICR-20K and ECR, produce much higher performance than the concept representations learned from low-level features including Classemes and FCR for most of the events. This is reasonable since CNN model can extract learning based features that have been shown to achieve strong performance. (3) Although all are trained with deep learning features, ECR generated by our proposed EventNet concept library performs significantly better than ICR-1K and ICR-20K, which are generated by deep learning models trained on ImageNet images. The reason is that concepts in EventNet are more relevant to events than the concepts in ImageNet which are mostly objects independent of events. From this result, we can see that our EventNet concepts even beat the concepts from the state-of-the-art visual recognition system, and is believed to be a powerful concept library for the task of zero-shot event retrieval.

Notably, our ECR achieves significant performance gains over the best baseline ICR-20K where the mAP on TRECVID MED increases from 2.89% to 8.86% with 207% relative improvement. Similarly, the mAP on CCV increases from 30.82% to 35.58% (15.4% relative improvement). Moreover, our ECR achieves the best performances on most of the event categories on each dataset. For instance, on event "E02: *changing a vehicle tire*" of TRECVID MED dataset, our method outperforms the best baseline ICR-20K by 246% relative improvement. On TRECVID MED dataset, the reason of large improvement on "E13: *dog show*" is because the matched events contain exactly the same event "dog show" as the event query. The performance on E10 and E11 is not so good since the automatic event matching method matched them to wrong events. When we use EventNet structure to correct the matching errors as described in Section 8.4, we achieve higher performance on these events.

In Figure 7, we show the impact on zero-shot event retrieval performance when the number of concepts changes by using the concept matching method described in Section 7, i.e., we first find the matched events, and then pick up the top ranked concepts belonging to these events. We select the number of events until the desired number of concepts is reached. On TRECVID MED, we can see consistent and significant performance gains of our proposed ECR method over others. However, on CCV dataset, ICR-20K achieves similar or even better performance when a large number of concepts is adopted. We conjecture this is due to the fact that CCV dataset contains a number of object categories such as "E8: cat" and "E9: dog", which might be better described by the visual objects contained in ImageNet dataset. Alternatively, all events in TRECVID MED are highly complicated events, which may be better described by EventNet. It is worth mentioning that the mAP first increases and then decreases as we choose more concepts from EventNet. This is because our concept matching method always ranks the most relevant concepts on top of the concept list. Therefore, involving many less relevant concepts ranked at lower positions (after the 10th position in this experiment) in the concept list may decrease the performance. In Table 3, we compare our result with the state-of-the-art results reported on TRECVID MED 2013 test set with the same experiment setting. We can see that our ECR method outperforms these results by a large margin.

Method	mAP (%)
Selective concept [9, 22]	4.39
Bi-concept [9, 26]	3.45
Composite concept [9]	5.97
Weak concept [32]	3.48
Annotated concept [15]	6.50
Our EventNet concept	**8.86**

Table 3: Comparisons between our ECR with other state-of-the-art concept based video representation methods built on visual content. All results are obtained in the task of zero-shot event retrieval on TRECVID MED 2013 test set.

8.3 Task II: Semantic Recounting in Videos

Given a video, semantic recounting aims to annotate the video with the semantic concepts detected in the video. Since we have the concept based representation generated for the videos using the concept classifiers described earlier, we can directly use it to produce the recounting. Specifically, we rank the $4,490$ event specific concept scores on a given video in descending order and then choose the top ranked ones as the most salient concepts occurring in the video. Figure 8 shows the recounting results for some example videos from TRECVID MED and CCV datasets. As seen, the

Figure 8: Event video recounting results: each row shows evenly subsampled frames of a video and the top 5 concepts detected in the video.

concepts generated by our method precisely reveal the semantics presented in the videos.

It is worth noting that EventNet ontology also provides great benefits for developing a real time semantic recounting system which requires high efficiency and accuracy. Compared to other concept libraries that use generic concepts, EventNet allows selected execution of a small set of concepts specific to an event. Given a video to be recounted, it first predicts the most relevant events and then applies only concepts specific to these events. This unique two-step approach is able to greatly improve the efficiency and accuracy of multimedia event recounting since only a small number of event-specific concept classifiers need to be fired after event detection.

8.4 Task III: Effects of EventNet Structure for Concept Matching

As discussed in Section 7, due to the limitations of text based similarity matching, the matching result of an event query might not be relevant. In this case, the EventNet structure can help the users find relevant events and their associated concepts from EventNet concept library. Here we first carry out quantitative empirical study to verify this. Specifically, for each event query, we manually specify two suitable categories from the top 19 nodes of EventNet tree structure, and then match events under these categories based on semantic similarity. We compare the results obtained by matching all events in EventNet (i.e., without leveraging EventNet structure) with the results obtained by the method we described above (i.e., with leveraging EventNet structure). For each query, we apply each method to select 15 concepts from EventNet library and then use them to perform zero-shot event retrieval.

Method (mAP %)	MED	CCV
Without Leveraging EventNet Structure	8.86	35.58
With Leveraging EventNet Structure	**8.99**	**36.07**

Table 4: Comparison of zero-shot event retrieval using the concepts matched without leveraging EventNet structure (top row) and with leveraging EventNet structure (bottom row).

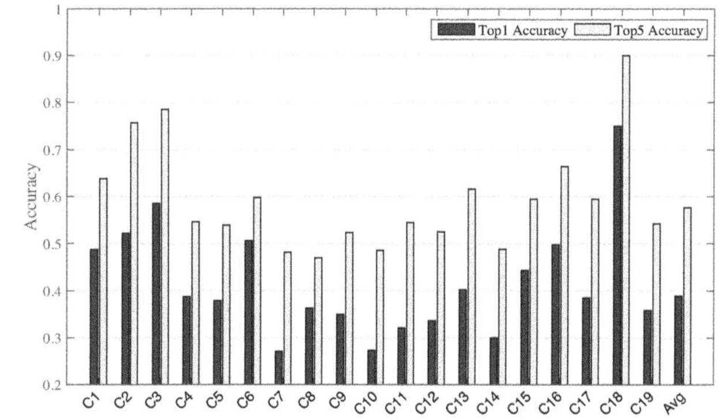

Figure 9: Top-1 and top-5 event classification accuracies over 19 high-level event categories of EventNet structure, in which the average top-1 and top-5 accuracy are 38.91% and 57.67%.

Table 4 shows the performance comparison between the two methods. From the results, we can see that event retrieval performance can be improved if we apply the concepts matched with the help of EventNet structure, which proves the usefulness of EventNet structure for the task of concept matching.

Figure 10: Event detection results of some sample videos. The 5 events with the highest detection scores are shown in the descending order. The bar length indicates the score of each event. Event with the red bar is the ground truth.

8.5 Task IV: Multi-Class Event Classification

The 95,321 videos over 500 event categories in EventNet can also be seen as a benchmark video dataset to study large scale event detection. To facilitate direct comparison, we provide standard data partitions and some baseline results over these partitions. It is worth noting that one important purpose of designing EventNet video dataset is to use it as a testbed for large scale event detection models such as deep convolutional Neutral Network. Therefore, in the following, we summarize a baseline implementation using the state-of-the-art CNN models like what was done in [27].

Data Split. Recall that each of the 500 events in EventNet has around 190 videos. In our experiment, we split videos and adopt 70% videos as training set, 10% videos as validation set, and 20% videos as test set. In all, there are roughly $70K$ training videos (2.8 million frames), $10K$ validation videos (0.4 million frames) and $20K$ test videos (0.8 million frames).

Deep Learning Model. We adopt the same network architecture and learning setting of the CNN model described in Section 6.1 as our multi-class event classification model. In the training process, for each event, we treat the frames sampled from training videos of an event as positive training samples and feed them into CNN model for model training. It takes seven days to finish $450K$ iterations of training. In the test stage, to produce predictions for a test video, we take the average of the frame-level probabilities over sampled frames in a video and use it as the video-level prediction result.

Evaluation Metric. Regarding evaluation metric, we adopt the most popular top-1 and top-5 accuracy commonly used in large scale visual recognition, where the top-1 (top-5) accuracy is the fraction of the test videos for which the correct label is among the top 1 (5) labels predicted to be most probable by the model.

Results. We report the multi-class classification performance by 19 high-level categories of events in the top layer of EventNet ontology. To achieve this, we collect all events under each of the 19 high-level categories in EventNet (e.g., 68 events under "home and garden"), calculate the accuracy of each event and then calculate their mean value over the events within this high-level category. As seen in Figure 9, most of the high-level categories show impressive classification performance. To illustrate the results, we choose four event video frames and show their top-5 prediction results in Figure 10.

9. CONCLUSION

We have introduced EventNet, a large scale structured event-driven concept library for representing complex event in video. The library contains 500 events mined from WikiHow and 4,490 event-specific concepts discovered from YouTube video tags, for which large margin classifiers are trained with deep learning feature over 95,321 YouTube videos. The events and concepts are further organized into a tree structure based on the WikiHow ontology. Extensive experiments on two benchmark event datasets have shown major superior performance of the proposed concept library over zero-shot event retrieval task. We also show that the tree structure of EventNet helps matching the event queries to semantically relevant concepts. For future work, we will continue to expand EventNet by continuously discovering more events from WikiHow, YouTube and other knowledge resources. We will also pursue a tree structured event modeling that incorporates the hierarchical relations of events in EventNet.

10. ACKNOWLEDGEMENT

Supported by the Intelligence Advanced Research Projects Activity (IARPA) via Department of Interior National Business Center contract number D11PC20071. The U.S. Government is authorized to reproduce and distribute reprints for Governmental purposes notwithstanding any copyright annotation thereon. Disclaimer: The views and conclusions contained herein are those of the authors and should not be interpreted as necessarily representing the official policies or endorsements, either expressed or implied, of IARPA, DOI-NBC, or the U.S. Government.

11. REFERENCES

[1] http://www.nist.gov/itl/iad/mig/med.cfm.

[2] http://www.wikihow.com/Main-Page.

[3] T. Berg, A. Berg, and J. Shih. Automatic Attribute Discovery and Characterization from Noisy Web Data. In *ECCV*, 2010.

[4] J. Chen, Y. Cui, G. Ye, D. Liu, and S.-F. Chang. Event-Driven Semantic Concept Discovery by Exploiting Weakly Tagged Internet Images. In *ICMR*, 2014.

[5] Y. Cui, D. Liu, J. Chen, and S.-F. Chang. Building A Large Concept Bank for Representing Events in Video. *arXiv:1403.7591*, 2014.

[6] L. Duan, D. Xu, I. W. Tsang, and J. Luo. Visual Event Recognition in Videos by Learning from Web Data. In *CVPR*, 2010.

[7] J. Deng, W. Dong, R. Socher, L.-J. Li, K. Li, and Li Fei-Fei. ImageNet: A Large-Scale Hierarchical Image Database. In *CVPR*, 2010.

[8] C. Fellbaum. WordNet: An Electronic Lexical Database. *Bradford Books*, 1998.

[9] A. Habibian, T. Mensink, and C. Snoek. Composite Concept Discovery for Zero-Shot Video Event Detection. In *ICMR*, 2014.

[10] L. Han, A. Kashyap, T. Finin, J. Mayfield, and Jonathan Weese. UMBC EBIQUITY-CORE: Semantic Textual Similarity Systems. In *ACL*, 2013.

[11] A. Krizhevsky, I. Sutskever, and G. Hinton. ImageNet Classification with Deep Convolutional Neural Networks. In *NIPS*, 2012.

[12] I. Laptev and T. Lindeberg. Space-Time Interest Points. In *ICCV*, 2003.

[13] I. Laptev, M. Marszalek, C. Schmid and B. Rozenfeld. Learning Realistic Human Actions from Movies. In *CVPR*, 2008.

[14] H. Liu and P. Singh. ConceptNet: A Pratical Commonsence Reasoning Toolkit. *BT Technology Journal*, 2004.

[15] J. Liu, H. Cheng, O. Javed, Q. Yu, I. Chakraborty, W. Zhang, A. Divakaran, H. Sawhney, J. Allan, R. Manmatha, J. Foley, M. Shah, A. Dehghan, M. Witbrock, J. Curtis, and G. Friedland. SRI-Sarnoff AURORA System at TRECVID 2013 Multimedia Event Detection and Recounting. In *NIST TRECVID Workshop*, 2013.

[16] J. Liu, Q. Yu, O. Javed, S. Ali, A. Tamrakar, A. Divakaran, H. Cheng, and H. Sawhney. Video Event Recognition Using Concept Attributes. In *WACV*, 2013.

[17] K.-T. Lai, D. Liu, M.-S. Chen, and S.-F. Chang, Recognizing Complex Events in Videos by Learning Key Static-Dynamic Evidences. In *ECCV*, 2014.

[18] Y. Jia. Caffe: An Open Source Convolutional Archtecture for Fast Feature Embedding. http://caffe.berkeleyvision.org, 2013.

[19] M. Jain, J. Gemert and C. Snoek. University of Amsterdam at THUMOS Challenge 2014. In *Thumos Challenge*, 2014.

[20] Y.-G. Jiang, Z. Wu, J. Wang, X. Xue, and S.-F. Chang. Exploiting Feature and Class Relationships in Video Categorization with Regularized Deep Neural Networks. *arXiv:1502.07209*, 2015.

[21] Y.-G. Jiang, G. Ye, S.-F. Chang, D. Ellis, and A. C. Loui. Consumer Video Understanding: A Benchmark Database and An Evaluation of Human and Machine Performance. In *ICMR*, 2011.

[22] M. Mazloom, E. Gavves, K. Sande, and C. Snoek. Searching Informative Concept Banks for Video Event Detection. In *ICMR*, 2013.

[23] G. Patterson and J. Hays. Sun Attribute Database: Discovering, Annotating, and Recognizing Scene Attributes. In *CVPR*, 2012.

[24] A. Ritter, Mausam, O. Etzioni, and S. Clark. Open Domain Event Extraction from Twitter. In *KDD*, 2012.

[25] K. Reddy and M. Shah, Recognizing 50 Human Action Categories of Web Videos. *Journal of Machine Vision and Applications*, 2012.

[26] M. Rastegari, A. Diba, D. Parikh, and A. Farhadi. Multi-Attribute Queries: To Merge or Not To Merge? In *CVPR*, 2013.

[27] O. Russakovsky, J. Deng, H. Su, J. Krause, S. Ma, Z. Huang, A. Karpathy, A. Khosla, M. Bernstein, Al. Berg and Li Fei-Fei. ImageNet Large Scale Visual Recognition Challenge. *arXiv:1409.0575*, 2014.

[28] K. Saenko, B. Kulis, M. Fritz, and T. Darrell. Adapting Visual Category Models to New Domains. In *ECCV*, 2010.

[29] K. Soomro, A. Zamir, and M. Shah. UCF101: A Dataset of 101 Human Action Classes From Videos in The Wild. *CRCV-TR*, 2012.

[30] S. Sadanand and J. Corso. Action Bank: A High-level Representation of Activity in Video. In *CVPR*, 2012.

[31] L. Torresani, M. Szummer, and A. Fitzgibbon. Efficient Object Category Recognition Using Classemes. In *ECCV*, 2010.

[32] S. Wu, S. Bondugula, F. Luisier, X. Zhuang, and P. Natarajan. Zero-shot Event Detection using Multi-modal Fusion of Weakly Supervised Concepts. In *CVPR*, 2014.

[33] H. Xu, G. Ye, Y. Li, D. Liu, and S.-F. Chang. Large Video Event Ontology Browsing, Search and Tagging (EventNet Demo). In *MM*, 2015.

[34] Z. Xu, I. Tsang, Y. Yang, Z. Ma, and A. Hauptmann. Event Detection using Multi-Level Relevance Labels and Multiple Features. In *CVPR*, 2014.

Modelling Human Factors in Perceptual Multimedia Quality: On The Role of Personality and Culture

Michael James Scott*†, Sharath Chandra Guntuku*‡,
Yang Huan‡, Weisi Lin‡, Gheorghita Ghinea†
† Department of Computer Science, Brunel University London, United Kingdom
‡ School of Computer Engineering, Nanyang Technological University, Singapore
michael.scott@brunel.ac.uk, sharathc001@e.ntu.edu.sg, hyang3@e.ntu.edu.sg,
wslin@ntu.edu.sg, george.ghinea@brunel.ac.uk

ABSTRACT

Perception of multimedia quality is shaped by a rich interplay between system, context and human factors. While system and context factors are widely researched, few studies consider human factors as sources of systematic variance. This paper presents an analysis on the influence of personality and cultural traits on the perception of multimedia quality. A set of 144 video sequences (from 12 short movie excerpts) were rated by 114 participants from a cross-cultural population, producing 1232 ratings. On this data, three models are compared: a baseline model that only considers system factors; an extended model that includes personality and culture as human factors; and an optimistic model in which each participant is modelled as a random effect. An analysis shows that personality and cultural traits represent 9.3% of the variance attributable to human factors while human factors overall predict an equal or higher proportion of variance compared to system factors. In addition, the quality-enjoyment correlation varied across the excerpts. This suggests that human factors play an important role in perceptual multimedia quality, but further research to explore moderation effects and a broader range of human factors is warranted.

Categories and Subject Descriptors

H.1.2 [**Models and Principles**]: User/Machine Systems—*Human Factors, Software Psychology*; H.5.1 [**Information Interfaces and Presentation**]: Multimedia Information Systems—*Evaluation/Methodology*

General Terms

Design; Experimentation; Human Factors

Keywords

Multimedia; Quality; QoE; Personality; Big-5; Culture; Hofstede; Enjoyment; Perception; Video

MM'15, October 26–30, 2015, Brisbane, Australia.
© 2015 ACM. ISBN 978-1-4503-3459-4/15/10 ...$15.00.
DOI: http://dx.doi.org/10.1145/2733373.2806254.

1. INTRODUCTION

The success of multimedia content and service providers is often determined by the 'perceived' quality of the content that their customers, the viewers, use and enjoy. Typically, this perception is dependent on the 'nature' of content (i.e., the affective narrative) and the parameters controlling how that content is delivered. The nature of content can only be manipulated by content creators, however providers have the ability to stream the content at the 'right' parameters to ensure adequate viewer satisfaction.

While it might seem obvious that nothing less than the highest possible parameters would satisfy viewers, there are occasions which necessitate streaming at lower parameters. For example, in the case of mobile streaming where bandwidth and transmission form a bottleneck [39]. Additionally, there is research which shows that it is not mandatory to stream videos at high parameters to convey satisfying experiences [7, 12].

Suppose that two viewers are both shown a video sequence each at {25fps, 480p} and {15fps, 720p}. Is it possible that one viewer's perceived quality on a video sequence with a lower parameter setting is broadly equivalent to the other viewer's perceptive quality on another sequence with higher parameters? If yes, what are the factors influencing perception of quality? Which of these factors contribute positively and which negatively? These are some of the questions which motivate the research discussed in this paper. Finding answers to these questions would help content providers to maintain adequete customer satisfaction in a personalized manner while optimally utilizing resources such as bandwidth.

The challenges associated with such personalization are very subtle, owing to the complexity associated with individual differences. Moreover, these differences occur both at a micro-cosmic level (i.e., specific to the individual) and at a macro-cosmic level (i.e., cultural influences). While the microcosmic traits can be analysed with personality (a series of "internal properties" that relate to overt behaviours [27]), the macroscopic traits can be captured using cultural dimensions (representing "the collective programming of the mind distinguishing the members of one [nation] or category of people from others" which subsequently leads to a "broad tendency [for members of a group] to prefer certain states of affairs over others" [18]).

* denotes equal contribution

Although a significant number of public video datasets for quality assessment exist, no dataset is suited to study the influence of the aforementioned human-factors. Without this subjective data, it is not possible to understand the impact of culture and personality on perceived quality and enjoyment, and whether it will be significant for practical applications. In addition, objective and subjective quality metrics are evaluated using existing public databases which do not take into account the human factors, or if they do they often draw participants from just the local population. This means that little is known about the generalisability of these quality metrics.

Therefore it is necessary to explore the impact that personality and culture has on Quality of Experience (QoE), as measured through the perceived quality of multimedia content and its associated subjective enjoyment. To answer this question, a novel video dataset consisting of 144 video sequences with a variety of movie-based content at different parameter settings is constructed (see Section 3.2 for detail). Then, a subjective experiment involving 114 participants is conducted to collect ratings on perceived quality and enjoyment. A set of regression models are developed to model the viewers' perception. Ratings on perceived quality and enjoyment (the dependent variables) are predicted given the movie excerpt, the quality parameters, and the participant's profile (the independent variables).

In summary, it is proposed that a model based on human factors could form the foundation for enabling multimedia content and service providers to optimise viewers' quality of experience under constrained conditions. As part of this work, the following research questions are addressed:

1. To what extent do human factors predict variance in ratings of quality and enjoyment?
2. What proportion of the variance attributable to human factors can be predicted by personality and culture (using the Big-5 and Hofestede models)?
3. Which aspects of the Big-5 Model and the Hofestede Model are key predictors of quality and enjoyment?
4. To what extent is quality related to enjoyment?

2. RELATED WORK

2.1 On Video Quality

Video quality and enjoyment evaluation has been widely investigated in the last few years, and numerous related video databases have been constructed. For example, the: VQEG HDTV database [13]; LIVE video database [36]; IVC video databases [23]; ReTRiEVED video database [31]; video enjoyment database [24], and aesthetic evaluation video database [29]. In these video quality assessment databases, the visual quality of videos derived from different distortion types (e.g., H.264 compression, packet loss and frame rate change) is evaluated by human beings. In video aesthetic evaluation databases, enjoyment (or appeal) levels are commonly given by participants. Generally, when performing the subjective tests, only four human factors (i.e., age, gender, vision and expertise levels) are reported. The obtained subjective scores are, then, analysed under the assumption that all participants have the same or similar perception to the visual quality of a video, irrespective of other human factors.

2.2 On Personality

We each possess traits which vary in systematic ways and these systematic differences can be explored. Consider personality, a series of "internal properties" that relate to overt behaviours [27]. Though there are many different theories which examine the predictive utility of personality, the Five Factor Model (FFM) [8] is one of the most parsimonious models. This consists of: openness to experience, conscientiousness, extroversion, agreeableness and neuroticism. These dimensions could map to perception of quality in many ways. For example, individuals with high neuroticism may be more sensitive to multimedia content that evokes negative emotions.

2.3 On Culture

The FFM can be considered as individual-level personality traits because they can be found to vary across a wide range of individuals [8]. However, there are also traits which are associated with the culture an individual is from. Perception and cognition are a product of the local environment in which someone lives and grows, which itself is shaped through shared conceptions and collective norms [20]. One theory in Psychology which studies such differences is the Hofstede's Six Factor Model (HM) [18], which includes: power distance; individualism; uncertainty avoidance index; masculinity; pragmatism; and indulgence [18]. Again, each of these dimensions could interact with the perception of quality and enjoyment. For example, individuals with high indulgence may become more critical of due to extended usage.

2.4 Background

It has been demonstrated that previous educational and socio-cultural backgrounds play important roles in such subjective rating [10, 34]. It has also been shown that cultural experience influences visual perception when viewing visual objects. In [30], it was found that there exists perceptual and attentional differences between Asians and Westerners, for example, Americans have more analytical visual perception (inclined to pay attention to details), while Asians have a more holistic visual perception (likely to be more sensitive to context). A more detailed investigation on the cultural differences in cognitive processes can be found in [28] where an analysis of the factors underlying the cultural differences can be found along with a multiple-level framework to integrate these factors to explore the cultural influences on cognitive processes. In [37], the cultural differences between American and Chinese individuals was studied on communication performance under audio and video conferencing conditions. In [9], the influence of culture on perception was investigated in many aspects, including optical illusion, colour perception, visual attention, and brain functioning. The correlation between culture and cognition was also studied in [1], by analysing the variation of word associations given by Japanese and American participants.

The experimental results across these studies indicate attentional variation in cross-cultural judgments. Previous research has also addressed factors which influence perception of quality (e.g. [4, 7, 32]) and emotions (e.g. [5, 25]). There has also been work which shows that personality influences media content preferences [3, 15].

As such, understanding, interpreting and evaluating content is dependent on previous experience, socio-cultural background, goals, and values. This may, consequently, influence what viewers consider to be of 'good' or 'bad' quality. Some works (for example [6, 21, 26, 32, 33, 38]) which do investigate the influence of above-mentioned human factors are often based on subjective tests applied to samples. However, it is seldom the case that samples are deliberately drawn from cross-cultural contexts.

Recently, there have been works which studied the influence of personality factors on perceived quality [40, 41]. However, one study involved about 59 users and their ratings on 6 YouTube videos covering three genres [41] and the other focussed on investigating the use of a multimodal remote control application in the context of IPTV [40]. However, such studies tend to draw their samples from only the local population.

Hence, it is meaningful to investigate, with a larger group of users from multiple demographic regions, the influences of individual and cultural variation with respect to the perceived quality and subsequent enjoyment video sequences, using a larger dataset, with various quality parameters. As such, it is important to involve participants from many different countries (as detailed in Section 3.5) in the subjective testing where culture and personality could potentially explain differences.

3. METHODOLOGY

3.1 Procedure

A lab-based subjective testing approach was taken. A set of video sequences were hosted on web server locally at each institution involved in the study (to avoid any latency issues over the Internet). Participants completed a questionairre and then watched several video sequences, rating the perceived quality and their enjoyment of each sequence immediately after viewing each. Informed consent and anonymity were assured at every stage of the study.

Participants started the survey by answering the VSM-2013 [19] and the BFI-10 [11] questionnaires to report cultural and personality traits respectively. Then each participant was shown 14 video sequences: 2 training video sequences (one at the beginning of the survey and another during the middle); and the 12 videos under assessment. The training video sequences showed participants what should be considered 'high' quality. They then had to respond to 12 further video sequences. Participants were randomly allocated quality parameters for each individual video sequence (except for the training videos).

Each participant was expected to rate all 12 video sequences. However, to maximise the ecological validity of participants' viewing behaviour, participants were left free and without any time-limit to complete the experiment. Of the 114 participants, 73.7% rated all 12. The minimum number of videos rated was 3, however the average was 10.8 ($\sigma = 2.56$). In total, 1232 ratings were recorded (90% of the maximum possible).

3.2 Video Dataset

This study is the first application of the CP-QAE-I video dataset (available from http://1drv.ms/1M1bnwU), after its validation in a previous study [16]. The dataset contains video sequences based on 12 excerpts from popular movies that were purposively selected to evoke different affects [35]. There were 3 ordinal parameters: bit-rate (384kb/s and 768kb/s); frame dimension (480p and 720p); and frame rate (5fps, 15fps and 25fps).

Table 1: Estimated Marginal Means of the Ratings for Each Movie Excerpt in the CP-QAE-I (z-Scores)

Movie Excerpt	Perceived Quality	Enjoyment
A_FISH_CALLED_WANDA	-.300	-.004
AMERICAN_HISTORY_X	-.121	-.560
CHILDS_PLAY_II	-.430	-.181
COPYCAT	-.022	-.443
DEAD_POETS_SOCIETY_1	-.105	-.437
DEAD_POETS_SOCIETY_2	.365	.782
FOREST_GUMP	.448	.747
SE7EN_1	.073	.402
SE7EN_3	-.229	-.312
SOMETHING_ABOUT_MARY	.220	.484
THE_PROFESSIONAL	.131	.330
TRAINSPOTTING	-.013	-.621

Covariates: Ext = 5.54; Agr = 7.22; Con = 6.55; Neu = 5.62; Ope = 6.75; PDI = -35.96; IDV = 18.73; MAS = -1.23; UAI = 44.61; PRG = 16.84; IVR = -16.97.

Thus, in the dataset, there were 144 conditions (resulting from the 3*2*2*12 settings of frame-rate, frame dimension, bit-rate, and content). Each video sequence has a length between 1 and 3 minutes. A review of the estimated marginal means show adequate distinction between the video sequences in terms of perceived quality and enjoyment as shown above in Table 1.

3.3 Measures

Participants responded to several measurement scales during the study in relation to: perception of quality; enjoyment; culture; and personality. These were previously validated and defined for participants.

3.3.1 Quality

To assess subjective perception of quality, the QoP-LoQ scale [14] was used. This consists of a single 5-point Likert-type rating item where participants indicate how they judged the quality of the video sequence. A low score indicates "no" satisfaction while a high score indicates "absolute" satisfaction.

3.3.2 Enjoyment

To assess enjoyment, a subjective measure was used. This consisted of a single 5-point Guttman-type rating item where participants indicated how much they enjoyed the video sequence. A low score indicates "no" enjoyment while a high score indicates "high" enjoyment.

3.3.3 Culture

Culture is a collective concept. Thus, when measured at the individual-level, traits associated with culture are being measured. The VSM-2013 questionnaire [19] was used to measure these traits according to the following dimensions: power distance (PDI); individualism (IDV); uncertainty avoidance (UAI); masculinity (MAS); pragmatism (PRG); and indulgence (IVR).

Table 2: Sample Descriptives

Human Factors	$\bar{x}(NTU)$	$\bar{x}(BUL)$	$\bar{x}(Pool)$	σ
Extroversion	5.61	5.46	5.54	1.689
Agreeableness	7.33	7.31	7.22	1.533
Conscientiousness	6.40	6.70	6.55	1.523
Neuroticism	5.56	5.68	5.62	1.716
Openness	6.60	6.91	6.75	1.424
Power Distance	-35.61	-36.32	-35.96	53.219
Individualism	25.79	11.67	18.73	50.619
Masculinity	3.68	-6.14	-1.23	53.483
Uncertainty Avoidance	52.54	36.67	44.61	47.182
Pragmatism	16.14	17.54	16.84	58.090
Indulgence	-22.63	-11.32	-16.97	65.522

$\bar{x}$: Sample Mean; σ: Standard Deviaton

3.3.4 *Personality*

To assess the personality of the participants, the BFI-10 [11] questionnaire was used. The personality is assessed according to the FFM [8], measuring: openness (Ope); conscientiousness (Con); Extroversion (Ext); Agreeableness (Agr); Neuroticism (Neu).

3.4 Sample Size

A power analysis was conducted, using G*Power 3, to determine the minimum sample size. Using the conventional error probabilities ($\alpha = .05$, $1 - \beta = 0.8$) while assuming that 'medium' effect sizes according to Cohen's benchmark will be detected ($f = 0.39$) and that the repeated measures will be correlated ($r = 0.8$), a minimum sample size of 64 was suggested. Due to the risk of error inflation associated with testing a large number of parameters, it was decided that a larger sample would be needed. A sample of 114 was obtained for this study.

3.5 Participants

The participants were 114 university students drawn from the two institutions the authors are affiliated with. Exactly 50% of the sample was drawn from each institution. In terms of nationality, there were: 43 British, 22 Indian, 16 Chinese, 15 Singaporean, 4 Nigerian, 2 Indonesian, 2 Pakistani, 2 Vietnamese, 1 Danish, 1 Dutch, 1 Latvian, 1 Myanmarian, 1 Polish, 1 Tanzanian, 1 Turkish, and 1 Zimbabwean. The proportion of female participants was 28.9% and the average age was 23.9 years ($\sigma = 3.68$).

Additional descriptives in terms of personality and cultural traits for each institution are shown above in Table 2. As would be expected, the means for the personality variables are consistent across the two institutions, following the expected normal distribution. However, several differences can be observed in terms of Hofestede's cultural dimensions. In particular, non-trivial differences can be seen in terms of: individualism; masculinity; uncertainty avoidance; and indulgence. It should be noted, however, that the full range of possible values were not observed for: extroversion (87.5% of expected range); openness (75% of expected range); and masculinity (67% of expected range).

These participants represent a non-probability sample. This sampling method tends to have two key weaknesses: lack of prototypicality (i.e., does the sample represent the target population?); and range restriction (i.e., is there sufficient variance in variables of interest to detect a relationship?). As the focus of this study is modelling rather than demography, only the latter presents a potential threat to validity. However, it can be seen that the participants varied in terms of personality and culture. There is little evidence of range restriction for most of the key variables of interest.

4. RESULTS

Analyses were conducted in PASW 18.0.3 for Windows. Due to the diverse range of nations represented in the sample and the overlap between each institution in terms of nationality of respondent, the geographic location of each institution could not be used as a proxy for culture. Hence, the two institutions are not compared. Instead, cultural variables were captured at the individual-level and a set of regression models are compared to examine differences in terms of these variables. Mixed linear regression has been used to account for repeated measures. The parameters in each model were estimated concurrently using the restricted maximum-likelihood method. Missing data was pair-wise excluded.

4.1 Baseline Model

The baseline model only considers system factors. In the context of the CP-QAE-I video dataset, there are 12 variations of the system factors which varied were: frame-rate (3 conditions); frame dimension (2 conditions); and bit-rate (2 conditions). Other system factors such as file format and delivery protocol were held constant as part of the experimental setup. Due to expected interactions between these conditions (e.g., an attempt to minimise bit-rate while maximising frame-rate and frame-dimension would likely create artefacts) these were modelled as factorial interactions. In addition, the movie excerpt itself is included as a parameter to reflect differences in cinematographic technologies and techniques used to create the movies. This was modelled as a main effect.

An analysis of this model can be seen in Table 3. It can be seen that all of the system factors and their interactions had a statistically significant effect on the perception of quality with the movie excerpt itself making a contribution. As expected, the movie excerpt itself had the largest impact on enjoyment. However, it is interesting to note that only a small number of the system factors had a statistically significant effect on enjoyment.

4.2 Extended Model

The extended model adds several fixed parameters to the baseline model as covariates with direct effects. These were cultural traits including: power distance; individualism; masculinity; uncertainty avoidance; pragmatism; and indulgence. Additionally, personality traits were also added, including: extroversion; agreeableness; conscientiousness; neuroticism; and openness.

Table 4 above show an analysis of the extended model. In addition, a more comprehensive overview of the parameters in the models can be found on the next page in Tables 6 and 7. It can be seen that several of personal and cultural traits are statistically significant predictors. Of particular interest are those which influence both perception of quality and overall enjoyment. These were:

Table 3: Baseline Model for Perception of Quality and Enjoyment

		Perceived Quality			Enjoyment		
Parameter	df_{num}	df_{den}	F	p	df_{den}	F	p
Movie Excerpt	11	191.387	8.880	.000	177.090	40.140	.000
Frame Rate (FR)	2	1152.788	23.540	.000	1131.230	5.173	.006
Frame Dimension (Dim)	1	1164.451	16.890	.000	1146.390	2.846	.092
Bit-Rate (BR)	1	1160.518	9.830	.002	1139.690	.474	.491
FR * Dim	2	1150.910	3.070	.047	1130.961	1.663	.190
FR * BR	2	1152.330	5.188	.006	1131.496	2.078	.126
Dim * BR	1	1165.993	8.240	.004	1137.742	1.364	.243
FR * Dim * BR	2	1154.080	5.714	.003	1130.448	.002	.998

Table 4: Extended Model for Perception of Quality and Enjoyment

		Perceived Quality			Enjoyment		
Parameter	df_{num}	df_{den}	F	p	df_{den}	F	p
Movie Excerpt	11	191.490	9.070	.000	171.956	39.733	.000
Frame Rate (FR)	2	1142.880	24.075	.000	1136.577	4.695	.009
Frame Dimension (Dim)	1	1153.771	13.578	.000	1151.402	3.336	.068
Bit-Rate (BR)	1	1148.206	12.677	.000	1145.171	.257	.612
FR * Dim	2	1145.057	3.748	.024	1145.206	1.057	.348
FR * BR	2	1144.258	5.262	.005	1138.177	1.856	.157
Dim * BR	1	1154.877	9.876	.002	1146.873	2.424	.120
FR * Dim * BR	2	1146.555	5.981	.003	1138.844	.057	.945
Extroversion	1	1151.392	.130	.718	1150.401	.024	.877
Agreeableness	1	1151.909	2.672	.102	1152.475	2.001	.157
Conscientiousness	1	1141.817	7.126	.008	1141.249	5.271	.022
Neuroticism	1	1149.100	11.708	.001	1146.479	.050	.823
Openness	1	1150.056	1.168	.280	1145.365	4.344	.037
Power Distance	1	1154.125	.290	.590	1152.465	9.138	.003
Individualism	1	1149.721	5.519	.019	1150.026	.674	.412
Masculinity	1	1147.422	5.578	.018	1141.312	3.312	.069
Uncertainty Avoidance	1	1144.686	.333	.564	1144.106	5.751	.017
Pragmatism	1	1152.021	4.889	.027	1160.700	.604	.437
Indulgence	1	1140.461	2.321	.128	1149.178	2.206	.138

Table 5: Optimistic Model for Perception of Quality and Enjoyment

		Perceived Quality			Enjoyment		
Parameter	df_{num}	df_{den}	F	p	df_{den}	F	p
Movie Excerpt	11	176.430	11.260	.000	179.877	46.990	.000
Frame Rate (FR)	2	1086.420	28.464	.000	1116.890	8.025	.000
Frame Dimension (Dim)	1	1100.669	17.950	.000	1120.818	3.130	.077
Bit-Rate (BR)	1	1092.200	13.052	.000	1121.960	.054	.816
FR * Dim	2	1091.110	2.892	.056	1117.780	.719	.487
FR * BR	2	1103.450	5.269	.005	1127.280	1.488	.226
Dim * BR	1	1114.040	7.513	.006	1128.860	1.466	.226
FR * Dim * BR	2	1087.310	7.143	.001	1113.480	.020	.980

Table 6: Standardised Parameter Estimates in the Extended Perceived Quality Model

Source	Parameter	Estimate	$SE_{\bar{x}}$	*df*	*t*	*p*	95% CI Lower	95% CI Upper	$\mathbf{r}_{y\lambda}$
System	5fps**	-.5568	.129	1086.514	-4.320	.000	-.810	.304	-.129
	384k**	-.8580	.134	1154.374	-6.377	.000	-1.122	-.594	-.184
	5fps * 384k**	.8026	.188	1145.181	4.268	.000	.433	1.171	.125
	15fps * 384k**	.7103	.182	1166.053	3.886	.000	.351	1.068	.113
	480p * 384k**	.8595	.191	1154.370	4.485	.000	.483	1.235	.130
	5fps * 480p * 384k**	-.8019	.262	1151.397	-3.061	.002	-1.316	-.287	-.089
	15fps * 480p * 384k**	-.7810	.260	1163.006	-3.003	.003	-1.291	-.270	-.087
Personality	Conscientiousness**	-.0747	.028	1141.817	-2.669	.008	-.130	-.020	-.078
	Neuroticism**	.0943	.028	1149.100	3.422	.001	.040	.148	.100
Culture	Individualism*	-.0636	.027	1149.721	-2.349	.019	-.117	-.010	-.069
	Masculinity*	.0659	.028	1147.422	2.362	.018	.011	.121	.069
	Pragmatism*	-.0653	.030	1152.021	-2.211	.027	-.123	-.007	-.065

Reference categories were: Frame Rate = 25fps, Frame Dimension = 720p, Bit Rate = 768k.
† $p < .10$, * $p < .05$, ** $p < .01$

Table 7: Standardised Parameter Estimates in the Extended Enjoyment Model

Source	Parameter	Estimate	$SE_{\bar{x}}$	*df*	*t*	*p*	95% CI Lower	95% CI Upper	$\mathbf{r}_{y\lambda}$
Personality	Conscientiousness*	-.0601	.026	1141.249	-2.296	.022	-.111	-.009	-.067
	Openness*	.0528	.025	1145.365	2.084	.037	-.003	.103	.061
Culture	Power Distance**	-.0795	.026	1152.465	-3.023	.003	-.131	-.028	-.088
	Masculinity†	.0474	.026	1141.312	1.820	.069	-.004	.099	.053
	Uncertainty Avoidance*	-.0661	.028	1144.106	-2.398	.017	-.120	-.012	-.070

Reference categories were: Frame Rate = 25fps, Frame Dimension = 720p, Bit Rate = 768k. All system interaction effects are non-significant and so are not shown.
† $p < .10$, * $p < .05$, ** $p < .01$

masculinity and conscientiousness. The regression coefficients for these parameters show that they have positive and negative impacts on overall ratings, respectively. Individualism, pragmatism, and neuroticism had, respectively, negative, negative, and positive impact on perceived quality. However, openness, power distance, and uncertainty avoidance respectively had positive, negative, and negative impacts on enjoyment respectively. The magnitudes of the effect sizes are also comparable with some system factors.

4.3 Optimistic Model

While the goal of a model is to predict the value of a dependent variable as accurately as possible, not all of the residual variance can be solely attributed to human factors which have not been measured. A non-trivial proportion of the residual variance can also, to name a few, be attributed to: random error; measurement error; and the limitations of the modelling technique (in this case, generalised linear regression). As such, an optimistic model can be used to estimate the proportion of this residual variance which can be reasonably attributed to human factors (and, to a small extent because of limitations to experimental control, context factors). This is achieved by modelling each participant as a "random effect". That is, the repeated measurements were used to vary the intercept of the regression for each individual participant.

An analysis of the optimistic models is shown in Table 5. There is only a small number of differences between the baseline and the optimistic model. As expected, the F-statistics for the intercepts are much larger, showing that they explain a larger proportion of the variance. Additionally, the borderline significant interaction between frame rate and frame dimension has become non-significant. The most notable difference, however, is a large increase in the variance explained as a result of including participants as random effects.

4.4 Model Comparison

The models are compared using paired t-tests on the Mean Squared Residuals (MSR), shown in Tables 8 and 9, and the proportional reduction in overall mean squared error of prediction is examined (see [2]).

4.4.1 Models for Perception of Quality

In the baseline model, the MSR is 1.2636 ($\sigma = 1.77$). The optimistic model reduces the MSR to 0.9085 ($\sigma = 1.63$) ($p < .000$). This represents 24.2% of the overall variance predicted (compared to 37.9% overall). However, culture and personality only predict a small proportion of this variance. The extended model predicts approximately 9.3% of variance attributable to human factors, reducing the baseline MSR to 1.2311 ($\sigma = 1.77$) ($p < .014$).

4.4.2 Models for Enjoyment

In the baseline model, the MSR is 1.3684 ($\sigma = 1.63$). The optimistic model reduces the MSR to 0.9481 ($\sigma = 1.22$) ($p < .000$). This represents 23.0% of the overall variance predicted (compared to 47.8% overall). However, again, culture and personality only predict a small proportion. The extended model predicts approximately 9.3% of variance attributable to human factors, reducing the baseline MSR to 1.3290 ($\sigma = 1.58$) ($p < .001$).

Table 8: Paired t-Test Comparing Models for Perceived Quality on MSR

Models	$\Delta\bar{x}$	σ	$SE_{\bar{x}}$	95% CI Lower	95% CI Upper	t	df	p
Baseline → Extended	.0325	.461	.013	.007	.058	2.472	1231	.014
Baseline → Optimistic	.3551	1.009	.029	.299	.412	12.350	1231	.000

Table 9: Paired t-Test Comparing Models for Enjoyment on MSR

Models	$\Delta\bar{x}$	σ	$SE_{\bar{x}}$	95% CI Lower	95% CI Upper	t	df	p
Baseline → Extended	.0394	.430	.012	.015	.063	3.219	1231	.001
Baseline → Optimistic	.4199	1.129	.032	.357	.483	13.069	1231	.000

4.5 Quality and Enjoyment

Descriptive statistics for each movie excerpt and parameter setting are presented alongside a correlation analysis between quality and enjoyment in Figures 2,4 and Table 10. These show how the parameters, the content, and level of enjoyment interact when human factors are not controlled. It can be seen that the overall correlation between quality and enjoyment is significant, however this is not consistent across all of the movie excepts. Additionally, the 'highest' quality parameters do not consistently perform well.

5. DISCUSSION

The results suggest that human factors play an important role in the way perception of quality and enjoyment are rated. The analysis of perceptual quality, in particular, reveals that a greater proportion of the variance can be predicted by human factors (24.3%) than by system factors (13.7%); although, all the system factors and most of their interactions have larger effect sizes than any individual human factor. This suggests that perceived quality and enjoyment are determined by humans as much as they are determined by the system itself. This is in line with previous work in the area [7], but more importantly shows that "lower" system factors may not automatically entail lower quality or enjoyment. To illustrate this the parameter setting {25fps, 480p, 384k} was ranked 4th for perceived quality and 1st for enjoyment, despite having a low bit-rate. Indeed, performance varied across different movie excerpts and participants. As such, understanding these factors could be used to prioritise limited resources while aiming to maintain minimally acceptable quality for a broad range of viewers.

It is important to recognise that the human factors explored in this study, namely personality and culture, represent a small portion of the variance which can be attributed to human factors overall. For both variables, they represented only 9.3% of the variance. While this is an important proportion, further study is needed to discover other contributing factors, which could include sensory impairments and expertise.

Nevertheless, a key facet to consider is moderation. That is, where the magnitude (and sign) of a relationship (e.g., perceived quality on enjoyment) depends on the value of a third variable (e.g., personality). A correlation analysis of the relationship between quality and enjoyment shows considerable inconsistency in effect size. It is interesting to note that the excerpts with objectionable content (i.e., graphic murders) had non-significant correlations while excerpts with widely acceptable content (i.e., romance) had much higher effect sizes. Presumably, this is because people do not enjoy objectionable experiences and so experiencing something they do not like in higher quality actually detracts from their enjoyment. As viewers tend to object to different content, such interactions could be used as a basis for managing quality parameters.

It is interesting to note that the indulgence cultural trait did not predict either perceived quality or enjoyment. This is interesting because habituation and sensitization effect were anticipated. That is, those with high indulgence scores tend to concentrate on individual well being and leisure time and so would likely seek to immerse themselves in multimedia content to a greater extent than those with lower indulgence scores. It is possible, however, that the indulgence may not correspond directly with the use and enjoyment of multimedia content. As such, whether or not participants regularly use multimedia content and services may be an important factor to consider in future studies.

Previous work [40] reports that agreeableness was a predictor for perceptual quality whereas extraversion was a predictor for enjoyment and [41] reports that there were no significant influence of personality in perceived quality. However, it should be noted that these differences are expected due to several reasons like a) stimuli-oreinted interaction effects (YouTube videos [41], IPTV [40] vs. Affective movie clips in our work), b) measurement instruments used (TIPI [11] for personality in [41] vs. BFI-10 in our work), variation in samples and the sampling method (users from the same university and living in the same country [40, 41] vs. users from different universities in different countries), analysis technique used (linear classifiers in [41] vs. statistical modeling in ours) and so on. To address these differences, building a comprehensive QoE model involving data from multiple datasets is encouraged.

It should be noted that due to the international nature of the research presented in this paper, participants did not use the same laboratories and therefore did not use the same devices. As such, system and contextual factors such

Table 10: Correlation Analysis Showing the Relationship Between Perceived Quality and Enjoyment

	C-I	C-II	C-III	C-IV	C-V	C-VI	C-VII	C-VIII	C-IX	C-X	C-XI	C-XII	Total[b]
Spearman's ρ	.252	.170	.377	.161	.242	.447	.507	.439	.367	.269	.391	.369	.375
p	.007	.082	.000	.095	.011	.000	.000	.000	.000	.007	-.000	.000	.000

[b] This aggregate is based on non-independent data due to repeated measures.
Movie Excerpts:- C-I: A_FISH_CALLED_WANDA; C-II: AMERICAN_HISTORY_X; C-III: CHILDS_PLAY_II; C-IV: COPYCAT; C-V: DEAD_POETS_SOCIETY_1; C-VI: DEAD_POETS_SOCIETY_2; C-VII: FOREST_GUMP; C-VIII: SE7EN_1; C-IX: SE7EN_3; C-X: SOMETHING_ABOUT_MARY; C-XI: THE_PROFESSIONAL; C-XII: TRAINSPOTTING.

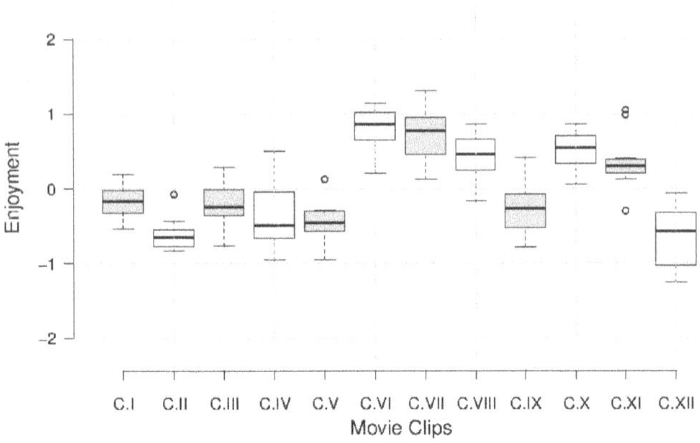

Figure 1: Box-Plot showing the distribution of Enjoyment of Each Movie Excerpt in the Dataset (z-Score)

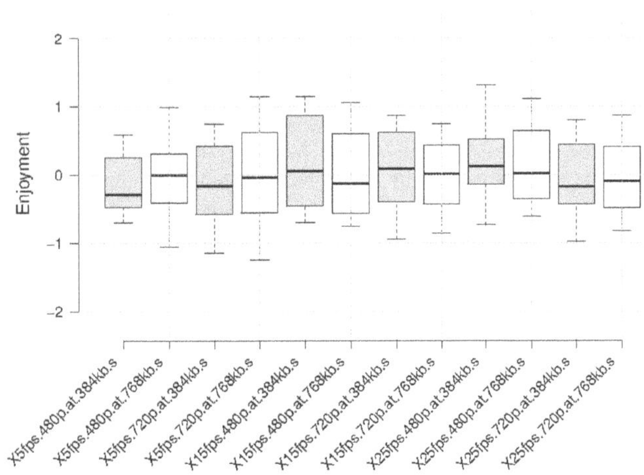

Figure 2: Box-Plot showing the distribution of Enjoyment of Each Parameter Setting in the Dataset (z-Score)

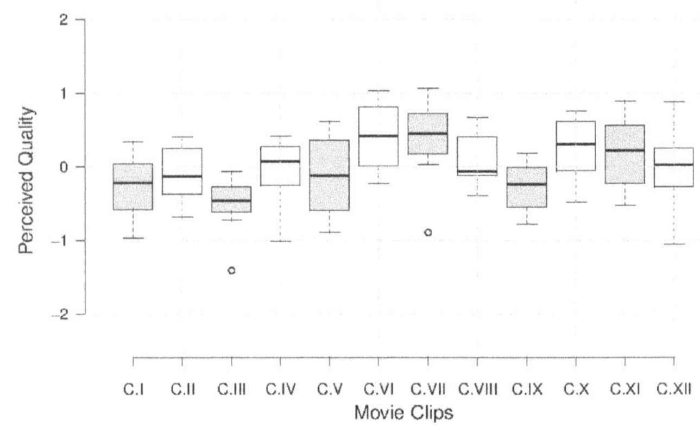

Figure 3: Box-Plot showing the distribution of Perceived Quality of Each Movie Excerpt in the Dataset (z-Score)

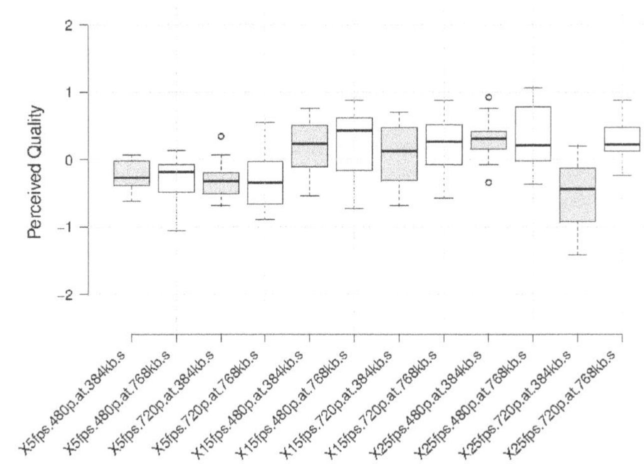

Figure 4: Box-Plot showing the distribution of Perceived Quality of Each Parameter Setting in the Dataset (z-Score)

as dead pixels, lighting conditions, and differences in computer hardware could have confounded any effect that has otherwise been attributed to the participants themselves. Consequently, this may over-estimate the variance attributable to human factors and so the relative 9.3% contribution of personality and culture may be an under-estimation.

6. CONCLUSION

Multimedia perception of quality and subsequent enjoyment is influenced by an intricate interplay between system, context, and human factors. Knowing the impact of these factors permits them to be exploited to optimise perceived quality and enjoyment under conditions where content delivery is constrained. As a step towards this goal, this paper presents a model of the role of human factors in perception of multimedia quality and its relationship to enjoyment.

Participants were drawn from a range of different nations to rate several video sequences under different conditions. It was found that: (i) approximately 13.7% of the variance in perceived quality could be predicted by system factors while 24.3% could be predicted by human factors; (ii) approximately 24.8% of the variance in enjoyment could be predicted by system factors while 23.1% could be predicted by human factors; (iii) approximately 9.3% of the variance attributable to human factors could be predicted by personal and cultural traits (for both perceived quality and enjoyment); (iv) the traits of masculinity and conscientiousness were important predictors for both perceived quality and enjoyment; (v) individualism, pragmatism, and neuroticism were important predictors for perceived quality; (vi) power distance, uncertainty avoidance, and openness were important predictors for enjoyment; and (vii) the quality-enjoyment correlation varied in magnitude across the movie excerpts.

These findings confirm that human factors play a key role in perceptual multimedia quality and enjoyment. Of particular note, the variance attributable to human factors had an equivalent or greater impact on predicting the ratings compared to the system factors. This reveals that perceptual quality and enjoyment are as much human constructs as they are the result of objective technological differences. This offers several opportunities in terms of reducing bandwidth using human-centred quality of service algorithms. Based on the results of this study, such an algorithm could incorporate individualism, masculinity, pragmatism, neurotism and conscientiousness as paramaters (based on their ability to predict perceived quality) and individual preference for different genres (based on the differing correlations between quality and enjoyment across content).

However, further work is encouraged to model human factors because the personal and cultural traits selected in this study only represent a small proportion of the variance. Additionally, several limitations exist. Firstly, only the main effects of personality and culture were explored. It is possible that these traits interact with other factors and so more complex relationships could be identified. Secondly, the scope of the study was limited to a small subset of human and system factors. Broader investigations of system and context factors are needed. Thirdly, those recruited in this study were university students attending the authors' respective institutions. While there is no evidence to suggest that students are different to the general population in terms of quality of experience, additional work is encouraged to ensure that the full range of each human factor is considered (see [17, 22]) and any potential confounds are identified.

7. REFERENCES

[1] A. Acar, T. Taura, E. Yamamoto, and N. Yusof. Object vs. relation: understanding the link between culture and cognition with the help of wordnet. *International Journal on Asian Language Processing*, 21(9):199–208, 2011.

[2] R. Bosker and T. Snijders. Multilevel analysis: An introduction to basic and advanced multilevel modeling, 2nd ed. *New York*, 2012.

[3] M. Cristani, A. Vinciarelli, C. Segalin, and A. Perina. Unveiling the multimedia unconscious: Implicit cognitive processes and multimedia content analysis. In *Proceedings of the 21st ACM international conference on Multimedia*, pages 213–222. ACM, 2013.

[4] M. Fiedler, T. Hossfeld, and P. Tran-Gia. A generic quantitative relationship between quality of experience and quality of service. *Network, IEEE*, 24(2):36–41, 2010.

[5] X.-P. Gao, J. H. Xin, T. Sato, A. Hansuebsai, M. Scalzo, K. Kajiwara, S.-S. Guan, J. Valldeperas, M. J. Lis, and M. Billger. Analysis of cross-cultural color emotion. *Color Research & Application*, 32(3):223–229, 2007.

[6] G. Ghinea and S. Y. Chen. The impact of cognitive styles on perceptual distributed multimedia quality. *British Journal of Educational Technology*, 34(4):393–406, 2003.

[7] G. Ghinea and J. P. Thomas. Qos impact on user perception and understanding of multimedia video clips. In *Proceedings of the sixth ACM international conference on Multimedia*, pages 49–54. ACM, 1998.

[8] L. R. Goldberg. An alternative" description of personality": the big-five factor structure. *Journal of personality and social psychology*, 59(6):1216, 1990.

[9] E. Goldstein. *Cultural effects on visual perception.* SAGE Publications, Inc., Encyclopedia of Perception, 2010.

[10] E. Goldstein. *Sensation and Perception.* Cengage Learning, 2013.

[11] S. D. Gosling, P. J. Rentfrow, and W. B. Swann. A very brief measure of the big-five personality domains. *Journal of Research in personality*, 37(6):504–528, 2003.

[12] V. Q. E. Group et al. Final report from the video quality experts group on the validation of objective models of video quality assessment, phase ii (fr_tv2). *ftp://ftp. its. bldrdoc. gov/dist/ituvidq/ Boulder_VQEG_jan_04/VQEG_PhaseII_FRTV_Final _Report_SG9060E. doc, 2003*, 2003.

[13] V. Q. E. Group et al. Report on the validation of video quality models for high definition video content. *tech. re p., http://www. vqeg. org*, 2010.

[14] S. R. Gulliver and G. Ghinea. Defining user perception of distributed multimedia quality. *ACM Transactions on Multimedia Computing, Communications, and Applications*, 2(4):241–257, 2006.

[15] S. C. Guntuku, S. Roy, and W. Lin. Personality modeling based image recommendation. In *MultiMedia Modeling*, pages 171–182. Springer, 2015.

[16] S. C. Guntuku, M. J. Scott, H. Yang, G. Ghinea, and W. Lin. The CP-QAE-I: A video dataset for exploring the effect of personality and culture on perceived quality and affect in multimedia. In *QoMEX*. IEEE, 2015.

[17] J. Henrich, S. J. Heine, and A. Norenzayan. The weirdest people in the world? *Behavioral and brain sciences*, 33(2-3):61–83, 2010.

[18] G. Hofstede. Dimensionalizing cultures: The hofstede model in context. *Online readings in psychology and culture*, 2(1):8, 2011.

[19] G. Hofstede, G. J. Hofstede, M. Minkov, and H. Vinken. Values survey module 2013. *URL: http://www.geerthofstede.nl/vsm2013*, 2013.

[20] G. Hoftede, G. J. Hofstede, and M. Minkov. *Cultures and organizations: software of the mind: intercultural*

cooperation and its importance for survival. McGraw-Hill, 2010.

[21] M. Hyder, N. Crespi, M. Haun, C. Hoene, et al. Are qoe requirements for multimedia services different for men and women? analysis of gender differences in forming qoe in virtual acoustic environments. In *Emerging Trends and Applications in Information Communication Technologies*, pages 200–209. Springer, 2012.

[22] R. N. Landers and T. S. Behrend. An inconvenient truth: Arbitrary distinctions between organizational, mechanical turk, and other convenience samples. *Industrial and Organizational Psychology*, pages 1–38, in press.

[23] M. Leszczuk, L. Janowski, and M. Barkowsky. Freely available large-scale video quality assessment database in full-hd resolution with h.264 coding. In *IEEE Globecom 2013*, volume -, pages pp.1–6, Atlanta, United States, Dec 2013.

[24] Y. Luo and X. Tang. Photo and video quality evaluation: Focusing on the subject. In *In Eur. Conf. Comp. Vis. (ECCV)*, pages 386–399, 2008.

[25] B. Manav. Color-emotion associations and color preferences: A case study for residences. *Color Research & Application*, 32(2):144–150, 2007.

[26] W. A. Mansilla, A. Perkis, and T. Ebrahimi. Implicit experiences as a determinant of perceptual quality and aesthetic appreciation. In *Proceedings of the 19th ACM international conference on Multimedia*, pages 153–162. ACM, 2011.

[27] G. Matthews, I. J. Deary, and M. C. Whiteman. *Personality traits.* Cambridge University Press, 2003.

[28] Y. miyamoto. *Culture and analytic versus holistic cognition: toward multilevel analyses of culture influences.* Academic Press, Advances in Experimental Social Psychology, 2013.

[29] A. Moorthy, P. Obrador, and N. Oliver. Towards computational models of visual aesthetic appeal of consumer videos. In *In Eur. Conf. Comp. Vis. (ECCV)*, pages 1–14, 2010.

[30] R. Nisbett and Y. Miyamoto. The influence of culture: holistic versus analytic perception. *Trends in Cognitive Sciences*, 9(10):467–473, Oct 2005.

[31] P. Paudyal, F. Battisti, and M. Carli. A study on the effects of quality of service parameters on perceived video quality. In *Procs. of 5th European Workshop on Visual Information Processing, EUVIP*, 2014.

[32] B. Rainer, M. Waltl, E. Cheng, M. Shujau, C. Timmerer, S. Davis, I. Burnett, C. Ritz, and H. Hellwagner. Investigating the impact of sensory effects on the quality of experience and emotional response in web videos. In *QoMEX*, pages 278–283. IEEE, 2012.

[33] J. A. Redi, Y. Zhu, H. de Ridder, and I. Heynderickx. How passive image viewers became active multimedia users. In *Visual Signal Quality Assessment*, pages 31–72. Springer, 2015.

[34] U. Reiter, K. BrunnstrÃűm, K. D. Moor, M.-C. Larabi, M. Pereira, A. Pinheiro, J. You, and A. Zgank. *Factors Influencing Quality of Experience.* Springer, Quality of Experience, 2014.

[35] A. Schaefer, F. Nils, X. Sanchez, and P. Philippot. Assessing the effectiveness of a large database of emotion-eliciting films: A new tool for emotion researchers. *Cognition and Emotion*, 24(7):1153–1172, 2010.

[36] K. Seshadrinathan, R. Soundararajan, A. C. Bovik, and L. K. Cormack. Study of subjective and objective quality assessment of video. *Image Processing, IEEE transactions on*, 19(6):1427–1441, 2010.

[37] L. Setlock, P.-A. Quinones, and S. Fussell. Does culture interact with media richness? the effect of audio vs video conferencing on chinese and american dyads. In *Proceedings of the 40th Annual Hawaii International Conference on System Sciences*, 2007.

[38] E. Siahaan, J. Redi, and A. Hanjalic. Beauty is in the scale of the beholder: Comparison of methodologies for the subjective assessment of image aesthetic appeal. In *QoMEX*, pages 245–250, Sept 2014.

[39] W. Song, D. Tjondronegoro, and M. Docherty. Saving bitrate vs. pleasing users: where is the break-even point in mobile video quality? In *Proceedings of the 19th ACM international conference on Multimedia*, pages 403–412. ACM, 2011.

[40] I. Wechsung, M. Schulz, K.-P. Engelbrecht, J. Niemann, and S. Möller. All users are (not) equal-the influence of user characteristics on perceived quality, modality choice and performance. In *Proceedings of the Paralinguistic Information and its Integration in Spoken Dialogue Systems Workshop*, pages 175–186. Springer, 2011.

[41] Y. Zhu, I. Heynderickx, A. Hanjalic, and J. A. Redi. Towards a comprehensive model for predicting the quality of individual visual experience. In *IS&T/SPIE Electronic Imaging*, pages 93940A–93940A. International Society for Optics and Photonics, 2015.

Biologically Inspired Media Quality Modeling

Luming Zhang[†‡], Meng Wang[†], Liqiang Nie[‡], Richang Hong[†],
Yingjie Xia[*] and Roger Zimmermann[†]
[†]Department of CSIE, Hefei University of Technology, China
[‡]School of Computing, National University of Singapore, Singapore
[*]College of Computer Sciences, Zhejiang University, China
{zglumg,eric.mengwang,nieliqiang,hongrc.hfut}@gmail.com,
xiayingjie@zju.edu.cn rogerz@comp.nus.edu.sg

ABSTRACT

In this paper, we propose a biologically inspired quality model, focusing on interpreting how humans perceive visually and semantically important regions in an image (or a video clip). Particularly, we first extract local descriptors (graphlets in this work) from an image/frame. They are projected onto the perceptual space, which is built upon a set of low-level and high-level visual features. Then, an active learning algorithm is utilized to select graphlets that are both visually and semantically salient. The algorithm is based on the observation that each graphlet can be linearly reconstructed by its surrounding ones, and spatially nearer ones make a greater contribution. In this way, both the local and global geometric properties of an image/frame can be encoded in the selection process. These selected graphlets are linked into a so-called biological viewing path (BVP) to simulate human visual perception. Finally, the quality of an image or a video clip is predicted by a probabilistic model. Experiments shown that 1) the predicted BVPs are over 90% consistent with real human gaze shifting paths on average; and 2) our quality model outperforms many of its competitors remarkably.

Keywords

Biological; Gaze shifting; Path; Active learning; Geometry, Preservation; Human perception

1. INTRODUCTION

The volume of media data[1] we handle on a daily basis is growing exponentially due to the availability of ubiquitous and cheap sensors, sharing platforms, and new social trends. Artificial intelligence has proven useful for interpreting this preponderance of data. In the last decades, many models have been proposed to evaluate the quality of an image or a video clip. A successful quality model can facilitate many multimedia applications. For example, by quantifying the saliency of different image regions, a higher accuracy can be achieved if we employ only the salient regions from each image for retrieval. Moreover, video summarization algorithms typically extract key frames from one or multiple video clips. A well-designed quality model can generate a set of semantically representative and low redundant key frames.

In the literature, various media quality models have been proposed by utilizing both low-level (*e.g.*, texture and structure) and high-level visual features, (*e.g.*, portrait and architecture). As far as we know, however, none of them can capture the movement of the human eye and the mechanism of of visual cortex in aesthetic perception. Recent reports from both neuroscience and computer vision have demonstrated that biologically plausible features perform impressively in visual recognition. Thus, we propose a biological inspired quality model containing two modules: 1) engineering biological viewing paths (BVPs) that reflect how human perceive regions salient in an image/frame; and 2) a mathematical model that combines the BVPs of multiple users to assess media quality. It is worth emphasizing that developing such two modules encounters the following challenges:

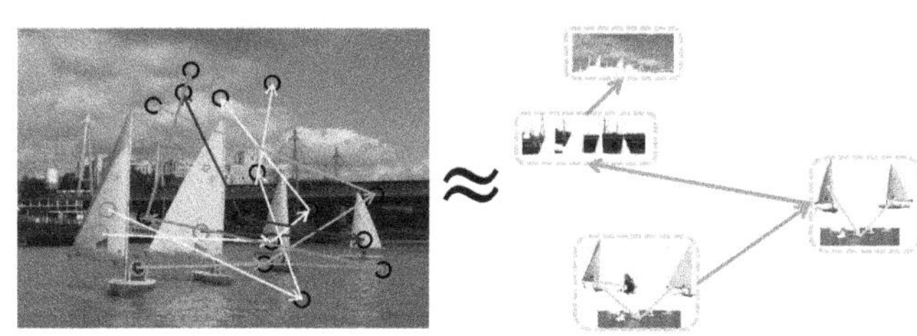

Figure 1: The gaze shifting paths recorded from five observers (left) and the BVP predicted by our algorithm (right)

- To mimick human gaze shifting, the predicted BVP should maximally reflect human perception of image/frame geometric attributes. However, current models cannot ensure that the detected salient regions can best recover an image/frame both locally and globally. This is because of the difficulty to establish a mathematical model that optimizes the local and global descriptiveness of a BVP simultaneously.

[1]The media data in this work specifically denotes images or video clips. The training media means the training images or video clips; and the test media denotes a test image or video clip.

MM '15, October 26–30, 2015, Brisbane, Australia.

http://dx.doi.org/10.1145/2733373.2806255.

- Psychophysics studies have demonstrated that object-level visual cues dominate over the deployment of attention [1]. That is to say, observers are more likely to attend to the "interesting" objects, rather than the highly contrasted non-object regions. However, current computational saliency models have limited capabilities to exploit object-level cues. One common scheme is to integrate object detectors, but this does not scale well and in practice, only a few pre-specified categories such as human faces can be well detected.

- We target a quality model that can simulate human visual perception. That means the model should convey some subjective factors. As shown in Fig. 1, observers with different backgrounds, education, and nationalities might generate slightly different gaze shifting paths on a same image (or a video clip). Toward a fair gaze shifting prediction, we expect that a BVP is maximally similar to the gaze shifting paths recorded from multiple observers. The challenge is how to implement such a "maximally similar" mechanism.

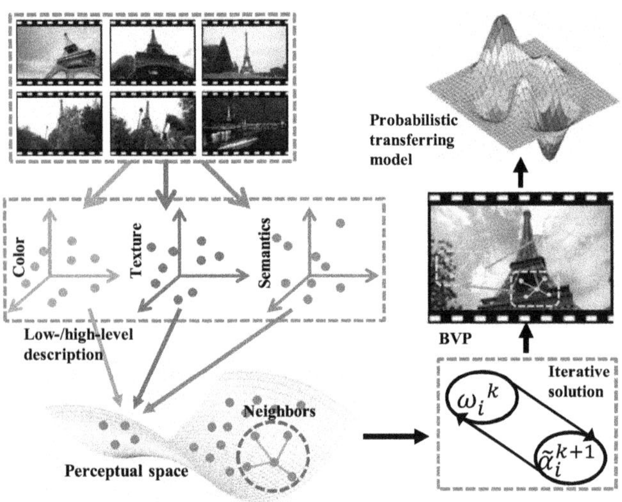

Figure 2: The pipeline of the proposed biological inspired media quality model

To solve the above problems, we propose a novel media quality model. The key is a geometry-preserving active learning (GPAL) that constructs BVPs in the perceptual space, which reflects both the low-level and high-level features. An overview of the proposed framework is presented in Fig. 2. By transferring semantics of media tags (*i.e.*, image/video-level labels) into different graphlets in an image, we represent each graphlet by a number of low-level and high-level visual features. Thereby, each graphlet can be deemed as a point in the perceptual space. To select those salient graphlets, a geometry-preserving active learning (GPAL) algorithm is utilized based on [9]. GPAL assumes that each graphlet can be linearly reconstructed by its spatially neighboring ones. To encode image/frame geometric properties both locally and globally, the nearer neighbors contribute a greater effect. To solve GPAL, an efficient two-stage iterative scheme is proposed. These detected salient graphlets are then linked into a biological viewing path (BVP) to mimick human gaze shifting. Based on the BVP, the media quality is predicted by probabilistically combining the BVPs learned from multiple observers. More specifically, we use GPAL to predict BVPs from both the training media recorded from multiple observers and the test media. Afterward, the media quality is quantified by the amount of BVPs that can be transferred from the training media data into a test one based on a probabilistic model.

2. RELATED WORK

Our approach assesses video quality by combining the quality scores of its constituent frames. Therefore, it is closely related to two topics in multimedia: image quality measurements based on human perception and human gaze estimation from an image.

2.1 Perceptual Image Quality Measure

Recently many image quality evaluation methods have been proposed, aiming at simulating how humans perceive an image. Ke *et al.* [6] developed a group of high-level visual features, such as the image simplicity based on the spatial distribution of edges, to imitate human perception of photo quality. Datta *et al.* [4] proposed 58 low-level visual features, *e.g.*, shape convexity, to capture photo quality. Dhar *et al.* [5] proposed a set of high-level attribute predictors to evaluate photo aesthetic quality. In [8], Luo *et al.* evaluated photo quality by utilizing a GMM-based hue distribution and a prominent line-based texture distribution. In [58], Cheng *et al.* proposed the omni-range context, *i.e.*, the spatial distribution of arbitrary pairwise image patches, to model photo aesthetic quality. Nishiyama *et al.* [10] assesses image quality by combining the SVM classifiers corresponding to a photo's internal subject regions. In [15], Nishiyama *et al.* proposed a color harmony-based photo quality model. The patch-level color distribution is converted into a bag-of-patches histogram, which is then classified by an SVM to identify photo quality. Luo *et al.* [29] attempted to use both photo-based aesthetic features and motion features for evaluating video quality. Moorthy *et al.* [30] introduced an approach to identify video quality based on 1) image-quality features, 2) motion features, and 3) single-photo aesthetic features. Yeh *et al.* [32] proposed to model video aesthetics by two modules: aesthetic features construction and temporal integration. Zhang *et al.* [7] learn human gaze shifting paths from image sub-regions to evaluate the quality of a candidate cropped photo. This model, however, discovers salient regions only in the semantic space. Comparatively, our approach detects salient regions in the perceptual space, reflecting both the low-level and high-level visual cues.

2.2 Human Gaze Prediction Techniques

The current gaze estimation can be categorized into two groups: model-based and appearance-based methods. Model-based methods use 3D eyeball models and estimate gaze direction using the geometric eye features [17, 44, 47]. They typically use infrared light sources and a high-resolution camera to locate the 3D eyeball position. Although this approach can estimate gaze directions accurately, its heavy reliance on the specialized hardware is a limitation. There exist methods relaxing this requirement by adopting only eye images to calculate the line of sight from the iris contour [42]. However, this is only effective within a short distance where high-resolution observations are available.

Appearance-based methods compute the non-geometric image features from the input eye image and then estimate gaze directions. The eye position is pre-computed for estimating the gaze target in the world coordinate system. With the popularity of monocular head pose tracking [49] and RGB-D head-tracking cameras [50], head poses can be captured accurately. Some appearance-based gaze estimation techniques use head poses as an auxiliary input for gaze estimation [51, 52]. Appearance variation of the eye images caused by head pose changes is another challenge. Usually they are tackled by a compensation function [51] or warping training images to new head poses [52]. While most of the existing appearance-based models adopt a person-dependent data set, Funes *et al.* proposed a cross subject training method for gaze estimation [53]. An RGB-D camera warps the training and test images to the frontal view. Then, an adaptive linear regression function is applied to compute gaze directions.

3. THE PROPOSED APPROACH

3.1 Perceptual Space Construction

3.1.1 The Concept of Graphlets

There are usually a number of of components within a photo. Among them, a few spatially neighboring ones and their spatial interactions capture the local features of a photo. Since graph is a powerful tool to describe the relationships among objects, we use it to model the spatial interactions of components in a photo. Particularly, we segment a photo into a set of atomic regions[2], and then construct graphlets to capture the local features of this photo. Formally, a graphlet is a small-sized graph defined as:

$$G = (V, E), \tag{1}$$

where V is a set of vertices representing those spatially neighboring atomic regions; and E is a set of edges, each of which connects pairwise spatially adjacent atomic regions. We call a graphlet with t vertices a t-sized graphlet. It is worth emphasizing that the number of graphlets within a photo is exponentially increasing with the graphlet size. Therefore, only small graphlets (*i.e.*, vertex number less than 10) are employed.

In this work, we characterize each graphlet in both color

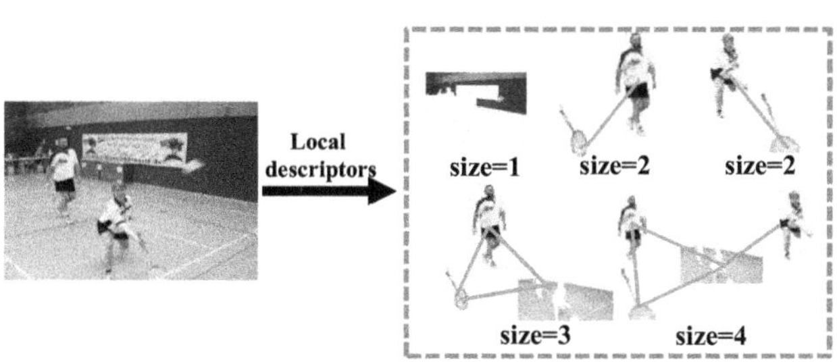

Figure 3: An example of differently sized graphlets

and texture channels. Given a t-sized graphlet, each row of matrix $\mathbf{M}_r^c$ represents the 9-dimensional color moment [2] and each row of matrix $\mathbf{M}_r^t$ denotes the 128-dimensional HOG [3] of an atomic region. To describe the spatial interactions of atomic regions, we employ a $t \times t$ adjacency matrix as:

$$\mathbf{M}_s(i,j) = \begin{cases} \theta(R_i, R_j) & \text{if } R_i \text{ and } R_j \text{ are adjacent} \\ 0 & \text{otherwise} \end{cases}, \tag{2}$$

where $\theta(R_i, R_j)$ is the horizontal angle of the vector from the centroid of atomic region R_i to that of atomic region R_j. Based on the three matrices $\mathbf{M}_r^c$, $\mathbf{M}_r^t$, and $\mathbf{M}_s$, we can describe a graphlet by $\mathbf{M} = [\mathbf{M}_r^c, \mathbf{M}_r^t, \mathbf{M}_s]$.

3.1.2 Semantically Encoding Graphlets

In addition to the color and texture channels description, high-level semantic cues should also be exploited for predicting human gaze shifting paths. In this paper, the semantic cues are integrated based on a weakly supervised algorithm. We transfer the semantics of image/video-level labels into different graphlets in an image/frame[3]. Particularly, the weakly supervised algorithm is implemented based on a manifold embedding described as:

$$\arg\min_{\mathbf{Y}} [\sum_{i,j} ||y_i - y_j||^2 l_s(i,j) - \sum_{i,j} ||y_i - y_j||^2 l_d(i,j)]$$
$$= \arg\min_{\mathbf{Y}} \mathrm{tr}(\mathbf{YRY}^T), \tag{3}$$

where $\mathbf{Y} = [y_1, y_2, \cdots, y_n]$ contains a collection of post-embedding graphlets; $\mathbf{R} = [\vec{\mathbf{e}}_{n-1}^T, -\mathbf{I}_{n-1}]\mathbf{W}_1[\vec{\mathbf{e}}_{n-1}^T, -\mathbf{I}_{n-1}] + \cdots + [-\mathbf{I}_{n-1}, \vec{\mathbf{e}}_{n-1}^T]\mathbf{W}_n[-\mathbf{I}_{n-1}, \vec{\mathbf{e}}_{n-1}^T]$; $\mathbf{W}_i$ is an $n \times n$ diagonal matrix whose h-th diagonal element is $[l_s(h,i) - l_d(h,i)]$.

$l_s(\cdot,\cdot)$ and $l_d(\cdot,\cdot)$ are functions measuring the semantic similarity and difference between graphlets respectively. Denoting $\mathbf{b}_i$ as a C-dimensional row vector containing the multiple labels of the media from which graphlet G_i is extracted; and $\vec{\mathbf{n}} = [n^1, n^2 \cdots, n^C]^T$ where n^c is the number of images (or video clips) with label c, then l_s and l_d are defined as:

$$l_s(i,j) = \frac{[\mathbf{b}_i \cap \mathbf{b}_j]\vec{\mathbf{n}}}{\sum_c n^c}, \tag{4}$$

$$l_d(i,j) = \frac{[\mathbf{b}_i \oplus \mathbf{b}_j]\vec{\mathbf{n}}}{\sum_c n^c}, \tag{5}$$

Based on the semantically aware embedding, we project graphlets onto the perceptual space, where each graphlet is described by $[\phi(\mathbf{M}_r^c), \phi(\mathbf{M}_r^t), y]$. $\phi(\cdot)$ is a row-wise matrix stacking operator. $\phi(\mathbf{M}_r^c)$, $\phi(\mathbf{M}_r^t)$, and y are three vectors describing each graphlet in color, texture, and semantic channels, respectively. For ease of expression, we again use $\mathbf{Y} = \{y_1, y_2, \cdots, y_n\}$ to represent the n graphlets in the perceptual space.

3.2 Biological Viewing Path Learning

Our proposed salient graphlets discovery is motivated by the transductive experimental design (TED) proposed by Yu *et al.* [18]. The key idea is to minimize the prediction variance of salient graphlets by a regularized linear regression function. In a geometrical view, it is equivalent to find

[2]The atomic regions are superpixels segmented using SLIC [46].

[3]Note that image/video-level labels are cheaply available nowadays. For example, many Flickr images and Youtube videos are associated with semantic tags. Also, image and video labels can be accurately predicted by an existing classification model, such as the spatial pyramid matching (SPM) [59].

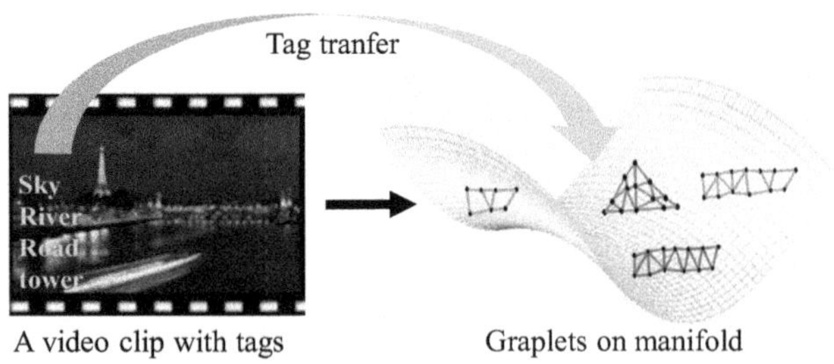

Figure 4: Projecting graphlets onto manifold by semantically encoding image/video-level labels

m salient (representative) graphlets $\mathbf{Z} = \{z_1, z_2, \cdots, z_m\} \in \mathbf{Y}$ in the perceptual space to maximally retain the information of $\mathbf{Y}$. This objective can be formulated as:

$$\min_{\mathbf{Z},\mathbf{A}} \sum\nolimits_{i=1}^{n} (||x_i - \mathbf{Z}a_i||_2^2 + \alpha||a_i||_2^2)$$
$$s.t.\ \ \mathbf{Z} = [z_1, z_2, \cdots, z_m] \in \mathbf{Y},$$
$$\mathbf{A} = [a_1, a_2, \cdots, a_n] \in \mathbb{R}^{m\times n}, \quad (6)$$

where α is a regularization parameter controlling the speed of shrinkage. To solve this problem, a sequential greedy strategy is proposed by Yu *et al.* [18].

3.2.1 Mathematical Formulation of GPAL

Obviously, TED reconstructs each graphlet via a linear combination of all the selected salient ones. Thus, it is reasonable to approximate a graphlet y_i by the linear combination of those salient graphlets, where the local and global geometric properties are preserved simultaneously as shown in Fig. 5. For any selected salient graphlet $z_j \in \mathbf{Z}$, we denote function $d(z_j, y_i)$ as the distance between z_j and y_i, where $d(\cdot,\cdot)$ can be any distance such as the geodesic distance. Intuitively, the smaller $d(z_j, y_i)$ is, the greater effect z_j will have for the reconstruction of y_i.

Motivated by this, we propose a new method called

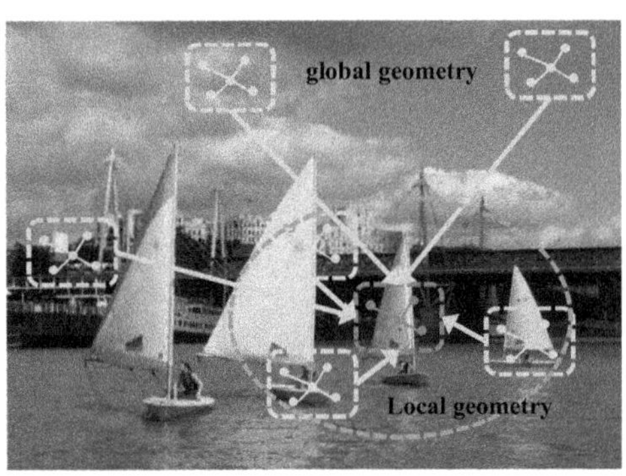

Figure 5: An illustration of the geometry-preserving mechanism in GPAL. The distance between a salient graphlet (red) and the rest non-salient ones (yellow) are well preserved in the salient graphlets discovery.

Geometr Preserving ctive Learning (GPAL) to select a few salient graphlets from an image/frame. For each graphlet y_i in an image/frame, we assume that the reconstruction is built upon the remaining graphlets. By penalizing the coefficients of the reconstruction, we formulate an objective function as:

$$\min_{\mathbf{Z},\mathbf{A}} \sum\nolimits_{i=1}^{n} (||y_i - \mathbf{Z}a_i||_2^2 + \mu||a_{ji}||d(z_j, y_i))$$
$$s.t.\ \ \mathbf{Z} = [z_1, \cdots, z_m] \in \mathbf{Y},$$
$$\mathbf{A} = [a_1, \cdots, a_n] \in \mathbb{R}^{m\times n}, \quad (7)$$

where a_{ji} is the j-th element of vector a_i and μ is a regularization parameter. In this objective function, the first term $||y_i - \mathbf{Z}a_i||_2^2$ means that y_i should be close to its approximation $\mathbf{Z}a_i$. The second term $\sum_{j=1}^{n} |a_{ji}|d(z_j, y_i)$ reflects that salient graphlets closer to y_i contribute more than those distant ones. This term encodes both the local and global geometric properties implicitly. The solution of the above algorithm is based on [9]'s theory.

The convergence can be guaranteed by the block-wise coordinate descent scheme. After obtaining the m salient graphlets, we link them into a biological viewing path (BVP). The first BVP vertex denotes the most salient graphlet, the second vertex represents the second most salient one, and so on.

3.3 Probabilistic Media Quality Measure

The learned BVPs capture the local and global geometric properties of an image/frame, at both the low-level and high-level. To effectively integrate them for measuring the quality of an image or a video clip, a probabilistic model is proposed.

As shown in Fig. 6, given a set of training images[4] $\{I^1, I^2, \cdots, I^L\}$ and a test media, they are highly correlated through their respective BVPs $\mathcal{P}$ and $\mathcal{P}^*$. The probabilistic model contains two types of nodes: observable nodes (green rectangles) and hidden nodes (blue rectangles). These two types of nodes form four layers. The first layer corresponds to all the training images with high quality; the second layer denotes all the BVPs learned from training media; the third layer represents all the BVPs learned from test media; and the last layer denotes the test media (I_*: an image, or $\{I_*^1, I_*^2, \cdots, I_*^F\}$: a video clip with F frames). The correlation between the first and the second layers is $p(\mathcal{P}|I^1, I^2, \cdots, I^L)$. The correlation between the second and the third layers is $p(\mathcal{P}_*|\mathcal{P})$. The correlation between the third and the fourth layers is $p(I_*|\mathcal{P}_*)$ (an image) or $p(I_*^1, I_*^2, \cdots, I_*^F|\mathcal{P}_*)$ (a video clip).

Intuitively, media quality can be quantified as the number of BVPs can be probabilistically transferred from the training media into the test one. Thus, the quality of a test video clip[5] can be formulated as a posterior probability as:

$$\gamma = p(I_*^1, I_*^1, \cdots, I_*^F|I_*^1, I_*^1, \cdots, I_*^L)$$
$$= p(I_*^1, I_*^1, \cdots, I_*^F|\mathcal{P}_*) \cdot p(\mathcal{P}_*|\mathcal{P}) \cdot p(\mathcal{P}|I^1, I^2, \cdots, I^L)$$
$$= p(\mathcal{P}_*|\mathcal{P}), \quad (8)$$

where the probability $p(\mathcal{P}_*|\mathcal{P})$ is calculated as:

$$p(\mathcal{P}_*|\mathcal{P}) = \prod\nolimits_{i=1}^{F} \prod\nolimits_{j=1}^{L} p(P_*^i|P^j)$$
$$= \prod\nolimits_{i=1}^{F} \prod\nolimits_{j=1}^{L} \prod\nolimits_{k=1}^{K} p(G_*^i(k)|G^j(k)), \quad (9)$$

where P_*^i and P^j denote the i-th and j-th BVP from the training and test media respectively; $G_*^i(k)$ and $G^i(k)$ are the k-th graphlet in BVP P_*^i and P^j respectively.

[4] A video clip can be treated as a sequence of frames.
[5] We simply set $F = 1$ for predicting the quality of an image.

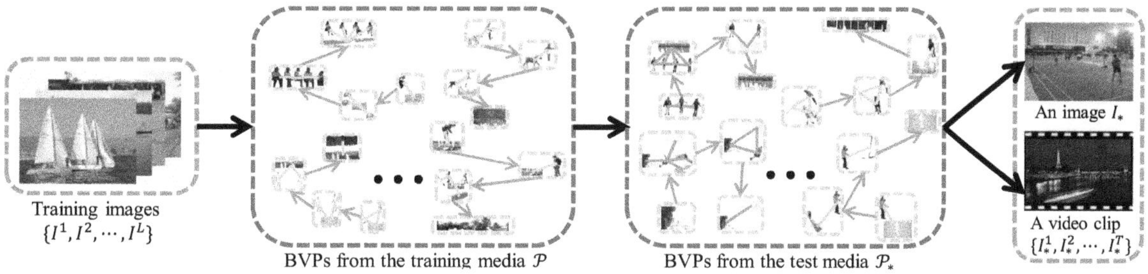

Figure 6: An illustration of the quality model by probabilistically transferring BVPs

Following many algorithms such as [20], we define the similarity between graphlets as a Gaussian kernel:

$$p(G|G') \propto \exp\left(-\frac{||y(G) - y(G')||^2}{2\sigma^2}\right), \qquad (10)$$

where $y(G)$ is the vector corresponding to graphlet G in the perceptual space, as elaborated in Sec 3.1.

4. EXPERIMENTS

This section evaluates the effectiveness of our biological inspired quality model based on four experiments. The first experiment compares our predicted BVP with the previous computational saliency models, as well as the real human gaze shifting paths. The second experiment compares our method with well-known quality models. The third part conducts user studies to evaluate our method. Finally, we analyze the influence of different parameters.

All the experiments were conducted on a PC equipped with an Intel X5482 CPU and 8GB RAM. The algorithms were implemented on the Matlab 2012 platform.

4.1 Effectiveness of the BVP

As the key component of our quality model, it is important to assert whether the learned BVPs can capture human visual saliency accurately. To the best of our knowledge, there are only a few public saliency data sets containing images with ground-truth human fixations. We experiment on the NUSEF [54] and the recent OSIE [1] data sets since they contain appropriate numbers of different semantic objects. The NUSEF consists of 758 images with 75 different objects, and the ground-truth human fixations are also provided. The OSIE is comprised of 700 images with eye-tracking data recorded from 15 viewers. The accompanied annotation data consists of 5,551 segmented objects with fine contours and 12 types of semantics. As the NUSEF and OSIE contain only hundreds of images, it is difficult to affirm our approach on them comprehensively. We thus collect 4,819 images from the PASCAL VOC series [55] and the Lotus Hill (LHI) data set [56]. For each image, we manually assign multiple semantic tags and collect the human fixation from five volunteers.

In our first experiment, we compare our learned BVP with ten well-known visual saliency models, including five low-level feature-based saliency models: Itti *et al.*'s saliency model [28], graph-based visual saliency by Harel *et al.* [26], image signature by Hou *et al.* [27], information-theory-based saliency model by Burce *et al.* [37], and hypercomplex fourier transform (HFT) saliency model by Li *et al.* [35]; as well as five high-level feature-based saliency models proposed by Judd *et al.* [33], Coferman *et al.* [25], Yang *et al.* [22], Yan *et al.* [23], and Zhang *et al.* [24] respectively. Toward a fair comparison, we have to convert our BVP into a saliency map. Specifically, we extract $m = 5$ salient graphlet. Then, we learn a Gaussian mixture model to describe the BVP distribution. Lastly, we calculate the probability of each graphlet $p(G_i)$, and then the saliency of the i-th pixel ρ is:

$$s(\rho_i) = \max_{G \supset \rho_i} p(G), \qquad (11)$$

where $G \supset \rho_i$ is the set of graphlets containing pixel ρ_i, and the "max" term mimicks the "winner-taken-all" mechanism in biological vision [16].

The AUC (area under the curve) scores of the NUSEF, the OSIE, and our own compiled data sets are presented in Table 2. Accordingly, the three ROC curves are shown in Fig. 7. To decide the threshold of saliency maps, for the training images, we use the Dice similarity coefficient to evaluate the overlap between the thresholded saliency map and the ground truth, wherein the peak value corresponds to the optimal threshold. Pixels whose saliency values falls below this threshold are deemed as non-salient, and vice versa. As shown in Table 2 and Fig. 7, the best performance is always achieved by our proposed BVP.

4.2 Comparison with the State-of-the-Art

4.2.1 Image Quality Evaluation

To the best of our knowledge, there exist three data sets for evaluating photo quality: the CUHK [6], the Photo.net [4], and the AVA [38]. A high-level description of the three data sets is as follows: 1) the CUHK [6] contains 12,000 photos collected from DPChallenge.com. We use a standard split of training/test sets on this data set; 2) the Photo.net consists of 3,581 images. Only URLs of the original photos are provided. Nearly half of the images have been removed from the websites, leaving only about 1,700 images available. They are randomly split into equal partitions, one for training and the rest for testing; and 3) the AVA [38] data set contains 25,000 highly- and low-aesthetic photos, each of which is associated with two semantic tags. The training and test photos of the AVA data set are pre-specified.

The first experiment compares our approach with five photo perceptual quality methods, including three global feature-based approaches by Dhar *et al.* [5], Luo *et al.* [8], and Marchesotti *et al.* [11], respectively; and two local patch integration-based methods by Cheng *et al.* [58] and Nishiyama *et al.* [15], respectively.

The source codes of the above five compared methods are not provided and some implementation details are ob-

Table 1: Comparative AUC Scores on the NUSEF, the OSIE, and our own compiled data set

Data set	Gofer. *et al*	Hou *et al*	GBVS	Judd *et al*	Yang *et al*	Itti *et al.*	Harrel *et al.*	Zhang *et al.*	Yan *et al.*	Li *et al.*	PM
NUSEF	57.64%	53.54%	50.37%	50.43%	53.19%	52.76%	52.11%	53.12%	54.22%	56.32%	**64.48%**
OSIE	67.65%	61.43%	58.89%	56.77%	53.37%	56.69%	54.42%	57.69%	55.64%	54.49%	**65.93%**
Ours	61.43%%	55.47%	56.32%	55.98%	54.12%	59.45%	56.64%	52.27%	57.76%	59.45%	**67.11%**

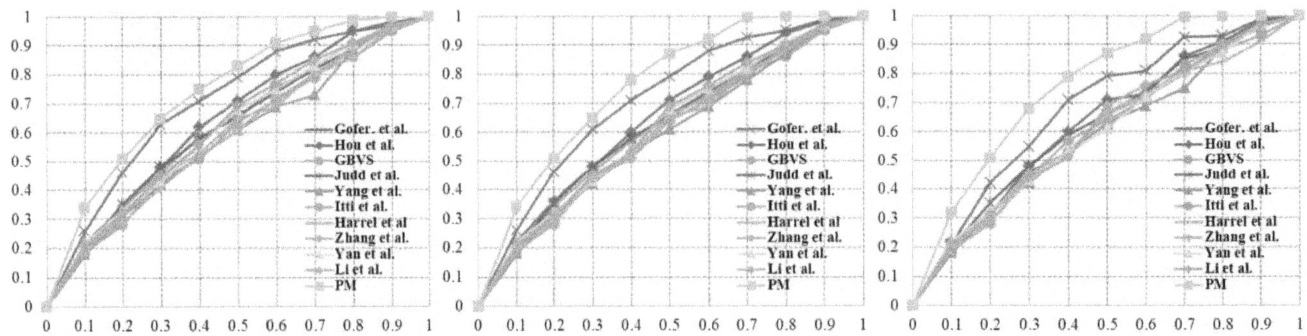

Figure 7: The ROC curves on the NUSEF (left), the OSIE (middle), and our own compiled data sets

Table 2: Comparison of aesthetics prediction accuracies

	CUHK	PNE	AVA
Dhar *et al.*	0.7386	0.6754	0.6435
Luo *et al.*	0.8004	0.7213	0.6879
Marchesotti *et al.* (FV-Color-SP)	0.8767	0.8114	0.7891
Cheng *et al.*	0.8432	0.7754	0.8121
Nishiyama *et al.*	0.7745	0.7341	0.7659
The proposed method	**0.9103**	**0.8595**	**0.8531**

scure. Therefore, it is difficult to strictly implement them. Our experiment adopts the following setups. For Dhar's approach, we use the public codes of Li *et al.* [12] to extract the attributes from each photo. These attributes are combined with the low-level features proposed by Yeh *et al.* [13] to train the quality classifier. For Luo *et al.*'s approach, not only the low-level and high-level features in their publication are implemented, but also the six global features from Getlter *et al.* [14]'s work are used to strengthen the quality prediction. For Marchesotti *et al.*'s approach, similar to the implementation of Luo *et al.*'s method, the six additional features are also employed. Cheng *et al.*'s approach is implemented by adopting only 2-sized graphlets for aesthetic quality measure. Noticeably, for the probabilistic model-based quality evaluation methods (*i.e.*, Cheng *et al.*'s method, Nishiyama *et al.*'s method, and our model), if the score is larger than 0.5, then an image is considered as a high quality one, and vice versa.

We present the aesthetics prediction accuracies on the CUHK, the PNE, and the AVA in Table 2. On the three data sets, our approach outperforms Marchesotti *et al.*'s method by nearly 4%, and exceeds the rest of the compared methods by over 6%, which demonstrates the advantage of our approach.

4.2.2 Video Quality Evaluation

The only publicly available benchmark for perceptual video quality evaluation is the Telefonica data set [30]. It contains 160 rated videos crawled from YouTube and is grouped into 16 categories. The categories include "baby laughing", "sky diving", and so on. Each video is cropped into a 15-seconds clip to reduce the potential biases of video length. The rating values of the Telefonica range from -2 to 2. If the quality score is above 0, then the video is deemed as high quality, and vice versa.

In the experiment, we compare our approach with three

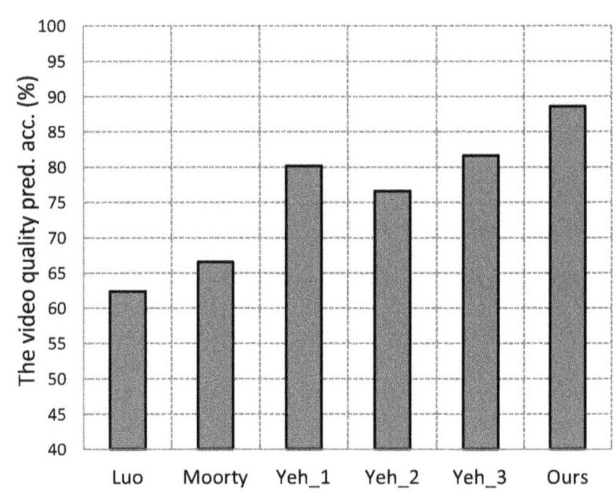

Figure 8: Performance comparison between our method and the other video quality models. Yeh_1, Yeh_2, and Yeh_3 denote the three best features selected in [32].

video quality models proposed by Luo *et al.* [29], Moorthy *et al.* [30], and Yeh *et al.* [32] respectively. We use half of the videos from Telefonica for training while leaving the rest for testing. The experiments were repeated five times and the average accuracies are presented in Fig. 8. Our approach achieves the best performance, which confirms the necessity of exploiting human gaze shifting paths in video quality prediction.

4.3 User Study

This experiment introduces subjective analysis. We apply different quality models for photo retargeting on the AVA data set [38], and then employ 30 volunteers to appraise the retargeted photos from different aspects. Specifically, as shown in Fig. 9, we learn the distribution of BVPs from the

	Lines/ edges	Faces/ people	texture	Fore. objects	Geometric structure	Symmetry	Aggregate
μ (with ref.)	0.103	0.191	0.193	0.154	0.123	0.212	0.111
μ (without ref.)	0.924	0.181	0.191	0.144	0.111	0.201	0.994

(a) Agreement of results from the paired comparison with/without a reference image

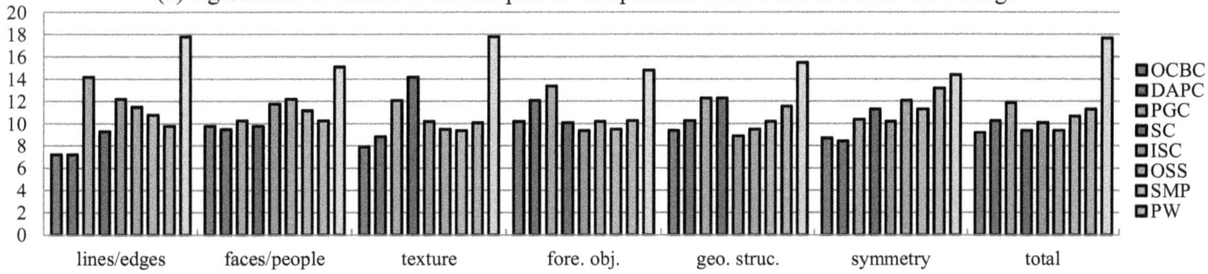

(b) The percentage of votes and total ranking of the nine compared method per attribute

Lines/edges:

PM PGC ISC SC OSS SMP PW OCBC DAPC

Faces/people:

PM OSS ISC SMP PGC SC PW OCBC DAPC

Texture:

PM SC PGC SMP ISC OSS PW OCBC DAPC

Foreground objects:

PM PGC DAPC SC OCBC PW OSS ISC SMP

Geometric structures:

PM PGC SC PW SMP DAPC OCBC OSS ISC

Symmetry:

PM PW OSS SC PGC SMP ISC OCBC DAPC

Aggregate:

PM PGC SMP PW ISC OCBC OSS SC DAPC

(c) Grouping of the compared retargeting model per attribute

Figure 10: A detailed subjective analysis of the comparative retargeted photos on the AVA data set

well-aesthetic training photos on the AVA [38], afterward the learned distribution guides the shrinking of 50 randomly selected photos. The baseline retargeting algorithms are from the survey article [36], including three cropping methods: omni-range context-based cropping (OCBC), probabilistic graphlet-based cropping (PGC), describable attribute for photo cropping (DAPC), and five content-aware retargeting algorithms: seam carving (SC) and its improved version (ISC), optimized scale-and sketch (OSS), saliency-based mesh parametrization (SMP), and the patch-based wrapping (PW).

The results in Fig. 10 are based on the subjective eval-

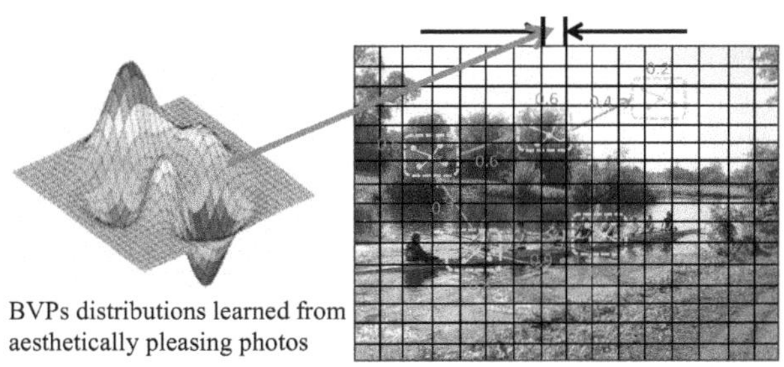

Figure 9: A illustration of photo retargeting based on the proposed BVP

uation of retargeting algorithms in [57]. First, we evaluate the degree of agreement when the volunteers vote for their favorite retargeted photos, where a high disagreement reflects the difficulty in decision making. In our experiment, we use the coefficient of agreement defined by Kendall and Babington-Smith [34]. The coefficients over all the four retargeted photos are shown in the last column of Fig. 10(a). Besides, we also collect the volunteers' votes on each attribute of the 50 sets of retargeted photos. As shown from the second column to the seventh column in Fig. 10(a), the volunteers are highly agreeable on the face/people, the texture, and the symmetry because these attributes are well preserved. Then, we present the votes on each attribute based on the four retargeted photos. As shown in Fig. 10(b), the proposed method consistently receives the most votes on all the attributes. Also, the probabilistic graphlet cropping proposed by Zhang *et al.* [31] performs competitively on several attributes. Based on the above votes, we rank all the compared retargeting algorithms as shown in Fig. 10(c), where the algorithms within a rectangle are statistically indistinguishable with respect to volunteer preferences. This again demonstrates the competitiveness of our model.

Next, we compare the proposed BVPs with real human gaze shifting paths quantitatively and qualitatively. We record the eye fixations from five observers by using EyeLink II[6], and then connect the fixations into a path sequentially. As can be seen from Fig. 11, in most images the proposed BVPs are consistent with human gaze shifting paths. Furthermore, the average proportion of overlap between the human gaze shifting path and the BVP is 90.89%. This shows that the proposed BVP can accurately predict the human gaze shifting process, leading to an excellent media quality prediction.

[6]http://www.sr-research.com/EL II.html

Figure 11: **Comparison between the learned BVPs (yellow paths) and real human gaze shifting paths recorded from five observers. The vertices in each BVP indicate the centroid of the BVP's constituent graphlets.**

4.4 Influence of Parameter Settings

The final experiment evaluates the influence of the three important parameters in our quality model: the graphlet number in a learned BVP m, and μ, λ in the GPAL optimization.

We first evaluate the quality prediction by varying m. As shown in Fig. 12, on all the four data sets, the quality prediction accuracy improves significantly when m increases from 1 to 4. Afterward, the accuracy fluctuates when m is tuned from 4 to 15. This is because humans typically fix on only $3 \sim 5$ objects when they view an image (free viewing without specific search tasks). Therefore, we set m to 4 in our model.

Then, we evaluate the performance under different values of μ, the regularization parameter. We tune the value of μ from $\{0.001,$
$0.005, 0.01, 0.05, 0.1, 0.2, 0.5\}$. As shown on the left of Fig. 13, on all the four data sets, the best accuracies were achieved when $\mu = 0.01$. Neither a too heavy nor a very slight penalty on the geometry preservation term yields a good quality prediction. Next, we evaluate the performance of our model by tuning the value of λ, a regularization parameter controlling the sparsity of $\hat{a}$. Similarly, we tune the value of λ from

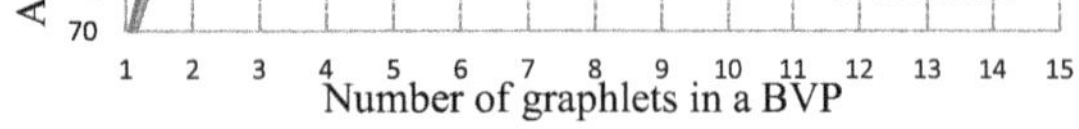

Figure 12: The quality prediction accuracies by tuning m on the four data sets

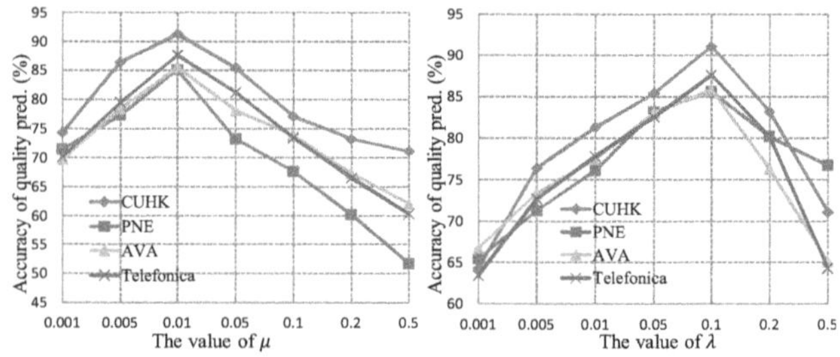

Figure 13: The quality prediction accuracies by tuning μ and λ respectively

$\{0.001, 0.005, 0.01, 0.05, 0.1, 0.2, 0.5\}$. As shown on the right of Fig. 13, the best accuracies were achieved when $\lambda = 0.1$ on all the four data sets.

5. CONCLUSIONS

This paper presents a perceptually aware quality model by mimicking how humans perceive low-level and high-level visual features from media. We first projected graphlets onto a pre-defined perceptual space. Then, an active learning algorithm GPAL is utilized to select graphlets both visually and semantically salient, and image/frame geometric attributes can be preserved optimally. Finally, these discovered graphlets are linked into a BVP, which is further integrated into a probabilistic model for predicting media quality. We also demonstrate that applications such as photo retargeting can be enhanced significantly by the learned BVPs.

6. ACKNOWLEDGMENTS

Thanks for the constructive comments of the three reviewers. Dr. Yingjie Xia is the correspondence author of this article.

7. REFERENCES

[1] Juan Xu, Ming Jiang, Shuo Wang, Mohan S. Kankanhalli, Qi Zhao, Predicting Human Gaze beyond Pixels, *Journal of Vision*, 14(1): 28, pages: 1–20 2014.

[2] Markus Stricker, Markus Orengo, Similarity of Color Images, *Storage and Retrieval of Image and Video Databases*, 1995.

[3] Navneet Dalal, Bill Triggs, Histograms of Oriented Gradients for Human Detection, *in Proc. of CVPR*, 2005.

[4] Ritendra Datta, Dhiraj Joshi, Jia Li, James Z. Wang, Studying Aesthetics in Photographic Images using a Computational Approach, *in Proceedings of ECCV*, pages: 288–301, 2006.

[5] Sagnik Dhar, Vicente Ordonez, Tamara L. Berg, High Level Describable Attributes for Predicting Aesthetics and Interestingness, *in Proceedings of CVPR*, pages: 1657–1664. 2011.

[6] Yan Ke, Xiaoou Tang, Feng Jing, The Design of High-level Features for Photo Quality Assessment, *in Proceedings of CVPR*, pages: 419–426, 2006.

[7] Luming Zhang, Yue Gao, Rongrong Ji, Qionghai Dai, Xuelong Li, Actively Learning Human Gaze Shifting Paths for Photo Cropping, *IEEE T-IP*, 21(5), pages: 2235–2245, 2014.

[8] Wei Luo, Xiaogang Wang, Xiaoou Tang, Content-based Photo Quality Assessment, *in Proceedings of ICCV*, pages: 2206–2213. 2011.

[9] Yao Hu, Debing Zhang, Zhongming Jin, Deng Cai, Xiaofei He, Active Learning Based on Local Representation, *IJCAI*, 2013.

[10] Masashi Nishiyama, Takahiro Okabe, Yoichi Sato, Imari Sato, Sensation-based Photo Cropping, *in Proceedings of ACM Multimedia*, pages: 669–672, 2009.

[11] Luca Marchesotti, Florent Perronnin, Diane Larlus, Gabriela Csurka, Assessing the Aesthetic Quality of Photographs using Generic Image Descriptors, *in Proceedings of ICCV*, pages: 1784–1791, 2011.

[12] Fei-Fei Li, Pietro Perona, A Bayesian Hierarchical Model for Learning Natural Scene Categories, *in Proceedings of CVPR*, pages: 524–531, 2005.

[13] Che-Hua Yeh, Yuan-Chen Ho, Brian A. Barsky, Ming Ouhyoung, Personalized Photograph Ranking and Selection System, *in Proceedings of ACM Multimedia*, pages: 211–220, 2010.

[14] Peter Gehler, Sebastian Nowozin, On Feature Combination for Multiclass Object Classification, *in Proceedings of ICCV*, pages: 221–228, 2009.

[15] Masashi Nishiyama, Takahiro Okabel, Imari Sato, Yoichi Sato, Aesthetic Quality Classification of Photographs based on Color Harmony, *in Proceedings of CVPR*, pages: 33–40, 2011.

[16] C. Koch, S. Ullman, Shifts in Selective Visual Attention: Towards the Underlying Neural Circuitry, *Human Neurobiology*, 4, pages: 219–227, 1985.

[17] Elias Daniel Guestrin, Moshe Eizenman, General Theory of Remote Gaze Estimation Using the Pupil Center and Corneal Reflections, *IEEE T-BE*, 53(6), pages: 1124–1133, 2006.

[18] Kai Yu, Jinbo Bi, Volker Tresp, Active Learning via Transductive Experimental Design, *in Proc. of ICML*, 2006.

[19] Yurii Nesterov, Gradient methods for minimizing composite objective function, *Technical Report*, 2007.

[20] Mingli Song, Dacheng Tao, Chun Chen, Jiajun Bu, Jiebo Luo, Chengqi Zhang, Probabilistic Exposure Fusion, *IEEE T-IP*, 21(1): 341–357, 2012.

[21] Honglak Lee, Alexis Battle, Rajat Raina, Andrew Y. Ng, Efficient Sparse Coding Algorithms, *in Proc. of NIPS*, 1996.

[22] Jimei Yang, Ming-Hsuan Yang, Top-down Visual Saliency via Joint CRF and Dictionary Learning, *in Proc. of CVPR*, pages: 2296–2303, 2012.

[23] Qiong Yan, Li Xu,Jianping Shi, Jiaya Jia, Hierarchical Saliency Detection, *in Proc. of CVPR*, pages: 1155–1162, 2013.

[24] Lingyun Zhang, Matthew H. Tong, Tim K. Marks, Honghao Shan, Garrison W. Cottrell, SUN: A Bayesian Framework for Saliency using Natural Statistics, *Journal of Vision*, 8(7), article 32, 2008.

[25] Stas Goferman, Lihi Zelnik-Manor, Ayellet Tal, Context-Aware Saliency Detection, *in Proc. of CVPR*, pages: 2376–2383, 2010.

[26] Jonathan Harel, Christof Koch, Pietro Perona, Graph-Based Visual Saliency, *in Proc. of NIPS*, pages: 545–552, 2007.

[27] Xiaodi Hou, Jonathan Harel, Christof Koch, Image Signature: Highlighting Sparse Salient Regions, *IEEE T-PAMI*, 34(1), pages: 194–201, 2011.

[28] Laurent Itti, Christof Koch, Ernst Niebur, A Model of Saliency-Based Visual Attention for Rapid Scene Analysis, *IEEE T-PAMI*, 20(11), pages: 1254–1259, 1998.

[29] Yiwen Luo, Xiaoou Tang, Photo and Video Quality Evaluation: Focusing on the Subject, *in Proc. of ECCV*, 2008.

[30] Anush K. Moorthy, Pere Obrador, Nuria Oliver, Towards Computational Models of the Visual Aesthetic Appeal of Consumer Videos, *in Proc. of ECCV*, 2010.

[31] Luming Zhang, Mingli Song, Qi Zhao, Xiao Liu, Jiajun Bu, Chun Chen, Probabilistic Graphlet Transfer for Photo Cropping, *IEEE T-IP*, 22(2), pages: 802–815, 2013.

[32] Hsin-Ho Yeh, Chun-Yu Yang, Ming-Sui Lee, Chu-Song Chen, Video Aesthetic Quality Assessment by Temporal Integration of Photo- and Motion-Based Features, *IEEE T-MM*, 15(8): 1944–1957, 2013.

[33] Tilke Judd, Krista A. Ehinger, Frédo Durand, Antonio Torralba, Learning to Predict Where Humans Look, *in Proc. of ICCV*, pages: 2106–2113, 2009.

[34] Michael Rubinstein, Ariel Shamir, Shai Avidan, Multi-operator Media Retargeting, *ACM TOG*, 28(3), 23, 2009.

[35] Jian Li, Martin D. Levine, Xiangjing An, Xin Xu, Hangen He, Visual Saliency Based on Scale-Space Analysis in the Frequency Domain, *IEEE T-PAMI*, 35(4), pages: 996–1010, 2013.

[36] Ariel Shamir, Olga Sorkine, Alexander Hornung, Modern Approaches for Media Retargeting, *SIGGRAPH Asia Courses*, 2012.

[37] Neil D. B. Bruce, John K. Tsotsos, Saliency, Attention, and Visual Search: An Information Theoretic Approach, *Journal of Vision*, 9(3), article 5, 2009.

[38] Naila Murray, Luca Marchesotti, Florent Perronnin, AVA: A Large-Scale Database for Aesthetic Visual Analysis, *in Proceedings of CVPR*, pages: 2408–2415, 2012.

[39] Jixu Chen, Qiang Ji, Probabilistic Gaze Estimation Without Active Personal Calibration, *in Proc. of CVPR*, 2011.

[40] Atsushi Nakazawa, Christian Nitschke, Point of Gaze Estimation through Corneal Surface Reflection in an Active Illumination Environment, *in Proc. of ECCV*, 2012.

[41] Han Liu, Mark Palatucci, Jian Zhang, Blockwise Coordinate Descent Procedures for the Multitask Lasso, with Applications to Neural Semantic Basis Discovery, *in Proc. of ICML*, 2009.

[42] Takahiro Ishikawa, Simon Baker, Iain Matthews, Takeo Kanade, Passive Driver Gaze Tracking with Active Appearance Models, *in Proc. of the 11th World Congress on Intelligent Transportation Systems*, 2004.

[43] Svetlana Lazebnik, Cordelia Schmid, Jean Ponce, Beyond Bags of Features: Spatial Pyramid Matching for Recognizing Natural Scene Categories, *in Proceedings of CVPR*, 2006.

[44] Jixu Chen, Qiang Ji, Probabilistic Gaze Estimation Without Active Personal Calibration, *in Proc. of CVPR*, 2011.

[45] Peng Zhao, Guilherme Rocha, Bin Yu, The Composite Absolute Penalties Family for Grouped and Hierarchical Variable Selection, *Annals of Statistics*, 37(6A): 3468–3497, 2009.

[46] Radhakrishna Achanta, Appu Shaji, Kevin Smith, Aurelien Lucchi, Pascal Fua, and Sabine SÍźsstrunk, SLIC Superpixels Compared to State-of-the-art Superpixel Methods, *IEEE T-PAMI*, 34(11): 2274–2282, 2012.

[47] Atsushi Nakazawa, Christian Nitschke, Point of Gaze Estimation through Corneal Surface Reflection in an Active Illumination Environment, *in Proc. of ECCV*, 2012.

[48] Rodolphe Jenatton, Julien Mairal, Guillaume Obozinski, Francis Bach, Proximal Methods for Hierarchical Sparse Coding, *in Proc. of ICML*, 2010.

[49] Erik Murphy-Chutorian, Mohan Manubhai Trivedi, Head Pose Estimation in Computer Vision: A Survey, *IEEE T-PAMI*, 31(4), pages: 607–626, 2009.

[50] Qin Cai, David Gallup, Cha Zhang, Zhengyou Zhang, 3D Deformable Face Tracking with a Commodity Depth Camera, *in Proc. of ECCV*, 2010.

[51] Feng Lu, Takahiro Okabe, Yusuke Sugano, Yoichi Sato, A Head Pose-free Approach for Appearance-based Gaze Estimation, *in Proc. of BMVC*, 2011.

[52] Kenneth Alberto Funes Mora, Jean-Marc Odobez, Gaze Estimation from Multimodal Kinect Data, *CVPR Workshop*, 2012.

[53] Kenneth Alberto Funes Mora, Jean-Marc Odobez, Person Independent 3d Gaze Estimation from Remote RGB-D Camera, *in Proc. of ICIP*, 2013.

[54] Subramanian Ramanathan, Harish Katti, Nicu Sebe, Mohan Kankanhalli, Tat-Seng Chua, An Eye Fixation Database for Saliency Detection in Images, *in Proc. of ECCV*, 2012.

[55] Mark Everingham, Luc Van Gool, Christopher K. I. Williams, John Winn, Andrew Zisserman, The PASCAL Visual Object Classes (VOC) Challenge, *IJCV*, 88(2), pages: 303–338, 2010.

[56] Benjamin Yao, Xiong Yang, Song-Chun Zhu, Introduction to a Large Scale General Purpose Ground Truth Dataset: Methodology, Annotation Tool, and Benchmarks, *EMMCVPR*, 2007.

[57] Michael Rubinstein, Diego Gutierrez, Olga Sorkine, Ariel Shamir, A Comparative Study of Image Retargeting, *ACM TOG*, 29(5),160, 2010.

[58] Bin Cheng, Bingbing Ni, Shuicheng Yan, Qi Tian, Learning to Photograph, *ACM Multimedia*, 2010.

[59] Jianchao Yang, Kai Yu, Yihong Gong, Thomas S. Huang, Linear Spatial Pyramid Matching using Sparse Coding for Image Classification, *in Proc. of CVPR*, 2009.

QoE Modelling for VP9 and H.265 Videos on Mobile Devices

Wei Song*, Yao Xiao*, Dian Tjondronegoro*, Antonio Liotta§
* Queensland University of Technology (QUT), Australia
§ Eindhoven University of Technology, The Netherland
{w1.song, dian}@qut.edu.au, pacifact@gmail.com, a.liotta@tue.nl

ABSTRACT

Current mobile devices and streaming video services support high definition (HD) video, increasing expectation for more contents. HD video streaming generally requires large bandwidth, exerting pressures on existing networks. New generation of video compression codecs, such as *VP9* and *H.265/HEVC*, are expected to be more effective for reducing bandwidth. Existing studies to measure the impact of its compression on users' perceived quality have not been focused on mobile devices. Here we propose new Quality of Experience (QoE) models that consider both subjective and objective assessments of mobile video quality. We introduce novel predictors, such as the correlations between video resolution and size of coding unit, and achieve a high goodness-of-fit to the collected subjective assessment data (adjusted R-square >83%). The performance analysis shows that H.265 can potentially achieve 44% to 59% bit rate saving compared to H.264/AVC, slightly better than VP9 at 33% to 53%, depending on video content and resolution.

Categories and Subject Descriptors

H.5.1 [Multimedia Information Services]: Evaluation/ methodology; **H.1.2 [User/Machine Systems]:** Human factor.

General Terms

Measurement, Performance, Human Factors and Verification.

Keywords

H.264/AVC, VP9, H.265/HEVC, video quality assessment, QoE modeling, mobile device.

1. INTRODUCTION

According to a recent report [1], global mobile video traffic has exceeded 55% of the total mobile data consumed in 2014. The majority of video contents are predicted to be mainly consumed on mobile devices such as tablets and smart phones on data network in the coming years [2]. This shift creates a sharp increase of demand for data bandwidth, pressuring the networks. To alleviate this problem, new video coding codecs are being developed, including VP9 by Google and H.265/HEVC (High Efficiency Video Coding) by the Joint Collaborative Team on Video Coding (JCT-VC) [3]. Accurate Quality of Experience (QoE) prediction models [4, 5] are crucial to estimate the potential benefits of using these new codecs to maintain or improve video quality on mobile devices, while using the same or less bandwidth compared to H.264/AVC.

The current research gaps are: 1) limited understanding on how much the new video codecs can increase the user's perceived quality on mobile settings; and 2) lack of QoE models for prediction of subjective quality based on objective measures. This paper aims to address both issues, which consequently will help to establish the potential benefits of VP9 and H.265 video codecs and inform future studies that use these codecs to achieve a scalable and user-centric HD video streaming [6-8]

We used subjective quality assessment method *Absolute Category Rating* (*ACR*), and objective quality assessments *SSIM* and *PSNR*, to benchmark H264, H.265 and VP9. We introduced novel predictors that define the characteristics of the video encoders, in addition to the existing video contents and encoding settings. These predictors were tested and selected to form two types of models using Linear Regression. One model uses objective quality measures as predictors, while the other does not. Both can explain over 83% of the total variation in subjective ACR scores. Our key contributions are:

- In-depth analysis on the subjective and objective assessment of VP9 and H.265 video quality on mobile devices, extending findings from existing studies, including the potential bitrate saving.
- Novel QoE models to predict users' perceived quality on mobile devices, across VP9, H.265 and H.264 codecs, as well as introduce some uniquely identified predictors.

2. RELATED WORK

The literature suggests that both H.265/HEVC [3] and VP9 video codecs are capable of saving approximately half of the required bandwidth while maintaining the same level of quality on conventional viewing devices such as TV, compared to the previous generation H.264/AVC [9] [10, 11]. However, the applicability of these findings on mobile devices is limited. For new codecs such as VP9, subjective quality assessment (sVQA) studies have been done mainly on conventional devices [12]. This limitation is due to the technical challenges of H.265 and VP9 videos playback on mobile devices because of the coding complexity. VP9 is a recent codec by Google and has only been adopted by few studies. Objective studies on VP9 bitrate saving performance [11, 13] have obtained inconsistent results, some of which are lower than the over 50% saving indicated in [11]. VP9 encoder was even shown to be inferior to the H.264 encoder with an average bitrate overhead of 8.4% at the same objective quality [13]. However, a subjective study [12] shows that VP9 performs

MM '15, October 26-30, 2015, Brisbane, Australia
© 2015 ACM. ISBN 978-1-4503-3459-4/15/10…$15.00
DOI: http://dx.doi.org/10.1145/2733373.2806256

the best for synthetic video content. Hence, further research is necessary to evaluate and verify the performance of VP9. QoE modelling for VP9 videos has not been done.

Compared to VP9, H.265 has attracted more attention and its performance has been investigated by both sVQA and oVQA assessments [12, 14, 15]. Current studies have established that H.265 can achieve high compression efficiency for Ultra High Definition (UHD) videos. However, only few studies have focused on mobile devices. One study [16] evaluated H.265 performance on a 4.5 inch mobile phone with video encoded at 360p and 200-400Kbps and suggested that H.265 has similar user experience to H.264 in low bandwidth settings. Yet this study cannot represent the current settings, as most of the new mobile devices can support much larger display resolution (e.g. 1920×1080pixels) and stream at higher rates (e.g., 4G, WiFi). Recent studies have modeled QoE for H.265 video content [17, 18] but not for mobile videos.

For objective video quality assessment (oVQA), the commonly used metrics are: peak signal-to-noise ratio (PSNR); Structural Similarity Index (SSIM); Multi-Scale SSIM index (MS-SSIM) Video Quality Matrix (VQM); and Motion-based Video Integrity Evaluation index (MOVIE). As PSNR only measures the signal distortions, many studies have found it to be significantly worse than all the other oVQA metrics for predicting subjective video quality. However, PSNR can still be a reliable metric if the impacts of video content and codec type are properly considered [19, 20]. SSIM can attain better prediction outcome because it makes use of the characteristic of human visual system (HVS), which is extremely sensitive to structural information of pictures, [21]. PSNR and SSIM are widely used for benchmark in various video quality studies. Using oVQA models on H.265 video quality assessment, study [14] found that all the existing models have underestimated the coding gain of H.265 compared to the increased scores from sVQA. This raises the need for future refinement of oVQA models.

For sVQA, the commonly used methods are set by ITU (International Telecommunication Union) [22, 23]. Single Stimulus Continuous Quality Evaluation (SSCQE) and Absolution Category Rating (ACR) ask viewers to rate one impaired video stream. Double stimulus continuous quality scale (DSCQS) and double stimulus comparison scale (DSCS) ask viewers to rate the quality or change in quality between two video streams (reference and impaired). Compared to DSCQS and DSCS, the results generated from ACR and SSCQE do not require the presence of reference video and are less resource and time consuming to carry out, but they are likely to be less accurate due to memory effect in test videos ordering. This drawback can be reduced by randomizing the video orders [24]. For mobile video assessment, double stimulus methods are not feasible for small-form factor display devices due to the lack of means to synchronize the screens from two mobile devices.

QoE models, as objective measurement of subjective video quality, are usually built upon the relationship of sVQA scores with some influencing factors/aspects, which are often considered as predictors. Generally, the predictors can be grouped into: Video signal distortion [21]; Encoding related parameters, such as spatial resolution, frame rate, bitrate and Quantization Parameter (QP) [18, 20]; Video content information, such as content type, and content characteristics of spatial and temporal complexity [18, 22]; Network parameters, such as packet loss rate, delay jitter and error rate [17, 25]; User interface information, such as screen resolution of mobile device or display resolution [20, 26]; and Codec information, such as codec type [26].

The abovementioned oVQA metrics (e.g., PSNR, SSIM, VQM, etc.) have been used in QoE models by many studies. These measurements are based on quality distortions of the received video relative to the original video, and how it can affect human visual system. However, these models do not incorporate knowledge about the video processing and delivery system, thereby more suitable for codec comparison and optimization [27]. Our study adopted the simplest models - PSNR and SSIM for comparing the performance of codecs, VP9, H.265 and H.264, and take further steps to improve their prediction accuracy.

Existing QoE models for H.265/HEVC videos have not leveraged much of other relevant information. For example, content-based video quality prediction (CVQP) model can be based on QP and content feature defined by motion and picture complexity index, which are extracted from the H.265 bit stream while encoding [18]. A further example is spatial-temporal characteristics of video content by using the weighted averages of coding unit quad-tree depth and prediction mode sequences [25]. Despite the benefits of incorporating these important factors of video content, the resulting models become codec dependent. A more generic method for defining video content characteristics is to calculate Temporal Information (TI) and Spatial Information (SI), which is recommended in ITU-T Rec. P.910 [22]. This method may not be profoundly accurate, but it is the most robust as it only associates with the original input video. Another study analyzed QoE for streamed H.265 videos from the impact of encoding bitrate, video content and transmission packet loss on subjective opinion [17]. It found that the combination of content type and packet loss has a significant impact on QoE. However, it has not provided a measurement of this impact.

Based on the literature, it is clear that many potential predictors still need to be verified for modeling the QoE of new generation codecs H.265 and VP9. In particular, in this paper we would identify the parameters to indicate codec types, and explore the potential correlations between video spatial resolution and codec-related information, which have not been discovered.

3. EXPERIMENT DESIGN

The study aims to construct a video quality prediction model for videos encoded by the latest codecs on mobile devices, using the data gathered from both subjective and objective video quality assessment methods. Figure 1 illustrates the study workflow.

Firstly, a set of master video sequences is selected from the IRCCyN 1080i HD video database [28] and prepared as reference sequences by scaling and de-interlacing. Secondly, compressing reference sequences into 5 different bitrates using 3 video encoders produce the distorted video sequences. Thirdly, commonly used sVQA method (ACR) and oVQA methods (PSNR and SSIM), are adopted to collect the video quality data, which subsequently is used to analyze the performance of the three codecs (H.265, VP9 and H.264). Finally, QoE models are constructed based on linear regression analysis, with the average ACR scores as the dependent variable and some encoding parameters and oVQA scores as the independent variables, i.e. the predictors. It should be noted that due to technical constraints (no available video player can directly playback H.265 smoothly), sVQA only assess H.264/AVC and VP9 encoders, while all three encoders will be assessed by oVQA. The subjective quality of H.265 are estimated based on the correlations between H.264, VP9 and H.265 in terms of objective quality and the correlations between H.264 and VP9 in terms of subjective quality. In our proposed QoE models, pixel format, frame rate and scanning mode are standardized, therefore will not be tested as predictors.

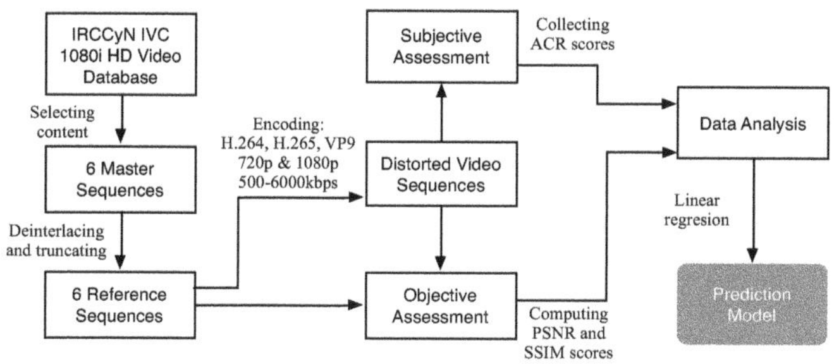

Figure 1. Overview of Video Quality Assessment Study Design

3.1 Video Source

We selected 6 videos as the master sequences to produce reference and distorted sequences. The selection was meant to cater the different scenes simulating real-life situations, which are described in Table 1. Table 1 also gives the average content complexity SI and TI value [22]. Refer to http://ivc.univ-nantes.fr/en/databases/1080i_Videos/ for more details about these video sources.

Table 1. Details of Selected Video Sequences

Seq	Source name	Description	Content Feature (SI&TI)
1	InsideMarathon	Large crowd runners moving from right to left without camera panning	Multiple fast moving objects with high spatial details in the still background (50,34)
2	Captain	Close-up of a captain looking through a monocular under heavy downpour	Close-up portrait with slow and minor zoom-in; low contrast (39,13)
3	Concert	A singer walking across the stage in spotlight with band members behind him.	Random panning and zooming; lowlight condition (43,16)
4	GroupDisorder	People running in different directions combined with camera movement	Fast random motion and panning camera (57,28)
5	Foot	Making a goal in a football match	Fast moving objects with wide angle camera panning and zooming (68,26)
6	DanceInTheWoods	People dancing on a trail in a forest	Random moving objects with camera zoom in; high contrast (57,18)

Master sequence 1 consists of extreme details and fast moving objects that will test the inter-frame compression capability of video encoders. Master sequence 2 contains close-up portrait, commonly seen in television drama series, talk shows, news broadcast and movies where protagonists' facial expressions are important. Master video sequence 3 was selected to demonstrate the recordings created under poorly and unprofessionally lit circumstances, such as candid shot, live music concert, and home videos created in uncontrolled environment. Such scene often contains dark background and gradient which will test the capability of encoders of dividing MBs. Master video sequence 5 was chosen as users often watch fast-paced sports games such as soccer, rugby and basketball where cameras are constantly panning with fast-moving players. Master video sequence 4 and 6 were selected to simulate video contents of high color contrast. Such contents are often seen in movies as they have been processed extensively by postproduction techniques such as colour correction to create the mood and atmosphere directors want to convey to audience. Despite such video contents are highly distorted due to editing and post-production, they are likely to be appealing to the eyes of audiences.

3.2 Reference and Distorted Video Sequences

Most online video contents are progressive scanned 4:2:0, therefore we de-interlaced and sub-sampled the 6 master sequences from YUV4:2:2 50i 1080p to YUV4:2:0 25p 1080p format by using FFmpeg [29] to generate the reference sequences. YUV4:2:0 sampling rate was adopted because existing literature suggests HVS is not as sensitive to pick color information as to pick up textual information [9], therefore, it is unlikely that end-users will be able to tell the difference in video quality between YUV4:2:0 and YUV4:2:2 sequences. Moreover, all online video content distributors, such *YouTube* and *DailyMotion,* currently deliver their videos in YUV4:2:0 sampling rate. YUV4:2:2 sampled sequences are neither easily available to end-users, nor sufficiently compact to be transmitted online.

The master sequences were de-interlaced in this study due to the decreasing number of video contents being delivered in interlaced scanning format to end-users, as modern flat panel displays on devices of all sizes are capable of displaying progressive scanning videos natively. Moreover, the latest generation of video encoders, such as the VP9 and H.265/HEVC have abandoned the support of field coding, as interlaced scanning is considered to be obsolete and no longer used for display devices and content distribution [3].

The 6 master sequences have at least ten seconds of duration. For standardization, we truncated them to be 10 seconds or 250 frames each to produce our reference sequences. The 6 reference sequences are then compressed into distorted sequences using the combinations of the following encoding settings:

- Bitrate (BR): 500kbps, 1Mbps, 2Mbps, 4Mbps, 6Mbps
- Resolution (RS): 720p and 1080p
- Coding Format (CF): H.264, H.265 and VP9

At the end, 180 distorted sequences in total were generated ($5BR \times 2RS \times 3CF \times 6Sequences = 180\ combinations$).

While all three encoders used in this study are capable of sub-sampling, FFmpeg was used to pre-subsample (/down-scale) the reference sequences to 720p resolution before encoding, in order to prevent inconsistency that might be caused by potential difference of the resizing arithmetic in different video encoders. After the distorted or compressed video sequences are decoded by their respective video decoders, the distorted raw YUV file in 720p resolution will then be up-scaled by using FFmpeg for the purpose of comparison with the reference sequences in oVQA.

We adopted Variable Bitrate (VBR) setting as bitrate control mode for encoding as most of the online videos are encoded in VBR mode. Unlike Constant Bitrate (CBR), which uses same amount of data (bits) to interpret every frame of a given video regardless of the frame complexity, VBR is able to adjust the amount of data allocated to represent each frame based on the level of image complexity. Consequently, a video content encoded with VBR setting is likely to be superior to those encoded by CBR if the sizes of the video files are kept the same. Allowing bitrates to vary significantly in a given sequence will affect the overall size of the encoded video; therefore, we allowed only marginal fluctuation of bitrates and make sure the final file sizes of distorted sequences are corresponding to their bitrates. For instance, a 10-seconds long distorted sequence produced from its reference sequence with a bitrate setting of 500kbps (kilobit per second) is expected to have a file size of 610.3kB (kilobyte) approximately. We allowed a tolerance of ±5% on the expected final size of distorted video sequences.

3.3 Encoder Settings

Three video encoders x264 0.120, VP9 v1.2.0, HM14 were used to generate three coding formats H.264/AVC, VP9 and H.265/HEVC respectively. These encoders were the latest at the time of this study. The default encoder settings are different; therefore, we made adjustments to the encoding parameters to ensure a fair comparison as much as possible. The summarized configuration options are described in Table 2.

Table 2. Encoder configurations

Coding Format	H.264/AVC	VP9	H.265/HEVC
Encoder Version	FFmpeg 0.9.4 with x264 0.120	VP9 v1.2.0	HM14
Encoding value	Very slow	Max	–
Pass	1	1	1
Maximum coding block Size (pixels)	16 × 16	64 × 64	64 × 64
Bitrate Control Mode	VBR (defined target bitrate)	VBR (defined target bitrate)	VBR (defined target bitrate)
GOP Length (Intra Period)	320	320	320
GOP Size	Auto	Auto	8
Internal Bit Depth	8	8	8

The Group of Pictures (GOP) size of H.265 encoder is set to the default value of 8 as it is a compulsory option to be turned on. Since the number of inter frames encoded are impossible to be kept constant for all three encoders due to their design differences, we only specified the maximum intra-frame distance for all three encoders. Intra-frame is usually introduced at a scene change or a start of video sequence. As each of our video sequences contains only one scene, only one I-frame is encoded in each of the distorted sequence. VP9 encoder includes a golden-frame, which functions the same as intra-frame, but is not displayed by the decoder and cannot be toggled off in the encoder settings.

3.4 sVQA Protocol

3.4.1 Test Environment

Video sequences were presented on a Microsoft Surface Pro 1st Generation which comes with 10.6-inch screen of native resolution 1920 × 1080 pixels, Intel i5 CPU, 4GB memory, 64GB Solid-State Drive, and the up-to-date Windows 8.1 Pro OS. The only third party software installed onto the device were *Google Chrome* for running our web-based sVQA application and *Combined Community Codec Pack* (CCCP) for detecting playback statistics. The web-based sVQA application and the test video sequences were copied into the solid-state hard drive for smooth playback. The device is selected for its capability of decoding both VP9 and H.264/AVC sequences smoothly without skipping frames and visual latency. A wireless mouse was used for a fuss-free operation and familiarity, despite the availability of touch screen as user input interface. The mobile device was disconnected from the Internet during the assessment sessions.

3.4.2 Participants

The sVQA study was conducted at a controlled lab environment as recommended by ITU-T Rec P.910 [22]. All the participants were asked to sit in an enclosed space where there was no source of distraction or strong window light, but florescence. The viewing distance was about 80cm and the viewing angle was about 30 degree. During assessment, the participant was left alone to complete his/her tasks while we kept a distance for observation without disruption, to minimize the unwanted effects of being supervised, such as tense and indecisive assessment [30].

The criteria for participants are:

- Adult, 18-50 age range
- No experience with video quality assessment study
- No visual impairment or illness associated with visual capabilities, e.g. colour blindness, severe myopic, etc.

We have recruited a total of 30 participants aged between 20-35 from university students and staff. The number of participants meets the common requirement for sVQA, prescribed by Video Quality Experts Group [28, 31] and ITU-R Rec. BT 500-13 [23]. To confirm that all our recruited participants do not have visual-associated illness or impairment, we asked them to describe the colors of the objects shown in the training videos and to make simple quality comparison during a demo session. Participants who are unable to fulfill these tasks would be deemed as unsuitable to sit for our study, and are therefore removed from the study. No invalid participation was found in our study.

Each sVQA session was separated into two parts: training and the actual evaluation. To get the participants familiar with the operation of our sVQA application and hardware, our facilitator explained in details about how our application and hardware function to each of the participants before they got started with 2 sets of training sequences during demo sessions. The participants were allowed to try the demo session as many times as they desired until they were confident with the application interface and sVQA operations. After the demo session, participants could start the actual sVOA session at anytime. Participants were informed that they were allowed to terminate the session anytime they intended should they felt uncomfortable or tired. Their scores, under such circumstances, would not be recorded.

3.4.3 Voting method

We adopted ACR method [22] to gather sVQA scores, which uses a 9-point scale (1-bad to 9-excellent) to give a more precise rating than 5-point scale. No hidden reference video sequence was shown to the participants during the sVQA sessions. In each sVQA session, a participant viewed one distorted sequence at a time and rated the video quality using a 9-point slider after viewing each sequence. A limited voting time of 10 seconds was applied. No score was recorded if the subject failed to make decision during the given time. Participants in this study have gone through a short training (demo) session to minimize the chance of failing to vote.

The sVQA study only assessed video sequences encoded by H.264 and VP9 encoders without reference video presented. In total, 120 distorted sequences were used. To alleviate participants' fatigues, we divided the 120 sequences into six groups to be watched in six sessions, and a short 5-10 minutes break was allowed between the sessions. Each session corresponds to one master sequence and has 20 distorted sequences arranged in a random manner regardless of their bitrate, resolution and encoder. The presentation order of distorted sequences is identical to all participants in each session. Although the viewing order of the six sessions was not restricted, it was observed that most participants viewed the sessions in the order from 1 to 6.

We have designed an HTML5 web-based application for this study. The application can playback both VP9 and H.264 sequences through Google Chrome browser in full screen [32] and store the ACR scores given by participants into CSV files. The first view of the web application is a list of the six testing sessions and the demo session with hyperlinks. Clicking on each hyperlink will start to play the corresponding videos one after another. A rating screen is displayed immediately after each video sequence is finished. This screen includes: a sliding-bar labeled as 9-excellent, 7-good, 5-fair, 3-poor, and 1-bad to allow the participant voting; a 'Next' button beneath the sliding bar to confirm the vote; a 'countdown timer' on the top right-hand corner to prompt the participants the remaining time.

3.5 oVQA Computing and Analysis Tools

We used Video Quality Measurement Tool (VQMT) from the Multimedia Signal Processing Group (MMSPG) [33] to generate the oVQA scores. The tool generates both frame-by-frame and average PSNR or SSIM scores. In this study, each of the 180 distorted sequences was firstly decoded into YUV format and up-scaled to the same resolution 1080p by FFMpeg, and then paired up with its corresponding reference sequence to generate average PSNR and SSIM scores. These oVQA scores were stored into CSV files for statistical analysis.

To compare coding efficiency of different codecs or different coding settings, Bjøntegaard model [34] is adopted to calculate average bit rate difference in percentage (BD-BR) or average PSNR different in dB between two rate distortion (RD) curves. We also computed the average MOS (instead of PSNR) and bit rate differences between two sets of subjective values pertinent to two codecs, based on the Subjective Comparison of ENcoders based on fItted Curves (SCENIC) model [35].

IBM SSPS Version 22 and R were used to tabulate and analyze the retrieved subjective and objective scores. The analysis includes: 1) Identification of sVQA data outliers that affect the consistency of the dataset; 2) Comparison between sVQA and oVQA scores; and 3) Discovery of potential predictors and test regression results for prediction models.

4. RESULTS

4.1 sVQA Analysis Results

A total of 3597 ACR scores were recorded with 3 fail-to-vote records (120 test sequences × 30 participants – 3 fails = 3597). Outliers were identified through Boxplot for each combination of video content, bitrate, resolution and codec. As a result, 148 entries out of 3597 were flagged out as outliers hence removed from our ACR score list.

Figure 2 depicts the average ACR scores of distorted sequences across the 6 video contents at two resolutions, 720p and 1080p. The results show that VP9 encoder performs significantly better than the H.264/AVC encoder across all 5 bitrates. Both encoders demonstrated similar performance patterns when bitrate increases. The correlation between bitrate and ACR scores is logarithmic. The wide error bars shown in Figure 2 are caused by the difference of mean scores for 6 different video contents, which can be further explained by Figure 3. Table 3 lists the percentages of the average ACR score differences throughout all five bitrates by comparing VP9 to H.264/AVC encoders. The *t-test* results show the significance of ACR score differences.

Based on Figure 2 and the *t*-test results shown in Table 3, the VP9 encoder is statistically significantly superior to the H.264/AVC encoder based on subjective quality (p<0.025, except bitrate at 4000kbps). The mean ACR score received by the VP9 encoder is 80% higher than that of generated by the H.264/AVC encoder under 500kbps bitrate. However, the advantage of VP9 encoder diminishes gradually as the bitrate increases. Under the highest bitrate of 6000kbps, the VP9 encoder only received 6.8% higher ACR score on average than the H.264/AVC encoder.

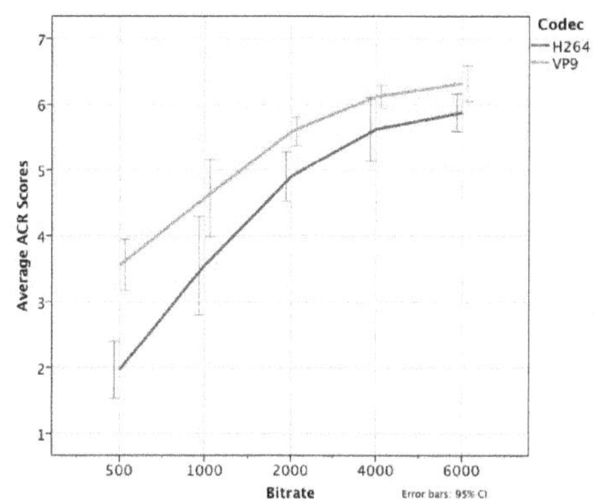

Figure 2. Average ACR scores of videos

Table 3. sVQA comparison between VP9 and H.264/AVC

Bitrate (kbps)	Mean Diff (%)	*t*-Test
500	+80	$t(11)=7.509, p<0.001$
1000	+27.8	$t(11)=3.248, p=0.008$
2000	+14.3	$t(11)=5.151, p<0.001$
4000	+8.9	$t(11)=1.909, p=0.083$
6000	+6.8	$t(11)=2.890, p=0.015$
Average	+19.1	

To analyze the impact of content and resolution on the subjective video quality, two separate diagrams are used for the six video contents and the two resolutions in Figure 3. Based on this figure, steep slopes are shown for content 1, 4 and 6, and relatively flat curves for content 2, 3 and 5. Based on the content description in Table 1, we conclude that higher bitrate contributing to better perceived quality is more for the videos with fast and large moving objects than for the videos with slow motion or small objects.

From the perspective of bit rate saving, the codec's performance (i.e. in terms of its subjective quality) is compared using the *SCENIC* model. Results in Table 4 show that the average bit rate reduction of VP9 relative to H.264 is 25.96% at 720p and 55.95% at 1080p, respectively. Moreover, H.264/AVC encoder appears to perform much better at 720p resolution than at 1080p resolution, gaining 62.65% of bit rate saving. VP9 encoder's performance is relatively consistent under the two resolutions and gains about 9.33% of more bit rate saving at 1080p than 720p. Their resolution related performance can be observed from Figure 4(a) and (b).

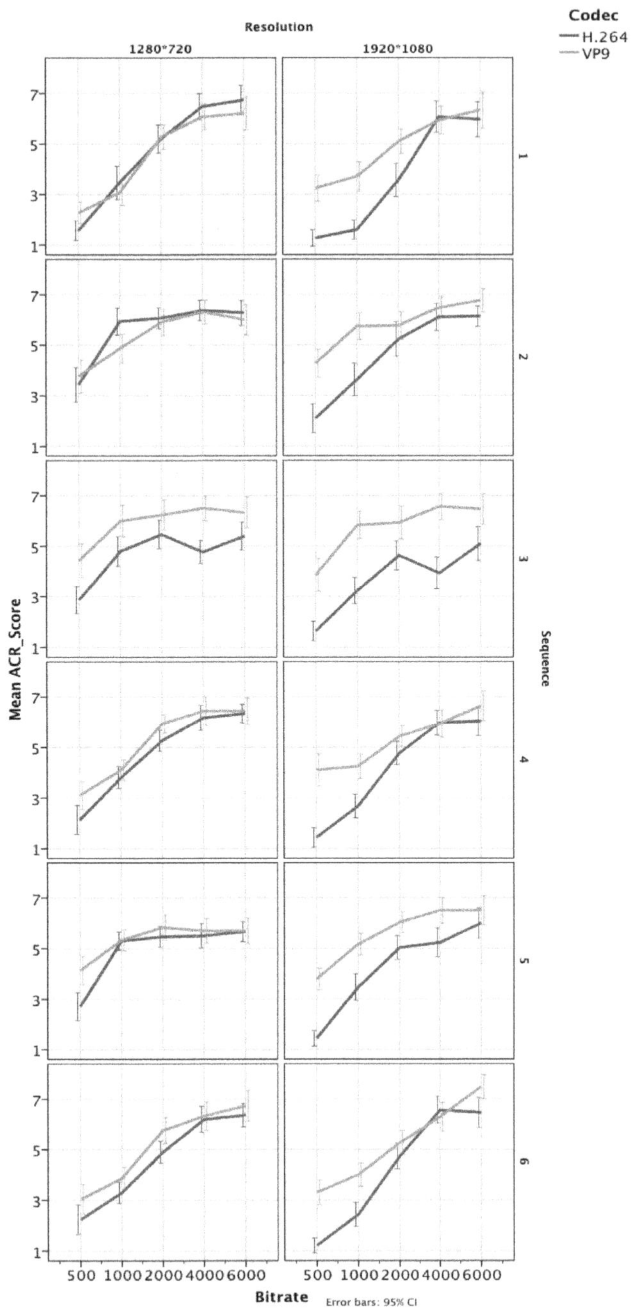

Figure 3. Average ACR scores for 6 contents and 2 resolutions

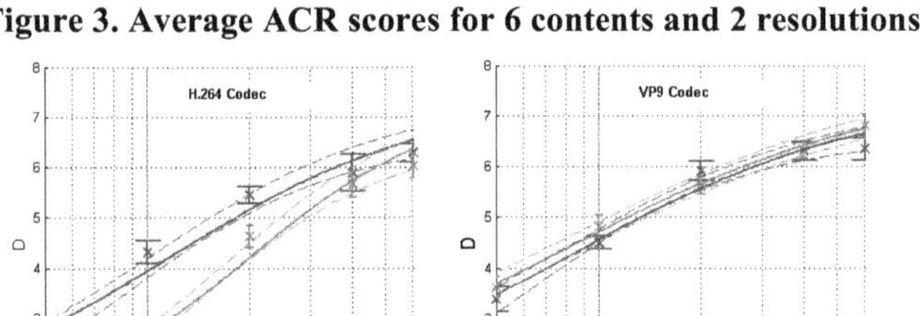

Figure 4. R-D curves of average subjective difference between two resolutions for (a) H.264/AVC and (b) VP9 codec

Table 4. Summary of bit rate saving with subjective comparisons between codecs and between resolutions

BD-MOS	H.264 vs. VP9		720p vs. 1080p	
	720p	1080p	H.264	VP9
Average	-25.96%	-55.95%	62.65%	-9.33%

4.2 oVQA Analysis Results

The PSNR and SSIM scores obtained are highly consistent and showing similar patterns, based on comparing Figure 5(a) with Figure 5(b). It can also be observed that: (1) The VP9 and H.265 have similar curves of oVQA vs bitrate for both 720p and 1080p resolutions, although the H.265 is overall marginally better than the VP9. (2) For both VP9 and H.265, the PSNR and SSIM scores under different resolutions are roughly equal (e.g., at 2000kbps, PSNR≈34.5dB, SSIM≈0.85). (3) The H.264 encoder performed poorly compared to the VP9 and H.265 encoders, especially at a relatively lower bitrate (e.g., 500kbps) and higher resolution. (4) The H.264 encoder at 720p performed significantly inferior to itself at 1080p. The observations of (2)-(4) are consistent with the sVQA results.

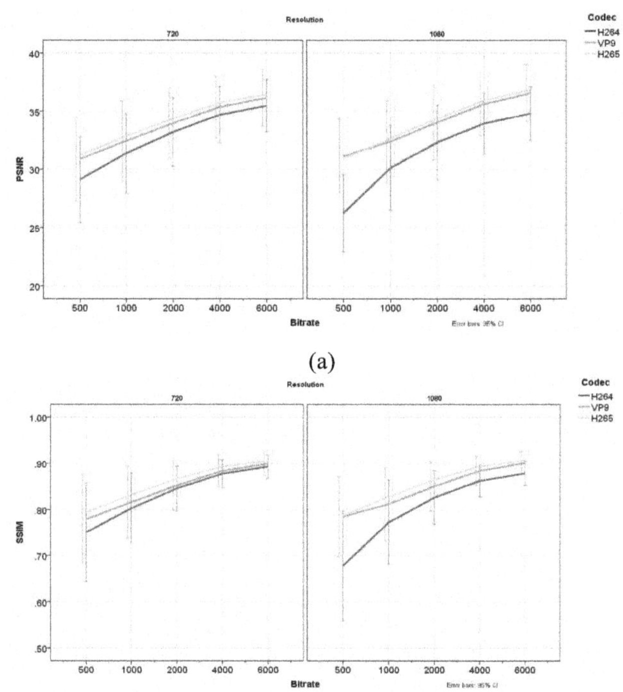

(a)

(b)

Figure 5. Averaged (a) PSNR and (b) SSIM for 6 contents

Further considering the observation (4), it is probably due to the fact that the H.264/AVC standard was designed in the early 2000s, before HD video contents became popular. It did not consider the spatial resolution in relation with the size of the supported MB and the data overhead caused by the number of MBs. The 16×16pixels MBs specified in the H.264/AVC standard will consume a big amount of MB overhead for a video with a large resolution; as a result, at a given encoding bitrate, more bits will be allocated in describing the MBs instead of storing actual frame information. For example, H.264 will generate a total number of 3600 (80 × 46 = 3600) MBs for a frame of 720p resolution, but 8160 (120 × 68 = 8160) MBs for the same video frame of 1080p, which is approximately 2.27 times of that of 720p. When the encoder allocates more binary bits to the overhead of MBs, it has to lower the amount of bits for the actual video information. Therefore, H.264/AVC encoder performed significantly worse at 1080p than 720p. Additionally, the negative effect caused by the MB overhead is more obvious under lower bitrate. On the other hand, to encode the video frame of 1080p, H.265 and VP9 will need only 510 (30×17=510) CUs/Superblock (64×64 pixels per block). This equates to approximately 15 times less bits for the overhead of a H.265/VP9 video stream than that of a H.264 video stream.

The PSNR and SSIM values are video content dependent, thus a wide error bars shown in Figure 5. Their trends of content dependency conform to those of ACR scores, that is, the PSNR or SIM value range becomes narrower with the lesser amount of motion and details in the videos. For example, The contents 1, 4 and 6 with a PSNR range of 25-37dB are distinguished from the contents 2, 3 and 5 with the range of 32-40dB across the bitrate from 500kbps - 6000kbps. Figure 6 compares the PSNR values of content 1 and 2 for different combinations of bitrates, resolutions and encoders.

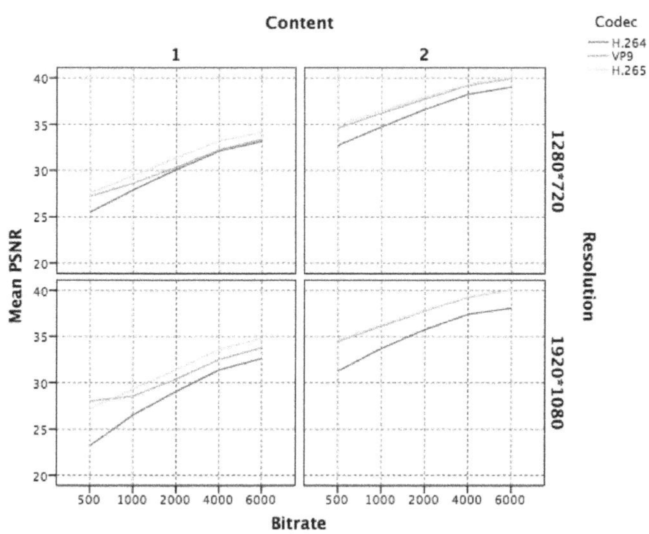

Figure 6. PSNR comparison between content 1 and 2

The Bjøntegaard metric was applied to calculate the bitrate saving achieved by the tested encoders based on the PSNR scores. The results, shown in Table 5, revealed that the average bitrate savings of the VP9 and H.265 encoders is 33% – 59% relative to the H.264 encoder. The bitrate saving varies with the video content type and the video resolutions. For example, video seq3 achieved the highest bitrate saving of 73.1% at 1080p resolution by using H.265 encoder; whereas seq1 achieved only 37.56% of bitrate saving. When the resolution increases from 720p to 1080p, the bit rate saving of H.265 or VP9 encoder versus H.264 encoder improves by about 15% or 19% consequently.

H.265 encoder is more efficient than VP9 encoder in terms of average bitrate saving: 5.85% at 1080p and 13.44% at 720p, especially for the video content that contains extreme motions and image details (e.g., seq1 and seq6). However, for less complex contents (e.g., seq2 and seq5), the advantage of the H.265 encoder over the VP9 encoder is very marginal, which is about 2-6% at 1080p. VP9 encoder outperformed the H.265 encoder by 2.3% under 1080p resolution for video that contains dark background, such as seq3. VP9 seems to have the performance advantage for high-resolution videos with low contrast images.

Table 5. Bitrate saving comparisons among three codecs

Parameter	Content	VP9 vs. H.264	H.265 vs. H.264	H.265 vs. VP9
720p @25fps	Seq1	13.94%	37.56%	28.91%
	Seq2	40.47%	46.16%	9.74%
	Seq3	57.04%	63.81%	0.33%
	Seq4	32.28%	38.36%	9.33%
	Seq5	31.84%	37.57%	9.23%
	Seq6	27.07%	43.12%	23.08%
	Ave	**33.77%**	**44.43%**	**13.44%**
1080p @25fps	Seq1	35.46%	52.83%	25.85%
	Seq2	57.83%	59.79%	3.93%
	Seq3	70.38%	73.13%	-2.32%
	Seq4	53.49%	56.38%	5.90%
	Seq5	54.45%	56.03%	1.79%
	Seq6	46.25%	55.88%	18.06%
	Ave	**52.98%**	**59.01%**	**5.85%**

5. QUALITY PREDICTION MODELS

Using the collected data from the sVQA and oVQA, we have constructed models to predict the user-perceived quality for the VP9 and H.265 encoders. The simplest mathematic model is a linear function, which is fast to compute and easy to use in real-world applications. Thus, we assumed the user-perceived quality, which values are the averaged ACR scores from 30 subjects (S_{ACR}), can be measured by a set of variables in a linear function. Linear regression analysis was applied in IBM SPSS tool for predictor testing and to generate the models. In linear regression, R^2 coefficient of determination is a common statistical measure of how well the regression line approximates the real data points. An R^2 of 1 indicates perfect goodness-of-fit. The pitfall of R^2 is that its value will only increase as more predictors are added to the regression model. To overcome this issue, adjusted R^2 should be used with models with more than one predictor variables. Another typical measure is standard error of the regression, also called the root mean square error RMSE. It indicates how close the observed data points are to the model's predicted values, of which lower value indicates a better fit. We also performed 3-fold cross validation for each model using R with 'DAAG' package 'cv.lm' function (http://www.stats.uwo.ca/DAAG). The prediction error is reported.

5.1 Potential Predictors

According to the logarithmic relationship between the ACR scores and bitrate, the ACR score could be represented as $S_{ACR} = a + b \cdot \log(bitrate)$, whereby the coefficient a determines the pass-through point of the curve $(1, a)$, while b determines the growth rate of the curve. Both coefficients may be influenced by encoder related characteristics and the video content and its encoding parameters, which have identified through the analysis in Section 4. To represent ACR scores as a linear model, the following potential predictors are considered based on their influences on video quality:

- *LBR*: the logarithmic bitrate with base 10. It converts the bitrate into a variable that is linearly related to ACR scores.
- *SR*: the spatial resolution of a given video divided by the resolution of 1280×720 pixels. (i.e., SR=1 for a 720p video).
- *LMB*: the largest size of macro block/coding unit that can be possibly allowed by a video encoder, divided by 16×16. (e.g., LMB equals to 16 for VP9, 1 for H.264).

- *RB*: the ratio of the SR to the LMB. It denotes the interactive influence between a video frame resolution and an encoder's coding characteristic.
- *TI*: the average value of temporal information over all frames of a video.
- *SI*: the average value of spatial information over all frames of a video.
- $LBR \times RB$ and $LBR \times TI$ are also considered to represent the impacts of the encoder and the video content characteristics on the curve of bitrate versus ACR scores.
- *PSNR*: the objective PSNR value divided by 30.
- *SSIM: the objective SSIM value.*

Then, ANOVA analysis is used to determine the significance of these potential predictors. The results in Table 6 show that SR, LMB and SI should be excluded because they did not significantly contribute to the model (p>.05).

Table 6. ANOVA results for the predictors

	Mean_sq	F	P
LBR	178.7	703.11	< 2e-16 ***
SR	0.3	1.11	0.29408
LMB	0.4	1.43	0.23480
RB	29.2	114.76	< 2e-16 ***
SI	0.7	2.80	0.09698
TI	4.8	18.73	3.4e-05 ***
LBRxRB	7.3	28.75	4.7e-07 ***
LBRxTI	3.4	13.57	0.00036 ***
PSNR	6.2	24.44	2.8e-06 ***
SSIM	4.0	15.86	0.00012 ***

*** Sig < .001

5.2 User-perceived Video Quality Modeling

When establishing the model for measuring the user-perceived video quality on small-form factor screen, we considered two situations: whether or not objective video quality measures (i.e., PSNR and SSIM) are available. We ran step-wise regression to build the final model. To ensure the model is robust, variables that have less than 1.5% of contribution to the model's R^2 change would be ignored.

For the situation of without oVQA parameters, after running step-wise regression, $LBR \times TI$, which increases the R^2 by 1.3%, is not included. Eventually, the model is generated as (1):

$$S'_{ACR} = 2.496LBR + 0.714RB \cdot LBR - 2.9RB - 0.028TI - 2.248 \quad (1)$$

For model (1), R = 0.916 indicates a close correlation between the predicted ACR scores (S'_{ACR}) and the subjective ACR scores. Adjusted R^2 that measures the goodness-of-fit for the model is 0.834, which means 83.4% of the variations in ACR scores are captured by model (1). RMSE is also low at about 0.6. Cross-validation residual sums of squares is 0.377, which is the measure of the prediction error averaged across all three folds.

When taking the oVQA scores into consideration, TI is no longer needed as a predictor (p>.05), which is possibly because its influence on subjective quality is reflected by the objective measures. The model using PSNR as a predictor is presented in (2), and the model using SSIM is in (3).

$$S'_{ACR} = 1.925LBR - 0.567RB \cdot LBR + 3.573PSNR - 2.288RB - 5.059 \quad (2)$$

$$S'_{ACR} = 1.786LBR + 0.502RB \cdot LBR + 6.691SSIM - 2.072RB - 6.244 \quad (3)$$

The prediction performance of Model (2) is indicated by R=.930, Adjusted R^2=.861, RMSE=.555. 3 fold cross-validation shows its prediction error is 0.306. Model (3) performs even better, whereby R=.943, Adjusted R^2=.885, RMSE =.532, and 3-fold cross-validation prediction error is 0.248. Figure 7 demonstrates each fold's predicted values against the actual ACR variable based on model (3).

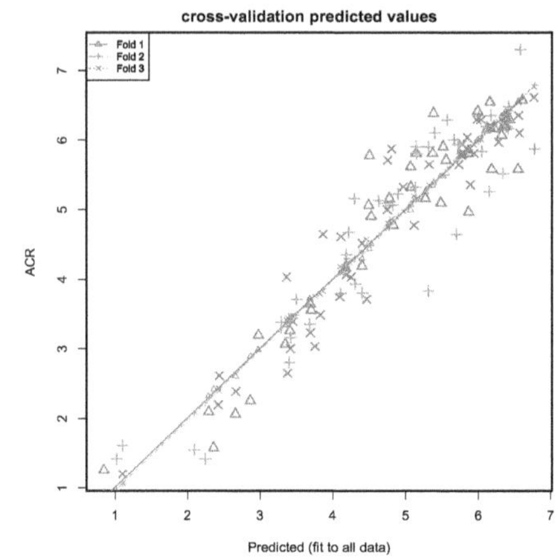

Figure 7. Scatter-plot of the predicted values by Model (3) versus subjective ACR scores

In all the three models, neither the video resolution (SR) nor the size of codec's largest macro block/coding unit (LMB) is significant for the user-perceived quality prediction, but their interaction (RB) shows as a significant predictor. The RB will increase as the video resolution increases while decrease as the size of LMB increases. Therefore, it is suggested to take this variable into consideration when developing subjective video quality prediction models across different codecs.

Although models (1) (2) and (3) are built with the ACR scores for VP9 and H.264 encoders, the format is applicable for other video codecs with similar block-based coding structure, because the predictor related to codec is generalized by the ratio of video frame resolution to the maximum size of the block. Only the coefficients of the model may be affected by the difference of codecs. Next, we will see this from the model for H.265 codec.

5.3 Subjective Video Quality Prediction for H.265

According to the oVQA result analysis, the objective performance of H.265 codec is similar to that of VP9, except it is marginally more efficient than VP9. Therefore, the subjective quality of H.265 videos is possibly predicted by using the correlation of the oVQA scores between the two codecs.

Based on the SSIM data, the SSIM values of videos encoded by H.265 can be represented by the values of VP9 in a close linear function (4), for which R^2 =.966, RMSE =0.01. The relationship is shown in Figure 8.

$$SSIM_{H265} = SSIM_{VP9} \times 0.885 + 0.11 \quad (4)$$

By plugging (4) into (3), we can get the model (5), in which $0.11 \times LBR \approx 0.33$. Model (5) can be used to estimate the user-perceived quality of H.265 videos.

$$S'_{ACR} = 1.786LBR + 0.502RB \cdot LBR + 5.921SSIM - 2.072RB - 6.134 \quad (5)$$

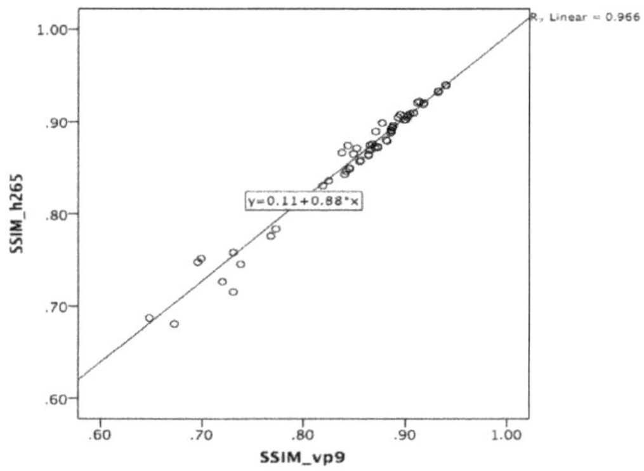

Figure 8. Correlations between the SSIM values from VP9 and H.265 video coding

6. DISCUSSION

In the sVQA and oVQA studies, we have examined the performance of VP9 and H.265/HEVC with the H.264/AVC as the baseline. Our quality assessment results are much different from the findings in [12], [13] and [16]. The detailed comparisons are show in Table 7. In [12, 13], H.265 shows dominant bit rate saving in comparison to VP9, which is about 35-43% in terms of objective PSNR and above 49% in terms of subjective score. Both studies state that VP9 is even worse than H.264/AVC with an average 5.1% of subjective loss or 8.4% of objective bit rate overhead. However, our study shows H.265 is only marginally superior to VP9, reaching an average of about 13% more bit rate saving at 720p resolution and downing to 6% when the resolution becomes 1080p. We concluded the same with [12, 13] in that H.265 is much better than H.264 with average 40-60% of bit rate saving according to Bjøntegaard Delta PSNR (BD-PSNR). This is different from [16], whereby no significant quality difference was perceived between the sequences compressed by H.265 and by H.264. This could be caused by the low bitrate 200-400Kbps as well as the small video resolution of 640×360 pixels used in [16].

We found that the advantage of VP9 and H.265/HEVC over H.264/AVC is dependent on both video content and video resolution, whereby videos with less motion and image complexity and bigger resolution will benefit more in bit rate saving than their counterparts. Content impact found in [12] shows HEVC is significantly better than the other codes in perceived quality of natural videos, while VP9 is the most efficient on synthetic video content. Our study used all natural videos; thus the advantage of VP9 on synthetic content is not captured. Instead, we discovered that VP9 performed the best on the content contains mostly dark or low contrast frames (e.g., seq3). The content dependency identified in [11] suggests that the number of points of visual attentions affects user experience. As the points of attention are related to the content complexity (e.g., SI and TI), this finding should be consistent with our result.

Interestingly, based on sVQA, the quality of H.264 video at a smaller resolution (e.g., 720p) is much better than it at a bigger resolution (e.g., 1080p), gaining an average 63% of bit saving. Therefore, if the H.264/AVC encoder has to be used for video compression, it is recommended to encode videos to 720p instead of full HD 1080p format at a given bitrate.

For QoE modeling, we considered two situations: without and with oVQA measurement as a predictor. The first situation is applicable for any cases; while the second can be regarded as further refinement of an existing oVQA metric (PSNR or SSIM) for QoE prediction. We determined the model predictors based on their significant impacts on subjective video quality. Except the bitrate related variable – logarithmic bitrate LBR, a special predictor RB was firstly identified as the ratio of a video resolution to the largest coding unit size supported by a video codec. This RB variable is used in both types of models, so is its interaction with LBR (RB×LBR). The QoE models involving such predictors can reflect codecs' performance variation with the changes of bitrate and video resolution. Thus, they are useful for predicting subjective quality of videos encoded by the codecs having block-based coding structure.

Table 7. Results comparisons with other studies

Items	[7]	[8]	[11]	Our Study
Study settings	4K UHD 1.5~20Mkbps 56" TV	832x480 ~ 2560x1600 QP: 22~37	640x360 200~400kbps 4.3'' mobile	720p, 1280p 500~6Mkbps 10.6" tablet
Method	Subjective Objective	– Objective	Subjective –	Subjective Objective
H.265/HEVC vs H.264	52.6% 39.6%	– 43.3%	Similar –	– 44%~60%
VP9 vs H.264	-5.1% 1.59%	– -8.4%	– –	26%~56% 34%~53%
H.265/HEVC vs VP9	49.4% 35.6%	– 39.3%	– –	– 6%~13%
Content dependency	H.265 is best for natural video; VP9 for synthetic video	–	Depend on points of attention	More bit rate saving on less motion and image complexity content
Resolution dependency	–	–	–	More bit rate saving on a bigger resolution

7. CONCLUSION AND FUTURE WORK

In this paper, we propose a set of novel subjective video quality prediction models based on the data from subjective and objective video quality assessment studies, which are applicable for mobile tablet and across the current and next generations of video codecs, i.e., H.264, H.265 and VP9. These models are presented as simple linear functions with only three predictor variables for each, but can explain more than 83% of variations of our collected subjective quality scores and have low standard errors (RMSE<.6).

To collect subjective and objective quality assessment scores, ACR method and PSNR and SSIM metrics were applied respectively on video sequences encoded with 500 – 6000kbps, 720p and 1080p, and VP9, H.265 and H.264 codecs. With the sVQA and oVQA results, we have evaluated the performance of these codecs. The results show that both VP9 and H.265 significantly outperform H.264 with average 26-56% of bit rate saving in terms of sVQA, and 33-59% of bit rate saving in terms of oVQA, whereby more bit rate saving is achieved at a higher video resolution. H.265 performs slightly better than VP9, with average 13% of bit rate saving at 720p resolution reduced to 6% at 1080p.

The limitation of this work is that the video ordering influence could not be avoided due to the nature of ACR study design. This can be improved by randomization of the video display orders across participants. As our subjective study was conducted with the assumption of perfect network transmission, our QoE models are not suitable for quality prediction under poor networks such as high packet loss. However, the SSIM or PSNR can still capture certain level of quality loss caused by network transmission.

In future work, we will carry out further subjective assessment study to evaluate the model for H.265 video quality prediction (eq. (5)) and take the frame rate parameter into consideration, which were not studied in this paper due to technical constraints (decoder availability). We will also make further comparisons with other QoE prediction models.

REFERENCE

1. Cisco. *Global mobile data traffic forecast update, 2014-2019.* Cisco white paper 2015. Available from: http://www.cisco.com/c/en/us/solutions/collateral/service-provider/visual-networking-index-vni/white_paper_c11-520862.html.
2. Ooyala, *Q1 2013 Video Index - TV is no longer a single screen in your living room.* 2013.
3. Sullivan, G.J., et al., 2012. *Overview of the high efficiency video coding (HEVC) standard.* IEEE Trans. Circuits Syst. Video Technol., 22,12, 1649-1668.
4. Brunnström, K., et al., 2013. *Qualinet White Paper on Definitions of Quality of Experience. Qualinet White Paper on Definitions of Quality of Experience Output from the fifth Qualinet meeti.*
5. Menkovski, V., Exarchakos, G. and Liotta, A. 2011. *The value of relative quality in video delivery.* Journal of Mobile Multimedia, **7**(3): p. 151-162.
6. Menkovski, V. and Liotta, A. 2013. *Intelligent control for adaptive video streaming.* In *Proceedings of Int. Conference on Consumer Electronics (ICCE2013), IEEE.* 2013.
7. Agboma, F. and Liotta, A. 2006. *User centric assessment of mobile contents delivery*, In *Proceedings of the 4th Int. Conf. Advances in Mobile Computing and Multimedia* (Yogyakarta, Indonesia). IEEE, 121-130.
8. Song, W., Tjondronegoro, D. and Himawan, I. 2014. *Acceptability-based QoE Management for User-centric Mobile Video Delivery: A Field Study Evaluation*, In *Proceedings of the ACM MM*, ACM. 267-276.
9. Sullivan, G.J., Topiwala, P.N. and Luthra, A. 2004. *The H. 264/AVC advanced video coding standard: Overview and introduction to the fidelity range extensions.* In *the SPIE 49th Annual Meeting Optical Science and Technology.*
10. Ohm, J.-R., et al., 2012. *Comparison of the Coding Efficiency of Video Coding Standards - Including High Efficiency Video Coding (HEVC).* IEEE Trans. Circuits Syst. Video Technol. 22,12, 1669-1684.
11. Bankoski, J., et al. 2013. *Towards a next generation open-source video codec.* In *IS&T/SPIE Electronic Imaging.* SPIE
12. Řeřábek, M. and Ebrahimi, T. 2014. *Comparison of compression efficiency between HEVC/H. 265 and VP9 based on subjective assessments*, In *Proceedings of SPIE Optical Engineering + Applications*, SPIE, San Diego, California, USA.
13. Grois, D., et al., 2013. *Performance Comparison of H. 265/MPEG-HEVC, VP9, and H. 264/MPEG-AVC Encoders*, In *Proceedings of the 30th PSC* (Dec 8-11 2013). IEEE .
14. Zeng, K., et al., 2013. *From H.264 to HEVC: Coding gain predicted by objective video quality assessment models*, In *Proceedings of the 7th VPQM* (Scottsdale, Arizona).
15. Sung-Ho, B., et al. 2013. *Assessments of Subjective Video Quality on HEVC-Encoded 4K-UHD Video for Beyond-HDTV Broadcasting Services.* IEEE Trans. Broadcast. 59, 2, 209-222.
16. Garcia, R. and Kalva, H. 2014. *Subjective evaluation of HEVC and AVC/H.264 in mobile environments.*, IEEE Trans. Consumer Electronics. 60, 1, 116-123.
17. Nightingale, J., et al. 2013. *Modeling QoE for streamed H. 265/HEVC content under adverse network conditions*, In *Proceedings of the 5th Int. Conf. on Wireless, Mobile and Multimedia Networks* (Beijing, China). IET. 249-253.
18. Anegekuh, L., Sun, L. and Ifeachor, E. 2013. *Encoding and video content based HEVC video quality prediction.* Multimedia Tools and Applications. 74:1795. Springer.
19. Huynh-Thu, Q. and Ghanbari, M. 2008. *Scope of validity of PSNR in image/video quality assessment.* Electronics letters, 44, 13, 800-801.
20. Song, W. and Tjondronegoro, D. 2014. *Acceptability-based QoE Models for Mobile Video.* IEEE Trans. Multimedia. 16, 3, 738 - 750.
21. Hore, A. and Ziou, D. 2010. *Image Quality Metrics: PSNR vs. SSIM.* In *Proceedings of ICPR 2010.*
22. ITU-T. 2008. *P. 910 Subjective Video Quality Assessment Methods For Multimedia Applications.*
23. ITU-R. 2012. Rec. *BT. 500-13: Methodology For The Subjective Assessment Of The Quality Of Television Pictures.*
24. Pinson, M. and Wolf, S. 2003. *Comparing subjective video quality testing methodologies*, In *Proceedings of SPIE Video Communications and Image Processing Conference*, SPIE. 573-582.
25. Nightingale, J., et al. 2014. *Deriving video content type from HEVC bitstream semantics.* In *Proceedings of SPIE Photonics Europe.*
26. ITU-T. 2007. *Opinion model for video-telephony applications* in *Quality of service and performance – Generic and user-related aspects.*
27. Takahashi, A., Hands, D. and Barriac, V. 2008. *Standardization activities in the ITU for a QoE assessment of IPTV.* IEEE Communications Magazine. 46, 2, 78-84.
28. Péchard, S., Pépion, R. and P. Le Callet. 2008. *Suitable methodology in subjective video quality assessment: a resolution dependent paradigm.* In *Proceedings of the 3rd IMQA.*
29. Bellard, F. and Niedermayer, M. 2012.*FFmpeg.*
30. Song, W., Tjondronegoro, D. and Docherty, M. 2010. *Exploration And Optimization Of User Experience In Viewing Videos On A Mobile Phone.* Int. J. Softw. Eng. Know. Eng. 20, 8, 1045-1075.
31. Hands, D. and Brunnstrom, K. 2007. *Multimedia Group Test Plan Draft Version 1.19*, Video Quality Experts Group.
32. Protalinski, E. 2013.*Google adds its free and open-source VP9 video codec to latest Chrome build.*
33. Hanhart, P. *VQMT: Video Quality Measurement Tool.* 2013 Available from: http://mmspg.epfl.ch/vqmt.
34. Bjontegaard, G. 2008. *Improvements of the BD-PSNR model.* ITU-T SG16 Q.6.
35. Hanhart, P. and Ebrahimi, T. 2014. *Calculation of average coding efficiency based on subjective quality scores.* J Vis Commun Image Represent. 25, 3, 555-564.

Towards Solving the Bottleneck of Pitch-based Singing Voice Separation

Bilei Zhu[1], Wei Li[1,2*], Linwei Li[1]

[1] School of Computer Science and Technology, Fudan University, Shanghai, China
[2] Shanghai Key Laboratory of Intelligent Information Processing, Fudan University, Shanghai, China
bileizhu@gmail.com, weili-fudan@fudan.edu.cn, lwli11@fudan.edu.cn

ABSTRACT

Singing voice separation from accompaniment in monaural music recordings is a crucial technique in music information retrieval. A majority of existing algorithms are based on singing pitch detection, and take the detected pitch as the cue to identify and separate the harmonic structure of the singing voice. However, as a key yet undependable premise, vocal pitch detection makes the separation performance of these algorithms rather limited. To overcome the inherent weakness of pitch-based inference algorithms, two novel methods based on non-negative matrix factorization (NMF) are devised in this paper. The first one combines NMF with the distribution regularities of vocals under different time frequency resolutions, so that many vocal unrelated portions are eliminated and the singing voice is hence enhanced. In consequence, the accuracy of vocal pitch detection is significantly improved. The second method applies NMF to decompose the spectrogram into non-overlapping and indivisible segments, which can be used as another cue besides the pitch to help identify the vocal harmonic structure. The two proposed methods are integrated into the framework of pitch-based inference. Extensive testing on the MIR-1K public dataset shows that both of them are rather effective, and the overall performances outperform other state-of-the-art singing separation algorithms.

Categories and Subject Descriptors

H.5.5 [Information Systems]: Information Interfaces and Presentation-*Sound and Music Computing*

General Terms

Algorithms; Experimentation

Keywords

Singing voice separation; pitch-based inference; singing pitch detection; non-negative matrix factorization (NMF)

MM'15, October 26-30, 2015, Brisbane, Australia
© 2015 ACM. ISBN 978-1-4503-3459-4/15/10…$15.00
DOI: http://dx.doi.org/10.1145/2733373.2806257

1. INTRODUCTION

Most music pieces people listen to in daily life are mixtures of singing voice and accompaniment. Compared with the instrumental accompaniment, the singing voice carries important information such as the main melody and lyrics, and is usually more impressive. Many applications in music information retrieval (MIR), e.g., melody extraction [1], singer identification [2], and automatic lyrics recognition [3], are mainly related to the singing voice, and in this case the musical accompaniment is treated as noise. Therefore, singing voice separation has emerged as a crucial technique in recent years.

Music recordings can be either monaural or stereo, and in the former case singing voice separation is generally considered more challenging because of the absence of spatial information. To tackle this problem, a few algorithms have been proposed in recent years and most of them are within the framework of pitch-based inference. It is known that singing voice is primarily comprised of voiced sounds (about 90%) [4], which are roughly harmonic, with frequencies of concurrent overtones being approximately integer multiples of the fundamental frequency. Pitch-based inference algorithms utilize the harmonic structure of the singing voice, and generally first extract the singing pitch from sound mixtures as the cue for subsequent separation.

Unfortunately, pitch-based inference algorithms have several intrinsic limitations. First of all, they highly rely on the technique of singing pitch detection from polyphonic music signals, which, however, remains an open problem and has not been maturely solved so far [5, 6, 7, 8]. As a premise, if the detected pitch is inaccurate, the harmonic structure of the singing voice cannot be correctly identified, so that the quality of vocal separation will be low. Next, singing voice is almost always accompanied by instrumental sounds, which in most cases are harmonic, broadband and strongly correlated with the vocals [9]. Spectral contents of the singing voice and accompaniment overlap in many time-frequency positions, which bring about great difficulties to vocal separation since it is nearly impossible to discriminate overlapping spectral contents using pitch as the only cue. Finally, although the majority of singing voice is voiced sounds, a small part of unvoiced sounds do exist. Having no underlying periodicity, unvoiced sounds cannot be characterized by pitch and further effectively separated from accompaniment using most of existing pitch-based inference algorithms [10].

This paper aims to solve the first two limitations of pitch-based inference to a certain degree, using two methods based on non-negative matrix factorization (NMF). In the first method, NMF is used to decompose the spectrogram of the input sound mixture, with long and short frames successively. Owing to the property of being fluctuant in frequency and short in time, singing voice exhibits certain continuity in the frequency axis and time axis when long and short frames are adopted, respectively. In consequence, NMF components reflecting the above phenomenon can be picked out and resynthesized to obtain an enhanced vocal signal, which will benefit for the subsequent singing pitch detection. In the second method, NMF is applied to the input sound mixture to obtain a set of non-overlapping time-frequency segments, each of which approximately originates from a single sound source. By virtue of the indivisible property, these segments provide additional information besides the periodicity information provided by the singing pitch, which is often inaccurate, for the identification of the vocal harmonic structure. The two proposed methods are integrated into the framework of pitch-based inference. Experiments carried out on the MIR-1K public dataset show the effectiveness of both methods, and the overall performances outperform two state-of-the-art methods.

The remainder of the paper is organized as follows. Section 2 reviews some related works on monaural singing voice separation. Section 3 introduces NMF briefly. Section 4 describes our singing voice separation algorithm. Experiment results and performance analysis are presented in section 5. Finally, section 6 concludes this paper.

2. RELATED WORK

In this section, related works on monaural singing voice separation are briefly reviewed. To our knowledge, the first attempt to comprehensively solve the problem of singing voice separation was made by Li and Wang [9]. Their algorithm is a typical method of pitch-based inference under the framework of computational auditory scene analysis (CASA) [11], where the predominant pitch is first extracted from the input sound mixture, and then applied as the cue to label the time-frequency units (T-F units). T-F units are obtained by decomposing the sound mixture via an auditory filterbank, and labeled as singing dominant if their local pitch values match that of the singing voice. Based on the labeled T-F units, the algorithm forms a binary mask and applies it to resynthesize the singing voice. This algorithm is later extended by Hsu and Jang [10], by combining an unvoiced sounds separation method and a spectral subtraction approach.

Obviously, the accuracy of singing pitch detection is critical for the performance of pitch-based singing separation. And meanwhile, it is also evident that enhanced singing voice is beneficial for singing pitch detection [12]. To utilize this interdependency, Hsu et al. proposed a tandem algorithm, which estimates the singing pitch and separates the singing voice jointly and iteratively [13]. Specifically, the algorithm first has a rough estimation for the pitch of the singing voice and then applies it to separate the singing voice by considering harmonicity and temporal continuity. The separated singing voice and estimated pitch are then iteratively fed back to each other for further refinement.

In contrast with the above three methods that represent the singing voice with a group of singing dominant T-F units, Ryynanen et al. proposed an alternative scheme which models the singing voice as a sum of time varying sinusoids [14]. Using this sinusoidal model, the task of singing voice separation resolves into first estimating the model parameters, i.e., frequency, amplitude and phase of each sinusoid per frame, and then interpolating them over time. To estimate these parameters, the singing pitch is first extracted, with its integer multiples as the constraints imposed on the frequencies of sinusoids. The amplitude and phase of each sinusoid are then estimated from the normalized cross-correlation between the analysis frame and a complex exponential having the frequency of the sinusoid. As above, singing pitch detection is the foundation of separation performance.

Virtanen et al. [15] first employed a pitch-based approach to extract the harmonic structure of the singing voice, and then applied NMF on the residual spectrogram. The factorization results in an estimation of the musical accompaniment, which is finally subtracted from the original mixture to achieve a better separation of the singing voice. On the surface, this method resembles our algorithm since they both integrate NMF into a pitch-based inference singing separation framework. However, the purposes of NMF are completely irrelevant. In other words, in [15] NMF is used to estimate the accompaniment, while in our algorithm it is used for singing enhancement and more precise identification of the vocal harmonic structure, respectively.

In addition to the above pitch-based inference separation algorithms, several algorithms outside this framework have also been proposed for monaural singing voice separation. Some of these algorithms are in accordance with the line of spectrogram factorization. In [16], Vembu and Baumann proposed using NMF to decompose the spectrogram of the input sound mixture into a set of components, which are then clustered into different sound sources using an unsupervised clustering approach based on spectral features. In [17], Chanrungutai and Ratanamahatana also applied NMF for spectrogram factorization, while the components are assigned to different sound sources by investigating the rhythmic and continuous events. Other algorithms for monaural singing separation include those based on the extraction of the repeating musical structure [18, 19], and those using robust principal component analysis [20, 21], etc.

3. NON-NEGATIVE MATRIX FACTORIZATION

Non-negative matrix factorization (NMF) [22] is an unsupervised technique employed for linear representation of non-negative data. Given a non-negative matrix $\mathbf{X}$ of dimensions $K \times T$ and a positive integer J, NMF finds an approximate factorization

$$\mathbf{X} \approx \mathbf{BG} \tag{1}$$

where $\mathbf{B}$ and $\mathbf{G}$ are non-negative matrices of dimensions $K \times J$ and $J \times T$ respectively. In contrast to many other linear representations such as independent component analysis (ICA) [23] and principal component analysis (PCA) [24], NMF imposes the non-negativity constraint, which leads to a parts based representation because the constraint allows only additive, not subtractive combinations of the original data.

Recently, NMF and its extensions have been successfully used in the field of audio analysis, for various problems such as polyphonic music transcription [25], audio-to-score alignment [26], and musical instrument classification [27]. In particular, NMF based algorithms have produced attractive results in sound source separation [28].

When using NMF for sound source separation, the observation matrix $\mathbf{X}$ is typically a phase-invariant time-frequency representation (e.g., magnitude spectrogram or power spectrogram), where K is the number of frequency channels and T is the number of time frames. The model matrices, $\mathbf{B}$ and $\mathbf{G}$ are basis matrix and gain matrix respectively, where the columns of $\mathbf{B}$ are basis functions and the rows of $\mathbf{G}$ are their gains in each frame.

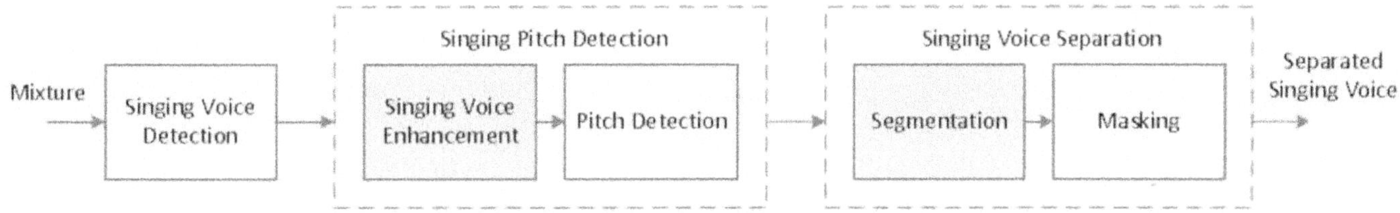

Figure 1: Overview of our singing voice separation algorithm.

The factorization, according to Eq. (1), is usually sought by minimizing a chosen cost function between **X** and **BG** while restricting their elements to nonnegative values. According to [28], the best performed cost function among several commonly used ones is the Kullback- Leibler divergence of Eq. (2)

$$\mathbf{D(X||BG)} = \sum_{k=1}^{K}\sum_{t=1}^{T}[\mathbf{X}]_{k,t}log\frac{[\mathbf{X}]_{k,t}}{[\mathbf{BG}]_{k,t}} - [\mathbf{X}]_{k,t} + [\mathbf{BG}]_{k,t} \quad (2)$$

Compared with other cost functions such as the Euclidean distance, the divergence is more sensitive to low energy observations, making it a better approximation of human auditory perception. To solve the minimization problem with respect to Eq. (2), Lee and Seung proposed a simple method [29], where **B** and **G** are initialized with random positive values and then alternatively updated with the following multiplicative update rules

$$\mathbf{B} \leftarrow \mathbf{B} \otimes \frac{\frac{\mathbf{X}}{\mathbf{BG}}\mathbf{G}^T}{\mathbf{1G}^T} \quad (3)$$

$$\mathbf{G} \leftarrow \mathbf{G} \otimes \frac{\mathbf{B}^T\frac{\mathbf{X}}{\mathbf{BG}}}{\mathbf{B}^T\mathbf{1}} \quad (4)$$

where $\mathbf{A}\otimes\mathbf{B}$ and $\frac{A}{B}$ are the element-wise multiplication and division of matrices **A** and **B**, respectively, and **1** is an all-one matrix of the same size as **X**. According to the proofs given in [29], the divergence Eq. (2) is non-increasing under the update rules Eq. (3-4). As a result of NMF, the observation matrix of the input sound mixture is decomposed into a set of repetitive components, each of which represents parts of a single sound source. A component here refers to a basis function (a column of **B**) and its time-varying gain (the corresponding row of **G**), and there are thus J components in total. Generally, each sound source is modeled as a sum of one or more components, and therefore the separation is done by grouping these components to sound sources.

4. ALGORITHM DESCRIPTION

As shown in Fig. 1, the overall pitch-based inference algorithm consists of three modules, i.e., singing voice detection, singing pitch detection, and singing voice separation. A sound mixture is first input into the singing voice detection module to locate the vocal portions by supervised classification. Then, such portions are used to calculate the singing pitch. To improve the precision of pitch estimation, a novel NMF-based singing enhancement method is designed and adopted as a preprocessing step. Finally, singing voice separation is done by decomposing the input mixture into T-F units and grouping singing dominant units to form a binary mask for resynthesizing. To correct the errors in identifying singing dominant units with only pitch as the cue, another NMF-based method, which decomposes the original mixture into time-frequency segments related to specific sound source, is designed to help improve the identification accuracy.

4.1 Singing Voice Detection

As a prerequisite of the following vocal separation, singing voice detection is first performed to partition the input sound mixture into vocal and nonvocal portions. To achieve this goal, we follow the typical solution of supervised classification. In training, each song in the training set is first divided into short-time overlapping frames, then Mel-frequency cepstral coefficients (MFCCs) are extracted from each frame. All pairs of MFCCs and pre-labeled tags (vocal/nonvocal) are assembled together frame by frame, and fed into the hidden Markov model (HMM) classifier to train its parameters. In testing, given a new song outside the training dataset, the MFCCs of each unlabeled frame are extracted and input to the classifier, with a decision made on whether vocal is present or not.

4.2 Singing Pitch Detection

The vocal portions obtained from the above module are normally mixed with music accompaniment, which brings great disturbance to singing pitch detection. Therefore, to weaken the negative effects of accompaniment, we first design a novel method to enhance the singing voice based on its unique time-frequency characteristic, and then integrate an existing method described in [30] to perform singing pitch detection.

The proposed method for singing voice enhancement is inspired by the observation that singing voice is a temporally variable signal with distinctive characteristics, i.e., fluctuation and shortness [12]. Due to the intrinsic features, singing voice exhibits distinct temporal and spectral properties in spectrograms calculated with different frame lengths. To be specific, in the case of long (short) frame length, the frequency (time) resolution is relatively high, thus the vocal signals appear more smoothly and continuously in the frequency (time) axis, as illustrated in Fig. 2.

Motivated by the above observation, a two-stage NMF based procedure is naturally conceived to screen out the vocal portions from spectrograms of different time-frequency resolutions. As shown in Fig. 3, a magnitude spectrogram is first constructed from the input song using long-frame (e.g., 256 ms) short-time Fourier transform (STFT), and then decomposed into a set of NMF components. Generally speaking, each component approximately originates from a single sound source. As a result, the problem of how to select and retain vocal portions that are relatively continuous along the frequency axis is equivalently converted to

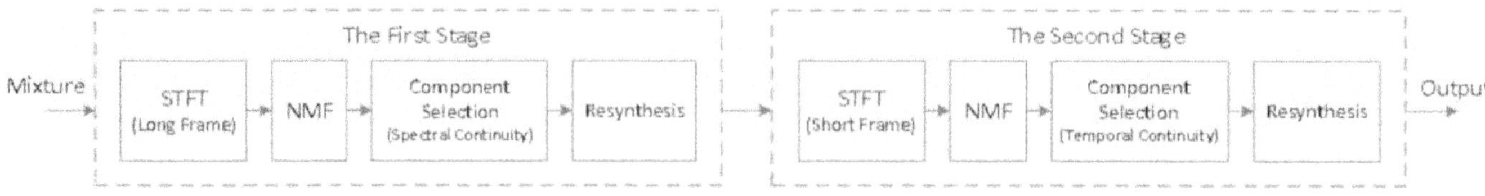

Figure 3: Overview of the proposed singing voice enhancement method.

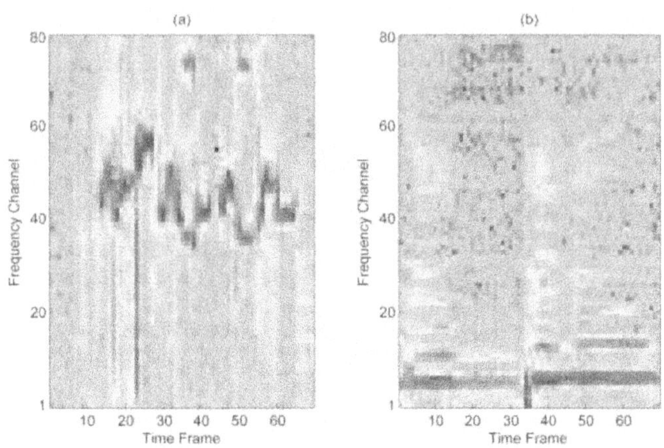

Figure 2: Magnitude spectrograms of a singing voice signal. (a) A part of a long-frame spectrogram (frame length = 256 ms, frame overlap = 128 ms). (b) A part of a short-frame spectrogram (frame length =32 ms, frame overlap = 16 ms).

how to pick out the NMF components which are continuous in the same direction. After eliminating unwanted components, a new spectrogram is reconstructed from the retained ones, and used to resynthesize the preliminarily enhanced singing signal via inverse STFT. Next, the resynthesized signal is input into the second stage which is completely similar to the above procedures except that the short-frame (e.g., 32 ms) STFT is adopted to pick out vocal signals that are relatively continuous along the time axis. After the two-stage of filtering, accompaniment is significantly attenuated, namely the singing content is greatly enhanced which will be beneficial for the subsequent singing pitch calculation.

As a key technical problem, the selection of NMF components is solved by applying a spectral or temporal continuity thresholding method, formalized as below. Given the spectrogram **X** of dimensions $K \times T$, the number of components J, and the factorization $\mathbf{X} \approx \mathbf{BG}$, spectral continuity of each component is measured by assigning a cost to large changes between adjacent elements in the corresponding column of the basis matrix **B**. Specifically, for component $\boldsymbol{X}^j$, $j = 1,\ldots, J$ being the component index, the spectral continuity measure $c_s(\boldsymbol{X}^j)$ is defined as

$$c_s(\boldsymbol{X}^j) = \frac{1}{\sigma_j^2}\sum_{k=2}^{K}([\boldsymbol{B}]_{k,j} - [\boldsymbol{B}]_{k-1,j})^2, \qquad (5)$$

where $\sigma_j = \sqrt{\frac{1}{K}\sum_{k=1}^{K}[B]_{k,j}^2}$ is a normalization factor. And if $c_s(\boldsymbol{X}^j)$ satisfies

$$c_s(\boldsymbol{X}^j) \le \theta_s, \qquad (6)$$

where θ_s is a threshold, the component is considered to be continuous in the frequency axis.

As for temporal continuity of each component, it is measured using the criteria described in [28], which assigns a cost to large changes between adjacent elements in the corresponding row of the gain matrix **G**. Specifically, for component $\boldsymbol{X}^j, j = 1,\ldots,$ J being the component index, the temporal continuity measure $c_t(\boldsymbol{X}^j)$ is written as

$$c_t(\boldsymbol{X}^j) = \frac{1}{\epsilon_j^2}\sum_{t=2}^{T}([\boldsymbol{G}]_{j,t} - [\boldsymbol{G}]_{j,t-1})^2, \qquad (7)$$

where $\epsilon_j = \sqrt{\frac{1}{T}\sum_{t=1}^{T}[\boldsymbol{G}]_{j,t}^2}$ is a normalization factor. And if $c_t(\boldsymbol{X}^j)$ satisfies

$$c_t(\boldsymbol{X}^j) \le \theta_t, \qquad (8)$$

where θ_t is a threshold, the component is considered to be continuous in the time axis.

4.3 Singing Voice Separation

In this stage, singing voice is to be separated from the input sound mixture based on the detected singing pitch. First, the input song is passed through a 128-channel Gammatone filterbank, whose center frequencies are equally distributed on the equivalent rectangular bandwidth (ERB) scale between 80 Hz and 5 kHz. The output signal of each filter is then divided into short-time overlapping frames. As a result, the input sound mixture is decomposed into a collection of T-F units. A T-F unit here is denoted as u_{cm}, where c and m are the indexes of filter channel and time frame, respectively. Given these T-F units, the singing voice separation is done by first estimating the ideal binary time frequency mask and then resynthesizing.

An ideal binary mask is a binary matrix, where 1 means that the energy of the singing voice is stronger than that of the accompaniment within the corresponding T-F unit and 0 indicates weaker [31]. To estimate the mask, a natural choice is to perform unit labeling, i.e., to label each individual T-F unit with 1 if it is identified as singing dominant or 0 if otherwise. Given the detected singing pitch, this is usually done by matching the local periodicity of each T-F unit, obtained by finding the maximum of the autocorrelation within plausible pitch range, with the pitch period of the present frame. If the match occurs, the T-F unit is identified as singing dominant [9, 10]. However, due to the inaccuracy of detected singing pitch, the pitch-based unit labeling often results in errors, especially false negatives for labeling singing-dominant T-F units.

To deal with the errors occurred in pitch-based unit labeling, we devise a NMF-based rectification method specified as follows.

1. Construct an energy matrix **E** of T-F units, the matrix element $[\mathbf{E}]_{c,m}$ is calculated as

$$[\mathbf{E}]_{c,m} = \sum_{n=1}^{N} u_{cm}^2(n), \quad (9)$$

where $u_{c,m}(n)$ is the nth sample in $u_{c,m}$, N is frame length in number of samples. Obviously, **E** is a nonnegative matrix of dimensions $C \times M$, where $C = 128$ is the number of filter channels, and M is the number of time frames.

2. Next, perform NMF on the obtained matrix **E** to decompose it into a set of components. Given the factorization $\mathbf{E} \approx \mathbf{WH}$ and the number of components R, a component here is denoted as $\boldsymbol{E}^r$, r = 1, R, and represented as a time-frequency matrix. Specifically, the matrix element at position (c, m) is calculated as

$$[\boldsymbol{E}^r]_{c,m} = [\mathbf{W}]_{c,r}[\mathbf{H}]_{r,m} \quad (10)$$

Generally, each of the obtained components originates from a single sound source.

3. Finally, a segment is generated from each component obtained above. Specifically, for a given component $\boldsymbol{E}^r$, its time-frequency representation is compared with those of other components, with the matrix elements satisfying Eq. (11) selected.

$$[\boldsymbol{E}^r]_{c,m} = \max_{i=1\sim R}[\boldsymbol{E}^i]_{c,m} \quad (11)$$

In general, each selected element $[\boldsymbol{E}^r]_{c,m}$ corresponds to a T-F unit $u_{c,m}$, and all these T-F units form a segment S^r corresponding to $\boldsymbol{E}^r$.

Fig. 4 gives an illustration of how to generate segments from NMF components. For a given component, red elements in its time-frequency representation are those satisfying Eq. (11), meaning that they are larger than all the green elements in the same positions of other time-frequency representations. Typically, each red element corresponds to a T-F unit with the same time frequency index with it, and all these units form the segment corresponding to the given component.

As a result of the above procedure, the input sound mixture is decomposed into a set of time-frequency segments, each of which is indivisible, with primary energy originating from a single sound source. With the constraint of Eq. (11), these segments are non-overlapping, i.e., a T-F unit only belongs to a single segment. In other words, segments are disjoint clusters of T-F units, and all the T-F units included in a segment are dominated by the same sound source. Given this property, a T-F unit can be labeled based on not only the periodicity information provided by the singing pitch, but also the origination of the segments that it belongs to.

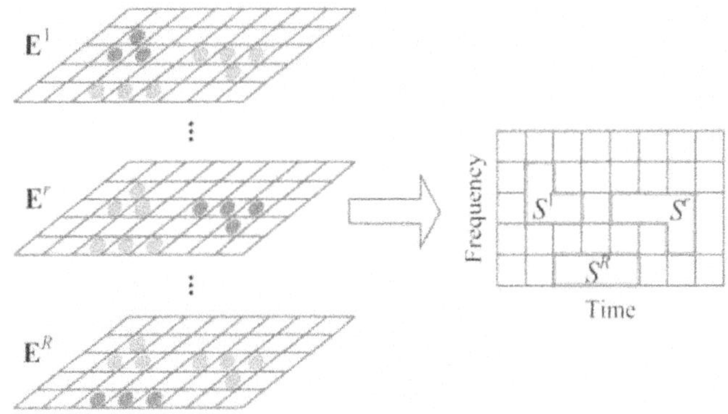

Figure 4: Illustration of segment generation.

Given the time-frequency segments, we now describe how to estimate the ideal binary mask using pitch and segment as two complementary cues. First, let $\boldsymbol{M}^0$ be the masking result for singing voice of conventional pitch-based unit labeling method. Then, the segment cue is considered to get additional masking information. To be specific, for each segment, if more than a certain percentage (20% for example) of its units have been identified as singing dominant, the whole segment is considered to be originated from vocals. All these segments are assembled together and form another masking matrix, denoted as $\boldsymbol{M}^1$. The final estimation result **M** is the combination of $\boldsymbol{M}^0$ and $\boldsymbol{M}^1$, i.e.,

$$\mathbf{M} = \boldsymbol{M}^0 || \boldsymbol{M}^1, \quad (12)$$

where **A**||**B** is the element-wise OR operation of matrices **A** and **B**. In this way, provided located in a same segment, scattered unit label mistakes in $\boldsymbol{M}^0$ have a great chance to be rectified by the successive unit labels in $\boldsymbol{M}^1$.

Given **M**, the singing voice is finally resynthesized from the input sound mixture, by applying the inverse of the Gammatone filterbank and the technique of overlap and addition.

5 EVALUATION

In this section, we thoroughly evaluate each of the above three modules as well as the overall singing voice separation algorithm. The dataset used for evaluation is MIR-1K published in [10], which contains 1000 song clips recorded at 16 kHz sampling rate and 16 bit quantization, with durations ranging from 4 to 13 s. These clips are extracted from 110 karaoke Chinese pop songs performed by male and female amateurs, with accompaniment and vocals recorded in the left and right channels, respectively. To provide the ground truth, some useful information such as manual annotations of the singing pitch contours, indices of the vocal/nonvocal frames, indices and types for unvoiced frames, and lyrics etc., are included in the dataset. On the basis of MIR-1K dataset, we create three sets of sound mixtures at different qualities for evaluation. To be exact, for each original music clip in MIR-1K, the singing voice and music accompaniment are mixed into a monaural signal under three different signal-to-noise ratios (SNRs), i.e., -5 dB (accompaniment is louder), 0 dB (same level), and 5 dB (singing voice is louder). Note that in this circumstance, signal refers to the singing voice, while the accompaniment is deemed as noise.

5.1 Evaluation of Singing Voice Detection

(1) Dataset Description

All 1000 song clips of the MIR-1K dataset are used to evaluate the performance of singing voice detection described in subsection 4.1. Since this approach is based on supervised classification, the whole dataset is further partitioned into two nonintersecting subsets with nearly equal size (483 vs. 517) for training and testing. The final results are given through a two-fold cross validation.

(2) Performance Measure

The performance of singing voice detection is measured with frame-level precision and recall of the vocal and nonvocal portions. Take vocal frame detection as an example, suppose $N_{classified}$ be the number of frames that are alleged to be vocal by classifier, $N_{correct}$ be the number of frames that are correctly classified as vocals, and $N_{reference}$ be the number of total true vocal frames, then the precision and recall are defined as $N_{correct}=N_{classified}$ and $N_{correct}=N_{reference}$, respectively.

(3) Experimental Settings and Results

In experiment, the input song clip is first segmented into frames of 40 ms long with 50% overlap, and a 39-dimensional MFCC feature vector (12 cepstral coefficients and the log energy, together with their first and second order derivations) is extracted from each frame to characterize the audio content. Then, a Gaussian mixture model (GMM) with 32 components, each having a diagonal covariance matrix, is trained to model the MFCC distribution of vocal and nonvocal frames, respectively. Parameters of the GMMs are initialized using the K-means algorithm and iteratively adjusted via the expectation-maximization (EM) algorithm. Each of the GMMs is considered as a state in a fully connected HMM. The transition probabilities of the HMM are obtained by frame counting in the training set, and the Viterbi algorithm is used to decode the sound mixture into vocal and nonvocal portions.

Fig. 5 illustrates the results of frame-level singing voice detection in the precision-recall space at different SNRs of -5, 0 and 5 dB. As can be seen, precisions and recalls keep going upwards with the increase of SNR, no matter for vocal or nonvocal frames. Meanwhile, the performances of vocal frame detection are notably better than those of nonvocal frame detection in all three SNRs. We claim that both of the observations are reasonable, as song clips in the dataset involve significantly more vocal portions (beyond 70%) than nonvocal portions. In the circumstance of singing separation, what to be considered is mainly the precisions and recalls of vocal frames, and in Fig. 5 they have been shown to be high enough (e.g., 93% precision and 83% recall under 5 dB SNR) for further singing voice processing.

5.2 Evaluation of Singing Pitch Detection

(1) Dataset Description

All 1000 music clips of the MIR-1K dataset are used to evaluate the performance of singing pitch detection.

(2) Performance Measure

The performance of singing pitch detection is measured using the frame-level gross error rate, which occurs if the absolute difference between the detected pitch and the ground truth is more than a semitone.

(3) Experimental Settings and Results

As shown in Fig. 1, the singing pitch detection module consists of two steps. The parameter values used in singing voice enhancement are experimentally set and summarized in Table 1. The parameters θ_t(time axis) and θ_s(frequency axis) are obtained by grid search, that is, adjust the parameters step-by-step within a specific range determined in experiment, and select the ones that make the results best. And the pitch detection step follows the default settings of Praat [30], except that the plausible pitch range is set to [80, 500] Hz, and the frame length is set to 40 ms with an overlap of 20 ms.

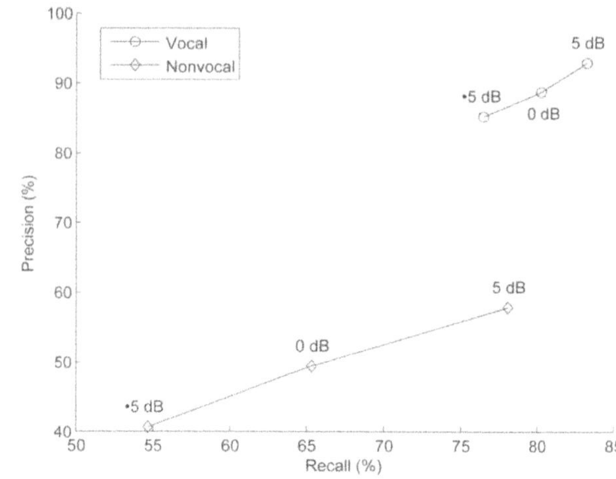

Figure 5: Performance of singing voice detection.

Table 1: Parameter values used for singing voice enhancement

The first stage	The second stage
Frame length = 256 ms	Frame length = 32 ms
Frame overlap = 128 ms	Frame overlap = 16 ms
# NMF component = 30	# NMF component = 30
$\theta_s = 1200$	$\theta_t = 300$

To get a direct impression on the effect of singing voice enhancement, Fig. 6 shows a typical example taking a snippet extracted from the MIR-1K dataset as input. The spectrograms of the original song mixture, the original clean singing voice, and the enhanced singing voice are shown in Fig. 6(a), (b), and (c), respectively. As can be obviously seen, Fig. 6(c) resembles Fig. 6(b) pretty much, while is quite dissimilar with Fig. 6(a). In other words, the proposed method retains most of the singing components in the mixture, while eliminates lots of the non-singing ones.

In light of the introduction of section 4.2, singing enhancement includes two NMF-based decompositions that are consecutively performed with long-frame and short-frame spectrograms, respectively. To quantitatively assess the effect of singing enhancement on subsequent pitch detection, four groups of experiments under different conditions are designed as below,

- *Without SVE*: Pitch detection without singing voice enhancement (abbreviated as SVE here).
- *With SVE1*: Pitch detection with only the first stage of singing voice enhancement (long-frame type of NMF based enhancement).
- *With SVE2*: Pitch detection with only the second stage of singing voice enhancement (short-frame type of NMF based enhancement).
- *With SVE*: Pitch detection with two-stage singing voice enhancement.

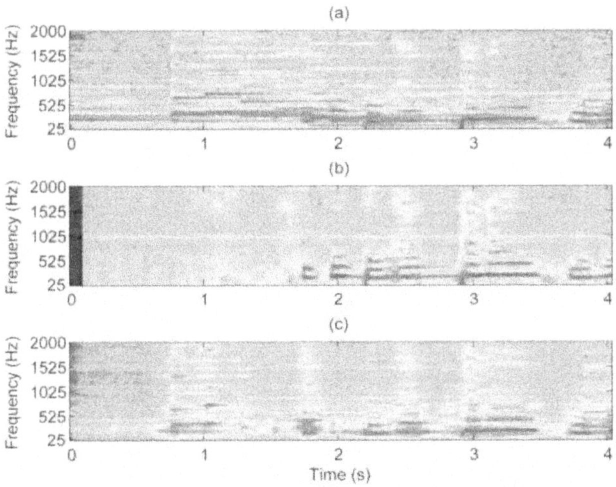

Figure 6: Singing voice enhancement for a snippet of the song clip Ani_4_01 in the MIR-1K dataset at 0-dB SNR. (a) Spectrogram of the original song mixture. (b) Spectrogram of the clean singing voice. (c) Spectrogram of the singing-voice-enhanced signal.

Results of the above comparative experiments are illustrated in Fig. 7. Obviously, all three enhancement mechanisms, i.e., experiments of *With SVE1*, *With SVE2*, and *With SVE*, show their effectiveness in improving the performance of singing pitch detection. Particularly, applying the entire two-stage process (*With SVE*) achieves the best results (or the minimum pitch detection error rates) in all SNRs, indicating that the two stages are complementary. As for the comparison of the two individual stages, applying only the first stage of the enhancement method (*With SVE1*) achieves better results than applying only the second stage (*With SVE2*). This result is reasonable and expectable. The long-frame based enhancement stage gives emphasis to the spectral smoothness, and therefore attenuates the energy of harmonic chordal sounds which usually create much difficulty for singing pitch detection. In contrast, the short-frame based enhancement stage highlights the temporal smoothness, and hence weakens the energy of percussive sounds, which are aperiodic and do not do as much damage as chordal sounds for singing pitch detection.

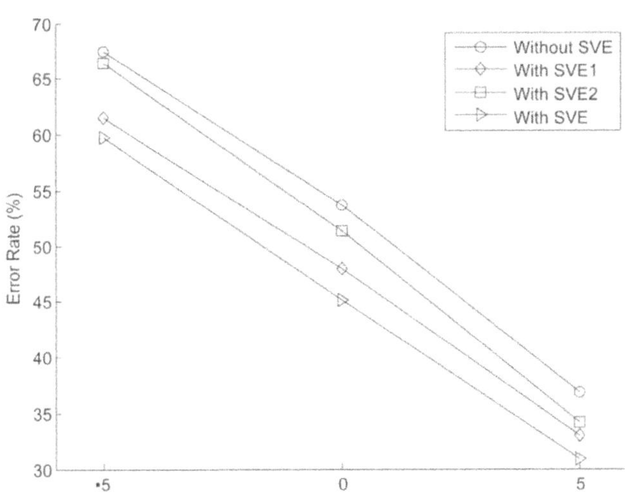

Figure 7: Performance of singing pitch detection.

5.3 Evaluation of Singing Voice Separation

(1) Dataset Description

All 1000 song clips of the MIR-1K dataset are used to evaluate the performance of singing voice separation.

(2) Performance Measure

Given a resynthesized singing voice $\hat{\boldsymbol{v}}$ and the original clean singing voice $\boldsymbol{v}$, the signal-to-distortion ratio (SDR) is first defined as below to measure the quality difference between them.

$$\mathbf{SDR}(\hat{\boldsymbol{v}}, \boldsymbol{v}) = \mathbf{10}\ \boldsymbol{log}_{10}\left[\frac{\langle\hat{\boldsymbol{v}}, \boldsymbol{v}\rangle^2}{\|\hat{\boldsymbol{v}}\|^2\|\boldsymbol{v}\|^2 - \langle\hat{\boldsymbol{v}}, \boldsymbol{v}\rangle^2}\right], \qquad (13)$$

where $\langle\hat{\boldsymbol{v}}, \boldsymbol{v}\rangle$ is the inner product of vectors $\hat{\boldsymbol{v}}$ and $\boldsymbol{v}$, and $\|\boldsymbol{v}\|^2$ is the energy of $\boldsymbol{v}$.

Next, normalized SDR (NSNR) is defined in Eq. (14) following the suggestion in [10]. It is the improvement of the SDR between the original mixture **x** and the estimated voice $\hat{\boldsymbol{v}}$, and used to assess the separation performance of each mixture.

$$\mathbf{NSDR}(\hat{\boldsymbol{v}}, \boldsymbol{v}, \boldsymbol{x}) = \mathbf{SDR}(\hat{\boldsymbol{v}}, \boldsymbol{v}) - \mathbf{SDR}(\boldsymbol{x}, \boldsymbol{v}) \qquad (14)$$

Finally, the global NSDR (GNSDR) is calculated in terms of Eq. (15) as the final measure of evaluating the overall separation performance.

$$\mathbf{GNSDR} = \frac{\sum_{n=1}^{N} \omega_n \mathbf{NSDR}(\hat{\boldsymbol{v}}_n, \boldsymbol{v}_n, \boldsymbol{x}_n)}{\sum_{n=1}^{N} \omega_n} \qquad (15)$$

where n is the index of a song, N is the total number of the songs, and ω_n is the length of the nth song. Generally speaking, a higher GNSDR value indicates better separation quality.

(3) Experimental Settings and Results

The frame length used in the separation is 40 ms with an overlap of 50%.

To intuitively show the effectiveness of our singing separation algorithm, a song clip in the MIR-1K dataset at 0-dB SNR is taken as an example for testing and illustration. The waveform of the original clean singing voice, and three signals that are separately resynthesized from the ideal binary mask, the result of pitch-based unit labeling, and our separation algorithm (with 60 segments used in experiment) are drawn together in Fig. 8. Apparently, compared with the signal resynthesized from the result of unit labeling, the output waveform of our algorithm better matches that resynthesized from the ideal binary mask. And it also matches the original clean singing voice better.

Apart from observing the visualized time-domain separated waveforms, the binary masking matrices related to Fig. 8 (b, c, d) are also drawn in Fig. 9 for a more specialized comparison. Specifically, Fig. 9(a) is the ideal binary mask estimated from the premixed singing voice and musical accompaniment, Fig. 9(b) is the mask estimated by pitch based unit labeling, and Fig. 9(c) is the mask estimated by our separation algorithm. It can be clearly observed that, the binary mask estimated by our separation algorithm looks more like the ideal binary mask than that estimated by unit labeling. It retains more energy of the singing voice, which indicates the effectiveness of the proposed method.

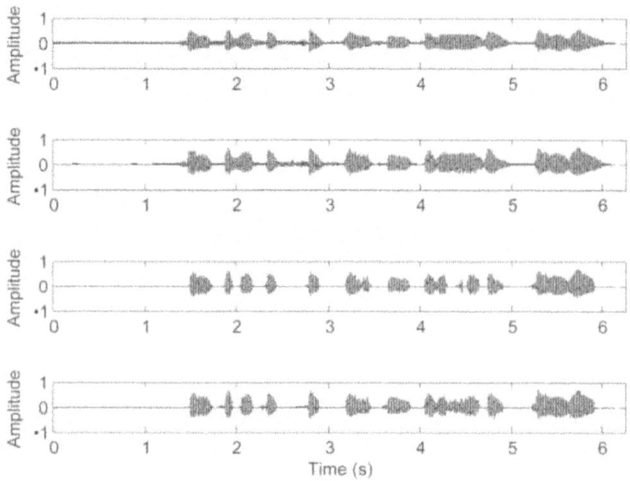

Figure 8: Singing voice separation for the song clip Ani_1_03 in the MIR-1K dataset at 0-dB SNR. (a) Clean singing voice. (b) Signal resynthesized from the ideal binary mask. (c) Signal resynthesized from the result of pitch-based unit labeling. (d) Output of our separation algorithm (number of segments =60).

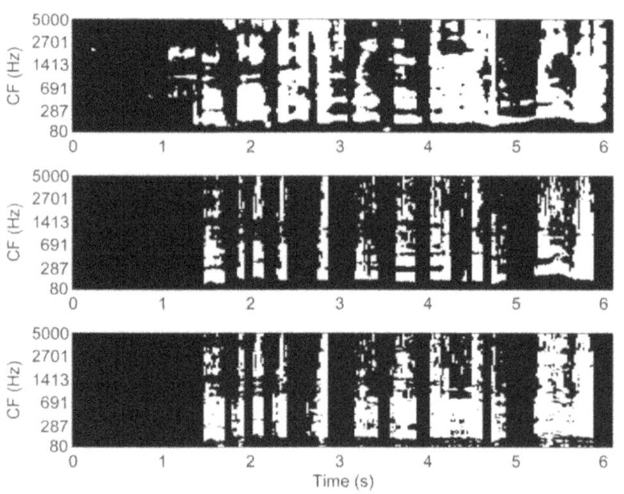

Figure 9: Mask comparison for the song clip Ani_1_03 in the MIR-1K dataset at 0-dB SNR. (a) Ideal binary bask obtained from the premixed singing voice and musical accompaniment. White pixels indicate 1 and black ones indicate 0. (b) The mask estimated by pitch-based unit labeling (3) The mask estimated by our separation algorithm (number of segments = 60).

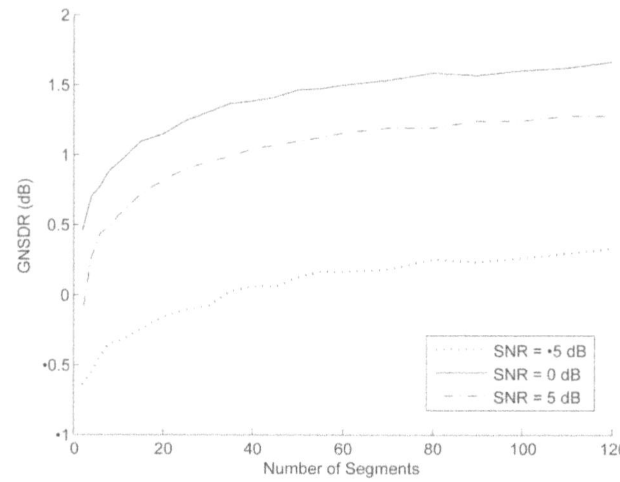

Figure 10: Performance of singing voice separation as a function of the number of segments.

Next experiment is to investigate the relationship between the performance of singing voice separation and the number of NMF segments used in section 4.3. As shown in Fig. 10, increasing the number of segments makes the GNSDRs for all SNRs monotonically rise up until even out after certain points. This phenomenon is as expected. Remind that the task of our segmentation method is to generate a set of indivisible time-frequency segments as another cue to facilitate the singing separation. When the number of segments is small, the size of each segment tends to be large. The larger the segments are, the more difficult to ensure the indivisibility. In contrast, when the number of segments increases, their indivisibility is also increased. And after certain points, the indivisibility converges.

The effects of the two designed improvement approaches, namely singing enhancement and segmentation, are also comparatively studied in the following experiments under different conditions described below, and illustrated in Fig. 10.

- *Without SVE*, without segmentation: Singing voice separation without singing voice enhancement and segmentation. The pitch of the singing voice is extracted from the original sound mixture. The mask for the singing voice is estimated by pitch-based unit labeling only.
- *With SVE*, without segmentation: Singing voice separation with singing voice enhancement, without segmentation. The pitch of the singing voice is extracted from the signal where singing voice is enhanced.
- *Without SVE*, with segmentation: Singing voice separation without singing voice enhancement, with segmentation (number of segments = 60). The mask for the singing voice is estimated by combining $\boldsymbol{M}^0$ and $\boldsymbol{M}^1$.
- *With SVE*, with segmentation: Singing voice separation with both singing voice enhancement and segmentation (number of segments = 60).

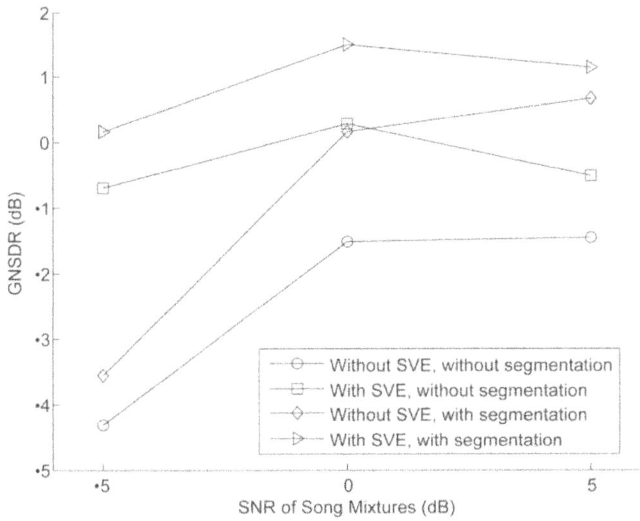

Figure 11: Illustration the effects of the two proposed methods for the performance of singing voice separation.

As demonstrated in the figure, when other factors are fixed (e.g., with or without segmentation), applying the proposed singing voice enhancement method achieves better separation results in all SNRs than not applying it, indicating the importance of accurate singing pitch detection for the performance of pitch-based singing voice separation. Besides, applying the proposed segmentation method also improves the performance of separation in all SNRs, which shows its effectiveness. In other words, the information provided by the segments is reliable, and can be used for more accurate estimation of the ideal binary mask.

Finally, our algorithm is compared with two state-of-the-art singing voice separation algorithms, i.e., the Hsu method [10] and the Rafii method [19]. The result of the comparison is illustrated in Fig. 12. As can be seen, our algorithm significantly outperforms the Hsu method in all three SNRs. It also outperforms the Rafii method in SNRs of 0 dB and 5 dB.

6 CONCLUSION

This paper presents a pitch-based inference algorithm for monaural singing voice separation. To address the limitation caused by inaccurate vocal pitch detection, two methods based on NMF are proposed and integrated into the framework. Specifically, the first method enhances the singing voice in sound mixtures for more accurate singing pitch detection. It utilizes the fluctuation and shortness of the singing voice, and enhances the vocals by sequentially applying NMF on spectrograms of different frame lengths. As for the second method, it decomposes the sound mixture into a set of segments, each of which originates from a single sound source. With these segments, singing-dominant T-F units can be identified based on not only the pitch, but also the origination of the segments they belong to. Quantitative evaluation shows that both of the proposed methods are effective in improving the performance of singing voice separation. In future, experiments should be moved from the manually mixed simple MIR-1K dataset to real CD songs. And in this condition, other long-term mechanisms such as music structure analysis and melody contour similarity etc. can be integrated into the current preliminary framework.

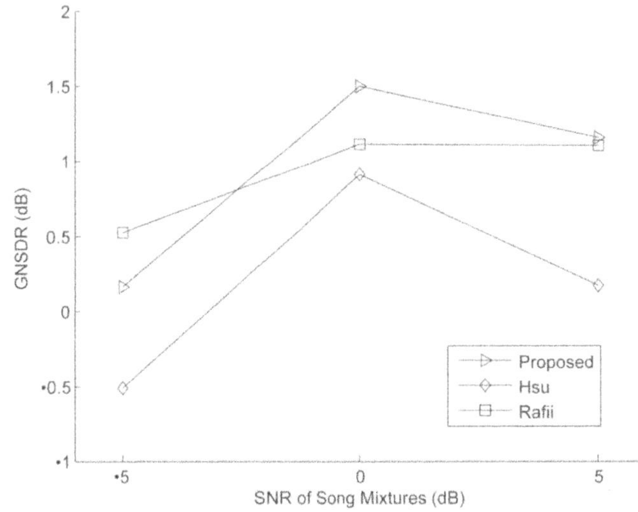

Figure 12: Comparison of our algorithm (number of segments = 60) with the Hsu method and the Rafii method.

7 ACKNOWLEDGEMENTS

This work is supported by NSFC (61171128).

8 REFERENCES

[1]. J. L. Durrieu, G. Richard, B. David and C. Ffievotte. Source/filter model for unsupervised main melody extraction from polyphonic audio signals. IEEE Transactions on Audio, Speech, and Language Processing, 18(3): 564-575, 2010.

[2]. H. Fujihara, M. Goto, T. Kitahara and H. G. Okuno. A modeling of singing voice robust to accompaniment sounds and its application to singer identification and vocal-timbre-similarity-based music information retrieval. IEEE Transactions on Audio, Speech, and Language Processing, 18(3): 638-648, 2010.

[3]. A. Mesaros and T. Virtanen. Automatic recognition of lyrics in singing. EURASIP Journal on Audio, Speech, and Music Processing, 2010, Article ID 546047.

[4]. Y. E. Kim. Singing voice analysis/synthesis. PhD thesis, Massachusetts Institute of Technology, 2003.

[5]. J. Salamon, E. Gomez, D. P. W. Ellis and G. Richard. Melody extraction from polyphonic music signals: Approaches, applications, and challenges. IEEE Signal Processing Magazine, 31(2): 118- 134, 2014.

[6]. J. Salamon and E. Gomez. Melody extraction from polyphonic music signals using pitch contour characteristics. IEEE Transactions on Audio, Speech, and Language Processing, 20(6): 1759-1770, 2012.

[7]. C. L. Hsu and J. S. Roger Jang. Singing pitch extraction by voice vibrato/tremolo estimation and instrument partial deletion. The International Society of Music Information Retrieval Conference (ISMIR), pp. 525-530, 2010.

[8]. T. C. Yeh, M. J. Wu, J. R. Jang, W. L. Chang and I. B. Liao. A hybrid approach to singing pitch extraction based on trend estimation and hidden markov models. IEEE International Conference on Acoustics, Speech, and Signal Processing (ICASSP), pp. 457-460, 2012.

[9]. Y. Li and D. L. Wang. Separation of singing voice from music accompaniment for monaural recordings. IEEE

Transactions on Audio, Speech, and Language Processing, 15(4): 1475-1487, 2007.

[10]. C. L. Hsu and J. S. R. Jang. On the improvement of singing voice separation for monaural recordings using the MIR-1K dataset. IEEE Transactions on Audio, Speech, and Language Processing, 18(2): 310-319, 2010.

[11]. D. L. Wang and G. J. Brown, Computational auditory scene analysis: principles, algorithms, and applications. Wiley, New York, 2006.

[12]. H. Tachibana, T. Ono, N. Ono and S. Sagayama. Melody line estimation in homophonic music audio signals based on temporal-variability of melodic source. IEEE International Conference on Acoustics, Speech, and Signal Processing (ICASSP), pp. 425-428, 2010.

[13]. C. L. Hsu, D. L. Wang, J. S. R. Jang and K. Hu. A tandem algorithm for singing pitch extraction and voice separation from music accompaniment. IEEE Transactions on Audio, Speech, and Language Processing, 20(5): 1482-1491, 2012.

[14]. M. Ryynanen, T. Virtanen, J. Paulus and A. Klapuri. Accompaniment separation and karaoke application based on automatic melody transcription. IEEE International Conference on Multimedia and Expo (ICME), pp. 1417-1420, 2008.

[15]. T. Virtanen, A. Mesaros and M. Ryynanen. Combining pitch-based inference and non-negative spectrogram factorization in separating vocals from polyphonic music. ISCA Tutorial and Research Workshop on Statistical and Perceptual Audio Processing, pp. 17-22, 2008.

[16]. S. Vembu and S. Baumann. Separation of vocals from polyphonic audio recordings. The International Society of Music Information Retrieval Conference (ISMIR), pp. 337-344, 2005.

[17]. A. Chanrungutai and C. A. Ratanamahatana. Singing voice separation in mono-channel music. International Symposium on Communications and Information Technologies, pp. 256-261, 2008.

[18]. A. Liutkus, Z. Rafii, R. Badeau, B. Pardo and G. Richard. Adaptive filtering for music/voice separation exploiting the repeating musical structure. IEEE International Conference on Acoustics, Speech and Signal Processing (ICASSP), pp. 53-56, 2012.

[19]. Z. Rafii and B. Pardo. A simple music/voice separation method based on the extraction of the repeating musical structure. IEEE International Conference on Acoustics, Speech and Signal Processing (ICASSP), pp. 21-224, 2011.

[20]. P. S. Huang, S. D. Chen, P. Smaragdis and M. Hasegawa-Johnson. Singing-voice separation from monaural recordings using robust principal component analysis. IEEE International Conference on Acoustics, Speech and Signal Processing (ICASSP), pp. 57-60, 2012.

[21]. Y. H. Yang. On sparse and low-rank matrix decomposition for singing voice separation. ACM international conference on Multimedia (ACM MM), pp. 757-760, 2012.

[22]. D. D. Lee and H. S. Seung. Learning the parts of objects by non-negative matrix factorization. Nature, 401(6755): 788-791, 1999.

[23]. A. Hyvarinen, J. Karhunen and E. Oja. Independent component analysis. Wiley, New York, 2001.

[24]. I. T. Jollifie. Principal component analysis. Springer-Verlag, New York, 1986.

[25]. P. Smaragdis and J. C. Brown. Non-negative matrix factorization for polyphonic music transcription. IEEE Workshop on Applications of Signal Processing to Audio and Acoustics (WASPAA), pp. 177-180, 2003.

[26]. A. Cont. Realtime audio to score alignment for polyphonic music instruments, using sparse non-negative constraints and hierarchical HMMs. IEEE International Conference on Acoustics, Speech and Signal Processing (ICASSP), 2006.

[27]. E. Benetos, M. Kotti and C. Kotropoulos. Musical instrument classification using non-negative matrix factorization algorithms and subset feature selection. IEEE International Conference on Acoustics, Speech and Signal Processing (ICASSP), 2006.

[28]. T. Virtanen. Monaural sound source separation by nonnegative matrix factorization with temporal continuity and sparseness criteria. IEEE Transactions on Audio, Speech, and Language Processing, 15(3): 1066-1074, 2007.

[29]. D. D. Lee and H. S. Seung. Algorithms for non-negative matrix factorization. Advances in Neural Information Processing Systems, 2001.

[30]. P. Boersma and D. Weenink. Praat: Doing Phonetics by Computer, Ver. 4.0.26. http://www.fon.hum.uva.nl/praat, 2002.

[31]. D. L. Wang. On ideal binary mask as the computational goal of auditory scene analysis. In P. Divenyi, editor, Speech Separation by Humans and Machines, pp. 181-197. Kluwer, Norwell MA, 2005

Enhancing the Quality of Interactive Multimedia Services by Proactive Monitoring and Failure Prediction

Mohammed Shatnawi
Microsoft, Redmond, WA, and
Simon Fraser University
Burnaby, BC, Canada

Mohamed Hefeeda
Qatar Computing Research Institute
Hamad Bin Khalifa University
Doha, Qatar

ABSTRACT

Online multimedia communication services, such as Skype and Google Hangout, are used by millions of users every day. Although these services provide acceptable quality on average, users occasionally suffer from reduced audio quality, dropped video streams, and even failed sessions. To mitigate some of these problems, service providers closely monitor the performance of different parts of the system. However, most current techniques for monitoring and managing the quality of service (QoS) of online multimedia communication services are reactive and lack the ability to adapt to dynamic changes in real time. We propose a novel *roactive* approach for continuously monitoring the health of large-scale multimedia communication services, and dynamically managing and improving the quality of the multimedia sessions. The proposed approach, called Proactive QoS Manager, has novel light-weight methods for estimating the capacity of different components of the system and for using this capacity estimation in allocating resources to multimedia sessions in *real time*. We implement the proposed approach in one of the largest online multimedia communication services in the world and evaluate its performance on more than 100 million audio, video, and conferencing sessions. Our empirical results show that substantial quality improvements can be achieved using our proactive approach, without changing the production code of the service or imposing significant overheads. For example, in our experiments, the Proactive QoS Manager reduced the number of failed sessions by up to 25% and improved the quality (in terms of the Mean Opinion Score (MOS)) of the succeeded sessions by up to 12%. These improvements are achieved for the well-engineered and highly-provisioned online service examined in this paper; we expect higher gains for other similar services.

Categories and Subject Descriptors

H.4.3 [**Information Systems**]: Information Systems Applications: Communications Applications

MM'15, October 26–30, 2015, Brisbane, Australia.
© 2015 ACM. ISBN 978-1-4503-3459-4/15/10 ...$15.00.
DOI: http://dx.doi.org/10.1145/2733373.2806275.

Keywords

Online multimedia communications; quality of service; failure prediction; dynamic monitoring

1. INTRODUCTION

Interactive multimedia communication services such as Skype, Viber, Whatsapp, and Google Hangout offer a wide variety of services including calling, media sharing, and conferencing services. There are over a billion customers who use online communication and media sharing services everyday [21]. These social and multimedia communication services compete in the features they provide, as well as the quality of their services. They have Service Level Agreements (SLAs) covering various aspects such as call quality, media quality, content sharing latency, reliability, response times, and up-times. Failure to adhere to SLAs results not only in low customer satisfaction, but also comes with a heavy price tag due to fines and loss of business. For example, the estimated cost of the annual downtime of IT systems in North America is about $26.5 billion [2].

A typical interactive multimedia communication service includes client applications and an online cloud infrastructure deployed in multiple data centers around the world, and it uses the Internet as the backbone for communications. When a user calls another user, a client application initiates the session and invokes an online service endpoint in one of the data centers. This end point manages the session by invoking many other sub-services, referred to as components, including identity verification, call management, media adaptation, session routing, experimentation, and advertising. Instances of these components are created and provisioned on different data centers. The perceived quality of session is directly impacted by the performance of these components. Therefore, if we are able to monitor these various components in real-time to assess their current performance and predict any failures before they happen, we can significantly improve the quality observed by users, by routing the sessions and multimedia content through the components and data centers that currently have the highest performance and reliability.

We define a failure as an observed deviation of a component from its expected behavior. For example, some users may be having a video conference call using Skype, sharing a presentation, and exchanging messages. Users expect the audio and video streams and the shared presentation to work properly without failures such as intermittent audio, video glitches, and lost slides. Failure management, a term we use to refer to all aspects of dealing with failures, plays a key role in the reliability of online multimedia communication services. It includes service monitoring, failure prediction and detection, root-cause analysis, all the way to failure handling and prevention. We focus in this paper on end-to-end (e2e) real-time service health monitoring, failure prediction, and making real-time decisions about component selection and routing paths to enhance the reliability and quality of interactive multimedia communication services.

Current approaches to health monitoring and failure prediction in multimedia communication services, and online services in general, are mostly reactive [17, 11]. For example, Monitoring in Hystrix of Netflix takes place in real-time but failures are noted after they happen. Also, the creation of a failure predictor is complex and time consuming and thus not suitable for real-time management [25, 12]. Thus, failure prediction generation takes place before the run-time lifecycle of the online service. Also, the resulting predictor is built for certain configurations and working conditions like the number and performance of audio de-jitters and video transcoders. If these configurations change, the predictor may no longer be accurate. For example, the predictor could be designed for a video encoder that is able to encode N videos per minute and it fails beyond that. If the administrator adds more resources to the encoder so that it can handle $2 \times N$ videos per minute, the predictor would likely continue to predict failure if the number of videos per minute approaches N, not $2 \times N$. In this paper, we call these predictors **static predictors**, because they do not adapt to changes in the service functionality or the provisioned resources.

We propose a novel approach to monitoring the health and improving the quality of interactive multimedia communication services **in real-time**. Real-time refers to the runtime lifecycle of the service, where the service is in production and being used by real customers. We use *s nthetic transactions* to monitor the service by exercising it like real customers, generate current data about it, and then use this *resh* data to create and maintain up-to-date failure predictors for the service. The results of the synthetic transactions and the failure predictors are used to make decisions, in real-time, on which services and which paths to route audio and video sessions to.

We implement and evaluate the effectiveness of the proposed approach in a large interactive multimedia communication service in Microsoft[13]. The service handles around 2.5 million transactions per second at peak time. We run our experiments for 5 days in a test cluster that gets 1% of the traffic in a data center, and we process more than 100 million audio, video, and conferencing sessions. Our results show that our proactive approach not only substantially improves the quality of interactive multimedia communication services, but it also saves network and computing resources. This allows the service to admit more sessions and/or allow current sessions to further improve their quality by adding more streams.

The contributions of this work are as follows:

- Novel approach to proactively monitor the health and quality of interactive multimedia communication services.

- Light weight algorithm for building dynamic failure predictors in online multimedia communication services, and using these predictions to estimate the available capacity of different components of the service.

- Algorithm to provide service configuration and routing path recommendations in real-time for the sessions in multimedia communication services.

- Insights and experiences from our actual implementation and deployment of the proposed approach in a large online service.

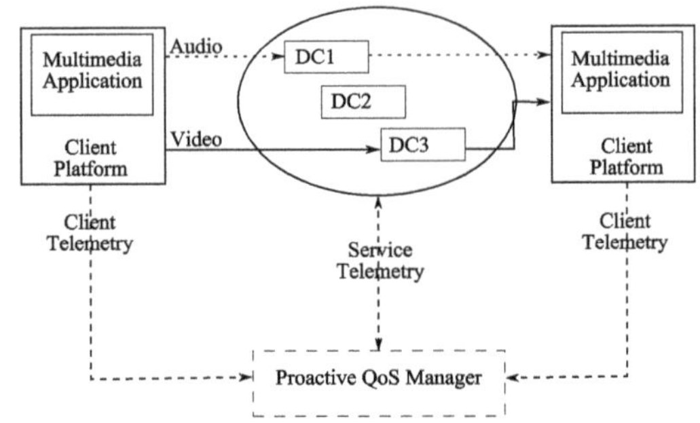

Figure 1: High-level architecture of multimedia communication services.

The rest of this paper is organized as follows: Section 2 discusses the background of our work and the related works. Section 3 presents our approach. Section 4 describes the evaluation of the proposed approach, and Section 5 concludes the paper.

2. BACKGROUND AND RELATED WORK

In this section, we present a high level overview of interactive multimedia communication services, describe how audio and video sessions are created, the points of failure we try to address, and the current research methods that attempt to handle them.

2.1 Background

A high level diagram of an interactive multimedia communication service is depicted in Figure 1. When a user calls another user, the session is routed to the closest data center. The session may be composed of audio, image, and video streams. Each data center implements an instance of the multimedia communication service that is able to handle all streams in a session. Each data center also implements a service routing and selection component. If the data center is able to handle the session, it routes all aspects of the session to its internal components. If the data center is able to handle part of the session, e.g., the audio but not the video stream, it routes the video stream to another data center. Thus, a multimedia communication session may have all its streams going through the same path from the source to the destination, or may have some of the streams of the session go through different paths. An example is shown in Figure 1, where the audio from the source client on the left is processed by DC1, and the video is processed by DC3.

Figure 2 provides a more detailed look at the components in each data center as well as the components of the proposed approach, shown in the dotted rectangle. We describe the proposed approach in the next section. For now, we describe the various components in each data center, and how

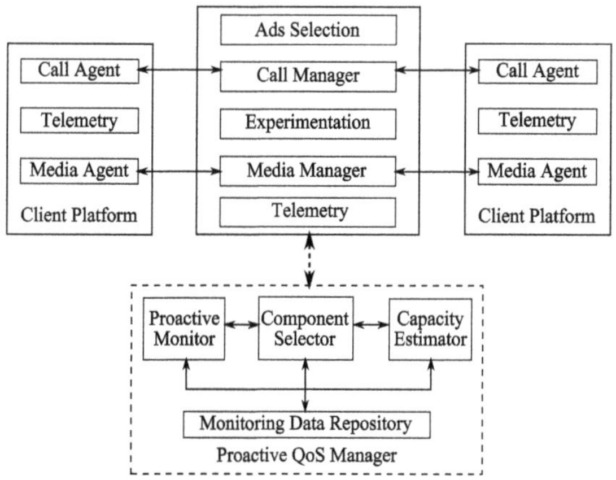

Figure 2: The components of the multimedia communication service and the Proactive QoS Manager.

a session is created between two client applications. The service has challenging requirements, and operates under strict SLAs. It receives multimedia communication requests from applications running on mobile devices, Web, and PCs. It processes each request, determines the source device, identifies ads and experimentation configurations based on app categories, device types, user information if available with user permission to use, and user location. It processes the media, and makes a call to the destination client app with the target media, ads, and experimental parameters. Each of the components in the multimedia communication service is comprised of many geo-located instances so that the client call is routed to the most suitable, geo-location and performance wise, data center. The service is composed mainly of Call Manager, Experimentation, Ads Selection, Media Manager, and Telemetry components. The Media Manager estimates the available compute and network resources to maximize the session quality. The Media Manager enables image, audio, and video content to be transported from one endpoint to another as part of a session using UDP or TCP. It implements audio and video encoding and decoding, and packet loss compensation. The Ads Selection component finds relevant ads for the session. The Experimentation component identifies sessions that are suitable for new experiments like new app functionality and/or new color schemes. The Telemetry component collects system performance indicators like available memory and compute resources, as well as functionality measurements like the quality of a video in a multimedia session and number of calls made per minute.

When a user makes a call from an application, the Call Agent tries to connect to the multimedia communication service. The Call Manager of the service handles the incoming session request. It breaks down the multimedia session into its constituents (i.e., audio, video, conferencing, ads, experiments) and tries to identify the best instances in the available data centers that are able to handle the multimedia session. Depending on the used transport protocol (UDP vs TCP) the packets of the session are routed to the selected components, and the connection is established between the two ends of the multimedia session. During the session, the selected components and routing paths do not change.

As can be noted from this high-level description, the quality of the multimedia calling experience has complex dependencies including the selection of components, the routing paths to get to the destination, and the scale and performance characteristics of the Media Manager. There is high demand on the Media Manager component, which may lead the Media Manager to reduce the quality of multimedia streams to ensure that communication sessions do not get dropped. So if we can, in real-time, continuously know the components that have the highest available resources, the highest performance characteristics, and the highest multimedia throughput quality as well as predict how these factors will change over the coming short period of time, we can make component selection and path routing decisions in real-time that will result in high quality multimedia communication sessions.

2.2 Related Work

Several works have tried to address the reduced quality stemming from contention in multimedia communication services. For example, Trajkovska et al. [24] propose an algorithm to join P2P and cloud computing to enhance the Quality of Service (QoS) of multimedia streaming systems. They investigate cloud APIs with built-in functions that allow the automatic computation of QoS. This enables negotiating QoS parameters such as bandwidth, jitter and latency. The work in [24] deals with the limitations caused by the platforms where the multimedia streaming takes place. Tasaka et al. [22] study the feasibility of switching between error concealment and frame skipping to enhance the Quality of Experiences (QoE). This approach utilizes a tradeoff between the spatial and temporal quality that is caused by error concealment and frame skipping. The algorithm they suggest switches between error concealment to frame skipping depending on the nature of errors encountered in the video output. Ito et al. [5] study the tradeoff between quality and latency in interactive audio and video applications with the Internet being the medium of communications. They note that the temporal structure of audio-video communication is disturbed by the delay jitter of packets. They study the impact of de-jittering on latency, and the impact of improved latency on quality, which is how the temporal structure is preserved. Through the adoption of psychometric methods, they adjust the initial buffering to enhance latency and quality.

To study the impact of geographical distribution of multimedia services and distributed peers, Rainer and Timmerer [14] suggest a self-organized distributed synchronization method for multimedia content. They adapt IDMS MPEG-DASH to synchronize multimedia playback among the geographically distributed peers. They introduce session management to MPEG-DASH and propose a new distributed control scheme that negotiates a reference for the playback time-stamp among participating peers in the multimedia session. The goal is to improve synchronization, enhance quality, reduce jittering, and enhance latency.

A number of works have attempted to address video rendering problems in real-time. Li et al. [9] propose a new rendering technique, LiveRender, that addresses the problems of bandwidth optimization techniques like inter-frame compression and caching. They address problems of latency and quality by introducing compression in graphics streaming. Shi et al. [20] propose a video encoder to select a set of key frames in the video sequence which uses a 3D image warping algorithm to interpolate non-key frames. This approach takes advantage of the run-time graphics rendering contexts to enhance the performance of video encoding.

The aforementioned approaches work on the limitation of the systems, and try to make the best of available resources to enhance the multimedia communication experiences. These schemes aim at controlling QoS, and managing latency and lack of quality. They come short of addressing the actual cause of the problem, which is knowing the state of the services, identifying the services and components that are not performing well, and/or will not perform well in the coming period, and trying to avoid contention and congestion before they happen. We propose a different approach to enhancing the quality in multimedia communication services. We proactively and dynamically monitor the multimedia services to get an insight into their state, and continuously know the best available components where there is minimal contention and congestion, best quality, and least jitter and delay.

3. PROACTIVE QOS MANAGER

We define three terms that we use in this paper: **Application**, **Service**, and **Platform**. Application refers to the software used by real customers to make calls. Service is the online backend system that applications invoke to accomplish the required functionality such as calling other parties and sharing media with them. A service may be comprised of one or more online services. To avoid confusion, we refer to these other services as components of the main service. Platform refers to the stack of software, hardware, and operating system that is used to run the applications and services. For example an Apple iPhone is a client platform, and Microsoft Azure is a service platform.

3.1 Overview

The proposed approach, denoted by Proactive QoS Manager in Figure 2, monitors the health and QoS of multimedia communication services and predicts failures in real-time. We use synthetic transactions to proactively and continuously test the services and platforms and generate current data about them. The data is used in its ephemeral state to: (1) provide situational awareness about the whole service, (2) correlate failures between applications, services, and platforms, and (3) build a failure prediction algorithm that predicts future failures. The data is used to keep the failure prediction system up to date with the changes of the services and platforms. These three steps result in the ability to make decisions about which components to use that result in the best possible multimedia session experiences.

Before getting into the details of the proposed approach, we describe the Testing in Production (TiP) concept, because our approach uses it. TiP entails software testing techniques that utilize real production environments, while mitigating risks to end users [16, 3, 23]. Online service providers such as Facebook, Google, Microsoft, and Yahoo use TiP to perform functional, stress and performance testing in real-time [23]. Synthetic transactions are used in TiP to generate testing loads, and they are marked with special moniker(s) so that they are distinguished from real transactions. Synthetic Transactions should not interfere with the service destructively, or result in an incorrect state of the service like product inventory reduction due to test purchases. Synthetic transactions in TiP do use the computing resources of the tested service. Service designers account for such an impact due to the importance of TiP; without it the service would be flying blind [16, 23]. We add our synthetic transactions for QoS management to the existing TiP transactions as described in the next section. No code is instrumented in the production code of the service to generate the data for our approach. This is an important advantage for our approach, because we do not impact the production code, and thus no extra testing is needed. Also, updates to the service monitoring and failure predictor do not require production code update or redeployment.

Figure 2 shows the high-level diagram of the multimedia communication service with the proposed approach in the dotted rectangle. The proposed approach consists of four components: (1) Proactive Monitor, (2) Capacity Estimator, (3) Component Selector, and (4) Monitoring Data Repository. The first three components are implemented for each service instance deployed in a single data center, and the Monitoring Data Repository is centralized to all instances; i.e., one instance for the whole system. The Proactive Monitor tests the individual components of the service as well as the whole service e2e. It collects the test results and makes them available to the Capacity Estimator and the Component Selector. The Capacity Estimator uses this data to implement a dynamic failure predictor and to keep it up to date to handle any changes. It predicts the capacity of individual components of the service and the loads at which the components will start to violate their SLAs. The Component Selector collects the current status of the service and its components from the Proactive Monitor, and the capacity limits that will result in SLA violations for the coming monitoring period from the Capacity Estimator. It then creates a **Service Capacity Plan** for the coming monitoring period. The plan contains the available components in the service, their current state, and their projected capacity before SLA violations start to happen. It pushes this plan to the Monitoring Data Repository which gets the service capacity plans from all service instances from all data centers. It combines these plans into one **Global Capacity Plan**, and makes it available to each service instance to pull through an API. The plans are updated regularly; the frequency of update depends on the service at hand, typically this would range from 30 seconds to a few minutes. The following subsections describe each of the elements of the proposed approach.

3.2 Proactive Monitor

The goal of the Proactive Monitor is to provide real-time insights into the state of the multimedia communication service. We define two concepts: **Local System** and **Scenario**. Local System refers to the stack of software, hardware, and operating system used to perform a specific functionality in the online service. Scenario refers to the collaboration of the set of local systems that are used to implement an e2e user scenario. As an example, assume a multimedia communication service that allows users to invite other users to watch a video together. The e2e scenario is the process of calling others and sharing videos with them. Assume the event of interest is video quality. The video quality SLA for the e2e transaction could be 4, i.e., good quality, using the Mean Opinion Score (MOS) [10]. The video sharing process meets its SLA if the video MOS quality is 4 or 5, and fails otherwise. Assume that the sharing service makes the following calls behind the scene: buffer and encode video, transmit video, receive video, decode video, and de-jitter video. Each of these calls represents a local system. The collaboration of these local systems to implement the video sharing process represents the e2e scenario.

We define three levels of monitoring: (1) local system level, (2) scenario level, and (3) platform level. The Proactive Monitor implements the first level by regularly performing Local System synthetic transaction Tests (LSTs), to continuously monitor the health of each local system. For example, this would be calling the video buffer and encode function and passing it a video, and noting its output video and the time it took to perform the encoding. The Proactive Monitor implements the scenario level of monitoring by performing an e2e Scenario Synthetic Transaction Tests (SSTs) that implement the functionality provided to customers, i.e., sharing a video between two clients. The SST test calls all the local systems that collaborate to perform the functionality, and notes the e2e output of the scenario. These two sets of tests, the LSTs and SSTs, are used to monitor the individual local systems and the e2e scenarios. The Proactive Monitor also implements Platform Synthetic Transaction Tests (PSTs) to collect performance indicators like CPU utilization, memory consumption, and process count to correlate with the observed failures. We do not implement application synthetic transactions, i.e., test calls to the applications, as applications are generally installed on user devices and are mostly on metered networks. We use the default client telemetry implemented on these devices that provide information about the application usage. We combine this information with the service and platform synthetic transaction information to monitor the service e2e, and to generate failure prediction systems.

The Proactive Monitor makes LST and SST calls using test loads, which are similar to real loads. The real user behavior, loads and call distributions, is found from logs of previous deployments of the service, or from field/market studies about the service. For example, it would be known, based on previous production logs and/or estimated from market research, that the average user of a multimedia communication service shares a video of 60 seconds with 2-5 friends at a time, and that the service gets around 1,000 concurrent users at peak times. The SSTs made by the Proactive Monitor start with these loads, and progressively add more loads until the failure causing loads are found. If the SLA of video quality is, say, a minimum MOS value of 4, then any video quality of MOS value less than 4 is considered a failure. The test loads are executed on the current service, thus they generate information that represent the current state of the service and its performance characteristics. The synthetic transactions are run for a short period of time, e.g., 5 seconds every couple of minutes. Thus, they do not increase the load on the service considerably.

The LST, SST, and PST calls are made at equidistant time series; once every M seconds. The value of M is configurable, depending on the service, and it varies during run time, depending on the state of the service. If the service is churning and failures are happening more, then M is reduced to get a better pulse of the service. The event, i.e., video quality, is captured after each of these tests, and its value is compared to the result of the prediction. If the accuracy of the predictor starts to drop, the tests are done at a higher rate to generate data to build a new predictor.

The set of tests performed every M seconds need not be exactly like those of customer behavior. However, if the service at hand requires an exact replica of the user behavior, then parts of previous production logs representing real user behavior can be replayed as suggested by [15, 7, 18].

3.3 Capacity Estimator

The Capacity Estimator tries to find the maximum capacity that the service and its components can handle before SLA violations start to happen. It does so by predicting the capacity at which failure starts to happen. It implements a dynamic failure predictor that is able to cope with the service and component changes in real-time. The failure predictor is an independent module that runs in the same environment where the online multimedia service runs. It is part of the TiP system. It has access to the same resources as the production service, but is not part of the online service code. Updates and re-deployments of the predictor code can be done anytime without interfering with the service production system.

Failure predictors are designed to predict the outcome of an event [4, 6]. In multimedia communication applications and services, events represent a variety of measurable aspects of the service, such as the call quality, the response time of the service, and the availability of the service. In this paper, failure prediction means predicting when the outcome of an event does not meet its SLA. For example, if the event of interest is multimedia quality, then failure prediction means predicting the cases where the quality of the shared media drops below the MOS value specified in the SLA. We need a dynamic failure predictor that can be created and updated in real-time. We implement one of the latest failure predictors called Real-Time Dynamic Failure Prediction (RTDFP) algorithm [19]; other predictors can be used in our approach as well. We choose RTDFP because it can be created and maintained in real-time in a short amount of time, and has high prediction accuracy. We customize RTDFP for our Proactive QoS Management approach. The main steps of the Capacity Estimator are summarized as follows:

- Step 1: Use the Proactive Monitor to exercise the service and generate current data about it.
- Step 2: Collect, from the Proactive Monitor, the synthetic transactions and applications' inputs, service and platform outputs, e2e scenario outputs, such as media quality and response times, and events of interest. This data is collected into in-memory constructs with a predefined dimensional model (explained below).
- Step 3: Build a real-time predictor, from the data collected from the applications, services, and platforms and the events of interest.
- Step 4: Estimate the available capacity based on the outcomes from the failure predictor.

The data collected in Step 2 includes the current load and state of the service like the number of videos to process, and the used resources like media processors and call de-jitters. Service and platform related data such as memory utilization, number of processes, and CPU utilization are also collected. We describe in the evaluation section how we capture such data in our experiments. The data is collected and hosted in memory in an array with a dimensional model schema [8]. Dimensional modeling refers to a set of techniques used in data analysis to provide insights into the cause-effect relationships between entities. Data is organized into two sets, a set of measured or monitored data, called **facts**, and a set of parameters, called **dimensions** that define and control the facts. For this paper, the fact is the event of interest that is to be predicted, such as media quality. The dimensions are the other sets of data that impact the event, such as:

- The **LST** that is called: this allows us to know which test is run.
- The **time** that LST is called: the time stamp allows us to relate the cause and effect in the service calls, i.e., at a specific time there were that many function calls and tasks, which caused the observed response time.
- The **number of tasks**: the number of media processing jobs in the service.
- The **component**: the specific component, like Ads Selection or Experimentation, in the service instance.
- The **data center**: where the components are deployed; this could include more details such as the deployment ID.

Table 1: Dimensional Model for the online Multimedia Service.

Dimensions					Fact
Dim1 LST	Dim2 Tasks	Dim3 Data center	Dim4 Component	Dim5 LST time	Fact1 Video Quality (MOS)
1	53	3	5	23	4
2	53	3	2	17	4
3	53	3	3	31	3
4	53	3	1	19	5

Table 1 represents a service QoS dimensional model. Note that we use surrogate keys [8] to represent non-measured and non-numeric values. A surrogate key is a unique identifier of an entity; it is an integer and it is not derived. This makes a table with smaller footprint in memory, as only integers are used, and enhances the performance of operations done on it. The map between the surrogate keys and the actual values is stored in a local table that has the actual dimension values and the corresponding surrogate keys. For example, the service instance in the US western data center maps to "Dim3 Service" surrogate key value 3.

The collected data is used for two purposes. The first purpose is to feed the Monitoring Data Repository to build reports and dashboards that represent the current state of the service such as how many users are making multimedia calls in a given data center and the average quality of shared media over time. This provides situational awareness about the service on an ongoing basis. The other purpose that we use this data for is to generate a real-time failure predictor, and maintain its accuracy over time (Step 3).

A predictor is a classification system [4, 6] that defines and monitors boundaries of working conditions that result in an event success or failure. The event could be the MOS quality. The working conditions are the independent and dependent variables that control the outcome of the event. We use the load of each component as the independent variable, and the CPU utilization as the dependent variable; because it is dependent on the load of each component, yet it plays a key role in controlling the event outcome. We implement a light-weight predictor based on RTDFP that uses the load and the CPU utilization of each component as a logical expression model [19]. The logical expression model is a set of conditions defining the safe component working-conditions that result in the success of the event. We define the following model for the MOS value to be successful:

- MOS Quality Condition for Success for Component N:
  - Independent Variable for Component $N <$ $IndependentVariableMaxValue$ found by the Proactive Monitor
  - Dependent Variable For Component $N <$ $DependentVariableMaxValue$ found by the Proactive Monitor

The Capacity Estimator (Step 4) gets the maximum values for the independent and dependent variables that are found by the Proactive Monitor LST and SST tests, builds the Service Capacity Plan for the coming monitoring period, and passes it to the Component Selector. In other words, the Capacity Estimator utilizes the RTDFP failure prediction to build the component capacity for the coming monitoring period that will not result in SLA violations.

3.4 Component Selector

The Component Selector combines the current data about the service from the Proactive Monitor with the projected capacity that the service and its components can handle from the Capacity Estimator. Table 2 shows an example of this combined data that represents the Service Capacity Plan for the coming monitoring period. The Component Selector pushes Table 2 to the Monitoring Data Repository to be combined with similar data about the components of the rest of the data centers. The Component Selector pulls the Global Capacity Plan from the Monitoring Data Repository into a new instance of Table 2.

The Service and Global Capacity Plans are computed at the beginning of each monitoring period. Each Component Selector reads these plans from the Monitoring Data Repository, and makes them available for its local service instance in its data center. The local service reads the Global Capacity Plan from the Component Selector into an in-memory array to make access to it fast and suitable for routing every session in real-time. When a client invokes the local service, the local service finds the most suitable component to handle the session from its in-memory copy of Table 2, and routes the session to it. Two factors are used in determining the most suitable component: (1) geo-graphical location; the Data Center dimension in Table 2 is used to find the closest component that can be used, so locally first then the same region, and (2) the component that has the highest available capacity; the Projected Extra Media Jobs fact in Table 2 provides this information. Once a session is committed to a component, it remains there until completed. In other words, session routing to components using

Procedure 1 Component Selector Algorithm

COMPONENT SELECTION

function GETCURRENTSTATEOFSERVICES
Select Service, Component, ProcessingJobCount, AvgMOS
from Table1
orderdescendingby AvgMOS
groupby Service and Component;
end function

function GENERATESERVICECAPACITYPLAN
GetCurrentStateOfServices();
Use RTDFP to get Predicted JobCount until failure;

MergeJoin Ordered list with Predicted JobCount until failure
orderdescendingby Service and Component;

Select Service, Component, ProcessingJogCount,
AvgMOS, JobCountUntilFailure
orderdescendingby AvgMOS and JobCountUntilFailure;

Populate Service Capacity Plan instance of Table 2;
end function

function GETGLOBALCAPACITYPLAN
Push Service Capacity Plan to Monitoring Data Repository;
Wait until Monitoring Data Repository builds Global Capacity Plan;
Pull Global Capacity Plan from Monitoring Data Repository;
Push Global Capacity Plan to local service Configurations component;
end function

the Global Capacity Plan affects new sessions only. This prevents session oscillation between components.

As shown in Procedure 1, the Component Selector implements three functions: GetCurrentStateOfServices(), GenerateServiceCapacityPlan(), and GetGlobalCapacityPlan(). GetCurrentStateOfServices() gets the current loads and status of each component in the system from the Proactive Monitor. This function returns an instance of Table 1. GenerateServiceCapacityPlan() uses the failure predictor to predict the loads that will result in SLA violations. These loads are used to determine the available capacities in the components for the next monitoring period. The available capacities are combined with the instance of Table 1 to produce an instance of Table 2, which is the Service Capacity Plan. GetGlobalCapacityPlan() pushes the Service Capacity Plan to the Monitoring Data Repository which gets all such plans from all Component Selectors. The Monitoring Data Repository combines all these instances into the Global Capacity Plan. GetGlobalCapacityPlan() pulls the Global Capacity Plan from the Monitoring Data Repository and pushes it to the service configurations so that the service can use it in routing sessions.

Table 2: Service Capacity Plan.

Data Center	Component	Current Processing Jobs	Current Avg MOS at Service	Projected Extra Media Jobs
4	5	36	5	28
2	6	41	5	23
3	2	27	5	19
7	4	17	5	17

3.5 Monitoring Data Repository

The main function of the Monitoring Data Repository is to combine the local Service Capacity Plans into one Global Capacity Plan that represents the whole system, and to make it available to all components to pull as needed. This is an important functionality that prevents excessive communication between the Component Selectors of each data center instance of the Proactive QoS Manager. With the Monitoring Data Repository, every Component Selector computes the Service Capacity Plan, and communicates twice with the Monitoring Data Repository. The first is to send its Service Capacity Plan, and the second is to get the Global Capacity Plan. The Monitoring Data Repository gets all Capacity Plans, merges them, and generates one Global Capacity Plan that represents the current usage of all components as well as their projected capacities. The Monitoring Data Repository is implemented as a single instance. It is part of the TiP system, so it does not have the high availability requirements that production systems have. In case it is down, each Component Selector continues to use its own Service Capacity Plan until the Global Capacity Plan is built. The production service uses the suggested Proactive QoS Monitor as a heuristic agent to enhance its component selection and routing functionality. The production system is designed to survive and function well, even if the whole TiP system is down.

4. EVALUATION

We implement the proposed approach in an operational online multimedia communication service offered by Microsoft [13] and we present results from more than 100 million video and audio sessions.

4.1 Implementation and Setup

We implement LSTs for four local systems: Call Manager, Experimentation, Ads Selection, and Media Manager. The geo-distributed multimedia communication service processes about 2.5 million requests per second at the peak. It is deployed in 8 data centers in 3 continents. LSTs are API calls to each of these components, with loads as explained in the Proactive Monitor section. The setup we implement is based on the model shown in Figure 2. We use a small test cluster of 10 servers in the data center, which gets about 1% of the data center traffic to run our experiments. Each server is a quad-core intel Xeon server with 12 GB RAM. We implement a Proactive Monitor that makes LST, SST, and PST calls to exercise each component and we capture the inputs to the LSTs and the outputs of the Local systems. Similarly, we record the output of SSTs and PSTs. An SST is composed of the LSTs that represent the scenario; so a session with audio and video is composed of Call Manager, Experimentation, Ads Selection, and Media Manager LSTs with parameters that specify the audio and video characteristics like length and encoding. We measure the SST response time and quality of the multimedia session using a proprietary automated MOS algorithm. PSTs are implemented in an infinite loop that reads CPU utilization, memory utilization, and number of processes from the performance monitoring APIs of the operating system of each component every 30 seconds.

The Proactive Monitor makes the calls to each of the local systems and controls the various aspects of the multimedia communication request, including media type, media size, location, and automated user information. The Proactive Monitor also simulates multimedia sessions made by multiple clients, by making simultaneous calls with different user agent information. It controls the load in two ways: the number of media sessions made by each simulated client in a given time, and the number of simultaneous media sessions representing multiple client calls. The data is collected into in-memory arrays with a schema similar to Table 1. The synthetic transactions are designed to run 100 concurrent LSTs every minute. The accuracy of the predictor is measured by comparing its predictions with the actual results and monitored event value from running LSTs and SSTs. Each LST set of tests takes about 5 seconds to complete. The resulting data from the Proactive Monitor synthetic transactions are collected by the Capacity Estimator and Component Selector. The Capacity Estimator makes capacity estimates for the coming monitoring period of one minute. The Component Selector builds the Service Capacity Plan every minute, and communicates with the Monitoring Data Repository to get the updated Global Capacity Plan.

4.2 Performance Metrics

We study the quality of media during the multimedia session and the number of shared media streams, i.e., video, audio, and image. We use the following metrics in our experiments:

- **Media Quality**: the quality of media (audio, video, and image) that is shared between clients. We use MOS for this metric. We use a proprietary *automated* MOS algorithm. Other automated MOS test software is commercially available, e.g., [1]. These automated MOS algorithms enable quality measurements in test environments, where sessions are generated programmatically between test clients.
- **Number of Failures**: the number of sessions that failed to meet the required MOS quality as specified by the service SLAs.
- **Increase in Service Capacity**: the number of additional sessions that the service can handle. This value is found by the Capacity Estimator and using the Proactive Monitor tests to verify its accuracy. We measure the service capacity, by finding the loads that the service can handle until failure, with and without the proposed approach.
- **CPU Utilization**: this reflects how much of the total available resources are freed up due to better resource utilization and load balancing. We get this as part of running the PSTs, through an operating system API call every 30 seconds. This is extracted for each component.
- **Overhead**: We measure the CPU utilization of the service with and without the TiP system, to find the overhead of TiP.

4.3 Results

The service we test our approach in has a high track record for meeting its strict SLAs; on average and over a period of almost three years, the service is able to meet its multimedia communication quality SLA more than 99.9% of the time. The service strives to do better, as a 0.1% failure rate is

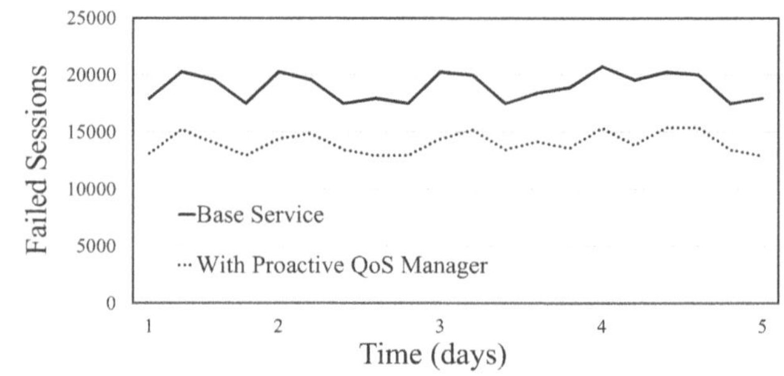

Figure 3: Failure reduction with proposed approach.

still high and costs a lot of money for a service that manages 2.5 million transactions per second at peak. That's 25,000 transactions per second at peak that potentially did not meet SLA. To provide an idea of the monetary impact alone of such a failure rate, note that the ads monetization for such a service runs at a rate higher than $10 per a thousand ad impressions. That is, advertisers pay $10 for every 1,000 ads shown to customers. So that's an opportunity loss of minimally $250 *er second*, let alone the negative impact of the lower customer satisfaction, which can lead to losing customers to competitors.

Our test cluster gets about 3,000 transactions per second at peak. We ran the experiment for 5 days, and we divide the test time into two alternating parts: (1) the base or reference part, where we run the traffic over the service without the proposed solution for one hour, and (2) the updated service or optimized part, where we run the traffic over the service with the proposed solution for another hour. We aggregate the results of our tests at a granularity of 6 hours; i.e., each point in the graphs we show in this section represents a 6-hour aggregation, unless otherwise mentioned. In each 6-hour period, 3 hours have the results for the base service, and the other 3 hours have the results for the optimized service with our Proactive QoS monitoring approach.

We processed more than 100 million sessions over the 5-day period. For each period of 6 hours, the average number of multimedia sessions we get is about 5 million, half of them with our approach and the other half without it.

Number of Failures: We measure the number of failed sessions with and without our approach, and we plot the results in Figure 3. As the figure shows, the average number of failed sessions is about 19,000 failures without our approach. Using the proposed approach to monitor, estimate capacity, predict failures, and route to components with higher capacity and better performance, the failed sessions count drops to an average of 14,000. Therefore, the proposed approach manages to drop the failed sessions by about 26%, on average. The average is fairly smooth because it is measured across a large period of 3 hours. The gain from our approach is much higher during peak times, where resources are constrained.

Media Quality: We measure the media quality of the succeeded sessions. Our results show that not only did the failed session count drop by about 26%, but the quality of the sessions that meet SLA have seen an improvement as well. Figure 4 shows that, on average, around 12% of the sessions that used to meet SLA with MOS 4, are now meeting their SLA with MOS 5, Excellent Quality. We study

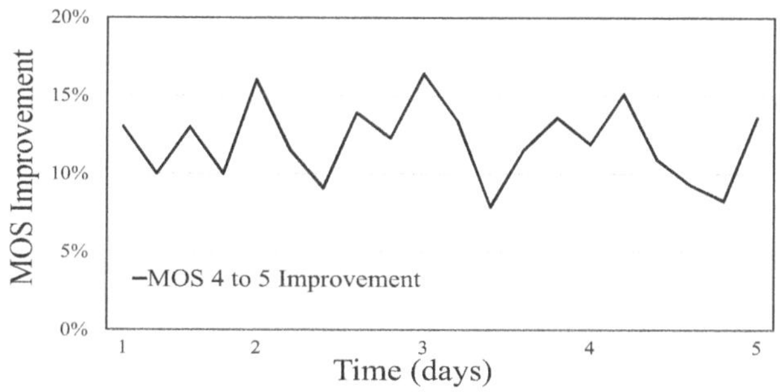

Figure 4: MOS increase from 4 to 5 over 5 days.

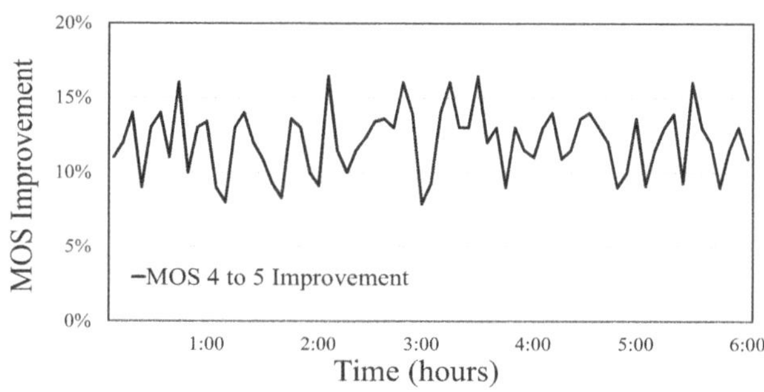

Figure 5: MOS increase from 4 to 5 over 6 hours.

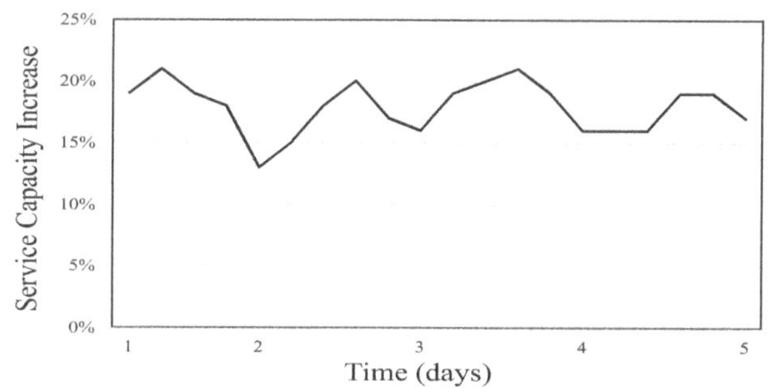

Figure 6: Increase in the available capacity.

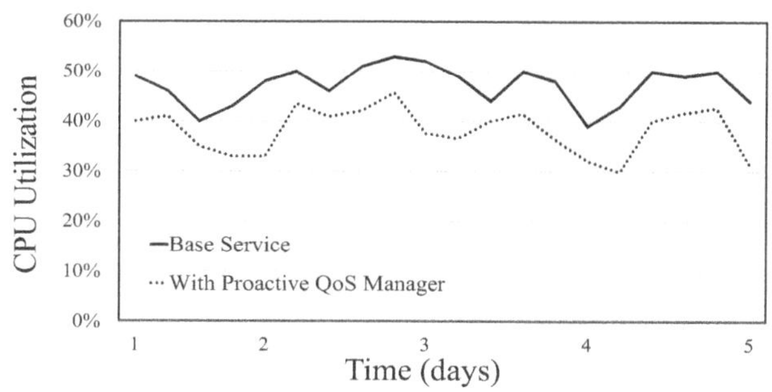

Figure 7: Reduction of CPU utilization.

the MOS improvement from 4 to 5 in more details over 12 hours, while alternating between using the service with and without our approach every hour. We average the MOS measurement every 5 minutes. We see an improvement of about the same average, around 12%, as we see in the 5 days experiment with 6 hour aggregation; please refer to Figure 5. This shows the stability and predictability of the proposed approach over different time ranges and aggregation periods.

Increase in Service Capacity: The average available service capacity has also seen an improvement. This is the number of extra multimedia sessions the service can handle. Because of the enhanced component selection, the service is seeing less bottlenecks and delays, and so is able to handle more multimedia sessions. Figure 6 shows that the service has an average of about 17% session capacity increase over the 5 day experiment, and a maximum of up to 21% increase can be achieved.

CPU Utilization: The service CPU utilization has seen a drop of an average of 10% over the 5 day experiment, as shown in Figure 7. This is closely related to the increase in service capacity. Because of the optimized component selection, the components are observing better load distribution and so less congestion. The demand on their CPUs has dropped by about 10%, which allows the components to handle more sessions, by about 17%, with the same resources.

Overhead: we measure the overhead of the TiP system on the production system to determine the cost of the proposed approach. We measure the service CPU utilization with and without TiP. We find that the average service CPU impact caused by the whole TiP system is around 3% over 5 days, as seen in Figure 8. This includes the proposed Proactive QoS Manager approach as well as all other testing in production functionality. All computations of our approach are done on the TiP system, not the production system. The improved multimedia quality, reduced failures, enhanced service session capacity, and reduced CPU usage are gains made by the proposed approach that make the overall investment in the TiP system more than justified.

5. CONCLUSIONS AND FUTURE WORK

Current approaches to the management of the health and quality of service in online multimedia communication services are mostly static and can not keep up with the frequent changes that happen during the real-time lifecycle of the services. Monitoring the services and waiting for real sessions to fail in order to gain insights into the state of the service is a not an efficient solution. Online services have dynamic situations that require them to change often, and the cost of failures is higher. We presented a dynamic approach to monitoring the health and quality of multimedia communication services. We use *s nthetic transactions* to monitor the service by exercising it like real customers, generate current data about it, and then use this *resh* data to create and maintain up-to-date capacity predictions of different components of the multimedia communication service. We then take component selection and routing path actions in real-time to enhance the quality of multimedia sessions. On average, the proposed approach increased the overall media sharing quality by 12%, decreased the percentage of failures by 25%, reduced the CPU usage by 10%, and increased the session capacity in the service by 17%.

A potential future work is to apply the proactive QoS management approach to other multimedia services, such as on-demand and live streaming systems.

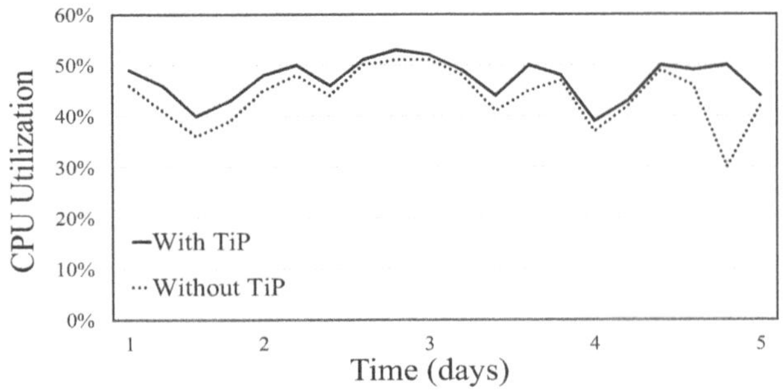

Figure 8: TiP impact on CPU utilization.

6. REFERENCES

[1] Automated mean opinion score. http://voip.about.com/od/voipbasics/a/MOS.htm.

[2] IT Channel. http://www.itchannelplanet.com/.

[3] E. Elliot. Testing in production A to Z - tip methodologies, techniques, and examples. In *Proc. o So t are est Pro essionals (S P' 2)*, New Orleans, LA, March 2012.

[4] J. Han, M. Kamber, and J. Pei. *Data Mining Conce ts and echni ues.* Morgan Kaufmann, 3rd edition, 2011.

[5] Y. Ito, S. Tasaka, and Y. Fukuta. Psychometric analysis of the effect of buffering control on user-level QoS in an interactive audio-visual application. In *Proc. o CM Multimedia Worksho on Ne t generation Residential Broad and Challenges (NRBC'04)*, New York, NY, October 2004.

[6] M. Kantarczic. *Data Mining Conce ts Models Methods and lgorithms.* Wiley and IEEE Press, 2nd edition, 2011.

[7] C. Killian, J. W. Anderson, R. Jhala, and A. Vahdat. Life, death, and the critical transition: Detecting liveness bugs in systems code. In *Proc. o US NIX S m . on Net orked S stems Design and Im lementation (NSDI'07)*, pages 243–256, Cambridge, MA, April 2007.

[8] R. Kimball and M. Ross. *he Data Warehouse oolkit: he De nitive Guide to Dimensional Modeling.* Wiley Computer Publishing, 3rd edition, 2013.

[9] L. Lin, X. Liao, G. Tan, H. Jin, X. Yang, W. Zhang, and B. Li. Liverender: A cloud gaming system based on compressed graphics streaming. In *Proc. o CM International Con erence on Multimedia (MM' 4)*, pages 347 – 356, Orlando, Florida, November 2014.

[10] Mean opinion score. https://technet.microsoft.com/en-us/library/bb894481(v=office.12).aspx.

[11] Real-time monitoring. http://techblog.netflix.com/2012/11/hystrix.html. and https://github.com/Netflix/Hystrix.

[12] K. Nagaraj, C. Killian, and J. Neville. Structured comparative analysis of systems logs to diagnose performance problems. In *Proc. o US NIX Con erence on Net orked S stems Design and Im lementation (NSDI' 2)*, pages 353–366, San Jose, CA, April 2012.

[13] Microsoft application and services group. http://www.microsoft.com.

[14] B. Rainer and C. Timmerer. Self-organized inter-destination multimedia synchronization for adaptive media streaming. In *Proc. o CM International Con erence on Multimedia (MM' 4)*, pages 327–336, Orlando, FL, November 2014.

[15] P. Reynolds, C. Killian, J. L. Wiener, J. C. Mogul, M. A. Shah, and A. Vahdat. Pip: Detecting the unexpected in distributed systems. In *Proc. o S m . on Net orked S stems Design and Im lementation (NSDI'06)*, pages 115–128, San Jose, CA, May 2006.

[16] L. Riungu-Kalliosaari, O. Taipale, and K. Smolander. *esting in the Cloud: loring the Practice.* IEEE Software Magazine, 2012.

[17] F. Salfner, M. Lenk, and M. Malek. A survey of online failure prediction methods. In *Proc. o CM Com uting Surve s Vol. 42 No. 3 rticle 0*, March 2010.

[18] F. Salfner and S. Tschirpke. Error log processing for accurate failure prediction. In *Proc. o US NIX Worksho on nal sis o S stem Logs (W SL'08)*, San Diego, CA, December 2008.

[19] M. Shatnawi and M. Hefeeda. Real-time failure prediction in online services. In *Proc. o I IN OCOM' 5*, Hong Kong, April 2015.

[20] S. Shi, C. Hsu, K. Nahrstedt, and R. Campbell. Using graphics rendering contexts to enhance the real-time video coding for mobile cloud gaming. In *Proc. o CM International Con erence on Multimedia (MM')*, pages 103–112, Scottsdale, AZ, November 2011.

[21] Social networking statistics. http://www.statisticbrain.com/social-networking-statistics.

[22] S. Tasaka, H. Yoshimi, A. Hirashima, and T. Nunome. The effectiveness of a qoe-based video output scheme for audio-video ip transmission. In *Proc. o CM International Con erence on Multimedia (MM'08)*, pages 259–268, Vancouver, BC, Canada, October 2008.

[23] Testing in production. http://blogs.msdn.com/b/seliot/archive/2011/06/07/testing-in-production-tip-it-really-happens-and-that-s-a-good-thing.aspx.

[24] I. Trajkovska, J. Rodriguez, and A. Velasco. A novel p2p and cloud computing hybrid architecture for multimedia streaming with QoS cost functions. In *Proc. o International Con erence on Multimedia (MM' 0)*, pages 1227–1230, Firenze, Italy, October 2010.

[25] W. Xu, L. Huang, A. Fox, D. Patterson, and M. Jordan. Detecting large-scale system problems by mining console logs. In *Proc. o CM S m . on O erating S stems Princi les (SOSP'09)*, pages 117–132, Big Sky, MT, October 2009.

Distributed Optimal Datacenter Bandwidth Allocation for Dynamic Adaptive Video Streaming

Fanxin Kong[1], Xingjian Lu[1,2], Mingyuan Xia[1], Xue Liu[1] and Haibing Guan[3]
[1]School of Computer Science, McGill University
[2]School of Information Science and Engineering, East China University of Science and Technology
[3]Department of Computer Science and Engineering, Shang Hai Jiao Tong University
fanxin.kong@mail.mcgill.ca, luxj@ecust.edu.cn, mingyuan.xia@mail.mcgill.ca
xueliu@cs.mcgill.ca, hbguan@sjtu.edu.cn

ABSTRACT

Video streaming systems such as YouTube and Netflix are usually supported by the content delivery networks and datacenters that can consume many megawatts of power. Most existing works independently study the issues of improving quality of experience (QoE) for viewers and reducing the cost and emissions associated with the enormous energy usage of datacenters. By contrast, this paper addresses them both, and jointly optimizes the QoE, the energy cost and emissions by intelligently allocating datacenter bandwidth among different client groups. Specially, we propose a distributed algorithm for achieving the optimal bandwidth allocation. The algorithm novelly decomposes the optimization process into separate ones, which are solved iteratively across datacenters and clients. We demonstrate its convergence by both theoretical proof and experimental validation. The experimental results show that the proposed algorithm converges very fast and achieves much better QoE-cost balance than existing approaches.

Categories and Subject Descriptors

C.2.4 [**Computer-Communication Networks**]: Distributed Systems

Keywords

Datacenter; video streaming; bandwidth allocation; quality of experience; energy cost

1. INTRODUCTION

Dynamic Adaptive Streaming over HTTP (DASH) is an adaptive streaming technique that dynamically adjusts media quality levels according to network conditions [1,2]. This technique is widely-used by streaming service providers such as YouTube and Netflix [3]. Many research efforts have been made on improving quality of experience (QoE) based on DASH. For example, Google publishes its technical basis about how YouTube streams videos [4]. Works in academia such as [5–8] develop various quality adaptation algorithms for the video player.

On the other hand, the large-scale streaming systems are provided by massive geographically distributed content delivery networks and datacenters, each with hundreds to thousands of servers and requiring megawatts of power for streaming. The enormous energy usage has motivated research both in academia and industry on economic and environmental aspects, e.g., [9–14]. However, most of the existing works focus on each individual issue, either on improving QoE for viewers or reducing energy cost and emissions for datacenters. In this work, we study both issues and jointly optimize QoE, energy cost and emissions.

Challenge arises due to the conflict between these objectives. To be specific, better quality of experience usually appeals more users and thus benefits the service providers with higher revenues. Meanwhile, this requires high quality video and thus needs more network resources for streaming. Allocating more datacenter bandwidth results in larger probability of streaming high quality videos, but causes increased energy usage and emissions to datacenters. We address this challenge and design an intelligent datacenter bandwidth allocation scheme to balance QoE, energy cost and emissions.

Existing works on datacenter cost/emission reduction make the allocation decision based on the arrival rate of user requests, e.g., [9–14]. However, these request-level methods may cause significant unbalanced allocation of datacenter bandwidth. In a DASH-based streaming system, different requests can demand different video quality levels and thus have different bandwidth requirements. For example, a request for high definition video (1080p) requires as much as 10 times more bandwidth than a request for lower definition (240p) does [15]. Hence, unlike these existing works, we propose a flow-based solution that particularly aims at traffic routing for DASH-based streaming systems. Specially, we make the following three contributions.

First, it is observed that a typical DASH-based streaming system has the following three characteristics [16–21]: (i) The QoE increases in a non-linear manner as the video quality rises; (ii) The streaming system prefers to route user requests to datacenters with shorter network delay; (iii) Datacenters in such a system are geographically distributed into different regions with diversities in electricity price and emission factor. We present a system model that fully captures these unique characteristics.

Second, we develop a distributed algorithm that provably computes the optimal bandwidth allocation. The algorithm novelly decomposes the optimization process. The separate

MM'15, October 26–30, 2015, Brisbane, Australia.

DOI: http://dx.doi.org/10.1145/2733373.2806263.

processes are solved iteratively across datacenters and client groups. We prove that the algorithm surely converges to the optimum if with a bounded interval between iterations.

Third, we evaluate the distributed algorithm using trace-driven simulations. The experimental results demonstrate the fast convergence and better QoE-cost balance of our algorithm. Interesting findings are also provided through extensive sensitivity analysis.

The rest of the paper is organized as follows. Section 2 presents models and problem formulations. Section 3 proposes the distributed algorithm and proves its optimality and convergence. Section 4 evaluates the proposed algorithm. Section 5 describes the related work. Section 6 concludes the paper and gives the future work.

2. MODEL AND PROBLEM STATEMENT

In this section, we first present an overview of DASH, then give the modelling for the clients and datacenters, and finally formulate the bandwidth allocation problem.

2.1 Overview of DASH

By DASH [1,2], each video clip is first encoded into multiple quality levels or bitrates, by varying the resolution, frame size, etc. The video clip is then cut into multiple equal chunks. The chunk size is usually from two to ten seconds of video. A media presentation description file or manifest file, along with each video clip, describes the mapping of the chunk position to video time. When a client attempts to watch a video, the front-end server first delivers a DASH-capable video player and the video's manifest file to the client's device. The manifest file also includes URL for the video and the player uses this URL to get video chunks from datacenters (or CDNs) via standard HTTP GET requests. The video player decides the quality level of next video chunk to download according to the downloading information (e.g., measured throughput using downloading bytes divided by downloading time) of the previous chunk or previous few chunks. The player approximates this information as the current network conditions. By continuously playing consecutive video chunks, the video player can reassemble the chunks (even with different quality levels) into a seamless video playback. We now model a DASH-based streaming system.

2.2 Client Side Model

We consider that there are M front-end portals in a DASH-based streaming system, each of which receives requests from a group of clients. Front-end portals dispatch client requests to N datacenters. Without loss of generality, we assume that each client group can source from any of the N datacenters. Fig. 1 depicts all of the $N \cdot M$ possible flows. We consider a discrete-time model, where the time line is partitioned into equal timeslots. In practice, the length of the timeslot could be from minutes to hours[1]. At the beginning of each timeslot τ, routing and capacity provisioning decisions are updated. For each timeslot τ, we define $r_{ij}(\tau)$ as the flow rate of the traffic from datacenter i to group j. Each flow has a bandwidth limit of $r_{ij}(\tau) \leq \overline{R}_{ij}(\tau)$.

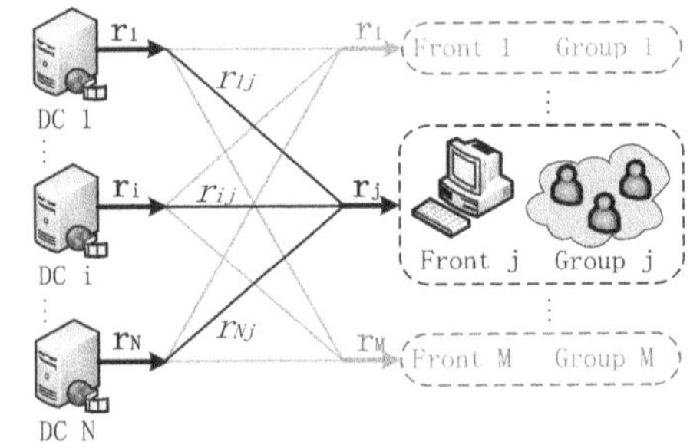

Figure 1: M client groups sourcing from all N datacenters. DC i: datacenter i; Front j: front-end portal j; Group j: client group j.

Revenue gain and loss. There are several metrics to define different aspects of quality of experience in a DASH-based streaming system, such as start-up time, freeze and video quality [21]. The performance on these metrics has significant impact on viewers' behavior. For example, according to [21], viewers start to abandon a video if it takes more than 2 seconds to start up or if its quality degrades. Network delay and bandwidth largely determines the performance on these metrics of such a system. Hence, we design a revenue model that involves the network delay and flow rate to reflect the quality of experience in a DASH-based streaming system[2].

In general, there are two approaches for modeling revenue: revenue gain and revenue loss. First, revenue gain can be modeled as the sum of clients' utility as in Network Utility Maximization (NUM) problem [22,23]. The utility function is usually assumed to be continuously differentiable, non-decreasing and strictly concave, such as logarithm functions. Second, revenue loss can be modeled as the sum of clients' disutility such as [24,25]. We present the algorithm design and proofs for the revenue loss model in the main part and put that for the revenue gain model in Appendix.

The definition of the revenue loss or disutility by serving client group j is given by

$$g_j(\tau, \mathbf{r}_j(\tau)) = w \cdot \sum\nolimits_i e^{-\beta_{ij} r_{ij}}, \tag{1}$$

where $\mathbf{r}_j(\tau) = (r_{1j}(\tau), ..., r_{Nj}(\tau))$ is the vector of flow rate r_{ij} to client group j; $\beta_{ij} \geq 0$ denotes the preference of flow r_{ij} among all of the N flows; $w \geq 0$ is for conversion from flow rate to revenue. Existing works such as [13,14] employ average queueing delay or end-to-end delay of user requests to model the revenue. By contrast, this work adopts flow rate, which is more suitable to streaming systems. Note that we take Eqn. (1) as an exemplary disutility function to ease our presentation, but the proposed algorithm applies to any disutility function respecting the following three aspects.

The rationale behind this model comes from three aspects.

(i) The revenue loss increases as the video quality level decreases, as viewers have better QoE with high quality video.

(ii) The rate of revenue loss increases as the video quality level decreases. For example, when watching a video on YouTube, viewers feel more quality degradation from

[1] The length can be chosen based on workload conditions: short (e.g., 5 minutes) if with frequent fluctuations; long (e.g., 1 hour), otherwise. It can be also chosen according to the electricity market that datacenters participate. The electricity price changes every few minutes in the real-time market and every one hour in the wholesale market. Thus, a typical length is several minutes for the former market and one hour for the latter market.

[2] Although streaming providers may have different business models such as advertisement-based and flat-rate payment, they all rely on the quality of experience of users. Thus, we use a general model that is dependent on the quality of experience in this paper.

480p to 360p than from 720p to 480p if keeping the window of the video player at the same size. This quality change corresponds to the video bitrate varying from $1000Kbps$ to $750Kbps$ than $2500Kbps$ to $1000Kbps$ [15]. Note that from the angle of revenue gain, that is, as the video quality level increases, the revenue increases but the increasing rate decreases. In addition, a lower (higher) quality level or video bitrate require lower (larger) flow rates [15]. To capture the above two aspects, Eqn. (1) adopts an exponential function (e.g., $e^{-r_{ij}}$) in the model.

(iii) We use β_{ij} to define the preference of a client group j to all N datacenters. A larger β_{ij} means higher preference of datacenter i serving client group j (or higher preference of traffic from datacenter i to client group j). The preference can be determined by the network delay. For example, a larger network delay corresponds to smaller β_{ij}. Moreover, it could be 0 if with unacceptably large network delay, and then there is no traffic from the corresponding datacenter. The network delay can be estimated by mapping and coordinate based approaches, e.g., [26,27] or simply approximated by geographical distance [12].

Note that though this kind of disutility modeling approach (and utility modeling approach in Appendix) may seem to be restrictive, it is standard in network economics literature, e.g., [22–25], where its good applicability has been proved.

2.3 Datacenter Side Model

We consider N geographically distributed datacenters (or CDNs) and they only draw power from the electrical grid. Each datacenter i is modeled as a collection of n_i homogeneous servers for streaming. These servers support a maximum egress bandwidth of $\overline{B}_i$. Our model for datacenter cost focuses on the operational cost, which includes the energy cost and emission cost.

Datacenter cost. There are geographical diversities for both the electricity price and emission factor of the electrical grid [12]. To capture these diversities, for each datacenter i, we first use $p_i(\tau)$ to denote the unit energy cost, which is normalized to the maximum egress bandwidth that datacenter i supports. The normalization is the product of the peak power of the n_i servers and electricity price, divided by the maximum bandwidth $\overline{B}_i$. And thus, the energy cost of datacenter i is $p_i(\tau) \cdot (\sum_j r_{ij}(\tau))$. We then let $q_i(\tau)$ denote the unit emission cost, which is also normalized to the maximum egress bandwidth. We employ the emission factor [12] in timeslot τ and carbon tax policy [28] for the normalization. Thus, the emission cost of datacenter i is $q_i(\tau) \cdot (\sum_j r_{ij}(\tau))$. Therefore, the operational cost of datacenter i is the sum of its energy cost and emission cost:

$$f_i(\tau, \mathbf{r}_i(\tau)) = c_i(\tau) \cdot (\sum_j r_{ij}(\tau)) \tag{2}$$

where $\mathbf{r}_i(\tau) = (r_{i1}(\tau), ..., r_{iM}(\tau))$ denotes the vector of flow rate r_{ij} from datacenter i; $c_i(\tau) = p_i(\tau) + q_i(\tau)$ is the unit operational cost of datacenter i. Note that our approach can be easily extended to include any kind of cost that can be approximated a convex relation with the flow rate.

2.4 Problem Statement

Based on the revenue and cost model given in the previous subsections, our goal is to determine optimal flow rate $r_{ij}(\tau)$ that minimizes the sum of revenue loss and operational cost for each timeslot τ. We formulate the bandwidth allocation problem (BAP) as follows:

$$\min_{r_{ij}(\tau)} Z(\tau, \mathbf{r}(\tau))) = \sum_j g_j(\tau, \mathbf{r}_j(\tau)) + \sum_i f_i(\tau, \mathbf{r}_i(\tau)), \tag{3a}$$

$$s.t.\ 0 \le \mathbf{r}_j(\tau) \le \overline{\mathbf{R}}_j(\tau),\ \ \forall j \in \{1, ..., M\}, \tag{3b}$$

$$\sum_i r_{ij}(\tau) \le A_j(\tau),\ \ \forall j \in \{1, ..., M\}, \tag{3c}$$

$$\sum_j r_{ij}(\tau) \le \overline{B}_i,\ \ \forall i \in \{1, ..., N\}, \tag{3d}$$

where $\overline{\mathbf{R}}_j(\tau) = (\overline{R}_{1j}, ..., \overline{R}_{Nj})$ is the vector of bandwidth limits of flows to client group j; $A_j(\tau)$ is the bandwidth required by client group j in timeslot τ when assuming maximum video quality level for all requests. In the above optimization problem, the objective Eqn. (3a) is to balance QoE, the energy cost and emissions. The constraint Eqn. (3b) limits each flow. The constraint Eqn. (3c) limits the sum flow rate of each client group. The constraint Eqn. (3c) restricts that the sum egress flow rate of a datacenter is less than or equal to its maximum bandwidth. Further, the optimization problem employs the predicted bandwidth requirement for each time slot. It uses fixed workload within timeslots and considers fluctuations between timeslots. Note that using historical data, factors such as the requirement and network conditions in the short term can be predicted accurately [10, 12, 29]. Thus, its result is enough accurate for practical deployment. We consider the optimization for a single timeslot and omit time index in the rest of this paper.

For constraint Eqn. (3c), we use $A_j(\tau)$ that is calculated based on the assumption that every request needs maximum quality level, instead of the requirement calculated using what exactly clients need. This is because the latter calculation can cause significant quality degradation, for DASH enables dynamic video quality adaptation. A DASH-capable video player dynamically adapts video quality levels mainly according to network conditions. However, datacenters are not aware of this adaption process and only serve clients with the requested quality levels. Hence, problems arise when network conditions vary. When network conditions become worse, the player will request video chunks of lower quality levels. The bandwidth requirement will also decline if using the latter calculation. And thus, there is less datacenter bandwidth allocated to the client group. Even when other network conditions become better, the player can not increase video quality levels since the allocated datacenter bandwidth becomes the bottleneck now. In the worst case, it can degrade to the lowest quality level and never come back. By contrast, the former calculation gives a safe upper bound for the bandwidth requirement.

3. DISTRIBUTED ALGORITHM DESIGN

In this section, we first propose a distributed algorithm to solve the BAP problem in Eqn. (3). The algorithm decomposes the optimization process into separate ones, which are solved iteratively across the datacenters and front-end portals. We then prove that the iteration process converges to the unique optimal solution.

3.1 The Dual Problem

For the primal problem given by Eqn. (3), flow rates r_{ij}s are coupled by constraints Eqn. (3c) and (3d). It is difficult to decompose them as to the primal problem. The key idea to a distributed solution is to look at the dual problem.

Define the Lagrangian as:

$$\begin{aligned} L(r,\theta,\delta) &= \sum_j w\cdot(\sum_i e^{-\beta_{ij}\cdot r_{ij}}) + \sum_i c_i\cdot(\sum_j r_{ij}) \\ &+ \sum_j \theta_j\cdot(\sum_i r_{ij} - A_j) \\ &+ \sum_i \delta_i\cdot(\sum_j r_{ij} - \bar{B}_i), \end{aligned} \tag{4}$$

where $\theta_j s$ and $\delta_i s$ are Lagrange multipliers corresponding to Eqn. (3c) and (3d), respectively.

By manipulating Eqn. (4), we observe that the first item in Eqn. (5) is separable in flow rate vector $\mathbf{r}_j$ as follows:

$$\begin{aligned} L(r,\theta,\delta) &= \sum_j \left[\widehat{Z}_j(\mathbf{r}_j) + \theta_j\cdot\sum_i r_{ij} + \sum_i \delta_i\cdot r_{ij}\right] \\ &- \sum_j \theta_j\cdot A_j - \sum_i \delta_i\cdot \overline{B}_i, \end{aligned} \tag{5}$$

where $\widehat{Z}_j(\mathbf{r}_j) = w\cdot(\sum_i e^{-\beta_{ij}\cdot r_{ij}}) + \sum_i c_i\cdot r_{ij}$. This separability allows datacenters and front-end portals to iteratively solve flow rate $\mathbf{r}_j$ in a distributed manner.

Before giving the distributed solution, we define the dual problem to the primal BAP problem as follows. Given Eqn. (5), the objective function of the dual problem is thus:

$$D(\theta,\delta) = \min_{\mathbf{r}_j\in\Lambda_j} L(r,\theta,\delta), \tag{6}$$

where Λ_j is the feasible set defined by Eqn. (3b). And the dual problem is:

$$\max_{\theta\geq 0,\delta\geq 0} D(\theta,\delta). \tag{7}$$

Since Eqn. (3a) is convex and the constraints Eqn. (3b)(3c)(3d) are linear, there is no gap between the primal and dual problem according to Slater's condition [30], i.e., the primal and dual problem has the same optimum.

3.2 Distributed Gradient Projection

We solve the dual problem by gradient projection method in a distributed manner. In each iteration, datacenters and front-end portals perform the following updates separately.

Updates for datacenter i. We adjust each $\delta_i \geq 0$ along the direction of the gradient $\frac{\partial D}{\partial \delta_i}$:

$$\delta_i(t+1) = \left[\delta_i(t) + \gamma\cdot\frac{\partial D}{\partial \delta_i}(\delta_i(t))\right]^+,$$

where $[x]^+ = \max\{x,0\}$, and $\gamma > 0$ is a step size. Let $\mathbf{r}(\delta,\theta)$ be the unique minimizer in Eqn. (6). Then, we have:

$$D(\delta,\theta) = L(\mathbf{r}(\delta,\theta),\delta,\theta).$$

Since $Z(\mathbf{r})$ is strictly convex, $D(\delta,\theta)$ is continuously differentiable. Hence, we have:

$$\frac{\partial D}{\partial \delta_i}(\delta) = \sum_j r_{ij}(\delta) - \overline{B}_i. \tag{8}$$

Thus, the update for δ_i is:

$$\delta_i(t+1) = \left[\delta_i(t) + \gamma\cdot(\sum_j r_{ij}(\delta_i(t)) - \overline{B}_i)\right]^+. \tag{9}$$

Each datacenter i communicates the updated δ_i to all M front-end portals. These front-end portals then carry out the following updates.

Updates for front-end portal j. Each front-end portal includes two kinds of updates. One is for each θ_j; the other is for flow rate vector $\mathbf{r}_j$. First, we adjust each θ_j along the direction of the gradient $\frac{\partial D}{\partial \theta_i}$:

$$\theta_j(t+1) = \left[\theta_j(t) + \gamma\cdot\frac{\partial D}{\partial \theta_j}(\theta_j(t))\right]^+,$$

Since $D(\delta,\theta)$ is continuously differentiable, we have:

$$\frac{\partial D}{\partial \theta_j}(\theta) = \sum_i r_{ij}(\theta) - A_j. \tag{10}$$

Thus, the adjustment for θ_j is:

$$\theta_j(t+1) = \left[\theta_j(t) + \gamma\cdot(\sum_i r_{ij}(\theta_j(t)) - A_j)\right]^+. \tag{11}$$

Second, by Karush-Kuhn-Tucker (KKT) conditions [30], setting $\frac{\partial L}{\partial r} = 0$ derives the unique minimizer of Eqn. (6) for a given (δ,θ). For each flow r_{ij}, we have:

$$\frac{\partial L}{\partial r_{ij}} = w\cdot\beta_{ij}\cdot e^{-\beta_{ij}\cdot r_{ij}} - c_i - \theta_j - \delta_i = 0, \tag{12}$$

which is equivalent to

$$r_{ij} = -\ln\frac{c_i+\theta_j+\delta_i}{w\cdot\beta_{ij}} \Big/ \beta_{ij}. \tag{13}$$

Hence, the update for flow rate vector $\mathbf{r}_j$ is:

$$\mathbf{r}_j(t+1) = \begin{pmatrix} \left[-\ln\frac{c_1+\theta_j(t+1)+\delta_1(t+1)}{w\cdot\beta_{1j}} \Big/ \beta_{1j}\right]_0^{\overline{R}_{1j}} \\ \vdots \\ \left[-\ln\frac{c_i+\theta_j(t+1)+\delta_i(t+1)}{w\cdot\beta_{ij}} \Big/ \beta_{ij}\right]_0^{\overline{R}_{ij}} \\ \vdots \\ \left[-\ln\frac{c_N+\theta_j(t+1)+\delta_N(t+1)}{w\cdot\beta_{Nj}} \Big/ \beta_{Nj}\right]_0^{\overline{R}_{Nj}} \end{pmatrix}, \tag{14}$$

where $[x]_a^b = \min\{\max\{x,a\},b\}$.

Each front-end portal uses θ_j locally, and thus there is no need to send it to datacenters or other front-end portals. Moreover, from Eqn. (9), the adjustment of δ_i relies on the total traffic of all front-end portals assigned to datacenter i, not on each individual flow. Hence, front-end portals do not have to communicate r_{ij}s to datacenters, if datacenters can measure their total egress flow rates.

The convergence property of the distributed algorithm is stated by Theorem 1. According to the theorem, large step sizes can be chosen to accelerate convergence. The convergence rate is illustrated with a setting on realistic data traces in Section 4.

Theorem 1. *Let $(\delta(t),\theta(t),\mathbf{r}(t))$ be a sequence generated by Eqn. (9)(11)(14). If $0 < \gamma < \frac{w\cdot\underline{\beta}^2\cdot e^{-\overline{\beta}\cdot\overline{\mathfrak{R}}}}{U}$, then*

(i) Every limit point of $(\delta(t),\theta(t),\mathbf{r}(t))$ is primal-dual optimal;

(ii) $D(\delta(t),\theta(t))$ and $Z(\mathbf{r}(t))$ converge to the optimal value, respectively;

where $U = \max\{M,N\}$, $\underline{\beta} = \min_{ij}\{\beta_{ij}\}$, $\overline{\beta} = \max_{ij}\{\beta_{ij}\}$ and $\overline{\mathfrak{R}} = \max_{i,j}\{\mathfrak{R}_{ij}\}$.

3.3 Convergence to the Unique Optimum

We first show the uniqueness of the optimal solution, and then prove the convergence property given by Theorem 1.

3.3.1 Uniqueness of the Optimal Solution

First, the BAP problem in Eqn. (3) has at least one optimal solution. This existence property can be derived by applying the Weierstrass extreme value theorem [31]. The reason is that the objective function $Z(\mathbf{r})$ is continuous and the feasible set given by Eqn. (3b)-(3d) is a compact subset. Second, the BAP problem has a unique optimal solution. The uniqueness property can be seen from the strict convexity of the objective function $Z(\mathbf{r})$. This is because that its second-order derivative with respect to flow r_{ij} is $\frac{\partial Z}{\partial r_{ij}} = w \cdot \beta_{ij}^2 \cdot e^{-\beta_{ij} \cdot r_{ij}}$, which is positive. Hence, if the distributed algorithm converges to an optimum, it must be the unique optimum.

3.3.2 Proof for convergence

We first give some useful definitions and lemmas, and then present the proof for the convergence property stated in Theorem 1.

Definitions. (i) Define a $(N+M) \times (N \cdot M)$ matrix $\mathbf{X}$ as the routing matrix for the BAP problem in Eqn. (3). The matrix is as follows:

$$\begin{array}{c} \\ \delta_1 \\ \delta_2 \\ \vdots \\ \delta_N \\ \theta_1 \\ \theta_2 \\ \vdots \\ \theta_M \end{array} \begin{array}{c} \begin{array}{cccccccc} r_{11} & r_{21} & \cdots & r_{N1} \cdots\cdots & r_{1M} & r_{2M} & \cdots & r_{NM} \end{array} \\ \begin{pmatrix} 1 & 0 & \cdots & 0 & \cdots\cdots & 1 & 0 & \cdots & 0 \\ 0 & 1 & \cdots & 0 & \cdots\cdots & 0 & 1 & \cdots & 0 \\ \vdots & \vdots & \ddots & \vdots & \cdots\cdots & \vdots & \vdots & \ddots & \vdots \\ 0 & 0 & \cdots & 1 & \cdots\cdots & 0 & 0 & \cdots & 1 \\ 1 & 1 & \cdots & 1 & \cdots\cdots & 0 & 0 & \cdots & 0 \\ 0 & 0 & \cdots & 0 & \cdots\cdots & 0 & 0 & \cdots & 0 \\ \vdots & \vdots & \ddots & \vdots & \cdots\cdots & \vdots & \vdots & \ddots & \vdots \\ 0 & 0 & \cdots & 0 & \cdots\cdots & 1 & 1 & \cdots & 1 \end{pmatrix} \end{array}$$

The rows denote all possible flows between the N datacenters and M front-end portals; while the columns represent these datacenters and front-end portals. One entry of $\mathbf{X}$ equals 1 if there is a possible flow between the datacenter and the front-end portal.

(ii) Define a $(N \cdot M) \times (N \cdot M)$ diagonal matrix $\mathbf{H}(\delta, \theta)$, whose diagonal element equals:

$$h_{kk}(\delta, \theta) = \frac{1}{\frac{\partial^2 L}{\partial r_{ij}}(r(\delta, \theta))},$$

where $i = (k-1)\%N + 1$, $j = \lfloor (k-1)/N \rfloor + 1$; the second-order partial derivative of L is:

$$\frac{\partial^2 L}{\partial r_{ij}} = w \cdot \beta_{ij}^2 \cdot e^{-\beta_{ij} \cdot r_{ij}} \in \left[w \cdot \beta_{ij}^2 \cdot e^{-\beta_{ij} \cdot \overline{\Re}_{ij}}, w \cdot \beta_{ij}^2 \right]. \tag{15}$$

Hence, we have the range of h_{kk}:

$$h_{kk} \in \left[\frac{1}{w \cdot \beta_{ij}^2}, \frac{1}{w \cdot \beta_{ij}^2 \cdot e^{-\beta_{ij} \cdot \overline{\Re}_{ij}}} \right]. \tag{16}$$

(iii) Matrix norm definitions. The norm $\|\mathbf{Y}\|_1$ is the maximum absolute column sum of the matrix $\mathbf{Y}$. The norm $\|\mathbf{Y}\|_\infty$ is the maximum absolute row sum of the matrix $\mathbf{Y}$. The norm $\|\mathbf{Y}\|_2$ is the square root of the largest eigenvalue of the positive-semidefinite matrix $\mathbf{YY}$.

Lemma 1. *The Hessian matrix of the objective function $D(\delta, \theta)$ in Eqn. (6) is $\nabla^2 D(\delta, \theta) = \mathbf{XHX}^T$.*

PROOF. From Eqn. (12), we have:

$$\frac{\partial^2 L}{\partial r_{ij} \partial \delta_i} = \frac{\partial^2 L}{\partial r_{ij}} \cdot \frac{\partial r_{ij}}{\partial \delta_i} = 1, \textit{ and}$$

$$\frac{\partial^2 L}{\partial r_{ij} \partial \theta_i} = \frac{\partial^2 L}{\partial r_{ij}} \cdot \frac{\partial r_{ij}}{\partial \theta_i} = 1.$$

Thus, the Jacobian matrix of $D(\delta, \theta)$ is:

$$\nabla D(\delta, \theta) = \mathbf{HX}^T.$$

From Eqn. (8)(10), the Hessian matrix is thus:

$$\nabla^2 D(\delta, \theta) = X \nabla D(\delta, \theta) = \mathbf{XHX}^T,$$

which completes the proof. □

Lemma 2. *The Hessian matrix of the objective function $D(\delta, \theta)$ has the property of $\left\|\nabla^2 D(\delta, \theta)\right\|_2 \le \frac{2U}{w \cdot \underline{\beta}^2 \cdot e^{-\overline{\beta} \cdot \overline{\Re}}}$.*

PROOF. Let a $(N+M) \times (N+M)$ matrix $\mathbf{Y} = \mathbf{XHX}^T$. Since the matrix $\mathbf{H}$ is diagonal, the entry of $\mathbf{Y}$ equals:

$$y_{ij} = \sum\nolimits_{k=1}^{N \cdot M} x_{ik} \cdot x_{jk} \cdot h_{kk}.$$

Hence, we have:

$$\begin{aligned} \|\mathbf{Y}\|_\infty &= \max_i \sum\nolimits_{j=1}^{N+M} y_{ij} \\ &= \max_i \sum\nolimits_{j=1}^{N+M} \left(\sum\nolimits_{k=1}^{N \cdot M} x_{ik} \cdot x_{jk} \cdot h_{kk} \right) \\ &\le \max_k |h_{kk}| \cdot \max_i \sum\nolimits_{j=1}^{N+M} \left(\sum\nolimits_{k=1}^{N \cdot M} x_{ik} \cdot x_{jk} \right) \\ &= \frac{2U}{w \cdot \underline{\beta}^2 \cdot e^{-\overline{\beta} \cdot \overline{\Re}}}. \end{aligned}$$

According to Proposition A.25(e) in [32], we have:

$$\|\mathbf{Y}\|_2^2 \le \|\mathbf{Y}\|_\infty \|\mathbf{Y}\|_1.$$

Since $\mathbf{Y}$ is a symmetric matrix, $\|\mathbf{Y}\|_\infty = \|\mathbf{Y}\|_1$. Thus,

$$\|\mathbf{Y}\|_2 \le \|\mathbf{Y}\|_\infty \le \frac{2U}{w \cdot \underline{\beta}^2 \cdot e^{-\overline{\beta} \cdot \overline{\Re}}}.$$

The lemma holds. □

Lemma 3. *The Jacobian matrix ∇D is Lipschitz continuous with*

$$\|\nabla D(\mathbf{v}_1) - \nabla D(\mathbf{v}_2)\|_2 \le \frac{2U}{w \cdot \underline{\beta}^2 \cdot e^{-\overline{\beta} \cdot \overline{\Re}}} \|\mathbf{v}_1 - \mathbf{v}_2\|_2,$$

where $\mathbf{v}_1$ and $\mathbf{v}_2$ are vectors of $(\delta_1, ..., \delta_N, \theta_1, ..., \theta_M)^T$.

PROOF. Based on Lemma 2, the lemma follows from Theorem 9.19 in [33] or Lemma 3 in [22]. □

Lemma 4. *Under the Lipschitz condition in Lemma 3, γ is positive, Φ is the feasible set of $(\delta_1, ..., \delta_N, \theta_1, ..., \theta_M)^T$, $\mathbf{v} \in \Phi$, $K = \frac{2U}{w \cdot \underline{\beta}^2 \cdot e^{-\overline{\beta} \cdot \overline{\Re}}}$, then*

(i) $D(\mathbf{v}(t+1)) \le D(\mathbf{v}(t)) - (\frac{1}{\gamma} - \frac{K}{2}) \|\mathbf{v}(t+1) - \mathbf{v}(t)\|_2$;

(ii) $\mathbf{v}(t+1) = \mathbf{v}(t)$ if and only if $(\mathbf{u} - \mathbf{v}(t))^T \nabla D(\mathbf{v}(t)) \ge 0$ for all $\mathbf{u}$ in Φ, i.e., $\mathbf{v}(t)$ minimizes D.

PROOF. (i) By the projection theorem of Proposition 3.2(b) in [32] and with the mapping in Eqn. (9)(11), we have

$$(\mathbf{u} - \mathbf{v}(t+1))^T (\mathbf{v}(t) - \gamma \nabla D(\mathbf{v}(t)) - \mathbf{v}(t+1)) \le 0, \forall \mathbf{u} \in \Phi. \tag{17}$$

Letting $\mathbf{u} = \mathbf{v}(t)$, we have

$$(\mathbf{v}(t) - \mathbf{v}(t+1))^T (\mathbf{v}(t) - \gamma \nabla D(\mathbf{v}(t)) - \mathbf{v}(t+1)) \leq 0, \quad (18)$$

which is equivalent to

$$\gamma(\mathbf{v}(t+1) - \mathbf{v}(t))^T \nabla D(\mathbf{v}(t)) \leq - \|\mathbf{v}(t+1) - \mathbf{v}(t)\|_2^2 . \quad (19)$$

Then, using Descent Lemma (Lemma 2.1 in [32]), we have

$$D(\mathbf{v}(t+1)) = D(\mathbf{v}(t) + \mathbf{v}(t+1) - \mathbf{v}(t)) \leq$$
$$D(\mathbf{v}(t)) + (\mathbf{v}(t+1) - \mathbf{v}(t))^T \nabla D(\mathbf{v}(t)) + \frac{K}{2} \|\mathbf{v}(t+1) - \mathbf{v}(t)\|_2^2 . \quad (20)$$

Manipulating Eqn. (19) and (20), we have

$$D(\mathbf{v}(t+1)) \leq D(\mathbf{v}(t)) - (\frac{1}{\gamma} - \frac{K}{2}) \|\mathbf{v}(t+1) - \mathbf{v}(t)\|_2^2 ,$$

which proves part (i).

(ii) For sufficiency, by Eqn. (17), if $\mathbf{v}(t+1) = \mathbf{v}(t)$, then

$$(\mathbf{u} - \mathbf{v}(t))^T \gamma \nabla D(\mathbf{v}(t)) \geq 0.$$

For necessity, substituting $\mathbf{u}$ by $\mathbf{v}(t+1)$, we have

$$(\mathbf{v}(t+1) - \mathbf{v}(t))^T (\mathbf{v}(t) - \gamma \nabla D(\mathbf{v}(t)) - \mathbf{v}(t)) \leq 0. \quad (21)$$

Adding Eqn. (18) and (21), we have

$$(\mathbf{v}(t) - \mathbf{v}(t+1))^T (\mathbf{v}(t) - \mathbf{v}(t+1)) \leq 0,$$

which holds only when $\mathbf{v}(t) = \mathbf{v}(t+1)$.

In addition, according to optimal conditions of Proposition 3.1 in [32], $\mathbf{v}(t)$ minimizes $D(\mathbf{v})$ over the set Φ. Therefore, part (ii) holds. □

Proof of Theorem 1. First, let $\{\mathbf{v}(t)\}$ be the vector sequence by the algorithm. By part (i) of Lemma 4, if $0 < \gamma < \frac{2}{K}$, the sequence $\{D(\mathbf{v}(t))\}$ is non-increasing. And, the objective $D(\mathbf{v})$ is lower bounded, hence $\{D(\mathbf{v}(t))\}$ converges, i.e., $\mathbf{v}(t+1) - \mathbf{v}(t)$ converges to zero. Let $\mathbf{v}^*$ be a limit point of $\{\mathbf{v}(t)\}$. The sequence $\{\mathbf{v}(t)\}$ converges to $\mathbf{v}^*$ due to the continuity of the mapping by Eqn. (9)(11). Then, by part (ii) of Lemma 4, $\mathbf{v}^*$ minimizes $D(\mathbf{v})$, i.e., is dual-optimal. Moreover, the sequence $\{\mathbf{r}(\mathbf{v}(t))\}$ also converges to the limit point of $\{\mathbf{r}(\mathbf{v}^*)\}$, due to the continuity of the mapping by Eqn. (14). Hence, it is also primal-optimal. The theorem holds. The proof is parallel to that of Proposition 3.4 in [32].

3.4 Practical Considerations

The above distributed algorithm yields the optimal result for bandwidth allocation, i.e., the traffic from each front-end portal/client group to each datacenter. We discuss two ways on how to deploy the resulting allocation into a DASH system as follows. The two approaches both use round-robin scheduling. The first one is to configure DNSes in front-end portals by resolving video chunk requests from the same client group to different datacenters. For example, if a client group's requests are mapped to two datacenters and the bandwidth allocation is $\{b_1, b_2\}$, in each round, the traffic (number of requests multiplied by the recommended bandwidth of the corresponding quality level) to the two datacenters should have a ratio of $b_1 : b_2$. This approach works well in a video streaming system who owns private DNSes, such as YouTube. The second approach is to implement the round-robin scheduling in the video player. The manifest file returned to clients is augmented to include the information of the bandwidth allocation. With this information,

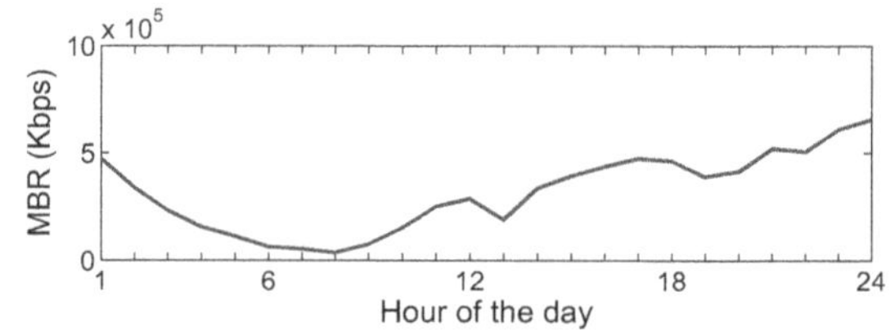

Figure 2: Hourly maximum bandwidth requirements.

video players download video chunks in a round-robin manner similar to the above example. This approach applies to video streaming systems using public DNSes such as Netflix or those using private DNSes such as YouTube. Note that this approach should work with the rate adaptation schemes that are embedded in video players, in order to guarantee to satisfy the bandwidth allocation.

4. EVALUATION

In this section, we evaluate the proposed algorithm using trace-driven simulations. We demonstrate four different kinds of results: the convergence of our approach, comparison on revenue loss and cost, trade-off between cost and QoE or video quality, and sensitivity analysis.

4.1 Experimental Setup

Workload and front-end portals. We consider traces of video requests from YouTube, which were collected in a campus network [35]. Our evaluation chooses to use the 24-hour trace on March 12, 2008. We assume that each video has 100 chunks on average. The highest video quality level has a recommended bandwidth of $4500Kbps$ [15]. Fig. 2 shows the adjusted trace of hourly maximum bandwidth requirement (MBR). MBR is relative to the recommended bandwidth of the highest video quality level, not to the network conditions. Based on this trace, we build our experimental workload by sitting one front-end portal in each US state. Each state's bandwidth requirement is proportionally scaled by the population of the state [36], that is, (the campus network bandwidth requirement)×(the state population/the campus population). The resulting trace is then shifted to the time-zone of the corresponding state.

Datacenter. We model a DASH-based streaming system with 10 datacenters, which locate at each US state known to have Google datacenters. The capacity of a datacenter is proportional to the number of Google datacenters in that state. We assume that servers in all datacenters are homogeneous and each has a power of $300w$ and bandwidth of $1Gbps$. One unit datacenter has 400 servers for video streaming, and thus its unit egress bandwidth is $0.4Tbps$ and unit peak power consumption is $0.12Mw$. The bandwidth limit of each flow is set as $1Tbps$. Table 1 shows the setting for the 10 datacenters.

Unit cost. Our algorithm performs an optimization for each timeslot. Thus, for each timeslot, we use constant electricity price for each data center. The average on-peak spot electricity price in 2012 [37] is used here. The regional emission factor is calculated using the fuel mix that generates electricity in each state [38] and the emissions that are produced when generating electricity using those fuels [39]. Our experiment is easily adapted to the case when different time slots have different the electricity prices and emission factors. Table 1 shows the electricity price and emission factor in each state. We use carbon-tax policy and assume the

Table 1: **The number of Google datacenters in each US state [34], the capacity in $Tbps$ of experimental datacenter setting, and the electricity price in $\$/Mwh$ and the emission factor in ton/Mwh of each state.**

	CA	VA	OR	GA	IL	WA	TX	FL	NC	SC
Number	5	3	2	1	1	1	1	1	1	1
Capacity	2	1.2	0.8	0.4	0.4	0.4	0.4	0.4	0.4	0.4
Elec. Prc.	34.57	32.65	26.61	27.77	32.12	22.22	35.46	34.46	32.65	32.65
Emis. Fa.	0.48	1.20	0.48	1.20	1.36	0.48	1.30	1.20	1.20	1.20

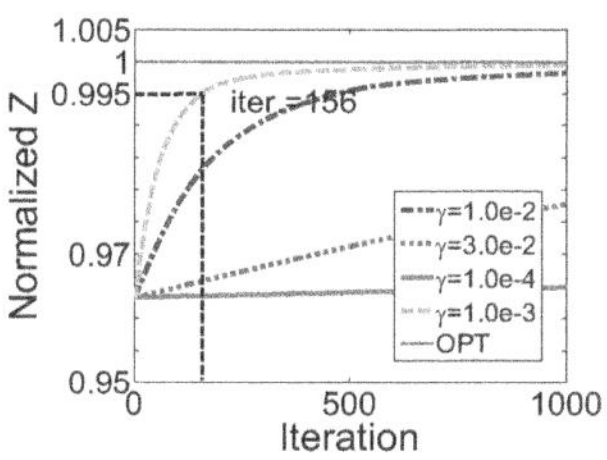

(a) Iteration vs objective Z in Eqn. (3a)

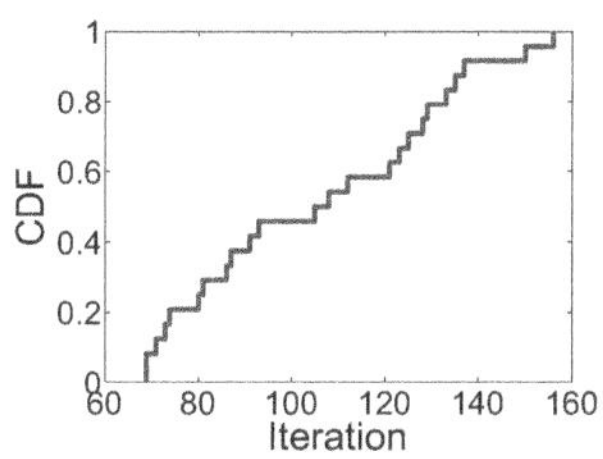

(b) Iteration CDF

Figure 3: Convergence of the distributed algorithm. Y-axis is normalized to the maximum objective (Z).

emission price to be $15\$/ton$ [28]. These two unit costs are then converted to $\$/Tbps$ using the method mentioned in Section 2.3.

4.2 The convergence of our approach

This experiment sets equal preference ($\forall i, j, \beta_{ij}$ =1) and weight as w = 20. Fig. 3(a) depicts the convergence of the distributed algorithm with different step sizes, as to the first hour of the trace in Fig. 2. The result validates the convergence analysis for our algorithm. As the step size γ increases (and varies inside the proved range in Theorem 1), the convergence speed rises. It takes only 156 iterations for $\gamma = 3.0e-2$ to converge to 99.5% of the optimal value. By contrast, when $\gamma = 1.0e-4$, the intermediate result changes only a little after 1000 iterations. Fig. 3(b) illustrates the number of iterations for each of the 24 hours, when the algorithm converges to 99.5% of the optimal value. The step size is $3.0e-2$. All have iterations less than 156. This figure shows the algorithm converges fast enough to provide near-optimal solution. Hence, we show only the optimal solution in the plots of the following subsections.

Fig. 4 demonstrates the impact of disconvergence on both objective value and flow rate, when the step size does not satisfy Theorem 1. We set step size $\gamma = 10$ and plot the value point for each iteration. First, the resulting value in both subfigures turns to regular oscillation after about 780 iterations, which illustrates that the algorithm (with $\gamma = 10$) is indeed disconvergent. Second, different with Fig. 3(a), Fig. 4(a) shows that the resulting objective value oscillates and never comes close to the optimal as the number of iterations grows. A more serious impact of the disconvergence can be observed from Fig. 4(b), where we take the resulting flow rate of datacenter CA as an example. The flow rate oscillates a lot, i.e., the difference between the maximum and minimum is more than 100%. This oscillation means that the datacenter has to adjust its bandwidth and server status frequently and significantly.

4.3 Revenue loss and cost comparison

Fig. 5 demonstrates the comparison on revenue loss and cost among the three different approaches. (i) *OPT*. Our

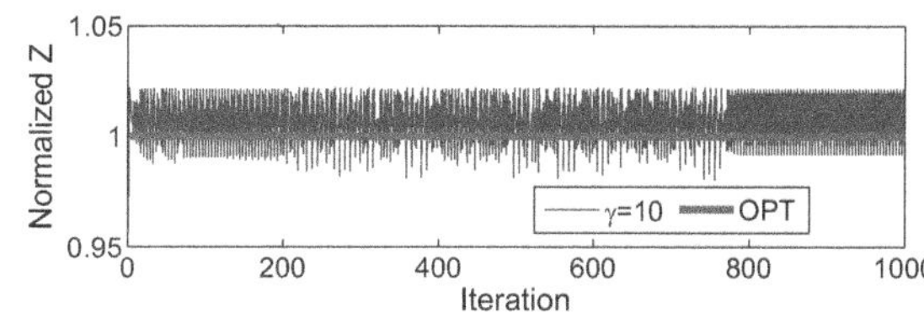

(a) Iteration vs objective Z

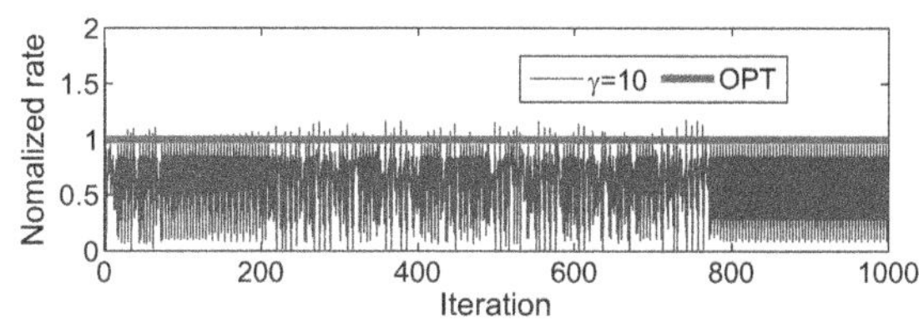

(b) Iteration vs flow rate of CA

Figure 4: Impact of disconvergence on objective and flow rate when step size $\gamma = 10$. (a) Y-axis is normalized to the maximum objective Z in Eqn. (3a); (b) Y-axis is normalized to the optimal flow rate of the datacenter in CA.

optimal algorithm. (ii) *GLB*. This approach performs geographical load balancing for requests as [10, 11] do, and assumes that each request requires the highest video quality level. (iii) *PLB*. This approach employs proportional load balancing, that is, datacenters service video streams in proportion to the datacenters' capacities. It uses flexible video quality levels as *OPT* does. This experiment set all β_{ij} to 1 and w to 20. Analysis on varying w and β_{ij}s is given in Section 4.4 and 4.5, respectively.

We choose 5 out of 24 hours to represent heavy (hour 1 and 24), middle (hour 16) and light (hour 4 and 7) maximum bandwidth requirement (MBR). First, *OPT* always has the smallest sum of revenue loss and cost, among all the three approaches from light to heavy MBR. It achieves up to 25% saving compared to *GLB* and up to 10% compared to *PLB*. The reason is that *OPT* jointly minimizes revenue loss and cost, and better strikes a balance between them. By contrast, the other two algorithms optimize either of the two. Second, *GLB* always comes with the least revenue loss. This is because that *GLB* assumes highest video quality level and the resulting flow rates always equal MBR.

Third, interestingly, *GLB* has larger cost than *PLB* for heavy MBR and lower cost for light MBR. The reason is two-fold. When MBR is heavy, *PLB* reduces the flow rates (less than MBR) in order to cut the cost. By contrast, *GLB* guarantees the MBR and thus results in higher cost. The sizes of flow rates dominate in this case. When MBR is light, both *PLB* and *GLB* can meet the MBR and thus datacenters' electricity and emission price dominate. Since *GLB* prefers to assign requests to datacenters where the price is cheaper, its cost becomes lower than *PLB*. This observation also validates the significance of jointly optimizing revenue loss and cost.

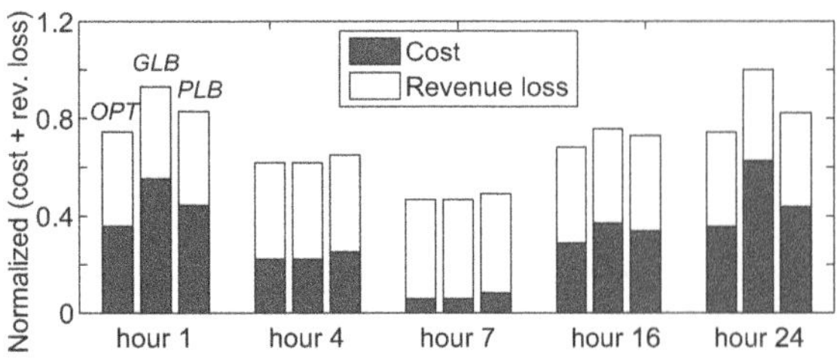

Figure 5: Comparison on revenue loss and cost among OPT, GLB, and PLB. Y-axis is normalized to the maximum sum of revenue loss and cost. Each blue and white bar represent revenue loss and cost respectively, and each combined bar is their sum.

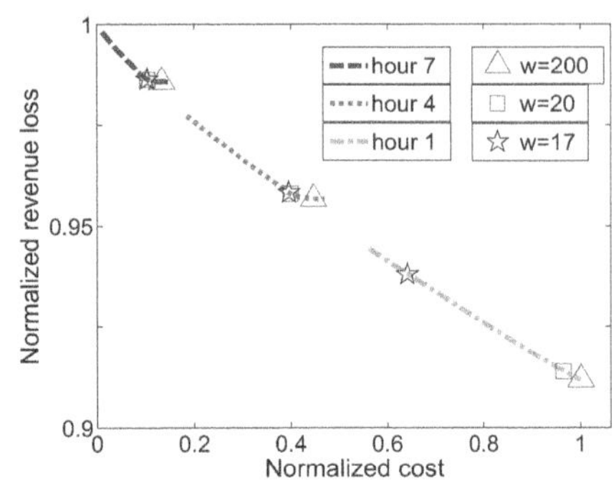

Figure 6: Pareto efficient frontier of the revenue loss and cost minimization problem (Eqn. (3)) as a function w for three different hours. Note that we plot only a section of the frontier for each hour in order to avoid overlapping of the three curves. Y-axis is normalized to the maximum revenue loss; while X-axis is normalized to the maximum cost.

4.4 Cost vs QoE

The objective function $Z(\mathbf{r})$ (Eqn. (3)) imposes a tradeoff between the cost and QoE or video quality (revenue), which is captured by weight w (Eqn. (1)). It is important to understand the impact of this weight. Thus, we plot the Pareto efficient frontier in Fig. 6. The Pareto efficient frontier in this paper is the set of allocations (i.e., resulting flow rates) that are all Pareto efficient. Pareto efficiency is a state of allocation, in which it is impossible to make any individual flow better off without making at least one individual flow worse off. The three frontiers have different ranges because of their different MBRs. Heavier MBRs (e.g., hour 1) have larger ranges while lighter ones (e.g., hour 7) come with smaller ranges. We observe that as w increases, the revenue loss decreases and QoE or video quality goes up, and vice versa. For example, for hour 1, $w = 200$ has 56% more cost and 3% less revenue loss than $w = 17$ does. It is worth to note that the video quality improves significantly even with a little reduction in revenue loss, because the revenue loss is modeled as an exponential function.

4.5 Sensitivity analysis

We conduct sensitivity analysis to see the impact of emissions and preference β_{ij}s on revenue loss and cost.

Impact of emissions. This analysis shows the importance of incorporating emission cost when conducting optimization for the bandwidth allocation. We compare the revenue loss and cost for two cases. (i) *Emis+*. We perform the optimization using the emission price in Table 1. (ii) *Emis-*.

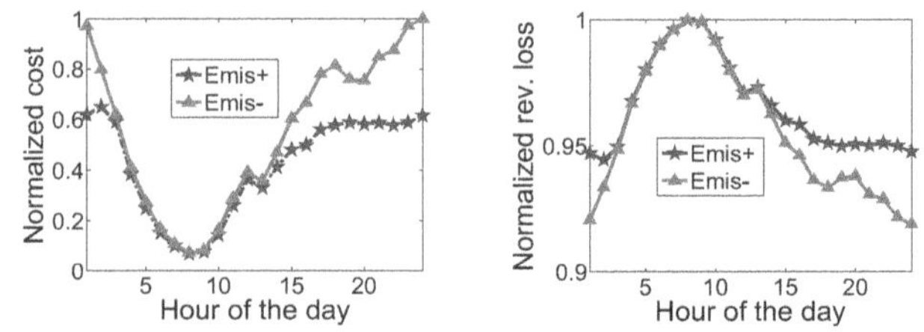

(a) Cost comparison (b) Revenue loss comparison

Figure 7: Sensitivity analysis on emissions for the 24 hours. Y-axis is normalized to the maximum.

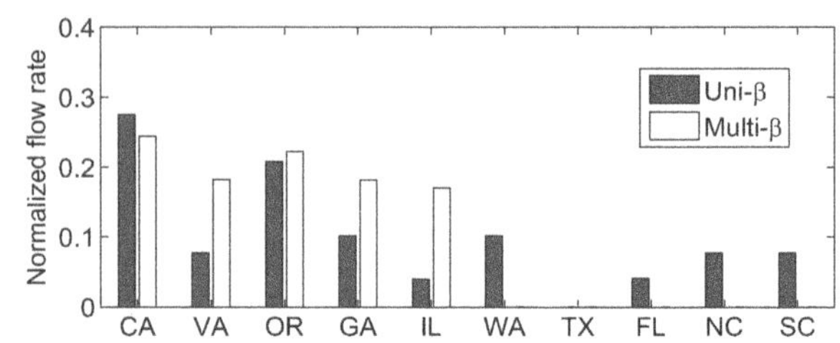

Figure 8: Sensitivity analysis on preference β. Y-axis is normalized to the total traffic to the front-end portal in CA. X-axis is the flow rate from each google datacenter to the front-end portal.

We first do the optimization by setting emission price as 0; then use the resulting flow rates to calculate emission cost based on the price in Table 1; finally, add the emission cost and the energy cost. We set all β_{ij} to 1 and w to 20. Fig. 7 depicts the result for all of the 24 hours. For heavy MBRs, compared to $Emis+$, $Emis-$ has larger cost (Fig. 7(a)) but smaller revenue loss (7(b)). This is because $Emis-$ sets emission price to 0 and thus results in larger flow rates than $Emis+$. For light MBRs, the flow rates of both cases equal to the MBR and thus they have the same revenue loss and cost. It is worth to note that $Emis-$ never has smaller sum of revenue loss and cost than $Emis+$. Hence, emission cost should be counted when doing the optimization in order to minimize the sum.

Impact of preference β_{ij}s. This analysis is to demonstrate the impact of preference $\beta_{ij}s$ on the flow rates. We use the front-end portal in CA as an example. We consider two cases by setting β_{ij}s of the portal CA to different values. (i) *Uni-β*. All portal CA's β_{ij}s are set to 1. (ii) *Multi-β*. The β_{ij}s from datacenter CA, VA, OR, GA and IL to portal CA are set as 2; while those from the other five datacenters to portal CA are set as 1. All other front-end portals' β_{ij}s are set to 1. Moreover, to do a fair comparison, we let the total traffic to portal CA for the two cases be the same. Fig. 8 plots the flow rate comparison between the two cases for hour 1. By *Multi-β*, portal CA sources from only the five preferred datacenters (with $\beta_{ij} = 2$), and the flow rates from datacenter VA, OR, GA and IL increase. In contrast, *Uni-β* imposes no preference across these datacenters, and thus portal CA sources from nice datacenters (no datacenter TX due to its very high price (c_i)). Hence, using β_{ij} makes front-end portals able to choose preferred datacenters according to network conditions such as network delay.

5. RELATED WORK

In this section, we discuss the related work most pertinent to our study. Our discussion focuses on two topics: quality of experience improvement for viewers, and cost and emission reduction for datacenters.

Improvement on QoE. The authors in [5] propose a rate adaptation algorithm that detects network conditions using a smoothed HTTP throughput. The throughput is measured based on segment fetch time instead of the instantaneous TCP transmission rate. The authors in [6] present QDASH, a rate adaptation algorithm that determines the most suitable quality level for users based on a measurement proxy architecture. The authors in [7] study the responsiveness and smoothness trade-off for DASH, and propose rate adaptation algorithms to strike a balance for the trade-off. The authors in [40] design two rate adaption methods based on serial chunk fetching and parallel chuck fetching respectively. All of these works focus on local tuning on how play videos, i.e., design rate adaptation algorithms to improve quality from only the video player end. Different with them, our work studies global traffic routing between datacenters and client groups. Furthermore, our work jointly manages QoE (or revenue), energy cost and emissions for DASH-based streaming systems. The local and global problems are both important for QoE improvement.

Cost and emission reduction for datacenters. There are many works that study the cost reduction problem in an intra-datacenter setting. By contrast, our work focuses on the inter-datacenter setting. Thus, we confine to the discussion of related works explicitly dealing with geographically distributed datacenters. The authors in [9] first observe the temporal and spatial diversities of electricity price in the electricity market. They design new load balancers that place workload from clients to datacenters located at regions with cheaper price. This method makes significant economic gain to datacenter operators. The authors in [10] propose distributed algorithms to solve the cost minimization problem for datacenters. The authors in [11] and [12] propose request distributing frameworks that optimize energy cost and emissions together. The authors in [14, 41] consider energy and bandwidth cost and jointly manage request mapping and request routing. The authors in [42] optimize datacenter emissions under monthly operating budgets. The authors in [43] make a joint optimization of electricity cost and carbon footprint across multiple datacenters. There are also a great deal of other research efforts addressing this topic. Interested readers can refer to the extensive survey [44] for more discussion on this topic. These above work focuses on request-level methods, where user requests are equally treated. However, in DASH-based streaming systems, requests for video chunks show extremely different bandwidth requirement. And thus, request-level methods does not apply here because they may cause highly unbalanced datacenter bandwidth allocation. Hence, specially targeting DASH-based streaming systems, our work employs flow based approaches, which makes it different with these existing research efforts.

6. CONCLUSION

In this paper, we study an important and novel problem on how to optimally allocate datacenter bandwidth for DASH-based streaming systems to balance QoE, energy cost and emissions. We first present a revenue and cost model that captures the unique characteristics of such systems. Then, we formally define the datacenter bandwidth allocation problem and propose a distributed algorithm with provable optimality guarantee. The algorithm decomposes the optimization process into separate ones that are solved iteratively across datacenters and client groups. Its convergence is demonstrated by theoretical proof and experimental validation. We finally evaluate our algorithm based on simulations using real-world data traces. The result demonstrates that the proposed algorithm has very fast convergence speed and achieves bandwidth allocation with much better QoE-cost balance.

For the future work, we will study the datacenter bandwidth allocation problem in presence of renewable energy. Many modern datacenters are beginning to incorporate renewable energy into their power supply [45]. Renewable generation usually depends on external conditions (e.g., wind speed and solar irritation) and thus possesses much uncertainty. This uncertainty brings much difficulty to the bandwidth allocation problem. Facing such difficulty, we will study how to design and analyze stochastic optimization based algorithms for the problem.

Acknowledgments

We would like to thank the anonymous reviewers for their constructive comments. This work was supported in part by the NSERC Discovery Grant 341823, Canada Foundation for Innovation (CFI)'s John R. Evans Leaders Fund 23090, and McGill Tomlinson Scientist Award.

7. REFERENCES

[1] T. Stockhammer, "Dynamic adaptive streaming over HTTP–: standards and design principles," in *MMSys*. ACM, 2011.

[2] A. Begen, T. Akgul, and M. Baugher, "Watching video over the web: Part 1: Streaming protocols," *IEEE Internet Computing*, 2011.

[3] comScore, "comScore releases may 2010 U.S. online video rankings," http://www.comscore.com/Insights/Press-Releases/2010/6/comScore-Releases-May-2010-US-Online-Video-Rankings, [Online accessed Jun., 2014].

[4] M. Ward and S. Robertson, "Google i/o 2013 - adaptive streaming for you and youtube," https://www.youtube.com/watch?v=UklDSMG9ffU&feature=share, [Online accessed Jun., 2014].

[5] C. Liu, I. Bouazizi, and M. Gabbouj, "Rate adaptation for adaptive HTTP streaming," in *MMSys*. ACM, 2011.

[6] R. K. Mok, X. Luo, E. W. Chan, and R. K. Chang, "QDASH: a QoE-aware DASH system," in *MMSys*, 2012.

[7] G. Tian and Y. Liu, "Towards agile and smooth video adaptation in dynamic HTTP streaming," in *CoNEXT*. ACM, 2012.

[8] K. Miller, E. Quacchio, G. Gennari, and A. Wolisz, "Adaptation algorithm for adaptive streaming over HTTP," in *PV*. IEEE, 2012.

[9] A. Qureshi, R. Weber, H. Balakrishnan, J. Guttag, and B. Maggs, "Cutting the electric bill for Internet-scale systems," in *SIGCOMM*. ACM, 2009.

[10] Z. Liu, M. Lin, A. Wierman, S. H. Low, and L. L. Andrew, "Greening geographical load balancing," in *SIGMETRICS*. ACM, 2011.

[11] K. Le, O. Bilgir, R. Bianchini, M. Martonosi, and T. D. Nguyen, "Managing the cost, energy consumption, and carbon footprint of Internet services," in *SIGMETRICS*. ACM, 2010.

[12] P. X. Gao, A. R. Curtis, B. Wong, and S. Keshav, "It's not easy being green," in *SIGCOMM*. ACM, 2012.

[13] M. Ghamkhari and H. Mohsenian-Rad, "Energy and performance management of green data centers: a profit maximization approach," *IEEE Transactions on Smart Grid*, 2013.

[14] H. Xu and B. Li, "Joint request mapping and response routing for geo-distributed cloud services," in *INFOCOM*. IEEE, 2013.

[15] YouTube, "Live encoder settings, bitrates and resolutions," https://support.google.com/youtube/answer/2853702?hl=en, [Online accessed Jun., 2014].

[16] V. K. Adhikari, S. Jain, and Z.-L. Zhang, "YouTube traffic dynamics and its interplay with a tier-1 ISP: an ISP perspective," in *IMC*. ACM, 2010.

[17] R. Torres, A. Finamore, J. R. Kim, M. Mellia, M. M. Munafo, and S. Rao, "Dissecting video server selection strategies in the YouTube CDN," in *ICDCS*. IEEE, 2011.

[18] V. K. Adhikari, S. Jain, Y. Chen, and Z.-L. Zhang, "Vivisecting YouTube: An active measurement study," in *INFOCOM (Mini conferecne)*. IEEE, 2012.

[19] V. K. Adhikari, Y. Guo, F. Hao, M. Varvello, V. Hilt, M. Steiner, and Z.-L. Zhang, "Unreeling Netflix: Understanding and improving multi-CDN movie delivery," in *INFOCOM*. IEEE, 2012.

[20] A. Finamore, M. Mellia, M. M. Munafò, R. Torres, and S. G. Rao, "YouTube everywhere: Impact of device and infrastructure synergies on user experience," in *IMC*. ACM, 2011.

[21] S. S. Krishnan and R. K. Sitaraman, "Video stream quality impacts viewer behavior: inferring causality using quasi-experimental designs," in *IMC*. ACM, 2012.

[22] S. H. Low and D. E. Lapsley, "Optimization flow control-I: basic algorithm and convergence," *IEEE/ACM Transactions on Networking*, 1999.

[23] S. Shakkottai and R. Srikant, *Network optimization and control*. Now Publishers Inc, 2008.

[24] X. Liu, Q. Wang, W. He, M. Caccamo, and L. Sha, "Optimal real-time sampling rate assignment for wireless sensor networks," *ACM Transactions on Sensor Networks*, 2006.

[25] W. Shu, X. Liu, Z. Gu, and S. Gopalakrishnan, "Optimal sampling rate assignment with dynamic route selection for real-time wireless sensor networks," in *RTSS*. IEEE, 2008.

[26] T. E. Ng and H. Zhang, "Predicting Internet network distance with coordinates-based approaches," in *INFOCOM*. IEEE, 2002.

[27] R. Krishnan, H. V. Madhyastha, S. Srinivasan, S. Jain, A. Krishnamurthy, T. Anderson, and J. Gao, "Moving beyond end-to-end path information to optimize CDN performance," in *SIGCOMM*. ACM, 2009.

[28] Carbon Tax Center, "Pricing carbon efficiently and equitably," http://www.carbontax.org/, [Online accessed Jun., 2014].

[29] Z. Liu, Y. Chen, C. Bash, A. Wierman, D. Gmach, Z. Wang, M. Marwah, and C. Hyser, "Renewable and cooling aware workload management for sustainable data centers," in *SIGMETRICS*. ACM, 2012.

[30] S. P. Boyd and L. Vandenberghe, *Convex optimization*. Cambridge university press, 2004.

[31] D. P. Bertsekas, *Nonlinear programming*. Athena scientific Belmont, 1999.

[32] D. P. Bertsekas and J. N. Tsitsiklis, *Parallel and distributed computation*. Old Tappan, NJ (USA); Prentice Hall Inc., 1989.

[33] W. Rudin, *Principles of mathematical analysis*. McGraw-Hill New York, 1976.

[34] R. MILLER, "Google data center FAQ," http://www.datacenterknowledge.com/archives/2012/05/15/google-data-center-faq/, [Online accessed Jun., 2014].

[35] M. Zink, K. Suh, Y. Gu, and J. Kurose, "Characteristics of youtube network traffic at a campus network–measurements, models, and implications," *Computer Networks*, 2009.

[36] Wikipedia, "List of U.S. states and territories by population," http://en.wikipedia.org/wiki/List_of_U.S._states_and_territories_by_population, [Online accessed Jun., 2014].

[37] Federal Energy Regulatory Commission, "Electric power markets," *http://www.ferc.gov/market-oversight/mkt-electric/overview.asp*.

[38] Edison Electric Institute, "Fuel diversity," http://www.eei.org/issuesandpolicy/generation/fueldiversity/Pages/default.aspx, [Online accessed Jun., 2014].

[39] U.S. Energy Information Administration, "How much carbon dioxide (CO_2) is produced per kilowatthour when generating electricity with fossil fuels?" http://www.eia.gov/tools/faqs/faq.cfm?id=74&t=11, [Online accessed Jun., 2014].

[40] C. Liu, I. Bouazizi, M. M. Hannuksela, and M. Gabbouj, "Rate adaptation for dynamic adaptive streaming over http in content distribution network," *Signal Processing: Image Communication*, 2012.

[41] B. Aksanli, J. Venkatesh, I. Monga, and T. S. Rosing, "Renewable energy prediction for improved utilization and efficiency in datacenters and backbone networks," in *Computational Sustainability*. Springer, 2015.

[42] Y. Zhang, Y. Wang, and X. Wang, "GreenWare: Greening cloud-scale data centers to maximize the use of renewable energy," in *Middleware*. ACM/IFIP/USENIX, 2011.

[43] Z. Abbasi, M. Pore, and S. K. Gupta, "Online server and workload management for joint optimization of electricity cost and carbon footprint across data centers," in *IPDPS*. IEEE, 2014.

[44] A. Rahman, X. Liu, and F. Kong, "A survey on geographic load balancing based data center power management in the smart grid environment," *IEEE Communications Surveys & Tutorials*, 2014.

[45] F. Kong and X. Liu, "A survey on green-energy-aware power management for datacenters," *ACM Computing Surveys*, 2014.

APPENDIX

A. Algorithm Design for Revenue Gain

A.1 Problem Formulation

We define the revenue gain by serving client group j as

$$g_j(\mathbf{r}_j) = w \cdot \sum\nolimits_i \beta_{ij} \log(r_{ij} + 1), \tag{22}$$

where $\mathbf{r}_j = (r_{1j}, ..., r_{Nj})$ is the vector of flow rate r_{ij} to client group j; $\beta_{ij} \geq 0$ denotes the preference of flow r_{ij} among all of the N flows; $w \geq 0$ is for conversion from flow rate to revenue; "+1" lets flow rate r_{ij} can be zero. Logarithm function is usually employed as in most work that discusses Network Utility Maximization (NUM). Note that we take Eqn. (22) as an exemplary utility function, but the proposed algorithm applies to any utility function that respects the following three aspects.

Using the above revenue gain model and cost model in Eqn. (2), we formulate an optimization problem as follows. The objective is to choose flow rate r_{ij} in order to maximize the revenue minus operational cost.

$$\begin{aligned} \max_{r_{ij}} \quad & Z = \sum\nolimits_j g_j(\mathbf{r}_j) - \sum\nolimits_i f_i(\mathbf{r}_i), \\ s.t. \quad & Eqn.\ (3b)(3c)(3d). \end{aligned} \tag{23}$$

A.2 The Dual Problem

Define the Lagrangian as follows:

$$\begin{aligned} L(r, \theta, \delta) = & \sum\nolimits_j w \cdot (\sum\nolimits_i \beta_{ij} \log(r_{ij} + 1)) \\ & - \sum\nolimits_i c_i \cdot (\sum\nolimits_j r_{ij}) - \sum\nolimits_j \theta_j \cdot (\sum\nolimits_i r_{ij} - A_j) \\ & - \sum\nolimits_i \delta_i \cdot (\sum\nolimits_j r_{ij} - \bar{B}_i), \end{aligned} \tag{24}$$

where $\theta_j s$ and $\delta_i s$ are Lagrange multipliers corresponding to Eqn. (3c) and (3d), respectively.

By manipulating Eqn. (24), we observe that the first item in Eqn. (25) is separable in vector $\mathbf{r}_j$ as follows:

$$\begin{aligned} L(r, \theta, \delta) = & \sum\nolimits_j \left[\widehat{Z}_j(\mathbf{r}_j) - \theta_j \cdot \sum\nolimits_i r_{ij} - \sum\nolimits_i \delta_i \cdot r_{ij} \right] \\ & + \sum\nolimits_j \theta_j \cdot A_j + \sum\nolimits_i \delta_i \cdot \overline{B}_i, \end{aligned} \tag{25}$$

where $\widehat{Z}_j(\mathbf{r}_j) = w \cdot (\sum_i \beta_{ij} \log(r_{ij} + 1)) - \sum_i c_i \cdot r_{ij}$. This separability allows datacenters and front-end portals to iteratively solve $\mathbf{r}_j$ in a distributed manner.

We now define the dual problem. The objective function of the dual problem is thus:

$$D(\theta, \delta) = \max_{\mathbf{r}_j \in \Lambda_j} L(r, \theta, \delta), \tag{26}$$

where Λ_j is the feasible set defined by Eqn. (3b). And the dual problem is:

$$\min_{\theta \geq 0, \delta \geq 0} D(\theta, \delta). \tag{27}$$

Since Eqn. (23) is concave and constraints Eqn. (3b)(3c)(3d) are linear, there is no gap between the primal and dual problem according to Slater's condition [30], i.e., the primal and dual problem has the same optimum.

Based on the above dual problem, the distributed algorithm for this revenue gain model is similar that presented in Section 3.2. The corresponding convergence proof is similar to that presented in Section 3.3. Thus, we omit the detail for the algorithm design and convergence analysis due to the space limit.

HTTP/2-Based Methods to Improve the Live Experience of Adaptive Streaming

Rafael Huysegems, Tom Bostoen, Patrice Rondao Alface
Bell Labs, Alcatel-Lucent
Copernicuslaan 50
B-2018 Antwerp, Belgium
rafael.huysegems@alcatel-lucent.com

Jeroen van der Hooft, Stefano Petrangeli, Tim Wauters, Filip De Turck
Ghent University - iMinds
Gaston Crommenlaan 8/201
B-9050 Ghent, Belgium
jeroen.vanderhooft@intec.ugent.be

ABSTRACT

HTTP Adaptive Streaming (HAS) is today the number one video technology for over-the-top video distribution. In HAS, video content is temporally divided into multiple segments and encoded at different quality levels. A client selects and retrieves per segment the most suited quality version to create a seamless playout. Despite the ability of HAS to deal with changing network conditions, HAS-based live streaming often suffers from freezes in the playout due to buffer under-run, low average quality, large camera-to-display delay, and large initial/channel-change delay. Recently, IETF has standardized HTTP/2, a new version of the HTTP protocol that provides new features for reducing the page load time in Web browsing. In this paper, we present ten novel HTTP/2-based methods to improve the quality of experience of HAS. Our main contribution is the design and evaluation of a push-based approach for live streaming in which *super-short* segments are pushed from server to client as soon as they become available. We show that with an RTT of 300 ms, this approach can reduce the average server-to-display delay by 90.1 % and the average start-up delay by 40.1 %.

Categories and Subject Descriptors

H.m [**Information Systems**]: Miscellaneous

Keywords

HTTP adaptive streaming, DASH, HTTP/2, SPDY, video streaming, live streaming, latency, server push

1. INTRODUCTION

Over the last years, the delivery of multimedia content became more prominent than ever. Particularly, video streaming applications are now responsible for more than half of the Internet traffic [30]. To enable video streaming over the best-effort Internet, the concept of HTTP Adaptive Streaming (HAS) was introduced. As shown in Figure 1, video content is encoded at different quality levels. Each quality level is determined by its corresponding average bitrate. In addition, the content is divided in segments that have a typical duration of one to ten seconds. Each segment can be decoded independently of other segments. A HAS client initiates a new session by downloading a manifest file. This manifest file provides a description of the different available quality levels and segments. Based on the network conditions and the current buffer-filling level, the Rate Determination Algorithm (RDA) in the HAS client determines the quality for the next segment download. The objective of the RDA is to optimize the global Quality of Experience (QoE) determined by the occurrence of video freezes, the average quality level, and the frequency of quality changes. The main advantage of HAS over progressive download and traditional real-time streaming is its ability to adapt the video quality to the available bandwidth in order to avoid video freezes. As a consequence, HAS facilitates video streaming over a best-effort network. In addition, HTTP-based video streams can easily traverse firewalls and reuse the already deployed HTTP infrastructure such as HTTP servers, HTTP proxies, and Content Delivery Network (CDN) nodes. Because of these advantages, major players such as Microsoft, Apple, Adobe and Netflix massively adopted the adaptive streaming paradigm. As most HAS solutions use the same architecture, the Motion Picture Expert Group (MPEG) proposed a standard called Dynamic Adaptive Streaming over HTTP (DASH) [31].

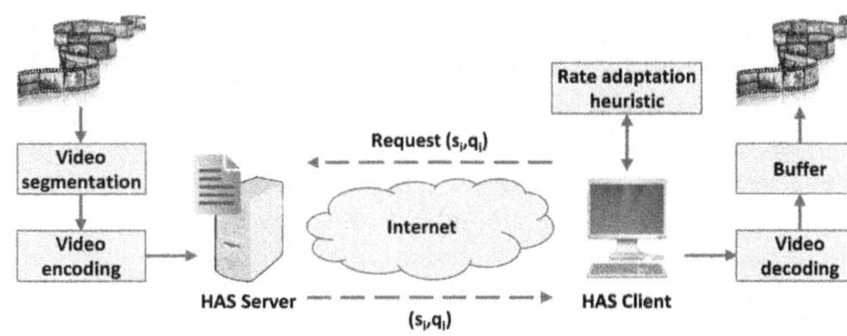

Figure 1: The concept of HTTP Adaptive Streaming.

Despite the many HAS advantages, several inefficiencies still have to be solved to improve the user's QoE, especially in live video streaming.

- Video freezes caused by rebuffering: Dobrian et al. [11] show that rebuffering has the largest impact on user engagement. Conviva [10] estimates the number of HAS sessions that suffer from video freezes at 27

MM '15, October 26-30, 2015, Brisbane, Australia
© 2015 ACM. ISBN 978-1-4503-3459-4/15/10 ...$15.00.
DOI: http://dx.doi.org/10.1145/2733373.2806264.

percent. Especially in environments with rapid bandwidth changes such as mobile networks, the client may have insufficient time to adapt and may need to rebuffer [24]. Rebuffering could be avoided by using larger client buffers but unfortunately this increases also the end-to-end delay for live streaming.

- Low average video quality: In [10], the number of sessions impacted by low resolution is estimated at 43 percent.

- Frequent video-quality changes: Subjective tests described in [22] and [32] show that frequent and abrupt fluctuations in the selected video-quality levels as well as video-quality oscillations have a negative impact on the QoE.

- Large camera-to-display delay: Lohmar et al. [21] show that the total delay from camera to display in live streaming should be kept as small as possible. The viewing experience of a live soccer game can be spoiled by social media or neighbors cheering for a goal when this goal was not yet shown on the screen. In current HAS deployments, this camera-to-display delay is in the order of tens of seconds.

- Large interactivity delay: Such delay is defined as the waiting time for the viewer when interacting with the HAS client. We distinguish start-up delay, seeking delay, and channel change delay.

Our goal is to reduce the number of video freezes, increase the average video quality, reduce the number of quality-level changes, reduce the latency for live streaming, and reduce the interactivity delay by using new HTTP/2 features. Early 2012, the IETF httpbis working group [18] started the standardization of HTTP/2, to address a number of deficiencies in HTTP/1.1. In February 2015, the new HTTP/2 standard was published as an IETF RFC [2] and is now supported by major browsers such as Chrome, Firefox and Internet Explorer. The main focus of HTTP/2 is to reduce the latency in Web delivery, using four new features that provide possibilities to terminate the transmission of certain content, multiplex several requests, prioritize more important content, and push content from server to client.

The main contributions of this paper are threefold. As a first contribution, we propose ten novel methods to improve the QoE of HAS, based on HTTP/2 features. Two methods are based on request/response multiplexing and prioritization. These HTTP/2 features enable simultaneous requests for subsequent segments or segment layers in the case of Scalable Video Coding (SVC) to avoid the per-segment/per-layer round-trip time (RTT). Another two methods are based on the cabability of HTTP/2 to abort a stream (and the corresponding segment retrieval). This capability is used when a channel change is detected or when the bandwidth suddenly drops while downloading a too high quality segment. Six more methods use HTTP/2's server push. To avoid RTT cycles, an HTTP/2-based server can push manifests, segments, or segment layers to the client when the server knows the client will request these in the near future. The server can also push segments or segment layers additional to or as an alternative for segments or segment layers requested by the client as network conditions require. In the *full push* method, the server continuously pushes new segments to the client when they become available. The client sends HTTP messages to the server to start, stop, pause, or resume the stream or to request a quality-level change. By eliminating wait cycles such as the RTT between subsequent segment retrievals and the client polling time, this method improves the average selected video quality. As a second contribution, we show that HTTP/2 server-push can also be used to improve the QoE for live streaming by alleviating the disadvantages linked to the use of super-short segments. This allows us to bring the segment duration to a sub-second level. In addition, we propose a method to solve the encoding overhead induced by super-short segments. This combination results in a significantly reduced start-up and end-to-end delay for live video. As a third contribution, we present detailed experimental results based on an emulation-based setup with full push and super-short segments to characterize the potential of the presented solution compared to traditional HAS clients.

The remainder of this paper is organized as follows. Section 2 gives an overview of the related work on HAS and HTTP/2. In Section 3, we provide a root-cause analysis of the HAS QoE problems. Section 4 introduces ten novel methods to improve the QoE of HAS and describes how a combination of the full-push method and super-short-segments results in a superior QoE for live HAS streaming. An evaluation of the results is presented in Section 5. Next, section 6 defines future work, before coming to final conclusions in Section 7.

2. RELATED WORK

2.1 HTTP Adaptive streaming

Techniques to improve the QoE for HAS can be divided in three main classes.

The first class focuses on the client's RDA. E.g., Benno et al. [3] propose a more robust RDA for wireless live streaming. Claeys et al. [9] propose an RDA that dynamically learns the optimal behavior for the corresponding network environment.

The second class uses SVC to encode the segments. Famaey et al. [14] and Sanchez et al. [29] compare SVC-based HAS to AVC-based HAS. Because an SVC client has an increased number of decision points, such a client copes better with a highly variable bandwidth as in mobile scenarios. Although SVC reduces the footprint for storage, caching, and transport compared to a complete simulcast AVC system, the SVC coding adds an overhead of 12 percent for a single medium-quality stream and 26 percent when delivering a single high-quality stream. For VoD, Sánchez et al. [28] show that when both the cache feeder link and the access links are congested, SVC-based HAS leads to an improved QoE. Muller et al. [25] compare AVC-based DASH with SVC-based DASH in a constrained environment such as a mobile network. They conclude that the flexibility of SVC's layered coding structure allows for a more aggressive buffer model. Bouten et al. [6] use Differentiated Services (DiffServ) in the IP network to give priority to the base-layer (BL) segments. Because the SVC-based client is more robust to video freezes, it is possible to reduce the client buffer from 6 to 30 seconds in AVC-based HAS to 2 seconds. However, the practical application of SVC in live streaming is still under question because SVC introduces a significant encoding overhead and increases the complexity of the decoder.

The third class explores how the QoE can be improved by making the network and server HAS aware. In current HAS deployments, the greedy QoE optimization prevents clients to reach a globally optimal distribution of resources and QoE. Bouten et al. [7] and Petrangeli et al. [26] avoid such suboptimal distribution by introducing intelligence in the service-provider network that can help the client's local RDA decisions. Akhshabi et al. [1] propose to use server-based traffic shaping to reduce video quality oscillations at the client.

2.2 HTTP/2

In this paper, we target an improved QoE of HAS by using HTTP/2. This new version of HTTP is based on SPDY. The main objective of SPDY is to speed up Web browsing. According to Google [16], a reduction in page load time of up to 64 percent can be achieved. Other studies show that the mere replacement of HTTP by SPDY helps only marginally. Cardaci et al. [8] evaluate SPDY over high latency satellite channels. On average, SPDY slightly outperforms HTTP. Erman et al. [13] provide a detailed measurement study to understand the benefits of using SPDY over cellular networks. They report that SPDY does not clearly outperform HTTP due to cross-layer dependencies between TCP and the cellular network technology. Elkhatib et al. [12] conclude that SPDY may both decrease as well as increase page load times. SPDY's multiplexed connections last much longer than HTTP's. Such long-lasting connections make SPDY more susceptible to packet loss, which gives rise to problems with TCP backoff.

2.3 HAS over HTTP/2

Mueller et al. are the first to evaluate the performance of adaptive streaming over SPDY, more specifically for the DASH standard [23]. The existing HTTP/1.0 or HTTP/1.1 layer is replaced by SPDY, without any further modifications to the HAS client or server. The authors show that if SPDY is used over SSL, the gains obtained by using header compression, a persistent connection, and pipelining are almost completely cancelled out by the losses due to the SSL and framing overhead.

Wei et al. are the first to explore how new HTTP/2 features can be used to improve HAS [37]. By reducing the segment duration from five seconds to one second, they manage to reduce the camera-to-display delay by about ten seconds. They avoid an increased number of GET requests by pushing k segments after each request, using HTTP/2 server push. This approach has the disadvantage that when a client switches to another quality level, the pushed stream using the old quality level is in competition with the segments downloaded at the new quality level. This increases the switching delay for the client and the bandwidth overhead in the network. In later work, the authors show that the induced switching delay is about two segment durations and independent of the value of k, while the introduced bandwidth overhead heavily depends on this value [36]. Moreover, HTTP/2 functionalities are used to push audio segments upon receiving a request for the associated video segments.

3. ROOT CAUSES OF HAS QOE PROBLEMS

To better understand possible HAS improvements, we first identify four root causes of the HAS QoE problems that are presented in Section 1.

A first deficiency of HAS is its susceptibility to large RTTs. Because segments are fetched sequentially, an RTT is lost between subsequent transfers. This has following effects: (1) At start-up, the HAS client has to retrieve several objects (manifest, segment, ...) before the playout can be started. When the RTT is large, the lost RTT cycles significantly increase the initial playout delay. (2) One RTT is lost between subsequent segment retrievals, possibly leading to a poor link utilization and average quality level. Both effects are stronger for short segments and large RTTs. In 2013, [15] measured an average RTT during peak periods of 18 ms for fiber-to-the home, 26 ms for cable, and 44 ms for DSL connections. When using a Content Delivery Network (CDN), [19] estimates the RTT as 51 ms for fiber-to-the home, 67 ms for cable, 238 ms for DSL, 250 ms for 4G, and 550 ms for 3G. If the requested object is not found in the CDN node, an additional 135 ms must be added, e.g., when the CDN node is located on the US West Coast and the origin server on the US East Coast. For Wi-Fi, 6 ms to 100 ms must be added. These figures indicate that the RTT can have a significant impact on the QoE for HAS, especially for wireless connections.

A second deficiency is the pull-based nature of HAS for live streams. At the client, the polling for new segments introduces an additional wait time during which the available bandwidth remains unused. This idle time reduces the link utilization and increases the live delay.

A third HAS deficiency is caused by the client buffer. For live streaming, this buffer is typically 3 to 5 times the segment duration and accounts for a significant part of the end-to-end delay.

A fourth HAS deficiency is the inability of HAS (and HTTP/1.1 in general) to terminate an ongoing segment transfer. This affects the QoE in two situations: (1) If a client just started a segment download when the user requests a channel change, the client must first complete the entire download of the obsolete segment causing significant channel change delay. (2) If a client started the download of a high-quality segment when the available bandwidth suddenly decreases, the client must first complete the entire download. This condition often leads to video freezes.

4. HTTP/2-BASED QOE-IMPROVEMENT METHODS

In this section, we propose ten novel or improved HTTP/2 based methods that enhance the QoE of HAS as presented in Table 1. To implement these methods, it may be required to modify the server, the client, or both. In this paper, the term *server* may refer to an origin server, an HTTP proxy, or a CDN node.

4.1 Stream Termination

HTTP/2 enables the use of multiple streams within one TCP connection. This feature makes it possible to use a separate stream per segment download. At any moment, the client can terminate an active stream by sending an RST_STREAM frame to indicate that the stream is no longer needed [2]. Upon reception of such a frame, the server stops

Method	HTTP/2 features used	QoE impact	Relation with other methods	Required updates
High-quality segment termination	stream termination	freeze	none	client
Obsolete segment termination	stream termination	channel change delay	none	client
Pull many	request/response multiplex, stream prioritization	average quality, freeze	none	client
Pull many with termination	request/response multiplex, stream prioritization, stream termination	average quality, freeze	on top of pull-many method	client
Safety push	push, stream prioritization	freeze	none	server, (client)
Initial push	push	initial delay, channel change delay	none	server, (client)
Layered push	push, stream prioritization	average quality	none	server
Manifest push	push	average quality	none	server
Overruling push	push	freeze	none	server, client
Full push	push	average quality, initial delay, channel change delay, live delay	includes methods: initial push, manifest push	server, (client)

Table 1: Overview of the different methods to improve the QoE for live HAS streams.

the ongoing transmission and closes the stream. This feature is actively exploited in the methods detailed in the following sections. Note that the advantages of these methods increase when the RTT is small, because the terminate message is conveyed faster from the client to the server. As a result, the occupied resources are released earlier and can be reused for the transport of a new segment.

4.1.1 High-Quality-Segment Termination

When the network conditions deteriorate severely, the continuation of a high-quality segment download takes a long time. Such a slow download could lead to a video freeze. By using HTTP/2 stream termination, the client can actively terminate the ongoing high-quality segment transfer. This way, network resources are released sooner and the client can start the download of a segment encoded at a lower quality level faster.

4.1.2 Obsolete-Segment Termination

When a user switches between video channels, the segment that is currently under transfer can no longer be used in the video playout. By terminating the transfer of the obsolete segment, the client can immediately request the first segment(s) of the new channel. Because network resources are released sooner, the channel change delay can be significantly reduced.

4.2 Request/Response Multiplexing and Stream Prioritization

In HTTP/2, multiple streams can be used to download segments in parallel over one TCP connection. To orchestrate the segment delivery, the client can specify that a new stream depends on a previous one. In this way, the client expresses a preference to allocate server processing and bandwidth resources to the parent stream rather than to the dependent stream. In the methods described below, the HAS client requests multiple segments at once to avoid lost RTT cycles between subsequent retrievals. Via HTTP/2 dependencies, the client ensures that segments that are required first for playout will be received first. Because lost RTT cycles are avoided, such methods increase the link utilization and the average video quality.

4.2.1 Pull Many

In this method, the client sends simultaneously requests for n subsequent segment requests. The delivery order is imposed by the client using HTTP/2 stream dependencies.

When SVC encoding is applied, the client downloads different quality layers to reconstruct one playable segment. As a result, multiple RTTs are lost per playable segment, leading to a lower link utilization and a lower average quality. In the *pull many* method, the different layers composing a segment are requested all at once. Using stream dependencies, the client makes sure that the base layer and the different enhancement layers are received in the correct order. Just as for standard SVC, the main advantage of this approach is that when a segment is urgently required for playout, and a higher layer is still under transfer, the base layer is already available. This way, playout freezes can be avoided.

4.2.2 Pull Many with Termination

This method builds on the pull-many method. Traditional RDAs predict the most appropriate quality level for the next segment download. In our approach, the client requests both the base layer and all enhancement layers for each segment. This triggers the server to send all the quality layers in a back-to-back fashion. The advantage is that at any moment during the transfer of the segments, the client can cancel the download of additional enhancement layers via stream termination. This happens if the bandwidth is not sufficient to transport all layers in time for playout. With this method, instead of predicting the optimal quality one segment in advance, the client simply adapts to the current bandwidth conditions with a delay of one RTT required to terminate the stream.

4.3 Server Push

HTTP/2 enables a server to preemptively send (push) responses to a client based on a previous request from the client. Especially for live streaming, using a push-based approach has multiple advantages. First, because subsequent segments can be pushed back-to-back, lost RTT cycles between such segments are avoided, increasing the average link utilization and video quality. Second, a reduction of the live

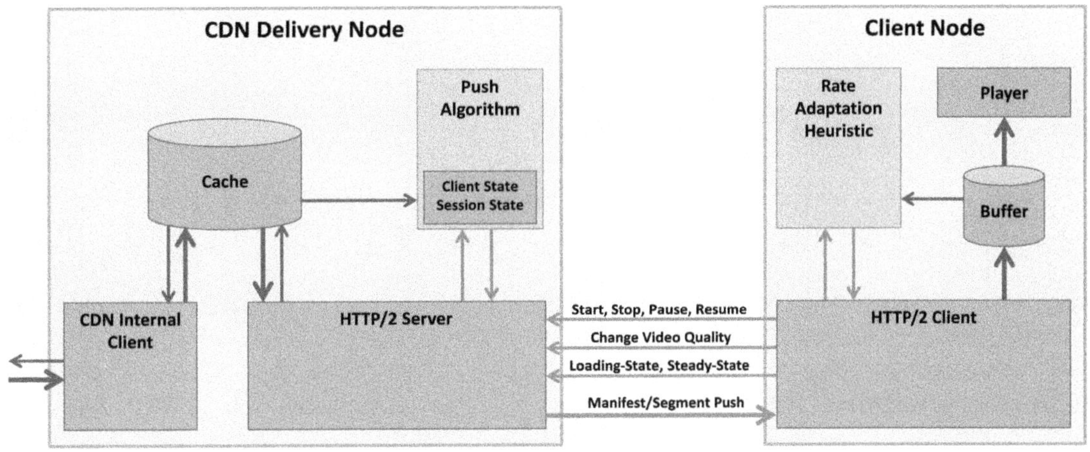

Figure 2: Implementation of the full push method in a CDN environment with the modified RDA at the client and the added push algorithm at the CDN delivery node.

delay can be obtained, because video data is pushed as soon as it becomes available at the server. This is in contrast with traditional pull-based HAS approaches, where client-based polling is required to retrieve new segments. However, a legacy browser architecture using client plug-ins can pose restrictions on the application of push methods for HAS because the browser's API does not offer push support. When a video segment or manifest is received by the browser via push, the client plug-in is not informed. This has two possible effects. First, if the client's RDA selects another quality level for the same segment, the already pushed segment can't be used. Second, transfers are still performed based on client polling but with the advantage that already pushed objects are served immediately from the local cache in the browser as soon as the client issues a new HTTP GET request.

4.3.1 Safety Push

When the client buffer drops below a certain threshold, the client typically enters the panic mode, in which the lowest quality level is retrieved. Using the *safety push* method, the server pushes the lowest quality level of a requested segment. This push is performed before the transfer of the segment at the requested quality level. Consequently, if the client enters the panic mode, the lowest quality is already available, avoiding buffer starvation and the related video freeze. The overhead introduced by this method is only acceptable if the bit rate of the highest quality is several orders of magnitude higher than the bit rate of the lowest quality. The *safety push* may be applied (1) continuously, (2) only when the client recently reduced the requested quality level, or (3) only when the client's buffer filling drops below a certain threshold. The buffer filling can be conveyed from the client to the server in the HTTP request or deduced by the server via session reconstruction [17].

4.3.2 Initial Push

In this method, all objects required to start the playout of the content such as (an) additional manifest file(s), DRM objects and the first segment(s) are pushed when the client requests a manifest from the server. For this purpose, the server is aware of the relationship between the different HAS objects. Instead of requesting objects sequentially and losing one RTT per object, the client receives all the required data together and starts the playout immediately, resulting in a significant reduction of the start-up time. For VoD streaming, the server pushes the first segment. For live streaming, the server pushes a segment that was made available d seconds ago such that the client can build a buffer that is maximum d seconds long. The value of d used by the server can be fixed for a particular type of client or specified by the client in the manifest request.

4.3.3 Layered Push

In the *layered push* method, an SVC-based client requests only the highest enhancement layer required for the desired quality level. By knowing the dependencies between the different layers, the server pushes the required lower layers autonomously. As a result, all layers are delivered using one RTT cycle, increasing the link utilization and the average video quality.

4.3.4 Manifest Push

This method is applicable to live clients that require a regular update of the manifest file such as Apple HLS clients. These clients rely on polling to periodically fetch a new manifest file. The client parses the manifest file and checks if a new segment was added. If so, the client downloads the new segment. Every segment cycle, the line remains idle for two RTT cycles (manifest and segment retrieval) and the polling time for the manifest (time between the availability of the new manifest at the server and the retrieval of the manifest by the client). Using the *manifest push* method, the server pushes the manifest as soon as a new version becomes available at the server. As a result, the idle time per cycle is reduced to one RTT to retrieve the segment. Based on previous segment retrievals, the server identifies clients that benefit from this method. For this reason, the server has to keep state about the ongoing sessions.

4.3.5 Overruling Push

In HAS, the decision on which quality level to download is made by the client's RDA. The RDA takes this decision based on the current buffer filling and a prediction of the available bandwidth for the next download. This prediction is based on the perceived bandwidth from server to client during the download of previous segments. However, there

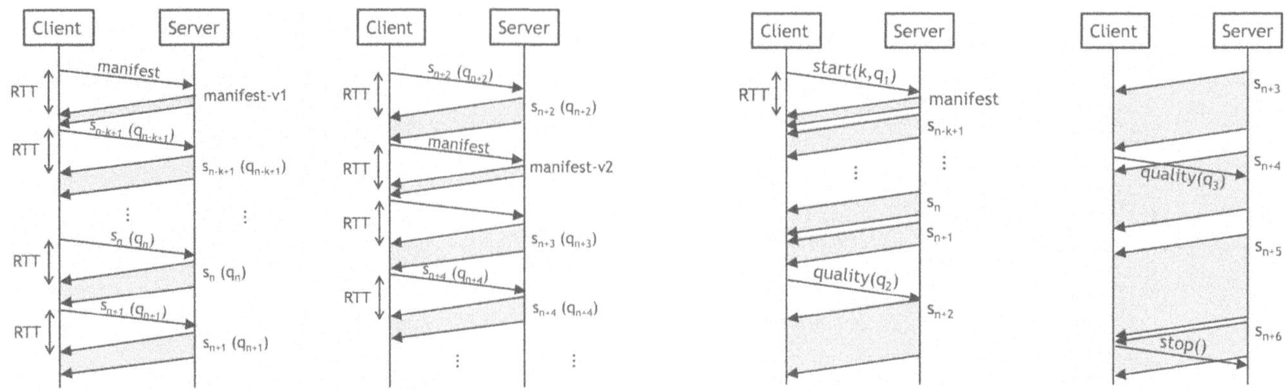

(a) HAS using traditional HTTP/1.1.

(b) HAS using the HTTP/2-based full-push method.

Figure 3: Sequence diagram for HAS live streaming with and without the HTTP/2-based full-push method.

are situations where the previously perceived bandwidth is a poor estimation of the future bandwidth. It is also possible that the server (e.g., a CDN delivery node) has better information on the available bandwidth. The goal of the *overruling push* method is to provide a possibility for the server to influence the quality selection process of the client. This can be done by pushing a segment to the client at a (typically lower) quality level. In this case, the client adds the segment to the playout buffer and refrains from requesting the same segment in another (higher) quality level.

4.3.6 Full Push

Figure 2 shows an application of the *full-push* method whereby segments (and manifests) are continuously pushed from the server (CDN delivery node) to the client. The client controls the session by sending start, stop, pause, or resume messages under the form of an HTTP GET or HTTP POST to the server. Each time a segment is completely received by the client, the RDA determines the perceived bandwidth and the actual buffer filling level. Based on these parameters, it can send a request to change the applied quality level for the pushed segments. As soon as the server receives such a request, it will change the quality starting with the next segment to be pushed. In case of VoD, the client also informs the server about the state of its buffer by sending loading-state or steady-state messages, indicating respectively that segments must be sent back-to-back or that segments must be sent at the playout rate to avoid buffer overflow. In case of live streaming as illustrated in Figure 3, the client can specify in the start-message the initial quality level and the start segment in terms of a number of segments k before the last available segment. The server will then push back-to-back all segments from the start segment s_{n-k+1} up to the last available segment s_n of the live stream. From that moment, the server will send a new segment each time when it becomes available. To do this, the server keeps track of clients and sessions.

4.4 Application in Live Streaming

Compared to traditional UDP-based video streaming such as RTP, HAS exhibits advantages such as easy firewall traversal, reuse of existing HTTP infrastructure, and adaptability. However, real-time UDP-based streaming still exhibits some advantages over HAS: a higher bandwidth utilization, the capability to use multicast to reduce the network load, a lower start and channel-change delay, and a lower end-to-end delay for live streaming.

To improve the QoE for HAS live streaming, a shorter segment duration could be used. This has following advantages: (1) Short segments are sooner available at the client because less time is required for encoding at the head-end and for transport. This results in a reduced live delay. (2) When the client starts a session, the first segment needs less time for transport, resulting in a reduced initial delay and a faster response to channel change. (3) At a channel change, there is less obsolete video data in the pipeline from server to client that still needs to be received by the client. As a result, the channel-change delay is further reduced. (4) Short segments increase the number of measuring and decision points for the RDA. In case of deteriorating network conditions, the RDA is able to react faster, possibly preventing a freeze.

Unfortunately, it is generally infeasible to use super-short segments in current HAS systems because of the following reasons: (1) More HTTP-GET messages are required to retrieve the segments, resulting in a larger overhead for the server and network. (2) Because more segments must be retrieved, more RTT cycles are lost between subsequent requests. This reduces the link utilization and the average quality. (3) In HAS, every segment starts with an IDR frame in order to be decoded independently of other segments. For video coding standards such as H.264/AVC and High Efficiency Video Coding (HEVC), the encoding efficiency of an IDR frame is significantly lower than the efficiency of frames composed of P or B slices. As a result, a higher bitrate is required to reach the same quality as for longer segments. A standard way to estimate this bitrate overhead required to achieve an equivalent average PSNR score over a set of segments is to measure the Bjontegaard Delta rate [5] for several test sequences. The estimated overheads for various segment lengths are reported in Section 5.

However, the drawbacks of short segments can be mitigated by applying additional methods. (1) The increased overhead of HTTP-GET messages can be avoided by using the *full-push* method. (2) Similarly, the problem caused by the additional lost RTT cycles between subsequent segment retrievals can be avoided by using full push since segments are pushed back-to-back. (3) The problem of the lost encoding efficiency could be mitigated by using *quality-level dependent encoding*. Using this type of encoding, the high quality levels contain less IDR frames than the lower quality levels. Since all segments have the same duration in every level, not every segment in the highest level starts with an IDR frame. Consequently, upwards quality switching requires a high quality segment that starts with an IDR frame. Downward quality switching can be done at every segment since every low-quality segment starts with an IDR frame. This type of encoding matches very well with the HAS characteristics since a HAS client must be able to switch down quickly to avoid a freeze. However, clients act very conservatively when increasing the quality. Typically, a client waits several seconds, evaluating the available bandwidth, before it decides to increase the quality. For now, quality-level dependent encoding was left as future work. Instead, we based our evaluation on the typical HAS encoding scheme where every segment starts with an IDR frame.

5. EVALUATION

To illustrate the possible gains of an HTTP/2-based push approach with super-short segments, we implemented the full-push scheme proposed in Section 4 and evaluated results for different network conditions and segment durations. The experimental setup is discussed below, followed by a detailed overview of the obtained results.

5.1 Experimental Setup

The applied video sequence is the *Big Buck Bunny* video, which has a total length of 596.4 seconds. This video is segmented using five segment durations: 133, 266, 500, 1000, and 2000 ms. Furthermore, the video is encoded in H.264 using seven quality levels: 1, 1.7, 3, 5, 8, 12.5, and 20 Mb/s. Because shorter segments are encoded less efficiently compared to the 2 second segments, we modified these nominal bit rates to reflect the overhead of the additional IDR encoded frames. Considering segments of 2 seconds as the reference, the estimated average bit rate was increased with 0.5% for 1 second segments, 2.16% for 500 ms segments, 4.89% for 266 ms segments and 9.84% for 133 ms segments, respectively. While these overheads enable to encode the segments at the same average PSNR level, the perceived quality impact of experiencing a higher frequency of IDR frames can be investigated in future work. For a fair comparison of the obtained average quality levels in experiments that use a different segment duration, we refer in our results to the normalized bit rate, since this value represents the quality level as perceived by the user.

To evaluate the proposed approach, the network topology in Figure 4 is emulated using the MiniNet framework on the Virtual Wall, a testbed containing 300 physical servers [33, 20]. The topology consists of a single HAS client, streaming video from a dedicated HAS server. The bandwidth between client and server is limited to 25 Mb/s on link 2, which is sufficient to provide the content at the highest quality level. To use HTTP/2's server push, modifications to the server and client are required, which are summarized below.

5.1.1 Server-Side Implementation

The HAS server implementation is based on the Jetty web server, which was extended to provide support for HTTP/2 [35]. Jetty's HTTP/2 component allows to setup a push-based strategy, which defines all resources that need to be pushed along with the requested resource. Such a strategy is ideal for web-based content, where the required JavaScript and CSS files, images, and other content can immediately be

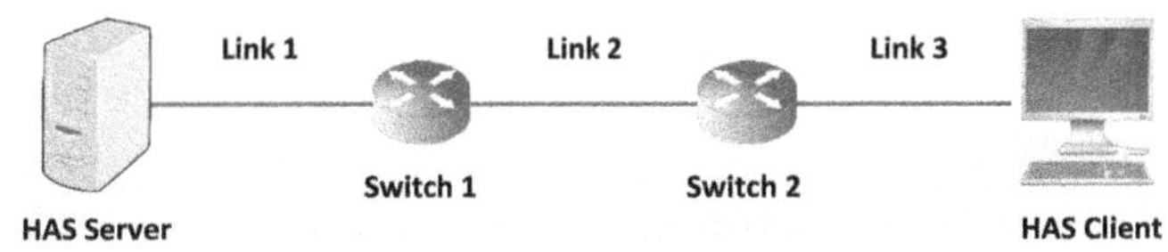

Figure 4: Emulated network topology.

pushed. However, since we target a live-stream scenario, not all segments are available when a request is issued. Therefore, we defined a new request handler that processes GET requests issued by the client. This handler allows a client to issue a live-stream request, passing along parameters such as the preferred buffer size and quality level. When this request corresponds to a new session, the server starts a push thread that pushes instantly the five last released video segments at the lowest quality. This way, the client can ramp up its buffer quickly, while not overloading the network. In order to simulate a live stream scenario, a release thread makes new segments available every segment duration. As soon as new segments are available, the push thread is notified and a segment is pushed to the corresponding client. When the client wants to change the quality level at which the segments are pushed, a new GET request is issued and the quality level is updated at server side accordingly.

5.1.2 Client-Side Implementation

The HAS client is implemented on top of the libdash library, the official reference software of the ISO/IEC MPEG-DASH standard [4]. To make use of HTTP/2's server pushing feature, a number of changes is made. First, an HTTP/2-based connection is added to enable the reception of pushed segments. The nghttp2 library is used to set up an HTTP/2 connection over SSL [34]. Note that the reference software uses curl to issue all GET requests, yet this library does not yet support HTTP/2 push. Second, the RDA is modified to recalculate the quality level every time a segment is received and the corresponding push stream is closed. While in HTTP/1.1 a GET request is required for every segment, no request is sent in the HTTP/2-based scheme if no quality change is required. Third, the perceived bandwidth is estimated based on the elapsed time between the reception of the push promise and the time the segment is available. In HTTP/1.1, this estimation is based on the total download time, which includes the time to send the GET request.

The used RDA is the FINEAS RDA[1], developed by Petrangeli et al. [27]. It can deal with low buffer sizes and has shown to outperform well-known RDA's such as MSS. The used RDA parameters are a quality window of 70 seconds, a panic threshold of two segments and a buffer target of 80%. These values were selected after tweaking the RDA for a buffer size of five segments. Note that our main goal is to show the possible gain obtained by using HTTP/2 with super-short segments instead of HTTP/1.1; a comparison of the performance of different RDA's using HTTP/2 will be left as future work.

5.2 Evaluation Metrics

The following evaluation metrics are considered: (i) the average video quality, expressed as the average normalized bit rate of all video segments; (ii) the server-to-display delay, defined as the time between the release of a segment and its

[1]The in-network computation proposed by the authors has not been implemented in this work.

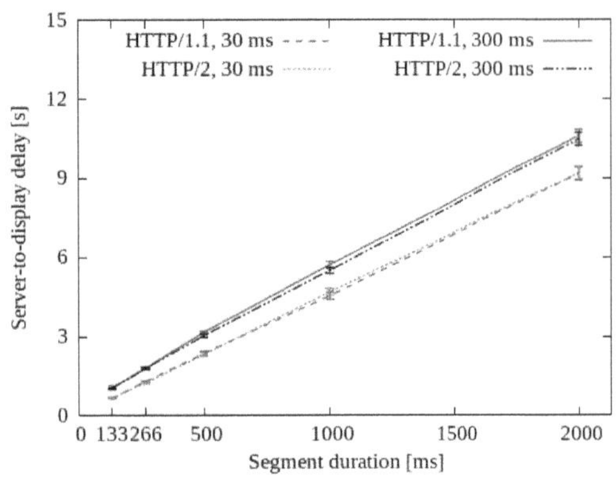

(a) Average server-to-display delay

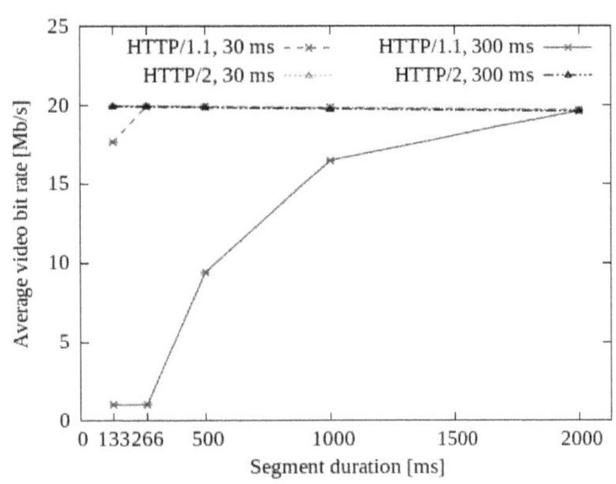

(b) Average video bit rate

Figure 5: Impact of the segment duration on the average normalized bit rate and the average server-to-display delay, both for an RTT of 30 ms and 300 ms.

playout at client-side. Note that this is not the same as the camera-to-display delay, as no real live event is captured in our experiments; (iii) the initial start-up delay, which is defined as the time between requesting the live video at client-side and the playout of the first video segment.

To properly evaluate the impact of the segment duration and the RTT on these metrics, the *Big Buck Bunny* video was streamed multiple times. In our experiments, all five segment durations were tested using HTTP/1.1 and HTTP/2 over SSL, with realistic RTTs in the range of 30 ms to 300 ms. To account for possible outliers, experiments were repeated multiple times for every configuration. Results are therefore shown using the observed averages and the appropriate 95% confidence intervals.

5.3 Detailed Results

5.3.1 Segment Duration and Round-Trip Time

Figure 5 shows the impact of an increasing segment duration for an RTT of 30 ms and 300 ms. Figure 5a shows the average server-to-display delay, defined as the time between the release of a segment and its playout at client-side. Both for an RTT of 30 ms and 300 ms, a clear increase is observed for higher segment durations. This is because the selected buffers are designed to hold five video segments, and the playout delay is directly proportional to the buffer size. While this increase is observed both for HTTP/1.1 and HTTP/2, results for the latter are slightly better. This is because, using a push-based approach, an average decrease of half an RTT cycle is achieved. Using a segment duration of 133 ms, the initial server-to-display delay is reduced to 0.87 s and 0.77 s for HTTP/1.1 and HTTP/2 respectively. A naive and straightforward way to lower the playout delay is thus to simply use super-short segments. However, as shown by Figure 5b, the average video bit rate is significantly lower when short segments of 133 ms and 266 ms are used. This is especially true for an RTT of 300 ms, where the lowest video bit rate is always selected. This is because it is impossible to get a segment in time, as its duration is even lower than the RTT. For every requested segment, a playout freeze is thus observed. For larger segment durations, the average bit rate increases because of a higher bandwidth utilization. Using HTTP/2's server push however, the average video bit rate is always around 20 Mb/s. This indicates that the proposed approach results in a higher bandwidth utilization and selected quality level, which is attributed to the gain of an RTT cycle for every segment request.

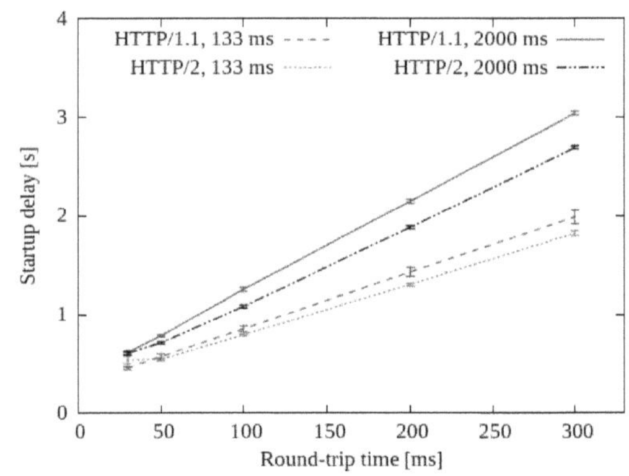

Figure 6: Impact of the RTT on the average startup delay, both for a segment duration of 133 ms and 2 s.

Figure 6 shows the impact of an increasing RTT on the client's startup delay, for a segment duration of 133 ms and 2 s. While differences are small for an RTT of 30 ms, a clear increase is shown for higher RTTs. This is the consequence of the TCP slow-start phase, which requires multiple RTT cycles to send the manifest and the first segment from server to client. For both segment durations, results for HTTP/1.1 are clearly inferior to those for HTTP/2. The average gain is one RTT cycle, attributed to the fact that no additional requests are required to get the first video segments. From these results, we can conclude that using HTTP/2's server push is indeed beneficial when the manifest and video segments are stored on the same server. Using HTTP/2 with a segment duration of 133 ms, instead of HTTP/1.1 with a duration of 2 s, the average startup delay for an RTT of 300 ms can actively be reduced from 3.04 s to 1.82 s. It is worth noting that, if the user would switch from one videostream to another, the channel change delay would be reduced by exactly one RTT cycle if the existing TCP connection is reused.

A summary of results for HTTP/1.1 and HTTP/2 with an RTT of 300 ms is presented in Table 2, for a segment duration of 133 ms and 2 s. These results indicate that using super-short segments to limit the server-to-display delay, is not feasible when HTTP/1.1 is used in a scenario with high RTTs: when the RTT exceeds the segment duration, the lowest bit rate is always selected. Using the push-based ap-

Configuration	Segment duration [ms]	Bit rate [Mb/s]	Server-to-display delay [s]	Startup delay [s]
HTTP/1.1	133	1.00 ± 0.00	1.07 ± 0.07	1.99 ± 0.07
	2000	19.62 ± 0.00	10.59 ± 0.25	3.04 ± 0.02
HTTP/2	133	19.94 ± 0.00	1.05 ± 0.02	1.82 ± 0.03
	2000	19.61 ± 0.00	10.48 ± 0.25	2.69 ± 0.01

Table 2: Performance summary for HTTP/1.1 and HTTP/2, for an RTT of 300 ms. The average values are reported, together with the 95% confidence intervals.

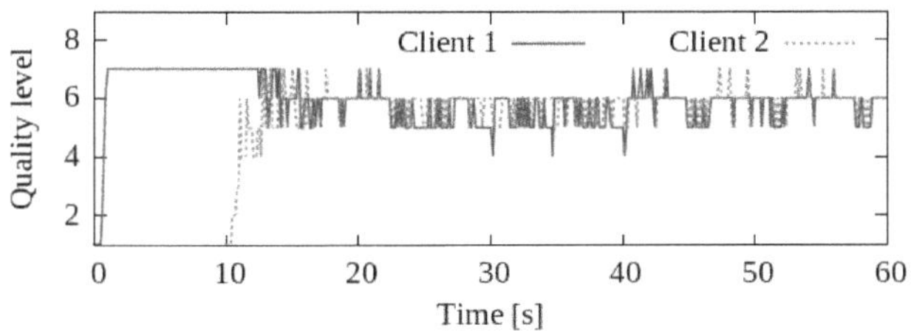

(a) Streaming over HTTP/1.1

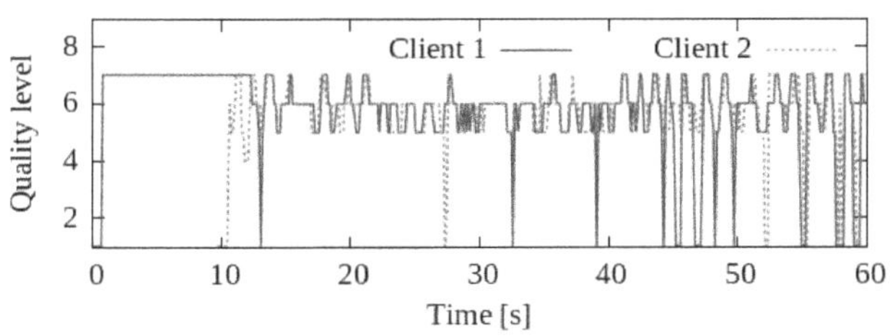

(b) Streaming over HTTP/2

Figure 7: Played quality level for two clients streaming video with a segment duration of 133 ms and an RTT of 30 ms, both for HTTP/1.1 and HTTP/2.

proach however, segment durations as low as 133 ms can be used with an RTT of up to 300 ms. In contrast to streaming over HTTP/1.1, the video content is delivered at the highest quality when the perceived bandwidth is sufficiently high. Comparing the server-to-display delay for HTTP/1.1 with a segment duration of 2 s and HTTP/2 with a segment duration of 133 ms, a reduction of 90.1% is observed. This means that the client is capable of following the live signal more closely, resulting in a better user experience. Furthermore, a reduction of 40.1% is achieved for the start-up delay, indicating that the client can start the playout of the video significantly faster. Overall, results for the traditional HTTP/1.1 approach are inferior to those for HTTP/2, showing the potential of the proposed push-based approach.

6. FUTURE WORK

Future work will focus on (1) a more elaborate evaluation of full push and super-short segments using time-varying bandwidth bottlenecks, competing clients, and the combination of HAS and non-HAS traffic, (2) the application of the quality-level dependent encoding technique, and (3) an evaluation of the other proposed methods.

To demonstrate possible challenges with competing clients, we performed a simple experiment where we expanded the topology in Figure 4 with one additional client. In Figure 7a, the two competing clients use traditional HTTP/1.1. When the first client starts, the RDA almost immediately increases the selected quality to 20 Mb/s. Once the second client starts, the first client lowers its video quality and the clients further compete for the available bandwidth (25 Mb/s). In Figure 7b, both clients use the proposed full-push approach over HTTP/2. Again, the RDA immediately increases the selected quality to 20 Mb/s. However, once the second client starts streaming, upward peaks are wider and short peaks to the lowest quality level are observed. This is explained as follows. While a segment n is being received by the client, new segments $n+1, ..., n+k$ are already pushed to the client at the same video quality as segment n. Because under the influence of the competing clients, the network is not always capable to provide the necessary bandwidth, the download of the segments might take longer. As a result, the RDA's panic threshold for the buffer filling is hit more frequently, leading to the selection of the lowest video quality. More work is required to evaluate possible solutions such as the use of a more frequent update signal from client to server or a limitation of the number of segments in flight between server and client.

7. CONCLUSIONS

In this paper, we proposed ten HTTP/2 based methods to improve the QoE for HAS streaming. Furthermore, we presented a new streaming concept for live streaming that combines the advantages of push-based real-time streaming and the advantages of HTTP adaptive streaming. This concept is based on the combination of super-short segments and our HTTP/2-based full-push method. To quantify the advantages, we implemented a working prototype based on the MiniNet framework. We used a modified Jetty server that is HTTP/2-push-enabled and a modified libdash client. To perform an initial evaluation of both methods, we used a constant network bandwidth sufficient to support the highest quality levels in the HAS setup.

First, we showed that high RTT values significantly reduce the average quality of the HAS sessions, especially when segment durations are short. Next, we showed that with an RTT of 300 ms, super-short segments can reduce the server-to-display delay for live streaming with 89.9 %. However, it was also demonstrated that the use of super-short segments causes an unacceptable degradation of the average HAS quality. Finally, we evaluated the combination of super-short segments with the full-push method. We demonstrated that HTTP/2-based full push is able to eliminate the disadvantages inherent to the use of super-short segment durations such as the HTTP message overhead and the reduced average quality. Moreover, the combination of the two methods was able to reduce the server-to-display delay for live streams by 90.1% and the start-up delay by 40.1%.

8. ACKNOWLEDGMENTS

This research was performed partially within the iMinds V-FORCE (Video: 4K Composition and Efficient streaming) project under an Agency for Innovation by Science and Technology in Flanders (IWT) grant agreement no. 130655 and by FLAMINGO, a Network of Excellence project (318488) supported by the European Commission under its Seventh Framework Programme. Jeroen van der Hooft is funded by grant of the IWT."

9. REFERENCES

[1] S. Akhshabi, L. Anantakrishnan, C. Dovrolis, and A. C. Begen. Server-Based Traffic Shaping for Stabilizing Oscillating Adaptive Streaming Players. In *NOSSDAV*, 2013.

[2] M. Belshe, R. Peon, and M. Thomson. Hypertext Transfer Protocol Version 2. Technical Report Internet-Draft, 2015.

[3] S. Benno, A. Beck, J. Esteban, L. Wu, and R. Miller. WiLo: A Rate Determination Algorithm for HAS Video in Wireless Networks and Low-Delay Applications. In *Globecom Workshops*, 2013.

[4] bitmovin. libdash. https://github.com/bitmovin/libdash/.

[5] G. Bjontegaard. Calculation of Average PSNR Differences between RD-Curves. In *ITU-T SG16/Q.6, Doc. VCEG-M033*, 2001.

[6] N. Bouten, M. Claeys, S. Latré, J. Famaey, W. Van Leekwijck, and F. De Turck. Deadline-Based Approach for Improving Delivery of SVC-Based HTTP Adaptive Streaming Content. In *NOMS*, 2014.

[7] N. Bouten, J. Famaey, S. Latré, R. Huysegems, B. Vleeschauwer, W. Leekwijck, and F. De Turck. QoE Optimization Through In-Network Quality Adaptation for HTTP Adaptive Streaming. In *CNSM*, 2012.

[8] A. Cardaci, L. Caviglione, A. Gotta, and N. Tonellotto. Performance Evaluation of SPDY over High Latency Satellite Channels. Institute for Computer Sciences, Social Informatics and Telecommunications Engineering. 2013.

[9] M. Claeys, S. Latré, J. Famaey, T. Wu, W. Van Leekwijck, and F. De Turck. Design of a Q-Learning-Based Client Quality Selection Algorithm for HTTP Adaptive Video Streaming. In *AAMAS*, 2013.

[10] Conviva. Viewer Experience Report 2014. 2014.

[11] F. Dobrian, V. Sekar, A. Awan, I. Stoica, D. Joseph, A. Ganjam, J. Zhan, and H. Zhang. Understanding the Impact of Video Quality on User Engagement. *SIGCOMM*, 2011.

[12] Y. Elkhatib, G. Tyson, and M. Welzl. Can SPDY Really Make the Web Faster? In *IFIP*, 2014.

[13] J. Erman, V. Gopalakrishnan, R. Jana, and K. K. Ramakrishnan. Towards a SPDY'Ier Mobile Web? In *CoNEXT*, 2013.

[14] J. Famaey, S. Latré, N. Bouten, W. Van de Meerssche, B. De Vleeschauwer, W. Van Leekwijck, and F. De Turck. On the Merits of SVC-based HTTP Adaptive Streaming. In *IFIP*, 2013.

[15] FCC. Measuring Broadband America. http://transition.fcc.gov/cgb/measuringbroadbandreport/2013/Measuring-Broadband-America-feb-2013.pdf, 2013.

[16] Google. SPDY: An Experimental Protocol for a Faster Web. Technical report, 2009.

[17] R. Huysegems, B. De Vleeschauwer, K. De Schepper, C. Hawinkel, T. Wu, K. Laevens, and W. Van Leekwijck. Session Reconstruction for HTTP Adaptive Streaming: Laying the Foundation for Network-Based QoE Monitoring. In *IWQoS*, 2012.

[18] IETF. Hypertext Transfer Protocol (httpbis). 2012.

[19] Igvita. *High Performance Browser Networking.* O'Reilly, 2014.

[20] iMinds. Virtual Wall. http://ilabt.iminds.be/iminds-virtualwall-overview/.

[21] T. Lohmar, T. Einarsson, P. Frojdh, F. Gabin, and M. Kampmann. Dynamic Adaptive HTTP Streaming of Live Content. In *WoWMoM*, 2011.

[22] R. K. P. Mok, X. Luo, E. W. W. Chan, and R. K. C. Chang. QDASH: A QoE-aware DASH System. In *MMsys*, 2012.

[23] C. Mueller, S. Lederer, C. Timmerer, and H. Hellwagner. Dynamic Adaptive Streaming over HTTP/2.0. In *ICME*, 2013.

[24] C. Müller, S. Lederer, and C. Timmerer. An Evaluation of Dynamic Adaptive Streaming over HTTP in Vehicular Environments. In *MoVid*, 2012.

[25] C. Müller, D. Renzi, S. Lederer, S. Battista, and C. Timmerer. Using Scalable Video Coding for Dynamic Adaptive Streaming over HTTP in Mobile Environments. In *EUSIPCO*, 2012.

[26] S. Petrangeli, M. Claeys, S. Latré, J. Famaey, and F. De Turck. A Multi-Agent Q-Learning-Based Framework for Achieving Fairness in HTTP Adaptive Streaming. In *NOMS*, 2014.

[27] S. Petrangeli, J. Famaey, M. Claeys, S. Latré, and F. De Turck. QoE-driven Rate Adaptation Heuristic for Fair Adaptive Video Streaming. *ACM TOMM*, 2015.

[28] Y. Sánchez de la Fuente, T. Schierl, C. Hellge, T. Wiegand, D. Hong, D. De Vleeschauwer, W. Van Leekwijck, and Y. Le Louédec. iDASH: Improved Dynamic Adaptive Streaming over HTTP Using Scalable Video Coding. In *MMSys*, 2011.

[29] Y. Sánchez de la Fuente, T. Schierl, C. Hellge, T. Wiegand, D. Hong, D. De Vleeschauwer, W. Van Leekwijck, and Y. Le Louédec. Efficient HTTP-Based Streaming Using Scalable Video Coding. In *MMSys*, 2012.

[30] Sandvine. Global Internet Phenomena Report, 1H 2014. 2014.

[31] T. Stockhammer. Dynamic Adaptive Streaming over HTTP: Standards and Design Principles. In *ACM MM*, 2011.

[32] S. Tavakoli, J. Gutierrez, and N. Garcia. Subjective Quality Study of Adaptive Streaming of Monoscopic and Stereoscopic Video. *Journal of Selected Areas in Communications*, 2014.

[33] M. Team. MiniNet. http://mininet.org/.

[34] T. Tsujikawa. nghttp2. https://nghttp2.org/.

[35] Webtide. Jetty. https://webtide.com/.

[36] S. Wei and V. Swaminathan. Cost Effective Video Streaming Using Server Push over HTTP 2.0. In *MMSP*, 2014.

[37] S. Wei and V. Swaminathan. Low Latency Live Video Streaming over HTTP 2.0. In *NOSSDAV*, 2014.

Bandwidth-aware Prefetching for Proactive Multi-video Preloading and Improved HAS Performance

Vengatanathan Krishnamoorthi[†] Niklas Carlsson[†] Derek Eager[‡]
Anirban Mahanti[§] Nahid Shahmehri[†]
[†] Linköping University, Sweden, firstname.lastname@liu.se
[‡] University of Saskatchewan, Canada, eager@cs.usask.ca
[§] NICTA, Australia, anirban.mahanti@nicta.com.au

ABSTRACT

This paper considers the problem of providing users playing one streaming video the option of instantaneous and seamless playback of alternative videos. Recommendation systems can easily provide a list of alternative videos, but there is little research on how to best eliminate the startup time for these alternative videos. The problem is motivated by services that want to retain increasingly impatient users, who frequently watch the beginning of multiple videos, before viewing a video to the end. We present the design, implementation, and evaluation of an HTTP-based Adaptive Streaming (HAS) solution that provides careful prefetching and buffer management. We also present the design and evaluation of three fundamental policy classes that provide different tradeoffs between how aggressively new alternative videos are prefetched versus the importance of ensuring high playback quality. We show that our solution allows us to reduce the startup times of alternative videos by an order of magnitude and effectively adapt the quality such as to ensure the highest possible playback quality of the video being viewed. By improving the channel utilization we also address the discrimination problem that HAS clients often suffer from, allowing us to in some cases simultaneously improve the playback quality of the video being viewed and provide the value-added service of allowing instantaneous playback of the prefetched alternative videos.

Categories and Subject Descriptors

C.4 [**Information Systems Organization**]: Performance of Systems; C.2.2 [**Network Protocols**]: Applications; H.5.1 [**Multimedia Information Systems**]: Video

Keywords

HTTP-based adaptive streaming (HAS); Bandwidth-aware prefetching; Multi-video preloading; Seamless playback

MM'15, October 26–30, 2015, Brisbane, Australia.
© 2015 ACM. ISBN 978-1-4503-3459-4/15/10 ...$15.00.
DOI: http://dx.doi.org/10.1145/2733373.2806270.

1. INTRODUCTION

Today's users are highly impatient and frequently switch movies or channels within a few minutes of viewing. For example, analysis of 540 million video-on-demand sessions has shown that users often view the beginning of a few videos (5 on average) before finally viewing one video to the end [6]. To retain users and help minimize the chance that users decide to use competing providers, it is therefore important to quickly provide these users with attractive alternative video choices that they can view next. For example, a selection of alternative videos could be presented to the user as thumbnails, or the user could be presented previews or ads whenever pausing playback. We argue that to maximize retention rates, these alternative videos ideally should be proactively preloaded or prefetched to the client in a manner that allows the videos to be available for instantaneous viewing at the time when the client decides to terminate playback of the originally viewed video or to switch video to view.

While there is much work on recommendation algorithms for determining the best set of alternative videos that the user is likely to want to view next [7, 8, 28], there is a lack of research on the best ways to prefetch these alternative videos. In order to maximize the user perceived Quality of Experience (QoE), such techniques must balance the importance of high-quality uninterrupted playback against the desire to allow instantaneous playback of the alternative videos. This problem is both important and challenging, as users often are highly heterogeneous with time-varying bandwidth conditions and the alternative videos must be carefully prefetched in parallel with the video being streamed such as to ensure timely preloading of these videos, while at the same time minimizing the impact on the streamed video.

In this paper we present the design, implementation, and evaluation of an HTTP-based Adaptive Streaming (HAS) solution that provides prefetching and buffer management such as to ensure instantaneous playback of alternative videos whenever a user selects one of the alternative videos or interrupts playback. The use of HAS allows the quality of both the streaming video (currently being viewed) and the prefetched alternative videos (that are cached for potential future viewing) to be adapted such as to make the best use of the available bandwidth. Within our framework, carefully designed prefetching policies are used to ensure interruption free playback, while allowing the player different (policy dependent) means to control when each alternative video is expected to be ready for instantaneous playback.

Typical HAS players are designed to interrupt download when the buffer is sufficiently full, as measured by an upper buffer threshold T_{max}, for example, and not resume download again until the buffer has drained to some lower buffer threshold T_{min}. While the use of an upper threshold T_{max} helps limit the wasted resources associated with users not watching the full video, it has been shown that the resulting *on-off behavior* [5, 21, 24] can lead to poor performance under conditions with competing traffic [3, 13]. Our solution carefully schedules prefetching during off-periods, obtaining improved download rates, while also ensuring that the prefetching does not negatively impact the user playback experience. In fact, we show that under some circumstances, prefetching of alternative videos can even improve the playback quality of the streaming video itself.

It is likely that the criticality of preloading alternative videos will differ both across services and between users within a service. For example, for some users, timely preloading of alternative videos may be very important such as to allow seamless "video browsing", whereas for other users that are less likely to change videos, the preloading is simply a value added service used occasionally.

Motivated by a diverse set of use cases, and user behaviors, within our framework, we present the design and evaluation of three fundamental policy classes used for multi-file prefetching. The first two policy classes use opportunistic prefetching only during off periods, but differ in how aggressively they prefetch new alternative videos versus ensuring that the prefetched videos are relatively evenly paced. The third class uses strict prefetch deadline targets for when the beginning of the different alternative videos should have been prefetched. In bandwidth restricted scenarios, this policy class must therefore sometimes trade a lower quality level of the streaming video for more reliable delivery of the prefetched alternative videos. We use an optimization framework to balance the importance of the different deadlines associated with this policy. Within each policy class, we consider both non-adaptive and adaptive quality selection versions.

We implement a proof-of-concept solution on top of the Open Source Media Framework (OSMF), within which we combine the OSMF Ad insertion plugin (to allow playback of multiple videos in the same video container) and a download-manager extension based on Krishnamoorthi et al.'s [19] branched video framework (that supports prefetching and caching). Our implementation allows the user to seamlessly switch to viewing an alternative video with negligible startup delay, as soon as the player has prefetched the beginning of the alternative video(s). Moreover, the use of the ad plugin to stitch together multiple videos within a single container and cache management allow the currently played video to be quickly replaced by an already prefetched video. In experiments assuming a 4 Mb/s link, for example, the startup time of an alternative video (at lowest playback quality) is reduced from about 6 seconds (without prefetching but using the ad plugin for faster playout) to 0.6 seconds (needed to switch and load containers).

In summary, the primary contributions of the paper are (i) a prefetching framework that simultaneously allows adaptive prefetching and playback of alternative videos, while addressing the on-off problem typically associated with HAS, (ii) a novel proof-of-concept implementation that we show implements effective prefetching policies and provides close to instantaneous playback of alternative videos, and (iii) the design and evaluation of three candidate policy classes, including both non-adaptive and quality adaptive versions. Our experimental results highlight and validate the basic properties associated with the different policy classes and characterize their performance tradeoffs.

The remainder of the paper is organized as follows. Sections 2 and 3 set the context and describe our system framework, respectively. We then define the policy classes and their variations (Section 4), describe our system implementation (Section 5), and present our validation and performance results (Section 6). Finally, related work (Section 7) and conclusions (Section 8) are presented.

2. BACKGROUND

HTTP-based Adaptive Streaming (HAS) is the most popular means of providing streaming services today [2]. HAS is client driven and allows the use of stateless Web servers and caches. Typically, the players either use byte-range requests or request each individual file "chunk" with a unique URL [5]. The use of multiple files with different video qualities, with aligned chunks, allows the player to adapt the playback media streaming rate based on current buffer and network conditions.

Commonly, the client-side scheduling of chunk requests by HAS players results in on-off periods in the bandwidth usage [24]. To understand why, note that players must balance the need to buffer sufficiently many chunks such as to account for jitter and bandwidth variations against the desire to avoid wasting unnecessary resources on clients terminating playback early. For these reasons, HAS players typically try to maintain some minimum desired buffer occupancy T_{min} (measured in second of playback) without exceeding some maximum desired buffer occupancy T_{max}. For example, with the simplest policies, as used by the OSMF player, for example, playback begins whenever T_{min} data is buffered and the player continues to make requests until T_{max} is reached. Then, the player does not make any new requests until the buffer occupancy falls below T_{min} again.

Similar on-off patterns have been observed with other players [5, 21, 24]. One noticeable difference between players is the size of the buffer thresholds. For example, among general video streaming frameworks, OSMF uses much smaller default values ($T_{min}/T_{max} = 4/6$) compared to Microsoft Smooth Streaming ($T_{min}/T_{max} = 12/30$) [5]. Even more extreme is the $T_{max} = 240$ second buffer that Netflix tries to maintain in steady state [14]. A larger buffer provides additional protection against errors in rate estimation, and can in some cases allow clients to recover from temporary network outages. Note that OSMF may be designed for short duration videos played on mobile devices, whereas Netflix focuses on delivering full-length movies and TV shows. Yet, despite the large differences in the desired buffer size, the on-off behavior is common across the players.

Coupled with TCP congestion control mechanisms, the on-off periods can result in clients not obtaining their fair bandwidth share [13, 15]. To understand why, note that the overall throughput of HAS depends on the underlying end-to-end congestion mechanism of TCP. For example, consider the case in which the congestion window timer times out during an off period. In this case, the sender will reset its congestion window to a predefined minimum and begin slow-start at the start of the on-period. More generally, the use of on-off periods can cause a user to pick a lower quality than it otherwise would, resulting in increasingly bigger off-periods, thus allowing other users to grab a bigger bandwidth share. This behavior is self-feeding and HAS users can get increasingly smaller bandwidth share [13].[1]

In this paper, we present a novel system design that utilizes the otherwise unused bandwidth during off periods to prefetch the initial chunks of alternative videos. This allows the player to simultaneously preload alternative videos and maintain its fair bandwidth share.

3. SYSTEM OVERVIEW

3.1 Basic Approach

We assume that each user has been assigned a set of alternative videos that the content provider would like to preload at the client. This list could include, for example, videos that the user is likely to view next or ads that the provider may want to show when the user pauses playback. We will refer to the video being streamed as the *streaming video*, and the videos to be preloaded as *alternative videos*. To allow instantaneous playback of an alternative video, its initial chunks must be prefetched and cached locally on the client.

Our solution leverages HAS chunking and adaptivity. To allow instantaneous playback of alternative videos, the initial chunks of these videos are downloaded in parallel with the chunks of the currently streamed video. By prefetching the initial chunks of the alternative videos, the player can allow the user to seamlessly switch between multiple videos without enduring noticeable playback interruption. To ensure interruption free streaming of the currently viewed video, the video qualities of both the streamed video and of the prefetched alternative videos are adapted based on current conditions.

Our solution utilizes the off periods associated with typical HAS players to perform prefetching. Using opportunistic and adaptive prefetching of the alternative videos during time periods when connections otherwise would be idle allows us to make use of the otherwise wasted bandwidth. By eliminating off periods, the player also avoids TCP congestion window timeouts and other throughput problems associated with the on-off pattern of typical HAS systems, allowing the client to maintain its fair bandwidth share and improve download speeds.

In Figure 1(a) we use example traces to illustrate how prefetching of alternative videos can help improve the client's overall download throughput during on periods, and hence also the playback quality of the streaming video itself. Note that after the off period (during which the regular HAS player would not be downloading chunks), there is a non-negligible ramp-up period required by TCP before the regular HAS player reaches the original download rate, resulting in a slower average download rate during the following on period. This is clearly illustrated by the difference in the slope of the cumulative download curves (Figure 1(b)) between 28 and 37 seconds. The higher download rate also results in T_{max} being reached sooner, illustrated by the streaming video curve of our player plateauing three seconds before the native HAS player without prefetching.

[1]While the impact of on-off periods differs between TCP implementations, typically TCP enters slow start when the idle period exceeds the RTO threshold. Section 6.7 takes a closer look at the impact of TCP version and slow start.

3.2 Simple Prefetch Example

Figure 2 illustrates the operation of a basic "best effort" prefetching policy that prefetches the first two chunks of each of the two alternative videos. In this example there are only two quality encodings, and the player downloads the initial chunks of the alternative videos, at the lower quality, whenever there would otherwise be an off period.

As with regular HAS, the client starts downloading the first few chunks of the streaming video at a low quality and then increases quality as network conditions permit. The player continues to download chunks back-to-back until the buffer occupancy reaches or exceeds T_{max}. At this time, rather than entering an off period, our modified player now downloads the chunks of the alternative video, starting with the first chunk of the first alternative video.

Chunks of the alternative videos are downloaded into a separate cache and are not loaded directly into the player. Therefore, the playback buffer is drained at exactly the same rate as for a regular HAS player. The modified player continues downloading alternative chunks until the next expected completion time would be after the playback buffer reaches T_{min}. For example, in the case that the current download rate is r and the current playback buffer is T, the player should no longer initiate new downloads of alternative chunks whenever $r(T - T_{min})$ is smaller than the size S of the next alternative chunk. Instead, the player switches back to downloading chunks from the streaming video, and the download pattern is repeated.

4. PREFETCH POLICIES

All considered prefetch policy classes (Section 4.1) assume an ordered list of alternative videos, but differ with respect to how many chunks are downloaded of each alternative video, the timing of when alternative video chunks are downloaded, and how strictly potential chunk deadlines are applied. Variants of the policy classes (Section 4.3) are defined based on their quality adaptation.

4.1 Policy Classes

Best-effort: This is the simplest policy class. When the buffer occupancy reaches T_{max}, the player starts downloading chunks of the alternative videos, and continues doing so until it estimates the download rate to be insufficient to allow another such chunk download before the buffer falls below T_{min}. At this time, the player goes back to downloading chunks of the streaming video. When given a prefetch opportunity, this policy always prefetches the first n chunks of the alternative video next on the list of alternative videos, one after the other. Here, n is a policy parameter controlling how much of each video should be prefetched before being presented as a preloaded alternative.

This policy class is well suited for network conditions where the buffer size periodically reaches T_{max}. Naturally, T_{max} is reached most frequently under high-bandwidth scenarios. However, interestingly, due to the quality adaptation of typical HAS players, alternative chunks will also be downloaded relatively frequently also under low bandwidths scenarios, as long as the download rate exceeds the minimum encoding rate. Perhaps the biggest downside with this policy class is that it does not provide the content provider with any control of how quickly new alternative videos are prefetched. The following two policy classes address this shortcoming.

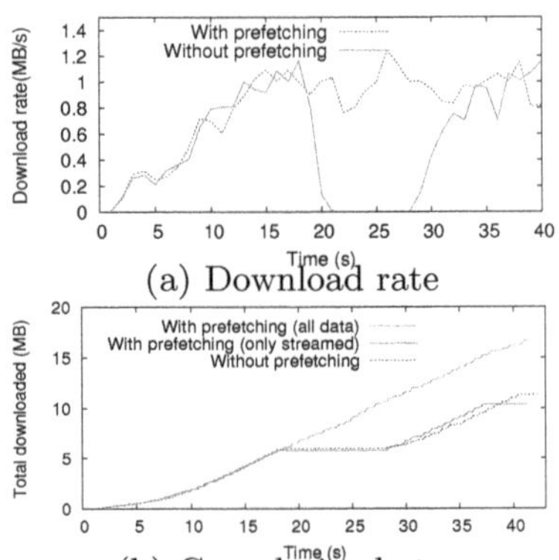

Figure 1: Transfer during example experiment.

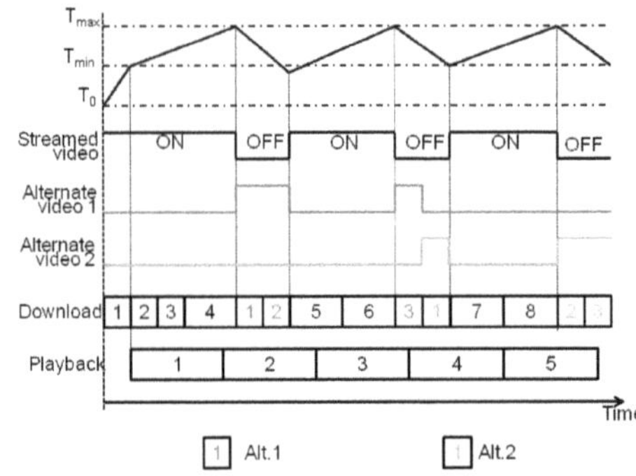

Figure 2: Prefetch framework overview.

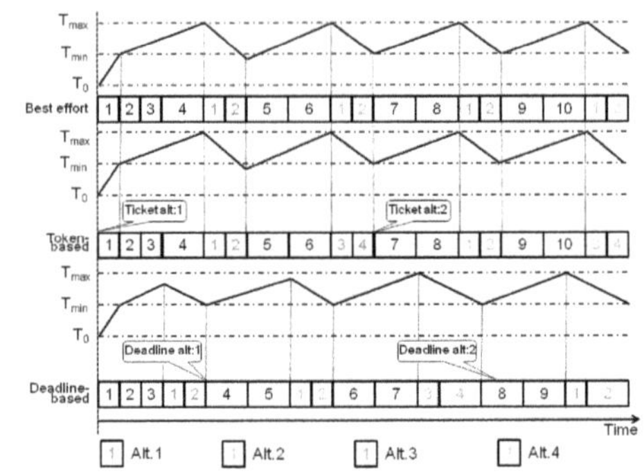

Figure 3: High-level comparison of prefetching classes.

Token-based: This policy class provides greater control of the earliest time new alternative videos should be prefetched, allowing the client to pace the rate that such videos are prefetched. These policies download chunks from the alternative videos at exactly the same instances as the *best-effort* policies, but differ in how they decide from which video to download next. To achieve an even pacing without impairing the playback quality of the streaming video, these policies implement a token-bucket approach in which new video tokens are generated and placed in a queue every Δ seconds. Each token is associated with a new alternative video, and the player always downloads the first n chunks of the video next in the token-bucket queue, unless the queue goes empty, in which case the player continues to select chunks of the video associated with the most recent token. The policy parameter Δ determines the pacing, and n the minimum amount of prefetching of each video. With $\Delta = 0$, the token-based policy is equivalent to best-effort.

Except for a much more even pacing of alternative videos, the performance of the *token-based* policies is the same as for the corresponding *best-effort* policies. Both these policy classes only download alternative video chunks when given an opportunity to do so without adapting the downloads of the streaming video, ensuring that the playback quality of the streaming video is not negatively impacted.

Deadline-based: For some video browsing users [6], stall-free switching between videos may be more important than achieving the highest possible streaming rate of the currently streamed video. To further prioritize the download of alternative videos and enforce an even pacing of the alternative videos, the third policy class associates deadlines with each alternative video and applies an optimization framework to find the best tradeoff between video quality and ensuring that the alternative videos are prefetched in time of their respective deadlines.

For simplicity, we define relative playback deadlines, such that the deadline of the next alternative video a always occurs when m_a chunks of the streaming video have been played either since the deadline for the previous alternative video or since playback began (in the case there are no prior deadlines). At each such deadline the player is expected to have downloaded the first n chunks of the alternative video. Assuming that the m_a chunks of the streaming video are downloaded ahead of the n chunks of the alternative video, we can now determine an optimized download schedule by solving the following optimization problem:

$$\text{maximize} \sum_{i=1}^{m_a+1} q_i^s l_i^s + \sum_{j=1}^{n} q_j^a l_j^a, \tag{1}$$

subject to

$$t_i^s \leq \tau + \sum_{j=1}^{i-1} l_j^s, \quad 1 \leq i \leq m_a + 1 \tag{2}$$

$$t_j^a \leq \tau + \sum_{i=1}^{m_a} l_j^s, \quad 1 \leq j \leq n \tag{3}$$

$$r_i^s(t_i^s - t_{i-1}^s) = q_i^s l_i^s, \quad 2 \leq i \leq m_a + 1 \tag{4}$$

$$r_1^a(t_1^a - t_{m+1}^s) = q_1^a l_1^a, \tag{5}$$

$$r_j^a(t_j^a - t_{j-1}^a) = q_j^a l_j^a, \quad 2 \leq j \leq n \tag{6}$$

The structure of this optimization model is similar to that used by Krishnamoorthi et al. [19] to address a different prefetching problem, concerning "branched video". Here, q_i^s, l_i^s, and t_i^s are the quality, chunk size, and download completion time of the ith chunk of the streaming video; q_j^a, l_j^a and t_j^a are the corresponding values for the next alternative video. Furthermore, r_i^s and r_j^a are the estimated download rates for chunks i and j of the two videos, respectively, and the startup delay τ is equal to the most recent deadline, or the playback start of the first downloaded chunk.

The objective function (1) tries to maximize the playback quality of the streaming video, conditioned on the individual playback deadlines of the streaming video (2), the n alternative chunks being downloaded before their deadline (3), and bandwidth flow conservation assuming that the n alternative chunks (5 and 6) are downloaded after the m_a chunks of the streaming video (4). This prioritization ensures that the client does not experience unnecessary stall times for the streaming video. However, as chunks from alternative videos may be prefetched even when the player is not in an off-period, it may potentially impair the playback quality of the streaming video.

Whenever the deadline of an alternative video is passed, we simply move on to the next deadline. Furthermore, in the case that n chunks of the alternative video have been downloaded but the deadline of the alternative video is not passed, chunks from the streaming and alternative videos are downloaded in round-robin order. This approach therefore paces the downloads of alternative videos and naturally limits the workahead of the streaming video.

4.2 High-level Comparison

Figure 3 presents a high-level comparison between the three policy classes. In this example, we have assumed $n = 2$ and that the prefetched chunks are of the lower of two qualities. We note that the best-effort policy consistently downloads the first two chunks of each alternative video, whereas the token-based policy uses exactly the same opportunities to build up a larger buffer (workahead) for the video associated with the tokens generated thus far. This illustrates the differing policy tradeoffs between prioritizing pacing the prefetching of new alternative videos (potentially building up additional workahead for the current video that the client may be more likely to start viewing) and prefetching the largest possible set of alternative videos.

The biggest differences are observed for the deadline-based policy class. In contrast to the first two policy classes, this policy class uses deadlines to enforce downloads of alternative videos. Of course, this can come at the expense of the streaming video itself. For example, in Figure 3 the more aggressive prefetching required to meet the download deadlines of the alternative video chunks results in earlier downloads of these chunks and the playback buffer of the streaming video does not reach T_{max} until after the first such deadline. Note also that the more aggressive use of prefetching results in tighter buffer conditions. As seen in our experimental results (Section 6), this often results in the streaming video being streamed at a lower overall average quality compared to with the other two policies.

4.3 Fixed vs. Adaptive Prefetching

Thus far, for each policy class, we have described a simple policy variant that always prefetches chunks of the alternative videos at the lowest quality. We call these policy variants *lowest quality*. We also consider variants that adapt the quality of the alternative chunks based on the current buffer conditions and download rates. With our *adaptive quality* variants the quality of each prefetched chunk is selected at the time of the download request. At this time, the client greedily maximizes the quality of the next prefetched chunk, based on the estimated bandwidth and conditioned on the download being completed before the buffer occupancy falls below T_{min} and any other download deadline constraints associated with the *deadline-based* policy, for example.

5. SYSTEM IMPLEMENTATION

We have implemented a prototype of our system on top of the OSMF framework. Although the general policies described here are applicable to any HAS system, one advantage of the OSMF framework is that it is open source and we can share our implementation with the research community.[2] To simplify the head-to-head comparison of the prefetching policy classes, and to help ensure that our results are not determined by some quirk of OSMF, we use a somewhat simplified rate switching algorithm which does not leverage OSMF specific rules such as `DroppedFPSRule` or `EmptyBufferRule`. This algorithm consistently determines the quality of the next chunk as the highest chunk encoding rate that is lower than 0.8 times the current estimated bandwidth. An EWMA on the chunk download rates with α=0.4 is used to estimate the current download rate. The specific rate switching algorithm used was found to not significantly impact the relative policy comparisons.

The prefetching policies are implemented in a separate `HTTPDownloadManager` class that we incorporate in the OSMF framework. To facilitate seamless playback of multiple separate videos within the same container (e.g., to show snippets) we leverage the OSMF Ad insertion plugin.

Multi-file prefetching: Our `HTTPDownloadManager` class is responsible for (i) estimating download rates, (ii) updating buffer occupancies, (iii) regulating on-off periods, and (iv) managing the download schedule of chunks from the streaming video and alternative videos. This class integrates with the original OSMF libraries, thereby facilitating transparent operations between the original and custom components of the player. Chunks which are downloaded by this class are placed in the browser cache. When initiating playback of an alternative video these chunks are then requested by the player, resulting in a browser cache hit, from which the chunks can be quickly retrieved and subsequently played.

Browser cache: In our experiments, we make use of the browser cache as a temporary store for prefetched data rather than holding this data internally within the player. This circumvents limitations within the OSMF platform. For our experiments we place the browser cache on the RAM as it provides the fastest retrieval times. In the case a larger cache is needed, the cache may also be placed on the hard disk. The difference between these two configurations was verified to be minimal in our system.

Multi-file playback: The OSMF Ad insertion plugin was originally designed to play advertisements without having to load a new player/webpage each time, and allows multiple separate videos to be played within the same video container. We modified this plugin to allow different videos to be seamlessly stitched together at the time instance when the user selects to view the alternative video.

User interaction: There are multiple ways for the alternative videos to be displayed to the user. First, the user can be presented with a list of alternative videos that currently have been prefetched and are available for instantaneous playback. As new alternative videos are prefetched, they are added to the list. Second, when the streaming video is paused, the container can be replaced with a different instance of the video player, which plays one or more alternative videos. In this case, upon completion, playback of the original streaming video is automatically resumed.

The plugin also supports overlaying videos to be displayed. In this case, both the streaming video currently being viewed by the user, and one or more alternative videos can be displayed simultaneously in the same container. Other content providers may want to just display a thumbnail image or example frame of the alternative video. In this paper, we focus on the performance aspects of our framework, and leave user interface design issues for future work.

6. VALIDATION AND PERFORMANCE

6.1 Experimental Setup

Our experiments have been performed using a high-speed LAN. Dummynet [26] is used to control available bandwidths and round-trip times (RTTs). Our videos are hosted on a Windows 7 machine running Flash Media Server (FMS) 4.5 on top of TCP Reno. We also cross validate our results with FMS running on a Linux machine with TCP CUBIC

[2]Our data, source code, and system framework are available at `http://www.ida.liu.se/~nikca89/papers/mm15.html`.

and TCP Reno as the congestion control algorithm. The client machine runs Windows 7 and the player is embedded on a webpage within a Mozilla Firefox version 25.0.1 browser. The streaming video is the Big Buck Bunny video, each chunk is four seconds long, and has been encoded at 1,300 Kb/s, 850 Kb/s, 500 Kb/s and 250 Kb/s. The alternative videos are encoded using the same parameters.

In the following experiments, we present results which show how different policies perform under different network conditions. For all experiments we use two servers. One server hosts all the videos and the other hosts large files that are downloaded in parallel to generate between one and four competing flows. Dummynet runs on the end hosts.

To evaluate the impact RTTs have on the performance of the policies we keep the RTTs for the competing flow(s) fixed, while running experiments with different RTTs between the client and the streaming service. By running experiments with different number of competing flows, we can capture the bandwidth degradation while experiencing increased competition [13, 15]. In our default experiments we use a single competing flow. Both the video flow and the competing flow experience an RTT of 150ms, as motivated by the average ping latency observed from our university network to the top-million websites (per Alexa.com).

To capture both good and bad network conditions for the encodings and setup above, we evaluate the system for different shared available bandwidths, with 4,000 Kb/s being our default bandwidth. In our experiments, we also take a closer look at the impact of the buffer size and TCP version.

Our instrumented player continually records information about player states and events to a log file. These log files are then processed to generate our results. Unless specifically mentioned, in each experiment the streaming video plays for 90 seconds and each experiment is repeated 20 times.

We also include results using the naive OSMF player without any modifications, which does not do any prefetching of alternative videos, to provide a baseline for comparison. The prefetch policies are all implemented using this as a baseline.

6.2 Playback Initiation of Alternative Videos

Before comparing prefetching policies, we show the potential impact of prefetching on the startup times of alternative videos. For this purpose we compare the startup delays of an implementation that does not perform any prefetching with one that has already prefetched the videos.

In both cases, when the user initiates the playback of an alternative video, the currently streaming video is paused, removed from the playback container, and a new player instance is created and added to the container. The player then initializes parameters using the manifest file (assumed available to the player), and then places a request for the first chunk of the alternative video. In the case the chunk has been prefetched it typically takes our player less than 0.1 seconds to load this chunk from the cache, resulting in a total startup time of 0.6 seconds (with a standard deviation of 0.15 seconds). In contrast, for the case without prefetching the chunk must first be downloaded from the origin server which takes considerable time. For example, in our default scenario (with $B = 4,000Kb/s$, $RTT = 150$ ms, and one competing flow) we had a startup delay of 5.8 ($\sigma = 2.3$) seconds, an order of magnitude larger. With $B = 2,000Kb/s$ the startup delay without prefetching was 10.0 (4.1) seconds, and with $B = 8,000Kb/s$ was 3.6 (1.4) seconds.

While these delays due to downloading the first chunk of the alternative video at first may seem larger than the download of a typical chunk during playback, it is important to remember the state of the system when the client selects to play a different video. In the case the chunk must be retrieved from the origin server, one of two different scenarios typically takes place. First, if there is an ongoing download the client must either make the request over the same connection as the ongoing download (requiring some waiting time before the download can begin) or open up a new parallel connection (in which case the client typically must endure connection establishment, slow start, and simultaneously share the bandwidth with the original connection). Which of these cases takes place is determined by the OSMF download manager, but both result in non-negligible delays as even the lowest-quality chunks typically consist of more than one hundred 1,500 byte packets. While the download typically is faster in the case there is no ongoing download, this case also requires substantial startup delays, especially if having to endure slow start due to timeouts, for example.

6.3 Policy Comparison, Default Scenario

Some of the qualitative differences among the policies are captured by the cumulative distribution function (CDF) of the time stamps at which the different policies have downloaded the first two chunks of the different alternative videos. Figure 4 shows the CDFs of the *lowest quality* policy variants for our default scenario with $B = 4,000Kb/s$, $RTT = 150ms$, $T_{min}/T_{max} = 8/12$, and a single competing flow (also with an RTT of 150ms). The results for the *adaptive quality* variants are qualitatively similar.

Note that while the first CDF with the *best effort* policy and that with the *token-based* policy are similar (as the policies are identical to this point), their characteristics differ substantially for later alternative videos. The *best effort* policy quickly tries to download as many alternative chunks as possible. In contrast, the *token-based* policy paces itself, and downloads a few extra chunks of each video. For this policy a new token was released every 20 seconds, starting at time 0. Most even is the pacing of the *deadline-based* policy. For this policy a deadline was placed every 20 seconds, starting at time 20s. For the default scenario considered here none of the policies experienced playback stalls.

As noted previously, the deadline-driven pacing of the *deadline-based* policy class comes at the cost of a somewhat lower playback quality than for the other policies. Figure 5 quantifies these playback quality differences, and includes results for both the *lowest quality* and *adaptive quality* policy variants. The figure shows the percentage of time the streaming video is playing at different video encodings, as well as the quality of the chunks of the alternative videos downloaded. We note that the *best-effort* and *token-based* policies achieve slightly higher playback quality for the streaming video than the naive player, whereas there are only small differences in the playback quality observed for the *deadline-based* policy class. This difference is due to the optimization framework's need to take into account tighter deadlines to ensure small stall probabilities for the *deadline-based* policies.

6.4 Impact of Network Conditions

We next take a closer look at the impact of the available bandwidth (B), round-trip time (RTT), and the amount of

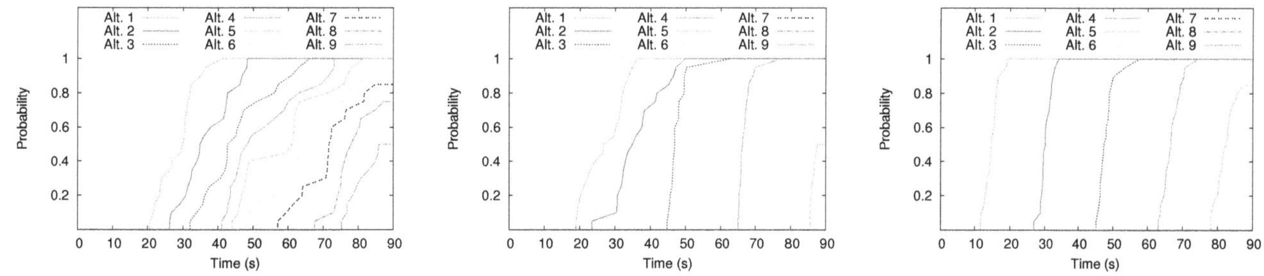

(a) Best effort (b) Token-based (c) Deadline-based

Figure 4: CDF of prefetch completion times for alternative videos under default scenario ($B = 4,000$ Kb/s).

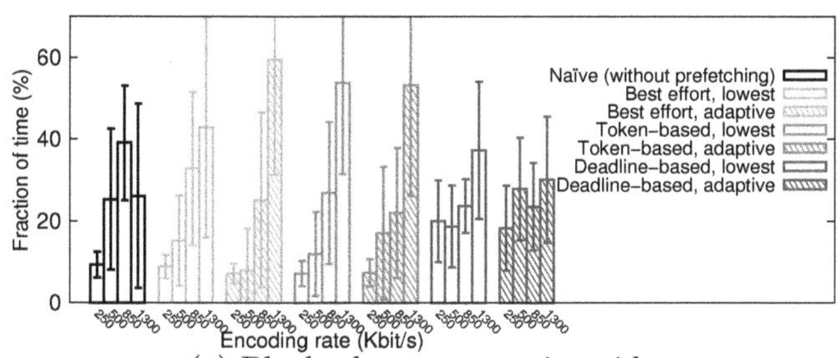

(a) Playback rate streaming video

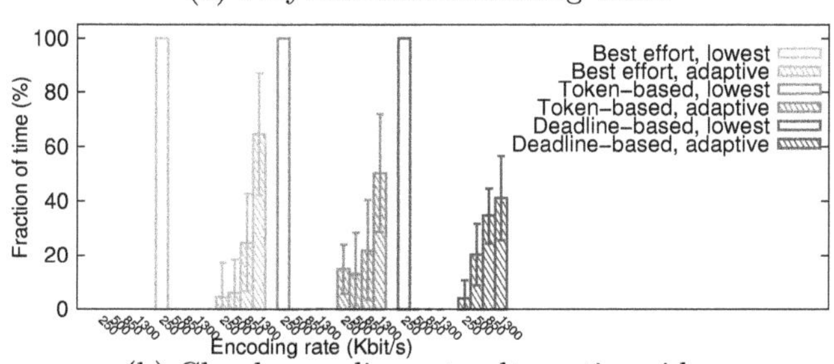

(b) Chunk encoding rate alternative video

Figure 5: Encoding rates under default scenario.

competing traffic. For this analysis we consider (a) the average stall probability, (b) the playback rate for the streaming videos, and (c) the average encoding rate for the alternative videos downloaded. While we have omitted the number of stalls and stall duration, the Pearson correlation coefficients between the stall probability and these two metrics are 0.94 and 0.71, respectively, for the cases we observe stalls.

Shared available bandwidth: As expected, all policies adapt the streaming quality based on the available bandwidth (Figure 6(b)), and for the *adaptive quality* variant also the chunk quality is adapted (Figure 6(c)).

Referring to Figure 6(b), we can also see that the player performance of all policies (with one competing flow) flattens out somewhere between 6,000 and 8,000 Kb/s shared available bandwidth, and that not much additional performance is gained beyond this point, as the client achieves close to the maximum encoding rate of 1,300 Kb/s.

Naturally, with the *best effort* and *token-based* policies, prefetching will only take place when there is sufficient bandwidth to fill the buffer. In contrast, the *deadline-based* policy prioritizes downloading the initial chunks of the alternative videos by their respective deadlines at the cost of somewhat lower streaming quality (Figure 6(b)).

In general, the stall probabilities (Figure 6(a)) are low or zero, except for the low-bandwidth scenario (with $B = 1,000$ Kb/s). The higher stall probabilities for the case when $B = 1,000$ Kb/s are in large part due to the lack of lower qualities (below 250 Kb/s) causing a smaller error margin, and the coarser chunk granularity at this bandwidth causing a higher penalty of selecting the wrong quality. In this scenario, many of the stalls occur due to clients switching to a higher quality (typically from 250 Kb/s to 500 Kb/s, with all policies having an average playback rate, in this case, of between 259 and 277 Kb/s) and then not getting the next chunk in time, due to a (temporary) degradation of the download speed (e.g., due to the competing flow).

While non-negligible when $B = 1,000$ Kb/s, the stall probabilities of the *best effort* and *token-based* policies are comparatively (slightly) lower than those of the *naive* player. The higher stall probabilities for the *deadline-based* policy (40%) observed for this scenario are due to very tight conditions. For example, to meet the first deadline, more than 28s of video must be downloaded in 16s, and the competing flow hogs much of the shared bandwidth and complicates the bandwidth prediction used in the optimization framework. This shows that the policy is somewhat optimistic for these circumstances, and that prioritizing the alternative videos under conditions with limited and variable available bandwidth can come at the cost of increased stall probabilities.

While we expect that the results could be improved with the help of better prediction algorithms for the available bandwidth, the use of bigger buffers, or by increasing the distance between download deadlines of alternative videos, clearly, giving too high priority to the alternative videos may not be ideal in these constrained (and hard-to-predict) cases. In such cases the simpler *token-based* approach may be preferable.

Finally, for all of the bandwidths, the *adaptive-quality* policy variants are able to download the alternative videos at a much higher quality than the *lowest-quality* variants (Figure 6(c)), without negatively impacting the streaming quality of the streaming video as measured by the stall probabilities (Figure 6(a)) and the playback encoding rate of the streaming video (Figure 6(b)) These results suggest that these relatively simple *adaptive-quality* variants do a good job adjusting to the current network conditions.

Round-trip times: TCP throughput is greatly impacted by RTTs. We run experiments for different RTTs (between 50ms and 250ms) for our application, while keeping the RTT of the competing flows fixed at 50ms. The results in Figure 7 shows that the policies in general adapt well to the varying network conditions, adjusting the streaming playback rate (Figure 7(b)) to maintain low (typically zero) stall probabilities (Figure 7(a)).

As expected, there is a clear decrease in the playback rate (Figure 7(b)) of the streaming video as the RTT of the video application increases. This trend matches well with the in-

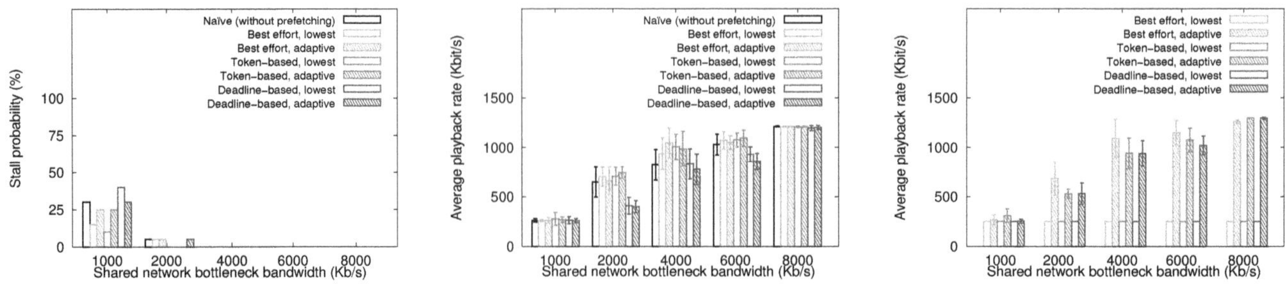

(a) Stall probability (b) Streaming encoding rate (c) Alternative encoding rate

Figure 6: Impact of the shared available bandwidth.

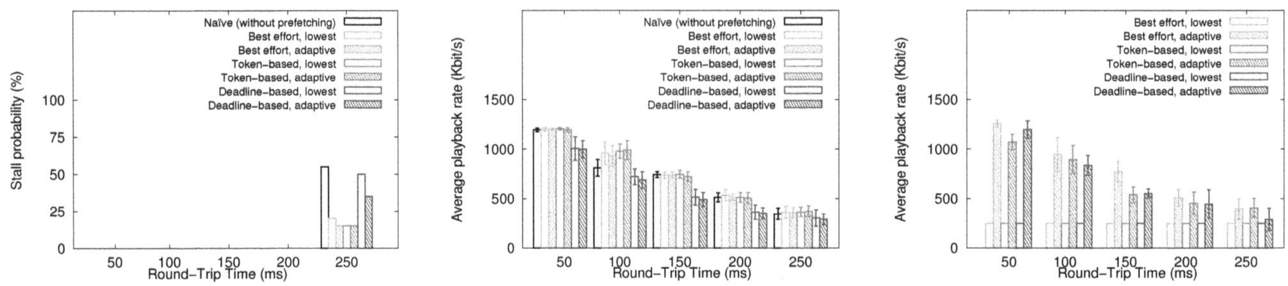

(a) Stall probability (b) Streaming encoding rate (c) Alternative encoding rate

Figure 7: Impact of the round-trip times (RTTs).

verse relationship typically observed between TCP throughput and RTTs. For the case for which we observe stalls, note that the stall probabilities of all policies are similar or lower than for the naive player. This is particularly encouraging for the *adaptive-quality* variants which are able to download alternative videos at a higher quality (Figure 7(c)) than the *lowest-quality* variants without sacrificing playback quality of the streaming video (Figure 7(b)).

Competing flows: The effective bandwidth share of the application decreases with increasing numbers of competing flows traversing the bottleneck, giving similar results (omitted) to those seen with decreasing available bandwidth in Figure 6. Our prefetching policies adapt by adjusting the playback quality, and with the adaptive variants also the encoding of the alternative videos.

Alternative videos downloaded: Another important consideration when selecting which type of policy to use is the number of alternative videos that the policy is able to download (in the case of the *deadline-based* policy, by their individual deadlines). Figure 8 shows this metric for the first 90 seconds of our experiments.

As expected, the *best-effort* policy typically downloads the first two chunks of more alternative videos than the other policies; the differences being particularly apparent when considering the *lowest-quality* variants. For the other policies the *lowest-quality* and *adaptive-quality* variants are able to complete approximately the same number of preloads. Given the higher quality seen with *adaptive-quality* (Figures 6(c) and 7(c)), these results may suggest that the *adaptive-quality* variants are more attractive than the corresponding *lowest-quality* policies.

6.5 High-bandwidth Variation Scenarios

We have also evaluated the different policies under real-world commuter traces with widely varying available bandwidths, collected while using different modes of transport in Oslo [25]. The *ferry trace* has an average bandwidth $\overline{B}$ of 2,026 Kb/s and a standard deviation (σ) of 1,020. The *bus trace* has $\overline{B}$ = 2,031 Kb/s and σ = 432; the *metro trace* has $\overline{B}$ = 1,014 Kb/s and σ = 470; and finally the *tram trace* has $\overline{B}$ = 1,082 Kb/s and σ = 286.

Among these traces, the ferry trace is perhaps the most extreme as the available bandwidth varies widely depending on the distance to land. The variation is high also for the metro trace. For these two traces, all policies (including the naive player) have stall probabilities above 75%. The *deadline-based* policies also suffer from significant stall probabilities (around 50%) for the tram trace. For all other policies and scenarios we observe only negligible stall probabilities. In general, as for the previous scenarios, both the *best-effort* and *token-based* policies are able to achieve similar or better performance than the naive player, while also prefetching alternative videos for instantaneous playback. This is examplified by the playback encoding rates shown in Figure 9.

6.6 Buffer Size

HAS clients make use of a playback buffer to accommodate for network jitter and short-term variations in the available bandwidth. The typical buffer size varies between applications, playback device, and in some cases also on the network in which the application and device are deployed. We have validated our conclusions for T_{min}/T_{max} = 4/6, 8/12, 8/16, 12/24, 12/30 (seconds). Note that as $T_{max} - T_{min}$ increases in these configurations, there will be fewer off-periods, but of greater duration (equal to 2, 4, 8, 12, and 18 seconds, respectively). While we observed much fever stalls for bigger buffer sizes, the relative performance across policies and against the naive player are consistent with the results presented earlier in the paper. (Figures omitted.)

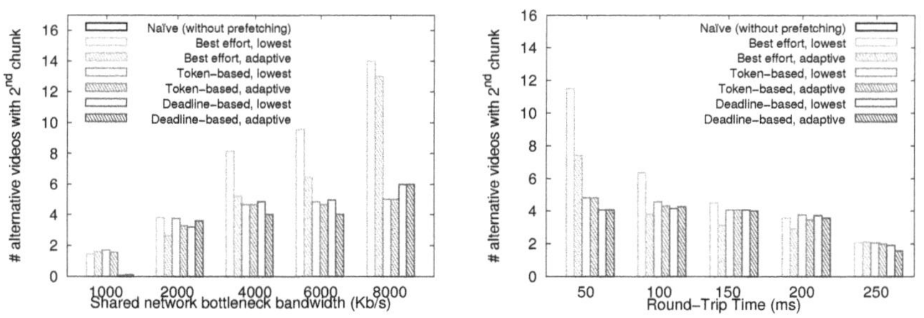

(a) Bandwidth (b) RTT

Figure 8: Number of alternative videos with at least two chunks.

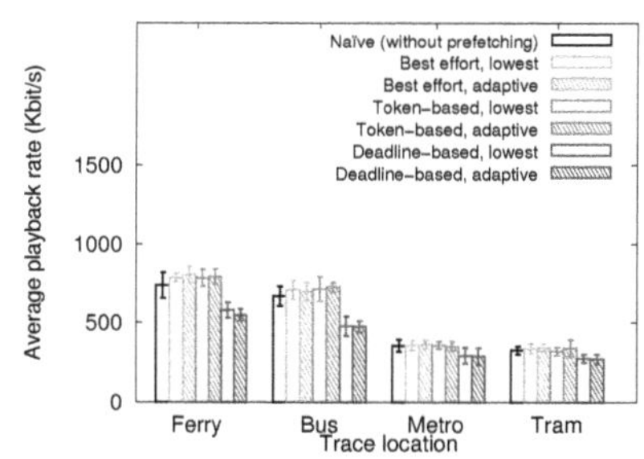

Figure 9: Streaming encoding rate in trace-driven scenarios.

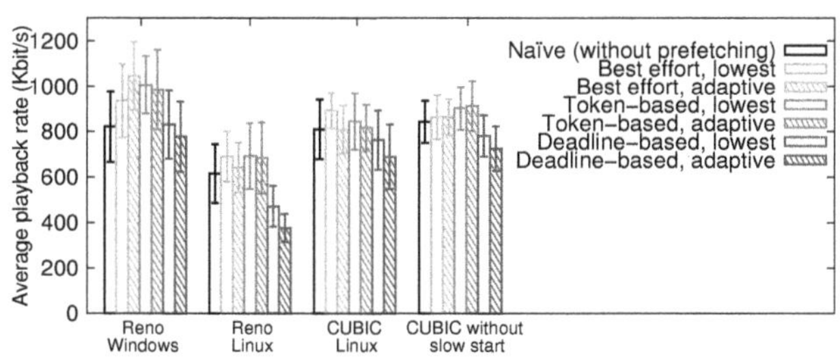

Figure 10: TCP version comparison.

6.7 Slow Start and TCP Configurations

The performance under competing traffic also varies between TCP versions. The impact of off periods is particularly apparent in cases when slow start is invoked after the off periods, or the congestion window, due to other reasons, takes more time to reach its fair-share bandwidth.

To understand the impact of TCP slow start and congestion control in general, we compared the performance of four alternative TCP implementations: (i) Reno on Windows, (ii) Reno on Linux, (iii) CUBIC on Linux, and (iv) a modified version of CUBIC on Linux that retains its window size during off periods. We note that the three first versions by default reduce the number of segments that the server can send at a time whenever the flow has remained inactive for duration that is longer than a timeout threshold.

While the performance improvements achieved by the *best-effort* and *token-based* policies are largest with the two Reno implementations, our conclusions are consistent across TCP implementations. Both these policies consistently give the same or better performance than the naive player. For example, Figure 10 shows the average playback rate for the default scenario (with $B = 4,000$ Kb/s). Here, the *best-effort* policy achieve average improvements in the playback rate (relative to the naive player) of 20.5% and 8.1% with the two Reno implementations, respectively, 5.1% with CUBIC, and 2.6% using CUBIC without slow start. Not surprisingly, the smallest improvements are seen when using CUBIC without slow start. These observations are expected as CUBIC ramps up faster than Reno, but not as quickly as the CUBIC implementation that avoids slow start after inactive periods. The prefetch policies, on the other hand, effectively avoid off periods altogether.

7. RELATED WORK

Playback stalls and frequent quality switches have been shown to have the most significant impact on user satisfaction and video abandonment during playback [10, 11]. The HAS player adaptation algorithm plays an important role here [5]. Inaccuracies in the rate estimations [17] and interaction with other competing flows [3, 13] have been found to negatively impact the performance of many HAS players. TCP is often part of the problem, as clients may be forced to resume the download from slow start after an idle period. Although observed as a problem already for traditional web workloads [22], this feature remains the default in several TCP implementations.

For long duration content, others have suggested that rate estimates are only important for the initial transient period, when building up a playback buffer, and that buffer-based policies that track changes in buffer size can be used in steady-state [9, 14]. Rather than looking at the steady-state period of such large-buffer and long-duration video systems we consider preloading during the transient period, when users are more likely to switch to an alternative video.

In order to be fair to multiple competing clients, server-based traffic shaping has been proposed [4]. Other solutions have relied on optimized chunk scheduling, bandwidth estimation, and quality selection that ensures fair and stable playback characteristics [15].

Prefetching has long been used to improve Web performance [23], but has also been applied in the context of HAS-aware proxies that preemptively try to download chunks that the clients are likely to download next [18]. Others have observed that some players may re-download chunks that have already been downloaded, at a higher quality [27]. In this paper, we show how careful prefetching can be used to improve HAS performance, by stabilizing the client's bandwidth share and simultaneously allowing preloading of alternative videos, but do not consider policies that use the extra bandwidth to re-download chunks at higher quality. Combining these ideas could be interesting future work.

Many recommendation algorithms and systems have been proposed, including to determine which video a user is likely to want to view next [7, 8, 12, 28]. In addition to client-side recommendations, video recommendations have also been used to improve cache efficiency [20].

While both the prefetching framework and the implementation to allow quick preloading of alternative videos are novel, we are not the first to combine multiple videos into a seamless playback experience. For example, Johansen et al. [16] use a modified player to combine video snippets based on tagged videos and user search queries into a single personalized video stream. Krishnamoorthi et al. [19] implement an OSMF-based client that is able to provide seamless playback of interactive branched video. The DASH specification also allows ad insertion into live and VoD streams [1].

8. CONCLUSIONS

This paper presents the design, implementation, and evaluation of a HAS-based framework that uses careful prefetching and buffer management to preload the initial chunks of alternative videos. We show that our design and implementation allows prefetching and instantaneous playback of prefetched alternative videos without any playback quality degradation of the currently streamed video. To capture a wide range of objectives, three classes of prefetching policies are designed and evaluated.

The design, characteristics, and performance of the three policy classes (i.e., *best-effort*, *token-based*, and *deadline-based*), and their variations (i.e., *lowest-quality* and *adaptive-quality*), are compared against each other and the naive player on top of which they are all implemented. As the policy classes are designed with different objectives, these comparisons provide insights into desirable policy choices for providers with different objectives. Perhaps most encouraging is the performance of the *token-based, adaptive-quality* policy. This policy (i) allows the download of alternative videos to be relatively well paced for a wide range of network conditions, (ii) nicely adapts the quality of the prefetched chunks based on the current conditions, and (iii) provides as good, and often better, playback quality as the naive player, as exemplified by similar stall probabilities and better playback encoding rate. The *best-effort, adaptive-quality* policy performs similarly except does not pace alternative video downloads. Finally, the *deadline-based* policies trade some of the playback quality of the streaming video for prefetch deadlines and more even pacing.

Much of the improvements in bandwidth utilization and streaming performance shown in this paper are achieved by leveraging the off periods typically observed with HAS players. In this paper we have leveraged rate estimates to decide when and at what quality to download chunks of the alternative videos. Recent work has suggested that in steady state buffer-based policies (rather than rate-based policies) should be used to adapt the playback quality [14]. Future work will consider such generalizations.

9. REFERENCES

[1] 3gpp tr 26.938 version 12.0.0 release 12, 2014.

[2] Sandvine global internet phenomena report- 2h2014-technical report, 2014.

[3] S. Akhshabi, L. Anantakrishnan, A. C. Begen, and C. Dovrolis. What happens when HTTP adaptive streaming players compete for bandwidth? In *Proc. ACM NOSSDAV*, 2012.

[4] S. Akhshabi, L. Anantakrishnan, C. Dovrolis, and A. C. Begen. Server-based traffic shaping for stabilizing oscillating adaptive streaming players. In *Proc. ACM NOSSDAV*, 2013.

[5] S. Akhshabi, A. C. Begen, and C. Dovrolis. An experimental evaluation of rate-adaptation algorithms in adaptive streaming over HTTP. In *Proc. ACM MMsys*, 2011.

[6] L. Chen, Y. Zhou, and D. Chiu. A study of user behavior in online vod services. *Computer Communications*, 2014.

[7] P. Cui, Z. Wang, and Z. Su. What videos are similar with you?: Learning a common attributed representation for video recommendation. In *Proc. ACM Multimedia*, 2014.

[8] J. Davidson, B. Liebald, J. Liu, P. Nandy, T. Van Vleet, U. Gargi, S. Gupta, Y. He, M. Lambert, B. Livingston, and D. Sampath. The YouTube video recommendation system. In *Proc. ACM RecSys*, 2010.

[9] L. De Cicco, V. Caldaralo, V. Palmisano, and S. Mascolo. ELASTIC: A client-side controller for dynamic adaptive streaming over HTTP (DASH). In *Proc. IEEE Packet Video Workshop*, 2013.

[10] F. Dobrian, V. Sekar, A. Awan, I. Stoica, D. Joseph, A. Ganjam, J. Zhan, and H. Zhang. Understanding the impact of video quality on user engagement. In *Proc. ACM SIGCOMM*, 2011.

[11] T. Hossfeld, M. Seufert, C. Sieber, T. Zinner, and P. Tran-Gia. Identifying QoE optimal adaptation of HTTP adaptive streaming based on subjective studies. *Computer Networks*, 2015.

[12] Q. Huang, B. Chen, J. Wang, and T. Mei. Personalized video recommendation through graph propagation. *ACM TOMM*, 2014.

[13] T. Huang, N. Handigol, B. Heller, N. McKeown, and R. Johari. Confused, timid, and unstable: Picking a video streaming rate is hard. In *Proc. ACM IMC*, 2012.

[14] T. Huang, R. Johari, N. McKeown, M. Trunnell, and M. Watson. A buffer-based approach to rate adaptation: Evidence from a large video streaming service. In *Proc. ACM SIGCOMM*, 2014.

[15] J. Jiang, V. Sekar, and H. Zhang. Improving fairness, efficiency, and stability in HTTP-based adaptive video streaming with festive. In *Proc. ACM CoNEXT*, 2012.

[16] D. Johansen, P. Halvorsen, H. Johansen, H. Riiser, C. Gurrin, B. Olstad, C. Griwodz, Å. Kvalnes, J. Hurley, and T. Kupka. Search-based composition, streaming and playback of video archive content. *MTA*, 2012.

[17] Z. Kelvin, J. Erman, V. Gopalakrishnan, E. Halepovic, R. Jana, X. Jin, J. Rexford, and R. Sinha. Can accurate predictions improve video streaming in cellular networks? In *Proc. ACM HotMobile*, 2015.

[18] V. Krishnamoorthi, N. Carlsson, D. Eager, A. Mahanti, and N. Shahmehri. Helping hand or hidden hurdle: Proxy-assisted http-based adaptive streaming performance. In *Proc. IEEE MASCOTS*, 2013.

[19] V. Krishnamoorthi, N. Carlsson, D. Eager, A. Mahanti, and N. Shahmehri. Quality-adaptive prefetching for interactive branched video using http-based adaptive streaming. In *Proc. ACM Multimedia*, 2014.

[20] D. Krishnappa, M. Zink, C. Griwodz, and P. Halvorsen. Cache-centric video recommendation: An approach to improve the efficiency of YouTube caches. In *Proc. ACM MMSys*, 2013.

[21] T. Kupka, P. Halvorsen, and C. Griwodz. Performance of on-off traffic stremming from live adaptive segmented HTTP video streaming. In *Proc. IEEE LCN*, 2012.

[22] V. Padmanabhan and R. Katz. Tcp fast start: A technique for speeding up web transfers. In *Proc. IEEE Globecom*, 1998.

[23] V. Padmanabhan and J. Mogul. Using predictive prefetching to improve world wide web latency. *ACM CCR*, 1996.

[24] A. Rao, A. Legout, Y. Lim, D. Towsley, C. Barakat, and W. Dabbous. Network characteristics of video streaming traffic. In *Proc. ACM CoNEXT*, 2011.

[25] H. Riiser, H. S. Bergsaker, P. Vigmostad, P. Halvorsen, and C. Griwodz. A comparison of quality scheduling in commercial adaptive HTTP streaming solutions on a 3G network. In *Proc. Workshop on Mobile Video*, 2012.

[26] L. Rizzo. Dummynet: A simple approach to the evaluation of network protocols. *ACM CCR*, 1997.

[27] C. Sieber, A. Blenk, M. Hinteregger, and W. Kellerer. The cost of aggressive HTTP adaptive streaming: Quantifying YouTube's redundant traffic. In *Proc. IFIP/IEEE IM*, 2015.

[28] A. Xavier. Mining large streams of user data for personalized recommendations. *ACM SIGKDD Explor. Newsl.*, 2012.

Multi-View Visual Recognition of Imperfect Testing Data

Qilin Zhang[1]
[1]Stevens Institute of Technology
1 Castle Point Terrace
Hoboken, NJ, USA, 07030
qzhang5@stevens.edu

Gang Hua[1,2]
[2]Microsoft Research Asia
No. 5 Danling Street,Haidian District
Beijing, P.R. China 100080
ganghua@gmail.com

ABSTRACT

A practical yet under-explored problem often encountered by multimedia researchers is the recognition of imperfect testing data, where multiple sensing channels are deployed but interference or transmission distortion corrupts some of them. Typical cases of imperfect testing data include missing features and feature misalignments. To address these challenges, we choose the latent space model and introduce a new similarity learning canonical-correlation analysis (SLC-CA) method to capture the semantic consensus between views. The consensus information is preserved by projection matrices learned with modified canonical-correlation analysis (CCA) optimization terms with new, explicit class-similarity constraints. To make it computationally tractable, we propose to combine a practical relaxation and an alternating scheme to solve the optimization problem. Experiments on four challenging multi-view visual recognition datasets demonstrate the efficacy of the proposed method.

Categories and Subject Descriptors

H.3.3 [**Information Storage and Retrieval**]: Information Search and Retrieval; I.2.10 [**Artificial Intelligence**]: Vision and Scene Understanding

Keywords

similarity learning; CCA; missing data; misalignment

1. INTRODUCTION

Thanks to the recent popularity of multi-sensory and multi-spectrum imaging, such as depth-sensing and infrared (IR) sensing cameras, visual recognition with multiple views of information attracts the attention of many multimedia and computer vision researchers. However, the pronounced reliability issues and data integrity concerns of multiple sensors plague the adoption of these systems in real world applications, especially in harsh or adversarial sensing environments.

MM'15, October 26–30, 2015, Brisbane, Australia.

ACM 978-1-4503-3459-4/15/10 ...$15.00.
DOI: http://dx.doi.org/10.1145/2733373.2806224.

In particular, this paper addresses two common obstacles in these sensing systems, i.e., the missing feature problem and the feature misalignment problem in testing data. For both problems, the system is typically trained with labeled multi-view data in advance, but the testing data could be imperfect: the secondary view can be completely missing, or both views can be randomly missing, possibly caused by sensor malfunction, predominant interferences or limited transmission bandwidth. The feature misalignment problem could arise when the semantic correspondences between two views (i.e., sensing channels) are corrupted during testing data acquisition or transmission, thus cross-view verification is required to recover these correspondences.

For these problems, the major challenge lies in how to effectively leverage the semantic consensus across all views, so as to facilitate the training of a stronger classifier that works solely on a single view, or a verification algorithm that captures the cross-view similarity information. In particular, we propose to seek a common semantic space to capture the relevance among multiple views, and further incorporate the discriminative information embedded in the class labels.

This is achieved by a new similarity learning canonical-correlation analysis algorithm, namely, the similarity learning canonical-correlation analysis (SLCCA) algorithm, inspired by [34, 35], which constructs projection matrices for a common latent space, where the intra-class and inter-class relationships are preserved. These learned projection matrices are subsequently used to discriminatively transfer all observations from all views to this common semantic space.

After obtaining the projected training samples in the common space, conventional supervised classifiers (e.g., the SVM classifier [5]) or verification algorithm (e.g., the joint Bayesian verification algorithm [6, 18, 19]) can be trained in this space. For the recognition problem, the testing data from the available view is projected onto this space before applying the aforementioned classifier[1]. For the cross-modal verification problem, both modalities are first projected onto this space before learning their pairwise similarity.

The primary contributions of this paper are: (1) we investigate two common data integrity difficulties in multi-view recognition systems (i.e., the missing feature problem and the feature misalignment problem), and propose a unified solution by leveraging the semantic consensus; (2) we propose the new SLCCA algorithm, whose performance enhancements on various recognition/verification asks are validated on four different real world datasets; (3) after formulating the problem as a generic quadratically constrained

[1]An overview of this approach is presented in Fig. 1.

quadratic program (QCQP), we relax it and approximate it with an alternating optimization of a linear program and a decomposition procedure, and finally efficiently solve it.

The rest of the paper is organized as follows. Related works are briefly discussed in Section 2. Section 3 formulates the proposed SLCCA algorithm, followed by Section 4 with the solution to it. Experimental datasets and settings are summarized in Section 5. Section 6 presents the experimental results, and Section 7 concludes the paper.

2. RELATED WORK

In this section, related work is summarized, then brief comparisons between these related works and the focused problem of this paper are provided.

Inspired by the human cognition and psychology studies with multi-sensory/uni-sensory experiments in [25] (where human volunteers performing the uni-sensory recognition tasks with prior multi-sensory learning significantly outperforms their counterparts with uni-sensory learning), we make the hypothesis that there should be an underlying common semantic space representing some consensus between multiple views/sensory channels. This hypothesis is capable of justifying the phenomenon in [25], and the remaining challenge is to design at least one method to recover this semantic latent space. Once this latent space is obtained, the missing data resilient multi-view recognition problem and the cross-modal verification problem can be readily solved, following Fig. 1.

In order to construct such a semantic common space, information transfer with preserved discriminative power is crucial. There are plenty of work in the transfer learning literature (e.g., [10, 24, 15]), however, they generally focus on transferring the label information from the source domain to the target domain, instead of preserving the congruent information embedded in the labeled, paired multi-view training samples.

As for preserving the cross-view consensus, the early semi-supervised co-training framework [2] and the later multi-view/multi-task learning work [11, 37, 22, 32, 1] are examples of synergistically modeling multiple views and fusing the information from all views. However, it is worth noting that there are no missing data (missing view or missing observations) involved, and there are no easy extension to address the cross-view verification problem (as defined in Section 1). A recent work [8] addresses both the missing view recognition and domain transfer problems, by imposing additional regularization terms on a multi-view classifier, but without explicitly modeling the discriminative label information.

Another line of research involves methods that also assume a common semantic space model, such as different variants of the CCA algorithms [29, 14, 13, 30, 38]. They either focus on variants of cross-view correlations considering the discriminative label information [13, 30], or incorporate the label information in an ad-hoc way [38]. In [14], the image set recognition requires abundant views, which is not always available in generic multi-view recognition problems. In [29], the second view of multi-dimensional training labels is nevertheless incompatible with generic multi-view recognition problems or missing data recognition problems. In [31], Tommasi *et al.* address a different problem (the bias between datasets) also with a latent space model.

In addition, there are previous papers addressing related problems [7, 12, 28]. They either focus only on the missing

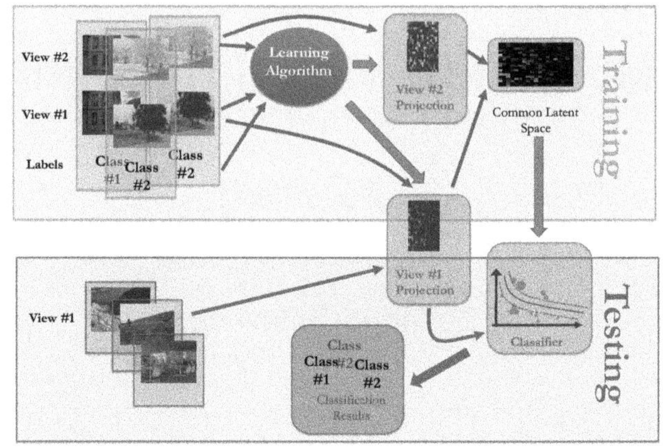

Figure 1: A latent space framework, with the training and testing processes shown in blue and yellow, respectively.

view case [7], or the random missing features case [12], or adopt a totally different learning concept such as the multi-modal deep learning [28].

On the contrary, our proposed method directly seeks two similarity preserving projections to reveal the common semantic latent space, thus it is capable of addressing both the systematic and random missing feature problems as well as the cross-view verification problem.

3. FORMULATION

In this section, the recognition problems are first formalized, followed by the overview of the latent space model as well as the proposed SLCCA algorithm.

3.1 Problem Formalization

Let $\mathbf{X}^{(1)} \in \mathcal{R}^{p\times n}$ and $\mathbf{X}^{(2)} \in \mathcal{R}^{q\times n}$ denote the observations from the first and the second view of n training pairs, with each column of the $\mathbf{X}^{(1)}$ and $\mathbf{X}^{(2)}$ representing a p-dimensional and q-dimensional feature, $\mathbf{X}^{(1)} = [\mathbf{x}_1^{(1)}, \cdots, \mathbf{x}_n^{(1)}]$ and $\mathbf{X}^{(2)} = [\mathbf{x}_1^{(2)}, \cdots, \mathbf{x}_n^{(2)}]$. The training label vector is $\mathbf{y} = [y_1, y_2, \cdots, y_n]^T$, $y_i \in \{1, \cdots, c\}$, with c denoting the number of classes. In summary, the multi-view training features and labels are denoted as triplets[2] $\{\mathbf{x}_i^{(1)}, \mathbf{x}_i^{(2)}, y_i\}_{i=1}^n$. Unlike classical multi-view problems with testing data in pairs like $\{\tilde{\mathbf{x}}_i^{(1)}, \tilde{\mathbf{x}}_i^{(2)}\}_{i=1}^{n_t}$, three special cases of recognition tasks with incomplete or misaligned n_t testing samples are considered: (1) testing data lacks the 2nd view, $\{\tilde{\mathbf{x}}_i^{(1)}\}_{i=1}^{n_t}$; (2) testing data is a single view observation taken randomly from the 1st or 2nd view, $\{\tilde{\mathbf{x}}_i^{(v_i)}\}_{i=1}^{n_t}$, where random variable v_i satisfies $\Pr(v_i = 1) = \Pr(v_i = 2) = 0.5$; (3) testing data has both views, but misaligned, $\{\tilde{\mathbf{x}}_i^{(1)}\}_{i=1}^{n_t}$ and $\{\tilde{\mathbf{x}}_j^{(2)}\}_{j=1}^{n_t}$, but $\tilde{\mathbf{x}}_k^{(1)}$ and $\tilde{\mathbf{x}}_k^{(2)}$ are not guaranteed to come from the same source for any specific k.

3.2 Latent Space

To address the aforementioned challenges, we propose to construct a semantic latent space where the imperfect testing data can be projected onto. Ideally, the projections retain the discriminative information and assimilate the

[2]Both measurements $\mathbf{x}_i^{(1)}$ and $\mathbf{x}_i^{(2)}$come from the same source i, but in distinctive view (1) and view (2).

view differences, converting the aforementioned problems into conventional classification/verification tasks as outlined in Fig. 1.

Let $\mathbf{A}^{(1)} \in \mathcal{R}^{n\times d}$ and $\mathbf{A}^{(2)} \in \mathcal{R}^{n\times d}$ denote projection matrices for the 1st and 2nd view, respectively. Kernelization and centralization are applied to all available training data, which leads to the Gram matrices $\mathbf{K}^{(1)}$ and $\mathbf{K}^{(2)}$,

$$\mathbf{K}^{(v)} = [\boldsymbol{\kappa}_1^{(v)}, \cdots, \boldsymbol{\kappa}_n^{(v)}],\ v = 1, 2. \tag{1}$$

with the element at the ith row and jth column being,

$$\mathbf{K}^{(v)}(i,j) = \langle \mathbf{x}_i^{(v)}, \mathbf{x}_j^{(v)} \rangle_{\mathcal{H}},\ i,j = 1, \cdots, n$$

where $\langle \cdot, \cdot \rangle_{\mathcal{H}}$ denotes the inner product defined in a Reproducing Kernel Hilbert space.

3.3 Similarity Measure

After kernelization, we continue to project these observations onto a latent space, which captures the common semantics with relatively low dimension. This is realized by multiplying the kernel matrices with the projection matrices $\mathbf{A}^{(v)} \in \mathcal{R}^{n\times d}$, $v = 1, 2$. Consider the matrix $\mathbf{R}^{vv'}$ with its (i,j)th element being

$$\begin{aligned}\mathbf{R}^{vv'}(i,j) &= \langle \mathbf{A}^{(v)T}\boldsymbol{\kappa}_i^{(v)}, \mathbf{A}^{(v')T}\boldsymbol{\kappa}_j^{(v')} \rangle \\ &= \boldsymbol{\kappa}_i^{(v)T}\mathbf{A}^{(v)}\mathbf{A}^{(v')T}\boldsymbol{\kappa}_j^{(v')}.\end{aligned} \tag{2}$$

In the normalized latent subspace, the inner product serves as a natural criterion for measuring distances, i.e., larger inner products indicate smaller angles[3] between projected vectors $\mathbf{A}^{(v)T}\boldsymbol{\kappa}_i^{(v)}$ and $\mathbf{A}^{(v')T}\boldsymbol{\kappa}_j^{(v')}$, and vice versa. Inspired by [34, 35], the angles between the projected vectors are utilized to estimate the similarity between the vectors in this paper. Therefore, if the following constraints are imposed,

$$\mathbf{R}^{vv'}(i,j) \begin{cases} \geq c_{ij} & \text{if } y_i = y_j \\ \leq c'_{ij} & \text{if } y_i \neq y_j \end{cases}, \tag{3}$$

where the thresholds c_{ij}, c'_{ij} are properly selected to match the dataset[4], the similarity between the projected vectors $\mathbf{A}^{(v)T}\boldsymbol{\kappa}_i^{(v)}$ and $\mathbf{A}^{(v')T}\boldsymbol{\kappa}_j^{(v')}$ can be regulated with respect to their labels, i.e., keeping pairs close if they share the same class label and simultaneously separating pairs apart if they differ in class labels.

3.4 Similarity Learning CCA

For notational simplicity, we define the aggregated projection matrices $\mathbf{G} = \left[\mathbf{A}^{(1)T}, \mathbf{A}^{(2)T}\right]^T$. The optimization target of the SLCCA algorithm is,

$$\max_{\mathbf{G}}\ \mathrm{tr}\left(\mathbf{K}^{(1)}\mathbf{K}^{(2)T}\mathbf{L}_2\mathbf{G}\mathbf{G}^T\mathbf{L}_1^T\right) \tag{4}$$

$$\text{s.t. } \boldsymbol{\kappa}_i^{(1)T}\mathbf{L}_1\mathbf{G}\mathbf{G}^T\mathbf{L}_2^T\boldsymbol{\kappa}_j^{(2)} \begin{cases} \geq c_{ij} \text{ if } y_i = y_j \\ \leq c_{ij} \text{ otherwise} \end{cases} \tag{5}$$

$$\boldsymbol{\kappa}_i^{(1)T}\mathbf{L}_1\mathbf{G}\mathbf{G}^T\mathbf{L}_1^T\boldsymbol{\kappa}_j^{(2)} \begin{cases} \geq c_{ij} \text{ if } y_i = y_j \\ \leq c_{ij} \text{ otherwise} \end{cases} \tag{6}$$

$$\boldsymbol{\kappa}_i^{(1)T}\mathbf{L}_2\mathbf{G}\mathbf{G}^T\mathbf{L}_2^T\boldsymbol{\kappa}_j^{(2)} \begin{cases} \geq c_{ij} \text{ if } y_i = y_j \\ \leq c_{ij} \text{ otherwise} \end{cases} \tag{7}$$

$$\mathbf{G}^T\boldsymbol{\Gamma}(\mathbf{K})\mathbf{G} = \mathbf{I} \tag{8}$$

where $\mathbf{L}_1 \stackrel{\text{def}}{=} [\mathbf{I}_n, 0_n]$, $\mathbf{L}_2 \stackrel{\text{def}}{=} [0_n, \mathbf{I}_n]$, and

$$\boldsymbol{\Gamma}(\mathbf{K}) = \begin{bmatrix} \mathbf{K}^{(1)}\mathbf{K}^{(1)T} + \lambda\mathbf{I} & \mathbf{0} \\ \mathbf{0} & \mathbf{K}^{(2)}\mathbf{K}^{(2)T} + \lambda\mathbf{I} \end{bmatrix}, \tag{9}$$

and λ is a small constant number added to eliminate numerical issues.

Note that Eq. (4) and Eq. (8) are equivalent to the standard CCA [13] target, i.e., maximizing the correlations, because in Eq. (4),

$$\mathrm{tr}\left(\mathbf{K}^{(1)}\mathbf{K}^{(2)T}\mathbf{L}_2\mathbf{G}\mathbf{G}^T\mathbf{L}_1^T\right) \tag{10}$$

$$= \mathrm{tr}\left(\mathbf{G}^T\mathbf{L}_1^T\mathbf{K}^{(1)}\mathbf{K}^{(2)T}\mathbf{L}_2\mathbf{G}\right) \tag{11}$$

$$= \mathrm{tr}\left(\mathbf{A}^{(1)T}\mathbf{K}^{(1)}\mathbf{K}^{(2)T}\mathbf{A}^{(2)}\right) \tag{12}$$

$$= \sum_{i=1}^{d} \boldsymbol{\alpha}_i^{(1)T}\mathbf{K}^{(1)}\mathbf{K}^{(2)T}\boldsymbol{\alpha}_i^{(2)} \tag{13}$$

$$= \sum_{i=1}^{d} \boldsymbol{\alpha}_i^{(1)T}\boldsymbol{\Sigma}^{(1,2)}\boldsymbol{\alpha}_i^{(2)}, \tag{14}$$

where $\boldsymbol{\alpha}_i^{(1)}$ and $\boldsymbol{\alpha}_i^{(2)}$ in Eq. (13)–(14) denote the ith column of $\mathbf{A}^{(1)}$ and $\mathbf{A}^{(2)}$, respectively. Therefore, $\boldsymbol{\alpha}_i^{(1)T}\mathbf{K}^{(1)}$ and $\boldsymbol{\alpha}_i^{(2)T}\mathbf{K}^{(2)}$ in Eq. (13) denote the ith pair of canonical variables. $\boldsymbol{\Sigma}^{(1,2)} = \mathbf{K}^{(1)}\mathbf{K}^{(2)T}$ denotes the cross-covariance matrix between the two views. Note similar to the standard CCA, normalization of the variables is also required. Plugging Eq. (9) into Eq. (8) leads to

$$\begin{aligned}&\mathbf{G}^T\boldsymbol{\Gamma}(\mathbf{K})\mathbf{G} \\ &= \begin{bmatrix}\mathbf{A}^{(1)T} & \mathbf{A}^{(2)T}\end{bmatrix}\boldsymbol{\Gamma}(\mathbf{K})\begin{bmatrix}\mathbf{A}^{(1)} \\ \mathbf{A}^{(2)}\end{bmatrix} \\ &= \mathbf{A}^{(1)T}\left(\mathbf{K}^{(1)}\mathbf{K}^{(1)T} + \lambda\mathbf{I}\right)\mathbf{A}^{(1)} \\ &+ \mathbf{A}^{(2)T}\left(\mathbf{K}^{(2)}\mathbf{K}^{(2)T} + \lambda\mathbf{I}\right)\mathbf{A}^{(2)} = \mathbf{I},\end{aligned} \tag{15}$$

which is a relaxed version of the following two constraints Eq. (16)–(17) (ignoring the scaling constant),

$$\mathbf{A}^{(1)T}\left(\mathbf{K}^{(1)}\mathbf{K}^{(1)T} + \lambda\mathbf{I}\right)\mathbf{A}^{(1)} = \mathbf{I}, \tag{16}$$

$$\mathbf{A}^{(2)T}\left(\mathbf{K}^{(2)}\mathbf{K}^{(2)T} + \lambda\mathbf{I}\right)\mathbf{A}^{(2)} = \mathbf{I}. \tag{17}$$

Eq. (16)–(17) are the standard CCA orthogonal constraints in matrix equations form. For example, Eq. (16) is equiva-

[3] Assuming unit vector norms.

[4] The choices of c_{ij}, c'_{ij} are subtle, which need to strike a balance between the feasibility of the optimization and the effects of similarity learning. Details are provided in the following Section 5.

lent to

$$\boldsymbol{\alpha}_i^{(1)T}\hat{\boldsymbol{\Sigma}}^{(1,1)}\boldsymbol{\alpha}_i^{(1)} = 1,\ i = 1, \cdots, d \tag{18}$$

$$\boldsymbol{\alpha}_i^{(1)T}\hat{\boldsymbol{\Sigma}}^{(1,1)}\boldsymbol{\alpha}_j^{(1)} = 0,\ i, j = 1, \cdots, d, i \neq j, \tag{19}$$

where $\boldsymbol{\alpha}_i^{(1)}$ and $\boldsymbol{\alpha}_j^{(1)}$ denote the ith and jth column of $\mathbf{A}^{(1)}$, respectively, and $\hat{\boldsymbol{\Sigma}}^{(1,1)} = \mathbf{K}^{(1)}\mathbf{K}^{(1)T} + \lambda\mathbf{I}$ is the regularized covariance matrices in the first view.

The compact format of Eq. (15) is preferable to Eq. (16)–(17) due to it is easier to optimize with respect to $\mathbf{G}$ using a LP solver. Empirically, Eq. (15) gives highly similar results to that produced by Eq. (16)–(17).

In addition to the standard CCA target Eq. (4) and constraint Eq. (8), additional constraints of Eq. (5)–(7) are included to impose the cross-view similarity and intra-view similarity conditions. Plugging the equations $\mathbf{A}^{(1)} = \mathbf{L}_1\mathbf{G}$ and $\mathbf{A}^{(2)} = \mathbf{L}_2\mathbf{G}$ into Eq. (5)–(7) leads to the aforementioned similarity preserving constraints detailed in Eq. (3).

Unfortunately, the optimization problem in Eq. (4)–(8) is a generic quadratically constrained quadratic program (QCQP) problem and it is NP-hard [23, 26]. In order to approximate the solution with reasonable computational complexity, in the following Section 4 we first adopt relaxations to the problem, and subsequently develop an efficient iterative solution to it.

4. RELAXATION AND SOLUTION

To alleviate the computational difficulty of optimizing the objective function in Eq. (4)–(8), we apply the SDP relaxation techniques presented in [23] and propose the approximate solutions, accordingly.

As a standard step of SDP relaxation, an extra positive semidefinite matrix $\mathbf{M}_G$ relevant to the original optimization variable $\mathbf{G}$ need to be defined. The definition of $\mathbf{M}_G$ determines how the original constraint in Eq. (8) is relaxed. As later shown in Eq. (26), we choose a conservative definition of $\mathbf{M}_G$ with dimension[5] of $2n \times 2n$. Ideally,

$$\mathbf{M}_G = \mathbf{G}\mathbf{G}^T = \begin{bmatrix} \mathbf{A}^{(1)}\mathbf{A}^{(1)T} & \mathbf{A}^{(1)}\mathbf{A}^{(2)T} \\ \mathbf{A}^{(2)}\mathbf{A}^{(1)T} & \mathbf{A}^{(2)}\mathbf{A}^{(2)T} \end{bmatrix}. \tag{20}$$

However, if Eq. (20) holds exactly, the optimization is identical to (i.e., as difficult as) the original QCQP problem. Hence in stead of requiring $\mathbf{M}_G = GG^T$, we relax it to $\mathbf{M}_G - GG^T \succeq 0$ (following [23]), and using the Schur's complement, this constraint is equivalent to

$$\begin{bmatrix} \mathbf{M}_G & \mathbf{G} \\ \mathbf{G}^T & \mathbf{I}_d \end{bmatrix} \succeq 0. \tag{21}$$

With Eq. (21) defined, the original constraint in Eq. (8) can be readily relaxed to Eq. (26), where only the trace[6] of $\boldsymbol{\Gamma}(\mathbf{K})\mathbf{M}_G$ is fixed instead of a series of constraints on each element of the $\mathbf{G}^T\boldsymbol{\Gamma}(\mathbf{K})\mathbf{G}$. Empirically, a large number of constraints drastically increase the computational burden and even make the optimization infeasible, and this relaxation reduces the number of constraints[7], which makes the practical solution of Eq. (22)–(28) possible.

[5] Alternative relaxations are presented in the appendix.

[6] It is also the trace of $\mathbf{G}^T\boldsymbol{\Gamma}(\mathbf{K})\mathbf{G}$.

[7] From d^2, the total number of element in matrix $\mathbf{G}^T\boldsymbol{\Gamma}(\mathbf{K})\mathbf{G}$ down to 1.

$$\max_{\mathbf{G},\mathbf{M}_G} \operatorname{tr}\left(\mathbf{K}^{(1)}\mathbf{K}^{(2)T}\mathbf{L}_2\mathbf{M}_G\mathbf{L}_1^T\right) \tag{22}$$

$$\text{s.t. } \boldsymbol{\kappa}_i^{(1)T}\mathbf{L}_1\mathbf{M}_G\mathbf{L}_2^T\boldsymbol{\kappa}_j^{(2)} \begin{cases} \geq c_{ij} & \text{if } y_i = y_j \\ \leq c_{ij} & \text{otherwise} \end{cases} \tag{23}$$

$$\boldsymbol{\kappa}_i^{(1)T}\mathbf{L}_1\mathbf{M}_G\mathbf{L}_1^T\boldsymbol{\kappa}_j^{(2)} \begin{cases} \geq c_{ij} & \text{if } y_i = y_j \\ \leq c_{ij} & \text{otherwise} \end{cases} \tag{24}$$

$$\boldsymbol{\kappa}_i^{(1)T}\mathbf{L}_2\mathbf{M}_G\mathbf{L}_2^T\boldsymbol{\kappa}_j^{(2)} \begin{cases} \geq c_{ij} & \text{if } y_i = y_j \\ \leq c_{ij} & \text{otherwise} \end{cases} \tag{25}$$

$$\operatorname{tr}(\boldsymbol{\Gamma}(\mathbf{K})\mathbf{M}_G) = d \tag{26}$$

$$\mathbf{M}_G = \mathbf{M}_G^T \tag{27}$$

$$\begin{bmatrix} \mathbf{M}_G & \mathbf{G} \\ \mathbf{G}^T & \mathbf{I}_d \end{bmatrix} \succeq 0, \tag{28}$$

Note that the problem in Eq. (22)–(28) takes the standard form of an SDP, hence it is convex and theoretically solvable with the standard interior point methods. However, in common visual recognition scenarios, the total dimension of variables in $\mathbf{M}_G$ and $\mathbf{G}$ are too large for the off-the-shelf SDP solvers, and it is known that a large scale SDP problem is computational prohibitive [23]. Therefore we further relax the problem in Eq. (22)–(28) to the following alternating optimization where a computational efficient linear program is adopted instead.

$$\max_{\mathbf{M}_G} \operatorname{tr}\left(\mathbf{K}^{(1)}\mathbf{K}^{(2)T}\mathbf{L}_2\mathbf{M}_G\mathbf{L}_1^T\right) + \mu\operatorname{tr}\left(\mathbf{G}^T\mathbf{M}_G\mathbf{G}\right) \tag{29}$$

$$\text{s.t. } \boldsymbol{\kappa}_i^{(1)T}\mathbf{L}_1\mathbf{M}_G\mathbf{L}_2^T\boldsymbol{\kappa}_j^{(2)} \begin{cases} \geq c_{ij} & \text{if } y_i = y_j \\ \leq c_{ij} & \text{otherwise} \end{cases} \tag{30}$$

$$\boldsymbol{\kappa}_i^{(1)T}\mathbf{L}_1\mathbf{M}_G\mathbf{L}_1^T\boldsymbol{\kappa}_j^{(2)} \begin{cases} \geq c_{ij} & \text{if } y_i = y_j \\ \leq c_{ij} & \text{otherwise} \end{cases} \tag{31}$$

$$\boldsymbol{\kappa}_i^{(1)T}\mathbf{L}_2\mathbf{M}_G\mathbf{L}_2^T\boldsymbol{\kappa}_j^{(2)} \begin{cases} \geq c_{ij} & \text{if } y_i = y_j \\ \leq c_{ij} & \text{otherwise} \end{cases} \tag{32}$$

$$\operatorname{tr}(\boldsymbol{\Gamma}(\mathbf{K})\mathbf{M}_G) = d \tag{33}$$

$$\mathbf{M}_G = \mathbf{M}_G^T,\ \mathbf{G}^T\mathbf{M}_G\mathbf{G} = \mathbf{I} \tag{34}$$

and

$$\max_{\mathbf{G}} \operatorname{tr}\left(\mathbf{G}^T\mathbf{M}_G\mathbf{G}\right) \tag{35}$$

$$\text{s.t. } \mathbf{G}^T\mathbf{G} = \mathbf{I} \tag{36}$$

By alternating optimizing with respect to $\mathbf{M}_G$ and $\mathbf{G}$ using Eq. (29)–(34) and Eq. (35)–(36), respectively, the aggregated projection matrix $\mathbf{G}$ can be obtained. As for the selection of parameters and initialization, these details are given in the following Section 5. Whilst this alternating process could not necessarily find the global optimum $\mathbf{G}$ specified in Eq. (4)–(8), it is guaranteed to find at least a strong local minimum such that no further perturbations increase Eq. (29) and Eq. (35).

5. DATASETS AND SETTINGS

The experiments are conducted on four different multi-view datasets, i.e., the RGBD Object dataset [16], the NYU Depth V1 Indoor Scenes dataset [27], the multi-spectral

Figure 2: Examples of multi-view image pairs. Left to right, top to bottom, [16] RGB/depth, [27] RGB/depth; [4] RGB/infrared, [36] grayscale/depth.

scene dataset [4] and Binghamton University 3D Facial Expression dataset [36]. Examples are shown in Fig. 2.

For the missing data recognition task, two types of missing schemes are considered. First the systematic missing scheme is included, where both views are present in the training phase, but the second view is nonexistent in the testing phase. The alternative type is the random missing scenario, where both views are present in the training phase, but the testing data contains only a single view (either the first view or the second view), chosen randomly according to a Bernoulli distribution with probability $p = 0.5$.

With all four datasets, we test our proposed method against competing ones in both missing data scenarios, i.e., the complete missing of second view case and the random missing case. In addition, with the Binghamton University 3D Facial Expression dataset, we also conducted the cross-view identity verification task, whose target is to determine whether the "depth-face" and "image-face" pairs come from the same person. Regarding the off-the-shelf recognition algorithms, the LIBSVM [5] is adopted for classification while the joint Bayesian verification algorithm [6, 18, 19] is adopted for verification.

While evaluating the performance, we adopted five competing algorithms, namely, SVM/Raw, SVM-2K*, KCCA, RGCCA, and DCCA. With both missing data recognition tasks, the baseline is the direct application of the SVM. For the complete missing of second view scenario, one SVM is learned only on the first view training data, and tested on the first view testing data. For the random missing scenario, two SVM are separately learned on two views, and the testing data is processed by the corespondent SVM. For the cross-modal verification task with the Binghamton University 3D Facial Expression dataset, the "Raw" approach directly trains a joint Bayesian verification algorithm based on the similar/dis-similar cross-view pairs without any latent space projections.

Termed as the "SVM-2K*", this approach is a naive extension of "SVM-2K" [11] to the missing data scenario of multi-view learning, in which we train with both views, but test with only the first view classifier or corresponding single view classifier, in the "missing 2nd view" and "missing randomly" scenarios, respectively. The "KCCA" approach also adopts the latent space framework in Fig. 1, however, it maximizes the nonlinear correlation between the first view and the second view so as to construct a pair of projection vectors iteratively using the standard kernelized CCA [13]. After obtaining the latent space, subsequent SVM or joint Bayesian verification algorithm is applied in this latent space. "RGCCA" and "DCCA" are two extended versions of the "KCCA", they are different from "KCCA" only in replacing the standard kernelized CCA [13] with the algorithms proposed in [30] and [38], respectively.

In the following experiments, the RBF kernel is applied to both the KCCA algorithm and the SVM algorithms. The bandwidth parameter in the RBF kernel, the parameters in the SVM-2K* algorithm, λ and μ in the proposed approach are all determined by a 4-fold cross validation. The data dependent thresholds c_{ij} in Eq. (30)–(32) are determined as follows. First, the proposed algorithm is initialized with the projection matrix $\mathbf{G}_0$ learned by the KCCA algorithm [8], and $\mathbf{M}_{G0} = \mathbf{G}_0\mathbf{G}_0^T$. Then the initial original values c_{0ij} are computed using the Eq. (30)–(32), respectively (e.g., with Eq. (30), $c_{0ij} = \mathrm{tr}(\boldsymbol{\kappa}_i^{(1)T}\mathbf{L}_1\mathbf{M}_{G0}\mathbf{L}_2^T\boldsymbol{\kappa}_j^{(2)})$). After obtaining the c_{0ij} values, a contraction/expansion process is applied as follows. $c_{ij} = (1+\epsilon)c_{0ij}$ if $y_i = y_j$, and $c_{ij} = (1-\epsilon)c_{0ij}$ otherwise, where the scalar $\epsilon \in [0 : 0.05 : 0.5]$ is determined by a cross validation.

6. EXPERIMENTAL RESULTS

In this section, the proposed method is tested against competing algorithms on four real world datasets with two missing data recognition tasks and one cross-modal verification task.

6.1 UW RGBD Dataset

The RGBD object dataset [16, 3] consists of paired RGB images and depth maps of multiple object instances from 51 categories. Without loss of generality, we assign the RGB images as the first view, and the depth maps as the second view. We focus on the instance level object recognition within each of the categories, and demonstrate that the proposed SLCCA paired with the discriminative latent space model can facilitate better recognition based on the single view data, or randomly interlaced single view data. We follow [16] to construct the "leave-sequence-out" training/testing split[9], and [3] to extract the HMP-based features from both views.

The recognition results under the "missing 2nd view" scenario and "missing randomly" scenario are illustrated in Fig. 3 and also summarized in Table 1. Due to the drastic change of recognition difficulties among the categories[10], the recognition accuracies fluctuate significantly. To alleviate the difficulty of comparison, the SVM is selected as a baseline with its accuracies plotted at the bottom in both the "Missing 2nd View" and "Missing Randomly" cases. The recognition accuracies of the remaining algorithms are first subtracted by the SVM baseline and the differences are situated at the top in both cases.

With the case of missing the second view (Fig. 3(a)), the SVM-2K* variant offers no significant improvements against the baseline SVM approach, while the KCCA and RGCCA both offer marginally better recognition results. The DCCA approach is better with an average recognition accuracy of 94.6%, but not as high as our proposed SLCCA approach, which achieves 95.1% accuracy. Again with the random missing scheme, in Fig. 3(b), although the recognition ac-

[8]The KCCA algorithm is needed both for a reasonable initialization and also for faster practical convergence.

[9]This is a fixed split scheme, hence neither standard deviation nor t-test is applicable.

[10]For example, it is much harder to distinguish three tomatoes than distinctive brands of cellphones.

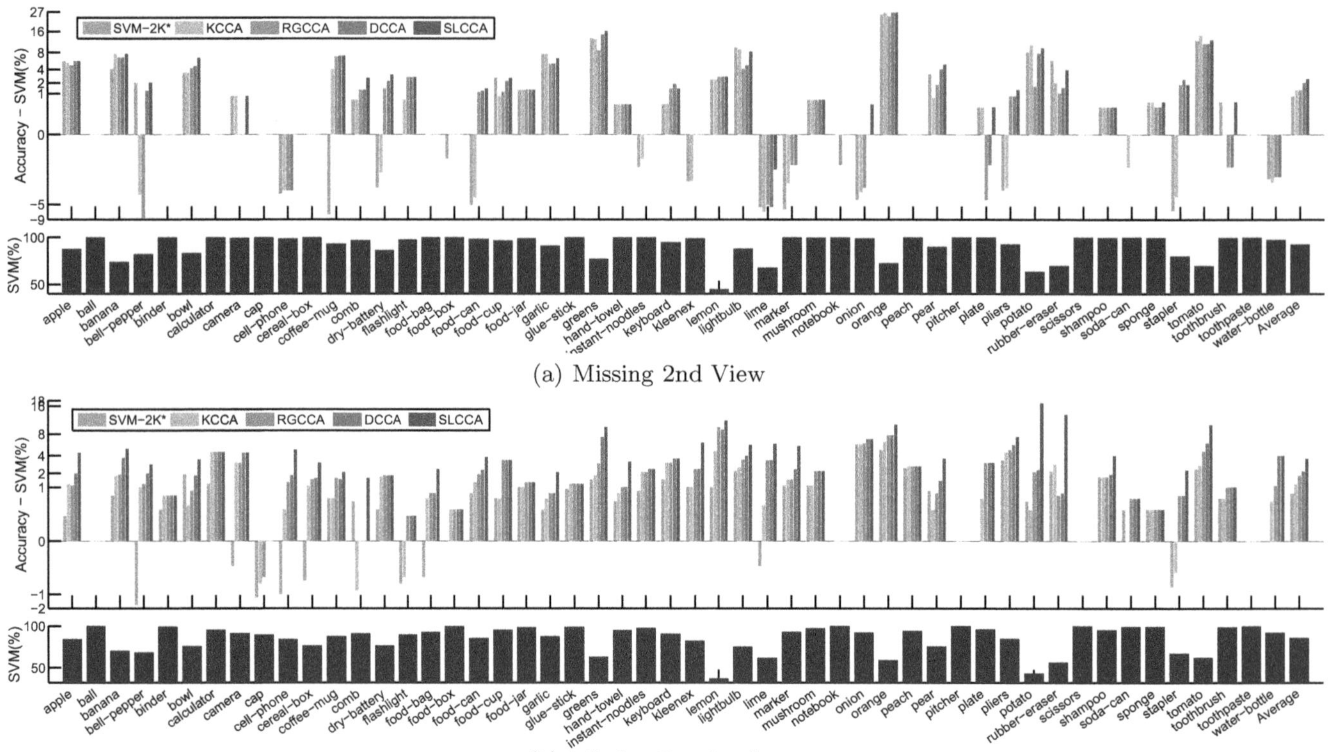

(a) Missing 2nd View

(b) Missing Randomly

Figure 3: Multi-View RGBD Object Instance Recognition from all 51 categories and average results (in percentage). For both case (a) Missing 2nd View and case (b) Missing 2nd View, the accuracies of SVM baseline are situated at the bottom, while the differences of subtracting SVM accuracies from the corresponding, remaining algorithms are situated at the top. The Average accuracies across all 51 categories for both cases are situated furthest to the right.

curacy varies a lot across categories, the proposed approach offers obvious performance boost against competing algorithms, achieves an average accuracy of 90.0%.

Table 1: Multi-View RGBD Object Instance Recognition, average results across all 51 categories.

Missing	SVM	SVM-2K*	KCCA	RG-CCA	DCCA	SLCCA
2nd View	92.6	93.4	93.9	93.9	94.6	95.1
Randomly	86.4	87.1	87.6	88.2	88.6	90.0

6.2 NYU Indoor Scenes Dataset

Collected by a custom made Kinect sensor, the NYU-Depth-V1-Indoor Scene Dataset [27] consists of RGB-depth image pairs of 7 classes of indoor scenes. This multi-channel capturing scheme enables us to examine a wide range of missing-data recognition scenarios. First, two types of view assignments are considered. As shown in Table 2, *L+D* denotes the case where the luminance channel (i.e., the grayscale image, which is obtained by converting from the RGB channels) feature is assigned as the first view, while the depth channel as the second view, and *RGB+D* denotes the case where the first view consists of features extracted independently from all the R,G and B channels and then concatenated, while the depth channel feature is regarded as the second view.

For the missing data profile, we consider both the systematic missing scheme and the random missing scheme detailed in Section 5, which are denoted as "Missing 2nd View" and "Missing Randomly" in Table 2, respectively. We consider two types of features: both the lower dimensional GIST [21] features and the higher dimensional spatial pyramid bag-of-feature representation [17]. All these features are firstly extracted independently from the respective channel (luminance, R, G, B or depth channel). For the spatial pyramid bag-of-feature representation, we densely extract SIFT descriptors from 40×40 patches with a stride of 10 pixels, and use two dictionary of size (200 and 800) for the k-means clustering. We denote these two feature extraction schemes as SP200 and SP800 in Table 2, respectively.

The experimental data are randomly split into 50 folds of training data and testing data with comparable number of samples (following [27]). The proposed and the competing algorithms are tested and the mean and the standard deviation of the recognition accuracies (in percentage) are summarized in Table 2, with three different kinds of feature matching schemes, two types of missing data scenarios and two sets of view assignments.

It can be observed that the higher dimensional and more sophisticated spatial pyramid bag-of-feature representation is capable of achieving higher recognition accuracies than the lower dimensional GIST features. Also, the random missing scheme generally poses a more challenging problem than the systematic missing scheme, due to the phenomenon that the first view (grayscale or RGB images) is intrinsically more informative than the second view (depth maps) in determining

Table 2: NYU Depth V1 Indoor Scenes

Settings	GIST, Missing 2nd View		GIST, Missing Randomly	
Views	L+D	RGB+D	L+D	RGB+D
SVM	59.61±3.42	61.33±3.32	42.17±4.72	43.43±5.87
SVM-2K*	58.26±3.71	60.92±3.80	42.47±4.33	43.51±4.82
KCCA	59.33±6.92	61.58±6.28	43.43±5.44	43.67±4.32
RGCCA	58.97±5.83	62.15±4.85	44.43±4.52	45.22±5.11
DCCA	60.37±4.23	62.98±4.37	44.88±6.10	45.52±4.08
SLCCA	60.45±6.89	62.87±5.92	46.22±5.12	47.08±4.71
Settings	SP200, Missing 2nd View		SP200, Missing Randomly	
Views	L+D	RGB+D	L+D	RGB+D
SVM	63.24±3.61	65.01±4.05	45.59±4.12	46.60±3.88
SVM-2K*	60.37±4.25	61.23±4.93	44.52±5.25	46.76±4.65
KCCA	63.37±5.29	64.22±5.41	46.02±4.30	46.68±5.31
RGCCA	63.04±4.83	63.85±5.37	46.22±5.31	46.70±5.27
DCCA	65.90±4.76	65.22±5.69	47.02±6.20	46.98±4.82
SLCCA	66.02±7.69	66.29±6.49	48.98±5.13	49.92±4.98
Settings	SP800, Missing 2nd View		SP800, Missing Randomly	
Views	L+D	RGB+D	L+D	RGB+D
SVM	64.63±3.13	65.72±3.75	46.80±3.37	48.59±4.62
SVM-2K*	59.73±4.32	61.82±4.49	45.47±4.38	47.65±5.73
KCCA	65.14±5.72	65.56±6.23	48.20±3.31	48.60±3.28
RGCCA	65.09±5.39	66.16±5.43	48.60±4.69	48.88±5.88
DCCA	65.76±5.07	66.44±5.02	48.92±5.34	49.06±6.21
SLCCA	66.79±5.94	67.26±6.54	51.46±4.33	52.02±4.27

the scene types, especially the highly clutter indoor scenes in this dataset.

Comparing the results from these algorithms, we note that the variant of SVM-2K* fails to achieve significant performance advantage over the baseline SVM algorithm. We would like to point out that SVM-2K [11] was formulated as a multi-view learning algorithm without considering the missing data case, and the simple extension to the missing data case may not satisfy the assumption of the "prediction consistency" regularization. The competing KCCA, RGCCA and DCCA algorithms provide various degrees of performance enhancements but not as significant as the proposed SLCCA approach. Conducting the t-tests for the 12 settings in Table 2, the proposed SLCCA approach significantly outperforms the baseline SVM algorithm 8 and 2 times with confidence level 0.95 and 0.90, respectively.

6.3 Multi-Spectral Scene Dataset

With these experimental results on the multi-spectral scene dataset [4], we demonstrate the efficacy of our proposed approach in missing-data resilient scene recognition, with both the systematic missing scheme ("Missing 2nd View") and the random missing scheme ("Missing Randomly"). The multi-spectral scene dataset [4] consists of 477 paired RGB and near-infrared (IR) images from 9 different scene categories.

In line with [4], the RGB images are first converted to the **LAB** color space, subsequently the GIST [21] features are extracted independently on each of the L, A, B and IR channels. Two view assignments are considered, i.e., $L{+}I$ denotes GIST features extracted from the luminance channel and the IR channel are assigned as the first view and the second view, respectively; and $LAB{+}I$ denotes GIST features extracted independently from the L, A and B channels are concatenated to form the first view, while those extracted from the IR channel are considered as the second view. Following [4], we construct 50 random training/testing splits, and the mean and the standard deviation of the recognition accuracies (in percentage) are reported in Table 3.

From Table 3, despite the large standard deviations (due to the large intra-class variations [4]), we note that the

Table 3: Multi-Spectral Scenes

Settings	Missing 2nd View		Missing Randomly	
Views	LAB+I	L+I	LAB+I	L+I
SVM	67.78±5.25	61.82±3.77	42.11±5.56	38.02±4.69
SVM-2K*	67.17±5.58	61.82±4.59	42.80±5.42	38.22±4.30
KCCA	67.87±4.76	62.32±4.81	44.21±4.89	39.08±5.61
RGCCA	68.59±3.94	62.22±3.96	46.02±3.36	40.73±5.28
DCCA	70.51±2.37	65.66±4.57	46.60±5.40	41.22±4.61
SLCCA	71.22±3.26	66.12±4.68	49.18±4.92	43.64±5.21

$LAB{+}I$ assignments are generally better than the $L{+}I$, which is consistent with the $LAB{+}I$ assignment being more informative. Again, the random missing scheme is generally more challenging than the systematic missing scheme, also due to the limited discriminative power in the second view. With the competing algorithms, neither the KCCA nor the SVM-2K* algorithm achieves a significant advantage over the SVM baseline. The more flexible RGCCA and DCCA algorithms marginally outperform the baseline SVM algorithm. As anticipated, the proposed SLCCA achieves the highest accuracies and it significantly outpeforms the SVM baseline in all four cases of Table 3 in t-tests at confidence level 0.99.

6.4 Binghamton 3D Facial Expression dataset

For the experiment on this Binghamton 3D Facial Expression dataset [36], we demonstrate the efficacy of our proposed approach in both the missing data recognition problems and the cross-modal verification problem. We show that by collegially modeling the discriminative model based on two views, various visual recognition tasks (expression, gender, and race recognition) with missing data could be improved. In addition, we demonstrate the effectiveness of the proposed approach in recover the semantic correspondences with cross-modal identity verification (determining whether a pair of image-face and depth-face come from the same person).

The Binghamton dataset [36] consists of 3D face models as well as face images of 100 subjects (with both genders and a variety of ethnic/racial ancestries, i.e., White, Black, East-Asian, Middle-east Asian, Indian, and Hispanic Latino) of 7 facial expressions (happiness, disgust, fear, angry, surprise, sadness and neutral). We extract all the frontal face images and the frontal face depth maps from the 3D point clouds, and feed them to the Eigen-PEP model [6, 18, 19] to extract features independently on the grayscale images and on the depth maps, respectively. Unlike 3D face features such as [33, 20] that require manual labelling of facial landmarks, our features are automatically generated without the need of these facial landmark labels.

Following conventions, we assign the image features as the first view and the depth features as the second view. For statistical stability, 50 random training/testing splits are constructed, with equal number of subjects as training and testing samples. While constructing these splits, we adopt an exclusive-identity protocol, i.e., we make sure that any individual appearing in the training set never simultaneously appears in the testing set, and vice versa. The classification algorithm is SVM using the LIBSVM [5], and the target is to recognize the expression, gender, ethnic/racial ancestries of the testing samples. The target of the verification is to verify whether a facial image and a facial depth map come from the same individual (regardless of expression variations), and the algorithm is based on the joint Bayesian verification algorithm in [6, 18, 19], where 10000 pairs of similar and dissimilar pairs are sampled and fed to the training process.

Table 4: Binghamton 3D Facial Expression

Settings	Recognition:Missing 2nd View			
Algorithms	SVM	KCCA	DCCA	SLCCA
expression	72.2±4.1	73.1±3.7	74.5±4.1	75.8±3.2
gender	92.1±3.2	89.4±4.1	92.6±5.3	92.8±3.8
race	72.0±3.9	74.1±4.2	75.2±5.2	78.1±4.3
Settings	Recognition:Missing Randomly			
expression	69.1±3.9	69.5±3.3	71.9±5.9	73.8±4.2
gender	87.4±4.2	88.6±3.5	89.5±4.4	89.6±3.5
race	64.0±4.2	66.2±3.7	66.5±5.3	68.4±4.3
Settings	Cross-modal Verification			
Algorithms	Raw	KCCA	DCCA	SLCCA
Accuracy	81.1±4.2	82.3±3.9	82.6±4.4	86.4±5.4

The recognition/verification accuracies (in percentage) are summarized in Table 4. The missing data recognition results are shown in the upper part of Table 4, with the systematic missing scheme followed by the random missing scheme. In both scenarios, we carried out recognition based on the expression, gender and race labels. In both the expression and race recognition tasks, the proposed algorithm outperforms the baseline SVM algorithm significantly in t-tests at confidence level 0.99. The gender recognition task is different in that only two classes (male and female) are present with potentially larger intra-class variations, which could limit the effectiveness of discriminative similarity learning algorithms.

In summary, the proposed algorithm achieves the highest verification accuracy in the cross-modal identity verification task, and it significantly outperforms the Raw method (detailed in Section 5) in the t-test at confidence level 0.99.

6.5 Comparison of Algorithms

KCCA finds the latent space without explicitly resorting to the labels; DCCA first encodes an extra view based on training labels, and subsequently incorporates the label information by maximizing correlations between existing views and the encoded view; unlike the previous two-step way, the proposed SLCCA explicitly incorporates similarity constraints inside the optimization target, which leads to the best performance benchmarks in the aforementioned experiments.

7. CONCLUSION

We have proposed a recognition framework casting the multi-view information into a single semantic latent space and developed the SLCCA algorithm to construct such a latent space for the missing data recognition / verification problem. The proposed algorithm explicitly preserves the intra-class and inter-class relationships, and it is implemented with relaxation and alternating optimization. Experiments with four different datasets demonstrate that the proposed method outperforms the competing ones.

8. ACKNOWLEDGMENTS

Research reported in this publication was partly supported by the National Institute Of Nursing Research of the National Institutes of Health under Award Number R01NR015371. The content is solely the responsibility of the authors and does not necessarily represent the official views of the National Institutes of Health. This work is also partly supported by US National Science Foundation Grant IIS 1350763, Gang Hua's start-up funds and Qilin Zhang's Innovation & Entrepreneurship Doctoral Fellowship from Stevens Institute of Technology.

9. REFERENCES

[1] A. Argyriou, T. Evgeniou, M. Pontil, A. Argyriou, T. Evgeniou, and M. Pontil. Convex multi-task feature learning. In *Machine Learning*. press, 2007.

[2] A. Blum and T. Mitchell. Combining labeled and unlabeled data with co-training. In *Proceedings of the eleventh annual conference on Computational learning theory*, pages 92–100. ACM, 1998.

[3] L. Bo, X. Ren, and D. Fox. Unsupervised feature learning for rgb-d based object recognition. In *Experimental Robotics*, pages 387–402. Springer, 2013.

[4] M. Brown and S. Susstrunk. Multi-spectral sift for scene category recognition. In *Computer Vision and Pattern Recognition (CVPR), 2011 IEEE Conference on*, pages 177–184. IEEE, 2011.

[5] C.-C. Chang and C.-J. Lin. Libsvm: a library for support vector machines. *ACM Transactions on Intelligent Systems and Technology (TIST)*, 2(3):27, 2011.

[6] D. Chen, X. Cao, L. Wang, F. Wen, and J. Sun. Bayesian face revisited: A joint formulation. In *Computer Vision–ECCV 2012*, pages 566–579. Springer, 2012.

[7] J. Chen, X. Liu, and S. Lyu. Boosting with side information. In *Computer Vision–ACCV 2012*, pages 563–577. Springer, 2013.

[8] L. Chen, W. Li, and D. Xu. Recognizing rgb images by learning from rgb-d data. In *Computer Vision and Pattern Recognition (CVPR), 2014 IEEE Conference on*, pages 1418–1425. IEEE, 2014.

[9] J. Currie and D. I. Wilson. Opti: lowering the barrier between open source optimizers and the industrial matlab user. *Foundations of computer-aided process operations, Savannah, Georgia, USA*, pages 8–11, 2012.

[10] J. V. Davis, B. Kulis, P. Jain, S. Sra, and I. S. Dhillon. Information-theoretic metric learning. In *Proceedings of the 24th international conference on Machine learning*, pages 209–216. ACM, 2007.

[11] J. Farquhar, D. Hardoon, H. Meng, J. S. Shawe-taylor, and S. Szedmak. Two view learning: Svm-2k, theory and practice. In *Advances in neural information processing systems*, pages 355–362, 2005.

[12] A. Globerson and S. Roweis. Nightmare at test time: robust learning by feature deletion. In *Proceedings of the 23rd international conference on Machine learning*, pages 353–360. ACM, 2006.

[13] D. R. Hardoon, S. Szedmak, and J. Shawe-Taylor. Canonical correlation analysis: An overview with application to learning methods. *Neural Computation*, 16(12):2639–2664, 2004.

[14] T.-K. Kim, J. Kittler, and R. Cipolla. Discriminative learning and recognition of image set classes using canonical correlations. *Pattern Analysis and Machine*

Intelligence, IEEE Transactions on, 29(6):1005–1018, 2007.
[15] B. Kulis, K. Saenko, and T. Darrell. What you saw is not what you get: Domain adaptation using asymmetric kernel transforms. In *Computer Vision and Pattern Recognition (CVPR), 2011 IEEE Conference on*, pages 1785–1792. IEEE, 2011.
[16] K. Lai, L. Bo, X. Ren, and D. Fox. A large-scale hierarchical multi-view rgb-d object dataset. In *Robotics and Automation (ICRA), 2011 IEEE International Conference on*, pages 1817–1824. IEEE, 2011.
[17] S. Lazebnik, C. Schmid, and J. Ponce. Beyond bags of features: Spatial pyramid matching for recognizing natural scene categories. In *Computer Vision and Pattern Recognition, 2006 IEEE Computer Society Conference on*, volume 2, pages 2169–2178. IEEE, 2006.
[18] H. Li, G. Hua, Z. Lin, J. Brandt, and J. Yang. Probabilistic elastic matching for pose variant face verification. In *Computer Vision and Pattern Recognition (CVPR), 2013 IEEE Conference on*, pages 3499–3506. IEEE, 2013.
[19] H. Li, G. Hua, Z. Lin, J. Brandt, and J. Yang. Probabilistic elastic part model for unsupervised face detector adaptation. In *Computer Vision (ICCV), 2013 IEEE International Conference on*, pages 793–800. IEEE, 2013.
[20] A. Maalej, B. B. Amor, M. Daoudi, A. Srivastava, and S. Berretti. Shape analysis of local facial patches for 3d facial expression recognition. *Pattern Recognition*, 44(8):1581–1589, 2011.
[21] A. Oliva and A. Torralba. Modeling the shape of the scene: A holistic representation of the spatial envelope. *International journal of computer vision*, 42(3):145–175, 2001.
[22] Z. Qi, M. Yang, Z. M. Zhang, and Z. Zhang. Mining noisy tagging from multi-label space. In *Proceedings of the 21st ACM international conference on Information and knowledge management*, pages 1925–1929. ACM, 2012.
[23] A. Qualizza, P. Belotti, and F. Margot. Linear programming relaxations of quadratically constrained quadratic programs. In *Mixed Integer Nonlinear Programming*, pages 407–426. Springer, 2012.
[24] K. Saenko, B. Kulis, M. Fritz, and T. Darrell. Adapting visual category models to new domains. In *Computer Vision–ECCV 2010*, pages 213–226. Springer, 2010.
[25] L. Shams, D. R. Wozny, R. Kim, and A. Seitz. Influences of multisensory experience on subsequent unisensory processing. *Frontiers in psychology*, 2, 2011.
[26] H. D. Sherali and B. M. Fraticelli. Enhancing rlt relaxations via a new class of semidefinite cuts. *Journal of Global Optimization*, 22(1-4):233–261, 2002.
[27] N. Silberman and R. Fergus. Indoor scene segmentation using a structured light sensor. In *Computer Vision Workshops (ICCV Workshops), 2011 IEEE International Conference on*, pages 601–608. IEEE, 2011.
[28] N. Srivastava and R. Salakhutdinov. Multimodal learning with deep boltzmann machines. In *Advances in neural information processing systems*, pages 2222–2230, 2012.
[29] L. Sun, S. Ji, and J. Ye. Canonical correlation analysis for multilabel classification: A least-squares formulation, extensions, and analysis. *Pattern Analysis and Machine Intelligence, IEEE Transactions on*, 33(1):194–200, 2011.
[30] A. Tenenhaus and M. Tenenhaus. Regularized generalized canonical correlation analysis. *Psychometrika*, 76(2):257–284, 2011.
[31] T. Tommasi, N. Quadrianto, B. Caputo, and C. H. Lampert. Beyond dataset bias: Multi-task unaligned shared knowledge transfer. In *Computer Vision–ACCV 2012*, pages 1–15. Springer, 2013.
[32] V. Vapnik, A. Vashist, and N. Pavlovitch. Learning using hidden information (learning with teacher). In *Neural Networks, 2009. IJCNN 2009. International Joint Conference on*, pages 3188–3195. IEEE, 2009.
[33] J. Wang, L. Yin, X. Wei, and Y. Sun. 3d facial expression recognition based on primitive surface feature distribution. In *Computer Vision and Pattern Recognition, 2006 IEEE Computer Society Conference on*, volume 2, pages 1399–1406. IEEE, 2006.
[34] K. Q. Weinberger, J. Blitzer, and L. K. Saul. Distance metric learning for large margin nearest neighbor classification. In *Advances in neural information processing systems*, pages 1473–1480, 2005.
[35] E. P. Xing, M. I. Jordan, S. Russell, and A. Y. Ng. Distance metric learning with application to clustering with side-information. In *Advances in neural information processing systems*, pages 505–512, 2002.
[36] L. Yin, X. Wei, Y. Sun, J. Wang, and M. J. Rosato. A 3d facial expression database for facial behavior research. In *Automatic face and gesture recognition, 2006. FGR 2006. 7th international conference on*, pages 211–216. IEEE, 2006.
[37] D. Zhang, J. He, Y. Liu, L. Si, and R. D. Lawrence. Multi-view transfer learning with a large margin approach. In *Proceedings of the 17th ACM SIGKDD international conference on Knowledge discovery and data mining*, pages 1208–1216, 2011.
[38] Q. Zhang, G. Hua, W. Liu, Z. Liu, and Z. Zhang. Can visual recognition benefit from auxiliary information in training? In *Computer Vision – ACCV 2014*, volume 9003 of *Lecture Notes in Computer Science*, pages 65–80. Springer International Publishing, 2015.

APPENDIX

A. ALTERNATIVE RELAXATIONS

In this appendix, two alternative relaxations to the one presented in Section 4 are first presented, and followed by brief comparisons.

Indeed, the relaxations proposed in Section 4 are not tight; abundant works have been devoted to the QCQP relaxations [23, 26] and many tighter relaxations exist, but they are computational prohibitive while solving the practical scale optimization problem in multimedia recognition. These alternative relaxations are tighter approximations[11], but they

[11] In the sense of enforcing Eq. (8).

are not chosen for computational reasons and numerical issues.

A.1 Alternative Relaxation 1

In stead of Eq. (26) in Section 4, this alternative relaxation defines d distinctive $\mathbf{M}_{Gj}$, where $j = 1, 2, \cdots, d$ to make the constraints in Eq. (39) possible. Ideally,

$$\mathbf{M}_{Gj} = \mathbf{G}(:, j)\mathbf{G}(:, j)^T, \ j = 1, \cdots, d, \tag{37}$$

where $\mathbf{G}(:, j), j = 1, \cdots, d$ denotes the jth column of matrix $\mathbf{G}$. However, the SDP relaxation only enforces Eq. (40) instead of Eq. (37). Therefore, the optimization target is,

$$\max_{\mathbf{G},\mathbf{M}_{G1},\cdots,\mathbf{M}_{Gd}} \sum_{j=1}^{d} \operatorname{tr}\left(\mathbf{K}^{(1)}\mathbf{K}^{(2)T}\mathbf{L}_2\mathbf{M}_{Gj}\mathbf{L}_1^T\right) \tag{38}$$

$$\begin{aligned}
\text{s.t.} \ & \sum_{j=1}^{d} \boldsymbol{\kappa}_i^{(1)T}\mathbf{L}_1\mathbf{M}_{Gj}\mathbf{L}_2^T\boldsymbol{\kappa}_j^{(2)} \begin{cases} \geq c_{ij} & \text{if } y_i = y_j \\ \leq c_{ij} & \text{otherwise} \end{cases} \\
& \sum_{j=1}^{d} \boldsymbol{\kappa}_i^{(1)T}\mathbf{L}_1\mathbf{M}_{Gj}\mathbf{L}_1^T\boldsymbol{\kappa}_j^{(2)} \begin{cases} \geq c_{ij} & \text{if } y_i = y_j \\ \leq c_{ij} & \text{otherwise} \end{cases} \\
& \sum_{j=1}^{d} \boldsymbol{\kappa}_i^{(1)T}\mathbf{L}_2\mathbf{M}_{Gj}\mathbf{L}_2^T\boldsymbol{\kappa}_j^{(2)} \begin{cases} \geq c_{ij} & \text{if } y_i = y_j \\ \leq c_{ij} & \text{otherwise} \end{cases} \\
& \operatorname{tr}(\boldsymbol{\Gamma}(\mathbf{K})\mathbf{M}_{Gj}) = 1, \qquad j = 1, \cdots, d \qquad (39) \\
& \mathbf{M}_{Gj} = \mathbf{M}_{Gj}^T, \qquad j = 1, \cdots, d \\
& \begin{bmatrix} \mathbf{M}_{Gj} & \mathbf{G}(:, j) \\ \mathbf{G}(:, j)^T & 1 \end{bmatrix} \succeq 0, \qquad j = 1, \cdots, d \qquad (40)
\end{aligned}$$

The specific definition in Eq. (37) leads to Eq. (39), where the d^2 scalar equations in Eq. (8) are reduced to d scalar equations in Eq. (39). Compared with Eq. (26), the number of constraints d are still to large to practically enforce. Worse still, there are d times more elements in $\mathbf{M}_{Gj}, j = 1, \cdots, d$ of Eq. (37) than the $\mathbf{M}_G$ in Eq. (20).

A.2 Alternative Relaxation 2

Similar to Eq. (37), the ideal value of $\mathbf{M}_G$ is $\text{vec}(\mathbf{G})\text{vec}(\mathbf{G})^T$, and it is similarly relaxed and enforced in Eq.(43). Therefore, the optimization target is:

$$\max_{\text{vec}(\mathbf{G}),\mathbf{M}_G} \sum_{j=1}^{d} \operatorname{tr}\left(\mathbf{K}^{(1)}\mathbf{K}^{(2)T}\mathbf{L}_2\mathbf{M}_G(jj)\mathbf{L}_1^T\right) \tag{41}$$

$$\begin{aligned}
\text{s.t.} \ & \sum_{j=1}^{d} \boldsymbol{\kappa}_i^{(1)T}\mathbf{L}_1\mathbf{M}_G(jj)\mathbf{L}_2^T\boldsymbol{\kappa}_j^{(2)} \begin{cases} \geq c_{ij} & \text{if } y_i = y_j \\ \leq c_{ij} & \text{otherwise} \end{cases} \\
& \sum_{j=1}^{d} \boldsymbol{\kappa}_i^{(1)T}\mathbf{L}_1\mathbf{M}_G(jj)\mathbf{L}_1^T\boldsymbol{\kappa}_j^{(2)} \begin{cases} \geq c_{ij} & \text{if } y_i = y_j \\ \leq c_{ij} & \text{otherwise} \end{cases} \\
& \sum_{j=1}^{d} \boldsymbol{\kappa}_i^{(1)T}\mathbf{L}_2\mathbf{M}_G(jj)\mathbf{L}_2^T\boldsymbol{\kappa}_j^{(2)} \begin{cases} \geq c_{ij} & \text{if } y_i = y_j \\ \leq c_{ij} & \text{otherwise} \end{cases} \\
& \operatorname{tr}(\boldsymbol{\Gamma}(\mathbf{K})\mathbf{M}_G(ji)) = \delta_{ji}, i, j = 1, \cdots, d \qquad (42) \\
& \mathbf{M}_G = \mathbf{M}_G^T, \\
& \begin{bmatrix} \mathbf{M}_G & \text{vec}(\mathbf{G}) \\ \text{vec}(\mathbf{G})^T & 1 \end{bmatrix} \succeq 0, j = 1, \cdots, d \qquad (43)
\end{aligned}$$

where δ_{ji} denotes the Kronecker delta and $\text{vec}(\mathbf{G})$ denotes the vectorization (column by column) of matrix $\mathbf{G}$.

With this relaxation, the d^2 scalar equations in Eq. (8) are all kept in Eq. (42). Compared with Eq. (26), the number of constraints d^2 are so large that it is practically intractable. Worse still, as defined in this relaxation, the $\mathbf{M}_G$ is a huge rank-one matrix of size $2nd \times 2nd$, which is well beyond the capacity of current solvers.

B. ALTERNATING OPTIMIZATION

In this section, the derivation details of the proposed alternating optimization method in Section 4 are presented.

B.1 Updating $\mathbf{M}_G$

After obtaining the large scale SDP problem, the following modified **EXT** relaxation [23] is obtained by dropping the last positive semidefinite constraint. We modify the **EXT** relaxation to include an extra $\operatorname{tr}(\mathbf{G}^T\mathbf{M}_G\mathbf{G})$ term, which links the constraints between the augmented variable $\mathbf{M}_G$ and the original variable $\mathbf{G}$. Even with the extra term, the modified **EXT** retains the property of a linear program and can be efficiently solved by an off-the-shelf solvers such as [9]. $\mathbf{M}_G$ is obtained by solving the following linear program,

$$\begin{aligned}
\max_{\mathbf{M}_G} \ & \operatorname{tr}\left(\mathbf{K}^{(1)}\mathbf{K}^{(2)T}\mathbf{L}_2\mathbf{M}_G\mathbf{L}_1^T\right) \\
& + \mu\operatorname{tr}\left(\mathbf{G}^T\mathbf{M}_G\mathbf{G}\right) \qquad (44) \\
\text{s.t.} \ & \boldsymbol{\kappa}_i^{(1)T}\mathbf{L}_1\mathbf{M}_G\mathbf{L}_2^T\boldsymbol{\kappa}_j^{(2)} \begin{cases} \geq c_{ij} & \text{if } y_i = y_j \\ \leq c_{ij} & \text{otherwise} \end{cases} \qquad (45) \\
& \boldsymbol{\kappa}_i^{(1)T}\mathbf{L}_1\mathbf{M}_G\mathbf{L}_1^T\boldsymbol{\kappa}_j^{(2)} \begin{cases} \geq c_{ij} & \text{if } y_i = y_j \\ \leq c_{ij} & \text{otherwise} \end{cases} \qquad (46) \\
& \boldsymbol{\kappa}_i^{(1)T}\mathbf{L}_2\mathbf{M}_G\mathbf{L}_2^T\boldsymbol{\kappa}_j^{(2)} \begin{cases} \geq c_{ij} & \text{if } y_i = y_j \\ \leq c_{ij} & \text{otherwise} \end{cases} \qquad (47) \\
& \operatorname{tr}(\boldsymbol{\Gamma}(\mathbf{K})\mathbf{M}_G) = d \qquad (48) \\
& \mathbf{M}_G = \mathbf{M}_G^T \qquad (49) \\
& \mathbf{G}^T\mathbf{M}_G\mathbf{G} = \mathbf{I}. \qquad (50)
\end{aligned}$$

The optimization problem presented in Eq. (44)–(50) is a linear program [23], hence a global optimal solution is guaranteed. In our experiments, we use the OPTI toolbox [9] to solve this LP problem.

B.2 Updating $\mathbf{G}$

Discarding irrelevant terms, the $\mathbf{G}$ is updated by the following optimization,

$$\max_{\mathbf{G}} \operatorname{tr}\left(\mathbf{G}^T\mathbf{M}_G\mathbf{G}\right) \ \text{ s.t. } \mathbf{G}^T\mathbf{G} = \mathbf{I}. \tag{51}$$

Note that this is exactly the canonical correlation analysis problem [13]. Note that $\mathbf{G} = \left[\mathbf{A}^{(1)T}, \mathbf{A}^{(2)T}\right]^T$ and $n > d$, $\mathbf{G}$ can be obtained by Incomplete Cholesky factorization of $\mathbf{M}_G$. Denote the SVD of $\mathbf{M}_G$ be

$$\mathbf{M}_G = \mathbf{U}\Sigma\mathbf{U}^T = \mathbf{U}\Sigma_1\mathbf{U}^T + \mathbf{U}\Sigma_2\mathbf{U}^T, \tag{52}$$

where $\Sigma, \Sigma_1, \Sigma_2$ are diagonal matrices with corresponding non-negative singular values on their diagonals, and Σ_1 contains the largest d singular values while Σ_2 containing the remaining ones. $\mathbf{G} = \mathbf{U}\Sigma_1^{1/2}$. In practise, an incomplete Cholesky factorization is favored due to its computational efficiency.

If You Can't Beat Them, Join Them: Learning with Noisy Data

Pravin Kakar
Institute for Infocomm Research
#21-01, 1 Fusionopolis Way
Singapore 138632
kakarpv@i2r.a-star.edu.sg

Alex Yong-Sang Chia
Rakuten Institute of Technology
1 George Street
Singapore 049145
alex.a.chia@rakuten.com

ABSTRACT

Vision capabilities have been significantly enhanced in recent years due to the availability of powerful computing hardware and sufficiently large and varied databases. However, the labelling of these image databases prior to training still involves considerable effort and is a roadblock for truly scalable learning. For instance, it has been shown that tag noise levels in Flickr images are as high as 80%. In an effort to exploit large images datasets therefore, extensive efforts have been invested to reduce the tag noise of the data by refining the image tags or by developing robust learning frameworks. In this work, we follow the latter approach, where we propose a multi-layer neural network-based noisy learning framework that incorporates noise probabilities of a training dataset. These are then utilized effectively to perform learning with sustained levels of accuracy, even in the presence of significant noise levels. We present results on several datasets of varying sizes and complexity and demonstrate that the proposed mechanism is able to outperform existing methods, despite often employing weaker constraints and assumptions.

Categories and Subject Descriptors

I.5.1 [**Pattern Recognition**]: Models—*Neural nets*; I.5.4 [**Pattern Recognition**]: Applications—*Computer vision*

Keywords

Label noise; probabilistic learning

1. INTRODUCTION

Great strides have been made in recent years in computer vision and machine learning due to the availability of powerful computing hardware such as general-purpose GPUs and cluster and cloud computing. This has been accompanied with an explosion in the availability of "big data" in vision as well as other fields. For example, benchmarking datasets in computer vision have gone from relatively small sizes of hundreds to a few thousand images (Graz 02 [33], Caltech 101 [14], etc.) to datasets containing tens of thousands of images (PASCAL Visual Object Challenge [13], CIFAR-10 [23]) to datasets containing hundreds of thousands of images (ImageNet Large Scale Visual Recognition Challenge [37]).

Considerable effort is involved in creating these datasets to ensure that the noise level present in them is reasonably low. For instance, Pammer, Kump and Lindstaedt [35] found that only 20% of the tags for Flickr[1] images correspond to visible concepts. This presents an obstacle to truly "on-demand" scalable learning from noisily annotated web sources. For instance, Fig. 1 shows some sample images obtained from a web search engine by querying for "bike" and "not bike". As observed, there are mislabelled instances in both cases which are likely to confuse the classifier during the training process. More generally for the on-demand setting, learning a new image category requires that: 1) the set of images for the new category be clean and 2) images corresponding to the positive class not be found in large numbers in the negative set. Either or both of these conditions involve some form of verification of the image labels to ensure acceptable levels of purity. If this requirement is somehow circumvented i.e. if it is possible to perform learning with little concern about the correctness of individual labels, it would result in a learning mechanism that is capable of ignoring noisy labels without any human intervention. In this paper, we present just such a technique.

Our main contribution in this work is the formulation of a novel neural network-based learning framework that incorporates *apriori* estimates of the noise probabilities in the training sets. We focus on noise in the output labels rather than noise in the input data (e.g. missing features). We show that these noise estimates need not be robustly determined for good performance, in general. These noise probability estimates are used to optimize the weights of the network, in which as the classifier becomes more confident about the output label of a training sample, the sample's influence on the learning process decreases, regardless of its class label. Experimental results demonstrate the efficacy of our technique where we outperform existing methods on several benchmarking datasets.

The rest of this paper is organized as follows. Learning with label noise in data has been studied from various perspectives and we review some of these in Section 2. We describe our proposed learning mechanism in Section 3. Finally, we describe the results of experiments on various

MM'15, October 26–30, 2015, Brisbane, Australia.

ACM 978-1-4503-3459-4/15/10 ...$15.00.
DOI: http://dx.doi.org/10.1145/2733373.2806231 .

[1]`http://www.flickr.com`

(a) Bike

(b) Not bike

Figure 1: Sample images from WebSearch Dataset [5]. Red borders indicate mislabelled images. Figures in this paper are best viewed in color.

datasets in Section 4 that demonstrate the efficacy of our technique.

2. RELATED WORK

Various approaches have been devised for learning with noisy data. A detailed review of these approaches can be found in [15] and we review some of the more relevant methods here.

Kernel methods: These approaches incorporate probabilistic models of label noise in kernel functions. For example, Lawrence and Schölkopf [24] utilize a robust Fisher kernel discriminant, but assume symmetric (equal across classes) noise. This causes the mean proportion of true positives to true negatives in the data to be very close to the same proportion in the original noise-free data, thus simplifying the learning process. In [27], the symmetry assumption is eliminated. Bootkrajang and Kabán [4] extend quadratic normal discriminant analysis to deal with mislabelled data, and show better performance than [24, 27]. The work of [31] modifies existing kernelizable loss functions to be robust to noisy labels and provides limited experimental results. We highlight here that most of the works in this class of approaches restrict themselves to datasets containing a few hundred samples due to computational complexity issues associated with the kernelization process. This makes them unsuitable for many modern computer vision datasets such as [23, 38].

Bagging/boosting: Another class of approaches learns an ensemble of weak classifiers via bagging and/or boosting. The inspiration here is that weak classifiers, though performing only slightly better than average, can give robust classification when combined together. However, common boosting approaches like AdaBoost [16] perform notoriously weakly when faced with outliers in the data [10]. Similarly, bagging approaches tend to average out the noise along with the signal and they generally perform slightly better than boosting alone in the presence of significant noise [10]. The authors of [22] propose a method that utilizes boosting followed by bagging and show significant improvements over both of the previous types of approaches. However, their technique assumes a symmetric distribution of noise in the data. We make no such assumptions in this paper and demonstrate that our method can handle both symmetric and asymmetric noise effectively. The work presented in [6] relaxes the symmetry condition of [22]. While good results are obtained for low-dimensional data, the authors assume that the true noise distribution is known. In contrast, our proposed method does not require accurate knowledge of the label noise distribution.

Active learning: Another widely-researched set of approaches use active learning or learning with an oracle [39]. These approaches begin learning with a small, clean dataset and query an oracle for the ground-truth class of a subset of unlabelled examples that will maximize the information gained about the training data. While various techniques have been proposed that employ different methods of deciding which unlabelled examples need to be queried, the emphasis on the cleanliness of the initial dataset and possibly, subsequent examples, make these interactive and therefore unsuitable for scalable learning.

Multiple-instance learning: A popular class of techniques that are specifically intended to deal with large amounts of asymmetric noise in the training data is multiple-instance learning. The original problem for this set of techniques was for drug activity prediction [11]. This was formulated as a set of positive and negative "bags" containing subsets of the training data as instances. The assumption is that positive bags contain *at least* one positive instance, whereas the negative bags contain only negative training data. Image classification has also been studied using various multiple-instance learning frameworks. In [29], a method using diverse density is discussed for natural scene classification. The work of [45] presents a multiple-instance version of boosting for image classification. Additionally, they also present a multiple-instance version of support vector machines in the same spirit as [2, 42]. While good results were reported, all these techniques follow the standard assumptions of multiple-instance learning above. This results in significant under-utilization of positive data at low noise levels in the positive data and suboptimal performance in the case of even low levels of noise in the negative data. The work of [25] relaxes the assumption on positive data allowing for a variable proportion of noise, but does not address noise in the negative dataset. Moreover, in order to enable the solution to be computationally feasible, the technique restricts itself to the use of only a few hundred images split into bags. The work of [44] uses multiple instance learning by modifying the error function used to train a neural network. This function uses the minimum (maximum) confidence of a positively (negatively) classified instance in a positive (negative) bag. Therefore, it underutilizes both positive and negative training data, with difficult instances from the latter not being used to determine the decision boundary. Our method does not impose such restrictions and utilizes all available data. [43] is a variation on the multiple-instance learning theme, that generalizes to completely unknown instance labels per bag. Nevertheless, it assumes knowledge of bag-level label distribution in training, while our proposed method does not need such assumptions about the data.

Neural network-based techniques: In this work, we use a neural network architecture to learn with noisy data. There are few works that consider noise-robust neural networks. [19] reviews some techniques inspired by the λ-trick [20] and the α-bound [9] in the context of neural networks. Additionally, variants of perceptron learning with margin τ [21, 26] are discussed, both independently and when combined with the above bounds. Experiments on several real and synthetic datasets reveal that perceptron learning with margin surprisingly performs the best in general, despite not having been explicitly designed for dealing with noisy labels. In the preprint work of [40], a similar noisy learning algorithm to ours is utilized and state-of-the-art results are obtained by using it as a single layer add-on while training entire deep convolutional neural networks (CNNs). The method also assumes the availability of significantly large clean training data which is used to switch between noisy and traditional learning during training in many scenarios. Our proposed technique does not make such an assumption as it has a different objective. We aim to recover the noise-free performance of a classifier by using only corrupted data, rather than improve the performance by augmenting the noise-free data as in [40]. A closely-related technique based on robust logistic regression (including a sparse realization for high-dimensional data) by alternating between updating parameters and noise estimates is discussed in [5]. In contrast to their method, we use a multi-layer architecture and demonstrate its effectiveness even in scenarios where the noise distribution is not robustly estimated. Additionally, unlike [40], we do not need to retrain the preceding feature extraction process, making it less computationally expensive to achieve similar or better performance. The very recent work of [8] presents an interesting approach to visual understanding, by using a clean seed dataset for training a CNN, and following it with a controlled fine-tuning on a possibly noisy dataset. Hence, it is similar in spirit to some aspects of the work of [40]. Additionally, by training an entire CNN from scratch using clean initial training data, it is not directly comparable to our proposed approach, which does not retrain any underlying "feature extraction" systems.

Although the above methods are often developed as general machine learning techniques, many of them have been applied to computer vision tasks of varying complexity. Examples of datasets used include [6, 23, 38]. Learning with noisy data also features in other fields where correspondences between input data and labels often tend to be noisy. Our technique presented in this paper is inspired by the work of Mnih and Hinton [30] which uses a similar noise model to correlate map and image data. As they focus on an image registration problem in their work, they incorporate translational noise along with the spatial smoothness of such data in their optimization framework. Our work, on the other hand, focuses on discriminative classification and does not impose such constraints. The authors of [34] also apply a similar noise model in the case of localizing events from natural text on the web.

3. PROPOSED TECHNIQUE

In this section, we discuss the noise model we employ and the proposed neural network-based learning architecture.

3.1 Modelling Noisy Data

Traditionally, discriminative classification of data models the conditional probability distribution $p(y|x)$, where x is the input data and y is the corresponding label. Generative models model the joint probability distribution $p(y,x)$ which can be used to retrieve the conditional distribution via Bayes' rule. Both these distributions implicitly assume that there is a noise-free correspondence between the input data and their labels. As discussed earlier, this assumption may not always hold. Hence, in this work, we consider the case of label noise where the labels of input data may be corrupted. For example, a keyword search for "boxer" images may return images of dogs or sportspersons, thus corrupting the positive training set. Similarly, noisy labels can also be found in negative datasets. Pruning such erroneous images manually requires considerable effort.

In our technique, we employ a different model to account for noise. In particular, we assume that the labels of the training set are *observed labels* $\hat{y}$ and assume the actual, unobserved *latent labels* y to be noise-free. The conditional probability of an observed label can then be represented as:

$$p(\hat{y}|x) = \sum_y p(\hat{y}|y)p(y|x) \tag{1}$$

For ease of exposition, we only analyse the case of binary classification below, although it can readily be extended to the multi-class case.

We denote the probability $p(\hat{y}=1|y=0)$ by q_0 and $p(\hat{y}=0|y=1)$ by q_1. Also, let the classifier output be denoted as $p(y|x)$. Then, we can denote $p(\hat{y}|x)$ as:

$$p(\hat{y}=1|x) = \quad q_0(1-p(y|x)) + (1-q_1)p(y|x) \tag{2}$$

$$p(\hat{y}=0|x) = \quad (1-q_0)(1-p(y|x)) + q_1 p(y|x) \tag{3}$$

We model $p(y|x)$ as the output $g(x)$ of a log sigmoid function i.e. $p(y|x) = g(x) = 1/(1+\exp(-\sum_j w_j x_j))$, where w_j is the weighting factor of the x_j input.

Learning a classifier generally involves the use of a cost or error function. However, noise in the observed training labels precludes the direct use of such an option in our case. We therefore choose to maximize the log likelihood of the observed labels, thus employing a probabilistic objective function. It is to be noted that [6] does utilize a boosting cost function modified in a probabilistic fashion. However, this penalizes very confident predictions to avoid overfitting which we do not observe to be a significant problem in our technique.

The log likelihood of $p(\hat{y}=1|x)$ can be written as:

$$\log p(\hat{y}=1|x) = \log\left(1+\frac{1-g(x)}{g(x)}q_0 - q_1\right) + \log g(x) \tag{4}$$

Differentiating this with respect to the weight to be learned, w_j, results in:

$$\frac{\partial \log p(\hat{y}=1|x)}{\partial w_j} = (1-g(x))\,x_j \frac{1-q_0-q_1}{1+\frac{1-g(x)}{g(x)}q_0 - q_1} \tag{5}$$

Similarly, we can write the equivalent derivative for $p(\hat{y}=0|x)$ as:

$$\frac{\partial \log p(\hat{y}=0|x)}{\partial w_j} = -g(x)x_j \frac{1-q_0-q_1}{1+\frac{g(x)}{1-g(x)}q_1 - q_0} \tag{6}$$

There are several interesting observations to be made from eqns. (5) and (6). For the noise-free case (i.e. $q_0 = q_1 = 0$),

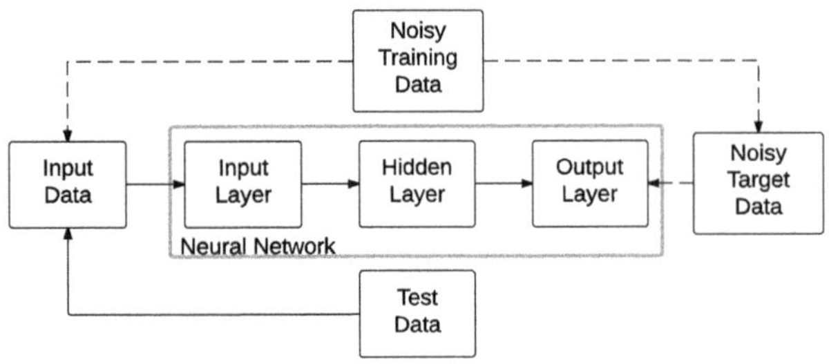

Figure 2: Graphical representation of neural network. Dashed lines indicate components active only during training phase.

eqns. (5) and (6) reduce to the case of standard logistic regression as expected. It can also be observed that for cases where $q_0 + q_1 = 1$, the derivatives are zero and from eqns. (2) and (3), $p(\hat{y} = 1|x) = q_0$ and $p(\hat{y} = 0|x) = 1 - q_0$. Correspondingly, no learning takes place as $\hat{y}$ becomes independent of x. For cases where $q_0 + q_1 > 1$, the derivatives switch signs for the same value of $g(x)$ as compared to $q_0 + q_1 < 1$, indicating that the weights are being moved in the opposite direction of the observed labels. This makes intuitive sense because $q_0 + q_1 > 1$ implies that at least one of q_0 or q_1 is greater than 0.5 causing at least one of the labels to be more likely due to noise than the data. In particular, we note that if $q_0 > 0.5$ and $q_1 > 0.5$, better classification performance can be achieved by naively switching the labels for the entire dataset.

3.2 Learning Architecture

We employ the above formulation of noisy labels in a two-layer feedforward neural network with log sigmoid units. A representation of this network for the training and test phases is shown in Figure 2. The input and hidden layers also include bias terms in order to improve the expression capability of the network. The gradients calculated in eqns. (5) and (6) can be easily backpropagated through the network. The weight update rule for the last layer of weights that we use is:

$$w_j \leftarrow w_j + \alpha \frac{\partial \mathcal{L}}{\partial w_j} - \lambda w_j \tag{7}$$

$$b \leftarrow b + \alpha \frac{\partial \mathcal{L}}{\partial b} \tag{8}$$

Here, $\mathcal{L}$ is the appropriate log likelihood chosen on the basis of the observed label $\hat{y}$. w_j and b represent the weights connecting the hidden (non-bias) and bias units to the output respectively. α is the learning rate that controls the rate of change of the weights. λ represents a regularization parameter imposing a l_2-norm constraint on the weights of the hidden units preventing them from growing too big. This helps the learning method to avoid overfitting the training data. Note that the bias term is not regularized as is typical in neural networks.

Initialization of the network is done with small random values for each weight. Training of this network is performed using a batch gradient ascent algorithm, summing the gradients of the log likelihood for all the instances in the batch. With noisy labels, it is difficult to determine when training should be stopped. While using a clean validation set may be a viable option (e.g. [6, 40]), it is not always the case that such a set is available. However, we empirically observe that our network is generally able to learn the labels of the clean training data first before trying to learn the labels of the noisy data, if at all. A probable explanation for this is that the network's weights are initially determined by the commonality of the clean data and then tuned to allow the noisy data to achieve their latent outputs. Therefore, in practice, we find that stopping training when the training label error stops changing or continues changing very slowly over a sufficiently large number of iterations yields good performance.

3.3 Network Parameters

As mentioned above, we use a two-layer neural network architecture with log sigmoid units and bias elements. The input layer is of size $n + 1$ where n is the number of input features, and the extra element is the bias. The number of input features depends on the dataset being tested on to showcase the versatility of our proposed technique. For non-image datasets, the data are already presented in feature form, so no processing is required. We manually decide the number of features for image datasets, where we employ the features from the fully-connected layer fc_7 of [18] that yield a 4096-dimensional feature vector. For the CIFAR-10 dataset, we use a similar principle using a 10-dimensional feature vector from the penultimate layer of [18]'s implementation. All feature vectors are normalized in the range of $[0, 1]$ over the training dataset. To ensure a fair evaluation, for all experiments in Sec. 4, we use the same types of features to evaluate our method and the existing methods.

We use a hidden layer of 101 units for all but two of our experiments, which consists of 100 units fully connected to the input layer and 1 bias element. The exceptions are Secs. 4.6 and 4.7 where we use 201 units to account for the larger number of classes being dealt with. This hidden layer is then connected to the output layer that consists of 1 unit for binary classification, and the number of classes in the data otherwise.

We use a regularization parameter $\lambda = 0.001 \times |m|$, where $|m|$ represents the size of the training batch. In our case, we split each dataset into ten minibatches for training. We use an initial learning rate of $\alpha = \frac{0.6}{|m|}$ for each dataset, and adapt it based on the magnitude of change in the training error. The extremely small learning rate is balanced by the minibatch learning process where the errors are aggregated prior to changes in the network weights. The learning process is terminated when the rate of change of the training label error decreases to less than 0.5% of the size of the training set over 1000 iterations, or the direction of change is reversed. In order to deal with the slightly noisy nature of minibatch learning, we compute the rate of change by averaging it over the last 50 iterations. The above parameters are determined empirically, and we find the performance to be only mildly sensitive to the parameter settings. For instance, varying the number of minibatches between 5 and 100 at 50% noise in Sec. 4.6 causes the accuracy to vary only by 0.3%.

4. EXPERIMENTAL RESULTS

In this section, we provide results and observations from testing the network on several datasets, and compare its

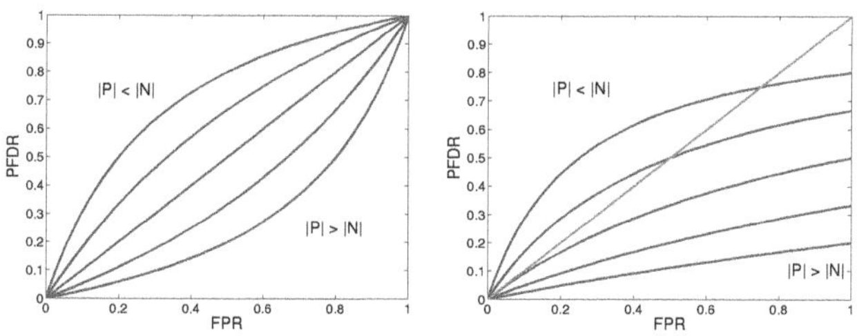

(a) (b)

Figure 3: Plotting positive false discovery rate (PFDR) versus false positive rate (FPR) for various relative dataset sizes and (a) symmetric noise, (b) asymmetric noise. Red line indicates corresponding FPR for visual comparison.

performance with existing techniques. Label noise is introduced in the experiments by randomly switching the labels of the clean data with the noise probability being evaluated. By doing this, we aim to decouple the dataset characteristics from the label noise and present results that are more relevant in exploring the effects of the latter.

We evaluate the performance of two versions of our proposed network architecture. The first version is used in all the experiments below and is called the *constant noise* (CN) version. In this version, we used fixed values for q_0 and q_1. In the case of noise in only the positive class (asymmetric), we set $q_0 = 0.5$ and $q_1 = 0$, whereas in the case of noise in both classes (symmetric), $q_0 = q_1 = 0.25$. These values are chosen as the mean of their feasible ranges i.e. $0 \leq q_0, q_1, q_0 + q_1 \leq 1$. Thus, q_0 and q_1 are the only parameters of this method and we use the above fixed values for all the experiments. The second version is additionally used in Secs. 4.4 and 4.5 and is called the *dynamic noise* (DN) version. Here, we approximate the true values of q_0 and q_1 in our experiments to observe how *apriori* knowledge may be used in improving the efficacy of the learning process. In order to avoid exact estimates of the noise present in the training dataset, we set q_0 and q_1 as the positive and negative false discovery rates (PFDR/NFDR) respectively, whereas they actually correspond to the false positive and negative rates (FPR/FNR) in eqns. (6) and (5) respectively. Note that FPR = FP/(FP+TN), while PFDR = FP/(FP+TP), and similarly for FNR and NFDR. The relationship between the two can be observed in Fig. 3. As can be seen, except when the positive and negative classes equal in size and have the same amount of noise, PFDR underestimates or overestimates FPR. In sum, we use fixed values based on feasible ranges for the noise probabilities in all our experiments, and also provide results that utilize optional, approximate, apriori noise estimates to possibly further refine results.

We use the default parameters of all the evaluated techniques in this section. This is because: a) we do not presuppose the availability of a clean validation set for parameter tuning and b) some parameters may be sensitive to the generally unknown noise level. For example, in Sec. 4.5, linear SVMs in the case of symmetric noise have their best accuracy (0.968) at a cost $c = 10^{-2}$ for 10% noise, but at $c = 10^{-4}$ (0.896) for 40% noise. At the higher noise, $c = 10^{-2}$ gives accuracy 0.728.

Method \ q	0	0.05	0.1	0.15	0.25
$\tau \times \lambda$ Last	0.968	0.897	0.849	0.816	0.711
$\tau \times \lambda$ Longest	**0.973**	0.899	0.846	0.807	0.704
$\tau \times \lambda$ Voted	0.968	0.897	0.849	0.821	0.706
$\tau \times \alpha$ Last	0.97	0.899	0.858	0.817	0.711
$\tau \times \alpha$ Longest	0.968	0.899	0.855	0.817	0.706
$\tau \times \alpha$ Voted	0.97	0.902	0.856	0.816	0.711
SNN	0.953	0.895	0.850	0.807	0.742
Proposed (CN)	0.955	**0.933**	**0.903**	**0.873**	**0.832**

Table 1: Accuracy on synthetic dataset of [19]. Gray cells indicate best performance of all techniques in [19]; bold text indicates best performance overall.

4.1 50-dimensional synthetic data

First, we evaluate the performance of our technique on a dataset with synthetic noise. This is done on the dataset of [19] which compares multiple noisy perceptron learning techniques as well as their combinations and variants (last state, longest survivor and voted perceptron). The authors provide detailed results for the case of 50-dimensional data and we report the performance of our proposed technique on the same data. We also compare the performance of a standard neural network (SNN) that uses the same architecture as in our case, but effectively sets $q_0 = q_1 = 0$, reducing it to typical logistic regression in this and subsequent experiments.

The dataset consists of $n = 600$ 50-dimensional samples with a 540/60 training/testing split. For a sample x_i, each attribute is a random integer selected uniformly in the range [-10,10]. A weight vector w is generated by a Bernoulli process with parameter $p = 0.5$. A separation threshold $\theta = \frac{0.5}{n} \sum_i |\langle w, x_i \rangle|$ is also determined. The labels of the data are randomly corrupted by switching them with the desired probability.

The performance of our proposed technique is presented in Table 1. The accuracy for different levels of noise in the data is reported in our case for the CN version of our architecture. This is compared against the results of combinations and variants from the evaluation reported in [19] as well as the SNN. We note that [19] obtained their results by searching across combinations of parameters on the test data, and no single technique is able to provide the best result at every noise level. Our proposed method on the other hand, is able to achieve the best performance on all cases with noise, degrading gracefully as the noise levels increase. Note that, unlike [19], we do not search for optimal parameters on the test data, and we use the CN version of our proposed technique. For the noise-free case, the fixed values of q_0 and q_1 likely eliminate a significant amount of noise-free samples, but the performance of the CN version still remains quite competitive and comparable to the SNN.

4.2 UCI Datasets

In this subsection, we compare the performance of the CN version of our proposed technique against that of [6] over several datasets and configurations from the latter. The datasets that we use are from the popular UCI repository [3] where we use the Banana, Diabetes and Heart datasets from the repository for comparison.

Dataset	+ve samples	-ve samples	Dimensions	Noise	[6]	SNN	Proposed (CN)
Banana	2375	2924	2	10% asym.	**12.55**	14.82	14.87
				30% asym.	**14.27**	16.54	14.28
				10% sym.	**12.94**	15.13	14.12
				30% sym.	**14.47**	16.57	16.06
Diabetes	268	500	8	10% asym.	25.57	25.32	**25.07**
				30% asym.	30.20	32.90	**22.73**
				10% sym.	25.63	25.54	**23.64**
				30% sym.	29.57	27.27	**27.01**
Heart	120	150	13	10% asym.	22.20	**19.14**	20.74
				30% asym.	24.30	32.10	**14.07**
				10% sym.	20.30	17.90	**14.81**
				30% sym.	22.60	24.07	**17.04**

Table 2: Errors on UCI datasets compared with [6]

Dataset	Noise	$\tilde{\ell}_{log}$[31]	C-SVM [31]	Proposed (CN)
Diabetes	20% sym.	76.04	66.41	**76.62**
	40% sym.	65.89	65.89	**66.09**
	30%+,10%-	**75.52**	66.41	74.46
Heart	20% sym.	**82.96**	61.48	80.67
	40% sym.	57.04	54.81	**64.04**
	30%+,10%-	**84.44**	57.04	78.93

Table 3: Accuracy on UCI datasets compared with [31]

The results for [6] are provided for their robust boosting with robust learner configuration where [6] assumes that the noise probabilities are accurately known. On the other hand, in our case, we use fixed values for q_0 and q_1 as discussed above. We report the comparison results in Table 2. As can be seen, we significantly improve the classification accuracy on two of the datasets and achieve comparable performance on the remaining two-dimensional one, despite not incorporating knowledge of noise probabilities in our CN learning framework. It is also to be noted that we perform better than SNN across most noise levels, despite our method adopting an identical network architecture, but with the proposed objective function. This demonstrate the effectiveness of our proposed method to be robust against noise.

It is to be noted that the authors of [31] also perform a few experiments on these datasets, but with different noise levels and train/test splits. Moreover, they tune the parameters of their algorithms using cross-validation, whereas we maintain fixed noise level estimates in all our experiments with the CN version of our proposed architecture. The comparative performance can be found in Table 3. It can be seen that despite the weaker constraints of our method, its accuracy remains quite competitive with that of [31].

4.3 WebSearch Dataset

We compare the performance of our proposed method against that of [5] when applied to images. For this, we utilize their WebSearch dataset that consists of 1030 images obtained by searching for "bike" and "not bike" on the internet. Manual inspection of the retrieved images shows that 183 of them are mislabelled, corresponding to about 20% symmetric noise in the dataset. In other words, the dataset contains about 20% label noise in its original form with no synthetic noise added.

In the original work of [5], the authors used a combination of SIFT [28] and LBP [32], but do not provide details about the parameter configuration. In order to ensure fairness in evaluation of the algorithms, we extract deep learning features (4096-dimensional output of fc_7 layer from [18]'s deep network) from the training data. We apply our proposed method as well as the algorithm of [5] on these features. 50 independent repetitions of the experiment are performed, with 90% of the data randomly selected for training and the remaining for testing. The label knowledge obtained by manual inspection is only used during the testing phase for evaluation. While [5] achieves an error of 15.67%±0.04 with the original features, this improves to 11.94%±0.03 by using deep learning features. Our proposed method's CN version attains a lower error of 9.81%±0.03. This is also found to be statistically significant at the 5% level from a 2-sample t-test. In the same setting, the SNN achieves an error of 11.41%±0.02, which is comparable to that of [5].

For a more thorough analysis, we modify this dataset further by adding synthetic label noise and/or correcting the mislabelled images. This allows us to observe the performance of the techniques on other noise levels as well, as shown in Table 4. It can be seen that our proposed method significantly outperforms the other techniques at both lower and higher levels of noise. It is significant that the proposed method is able to outperform the SNN, which has the same network architecture but a standard objective function, thus highlighting the robustness of our proposed method to label noise.

4.4 Graz 02 Dataset

We compare the performance of our proposed architecture with that of standard neural network (SNN) learning on the widely used Graz 02 image dataset [33]. SNN learning uses the same architecture as in our case, but effectively sets $q_0 = q_1 = 0$, reducing it to typical logistic regression.

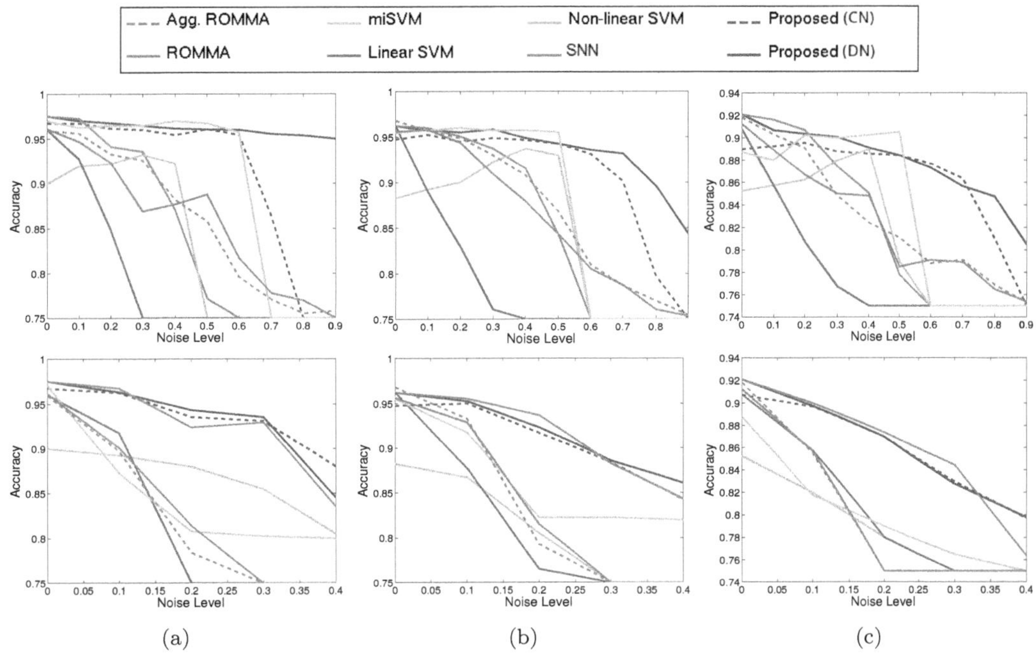

Figure 4: Results on Graz 02 dataset. Top row: Asymmetric noise. Bottom row: Symmetric noise (a) bike (b) person (c) car.

Noise	[5]	SNN	Proposed (CN)
10%	8.74%±0.02	8.09%±0.02	**5.83%±0.01**
20%	11.94%±0.03	11.41%±0.02	**9.81%±0.03**
30%	21.36%±0.04	11.00%±0.01	**8.09%±0.01**

Table 4: Errors on WebSearch dataset. Gray row indicates performance with existing, non-synthetic label noise.

We also compare results from support vector machines using the RBF and linear kernels, and multiple-instance support vector machines [2] with a linear kernel and bags containing ten instances each. We use implementations from [7] and [12] for these cases respectively. Finally, we evaluate the best performer of [19] on this dataset. We use a generalized version of perceptron learning with margin, ROMMA [26], that takes into account unbalanced data. As this is an online algorithm, we convert it to batch mode by the usual technique of running it sequentially multiple times over the data until convergence. We evaluate two versions of this algorithm - ROMMA and aggressive ROMMA. The latter penalizes weakly confident predictions more severely and is shown to provide a boost in performance.

The Graz 02 dataset consists of three categories of objects - bikes, persons and cars - with varied poses and occlusion levels and one "background" category consisting of images containing none of the above three objects. As mentioned earlier, 4096-dimensional image features obtained from a deep neural network are utilized. In order to improve performance and be consistent with the underlying deep neural network, a modified version of dropout [17] is also utilized that randomly sets a fraction of the hidden units to zero in each training epoch for all classifiers using neural networks. This has been shown to reduce overfitting and impact the performance positively.

We create a test set of 400 images from the four categories and use the remaining images for training. The results for training classifiers on this set of data are shown in Fig. 4. For the case of asymmetric noise, we observe that at low levels of noise, all of the evaluated techniques perform comparably. However, as the level of noise increases, standard classifiers such as SVMs start degrading rapidly in performance. Multiple-instance SVMs [2] show strong resilience to noise until moderate noise levels, but are observed to be trapped in local minima in solution space at higher noise levels. This limits their utility. We evaluate the DN and CN versions of our proposed method on the dataset and observe both versions to have equal performance until about 50% noise level. Beyond this, the CN version's performance rolls off quickly as it underestimates the level of noise in the data thereby allowing corrupt data to influence the learning process. On the other hand, the DN version gracefully degrades in performance.

For the case of symmetric noise which is widely acknowledged as a simpler problem than asymmetric noise, we observe that violation of the multiple-instance assumption causes [2] to almost immediately drop in performance at low levels of noise. We notice that the standard neural network performs reasonably well in the case of symmetric noise. This is due to the use of dropout which reduces overfitting and thus compensates for some of the noisy data. However, it is still not as effective as using either the DN or CN versions of our proposed noise-robust technique in most cases, and also does not perform comparably in the case of asymmetric noise.

4.5 Oxford-IIIT Pets Dataset

We also evaluate the performance of the above techniques on a more challenging image dataset [36]. The dataset consists of approximately 2500 images of cats and 5000 images of dogs of several breeds and in various poses. We create train-

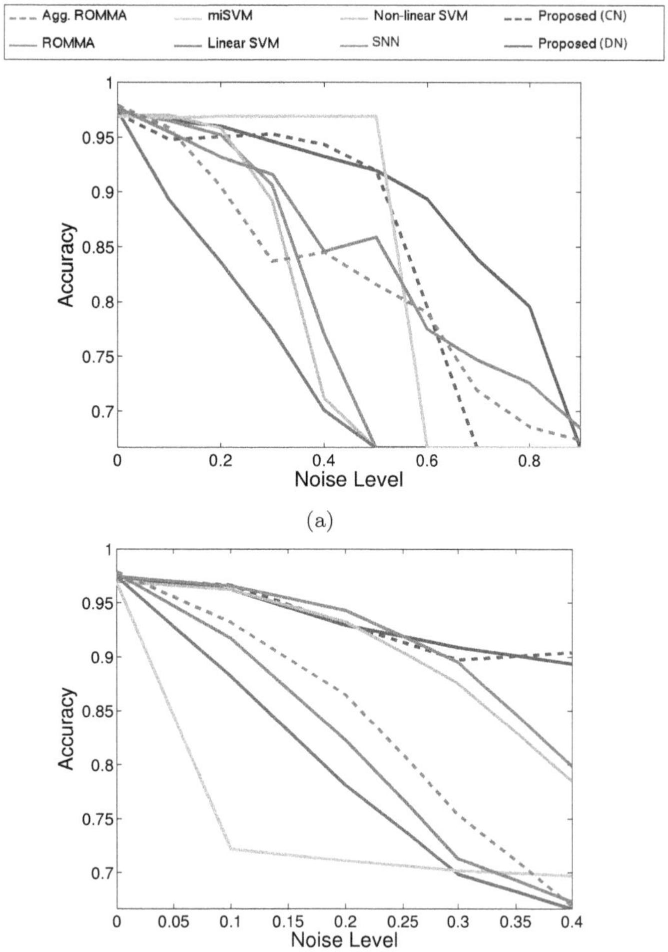

(a)

(b)

Figure 5: Results on pets dataset (a) asymmetric (b) symmetric.

ing and testing sets of 3000 images each from this dataset through random sampling, and the ratio of cats to dogs being 1:2. Then, we randomly flip the labels of a fraction of the cats or both cats and dogs to create the noisy data. The results of learning classifiers on such data are shown in Fig. 5.

It can be seen that in the case of asymmetric noise, both standard and multiple-instance classifiers perform weakly beyond moderate levels of noise. Although the performance of our DN version also degrades to a baseline, it does so in a graceful manner. Finally, it can be seen again similar to Sec. 4.4 that underestimating the noise level by a significant margin causes a sharp roll-off in performance. For the symmetric case, both our versions outperform other classifiers by considerable margins, especially at high levels of noise. Favorably, the two versions do not show much difference in their overall accuracies indicating that a weak approximation of the estimated noise in the data is sufficient to achieve good accuracy.

4.6 CIFAR-10 Dataset

We evaluate the performance of our technique on the CIFAR-10 dataset [23] consisting of 50,000 32×32 pixel color images distributed uniformly across ten categories as a training set, and a separate testing set of 10,000 images. The recent work of [40] presents a few variations of experiments on this dataset, including performance improvement by augmenting data from the TinyImages dataset [41] and learning the noise distribution of the data or estimating it using additional clean data. Their technique uses their linear noisy learning module as an add-on to Krizhevsky's 18% architecture [1] and then proceeds to essentially retrain the entire network to achieve their results. In our technique we use a multi-layer neural network add-on to [18]'s implementation of the architecture but only train our proposed module without modifying the rest of the network, thus incurring much less training cost.

We compare the performance of our CN technique against [40] in their noisy+clean data setting, where our technique should be weaker because it is agnostic to the split of the noisy and clean data. First, a deep neural network is trained using 10,000 images as clean data. This achieves 30% test error on the CIFAR-10 testing set of 10,000 images. Following this, another 30,000 images from the training set are selected and their labels are switched randomly to evaluate on various tested noise values (50% and 70%). Specifically, this involves selecting a label to be corrupted with a probability equal to the noise value being evaluated, and then changing the label to one of the other classes with a uniform probability. We then pass these images through the deep neural network, retrieve the raw scores from the penultimate layer and use these as 10-dimensional features for our noisy learning module. We use a 11-201-10 architecture incorporating bias elements and using the noisy labels from above for training. We still employ the CN version of our training, but with an important modification. For the multi-class case, q_0 is still estimated at 0.5, but because there are nine negative classes for a given positive class, q_1 is set to be $\frac{0.5}{9}$. Note that this is not adapting the noise estimates beyond acknowledging the multi-class scenario. In general for multi-class label noise, x% noise can be interpreted as x% of all training labels being incorrect. For n classes, this corresponds to a false negative rate of x%, and a false positive rate of $\frac{x}{n-1}$% per class. Note that this formulation reduces to the standard case of $q_0 = q_1$ for a binary classification scenario ($n = 2$).

In [40], results for three scenarios of the noise estimates are reported. The "true" scenario assumes that the noise distribution is exactly known. The "estimated" scenario uses the performance difference between the above noisy training set and the remaining 10,000 clean images to estimate the noise distribution before proceeding with training using only the noisy training set. The "learned" scenario attempts to separate the effects of noisy labels and the underlying classifier without using any clean data in the manner of the "estimated" scenario, and is thus conceptually the closest to our proposed method.

The performance comparison results are shown in Table 5. At 50% noise, the performance of our CN technique is comparable to their learned version despite not training the entire network with the additional images and using fixed values of q_0 and q_1. At 70% noise, our method achieves better performance as compared to [40], even against the estimated and true scenarios. Also, the significantly lower drop in performance of our method between the two levels of noise showcases its robustness to noise in the data.

Method	50% noise	70% noise
True [40]	**28%**	35%
Estimated [40]	29%	35%
Learned [40]	30%	40%
SNN	35%	36%
Proposed (CN)	33%	**34%**

Table 5: Test errors on CIFAR-10 dataset using 30,000 images at different levels of noise

4.7 ImageNet Dataset

Finally, we evaluate the performance of our technique on the ImageNet Large Scale Visual Recognition Challenge (ILSVRC) dataset [38] which contains 1000 distinct object classes against that of the SNN to demonstrate the effectiveness of our proposed technique even when dealing with a large number of classes. We conduct a preliminary examination using a smaller training set than the actual ILSVRC classification subtask, but still test the performance on the actual task test set. Specifically, we use the 50,000 image validation set as a training set and corrupt the labels by randomly reassigning them to other classes with a probability of 70%. Again, we use 4096-dimensional features extracted from a pre-trained deep network and use them to train our proposed two-layer network architecture in the CN setting. As in the case of CIFAR-10 above, we adapt q_1 to the multi-case scenario by setting it to $\frac{0.5}{999}$.

The performance is then evaluated on the 100,000-image ILSVRC test dataset. The SNN achieves a top-5 error of 0.700, whereas our proposed method obtains a top-5 error of 0.643, showing a significant improvement over using a standard neural network classifier when dealing with a significant amount of label noise across a large number of classes.

5. CONCLUSIONS

In this work, we develop a novel technique to incorporate the inherent noise in the labels of training data for learning a classifier. We assume the presence of latent class labels, thus separating the noise in the labels from the actual class distribution. We cast this into a log-likelihood optimization framework and use a multi-layer neural network to learn the classifier using backpropagation. Results are shown on multiple datasets and comparisons with several techniques are provided to show the effectiveness of the proposed technique. We observe that the proposed method outperforms several widely used techniques, performs robustly at significant levels of noise and often achieves state-of-the-art performance with lower computational requirements. We plan to investigate the use of larger datasets, alternative methods of noise estimation and deeper neural architectures to enhance learning in the future.

6. REFERENCES

[1] Cuda-convnet: High-performance c++/cuda implementation of convolutional neural networks. `https://code.google.com/p/cuda-convnet`.

[2] S. Andrews, I. Tsochantaridis, and T. Hofmann. Support vector machines for multiple-instance learning. In *Advances in Neural Information Processing Systems*, pages 561–568, 2002.

[3] K. Bache and M. Lichman. UCI machine learning repository. `http://archive.ics.uci.edu/ml`, 2013.

[4] J. Bootkrajang and A. Kabán. Multi-class classification in the presence of labelling errors. In *European Symposium on Artificial Neural Networks, Computational Intelligence and Machine Learning*, 2011.

[5] J. Bootkrajang and A. Kabán. Label-noise robust logistic regression and its applications. In *Machine Learning and Knowledge Discovery in Databases*, pages 143–158. Springer, 2012.

[6] J. Bootkrajang and A. Kabán. Boosting in the presence of label noise. *arXiv preprint arXiv:1309.6818*, 2013.

[7] C.-C. Chang and C.-J. Lin. LIBSVM: a library for support vector machines. *ACM Transactions on Intelligent Systems and Technology*, 2(3):27, 2011.

[8] X. Chen and A. Gupta. Webly supervised learning of convolutional networks. *arXiv preprint arXiv:1505.01554*, 2015.

[9] N. Cristianini and J. Shawe-Taylor. *An introduction to support vector machines and other kernel-based learning methods.* Cambridge university press, 2000.

[10] T. G. Dietterich. An experimental comparison of three methods for constructing ensembles of decision trees: Bagging, boosting, and randomization. *Machine Learning*, 40(2):139–157, 2000.

[11] T. G. Dietterich, R. H. Lathrop, and T. Lozano-Pérez. Solving the multiple instance problem with axis-parallel rectangles. *Artificial Intelligence*, 89(1):31–71, 1997.

[12] G. Doran and S. Ray. A theoretical and empirical analysis of support vector machine methods for multiple-instance classification. *Machine Learning*, pages 1–24, 2013.

[13] M. Everingham, L. Van Gool, C. K. I. Williams, J. Winn, and A. Zisserman. The PASCAL Visual Object Classes Challenge 2011 (VOC2011) Results. `http://www.pascal-network.org/challenges/VOC/voc2011/workshop/index.html`.

[14] L. Fei-Fei, R. Fergus, and P. Perona. Learning generative visual models from few training examples: An incremental bayesian approach tested on 101 object categories. *Computer Vision and Image Understanding*, 106(1):59–70, 2007.

[15] B. Frénay, M. Verleysen, et al. Classification in the presence of label noise: a survey. *IEEE Transactions on Neural Networks and Learning Systems*, 25(5):845–869, 2014.

[16] Y. Freund, R. E. Schapire, et al. Experiments with a new boosting algorithm. In *International Conference on Machine Learning*, pages 148–156, 1996.

[17] G. E. Hinton, N. Srivastava, A. Krizhevsky, I. Sutskever, and R. R. Salakhutdinov. Improving neural networks by preventing co-adaptation of feature detectors. *arXiv preprint arXiv:1207.0580*, 2012.

[18] Y. Jia. Caffe: An open source convolutional architecture for fast feature embedding. `http://caffe.berkeleyvision.org/`, 2013.

[19] R. Khardon and G. Wachman. Noise tolerant variants of the perceptron algorithm. *The Journal of Machine Learning Research*, 8:227–248, 2007.

[20] A. Kowalczyk, A. J. Smola, and R. C. Williamson. Kernel machines and boolean functions. In *Advances in Neural Information Processing Systems*, pages 439–446, 2001.

[21] W. Krauth and M. Mézard. Learning algorithms with optimal stability in neural networks. *Journal of Physics A: Mathematical and General*, 20(11):L745, 1987.

[22] A. Krieger, C. Long, and A. Wyner. Boosting noisy data. In *International Conference on Machine Learning*, pages 274–281, 2001.

[23] A. Krizhevsky. Learning multiple layers of features from tiny images. Technical report, University of Toronto, 2009.

[24] N. D. Lawrence and B. Schölkopf. Estimating a kernel fisher discriminant in the presence of label noise. In *International Conference on Machine Learning*, pages 306–313, 2001.

[25] W. Li, L. Duan, D. Xu, and I. W.-H. Tsang. Text-based image retrieval using progressive multi-instance learning. In *IEEE International Conference on Computer Vision*, pages 2049–2055. IEEE, 2011.

[26] Y. Li and P. M. Long. The relaxed online maximum margin algorithm. *Machine Learning*, 46(1-3):361–387, 2002.

[27] Y. Li, L. F. Wessels, D. de Ridder, and M. J. Reinders. Classification in the presence of class noise using a probabilistic kernel fisher method. *Pattern Recognition*, 40(12):3349–3357, 2007.

[28] D. G. Lowe. Distinctive image features from scale-invariant keypoints. *International Journal of Computer Vision*, 60(2):91–110, 2004.

[29] O. Maron and A. L. Ratan. Multiple-instance learning for natural scene classification. In *International Conference on Machine Learning*, pages 341–349, 1998.

[30] V. Mnih and G. E. Hinton. Learning to label aerial images from noisy data. In *International Conference on Machine Learning*, pages 567–574, 2012.

[31] N. Natarajan, I. S. Dhillon, P. K. Ravikumar, and A. Tewari. Learning with noisy labels. In *Advances in Neural Information Processing Systems*, pages 1196–1204, 2013.

[32] T. Ojala, M. Pietikainen, and T. Maenpaa. Multiresolution gray-scale and rotation invariant texture classification with local binary patterns. *IEEE Transactions on Pattern Analysis and Machine Intelligence*, 24(7):971–987, 2002.

[33] A. Opelt, A. Pinz, M. Fussenegger, and P. Auer. Generic object recognition with boosting. *IEEE Transactions on Pattern Analysis and Machine Intelligence*, 28(3):416–431, 2006.

[34] C. Pal, G. Mann, and R. Minerich. Putting semantic information extraction on the map: Noisy label models for fact extraction. In *AAAI Workshop on Information Integration on the Web*, 2007.

[35] V. Pammer, B. Kump, and S. Lindstaedt. On the feasibility of a tag-based approach for deciding which objects a picture shows: an empirical study. In *Semantic Multimedia*, pages 40–51. Springer, 2009.

[36] O. M. Parkhi, A. Vedaldi, A. Zisserman, and C. V. Jawahar. Cats and dogs. In *IEEE Conference on Computer Vision and Pattern Recognition*, pages 3498–3505, 2012.

[37] O. Russakovsky, J. Deng, Z. Huang, A. C. Berg, and L. Fei-Fei. Detecting avocados to zucchinis: what have we done, and where are we going? In *IEEE International Conference on Computer Vision*, pages 2064–2071. IEEE, 2013.

[38] O. Russakovsky, J. Deng, H. Su, J. Krause, S. Satheesh, S. Ma, Z. Huang, A. Karpathy, A. Khosla, M. Bernstein, A. C. Berg, and L. Fei-Fei. ImageNet Large Scale Visual Recognition Challenge, 2014.

[39] B. Settles. Active learning. *Synthesis Lectures on Artificial Intelligence and Machine Learning*, 6(1):1–114, 2012.

[40] S. Sukhbaatar and R. Fergus. Learning from noisy labels with deep neural networks. *arXiv preprint arXiv:1406.2080*, 2014.

[41] A. Torralba, R. Fergus, and W. T. Freeman. 80 million tiny images: A large data set for nonparametric object and scene recognition. *IEEE Transactions on Pattern Analysis and Machine Intelligence*, 30(11):1958–1970, 2008.

[42] S. Vijayanarasimhan and K. Grauman. Keywords to visual categories: Multiple-instance learning forweakly supervised object categorization. In *IEEE Conference on Computer Vision and Pattern Recognition*, pages 1–8. IEEE, 2008.

[43] F. Yu, D. Liu, S. Kumar, T. Jebara, and S. Chang. $\propto$-SVM for learning with label proportions. In *Proceedings of the 30rd International Conference on Machine learning*, 2013.

[44] Z.-H. Zhou and M.-L. Zhang. Neural networks for multi-instance learning. In *International Conference on Intelligent Information Technology*, pages 455–459, 2002.

[45] Z.-H. Zhou and M.-L. Zhang. Multi-instance multi-label learning with application to scene classification. In *Advances in Neural Information Processing Systems*, pages 1609–1616, 2006.

Searching Persuasively: Joint Event Detection and Evidence Recounting with Limited Supervision

Xiaojun Chang[1,2], Yao-Liang Yu[3], Yi Yang[1] and Alexander G. Hauptmann[2]
[1]Centre for Quantum Computation and Intelligent Systems, University of Technology Sydney
[2]Language Technologies Institute, Carnegie Mellon University
[3]Machine Learning Department, Carnegie Mellon University
{cxj273, yee.i.yang}@gmail.com,{yaoliang,alex}@cs.cmu.edu

ABSTRACT

Multimedia event detection (MED) and multimedia event recounting (MER) are fundamental tasks in managing large amounts of unconstrained web videos, and have attracted a lot of attention in recent years. Most existing systems perform MER as a post-processing step on top of the MED results. In order to leverage the mutual benefits of the two tasks, we propose a joint framework that simultaneously detects high-level events and localizes the indicative concepts of the events. Our premise is that a good recounting algorithm should not only explain the detection result, but should also be able to assist detection in the first place. Coupled in a joint optimization framework, recounting improves detection by pruning irrelevant noisy concepts while detection directs recounting to the most discriminative evidences. To better utilize the powerful and interpretable semantic video representation, we segment each video into several shots and exploit the rich temporal structures at shot level. The consequent computational challenge is carefully addressed through a significant improvement of the current ADMM algorithm, which, after eliminating all inner loops and equipping novel closed-form solutions for all intermediate steps, enables us to efficiently process extremely large video corpora. We test the proposed method on the large scale TRECVID MEDTest 2014 and MEDTest 2013 datasets, and obtain very promising results for both MED and MER.

Categories and Subject Descriptors

H.3.1 [**Information Search and Retrieval**]: Content Analysis and Indexing; I.2.10 [**Vision and Scene Understanding**]: Video analysis

Keywords

Video Analysis; Multimedia Event Detection; Multimedia Event Recounting

MM'15, October 26–30, 2015, Brisbane, Australia.
© 2015 ACM. ISBN 978-1-4503-3459-4/15/10 ...$15.00.
DOI: http://dx.doi.org/10.1145/2733373.2806218.

1. INTRODUCTION

To deal with the rapidly growing amount of internet videos, this work is focused on two basic tasks in video analysis, event detection and event recounting, and we aim at addressing the two *simultaneously* in a joint framework so that they will greatly benefit from each other. As we will see, the joint framework is particularly advantageous when training data is scarce, because of the information sharing between the two tasks.

In ***event detection***, a sequence of unseen videos is presented and the algorithm must rank them according to their likelihood of belonging to, say the *birthday party* event. Obvious applications of event detection include, but are not limited to, video categorization and retrieval. Here, we are interested in complex events, which may be characterized by several scenes, objects, actions and the rich interactions between them. Because complex events can be extremely complicated or even abstract, their detection, despite a lot of recent progress [5, 11, 16, 22, 41], is still in its infancy. Factors that add to the difficulty include: 1). Web videos are usually unstructured and do not follow any particular distribution; 2). Only a few positive exemplars are available for a certain event during training; 3). The evidences of a certain event can scatter anywhere in a video, and each can be hard to reliably detect.

The most commonly used technique for complex event detection is to aggregate low-level visual features and then feed them to sophisticated statistical classification machines. A recent trend is to employ, instead, semantic *concept* representations [11, 12, 23, 24, 34, 36], which are found to be more discriminative and interpretable. Since not all concepts are related to a certain event, and their representation could be imprecise, our first goal in this paper is to be able to automatically identify the few relevant semantic concepts for detecting a particular complex event.

Event recounting refers to the task of providing *comprehensible* evidences to justify a detection result, *e.g.*, why is this video classified as a "birthday party" event? Low-level features are less useful for event recounting since they are not interpretable, while high-level concepts can provide very useful cues, *e.g.*, this video is a "birthday party" event because semantic concepts like "birthday cake" and "blowing candle" appeared. While most existing works [18, 39] perform event recounting only as a post-processing step after the detection phase, we believe that a good recounting algorithm should not only explain the detection, but also be able to assist detection in the first place.

To this end, we propose a joint framework, illustrated in Figure 1, to simultaneously classify high-level events and locate semantic evidences for each complex event. After extracting a semantic, albeit noisy, video representation, we introduce a recounting model based on recent sparse regularizers [6, 32, 45] that can localize key evidences both concept-wise and temporal-wise, and

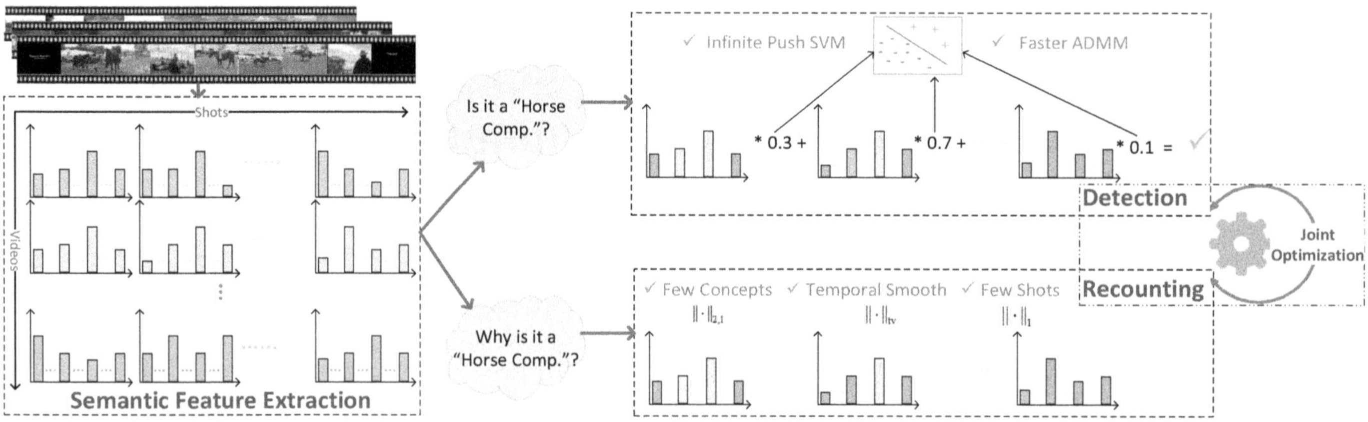

Figure 1: The proposed framework simultaneously conducts event detection and evidence recounting. Illustrated on the particular *Horse Competition* event. We first segment each video into multiple shots upon which we extract *semantic* features. Then we iterate between the detection model and the recounting model. We employ the infinite push SVM [31] for detection and develop a fast ADMM algorithm for it. Sparse regularizers are used to localize indicative concepts for recounting.

a detection model based on the infinite push support vector machine (SVM) [31] that greatly enhances the discriminative power. In a nutshell, our recounting model assists detection by filtering out noisy irrelevant information while simultaneously our detection model guides recounting by directing it to the most discriminative evidences. We further segment each video into multiple shots to exploit the rich temporal information, although this in turn creates a severe computational challenge, especially on large-scale datasets. Therefore, our second contribution is a significantly improved alternating direction method of multiplier (ADMM) algorithm. In contrast to existing works *e.g.* [18, 30], we prove novel closed-form solutions for all intermediate updates that allow us to remove all inner loops, resulting in tremendously improved efficiency. The per-step complexity of our algorithm scales only *linearly* with the problem size. We test our algorithm on the recent TRECVID MEDTest 2013 dataset [25] and MEDTest 2014 dataset [26], and achieve very promising results for both detection and recounting.

We summarize our contributions as follows:

(a). Unlike most previous works that address detection and recounting separately, we integrate event detection and recounting into a joint optimization framework, allowing us to exploit the mutual benefits of the two tasks, particularly when training data is scarce.

(b). We propose a very efficient ADMM algorithm that is key to perform recounting and detection jointly on large scale shot-level video representations.

(c). We conduct extensive experiments on the recent large-scale MEDTest 13 and MEDTest 14 datasets, and obtain very promising results for both detection and recounting.

Paper organization: We first review some related works on event detection and recounting in §2. Then we introduce our semantic representation in §3.1. The joint framework is presented in §3.2, and its optimization scheme is detailed in §4. Experiments are conducted in §5. Finally we conclude in §6.

Notations: We use $\|\cdot\|_F$, $\|\cdot\|_1$, $\|\cdot\|_2$ for the Frobenius norm, 1-norm, and 2-norm, respectively. For matrix A, we use the notation $A_{i,j}$, $A_{i,:}$, $A_{:,j}$ for its ij-th entry, i-th row, and j-th column, respectively. We split our m training videos into p positive exemplars $\mathfrak{P}$ and n negative exemplars $\mathfrak{N}$, where of course $m = p + n$. Frequently we will use A_+ to denote the positive part, *i.e.* $\max\{A, 0\}$, understood componentwise for vectors or matrices. The standard inner product $\langle A, B\rangle = \sum_{ij} A_{i,j} B_{i,j}$ is used throughout.

2. RELATED WORK

Complex event detection on unconstrained web videos has attracted wide attention in the field of multimedia and computer vision. A decent video event detection system usually consists of a good feature extraction module and a highly effective classification module (such as large margin support vector machines and kernel methods). Various low-level features (static, audio, *etc.*), *e.g.* the improved dense trajectories [40], already achieve good performances under the bag-of-words representation [35, 37]. Further improvements are obtained by aggregating complementary features in the video level, such as Fisher vector coding [27] and pooling [18, 19]. The latter approaches also try to exploit temporal information by decomposing an event video into short segments and selecting the most informative one for pooling. Unlike these methods, we aim at localizing *semantic* evidences that goes beyond feature pooling, and through a joint detection and recounting framework we achieve better performance.

A recent trend in complex event detection is to employ some high-level semantic representation, which can be advantageous in multiple aspects: 1). It leads to improved generalization capability and allows zero-shot learning (*i.e.* recognizing new events that are never seen in the training phase) [4, 12, 23, 24]. 2). It provides a meaningful way to aggregate low-level features. 3). It yields more interpretable results [11, 34, 36], hence may facilitate other video analysis tasks such as retrieval and recounting. Such semantic representations are usually trained on top of many low-level features, and have roots in object and action recognition [8, 14, 20, 42].

Although much progress has been made for complex event detection and video retrieval, semantic event recounting, which refers to the task of "explaining" a certain detection result, is relatively less addressed. A rule based approach was proposed in [36] to collect evidences, however, it worked on a tailored concept set which heavily relies on human knowledge. In a more controlled setting, [2] adopted object tracks and body-postures to generate textual evidences. By weighing the contributions of the individual concepts to the final detection score and mining the co-occurrence of different concepts, [18, 21, 39] performed event recounting only as a post-processing step after the detection phase. Interestingly, [21] obtained slightly worse detection accuracy when using the recounted key evidences to re-train the detection classifier. We believe this is because the event detection and recounting in [21] are not conducted *jointly* but in two separate stages. The recent work [34], which also considered simultaneous detection and recounting, is the most similar to our work. However, [34] modeled the evidence location as latent variables, which are harder to train when only few unconstrained videos are available. In contrast, our recounting model is much simpler and appears to be more efficient.

We would also like to mention some recent works on video summarization, *e.g.* [7, 10]. Unlike event recounting, video summarization is not oriented towards event detection: It merely aims at summarizing the vast information in a given video, a significant portion of which can be actually irrelevant to detection or recounting, though. How to effectively incorporate summarization information is an interesting direction yet to be explored.

3. JOINT DETECTION AND RECOUNTING

We start by introducing our semantic representation of the video ensemble, which unfortunately is usually noisy and not directly applicable for the recounting task. Then, we motivate our joint training protocol by separately detailing the recounting model and the detection model. The two models are combined into a joint framework to allow *simultaneous* detection and recounting.

3.1 Semantic Concept Representation

Videos, in their raw format, are represented by pixel values of each frame, which are not robust against small variations. Thus, in many video analysis tasks it is a common practice to first extract low level features, such as the improved dense trajectories [40]. To reduce the high dimensionality of low level features and increase their discriminative power, various pooling procedures can be applied on top [14, 35]. However, low level features usually do not have semantic meanings, thus are not suitable for interpretation purposes, such as the recounting task we consider in this work. In recent years, semantic representations based on *concepts, attributes,* and *actions* have been popular in video event detection, recognition and recounting [11, 21, 23, 24, 34, 36]. Usually, these semantic representations are trained on top of low level features.

In this work we represent each video by its confidence scores on c pre-defined concept classes $\mathcal{C} = \{C_1, C_2, \dots, C_c\}$. The construction of these concepts is detailed in Section 5 below. In order to identify the key *temporal* evidences, we further split each video into s shots/clips. Here, for simplicity, we assume each video has the same number of shots, but the algorithm can be easily extended to the heterogeneous setting. Each shot (in the i-th video) is encoded by a confidence score vector $\mathbf{v}_t \in [0,1]^c, t = 1, \dots, s$, where for each $k = 1, \dots, c$, $(\mathbf{v}_t)_k$ indicates the confidence of the k-th concept being present in the t-th shot. Thus, the i-th video is encoded as the matrix $V^i = [\mathbf{v}_1, \dots, \mathbf{v}_s] \in [0,1]^{c \times s}$, and we use $V = [V^1, \dots, V^m] \in [0,1]^{c \times sm}$ to represent the entire video ensemble. Here m is the total number of videos. Building on this semantic representation, our goal is to decide whether or not each video V^i belongs to a certain event, and also identify the key evidences to support our classification results, i.e., based on what concepts appeared in which shots our detection algorithm made its judgment.

3.2 The Joint Training Protocol

Motivations: Our joint training protocol for simultaneous event detection and recounting is motivated by the following observations: 1). The concept detectors we use are far from perfect, partly because of the relatively small number of positive exemplars and partly because of the cross-domain training. Therefore, there is a considerable amount of noise in our semantic representation, hence it is only reasonable to treat each semantic representation V^i as a noisy perturbation of some ground truth R^i. 2). Usually, only a few concepts are relevant for detecting a certain event [3]. For instance, in detecting the birthday party event, we would expect concepts like "birthday cake" or "blowing candle" to be highly discriminative while others would be less useful or even misleading (worsened by the imperfections of our semantic representation). Thus it makes sense to find a clean and discriminative representation R^i that has many zero rows, *i.e.* containing only few relevant concepts. Moreover, since each relevant concept likely appears only in very few shots and in a temporally smooth way, we expect each row of R^i to contain only few *consecutive* nonzero entries. 3). Event recounting is different from video summarization (*e.g.* [7, 10]), in the sense that not all concepts appearing in our video are equally useful. In particular, event recounting is detection oriented: We are only interested in identifying the few concepts, along with their temporal positions, that are highly discriminative for our detection module. In other words, event recounting acts more like a recurrent supervised learning task: It aims at both explaining and serving the detection module. Ideally, we would like our "clean" representation R^i to be highly discriminative.

Our recounting model and detection model take the above observations into account. Specifically, our recounting model "denoises" the semantic representation so that it only contains few concepts appearing in few shots in a temporally smooth manner. This denoised representation localizes key evidences and is fed into the infinite push support vector machine (SVM) [1, 30, 31] to gain more discriminative power. Unlike previous recounting works [21, 39], we conduct event detection and event recounting *simultaneously* in a joint framework.

Recounting Model: Our recounting model finds the latent "clean" representation (*i.e.*, ground truth) $R = [R^1, \dots, R^m]$ by solving the following denoising problem:

$$\min_R \tfrac{1}{2}\|V - R\|_{\mathsf{F}}^2 + \Omega(R), \tag{1}$$

where the regularizer Ω encodes our observation that only few concepts are relevant and they appear in few shots in a temporally smooth manner. Specifically, we use

$$\Omega(R) = \alpha\|R\|_{2,1} + \beta\|R\|_1 + \gamma\sum_{i=1}^{m}\|R^i\|_{\mathsf{tv}}, \tag{2}$$

where the group norm [45]

$$\|R\|_{2,1} = \sum_{k=1}^{c}\|R_{k,:}\|_2 \tag{3}$$

encourages many rows of R to be zeroed out (*i.e.* few concepts are relevant); the total variation semi-norm [32]

$$\|R^i\|_{\mathsf{tv}} = \sum_{k=1}^{c}\sum_{t=2}^{s}|R^i_{k,t} - R^i_{k,t-1}| \tag{4}$$

encourages piecewise constant entries (i.e. temporally smooth) in each row of R^i; and finally the 1-norm $\|R\|_1$ encourages sparsity [6] (i.e., relevant concepts appear only in few shots). By inspecting the support patterns (*i.e.* nonzero entries) of the "clean" representation R we can localize the key evidences hence perform recounting. However, so far the recounting model (1) is purely unsupervised hence may not be helpful for event detection. To enhance its discriminative power, we will couple it with our supervised detection model below. Note that we detect each event separately (as required in the NIST standard [25, 26]). Therefore, each event will have its own clean representation R, and may choose different indicative concepts. To our best knowledge, the formulation of our recounting model is new.

Detection Model: Our detection model follows the usual approach. It finds a discriminative linear classifier, parameterized by an appropriate matrix W, to distinguish the positive and negative "clean" representations R. From now on we split the m training videos into positive exemplars $\mathfrak{P}$ and negative exemplars $\mathfrak{N}$, with size respectively p and n. For each negative exemplar $j \in \mathfrak{N}$, the quantity $\sum_{i\in\mathfrak{P}} \mathbb{1}(\langle W, R^i\rangle < \langle W, R^j\rangle)$ counts the number of positive exemplars i that are ranked below j by the linear classifier W. These ranking errors with respect to each negative exemplar are combined to yield a loss that we aim to minimize. For computational tractability we upper bound the discrete 0-1 loss $\mathbb{1}(\delta < 0)$ by the *convex* hinge loss $(1-\delta)_+$, where as usual $(\delta)_+ := \max\{\delta, 0\}$ is the positive part. Since we usually pay more attention, if not exclusively, to the *top* of the rank list, we focus on minimizing the maximum ranking error among all negative exemplars $j \in \mathfrak{N}$:

$$\ell(W; R) := \max_{j\in\mathfrak{N}} \frac{1}{p} \sum_{i\in\mathfrak{P}} (1 - \langle W, R^i - R^j\rangle)_+. \quad (5)$$

Adding an appropriate regularizer Φ to control the model complexity, we obtain the infinite push support vector machine [1, 30, 31]:

$$\min_W \ \ell(W; R) + \Phi(W). \quad (6)$$

Usual choices for Φ include the (squared) 2-norm $\Phi(W) = \lambda\|W\|_{\mathsf{F}}^2$ [1] and the sparse 1-norm $\Phi(W) = \lambda\|W\|_1$ [30]. Since our "clean" representation R is already sought to be sparse, we will mostly use the 2-norm in our experiments, due to its better performance. If desired, loss functions other than the worst ranking error ℓ in (5) can also be used.

Joint Framework: So far the recounting model and the detection model are separate hence not helping each other. To integrate them, we propose the following joint optimization framework:

$$\min_{W,R} \ \ell(W; R) + \tfrac{1}{2}\|V - R\|_{\mathsf{F}}^2 + \Phi(W) + \Omega(R), \quad (7)$$

where ℓ and Ω are given respectively in (5) and (2) above. By coupling the two models jointly in the ranking loss ℓ, we expect to exploit the mutual benefits of the two tasks. Indeed, the detection model works on the clean representation R that is supplied by the recounting model, avoiding any noisy or irrelevant concepts. Conversely, the detection model also directs the recounting model to find discriminative evidences that are tailored for detection. More conveniently, the joint optimization problem (7) is biconvex, meaning that fixing either one of W and R results in a convex problem that is immune to local minima. Thus we will use a coordinate descent algorithm to learn W and R, one at a time and iteratively. However, standard convex optimization toolboxes cannot be naively applied here for two reasons: 1). The training ensemble has a large size $c \times s \times m$, putting a stringent time complexity on the numerical algorithm (preferably linear-time); 2). The regularizer Ω is a highly non-smooth function, leading to extremely slow convergence if not properly handled. One obvious remedy for the first issue is to apply a pooling procedure to aggregate the s shot-level information, but it leads to a significant loss of temporal information. Instead, we circumvent the computational difficulties by developing a significantly improved alternating direction method of multipliers (ADMM) algorithm in the next section.

4. THE OPTIMIZATION SCHEME

In this section we develop a much improved linear time ADMM algorithm for our joint model (7). First, we rewrite the ranking loss ℓ by introducing an auxiliary variable A for decoupling:

$$\min_{W,R,A} \ g(A) + \tfrac{1}{2}\|V - R\|_{\mathsf{F}}^2 + \Phi(W) + \Omega(R), \quad (8)$$

$$\text{s.t.} \quad \forall i \in \mathfrak{P}, j \in \mathfrak{N}, \ A_{i,j} = 1 - \langle W, R^i - R^j\rangle, \quad (9)$$

where $g(A) = \frac{1}{p} \max_{j\in\mathfrak{N}} \sum_{i\in\mathfrak{P}} (A_{i,j})_+$. Next we introduce the Lagrangian multiplier matrix Γ and a quadratic penalty term to eliminate the linear constraint (9):

$$\min_{W,R,A} \ \langle \Gamma, A + \mathcal{R}(W) - E\rangle + \tfrac{1}{2}\|A + \mathcal{R}(W) - E\|_{\mathsf{F}}^2 + \tfrac{1}{2}\|V - R\|_{\mathsf{F}}^2 + \Phi(W) + \Omega(R) + g(A), \quad (10)$$

where E is the all 1's matrix and $\mathcal{R}(W) = \mathcal{W}(R)$ is the matrix whose ij-th entry is $\langle W, R^i - R^j\rangle$. We use $\mathcal{R}(W)$ to emphasize the linearity in W when R is fixed and use $\mathcal{W}(R)$ to highlight the linearity in R when W is fixed.

The optimization variables in (10) are now uncoupled, and the usual ADMM algorithm iteratively solves them one at a time. At a high level, we switch iteratively between the detection model (parameterized by W, A) and the recounting model (parameterized by R), until they collaboratively reach a consensus. Interestingly, the subproblems w.r.t. W, A and w.r.t. R are completely analogous, thus largely simplifying the subsequent developments. We discuss each subproblem in more details below, and address some severe computational challenges there.

4.1 Optimizing W while fixing R

In this step we fix R as a constant and solve for W and A. The updates from the vanilla ADMM algorithm are as follows:

$$W \leftarrow \arg\min_W \tfrac{1}{2}\|A + \mathcal{R}(W) - E + \Gamma\|_{\mathsf{F}}^2 + \Phi(W) \quad (11)$$

$$A \leftarrow \arg\min_A \tfrac{1}{2}\|A + \mathcal{R}(W) - E + \Gamma\|_{\mathsf{F}}^2 + g(A) \quad (12)$$

$$\Gamma \leftarrow A + \mathcal{R}(W) - E + \Gamma. \quad (13)$$

Unfortunately, executing the above steps is not easy (except for the Lagrangian multiplier Γ). Previous work [30] proposed two dedicated iterative subroutines for the W-step (11) and the A-step (12), respectively. However, the whole algorithm requires three nested loops, significantly slowing down the convergence. Moreover, the numerical errors in the inner loops may also accumulate and affect the outer loop. Essentially the same algorithm (hence same drawback) was adopted in [18]. Here we eliminate all inner loops based on two novel ideas.

Firstly, the difficulty in the W-step (11) is mostly due to the (non-diagonal) quadratic term induced by the linear map $\mathcal{R}(W)$ (recall that R is fixed). Fortunately, we can bypass this difficulty by linearizing the quadratic term at the current iterate W, which is known as the inexact Uzawa step in the ADMM literature [13]. Namely, we replace (11) with two steps:

$$\tilde{W} \leftarrow W - \tfrac{1}{\mu}\mathcal{R}^\top[A + \mathcal{R}(W) - E + \Gamma] \quad (14)$$

$$W \leftarrow \mathsf{P}_\Phi^\mu(\tilde{W}), \quad (15)$$

where the first step is a simple gradient update with step size $1/\mu$ while the second step is a proximal update with respect to the regularizer Φ. The latter, usually referred to as the proximal map [44], is defined for any function f with parameter μ as

$$\mathsf{P}_f^\mu(\mathbf{x}) = \arg\min_{\mathbf{z}} \tfrac{\mu}{2}\|\mathbf{x} - \mathbf{z}\|_2^2 + f(\mathbf{z}). \quad (16)$$

It is a strict and natural generalization of the usual Euclidean projection operator (where f is the indicator function of some constraint set). For "simple" functions, the proximal map admits a closed-form solution, for instance,

$$\mathsf{P}^{\mu}_{\Phi}(W) = \begin{cases} \frac{\mu}{\lambda+\mu} W, & \text{if } \Phi = \frac{\lambda}{2}\|\cdot\|_{\mathsf{F}}^2 \\ \operatorname{sign}(W) * (|W| - \frac{\lambda}{\mu})_+, & \text{if } \Phi = \lambda\|\cdot\|_1 \end{cases}, \quad (17)$$

where the algebraic operations are componentwise. Thus, the W-step (14) and (15) can now be performed in linear time, without the need of any nested loop at all.

Secondly, using the proximal notation in (16) we note that the A-step in (12) is simply the proximal update $\mathsf{P}^1_g(-\mathcal{R}(W) + E - \Gamma)$. Surprisingly, we prove here that this proximal update in fact admits a closed-form solution, which, to our best knowledge, has not been derived previously. Our result is based on the following new theorem, where we recall that $\mathbf{z}_+$ denotes the positive part, i.e., $(\mathbf{z}_+)_i = \max\{z_i, 0\}$.

THEOREM 1. *If the function* $f : \mathbb{R}^d \to \mathbb{R} \cup \{\infty\}$ *satisfies*

$$\forall i,\ \forall \mathbf{z},\ \ f(\mathbf{z}) \geq f(z_1, \ldots, z_{i-1}, 0, z_{i+1}, \ldots, z_d), \quad (18)$$

then for all $\mu > 0$,

$$\mathbf{w} - \mathbf{w}_+ + \mathbf{u} \in \arg\min_{\mathbf{z}} \tfrac{\mu}{2}\|\mathbf{w} - \mathbf{z}\|_2^2 + f(\mathbf{z}_+) \quad (19)$$

$$\textit{if and only if} \quad \mathbf{u} \in \arg\min_{\mathbf{z}} \tfrac{\mu}{2}\|\mathbf{w}_+ - \mathbf{z}\|_2^2 + f(\mathbf{z}). \quad (20)$$

Note that Theorem 1 does not even require the function f to be convex: The condition (18) basically says that on each coordinate i, f attains its minimum at 0. Many familiar functions, for instance p-norms for all $p \geq 0$, satisfy this condition. The significance of the established equivalence in Theorem 1 is that it allows us to swap the positive part (a nonlinear operation) from an *optimization variable* $\mathbf{z}$ in (19) to a *fixed input variable* $\mathbf{w}$ in (20). This simple swapping can lead to enormous computational savings, especially when f is "simple". Indeed, for the A-step in (12), $g = f(A_+)$, where $f(A) = \frac{1}{p}\|A\|_{\infty,1}$ is the max norm of the 1-norms of each column of A. Since the proximal map $\mathsf{P}^{\mu}_{\|\cdot\|_{\infty,1}}$ has been derived in (nearly) closed-form in *e.g.* [29], applying Theorem 1 we immediately have a closed-form for the A-step (12):

$$A \leftarrow \mathsf{P}^1_g(\tilde{A}) = \tilde{A} - \tilde{A}_+ + \mathsf{P}^p_{\|\cdot\|_{\infty,1}}(\tilde{A}_+), \quad (21)$$

where $\tilde{A} = -\mathcal{R}(W) + E - \Gamma$. The computational complexity is linear after sorting [29], without any nested loop at all. In §5.1 below we empirically verify that our closed-form solution (21) significantly improves the nested loops in [18, 30]. We expect Theorem 1 to be useful for other applications involving the infinite push ranking loss.

To summarize, for fixed R we can perform the update w.r.t. W and A in linear time in a single step. The same idea can be recycled to update R, which we discuss next.

4.2 Optimizing R while fixing W

This step is analogous to the previous step where W is optimized. For brevity we only mention the few differences. Again we linearize the quadratic term induced by $\mathcal{W}(R) = \mathcal{R}(W)$ at the current iterate R, and we perform the following updates (for some step size $\mu > 1$):

$$\tilde{R} \leftarrow R - \tfrac{1}{\mu}\mathcal{W}^\top[A + \mathcal{W}(R) - E + \Gamma] + \tfrac{1}{\mu}(V - R) \quad (22)$$

$$R \leftarrow \mathsf{P}^{\mu}_{\Omega}(\tilde{R}) \quad (23)$$

$$A \leftarrow \arg\min_{A} \tfrac{1}{2}\|A + \mathcal{W}(R) - E + \Gamma\|_{\mathsf{F}}^2 + g(A) \quad (24)$$

$$\Gamma \leftarrow A + \mathcal{W}(R) - E + \Gamma, \quad (25)$$

Algorithm 1: Faster ADMM for solving JEDaR (7)

Input: $V, \alpha, \beta, \gamma, p, \Phi$. Initialize: $W, R, A, \Gamma, \mu > 1$.
repeat
  $W \leftarrow W - \frac{1}{\mu}\mathcal{R}^\top[A + \mathcal{R}(W) - E + \Gamma]$;
  $W \leftarrow \mathsf{P}^{\mu}_{\Phi}(W)$; // Equation (17)
  $A \leftarrow -\mathcal{R}(W) + E - \Gamma$;
  $A \leftarrow A - A_+ + \mathsf{P}^p_{\|\cdot\|_{\infty,1}}(A_+)$;
  $\Gamma \leftarrow A + \mathcal{R}(W) - E + \Gamma$;
  $R \leftarrow R - \frac{1}{\mu}\mathcal{W}^\top[A + \mathcal{W}(R) - E + \Gamma] + \frac{1}{\mu}(V - R)$;
  $R \leftarrow \mathsf{P}^{\mu}_{\alpha\|\cdot\|_{2,1}}\left(\mathsf{P}^{\mu}_{\beta\|\cdot\|_1}\left(\mathsf{P}^{\mu}_{\gamma\|\cdot\|_{\mathsf{tv}}}(R)\right)\right)$;
until *convergence*;

where the first step is a simple gradient update; the third A-step is solved using (21) as before; the fourth Γ-step is also straightforward (standard matrix operations). The second proximal update w.r.t. the regularizer Ω in our recounting model is more involved, and has not been considered in previous work. Fortunately, we prove that it can still be easily computed by decomposing the individual regularizers as follows:

THEOREM 2. $\mathsf{P}^{\mu}_{\Omega}(R) = \mathsf{P}^{\mu}_{\alpha\|\cdot\|_{2,1}}\left(\mathsf{P}^{\mu}_{\beta\|\cdot\|_1}\left(\mathsf{P}^{\mu}_{\gamma\|\cdot\|_{\mathsf{tv}}}(R)\right)\right)$.

Very crucially, all three proximal maps on the right-hand side of Theorem 2 have known exact linear time algorithms. By composing them we immediately obtain the proximal map for the sum regularizer Ω, completing the R-step in (23).

To summarize, for fixed W we can again update w.r.t. R in linear time in a single step, without any nested loop at all.

4.3 Combining the W and R steps

For fixed R, iterating (14), (15), (21), (13) by at most $O(\frac{1}{\epsilon})$ steps yields an ϵ-optimal solution for W [13]. Similarly, for fixed W, iterating (22), (23), (24), (25) by at most $O(\frac{1}{\epsilon})$ steps yields an ϵ-optimal solution for R. The two procedures can be alternated until convergence, however, we notice that they share the same A-step and Γ-step. Therefore it seems reasonable to combine the two procedures into one. Another way of thinking about the combination is that since we are alternating the two procedures it would be wasteful to wait until each procedure completely converges. Instead, we simply run each procedure for a *single* iteration and then switch to another immediately. As we observed in the experiments, this "eager" switching strategy works very well.

We summarize the combined and improved ADMM algorithm for solving our joint training protocol (7) in Algorithm 1, and we wish to point out that Algorithm 1 is very general and accommodates various regularizers Φ (*e.g.* those in (17)). Computationally, Algorithm 1 is very appealing since each iteration incurs only a cost linear in the size of the training data. To appreciate the efficiency of our algorithm, we compared it with the full algorithm in [30] (whose model requires $\alpha = \beta = \gamma = 0$ and $\Phi = \lambda\|\cdot\|_1$). In general 400x speedups were achieved even on moderate problem sizes (*e.g.* $m = 800, cs = 100$). This tremendous speedup is the key for us to train our joint framework on large real multimedia datasets.

5. EXPERIMENTS

In this section we conduct thorough experimental evaluations of the proposed **J**oint **E**vent **D**etection **a**nd **R**ecounting framework, abbreviated as **JEDaR**.

Datasets: We test on two real-world datasets: the TRECVID MEDTest 2013 [25] and the TRECVID MEDTest 2014 [26]. Both are collected by the NIST for the TRECVID competition. Each dataset consists of 20 complex events with 10 events in common. Specifically, the MEDTest 2013 dataset has events E006 to E015 and E021 to E030, while the MEDTest 2014 contains events E021 to E040. These events include *changing a vehicle tire*, *grooming an animal*, *etc*. Please refer to [25, 26] for the complete list of event names.

Setup: For all our experiments we strictly follow the ***10Ex evaluation procedure*** outlined by the NIST TRECVID event kit. According to the rules, we ***detect each event separately***, totaling 20 individual detection tasks for each dataset. For each event, we have ***10*** positive videos from the event kit training data, along with approximately 5,000 negative videos from the background training data. The testing data has about 23,000 videos. We report both event detection and recounting results for each event.

Competitors: We compare our method JEDaR against current state-of-the-art alternatives. Support Vector Machine (SVM) and Ridge Regression (RR) are the most widely used classifiers in the TRECVID MED 2014 competition among the top ranked teams and recent research reports. Therefore, the two algorithms are used as the baseline. We also compare to more recent state-of-the-art alternative methods, including dynamic pooling with segment-pairs (DPSP) [19], VD-HMM [37], and ELM [34]. All comparisons follow the same rules of the official TRECVID MEDTest 2013 and MEDTest 2014 data splits.

Concept detectors: 3,135 concept detectors are pre-trained using the TRECVID SIN dataset (346 categories), google sports (478 categories) [15, 17], ucf101 dataset (101 categories) [15, 33], YFCC dataset (609 categories) [15, 38] and DIY dataset (1,601 categories) [15, 43]. The improved dense trajectory features are extracted with the code provided in [40] and encoded them with the fisher vector representation [28]. Then, on top of the extracted low-level features the cascade SVM [9] was trained for each concept detector. We further split each video in the TRECVID MEDTest 2013 and 2014 datasets into s shots, using the color histogram difference as an indication of the boundary. We applied the pre-trained concept detectors to each shot and obtained a 3135-dimensional representation. The average accuracy of the concept detectors is relatively low due to the small number of positive training examples, therefore justifying our recounting model (1) which tries to *denoise* the noisy concept representations.

Parameter Tuning: Our Algorithm 1 has a few parameters and we tune them as follows. We use the recounting model (1) alone, without coupling with the detection model (2), to first tune the regularization constant α so that roughly $5 \sim 10$ rows of the semantic representation R are nonzero. Then we further tune β so that each row contains roughly 10 nonzero entries. These two parameters are fixed in our subsequent experiments. Next we cross-validate the parameter λ from the range $\{0.01, 0.1, 1, 10, 100\}$, and similarly for the parameter γ from the same range. We have conducted a sensitivity analysis and found the results to be relatively robust once the parameters are in a reasonably large region. The parameters for other competing algorithms are set according to their respective implementations.

5.1 Efficiency of our closed-form solution

We first demonstrate the efficiency of our ADMM Algorithm 1, where the key is Theorem 1 that provides a closed-form solution in (21) for the A-step in (12). Previous work [18, 30] dedicated a nested loop iterative subroutine for this step. We randomly generated the input (fixed) square matrix W with varying sizes, and compared the objective values in the A-step (12) (the smaller the better). In this section we set $\alpha = \beta = \gamma = 0$ since this is the

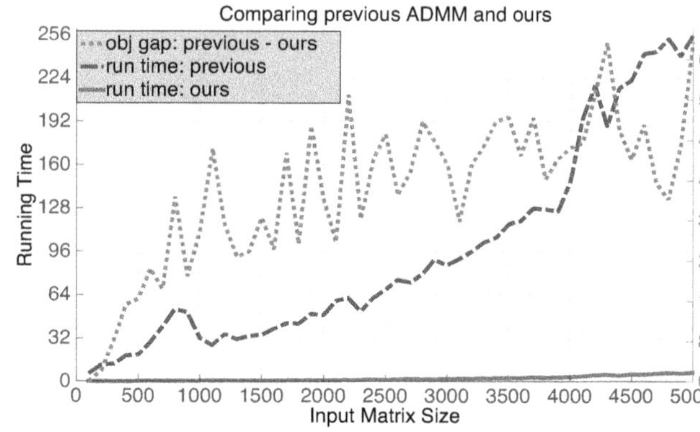

Figure 2: Comparison between our closed-form solution (21) and the previous nested loop iterative subroutine in [30]. Even after spending significantly more time (blue dashed vs. solid green), the latter still has not converged yet (red dot).

setting that [18, 30] can handle, although our algorithm efficiently extends to any α, β, γ, thanks to the new Theorem 2. We used the default setting in [30]: The maximum number of outer and inner iterations are 200 and 50, respectively. Figure 2 confirms the huge computational saving we enjoy thanks to Theorem 1. As can be seen from Figure 2, the running time of [30] increased sharply with the input size, but still failed to converge to the optimum. In comparison, our closed-form solution (21) only took a negligible time and returned a much smaller (in fact optimal) objective value. For the full ADMM algorithm, the difference is even larger, since we chose to linearize the W-step while [18, 30] used another nested loop. This tremendous speedup is the key to train our joint framework on the large TRECVID MEDTest datasets, especially when we segment each video into multiple shots to exploit temporal information and to perform recounting (see below).

5.2 Event Detection Result

As the common practice, we evaluate the event detection performance using the (mean) average precision. The results of our method JEDaR and the competitors (quoted from the respective papers) on both the MEDTest 2013 and MEDTest 2014 datasets are recorded in Table 1. It is clear that the proposed method JEDaR performs the best on both datasets. Comparing against the SVM baseline, we see that JEDaR significantly improves the detection performance for nearly all events, with mAP of 30.95% vs SVM's 20.73% on the MEDTest 2013 dataset and mAP of 25.21% vs 18.32% on the MEDTest 2014 dataset. We attribute the improvement to our joint training framework that integrates recounting with detection. Thanks to our recounting model, many irrelevant noisy concepts are pruned away, which in turn largely improves the detection performance.

Next we discuss the state-of-the-art alternatives that we were able to compare against. From Table 1, we have the following observations: 1). RR performs similar to SVM for most events, achieving for instance mAP of 18.78% vs 18.32% on the MEDTest 2014 dataset. This is in accordance with past experiences of several research groups in the TRECVID MED competition. 2). DPSP [19] improves RR (and SVM), with mAP 20.47% vs 18.78% on the MEDTest 2014 dataset. This is probably because DPSP identifies the segments that are most informative for detecting a given event and also dynamically determines the pooling operator most suited for each sequence. 3). VD-HMM [37] further improves the performance by discovering and assigning sequences of states that are most discriminative for a given event. Note that none of the above methods considered detection and recounting in a joint

Table 1: Experimental comparisons for 10Ex event detection on TRECVID MEDTest 2013 and TRECVID MEDTest 2014 datasets. Mean average precision (mAP) is used as the evaluation metric. Results are presented in percentages. Larger mAP indicates better performance. From the results we observe that the proposed algorithm outperforms the state-of-the-art competitors on both datasets, indicating the superiority of the proposed JEDaR.

	MEDTest 2013							MEDTest 2014					
Event ID	SVM	RR	DPSP	VDHMM	ELM	JEDaR	Event ID	SVM	RR	DPSP	VDHMM	ELM	JEDaR
E006	26.54	27.68	31.29	35.74	38.25	44.66	E021	11.96	12.58	11.24	15.57	14.75	19.53
E007	38.75	39.85	44.48	50.86	54.39	57.63	E022	2.76	2.87	2.72	4.84	7.54	8.77
E008	47.29	48.78	54.82	61.62	65.17	64.22	E023	27.47	27.72	30.75	38.32	41.29	46.26
E009	37.76	36.82	38.75	41.88	45.54	47.94	E024	3.17	2.98	3.12	2.86	3.16	3.98
E010	17.12	17.47	20.64	23.56	26.38	28.49	E025	0.81	0.92	0.87	1.05	1.12	1.27
E011	8.88	9.53	11.28	13.34	14.29	16.77	E026	4.16	4.48	4.85	5.42	5.88	6.23
E012	25.34	25.57	30.66	34.82	38.14	39.38	E027	10.58	10.29	12.56	11.25	13.96	15.62
E013	56.82	57.24	62.53	67.44	66.58	68.25	E028	16.91	18.64	20.82	22.43	25.25	27.41
E014	37.76	38.11	42.48	47.26	47.41	52.33	E029	11.78	12.47	14.28	15.12	17.84	19.63
E015	17.68	18.72	22.69	27.85	31.82	35.34	E030	10.96	11.26	13.65	14.88	15.92	15.26
E021	11.96	12.58	11.24	15.57	14.75	19.53	E031	55.98	56.74	61.82	64.24	67.85	69.41
E022	2.76	2.87	2.72	4.84	7.54	8.77	E032	22.89	23.57	24.64	26.48	27.43	28.28
E023	27.47	27.72	30.75	38.32	41.29	46.26	E033	38.74	39.85	41.47	44.28	46.54	46.27
E024	3.17	2.98	3.12	2.86	3.16	3.98	E034	25.88	26.59	27.83	28.74	29.78	31.63
E025	0.81	0.92	0.87	1.05	1.12	1.27	E035	34.85	35.28	38.86	40.63	42.86	45.32
E026	4.16	4.48	4.85	5.42	5.88	6.23	E036	13.28	13.75	15.28	16.45	16.52	19.27
E027	10.58	10.29	12.56	11.25	13.96	15.62	E037	33.15	33.74	35.87	36.12	47.81	49.25
E028	16.91	18.64	20.82	22.43	25.25	27.41	E038	0.92	0.85	0.78	0.91	1.14	1.43
E029	11.78	12.47	14.28	15.12	17.84	19.63	E039	26.94	27.36	31.43	23.22	28.72	30.58
E030	10.96	11.26	13.65	14.88	15.92	15.26	E040	13.25	13.67	16.54	21.41	15.83	18.62
mean	20.73	21.19	23.72	26.81	28.73	30.95	mean	18.32	18.78	20.47	21.71	23.56	25.21

framework. 4). Similar to our method, ELM [34] also considers detection and recounting jointly, and it achieves the second best performance, *e.g.*, with mAP 23.56% on the MEDTest 2014. However, it explicitly models the evidence locations which involve a large number of latent variables, making learning less efficient especially when training data is scarce. Overall, the advantage of DPSP, VD-HMM and ELM over RR and SVM suggests that finding important segments generally leads to better performance. 5). Lastly, the proposed method JEDaR achieves the best performance on both datasets. This confirms the benefits of our joint training framework, in which recounting improves detection by pruning irrelevant noisy concepts while detection directs recounting to the most discriminative evidences.

5.3 Event Recounting Result

In the TRECVID Multimedia Event Recounting (MER) task, a video description is defined as a video shot with a starting frame, an ending frame and a textual description. We use the proposed method to obtain such results as follows: We average the SVM weight W along the shot dimension and pick few top concepts for each event. These concepts are highly discriminative. Then, for each shot of the test video, we examine its top concept scores and decide if it is useful for recounting. The evaluation of event recounting is not easy, since a). there is no ground truth information, and b). few previous works can be compared with. Here we compare to the natural baseline which conducts detection and recounting in separate stages. Following the NIST evaluation pipeline [25, 26], we invited 10 volunteers to serve as judges. Before evaluation, we showed each judge the event category descriptions in text, in addition to five positive videos in the training set. Then, we randomly picked 10 positive videos from the test set, and presented informative shots generated by the baseline and the proposed method. The judges were asked to determine which shots are more discriminative. To make a fair comparison, we do not tell the judges which shot is generated by which method during evaluation. Two evaluation metrics are employed: 1). average accuracy, which measures the percentage of correctly labeled shots; and 2). relative performance, which counts judges' preferences of the baseline or the proposed method.

Table 2: Average video length, average shot length generated by the proposed method, and average accuracy derived from the judges' labels.

	MEDTest 2013	MEDTest 2014
Average Video Length	164.3 seconds	188.4 seconds
Average Shot Length	6.4 seconds	8.6 seconds
Average Accuracy	89.7 %	83.2 %

Table 2 summarizes the average length of the test videos, the average length of shots generated by the proposed method, and the average accuracy derived from the judges' labels. We observe that the proposed method achieves 89.7% and 83.2% average accuracy by selecting only 3.8% and 4.5% of shots in the original videos, respectively. This clearly demonstrates that our method is capable of localizing reasonable evidences that are accountable to the (positive) detection outcome and are comprehensible to humans. The results seem to indicate that the MEDTest 2014 dataset is more challenging than the MEDTest 2013 dataset.

The judges' preferences between the proposed method and the baseline are averaged and recorded in Table 3. It is clear that the proposed method is subjectively better for most of the events on both datasets. To verify, we show some of the recounting results in Figure 3 for the MEDTest 2014 dataset. These results again confirm that the proposed method successfully localizes the key evidences that also match human's intuition, for instance, as one would expect, "horse", "show jumping" and "animal" are all very indicative evidences for the *horse riding competition* event.

5.4 Sensitivity Analysis

We conduct some sensitivity analysis in this section, to draw further insights of the proposed joint training framework.

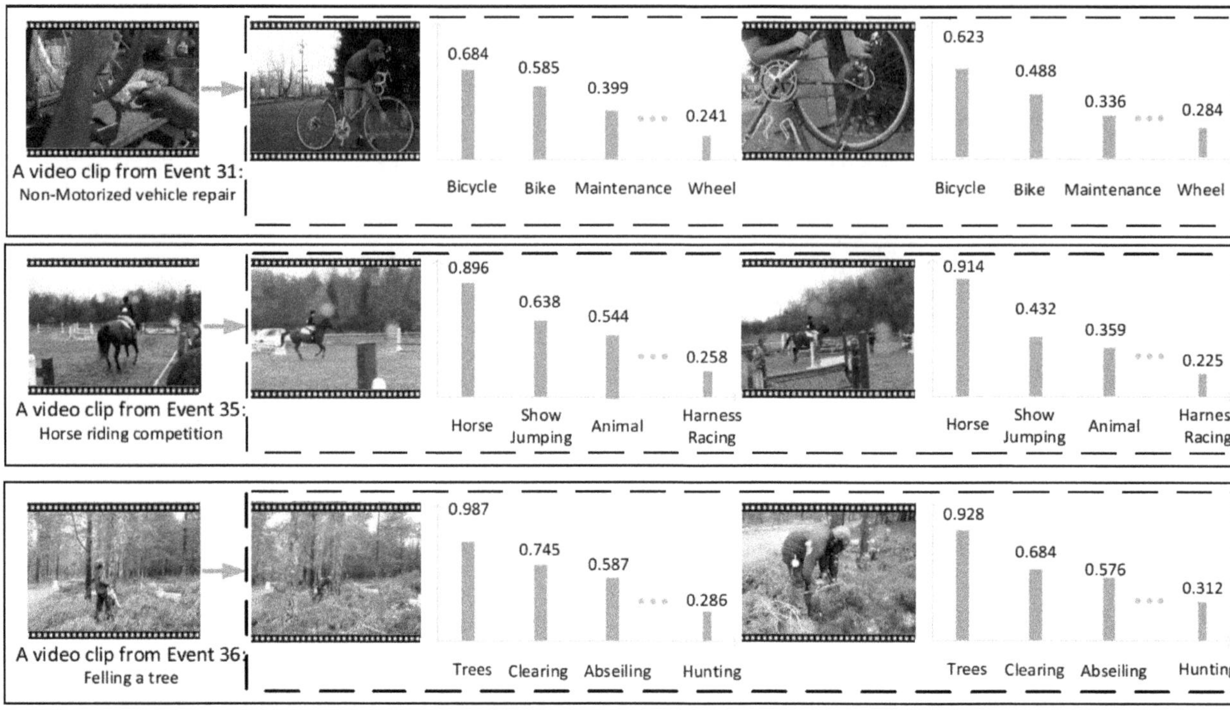

Figure 3: Example recounting results generated by the proposed method on the TRECVID MEDTest 2014 dataset. The video events are *non-motorized vehicle repair*, *horse riding competition* and *felling a tree*. The first two relevant shots are displayed.

Table 3: Event recounting results on the TRECVID MEDTest 2013 and 2014 datasets. For each event, we randomly pick 10 positive test videos and ask 10 judges to rate *better, similar, or worse* between the proposed method and the baseline. The results among judges are aggregated via averaging.

MEDTest 2013				MEDTest 2014			
ID	Better	Worse	Similar	ID	Better	Worse	Similar
E006	6	2	2	E021	8	1	1
E007	8	1	1	E022	2	5	3
E008	7	2	1	E023	4	4	2
E009	5	2	3	E024	7	0	3
E010	9	1	0	E025	5	2	3
E011	7	1	2	E026	6	2	2
E012	5	2	3	E027	7	2	1
E013	3	6	1	E028	5	3	2
E014	7	1	2	E029	4	2	4
E015	3	1	6	E030	3	1	6
E021	8	1	1	E031	8	0	2
E022	2	5	3	E032	6	2	2
E023	4	4	2	E033	6	1	3
E024	7	0	3	E034	5	0	5
E025	5	2	3	E035	3	1	6
E026	6	2	2	E036	4	1	5
E027	7	2	1	E037	6	2	2
E028	5	3	2	E038	3	6	1
E029	4	2	4	E039	3	0	7
E030	3	1	6	E040	7	1	2
Total	111	41	48	Total	102	36	62

Effects of Ω in recounting model: We first study the influence of different norms in the sparse regularizer Ω on MEDTest 2014 dataset. Recall that $\Omega(R) = \alpha\|R\|_{2,1} + \beta\|R\|_1 + \gamma\sum_i \|R^i\|_{\text{tv}}$ is used in our recounting model to enforce different structured sparse information about the evidences. We drop one of the three terms in Ω and record its influence on the detection accuracy. In details, we compare: a). without the group norm, *e.g.* $\alpha = 0$; b). without the ℓ_1 norm, *e.g.* $\beta = 0$; and c). without the total variation norm, *e.g.* $\gamma = 0$. The results are summarized in Figure 4. We see that the full method (*i.e.*, none of α, β, γ is set 0) consistently performs the best, indicating the usefulness of all three sparse regularizers. Dropping the total variation norm (*i.e.* $\gamma = 0$) deteriorates the performance the most, indicating the utter importance of temporal smoothness. Dropping the group norm (*i.e.* $\beta = 0$) affects the performance the least (on average). This is because the ℓ_1 norm also has the effect of zeroing out irrelevant concepts. The comparison against the separate training model, *i.e.* $\alpha = \beta = \gamma = 0$, is performed below. Overall the benefits of incorporating these sparse regularizers in our joint detection and recounting framework are significant.

Effects of Φ in detection model: As discussed in Section 3.2, the proposed algorithm directly applies to different regularizers Φ in the infinite push SVM detection model (6), including the usual (squared) ℓ_2-norm and the sparse ℓ_1-norm. We conduct experiments to compare their performances on MEDTest 2014 dataset. The results are summarized in Figure 5. We observe that $\Phi = \ell_2^2$ outperforms $\Phi = \ell_1$ for all events, leading to a significantly higher mAP. This is because the "clean" representation R is already sought to be sparse in our recounting model, thus imposing further sparsity in the detection model often hurts the detection performance. On the other hand, the learned SVM weight W for $\Phi = \ell_1$ is much sparser than $\Phi = \ell_2^2$, and may be advantageous when testing time is a bigger concern.

Joint vs. Separate: In our last experiment we validate the effectiveness of the proposed joint detection and recounting framework. By setting $\alpha = \beta = \gamma = 0$, we obtain a separate model that first performs event detection then followed by recounting. The results, summarized in Table 4, clearly demonstrate that the proposed joint training method consistently outperforms the separate training method on all events, usually by a large margin. We attribute this significant improvement to the coupling between detection and recounting: recounting helps detection by pruning irrelevant noisy concepts while detection directs recounting to more discriminative concepts.

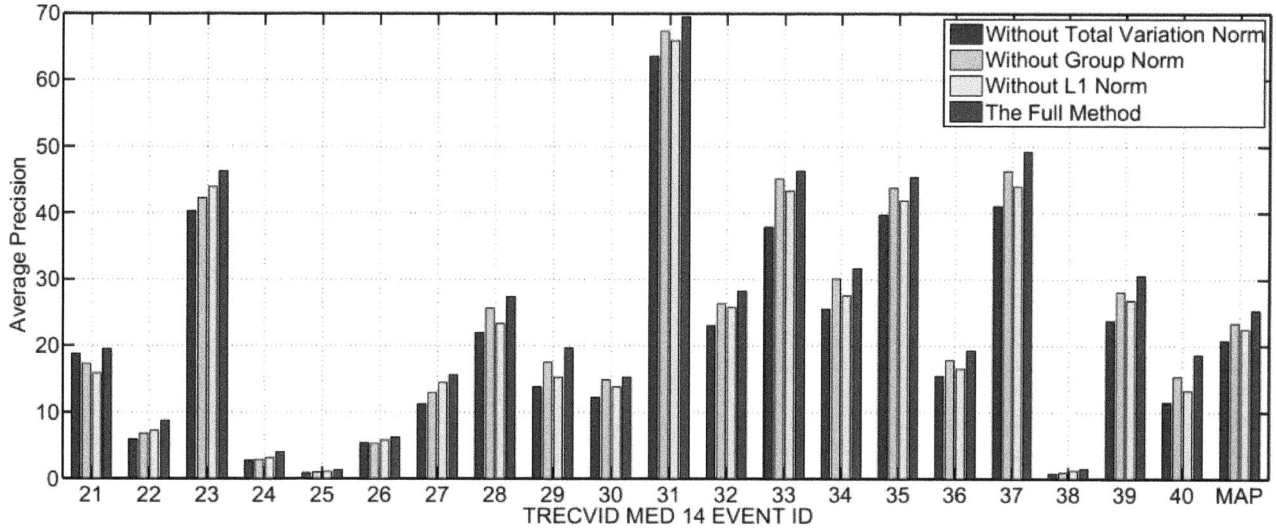

Figure 4: The average precisions of different sparse regularizers Ω on the TRECVID MEDTest 2014 dataset. Comparisons are made among our method by a) dropping group norm ($\alpha = 0$); b) dropping the ℓ_1 norm ($\beta = 0$); c) dropping total variation norm ($\gamma = 0$); and d) the full method.

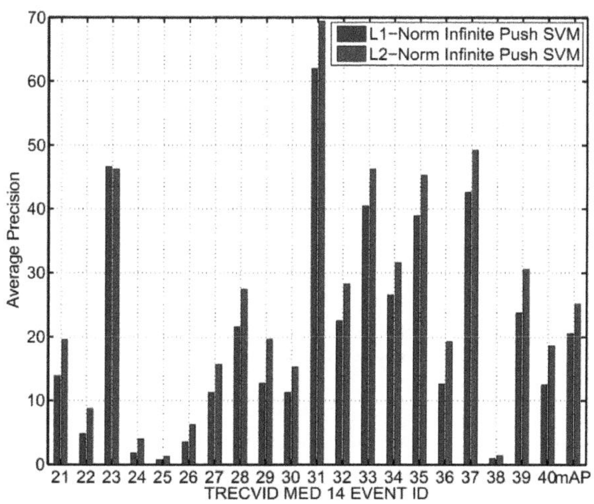

Figure 5: Performance comparison for the infinite-push SVM with $\Phi = \ell_2^2$ and $\Phi = \ell_1$ on the TRECVID MEDTest 2014 dataset. Results are presented in percentages.

6. CONCLUSION

We have proposed a novel joint training protocol to *simultaneously* conduct event detection and recounting. Based on a noisy semantic video representation, we couple a recounting model which aims at localizing the key evidences with a detection model which aims at enhancing the discriminative power. The recounting model assists detection by filtering out noisy irrelevant information while simultaneously the detection model guides recounting by directing it to the most discriminative evidences, conceptual-wise and temporal-wise. The two models are optimized *jointly* hence benefit greatly from each other. To address the computational challenge due to operating on the shot level, we significantly improve the existing ADMM algorithm by proving closed-form solutions for the intermediate proximal updates. Augmented with the Uzawa linearization trick we are able to remove all inner loops in previous ADMM implementations, without affecting the convergence properties at all. The proposed method is tested on the large-scale and challenging TRECVID MEDTest 2013 and 2014 datasets, achieving very promising results in both detection and recounting. In the future we intend to incorporate domain knowledge and supplementary information such as text and audio.

Table 4: Performance comparison of the separate training method (*i.e.* event detection only with $\alpha = \beta = \gamma = 0$) and our joint training method. Mean average precision (mAP) is used as the evaluation metric. Results are presented in percentages. A larger mAP indicates better performance.

	MEDTest 2013			MEDTest 2014	
ID	Separate	Joint	ID	Separate	Joint
E006	38.25	44.66	E021	12.68	19.53
E007	49.26	57.63	E022	5.86	8.77
E008	57.45	64.22	E023	41.35	46.26
E009	41.58	47.94	E024	2.73	3.98
E010	22.69	28.49	E025	0.76	1.27
E011	11.58	16.77	E026	4.46	6.23
E012	31.86	39.38	E027	10.26	15.62
E013	61.59	68.25	E028	21.48	27.41
E014	43.87	52.33	E029	11.64	19.63
E015	27.43	35.34	E030	9.58	15.26
E021	12.68	19.53	E031	61.58	69.41
E022	5.86	8.77	E032	22.57	28.28
E023	41.35	46.26	E033	39.58	46.27
E024	2.73	3.98	E034	25.57	31.63
E025	0.76	1.27	E035	38.58	45.32
E026	4.46	6.23	E036	12.74	19.27
E027	10.26	15.62	E037	41.84	49.25
E028	21.48	27.41	E038	0.98	1.43
E029	11.64	19.63	E039	24.86	30.58
E030	9.58	15.26	E040	13.98	18.62
mean	25.32	30.95	mean	21.28	25.21

Acknowledgment

We thank the reviewers for their valuable comments. This work was partially supported by the US Department of Defense, the U.S. Army Research Office (W911NF-13-1-0277), partially supported by the Intelligence Advanced Research Projects Activity (IARPA) via Department of Interior National Business Center contract number D11PC20068, and partially supported by the ARC DECRA project. The U.S. Government is authorized to reproduce and distribute reprints for Governmental purposes notwithstanding any copyright annotation thereon. Disclaimer: The views and conclusions contained herein are those of the authors and should not be interpreted as necessarily representing the official policies or endorsements, either expressed or implied, of IARPA, DoI/NBC, ARO, or the U.S. Government.

References

[1] S. Agarwal. The infinite push: A new support vector ranking algorithm that directly optimizes accuracy at the absolute top of the list. In *SDM*, 2011.

[2] A. Barbu et al. Video in sentences out. In *UAI*, 2012.

[3] S. Bhattacharya, F. X. Yu, and S.-F. Chang. Minimally needed evidence for complex event recognition in unconstrained videos. In *ICMR*, 2014.

[4] X. Chang, Y. Yang, A. G. Hauptmann, E. P. Xing, and Y.-L. Yu. Semantic concept discovery for large-scale zero-shot event detection. In *IJCAI*, 2015.

[5] X. Chang, Y. Yang, E. P. Xing, and Y.-L. Yu. Complex event detection using semantic saliency and nearly-isotonic SVM. In *ICML*, 2015.

[6] S. S. Chen, D. L. Donoho, and M. A. Saunders. Atomic decomposition by basis pursuit. *SIAM Review*, 43(1):129–159, 2001.

[7] P. Das, C. Xu, R. Doell, and J. Corso. A thousand frames in just a few words: Lingual description of videos through latent topics and sparse object stitching. In *CVPR*, 2013.

[8] A. Farhadi, I. Endres, D. Hoiem, and D. Forsyth. Describing objects by their attributes. In *CVPR*, 2009.

[9] H. P. Graf, E. Cosatto, L. Bottou, I. Durdanovic, and V. Vapnik. Parallel support vector machines: The cascade SVM. In *NIPS*, 2004.

[10] A. Gupta, P. Srinivasan, J. Shi, and L. S. Davis. Understanding videos, constructing plots: Learning a visually grounded storyline model from annotated videos. In *CVPR*, 2009.

[11] A. Habibian, K. E. van de Sande, and C. G. Snoek. Recommendations for video event recognition using concept vocabularies. In *ICMR*, 2013.

[12] A. Hauptmann, R. Yan, W.-H. Lin, M. Christel, and H. Wactlar. Can high-level concepts fill the semantic gap in video retrieval? a case study with broadcast news. *IEEE Transactions on Multimedia*, 9(5):958–966, 2007.

[13] B. He and X. Yuan. On the $O(1/n)$ convergence rate of Douglas-Rachford alternating direction method. *SIAM Journal on Numerical Analysis*, 50(2):700–709, 2012.

[14] N. Ikizler-Cinbis and S. Sclaroff. Object, scene and actions: Combining multiple features for human action recognition. In *ECCV*, 2010.

[15] L. Jiang, D. Meng, S. Yu, Z. Lan, S. Shan, and A. G. Hauptmann. Self-paced learning with diversity. In *NIPS*, 2014.

[16] Y.-G. Jiang, S. Bhattacharya, S.-F. Chang, and M. Shah. High-level event recognition in unconstrained videos. *International Journal of Multimedia Information Retrieval*, 2(2):73–101, 2013.

[17] A. Karpathy, G. Toderici, S. Shetty, T. Leung, R. Sukthankar, and L. Fei-Fei. Large-scale video classification with convolutional neural networks. In *CVPR*, 2014.

[18] K.-T. Lai, D. Liu, M.-S. Chen, and S.-F. Chang. Recognizing complex events in videos by learning key static-dynamic evidences. In *ECCV*, 2014.

[19] W. Li, Q. Yu, A. Divakaran, and N. Vasconcelos. Dynamic pooling for complex event recognition. In *ICCV*, 2013.

[20] J. Liu, B. Kuipers, and S. Savarese. Recognizing human actions by attributes. In *CVPR*, 2011.

[21] J. Liu, Q. Yu, O. Javed, S. Ali, A. Tamrakar, A. Divakaran, H. Cheng, and H. Sawhney. Video event recognition using concept attributes. In *WACV*, 2013.

[22] Z. Ma, Y. Yang, Y. Cai, N. Sebe, and A. G. Hauptmann. Knowledge adaptation for ad hoc multimedia event detection with few exemplars. In *ACM MM*, 2012.

[23] M. Mazloom, A. Habibian, and C. G. Snoek. Querying for video events by semantic signatures from few examples. In *ACM MM*, 2013.

[24] M. Merler, B. Huang, L. Xie, G. Hua, and A. Natsev. Semantic model vectors for complex video event recognition. *IEEE Transactions on Multimedia*, 14(1):88–101, 2012.

[25] NIST. The TRECVID MED 2013 evaluation plan. `http://nist.gov/itl/iad/mig/med13.cfm`, 2013.

[26] NIST. The TRECVID MED 2014 evaluation plan. `http://nist.gov/itl/iad/mig/med14.cfm`, 2014.

[27] D. Oneaţă, J. Verbeek, and C. Schmid. Action and event recognition with fisher vectors on a compact feature set. In *ICCV*, 2013.

[28] F. Perronnin, J. Sánchez, and T. Mensink. Improving the fisher kernel for large-scale image classification. In *ECCV*, 2010.

[29] A. Quattoni, X. Carreras, M. Collins, and T. Darrell. An efficient projection for $l_{1,\infty}$ regularization. In *ICML*, 2009.

[30] A. Rakotomamonjy. Sparse support vector infinite push. In *ICML*, 2012.

[31] C. Rudin. The p-norm push: A simple convex ranking algorithm that concentrates at the top of the list. *Journal of Machine Learning Research*, 10:2233–2271, 2009.

[32] L. I. Rudin, S. Osher, and E. Fatemi. Nonlinear total variation based noise removal algorithms. *Physica D*, 60:259–268, 1992.

[33] K. Soomro, A. R. Zamir, and M. Shah. UCF101: A dataset of 101 human actions classes from videos in the wild, 2012.

[34] C. Sun and R. Nevatia. DISCOVER: Discovering important segments for classification of video events and recounting. In *CVPR*, 2014.

[35] A. Tamrakar, S. Ali, Q. Yu, J. Liu, O. Javed, A. Divakaran, H. Cheng, and H. Sawhney. Evaluation of low-level features and their combinations for complex event detection in open source videos. In *CVPR*, 2012.

[36] C. C. Tan, Y.-G. Jiang, and C.-W. Ngo. Towards textually describing complex video contents with audio-visual concept classifiers. In *ACM MM*, 2011.

[37] K. Tang, L. Fei-Fei, and D. Koller. Learning latent temporal structure for complex event detection. In *CVPR*, 2012.

[38] B. Thomee, D. A. Shamma, G. Friedland, B. Elizalde, K. Ni, D. Poland, D. Borth, and L. Li. The new data and new challenges in multimedia research. *CoRR*, abs/1503.01817, 2015.

[39] C. Tsai, M. L. Alexander, N. Okwara, and J. R. Kender. Highly efficient multimedia event recounting from user semantic preferences. In *ICMR*, 2014.

[40] H. Wang and C. Schmid. Action recognition with improved trajectories. In *ICCV*, 2013.

[41] Y. Yang, Z. Ma, Z. Xu, S. Yan, and A. G. Hauptmann. How related exemplars help complex event detection in web videos? In *ICCV*, 2013.

[42] B. Yao, X. Jiang, A. Khosla, A. Lin, L. Guibas, and L. Fei-Fei. Human action recognition by learning bases of action attributes and parts. In *ICCV*, pages 1331–1338, 2011.

[43] S. Yu, L. Jiang, and A. G. Hauptmann. Instructional videos for unsupervised harvesting and learning of action examples. In *ACM MM*, 2014.

[44] Y. Yu. On decomposing the proximal map. In *NIPS*, 2013.

[45] M. Yuan and Y. Lin. Model selection and estimation in regression with grouped variables. *Journal of the Royal Statistical Society, Series B*, 68:49–67, 2006.

Beyond Doctors: Future Health Prediction from Multimedia and Multimodal Observations

Liqiang Nie[†], Luming Zhang[‡], Yi Yang[§], Meng Wang[‡], Richang Hong[‡] and Tat-Seng Chua[†]

[†] School of Computing, National University of Singapore, Singapore

[‡] Department of Electric Engineering and Information System, Hefei University of Technology, China

[§] Centre for Quantum Computation and Intelligent Systems (QCIS), University of Technology Sydney, Australia

{nieliqiang, zglumg, yee.i.yang, eric.mengwang, hongrc.hfut}@gmail.com, dcscts@nus.edu.sg

ABSTRACT

Although chronic diseases cannot be cured, they can be effectively controlled as long as we understand their progressions based on the current observational health records, which is often in the form of multimedia data. A large and growing body of literature has investigated the disease progression problem. However, far too little attention to date has been paid to jointly consider the following three observations of the chronic disease progression: 1) the health statuses at different time points are chronologically similar; 2) the future health statuses of each patient can be comprehensively revealed from the current multimedia and multimodal observations, such as visual scans, digital measurements and textual medical histories; and 3) the discriminative capabilities of different modalities vary significantly in accordance to specific diseases. In the light of these, we propose an adaptive multimodal multi-task learning model to co-regularize the modality agreement, temporal progression and discriminative capabilities of different modalities. We theoretically show that our proposed model is a linear system. Before training our model, we address the data missing problem via the matrix factorization approach. Extensive evaluations on a real-world Alzheimer's disease dataset well verify our proposed model. It should be noted that our model is also applicable to other chronic diseases.

Categories and Subject Descriptors

J.3 [**Life and Medical Sciences**]: Health, Medical Information Systems

General Terms

Algorithms, Performance, Experimentation

Keywords

Chronic Diseases; Multimodal Analysis; Disease Progression; Adaptive Multimodal Multi-Task Learning

MM'15, October 26–30, 2015, Brisbane, Australia.

DOI: http://dx.doi.org/10.1145/2733373.2806217.

1. INTRODUCTION

Many health conditions can be classified under the broad heading of chronic diseases, such as asthma, depression, stroke and Alzheimer's Disease (AD). They are mostly characterised by complex casuality, long latency periods, a prolonged course of illness and functional impairment. Besides financial burden, chronic diseases have profound effects on sufferers' physical and mental well-being, which often makes them difficult to carry on with daily routines[1]. Even though chronic disease does not often resolve spontaneously and is rarely cured completely[2], they progress over a long period of time to become fully established. Hence it offers us a chance for progression prediction, which is the key to moving from episodic and reactive care to a planned and proactive management [1, 14].

Disease progression prediction aims to estimate the disease statuses at some future time points, given the current multimodal observations of the patients. The severity of disease status can be measured by some clinical scores, which are designed by professionals and used as essential criteria for clinical diagnosis. Proactive care of chronic diseases would benefit from the prediction of disease progression in terms of these clinical measures. However, progression prediction in the real world faces the following challenges,

1. **Multimedia and Multimodal Observations.** Recent advances in medical technologies have made it possible to collect multimedia and multimodal data to describe the same patients [7]. For example, an echocardiogram video is acquired to provide dynamic information about the function of the heart; pictures made from Magnetic resonance imaging (MRI) scans visually show the structure problems inside the heart organs; while textual complains collected from the patients signal their symptoms. These multimedia observations, which are often multimodal data, collectively reveal the health conditions from different perspectives. Figure 1 shows a typical example of multimedia and multimodal observations for the same patient. How to effectively uncover the information embedded in the multimodal data remains a largely unaddressed research problem.

2. **Modality Confidences.** The discriminative capability of each modality differs from one to another and is heavily dependent on the type of disease. For instance, in the progression of cancer, the modality of

[1] http://www.forahealthieramerica.com/ds/impact-of-chronic-disease.html

[2] http://www.aihw.gov.au/WorkArea/DownloadAsset.aspx?id=10737421546

positron emission tomography (PET) scan, as compared to others, plays a more important role to spot a cancer, identify the stage of the cancer, show whether it has spread and help doctors make treatment plans. On the other hand, the modality of cerebrospinal fluid (CSF) measurement is more critical to multiple sclerosis.

3. **Task Relatedness.** Assume that each task concerns the prediction of a health status at one time point. Multiple tasks along a sequential timeline are not independent. Identifying and modelling their intrinsic relatedness are of vital importance, which enables the sharing of training instances among the tasks.

In addition to these three challenges, medical observations of a patient are missing at times, which could be caused by dropout or partial absence in a longitudinal study, and other private reasons. The problem of missing data may sometimes affect the prediction profoundly, and should thus be carefully addressed.

The research in disease progression modelling has been active in recent years, which can generally be divided into three categories. One is mono-modal mono-task learning. In this context, disease statuses at different time points are estimated separately by exploring a single modality [22, 10]. Neither the correlation among tasks nor the collective information across modalities is explored. Another line of efforts is the multiple task learning [35, 31]. They formulate the prediction of health statuses at a sequence of time points as a multi-task regression problem. Multi-task learning improves the learning performance by somewhat sharing the training instances among related tasks. The relatedness is modeled by assuming that they either share a common representation space or share some parameters. However, they disregard the relatedness among different modalities of a single task. The third category of approaches is the multimodal analysis [28, 30, 25]. They work towards discovering comprehensive information from several clinical modalities of the same patients for disease status prediction at one time point. Existing multimodal analysis, however, ignores the label information from other related tasks.

As an improved work, we propose a novel regression model, adaptive multimodal multi-task learning ($\mathbf{aM^2L}$), to predict chronic disease progression. Our model takes three types of prior knowledge into consideration. The first is modality agreement. Specifically, the disagreement among multi-modalities are penalized, since they are supposed to reflect the same disease status. The second is adaptive modality weighting. Namely, different modalities should have different weights, which are disease specific. The last is temporal progression. In particular, the disease status progresses smoothly, and sudden changes between nearby time points should be penalized. Our model differs from [32, 11], where multi-view learning mainly focuses on semi-supervised configurations and uniformly regularizes the task relatedness instead of temporal prior. In this work, we focus on multimodal analysis in the supervised settings and we do not assume that there are abundant unlabeled data available. Before training our model, we utilize the matrix factorization approach to complete the missing data.

The contributions of this work are threefold: 1) we propose an adaptive multimodal multi-task learning approach to model the chronic disease progression from multimedia observations. The proposed method simultaneously considers modality agreement, adaptive modality weights and the temporal progression; 2) we theoretically demonstrate that our proposed model is a linear model and practically analyze its computational complexity; and 3) we validate our model on a real-world AD dataset. Our model is also applicable to other chronic diseases.

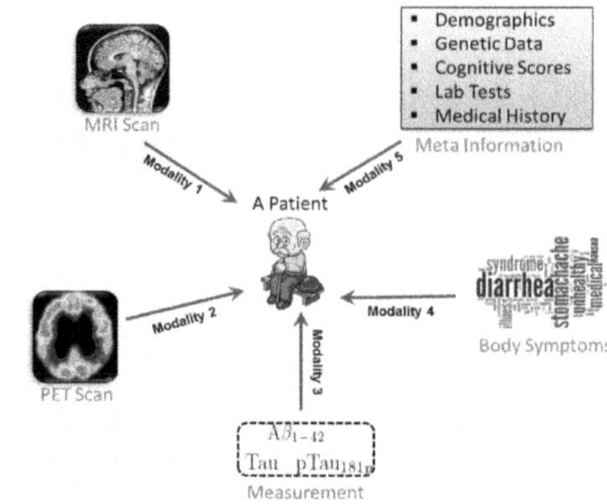

Figure 1: Illustration of multimedia and multimodal descriptions for the same patient. The modalities can be in various forms, such as visual images, digital measurements, textual descriptions, and even video records. Heterogeneous modalities reflect the health status of the same patient from diverse perspectives.

The remainder of the paper is structured as follows. Section 2 reviews the related work. Sections 3 and 4 respectively detail our data collection and the proposed disease progression model. Experimental settings and results are reported in Section 5, followed by conclusion and future work in Section 6.

2. RELATED WORK

2.1 Disease Progression modelling

Computational wellness has attracted increasing research attentions from computer science communities [19, 21, 17, 16]. Progression modeling of chronic diseases is part of the computational wellness research and it aims to predict the future disease statuses, which can be measured by the clinically defined categories [2, 5] or the continuous clinical scores [23, 6]. Broadly speaking, the existing efforts on disease progression modelling can be grouped into three categories: mono-modal mono-task learning, multi-task learning, and multimodal analysis.

Mono-modal mono-task learning in the past decade dominated the community of disease progression modelling. They estimated the disease status separately on a single modality of data, such as exploring the MRI scans to infer the targets at a future time point [23, 6]. Besides regression models, survival models were introduced in [22] to predict the future disease status of liver transplant patients by considering historical clinical variables individually. In addition, some approach [10] considered a small number of input features, and each feature was individually added to the model to examine its effectiveness. However, when the number of features is large and significant correlations among features exist, these approaches are usually suboptimal. Meanwhile, they neither considered the intrinsic correlation among tasks, nor utilized the complementary information embedded in different modalities. Their performance is thus far from satisfactory to be clinically useful.

Multi-task learning was recently proposed to model the disease progression, which utilizes the correlations among different tasks and simultaneously learns a problem together with other related problems. This often leads to a better model than learning each task separately. The key issue in multi-task learning is how to characterize and use the relatedness among multiple tasks. Two kinds of relatedness have been studied in the disease progression modelling. One is that the multiple tasks are assumed to share parameters or prior distributions of the hyper parameters. For example, Zhou et al. [35] formulated the prediction of clinical scores at a sequence of time points as a multi-task regression problem and captured the intrinsic relatedness among different tasks by a temporal group lasso regularizer. The other way of modelling the inter-task relatedness is to assume that they share a common underlying representation. For instance, the work in [31] constrained the models to share a common set of features. The work in [34] proposed a novel sparse group lasso formulation to select task-sharing and task-specific features in parallel.

Multimodal analysis was proposed to integrate clinical data from multiple channels, such as genetic, imaging and medical history. Ye et al. [28] proposed a multiple kernel learning method for integrating imaging and non-imaging data for AD study and extended the kernel framework to selecting features from heterogeneous modalities. Experiments showed that the integration of multimedia data leads to a considerable improvement in prediction accuracy. One common problem that hampers the use of multimodal analysis is the problem of missing data. To address this issue, two novel methods were introduced in [30] for joint analysis of incomplete multimodal neuroimaging data, where patients with missing measures were also kept for training. One year later, Xiang et al. [25] presented a "bi-level" learning model for multimodal block-wise missing data. It is capable of handling both feature-level and modality-level analysis.

2.2 Multi-View Multi-Task Learning

Disease progression modelling exhibits dual heterogeneities. In particular, a single learning task could have features from multiple modalities and multiple learning tasks could be related to each other through some shared components. Existing multi-task learning or multimodal analysis only captures one of the dual heterogeneities. Our proposed **aM^{2}L** approach well-addressed both by jointly regularizing task and modality relatedness. In fact, our model falls into the community of multi-view multi-task learning.

There are relatively sparse literatures so far on multi-task problem with multi-view data [31]. For example, He and Lawrence [9] proposed a graph-based iterative framework for multi-view multi-task learning ($IteM^2$) and applied it to text classification. $IteM^2$ projects task pairs to a new Reproducing Kernel Hilbert Space based on the common views shared by them. However, it can only deal with problems with only non-negative feature values. In addition, it is a transductive model. Hence it is unable to generate predictive models for independent and unseen testing samples. To address the intrinsic limitations of transductive models, an inductive multi-view multi-task learning model regMVMT was introduced in [32]. regMVMT regulates the view consistency on the unlabeled samples. Additional regularization functions are utilized to ensure that the learned functions are similar to each other across multiple tasks. However, without prior knowledge, simply restricting all the tasks to be similar is often inappropriate. As an extension of regMVMT, an inductive convex shared structure learning algorithm for multi-view multi-task problem (CSL-MTMV) was developed in [11]. Compared to regMVMT, CSL-MTMV considers the shared predictive structure among multiple tasks.

However, none of the methods mentioned above have been successfully applied to disease progression modelling except the one in [31]. This may be due to the facts that: 1) $IteM^2$, regMVMT and CSL-MTMV are all binary classification models, for which the extension to multi-class or regression problem is nontrivial, especially when the number of classes is large; and 2) the tasks in disease progression prediction are temporally related rather than uniformly or structurally related. Uniform and structural relations are considered in the three methods. The work in [31] treated the estimation of multiple clinical scores as different tasks and adopted the multi-task learning model [27] to learn a common feature subset. They then utilized a kernel-based multimodal data fusion method to fuse features from individual modality. They finally trained a support vector regression model to predict multiple clinical scores. However, this work does not consider the chronological progression of diseases and the separate tri-stages are hardly to reinforce each other. As a complement, we propose a unified multimodal multi-task learning framework for disease progression modelling, which regularizes task relatedness, modality agreement, and adaptive modality weights at the same time.

3. DATA COLLECTION

In this work, we selected one chronic disease, AD, due to following reasons: 1) **Prevalence**. It is the most common type of dementia, accounting for 60-80% of age-related dementia cases. It affects about 5.2 million people in the US, with a significant increase predicted in the near future if no disease-altering therapeutics are developed[3]. 2) **Mystery**. The cause of AD is poorly understood to date, especially the discriminant modality of AD. 3) **Accessibility**. The representative study data of AD can be requested from the Alzheimer's Disease Neuroimaging Initiative[4] (ADNI). ADNI is an ongoing and longitudinal study designed to develop clinical, imaging and genetic biomarkers for the early detection and tracking of AD.

To verify our model, we officially requested all the data of ADNI-1. ADNI-1 began in *2004* and its 822 participants were recruited from 59 sites across U.S. and Canada. The gender, diagnostic, ethnic and racial distributions of these enrolled participants are summarized in Table 1. We can see that the white patients dominate the participants. In addition, the distributions over age and years of education are respectively illustrated in Figure 2. It can be seen that the majorities range from 70 to 80 years old, and were well-educated before. In our study, the date recorded when the patient performed the screening in the hospital for the first time is called baseline, and the time point for the follow-up visits is denoted by the duration starting from the baseline. Taking the notation "M06" as an example, it denotes the time point six months after the first visit.

[3] https://www.alz.org/downloads/Facts_Figures_2014.pdf
[4] http://adni.loni.usc.edu/
[5] http://surfer.nmr.mgh.harvard.edu/
[6] http://www.fil.ion.ucl.ac.uk/spm/
[7] http://www.biomarkersconsortium.org/projects.php

Table 1: **Demographic statistics of the 822 ADNI-1 participants, including distribution of gender, diagnostic, ethnic and racial categories. "Unkn" refers to "unknown".**

Gender		Diagnostic			Ethnic Categories			Racial Categories					
Male	Female	NL	MCI	AD	Hispanic or Latino	Not Hispanic or Latino	Unkn	American Indian or Alaskan Native	Asian	Back or African American	White	More than one	Unkn
478	344	229	405	188	21	792	9	1	14	39	764	3	1

Table 2: Statistics of modalities, number of patients, and extracted features at the baseline time.

Modality	Number of patients	Feature Dimension	Feature Extractor
MRI	818	305	Image Analysis Suite FreeSurfer[5]
PET	419	116	SPM Software for visual scan[6]
CSF	415	5	ADNI Biomarker Core Lab [24]
PROT	566	147	Biomarkers Consortium Project[7]
META	818	51	Combination of Four Types[8]

The patients in ADNI-1 at their enrolment time can be in one of three diagnostics: normal elder (NL), mild cognitive impairment (MCI), and AD. NL and MCI could progress to AD. In this work, we selected 818 patients (229 NL, 401 MCI and 188 AD). Meanwhile, we utilized five modalities to collectively describe each patient, including 1.5T MRI scans (MRI), PET, CSF, proteomics (PROT) and META. Statistics over modalities, number of patients, and extracted features at the baseline time are shown in Table 2. It can be seen that each of our selected patients has at least two modalities at the same time: MRI and META. 624-D visual and textual features in total were extracted for those patients with all the five modalities available. We will detail how to complete the missing data in the experiments.

We aim to harvest their modalities at the baseline time of the given patients to predict their future health statuses in terms of MMSE and ADAS-cog scores. MMSE and ADAS-Cog are respectively the short names of Mini Mental State Examination and Alzheimer's Disease Assessment Scale cognitive subscale. They have been shown to be correlated with the underlying AD pathology and progressive deterioration of functional ability [12]. MMSE is a sensitive, valid and reliable 30-point questionnaire that is commonly used to estimate the severity and progression of cognitive impairment of AD. The ADAS-Cog is scored from 0 to 70. A larger MMSE and a smaller ADAS-Cog score usually indicates a better health status. Table 3 summarizes the number of patients available for MMSE and ADAS-Cog at different time points in our dataset. These cognitive scores are used as groundtruth to verify our model. We do not predict the health statuses at the time point M18 and M48 because of the severe data loss. Figure 3 illustrates the average evolution of health status. For ADAS-Cog cognitive progression, the AD curve grows up very fast while the MCI curve slightly rises within four years. When it comes to the NL curve, it is relatively stable. A similar pattern can be observed for the MMSE.

[8] The META modality is a fusion of 3-D demographic(age, years of education, gender), 7-D genetic (ApoE-$\varepsilon 4$, etc.), 23-D baseline cognitive scores (CDR, FAQ, GDS, etc.), 18-D lab tests(RCT1, RCT11, RCT12, etc.)

Table 3: The number of AD, MCI, and NL patients under MMSE/ADAS-Cog at different time points.

Type	baseline	M06	M12	M18	M24	M36	M48
AD	188	176	158	0	139	11	2
MCI	401	384	362	328	304	252	33
NL	229	221	212	0	203	187	56
Total	818	781	732	328	646	450	111

4. ADAPTIVE MULTIMODAL MULTI-TASK LEARNING

In this section, we first detail the formulation of our proposed **aM²L** approach and its optimization. We then demonstrate its linear property followed by the analysis of its computational complexity.

Before stepping into the model, we first define the notations that will be used. Assume that we have N training patients at the baseline time $\mathbf{X} = [\mathbf{x_1}, \mathbf{x_2}, ..., \mathbf{x_N}]^T$, and their corresponding disease statuses of the following M time points $\mathbf{Y} = [\mathbf{y^1}, \mathbf{y^2}, ..., \mathbf{y^M}] \in \mathbb{R}^{N\times M}$. Each patient is characterized by S collective modalities. For example, the i-th patient can be represented by $\mathbf{x_i} = [\mathbf{x_{i1}^T}, \mathbf{x_{i2}^T}, ..., \mathbf{x_{iS}^T}]^T$, where $\mathbf{x_{is}} \in \mathbb{R}^{D_s}$, and D_s denotes the feature dimension of the s-th modality. All the training patients on the s-th modality and on all the modalities are respectively represented as $\mathbf{X_s} = [\mathbf{x_{1s}}, \mathbf{x_{2s}}, ..., \mathbf{x_{Ns}}]^T \in \mathbb{R}^{N\times D_s}$ and $\mathbf{X} = [\mathbf{X_1}, \mathbf{X_2}, ..., \mathbf{X_S}] \in \mathbb{R}^{N\times D}$, where $D = \sum_{s=1}^{S} D_s$. The involved notations of this work are summarized in Table 4. Our objective is to design and learn a disease progression model, which is capable of predicting the future disease statues of new incoming patients given their multiple health descriptions at the baseline. In future, we can also incorporate the followup observations to enhance the prediction model. For example, we can merge the observations at baseline, M06 and M12 as input to predict the health status at M24. However, integrating the observational data at various time points are much more challenging. This is because the data is changing and simple fusion is unable to capture the data evolution.

4.1 Problem Formulation

In a vector-wise form, we linearly define the predictive function for all patients at the time point t with the knowledge from modality s as,

$$\mathbf{f_s^t}(\mathbf{X_s}) = \mathbf{X_s}\mathbf{w_s^t}, \tag{1}$$

where $\mathbf{w_s^t} \in \mathbb{R}^{D_s}$ is the parameter vector we aim to learn. In fact, $\mathbf{w_s^t}$ explicitly reveals the weight of features extracted from modality s. To learn $\mathbf{w_s^t}$, we jointly consider the following three kinds of prior knowledge:

1. **Modality Agreement.** Heterogeneous modalities of the same patients describe their health from various perspectives, but they coherently express the same disease status. In particular, for a given patient at each

Table 4: **Summary of key symbols and notations used in this work.**

Notations	Descriptions
N, S, M	number of training patients, modalities and tasks/time points, respectively.
D_s, $D = \sum_{s=1}^{S} D_s$	feature dimension on the s-th modality and on all the modalities, respectively.
$\mathbf{X_s} \in \mathbb{R}^{N\times D_s}$, $\mathbf{X} = [\mathbf{X_1}, \mathbf{X_2}, ..., \mathbf{X_S}] \in \mathbb{R}^{N\times D}$	N training patients on the s-th modality and on all the modalities, respectively.
$\mathbf{y^t} \in \mathbb{R}^{N}$, $\mathbf{Y} = [\mathbf{y^1}, \mathbf{y^2}, ..., \mathbf{y^M}] \in \mathbb{R}^{N\times M}$	disease statuses of all the training samples on the t-th and on the all time points, respectively.
$f_s^t(\mathbf{x_{ns}})$, $\mathbf{f_s^t}(\mathbf{X_s}) \in \mathbb{R}^N$	the predictive function for patient n at time point t with the knowledge from the modality s, and its vector-wise form for all patients.
$\mathbf{w_s^t} \in \mathbb{R}^{D_s}$, $\mathbf{W_s} = [\mathbf{w_s^1}, \mathbf{w_s^2}, ..., \mathbf{w_s^M}] \in \mathbb{R}^{D_s\times M}$	the parameter vector for modality s at time point t, and the parameter matrix for modality s at all time points. They are what we aim to learn.
α_s, $\boldsymbol{\alpha} \in \mathbb{R}^S$	the weight of the s-th modality and its vector-wise form for all the modalities.
Φ, L, C, T, Ω, Ψ	overall objective function, loss function, modality agreement regularizer, temporal progression regularizer, regularization on feature weight and modality weight.
θ_1, θ_2, θ_3, θ_4	the corresponding parameters involved for C, T, Ω, and Ψ in our model.

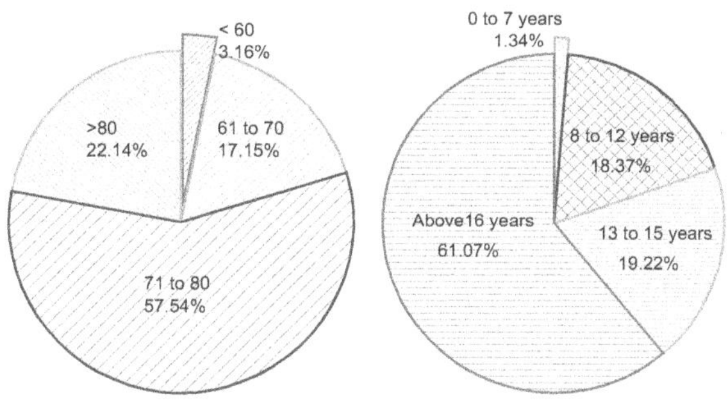

Figure 2: Distributions over age and education years of the 822 patients at the baseline time. Majorities of the enrolled patients are senile and well-educated.

specific time point t, the disease status estimated via exploring different modalities should be consistent.

2. **Adaptive Modality Weights.** The discriminative capabilities of each modality is disease specific. Instead of manually fixing the modality weights, which requires painful tuning, we incorporate the weighting parameters into our model as an variable and adaptively learn them via a statistical approach. Mathematically, the disease statuses for all patients at time point t are modeled by weighted fusion of the prediction results from all modalities,

$$\mathbf{f^t}(\mathbf{X}) = \sum_{s=1}^{S} \alpha_s \mathbf{f_s^t}(\mathbf{X_s}) = \sum_{s=1}^{S} \alpha_s \mathbf{X_s} \mathbf{w_s^t}, \qquad (2)$$
$$\text{s.t.} \quad \sum_{s=1}^{S} \alpha_s = 1,$$

where α_s is the weight for the s-th modality of the given disease. We intentionally do not constrain α_s to be larger than zero, because in this way we can infer which modality is negatively correlated with the given chronic disease.

3. **Temporal Progression.** Chronic disease is of long duration and generally in smooth progression[9]. Hence the sudden changes of disease statuses between neighbouring time points should be penalized.

To unify the aforementioned prior knowledge, we formulate our objective function $\Phi(\mathbf{w_s^t}, \boldsymbol{\alpha})$ as,

$$L(\mathbf{w_s^t}, \boldsymbol{\alpha}) + \theta_1 C(\mathbf{w_s^t}) + \theta_2 T(\mathbf{w_s^t}) + \theta_3 \Omega(\mathbf{w_s^t}) + \theta_4 \Psi(\boldsymbol{\alpha}). \quad (3)$$

[9] http://www.hpb.gov.sg/HOPPortal/health-article/3396

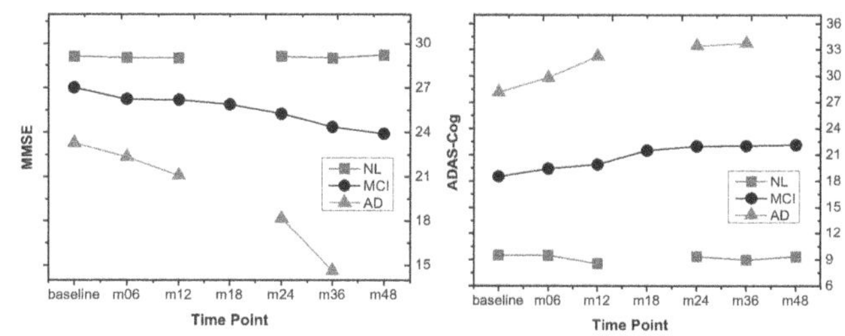

Figure 3: Cognitive score progression along time in terms of MMSE and ADAS-Cog. It is noted that some time points do not have cognitive scores.

The first term is a squared loss function that measures the empirical error on the training patients. As reported in [26], the squared loss usually yields good performance as other complex loss functions. We thus adopt the squared loss in our algorithm for simplicity and efficiency,

$$L(\mathbf{w_s^t}, \boldsymbol{\alpha}) = \frac{1}{2}\sum_{t=1}^{M} \parallel \mathbf{y^t} - \sum_{s=1}^{S} \alpha_s \mathbf{X_s} \mathbf{w_s^t} \parallel^2 . \qquad (4)$$

In Eqn.(3), the second and third term respectively controls the consistency among various modalities and progressive changes between adjacent time points,

$$\begin{cases} C(\mathbf{w_s^t}) = \frac{1}{2}\sum_{t=1}^{M}\sum_{s=1}^{S}\sum_{s'\neq s}^{S} \parallel \mathbf{X_s}\mathbf{w_s^t} - \mathbf{X_{s'}}\mathbf{w_{s'}^t} \parallel^2, \\ T(\mathbf{w_s^t}) = \frac{1}{2}\sum_{t=1}^{M}\sum_{s=1}^{S} \parallel \mathbf{w_s^t} - \mathbf{w_s^{t+1}} \parallel^2 . \end{cases} \qquad (5)$$

We set $\mathbf{w_s^{M+1}} = \mathbf{0}$ for the temporal progression term $T(\mathbf{w_s^t})$, since we only consider M time points in total. In addition, to facilitate the optimization of the temporal progression term, we restate $T(\mathbf{w_s^t})$ in an equivalent form as follows,

$$\sum_{t=1}^{M}\sum_{s=1}^{S} \parallel \mathbf{w_s^t} - \mathbf{w_s^{t+1}} \parallel^2$$
$$= \sum_{s=1}^{S} \parallel \mathbf{W_s}\mathbf{H} \parallel^2 = \sum_{s=1}^{S} \parallel \sum_{t=1}^{M} \mathbf{w_s^t}\mathbf{h_t^{\mathit{T}}} \parallel^2, \qquad (6)$$

where matrix $\mathbf{W_s} = [\mathbf{w_s^1}, \mathbf{w_s^2}, ..., \mathbf{w_s^M}] \in \mathbb{R}^{D_s\times M}$ and matrix $\mathbf{H} = [\mathbf{h_1}, \mathbf{h_2}, ..., \mathbf{h_T}]^T \in \mathbb{R}^{M\times(M-1)}$. The matrix $\mathbf{H}$ is pre-calculated by the following definition,

$$H_{ij} = \begin{cases} 1 & \text{if } i = j; \\ -1 & \text{if } i = j+1; \\ 0 & \text{otherwise.} \end{cases} \qquad (7)$$

The last two terms in Eqn.(3) penalize the generalization errors to avoid overfitting.

$$\begin{cases} \Omega(\mathbf{w_s^t}) = \frac{1}{2}\sum_{t=1}^{M}\sum_{s=1}^{S} \parallel \mathbf{w_s^t} \parallel^2, \\ \Psi(\boldsymbol{\alpha}) = \frac{1}{2} \parallel \boldsymbol{\alpha} \parallel^2 . \end{cases} \quad (8)$$

Overall, our proposed model has four parameters as shown in Eqn.(3). Parameters θ_1 and θ_2 respectively regularize the disagreement of different modalities for the same task and changes of health status between chronologically adjacent time points on the same modality. θ_3 and θ_4 regulate the strength of the l_2-norm regularization on multimodal multi-task learning and modality weights, respectively. We will detail the parameter tuning procedure in the experiments.

4.2 Alternative Optimization

We alternatively optimize $\boldsymbol{\alpha}$ and $\mathbf{w_s^t}$ via fixing the other one first. We will show that both of them admit analytic solutions.

4.2.1 *Optimizing $\boldsymbol{\alpha}$ with $\mathbf{w_s^t}$ Fixed*

We first fix $\mathbf{w_s^t}$ and optimize $\boldsymbol{\alpha}$. In such context, our objective function $\Phi(\mathbf{w_s^t}, \boldsymbol{\alpha})$ can be re-stated as $\Phi(\boldsymbol{\alpha})$,

$$\frac{1}{2}\sum_{t=1}^{M} \parallel \mathbf{y^t} \boldsymbol{e}^T\boldsymbol{\alpha} - \mathbf{X}\boldsymbol{\Lambda}\boldsymbol{\alpha} \parallel^2 + \frac{\theta_4}{2} \parallel \boldsymbol{\alpha} \parallel^2 + \xi(1 - \mathbf{e}^T\boldsymbol{\alpha}), \quad (9)$$

where $\boldsymbol{\Lambda} \in R^{D\times S}$ is a block matrix with its s-th diagonal block as $\mathbf{w_s^t}$; $\boldsymbol{e}$ is a vector with all elements being 1, and hence $\boldsymbol{e}^T\boldsymbol{\alpha}$ equals to 1; and ξ is the nonnegative Lagrange multiplier, which is frequently utilized in the optimization problem [33]; By setting the derivative of $\Phi(\boldsymbol{\alpha})$ with respect to $\boldsymbol{\alpha}$ to zero, we obtain,

$$\boldsymbol{\alpha} = \xi\boldsymbol{\Delta}^{-1}\boldsymbol{e}, \quad (10)$$

where $\boldsymbol{\Delta}$ is a positive definite and invertible matrix defined as,

$$\boldsymbol{\Delta} = (\mathbf{y}\boldsymbol{e}^T - \mathbf{X}\boldsymbol{\Lambda})^T(\mathbf{y}\boldsymbol{e}^T - \mathbf{X}\boldsymbol{\Lambda}) + \theta_4\mathbf{I} \quad (11)$$

In addition, based upon $\boldsymbol{e}^T\boldsymbol{\alpha} = 1$, we multiply both sides of Eqn.(10) with $\boldsymbol{e}^T$ to obtain,

$$\begin{cases} \xi = \frac{1}{\boldsymbol{e}^T\boldsymbol{\Delta}^{-1}\boldsymbol{e}}, \\ \boldsymbol{\alpha} = \frac{\boldsymbol{\Delta}^{-1}\boldsymbol{e}}{\boldsymbol{e}^T\boldsymbol{\Delta}^{-1}\boldsymbol{e}}. \end{cases} \quad (12)$$

4.2.2 *Optimizing $\mathbf{w_s^t}$ with $\boldsymbol{\alpha}$ Fixed*

We then fix $\boldsymbol{\alpha}$ and optimize $\mathbf{w_s^t}$. We take the derivative of $\Phi(\mathbf{w_s^t})$ with respect to $\mathbf{w_s^t}$,

$$\frac{\partial\Phi(\mathbf{w_s^t})}{\partial\mathbf{w_s^t}} = \alpha_s\mathbf{X_s}^T(\sum_{s=1}^{S}\alpha_s\mathbf{X_s}\mathbf{w_s^t} - \mathbf{y^t}) + \theta_1\mathbf{X_s}^T\sum_{s'\neq s}^{S}(\mathbf{X_s}\mathbf{w_s^t} - \mathbf{X_{s'}}\mathbf{w_{s'}^t}) + \theta_2\sum_{j=1}^{M}\mathbf{w_s^j}\mathbf{h_j}^T\mathbf{h_t} + \theta_3\mathbf{w_s^t}. \quad (13)$$

We set Eqn.(13) to zero and rearrange its terms. We arrive at the following equation,

$$\alpha_s\mathbf{X_s}^T\mathbf{y^t} = \left\{\alpha_s^2\mathbf{X_s}^T\mathbf{X_s} + \theta_1(S-1)\mathbf{X_s}^T\mathbf{X_s} + \theta_3\mathbf{I} + \theta_2\mathbf{h_t}^T\mathbf{h_t}\mathbf{I}\right\} \mathbf{w_s^t} + \sum_{s'\neq s}^{S}(\alpha_s\alpha_{s'} - \theta_1)\mathbf{X_s^T}\mathbf{X_{s'}}\mathbf{w_{s'}^t} + \theta_2\sum_{t'\neq t}^{M}\mathbf{h_t}^T\mathbf{h_{t'}}\mathbf{w_s^{t'}}, \quad (14)$$

where $\mathbf{I} \in \mathbb{R}^{D_s\times D_s}$ is an identity matrix. To ease the analysis, we align Eqn.(14) with the following form,

$$\mathbf{A_s^t} = \mathbf{B_s^t}\mathbf{w_s^t} + \sum_{s'\neq s}^{S}\mathbf{C_{ss'}}\mathbf{w_{s'}^t} + \sum_{t'\neq t}^{M}\mathbf{D^{tt'}}\mathbf{w_s^{t'}}. \quad (15)$$

By aligning Eqn.(14) with Eqn.(15), we derive the following set of equations,

$$\begin{cases} \mathbf{A_s^t} = \alpha_s\mathbf{X_s}^T\mathbf{y^t}; \\ \mathbf{B_s^t} = \alpha_s^2\mathbf{X_s}^T\mathbf{X_s} + \theta_1(S-1)\mathbf{X_s}^T\mathbf{X_s} + \theta_3\mathbf{I} + \theta_2\mathbf{h_t}^T\mathbf{h_t}\mathbf{I}; \\ \mathbf{C_{ss'}} = (\alpha_s\alpha_{s'} - \theta_1)\mathbf{X_s^T}\mathbf{X_{s'}}; \\ \mathbf{D^{tt'}} = \theta_2\mathbf{h_t}^T\mathbf{h_{t'}}\mathbf{I}. \end{cases} \quad (16)$$

Eqn.(15) and Eqn.(16) explicitly indicate that we must jointly learn $\mathbf{w_s^t}$ and $\mathbf{w_{s'}^{t'}}$ from a large set of equations, where $s' \neq s$ and $t' \neq t$. After combining the equations for all tasks on all modalities, we obtain a linear system as illustrated in Eqn.(17). It is worth noting that we can equivalently simplify this linear system as,

$$\mathbf{L}\mathbf{w} = \mathbf{a}, \quad (18)$$

where each entry in $\mathbf{L} \in \mathbb{R}^{(S\times M)\times(S\times M)}$ is a block matrix. Each block corresponds to a specific task on a specific modality, and its size is the dimensionality of the feature extracted from the corresponding modality. Similarly, $\mathbf{w}$ and $\mathbf{a}$ are block vectors with $S\times M$ blocks. So far, we have successfully transferred our proposed $\mathbf{aM^2L}$ model to a linear model. As we will show in the next subsection, $\mathbf{L}$ is positive definite, and thus invertible. Therefore, $\mathbf{w}$ can be obtained by solving the linear system shown in Eqn.(18).

4.2.3 *Linear Model Demonstration*

Before theoretically proving the invertible property of $\mathbf{L}$, we introduce three theorems.

Theorem 1: We consider multiple modalities and utilize S to denote the number of modalities. It is thus reasonable to assume that $S \geq 2$, and hence $\theta_1(S-1) \geq \theta_1$ when $\theta_1 > 0$.

Theorem 2: Without loss of generality, we assume $\mathbf{v_i}$ is an arbitrary block vector. We can then derive the following result,

$$\sum_{i=1}^{K}\mathbf{v_i}^T\mathbf{v_i} + \sum_{i=1}^{K}\sum_{j\neq i}^{K}\mathbf{v_i}^T\mathbf{v_j} = \frac{1}{2}\sum_{i=1}^{K} \parallel \mathbf{v_i} \parallel^2 + \frac{1}{2} \parallel \sum_{i=1}^{K}\mathbf{v_i} \parallel^2 \geq 0. \quad (19)$$

Theorem 3: Let's denote $\mathbf{z_i}$ as an arbitrary block vector. We will have the following inequality,

$$\sum_{i=1}^{K}\mathbf{z_i}^T\mathbf{z_i} - \sum_{i=1}^{K}\sum_{j\neq i}^{K}\mathbf{z_i}^T\mathbf{z_j} = \frac{1}{2} \parallel \mathbf{z_1} - \mathbf{z_K} \parallel^2 + \frac{1}{2}\sum_{i=2}^{K} \parallel \mathbf{z_i} - \mathbf{z_{i-1}} \parallel^2 \geq 0. \quad (20)$$

Next, we show that $\mathbf{L}$ is invertible by proving that $\mathbf{L}$ is a positive definite matrix. We define a $S\times M$ non-zero block vector, $\mathbf{g}^T = [\mathbf{g}_{11}^T, \mathbf{g}_{21}^T, ..., \mathbf{g}_{S1}^T, \mathbf{g}_{12}^T, ..., \mathbf{g}_{st}^T, ..., \mathbf{g}_{1M}^T, ..., \mathbf{g}_{SM}^T]$.

$$
\begin{pmatrix}
B_1^1 & C_{12} & C_{13} & \cdot\cdot & C_{1S} & D^{12} & 0 & 0 & \cdot\cdot & 0 & D^{13} & 0 & 0 & \cdot\cdot & 0 & \cdots & D^{1M} & 0 & 0 & \cdot\cdot & 0 \\
C_{21} & B_2^1 & C_{23} & \cdot\cdot & C_{2S} & 0 & D^{12} & 0 & \cdot\cdot & 0 & 0 & D^{13} & 0 & \cdot\cdot & 0 & \cdots & 0 & D^{1M} & 0 & \cdot\cdot & 0 \\
\vdots & \vdots & \vdots & \vdots & \vdots & \vdots & \vdots & \vdots & \vdots & \vdots & \vdots & \vdots & \vdots & \vdots & \vdots & \vdots & \vdots & \vdots & \vdots & \vdots & \vdots \\
C_{S1} & C_{S2} & C_{S3} & \cdot\cdot & B_S^1 & 0 & 0 & 0 & \cdot\cdot & D^{12} & 0 & 0 & 0 & \cdot\cdot & D^{13} & \cdots & 0 & 0 & 0 & \cdot\cdot & D^{1M} \\
D^{21} & 0 & 0 & \cdot\cdot & 0 & B_1^2 & C_{12} & C_{13} & \cdot\cdot & C_{1S} & D^{23} & 0 & 0 & \cdot\cdot & 0 & \cdots & D^{2M} & 0 & 0 & \cdot\cdot & 0 \\
0 & D^{21} & 0 & \cdot\cdot & 0 & C_{21} & B_2^2 & C_{23} & \cdot\cdot & C_{2S} & 0 & D^{23} & 0 & \cdot\cdot & 0 & \cdots & 0 & D^{2M} & 0 & \cdot\cdot & 0 \\
\vdots & \vdots & \vdots & \vdots & \vdots & \vdots & \vdots & \vdots & \vdots & \vdots & \vdots & \vdots & \vdots & \vdots & \vdots & \vdots & \vdots & \vdots & \vdots & \vdots & \vdots \\
0 & 0 & \cdot\cdot & 0 & D^{21} & C_{S1} & C_{S2} & C_{S3} & \cdot\cdot & B_S^2 & 0 & 0 & 0 & \cdot\cdot & D^{32} & \cdots & 0 & 0 & \cdot\cdot & 0 & D^{2M} \\
\vdots & \vdots & \vdots & \vdots & \vdots & \vdots & \vdots & \vdots & \vdots & \vdots & \vdots & \vdots & \vdots & \vdots & \vdots & \vdots & \vdots & \vdots & \vdots & \vdots & \vdots \\
D^{M1} & 0 & 0 & \cdot\cdot & 0 & D^{M2} & 0 & 0 & \cdot\cdot & 0 & \cdots & D^{M(M-1)} & 0 & 0 & \cdot\cdot & 0 & B_1^M & C_{12} & C_{13} & \cdot\cdot & C_{1S} \\
0 & D^{M1} & 0 & \cdot\cdot & 0 & 0 & D^{M2} & 0 & \cdot\cdot & 0 & \cdots & 0 & D^{M(M-1)} & 0 & \cdot\cdot & 0 & C_{21} & B_2^M & C_{23} & \cdot\cdot & C_{2S} \\
\vdots & \vdots & \vdots & \vdots & \vdots & \vdots & \vdots & \vdots & \vdots & \vdots & \vdots & \vdots & \vdots & \vdots & \vdots & \vdots & \vdots & \vdots & \vdots & \vdots & \vdots \\
0 & 0 & \cdot\cdot & 0 & D^{M1} & 0 & 0 & 0 & \cdot\cdot & D^{M2} & \cdots & 0 & 0 & 0 & \cdot\cdot & D^{M(M-1)} & C_{S1} & C_{S2} & C_{S3} & \cdot\cdot & B_S^M
\end{pmatrix}
\begin{pmatrix} w_1^1 \\ w_2^1 \\ \vdots \\ w_S^1 \\ w_1^2 \\ w_2^2 \\ \vdots \\ w_S^2 \\ \vdots \\ w_1^M \\ w_2^M \\ \vdots \\ w_S^M \end{pmatrix}
=
\begin{pmatrix} A_1^1 \\ A_2^1 \\ \vdots \\ A_S^1 \\ A_1^2 \\ A_2^2 \\ \vdots \\ A_S^2 \\ \vdots \\ A_1^M \\ A_2^M \\ \vdots \\ A_S^M \end{pmatrix}. \quad (17)
$$

We then derive that $\mathbf{g}^T\mathbf{L}\mathbf{g}$ equals to

$$
= \sum_{s=1}^{S}\sum_{t=1}^{M} \mathbf{g}_{st}^T \mathbf{B}_s^t \mathbf{g}_{st} + \sum_{s=1}^{S}\sum_{t=1}^{M} \mathbf{g}_{st}^T \sum_{s' \neq s}^{S} \mathbf{C}_{ss'} \mathbf{g}_{s't} +
$$

$$
\sum_{s=1}^{S}\sum_{t=1}^{M} \mathbf{g}_{st}^T \sum_{t' \neq t}^{M} \mathbf{D}^{tt'} \mathbf{g}_{st'}. \quad (21)
$$

By substituting Eqn.(16) into Eqn.(21), we obtain $\mathbf{g}^T\mathbf{L}\mathbf{g}$,

$$
= \sum_{s=1}^{S}\sum_{t=1}^{M} \mathbf{g}_{st}^T \Big\{ \alpha_s^2 \mathbf{X}_s^T \mathbf{X}_s + \theta_1 (S-1) \mathbf{X}_s^T \mathbf{X}_s + \quad (22)
$$

$$
\theta_3 \mathbf{I} + \theta_2 \mathbf{h}_t^T \mathbf{h}_t \mathbf{I} \Big\} \mathbf{g}_{st} + \sum_{s=1}^{S}\sum_{t=1}^{M}\sum_{s' \neq s}^{S} \mathbf{g}_{st}^T \Big\{ (\alpha_s \alpha_{s'} -
$$

$$
\theta_1) \mathbf{X}_s^T \mathbf{X}_{s'} \Big\} \mathbf{g}_{s't} + \theta_2 \sum_{s=1}^{S}\sum_{t=1}^{M}\sum_{t' \neq t}^{M} \mathbf{g}_{st}^T \mathbf{h}_t^T \mathbf{h}_{t'} \mathbf{g}_{st'}. \quad (23)
$$

As stated in ***theorem 1***, $\theta_1(S-1) \geq \theta_1$, we can thus further derive that $\mathbf{g}^T\mathbf{L}\ \mathbf{g}$ is greater than or equal to the followings,

$$
\sum_{t=1}^{M} \Big\{ \sum_{s=1}^{S} \mathbf{g}_{st}^T (\alpha_s^2 \mathbf{X}_s^T \mathbf{X}_s + \theta_1 \mathbf{X}_s^T \mathbf{X}_s) \mathbf{g}_{st} + \sum_{s=1}^{S}\sum_{s' \neq s}^{S} \mathbf{g}_{st}^T
$$

$$
(\alpha_s \alpha_{s'} \mathbf{X}_s^T \mathbf{X}_{s'} - \theta_1 \mathbf{X}_s^T \mathbf{X}_{s'}) \mathbf{g}_{s't} \Big\} + \theta_2 \sum_{s=1}^{S} \Big\{ \sum_{t=1}^{M} \mathbf{g}_{st}^T \mathbf{h}_t^T \mathbf{h}_t \mathbf{g}_{st}
$$

$$
+ \sum_{t=1}^{M}\sum_{t' \neq t}^{M} \mathbf{g}_{st}^T \mathbf{h}_t^T \mathbf{h}_{t'} \mathbf{g}_{st'} \Big\} + \theta_3 \sum_{s=1}^{S}\sum_{t=1}^{M} \mathbf{g}_{st}^T \mathbf{g}_{st}. \quad (24)
$$

Let's respectively denote block vector $\mathbf{v}_s = \alpha_s \mathbf{X}_s \mathbf{g}_{st}$, block vector $\mathbf{u}_t = \mathbf{h}_t \mathbf{g}_{st}$, and block vector $\mathbf{z}_s = \sqrt{\theta_1} \mathbf{X}_s \mathbf{g}_{st}$. We can rewrite the above formulas as follows,

$$
= \sum_{t=1}^{M} \Big\{ \{ \sum_{s=1}^{S} \mathbf{v}_s^T \mathbf{v}_s + \sum_{s=1}^{S}\sum_{s' \neq s}^{S} \mathbf{v}_s^T \mathbf{v}_{s'} \} + \{ \sum_{s=1}^{S} \mathbf{z}_s^T \mathbf{z}_s -
$$

$$
\sum_{s=1}^{S}\sum_{s' \neq s}^{S} \mathbf{z}_s^T \mathbf{z}_{s'} \} \Big\} + \theta_2 \sum_{s=1}^{S} \Big\{ \sum_{t=1}^{M} \mathbf{u}_t^T \mathbf{u}_t + \sum_{t=1}^{M}\sum_{t' \neq t}^{M} \mathbf{u}_t^T \mathbf{u}_{t'} \Big\}
$$

$$
+ \theta_3 \sum_{s=1}^{S}\sum_{t=1}^{M} \mathbf{g}_{st}^T \mathbf{g}_{st}. \quad (25)
$$

According to ***theorems 2*** and ***3***, we derive that Eqn.(25) is larger than or equal to,

$$
\theta_3 \sum_{s=1}^{S}\sum_{t=1}^{M} \mathbf{g}_{st}^T \mathbf{g}_{st} = \theta_3 \sum_{s=1}^{S}\sum_{t=1}^{M} \parallel \mathbf{g}_{st} \parallel^2 > 0. \quad (26)
$$

So far we have proven that $\mathbf{L}$ is a positive definite matrix. From the definition of positive definite matrix, we know that $\mathbf{L}$ is invertible.

4.3 Discussion

In the whole process of our alternative optimization, each step decreases the objective function value Φ, whose lower bound is zero and hence the convergence of our model is guaranteed [15].

The computational complexity of the training process is $O(T \times (O_1 + O_2))$, where O_1 and O_2 respectively equals to $(NS^2 + NDS + S^3)$ and (D^3M^3). T is the iteration times of the alternative optimization. S, N, M and D respectively refer to the number of modalities, patients, tasks, and the total feature dimensions over all the modalities. Usually, we consider less than 10 time points and modalities, hence both M and S are very small. D is in the order of a few hundreds. In our experiments, we studied less than one thousand patients in the training set. The process can be completed in less than five seconds excluding feature extraction on a desktop (3.4GHz and 16G memory). Therefore, our model can be easily scaled to other Web-scale or real-time applications, such as predicting the consumer taste progressions and event evolution modelling.

5. EXPERIMENTS

In this section, we verified our proposed model from various angles.

5.1 Experimental Settings

To facilitate the comparison among regression models, we employed the R-value to estimate the correlation coefficient between the predicted values and the ground truths [18],

$$
R - value = \frac{\sum_{i=1}(p_i - \bar{p})(r_i - \bar{r})}{\sqrt{\sum_{i=1}(p_i - \bar{p})^2}\sqrt{\sum_{i=1}(r_i - \bar{r})^2}}, \quad (27)
$$

where p_i is the predicted value and $\bar{p}$ is the average predicted value; r_i and $\bar{r}$ is the target value and the average target value, respectively. R-value always takes a value between -1 and 1, with 1 and -1 respectively indicating perfect positive and negative correlation. A correlation value close to 0 indicates no association between the variables. Besides, we also measured the regression performance by normalized

Mean Squared Error (nMSE) [29], which is the mean squared error divided by the variance of the target,

$$nMSE = \frac{\sum_{i=1}(p_i - r_i)^2}{\sum_{i=1}(r_i - \bar{r})^2}. \quad (28)$$

A better regression model usually has a higher R-value and a lower nMSE value.

Considering the small data size, the experimental results reported in this paper are based on 10-fold cross-validation. Note that patients with missing labels in the testing set are not utilized to assess our model, even their labels are estimated by our data completion method. Takeing "M36" as an example, 10-fold cross-validation assigns the testing set with approximately 81 patients. Thereinto, about 45 patients with real labels are taken for testing.

5.2 On Data Missing Issues

Due to the nature of longitudinal and periodic data collection, real chronic disease datasets usually contain a certain percentage of missing data, which greatly hampers the learning performance. Generally speaking, there exist two kinds of missing data. One is missing label (disease status), which is estimated by clinical measures, such as MMSE and ADAS-Cog. This is because some patients may be dead or absent at some time points. The other one is missing modality. In particular, the patients may not provide their complete health modalities at the baseline owing to privacy and security concerns. In fact, Tables 2 and 3 respectively show the details of missing modality and missing label in our dataset.

On the other hand, the mature matrix factorization technique that is able to deal with missing data in a principled way, has attracted a lot of attentions from diverse communities [4, 13, 3]. Basically, matrix factorization factorizes a given matrix into two latent matrices, such that their multiplication approximates the original one. The entries in the two latent matrices are inferred by the observed values in the original matrix only, and overfitting is avoided through an appropriate regularized model. In this work, we merge modality matrix and the disease status matrix as the original matrix $\mathbf{O} = [\mathbf{X}, \mathbf{Y}] \in \mathbb{R}^{N \times (D+M)}$, and aim to infer the missing entries in $\mathbf{O}$. Based on this framework[10], we implemented a flexible learning rate adjuster to monitor and adjust the learning rate in matrix factorization. This adjuster is triggered on each epoch. It will shrink the learning rate if the value of the objective function goes up. The idea is that in this case the learning algorithm is overshooting the bottom of the objective function. On the other hand, the adjuster will increase the learning rate if the value of the objective function decreases too slowly. This makes our learning rate parameter less dependent to the initial value. Though it is not a very mathematically principled approach, it works well in practice and really accelerates the learning process.

To examine the necessity, effectiveness and efficiency of our proposed data completion method, we evaluated our **aM^{2}L** model under the following settings.

- **REM**: We simply removed the patients with either missing modality or missing label.
- **NN**: We replaced the missing values in $\mathbf{O}$ with the corresponding values from the nearest column based on META and MRI modality. Gaussian kernel function [20] was employed to estimate the pairwise similarity.
- **MF**: The missing data was completed by a matrix factorization method. The learning rate was set as a sufficient small value of 0.00001 to avoid oscillation. This value was fixed across the training process.
- **aMF**: The missing data was inferred by a matrix factorization method with adaptive learning rate adjuster. The initial learning rate was set as 0.01.

[10] http://www.quuxlabs.com/blog/2010/09/matrix-factorization-a-simple-tutorial-and-implementation-in-python/

Table 5: Performance comparison among different data completion methods. Time refers to the time cost of data completion in terms of epoch.

Method	Predicted by MSMT Learning				Time
	MMSE		ADAS-Cog		
	R-value	nMSE	R-value	nMSE	
DEL	0.6587	0.1736	0.6944	0.0602	–
KNN	0.8597	0.1375	0.8784	0.0413	–
MF	0.8901	0.1181	0.9168	0.0318	3174
aMF	0.8901	0.1181	0.9168	0.0318	32

In Table 5, we show the performance of our model with different data completion methods. From this table, we have the following observations: 1) nMSE under ADAS-Cog is much smaller as compared against that under MMSE. That is because the variance of ADAS-Cog is very large. ADAS-Cog scores range from 0-70, while MMSE scores range from 0-30. But this does not affect the comparison among models under the same cognitive score. 2) **REM** achieves the worst performance across different cognitive measures and evaluation criteria. A possible reason is that it substantially reduces the training size and patients with incomplete data cannot be leveraged to train the regression model. According to our statistic, only 184 patients have all the five modalities and 429 patients have all the labels at M06, M12, M24 and M36. Worse still is only 93 patients having all the labels and five sources simultaneously. This indicates that the data completion procedure is critical. 3) **aMF** exhibits better performance than **NN** and **MF**, in terms of effectiveness and efficiency, respectively. This is because **NN** is unable to explore global information for missing data inference, and **MF** is unable to flexibly adjust its learning rate and thus it takes a long time to reach convergence.

5.3 On Parameter Tuning

We have four key parameters as shown in Eqn.(3). The optimal values of these parameters were carefully tuned with 5-fold cross-validation in the training data. In particular, based upon the 10-fold cross-validation, we have around 736 patients during each training round. We performed 5-fold cross-validation on the 736 patients to learn the optimal parameters by grid search between 10^{-2} to 10^{2} with small but adaptive step size. In particular, the step size was 0.01, 0.05, 1, and 5 for the range of [0.01,0.1], [0.1,1], [1,10] and [10,100], respectively. The parameters corresponding to the best R-value were used to report the final results. For other competitors, the procedures to tune the parameters are analogous to ensure fair comparison.

5.4 On Component-wise Analysis

To verify how effective each component is in the proposed **aM^{2}L** model, we compared the performance of the following

Table 6: **Effectiveness evaluation of each involved component in our proposed model.**

Methods	MMSE		ADAS-Cog		P-value
	R-value	nMSE	R-value	nMSE	
Ridge	0.7982	0.1577	0.8485	0.0433	3.2e-12
noTP	0.8245	0.1496	0.8613	0.0429	4.8e-10
noMA	0.8706	0.1275	0.9017	0.0362	5.9e-4
M²L	0.8794	0.1233	0.9094	0.0347	1.1e-3
aM²L	**0.8901**	**0.1181**	**0.9168**	**0.0318**	–

methods, which can be derived from our model by removing some terms:

- **Ridge**: Ridge regression is a simple approach to estimate the future health statuses by modelling modalities and tasks at different time points separately [8]. It is typically formulated as $(\mathbf{y^t} - \mathbf{X}\mathbf{w^t})^2 + \delta \parallel \mathbf{w^t} \parallel_F^2$, and admits an analytical solution given by $\mathbf{w^t} = (\mathbf{X}^T\mathbf{X} + \delta\mathbf{I})^{-1}\mathbf{X}^T\mathbf{y}$. It is a special case of our model, when $\theta_1 = 0$, $\theta_2 = 0$, $\theta_4 = 0$, and $\alpha_s = 0.2$ ($\alpha_s = \frac{1}{S}$ and $S = 5$).
- **noTP**: We did not consider temporal progression by setting $\theta_2 = 0$.
- **noMA**: We did not take modality agreement into consideration by setting $\theta_1 = 0$.
- **M²L**: Our proposed regression model without considering the confidence of each modality. This can be derived by setting $\theta_4 = 0$ and $\alpha_s = \frac{1}{S}$.
- **aM²L**: Our proposed regression model.

The results of component-wise analysis are reported in Table 6. From this table, the following observations can be made: 1) **Ridge** achieves the most unsatisfactory results. This may be caused by the fact that **Ridge** neither explores the temporal smoothness among tasks, nor considers the consistency relatedness among modalities. This results imply that jointly modelling the dual-heterogeneities of disease progression is of vital importance: the prediction task at each time point has features from multiple modalities, and multiple tasks are related to each other in chronological order. 2) **noMA** and **M²L** perform better than **noTP**. This demonstrates that multi-task learning has even more encouraging effects as compared to multimodal analysis. This is because multi-task learning effectively increases the number of samples by learning multiple related tasks simultaneously and our data size is not very large. 3) **aM²L** is superior to others. This further demonstrates that every involved component in our proposed model is indispensable. For instance, as compared to **M²L**, **aM²L** shows its advantage of adaptive modality confidences.

We also conducted the analysis of variance (known as ANOVA) based on R-value under MMSE. In particular, we performed paired t-test between our **aM²L** model and each of the benchmarks based on 10-fold cross validation. We found that all the p-values are much smaller than 0.05, which shows that the improvements of our proposed model are statistically significant.

5.5 On Model Performance Comparison

Beside component analysis, we carried out experiments to compare the overall effectiveness of our proposed **aM²L** model with other state-of-the-arts regression models in the disease progression domain, and other multi-view multi-task learning models:

- **TGL**: A Temporal Group Lasso model proposed in [35] to predict the chronic disease progression. It captures the relatedness among tasks at sequential time points by a temporal group lasso regularizer.
- **cFSGL**: A novel Convex Fused Sparse Group Lasso formulation introduced in [34] to model the disease progression. It simultaneously selects task-shared and task-specific features using the sparse group Lasso penalty.
- **nFGL**: A non-Convex Fused Group Lasso method proposed to model the disease progression in Eqn.17 of [34]. It is a composite $l_{0.5,1}$-like penalty. The difference of convex programming technique was employed to solve the non-convex formulations.
- **regMVMT**: A semi-supervised inductive multi-view multi-task learning model introduced in [32]. As reported in [32], this model outperforms most of the prevailing multi-view multi-task learning approaches. That is why we did not selected other multi-view multi-task learning models as competitors.

Table 7 shows the performance of various disease progression models in terms of nMSE and R-value. From this table, we observed the following points: 1) Our proposed **aM²L** model is remarkably and consistently better than the first three prevailing disease progression models. The reason could be that none of the disease progression models jointly leverage the prior knowledge of modality agreement and their confidences while modelling the task relatedness. This observation manifests the consistent relations among modalities and their confidences are able to appropriately reinforce the descriptions of health conditions and hence enhance the prediction performance of disease progression. 2) **aM²L** outperforms **regMVMT**. This is because the latter does not flexibly consider the modality weights and is unable to make full advantage of the labeled samples. Meanwhile, it assumes that the relations among tasks are uniformly distributed, which is often not true in the real world. 3) Some learning models on some tasks, where the real labeled samples are relatively less, surprisingly achieve a better performance. For example, the learning performance on M24 is greater than that on M06. Though we estimated the missing labels before the training, there exists a certain bias between the estimated labels and the true labels. After inspecting the distribution of patients, we found it is reasonable. The percentage of NL changed from 28.3% in M06 to 31.4% in M24, which results in a smaller variance and hence a possible larger nMSE.

5.6 On Multimodal Analysis

We also studied the effectiveness of different modality combination. Recall that each patient after data completion is represented by five modalities in our work. Instead of exhaustively examining all possible modality combinations, we fed the following representative combinations into our proposed model and validated their description power:

- **IMG**: Imaging set comprises of MRI and PET.
- **nIMG**: Non-imaging set has CSF, PROT, and META.
- **ALL**: We incorporated all the five modality into our model simultaneously.

Table 7: Comparison of our proposed model with other state-of-the-art disease regression models and multi-view multi-task learning models on longitudinal MMSE and ADAS-Cog prediction.

Models	MMSE						ADAS-Cog					
	All Tasks		Individual Task (nMSE)				All Tasks		Individual Task (nMSE)			
	R-value	nMSE	M06	M12	M24	M36	R-value	nMSE	M06	M12	M24	M36
TGL	0.8464	0.1416	0.1610	0.1485	0.1072	0.1459	0.8793	0.0412	0.0408	0.0380	0.0412	0.0469
cFSGL	0.8523	0.1403	0.1586	0.1479	0.1073	0.1434	0.8906	0.0389	0.0406	0.0356	0.0377	0.0430
nFGL	0.8557	0.1382	0.1581	0.1462	0.1041	0.1394	0.8928	0.0383	0.0407	0.0352	0.0370	0.0409
regMVMT	0.8687	0.1284	0.1467	0.1324	0.0991	0.1315	0.8975	0.0363	0.0381	0.0344	0.0356	0.0399
aM^{2}L	**0.8901**	**0.1181**	**0.1313**	**0.1159**	**0.0804**	**0.1143**	**0.9168**	**0.0318**	**0.0332**	**0.0298**	**0.0309**	**0.0338**

Table 8: Performance comparison among different multimedia and multi-modal combinations.

Sources	Predicted by MSMT Learning				p-value
	MMSE		ADAS-Cog		
	R-value	nMSE	R-value	nMSE	
IMG	0.8694	0.1281	0.8993	0.0375	1.3*e*-5
nIMG	0.8804	0.1205	0.9081	0.0353	2.6*e*-3
ALL	**0.8901**	**0.1181**	**0.9168**	**0.0318**	–

Table 8 summarizes the multimodal analysis and the paired t-test results. We observed that: 1) The model trained on **nIMG** outperforms that trained on **IMG**. This tells us the non-imaging modality combination is much more informative as compared against the imaging scans. 2) The paired t-test results show that the model on all the five modalities is significantly better than those trained on others. This implies that the visual features from imaging set can enhance the learning performance. 3) We examined the modality confidence α_s during training on **ALL**. We found that the weight on META, PROT, MRI, PET, CSF in turn goes down. This reveals that META is the most discriminative modality for AD characterization.

6. CONCLUSION AND FUTURE WORK

In this paper, we presented a new approach to model the progression of chronic diseases based on multimedia and multimodal observational data. It seamlessly unifies the modality agreement, temporal progression and the modality confidences. Extensive experiments on a publicly acquirable dataset have well verified the effectiveness of our proposed model and each of its components.

In future, we plan to further improve the model in the following directions. First of all, we will further consider the structural relations between tasks, instead of just linear relations. Secondly, beyond modality agreement, we will extend our model to incorporate the complementary relations among modalities. At last, we plan to apply our model to other diseases.

7. ACKNOWLEDGEMENTS

This research is supported by the Singapore National Research Foundation under its International Research Centre @ Singapore Funding Initiative and administered by the IDM Programme Office.

8. REFERENCES

[1] A. Bogomolov, B. Lepri, M. Ferron, F. Pianesi, and A. S. Pentland. Daily stress recognition from mobile phone data, weather conditions and individual traits. In *ACM MM*, 2014.

[2] Y. F. C. Misra and C. Davatzikos. Baseline and longitudinal patterns of brain atrophy in mci patients, and their use in prediction of short-term conversion to ad: results from adni. *NeuroImage*, 2009.

[3] C.-M. Chen, M.-F. Tsai, J.-Y. Liu, and Y.-H. Yang. Using emotional context from article for contextual music recommendation. In *ACM MM*, 2013.

[4] P. Cui, Z. Wang, and Z. Su. What videos are similar with you?: Learning a common attributed representation for video recommendation. In *ACM MM*, 2014.

[5] R. Desikan, H. Cabral, F. Settecase, C. Hess, W. Dillon, C. Glastonbury, M. Weiner, N. Schmansky, D. Salat, and B. Fischl. Automated mri measures predict progression to alzheimer's disease. *Neurobiology of aging*, 2010.

[6] S. Duchesne, A. Caroli, C. Geroldi, D. Collins, and G. Frisoni. Relating one-year cognitive change in mild cognitive impairment to baseline mri features. *NeuroImage*, 2009.

[7] S. Ebadollahi, A. R. Coden, M. A. Tanenblatt, S.-F. Chang, T. Syeda-Mahmood, and A. Amir. Concept-based electronic health records: Opportunities and challenges. In *ACM MM*, 2006.

[8] M. Eliot, J. Ferguson, M. P. Reilly, and A. S. Foulkes. Ridge regression for longitudinal biomarker data. *JMLR*, 2011.

[9] J. He and R. Lawrence. A graph-based framework for multi-task multi-view learning. In *ICML*, 2011.

[10] K. Ito, B. Corrigan, Q. Zhao, J. French, R. Miller, H. Soares, E. Katz, T. Nicholas, B. Billing, R. Anziano, and T. Fullerton. Disease progression model for cognitive deterioration from alzheimer's disease neuroimaging initiative database. *Alzheimer's and Dementia*, 2010.

[11] X. Jin, F. Zhuang, S. Wang, Q. He, and Z. Shi. Shared structure learning for multiple tasks with multiple views. In *MLKDD*. 2013.

[12] P. JR, C. RE, and D. PM. Neuroimaging and early diagnosis of alzheimer disease: a look to the future. *Radiology*, 2003.

[13] Z. Li, J. Liu, X. Zhu, T. Liu, and H. Lu. Image annotation using multi-correlation probabilistic matrix factorization. In *ACM MM*, 2010.

[14] H. Lin, J. Jia, Q. Guo, Y. Xue, Q. Li, J. Huang, L. Cai, and L. Feng. User-level psychological stress detection from social media using deep neural network. In *ACM MM*, 2014.

[15] Z. Ma, Y. Yang, F. Nie, J. Uijlings, and N. Sebe. Exploiting the entire feature space with sparsity for automatic image annotation. In *ACM MM*, 2011.

[16] L. Nie, M. Akbari, T. Li, and T.-S. Chua. A joint local-global approach for medical terminology assignment. In *SIGIR, MIR Workshop*, 2014.

[17] L. Nie, T. Li, M. Akbari, J. Shen, and T.-S. Chua. Wenzher: Comprehensive vertical search for healthcare domain. In *SIGIR*, 2014.

[18] L. Nie, M. Wang, Z.-J. Zha, and T.-S. Chua. Oracle in image search: A content-based approach to performance prediction. *TOIS*, 2012.

[19] L. Nie, M. Wang, L. Zhang, S. Yan, B. Zhang, and T.-S. Chua. Disease inference from health-related questions via sparse deep learning. *TKDE*, 2015.

[20] L. Nie, S. Yan, M. Wang, R. Hong, and T.-S. Chua. Harvesting visual concepts for image search with complex queries. In *ACM MM*, 2012.

[21] L. Nie, Y.-L. Zhao, M. Akbari, J. Shen, and T.-S. Chua. Bridging the vocabulary gap between health seekers and healthcare knowledge. *TKDE*, 2015.

[22] R. K. Pearson, R. J. Kingan, and A. Hochberg. Disease progression modeling from historical clinical databases. In *SIGKDD*, 2005.

[23] C. Stonnington, C. Chu, S. Klöppel, C. Jack, J. Ashburner, R. Frackowiak, and the Alzheimer Disease Neuroimaging Initiative. Predicting clinical scores from magnetic resonance scans in alzheimer's disease. *NeuroImage*, 2010.

[24] N. Tzourio-Mazoyer, B. Landeau, D. Papathanassiou, F. Crivello, O. Etard, N. Delcroix, B. Mazoyer, and M. Joliot. Automated anatomical labeling of activations in spm using a macroscopic anatomical parcellation of the mni mri single-subject brain. *NeuroImage*, 2002.

[25] S. Xiang, L. Yuan, W. Fan, Y. Wang, P. M. Thompson, and J. Ye. Multi-source learning with block-wise missing data for alzheimer's disease prediction. In *SIGKDD*, 2013.

[26] Q. Xu, Q. Huang, and Y. Yao. Online crowdsourcing subjective image quality assessment. In *ACM MM*, 2012.

[27] X. Yang, S. Kim, and E. P. Xing. Heterogeneous multitask learning with joint sparsity constraints. In *NIPS*, 2009.

[28] J. Ye, K. Chen, T. Wu, J. Li, Z. Zhao, R. Patel, M. Bae, R. Janardan, H. Liu, G. Alexander, and E. Reiman. Heterogeneous data fusion for alzheimer's disease study. In *SIGKDD*, 2008.

[29] Z. Yu and D.-Y. Yeung. Multi-task learning using generalized t process. *JMLR*, 2010.

[30] L. Yuan, Y. Wang, P. M. Thompson, V. A. Narayan, and J. Ye. Multi-source learning for joint analysis of incomplete multi-modality neuroimaging data. In *SIGKDD*, 2012.

[31] D. Zhang and D. Shen. Multi-modal multi-task learning for joint prediction of clinical scores in alzheimer's disease. In *Multimodal Brain Image Analysis*. 2011.

[32] J. Zhang and J. Huan. Inductive multi-task learning with multiple view data. In *SIGKDD*, 2012.

[33] X. Zhao, G. Li, M. Wang, J. Yuan, Z.-J. Zha, Z. Li, and T.-S. Chua. Integrating rich information for video recommendation with multi-task rank aggregation. In *ACM MM*, 2011.

[34] J. Zhou, J. Liu, V. A. Narayan, and J. Ye. Modeling disease progression via fused sparse group lasso. In *SIGKDD*, 2012.

[35] J. Zhou, L. Yuan, J. Liu, and J. Ye. A multi-task learning formulation for predicting disease progression. In *SIGKDD*, 2011.

Multi-sensor Self-Quantification of Presentations

Tian Gan[1,2,3], Yongkang Wong[2], Bappaditya Mandal[3], Vijay Chandrasekhar[3], Mohan S. Kankanhalli[1,2]

[1]School of Computing, National University of Singapore
[2]Interactive & Digital Media Institute, National University of Singapore
[3]Institute for Infocomm Research, Singapore

gantian@comp.nus.edu.sg, yongkang.wong@nus.edu.sg, {bmandal,vijay}@i2r.a-star.edu.sg, mohan@comp.nus.edu.sg

ABSTRACT

Presentations have been an effective means of delivering information to groups for ages. Over the past few decades, technological advancements have revolutionized the way humans deliver presentations. Despite that, the quality of presentations can be varied and affected by a variety of reasons. Conventional presentation evaluation usually requires painstaking manual analysis by experts. Although the expert feedback can definitely assist users in improving their presentation skills, manual evaluation suffers from high cost and is often not accessible to most people. In this work, we propose a novel multi-sensor self-quantification framework for presentations. Utilizing conventional ambient sensors (i.e., static cameras, Kinect sensor) and the emerging wearable egocentric sensors (i.e., Google Glass), we first analyze the efficacy of each type of sensor with various nonverbal assessment rubrics, which is followed by our proposed multi-sensor presentation analytics framework. The proposed framework is evaluated on a new presentation dataset, namely NUS Multi-Sensor Presentation (NUSMSP) dataset, which consists of 51 presentations covering a diverse set of topics. The dataset was recorded with ambient static cameras, Kinect sensor, and Google Glass. In addition to multi-sensor analytics, we have conducted a user study with the speakers to verify the effectiveness of our system generated analytics, which has received positive and promising feedback.

Categories and Subject Descriptors

I.2.10 [**Vision and Scene Understanding**]: Video analysis; I.5.4 [**Applications**]: Signal processing

Keywords

Quantified Self; Multi-modal Analysis; Presentations; Sensors; Egocentric Vision

MM'15, October 26–30, 2015, Brisbane, Australia.
© 2015 ACM. ISBN 978-1-4503-3459-4/15/10 ...$15.00.
DOI: http://dx.doi.org/10.1145/2733373.2806252.

1. INTRODUCTION

Presentation is one of the most important methods to convey ideas to an audience, where the ideas have generally been researched, organized, outlined and practiced [41]. The circumstances of a presentation can range from a public speech to an academic seminar. Studies have shown that effective oral communication skills are important in a variety of areas, such as politics, business, and education [9]. Similarly, nonverbal communication, such as gesture, facial expression, posture, and interaction with the audience, also plays a predominant role in effective delivery [33]. Nowadays, presentation software (e.g., PowerPoint, Keynote, *etc.*) is widely used to create quality slides and content for a presentation. Nevertheless, the speaker's presentation skills are still critical to convey ideas.

A bad presentation could be a result of speech anxiety, lack of confidence, insufficient preparation, communication apprehension, lack of practice, etc. Studies from the clinical psychology show that a good presentation is "not a gift bestowed by providence on only a few rarely endowed individuals" but rather a skill to be taught and learned [12]. In order to improve presentation skills, many works in the communication literature have designed various scoring rubrics as guidance for presentation evaluation [9, 24, 25, 29, 32, 36]. Cognitive learning theory suggests that the feedback from an expert facilitates deliberate practice, and these trial-and-error attempts allow for the successful approximation of the target performance [23]. These assessments can be used for individual diagnostic purposes, where this feedback loop serves as effective information for training in making of effective presentations [2, 12]. In spite of that, the manual assessment process requires a human evaluator which is not always feasible in most real-world settings.

In recent years, the advancement of sensor technologies has enabled the development of automated presentation analytics algorithms. These algorithms are designed for various ambient type of sensors, such as microphone, RGB camera, depth sensor, *etc.*, and can be categorized into single modality analysis and multi-modal analysis. Examples of single modality analysis include speech fluency analysis [1] and speech rate detection [8], whereas works on multi-modal analysis include body language analysis with RGB camera and depth sensor [6, 7, 44]. Recently, wearable sensing devices have enabled both opportunities and challenges for user behavior analytics [13, 16, 20]. These devices are equipped with multiple sensors, which include First-Person-View (FPV) visual sensor, microphone, proximity sensor, ambient light sensor, accelerometer, and magnetometer. For example, wearable fitness devices are being increasingly deployed to record the physical activity of a user, where a comprehensive activity report (i.e., quantified self) is automatically generated [15]. In contrast, the use of wearable sensing device has not yet been explored for self-quantification of presentations. This is in spite of the fact that a wearable sensor will provide a constraint-free setting for the speaker's movement, which makes it an ideal device for self-quantification of presentations.

In this work, we propose a multi-sensor self-quantification framework for presentations, where the framework can work with only a wearable sensor or can be combined with existing ambient sensors for improved precision. To the best of our knowledge, this is the first time that the wearable sensor is used to quantify the performance of presentations. Our contributions are as follows:

- We review the past studies in communication, cognitive science, and psychology along with the speech analysis literature, and formalize an assessment rubric suitable for presentation self-quantification.
- We propose a multi-sensor analytics framework for presentations, which analyzes both the conventional ambient sensors (audio, visual, and depth sensor) and wearable sensors (audio, visual, and motion sensor). We quantitatively evaluated our proposed framework on the assessment rubric under single sensor and multi-sensor scenarios. These findings provide an insightful benchmark for multi-sensors based self-quantification research.
- We recorded a new multi-sensor presentation dataset, namely NUS Multi-Sensor Presentation (NUSMSP) dataset, which consists of web cameras, Kinect sensor, and multiple Google Glasses. It consists of 51 presentations of varied durations and topics. In addition, we manually annotated each presentation based on the proposed assessment rubric. The dataset is now publicly available for the research community.
- We have conducted a user study with the presenters in this dataset. For each presenter, we provided our system generated feedback and then the presenter was asked to verify the effectiveness of this feedback. The study shows positive results of our proposed system and provides several useful insights for future research.

The remainder of the paper is organized as follows. Section 2 provides an overview of the related literature for presentations. Section 3 provides the assessment rubrics for self-quantification of presentations. Section 4 elaborates on the sensor configuration and the proposed analytics framework. Section 5 contains the details of new dataset, experimental results and discussion, whereas Section 6 discusses the feedback from the user study. Section 7 concludes the paper.

2. RELATED WORK

In the psychology of learning, presentation in a small group or large public environment is one of the well-studied areas in the last few decades [5, 9, 12, 24, 25, 29, 32, 36]. Generally, the communication skills of a presentation are often assessed using certain rubrics [5, 9]. In the late 1970s, the National Communication Association (NCA) conducted a large scale study to identify the core competencies (including speaking and listening skills) for students. Quianthy [29] identified eight competencies: purpose determination, topic selection, organization, vocal variety, articulation, nonverbal behavior, language use, and use of supporting material. Following the study in [29], Morreale *et al.* [25] developed the "Competent Speaker Speech Evaluation Form", which evaluates eight items in a two-stage assessment process (i.e., *preparation and content* and *presentation and delivery*). Several other assessment rubrics have also been separately developed by different research groups [24, 32, 36]. Across these assessment rubrics, the core competencies only differ subtly where several items were adjusted to meet the respective analytic requirements [32].

In the computing literature, a variety of computational models have been proposed to analyze various types of competencies in presentation delivery, e.g., speech rate measurement [8], speech liveliness measurement [17], and social phobia analysis [34]. Kurihara *et al.* [19] proposed a presentation training system, which analyzes the speaking rate, eye contact with the audience, and timing during the presentation. The proposed system consists of only two sensors: "microphone" and "web camera". As the performance of the training system is mainly restricted by the analysis algorithms, the early prototype required the presenter to wear a special visual marker over the head to enhance the performance. Pfister and Robinson [28] proposed a system to analyze the speech emotion for the same application. The audio-based system focuses on the analysis of the various types of speech emotions (i.e., competent, credible, dynamic, persuasive, and pleasant). Recently, more modalities have been included in the analysis, especially the depth channel from Kinect sensor due to its robustness in tracking human body's motion. Several researchers have exploited the multi-modality data from the visual data, audio data and depth information [6, 7, 10, 27]. Nguyen *et al.* [27] used the Kinect sensor to recognize the bodily expressions and provide feedback on a scale of five degrees (i.e., bad, not bad, neutral, good, and excellent). Similarly, Echeverría *et al.* [10] proposed the use of the same sensor to grade the presenters' performance using eye contact score and body posture language score. Chen *et al.* [6] presented their initial study on the development of an automated scoring model, where they predict a singular score based on the analysis of the multi-modal features. In comparison, their later work [7] provides scores for the *delivery skills* and *slides quality*.

The technological advancements in microelectronics and computer systems have enabled new sensors and mobile devices with unprecedented characteristics. One of the new categories is the wearable sensing device, which has reduced size, weight and power consumption, and is generally equipped with multiple sensors. Examples of wearable sensing device include Fitbit, smartwatch, GoPro, and Google Glass. In contrast to the aforementioned sensors, denoted as ambient sensors in this work, the wearable sensor enables high precision in tracking the user's motion, and allows for continuous usage for daily activities [16]. For example, the skeleton data extracted with depth sensor is unreliable if the profile view of a user is given. But the Fitbit can provide activity data continuously. Another key difference resides in how the user interacts with the sensor [20]. The ambient sensors are pre-configured with a pre-determined region-of-interest, which restrict user interaction in a specific spatial location [14]. In contrast, the wearable sensor has no such constraints and user can perform the desired action in any location. There arise several new research problems with the wearable sensors. Ermes *et al.* [11] proposed the use of wearable sensors for detecting daily activities and sports under both controlled and uncontrolled conditions. Similarly, Hernandez *et al.* [16] estimates the physiological signals of the wearer using a head-mounted wearable device. Gan *et al.* [13] proposed a framework that used multiple egocentric visual sensors to recover the spatial structure of a social interaction. To the best of our knowledge, this is the first time that the wearable sensor has been used to quantify the performance of presentations.

3. THE ASSESSMENT RUBRIC

In this section, we detail the assessment rubric for multi-sensor self-quantification of presentations. Different from the assessment rubrics in the literature, the new rubric does not contain high level semantic concepts such as *topic selection* and *organization of ideas*, which makes it more suitable for data-driven analytics with sensors. This is motivated by the intention to make such self-quantification process automated, cheap yet useful. In the following sections, we first provide the overview of the proposed assessment rubric, followed by detailed discussion of each category.

3.1 Overview

In the psychology of learning and cognitive learning literature, the evaluation of presentation skills is always associated with the guidance of an assessment rubric [9, 24, 25, 29, 32, 36]. A rubric is a coherent set of criteria that includes descriptions of levels of performance quality on the criteria [5]. The human evaluator, based on speaker's behavior and the rubric, will decide the presentation quality and provide feedback to the speaker.

The computing literature follows a similar process and provides a *score* for each concept [6, 7, 10, 27]. However, these scores do not provide sufficient semantic cue to the speaker. For example, the system provides a speaking rate of 2 rather than a semantically meaningful label like "slow". Therefore, we have reviewed the prior work in the literature, and have proposed a new assessment rubric which is not only semantically meaningful, but is also more suitable for automated sensor-based analytics algorithms. The overview diagram of the proposed assessment rubric for multi-sensor self-quantification of presentations is shown in Figure 1.

The proposed assessment rubric consists of a three layered hierarchical structure, namely **category**, **concept** and **state**. The category layer contains the high level separation of behavior type in presentation, which consists of *vocal behavior*, *body language*, *engagement*, and *presentation state*. The concept layer further segments each category into a more detailed behavior. For example, the vocal behavior category contains the *speaking rate*, *liveliness*, and *fluency* concepts. The state layer provides the semantically meaningful state/class for each concept. For example, the gesture concept can be divided into three states (i.e., *normal*,

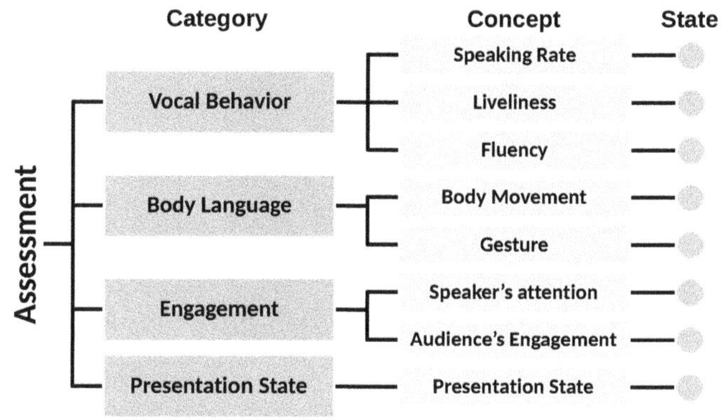

Figure 1: Proposed assessment rubric for multi-sensor self-quantification of presentations.

excessive, and *insufficient*). The detailed descriptions can be found in the next section.

3.2 Assessment Categories

3.2.1 Vocal Behavior

Presentation skill is multifaceted in nature, including lexical usage, fluency, pronunciation, and prosody [7]. This work focuses on the nonverbal vocal behaviors, where the prosodic features (e.g., pitch, tempo, energy, *etc.*) correspond to the voice quality [37]. We have identified three concepts which are frequently used in the assessment rubric [9, 24, 25, 29, 32, 36]: *speaking rate*, *liveliness*, and *fluency*. The speaking rate is a good predictor of the subjective concept fluency and liveliness. Liveliness is defined as the variation in intonation, rhythm and loudness. Fluency is a speech language pathology term that means the smoothness or flow with which sounds, syllables, words and phrases are joined together when speaking quickly. These three cognitive concepts can be interpreted in the computational measurement such as the number of syllables per minute, variation in pitch, and the number of filled pauses per minute. In our work, we quantify these concepts into three states: *insufficient*, *normal* and *excessive*.

3.2.2 Body Language

Body language is a form of nonverbal delivery method to strengthen the messages during presentation [18], where the messages are expressed by physical behavior, such as facial expression, body posture, gesture, and eye contact. As the facial analysis techniques are still far from perfect for real-world applications [43], we deliberately exclude facial expression and eye contact in this work. In addition, the speaker is often far away from the audience, resulting in low facial image resolution in the video footage. Two concepts, namely *body movement* and *gestures*, are included in the proposed rubric. The body movement relates to the usage of space and posture of the body. On the other hand, gestures, which are movements of the head, hands, and arms, can be used to convey specific messages that have linguistic translations. In our work, we quantify these concepts into three states: *insufficient*, *normal* and *excessive*.

3.2.3 Engagement

Engagement with audience in training or educational presentations is the key factor for effective idea delivery [38].

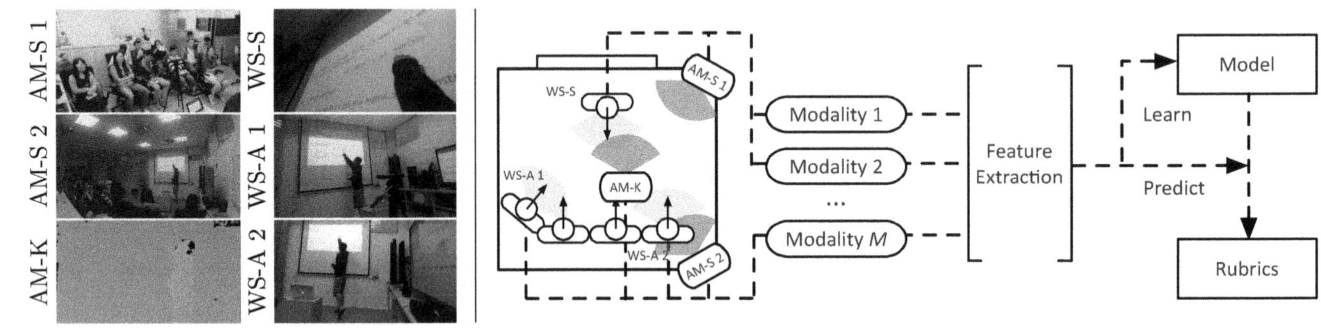

Figure 2: The sensor configuration and the proposed framework. AM-S and AM-K are the ambient static camera and ambient Kinect sensor. WS indicate the wearable sensor, where WS-S and WS-A represent WS from speaker and audience, respectively.

In this category, we evaluate both the speaker's and audience's attention, which are useful to characterize the engagement. During the presentation, the speaker may pay attention to the script, the audience, or the computer. Therefore, we list out the most common objects/scenes in a presentation and include an "others" category for completeness. Formally, the states for speaker's attention concept are *audience*, *screen*, *computer*, *script* and *others*. For the audience's engagement, we have formalized three states which are *no attention*, *attention without feedback*, and *attention with feedback*. The feedback can be reflected in the form of behavior like nodding of head to show acknowledgement, or involvement in the interaction between the audience and the speaker. For each state, the classifier will provide a binary decision for the presence of the state.

3.2.4 Presentation State

Question Answering (QA) is the interactive element of presentations. It provides speaker an opportunity to learn the current state of comprehension of the audience, and provides the audience a chance to convey their concerns. For this category, we have designed two states in the proposed assessment rubric, namely *presentation* and *QA*. The *presentation* characterizes the period where the speaker is the dominant person in the presentation, whereas *QA* characterizes the interval where the audience is asking questions or is having some discussion. The analytics on the presentation state mainly reflects the transition and flow of the presentation.

4. PROPOSED METHOD

In this section, we first provide an overview of the sensor configuration, followed by the proposed multi-sensor self-quantification framework and the details of the sensor analytics components.

4.1 Sensor Configuration

We set up our experiment environment in a meeting room with a Kinect sensor (denoted as AM-K) and two static RGB cameras with microphone (denoted as AM-S 1 and AM-S 2). AM-S 1 and AM-S 2 capture the speaker and audience from two different locations, whereas AM-K is configured to capture the behavior of the speaker with both RGB and depth channel. For each presentation, three Google Glasses are deployed, where one is worn by the speaker (denoted as WS-S) and the remaining two are worn by two randomly chosen audience members (denoted as WS-A 1 and WS-A 2). The overview of the sensor configuration and the approximate spatial location of the speaker and the audience are shown in Figure 2.

4.2 Multi-Sensor Analytics Framework

In the context of multi-sensor and multi-modal analysis, we assume that the data from each sensor can be modeled as a collection of feature set $\mathbb{X}$, where each member $\boldsymbol{X}^{m,i}$ is the feature extracted from the m modality and i feature type. In this work, we consider the *acoustic*, *visual*, *depth*, and *motion* modality, where the corresponding features of each modality are presented in the following sections. The feature $\boldsymbol{X}^{m,i}$ is further divided into N segments with an interval of T seconds: $\boldsymbol{X}^{m,i} = \{\boldsymbol{x}_1^{m,i}, \boldsymbol{x}_2^{m,i}, \ldots, \boldsymbol{x}_N^{m,i}\}$. Given the extracted feature, the task is to learn the respective classifier $\mathcal{F}_c : \boldsymbol{x}_n^{m,i} \mapsto r_n^c$ to produce r_n^c, where r_n^c is the predicted state/class for the corresponding c concept. The overview of our proposed framework is shown in Figure 2.

4.3 Feature Representation and Classification

4.3.1 Acoustic Feature

Four types of acoustic feature accounting for the speaking style are extracted from raw audio data using the Praat script [3]. The selected acoustic features are *pitch*, *intensity*, *formants*, and *syllables*.

Pitch is an auditory sensation which allows the ordering of sounds on a frequency-related scale. It is defined in the music literature as a stretch of sound whose frequency is clear and stable enough to be heard as not noise [30]. Following the work in [17], we compute the Pitch Variation Quotient (PVQ) feature as follows:

$$\boldsymbol{x}_n^{A,pitch} = \mu(\boldsymbol{p})_n / \sigma(\boldsymbol{p})_n \tag{1}$$

where $\boldsymbol{p}$ is the pitch feature computed from a T seconds interval.

The second feature is called the acoustic intensity and is defined as the sound power per unit area. The sound intensity is highly related to the subjective measure of loudness. The n acoustic intensity feature, $\boldsymbol{x}_n^{A,intensity}$, is defined as the mean and standard deviation of intensity over T seconds. These two features $\boldsymbol{x}^{A,pitch}$ and $\boldsymbol{x}^{A,intensity}$ are used to predict the liveliness concept. In this work, T is set to 10 seconds as it guarantees the inclusion of a fair amount of speech at the normal pausing rates [17].

Formant is a concentration of acoustic energy around a particular frequency in the speech wave. The fluency of speech is related to the presence of filled pauses, which are the hesitation sounds that speakers employ to indicate uncertainty or to maintain control of a conversation while thinking of what to say next. The formant information is used to characterize the fluency of a speech due to its ability of detecting filled pauses [1]. Based on the work in [1], we first compute the formant at a frame rate of 10 ms. Then the standard deviation of the first and second formant, $\sigma(F1)$ and $\sigma(F2)$, are computed over a window of T seconds centered on the current frame. The distribution of the $\sigma(F1)$ and $\sigma(F2)$ are discretized into 51 bins over the range from 0 to 200, which leads to a 51-point probability mass function $F_1 = f_{\sigma_{F1}}(i)$ and $F_2 = f_{\sigma_{F2}}(i)$ for $i = 1, 2, \ldots, 51$. We follow the work [21] to extract the feature $r(F)$, which is the ratio of the sum of the frequencies at the left side of a given frequency point. This feature is extracted for both F1 and F2 when the frequency point is 100Hz, $r_1(F)$, and 40Hz, $r_2(F)$, and is used to predict the fluency concept:

$$\boldsymbol{x}^{A,fluency} = [r_1(F_1), r_1(F_2), r_2(F_1), r_2(F_2)]. \quad (2)$$

The last feature, syllables, is used to predict the state of the speaking rate concept, which is a critical component of speech delivery. The speaking rate can be measured as the total number of words or syllables per minute. Generally, speech with a slower speaking rate is more intelligible than faster one. However, the variation in speaking rate may also contribute to the liveliness of speech [8, 35]. Using the method in [8], we extracted the location of the syllables for audio segment. For each n-th segment, we further count the number of syllables $||syl^n||$ within every one second, and discretize this distribution into 4 bins, which results in:

$$\boldsymbol{x}^{A,speakingrate} = \text{hist}(||syl^n||). \quad (3)$$

In order to detect the presentation state, it is important to understand the dominant role in a conversation (i.e., who is currently speaking?), as well as the identity of the speaker (i.e., who is the presenter and who are the audience?). In this work, we first utilize the open-source speaker diarization toolkit LIUM [31] to learn the identity (i.e., speaker or audience) from the audio data of the whole presentation. Conceptually, we perform an audio clustering where each cluster represents a unique person. Then, under the assumption that the presenter is the person who speaks for the longest duration, we label the audio data from this person as the presenter and the rest are labeled as audience. Given this information, the diarization feature is computed as a binary T-dimensional vector $\boldsymbol{x}^{A,speakerID}$ that indicates the speaker is currently speaking, where the t dimension corresponds to t seconds of the segmented data. This feature is used to predict the presentation state concept.

4.3.2 Visual Feature

The class of scene (e.g., audience, computer, script, *etc.*) from the speaker's FPV image is a good indicator of where the speaker is paying attention to. Given an image set $\mathbb{I}_n$ from the n-th segment, we first extract the pyramid histograms of visual words (PHOW) features [4] from each image and represent it as a Bag-of-Words (BoW) descriptor with vector quantization. Due to the scalability to perform scene classification in each frame, we pool all the frames from each second into a BoW descriptor $\boldsymbol{d}_n^t$. Inspired by the multi-instance learning problem, the n-th video segment is represented as $\boldsymbol{D}_n = [\boldsymbol{d}_n^1, \boldsymbol{d}_n^2, \ldots, \boldsymbol{d}_n^T]$, where each $\boldsymbol{d}_n^t$ is considered as an instance. Adopting a recent multi-instance learning approach [40], the BOW descriptor $\boldsymbol{D}_n$ is mapped into Fisher Vector to represent the n video segment:

$$\boldsymbol{x}_n^{V,scene} = M_f(\boldsymbol{D}_n, p), \quad (4)$$

where M_f is the mapping function proposed in [40], and p is the Gaussian Mixture Model (GMM).

4.3.3 Depth Feature

The recent advancements in depth sensing have created many opportunities for human behavior analysis [44]. By using Kinect sensor and the provided API, the Kinect skeletal tracking can represent the human body by a number of joints such as head, neck, shoulders. The skeleton information is useful in characterizing the behavior of the speaker, for example the body language. To differentiate the body movement and gesture, we use two kinds of features. First, the movement of the body, which is calculated by the average and standard deviation of the displacement of 12 upper body joints[1] *disUpper* over T seconds, are used to describe the body movement; second, an average and standard deviation of relative displacement of the selected joints[2] with respect to the human body center over T seconds are used to describe the gesture. In addition, the facial features like the landmarks of the face and orientation of the face can be obtained more efficiently and robustly with depth images when compared to extracting using only RGB images. Specifically, the head direction vector ori^{XYZ} are used:

$$\begin{aligned} \boldsymbol{x}^{D,body} &= [\mu(disUpper), \sigma(disUpper)] \\ \boldsymbol{x}^{D,gesture} &= [\mu(disUpper^{relative}), \sigma(disUpper^{relative})] \\ \boldsymbol{x}^{D,head} &= [\mu(ori^{XYZ}), \sigma(ori^{XYZ})] \end{aligned} \quad (5)$$

4.3.4 Motion Feature

In addition to the visual RGB sensor, Google Glass is also equipped with sensors like gyroscope, magnetometer, and accelerometer. These inertial motion sensors provide information about the device wearer's viewing direction and motion pattern. In contrast with the use of visual information to track human's head, which will fail in the non-frontal view, the sensor data is more accurate and robust. Two features, the mean and standard deviation of the camera viewing direction vector ori^{XYZ}, and the linear acceleration of the camera acc^{XYZ} over T seconds are used:

$$\boldsymbol{x}^{M} = [\mu(ori^{\text{XYZ}}), \sigma(ori^{\text{XYZ}}), \mu(acc^{\text{XYZ}}), \sigma(acc^{\text{XYZ}})] \quad (6)$$

4.4 Multi-Modal Analytics

For every single feature, we employ machine learning approach to predict the state of the concept. The multi-class SVM using a polynomial kernel was utilized as the machine learning tool. For multiple features, for example x^A and x^B, where A and B can be cross-sensors with the same type of feature, or cross-modalities from the same sensor, decision level fusion is done by training-based super-kernel fusion [42].

[1]The upper joints are HipCenter, Spine, ShoulderCenter, Head, ShoulderLeft, ElbowLeft, WristLeft, HandLeft, ShoulderRight, ElbowRight, WristRight, HandRight, and HipLeft.

[2]ElbowLeft, WristLeft, HandLeft, ElbowRight, WristRight, and HandRight.

5. EXPERIMENTS

In this section, we first describe the new multi-sensor presentation dataset, followed by the quantitative evaluation and discussion of the sensor performance using the assessment rubric.

5.1 Multi-Sensor Presentation Dataset

We have collected a new presentation dataset, namely NUS Multi-Sensor Presentation (NUSMSP) dataset[3], which is designed for experiments in multi-sensor self-quantification of presentations under real-world conditions. The dataset is recorded in a meeting room with two static cameras (with built-in microphone), one Kinect sensor, and three Google Glasses. Figure 2 shows the sensor configuration. The NUSMSP dataset consists of 51 unique speakers (32 male and 19 female), where each speaker was asked to prepare and deliver a 15 minutes presentation with no restriction on the topic and content. The number of audience ranged from 4 to 8. For each presentation, the speaker and two randomly chosen audience were asked to wear Google Glass. In total, we have about 10 hours of presentation data. Due to unforeseen technical issues in the recording devices, a small portion of presentation has not been recorded.

We manually annotated the NUSMSP dataset based on the proposed assessment rubric (see Figure 1 for details). The video data are segmented into multiple clips of 10 seconds duration. To remove the subjective bias in the annotation, each clip was annotated with a minimum of five human annotators and the final groundtruth is determined by majority voting.

5.2 Result and Discussion

In this section, we present the single modality and multi-modality based evaluation on *body language*, *engagement*, and *presentation state* category. The analytics are evaluated with depth information (D), motion information (M), visual information (V), and audio data. As the analytics of vocal behavior category are achieved with existing methods [1, 8, 17], it is not reported in this section. The classification performance is reported with 5-fold cross-validation. In the remaining section, we denote ambient static camera and ambient Kinect sensor as Am-S and Am-K, where the wearable sensor on speaker and audience are denoted as WS-S and WS-A, respectively. An overview of the configuration of sensor type, data modality, and the respective concept are listed in Table 1.

Table 2 shows the classification result on the body language category. The "Body Movement" and "Gesture" concept have three states: "In", *insufficient*; "Norm", *normal*; and "Exc", *excessive*. Am-K's depth sensor data and WS-S's motion sensor data are used for the classification. The depth modality performs the best for the *insufficient* state in both body movement and gesture concept. However, it does not perform well on the *normal* and *excessive* states. The reason is because the *insufficient* state mostly has little amount of joint location displacement, and is comparatively easier to differentiate from *normal* or *excessive* states. In comparison, the distinction between *normal* and *excessive* is less obvious, even in the human annotated ground truth. The motion data performs average on the three states, in which the performance on the gesture concept is comparatively worse than body movement. This is because the motion information from the head-mounted wearable sensors have less relation with the gesture as compared to the body movement. The fusion of depth data and motion data indeed helps in the classification of the *insufficient* and *excessive* state in body movement concept. The poor performance on the *normal* state further validates the ambiguous boundary between two consecutive states.

The results on speaker's attention are shown in Table 3. The classification on four states *script*, *audience*, *computer*, and *screen* are evaluated. The head tracking information extracted from Am-K's depth sensor and the visual and motion information from WS-S are used for the classification. In general, the visual modality performs best among the three modalities. The superiority is less prominent for the *audience* state. This is because compared to *script*, *computer*, and *screen* state, the *audience* state has more visual variations. The depth information performs the worst among these three modalities. This is because the depth head tracking which provides the head orientation works well only when the human shows the frontal view. The performance on the motion sensor data which also provide the orientation information is much more accurate than on the depth data. The fusion of these modalities

[3]http://mmas.comp.nus.edu.sg/NUSMSP.html

Table 1: The configuration of sensor type, data modality, and the respective concept to be analyzed. The red, blue, and green columns represent concepts from the body language, engagement, and presentation state, respectively. Am-S and Am-K denote the ambient static camera and ambient Kinect sensor, where WS-S and WS-A represent the wearable sensor on Speaker and Audience, respectively.

Sensor Type	Modality	Body Movement	Gesture	Speaker's Attention	Audience Engagement	Presentation State
Am-S	Visual					
	Audio					✓
Am-K	Depth	✓	✓	✓		
WS-S	Motion	✓	✓	✓		
	Visual			✓		
	Audio					✓
WS-A	Motion				✓	
	Visual				✓	
	Audio					✓

Table 2: Average classification accuracy on the body language category. D and M represent Am-K-Depth and WS-S-Motion, respectively.

Modality	Body Movement			Gesture		
	In	Norm	Exc	In	Norm	Exc
D	81.28	26.73	36.28	80.13	38.59	30.65
M	52.07	42.04	65.13	48.58	53.77	34.18
D+M	84.33	10.10	63.46	67.69	29.73	51.27

Table 3: Average classification accuracy on the speaker's attention concept. D, V, M represent Am-K-Depth, WS-S-Visual and WS-S-Motion, respectively.

Modality	Script	Audience	Computer	Screen
D	65.83	56.35	62.67	66.15
V	96.25	78.94	86.21	85.03
M	77.36	71.97	66.30	79.44
V + M	95.97	82.71	84.26	83.36
D + V	95.97	82.71	84.96	84.76
D + M	77.36	73.08	67.13	80.28
D + V + M	95.97	82.71	84.54	83.50

Table 4: Average classification accuracy on the audiences' engagement concept. V and M represent WS-A-Visual and WS-A-Motion, respectively.

Modality	No	Yes without Feedback	Yes with Feedback
V	59.28	63.73	65.07
M	42.94	68.95	65.80
V+M	68.37	62.85	64.48

performs similar with their corresponding single modality on *script*, *computer*, *screen* state, in which V is the dominating modality. In comparison, fusion on *audience* state helps improve the performance.

Table 4 reports the result of the audience's engagement. The three states are *no*, *yes without feedback*, and *yes with feedback*. The performance on the *no* state is worse than the other two states. This is because the audience mostly focus on the other audience, screen, or are engaged in the discussion with speaker and other audience mentioned in the *yes* states. In comparison, the *no* state has more variations. The fusion of V and M helps improve the performance on *no* state, with slight decrement on the two other states.

The presentation state is detected based on the speaker diarization information using the audio modality: the audio from the ambient static sensor, the speaker's wearable sensor, and the audience's wearable sensors. As shown in Table 5, the ambient sensor's performance on the "QA" state is significantly worse than the performance using wearable sensors' data. By analyzing the result we found out that the audio from the speaker's and audience's FPV sensor achieves better performance on the speaker diarization than the ambient sensor. The speaker's and audience's FPV sensor helps diarize the speaker and audience better.

To summarize, in terms of the cross-sensor analysis, based on the sensor configuration in Table 1, the speaker's wearable sensor WS-S can classify the speaker's attention and the presentation state well. The performance on the body language is not satisfying on our selected head-mounted wearable sensor. This may be improved by other new types of sensors such as smart watches. The conventional ambient sensors can also classify the same set of concepts, with better performance on analyzing human body language during presentations. However, the performance of the ambient sensors on tracking the speaker's attention is poor, due to its speaker frontal view restriction. Also, the performance on the presentation state is lower when using the ambient audio data when compared to the wearable sensors' audio data. Due the low facial image resolution in the speaker view camera, conventional methods that detects and tracks audience's faces to predict audience's engagement are unreliable in the unconstrained environment [22, 26, 39]. In contrast, wearable sensors on the audience can provide more accurate and detailed information about the audience's engagement state and the presentation state. However, the audience's engagement is based on the selected audience who wear the sensor. It is difficult to equip every audience with a wearable sensor and to expect them to share their data.

Table 5: Average classification accuracy on presentation state.

Modality	Presentation	QA
Am-S-Audio	87.31	58.16
WS-S-Audio	81.19	80.91
WS-A-Audio	80.81	80.75

6. USER STUDY

In this section, we elaborate the details of user study with the speakers in our dataset. We first describe the system generated self-quantification report, followed by discussion of the presenters' feedback.

6.1 Analytics

Using the analytic model for each proposed assessment rubric, a system generated analytics report is generated for each presentation. The report consists of three main components: **(1)** footage from all video capturing devices, **(2)** time-series analytics, and **(3)** cumulative sum of the analytic result. Snapshots of two system-generated reports are shown in Figure 3.

The top section of the generated feedback shows the video footage from each device. The current frames correspond to the moment highlighted in the time-series analytics section. The bottom left section shows the time-series result, in which the first five concepts, i.e., speaking rate, fluency, liveliness, body movement, and gesture, are shown with the *insufficient*, *normal*, and *excessive* state quantified into three regions (bottom, middle, and top portion for each horizontal bar). The speaker's attention concept is shown as the red occupation mark at each time point. For example, if the speaker is paying attention on *audience* in the *t*-th segment, the corresponding location on the *audience*'s row will be marked as red. It is common that multiple attention states can co-exist in the same segment, e.g., the audience state and the screen state are marked with attention when the speaker switches between audience and screen. If none of the state in *audience*, *screen*, *computer*, or *script*, the attention will be shown as *others*. The last two concepts are audience's engagement, in which the corresponding states are *no attention*, *attention without feedback* and *attention with feedback* from bottom to top. These concepts (except for the speaker's attention) are highlighted in red, purple, and grey, representing *presentation* state, *QA* state, and unavailable state (this may due to the error of the sensor). The number of the audience's engagement concepts can vary depend on the available audience's FPV devices. The bottom right section shows the cumulative sum of the analytic result.

The analytics feedback allows the user to quickly examine their performance. From Figure 3, we can see that Speaker A and Speaker B have very different behaviors during the presentation. From the time-series results, we notice that

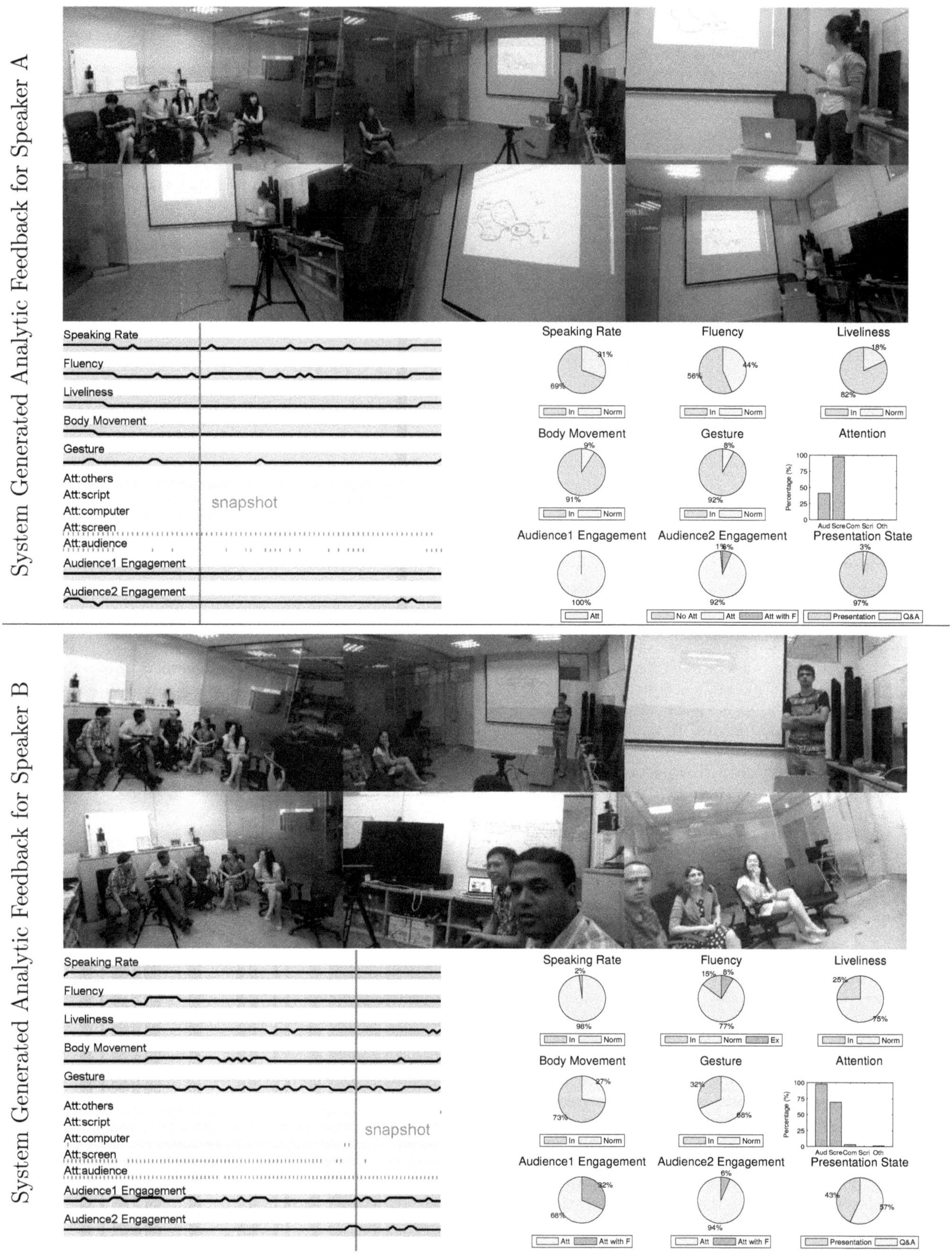

Figure 3: Example of two system generated analytic feedbacks. For each feedback, the six snapshots are taken from the ambient sensors (top row) and wearable first-person-view sensors (bottom row).

Speaker A spent a significant of time on the screen, without interacting or even looking at the audience. In contrast, although Speaker B spent around 70% of the time looking at the screen, we can see that he kept switching between the screen and the audience. Also, Speaker B's presentation involves significant time in the *QA* state. For example, the snapshot in this example is in the state where a question triggers the audience members to discuss among themselves.

6.2 Feedback from the Speakers

In order to further validate the efficacy of our system generated analytics report, we presented the results to the speakers and requested them to complete the following survey:

1. Are the analytics results surprising to you?
2. Are the analytics results useful to you?
3. Can these results help you improve your presentation skills? If so, could you please precisely explain how they can do so?
4. Do you find it intrusive to use the wearable sensor during the presentation? Please elaborate on your experience.
5. If the technology is mature and non-intrusive enough to provide such feedback with good accuracy, would you like to use it?
6. Do you have any other suggestions for improving this analytics feedback?

The first five questions are to be answered using a score from 1 to 5, ranging from "strongly disagree" to "strongly agree". Question 3, 4 and 6 require speaker to elaborate their opinions. In total, we received 21 responses from the speakers, with an average score of 3.59, 4.27, 4.36, 2.79, 4.58 for the first five questions.

Generally speaking, we found that the speakers held a positive attitude towards our summarized feedback. One of the speakers who was "surprised" by the results responded with "I was not aware that I have spent so many time looking at the screen." Most of the speakers found the presentation behavior patterns identified by the system to be accurate, and agreed that the feedback is useful (4.27) as well as helpful for improvement (4.36). Their feedback for the results are: "Avoid excessive gestures and have more eye contact with the audience." By the synchronization with the presentation state, one speaker responded that "Also, maybe more gestures during the presentation (not only during QA session) will be beneficial.", which implies the actual usage of the combination of presentation concept and gesture concept. The opinions about the "intrusiveness" of the Google Glass are mostly neutral or positive, except that three of the speakers criticized the design of the Google Glass: " I just could not help looking at the small screen of Google Glass. It's not comfortable since I have to roll my eyes to one side to see it clearly.", " Very intrusive, the Google glass blocks my view and is very heavy.", "Not convenient especially for people who wear glasses". The answers for trying this type of system are positive (4.58), with all the responses from ranging from agree to strongly agree.

The suggestions from the speakers can be summarized as follows: (1) comparison with the average performance or good performance will be helpful as one speaker mentioned that "A reference frame would be useful, e.g., the average score of all participants or the best score for a good presentation. If I don't know what I am compared with, I won't know how I could improve."; (2) timely feedback after the presentation: "If I am given the results right after the presentation, I can remember what I did to lose my audience's attention, or why I had a bad body expression, etc."; (3) showing the examples of the typical behavior: "Maybe examples of 'insufficient', 'normal', and 'excessive' behaviors will be useful, in form of short video clips?" We can see that the speakers all agree that this kind of information is useful, however, timely feedback immediately after the presentation and reference statistics can help them better interpret the data. Also, they are interested in observing their actual behavior for each concept.

7. CONCLUSIONS AND FUTURE WORKS

In this work, we have proposed a multi-sensors analytics framework to provide the analysis of a presentation. The proposed framework consists of ambient sensors (e.g., visual sensors and depth sensors), First-Person-View (FPV) sensor on speaker, and multiple FPV sensors by the audience. Based on the literature from both social science and computing, we have developed a novel assessment rubric for presentations. We evaluate the performance of existing computational models and analyze the efficacy by combining multiple sensors. To complement the research, we have recorded a new dataset, *NUSMSP*, which consists of 51 subjects giving presentations on diverse topics. We have conducted user studies on the speakers with our generated analytics report, which provides good insights for future research directions.

For the future work, we plan to conduct user studies with our system to measure the individual improvement over multiple presentation sessions. This process will include presentation coaches for validation purposes. In addition, we would like to generalize the current framework with an online learning approach so that the system can adapt to new speakers and new environments efficiently. Last, we aim to improve the visualization of our system generated analytics feedback with richer information.

8. ACKNOWLEDGMENT

This research was carried out at the SeSaMe Centre. It is supported by the Singapore NRF under its IRC@SG Funding Initiative and administered by the IDMPO.

9. REFERENCES

[1] K. Audhkhasi, K. Kandhway, O. Deshmukh, and A. Verma. Formant-based technique for automatic filled-pause detection in spontaneous spoken english. In *Proceedings of the IEEE International Conference on Acoustics, Speech, and Signal Processing*, pages 4857–4860, 2009.

[2] T. W. Banta. *Assessing Student Achievement in General Education: Assessment Update Collections*, volume 5. John Wiley & Sons, 2007.

[3] P. Boersma and D. Weenink. Praat, a system for doing phonetics by computer. *Glot International*, pages 341–345, 2002.

[4] A. Bosch, A. Zisserman, and X. Muñoz. Image classification using random forests and ferns. In *International Conference on Computer Vision*, pages 1–8, 2007.

[5] S. M. Brookhart and F. Chen. The quality and effectiveness of descriptive rubrics. *Educational Review*, pages 1–26, 2014.

[6] L. Chen, G. Feng, J. Joe, C. W. Leong, C. Kitchen, and C. M. Lee. Towards automated assessment of public speaking skills using multimodal cues. In *Proceedings of the International Conference on Multimodal Interaction*, pages 200–203, 2014.

[7] L. Chen, C. W. Leong, G. Feng, and C. M. Lee. Using multimodal cues to analyze mla'14 oral presentation quality corpus: Presentation delivery and slides quality. In *Proceedings of the ACM Workshop on Multimodal Learning Analytics Workshop and Grand Challenge*, pages 45–52, 2014.

[8] N. De Jong and T. Wempe. Praat script to detect syllable nuclei and measure speech rate automatically. *Behavior Research Methods*, 41(2):385–390, 2009.

[9] N. E. Dunbar, C. F. Brooks, and T. Kubicka-Miller. Oral communication skills in higher education: Using a performance-based evaluation rubric to assess communication skills. *Innovative Higher Education*, 31(2):115–128, 2006.

[10] V. Echeverría, A. Avendaño, K. Chiluiza, A. Vásquez, and X. Ochoa. Presentation skills estimation based on video and kinect data analysis. In *Proceedings of the ACM Workshop on Multimodal Learning Analytics Workshop and Grand Challenge*, pages 53–60, 2014.

[11] M. Ermes, J. Pärkkä, J. Mäntyjärvi, and I. Korhonen. Detection of daily activities and sports with wearable sensors in controlled and uncontrolled conditions. *IEEE Transactions on Information Technology in Biomedicine*, 12(1):20–26, 2008.

[12] S. B. Fawcett and L. K. Miller. Training Public-Speaking Behavior: An Experimental Analysis and Social Validation. *Journal of Applied Behavior Analysis*, (2):125–135, 1975.

[13] T. Gan, Y. Wong, B. Mandal, V. Chandrasekhar, L. Li, J.-H. Lim, and M. S. Kankanhalli. Recovering social interaction spatial structure from multiple first-person views. In *Proceedings of International Workshop on Socially-Aware Multimedia*, pages 7–12, 2014.

[14] T. Gan, Y. Wong, D. Zhang, and M. S. Kankanhalli. Temporal encoded F-formation system for social interaction detection. In *Proceedings of ACM International Conference on Multimedia*, pages 937–946, 2013.

[15] F. Guo, Y. Li, M. S. Kankanhalli, and M. S. Brown. An evaluation of wearable activity monitoring devices. In *Proceedings of ACM International Workshop on Personal Data Meets Distributed Multimedia*, pages 31–34, 2013.

[16] J. Hernandez, Y. Li, J. M. Rehg, and R. W. Picard. BioGlass: Physiological parameter estimation using a head-mounted wearable device. In *International Conference on Wireless Mobile Communication and Healthcare: "Transforming healthcare through innovations in mobile and wireless technologies"*, pages 55–58, 2014.

[17] R. Hincks. Measures and perceptions of liveliness in student oral presentation speech: A proposal for an automatic feedback mechanism. *System*, 33(4):575 – 591, 2005.

[18] E. S. Klima. *The signs of language.* Harvard University Press, 1979.

[19] K. Kurihara, M. Goto, J. Ogata, Y. Matsusaka, and T. Igarashi. Presentation sensei: a presentation training system using speech and image processing. In *Proceedings of the International Conference on Multimodal Interfaces*, pages 358–365, 2007.

[20] O. D. Lara and M. A. Labrador. A survey on human activity recognition using wearable sensors. *IEEE Communications Surveys and Tutorials*, 15(3):1192–1209, 2013.

[21] G. Luzardo, B. Guamán, K. Chiluiza, J. Castells, and X. Ochoa. Estimation of presentations skills based on slides and audio features. In *Proceedings of the ACM Workshop on Multimodal Learning Analytics Workshop and Grand Challenge*, pages 37–44, 2014.

[22] W. Mansell, D. M. Clark, A. Ehlers, and Y.-P. Chen. Social anxiety and attention away from emotional faces. *Cognition and Emotion*, 13(6):673–690, 1999.

[23] R. E. Mayer. *Learning and instruction.* Prentice Hall, 2003.

[24] S. Morreale and P. Backlund. Large-scale assessment in oral communication: K-12 and higher education, washington. *National Communication Association*, 2007.

[25] S. P. Morreale, M. R. Moore, K. P. Taylor, D. Surges-Tatum, and R. Hulbert-Johnson. *The competent speaker speech evaluation form.* National Communication Association, 1993.

[26] J. Müller, J. Exeler, M. Buzeck, and A. Krüger. Reflectivesigns: Digital signs that adapt to audience attention. In *International Conference on Pervasive Computing*, pages 17–24, 2009.

[27] A.-t. Nguyen, W. Chen, and M. Rauterberg. Online feedback system for public speakers. In *IEEE Symposium on E-Learning, E-Management and E-Services*, pages 1–5, 2012.

[28] T. Pfister and P. Robinson. Speech emotion classification and public speaking skill assessment. In *Human Behavior Understanding Workshop*, pages 151–162. Springer, 2010.

[29] R. L. Quianthy. *Communication is life: Essential college sophomore speaking and listening competencies.* Speech Communication Association, 1990.

[30] D. M. Randel. *The Harvard dictionary of music*, volume 16. Harvard University Press, 2003.

[31] M. Rouvier, G. Dupuy, P. Gay, E. el Khoury, T. Merlin, and S. Meignier. An open-source state-of-the-art toolbox for broadcast news diarization. In *INTERSPEECH*, pages 1477–1481, 2013.

[32] L. M. Schreiber, G. D. Paul, and L. R. Shibley. The development and test of the public speaking competence rubric. *Communication Education*, 61(3):205–233, 2012.

[33] A. W. Siegman and S. Feldstein. *Nonverbal behavior and communication.* Psychology Press, 2014.

[34] M. Slater, D. Pertaub, C. Barker, and D. M. Clark. An experimental study on fear of public speaking using a virtual environment. *Cyberpsychology, Behavior, and Social Networking*, 9(5):627–633, 2006.

[35] S. M. Tasko and K. Greilick. Acoustic and articulatory features of diphthong production: A speech clarity study. *Journal of Speech, Language, and Hearing Research*, 53(1):84–99, 2010.

[36] S. Thomson and M. L. Rucker. The development of a specialized public speaking competency scale: Test of reliability. *Communication Research Reports*, 19(1):18–28, 2002.

[37] A. Vinciarelli, M. Pantic, and H. Bourlard. Social signal processing: Survey of an emerging domain. *Image and Vision Computing*, 27(12):1743–1759, 2009.

[38] J. Webster and H. Ho. Audience engagement in multimedia presentations. *ACM SIGMIS Database*, 28(2):63–77, 1997.

[39] X. Wei and Z. Yang. Mining in-class social networks for large-scale pedagogical analysis. In *Proceedings of ACM International Conference on Multimedia*, pages 639–648, 2012.

[40] X.-S. Wei, J. Wu, and Z.-H. Zhou. Scalable multi-instance learning. In *IEEE International Conference on Data Mining*, pages 1037–1042, 2014.

[41] J. S. Wrench, A. Goding, D. I. Johnson, and B. A. *Stand Up, Speak Out: The Practice and Ethics of Public Speaking.* 2011.

[42] Y. Wu, E. Y. Chang, K. C.-C. Chang, and J. R. Smith. Optimal multimodal fusion for multimedia data analysis. In *Proceedings of ACM International Conference on Multimedia*, pages 572–579, 2004.

[43] Z. Zeng, M. Pantic, G. I. Roisman, and T. S. Huang. A survey of affect recognition methods: Audio, visual, and spontaneous expressions. *IEEE Transactions on Pattern Analysis and Machine Intelligence*, 31(1):39–58, 2009.

[44] Z. Zhang. Microsoft kinect sensor and its effect. *IEEE MultiMedia*, 19(2):4–10, 2012.

HyperMeeting: Supporting Asynchronous Meetings with Hypervideo

Andreas Girgensohn[1], Jennifer Marlow[1], Frank Shipman[2], Lynn Wilcox[1]

[1]FX Palo Alto Laboratory
3174 Porter Drive
Palo Alto, CA 94304
{andreasg,marlow,wilcox}@fxpal.com

[2]Department of Computer Science
Texas A&M University
College Station, TX 77843-3112
shipman@cs.tamu.edu

ABSTRACT

While synchronous meetings are an important part of collaboration, it is not always possible for all stakeholders to meet at the same time. We created the concept of hypermeetings for meetings with asynchronous attendance. Such hypermeetings consist of a chain of video-recorded meetings with hyperlinks for navigating through them. Our HyperMeeting system supports the viewing of prior meetings during a videoconference. Natural viewing behavior such as pausing video generates hyperlinks between previous and current meetings. During playback, automatic link-following guided by playback plans present the relevant content to users. Playback plans take into account the user's meeting attendance and viewing history and match them with features such as topic and speaker segmentation. A user study showed that participants found hyperlinks useful but did not always understand where the links would take them. Experiences from longer-term use and the study results provide a good basis for future system improvements.

Categories and Subject Descriptors

H.4.3 [**Information Systems Applications**]: Communications Applications – *computer conferencing, teleconferencing, and videoconferencing*. H.5.1 [**Information Interfaces and Presentation**]: Multimedia Information Systems – *hypertext navigation and maps, video.*

Keywords

Hypervideo; hypermeeting; meeting capture; asynchronous meetings; teleconferencing.

1. INTRODUCTION

Meetings are an important part of collaboration. Although it is well known that people prefer face-to-face meetings, this is not always possible. For the case where attendees are remote but a synchronous meeting can be arranged, Skype or Google Hangouts can be used. However, when users are in different time zones or are traveling, finding a time for a synchronous meeting among all members is frequently difficult and sometimes impossible. One option is to record the meeting so that missing members can review it asynchronously. While there are third-party tools for recording such videoconferences, experience indicates that people rarely go back and listen to the recordings, resulting in the need for participants to bring missing members up to speed by repeating parts of the past meeting. It can also be burdensome to review the entirety of previous meetings for a few key action items or takeaway points [14]. Formal meetings have minutes but those are not a replacement for access to the meeting discussion as they tend to record decisions and not why the decision was made.

MM'15, October 26-30, 2015, Brisbane, Australia
© 2015 ACM. ISBN 978-1-4503-3459-4/15/10...$15.00
DOI: http://dx.doi.org/10.1145/2733373.2806258

We propose the notion of a hypermeeting as a means to capture and review meetings in an asynchronous manner. Synchronous participants record the meeting, while later participants simultaneously review the meeting and add comments. We hypothesize that the ability to add comments will encourage members who missed it to actually listen to the meeting. In turn meeting attendees will be interested enough to review the comments made about their meeting. Thus rather than isolated recordings, these hypermeetings will allow a single meeting to be held asynchronously. We pose the following research questions:

1. How can technology support the creation, continuation and review of asynchronous, distributed discussions over time?
2. How does allowing people to review content in a non-linear way influence the process of navigating through and understanding a series of past meetings?

The HyperMeeting system combines meeting capture with generating and viewing hypervideo. Video from multiple synchronous videoconferencing attendees is recorded and indexed by speaker and topic. During subsequent meetings, this video is viewed synchronously by potentially geographically separated attendees, and discussions of topics in the previous meeting or new topics are recorded. Pausing prior recordings usually leads to further discussions of the same content so that we chose this interaction as the trigger for automatic hyperlink creation. We use the terms *hypermeeting* and *meeting chain* to describe such a series of interlinked meetings.

These linked video recordings form a hypervideo that can be navigated in different ways. Our novel concept of a playback plan infers information needs of watchers from their roles in a meeting chain to support automatic playback behavior. Plans can take into account features of the current meeting and attendee actions, involvement in prior meetings by current meeting attendees, and topics attached to meeting content to decide which links to follow automatically in a set of interlinked meetings. Plans can include filters to skip undesired content such as silence or previously watched video segments.

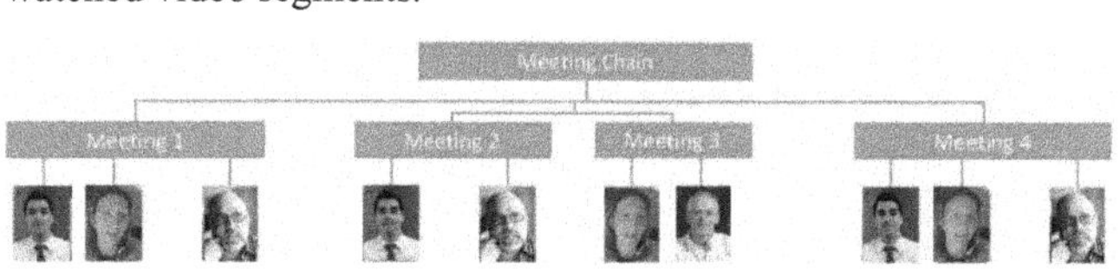

Figure 1. Example of sequence of project meetings.

The novel contributions of our work are the support for a chain of synchronous meetings forming an asynchronous hypermeeting, the synchronized playback of video streams by attendees of follow-up meetings, the ease of creating hyperlinks from recorded to live video, and automatic playback guided by playback plans.

The next sections present a usage scenario, the conceptual framework, and related work. Section 4 describes the HyperMeeting architecture and its components. Sections 5 and 6 present experiences gained from longer-term use and the results of an initial user evaluation of HyperMeeting. The conclusions in Section 7 indicate directions for future work.

2. SCENARIO AND FRAMEWORK

HyperMeeting can record and support access to meeting content in many contexts but our focus is enabling project teams distributed over multiple time zones. Figure 1 shows an example of such a situation. Consider the case where periodic meetings occur for a project involving a distributed team, John and Ann in San Francisco and Anders in Munich. As such, remote meeting software is required because members of the team have other responsibilities and are not available for every scheduled meeting. Additional team members at both sites are involved in the meetings. This scenario and our first system design focus on egalitarian meetings – the type of meetings most valuable to our initial user community.

In Figure 1, a kickoff videoconference (Meeting 1) occurs with John, Ann and Anders each recorded in their own video (although John and Ann could have been in the same room). The next week, Ann is not available at the normal meeting time but John and Anders meet to discuss progress and look back at the recordings from the prior week's meetings to make sure they remember Ann's perspective on some of the design issues (Meeting 2). As they replay and comment on the prior recordings, links are automatically generated between the original and later meeting and, sometimes, John and Anders attach labels to the links to indicate the subject of the discussion. Later, Ann meets with Bob to further discuss the project (Meeting 3). Their meeting is initially a set of reactions and responses to Meeting 2 but moves on to other topics as well. The regularly scheduled distributed meeting (Meeting 4) reviews the recordings and links from the previous meetings to guide further discussions of the main subjects.

An important aspect of supporting both those attending and missing meetings is to establish relations among meetings as new meeting content is recorded. We define a *meeting chain* or *hypermeeting* to be a recurring meeting or a set of interrelated meetings. Each meeting is composed of synchronized video streams and other associated data. A meeting may consist of just a single video stream in cases when an individual is recording responses to a previously recorded meeting that they could not attend or if an in-person meeting was recorded by a single camera.

Metadata about the meeting series include the list of attendees for each meeting, the topics assigned to segments of the meetings, and the links between meetings. Segmentation of the meetings based on who is speaking and the topics being discussed is used to provide finer access into the recordings. The framework allows for a variety of automatic, semi-automatic, and manual techniques to be used for segmentation, indexing, linking, and playback.

3. RELATED WORK

Previous research has employed a variety of approaches to address the issue of allowing people to asynchronously revisit and review content from discussions or meetings.

One class of systems aimed at addressing this problem focuses on capturing the content of meetings for later consumption. Meeting capture systems [6][7][10][13] record content for later playback and browsing, taking advantage of natural activity during meetings (e.g., slide presentations or activities on an electronic whiteboard) to generate navigation points back into the record. These systems allow users to review and find information in a meeting but do not incorporate the ability to extend a previous meeting or create links between meetings.

A second class of systems have been designed to support asynchronous participation in meetings, e.g., Time Travel Proxy [19] and Video Threads [1], by having meeting attendees record and view short videos on topics with responses. In Time Travel Proxy, an absent meeting attendee pre-records a video message that is played in the meeting and the attendees' reaction is recorded. Video Threads puts asynchronous video recordings into a conversation thread similar to an email discussion. These recordings form a discussion thread that supports responses on individual topics but loses the connections between the responses, i.e., the fact that they came from the same meeting.

A third class of systems allow viewers and creators of content to make video more interactive by creating navigable links or annotations within the video itself, e.g., hypervideo. This has been viewed as particularly valuable for education [20]. For example, recent work by [5] in the educational domain allows viewers to annotate and embed discussions at particular locations and times within a video, and to peruse and continue the discussion asynchronously using these "spatiotemporal links." The economic viability for enterprise use of interactive video to support decision making is explored in [11].

General purpose hypervideo systems (e.g., [17][18]) enable rich linking between video content but prior work on hypervideo has focused on authored content. A video-recorded meeting could be taken as the starting point for such authoring but prior systems lack the ability to identify topics and relations among topics as a way of authoring or generating the hypervideo. Also, they do not include features to support the meeting-specific nature of the video (e.g., attachment of metadata indicating attendees, topics, and time/date indexing). Hypermedia models like CHM [16] represent relationships between content elements and definition of presentation arrangements. Such models could be used to represent speaker, topic, and link information. Finally, none of these systems support geographically distributed synchronous viewing of hypervideos although there has been work to optimize prefetching of video content in anticipation of user-driven navigation [9].

A last class of related systems support the synchronous viewing of video content on distributed devices [3][15]. These systems can include additional channels of communication (e.g., chat) for synchronous viewers to discuss what they are watching but these records of communication are, at best, attached as metadata to the video content. In our context, it is important that each meeting be treated as primary content whether or not it is the first meeting in a meeting chain.

4. HYPERMEETING SYSTEM

We designed the HyperMeeting system to address the research question of *how technology can support the creation, continuation and review of asynchronous, distributed discussions over time.* The system provides two main functionalities, a video conferencing system with recording capability and an environment for collaboratively viewing a chain of previously recorded meetings. Figure 2 shows the user interface. During a meeting, any attendee

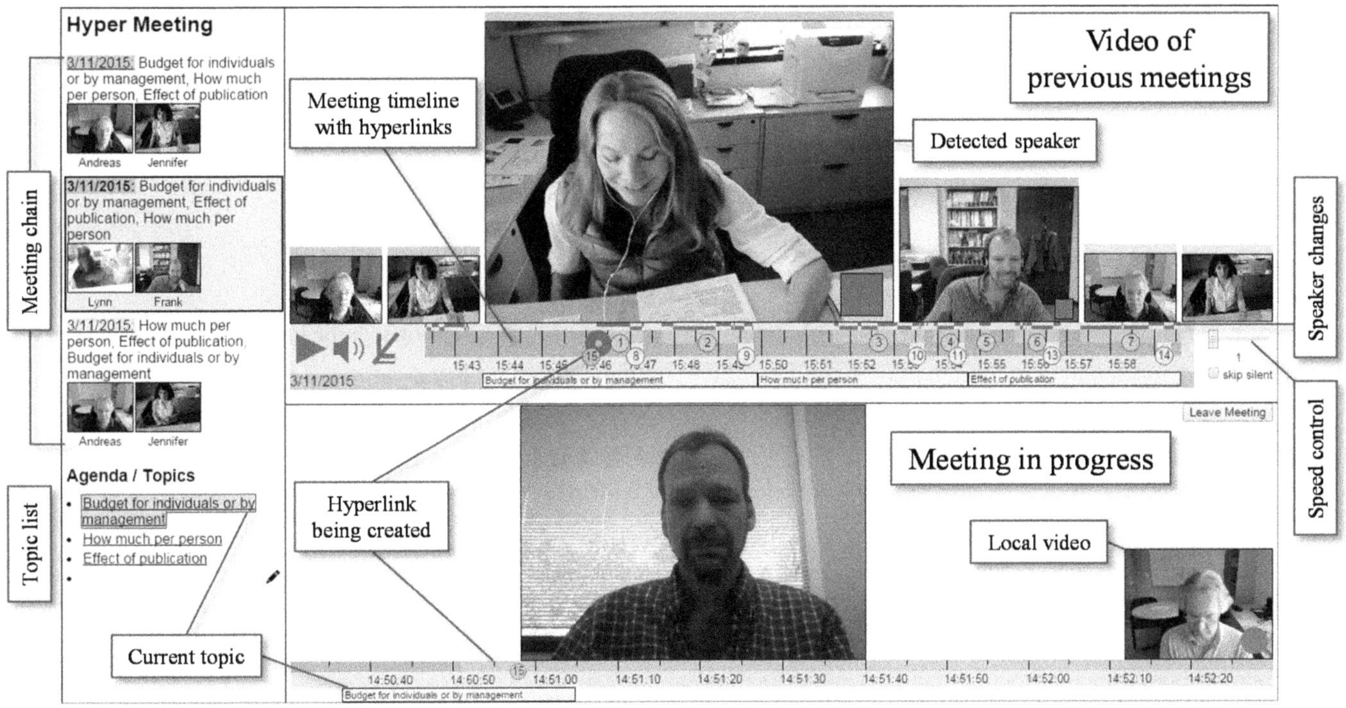

Figure 2. HyperMeeting recording interface continuing a chain of three previous meetings.

may navigate hyperlinks connecting video recordings of previous meetings, while keeping the view of all attendees synchronized.

In the following subsections, we cover how a chain of meetings is recorded and hyperlinks are created to form an asynchronous hypermeeting. We then describe synchronized playback of multiple video streams by multiple attendees of follow-up meetings. We introduce the novel features of automatic link-following and of playback plans that adapt playback for different contexts of use. Finally, we describe the web-based architecture of the HyperMeeting system.

4.1 Meeting Recording

A unique characteristic of HyperMeeting is that video playback and annotation can be a collaborative activity. Previously recorded meetings can be continued in a new synchronous video meeting that is added to the meeting chain. Video players showing oneself and the other attendees of the current meeting are displayed in the bottom right portion of the interface (see "Meeting in progress" in Figure 2). A red circle on top of the local video display in the bottom-right indicates that the video is being recorded. The video of each meeting participant is time-stamped and uploaded to a central server for further processing.

Meeting attendees may collaboratively edit a list of topics (see "Topic list" in Figure 2). Topics can be assigned during the initial recording by attendees, by those watching the videos later, and potentially through automated mechanisms that match the elements of predefined agendas based on content processing. The topics are started and ended during the meeting by clicking in the list. In the recording of the meeting, those topics are attached to the timeline to segment the meeting and to allow for easy navigation to a particular topic. Topics visited during playback of prior meetings are automatically inherited unless a different topic is manually selected. In Figure 2, the topic "Budget for individuals or by management" was started when playback of the recorded meeting entered that topic and would end either when playback moved to a different topic or when a meeting attendee selected a different topic.

4.2 Creating Hyperlinks

Having a record of the relationships among meetings is valuable for following discussions across meetings. The playback activity provides insight into these relations. Consider a later meeting, with different attendees, watching a previously recorded meeting. We observed that attendees in such a context pause the recording of the previous meeting to discuss the topic being presented. We support this behavior by creating a hyperlink between the previous recording and the meeting being recorded whenever playback is paused. At a later time, when both meetings are reviewed together, the hyperlink enables the later watcher to see the continued discussion in the context of the earlier meeting.

Such hyperlinks consist of a video segment in both the older and newer video. We call those segments source and destination link anchors. The destination link anchor in the current video recording starts when video playback is paused and ends when playback resumes (see circle "15" in Figure 2). The source link anchor in the prior meeting ends at the playback position. To provide context for the older meeting, the source anchor starts a fixed duration prior to the playback position. Because playback is sometimes paused without the intention to create a hyperlink, we provide a link-cancel button that removes the automatically created hyperlink with the option to add it later. Users may add a caption to a hyperlink that is displayed as a tooltip during video playback.

There are multiple ways to determine the source link anchor. The obvious solution is to use the point in the older meeting where the link was created. This is likely to be in the middle of a statement and also misses the discussion in the prior meeting that was the impetus for the newer content. Currently, HyperMeeting starts the source link anchor 20 seconds prior to the paused point. Future versions can improve on this by adjusting the start to be at the

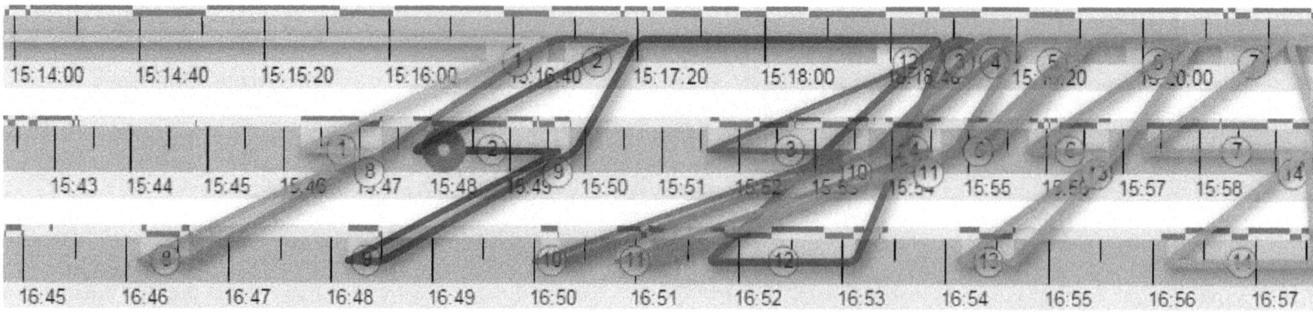

Figure 3. Playback plan for the oldest meeting with automatic link following. Gradient color indicates playback progression.

beginning of a speaker's turn, the beginning of a topic, or some combination of these features.

4.3 HyperMeeting Playback

Any meeting attendee can initiate playback for all current attendees, navigate among the previously recorded meetings in the meeting chain, and pause or skip through the recorded video streams. This synchronization ensures a common context for current attendees continuing discussions based on prior meeting content. All video streams belonging to the same meeting are synchronized as well during playback.

The meeting chain shown at the left of Figure 2 visualizes the context of the synchronous meetings in the chain. Meetings are represented by a combination of the date of the recording, the most-used topics, and the attendees at the meeting. Meetings are color-coded by age in a range from blue to red. Clicking on a meeting in the chain displays the corresponding timeline and starts playback at the start of that meeting. The timeline visualizes the context of the selected meeting with the time-of-day, links to earlier and later meetings, and the selected topics.

Topics are highlighted when the player reaches a segment of the meeting noted as being concerned with a topic. In Figure 2, the current topic is "Budget for individuals or by management". Users viewing the recorded meeting can add or change the topic selected by clicking on the topic in the topic list that is then attached to the timeline. Topics attached to the timeline can be used for navigation. Clicking on one of those topics skips the video playback to the start of the topic. As described earlier, topics encountered during playback are automatically assigned in the live meeting unless the attendees selected a different topic.

The top right portion of the interface is for watching and navigating within the video streams associated with the playback of a recorded meeting (see "Video of previous meetings" in Figure 2). Video players for all videos across all meetings in the meeting chain are available to the user. Each of these video players is color coded above the video frame to indicate the corresponding meeting.

In Figure 2, the middle meeting (with the green color code above the frames) is currently playing. Its video players are larger than the others and show the speaker color in the corner. Speaker transitions are animated with the player associated with previous speaker shrinking as the player of the new speaker grows in size.

The timeline shows the meeting progressing as the time-of-day with a 24-hour clock. Above the timeline, the progression of speakers is color-coded. Topic tags are presented below the timeline next to the date and color-coding of the meeting. Controls to the left of the timeline let the user pause or mute the playback. The link cancel button is only present in live meetings. To the right of the timeline is a slider to speed the playback up to three times the normal speed.

4.4 Link Following

Hyperlinks are shown in the timeline as numbered circles with colors indicating the meeting at the other end of the link. Figure 3 shows timelines of a meeting chain with the newest meeting at the bottom. The middle timeline is also shown in Figure 2, labeled "Meeting timeline with hyperlinks." The vertical position of the link circle indicates whether it is a source link anchor pointing down to a newer meeting or a destination link anchor pointing up.

Links can be followed in both directions by clicking on the numbered circle identifying a link. When following a link, first the link anchor in the older meeting is played to provide context and then the link anchor in the newer meeting is played. In Figure 4, after clicking the green "1", first the green source link anchor around the circle would be played and then the destination link around the blue "1", as indicated by the solid line. The playback would stop at the end of the destination link anchor. Clicking on the blue "1" would cause the same playback sequence. A second click on a link circle advances the playback to the destination link anchor. Our user study described later in this paper uncovered some issues with the sequence of playing the two link anchors.

4.5 Automatic Link-Following

Viewing a hypermeeting can be a purely manual interaction where the user selects which hyperlinks should be followed and which parts of the video should be skipped. However, the system's knowledge of the viewing users' participation and interests can be used to automate the navigation through the hypermeeting.

In addition to user-initiated link traversal, links may also be automatically traversed as they are encountered. Continuous playback of the multipart meeting can move back and forth between the original and additional video content as links are encountered. For example, as links to newer meetings are encountered, the playback automatically follows that link and returns to the original position after playing the destination link anchor.

If the linked video contains a link to a more recent meeting, that link is followed in the same fashion. The dashed line in Figure 4 provides an example of this behavior. While the user played the destination anchor of link "1", link "8" was encountered and automatically followed. Because the ends of the link anchors of links "1" and "8" line up, playback would stop at the end of the green segment depicting the destination anchor of link "8".

4.6 Playback Plans

Depending on the information need of the user, there are different ways links could be followed automatically. We created the abstraction of playback plans to describe such automatic behavior.

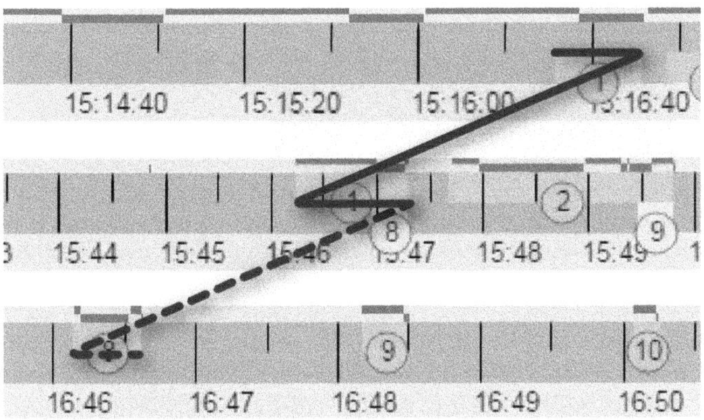

Figure 4. Playback plan for link following. The dashed part indicates automatic link following.

4.6.1 Types of Playback Plans

Playback plans are computed when a user clicks on a link, navigates to a different meeting in the chain, or navigates outside the current plan. Playback plans can be used to filter recorded content and are interactive (i.e., users can navigate within a playback plan).

The result of a specific playback plan applied to a specific hypermeeting is similar to an edit decision list for video editing. It consists of a sequence of video segments from multiple videos that are played in order. Unlike edit decision lists, playback plans are computed automatically based on available links, filter conditions, and previous behavior of the user. The playback plans themselves encode logic for deciding when to follow links and when not to. Some plans are a generalization of hypervideo link behaviors [8] – that is they determine what happens when the beginning or ending of a source or destination link anchor is encountered during playback. Other plans may represent filters that skip over undesired portions of a video such as silence. More complex plans can be combinations of such behaviors. Playback plans may also alter the playback speed.

We identified playback plans that are appropriate to particular use scenarios. Table 1 details six expected contexts of use for playback plans, the information goals of the user in these contexts, and the playback plan behavior. This is not meant as a complete list of use contexts. Currently, HyperMeeting only implements playback plans for the more common scenarios that include automatically following links to newer meetings, either for a whole meeting or a single link, in combination with a filter for silence. Additional plans require improved detectors for the context of use.

Selecting a playback plan takes into account participation in previous meetings. For a user who has not participated in the meeting chain, one could play the video of the meeting that started the chain and automatically follow all links to subsequent meetings such that those comments can be viewed in context. Such a traversal through the hypervideo would skip the parts of the subsequent meetings that are not linked, presumably because the content in these portions is not related to the older meetings.

Another default plan would be for people who participated in a series of meetings and wished to review comments linked to meeting they attended. In this case the source anchors in the meeting they attended would be played before playing the linked comment, but any links to previous meetings encountered while playing the source anchors would be ignored.

Figure 4 shows a playback plan for playing both halves of link "1" and then stopping, as would happen if a user clicked on the link without automatic link-following enabled. If automatic link-following were enabled, link "8" would be played, too, as indicated by the dashed line.

Context of Use	Likely Viewing Behavior	Plan Behavior
Reviewing a meeting that one participated in	Look for specific segments based on topic	Play segments on a topic
Reviewing multiple meetings that one participated in or has viewed	Look for related segments across meetings based on topic	Play segments on a topic with embedded links to additional related discussions
Viewing a meeting where one was absent	View the whole meeting	Play the meeting
Viewing a meeting where one was absent but at prior meetings	View the whole meeting in the context of prior meetings	Play the meeting with contextual segments from prior meetings
Viewing multiple related meetings where one was absent	View all the meetings with an understanding of relations between meetings	Play the oldest meeting in its entirety along with links to related content in newer meetings, then play additional content in newer meetings
Viewing multiple related meetings where one was absent but at some prior meeting	View all the unseen meetings with an understanding of relations between these meetings and their relations to prior meetings	Play the absent meeting in its entirety along with links to related content in newer meetings, then play additional content in newer meetings together with contextual segments from prior meetings

Table 1. Types of playback plans.

All playback plans can include filter criteria. A common filter can skip silence in the video. Such a filter is useful in situations where meeting attendees are listening to an older meeting without speaking at the same time. Attendees of a future meeting would want to skip that period of silence. Other filters could focus on particular topics or speakers.

Plans can also be personalized based on who is speaking in each segment. Thus, a plan could play any responses to segments in which the current user was a speaker, first playing the original segment followed by the responses. Similarly, topic-oriented plans can play through segments tagged with particular topics and any content attached to those segments.

4.6.2 Execution of Playback Plans

Figure 3 shows the execution order of a plan for playing the oldest meeting and all links to newer meetings. The circles indicate hyperlinks with the numbers matching the two halves of a link. The colored areas surrounding the circles are the link anchors. Superimposed as a gradient line to indicate playback progress is a plan for playing the oldest meeting in the chain while automatically following all links to newer meetings. Note that link "12" to the newest meeting at 16:52 causes out-of-order playback. After returning from link "9", link "12" is followed, then links "3", "10", "4", and "11"

Manual navigation within a playback plan, i.e., skipping to a part of the video that is covered by the plan, just continues the plan from that position in the video. Other user interaction could include clicking on a link circle while playing the source of that link. Such an interaction skips the playback to the destination of that link and continues the plan from there. Navigation to a part of the video not covered by the current playback plan leads to the computation of a new playback plan including that part of the video, by default a plan that plays the video of the current meeting and follow links to all later meetings.

4.7 System Architecture

For the first version of our system, we focus on distributed meetings conducted as a video conference. That approach makes it easy to get a video recording of each attendee and allows for simple speaker segmentation. In such a scenario, multiple video streams are recorded that are played together when the recorded meeting is being watched at a later time. In the future, we plan to support other types of meetings such as local meetings recorded by a single video camera or video conferences between two hubs. Presenting slides to remote attendees is important (e.g., [12]). Such a feature could be integrated into HyperMeeting via screen sharing similar to [4].

Figure 5 shows the primary components of the system. The HyperMeeting client runs in standard web browsers as a single page application. Meetings are visualized by manipulating the web page with JavaScript. Recorded video is displayed in HTML5 video tags and timelines are drawn in canvases. The live video conference among the distributed meeting attendees is maintained with WebRTC (Web Real-Time Communication)[1] peer-to-peer connections. Our HyperMeeting server manages the initial signaling to set up those connections. Clients keep a Websocket connection open to the HyperMeeting Manager on the server to maintain meeting state. Initially, each user is in a separate meeting and may join another existing meeting. Video playback is synchronized among users in the same meeting by clients sending playback change messages to the HyperMeeting Manager that are forwarded to other clients in the same meeting. Between changes, each client maintains the requested playback speed.

The HyperMeeting server stores the recorded video and images in the file system to support random access during playback. Other metadata such as the list of participants of a meeting is stored in a database. WebRTC is still an evolving standard that is currently supported in the Chrome and Firefox web browsers. Only Firefox currently provides an implementation of the Media Recorder API.[2] We created a workaround for Chrome to record audio with the Web Audio API[3] and video as a sequence of images. Chunks of the recorded media streams are uploaded to the HyperMeeting server and appended to the video files. After recording is completed, video is transcoded to a more compressed format. In the future, we may use a video conference multi-point control unit with recording capability to avoid the need for sending video content twice. However, it would be important in such a setup to get accurate timestamps to synchronize later playback.

There are several challenges when using a web-based architecture. While the HTML5 video tag as implemented in modern web browsers offers good video playback capabilities, it does not offer as much control as a standalone video player. In particular, it is difficult to control the caching behavior. Preloaded videos may tie up all socket connections to the server until they are completely downloaded. Instead, the system repeatedly attempts to play each video and pauses it in response to the "playing" event. We switched to using a Websocket for communication with the server in part because it works even if all socket connections are tied up.

We also encountered audio clipping at higher playback rates. It is unclear whether the problems were caused by the video player or by our speaker segmentation that muted all but one player. The latter was necessary because there is no echo cancelation for other sources, i.e., the playback of recorded video during a video conference. Also, too frequent synchronization negatively impacts playback. Only correcting drift of more than two seconds is a reasonable compromise. The user evaluation described later in the paper shows that improvements in these areas would be desirable.

4.7.1 Speaker Segmentation

Speaker segmentation serves a utility role in several parts of the system. We currently assume that each attendee has a microphone set up such that the audio from the meeting playback or co-located speaker is not picked up by the microphone. Thus the task of segmenting the audio based on speaker is reduced to determining when each speaker is not silent. We use a low-pass filter and a sampling window for audio energy to eliminate short noise artifacts. We compare the audio energy windows for all attendees and require a minimum speech duration to allow a speaker change.

In the user interface, it is useful to display a timeline showing when each of the attendees is speaking. This allows the viewer, for example, to skip to comments made by a particular person. The speaker segmentation is visualized as red and green lines above the timeline in Figure 2. The "skip silent" check box lets users control whether to automatically skip segments where nobody is speaking (e.g., 15:43:20 to 15:46:15 in Figure 2).

Speaker segmentation is also useful when playing several video streams depicting meeting attendees in parallel. Unless all recorded attendees wore headphones, sounds from the playback of even earlier meetings may be included in the recording. Current echo

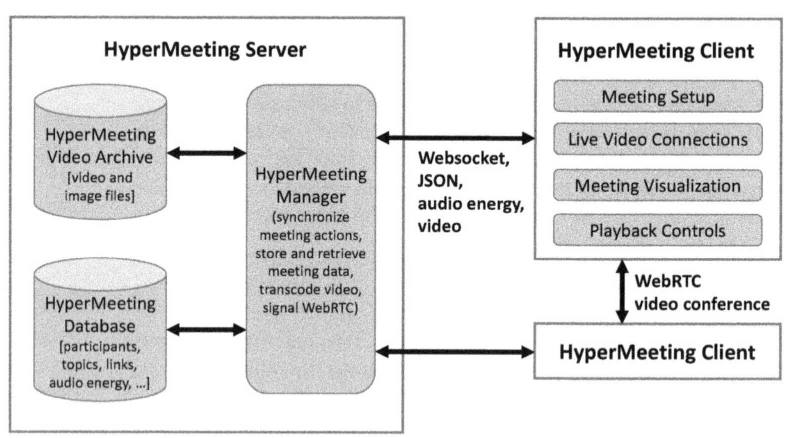

Figure 5. HyperMeeting Architecture

[1] http://www.w3.org/TR/webrtc/
[2] http://www.w3.org/TR/mediastream-recording/
[3] http://www.w3.org/TR/webaudio/

cancelation systems in web browsers remove sounds from the other end of a video conference but not those produced by a video player running at the same time. If several of those "tainted" video streams are played in parallel, slight differences in timing may cause echoes that can be suppressed by unmuting only the video player of the detected speaker.

5. Experience from Longer-Term Use

Our project team has used HyperMeeting over the course of its development. Since one of the members of our team was remote and other members had significant amounts of travel, it was not always possible to hold synchronous meetings. We used the HyperMeeting system to record design meetings so that people who did not attend could later review and add their comments. All team members attended at least some of the meetings, and there was typically a conclusion meeting in which all members were present.

Our experiences showed that there is a significant learning curve in the use of HyperMeeting. One problem is due to differences with common videoconferencing software such as Skype and Google Hangouts. In particular, these other tools provide no insight into the shared synchronized watching of previously recorded content. Issues such as who will drive the playback controls lead to communication among participants about this control. For example, it was common to explicitly say *"I will pause now"* when one of the participants wanted to add a link to a meeting they were reviewing. Similarly, when resuming playback of a recorded meeting after making comments, *"let's take that link to see what they said"* was a common utterance.

However, within a few months of experience, use of HyperMeeting changed distributed group interaction. One example of this is that meeting participants took advantage of knowing that others would review the current meeting. They called out expected future viewers to ask them questions or to respond to some opinion. For example, *"[Name], can you remind me why the system does this when I do that?"* or *"[Name], how can we examine the effect of the hyperlinks on information seeking?"* The request for feedback from someone not in the current meeting became natural in this context. This is something that the system could support more directly by either having people tag such questions/responses or have the system automatically detect mention of non-participating team members.

Due to the learning curve we experienced in recording and linking meetings with HyperMeeting, we decided to focus our first user study on the review of previously recorded meetings. We were aware of issues with link traversal. Through the study, we hoped to better understand their utility and usability. Once these issues are solved we plan to do a longitudinal study of the system that will cover both the creation and review of HyperMeeting.

6. User Evaluation

One research question focused on *how does allowing people to review content in a non-linear way influence the process of navigating through and understanding a series of past meetings.* To gain insights into user behavior with the system, we conducted an evaluation of HyperMeeting that focused just on the playback of a meeting chain. The participants were placed in the role of a decision maker who did not attend any meetings in the chain. We chose to look only at that part of the system because it covers features novel to most users and is amenable to a controlled study.

We particularly wanted to examine the effects of two novel design decisions described in Section 4:

1. The inclusion of hyperlinks between meetings rather than just facilitating synchronized distributed viewing of prior meetings and recording of new content.
2. The inclusion of playback plans (notably automatic link-following) rather than requiring users to control all navigation.

6.1 Evaluation Method

We recorded hypermeetings for training and for two study tasks. Each hypermeeting consisted of a chain of three meetings with an attendee pattern of AB, CD, AB. The training hypermeeting and one of the task hypermeetings included hyperlinks. We edited a copy of the training hypermeeting to remove links and periods of silence so that it could be used for training the no-link condition.

Two pilot participants helped us refine the study setup. In response to their interaction with the study materials, we modified some hyperlinks to avoid overlapping links. Because they had issues with automatic link-following, we decided to turn that feature off for half the participants. We also divided tasks into browsing and question-answering parts, improved the instructions, and added questions about the meeting content to test the participants' retention of the presented material. There was no significant effect of the conditions on retention so we do not further discuss that aspect of the study.

Eight participants (three female; ages 30 to 60) were selected from members of the research lab with no connection to and no experience with HyperMeeting. For their participation they received a chocolate bar. These participants were asked to view two series of three interrelated meetings with a goal of understanding the content of the meetings and answering questions about who said what. The study was a within-subjects design where each participant used both versions of HyperMeeting (with and without links). The order of the versions was counterbalanced. Only half the participants were given a system with automatic link-following enabled.

Each session lasted about 1½ hours consisting of two halves. In each half, participants were given 10 minutes to read written training materials and to play with the user interface to explore training meeting content unrelated to later tasks. They then performed a task with one version of HyperMeeting. In each task, the participants spent up to 15 minutes to review a series of three meetings related to topics that they would have interest in (policy decisions for the research lab related to employee bonuses and travel funding). They then had 15 minutes to answer questions about the meeting contents and could use HyperMeeting to help locate particular content. No note-taking was allowed during the first 15 minutes to better observe navigation behavior during the second 15 minutes. Finally, they answered a questionnaire with the ten-item System Usability Scale [2] to assess overall usability of the system. It also included two Likert-scale questions about the ease and enjoyability of performing the task using the system (i.e., "It was easy to perform the task using this tool to review meetings" and "I enjoyed performing the task using this tool."). Finally, to assess the utility of the hyperlinks in particular, in the condition with links, participants rated the question "Were hyperlinks useful?" on a Likert scale. The questionnaire also contained open-ended questions about the likes and dislikes of the system, and of hyperlinks in particular.

The software was configured to generate a log of user activity in the interface and associated video playback. Finally, one or two team members observed each activity to note behaviors and difficulties that might not come up in user comments.

6.2 Evaluation Results

We compared the participants' experience using the linked version of the system (either with or without automatic link following) with their experience viewing an unlinked series of meeting videos. Here we report results from the questionnaire responses given, open-ended feedback on the two system versions, and behavioral patterns observed in the logs and during the evaluation.

6.2.1 Reactions to hyperlinks and playback plans

A primary evaluation goal was to examine the utility of the hyperlinks and playback plans as a mechanism for navigating content in a new way. Participants' responses to the question "What did you like and dislike about the hyperlinks for reviewing this meeting?" yielded insights into positive and negative aspects of the design of hyperlinks.

Study participants clearly found the hyperlinks useful — 7 of the 8 participants agreed or strongly agreed with the statement about the usefulness of the hyperlinks. Two participants who were given the meeting with hyperlinks first complained about not having them in the second series of meetings: "*Felt like I watched three unrelated meetings. Threads weren't there and I couldn't feel consensus*" (P8) and "*It gets boring to listen through each topic without getting a direct response on each point. Harder to follow each discussion point when chunks of discussion is larger*" (P2).

Other positive comments showed that links allowed users to follow the discussion on a topic. For example, "*It supported topic to speaker navigation very fluidly and helped identify who said what much more easier and in context*" (P4). Links also highlighted important parts of the discussion: "*could easily move to related comments*" (P7) and "*I felt if I listened to linked material, I covered what was important*" (P8).

Although users tended to like hyperlinks, there were clear problems with usability across the different playback plans. A common complaint was feeling lost, meaning not knowing where in the meeting chain you were after following hyperlinks. This was commonly mentioned among users with the automatic link following, and well-summarized by the comment that "*Automatic link following is good for getting related thoughts together, but also leads to a feeling of being lost*" (P1).

Users with manual link-following also felt uncertain about where they were taken when following a link. "*I couldn't tell when the system would jump back out of a hyperlink or when it would pause playback*" (P4). Another explained that "*initially what happened when you click on a future link was counter-intuitive. Not obvious which part of time-line is sensitive to what (what the action will be when you click)*" (P7). P4 suggested. "*Maybe in sequential play / hyperlink do not start from start of segment*" and "*Indicator when a jump back is about to go.*"

Users made other interesting suggestions for improvements to link behavior. One user mentioned visualizing parts of the video that had been seen and optionally skipping already seen material: "*First time viewing, not showing what has been seen or skipping those parts*" (P5). They also suggested a back button for the automatic case because "*Sometimes want to go back to a previous point in the thread, not easy*" (P5).

Two users suggested another visualization of links besides the current numbering system. As one said, "*The links could be visualized differently. They keep on changing numbers which was kind of confusing. Maybe just a different numbering system*" (P2). Another user suggested alternative ways of visualizing the navigation such as using text "*What does the number represent? Perhaps a textual link might be more descriptive*" or a graph "*Need a graph for the links. Could not make sense of the structure*" (P6).

6.2.2 Usability of linked and unlinked versions

Participants rated the overall usability of their experience using the system with and without links. On the 100-point System Usability Scale (where a higher score means greater usability), the mean rating of the non-linked version was 74.38 (SD=14.19) and the mean rating of the linked version was 66.56 (SD=9.06). However, this difference was not statistically significant ($t(1,15)=1.80$, $p=.20$). There were no statistically significant differences between the linked and unlinked versions on individual scale sub-items (scale 0 to 4), with the exception of the rating of complexity. Here, the linked version of the system was deemed to be significantly more complex (M=3.375) than the unlinked version (M=2.625) ($t(1,15)=5.47$, $p=.03$). The difference in the rating of complexity comes from the condition with automatic link-following (M=3.50 vs. M=2.25). There is no significant difference in the other condition. There were no significant differences between linked and unlinked systems in terms of rating of ease of use and enjoyability. There were no significant order effects in the usability ratings with respect to performing the task with hyperlinks first.

Given that participants only used the systems for a short amount of time, it is possible that initial attitudes about usability and complexity could evolve and change over time. However, responses to the open-ended questions about what participants liked and disliked about each version of the system provided more information about how the links (or lack thereof) influenced the experience of reviewing meetings.

6.2.3 Other usability observations

Participants liked several features of the system particularly those that allowed for speedup and skip silences (P1, P3, P5, P8) and those that allowed for color-coding to identify speakers (P1, P6).

There was disagreement on the animation that zoomed in on the video of the speaker: this was mentioned as both a "like" "*Resizing speaker video to highlight who is talking*" (P6) and a "dislike" "*changing video size seemed to busy*" (P1), "*Video Zoom for active speaker was distracting*" (P4).

Several participants requested more fine-grained topics in the non-link condition: "*Topics not fine enough in granularity*" (P5), and in particular they "*would like to search for keywords*" (P7).

Finally, several participants had issues with audio clipping: "*Sometimes on change of speaker it seemed like I lost a bit of audio*" (P1), "*In fast forward mode, some of the audio is skipped*" (P6), "*Audio clipped too much so parts missing*" (P7). There was also some lag: "*lag in playing video, unable to scrub*" (P7)

6.3 Log Analysis

The analysis of the usage log revealed how and when participants used the different features of the system. All but one participant used the "skip silent" feature, and all participants increased the playback speed. There were differences in using the content navigation-based system features (links, topics, and directly clicking on the timeline) depending on what was available. Because each task was separated into two halves, the exploration of the meeting chain and goal-oriented navigation to answer questions, the strategies and features used differ in those halves.

Navigation with links: Links were used more frequently for exploration than for answering specific questions. In the exploration phase, two participants with automatic link-following (P1 and P6) started playback at the beginning of the oldest meeting and watched the complete link chain without manual navigation while automatically following 23 links. The other six participants clicked on links about the same number of times in that half (M=9.0; SD=2.4). In the goal-oriented (question answering) phase, links were used sparingly (M=1.1; SD=0.9). In that half, automatic link-following happened unevenly among the participants that had it (M=3.3; SD=2.2).

Navigation by topics: In the no-link condition, navigation by clicking on a topic was used more. It occurred more in the exploration phase (no link: M=5.3; link: M=1.3) than in the question-answering phase (no link: M=2.1; link: M=1.3).

Navigation by clicking on the timeline: Directly clicking on the timeline to jump to various points in the discussion was about twice as frequent in the question-answering phase (no link: M=21.7; link: M=27.3) compared to the exploration phase (no link: M=10.9; link: M=14.3).[4]

In summary, links were used frequently in the exploration phase. In their absence, navigation by topics was used instead. Links and topics were only used sparingly in the question-answering phase. As with links, topics seem to be better suited for exploration. In the question-answering phase, clicking on the timeline was twice as frequent as in the earlier phase. This seemed to be preferred for finding specific answers. That may explain the comments of some participants that topics were not fine-grained enough.

6.4 Discussion

It is encouraging that the study participants found hyperlinks useful for navigating the video recording of a meeting chain. Several participants commented that they missed them in the condition without hyperlinks. Log analysis shows that links were used for exploration if present and that otherwise topics were used as proxy. At the same time, the study uncovered usability issues with hyperlinks and automatic link-following in particular. To address this issue, several participants suggested visualizations of the link network or of content that they already watched. One participant requested a back button similar to that in a web browser. Such a feature is similar to the navigation stack described in [18].

For visualizing the link network, our first idea can be seen in Figure 3. However, the many crossed paths would make such a visualization non-intuitive. An alternative would be to make the timelines nonlinear such that most corresponding link anchors line up and connecting lines would be mostly vertical. Such a visualization may make the link behavior more intuitive because the users could predict where the link would go and whether playback would stop at the end of the link anchor. Indicating previously watched content or even skipping it by default are good suggestions from our participants. We will integrate this into a future version of the system.

The labeling of links with numbers turned out to be another issue. Our system supports link labels that appear as tooltips on mouse-over but we did not create link labels when we recorded the meeting chains. We believe that many other users will not create link labels, either, so that a less laborious solution would be desirable, maybe using automatic speech recognition. One participant expected the links covering the same content to have the same number. Currently, numbers are assigned sequentially so that a link from the second to the third meeting would not have the same number as a link from the first to the second meeting even if the links line up at the second meeting. Clustering links by time may be a solution for this issue.

Some participants made extensive use of topics for navigation, especially in the condition without links. However, several participants commented that the topics were too coarse. Displaying keywords determined by automatic speech recognition might be an approach for more fine-grained navigation support.

Several participants noticed problems with audio clipping. We decided to use our speaker segmentation to mute all but one video player. That deals with an issue where background audio from playing previous meetings may be present in the recording, leading to echo if more than one instance is played. This can be avoided if all participants wear headphones but it would be challenging to remove it with echo cancelation because of variable latency. It appears that our speaker segmentation is not precise enough to avoid audio clipping. One possible solution would be to unmute the next speaker slightly earlier than muting the current speaker.

The lag observed by a pilot participant and one of the other participants is likely due to caching and network latency. Worse network connectivity would impact it negatively. Unfortunately, our web-based solution does not offer much control over video caching. Keeping a second video player in the background that skips ahead to likely playback positions may be a possible solution. This lag is also a reason why we did not implement video scrubbing requested by some participants.

Finally, as mentioned in Section 5, the current HyperMeeting system seemed to best support a series of three or four meetings. Issues of scalability could arise as the historical record grows beyond this number of meetings, making navigation and information finding more complex and difficult. Designing for longer-term archiving and use of the hypervideo system will require adaptation of the interface and is out of the scope of this initial study, but remains a fruitful area for future work.

7. Conclusions

Meetings often overlap in terms of content. This causes difficulties as meetings that build on what was discussed in prior meetings result in barriers for those not at prior meetings and meetings that re-discuss topics are often viewed as unproductive by the participants that were at prior meetings. HyperMeeting was designed to support geographically-distributed teams that need meetings to make decisions and coordinate without requiring them to be available and on-line at the same time.

HyperMeeting combines in a single interface several novel features that integrate meeting capture, synchronous playback of meeting content, and the recording of new meetings and extensions to prior meetings. As a result, it is possible to use the playback activities (e.g., pausing a recorded meeting) to automatically generate hyperlinks between recordings. A critical component of this is the ability to synchronize playback and annotation by distributed participants.

During playback, automatic link-following guided by playback plans present the relevant content to the users. An analysis of usage scenarios identified a variety of viewing behaviors appropriate as responses to navigational actions based on the user's meeting attendance and viewing history. Playback plans take into account

[4] Excludes outlier P8 who clicked the timeline in one half seven times as often as the mean of the others.

features of the user along with features of the content to present just enough previously viewed content to contextualize new content.

Multiple months of use of HyperMeeting within our own geographically-distributed team showed that users developed new meeting practices based on the ability to review prior meetings and call out to attendees of future meetings. These practices improved understanding of meetings that group members were not at and increased shared understanding within the group.

A user study examined the viewing of hypermeetings. The results show that participants generally liked having links. Log analysis supported user feedback of the value of links. Without them, users relied on topics but found them too coarse-grained. Users found navigating back-and-forth between multiple videos disorienting as documented in prior reports on the evolution of hypervideo playback interfaces [8].

HyperMeeting is a promising option for people who cannot attend synchronous meetings. Future work will address issues uncovered in the user study such as the need for refinements to the interface cues surrounding navigation. A future study will more formally assess the process of synchronously viewing prior meetings and recording extensions to that content. Longer term future work will explore the inclusion of roles for meeting participants (e.g., meeting chairs) and formal or informal results (e.g., official minutes and individual's notes).

8. REFERENCES

[1] J. Barksdale, K. Inkpen, M. Czerwinski, A. Hoff, P. Johns, A. Roseway, and G. Venolia. Video threads: asynchronous video sharing for temporally distributed teams. *Proc. CSCW '12,* 1101-1104.

[2] J. Brooke. SUS: A Quick and Dirty Usability Scale. In: P. Jordan, B. Thomas, B. Weerdmeester, and I. McClelland (Eds.), *Usability Evaluation in Industry*. London: Taylor & Francis, 1996.□

[3] J.J. Cadiz, Anand Balachandran, Elizabeth Sanocki, Anoop Gupta, Jonathan Grudin, and Gavin Jancke. Distance learning through distributed collaborative video viewing. *Proc. CSCW '00,* 135-144.

[4] L. Denoue, S. Carter, A. Girgensohn, and M. Cooper. Building digital project rooms for web meetings. *Proc. DocEng '14,* 135-138.

[5] B. Dorn, L.B. Schroeder, and A. Stankiewicz. Piloting TrACE: Exploring Spatiotemporal Anchored Collaboration in Asynchronous Learning. *Proc. CSCW '15,* 393-403.

[6] L. Gericke, M. Wenzel, and C. Meinel. Asynchronous understanding of creative sessions using archived collaboration artifacts. *Proc. Collaboration Technologies and Systems 2014,* 41–48.

[7] W. Geyer, H. Richter, and G.D. Abowd. Towards a Smarter Meeting Record—Capture and Access of Meetings Revisited. *Multimedia Tools Appl.* 27(3), 2005, 393-410.

[8] A. Girgensohn, L. Wilcox, F. Shipman, and S. Bly. Designing affordances for the navigation of detail-on-demand hypervideo. *Proc. AVI '04,* 290-297.

[9] R. Grigoras, V. Charvillat, and M. Douze. Optimizing Hypervideo Navigation Using a Markov Decision Process Approach. *Proc. MM '02,* 39-48.

[10] S. Hunter, P. Maes, S. Scott, and H. Kaufman. MemTable: an integrated system for capture and recall of shared histories in group workspaces. *Proc. CHI '11,* 3305-3314.

[11] F. Lehner, M. Langbauer, and N. Amende. Measuring success of enterprise social software: the case of hypervideos. *Proc. i-KNOW '14,* Article 3, 9 pages.

[12] G. Mark, J. Grudin, and S.E. Poltrock. Meeting at the desktop: an empirical study of virtually collocated teams. *Proc. ECSCW '99,* 159-178.

[13] T.P. Moran, L. Palen, S. Harrison, P. Chiu, D. Kimber, S. Minneman, W. van Melle, and P. Zellweger. "I'll get that off the audio": a case study of salvaging multimedia meeting records. *Proc. CHI '97,* 202-209.

[14] M. Nathan, M. Topkara, J. Lai, S. Pan, S. Wood, J. Boston, and L. Terveen. In case you missed it: benefits of attendee-shared annotations for non-attendees of remote meetings. *Proc. CSCW '12,* 339–348.

[15] J. Pan, L. Li, and W. Chou. Real-Time Collaborative Video Watching on Mobile Devices with REST Services. *Proc. MUSIC '12,* 29-34.

[16] M. Sadallah, O. Aubert, and Y. Prié. CHM: an annotation- and component-based hypervideo model for the Web. *Multimedia Tools Appl.* 70(2), 2014, 869-903.

[17] N. Sawhney, D. Balcom, I. Smith, HyperCafe: narrative and aesthetic properties of hypervideo. *Proc. HT '96,* 1-10.

[18] F. Shipman, A. Girgensohn, and L. Wilcox. Authoring, viewing, and generating hypervideo: An overview of Hyper-Hitchcock. *ACM Trans. Multimedia Comput. Commun. Appl.* 5(2), 2008, Article 15, 19 pages.

[19] J. Tang, J. Marlow, A. Hoff, A. Roseway, K. Inkpen, C. Zhao, and X. Cao. Time travel proxy: using lightweight video recordings to create asynchronous, interactive meetings. *Proc. CHI '12,* 3111-3120.

[20] C.A.B. Tiellet, A. Grahl Pereira, E.B. Reategui, J.V. Lima, and T. Chambel. Design and evaluation of a hypervideo environment to support veterinary surgery learning. *Proc. HT '10,* 213-222.

MMToC: A Multimodal Method for Table of Content Creation in Educational Videos

Arijit Biswas *
Xerox Research Centre India, Bangalore, India
Arijit.Biswas@xerox.com

Ankit Gandhi *
Xerox Research Centre India, Bangalore, India
Ankit.Gandhi@xerox.com

Om Deshmukh
Xerox Research Centre India, Bangalore, India
Om.Deshmukh@xerox.com

ABSTRACT

In this paper we propose a multimodal method called MMToC for automatically creating a table of content for educational videos. MMToC defines and quantifies word saliency for visual words extracted from the slides and spoken words obtained from the speech transcript. The saliency scores from these two modalities are combined to obtain a ranked list of salient words. These ranked words along with their saliency scores are used to formulate a topic segmentation cost function. The cost function is optimized using a dynamic program framework to obtain the topic segments of the video. These segments are labelled with their corresponding topic names for creating the table of content. We perform experiments on 24 hours of lectures spread across 23 videos ranging over 20-75 minutes duration each. We compare the proposed method with LDA-based video segmentation approaches and show that the proposed MMToC method is significantly better (F-score improvement of 0.19 and 0.24 on two datasets). We also perform a user study to demonstrate the effectiveness of MMToC for navigating educational videos.

Categories and Subject Descriptors

I.7.3 [**Computing Methodologies**]: Document and Text Processing—*Index Generation*; I.4 [**Computing Methodologies**]: Image Processing and Computer Vision

Keywords

Multimodal; table of content; educational videos; visual saliency; text saliency; temporal segmentation; dynamic program

1. INTRODUCTION

Online courses and Open Educational Resources (OER) have emerged as one of the most popular modes of learning in the recent years. Many top-ranked universities and educational technology companies are making numerous video lectures available online for free of cost. As the amount of online educational content increases (tens of thousands of hours of video currently), it is important to develop methods for efficient consumption of this multimedia content. Developing methods for summarization [7, 17], navigation [35] and topic transition [15, 23, 24, 25], for educational videos are now active areas of research.

One of the most challenging research area is to automatically segment an educational video into relevant topics and label each segment with the corresponding topic. Such labelled partitioning of videos can help students to efficiently navigate to the required segments in the videos. For example, in a 1 hour long lecture video on support vector machine (SVM), a professor might cover the definition of version space, motivation for SVM, primal formulation, dual formulation, support vectors and perhaps end the lecture with kernel formulation. When a student is going through this lecture before an assessment, s/he might only be interested in the dual formulation of SVM, which s/he might have found hard to comprehend earlier. It might be very tedious to find out the part where dual formulation had been discussed. In such a situation the student would typically 'guesstimate' the location with multiple back and forth navigations of the video. [Indeed, in a large-scale study on the EdX platform, authors in [12] found that certificate earning students, on an average, spend only about 4.4 minutes on a 12-15 minute-long video and skip about 22% of the content.] If the lecture video can be accompanied by a table of content (like the ones used in textbooks), which contains the beginning times of different topic segments in the video along with the topic labels, that will help the student to quickly navigate to the topic of interest. This could also help instructors who are browsing through a collection of videos to decide which videos are relevant for students.

A human expert can manually go through each lecture video and can create a table of content. However as the amount of online video lectures increase in the next few years, manually creating table of contents for all of them will be an impossible task. The goal of this work is to automatically segment an educational video into topics and creating a table of content for the video. Demarcating these topic segments is straightforward in written documents as the authors tend to create table of contents or sections and subsections. But no such facility is readily available when video lectures are created.

In this paper, the text from visual and speech modalities[1]

*Equal contribution.

MM'15, October 26 - 30, 2015, Brisbane, Australia

ACM 978-1-4503-3459-4/15/10 ...$15.00
DOI: http://dx.doi.org/10.1145/2733373.2806253.

[1]Throughout the paper we will use visual words to refer to the words obtained from slides and spoken words to refer to the words obtain from the speech-to-text transcript.

are combined in a dynamic program framework to estimate the time instants of topic changes in an educational video. A set of key-phrases indicating the topic of each segment is extracted to create the table of content. The main novel contributions of this paper:

1. **Visual saliency of words (Section 3):** Our first major contribution is to define and quantify saliency of words present on slides and use these saliency scores to improve topic partition. We establish that the identity of the words and the manner in which the words are rendered on the slides provide significant cues regarding the words' significance in topic change. For example, a word in bold and located towards the top left of the slide contributes more in the topic partition than a word located at the bottom right corner of a slide. To capture these visual characteristics, we propose seven novel mid-level features for the words present in educational videos. These features are called *underlineness, boldness, size, capitalization, isolation, padding,* and *location.* These features are combined using a weight vector to create a saliency score for every word in the video. The optimal weight vector is learnt using a novel formulation of the Rank-SVM algorithm [5] on human-annotated salient words.
2. **Multimodal words and saliency (Section 5):** The Speech-to-text transcript of the lecture is processed to estimate the saliency of the spoken words. A novel combination of graph-based and unsupervised text processing algorithms in conjunction with the visual saliency is proposed to generate a ranked list of multimodal salient words. These words along with their saliency scores are used to estimate the topic segmentation.
3. **Dynamic program formulation (Section 6.2 and 6.3):**
The topic segmentation problem is formulated as a dynamic program. The cost function in the dynamic program is defined in such a way that it simultaneously minimizes saliency-based metric of words common to two adjacent segments and maximizes the saliency-based metric of words unique to either of the two segments.
4. **Table of Content creation (Section 7 and 8):**
We generate a representative 'title' for each topic and present a video navigation interface that allows the end user to efficiently navigate through the video. Automatic assessment and user studies are presented to demonstrate the superiority of the proposed technique.

The proposed multimodal table of content (referred as MMToC from now on) generation method is compared with different LDA [4] based video segmentation approaches. We show that MMToC significantly outperforms the baselines. For example, using the videos from NPTEL [1], we obtain an improvement of F-score by 0.19 (relative improvement is 37%). We also demonstrate the effectiveness of MMToC on real-life user studies. A user takes 45 seconds on an average to find the topic segments in hour long videos using MMToC, whereas for the same task the time taken using the standard scrubbing + baseline transcript (used in several leading MOOC platforms) is about 90 seconds.

2. RELATED WORK

We outline previous research in the following three broad categories.

- **Text segmentation:** Several supervised and unsupervised algorithms have been presented to partition written text into multiple topic segments. The TextTiling approach [13] detects topic changes by comparing adjacent blocks of fixed size of text and estimating introduction of new vocabulary and between-block similarity of words. In [30], authors propose an approach based on TextTiling and LDA [4]. This approach however requires a trained LDA model on a large corpus from similar domain. Authors in [8] propose a hierarchical Bayesian model for unsupervised topic segmentation. This model integrates a point-wise boundary sampling algorithm used in Bayesian segmentation into a structured topic model that can capture the hierarchical topic structure in the documents. Authors in [26] focus on documents with relatively small segment sizes and for which within-segment sentences have relatively few words. Query expansion techniques are used to find common features for robust topic segmentation. In [6] the relative ranking of similarity measures across sentences, rather than their actual values, is used to segment short written text. [3] presents a supervised approach where an exponential model is incrementally built to extract features that are correlated to the text boundaries in the labelled text. [29] treats the process of creating documents as an instance of the noisy channel model and the topic segmentation task as a labeling task.
- **Speech segmentation:** Authors in [9] present a domain-independent topic segmentation algorithm for multi-party speech. The text is processed to analyze the content while the acoustic signal is processed to analyze the form. These streams are combined using automatically induced decision rules. In [18], the spoken lecture segmentation problem is modeled as a multi-way normalized cut problem and a dynamic program is used to get the final segmentation. The cost formulation part of MMToC is motivated by this work. However the cost in [18] computes the normalized cut of each segment with the rest of the spoken lecture whereas our cost only compares adjacent segments for salient common and novel words. In [20], the authors use word co-occurrence statistics to evaluate coherence between pairs of adjacent windows over the speech or text stream and find out the segment boundaries at extrema in the similarity signal.
- **Vision-based segmentation:** Authors in [24] proposed a method for high level segmentation of topics in an instructional video using the variation in the content density function. The key contributing factors which manipulate the content density function are shot length, motion and sound energy. This work is extended in [25], where a thematic function is introduced to capture the frequency of appearance of the narrator, frequency of the superimposed text and narrator's voice over. The thematic function is used along with the content density function in a two tiered hierarchical algorithm for segmenting the topics. The authors in [23] propose a two-level hidden markov model (HMM) based approach for topic change detection. All of these approaches were developed mainly for videos used in industries to train people and to convey instructions and practices, e.g., fire safety video. However OER videos, where the teacher goes over the content of slides, are very different from these kinds of videos. More importantly, none of these methods capture the actual content

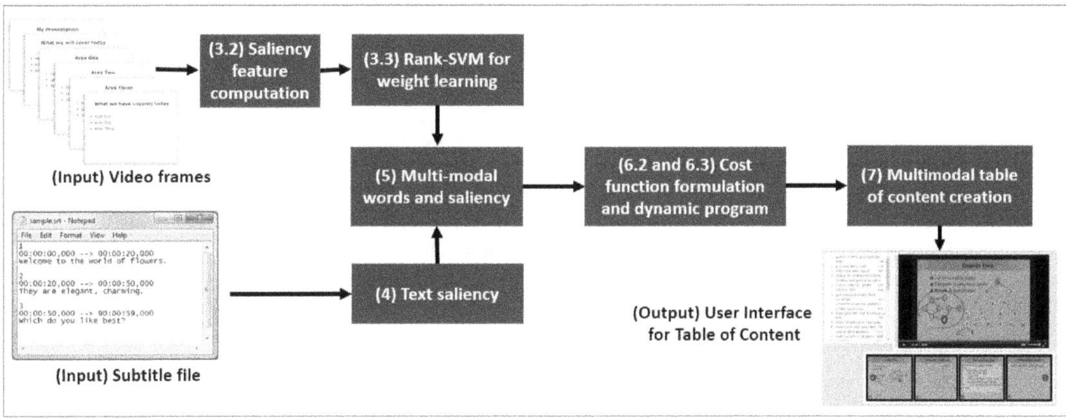

Figure 1: Pipeline of the proposed method MMToC. MMToC takes the video frames and the speech-to-text transcript from an educational video as inputs and automatically creates a table of content.

or their characteristics like saliency to model the topic partition. Authors in [2] proposed a novel method for creating a searchable text index which allows users to locate materials within lecture videos. The index is created from words on the presentation slides appearing in the video along with any associated metadata when available. However this method does not partition a video into segments corresponding to the topics discussed in the video.

Our work addresses the problem of topic segmentation in educational videos by defining and quantifying word saliencies across the visual and the spoken content, combining these saliency scores in a dynamic programming formulation to estimate the topic boundaries and presents a user interface for easy navigation through the videos.

Figure 1 shows the main building blocks of the proposed MMToC method. The method takes a set of uniformly sampled video frames and the speech transcript of the educational video as inputs and generates a list of topics along with their beginning times and title keyphrases. Sections 3.2 and 3.3 describe how the visual saliency is quantified. The estimation of initial set of likely topic partition points is described in 3.4. Section 4 describes the computation of saliency of the spoken words. The novel mechanism to combine the saliency of these two modalities is described in section 5. The cost function for topic segmentation and the dynamic programming formulation is described in section 6. Section 7 explains how the title keyphrases for each of the topic segments are generated. Finally, section 8 compares the performance of the proposed MMToC method with other state of the art techniques.

3. VISUAL SALIENCY

In this section we describe how the visual saliency features are computed and combined to obtain a saliency score.

3.1 Word Recognition and Text Post-processing

Recognizing text from images [33] is an extremely hard problem and continues to be an active area of computer vision research. Word recognition usually involves two steps, first, localization of text in the frame, and then identification of the text in the localized regions. In our proposed method, we use the algorithm proposed by Neumann *et al* [21] for localizing text in frames and the open source OCR engine Tesseract to recognize the words in the localized regions. Non-slide frames which do not have any detected text regions are ignored from any further visual processing. The recognized words and their corresponding locations serve as the input to the next part of MMToC, where the visual saliency features are extracted. Stop words ('and', 'it', 'the',...) are removed and the rest of the words are stemmed [27] (e.g., 'played', 'playing', 'player' become 'play').

3.2 Saliency Feature Computation

Location, font size and other visual effects are routinely used to highlight the significant words in a slide. We quantify this significance into word-saliency-score which contains two steps: feature computation and feature combination. First, several mid-level visual features are computed for all the words present on a slide and then they are combined using a weight vector learned from rank-SVM [5]. For computing the visual features, OCR outputs, i.e., the recognized words and their locations (bounding boxes) are used. Based upon the analysis of several educational videos (different from the ones used in the final evaluation) taken from NPTEL and edX, we formulated several visual features such as location, boldness, underlineness, capitalization, isolation, padding and size, that are indicative of visual saliency. In this section, we provide a way to quantize them and in the next section, a formal framework is proposed that combines them to predict the overall visual saliency of a word. The visual feature extraction procedure for each of the words is described below:

- **Location feature (u_1):** This feature captures the location information of a word in a slide. Generally, words which are located towards the top and left of a page are more important than the words located at the bottom and right corner of a page. We use two one dimensional Gaussian distributions ($f(x, \mu, \sigma) = \frac{1}{\sigma\sqrt{2\pi}} e^{\frac{-(x-\mu)^2}{2\sigma^2}}$) to compute this feature. The mean of the first Gaussian distribution is set to be the left most point of an image (giving maximum score to left-most words) and the mean of the second Gaussian distribution is set to be the top most point of an image (giving maximum score to the top most words). For each word, top-left corner (X-Y coordinate) of its bounding box is chosen as the variables in the Gaussian distributions. The location feature is given by the product of the scores obtained from the two Gaussian distributions.
- **Boldness feature (u_2):** The number of foreground pixels (i.e., the pixels which are part of the written text) nor-

malized with the number of characters present in a word is used to obtain the boldness feature. Thus, the boldness feature captures the average number of pixels occupied per character in a word.

- **Underlineness feature (u_3):** In this work, we use Hough Transform [32] of an image to detect horizontal or near-horizontal line segments present in that image. We also ignore all the horizontal line segments which are too close to the margin. Then, all the words which are immediately above the remaining horizontal/near-horizontal line segments are assigned a non-zero score for the underlineness feature. The underlineness feature for a word is binary denoting whether the word is underlined or not.
- **Capitalization feature (u_4):** If all the characters of a word are in upper case, then a word is assigned a non-zero score for the capitalization feature. This feature is also binary.
- **Isolation feature (u_5):** The isolation feature represents how isolated a word is in the slide. The hypothesis is that fewer the number of words in a slide, the more important the words present in it and similarly, the fewer the number of words in a line of a slide, more important the words in that line. For example, often in title slides, only a title word or a phrase is present in the center of the slide. And, the title word instances are more important than their corresponding instances elsewhere. Suppose, a word w is present in line l of a slide, then the isolation feature for word w is computed as follows -

$$u_5(w) = \frac{1}{\text{No. of lines in the slide} \times \text{No. of words in line } l}$$

- **Padding feature (u_6):** Past studies [16] have shown that line-spacing has a direct impact on readability and memorization of content. Also in educational videos teachers tend to keep some empty space while ending a concept and beginning a new concept in the same slide. We introduce a novel feature called padding to capture that information. For a word, padding feature is computed as the amount of empty space available below and above the line in which the word is present. Free space above is computed as number of pixels present between the current line and the previous line. Similarly, free space below is computed as the number of pixels present between the considered line and the next line. The sum is then normalized by the height of the image (slide) and the average line gap in the slide.
- **Size feature (u_7):** This feature captures the size of word in the slide. We denote the size of a word (size feature) as the height of the smallest character present in that word.

We normalize each of the visual features using 0-1 normalization across the entire video. The weighted sum of the normalized scores represents the overall saliency of the words in the frame. The weights are obtained using Rank-SVM [5], which we describe in the next subsection.

3.3 Learning to Rank Using Rank-SVM

In this subsection, we learn the relative importance of the visual features to predict the overall saliency of words. The weights determine the relative contribution of each visual feature to the overall saliency. The weights were learnt by collecting a training dataset from 10 users over 5 videos. 10 slides were randomly selected from each video (hence, total of 50 slides) to collect the training set. Each slide has been shown to 3 users and thus, a single user provides data for 15 unique slides. For each slide, the user was asked the following question - '*What are the salient words present in the slide that describe the overall content of the slide?*'. Generally, the number of selected salient words per slide vary between $2-12$ depending upon the user and the slide. To overcome inter-user subjectivity, a word is accepted as salient only if it is marked as salient by at least 2 users. Since in each slide users considered the selected words more salient than the words which were not selected, we consider them as pairwise preferences. These pairwise preferences can naturally be used in a Rank-SVM framework to learn the corresponding feature weights. We found that combining the visual features with equal weights often do not match the human provided ordering of salient words in a slide. Hence gathering training data from humans and using that in a discriminative learning framework to find the weights was required to accurately determine the saliency scores of words in a slide.

Let $\boldsymbol{u} = [u_1 u_2 \dots u_7]$ denotes the visual saliency feature vector and $\boldsymbol{w} = [w_1 w_2 \dots w_7]$ denotes the weight vector to be learnt for a particular word. Also, let $\mathcal{D}$ denotes the set of words and $\mathcal{D}_s$ (subscript 's' is used to imply salient) denotes the set of salient words present in a slide S. Consider two words i and j such that $i \in \mathcal{D}_s$ and $j \in \mathcal{D} - \{\mathcal{D}_s\}$ and their visual features are $\boldsymbol{u}_i$ and $\boldsymbol{u}_j$ respectively. Then the weights learnt should satisfy the saliency ordering constraints (pairwise preferences by users): $\boldsymbol{w}^T \boldsymbol{u}_i > \boldsymbol{w}^T \boldsymbol{u}_j$, $\forall i, j$. For each slide S, we will have $|\mathcal{D}_s| \times |\mathcal{D} - \{\mathcal{D}_s\}|$ number of constraints. Our goal is to learn a saliency ranking function $r(\boldsymbol{u}) = \boldsymbol{w}^T \boldsymbol{u}$ such that the maximum number of the following pairwise constraints are satisfied:

$$\boldsymbol{w}^T \boldsymbol{u}_i > \boldsymbol{w}^T \boldsymbol{u}_j, \forall (i,j) \in (\mathcal{D}_s, \mathcal{D} - \{\mathcal{D}_s\}), \forall S \quad (1)$$

While the above optimization problem is a NP-hard problem, it can be solved approximately by introducing negative slack variables similar to SVM classification. This leads to the following optimization problem:

$$\begin{aligned} &\min \ (\frac{1}{2}||\boldsymbol{w}^T||_2^2 + C \sum \xi_{ij}^2) \quad (2) \\ &\text{s.t. } \boldsymbol{w}^T \boldsymbol{u}_i > \boldsymbol{w}^T \boldsymbol{u}_j + 1 - \xi_{ij}; \forall (i,j) \in (\mathcal{D}_s, \mathcal{D} - \{\mathcal{D}_s\}), \forall S \\ &\xi_{ij} \geq 0 \end{aligned}$$

The above formulation is very similar to the SVM classification problem but on pairwise difference vectors, where C is the trade-off between maximizing the margin and satisfying the pairwise relative saliency constraints. The primal form of above optimization problem is solved using Newton's method [5, 22]. It should be noted that the above optimization problem learns a function that explicitly enforces a desired ordering on the saliency of words provided as training data. Now for any new word with feature vector $\boldsymbol{u}$, the saliency score can be obtained by computing the dot product of $\boldsymbol{u}$ with $\boldsymbol{w}$ (i.e., $\boldsymbol{w}^T \boldsymbol{u}$).

Some example frames from different videos with the detected words and their corresponding saliency scores are shown in Figure 2. Note that the words 'Torsional' and 'Waves' are part of the title of the slide in Figure 2a and are visually more salient. Hence, they have received higher scores. Similarly, in Figure 2b, the word 'Concepts' has received the highest saliency score. When we set equal weights for all the features, sometimes the computed saliency scores are counter-intuitive, e.g.: in 2b, the word 'Manipulative' is found to be more salient than 'inputs' because of the wide

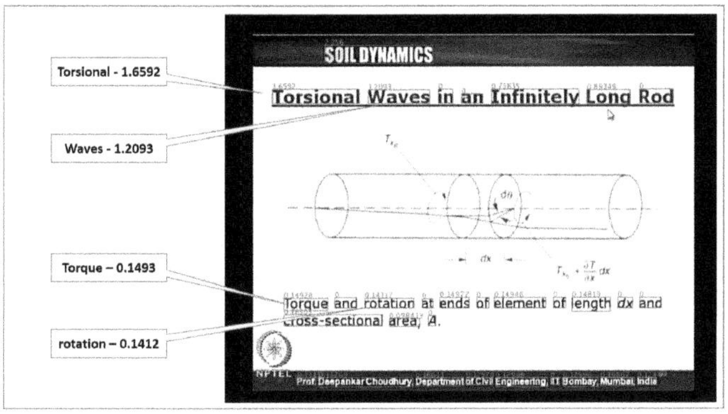

(a) Example frame 1

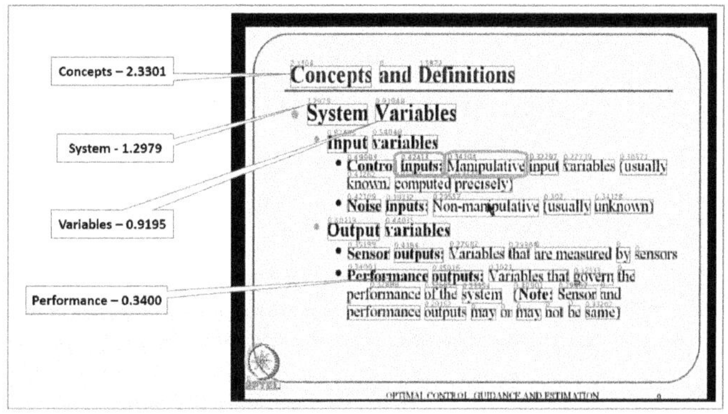

(b) Example frame 2

Figure 2: Figure showing the visual saliency scores of words on a few slides sampled from NPTEL educational videos. Note that the words which are visually more salient based on boldness, underlineness, size, location, isolation, padding and capitalization have received higher scores.

space above the word 'Manipulative'. Using Rank-SVM, we can get rid of such inconsistencies. For further details on visual saliency extraction refer to [10].

3.4 Unique Frame Extraction

Unique frames are identified from uniformly sampled frames of a video based on a criterion defined using (a) pixel difference, and (b) the proportion of words matched. Each frame is compared with all the previous frames of the video and is marked as duplicate if the pixel difference threshold between the current frame and any of the previous frames is less than γ or, more importantly, if the proportion of word overlap in the two frames is greater than a threshold ρ. The duplicate frames are dropped from any further processing. Once we find the final set of unique slides, we note the time instances $\mathcal{T}_u^{vis} = \{t_{u_1}^{vis}, t_{u_2}^{vis}, \ldots, t_{u_M}^{vis}\}$ when each of the unique slide appears for the first time, where $t_{u_m}^{vis}$ is the time instant when the m-th slide begins and there are total M slides. We observe that the beginning of a new topic is typically in the vicinity of these time instances ($\mathcal{T}_u^{vis}$). We empirically find that this restriction improves the run time as well as the segmentation accuracy of the MMToC method. This is explained in more detail in section 6.1.

4. SPOKEN WORD SALIENCY

This section describes the estimation of the salient spoken words and the computation of their corresponding saliency scores.

4.1 Candidate Salient Word Selection

The discourse in a video lecture is different from that in a text document in multiple obvious dimensions: the sentence structure is more disfluent, there is more repetition and a lesser degree of formalism. We make a further interesting observation based on our analysis of several video lectures: The instructors rely on the availability of the visual channel and thus make plenty of visual coreferences while teaching (i.e., referring to terms/equations as 'this', 'it' and so on). Encouraged by this observation, we compared the proportion of coreferencing in a random subset of six videos from three courses with that in corresponding six sections in the textbooks of those courses. The per-word coreferencing in video lectures is 0.78 whereas for written textbooks it is 0.55. The Stanford CoreNLP [28] implementation of the coreference resolution system was used in our work. Note that this coreference resolution method is optimized for a text-only coreference scenario and misses out on several visual coreferences. The coreferred pronouns are then expanded to their corresponding noun form.

In the next step, the standard stop words (typical function words such as 'a', 'an', 'the', 'of') are removed. In the Term Frequency - Inverse Document Frequency (TF-IDF) parlance, these are the words that may have high term frequency in a given document but also occur in almost every document thus reducing their inverse document frequency count (i.e., specificity). As a result, they are not discriminative about the document. Formally, TF-IDF of a term t in a document d in a corpus of documents D is defined as follows:

$$TF(t,d) = (\text{frequency of t in d})/(\text{total terms in d})$$

$$IDF(t,D) = log\frac{|D|}{|\{d \in D : t \in d\}|}$$

$$TF - IDF(t,d,D) = TF(t,d) * IDF(t,D)$$

We extend this TF-IDF computation to the document-dependent stop words defined in [14] but estimate them in a way that is consistent with the TF-IDF formulation: The lecture transcript is split into chunks of one minute each. Each chunk is treated as a separate document and words with low IDF are identified as document-dependent stop words. For example in a video lecture on algorithms the words 'algorithm' and 'complexity' are found to be the document dependent stop words. These document-dependent stop words are also removed from further processing. To reduce the dimensionality, the Part of Speech (PoS) tag of the rest of the words is identified (using [31]) and only the nouns and adjectives are considered for further processing. Finally, these words are stemmed using the Porter stemmer [27]. The resultant words are referred to as the content words. The steps outlined above reduce the computational complexity without affecting the topic segmentation accuracy.

4.2 Text Saliency Computation

To quantify the relative saliency of the content words, we build on the graph-based ranking model, TextRank, proposed in [19]: Assume $G = (V, E)$ is a weighted graph with the set of vertices V and set of edges E. The weight of the edge connecting V_i and V_j is denoted as E_{ij}. For a given

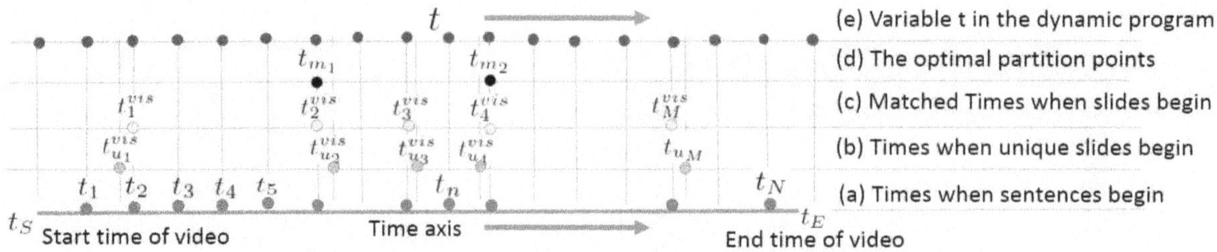

Figure 3: Visualization of different time instants used in our cost formulation. (a) Times instants when the new sentences begin. (b) Time instants when unique slides begin. (c) Unique slide times mapped to the nearest sentence beginning times. (d) The optimal video partition points (subset of the matched slide times). (e) The variable t which is used in the DP.

vertex V_i if $I(V_i)$ is the set of vertices that point to it and $O(V_i)$ is the set of vertices that V_i points to, then the score of the vertex V_i is defined as:

$$S(V_i) = (1-d) + d \sum_{V_j \in I(V_i)} \frac{E_{ji}}{\sum_{V_k \in O(V_j)} E_{jk}} S(V_j)$$

where d is the damping factor which signifies the probability of jumping from one vertex to another.

Each vertex V_i is a content word w_i and E_{ij} is defined as the proportion of the times w_i and w_j co-occured within a window of $\pm l$ words ($l = 5$ experimentally). The graph is an undirected graph and thus $I(V_i) = O(V_i)$. Also note that this vertex scoring is an iterative mechanism. We start with a uniform score of one for all the vertices and stop when the difference between the scores computed at two successive iterations is below a threshold. Words (i.e., vertices) with a score greater than one are chosen as the salient spoken words and the corresponding vertex score is the saliency score. Intuitively, higher vertex score implies the corresponding word co-occurs in a broader context and is thus more relevant for the discourse.

5. MULTIMODAL WORDS

Typically, far fewer words are displayed prominently on slides than are spoken. Thus, the list of visual salient words is a good 'seed set' of words to identify topic changes. But at the same time, a given visual word or phrase may be referred to differently in the spoken discourse (e.g., "support vector machines" vs. "SVM") and thus restricting the topic analysis to only visual words can be limiting. The other extreme of using all the spoken words for topic analysis can introduce unwanted noise. To strike a balance between the two modalities of salient words, we use a local context analysis based method ([34, 11]) to identify the synonyms of the visual words in the spoken content.

The method works as follows: Each visual word (w_v) is represented by a vector of context words C_{w_v}. The entry for a context word w_c in this vector is the number of times w_c was spoken in the context of w_v, i.e., spoken in a $\pm l$ word window centred around w_v, normalized by the frequency of w_c in the entire video. Similar context vectors are also formed for all the words in the spoken content. Cosine similarity between the context vector of the given visual word and each spoken word (w_s) is computed ($S(C_{w_v}, C_{w_s})$). The spoken content words are ranked based on their cosine similarity with the given visual word and top N (=5) words are chosen as the synonym candidates to expand the visual word. For example, corresponding to the word 'method' in a slide, we get 'system', 'technique','approach','algorithm' and 'process' as the synonyms in the spoken content. The new saliency score for the visual word and each of its synonyms is the average of the saliency scores of the visual word and that of all the synonyms in the spoken content. These visual words along with their synonyms and the new saliency scores are used in the cost formulation in the next section. While comparing two video segments the synonymous relationship is considered, i.e., if 'method' is present in one segment and 'approach' is present in another segment, we take their similarity into account.

6. COST AND DYNAMIC PROGRAM

Given an educational video our objective is to partition it into several segments such that each segment discusses about a single coherent topic.

6.1 Initial candidates for topic boundaries

Visual events such as change of slides or panning from the lecturer's face to the slide view are not necessarily synchronized with the spoken events such as the beginning of a new sentence. Thus the potential time instances as candidates for a multimodal topic partition can be infinitely many. In MMToC we narrow down this initial list to a few instances and restrict the final topic boundaries to be among these instances as follows: The first assumption is that a new topic begins at the beginning of a new sentence. Indeed, human annotators and end users are highly likely to mark the beginning of a topic at the beginning of a new sentence rather than in the middle of a sentence. The second reasonable assumption is that the duration of individual sentences is, on an average, much smaller than the duration of display of individual slides. Figure 3(a) shows the time instances when different sentences begin: $\mathcal{T} = \{t_1, t_2, \ldots, t_N\} \in [t_S, t_E]$, where t_S and t_E are start time and end time of a video and t_n is the start time of the n-th spoken sentence. The search space of the final segmentation points is restricted to be from $\mathcal{T}$.

The time instances when the unique slides are displayed for the first time are computed in Section 3.4. These time instances $\mathcal{T}_u^{vis} = \{t_{u_1}^{vis}, t_{u_2}^{vis}, \ldots, t_{u_M}^{vis}\}$ are shown in Figure 3(b). They are are matched to the closest times in $\mathcal{T}$ to avoid any audio-visual confusion such as beginning to play a video segment from the middle of a sentence. Let us assume that these matched time instances are $\mathcal{T}^{vis} = \{t_1^{vis}, t_2^{vis}, \ldots, t_M^{vis}\} \in \mathcal{T}$, (see Figure 3(c)). As discussed in Section 3.4, the search space of the topic partition points is further restricted to be from $\mathcal{T}^{vis}$.

6.2 Cost function formulation

Our objective is to find out K (where K is also unknown) partition points in the video such that each segment in the video represents one of the topics discussed. The proposed method tries to optimize an objective function that minimizes a metric based on the salient words which are common between the two adjacent segments, and maximizes a metric based on the salient words which are unique to either of the two segments. We find the set of optimal partition points $\mathcal{T}^{opt} = \{t_{m_1}, t_{m_2}, \cdots, t_{m_K}\}$, where $t_{m_k} \in \mathcal{T}^{vis}$ $\forall k$ (see Figure 3(d)), by optimizing the below cost function in equation 3. We define an indicator function $\mathbb{1}(w_p \in A)$, which is 1 if w_p belongs to the set A and zero, otherwise. Note that S_{m_{k-1},m_k} denotes the video segment and $\mathcal{W}_{m_{k-1},m_k}$ denotes the words present between the time instants $t_{m_{k-1}}$ and t_{m_k}. Also note that s_p denotes the saliency score of the p-word present in $\mathcal{W}_{m_{k-1},m_k}$.

Cost Function:

$$\mathcal{T}^{opt} = \underset{\mathcal{T}^{vis}}{\text{argmin}} \sum_{k=1}^{K} (\alpha \cdot C(S_{m_{k-1},m_k}, S_{m_k,m_{k+1}}) - (1-\alpha) \cdot D(S_{m_{k-1},m_k}, S_{m_k,m_{k+1}})) \quad (3)$$

Where,

$$C(S_{m_{k-1},m_k}, S_{m_k,m_{k+1}}) = \frac{\sum_{w_p} s_p \cdot \mathbb{1}(w_p \in \mathcal{W}_{m_{k-1},m_k} \cap \mathcal{W}_{m_k,m_{k+1}})}{\sum_{w_p} s_p \cdot \mathbb{1}(w_p \in \mathcal{W}_{m_{k-1},m_k})} + \frac{\sum_{w_p} s_p \cdot \mathbb{1}(w_p \in \mathcal{W}_{m_{k-1},m_k} \cap \mathcal{W}_{m_k,m_{k+1}})}{\sum_{w_p} s_p \cdot \mathbb{1}(w_p \in \mathcal{W}_{m_k,m_{k+1}})} \quad (4)$$

$$D(S_{m_{k-1},m_k}, S_{m_k,m_{k+1}}) = \frac{\sum_{w_p} s_p \cdot \mathbb{1}(w_p \in \mathcal{W}_{m_{k-1},m_k} \setminus \mathcal{W}_{m_k,m_{k+1}})}{\sum_{w_p} s_p \cdot \mathbb{1}(w_p \in \mathcal{W}_{m_{k-1},m_k})} + \frac{\sum_{w_p} s_p \cdot \mathbb{1}(w_p \in \mathcal{W}_{m_k,m_{k+1}} \setminus \mathcal{W}_{m_{k-1},m_k})}{\sum_{w_p} s_p \cdot \mathbb{1}(w_p \in \mathcal{W}_{m_k,m_{k+1}})} \quad (5)$$

Dynamic Program:

$$Cost(t) = \min_{u \in [t_{min}, t_{max}]} [Cost(t-u) + (\alpha \cdot C(S_{Seg(t-u),t-u}, S_{t-u,t}) - (1-\alpha) \cdot D(S_{Seg(t-u),t-u}, S_{t-u,t}))] \quad (6)$$

$$Seg(t) = \underset{u \in [t_{min}, t_{max}]}{\text{argmin}} [Cost(t-u) + (\alpha \cdot C(S_{Seg(t-u),t-u}, S_{t-u,t}) - (1-\alpha) \cdot D(S_{Seg(t-u),t-u}, S_{t-u,t}))] \quad (7)$$

- $C(S_{m_{k-1},m_k}, S_{m_k,m_{k+1}})$ (equation 4) captures the commonality of salient words between two segments. The first factor denotes the sum of saliency scores (computed for S_{m_{k-1},m_k}) of the words which are common between S_{m_{k-1},m_k} and $S_{m_k,m_{k+1}}$ normalized by the total saliency of all the words present in S_{m_{k-1},m_k}. The second factor denotes the sum of saliency scores (computed for $S_{m_k,m_{k+1}}$) of the words which are common between S_{m_{k-1},m_k} and $S_{m_k,m_{k+1}}$ normalized by the total saliency of all the words present in $S_{m_k,m_{k+1}}$.
- $D(S_{m_{k-1},m_k}, S_{m_k,m_{k+1}})$ (equation 5) captures the difference in the salient words in the two segments. The first factor denotes the sum of saliency scores (computed for S_{m_{k-1},m_k}) of the words which are present in S_{m_{k-1},m_k} but not in $S_{m_k,m_{k+1}}$ and normalized by the total saliency of all the words present in S_{m_{k-1},m_k}. The second factor is also defined in a similar way for $S_{m_k,m_{k+1}}$.
- α is a parameter which decides how much relative weight should be given to each of the factors in our optimization problem.

6.3 Dynamic Program for Optimization

We now optimize the cost function in equation 3 to obtain the topic based partition points in a video. Since the segmentation of a video into topics preserves linearity, i.e., all of the time instants between the first and the last time instants of a particular segment must belong to the same topic, we can optimize the cost function in equation 3 using DP described below. Let us assume that $Cost(t)$ (see t in Figure 3(e)) denotes the cost of the optimal segmentation of the video till the t-th time instant and shown in equation 6. $Seg(t)$ stores the last partition point of the optimal segmentation till the t-th time instant and is also used to backtrack the optimal set of partition points (shown in equation 7).

- t_{min} and t_{max} (t in Figure 3(e)) denote the minimum and maximum possible number of time instants considered for a topic respectively.
- The number of final partition points K varies in the range: $\frac{|\mathcal{T}|}{t_{max}} - 1 \leq K \leq \frac{|\mathcal{T}|}{t_{min}} - 1$, where $|\mathcal{T}|$ denotes the number of elements in $\mathcal{T}$.
- Initialization: $Cost(t) = \infty$, $t \in \mathcal{T}$, $Seg(t) = 1$, $t \in \mathcal{T}$.
- We restrict the final solution $\mathcal{T}^{opt}$ to be from the subset $\mathcal{T}^{vis}$ by assigning a very high value to $Cost(t)$, $\forall t \in \mathcal{T} \setminus \mathcal{T}^{vis}$.
- Complexity: the complexity of the proposed dynamic program approach is $O((t_{max} - t_{min})|\mathcal{T}^{vis}|)$, i.e., $O(t_{max}|\mathcal{T}^{vis}|)$.

Once the video is partitioned using the dynamic program, each segment represents one coherent topic. The next step is to label these partitions.

7. TABLE OF CONTENT CREATION

Given the topic segments, the next step is to automatically assign a representative name to each of the topics. The following steps summarize this process:

All the visually salient keywords in the given segment are identified. The spoken saliency score for these keywords, if any, is added to the visual saliency score. The keyword list is ranked based on this combined saliency score and the five most salient words are retained. The text transcript is then analysed to identify the salient words that are most co-occurring (within a window of ±3 words). Up to three most common phrases of these salient words are chosen as the representative name for the topic.

The perfect algorithm for table of content creation should select only one keyphrase for each segment. However, in real life, the best phrase selected by the algorithm may not be fully indicative of the actual topic of that segment. Thus, we choose multiple top key-phrases for each segment in the hope that the combination reflects the true topic in that segment. This also creates a more meaningful and complete table of content for the educational video. Some example keyphrases generated by MMToC are highlighted in the table of content in Figure 5.

8. EXPERIMENTAL RESULTS

In this section we describe the experimental results and the user study.

8.1 Datasets

We perform experiments on two different datasets. The ground truth annotation of partition points in each video is obtained from two annotators who are experts in the concepts discussed in that video. The annotators were asked to go through each video carefully to annotate the topic segmentation points and on average it took 1.5 hours to annotate an hour long video. Only the partition points that are selected by both the annotators are chosen to be part of the final ground truth partition points.

1. **NPTEL dataset:** NPTEL [1] records video lectures from tier-1 colleges in India and makes them freely available on their website for other institutions where recruiting and retaining high quality teachers may not be possible due to the lack of infrastructure. The NPTEL repository has a large number of educational videos available. We choose a random subset of 14 educational videos from this repository to perform our experiments. Obtaining annotation for each video is a time intensive process and identifying annotators with the required expertise in the subject of the video is also a challenging task. These two factors dictate the dataset used for evaluation. The duration of each of these videos is around $1 - 1.5$ hours. NPTEL videos are recorded under a diverse set of conditions: Slide orientations and style, camera angle, ambience light, video resolution, and lecturer positioning in the slides vary significantly across the NPTEL videos, e.g., on few occasions the lecturer occupies bottom right part of the slide and sometimes full frame. In few of the videos, the lecturer uses printed text instead of using slides. All these scenarios make the video partitioning a challenging task.
2. **Youtube dataset:** We also perform experiments on nine randomly chosen lecture videos downloaded from Youtube. Six of these were 20-30 minute long Coursera video lectures. The other three videos were $1 - 1.25$ hours long.

The NPTEL and the three longer youtube videos have 16 ground truth partition points on average, whereas the remaining six shorter youtube videos have 5 ground truth partition points on average.

System Parameters: We have used several parameters while developing the components of MMToC. Now we describe them. These parameters are chosen using a validation set of 6 videos (different from the NPTEL and youtube video dataset described earlier) and usually remain the same for all test videos. The variance of two Gaussian distributions used to compute the location features are chosen as 0.25 times the width of an image and 0.16 times the height of an image respectively (Section 3.2). The parameters γ and ρ for unique slide detection are chosen as 0.98 and 0.9 respectively (Section 3.4). t_{min} and t_{max} are set to be 5 and 100 time instants (in $\mathcal{T}$) respectively in our DP formulation (Section 6.3). In Section 6.2, we have used a parameter α that defines the relative weight of the two terms in our cost function in equation 3. We find that using $\alpha = 0.25$ and $\alpha = 0.65$, we get top two highest F-measures (0.69 & 0.68) on the validation set (the third highest is 0.54). While running MMToC on our test videos we try both $\alpha = 0.25$ and $\alpha = 0.65$ and report the better F-score. Automatically determining which one of these two α values to use for a new test video could be an interesting future work.

8.2 Baseline methods

The performance of the proposed MMToC method is compared with different state-of-the-art methods described below:

1. **LDA [4]:** Latent Dirichlet Allocation (LDA) is a generative model that explains the set of observations using hidden topics. In LDA, each document is considered as a mixture of topics. In our work, we consider each segment between two unique slides as a different document. Union of the visual and spoken words in each segment is considered as the vocabulary in the LDA approach. Each segment is assigned a topic by maximizing over the topic likelihoods obtained from LDA. Time instances of segments where the topic changes are the final topic segmentation points.
2. **LDA + proposed saliency:** In this approach instead of using the union of words in the visual and spoken domain, we use the set of multimodal words and their corresponding saliency scores produced by MMToC as described in section 5. The saliency scores are used as weights of the words in LDA.
3. **MMToC with only visual:** The proposed dynamic program formulation (Section 6.3) is used with only the visual words and their corresponding visual saliency scores (Section 3).
4. **MMToC with only speech:** The proposed dynamic program formulation (Section 6.3) is used with only the spoken words and their corresponding saliency in the spoken domain (Section 4).
5. **MMToC:** This is the proposed multimodal method.

8.3 Evaluation Criterion

If a time instant obtained by MMToC is within ± 10 seconds of a ground truth partition point, we consider that MMToC has successfully retrieved that partition point. We evaluate the proposed method by computing the F-score of the set of partition points obtained using MMToC with respect to the ground truth. F-score is computed as the harmonic mean of precision and recall. Recall measures how well the system can retrieve the true ground truth partition points, and high precision ensures that it does not overpredict the true topic partitions. F-Score is 1 in the ideal case, i.e., when the algorithm is perfect and both precision and recall are 1.

8.4 Discussion

The visual features extracted in Section 3.2 are combined using the weight vector obtained in Section 3.3. The weights learned are 1.1250 (boldness), 1.0015 (location), 0.6605 (underlineness), 0.6050 (size), 0.4612 (capitalization), 0.2291 (isolation), 0.0232 (padding). We observe that boldness and location features have higher weights compared to the other

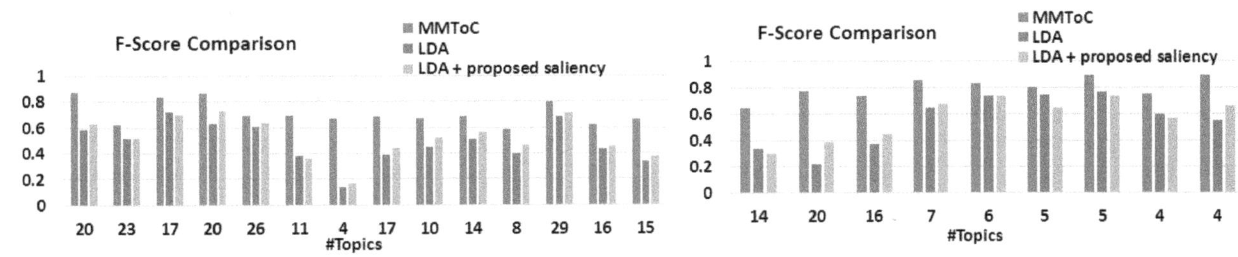

(a) NPTEL dataset (b) Youtube video dataset

Figure 4: Comparison of the proposed approach with LDA [4] and LDA + proposed saliency on 14 NPTEL and 9 youtube videos. The number of ground truth topics in each video are shown along the x-axis. Average results on MMToC with only visual and only speech are provided in Table 1 to avoid clutter in this Figure.

Table 1: Average F-score on all the videos for NPTEL and youtube dataset.

F-score	LDA [4]	LDA + proposed saliency	MMToC with only visual	MMToC with only speech	MMToC
NPTEL dataset	0.48	0.52	0.68	0.55	**0.71**
Youtube dataset	0.55	0.57	0.77	0.59	**0.81**

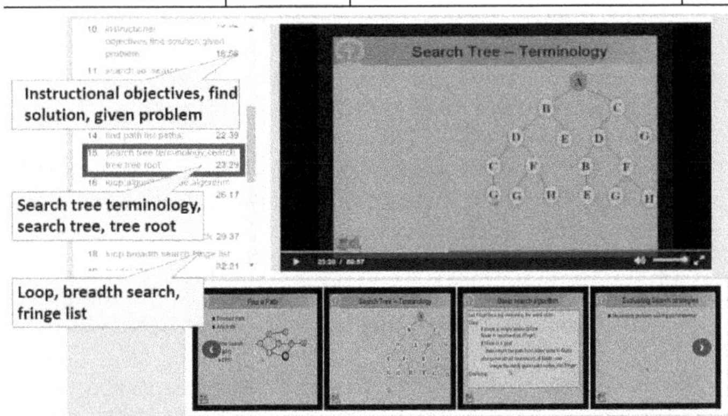

Figure 5: Screen-shot of the user interface for displaying the table of content. Along with the generated table of content the interface also displays the corresponding slides, such that users can look into the figures, equations and hand-written content which are not included in the table of content.

weights indicating that these two features are perhaps more important in determining the overall visual saliency.

The results on NPTEL and youtube datasets are provided in Figure 4 and Table 1. The proposed method MMToC significantly outperforms the state-of-the-art topic analysis methods LDA and LDA+proposed saliency. For the NPTEL dataset the proposed method is better than LDA+proposed saliency by an F-score of 0.19 (relative improvement is 37%, $t(14) = 3.88$ and $p = 0.0004$). Similarly for the youtube dataset MMToC is better than LDA+proposed saliency by an F-score of 0.24 (relative improvement is 42%, $t(9) = 3.76$ and $p = 0.001$). We also observe that using only the visual words and their corresponding saliency, we outperform LDA+proposed saliency. The improvement in F-score and the t-test results clearly indicate that MMToC is statistically better than previous topic segmentation methods.

8.5 User Study

Although quantitatively our method is superior to other state-of-the-art approaches, we further evaluated how good MMToC is for non-linear navigation with real users. We create a user interface (UI) such that users can easily navigate through a video using MMToC. A screen-shot of the UI is displayed in Figure 5. There are two major components of the UI other than the actual video. First, the table of content generated by MMToC is displayed at the left of the video. Second, the beginning slides corresponding to each segment in the table of content are displayed below such that users can also scroll through them to find a topic. The slides were included in the UI to provide users the visual information such as figures, equations or text written in hand, which cannot be captured in the table of content. These components are hyperlinked to their corresponding time instances in the video for ease of navigation.

We conducted a preliminary user study consisting of 18 participants and 3 videos where we compared the MMToC with several baseline interfaces: (a) transcript+youtube style rendering based interface (similar to the EdX interface) where the text is hyperlinked with the corresponding location in the video where it is spoken, (b) all the unique slides were shown to the users without the Table of Content and (c) only ToC list was shown and the beginning slides were not shown. All the 18 participants (ten male and eight female) had engineering degrees, exposure to MOOC videos and had not seen any of these videos earlier. The three videos used were of 60, 55 and 56 minutes long. Each participant was presented two videos with two different interfaces (out of the fours UIs we considered). Thus each video+interface combination was evaluated by three different users. For each video, each user was asked the question *'Where in the video does the teacher start talking about topic X?'*: Five times with five different *'X'*. The users were allowed to go back and forth in the video multiple times to identify these topic locations. These 5 topics (*'X'*) were randomly chosen from the ground truth topics given by the human experts (Section 8.1). We measured the total time taken by the participant to answer all the questions along with the number of questions which were correctly answered. We considered an answer to be correct if it is within a window of ± 10 seconds of the corresponding ground truth topic start point.

We found that the average time taken by the participants to find a topic in a video was 45 ± 14.62 seconds using MMToC, 90 ± 36.47 seconds using the interface (a), 68 ± 27.54 seconds using the interface (b) and 54 ± 24.12 seconds using the interface (c). The proposed interface shows statistically significant time saving compared to the baseline interface (a) ($t(9) = -3.41$ and $p = 0.003$). The percentage of correctly answered questions were 79% and 69% respectively using MMToC interface and the interface (a). That clearly shows the effectiveness and efficiency of our proposed method.

9. CONCLUSION

A Multimodal method for table of content creation for instructional videos (MMToC) is proposed in this paper. Salient words obtained from slides and speech transcript are used to formulate a cost function and is optimized using a dynamic program formulation to get the optimal partitioning of a video into topics. MMToC significantly outperforms the LDA based baseline topic partition approaches. Also a preliminary user study demonstrates the effectiveness of our method with real users. The proposed MMToC method along with the keyword based navigation technique proposed in [35] provide text-book-like navigation capabilities for instructional videos through our e-learning platform called the TutorSpace Personalized Learning Platform. Finally, although MMToC is developed for educational videos, it can be applied to other kinds of videos such as news and movies for temporal segmentation and creating table of contents.

10. REFERENCES

[1] `http://nptel.ac.in/`.

[2] J. Adcock, M. Cooper, L. Denoue, H. Pirsiavash, and L. A. Rowe. Talkminer: a lecture webcast search engine. In *ACM MM*, 2010.

[3] D. Beeferman, A. Berger, and J. Lafferty. Statistical models for text segmentation. *Machine Learning*, 1999.

[4] D. M. Blei. Probabilistic topic models. *Commun. ACM*, 55(4), 2012.

[5] O. Chapelle and S. S. Keerthi. Efficient algorithms for ranking with SVMs. *Inf. Retr*, 13(3), 2010.

[6] F. Y. Choi. Advances in domain independent linear text segmentation. In *ACL*, 2000.

[7] C. Choudary and T. C. Liu. Summarization of visual content in instructional videos. *IEEE Transactions on Multimedia*, 9(7), Nov. 2007.

[8] L. Du, W. L. Buntine, and M. Johnson. Topic segmentation with a structured topic model. In *HLT-NAACL*, 2013.

[9] M. Galley, K. McKeown, E. Fosler-Lussier, and H. Jing. Discourse segmentation of multi-party conversation. In *ACL*, 2003.

[10] A. Gandhi, A. Biswas, and O. Deshmukh. Topic transition in educational videos using visually salient words. In *EDM*, 2015.

[11] S. Godbole, I. Bhattacharya, A. Gupta, and A. Verma. Building re-usable dictionary repositories for real-world text mining. In *CIKM*. ACM, 2010.

[12] P. J. Guo and K. Reinecke. Demographic differences in how students navigate through moocs. In *LAS*. ACM, 2014.

[13] M. A. Hearst. Texttiling: A quantitative approach to discourse segmentation. *Computational Linguistics*, 23(1), Mar. 1997.

[14] X. Ji and H. Zha. Domain-independent text segmentation using anisotropic diffusion and dynamic programming. In *SIGIR*. ACM, 2003.

[15] Y. Li, Y. Park, and C. Dorai. Atomic topical segments detection for instructional videos. In *ACM Multimedia*. ACM, 2006.

[16] J. Ling and P. van Schaik. The influence of line spacing and text alignment on visual search of web pages. *Displays*, 28(2), 2007.

[17] T. C. Liu and C. Choudary. Content extraction and summarization of instructional videos. In *ICIP*, 2006.

[18] I. Malioutov and R. Barzilay. Minimum cut model for spoken lecture segmentation. In *ACL*. Association for Computational Linguistics, 2006.

[19] R. Mihalcea and P. Tarau. Textrank: Bringing order into text. In *EMNLP*. ACL, 2004.

[20] M. Mohri, P. Moreno, and E. Weinstein. Discriminative topic segmentation of text and speech. In *AISTATS*, 2010.

[21] L. Neumann and J. Matas. Scene text localization and recognition with oriented stroke detection. In *ICCV*. IEEE, 2013.

[22] D. Parikh and K. Grauman. Relative attributes. In *ICCV*. IEEE, 2011.

[23] D. Q. Phung, T. V. Duong, S. Venkatesh, and H. H. Bui. Topic transition detection using hierarchical hidden markov and semi-markov models. In *ACM Multimedia*. ACM, 2005.

[24] D. Q. Phung, S. Venkatesh, and C. Dorai. High level segmentation of instructional videos based on content density. In *ACM Multimedia*, 2002.

[25] D. Q. Phung, S. Venkatesh, and C. Dorai. Hierarchical topical segmentation in instructional films based on cinematic expressive functions. In *ACM Multimedia*, 2003.

[26] J. M. Ponte and W. B. Croft. Text segmentation by topic. *Lecture Notes in Computer Science*, 1324, 1997.

[27] M. F. Porter. An algorithm for suffix stripping. *Program*, 14(3), 1980.

[28] M. Recasens, M. de Marneffe, and C. Potts. The life and death of discourse entities: Identifying singleton mentions. In *HLT-NAACL*, 2013.

[29] J. C. Reynar. Statistical models for topic segmentation. In *ACL*. Association for Computational Linguistics, 1999.

[30] M. Riedl and C. Biemann. Topictiling: a text segmentation algorithm based on lda. In *Proceedings of ACL 2012 Student Research Workshop*, 2012.

[31] K. Toutanova, D. Klein, C. D. Manning, and Y. Singer. Feature-rich part-of-speech tagging with a cyclic dependency network. In *HLT-NAACL*. Association for Computational Linguistics, 2003.

[32] R. S. Wallace. A modified hough transform for lines. In *CVPR*, 1985.

[33] K. Wang, B. Babenko, and S. Belongie. End-to-end scene text recognition. In *ICCV*, 2011.

[34] J. Xu and W. B. Croft. Query expansion using local and global document analysis. In *ACM SIGIR*. ACM, 1996.

[35] K. Yadav, K. Shrivastava, M. Prasad, H. Arsikere, S. Patil, R. Kumar, and O. Deshmukh. Content-driven multi-modal techniques for non-linear video navigation. In *ACM IUI*, 2015.

Interactive Scene Flow Editing for Improved Image-based Rendering and Virtual Spacetime Navigation

Kai Ruhl[1], Martin Eisemann[1,2], Anna Hilsmann[3], Peter Eisert[3] and Marcus Magnor[1]
[1]TU Braunschweig, Germany [2]TH Koeln, Germany [3]Fraunhofer HHI, Berlin, Germany
ruhl@cg.cs.tu-bs.de, martin.eisemann@th-koeln.de, anna.hilsmann@hhi.fraunhofer.de *
peter.eisert@hhi.fraunhofer.de, magnor@cg.cs.tu-bs.de

ABSTRACT

High-quality stereo and optical flow maps are essential for a multitude of tasks in visual media production, e.g. virtual camera navigation, disparity adaptation or scene editing. Rather than estimating stereo and optical flow separately, scene flow is a valid alternative since it combines both spatial and temporal information and recently surpassed the former two in terms of accuracy. However, since automated scene flow estimation is non-accurate in a number of situations, resulting rendering artifacts have to be corrected manually in each output frame, an elaborate and time-consuming task. We propose a novel workflow to edit the scene flow itself, catching the problem at its source and yielding a more flexible instrument for further processing. By integrating user edits in early stages of the optimization, we allow the use of approximate scribbles instead of accurate editing, thereby reducing interaction times. Our results show that editing the scene flow improves the quality of visual results considerably while requiring vastly less editing effort.

Categories and Subject Descriptors

I.4.8 [**Image Processing and Computer Vision**]: Scene Analysis—*Depth cues*; I.4.8 [**Image Processing and Computer Vision**]: Scene Analysis—*Motion*; H.5.2 [**Information Interfaces and Representation**]: User Interfaces—*Interaction styles*

Keywords

scene flow; stereo; optical flow; interactivity; user interface; image-based rendering; view interpolation

1. INTRODUCTION

In visual media productions, several editing operations in post-production require information about scene depth and/or motion. Due to the current popularity of stereoscopic 3D movies, depth has taken a prominent role for all manner of stereo post production tasks [21], while motion is used primarily for slow-motion, frame upsampling and motion-based effects such as motion blur.

*Video and further paper details available under:
`http://graphics.tu-bs.de/publications/ruhl2015acmmm/`

MM'15, October 26 - 30, 2015, Brisbane, Australia

ACM 978-1-4503-3459-4/15/10...$15.00
DOI: http://dx.doi.org/10.1145/2733373.2806251

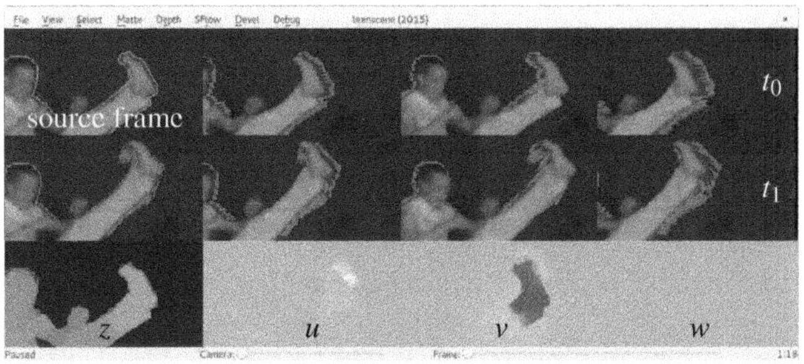

Figure 1: User interface for a scene recorded by four cameras. Top and middle row: View interpolation towards the cameras at times t_0 and t_1 using one source frame and the current scene flow. The user can toggle the warped vs. recorded frames to identify visual artifacts. Bottom row: color-coded visualization of the current depth z and 3D motion u, v, w estimate.

Up to now, multimedia authoring tools have estimated depth and motion separately using only two images each, an under-determined and ill-posed problem. Since there are strong links between spatial and temporal image correspondences, i.e. object texture and boundaries are present in both, using joint optimization in the form of scene flow [15] is a promising direction to improve the robustness of the estimation; stereo and optical flow are then mere reprojections of the scene flow into specific cameras at specific times.

Surprisingly, for over a decade scene flow has not been able to reach the quality of dedicated stereo and optical flow methods. Only recently, scene flow algorithms have begun to outperform the former two [16]. This gives rise to the idea of multimedia content production tools based on scene flow.

However, similar to stereo/optical flow, scene flow algorithms are not perfect, showing typical failure cases e.g. for repeating structures, occlusions and violations of the color constancy assumption. Flow field artifacts manifest themselves as visual artifacts in rendered output frames, e.g. for virtual camera views. Usually, visual artists employ image editing tools such as Adobe Photoshop to repair those visual artifacts frame-by-frame. Alternatively, they can use keyframe animation in tools such as TheFoundry NUKE or Adobe AfterEffects to model spatiotemporal transitions manually. Both are elaborate and time-consuming tasks whose effort is linear in the number of output frames or transitions.

For this reason, first editing tools for stereo and optical flow fields have recently been developed. They range from relatively direct cut&paste tools [6] to shape-fitting approaches [23]. However, to the best of our knowledge, no existing multimedia authoring tool includes scene flow yet. Our contribution is the first workflow that provides scene flow editing capabilities, allowing *interactive* manipulation of an *ongoing* scene flow estimation.

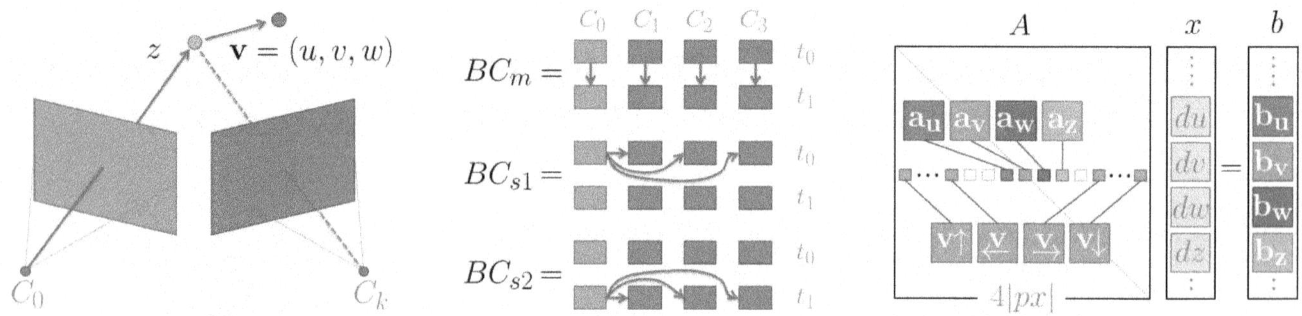

(a) scene flow variables

(b) data term components

(c) inner $Ax = b$ equations; some row for v

Figure 2: Optimization details. (a) The 4D flow components z, u, v, w are modeled in world space, allowing for an arbitrary number of cameras to support the "hero camera" C_0; arrows denote depth and motion. (b) The data term comprises a motion term $BC_m(z, \mathbf{v})$, a depth term $BC_{s1}(z)$ and a depth-after-motion term $BC_{s2}(z, \mathbf{v})$; arrows denote the frames used for data term evaluation. (c) The $A\mathrm{x} = \mathrm{b}$ system of linear equations links u, v, w and z and retrieves support information from the 4-neighborhood, here: a row for v.

1.1 Related Work

In multimedia authoring, depth map editing has become popular with the latest recurrence of stereoscopic 3D movies, having two complementary approaches: stereo conversion for videos shot with a single camera, and stereo estimation for footage recorded by two cameras. In stereo conversion, 2D video is converted to 3D video by manually creating a depth map for each input frame. Current approaches use scribble-based interfaces to draw depth scribbles and interpolate for the remaining pixels [5, 18], or use a set of sparse depth (in)equalities to add depth to cartoons [14]. For footage captured with stereo cameras, user interaction is often used to guide stereo matching. Current approaches provide sparse ground truth initializations in the form of point correspondences [17] or matching splines [9] while we use matching regions; remove outliers for better depth interpolation [3] or restrict the cost volume and enhance local depth resolution [10]; use geometric model fitting and discontinuity brushes in a belief propagation framework [23] where we use discontinuity scribbles; or modify local weights in a variational energy functional [4], which is part of our approach too.

Optical flow editing is useful for all manner of temporal effects, or when employing multiple non-synchronized cameras [7]. Current approaches use cut&paste on a flow field to match regions via perspective transformation and to recompute optical flow locally [6], or provide approximate correspondence regions which are then refined within further optimization [11], similar to our method.

To the best of our knowledge, no approach for *scene flow editing* exists. The closest in spirit to our method are the *stereo editing* approach by Doron et al. [4] and the *optical flow editing* approach by Ruhl et al. [11] in the sense that both modify a variational energy functional, and the latter exploits the image pyramid for refining approximate user input.

1.2 User Interface

Our objective is the creation of smooth spatiotemporal view interpolation. Fig. 1 shows our user interface: A scene has been recorded with four cameras C_k at two time steps t_0 and t_1, yielding frames I_t^k. One source frame has been selected (I_0^0 in the following, w.l.o.g.) and warped fully towards all other cameras and time steps using the scene flow. Ideally, the interpolated frames are equal to the recorded frames I_t^k; the user can check this by toggling between recorded/interpolated frames.

The scene flow is estimated in the background using a coarse-to-fine image pyramid with levels $L = L_{\max}..0$, where 0 is the finest resolution level. At each step of the optimization, the user interface is updated to show the warped frames at increasingly higher resolutions and warped using better scene flow estimates. The user observes the optimization and identifies visual artifacts in the warped frames as soon as they become apparent on some (early) level L. Once such an error has been identified, the user pauses the estimation and uses our editing operations to guide the algorithm.

This guidance is taken as coarse initialization or soft constraint while the ongoing optimization determines the subpixel-precise final solution. In this manner, we benefit from both human scene recognition and subsequent algorithmic refinement.

2. PROBLEM FORMULATION

In order to develop appropriate editing operations, we first have to analyze the failure modes of scene flow estimation. We base our analysis on the well-known multi-view scene flow by Basha et al. [1, 8]. Scenes are recorded with an arbitrary number K of cameras $C_{0..K-1}$, one of which is designated as the so-called "hero" camera, at two frames t_0 and t_1, making it usable not only for stereo cameras but also e.g. for trifocal cameras [12]. For the hero camera (C_0 in the following, w.l.o.g.), we reconstruct the per-pixel depth z and the 3D motion $\mathbf{v} = (u, v, w)$ in world space, Fig. 2 (a). Assuming brightness constancy, we use a variational energy minimization:

$$E(z, \mathbf{v}) = \int_\Omega \underbrace{(BC_m + BC_{s1} + BC_{s2})}_{\text{data term}} + \alpha \underbrace{(S_m + \mu S_s)}_{\text{smoothness term}} \, dxdy \quad (1)$$

with α balancing data vs. smoothness and μ balancing motion vs. depth smoothness. Using recorded frames I_t^k from cameras C_k at time steps $t = 0..1$, the subterms are, Fig. 2 (b):

$$BC_m(z, \mathbf{v}) = \sum_{k=0}^{K-1} o_m^k \cdot \psi(|I_0^k(\mathbf{p}_0^k) - I_1^k(\mathbf{p}_1^k)|^2) \quad (2)$$

$$BC_{s1}(z) = \sum_{k=1}^{K-1} o_{s1}^k \cdot \psi(|I_0^0(\mathbf{p}_0^0) - I_0^k(\mathbf{p}_0^k)|^2) \quad (3)$$

$$BC_{s2}(z, \mathbf{v}) = \sum_{k=1}^{K-1} o_{s2}^k \cdot \psi(|I_1^0(\mathbf{p}_1^0) - I_1^k(\mathbf{p}_1^k)|^2) \quad (4)$$

$$S_m(\mathbf{v}) = \psi(|\nabla u|^2 + |\nabla v|^2 + |\nabla w|^2) \quad (5)$$

$$S_s(z) = \psi(|\nabla z|^2) \quad (6)$$

with $BC_{m,s1,s2}$ the brightness constancy data terms for motion, depth and depth-after motion, $S_{m,s}$ the smoothness terms for mo-

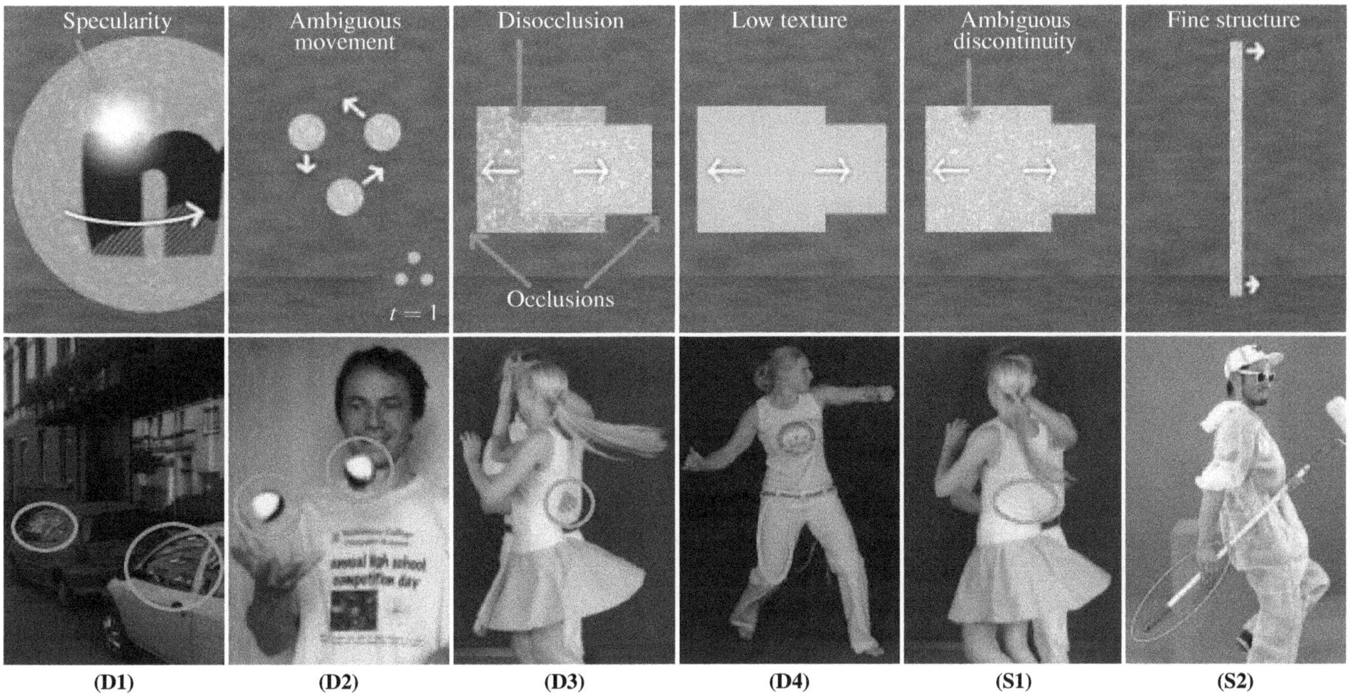

Figure 3: Common artifact causes. (D1) color constancy violation: the ball rotates to the right while the specularity stays in place. (D2) ambiguous displacements of three spheres (D3) disoccluded region without proper source region (D4) low-textured regions (S1) ambiguous discontinuities: not all image gradients are discontinuities. (S2) fine-scale objects. See Fig. 4–7 for artifact details.

tion and depth; occlusion maps $o_{m,s1,s2}$ deactivating the data term locally, image space points $\mathbf{p}^k_{t=0}(z)$ and $\mathbf{p}^k_{t=1}(z, \mathbf{v})$ reprojected from world space points $\mathbf{P}_0$ and $\mathbf{P}_1$ into a camera k, and the non-quadratic robust Charbonnier penalty $\psi(s^2) = \sqrt{s^2 + \varepsilon^2}$ [13].

Now where does this model have failure cases? We identified six typical situations, exemplified in Fig. 3 by both synthetic and real-world scenes. Row 1 shows input frames leading to artifacts; row 2 additionally motivates the scenarios. Four problems arise from the data term **(D1–4)** and two from the smoothness term **(S1–2)**:

(**D1**) Violations of brightness or color constancy assumption. Any reflectance, specularity or other non-Lambertian property such as shadows can cause pixels in one image to simply not look the same in other images, invalidating the data terms $BC_{s1,s2}$ spatially and/or BC_m temporally. Thus, we would like to deactivate the data term locally, leaving the region to the smoothness term.

(**D2**) Spatial ambiguities or large displacements. Repeating or similar structures have multiple local minima and can be incorrectly matched in the energy minimization. Also, since variational approaches such as ours handle large displacements on coarse image pyramid levels, an object smaller than its motion between t_0 and t_1 might be oversmoothed in the pyramid during downsampling, effectively vanishing. In these cases, we would like to give the algorithm some correspondence hint.

(**D3**) Occluded regions. Between two images I^k_t, occluded pixels have no proper target in $BC_{m,s1,s2}$, violating the color constancy assumption. Other images might still contain the same region, so in this case we would like a highly selective version of data term deactivation. Additionally, should no image contain the occluded region, smoothness will now fill the region from all sides, which is usually not the desired effect, so we would like to be able to influence the smoothness propagation direction.

(**D4**) Low-textured regions. A uniform case of ambiguous matching, low texture is ideally resolved by the smoothness terms $S_{m,s}$, since the data term has equal penalties everywhere. However, noise has a comparatively large influence in $BC_{m,s1,s2}$. Thus, we would like to either provide some hint regarding matching regions, or promote uniform z and $\mathbf{v}$ for that region.

(**S1**) Discontinuities. The smoothness terms $S_{m,s}$ do not actively detect object boundaries, and uniformely demand e.g. $|\nabla u|$ in Eq. 5 to be low. Robust approaches like ours avoid over-penalization of discontinuities when compared to quadratic terms but still require smoothness everywhere. Furthermore, Vogel at al. [16] argue that w motion around discontinuities can often be "simulated" by u and v motion to avoid a smoothness penalty, circumventing correct discontinuity formation. Heuristics like anisotropic regularization [20] explicitly encourage the formation of discontinuities along image gradients, but cannot differentiate between true object boundaries and texture gradients (e.g. striped shirt). Thus, we would like to specify "true" discontinuities manually, either as sharp boundary or as broad brush indicating boundary candidates.

(**S2**) Inappropriate smoothness weight. Weighting the smoothness term vs. the data term is usually done globally, here with α and μ. Depending on the image content, applying different weights to different regions may be more appropriate. Setting one global weight too high results in oversmoothing, preventing deformations and glueing objects together. Setting the weight too low results in non-smooth objects distorted by ambiguities in the data term. Therefore, we would like to control the smoothness weights α and μ per image region.

3. APPROACH

We distill the above analysis into four interactive editing tools that can be used in conjunction with each other: An edge tool (**ET**) in Sec. 3.1, an occlusion tool (**OT**) in Sec. 3.2, a smoothness

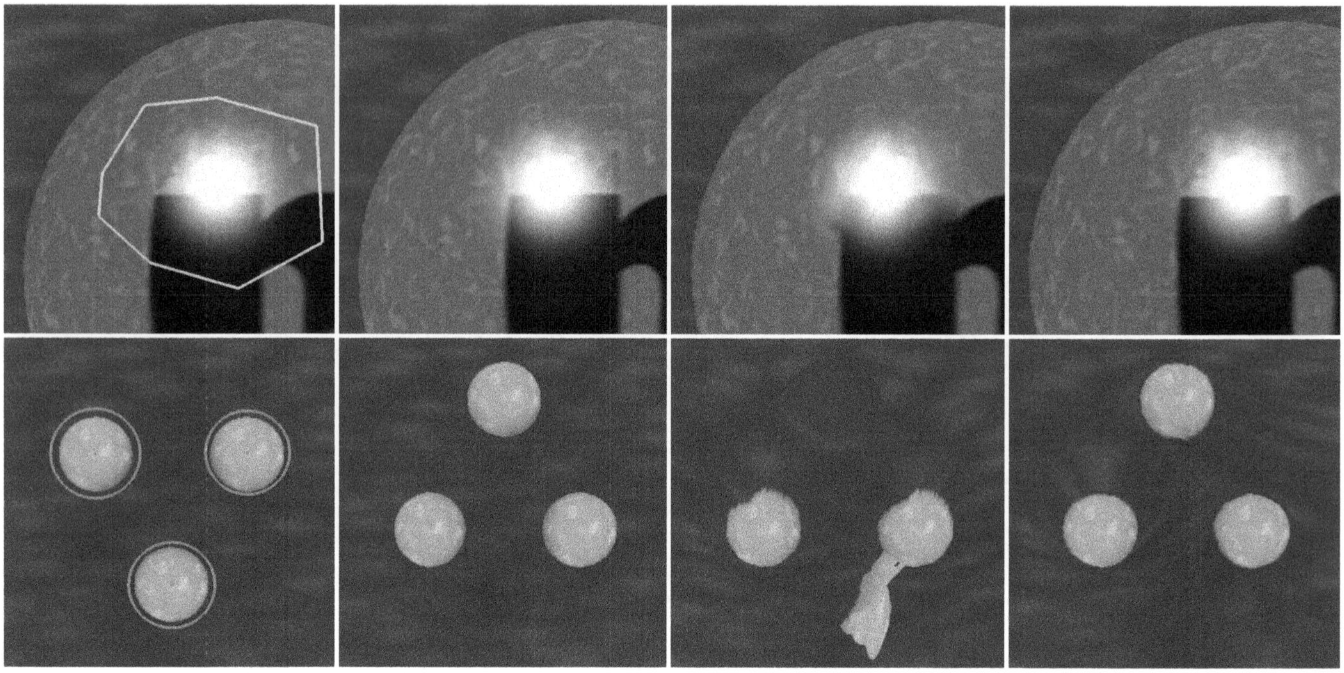

(a) user interaction at t_0 (b) reference image at t_1 (c) without user interaction (d) with user interaction

Figure 4: Avoiding artifacts in warped images. Row 1: Correcting a brightness constancy violation (D1). The specular region is marked as "occluded", deactivating the data term (a). Warped images should look like the reference (b). Automated scene flow produces distorted results around the specularity (c). User interaction preserves the sphere's shape (d). Row 2: Correcting ambiguous matching (D2). Circular matches provide a local initialization (a). Compared to the reference (b), automated scene flow cannot determine which ball belongs to which (c). The user's local initialization is enough to converge to the correct result (d).

tool (**ST**) in Sec. 3.3, and a match tool (**MT**) in Sec. 3.4. We ported the scene flow by Basha et al. [1] to the GPU, yielding a speedup factor of 3–5 and enabling interactive feedback to the user. Our video[1] shows all presented tools in action.

To integrate the tools into the scene flow estimation, we need to consider the optimization algorithm, detailed in Sec. 2.3 of [1]. It couples the multi-resolution levels with two nested fixed-point iterations, where outer iterations update z and $\mathbf{v}$ and re-warp the images accordingly, while inner iterations compute small increments dz and $\mathbf{dv} = (du, dv, dw)$. At each inner fixed-point iteration, the Euler-Lagrange equations for the variables z, u, v and w are solved by posing an $A\mathbf{x} = \mathbf{b}$ problem, Fig. 2 (c). A is sparse and has 4 times the number of pixels rows and columns, with elements close to the diagonal referencing the other variables (e.g. v references u, w and z at the same pixel) and receiving support information from the 4-neighborhood.

3.1 Edge Tool (ET)

Human scene understanding can easily distinguish true discontinuities from in-object gradients (e.g. recognizing a striped shirt as such), so we allow the user to draw a polygon using the mouse to form an undirected edge scribble on object discontinuities in the hero camera image I_0^0, Fig 5– 7. Pixel neighborhood across such a scribble will be ignored in the smoothness term, addressing problems (**S1**) and (**D3**). This unfortunately requires precise user input. Ideally, a broad stroke could be used to define a region in which anisotropic filtering would find the exact edge location, however in practice failure cases occur mostly around less visible discontinuities (note that e.g. in [4], Fig. 2 (b) vs. (h), the discontinuity brush on the desk edge is rather ineffective). Therefore, we keep using exact scribbles.

For integration into the scene flow, we cannot modify the energy functional directly since α is applied omnidirectionally, while we desire a discontinuity perpendicular to the user defined edge. Instead, consider the realization of S_m, Eq. 5, into the neighborhood coefficients $v_{\leftarrow}$, $v_{\rightarrow}$, $v_{\uparrow}$ and $v_{\downarrow}$ in Fig. 2 (c). For a pixel $\mathbf{p} = [x,y]^T$, e.g. $v_{\leftarrow}$ is defined as (derived from Eq. 35 in Appendix C of [1]):

$$v_{\leftarrow} = -\alpha \cdot \mu_v \cdot \frac{1}{2}(\mathrm{div}^{uvw}(x,y) + \mathrm{div}^{uvw}(x-1,y)) \tag{7}$$

with div^{uvw} the divergence coefficients for u, v and w derived from S_m (div^z is used analoguously for realizing S_s, Eq. 6, into $z_{\leftarrow}$). In order to deactivate the neighborhood relation, we test whether a segment of the edge scribble intersects the line between the center points of the current pixel and the left neighbor pixel, and if so, set $v_{\leftarrow}$ to zero. The user can also enter a small numerical weight using the keyboard to produce a less sharply pronounced discontinuity.

3.2 Occlusion Tool (OT)

Within a mouse-clicked closed polygon on the source image I_0^0, the user can deactivate the data term w.r.t. a number of images I_t^k by selecting those images using the mouse or keyboard, Fig 4–7, making this tool useful both for true occlusions as well as for color constancy violations, addressing (**D1**) and (**D3**). As long as other cameras can see the region, the scribble can be defined very approximately. For a complete data term deactivation, the region can also be approximately defined but expected smoothness propagation must be considered; in practice, an additional edge can be used to stop unwanted propagation directions.

Regarding integration into the scene flow, consider the realiza-

[1]Video and further paper details available under: http://graphics.tu-bs.de/publications/ruhl2015acmmm/

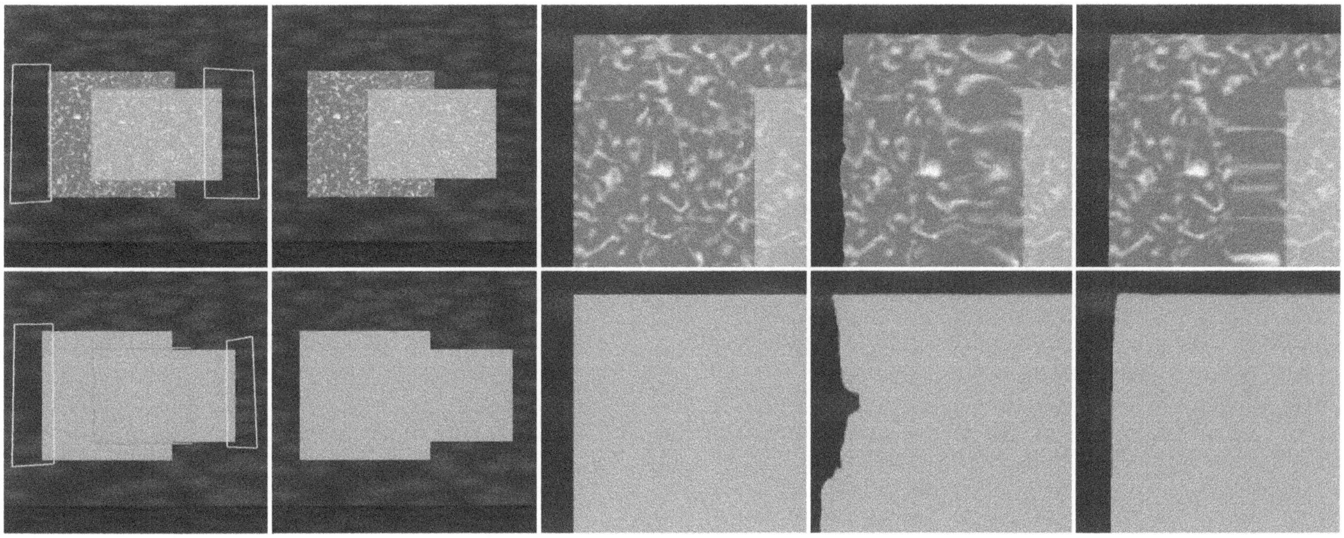

(a) user interaction at t_0 (b) reference image at t_1 (c) zoomed at t_1 (d) without user interaction (e) with user interaction

Figure 5: Warped images. Row 1: Correcting occluded regions to the left and right, and a disoccluded region in the middle (D3), all under good texturing conditions. Occluded regions are marked as such, and an edge allows the formation of a discontinuity (a). Warped images should look like the reference at t_1 (b, c). Automated scene flow produces uneven results around the discontinuity (d), whereas the corrected version pulls the flow field apart very evenly (e). Row 2: Correcting low-textured regions (D4). Same input as above, but the edge can be placed almost arbitrarily (a). Compared to the reference (b, c) and to above, automated scene flow suffers from uneven smoothness propagation (d). The edge scribble allows for a uniform smoothness propagation towards the left (e).

tion of BC_m and BC_{s2}, Eq. 2,4, into the diagonal coefficient a_v in Fig. 2 (c). For a pixel $\mathbf{p}$, a_v is defined as (derived from Eq. 35 in Appendix C of [1]):

$$a_v = \alpha \cdot \mu_v \sum_{\mathbf{q} \in N(\mathbf{p})} \frac{1}{2}(\mathrm{div}^{uvw}(\mathbf{p}) + \mathrm{div}^{uvw}(\mathbf{q})) \tag{8}$$
$$+ \sum_{k=0}^{K-1} o_m^k \psi_m^k(.) \cdot (\mathrm{Iw}_{t[v]}^k)^2 + \sum_{k=1}^{K-1} o_{s2}^k \psi_{s2}^k(.) \cdot (\mathrm{Iw}_{t[v]}^k - \mathrm{Iw}_{t[v]}^0)^2$$

with N the 4-neighborhood; ψ_m and ψ_{s2} derived from $BC_{m,s2}$; $\mathrm{Iw}_{t[v]}^k$ the relevant images (c.f. Fig. 2 (b)) warped with the current $z/\mathbf{v}$ solution and differentiated w.r.t. v; and $\mathbf{p}$ only noted where necessary to improve readability.

The occlusion variables o_m and o_{s2} are from Eq. 2 – 4 (o_{s1} is used for calculating a_z). We locally replace o_{s1} for spatial occlusions and o_m and o_{s2} for temporal occlusions, or all for total data term deactivations, e.g. for a moving specular region. When set to zero, the data terms $BC_{m,s1,s2}$ are effectively omitted and do not factor into a_v at all, leaving the smoothness $S_{m,s}$ as the only influence.

3.3 Smoothness Tool (ST)

Within a mouse-clicked closed polygon on the source image I_0^0, the user can assign stronger or weaker smoothness weights α and μ using the keyboard, Fig 7 row 2, addressing (**D4**) and (**S2**). Undersmoothing can be easily solved by selecting a region and increasing α and/or μ. Oversmoothing can be solved either by decreasing α/μ or by providing an edge scribble. In practice, a common strategy is to define regions with increased smoothness as slightly too large and then using the edge tool to encourage discontinuity formation.

For integration into the scene flow, consider a_v in Eq. 8 and $v_{\leftarrow}$ in Eq. 7 again. To modify the smoothness, we locally replace α and μ by custom user values defined within the closed smoothness scribble. It is also possible to define α_Z, α_u, α_v and α_w separately (same for μ), but in practice this is rarely needed.

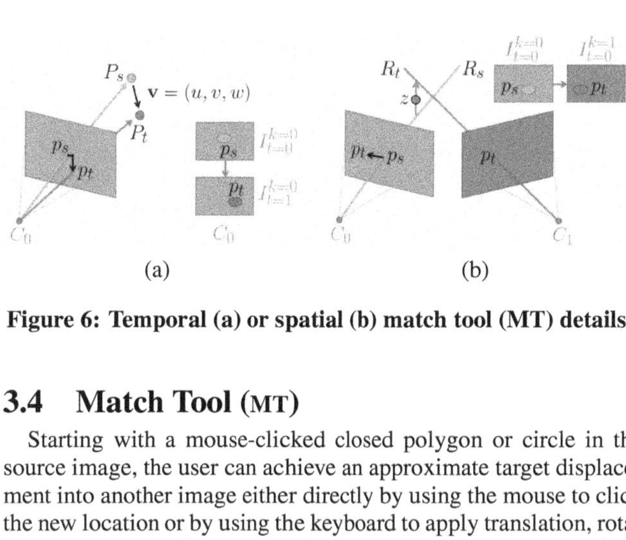

(a) (b)

Figure 6: Temporal (a) or spatial (b) match tool (MT) details.

3.4 Match Tool (MT)

Starting with a mouse-clicked closed polygon or circle in the source image, the user can achieve an approximate target displacement into another image either directly by using the mouse to click the new location or by using the keyboard to apply translation, rotation, and scaling, Fig. 4 row 2, similar to [6] and addressing (**D2**) as well as (**D1**) and (**D4**). For spatial matches at the same time, a guide along the epipolar line is provided to the user. For temporal matches, no guides are possible since movement is not constrained in 3D space. The match does not need to be very precise, since it is used merely as initialization that is further refined by the data term. In practice, matches are often necessary for large displacements, and subsequently incur a strong smoothness penalty S_m, Eq. 5; this can be ameliorated by an additional edge scribble. It is also a good strategy to define matches on a coarse pyramid level L as early as possible to allow the data term to refine the match on finer levels.

For integration into the scene flow, each pixel $\mathbf{p}_s$ inside the source region is first related to a target pixel $\mathbf{p}_t$, Fig. 6, using an affine transform based on the user-defined translation, rotation and scale. In the case of motion, we project both source and target pixel into world space using the current z solution, yielding world space points $\mathbf{P}_s$ and $\mathbf{P}_t$, Fig. 6 (a); the difference between them is the new motion

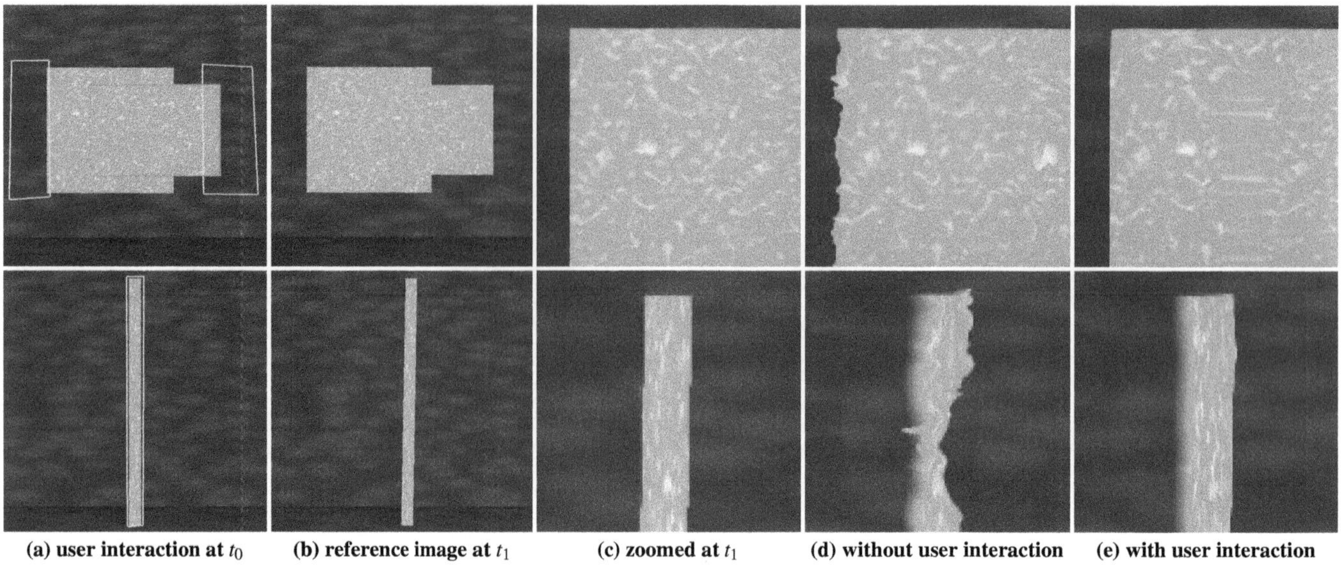

Figure 7: Warped images. Row 1: Correcting an ambiguous discontinuity (S1). As in Fig. 5 row 1, occluded regions are marked, and the edge allows formation of the discontinuity (a). Warped images should look like the reference at t_1 (b, c). Unaided scene flow results in craggedness around the discontinuity (d), while the corrected discontinuity is very even (e). Row 2: Preserving fine structures (S2). The stick receives an increased smoothness weight (a). Compared to the reference (b, c), automated scene flow often smooths the background flow over the stick (d). The corrected version preserves the stick structure (e).

vector $\mathbf{v}$. In the 1D constrained case of depth, we project camera rays $\mathbf{R}_s$ and $\mathbf{R}_t$ into world space, Fig. 6 (b), calculate the shortest line between the rays via closed form solution, and take the z component in the middle of the line.

At each outer fixed-point iteration, we locally set the current z and/or $\mathbf{v}$ solution to the calculated value. During matching, we repeat this up to a level L_d chosen by the user; this leads to a stable and predictable influence on the surrounding region similar to the strategy in [11] (however, we do not use an anisotropic term; note how the user displacements in [11] are only shown for regions with good object/background image gradients). The lower (finer) L_d, the less iterations will be performed to refine the match. Depending on the situation, this allows the user to specify either refined approximate or enforced precise matches.

3.5 Direct Matching

In addition to the intra-optimization tools above, we also allow the user to match regions after the estimation has finished, effectively emulating [6] for scene flows. However this is only needed for rare intractable cases (e.g. two grids moving against each other), requires very precise user input and was not used for our results. It also requires waiting for the final scene flow, whereas we usually run the last refinement levels unattended.

3.6 View Propagation Tools

When scene flows for multiple hero cameras are desired (e.g. to produce the morphed frames in our results), the first solution is to reproject our world space scene flow into the other cameras. However, pixels disoccluded in the target camera will be undefined, necessitating a new scene flow calculuation.

We therefore implemented the propagation of scribbles towards other cameras and time steps according to the estimated scene flow. Smoothness and matching regions are reprojected using z and $\mathbf{v}$ obtained at the centroid of the region. Edges must either partially enclose some region or be defined in pairs that, when connected, form a closed region whose centroid can be taken. Occlusion regions are often on the background, near a discontinuity; they must either be redefined or can be transferred by taking the centroid of a nearby smoothing or matching scribble.

In all cases, we allow further translation/rotation via mouse clicks and numpad keys. For spatially propagated scribbles, usually only a minority must be corrected and even fewer redefined. Temporally propagated scribbles suffer from missing temporal symmetry more often and thus need redefinition more frequently. Compared to manual redefinition of all scribbles, the propagation approach saved considerable time in the creation of our results.

4. RESULTS

Our results are presented in two parts, and shown in motion in our video[2]. Sec. 4.1 shows the hero camera frame at t_0 *warped* towards t_1. This approach is best suited for quality assessment because artifacts in the scene flow are directly identifiable. Sec. 4.2 presents results *morphed* from all cameras at both t_0 and t_1 towards a virtual camera position k_{vrt} and a time t_{vrt}, i.e. all images are warped towards the same virtual spatiotemporal location and then blended. This method produces the visually most pleasing results. We conclude with a quantitative evaluation of the rendered output and a summative user study.

4.1 Warps for Quality Assessment

For a visual assessment of flow field quality, we present the hero camera's t_0 frame warped fully towards t_1. By comparing the warped frame to the reference frame at t_1, flow field artifacts become directly visible. For warping, we use a fully connected mesh with one vertex in the center of each pixel; we also use nearest neighbor interpolation because single pixels can be discerned that way. To clearly demonstrate cause and effect, we present 6 synthetic examples with minimal user interaction, each addressing one of the failure cases identified in Sec. 2. Often, e.g., an additional

[2]Video and further paper details available under: `http://graphics.tu-bs.de/publications/ruhl2015acmmm/`

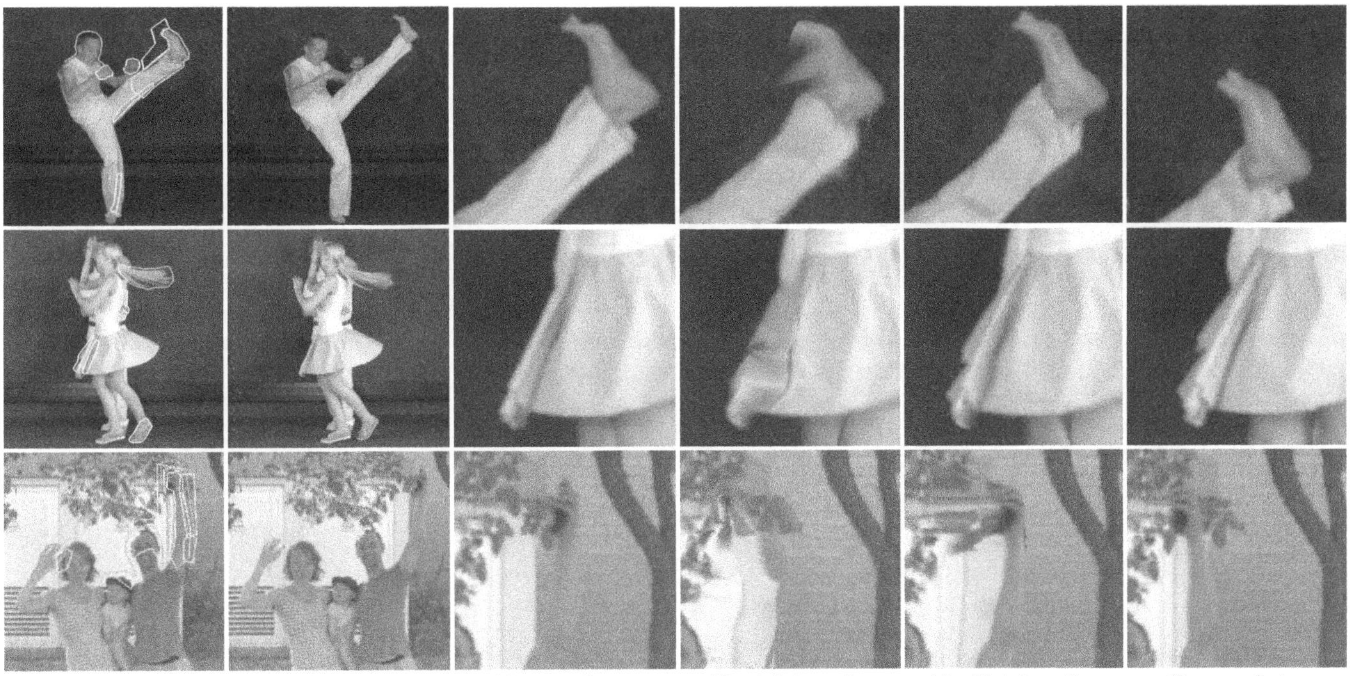

(a) interaction at t_0 (b) reference at t_1 (c) zoomed at t_1 (d) w/o interaction (e) with interaction (f) zoomed at t_0

Figure 8: Warped images. Row 1: Capoeira scene with large displacements, low texture and shadows. The foot is matched, shadows and creases marked as occluded, smoothness increased (a). Compared to the reference at t_1 (b, c), the foot motion leads to streaking artifacts (d). The corrected version forms the foot better (e) given the large displacement from (f). Row 2: Dancing scene with creases in low textured clothing. A large crease is matched, the outer side marked occluded, smoothness increased (a). Compared to the reference (b, c), the skirt is not solved well at all (d). The corrected version resolves the motion plausibly (e), with some of the left border from t_0 (f) remaining. Row 3: Family scene with fine structures under complex background. The arm is matched, smoothed, and marked as occluded where color constancy violations remain (a). Compared to the reference (b, c), the arm is completely destroyed in (d). The corrected version preserves the shape of the arm (e) and stretches the disocclusion stemming from (f) evenly.

edge scribble could improve the result further but would reduce clarity. Additionally, we present 3 real-world examples, where all tools have been applied in combination.

Synthetic Examples. Fig. 4 row 1 shows a rotating textured sphere with a large specularity, addressing (**D1**). The color constancy violation is treated by specifying a full spatiotemporal occlusion (**OT**) that deactivates all brightness constancy terms $BC_{m,s1,s2}$, Eq. 2–4. Since the scene flow model does not separate light transport and object surface, moving the specularity with the object is the geometrically correct choice and the desired effect; alternatively, preserving the specular location would be possible with an edge scribble (**ET**) to separate it from the surrounding motion. The corrected sphere shows intact letters where the automated version shows distorted ones.

Fig. 4 row 2 shows three diffuse balls with the same texture, all moving to new locations, addressing (**D2**). The ambiguous matching problem is mitigated by providing three manual matches (**MT**), which are then refined automatically. Note that as no further edge scribbles have been applied to the example, the background is partly drawn with the balls. The corrected balls move to the correct location where the automated version shows severe misplacement.

Fig. 5 row 1 shows two textured boxes horizontally moving apart from each other, leading to occlusions of the background and a disocclusion of the red box, addressing (**D3**). The occlusion problem is solved by applying the temporal occlusion tool (**OT**) on the background. The scribbles may well encompass part of the foreground, as long as the marked foreground is spatially visible in other cameras. An additional edge scribble (**ET**) around the green box targets the disocclusion problem, and leads to a consistent discontinuity formation at the purple line. Note that had we relied on anisotropic smoothness, it would have lead to wavy edges as in (d) due to irregular brightness coincidences e.g. between box and background. The corrected boxes show straight borders and discontinuities where the automated version shows distorted ones.

Fig. 5 row 2 shows the same two moving boxes from row 1 but this time untextured, addressing (**D4**). While it is impossible to determine the scene flow quality visually in the middle of the image, the same two temporal occlusion scribbles (**OT**) and one edge scribble (**ET**) at some plausible box boundary solve the problem. Our tests confirm that the edge scribble is indeed necessary; without it, irregular smoothness propagation from the top and bottom of the boxes arrives as incoherent horizontal u motion at the left and right rectangle borders. The corrected box preserves the straight border where the automated version produces irregular curvature.

Fig. 7 row 1 is almost identical to Fig. 5 row 1 but this time the two boxes have the same texture and are much more difficult to disambiguate, addressing (**S1**). The same user interaction from Fig. 5 solves the issue here as well, since it allows flow field divergence at the correct location (**ET**) and disallows impossible pixel matches in the regions occluded at t_1 (**OT**). The corrected boxes preserve straight borders and discontinuity where the automated version shows distorted results.

Fig. 7 row 2 shows a thin, slowly moving structure that is prone to being overridden by the surrounding background due to its rela-

(a) without user interaction **(b) with user interaction** **(c) w/o interaction, zoomed** **(d) w/ interaction, zoomed**

Figure 9: Morphed images from 8 views (4 cameras, 2 time steps). Row 1: Capoeira scene. Different artifacts in the views produce a halo streaking effect around the foot (c), while the corrected version features only minor motion blur (d). Row 2: Dancers scene. The blended skirt artifact (c) has vanished in the repaired version (d). Row 3: Family scene. Widely differing failure modes make the blended arm almost invisible (c), while the correct version preserves the arm's shape.

tively small influence in the smoothness term evaluation, addressing (**S2**). The problem is solved by demanding a large smoothness weight for the stick, using a region scribble around the structure (**ST**). Note that an additional edge scribble would reduce the impact of brightness coincidences between stick and background texture further. The corrected stick retains its shape while the automated version deforms its shape considerably.

Real-World Examples. We use all four tools in combination on our real-world footage, which was recorded with 4 RED Scarlet-X at 4K resolution and 15cm interocular baseline, only approximately color-graded, and downsampled to 540p to reduce noise.

Fig. 8 row 1 shows a Capoeira scene with fast motion and low-textured clothing featuring crease deformations and shadows. Consider the high-kicking leg. Foot and lower leg receive increased smoothness (**ST**) and an edge (**ET**) to allow large motions against a static background. The background above the leg is marked as temporally occluded (**OT**). An additional match (**MT**) around the ankle is required to overcome an incorrect local minimum. A clothing crease on the thigh not visible at t_1 is also marked as occluded (**OT**). Further edits include the standing leg with match and smoothing, the dark hair being edge-protected from the equally dark background, and hands being smoothed. The corrected foot shows a consistent shape where the automated version shows severe streaking artifacts.

Fig. 8 row 2 shows a pair-dance scene with actress/actor occlusions under same-colored clothing, a classic failure case for anisotropic smoothness, and deep clothing creases. Consider the left side of the skirt. The shadowed and deforming crease is matched (**MT**) and left and right side marked as occluded (**OT**) for true temporal occlusion and color constancy violation respectively. Further edits include smoothing the flowing hair and edge-protecting it against the background; edges around the female dancer's upper arm; increased smoothness and temporal occlusion at the male dancer's hand; and smoothing and matching around the foot and ankle. The corrected skirt shows a plausible shape where the automated version shows unrealistic folding.

Fig. 8 row 3 shows a complex outdoor family scene with sharp depth discontinuities as well as fine structures with large motions, which are usually lost in the downsampling of the image pyramid. Consider the rightmost arm, its color similarity to the right

Dataset	auto	user	RRE	Fig. 8
Capoeira (foot)	0.937	0.944	+12%	row 1 (c)–(e)
Dancers (skirt)	0.919	0.940	+26%	row 2 (c)–(e)
Family (right arm)	0.879	0.880	+1%	row 3 (c)–(e)

Table 1: Structural similarity index [19] between the reference frame at t_1 and the images warped to t_1 either without (auto) or with (user) correction. While both scores are already very good, user interaction yields a further reduction of the remaining error (RRE) of up to 26%.

background, and the hand's large displacement relative to its size. The arm is matched (**MT**), smoothness increased (**ST**), and edge-protected (**ET**). Due to the texture similarity of arm and background, data term refinement after matching can still produce artifacts, which are suppressed with the occlusion tool (**OT**). Note that the smearing artifacts in the disoccluded region on the left side of the arm are caused by the fully connected mesh used in our warping approach. Further edits include smoothness and edge-protection around the heads; and match, small edge and data term deactivation via occlusion to repair the leftmost hand. The corrected arm preserves its shape where the uncorrected version tears the arm apart.

In all examples, editing times are on the order of minutes; applying the scribbles is a matter of seconds, and observing the effect forming in the ongoing optimization takes tens of seconds over several re-warp iterations. While we already run a GPU scene flow to achieve interactive feedback, an even faster scene flow algorithm or faster GPUs would reduce total editing time further.

4.2 Morphs for Rendering

In the following, we present how our tools can be used to improve image-based rendering quality, morphing 8 views (4 cameras at 2 time steps) based on Lumigraph rendering [2]. The virtual camera is defined by a virtual camera position $k_{\text{vrt}} = 0..3$ and virtual time $t_{\text{vrt}} = 0..1$. Frames are blended with linear temporal weighting and spatial weighting depending on the viewing angle per pixel (details in [2]). The best virtual spatiotemporal position to observe artifacts is in the middle between two cameras and times, i.e., $t_{\text{vrt}} = 0.5$ and $k_{\text{vrt}} = 0.5$, 1.5 or 2.5 respectively, where input from the 4 adjacent views are maximally warped before being blended. Below, we show results at $t_{\text{vrt}} = 0.5$ and $k_{\text{vrt}} = 0.5$.

Fig. 9 row 1 shows the improved visual quality of morphs with user interaction compared to morphs without user interaction, mirroring the improvements of warped results, c.f. Fig. 8. On the Capoeirista's high foot, the 4 involved views all have differing artifacts, each of which are 25% visible as a halo artifact when blended. The corrected version is spatiotemporally consistent and therefore able to provide high-quality blending.

Fig. 9 row 2 again shows that user interaction, here on the skirt, solves the shortcomings of automated estimation. The left side of the Dancer's skirt blends 4 different artifacts in the unaided case, which are replaced with a consistent appearance in the corrected version.

Fig. 9 row 3 shows the most extreme example. Due to widely differing arm motions in the 4 automated estimates, the arm effectively vanishes during blending. In contrast, the corrected version leaves the arm entirely intact. Note that the smearing artifacts in the disoccluded region left of the arm are rendering artifacts due to warping with a fully connected mesh. In future work, a more sophisticated rendering removing these regions in the relevant views will improve morphing results.

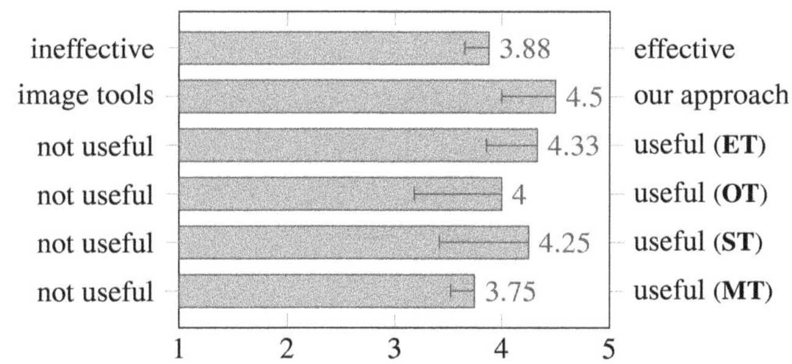

Figure 10: User study with scores 1..5; mean values and standard deviation are shown. Sample size was 4 experts with both image editing and stereo and/or optical flow experience. Questions were general usefulness, relative usefulness of our tool compared to image-based tools, and usefulness per tool.

4.3 Quantitative Evaluation

In addition to the visual quality, we assess the numerical quality of our corrected scene flows compared to uncorrected ones based on the structural similarity index method (SSIM) [19], comparing fully-warped images to the reference image at t_1, Table 1. We report scores calculated on the partial images shown in Fig. 8 (c)–(e).

User interaction for the Capoeira and Dancers scenes removes 12–26% of the remaining error. In contrast, the Family scene shows only a 1% reduction, though the right-arm artifact is the visually most obvious and disturbing of all examples. The close scoring is probably caused by the color similarity of arm and background.

4.4 Summative Evaluation

Since there are no multimedia authoring tools using interactive scene flow estimation, we evaluate the relative attractiveness of our approach against the industry standard, fixing rendered frames with image-space tools. Our tools are meant for trained visual artists and not for the general public. As such, we undertook a summative evaluation with 4 experts in the age range 25–35 with at least 5 years of image processing experience as well as exposure to stereo and/or optical flow. They were coached in the use of our tools for up to 20 minutes each, on training footage not used for subsequent evaluation, the latter of which used the Capoeira scene, Fig. 8–9 row 1. Assuming a moderate number of 10 frames rendered from an automatically estimated scene flow at $t_{0.0}$, $t_{0.1}$, $t_{0.2}$, .., $t_{1.0}$, we asked our experts to repair the scene flow for subsequent re-rendering. For the alternative workflow, we asked them to repair the 10 originally rendered frames instead, using an image-space tool of their choice (all chose Adobe Photoshop). At 10 minutes into either task, the experts were instructed to finish their last operation. Afterwards, the results of both workflows were compared and the experts were asked to rate both with 1 (not useful) to 5 (very useful) on the MOS (mean opinion score) scale.

As shown in Fig. 10, the general usefulness of our approach for the given task was confirmed with a mean score of 3.88. All experts expressed the wish for real-time scene flow recomputation after each scribble, which is not yet possible with state-of-the-art algorithms. Single wishes included using scribbles on target frames instead of the source frame, and instant comparison against the effect of previous scribbles. Compared to image-space tools, the relative attractiveness of our method increased to a mean score of 4.50, with all experts seeing the built-in spatiotemporal consistency between frames as a key advantage of our method.

The experts found all four tools similarly useful with mean scores ranging from 3.75–4.33; all noted that 20 minutes of coaching were sufficient to use the tools effectively. Given the fact that they are used to Photoshop, all experts noted that an increasing familiarity with our tools would probably allow even better results.

5. DISCUSSION

All experts agreed on the effectiveness of our approach as demonstrated by the improved visual quality of the output frames. The most desired improvement were instant response times, which requires realtime scene flow algorithms. With respect to the latter, our scene flow optimization could potentially benefit from a primal-dual approach in the style of [22], left for future work.

Our scene flow estimation algorithm is a GPU-based re-implementation of [1]. By integrating user guidance, we expect similar gains for other scene flow approaches since the failure modes are based on commmon assumptions and scene properties rather than algorithmic intricacies.

When used for visual media production, our approach does not preclude the use of image-based tools; it optionally preceeds it, reducing but in some cases not fully mitigating image-space work.

Our content production approach has two time savers: First the approximate way most scribbles can be defined (edges between two salient regions being the sole exception), and second the arbitrary number of frames that can be rendered using a single scene flow field. Additionally, when going from traditional multimedia production towards free spacetime navigation, "post-production frame correction" is not possible because the number of frames is arbitrary. In this case, editing depth and motion itself is the only viable way to produce artifact-free output frames.

6. CONCLUSIONS

In this paper we presented a workflow for high-quality view interpolation with interactive scene flow estimation, useful for spatiotemporal multimedia content authoring. We analyzed common artifacts during scene flow estimation and presented four interactive tools to overcome these. By refining the coarse user input to subpixel precision using a variational formulation, we ease the user of the burden of precise and time-consuming interaction. This vastly decreases the required effort compared to the common technique of repairing each rendered output frame by hand. Output rendered with our corrected scene flow appears plausible to a human observer, making our approach suitable for applications such as virtual spacetime navigation or high-quality image-based rendering.

7. ACKNOWLEDGMENTS

The research leading to these results has received funding from the European Union's Seventh Framework Programme FP7/2007-2013 under grant agreement no. 256941, Reality CG. We would also like to thank Basha et al. [1] for making the multi-view scene flow C++ source code and part of their data sets openly available.

8. REFERENCES

[1] T. Basha, Y. Moses, and N. Kiryati. Multi-view scene flow estimation: A view centered variational approach. *International journal of computer vision*, 101(1):6–21, 2013.

[2] C. Buehler, M. Bosse, L. McMillan, S. Gortler, and M. Cohen. Unstructured lumigraph rendering. In *Proc. of 28th SIGGRAPH*, pages 425–432. ACM, 2001.

[3] G. Chaurasia, O. Sorkine, and G. Drettakis. Silhouette-aware warping for image-based rendering. In *22nd Eurographics conference on Rendering*, pages 1223–1232, 2011.

[4] Y. Doron, N. D. Campbell, J. Starck, and J. Kautz. User directed multi-view-stereo. In *2nd Workshop on User-Centred Computer Vision (at ACCV)*, 2014.

[5] M. Guttmann, L. Wolf, and D. Cohen-Or. Semi-automatic stereo extraction from video footage. In *Intl. Conference on Computer Vision (ICCV)*, pages 136–142, 2009.

[6] F. Klose, K. Ruhl, C. Lipski, and M. Magnor. Flowlab - an interactive tool for editing dense image correspondences. In *European Conf. on Visual Media Production (CVMP)*, 2011.

[7] C. Linz, C. Lipski, L. Rogge, C. Theobalt, and M. Magnor. Space-time visual effects as a post-production process. In *ACM Multimedia 2010 - 1st Intl. 3DVP Workshop*, 2010.

[8] P. Mordohai. On the evaluation of scene flow estimation. In *Computer Vision – ECCV 2012. Workshops and Demonstrations*, pages 148–157. Springer, 2012.

[9] D. Ring and A. Kokaram. User-assisted feature correspondence matching. In *Proc. European Conference on Visual Media Production*, pages 214–219, 2009.

[10] K. Ruhl, M. Eisemann, and M. Magnor. Cost volume-based interactive depth editing in stereo post-processing. In *Euro. Conference on Visual Media Production (CVMP)*, 2013.

[11] K. Ruhl, B. Hell, F. Klose, C. Lipski, S. Petersen, and M. Magnor. Improving dense image correspondence estimation with interactive user guidance. In *Proc. ACM Multimedia 2012*, pages 1129–1132. ACM, Oct. 2012.

[12] J. Steurer. Tri-focal rig (practical camera configurations for image and depth acquisition). *SMPTE Conferences*, 2013(10):1–15, 2013.

[13] D. Sun, S. Roth, and M. J. Black. Secrets of optical flow estimation and their principles. In *Computer Vision and Pattern Recognition (CVPR)*, pages 2432–2439. IEEE, 2010.

[14] D. Sykora, D. Sedlacek, S. Jinchao, J. Dingliana, and S. Collins. Adding depth to cartoons using sparse depth (in)equalities. *Computer Graphics Forum*, 29(2), 2010.

[15] S. Vedula, S. Baker, P. Rander, R. Collins, and T. Kanade. Three-dimensional scene flow. In *7th Intl. Conf. Computer Vision (ICCV)*, volume 2, pages 722–729. IEEE, 1999.

[16] C. Vogel, K. Schindler, and S. Roth. Piecewise rigid scene flow. In *International Conference on Computer Vision (ICCV)*, pages 1377–1384. IEEE, 2013.

[17] L. Wang and R. Yang. Global stereo matching leveraged by sparse ground control points. In *Conf. on Computer Vision and Pattern Recognition (CVPR)*, pages 3033–3040, 2011.

[18] O. Wang, M. Lang, M. Frei, A. Hornung, A. Smolic, and M. Gross. Stereobrush: interactive 2d to 3d conversion using discontinuous warps. In *8th Eurographics Symposium on Sketch-Based Interfaces and Modeling*, pages 47–54, 2011.

[19] Z. Wang, A. Bovik, H. Sheikh, and E. Simoncelli. Image quality assessment: from error visibility to structural similarity. *IEEE Trans. Image Processing*, 13(4), 2004.

[20] M. Werlberger, W. Trobin, T. Pock, A. Wedel, D. Cremers, and H. Bischof. Anisotropic Huber-L1 optical flow. In *British Machine Vision Conference (BMVC)*, volume 34, 2009.

[21] L. Wilkes. The role of Ocula in stereo post production. *The Foundry, Whitepaper*, 2009.

[22] C. Zach, T. Pock, and H. Bischof. A duality based approach for realtime TV-L1 optical flow. In *Pattern recognition: 29th DAGM symposium*, volume 29, pages 214–223, 2007.

[23] C. Zhang, B. Price, S. Cohen, and R. Yang. High-quality stereo video matching via user interaction and space-time propagation. In *Intl. Conf. 3DV*, pages 71–78. IEEE, 2013.

Real-Time Assistance in Multimedia Capture Using Social Media

Yogesh Singh Rawat
School of Computing
National University of Singapore
Singapore, 117417
yogesh@comp.nus.edu.sg

ABSTRACT

In the last decade, we have seen significant improvement in the ease and cost of capturing multimedia content. However, the aesthetic quality of the content captured by an amateur user still needs substantial improvement. This doctoral research aims at providing real-time assistance to amateur users so that they can capture high quality photographs and home videos. Our approach is focused on learning the art of photography and videography from multimedia content shared on social media. We have proposed a context-based photography learning method which can assist a user in capturing high quality photographs. The photography learning is augmented with contextual information such as time, geo-location, environmental conditions and type of image, which have an impact on photography. The proposed method can provide real-time feedback to the user regarding scene composition, camera parameters, camera movement and viewpoint. We have presented some preliminary results and also described the planned future work.

Categories and Subject Descriptors

H.4 [**Information Systems Applications**]: Miscellaneous

General Terms

Photography, Videography, Camera Parameters, Scene Composition, Viewpoint

Keywords

Photography Assistance, Recommendation, Context, Social Media, Aesthetics, Machine Learning

1. INTRODUCTION AND MOTIVATION

We all love to capture important moments in our life and share them with our dear ones. With the advancement in digital photography, digital cameras have become more affordable and people have started taking more photos and

MM'15, October 26-30, 2015, Brisbane, Australia
ACM 978-1-4503-3459-4/15/10
http://dx.doi.org/10.1145/2733373.2807992

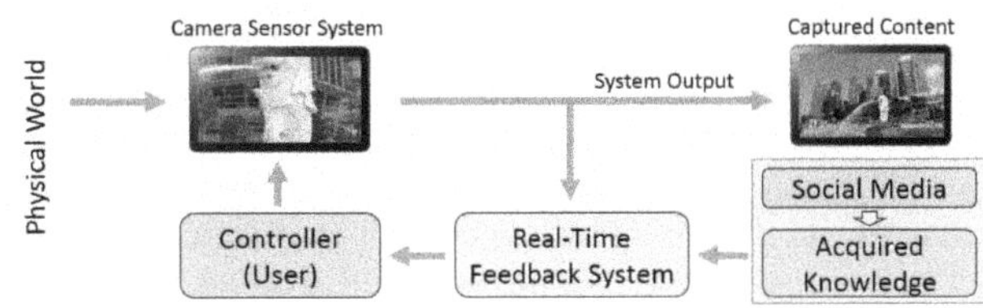

Figure 1: Overview of our approach

videos to capture their experiences. Development in wireless technology allow us to share our experience on the move. Thus, technology has make it easier for us to capture and share our experiences with family and friends. However, devices with advance features cannot always guarantee high quality media capture. Professional users utilize their training and experience and exploit various other parameters based on the context to capture high quality multimedia content. Although, digital cameras have advanced facilities like auto-focus, face detection, etc, for assisting users in capturing better photos and videos, these are not sufficient considering the complex nature of photography and videography. Therefore, it remains a challenge for amateur users to capture high quality multimedia content. We have many post processing tools which can be used for improving the quality of already captured multimedia content. However, these are not an option for mobile users who love to capture and share on the go as it delays the real-time sharing. Moreover, post processing tools cannot do much in case of poorly captured content and not all the information lost during capture is recoverable using these tools.

In the last decade, we have seen an increasing trend in people's photo and video capturing and sharing behavior. There are many social media services such as *Flickr, Panoramio, Youtube* and *Photo.net*, with large collection of photographs and videos shared by professional and other users. Moreover, this social media content is augmented with contextual information such as, geo-location, time of capture, tags, etc., and social media cues such as, comments, likes, shares, etc. The growth of social media content and advancement in sensor technology provides us an opportunity to enhance the experience of amateur users in capturing multimedia content. We believe that the social media data along with the associated meta-content can be utilized for learning the art of photography and videography to assist amateur users in capturing high quality multimedia content.

In this doctoral research we aim to exploit the available social media content for providing real-time feedback to a user for capturing high quality photographs and home videos.

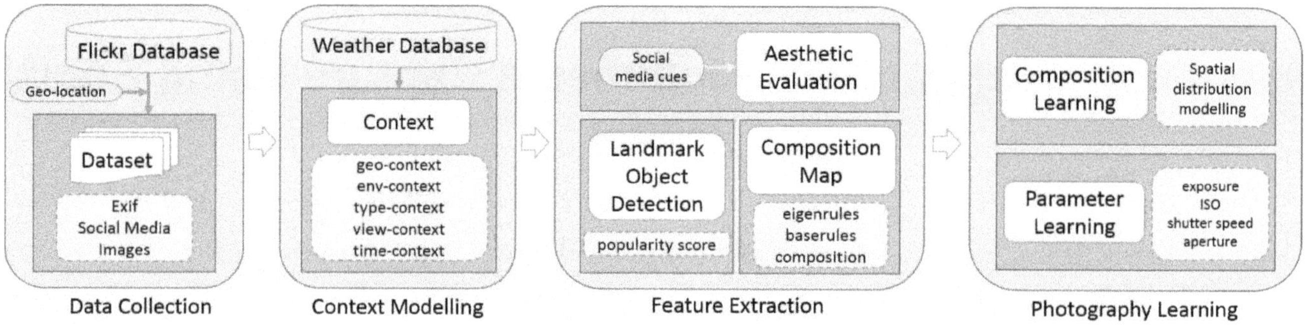

Figure 2: Proposed Framework for Photography Learning [26]

Figure 1 shoes an overview of our approach. The complex nature of photography and videography makes this problem challenging. The main focus of this work will be to investigate the compositional aspect of photographs and videos for providing real-time feedback to the user. Moreover, the role of context in photography makes this problem even more complex [10], therefore, quantization of context will be another point of focus in this research.

The rest of the paper is organized as follows. We begin by discussing the related work in section 2. Section 3 presents an overview of our approach. The preliminary results and corresponding contributions are presented in section 4 along with ongoing research work. Finally, in section 5 we will conclude the paper with a summary.

2. STATE OF THE ART

In recent years, researchers have shown some interest in the field of photography assistance. This is closely related to the research in aesthetic evaluation of multimedia content. However, the role of user context and real-time feedback to the user differentiate this area from existing work in aesthetic evaluation of photographs [7] and videos [6].

Professional photographers follow some widely accepted principles such as *rule of thirds, leading lines, repeating patterns, layering, horizon lines, relative scale, etc.* as they compose a scene [10]. Based on this fact the authors of [5, 4, 19, 30, 17] proposed photography assistance based on image composition and make use of some well known photography rules along with some heuristics (clear theme, position of main object, region of interest, etc.) to assist users in capturing photographs. However, these methods are limited to some well known heuristic rules and also lack contextual knowledge which plays a vital role in photography.

In contrast to rule based approaches, the authors of [29, 23, 16, 22] proposed data driven approach and make use of crowd-sourced images to build aesthetic evaluation models which can provide feedback regarding image quality. However, the proposed methods do not make use of any context information. Yin et al. [35] proposed a more comprehensive photography learning model which make use of context information and also make suggestions regarding camera parameters. However, the proposed method does not consider presence of people in images and the composition recommendation is based on one iconic image selected for a given view. In portrait photography, the quality of captured image also depends on the pose and position of the person present in the photograph. Motivated by this, the authors of [11] [18] [33] and [32] proposed photography assistance methods which provide suggestions for the person in the photograph. However, their method considers only a single person and does not provide any feedback regarding scene composition.

The works discussed so far mainly focus on improving the image composition based on the preview on user's camera. The recommendation provided by these proposed methods assumes that the user is already standing at a good viewpoint. Therefore authors have also proposed methods for providing location recommendation using publicly available photographs. These methods are focused on studying the photo taking behavior of people at well known tourist locations and providing point-of-interest recommendation to the user [28, 15, 14, 34]. In [36, 27] and [24] the authors have proposed methods which recommend photo-shooting location based on photo taking behavior extracted from community contributed images. However, the recommendation provided by these methods is not generated at the time of capture and is static irrespective of the context and the view user is trying to capture.

Existing research related to quality of user videos is mainly focused on either post-processing [3], [1], [12] or aesthetics evaluation [21], [6], [31]. Although, there are some works which attempted to provide guidance to the user for capturing high quality videos [9], [2], [8], [20], the proposed methods make use of few known principles of cinematography and are limited to specific scene types. To the best of our knowledge, there is no work so far which aims at assisting a user in real-time to capture high quality home videos from aesthetics perspective via social media.

3. PROPOSED APPROACH

As discussed in the previous section, the methods proposed so far for photography assistance have addressed some of the challenges but there are still many open problems. In this doctoral research we aim to address some of these open problems along with videography assistance. One of the objectives of this research is to understand the art of photography and videography from composition perspective and utilize it further in assisting amateur users to capture high quality photographs and home videos. Since, context plays an important role in photography, we also aim to quantify user context for photography. In our approach, we will utilize social media data for learning the art of photography and videography instead of using known set of rules. This is because knowledge learned from social media data will not be restricted to some known set of rules and also the associated meta-information in social media data can be used to infer the user context, which is important from photography perspective.

We aim at overcoming the limitations of current approaches

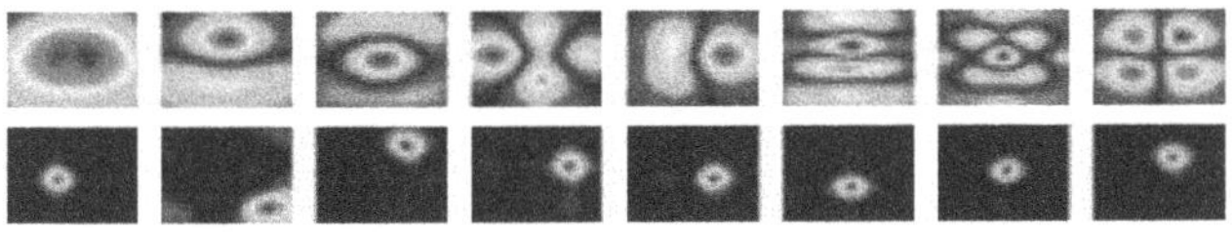

Figure 3: Visualization of *Eigenrules* and *Baserules* [25]

in photography assistance by addressing the following problems:

1. **General yet Context-Aware Approach** - A framework for context aware composition and camera parameter learning which accounts for the presence of multiple human objects in the photograph and is not limited by the number of main objects in the scene.

2. **Camera Movement** - A system which can guide a user to control the camera for pan, tilt and zoom motion to achieve better composition of the scene.

3. **Viewpoint** - Capturing a photograph from a good viewpoint is necessary to take a high quality image, therefore making viewpoint recommendation to the user before capturing a photograph is important from photography perspective.

In our first objective (**OBJ-1**) the goal is to address the above challenges (1 & 2) and develop a framework which can provide assistance to amateur users for capturing high quality photographs at popular tourist locations. Moreover, the system should perform in real-time to ensure instantaneous feedback to the user. In our second objective (**OBJ-2**), we aim to extend this framework and address the problem of viewpoint recommendation. In this objective, we will attempt to bridge the gap between view-based and location-based recommendation. Finally, in our last objective (**OBJ-3**), we will focus on videography assistance from composition perspective. The framework of composition learning for photography will be extended to investigate the role of scene composition in aesthetics of home videos and will further be utilized for user guidance.

4. RESULTS AND CONTRIBUTIONS

In our preliminary work, we focused on **OBJ-1** and **OBJ-2** and proposed a framework for photography model which address the challenges discussed in previous section.

4.1 Context-Aware Photography Learning

Scene composition and camera parameter settings are considered to be the most important factors in the art of photography [13]. Motivated by this, in our first contribution (**OBJ-1**), we have proposed a context-aware photography learning model which provides feedback to the user regarding scene composition and camera parameters [25]. The details of the framework are presented in figure 2. We employ machine learning to build the models for image composition and camera parameters using social media images. The context for photography is quantized using factors such as time, geo-location, environmental conditions and type of image, which have an impact on photography (figure 4). We extended this photography model further to provide camera movement suggestions to the user for improving the scene composition [26].

We evaluated the proposed framework with extensive experiments and user studies. In summary our primary contributions are: 1) We proposed a context based composition

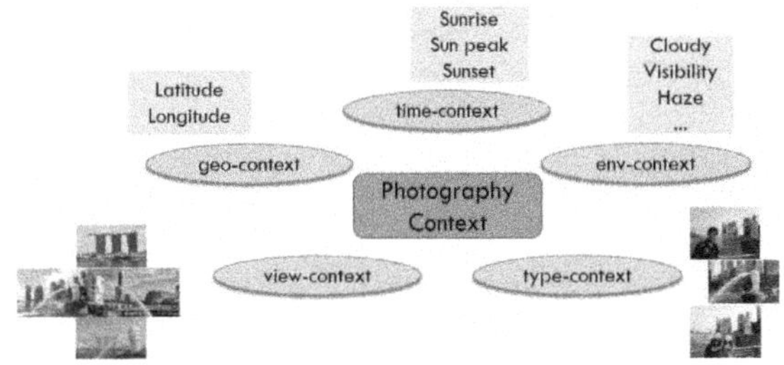

Figure 4: Context for Photography

and camera parameter learning system which accounts for the presence of human objects in the photograph and is not limited by the number of main objects in the scene. 2) We introduced the concepts of *eigenrules* and *baserules* to investigate the role of image composition in aesthetics (figure 3). 3) The proposed system can guide the user to control the camera for pan, tilt and zoom motion to achieve better composition of the scene.

4.2 Viewpoint Recommendation

Considering the importance of viewpoint in photography, we propose *ClickSmart*, a novel viewpoint recommendation system which can assist a user in capturing high quality photographs at well known tourist locations. This work addresses the second objective (**OBJ-2**) of our proposal. *ClickSmart* makes use of publicly available geo-tagged images along with associated meta data for learning a recommendation model. We define *geo-pixels*, macro blocks in geo-space, and propose the idea of *popularity*, *quality* and *uniqueness* of geo-pixels from viewpoint perspective. Viewpoint recommendation is generated at a granularity of *geo-pixel* and is based on its *popularity*, *quality* and *uniqueness*, which are estimated using social media cues associated with images.

ClickSmart can provide real-time viewpoint recommendation based on the preview on user's camera, current time and geo-location. It can provide two kinds of recommendations, quality-based and *uniqueness*-based. Although, both were found effective in experimental evaluation, user study showed that *uniqueness* based recommendation was preferred more by skilled photographers as compared to amateur users. In summary our primary contributions are: 1) We proposed a novel viewpoint recommendation system for photography assistance which make use of publicly available photographs via social media. We proposed the idea of *uniqueness* of geo-pixels which is further utilized in recommending rare but interesting viewpoints for photography. 2) We investigated the impact of context such as time and weather conditions on viewpoint recommendation. 3) The proposed recommendation system also considers the presence of people in photographs.

4.3 Work in Progress

We are currently working on **OBJ-3** where we aim to extend the composition model so that it can be applied for home videos. The earlier proposed *eigenrules* and *baserules* will be investigated further to understand various types of scene categories and an extensive composition model will be proposed. We have categorized this problem into two stages. First we will focus on videos with static camera and later it will be extended to videos with moving camera. Although we have done some extensive experiments and also conducted user studies to evaluate our proposed methods, we are also developing a mobile application which can be utilized for further evaluation of our system.

5. CONCLUSION

In this paper we discussed our approach for real-time assistance in multimedia capture using social media. In our first contribution (**OBJ-1**), we proposed a context-aware photography assistance system which can guide a user in capturing high quality photographs. After that, we focused on our second objective (**OBJ-2**) and proposed a viewpoint recommendation system which can provide real-time assistance to the user based on the preview on user's camera, time and geo-location. We are currently working on our next objective (**OBJ-3**) where we aim to develop a videography assistance system for home videos.

6. ACKNOWLEDGMENT

This research was carried out at the SeSaMe Centre. It is supported by the Singapore NRF under its IRC@SG Funding Initiative and administered by the IDMPO.

7. REFERENCES

[1] R. S. V. Achanta, W.-Q. Yan, and M. S. Kankanhalli. Modeling intent for home video repurposing. In *IEEE MultiMedia*, pages 46–55, 2006.

[2] B. Adams and S. Venkatesh. Situated event bootstrapping and capture guidance for automated home movie authoring. In *ACM MM*, 2005.

[3] B. Adams, S. Venkatesh, and R. Jain. IMCE: integrated media creation environment. *ACM TOMM*, 2005.

[4] S. Banerjee and B. L. Evans. In-camera automation of photographic composition rules. *IEEE TIP*, 2007.

[5] W. Bares. A photographic composition assistant for intelligent virtual 3d camera systems. In *Smart Graphics*. Springer Berlin Heidelberg, 2006.

[6] S. Bhattacharya, B. Nojavanasgheri, T. Chen, D. Liu, S.-F. Chang, and M. Shah. Towards a comprehensive computational model for aesthetic assessment of videos. In *ACM MM*, 2013.

[7] S. Bhattacharya, R. Sukthankar, and M. Shah. A framework for photo-quality assessment and enhancement based on visual aesthetics. In *ACM MM*, 2010.

[8] S. Carter, J. Adcock, J. Doherty, and S. Branham. Nudgecam: Toward targeted, higher quality media capture. In *ACM MM*, pages 615–618, 2010.

[9] M. Davis, J. Heer, and A. Ramirez. Active capture: Automatic direction for automatic movies. In *ACM MM*, pages 88–89, 2003.

[10] M. Freeman. *The Photographer's Eye: Composition and Design for Better Digital Photos*. Focal Press, 2007.

[11] H. Fu, X. Han, and Q. H. Phan. Data-driven suggestions for portrait posing. In *ACM SIGGRAPH Asia*, New York, NY, USA, 2013.

[12] M. L. Gleicher and F. Liu. Re-cinematography: Improving the camerawork of casual video. *ACM TOMM*, Oct. 2008.

[13] S. Kelby. *The digital photography book*. Peachpit Press, [Berkeley, CA], 2006.

[14] I. Lee, G. Cai, and K. Lee. Points-of-interest mining from people's photo-taking behavior. In *HICSS*, 2013.

[15] J. Liu, Z. Huang, L. Chen, H. T. Shen, and Z. Yan. Discovering areas of interest with geo-tagged images and check-ins. In *ACM MM*, 2012.

[16] K.-Y. Lo, K.-H. Liu, and C.-S. Chen. Intelligent photographing interface with on-device aesthetic quality assessment. In *ACCV*. 2012.

[17] C. Lujun, Y. Hongxun, S. Xiaoshuai, and Z. Hongming. Real-time viewfinder composition assessment and recommendation to mobile photographing. In *PCM*. Springer, 2012.

[18] S. Ma, Y. Fan, and C. W. Chen. Pose maker: A pose recommendation system for person in the landscape photographing. In *ACM MM*, 2014.

[19] H. Mitarai, Y. Itamiya, and A. Yoshitaka. Interactive photographic shooting assistance based on composition and saliency. In *ICCSA*. Springer, 2013.

[20] H. Mitarai and A. Yoshitaka. Interactive video cam system for emotive video production. In *IEEE ICME*, pages 1–6, July 2011.

[21] A. K. Moorthy, P. Obrador, and N. Oliver. Towards computational models of the visual aesthetic appeal of consumer videos. In *ECCV*. Springer, 2010.

[22] B. Ni, M. Xu, B. Cheng, M. Wang, S. Yan, and Q. Tian. Learning to photograph: A compositional perspective. *IEEE TMM*, Aug. 2013.

[23] J. Park, J.-Y. Lee, Y.-W. Tai, and I. S. Kweon. Modeling photo composition and its application to photo re-arrangement. In *ICIP*, 2012.

[24] T. Phan, J. Zhou, S. Chang, J. Hu, and J. Lee. Collaborative recommendation of photo-taking geolocations. In *ACM GeoMM*, 2014.

[25] Y. S. Rawat and M. S. Kankanhalli. Context-based photography learning using crowdsourced images and social media. In *ACM MM, Grand Challenge*, 2014.

[26] Y. S. Rawat and M. S. Kankanhalli. Context-aware photography learning for smart mobile devices. *ACM TOMM*, 2015.

[27] M. Shirai, M. Hirota, H. Ishikawa, and S. Yokoyama. A method of area of interest and shooting spot detection using geo-tagged photographs. In *ACM SIGSPATIAL*, 2013.

[28] M. Shirai, M. Hirota, S. Yokoyama, N. Fukuta, and H. Ishikawa. Discovering multiple HotSpots using geo-tagged photographs. In *ACM SIGSPATIAL*, 2012.

[29] H.-H. Su, T.-W. Chen, C.-C. Kao, W. Hsu, and S.-Y. Chien. Preference-aware view recommendation system for scenic photos based on bag-of-aesthetics-preserving features. *IEEE TMM*, (3):833–843, 2012.

[30] P. P. Wang, W. Zhang, J. Li, and Y. Zhang. Online photography assistance by exploring geo-referenced photos on MID / UMPC. In *IEEE MSP*, 2008.

[31] Y. Wang, Q. Dai, R. Feng, and Y.-G. Jiang. Beauty is here: Evaluating aesthetics in videos using multimodal features and free training data. In *ACM MM*, 2013.

[32] Y. Wang et al. Where2stand: A human position recommendation system for souvenir photography. In *ACM TIST*, 2015.

[33] P. Xu et al. Where should i stand? learning based human position recommendation for mobile photographing. In *MTAP*. Springer, 2014.

[34] Y. Yang, Z. Gong, and L. H. U. Identifying points of interest by self-tuning clustering. In *ACM SIGIR*, 2011.

[35] W. Yin, T. Mei, C. W. Chen, and S. Li. Socialized mobile photography: Learning to photograph with social context via mobile devices. *IEEE TMM*, 2014.

[36] Y. Zhang and R. Zimmermann. Camera shooting location recommendations for landmarks in geo-space. In *IEEE MASCOTS*, 2013.

Intuitive Input Methods for Interactive Segmentation on Mobile Touch-Based Devices

Christoph Korinke
OFFIS - Institute for Information Technology
Oldenburg, Germany
korinke@offis.de

ABSTRACT

Existing interactive image segmentation approaches mainly focus on the algorithms rather than the input methods. The literature regarding the input methods is mainly applied to desktop PCs. However, there is a transition to mobile touch-based devices. In this paper we describe our approach to identify a set of intuitive input methods for interactive segmentation on mobile devices. Preliminary results of two user studies are presented. A description of our planned research is given, divided into *initial* and *refinement input methods* and the exploitation of the input for segmentation algorithms.

Categories and Subject Descriptors

H.5.2 [**Information Systems**]: User Interfaces—*evaluation/methodology, interaction styles, user-centred design*; I.4.6 [**Computing Methodologies**]: Segmentation

General Terms

Human Factors, Design

Keywords

Interactive Image Segmentation, Input Methods Evaluation, Mobile touch-based Devices

Figure 1: Example of Challenge: Segmenting an image on a mobile device to gray out the background

1. MOTIVATION

In recent years, the number of owners of mobile phones with an integrated camera increased steadily. Contemporary, a large percentage using the camera is also increasing [14]. Photos taken with mobile phones are not only for personal use but rather, with the advent of social networks, people start to share them to show special moments and interesting things. New applications and networks arose like Snapchat and Instagram as well as messenger applications like WhatsApp. They are heavily used to share photos as depicted in table 1. Instagram, Snapchat and WhatsApp are mobile applications and have a wide distribution. Consequently, photos are used directly on mobile phones and if a photo should be beautified, for example with filters, a direct and fast edit process is necessary. Many of the existing programs provide only filters for the whole photo. But sometimes single objects in a photo should be treated with other filters. Many approaches for selecting a single object in an image exist. A small overview is given in section 2. However, these approaches mainly focus on the algorithms and the input methods are just a means of the algorithms. Therefore cutting things out or editing a single object is still a tedious process which often needs a lot of attention and time by the user to get good results. There is hardly any literature which is regarding the input process for interactive image segmentation. Furthermore the existing approaches focus mainly on desktop PC environments. But input with fingers on mobile devices is not as precise as with a mouse on desktop PCs.

The purpose of my research is to determine suitable input methods for interactive image segmentation processes on touch-based mobile devices and how this methods can be exploited as a-priori knowledge for segmentation algorithms.

2. STATE OF THE ART

Algorithms for interactive image segmentation are studied intensively. This section gives a short selection of different approaches.

Reese and Barrett [10] characterize interactive image segmentation as an iterative adjustment of cues and parameters to incrementally refine a selection until the desired result is reached. Li et al. categorize the approaches in two main methods in [5]: boundary based and region based.

MM'15 October 26-30, 2015, Brisbane, Australia
ACM 978-1-4503-3459-4/15/10.
DOI: http://dx.doi.org/10.1145/2733373.2807993 .

With boundary based methods the users surround an object with a curve. An example of this approach is Intelligent Scissors [8] from Mortensen and Barrett, also called as Magnetic Lasso. The algorithm tries to link seed points, given by a user, with a boundary adjusted line. Direct feedback is given by showing the actual line between the last seed point and the position of the mouse pointer. In texture rich regions many alternative paths exist which is a weakness of this approach. To enhance the results the user often has to zoom in which can lead to a loss of overview. Further, to finish the process the user has to enclose the object entirely. In general, increased user interaction is required with boundary based input methods. Another boundary based approach is Image Snapping [2] which moves the mouse cursor to nearby features, e.g. edges.

Region based methods are based on loose hints of foreground objects and background parts of an image often given by clicking or strokes. An algorithm handles this hints to extract the object boundary. The result can be improved step-by-step with additional hints given by the user. Rother et al. describe a region based method in [11], called GrabCut, using a graphcut algorithm. A first estimation will be given by a bounding box around an object. Everything outside the box is defined as background, everything inside as unknown. The unknown pixels are then classified into fore- and background with the given graphcut algorithm. Wrong classified pixels can be marked with strokes to improve the result in further iterations. [9] gives an overview of graph theoretical approaches.

A combination of both methods, boundary and region based, is used with Lazy Snapping [5] from Yin Li et al. It is divided in two steps. In the first object marking step the object is specified by strokes. In the second boundary editing step, the result can be enhanced by dragging polygon vertices with a boundary based method.

In [6] an algorithm orientated towards mobile phones is described. At first a bounding box must be drawn. This region is then oversegmented with the mean shift algorithm. The user then gives hints with strokes marking the foreground object and background. With neighbourhood information and the given hints, the segmented parts are clustered.

In [1] the user gives spare and incomplete boundary hints. Thereby the user doesn't have to switch between foreground and background input. In the opinion of Bagon, this approach lead to a minimal interaction effort and is suitable for touch-based devices. Another approach to reduce user interaction can be found in [12]. Scheuermann and Rosenhahn show that their approach, based on level-sets and on Dempster-Shafer theory of evidence, need less interaction than two other approaches by exploiting user interaction.

Sener et al. investigate an error-tolerance approach of user input for interactive image segmentation on small touch devices in [13]. The user can only correct false classified foreground by using strokes. False classified background is solved through an algorithm trying to correct erroneous interaction.

The performance of four interactive segmentation algorithms for desktop PCs is evaluated via user experiments by McGuinness and Noel in [7]. The three criteria accuracy, efficiency (amount of time) and repeatability are considered for four algorithms: Seeded Region Growing, Interactive Graph Cuts, Simple Interactive Object Extraction and Interactive Segmentation using Binary Partition Trees. The results show that interactive graph cut and binary partition tree algorithms are the most effective techniques. The most popular is interactive graph cuts. The participants dislike algorithms with difficult refinement methods. On the other hand, algorithms with easy to use iterative improvements are preferred even if they require more time to segment an object.

	Year		
	2012	2013	2014
Instagram	9	51	60
Snapchat	51	394	703
WhatsApp	-	394	703
Flickr	3	2	2
Facebook	300	343	351
Total	363	1184	1819

Table 1: Daily shared photos on social networks worldwide in the years 2012 to 2014 (in millions) [15]

An evaluation of input methods for interactive segmentation algorithms on desktop PCs is presented in [3]. The amount of user interactions, average time taken, number of strokes per segmentation, accuracy, efficiency and repeatability are compared. The three evaluated approaches are all based on a graph cut algorithm and only vary in the input gestures: 1. only strokes, 2. bounding box + strokes, 3. outline / free form of the object contour. The results show that the interaction method affects segmentation accuracy and the most popular method was bounding box + strokes.

Quite few interactive image segmentation approaches exist. Most of them have in common the focus on the algorithms, whereas the way of input is only considered as a means for the algorithms. The few literature regarding the input methods are mainly for Desktop PCs. Through the shift to mobile devices, it is crucial to investigate the existing approaches on their suitability for mobile touch-based devices and if necessary to evaluate new approaches.

3. APPROACH

We aim to show that intuitive usable input methods with good user experience can improve the results of interactive segmentation. Because of the difference of computer systems and the increasing amount of mobile touch-based devices we want to focus on these. The following steps have to be considered:

1. Identification of intuitive input methods for interactive segmentation on mobile devices.
2. Derivation of guidelines for input methods.
3. Identification of features exploitable by segmentation algorithms.

To gain first insights into intuitive input methods, we start to investigate how users segment objects from background from scratch on mobile touch-based devices, i.e. without any instructions. These findings form the basis of the next steps. The initial input methods, i.e. for the first iteration, can differ from the refinement input methods, i.e. further iterations, that is why we plan to treat them separately. Both method types are going to be evaluated in a user-centred design process. Within this process, we plan to investigate the user experience with different forms like the System Usability Scale and also interviews to get qualitative feedback. Beside this user-driven data we plan also to collect quantitative data as e.g. input time and accuracy.

In this design process we want to gain a set of intuitive input methods, which can be used for interactive image segmentation on mobile touch-based devices. Because this set will probably not cover every suitable method, we aim to derive general guidelines based on the study results of these methods.

Finally, we plan to identify features of the set of input methods and guidelines exploitable for segmentation algorithms. As a result not only the input itself but also its features are supposed the improve the overall result of the interactive image segmentation.

4. PRELIMINARY FINDINGS

4.1 Segmentation from Scratch

To get an impression on how users select intuitively a foreground object in an image on mobile touch-based devices, we conducted a pilot-study. We started from scratch and asked 13 participants to use any touch gestures to segment the foreground object in a simple paint application. No segmentation algorithm was applied in this application. This task had to be done on nine different images by the participants, whereas the size of the foreground object and the given time frame to select the object is varied on each of the nine images. This variation was done to identify if the participants use different gestures for different object sizes and time frames. To avoid learning effects, the scenarios where counter-balanced by Latin Square. Beside capturing the input times and gestures, a structured interview has been carried out to identify, which other input methods the participants can imagine than the used ones. The average selection time with no time constraints was 76 seconds. However, the participants remarked they would spend more time on editing private photos to get better results. The gestures used by the participants can be grouped in three groups: *Outline*, *Colouring* and *Other*. In *Outline* the participants traced the contour of the object. With an amount of 76.07% *Outline* is the most used method. The second group with 14.53% is *Other*. This group contains single strokes as well as different forms of bordering the foreground object like circles or rectangles. Despite the low usage of *Colouring* (9,4%), 8 of the 13 participants can imagine to colour out or click the foreground object to select it.

4.2 Field Study

With these findings we conducted an additional study based on a real interactive image segmentation application. In this study the participants segmented ten images with three input methods respectively. The input methods we have chosen are *Outline* and *Colouring* based on the previous study. The third method is *Bounding Box + Scribble* based on the results of [3] as described in section 2. The *Outline* Method is extended with *Scribble* for the refinement steps based on *Bounding Box + Scribble*.

a) Outline + Scribble: Drawing a loose contour around the foreground object. In the next iterations giving strokes to refine the result,

b) Colouring: Colouring out the object,

Figure 2: Input methods of the field study.

c) Bounding Box + Scribble: Drawing a bounding box and refining the result in further iterations with strokes.

Examples of the methods are depicted in figure 2. Subsequent to the practical task, the participants were interviewed and had to rank the methods. As a result, the ratings show that there is no favourite of the three methods. Whereas, *Outline + Scribble* and *Bounding Box + Scribble* are rated nearly the same and *Colouring* is generally rated lower. One problem mentioned by the participants of *Outline + Scribble* is the coverage of the finger which leads to overdrawing the object border. With *Bounding Box + Scribble* the users had difficulties to set the right start point so that the box is near the border, because the box had to be drawn from beginning to correct it. Further, the participants had the feeling *Outline + Scribble* took much effort. On the other hand they mentioned a loss of control with *Bounding Box + Scribble*, because it was not clear for them which parts the algorithm will choose. The refinement with *Scribble* is unsuitable because of the well known fat finger problem. With these findings we could establish first guidelines for interaction methods for image segmentation on mobile devices: **1.** The initial input should be outside the object. **2.** The initial selection may not be too loose as with bounding box and not too accurate as with outlining. **3.** The fat finger problem plays an important role, therefore strokes are not applicable.

5. PLANNED WORK

Initial Input Methods: Based on the first established guidelines we prepare a study to improve the initial input. As the initial input and the refinement input have different requirements, we regard these inputs separated. In the planned study, we are going to evaluate two methods. The first method *Dynamic Outline* pick up the conclusions of *Outline + Scribble* from the previous study. Because the finger covers the input line and the users tend to draw the line too accurately and thereby have the feeling of much effort, a straight line is drawn from the last position to the position of the finger on the touch screen. The user can move the finger in every direction to change the length and position of the line. Thereby, the line is not covered by the finger and the contour can be roughly traced. At any time, the user can add new anchor points to adapt lines and also can move every point in any direction. The second method *Dynamic Bounding Box* is inspired by *Bounding Box + Scribble* from the previous study. The users can draw a rectangle by moving the finger from one corner to the diagonal corner. Then, the edges and corners can be corrected. Afterwards, the shape of the rectangle can be adjusted by moving and adding single anchor points. Consequently, the same shapes can be created with both methods with respect to the three first guidelines described at the end of section 4. In the study, we want to verify the usability and user experience of the methods as well as reveal first indications of exploitable features as a-priori knowledge for segmentation algorithms. An example input result of both methods is depicted in figure 5.

Figure 3: Example result of the suggested input methods for the planned study

Depending on the results, we want to improve the input methods or investigate new approaches to gain a set of intuitive input methods and guidelines for the initial step of interactive image segmentation.

Refinement Input Methods: The previous findings show that the often used *Strokes* are not suitable on touch-based devices because of the *Fat Finger Problem*. Therefore, new approaches have to be investigated. We want to investigate different approaches for *direct* as well as *indirect* input methods. *Direct* input means drawing directly on the image and *indirect* input is done on visualized image features shown not directly on the image. Early approaches for indirect input methods based e.g. on histograms and superpixels are investigated and tested by us.

Exploiting the Input: The approach in [4] from Lempitsky et al. shows that the input can be exploited to improve the segmentation algorithms. We plan to investigate the resulting initial and refinement methods from our research of possible exploits in conjunction with existing segmentation algorithms. For example, in the preliminary findings we identified that users have the tendency to trace the contour of objects. This could be exploited e.g. in form of shape matching or the distance to the object contour.

6. REFERENCES

[1] S. Bagon. Boundary driven interactive segmentation. In *Information Science and Applications (ICISA), 2012 International Conference on*, pages 1–5. IEEE, 2012.

[2] M. Gleicher. Image snapping. In *Proceedings of the 22nd annual conference on Computer graphics and interactive techniques*, pages 183–190. ACM, 1995.

[3] R. Hebbalaguppe, K. McGuinness, J. Kuklyte, G. Healy, N. O'Connor, and A. Smeaton. How interaction methods affect image segmentation: User experience in the task. 2013.

[4] V. Lempitsky, P. Kohli, C. Rother, and T. Sharp. Image segmentation with a bounding box prior. In *Computer Vision, 2009 IEEE 12th International Conference on*, pages 277–284. IEEE, 2009.

[5] Y. Li, J. Sun, C.-K. Tang, and H.-Y. Shum. Lazy snapping. In *ACM SIGGRAPH 2004 Papers*, SIGGRAPH '04, pages 303–308, New York, NY, USA, 2004. ACM.

[6] D. Liu, K. Pulli, L. G. Shapiro, and Y. Xiong. Fast interactive image segmentation by discriminative clustering. In *Proceedings of the 2010 ACM multimedia workshop on Mobile cloud media computing*, pages 47–52. ACM, 2010.

[7] K. McGuinness and N. E. O'Connor. A comparative evaluation of interactive segmentation algorithms. *Pattern Recognition*, 43(2):434–444, 2010.

[8] E. N. Mortensen and W. A. Barrett. Intelligent scissors for image composition. In *Proceedings of the 22nd annual conference on Computer graphics and interactive techniques*, SIGGRAPH '95, pages 191–198, New York, NY, USA, 1995. ACM.

[9] B. Peng, L. Zhang, and D. Zhang. A survey of graph theoretical approaches to image segmentation. *Pattern Recognition*, 2012.

[10] L. Reese and W. Barrett. Image editing with intelligent paint. In *Proceedings of Eurographics*, volume 21, pages 714–724, 2002.

[11] C. Rother, V. Kolmogorov, and A. Blake. Grabcut: interactive foreground extraction using iterated graph cuts. In *ACM SIGGRAPH 2004 Papers*, SIGGRAPH '04, pages 309–314, New York, NY, USA, 2004. ACM.

[12] B. Scheuermann and B. Rosenhahn. Interactive image segmentation using level sets and dempster-shafer theory of evidence. In *Image Analysis*, pages 656–665. Springer, 2011.

[13] O. Sener, K. Ugur, and A. A. Alatan. Error-tolerant interactive image segmentation using dynamic and iterated graph-cuts. In *Proceedings of the 2nd ACM international workshop on Interactive multimedia on mobile and portable devices*, pages 9–16. ACM, 2012.

[14] A. V. und Medienanalyse. Verbrauchs- und medienanalyse - vuma 2015. Statista, 2014. http://de.statista.com/statistik/daten/studie/290051/umfrage/umfrage-in-deutschland-zur-nutzung-der-foto-video-funktion-von-handys/, Accessed Mai 8th 2015.

[15] WirtschaftsWoche. Internet trends 2014. Statista, 2014. http://de.statista.com/statistik/daten/studie/312208/umfrage/taegliche-foto-uploads-ueber-ausgewaehlte-soziale-netzwerke-und-apps/, Accessed Mai 8th 2015.

Exploiting Contextual Information to Enable Efficient Content Delivery for 3D Tele-Immersion Applications

Shannon Chen
University of Illinois at Urbana-Champaign
cchen116@illinois.edu
Advised by Klara Nahrstedt

ABSTRACT

The tradeoff relationship between resource requirement, content complexity, and user satisfaction is magnified when more and more modern 3D Tele-immersive (3DTI) applications with higher quality demands and/or scalability requirements come into the picture. These demanding applications introduce challenges in different phases throughout the delivery chain of 3DTI systems. To tackle them, we propose to exploit contextual information of 3DTI systems, such as contextual information on resource, content, and satisfaction aspects. Understanding contextual information will improve the utilization of different computing environments to fulfill the objectives of targeted application.

Categories and Subject Descriptors

H.4.3 [**Information Systems**]: Information Systems Applications – *Communication Applications*

Keywords

3D Tele-immersion, Contextual information.

1. INTRODUCTION

3D Tele-immersion (3DTI) technology allows full-body, multimodal interaction among geographically dispersed users, which opens a variety of possibilities in cyber collaboration. Users of 3DTI systems are captured by 3D camera array surrounding their user spaces along with other application-specific sensors. The captured 3D models with 360° coverage of users' bodies are put into a shared virtual space where activities such as art performance, exergaming, and physical rehabilitation happen.

However, with its great potential, the resource and quality demands of 3DTI rise inevitably, especially when some advanced applications target resource-limited computing environments (e.g., mobile or home environments) with stringent scalability requirements (e.g., multi-site interaction or large-scale broadcasting). Under these circumstances, the tradeoffs between (1) resource requirements, (2) content complexity, and (3) user satisfaction in delivery of 3DTI are magnified. Intuitively, when resource budget is low and content complexity is high, user's perceptual quality will be sacrificed. For example, watching live broadcasting 3DTI sport events on limited bandwidth budget incurs bad viewing experience. On the other hand, when the computing resource is scarce and the service quality is demanded, the system can only support low complexity activities as its content. For example, a 3DTI client running on a smart phone over 3G network will not support telehealth applications.

MM'15, October 26-30, 2015, Brisbane, Australia
ACM 978-1-4503-3459-4/15/10.
http://dx.doi.org/10.1145/2733373.2807994

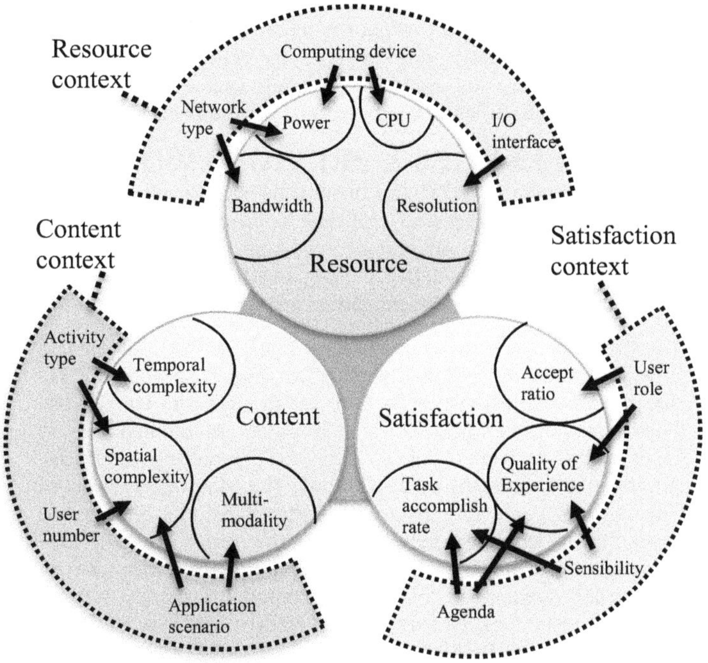

Figure 1. Contextual information.

In this proposal, we argue that these tradeoffs of 3DTI applications are actually avoidable when the underlying delivery chain takes contextual information into consideration. We propose the concept of *contextual information* in 3DTI, which spans across the three factors: resource, content, and satisfaction in 3DTI systems. With contextual information, we expect 3DTI systems to be able to (1) identify the characteristics of its computing environment to allocate computing power and bandwidth to delivery of prioritized contents, (2) pinpoint and discard the dispensable, unnoticeable details in content capturing according to properties of target application, and (3) differentiate contents by their contributions on fulfilling user's expectation so that the adaptation module can allocate resource budget accordingly. With these capabilities we can change the tradeoffs into synergy between resource, content, and user satisfaction. For example:

- **In 3DTI capturing**, when delivering activity involving only little user movement (e.g., storytelling), the system could tune down the temporal resolution of video capturing to save extra bandwidth without degrading perceptual quality and vice versa.
- **In 3DTI dissemination**, when the preferences of viewer towards each 3DTI performer are acquired by the system, streams can be prioritized on their delivery to reach maximum service satisfaction under bounded bandwidth.
- **In 3DTI receiving**, when targeting on mobile devices with limited power and display resolution, computation-intensive render functions should be automatically offloaded.

We implement contextual-information-aware 3DTI systems to verify the performance gain on the three phases in 3DTI systems' delivery chain: capturing phase, dissemination phase, and receiving phase. The implemented systems are tested with various applications including gross/fine motor activities (e.g., physical rehabilitation/storytelling); high/low motion user movements (e.g., exergaming/lecturing); and small/large scale applications (e.g., telehealth/broadcasting).

To sum up, in this proposal, we aim to change the tradeoff between resource, content, and satisfaction in 3DTI by exploiting the contextual information about the three factors. We expect the proposed mechanisms will enhance the efficiency of 3DTI systems targeting on serving different user activities, and applications with different computational requirements and scales.

2. CHALLENGES & PREVIOUS WORKS

A delivery chain of 3DTI lies behind the media-enriched cyber collaborations to cope with real-time constraint of interaction, processing complexity of graphic rendering, and heavy load of data transmission. The delivery chain can be broken down into three phases: capturing, dissemination, and receiving.

Capturing phase and its challenges. Equipped with 3D camera array, microphone, and other application-specific sensors, a 3DTI site captures the activity of its user and digitize it to enable full-body, free viewpoint experience. However, as pointed out by many previous works [1][2][3] on 3DTI capturing interfaces, bitrate of the captured content bundle (i.e., the aggregation of heterogeneous content streams) is oftentimes too high to be supported by common networking environments. An empirical calculation provided by Yang et al. [1] reports a 300 Mbps bitrate for visual streams in 3DTI with minimum quality setting (320x240 resolution, 10 fps). A more modern hardware setting in interface proposed by Mekuria et al. [2] introduces an even higher 1,032 Mbps bitrate with Kinect camera (assuming 640x480 resolution, 30 fps) without compression. Yet, advanced applications of 3DTI such as event broadcasting [4], remote healthcare [5][6], and mobile communication [7] all picture modest CPU/GPU and low bandwidth budget in their computing environments in order to enable them on home or mobile devices.

Thus, in the capturing phase of 3DTI, the tradeoffs happen between outbound bandwidth of the capturing site (resource); temporal/spatial resolutions of the captured stream (content); and the perceptual quality of streams (satisfaction). It is necessary to identify the dispensable details in the content bundle to reduce the total bitrate to a manageable level.

Dissemination phase and its challenges. On dissemination of the captured content, stream bundles captured by multiple performer sites (3DTI sites that capture their users' activity) are exchanged and shared between viewer sites (all participating site regardless of whether its user is been captured) via P2P network. With the received content, a synchronous, shared virtual space is rendered locally in each site. In this process, the first challenge comes from 3DTI's multi-view characteristic. The multi-source (multi-performer), multi-content (multi-camera) dissemination becomes a content distribution forest construction problem in the P2P network formed by all participating sites. Multiple viewers subscribing to multiple streams from multiple performers introduces massive bandwidth consumption, especially when the user number scales up. Platform for 3DTI broadcasting envisioned by Ahsan et al. [4] aims to serve 1,000 concurrent viewers. The system is estimated to consume up to 6 Gbps out-bound bandwidth of the content sources. The second challenge is efficient delivery of the multi-view content. Streams produced by all performer sites are not equally important in a viewer's rendering. Yang et al. [1] first identifies the relationship between a camera stream's shooting angle and its contribution to the field of view (FOV) of a viewer. The work identifies the importance of content differentiation in the dissemination phase. However, in multi-site settings [4][8], Yang's dissemination only brings marginal (<5%) improvement on scalability.

Thus, in the dissemination phase of 3DTI, the tradeoffs happen between bandwidth/delay restrictions of the dissemination network (resource); size of the stream bundle and user group (content); and the acceptance ratio for user subscriptions (satisfaction). We need an efficient prioritization scheme to enable efficient utilization of the overlay network to create a manageable environment for large-scale applications.

Receiving phase and its challenges. Depending on the characteristic of application, a 3DTI site may receive the content bundle for immediate display (for live interactive applications) or for storage and later retrieval (for asynchronous on-demand viewing). For these different purposes, the challenges of receiving phase lie in (1) efficient storage, (2) review summary generation, and (3) adaptive rendering. On efficient storage, Mekuria et al. [2] proposed a mesh-based compression scheme for 3DTI content which reaches 1:10 compression ratio. However, this is still far from being comparable to video codecs for conventional 2D content (e.g., 1:100 for MPEG). On review summary generation, Jain et al. [9] propose a metadata analysis module in their 3DTI system for activity recognition. Yet, training and tuning phase of the module make it impractical for most applications in home environment. On adaptive rending, previous 3DTI clients proposed are all designed for specific computing environments (mobile: [7], PC: [3]) and platforms (Windows: [3], Linux: [1], Android [7]). However, in modern use cases, many applications require the flexibility to run under different resource limitations and the capability of crossing platforms.

Thus, in the receiving phase of 3DTI, the tradeoff happen between power/bandwidth limits of the client (resource); total size of the streamed data (content); and controllability/accessibility of service (satisfaction). We need an adaptive, cross-platform client and a database entity with efficient storage and retrieval features.

3. PROPOSED APPROACHES

To tackle these identified challenges, we propose the concept of contextual information, which spans across resource, content, and satisfaction. We argue that, a 3DTI system should reference the contextual information of these three factors throughout its delivery chain in order to avoid the tradeoff situation between them. In the following sections, we formally define the scope of contextual information and then we discuss where and how different contextual information will help improving each phase in the delivery chain of various 3DTI systems of different scales and purposes.

3.1 Contextual Information

As illustrated in Figure 1, contextual information spans across resource, content, and satisfaction. Thus, we start from formalizing the scope of these three factors.

- Resource: The computing resources that can be utilized for delivering 3DTI contents. This covers the capabilities of computing device and I/O devices in each 3DTI site as well as the network connecting them. For example: network bandwidth, display resolution, CPU/GPU capability, and power limitation.

- Content: The complexity of the captured content bundle throughout an application session. This covers the complexity of the bundle itself as well as the complexity of each data stream inside the bundle. For example: number of heterogeneous streams inside the bundle (i.e., multimodality), temporal resolution of bio-sensing streams, and spatial variance (i.e., frame difference) of 3D video stream.
- Satisfaction: The achievement level of application's objectives and user's expectation. The scope of satisfaction is application-dependent but it can cover both subjective opinions and objective metrics. For example: quality of experience, subscription acceptance ratio, and task accomplishment rate.

With the scopes formalized, we define contextual information as:

> *"The aggregation of information about the three factors - resource, content, and satisfaction - of a 3DTI system and its application."*

For example, contextual information of resource includes the targeting environment of the 3DTI application (e.g., home, mobile, or dedicated facilities). From the environment, we can infer the connection type (e.g., 3G, home cable network, or dedicated optical connection), computation budgets (e.g., CPU rate, RAM size) and I/O interfaces (e.g., desktop screen or phone screen). This help the underlying system adapts its content complexity to avoid wasting unnecessary resource, or offloads/un-offloads computation intensive functions to more powerful entities in the delivery chain. Similarly, contextual information of content and satisfaction (illustrated in Figure 1) helps the underlying system to enhance the efficiency on utilizing the computing environment to fulfill the objectives of users. In the following sections, we will introduce our design which utilizes different contextual information in each phase of the delivery chain of 3DTI systems. In the rest of this proposal, we use the terms resource context, content context, and satisfaction context for contextual information of resource, content, and satisfaction, respectively.

3.2 Content Context in Capturing Phase

Preface. From user studies of Wu et al. [10] and Schulte et al. [11], we see that 3DTI users can have very different quality preferences when participating in different user activities. Thus, in the capturing phase of 3DTI system, we propose the Activity-Aware Adaptive Compression (A3C) [12], which is a real-time compression scheme that utilizes content context to dynamically adjust its compression ratio and quality.

Solution. A3C adopts the Morphing-based Frame Synthesis (MBFS) [13] as its core function. Taking advantage of the unique properties of 3DTI scenes, MBFS allows content receiver to boost up video framerate by injecting synthesized frames. Thus, the capturing frame rate of the performer site can be reduced to save substantial bandwidth for content delivery.

To maximize the effectiveness of MBFS compression, we apply activity recognition to identify content context: the motion characteristics of current user activity. We assign compression settings according to the activity type to adjust the compression ratio and spatial quality of captured content. The quality of synthesized frames depends heavily on the motion level of the activity. For high motion activities, the graphical difference between frames is large and the sharpness degrades due to motion blur. These effects increase the artifacts introduced by feature-based morphing, making the synthesis unnatural and noticeable to viewers. Therefore, we propose to combine the compression

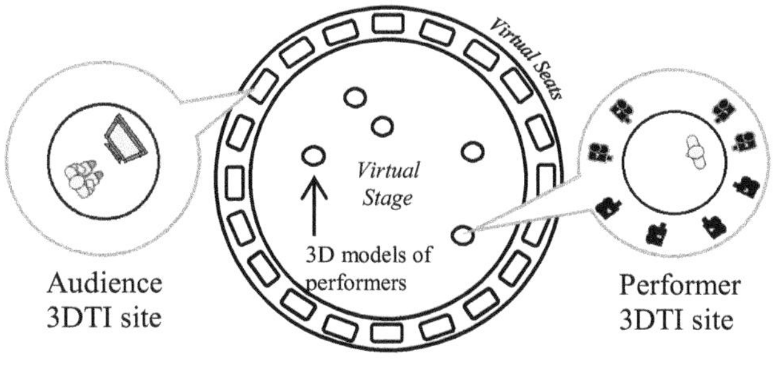

Figure 2. 3DTI Amphitheater.

scheme with user activity recognition to dynamically tune the compression and achieve quality preservation and resource saving.

Verification. To verify our design, we implement the A3C scheme on our 3DTI platform: the TEEVE Endpoint [3], which includes a general purpose capturing interface that does not target specific application. We will evaluate A3C via objective compression ratio as well as subjective user study. Objective evaluation will focus on the bandwidth saving (resource factor) with A3C under different application scenarios, e.g., gaming, exercise, lecture, and storytelling. Subjective evaluation will be conducted via interviewing player of our 3DTI virtual fencing game built upon the TEEVE Endpoint with the A3C module embedded (satisfaction factor).

3.3 Satisfaction context in Dissemination

Preface. Due to the high bandwidth demand in dissemination phase, previous 3DTI applications are restricted with a small user group (fewer than four [1]). In order to promote 3DTI to applications with more flexible scalability, we propose the 3DTI Amphitheater, a broadcasting platform which renders a shared virtual space (Figure 2) that accommodates hundred-scale users.

Solution. Users in the 3DTI Amphitheater are divided into two groups: performers and the audience. A user is a performer when she is captured by a camera array. The 3D models of performers interact on the virtual stage while actual users can be physically dispersed. A user is in the audience when she passively view the 3D streams created by the performers without involvement.

We propose to tackle the challenge of high bandwidth demand by content differentiation. We argue that not all streams in the amphitheater are equally important. Content's importance to a viewer can be affected by two types of satisfaction context: view-based priority and role-based priority. For example, when the shooting angle of the visual content complies with the chosen view of a user, the stream should have higher view-based priority to her. We propose to adopt the contribution factor (CF) [1] to quantify the view-based importance of streams. As for role-based priority, we argue that: to a particular viewer, not all performers are equally important. The importance of a particular performer depends on her role in the performance. For example the audience may be more interested in the vocalist of a rock band. Also note that the importance of a performer is not universal. A viewer who is an audience and a viewer who is a performer have different viewing preferences. The amphitheater constructs its content dissemination forest based on these satisfaction context to allocate bandwidth to the prioritized streams.

Verification. We propose to verify the performance of 3DTI Amphitheater by emulation with real-world network topology and the configurations of our 3DTI platform. The verification is two-fold. First, we evaluate the effectiveness of our semantic stream prioritization by examining the application quality of service (AQoS) of user sites. The AQoS is defined as a weighted acceptance ratio of stream subscription request, where the weight of a request is the semantic priority. Second, we investigate the bandwidth saving brought by content dissemination scheme in the amphitheater. We compare its bandwidth usage (resource factor) and its sustainable performer crew size (content factor) with other multi-site/broadcasting platforms [4][8].

3.4 Resource context in Receiving Phase

Preface. Challenges in the receiving phase are (1) efficient storage, (2) review summary generation, and (3) adaptive rendering. To approach them, we focus on 3DTI application with asynchronous service model (i.e., on-demand service for offline reviewing) because its storage and retrieval features make these challenges inevitable in the receiving phase. As a platform for investigating resource context in the receiving phase, we implement an asynchronous 3DTI system for physiotherapy session reviewing: the CyPhy (Cyber-Physiotherapy) system.

Solution. The envisioned use case model of CyPhy is as follows. As part of the prescription given in the end of at-clinic face-to-face meeting between therapist and patient, a "CyPhy kit" will be provided to the patient. The kit includes required devices (e.g., Kinect cameras) for the patient to set up a light-weighted 3DTI recording studio at home. On a daily basis, CyPhy will stream to the patient a pre-recorded exercise demonstration prescribed by the therapist. Patient will follow the video to conduct correct therapeutic exercises and have this rehabilitation session recorded with the CyPhy kit. The recorded session is upload to an electronic health record (EHR) cloud to be archived. Recorded sessions will be played out by the therapist whenever and wherever she is available on mobile device or PC. Therapist can supervise the correctness of patient's moves by viewing the streamed content bundle and provide professional feedbacks.

On efficient storage in the EHR cloud, we propose a new compression scheme for 3D videos that reaches a compression ratio close to 2D video codecs. We identify the likeliness of everyday rehabilitation video and exploit this property for inter-3D-video coding. On review summary generation, we propose to analyze the metadata of inter-video coded frame sizes to detect anomaly events (i.e., patient fall or injured). This non-intrusive analysis shortens the detection time, which is a crucial improvement due to the large size and quantity of 3DTI recordings in the EHR cloud. On adaptive rendering, CyPhy references the resource context for bitrate adjustment and offloaded rendering. First, we propose to adopt the DASH [14] standard in CyPhy client to accommodate with different network capabilities in heterogeneous environments. Second, to enable different computing environments (e.g., PC, mobile) as CyPhy clients, we propose an offloading mechanism to offload the 3D rendering to DASH server. These features allow the CyPhy system to adaptively adjust its streaming content complexity and provide different levels of user control.

Verification. We generate a series of rehabilitation session recordings in our lab as our dataset to test CyPhy's archiving feature. Preliminary results show our storage compression scheme achieves 1:1255 compression ratio. The same dataset will be used in the verification of metadata-based anomaly detection. For adaptive rendering, the DASH-based design will be verified against bandwidth fluctuations under different network environments. The offloading feature will be verified on mobile devices with power limitation. We expect CyPhy will adjust its streaming quality and user controllability according to bandwidth dimension and power dimension of resource context.

4. CONCLUSION

The core idea of this proposal is to leverage the contextual information in resource, content, and satisfaction throughout the three phases of delivery chain of 3DTI applications. In summary our expected contributions are:

1-1. Identifying the dispensable details in content capturing phase according to content context.
1-2. Validating the utilization of content context in capturing phase by implementation of an adaptive compression module.

2-1. Enabling efficient utilization of the overlay network in dissemination phase by differentiating streams according to satisfaction context.
2-2. Recognizing the satisfaction context in dissemination phase by validating a manageable large-scale 3DTI platform.

3-1. Proposing 3DTI client which adapts with the resource context in the receiving phase.
3-2. Devising an asynchronous 3DTI system which realizes the adaptation to resource context in bandwidth and power.

The expected contributions combined will lead to 3DTI frameworks that are capable of sustaining advance applications with higher quality and scalability requirements. Preliminary results of our ongoing researches indicate optimistic expectations on various aspects (e.g., scalability [15][16], compression [13][17], activity recognition [9][12]). The outcomes thus far persuade us to continue on extending the utilization of contextual information and on verifying them in actual 3DTI prototypes.

5. REFERENCES

[1] Z. Yang, W. Wu, and K. Nahrstedt et al., "Enabling multi-party 3D tele-immersive environments with ViewCast," ACM TOMM, 2010
[2] R. Mekuria, M. Sanna, S. Asioli et al., A 3D Tele-Immersion System Based on Live Captured Mesh Geometry, ACM MMSys 2013
[3] P. Xia and K. Nahrstedt, "TEEVE endpoint: towards the ease of 3D tele-immersive application development", ACM MM, 2013
[4] A. Arefin, Z. Huang, K. Nahrstedt et al., 4D TeleCast: towards large scale multi-site and multi-view dissemination of 3DTI contents, IEEE ICDCS, 2012
[5] J. J. Han, G. Kurillo, R. T. Abresch, E. de Bie, A. Nicorici, R. Bajcsy, Upper extremity 3D reachable workspace analysis in dystrophinopathy using Kinect, Muscle Nerve. 2015.
[6] D. Sonnenwald, H. Söderholm, G. Welch, Illuminating collaboration in emergency healthcare: paramedic-physician collaboration and 3D telepresence technology. Information Research, 2014
[7] S. Shi, K. Nahrstedt, R. Campbell, A Real-Time Remote Rendering System for Interactive Mobile Graphics, ACM TOMCCAP, 2012.
[8] W. Wu, Z. Yang, and I. Gupta et al., "Towards multi-site collaboration in 3D tele-immersive environments," ICDCS, 2008
[9] A. Jain, A. Arefin, R. Rivas, et al. 3DTI Activity Classification Based on Application-System Metadata, ACM Multimedia, 2013.
[10] W. Wu, A. Ahsan, G. Kurillo et al., Color-plus-depth level-of-detail in 3D tele-immersive video: a psychophysical approach", MM 2011
[11] S. Schulte, S. Chen, and K. Nahrstedt, "Stevens' Power Law in 3D tele-immersion: towards subjective modeling of multimodal cyber interaction", Proc. ACM MM, 2014
[12] S. Chen, P. Xia, and K. Nahrstedt, "Activity-aware adaptive compression: a morphing-based frame synthesis application in 3DTI", Proc. ACM MM, 2013
[13] S. Chen and K. Nahrstedt, "Activity-based Synthesized Frame Generation in 3DTI Video", IEEE ICME, 2013.
[14] ISO/IEC 23009-1, Information technology -- Dynamic adaptive streaming over HTTP (DASH), 2014.
[15] S. Chen, K. Nahrstedt, and I. Gupta, "3DTI Amphitheater: a manageable 3DTI environment with hierarchical stream prioritization", Proc. ACM MMSys, 2014
[16] S. Chen, Z. Gao, K. Nahrstedt, and I. Gupta, "3DTI Amphitheater: Towards 3DTI Broadcasting", ACM TOMM, 2015
[17] S. Chen, K. Nahrstedt, "Impact of morphing-based frame synthesis on bandwidth optimization for 3DTI video", Proc. IEEE ISM, 2013

Socializing Multimodal Sensors for Information Fusion

Yuhui Wang
NUS Graduate School for Integrative Sciences and Engineering
National University of Singapore, Singapore
wangyuhui@u.nus.edu

ABSTRACT

In the modern big data world, development of a huge number of physical or social sensors provides us a great opportunity to explore both cyber and physical situation awareness. However, social sensor fusion for situation awareness is still in its infancy and lacks a unified framework to aggregate and composite real-time media streams from diverse sensors and social network platforms. We propose a new paradigm where sensor and social information are fused together facilitating event detection or customized services. Our proposal consists of **1)** a tweeting camera framework where cameras can tweet event related information; **2)** a hybrid social sensor fusion algorithm utilizing spatio-temporal-semantic information from multimodal sensors and **3)** a new social-cyber-physical paradigm where human and sensors are collaborating for event fusion. Our research progress and preliminary results are presented and future directions are discussed.

Categories and Subject Descriptors

H.4.m [**Information Systems Applications**]: Miscellaneous

Keywords

social sensor network; multimodal fusion; information fusion;

1. INTRODUCTION

We are witnessing a world of big social and sensor data explosion. All kinds of sensors that are constantly monitoring our surrounding situations. ***Physical sensors*** like visual sensors, humidity sensors, GPS sensor, mobile phones are widely used in capturing ambient signals. ***Social sensors*** such as Twitter, Facebook, Sina Weibo, Flickr are fed with exploding voluntarily user-generated data. These sensors, though working in different way, often provide complementary event related information. Their ambient sensing capabilities provide the opportunity that allows humans and machines working together to make sense of real-time situation. This has provided us an opportunity to socialize sensors with humans by which human can establish connections with sensors in social network and "follow", interact or get updates from them. Socializing physical sensors with human and fusing social sensor would not only lead to a better understanding of dynamically occurring situations but also a new social-cyber-physical ecosystem that connects sensors and people for human's needs as their situations evolve.

However, due to the diversity of these sources, currently physical sensors and social sensors are capturing information separately in their individual silos. The information captured by sensors of different modalities are residing as heterogeneous data. They are not combined or fused which impedes event detection and understanding in a comprehensive manner. Without aggregating relevant these multimodal sensors signals, it is hard to obtain a holistic and comprehensive event or situation overview. Moreover, though these sensors are observing and monitoring our physical world, there is a lack of effective interaction between them and humans for situation information retrieval and propagation.

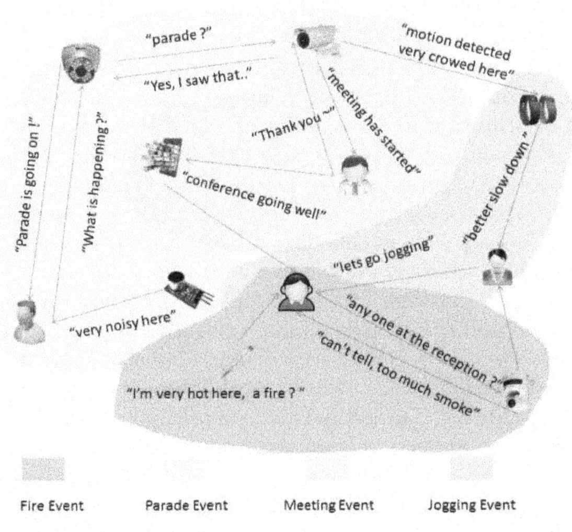

Figure 1: Social Sensors Fusion for Event Detection

This thesis proposes to extend the traditional sensing paradigm by combining sensors of different modality and socializing them with human so as to facilitate real-world event information fusion and analysis. Our conceptual idea is shown in 1. Specifically, we propose to socialize multimodal sensors for information fusion such that **1)** camera network-

MM'15, October 26–30, 2015, Brisbane, Australia.
ACM 978-1-4503-3459-4/15/10.
DOI: http://dx.doi.org/10.1145/2733373.2807995.

s "tweet" information when things of interest happens; **2)** spatio-temporal semantic information is fused in a pseudo-image representation when particular physical event happens, giving more precise and complementary information; **3)** humans interact with sensors through social networks by following sensors, receiving event related alert or notification from sensors, and providing semantic knowledge to sensors, making them smart so that useful information could be best gathered, utilized and disseminated through the whole human-sensor social network.

2. RELATED WORK

With an increasing number of sensors having capabilities of sensing, processing, communicating, usage of sensors in event detection and situation awareness is spreading. Massively distributed visual sensors (webcams) are utilized for environment understanding [8]. A multi-tier network SensEye of heterogeneous cameras has been proposed to overcome the disadvantage of single-tier networks in surveillance application, performing object detection, recognition and tracking tasks [11]. Distributed smart cameras [4] are also being widely used in camera sensor networks to produce alerts if certain types of unusual behaviour or abnormal events occur. To bridge the gap between machine-oriented low level features and human readable high level semantics, a number of works concern image captioning [6] and video concept detection [9, 3], where the task is to assign concept labels to an input image/video along with their associated probabilities. Moreover, multi-modal sensor fusion has been studied for combining multiple level of information for various multimedia tasks [1]. Fusion of mobile computing and social networking services for traffic anomaly detection has been proposed in [12]. Crowd-sourced sensing and collaboration systems over Twitter are designed and implemented which opens publish-subscribe infrastructure for sensors to be combined with social platform [5].

Many online social network services are prevalent nowadays where users share personal opinions, breaking news. Twitter, as one of the most important social sensors, has been leveraged to generate a large number of event detection or situation understanding systems such as Twitris [14] and Evenshop [15]. It is regarded as a social sensor [13] in detecting and tracking earthquakes, typhoons or traffic jams. Also a situation awareness algorithm is proposed to detect geo-spatial events in a given monitored geographic area, which offers good summary of events [16] .

With the Internet of things (IoT), everyday objects now have the ability to interconnect not only among themselves but also humans. Social networking concepts have been integrated into IoT [2], which establishes Social Internet of Things (SIoT). Things not only sense but start to update their status in social networks. Kranz et al. [10] make both humans and technical systems together to form a socio-technical network by describing cognitive office, where the states of the plant, windows and doors are posted via Twitter accounts. Many other such accounts have been created. For example, @VedamsIoTEdison tells if room lights are off or on; @VedamsIoTRPi tweets when there was a power cut in office hours; @MoneyPlantTrack posts not only plants temperature, humidity, status but also uploads images captured by camera when there are abnormal situations.

Summing up, aforementioned works consider information from either physical sensors or social sensors and do not deal with fusing these two types of sources in a unified framework and there is lack of interaction between humans and sensors which impede information fusion and processing for event recognition. Also, sensors or smart things tweet information related to predefined tasks and have limitations in application wise extension. We contribute to this part by proposing a new sensing paradigm where both social and physical sensor information are represented through unified data structure which enable multimodal information fusion and user customized situation understanding.

3. APPROACH

In order to socialize multimodal sensors and establish connections among them for event detection and fusion, we propose to first combine and process information from different sensor modalities, particular from visual sensor and social sensors to enhance event detection and situation understanding by building tweeting cameras, which tweet useful information among sensor networks or to the social networks. Second, we fuse spatio-temporal-semantic information from different modalities via a unified image-like representation named Cmage (Concept Image), so as to filter out sensor noise and give precise event situation. Third, we propose a new paradigm of sensing mechanism where people and physical sensors are collaborating for information mining, propagation and knowledge learning.

3.1 Tweeting Cameras for Event Detection

Combining these two complementary sensor streams can significantly improve the task of event detection and aid in comprehending evolving situations. However, the different characteristics of these social and sensor data make such information fusion for event detection a challenging problem. To tackle this problem, we have established connection between information from visual sensors (camera) and social sensors (Twitter), and have proposed an innovative multi-layer tweeting cameras framework integrating both physical sensors and social sensors to detect various concepts of real-world events [17]. In this framework, shown in Figure 2, visual concept detectors are applied on camera video frames and these concepts can be construed as "camera tweets" posted regularly. These tweets are represented by a unified probabilistic spatio-temporal (PST) data structure which is then aggregated to a concept-based image (Cmage) as the common representation for visualization. To facilitate event analysis, we have defined a set of operators and analytic functions that can be applied on the PST data by the user to discover occurrences of events and to analyse evolving situations. We further leveraged on geo-located social media data by mining current topics discussed on Twitter to obtain the high-level semantic meaning of detected events. The information captured by sensors of different modality is then combined to facilitate situation awareness in a comprehensive manner.

3.2 Hybrid Social Sensor Fusion

As geo-tagging techniques and mobile sensors become prevalent, spatial temporal and semantic patterns of various multimedia sensor data are now available for event detection and situation understanding. Therefore, we propose to extract spatial temporal and semantic patterns from information captured by sensors of different modalities, and represent those information in a pseudo-image based structure, where

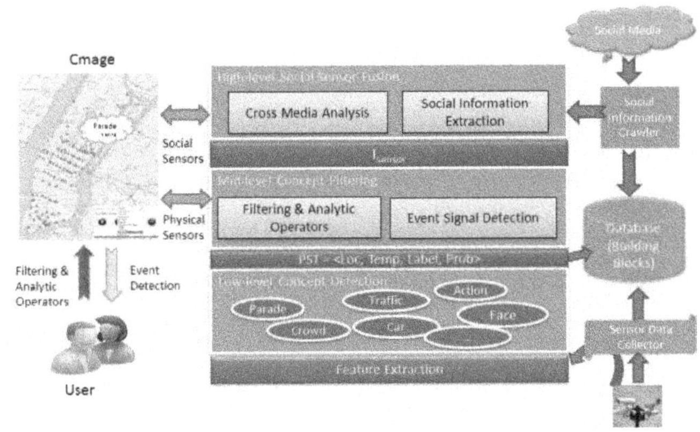

Figure 2: Multi-layer Tweeting Cameras Framework

data structure from multi-sensor streams is expressed in a unified format and easy to be fused in a way similar to image fusion. We conceive each "pixel" in an image presents an event or concept "signal" with semantic meaning, and consider semantic relatedness among signals when fusing situation images provided by particular sensor streams.

3.3 New Paradigm of Social Sensor Network

Establishing connections between people and the resources they need is a fundamental task in society, which leads to the problem of "Social Life Networks" (SLN) [7]. We imagine and propose a new paradigm where people are not only connected to people through social network, but also have access to customized services provided by all kinds of widely used physical sensors. Node pairs in these network are temporally, spatially, semantically or information-wise close to them. E.g., as in Figure 1, a sensor could directly tell a person a parade in going on at some specific place; a meeting has started or abnormal things are detected. An end user could specify their information needs from sensors by assigning customized tasks or share personal information to sensors making them learn to be smarter for future event detection or fusion tasks. Such a new sensor-involved social network would greatly improve our situation understanding and effectively satisfy people's information and resources needs through human sensor interaction and collaboration.

4. EXPERIMENT RESULTS

We have crawled live feeds from 150 public CCTV traffic cameras distributed on the roads all over the Manhattan district of New York City as well as Manhattan geotagged tweets from October 08, 2014 onwards, and also collected NUS campus foodcourts video dataset consisting of video feeds from 73 cameras located at 9 different foodcourts. We quantitatively evaluated proposed tweeting cameras framework in Figure 2 with this large-scale dataset.

4.1 Events Ground Truth

We use the notices posted on the "Weekend Traffic Advisory" website of the New York City Department of Transportation for obtaining the ground truth.[1] The ground truths for the events that we try to detect are shown in Table 1.

4.2 Applying Analytic Functions

We apply concept detectors on raw camera feeds and we defined a set of analytic functions and operators such as

[1]http://www.nyc.gov/html/dot/html/motorist/wkndtraf.shtml

Table 1: Real-world Events Ground Truth

Event	*Date*	*Time*	*Location*
CBGB Music Festival	12 Oct	10am-7pm	Broadway 51 Street
Hispanic Parade	12 Oct	12pm-5pm	5th Avenue
Columbus Day Parade	13 Oct	11am-5pm	5th Avenue
Saint Patrick's Day Parade	17 Mar	12pm-5pm	5th Avenue
Million March NYC Protest	13 Dec	2pm-5pm	Washington Square Park, 5th Avenue, Foley Square

"smooth" , "extreme", "trend" that can be applied to obtain meaningful information such as event pattern, concept trending etc. Results of "smooth" and "trend" function is shown in Figure 3 and Figure 4 which reduce sensor noise in "St Patrick's Data Parade" event data and describes university Foodcourt crowdedness trend respectively.

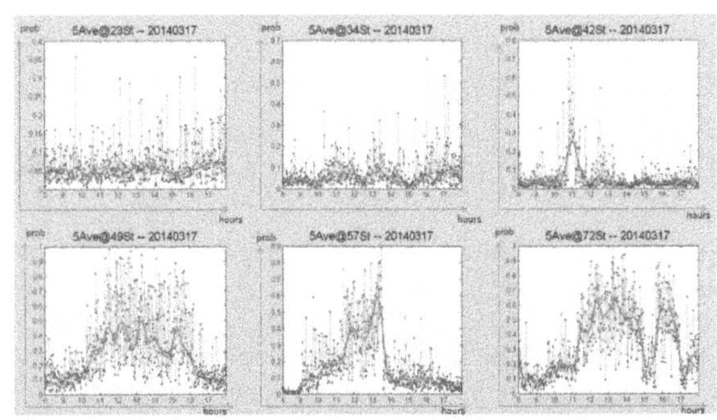

Figure 3: *People Marching* Concept Results from 8:00 to 18:00 in March 17th, during Saint Patrick's Day Parade Event

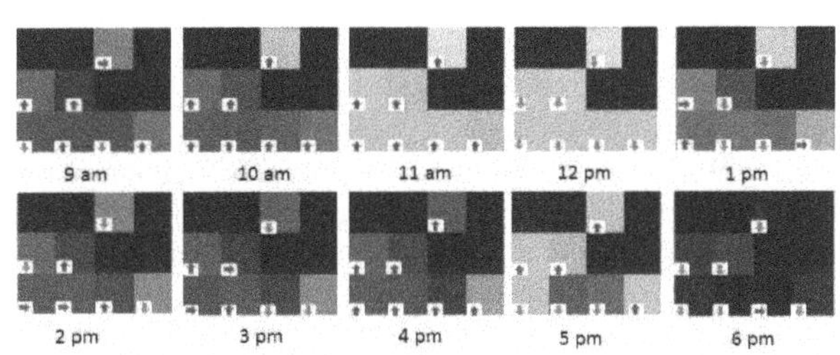

Figure 4: A Campus Foodcourt Cmage *Crowdness* with Arrows indicating Ascending, Descending and Plateau Trend.

4.3 Social Sensor Fusion

To fuse sensor and social information, we detect events spatial and temporal information from sensors and then generate related representative terms from social media by using tweets posted nearby the places where an event occurs. Results are shown in Figure 5. As can be seen, social tweets posted near an event location are able to give high-level semantic meaning of the event, which enhance the understanding of situations.

The results demonstrates the feasibility and effectiveness of our proposed framework and the idea of combining camera tweets (with spatial and temporal information) and social tweets (high level semantic meanings) are shown to be promising for detecting real-world events.

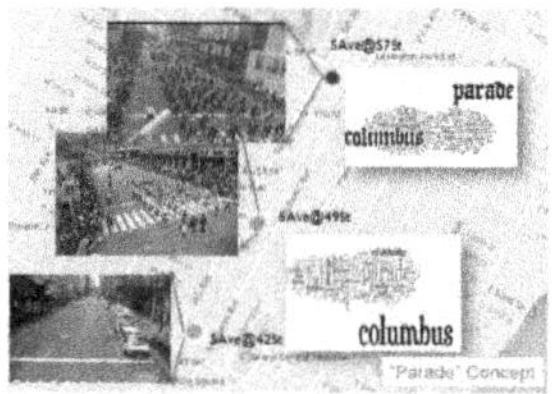

(a) Social Sensor Fusion for "Columbus Day Parade"

(b) Social Sensor Fusion for "Hispanic Parade" Event

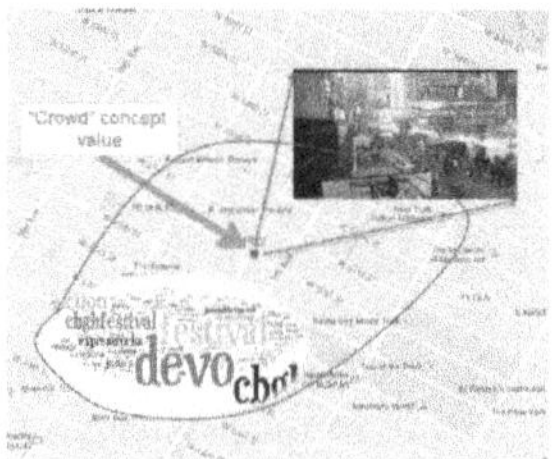

(c) Crowd Concept and Salient Topic Words during "CBGB Musical Festival"

(d) Sensor and Social Information of "Million March NYC" Protest Event

Figure 5: Social Sensor Fusion for Real-world Events

5. CONCLUSIONS AND FUTURE WORK

We propose an new paradigm that extend traditional sensor sensing mechanism by combining sensor of different modality and socializing them with human to facilitate real-world event information fusion. The work includes a novel tweeting camera frame that combines both physical sensor and social sensor together for event detection, which is demonstrated through data analysis in real-world events, and a pseudo-image based social sensor fusion algorithm.

Future directions:

As we are solving multimodal fusion problem, our future works mainly direct in two folds: 1) In social sensor fusion, we will explore how social sensors information is diffusing spatially and temporally in social network and how this diffusion should improve physical sensors detection task. The reliability of social sensors for event detection and the system scalability issues will also be explored. 2) We will build a new social-cyber-physical paradigm where human and sensor are interacting in information sharing, fusion and recommendation. Besides spatial and temporal correlation, we will explore semantic correlation among event related signals from different sensing modalities to provide deeper understanding of going situation. Such spatio-temporal-semantic pattern mining using multi-modal and complementary sensors could offer more proper, prompt and accurate recommendation for action takings.

6. ACKNOWLEDGEMENT

This research was conducted at NUS-ZJU SeSaMe Centre, which is supported by the Singapore NRF under its IRC@SG Funding Initiative and administered by the IDMPO.

7. REFERENCES

[1] P. Atrey, M. Hossain, A. El Saddik, and M. Kankanhalli. Multimodal fusion for multimedia analysis: a survey. *Multimedia Systems*, 16(6):345–379, 2010.

[2] L. Atzori, A. Iera, and G. Morabito. From "smart objects" to "social objects": The next evolutionary step of the internet of things. *Communications Magazine, IEEE*, 52(1):97–105, January 2014.

[3] C. A. Bhatt, P. K. Atrey, and M. S. Kankanhalli. A reward-and-punishment-based approach for concept detection using adaptive ontology rules. *ACM Transactions on Multimedia Computing, Communications and Applications*, 9(2):10:1–10:21, 2013.

[4] M. Bramberger, A. Doblander, A. Maier, B. Rinner, and H. Schwabach. Distributed embedded smart cameras for surveillance applications. *Computer*, 39(2):68–75, 2006.

[5] M. Demirbas, M. Bayir, C. Akcora, Y. Yilmaz, and H. Ferhatosmanoglu. Crowd-sourced sensing and collaboration using twitter. In *International Symposium on a World of Wireless Mobile and Multimedia Networks (WoWMoM)*, pages 1–9, 2010.

[6] C. Farabet, C. Couprie, L. Najman, and Y. LeCun. Learning hierarchical features for scene labeling. *PAMI*, 35(8):1915–1929, 2013.

[7] A. Gupta and R. Jain. Social life networks: A multimedia problem? In *ACM MM*, pages 203–212, 2013.

[8] N. Jacobs, W. Burgin, N. Fridrich, A. Abrams, K. Miskell, B. H. Braswell, A. D. Richardson, and R. Pless. The global network of outdoor webcams: Properties and applications. In *ACM SIGSPATIAL*, pages 111–120, 2009.

[9] Y.-G. Jiang, J. Yang, C.-W. Ngo, and A. Hauptmann. Representations of keypoint-based semantic concept detection: A comprehensive study. *IEEE Transactions on Multimedia*, 12(1):42–53, 2010.

[10] M. Kranz, L. Roalter, and F. Michahelles. Things that twitter: Social networks and the internet of things. In *CIoT Workshop*, 2010.

[11] P. Kulkarni, D. Ganesan, P. Shenoy, and Q. Lu. Senseye: A multi-tier camera sensor network. In *ACM MM*, pages 229–238, 2005.

[12] B. Pan, Y. Zheng, D. Wilkie, and C. Shahabi. Crowd sensing of traffic anomalies based on human mobility and social media. In *ACM SIGSPATIAL*, pages 344–353, 2013.

[13] T. Sakaki, M. Okazaki, and Y. Matsuo. Earthquake shakes twitter users: Real-time event detection by social sensors. In *WWW*, pages 851–860, 2010.

[14] A. Sheth, A. Jadhav, P. Kapanipathi, C. Lu, H. Purohit, G. A. Smith, and W. Wang. 'twitris- a system for collective social intelligence'. Encyclopedia of Social Network Analysis and Mining, 2013.

[15] V. K. Singh, M. Gao, and R. Jain. Social pixels: Genesis and evaluation. In *ACM MM*, pages 481–490, 2010.

[16] M. Walther and M. Kaisser. Geo-spatial event detection in the twitter stream. In *European Conference on Advances in Information Retrieval*, pages 356–367, 2013.

[17] Y. Wang and M. S. Kankanhalli. Tweeting cameras for event detection. In *WWW*, pages 1231–1241, 2015.

Learn to Recognize Actions Through Neural Networks

Zhenzhong Lan
School of Computer Science, Carnegie Mellon University
lanzhzh@cs.cmu.edu

ABSTRACT

This research seeks to develop neural network techniques to effectively recognize actions in videos. The proposed study will lead to a deeper understanding of how neural network algorithms can help AI systems to understand motions. It will also realize an action recognition system that significantly outperforms current state-of-the-art. In addition, we will investigate the extent to which our work can be beneficial to understanding how brains perceive and analyze actions.

Recent data-driven neural network approaches such as convolutional neural networks have been successful for object recognition. However, learning to recognize actions has proven to be quite a challenge due to the difficulty of getting enough labels, processing large-scale video data, and capturing motion information from videos. Therefore, we leverage effective techniques from local hand-crafted methods to help neural network algorithms learn motion features. These techniques include learning from video and optical flow volumes that follow motion trajectories, pooling features from videos played at multiple frame rates to achieve speed invariance, extending the local descriptors with normalized locations to incorporate spatial-temporal information, and a training-free re-ranking technique to exploit the relationship among classes. We also discuss a fundamental problem of whether should we learn time-aware models and what our models actually capture when we feed them temporal data. Finally, we discuss the connection of our research with how brains perceive and recognize motions.

Categories and Subject Descriptors

H.4 [**Information Systems Applications**]: Miscellaneous

General Terms

Algorithms; Experimentation

Keywords

Feature; Action Recognition; Neural Networks; Learning

MM'15, October 26–30, 2015, Brisbane, Australia.
ACM 978-1-4503-3459-4/15/10.
DOI: http://dx.doi.org/10.1145/2733373.2807996 .

1. INTRODUCTION

The past decade has witnessed an explosion of video data. To use this enormous and ever-growing multimedia data, we need an automatic way of indexing it. Such indexing requires recognition of objects, scenes and actions. Recent progress on action recognition has mainly focused on improving features, which can be categorized into two broad classes: 1) more traditional hand-crafted local features [18] and their corresponding bag-of-feature encoding methods [13], and 2) learning based features that are mainly inspired by the success of convolutional neural networks (CNNs) for image recognition [6, 14, 5]. State-of-the-art hand-crafted methods, which use optical flow and tracking, are good at detecting motion information but rely on simple hand-crafted descriptors. In contrast, neural networks methods, with their powerful modeling ability, have difficulty in capturing motion information and require a large amount of data labeling. With limited data, the learned features are generally not discriminative enough to outperform the state-of-the-art hand-crafted features such as Improved Dense Trajectories (IDT)[18]. In this paper, we leverage the advantages of both groups of methodologies by selecting effective techniques from hand-crafted features to improve the performance of learning based methods.

First, we propose to learn from video and optical flow volumes detected by IDT, instead of learning from videos clips [5] or video cuboids [10]. We show that the proposed two-stream (video and optical flow streams) framework combined with unsupervised learning methods can boost the overall performance. In specific, we use Stacked Convolutional Independent Subspace Analysis (ConvISA), a state-of-the-art unsupervised feature learning method. We give an in-depth discussion about what ConvISA really learn from the given temporal data. Second, we enhance the inputs of two-stream stacked ConvISA to achieve speed invariance through pooling data from videos played at multiple frame rates. Our novel technique, referred to as Multi-skIp Feature Stacking (MIFS) [7], stacks data extracted by a family of differential filters parameterized with multiple time skips and encodes shift-invariance into the frequency space. MIFS allows us to match actions at different speeds and ranges of motion. Third, in order to incorporate spatio-temporal information into the learned descriptors and keep resulting feature dimensions relatively low at the same time, we augment those descriptors with normalized spatio-temporal location information. This augmented descriptors are called Space-Time Extended Descriptors (STED). Finally, to capture the relationship among action classes, we design a Multi-class Iterative Re-ranking (MIR) method that exploits the relationship among classes. MIR requires no training yet can significantly improve the ranking performance measured by mean average precision (MAP).

We use the above four complementary methods to improve the performance of our learned motion features. However, despite the overall superior performance, the way we build our model contradicts with the biological fact that human do not have separate receptive fields for inputs with different time stamps. We will investigate on this contradiction and discuss whether it is necessary to learn time-aware networks and how our observation can be beneficial for neural science research.

2. RELATED WORK

Features and encoding methods are the major sources of considerable breakthroughs in conventional video representations. Among them the trajectory based approaches [18, 4], especially the Dense Trajectory (DT) and IDT [16, 18], are the basis of current state-of-the-art hand-crafted algorithms. These trajectory-based methods are designed to address the flaws of image-extended video features. Their superior performance validates the need for a unique representation of motion features.

There have been many works trying to improve IDT due to its popularity. Peng et al. [12] improved the performance of IDT by increasing codebook sizes and fusing multiple coding methods. Hoai & Zisserman [2] achieved state-of-the-art performance on several action recognition datasets through applying three techniques including data augmentation, modeling score distribution over video subsequences, and capturing the relationship among action classes. Fernando et al. [1] modeled the evolution of appearance in the video and achieved state-of-the-art results on the Hollywood2 dataset. Despite those improvements, none of them dealt with the fact that IDT relies on very simple hand-crafted descriptors. In contrast, data-driven approaches have demonstrated their modeling power over image recognition [6] and are gradually replacing traditional hand-crafted image recognition methods.

Motivated by the success of CNNs in image recognition, researchers are working intensely towards developing CNN equivalents for learning video features. Some accomplishment has been reported from using CNNs for action recognition in videos. Karpathy et al. [5] trained deep CNNs through one million weakly labeled YouTube videos and reported moderate success on using it as a feature extractor. Simonyan & Zisserman [14] reported a result competitive to IDT [18] through training deep CNNs using both sampled frames and stacked optical flows. All of the above relied on a large amount of labels which are expensive to get and generally perform worse than hand-crafted features among small datasets.

There is limited number of works on applying unsupervised methods to learn video features. Among them Independent Component Analysis (ICA) [3] was the first approach to learn representations of videos in an unsupervised way. Le et al. [10] approached the problem using stacked ConvISA. Srivastava et al. [15] tried unsupervised feature learning through long-short term memory. Because those methods rely purely on pixel data, they struggled to capture motion information and mostly performed no better than state-of-the-art hand-crafted methods. Also, none of them touch the fundamental question of what it means to learn from temporal data.

In this study, we overcome limitations of previous methods by applying unsupervised feature learning methods on video and optical flow volume detected by IDT. Our new learning paradigm does not rely on any label, hence can work well on small datasets. It works better in capturing motion information due to the usage of optical flow and tracking. As illustrated by MIFS, it can also use data enhancing techniques developed for hand-crafted features. Also, we show that learning from temporal data is a process of learning de-noising filters rather than time-aware filters.

3. TWO-STREAM STACKED CONVISA

The initial stacked ConvISA was designed to learn appearance and motion together, but spatio-temporal features learned from fixed size cuboids do not capture the motion part well, as shown in [5, 14]. To explicitly learn the motion information, we propose a two-stream stacked ConvISA that captures appearance information and motion information separately. Demonstrated in Figure 1, the appearance stream learns from video volumes that follow the trajectories detected by IDT and the motion stream learns to describe the corresponding optical flow volumes. Since the trajectories follow motion, the inputs of our learning models, being video volumes or optical flow volumes, explicitly encode motion information. For the learning model we use a two-layer stacked ConvISA as in Le et al. [10]. Figure 2 shows some randomly chosen filters learned from two stream stacked ConvISA. As can be seen in Figure 2, filters from optical flow volumes have much more complex shapes than those from video volumes, indicating that motion signals are more difficult to learn. This is because patches in video volumes are temporally coherent due to brightness constancy constraint by tracking while patches in optical flow volumes have much less correlation due to the flow estimation error. To quantify the correlation difference between image patches and flow patches, we randomly sample 200000 volumes for each stream of data from HMDB51 dataset and calculate the average correlation coefficient of randomly selected patch pair within volumes. The average correlation coefficient of video volumes and flow volumes are 0.80 and 0.28, respectively. These correlation measurements show that optical flow volumes along trajectories are too noisy to learn robust filters. To address this problem, we sample optical flow volumes inside each frame according to the spatial location of the trajectory. In another word, we compress the time dimension of the trajectory into 1 to reduce the temporal variation of the flow volumes. This alternative way of sampling increase the temporal correlation of flow patches from 0.28 to 0.75 and help us to learn better filters. By using this technique, we can improve our flow net's performance on HMDB51 from 44.2% accuracy to 53.1%. This result show that learning from temporal data is a process of learning de-noising filters rather than time-aware filters. If the noise level out-weight the real action signals or the model's learning capability, then it becomes difficult to learn meaningful model. More discussion of this observation can be found in [8].

Table 1 compares our two-stream stacked ConvISA to the recent two-stream CNNs [14]. We see that two-stream ConvISA has better performance to two-stream CNNs on both

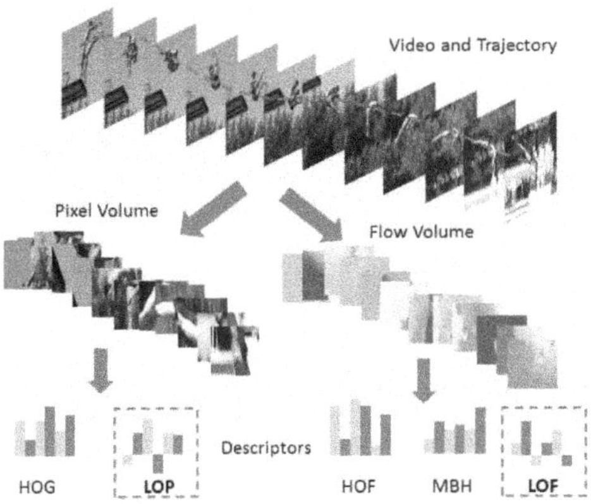

Figure 1: Illustration of our novel local video descriptors. LOP and LOF describe gray pixel and optical flow volumes, respectively. They resemble HOG/HOF/MBH in a data-driven learning framework.

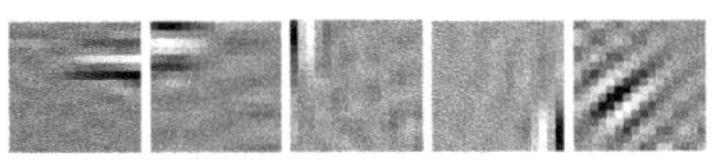

(a) Filters learned from gray pixels.

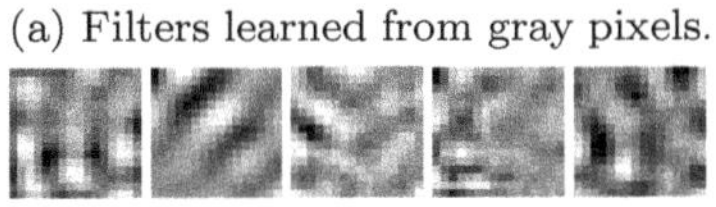

(b) Filters learned from optical flow

Figure 2: Example filters learned using two-stream stacked ConvISA.

UCF101 and HMDB51 datasets, yet it is computationally much cheaper and label-free.

4. MULTI-SKIP FEATURE STACKING

Filters that have been used in IDT and other hand-crafted features often involve differential operators through time, which act as highpass filters and tend to attenuate low frequency action information. This attenuation introduces bias to the resulting features and generates ill-conditioned feature matrices. In order to address the issue, we propose MIFS which stacks features with different frequencies to achieve invariance in the frequency domain. We prove that MIFS exponentially enhances the learnability of resulting feature matrices [7] because it simultaneously reduces the expectation and variance of condition numbers from the feature matrices.

5. SPACE-TIME EXTENDED DESCRIPTORS

The spatial pyramid [9] and its variants have been very popular feature models due to their success in balancing spatial location encoding and spatial invariance. Although it seems straightforward to extend spatial pyramid to the temporal domain, the large spatio-temporal diversity of unconstrained videos and the resulting significantly higher dimensional features make it less appealing. STED is a simple yet efficient alternative to include the spatio-temporal location into the video features. Instead of just coding motion information and leaving locations to be represented at the pooling stage, location information is used as part of the encoding step. This method avoids the danger of over committing to artificial boundaries and its dimension is relatively low.

	Two-stream ConvISA	Two-stream CNNs
Size	1 millions	60 millions
Label	Not needed	Needed
UCF101	88.3%	88.0%
HMDB51	61.5 %	59.4 %

Table 1: Comparison of two-stream ConvISA to two-stream CNNs

Algorithm 1 Multi-class Iterative Re-ranking

1: **Input:** The prediction scores of K class $P \in \mathbb{R}^{N\times K}$; Re-ranking annealing parameter η; Re-ranking weighting coefficient $\alpha > 0$; Total iteration steps W.
2: **Init:**$P^{(0)} = P$
3: **for** $w = 1, 2, \cdots, W-1$ **do**
4: For any instance index $i \in \{1, 2, \cdots, N\}$ and class index $j \in \{1, 2, \cdots, K\}$,

$$\Delta_{i,j}^{(w)} = \mathrm{sort}(\{P_{i,1}^{(w)}, P_{i,2}^{(w)}, \cdots, P_{i,K}^{(w)}\} \backslash P_{i,j}^{(w)}, \downarrow)$$

$$P_{i,j}^{(w+1)} = P_{i,j}^{(w)} - \eta^{w-1} \sum_{\substack{r=1 \\ r\neq j}}^{K} \mathrm{e}^{-\alpha r} \Delta_{i,j}^{(w)}(r)$$

5: **end for**
6: **Output:** $P^{(W)}$

6. MULTI-CLASS ITERATIVE RE-RANKING

Algorithm 1 shows our MIR algorithm. Given a score matrix $P \in \mathbb{R}^{N\times K}$ that contains K classifiers' predictions on N instances. We update each score $P_{i,j}$ iteratively by looking at other classifiers' predictions on the same instance and reducing the score using the predictions from the other classifiers. The reduction is carried out by first sorting other classifiers' predictions $\{P_{i,1}^{(w)}, P_{i,2}^{(w)}, \cdots, P_{i,K}^{(w)}\} \backslash P_{i,j}^{(w)}$ in a descending order and then subtracting the weighted sum of the sorted scores from $P_{i,j}$. We use exponential decaying weight and the weighting coefficient α has been set to 1 in this paper. For designing MIR, we assume that most of the instances only belong to one class. However, our experiments show that MIR is quite useful for improving ranking performance even in the case where each instance has multiple labels. Algorithm 1 can only improve the ranking performance. To make this improvement on ranking be beneficial for classification accuracy measurement, we propose to fuse the improved ranking, a flat version of scores with the original score matrix. Specifically, after getting the improved ranking matrix P_R, we do a z-score normalization to get $\hat{P}_R$, which becomes comparable to the original score matrix P. Our final prediction would be $P = \hat{P}_R + P$.

7. EXPERIMENTS

We examine our proposed algorithms on several benchmark datasets. The experimental setting is the same as in [7, 8]. The results are shown in Table 2, also compared to those from the state-of-the-art. The best results are highlighted in bold. Though our two-stream method is inferior to [18], the performance improves when we combine the learned descriptors from the two-stream method with the hand-crafted descriptors from IDT (hybrid). We further en-

HMDB51 (MAcc. %)		Hollywood2 (MAP %)		UCF101(MAcc. %)		UCF50 (MAcc. %)	
Wang *et al.* [18]	57.2	Wang *et al.* [18]	64.3	Karpathy et al. [5]	65.4	Oneata *et al.* [11]	90.0
Simonyan *et al.* [14]	59.4	Hoai *et al.* [2]	**73.6**	Wang *et al.* [17]	85.9	Wang *et al.* [18]	91.2
Peng *et al.* [13]	**66.8**	Fernando *et al.* [1]	**73.7**	Simonyan *et al.* [14]	88.0	Peng *et al.* [12]	92.3
Two-stream	56.1	Two-stream	61.1	Two-stream	85.9	Two-stream	89.3
Our best	**67.0**	Our best	71.9	Our best	**90.2**	Our best	**95.4**

Table 2: Comparison of our results to the state-of-the-art. Our best results using all of the four techniques presented in the papers

hance performance through three other techniques that have been proposed for the hybrid descriptors. Overall, we observe improvement on the state-of-the-art in three out of the four datasets. Note that although we list several most recent approaches here for comparison purposes, most of them are not directly comparable to our results due to the use of different data augmentation, features, and encoding methods. The most comparable method is [18], from which we build our approaches and serve as our baseline method.

8. DISCUSSION AND FUTURE WORK

It is difficult to learn video features using the CNN framework since it is computationally intensive and label demanding. To address such a problem, we revisit the unsupervised feature learning framework. In order to learn motion features, we use video and optical flow volumes extracted by IDT. We also apply MIFS to achieve speed invariance; use STED to incorporate spatio-temopral information and MIR to exploit relationships among multiple action classes. Despite our overall superior performance, the randomly chosen filters in Figure 2 show that current state-of-the-art learning methods which were designed to model pixels do not model motion well. Our next step is to customarily design models for motion inputs. Such exploration will be guided by neural research on how human perceive and understand motion. Our research can significantly improve the performance of current state-of-the-art action recognition system.

9. ACKNOWLEDGEMENT

This work was partially supported by Intelligence Advanced Research Projects Activity (IARPA) via Department of Interior National Business Center contract number D11PC20068. The U.S. Government is authorized to reproduce and distribute reprints for Governmental purposes notwithstanding any copyright annotation thereon. Disclaimer: The views and conclusions contained herein are those of the authors and should not be interpreted as necessarily representing the official policies or endorsements, either expressed or implied, of IARPA, DoI/NBC, or the U.S. Government. The work was also supported in part by the U. S. Army Research Office (W911NF- 13-1-0277). Any opinions, findings, and conclusions or recommendations expressed in this material are those of the authors and do not necessarily reflect the views of ARO.

10. REFERENCES

[1] B. Fernando, E. Gavves, et al. Modeling video evolution for action recognition. In *CVPR*, 2015.

[2] M. Hoai and A. Zisserman. Improving human action recognition using score distribution and ranking. In *ACCV*, 2014.

[3] J. Hurri and A. Hyvärinen. Simple-cell-like receptive fields maximize temporal coherence in natural video. *Neural Computation*, 15(3):663–691, 2003.

[4] Y.-G. Jiang, Q. Dai, X. Xue, W. Liu, and C.-W. Ngo. Trajectory-based modeling of human actions with motion reference points. In *ECCV*. 2012.

[5] A. Karpathy, G. Toderici, S. Shetty, T. Leung, R. Sukthankar, and L. Fei-Fei. Large-scale video classification with convolutional neural networks. In *CVPR*, 2014.

[6] A. Krizhevsky, I. Sutskever, and G. E. Hinton. Imagenet classification with deep convolutional neural networks. In *NIPS*, 2012.

[7] Z. Lan, M. Lin, X. Li, A. G. Hauptmann, and B. Raj. Beyond gaussian pyramid: Multi-skip feature stacking for action recognition. *CVPR*, 2015.

[8] Z. Lan, D. Yao, M. Lin, S.-I. Yu, and A. Hauptmann. The best of both worlds: Combining data-independent and data-driven approaches for action recognition. *arXiv preprint arXiv:1505.04427*, 2015.

[9] S. Lazebnik, C. Schmid, and J. Ponce. Beyond bags of features: Spatial pyramid matching for recognizing natural scene categories. In *CVPR*, 2006.

[10] Q. V. Le, W. Y. Zou, et al. Learning hierarchical invariant spatio-temporal features for action recognition with independent subspace analysis. In *CVPR*, 2011.

[11] D. Oneata, J. Verbeek, C. Schmid, et al. Action and event recognition with fisher vectors on a compact feature set. In *ICCV*, 2013.

[12] X. Peng, L. Wang, X. Wang, and Y. Qiao. Bag of visual words and fusion methods for action recognition: Comprehensive study and good practice. *arXiv preprint arXiv:1405.4506*, 2014.

[13] X. Peng, C. Zou, Y. Qiao, and Q. Peng. Action recognition with stacked fisher vectors. In *ECCV*. 2014.

[14] K. Simonyan and A. Zisserman. Two-stream convolutional networks for action recognition in videos. In *NIPS*, 2014.

[15] N. Srivastava, E. Mansimov, and R. Salakhutdinov. Unsupervised learning of video representations using lstms. *arXiv preprint arXiv:1502.04681*, 2015.

[16] H. Wang, A. Klaser, C. Schmid, and C.-L. Liu. Action recognition by dense trajectories. In *CVPR*, 2011.

[17] H. Wang and C. Schmid. Lear-inria submission for the thumos workshop. In *ICCV Workshop*, 2013.

[18] H. Wang, C. Schmid, et al. Action recognition with improved trajectories. In *ICCV*, 2013.

Challenge for Manga Processing: Sketch-based Manga Retrieval

Yusuke Matsui
The University of Tokyo
7-3-1, Hongo, Bunkyo-ku
Tokyo, Japan
matsui@hal.t.u-tokyo.ac.jp

ABSTRACT

We propose a sketch-based system for manga image retrieval. In the system, users simply draw sketches, and similar images are retrieved in real time from a manga database. The results are updated every time the user draws a stroke and therefore users can intuitively interact with the system. The proposed method consists of a simple and efficient sliding window-based feature description framework and interactive re-ranking schemes, which are introduced because the characteristics of manga images are different from those of naturalistic images, and thus, traditional image retrieval methods are not effective. Additionally, the future directions of improving the current retrieval system, including by using a combination of text features and image features, and the construction of a large database are discussed.

Categories and Subject Descriptors

I.4.9 [**Image Processing and Computer Vision**]: Applications

General Terms

ALGORITHMS

Keywords

Image retrieval; sketch; manga

1. INTRODUCTION

Manga (Japanese comics) are popular in many parts of the world. Nowadays, manga are being distributed not only in print but also electronically via online stores, such as Amazon, and are viewed on electronic devices, including Kindles, iPads, and PCs. Some of the e-manga archives are very large, e.g., the Amazon Kindle store sells more than 30,000 e-manga titles[1], but offer very limited search support, i.e., a keyword-based search by title or author and tag-based suggestions. For this reason, the application of content-based techniques has the potential to render the manga search experience more intuitive, efficient, and enjoyable.

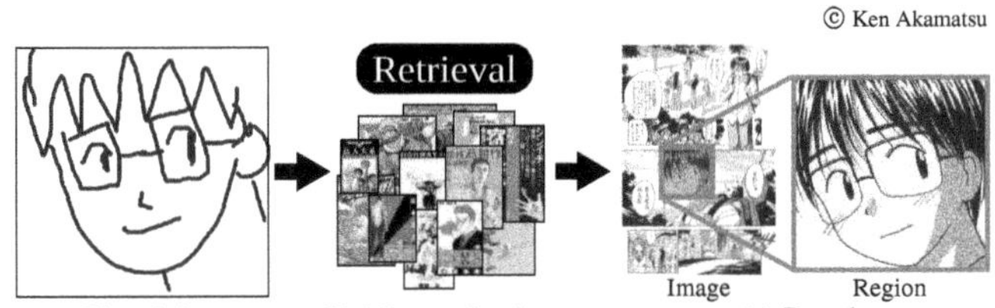

(a) Sketch input (b) Manga database (c) Result

Figure 1: Processing flow. (a) A user draws a rough sketch. (b) Similar images are retrieved from a manga database. (c) An image containing a region that best matches the sketch is retrieved.

Two unique challenges are associated with content-based manga retrieval. First, the visual characteristics of manga images are very different from those of naturalistic images. For example, as shown in Figure 1(c), manga images are usually line drawings comprising black lines on a flat white ground. Local feature characterization systems, such as SIFT, are not suited to describing manga images, which do not have varying gradient intensities. Furthermore, a manga image (page) comprises several frames, i.e., rectangular areas. It is therefore necessary to retrieve not only an image but also a part of an image, as shown in Figure 1(c), where the red square region within the image is detected.

The second challenge is to avoid limitations in the query modality. Because manga images are mostly black-and-white drawings, users should have access to some form of drawing, such as examples of manga images or sketches of their own. For this reason, it is important to provide a natural sketch-based interface for manga retrieval.

2. GOALS

The purpose of the study presented in my dissertation is to design a content-based manga retrieval system that addresses the above two challenges. The proposed system is divided into three steps.

- **(S1)** Sketch-based retrieval: We proposed a method for sketch-based manga image retrieval, that has already been presented in [9]. Fig. 1 shows the workflow of the system. To achieve the retrieval, the edge histograms of local patches are extracted from manga pages in a database, hashed to binary codes, and com-

[1]Amazon.co.jp Kindle Comic. Retrieved from January 28, 2014, from `http://amzn.to/WWXSuw`

MM'15, October 26–30, 2015, Brisbane, Australia.
ACM 978-1-4503-3459-4/15/10.
DOI: http://dx.doi.org/10.1145/2733373.2807997 .

pared to an input query sketch. Additionally, we proposed new interactive retrieval schemes, **relevance feedback** and **query retouch**, which facilitate manga retrieval tasks, such as character retrieval. These sketch-based retrieval and interactions serve as key components of the content-based manga retrieval system.

- (**S2**) Combining text with image features: Although sketch-based interactions are useful for querying manga images, it remains important to take text information into consideration for the purpose of retrieval. In addition to simply assigning title or author information to images for querying, we are seeking a method to mine also text information from manga images and combine this information with image features.
- (**S3**) Construction of a large scale database: Benchmarking and user studies are essential for evaluating the proposed system. However, presently there is no publicly available large scale manga image dataset. The construction of such a database would not only be useful for evaluating the retrieval system, but also would be an important contribution to all types of research that focus on manga images.

3. RELATED WORK

Sketch-based retrieval: Several methods have been proposed to address the sketch-based retrieval of naturalistic images, where queries constitute sketches drawn by users. Because a sketch consists of lines, edges are useful for representing images. Methods based on histograms of oriented gradients [5] have therefore been proposed [6]. Because the contours of objects are usually described by sketches, contour-based matching using chamfer distances have also been actively researched [3, 15].

Manga image processing: Several methods for processing manga images have been proposed, e.g., colorization [10, 13], layout recognition [16], layout generation [1], element composition [2], speech balloon detection [12], face tailored features [4], and screentone detection [7]

4. APPROACH

Currently, the first step of the study toward my dissertation, sketch-based retrieval (**S1**), has been completed and presented in [9]. In this section, we briefly review the proposed algorithm. Fig. 2 shows the framework of our method.

4.1 Feature representation

In content-based image retrieval, the basic form of image representation is the bag-of-features (BoF), whereby local features such as SIFT are extracted from the image and quantized into a sparse vector [14]. When a manga image is represented as a BoF, two problems arise. First, local features are not suitable, because the intensity gradients of a manga image are low. Second, because BoF discards spatial information, it is difficult to locate the part of the image containing the similarity.

To solve these problems, we propose a simple and efficient approach: sliding windows. After pre-processing, i.e, labeling unnecessary areas, we define spatial areas in terms of a multi-scale sliding window, and create a histogram of the edge orientation for each area [8]. Therefore, a set of histogram features are extracted from an input manga image,

(a) Querying by "two boys"

©Ken Akamatsu

(b) The result of the manga page corresponding to the 1st ranked in (a)

Figure 3: (a) Interface for the retrieval. The left area is the canvas for the user's sketch. In this case, two boys are drawn. The right area shows the retrieved results. (b) When the user clicks on one of the results, the page containing it is shown.

i.e., a page, where each feature denotes a region in the image. A feature from the query sketch and features from database images are compared, and the database feature that most closely matches the query feature is selected. The interface of the system is shown in Fig. 3.

This sliding-window-based representation is simple and efficient for finding the area in the image that matches one in the database, because the feature implicitly describes the position of the area in the image. This property is particularly useful for retrieving manga pages. Its disadvantage is that feature comparison can require a significant amount of memory and computation time.

To reduce computational cost and memory consumption, we employ an approximate nearest neighbor technique; features are converted into bit strings to achieve efficient computation and to save memory [11]. After the features are converted to binary strings, the Hamming distance between two strings, which approximates well their original Euclidean distance, can be computed quickly using low-level machine operations. The search can therefore be performed efficiently even for large numbers of database vectors.

4.2 Querying by Sketch

To achieve a natural and intuitive interface, we leveraged a sketch-based query. Because a manga itself comprises sketches drawn by authors, sketching is compatible with manga querying. The method is fully implemented on the Amazon EC2 platform and the interface is provided by

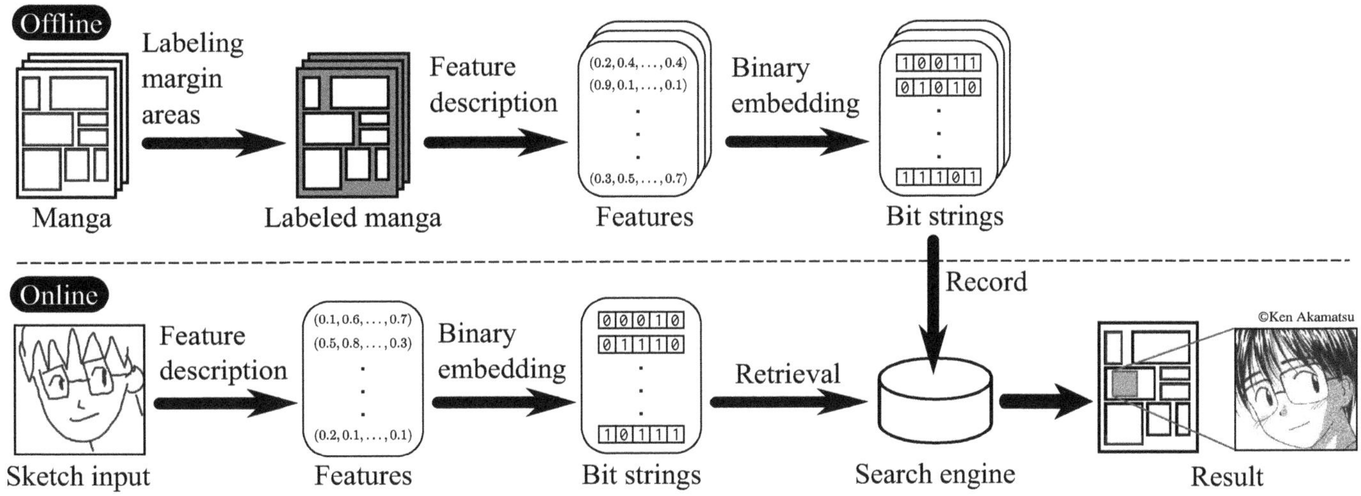

Figure 2: Framework of the proposed method.

a Web browser. The retrieval is performed automatically after each stroke is completed.

In addition, users can utilize sketching not only for the initial query but also for additional interaction with the retrieved results. The queries that can be performed using the proposed framework are summarized as follows. (1) Sketch querying, the proposed sketch-based retrieval described above, (2) *relevance feedback*, which reuses the retrieved results, (3) *query retouch*, where the result of relevance feedback is modified, and (4) combinations of the above.

Relevance feedback extends the existing method. Users can reuse a retrieved result simply by dragging the result to the canvas, as shown in Figure 4. By using relevance feedback, even novice users can use professional manga images as queries. Query retouch is a new method for interactive querying. In query retouch, users can modify either the initial sketch or a query taken from the results of a retrieval (Figure 5). As the query is changed by the addition of lines or partial erasure, the results change immediately. As a result, users can intuitively change the results of the retrieval in the desired direction.

5. WORK IN PROGRESS

As discussed in Section 4, the first step in the study toward the dissertation has been achieved. Current work in progress is related to (**S2**) and (**S3**).

5.1 Toward multi-modal manga image retrieval

Although sketch-based image retrieval is very effective, text information is still useful. For example, if a user wishes to find a character who is difficult to draw but can be easily specified by the character's name, querying should be performed first by a keyword-based search using the name. Then, sketch-based interactions, including relevance feedback and query retouch, can be applied as re-ranking. This kind of querying using both text and image features is known as a **multimodal search**, which can be the next step in a content-based manga image search (**S2**).

The challenge here is to find, collect, and assign labels automatically. To achieve the multimodal search, associated labels must be assigned to each image feature. For example, to find the face image patch in Fig. 1(c) using a keyword-based search by inputting, e.g., "boy," "glasses," or "Keitaro (the name of this character)," such labels need to be assigned to the image patch in advance. This seems easy when considering a Web image search; e.g., querying by "orange" in Google Image Search returns many images of oranges. However, such a keyword-based search is successful because the images on the Web are crawled from Web sites that contain much text information, and relevant labels are automatically extracted from the texts and assigned to each image. Usually, manga images do not have such rich sources of text information, and methods to find, collect, and assign correct labels automatically are not known. This is a work in progress in the study toward my dissertation.

5.2 Manga Image Database

After the content-based manga image retrieval system using multimodal queries has been realized, the next step is to evaluate the system (**S3**). Currently, no large scale manga image database is publicly available, which prevents researchers from conducting a large scale evaluation and a fair comparison of the methods proposed by various research groups. Because manga images are artwork and they are protected by copyrights, researchers should not reproduce them in their papers unless they have permission to do so; however, obtaining permission is a time-consuming task.

Therefore, the construction of a publicly available manga image dataset is important. Cooperating with members of our group and an organization of creators, we are in the process of building a large dataset. If a large scale manga image dataset is constructed, it will be useful for not only manga image retrieval but also any research studies related to manga, including those addressing colorization [10, 13], layout recognition [1], element composition [2], etc.

6. CONCLUSIONS

We proposed a sketch-based method for manga image retrieval, where users simply draw sketches via a Web browser and similar images are retrieved in real time from a manga database, with real-time updating for every stroke. We also proposed interactive querying schemes, relevance feedback

©Ken Akamatsu

(a) First sketch (b) Dragging a result to the canvas (c) Retrieval by reusing the result (d) 4th result

Figure 4: Relevance feedback. (a) A user draws strokes and finds the target building in the 11-th result (red colored). (b) By dragging it to the canvas, another retrieval is performed automatically using this result as the query. (c) A wide range of images of the target building is obtained. (d) The 4-th result is shown.

©Ken Akamatsu

(a) Results of relevance feedback (b) Draw a glass (c) Relevance feedback, again (d) 4th result

Figure 5: Query retouch. (a) Results of relevance feedback where target characters are colored red. (b) The user adds strokes to and draws glasses on the target character. Other target characters with glasses are then retrieved (red colored). Note that users can erase lines using an eraser tool. (c) Both relevance feedback and query retouch can be conducted multiple times. (d) The 4-th resultant image is shown.

and query retouch, using which users can interactively re-rank the results. Future research directions are (1) combining text features with the image-based retrieval system, and (2) construction of a large scale database for evaluation.

Acknowledgments

This work is partially supported by the Strategic Information and Communications R&D Promotion Programme (SCOPE) and JSPS KAKENHI Grant Number 257696.

7. REFERENCES

[1] Y. Cao, A. B. Chan, and R. W. H. Lau. Automatic stylistic manga layout. In *Proc. SIGGRAPH Asia*. ACM, 2012.

[2] Y. Cao, R. W. H. Lau, and A. B. Chan. Look over here: Attention-directing composition of manga elements. In *Proc. SIGGRAPH*. ACM, 2014.

[3] Y. Cao, C. Wang, L. Zhang, and L. Zhang. Edgel index for large-scale sketch-based image search. In *Proc. CVPR*. IEEE, 2011.

[4] W.-T. Chu and Y.-C. Chao. Line-based drawing style description for manga classification. In *Proc. MM*. ACM, 2014.

[5] N. Dalal and B. Triggs. Histograms of oriented gradients for human detection. In *Proc. CVPR*. IEEE, 2005.

[6] M. Eitz, K. Hildebrand, T. Boubekeur, and M. Alexa. Sketch-based image retrieval: Benchmark and bag-of-features descriptors. *IEEE TVCG*, 17(11):1624–1636, 2011.

[7] K. Ito, Y. Matsui, T. Yamasaki, and K. Aizawa. Separation of line drawings and screentones of manga. In *Proc. Eurographics*, 2015.

[8] K. Levi and Y. Weiss. Learning object detection from a small number of examples: the importance of good features. In *Proc. CVPR*. IEEE, 2004.

[9] Y. Matsui, K. Aizawa, and Y. Jing. Sketch2manga: Sketch-based manga retrieval. In *Proc. ICIP*. IEEE, 2014.

[10] Y. Qu, T.-T. Wong, and P.-A. Heng. Manga colorization. In *Proc. SIGGRAPH*. ACM, 2006.

[11] M. Raginsky and S. Lazebnik. Locality-sensitive binary codes from shift-invariant kernels. In *Proc. NIPS*, 2009.

[12] C. Rigaud, J.-C. Burie, J.-M. Ogier, D. Karatzas, and J. V. de Weijer. An active contour model for speech balloon detection in comics. In *Proc. ICDAR*. IEEE, 2013.

[13] K. Sato, Y. Matsui, T. Yamasaki, and K. Aizawa. Reference-based manga colorization by graph correspondence using quadratic programming. In *Proc. SIGGRAPH Asia Technical Brief*. ACM, 2014.

[14] J. Sivic and A. Zisserman. Video google: A text retrieval approach to object matching in videos. In *Proc. ICCV*. IEEE, 2003.

[15] X. Sun, C. Wang, C. Xu, and L. Zhang. Indexing billions of images for sketch-based retrieval. In *Proc. MM*. ACM, 2013.

[16] T. Tanaka, K. Shoji, F. Toyama, and J. Miyamichi. Layout analysis of tree-structured scene frames in comic images. In *Proc. IJCAI*, 2007.

Captioning Images Using Different Styles

Alexander Mathews
The Australian National University
Acton, Canberra, ACT
alex.mathews@anu.edu.au

ABSTRACT

I develop techniques that can be used to incorporate stylistic objectives into existing image captioning systems. Style is generally a very tricky concept to define, thus I concentrate on two specific components of style. First I develop a technique for predicting how people will name visual objects. I demonstrate that this technique could be used to generate captions with human like naming conventions. Full details are available in a recent publication [16]. Second I outline a system for generating sentences which express a strong positive or negative sentiment. Finally I present two possible future directions which are aimed at modelling style more generally. These are learning to imitate an individuals captioning style and generating a diverse set of captions for a single image.

Categories and Subject Descriptors

I.2 [**Artificial Intelligence**]: Vision and Scene Understanding; I.2 [**Artificial Intelligence**]: Natural Language Processing—*Language generation*

Keywords

caption generation; image description; object naming; sentiment

1. INTRODUCTION

Many of the photographs available on the Internet are not annotated with textual descriptions this makes them less easily accessible, to search engines and people with vision impairments. To alleviate this problem automatic annotations methods are needed. One area that has been receiving a lot of attention recently is the generation of natural language sentences to describe images.

Producing natural language captions for general web images is a very challenging problem; one which is strongly linked to the general image understanding problem. A system that can generate captions would ideally incorporate both a working model for natural language and a strong vision model capable of reliably detecting thousands of concepts. Unfortunately no reliable models for either of these tasks exist. Nevertheless, a range of approaches to automatic caption generation have been put forward.

The focus of my research is on improving systems for generating natural language captions for images. Unlike other researchers working on caption generation my aim is to improve the stylistic properties of captions, rather than focus exclusively on visual relevance. Although visual relevance is important, there are always many different ways to describe the same image. My goal is to select between these possible ways in order to optimise a set of stylistic objectives.

Writing style is strongly effected by the goal, whether it is to inform, persuade or entertain. When people write captions they typically have a goal in mind such as to describe the content of the image clearly. The clarity of a description can be strongly affected by the choice of words – a description dense in very specific scientific names is not suitable for a general audience. A caption author may also wish to encourage the reader to respond to the image in a particular way.

I focus my efforts on these two stylistic goals. First I investigate, and try to predict, how people name visual objects. Through this exploration I gain insights into generating captions with human like naming conventions. The result is a choice of names which are more easily understood by a general audience. Next I tailor a caption generation approach to express strong sentiment. The goal is to produce captions that encourage viewers to respond either positively or negatively towards an image. In my future work section I explore a couple of promising directions for allowing richer and more complex style domains to be used.

2. RELATED WORK

My thesis involves three main areas, caption generation as a whole, naming visual objects and sentiment in image captions. Caption generation is the framework in which my research fits, while the other two areas are the stylistic domains I have chosen to focus on.

2.1 Caption Generation

Over the last few years the challenging task of automatically generating natural language captions for images has grown in popularity; though it is still a very difficult problem. In fact two necessary components, visual concept detection and Natural Language Generation (NLG) are both unsolved research problems in their own right. A variety of attempts have been made to build complete caption generation systems, these tend to fall into one of three categories:

MM'15, October 26-30, 2015, Brisbane, Australia
ACM 978-1-4503-3459-4/15/10.
http://dx.doi.org/10.1145/2733373.2807998

Figure 1: (Left)An example of the same object being named differently because of the visual context. (Right)The per-concept accuracy improvement of my context enriched method over a baseline which selects the most frequent name for each concept.

detection and generation, caption retrieval and generative deep networks.

Detection and generation approaches [27, 13, 20] employ a pipeline of independently trained object and attribute detectors; they typically follow a similar formula. First a fixed set of object and attribute detectors are used to identify visual concepts, these are then mapped into some intermediate representation, where smoothing is applied to enhance coherency. The smoothed intermediate representation is then realised as natural language text by a NLG system. A major problem with these approaches is that they use rigid intermediate representations and rely heavily on template systems for NLG; resulting in text which sounds very formulaic and un-natural.

Caption retrieval approaches [18, 8, 14] are designed to address the narrow scope and formulaic language that affects detection and generation approaches. Intuitively, transferring captions, or parts of captions [14], from other images should produce very natural image descriptions because most of the human imposed structure is kept in place. The challenge for caption retrieval approaches is ensuring that the relevance of the caption to the image.

Generative deep networks for natural language caption generation have recently become very popular [5, 10, 11, 15, 26]; quickly becoming the state of the art for caption generation. Generative deep networks consist of at least two components, a vision component, which is typically a Convolution Neural Network (CNN) [12], and a language component which is typically a Recurrent Neural Network (RNN). These two components are trained simultaneously using back-propagation.

In the related works mentioned above the primary aims were to improve the visual relevance or linguistic fluency of generated captions. Whereas, the aim of my thesis is to incorporate stylistic objectives into existing caption generation approaches.

2.2 Naming Visual Objects

A model for how people name objects was introduced in the psychology literature by Rosch [22]; this model revolved around the idea of basic-level categories. The basic-level category represents the ideal trade-off between low in-category visual variability and high between-class visual variability. Work by Rosch [21] notes that there are contextual effects on both the level of abstraction used to name an object and even if it will be named. Chaigneau et al. [2] demonstrate, using adult subjects, that situational information changes the way subjects categorize unfamiliar objects into familiar categories.

Recently there has been interest in developing machine learning techniques to choose the most appropriate name to give to a visual object. One approach taken by Deng et al. [4] is to optimise the accuracy-specificity trade off by using a semantic hierarchy to select the appropriate name. This technique does not take into account how people actually describe objects. Ordonez et al. [17] present a model predicting the labels people will actually use to name objects. Their model uses a text based component which trades off name frequency with linguistic proximity and a visual component that assesses the visual saliency of names to the image. This model does not capture the important affects of visual context. In section 3.1 I present my model which both incorporates visual context and works on a much larger scale than previous approaches.

2.3 Sentiment in Image Captions

Identifying the sentiment conveyed by both text and images is an active area of research. In contrast automatically generating text which conveys a strong sentiment has not been explored in great detail, though it is an emerging subfield of Natural Language Generation (NLG) called affective NLG.

Many techniques for text based sentiment analysis rely on aggregating known sentiment estimates for individual phrases. Two well know sources for phrase sentiments are SentiWordNet [6] and SentiStrength [25]; though many approaches learn phrase sentiments directly from the target domain. More recently authors such as Socher et al. [24] have shown how to jointly learn phrase sentiments and composition rules, allowing constructs such as negations to be captured.

Research towards identifying the sentiment in images has mostly been focused on using low level visual features such as color and contrast [9]. More recently Borth et al. [1] have made use of visual concept detectors to identify the sentiments expressed in images. They trained concept detectors for over 1200 adjective noun pairs identified as expressing a strong sentiment.

Work on affective NLG system [23, 19, 7] show that it is possible to generate sentences which convey a strong sentiment. Of particular interest is the work of Gatti et al. [7] which presents a way to automatically modify an existing sentence to achieve a sentiment goal. Their approach uses constituent re-ordering to emphasise or de-emphasise parts of a sentence. They also swap short phrases with similar ones that align better with the sentiment goal. Although these techniques have been shown to apply to domains such as restaurant reviews [7] and medical reports [23], the image captioning domain has not been explored. My research is the first to investigate the possibility of using affective NLG for image caption generation.

3. APPROACH

My research so far has considered two specific style domains. The first is how to choose names for visual concepts in a way that is consistent with human judgements, while the second relates to generating sentences that exhibit a strong sentiment. The work on naming visual concepts is published [16], while the research into sentence generation with sentiment is ongoing.

3.1 Choosing the Most Appropriate Names

There are often many different names that can be used to describe a visual concept, for example Figure 1 presents a visual concept, in this case an *apple*. Other names that may be used include *fruit* and *Gala apple*. Depending upon the visual context some names are more likely than others, for example when there are other fruit in the image it is more common to name the *apple* as a *fruit*. There are many situations, other than collective naming, were visual context changes how a concept is described.

I propose a three step approach to automatically determine the context dependent basic-level names of visual objects. First I use ImageNet [3], a large dataset of manually categorised images, to learn over 2600 visual concept detectors. I then fit a model for selecting a basic-level name for each of these concepts, while taking into account visual context, object importance and object appearance. Finally, I fine-tune the obtained descriptions for an image using language context – this is done via a model for ranking descriptions from different visual concepts.

The first step towards deciding on descriptive names for a visual scene is to identify concepts. I define my concept domain using the well-known ImageNet [3] database which illustrates thousands of concepts (otherwise known as synsets) with a few hundred images each. I capture visual semantics by learning a visual representation of each synset from ImageNet.

The second step is to identify a set of descriptive names which can be used to describe a visual concept. In this work, I obtain a set of descriptive names for each concept by searching up the WordNet hypernym hierarchy (i.e., expanding parent concepts). Next I learn a classifier for each concept, to infer the most likely name given the visual context. I use Convolution Neural Network features as visual context and linear classifiers to select the most likely name. The ground-truth is constructed by matching the set of possible descriptive names to human generated captions.

I apply a linear ranking function based on the RankSVM formulation to rank descriptive names using four different types of features which capture both visual saliency and linguistic context. The most important of which are the *Score* features which include visual classifier confidences and the *Word2Vec* features that capture the word context.

3.2 Generating Descriptions with Sentiment

Original: a cat on a desk next to a laptop
Sentiment: a happy cat sleeping on a desk next to an open laptop

Figure 2: An example where positive sentiment is added to a descriptive caption.

Generating captions which exhibit a strong positive or negative sentiment is challenging because it combines the difficulties of caption generation with the added challenge of incorporating sentiment in very short texts. In light of this I have based my system on a state-of-the-art generative deep network model. This deep network, by itself, does not produce captions with a strong sentiment.

The first step towards generating descriptions with strong sentiment is to construct a dataset of human generated captions with strong sentiment. Since sentiment can be difficult to impose or even identify in short texts, I focus on sentences with sentimental adjective noun pairs. Mechanical Turk workers are asked to write image captions containing one of several adjective noun pairs that have been identified as having a strong sentiment. The resulting dataset consists of captions that are both visually relevant and exhibit a strong sentiment.

The primary problem with training a generative deep network on the sentiment dataset is controlling over-fitting. In particular I want to retain the general properties of the generative deep network trained on the purely descriptive sentences, but introduce the most important aspects of the sentiment dataset. To this end I train a new model that dynamically weights the contribution of the pre-trained network and a new network. This new network incorporates additional features such as a sentiment alignment objective and domain specific visual features.

4. RESULTS TO DATE

Here I present a summary of my previously published results on selecting the most appropriate name for a visual concept.

I evaluated my method, which takes into account visual context, against a baseline that always selects the most common name for a visual concept. In Figure 1 I show the results for cross-validation on a dataset consisting of 760000 image caption pairs collected from Flickr [18]. Among the 2,633 visual concepts my method improves upon the *Most frequent name* baseline for 1,222 concepts, among which 783 improved by more than 1%. No change in accuracy is measured for 1190, and 221 concepts exhibited a small accuracy decrease. I found that my method provides the most improvement for visual concepts with ambiguous basic-level names – two or more names used with similar frequency. The 221 concepts that exhibit an accuracy decrease are characterised by ambiguous basic-level names and fewer than average training examples.

My system produces natural names for hundreds of concepts by taking visual context into account. This highlights visual context as a feature for inclusion in visual naming systems and verifies the arguments laid out in the psychology literature on a scale that is difficult to achieve with human subjects. My approach is targeted towards caption generation where it can be used to impose human like naming conventions. This will improve the overall naturalness and fluency of captions generated by existing systems.

5. SUMMARY AND OUTLOOK

In my current and past research I have been working towards generating captions which optimise a specific style attribute – either object naming style or positive/negative sentiment. A set of discreet attributes, such as these, is a clear way of defining the style for the generated caption. It is also a very useful method when there is a style attribute that you know you want to optimise for.

5.1 Imitating Captioning Style

Another method for specifying the style of a caption is to provide examples of the style of writing you would like to produce, and then have the system imitate. For example, given a sample of captions written by an individual author the aim would be to generate captions in that authors style. Such a system would need to learn how to represent style compactly and then be able to generate captions from that representation. The system would also need to make use of more general information about caption construction. To train this system I would start by trying to build a style representation that is similar for captions generated by the same author, but different for captions generated by separate authors. Existing datasets can be used for this provided authorship information can be obtained.

5.2 Generating a Diverse Set of Captions

Current state of the art caption generation systems are designed to produce a single caption for an image. In reality there may be many different ways to describe the same image, which are all of a similar quality. A model which is able to enumerate a diverse selection of these sentences could be very useful. It would effectively allow the user to choose the style that they wish to use for a particular caption. In addition, using multiple different ways to describe a scene could be a more effective way to communicate than a single caption. The main challenge would be maintaining visual accuracy while increasing caption diversity.

6. REFERENCES

[1] D. Borth, R. Ji, T. Chen, T. Breuel, and S.-F. Chang. Large-scale visual sentiment ontology and detectors using adjective noun pairs. *ACMMM*, 2013.

[2] S. E. Chaigneau, L. W. Barsalou, and M. Zamani. Situational information contributes to object categorization and inference. *Acta psychologica*, 2009.

[3] J. Deng, W. Dong, R. Socher, L.-J. Li, K. Li, and L. Fei-Fei. ImageNet: A large-scale hierarchical image database. In *CVPR*, 2009.

[4] J. Deng, J. Krause, a. C. Berg, and L. Fei-Fei. Hedging your bets: Optimizing accuracy-specificity trade-offs in large scale visual recognition. *CVPR*, 2012.

[5] J. Donahue, L. A. Hendricks, S. Guadarrama, M. Rohrbach, S. Venugopalan, K. Saenko, and T. Darrell. Long-term recurrent convolutional networks for visual recognition and description. *CoRR*, 2014.

[6] A. Esuli, F. Sebastiani, and V. G. Moruzzi. SENTIWORDNET : A Publicly Available Lexical Resource for Opinion Mining. *LREC*, 2006.

[7] L. Gatti, M. Guerini, O. Stock, and C. Strapparava. Sentiment Variations in Text for Persuasion Technology. *Persuasive Technology*, 2014.

[8] M. Hodosh, P. Young, and J. Hockenmaier. Framing image description as a ranking task: data, models and evaluation metrics. *JAIR*, 2013.

[9] D. Joshi, R. Datta, E. Fedorovskaya, Q.-T. Luong, J. Wang, J. Li, and J. Luo. Aesthetics and emotions in images. *Signal Processing Magazine, IEEE*, 2011.

[10] A. Karpathy, A. Joulin, and F. F. F. Li. Deep fragment embeddings for bidirectional image sentence mapping. *NIPS*, 2014.

[11] R. Kiros, R. Salakhutdinov, and R. Zemel. Unifying Visual-Semantic Embeddings with Multimodal Neural Language Models. *arXiv*, 2014.

[12] A. Krizhevsky, I. Sutskever, and G. Hinton. Imagenet classification with deep convolutional neural networks. *NIPS*, 2012.

[13] G. Kulkarni, V. Premraj, and S. Dhar. Baby talk: Understanding and generating simple image descriptions. *CVPR*, 2011.

[14] P. Kuznetsova, V. Ordonez, and A. Berg. Collective generation of natural image descriptions. *ACL*, 2012.

[15] J. Mao, W. Xu, Y. Yang, J. Wang, and A. L. Yuille. Explain Images with Multimodal Recurrent Neural Networks. *NIPS*, 2015.

[16] A. Mathews, L. Xie, and X. He. Choosing basic-level concept names using visual and language context. *WACV*, 2015.

[17] V. Ordonez, J. Deng, and Y. Choi. From large scale image categorization to entry-level categories. *ICCV*, 2013.

[18] V. Ordonez, G. Kulkarni, and T. Berg. Im2text: Describing images using 1 million captioned photographs. *NIPS*, 2011.

[19] G. Özbal, D. Pighin, and C. Strapparava. BRAINSUP: Brainstorming Support for Creative Sentence Generation. *ACL*, 2013.

[20] M. Rohrbach, W. Qiu, I. Titov, and S. Thater. Translating Video Content to Natural Language Descriptions. *ICCV*, 2013.

[21] E. Rosch. *Principles of categorization.* 1999.

[22] E. Rosch, C. Mervis, and W. Gray. Basic objects in natural categories. *Cognitive Psychology*, 1976.

[23] F. D. Rosis and F. Grasso. Affective natural language generation. *Affective interactions*, 2000.

[24] R. Socher, A. Perelygin, and J. Wu. Recursive deep models for semantic compositionality over a sentiment treebank. *EMNLP*, 2013.

[25] M. Thelwall, K. Buckley, G. Paltoglou, D. Cai, and A. Kappas. Sentiment strength detection in short informal text. *JASIST*, 2010.

[26] O. Vinyals and A. Toshev. Show and Tell: A Neural Image Caption Generator. *arXiv*, 2014.

[27] Y. Yang, C. Teo, H. D. III, and Y. Aloimonos. Corpus-guided sentence generation of natural images. *EMNLP*, 2011.

Weakly Supervised Learning of Part-based Models for Interaction Prediction via LDA

Jia-Lin Chen
DSP/IC Design Lab,
Graduate Institute of Electrical Engineering,
National Taiwan University
jocelyn@video.ee.ntu.edu.tw

ABSTRACT

In this paper, we focus on interaction prediction which infers to what interaction might happen in the near future. Each interaction is modeled by mixtures of deformable parts in order to provide higher tolerance to part configurations. In our weakly supervised learning setting, part detectors are learned from training data without bounding boxes around the true locations of the people in each frame. The discriminating features are obtained using a two-layer Linear Discriminant Analysis (LDA) classification to promise maximal separability for parts and interactions respectively. Experimental results demonstrate that the proposed system is effective in learning part-based models in less annotated information and achieves comparable performance to state-of-the-art fully supervised approaches.

Categories and Subject Descriptors

I.2.10 [**ARTIFICIAL INTELLIGENCE**]: Vision and Scene Understanding—*motion, video analysis*; I.5.4 [**PATTERN RECOGNITION**]: Applications—*computer vision*

General Terms

Multimedia Systems

Keywords

Action prediction; weakly supervised learning; linear discriminant analysis

1. INTRODUCTION

When a violence event is going to happen, some people yelling, "here comes the police!" may hold back the perpetrator and stop making things worse. An intelligence surveillance system with interaction prediction is needed to detect violence event as early as possible and send warning to the perpetrator that he has gotten attention. Such an interaction prediction system have variety applications ranging from intelligence surveillance system, driver assistance system, marker-less augmented reality and autonomous robot system.

MM'15, October 26–30, 2015, Brisbane, Australia.
ACM 978-1-4503-3459-4/15/10.
DOI: http://dx.doi.org/10.1145/2733373.2807999.

Our goals are quite in common with previous works on recognizing an action before it is completely executed as action prediction. Ryoo et al. [1] introduce the interaction prediction task of recognition ongoing interactions at their early stage as opposed to the after-the-fact classification of completed activities. They represent an activity as an integral histogram of spatio-temporal features based on provided space and time locations. Raptis et al. [2] model an action as a sparse sequence of temporally local keyframes with spatially annotated poselets. The proposed approach has the ability to localize the action and deal with partial video observation to predict actions. Lan et al. [3] propose hierarchical movemes for predicting future action in natural scenarios (e.g. TV series) from still images or short video clips. Different movemes trained from annotated videos describe human movements at different levels of granularities, ranging from fine-grained details to coarser movements that cover a larger temporal extent.

Most previous works are supposed to be given annotated local patches for training. This is not practical since the supervision costs lots of time and manual labour. Many researchers have proposed weakly supervised learning algorithms to discover distinctive parts for an object or scene class [4] [5] [6]. This paper is inspired by their methods but we extent the learning algorithm to interaction prediction which considers both spatial and temporal domains. The part-based models representing different interactions are obtained from an initial exemplar then refined in an iterative scheme. A two-layer LDA classification is then adopted for interaction prediction.

The remainder of this paper is organized as follows. In the following section, we introduce the proposed action prediction system. Section 3 shows our experiment results and analysis. We conclude with discussion in Section 4.

2. PROPOSED SYSTEM

In the scenario we focus on, each interaction is the action between two people. If a person extends his hand and another person keeps closing and extends his hand too, we can expect they are going to shake hands. However if a person extends his hand and another person tries to dodge, a punching is more likely to happen. Based on the observation, we model each interaction by mixtures of deformable parts [7]. Each part of an interaction represents an action executed by a person.

A two-layer LDA classification framework for interaction prediction is proposed. Firstly, a weakly labeled training set is given. Part detectors are trained from a single positive exemplar using the accelerated LDA [8]. Secondly, the interaction models defined by mixtures of deformable part are trained. Response of all part models are projected to the whitened space by LDA again for promising maximal separability. The details of each stage are described below.

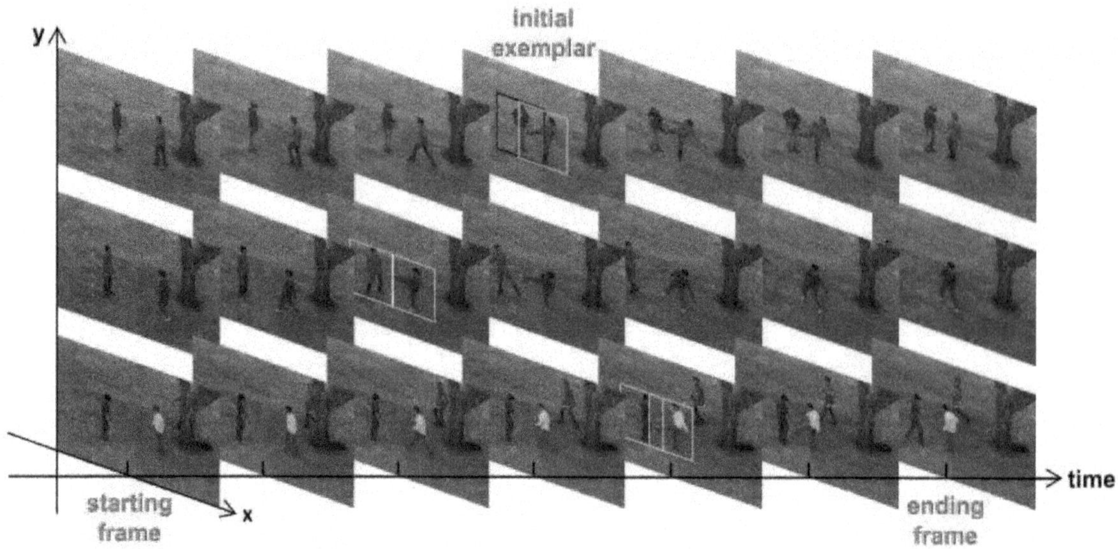

Figure 1: Weakly supervised learning scheme.

2.1 Weakly Supervised Learning Scheme

In the training stage, the part learning problem is addressed as part alignment both in spatial and temporal domains. Our goal is to find a discriminative part collection of each interaction. In Fig. 1, there are some sampled frames from three videos of interaction "kicking" illustrated. Each segmented video is truncated with the annotated starting frame and ending frame.

In our weakly supervised setting, we assume that we are given a collection of videos annotated only by the interaction classes they contain, not by their location in the frame. In addition to giving indistinct starting frames and ending frames of interactions, the executing frames are annotated for temporal cues. The dimension of the problem is then reduced from 3D to 2D part alignment only in spatial domain.

The weakly supervised learning scheme starts from an initial exemplar given from an executing frame. An example of initial exemplar is shown in Fig. 1. Two parts of an interaction are bounded by the blue and orange boxes respectively in the first row. Part models are built for each part and used for pooling the maximum response in other executing frames of the same interaction class. More positive examples correspond to the initial exemplar are then found as shown by the light green and yellow bounding boxes in the second and third rows. The part models are refined by all positive examples which can significantly improve the reliability of the part detector.

It is noticed that the overlap area of two bounding boxes varies from video to video. This indicates that the distance between each part is different. The mixtures of deformable parts adopted in our system can describe the variation of the distance and give enough tolerance. Some examples of part collection found by our weakly supervised learning scheme are shown in Fig. 2. In each column, the color images are shown on the left side while the corresponding optical flow images are shown on the right side.

2.2 Two-layer LDA Classification

For describing each part, we train three models with Histogram of Oriented Gradients (HoG) [9], Histogram of Optical Flow (HoF) and Histogram of Motion Boundaries (HoMB) [10], respectively. HoG directs the shape cue while HoF and HoMB represent the motion cue from the previous frame to the current frame. We used "unsigned gradients" for HoG and HoMB while used "signed gradients" for HOF since the direction of optical flow is important information.

LDA is a generative model for classification. This technique maximizes the proportion of the between-class variance to the within-class variance and promise maximal separability. After applying LDA to obtain the projected feature, the contours of action part, the important motion and the boundaries of motion are stressed, while the background gradients are suppressed.

Given a training dataset of features x annotated with class label, we define the between-class covariance matrix is Sb and the within-class covariance matrix is Sw. Sb indicates the deviation between the feature mean for each pair of classes, while Sw shows the scatter of samples around the feature mean of their own class. In order to maximize the ratio of the between-class variance to the within-class variance, the projection matrix W can be obtained by calculating the eigenvectors of the discrimination matrix $Sw^{-1}Sb$. The projected feature x' with higher separability is then obtained by $x' = Wx$. The nearest mean methods is finally applied to determine the classification result.

The LDA accelerated version [8] is used in our system. Under the assumption that the number of instances of any class is small compared to the number of all instances, the covariance matrix and mean of the background can be pre-computed across the entire training set, ignoring class labels. This step can be done just once and reused for all classes.

In our system we apply two-layer LDA classification for parts classification and interaction classification respectively. In the first layer, the inputs are HoG, HoF and HoMB features of each part collection found from the previous step. Each part's appearance is modeled as a LDA classifier. In the second layer, the input are the distance between the projected feature and the center of each part model. Each interaction's appearance is modeled as a LDA classifier again. The classification result is determined by minimum

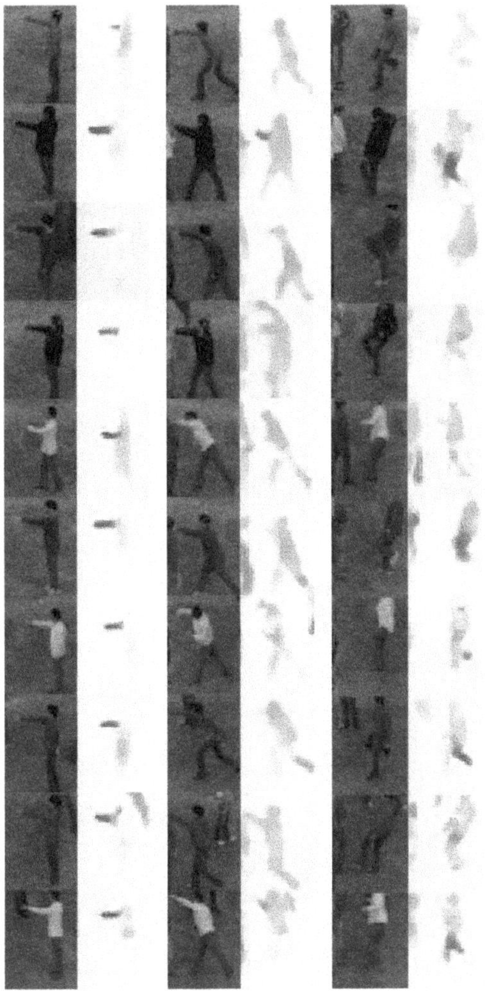

Figure 2: Some examples of part collection found by our weakly supervised learning scheme.

distance between projected feature of the second layer and the center of each interaction.

3. EXPERIMENTS

We validate the proposed system on the UT-Interaction benchmark dataset [11] using the segmented versions for learning and detection setting. The segmented versions of the dataset contains one human-human interaction in each video. There is a total of 120 videos including 6 classes of interactions: handshake, point, hug, push, kick and punch. Based on the 10-fold leave-one-out cross-validation, our method is evaluated and compared with the previous action prediction works in Table 1. The second and third columns report the accuracies using the first half and the entire video, respectively. Our method achieves an accuracy of 81.7% when only the first half of the video is available and 88.3 % when entire video observed. This is slightly lower than the state-of-the-art performance, but our system is learned in the weakly supervised setting and neither requires access to large annotated information.

4. CONCLUSION

We propose an interaction prediction system to recognize interaction before it is fully executed. The flexible part-based model of interactions gives tolerance for the distance between each part. The two-layer LDA classification proposed promises maximal separability for parts and interactions respectively. Our experiments demonstrate that the proposed weakly supervised learning scheme is effective in learning the discriminative parts and achieves comparable performance to state-of-the-art fully supervised approaches.

Table 1: Performance comparison on the UT-Interaction Dataset.

Method	Accuracy w. half videos	Accuracy w. full videos
`Our Model`	81.7%	88.3%
`Lan[3]`	83.1%	88.4%
`Raptis[2]`	73.3%	93.3%
`Ryoo[1]`	70%	85%

5. REFERENCES

[1] M. Ryoo, "Human activity prediction: Early recognition of ongoing activities from streaming videos," in *Computer Vision (ICCV), 2011 IEEE International Conference on*. IEEE, 2011, pp. 1036–1043.

[2] M. Raptis and L. Sigal, "Poselet key-framing: A model for human activity recognition," in *Computer Vision and Pattern Recognition (CVPR), 2013 IEEE Conference on*. IEEE, 2013, pp. 2650–2657.

[3] T. Lan, T.-C. Chen, and S. Savarese, "A hierarchical representation for future action prediction," in *Computer Vision–ECCV 2014*. Springer, 2014, pp. 689–704.

[4] I. Endres, K. Shih, J. Jiaa, and D. Hoiem, "Learning collections of part models for object recognition," in *Computer Vision and Pattern Recognition (CVPR), 2013 IEEE Conference on*. IEEE, 2013, pp. 939–946.

[5] M. Juneja, A. Vedaldi, C. Jawahar, and A. Zisserman, "Blocks that shout: Distinctive parts for scene classification," in *Computer Vision and Pattern Recognition (CVPR), 2013 IEEE Conference on*. IEEE, 2013, pp. 923–930.

[6] C. Doersch, A. Gupta, and A. A. Efros, "Mid-level visual element discovery as discriminative mode seeking," in *Advances in Neural Information Processing Systems*, 2013, pp. 494–502.

[7] Y. Yang and D. Ramanan, "Articulated pose estimation with flexible mixtures-of-parts," in *Computer Vision and Pattern Recognition (CVPR), 2011 IEEE Conference on*. IEEE, 2011, pp. 1385–1392.

[8] B. Hariharan, J. Malik, and D. Ramanan, "Discriminative decorrelation for clustering and classification," in *Computer Vision–ECCV 2012*. Springer, 2012, pp. 459–472.

[9] N. Dalal and B. Triggs, "Histograms of oriented gradients for human detection," in *Computer Vision and Pattern Recognition, 2005. CVPR 2005. IEEE Computer Society Conference on*, vol. 1. IEEE, 2005, pp. 886–893.

[10] H. Wang and C. Schmid, "Action recognition with improved trajectories," in *Computer Vision (ICCV), 2013 IEEE International Conference on*. IEEE, 2013, pp. 3551–3558.

[11] M. S. Ryoo and J. K. Aggarwal, "UT-Interaction Dataset, ICPR contest on Semantic Description of Human Activities (SDHA)," http://cvrc.ece.utexas.edu/SDHA2010/Human_Interaction.html, 2010.

Author Index

www.ingramcontent.com/pod-product-compliance
Ingram Content Group UK Ltd.
Pitfield, Milton Keynes, MK11 3LW, UK
UKHW051420290926
15471UKWH00009B/1696